The New York Times 2011 ALMANAC

Edited by John W. Wright

WITH EDITORS AND REPORTERS OF

The Times

PENGUIN REFERENCE

PENGUIN BOOKS

Published by the Penguin Group

Penguin Group (USA) Inc., 375 Hudson Street, New York, New York 10014, U.S.A.

Penguin Group (Canada), 90 Eglinton Avenue East, Suite 700, Toronto, Ontario, Canada M4P 2Y3 (a division of Pearson Penguin Canada Inc.)

Penguin Books Ltd, 80 Strand, London WC2R 0RL, England

Penguin Ireland, 25 St Stephen's Green, Dublin 2, Ireland (a division of Penguin Books Ltd)

Penguin Group (Australia), 250 Camberwell Road, Camberwell, Victoria 3124, Australia (a division of Pearson Australia Group Pty Ltd)

Penguin Books India Pvt Ltd, 11 Community Centre, Panchsheel Park, New Delhi – 110 017, India

Penguin Group (NZ), 67 Apollo Drive, Rosedale, North Shore 0632, New Zealand (a division of Pearson New Zealand Ltd)

Penguin Books (South Africa) (Pty) Ltd, 24 Sturdee Avenue, Rosebank, Johannesburg 2196, South Africa

Penguin Books Ltd, Registered Offices: 80 Strand, London WC2R 0RL, England

Published in Penguin Books, a member of Penguin Group (USA) Inc. 2009

10 9 8 7 6 5 4 3 2 1

ISBN 978-0-14-311894-7
ISSN 1523-7079

Printed in the United States of America
Set in Utopia and Optima
Designed by Virginia Norey

Please direct all comments to:
John W. Wright
The New York Times Almanac
1133 Broadway (1124)
New York, NY 10010

CONTRIBUTORS AND STAFF

General Editor
John W. Wright

Executive Editor
Lisette E. Johnson

Senior Executive Editor
Matt Fisher

Senior Writers
Ariana Brookes, Bryan Bunch, Ellen Chodosh, John Connelly, Philip Francis, Andrea Galyean, Alan Joyce, David Major, John Major, Allison Paxton Paine, Lincoln Paine, John Rosenthal, Patricia Szczerba, Jenny Tesar

Contributing Editors
Alice Finer, Glen Gendzel, Deborah Kaple, Jerold Kappes, Michael Kaufman, James McCaffrey, Thomas LaRosa, Mary Quigley, Frederic Riccardi

Researchers and Fact Checkers
Robert L. Spring, Victoria Vine

Data Entry
Arlene Jacks, Dorothy Green

The New York Times
Michael S. Greenspon, General Manager, News Services; Nancy Lee, Executive Editor and Vice President, News Service and Syndicate; Alex Ward, Editorial Director, Book Development

Correspondents
Binyamin Appelbaum, Randal C. Archibold, Al Baker, Peter Baker, Anne Barnard, Alexei Barrionuevo, James Barron, Ellen Barry, Pascale Bonnefoy, Graham Bowley, Ethan Bronner, Nick Bunkley, John Burns, Sewell Chan, Nicola Clark, Alan Cowell, James Dao, Monica Davey, Michael J. de la Merced, Shaila Dewan, Larry Dorman, Eric Eckholm, Andrea Elliott, Steven Erlanger, Martin Fackler, Carlotta Gall, Laurie Goodstein, Denise Grady, Gardiner Harris, Miguel Helft, David M. Herszenhorn, David Johnston, Gina Kolata, Andrew Kramer, Clifford Krauss, Nicholas Kulish, Marc Lacey, David Leonhardt, Clifford J. Levy, Adam Liptak, Jere Longman, Salman Masood, Mark Mazzetti, Robert D. McFadden, Jesse McKinley, Gretchen Morgenson, Jad Mouawad, Seth Mydans, Steven Lee Myers, Robert Pear, Bill Pennington, Michal Piotrowski, William Rashbaum, Campbell Robertson, Choe Sang-Hun, Susan Saulny, Michael S. Schmidt, John Schwartz, Scott Shane, Deborah Sontag, Brian Stelter, Sheryl Gay Stolberg, Louise Story, Landon Thomas Jr., Ian Urbina, Nicholas Wade, Duff Wilson, Michael Wines, Robert F. Worth, Edward Wyatt, Kate Zernike

Maps
Steve Hadermeyer, John Papasian

CONTENTS

Late Breaking News

Standoff in Ecuador Ends With Leader's Rescue

On September 30, 2010, Ecuadorean soldiers stormed a police hospital in the capital city of Quito where President Rafael Correa was held by rebellious elements of the police forces, and rescued him amid an exchange of gunfire in an effort to end a tense standoff between Mr. Correa and hundreds of protesting police officers and military personnel.

The operation came during a state of emergency declared that day in Ecuador after Mr. Correa was caught at one point earlier in the day in an angry scrum of officers at a barracks in Quito and was physically assaulted. He was tear-gassed, shoved, insulted and pelted with water, and emerged gasping for air.

He sought refuge in the police hospital, which was surrounded by protesting officers. Speaking to the news media by telephone, the president said that he was "practically captive," while hundreds of his supporters marched on the police compound, demanding his release.

The military leadership appeared to support the president. Gen. Ernesto González, the highest-ranking military official, called on the protesting police officers and troops to stand down. "We are a state of law," he said in comments broadcast on Ecuadorean radio.

On the following day, soldiers patrolled the major cities. Five peoplpe had been killed and 200 hurt.

—SIMON ROMERO

U.S. Infected Guatemalans With Syphilis in 1940s

In September 2010, Secretary of State Hillary Rodham Clinton and Health and Human Services Secretary Kathleen Sebelius revealed that from 1946 to 1948, American public health doctors deliberately infected nearly 700 Guatemalans—prison inmates, mental patients and soldiers—with venereal diseases in what was meant as an effort to test the effectiveness of penicillin. American tax dollars, through the National Institutes of Health, even paid for syphilis-infected prostitutes to sleep with prisoners, since Guatemalan prisons allowed such visits.

If the subjects contracted the disease, they were given antibiotics.

Ms. Clinton and Ms. Sibelius apologized to the government of Guatemala and the survivors and descendants of those infected. They called the experiments "clearly unethical."

President Álvaro Colom of Guatemala, who first learned of the experiments in a phone call from Mrs. Clinton, called them "hair-raising" and "crimes against humanity."

—*TIMES* STAFF

Pioneer of in Vitro Fertilization Wins Nobel Prize

The Nobel prize in physiology or medicine was awarded this year to Robert G. Edwards, an English biologist who with a physician colleague, Dr. Patrick Steptoe, developed the in vitro fertilization procedure for treating human infertility.

Since the birth of the first test tube baby, Louise Brown, on July 25, 1978, some four million babies worldwide have been conceived by mixing eggs and sperm outside the body and returning the embryo to the womb to resume the normal development. The procedure overcomes many previously untreatable causes of infertility and is used in 3 percent of all live births in developed countries.

Research with human embryonic stem cells, made possible by Dr. Edwards's development of in vitro fertilization, has aroused public outrage, but so far there are no offsetting practical benefits like the birth of healthy babies to eager parents. Because of the difficulty of stem cell research, such benefits may not be seen for many years, if ever.

—NICHOLAS WADE

Obituaries

Blanda, George, 83, NFL Hall of Fame quarterback and place-kicker whose career spanned four decades, 1949–75 in both the NFL (Chicago Bears, Oakland Raiders) and the AFL (Houston Oilers, Oakland Raiders); his 26 seasons are the most in league history; all-time scoring leader at the time of his retirement. After a brief illness, Sept. 27, 2010.

Curtis, Tony, 85, Bronx-born Bernie Schwartz was best known for donning a dress in *Some Like It Hot* (1959) and being cuffed to Sidney Poitier in *The Defiant Ones* (1958); equally adept in comedy and drama; other notable films include *Spartacus* (1960) and *Sweet Smell of Success* (1967). Of cardiac arrest, Henderson, Nev., Sept. 29, 2010

Fisher, Eddie, 82, 1950s pop singer who headlined with No. 1 hits like "Wish You Were Here" and "Oh! My Pa-Pa" as well as nightclub and TV shows; career dimmed by tabloid headlines when he dumped Debbie Reynolds for Elizabeth Taylor, who dumped him for Richard Burton. Of hip surgery complications, Berkeley, Calif., Sept. 22, 2010.

Penn, Arthur, 88, Philadelphia-born film, stage, and TV director who brought Method acting and New Wave sensibility to movies with his best-known work, *Bonnie and Clyde* (1967); TV's The *Miracle Worker* (1957) was Emmy winner as well as Tony and Oscar winner in stage and screen versions; other films include *Mickey One* (1965), *Alice's Restaurant* (1969), *Little Big Man* (1970), and *Missouri Breaks* (1976). Of congestive heart failure, New York, Sept. 28, 2010.

Stuart, Gloria, 100, 1930s movie actress in supporting roles with stars like Boris Karloff, James Cagney, and Shirley Temple; returned to Hollywood and Oscar nomination for *Titanic* (1997) as the 101-year-old survivor Rose Calvert. Of old age, Los Angeles, Sept. 26, 2010.

THE ALMANAC OF THE YEAR
Chronology of the Year Nov. 1, 2009–Sept. 30, 2010

NOVEMBER 2009

2 Hamid Karzai is officially declared the winner of the much-disputed presidential election in Afghanistan. Pres. Obama places a congratulatory call and also admonishes Mr. Karzai to take on the rampant corruption and drug trade that have fueled the resurgence of the Taliban.

A federal appeals court in Manhattan rules that Maher Arar, a Canadian man who claims that American officials sent him to Syria in 2002 to be tortured, cannot sue for damages because Congress has not authorized such suits.

3 Pres. Vaclav Klaus of the Czech Republic signs the Treaty of Lisbon, an agreement aimed at giving the European Union a global stature on par with major powers like the U.S. and China. The treaty, which required ratification by all 27 member states, will try to increase Europe's clout on foreign policy issues and will streamline the organization's decision-making.

4 The New York Yankees win the World Series, defeating the Philadelphia Phillies in Game 6 at Yankee Stadium. It is their 27th World Series victory and their first title since 2000.

The Senate votes unanimously to offer up to 20 more weeks of unemployment benefits, after weeks of delay in which hundreds of thousands of Americans exhausted their government aid. The measure increases to 99 weeks, the maximum length of time that a jobless worker can get benefits in some states.

5 Maj. Nidal Malik Hasan, an Army psychiatrist facing deployment, kills 12 people and wounds 31 others in a shooting rampage at the Fort Hood Army post in central Texas. The gunman is still alive after being shot four times by first-responders.

Democrats on the Environment and Public Works Committee push through a climate bill without any debate or participation by Republicans. The seven Republicans boycotted the committee meetings saying they had not had sufficient time to study the bill.

6 The Labor Department reports that the unemployment rate for October was 10.2 percent, up from 9.8 percent in September. More than one out of every six workers—17.5 percent—is unemployed or underemployed. The previous recorded high was 17.1 percent, in December 1982.

7 The House of Representatives votes 220 to 215 to approve a sweeping overhaul of the nation's health care system, in a measure that will cost $1.1 trillion over 10 years and will extend coverage to 36 million people now without insurance.

8 Iraq approves a law to administer a national election in January, a step that will allow the rapid withdrawal of American combat forces in early 2010. The compromise, which satisfied Kurds, Arabs, and Turkmens, is hailed as a demonstration of Parliament's ability to resolve sectarian disputes for the national benefit.

9 More than five months after holding parliamentary elections, Lebanon forms a new cabinet which includes 15 seats for the Western-aligned majority, 10 for the Hezbollah-led opposition, and five for Pres. Michel Suleiman, who has struggled to maintain neutrality.

The New York Times reports that U.S. intelligence agencies intercepted communications between the military psychiatrist accused of shooting 13 people at Fort Hood, Texas, and Anwar al-Awlaki, a radical cleric in Yemen known for his incendiary anti-American teachings. Federal authorities dropped an inquiry into the matter after deciding that the messages did not suggest any threat of violence.

12 The Immigration and Customs Enforcement office reports that federal authorities have identified more than 111,000 immigrants with criminal records being held in local jails. Among the immigrants identified through the program, known as Secure Communities, more than 11,000 had been charged with or convicted of the most serious crimes, and about 1,900 of those have been deported.

13 The Obama administration says that it will prosecute Khalid Shaikh Mohammed, the self-described mastermind of the Sept. 11 attacks, in a Manhattan federal courtroom. The decision is announced by Attorney General Eric H. Holder Jr., who says he will instruct prosecutors to seek death sentences for Mr. Mohammed and four accused co-conspirators.

NASA reports that their Lunar Crater Observation and Sensing Satellite (LCROSS) has found water on the moon. The satellite crashed into a crater near the Moon's south pole and carved out a hole 60 to 100 feet wide, kicking up at least 26 gallons of water.

16 The U.S. Preventative Services Task Force issues new guidelines stating that most women should start regular breast cancer screening at age 50, not 40. The new recommendations, which do not apply to women with unusual risk factors for breast cancer, reverse longstanding guidelines and are aimed at reducing harm from overtreatment. It also says women age 50 to 74 should have mammograms every two years, rather than every year.

Inspectors for the International Atomic Energy Agency, who gained access to Iran's newly revealed underground nuclear enrichment plant, release a report voicing strong suspicions that Iran is concealing other atomic facilities. Iran denies that it has built other hidden sites.

17 Israel says that it has advanced plans to expand a Jewish district of Jerusalem in territory that the Palestinians claim as part of their future state. The announcement comes as the Palestinians have begun seeking support for a plan to win the U.N. Security Council's recognition of a Palestinian state, without Israel's agreement, in the lands Israel won in 1967.

18 In an unannounced visit to Kabul, Sec. of State Hillary Rodham Clinton warns Pres. Hamid Karzai that future civilian aid will depend in part on how his government performs in areas like developing an effective army and curbing cronyism, saying that Mr. Karzai had begun to tackle corruption, but "not nearly enough."

Kathleen Sebelius, the secretary of health and human services, acknowledges that the recent recommendations regarding mammograms have "caused a great deal of confusion and worry," and says that government insurance programs will continue to cover routine mammograms for women starting at age 40.

A federal judge finds that poor maintenance of a major navigation channel by the Army Corps of Engineers led to some of the worst flooding after Hurricane Katrina. If upheld, the ruling could force the federal government to pay tens of millions of dollars to homeowners whose property was lost or damaged by water from the Mississippi River–Gulf Outlet.

19 On the heels of the hotly disputed guidelines regarding mammograms The American College of Obstetricians and Gynecologists releases new guidelines for cervical cancer screening which say that women should delay their first Pap test until age 21, and be screened less often than in the past.

Leaders of the 27 countries of the European Union choose Herman Van Rompuy, the Belgian prime minister, as the European Union's first president, and Catherine Ashton of Britain as its high representative for foreign policy.

Pres. Hamid Karzai of Afghanistan is inaugurated for a second term, promising to remedy the country's problems and to have the Afghan Army assume full control of security within five years. Mr. Karzai promises to create a transparent and accountable government and to fight corruption.

20 Scientists at CERN, the European Center for Nuclear Research, succeed in sending beams of protons clockwise around the 17-mile underground magnetic racetrack known as the Large Hadron Collider, the world's biggest and most expensive physics experiment. Physicists and engineers have spent the past year making repairs on the collider which was unable to handle the high currents required to run the collider at its intended energy.

21 The Senate votes to begin full debate on major health care legislation. The 60-to-39 vote, along party lines, clears the way for floor proceedings that will begin after Thanksgiving.

23 Iraq's effort to hold its parliamentary election in January collapses, raising the prospect of a political and constitutional crisis as the U.S. begins withdrawing the majority of its troops. The failure to agree on the terms of the election has inflamed ethnic and sectarian tensions.

24 Pres. Obama says that he is determined to "finish the job" in Afghanistan, and his aides signal to allies that he will send as many as 25,000 to 30,000 additional American troops there.

25 Pres. Obama pledges a provisional target for reductions in greenhouse gas emissions in the U.S., saying that the U.S. intends to reduce its greenhouse gas emissions "in the range of" 17 percent below 2005 levels by 2020 and 83 percent by 2050.

Prime Minister Benjamin Netanyahu of Israel announces his intention to halt new residential construction in West Bank settlements for 10 months as part of an effort to revive stalled Middle East peace talks. A top Palestinian official says the plan is not enough and the U.S. offers a mixed response.

26 The Chinese government announces that it has set a target to slow the growth of its greenhouse gas emissions by 2020 proposing to reduce carbon intensity—the amount of carbon dioxide emitted per unit of economic output—by 40 to 45 percent compared with 2005 levels.

27 The International Atomic Energy Agency demands that Iran immediately freeze operations at a once-secret uranium enrichment plant, a sharp rebuke that is endorsed by Russia and China.

28 The Obama administration announces a campaign to pressure mortgage companies to reduce payments for troubled homeowners, as evidence mounts that a $75 billion taxpayer-financed effort aimed at stemming foreclosures is foundering.

29 Iran refuses to comply with a demand by the U.N. nuclear agency to cease work on its nuclear fuel enrichment plant, and declares it will construct 10 more such plants. Iran's president, Mahmoud Ahmadinejad says his cabinet will also order a study of what it will take for Iran to enrich its existing stockpile of nuclear fuel.

The United Arab Emirates says that it will lend money to banks operating in Dubai in an effort to head off the kind of crisis of confidence that froze credit markets last year and brought the global economy to the brink of failure.

The Swiss overwhelmingly impose a national ban on the construction of minarets, the prayer towers of mosques. The referendum passed with a clear majority of 57.5 percent of voters, and in 22 of Switzerland's 26 cantons.

José Mujica, a former guerilla fighter, is elected president of Uruguay, cementing the hold of the Broad Front, a leftist movement credited with improving economic conditions in that country.

30 The Congressional Budget Office says that the Senate health bill could significantly reduce costs for many people who buy health insurance on their own, and that it will not substantially change premiums for the vast numbers of Americans who receive coverage from large employers.

Pres. Obama issues orders to send about 30,000 additional American troops to Afghanistan, conveying his decision to military leaders during a meeting in the Oval Office. The troop buildup will nearly triple the American military presence in Afghanistan that Mr. Obama inherited when he took office.

In an unsigned decision, the Supreme Court rules unanimously that a death penalty lawyer's failure to present evidence of the trauma his client suffered in combat in the Korean War requires a new sentencing hearing.

The Supreme Court vacates a lower court ruling that would have required the government to release photographs showing the abuse of prisoners in Iraq and Afghanistan. The decision follows the enactment of a law allowing the secretary of defense to block release of the pictures.

DECEMBER 2009

2 Less than a year after receiving two multibillion-dollar bailouts from Washington, Bank of America announces that it will repay all of its federal aid—$45 billion—underscoring the banking industry's swift recovery from the gravest financial crisis since the Depression.

3 The White House authorizes an expansion of the C.I.A.'s drone program in Pakistan's lawless tribal areas to parallel the president's decision to send 30,000 more troops to Afghanistan. Officials hope to eliminate any haven for militants in the region.

4 In the best report since the recession began two years ago, the Labor Department reports that the unemployment rate for November dipped to 10 percent, from 10.2 percent the previous month, and that only 11,000 jobs were lost.

NATO announces that it plans to commit an additional 7,000 soldiers to the coalition in Afghanistan, portraying the pledge as a powerful vote of support for the American-led effort. NATO's secretary general declined to specify which countries will be sending troops, or when.

7 David C. Headley of Chicago is charged with helping plot the 2008 rampage in Mumbai, India, that left 163 people dead. The suspect is accused of helping identify targets for the Pakistani-based terrorist group called Lashkar-e-Taiba.

The Environmental Protection Agency issues a final ruling that greenhouse gases pose a danger to human health and the environment, paving the way for regulation of carbon dioxide emissions from vehicles, power plants, factories, refineries, and other major sources.

8 The federal government announces that it intends to pay $3.4 billion to settle claims that it has mismanaged the revenue in American Indian trust funds, potentially ending one of the largest class-action lawsuits ever brought against the U.S. The tentative agreement will resolve a 13-year-old lawsuit over hundreds of thousands of land trust accounts that date to the 19th century.

Pres. Hamid Karzai says that Afghanistan will not be able to pay for its own security until at least 2024, underscoring the government's long-term financial dependence on the U.S. and NATO.

11 The House of Representatives approves a Democratic plan to tighten federal regulation of Wall Street and banks, voting 223 to 202 to approve the measure which will create an agency to protect consumers from abusive lending practices, set rules for the trading of some of the sophisticated financial instruments that fueled the crisis, and take steps to reduce the threat that the failure of one or two huge banks or investment firms could topple the entire economy.

12 The U.S. begins talks with Russia and a U.N. arms control committee about strengthening Internet security and limiting military use of cyberspace. Officials familiar with the talks say the Obama administration realizes that more nations are developing cyberweapons and that a new approach is needed to blunt an international arms race.

13 The Senate approves a $446.8 billion spending package that will keep much of the federal government running through next September, but Democrats are deeply divided over efforts to substantially raise the federal debt limit before Congress quits for the year.

14 China and the U.S. are at an impasse at the U.N. climate change conference in Copenhagen over how compliance with any treaty can be monitored and verified. China is refusing to accept any kind of international monitoring, and the U.S. insists that without stringent verification, it cannot support any deal.

16 The Palestine Liberation Organization indefinitely extends the term of Pres. Mahmoud Abbas. Mr. Abbas had called for presidential and parliamentary elections to be held on Jan. 24, but Pales-

tinian election officials said the voting could not be held because Hamas, the Islamic group that controls Gaza, will not allow them to begin preparations for the elections there.

The House approves a short-term $200 billion increase in federal borrowing power and also approves a $626 billion Pentagon spending measure. The Pentagon measure, which passed on a vote of 395 to 34, pays for continuing operations in Iraq and Afghanistan.

18 In Copenhagen, Pres. Obama announces that five major nations have together forged a climate deal. The agreement negotiated between the U.S., China, India, Brazil, and South Africa provides a system for monitoring and reporting progress toward national pollution-reduction goals and sets a goal of limiting the global temperature rise to 2 degrees Celsius above preindustrial levels by 2050.

19 Senate Democrats say that they have clinched an agreement on a far-reaching overhaul of the nation's health care system, and forge ahead with efforts to approve the legislation by Christmas. Sen. Ben Nelson, Democrat of Nebraska, agreed to back the bill after 13 hours of negotiations, making him the pivotal 60th vote for the measure.

21 Transportation Secretary Ray LaHood announces stiff penalties on airlines that keep passengers waiting too long on the tarmac without feeding them or letting them off the plane. Under the new rules, airlines that do not provide food and water after two hours, or a chance to disembark after three hours, will face penalties of $27,500 a passenger.

A U.N. panel investigating the massacre and rape of unarmed protesters in Guinea three months ago says that the nation's military ruler and some of his adjutants should be referred to the International Criminal Court for "crimes against humanity." The violence, which occurred on September 28, left at least 156 people dead or missing and about 109 women raped or sexually abused.

22 Jordan's King Abdullah II dismisses the prime minister and replaces him with a palace aide and loyalist, then dissolves Parliament and postpones legislative elections for a year. The decisions are widely seen as an effort to push through financial measures to shore up an economy burdened by debt, but the moves demonstrate the leadership's continued intention to suppress the political process.

24 The Senate votes, in a 60-to-39 party line vote, to reinvent the nation's health care system, passing a bill to guarantee access to health insurance for tens of millions of Americans and to rein in health costs.

25 A Nigerian man with possible terrorist ties sneaks an explosive onto a trans-Atlantic Northwest Airlines flight from Amsterdam and tries to ignite it as the plane prepared to land in Detroit. The device failed to fully detonate.

26 Federal authorities charge Umar Farouk Abdulmutallab, a 23-year-old Nigerian man, with trying to blow up a Detroit-bound airliner saying that he had obtained the elements of the device from a bomb expert in Yemen associated with Al Qaeda. The man's father had recently told officials at the U.S. Embassy in Nigeria that he was concerned about his son's increasingly extremist religious views.

27 Thai military officers begin to forcibly return 4,000 Hmong asylum seekers to Laos. The tribe aided the U.S. in its secret war in Laos and the asylum seekers say they fear retribution by the Laotian government. Thailand is moving ahead with the repatriation despite complaints from the U.S., the U.N., and human rights groups.

28 Israel announces that it will build nearly 700 housing units in Jewish areas of Jerusalem, on territory won in the 1967 war that Palestinians claim for their future state. The move is criticized by Washington and condemned by Palestinian leaders, who cite it as evidence that the Israelis are undermining efforts to restart peace talks.

29 Pres. Obama declares that there had been a "systemic failure" of the nation's security apparatus after being told about missed signals and uncorrelated intelligence that should have prevented a would-be bomber from boarding a flight for the U.S.

31 In a significant blow to the Justice Department, a federal judge throws out the indictment of five former Blackwater security guards over a shooting in Baghdad in 2007 that left 17 Iraqis dead and about 20 wounded. The judge cited misuse of statements made by the guards writing that the government's mishandling of the case "requires dismissal of the indictment against all the defendants."

JANUARY 2010

1 A suicide bomber rams a truck loaded with hundreds of pounds of explosives into families and children crowded on a playground in northwest Pakistan, underscoring their determination to prevent Pakistani citizens from forming armed militias to keep the Taliban at bay.

Police in Copenhagen foil an attempt to kill an artist who drew a cartoon depicting the Prophet Muhammad that sparked outrage in the Muslim world. Police say a Somali man armed with an axe and a knife tried to enter the home of the artist, Kurt Westergaard.

2 Lawmakers in Afghanistan resoundingly reject most of Pres. Hamid Karzai's nominees for cabinet posts and express discontent with the candidates' competence. Of Mr. Karzai's 24 nominees, 17 are rejected and 7 approved.

3 The U.S. and Britain close their embassies in the capital of Yemen, citing continuing threats from Al Qaeda in the Arabian Peninsula.

Ben S. Bernanke, the Federal Reserve chairman, says that regulatory failure, not low interest rates, is responsible for the housing bubble of the last decade and subsequent financial crisis, stating that stronger regulation aimed at underwriting practices and risk management would have been more effective to constraining the housing bubble than an increase in interest rates.

5 The U.N. World Food Program announces that it is suspending food deliveries to one million people in southern Somalia indefinitely after weeks of intimidation, threats, and harassment.

The U.S. reopens its embassy in Yemen a day after Yemeni security forces kill two people suspected of being member of Al Qaeda and linked to the threats against several diplomatic outposts.

The U.S. court of appeals for the District of Columbia Circuit backs the powers of the government to hold Guantánamo detainees and other noncitizens suspected of committing terrorist acts, finding that the presidential war power to detain those suspected of terrorism is not limited, even by international law of war.

7 The E.P.A. proposes a stricter standard for smog-causing pollutants that will bring substantial health benefits to Americans while imposing large costs on industry and local governments. The standard will replace one set by the Bush administration which has been challenged in court as too weak to adequately protect human health and the environment.

Pres. Obama orders intelligence agencies to take a series of steps to streamline how terrorism threats are pursued and analyzed, and directs the Homeland Security Department to speed the installation of $1 billion in advanced-technology equipment for the screening of passengers.

8 The Labor Department reports that the nation lost 85,000 jobs in December and that the unemployment rate held steady at 10 percent.

10 North Korea proposes talks with the U.S. to reach a formal peace treaty that will replace the truce that halted the Korean War 57 years ago, indicating that it will not give up its nuclear weapons until Washington signs such an accord.

11 Google says it will stop cooperating with Chinese Internet censorship and will consider shutting down its operations in the country altogether. Since 2006, Google had an arrangement with the government that purged its Chinese search results of banned topics, but came under fire for abetting a system that restricts what citizens can read online.

A fierce earthquake strikes Haiti, leveling countless buildings and dwellings. The earthquake, the worst in the region in more than 200 years, leaves the country in shambles with no electricity or telephones. In the chaos it is impossible for officials to determine how many people have been killed and injured.

12 Haiti lies in ruins as Pres. René Préval calls the death toll "unimaginable" in the wake of a 7.0 magnitude earthquake. Relief agencies around the world begin to marshal resources to send to the devastated nation.

The Obama administration appoints Michael R. Taylor, a veteran food expert, as deputy commissioner for foods at the Food and Drug Administration, a newly created position designed to oversee the agency's food and nutrition programs.

14 The White House, Congressional leaders, and labor unions say they have reached agreement on a proposal to tax high-cost health insurance policies. The changes will lessen and delay the impact of the tax on workers and will reduce the amount of revenue collected, resolving one of the key issues in the overhaul of the U.S. health-care system.

15 The Obama administration extends special immigration status to Haitians living illegally in the U.S. that protects them from deportation for 18 months, because their safety would be at risk if they returned to Haiti. The special status will cover at least 100,000 Haitians living in the U.S. illegally, as well as 30,000 Haitians who had been ordered deported.

A Pentagon review of the shooting rampage at Fort Hood, Texas in November concludes that the Department of Defense was poorly prepared to defend itself from internal threats and that the government has not achieved the communication and agility among intelligence agencies that has been sought since the attacks of Sept. 11.

16 International officials and aid workers admit that only a small part of the aid is reaching Haitians without food, water, or shelter. Reports of isolated looting and violence intensify and there are reports of Haitians streaming out of the capital.

17 Sebastián Piñera, a billionaire businessman and former senator, breaks the 20-year hold on power of a leftist coalition, becoming the first right-wing president to be elected in Chile since the dictatorship ended in 1990.

18 A team of Taliban militants launch a spectacular assault at the heart of the Afghan government with two men detonating suicide bombs and the rest fighting to the death only yards away from the presidential palace.

19 Scott Brown, a little-known Republican state senator decisively defeats Martha Coakley, the state's attorney general, in an election to fill the Senate seat that was long held by Edward M. Kennedy in the overwhelmingly Democratic state of Massachusetts.

21 Overruling two precedents about the First Amendment rights of corporations, the Supreme Court rules that the government may not ban political spending by corporations in candidate elections. The 5-to-4 decision in *Citizens United v. Federal Election Commission*, will have major political and practical consequences and is likely to reshape the way elections are conducted.

23 Vice President Joseph R. Biden promises Iraqi leaders that the U.S. will appeal the dismissal of manslaughter charges against five Blackwater Worldwide security contractors involved in a deadly shooting that has inflamed anti-American tensions.

25 Ali Hassan al-Majid, a symbol of the former government of Saddam Hussein who ordered a poison gas attack on a Kurdish village in northern Iraq is executed. Mr. Majid was sentenced to death for his role in the 1988 attack in which more than 5,000 Kurds died.

The Supreme Court refuses the block the extradition to France of Manuel Antonio Noriega, the deposed Panamanian dictator. Mr. Noriega completed his prison sentence for drug crimes in the U.S. but has been convicted in absentia in France of money-laundering offenses.

26 Pres. Obama plans to establish, by executive order, a bipartisan commission to press for tax increases and spending cuts. The panel will make recommendations to reduce annual budget deficits and slow or reverse the growth of the national debt but cannot force Congress to vote on their suggestions.

27 In his State of the Union address, Pres. Obama vows not to give up on his ambitious legislative agenda, focusing on job creation, health care, new regulations on banks, and energy legislation.

The deposed former Honduran president, Manuel Zelaya, flies into exile as the country inaugurates a new president, Porfirio Lobo. Mr. Zelaya's departure to the Dominican Republic ends a protracted political crisis that began in June 2009.

28 The Senate gives Ben S. Bernanke a second four-year term as the head of the Federal Reserve after critics excoriated the central bank's conduct in the years leading up to the financial crisis. The 70-to-30 vote is the weakest endorsement ever extended to a chairman in the Fed's 96-year history.

29 The Obama administration gives up on its plan to try the Sept. 11 plotters in Lower Manhattan, bowing to almost unanimous pressure from New York officials and business leaders to move the terrorism trial elsewhere.

A new report reveals that the U.S. economy grew at its fastest pace in more than six years at the end of 2009. Gross domestic product, the broadest measure of economic activity, expanded at an annual rate of 5.7 percent in the fourth quarter, after a 2.2 percent increase the previous quarter.

The Obama administration approves an arms sales package to Taiwan worth more than $8 billion, a move that enrages China and may complicate Pres. Obama's effort to enlist Beijing's cooperation on Iran.

30 The Obama administration accelerates the deployment of new defenses against possible Iranian missile attacks in the Persian Gulf, placing special ships off the Iranian coast and antimissile systems in at least four Arab countries.

Pres. Obama sends a $3.8 trillion budget to Congress for the coming fiscal year that will increase financing for education and for civilian research programs by more than 6 percent and provide $25 billion for cash-starved states.

31 The Obama administration proposes a sweeping overhaul of Pres. Bush's signature education law, No Child Left Behind, and calls for broad changes in how schools are judged to be succeeding or failing, as well as for the elimination of the law's 2014 deadline for bringing every American child to academic proficiency.

The White House says that it will resume a U.S. military airlift of Haitians seriously injured in the Jan. 12 earthquake, reversing a five-day suspension that doctors worried would strand patients with devastating injuries. The flights were halted after Florida officials complained that their hospitals were overwhelmed.

FEBRUARY 2010

1 Fifty-five developed and developing countries submit their emission reduction plans to the U.N. Framework Convention on Climate Change, in accordance with an agreement reached in Copenhagen in December, restating earlier pledges to curb emissions by 2020. Mexico and Russia did not submit plans by the Jan. 31 deadline.

2 Defense Secretary Robert Gates and Adm. Mike Mullen, the chairman of the Joint Chiefs of Staff call for an end to the 17-year-old "don't ask, don't tell" law, a major step toward allowing openly gay men and women to serve in the U.S. military.

3 Ten Americans who tried to take 33 Haitian children out of the country without the government's consent are charged with child abduction and criminal conspiracy. The Americans intended to take the children to an orphanage in the Dominican Republic but acknowledge that they failed to get approval and that several of the children have one living parent.

Romanian officials approve an American proposal to base missile interceptors there, saying the system would be working by 2015.

4 The Labor Department reports that the unemployment rate for January dipped to 9.7 percent from 10 percent in December. The economy lost 20,000 net jobs during the month.

The prime ministers of Britain and Ireland announce a breakthrough agreement to transfer Northern Ireland's police and justice system from Britain to local control on April 12. Transfer of power has been the most contentious issue still outstanding in the effort to bring peace to the six British-ruled counties of Northern Ireland.

5 Finance ministers from the Group of 7 conclude a meeting in Canada with pledges to maintain their fiscal stimulus programs, despite worries among investors about the mounting debts of some European governments.

7 Iran's president, Mahmoud Ahmedinejad orders his atomic scientists to begin enriching their stockpile of uranium in order to power a medical reactor. The order is the latest in a series of signals about Iran's intentions regarding the country's uranium stockpile.

9 Nigeria's National Assembly votes to make Vice President Goodluck Jonathan the acting president, filling a power vacuum that has existed in Africa's most populous nation since Pres. Umaru Yar'Adua left the country for medical treatment in November.

The F.D.A. says it will take steps to more stringently regulate three of the most potent forms of medical radiation, including CT scans, some of which deliver the radiation equivalent of 400 chest X-rays. The move follows a report that more than 300 patients in four hospitals were over-radiated.

11 The Senate reaches a rare bipartisan agreement on steps to spur job creation. Sen. Harry Reid, the majority leader, says he will take four core job-creating initiatives from the proposal—including tax breaks for businesses that hire unemployed workers and increased public works spending—and seek to move those rapidly through the Senate.

The Senate unanimously confirms more than two dozen of Pres. Obama's nominees to federal positions after threats that the president might use the President's Day break to make recess appointments.

12 A force of 6,000 American, Afghan, and British troops attack the Taliban fortress of Marja, moving to destroy the insurgency's largest haven and begin a campaign to reassert the dominance of the Afghan government.

14 On the second day of a major allied offensive around Marja, an errant American rocket strikes a compound crowded with Afghan civilians, killing at least 10 people, including five children. Avoiding such civilian deaths is a cornerstone of the war strategy of Gen. Stanley A. McChrystal, who apologizes to Pres. Hamid Karzai for the tragic loss of life.

15 Mullah Abdul Ghani Baradar, the Taliban's top military commander, is captured in Karachi, Pakistan, in a secret joint operation by Pakistani and American intelligence forces.

Senator Evan Bayh of Indiana announces that he will not seek reelection, describing the Senate as frozen by partisan politics and incapable of passing even basic legislation. This is the latest in a series of setbacks for the Democrats since Pres. Obama came into office.

16 A study released by the Inter-American Development Bank says that the devastating earthquake in Haiti has caused between $7.2 billion and $13.2 billion in damage. Earlier estimates hovered around $5 billion.

17 A Haitian judge orders the release of eight of the 10 Americans arrested on child abduction charges but decide that two members of the group, including its leader, will remain in jail for additional questioning.

18 More than eight years after anthrax-laced letters killed five people the F.B.I closes its investigation, adding new details to its case that the 2001 attacks were carried out by Bruce E. Ivins, an Army biodefense expert who killed himself in 2008.

19 The Sunni political party whose two most prominent leaders were disqualified from next month's parliamentary elections in Iraq call for a boycott of the vote, raising fears of worsening sectarian tensions in the campaign.

20 A last-ditch effort to keep Dutch troops in Afghanistan brings down the government in the Netherlands. Dutch leaders had promised to bring home most of the troops this year, but Prime Minister Jan Peter Balkenende tried to find a compromise to extend the Dutch presence on a scaled-back basis, leading the Labor Party to pull out of the government.

The U.S. lifts an advisory that warned American travelers about security concerns in Syria as Washington tries to thaw relations with the Syrians, who are seen as crucial to peace in the Middle East.

21 Pres. Obama proposes giving the federal government new power to block excessive rate increases by health insurance companies. Mr. Obama is seizing on outrage about recent premium increases of up to 39 percent announced by Anthem Blue Cross of California.

The Obama administration proposes a change to the No Child Left Behind law that will require states to adopt "college-and career-ready standards" in reading and mathematics to qualify for federal money from a $14 billion program that concentrates on impoverished students.

22 Najibullah Zazi, the Afghan immigrant at the center of an Al Qaeda plot to detonate a bomb in the New York subway pleads guilty to terrorism charges, characterizing the plot as a "martyrdom operation" that he was just days away from executing when he was arrested.

Five Republican senators break ranks with their party to advance a $15 billion job-creation measure put forward by Democrats, clearing the way for a Senate vote on a measure which is expected to create tens of thousands of jobs.

24 The Supreme Court rules that police can request a suspect who has invoked his Miranda rights, but they must wait until 14 days after the suspect has been released from custody. Justice Antonin Scalia wrote for seven justices in *Maryland v. Shatzer*. The ruling does not dispose of the case.

25 China reaffirms its resolve to punish the U.S. over its decision to sell weapons to Taiwan and suggests that there will be even greater consequences if Washington fulfills a long-standing request by Taiwan for advanced fighter jets.

India and Pakistan take a first step toward rebuilding confidence after a wide-ranging meeting between high-level diplomats of both countries that included discussions on terrorism, the Mumbai attacks, the border region of Kashmir, and competing water claims.

26 Sen. Jim Bunning of Kentucky refuses to allow the Senate to take up a House measure that provides another 30 days of unemployment benefits, insisting the money be offset by other savings. The impasse will cause benefits to run out for thousands of Americans.

27 A deadly 8.8-magnitude earthquake strikes central Chile, killing at least 200 people, and displacing more than 1.5 million. Pres. Michelle Bachelet calls the quake "one of the worst tragedies in the last 50 years," and declares a state of emergency.

MARCH 2010

1 The Chilean government asks for outside aid in the wake of a devastating earthquake, requesting generators, water filtration equipment and field hospitals, as well as expert help to assess the damage.

2 Radovan Karadzic, the Bosnian Serb wartime leader, denies charges that his troops committed large-scale atrocities during the Bosnian war in 1995, saying that the war crimes tribunal in The Hague should withdraw his indictment and throw out the prison sentences given to some of his generals.

The Senate ends a politically charged impasse over unemployment pay, voting to provide another month of benefits to jobless Americans. The bipartisan 78-to-19 vote will also allow 2,000 federal workers furloughed from the Dept. of Transportation to return to work.

3 Rep. Charles B. Rangel of New York steps down as chairman of the House Ways and Means Committee after losing support within his party because of ethics violations, saying he is leaving the post to prevent Republicans from forcing a vote on ousting him from the position.

The Parliament in Ukraine passes a vote of no confidence in Prime Minister Yulia V. Tymoshenko, ousting the last of the Orange Revolution leaders from power.

Washington D.C. becomes the sixth place in the nation where same-sex marriages can take place. The mayor signed the measure into law in December, but because the District of Columbia is not a state, the law had to undergo Congressional review.

4 The House approves a $15 billion measure intended to spur job creation by granting tax breaks to businesses that hire workers. The measure was pushed through on mainly party lines.

The House Foreign Affairs Committee votes to condemn as genocide the mass killings of Armenians early in the last century, defying a last-minute plea from the Obama administration to forgo a vote that is likely to jeopardize Turkish-Armenian reconciliation.

5 The Labor Department reports that the American economy lost 36,000 jobs in February, while the unemployment rate remains unchanged at 9.7 percent. Compared with earlier monthly job losses, most economists construe the report as a sign that a tenuous recovery is gaining momentum.

7 In spite of deadly attacks in Baghdad and other cities, Iraqis go to the polls to choose a new Parliament. At least 38 people are killed in Baghdad, but voter turnout was higher than expected, and

could signal a fundamental weakening of the insurgency's power.

The Palestine Liberation Organization agrees to hold U.S.-mediated peace talks with Israel for four months, effectively ending a 14-month breakdown in communications between the two sides. The decision follows an agreement by the Arab League in Cairo to endorse indirect talks between the Palestinians and Israelis.

8 Officials and human rights groups in Nigeria increase the count of the dead after a weekend of vicious ethnic violence, saying that as many as 500 people may have been killed as a result of tensions between Christians and Muslims.

Vice President Joseph R. Biden, begins a five-day visit to the Middle East as part of an American effort to restart Israeli-Palestinian peace talks and to keep Israel focused on relying on sanctions against Iran's nuclear program rather than on unilateral military action.

9 Hours after Vice President Joseph R. Biden vowed American support for Israel's security, Israel's Interior Minister, Eli Yishai, announces 1,600 new housing units for Jews in East Jerusalem. Mr. Biden condemns the move as "precisely the kind of step that undermines the trust we need right now."

China and India formally agree to join the international climate change agreement reached in December in Copenhagen, Denmark, the last two major economies to sign on. They join nearly 200 countries that have signed the accord.

Colleen R. LaRose, a Pennsylvania woman who on the Internet calls herself JihadJane, is indicted in an alleged assassination plot against a Lars Vilks, a Swedish cartoonist who depicted the prophet Muhammad atop the body of a dog. A group linked to Al Qaeda had put a $100,000 bounty on his head for the cartoon.

10 House Democratic leaders ban budget earmarks to private industry, ending a practice that has steered billions of dollars in no-bid contracts to companies and set off corruption scandals. The ban is the most forceful step yet in an effort by Congress to curb abuses in the use of earmarks.

In a strong bipartisan endorsement of the Obama administration's policy in Afghanistan, the House of Representatives rejects a call to withdraw American troops by the end of the year. After a three-hour debate, the House votes 356–65 to reject the withdrawal proposal.

11 Chile's first right-wing leader in 20 years, Sebastián Piñera, is sworn in as its new president as the earthquake-ravaged country suffers from strong aftershocks which almost overshadow the inauguration.

Pres. Obama makes good on his promise to give his $1.4 million in Nobel Peace Prize money to charity and releases the names of the organizations that will benefit, including Fisher House, the Clinton Bush Haiti Fund, and the Posse Foundation.

12 After three days of turbulent meetings, the Texas Board of Education approves a social studies curriculum that will put a conservative stamp on history and economics textbooks, stressing the superiority of American capitalism, questioning the Founding Fathers' commitment to a purely secular government, and presenting Republican political philosophy in a more positive light.

13 The Obama administration calls for a broad overhaul of Pres. George W. Bush's No Child Left Behind law, proposing to reshape provisions that encourage instructors to teach to tests, narrow the curriculum, and label one in three American schools as failing.

14 Prime Minister Benjamin Netanyahu of Israel tells his cabinet that the ill-timed announcement of new housing plans for a Jewish neighborhood in East Jerusalem during a visit by Vice President Joseph R. Biden had been "regrettable" and "hurtful," but he did not indicate that the building project would be cancelled.

Tens of thousands of protesters pour into Bangkok demanding that the government step down. Prime Minister Abhisit Vejjajiva came to power in December 2008 after a court forced the dissolution of the previous government by disbanding a political party loyal to Thaksin Shinawatra, who had been ousted in a military coup four years ago. Mr. Abhisit called the protesters' demands "impractical."

15 Gen. Stanley A. McChrystal, the top American commander in Afghanistan tells Afghan officials that he has brought most American Special Operations forces under his direct control, out of concern over continued civilian casualties and disorganization among units in the field. Afghan official and others say that Special Operations forces have been responsible for a large number of civilian casualties, and operate by their own rules.

Peter Hullermann, the priest at the center of a German sexual-abuse scandal, is suspended from his duties after continuing to work with children for more than 30 years after being convicted by a German court of molesting boys.

17 In a rare bipartisan vote, the Senate approves and sends to Pres. Obama a bill intended to spur employment by providing businesses with incentives to hire new workers. The legislation, approved 68–29, will give employers an exemption from payroll taxes through the end of 2010 on workers they hire who have been unemployed for at least 60 days, and also extends the federal highway construction program, and takes other steps to bolster public improvement projects.

18 Delegates at a U.N. conference on endangered species in Doha, Qatar, defeat American-supported proposals to ban international trade in bluefin tuna and to protect polar bears. Juan Carlos Vásquez, a spokesman for the U.N. says "It wasn't a very good day for conservation."

Sen. Charles E. Schumer, Democrat of New York, and Lindsey Graham, Republican of South Carolina, unveil the outlines of a proposal to overhaul the immigration system, which would require illegal immigrants to admit they broke the law before they could gain legal status and require all workers in the United States to carry a biometric identity card to prove that they are eligible to work.

20 Pres. Obama delivers his second message to the Iranian people for the festival of Nowruz, which marks the Iranian New Year, releasing a video in which he again offers Iran's leaders engagement with the U.S. The Obama administration has recently pushed for a new round of international sanctions.

Faced with a church sexual abuse scandal spreading across Europe, Pope Benedict XVI apologizes directly to victims and their families in Ireland, expressing "shame and remorse" for what he calls "sinful and criminal" acts committed by members of the clergy.

21 House Democrats approve a far-reaching overhaul of the nation's health system, voting over unanimous Republican opposition to provide medical coverage to tens of millions of uninsured Americans after an epic political battle. With the 219–212 vote, in which 34 Democrats voted against the bill, the House gives final approval to legislation passed by the Senate on Christmas Eve.

Prime Minister Nuri Kamal al-Maliki endorses calls for a recount of Iraq's parliamentary election, as the latest results show his main competitor with a slight lead. Pres. Jalal Talabani also calls for a recount. The appeals by Iraq's two highest government officials add to the rash of complaints related to how the March 7 election was conducted. With 95 percent of the vote counted, former Prime Minister Ayad Allawi's Iraqiya alliance lead Mr. Maliki's State of Law coalition by about 11,000 votes, out of 12 million

Ayatollah Ali Khamenei, Iran's supreme leader, sharply denounces the U.S., accusing it of plotting to overthrow the clerical leadership in a chilly response to an overture by Pres. Obama for better cultural ties.

22 Google closes its Internet search service in China and begins directing users to its uncensored search engine in Hong Kong, in an effort to skirt Chinese censorship requirements and intrusions by hackers.

During a flurry of meetings in the U.S., Prime Minister Benjamin Netanyahu of Israel serves notice that his government will not yield easily to American demands regarding the construction of Jewish housing in Jerusalem. In a speech to a pro-Israel lobbying group, Mr. Netanyahu reiterates that Israel has no plans to freeze housing in Jerusalem.

Members of Parliament from Turkey's religious conservative governing party propose constitutional changes that will make it harder to ban political parties and easier to prosecute military officials in civilian courts. The military has been the enforcer of a strong separation between Islam and the state, but there have been accusations that current and former military officers plotted a coup against the governing Justice and Development Party, in 2003.

23 Pres. Obama, with 20 pens, signs health care reform into law at ceremonies in the East Room of the White House. The Patient Protection and Affordable Care Act is the most expansive social legislation enacted in decades, which enshrines "the core principle that everybody should have some basic security when it comes to their health care."

24 Russia discloses that Russian and Chinese envoys have pressed Iran's government to accept a U.N. plan on uranium enrichment, but that Iran has refused, leaving "less and less room for diplomatic maneuvering." An official in the Russian Foreign Ministry says that Russia will consider supporting sanctions tailored to prevent the spread of nuclear weapons.

Democratic lawmakers receive death threats and are the victims of vandalism because of their votes in favor of the new health care bill. Rep. Steny H. Hoyer, Democrat of Maryland, and the majority leader, says at least 10 House members have raised concerns about their personal safety and at least two Congressional district offices were vandalized.

25 The Obama administration announces broad new initiatives to help troubled homeowners, potentially refinancing several million of them into fresh government-backed mortgages with lower payments.

Pakistan and the U.S. wrap up two days of high-level talks with a raft of economic development initiatives, an agreement to hasten deliveries of military hardware, and a promise to put their often mistrustful relationship on a new footing. The countries also say they will "redouble efforts to deal effectively with terrorism, and will work together for peace and stability in Afghanistan."

Congress votes to force commercial banks out of the federal student loan market, cutting off billions of dollars in profits in a sweeping restructuring of financial-aid programs and redirecting most of the money to new education initiatives. Republicans unanimously opposed the bill in both chambers.

26 The secular party of Ayad Allawi, a former interim prime minister, wins a wafer-thin victory in Iraq's election. The outcome is immediately challenged by Prime Minister Nuri Kamal al-Maliki and his supporters. Iraqi political experts say they doubt that Mr. Allawi will succeed in assembling a governing coalition.

A South Korean Navy patrol ship sinks near the disputed western maritime border with North Korea after suffering damage to its hull, raising suspicions about the possible involvement of North Korea, whose navy has skirmished with South Korean ships in the waters off the Korean Peninsula.

Maj. Gen. Robert A. Harding, a retired Army intelligence officer and Pres. Obama's choice to lead the Transportation Security Administration, abruptly withdraws his nomination amid questions about his work as a defense contractor. This is the second time the White House has lost a nominee for this critical security post.

27 Pres. Obama says he will bypass the Senate and install 15 appointees during Congress's spring recess, including a union lawyer whose nomination to the National Labor Relations Board was blocked last month with the help of two Democrats. The White House said the 15 nominees had been waiting, on average, seven months to be confirmed.

28 Pres. Obama makes an unannounced visit to Kabul, Afghanistan to personally deliver criticism to Pres. Hamid Karzai regarding corruption within his administration, and the pace of fulfilling promises regarding possible reintegration with certain reconcilable members of the Taliban insurgency.

29 Explosions set off by female suicide bombers during the morning rush hour in two landmark subway stations in Moscow kill at least 38 people and wound scores of others, raising fears that the Muslim insurgency in southern Russia, including Chechnya, is being brought to the heart of the country.

Members of the party of Daw Aung San Suu Kyi, the long-detained pro-democracy leader, defy Myanmar's junta by announcing that they will boycott the country's first elections in two decades. Western governments say that Mrs. Aung San Suu Kyi's participation and that of her party are prerequisites for legitimate elections.

30 The Obama administration proposes to open vast expanses of water along the Atlantic coastline, the eastern Gulf of Mexico and the north coast of Alaska to oil and natural gas drilling for the first time. The proposal ends a longstanding moratorium on oil exploration along the East Coast, covering 167 million acres of ocean.

A report published by Amnesty International says that China executed more people last year than the rest of the world combined, saying that there were "thousands" of Chinese executions in 2009. By comparison, 714 people were executed in 17 other countries, led by Iran, Iraq, Saudi Arabia, and the United States.

Pres. Obama signs legislation to expand college access for millions of young Americans by revamping the federal student loan program. The new law will eliminate fees paid to private banks to act as intermediaries in providing loans to college students, and use much of the nearly $68 billion in savings over 11 years to expand Pell grants and make it easier for students to repay outstanding loans after graduating.

31 A federal judge in the Federal District Court in San Francisco rules that the National Security Agency's program of surveillance without warrants is illegal. In a 45-page opinion, the judge states that the government violated a 1978 federal statute requiring court approval for domestic surveillance when it intercepted phone calls of Al Haramain, a now-defunct Islamic charity in Oregon, and of two lawyers representing it, in 2004.

Doku Umarov, a former Chechen separatist and a proponent of global jihad, takes responsibility for two suicide bombings on Moscow's subway. His announcement may provide Prime Minister Vladimir V. Putin with a fresh rationale to pursue a take-no-prisoners policy in the Caucasus because of its threat to Russia's security.

The secretary of the Army, John M. McHugh, says that he is effectively ignoring the "don't ask, don't tell" law because he has no intention of pursuing discharges of active-duty service members who have recently told him that they are gay. Pres. Obama, Defense Secretary Robert M. Gates, and Adm. Mike Mullen, the chairman of the Joint Chiefs of Staff, have all called on Congress to repeal the 17-year-old law and allow gay service members to serve openly.

APRIL 2010

1 Pres. Obama signs off on new security protocols for people flying to the U.S., establishing a system that uses intelligence information and assessment of threats to identify passengers who could have links to terrorism. The new approach will replace a broader layer of extra scrutiny that has been imposed recently on all passengers from 14 countries, most of which are Muslim.

Sen. John Kerry, a Massachusetts Democrat and chairman of the Senate Foreign Relations Committee meets with Pres. Bashar al-Assad of Syria in Damascus, another indication that the U.S. is moving to reengage with Syria as the Obama administration works to resuscitate Middle East peace talks.

2 The Labor Department reports that employers added 162,000 non-farm jobs in March, while the nationwide unemployment rate held steady at 9.7 percent. The economy needs to add more than

100,000 jobs a month just to absorb new entrants into the labor market, let alone provide a livelihood for the 15 million Americans looking for work.

3 Twenty-five members of a prominent Sunni family are killed in the Iraqi village of Hawr Rajab by killers passing as American military personnel. Most of the 19 male victims were members of Iraqi security forces or of Awakening Councils, groups that partner with American forces, but who are often branded by Al Qaeda as traitors.

4 Salvage experts and a tugboat crew struggle to save a large Chinese freighter that slammed into the Great Barrier Reef off Australia over the weekend, trying to prevent the vessel from breaking apart as some of the 1,075 tons of engine fuel in its tanks begins oozing from the hull, threatening the world's largest collection of coral.

5 The U.S. Transportation Department says it will seek a $16.4 million fine against Toyota because the company had failed to promptly notify the government about potential problems with accelerator pedals. The fine would be the largest civil penalty assessed by the government against a car company.

Pres. Obama says he is revamping American nuclear strategy to substantially narrow the conditions under which the U.S. would use nuclear weapons, but said that he is carving out an exception for "outliers like Iran and North Korea" that have violated or renounced the main treaty to halt nuclear proliferation.

A blast at a W. Virginia coal mine leaves at least 12 miners dead, and 10 unaccounted for. The blast occurred at the Upper Big Branch mine, 30 miles south of Charleston. Federal records indicate that the Upper Big Branch mine has recorded an injury rate worse than the national average for similar operations for at least 6 of the past 10 years.

6 The U.S. court of appeals for the District of Columbia Circuit rules that regulators have limited power over Web traffic under current law. The decision, which is a setback to efforts by the F.C.C. to require companies to give Web users equal access to all content, allows Internet service companies to block or slow specific sites, and to charge sites like YouTube to deliver their content faster to users.

The Obama administration authorizes the targeted killing of the radical Muslim cleric Anwar al-Awlaki. Mr. Awlaki, who was born in New Mexico, is in hiding in Yemen and has been under scrutiny since he was linked to Maj. Nidal Malik Hasan, the Army psychiatrist accused of killing 13 people at Fort Hood, Tex. in November, and then to Umar Farouk Abdulmutallab, the man charged with trying to blow up a Detroit-bound airliner in December.

7 Kurmanbek Bakiyev, the president of Kyrgyzstan, is forced to flee the capital of Bishkek after bloody protests erupt across the country over his repressive rule. Opposition politicians take control over the government, and demand that the president sign a formal letter of resignation.

Prime Minister Abhisit Vejjajiva of Thailand declares a state of emergency in the Bangkok area after antigovernment demonstrators break into the Parliament building, forcing government ministers to flee by helicopter. The announcement comes after nearly a month of street demonstrations in defiance of government restrictions.

8 The U.S. and Russia open what they call a new era in their tumultuous relationship as they sign an arms control treaty and present a largely united front against Iran's nuclear program, marking a sharp change since they broke over the Georgia war two years ago. The New Start pact, signed in Prague, Czech Republic, will pare back the nations' nuclear arsenals.

9 Justice John Paul Stevens announces his resignation from the Supreme Court after 34 years, giving Pres. Obama the rare opportunity to make back-to-back appointments during the first two years of his presidency. Stevens was nominated in 1975 by Pres. Gerald R. Ford, who said all he wanted was "the finest legal mind I could find."

10 A plane carrying the Polish president Lech Kaczynski, his wife, and dozens of the country's top political and military leaders, crashes in Western Russia, killing everyone on board. The flight was headed to a commemoration ceremony at Katyn Woods, the site of a Soviet massacre of Polish officers in World War II.

11 European leaders provide a long-awaited financial rescue line to Greece by offering the country up to $40 billion in aid to meet its giant debt obligations. Concerns about a potential Greek default had caused anxiety among markets worldwide and raised fears that the euro would be severely undermined if other struggling countries like Spain, Portugal, and Italy follow Greece to the financial precipice.

12 Pres. Obama secures a promise from Pres. Hu Jintao of China to join negotiations on a new package of sanctions against Iran. Mr. Obama assures Mr. Hu that he will work to make sure that Beijing has a steady supply of oil if Iran cuts China off in retaliation for joining in severe sanctions.

The Senate agrees to consider a temporary extension of unemployment benefits after four Republicans join Democrats in voting to debate the proposal. The Senate votes 60–34 to move ahead with a measure that will keep checks flowing to jobless Americans who are exhausting their benefits and maintain federal subsidies for health insurance for the unemployed.

13 Kurmanbek Bakiyev, the deposed president of Kyrgyzstan, says he will formally step down if there are guarantees of safety for him and his family. The leader of the interim government, Roza Otunbayeva, says the government would "guarantee only his personal security," but that the guarantee does not extend to his family, some of whom have been accused of corruption.

14 Lt. Gen. Ronald L. Burgess Jr., the director of the Defense Intelligence Agency, and Gen. James E. Cartwright, the vice chairman of the Joint Chiefs of Staff, present testimony to the Senate Armed Services Committee stating that Iran could produce bomb-grade fuel for at least one nuclear weapon within a year, but would most likely need two to five years to manufacture a workable atomic bomb.

15 The ash from a volcanic eruption in Iceland forces airlines to cancel thousands of flights in northern Europe. The ash cloud, made up of minute particles of silicate that can severely damage jet engines was caused by the eruption of Eyjafjallajokull, is directly in the way of commercial airliners but not an immediate health threat to people on the ground.

Pres. Obama orders his health secretary to issue new rules aimed at granting hospital visiting rights to same-sex partners, and to make it easier for gay men and lesbians to make medical decisions on behalf of their partners.

16 Goldman Sachs is accused of securities fraud in a civil lawsuit filed by the Securities and Exchange Commission, which claims the bank created and sold a mortgage investment that was secretly intended to fail.

The Census Bureau reports that nearly one in three Americans failed to return their census questionnaires by the official April 16 deadline. The mail participation rate is at 68 percent, with Wisconsin logging the highest rate of any state, 78 percent. The lowest rate is in New Mexico (59 percent).

17 Defense Secretary Robert M. Gates warns in a secret three-page memorandum to top White House officials that the U.S. does not have an effective long-range policy for dealing with Iran's steady progress toward nuclear capability. The analysis comes in the midst of an effort to develop new options for Mr. Obama, including a set of military alternatives, should diplomacy and sanctions fail to force Iran to change course.

Volcanic ash from the Icelandic volcano hobbles air traffic for a third day with no signs of letting up. The disaster is estimated to be costing airlines $200 million a day and is raising concerns about the longer term consequences for public health, military operations, and the world economy.

Pres. Hamid Karzai chooses a new head of Afghanistan's election commission, who receives the immediate endorsement of the U.N. The U.N. also endorses a plan that will weaken a separate election-fraud monitoring body, but would give Western representatives veto power over its decisions.

18 As Europe grounds most airline flights for a fourth day because of a volcanic ash cloud, airlines run test flights to show that flying is safe, and press aviation authorities to loosen the flight ban. Airlines complain that European governments are overreacting to the threat.

Pres. Hugo Chávez says that China has agreed to extend $20 billion in loans to Venezuela, pointing to deepening ties between the two countries as China seeks to secure oil supplies from that nation. The announcement of the loans follows other financing agreements with China that have softened a sharp economic downturn in Venezuela.

19 *The New York Times* reports that an investigation of Internet hackers who had stolen information from Google's computers in January reveals that the losses included Google's password system that controls access to almost all of the company's Web services, including e-mail and business applications.

20 In a major First Amendment ruling, the Supreme Court strikes down a federal law that made it a crime to create or sell dogfight videos and other depictions of animal cruelty. Chief Justice John G. Roberts Jr., writes for the majority in the 8-to-1 decision, saying that the law had created "a criminal prohibition of alarming breadth." Justice Samuel A. Alito Jr. dissents.

21 An explosion on an oil drilling rig off the coast of southeast Louisiana leaves at least three people critically injured and 11 other missing. Officials say the pollution is considered minimal so far because most of the oil and gas was being burned up in the fire.

22 A German bishop accused of beating children decades ago when he was a priest, tenders his resignation to Pope Benedict XVI, the latest jolt to the Roman Catholic Church in Germany as it grapples with a swirling sexual abuse scandal.

The Deepwater Horizon, the oil rig burning out of control in the Gulf of Mexico sinks, with 11 workers still missing and the authorities fearing a potential environmental disaster. The sinking of the rig, which is leased by BP, leaves a one-by-five mile sheen of what the authorities say is "crude oil mix."

23 Gov. Jan Brewer of Arizona signs the nation's toughest bill on illegal immigration into law. Its aim is to identify, prosecute, and deport illegal immigrants, making the failure to carry immigration documents a crime and giving the police broad power to detain anyone suspected of being in the country illegally. The move is strongly criticized by Pres. Obama.

24 Robotic devices monitoring the deepwater well where a giant oil rig exploded and sank the week before discover oil leaking from the well. Roughly 1,000 barrels of oil a day are estimated to be emanating from the pipe that connects the well at the ocean floor to the drilling platform on the surface.

25 Senate Democrats say that they have bridged internal party differences and coalesced around a plan to tighten regulation of derivatives, the complex financial instruments that were a major factor in the 2008 economic crisis. The agreement among Democrats combines overlapping proposals on derivatives by the banking and agriculture committees, and raises the pressure on Senate Republicans who plan to block the start of floor debate.

26 Seven weeks after Iraqis went to the polls a special elections court disqualifies a winning parliamentary candidate, most likely reversing the narrow defeat of Prime Minister Nuri Kamal al-Maliki's alliance and possibly allowing him the first chance to form a new coalition government. If upheld by the court, the disqualification will erase the two-seat victory by a largely secular coalition led by Ayad Allawi.

Sudan's incumbent president, Omar Hassan al-Bashir, wins the country's first multiparty election in more than 20 years, receiving 68 percent of the vote, though many international observers say the election was marred by intimidation, gerrymandering, and fraud. In southern Sudan, which is preparing to vote on whether to become its own country, the incumbent there, Salva Kiir, prevails, winning 93 percent of the vote to remain president of that semiautonomous region.

28 After nine years of regulatory review, the Dept. of Interior gives the green light to the nation's first offshore wind farm off the coast of Cape Cod. Interior Sec. Ken Salazar says he is requiring the developer, Cape Wind Associates, to take several steps to mitigate possible adverse effects on the environment.

Government officials say that oil might be leaking from a well in the Gulf of Mexico at a rate five times as large as initial estimates have suggested. Rear Adm. Mary E. Landry of the Coast Guard says that a scientist from the National Oceanic and Atmospheric Administration has concluded that oil is leaking at a rate of 5,000 barrels a day, not 1,000 as had been originally estimated.

A badly fractured Supreme Court, with six justices writing opinions, reopens the possibility that a large cross serving as a war memorial in a remote part of the Mojave Desert may be permitted to remain there. The 5-to-4 decision, in *Salazar v. Buono*, shows how deeply divided the court is on the role religious symbols may play in public life. Justice Anthony M. Kennedy writes the plurality opinion.

29 Florida governor Charlie Crist announces that he will run as an independent for the U.S. Senate seat, saying that his decision to leave the Republican Party is "the right thing for America," after Marco Rubio, former speaker of the Florida House wins the support of Tea Party activists and the G.O.P. establishment.

30 The police discover a car bomb in a smoking Nissan Pathfinder in the heart of Times Square, in New York City, prompting the evacuation of thousands of tourists and theatergoers from the area. The device included propane tanks, some kind of powder, gasoline, and a timing device.

Arab ministers gathered at the offices of the Arab League in Cairo again endorse staging indirect talks between Palestinians and Israelis, formally resurrecting an American proposal that collapsed last month after Israel announced plans to build new housing in East Jerusalem. The ministers did not give ground on the issue of the settlements.

A unit of Johnson & Johnson voluntarily begins a recall of children's Tylenol, Motrin, Zyrtec, and Benadryl because of manufacturing deficiencies. The F.D.A says the deficiencies may affect the potency, purity, or quality of the products and may contain more of the active drug ingredients than specified.

Tens of thousands of demonstrators join marches and rallies in cities across the country to protest Arizona's tough anti-illegal immigrant law, calling on Congress to pass an immigration overhaul. The demonstrations are far larger than planners had anticipated: in Los Angeles alone, the crowd peaked at 50,000.

MAY 2010

2 United Airlines and Continental Airlines agree to a $3 billion merger that will create the world's biggest airline. United is buying Continental and the combined company will keep the United name and be based in Chicago.

Pres. Obama visits Louisiana for a firsthand look at the response effort to the oil spill that he calls a "potentially unprecedented environmental disaster," as officials for BP describe in detail their desperate efforts to seal the gushing well.

3 Federal agents and police detective arrest Faisal Shahzad, a naturalized U.S. citizen from Pakistan, in connection with the failed Times Square car bombing. Mr. Shahzad is taken into custody at Kennedy Airport, apparently trying to flee the country.

Ajmal Kasab, the only surviving gunman in the 2008 terrorist attack in Mumbai, is convicted of murder, conspiracy, and waging war against India during a three-day assault that killed more than 160 people. Mr. Kasab, 22, is sentenced to death by hanging.

4 Faisal Shahzad, the Pakistani-American man arrested in the failed Times Square car bombing admits his role in the attempted attack and says he received explosives training in Pakistan. There are

reports that seven or eight people have been arrested in Pakistan, as officials in both countries seek to determine the origins and scope of the plot.

Pres. Mahmoud Ahmadinejad of Iran says that relations with the U.S. might never be repaired if new sanctions are imposed against his country, that the U.N. atomic agency has no authority over matters like missiles, and that despite his contested reelection last year, Iran has not become a republic of fear.

The E.P.A. issues a long-awaited proposal to regulate coal ash, the toxic byproduct of burning coal to produce power. The agency defers the decision on whether to treat it as hazardous waste, or under the same framework that governs household garbage. The agency will choose between the options after a 90-day comment period.

5 American officials say that it is very likely that the Pakistani Taliban, a radical group once thought unable to attack the U.S., had played a role in the bombing attempt in Times Square. The Dept. of Homeland Security also directs airlines to speed up their checks of new names added to the no-fly list, a requirement that might have prevented Mr. Shahzad from boarding a flight to Dubai before his arrest at Kennedy airport.

6 The Dow Jones industrial average falls 1,000 points, in a plunge that recalls the panic of 2008. It lasts just 16 minutes, leaving Wall Street experts groping for explanations. At the end of the day, the Dow ended down 347.80 points, at 10,520.32.

The political party of Myanmar's detained opposition leader, Daw Aung San Suu Kyi, is officially dissolved after more than 20 years as the core of pro-democracy resistance to Myanmar's military junta. The National League for Democracy says it will continue to perform social work as a nonpolitical group.

A team of biologists at the Max Planck Institute for Evolutionary Anthropology in Leipzig, Germany, who have been decoding the genome of Neanderthals, reports that Neanderthals mated with some modern humans and left their imprint in the human genome. This inter-breeding theory undercuts the present belief that all human populations today draw from the same gene pool that existed 50,000 years ago.

7 The British public fails to elect a clear winner in the national election, leaving the Conservatives and Liberal Democrats in intensive talks to try to fashion a coalition that will allow them to form a government quickly. David Cameron, the Conservative leader, says that talks with Nick Clegg, the Liberal Democrat leader, have been "constructive."

8 The Election Assistance Commission proposes new regulations that will allow nearly three million overseas and military voters from at least 33 states, to cast ballots over the Internet using email or fax. Critics of the increased use of Internet voting say the commission is violating federal law by circumventing the technical board that is supposed to review any such new regulations.

9 Pres. Obama nominates Solicitor General Elena Kagan as the nation's 112th justice to the Supreme Court, selecting his own chief advocate to succeed the retiring Justice John Paul Stevens. Ms. Kagan has served as a staff member in all three branches of government and was the first woman to be dean of the Harvard Law School.

European leaders agree to provide a rescue package of nearly $1 trillion in a sweeping effort to combat the debt crisis that has engulfed Europe and threatens markets around the world, announcing that the International Monetary Fund is prepared to give up to $321 billion separately.

The Obama administration says it will seek a law allowing investigators to interrogate terrorism suspects without informing them of their rights. Attorney General Eric H. Holder Jr., proposes carving out a broad new exception to Miranda rights, saying interrogators need greater flexibility to question terrorism suspects than is provided by existing exceptions.

10 A series of attacks in Baghdad and other cities across Iraq strike police and army checkpoints, as well as markets, a mayor's office and a textile factory, killing at least 100 people and wounding hundreds more. The attacks occur amid a protracted dispute over the results of the country's election more than two months ago. Officials blame the political impasse for creating a security vacuum that extremists hope to exploit.

Prime Minister Gordon Brown of Britain announces that he will resign as Labour Party leader as part of a bid to lure the Liberal Democrats into rejecting the Conservatives and joining a rejuvenated Labour in a left-of-center governing coalition. Mr. Brown says he would stand down as Labour's leader when a successor is elected sometime before the party's annual conference in September.

The Organization for Economic Cooperation and Development, a 31-country group seen as an exclusive club of rich countries, votes unanimously to admit Israel. Estonia and Slovenia were also accepted into the O.E.C.D.

11 Britain's Conservatives return to power after 13 years in opposition as David Cameron takes over as prime minister from Labour's Gordon Brown. Mr. Cameron cobbled together an awkward alliance with the Liberal Democrats to form the first coalition government since World War II.

Pope Benedict XVI issues his most forceful remarks on the sexual abuse crisis sweeping the Catholic Church, suggesting that its origins lay with abusive priests and with highly placed church officials who for decades concealed or minimized the problem.

Sen. Benigno S. Aquino III appears almost certain to become the next president of the Philippines. The nearly complete results of Monday's election show that Mr. Aquino is winning by the widest margin in a presidential election since his mother, Corazon C. Aquino, overthrew the longtime dictator Ferdinand E. Marcos in a "people power" movement in 1986.

14 Iraq's election commission announces that it has completed a partial recount of ballots from the country's election two months ago and finds no widespread fraud or irregularities. Prime Minister Nuri Kamal al-Maliki's electoral bloc demanded the recount after finishing narrowly behind the secular and Sunni coalition led by a former interim prime minister, Ayad Allawi.

The space shuttle *Atlantis*, carrying a crew of six, a Russian docking module, and critical spare parts, vaults into orbit on a 12-day space station assembly mission. This is its 32nd and final planned flight after a quarter-century of service.

16 After more than three weeks of efforts to stop a gushing oil leak in the Gulf of Mexico, BP engineers achieve some success as they use a mile-long pipe to capture some of the oil and divert it to a drill shop on the surface, some 5,000 feet above the wellhead.

17 The Supreme Court rules in a 6–3 decision, that juveniles who commit crimes in which no one is killed may not be sentenced to life in prison without the possibility of parole. The majority opinion in *Graham v. Florida* is written by Justice Anthony M. Kennedy. Justice Clarence Thomas writes the dissent which is joined by Justices Scalia and Alito.

In a broad endorsement of federal power, the Supreme Court rules, 7–2, that Congress has the authority under the Constitution, to allow the continued civil commitment of sex offenders after they have completed their criminal sentences. Justice Stephen G. Breyer writes the opinion for four justices in *U.S. v. Comstock*. Justices Alito and Kennedy voted to uphold the law, but did not join the opinion. Justices Thomas and Scalia dissented.

18 Sen. Arlen Specter of Pennsylvania, who left the Republican Party in hopes of salvaging a 30-year career, is rejected by Democratic primary voters, who selected Rep. Joe Sestak as the party's nominee. Mr. Sestak is riding an anti-incumbent wave that is defining the mid-term elections.

The Obama administration announces an agreement with other major powers, including Russia and China, to impose a fourth set of sanctions on Iran over its nuclear program. The announcement comes the day after Iranian leaders announced their own tentative deal with Turkey and Brazil, to turn over about half of Iran's nuclear fuel for a year.

19 Britain's new coalition government of Conservatives and Liberal Democrats unveils an ambitious plan for upending the highly-centralized and often intrusive way the country is governed. The plan will roll back many "nanny state" laws, nonelected administrative bodies and surveillance systems that critics say have curbed individual freedoms, and enlarged state powers to a degree unrivaled by most other democratic societies.

20 The Senate approves a far-reaching financial regulatory bill, putting Congress on the brink of approving a broad expansion of government oversight of the increasingly complex banking system and financial markets. The vote was 59—39 with four Republicans joining the majority in favor of the bill, and two Democrats opposing the measure, saying it is not tough enough.

The House Armed Services Committee deals a blow to Pres. Obama's hopes to shut the military prison at Guantánamo Bay, Cuba by approving legislation that will prohibit creating a detention center inside the U.S. The administration had asked Congress to approve about $350 million to buy and renovate a nearly empty prison in Thomson, Illinois.

21 A federal appeals court rules that three men, two Yemenis and one Tunisian, who have been detained by the U.S. military for years without trial in Afghanistan, have no recourse to American courts. The decision is a broad victory for the Obama administration in its efforts to hold terrorism suspects overseas for indefinite periods without judicial oversight.

23 Pres. Lee Myung-bak says that South Korea will cut nearly all trade with North Korea, deny North Korean merchant ships use of South Korean sea lanes and ask the U.N. Security Council to punish the North for what he called the deliberate sinking of a South Korean warship two months ago.

Prime Minister Yukio Hatoyama tells outraged residents of Okinawa that an American air base will be moved only to the north side of the island rather than off the island. The announcement is a victory for the Obama administration and a humiliating setback for Mr. Hatoyama who used the relocation as a major campaign issue.

The Jamaican government declares a state of emergency in portions of Kingston, the capital, after supporters of Christopher Coke, a gang leader who is wanted in the U.S. on gun and drug charges, attack three police stations in an attempt to pressure the government to let him remain free.

24 The U.S. and its allies announce naval exercises to detect submarines of the kind suspected of sinking a South Korean warship, putting new pressure on North Korea. American officials acknowledge that the announced steps, including the threat of U.N. Security Council sanctions, and military maneuvers, have been tried before, and have failed to deter North Korea's actions.

The F.B.I releases a report showing that crime rates fell significantly across the U.S. in 2009. Compared with 2008, violent crimes declined by 5.5 percent, and property crimes decreased 4.9 percent. There was an overall decline in reported crimes for the third straight year.

25 Pres. Obama orders the deployment of up to 1,200 National Guard troops to the Southwest border and seeks increased spending on law enforcement there to combat drug smuggling, after Republican and Democratic lawmakers demand that border security be tightened. The troops will be stationed in the four border states for a year.

26 Britain discloses that it has a stockpile of 225 nuclear warheads, its first public accounting of its total nuclear arsenal. The announcement follows the Obama administration's recent disclosure that the U.S. has 5,113 nuclear warheads in its arsenal and "several thousand" more retired warheads awaiting the junk pile.

Iraq's election commission sends the final results of the March 7 elections to the Supreme Court for certification, which could clear a major obstacle in forming the new government after weeks of delay. The results of the election have been in dispute, heightening tensions in Iraq's fragile democracy at a time when American forces are preparing to depart.

BP begins a maneuver known as a top kill on the stricken well in the Gulf of Mexico. The process involves injecting heavy fluids, known as "drilling mud," down through drill pipes and hoses attached to the five-story-high blowout preventer sitting on top of the well. Once the liquids have forced the oil back, the well can be cemented and shut off.

27 The House of Representatives votes to let the Defense Department repeal the ban on gay and bisexual people from serving openly in the military, a major step toward dismantling the 1993 law widely known as "don't ask, don't tell." The provision was adopted as an amendment to the annual Pentagon policy bill. The House vote was 234 to 194, with 229 Democrats and 55 Republicans in favor.

28 Nepal averts political chaos when the leading political parties reach a last-minute agreement that prevents the dissolution of Parliament and

provides another year for the nation to complete a new national constitution.

Israel's military partly opens a major highway that runs through the West Bank to local Palestinian traffic. The military was forced to do so by an Israeli Supreme Court ruling that deemed its continued closing to Palestinians inconsistent with the rules of international law regarding a belligerent occupation.

29 BP engineers say that the "top kill" technique has failed to stem the flow of oil gushing from a well beneath the Gulf of Mexico, and they have decided to move on to another strategy. The abandonment of the top kill technique is the latest in a series of failed efforts.

The American military releases a scathing report on the deaths of 23 Afghan civilians, saying that "inaccurate and unprofessional" reporting by Predator drone operators helped lead to an airstrike in February on a group of innocent men, women and children. Gen. Stanley A. McChrystal announces a series of training measures intended to reduce the changes of similar events.

31 Israel faces intense international condemnation and growing domestic questions after a raid by naval commandos that killed nine people, many of them Turks, on an aid flotilla bound for Gaza. Israel says the violence was instigated by pro-Palestinian activists who presented themselves as humanitarians. Turkey, Israel's most important friend in the Muslim world, recalls its ambassador, and street protests erupt around the world.

JUNE 2010

1 The Obama administration says that it has begun civil and criminal investigations into the oil spill in the Gulf of Mexico. Attorney General Eric H. Holder Jr. says that he plans to "prosecute to the fullest extent of the law" any person or entity that the Justice Department determines has broken the law in connection with the oil spill.

Prime Minister Yukio Hatoyama of Japan announces that he will step down after facing growing pressure to quit amid criticism that he has squandered an electoral mandate to change Japan's sclerotic postwar political order. He was strongly criticized for breaking his campaign pledge to remove an American military base from Okinawa.

In a 5-to-4 ruling, the Supreme Court refines the court's landmark 1966 ruling in *Miranda v. Arizona* by finding that criminal suspects seeking to protect their right to remain silent, must speak up to invoke it. Justice Anthony M. Kennedy, writing for the majority, says that the decision does not disturb Miranda's requirement that suspects be told they have the right to remain silent, but that courts need not suppress statements made by defendants who received such warnings, did not expressly waive their rights, and spoke only after remaining silent through hours of interrogation. Justice Sonia Sotomayor wrote the dissent in *Berghuis v. Thompkins*.

2 Israel agrees to a rapid release of all detainees, including those suspected of attacking its soldiers, taken after the deadly nighttime raid of six ships seeking to break its blockade of the Gaza Strip. Planes carrying hundreds of activists fly to Turkey and Greece, as others are released through Jordan.

A 29-page report to the U.N. Human Rights Council, says that the growing use of armed drones by the U.S. to kill terrorism suspects is undermining global constraints on the use of military force. Philip Alston, the U.N. special representative on extrajudicial executions, calls on the U.S. to exercise greater restraint in its use of drones, warning that the American example could lead to a chaotic world as the new weapons technology inevitably spreads.

3 While still insisting that its blockade of Gaza is essential to its security, the Israeli government is shifting its position, "exploring new ways" of allowing goods to reach the coastal enclave. A government official says Israel is determined to have every ship heading to Gaza inspected to prevent the smuggling of rockets and other weapons, but the government wants to facilitate the entry of civilian goods into the region.

The E.P.A. issues a new health standard for sulfur dioxide emissions, the first such revision in nearly 40 years. The agency says the new standard, adopted under the Clean Air Act, will prevent 2,300 to 5,900 premature deaths and 54,000 asthma attacks each year.

4 Pres. Obama picks Lt. Gen. James R. Clapper Jr. as director of national intelligence, two weeks after forcing Adm. Dennis C. Blair out of the job. With this selection, Pres. Obama taps a retired officer with decades of experience to improve coordination of the nation's sprawling spy apparatus amid increasing threats at home and escalating operations abroad.

The Labor Department's monthly report shows that job growth was weak in the private sector in May. Employers added 431,000 jobs and the jobless rate fell to 9.7 percent, from 9.9 percent in April, but almost all the growth came from the 411,000 workers hired by the federal government to help with the Census.

5 Israel prevents a new attempt to break its blockade of Gaza when its naval commandos board an Irish-owned vessel carrying humanitarian supplies and prominent activists, and steered it to Ashdod, an Israeli port. There are no attempts at resistance or reports of violence.

6 Two New Jersey men who were bound for Somalia with the intention of joining an Islamic extremist group are arrested at Kennedy International Airport. The men, Mohamed Mahmood Alessa and Carlos Eduardo Almonte were seeking to join Al Shabab which has provided a haven for Al Qaeda operatives wanted for bombings of U.S. embassies in Kenya and Tanzania.

7 More than 25 years after a plume of fatal toxic gas from a Union Carbide chemical plant wafted over the city of Bhopal, India, eight former executives of the company's Indian subsidiary are convicted of negligence. One executive has since died, but the seven surviving defendants are sentenced to two years in prison and fined 100,000 rupees, or $2,100. The leak killed more than 3,000 people instantly and roughly 1,000 more died later from the after effects of the toxic gas. These are the first criminal convictions stemming from the disaster.

Secretary of State Hillary Rodham Clinton pleads with Latin American countries to readmit Honduras to the Organization of American States, a year after the country's left-leaning president was ousted in a coup. Argentina, Brazil, Ecuador, Nicaragua, and other nations refuse to recognize the new Honduran leader, Porfirio Lobo.

8 The Supreme Court bars officials in Arizona from providing matching funds to candidates for state office who accept public financing, a program meant to help them keep pace with the unlimited spending of candidates who do not take public financing. In an unsigned order without noted dissents, the justices reinstated a trial court injunction that barred those additional payments.

9 The U.N. Security Council levels a fourth round of sanctions against Iran's nuclear program. Twelve of the 15 nations on the Council voted for the measures which are aimed at the military purchases and trade and financial transactions carried out by the Islamic Revolutionary Guards Corps, which controls the nuclear program.

10 A government panel doubles its estimate of how much oil has been spewing from the out-of-control BP oil well, with a new calculation suggesting that 25,000 to 30,000 barrels a day could be flowing into the Gulf of Mexico. The estimate is far above the previous estimate of 12,000 to 19,000 barrels a day.

John McHugh, Secretary of the Army, says that the remains in more than 200 graves at Arlington National Cemetery may be incorrectly identified, and announces a shake-up in the cemetery's management. The majority of the mismarked graves are in the sections that include the graves of Marines killed in a 1983 bombing in Beirut.

The Senate defeats a Republican-led effort to prevent the E.P.A. from curbing greenhouse gases. The Senate voted 53–47 to reject an attempt by Sen. Lisa Murkowski of Alaska, to block the E.P.A. from imposing new limits on carbon emissions based on its 2009 finding that such gases represent a threat to human health and the environment.

11 Addressing the sexual abuse crisis from the seat of the Roman Catholic Church before thousands of priests, Pope Benedict XVI begs forgiveness, saying the church would do "everything possible" to prevent priests from abusing children. It is the first time that Benedict has asked forgiveness for the crisis.

12 After a third day of violence, the Kyrgyz provisional government asks Russia to send in troops. The government, headed by acting president Roza Otunbayeva acknowledges that its efforts to end the violence have been fruitless. It remains unclear what started the violence, which threatens to undermine the fragile provisional government that took power in April.

13 Senior American government officials report that the U.S. has discovered nearly $1 trillion in untapped mineral deposits in Afghanistan. The previously unknown deposits—including huge veins of iron, copper, cobalt, gold, and industrial metals like lithium—are so big that Afghanistan could eventually be transformed into one of the most important mining centers in the world.

The move to break up Belgium gathers momentum as Bart de Wever's Flemish nationalist party wins an emphatic election victory in Flanders, the more prosperous Dutch-speaking region of the divided nation. Belgium is due to assume the rotating presidency of the European Union in the next three weeks.

Israel announces the composition of a government-appointed commission with foreign participation to investigate the circumstances surrounding its deadly commando raid on a flotilla bound for Gaza in late May. The panel, called the Independent Public Commission, will be led by a retired Israeli Supreme Court justice,

Jacob Turkel, and will include two foreign observers in addition to two Israeli experts in international law.

14 German Chancellor Angela Merkel faces calls from opposition leaders for new elections, as bickering within her governing coalition leads to growing speculation that a collapse of her government could be imminent.

15 Speaking to a national television audience for the first time from the Oval Office, Pres. Obama summons Americans to a "national mission" to move away from reliance on oil and develop alternative sources of energy. He also promises a long-term plan to make sure that states suffering from the oil spill are made whole again, and is appointing Ray Mabus, the former governor of Mississippi to develop a Gulf Coast restoration plan.

British Prime Minister David Cameron offers an extraordinary apology for the 1972 killings of 14 unarmed demonstrators by British soldiers in Northern Ireland, saying that a long-awaited judicial inquiry had left no doubt that the "'Bloody Sunday' shootings were both unjustified and unjustifiable."

Gen. David H. Petraeus, commander of American forces in the Middle East, confronts intense bipartisan challenges to the Obama administration's decision to set a deadline of July 2011 to start pulling troops out of Afghanistan. Lawmakers asked if the administration's timetable for withdrawal helps the mission, or hurts the changes for success by undermining confidence that the U.S. has the will to see it through.

16 After intense negotiations between the White House and BP lawyers, Pres. Obama announces that the oil giant will create a $20 billion fund to pay damage claims to thousands of fishermen and others along the Gulf Coast. The fund will be administered by Kenneth R. Feinberg, the lawyer who ran the fund for victims of the Sept. 11 attacks.

17 Israel announces what it calls "adjustments" in its policy regarding the blockade of Gaza, promising to ease the entry of civilian goods by land while maintaining its naval blockade.

The Supreme Court rules 8–0 in *Stop the Beach Renourishment v. Florida Department of Environmental Protection* that a project to restore eroded beaches in the Florida Panhandle did not violate the Constitution's takings clause even though the state claimed ownership of the strip of land the project created next to the ocean. Although the decision was unanimous, the case generated three separate decisions written by Justices Scalia, Kennedy, and Breyer. Justice John Paul Stevens did not participate.

The Supreme Court rules unanimously in *City of Ontario v. Quon* that a California police department did not violate the constitutional privacy rights of an employee when it audited the text messages on a pager the city had issued him. Justice Anthony M. Kennedy wrote for the court.

Republican representative Joe L. Barton of Texas apologizes to BP for what he calls a $20 billion "shakedown" by Pres. Obama for loss claims in the gulf oil spill, and four hours later apologizes for his apology, after being pummeled in the blogosphere and assailed by members of both parties.

18 The Obama administration decides to file a lawsuit to strike down a new Arizona law aimed at deporting illegal immigrants, thrusting itself into the national debate over how the U.S. should enforce immigration policies.

19 China announces that it will allow greater flexibility in the value of its currency, a move that would deflect growing international criticism of its economic policies. The statement, by China's central bank, is the clearest sign yet that the country will allow its currency to appreciate gradually against the dollar.

20 Israel formally announces an eased blockade of Gaza that could significantly expand the flow of goods overland into the impoverished coastal Palestinian enclave. The announcement comes three weeks after the deadly Israeli naval commando raid that thwarted a breach of the blockade by a flotilla of pro-Palestinian aid activists.

21 In a 6-to-3 decision, the Supreme Court upholds a federal law that makes it a crime to provide "material support" to foreign terrorist organizations, even if the help takes the form of training for peacefully resolving conflicts. Chief Justice John G. Roberts wrote for the majority in *Holder v. Humanitarian Law Project*.

Faisal Shahzad, the suspect in the failed Times Square bombing, pleads guilty. Mr. Shahzad recounts how and why he conceived the plot, and despite his admission of guilt, was unapologetic.

22 After only six weeks in office, the government of Prime Minister David Cameron unveils the most severe package of spending cuts and tax increases since the early days of Margaret Thatcher's era. The government hopes that austerity measures will help balance the books without pitching the country into a double-dip recession.

23 Pres. Obama fires Gen. Stanley A. McChrystal, his top Afghanistan war commander, after McChrystal and his staff made remarks in an article published in *Rolling Stone* magazine that were contemptuous of senior administration officials. Gen. David H. Petraeus is put in charge of the Afghanistan war effort.

24 In a unanimous ruling, the Supreme Court significantly narrows the scope of a law often used by federal prosecutors in corruption cases and calls into question the fraud conviction of Jeffrey K. Skilling, a former chief executive of Enron, and Conrad M. Black, a newspaper executive convicted of defrauding his media company.

In an 8-to-1 decision, the Supreme Court rules that people who sign petitions to put referendums on state ballots do not have a general right under the First Amendment to keep their names secret. Chief Justice John G. Roberts Jr. wrote for the majority. Justice Clarence Thomas dissented in *Doe v. Reed*.

A Pakistani court sentences five American Muslim men who had been arrested in Punjab Province to 10 years of labor in prison for conspiring to carry out terrorist attacks. The men, all in their 20s and all from Virginia, are believed to have traveled to Pakistan to join the fight against American forces in Afghanistan.

25 The House and Senate reach an accord for an overhaul of finance rules, expanding federal authority to curb risky Wall Street practices and exotic investment instruments. The deal will levy fees on the financial services industry, forcing big banks and hedge funds to pay the projected $20 billion, five-year cost of the new oversight that they will face.

27 At the Group of 20 summit meeting in Toronto, leaders of the world's biggest economies agree on a timetable for cutting deficits and halting the growth of their debt. The action underscores the conviction of European nations that deficits represent the biggest threat to their economic stability.

28 In a 5-to-4 decision, the Supreme Court rules that the Second Amendment's guarantee of an individual right to bear arms applies to state and local gun control laws. Justice Samuel A. Alito Jr., writes for the majority in *McDonald v. Chicago.* Justice John Paul Stevens writes the dissent.

Federal prosecutors accuse 11 people of being part of a Russian espionage ring, living in deep cover in a patient scheme to penetrate what one coded message called American "policy making circles." The F.B.I. investigation began seven years ago and culminated in the arrest of 10 people in Yonkers, Boston, and northern Virginia.

In a 5-to-4 decision, the Supreme Court rules that a public law school did not violate the First Amendment by withdrawing recognition from a Christian student group that excluded gay students. Justice Ruth Bader Ginsburg writes for the majority in *Christian Legal Society v. Martinez.* Justice Samuel A. Alito Jr. writes the dissent.

The Obama administration unveils a space policy that emphasizes international cooperation, including the possibility of an arms control treaty that will limit the development of space weapons. The new policy states that Washington will "consider proposals and concepts for arms control measures if they are equitable, effectively verifiable and enhance the national security of the U.S. and its allies."

30 The House Agriculture Committee votes to reverse a decades-long ban on U.S. citizens traveling to Cuba and to ease restrictions on the sale of American commodities there. Though the vote is only a first step toward Congressional approval of the changes, supporters view it as a significant step toward normalization of the relationships between the countries.

JULY 2010

1 British Prime Minister David Cameron cancels longstanding plans to build a third runway at Heathrow Airport stating that enabling more flying is incompatible with Britain's stated goal of curbing emissions. The country's 2008 Climate Change Act requires it to reduce emissions by at least 34 percent by 2020.

A senior Communist Party official says that reincarnations of Tibetan spiritual leaders, including the Dalai Lama, must be approved by the Chinese central government, the clearest indications yet that China will appoint a reincarnation of the Dalai Lama after the current Dalai Lama dies.

Pres. Obama presses Congress to adopt a sweeping plan to fix a "fundamentally broken" immigration system. In his first speech devoted entirely to immigration policy, Mr. Obama tries to navigate between the two extremes of the debate, defending his efforts to strengthen border security while promoting a path to citizenship for many of the 11 million people in the U.S. illegally.

2 The monthly snapshot released by the Labor Department reveals that the U.S. added just 83,000 private sector jobs in June, far less than the number needed to reduce the numbers of unemployed Americans. The unemployment rate declined to 9.5 percent, from 9.7 percent in May, but that is an illusory decline, as 652,000 Americans left the workforce.

Defense Secretary Robert M. Gates issues orders requiring top-level Pentagon and military leaders to notify the office of the Defense Department's assistant secretary for public affairs "prior to interviews or any other means of media and public engagement with possible national or international implications." The orders come nine days after Gen. Stanley A. McChrystal was relieved of command for comments made to *Rolling Stone* magazine.

5 British Deputy Prime Minister Nick Clegg outlines a package of measures designed to restore public confidence in the government. The bill provides for a fixed five-year term for parliaments and requires a two-thirds vote by members of the House of Commons to force a new election when a government loses a confidence vote within those five years. An election would also be called if a government falls and no new government is formed within 14 days.

6 Pres. Obama says that he expects direct negotiations between Israelis and Palestinians to begin well before a moratorium on settlement construction expires at the end of September, and Israeli Prime Minister Benjamin Netanyahu pledges to take "concrete steps" in the coming weeks to get talks moving.

The Justice Department files a lawsuit against Arizona to challenge a new state law intended to combat illegal immigration, arguing that it will undermine the federal government's pursuit of terrorists, gang members and other criminal immigrants. The suit says, "The Constitution and the federal immigration laws do not permit the development of a patchwork of state and local immigration policies throughout the country."

7 Turkey's highest court strikes down parts of a controversial government package aimed at restructuring the country's constitution, clearing the way for a referendum on the measures in September. The governing Justice and Development Party contends that the overhaul is necessary to bring Turkey's constitution in line with those of Western European democracies, but the opposition Republican People's Party argues that they are an attempts to breach the separation of the state and the judiciary by giving it more control over military and legal appointments.

8 The U.S. seals an agreement to trade 10 Russian agents arrested last month for four men imprisoned in Russia for alleged contacts with Western intelligence agencies. The 10 sleeper agents plead guilty to conspiracy after revealing their true identities and are sentenced to time served. They will be transferred to Russian custody and flown out of the country.

A federal judge in Massachusetts finds that the 1996 law, known as the Defense of Marriage Act, barring the federal government from recognizing same-sex marriage is unconstitutional, ruling that gay and lesbian couples deserve the same federal benefits as heterosexual couples.

Three men are found guilty in a London court of plotting to commit murder in a case that centered on a 2006 conspiracy, with links to Al Qaeda, to attack seven trans-Atlantic airliners bound for the U.S. and Canada with "liquid bombs." In all, 10 men faced charges in the case over three trials and all but two were convicted.

A federal court turns down the Obama administration's effort to enforce a six-month moratorium on deepwater drilling in the Gulf of Mexico. A three-judge panel of the U.S. court of appeals for the fifth circuit, in New Orleans ruled after a hearing in a lawsuit filed by companies that claim they are being financially crippled by the suspension of drilling.

11 Japan's governing Democratic Party suffers a setback in midterm elections that shows growing voter disappointment with the party's apparent inability to revamp the country's postwar order. Democrats trail the opposition Liberal Democrats, failing to win enough of the contested seats to gain a controlling majority in the chamber.

BP says it has made progress toward installing a new cap that could contain all of the oil spewing from its out-of-control well in the Gulf of Mexico, and that a flotilla of skimmers is helping to collect the additional oil leaking while the procedure is underway.

12 The International Criminal Court in The Hague says it has issued a second arrest warrant for Pres. Omar Hassan al-Bashir of Sudan, this time for three counts of genocide. All of the charges against Mr. Bashir are linked to the conflict in the western Darfur region of Sudan where an estimated 300,000 people have died and more than two million have been uprooted by a decade of fighting between the government and rebels.

13 Six months after the British government handed control of the police in Northern Ireland to local officials, the worst rioting in years leaves 82 police officers injured in Belfast. The rioting was set off by the annual July 12 marches by the Orange Order, a Protestant fraternal organization.

14 The Senate Foreign Relations Committee releases more than 1,100 pages of previously classified Vietnam-era transcripts that show senators of the time sharply questioning whether they had been deceived by the White House and the Pentagon over the 1964 Gulf of Tonkin incident. Pres. Lyndon B. Johnson cited the attacks to persuade Congress to authorize broad military action in Vietnam, but historians have concluded that the Aug. 4 attack never happened.

The White House issues new rules requiring health insurance companies to provide free coverage for dozens of screenings, laboratory tests and other types of preventive care. The rules eliminate co-payments, deductibles and other charges for blood pressure, diabetes and cholesterol tests; many cancer screenings; routine vaccinations, prenatal care; and wellness visits for infants and children.

15 Congress approves a sweeping expansion of federal financial regulation. The bill subjects more financial companies to federal oversight, regulates many derivatives contracts, and creates a panel to detect risks to the financial system along with a consumer protection regulator.

BP says it has capped its hemorrhaging well, marking the first time in 86 days that oil is not gushing into the Gulf of Mexico. The announcement comes after a series of failed attempts to contain the runaway well.

Argentina's senate narrowly approves a law authorizing same-sex marriages, making it the first country in Latin America to allow gay couples to wed. The senate voted 33 to 27 in favor of the measure after the president Cristina Fernández de Kirchner waged a war of words with the Catholic Church over the issue.

BP confirms that it had lobbied the British government to conclude a prisoner-transfer agreement that the Libyan government wanted to secure the release of the only person convicted for the 1988 Lockerbie airliner bombing over Scotland, which killed 270 people, 189 of them Americans.

19 The Defense Department announces that an aircraft carrier, the *George Washington*, will arrive in the South Korean port of Busan as the U.S. and South Korea prepare for joint military exercises meant to be a show of strength against North Korea. Defense Secretary Robert M. Gates says the military exercises will be a "signal of deterrence to the North."

20 The Senate Judiciary Committee votes to forward the nomination of Solicitor General Elena Kagan for a seat on the Supreme Court, to the full Senate for consideration. The 13-to-6 vote was almost entirely along party lines.

The Senate clears the way for more unemployment pay to reach millions of Americans who have been out of work for six months or more, voting 60–40 to break a partisan logjam and end debate over the jobless pay. The vote overrides Republican objections that the $34 billion cost of the additional compensation should not be added to the deficit.

21 *The New York Times* reports that a confidential survey of workers on the Deepwater Horizon in the weeks before the oil rig exploded showed that many of them were concerned about safety practices and feared reprisals if they reported mistakes or other problems. In the survey, commissioned by the rig's owner, Transocean, workers said that company plans were not carried out properly and that they "often saw unsafe behaviors on the rig."

The White House and Agriculture Secretary Tom Vilsack apologize to Shirley Sherrod, a black mid-level official, for the way she had been forced to resign her Agriculture Department job after a conservative blogger put out a misleading video clip that seemed to show her admitting antipathy toward a white farmer. In fact, the full video shows that it was a consciousness-raising story, and the white farmer who was the subject of the video rose to Ms. Sherrod's defense.

22 A House investigative panel finds "substantial reason to believe" that Rep. Charles B. Rangel violated a range of ethics rules, dealing a serious blow to the Harlem Democrat in the twilight of his political career. The finding means that he must face a public trial before the House ethics committee, the first member of Congress to be forced to do so since 2002.

The International Court of Justice—the U.N.'s highest court—says that Kosovo's unilateral declaration of independence from Serbia in 2008 did not violate international law. The ruling avoids saying that the state of Kosovo is legal under international law, a narrow and carefully calibrated compromise that could allow both sides to declare victory in a dispute that remains raw even 11 years after the war there. Only 69 countries in the U.N. General Assembly have recognized Kosovo so far.

A report from the College Board warns that the growing gap between the U.S. and other countries in college-completion rates, threatens to undermine American economic competitiveness. The U.S. used to lead the world in the number of 25-to 34-year-olds with college degrees. It now ranks 12th among 36 developed nations.

25 BP's board names an American, Robert Dudley, as its chief executive, replacing Tony Hayward, whose repeated stumbles during the company's three-month oil spill in the Gulf of Mexico alienated federal and state officials as well as residents of the Gulf Coast. About one-third of the company's wells, refineries and other business interests are in the U.S. and 40 percent of its shareholders are Americans.

A U.N.-backed tribunal finds Kaing Guek Eav, a former prison warden of the Khmer Rouge, guilty of crimes against humanity and war crimes for overseeing the torture and killing of more than 14,000 prisoners. He is the first major figure to be tried since the regime was toppled 30 years ago. The court sentences him to serve 19 years in prison. There is no death penalty in Cambodia.

26 The White House seeks to reassert control over the public debate on the Afghanistan war following the disclosure of a six-year archive of classified military documents is released on the Internet by Wikileaks. The documents reveal that the war is going more poorly than two administrations have portrayed.

The Chinese government reacts angrily to an announcement by Secretary of State Hillary Rodham Clinton that Washington might step into a long-simmering territorial dispute between China and its smaller neighbors in the South China Sea. Mrs. Clinton says that the U.S. has an interest in mediating the dispute which involves roughly 200 islands that are claimed by China, Vietnam, Brunei, Malaysia, Taiwan, Indonesia, and the Philippines, while Foreign Minister Yang Jiechi of China warns the U.S. against wading into the conflict.

27 The House of Representatives agrees to provide $59 billion to continue financing America's two wars, but the vote shows deepening divisions among Democrats over the course of the nearly nine-year-old conflict in Afghanistan. The 308-to-144 vote, with strong Republican support comes after the leak of an archive of classified battlefield reports from Afghanistan that fueled new debate over the course of the war.

28 A federal judge blocks the most controversial parts of Arizona's immigration enforcement law from going into effect, a ruling that temporarily squashes a state policy that had inflamed the national debate over immigration. Judge Susan Bolton issues a preliminary injunction against sections of the law that call for police officers to check a person's immigration status while enforcing other laws and required immigrants to prove that they are authorized to be in the country.

29 The House ethics committee lays out 13 charges of ethical violations committed by Rep. Charles B. Rangel, accusing him of a pattern of "indifference and disregard" for the law and the rules of the House. Mr. Rangel's lawyers suggest they are still trying to reach a settlement to avoid a public trial by the committee this fall.

Senate Republicans reject a bill to aid small businesses with expanded loan programs and tax breaks in a procedural blockade that underscores how determined the party's leaders are to deny Democrats any further legislative accomplishments before the midterm elections. Republican leaders filibustered over the number of amendments they would be able to offer.

30 The panel that oversaw the two-year ethics inquiry into Rep. Charles B. Rangel's conduct recommends that the congressman be punished with a reprimand, rather than a more serious censure or expulsion from office. The recommendation appears to be carrying significant weight with the full 10-member House ethics committee.

The Anti-Defamation League announces its opposition to a proposed Islamic center and mosque two blocks north of Ground Zero in Lower Manhattan, intensifying a fierce national debate about the limits of religious freedom and the meaning of the Sept. 11 terrorist attacks. The unexpected move by the A.D.L. may be a turning point in the battle over the project for which national opposition is mounting.

A Commerce Department report shows that economic growth slipped sharply in the latest quarter from a much brisker pace earlier, an annual rate of five percent at the end of 2009 and 3.7 percent in the first quarter of 2010.

Rep. Maxine Waters, Democrat of California faces charges of misusing her office and is expected to contest the claims in a House trial. A House ethics subcommittee has charged Ms. Waters in a case involving communications that she had with the top executive of a bank that her husband owned stock in while it was applying for a federal bailout in 2008.

31 Floods driven by record-breaking rainfall have killed at least 800 people and destroyed thousands of homes, in the latest disaster to test Pakistan's already strained government, which is struggling to fight an Islamic insurgency and to cope with the aftermath of a plane crash in which 152 people died.

AUGUST 2010

1 The United Arab Emirates says that it will suspend BlackBerry mobile services in the latest clash between governments and communications providers. The Emirates have been in a dispute with Research in Motion, the smartphone's producer, over the BlackBerry's highly encrypted data system, which offers security to users but makes it more difficult for governments to monitor communications.

2 A federal jury finds Russell M. Defreitas and Abdul Kadir, two Guyanese men, guilty of conspiring to attack Kennedy International Airport. The month-long trial focused on their plan to blow up fuel tanks and set off a series of explosions along a pipeline that cuts through New York City. Two other men plead guilty to participating in the plot and another man is awaiting trial.

3 The National Oceanic and Atmospheric Administration reports that three-quarters of the oil from the Deepwater Horizon leak has already evaporated, dispersed, been captured or otherwise eliminated, and that much of the rest is so diluted that it does not seem to pose much additional risk of harm. About 26 percent of the oil released from the well could, in principle, cause new problems.

Pakistan's president, Asif Ali Zardari, is quoted in a French newspaper as saying that coalition forces are losing the war in Afghanistan because they had "lost the battle to win hearts and minds" of Afghans, and that the Taliban's success lay "in knowing how to wait" for NATO forces to withdraw.

The Centers for Disease Control and Prevention issues a report stating that 2.4 million more people in America became obese from 2007 to 2009, bringing the total to 72.5 million, or 26.7 percent of the population. The rates are probably underestimated because they are based on a phone survey in which 400,000 participants were asked their weight and height instead of having it measured by someone else.

4 A federal judge in San Francisco strikes down California's voter-approved ban on same-sex marriage. Vaughn R. Walker, the chief judge of the court immediately stayed his own decision, pending appeals by proponents of Proposition 8, who seem confident that higher courts will hear and favor their position. Judge Walker writes that "Proposition 8 cannot withstand any level of scrutiny under the Equal Protection Clause."

Kenya's new constitution, which addresses the political issues that have dogged the nation since independence in 1963, appears headed toward approval after a peaceful nationwide referendum. Pro-constitution votes are leading 66 percent to 34 percent with about half the votes counted.

5 Russian Prime Minister Vladimir V. Putin bans all exports of grain after millions of acres of Russian wheat withered in a severe drought, driving up prices around the world and pushing them to their highest level in two years in the U.S. The move is the latest intervention in the Russian economy by Mr. Putin, who called the ban necessary to curb rising food prices in the country.

The Senate confirms Elena Kagan to a seat on the Supreme Court in a 63-to-37 vote. Ms. Kagan becomes the fourth woman to serve on the court and will be the only justice on the court not to have served previously as a judge.

The Senate approves $26 billion in aid to states and school districts to prevent the layoffs of tens of thousands of teachers and government workers while allocating $600 million to strengthen border security. Both measures require approval by the House, which will be reconvened to approve the bill.

BP completes pumping cement into its runaway well in hope of plugging its flow for good. In an operation called a static kill, cement followed the tons of mud already poured into the well, which was tightly capped on July 15. Crews are still drilling relief wells which will be completed in late August.

6 The Department of Labor reports that the nation lost 131,000 jobs in July and that the unemployment rate remains stuck at 9.5 percent. Private employers added 71,000 jobs, but 143,000 people temporary Census workers were let go by the government.

Investigators in the United Arab Emirates say that a terrorist attack caused the mysterious damage to a Japanese oil tanker that was passing through the Strait of Hormuz last week. The Abdullah Azzam Brigades, a militant group with ties to Al Qaeda, claimed it had carried out the attack.

7 Afghan gunmen kill an aid team working in northern Afghanistan, which included six Americans, a Briton, a German and four Afghans. The Taliban claims responsibility for the killings, accusing the group of being spies and Christian missionaries.

Former President Fidel Castro of Cuba addresses a session of Parliament for the first time in four years, warning that the confrontation between Iran and the U.S. and its allies over the issue of nuclear weapons has pushed the world to the brink of nuclear war. The speech marks the first time Mr. Castro has participated in a public government meeting since he underwent intestinal surgery in 2006.

Elena Kagan is sworn in as the 112th person to serve on the Supreme Court. The low-key formal ceremony comes two days after she was confirmed by the Senate. She is Pres. Obama's second successful nominee to the court.

8 F.B.I agents and their counterparts from Britain, Germany and Afghanistan confirm that the 10 aid workers murdered in northern Afghanistan were members of the Nuristan Eye Camp Expedition, a medical team from the International Assistance Mission.

A landslide buries and floods hundreds of homes in a remote mountainous region of Gansu Province in China. Officials say that 127 bodies have been recovered and that nearly 2,000 people are missing.

9 Health officials in Moscow say that the death toll from the heat wave has doubled in recent days because of increases in heart and lung ailments and strokes. The heat and smoke from wildfires are creating a toxic mixture of fine particles and carbon monoxide in Moscow's smoky atmosphere. Weather forecasters say there is no relief in sight from the hot weather.

Researchers report that a spinal fluid test can be 100 percent accurate in identifying patients with significant memory loss who are on their way to developing Alzheimer's disease. Although there has been evidence of the value of this and other tests, the study shows how accurate they can be.

10 Federal Reserve officials plan to use proceeds from the Fed's huge mortgage-bond portfolio to buy long-term government debt, a move that may put downward pressure on long-term interest rates and stimulate borrowing, and will maintain mortgage rates at record lows for some time.

Prime Minister Naoto Kan of Japan offers a renewed apology to South Korea for Japan's brutal colonial rule, as part of a statement marking the 100th anniversary of the nation's annexation of the Korean Peninsula in 1910.

Former Senator Ted Stevens of Alaska is among five people who died in a plane crash in remote southwest Alaska while on a fishing trip. Sen. Stevens served in the Senate for 40 years until he lost his bid for a seventh term after he was found guilty of corruption charges.

The House approves $26 billion in aid to school districts and states to prevent large-scale layoffs of teachers and public employees. The vote was 247–161 in favor of the legislation.

11 Russia announces that it has deployed an advanced surface-to-air missile system in the breakaway Georgian enclave of Abzhazia, a sign that Russian forces are becoming more entrenched in a disputed region at the focal point of Russia's brief war with Georgia two years ago.

The U.N. appeals for donations of nearly half a billion dollars to aid flood victims in Pakistan as the magnitude of the disaster widens with about one-fifth of the country submerged and the annual monsoon season still potent.

General Motors reports its best quarterly earnings in six years and announces that its chief executive, picked by the Obama administration last year to lead it after bankruptcy, will step down next month. The success of G.M.'s upcoming initial public stock offering will determine how much American taxpayers will recoup from their 61 percent investment stake in G.M., which resulted from the government bailout of the company a year ago.

The Canadian Navy and Coast Guard intercept a ship off the coast of British Columbia thought to be carrying hundreds of Tamil migrants from Sri Lanka. Authorities have been tracking the ship since it left Sri Lanka saying that some of the ship's 490 passengers are "suspected human smugglers and terrorists."

13 The F.D.A. approves a new form of emergency contraceptive pill that prevents pregnancies if taken as many as five days after unprotected intercourse. Developed in government laboratories, it is more effective than Plan B, the morning-after pill now available.

Pres. Obama signs into law a $600 million bill to pay for 1,500 new border agents, additional unmanned surveillance drones, and new Border Patrol stations along the southwest border. The measure sailed through Congress with broad bipartisan support.

The Indus River breaches its banks again bringing further devastation to southern Pakistan as health officials confirm the first cases of cholera caused by the worst flooding in the nation's history.

14 Gen. David H. Petraeus, the commander of American and NATO forces in Afghanistan, begins a campaign to convince an increasingly skeptical public that the American-led coalition can still succeed despite months of setbacks. He says he did not come to Afghanistan to preside over a "graceful exit."

15 The Obama administrations says that it will require significantly more environmental review before approving new offshore drilling permits, ending a practice in which government regulators essentially rubber-stamped potentially hazardous deepwater projects like BP's out-of-control well.

The Taliban order their first public execution by stoning in nine years, killing a young couple who had eloped. The punishment was carried out by hundreds of the victims' neighbors in a village in northern Afghanistan.

16 Tom DeLay, a Texas Republican and former House majority leader who fell from power in 2006, will not face federal corruption charges over his dealings with the disgraced lobbyist Jack Abramoff. After a six-year investigation, the Justice Department is closing its file, although Mr. DeLay still faces a trial in Texas on charges of money laundering.

17 After deliberating for two weeks, a Chicago jury finds Rod R. Blagojevich, the former governor of Illinois, guilty of a single criminal count—making false statements to the F.B.I. The jurors could not reach a unanimous verdict on 23 of the 24 counts against him, including an accusation that he tried to sell an appointment to fill the Senate seat once held by Pres. Obama.

Lebanon passes a law granting Palestinian refugees the same rights to work as other foreigners, a step in ending years of discrimination that had restricted them to the most menial of jobs. An estimated 400,000 refugees live in Lebanon, where their status has long divided lawmakers.

18 New research confirms the existence of a large plume of dispersed oil deep in the Gulf of Mexico and suggests that it has not broken down rapidly, raising the possibility that it might pose a threat to wildlife for months or years to come.

20 Palestinian president Mahmoud Abbas agrees to resume direct negotiations with Israel after intense pressure from the U.S. and Europe, as the Obama administration seeks to restart the Middle East peace process. Secretary of State Hillary Rodham Clinton formally announces the new talks.

Blackwater Worldwide, the private security company plagued by accusations of impropriety, reaches an agreement with the State Department for the company to pay $42 million in fines for hundreds of violations of U.S. export control regulations, including illegal weapons exports to Afghanistan.

21 A Lebanese aid ship destined for Gaza delays its departure after Cyprus refuses to allow the ship to sail through its waters or to use its ports. Cyprus's refusal comes after Israel said it would use force against the vessel.

Australia's Parliament faces the prospect of a stalemate after voters apparently fail to deliver a clear majority to either the governing center-left Labor Party or a conservative opposition coalition in the tightest race in decades.

22 More than 127,000 people are evacuated in northeastern China after torrential rains batter the area and lead to severe flooding along the border with North Korea.

Thirty-three miners trapped underground for 17 days in a gold and copper mine in northern Chile send up a message tied to a drill telling rescuers they are all alive. Pres. Sebastián Piñera says it will take months to get the trapped men out.

Floodwaters surge deeper into areas of southern Pakistan forcing thousands more people to abandon their homes. Nearly five million people have been displaced from the worst flooding ever recorded in Pakistan.

23 A federal district judge blocks Pres. Obama's 2009 executive order that expanded embryonic stem cell research, say it violates a ban on federal money being used to destroy embryos. Chief Judge Royce C. Lamberth writes that his temporary injunction returns federal policy to the "status quo."

Nepal's Parliament fails for a fifth time to select a new prime minister, in a deepening political stalemate that is crippling the government and the economy.

24 The National Association of Realtors reports that housing sales in July plunged 25.5 percent below the level of a year ago. The steep decline surprises nearly every analyst and drives down the Dow Jones industrial average by 134 points.

The Obama administration says it will appeal a court ruling challenging the legality of Pres. Obama's rules governing human embryonic stem cell research. Dr. Francis S. Collins, director of the

National Institutes of Health says if upheld, the decision would most likely force the cancellation of dozens of experiments in diseases ranging from diabetes to Parkinson's.

Shirley Sherrod, who was ousted from the Agriculture Department during a racial firestorm that embarrassed the Obama administration, rejects an offer to return to the department, though she left open the possibility that she might do consulting work for Agriculture Secretary Tom Vilsack on racial issues.

25 *The New York Times* reports that Mohammed Zia Salehi, the aide to Pres. Hamid Karzai at the center of a corruption investigation, has been on the C.I.A. payroll for a number of years. It is unclear what he does in exchange for the money.

Terry Jones, pastor of a small church in Gainesville, Florida, announces that he plans to memorialize the Sept. 11 attacks with a bonfire of Korans. Muslim leaders in several countries formally condemn him and his church, the Dove World Outreach Center.

26 Scientists working with NASA's Kepler satellite report that they might have spotted a planet just 1.5 times the diameter of Earth around a Sunlike star 2,000 light-years away. The Kepler team is in the process of confirming that this is a planet.

27 The National Center for Health Statistics reports that the U.S. birthrate has fallen to its lowest level in at least a century, dropping for the second year in a row. Births fell 2.6 percent last year.

28 Pres. Hamid Karzai fires one of Afghanistan's most senior prosecutors because he refused to block corruption investigations at the highest levels of Mr. Karzai's government. Fazel Ahmed Faqiryar says investigations of more than two dozen senior officials are being thwarted by Mr. Karzai, an account corroborated by Western officials.

An enormous crowd rallies at the steps of the Lincoln Memorial, summoned by Glenn Beck, a conservative broadcaster who called for a religious rebirth in America. The rally took place at the site where the Rev. Dr. Martin Luther King Jr. delivered his "I Have a Dream" speech 47 years ago to the day.

30 The ACLU and the Center for Constitutional Rights go to court to challenge to Obama administration's decision to authorize the killing of Anwar al-Awlaki, the American-born radical Muslim cleric now hiding in Yemen. The lawsuit is filed in federal court in Washington on behalf of Mr. Awlaki's father, arguing that the U.S. government should not be permitted to kill an American citizen away from the battlefield and without judicial review.

Vice President Joseph R. Biden arrives in Baghdad to commemorate the official end of the U.S. combat mission and to meet with Iraqi political leaders who have yet to form a government more than five months after the election.

31 Pres. Obama declares an end to the seven-year American combat mission in Iraq, saying that the U.S. has met its responsibility to that country and that it is now time to turn to pressing problems at home.

SEPTEMBER 2010

1 Pres. Obama begins his Middle East peace initiative as the Israeli and Palestinian leaders, Prime Minister Benjamin Netanyahu and Pres. Mahmoud Abbas, commit to work to end the conflict that has endured for six decades.

2 The Labor Department reports that American businesses added more jobs in the last three months than originally estimated, with the private sector adding 67,000 jobs in August. The jobless rate for August was 9.6 percent.

4 The Afghan government injects funds into the privately owned Kabul Bank in an effort to head off the run on the bank by its customers who have withdrawn more than $200 million in the past few days amid fears of a wider economic collapse.

5 Bahraini officials announce that they are charging 23 people, most of them activists from the Shiite majority, with coordinating a violent campaign to overthrow the minority Sunni government. Prosecutors describe the men as being part of a sophisticated terrorist network with international support.

6 Pres. Obama calls for Congress to approve major upgrades to the nation's roads, rail lines, and runways—part of a six-year plan that would spur job growth. Central to the plan is an "infrastructure bank," which would finance innovative transportation projects.

7 Prime Minister Julia Gillard of Australia retains power by the slimmest margin, forging a tenuous coalition with three independents and one legislator from the Greens Party that gives her Labor Party a one-seat majority in the House of Representatives.

Prominent Christian, Jewish, and Muslim leaders hold an "emergency summit" in Washington to denounce what they call "the derision, misinformation, and outright bigotry" aimed at American Muslims during the controversy over the proposed Islamic community center in Manhattan.

8 A federal appeals court rules that former prisoners of the C.I.A. cannot sue over their alleged torture in overseas prisons because such lawsuits might expose secret government information. The 6-to-5 ruling is a major victory for the Obama administration's efforts to advance a sweeping view of executive secrecy powers.

9 Judge Virginia A. Phillips of the Federal District Court in California rules that the "don't ask, don't tell" policy toward gay members of the military is unconstitutional.

A federal appeals court in Washington rules that federal financing of embryonic stem cell research can continue while the court considers a judge's order that banned the government from underwriting the work

10 Pres. Obama calls for Israel to extend its moratorium on settlement construction in the West Bank as a good-will gesture to move peace talks with the Palestinians forward. The settlement construction moratorium is scheduled to expire on Sept. 26.

12 House Republican leader, John A. Boehner, opens the door to compromise on the issue of the Bush-era tax cuts, saying he would vote to maintain lower rates for families earning less than $250,000 even if the Democrats insist on ending the cuts for wealthier Americans.

Turkish voters approve a sweeping package of constitutional reforms by a wide margin. The changes are intended to bring Turkey's military-imposed Constitution in line with European standards of law and democracy.

14 The United Nations reports that the number of undernourished people in the world decreased this year for the first time in 15 years. The number of hungry people fell to 925 million from a record high of 1.02 billion in 2009, with most of the improvement in the Asia–Pacific region.

Iran releases Sarah E. Shourd, one of three American hikers who had been held on espionage charges since their arrest more than a year ago. She is freed on $500,000 bail after concerns were voiced about her health. There is no talk of releasing her two companions.

15 A U.N.-backed court in Cambodia formally indicts four surviving leaders of the Khmer Rouge on charges of genocide, war crimes, crimes against humanity, and murder. The defendants are charged with being involved in the deaths of 1.7 million people between 1975 and 1979.

16 The Census Bureau reports that 14.3 percent of Americans were struggling below the poverty line in 2009—the highest number since 1994. Four million additional Americans found themselves in poverty, with the total reaching 44 million.

The Senate Foreign Relations Committee votes 14–4 to approve an arms control treaty with Russia, known as New Start, after negotiating a resolution addressing conservative concerns about missile defense and modernization of the nuclear arsenal.

18 Voter turnout is light for Afghanistan's parliamentary elections as the Taliban attacks polling centers, fulfilling a vow to disrupt the election process. At least 10 people are killed, although Afghan officials insist that in most places the election went ahead without major incident.

19 Pope Benedict XVI ends his historic and contentious visit to Britain by beatifying Cardinal John Henry Newman, a 19th-century thinker and writer who left the Church of England to convert to Catholicism.

The federal government declares BP's Macondo oil well dead, nearly five months after it blew out of control, unleashing an environmental calamity in the Gulf of Mexico. The well and the two relief wells will now be abandoned following standard industry practice.

21 The Senate votes against taking up a major military bill that would allow the repeal of the "don't ask, don't tell" policy with Senate Republicans voting unanimously to block debate after majority leader Harry Reid says he will move to limit the amendments offered by Republicans.

The White House says that Lawrence H. Summers, the chief architect of Pres. Obama's economic policy, will leave at the end of the year, saying the departure has been long planned because Mr. Summers must return to his professorship at Harvard by January to keep his tenure.

Italian monetary authorities say that they have impounded $30 million from the Vatican bank and placed its top two officers under investigation in connection with a money-laundering inquiry.

22 In a speech before the U.N. General Assembly, Turkish president Abdullah Gul defends Turkey's close ties to Iran and proclaims his nation's intention to become a leader in the Muslim world, saying Turkey will adhere to the U.N. sanctions but will not allow the measures to constrict its broader trade with Iran.

23 Pres. Obama increases pressure on China to immediately revalue its currency, devoting most of a two-hour meeting with China's prime minister to the issue. Democrats in Congress have been threatening to pass legislation that would slap huge tariffs on Chinese goods to undermine the advantages they enjoy from a currency that experts say is artificially weakened.

24 According to Afghan and international election observers and diplomats, evidence is mounting that fraud in last week's parliamentary election is so widespread that it could affect the results in a third of the provinces, calling into question the credibility of the vote. The fraud appears to cut both for and against the government of Pres. Hamid Karzai.

The Obama administration completes a legal brief that asks a federal judge to throw out a lawsuit seeking to stop the government from killing Anwar Al-Awlaki, a radical Muslim cleric born in New Mexico who is accused of ties to Al Qaeda. The brief argues that litigating the matter could reveal state secrets.

25 The Atomic Energy Organization, the Iranian agency that runs the country's nuclear facilities, reports that its engineers are trying to protect their facilities from Stuxnet, a sophisticated computer worm that has infected industrial plants across Iran. The worm is a self-replicating malware computer program which is aimed solely at industrial equipment made by Siemens.

26 Israel allows a politically-charged freeze on Jewish settlement building in the West Bank to expire, but the Palestinians do not carry out a threat to quit peace negotiations.

27 Kim Jong-un, the youngest son of Kim Jong-il, North Korea's leader, is promoted to a military general, the clearest sign yet that he is in line to succeed his father as the country's leader. Little is known about Kim Jong-un, who is either 27 or 28 years old.

The opposition party in Venezuela wins one-third of the seats in the National Assembly and about half of the popular vote which will allow it to block legislation and play a role in determining the makeup of the Supreme Court which is now packed with supporters of Pres. Hugo Chávez.

28 Pres. Hamid Karzai names a 70-member peace council, an announcement that is the Afghani government's first concrete step to open formal contacts with the Taliban. The U.S. indicates support for the reconciliation process and says high-level members of the Taliban have already reached out to the government.

29 The Obama administration puts eight Iranian officials on a blacklist for their role in the bloody suppression of antigovernment activists after the disputed election last year, citing human-rights abuses for the first time as a basis for sanctions. The U.S. will freeze foreign assets and deny visas to officials, including the commander of the Islamic Revolutionary Guard Corps and the minister of welfare and social security.

Astronomers say that NASA's Kepler satellite has found a very distant planet capable of harboring water on its surface, thus potentially making it a home for plant or animal life. The planet, known as Gliese 581g, is orbiting a star about 20 light-years away in the constellation Libra.

30 Pres. Obama appoints Peter Rouse as White House chief of staff, replacing Rahm Emanuel who is moving back to Chicago to run for mayor.

Major News Stories of 2009–10

By Correspondents of The New York Times

National

Rig Explodes in Gulf of Mexico, Causing Catastrophic Oil Spill

On the night of April 20, an explosion on an offshore drilling rig in the Gulf of Mexico killed 11 workers and set off the largest marine oil spill in U.S. history. The spill, which would eventually dump 4.1 million barrels of oil into the Gulf over nearly three months, drew attention to years of lax federal oversight, prompted an enormous and costly spill response operation and triggered severe economic anxiety along the entire Gulf coast.

The rig sank two days after the explosion, detaching from the well itself, which continued to spew oil 5,000 feet below the surface of the gulf. The Coast Guard and BP, the company that had been leasing the rig, began a series of complicated attempts to stop the flow of oil. These attempts involved complex engineering and added exotic new phrases to the national vocabulary, like top kill and junk shot, but they repeatedly resulted in failure.

The explosion was caused by a blowout, or a sudden, unexpected release of hydrocarbons. A variety of safety devices, including a large set of valves called a blowout preventer, either did not work, were not activated or had not been installed in the first place.

While blame was cast among various companies involved—including BP and Transocean, which owned the rig—the explosion revealed clear failures of oversight by the Minerals Management Service, an agency within the Department of the Interior that regulated offshore drilling.

In the wake of the disaster, that agency was split into three parts: one responsible for leasing offshore wells, another for fee collections and a separate division for environmental oversight. More controversially, the Obama administration declared a moratorium on exploratory offshore drilling until the causes of the Deepwater Horizon blowout were determined and safety regulations for existing rigs were tightened. Throughout the summer, beaches sat empty and fishermen sat idle as the oil showed up onshore on hundreds of miles of coastline from Louisiana to the Florida panhandle.

Under federal law, the Coast Guard was in charge of the clean-up while BP, as the party deemed responsible for the spill, had to execute and pay for it. Tens of thousands of workers and thousands of boats, including those belonging to fishermen who were left unemployed by the spill, were put to work trying to corral the oil or prevent it from hitting shore. Nearly two million gallons of chemical dispersant were used to break the spill apart, a procedure that drew criticism from environmentalists and fishermen who worried about the effects of the dispersant on wildlife.

While the long term effects were still being studied, the dispersant, combined with the warm, microbe-rich waters of the Gulf, appeared to have broken down the oil faster than initially anticipated. Concerns about the long term health of crab, fish and shrimp larvae remained, however.

BP early on said it would pay all legitimate claims to people affected by the spill, regardless of a $75 million cap on liability in the federal Oil Pollution Act. In June, BP and the White House announced the creation of a $20 billion fund dedicated to such claims. In late August, Kenneth R. Feinberg, who administered the settlement fund for 9/11 victims, took control of that fund and began dispensing payments to those were affected along the Gulf coast.

The Justice Department also began to investigate possible criminal charges, and hundreds of lawsuits were filed against BP, Transocean and others involved in the accident, promising years of litigation

On July 15, 86 days into the spill, the oil was finally contained when a new set of valves were lowered on top of the well, shutting it in entirely. In September, the spill was killed for good by a relief well, a separate well that was drilled into the original one, which it filled with cement.

—CAMPBELL ROBERTSON

Declining Public Support for Obama Overshadows Legislative Victories

It was a rocky second year in office for President Obama, who weathered plummeting poll numbers, a brutal economy and a massive oil spill even as he scored major legislative victories on Capitol Hill. The tide of hope and good will that accompanied his 2009 inaugural evaporated in 2010, as the nation's 44th president became just as divisive a figure as his predecessor, George W. Bush.

"Jobs must be our number one focus in 2010," Mr. Obama declared in his State of the Union address in January. But the unemployment rate remained stuck above 9 percent, driving down Mr. Obama's approval ratings and hurting Democrats as they headed into the November mid-term re-elections.

The year opened with a political bombshell: Scott Brown, a Republican, won a special Senate election to succeed the late Massachusetts Democrat, Edward M. Kennedy, costing Democrats their 60-vote supermajority. Mr. Obama's long-held dream of expanding health coverage to millions of Americans seemed doomed. Emboldened Republicans demanded Mr. Obama throw out his health bill and start over.

But Mr. Obama managed to revive the measure. He convened an all-day, televised bipartisan health care summit, insisting Republicans offer their own ideas. He barnstormed the nation and twisted arms on Capitol Hill. On March 22, in a raucous ceremony in the White House East Room, he signed it into law, citing "the core principle that everybody should have some basic security when it comes to their health care." It was a stunning victory for a president who sorely needed one. The White House also succeeded in its push for Wall Street oversight; in July Mr. Obama signed into law the most sweeping expansion of financial regulations since the Great Depression. The president's hopes for a broad energy package, however, were dashed in 2010 when a bipartisan bill fell apart. Another high priority for Mr. Obama, immigration reform, stalled in Congress, a victim of election year politics.

One high point for Mr. Obama was Senate confirmation of his solicitor general, Elena Kagan, to the Supreme Court.

On foreign policy, Mr. Obama hosted world leaders in Washington for a nuclear proliferation summit; they endorsed his call to secure all nuclear materials around the globe within four years. He stepped up his Mideast peace efforts, convening Israeli and Palestinian leaders in Washington for high-level talks. He grappled with declining public support for the war in Afghanistan and fired his top general there, Stanley McChrystal, after the general made disparaging remarks about the president's team in a magazine interview. And he made good on his promise to withdraw combat troops from Iraq, using a rare Oval Office address in late August to explain his policy to the nation.

But the president scaled back the aggressive foreign travel schedule he had pursued in 2009. He twice postponed a trip to Indonesia, where he had lived as a boy, citing pressing domestic matters. One was the explosion in April of a BP oil rig, which sent millions of gallons of oil spewing into the Gulf of Mexico, testing the administration's ability to respond to a complicated environmental disaster. The even-tempered Mr. Obama faced withering criticism that he lacked outrage and was slow to respond. In May, five weeks after the spill, he called a rare news conference, insisting, "I'm fully engaged."

Throughout the summer and fall, as Mr. Obama's approval ratings sank below 50 percent and the economic recovery seemed ever more tentative, the president became a political liability for Democrats seeking reelection. He continued to raise money; in speeches, he cast the midterms as a choice between going forward and going back to the era of Republican control. Using a car as a metaphor for the economy, Mr. Obama often said Republicans "drove the car into the ditch," adding, "now they want the keys back." But his campaign appearances were restricted as some Democrats refused to be seen with him—a stark contrast to the heady days of his own run for the White House just two years earlier.

—SHERYL GAY STOLBERG

Landmark Healthcare Overhaul Passes

House Democrats approved a far-reaching overhaul of the nation's health system on March 21, 2010, voting over unanimous Republican opposition to provide medical coverage to tens of millions of uninsured Americans after an epic political battle that could define the differences between the parties for years. President Obama, whose yearlong push for the legislation was the centerpiece of his agenda and a test of his political power, signed it into law two days later, taking the final step in a bitter legislative fight that highlighted the nation's deep partisan and ideological divisions.

On the sun-splashed day of the House vote, protesters outside the Capitol, urged on by House Republicans, chanted "Kill the bill" and waved yellow flags declaring "Don't Tread on Me." They carried signs saying "Doctors, Not Dictators." Inside, Democrats hailed the votes as a historic advance in social justice, comparable to the establishment of Medicare and Social Security. They said the bill would also put pressure on rising health care costs and rein in federal budget deficits.

After a year of combat and weeks of legislative brinksmanship, House Democrats and the White House clinched their victory only hours before the voting started. They agreed to a deal with opponents of abortion rights within their party to reiterate in an executive order that federal money provided by the bill could not be used for abortions, securing for Democrats the final handful of votes needed to assure passage.

Republicans said the plan would saddle the nation with unaffordable levels of debt, leave states with expensive new obligations, weaken Medicare and give the government a huge new role in the health care system.

The debate on the legislation set up a bitter midterm campaign season, with Republicans promising an effort to repeal the legislation, challenge its constitutionality or block its provisions in the states.

The health care bill would require most Americans to have health insurance, would add 16 million people to the Medicaid rolls and would subsidize private coverage for low- and middle-income people, at a cost to the government of $938 billion over 10 years, the Congressional Budget Office said. The bill would require many employers to offer coverage to employees or pay a penalty. Each state would set up a marketplace, or exchange, where consumers without such coverage could shop for insurance meeting federal standards.

The budget office estimates that the bill would provide coverage to 32 million uninsured people, but still leave 23 million uninsured in 2019. One-third of those remaining uninsured would be illegal immigrants. The new costs, according to the budget office, would be more than offset by savings in Medicare and by new taxes and fees, including a tax on high-cost employer-sponsored health plans and a tax on the investment income of the most affluent Americans.

Cost estimates by the budget office, showing that the bill would reduce federal budget deficits by $143 billion in the next 10 years, persuaded some fiscally conservative Democrats to vote for the bill. Republicans criticized the budget office estimates as overly rosy, because the new taxes and fees would start immediately, while the major costs would not show up for years.

Democrats said Americans would embrace the bill when they saw its benefits, including some provisions that take effect later this year. Health insurers, for example, could not deny coverage to children with medical problems or suddenly drop coverage for people who become ill. Insurers must allow children to stay on their parents' policies until they turn 26. Small businesses could obtain tax credits to help them buy insurance.

—ROBERT PEAR
and DAVID M. HERSZENHORN

After a Promising Start, the Economy Struggles As the Stimulus Expires

The United States economy struggled for much of 2010 to emerge from the deepest recession in at least a generation. In the early months of the year, the economy seemed headed for a solid recovery. Monthly job losses had shrunk throughout most of 2009 and by the beginning of 2010, the economy was adding jobs again. The pace of economic activity in the spring—consumer spending, business investment, hiring—was faster than many forecasters had expected. But it began to slow noticeably in the summer. By the end of the summer, employment was shrinking again, though not nearly as rapidly as it had been in 2009.

The 2010 slowdown was in some ways typical. Recoveries from financial crises tend to be halting, and the financial crisis of 2007–09 was widely considered to be the most severe since the Great Depression. Indebted consumers did not rush back to stores and began spending lavishly. The housing market was still recovering from the bubble in prices, and sales remained subdued. Banks, trying to rebuild their balance sheets, remained reluctant to lend, especially to small businesses. The relatively high level of the dollar hampered the attempts of businesses to increase exports.

But the slowdown was also a result of the sunset of the federal government's stimulus program. Passed in February 2009, that program lifted employment by more than 2.5 million jobs, according to analyses by the Congressional Budget Office and various private research firms. By mid-2010, many parts of the program began to expire. The lapsing of fiscal aid to states led to layoffs of state and local government workers, including firefighters and teachers. After a tax credit for house purchases expired in June, home sales plunged.

The House of Representatives passed a fairly large bill to stimulate the economy further in the summer of 2010, but the bill was not able to get the support of 60 senators, which was necessary to overcome a filibuster. The Senate instead passed several much smaller bills, which President Obama signed.

The Fed, meanwhile, was caught somewhat unaware by the slowdown. Into the summer, some Fed officials continued to warn that the government's extraordinary efforts to help the economy in 2008 and 2009 could have led to overly rapid growth and accelerating inflation. Instead, inflation fell near zero in 2010, and Ben S. Bernanke, the Fed chairman, began to warn of the risk of a destabilizing cycle of falling prices, known as deflation. In August, the Fed took some modest steps to lift growth, by buying bonds to reduce interest rates and encourage spending.

There were some positive signs late in 2010. The stock market and corporate profits had both rebounded strongly from their 2009 lows. Wages had outpaced inflation for most workers since the start of the recession in 2007—which was not the case in the other deep slumps of the last half-century.

But no matter how quickly the economy grows in 2011, it will have to dig out of a very large hole. To return the unemployment rate to its pre-recession level of less than 5 percent, the economy would have to add jobs at the rapid pace of the late 1990s—for almost five straight years.

—DAVID LEONHARDT

Kagan, Succeeding Stevens, Sworn In on Supreme Court

Elena Kagan was sworn in on Aug. 7 as the 112th person, and fourth woman, to serve on the Supreme Court, continuing a generational and demographic transformation of the nation's highest bench.

The low-key formal ceremony in the Supreme Court Building came two days after she was confirmed by the Senate and a day after President Obama marked her ascension with a jubilant televised celebration in the White House. She was Mr. Obama's second successful nominee to the court, and her approval by the Senate was taken as a jolt of validation for a White House battered by political and economic troubles.

Succeeding Justice John Paul Stevens, the court's retiring liberal leader, Justice Kagan, 50, presumably will not drastically change the philosophical balance on the divided court. But if she were to serve until she was 90, as Justice Stevens has, she would have four decades to shape the nation's legal architecture, long after the man who appointed her left the White House. Even a shorter tenure would give her time to leave her mark.

Justice Kagan is the third woman on the current court, joining Justices Ruth Bader Ginsburg and Sonia Sotomayor. She is also the fifth justice born after World War II, making that group a majority, and she brings down the average age on the court to 64, from nearly 69. And she is the first person since William H. Rehnquist, 38 years ago, to join the court without experience as a judge.

If her installation added diversity in some ways, though, it reinforced the court's lack of it in other areas. Her addition means the court now includes neither Protestants nor anyone without an Ivy League background. Justice Kagan joins two other Jewish justices and six Catholics. She is the sixth justice to have studied at Harvard Law School (although Justice Ginsburg later transferred to and graduated from Columbia Law School); the other three graduated from Yale Law School. And she is the fourth justice to have grown up in New York City.

Justice Kagan served as a lawyer and domestic policy aide in the Clinton White House, was dean of Harvard Law School and in 2009 was appointed by Mr. Obama as solicitor general, the government's lawyer before the Supreme Court.

She was confirmed on a 63-to-37 Senate vote, with most Republicans opposing her, citing her lack of judicial experience and liberal views on issues like abortion, guns and gay rights.

—PETER BAKER

Supreme Court Rules On Campaign Finance, Guns and Gay Rights

The blockbuster Supreme Court cases tend to arrive at the end of the term, but this year the court's biggest decision came early. In January 2010, the court ruled that corporations and unions may spend freely in candidate elections, striking down a central part of the 2002 McCain-Feingold campaign finance law and overturning two important precedents. The 5-to-4 ruling in the case, *Citizens United v. Federal Election Commission*, resonated through the balance of the term. President Obama criticized it days later at the State of the Union address with six justices in attendance, eliciting a mouthed "not true" from Justice Samuel A. Alito Jr.

Justice John Paul Stevens cited his halting performance in summarizing his dissent from the bench in *Citizens United* as a reason for his retirement at the end of the term. Elena Kagan, nominated to succeed Justice Stevens, argued the losing side of the case as United States solicitor general and was questioned about it at her confirmation hearings in June.

There were other notable decisions, of course, with many piled up at the end of the term in June. The most important was probably *McDonald v. Chicago*, a sequel to the 2008 decision in *District of Columbia v. Heller*, which ruled that the Second Amendment protects an individual right to own guns, at least where federal laws are at issue. The McDonald case extended that right to state and local laws as well and suggested that Chicago's almost total gun ban is unconstitutional.

The court issued rulings in three cases touching on gay rights. In one, *Christian Legal Society v. Martinez*, the court ruled that a public law school could withdraw recognition from a Christian student group that would not accept gay and lesbian members. In *Doe v. Reed*, the court said the names of people who signed a petition to put an anti-gay-rights measure on the ballot in Washington State could be made public. And, in *Hollingsworth v. Perry*, the court blocked camera coverage of a trial over same-sex marriage in San Francisco.

The court issued three decisions limiting the Miranda rule, which requires the police to warn suspects in custody of their rights before interrogating them. The court allowed the police to vary the language of the warning, insist that suspects speak in order to protect their right to remain silent and resume questioning after suspects have invoked their rights.

In other cases, however, the court ruled in favor of criminal defendants. In a pair of decisions in June involving two former corporate executives, Jeffrey K. Skilling of Enron and Conrad M. Black of Hollinger International, the court significantly limited the sweep of a federal law that made it a crime to deprive another of "honest services." In *Graham v. Florida*, the court ruled that sentencing juvenile offenders to life in prison without the possibility of parole for crimes in which no one was killed violated the Eighth Amendment's ban on cruel and unusual punishment.

The court upheld a federal law allowing the continued civil commitment of sex offenders who had completed their criminal sentences. The law was challenged on the ground that Congress did not have the constitutional authority to enact it, and the broad ruling in the case, *United States v. Comstock*, suggested that the court may not be prepared to strike down the recent health care legislation when challenges based on similar theories reach it.

Citizens United was not the only case involving a First Amendment challenge to a federal law. In *United States v. Stevens*, the court struck down a federal law that made it a crime to sell videos of dog fights and other depictions of animal cruelty.

But, in *Holder v. Humanitarian Law Project*, it upheld a law making it a crime to provide even benign advice to groups designated as foreign terrorist organizations by the State Department.

One of the most heated dissents of the term did not involve a legal issue at all. In May, the court announced that visitors could no longer enter the Supreme Court's courthouse through the front door at the top of its grand staircase but would instead be sent through ground-level side entrances. Justice Stephen G. Breyer, joined by Justice Ruth Bader Ginsburg, issued a statement expressing regret over the decision.

"This court's main entrance and front steps," Justice Breyer wrote, "are not only a means to, but also a metaphor for, access to the court itself."

—ADAM LIPTAK

Judge Blocks Stringent Law on Immigration

Gov. Jan Brewer of Arizona signed the nation's toughest bill on illegal immigration into law on April 23, 2010. Its aim is to identify, prosecute and deport illegal immigrants. The law unleashed immediate protests and reignited the divisive battle over immigration reform nationally. Pres. Obama strongly criticized the bill and in early July the U.S. Justice Department filed suit to challenge the law. Later that month, on the day before the law was to go into effect, a federal judge in Washington issued a preliminary injunction that blocked its most controversial sections, including one calling for police officers to check a person's immigration status when enforcing another law or ordinance.

The political debate leading up to Ms. Brewer's signing the bill underscored the power of the immigration debate in states along the Mexican border. Hispanics, in particular, who were not long ago courted by the Republican Party as a swing voting bloc, railed against the law as a recipe for racial and ethnic profiling. The law also opened a deep fissure in Arizona, with a majority of the thousands of callers to the governor's office urging her to reject it, while other residents called it a sensible approach to control immigration locally.

Ms. Brewer and other elected leaders have come under intense political pressure in Arizona, made worse by the killing of a rancher by a suspected smuggler a couple of weeks before the State Legislature voted on the bill. His death was invoked by Ms. Brewer as she announced a plan urging the federal government to post National Guard troops at the border. In May, Pres. Obama ordered the deployment of 1,200 National Guard troops to patrol the Southwest border, but they did not begin arriving until September.

In issuing the injunction, Judge Susan Bolton of the Federal District Court did allow some less-debated provisions of the law to go into effect, including one that bans cities from refusing to cooperate with federal immigration agents. Governor Brewer appealed the injunction almost immediately but her request for an expedited review was rejected and was scheduled for November. Legal experts predicted that the case could end up before the Supreme Court.

—RANDAL C. ARCHIBOLD

Army Officer Kills 13, Wounds More Than 30 In Fort Hood Shooting

An Army psychiatrist trained to counsel troubled soldiers killed 13 people and wounded more than 30 others on Nov. 5, 2009 in a shooting rampage at the Fort Hood Army post in central Texas. Maj. Nidal Malik Hasan, 39, who had reported for duty at Fort Hood's medical center in July, allegedly sprayed bullets from two handguns inside a crowded screening area of the post's processing center, where personnel are readied for overseas deployment, and then continued to fire as the occupants fled.

The victims—12 soldiers and 1 civilian employee—ranged in age from 19 to 62. Three were women and 10 were men. As the shooting unfolded, Major Hasan was confronted by two civilian police officers posted on the base. He was shot four times and left paralyzed from the chest down.

Major Hasan, a Virginia-born Muslim of Palestinian descent, had served two years as an enlisted soldier before rejoining the Army in 1997 to attend medical school at the Uniformed Services University of the Health Sciences in Bethesda, graduating in 2003. He did his internship and psychiatric residency at Walter Reed Army Medical Center in Washington.

Initial investigations into the attack concluded that Major Hasan acted alone, and that his actions were not part of a terrorist plot. Officials said that he had suffered from emotional pressures that were exacerbated by his work with war veterans who returned home with serious psychological problems. Colleagues and acquaintances portrayed him as a troubled man, inclined toward increasingly extreme religious beliefs, and concerned about being sent to a war zone. He was scheduled to be deployed to Afghanistan in November.

On April 9, 2010, Major Hasan was discharged from a military hospital in San Antonio and airlifted to the county jail in Belton, Texas. He was isolated from other inmates and kept under a 24-hour watch while awaiting a hearing to determine whether his case would go to trial. A military hearing similar to a civilian grand jury proceeding, was scheduled to start in June at Fort Hood. But Major Hasan's defense team requested more time and the hearing was postponed to Oct. 4.

Under the Uniform Code of Military Justice, prosecutors have charged Major Hasan with 13 counts of premeditated murder and 32 counts of attempted premeditated murder. If he is convicted of murder the minimum sentence is life with the possibility of parole. The maximum sentence is death.

—ROBERT D. MCFADDEN,
CLIFFORD KRAUSS, JAMES DAO,
DAVID JOHNSTON and OTHERS

Times Square Device Fails To Detonate, Bomber Arrested

An explosive device was found in a sport utility vehicle in the Times Square district of New York City on the evening of May 1, prompting the evacuation of thousands of tourists and theatergoers.

Inside the S.U.V. emergency responders discovered gasoline canisters, propane tanks, bags of fertilizer, fireworks, and alarm clocks connected to wires. The items were smoldering, as if the occupant of the car had attempted to initiate an explosion. Officials said the device would have been deadly had it detonated.

Investigators quickly traced the ownership of the vehicle to a Connecticut man, Faisal Shahzad, a 30-year-old naturalized U.S. citizen from Pakistan. On May 3, Mr. Shahzad was arrested at John F. Kennedy Airport as he tried to flee in a Dubai-bound jet. He had boarded the plane but was captured minutes before it taxied away.

Mr. Shahzad waived his right to remain silent and readily confessed to federal agents that he had assembled the dud bomb. But even more shocking was his admission that he had been trained to build the bomb in Waziristan, a tribal region in northwest Pakistan that is a stronghold of the Taliban. While authorities had treated the failed bombing as a potential terrorist attack, Mr. Shahzad's acknowledgment that the Pakistani Taliban had aided and directed him meant that a radical group once thought unable to attack the United States had delivered at least a glancing blow on American soil.

In 10 years in the U.S., Mr. Shahzad had given no outward sign that he had connections to terrorists. Born and raised in Pakistan as the privileged son of a senior military officer, he left home at the age of 19 to study computer science at the University of Bridgeport. In 2009 he became an American citizen. But people who knew him, both in Connecticut and Pakistan, said he had changed in recent years, showing signs of a profound, religiously infused alienation.

Mr. Shahzad had been critical of American foreign policy, and angered by the war in Iraq. He wrote e-mail messages to friends arguing that the West was at war with Islam and that Muslims had a religious duty to fight back. But the triggering event in his radicalization, officials say, was the July 10, 2007 storming of the Red Mosque in Islamabad by Pakistani commandos that ended a standoff with militants and left more than 100 dead. Mr. Shahzad had prayed at the mosque during visits home, and was said to be outraged. In June 2009 he moved back to Pakistan. By then, according to federal investigators, he had set himself on a course to attack Times Square.

On June 17 Mr. Shahzad was indicted by a federal grand jury in Manhattan and charged with 10 crimes, including attempted use of a weapon of mass destruction, acts of terrorism, and conspiracy. The first two charges carry a maximum sentence of life in prison. Four days later he abruptly and unapologetically pleaded guilty to all the charges. He told U.S. District Judge Miriam Goldman Cedarbaum that he was a "Muslim soldier" and that he did not consider what he had done to be a crime. His sentencing was scheduled for Oct. 5.

Some analysts suggested that Mr. Shahzad's statements were meant to rehabilitate his image among jihadists, given his amateurish bombing attempt. But one expert noted that his recruitment was probably worth the effort of his terrorist handlers who, he said, were more than willing to "trade experience for people who simply are less likely to be caught." Mr. Shahzad was sentenced to life imprisonment on Oct. 5.

—AL BAKER, WILLIAM RASHBAUM,
MARK MAZZETTI, JAMES BARRON
and ANDREA ELLIOTT

Recession Raises Poverty Rate In U.S. To a 15-Year High

The percentage of Americans struggling below the poverty line in 2009 was the highest it has been in 15 years, the Census Bureau reported in September, and interviews with poverty experts and aid groups said the increase appeared to be continuing in 2010.

With the country in its worst economic crisis since the Great Depression, four million additional Americans found themselves in poverty in 2009, with the total reaching 44 million, or one in seven residents. Millions more were surviving only because of expanded unemployment insurance and other assistance.

And the numbers could have climbed higher: One way embattled Americans have gotten by is sharing homes with siblings, parents or even non-relatives, holding down the rise in the national poverty rate, according to the report.

The share of residents in poverty climbed to 14.3 percent in 2009, the highest level recorded since 1994. The rise was steepest for children, with one in five affected, the bureau said.

The report provides the most detailed picture yet of the impact of the recession and unemployment on incomes, especially at the bottom of the scale. It also indicated that the temporary increases in aid provided in last year's stimulus bill eased the burdens on millions of families.

For a single adult in 2009, the poverty line was $10,830 in pretax cash income; for a family of four, $22,050.

There are strong signs that the high poverty numbers have continued into 2010 and are probably still rising, some experts said, as the recovery sputters and unemployment remains near 10 percent.

One indirect sign of continuing hardship is the rise in food stamp recipients, who now include nearly one in seven adults and an even greater share of the nation's children. While other factors as well as declining incomes have driven the rise, by mid-2010 the number of recipients had reached 41.3 million, compared with 39 million at the beginning of the year.

The Census report showed increases in poverty for whites, blacks and Hispanic Americans, with historic disparities continuing. The poverty rate for non-Hispanic whites was 9.4 percent, for blacks 25.8 percent and for Hispanics 25.3 percent. The rate for Asians was unchanged at 12.5 percent.

The median income of all households stayed roughly the same from 2008 to 2009. It had fallen sharply the year before, as the recession gained steam and remains well below the levels of the late 1990s—a sign of the stagnating prospects for the middle class.

The number of United States residents without health insurance climbed to 51 million in 2009, from 46 million in 2008, the Census said. Their ranks are expected to shrink in coming years as the health care overhaul adopted by Congress in March begins to take effect.

—ERIC ECKHOLM

29 Die in West Virginia Mine Disaster

On April 5, 2010, a massive explosion about 1,000 feet underground at Massey Energy's Upper Big Branch coal mine in Raleigh County, West Virginia trapped and eventually killed 29 coal miners. It was the deadliest coal mining accident in the United States since 1970, when 38 miners were killed at a mining accident in Hyden, Kentucky

The mine was operated by the Performance Coal Company, a subsidiary of Massey Energy. State investigators found indications of high methane levels in the mine at the time of the explosion. The ignition source of the explosion, however, remained unclear while the investigation was ongoing. Immediately after the explosion, 25 men were identified as killed. Four days later, four missing men were also found dead.

State and federal mining regulators launched investigations of the incident. The FBI has also launched a criminal probe.

The mine owner, Massey Energy, has repeatedly stated its commitment to safety. Massey officials also released information about a massive crack in the mine's floor that they said may have been a source of methane that exploded in the mine. But federal officials said they were skeptical that this was the cause. They instead pointed to a number of dangerous adjustments the company made to the mine's ventilation system which may have instead led to the dangerous buildup of the explosive gases.

In 2009, the company was fined more than $350,000 for "serious" violations, many of them relating to the mine's ventilation and safety systems. At the time of the accident, the company had paid a small percentage of its federal fines because it made a habit of appealing and litigating them instead. Don Blankenship, the chairman and CEO of Massey, has been a controversial figure in the coal industry, taking an unusually strong antiunion stand and spending large sums of money to sway political and judicial campaigns in West Virginia.

The Upper Big Branch Mine-South, which is the section where the explosion occurred, has been in operation since October 1994. In the months before the explosion production at the mine had kicked into overdrive, as the company tried to keep up with growing demand for the mine's valuable type of coal, which is used to make steel. Federal data indicates that in the fourth quarter of 2009, coal production at Upper Big Branch almost doubled from the previous three months.

—IAN URBINA

U.S. Arrests, Then Exchanges, 10 Spies Who Found No Secrets

It may not have been quite, in the words of Karl Marx, history repeating itself as farce. But the arrest in late June of 10 suspected Russian spies who had spent years burrowing into American life, and their exchange just two weeks later for four Russians accused of spying for the West, had the trappings of cold war drama without the high stakes.

The "illegals" in the United States—intelligence officers posing not as diplomats but as private citizens—had evidently managed to obtain no real secrets. They were charged not with espionage but with failing to register as foreign agents. And the Obama administration had begun to ponder making a deal to send them home months before the arrests.

The tone of the whole affair was perhaps caught best by American tabloids, in their gleeful infatuation with the most comely of the spies, Anna Chapman, the 28-year-old businesswoman whose jet-setting lifestyle had produced an inexhaustible supply of sexy photos. On NBC's *Tonight Show*, Vice President Joseph Biden quipped, "Let me be clear. It was not my idea to send her back."

The biggest puzzle was why the Russian intelligence service had gone to such trouble to plant the spies, most of whom posed as married couples, raising children and holding ordinary jobs. Messages intercepted in the F.B.I.'s decade-long surveillance operation revealed a squabble between "Moscow Center," or "C," and two spies, known as Richard and Cynthia Murphy, buying a house in pricey Montclair, N.J.

"From our perspective purchase of the house was solely a natural progression of our prolonged stay here," the couple wrote. " It was a convenient way to solving the housing issue, plus 'to do as the Romans do' in a society that values home ownership."

The spies' assignment was described most fully in another message from Moscow Center: "Your education, bank accounts, car, house etc.—all these serve one goal: fulfill your main mission, i.e. to search and develop ties in policymaking circles and send intels," or intelligence reports. In fact, the Russians collected decidedly low-grade information—speculation about President Obama's goals for a summit meeting, tips on the world gold market. But they nevertheless used every cold war trick and more: lookalike bags exchanged in a train-station stairway, money buried in a rural field, messages sent by shortwave burst transmission, and information hidden inside ordinary-looking Internet images.

All that tradecraft had produced such meager results that few protested when the Obama administration sent the Russians home. They pleaded guilty and were swapped in Vienna—another spy-movie touch—for four other Russians imprisoned by Moscow for spying for the West. The whole anachronistic intrigue was over so fast that it barely made a ripple in improving relations between Russia and the United States.

—SCOTT SHANE

Blagojevich Found Guilty On 1 of 24 Counts

Prosecutors in Chicago once said that the conduct of Rod R. Blagojevich, the former governor of Illinois, was so despicable it would make Abraham Lincoln "roll over in his grave," but 12 jurors in the federal corruption case against him were apparently not all so certain. After deliberating for 14 days, the jury found Mr. Blagojevich guilty of a single criminal count—making false statements to the F.B.I., which carries a maximum sentence of five years in prison, one of the least severe penalties in the charges against him.

The jurors also said they could not reach a unanimous verdict on 23 of the 24 counts against him, including an accusation that he had tried to sell an appointment to fill the Senate seat once held by President Obama. On that count, one juror said, the group was split 11 to 1 in favor of convicting him.

Prosecutors immediately announced plans for a retrial, but the outcome was seen as something of a victory, at least for now, for Mr. Blagojevich, 53, a Democrat and lifelong politician from this city, who had always proclaimed his innocence and did so again as he left court.

As for the more serious counts against Mr. Blagojevich, the jurors, who had seemed during the trial to be a particularly attentive, studious bunch, had trouble right from the start of their deliberations in reaching much agreement, said one juror, Erik Sarnello.

The group was split 11 to 1, he said, in favor of convicting Mr. Blagojevich on charges that he tried to trade or sell the Senate seat, but was divided in various ways at various moments on the rest of the counts.

—MONICA DAVEY and SUSAN SAULNY

Black Official Receives a Firing And Then a Flurry of Apologies

The White House and Agriculture Secretary Tom Vilsack apologized profusely and repeatedly on July 21, 2010, to a black midlevel official for the way she had been humiliated and forced to resign her Agriculture Department job after a conservative blogger put out a misleading video clip that seemed to show her admitting antipathy toward a white farmer.

By the end of the day, the official, Shirley Sherrod, the Agriculture Department's rural development director in Georgia, had gained instant fame and emerged as the heroine of a compelling story about race and redemption.

Pretty much everyone else had egg on his face—from the conservative bloggers and pundits who first pushed the inaccurate story to Mr. Vilsack, who looked stricken as he told reporters that he had ordered Ms. Sherrod's firing in haste, without knowing that the video clip, from a speech she gave to the N.A.A.C.P., had been taken out of context. He said that he had acted on his own, and that there was "no pressure from the White House."

This capped a humiliating and fast-paced few days not only for the White House, but also for the N.A.A.C.P. and the national news media, especially the Fox News Channel and its hosts Bill O'Reilly and Sean Hannity, all of whom played a role in promoting the story about Ms. Sherrod.

The controversy illustrates the influence of right-wing Web sites like the one run by Andrew Breitbart, the blogger who initially posted the misleading and highly edited video, which he later said had been sent to him already edited.

The full video of Ms. Sherrod's March speech to an N.A.A.C.P. gathering in Douglas, Ga., showed that it was a consciousness-raising story. Ms. Sherrod's father was murdered in 1965 by white men who were never indicted; she spoke about how in response, she vowed to stay in the South and work for change. She married the Rev. Charles Sherrod, a civil rights leader and co-founder of the Student Nonviolent Coordinating Committee.

Later, as director of a nonprofit group in Georgia formed to help black farmers, long before she went to work for the Agriculture Department, Ms. Sherrod received a request to help a white farm couple, Roger and Eloise Spooner, and she confessed in the speech that the request had given her pause. She did help them, however, and as the fracas over her firing became public, the Spooners came to her defense, saying Ms. Sherrod had gone out of her way to accompany them to see a lawyer and, in effect, had helped them save their farm.

—SHERYL GAY STOLBERG, SHAILA DEWAN and BRIAN STELTER

Judge Strikes Down California's Gay Marriage Ban

Saying that it discriminates against gay men and women, a federal judge in San Francisco struck down California's voter-approved ban on same-sex marriage on Aug. 4, handing supporters of such unions at least a temporary victory in a legal battle that seems all but certain to be settled by the Supreme Court.

The decision was just the latest chapter in what is expected to be a long battle over the ban—Proposition 8, which was passed in 2008 with 52 percent of the vote. Indeed, while striking down Proposition 8, the decision did not immediately lead to any new same-sex marriages being performed in California. Vaughn R. Walker, the chief judge of the Federal District Court in San Francisco, immediately stayed his own decision, pending appeals by proponents of Proposition 8, who seem confident that higher courts would hear and favor their position.

But for the time being the winds seemed to be at the back of those who feel that marriage is not, as the voters of California and many other states have said, solely the province of a man and a woman.

"Proposition 8 cannot withstand any level of scrutiny under the Equal Protection Clause," wrote Judge Walker. "Excluding same-sex couples from marriage is simply not rationally related to a legitimate state interest."

Supporters of Proposition 8 said that the decision defied the will of the people of California, and could well be an issue in November's midterm elections.

The decision applied only to California and not to the dozens of other states that have either constitutional bans or other prohibitions against same-sex marriage. Nor does it affect federal law, which does not recognize such unions.

The plaintiffs' case was argued by David Boies and Theodore B. Olson, ideological opposites who once famously sparred in the 2000 Supreme Court battle between George W. Bush and Al Gore over the Florida recount and the presidency. The lawyers brought the case—Perry v. Schwarzenegger—in May 2009 on behalf of two gay couples who said that Proposition 8 impinged on their constitutional rights to equal protection and due process.

—JESSE MCKINLEY and JOHN SCHWARTZ

Tea Party Moves From Protesting To Helping Elect Candidates

In 2010, the Tea Party movement channeled the anger that had triggered its street protests the year before into electoral energy. In January, Tea Party activists from across the country flooded Massachusetts to help Scott Brown, a Republican, win the United States Senate seat that had been held for nearly 50 years by the late Edward M. Kennedy, a scion of the nation's most storied Democratic dynasty. Mr. Brown was an unlikely candidate for the small government movement, having voted as a state senator for a health care overhaul that was considered a model for federal legislation the Tea Party hoped to defeat. But activists realized that he would give Republicans a 41st vote in the Senate, denying Democrats the supermajority they needed to pass key legislation.

In March, as Congress held a final vote on the health care bill, thousands of Tea Party protesters descended on Washington. Democrats, including Representative John Lewis of Georgia, a veteran of the civil rights movement, accused demonstrators of spitting and shouting epithets at black or gay congressmen as they marched to the House chamber to vote.

In a *New York Times*/CBS News poll in April, 18 percent of Americans identified themselves as supporters of the movement. They tended to be white, male, older than 65, and to have higher incomes and levels of education than other Americans. They were also more likely to describe themselves as "angry" with Washington.

In May, the Tea Party had its most significant electoral victory, when Republican primary voters in Kentucky overwhelmingly chose Rand Paul as their Senate nominee. Mr. Paul, the son of Ron Paul, the Texas congressman and 2008 presidential candidate, had begun his campaign at Tea Party rallies and embraced the libertarian philosophy of the movement. He created immediate controversy when he said that he disagreed on principle with the provisions of the 1964 Civil Rights Act that forbid business owners from refusing service to blacks.

Republican leaders in Washington worried that Tea Party candidates were too polarizing to win general election contests. But Republican voters continued to choose them over more moderate, establishment-backed candidates. Tea Party candidates had soon won primary victories in many congressional districts across the country. And there were Tea Party nominees in several Senate contests: Ken Buck in Colorado, Ron Johnson in Wisconsin, and Sharron Angle running to replace Senator Harry Reid, the leader of the Democratic majority, in Nevada.

In the Delaware Republican primary, Christine O'Donnell rode Tea Party support to beat Representative Michael N. Castle, a moderate who had won statewide election a dozen times as a congressman and governor. Her victory was a sign of strength from local grassroots activists; even Washington groups that support the Tea Party did not back Ms. O'Donnell, believing she would lose to the Democrat in the general election.

Tea Party supporters helped move the discussion on the campaign trail away from social issues like gay marriage and abortion, by arguing that the Republican Party needed to talk more about economic conservatism. But the traditional conservative tenets of faith and family continued to hold sway over many Tea Party supporters. On a hot August day, the Fox News personality Glenn Beck summoned a large and impassioned crowd to the National Mall in Washington and issued a call for a religious revival.

—KATE ZERNIKE

Plans for Islamic Center Near Ground Zero Set Off National Debate

The ninth anniversary of the Sept. 11, 2001 attacks was unusually tinged with political disagreement and acrimony, amid a national debate over plans by a group of New York Muslims to build a community center, including a mosque somewhere within its envisioned 13 to 15 stories, two blocks from the World Trade Center site.

Opponents said it was insensitive to build a Muslim worship space close to the scene of deadly attacks by people claiming to represent Islam; supporters said that view implied Muslims were collectively responsible for 9/11 and ignores the fact that they were also victims of the attacks.

The idea began with Feisal Abdul Rauf, 61, the imam of a small Sufi mosque 12 blocks from the World Trade Center site, and Sharif el-Gamal, 37, a real estate developer who worshipped there. The two men wanted to combine a new mosque with a community center modeled on the YMCA or YMHA—open to all, including educational programs, interfaith outreach, a swimming pool, a theater and day care. Mr. Gamal and a group of investors purchased property and on May 5, 2010, with the support of local politicians and interfaith groups, a committee of Community Board 1 approved the project unanimously.

But a second committee meeting on May 25th drew opponents led by Pamela Geller and her organization Stop Islamization of America, as well as some 9/11 victims' families. They branded the project the "Ground Zero mosque," a term adopted by tabloids and television news.

Opposition ignited, merging with discontent among Tea Party conservatives with President Obama and immigration issues. The debate tapped into broader tensions, as proposed mosques in Staten Island, Brooklyn, Tennessee, and California faced opponents not just concerned about traffic and zoning but afraid that mosques would become hubs of extremism. Muslim leaders said the climate made American Muslims more insecure about their place in the country than at any time since 9/11.

Debate accelerated in early August when the center cleared its only legal hurdle, approval from the city's landmarks commission. Politicians weighed in, with Mayor Bloomberg and Pres. Obama defending the center on the grounds of religious freedom and Newt Gingrich and Sarah Palin opposing it.

Opponents painted Mr. Abdul Rauf, a prominent speaker on moderate Islam after 9/11, as a radical, in part because of critical statements he had made about American policy. They raised concerns that hostile states or groups might fund the center. The planners promised to vet and disclose all donations and accept none tied to "un-American values." They changed the name from Cordoba House, named after Mr. Abdul Rauf's Cordoba Initiative and the medieval Spanish city that was home to a scholarly golden age for Muslims, Jews and Christians under Muslim rule, to the more anodyne Park51 after some opponents suggested Cordoba represented Muslim domination.

On Sept. 11, 2010, demonstrators for and against the center gathered near Ground Zero. Meanwhile, the planners lacked the $100 million needed to start building, and it remained unclear if it would ever be built.

—ANNE BARNARD

Sex Scandal Wrecks Tiger Woods' Image, Ends His Marriage and Rattles His Game

On Nov. 25, 2009, a tabloid leaked word it was about to publish a story about Tiger Woods, the biggest name in golf if not all of sport, having cheated on his wife. Two days later, the once unassailable Woods image was shaken when police were called to a wealthy Orlando, Fla. enclave just after 2 a.m. to find the golfer lying in the street with his face bloodied not far from his Cadillac Escalade, which he had crashed into a neighbor's tree. Woods was slipping in and out of consciousness as his wife, Elin, hovered over him, holding a golf club that some reports would later wrongly suggest she had used to strike her husband.

The accident and injuries, though minor, were shockingly out of character for the seemingly squeaky-clean Woods and they immediately set off a flurry of wild rumors, some confirmed by the tabloid report. Two days of silence prompted more rumors, fueled further by the release of a statement signed by Woods that accepted blame and requested privacy.

The request backfired. The wall of privacy surrounding the couple was breached, with a flurry of women subsequently alleging affairs. Woods became the butt of skits on network TV and comedy clubs. His popularity plummeted and his silence continued until Dec. 2, when a damaging voicemail he had left on the phone of one of his alleged female consorts prompted the release of another statement, this one admitting, "I have let my family down and I regret those transgressions with all of my heart."

Corporate sponsors, a huge source of Woods' income and visibility, fled. After Woods's Dec. 11 announcement that he would be taking "an indefinite leave from golf," Gillette said it would be limiting his role in future advertising and long-time sponsor Accenture dropped him. So did AT&T and Gatorade.

Woods entered a Hattiesburg, Miss., rehabilitation center for the treatment of sex addictions, and in a nationally televised appearance on Feb. 19 apologized to his wife and made an emotional reiteration of a previous denial that she had ever struck him.

Woods, who has won 24 PGA Tour championships including the four major championships comprising the Grand Slam, returned to competitive golf at the Masters Tournament in April of 2010, scraping out a tie for fourth despite sometimes erratic play. By summer's end, after adding a tie for fourth at the U.S. Open and credible but lackluster performances at the British Open and PGA Championship, he parted with his longtime swing coach Hank Haney. The week that the season-ending PGA Tour Playoffs for the FedEx Cup started, his divorce became final.

—LARRY DORMAN

International

Cataclysmic Earthquake in Haiti Leaves 300,000 Dead; Recovery Efforts Slow

On Jan. 12, just before 5 p.m., Haiti, the poorest country in the Western Hemisphere, was struck by a massive earthquake measuring 7.3 on the Richter scale. The earthquake violently shook the heart of the Caribbean nation for just under 35 seconds but its devastating repercussions are expected to be long-lasting.

In the immediate aftermath of the earthquake, the disaster scene was nightmarish, with corpses dangling from flattened buildings or lying caked in the white powder of limestone ash on rubble-strewn streets. A blanket of bodies—dead, dying and wounded—covered the grounds of the capital's main public hospital as doctors did triage by the light of their cell phones. Twelve hours after the earthquake, the central morgue was filled to capacity; the death toll eventually rose to 300,000 by the government's estimate. Another 300,000 were injured. More than 1.5 million were displaced by the wreckage or damage of their homes and neighborhoods; some fled into the countryside, others moved into the 1,200 ragged encampments that soon dotted the vast disaster zone and grew entrenched.

Haiti's earthquake was, proportionate to the size of its population and economy, the worst natural disaster in modern history, the Inter-American Development Bank said. Its epicenter lay near Leogane, just 10 miles southwest of the capital city of Port-au-Prince, which is the center of Haiti's population, economy and government.

A lingering symbol of the destruction was the crumpled presidential palace, its three domes toppled. Seven months after the earthquake, the palace had not been torn down or propped up and, as it sunk further into its foundation, it came to represent the paralysis of the recovery process. Debris removal, so essential to progress, was moving forward at a snail's pace, with estimates that it would take five years or longer for the clean-up operation.

Established humanitarian organizations greatly expanded their operations in Haiti and new ones flocked there from around the world. Further disaster, initially feared, was largely averted; there was no significant starvation, outbreak of disease or breakdown of security. Hurricane season, though, raised new worries. At the end of March, the international community pledged $5.3 billion over the following 18 months to begin Haiti's path to recovery. The money was slow to arrive as it worked its way through the appropriations process in several countries and as many donors awaited a more developed plan of action from Haiti's interim reconstruction commission.

The commission—co-chaired by Prime Minister Jean-Max Bellerive and Bill Clinton, the former president and United Nations special envoy to Haiti—did not hold its first meeting until June. At the end of the summer, its office—a giant, high-tech tent—was filled with rows of new computers, mostly unmanned; an executive director for a half-year term had been named but 30 staff positions remained to be filled. In August, the reconstruction commission approved $1.6 billion in reconstruction work, most of it Inter-American Development Bank-financed projects to build roads, overhaul the education system and support agriculture.

Also in August, the election season began as 19 candidates for the presidential elections to be held on Nov. 28 were approved. Wyclef Jean, the Haitian-born hip-hop star whose potential candidacy made the biggest splash, was disqualified from running because he had not lived in Haiti for the previous five years, as required.

—DEBORAH SONTAG

Devastating Floods Hit Pakistan, With No Region Unaffected

In late July, 2010, unprecedented monsoon rains devastated Pakistan as floodwaters surged over about one-fifth of the country—about 62,000 square miles, an area larger than England. Nearly 20 million people, an eighth of the population, were affected and at least 1,700 lost their lives. The extensive damage stretched from the northern parts of the country to the southern as millions lost their livelihoods.

The catastrophe is estimated to have set back Pakistan, an already fragile country with a weak economy, many years if not decades. Millions of dollars' worth of crops and livestock were lost and no region escaped destruction.

There was bitterness in the country over the slow pace of relief efforts and an equal dismay over the inept response by the civilian government. President Asif Ali Zardari, whose popularity has been plummeting since he became the head of the country in 2008, was heavily criticized for going ahead with foreign visits while the country was literally drowning. Meanwhile, Taliban militants affiliated with Al Qaeda continued to target civil and military installations, places of worship belonging to Shiite Muslims and minorities like Ahmadis and Christians. The Pakistan military, however, which had come under sharp criticism during the rule of former president and military dictator General Pervez Musharraf, managed to burnish its credentials due to its relief and rescue work.

Earlier in the year it was clear that the military remained the real arbiter of control in Pakistan. In April, parliament approved a raft of constitutional amendments that took powers away from the office of the president, and in July the government gave Gen. Ashfaq Pervez Kayani, the powerful army chief since 2007, a three-year extension. General Kayani has won praise from American officials for his professionalism and is credited with salvaging the army's public image. Also in July, the role of Pakistan's powerful intelligence agency, Inter-Services Intelligence (ISI), came under the spotlight after the whistle-blowing website WikiLeaks released reports that suggested low-level Pakistani intelligence support for the Taliban in Afghanistan.

Making public the trove of intelligence reports caused embarrassment in Washington and Islamabad as high-ranking officials from both sides stressed that these leaked documents would not affect the existing level of cooperation between the United States and Pakistan.

In May, Faisal Shahzad, a naturalized American of Pakistani origins, was arrested in New York after he tried unsuccessfully to detonate a crude bomb in Times Square. Mr. Shahzad—like many aspiring militants—had received militant training in the country's restive tribal regions, according to Pakistan and American officials. The son of a retired air vice marshal of Pakistan's Air Force, Mr. Shahzad had traveled to Pakistan frequently and as recently as February.

In what was seen as the most decisive blow to the Taliban leadership since 2001, American and Pakistani intelligence agents raided a house in the southern port city of Karachi and arrested Mullah Abdul Ghani Baradar, who had long overseen the Taliban insurgency against American, NATO and Afghan troops in Afghanistan. The following month Pakistani agents captured Mullah Abdul Kabir, a member of the Quetta Shura, a small group of Taliban leaders who report to Mullah Muhammad Omar, the group's founder.

—SALMAN MASOOD

Afghan War Grows As Relations With Karzai Government Worsen

The war in Afghanistan grew in momentum and casualties in 2010 after the Obama administration decided to enhance its counterinsurgency operations against Taliban militants and ordered a mini-surge of 30,000 extra troops into the country after a strategic review in December 2009. By August 2010, after a steady buildup of troops, the combined United States and coalition forces in the NATO-led International Security Assistance Force reached 120,000, with 78,000 (60 percent) of them American.

Under Gen. Stanley A. McChrystal, the United States Marines in February mounted a large-scale operation against a Taliban stronghold in the district of Marja in the southern province of Helmand. The operation was heralded as an important step in turning around the war against Taliban insurgents and ending the thriving narcotics business in Marja, but despite early claims of success, the campaign became dogged by daily attacks and skirmishes with guerrilla fighters that continued through the summer.

American forces also began building up forces to secure the adjoining province of Kandahar, the most critical region in southern Afghanistan and traditional territory of the Taliban. Yet operations against militants in districts around the city of Kandahar were revised and delayed several months and only got underway properly in September.

Taliban militants continued to expand their presence, reaching into new areas in northern and western Afghanistan, and attacking the capital, Kabul, with spectacular raids with multiple suicide bombers against central government buildings in January and Indian nationals in February. They also disrupted a peace convention called by Afghan President Hamid Karzai in June with a rocket attack.

With the increase of troops and activity, foreign troop casualties reached their highest levels in the Afghan theater since the intervention of western troops in 2001 and reached the 2,000 mark by mid-August, 1,226 of them American. Afghan civilian casualties continued to be a source of public discontent. In June General McChrystal resigned as commander of American and NATO forces in Afghanistan after he was quoted as criticizing members of the Obama administration in a *Rolling Stone* article and Gen. David Petraeus took over the following month.

President Karzai, who was elected to a second five-year term in 2009 in an election marred by large-scale fraud, ran into several confrontations with parliament when the lower house rejected the majority of his cabinet appointments, and threw out his proposed changes to the electoral law. New parliamentary elections went ahead Sept. 18 despite worsening security and widespread voter apathy, but according to early reports less wholesale fraud.

Despite showcase events such as an international conference on Afghanistan in London in January, and a gathering of 34 foreign ministers to show support for Afghanistan in Kabul in July, frustrations among Afghans and Western governments over the lack of progress became increasingly apparent.

Relations between Mr. Karzai and the United States also deteriorated in the aftermath of the disputed election. President Obama paid a short visit to Kabul in April—his first since his own election—to press for more action from the Afghan government on reforms to the election commission and laws, and against corruption. Just days after the visit, Mr. Karzai accused the international community of instigating the election fraud in order to discredit him, and warned that the international troop presence was becoming increasingly close to that of an invading force and could spark a national resistance against it.

Relations eased up when Mr. Karzai was given red carpet treatment during a visit to Washington in May, but deteriorated again over corruption issues, in particular after the arrest of an aide of Mr. Karzai. In August the near collapse of Kabul Bank, of which the president's brother Mahmoud Karzai is a shareholder, forced the Central Bank to impose its own administrators.

—CARLOTTA GALL

Iraqis Hold a National Election While U.S. Withdraws Troops

The United States declared an official end to combat operations in Iraq at the end of August 2010, leaving only 50,000 American troops in a largely advisory role as President Obama began to fulfill his pledge to bring an unpopular war to a gradual end.

The steady withdrawal, which left fewer American soldiers in Iraq than at any point since the invasion in 2003, proceeded over the course of the year despite a protracted political struggle that paralyzed the government, inflamed tensions and fueled public apathy and disillusion. A national election in March, though already three months behind schedule, raised hopes that a new 325-member parliament would solidify the country's democracy and repair some of the ethnic and sectarian hatreds that have ravaged the country since the fall of Saddam Hussein.

It was the most open and competitive election in Iraq's history and, arguably, the entire region. Despite threats and violence, including a series of bombings on election day, 62 percent of eligible voters cast ballots for thousands of candidates representing each of the country's 18 provinces.

The results, though, illustrated how deeply divided—and distrustful—the country's political and social factions remain. A coalition lead by a former interim prime minister, Ayad Allawi, narrowly defeated Prime Minister Nuri Kamal al-Maliki's bloc by luring Sunni and Shiite voters under a largely secular banner. Mr. Allawi's coalition, Iraqiya, won 91 seats compared to Mr. Maliki's 89, but neither could quickly assemble the 163-seat majority needed to elect a new prime minister and form a government.

Mr. Maliki's supporters challenged the results, insisting on a recount in Baghdad, while a secretive commission revived accusations that candidates should be disqualified because of ties to Saddam Hussein's Baath Party. The challenges delayed the final certification of the results for weeks but did not change the outcome. What followed was months of inscrutable, behind-the-scenes negotiations as distrustful Iraqi leaders jockeyed for advantage and power. A merger announced in May between Mr. Maliki's supporters and a second Shiite coalition, the Iraqi National Alliance, stalled because of fierce opposition by followers of the prominent anti-American cleric, Moktada al-Sadr, to giving Mr. Maliki a second term as prime minister.

Public anger rose as the political impasse dragged on and the summer's heat worsened the chronic electricity outages afflicting most cities. Violence, though far lower than in the worst years of the war, simmered relentlessly, as insurgents appeared intent on further disrupting the political process.

In April, an American-Iraqi raid killed the two leaders of the Islamic State of Iraq, the insurgent front that includes the Iraqi franchise of Al Qaeda. The raid was part of a series of arrests and killings that American and Iraqi commanders said had decimated the group. And yet daily attacks persisted, punctuated by spectacular attacks that killed dozens in Baghdad and other cities.

In early October, after seven months of bare-knuckle backroom bargaining, Mr. Maliki appeared assured of a second term after securing the support of the anti-American Shiite Islamic movement whose return to power could profoundly complicate relations with the United States. The deal splintered a broad Shiite alliance and threatened to raise tensions with Sunnis who largely supported Mr. Allawi.

—STEVEN LEE MYERS

In Iran, Opposition Quieted As West Steps Up Sanctions

In late 2009, Iran still seemed a country in the midst of profound domestic turmoil, after the disputed presidential election set off the country's worst internal dissent since the Islamic revolution in 1979. Large and bloody street demonstrations persisted until the end of the year, despite a fierce government crackdown and mass trials of opposition figures. The Ashura holiday in late December saw violent protests and chants of "death to the dictator" across the country, as Iran's "green" opposition movement—led by presidential candidate Mir-Hussein Moussavi—continued to maintain that Mahmoud Ahmadinejad's landslide electoral victory in June 2009 had been marred by massive fraud. The government's continuing crackdown, in which dozens of people were tortured and killed, provoked criticism even among some political conservatives.

But by early 2010, the opposition's momentum began to fade, thanks in part to its own lack of clear leadership and the government's increasingly effective intimidation measures. A protest rally planned to commemorate the 31st anniversary of the Islamic revolution in mid-February largely failed to materialize, and generated a flood of self-criticism. The movement was too fragmented, and too dependent on expatriate figures and the Internet, many members said; it lacked the social depth and commitment to force real change. Meanwhile, the government continued to shut down reformist newspapers and magazines and jail many opposition figures, and protests virtually came to an end.

At the same time, intra-conservative tensions revived, as rivals to Mr. Ahmadinejad in Iran's Parliament—including Parliament speaker Ali Larijani—began to accuse him more harshly than ever of ignoring both the legal process and the clerical establishment as he concentrated power in his own hands.

On the international front, Iran had rejected a United Nations-sponsored proposal in late 2009 under which Iran would have shipped most of its supply of low-enriched uranium abroad for processing, buying time for a longer-term solution to the nuclear standoff. For months afterward, Iranian officials continued to signal their willingness to make a watered-down deal, and in June 2010, Brazil and Turkey offered to broker an arrangement that would allow Iran to keep a larger supply of uranium.

But that proposal was widely viewed as a time-buying ploy in the West, where pressure had been building for more economic sanctions. In June, the United Nations Security Council imposed its fourth round of sanctions on Iran. A week later, the United States and the European Union imposed further sanctions putting greater restrictions on Iranian banks and the insurance and transport sector, with special measures aimed at Iran's elite Revolutionary Guard Corps.

By August, American officials were already expressing confidence that the new sanctions were having an effect on Iran's economy, long troubled by high inflation and unemployment. In September, the direction of his country's relations with the West seemed less clear and more fraught with risks than ever. The possibility of an airstrike on Iran's uranium enrichment plants—whether by Israel or the United States—continued to loom, even as Iranian leaders offered mixed signals on their willingness to return to negotiations.

—ROBERT F. WORTH

For Israel, Prosperity But Increased Isolation

Israel inhabited two distinct realities in 2009-2010—growing prosperity and sophistication at home combined with increased censure abroad. It was inducted into the Organization for Economic Cooperation and Development, a club of rich countries, and it discovered large amounts of natural gas off its coast. One of its chemists was awarded a Nobel Prize – the country's ninth—and its technological innovations and artistic output drew wide praise. Tel Aviv marked its centenary. But its actions in Gaza, East Jerusalem and the West Bank led to increased international isolation. Its relations with Washington chilled to their coolest in two decades and Israel seemed on the verge of losing its most important Muslim ally, Turkey.

Its difficulties with the United States stemmed from the gap between its rightist government, led by Prime Minister Benjamin Netanyahu of Likud, and that of the left-leaning Obama administration. President Obama was recalibrating America's relations with the Muslim world after eight years of the Bush administration's war on terror partly by pressing Israel to halt settlement activity in lands it had captured in the 1967 Middle East War.

Mr. Netanyahu resisted but did announce a 10-month settlement building moratorium in November 2009. It did not include East Jerusalem and was preceded by a building boom.

During a visit in March 2010 by Vice President Joseph R. Biden, Israel announced 1,600 new Jewish housing units in East Jerusalem which the Palestinians want for their future capital. This embarrassed Mr. Biden and angered the administration.

Another crisis for Israel occurred in May and it had to do with Gaza. Since Hamas, the Islamist group, had come to power there in 2006, Israel—and Egypt—had isolated it by severely limiting the goods and people going in and out of the coastal Palestinian strip. In late 2008, in response to rockets fired from Gaza, Israel had invaded, destroying thousands of houses and killing some 1,300 people. A United Nations report issued by a South African judge, Richard Goldstone, in September 2009 accused Israel—and Hamas—of likely war crimes. Groups and countries opposed to Israel's Gaza policy sent shipments to Gaza. Israel let some through and stopped others.

In late May 2010, a six-ship flotilla, with Turkish sponsorship and hundreds of activists, set sail for Gaza. Israel offered to let the goods onboard pass through its port of Ashdod. The activists refused and Israeli naval commandos boarded the boats in international waters. On a Turkish vessel named the Mavi Marmara, men with sticks and poles fought off the Israeli soldiers descending from helicopters. The Israelis responded with live fire, killing nine men, all Turkish, including one with dual American citizenship. Turkey withdrew its ambassador from Tel Aviv and led an international campaign of condemnation.

The Obama administration came to the aid of Israel. The two had also found common ground in their mutual concern over Iran's regional ambitions and nuclear program. By late summer, American–Israeli ties were back to normal and Washington pushed the Palestinian Authority under President Mahmoud Abbas to enter direct peace talks with Mr. Netanyahu. Mr. Abbas balked. He wanted a promise of an ongoing settlement construction freeze, saying the Jewish population of the West Bank was growing so large as to make a Palestinian state there impossible. The Israelis refused but made promises of other concessions. On Sept. 1, Israeli and Palestinian leaders, joined by President Hosni Mubarak of Egypt and King Abdullah II of Jordan, gathered for dinner at the White House to launch direct peace talks, the first in 20 months.

Mr. Abbas and Mr. Netanyahu planned to meet every two weeks for a year and put together a framework for two states covering all outstanding issues—borders, Palestinian refugees, settlements, Jerusalem and security. People on both sides said that after 17 years of mutual mistrust, the talks would likely fail. The growing divide between the Palestinian Authority in the West Bank and Hamas in Gaza also threatened to doom the effort.

—ETHAN BRONNER

For China, Growing Economic Clout Plus Natural and Man-made Disasters

The year 2010 in China began with a singular example of the mixed emotions with which Beijing's partners greeted its increasing economic clout and rising global profile. On Jan. 12, Google Inc. stunned the business world—and miffed Beijing—by ceasing cooperation with Chinese Internet censors after detecting China-based cyberattacks on its computer systems. The attacks, which struck 33 other Western targets, were traced to two Chinese universities, but were not definitively linked to the government, which denied any role.

The affair epitomized concerns that an increasingly restrictive China was hamstringing both corporate and personal freedoms. On Jan. 21, Secretary of State Hillary Rodham Clinton condemned the attacks and Chinese censorship, saying it threatened information freedom. The Communist Party's *Global Times* newspaper, bristling in response, labeled an uncensored Internet an American plot to maintain "hegemonic domination" of information.

Google eventually shuttered its mainland China-based search engine, directing customers to uncensored Google servers in Hong Kong. But information from those servers was censored anyway, by Chinese government computers that intercepted traffic as it flowed to mainland computer users. Privately, Western business officials commended Google's withdrawal on principle from China's vast, increasingly lucrative pool of Internet users. Publicly, none followed.

And China's economic rise continued apace. In July, the state-owned Agricultural Bank of China floated history's largest initial public stock offering, $22.1 billion, despite a history of poor management and vast government bailouts. In August, statisticians said China's gross domestic product had passed Japan's, wresting away the title of the world's second largest economy. Premier Wen Jiabao explained China's success: "The socialist system's advantages," he said in March, "enable us to make decisions efficiently, organize effectively and concentrate resources to accomplish large undertakings."

China's elevated global profile did not impact its traditionally cautious diplomacy. The world condemned North Korea after a March 26 blast, traced by investigators to a North Korean torpedo, sank a South Korean naval vessel, the Cheonan, killing 46. But China quashed calls for new United Nations sanctions against its ally, declined to endorse the investigators' conclusions, and twice hosted North Korea's leader Kim Jong-Il, just six weeks after the sinking in May, and in August.

On June 10, China reluctantly joined major powers in backing strengthened United Nations economic sanctions against Iran, an ally and energy supplier that had refused to open its nuclear program to international inspection. But behind the scenes, the Chinese worked hard to water down the latest sanctions so that critical goods like gasoline were excluded.

On April 13, a magnitude 6.9 earthquake struck mountainous Qinghai Province, devastating the Yushu County seat, Jiegu, close to the Sichuan Province site of a 2008 quake. In the thin air at 13,000 feet on the Tibetan plateau, altitude sickness felled rescuers and even rescue dogs, and cold claimed wreckage-trapped victims before injuries did. At least 2,698 died.

Summer brought more grief: In Dalian, a sprawling northeastern port, a July 16 pipeline rupture triggered China's largest-ever oil spill, fouling a bay with 11,000 barrels by government reckoning, and at least five times that by outsiders' estimates. Summer-long floods displaced 12 million people, mostly in northern China, and left more than 2,000 dead or missing. An Aug. 8 landslide in northwestern Gansu Province wrecked a small city, killing at least 1,467 and 298 missing.

But the year's most shocking tragedy was a series of attacks—six, from March 23 to Aug. 10—on children in kindergartens and schools, largely in urban eastern China. At least 18 children and five adults perished, all by young men wielding knives and, once, a hammer. The government convened an investigative panel, and panicked officials installed cameras and posted guards at schools nationwide. But the assaults lacked any theme, leaving analysts to speculate that China's breakneck social change and inadequate mental-health care were at fault.

—MICHAEL WINES

Searing Heat Wave Causes A Summer of Russian Misery

Russia is known for its brutal winters, but in 2010, it was the summer that brought misery. Here is how extreme it became: there is an area in Siberia that is considered one of the coldest places on earth, with temperatures dropping to as low as minus 90 degrees Fahrenheit. During the heat wave, the thermometer there also read 90 degrees. Plus 90. In the evening. Temperatures soared to records. Wheat fields withered. Wildfires consumed swaths of forests. And smoke from smoldering blazes in peat bogs around Moscow blanketed the city.

Most Russians do not have air conditioners or even fans because those items are considered to be not worth the expense, so they had difficulty coping. Death rates, especially among the elderly and disabled, climbed in major cities. Thousands died from drowning in rivers, reservoirs and elsewhere, often after seeking relief from the heat while intoxicated. In Moscow alone, the number of such deaths tripled.

As if the heat were not bad enough, smoke from fires in peat bogs in the suburbs of Moscow made life in the city especially unpleasant. Many of the bogs had been drained early in the Soviet era when the peat was mined and used for fuel. They were thus dry and prone to fires, which burned below the surface and were hard to extinguish. Russian health officials expressed concern that the effect of the fine particles and carbon monoxide in the smoke was comparable to smoking a pack of cigarettes a day. People tried to flee Moscow, but space on trains and planes was soon unavailable.

The drought caused Russian grain production to drop by roughly a third. In response, Prime Minister Vladimir V. Putin banned exports of grain, hoping to stabilize prices on the domestic market. Since rebounding from inefficient Soviet policies, Russia has played an increasingly important role in the world grain market. In 2009, it was the world's third largest exporter of wheat, after the United States and Canada. The ban helped to drive up prices. That in turn led to food speculation and fears of shortages in Russia, rekindling, especially among the elderly, a tendency from Soviet times toward hoarding.

The country grew jittery because of rising prices for meat, flour, pasta and other staples. The Kremlin ordered a crackdown on speculators, concerned that discontent over prices could influence the 2012 presidential election, when either Mr. Putin or his protégé, President Dmitri A. Medvedev, was expected to run.

—CLIFFORD J. LEVY

Sex Abuse Charges Multiply, Engulfing the Vatican

Scandals over child sexual abuse by Roman Catholic priests have been cropping up in the United States and other countries for decades, but 2010 was the year that the scandal spread across Europe, engulfed the Vatican and put two popes under scrutiny.

Abuse cases emerged in Belgium, Germany, Ireland, the Netherlands, Switzerland, Italy, and Austria, as well as in Brazil, Chile, and India. In March, a newspaper revealed that when Pope Benedict XVI was archbishop of Munich in 1980, he had permitted a priest undergoing psychological treatment for abusing children to be transferred to work in another parish. That priest, the Rev. Peter Hullerman, abused more victims and was convicted in 1986, but was still serving in a Bavarian parish when the story broke in 2010. The Vatican said Benedict had had no knowledge of the transfer, but *The New York Times* reported that Benedict, as archbishop, had led a meeting and was copied on a memo in which the priest's assignment was discussed.

The controversy snowballed. Europeans flooded hotlines set up by the church or by prosecutors to report abuse by priests. Documents surfaced in the United States showing that Benedict, in his previous role as head of the Vatican's Congregation for the Doctrine of the Faith, and his subordinates postponed requests from bishops to defrock clergy abusers in the 1980s and 1990s. One case involved a priest in Milwaukee accused of abusing more than 200 deaf boys at a school he ran. Another involved a California priest who was a convicted sex offender.

The Vatican and many bishops vigorously defended the pope's record, with some casting the media coverage as anti-Catholic persecution. Benedict attempted to change the tone, meeting privately with abuse victims on a trip to Malta in April. In Portugal in May he called the problem "truly terrifying," and said that "forgiveness is not a substitute for justice." The Vatican took the dramatic step of overhauling the leadership of the Legionaries of Christ, a religious order whose founder, the Rev. Marcial Maciel Degollado (who died in 2008), was found to have sexually abused young seminarians, fathered children, and misappropriated large sums of money.

But Benedict's efforts to address the scandal did not quiet it. In June, Belgian police raided church offices, detaining the country's bishops while the police searched for documents. They drilled into the tombs of two cardinals buried in the Brussels Cathedral. Police were investigating whether church officials covered up for the Bishop of Bruges, Roger Vangheluwe, accused of having sexually abused his young nephew years ago for eight years. (Bishop Vangheluwe had resigned suddenly in April.) The Vatican issued a formal complaint about the raid.

On July 15, the Vatican released long-awaited changes to its internal canon laws, streamlining the process for handling cases of sexual abuse. But the Vatican caused an uproar by adding to its list of grave offenses, which includes sexual abuse of minors, the ordination of women as priests.
—LAURIE GOODSTEIN

Tories in Britain Reclaim Power With a Coalition

Britain's Conservatives returned to power on May 11 after 13 years in opposition when David Cameron, who claimed to have recast the party of Margaret Thatcher for a new century as more compassionate and less class-bound, took over as prime minister from Labour's Gordon Brown.

Five days after a general election that left the Conservatives 20 seats short of a majority, Mr. Cameron, 43, cobbled together an awkward alliance with the Liberal Democrats to form the first coalition government since World War II. Nick Clegg, the Liberal Democrats' leader, became deputy prime minister. The Conservatives and Liberal Democrats are far apart on many issues, from immigration to relations with Europe, but five ministers in the new government were Liberal Democrats, including Vince Cable, a former oil economist who has called for sharp spending cuts.

The transfer of power took place with the swiftness characteristic of Britain's parliamentary system. Less than 75 minutes after Mr. Brown fast-forwarded events by an earlier-than-expected resignation announcement at a lectern in Downing Street, Mr. Cameron stood at the same lectern as Britain's new leader. In between, both men had met with Queen Elizabeth II to make the transfer formal.

Facing a $240 billion black hole in the government's annual accounts, largely a result of prodigious levels of deficit spending by Labour during the global recession of the past two years, Mr. Cameron in his Downing Street remarks made clear that fiscal toughness would be a hallmark of his government.

The new prime minister quickly followed through on that. An emergency budget unveiled in June proposed an austerity campaign of extraordinary severity, increasing taxes and setting across-the-board cuts over the next five years of 25 percent and more, amounting to $130 billion. The result, said the Institute for Fiscal Studies, a research group, will be "the longest, deepest sustained period of cuts to public services spending" since World War II.
—JOHN BURNS

Japan Elects a New Premier, The Fifth in Four Years

Naoto Kan, a plain-spoken finance minister with activist roots, was elected prime minister on June 4, 2010, making him the fifth Japanese leader in four years. Mr. Kan, 63, succeeded Yukio Hatoyama, and will face an uphill task in trying to win back the public support that Mr. Hatoyama had squandered in months of indecision over the fate of an American military base. He must also help the governing Democratic party—which chose him—regain the momentum it had after winning a landslide election victory in 2009 that ended a half-century of virtual one-party rule.

Known for his quick temper, Mr. Kan gained national attention in the mid-1990s when, as health minister, he exposed his own ministry's use of blood tainted with H.I.V. In the Hatoyama administration, he also served as deputy prime minister and was a point man in the party's push to rein in the secretive central ministries that have run Japan since World War II.

Mr. Kan vowed to refocus the party on its original goal of ending Japan's two-decade stagnation. He said he would do this by tackling two of Japan's most daunting problems, its anemic growth rates and ballooning public debt. Touching on his predecessor's difficulties, he said he would honor an agreement to relocate a United States Marine air base on Okinawa and work to rebuild trust between the allies. But he also said he would place equal emphasis on improving ties with China, with whom Japan now has larger trade relations.

By choosing Mr. Kan, the Democratic party was apparently betting that his background as a former civil rights activist and veteran battler of Japan's powerful bureaucrats would make him a more forceful leader than the indecisive and professorial Mr. Hatoyama.

Mr. Kan is the latest in what has been nearly a turnstile procession of prime ministers in recent years. Shinzo Abe served exactly one year, resigning under pressure in September 2007. He was succeeded by Yasuo Fukuda and then Taro Aso, each of whom served about one year. Mr. Hatoyama took office on Sept. 16, 2009.
—MARTIN FACKLER

Amid Signs of Internal Trouble, North Korea Remains Strident

North Korea says officially that it seeks to end "the hostile relationship" with the United States by signing a peace treaty and normalizing ties. But it stands accused of continuing to develop its nuclear weapons and missile programs, financing them with the profits from arms trade, money laundering and other illicit activities.

As doubt grows that North Korea will ever give up its nuclear weapons, so does international pressure on the isolated country. South Korea has cut off aid for North Korea. The North, which pursues "military-first politics," has responded with belligerent rhetoric and tension-raising maneuvers like missile and nuclear tests, which in turn have compelled the United Nations Security Council to urge the tightening of an arms embargo against the North.

This long-running pattern repeated itself in 2010.

In December 2009, an air cargo of North Korean weapons bound for an airport in Iran was seized in Bangkok. In January, North Korea fired 400 artillery shells and rockets in waters near a disputed western sea border with the South.

The North's strident posture came amid signs of internal trouble. In late 2009, it introduced new banknotes in a currency reform aimed at fighting inflation and controlling the spread of private markets. By early 2010, however, inflation had returned and officials in charge of implementing the reform were reportedly fired or executed.

In March, the *Cheonan*, a 1,200-ton South Korean warship, was sunk, killing 46 crewmen. A South Korea-led international investigation concluded in May that a North Korean submarine had torpedoed the ship and Seoul cut off most of its trade with the North. In a show of force, the United States and South Korea conducted naval exercises in late July and August. Washington vowed to slap more financial penalties on the North.

As his government's relations with South Korea and the U.S. chilled, Mr. Kim traveled to China in May, his first trip outside North Korea since reportedly suffering a stroke in 2008, courting the support of his government's last remaining major ally. In June, he presided over a session of the rubber-stamp Supreme People's Assembly where Jang Song-taek, his brother-in-law and a potential caretaker for his son, was elevated to the No. 2 post in the ruling hierarchy. In late September, Mr. Kim made his son, Kim Jong-un, a member of the Central Committee of the ruling Workers' Party.

A bizarre twist in U.S. relations with North Korea came in January when Aijalon Mahli Gomes, an American from Boston, was arrested in North Korea for illegally entering the country. His detention followed that of Robert Park, a Christian missionary from Tucson, who illegally entered North Korea on Dec. 25 carrying a letter urging Mr. Kim to free political prisoners. North Korea released Mr. Park in February. Mr. Gomes, who was believed to have entered North Korea in support of Mr. Park, was freed in August when former President Jimmy Carter visited the country to gain his release.

—CHOE SANG-HUN

Kyrgyzstan President Ousted, And Ethnic Violence Ensues

In 2010, Kyrgyzstan, a former Soviet republic in Central Asia, endured a tumultuous year that included the overthrow of its president and ethnic violence that left thousands of people dead and wounded. The instability attracted widespread attention because Kyrgyzstan has been the site of an important American military base that has supported the NATO mission in nearby Afghanistan. While the base was not threatened, it had to halt some operations temporarily at one point. Russia has also maintained a military base in Kyrgyzstan, and the unrest occurred even as both powers continued a longstanding struggle to retain influence there.

Political tensions in Kyrgyzstan had been brewing for months over the autocratic rule of the president, Kurmanbek Bakiyev, when demonstrations in April in the capital, Bishkek, erupted into violence and he was forced to flee. Mr. Bakiyev later resigned and went into exile, and an interim government took over, but it proved to have a shaky hold on the country.

In June, rioting broke out in the south between the majority Kyrgyz and ethnic Uzbeks, who form a prosperous minority around Osh, the second largest city in Kyrgyzstan. The spark has remained unclear, but for days, Kyrgyz mobs rampaged through Uzbek areas, attacking people and setting fires that destroyed numerous neighborhoods. Uzbeks later recounted how Kyrgyz assailants were assisted and sometimes even led by Kyrgyz soldiers and police officers who were riding armored vehicles and using military weapons. The interim government at first denied that government personnel took part in the violence, but later acknowledged that it may have lost control over some units.

Hundreds of thousands of ethnic Uzbeks fled across the border to Uzbekistan, the vast majority of them women and children, in one of the largest refugee crises in the post-Soviet space since the fall of Communism nearly two decades ago. They were sheltered in camps for weeks before returning to Kyrgyzstan after the violence subsided.

—CLIFFORD J. LEVY

Debt Level in Greece Sets Off A Financial Crisis in Europe

The sovereign debt crisis in Europe began in the fall of 2009 when the new Greek government announced that its budget deficit for the year would not be six percent of G.D.P. but twice that figure. The disclosure came as a shock to investors, especially since Greece had one of the highest debt levels in Europe at about 120 percent of G.D.P. With government deficits on the rise due to the extraordinary spending programs put into effect to counter the 2008 financial crisis, investors were becoming increasingly skeptical about their ability to continue to borrow from financial markets.

Within a few months, interest rates in Greece soared and when the government finally ran out of money it was forced to strike a deal in May with the International Monetary Fund and the European Union which provided $140 billion in funds in exchange for Greece implementing tough austerity measures.

But instead of calming markets, the Greece rescue prompted fears that Spain, a much larger economy than Greece that had a lower debt ratio but had suffered a terrible real estate collapse, would meet a similar fate. Panic spread through Europe and affected the U.S. markets as well, pushing interest rates up and causing the euro to plummet to a low of about 1.21 to the dollar as fears built that the community of 16 nations bound by a single currency would be forced to break apart. Finally, under pressure from an impatient U.S. government, French president Nicolas Sarkozy and German chancellor Angela Merkel, with the assistance of the European Central Bank and the I.M.F. cobbled together a nearly trillion-dollar rescue package that would be available for any European country or countries that needed it.

The crisis highlighted a crucial flaw of the currency zone. Designed a decade earlier as the final step toward finally unifying Europe under a common monetary and fiscal banner, the eurozone failed in one of its primary missions—to persuade all economies that adopted the euro to adopt responsible fiscal policies. Countries like Greece and Portugal financed their deficits with cheap debt and saw their competitiveness suffer when compared to more fiscally responsible nations like Germany. But in the midst of a global liquidity boom, no attention was paid to their high debt levels until after 2008 when Lehman Brothers collapsed.

The crisis has pushed once spendthrift European economies hard into the austerity camp. From Ireland, to Portugal, to Spain and even to Italy, Germany, and France, European governments have become ruthless in cutting back spending, raising taxes and paring the generous social benefits that for decades had served as a safety net for Europeans.

Britain, while not a member of the eurozone, has led the way in this regard, with the new conservative government introducing a severe program of cuts designed to bring down its own very high debt level.

While fears of a breakup of the eurozone have waned, the broader debate of whether an economic program of spending cuts and restraint at a time of broad economic weakness continues.
—LANDON THOMAS, JR.

Yemen Emerges As New Theater For America's "Secret War"

It was on Christmas Day 2009, when most Americans were celebrating or taking a nap, that Yemen burst back into the headlines. A young Nigerian, Umar Farouk Abdulmutallab, then 23, tried to blow up a Detroit-bound airliner by setting fire to explosives hidden in his underwear. Mr. Abdulmutallab alone was hurt, with burns, but his bomb did not go off.

The near-miss set the American security establishment scrambling, and Mr. Abdulmutallab reportedly started talking to interrogators. The plot was initiated in the lawless territories of Yemen, by an offshoot of Al Qaeda—Al Qaeda in the Arab Peninsula, a new combination of the terrorist group's branches in Yemen and neighboring Saudi Arabia.

Impoverished, corrupt Yemen is considered a new theater for America's "secret war" against Islamic terrorism. Osama bin Laden's ancestral homeland, from where his father emigrated to Saudi Arabia to make a fortune, Yemen has been run for decades by Ali Abdullah Saleh, who initially took power in 1977 in what was then North Yemen. He became president of the Republic of Yemen when North Yemen united with socialist South Yemen in 1990, and he was elected as president in 1999 and again in 2006. But Mr. Saleh has been preoccupied by an internal rebellion in the north; by civilian dissent and protests by secessionists in the south; by keeping the loyalty of tribal chiefs; and by an effort to ensure that his son Ahmed succeeds him.

Al Qaeda took advantage of the chaos to establish a regional network in Yemen's large and rugged tribal territories, creating training camps, attacking Western targets and receiving increased public sympathy. Al Qaeda in an older form was responsible for bombing the USS Cole in 2000, and the Saleh government, pressured by the U.S., cracked down on it then.

Some of the organizers of that attack escaped from prison in 2006, and were joined by men released from detention at Guantanamo Bay, Cuba, after having fought with Osama Bin Laden in Afghanistan. Others fought the Americans in Iraq. They were also joined by a young, radical, American-born Yemeni cleric, Anwar al-Awlaki, a preacher on the Internet who returned to Yemen in the spring of 2009. Mr. Awlaki, fluent in English, was an inspiration for Nidal Malik Hassan, the U.S. army major who went on a shooting spree at Ft. Hood, Tex. in November 2009. Mr. Awlaki is also said by American officials to have helped to recruit Mr. Abdulmutallab. Washington later put Mr. Awlaki, who has joint Yemeni-American citizenship, on a list allowing him to be killed, a rarity for an American citizen.

The United States sent Special Forces to help train and equip Yemeni forces and provided satellite and communications intelligence. American forces have also pinpointed Al Qaeda targets for Yemeni forces to strike, and sometimes struck them, quietly, themselves. While initial reports of the strikes were uniformly positive, it emerged that sometimes targeted individuals had left the area, or the wrong targets were hit, and sometimes innocent people died, creating more support for Al Qaeda.

As he fights Al Qaeda, Mr. Saleh continues to try to negotiate with them, while trying to keep his distance from Washington. In this manner, too, fragile Yemen reminds many analysts of Pakistan.
—STEVEN ERLANGER

After Two Months, Thai Army Crushes Anti-Government Protests in Bangkok

This was the year of the "red shirts" in Thailand as protesters occupied parts of Bangkok for more than two months until they were crushed by the military on May 19. It was one of the worst eruptions of political violence in recent history, involving deep social divisions that remained unresolved.

The protesters, many of them rural and urban poor, began a sit-in at the Phan Fa bridge on March 14, demanding that Prime Minister Abhisit Vejjajiva dissolve his government, which they called illegitimate, and hold a new election. Many were angered by the Supreme Court's confiscation on Feb. 27 of $1.4 billion in frozen assets belonging to former Prime Minister Thaksin Shinawatra, who was ousted in a coup in 2006 and remained abroad evading arrest on a corruption charge.

On April 10 the military attempted to clear the Phan Fa area, leading to a pitched battle in which at least 26 soldiers and civilians were killed. The protests then consolidated in a mass occupation that turned Bangkok's central commercial area into a tent city, forcing major malls and hotels to shut down. Though the sit-in was mostly peaceful, there were sporadic outbreaks of violence outside the protest site that included M-79 grenade attacks. On May 3, Mr. Abhisit offered a reconciliation plan that included an election on Nov. 12. An initial agreement by the protesters collapsed as they added new conditions.

The prime minister then ordered the military to surround and squeeze the protest site, leading to further violent confrontations. On May 13, the leader of a militant wing of red shirts, Maj. Gen. Khattiya Sawatdiphol, was shot in the head and killed, apparently by a sniper, as he was giving an interview to The New York Times. On the morning of May 19, 2010, the army moved in with armored vehicles and crushed the protest site. The attack set off a spate of arson attacks around the city and the destruction of municipal halls in three provinces sympathetic to the red shirts. Altogether about 90 people died in the protests and up to 2,000 were injured.

The government charged 27 protest leaders with terrorism, including Mr. Thaksin, whom it accused of directing and helping to pay for the protests. The bank accounts of scores more alleged supporters were frozen, a state of emergency was extended in 22 provinces as well as Bangkok, later reduced to seven provinces, and a wide campaign of censorship forced the closure of scores of opposition radio stations and thousands of web sites and pages.

Throughout the crisis, King Bhumibol Aduljadej, 82 years old and confined to a hospital, made no statement to halt the bloodshed as he had done during past crises.

—SETH MYDANS

Khmer Rouge Sentence Leaves Many Dissatisfied

For 30 years since the brutal Khmer Rouge regime was driven from power, Cambodians have lived with unresolved trauma, with skulls and bones from killing fields still lying in the open and with parents hiding the pain of their past from their children.

On July 26, 2010, Cambodia took a significant step toward addressing its harsh past with the first conviction of a major Khmer Rouge figure in connection with the deaths of 1.7 million people from 1975 to 1979. But some survivors were distraught over what they saw as a lenient sentence, one that could possibly allow the defendant, Kaing Guek Eav, 67, commonly known as Duch, to walk free one day.

A United Nations-backed court found Duch (pronounced DOIK), the commandant of the central Khmer Rouge prison, Tuol Sleng, guilty of war crimes and crimes against humanity and sentenced him to 35 years in prison for overseeing the torture and killing of more than 14,000 people. The court reduced that term to 19 years because of time already served and in compensation for a period of illegal military detention.

It was the first time in Cambodia's modern history that a senior government official had been made accountable for serious human rights violations and the first time such a trial had been held that met international standards of justice.

The verdict took into account mitigating circumstances that a court spokesman, Lars Olsen, said included Duch's cooperation, his admission of responsibility and limited expressions of remorse, the coercive environment of the Khmer Rouge period and the possibility of his rehabilitation.

There is no death penalty in Cambodia and prosecutors had sought a 40-year sentence, but many people said they would accept nothing less than a term of life in prison.

—SETH MYDANS

Polish President Killed in Jet Crash in Russia

A plane carrying the Polish president and dozens of the country's top political and military leaders to the site of a Soviet massacre of Polish officers in World War II crashed in western Russia on April 10, killing everyone on board.

President Lech Kaczynski's plane tried to land in a thick fog, missing the runway and snagging treetops about half a mile from the airport in Smolensk, scattering chunks of fuselage across a bare forest.

The crash came as a stunning blow to Poland, wiping out a large portion of the country's leadership in one fiery explosion. And in a chilling twist, it happened at the moment that Russia and Poland were beginning to come to terms with the killing of more than 20,000 members of Poland's elite officer corps in the same place 70 years ago.

Those killed included Poland's deputy foreign minister and a dozen members of Parliament, the chiefs of the army and the navy, and the president of the national bank. They included Anna Walentynowicz, 80, the former dock worker whose firing in 1980 set off the Solidarity strike that ultimately overthrew Polish Communism, as well as relatives of victims of the massacre that they were on their way to commemorate.

Poles united in their grief in a way that recalled the death of the Polish pope, John Paul II, five years ago. Thousands massed outside the Presidential Palace, laying flowers and lighting candles.

The crash happened days after Prime Minister Vladimir V. Putin became the first Russian leader to join Polish officials in commemorating the 1940 massacre at Katyn Woods, a wound that has festered between the two countries for decades and to Poles was a symbol of Russian domination.

Mr. Kaczynski, 60, a pugnacious nationalist who often clashed with Russia, was on his way to Katyn, where members of the Soviet secret police executed Polish officers captured after the Red Army invaded Poland in 1939.

In July, the centrist Bronislaw Komorowski narrowly defeated Mr. Kaczynski's twin brother, Jaroslaw, in the election to become Poland's new president.

—NICHOLAS KULISH, ELLEN BARRY and MICHAL PIOTROWSKI

Signs of Growing Tension Between U.S. and Mexico As Drug Violence Continues

The violence in Mexico continued unabated in 2010 even as the Obama administration backed President Felipe Calderon's anti-drug offensive with a multi-million-dollar aid package that funds everything from helicopters to training for prosecutors and prison guards. In both countries, officials on the front lines of the effort to rein in Mexico's drug trafficking organizations offered the same warning: no quick end to the bloodshed was expected.

The headlines were grim. In August, authorities discovered the dead bodies of 72 migrants in a ranch in Tamaulipas State in northeast Mexico. The victims, who had been heading to the United States, were believed to have been killed by members of organized crime groups, which have branched out as their drug business has been targeted by law enforcement. Kidnapping migrants, demanding protection money from business owners and selling counterfeit merchandise are all new activities used by drug gangs to supplement their illicit profits.

The Tamaulipas case grew worse when two investigators went missing. Their remains were later found about 30 miles away in what was viewed as a chilling warning from the criminals about who was in charge.

The Obama administration has acknowledged that the demand for drugs in the United States fuels the violence. On top of that, American border states are regarded as a prime source for the weaponry used by Mexican criminals. But despite the two countries' talk of shared responsibility, there were signs of growing tensions between Washington and Mexico City, as well.

In September, the United States said it would withhold about $26 million in anti-drug assistance because of concerns that Mexico had not done enough to rein in police and military abuse. It was the first time that the State Department had cited human rights concerns to hold back some of the $1.4 billion in aid allocated under the so-called Merida Initiative.

The Mexican government was livid, calling the findings an affront to its sovereignty. "The Merida Initiative is based on shared responsibility, mutual trust and respect for each other's jurisdiction," the government said.

Mexico also reacted strongly to Arizona's tough immigration law. A federal judge blocked much of the law from going into effect but Mexico still warned its citizens about traveling to Arizona and Mexican governors boycotted a conference of governors from both sides of the border that was to be held in Phoenix. It was rescheduled for Santa Fe, N.M. The Mexican governors attended but Governor Jan Brewer of Arizona was a no show.
—MARC LACEY

Icelandic Volcano Spews Ash, Disrupts European Air Travel

An ash cloud drifting south and east from an erupting volcano in Iceland shrouded much of northern Europe for six days in April 2010, forcing airlines to ground thousands of flights and creating scenes of travel chaos.

The eruption occurred under the Eyjafjallajokull glacier, in a rural area 100 miles southeast of Iceland's capital, Reykjavik. The Eyjafjallajokull volcano (pronounced EY-ya-fyat-lah-YOH-kuht) began erupting in March for the first time since 1821. The initial phase was brief but spectacular "lava falls" that made the volcano a tourist attraction. On April 12, scientists at the Icelandic Meteorological Office declared that volcanic activity at the site had essentially stopped. But two days later the volcano erupted again, much more violently, and melted a hole in the ice cap at its summit, sending floodwater coursing down the glacier into lowland areas. Hundreds of residents were evacuated.

Clouds of ash soaring as high as 30,000 feet—an altitude commonly used by jetliners—moved with prevailing winds over Britain and across continental Europe, expanding a massive transportation gridlock.

The plume presented a severe challenge to aviation. Volcanic ash consists of glass-like particles that can enter a jet engine and liquefy, causing a plane to stall in midflight. The threat was great enough to close airports from Ireland to Ukraine, and Norway to Spain. The shutdown of airspace was the worst disruption in international air travel since the attacks of Sept. 11, 2001.

As the crisis entered a fourth day, increasingly desperate airlines ran test flights to show that flying was safe, and pressed European regulators to loosen the flight bans. Some criticized the authorities for overreacting and needlessly stranding millions of passengers and tons of cargo.

On April 20, after new data from engine manufacturers indicated that aircraft could safely fly through greater levels of ash, restrictions began to be lifted. Ash plume hazards continued for the next month, however, forcing new closures of airports including London Heathrow. Release of ash gradually declined in frequency and magnitude and by May 23 very little volcanic activity was observed at Eyjafjallajokull.

The long-term economic impact of the eruption was difficult to calculate. The International Air Transport Association estimated lost revenues of $1.7 billion for airlines alone.
—NICOLA CLARK, ALAN COWELL, STEVEN ERLANGER, and JAD MOUAWAD

Suicide Bombers Kill 40 On Moscow Subway

Two female suicide bombers blew themselves up in the Moscow subway during the morning rush on March 29, 2010, killing 40 people and raising the specter of a return to a time when the city, including the subway, was hit with several terrorist attacks. The coordinated bombing at two separate stations was the sixth such incident in the subway since 1996 and the first since August 2004.

Officials said the first bomb struck at about 8 a.m. on a train that had just arrived at Lubyanka station. Within 40 minutes a second explosion went off in the Park Kultury station, four stops away on the same line. Both attackers detonated their explosive belts as the train doors opened, taking the lives of passengers both inside the trains and on the station platforms.

Federal Security Service officials quickly identified the bombers as two women from Dagestan—a volatile, predominantly Muslim region bordering Chechnya where an Islamist insurgency is raging. One was the 17-year-old bride of a militant killed by federal forces in December, and the other was a 28-year-old teacher married to an insurgent leader. They fit the profile of "Black Widows," young women who are deployed as human bombs to avenge the deaths of loved ones.

Two days after the attacks, one of Russia's most-wanted rebel commanders, Doku Umarov, issued a video statement taking responsibility for the bombings, claiming they were in response to the killing by Russian forces of four local civilians. In 2007 Mr. Umarov adopted the title "Emir" with the aim of creating an independent state under Sharia law in the North Caucasus, spanning the republics of Chechnya, Ingushetia, North Ossetia and Dagestan.

The bombings came at an uncertain moment for Russia's Caucasus policy, which had been wavering between the muscular clampdown championed by hardliners and the cautious overtures of President Dmitri Medvedev who has spoken in favor of increasing political pluralism. The worst fears of liberals were realized in July, when President Medvedev signed legislation authorizing the F.S.B., the successor to the KGB, to take "preventive measures" against individuals only suspected of criminal activity, reviving a Soviet-era practice that was often used against dissidents. Civil rights advocates condemned the legislation as a violation of the presumption of innocence.
—CLIFFORD J. LEVY, ANDREW KRAMER and ELLEN BARRY

Chilean Miners Found Alive 17 Days After Cave-In; Long Rescue Anticipated

Thirty-three miners trapped 2,300 feet down in a gold and copper mine in northern Chile that collapsed on Aug. 5 sent up a message 17 days later saying they were miraculously all alive. The message, in a bag tied to a drilling hammer used to try and reach the men, came when hope for their survival was all but gone, and set off jubilance among their rescuers and teary-eyed relatives who had encamped outside the mine. The miners later used a modified telephone to sing Chile's national anthem and in Santiago, the capital, motorists honked their horns and people cheered wildly on subway platforms.

Officials began boring a rescue hole that was expected to take three to four months to complete, and in plastic tubes were able to get to the miners a gel-like vitamin and protein substance to keep them alive, as well as tiny lights to illuminate the darkness and encouraging notes from their families. Before they were found, the miners had survived on two spoonfuls of tuna, a cup of milk, one cracker and a bit of a peach topping eaten every two days, family members said.

The miners, who are trapped in a hot, stuffy chamber about 33 feet by 20 feet, were not told how long the rescue was expected to take, for fear of breaking their spirit.

"Psychologically, we have to try to keep them on the right track," said Laurence Golborne, Chile's mining minister. "They are miners, so they understand that we have to go through 700 meters of solid rock to rescue them." But even so, he added, "we don't want them to suffer ups and downs."

Questions swirled about the cause of the mine collapse. The owner, the San Esteban Mining Company, tried to deflect discussion of blame, saying this was not the proper time to discuss responsibility. But mining unions, lawmakers and even some who have worked for the company said it had a long history of disregarding safety.

Mr. Golborne said the Chilean government is committed to punishing those responsible. "There is not going to be any impunity here, neither public nor private," he said.

—ALEXEI BARRIONUEVO
and PASCALE BONNEFOY

Vancouver Olympics Prevail After an Early Tragedy

Unlike many recent Olympics, there was little controversy in the build-up to the 2010 Vancouver Winter Olympics. But hours before the opening ceremonies, tragedy brought an ominous tone to the event's feel-good atmosphere when Nodar Kumaritashvili, a luger from Georgia, was killed in a training run. Changes were made in the ultra-fast luge and bobsled track, but days later, more safety concerns were raised after several frightening crashes in the women's alpine downhill. There were minor modifications made in that course as well.

After the heartrending and bumpy start, the Vancouver Olympics evolved into a celebration of something culturally significant to the host country: traditional winter sports. By the end, Canada led all countries with 14 gold medals. Most importantly to Canadians, the home side won both the men's and women's ice hockey gold medals—with national sporting icon Sidney Crosby scoring the winning goal in overtime of the men's gold-medal game. In its other winter sports passion, the obscure medieval sport of curling, Canada won the men's competition and the women's team won the silver medal.

So all things were right with the world through a Canadian's eyes and it revealed itself in large, convivial street celebrations in Vancouver and Whistler, the mountain village and ski resort that hosted several events.

The Vancouver Olympics were very good to North American athletes as the United States received 37 medals, the most by a single nation in a Winter Games. It was also an Olympics that featured the continued rise of Asian athletes in winter sports like figure skating, where athletes from China, South Korea, and Japan won five medals, and speed skating and short track speed skating, where China and South Korea, combined for 18 medals. In figure skating singles, Evan Lysacek of the United States won the men's gold medal and South Korea's Kim Yu-Na won the women's gold medal.

The United States had its best showing ever in alpine skiing, winning eight medals. Lindsey Vonn became the first American woman to win the downhill. Her teammate Julia Mancuso was second, one of her two silver medals at the Games.

After an ignominious 2006 Olympics in Italy, American Bode Miller came back to win three skiing medals—one of every shade. Norway's Aksel Lund Svindal, a former world champion recovering from a near-fatal injury, matched Miller's medal total.

Among other firsts for the United States team, Bill Demong and Johnny Spillane won multiple Nordic combined medals. And short track speed skater Apolo Anton Ohno won three medals which gave him eight for his career, the most by an American winter Olympian. Shaun White reprised his famed gold medal performance at the 2006 Olympics in snowboarding's halfpipe, with a record number of twists and flips that only added to his already considerable marketing appeal.

The emotional high point was a mix of triumph and sorrow. Canadian figure skater Joannie Rochette, whose mother died in Vancouver of a heart attack during the Games, won the bronze medal in women's singles.

—BILL PENNINGTON

Spain Wins the World Cup, South Africa Wins Plaudits as Host

In effect, two World Cups took place in 2010. One was the soccer tournament. The other was a referendum on whether Africa was prepared to host the world's most popular sporting event for the first time. Spain proved to be the world's best team with its elegant passing, while host South Africa succeeded in allaying fears that it was not yet capable of handling security, crime and logistical concerns 16 years after the dismantling of apartheid. "All the concerns people had about Africa were dispelled," said Sunil Gulati, president of the United States Soccer Federation.

The soccer itself was not spectacular as a whole, perhaps because of the altitude, the Southern Hemisphere winter or the weariness of many international players after enervating European club seasons. And crucial errors by the referees led FIFA, soccer's world governing body, to begin considering the use of instant replay in the future.

France, the 1998 champion and 2006 runner-up, left embarrassingly early after its players mutinied against unpopular coach Raymond Domenech. Italy, a four-time champion, also exited meekly, too many of its stars aged and ineffective. Brazil, a five-time winner, left in the quarterfinals, the beautiful game it once played replaced by a brawniness that was both insufficiently graceful and muscular.

The United States reached the second round, displaying a persistence and resilience that compelled it to play on in belief that unyielding commitment would prevail even when skill and tactics would not. Yet, the Americans also missed a great opportunity to advance as far as the semifinals, squandering an inviting draw with a listless performance against Ghana in the round of 16.

Instead, Ghana emerged as a revelation, becoming only the third African team to reach the quarterfinals (its bid for the semis was waylaid in a controversial finish against Uruguay). Germany, too, made an indelible mark into the semifinals with style and imagination and multiculturalism.

In the end, Spain, long considered an underachiever, proved the most complete and graceful team in winning its first World Cup. It overcame a shocking loss to Switzerland in its opener, prevailing with patience and the beautiful geometry of its triangular passing. The Netherlands tried to disrupt this refined style with brutish fouling in the final, but Spain received a goal from Andres Iniesta in overtime, and its 1–0 victory provided a triumph of flair over cynicism.

—JERE LONGMAN

BUSINESS & ECONOMY

Congress Passes Overhaul Of Financial Regulations

Congress approved a sweeping expansion of federal financial regulation on July 15, reflecting a renewed mistrust of financial markets after decades in which Washington stood back from Wall Street with wide-eyed admiration.

The bill, heavily promoted by President Obama —who signed it a week later—and Congressional Democrats as a response to the 2008 financial crisis, cleared the Senate by a vote of 60 to 39, largely along party lines, after weeks of wrangling that allowed Democrats to pick up the three Republican votes to ensure passage.

The vote was the culmination of nearly two years of fierce lobbying and intense debate over the appropriate response to the financial excesses that dragged the nation into the worst recession since the Great Depression. The result was a catalog of repairs and additions to the rusted infrastructure of a regulatory system that has failed to keep up with the expanding scope and complexity of modern finance.

The bill subjects more financial companies to federal oversight, regulates many derivatives contracts, and creates a panel to detect risks to the financial system along with a consumer protection regulator. It leaves a vast number of details for

regulators to work out, inevitably setting off another round of battles that could last for years.

Democrats argue that the government's expanded role will improve the stability of the financial system without sapping its vitality. But that project faces considerable challenges. Many investors have withdrawn from markets like commercial paper that were once seen as safe. Lenders have lost faith in borrowers. Politicians and central bankers are struggling to repair economies and restore the flow of credit.

Even the bill's political luster no longer seems certain. Despite public anger at Wall Street, the vast majority of Republicans opposed the bill with loud confidence.

The bill expands federal banking and securities regulation from its focus on banks and public markets, subjecting a wider range of financial companies to government oversight, and imposing regulation for the first time on "black markets" like the enormous trade in credit derivatives.

It creates a council of federal regulators, led by the Treasury secretary, to coordinate the detection of risks to the financial system, and it provides new powers to constrain and even dismantle troubled companies.

It also creates a powerful new regulator, appointed by the president, to protect consumers of financial products, which will be housed in the Federal Reserve.

The legislation is painted in broad strokes, so regulators have broad leeway to shape its meaning and its impact. The legislation, for example, requires many derivatives to be traded through clearinghouses, a form of insurance for the traders, and it requires traders to disclose pricing data to encourage competition. But regulators will decide which derivatives, and how long traders can wait to disclose pricing information.

—BINYAMIN APPELBAUM
and DAVID M. HERSZENHORN

Apple's Highly Anticipated iPad Even More Popular Than Expected

After months of fevered anticipation, Steven P. Jobs, the chief executive of Apple, in January unveiled the iPad, a tablet computer that gave renewed momentum to what was already the most remarkable comeback in American business. While it seemed improbable that the device could match the high expectations that preceded it, the iPad turned into a blockbuster success for Apple and helped to reshape the consumer electronics industry as scores of would-be competitors rushed to develop rival products.

The 9.7-inch iPad, which ranges in price from $499 to $829, looks like an oversized iPhone. It has proven to be ideally suited for consuming such media as books, Web pages, photos and videos, as well as for playing games. With its ability to run most of the more than 200,000 apps written for the iPhone, it piggybacked on the success of that device.

And the iPad's success surpassed even the most optimistic forecasts. By the end of June, three months after the iPad became available, Apple had sold nearly 3.3 million, generating $2.1 billion in revenue for Apple. Apple had difficulty keeping up with demand through much of the summer.

With the iPad, Mr. Jobs succeeded where many, including his rival Bill Gates, had failed. In 2001, Mr. Gates predicted that tablet computers would outsell PCs within five years, and Microsoft helped to develop several tablet computers. But burdened by a complicated user interface and software, those devices failed to catch on with consumers.

The success of the iPad helped to propel Apple's stock ever higher. On May 26, Apple reached a market value of $222.12 billion, surpassing Microsoft as the most valuable technology company, and the second most valuable American company behind Exxon Mobil. The highly symbolic milestone represented the culmination of a turnaround that began in 1996, when Mr. Jobs returned to a nearly bankrupt Apple after a more than 10-year absence.

The iPad was well timed to ride the wave of popularity of e-books and was embraced by publishers. But no other sector put more faith in the iPad's potential to revive its fortunes than the newspaper and magazine industries. Suffering from a decline in advertising and print subscriptions, news publishers viewed the iPad as an opportunity to correct mistakes from the past, and in particular, to begin charging for customized versions of their publications. While many publishers developed paid iPad apps, it was too early to tell whether the revenue generated by them will prove to be significant.

—MIGUEL HELFT

Massive Recall Puts a Crack In Toyota's Reputation

Toyota Motor, the world's largest automaker, recalled more than eight million vehicles and paid a record fine to United States safety regulators in a crisis that threatened to undermine the company's reputation for building safe and reliable vehicles.

The recalls, in late 2009 and early 2010, related to problems with the accelerator pedals on many of Toyota's most popular models, including the Camry and Corolla sedans. The National Highway Traffic Safety Administration accused Toyota of waiting too long to initiate the recalls and ordered the company to pay $16.4 million, the maximum allowed by law.

Toyota said some of the models were designed in a way that the accelerator pedal could be trapped under the floor mat, causing the vehicle to speed out of control. Others were built using a pedal that in rare cases could become stuck when partially depressed or spring back too slowly, the company said.

The issues first received widespread attention after a fiery crash near San Diego killed an off-duty California Highway Patrol officer driving a Lexus sedan and three of his family members. One of the passengers called 911 from the back seat saying the officer was unable to stop the car because the accelerator pedal was stuck.

In more than 3,000 complaints to the safety agency, many of which were filed in the months after the recalls started, consumers alleged that 93 deaths were caused by Toyota and Lexus vehicles accelerating suddenly. Toyota argued that many of the incidents were actually caused by drivers mistakenly flooring the accelerator pedal instead of the brake, and it dismissed widespread speculation that the vehicles' electronic throttle control systems were to blame.

An initial investigation by the highway safety agency into 58 complaints about Toyota and Lexus vehicles that crashed after accelerating suddenly found no evidence of a glitch in the electronics. On-board data recorders in 35 of the vehicles showed no signs that the driver had depressed the brake, supporting Toyota's "pedal misapplication" argument. But the regulators said they were continuing to study the matter, and the National Aeronautics and Space Administration was investigating the possibility that electromagnetic interference could be responsible. The carmaker also was being investigated by several congressional committees and Japan's transport ministry.

The recalls caused Toyota's sales in the United States to fall for several months, and the company began an aggressive campaign to mend its reputation by offering free maintenance and some of the largest discounts it ever had offered.

Executives in Japan estimated the lost sales and repairs could cost the company $2 billion. In addition, class-action lawsuits filed by Toyota owners, including crash victims and relatives of drivers and passengers who were killed, were seeking billions of dollars in damages.

In August, Toyota said it would recall 1.13 million compact cars after federal safety regulators upgraded an investigation into numerous complaints that the cars were stalling. That recall, which involved the 2005 through 2008 Corolla sedan and Matrix hatchback, was not related to the accelerator pedal and floor-mat problems.

—NICK BUNKLEY

United–Continental Merger Said to Create Largest Airline

United Airlines and Continental Airlines agreed in May 2010 to a $3 billion merger that would create the world's biggest airline.

The deal would form a coast-to-coast behemoth with a leading presence in the top domestic markets, including New York, Chicago, and Los Angeles, along with an extended network to Asia, Latin America and Europe. The deal would give the airlines the muscle to fend off low-cost rivals at home and to take on foreign carriers abroad.

United is buying Continental, and the combined company will keep the United name and be based in Chicago. Jeffery A. Smisek, Continental's chief executive, would run the company. The merged airline would replace Delta Air Lines as the top carrier.

The merger was an all-stock deal, with the acquisition valued at $3.17 billion based on the April 30 closing price. The merger is expected to be completed before the end of the year.

For consumers, the merger could eventually result in higher prices. Though the new company does not intend to raise fares, according to the people briefed on the matter, one of the rationales for airline mergers is to cut capacity. That reduces the number of seats in the industry and allows airlines to increase fares.

In addition, United and Continental will no longer be competing against each other on some routes, allowing them to save money but offering travelers fewer options.

Combined, United and Continental have 21 percent of domestic capacity, in terms of so-called available seat miles, or one seat flown one mile. Delta has a market share of 20 percent. Globally, the merged companies would have a 7 percent market share.

In late August, the airlines won swift approval from the Justice Department, lifting the biggest regulatory hurdle to the merger. Seeking approval from their respective pilots' unions, the two airlines also had an agreement in principle with their pilots on how to manage talks that would merge their seniority lists.

—JAD MOUAWAD
and MICHAEL J. de la MERCED

Dow Falls 1,000 Points in Minutes, Then Rebounds, Shaking Market

A bad day in the stock market turned into one of the most terrifying moments in Wall Street history on May 6, 2010, with a brief 1,000-point plunge that recalled the panic of 2008. It lasted just 16 minutes but left Wall Street experts and ordinary investors alike struggling to come to grips with what had happened—and fearful of where the markets might go from there.

The speed and scale of the plunge—the largest intraday decline on record—seemed to feed fears that the financial troubles gripping Europe were at last reaching across the Atlantic.

Traders and Washington policy makers struggled to keep up as the Dow Jones industrial average fell 1,000 points shortly after 2:30 p.m. and then mostly rebounded in a matter of minutes. For a moment, the sell-off seemed to overwhelm computer and human systems alike, and some traders began referring grimly to the day as "Black Thursday."

In the end, it was not as black as it had seemed. After briefly sinking below 10,000, the Dow ended down 347.80, or 3.2 percent, at 10,520.32. The Standard & Poor's 500-stock index dropped 37.75 points, or 3.24 percent, to close at 1,128.15, and the Nasdaq was down 82.65 points, or 3.44 percent, at 2,319.64.

But on Wall Street and across the nation, many investors were dumbstruck. Experts groped for explanations as blue-chip stocks like Procter & Gamble, Philip Morris, and Accenture plunged. At one point, Accenture fell more than 90 percent to a penny. P.& G. plunged to $39.37 from more than $60 within minutes.

On the trading floor of the New York Stock Exchange, traders shouted or watched open-mouthed as the screens lighted up with plummeting prices and as phones rang off the hook. Wall Street managers wandered their trading floors, trying to calm their people and figure out what was going on. They began to notice wild movements in stocks like P.& G. and Philip Morris. Many traders said computer program trades accelerated the slide as market indexes fell through crucial levels.

In the days after, regulators searching for the causes focused closely on the heavy selling of stock-index futures by a single trader, beginning 10 minutes before stock prices began to plummet. According to Gary Gensler, the chairman of the Commodity Futures Trading Commission, the futures trader, who was not identified, accounted for about 9 percent of trading volume in the most actively traded stock-index derivative contract, known as the 500 e-mini futures contract.

Three rival exchanges stopped routing trades to the exchange's electronic market after they perceived technical problems there. Market experts said they believed this prompted high-frequency computer traders, who account for a vast swath of trading, to withdraw from the market.

In early October, in a long-awaited report, regulators said that the cause was an automated sale of a large block of futures by a mutual fund – not named in the report but identified as Waddell & Reed Financial, of Overland, Kan. The fund started a program at about 2:32 p.m. to sell $4.1 billion of futures contracts, using a computer sell algorithm that over the next 20 minutes dumped 75,000 contracts onto the market, even automatically accelerating its selling as prices plunged.

The regulators hoped the report would lift the uncertainty that hung over the nation's exchanges, but it left lingering questions among many who felt it did not explain why the crash took place on that particular day, or provide any assurance that it would not occur again.

—GRAHAM BOWLEY and EDWARD WYATT

Goldman Settles S.E.C. Suit For Fraud in Housing Deal

Goldman Sachs, the Wall Street powerhouse, agreed in July to pay $550 million to settle a civil lawsuit for securities fraud filed three months earlier by the Securities and Exchange Commission, which claimed the bank created and sold a mortgage investment that was secretly intended to fail.

The suit represented the first time that regulators had taken action against a Wall Street deal that helped investors capitalize on the collapse of the housing market. The suit also named Fabrice Tourre, a vice president at Goldman who helped create and sell the investment, but who was not included in the settlement.

The focus of the S.E.C. case, an investment vehicle called Abacus 2007-AC1, was one of 25 such vehicles that Goldman created so the bank and some of its clients could bet against the housing market. Those deals initially protected Goldman from losses when the mortgage market disintegrated and later yielded profits for the bank.

As the Abacus portfolios in the S.E.C. case plunged in value, a prominent hedge fund manager made money from his bets against certain mortgage bonds, while investors lost more than $1 billion.

According to the complaint, Goldman created Abacus 2007-AC1 in February 2007 at the request of John A. Paulson, a prominent hedge fund manager who earned an estimated $3.7 billion in 2007 by correctly wagering that the housing bubble would burst. Mr. Paulson was not named in the suit.

Goldman told investors that the bonds would be chosen by an independent manager. In the case of Abacus 2007-AC1, however, Goldman let Mr. Paulson select mortgage bonds that he believed were most likely to lose value, according to the complaint. Goldman then sold the package to investors like foreign banks, pension funds and insurance companies, which would profit only if the bonds gained value. The European banks IKB and ABN Amro and other investors lost more than $1 billion in the deal, the commission said.

Though Goldman did not formally admit to the S.E.C.'s allegations, it agreed to a judicial order barring it from committing intentional fraud in the future under federal securities laws. In addition, Goldman acknowledged that the marketing materials for Abacus "contained incomplete information" and that it was "a mistake" not to have disclosed Mr. Paulson's role. As a part of the agreement, the bank also said it "regrets that the marketing materials did not contain that disclosure."

—LOUISE STORY, GRETCHEN MORGENSON and SEWELL CHAN

SCIENCE & MEDICINE

Judge Halts Stem Cell Aid Backed by Obama

On August 23, 2010, a federal district judge blocked President Obama's 2009 executive order that expanded embryonic stem cell research, saying it violated a ban on federal money being used to destroy embryos. The ruling on Aug. 23 came as a shock to scientists at the National Institutes of Health and at universities across the country, which had viewed the Obama administration's new policy and the grants provided under it as settled law.

In his ruling, Chief Judge Royce C. Lamberth of Federal District Court for the District of Columbia wrote that his temporary injunction returned federal policy to the "status quo," but few officials, scientists or lawyers in the case were sure what that meant.

The judge ruled that the Obama administration's policy was illegal because the administration's distinction between work that leads to the destruction of embryos—which cannot be financed by the federal government under the current policy—and the financing of work using stem cells created through embryonic destruction was meaningless. In his ruling, he referred to embryonic stem cell research as E.S.C.

"If one step or 'piece of research' of an E.S.C. research project results in the destruction of an embryo, the entire project is precluded from receiving federal funding," wrote Judge Lamberth, who was appointed to the federal bench in 1987 by President Ronald Reagan.

In other words, the neat lines that the government had drawn between the process of embryonic destruction and the results of that destruction are not valid, the judge ruled.

For scientists, the problem with the judge's reasoning is that it may render all scientific work regarding embryonic stem cells illegal—including work allowed under the more restrictive policy adopted by Pres. George W. Bush in 2001.

The Obama administration appealed and on Sept. 10 a federal appeals court in Washington ruled that federal financing of embryonic stem cell research could continue while the court considers Judge Lamberth's ruling.

For years, private financing has been used to create embryonic stem cell lines, mostly from discarded embryos from fertility clinics. The process destroys the embryos. President Bush agreed to finance embryonic stem cell research, but limited federally financed research to 21 cell lines already in existence by 2001.

Under the Obama administration, private money was still needed to obtain the embryonic stem cells, but federal money could be used to conduct research on hundreds more stem cell lines, as long as donors of embryos signed consent forms and complied with other rules.

In rules announced in 2009, the Obama administration allowed financing of research into any embryonic stem cell lines that either were allowed by the Bush administration or had been created using embryos discarded after fertilization procedures and in which unpaid donors had given clear consent for the embryos to be used for research purposes.

—GARDINER HARRIS

Maternal Deaths in Sharp Decline Globally

For the first time in decades, researchers are reporting a significant drop worldwide in the number of women dying each year from pregnancy and childbirth, to about 342,900 in 2008 from 526,300 in 1980. The findings, published in April 2010 in the medical journal The Lancet, challenge the prevailing view of maternal mortality as an intractable problem that has defied every effort to solve it.

"The overall message, for the first time in a generation, is one of persistent and welcome progress," the journal's editor, Dr. Richard Horton, wrote.

The study cited a number of reasons for the improvement: lower pregnancy rates in some countries; higher income, which improves nutrition and access to health care; more education for women; and the increasing availability of "skilled attendants"—people with some medical training —to help women give birth. Improvements in large countries like India and China helped to drive down the overall death rates.

Dr. Richard Horton, The Lancet's editor, said the new study was based on more and better data, and more sophisticated statistical methods than were used in a previous analysis by a different research team that estimated more deaths, 535,900 in 2005.

The new report comes from the University of Washington and the University of Queensland in Brisbane, Australia, and was paid for by the Bill and Melinda Gates Foundation.

The researchers analyzed maternal mortality in 181 countries from 1980 to 2008, using whatever information they could glean from each country: death records, censuses, surveys and published studies. They ultimately gathered about three times as much data as the previous researchers had found.

Among poor countries with longstanding high death rates, progress varied considerably. For instance, from 1990 to 2008, the maternal death rate dropped 8.8 percent a year in the Maldives, but rose 5.5 percent in Zimbabwe. Sub-Saharan Africa has the highest maternal death rates. Brazil improved more than Mexico, Egypt more than Turkey. Six countries accounted for more than half of all the maternal deaths in 2008: India, Nigeria, Pakistan, Afghanistan, Ethiopia, and the Democratic Republic of Congo.

But India has made steady progress, and because its population is so large, its improvements have helped considerably to decrease the worldwide rate of maternal deaths. China has also made considerable progress. In India, there were

408 to 1,080 maternal deaths per 100,000 live births in 1980, and by 2008, there were 154 to 395, the new study found. In China, there were 144 to 187 deaths per 100,000 live births in 1980, and 35 to 46 in 2008.

—DENISE GRADY

Guidelines Seek Early Detection of Alzheimer's

For the first time in 25 years, medical experts are proposing a major change in the criteria for Alzheimer's disease, part of a new movement to diagnose and, eventually, treat the disease earlier. The new diagnostic guidelines, presented in July 2010, would mean that new technology like brain scans would be used to detect the disease even before there are evident memory problems or other symptoms.

If the guidelines are adopted, as expected, some experts predict a two- to threefold increase in the number of people with Alzheimer's disease. Many more people would be told they probably are on their way to getting it. The Alzheimer's Association says 5.3 million Americans now have the disease.

The changes could also help drug companies that are, for the first time, developing new drugs to try to attack the disease earlier. So far, there are no drugs that alter the course of the disease.

Development of the guidelines, by panels of experts convened by the National Institute on Aging and the Alzheimer's Association, began a year ago because, with a new understanding of the disease and new ways of detection, it was becoming clear that the old method of diagnosing Alzheimer's was sorely outdated. The current formal criteria for diagnosing Alzheimer's require steadily progressing dementia—memory loss and an inability to carry out day-to-day activities, like dressing or bathing—along with a pathologist's report of plaque and another abnormality, known as tangles, in the brain after death.

But researchers are now convinced that the disease is present a decade or more before dementia. The new guidelines include criteria for three stages of the disease: preclinical disease, mild cognitive impairment due to Alzheimer's disease and, lastly, Alzheimer's dementia. The guidelines should make diagnosing the final stage of the disease in people who have dementia more definitive. But, the guidelines also say that the earlier a diagnosis is made the less certain it is. And so the new effort to diagnose the disease earlier could, at least initially, lead to more mistaken diagnoses.

Under the new guidelines, for the first time, diagnoses will aim to identify the disease as it is developing by using results from so-called biomarkers—tests like brain scans, M.R.I. scans and spinal taps that reveal telltale brain changes.

The biomarkers were developed and tested only recently and none have been formally approved for Alzheimer's diagnosis. One of the newest, a PET scan, shows plaque in the brain—a unique sign of Alzheimer's brain pathology. The others provide strong indications that Alzheimer's is present, even when patients do not yet have dementia or even much memory loss.

—GINA KOLATA

In Spinal Test, Early Warning On Alzheimer's

Researchers report that a spinal fluid test can be 100 percent accurate in identifying patients with significant memory loss who are on their way to developing Alzheimer's disease. Although there has been increasing evidence of the value of this and other tests in finding signs of Alzheimer's, the study, which appeared in August 2010 in the *Archives of Neurology*, shows how accurate they can be. The new result is one of a number of remarkable recent findings about Alzheimer's.

After decades when nothing much seemed to be happening, when this progressive brain disease seemed untreatable and when its diagnosis could be confirmed only at autopsy, the field has suddenly woken up.

Alzheimer's, medical experts now agree, starts a decade or more before people have symptoms. And by the time there are symptoms, it may be too late to save the brain. So the hope is to find good ways to identify people who are getting the disease, and use those people as subjects in studies to see how long it takes for symptoms to occur and in studies of drugs that may slow or stop the disease.

Researchers are finding simple and accurate ways to detect Alzheimer's long before there are definite symptoms. In addition to spinal fluid tests they also have new PET scans of the brain that show the telltale amyloid plaques that are a unique feature of the disease. And they are testing hundreds of new drugs that, they hope, might change the course of the relentless brain cell death that robs people of their memories and abilities to think and reason.

The new study included more than 300 patients in their 70s, 114 with normal memories, 200 with memory problems and 102 with Alzheimer's disease. Their spinal fluid was analyzed for amyloid beta, a protein fragment that forms plaques in the brain, and for tau, a protein that accumulates in dead and dying nerve cells in the brain. To avoid bias, the researchers analyzing the data did not know anything about the clinical status of the subjects. Also, the subjects were not told what the tests showed.

Nearly every person with Alzheimer's had the characteristic spinal fluid protein levels. Nearly three quarters of people with mild cognitive impairment, a memory impediment that can precede Alzheimer's, had Alzheimer's-like spinal fluid proteins. And every one of those patients with the proteins developed Alzheimer's within five years. And about a third of people with normal memories had spinal fluid indicating Alzheimer's. Researchers suspect that those people will develop memory problems.

—GINA KOLATA

Citing Heart Risk, F.D.A. To Restrict Diabetes Drug

In a highly unusual coordinated announcement, drug regulators in Europe and the United States said Sept. 23 that Avandia, the controversial diabetes medicine, would no longer be widely available.

The drug's sales will be suspended entirely in Europe, while patients in the United States will be allowed access to the medicine only if they and their doctors attest that they have tried every other diabetes medicine and that patients have been made aware of the drug's substantial risks to the heart. Patients now taking Avandia may continue to do so.

The Food and Drug Administration's decision showed that the Obama administration is taking a harder line on drug safety issues, even in the face of scientific uncertainty. Along with its announcement, the agency for the first time immediately posted on its Web site internal memorandums from top staff members that in some cases offered entirely contradictory advice.

The decision on Avandia signals a new era in the treatment of diabetes, a disease that is reaching epidemic proportions in much of the industrialized world. Because of Avandia, the F.D.A. announced in 2008 that it would no longer approve medicines simply because they help diabetics control blood sugar levels—the standard for more than 80 years. Instead, the F.D.A. now insists that drugmakers conduct trials lasting at least two years to show that their medicines do not hurt the heart and that they improve the quality or length of diabetics' lives, far tougher tests.

The Avandia story also begins a new and unsettling period for pharmaceutical companies because Avandia's risks became known only after Dr. Steven Nissen, a cardiologist at the Cleveland Clinic, analyzed data from clinical trials that GlaxoSmithKline, the maker of the drug, had been forced to post on its Web site as a result of a legal settlement. Such public postings are increasingly the norm, which means that drugmakers can no longer easily hide or control scientific information about their medicines.

The agency's decision to order restrictions on Avandia's sales also demonstrates that the F.D.A. given new powers over drugmakers and drug distribution in a 2007 law—intends to use those powers. The agency has now ordered that dozens of drugs be sold only with special restrictions.

The suspension and restrictions all but ensure that Avandia's sales—$1.19 billion last year and $3.2 billion as recently as 2006—will plunge as regulatory authorities around the world are bound to follow with similar restrictions.

GlaxoSmithKline responded that "the company continues to believe that Avandia is an important treatment for patients with Type 2 diabetes" and is working with the F.D.A. and European regulators "to implement the required actions." The company promised that it would end Avandia promotions around the world.

—GARDINER HARRIS

Plan to Widen Statin Use Has Skeptics

With the government's blessing, a drug giant is about to expand the market for its blockbuster cholesterol medication Crestor to a new category of customers: as a preventive measure for millions of people who do not have cholesterol problems.

Some medical experts question whether this is a healthy move. They point to mounting concern that cholesterol medications—known as statins and already the most widely prescribed drugs in the United States—may not be as safe a preventive medicine as previously believed for people who are at low risk of heart attacks or strokes.

Statins have been credited with saving thousands of lives every year with relatively few side effects, and some medical experts endorse the drug's broader use. But for healthy people who would take statins largely as prevention—which would be the case for the new category of Crestor patients—other experts suggest the benefits may not outweigh any side effects.

Among the risks raising new concerns, recently published evidence indicates that statins could raise a person's risk of developing Type 2 diabetes by 9 percent. There is also debate over the blood test being used to identify the new statin candidates. Instead of bad cholesterol, the test measures the degree of inflammation in the body, but there is no consensus in the medical community that inflammation is a direct cause of cardiovascular problems.

The Food and Drug Administration approved the new criteria in February for Crestor, which is made by AstraZeneca and is the nation's second best-selling statin, behind Lipitor by Pfizer. AstraZeneca plans to begin a new marketing and advertising campaign for Crestor, based on the new F.D.A.-approved criteria.

Under those criteria, an estimated 6.5 million people in this country who have no cholesterol problems and no sign of heart problems will be deemed candidates for statins. That is in addition to the 80 million who already meet the current cholesterol-based guidelines, about half of whom now take statins.

The F.D.A. acknowledged the diabetes risk, and told AstraZeneca to add it to Crestor's label. But the agency nonetheless approved the new use on the basis of the clinical study, which showed a small but measurable reduction of strokes, heart attacks and other "cardiovascular events" among people taking the statin, compared with patients taking a placebo.

—DUFF WILSON

Rapid Change Found In Male Chromosome

A new look at the human Y chromosome has overturned longstanding ideas about its evolutionary history. Far from being in a state of decay, the Y chromosome is the fastest-changing part of the human genome and is constantly renewing itself.

The Y chromosome makes its owner male because it carries the male-determining gene. Boys are born with one Y and one X chromosome in all their body's cells, while girls have two X's. The other 22 pairs of chromosomes in which the human genome is packaged are the same in both sexes.

The Y chromosome's rapid rate of evolutionary change does not mean that men are evolving faster than women. But its furious innovation is likely to be having reverberations elsewhere in the human genome.

The finding was reported in January 2010 in the journal *Nature* by a team led by Jennifer Hughes and David Page of the Whitehead Institute in Cambridge, Mass. In 2003, Dr. Page, working with scientists at the Washington University School of Medicine, decoded the DNA sequence of the human Y chromosome. He and the same Washington University genome team have now decoded the chimpanzee Y chromosome, providing for the first time a reference against which to assess the evolutionary history of the human Y.

Over all, the genomes of the two species are very similar and differ in less than 1 percent of their DNA. But the Y chromosomes differ in 30 percent of their DNA, meaning that these chromosomes are changing far faster in both species than the rest of the genome.

In the case of chimps, their mating habits are probably the source of the fierce evolutionary pressure on their Y chromosome. Many genes that govern sperm production are situated on the Y chromosome, and any genetic variation that improves a chimp's chances of fatherhood will be favored and quickly spread through the population. Sperm competition may have been important in the earliest humans, too.

Another reason for the intensity of selective pressures on the Y chromosome in both chimps and humans may be that natural selection sees it as a single unit, so a change in any one of its genes affects the survival of all the rest. On the other chromosomes, selection is more focused on individual genes because chunks of DNA are swapped between the members of each pair of chromosomes before the generation of eggs and sperm.

This DNA swapping process is forbidden between the X and the Y pair, keeping the male-determining gene from being transferred into the X chromosome, creating gender chaos and causing most of the genes on the Y chromosome to decay for lack of fitness. Until now, many biologists have assumed either that the Y chromosome was headed for eventual extinction, or that its evolutionary downslide was largely over and it has sunk into stagnation.

Dr. Page's new finding shows that the Y chromosome has achieved an unexpected salvation. The hallmark of the Y chromosome now turns out to be renewal and reinvigoration, once the unnecessary burden of X-related genes has been shed.

—NICHOLAS WADE

Analysis of Neanderthal Genome Points To Interbreeding With Modern Humans

Neanderthals mated with some modern humans and left their imprint in the human genome, a team of biologists reported in the journal *Science* in May 2010. It is the first detailed analysis of the Neanderthal genetic sequence.

The biologists, led by Svante Paabo of the Max Planck Institute for Evolutionary Anthropology in Leipzig, Germany, have been slowly reconstructing the genome of Neanderthals, the stocky hunters that dominated Europe until 30,000 years ago, by extracting the fragments of DNA that still exist in their fossil bones.

Scientists say they have recovered 60 percent of the genome so far and hope to complete it. By comparing that genome with those of various present day humans, the team concluded that about 1 percent to 4 percent of the genome of non-Africans today is derived from Neanderthals. But the Neanderthal DNA does not seem to have played a great role in human evolution, they said.

Experts believe that the Neanderthal genome sequence will be of extraordinary importance in understanding human evolutionary history since the two species split some 600,000 years ago.

So far, the team has identified only about 100 genes—surprisingly few—that have contributed to the evolution of modern humans since the split. The nature of the genes in humans that differ from those of Neanderthals is of particular interest because they bear on what it means to be human, or at least not Neanderthal. Some of the genes seem to be involved in cognitive function and others in bone structure.

The Leipzig team's conclusion that there was probably interbreeding between Neanderthals and modern humans before Europeans and Asians split, was met with reserve by some archaeologists.

A degree of interbreeding between modern humans and Neanderthals in Europe would not be greatly surprising given that the species overlapped there from 44,000 years ago when modern humans first entered Europe to 30,000 years ago when the last Neanderthals fell extinct. Archaeologists have been debating for years whether the fossil record shows evidence of individuals with mixed features.

But the new analysis, based solely on genetics and statistical calculations, is more difficult to match with the archaeological record. The Leipzig scientists assert that the interbreeding did not occur in Europe but in the Middle East and at a much earlier period, some 100,000 to 60,000 years ago, before the modern human populations of Europe and East Asia split. There is much less archaeological evidence for an overlap between modern humans and Neanderthals at this time and place.

—NICHOLAS WADE

Obituaries November 15, 2009–September 30, 2010

Adler, Jerry, 91, Baltimore-born harmonica master whose soulful sounds underscored the emotions of Hollywood classics *High Noon* (1952), *Shane* (1953), and other films; brother to classical harmonicist Larry Adler. Of prostate cancer, Ellenton, Pa., March 13, 2010.

Archer, Lee A. Jr., 90, World War II pilot with Tuskegee Airmen, the unit of black fliers whose daring skills flew in the face of military segregation of the time; he shot down four German planes, three in one day. Cause undisclosed, New York, Jan. 27, 2010.

Auchincloss, Louis, 92, New York writer who also practiced law; many novels depict the money/morality clash of wealthy WASP world of his birth, from best-selling *The Rector of Justin* (1964) to *The Headmaster's Dilemma* (2007). After a stroke, New York, Jan. 26, 2010.

Ayala, Francisco, 103, Spanish writer highly regarded in Spain, though banned during Franco regime, and little known in U.S. except for *Death as a Way of Life* (transl. 1964) and *Usurpers* (transl. 1987); left Spain in 1939 and lived in U.S. from 1950s teaching at several universities until 1978 return to Spain. Of old age, Madrid, Nov. 3, 2009.

Bachrach, Fabian, 92, U.S. photographer of Kennedy and Nixon, DiMaggio and Ali, socialites and world leaders—as well as wedding parties; his grandfather founded company and photographed Lincoln. Of pneumonia, Newton, Mass., Feb. 26, 2010.

Bainbridge, Beryl, 77, British writer who turned from acting to create a series of sharply caustic novels, including *The Dressmaker* (1973) and *The Bottle Factory Outing* (1977); also wrote fiction based on history, such as *Young Adolf* (1978). Of cancer, London, July 1, 2010.

Barry, Gene, 90, New York–born actor of many TV roles, most notably Bat Masterson (1958–61) and Amos Burke (1963–66); also starred on Broadway in *La Cage aux Folles* (Tony nomination, 1984). Of natural causes, Woodland Hills, Calif., Dec. 9, 2009.

Bell, Glen, W., 86, California entrepreneur, the man behind Taco Bell, the fast-food chain that made Mexican fare a U.S. staple for millions of tacos fans; first drive-in stand opened late 1940s, now 5,600-chain worldwide. Cause undisclosed, Rancho Santa Fe, Calif., Jan. 17, 2010.

Black, James, 85, Scottish scientist, co-winner of 1988 Nobel Prize for development of two life-saving drugs for millions of patients: propanolol (Inderal) for angina and cimetidine (Tagamet) for ulcers. Cause undisclosed, reported by University of Dundee, March 20, 2010.

Bourgeois, Louise, 98, French-born U.S. artist whose sculptures and drawings often depict sexuality and pain; notable are latex phallus *Fillette* (1968) and bronze *Arch of Hysteria* (1993); influential feminist who only achieved fame in her 70s. Of a heart attack, New York, May 31, 2010.

Bourjaily, Vance, 87, U.S. novelist of Mailer postwar generation whose first work, *The End of My Life* (1947), dealt with young angst in World War II; other novels less widely known; influential teacher at Iowa Writers' Workshop. After a fall, Greenbrae, Calif., Aug. 31, 2010.

Braun, Carl, 82, New York Knicks guard 1947–61, high-scoring All-Star 1953–57; set record of 47 points in one game as a rookie in the young N.B.A. league. Cause undisclosed, Stuart, Fla., Feb. 10, 2010

Brookshier, Tom, 78, Philadelphia Eagles defensive back 1953–61, part of N.F.L. 1960 championship team; played on '59 and '60 Pro Bowl teams; later did TV for CBS through 1980s, covering three Super Bowls with Pat Summerall. Of cancer, Wynnewood, Pa., Jan. 29, 2010.

Bryan C. D. B., 73, U.S. writer best known for *Friendly Fire* (1976), later a TV movie, which portrays the disillusion and anger of patriotic parents turned antiwar activists when their son is killed accidentally in the Vietnam War. Of cancer, Guilford, Conn., Dec. 15, 2009.

Byrd, Robert C., 92, West Virginia Democratic senator since 1958, all-time Senate record, served as both majority and minority leader as well as chairman of purse-powerful Appropriations Committee, delivering billions of federal dollars to impoverished state; early on Klan member, later supported civil rights; zealous guardian of Senate rules and institution. Of old age, Fairfax, Va., June 28, 2010.

Carpenter, Liz, 89, Texas-born newspaper reporter who became press secretary to Lady Bird Johnson during LBJ presidency; strong supporter of failed Equal Rights Amendment. Of pneumonia, Austin, Tex., March 20, 2010.

Carter, Dixie, 70, Tennessee-born TV actress best known for playing *Designing Women's* sweetly barbed Julia Sugarbaker, as well as a hellish mother-in-law on *Desperate Housewives*; drew rave notices singing at New York's stylish Café Carlyle. Of cancer, Houston, April 10, 2010.

Chabrol, Claude, 80, French New Wave pioneer, film critic turned director of more than 50 movies, including *Les Cousins* (1958), *Le Boucher* (1969), *Madame Bovary* (1990), and his final film, *Bellamy* (2009). Of severe anemia, Paris, Sept. 12, 2010.

Coleman, Gary, 42, little Arnold of TV's *Diff'rent Strokes* (1978–86), whose cutie-pie personality masked an unhappy real life of kidney disease, parental manipulation, and financial problems. Of brain hemorrhage after a fall, Provo, Utah, May 28, 2010.

Conrad, Paul, 86, Pulitzer Prize–winning cartoonist, since 1950 the scourge of the pompously powerful, especially politicians such as Reagan and Nixon as well as Johnson and Carter. Of natural causes, Rancho Palos Verdes, Calif., Sept. 4, 2010.

Coryell, Don, 85, NFL and College football coach; San Diego State Aztecs (1961-1972) St Louis Cardinals (1973-1977); San Diego Chargers (1978-1986); one of the founding fathers of the passing game whose Air Coryell set records and led the NFL in passing almost every season; member of the College Football Hall of Fame who is the only coach to win 100 games in both college and professional football. Cause undisclosed, La Mesa, Calif., July 1, 2010.

Culp, Robert, 79, California-born actor best known for *I Spy* (1965–68), paired with Bill Cosby in an interracial first for TV, for which he also wrote seven episodes; several movies include *Bob*

& Carol & Ted & Alice (1969). Of a heart attack, Los Angeles, March 24, 2010.

Curtis-Verna, Mary, 88, U.S. soprano who won good notices at the Met 1956–66, especially when she took over at short notice for "indisposed" divas such as Renata Tebaldi, Eleanor Steber, and Leonie Rysanek. After suffering broken hip, Seattle, Dec. 4, 2009.

Dean, Jimmy, 81, Texas-born singer/salesman, host of his own TV show (1963–66), who delivered homey country music with the same appeal in later TV ads that charmed America to buy his "homemade" breakfast sausages. Cause undisclosed, Varina, Va., June 13, 2010.

Disney, Roy E., 79, nephew to Walt Disney, he grew up with *Pinocchio* (1940) and later revived famed animation studio with success of *The Little Mermaid* (1989) and *The Lion King* (1994), frequently at odds with studio executives. Of stomach cancer, Newport Beach, Calif., Dec. 16, 2009.

Dobrynin, Anatoly F., 90, U.S.S.R. ambassador to Washington, 1962–86, representing six Soviet leaders to six U.S. presidents, most notably at start of tenure in diplomatic settlement of Cuban nuclear missile crisis; known for tough-minded charm. Cause undisclosed by Kremlin, April 6, 2010.

Dominy, F. E., 100, commissioner of Interior Department's Bureau of Reclamation, 1959–69, he tamed the Colorado and Trinity Rivers with dams that generate electricity and bring deserts to life, often to environmentalists' dismay. Of old age, Boyce, Va., April 20, 2010.

Dudley, Bill, 88, University of Virginia and N.F.L. running back, though slim and slow, had successful career in 1940s and 1950s, elected to Hall of Fame 1966. After a stroke, Lynchburg, Va., Feb. 4, 2010.

Foot, Michael, 96, British Socialist politician elected head of Labour Party in 1980 but unable to bring unity to party factions; forced to step down in wake of overwhelming Thatcher victory in 1983. Of old age, London, March 3, 2010.

Forsythe, John, 92, New Jersey–born actor of TV, stage, and film; best known as silver-tongued and silver-haired Blake Carrington of *Dynasty* (1981–89), which reflected the tinsel charm of Reagan era. Of pneumonia, Santa Ynez, Calif., April 1, 2010.

Francis, Dick, 89, British writer who turned early career as champion jockey into more than 40 best-selling mystery novels, from *Dead Cert* (1962) to *Crossfire* (2010), wherein jockeys and horses are often killed by pitiless wretches. Cause undisclosed, Cayman Islands, Feb. 14, 2010.

Frankel, Bobby, 68, Brooklyn-born thoroughbred trainer whose champions include Bertrando and Empire Maker; five-time winner of Eclipse trainer award and had six Breeders' Cup winners. Of cancer, Pacific Palisades, Calif., Nov. 16, 2009.

Gardner, Martin, 95, U.S. writer best known for annotated editions of *Alice in Wonderland* and *Casey at the Bat,* as well as wide range of books on math, puzzles, and philosophy. Of old age, Norman, Okla., May 22, 2010.

Gates, Daryl F., 83, Los Angeles police chief since 1978, compelled to resign in 1992 after acquittal of officers accused of beating Rodney King; credited with launching first helicopter and SWAT units in police work. Of cancer, Dana Point, Calif., April 16, 2010.

Gelfand, Israel, 96, Ukraine-born mathematician who came to U.S. universities in 1989; focused on foundations of math, aiding physicists in quantum mechanics, also leading to development of CAT scans. Of old age, New Brunswick, N.J., Oct. 5, 2009.

Gies, Miep, 100, Vienna-born woman whose family settled in Amsterdam; she helped hide Anne Frank and her family from Nazi persecution in World War II, then retrieved Anne's diary after their arrest, to the gratitude of readers worldwide. After a fall, Amsterdam, Jan. 11, 2010.

Ginzburg, Vitaly, 93, Russian physicist, co-winner of 2003 Nobel Prize for work in developing superconductors, which make magnetic resonance imaging possible; teamed with Andrei Sakharov in developing first Soviet hydrogen bomb. Of a heart attack, Moscow, Nov. 8 2009.

Gould, Harold, 86, U.S. actor, a familiar face in TV shows from 1960s on, most notably as Rhoda's father on *The Mary Tyler Moore Show* and *Rhoda,* and as Rose's beau on *The Golden Girls.* Of prostate cancer, Woodland Hills, Calif., Sept. 11, 2010.

Graham, Bruce J., 84, Chicago architect whose imprint on city's skyline is broad: Hancock Center (1970), 110-story Sears (now Willis) Tower (1974), Madison Plaza (1982), as well as other buildings and city design plans. Of Alzheimer's disease, Hobe Sound, Fla., March 6, 2010.

Graves, Peter, 83, Minneapolis-born actor best known as unflappable Jim Phelps of TV's *Mission: Impossible* (1967–73, 1988–90); many films include *Airplane!* (1980), parodying his straight-arrow image, and *Stalag 17* (1953). Of a heart attack, Los Angeles, March 14, 2010.

Grayson, Kathryn, 88, Hollywood star whose clear soprano voice and heart-shaped lips made music in *Anchors Aweigh* (1945) with Frank Sinatra, *That Midnight Kiss* (1949) with Mario Lanza, *Show Boat* (1951) with Howard Keel, and many other MGM musicals. Cause undisclosed, Los Angeles, Feb. 16, 2010.

Haig, Alexander M. Jr., 85, Army general who served as Pres. Nixon's chief of staff, virtually in charge at White House as Nixon was forced to resign in 1974, then served as Pres. Reagan's secretary of state, mistakenly proclaiming himself in charge at White House when Reagan was shot in 1981. Cause undisclosed, Baltimore, Feb. 20, 2010.

Haney, Chris, 59, Canadian inventor of Trivial Pursuit with partner Scott Abbott; the game of challenging insignificance, introduced in 1981, tapped into boomer nostalgia and has sold more than 100 million copies worldwide. Cause undisclosed, Toronto, May 31, 2010.

Harwell, Ernie, 92, Georgia-born baseball announcer known for easygoing style and accurate calls, first with N.Y. Giants (including famous 1951 pennant win), then with Detroit Tigers 1960–2002. Of bile duct cancer, Novi, Mich., May 4, 2010.

Havoc, June, 97, "Baby June" of *Gypsy* fame, who in real life achieved stage and screen stardom; the original Gladys Bumps in *Pal Joey* (1940); Tony nominated for directing *Marathon 33,* based on her memoir of Depression-era marathon dances. Of old age, Stamford, Conn., March 28, 2010.

Height, Dorothy, 98, Virginia-born women's rights pioneer praised by Pres. Obama as "the godmother of the civil rights movement"; though never as famous as major male civil rights leaders, awarded Presidential Medal of Freedom. Of old age, Washington, April 20, 2010.

Henrich, Tommy, 96, last of storied 1930s Yankees, right fielder played alongside Gehrig and

DiMaggio, retired in 1950; Old Reliable's timely hits helped Yankees to seven World Series triumphs. Of old age, Dayton, Ohio, Dec. 1, 2009.

Hickel, Walter J., 90, Alaska Republican governor 1966–68, 1990–94, and Pres. Nixon's interior secretary 1969–70; never afraid to rattle critics, he promoted development as governor and the environment as interior secretary. Of natural causes, Anchorage, May 7, 2010.

Hooks, Benjamin L, 85, N.A.A.C.P. president 1977–92, led the civil rights association during time of declining membership and increasingly hostile conservatism, focusing on employment and education for blacks. Of heart failure, Memphis, Tenn., April 15, 2010.

Hopper, Dennis, 74, U.S. actor of oddball roles, notably in *Easy Rider* (1969), which he co-wrote, and *Apocalypse Now* (1979); after overcoming addictions in 1980s, made many movies, including *Hoosiers* (1986, Oscar nomination). Of prostate cancer, Venice, Calif., May 29, 2010.

Horne, Lena, 92, Brooklyn-born African-American singer/actress and fierce civil rights advocate; with exception of *Cabin in the Sky* (1943), her MGM roles were inserted specialty numbers that could be cut for showings in the South; triumphed on Broadway in *Jamaica* (1957) and *The Lady and Her Music* (1981); many recordings keep her eloquent voice alive. Cause undisclosed, New York, May 9, 2010.

Houk, Ralph, 90, baseball manager whose leadership ability as decorated major in World War II served him well at the helm of the Yankees (two World Series championships), Tigers, and Red Sox. Of old age, Winter Haven, Fla., July 21, 2010.

Hoving, Thomas, 78, New York's Metropolitan Museum dynamic director 1967–77, he remade the staid landmark into a "happening" place with blockbuster shows, headline acquisitions such as the Temple of Dendur, as well as an expanded "front porch," now a prime N.Y. people place. Of lung cancer, New York, Dec. 10, 2009.

Jacobi, Lou, 95, Toronto-born actor adept at both comic and dramatic roles; 10 Broadway plays include *The Diary of Anne Frank* (1955) and its film version, 1959; many other movies include *My Favorite Year* (1982). Of old age, New York, Oct. 23, 2009.

Jeanne-Claude, 74, French environmental artist who with husband, Christo, wrapped Berlin's Reichstag and Paris's Pont Neuf in fabric, and installed thousands of vinyl "gates" in Central Park, visited by millions of the curious. Of an aneurysm, New York, Nov. 18, 2009.

Jellinek, George, 90, Budapest-born radio M.C. whose Vocal Scene and First Hearing programs on WQXR charmed New York–area opera lovers for 36 years. Of old age, Sleepy Hollow, N.Y., Jan. 16, 2010.

Jones, Jennifer, 90, Hollywood star of 1940 and '50s best remembered for Oscar-winning saintly debut in *The Song of Bernadette* (1943) and as sensuous Pearl Chavez in *Duel in the Sun* (1946) in a career dominated by husband David O. Selznick. Of natural causes, Malibu, Calif., Dec. 17, 2009.

Judt, Tony, 62, British historian and essayist on wide variety of subjects, including French politics, U.S. foreign policy, social democracy, and Israel as secular state; notable work is *Postwar: A History of Europe Since 1945* (2005). Of Lou Gehrig's disease, New York, Aug. 6, 2010.

Kaczynski, Lech, 60, president of Poland since 2005, former child actor who with twin brother, Jaroslaw, rose in politics with Solidarity movement but later broke with it, pressing nationalist, anti–E.U. views. Killed in plane crash, Russia, April 10, 2010.

Kamenshek, Dorothy, 84, played first base with Rockford Peaches in World War II professional female league, batting over .300 in '46 and '47; one of the originals for Geena Davis as "Dotty" in *A League of Their Own* (1992). Of natural causes, Palm Desert, Calif., May 17, 2010.

Kaysen, Carl, 89, Harvard and M.I.T. economist whose wide-ranging intellect also covered law and national security; served as Pres. Kennedy's point man in 1963 nuclear test ban negotiations. Of old age, Cambridge, Mass., Feb. 8, 2010.

Kermode, Frank, 90, British literary critic highly respected for clear style and disdain for trendy theories, notably in *The Sense of an Ending* (1967) and *Shakespeare's Language* (2000); influential teacher at Cambridge and Columbia. Of old age, Cambridge, England, Aug. 17 2010.

Kilpatrick, James, J., 89, Oklahoma-born journalist who promoted conservative views in newspaper columns and on TV, whether in defense of segregation and state sovereignty or against sloppy prose style. Of congestive heart failure, Washington, Aug. 15, 2010.

Kluge, John W., 95, German-born media baron whose billions came from Metromedia, the independent communications giant; relished making the deals that allowed him to make huge gifts to alma mater Columbia and other causes. Of old age, Charlottesville, Va., Sept. 7, 2010.

Knox, Bernard, 95, British-born U.S. classics professor who saw action with the O.S.S. in World War II and went on to become a preeminent authority on Sophocles and establish Harvard's Hellenic Studies Center. Of a heart attack, Bethesda, Md., July 22, 2010.

Krebs, Edwin G., 91, U.S. physician, co-winner of 1992 Nobel Prize for discovery of cell regulation process in which hormone release can affect development of heart disease, diabetes, and cancer. Of heart failure, Seattle, Dec. 21, 2009.

Lee, Fran, 99, New York TV personality turned forceful grandmotherly gadfly whose loud advocacy prompted the city to enact 1978 "pooper-scooper" law. Of old age, Jerusalem, Feb. 13, 2010.

Levi-Strauss, Claude, 100, French anthropologist whose groundbreaking studies of myth and culture revolutionized Western views of the "primitive," showing universal structures in all human societies; many books include four-volume *Mythologiques* (1964–71). Of cardiac arrest, Paris, Oct. 31, 2009.

Levine, David, 83, Brooklyn-born artist whose satiric drawings of the political and literary famous and infamous captured their souls with sharp pen strokes and big heads; Presidents Johnson and Nixon were favorite targets. Of prostate cancer, New York, Dec. 29, 2009.

Lincoln, Abbey, 80, born Anna Marie Wooldridge in Chicago, she became influential jazz singer and composer, notably in *Abbey Sings Abbey* (Verve, 2007) as well as voice for civil rights; early film career included *For Love of Ivy* (1968). Cause undisclosed, New York, Aug. 14, 2010.

Linkletter, Art, 97, amiable M.C. of *People Are Funny* and *House Party*, first on radio from 1940s on, then on TV into 1960s; honed ad-libbing skill on radio, getting people to do zany stunts and kids to "say the darndest things." Of old age, Los Angeles, May 26, 2010.

Mackerras, Charles, 84, Australian conductor best known for promoting the operas of Janacek in the West after studying in Prague; his astute research influential in establishing authentic period style in works of Handel and Mozart. Cause undisclosed, London, July 14, 2010.

Martino, Al, 82, born Jasper Cini, Philadelphia, he sang sweet pop ballads from the 1950s on, despite rock's reign; hits include "Here in My Heart" and "Volare"; played Johnny Fontane, Sinatra-like singer, in Godfather films. Cause undisclosed, Springfield, Pa., Oct. 13, 2009

Mathias, Charles, 87, Maryland Republican, congressman 1961–69, senator 1969–87, advocate of civil rights and campaign finance reform legislation, often sparring with conservative policies of Reagan and Nixon administrations. Of Parkinson's disease, Chevy Chase, Md., Jan. 25, 2010.

McCarthy, Kevin, 96, U.S. actor, brother of acerbic writer Mary McCarthy, played many stage and TV roles but is perhaps best remembered for cult film Invasion of the *Body Snatchers* (1956). Of old age, Hyannis, Mass., Sept. 11, 2010.

McClanahan, Rue, 76, U.S. actress best known as one of TV's *Golden Girls* (1985–92), funny, drawling, man-crazy Blanche, a modern-day Wife of Bath who could date a new man at her husband's funeral. Of a brain hemorrhage, New York, June 3, 2010.

McGuire, Dick, 84, New York Knicks guard, known for passing and feinting skills as a player, 1949–57; later became respected coach and scout for the team; inducted in Hall of Fame 1993. Of an aortic aneurysm, Huntington, N.Y., Feb. 3, 2010.

McQueen, Alexander, 40, British fashion outlaw who dressed his models in outrageous "shreds and patches," successfully calling attention to his style of expertly tailored brutality. A suicide, London, Feb. 11, 2010.

Miller, Alice, 87, Polish-born psychoanalyst whose many books, notably *The Drama of the Gifted Child* (1981), blame coercive parenting as the cause of neuroses in children and the scarred adults they become. Cause undisclosed, at home in Provence, April 14, 2010.

Miller, Mitch, 99, U.S. music man who coaxed America to sing old favorites along with him on '60s TV; as influential record producer, guided careers of Rosemary Clooney, Tony Bennett, and others. Cause undisclosed, New York, July 31, 2010.

Mitchell, Willie, 81, Mississippi-born maestro of soul music, his Hi Records of Memphis created hits for singer Al Green and others—sweet guitar and organ with light drums—starting with "Let's Stay Together" in 1971. Of cardiac arrest, Memphis, Tenn., Jan. 5, 2010.

Morrison, Fred, 90, U.S. entrepreneur whose Frisbee invention started as a tossed popcorn lid in 1937, then pie tins, later the Pluto Platter, ultimately the millions of familiar plastic discs tossed worldwide. Of cancer, Monroe, Utah, Feb. 9, 2010.

Murtha, John P., 77, Pennsylvania Democrat first elected to Congress 1974; tough, decorated Marine who initially supported Iraq war, but later came out against it; adept at bringing home federal "pork" to his district. Of gallbladder surgery complications, Arlington, Va., Feb. 8, 2010.

Neal, Patricia, 84, U.S. actress whose sexy, viola-like voice was silenced after 1965 strokes, which she overcame to star in *The Subject Was Roses* (1968); she could play earthy (Oscar for *Hud*, 1984) or elegant (*The Fountainhead*, 1949; *Breakfast at Tiffany's*, 1961). Of lung cancer, Edgartown, Mass., Aug. 8, 2010.

Newman, Edwin, 91, New York journalist whose radio and TV beat included *Today* and *Meet the Press* as well as moderating 1976 and 1984 presidential debates; guardian of language against "hopefully," "y'know," and other felonies in *A Civil Tongue* (1976). Of pneumonia, Oxford, England, Aug. 13, 2010.

Nirenberg, Marshall, 82, Brooklyn-born biologist, co-winner of 1968 Nobel Prize for experiments that unraveled the genetic code, which governs how DNA is converted into the proteins of living cells. Of cancer, New York, Jan 15, 2010.

Nissen, George, 96, Iowa-born gymnast whose homemade "bouncing rig" became his invention of the trampoline (*trampolino,* "springboard") much to the delight of high-spirited tumblers worldwide, as well as Olympic champions. Of old age, San Diego, April 7, 2010.

Noland, Kenneth, 85, U.S. artist, influenced by works of Matisse and Klee, took Abstract Expressionism into a realm of geometric shapes and dazzling color, called Color Field painting. Of cancer, Port Clyde, Me., Jan 5, 2010.

Olsen, Merlin, 69, N.F.L. Hall of Famer with L.A. Rams 1962–77, one of the "Fearsome Foursome," he then did TV coverage as well as major roles in *Little House on the Prairie* and *Father Murphy.* Of mesothelioma, Duarte, Calif., March 11, 2010.

Palevsky, Max, 85, Chicago-born philosophy teacher turned entrepreneur who founded Intel, the computer-chip megacorporation; supported liberal politicians and campaign finance reform. Of heart failure, Beverly Hills, Calif., May 5, 2010.

Parker, Fess, 85, Texas-born actor, TV's Davy Crockett, he inspired America's children to don coonskin caps in mid-1950s; Disney heeded history and had the hero die at the Alamo, only to resurrect him for another season. Of natural causes, Santa Ynez, Calif., March 18, 2010.

Parker, Robert B., 77, U.S. novelist best known for his detective mysteries featuring Spenser: cunning and cocky against the cold-blooded and corrupt; many novels adapted for TV and film, notably *Spenser: For Hire* (1985–88). Of a heart attack, Cambridge, Mass., Jan 18, 2010.

Patz, Arnall, 89, U.S. physician whose discoveries helped avert blindness in premature infants by lowering doses of oxygen to help breathing and in diabetic adults with development of argon lasers. Of heart disease, Pikesville, Md., March 10, 2010.

Pekar, Harvey, 70, Cleveland-born writer of *American Splendor,* the cult comic book with illustrations by R. Crumb and others that depicted life as dull drudgery; 2003 film version drew wider praise. Cause undisclosed, Cleveland Heights, Ohio, July 12, 2010.

Penn, Irving, 92, U.S. photographer best known for elegantly composed fashion spreads in *Vogue* magazine and close-ups of celebrities as well as cooks and other workers; many of his prints are exhibited in museums. Of old age, New York, Oct. 7, 2009.

Redgrave, Lynn, 67, British actress of the celebrated theater clan, she made her own way in film and TV, as well as in classic stage roles; notable movies are *Georgy Girl* (1966) and *Gods and Monsters* (1998); also wrote plays about her family. Of cancer, Kent, Conn., May 2, 2010.

Redgrave, Corin, 70, British actor of famed theatrical family, who promoted leftist causes; films include *Four Weddings and a Funeral* (1994). Cause undisclosed, London, April 6, 2010.

Reed-Amini, Alaina, 63, Ohio-born theater and TV performer best known as Olivia the photographer on *Sesame Street* (1976–88); also played Rose Lee on 227. Of cancer, Santa Monica, Calif., Dec. 17, 2009.

Roberts, H. Edward, 68, Miami-born physician who as a young man in mid-1970s devised the MITS Altair, regarded as the first personal computer; sold his company to become a country doctor. Of pneumonia, Macon, Ga., April 1, 2010.

Roberts, Oral, 91, Oklahoma-born televangelist whose powerful preaching and claims of faith healing inspired millions to give millions to support his worldwide religious and educational enterprise. Of pneumonia, Newport Beach, Calif., Dec. 15, 2009.

Roberts, Pernell, 81, Georgia-born actor who made his mark in Shakespeare roles before playing Adam Cartwright on TV's *Bonanza* from 1959 to 1965, when he quit what he called "junk TV." Of pancreatic cancer, Malibu, Calif., Jan. 24, 2010.

Roberts, Robin, 83, Hall of Fame pitcher for Philadelphia Phillies 1948–61, notably with 1950 "Whiz Kids," winning N.L. pennant; played 19 seasons in all, six with 20+ wins, striking for his steady control and motion. Of natural causes, Temple Terrace, Fla., May 6, 2010.

Rohmer, Eric, 89, French film director, one of the New Wave auteurs; his movies focus on quiet conversation that can turn alluring, notably in *My Night at Maud's* (1969) and *Claire's Knee* (1970). Cause undisclosed, Paris, Jan. 11, 2010.

Rolfe Johnson, Anthony, 69, British opera singer who first worked as a farmer and went on to a prominent career notable for Bach and Handel works and searing Met Opera performances in title role of Britten's Peter Grimes. Of Alzheimer's complication, London, July 21, 2010.

Rosen, Moishe, 78, U.S. Baptist minister born and raised in Orthodox Jewish family, in 1973 established Jews for Jesus, the contentious organization of Jews who accept Jesus as the Messiah. Of prostate cancer, San Francisco, May 19, 2010.

Rostenkowski, Dan, 82, Illinois Democratic congressman 1958–94; rose to power as chairman of House Ways and Means Committee 1981–94, skillfully influencing tax and welfare law; fell from power amid financial accusations, later imprisoned for mail fraud. Of lung cancer, Benedict Lake, Wis., Aug. 11, 2010.

Sales, Soupy, 83, born Milton Supman, TV comic whose eponymous show raised pie throwing to its zaniest zenith, for kids, adults, and even stars like Jerry Lewis and Frank Sinatra. Cause undisclosed, New York, Oct. 22, 2009.

Salinger, J(erome) D(avid), 91, famously reclusive author of *The Catcher in the Rye* (1951), the best-selling novel that captured adolescent angst in the unmistakably cheeky voice of Holden Caulfield; equally compelling are *Nine Stories* (including "A Perfect Day for Bananafish") (1953) and the Glass family novellas *Franny and Zooey* (1961), *Raise High the Roof Beam, Carpenters*

(1963), and *Hapworth 16, 1924* (1965). Of natural causes, Cornish, N.H., Jan. 27, 2010.

Samaranch, Juan Antonio, 89, International Olympic Committee president 1980–2001; Spanish diplomat who brought financial stability and greater inclusion to the modern Olympic Games, ending boycotts and fake amateurism. Of heart failure, Barcelona, April 21, 2010.

Samuelson, Paul A., 94, dominant 20th-century U.S. economist, influential M.I.T. professor, awarded 1970 Nobel Prize for adding mathematical precision to economic thinking; in many editions of his best-selling textbook, *Economics* (1948), he argues for Keynesian theory that government can prevent depressions by deficit spending or tax reduction. Of old age, Belmont, Mass., Dec. 13, 2009.

Saramago, Jose, 87, Portuguese journalist turned novelist, staunch Communist, awarded 1998 Nobel Prize for works at once realistic, fantastic, and ironic; notable are *Baltasar and Blimunda* (1982), *Blindness* (1995), and posthumous *The Elephant's Journey* (2010). Of multiple organ failure, Canary Islands, June 18, 2010.

Saxbe, William, 94, Ohio Republican who served in state legislature and U.S. Senate but became voice of integrity as disgraced Pres. Nixon's fourth attorney general after "Saturday night massacre" firings during Watergate scandal. Of old age, Mechanicsburg, Ohio, Aug. 24, 2010.

Schorr, Daniel, 93, Bronx-born journalist, first with CBS News in 1955 reporting from Moscow, then with CNN 1979–85, finally as NPR commentator until his death; won three Emmys for Watergate reports and proud to be on Nixon's enemies list. Cause undisclosed, Washington, July 23, 2010.

Segal, Erich, 72, Brooklyn-born novelist and classics professor who was never sorry he wrote *Love Story* (1970), best seller in millions and blockbuster movie, confounding critics; classical studies include *The Death of Comedy* (2001). Of a heart attack, London, Jan. 17, 2010.

Sheppard, Bob, 99, New York Yankees public-address voice 1951–2008, he was as much a part of the old stadium as the many famous players whose names he always carefully announced with what some called the "Voice of God." Of old age, Baldwin, L.I., N.Y., July 11, 2010.

Siepi, Cesare, 87, Italian opera singer, popular Met basso after 1950 debut as King Philip in Verdi's *Don Carlo*, going on to 500 Met performances over 23 years, most notably as Mozart's stylishly sexy Don Giovanni, as well as Gurnemanz in Wagner's *Parsifal*. Cause undisclosed, Atlanta, Ga., July 5, 2010.

Sillitoe, Alan, 82, British author of more than 50 books; best known for 1950s fiction: *Saturday Night and Sunday Morning* (1960 film) and *The Loneliness of the Long Distance Runner* (1962 film), both about class conflict. Cause undisclosed, London, April 25, 2010.

Simmons, Jean, 80, British actress who early in career played Ophelia in Olivier's *Hamlet* (1948); other notable films are *The Actress* (1953), *Guys and Dolls* (1955) and *Elmer Gantry* (1960); TV work includes *The Thorn Birds*. Of lung Cancer, Santa Monica, Calif., Jan. 22, 2010.

Sizer, Theodore R., 77, U.S. educator whose reform-minded Essential Schools movement champions high schools in which students and teachers work together on core subjects; served as

Harvard education dean and Phillips Exeter Academy headmaster. Of colon cancer, Cambridge, Mass., Oct. 21, 2009.

Soderstrom, Elisabeth, 82, Swedish soprano highly esteemed for impeccable musical/dramatic talent, notably in Mozart, Strauss, and Janacek operas; acclaimed Met Opera star 1950s and '80s. Of stroke complications, Stockholm, Nov. 20, 2009.

Stang, Arnold, 91, New York actor whose "Noo Yawk" accent was memorable on radio and TV from the 1930s on, often as kvetching pal of comics Henry Morgan and Milton Berle; films include *The Man With the Golden Arm* (1955). Of pneumonia, Newton, Mass., Dec. 20, 2009.

Steinbrenner, George, 80, New York Yankees owner 1973–2008, his big mouth and deep pockets brought team seven World Series wins, 11 pennants, multiple managers, and a brand-new stadium; beloved by some for charities; berated by many others like Yogi Berra for insults. Of a heart attack, Tampa, Fla., July 13, 2010.

Stevens, Ted, 86, Alaska Republican senator 1968–2008, zealous advocate who brought billions in federal funds to 49th state, but who was defeated after conviction for failure to report gifts for home renovation, later dismissed. Killed in plane crash, southwest Alaska, Aug. 9, 2010.

Sutton, Percy, 89, Texas-born New York politician and civil rights advocate; Manhattan borough president 1966–77; close ally of Mayor Dinkins and Representative Rangel. Of old age, New York, Dec. 26, 2009.

Syms, Sy, 83, Brooklyn-born clothing merchant whose ads persuaded customers they were "educated consumers," savvy enough to buy brand-name apparel at discounts. Of heart failure, New York, Nov. 17, 2009.

Thebom, Blanche, 94, U.S. mezzo-soprano whose more than 350 Met Opera performances, 1944–67, were highly acclaimed, notably in Wagner roles such as Brangäne and Ortrud, as well as Amneris in *Aida* and title role in *Carmen*. Of old age, San Francisco, March 23, 2010.

Thomson, Bobby, 86, born in Scotland, raised in Staten Island, N.Y., he hit baseball's immortal home run—the "shot heard round the world," Oct. 3, 1951—wresting the pennant from Brooklyn Dodgers for N.Y. Giants; event commemorated in 1999 U.S. stamp. After a fall, Savannah, Ga., Aug. 16, 2010.

Todd, Richard, 90, British film actor who often played upstanding, self-possessed characters, notably in *The Hasty Heart* (1949), *A Man Called Peter* (1955), and *The Longest Day* (1962). Of cancer, Little Humby, England, Dec. 3, 2009.

Udall, Stewart L, 90, U.S. secretary of the interior under Presidents Kennedy and Johnson; championed conservation of natural resources and clean environment, notably with new national parks and the first national seashores. After a fall, Santa Fe, N.M., March 20, 2010.

Wagner, Wolfgang, 90, German opera director, grandson of composer Richard Wagner, co-director of Bayreuth festival 1951–1966 with brother, Wieland, then solely in charge after Wieland's death until 2008 retirement; some critics found his productions dull compared to Wieland's innovative ideas. Of old age, Bayreuth, March 20, 2010.

Wahid, Abdurrahman, 69, president of Indonesia 1999–2001, a tumultuous period after 32-year Suharto presidency, he failed to end disorder with advocacy of an inclusive, liberal Islamic outlook. Of kidney disease and strokes, Jakarta, Dec. 30, 2009.

Warren, David, 85, Australian inventor who made the prototype for what became known as the "black box" (actually red or orange for visibility), the universally used flight data recorder that provides essential information in plane crashes. Of old age, Melbourne, July 19, 2010.

Whitcomb, Richard T., 88, U.S. engineer who redesigned the fuselage shape and wing curvature of jet planes, making supersonic speed practical while lessening fuel and flying time cost. Of pneumonia, Newport News, Va., Oct. 13, 2009.

Wild, Earl, 94, Pittsburgh-born pianist was master of the Romantic repertory, notably Liszt and Rachmaninoff, played with dazzling yet solid technique; influential teacher. Of old age, Palm Springs, Calif. Jan. 23, 2010.

Wilson, Charlie, 76, Texas Democrat, congressman 1973–96, outdid his playboy image by setting up secret aid in billions in support of Afghans fighting Soviet invaders in the 1980s; inspired 2007 film *Charlie Wilson's War*. Of heart failure, Lufkin, Tex., Feb. 10, 2010.

Wirtz, W. Willard, 98, U.S. secretary of labor 1962–69, he focused on job training, unemployment aid, and workplace discrimination; leader in Pres. Johnson's war on poverty, but disagreed with Vietnam War policy. Of natural causes, Washington, April 24, 2010.

Wolper, David L, 82, Manhattan-born TV and movie producer best known for mini-series *Roots* (1977), which won nine Emmys and made cultural headlines; other notable work includes *The Thorn Birds* (1983) and 1984 Olympic Games ceremonies. Of Parkinson's complications, Beverly Hills, Calif., Aug. 10, 2010.

Wooden, John, 99, Indiana-born basketball coach who started at U.C.L.A. in 1948 and had 10 national championship teams 1964–75; beloved by players such as Abdul-Jabbar and Walton to whom he taught the simple truths of life as well as the game. Of old age, Los Angeles, June 4, 2010.

Yar'Adua, Umaru, 58, Nigeria president elected 2007 with promise to end corruption and civil wars in oil-rich, poverty-stricken nation; chronic ailments led to constitutional impasse that ended with his death in the capital, Abuja, May 5, 2010.

Yohai, Morrie, 90, New York merchant who gave us in late 1950s the snack Cheez Doodles, and it's been hard to stop munching ever since. Of old age, Kings Point, N.Y., July 27, 2010.

Zinn, Howard, 87, Brooklyn-born historian whose best-selling *A People's History of the United States* (1980) focuses on the dark side of the usual U.S. heroes from what he called "the perspective of the slaughtered and the mutilated." Of a heart attack, Santa Monica, Calif., Jan. 27, 2010.

Calendar of the Year

UNDERSTANDING CALENDARS

The day Earth turns at a fairly steady pace about the imaginary line that defines the North and South Poles. This line through the poles is called Earth's *axis*. Each turn about the axis, called a *rotation*, takes slightly less than 24 hours. Since Earth is also traveling around the Sun, however, the time from noon to noon is longer than the time it takes for one rotation—about three minutes and 56 seconds longer, or almost exactly 24 hours. The time from noon to noon changes slightly during the year, depending on where Earth is in its path. If you average all the days in a year, the mean time from noon to noon is exactly 24 hours.

The year All the planets of the solar system travel in nearly circular paths, called *orbits*, around the Sun. Each trip around the Sun is called a *revolution*. The planets all revolve in the same direction, which can be observed from Earth by noting the position the Sun has among the background stars, which are traditionally grouped into constellations. (Since you can't see the Sun and stars at the same time, you can observe where the Sun rises or sets each day and then note the stars that appear in the same region.) Over the course of a year, the Sun appears to pass through the 12 constellations that make up the zodiac.

Earth's trip around the Sun, reflected in the Sun's trip through the zodiac, takes about 365.25 days. This varies slightly from time to time, so astronomers add or delete a second in some years to keep their records in tune with Earth's motion. (See also "Precession of the equinoxes" below).

Seasons The seasons mark the change in the pattern of daylight over the course of the year. Because the Earth is tilted with respect to its path around the Sun, different parts receive different amounts of sunlight during Earth's annual orbit, the time we know as a year. Between late September (around the 21st) and late March, Earth's Northern Hemisphere is tilted away from the Sun. This period constitutes the fall and winter seasons for the Northern Hemisphere, during which there are fewer than 12 hours of daylight each day. For the rest of the year, spring and summer, the Northern Hemisphere is tilted toward the Sun, and daylight hours constitute more than half of each day. In the Southern Hemisphere, this situation is reversed: spring and summer last from late September to late March, while fall and winter make up the other half of the year.

At the points of transition from long days and short nights to short days and long nights and vice versa, the *equinoxes* occur—the two days of the year when periods of daylight and darkness are equal. The *vernal equinox*, marking the first day of spring, takes place on or around March 21 in the Northern Hemisphere, while the *autumnal equinox*, marking the beginning of fall, is on or around September 21. Officially, summer begins on the day of the longest daytime during the year, about June 21 in the Northern Hemisphere, called the *summer solstice*. The *winter solstice*, about December 21 in the Northern Hemisphere, has the shortest amount of daylight and the longest night of the year. The word *solstice* means "standing still Sun." These two days are so called because the apparent movement of where the Sun rises or sets reaches its extreme positions on the solstices and then reverses direction.

Precession of the equinoxes Ancient Greek astronomers determined that the direction of Earth's axis is constantly, but very slowly, changing in a regular pattern. The kind of change is similar to the way a spinning top slowly leans one way then another as its axis changes direction. This movement of the Earth is caused by several factors, the most dominant being one called *precession*. The precession of the Earth results from its not being a perfect sphere. Earth's diameter is about 27 miles greater from one side of the equator to the other than it is from one pole to the other. (Earth is oblate, or fat around the middle, as a result of its rotation.)

Picture Earth without considering its revolution. Keep Earth's center in the same place mentally, and think about how the axis changes position during precession. Any point on Earth's axis (except the center of the planet) moves in a slow circle as a result of precession. This movement is so slow that it takes 26,000 years for a point to return to its original spot. In the meantime, the axis gradually changes its position in relation to the stars. While what we call the North Star (officially known as Polaris) is currently positioned above the North Pole about one degree off center, over time the axis will shift, so that about A.D. 15,000 the star Vega will be above the North Pole within about four degrees of that axis. By about A.D. 28,000, Polaris will have returned to its present position.

As the precession continues, one of its effects is to change the times of the year that seasons occur. Our calendar is corrected for this; if it were not, the vernal equinox would, over 13,000 years, shift from around March 21 to about September 21, the date at which the autumnal equinox is now. For this reason, the precession of the Earth is generally known as the precession of the equinoxes.

Although the precession of the equinoxes is slow, it can be easily observed. The year of about 365.25 days is the time it takes from one vernal

Solar Phenomena: The Seasons, 2011

Solar phenomenon	Month	Day	Hour	Min
Perigee[1]	Jan.	3	19	N.A.
Vernal equinox	Mar.	20	23	21
Summer solstice	June	21	17	16
Apogee[2]	July	4	5	N.A.
Autumnal equinox	Sept.	23	09	05
Winter solstice	Dec.	22	05	30

Notes: Shown in Universal time (UT). To convert to local time, see "Timing Planetary Phenomena." 1. Sun closest to the Earth (91.4 million miles). 2. Sun farthest from the Earth (94.5 million miles). **Source:** U.S. Naval Observatory, *Astronomical Phenomena for the Year 2011* (2010).

equinox to the next. Because of the precession of the equinoxes, however, the time it takes the Sun to appear in the same position with respect to the stars is 20 minutes, 24 seconds longer than the period from one equinox to the next. For this reason, accurate star maps have to specify both the date and the year for which they are intended.

Lunar Calendar There is some evidence that very early humans (c. 25,000 B.C.) used marks on bone to indicate the passage of time, which they may have measured by the Moon's phases. A calendar for the year can be based upon the Moon's phases, which gives a year of 12 periods from new moon to new moon (hence the word *month*) lasting about 354 days. This is about 11 days shorter than the time it takes Earth to revolve around the Sun. The Chinese, who still use a version of this calendar, resolve the discrepancy by inserting extra months at fixed intervals to bring the lunar and solar years into alignment. The Chinese year is divided into months that are either 29 or 30 days long, since the time from new moon to new moon is approximately 29.5 days. The New Year begins at the first new moon over China between Jan. 21 and Feb. 19, and is celebrated for a four-day period. Each year has both a number and a name. The year 2011, or 4709 in the Chinese era, is the Year of the Rabbit.

Solar Calendar The ancient Egyptians were the first people known to have instituted a solar calendar. In actuality, their calendar might be called a stellar calendar, since the year began with the rising of Sirius (the brightest star in the sky) at the same place the Sun rises, which generally happened at the same time the Nile flooded. The Egyptians determined that a year was 365 days, about one-quarter of a day short of the true solar year, so gradually the Egyptian calendar no longer coincided with the seasons. Historical records reveal when the Egyptian calendar and the rising of Sirius coincided, from which astronomers inferred that the Egyptian calendar must have been instituted in either 4241 B.C. or 2773 B.C. The Egyptian calendar had 12 months of 30 days and five days of festival, a system adopted by various early cultures, although some continued to use lunar calendars.

Julian Calendar In 46 B.C., Julius Caesar realized that various parts of the land controlled by Rome used different calendars, so he asked the astronomer Sosigenes to develop a uniform calendar. Sosigenes proposed that since the year was 365.25 days long (though not exactly), a 365-day calendar be kept with one day added (a leap day) every fourth year. When Caesar introduced the new system, he also added days to the year 46 B.C. to bring the seasons in line with the calendar. With a total of 445 days, 46 B.C. is the longest calendar year on record. A year at that time began in what we call

March, and the months were numbered. *September, October, November,* and *December* derive from this system and mean "seventh," "eighth," "ninth," and "tenth" months respectively.

There was a little further adjustment of the calendar, however, by Augustus Caesar, the first Roman emperor. The name of the fifth month was changed from Quintilis to July to honor Julius Caesar, and Augustus named the sixth month August after himself. So that August would not be shorter than 31-day July, Augustus borrowed a day from February. Because of the Roman Empire's great sphere of influence, the Julian calendar became the ordinary calendar of Western nations.

Julian Day Count A year after the Gregorian calendar was first instituted, Joseph Justus Scaliger developed a system of counting days instead of years, which is still used by astronomers. Called the Julian Day Count (after his father Julius Caesar Scaliger), it begins with 1 on Jan. 1, 4713 B.C. On this date, the Julian calendar, the lunar calendar and the Roman tax system (which had its own calendar) all coincided—something that won't happen again until A.D. 3267. Each day within such a 7,980-year period is numbered.

Gregorian Calendar From at least A.D. 730, it was known that the solar year—measured from vernal equinox to vernal equinox—was somewhat short of 365.25 days. Each century the solar year gets about half a second shorter. In 1990 the solar year was calculated at 365 days, 5 hours, 48 minutes, and 45.5 seconds long, not 365.25 days, which is what the Julian calendar assumes. Because the date of Easter was slipping, Pope Gregory XIII instituted calendar reform in 1582. He proclaimed that the day following Oct. 4 would be Oct. 15, which dropped 10 days from the year. Furthermore, on the advice of astronomer Christoph Clavius, the new calendar would be kept in line by omitting the leap year in century years unless they were divisible by 400. Thus 1900 was not a leap year, but 2000 was.

Most Roman Catholic countries and some other Western countries adopted the new system, but England did not. Finally, in 1752, England and its colonies adopted the Gregorian calendar, but they had to drop 11 days to fit common Western practice. It was at this time that New Year's Day in England was moved from Mar. 25 to Jan. 1, changing the number of the year for the almost three months affected. Thus George Washington was born according to the Julian calendar on Feb. 11, 1731, but he came to celebrate his birthday on Feb. 22, 1732 according to the Gregorian calendar.

Because the solar year is shortening, astronomers today keep the Gregorian calendar in line by making a one-second adjustment, as needed, usually on Dec. 31 at midnight, whenever the error's accumulation nears one second.

When Did the Third Millennium Begin?

Did the third millennium begin on January 1, 2000, January 1, 2001, or an entirely different day? The answer depends on how you count your years. If you believe that our calendar began in the year 1, rather than the year 0, then a thousand years did not pass until the end of the year 1000, and the third millennium didn't start until 2001.

But by that logic, the 1990s wouldn't have begun until 1991, and would have included the year 2000. Yet we routinely consider years ending in 0 to be the first year of a decade rather than the last, so why should it be any different for millennia? Also, calendars are an inexact science and plenty of shifting of days, months, and years, have been perpetrated over the years by kings, emperors and popes. The Jewish calendar counted more than 3,700 years before Western calendars counted their first, while the Chinese celebrated the third millennium more than 1,600 years ago.

Perpetual Calendar, 1775–2050

A perpetual calendar lets you find the day of the week for any date in any year. Since January 1 may fall on any of the seven days of the week, and may be a leap or non-leap year, 14 different calendars are possible. The number next to each year corresponds to one of the 14 calendars. For example, in 1776, calendar 9 (a leap year in which Jan. 1 fell on a Monday) was used; July 4 of that year was a Thursday. Calendar 1 was used in 2006; Calendar 7 will be used in 2011.

Year	No.	Year	No.	Year	No.	Year	No.	Year	No.	Year	No.	Year	No.
1775	1	1815	1	1855	2	1895	3	1935	3	1975	4	2015	5
1776	9	1816	9	1856	10	1896	11	1936	11	1976	12	2016	13
1777	4	1817	4	1857	5	1897	6	1937	6	1977	7	2017	1
1778	5	1818	5	1858	6	1898	7	1938	7	1978	1	2018	2
1779	6	1819	6	1859	7	1899	1	1939	1	1979	2	2019	3
1780	14	1820	14	1860	8	1900	2	1940	9	1980	10	2020	11
1781	2	1821	2	1861	3	1901	3	1941	4	1981	5	2021	6
1782	3	1822	3	1862	4	1902	4	1942	5	1982	6	2022	7
1783	4	1823	4	1863	5	1903	5	1943	6	1983	7	2023	1
1784	12	1824	12	1864	13	1904	13	1944	14	1984	8	2024	9
1785	7	1825	7	1865	1	1905	1	1945	2	1985	3	2025	4
1786	1	1826	1	1866	2	1906	2	1946	3	1986	4	2026	5
1787	2	1827	2	1867	3	1907	3	1947	4	1987	5	2027	6
1788	10	1828	10	1868	11	1908	11	1948	12	1988	13	2028	14
1789	5	1829	5	1869	6	1909	6	1949	7	1989	1	2029	2
1790	6	1830	6	1870	7	1910	7	1950	1	1990	2	2030	3
1791	7	1831	7	1871	1	1911	1	1951	2	1991	3	2031	4
1792	8	1832	8	1872	9	1912	9	1952	10	1992	11	2032	12
1793	3	1833	3	1873	4	1913	4	1953	5	1993	6	2033	7
1794	4	1834	4	1874	5	1914	5	1954	6	1994	7	2034	1
1795	5	1835	5	1875	6	1915	6	1955	7	1995	1	2035	2
1796	13	1836	13	1876	14	1916	14	1956	8	1996	9	2036	10
1797	1	1837	1	1877	2	1917	2	1957	3	1997	4	2037	5
1798	2	1838	2	1878	3	1918	3	1958	4	1998	5	2038	6
1799	3	1839	3	1879	4	1919	4	1959	5	1999	6	2039	7
1800	4	1840	11	1880	12	1920	12	1960	13	2000	14	2040	8
1801	5	1841	6	1881	7	1921	7	1961	1	2001	2	2041	3
1802	6	1842	7	1882	1	1922	1	1962	2	2002	3	2042	4
1803	7	1843	1	1883	2	1923	2	1963	3	2003	4	2043	5
1804	8	1844	9	1884	10	1924	10	1964	11	2004	12	2044	13
1805	3	1845	4	1885	5	1925	5	1965	6	2005	7	2045	1
1806	4	1846	5	1886	6	1926	6	1966	7	2006	1	2046	2
1807	5	1847	6	1887	7	1927	7	1967	1	2007	2	2047	3
1808	13	1848	14	1888	8	1928	8	1968	9	2008	10	2048	11
1809	1	1849	2	1889	3	1929	3	1969	4	2009	4	2049	6
1810	2	1850	3	1890	4	1930	4	1970	5	2010	6	2050	7
1811	3	1851	4	1891	5	1931	5	1971	6	2011	7		
1812	11	1852	12	1892	13	1932	13	1972	14	2012	8		
1813	6	1853	7	1893	1	1933	1	1973	3	2013	3		
1814	7	1854	1	1894	2	1934	2	1974	3	2014	4		

1

```
JANUARY                FEBRUARY               MARCH
S  M  T  W  T  F  S     S  M  T  W  T  F  S     S  M  T  W  T  F  S
1  2  3  4  5  6  7              1  2  3  4              1  2  3  4
8  9 10 11 12 13 14     5  6  7  8  9 10 11     5  6  7  8  9 10 11
15 16 17 18 19 20 21    12 13 14 15 16 17 18    12 13 14 15 16 17 18
22 23 24 25 26 27 28    19 20 21 22 23 24 25    19 20 21 22 23 24 25
29 30 31                26 27 28                26 27 28 29 30 31

APRIL                  MAY                    JUNE
S  M  T  W  T  F  S     S  M  T  W  T  F  S     S  M  T  W  T  F  S
               1           1  2  3  4  5  6              1  2  3
2  3  4  5  6  7  8     7  8  9 10 11 12 13     4  5  6  7  8  9 10
9 10 11 12 13 14 15     14 15 16 17 18 19 20    11 12 13 14 15 16 17
16 17 18 19 20 21 22    21 22 23 24 25 26 27    18 19 20 21 22 23 24
23 24 25 26 27 28 29    28 29 30 31             25 26 27 28 29 30
30

JULY                   AUGUST                 SEPTEMBER
S  M  T  W  T  F  S     S  M  T  W  T  F  S     S  M  T  W  T  F  S
               1              1  2  3  4  5                 1  2
2  3  4  5  6  7  8     6  7  8  9 10 11 12     3  4  5  6  7  8  9
9 10 11 12 13 14 15     13 14 15 16 17 18 19    10 11 12 13 14 15 16
16 17 18 19 20 21 22    20 21 22 23 24 25 26    17 18 19 20 21 22 23
23 24 25 26 27 28 29    27 28 29 30 31          24 25 26 27 28 29 30
30 31

OCTOBER                NOVEMBER               DECEMBER
S  M  T  W  T  F  S     S  M  T  W  T  F  S     S  M  T  W  T  F  S
1  2  3  4  5  6  7              1  2  3  4                 1  2
8  9 10 11 12 13 14     5  6  7  8  9 10 11     3  4  5  6  7  8  9
15 16 17 18 19 20 21    12 13 14 15 16 17 18    10 11 12 13 14 15 16
22 23 24 25 26 27 28    19 20 21 22 23 24 25    17 18 19 20 21 22 23
29 30 31                26 27 28 29 30          24 25 26 27 28 29 30
                                               31
```

2

```
JANUARY                FEBRUARY               MARCH
S  M  T  W  T  F  S     S  M  T  W  T  F  S     S  M  T  W  T  F  S
   1  2  3  4  5  6              1  2  3                 1  2  3
7  8  9 10 11 12 13     4  5  6  7  8  9 10     4  5  6  7  8  9 10
14 15 16 17 18 19 20    11 12 13 14 15 16 17    11 12 13 14 15 16 17
21 22 23 24 25 26 27    18 19 20 21 22 23 24    18 19 20 21 22 23 24
28 29 30 31             25 26 27 28             25 26 27 28 29 30 31

APRIL                  MAY                    JUNE
S  M  T  W  T  F  S     S  M  T  W  T  F  S     S  M  T  W  T  F  S
1  2  3  4  5  6  7           1  2  3  4  5                 1  2
8  9 10 11 12 13 14     6  7  8  9 10 11 12     3  4  5  6  7  8  9
15 16 17 18 19 20 21    13 14 15 16 17 18 19    10 11 12 13 14 15 16
22 23 24 25 26 27 28    20 21 22 23 24 25 26    17 18 19 20 21 22 23
29 30                   27 28 29 30 31          24 25 26 27 28 29 30

JULY                   AUGUST                 SEPTEMBER
S  M  T  W  T  F  S     S  M  T  W  T  F  S     S  M  T  W  T  F  S
1  2  3  4  5  6  7              1  2  3  4                    1
8  9 10 11 12 13 14     5  6  7  8  9 10 11     2  3  4  5  6  7  8
15 16 17 18 19 20 21    12 13 14 15 16 17 18    9 10 11 12 13 14 15
22 23 24 25 26 27 28    19 20 21 22 23 24 25    16 17 18 19 20 21 22
29 30 31                26 27 28 29 30 31       23 24 25 26 27 28 29
                                               30

OCTOBER                NOVEMBER               DECEMBER
S  M  T  W  T  F  S     S  M  T  W  T  F  S     S  M  T  W  T  F  S
   1  2  3  4  5  6              1  2  3                    1
7  8  9 10 11 12 13     4  5  6  7  8  9 10     2  3  4  5  6  7  8
14 15 16 17 18 19 20    11 12 13 14 15 16 17    9 10 11 12 13 14 15
21 22 23 24 25 26 27    18 19 20 21 22 23 24    16 17 18 19 20 21 22
28 29 30 31             25 26 27 28 29 30       23 24 25 26 27 28 29
                                               30 31
```

3

JANUARY

S	M	T	W	T	F	S
					1	2
6	7	8	9	10	11	12
13	14	15	16	17	18	19
20	21	22	23	24	25	26
27	28	29	30	31		

FEBRUARY

S	M	T	W	T	F	S
					1	2
3	4	5	6	7	8	9
10	11	12	13	14	15	16
17	18	19	20	21	22	23
24	25	26	27	28		

MARCH

S	M	T	W	T	F	S
					1	2
3	4	5	6	7	8	9
10	11	12	13	14	15	16
17	18	19	20	21	22	23
24	25	26	27	28	29	30
31						

APRIL

S	M	T	W	T	F	S
	1	2	3	4	5	6
7	8	9	10	11	12	13
14	15	16	17	18	19	20
21	22	23	24	25	26	27
28	29	30				

MAY

S	M	T	W	T	F	S
			1	2	3	4
5	6	7	8	9	10	11
12	13	14	15	16	17	18
19	20	21	22	23	24	25
26	27	28	29	30	31	

JUNE

S	M	T	W	T	F	S
						1
2	3	4	5	6	7	8
9	10	11	12	13	14	15
16	17	18	19	20	21	22
23	24	25	26	27	28	29
30						

JULY

S	M	T	W	T	F	S
	1	2	3	4	5	6
7	8	9	10	11	12	13
14	15	16	17	18	19	20
21	22	23	24	25	26	27
28	29	30	31			

AUGUST

S	M	T	W	T	F	S
				1	2	3
4	5	6	7	8	9	10
11	12	13	14	15	16	17
18	19	20	21	22	23	24
25	26	27	28	29	30	31

SEPTEMBER

S	M	T	W	T	F	S
1	2	3	4	5	6	7
8	9	10	11	12	13	14
15	16	17	18	19	20	21
22	23	24	25	26	27	28
29	30					

OCTOBER

S	M	T	W	T	F	S
		1	2	3	4	5
6	7	8	9	10	11	12
13	14	15	16	17	18	19
20	21	22	23	24	25	26
27	28	29	30	31		

NOVEMBER

S	M	T	W	T	F	S
					1	2
3	4	5	6	7	8	9
10	11	12	13	14	15	16
17	18	19	20	21	22	23
24	25	26	27	28	29	30

DECEMBER

S	M	T	W	T	F	S
1	2	3	4	5	6	7
8	9	10	11	12	13	14
15	16	17	18	19	20	21
22	23	24	25	26	27	28
29	30	31				

4

JANUARY

S	M	T	W	T	F	S
		1	2	3	4	5
6	7	8	9	10	11	12
13	14	15	16	17	18	19
20	21	22	23	24	25	26
27	28	29	30	31		

FEBRUARY

S	M	T	W	T	F	S
					1	
2	3	4	5	6	7	8
9	10	11	12	13	14	15
16	17	18	19	20	21	22
23	24	25	26	27	28	

MARCH

S	M	T	W	T	F	S
						1
2	3	4	5	6	7	8
9	10	11	12	13	14	15
16	17	18	19	20	21	22
23	24	25	26	27	28	29
30	31					

APRIL

S	M	T	W	T	F	S
		1	2	3	4	5
6	7	8	9	10	11	12
13	14	15	16	17	18	19
20	21	22	23	24	25	26
27	28	29	30			

MAY

S	M	T	W	T	F	S
				1	2	3
4	5	6	7	8	9	10
11	12	13	14	15	16	17
18	19	20	21	22	23	24
25	26	27	28	29	30	31

JUNE

S	M	T	W	T	F	S
1	2	3	4	5	6	7
8	9	10	11	12	13	14
15	16	17	18	19	20	21
22	23	24	25	26	27	28
29	30					

JULY

S	M	T	W	T	F	S
		1	2	3	4	5
6	7	8	9	10	11	12
13	14	15	16	17	18	19
20	21	22	23	24	25	26
27	28	29	30	31		

AUGUST

S	M	T	W	T	F	S
					1	2
3	4	5	6	7	8	9
10	11	12	13	14	15	16
17	18	19	20	21	22	23
24	25	26	27	28	29	30
31						

SEPTEMBER

S	M	T	W	T	F	S
	1	2	3	4	5	6
7	8	9	10	11	12	13
14	15	16	17	18	19	20
21	22	23	24	25	26	27
28	29	30				

OCTOBER

S	M	T	W	T	F	S
			1	2	3	4
5	6	7	8	9	10	11
12	13	14	15	16	17	18
19	20	21	22	23	24	25
26	27	28	29	30	31	

NOVEMBER

S	M	T	W	T	F	S
						1
2	3	4	5	6	7	8
9	10	11	12	13	14	15
16	17	18	19	20	21	22
23	24	25	26	27	28	29
30						

DECEMBER

S	M	T	W	T	F	S
	1	2	3	4	5	6
7	8	9	10	11	12	13
14	15	16	17	18	19	20
21	22	23	24	25	26	27
28	29	30	31			

5

JANUARY

S	M	T	W	T	F	S
			1	2	3	
4	5	6	7	8	9	10
11	12	13	14	15	16	17
18	19	20	21	22	23	24
25	26	27	28	29	30	31

FEBRUARY

S	M	T	W	T	F	S
1	2	3	4	5	6	7
8	9	10	11	12	13	14
15	16	17	18	19	20	21
22	23	24	25	26	27	28

MARCH

S	M	T	W	T	F	S
1	2	3	4	5	6	7
8	9	10	11	12	13	14
15	16	17	18	19	20	21
22	23	24	25	26	27	28
29	30	31				

APRIL

S	M	T	W	T	F	S
			1	2	3	4
5	6	7	8	9	10	11
12	13	14	15	16	17	18
19	20	21	22	23	24	25
26	27	28	29	30		

MAY

S	M	T	W	T	F	S
					1	2
3	4	5	6	7	8	9
10	11	12	13	14	15	16
17	18	19	20	21	22	23
24	25	26	27	28	29	30
31						

JUNE

S	M	T	W	T	F	S
	1	2	3	4	5	6
7	8	9	10	11	12	13
14	15	16	17	18	19	20
21	22	23	24	25	26	27
28	29	30				

JULY

S	M	T	W	T	F	S
			1	2	3	4
5	6	7	8	9	10	11
12	13	14	15	16	17	18
19	20	21	22	23	24	25
26	27	28	29	30	31	

AUGUST

S	M	T	W	T	F	S
						1
2	3	4	5	6	7	8
9	10	11	12	13	14	15
16	17	18	19	20	21	22
23	24	25	26	27	28	29
30	31					

SEPTEMBER

S	M	T	W	T	F	S
		1	2	3	4	5
6	7	8	9	10	11	12
13	14	15	16	17	18	19
20	21	22	23	24	25	26
27	28	29	30			

OCTOBER

S	M	T	W	T	F	S
				1	2	3
4	5	6	7	8	9	10
11	12	13	14	15	16	17
18	19	20	21	22	23	24
25	26	27	28	29	30	31

NOVEMBER

S	M	T	W	T	F	S
1	2	3	4	5	6	7
8	9	10	11	12	13	14
15	16	17	18	19	20	21
22	23	24	25	26	27	28
29	30					

DECEMBER

S	M	T	W	T	F	S
		1	2	3	4	5
6	7	8	9	10	11	12
13	14	15	16	17	18	19
20	21	22	23	24	25	26
27	28	29	30	31		

6

JANUARY

S	M	T	W	T	F	S
				1	2	3
4	5	6	7	8	9	10
11	12	13	14	15	16	17
18	19	20	21	22	23	24
25	26	27	28	29	30	31

FEBRUARY

S	M	T	W	T	F	S
1	2	3	4	5	6	7
8	9	10	11	12	13	14
15	16	17	18	19	20	21
22	23	24	25	26	27	28

MARCH

S	M	T	W	T	F	S
1	2	3	4	5	6	
7	8	9	10	11	12	13
14	15	16	17	18	19	20
21	22	23	24	25	26	27
28	29	30	31			

APRIL

S	M	T	W	T	F	S
				1	2	3
4	5	6	7	8	9	10
11	12	13	14	15	16	17
18	19	20	21	22	23	24
25	26	27	28	29	30	

MAY

S	M	T	W	T	F	S
						1
2	3	4	5	6	7	8
9	10	11	12	13	14	15
16	17	18	19	20	21	22
23	24	25	26	27	28	29
30	31					

JUNE

S	M	T	W	T	F	S
		1	2	3	4	5
6	7	8	9	10	11	12
13	14	15	16	17	18	19
20	21	22	23	24	25	26
27	28	29	30			

JULY

S	M	T	W	T	F	S
				1	2	3
4	5	6	7	8	9	10
11	12	13	14	15	16	17
18	19	20	21	22	23	24
25	26	27	28	29	30	31

AUGUST

S	M	T	W	T	F	S
1	2	3	4	5	6	7
8	9	10	11	12	13	14
15	16	17	18	19	20	21
22	23	24	25	26	27	28
29	30	31				

SEPTEMBER

S	M	T	W	T	F	S
			1	2	3	4
5	6	7	8	9	10	11
12	13	14	15	16	17	18
19	20	21	22	23	24	25
26	27	28	29	30		

OCTOBER

S	M	T	W	T	F	S
					1	2
3	4	5	6	7	8	9
10	11	12	13	14	15	16
17	18	19	20	21	22	23
24	25	26	27	28	29	30
31						

NOVEMBER

S	M	T	W	T	F	S
	1	2	3	4	5	6
7	8	9	10	11	12	13
14	15	16	17	18	19	20
21	22	23	24	25	26	27
28	29	30				

DECEMBER

S	M	T	W	T	F	S
			1	2	3	4
5	6	7	8	9	10	11
12	13	14	15	16	17	18
19	20	21	22	23	24	25
26	27	28	29	30	31	

7

JANUARY

S	M	T	W	T	F	S
					1	
2	3	4	5	6	7	8
9	10	11	12	13	14	15
16	17	18	19	20	21	22
23	24	25	26	27	28	29
30	31					

FEBRUARY

S	M	T	W	T	F	S
		1	2	3	4	5
6	7	8	9	10	11	12
13	14	15	16	17	18	19
20	21	22	23	24	25	26
27	28					

MARCH

S	M	T	W	T	F	S
		1	2	3	4	5
6	7	8	9	10	11	12
13	14	15	16	17	18	19
20	21	22	23	24	25	26
27	28	29	30	31		

APRIL

S	M	T	W	T	F	S
					1	2
3	4	5	6	7	8	9
10	11	12	13	14	15	16
17	18	19	20	21	22	23
24	25	26	27	28	29	30

MAY

S	M	T	W	T	F	S
1	2	3	4	5	6	7
8	9	10	11	12	13	14
15	16	17	18	19	20	21
22	23	24	25	26	27	28
29	30	31				

JUNE

S	M	T	W	T	F	S
			1	2	3	4
5	6	7	8	9	10	11
12	13	14	15	16	17	18
19	20	21	22	23	24	25
26	27	28	29	30		

JULY

S	M	T	W	T	F	S
					1	2
3	4	5	6	7	8	9
10	11	12	13	14	15	16
17	18	19	20	21	22	23
24	25	26	27	28	29	30
31						

AUGUST

S	M	T	W	T	F	S
	1	2	3	4	5	6
7	8	9	10	11	12	13
14	15	16	17	18	19	20
21	22	23	24	25	26	27
28	29	30	31			

SEPTEMBER

S	M	T	W	T	F	S
				1	2	3
4	5	6	7	8	9	10
11	12	13	14	15	16	17
18	19	20	21	22	23	24
25	26	27	28	29	30	

OCTOBER

S	M	T	W	T	F	S
						1
2	3	4	5	6	7	8
9	10	11	12	13	14	15
16	17	18	19	20	21	22
23	24	25	26	27	28	29
30	31					

NOVEMBER

S	M	T	W	T	F	S
		1	2	3	4	5
6	7	8	9	10	11	12
13	14	15	16	17	18	19
20	21	22	23	24	25	26
27	28	29	30			

DECEMBER

S	M	T	W	T	F	S
				1	2	3
4	5	6	7	8	9	10
11	12	13	14	15	16	17
18	19	20	21	22	23	24
25	26	27	28	29	30	31

8

JANUARY

S	M	T	W	T	F	S
1	2	3	4	5	6	7
8	9	10	11	12	13	14
15	16	17	18	19	20	21
22	23	24	25	26	27	28
29	30	31				

FEBRUARY

S	M	T	W	T	F	S
			1	2	3	4
5	6	7	8	9	10	11
12	13	14	15	16	17	18
19	20	21	22	23	24	25
26	27	28	29			

MARCH

S	M	T	W	T	F	S
				1	2	3
4	5	6	7	8	9	10
11	12	13	14	15	16	17
18	19	20	21	22	23	24
25	26	27	28	29	30	31

APRIL

S	M	T	W	T	F	S
1	2	3	4	5	6	7
8	9	10	11	12	13	14
15	16	17	18	19	20	21
22	23	24	25	26	27	28
29	30					

MAY

S	M	T	W	T	F	S
		1	2	3	4	5
6	7	8	9	10	11	12
13	14	15	16	17	18	19
20	21	22	23	24	25	26
27	28	29	30	31		

JUNE

S	M	T	W	T	F	S
					1	2
3	4	5	6	7	8	9
10	11	12	13	14	15	16
17	18	19	20	21	22	23
24	25	26	27	28	29	30

JULY

S	M	T	W	T	F	S
1	2	3	4	5	6	7
8	9	10	11	12	13	14
15	16	17	18	19	20	21
22	23	24	25	26	27	28
29	30	31				

AUGUST

S	M	T	W	T	F	S
			1	2	3	4
5	6	7	8	9	10	11
12	13	14	15	16	17	18
19	20	21	22	23	24	25
26	27	28	29	30	31	

SEPTEMBER

S	M	T	W	T	F	S
						1
2	3	4	5	6	7	8
9	10	11	12	13	14	15
16	17	18	19	20	21	22
23	24	25	26	27	28	29
30						

OCTOBER

S	M	T	W	T	F	S
	1	2	3	4	5	6
7	8	9	10	11	12	13
14	15	16	17	18	19	20
21	22	23	24	25	26	27
28	29	30	31			

NOVEMBER

S	M	T	W	T	F	S
				1	2	3
4	5	6	7	8	9	10
11	12	13	14	15	16	17
18	19	20	21	22	23	24
25	26	27	28	29	30	

DECEMBER

S	M	T	W	T	F	S
						1
2	3	4	5	6	7	8
9	10	11	12	13	14	15
16	17	18	19	20	21	22
23	24	25	26	27	28	29
30	31					

9

JANUARY
S M T W T F S
1 2 3 4 5 6
7 8 9 10 11 12 13
14 15 16 17 18 19 20
21 22 23 24 25 26 27
28 29 30 31

FEBRUARY
S M T W T F S
1 2 3
4 5 6 7 8 9 10
11 12 13 14 15 16 17
18 19 20 21 22 23 24
25 26 27 28 29

MARCH
S M T W T F S
1 2
3 4 5 6 7 8 9
10 11 12 13 14 15 16
17 18 19 20 21 22 23
24 25 26 27 28 29 30
31

APRIL
S M T W T F S
1 2 3 4 5 6
7 8 9 10 11 12 13
14 15 16 17 18 19 20
21 22 23 24 25 26 27
28 29 30

MAY
S M T W T F S
1 2 3 4
5 6 7 8 9 10 11
12 13 14 15 16 17 18
19 20 21 22 23 24 25
26 27 28 29 30 31

JUNE
S M T W T F S
1
2 3 4 5 6 7 8
9 10 11 12 13 14 15
16 17 18 19 20 21 22
23 24 25 26 27 28 29
30

JULY
S M T W T F S
1 2 3 4 5 6
7 8 9 10 11 12 13
14 15 16 17 18 19 20
21 22 23 24 25 26 27
28 29 30 31

AUGUST
S M T W T F S
1 2 3
4 5 6 7 8 9 10
11 12 13 14 15 16 17
18 19 20 21 22 23 24
25 26 27 28 29 30 31

SEPTEMBER
S M T W T F S
1 2 3 4 5 6 7
8 9 10 11 12 13 14
15 16 17 18 19 20 21
22 23 24 25 26 27 28
29 30

OCTOBER
S M T W T F S
1 2 3 4 5
6 7 8 9 10 11 12
13 14 15 16 17 18 19
20 21 22 23 24 25 26
27 28 29 30 31

NOVEMBER
S M T W T F S
1 2
3 4 5 6 7 8 9
10 11 12 13 14 15 16
17 18 19 20 21 22 23
24 25 26 27 28 29 30

DECEMBER
S M T W T F S
1 2 3 4 5 6 7
8 9 10 11 12 13 14
15 16 17 18 19 20 21
22 23 24 25 26 27 28
29 30 31

10

JANUARY
S M T W T F S
1 2 3 4 5
6 7 8 9 10 11 12
13 14 15 16 17 18 19
20 21 22 23 24 25 26
27 28 29 30 31

FEBRUARY
S M T W T F S
1 2
3 4 5 6 7 8 9
10 11 12 13 14 15 16
17 18 19 20 21 22 23
24 25 26 27 28 29

MARCH
S M T W T F S
1
2 3 4 5 6 7 8
9 10 11 12 13 14 15
16 17 18 19 20 21 22
23 24 25 26 27 28 29
30 31

APRIL
S M T W T F S
1 2 3 4 5
6 7 8 9 10 11 12
13 14 15 16 17 18 19
20 21 22 23 24 25 26
27 28 29 30

MAY
S M T W T F S
1 2 3
4 5 6 7 8 9 10
11 12 13 14 15 16 17
18 19 20 21 22 23 24
25 26 27 28 29 30 31

JUNE
S M T W T F S
1 2 3 4 5 6 7
8 9 10 11 12 13 14
15 16 17 18 19 20 21
22 23 24 25 26 27 28
29 30

JULY
S M T W T F S
1 2 3 4 5
6 7 8 9 10 11 12
13 14 15 16 17 18 19
20 21 22 23 24 25 26
27 28 29 30 31

AUGUST
S M T W T F S
1 2
3 4 5 6 7 8 9
10 11 12 13 14 15 16
17 18 19 20 21 22 23
24 25 26 27 28 29 30
31

SEPTEMBER
S M T W T F S
1 2 3 4 5 6
7 8 9 10 11 12 13
14 15 16 17 18 19 20
21 22 23 24 25 26 27
28 29 30

OCTOBER
S M T W T F S
1 2 3 4
5 6 7 8 9 10 11
12 13 14 15 16 17 18
19 20 21 22 23 24 25
26 27 28 29 30 31

NOVEMBER
S M T W T F S
1
2 3 4 5 6 7 8
9 10 11 12 13 14 15
16 17 18 19 20 21 22
23 24 25 26 27 28 29
30

DECEMBER
S M T W T F S
1 2 3 4 5 6
7 8 9 10 11 12 13
14 15 16 17 18 19 20
21 22 23 24 25 26 27
28 29 30 31

11

JANUARY
S M T W T F S
1 2 3 4
5 6 7 8 9 10 11
12 13 14 15 16 17 18
19 20 21 22 23 24 25
26 27 28 29 30 31

FEBRUARY
S M T W T F S
1
2 3 4 5 6 7 8
9 10 11 12 13 14 15
16 17 18 19 20 21 22
23 24 25 26 27 28 29

MARCH
S M T W T F S
1 2 3 4 5 6 7
8 9 10 11 12 13 14
15 16 17 18 19 20 21
22 23 24 25 26 27 28
29 30 31

APRIL
S M T W T F S
1 2 3 4
5 6 7 8 9 10 11
12 13 14 15 16 17 18
19 20 21 22 23 24 25
26 27 28 29 30

MAY
S M T W T F S
1 2
3 4 5 6 7 8 9
10 11 12 13 14 15 16
17 18 19 20 21 22 23
24 25 26 27 28 29 30
31

JUNE
S M T W T F S
1 2 3 4 5 6
7 8 9 10 11 12 13
14 15 16 17 18 19 20
21 22 23 24 25 26 27
28 29 30

JULY
S M T W T F S
1 2 3 4
5 6 7 8 9 10 11
12 13 14 15 16 17 18
19 20 21 22 23 24 25
26 27 28 29 30 31

AUGUST
S M T W T F S
1
2 3 4 5 6 7 8
9 10 11 12 13 14 15
16 17 18 19 20 21 22
23 24 25 26 27 28 29
30 31

SEPTEMBER
S M T W T F S
1 2 3 4 5
6 7 8 9 10 11 12
13 14 15 16 17 18 19
20 21 22 23 24 25 26
27 28 29 30

OCTOBER
S M T W T F S
1 2 3
4 5 6 7 8 9 10
11 12 13 14 15 16 17
18 19 20 21 22 23 24
25 26 27 28 29 30 31

NOVEMBER
S M T W T F S
1 2 3 4 5 6 7
8 9 10 11 12 13 14
15 16 17 18 19 20 21
22 23 24 25 26 27 28
29 30

DECEMBER
S M T W T F S
1 2 3 4 5
6 7 8 9 10 11 12
13 14 15 16 17 18 19
20 21 22 23 24 25 26
27 28 29 30 31

12

JANUARY
S M T W T F S
1 2 3
4 5 6 7 8 9 10
11 12 13 14 15 16 17
18 19 20 21 22 23 24
25 26 27 28 29 30 31

FEBRUARY
S M T W T F S
1 2 3 4 5 6 7
8 9 10 11 12 13 14
15 16 17 18 19 20 21
22 23 24 25 26 27 28
29

MARCH
S M T W T F S
1 2 3 4 5 6
7 8 9 10 11 12 13
14 15 16 17 18 19 20
21 22 23 24 25 26 27
28 29 30 31

APRIL
S M T W T F S
1 2 3
4 5 6 7 8 9 10
11 12 13 14 15 16 17
18 19 20 21 22 23 24
25 26 27 28 29 30

MAY
S M T W T F S
1
2 3 4 5 6 7 8
9 10 11 12 13 14 15
16 17 18 19 20 21 22
23 24 25 26 27 28 29
30 31

JUNE
S M T W T F S
1 2 3 4 5
6 7 8 9 10 11 12
13 14 15 16 17 18 19
20 21 22 23 24 25 26
27 28 29 30

JULY
S M T W T F S
1 2 3
4 5 6 7 8 9 10
11 12 13 14 15 16 17
18 19 20 21 22 23 24
25 26 27 28 29 30 31

AUGUST
S M T W T F S
1 2 3 4 5 6 7
8 9 10 11 12 13 14
15 16 17 18 19 20 21
22 23 24 25 26 27 28
29 30 31

SEPTEMBER
S M T W T F S
1 2 3 4
5 6 7 8 9 10 11
12 13 14 15 16 17 18
19 20 21 22 23 24 25
26 27 28 29 30

OCTOBER
S M T W T F S
1 2
3 4 5 6 7 8 9
10 11 12 13 14 15 16
17 18 19 20 21 22 23
24 25 26 27 28 29 30
31

NOVEMBER
S M T W T F S
1 2 3 4 5 6
7 8 9 10 11 12 13
14 15 16 17 18 19 20
21 22 23 24 25 26 27
28 29 30

DECEMBER
S M T W T F S
1 2 3 4
5 6 7 8 9 10 11
12 13 14 15 16 17 18
19 20 21 22 23 24 25
26 27 28 29 30 31

13

JANUARY
S M T W T F S
1 2
3 4 5 6 7 8 9
10 11 12 13 14 15 16
17 18 19 20 21 22 23
24 25 26 27 28 29 30
31

FEBRUARY
S M T W T F S
1 2 3 4 5 6
7 8 9 10 11 12 13
14 15 16 17 18 19 20
21 22 23 24 25 26 27
28 29

MARCH
S M T W T F S
1 2 3 4 5
6 7 8 9 10 11 12
13 14 15 16 17 18 19
20 21 22 23 24 25 26
27 28 29 30 31

APRIL
S M T W T F S
1 2
3 4 5 6 7 8 9
10 11 12 13 14 15 16
17 18 19 20 21 22 23
24 25 26 27 28 29 30

MAY
S M T W T F S
1 2 3 4 5 6 7
8 9 10 11 12 13 14
15 16 17 18 19 20 21
22 23 24 25 26 27 28
29 30 31

JUNE
S M T W T F S
1 2 3 4
5 6 7 8 9 10 11
12 13 14 15 16 17 18
19 20 21 22 23 24 25
26 27 28 29 30

JULY
S M T W T F S
1 2
3 4 5 6 7 8 9
10 11 12 13 14 15 16
17 18 19 20 21 22 23
24 25 26 27 28 29 30
31

AUGUST
S M T W T F S
1 2 3 4 5 6
7 8 9 10 11 12 13
14 15 16 17 18 19 20
21 22 23 24 25 26 27
28 29 30 31

SEPTEMBER
S M T W T F S
1 2 3
4 5 6 7 8 9 10
11 12 13 14 15 16 17
18 19 20 21 22 23 24
25 26 27 28 29 30

OCTOBER
S M T W T F S
1
2 3 4 5 6 7 8
9 10 11 12 13 14 15
16 17 18 19 20 21 22
23 24 25 26 27 28 29
30 31

NOVEMBER
S M T W T F S
1 2 3 4 5
6 7 8 9 10 11 12
13 14 15 16 17 18 19
20 21 22 23 24 25 26
27 28 29 30

DECEMBER
S M T W T F S
1 2 3
4 5 6 7 8 9 10
11 12 13 14 15 16 17
18 19 20 21 22 23 24
25 26 27 28 29 30 31

14

JANUARY
S M T W T F S
1
2 3 4 5 6 7 8
9 10 11 12 13 14 15
16 17 18 19 20 21 22
23 24 25 26 27 28 29
30 31

FEBRUARY
S M T W T F S
1 2 3 4 5
6 7 8 9 10 11 12
13 14 15 16 17 18 19
20 21 22 23 24 25 26
27 28 29

MARCH
S M T W T F S
1 2 3 4
5 6 7 8 9 10 11
12 13 14 15 16 17 18
19 20 21 22 23 24 25
26 27 28 29 30 31

APRIL
S M T W T F S
1
2 3 4 5 6 7 8
9 10 11 12 13 14 15
16 17 18 19 20 21 22
23 24 25 26 27 28 29
30

MAY
S M T W T F S
1 2 3 4 5 6
7 8 9 10 11 12 13
14 15 16 17 18 19 20
21 22 23 24 25 26 27
28 29 30 31

JUNE
S M T W T F S
1 2 3
4 5 6 7 8 9 10
11 12 13 14 15 16 17
18 19 20 21 22 23 24
25 26 27 28 29 30

JULY
S M T W T F S
1
2 3 4 5 6 7 8
9 10 11 12 13 14 15
16 17 18 19 20 21 22
23 24 25 26 27 28 29
30 31

AUGUST
S M T W T F S
1 2 3 4 5
6 7 8 9 10 11 12
13 14 15 16 17 18 19
20 21 22 23 24 25 26
27 28 29 30 31

SEPTEMBER
S M T W T F S
1 2
3 4 5 6 7 8 9
10 11 12 13 14 15 16
17 18 19 20 21 22 23
24 25 26 27 28 29 30

OCTOBER
S M T W T F S
1 2 3 4 5 6 7
8 9 10 11 12 13 14
15 16 17 18 19 20 21
22 23 24 25 26 27 28
29 30 31

NOVEMBER
S M T W T F S
1 2 3 4
5 6 7 8 9 10 11
12 13 14 15 16 17 18
19 20 21 22 23 24 25
26 27 28 29 30

DECEMBER
S M T W T F S
1 2
3 4 5 6 7 8 9
10 11 12 13 14 15 16
17 18 19 20 21 22 23
24 25 26 27 28 29 30
31

HOLIDAYS AND HOLY DAYS

▶ FEDERAL HOLIDAYS IN THE U.S.

Congress and the president have designated 10 days as federal holidays. Although these are so widely observed as to be considered "national" holidays, they technically apply only to federal employees and the District of Columbia. It is up to the individual states to designate their own holidays. When a federal holiday falls on a Saturday or a Sunday, it is observed on the preceding Friday or the following Monday.

New Year's Day (January 1)   The observance of the New Year dates back to pre-Christian times when rites were performed to ensure the return of spring.

Martin Luther King, Jr., Day (Third Monday in January)   Before his assassination in 1968, Martin Luther King, Jr., was the foremost civil rights leader of the 1950s and 1960s, and in 1964 he won the Nobel Peace Prize. In 1983, Congress set aside this day to celebrate his life and accomplishments.

Washington's Birthday (Third Monday in February)   Originally celebrated on the actual birthday of America's first president (February 22), this holiday was officially moved in 1971 to the third Monday in February to create a three-day weekend. It is sometimes known as Presidents' Day, because the birthday of Abraham Lincoln (Feb. 12) is so close.

Memorial Day (Last Monday in May)   Memorial Day (also known as Decoration Day) honors soldiers fallen in battle. Dating from the Civil War, it is traditionally marked with parades and memorial services.

Independence Day (July 4)   The most important U.S. holiday, Independence Day commemorates the signing of the Declaration of Independence on July 4, 1776, an event that marked America's birth as a free nation. The holiday was first observed in 1777 and is celebrated with fireworks, parades, and oratory.

Labor Day (First Monday in September)   The idea of Peter J. McGuire, president of the United Brotherhood of Carpenters and Joiners of America, the official observance of a day celebrating the American worker was signed into law on June 28, 1894.

Columbus Day (Second Monday in October)   On Oct. 12, 1492, Christopher Columbus and his crew landed in the Bahama Islands after sailing across the Atlantic. First celebrated in 1792, Columbus Day was not officially recognized until 1909. Its observance is of special national pride to Italian-Americans who claim the Genoese Columbus for their own.

Veterans' Day (November 11)   Armistice Day, which marked the end of World War I on Nov. 11, 1918, was made a legal holiday in 1938. The name was changed to Veterans' Day in 1954 to honor all of America's veterans.

Thanksgiving (Fourth Thursday in November)   Thanksgiving Day was first observed in Plymouth Colony (Massachusetts) in 1621, the year in which the Pilgrims landed in the New World and gave thanks for their first harvest and for the new land they had colonized. President Lincoln proclaimed Thanksgiving a national holiday in 1863.

Christmas (December 25) See "Christian Holy Days."

▶ U.S. MINOR HOLIDAYS AND OCCASIONS

April Fool's Day (April 1)   A day for practical jokes, the origins of April Fool's Day are obscure, but it bears some resemblance to an ancient Roman festival honoring the goddess of nature.

Arbor Day (Last Friday in April)   Dedicated to trees and their preservation. Internationally it is observed on December 22.

Armed Forces Day (Third Saturday in May)   A day to honor of the members of the United States Armed Forces.

Cinco de Mayo (May 5)   Regional holiday in Mexico and celebrated in communities of Mexican-Americans; commemorates the victory of the Mexican army over French forces in 1862.

Constitution/Citizenship Day (September 17)   First observed by presidential proclamation in 1952, Citizenship Day falls on the same day as the old Constitution Day.

Daylight Saving Time   The idea of moving clocks ahead one hour to capture more daylight on summer evenings dates back to colonial times—Benjamin Franklin first suggested it in a 1784 essay—but it did not become a nationwide practice until the Uniform Time Act of 1966 (effective April of 1967). During World War I, World War II, and the energy crisis of 1973–74, the U.S. adopted daylight saving time all year round to save money on fuel. Daylight saving time is not observed in Hawaii, most of Arizona (except on the Navajo Indian Reservation) or in the territories of American Samoa, Guam, Puerto Rico and the Virgin Islands. In 2007, the *Energy Act of 2005* went into effect, and changed daylight saving time to begin at 2 A.M. on the second Sunday in March and end at 2 A.M. on the first Sunday in November. Remember to "Spring ahead, Fall back."

Earth Day (April 22)   First celebrated in 1970, Earth Day marks the birth of the modern environmental movement. Its observance is meant to encourage preservation of the environment.

Election Day (Tuesday after first Monday in November)   In years evenly divisible by four, presidential elections are held; in years evenly divisible by two, elections for all members of the House of Representatives and for one-third of the members of the Senate are held.

Father's Day (Third Sunday in June)   Father's Day was first observed in West Virginia in 1908, but it was not until 1972 that the president signed a Congressional resolution designating its official

Important Dates in the U.S. and Canada, 2011–16

Event	2011	2012	2013	2014	2015	2016
New Year's Day[1]	Jan. 1	Jan. 1	Jan. 1	Jan. 1	Jan. 1	Jan. 1
Martin Luther King Day[1]	Jan. 17	Jan. 16	Jan. 21	Jan. 20	Jan. 19	Jan. 18
Groundhog Day	Feb. 2	Feb. 2	Feb. 2	Feb. 2	Feb. 2	Feb. 2
St. Valentine's Day	Feb. 14	Feb. 14	Feb. 14	Feb. 14	Feb. 14	Feb. 14
Susan B. Anthony Day	Feb. 15	Feb. 15	Feb. 15	Feb. 15	Feb. 15	Feb. 15
Washington's Birthday[1]	Feb. 21	Feb. 20	Feb. 18	Feb. 17	Feb. 16	Feb. 15
Mardi Gras	Mar. 8	Feb. 21	Feb. 12	Mar. 4	Feb. 17	Feb. 9
Daylight Saving begins	Mar. 13	Mar. 11	Mar. 10	Mar. 9	Mar. 8	Mar. 13
St. Patrick's Day	Mar. 17	Mar. 17	Mar. 17	Mar. 17	Mar. 17	Mar. 17
April Fool's Day	Apr. 1	Apr. 1	Apr. 1	Apr. 1	Apr. 1	Apr. 1
Earth Day	Apr. 22	Apr. 22	Apr. 22	Apr. 22	Apr. 22	Apr. 22
Arbor Day	Apr. 29	Apr. 27	Apr. 26	Apr. 25	Apr. 24	Apr. 29
Cinco de Mayo	May 5	May 5	May 5	May 5	May 5	May 5
National Teacher Day	May 3	May 8	May 7	May 6	May 5	May 3
Mother's Day	May 8	May 13	May 12	May 11	May 10	May 8
Armed Forces Day	May 21	May 19	May 18	May 17	May 16	May 21
Victoria Day[2]	May 23	May 21	May 20	May 19	May 18	May 23
National Maritime Day	May 22	May 22	May 22	May 22	May 22	May 22
Memorial Day[1]	May 30	May 28	May 27	May 26	May 25	May 30
Flag Day	June 14	June 14	June 14	June 14	June 14	June 14
Father's Day	June 19	June 17	June 16	June 15	June 21	June 19
Canada Day[2]	July 1	July 1	July 1	July 1	July 1	July 1
Independence Day[1]	July 4	July 4	July 4	July 4	July 4	July 4
Labor Day[1, 2]	Sept. 5	Sept. 3	Sept. 2	Sept. 1	Sept. 7	Sept. 5
Constitution/Citizenship Day	Sept. 17	Sept. 17	Sept. 17	Sept. 17	Sept. 17	Sept. 17
Columbus Day[1]	Oct. 10	Oct. 8	Oct. 14	Oct. 13	Oct. 12	Oct. 10
Thanksgiving Day[2] (Can.)	Oct. 10	Oct. 8	Oct. 14	Oct. 13	Oct. 12	Oct. 10
United Nations Day	Oct. 24	Oct. 24	Oct. 24	Oct. 24	Oct. 24	Oct. 24
Halloween	Oct. 31	Oct. 31	Oct. 31	Oct. 31	Oct. 31	Oct. 31
Daylight Saving ends	Nov. 6	Nov. 4	Nov. 3	Nov. 2	Nov. 1	Nov. 6
Election Day (U.S.)	Nov. 8	Nov. 6	Nov. 5	Nov. 4	Nov. 3	Nov. 8
Veterans' (Armistice) Day[1]	Nov. 11	Nov. 11	Nov. 11	Nov. 11	Nov. 11	Nov. 11
Remembrance Day[2]	Nov. 11	Nov. 11	Nov. 11	Nov. 11	Nov. 11	Nov. 11
Thanksgiving Day[1] (U.S.)	Nov. 24	Nov. 22	Nov. 28	Nov. 27	Nov. 26	Nov. 24
Christmas Day[1, 2]	Dec. 25	Dec. 25	Dec. 25	Dec. 25	Dec. 25	Dec. 25
Boxing Day[2]	Dec. 26	Dec. 26	Dec. 26	Dec. 26	Dec. 26	Dec. 26
Kwanzaa[3]	Dec. 26	Dec. 26	Dec. 26	Dec. 26	Dec. 26	Dec. 26
New Year's Eve	Dec. 31	Dec. 31	Dec. 31	Dec. 31	Dec. 31	Dec. 31

Note: 1. Federal holiday in U.S. 2. Federal holiday in Canada. 3. First day of seven-day holiday.

observance. Father's Day is a uniquely American institution.

Flag Day (June 14)   The first observance of Flag Day was in 1877, the centenary of the adoption of the Flag Resolution, which adopted the design of the American flag flown today. President Truman signed the Flag Day Bill in 1949.

Groundhog Day (February 2)   On this day the groundhog peeks out of his burrow to look for his shadow. If he sees his shadow, six weeks of winter will follow; if he doesn't, spring is just around the corner.

Halloween (October 31)   All Hallow's Eve (the day before the feast of All Saints in the Christian calendar) began as a pagan custom honoring the dead and a celebration of autumn. The wearing of costumes can be traced to medieval religious practice in which parishioners dressed as saints and angels and paraded through the churchyard. The modern practice of "trick or treat" is of American origin with no apparent historical basis.

Kwanzaa (or Kwanza)   This secular celebration by African-Americans commemorates their African heritage and emphasizes the role of family and community. It begins on Dec. 26 and lasts for seven days; on each day one candle of a candelabrum is lighted. Kwanzaa was developed by Maulana Karenga and was first observed in 1966.

Mother's Day (Second Sunday in May)   Conceived by Anne M. Jarvis of Philadelphia, where it was first observed, as a day for children to pay tribute to their mothers, this was declared a national holiday by presidential proclamation in 1914.

National Maritime Day (May 22)   Designated by presidential proclamation in 1935, this commemorates the anniversary of the departure of the SS *Savannah* on the first successful transoceanic voyage of a steam-powered vessel, in 1819. It is also a day of remembrance of merchant mariners who died in defense of their country.

National Teacher Day (Tuesday of first full week in May)   This is a day when students and communities around the country honor their teachers and the teaching profession.

St. Patrick's Day (March 17)   A day in honor of Ireland's patron saint, St. Patrick's Day is a religious, political and social event rolled into one. In Ireland, St. Patrick is honored by church ceremonies and a three-day period of devotion. In the

United States, March 17 is celebrated with parades and the "wearing of the green."

St. Valentine's Day (February 14) Originally an occasion to honor two Christian saints martyred by the Roman Emperor Claudius (A.D. 214–270), since the Middle Ages St. Valentine's Day has been dedicated to lovers, probably because it is believed to be the day that birds choose their mates.

Susan B. Anthony Day (February 15) Anthony (1820–1906) was one of the first women's rights advocates, working especially for equal suffrage—that is, the right to vote. She was a cofounder and later president of the National Woman Suffrage Association.

United Nations Day (October 24) This commemorates the ratification of the United Nations Charter on this date in 1945 by the five permanent members of the Security Council and a majority of the other Charter signatories.

▶ **CHRISTIAN HOLY DAYS**

Christmas is the celebration of Christ's birth. The exact date of his birth is unknown, but the date of December 25 was probably chosen because it coincided with the ancient mid-winter celebrations honoring pagan deities. The 12 days of Christmas fall between Christmas and Epiphany (January 6), the day the Wise Men visited the Christ child.

Advent, a religious season that begins on the Sunday nearest November 30 and lasts until Christmas, both celebrates the birth of Jesus and anticipates His second coming. At one time Advent was a solemn season observed by fasting, but this is no longer the case.

Easter is the most important holy day in the Christian religion. It is the celebration of Christ's Resurrection from the dead, which gave Christians the hope of salvation and eternal life. Although Easter is only one day, the full observance of the holy day spans from Septuagesima Sunday (70 days before Easter Sunday), which may fall as early as January, to Pentecost, which can occur as late as June.

Easter always falls on the first Sunday after the first full moon after the vernal equinox on March 21. Thus, Easter can fall no earlier than March 23 (if the first full moon is a Saturday March 22) and no later than April 24 (if the first full moon is a Sunday, April 17).

Mardi Gras (Shrove Tuesday; Fat Tuesday) Originally a day of penance, the last day before the beginning of Lent is now celebrated with feasting and merrymaking.

Ash Wednesday derives its name from the rite of burning the palms carried on the Palm Sunday of the year before and using the ashes to mark worshippers' foreheads with a cross.

Lent, a 40-day period of fasting and penitence beginning on Ash Wednesday and ending on Easter Sunday, Lent is traditionally observed by fasting, performing acts of charity, and by giving up certain pleasures and amusements.

Palm Sunday, the Sunday before Easter, celebrates Jesus'triumphant entry into Jerusalem where palm branches were spread before Him to honor His path.

Holy (Maundy) Thursday, is the anniversary of the Last Supper. The traditional services mark three events that occurred during the week before Jesus was crucified: He washed the feet of His 12 disciples; He instituted the Eucharist (the sacrament of Holy Communion); and He was arrested and imprisoned.

Good Friday marks the day of Christ's Crucifixion. The holy day is observed with fasting, mourning, and penitence.

Holy Saturday is the day that anticipates the Resurrection. In the Catholic church, special vigils are held on Holy Saturday evening.

Easter Sunday marks the day of Christ's Resurrection. Many worshippers celebrate the holy day with sunrise services, a custom believed to be inspired by the example of Mary Magdalene, who went to Christ's tomb "early, while it was yet dark."

Pentecost (literally, "fiftieth day") is the end of the full ecclesiastical observance of Easter. It takes place on the seventh Sunday after Easter Sunday and commemorates the descent of the Holy Spirit upon the Apostles.

The Annunciation This holy day marks the archangel Gabriel's announcement to Mary that she would conceive and give birth to Jesus. It is celebrated by Roman Catholics on March 25; it is not observed by Protestant denominations.

Trinity Sunday The Sunday after Pentecost, this occasion honors the Father, Son and Holy Spirit. It was declared a part of the church calendar in 1334 by Pope John XXII and is observed by Roman Catholics and by some Protestant denominations.

Corpus Christi This feast celebrates the presence of the body (*corpus*) of Christ in the Eucharist. At one time this was the principal feast of the church year, but today it is observed only by Catholic churches. Corpus Christi is celebrated on the Thursday following Trinity Sunday.

All Saints' Day, celebrated on November 1, honors all of the Christian saints. In America, many churches mark the Sunday nearest November 1 as a day to pay tribute to those who have died during the year. All Saints' Day is observed primarily by Roman Catholics.

Calendar of Christian Holy Days, 2011–16

Year A.D.	Ash Wednesday	Good Friday	Easter Sunday	Pentecost	Trinity Sunday	Advent
2011	Mar. 9	Apr. 22	Apr. 24	June 12	June 19	Nov. 27
2012	Feb. 22	Apr. 6	Apr. 8	May 27	June 3	Dec. 2
2013	Feb. 13	Mar. 29	Mar. 31	May 19	May 26	Dec. 1
2014	Mar. 5	Apr. 18	Apr. 20	June 8	June 15	Nov. 30
2015	Feb. 18	Apr. 3	Apr. 5	May 24	May 31	Nov. 29
2016	Feb. 10	Mar. 25	Mar. 27	May 15	May 22	Nov. 27

Source: www.godweb.org/christian_calendar

Holy Days of Obligation are feast days in the Catholic calendar observed by attendance at Mass and rest from unnecessary work. Six holy days of obligation are observed in the United States:

1. Solemnity of Mary, Jan. 1 (formerly, Christ's circumcision, the first shedding of his blood, was commemorated on this day).

2. Ascension (of Jesus to Heaven), 40 days after Easter

3. Assumption of the Blessed Virgin into Heaven, Aug. 15

4. All Saints' Day, Nov. 1

5. Mary's Immaculate Conception (honoring the Mother of God as the only person conceived without original sin), Dec. 8

6. Christmas, Dec. 25

▶ THE JEWISH CALENDAR

The months of the Jewish year are Tishri, Heshvan, Kislev, Tebet, Shebat, Adar, Nisan, Iyar, Sivan, Tammuz, Ab and Elul. The Jewish era dates from the year of the creation (*anno mundii* or A.M.), which is equal to 3761 B.C.), thus 5771 began in 2010 and ends in 2011 of the Gregorian calendar. (Tishri, the first month of the Jewish year, falls in either September or October of the Gregorian calendar.)

Because the Jewish calendar is a blend of solar and lunar calendars, there are intercalated months to keep the lunar and solar years in alignment. (Intercalation is the insertion of an extra day, month, or other unit—February 29 in a leap year, for example—into a calendar). The intercalated month is called Adar Sheni or Veadar—Second Adar.

▶ JEWISH HOLY DAYS

Sabbath is the first and most important Jewish holy day, occurring each week from sundown Friday to sundown Saturday. It is a day of rest and spiritual growth, given to men and women so they will remember the sweetness of freedom and keep it. Sabbath takes precedence over all other observances.

Rosh Hashanah (New Year) held to be the birthday of the world, is also called the Day of Judgment and Remembrance, and the day of the shofar—a ram's horn—which is blown to remind Jews of Abraham's willingness to sacrifice his son Isaac. The holiday takes place on the first and second days of Tishri (in September or October).

Yom Kippur (Day of Atonement) concludes the 10 days of repentance that Rosh Hashanah begins and takes place from sundown on the ninth day of Tishri until sundown on the 10th. The observance begins with the recitation of the most famous passage in the Jewish liturgy—*Kol Nidre*—which nullifies unfulfilled vows made in the past year. The entire day is spent praying and fasting.

Sukkoth (Tabernacles) is a harvest festival celebrated from the 15th through the 22nd of Tishri. Sukkoth also commemorates the journey of the Jewish people through the wilderness to the land of Israel. Jewish families take their meals this week in a roughly constructed *sukkah* (booth)—a reminder of an agricultural society, of the Exodus, and of how precarious and fragile life can be. On the Simchath Torah, the 23rd of Tishri, a congregation finishes reading the last book of the Torah and immediately starts again with the first.

Hanukkah (Chanukah, Feast of Dedication; Festival of Lights) The importance of the eight-day feast, which begins on the 25th day of Kislev, is its commemoration of the first war in human history fought in the cause of religious freedom. The Maccabees vanquished not just the military threat to Judaism, but the internal forces for assimilation into the Hellenistic culture of Israel's rulers. Jews light candles for eight nights to mark a miracle: a day's supply of oil found in the recaptured Temple which, according to religious myth, burned for eight days.

Purim (Feast of Lots) set on the 14th day of Adar, is another celebration of survival, noting the events described in the Book of Esther. At Purim, Jews rejoice at Queen Esther's and her cousin Mordecai's defeat of Haman, the Persian King Ahaseurus's advisor who plotted to slaughter all the Persian Jews around 400 B.C.

Pesach (Passover) beginning on the 15th day of Nisan and lasting seven days, commemorates the exodus of the Hebrews from Egypt in about 1300 B.C. The name Passover also recalls God's sparing (passing over) the Jewish first-born during the plagues upon the land brought by God through Moses. The holiday is marked by eating only unleavened foods, participating in a *seder*, or special meal, and reading the *Haggadah*, the story of the Hebrews' deliverance from Egypt.

Shavuoth (Feast of Weeks) is observed on the sixth or seventh day of Sivan. Originally an agricultural festival, Shavuoth is a celebration of the revelation of the Torah at Mt. Sinai, by which God established his covenant with the Jewish people.

▶ THE ISLAMIC CALENDAR

The 12 months of the Islamic year are: Muharram, Safar, Rab'i I, Rab'i II, Jomada I, Jomada II, Rajab, Sha'ban, Ramadan, Shawwal, Dhu al-Qa'dah, Dhu al-Hijja. The Islamic calendar is based on a lunar

Calendar of Jewish Holy Days, 5771–77

Year AM	Rosh Hashanah[1]	Yom Kippur	Sukkoth[1]	Hanukkah[1]	Purim	Pesach[1]	Shabuoth[1]
5771	Sept. 9, 2010	Sept. 18, 2010	Sept. 23, 2010	Dec. 2, 2010	Mar. 20, 2011	Apr. 19, 2011	June 8, 2011
5772	Sept. 29, 2011	Oct. 8, 2011	Oct. 13, 2011	Dec. 21, 2011	Mar. 8, 2012	Apr. 7, 2012	Mar. 27, 2102
5773	Sept. 17, 2012	Sept. 26, 2012	Oct. 1, 2012	Dec. 9, 2012	Feb. 24, 2013	Mar. 26, 2013	May 15, 2013
5774	Sept. 5, 2013	Sept. 14, 2013	Sept. 19, 2013	Nov. 28, 2013	Mar. 16, 2014	Apr. 15, 2014	June 4, 2014
5775	Sept. 25, 2014	Oct. 4, 2014	Oct. 9, 2014	Dec. 17, 2014	Mar. 5, 2015	Apr. 4, 2015	May 24, 2015
5776	Sept. 14, 2015	Sept. 23, 2015	Sept. 28, 2015	Dec. 7, 2015	Mar. 24, 2016	Apr. 23, 2016	June 12, 2016
5777	Oct. 3, 2016	Oct. 12, 2016	Oct. 17, 2016	Dec. 25, 2016	Mar. 12, 2017	Apr. 10, 2017	May 30, 2017

Note: The Jewish day begins and ends at sundown. Thus, all holidays begin at sundown of the day preceding the date shown. 1. Multiday holiday; first day of holiday shown. **Source:** B'nai B'rith.

year of 12 months of 30 and 29 days (alternating every month) and the year is equal to 354 days. It runs in cycles of 30 years, of which the 2nd, 5th, 7th, 10th, 13th, 16th, 18th, 21st, 24th, 26th, and 29th are leap years. Leap years have 355 days, the extra day being added to the last month, Dhu al-Hijja. There are no intercalated months or leap years, so the Islamic year does not keep a constant relationship to the solar year—which dictates the seasons—and months occur about 10 or 11 days earlier than in the year before.

The caliph Abu Bakr adopted A.D. 622, the year of the *hejira* (Mohammed's migration from Mecca to Medina), as the first year of Islam. However, dating of the Muslim era varies throughout the Islamic world. In some countries, the year of the Muslim era is obtained by subtracting 622 from the Gregorian year; 2011 A.D. equals 1389 A.H. (anno hegirae, in the year of the hejira).

Other countries (Saudi Arabia, Yemen, and the principalities of the Persian Gulf) continue to use a purely lunar year. To approximate the Muslim era equivalent of the Gregorian year, subtract 622 (the year of hejira in the Gregorian calendar) from the current year, and multiply the result by 1.031 (days in the year of the Gregorian calendar divided by days in the lunar year): 2011 A.D. = (2011–622) x 1.031 = 1432 A.H. The accompanying calendar uses this method of calculation.

▶ MUSLIM HOLY DAYS

Ramadan The ninth month of the Islamic calendar is the Islamic faith's holiest period. To honor the month in which the Koran was revealed, all adult Muslims of sound body and mind fast, eschewing food, water, or even a kiss between the hours of sunrise and sunset. Exempted from the fast are women in menstruation or childbirth bleeding, the chronically ill, or people on a journey, all of whom must make up the fast days at a later date.

Id al-Fitr This day of feasting is celebrated at the end of Ramadan. To mark the fast's break, worshippers also attend an early morning service, Salat-ul-'Id, at which they give alms in staple foodstuffs or their monetary value.

Id al-Adha The Feast of Sacrifice takes place on the 10th day of Dhu al-Hijja, the last month of the year and the season of the *haj*, or pilgrimage. The day begins with a service in the mosques or other places of gathering, and for those who are not pilgrims, continues with the ritual slaughter of a sheep in commemoration of God's ransom of Abraham's son from sacrifice. At least a third of the meat of the animal is to be given in charity.

Fridays At noontime, Muslims attend mosque or comparable gathering places to say the congregational Friday prayer that ends the week. While Friday is the holy day of the weekly Muslim calendar, it is not a Sabbath comparable to Christian Sundays or Jewish Saturdays, and there are no restrictions on work or other worldly enterprises.

▶ THE HINDU YEAR

The Hindu year consists of 12 months: Caitra, Vaisakha, Jyaistha, Asadha, Sravana, Bhadrapada, Asvina, Karttika, Margasivsa, Pansa, Magha and Phalguna. Calendrically, holidays are of two types, lunar and solar.

Solar holidays in the Hindu calendar include:

Mesasamkranti The beginning of the new astrological year, when the Sun enters the constellation Aries.

Makaraj-Samkranti The winter solstice, when the sun enters the constellation Capricorn.

Mahavisuva Day is New Year's Eve.

Lunar holidays in the Hindu calendar include:

Ramanavami (Caitra 9) celebrates the birth of Rama, in Hindu folklore, the epitome of chivalry, courage and obedience to sacred law. Considered an incarnation of Vishnu, his name is synonymous with God.

Rathayatra (Asadha 2) The pilgrimage of the chariot festival of Orissa.

Janmastami (Sravana 8) The birthday of Krishna, an incarnation of the supreme deity, Vishnu, celebrated as a philosopher-king and hero.

Dasahra (Asvina 7–10) commemorates Rama's victory over the demon Ravana.

Laksmipuja (Asvina 15) honors Laksmi, goddess of good fortune.

Dipavali (Karttika 15) Festival of lights and exchanging of presents.

Mahasivaratri (Magha 13) which honors the god Shiva, one of the three supreme Hindu gods. Shiva, whose name means "Auspicious One," is a god of both reproduction and destruction.

Calendar of Muslim Holy Days, 1432–36

Year A.H. (A.D.)	New Year's Day Muharram	Ramadan	Id al-Fitr, Shawwal	Id al-Adha, Dhu al-Hijja
1432 (2010–11)	Dec. 7, 2010	Aug. 1, 2011	Aug. 30, 2011	Nov. 6, 2011
1433 (2011–12)	Nov. 26, 2011	July 20, 2012	Aug. 19, 2012	Oct. 26, 2012
1434 (2012–13)	Nov. 15, 2012	July 9, 2013	Aug. 8, 2013	Oct. 15, 2013
1435 (2013–14)	Nov. 4, 2013	June 28, 2014	July 28, 2014	Oct. 4, 2014
1436 (2014–15)	Nov. 3, 2014	June 18, 2015	July 17, 2015	Sept. 23, 2015

Note: The Islamic calendar is based on calculation and depends on actual sighting of the moon. Therefore the dates above are estimates. For exact dates, contact your local masjid, organization, or scholar. **Source:** Islamic Shura Council of North America.

Months of the Year

Gregorian	Hebrew	Hindu	Muslim
January	Shebat	Magha	Muharram
February	Adar	Phalguna	Safar
March	Nisan	Caitra	Rab'i I
April	Iyar	Vaisakha	Rab'i II
May	Sivan	Jyaistha	Jomada I
June	Tammuz	Asadha	Jomada II
July	Ab	Sravana	Rajab
August	Elul	Bhadrapada	Sha'ban
September	Tishri	Asvina	Ramadan
October	Heshvan	Karttika	Shawwal
November	Kislev	Margasivsa	Dhu al-Qa'dah
December	Tebet	Pansa	Dhu al-Hijja

Note: The months of the traditional (lunar) Muslim calendar occur at different times every year. Months in *italics* indicate the first month of the year in the respective calendars.

Astrological Calendar

Dates	Sign
January 20–February 18	Aquarius, the water bearer
February 19–March 20	Pisces, the fishes
March 21–April 19	Aries, the ram
April 20–May 20	Taurus, the bull
May 21–June 20	Gemini, the twins
June 21–July 22	Cancer, the crab
July 23–August 22	Leo, the lion
August 23–September 22	Virgo, the virgin
September 23–October 22	Libra, the scales
October 23–November 21	Scorpio, the scorpion
November 22–December 21	Sagittarius, the archer
December 22–January 19	Capricorn, the goat

Birthstones

Month	Stone
January	Garnet
February	Amethyst
March	Aquamarine, Bloodstone
April	Diamond
May	Emerald
June	Alexandrite, Moonstone, Pearl
July	Ruby
August	Peridot, Sardonyx
September	Sapphire
October	Opal, Tourmaline
November	Topaz
December	Turquoise, Lapis Lazuli

Wedding Anniversaries

Anniversary	Type of gift	Anniversary	Type of gift
1st	Paper	14th	Ivory
2nd	Cotton	15th	Crystal
3rd	Leather	20th	China
4th	Fruit, flowers	25th	Silver
5th	Wood	30th	Pearl
6th	Sugar	35th	Coral
7th	Copper, wool	40th	Ruby
8th	Bronze, pottery	45th	Sapphire
9th	Pottery, willow	50th	Gold
10th	Tin	55th	Emerald
11th	Steel	60th	Diamond
12th	Silk, linen	70th	Platinum
13th	Lace		

Chinese Years, 1900–2019

The Chinese New Year is the second New Moon after the winter solstice. The Chinese Year 4708 began on February 14, 2010; Chinese Year 4709 begins on February 3, 2011 and ends January 22, 2012.

Year of the Rat	1900	1912	1924	1936	1948	1960	1972	1984	1996	2008
. . . Ox	1901	1913	1925	1937	1949	1961	1973	1985	1997	2009
. . . Tiger	1902	1914	1926	1938	1950	1962	1974	1986	1998	2010
. . . Hare (Rabbit)	1903	1915	1927	1939	1951	1963	1975	1987	1999	2011
. . . Dragon	1904	1916	1928	1940	1952	1964	1976	1988	2000	2012
. . . Snake	1905	1917	1929	1941	1953	1965	1977	1989	2001	2013
. . . Horse	1906	1918	1930	1942	1954	1966	1978	1990	2002	2014
. . . Sheep (Goat)	1907	1919	1931	1943	1955	1967	1979	1991	2003	2015
. . . Monkey	1908	1920	1932	1944	1956	1968	1980	1992	2004	2016
. . . Rooster	1909	1921	1933	1945	1957	1969	1981	1993	2005	2017
. . . Dog	1910	1922	1934	1946	1958	1970	1982	1994	2006	2018
. . . Pig	1911	1923	1935	1947	1959	1971	1983	1995	2007	2019

ASTRONOMICAL EVENTS, 2011

The main astronomical events included in this section are the phases of the Moon, the Moon's perigee (when it is closest to the Earth) and apogee (when it is farthest away), lunar and solar eclipses, and the visibility of the planets.

▶PHASES OF THE MOON

The relative position of the Earth, Moon and Sun affect what, if any, part of the Moon we can see il-luminated by the Sun during our night. A *new moon* occurs when the Moon is precisely aligned between the Earth and the Sun, making the Moon invisible from the Earth. When the Moon is at *first quarter* (90 degrees from the Sun relative to the Earth), its sunlit part appears in the shape of a D (in the Southern Hemisphere, a backward D). A *full moon*, when the Moon shows an almost fully illuminated face, occurs when the Moon is 180 degrees around the sky from the Sun. The *last quarter* (or third quarter) occurs when the Moon is again moving toward a position between the Earth and the Sun, and it appears as a backward D (a normal D in the Southern Hemisphere). Inter-

Phases of the Moon, 2011

New moon				First quarter				Full moon				Last quarter			
Month	d	h	m	Month	d	h	m	Month	d	h	m	Month	d	h	m
Jan.	04	09	03					Jan.	19	21	21	Jan.	26	12	57
Feb.	03	02	31	Jan.	12	11	31	Feb.	18	08	36	Feb.	24	23	26
Mar.	02	20	46	Feb.	11	07	18	Mar.	19	18	10	Mar.	26	12	07
Apr.	03	14	32	Mar.	12	23	45	Apr.	18	02	44	Apr	25	02	47
May	03	06	51	Apr.	11	12	05	May	17	11	09	May	24	18	52
June	01	21	03	May	10	20	33	June	15	20	14	June	23	11	48
July	01	08	54	June	09	02	11	July	15	06	40	July	23	05	02
July	30	18	40	July	08	06	29	Aug.	13	18	57	Aug.	21	21	54
Aug.	29	03	04	Aug.	06	11	08	Sept.	12	09	27	Sept.	20	13	39
Sept.	27	11	09	Sept.	04	17	39	Oct.	12	02	06	Oct.	20	03	30
Oct.	26	19	56	Oct.	04	03	15	Nov.	10	20	16	Nov.	18	15	09
Nov.	25	06	10	Nov.	02	16	38	Dec.	10	14	36	Dec.	18	00	48
Dec.	24	18	06	Dec.	02	09	52								

Note: Shown in Universal Time (UT). To convert to local time, see "Timing Planetary Phenomena."
Source: U.S. Naval Observatory, *Astronomical Phenomena for the Year 2011* (2010).

mediate phases are the *crescent moon*—between the new Moon and first quarter, and between the last quarter and new Moon; and the *gibbous moon*, occurring between the half and the full Moon. The full cycle from one phase through all the other phases takes about 29.53 days and is called a *lunation*.

▶ VISIBILITY OF THE PLANETS, 2011

Mercury can only be seen low in the east before sunrise, or low in the west after sunset (about the time of the beginning or end of twilight). It is visible in the mornings between the following approximate dates: January 1 to February 13, April 18 to June 5, August 25 to September 19, and December 10 to December 31. The planet is brighter at the end of each period (the best conditions in northern latitudes occur in the first half of January and in the second half of December, and in southern latitudes from late April to the end of the third week of May). It is visible in the evenings between the following approximate dates: March 7 to April 2, June 20 to August 9, and October 12 to November 28. The planet is brighter at the beginning of each period (the best conditions in northern latitudes occur in the second half of March and in southern latitudes in July from the beginning of the second week).

Venus is a brilliant object in the morning sky from the beginning of the year until near the end of second week of July when it becomes too close to the Sun for observation. During the second half of September it reappears in the evening sky where it stays until the end of the year. Venus is in conjunction with Jupiter on May 1 and with Venus on May 22.

Mars is too close to the Sun for observation until mid-April when it appears in the morning sky in Pisces. Its westward elongation gradually increases as it passes through Aries, Taurus, Gemini, Cancer, and into Leo. Mars is in conjunction with Mercury on April 19 and May 20, with Jupiter on May 1, and with Venus on May 22.

Jupiter can be seen at the beginning of the year in the evening sky in Pisces, moves in Cetus in late

Major Meteor Showers, 2011

Date[1]	Time (UTC)	Event	ZHR[2]
Jan. 4	01:14	Quadrantid Shower	120
Apr. 22	22:44	Lyrid Shower	20
May 5	11:59	Eta Aquarid Shower	60
July 28	13:47	Delta Aquarid Shower	20
Aug. 13	05:41	Perseid Shower	90
Oct. 21	21:59	Orionid Shower	20
Nov. 5	22:27	South Taurid Shower	10
Nov. 12	21:43	North Taurid Shower	15
Nov. 18	04:01	Leonid Shower	15
Dec. 14	17:11	Geminid Shower	120
Dec. 23	02:00	Ursid Shower	10

Note: Shown in Universal Coordinated Time (UTC). To convert to local time, see "Timing Planetary Phenomena." 1. Beginning of shower. Periods of showers vary in length, from several days to several weeks. 2. ZHR= Zenithal Hourly Rate, or maximum number of visible meteors per hour under ideal atmospheric conditions. Source: Sky Events Calendar, Fred Espenak and Sumit Dutta (NASA's GSFC).

February and back in Pisces in early March. From late March it becomes too close to the Sun for observation. It reappears in the morning sky in the second half of April and moves in Aries in early June. Its westward elongation gradually increases and from the beginning of August it can be seen for more than half the night. It is at opposition on October 29 when it is visible throughout the night. Its eastward elongation gradually decreases and at the end of the first week of December it passes once more into Pisces. Jupiter is in conjunction with Mercury on March 16 and May 10, with Mars on May 1 and with Venus on May 11.

Saturn rises shortly after midnight at the beginning of the year in Virgo and remains in this constellation throughout the year. Saturn is at opposition on April 4 when it can be seen throughout the night, and from early July until late September it is visible only in the evening sky. It then becomes too close to the Sun for observation until the end of October, after which it can be seen in the morning sky for the rest of the year.

Uranus is visible at the beginning of the year in the evening sky in Pisces and remains in this constellation throughout the year. From the beginning of March it becomes too close to the Sun for observation and reappears in the second wekk of April in the morning sky. Uranus is at opposition on September 26. Its eastward elongation gradually decreases and from late December it can only be seen in the evening sky.

Neptune is visible at the beginning of the year in the evening sky in Capricornus, moves into Aquarius in the second half of January and remains in his constellation for the rest of the year. In late January it becomes too close to the Sun for observation and reappears in the second week of March in the morning sky. Neptune is at opposition on August 22 and from late November can be seen only in the evening sky.

Do not confuse
(1) Jupiter with Mercury in mid-March and in the first half of May and with Mars in the late April to early May; on all occasions Jupiter is the brighter object. (2) Mercury with Mars in the second half of April when Mars is the brighter object. (3) Venus with Mercury from late April to late May and mid-October to late November, with Jupiter in the first half of May, with Mars from mid-May to early June and with Saturn in late September; on all occasions Venus is the brighter object. (4) Mercury with Mars in mid-May when Mercury is the brighter object.

▶ TIMING PLANETARY PHENOMENA
The times for astronomical data shown here are expressed in Universal Coordinated Time (UTC) which is the standard time of the Greenwich meridian (0 degrees of longitude) also known as Greenwich mean time (GMT). To convert to local time, determine your longitude and subtract 1 hour for every 15 degrees of longitude west of 0 degrees; or add 1 hour for every 15 degrees of longitude east of 0 degrees.

The first new moon of 2011 occurs Jan. 4 at 0903 hours in UTC. The equivalent time in New York (74°W) is five hours earlier at 0403 hours (4:03 A.M.); in Chicago (87°W), 6 hours earlier at 3:03 A.M.; in Denver (105°W), 7 hours earlier, or 2:03 A.M.; and in San Francisco (122°W), 8 hours earlier, or 1:03 A.M. (To obtain the P.M. equivalent of UTC times later than 1200, subtract 12.) Note that local times may differ from these standard times, especially when daylight savings time is in effect.

▶ ECLIPSES
Eclipses of the Moon
A lunar eclipse occurs when the Sun, Earth and Moon are in a straight line and the shadow of the Earth falls on the Moon. There are three kinds of lunar eclipse. A total eclipse occurs when the Moon passes completely into the Earth's total umbra, or shadow, so the Sun cannot be seen from the Moon. A partial eclipse occurs when only part of the Earth's umbra falls across the Moon and the Sun is partially visible from some places on the Moon. A penumbral eclipse occurs when only the Earth's penumbra (partial shadow) shades the Moon; and from the Moon one's view of the Sun would be only partially blocked by the Earth. It is usually difficult to detect a penumbral eclipse from the Earth.

During 2011, there will be to total eclipses of the Moon. (All times shown in universal coordinated time (UTC). To convert to local time, see *Timing Planetary Phenomena*.)

June 15, 2011 – Total eclipse
Eclipse begins at 17:23 and ends at 23:02; the total phase begins at 19:22 and ends at 21:03.
It is visible from South America, Africa, Europe, the Middle East, Asia, Australia, Antarctica, and the Atlantic, Indian, and southwestern Pacific Ocean.

December 10, 2011 – Total eclipse
Eclipse begins at 11:32 and ends at 17:32; the total phase begins at 14:06 and ends at 14:58.
It is visible from Africa, Europe, the Middle East, Asia, Australia, North America, Greenland, and the Indian, Pacific, and Arctic Oceans.

Eclipses of the Sun
A solar eclipse occurs when the Moon passes between the Earth and the Sun; there are three types. A *total eclipse* occurs when the Moon's shadow completely covers the Sun and the sky turns dark. Total eclipses occur along a narrow path (typically 100–200 miles wide) called the track of totality and last only a few minutes at any point on the track. A *partial eclipse* occurs when the Moon covers only a portion of the Sun. A total eclipse may be only partial in less than optimum viewing locations. An *annular* (ring-shaped) *eclipse* occurs when the Moon is too far from the Earth to completely cover the Sun, so that at the height of the eclipse, a ring of light surrounds the Moon. In 2011, there will be four partial eclipses of the Sun.

January 4, 2011 – Partial eclipse
Eclipse begins at 06:40 and ends at 11:01.
It is visible from Europea, northern Africa, the Middle East, and western Asia.

June 1, 2011 – Partial eclipse
Eclipse begins at 19:25 and ends at 23:07.
It is visible from eastern Asia, northern North America, Greenland, and the Arctic Ocean.

July 1, 2011 – Partial eclipse
Eclipse begins at 07:53 and ends at 09:23.
It is visible from the southern Indian Ocean.

November 25, 2011 – Partial eclipse
Eclipse begins at 04:23 and ends at 08:18.
It is visible from Antarctica, extreme southern Africa, New Zealand, and the extreme southern Atlantic, extreme southern Indian, and extreme southern Pacific Oceans.

Visibility of the Planets, 2011		
Planet	**Morning Twilight**	**Evening Twilight**
Venus	Jan. 1–July 11	Sept. 23–Dec. 31
Mars	Apr. 17–Dec. 31	N.A.
Jupiter	Apr. 21–Oct. 29	Jan. 1–Mar. 24
		Oct. 29–Dec. 31
Saturn	Jan. 1–Apr. 4	Apr. 4–Sept. 26
	Oct. 31–Dec. 31	

Source: U.S. Naval Observatory, *Astronomical Phenomena for the Year 2011* (2010).

The United States of America shares the North American continent with Canada, Mexico and the Central American nations. The 48 conterminous states lie in a broad land mass from approximately 24°N to 49°N from south to north, and 67°W to 124°W from east to west. It is bordered by Canada, on the south by Mexico and the Gulf of Mexico, on the east by the Atlantic Ocean, and on the west by the Pacific Ocean. The two nonconterminous states of Alaska and Hawaii are located to the northwest on the North American continent, and in the Pacific Ocean Basin approximately 2,400 miles southwest of the state of California, respectively.

▶ POLITICAL-GEOGRAPHIC DIVISIONS

The U.S. Census Bureau groups the states in a number of divisions and sub-divisions.

Northeast
New England Maine, New Hampshire, Vermont, Massachusetts, Rhode Island, Connecticut.
Middle Atlantic New York, New Jersey, Pennsylvania.

Midwest
East North Central Ohio, Indiana, Illinois, Michigan, Wisconsin.
West North Central Minnesota, Iowa, Missouri, North Dakota, South Dakota, Nebraska, Kansas.

South
South Atlantic Delaware, Maryland, District of Columbia, Virginia, West Virginia, North Carolina, South Carolina, Georgia, Florida.
East South Central Kentucky, Tennessee, Alabama, Mississippi.
West South Central Arkansas, Louisiana, Oklahoma, Texas.

West
Mountain Montana, Idaho, Wyoming, Colorado, New Mexico, Arizona, Utah, Nevada.
Pacific Washington, Oregon, California, Alaska, Hawaii.

▶ PHYSIOGRAPHIC REGIONS

The physiographic regions, or the primary geological features and landforms, of the United States are:

Atlantic and Gulf Coast Plains
These run from the islands of southern New England, Cape Cod, and Long Island, through New Jersey, Delaware, Maryland, Virginia, North Carolina, South Carolina, Georgia, Florida, Alabama, Mississippi, Louisiana, Texas; includes lower Mississippi Valley in Arkansas, Missouri, Tennessee.

Appalachian System
The Appalachian System is divided into five parts:
New England White Mountains (New Hampshire), Green Mountains (Vermont), Champlain Lowland and Hudson Valley (Vermont, New York), Catskill Mountains (New York).
The Piedmont Pennsylvania, Virginia, North Carolina, South Carolina, Georgia, Alabama.
Great Smoky and Blue Ridge Mountains Pennsylvania (Poconos), [discontinuous], Virginia, North Carolina, Georgia.
Ridge and Valley Pennsylvania, West Virginia, Virginia, Kentucky, Tennessee, Alabama.
Appalachian Plateau Pennsylvania, Ohio, West Virginia, Kentucky, Tennessee, Alabama.

Canadian (or Laurentian) Shield
This region covers much of eastern Canada and extends into the U.S. in two places:
Adirondack Mountains New York.
Superior Upland Upper Michigan, Wisconsin, Minnesota.

Central Lowland
The Central Lowland includes most of the U.S. interior, and is divided into four parts:
Interior Lowlands Ohio, Kentucky, Tennessee.
Mississippi Great Lakes Basin Ohio, Indiana, Illinois, Michigan, Wisconsin, Iowa, North Dakota, South Dakota.
Interior Highlands Ozark Mountains: Missouri, Arkansas, Oklahoma; Ouachita Mountains: Arkansas, Oklahoma.
Great Plains North Dakota, South Dakota, Nebraska, Kansas, Oklahoma, Texas, Montana, Wyoming, Colorado, New Mexico.

Cordilleran Province
Rocky Mountains New Mexico, Colorado, Wyoming, Montana.

Intermontane Range
This range is divided into four sections:
Colorado Plateau Colorado, Utah, New Mexico, Arizona (including Grand Canyon).
Basin and Range Plateau Nevada, Utah (including Wasatch Range).
Desert Basin and Range California (including Death Valley), Arizona.
Snake and Columbia River Basins Idaho, Washington, Oregon.

U.S. Geographic Extremes

Because the Aleutian Islands wrap around the Greenwich Meridian, Alaska technically contains both the easternmost and westernmost points in the United States.

Extreme	Contiguous 48 states (Long. or Lat.)	U.S. (Long. or Lat.)[1]
North	Northwest Angle Inlet, Minn. 49° 23' N	Point Barrow, Alaska, 71° 23' N
South	Key West, Fla. 24° 33' N	Ka Lae, Hawaii 18° 55' N
East	West Quoddy Head, Maine, 66° 57' W	Pochnoi Point, Alaska, 179° 52' E
West	Capa Alava, Wash. 124° 44' W	Amatignak Island, Alaska 179° 09' W

Note: 1. U.S. states only; does not include U.S. territories and possessions. **Source:** U.S. Geological Survey, Elevations and Distances in the United States, online edition. http://mapping.usgs.gov/isb/pubs/booklets/elvadist/elvadist.html.

Pacific Coastlands

This region is divided into four sections, three oriented north-south, the other east-west.
Cascade Mountains and Sierra Nevada Washington, Oregon, California, Nevada.
Puget Sound, Willamette Valley, and Central Valley Washington, Oregon, California.
Coast Ranges Washington, Oregon, California.
Los Angeles Extension Tehachapi Mountains (east-west), San Gabriel Mountains and San Bernardino Mountains.

▶ NATIONAL PARK SYSTEM

The National Park System of the U.S. began in March 1872 with the establishment of the Yellowstone National Park in the Territories of Montana and Wyoming, "as a public park or pleasuring ground for the benefit and enjoyment of the people" and was placed "under exclusive control of the Secretary of the Interior." The founding of Yellowstone began a worldwide national park movement and today more than 100 countries contain some 1,200 national parks or equivalent preserves.

President Woodrow Wilson created the National Park Service as a bureau within the Department of the Interior in 1916, and charged it with protecting the 35 national parks and monuments then in existence. Today, the U.S. National Park System comprises 392 units covering more than 84 million acres (3 percent of total U.S. area) across the country and U.S. territories. Additions to the National Park System are generally made through acts of Congress, and national parks can be created only through such acts. But under the Antiquities Act of 1906, the president has authority to proclaim national monuments on lands already under Federal jurisdiction.

The diversity of the parks managed by the National Park Service (NPS) is reflected in the variety of titles given to them. Although the system is best known for its scenic National Parks, more than half the areas of the National Park System preserve places, and commemorate persons, events, and activities important in the nation's history. Brief definitions of each type of park follow, together with the number of areas and total federal acreage. An additional 11 areas such as the White House, the National Mall, etc., totaling nearly 40,000 acres of federal land, are without designation. In 2009, over 20,000 Americans were employed by the N.P.S., including 743 firefighters and 2,342 law enforcement personnel.

National battlefields/battlefield parks/battlefield site/military parks cover a variety of areas associated with U.S. military history. (1 battlefield site, 1 acre; 9 military parks, 36,338 acres; 11 battlefields, 12,289 acres; 3 battlefield parks, 8,713 acres)

National capital parks include more than 346 sites (The Ellipse; Lafayette Park) throughout the Washington, D.C., area. (6,482 acres)

National historical parks are areas of greater physical extent and complexity than historic sites (Nez Perce, Idaho). (45; 173,709 acres)

National historic sites include areas of prehistoric and modern historical interest (Tuskegee Institute, Mississippi), archaeological sites, historic structures and the like. Because it is of importance to both the U.S. and Canada, St. Croix Island (28 acres) is designated an International Historic Site. (88, 77 administered by N.P.S.; 37,506 acres)

National Register of Historic Places is America's official list of cultural resources worthy of preservation. It administers 80,000 properties (buildings, sites, districts, structures, and objects). (varied acreage)

National lakeshores/seashores (Cape Cod NS, Massachusetts; Pictured Rocks NL, Michigan) preserve shoreline areas and offshore islands while providing water-oriented recreation. (4 lakeshores, 145,641 acres; 10 seashores, 594,014 acres)

National memorial designates an area or structure that is commemorative in nature (Mt. Rushmore, South Dakota). (44; 10,588 acres)

National monuments are intended to preserve at least one nationally significant resource (Rainbow Bridge, Utah). They are usually smaller than national parks and lack the diversity of attractions. (100, 75 administered by N.P.S.; 2,157,574 acres)

National parks contain a variety of resources and encompass large land and water areas (Grand Canyon, Arizona) to help provide adequate protection of resources. (58; 52,095,046 acres)

National parkways are ribbons of land flanking roadways (Natchez Trace, Mississippi, Alabama and Tennessee) that offer an opportunity for leisurely driving through areas of scenic interest. (4; 163,940 acres)

National preserves serve primarily to protect certain resources (Big Thicket, Texas). Activities like hunting and fishing or mineral extraction may be permitted. (18; 22,027,743 acres)

National recreation areas were originally areas surrounding reservoirs (Lake Mead, Nevada and Arizona), but now include other lands and waters set aside for recreational use. (18; 3,389,572 acres)

National reserves are similar to the preserves, but are administered by state or local authorities (City of Rocks, Idaho). (2, 1 affiliated; 11,440 acres)

National rivers/wild and scenic riverways preserve ribbons of land bordering free-flowing streams that have not been dammed, channelized, or otherwise altered (Delaware River, Pennsylvania and New Jersey). Activities such as hiking, boating and hunting may be permitted. (5 National Rivers; 312,161 acres; 10 National Wild & Scenic Riverways; 73,892 acres)

National scenic trails are usually long-distance footpaths winding through areas of natural beauty (Appalachian Trail, Maine to Georgia). (3; 166,922 acres)

National wilderness areas are designated under the Wilderness Act of 1964, and are largely untouched areas devoid of roads, mechanical transport, and structures. Wilderness areas are usually part of other larger entities. In addition to the National Park System, there are three groups of areas that are closely linked in importance and purpose to NPS-managed areas. (54 areas)

U.S. National Parks: Acreage, Visits, and Overnight Stays, 1990–2009

National Park, State	Acres under Federal protection, 2004	Visits ('000s)			Overnight stays ('000s)		
		1990	2000	2009	1990	2000	2009
Acadia, Maine	46,148	2,413	2,469	2,228	223	146	136
Arches, Utah	76,353	621	786	996	58	46	54
Badlands, South Dakota	232,822	1,326	1,106	934	35	54	46
Big Bend, Texas	775,279	257	262	364	215	186	17
Biscayne, Florida	170,955	573	393	439	29	N.A.	8
Black Canyon of the Gunnison, Colo.	30,750	[1]	192	171	[1]	14	15
Bryce Canyon, Utah	35,832	863	1,099	1,216	144	145	150
Canyonlands, Utah	337,570	277	402	436	78	108	90
Capitol Reef, Utah	241,234	562	613	617	48	42	35
Carlsbad Caverns, New Mexico	46,427	747	469	433	[3]	[3]	[3]
Channel Islands, California	79,018	144	483	349	32	101	56
Crater Lake, Oregon	183,223	385	427	447	45	73	80
Cuyahoga Valley, Ohio	19,559	[1]	3,325	2,589	[1]	6	2
Death Valley, California–Nevada	3,323,771	[1]	1,179	829	[1]	225	213
Denali, Alaska	4,724,790	547	364	358	118	121	90
Dry Tortugas, Florida	61,481	19	84	52	25	41	13
Everglades, Florida	1,398,657	958	995	901	128	106	33
Gates of the Arctic, Alaska	7,266,262	1	12	10	5	1	5
Glacier Bay, Alaska	3,223,018	204	385	438	36	44	17
Glacier, Montana	1,013,154	1,987	1,729	2,031	330	309	380
Grand Canyon, Arizona	1,180,862	3,777	4,460	4,348	908	1,085	1,270
Grand Teton, Wyoming	307,690	1,588	2,590	2,580	597	532	552
Great Basin, Nevada	77,180	65	81	85	44	32	30
Great Smoky Mountain, Tenn.–N.C.	521,122	8,152	10,176	9,490	463	421	401
Guadalupe Mountains, Texas	86,189	193	199	199	18	20	19
Haleakala, Hawaii	29,110	1,261	1,620	1,109	19	24	17
Hawaii Volcanoes, Hawaii	323,431	1,097	1,515	1,233	112	110	114
Hot Springs, Arkansas	4,932	1,123	1,338	1,285	8	4	10
Isle Royale, Michigan	539,281	23	21	15	56	61	43
Joshua Tree, California	769,175	[1]	1,234	1,304	[1]	245	266
Katmai, Alaska	405,432	41	72	43	12	29	5
Kenai Fjords, Alaska	601,839	66	255	218	1	4	2
Kings Canyon, California	461,845	1,063	529	609	302	217	182
Kobuk Valley, Alaska	1,669,912	[3]	[3]	2	[3]	[3]	2
Lake Clark, Alaska	2,226,807	10	6	10	1	2	3
Lassen Volcanic, California	106,368	461	375	366	113	79	99
Mammoth Cave, Kentucky	52,003	1,925	1,749	504	98	89	89
Mesa Verde, Colorado	51,890	611	452	550	159	82	92
Mount Rainier, Washington	235,625	1,327	1,345	1,152	184	196	169
North Cascades, Washington	504,633	456	26	27	97	19	15
Olympic, Washington	913,531	2,795	3,328	3,276	404	506	343
Petrified Forest, Arizona	93,532	845	605	631	1	2	6
Redwood, California	77,726	348	383	444	16	59	15
Rocky Mountain, Colorado	265,461	2,647	3,185	2,822	209	232	171
Saguaro, Arizona	87,526	[1]	765	665	[1]	2	2
Sequoia, California	403,875	1,064	839	965	345	252	259
Shenandoah, Virginia	198,250	1,772	1,420	1,121	323	284	293
Theodore Roosevelt, North Dakota	69,702	461	432	587	26	28	27
Virgin Island, U.S. Virgin Islands	12,916	665	704	416	173	215	103
Voyageurs, Minnesota	133,121	224	227	222	47	18	49
Wind Cave, South Dakota	28,295	586	669	588	11	10	2
Wrangell-St. Elias, Alaska	7,662,705	36	28	N.A.	3	2	N.A.
Yellowstone, Montana–Wyoming	2,219,789	2,824	2,838	3,295	1,345	1,191	1,276
Yosemite, California	759,530	3,125	3,401	3,737	2,220	1,633	1,701
Zion, Utah	143,073	2,102	2,432	2,735	292	243	307
Total National Parks	42,055,378	54,619	66,076	62,591	10,156	9,696	N.A.
Total National Parks System[2]	79,005,556	255,655	285,891	285,580	17,625	15,726	14,594

Notes: 1. Area was not a National Park in year shown. 2. Includes National Historic Sites, National Memorials, National Seashores, National Parkways, and other areas under the jurisdiction of the National Park Service. 3. Less than 1,000. Visit and overnight stay data often varies from year to year because of special events such as anniversaries and natural disasters. **Source:** National Park Service, Public Use Statistics Office, *National Park Service Statistical Abstract 2009* (2010).

Affiliated areas (designated by Act of Congress, 1970) are areas in the U.S. and Canada that preserve significant areas outside the National Park System but that rely on NPS assistance.

Wild and Scenic Rivers System (designated by Act of Congress, 1968) preserves undeveloped rivers as free-flowing streams accessible for public use. Wild rivers are free of dams and generally accessible only by trails; scenic rivers

State Parks and Recreation Areas by State, 2007–09

State	Total Acreage (000s)[2]	Recreation Visitors[1] (2009)	Recreation Visitors[1] (2008)	Percent change (2008–09)	Revenues 2007 ($1,000s)	Revenues as percent of operating expenses[2]
U.S. Total	13,922	285,579,941	274,852,949	3.9%	935,005	40.1%
Alabama	48	790,752	789,451	0.2%	22,567	57.0
Alaska	3,361	2,278,488	2,403,877	-5.2%	2,791	35.2
Arizona	64	10,713,122	10,681,127	0.3%	9,639	38.9
Arkansas	54	3,031,842	2,873,026	5.5%	22,332	48.3
California	1,566	35,318,711	34,374,981	2.7%	90,672	21.3
Colorado	420	5,443,039	5,383,786	1.1%	25,811	66.9
Connecticut	206	19,386	18,522	4.7%	5,104	29.9
Distrct of Columbia	N.A.	35,695,833	33,165,410	7.6%	N.A.	N.A.
Delaware	26	N.A.	N.A.	N.A.	12,397	53.6
Florida	700	9,495,437	7,937,737	19.6%	42,779	54.8
Georgia	86	6,475,874	6,425,910	0.8%	35,272	56.2
Hawaii	34	4,312,818	4,536,505	-4.9%	2,206	20.5
Idaho	46	494,196	543,485	-9.1%	3,608	20.9
Illinois	486	464,074	335,473	38.3%	6,804	11.9
Indiana	179	2,230,024	2,094,407	6.5%	41,379	78.1
Iowa	69	241,063	211,352	14.1%	3,864	25.1
Kansas	33	101,906	86,264	18.1%	5,998	57.1
Kentucky	49	1,828,340	1,708,529	7.0%	54,983	61.1
Louisiana	43	443,314	431,134	2.8%	7,669	24.6
Maine	100	2,227,698	2,075,857	7.3%	3,027	34.4
Maryland	133	3,445,530	3,544,992	-2.8%	16,694	49.4
Massachusetts	341	9,772,738	10,281,657	-4.9%	11,299	14.6
Michigan	273	1,628,704	1,420,947	14.6%	38,639	86.7
Minnesota	279	650,156	640,843	1.5%	15,694	44.9
Mississippi	24	6,582,890	5,898,917	11.6%	8,926	63.0
Missouri	204	3,933,043	3,436,201	14.5%	8,095	27.5
Montana	55	4,195,484	3,822,075	9.8%	4,952	55.3
Nebraska	135	273,444	265,858	2.9%	16,681	84.7
Nevada	139	5,836,491	5,770,632	1.1%	2,748	18.3
New Hampshire	233	34,558	29,819	15.9%	4,324	58.7
New Jersey	426	5,828,477	5,811,657	0.3%	10,388	26.9
New Mexico	93	1,659,574	1,556,586	6.6%	3,904	14.0
New York	1,348	17,327,234	16,913,720	2.4%	88,000	43.2
North Carolina	202	18,198,530	17,984,028	1.2%	5,317	13.8
North Dakota	18	631,459	553,135	14.2%	1,585	47.0
Ohio	174	2,882,593	3,121,019	-7.6%	27,530	37.3
Oklahoma	72	1,249,011	1,245,188	0.3%	36,368	78.7
Oregon	99	891,783	832,095	7.2%	17,187	36.1
Pennsylvania	292	8,885,894	9,189,257	-3.3%	17,176	20.6
Rhode Island	9	50,397	46,154	9.2%	4,322	47.6
South Carolina	84	1,504,680	1,441,433	4.4%	21,116	77.9
South Dakota	103	4,134,663	3,501,677	18.1%	11,530	82.0
Tennessee	174	8,061,848	7,733,827	4.2%	37,770	44.6
Texas	602	6,938,238	5,804,179	19.5%	38,172	43.8
Utah	151	8,755,401	8,451,252	3.6%	10,694	34.3
Vermont	69	31,129	37,121	-16.1%	6,124	79.9
Virginia	68	22,953,894	22,542,952	1.8%	14,214	45.5
Washington	117	7,559,552	7,140,553	5.9%	17,881	25.7
West Virginia	177	1,803,552	1,812,908	-0.5%	20,390	57.7
Wisconsin	139	452,365	424,669	6.5%	17,011	80.4
Wyoming	122	5,895,719	5,572,123	5.8%	1,371	19.0

Note: 1. Recreational visits are defined by the NPS as: "The entry of a person onto lands or waters administered by the NPS for recreational purposes, excluding government personnel, through traffic (commuters), trades-person, and a person residing within park boundaries." 2. Data is for 2007. **Sources**: National Park Service, Public Use Statistics Office, *National Park Service Statistical Abstract 2009*, "Recreation Visits by State." U.S. Census Bureau, *Statistical Abstract of the U.S., 2010*, "State Parks and Recreation Areas by State."

have relatively primitive shorelines and are largely undeveloped but may be accessible by road.

National Trails System
(designated by National Trails System Act of 1968) includes trails in both urban and rural settings for persons of all ages, interests, skills, and physical abilities. The Appalachian Trail and the Pacific Crest were the first two trails designated under the National Trails System. Today, the N.P.S. maintains 12,250 miles of unpaved trails and 763 miles of paved roads.

▶RIVERS AND LAKES
Major Navigable Waterways of the United States
The U.S inland and intracoastal waterway system handles over 500 million tons of traffic each year, carried by a fleet of more than 5,000 towboats and 31,000 barges on over 11,000 miles of primary channels. Ninety percent of these

channels have depths of between 9 and 14 feet. Maintenance and improvement of the waterways—including channel dredging, bridge and levee maintenance, and the construction of canals and locks—are in large measure the responsibility of the U.S. Army Corps of Engineers. The 522-mile New York State Barge Canal System is the only major non-federal waterway in the country.

Mississippi River System The major inland river transportation network is the Mississippi River and its tributaries. This north-south-oriented system includes the Mississippi River, the Ohio River System, the Illinois Waterway, and the Arkansas and Missouri rivers, among others. In this system there are about 7,000 miles of heavily used, improved navigable channels, 85 percent of which have at least nine-foot navigable channel depths.

Intracoastal Waterways At its mouth, the Mississippi River is intersected by the Gulf Intracoastal Waterway (GIWW), which parallels the Gulf Coast for 1,180 miles from St. Marks River, Florida, to Brownsville, Texas, at the Mexican border. The GIWW is intersected by a number of river systems in addition to the Mississippi, including the Mobile River, the Apalachicola and the Houston Ship Channel.

This network of major inland and coastal waterways connects some of the largest Gulf Coast ports—New Orleans, La.; Houston, Beaumont and Corpus Christi, Tex.; and Mobile, Ala.—with some of the largest inland ports—St. Louis, Mo.; Pittsburgh, Pa.; Huntington, W. Va.; Cincinnati, Ohio; Memphis, Tenn; and Chicago, Ill. The 40-foot controlling depth of the Mississippi River between the Gulf of Mexico and Baton Rouge allows ocean shipping to join the barge traffic, making this segment especially vital to both the domestic and foreign commerce of the United States.

The Atlantic Intracoastal Waterway provides 1,329 miles of protected channels for commercial and recreational navigation along the Atlantic Coast from Key West, Fla., to Norfolk, Va. Partially protected segments of the waterway continue north from Norfolk along the Delmarva Peninsula, the New Jersey coast and Long Island. Among the major Atlantic Coast ports located along this waterway are Miami, Savannah, Baltimore, Philadelphia and New York/New Jersey.

Pacific Coast In comparison with the Mississippi River system and the intracoastal waterways of the Atlantic and Gulf coasts, the inland and coastal waterways of the Pacific are few. Shallow draft waterways include the Columbia-Snake Waterway and the Willamette River above Portland, Oreg.; the Sacramento River above Sacramento, Calif.; the San Joaquin River above Stockton,

Calif.; and a few short navigable rivers stretching along the Washington and Oregon coasts.

The accompanying table shows the major navigable rivers in the United States, their total length, the distance commercially navigable, the body of water they flow into, and the head of navigation—the upriver point beyond which commercial ships cannot pass—and the states through or by which the rivers pass, from source to mouth.

Great Lakes and St. Lawrence Seaway The Great Lakes have been crucial to the development of the United States. They were the highways along which people and finished goods moved west, and along which raw materials such as lumber, minerals, and grains were transported to eastern markets. Later, the cities of the Great Lakes, such as Chicago, Duluth, Detroit and Buffalo, became important centers of finance, industry, and trade in their own right. So important was the maritime trade of the Lakes that in the 1890s, Chicago was the fourth-largest port in the world, despite being closed by ice for as many as five months a year.

An early obstacle to Great Lakes navigation was the fact that the lakes are not all at the same elevation: there is a difference of 354 feet between the level of the westernmost Lake Superior and easternmost Lake Ontario, and there is another 246 feet descent from Lake Ontario down the St. Lawrence River where it empties into the Atlantic Ocean. (It is 2,342 miles from Duluth, Minnesota, at the western end of Lake Superior, to the mouth of the St. Lawrence.)

The first canal (1799) was built on the St. Mary's River between Lake Superior and Lake Huron. (Today, there are two Sault Sainte Marie [or Soo] Canals—along the 70-mile river.) In 1825, the United States opened the way between the upper Lakes (all but Lake Ontario) and the Atlantic via the 175-mile Erie Canal between Buffalo, on Lake Erie, and Albany, on the Hudson River north of New York City. Canada followed with the 27-mile Welland Canal (1833) connecting Welland on Lake Erie and St. Catharine's on Lake Ontario.

The most ambitious undertaking was the construction of the St. Lawrence Seaway, a joint Canadian-American effort to open the entire length of the St. Lawrence and the Great Lakes to oceangoing navigation. Started in 1955 and opened to navigation in 1959, the seaway's system of canals and locks allows ships of up to 730 feet in length and 27 feet draft to sail the entire 2,342 miles from the mouth of the St. Lawrence to Duluth, Minn., at the western end of Lake Superior. The seaway continues to be an important artery of U.S. cargo shipping—total shipments increased 18 percent in the first part of 2010. The seaway also provides hydroelectric power for Canada and the United States.

The Great Lakes

Lake	Area		Depth		Height above sea level	
	(sq. mi)	(sq. km)	(feet)	(meters)	(feet)	(meters)
Erie	9,940	25,745	210	64	571	174
Huron	23,010	59,596	750	229	577	176
Michigan	22,400	58,016	923	281	577	176
Ontario	7,540	19,529	802	244	246	75
Superior	31,820	82,414	1,333	406	600	183

Source: U.S. Environmental Protection Agency and Environment Canada, *The Great Lakes: An Environmental Atlas and Resource Book* (1987).

The Panama Canal One of the great engineering feats of the world, the 44-mile Panama Canal bisects the continents of North and South America, making it possible for ships to sail between the Atlantic and Pacific oceans without rounding the treacherous Cape Horn at the tip of South America. The U.S. government began construction of the canal in 1904, and it was opened to commercial navigation Aug. 15, 1914. For interocean shippers, the savings in distance and time afforded by the canal are enormous. A ship sailing from New York to San Francisco via the Panama Canal travels a distance of 5,264 miles, a savings of more than 7,800 miles—or about 20 days— over the 13,100-mile route around Cape Horn. The mini-

mum depth of the canal is 41 feet, the minimum width 300 feet, and the highest elevation above sea level 85 feet.

The Canal Zone, a 10-mile-wide strip of land around the canal in the Republic of Panama was acquired in 1903 by the United States, who governed it until 1979. The Panama Canal Treaty of 1977 abolished the Canal Zone as an independent political entity, but the canal's maintenance and operation remained the responsibility of the U.S. Panama Canal Commission until 1999, when the Republic of Panama assumed full responsibility. Since then, the Panamanian Master Plan for the Canal proposes a third set of locks, to be constructed before 2025.

Land Cover and Use, by State, 2003 (thousands of acres)

State	Total surface area	Cropland	Rangeland	Forestland	State	Total surface area	Cropland	Rangeland	Forestland
AL	1,937,664	19.0%	20.9%	20.9%	NE	49,510	39.5%	46.6%	1.6%
AZ	33,424	7.5	0.2	64.4	NV	70,763	0.9	11.7	0.4
AK	34,037	22.1	0.1	44.1	NH	5,941	2.1	0	65.6
CA	101,510	9.3	17.5	13.7	NJ	5,216	10.1	0	30.8
CO	66,625	12.5	37.2	4.9	NM	77,823	2.0	51.3	7.0
CT	3,195	5.4	0	53.4	NY	31,361	17.1	0	56.1
DE	1,534	29.8	0	22.2	NC	33,709	16.4	0	45.9
FL	37,534	7.7	7.2	33.9	ND	45,251	53.6	24.5	1.0
GA	37,741	11.0	0	58.0	OH	26,445	42.5	0	27.3
ID	53,488	10.2	12.0	7.5	OK	44,738	20.1	31.6	16.5
IL	36,059	66.5	0	11.0	OR	62,161	6.0	15.1	20.5
IN	23,158	57.5	0	16.5	PA	28,995	17.7	0	53.9
IA	36,017	70.8	0	6.4	RI	813	2.5	0	45.9
KS	52,661	50.3	30.1	2.9	SC	19,939	11.9	0	56.0
KY	25,863	21.2	0	40.6	SD	49,358	34.6	44.7	1.0
LA	31,377	17.3	0.9	42.5	TN	26,974	17.6	0	44.3
ME	20,966	1.8	0	84.0	TX	171,052	14.9	56.2	6.2
MD	7,870	19.3	0	30.1	UT	54,339	3.1	19.6	3.5
MA	5,339	4.7	0	49.9	VT	6,154	9.5	0	67.1
MI	37,349	21.7	0	44.7	VA	27,087	10.6	0	48.7
MN	54,010	39.1	0	30.3	WA	44,035	14.7	13.3	28.9
MS	30,527	16.3	0	54.9	WV	15,508	5.3	0	68.1
MO	44,614	30.7	0.2	28.1	WI	35,920	28.7	0	40.4
MT	94,110	15.4	39.0	5.7	WY	62,603	3.5	44.0	1.5

Selected nonfederal rural land, percent of total

Notes: Excludes Alaska, District of Columbia, Hawaii, and island areas. **Source:** U.S. Department of Agriculture, National Resource and Conservation Service, Summary Report, 2003 *Annual National Resources Inventory*.

Land Cover and Use, by Type, 1982–2003

Year	Total surface area	Rural land, total[1]	Crop-land	Pasture land	Range-land	Forest land	Other rural land	Devel-oped land	Water areas	Fed-eral land
Land										
1982	1,937.	1,417.2	420.4	131.4	414.5	402.6	48.3	72.8	48.6	399.1
1992	1,937.6	1,400.2	381.2	125.1	406.6	404.0	49.3	86.5	49.4	401.5
2002	1,937.7	1,378.1	368.4	117.3	405.3	404.9	50.6	107.3	50.4	401.9
2003	1,937.7	1,377.3	367.9	117.0	405.1	405.6	50.2	108.1	50.4	401.9
Percent of total land										
1982	100.0%	73.1%	21.7%	6.8%	21.4%	20.8%	2.5%	3.8%	2.5%	20.6%
1992	100.0	72.3	19.7	6.5	21.0	20.9	2.5	4.5	2.5	20.7
2002	100.0	71.1	19.0	6.1	20.9	20.9	2.6	5.5	2.6	20.7
2003	100.0	71.1	19.0	6.0	20.9	20.9	2.6	5.6	2.6	20.7

Nonfederal rural land (thousands of acres)

Notes: 1. Includes Conservation Reserve Program land not shown separately. **Source:** U.S. Department of Agriculture, National Resources and Conservation Service, Summary Report, 2003 *Annual National Resources Inventory*.

Major Navigable Rivers in the U.S.

Ultimate outflow/river	Length (miles)	Navigable length (miles)	Mouth to head of navigation	States/provinces (from source to mouth)
ATLANTIC OCEAN				
St. Lawrence	760	760	Gulf of St. Lawrence to Lake Ontario	N.Y.; Ontario, Quebec (Canada)
Cape Cod Canal	17	17	Sandwich to Buzzards Bay, Mass.	Mass.
Connecticut	407	52	Long Island Sound to Hartford, Conn.	N.H., Vt., Mass., Conn.
Hudson	306	134	New York Bay to Troy Lock, N.Y. New York State Barge Canal links to Lake Erie (353 mi. Troy to Buffalo), and to Lakes Champlain, Ontario, Cayuga, Seneca.	N.Y.
Delaware	367	77	Delaware Bay to Trenton, N.J.	N.Y., Pa., N.J., Del.
Chesapeake and Delaware Canal	14	14	Delaware Bay to Chesapeake Bay	Del., Md.
Potomac	287	101	Chesapeake Bay to Washington, D.C.	Va., Md., D.C.
James	340	87	Chesapeake Bay to Richmond, Va.	Va.
Roanoke	410	112	Atlantic Ocean to Altavista, N.C.	Va., N.C.
Cape Fear	202	111	Atlantic Ocean to Fayetteville, N.C.	N.C.
Savannah	314	181	Atlantic Ocean to Augusta, Ga.	S.C., Ga.
Saint Johns	285	160	Atlantic Ocean to Lake Harney	Fla.
GULF OF MEXICO				
Chattahoochee	436	194	Apalachicola River to Columbus, Ga.	Ga., Ala.
Apalachicola	90	90	Gulf of Mexico to Chattahoochee, Fla.	Fla.
Mobile	45	45	Mobile Bay to confluence of Alabama and Tombigbee rivers	Ala.
Alabama	318	305	Mobile River to Montgomery, Ala.	Ala.
Tombigbee	362	362	Mobile River to Amory, Miss. Linked to Tennessee River by Tennessee-Tombigbee Waterway (253 mi.)	Ala., Miss.
Black Warrior	217	217	Tombigbee River to Birmingham, Ala.	Ala.
Houston Ship Channel	57	57	Galveston Bay to Houston, Tex.	Tex.
Rio Grande[1]	1,885	13	Gulf of Mexico to Brownsville, Tex.	Colo., N.Mex., Tex., Mexico
MISSISSIPPI RIVER SYSTEM				
Mississippi	2,348	1,807	Gulf of Mexico to Minneapolis, Minn.,	Minn., Wis., Iowa, Ill., Mo., Ky., Tenn., Ark., Miss., La
EASTERN TRIBUTARIES OF THE MISSISSIPPI				
Illinois	273	273	Mississippi River to Joliet. Also linked to Mississippi by Illinois and Mississippi Canal (La Salle to Rockport); and to Lake Michigan (at Chicago, Calumet, East Chicago Gary) by Illinois Waterway	Ill.
Ohio	981	981	Mississippi River to Pittsburgh, Pa.	Pa., Ohio, W.Va., Ind., Ky., Ill.
Monongahela	129	129	Ohio River to Fairmont, W.Va.	W.Va., Pa.
Allegheny	325	72	Ohio River to East Brady, Pa.	N.Y., Pa.
Kanawha	97	91	Ohio River to Charleston, W.Va.	W.Va.
Kentucky	259	82	Ohio River to Beattyville, Ky.	Ky.
Green	360	103	Ohio River to Bowling Green, Ky.	Ky.
Cumberland	694	387	Ohio River to Burnside, Ky.	Ky., Tenn.
Tennessee	652	648	Ohio River to Knoxville, Tenn.	Tenn., Ala., Miss., Ky.
Yazoo	169	165	Mississippi River to Greenwood, Miss.	Miss.
WESTERN TRIBUTARIES OF THE MISSISSIPPI				
Missouri	2,315	735	Mississippi River to Ponca, Nebr.	Mont., N.Dak., S.Dak., Nebr., Iowa, Kans., Mo.
Arkansas	1,396	448	McClellan-Kerr Arkansas River System from Mississippi River to Catoosa, Okla., incorporates sections of White, Arkansas, Verdigris rivers.	Colo., Kans., Okla., Ark.,
Ouachita[2]	605	351	Mississippi River to Camden, Ark.	Ark., La.
Red	1,018	236	Mississippi River to Shreveport, La.	N.Mex., Tex., Okla., Ark., La.
Atchafalaya[3]	220	220	Atchafalaya Bay to Mississippi River	La.
PACIFIC OCEAN				
San Joaquin	340	103	Sacramento River to Hills Ferry, Calif.	Calif.
Sacramento	374	163	San Francisco Bay to Chico Landing, Calif.	Calif.
Columbia	1,210	285	Pacific Ocean to Pasco, Wash.	British Col. (Can.), Wash., Oreg.
Snake	1,083	192	Columbia River to Johnson Bar Landing,	Wyo., Idaho, Oreg., Wash.
Willamette	294	133	Columbia River to Harrisburg, Oreg.	Oreg.

Notes: All distances given in nautical miles except for the Mississippi River and its tributaries: 1 nautical mile = 1.151 statute miles. 1. In Mexico known as the Río Bravo or Río Bravo del Norte. 2. Lower 57 miles known as the Black River. 3. Flows from the Mississippi River to the Gulf of Mexico. **Source:** National Oceanic and Atmospheric Administration, *Distances Between United States Ports, 1987* (1987).

Extreme Elevations of States and Outlying Areas

State	Highest Point Name	Elevation Feet	Elevation Meters	Lowest Point Name	Elevation Feet	Elevation Meters
United States	Mount McKinley, Alaska	20,320	6,198	Death Valley, Calif.	−282	−86
Alabama	Cheaha Mountain	2,405	733	Gulf of Mexico		Sea level
Alaska	Mount McKinley	20,320	6,198	Pacific Ocean		Sea level
Arizona	Humphreys Peak	12,633	3,853	Colorado River	70	21
Arkansas	Magazine Mountain	2,753	840	Ouachita River	55	17
California	Mount Whitney	14,494	4,419	Death Valley	−282	−86
Colorado	Mount Elbert	14,433	4,402	Arkansas River	3,315	1,011
Connecticut	Mount Frissell, South slope	2,380	726	Long Island Sound		Sea level
Delaware	Ebright Rd., New Castle Co.	448	137	Atlantic Ocean		Sea level
Dist. of Columbia	Tenleytown	410	125	Potomac River	1	0.3
Florida	Sec.30,T6N,R20W, Walton Co.	345	105	Atlantic Ocean		Sea level
Georgia	Brasstown Bald	4,784	1,459	Atlantic Ocean		Sea level
Hawaii	Mauna Kea	13,806	4,211	Pacific Ocean		Sea level
Idaho	Borah Peak	12,662	3,862	Snake River	710	217
Illinois	Charles Mound	1,235	377	Mississippi River	279	85
Indiana	Franklin Township, Wayne Co.	1,257	383	Ohio River	320	98
Iowa	Sec. 29, T100N, R41W Osceola Co.	1,670	509	Mississippi River	480	146
Kansas	Mount Sunflower	4,039	1,232	Verdigris River	679	207
Kentucky	Black Mountain	4,139	1,262	Mississippi River	257	78
Louisiana	Driskill Mountain	535	163	New Orleans	−8	−2
Maine	Mount Katahdin	5,267	1,606	Atlantic Ocean		Sea level
Maryland	Backbone Mountain	3,360	1,025	Atlantic Ocean		Sea level
Massachusetts	Mount Greylock	3,487	1,064	Atlantic Ocean		Sea level
Michigan	Mount Arvon	1,979	604	Lake Erie	571	174
Minnesota	Eagle Mountain, Cook Co.	2,301	702	Lake Superior	600	183
Mississippi	Woodall Mountain	806	246	Gulf of Mexico		Sea level
Missouri	Taum Sauk Mountain	1,772	540	St. Francis River	230	70
Montana	Granite Peak	12,799	3,904	Kootenai River	1,800	549
Nebraska	Johnson Township, Kimball Co.	5,424	1,653	Missouri River	840	256
Nevada	Boundary Peak	13,140	4,007	Colorado River	479	146
New Hampshire	Mount Washington	6,288	1,918	Atlantic Ocean		Sea level
New Jersey	High Point	1,803	550	Atlantic Ocean		Sea level
New Mexico	Wheeler Peak	13,161	4,014	Red Bluff Reservoir	2,842	867
New York	Mount Marcy	5,344	1,630	Atlantic Ocean		Sea level
North Carolina	Mount Mitchell	6,684	2,039	Atlantic Ocean		Sea level
North Dakota	White Butte, Slope Co.	3,506	1,069	Red River	750	229
Ohio	Campbell Hill	1,549	472	Ohio River	455	139
Oklahoma	Black Mesa	4,973	1,517	Little River	289	88
Oregon	Mount Hood	11,239	3,428	Pacific Ocean		Sea level
Pennsylvania	Mount Davis	3,213	980	Delaware River		Sea level
Rhode Island	Jerimoth Hill	812	248	Atlantic Ocean		Sea level
South Carolina	Sassafras Mountain	3,560	1,086	Atlantic Ocean		Sea level
South Dakota	Harney Peak	7,242	2,209	Big Stone Lake	966	295
Tennessee	Clingmans Dome	6,643	2,026	Mississippi River	178	54
Texas	Guadalupe Peak	8,749	2,668	Gulf of Mexico		Sea level
Utah	Kings Peak	13,528	4,126	Beaverdam Creek	2,000	610
Vermont	Mount Mansfield	4,393	1,340	Lake Champlain	95	29
Virginia	Mount Rogers	5,729	1,747	Atlantic Ocean		Sea level
Washington	Mount Rainier	14,410	4,395	Pacific Ocean		Sea level
West Virginia	Spruce Knob	4,861	1,483	Potomac River	240	73
Wisconsin	Timms Hill	1,951	595	Lake Michigan	579	177
Wyoming	Gannett Peak	13,804	4,210	Belle Fourche River	3,099	945
Puerto Rico	Cerro de Punta	4,390	1,339	Atlantic Ocean		Sea level
Amer. Samoa	Lata Mountain	3,160	964	Pacific Ocean		Sea level
Guam	Mount Lamlam	1,332	405	Pacific Ocean		Sea level
Virgin Islands	Crown Mountain	1,556	475	Atlantic Ocean		Sea level

Note: Sec. denotes section; T, township; R, range; N, north; W, west. **Source:** U.S. Geological Survey, *Elevations and Distances in the United States* (2000).

U.S. History

DOCUMENTS OF U.S. HISTORY

▶THE DECLARATION OF INDEPENDENCE

After a year of war with Britain, American patriots were driven to make the final break in 1776. On June 7, before the Continental Congress in Philadelphia, Richard Henry Lee of Virginia proposed a declaration that the colonies "are, and of right ought to be, free and independent States." A committee of five, headed by Thomas Jefferson, was appointed to draw up the formal Declaration of Independence on June 10. The committee brought its version, mainly the work of Jefferson, back to Congress on June 28. Congress voted unanimously to declare independence on July 2, and after making several changes in the Jefferson committee's draft, they unanimously adopted the Declaration of Independence on July 4. Copies of the Declaration were dispatched to the states for approval. Charles Carroll of Maryland was the last surviving signer of the Declaration when he died on November 14, 1832. The original document is on display today at the National Archives in Washington, D.C.

In Congress, July 4, 1776,
THE UNANIMOUS DECLARATION
OF THE
THIRTEEN UNITED STATES
OF AMERICA,

When in the Course of human events, it becomes necessary for one people to dissolve the political bands which have connected them with another, and to assume among the Powers of the earth, the separate and equal station to which the Laws of Nature and of Nature's God entitle them, a decent respect to the opinions of mankind requires that they should declare the causes which impel them to the separation.

We hold these truths to be self-evident, that all men are created equal, that they are endowed by their Creator with certain unalienable Rights, that among these are Life, Liberty and the pursuit of Happiness. That to secure these rights, Governments are instituted among Men, deriving their just powers from the consent of the governed. That whenever any Form of Government becomes destructive of these ends, it is the Right of the People to alter or to abolish it, and to institute new Government, laying its foundation on such principles and organizing its powers in such form, as to them shall seem most likely to effect their Safety and Happiness. Prudence, indeed, will dictate that governments long established should not be changed for light and transient causes; and accordingly all experience hath shown, that mankind are more disposed to suffer, while evils are sufferable, than to right themselves by abolishing the forms to which they are accustomed. But when a long train of abuses and usurpations, pursuing invariably the same Object evinces a design to reduce them under absolute Despotism, it is their right, it is their duty, to throw off such Government, and to provide new Guards for their future security. Such has been the patient sufferance of these Colonies; and such is now the ne-

cessity which constrains them to alter their former Systems of Government. The history of the present King of Great Britain is a history of repeated injuries and usurpations, all having in direct object the establishment of an absolute Tyranny over these States. To prove this, let Facts be submitted to a candid world.

He has refused his Assent to Laws, the most wholesome and necessary for the public good.

He has forbidden his Governors to pass Laws of immediate and pressing importance, unless suspended in their operation till his Assent should be obtained; and when so suspended, he has utterly neglected to attend to them.

He has refused to pass other Laws for the accommodation of large districts of people, unless those people would relinquish the right of Representation in the Legislature, a right inestimable to them and formidable to tyrants only.

He has called together legislative bodies at places unusual, uncomfortable, and distant from the depository of their Public Records, for the sole purpose of fatiguing them into compliance with his measures.

He has dissolved Representative Houses repeatedly, for opposing with manly firmness his invasions on the rights of the people.

He has refused for a long time, after such dissolutions, to cause others to be elected; whereby the Legislative Powers, incapable of Annihilation, have returned to the People at large for their exercise; the State remaining in the mean time exposed to all the dangers of invasion from without, and convulsions within.

He has endeavoured to prevent the population of these States; for that purpose obstructing the Laws of Naturalization of Foreigners; refusing to pass others to encourage their migration hither, and raising the conditions of new Appropriations of Lands.

He has obstructed the Administration of Justice, by refusing his Assent to Laws for establishing Judiciary Powers.

He has made Judges dependent on his Will alone, for the tenure of their offices, and the amount and payment of their salaries.

He has erected a multitude of New Offices, and sent hither swarms of Officers to harass our People, and eat out their substance.

He has kept among us, in times of peace, Standing Armies without the Consent of our legislature.

He has affected to render the Military independent of and superior to the Civil Power.

He has combined with others to subject us to a jurisdiction foreign to our constitution, and unacknowledged by our laws; giving his Assent to their acts of pretended legislation:

For quartering large bodies of armed troops among us:

For protecting them, by a mock Trial, from Punishment for any Murders which they should commit on the Inhabitants of these States:

For cutting off our Trade with all parts of the world:

For imposing taxes on us without our consent:

For depriving us in many cases, of the benefits of Trial by Jury:

For transporting us beyond Seas to be tried for pretended offences:

For abolishing the free System of English Laws in a neighbouring Province, establishing therein an Arbitrary government, and enlarging its Boundaries so as to render it at once an example and fit instrument for introducing the same absolute rule into these Colonies:

For taking away our Charters, abolishing our most valuable Laws, and altering fundamentally the forms of our Government:

For suspending our own legislature, and declaring themselves invested with Power to legislate for us in all cases whatsoever.

He has abdicated Government here, by declaring us out of his Protection and waging War against us.

He has plundered our seas, ravaged our Coasts, burnt our towns, and destroyed the lives of our people.

He is at this time transporting large armies of foreign mercenaries to compleat the works of death, desolation and tyranny, already begun with circumstances of Cruelty & perfidy scarcely paralleled in the most barbarous ages, and totally unworthy of the Head of a civilized nation.

He has constrained our fellow Citizens taken Captive on the high Seas to bear Arms against their Country, to become the executioners of their friends and Brethren, or to fall themselves by their Hands.

He has excited domestic insurrections amongst us, and has endeavoured to bring on the inhabitants of our frontiers, the merciless Indian Savages, whose known rule of warfare, is an undistinguished destruction of all ages, sexes and conditions.

In every stage of these Oppressions We have Petitioned for Redress in the most humble terms: Our repeated Petitions have been answered only by repeated injury. A prince, whose character is thus marked by every act which may define a Tyrant, is unfit to be the ruler of a free People.

Nor have We been wanting in attention to our British brethren. We have warned them from time to time of attempts by their legislature to extend an unwarrantable jurisdiction over us. We have reminded them of the circumstances of our emigration and settlement here. We have appealed to their native justice and magnanimity, and we have conjured them by the ties of our common kindred to disavow these usurpations, which would inevitably interrupt our connections and correspondence. They too have been deaf to the voice of justice and of consanguinity. We must, therefore, acquiesce in the necessity, which denounces our Separation and hold them, as we hold the rest of mankind, Enemies in War, in Peace Friends.

We, therefore, the Representatives of the United States of America, in General Congress, Assembled, appealing to the Supreme Judge of the world for the rectitude of our intentions, do, in the Name, and by Authority of the good People of these Colonies, solemnly publish and declare, That these United Colonies are, and of Right ought to be Free and Independent States; that they are Absolved from all Allegiance to the British Crown, and that all political connection between them and the State of Great Britain, is and ought to be totally dissolved; and that as Free and Independent States, they have full Power to levy War, conclude Peace, contract Alliances, establish Commerce, and to do all other Acts and Things which Independent States may of right do. And for the support of this Declaration, with a firm reliance on the Protection of Divine Providence, we mutually pledge to each other our Lives, our Fortunes and our sacred Honor.

▶ THE U.S. CONSTITUTION

During and after the Revolution, the United States was governed by the Continental Congress under the Articles of Confederation, which delegated very limited powers to the national government and reserved the rest to the states. Economic chaos, political confusion, and widespread dissatisfaction with the lack of central authority peaked after Shays's Rebellion in 1786. George Washington lent his prestige to the call for a convention to consider a new form of government. Congress endorsed the plan on February 21, 1787, "for the sole and express purpose of revising the Articles of Confederation." All states but Rhode Island sent delegates to the convention, which opened in Philadelphia on May 14. The delegates moved at once to discard the Articles, draw up a new Constitution, and conduct their meetings in secrecy, while Washington presided and James Madison took notes. A long summer of debate and compromise finally produced the document that most of the delegates signed on September 17. Congress ordered the Constitution sent to the states for ratification on September 28, requiring approval by at least nine of them to validate the new charter. Whether the Constitution would be adopted was in doubt until June 21, 1788, when New Hampshire became the ninth state to ratify it. The Constitution went into effect on March 4, 1789. All of the original 13 states eventually ratified the Constitution, ending with Rhode Island on May 29, 1790. The U.S. Constitution is the world's oldest written constitution.

Preamble

We, the People of the United States, in Order to form a more perfect Union, establish Justice, insure domestic Tranquillity, provide for the common defence, promote the general Welfare, and secure the Blessings of Liberty to ourselves and our Posterity, do ordain and establish this Constitution for the United States of America.

Article I

Section 1 All legislative powers herein granted shall be vested in a Congress of the United States, which shall consist of a Senate and House of Representatives.

Section 2 [1] The House of Representatives shall be composed of members chosen every second year by the people of the several States, and the electors in each State shall have the qualifications requisite for electors of the most numerous branch of the State legislature.

[2] No person shall be a Representative who shall not have attained to the age of twenty-five years, and been seven years a citizen of the United States, and who shall not, when elected, be an inhabitant of that State in which he shall be chosen.

[3] Representatives and direct taxes shall be apportioned among the several States which may be included within this Union, according to their respective numbers, which shall be determined by adding to the whole number of free persons, including those bound to service for a term of years, and excluding Indians not taxed, three-fifths of all other persons. The actual enumeration shall be made within three years after the first meeting of the Congress of the United States, and within every subsequent term of ten years, in such manner as they shall by law direct. The number of Representatives shall not exceed one for every thirty thousand, but each State shall have at least one Representative; and until such enumeration shall be made, the State of New Hampshire shall

Signers of the Declaration of Independence

Delegate	State	Born/Died	Delegate	State	Born/Died
Adams, John	Massachusetts	1735–1826	Lynch, Thomas, Jr.	South Carolina	1749–1779
Adams, Samuel	Massachusetts	1722–1803	McKean, Thomas	Delaware	1734–1817
Bartlett, Josiah	New Hampshire	1729–1795	Middleton, Arthur	South Carolina	1742–1787
Braxton, Carter	Virginia	1736–1797	Morris, Lewis	New York	1726–1798
Carroll, Charles	Maryland	1737–1832	Morris, Robert	Pennsylvania	1734–1806
Chase, Samuel	Maryland	1741–1811	Morton, John	Pennsylvania	1724–1777
Clark, Abraham	New Jersey	1726–1794	Nelson, Thomas Jr.	Virginia	1738–1789
Clymer, George	Pennsylvania	1739–1813	Paca, William	Maryland	1740–1799
Ellery, William	Rhode Island	1727–1820	Paine, Robert Treat	Massachusetts	1731–1814
Floyd, William	New York	1734–1821	Penn, John	North Carolina	1741–1788
Franklin, Benjamin	Pennsylvania	1706–1790	Read, George	Delaware	1733–1798
Gerry, Elbridge	Massachusetts	1744–1814	Rodney, Caesar	Delaware	1728–1784
Gwinnett, Button	Georgia	1732–1777	Ross, George	Pennsylvania	1730–1779
Hall, Lyman	Georgia	1724–1790	Rush, Benjamin	Pennsylvania	1745–1813
Hancock, John	Massachusetts	1737–1793	Rutledge, Edward	South Carolina	1749–1800
Harrison, Benjamin	Virginia	1726–1791	Sherman, Roger	Connecticut	1721–1793
Hart, John	New Jersey	d.1779	Smith, James	Pennsylvania	1713–1806
Hewes, Joseph	North Carolina	1730–1779	Stockton, Richard	New Jersey	1730–1781
Heyward, Thomas, Jr.	South Carolina	1746–1809	Stone, Thomas	Maryland	1743–1787
Hooper, William	North Carolina	1742–1790	Taylor, George	Pennsylvania	1716–1781
Hopkins, Stephen	Rhode Island	1707–1785	Thornton, Matthew	New Hampshire	1714–1803
Hopkinson, Francis	New Jersey	1737–1791	Walton, George	Georgia	1741–1804
Huntington, Samuel	Connecticut	1731–1796	Whipple, William	New Hampshire	1730–1785
Jefferson, Thomas	Virginia	1743–1826	Williams, William	Connecticut	1731–1811
Lee, Richard Henry	Virginia	1732–1794	Wilson, James	Pennsylvania	1742–1798
Lee, Francis Lightfoot	Virginia	1734–1797	Witherspoon, John	New Jersey	1723–1794
Lewis, Francis	New York	1713–1803	Wolcott, Oliver	Connecticut	1726–1797
Livingston, Philip	New York	1716–1778	Wythe, George	Virginia	1726–1806

be entitled to choose three; Massachusetts, eight; Rhode Island and Providence Plantations, one; Connecticut, five; New York, six; New Jersey, four; Pennsylvania, eight; Delaware, one; Maryland, six; Virginia, ten; North Carolina, five; South Carolina, five; and Georgia, three.

[4] When vacancies happen in the representation from any State, the executive authority thereof shall issue writs of election to fill such vacancies.

[5] The House of Representatives shall choose their Speaker and other officers, and shall have the sole power of impeachment.

Section 3 [1] The Senate of the United States shall be composed of two Senators from each State, chosen by the legislature thereof for six years; and each Senator shall have one vote.

[2] Immediately after they shall be assembled in consequence of the first election, they shall be divided as equally as may be into three classes. The seats of the Senators of the first class shall be vacated at the expiration of the second year, of the second class at the expiration of the fourth year, and of the third class at the expiration of the sixth year, so that one-third may be chosen every second year; and if vacancies happen by resignation or otherwise during the recess of the legislature of any State, the executive thereof may make temporary appointments until the next meeting of the legislature, which shall then fill such vacancies.

[3] No person shall be a Senator who shall not have attained to the age of thirty years, and been nine years a citizen of the United States, and who shall not, when elected, be an inhabitant of that State for which he shall be chosen.

[4] The Vice-President of the United States shall be President of the Senate, but shall have no vote, unless they be equally divided.

[5] The Senate shall choose their other officers and also a President pro tempore in the absence of the Vice-President, or when he shall exercise the office of President of the United States.

[6] The Senate shall have the sole power to try all impeachments. When sitting for that purpose, they shall be on oath or affirmation. When the President of the United States is tried, the Chief Justice shall preside; and no person shall be convicted without the concurrence of two-thirds of the members present.

[7] Judgment in cases of impeachment shall not extend further than to removal from office, and disqualification to hold and enjoy any office of honor, trust, or profit under the United States; but the party convicted shall, nevertheless, be liable and subject to indictment, trial, judgment, and punishment, according to law.

Section 4 [1] The times, places, and manner of holding elections for Senators and Representatives shall be prescribed in each State by the legislature thereof; but the Congress may at any time by law make or alter such regulations, except as to the places of choosing Senators.

[2] The Congress shall assemble at least once in every year, and such meeting shall be on the first Monday in December, unless they shall by law appoint a different day.

Section 5 [1] Each House shall be the judge of the elections, returns, and qualification of its own members, and a majority of each shall constitute a quorum to do business; but a smaller number may adjourn from day to day, and may be authorized to compel the attendance of absent members, in such manner, and under such penalties, as each House may provide.

[2] Each House may determine the rules of its proceedings, punish its members for disorderly behavior, and with the concurrence of two-thirds, expel a member.

[3] Each House shall keep a journal of its proceedings, and from time to time publish the

same, excepting such parts as may in their judgment require secrecy, and the yeas and nays of the members of either House on any question shall, at the desire of one-fifth of those present, be entered on the journal.

[4] Neither House, during the session of Congress, shall, without the consent of the other, adjourn for more than three days, nor to any other place than that in which the two Houses shall be sitting.

Section 6 [1] The Senators and Representatives shall receive a compensation for their services, to be ascertained by law and paid out of the Treasury of the United States. They shall, in all cases except treason, felony, and breach of the peace, be privileged from arrest during their attendance at the session of their respective Houses, and in going to and returning from the same; and for any speech or debate in either House they shall not be questioned in any other place.

[2] No Senator or Representative shall, during the time for which he was elected, be appointed to any civil office under the authority of the United States, which shall have been created, or the emoluments whereof shall have been increased during such time; and no person holding any office under the United States shall be a member of either House during his continuance in office.

Section 7 [1] All bills for raising revenue shall originate in the House of Representatives; but the Senate may propose or concur with amendments as on other bills.

[2] Every bill which shall have passed the House of Representatives and the Senate shall, before it becomes a law, be presented to the President of the United States; if he approves he shall sign it, but if not he shall return it, with his objections, to that House in which it shall have originated, who shall enter the objections at large on their journal and proceed to reconsider it. If after such reconsideration two-thirds of that House shall agree to pass the bill, it shall be sent, together with the objections, to the other House, by which it shall likewise be reconsidered, and if approved by two-thirds of that House it shall become a law. But in all such cases the vote of both Houses shall be determined by yeas and nays, and the names of the persons voting for and against the bill shall be entered on the journal of each House respectively. If any bill shall not be returned by the President within ten days (Sundays excepted) after it shall have been presented to him, the same shall be a law, in like manner as if he had signed it, unless the Congress by their adjournment prevent its return, in which case it shall not be a law.

[3] Every order, resolution or vote to which the concurrence of the Senate and House of Representatives may be necessary (except on a question of adjournment) shall be presented to the President of the United States; and before the same shall take effect shall be approved by him, or being disapproved by him, shall be repassed by two-thirds of the Senate and House of Representatives, according to the rules and limitations prescribed in the case of a bill.

Section 8 [1] The Congress shall have power to lay and collect taxes, duties, imposts and excises, to pay the debts and provide for the common defense and general welfare of the United States; but all duties, imposts and excises shall be uniform throughout the United States;

[2] To borrow money on the credit of the United States;

[3] To regulate commerce with foreign nations, and among the several States, and with the Indian tribes;

[4] To establish an uniform rule of naturalization, and uniform laws on the subject of bankruptcies throughout the United States;

[5] To coin money, regulate the value thereof, and of foreign coin, and fix the standard of weights and measures;

[6] To provide for the punishment of counterfeiting the securities and current coin of the United States;

[7] To establish post offices and post roads;

[8] To promote the progress of science and useful arts by securing for limited times to authors and inventors the exclusive right to their respective writings and discoveries;

[9] To constitute tribunals inferior to the Supreme Court;

[10] To define and punish piracies and felonies committed on the high seas and offenses against the law of nations;

[11] To declare war, grant letters of marque and reprisal, and make rules concerning captures on land and water;

[12] To raise and support armies, but no appropriation of money to that use shall be for a longer term than two years;

[13] To provide and maintain a navy;

[14] To make rules for the government and regulation of the land and naval forces;

[15] To provide for calling forth the militia to execute the laws of the Union, suppress insurrections, and repel invasions;

[16] To provide for organizing, arming and disciplining the militia, and for governing such part of them as may be employed in the service of the United States, reserving to the States respectively the appointment of the officers, and the authority of training the militia according to the discipline prescribed by Congress;

[17] To exercise exclusive legislation in all cases whatsoever over such district (not exceeding ten miles square) as may, by cession of particular States and the acceptance of Congress, become the seat of the Government of the United States, and to exercise like authority over all places purchased by the consent of the legislature of the State in which the same shall be, for the erection of forts, magazines, arsenals, dockyards, and other needful buildings;

[18] To make all laws which shall be necessary and proper for carrying into execution the foregoing powers, and all other powers vested by this Constitution in the Government of the United States, or in any department or officer thereof.

Section 9 [1] The migration or importation of such persons as any of the States now existing shall think proper to admit shall not be prohibited by the Congress prior to the year one thousand eight hundred and eight, but a tax or duty may be imposed on such importation, not exceeding ten dollars for each person.

[2] The privilege of the writ of habeas corpus shall not be suspended, unless when in cases of rebellion or invasion the public safety may require it.

[3] No bill of attainder or ex post facto law shall be passed.

[4] No capitation or other direct tax shall be laid, unless in proportion to the census or enumeration hereinbefore directed to be taken.

[5] No tax or duty shall be laid on articles exported from any State.

[6] No preference shall be given by any regulation of commerce or revenue to the ports of one State over those of another; nor shall vessels bound to

or from one State be obliged to enter, clear or pay duties in another.

[7] No money shall be drawn from the Treasury but in consequence of appropriations made by law; and a regular statement and account of the receipts and expenditures of all public money shall be published from time to time.

[8] No title of nobility shall be granted by the United States; and no person holding any office of profit or trust under them shall, without the consent of the Congress, accept of any present, emolument, office, or title of any kind whatever from any king, prince, or foreign state.

Section 10 [1] No State shall enter into any treaty, alliance, or confederation; grant letters of marque and reprisal; coin money, emit bills of credit, make anything but gold and silver coin a tender in payment of debts; pass any bill of attainder, ex post facto law or law impairing the obligation of contracts, or grant any title of nobility.

[2] No State shall, without the consent of the Congress, lay any imposts or duties on imports or exports, except what may be absolutely necessary for executing its inspection laws; and the net produce of all duties and imposts, laid by any State on imports or exports, shall be for the use of the Treasury of the United States; and all such laws shall be subject to the revision and control of the Congress.

[3] No State shall, without the consent of Congress, lay any duty of tonnage, keep troops and ships of war in time of peace, enter into any agreement or compact with another State or with a foreign power, or engage in war, unless actually invaded or in such imminent danger as will not admit of delay.

Article II

Section 1 [1] The executive power shall be vested in a President of the United States of America. He shall hold his office during the term of four years, and together with the Vice-President, chosen for the same term, be elected as follows:

[2] Each State shall appoint, in such manner as the legislature thereof may direct, a number of Electors, equal to the whole number of Senators and Representatives to which the State may be entitled in the Congress; but no Senator or Representative, or person holding an office of trust or profit under the United States shall be appointed an Elector.

[3] The Electors shall meet in their respective States and vote by ballot for two persons, of whom one at least shall not be an inhabitant of the same State with themselves. And they shall make a list of all the persons voted for, and of the number of votes for each; which list they shall sign and certify, and transmit sealed to the seat of government of the United States, directed to the President of the Senate. The President of the Senate shall, in the presence of the Senate and House of Representatives, open all the certificates, and the votes shall then be counted. The person having the greatest number of votes shall be the President, if such number be a majority of the whole number of Electors appointed; and if there be more than one who have such majority, and have an equal number of votes, then the House of Representatives shall immediately choose by ballot one of them for President; and if no person have a majority, then from the five highest on the list the said House shall in like manner choose the President. But in choosing the President the votes shall be taken by States, the representation from each

State having one vote; a quorum for this purpose shall consist of a member or members from two-thirds of the States, and a majority of all the States shall be necessary to a choice. In every case, after the choice of the President, the person having the greatest number of votes of the Electors shall be the Vice-President. But if there should remain two or more who have equal votes, the Senate shall choose from them by ballot the Vice-President.

[4] The Congress may determine the time of choosing the Electors and the day on which they shall give their votes, which day shall be the same throughout the United States.

[5] No person except a natural-born citizen, or citizen of the United States at the time of the adoption of this Constitution, shall be eligible to the office of President; neither shall any person be eligible to that office who shall not have attained to the age of thirty-five years, and been fourteen years a resident within the United States.

[6] In case of the removal of the President from office, or of his death, resignation, or inability to discharge the powers and duties of the said office, the same shall devolve on the Vice-President, and the Congress may by law provide for the case of removal, death, resignation, or inability, both of the President and Vice-President, declaring what officer shall then act as President, and such officer shall act accordingly until the disability be removed or a President shall be elected.

[7] The President shall, at stated times, receive for his services a compensation, which shall neither be increased nor diminished during the period for which he shall have been elected, and he shall not receive within that period any other emolument from the United States or any of them.

[8] Before he enter on the execution of his office he shall take the following oath or affirmation: "I do solemnly swear (or affirm) that I will faithfully execute the office of President of the United States, and will to the best of my ability preserve, protect, and defend the Constitution of the United States."

Section 2 [1] The President shall be Commander-in-Chief of the Army and Navy of the United States, and of the militia of the several States when called into the actual service of the United States; he may require the opinion, in writing, of the principal officer in each of the executive departments, upon any subject relating to the duties of their respective offices, and he shall have power to grant reprieves and pardons for offenses against the United States, except in cases of impeachment.

[2] He shall have power, by and with the advice and consent of the Senate, to make treaties, provided two-thirds of the Senators present concur; and he shall nominate, and, by and with the advice and consent of the Senate, shall appoint ambassadors, other public ministers and consuls, judges of the Supreme Court, and all other officers of the United States whose appointments are not herein otherwise provided for, and which shall be established by law; but the Congress may by law vest the appointment of such inferior officers, as they think proper, in the President alone, in the courts of law, or in the heads of departments.

[3] The President shall have power to fill up all vacancies that may happen during the recess of the Senate, by granting commissions which shall expire at the end of their next session.

Section 3 He shall from time to time give to the Congress information of the state of the Union, and recommend to their consideration such measures as he shall judge necessary and expedient;

he may, on extraordinary occasions, convene both Houses, or either of them, and in case of disagreement between them with respect to the time of adjournment, he may adjourn them to such time as he shall think proper; he shall receive ambassadors and other public ministers; he shall take care that the laws be faithfully executed, and shall commission all the officers of the United States.

Section 4 The President, Vice-President and all civil officers of the United States shall be removed from office on impeachment for and conviction of treason, bribery, or other high crimes and misdemeanors.

Article III

Section 1 The judicial power of the United States shall be vested in one Supreme Court, and in such inferior courts as the Congress may from time to time ordain and establish. The judges, both of the Supreme and inferior courts, shall hold their offices during good behavior, and shall, at stated times, receive for their services a compensation which shall not be diminished during their continuance in office.

Section 2 [1] The judicial power shall extend to all cases, in law and equity, arising under this Constitution, the laws of the United States, and treaties made, or which shall be made, under their authority; to all cases affecting ambassadors, other public ministers, and consuls; to all cases of admiralty and maritime jurisdiction; to controversies to which the United States shall be a party; to controversies between two or more States; between a State and citizens of another State; between citizens of different States; between citizens of the same State claiming lands under grants of different States, and between a State, or the citizens thereof, and foreign states, citizens, or subjects.

[2] In all cases affecting ambassadors, other public ministers and consuls, and those in which a State shall be party, the Supreme Court shall have original jurisdiction. In all the other cases before mentioned the Supreme Court shall have appellate jurisdiction, both as to law and fact, with such exceptions and under such regulations as the Congress shall make.

[3] The trial of all crimes, except in cases of impeachment, shall be by jury; and such trial shall be held in the State where the said crimes shall have been committed; but when not committed within any State, the trial shall be at such place or places as the Congress may by law have directed.

Section 3 [1] Treason against the United States shall consist only in levying war against them, or in adhering to their enemies, giving them aid and comfort. No person shall be convicted of treason unless on the testimony of two witnesses to the same overt act, or on confession in open court.

[2] The Congress shall have power to declare the punishment of treason, but no attainder of treason shall work corruption of blood or forfeiture except during the life of the person attained.

Article IV

Section 1 Full faith and credit shall be given in each State to the public acts, records, and judicial proceedings of every other State. And the Congress may by general laws prescribe the manner in which such acts, records, and proceedings shall be proved, and the effect thereof.

Section 2 [1] The citizens of each State shall be entitled to all privileges and immunities of citizens in the several States.

[2] A person charged in any State with treason, felony, or other crime, who shall flee from justice, and be found in another State, shall, on demand of the executive authority of the State from which he fled, be delivered up, to be removed to the State having jurisdiction of the crime.

[3] No person held to service or labor in one State, under the laws thereof, escaping into another, shall, in consequence of any law or regulation therein, be discharged from such service or labor, but shall be delivered up on claim to the party to whom such service or labor may be due.

Section 3 [1] New States may be admitted by the Congress into this Union; but no new State shall be formed or erected within the jurisdiction of any other State; nor any State be formed by the junction of two or more States or parts of States, without the consent of the legislatures of the States concerned as well as of the Congress.

[2] The Congress shall have power to dispose of and make all needful rules and regulations respecting the territory or other property belonging to the United States; and nothing in this Constitution shall be so construed as to prejudice any claims of the United States or of any particular State.

Section 4 The United States shall guarantee to every State in this Union a republican form of government, and shall protect each of them against invasion, and on application of the legislature, or of the executive (when the legislature cannot be convened), against domestic violence.

Article V

The Congress, whenever two-thirds of both Houses shall deem it necessary, shall propose amendments to this Constitution, or, on the application of the legislatures of two-thirds of the several States, shall call a convention for proposing amendments, which in either case shall be valid to all intents and purposes as part of this Constitution, when ratified by the legislatures of three-fourths of the several States, or by conventions in three-fourths thereof, as the one or the other mode of ratification may be proposed by the Congress; provided that no amendment which may be made prior to the year one thousand eight hundred and eight shall in any manner affect the first and fourth clauses in the Ninth Section of the First Article; and that no State, without its consent shall be deprived of its equal suffrage in the Senate.

Article VI

[1] All debts contracted and engagements entered into, before the adoption of this Constitution, shall be as valid against the United States under this Constitution as under the Confederation.

[2] This Constitution, and the laws of the United States which shall be made in pursuance thereof, and all treaties made, or which shall be made, under the authority of the United States, shall be the supreme law of the land; and the judges in every State shall be bound thereby, anything in the Constitution or laws of any State to the contrary notwithstanding.

[3] The Senators and Representatives before mentioned and the members of the several State legislatures, and all executive and judicial officers both of the United States and of the several States, shall be bound by oath or affirmation to support this Constitution; but no religious test shall ever be required as a qualification to any office or pub-

lic trust under the United States.

Article VII
The ratification of the conventions of nine States shall be sufficient for the establishment of this Constitution between the States so ratifying the same.

Amendments to the Constitution
[The first 10 amendments, known collectively as The Bill of Rights, were adopted in 1791.]

Amendment I
Congress shall make no law respecting an establishment of religion, or prohibiting the free exercise thereof; or abridging the freedom of speech or of the press; or the right of the people peaceably to assemble, and to petition the government for a redress of grievances.

Amendment II
A well-regulated militia being necessary to the security of a free State, the right of the people to keep and bear arms shall not be infringed.

Amendment III
No soldier shall, in time of peace, be quartered in any house without the consent of the owner, nor in time of war, but in a manner to be prescribed by law.

Amendment IV
The right of the people to be secure in their persons, houses, papers, and effects, against unreasonable searches and seizures, shall not be violated, and no warrants shall issue but upon probable cause, supported by oath or affirmation, and particularly describing the place to be searched, and the persons or things to be seized.

Amendment V
No person shall be held to answer for a capital, or otherwise infamous crime, unless on a presentment or indictment of a grand jury, except in cases arising in the land or naval forces, or in the militia, when in actual service in time of war or public danger; nor shall any person be subject for the same offense to be twice put in jeopardy of life or limb; nor shall be compelled in any criminal case to be a witness against himself, nor be deprived of life, liberty or property, without due process of law; nor shall private property be taken for public use without just compensation.

Amendment VI
In all criminal prosecutions, the accused shall enjoy the right to a speedy and public trial, by an impartial jury of the State and district wherein the crime shall have been committed, which district shall have been previously ascertained by law, and to be informed of the nature and cause of the accusation; to be confronted with the witnesses against him; to have compulsory process for obtaining witnesses in his favor, and to have the assistance of counsel for his defense.

Amendment VII
In suits at common law, where the value in controversy shall exceed twenty dollars, the right of trial by jury shall be preserved, and no fact tried by a jury shall be otherwise re-examined in any court of the United States, than according to the rules of the common law.

Amendment VIII
Excessive bail shall not be required, nor excessive fines imposed, nor cruel and unusual punishments inflicted.

Amendment IX
The enumeration in the Constitution of certain rights shall not be construed to deny or disparage others retained by the people.

Amendment X
The powers not delegated to the United States by the Constitution, nor prohibited by it to the States, are reserved to the States respectively, or to the people.

Amendment XI [Adopted Jan. 8, 1798]
The judicial power of the United States shall not be construed to extend to any suit in law or equity, commenced or prosecuted against one of the United States by citizens of another State, or by citizens or subjects of any foreign state.

Amendment XII [Adopted Sept. 25, 1804]
[1] The Electors shall meet in their respective States and vote by ballot for President and Vice-President, one of whom, at least, shall not be an inhabitant of the same State with themselves; they shall name in their ballots the person voted for as President, and in distinct ballots the person voted for as Vice-President, and they shall make distinct lists of all persons voted for as President and of all persons voted for as Vice-President, and of the number of votes for each; which lists they shall sign and certify, and transmit sealed to the seat of the government of the United States, directed to the President of the Senate. The President of the Senate shall, in the presence of the Senate and House of Representatives, open all the certificates and the votes shall then be counted. The person having the greatest number of votes for President shall be the President, if such number be a majority of the whole number of Electors appointed; and if no person have such majority, then from the persons having the highest numbers not exceeding three on the list of those voted for as President, the House of Representatives shall choose immediately, by ballot, the President. But in choosing the President the votes shall be taken by States, the representation from each State having one vote; a quorum for this purpose shall consist of a member or members from two-thirds of the States, and a majority of all the States shall be necessary to a choice. And if the House of Representatives shall not choose a President whenever the right of choice shall devolve upon them, before the fourth day of March next following, then the Vice-President shall act as President, as in the case of the death or other constitutional disability of the President.

[2] The person having the greatest number of votes as Vice-President shall be the Vice-President, if such number be a majority of the whole number of Electors appointed; and if no person have a majority, then from the two highest numbers on the list the Senate shall choose the Vice-President; a quorum for the purpose shall consist of two-thirds of the whole number of Senators, and a majority of the whole number shall be necessary to a choice. But no person constitutionally ineligible to the office of President shall be eligible to that of Vice-President of the United States.

Amendment XIII [Adopted Dec. 18, 1865]
Section 1 Neither slavery nor involuntary servitude, except as a punishment for crime whereof the party shall have been duly convicted, shall ex-

ist within the United States, or any place subject to their jurisdiction.

Section 2 Congress shall have power to enforce this article by appropriate legislation.

Amendment XIV [Adopted July 28, 1868]

Section 1 All persons born or naturalized in the United States, and subject to the jurisdiction thereof, are citizens of the United States and of the State wherein they reside. No State shall make or enforce any law which shall abridge the privileges or immunities of citizens of the United States; nor shall any State deprive any person of life, liberty or property, without due process of law; nor deny to any person within its jurisdiction the equal protection of the laws.

Section 2 Representatives shall be apportioned among the several States according to their respective numbers, counting the whole number of persons in each State, excluding Indians not taxed. But when the right to vote at any election for the choice of Electors for President and Vice-President of the United States, Representatives in Congress, the executive and judicial officers of a State, or the members of the legislature thereof, is denied to any of the male inhabitants of such State, being twenty-one years of age, and citizens of the United States, or in any way abridged except for participation in rebellion or other crime, the basis of representation therein shall be reduced in the proportion which the number of such male citizens shall bear to the whole number of male citizens twenty-one years of age in such State.

Section 3 No person shall be a Senator or Representative in Congress, or elector of President and Vice-President, or hold any office, civil or military, under the United States or under any State, who, having previously taken an oath as a member of Congress, or as an officer of the United States, or as a member of any State legislature, or as an executive or judicial officer of any State, to support the Constitution of the United States, shall have engaged in insurrection or rebellion against the same, or given aid or comfort to the enemies thereof. But Congress may, by a vote of two-thirds of each House, remove such disability.

Section 4 The validity of the public debt of the United States, authorized by law, including debts incurred for payment of pensions and bounties for services in suppressing insurrection or rebellion, shall not be questioned. But neither the United States nor any State shall assume or pay any debt or obligation incurred in aid of insurrection or rebellion against the United States, or any claim for the loss or emancipation of any slave; but all such debts, obligations, and claims shall be held illegal and void.

Section 5 The Congress shall have power to enforce, by appropriate legislation, the provisions of this article.

Amendment XV [Adopted Mar. 30, 1870]

Section 1 The right of citizens of the United States to vote shall not be denied or abridged by the United States or by any State on account of race, color, or previous condition of servitude.

Section 2 The Congress shall have power to enforce this article by appropriate legislation.

Amendment XVI [Adopted Feb. 25, 1913]

The Congress shall have power to lay and collect taxes on incomes, from whatever source derived, without apportionment among the several States, and without regard to any census or enumeration.

Amendment XVII [Adopted May 31, 1913]

Section 1 The Senate of the United States shall be composed of two Senators from each State, elected by the people thereof, for six years; and each Senator shall have one vote. The electors in each State shall have the qualifications requisite for electors of the most numerous branch of the State legislatures.

Section 2 When vacancies happen in the representation of any State in the Senate, the executive authority of such State shall issue writs of election to fill such vacancies: Provided, that the legislature of any State may empower the executive thereof to make temporary appointments until the people fill the vacancies by election as the legislature may direct.

Section 3 This amendment shall not be so construed as to affect the election or term of any Senator chosen before it becomes valid as part of the Constitution.

Amendment XVIII [Adopted Jan. 29, 1919]

Section 1 After one year from the ratification of this article the manufacture, sale or transportation of intoxicating liquors within, the importation thereof into, or the exportation thereof from the United States and all territory subject to the jurisdiction thereof, for beverage purposes, is hereby prohibited.

Section 2 The Congress and the several States shall have concurrent power to enforce this article by appropriate legislation.

Section 3 This article shall be inoperative unless it shall have been ratified as an amendment to the Constitution by the legislatures of the several States, as provided in the Constitution, within seven years from the date of the submission hereof to the States by the Congress.

Amendment XIX [Adopted Aug. 26, 1920]

Section 1 The right of citizens of the United States to vote shall not be denied or abridged by the United States or by any State on account of sex.

Section 2 Congress shall have power to enforce this article by appropriate legislation.

Amendment XX [Adopted Feb. 6, 1933]

Section 1 The terms of the President and Vice-President shall end at noon on the 20th day of January, and the terms of Senators and Representatives at noon on the 3d day of January, of the years in which such terms would have ended if this article had not been ratified; and the terms of their successors shall then begin.

Section 2 The Congress shall assemble at least once in every year, and such meeting shall begin at noon on the 3d day of January, unless they shall by law appoint a different day.

Section 3 If, at the time fixed for the beginning of the term of the President, the President-elect shall have died, the Vice-President-elect shall become President. If a President shall not have been chosen before the time fixed for the beginning of his term or if the President-elect shall have failed to qualify, then the Vice-President-elect shall act as President until a President shall have qualified; and the Congress may by law provide for the case wherein neither a President-elect nor a Vice-President-elect shall have qualified, declaring who shall then act as President, or the manner in which one who is to act shall be selected, and such person shall act accordingly until a President or Vice-President shall have qualified.

Section 4 The Congress may by law provide for the case of the death of any of the persons from whom the House of Representatives may choose a President whenever the right of choice shall have devolved upon them, and for the case of death of any of the persons from whom the Senate may choose a Vice-President whenever the right of choice shall have devolved upon them.

Section 5 Sections 1 and 2 shall take effect on the 15th day of October following the ratification of this article.

Section 6 This article shall be inoperative unless it shall have been ratified as an amendment to the Constitution by the legislatures of three-fourths of the several States within seven years from the date of its submission.

Amendment XXI [Adopted Dec. 5, 1933]

Section 1 The eighteenth article of amendment to the Constitution of the United States is hereby repealed.

Section 2 The transportation or importation into any State, territory, or possession of the United States for delivery or use therein of intoxicating liquors, in violation of the laws thereof, is hereby prohibited.

Section 3 This article shall be inoperative unless it shall have been ratified as an amendment to the Constitution by conventions in the several States, as provided in the Constitution, within seven years from the date of the submission hereof to the States by the Congress.

Amendment XXII [Adopted Feb. 26, 1951]

Section 1 No person shall be elected to the office of President more than twice, and no person who has held the office of President, or acted as President, for more than two years of a term to which some other person was elected President shall be elected to the office of President more than once. But this Article shall not apply to any person holding the office of President when this Article was proposed by the Congress, and shall not prevent any person who may be holding the office of President, or acting as President, during the term within which this Article becomes operative from holding the office of President or acting as President during the remainder of such term.

Section 2 This article shall be inoperative unless it shall have been ratified as an amendment to the Constitution by the legislatures of three-fourths of the several States within seven years from the date of its submission to the States by the Congress.

Amendment XXIII [Adopted Apr. 3, 1961]

Section 1 The District constituting the seat of Government of the United States shall appoint in such manner as the Congress may direct:

A number of electors of President and Vice President equal to the whole number of Senators and Representatives in Congress to which the District would be entitled if it were a State, but in no event more than the least populous State; they shall be in addition to those appointed by the States, but they shall be considered, for the purposes of the election of President and Vice-President, to be electors appointed by a State; and they shall meet in the District and perform such duties as provided by the twelfth article of amendment.

Section 2 The Congress shall have power to enforce this article by appropriate legislation.

Amendment XXIV [Adopted Jan. 23, 1964]

Section 1 The right of citizens of the United States to vote in any primary or other election for President or Vice-President, for electors for President or Vice-President, or for Senator or Representative in Congress, shall not be denied or abridged by the United States or any State by reason of failure to pay any poll tax or other tax.

Section 2 The Congress shall have power to enforce this article by appropriate legislation.

Amendment XXV [Adopted Feb. 10, 1967]

Section 1 In case of the removal of the President from office or of his death or resignation, the Vice-President shall become President.

Section 2 Whenever there is a vacancy in the office of the Vice-President, the President shall nominate a Vice-President who shall take office upon confirmation by a majority vote of both Houses of Congress.

Section 3 Whenever the President transmits to the President pro tempore of the Senate and the Speaker of the House of Representatives his written declaration that he is unable to discharge the powers and duties of his office, and until he transmits to them a written declaration to the contrary, such powers and duties shall be discharged by the Vice-President as Acting President.

Section 4 Whenever the Vice-President and a majority of either the principal officers of the executive departments or of such other body as Congress may by law provide, transmit to the President pro tempore of the Senate and the Speaker of the House of Representatives their written declaration that the President is unable to discharge the powers and duties of his office, the Vice-President shall immediately assume the powers and duties of the office as Acting President.

Thereafter, when the President transmits to the President pro tempore of the Senate and the Speaker of the House of Representatives his written declaration that no inability exists, he shall resume the powers and duties of his office unless the Vice-President and a majority of either the principal officers of the executive department or of such other body as Congress may by law provide, transmit within four days to the President pro tempore of the Senate and the Speaker of the House of Representatives their written declaration that the President is unable to discharge the powers and duties of his office. Thereupon Congress shall decide the issue, assembling within forty-eight hours for that purpose if not in session. If the Congress, within twenty-one days after receipt of the latter written declaration, or, if Congress is not in session, within twenty-one days after Congress is required to assemble, determines by two-thirds vote of both Houses that the President is unable to discharge the powers and duties of his office, the Vice-President shall continue to discharge the same as Acting President; otherwise the President shall resume the powers and duties of his office.

Amendment XXVI [Adopted June 30, 1971]

Section 1 The right of citizens of the United States, who are eighteen years of age or older, to vote shall not be denied or abridged by the United States or by any State on account of age.

Section 2 The Congress shall have power to enforce this article by appropriate legislation.

Amendment XXVII [Adopted May 18, 1992]

No law, varying the compensation for the services of the Senators and Representatives, shall take effect until an election of Representatives shall have intervened.

▶THE EMANCIPATION PROCLAMATION

On July 22, 1862, Abraham Lincoln read to his cabinet a preliminary draft of an emancipation proclamation. Secretary of State William Seward suggested that the proclamation not be issued until a military victory had been won. The battle of Antietam gave Lincoln his desired opportunity, and on Sept. 22, he read to his cabinet a second draft of the proclamation. After some changes this was issued as a preliminary proclamation; the formal and definite proclamation came Jan. 1, 1863.

A Proclamation.

Whereas on the 22nd day of September, A.D. 1862, a proclamation was issued by the President of the United States, containing among other things, the following, to wit:

"That on the first day of January, A.D. 1863, all persons held as slaves within any State or designated part of a State the people whereof shall then be in rebellion against the United States shall be then, thenceforward, and forever free; and the executive government of the United States, including the military and naval authority thereof, will recognize and maintain the freedom of such persons and will do no act or acts to repress such persons, or any of them, in any efforts they may make for their actual freedom.

"That the executive will on the first day of January aforesaid, by proclamation, designate the States and parts of States, if any, in which the people thereof, respectively, shall then be in rebellion against the United States; and the fact that any State or the people thereof shall on that day be in good faith represented in the Congress of the United States by members chosen thereto at elections wherein a majority of the qualified voters of such States shall have participated shall, in the absence of strong countervailing testimony, be deemed conclusive evidence that such State and the people thereof are not then in rebellion against the United States."

Now, therefore, I, Abraham Lincoln, President of the United States, by virtue of the power in me vested as Commander-in-Chief of the Army and Navy of the United States in time of actual armed rebellion against the authority and government of the United States, and as a fit and necessary war measure for suppressing said rebellion, do, on this 1st day of January, A.D. 1863, and in accordance with my purpose so to do, publicly proclaimed for the full period of one hundred days from the first day above mentioned, order and designate as the States and parts of States wherein the people thereof, respectively, are this day in rebellion against the United States the following, to wit:

Arkansas, Texas, Louisiana (except the parishes of St. Bernard, Plaquemines, Jefferson, St. John, St. Charles, St. James, Ascension, Assumption, Terrebonne, Lafourche, St. Mary, St. Martin, and Orleans, including the city of New Orleans), Mississippi, Alabama, Florida, Georgia, South Carolina, North Carolina, and Virginia (except the forty-eight counties designated as West Virginia, and also the counties of Berkeley, Accomac, Northhampton, Elizabeth City, York, Princess Anne, and Norfolk, including the cities of Norfolk and Portsmouth), and which excepted parts are for the present left precisely as if this proclamation were not issued.

And by virtue of the power and for the purpose aforesaid, I do order and declare that all persons held as slaves within said designated States and parts of States are, and henceforward shall be, free; and that the Executive Government of the United States, including the military and naval authorities thereof, will recognize and maintain the freedom of said persons.

And I hereby enjoin upon the people so declared to be free to abstain from all violence, unless in necessary self-defense; and I recommend to them that, in all cases when allowed, they labor faithfully for reasonable wages.

And I further declare and make known that such persons of suitable condition will be received into the armed service of the United States to garrison forts, positions, stations, and other places, and to man vessels of all sorts in said service.

And upon this act, sincerely believed to be an act of justice, warranted by the Constitution upon military necessity, I invoke the considerate judgment of mankind and the gracious favor of Almighty God.

▶THE GETTYSBURG ADDRESS

Abraham Lincoln's most famous and most eloquent words were delivered on Nov. 19, 1863, at the dedication of the cemetery that held the remains of the 45,000 soldiers who fell at the Battle of Gettysburg, a significant Union victory.

"Fourscore and seven years ago our fathers brought forth on this continent, a new nation, conceived in Liberty, and dedicated to the proposition that all men are created equal.

"Now we are engaged in a great civil war, testing whether that nation or any nation so conceived and so dedicated, can long endure. We are met on a great battle-field of that war. We have come to dedicate a portion of that field, as a final resting place for those who here gave their lives that that nation might live. It is altogether fitting and proper that we should do this.

"But, in a larger sense, we can not dedicate—we can not consecrate—we can not hallow—this ground. The brave men, living and dead, who struggled here, have consecrated it, far above our poor power to add or detract. The world will little note, nor long remember what we say here, but it can never forget what they did here. It is for us the living, rather, to be dedicated here to the unfinished work which they who fought here have thus far so nobly advanced. It is rather for us to be here dedicated to the great task remaining before us—that from these honored dead we take increased devotion to that cause for which they gave the last full measure of devotion—that we here highly resolve that these dead shall not have died in vain—that this nation, under God, shall have a new birth of freedom—and that government of the people, by the people, for the people, shall not perish from the earth."

▶PLEDGE OF ALLEGIANCE

The original version of the Pledge of Allegiance appeared in the September 8, 1892, issue of *Youth's Companion* magazine. Authorship was in dispute between magazine staffers Francis Bellamy and James B. Upham until 1939, when the United States Flag Association declared Bellamy the author, and the Library of Congress concurred in 1957. Congress mandated two wording changes in the original version by substituting "the flag of the United States of America" for "my flag" in 1923, and adding "under God" in 1954. Public schools throughout the United States made the daily Pledge of Allegiance obligatory, and students who refused were expelled until the Supreme Court ruled in *West Virginia Board of Education v. Barnette* (1943) that the First Amendment protected the "right of silence" as well as freedom of speech.

"I pledge allegiance to the flag of the United States of America, and to the Republic, for which it stands, one nation, under God, indivisible, with liberty and justice for all."

CHRONOLOGY OF U.S. HISTORY

c. 1000 Viking explorer Leif Ericson explores North American coast and founds temporary colony called Vinland.

1492 On first voyage to America, Christopher Columbus lands at San Salvador island in Bahamas.

1493 Pope Alexander VI divides New World between Spain and Portugal.

1497 John Cabot claims Newfoundland for King Henry VII of England.

1499 Florentine merchant Amerigo Vespucci visits New World and begins writing popular accounts of his voyages.

1506 Columbus dies poor and embittered, convinced he found a new route to Asia and refusing to believe he discovered new continent.

1507 German mapmaker Martin Waldseemüller, after reading Vespucci's descriptions of the New World, names it "America" after him.

1513 Juan Ponce de León discovers Florida. Vasco Nuñez de Balboa crosses Panama and sights Pacific Ocean.

1519 Hernán Cortés lands in Mexico.

1520 Ferdinand Magellan, leader of the first expedition to circumnavigate the globe, discovers the South American straits that bear his name. In 1521, he is killed in the Philippines by natives.

1522 Cortés captures Mexico City and conquers Aztec empire.

1524 Giovanni de Verrazano, commissioned by King Francis I of France, discovers New York harbor and Hudson River.

1534 Jacques Cartier of France explores coast of Newfoundland and Gulf of St. Lawrence.

1536 Traveling overland from Gulf of Mexico, Alvar Núñez Cabeza de Vaca reaches Gulf of California.

1539 Fernando de Soto conquers Florida and begins three-year trek across Southeast.

1540 Francisco Vásquez de Coronado explores Southwest, discovering Grand Canyon and introducing horses to North America.

1541 Coronado discovers Mississippi River.

1542 João Rodrígues Cabrilho explores coast of California, missing San Francisco Bay.

1565 Don Pedro Menéndez de Aviles founds first permanent European settlement in North America at St. Augustine, Florida.

1572 Sir Francis Drake of England makes first voyage to America, landing in Panama.

1576 English explorer Martin Frobisher searches for Northwest Passage.

1577 Drake begins voyage of plunder around the world.

1579 Drake lands north of San Francisco Bay and claims region for Queen Elizabeth I.

1584 Sir Walter Raleigh discovers Roanoke Island. He names land Virginia, after Queen Elizabeth.

1585 Raleigh establishes England's first American colony at Roanoke.

1586 Drake evacuates surviving Roanoke settlers.

1587 Raleigh resettles Roanoke with 150 new colonists. Virginia Dare first child of English parents born in America.

1591 Relief expedition returns to the Roanoke colony; all settlers disappeared without trace.

1602 Captain Bartholomew Gosnold, first Englishman to set foot in New England, explores Cape Cod and Martha's Vineyard.

1603 Samuel de Champlain of France explores St. Lawrence Seaway, later founds Quebec.

1607 First permanent English settlement in America established at Jamestown, Virginia. Only 32 of original 105 colonists survive first winter.

1608 Captain John Smith imprisoned by Indians and saved by Pocahontas, daughter of Chief Powhatan.

1609 Henry Hudson sets out in search of Northwest Passage. Champlain sails into Great Lakes.

1611 Hudson cast adrift by mutinous crewmen to die in bay named after him.

1612 First Dutch trading post appears on Manhattan Island.

1616 Smallpox epidemic decimates Indian tribes from Maine to Rhode Island.

1619 Dutch traders bring first African slaves to Virginia for sale. Americans hold first election when Virginia planters vote for House of Burgesses.

1620 Pilgrims and others arrive in Plymouth, Massachusetts, aboard Mayflower. They draw up the Mayflower Compact.

1622 Most of Virginia colony wiped out in an Indian attack.

1624 King James I revokes Virginia's charter and makes it royal colony.

1626 The Dutch colony of New Amsterdam founded on Manhattan Island, bought from Indians for about $24.

1630 John Winthrop sets sail for Massachusetts with 900 Puritans and others, beginning Great Migration to New England.

1632 King Charles I of England grants Lord Baltimore charter to establish colony in Maryland.

1634 Massachusetts adopts representative government. Jean Nicolet of France begins trading with Indians in Wisconsin.

1635 Roger Williams, banished from Massachusetts, founds dissident colony of Rhode Island.

1636 New Englanders massacre hundreds of Indians in Pequot War. Harvard College established.

1638 First Swedish colony founded in Delaware.

1639 "Oath of a Free Man" the first English document printed in America. First public school appears in Dorchester, first post office in Boston, and Connecticut writes first colonial constitution.

1644 Indians make last unsuccessful attempt to expel English settlers from Virginia. First American ship built in Boston.

1647 Margaret Brent of Maryland first American woman to demand right to vote. Massachusetts passes first compulsory education law. First witchcraft execution occurs in Hartford, Conn.

1648 Boston shoemakers and coopers establish first American labor unions.

1651 Parliament passes first Navigation Act regulating colonial trade.

1652 Rhode Island first colony to outlaw slavery. First American coins minted in Boston.

1654 Jacob Barsimon, first American Jew, arrives in New Amsterdam, followed by 23 more Jews from Brazil.

1655 Dutch colonists capture Swedish colony in Delaware. Lady Deborah Moody of Long Island first American woman to vote.

1656 First Quakers arrive in America; imprisoned in Boston, beaten, and deported.

1659 Massachusetts hangs two Quakers on Boston Common.

1660 Parliament forbids Americans to export goods to countries other than England. Massachusetts outlaws celebration of Christmas.

1661 Virginia becomes the first colony to recognize slavery as legal.

1662 Connecticut granted royal charter. Massachusetts appoints official press censors and institutes half-way covenant.

1663 Parliament requires colonial imports from Europe to pass first through England. King Charles II grants charters to Carolina and Rhode Island.

1664 New Amsterdam captured by Richard Nicolls, who renames it New York. New Jersey established.

1670 Charles Town, later called Charleston, first permanent settlement in Carolina.

1672 Parliament tightens trade restrictions on colonies and appoints American customs collectors.

1673 French explorers Jacques Marquette and Louis Joliet paddle down Mississippi River to Arkansas. Regular mail service begins between Boston and New York. Dutch forces recapture New York.

1674 Treaty of Westminster restores New York to England. King Louis XIV of France sends Sieur de La Salle to explore Mississippi River.

1675 Thousands die in King Philip's War between New Englanders and five Indian tribes.

1676 Bacon's Rebellion overthrows government of Virginia and burns down Jamestown.

1680 New Hampshire separated from Massachusetts and made royal colony.

1681 King Charles II names William Penn proprietor of Pennsylvania.

1682 Penn founds Philadelphia. Sieur de La Salle claims North American interior for France, naming it Louisiana.

1683 First German-Americans, group of Mennonites, arrive in Philadelphia.

1684 King Charles II revokes Massachusetts charter.

1686 King James II appoints Sir Edmund Andros governor-general of Dominion of New England, dissolving colonial governments.

1688 Quakers publish first anti-slavery tracts in Pennsylvania.

1689 Andros surrenders to Boston mobs and colonial self-government is reestablished. Jacob Leisler seizes power in New York uprising. King William's War begins in America.

1690 Massachusetts issues first colonial paper money. American campaigns against French Canada fail. French and Indians burn Schenectady, N.Y.

1691 Jacob Leisler surrenders and is hanged. Massachusetts rechartered with religious freedom.

1692 Witchcraft hysteria breaks out in Salem, Mass., leading to 20 executions.

1693 College of William and Mary chartered, the second college in America.

1695 New York City organizes public relief for poor and homeless.

1696 Parliament places more commercial restrictions on colonies. American merchants join slave trade.

1697 Treaty of Ryswick ends King William's War.

1701 Antoine de la Mothe Cadillac establishes French outpost at Detroit, Michigan. Yale College founded. Delaware separated from Pennsylvania.

1702 Queen Anne's War breaks out.

1704 Boston News-Letter first regularly published newspaper in America.

1710 German Migration to America begins. British and American forces capture Port Royal, Nova Scotia.

1711 Anglo-American attack on Quebec fails. Tuscarora Indian War breaks out in North Carolina.

1712 Militia quell slave rebellion in New York City. Pennsylvania prohibits importing slaves.

1713 Treaty of Utrecht ends Queen Anne's War.

1716 First American theater built in Williamsburg, Va. Slavery introduced to French Louisiana.

1718 Jean Baptiste le Moyne founds French city of New Orleans.

1721 Sir Robert Walpole loosens colonial trade restrictions with policy of "salutary neglect."

1722 France declares New Orleans capital of Louisiana.

1723 America's first business corporation chartered in Connecticut.

1724 France expels all Jews from Louisiana.

1728 First American synagogue built in New York City.

1729 North and South Carolina receive royal charters.

1731 Benjamin Franklin founds first American library in Philadelphia.

1732 King George II grants charter to Georgia. Only Catholic church in colonial America opens in Philadelphia. Benjamin Franklin begins publishing Poor Richard's Almanac. George Washington born in Virginia.

1733 Parliament passes the Molasses Act, taxing imports from non-British sugar islands.

1734 Beginning of Great Awakening, widespread religious revival.

1735 French begin settling in Illinois.

1737 Boston holds its first public celebration of St. Patrick's Day.

1739 War of Jenkin's Ear begins. South Carolina slaves mount Stono Rebellion. French explorers Pierre and Paul Mallet discover Rocky Mountains.

1741 Danish navigator Vitus Bering, hired by Peter the Great of Russia, explores coast of Alaska. American Magazine, first in colonies, begins publishing in Philadelphia. Slave insurrection panic sweeps New York City.

1742 First sugar cane planted in Louisiana.

1744 King George's War breaks out.

1745 British and Americans capture Fort Louisbourg on Cape Breton Island. French and Indians raid Maine.

1748 Treaty of Aix-la-Chapelle ends King George's War and returns Fort Louisbourg to France.

1751 Parliament forbids New England colonies to issue paper money.

1752 Benjamin Franklin conducts famous kite experiment. Liberty bell is cracked in Philadelphia.

1753 Governor Dinwiddie of Virginia sends George Washington into Ohio country to demand withdrawal of French. First steam engine arrives in America.

1754 Washington skirmishes with French patrol, touching off French and Indian War. Franklin presents Albany Plan of Union for colonies.

1755 Quakers withdraw from Pennsylvania assembly rather than vote for military spending. Washington leads retreat from Battle of the Wilderness.

1758 British and American forces lose Battle of Ticonderoga, but capture Louisbourg and Fort Duquesne. New Jersey sets aside first Indian reservation for Onami tribe.

1759 General Wolfe defeats General Montcalm as British capture Quebec. Both generals fall in battle.

1760 After fall of Montreal, all of New France surrenders to Britain. King George III crowned in England.

1762 King Louis XV of France secretly cedes Louisiana to Spain.

1763 Treaty of Paris ends French and Indian War. France cedes Canada to Britain. King George III prohibits Americans to settle in West. Conspiracy of Pontiac threatens frontier.

1764 Parliament passes Sugar Act and forbids all colonies to issue paper money. French settlers found St. Louis. "Paxton Boys" march on Philadelphia. In Boston, James Otis protests, "no taxation without representation."

1765 Parliament passes Stamp Act (tax on newspapers, legal documents, etc.) and Quartering Act (requiring housing of British soldiers in homes). Sons of Liberty organize resistance and non-importation throughout colonies. Stamp Act Congress meets in New York.

1766   Parliament repeals the Stamp Act, but passes Declaratory Act affirming its right to pass laws binding on colonies. Chief Pontiac makes peace.

1767   Parliament enacts Townshend Duties and suspends New York assembly for resisting Quartering Act.

1768   "Regulators" rebel in North Carolina. Boston riots against Townshend Duties.

1769   Daniel Boone explores Kentucky. Father Junipero Serra founds San Diego, first Spanish mission in California. Gaspar de Portola sails into San Francisco Bay.

1770   Five Americans perish in Boston Massacre (Mar. 5). Parliament repeals Townshend Duties, except tax on tea.

1772   Rhode Island mob burns British revenue ship *Gaspee*. Boston appoints first Committee of Correspondence.

1773   Parliament passes Tea Act, leading to Boston Tea Party (Dec. 16).

1774   Parliament passes "Intolerable Acts" punishing colonists for Tea Party. Boston is occupied by British forces. First Continental Congress meets in Philadelphia.

1775   American Revolution begins with Battle of Lexington and Concord (Apr. 19). Second Continental Congress appoints George Washington as commander of Continental Army. British win Battle of Bunker Hill. First abolition society organized in Pennsylvania.

1776   Tom Paine's *Common Sense* published. Declaration of Independence signed. Congress adopts name, "United States of America." British occupy New York City. Washington crosses Delaware to win Battle of Trenton, N.J.

1777   Americans win battles at Princeton and Saratoga. British occupy Philadelphia. Congress adopts Stars and Stripes flag and endorses Articles of Confederation. Washington's army spends winter at Valley Forge, Pa.

1778   France makes alliance with U.S. and declares war on Britain. When French fleet arrives, British evacuate Philadelphia.

1779   Congress offers to make peace in exchange for independence. British withdraw from New York City.

1780   Pennsylvania first state to abolish slavery. British occupy Charleston, S.C. Washington quells Continental Army mutiny. Benedict Arnold defects to British.

1781   French and American victory at Battle of Yorktown ends the American Revolution. Articles of Confederation take effect. Los Angeles founded by Spanish missionaries.

1782   Parliament votes for peace with U.S. Negotiations in Paris lead to provisional Anglo-American peace treaty. Virginia permits owners to free their slaves. First English Bible printed in America.

1783   Massachusetts, Connecticut, and Rhode Island abolish slavery. Treaty of Paris signed (Sept. 3), officially ending American Revolution . Washington retires to Mount Vernon, Va.

1784   Congress ratifies Treaty of Paris. Spain closes Mississippi River to American trade. First bale of American cotton shipped to Britain.

1785   First state university chartered in Georgia.

1786   Virginia proclaims religious freedom. Shays's Rebellion put down in Massachusetts. Annapolis Convention calls for revising Articles of Confederation. New Jersey abolishes slavery.

1787   Convention in Philadelphia writes Constitution. Congress passes Northwest Ordinance and submits Constitution for state approval.

1788   Constitution ratified by New Hampshire (June 21), the ninth state to do so thereby marking its final approval.

1789   Constitution takes effect (March 4). George Washington wins first presidential election

unopposed. Federal government begins meeting in New York City. Congress enacts first Federal tariff.

1790   First antislavery petitions are submitted to Congress. Temporary capital moved to Philadelphia. Pope Pius VI appoints John Carroll first Catholic bishop in U.S. First U.S. census lists population at 3,929,625.

1791   Congress sets up First Bank of the United States and first internal revenue law, a tax on whiskey. Vermont enters union as 14th state. Bill of Rights takes effect. Pres. Washington selects site of new U.S. capital on the Potomac River.

1792   New York stock traders begin meeting under a tree on Wall Street. Pres. Washington is unanimously reelected. Construction begins on White House.

1793   Eli Whitney invents cotton gin. Congress passes first Fugitive Slave Act. Pres. Washington holds first official cabinet meeting and lays cornerstone for Capitol. Britain begins confiscating American ships trading with France.

1794   Pres. Washington defeats Whiskey Rebellion in Pennsylvania. U.S. and Britain sign Jay's Treaty. Ohio Indians defeated at Battle of Fallen Timbers.

1795   Georgia stung by scandal of Yazoo land frauds. Senate ratifies Jay's Treaty with Britain.

1796   Pres. Washington delivers "Farewell Address." France begins to confiscate ships trading with Britain.

1797   France insults American diplomats in XYZ Affair. Spanish begin building Mission San Juan Capistrano in California.

1798   Georgia last state to abolish slave trade. Congress passes Alien and Sedition Acts. U.S. renounces alliance with France as unofficial naval war breaks out.

1799   Russian-American trading company set up in Alaska. New York abolishes slavery.

1800   Library of Congress founded. Convention of 1800 signed, ending quasi-war between U.S. and France. Spain secretly cedes Louisiana to France. Congress begins meeting in Washington.

1801   Election of Thomas Jefferson results in first transfer of executive power between rival parties. Congress takes jurisdiction over District of Columbia. Tripoli pirates declare war on U.S.

1802   U.S. Military Academy established at West Point, N.Y.

1803   Louisiana Purchase from France doubles size of the U.S. Federal outpost founded at Fort Dearborn, Illinois, future site of Chicago.

1804   Lewis and Clark expedition sets out from St. Louis. Alexander Hamilton killed in duel with Aaron Burr.

1805   Barbary War with Tripoli ends.

1806   Congress authorizes construction of Cumberland Road. Noah Webster's first dictionary published.

1807   Britain and France enact blockades in Europe, confiscating American trading ships. British attack USS Chesapeake. Embargo Act forbids all American exports.

1808   Congress declares end to African slave trade.

1809   Embargo Act replaced with Non-Intercourse Act, outlawing exports to Britain and France. First steamboat sea voyage made from New York City to Philadelphia.

1810   Pres. Madison annexes West Florida.

1811   Worst earthquake in U.S. history rocks Ohio-Mississippi valleys. Russians settle at Ft. Ross, California. First Bank of the United States fails to obtain recharter. Gen. William Henry Harrison defeats Indians at Battle of Tippecanoe.

1812   War of 1812 begins by close vote in Congress. New England resists war. British clamp blockade on U.S. ports, capture Detroit, and repel American attack on Canada at Queenston.

1813 Americans regain Detroit, attack Toronto and Ft. George in Canada, but surrender to British at Beaver Dams, Ontario. Captain Oliver H. Perry wins control of the Great Lakes. British and Indians burn Buffalo, N.Y.

1814 British destroy Fort Oswego, N.Y., and set fire to Washington, D.C. Francis Scott Key writes "The Star Spangled Banner." New Englanders opposed to war meet secretly at Hartford Convention. First textile mill established at Waltham, Mass. Treaty of Ghent ends War of 1812.

1815 General Andrew Jackson routs British at Battle of New Orleans, before news arrives that War of 1812 is over.

1816 Congress charters Second Bank of the U.S.

1817 Rush-Bagot Treaty between Britain and U.S. demilitarizes Great Lakes. New York Stock and Exchange Board organized. Work begins on Erie Canal. Indian attack starts Seminole War in Florida.

1818 Cumberland Road opens. Congress adopts present format for American flag. Canadian boundary dispute with Britain settled.

1819 Panic of 1819 plunges South and West into depression. U.S. obtains Florida from Spain in Adams-Onís Treaty, settling border of Louisiana. Savannah makes first successful trans-Atlantic crossing under steam power.

1820 Missouri Compromise solves crisis over admission of Missouri as slave state. Abolitionists begin colonizing freed slaves to Africa.

1821 First Catholic cathedral in U.S. built in Baltimore.

1822 Denmark Vesey and 36 others executed for organizing rebel slave conspiracy in Charleston, S.C.

1823 Monroe Doctrine, masterminded by Secy. of State John Quincy Adams, announced by Pres. Monroe.

1824 Russia and U.S. settle territorial disputes in Pacific Northwest. First presidential nominating convention held in Utica, N.Y.

1825 John Quincy Adams chosen president in infamous "Corrupt Bargain" with Henry Clay, who becomes Secy. of State. Erie Canal opened. Mexico invites Americans to settle in Texas.

1826 Anti-Mason party organized. John Adams and Thomas Jefferson die on 50th anniversary of Declaration of Independence. Jedediah Smith leads first overland expedition to California.

1827 U.S. and Britain agree to joint occupation of Pacific Northwest.

1828 Congress passes protectionist "Tariff of Abominations" over Southern protests.

1829 Mexico refuses Pres. Jackson's offer to buy Texas.

1830 Webster-Hayne Debate in U.S. Senate reveals sectional tension. Church of Latter-Day Saints (the Mormons) founded by Joseph Smith in Fayette, N.Y. Mexico forbids further American immigration to Texas.

1831 Nat Turner leads bloodiest of all slave rebellions, killing 57 whites in Virginia.

1832 Black Hawk War fought in Illinois and Wisconsin. First nationwide Democratic Party convention held in Baltimore. Pres. Jackson vetoes bill to recharter national bank. South Carolina nullifies "Tariff of Abominations."

1833 Massachusetts last state to end tax support for churches. Congress lowers tariff and passes "Force Bill" to pressure South Carolina, which rescinds nullification. American Anti-Slavery Society organized.

1834 Whig party organized by Senators Henry Clay and Daniel Webster in opposition to Pres. Jackson. Anti-abolitionist riots break out in New York and Philadelphia.

1835 Samuel Morse invents telegraph. National debt completely paid off. Pres. Jackson survives first attempt to assassinate a president. Second

Seminole War begins in Florida.

1836 Samuel Colt invents revolver. Texas declares independence from Mexico and requests U.S. annexation. Mexican army captures Alamo, but Texans are victorious at San Jacinto.

1837 Panic of 1837 begins lengthy depression.

1838 Joshua Giddings of Ohio is first abolitionist elected to Congress. Trans-Atlantic steamship service established. Congress blocks abolitionist petitions with "Gag Rule."

1839 Abner Doubleday of Cooperstown, N.Y., codifies rules of baseball. Congress outlaws dueling in Washington, D.C.

1840 "Log Cabin Campaign" between William Henry Harrison and Martin Van Buren begins era of mass political participation. Liberty Party founded by abolitionists in Albany, N.Y.

1841 First emigrant train of 48 covered wagons arrives in California. Pres. Harrison dies after month in office. First Japanese immigrant arrives in New Bedford, Mass.

1842 Webster-Ashburton Treaty settles Canada boundary disputes between U.S. and Britain. U.S. accidentally seizes California, then returns it with apology to Mexico.

1843 End of Second Seminole War. B'Nai B'rith founded in New York. Mormons begin practicing polygamy.

1844 Baptists first church to split North and South over slavery. Samuel Morse sends first telegraph message. James K. Polk, first "Dark horse" candidate, elected President.

1845 "Potato Famine" begins massive Irish immigration. U.S. annexes Texas, over Mexican protests. U.S. Naval Academy opens at Annapolis, Md.

1846 Mexican War begins when U.S. troops are attacked in disputed Texas territory. American settlers in California stage Bear Flag Revolt. Oregon Treaty gives U.S. sole possession of Pacific Northwest up to 49th parallel. First recorded baseball game played in Hoboken, N.J.

1847 Wilmot Proviso, forbidding slavery expansion, passes House and sets off wave of panic in South. General Winfield Scott conquers Mexico City. Brigham Young leads Mormons to Utah. Abraham Lincoln of Illinois arrives in Congress.

1848 Treaty of Guadalupe-Hidalgo ends Mexican War, ceding Southwest to U.S. Revolution of 1848 begins wave of German immigration. New York-Chicago telegraph line completed. Chicago Board of Trade established. Free Soil party organized. Gold discovered in California. First Chinese immigrants arrive in San Francisco. Lucretia Mott and Elizabeth Cady Stanton hold first Women's Rights Convention in Seneca Falls, N.Y.

1849 Gold Rush brings hundreds of thousands to California. Elizabeth Blackwell first American woman to receive medical degree.

1850 Sen. Henry Clay's Compromise of 1850 solves crisis over slavery expansion. Clayton-Bulwer Treaty pledges Anglo-American cooperation in building any Central American canal.

1851 Y.M.C.A. established. Northern mobs resist Fugitive Slave Act. Maine is first state to pass prohibition laws. New York Times founded. Herman Melville's Moby Dick published.

1852 Harriet Beecher Stowe's Uncle Tom's Cabin published.

1853 U.S. buys Gila River valley from Mexico in Gadsden Purchase. Native American, or "Know-Nothing," party founded. Commodore Matthew C. Perry opens trade with Japan.

1854 Congress passes Kansas-Nebraska Act, setting off mass protests across North. Republican Party founded. U.S. threatens to seize Cuba from Spain in Ostend Manifesto.

1855 "Bleeding Kansas" fighting begins as pro-slavery and anti-slavery settlers hold rival state conventions. First railroad train crosses Mississippi

River at Rock Island, Ill., into Davenport, Iowa.
1856   Cong. Preston Brooks of South Carolina beats Sen. Charles Sumner of Massachusetts unconscious on Senate floor. John Brown leads Pottawatomie massacre in Kansas. First Republican national convention in Pittsburgh, Pa., in February.
1857   New York-St. Louis railroad completed. Supreme Court hands down controversial Dred Scott decision protecting slavery. Panic of 1857 sends North into depression.
1858   Lincoln-Douglas Debates dramatize issue of slavery expansion in Illinois race for Senate. First trans-Atlantic telegraph cable laid.
1859   John Brown's raid on Harpers Ferry arsenal to launch abolitionist war against slavery ends in his capture and execution. Slave insurrection panic sweeps South. Comstock Silver Lode discovered in Nevada. First producing oil well in U.S. flows in Titusville, Pa.
1860   Democratic Party splits into Northern and Southern wings. South Carolina is first state to secede from Union after victory of Abraham Lincoln. Crittenden Compromise fails to preserve Union. Pony Express begins mail delivery between California and Missouri.
1861   Civil War begins with attack on Ft. Sumter, South Carolina (Apr. 12). Pres. Lincoln calls for 75,000 volunteers to suppress rebellion. Jefferson Davis of Mississippi elected President of Confederate States of America. New York-San Francisco telegraph link completed. Yale awards first American Ph.D. Congress enacts first federal income tax.
1862   Congress issues "greenbacks," subsidizes transcontinental railroad, abolishes slavery in District of Columbia, and passes Homestead Act. Pres. Lincoln issues Emancipation Proclamation after Battle of Antietam, bloodiest of Civil War.
1863   Emancipation Proclamation takes effect (Jan. 1). Union victories at Vicksburg, Miss., and Gettysburg, Pa., signal turning point of Civil War. West Virginia secedes from Virginia and rejoins Union. Hundreds killed in New York City draft riot. Pres. Lincoln proclaims Thanksgiving national holiday.
1864   Pres. Lincoln names General Ulysses S. Grant as commander of Union armies. General William T. Sherman destroys Atlanta and conducts "March to the Sea." Confederate army of General Robert E. Lee crippled in Wilderness Campaign. Cheyenne and Arapaho Indians slaughtered in Sand Creek Massacre in Colorado.
1865   General Lee surrenders to General Grant at Appomattox Court House, Virginia (Apr. 9). Pres. Lincoln assassinated by John Wilkes Booth in Washington, D.C. (Apr. 14). Confederacy dissolved, ending Civil War. Pres. Johnson proclaims amnesty for most rebels. Slavery outlawed by adoption of Thirteenth Amendment. Ku Klux Klan founded in Pulaski, Tenn.
1866   In the struggle over Reconstruction policy, Congress overrides Pres. Johnson's vetoes of Civil Rights Act and New Freedmen's Bureau Bill. Whites riot in New Orleans to protest black suffrage. Grand Army of the Republic organized by Union veterans.
1867   Congress takes control of Reconstruction in the South by passing First Reconstruction Act over Pres. Johnson's veto and Tenure of Office Act. U.S. purchases Alaska from Russia for $7.2 million (2¢ an acre). Farmers organize Patrons of Husbandry, beginning Granger movement.
1868   Pres. Johnson is impeached in the House (Feb. 24), but acquitted in the Senate by a single vote (May 16). U.S. and China sign Burlingame Treaty to allow immigration. Fourteenth Amendment grants equal citizenship and protection to freedmen (July 28). Half a million black votes help elect Gen. Ulysses S. Grant to the presidency. The typewriter invented.

1869   "Hard Money" prevails when Congress passes Public Credit Act, promising repayment of government debts in gold. Transcontinental railroad completed with golden spike between Union Pacific and Central Pacific lines at Promontory Point, Utah (May 10). Jay Gould and James Fisk cause financial panic by trying to corner gold market on "Black Friday" (Sept. 24). Knights of Labor union organized. National Women's Suffrage Association formed in New York. Wyoming Territory grants first U.S. women's suffrage.
1870   Fifteenth Amendment guarantees right to vote for all U.S. citizens, though only Wyoming and Utah territories allow women's suffrage (Mar. 30). Congress passes first Ku Klux Act to enforce Fifteenth Amendment. First black senator and black congressman are elected.
1871   Congress passes second Ku Klux Klan Act to enforce Fourteenth Amendment in the South. New York Times begins exposé of Boss William Marcy Tweed, leading to overthrow of Tammany Hall ring. Most of Chicago destroyed in the Great Fire (Oct. 8–11). Anti-Chinese race riots in Los Angeles.
1872   Crédit Mobilier scandal implicates Vice President Schuyler Colfax and embarrasses Grant administration. Yellowstone National Park created. Susan B. Anthony arrested for leading suffragists to the polls. Montgomery Ward opens for business in Chicago.
1873   Silver withdrawn from money supply in the "Crime of '73." Congressmen raise their own salaries 50 percent, and double president's pay in "Salary Grab" Act. Panic of 1873, triggered by failure of Jay Cooke's banking house, begins depression of 1870s. New York Stock Exchange forced to close for 10 days. Great Bonanza silver lode discovered in Nevada. San Francisco installs first cable cars.
1874   Granger movement begins passing railroad regulations in Midwestern states. Women's Christian Temperance Union founded in Cleveland, Ohio. Greenback Party formed in Indianapolis. Black rioters attack courthouse in Vicksburg, Miss. Chautauqua movement begins bringing educational speakers to rural communities across the country.
1875   Congress passes Specie Resumption Act to reduce money supply by redeeming greenbacks for gold, and Civil Rights Act to guarantee equal rights for freedmen. Whiskey Ring scandal casts further pall on Grant administration. Archbishop John McCloskey of New York first American bishop. Aristides wins first Kentucky Derby at Churchill Downs, Ky.
1876   U.S. awards patent to Alexander Graham Bell for the telephone. Gen. George A. Custer and 265 men are massacred by Sioux at Little Big Horn, S. Dak. (June 25). Democrat Samuel Tilden outpolls Republican Rutherford B. Hayes as presidential election is thrown into the House (Nov. 7). Baseball's National League established. Kappa Alpha opens first fraternity house at Williams College. Central Park in New York completed.
1877   Congress appoints Electoral Commission to solve impasse over disputed 1876 election. House votes 185 to 184 to declare Rutherford Hayes president, three days before his inauguration (Mar. 2). Reconstruction officially ends with withdrawal of federal troops from the South (Apr. 24). Pres. Hayes sends in troops as Great Railroad Strike paralyzes much of the country. Anti-Chinese riots break out in San Francisco.
1878   Sen. A. A. Sargent introduces Women's Suffrage Amendment in Congress (Jan. 10). Greenback-Labor Party formed in Toledo, Ohio. Limited coinage of silver resumes with Bland-Allison Act. American Bar Association organized in Saratoga, N.Y. Edison Electric begins operating in New York

City. New Haven, Conn. sets up first commercial telephone network.

1879 U.S. resumes specie payments for greenbacks. F.W. Woolworth opens his first store in Utica, N.Y. First Church of Christ, Scientist, founded in Boston. Thomas Edison invents light bulb. California adopts state constitution forbidding employment of Chinese labor.

1880 Pres. Hayes declares U.S. must control any Isthmian canal. U.S. and China agree to Chinese Exclusion Treaty. National Farmers' Alliance organized in Chicago. American branch of Salvation Army founded in Philadelphia, Pa. Census lists U.S. population over 50 million for first time (50,155,783).

1881 Pres. Garfield assassinated by Charles Guiteau in Washington, D.C. (July 2—dies Sept. 19). Clara Barton creates American Red Cross. Booker T. Washington founds Tuskegee Institute for black education in Alabama. Russian Jews begin immigrating to U.S. to escape pogroms.

1882 John D. Rockefeller organizes Standard Oil trust, first such combination. Congress passes first Chinese Exclusion Act (May 10), and legislates first immigration restrictions: no paupers, convicts, or mental defectives. Knights of Columbus founded with permission from Roman Catholic Church.

1883 Congress passes Pendleton Act, requiring civil service competition for Federal jobs. Brooklyn Bridge opened in New York. Supreme Court strikes down Civil Rights Act of 1875. New York-Chicago telephone service begins. Ohio River floods devastate Cincinnati. U.S. Navy builds its first steel ships. Railroads agree on Standard Time zones for North America.

1884 "Mugwumps" bolt Republican Party. Statue of Liberty cornerstone laid (Aug. 5). Belva A. Lockwood of Equal Rights Party first woman candidate for president. Grover Cleveland of New York first Democrat elected president since Civil War. Home Insurance Building of Chicago first skyscraper in the world. Moses Fleetwood Walker first black professional baseball player.

1885 Washington Monument completed after 36 years of construction. U.S. Marines land in Panama (Apr. 24). Senate refuses to ratify treaty for building a canal across Nicaragua. Congress outlaws building fences on public lands in the West. Josiah Strong's best-seller Our Country argues for American imperialism.

1886 Knights of Labor rail strike sets off national wave of strikes for eight-hour day. Haymarket Riot in Chicago leads to execution of seven anarchists. Statue of Liberty dedicated (Oct. 28). American Federation of Labor founded in Columbus, Ohio. Indian wars end with capture of Geronimo.

1887 Congress creates Interstate Commerce Commission, first federal regulatory agency, but with weak enforcement powers. Congress distributes reservation land to Indians, also bans opium imports. First electric trolley line built in Richmond, Va. U.S. Navy leases base at Pearl Harbor, Hawaii.

1888 Snow falls for 36 hours in New York, killing 400 people in "Great Blizzard of '88" (Mar. 12). First secret ballot election held in Louisville, Ky. George Eastman markets first Kodak camera. National Geographic Society founded in Washington, D.C. Edward Bellamy's utopian novel, Looking Backward, a sensational best-seller.

1889 Four new states—N.Dak., S.Dak., Mont., Wash.—all admitted in one day (Feb. 22). Oklahoma Land Rush results as former Indian territory is opened for settlement (Apr. 22). Johnstown Flood claims thousands of lives in Pennsylvania (May 31). Kansas passes first antitrust law. Jane Addams founds Hull House in Chicago.

1890 Congress passes Sherman Antitrust Act (July 2) and Sherman Silver Purchase Act. Wyoming admitted as first state with women's suffrage (July 10). Sioux uprising ends at Battle of Wounded Knee (Dec. 29). Yosemite National Park created. Mississippi leads South in disfranchising black voters. Jacob Riis's How the Other Half Lives awakens Americans to urban poverty. Navy wins 24-0 in first Army-Navy football game.

1891 New Orleans mob lynches 11 Italian immigrants. People's, or Populist, Party organized in Cincinnati. U.S. and Chile nearly go to war over death of two American sailors in Valparaiso (Oct. 16). Dr. James A. Naismith invents basketball in Springfield, Mass. Thomas Edison patents first American-made motion picture camera.

1892 Populist candidate James B. Weaver of Iowa receives over a million votes for president. Violent strikes break out among steel workers in Homestead, Pa., and silver miners in Coeur d'Alene, Idaho. Chinese immigrants forced to register with Federal government. First gasoline-powered American automobile built in Chicopee, Mass. Boll weevil first appears in Texas.

1893 U.S. gold reserve falls below $100 million (Apr. 21). Panic of 1893, touched off by New York stock market crash (June 27), begins second-worst depression in U.S. history. Congress repeals Sherman Silver Purchase Act (Oct. 30). Mormon Temple dedicated in Salt Lake City, Utah.

1894 Coxey's Army of unemployed march on Washington, D.C. (Apr. 30). U.S. Treasury issues two $50 million bond offerings to shore up dwindling gold reserves. Congress enacts first peacetime Federal income tax, denounced as "socialism, communism, devilism" (Aug. 27). Pullman strike paralyzes railroads across the country.

1895 J.P. Morgan bails out U.S. Treasury, faced with a gold drain. "Silver Democrats" appeal for unlimited silver coinage as way out of depression. Supreme Court rules income tax unconstitutional (May 20). First professional football game played in Latrobe, Pa.

1896 Supreme Court approves segregation (Plessy vs. Ferguson). William Jennings Bryan, "Silver Democrat" of Nebraska, wins nomination with "Cross of Gold" speech. Gold discovered in Klondike, Alaska, defusing the money question (Aug. 16). American athletes win nine of 12 events at first Olympics. Henry Ford builds his first automobile. First American motion pictures appear in theaters. "The Yellow Kid," first comic strip, begins running in New York World.

1897 U.S. offers to mediate Cuban rebellion, lodges official complaint against Spanish brutality. "Yellow press" newspapers keep up assault on Spain. First American subway completed in Boston.

1898 After mysterious explosion of battleship Maine in Havana (Feb. 15), Spanish-American War breaks out (Apr. 21). Commodore George Dewey destroys Spanish fleet at Manila Bay (May 1); U.S. takes Manila (Aug. 13). After Battle of San Juan Hill (July 1), Spanish garrison at Santiago, Cuba, surrenders (July 17). U.S. takes Cuba, Puerto Rico, Guam, Wake Island, and Philippines from Spain in Treaty of Paris (Dec. 10). Senate agrees to annex Hawaii.

1899 Philippine Revolt against U.S. rule erupts. Sec. of State John Hay issues Open Door notes to European powers and Japan, requesting no spheres of influence in China (Sept. 6). U.S. and Germany agree to partition Samoan Islands. Congress investigates incompetence in War Department, revealed during Spanish-American War.

1900 "Hard Money" triumphs as U.S. returns to single gold standard (Mar. 14). Puerto Rico and Hawaii become U.S. territories (Apr. 12 & Apr. 30). U.S. troops relieve foreign legations under siege in Peking, China, during Boxer Rebellion. Olds Company opens first Detroit auto factory. Carrie Nation leads hatchet-wielding women into Kansas saloons to smash liquor barrels.

1901 J.P. Morgan creates U.S. Steel, first billion-dollar corporation. U.S. retains control over Cuba with Platt Amendment. Pres. McKinley shot by anarchist Leon Czolgosz in Buffalo, N.Y. (Sept. 6—dies Sept. 14). Hay-Pauncefote Treaty secures British approval for a U.S.-built canal in Panama (Nov. 18). First great Texas oil strike made near Beaumont, Tex. Pres. Roosevelt promises to "speak softly and carry a big stick."

1902 End of Philippine Insurrection. Reclamation Act initiates Federal policy of conservation of natural resources (June 17). Congress declares Philippines an unorganized territory whose inhabitants are not U.S. citizens (July 1). First Rose Bowl game played. Pres. Roosevelt helps mediate Pennsylvania coal strike.

1903 Pres. Roosevelt helps Panama gain independence from Colombia, then negotiates treaty to build Panama Canal. Orville and Wilbur Wright conduct first powered flight near Kitty Hawk, N.C. (Dec. 17). The Great Train Robbery, first feature-length motion picture, released. Wisconsin holds first primary elections. Ford Motor Company formed. Boston defeats Pittsburgh in first baseball World Series.

1904 Supreme Court upholds antitrust dissolution of Northern Securities company (Mar. 14). "Roosevelt Corollary" to Monroe Doctrine justifies U.S. intervention to keep other powers out of Western hemisphere. New York state enacts first speed limit: 20 mph Deaf, dumb, and blind, Helen Keller graduates from Radcliffe College.

1905 Supreme Court disallows limits on length of working day. Industrial Workers of the World, a radical labor union, formed in Chicago. Pres. Roosevelt mediates Treaty of Portsmouth, ending Russo-Japanese War. Black leaders hold Niagara Falls Conference, calling for equal rights.

1906 San Francisco destroyed by earthquake and fire (Apr. 18–19). Congress passes Pure Food and Drug Act and Meat Inspection Act. Race riot breaks out in Atlanta (Sept. 22). Japan protests segregation of Asian students in California schools (Oct. 25). Pres. Roosevelt first American to win the Nobel Peace Prize, and first sitting president to leave U.S. on visit to Panama.

1907 Panic of 1907 triggers crash on Wall Street (Mar. 13) and run on banks across the country. Pres. Roosevelt orders exclusion of Japanese laborers (Mar. 14). Congress outlaws corporate contributions to political campaigns. Hundreds killed in coal mine explosions in Monongah, W. Va., and Jacobs Creek, Pa. All-time record 1,285,349 immigrants arrive in one year.

1908 U.S. and Japan conclude "Gentleman's Agreement" limiting immigration. Ford Model T appears on the market (Oct. 1). Root-Takahira Agreement promises U.S. and Japan will respect each other's interests in Pacific. Pres. Roosevelt appoints National Conservation Commission. Federal Bureau of Investigation established. New York City outlaws women smoking in public.

1909 Robert E. Peary plants American flag at North Pole (Apr. 6). Pres. Taft opens 700,000 acres for settlement in the West. W.E.B. DuBois founds National Association for the Advancement of Colored People (NAACP), advocating racial equality.

1910 Theodore Roosevelt calls for "New Nationalism" in a speech at Ossawatomie, Kans. Los Angeles Times building destroyed by terrorist bomb (Oct. 1). Glacier National Park created. Mann Act cracks down on "white slave" trade. Boy Scouts of America chartered.

1911 Pres. Taft orders U.S. troops to border during Mexican Revolution. Supreme Court upholds antitrust breakups of Standard Oil and American Tobacco. Calbraith P. Rodgers makes first transcontinental airplane flight. U.S. bankers take control of Nicaragua's finances. Steel magnate Andrew Carnegie donates $125 million for philanthropic purposes.

1912 *Titanic* sinks on maiden voyage from England (Apr. 15). Progressive, or "Bull Moose," Party founded by Theodore Roosevelt, who survives an assassination attempt by John Schrank in Milwaukee (Oct. 14). Massachusetts adopts first minimum wage law. U.S. Marines land in Honduras, Cuba, Nicaragua, and Santo Domingo. Textile strike in Lawrence, Mass.

1913 Sixteenth Amendment empowers Federal government to collect income taxes (Feb. 25). Seventeenth Amendment allows for popular election of U.S. senators (May 31). Congress creates Federal Reserve system. Ford Motor Company introduces assembly line. John D. Rockefeller donates $100 million to philanthropic Rockefeller Foundation. Grand Central Station opens in New York City.

1914 Pres. Wilson nearly goes to war with Mexico over arrests of American sailors in Tampico. U.S. Navy shells Vera Cruz and lands Marines in retaliation (Apr. 21). U.S. declares neutrality in World War I (Aug. 4). Congress passes Clayton Act, toughening antitrust standards. Congress proclaims Mother's Day.

1915 The Birth of a Nation, first movie blockbuster. Pres. Wilson strongly protests German sinking of Lusitania with 128 Americans aboard (May 7). U.S. Marines land in Haiti (July 28). Ku Klux Klan revived in Atlanta, Ga. Coast-to-coast long distance telephone service begins.

1916 House-Grey Memorandum warns Germany that refusal to negotiate may bring U.S. into World War I. Gen. John Pershing chases Pancho Villa into Mexico after border raid on Columbus, N.Mex. (Mar. 15). U.S. acquires Virgin Islands from Denmark for $25 million. Jeanette Rankin of Montana first woman elected to Congress. Louis D. Brandeis first Jewish member of Supreme Court. Margaret Sanger opens first birth control clinic in Brooklyn, N.Y. National Park Service created.

1917 Germany resumes unrestricted submarine warfare, leading U.S. to sever diplomatic relations (Feb. 3). Gen. John Pershing withdraws from Mexico. Zimmerman Telegram reveals German overtures to Mexico in case of war (Feb. 24). U.S. merchant ships armed for self-defense against German submarines (Mar. 13). After Pres. Wilson proclaims "the world must be made safe for democracy," Congress declares war on Germany (Apr. 6) and Austria-Hungary (Dec. 7). Prohibition begins as wartime conservation measure.

1918 Pres. Wilson announces U.S. war aims in "Fourteen Points" speech (Jan. 8). U.S. troops join Allied intervention in Russian Revolution (Aug. 2). Congress passes Sedition Act. Over a million U.S. troops participate in month-long Meuse-Argonne campaign (Sept. 26-Nov. 11). Republicans win control of Congress, a rebuke to Pres. Wilson. Armistice Day ends World War I (Nov. 11) as mass celebrations break out across the country. Pres. Wilson goes to Europe for peace conference. Supreme Court approves draft laws and strikes down child labor laws. Influenza epidemic takes hundreds of thousands American lives.

1919 Eighteenth Amendment establishes Prohibition (Jan. 29). Strike wave sweeps country, triggering "Red Scare." American Communist Party organized in Chicago. Race riots in Washington, D.C., and Chicago. Pres. Wilson suffers incapacitating stroke (Sept. 26). Volstead Act implements national Prohibition enforcement. Senate rejects Versailles Treaty and League of Nations (Nov. 19). Grand Canyon National Park created. New York-Chicago daily airmail service begins.

1920 Attorney General A. Mitchell Palmer stages "Palmer Raids," arresting and deporting thousands of radicals and immigrants. Sacco and Vanzetti are arrested for murder in Braintree, Mass. Supreme Court upholds Prohibition. Nineteenth Amendment establishes women's suffrage (Aug. 26). National League of Women Voters organized. First regular radio broadcasts begin in East Pittsburgh, Pa. Pres. Wilson receives Nobel Peace Prize. U.S. population, more urban than rural for first time, tops 100 million (105,710,620).

1921 Pres. Harding, promising a "return to normalcy," takes office. U.S. negotiates separate peace with Germany, Austria, and Hungary. Ku Klux Klan spreads terror in the South. Jack Dempsey defeats Georges Carpentier in first million-dollar prize fight.

1922 Washington Conference concludes with nine international treaties to limit naval arms race, relax tensions in the Pacific, and protect China. Supreme Court upholds women's suffrage. Lincoln Memorial dedicated in Washington, D.C. (May 30). Pres. Harding vetoes "Bonus Bill" for World War I veterans. Congress passes joint resolution in favor of Jewish homeland in Palestine (Sept. 21). First commercial radio show broadcast in New York.

1923 Last U.S. occupation troops leave Germany (Jan. 10). Senate begins investigating corruption in Veterans Bureau and Teapot Dome oil leases (Oct. 25). Pres. Harding dies mysteriously of "apoplexy" in San Francisco (Aug. 2). Pres. Coolidge's address to Congress, calling for economy in government, first radio broadcast of a presidential speech (Dec. 6). Oklahoma declares martial law to crack down on Ku Klux Klan. Yankee Stadium opens.

1924 Congress provides bonuses for World War I veterans over Pres. Coolidge's veto. Congress passes Immigration Act, imposing strict national quota system. European powers accept Dawes Plan for repayment of war debts and reparations. U.S. Marines withdraw from Santo Domingo. Coast-to-coast air mail service begins.

1925 Tennessee outlaws teaching evolution in school, leading to the Scopes Trial in Dayton, Tenn. (July 10-21). Ku Klux Klan marches on Washington, D.C. (Aug. 8) Nellie Tayloe Ross of Wyoming first woman governor. Florida land boom draws hordes of speculators. Chicago gang wars break out as Al Capone consolidates bootlegging operations.

1926 Treasury Sec. Andrew Mellon's drastic tax cuts approved. Admiral Richard E. Byrd and Floyd Bennett first to fly over North Pole (May 9). Henry Ford institutes 8-hour day and 5-day work week at Ford Motor Company factories. Hurricane sweeps Florida, killing 372 people. Book of the Month Club founded. U.S. Marines return to Nicaragua.

1927 Charles Lindbergh completes non-stop solo flight from New York to Paris (May 20-21), returns home to huge welcoming crowds. Sacco and Vanzetti executed in Massachusetts, despite international protests. The Jazz Singer with Al Jolson becomes first "talkie" motion picture (Oct. 6). Mississippi River floods causes $300 million damage. Ford Model A unveiled. Mechanical cotton picker invented. New York-London commercial telephone service begins.

1928 U.S. joins fourteen countries in signing Kellogg-Briand Pact for the "outlawry of war" (Aug. 27). Clark Memorandum disavows future U.S. interventions in Latin America. Pres. Coolidge refuses to aid American farmers mired in agricultural depression. Walt Disney creates "Steamboat Willie," first Mickey Mouse cartoon. George Eastman demonstrates color motion picture technology. Republicans promise "a chicken in every pot, a car in every garage."

1929 St. Valentine's Day Massacre claims six lives in Chicago gang wars. Young Plan replaces Dawes Plan for payment of war debts and reparations. Albert B. Fall, former secretary of the Interior,

found guilty in Teapot Dome scandal. Stock market crash on "Black Tuesday" (Oct. 29) ushers in Great Depression.

1930 Wave of bank failures sweeps U.S., wiping out millions of savings accounts and leading to private hoarding of gold. U.S., Britain, and Japan sign London Naval Treaty limiting naval arms race (Apr. 22). Hawley-Smoot Tariff raises barriers to world trade, worsening Depression. Congress creates Veteran's Administration (July 3).

1931 World War I veterans are offered "Bonus Loans" to combat Depression. "Star Spangled Banner" becomes national anthem. "Scottsboro Boys" arrested for rape in Alabama. Empire State Building, tallest building in the world, opens in New York City. Pres. Hoover declares moratorium on international debt and reparations payments.

1932 Stimson Doctrine condemns Japanese invasion of China. Congress approves Reconstruction Finance Corporation to help recovery. Norris-LaGuardia act restricts use of injunctions against labor strikes. Franklin D. Roosevelt wins presidential election in a landslide, promising a "New Deal." Stock market drops to 10% of its 1929 value. "Bonus Army" of poor veterans marches on Washington, D.C. Amelia Earhart first woman to fly solo across the Atlantic.

1933 Giuseppe Zangara kills Chicago Mayor Anton J. Cermak in a Miami, Fla., motorcade, narrowly missing president-elect Franklin D. Roosevelt (Feb. 15). Banks are closed for four days by presidential order (Mar. 5). During "Hundred Days" (Mar. 9-June 16), Pres. Roosevelt pushes New Deal through Congress, conducts first "Fireside Chat" on radio, and takes U.S. off gold standard. Prohibition repealed (Mar. 22). U.S. recognizes Soviet Union (Nov. 16). U.S. Marines withdraw from Nicaragua. Frances Perkins, Sec. of Labor, becomes first woman cabinet member.

1934 Dust storms inundate Southwest, driving "Okies" and "Arkies" to California. General strike paralyzes San Francisco (July 16). John Dillinger, public enemy number one, killed by FBI agents (July 22). Sen. Gerald P. Nye of North Dakota begins investigating role of U.S. munitions manufacturers in World War I. U.S. releases Cuba from Platt Amendment. U.S. troops withdraw from Haiti.

1935 Supreme Court invalidates National Industrial Recovery Act. Pres. Roosevelt pushes more "Second New Deal" legislation through Congress, notably the Wagner Act protecting unions, Social Security Act, and "Soak the Rich" Wealth Tax Act. Sen. Huey P. Long of Louisiana assassinated (Sept. 8). Congress of Industrial Organization (CIO) formed (Nov. 9). Congress passes first Neutrality Act. Alcoholics Anonymous founded.

1936 Congress passes second Neutrality Act. France, Britain, and U.S. sign New London Naval Treaty (Mar. 25). U.S. declares neutrality in Spanish Civil War (Aug. 7). CIO auto workers begin sit-down strikes in Flint, Mich. Life magazine begins publishing. Jesse Owens wins four gold medals at "Nazi Olympics" in Berlin.

1937 Congress passes third Neutrality Act. Pres. Roosevelt proposes controversial "court-packing" plan. German dirigible Hindenburg explodes and burns in Lakehurst, N.J. (May 6). Pres. Roosevelt angers isolationists with "Quarantine Speech" (Oct. 5). Japanese planes sink U.S. Navy gunboat Panay in China (Dec. 12). Slow recovery ends abruptly as Depression worsens.

1938 Pres. Roosevelt calls for military buildup. Mexico seizes U.S.-owned oil wells. Rep. Martin Dies of Texas begins House Un-American Activities Committee (HUAC) investigations of Communists and Fascists. Howard Hughes sets record for around-the-world flight in less than four days (July 14). "Invasion from Mars" radio broadcast by Orson

Welles causes widespread panic (Oct. 30). Hurricane devastates Atlantic coast, killing 700.

1939 Supreme Court upholds Tennessee Valley Authority. Pan Am begins first regular trans-Atlantic passenger service. U.S. declares neutrality in World War II (Sept. 5). Congress passes fourth Neutrality Act, approving Pres. Roosevelt's request for "cash-and-carry" arms sales to belligerents. First nylon stockings appear on the market.

1940 As World War II engulfs Europe, Pres. Roosevelt announces U.S. move from "neutrality" to "non-belligerency" (June 10). U.S. and Britain conclude Destroyers-for-Bases deal. Congress enacts peacetime draft (Sept. 16) and massive increases in military spending. Over 16 million men register for draft as embargo on strategic exports takes effect. Roosevelt, reelected to an unprecedented third term, calls for U.S. to, become "the arsenal of democracy" (Dec. 20).

1941 Congress appropriates $7 billion in Lend-Lease aid to Britain. German submarine sinks merchant ship *Robin Moor*, first U.S. casualty of war (May 21). Pres. Roosevelt responds by declaring "unlimited national emergency" (May 27), freezing German and Italian assets in U.S. (June 14), and promising aid to Soviet Union (June 24). Pres. Roosevelt freezes Japanese assets in retaliation for invasion of Indochina. U.S. Navy is ordered to "shoot on sight" at German warships. Japanese planes attack Pearl Harbor, Hawaii, killing 2,400 U.S. servicemen and civilians (Dec. 7). U.S. declares war on Japan (Dec. 8) and on Germany and Italy (Dec. 11).

1942 Roosevelt creates War Production Board, calls for mass mobilization, and puts New Deal on hold. U.S. troops land in North Ireland, first to arrive in Europe (Jan. 26). Pres. Roosevelt approves internment of Japanese-Americans for duration of war (Feb. 20). Japanese submarine shells an oil refinery in Santa Barbara, Calif. (Feb. 23). Maj. James H. Doolittle stages carrier-launched bombing raid on Tokyo (Apr. 18). U.S. armed forces surrender in Philippines (May 6), but win major naval victories over Japan in Coral Sea (May 4–8) and at Midway (June 3–6). U.S. offensive begins in Pacific with invasion of Guadalcanal Island (Aug. 7). First all-U.S. bombing attack launched against German forces at Rouen, France (Aug. 17). Congress approves "Victory Tax" on wartime incomes. Allies land 400,000 men in North Africa (Nov. 7–8). Eight German saboteurs apprehended in New York; six executed. Cocoanut Grove nightclub fire in Boston kills 492.

1943 Congress appropriates $100 billion for war effort. Roosevelt and Churchill demand "unconditional surrender" at Casablanca conference in Morocco. U.S. Marines drive last Japanese from Guadalcanal (Feb. 9). U.S. troops defeated in first battle with Germans at Kasserine Pass, Tunisia (Feb. 20). Pres. Roosevelt declares wage-and-price freeze to stem inflation. U.S. and Britain invade Sicily (July 10) and Italy proper (Sept. 3). Roosevelt and Churchill meet with Chiang Kai-Shek of China in Cairo, Egypt (Nov. 22), and with Josef Stalin of Soviet Union in Teheran, Iran (Dec. 4–6). Gen. Dwight D. Eisenhower named Supreme Commander of Allied forces in Europe.

1944 U.S. and British planes begin around-the-clock bombing of Berlin. Allied forces land at Anzio, Italy (Jan. 22). Congress approves $1.35 billion for United Nations Relief and Reconstruction Agency, first U.S. foreign aid (Mar. 29). Allied forces enter Rome (June 5) as reconquest of Europe begins with D-Day invasion of Normandy (June 6). Allied breakout from Normandy sends German forces reeling across France (July 25). Postwar financial arrangements made at an international conference in Bretton Woods, N.H. (July 1–22). Plans for U.N. made at Dumbarton Oaks conference (Aug. 21–Oct. 7). Gen. Douglas MacArthur begins reconquest of Philippines with landings at Leyte Gulf

(Oct. 20). Congress passes Servicemen's Readjustment Act, known as "GI Bill of Rights." Roosevelt wins fourth term.

1945 Roosevelt, Churchill and Stalin meet for last time at Yalta in Soviet Crimea to begin postwar planning (Feb. 4–11). Allied forces cross Rhine River and drive into heart of Germany (Mar. 7). U.S. air raids destroy Tokyo (Mar. 10–11). Pres. Roosevelt dies suddenly of cerebral hemorrhage in Warm Springs, Ga. (Apr. 12). Germany surrenders, ending war in Europe (May 7). Fifty nations sign United Nations Charter (June 26). First atomic explosion occurs in test at Alamagordo, N. Mex. (July 16). Pres. Truman meets with Churchill and Stalin at Potsdam, Germany (July 17–Aug. 2). Atomic bombs dropped on Hiroshima (Aug. 6) and Nagasaki (Aug. 9); Japan surrenders (Aug. 14), ending World War II. Council of Allied Foreign Ministers meets in London, unable to agree on peace treaty (Dec. 16–27). Empire State Building hit by B-25 bomber in heavy fog.

1946 Strike wave sweeps U.S., idling 4.6 million U.S. workers. Congress passes Employment Act, committing Federal government to postwar economic management. Churchill warns Americans about Communist expansion with "Iron Curtain" speech in Fulton, Mo. (Mar. 5). Pres. Truman seizes control of railroads and coal mines during strikes. U.S. presents Baruch Plan for international control of atomic energy, grants independence to Philippines (July 4), and agrees to loan Britain $3.5 billion for postwar reconstruction. Paris Peace Conference ends in failure (July 29–Oct. 15). Congress creates Atomic Energy Commission. U.N. General Assembly begins meeting in New York.

1947 Council of Foreign Ministers meets in Moscow, again unable to agree on peace treaty (Mar. 10–Apr. 24). Pres. Truman announces Truman Doctrine, promising aid to countries threatened by subversion (May 12). Sec. of State George C. Marshall announces Marshall Plan for reconstruction of Europe (June 5). Republican-dominated Congress restricts union organizing with Taft-Hartley Act. House Un-American Activities Committee (HUAC) begins investigating Communism in Hollywood (Oct. 20). Texas City, Tex., wiped out when a ship explodes, killing over 500. Jackie Robinson of Brooklyn Dodgers breaks color line in baseball.

1948 Postwar inflation keeps prices rising fast. Congress approves $5.3 billion for Marshall Plan aid to Europe with Foreign Assistance Act. U.S. recognizes new state of Israel (May 14) and admits 205,000 war refugees from Europe. Britain and U.S. begin airlifting supplies into West Berlin after Soviets cut off all traffic into city (June 26). Pres. Truman orders peacetime draft and desegregation of U.S. armed forces. HUAC charges Alger Hiss with spying for Soviet Union. Pres. Truman wins upset reelection victory over New York Gov. Thomas E. Dewey. Idlewild International Airport, world's largest, opens in New York.

1949 Pres. Truman calls for "Fair Deal" domestic programs and "Point Four" foreign aid programs. U.S., Canada, and 10 Western European nations sign treaty that will lead to North Atlantic Treaty Organization (NATO). Berlin Airlift ends when Soviets finally lift blockade (May 12). Pres. Truman announces Soviet atomic bomb test (Sept. 23). Eleven U.S. Communist leaders convicted of conspiring to overthrow government. Steel strike idles half a million workers (Oct. 1–Nov. 11). Lucky Lady II of U.S. Air Force completes first nonstop around-the-world flight.

1950 Sen. Joseph R. McCarthy of Wisconsin issues his first accusations of Communists in government at a speech in Wheeling, W. Va. North Korea invades South Korea, beginning Korean War (June 25). Pres. Truman orders U.S. intervention (June 27), obtains U.N. support (July 7), asks Congress for a $10 billion rearmament program (July 20), and calls up reserves (Aug. 4). Inchon landing begins rout of North Korean invaders (Sept. 15). U.N. troops recapture Seoul (Sept. 26) and invade North Korea (Oct. 7). Congress passes Internal Security Act, requiring registration of Communist organizations, over Pres. Truman's veto (Sept. 23). Puerto Rican nationalists nearly assassinate Pres. Truman in Washington (Nov. 11). After China intervenes in the Korean War, Pres. Truman proclaims a national emergency (Dec. 16).

1951 Gen. Dwight D. Eisenhower comes out of retirement to accept command of Allied forces in Europe (Apr. 4). Julius and Ethel Rosenberg sentenced to death for spying (Apr. 5). Pres. Truman removes Gen. Douglas MacArthur from command in Korea for insubordination (Apr. 11). MacArthur returns to the U.S., greeted by exultant crowds, to deliver address to Congress. Missouri River floods devastate Kansas City, causing over $1 billion in damages (July 11–25). U.S. concludes a mutual defense pact with Australia and New Zealand, and signs a peace treaty with Japan (Sept. 8). Congress passes the Mutual Security Act, providing $7 billion for foreign aid and military cooperation with pro-U.S. nations. CBS transmits first color television broadcast from New York.

1952 Pres. Truman seizes steel mills paralyzed by strikes (Apr. 8). U.S., Britain and France sign a peace treaty with West Germany (May 26). Construction begins on USS Nautilus, first atomic submarine. Supreme Court upholds barring subversives from teaching in schools. Sen. Richard M. Nixon of California, Republican candidate for Vice President, delivers "Checkers Speech" on national television to explain his "secret slush fund." Republicans win control of White House and both houses of Congress for first time since 1928. U.S. announces first successful hydrogen bomb test at Eniwetok Atoll in Marshall Islands (Nov. 16).

1953 Thirteen more Communist leaders are convicted of conspiring to overthrow the government. Julius and Ethel Rosenberg are executed in Ossining, N.Y. (June 19). Pres. Eisenhower lifts wage and price controls, increases U.S. support for French war effort in Indochina, negotiates armistice ending Korean War (June 27). Congress creates Department of Health, Education, and Welfare (Apr. 1). U.S. pledges aid to Spain in exchange for military bases (Sept. 26). Major Chuck Yeager of the U.S. Air Force sets new air speed record in rocket-powered X-1 jet plane.

1954 Sec. of State John Foster Dulles vows "massive retaliation" against Soviet aggression (Jan. 12). Puerto Rican nationalists shoot five Congressmen on the floor of the House of Representatives (Mar. 1). U.S. negotiates the Southeast Asia Treaty Organization (SEATO) security pact (Sept. 8). Supreme Court orders school desegregation in Brown v. Board of Education (May 17). CIA helps overthrow the Arbenz government in Guatemala (June 29). Senate censures Sen. Joseph McCarthy.

1955 Pres. Eisenhower promises to use atomic weapons in case of war and conducts first televised press conference. U.S., Soviet Union, and Allies agree on Austrian peace treaty to end occupation. Supreme Court orders school desegregation to proceed "with all deliberate speed." Interstate Commerce Commission orders desegregation on interstate trains and buses. AFL and CIO labor federations merge to form the AFL-CIO, with 15 million members. Dr. Jonas Salk perfects polio vaccine. Dr. Martin Luther King, Jr., leads bus boycott in Montgomery, Ala.

1956 Pres. Eisenhower refuses to intervene against Soviet invasion of Hungary and exerts pressure on Allies to withdraw from Suez. Congressmen signing Southern Manifesto promise "massive resistance" to school desegregation. Atomic Energy Commission approves commercial nuclear power plants. Congress passes Highway Act, appropriating $32 billion for construction of a vast nationwide road system. TWA and United airliners collide in midair and crash into Grand Canyon, killing 128 people. First trans-Atlantic telephone cable begins operating.

1957 Pres. Eisenhower announces Eisenhower Doctrine, promising aid to any Middle Eastern country threatened by Communism. McClellan Committee begins investigating corruption and racketeering in International Brotherhood of Teamsters union. Sen. J. Strom Thurmond of South Carolina sets all-time filibuster record (24 hours, 27 minutes) with speech against civil rights (Aug. 30). Congress nevertheless approves the first Civil Rights Act since Reconstruction (Sept. 9). Pres. Eisenhower sends troops to Little Rock, Ark., to enforce Federal desegregation order (Sept. 24). First underground atomic test conducted in Nevada (Sept. 19).

1958 In response to Soviet launch of Sputnik, U.S. launches Explorer I, first American satellite; Congress creates National Aeronautics and Space Administration (NASA). Vice President Richard M. Nixon nearly killed by angry mob in Caracas, Venezuela. At request of weak government in Beirut, Pres. Eisenhower orders U.S. Marines to land in Lebanon (July 15). Nuclear submarine Nautilus performs first undersea crossing of North Pole (Aug. 5). Presidential assistant Sherman Adams forced to resign in scandal over accepting favors (Sept. 22).

1959 Fidel Castro's takeover of Cuba begins rapid deterioration of U.S.-Cuba relations (Jan. 1). Alaska becomes 49th state (Jan. 3), and Hawaii becomes 50th state (Aug. 21). Joint U.S.-Canada St. Lawrence Seaway project completed. Congress passes the Landrum-Griffin Act to suppress racketeering in labor unions. Vice Pres. Richard M. Nixon holds impromptu "kitchen debate" in Moscow with Soviet Premier Nikita Khrushchev. Charles Van Doren testifies that his victory on the "$64,000 Question" TV game show was fixed.

1960 U.S. and Japan conclude new security treaty (Jan. 19). Black students stage first sit-in at a Woolworth's lunch counter in Greensboro, N.C. (Feb. 1). U-2 spy plane, with American pilot Francis Gary Powers, is shot down over the Soviet Union (May 1). Congress passes second Civil Rights Act since Reconstruction. Congress investigates "payola" in the radio industry, leading to the arrest of Alan Freed, "father of rock 'n' roll." After Cuba rejects American protests over confiscated property, Pres. Eisenhower imposes trade embargo. John F. Kennedy and Richard M. Nixon hold first televised presidential campaign debates. Kennedy wins election by 0.3 percent of popular vote, closest presidential election since 1884 (Nov. 8).

1961 Pres. Eisenhower breaks diplomatic relations with Cuba, warns Americans to beware of "military-industrial complex." CIA-backed Bay of Pigs invasion fails to overthrow Castro regime in Cuba (Apr. 17). Commander Alan B. Shephard, Jr., U.S. Navy, first American in space on Mercury rocket (May 5). Soviet construction of Berlin Wall creates temporary crisis (Aug. 13). Pres. Kennedy creates Peace Corps and Alliance for Progress. American families advised to build nuclear fallout shelters. "Freedom Rides" civil rights protests broken up by riots in Anniston and Birmingham, Ala. American Medical Association reports link between smoking and heart disease. National Council of Churches endorses birth control for families.

1962 Lt. Col. John H. Glenn, Jr., first American to orbit Earth. Pres. Kennedy convinces steel companies to rescind price increases. U.S. conducts first successful test of sea-launched long-range ballistic missile with nuclear warhead. Pres. Kennedy sends

U.S. marshals to protect James H. Meredith, a black student at University of Mississippi. U.S. extends a $100 million emergency loan to the United Nations. Threat of nuclear war during Cuban Missile Crisis averted when Soviet Union agrees to withdraw missiles from Cuba (Oct. 22–28). Rachel Carson's *Silent Spring* draws attention to environmental crisis.

1963 Pres. Kennedy proposes the Medicare program. U.S., Great Britain, and the Soviet Union conclude the Nuclear Test-Ban Treaty outlawing atmospheric testing (July 25). "Hot line" between Washington and Moscow put in place. Civil rights movement reaches a climax with mass demonstrations in Birmingham, Ala., and epic March on Washington, where Martin Luther King delivers his "I Have a Dream" speech (Aug. 28). Pres. Kennedy is assassinated in Dallas, Tex., by Lee Harvey Oswald (Nov. 22), who is murdered by Jack Ruby (Nov. 24).

1964 Pres. Johnson, taking up Pres. Kennedy's cause, calls for a "War on Poverty." Supreme Court orders states to redraw Congressional boundaries to ensure fair representation. Alaska declared disaster area after major earthquake rocks Anchorage (Mar. 28). Mississippi "Freedom Summer" begins with murder of three civil rights workers (June 22). Pres. Johnson pushes landmark Civil Rights and Economic Opportunity acts through Congress. After alleged North Vietnamese attack on U.S. Navy destroyers, Congress passes Tonkin Gulf Resolution giving Pres. Johnson free hand in Vietnam (Aug. 7). Warren Commission reports there was no conspiracy to assassinate Pres. Kennedy (Sept. 27). The Rev. Martin Luther King Jr. wins Nobel Peace Prize.

1965 Pres. Johnson calls for the "Great Society." Black nationalist Malcolm X is assassinated in New York City (Feb. 21). Pres. Johnson orders U.S. Marines into South Vietnam (Mar. 8) and into Santo Domingo (Apr. 38). U.S. troops authorized to undertake offensive operations in South Vietnam (June 8). Martin Luther King leads civil rights marches from Selma to Montgomery, Ala., and in white neighborhoods of Chicago. Congress approves Medicare (July 30) and Voting Rights Act (Aug. 6). The Watts Riot in Los Angeles leaves 34 dead and over $200 million in damage (Aug. 11–16), accelerating wave of ghetto riots. Tornadoes sweep Midwest, killing 271 and injuring 5,000.

1966 Pres. Johnson orders first B-52 strategic bombing raids on North Vietnam (Apr. 12). Supreme Court rules police must advise suspects of their rights. Cesar Chavez leads United Farm Workers strike and boycott against California grape growers. Stokeley Carmichael of Student Non-Violent Coordinating Committee demands "Black Power." Congress enacts safety standards for automobiles. U.S. troops in Vietnam increase from 215,000 to over 400,000.

1967 Green Bay defeats Kansas City in first ever Super Bowl. Hundreds of thousands of anti-war protesters march on Washington (Apr. 15 & Oct. 21–22). Pres. Johnson announces U.S. troop level will reach 525,000 by end of 1968. Worst race riot in U.S. history erupts in Detroit (July 23), leaving 43 dead, while riot in Newark, N.J., (July 12) kills another 26. Sen. Eugene McCarthy (D–Minn.) announces antiwar candidacy for president (Nov. 30). U.S. agrees to refrain from placing nuclear weapons in space and joins General Agreement on Tariffs and Trade (GATT). Thurgood Marshall becomes first black justice on Supreme Court.

1968 North Korea seizes *U.S.S. Pueblo*, holding 82 crewmen hostage (Jan. 23). North Vietnam and Viet Cong launch massive Tet Offensive (Jan. 30). Pres. Johnson makes surprise announcement that he will not seek re-election (Mar. 31). Martin Luther King assassinated by James Earl Ray in Memphis, Tenn. (Apr. 4). Washington-Hanoi peace talks begin in Paris (May 10). After winning California primary,

Sen. Robert F. Kennedy of New York murdered by Sirhan Sirhan in Los Angeles (June 5). U.S. signs Nuclear Non-Proliferation Treaty. Democratic Convention in Chicago marred by riots and police violence against antiwar demonstrators. Shirley Chisholm of New York is the first black woman elected to Congress. Apollo VIII completes first moon orbit.

1969 Oil spill off Santa Barbara, Calif., draws attention to need for environmental protection (Feb. 5). Pres. Nixon asks Congress to fund Anti-Ballistic Missile program as "safeguard" for strategic defense. U.S. losses in Vietnam exceed losses in Korean War. Sen. Edward M. Kennedy (D–Mass.) drives off a bridge at Chappaquiddick, Mass., killing Mary Jo Kopechne (July 18). Neil Armstrong and Buzz Aldrin of *Apollo XI* are first men to walk on the moon (July 20). Hurricane Camille claims over 300 victims in the South. Trial of Chicago Seven begins. Woodstock music festival near Bethel, N.Y., draws 400,000 young fans (Aug. 15–18). Vietnam Moratorium and "March Against Death" antiwar demonstrations draw hundreds of thousands to Washington. U.S. and the Soviet Union begin Strategic Arms Limitation Talks (S.A.L.T.) in Helsinki, Finland.

1970 Pres. Nixon calls for "Vietnamization" to decrease U.S. involvement in war. U.S. bombing of North Vietnam escalates dramatically; nationwide protests break out when U.S. invades Cambodia (Apr. 29). Four students are killed and nine wounded by National Guard units at Kent State University in Ohio (May 4). Lt. William L. Calley court-martialed for massacre of 102 civilians in My Lai South Vietnam (Nov. 12). Supreme Court upholds new 18-year-old voting age (Dec. 21). Congress creates Environmental Protection Agency, passes Water Quality Improvement Act, Air Quality Control Act, and Occupational Safety and Health Act.

1971 Pres. Nixon proposes federal revenue sharing with states. Charles Manson and three women followers convicted for Tate-LaBianca murders in Los Angeles (Jan. 25). Major earthquake rocks Southern California, killing 64 and injuring over 1,000 (Feb. 9). Supreme Court approves busing to achieve school integration. Indian occupation of Alcatraz Island in San Francisco Bay comes to an end. Prison riot in Attica, N.Y., kills 43 inmates and guards. *The New York Times* begins publishing "Pentagon Papers," top-secret history of Vietnam War (June 13). U.S. devalues dollar (Dec. 18). U.S. troops in Vietnam reach 139,000; U.S. air attacks are heaviest since 1968.

1972 Nixon first president to visit China (Feb. 21–28) and the Soviet Union (May 22–30). Airlines begin screening passengers to prevent hijackings. Congress passes Equal Rights Amendment and submits it to states for ratification. Gov. George Wallace of Alabama shot and seriously wounded by Arthur Bremer while campaigning for president in Laurel, Md. (May 15). Five men arrested for breaking into Democratic National Committee headquarters at the Watergate complex in Washington (June 17). Federal grand jury indicts five burglars and two former White House aides in Watergate break-in (Sept. 15). Pres. Nixon angers farmers with the "Great Grain Robbery," a secret deal to sell wheat at discount to Soviet Union. National Security Advisor Henry Kissinger announces "peace is at hand" in Vietnam in time for Pres. Nixon to carry 49 states in election. U.S. troops in Vietnam fall to 69,000 as Nixon orders resumed bombing of North Vietnam (Dec. 18).

1973 Supreme Court overturns state restrictions on abortions (*Roe v. Wade*). U.S. signs Paris peace accords ending Vietnam War (Jan. 27). Indians hold the town of Wounded Knee, S.D. in an armed standoff against Federal Marshals (Feb. 27–May 8). Trial of Watergate burglars reveals conspiracy to conceal White House involvement. Top presidential aides H.R. Haldeman, John Ehrlichman, John Dean, and Attorney General Richard Kleindienst resign amid charges of White House cover-up (Apr. 30). Sen. Sam Ervin of North Carolina chairs Senate investigation of Watergate scandal (May 17–Nov. 15). Pres. Nixon fires Watergate Special Prosecutor Archibald Cox and others in "Saturday Night Massacre" (Oct. 20). Vice President Spiro Agnew resigns after threat of prosecution for tax evasion (Oct. 10). Gasoline prices skyrocket after Arab nations embargo oil exports to U.S. in retaliation for U.S. aid to Israel in Yom Kippur War (Oct. 17). Pres. Nixon turns over first White House tapes, which include mysterious 18 1/2 minute gap (Nov. 26). Gerald R. Ford of Michigan sworn in as first vice president chosen under 25th Amendment (Dec. 6). Indians defy Federal authority in Wounded Knee, S.D.

1974 Arab oil embargo of U.S. lifted (Mar. 18). Supreme Court rules that Pres. Nixon must submit all White House tapes to Special Prosecutor Leon Jaworski (July 24). House Judiciary Committee votes three articles of impeachment (July 24–30). Pres. Nixon releases transcripts of tapes that show he ordered cover-up (Aug. 5). Citing "political" difficulties, Pres. Nixon resigns (Aug. 8), elevating Vice Pres. Ford to presidency (Aug. 9). Pres. Ford shocks nation by pardoning Nixon for all crimes (Sept. 8). Pres. Ford meets with Soviet Premier Leonid Brezhnev in Vladivostock to approve SALT treaty (Nov. 23–24). Newspaper heiress Patty Hearst kidnapped in Berkeley, Calif., by radical Symbionese Liberation Army.

1975 Nixon aides convicted of obstructing justice in Watergate investigation (Jan. 1). Last Americans evacuate Saigon as South Vietnam falls to North Vietnamese invasion (Apr. 30). Cambodia seizes USS Mayaguez (May 12), and Pres. Ford orders rescue operation (May 14). Apollo-Soyuz, joint Soviet-American space mission, achieves link-up in space (July 17). Lynette "Squeaky" Fromme and Sarah Jane Moore attempt to assassinate Pres. Ford in separate California incidents (Sept. 5 & Sept. 22). Congress votes to admit women to Army, Navy, and Air Force academies. House Democrats dismantle seniority system. Church Committee discovers CIA helped overthrow Salvador Allende of Chile and plotted to assassinate Fidel Castro of Cuba.

1976 Congress repeatedly overrides Pres. Ford's vetoes of bills providing for jobs, health, education, and welfare programs. Supreme Court upholds death penalty (July 3). Bicentennial of U.S. celebrated coast to coast. Jimmy Carter defeats Pres. Ford as voters hold Ford responsible for pardoning Nixon. Justice Department begins probing South Korean bribery of Congressmen and other officials. Viking I and Viking II space probes land on Mars, transmit scientific data and color photographs back to Earth. "Legionnaire's Disease" breaks out at Philadelphia American Legion convention, killing 29. Hundreds of West Point cadets found to have cheated on exams.

1977 Pres. Carter pardons Vietnam War draft evaders, threatens to reduce foreign aid for countries violating human rights, calls for "moral equivalent of war" in energy conservation, and signs Panama Canal treaty (Sept. 7). U.S. declares 200-mile sovereignty zone in Atlantic and Pacific oceans to exclude foreign fishing vessels. Power blackout sets off arson and looting spree in New York City (July 13–14). Oil begins flowing through the Alaska pipeline. Pres. Carter accuses oil industry of "the biggest rip-off in history" (Oct. 13). ABC mini-series Roots, draws 130 million viewers.

1978 Pres. Carter postpones production of neutron bomb. California voters approve Proposition 13, reducing property taxes and setting off a nationwide "taxpayers' revolt." Supreme Court gives limited approval to affirmative action programs, but disallows quotas for college admissions (June 28). In private talks with Anwar Sadat and Menachem Begin, Pres. Carter mediates peace between Egypt and Israel with landmark Camp David Accords (Sept. 17). Nearly one thousand American followers of the Rev. Jim Jones commit mass suicide in Jonestown, Guiana, after cult members murder Rep. Leo Ryan of California and others (Nov. 18). Federal loan guarantees rescue New York City from financial crisis.

1979 U.S. resumes diplomatic relations with China (Jan 1). Worst nuclear accident in U.S. history takes place at Three Mile Island power plant near Harrisburg, Pa. Pres. Carter and Soviet Premier Leonid Brezhnev sign SALT II treaty in Vienna (June 18). The Shah of Iran and Anastasio Somoza of Nicaragua, both U.S.-supported dictators, flee revolutions in their countries. Iranian militants seize U.S. Embassy in Teheran, taking 66 American hostages and demanding return of the Shah from U.S. (Nov. 4). They release 13 hostages, all blacks or women. Pres. Carter deports illegal Iranian students, freezes Iranian assets, and bars oil imports from Iran. Inflation reaches highest level in 33 years as Organization of Petroleum Exporting Countries doubles price of oil.

1980 Canadian embassy officials help six Americans escape from Iran (Jan. 29). In response to Soviet invasion of Afghanistan, Pres. Carter embargoes grain and high technology exports to Soviet Union, approves arms sales to China, and secures U.S. boycott of Olympics in Moscow. Congress grants Pres. Carter's request for Crude Oil Windfall Profits Tax and for resumption of Selective Service draft registration. Pres. Carter's secret rescue mission for American hostages in Iran fails when a U.S. Navy helicopter crashes in desert, killing eight servicemen (Apr. 24). Mt. St. Helens erupts in Washington state, killing 26 people (May 18). Banking and trucking industries deregulated. FBI's "Abscam" operation implicates over 30 public officials, including a senator and seven congressmen, for accepting bribes.

1981 Minutes after Pres. Reagan is sworn in, Iran releases 52 American hostages after 444 days in captivity. Pres. Reagan shot by John Hinckley in Washington (Mar. 30), but makes full recovery. Columbia completes first successful space shuttle mission (Apr. 12–14). Federal air traffic controllers go on strike and lose jobs when Pres. Reagan fires all 13,000 of them. Sandra Day O'Connor unanimously confirmed as first woman justice of Supreme Court. Pres. Reagan lifts grain embargo against Soviet Union, but imposes new sanctions after Poland declares martial law. Congress accepts Pres. Reagan's plans for tax cuts, lower domestic spending, and major defense buildup. U.S. sends military advisors and aid to El Salvador.

1982 Ending 13-year antitrust suit, AT&T agrees to surrender control of local Bell System phone companies in return for expansion into new businesses (Jan. 8). Pres. Reagan calls for "New Federalism," transferring programs to state and local control. Unemployment exceeds 10% for first time since Great Depression, and Federal budget deficit exceeds $100 billion a year for first time ever. After a decade, Equal Rights Amendment fails, falling three states short of ratification.

1983 Congress agrees to bail out the Social Security system, and admits internment of Japanese-Americans during World War II was unjust. Sally Ride is first American woman astronaut, aboard space shuttle Challenger. Pres. Reagan strongly condemns Soviet Union for shooting down Korean airliner with 269 people aboard (Sept. 1). U.S. Marines join peacekeeping force in Beirut, Lebanon, where Muslim terrorists kill 240 of them in suicide bombing (Oct. 23). U.S. invades Grenada to overthrow Cuban-backed regime (Oct. 25). Pres. Reagan calls for large-scale funding of Strategic Defense Initiative, or "Star Wars."

1984 Economic recovery begins as unemployment falls, inflation rate declines, and U.S. dollar soars on international markets. Pres. Reagan orders U.S. Marines out of Lebanon (Feb. 7). The Rev. Jesse Jackson mounts first major challenge by black candidate for major party nomination. Rep. Geraldine Ferraro, (D–N.Y.) becomes first woman to receive major party nomination for Vice president. Soviet bloc countries boycott Los Angeles Olympics. Pres. Reagan wins landslide re-election over Democratic challenger Walter Mondale.

1985 Pres. Reagan calls for more tax and budget cuts to sustain economic growth (Feb. 4–6). Despite worldwide protests, Pres. Reagan delivers address at Bitburg cemetery in West Germany, where Nazi SS troops are buried (May 5). Muslim terrorists hijack TWA airliner (June 14), kill one American hostage, then release rest in Beirut (June 30). Palestinian terrorists kill an American hostage aboard hijacked Italian cruise ship Achille *Lauro* (Oct. 9). Pres. Reagan and Soviet Premier Mikhail Gorbachev hold their first summit meeting in Geneva (Nov. 19–21). Pres. Reagan signs Gramm-Rudman Act, requiring spending cuts if Congress cannot reduce Federal deficit.

1986 Space shuttle *Challenger* explodes over Florida, killing six astronauts and a civilian passenger (Jan. 28). Investigations reveal NASA relaxed safety regulations to speed up launch date. U.S. Navy repels attack by Libyan forces during maneuvers in Gulf of Sidra (Mar. 24). Pres. Reagan blames Libya for death of two Americans in terrorist bombing of West Berlin disco, then orders retaliatory air raids on Tripoli and Benghazi (Apr. 14). Congress approves sweeping revision of U.S. tax structure. Democrats regain control of Senate. Pres. Reagan denies trading arms for hostages as Iran-Contra scandal breaks (Nov. 19). Wall Street financier Ivan Boesky fined $100 million for illegal insider trading on stock market.

1987 Pres. Reagan submits first trillion-dollar U.S. budget to Congress as national debt mounts. Stock market closes above 2000 for first time in U.S. history. After Pres. Reagan orders U.S. Navy into Persian Gulf to escort Kuwaiti oil tankers, an Iraqi warplane accidentally attacks *U.S.S. Stark*, killing 37 sailors (May 27). Bernhard Goetz acquitted of major charges in New York City "Subway Vigilante" shootings. Stock market crashes a record 508 points in one day, jolting markets around the world (Oct. 16). Third Reagan-Gorbachev summit in Washington produces agreement to dismantle medium-range missiles in Europe (Dec. 8).

1988 After Iran lays mines in Persian Gulf, U.S. Navy warships and planes destroy two Iranian oil platforms and repel Iranian counterattacks (Apr. 18–19). USS *Vincennes* accidentally shoots down Iranian passenger plane, killing 290 people (July 3). George Bush becomes first sitting vice president elected president since 1836. Terrorist bomb aboard Pan Am Flight 103 kills all 259 aboard, mostly Americans, and 11 on the ground in Lockerbie, Scotland (Dec. 21). Drexel Burnham Lambert agrees to pay all-time record $650 million penalty for securities fraud (Dec. 21).

1989 *Exxon Valdez* supertanker spills over 11 million gallons of oil off Alaska coast (Mar. 24). House speaker Jim Wright and Democratic majority whip Tony Coelho resign over ethics violations. Supreme Court upholds the right to burn U.S. flag. Pres. Bush signs $300 billion savings-and-loan bailout (Aug. 9). Earthquake, second worst in U.S. history, inflicts $6 billion damage and leaves 62 dead in San Francisco Bay area (Oct. 17). L. Douglas Wilder of Virginia is the first black elected governor (Nov. 7). Pres. Bush sends 24,000 U.S. troops to overthrow the Noriega regime and install a popularly elected government (Dec. 20).

1990 After Iraq invades Kuwait (Aug. 2), U.S. launches Operation Desert Shield: more than 200,000 U.S. troops move into Saudi Arabia. Pres. Bush works with U.N. Security Council to condemn invasion and impose stringent economic sanctions. Bush and Gorbachev meet twice: U.S. agrees to some economic aid, grants U.S.S.R. most favored nation trade status. Pres. Bush breaks campaign pledge of "no new taxes." A major flaw in the $1.5 bil. Hubble Space Telescope is discovered shortly after its deployment. Drexel Burnham Lambert defaults on $100 mil. in loans; Michael Milken, head of junk bond department, is fined $600 million and sentenced to jail.

1991 U.S. Operation Desert Storm quickly and decisively drives Iraq's armed forces out of Kuwait. The ground war lasts only 100 hours. Bush and Gorbachev sign first nuclear arms reduction treaty (July 31) as U.S.S.R. continues to crumble. Unemployment rate rises to highest level in a decade. Interest rates are cut to lowest levels in 20 years. Senate's confirmation of Clarence Thomas's nomination to the Supreme Court is delayed by Anita Hill's luridly detailed charges (Oct. 6) of sexual harassment. Oliver North and John Poindexter re exonerated in connection with the Iran-Contra scandal.

1992 The Americans with Disabilities Act takes effect, guaranteeing equal access for the disabled (Jan. 26). Pres. Bush and Russian Pres. Boris Yeltsin issue joint statement officially ending the cold war (Feb.1). Riots erupt in Los Angeles after an all-white jury acquits four L.A. police officers of beating Rodney King, a black man whose assault by police was captured on videotape (April 29–May 4); more than 50 people are killed, 2,000 injured, and over 7,000 arrested. Federal Reserve cuts discount rate to 3 percent, its lowest rate since 1963, after unemployment skyrockets to 7.8 percent, its highest level since 1983. Bill Clinton defeats Pres. George Bush and billionaire-populist third-party candidate Ross Perot to become the 42nd President. Pres. Bush commits at least 28,000 U.S. troops to protect the delivery of relief supplies to Somalia (Dec. 3). Pres. Bush pardons six Reagan Administration officials for their involvement in the Iran-Contra scandal.

1993 More than 120 nations, including the U.S. and Russia, agree to ban production, stockpiling, and use of all chemical weapons and to destroy them all within 10 years. Family Leave Act guarantees workers up to 12 weeks of unpaid leave for medical emergencies. A car bomb rips through the garage at New York's World Trade Center, killing 7, and injuring 1,000 (Feb. 26). Four federal agents are killed in a gunfight with cult leader David Koresh. After a 51-day standoff, Koresh sets the buildings on fire, killing himself and 86 followers (April 19). "The worst storm of the century" according to the National Weather Service pelts the mid-Atlantic and Northeast with as much as 40 inches of snow, killing at least 104 people. The Supreme Court rules (9–0) that public school systems must permit religious groups to use their buildings after hours. Law enforcement officials root out a Muslim extremist group plotting to bomb the U.N., federal office buildings, and to assassinate politicians (June 24). The Supreme Court rules (5–4) that legislative districts drawn to increase black representation can violate the constitutional rights of white voters. Pres. Clinton signs the Brady Bill, requiring background checks before gun purchases. The U.S. and Europe sign the General Agreement of Tariffs and Trade (GATT), substantially reducing tariffs on trade. The Pentagon rules that gays may serve in the military, but may not proclaim their sexual orientation.

1994 The Iran-Contra prosecutor finds no evidence that Pres. Reagan or Vice Pres. Bush broke the law. All four men on trial for the World Trade

Center bombing are found guilty. Rodney King wins $3.8 million in damages for his 1991 beating by the L.A. police. L.A. police charge former football star O.J. Simpson with murdering his ex-wife Nicole Brown and Ron Goldman. Simpson leads police on a bizarre 60-mile low-speed car chase before surrendering (June 17). Major league baseball players' strike results in the cancellation of the World Series (Aug. 11). The number of inmates in U.S. prisons tops 1 million. Republicans take control of both Houses of Congress for the first time in 40 years (Nov. 8).

1995   A federal judge issues an injunction against baseball owners for unfair labor practices, ending the longest players' strike in sports history. A massive car bomb blows up a Federal building in Oklahoma City, killing 169 people (April 19). The Supreme Court (5–4) overturns term limits on Congressional offices in 23 states. A federal grand jury indicts Timothy J. McVeigh and Terry L. Nichols on charges of blowing up the Oklahoma City Federal Building. Sheik Omar Abdel Rahman and nine militant Muslim followers are convicted of conspiring to blowup the U.N. and assassinate political leaders. A mostly black Los Angeles jury finds O.J. Simpson not guilty of murdering his ex-wife. (Oct. 3).

1996   Congress votes to return hundreds of thousands of workers to their jobs and to reopen nonessential government offices that had closed for three weeks in the budget impasse. The Hubble Space Telescope returns the first-ever images of Pluto, and pictures showing the existence of more than 50 billion galaxies; the Sun is one of 100 billion stars in the Milky Way. Congress approves a vast bill rewriting laws governing the telecommunications industries, deregulating cable television, and increasing competition among local phone companies. The worst drought since the Dust Bowl era of the 1930s plagues the southwest, bankrupting more than 10,000 farmers. (June 18). TWA Flight 800 explodes in midair over Long Island, killing all 230 aboard (July 17). Pres. Clinton signs welfare reform legislation, ending more than 60 years of federal cash assistance. Pres. Clinton signs the Defense of Marriage Act, denying Federal recognition to same-sex marriages.

1997   The Dow Jones Industrial Average breaks 7,000 in Feb., and 8,000 in July. Mergers and acquisitions by major corporations reach record levels. Madeleine Albright becomes the first woman Sec. of State. A civil jury finds O.J. Simpson liable in the killings of his ex-wife and Ronald Goldman and orders Simpson to pay $33.5 million in damages. The Supreme Court rules unanimously that a sitting president can be sued for actions outside the scope of his official duties thereby allowing the Paula Jones sexual harassment suit to proceed. Timothy J. McVeigh is found guilty in the 1995 bombing of the Federal building in Oklahoma City that killed 168. A separate jury convicts Terry L. Nichols of conspiracy and manslaughter. The tobacco industry agrees to pay $368.5 billion over 25 years to compensate states for the cost of smoking-related illnesses. Mars Pathfinder, a robotic spacecraft, arrives on Mars, and sends back panoramic pictures of the landscape. Thirty Wall Street brokerages agree to pay $900 million to end a civil suit contending they conspired for years to fix prices on the Nasdaq stock market.

1998   Bill Clinton becomes the first sitting president to submit as a defendant in civil court when he denies charges that he sexually harassed Paula Jones when he was governor of Arkansas. Under oath, and later in a national television address, Clinton also denies having sexual relations with White House intern Monica Lewinsky. Astronomers detect a titanic explosion in the outer reaches of the cosmos rivaled only by the Big Bang. Pictures from the Hubble Space Telescope show the first image of a planet outside our solar system. Two powerful bombs explode outside the U.S. Embassies in Kenya and Tanzania, killing at least 190 people and wounding nearly 5,000. Pres. Clinton testifies that he had an "inappropriate" relationship with Monica Lewinsky. Pres. Clinton announces a record budget surplus of about $70 billion, the first since 1969. The House of Representatives, along party lines, approves two articles of impeachment against Pres. Clinton (Dec. 19).

1999   The Senate acquits Pres. Clinton on both articles of impeachment (Feb. 12). NATO forces begin dropping bombs on Serbian forces occupying Kosovo (Mar. 24). Astronomers announce the detection of three large planets around a solar-type star, providing the first solid evidence that our solar system is no singular phenomenon (April 15). In the deadliest school massacre in U.S. history, two teenagers at Columbine High School in Littleton, Colo. kill 12 students and one teacher (April 20). The F.C.C. relaxes rules that had prevented a single company from owning multiple radio stations in the same city or from controlling too much of the cable industry. Congress repeals the 1933 Glass-Steagall Act, which had prevented the securities, banking, and insurance industries from expanding into one another's businesses. Jimmy Carter officially hands over control of the Panama Canal to Panama (Dec. 14).

2000   America Online buys Time Warner for $165 bil. in the biggest merger in history (Jan 10). Four white New York City police officers are acquitted of all charges in the shooting of unarmed African immigrant Amadou Diallo (Feb 25). Armed U.S. immigration agents storm a Miami house and remove six-year-old Cuban refugee Elián González so he can be returned to his father in Cuba (Apr 22). Two rival groups of scientists announce they have deciphered the human genome (June 26). The independent prosecutor in the Whitewater investigation concludes that there is insufficient evidence to show that Bill or Hillary Clinton committed any crimes (Sept. 20). The U.S.S. Cole, refueling in Yemen, is rocked by a terrorist bomb, killing 17 sailors (Oct. 12). Hillary Rodham Clinton wins the New York Senate race, becoming the only First Lady ever to hold public office. Despite losing the popular vote, George W. Bush wins a controversial presidential election after a recount in Florida is halted by the U.S. Supreme Court.

2001   A federal jury in New York convicts four men of conspiring with Osama bin Laden in the 1998 bombing of U.S. embassies in Kenya and Tanzania (May 29). In the worst terrorist attack in U.S. history, hijackers crash two U.S. airliners into the World Trade Center, destroying both buildings and killing nearly 3,000 people. A third hijacked plane crashes into the Pentagon, and a fourth crashes in western Pennsylvania (Sept. 11). Pres. Bush blames Osama bin Laden, calls up 35,000 military reservists, pledges an attack on Afghanistan, and warns of a long campaign against terrorism. The U.S. and Great Britain launch a series of air attacks against Afghanistan (Oct. 7). A letter filled with anthrax-laden powder contaminates a Senate office building and leads to 31 anthrax exposures (Oct. 15). Pres. Bush signs an executive order allowing foreigners accused of terrorism to be tried in special military tribunals. The Enron Corporation files the largest corporate bankruptcy in U.S. history (Dec. 2). Pres. Bush announces that America has formally withdrawn from the 1972 Antiballistic Missile treaty (Dec. 13).

2002   The U.S. begins transporting Taliban and Al Qaeda prisoners from Afghanistan to a detention center in Guantánamo Bay, Cuba. Defrocked priest John Geoghan, accused of molesting 130 children over three decades, is sentenced to 10 years in prison; the Boston Archdiocese agrees to pay $10 million to the victims. In his first State of the Union address, Pres. Bush calls Iran, Iraq and North Korea the "axis of evil" (Jan. 23). A federal jury in Houston convicts Arthur Andersen of obstruction of justice for shredding documents and impeding the Enron investigation (Jun. 15). The Supreme Court declares that the Constitution bars the execution of mentally retarded offenders, and that juries, rather than judges, must decide if a convicted murderer should get the death penalty. WorldCom submits the largest bankruptcy filing in U.S. history (Jul. 21). In two 5–4 decisions, the Supreme Court upholds a voucher plan to use public money for religious school tuition, and to permit random drug testing in public schools. (Jun. 27). The Senate votes (77–23) to authorize Pres. Bush to use military force against Iraq (Oct. 10). Republicans regain a majority control in the Senate, giving the G.O.P. control of all three branches of government. Congress approves creation of the Department of Homeland Security.

2003 Illinois Gov. George Ryan commutes all 167 death sentences in the state to life in prison, citing fundamental questions of fairness in the Illinois capital punishment system (Jan. 11). The space shuttle Columbia breaks up over Texas upon re-entry, killing all seven aboard (Feb. 1). Federal Reserve Chairman Alan Greenspan criticizes Pres. Bush's budget, saying the economy does not need tax cuts, and that the deficits could multiply rapidly (Feb. 11). Millions of demonstrators around the world protest the Bush administration's plans to invade Iraq (Feb. 15). Pres. Bush orders the invasion of Iraq (Mar. 19). Millions flood the streets of New York and other cities to protest the U.S. invasion (Mar. 22). Pres. Bush flies onto the deck of the *U.S.S. Abraham Lincoln* to declare "Mission Accomplished" in Iraq. The Supreme Court (5–4) backs affirmative action in a case involving admissions at the University of Michigan; and invalidates (6–3) a Texas sodomy law, thus legalizing gay sexual conduct (June 23–24). The White House projects a $455 billion budget deficit for 2003, the largest in U.S. history. The largest power blackout in American history hits eight Northeastern states and parts of Canada (Aug. 14). Congress approves a Medicare bill that adds prescription drug benefits and expands the role of private health plans (Nov. 25).

2004 *Spirit*, a 400-pound robotic rover, lands on Mars and immediately begins to transmit images; it is soon followed by a second rover, *Opportunity* (Jan. 4). At 115 airports U.S. immigration officers begin fingerprinting and photographing tens of thousands of foreign visitors (Jan. 5). David Kay, who led the American effort to find banned weapons in Iraq, concludes that Iraq had no stockpiles of chemical and biological weapons at the start of the war (Jan. 23). Senator John Kerry effectively captures the Democratic nomination (Mar. 2). Pres. Bush's former counterterrorism chief, Richard Clarke, testifies to the Sept. 11 commission that the Bush administration had largely ignored the threat from Al Qaeda. Officials confirm that Pres. Bush was told in a secret meeting on Aug. 6, 2001, that supporters of Osama bin Laden planned an attack "within the United States" and wanted to hijack airplanes (Apr. 9). U.S. legislators are shown hundreds of images of mistreatment of Iraqi prisoners at Abu Ghraib prison (May 12). Hundreds of gay and lesbian couples wed in Massachusetts, the first state to allow same-sex marriages (May 17). A March 2003 legal memo prepared for Defense Secretary Rumsfeld concluded that Pres. Bush was not bound by an international treaty prohibiting torture or by a federal antitorture law because he had the authority as commander in chief to approve any technique needed to protect the nation's security (June 7). The Supreme Court rules that those deemed enemy combatants by the Bush administration must be given the ability to challenge their detention before a judge or other "neutral decision-maker." (June 28). More than 500,000 demonstrators march through New York City on the eve of the Republican convention to protest the war in Iraq and the Bush presidency (Aug. 29). The Food and Drug Administration says that antidepressants appear to lead some children to become suicidal (Sept. 13). Pres. Bush is reelected, defeating Democratic nominee John Kerry with 51 percent of the popular vote (Nov. 2).

2005 The Supreme Court transforms federal criminal sentencing by restoring to judges much of the discretion Congress took away when it put sentencing guidelines in place over two decades ago (Jan. 12). Doctors remove the feeding tube of the brain-damaged woman Terry Schiavo despite efforts by Congress and Pres. Bush to halt the process (Mar. 18). General Motors and Ford Motor Co. lose their investment grade ratings and become junk bonds (May 5). Citigroup agrees to pay $2 billion to investors who accused the bank of aiding Enron in its accounting scandal. J.P. Morgan Chase agrees to pay $2.2 billion to Enron investors. The Supreme Court rules (5–4) that confiscating land for private development in the interest of economic development is an appropriate use of the government's power of eminent domain. The Supreme Court upholds the government display of the Ten Commandments monument in the Texas Capital but rules two Kentucky displays unconstitutional. Jack Abramoff, a Republican lobbyist linked to the ethics problems of House majority leader Tom DeLay, is indicted in Florida on charges of fraud (Aug. 11). Hurricane Katrina pounds the Gulf Coast, leaving over a million houses without power in Louisiana, Mississippi, and Alabama and flooding much of New Orleans (Aug. 28). A Texas grand jury indicts Tom DeLay on a charge of conspiring to violate Texas election laws (Sept. 28). The Senate confirms (78–22) John G. Roberts Jr. as the nation's 17th Chief Justice (Sept. 29). Pres. Bush names Harriet Miers, his White House counsel, to be a justice of the Supreme Court. Less than a month later she withdraws her name and Samuel J. Alito is nominated in her place. Vice Pres. Cheney's chief-of-staff, I. Lewis Libby Jr. is indicted by a federal jury on felony charges of lying to investigators. Pres. Bush admits he ordered the National Security Agency to conduct electronic eavesdropping without warrants and says that he will continue to do so.

2006 Vice Pres. Cheney accidentally shoots a friend in the face during a hunting trip in Texas (Feb. 12). Millions of immigrants and supporters protest in Washington D.C. and in other cities calling on Congress to offer legal status and citizenship to illegal immigrants. The Senate passes $70 billion in tax cuts mostly for the nation's wealthiest citizens. Pres. Bush vetoes a bill supported by his own party to expand federal support for embryonic stem cell research. The Food and Drug Administration approves over-the-counter sales of the morning-after pill to women over 18. The U.N. Security Council imposes sanctions on North Korea in the wake of that country's first nuclear test. Democrats gain control of both the House and Senate (Nov. 7). Nancy Pelosi of California becomes the first woman to be Speaker of the House. The Iraq Study Group, a bipartisan commission, warns that "the situation in Iraq is grave and deteriorating." Saddam Hussein is hanged in Bahgdad, Iraq (Dec. 30).

2007 Pres. Bush names Lt. General David Petraeus as the top military commander in Iraq and announces a "surge" of 20,000 additional American troops (Jan. 4). Intelligence officials reveal that the Pentagon and C.I.A. have obtained financial records of Americans (Jan. 13). Two Army leaders are fired following disclosure of dilapidated buildings and long delays in care for wounded soldiers at

Walter Reed Army Medical Center (Mar. 1). F.B.I. Director Robert Mueller concedes that the bureau improperly used the U.S.A. Patriot Act to obtain information about people and businesses (Mar. 9). A 23-year-old student gunman kills 32 people and injures 15 at Virginia Tech before shooting himself (Apr. 16). The Supreme Court rules that schools cannot seek integration through measures that take explicit account of a student's race (June 28). The White House admits to giving the C.I.A. approval to resume use of severe interrogation techniques on terrorism suspects held overseas (July 20). An Interstate highway bridge in Minneapolis collapses during rush hour, killing 12 people (Aug. 1). A federal jury finds Jose Padilla guilty of terrorism conspiracy charges five years after he was arrested (Aug. 16). Attorney General Alberto Gonzalez resigns after inquiries in Congress and the Justice Dept. find that federal prosecutors across the country were fired for political reasons (Aug. 27). Blackwater USA, a private American security provider, is charged with killing eight Iraqi civilians in Baghdad and is banned by the Iraqi government. The C.I.A. admits that it destroyed videotapes documenting harsh interrogations of two Al Qaeda operatives (Dec. 6).

2008 Democratic Senator Barack Obama and Republican Mike Huckabee win the Iowa caucuses (Jan 3). Citigroup, the nation's largest bank, reports a staggering fourth-quarter loss of $9.83 billion and warns that the housing market has still not bottomed out (Jan. 15). Senator Barack Obama wins decisive victories over Senator Hillary Clinton in three states. *The New York Times* reports that falling home prices and tighter lending standards are causing a rise in defaults on loans by people with good credit histories (Feb. 11). Oil prices hit a high of $100.88 a barrel, and gas prices are at their highest levels since 1981 (Feb. 26). Senator John McCain wins four primary contests to clinch the G.O.P. presidential nomination, while Senator Hillary Clinton wins major Democratic victories in Ohio and Texas to revive her campaign against Senator Barack Obama (Mar. 4). Pres. Bush vetoes a bill passed by Congress that would have limited the C.I.A.'s ability to use harsh interrogation tactics on terrorism suspects (Mar. 8). Stock prices rise as the Federal Reserve offers up to $200 billion in short-term loans to major Wall Street investment banks (Mar. 11). JPMorgan Chase agrees to buy all of Bear Stearns for $2 per share and to guarantee the obligations of the investment bank using a $30 billion credit line from the Federal Reserve (Mar. 16). A heavy mortar attack on the Green Zone in Baghdad kills 58 Iraqis and four Americans, pushing the number of U.S. military deaths in Iraq to over 4,000 (Mar. 23). The Congressional Budget Office projects that the number of Americans receiving food stamps will rise to a record 28 million in 2009 (Mar. 30). A *New York Times* / CBS News poll reports that 81 percent of Americans think that the country is "on the wrong track" (Apr. 4). *The New York Times* reports that Justice Dept. letters to Congress reveal that C.I.A. agents investigating charges of terrorism have been given latitude to legally use interrogation methods that would otherwise be prohibited under the Geneva Convention. The California Supreme Court overturns two state laws that ban gay marriage (May 15). In two decisions, the U.S. Supreme Court rules (7–2 and 6–3) that employees are protected from retaliation when they complain about discrimination in the workplace (May 27). The U.S. Supreme Court rebuffs the Bush Administration and rules (5–4) that detainees at Guantánamo Bay can challenge their detentions in federal court (June 12). Pres. Bush signs the sweeping housing bill passed by Congress that gives the Treasury Dept. broad authority to oversee the nation's two largest mortgage companies and allocates funding to rescue homeowners from foreclosure (Aug. 1). Nebraska Beef issues a recall of 1.2 million pounds of beef products just one month after the Dept. of Agriculture ended a previous recall of tainted meat from the same processor (Aug. 10). The U.S. and Poland reach a deal to place an American missile defense base on Polish territory (Aug. 14). The Treasury Dept. seizes control of Fannie Mae and Freddie Mac in a federal bailout that could cost an estimated $25 billion (Sept. 7). The Federal Reserve agrees to an $85 billion bailout of the insurance giant A.I.G. in the most radical intervention in private business in the central bank's history (Sept. 16). The White House proposes a vast bailout of the U.S. financial institutions, including full authority for the Treasury Dept. to buy up to $700 billion in mortgage-related assets from private firms (Sept. 20). The Federal Reserve announces that investment banks Goldman Sachs and Morgan Stanley will become bank holding companies, subject to much greater regulation (Sept. 21). Washington Mutual is seized by federal regulators and most of it is sold to JPMorgan Chase in the largest bank failure in U.S. history (Sept. 25). On the same day that the Labor Dept. reports that the U.S. lost 159,000 jobs in September, the worst month in five years, the House approves the bailout plan and Pres. Bush quickly signs it (Oct. 3). In anticipation of a Treasury Dept.'s announcement that it will invest $250 billion in U.S. banks, stock markets rally worldwide; the Dow gains 936 points (11 percent), the largest single-day gain in its history (Oct. 13). The stock market plunges, giving back over 700 of the 936 points it gained two days before as new evidence of economic deterioration is revealed (Oct. 15). Chinese regulators say that they have confiscated more than 3,600 tons of animal feed tainted with melamine, an industrial chemical that has contaminated food supplies in China and led to global recalls of Chinese dairy products. Barack Hussein Obama is elected the 44th president of the U.S. Democrats pick up at least six seats in the Senate, giving them a clear 59–41 seat majority. They also added 18 seats in the House, providing a margin of 252–173 over Republicans. Measures barring same-sex marriage passed in California, Arizona, and Florida. (Nov. 4). The nation's unemployment rate jumped to 6.5 percent, bringing the toll of lost jobs to 1.2 million for the year. The heads of the Big Three automakers of Detroit plead for emergency government aid to stave off potential collapse (Nov. 18). The stock market falls below 8,000 for the first time since early 2003. A federal judge issues the Bush administration a sharp setback, ruling that five Algerian men have been held unlawfully at the Guantánamo Bay detention camp for nearly seven years and orders their release (Nov. 20). The Federal Reserve and the Treasury announce $800 billion in new lending programs, sending the message that they will print as much money as needed to revive the nation's crippled banking system (Nov. 25). Bernard L. Madoff, an influential Wall Street trader, is arrested by federal agents who accuse him of running a multibillion-dollar Ponzi scheme. (Dec. 11). Pres. Bush announces the emergency bailout of General Motors and Chrysler (Dec. 19). The nation's largest spill of coal ash occurs at the Kingston Fossil Plant, a Tennessee Valley Authority generating plant about 40 miles west of Knoxville (Dec. 22).

2009 The Bureau of Labor Statistics reports that the nation lost 524,000 jobs in December, bringing the unemployment rate to a 16-year high of 7.2 percent. (Jan. 9) *The New York Times* reports that Pres. Bush deflected a secret request by Israel last year for specialized bombs it wanted for an attack on Iran's main nuclear complex. (Jan. 10) In a 5 to 4 decision, the Supreme Court rules that evidence obtained from an unlawful arrest based on careless record-keeping by the police, may be used against a criminal defendant. A US Airways jetliner, with 155 people aboard, lost power in both engines, after striking birds, having taken off from La Guardia Airport in New York. The pilot, Chesley B. Sullenberger III, ditched in the Hudson River and all on board were rescued by ferries and emergency boats. A secret federal appeals court says telecommunications companies must cooperate with the government to intercept international phone calls and e-mail of American citizens suspected of being spies or terrorists.(Jan. 15) Barack Hussein Obama is sworn in as the 44th president of the United States. (Jan. 20) Pres. Obama reverses the most disputed counterterrorism policies of the Bush administration, signing executive orders closing the detention compound at Guantánamo Bay; ending the C.I.A.'s secret prisons; and requiring all interrogations to follow the non-coercive methods of the Army Field Manual. The price tag for bailing out General Motors and Chrysler jumps to $39 billion, with the two automakers saying they will need the additional aid from the government to remain solvent. Pres. Obama says he will send an additional 17,000 American troops to Afghanistan in the spring and summer, adding nearly 50 percent to the 36,000 American troops already there. (Feb. 17) Pres. Obama announces that he will withdraw 142,000 combat troops from Iraq by August 2010, and all remaining troops by December 2011. Markets plunge around the world as investors bail out of stocks. In the United States, the Dow Jones industrial average falls 299.64 points, or 4.2 percent to 6,763.29, dropping below 7,000 for the first time since 1997. Government data reveals that 651,000 additional jobs were lost in the United States in February, pushing the unemployment rate to 8.1 percent, the highest level in 25 years. The Supreme Court erases a 2008 lower-court ruling that expanded the limits of executive authority to combat terrorism by allowing the president the power to order the indefinite military detention of legal residents of the United States. (Mar. 6) In a 5 to 4 ruling, the Supreme Court ruled that only election districts in which minorities make up at least half of the voting-age population are entitled to the protections of a part of the Voting Rights Act. The Obama administration says it has the authority to detain terrorism suspects at Guantánamo Bay, Cuba without criminal charges. A.I.G., which has received more than $170 billion in taxpayer bailout money, announces it plans to pay about $165 million in bonuses to executives in the same business unit that brought the company to the brink of collapse. (Mar. 15) The Federal Reserve announces that it will pump an extra $1 billion into the financial system by purchasing Treasury bonds and mortgage securities. Federal prosecutors issue a 19-count indictment against former Illinois governor Rod R. Blagojevich, stating that his aim was to "exercise and preserve power over the government of the State of Illinois for the financial and political benefit of Mr. Blagojevich, his family and friends." (Apr. 2) In a unanimous decision, the Iowa Supreme Courts finds unconstitutional a state law limiting marriage to a man and a woman. Pres. Obama begins his outreach to the Muslim world in a speech before Turkey's Parliament, saying that the U.S. "is not and will never be at war with Islam." (Apr. 6) The C.I.A. says that it will decommission the secret overseas prisons where it subjected Al Qaeda prisoners to brutal interrogation methods, bringing to a symbolic close the most controversial counterterrorism program of the Bush administration. (Apr. 9) Navy Seal snipers rescue Richard Phillips, the American cargo ship captain kidnapped by Somali pirates five days ago. The nation's two major labor unions, the A.F.L.–C.I.O., and the Change to Win federation, agree for the first time to join forces to support an overhaul of the immigration system. The Justice Department makes public detailed memos describing brutal interrogation techniques used by the C.I.A., and approved by the Bush administration, for extracting information from senior operatives of Al Qaeda. At the same time, Pres. Obama reassures the agency that the C.I.A. operatives involved would not be prosecuted. The Census Bureau reports that the number of people who changed residences declined to 35.2 million from March 2007 to March 2008, the lowest number since 1962. (Apr. 22) General Motors says it will eliminate another 21,000 factory jobs, close 13 plants, cut its network of 6,500 dealers, and close its Pontiac division. Congress gives final approval to its $3.5 trillion federal budget without a single Republican vote in either the House or Senate. The spending plan projects a $1.2 trillion deficit in 2010. Pres. Obama forces Chrysler into federal bankruptcy protection so it can pursue an alliance with the Italian automaker, Fiat, thereby allowing the United Auto Workers union, through their retirement plan, to take control of Chrysler, with Fiat and the U.S. as junior partners. (Apr. 30) Pres. Obama calls for curbing offshore tax havens and corporate tax breaks to collect billions of dollars more from multinational companies and wealthy individuals, estimating that the change would raise $210 billion over the next decade. (May 4) Releasing the results of the "stress tests" on American banks, federal regulators order 10 of them, including Wells Fargo, Morgan Stanley, and GMAC, to raise a total of $7 billion in extra capital. Other banking institutions are given a clean bill of health. (May 7) The Labor Department reports that another 539,000 jobs disappeared from the economy in April, and the unemployment rate jumped to 8.9 percent. Pres. Obama says he will fight to prevent the release of photographs documenting abuse of prisoners in Iraq and Afghanistan by U.S. military personnel, reversing his position after commanders warned that the images could set off a deadly backlash against American troops. (May 13) The White House says that the administration will prosecute some detainees being held at the prison in Guantánamo Bay, Cuba in a military commission system, but they are making changes that will grant detainees expanded legal rights. Pres. Obama announces tough new nationwide rules for automobile emissions and mileage standards. The Supreme Court rules in a 5 to 4 decision that a Pakistani Muslim who was arrested after the 9/11 attacks may not sue John Ashcroft, the former attorney general and Robert S. Mueller III, the director of the F.B.I., for abuses he suffered in a Brooklyn detention center. (May 18) The Supreme Court rules, in a 7 to 2 decision, that employers need not give women credit for some pregnancy leaves in calculating their pension benefits when they retire. In an abrupt shift, Senate Democratic leaders say they will not provide the $80 million that Pres. Obama requested to close the detention center at Guantánamo Bay, Cuba. (May 19) Four men are arrested in what the authorities say was a plot to bomb two synagogues in the Bronx, and to shoot down military planes at an Air National Guard base in Newburgh, New York. The California Supreme Court upholds a ban on same-sex marriage, ratifying a decision made by voters taken last year. (May 26) Pres. Obama pushes General Motors into bankruptcy protection, making a bet that by temporarily nationalizing the company, it can be brought back from the brink of insolvency. George Tiller, one of the only doctors in the nation who performed late-term abortions, was shot to death in Wichita, Kansas in the foyer of his longtime church. The New Hampshire legislature approves revisions to a same-sex marriage bill and Gov. John Lynch promptly signs the legislation, making the state the sixth to let gay couples wed. (June 3) In a bold overture to the Islamic world, Pres. Obama gives a speech in Cairo in which he confronts frictions between Muslims and the West, at once emphasizing America's unbreakable bond with Israel and expressing sympathy for the Palestinians. Angelo R. Mozilo, the man who built Countrywide Financial into the nation's largest mortgage lender, is charged with securities fraud and insider trading in a civil suit brought by the Securities and Exchange Commission. The Supreme Court rules in a 5 to 4 decision that elected judges must disqualify themselves from cases involving people who spent exceptionally large sums to put them on the bench. The Obama administration decides to let 10 big banks repay federal aid that had sustained them through the worst of the crisis. The companies, including American Express, Goldman Sachs, JPMorgan Chase, and Morgan Stanley plan to return a combined $68.3 billion. (June 9) Pres. Obama signs a presidential memorandum to extend benefits to same-sex partners of federal employees, but he stops short of pledging full health insurance coverage. The Supreme Court rules, in a 5 to 4 decision, prisoners have no constitutional right to DNA testing that might prove their innocence, emphasizing that 46 states already have laws that allow at least some prisoners to gain access to DNA evidence. The Supreme Court rules, in a 6 to 3 decision, that the Clean Water Act does not prevent the Army Corps of Engineers from allowing mining waste to be dumped into rivers, streams, and other waters. The Supreme Court rules in a 6 to 3 decision that parents of special education students may seek government reimbursement for private school tuition, even if they have never received special education services in public school. (June 22) Gov. Mark Sanford of South Carolina says that he has been having an extramarital affair with a woman in Argentina for the last year, ending the mystery surrounding his disappearance over Father's Day weekend. Michael Jackson, the pop superstar, dies at age 50 after arriving at U.C.L.A. Medical Center in a coma. The Supreme Court rules, in a 5 to 4 decision, that crime laboratory reports may not be used against criminal defendants at trial unless the analysts responsible for creating them give testimony and subject themselves to cross- examination. (June 25) The Centers for Disease Control and Prevention reports that swine flu has infected more than 1 million Americans and is infecting thousands more every week. About 3,000 Americans have been hospitalized and 127 have died. The Supreme Court rules that white firefighters in New Haven were subjected to race discrimination when the city threw out a promotional examination on which they had done well and black firefighters poorly. (June 29) A federal advisory panel votes narrowly to recommend a ban on Percocet and Vicodin, two of the most popular prescription painkillers in the world, because of their effects on the liver. The Labor Dept. reports that the U.S. economy lost 467,000 more jobs in June, bringing the unemployment rate to 9.5 percent. (July 2) Gov. Sarah Palin of Alaska abruptly announces that she is quitting, and has decided not to seek re-election. Pres. Obama signs an agreement to cut American and Russian strategic nuclear arsenals by at least one-quarter, a first step in a broader effort intended to reduce the threat of such weapons and to prevent their further spread to unstable regions. (July 6) Only one month after repaying billions of bailout dollars, Goldman Sachs posts $3.44 billion in profits, the richest quarterly profit in its 140-year history, and announces that it has earmarked $11.4 billion so far this year to compensate its employees. The government reports that the economy's long decline leveled off significantly from April to June, raising expectations of a turnaround in the second half of the year. (July 31) The Senate confirms Judge Sonia Sotomayor as the nation's first Hispanic Supreme Court justice. (Aug. 6) The White House, facing increasing skepticism over Pres. Obama's call for a public insurance plan, signals that it is willing to compromise and will consider a proposal for a non-profit health cooperative. Leaders of the Evangelical Lutheran Church in America, the largest Lutheran denomination, vote to allow gay men and lesbians in committed relationships to serve as members of the clergy. (Aug. 21) The C.I.A. refuses to make public hundreds of pages of internal documents about the agency's defunct detention and interrogation program, saying such disclosures would jeopardize national security. (Sept. 1) In a rare joint session of Congress, Pres. Obama confronts a skeptical nation, decrying the "scare tactics" of his opponents and presenting his most forceful case yet for a sweeping health care overhaul. (Sept. 9) The Census Bureau reports showing that in the recession, the nation's poverty rate climbed to 13.2 percent last year, up from 12.5 percent in 2007. The report also documents a decline in employer-provided health insurance and says 39.8 million residents lived below the poverty line, defined as a family income of $22,025 for a family of four. Median family incomes fell to $50,300, compared with $52,200 the year before. In a break with the trade policies of the Bush administration, Pres. Obama announces that he will impose a 35 percent tariff on automobile and light-truck tires imported from China. (Sept. 11) China increases pressure on the United States in a widening trade dispute, taking the first steps toward imposing tariffs on American exports of automotive products and chicken meat. The Tennessee Valley Authority says it will spend $43 million on economic development projects in Roane County, Tennessee, the site of a huge coal ash spill at one of the authority's power plants in December 2009. The F.B.I. reports an overall drop in violent crime for the second year in a row. In each of the four violent crime offenses, the 2008 rates were down from 2007. (Sept. 14) Pres. Obama scraps the Bush administration's proposed antiballistic missile shield in Eastern Europe and orders instead the development of a reconfigured system designed to shoot down short-and medium-range Iranian missiles. Gen. Stanley A. McChrystal, the top military commander in Afghanistan, warns in a confidential assessment of the war there that he needs additional troops within the next year or else the conflict "will likely result in failure." (Sept 20) The Labor Department reports that job seekers now outnumber job openings six to one, the worst ratio since the government began tracking open positions in 2000. The Nobel Prize Committee announces that Pres. Obama is the recipient of the Peace Prize for this year (Oct. 9). A U.S. army psychiatrist, who is a Muslim, goes on a shooting rampage at Fort Hood, Texas, killing 12 and wounding 31 (Nov. 5). The American College of Obstetricians and Gynecologists releases new guidelines for screening for cervical cancer that recommends fewer pap tests and none for women under 21 (Nov. 19). Pres. Obama announces he will send 30,000 or more soldiers to Afghanistan but vows to start bringing some troops home by Aug. 2011 (Dec. 1). The Senate approves a bill (60–39) to reinvent the nation's healthcare system, guaranteeing access to insurance for tens of millions of Americans (Dec. 24).

BIOGRAPHIES OF U.S. PRESIDENTS

1. George Washington (1789–97)

Born in Westmoreland County, Virginia, on Feb. 22, 1732, the first president, with a love for the land, trained as a surveyor in his teens. At age 16 he went to live with his brother Lawrence, who built Mount Vernon. Lawrence died only four years later, leaving his property to George, who went on to become one of Virginia's foremost landowners, ultimately acquiring more than 100,000 acres in Virginia and what is now West Virginia. In 1753 Washington joined the French and Indian War as an officer in the Virginia militia and fought bravely if poorly. The war provided Washington with the beginnings of his anti-British sentiments, exposing him to the arrogance of his British commanders. Upon returning to plantation life, and marrying Martha Custis, in 1759, Washington's resentment of the British was further fueled by their commercial restrictions. With the passage of the Stamp Act of 1765, Washington joined opposition to imperial rule in the Virginia House of Burgesses, becoming ever more active in resisting the British. He went as a delegate to the Continental Congress, which chose him to command the Continental Army when war with Britain broke out in 1775. Washington proved an uncommonly resourceful general, keeping his ragtag army together through years of defeat, retreat, and hard winters to outlast the British and finally prevail at Yorktown in 1781. Here, as in all his life, Washington earned respect for his judgment, dignity, and bearing. Retiring to Mount Vernon after the war, the general quashed suggestions that he assume military dictatorship of the fledgling republic, not wanting to subvert the very principles for which the Americans had fought. But because of his belief in a strong central government, Washington felt compelled to return to public life to salvage his country from the chaotic Articles of Confederation. In 1787 he presided over the Constitutional Convention in Philadelphia, which framed the presidency with him in mind, the only president ever elected unanimously in the electoral college (twice).

Washington's renowned judgment equaled the task of setting presidential precedent, for, as he wrote, "It is devoutly wished on my part, that these precedents may be fixed on true principles." His first act as president was to urge adoption of the Bill of Rights. Other notable achievements included national unity, quelling the Whiskey Rebellion, bolstering the treasury with a national bank, settling Jay's Treaty of commerce with Britain, and maintaining neutrality in the French Revolution. Washington successfully implemented executive power and quieted fears and suspicions of executive tyranny. But he regretted the rivalry between Thomas Jefferson and Alexander Hamilton, which led to the birth of political parties in his own cabinet; Washington feared that allegiance to "factions" would someday eclipse the guiding light of patriotism. After refusing a third term in 1796, Washington in his Farewell Address warned against party spirit, sectionalism, and "entangling alliances" with other nations. He died on Dec. 14, 1799, "first in war, first in peace, and first in the hearts of his countrymen," as his friend Henry Lee eulogized him.

2. John Adams (1797–1801)

A fifth-generation American directly descended from a Mayflower passenger, John Adams was born on Oct. 30, 1735, in Braintree, Massachusetts. At Harvard Adams considered the ministry but turned to law. He joined his cousin Sam Adams as an early opponent of the Stamp Act of 1765, organizing the Sons of Liberty and defending Americans accused of smuggling. Yet he also defended the British soldiers brought to trial for the Boston Massacre in 1770. In the Revolution, Adams persuaded the Continental Congress to commission George Washington as commander in chief, declare independence, and put stars and stripes on the flag. He wrote the Massachusetts state constitution in 1779 and negotiated peace with Britain in 1782. The first vice president, Adams called that position the "most insignificant office that ever the invention of man contrived or his imagination conceived."

Elected president as a Federalist in 1796, Adams retained Washington's cabinet, but Alexander Hamilton turned the party against him for refusing to make war on France. Adams built up the navy and kept the peace, but disaffecting the Federalists and signing the Alien and Sedition Acts (1798) politically weakened "His Rotundity." Adams lost the 1800 election to the increasingly popular Thomas Jefferson. The first president to reside in the White House, Adams lived to be 90, able to see his son John Quincy Adams elected the sixth president in 1824. John Adams died on the same day that Thomas Jefferson did: July 4, 1826, the 50th anniversary of the Declaration of Independence they both signed.

3. Thomas Jefferson (1801–09)

Thomas Jefferson was born on Apr. 13, 1743, in Albemarle County, Virginia, son of a self-made Virginian who died when Jefferson was 14. Jefferson graduated from William and Mary in 1762, began practicing law in 1767, and joined the Virginia House of Burgesses in 1769. With his pen Jefferson sharply criticized British rule, winning a place on Virginia's Committee of Correspondence to keep in touch with patriots in other colonies. His writings amassed great respect, earning him the right, as a delegate to the Continental Congress in 1776, to draft the Declaration of Independence. He then returned to Virginia as wartime governor, narrowly escaping capture when British troops destroyed his home. Congress sent Jefferson to Europe in 1784; he was minister to France during the Constitutional Convention and the early French Revolution, an event that affected him profoundly. As secretary of state under Washington, Jefferson's faith in democracy and states' rights clashed repeatedly with Alexander Hamilton's pursuit of central executive power. Jefferson resigned in 1793 and led opposition to the Federalists, whom Jefferson called "monarchists in principle." As vice president after 1796, Jefferson speeded the Federalists' downfall by secretly authoring the Kentucky Resolutions, critical of the Alien and Sedition Acts.

The House of Representatives chose Jefferson (ironically, with Hamilton's support) over Aaron Burr, whose electoral votes for president equaled his in 1800. "We are all Republicans—we are all Federalists," appealed Jefferson in his inaugural address, easing the transfer of power. In his first term, Jefferson slashed the budget, lowered taxes, reduced the national debt, and sent marines to fight Barbary pirates. Despite some concern over his constitutional authority to make the acquisition, Jefferson's greatest feat was the Louisiana Purchase from France in 1803, which doubled the size of the United States. "The less said about the constitutional difficulties, the better," wrote Jefferson, sending Lewis and Clark to explore the new lands. In his second term, Jefferson's unpopular Embargo Act (1807) was an attempt to avoid war with Britain or France, but it ruined American merchants. Retiring to Monticello in 1809, Jefferson busied himself with inventions and designing the University of Virginia. He died on the 50th anniversary of the Declaration of Independence, July 4, 1826. His broad interests spanned music, science, architecture, agronomy, and the classics, as well as politics and government.

4. James Madison (1809–17)

James Madison was born to a wealthy family on Mar. 16, 1751, in Port Conway, Virginia. A Princeton graduate, Madison attended the first Virginia state convention in 1776, drafting a bill that guaranteed religious liberty. As the youngest member of the Continental Congress in 1780, he led the movement to revise the Articles of Confederation. At the Constitutional Convention in Philadelphia in 1787, Madison's Virginia Plan became the pivot of discussion. Madison, dubbed the Father of the Constitution, tirelessly directed debate and applied his political wisdom. His voluminous notes provide the best record of the convention. Madison helped ratify the Constitution by coauthoring *The Federalist* (1787–88) with John Jay and Alexander Hamilton. A four-term congressman, Madison drafted the Bill of Rights and cofounded the Democratic-Republican party. In 1794 he married a young and ebullient widow, Dolley Payne Todd, an especially popular first lady. Madison led the opposition to the Federalists' Alien and Sedition Acts with the Virginia Resolutions, arguing the acts were unconstitutional attacks on liberty. Jefferson chose Madison as his secretary of state and later as his successor. Madison easily won the election of 1808. Britain and France preyed on American shipping throughout Madison's first term. Pushed by war hawks in Congress, Madison asked for a declaration of war to defend American rights against British outrages. Reelected despite numerous American defeats in the War of 1812, Madison barely escaped Washington as the British burned the White House. Yet he persisted in "Mr. Madison's War" until the Peace of Ghent (1814) and belated victory at New Orleans (1815) vindicated him. War expenses forced Madison to recharter the national bank and raise the tariff, contrary to his Jeffersonian principles. But by 1817 Madison could retire confident of secure independence, surging nationalism, and the total collapse of his Federalist opponents who had opposed the war. He died on June 28, 1836, having outlived all the Founding Fathers. Madison's presidency pales beside his greatest contributions—the Constitution and the Bill of Rights.

5. James Monroe (1817–25)

The last Revolutionary hero and member of the "Virginia Dynasty" to become president, James Monroe was born on Apr. 28, 1758, in Westmoreland County, Virginia. He left the College of William and Mary to answer the call to arms in 1775. Wounded at Trenton, Monroe fought courageously and rose to lieutenant colonel under Gen. Washington. He learned law as an aide to Thomas Jefferson, who helped Monroe into Congress and the Senate. Much diplomatic experience followed Monroe's appointment as minister to France in 1794. Governor of Virginia from 1799 to 1802, Monroe returned to Europe to negotiate the Louisiana Purchase and later served in Britain and Spain. James Madison appointed him secretary of state in 1811 and secretary of war in 1814. Chosen to succeed Madison, Monroe won the 1816 election and presided over the Era of Good Feeling, a period marked by minimal sectional or partisan discord. Monroe bought Florida from Spain in 1819, and his popularity survived the Panic of 1819 as well as rancorous debates over the admission of Missouri as a slave state. Monroe toured the nation to jubilant crowds, winning reelection with all but one electoral vote in 1820. John Quincy Adams, his secretary of state, suggested Monroe proclaim American opposition to European encroachment in the Western Hemisphere, which he did in 1823; decades later this became known as the Monroe Doctrine. After retiring, Monroe became a regent of the University of Virginia (1826) and a member of the Virginia constitutional convention of 1829. Because of lack of attention over the years, his private affairs had suffered greatly, and Monroe discovered he was lapsing into bankruptcy. He sold his plantation and died all but penniless on Independence Day, July 4, 1831.

6. John Quincy Adams (1825–29)

The first president's son to become president, John Quincy Adams was born on July 11, 1767, in Braintree, Massachusetts. A true child of the Revolution, Adams watched the Battle of Bunker Hill while holding his mother's hand, and he spent his teens in Europe with his father, John Adams, on diplomatic missions for the new nation. He entered Harvard in 1785, already an experienced diplomat fluent in seven languages. After a brief career as a Boston lawyer, Adams was minister to Holland in 1794 and to Prussia in 1797. As a Federalist, Adams was elected to the Senate in 1803, but after supporting Thomas Jefferson, he had to resign. James Madison made Adams minister to Russia in 1809, in time to witness Napoleon's invasion. Then Adams helped negotiate the Peace of Ghent (1814) before serving as ambassador to England, the second of three Adams generations to hold that post. James Monroe recalled Adams from Europe—where he had spent most of his life—to appoint him secretary of state in 1817, and in that post, Adams purchased Florida from Spain, patched relations with Britain, and conceived the Monroe Doctrine.

Running for president in 1824, Adams was beaten by Andrew Jackson in both popular and electoral votes; but with Henry Clay's support, the House of Representatives chose Adams for president. No one ever became president with less than Adams's 31 percent of the vote, yet he refused to conciliate his foes or even act like a politician. Adams posed above politics and made no effort to deal with Congress or use patronage. Consequently, elaborate plans for internal improvements and national academies came to naught. Adams, like his father, failed to win a second term, as Jackson gained revenge at the polls in 1828. Massachusetts rescued Adams from despair by sending him to Congress in 1830, and "Old Man Eloquent" remained a powerful antislavery leader until he collapsed on the floor of the House at age 80; he died in the Speaker's Room on Feb. 23, 1848. John Quincy Adams, who considered himself a failure as president, worked for the first 11 presidents and numbers among the most important architects of early American foreign policy.

7. Andrew Jackson (1829–37)

Born to Scotch-Irish immigrants in Waxhaw, South Carolina, on Mar. 15, 1767, Andrew Jackson was the first first-generation American to become president, as well as the first president from the western frontier and the first of seven to be born in a log cabin. Orphaned at 15, he was by then already a Revolutionary veteran, a former prisoner of war, and scarred by the saber of a British officer whose boots he refused to clean. Jackson read law and made his way to the Tennessee frontier, marrying Rachel Donelson Robards in 1791. She neglected to divorce her first husband, but Jackson challenged to a duel anyone who questioned his marriage, once even killing a man on the field of honor. Jackson's frontier law practice prospered, and Tennessee elected him its first congressman in 1796. He served only briefly in the Senate; Washington so disgusted the rough-hewn Jackson that he resigned. Back in Tennessee, Jackson became a respected judge and honorary major general of the militia. In the War of 1812, Jackson led troops to victory at the Battle of New Orleans (1815), his men routing British invaders twice their number.

"Old Hickory" was now a national icon, reentering the Senate in 1823 and running for president as a hero above party. Jackson won more popular and electoral votes than anyone in 1824 but lost when the election was thrown into the House and Henry Clay supported John Quincy Adams. Vowing revenge against the politicians, Jackson swept to victory in 1828 as the "people's choice" reform candidate. Jackson's wife died on the eve of his inauguration. As president, Jackson aggrandized the power of his office on behalf of the common man by expanding suffrage, rotating officeholders (the "spoils system"), and economizing in government. Under Jackson the Federal government completely paid off the national debt. Jackson vetoed Federal road-building and banking—yet he asserted Federal authority by ordering troops to South Carolina in the Nullification Crisis of 1832–33. The Whig party arose in opposition to "King Andrew I," especially to his high-handed veto of the national bank, but voters endorsed Jackson's war on privilege by reelecting him in 1832. In his second term, Jackson seized land from the Native Americans, ignoring the Supreme Court, and he recognized Texas in hopes of taking more land from Mexico. He became the first president to ride a train (1833) and to survive an assassination attempt (1835). After placing his friend Martin Van Buren in the White House, Jackson retired to the Hermitage, his plantation in Tennessee. He remained quite influential behind the scenes, persuading the Democrats to discard Van Buren and nominate James K. Polk in 1844. Jackson finally succumbed to dropsy and old wounds on June 8, 1845.

8. Martin van Buren (1837–41)

The first president to have played no part in the Revolution, Martin Van Buren was born to a Dutch family in Kinderhook, New York, on Dec. 5, 1782. Apprenticed to a lawyer at 14, Van Buren took to law and politics—so well, in fact, that he came to be called the Little Magician. By 1821 staunch party loyalty elevated him to the Senate, where Van Buren led northern supporters of Andrew Jackson and guided his victory in 1828. Brief service as New York governor ended when Jackson appointed him secretary of state in 1829. Van Buren helped build the Democratic party, and Jackson made him vice president in 1832. As Jackson's heir apparent, Van Buren won the 1836 election, but two months after he took office, the Panic of 1837 launched a severe depression that spoiled his presidency. "Martin Van Ruin" responded by creating the independent treasury system, but his lack of popularity was beyond repair. He made enemies in the North by protecting slavery and in the South by refusing to annex Texas. Though the self-made son of an innkeeper, Van Buren was cast by his opponents as an aristocrat. In 1844 Van Buren lost the Democratic nomination when Jackson abandoned him over the Texas issue. Then, in 1848 Van Buren guaranteed a Democratic defeat by founding the Free Soil party and running for president, which split the decisive New York vote. Van Buren died a Unionist on July 24, 1862, the only president whose life touched both the Revolution and the Civil War.

9. William Henry Harrison (1841)

Son of a signatory of the Declaration of Independence and grandfather of a president, William Henry Harrison was born in Charles City County, Virginia, on Feb. 9, 1773. Campaign legend held that his birthplace was a log cabin, but in fact it was a plantation mansion. Harrison left medical school to join the army and fight Native Americans in the Northwest in 1791. After an illustrious military career, he served in Congress (1816–19), the U.S. Senate (1825–28), and as ambassador to Colombia (1828–29) before falling victim to Andrew Jackson's spoils system. Harrison fit Whig designs of defeating Jacksonians with a war hero of their own and received the Whig nomination to face Martin Van Buren in 1840. Harrison's campaign sidestepped issues to cast him as a plain frontiersman who guzzled hard cider while Van Buren sipped champagne. In the first modern election full of hoopla and hype, "Tippecanoe and Tyler Too"—the Whig slogan—linked Harrison's most famous victory with his obscure running mate. A huge turnout gave Harrison the victory at age 67, the oldest person elected president until Ronald Reagan. Harrison delivered a record 8,500-word inaugural address hatless and coatless on a drizzly winter day. He caught a cold from which he never recovered and succumbed to pneumonia on Apr, 4, 1841. He was the first president to die in the White House—where he lived for only 31 days. His grandson, Benjamin Harrison, was the 23rd president.

10. John Tyler (1841–45)

The first vice president to become president by succession, the first president to see impeachment proposed against him, and the only president to change parties in office, John Tyler was born on Mar. 29, 1790, in Charles City County, Virginia. He was a Virginia legislator, congressman, senator, and governor before the Whigs chose him as William Henry Harrison's running mate in 1840. Though a strict constructionist and states' rights advocate, Tyler earned the Whigs' favor by opposing Andrew Jackson. But as president after Harrison's death, "His Accidency" earned their ire by vetoing, in mid-1842, two tariff bills vital to the Whig party. Eventually, his cabinet resigned and his party expelled him. Outraged members of Congress called for his impeachment. On July 10, 1842, John Minor Botts, a Whig representative from Richmond, Va., proposed the appointment of a special committee to investigate Tyler's conduct in office with an eye toward impeachment. The proposal was defeated on Jan. 10, 1843, by a vote of 127 to 83. This was the first time presidential impeachment proceedings were introduced in Congress. Tyler concluded the Webster-Ashburton Treaty (1842), which adjusted the northeastern boundary of the United States, and the Texas annexation (1845), but without popular or partisan support, he was powerless and decided against running for reelection. A veto on his last day in office became the first ever to be overridden. Tyler died on Jan. 18, 1862, awaiting his seat in the Confederate Congress.

11. James Knox Polk (1845–49)

The first dark-horse president, James Knox Polk was born in Mecklenburg County, North Carolina, on Nov. 2, 1795. A star orator in Tennessee politics, Polk idolized Andrew Jackson. "Young Hickory" took Jackson's old seat in Congress in 1825 and was reelected seven times. Polk was Speaker of the House from 1835 to 1839 and governor of Tennessee until 1841. He lost two bids for reelection, and his political career seemed over when the Democrats nominated him for president in 1844. Polk's name had not even appeared on the first seven ballots, but the deadlocked convention latched onto Polk as a pro-expansion dark horse. In the election he defeated Henry Clay by 1.5 percent of the vote on a platform that ignored slavery. From his inaugural address onward, Polk pursued expansion in the West. In 1846, he bluffed the British into believing the United States would go to war over Oregon, extracting a treaty for it. When Mexico attacked U.S. troops in disputed Texas territory, Polk called it an invasion and got a declaration of war. The ensuing Mexican War (1846–48) won California and the Southwest for the United States in the Treaty of Guadalupe-Hidalgo. Polk declined a second term, having fulfilled the nation's "Manifest Destiny" to span the continent. The last strong president before Abraham Lincoln, Polk added a million square miles to the United States. But the issue of slavery in the new territories split the Democrats and soon the whole country. "The presidency is not a bed of roses," complained Polk, who left the White House totally exhausted and died three months later, on June 15, 1849.

12. Zachary Taylor (1849–50)

Zachary Taylor, the first president to have no previous political experience, was born on Nov. 24, 1784, in Montebello, Virginia. His father was a colonel in the Revolutionary War, and Taylor—along with four brothers—served as a professional soldier for nearly 40 years. After distinguished service against the British and Native Americans, Gen. Taylor's finest hour came during the Mexican War, when he captured Monterrey and smashed Gen. Santa Ana's much larger army at the Battle of Buena Vista (1847). Though Taylor had never held office or even voted, the Whigs eagerly nominated "Old Rough and Ready" for president in 1848; Taylor, like William Henry Harrison, was an apolitical war hero above the slavery controversy. He won the election when the new Free Soil party siphoned off Democratic votes, but Taylor took office with Congress in chaos over the admission of California as a free state. Taylor opposed the Compromise of 1850 and probably would have vetoed it, but he died suddenly of acute indigestion on July 9, 1850. (A long, hot Fourth of July at Washington Monument ceremonies had no doubt contributed to his weakened state.) Backers of the compromise rejoiced that Taylor's death saved the Union. Taylor was both the last of eight slave owners and the last Whig to be elected president.

13. Millard Fillmore (1850–53)

Born in a log cabin on Jan. 7, 1800, Millard Fillmore was the son of a poor farmer in Locke Township, New York. Apprenticed to a cloth maker in his youth, Fillmore struggled for an education and got a job teaching even though he never attended college. Clerking for a judge taught Fillmore enough law to join the bar at age 23, and he became a prosperous New York attorney. Fillmore entered politics as an Anti-Mason and was a four-term congressman when the Whigs made him Zachary Taylor's vice president in 1848. Dignified good looks were Fillmore's main political asset; he was quite unprepared for the presidency when Taylor died suddenly in 1850. Fillmore delayed civil war another decade by signing the Compromise of 1850, but he lost the nomination in 1852 when the Whigs turned to Gen. Winfield Scott, yet another genial war hero and their last candidate. In 1856 Fillmore ran again for president as candidate of the American, or "Know Nothing," party. Fillmore hoped to unite the country behind anti-Catholicism and nativism, submerging the slavery issue, but he carried only Maryland. Though a Unionist in the Civil War, Fillmore denounced Abraham Lincoln and remained sharply critical of Republicans until his death on Mar. 8, 1874.

14. Franklin Pierce (1853–57)

Son of a Revolutionary War hero, Franklin Pierce was born in Hillsboro, New Hampshire, on Nov. 23, 1804—the first president born in the 19th century. A leader of Jacksonian Democrats in Congress in the 1830s, Pierce had been absent from national politics for a decade when the deadlocked Democratic convention nominated him for president on the 49th ballot in 1852. A dark horse candidate, Pierce won enough southern votes to defeat Gen. Winfield Scott, his Mexican War commander, becoming the youngest president as of that date. Pierce greatly hastened the coming of the Civil War by signing the Kansas-Nebraska Act (1854), which repealed the Missouri Compromise and reopened the dangerous issue of slavery expansion. He continually appeased the South by backing proslavery ruffians in "Bleeding Kansas," encouraging slavery expansionists who coveted Cuba, and buying the land known as the Gadsden Purchase from Mexico for a southern railroad. As a result Pierce's party lost elections to Republicans who charged that "slave power" controlled the White House. In 1856 Pierce became the only elected president to be denied his own party's renomination. During the Civil War, Pierce criticized the Emancipation Proclamation and was nearly lynched by angry New Englanders. He died a forgotten, depressed alcoholic, in Concord, New Hampshire, on Oct. 8, 1869, the only president from New Hampshire.

15. James Buchanan (1857–61)

Considered one of the worst presidents because of his lack of good judgment and moral courage, and also the only bachelor president, James Buchanan was born in Mercersburg, Pennsylvania, on Apr. 23, 1791. A lawyer and veteran of the War of 1812, Buchanan compiled more than 40 years of public service as legislator and diplomat. The Democrats nominated Buchanan in 1856 largely because he was in England during the Kansas-Nebraska debate and thus remained untainted by either side of the issue. Millard Fillmore's "Know-Nothing" candidacy helped Buchanan defeat John C. Frémont, the first Republican candidate for president. Buchanan favored "popular sovereignty" over slavery in the territories and was the last of the Doughfaces, or northern politicians submissive to the South. Few Americans shared Buchanan's faith that the Supreme Court's Dred Scott decision (1857) would end conflict over slavery expansion "speedily and finally." When it did not, Buchanan tried to close the issue himself by urging that Kansas be admitted as a slave state—an even worse miscalculation. Democrats deserted him, and Republicans won the House in 1858, but Buchanan's vetoes and southern votes in the Senate stalemated the government. He inadvertently helped Abraham Lincoln win in 1860 by refusing to conciliate his own party. The secession crisis paralyzed Buchanan, who denied both the southern right to secede and the Federal government's right to do anything about it; he was relieved to hand Lincoln the reins. Buchanan died on June 1, 1868. On the day before, he predicted that "history will vindicate my memory," but historians continue mainly to denigrate him.

16. Abraham Lincoln (1861–65)

A largely unpopular president until he was assassinated (the first assassinated president), Abraham Lincoln was born in a log cabin in Hodgenville, Kentucky, on Feb. 12, 1809. He accumulated barely a year's total education while growing up, though he did learn to write and developed a fondness for reading. Family moves took him to Indiana and then to Illinois by the time he was 21. At age 19 Lincoln had worked his way down the Mississippi and came away appalled at slavery. He served in the Black Hawk War (1832) before losing an election for the state legislature. A failed storekeeper, Lincoln worked odd jobs while he taught himself law, sometimes walking 20 miles to borrow books. He finally made the state legislature in 1834 as a Whig, and in 1842 married Mary Todd, having canceled their engagement once before.

Elected to Congress in 1846, Lincoln denounced James K. Polk for precipitating the Mexican War. He returned to his Springfield, Ill., law practice after only one term. But the repeal of the Missouri Compromise shocked Lincoln back into politics, and he helped organize the Illinois Republicans. An unsuccessful candidate for the Senate in 1858, Lincoln drew national attention in debates with Stephen A. Douglas, the nation's leading Democrat. Lincoln was rewarded with his party's nomination for president in 1860, the least objectionable candidate among several more prominent Republicans. He defeated three opponents in the election, though his name did not even appear on the ballot in the South. As Southern states left the Union, Lincoln preached conciliation and promised no harm to slavery—but he vowed to crush secession and forced the issue at Ft. Sumter. After early reverses in the Civil War, Lincoln decided slavery had to be abolished altogether to restore the Union, and he issued the Emancipation Proclamation (1862). Lincoln's management of the war was thwarted by incompetent generals, feuding politicians, and his own inexperience, which matched that of his troops. Yet, like them, Lincoln learned on the job, settling on Ulysses S. Grant as his top general by 1864. The powers of the presidency expanded dramatically under Lincoln, who stretched the Constitution on behalf of the war effort. Lincoln defeated Gen. George McClellan for reelection in 1864, vowing to "bind up the nation's wounds." Before he had the chance, Lincoln was shot on Good Friday, five days after the war's end, by John Wilkes Booth, an arch-Confederate. Lincoln died the next morning, on Apr. 15, 1865. Millions of Americans lined the 1,700-mile route of Lincoln's funeral train, their mournful cries resounding all the way back to Illinois. Lincoln's prestige has grown with time, until many have come to regard him as the greatest president.

17. Andrew Johnson (1865–69)

The first president to be impeached, Andrew Johnson was born in Raleigh, North Carolina, on Dec. 29, 1808, the son of a poor laborer. No president could claim humbler origins: Johnson's father died when he was three, his mother worked as a washerwoman, and he never attended a day of school in his life. As a teenager he ran away to Tennessee, opened a successful tailor's shop, and got elected mayor of Greeneville by age 21. A fiery Democratic stump speaker, Johnson's attacks on Whigs and rich planters won him a seat in the state legislature in 1835 and in Congress in 1843, made him governor in 1853, and took him to the Senate in 1857. Alone among 22 southern senators, Johnson stayed loyal to the Union in 1861, though a mob of Virginians nearly lynched him for it. Lincoln appointed Johnson military governor of Tennessee, and he was nominated for vice president on the "National Union" ticket in 1864. Suddenly made president by Lincoln's assassination, Johnson vowed to carry on Lincoln's policy of leniency toward the South, but radical Republican opposition and his own coarse ineptitude led to serious clashes with Congress. Johnson vetoed 29 bills and

was overridden 15 times, more than any other president to that time. A former slave owner, Johnson resisted Republican efforts to aid the freedmen. His only victory was the unpopular purchase of Alaska in 1867. Congress systematically stripped him of power until Johnson fought back by removing his disloyal secretary of war, Edwin M. Stanton. Impeached in the House for defying the Tenure of Office Act, Johnson was tried in the Senate and acquitted by a single vote on May 26, 1868. Few presidents were so stymied in office. Tennessee helped vindicate Johnson by making him the only former president elected to the Senate. He died a few months later, on July 31, 1875.

18. Ulysses S. Grant (1869–77)

A better general than president, Ulysses Simpson Grant was born in Point Pleasant, Ohio, on Apr. 27, 1822. Having barely passed West Point's height requirement for entrance, Grant attended the academy and graduated in the middle of his class in 1843. Fifty of Grant's classmates fought with or against him as Civil War generals. He served under Gen. Zachary Taylor in the Mexican War before marrying his sweetheart, Julia Dent, in 1848. Assigned to isolated posts after 1852, Grant grew bored away from his family and reportedly turned to heavy drinking. Finally resigning from the army in 1854, he went to Missouri, only to fail in farming and real estate. When the Civil War began, Grant was working in his younger brother's leather shop in Galena, Ill. He received a commission and rose rapidly to brigadier general. U.S. Grant acquired the nickname Unconditional Surrender for his string of western victories, notably at Vicksburg and Chattanooga in 1863. Once Abraham Lincoln made him supreme commander in 1864, Grant opened a relentless offensive that quickly ended the war. He personally accepted Gen. Robert E. Lee's surrender at Appomattox in 1865. After feuding with Andrew Johnson, Grant joined the Republicans and was elected president in 1868. Grant pressed radical Reconstruction in the South with mixed results. Corruption—notably the Jay Gould (1869), Crédit Mobilier (1872), and Whiskey Ring (1875) scandals—marred Grant's presidency; nevertheless, he easily won reelection in 1872. The Panic of 1873 triggered a deep economic depression that dissuaded Grant from a third term in 1876. Reconsidering in 1880, he sought the Republican nomination again and nearly succeeded. Afterward Grant retired and went bankrupt. To provide for his family, he began writing his memoirs. Developing cancer, Grant valiantly hung on to finish the project, which would earn him some literary fame and his family half a million dollars. He died on July 23, 1885, just four days after completing his autobiography.

19. Rutherford B. Hayes (1877–81)

Rutherford Birchard Hayes was born a frail child on Oct. 4, 1822, in Delaware, Ohio, where he was raised by his mother. After attending Harvard Law School, he set up a successful Cincinnati law practice in 1849. Hayes defended fugitive slaves and helped found the Ohio Republicans. In 1852 he married Lucy Ware Webb, the first college graduate first lady. A decorated Civil War veteran, Hayes was wounded five times and promoted to general. From 1868 to 1876 he served as governor of Ohio. Republicans turned to Hayes as a scandal-free hero in 1876 and nominated him for president. He lost the election to Samuel Tilden of the Democrats, but Republicans in Congress disputed enough state vote totals to connive "Rutherfraud" into office with the support of southern Democrats. Hayes's first acts were to appoint an ex-Confederate to his cabinet and to withdraw Federal troops from the South. He never overcame the resulting stigma of political bargain, and facing a Democratic Congress, Hayes seemed destined for a weak presidency. Yet he put the nation back on the gold standard, put down railroad strikes, reformed the civil service, and banished liquor from the White House before keeping his promise to serve only one term. Hayes viewed the return of prosperity and Republican majorities in Congress as personal triumphs. He worked quietly for charitable causes until his death on Jan. 17, 1893.

20. James A. Garfield (1881)

The last log cabin president, James Abram Garfield was born near Orange, Ohio, on Nov. 19, 1831, and like Rutherford B. Hayes, Garfield was raised by his mother. Garfield graduated from Williams College in 1856, became a classics professor, president of Hiram College, a lawyer, and at age 30 the youngest Union general in the Civil War. Garfield left the battlefield in 1864 to enter Congress, where he remained until the Republicans nominated him for president in 1880, a dark-horse compromise between Grant and James G. Blaine. Garfield defeated Gen. Winfield Scott Hancock of the Democrats by 0.1 percent of the vote in a campaign stressing tariffs. Republicans immediately swarmed to Garfield, demanding patronage for their rival "Stalwart" and "Half-Breed" factions. After only four months in office, Garfield was shot in a train station by Charles J. Guiteau, a disappointed Stalwart office-seeker. Garfield died 80 days later, on Sept. 19, 1881, the second presidential assassination ending the second-shortest presidency. When hordes of Republican hopefuls had besieged the White House begging for jobs, Garfield had exclaimed: "My God! What is there in this place that a man should ever want to get in it?"

21. Chester A. Arthur (1881–85)

Chester Alan Arthur was born a preacher's son on Oct. 5, 1829, in Fairfield, Vermont. He grew up in Vermont and in New York to become an ardent abolitionist like his father. A true machine politician, Arthur worked for Republican candidates in New York and enjoyed several patronage jobs during the Civil War. Ulysses S. Grant appointed him collector of the port of New York in 1871, and Arthur prospered there until 1879, when Rutherford B. Hayes removed him in the name of reform. In 1880 "Half-Breed" Republicans nominated Arthur for vice president in a conciliatory gesture to his "Stalwart" faction. "The office of Vice President is a greater honor than I ever dreamed of attaining," he said. But Arthur acceded to the presidency on Sept. 19, 1881, when another Stalwart assassinated James A. Garfield. Perhaps shamed into supporting civil service reform, Arthur signed the Pendleton Act (1883) and rooted out post office graft. Democrats in Congress thwarted the rest of Arthur's initiatives; Republicans, whose calls for spoils Arthur ignored, denied him renomination in 1884. He lost a Senate race in New York and died two years later, on Nov. 18, 1886. Arthur was the last of three presidents in the single year 1881.

22, 24. Grover Cleveland (1885–89; 1893–97)

The only president to serve two nonconsecutive terms, Stephen Grover Cleveland was a minister's son, born in Caldwell, New Jersey, on Mar. 18, 1837. The family moved to New York, where Cleveland's uncle made him a lawyer. He showed scant interest in politics until Buffalo elected him mayor in 1881, and the next year Cleveland became governor. His war on corrupt Tammany Hall made Cleveland the perfect Democratic reform candidate for president in 1884. During the election campaign, backers of James G. Blaine, the Republican candidate, accused Cleveland of fathering an illegitimate child. He admitted it and won anyway—by 0.3 percent of the vote—but not before the Republicans came up with the immortal campaign chant "Ma! Ma! Where's my Pa?/Gone to the White House,/Ha! Ha! Ha!" The first Democratic president after the Civil War, Cleveland pushed for civil service reform and lower tariffs. In the first White House wedding, Cleveland married Frances Folsom in 1886. Cleveland cast over 300 vetoes—more than twice the combined total of all previous presidents. He cut Civil War pensions, seized 81 million acres of unused land from railroads, and signed the Interstate Commerce Act (1887). Defeated in the 1888 election, Cleveland claimed there was "no happier man in the United States"; yet four years later he won a rematch with Benjamin Harrison. Back in the White House, Cleveland underwent a secret operation to remove his cancerous upper jaw. His tight-money policies did nothing to help the depression after the Panic of 1893. Cleveland sent Federal troops to break up the Pullman strike (1894) and supported William McKinley, a Republican, for president in 1896. "I have tried so hard to do right," Cleveland said on his deathbed on June 24, 1908.

23. Benjamin Harrison (1889–93)

Benjamin Harrison was born on Aug. 20, 1833, at the North Bend, Ohio, farm of his grandfather William Henry Harrison, the ninth president. He took up the law in Indiana before joining the Union Army in 1862. Harrison finished the Civil War a brigadier general and returned to Indiana, where he was a prominent Republican, defeated for governor in 1876 but elected senator in 1881. A colorless compromise candidate for president, Harrison won the 1888 election despite receiving fewer popular votes than Grover Cleveland. Harrison bowed to the "Billion Dollar Congress" of free-spending Republicans who escalated Civil War pensions, transportation subsidies, naval construction, and spoils patronage. The McKinley Tariff, the Sherman Anti-Trust Act, the Sherman Silver Purchase Act (all 1890), and Secretary of State James G. Blaine's vigorous foreign policy were hallmarks of Harrison's administration, which oversaw the admission of six new states. Democrats won back Congress in 1890 and the White House in 1892, when Harrison lost to Cleveland in their rematch. A legal expert, Harrison taught at Stanford University and defended Venezuela in a boundary dispute with Britain before his death, on Mar. 13, 1901. Harrison referred to the White House as "my jail."

25. William McKinley (1897–1901)

The last Civil War veteran to become president, William McKinley was born in Niles, Ohio, on Jan. 29, 1843, son of an iron founder. A college dropout, McKinley was a post office clerk when the Civil War began. He volunteered as a private and mustered out as a 22-year-old major. McKinley studied law and was elected to Congress in 1876. A longtime Republican floor leader, he authored the record-high McKinley Tariff of 1890, before losing his seat that same year. Ohio millionaire Marcus Hanna, McKinley's political manager, engineered two governor's terms for him and funded McKinley's run for the presidency in 1896. William Jennings Bryan opposed him on a free-silver platform, but McKinley's dignified front porch campaign stressed sound money, tariffs, and the "full dinner pail." He won the election with the first popular majority since Grant's reelection. Strongly probusiness, McKinley raised the tariff still higher and reluctantly led the country into the Spanish-American War (1898). By acquiring the Philippines and other islands, the country became a world power under McKinley, who went on to proclaim the open-door policy in China. McKinley defeated Bryan by an even larger margin in 1900 and was enjoying great popularity when anarchist Leon Czolgosz shot him in Buffalo, N.Y. McKinley died eight days later, on Sept. 14, 1901.

26. Theodore Roosevelt (1901–09)

Theodore Roosevelt was born in New York City on Oct. 27, 1858, the only president born there. A small, sickly child plagued by asthma, Roosevelt overcame a pampered youth to live the "strenuous life:" he boxed, hiked, hunted, rode horses, and climbed the Matterhorn. After graduating Phi Beta Kappa from Harvard in 1880, he attended Columbia Law School and became the youngest member of New York's legislature. Rich men of his day did not consider politics a suitable avocation, but Roosevelt desperately wanted "to be of the governing class." His first wife, Alice Hathaway Lee, died on the same day his mother died in 1884. Roosevelt wrote books and ran a cattle ranch in North Dakota until he married Edith Kermit Carow in 1886 and they moved to Oyster Bay, N.Y. During the Spanish-American War, Roosevelt left a job at the Navy Department in 1898 to lead the Rough Riders volunteer regiment in Cuba, achieving glory in the Battle of San Juan Hill. Elected governor of New York immediately upon returning home, Roosevelt was named William McKinley's running mate, in 1900. Roosevelt learned of McKinley's death while on a mountain-climbing expedition.

The youngest man to serve as president at 42 (though John F. Kennedy was the youngest elected president at 43), "T.R." promised a Square Deal to close the gap between capital and labor. He mounted well-publicized campaigns against big business and successfully arbitrated major strikes. "Teddy's" popularity soared when he humbled billionaire J.P. Morgan in the Northern Securities case, and a record plurality reelected him in 1904. Roosevelt signed progressive laws to regulate railroads, inspect food and drugs, and create more than 150 million acres of national parks and forests. No less vigorous in foreign policy, Roosevelt's corollary to the Monroe Doctrine asserted the country would intervene to prevent European involvement in Latin America. For helping to end the Russo-Japanese War, Roosevelt became the first American to win the Nobel Prize, but he considered the Panama Canal his greatest achievement. Roosevelt kept his pledge not to seek a third term in 1908—but in 1912 he ran against his chosen successor, William Howard Taft. Denied his party's nomination, Roosevelt survived an assassination attempt and won more than four million votes as the Progressive, or Bull Moose, candidate. During World War I, Roosevelt bitterly denounced the neutrality policy of Woodrow Wilson, who then denied Roosevelt's request to lead troops in France. While laying plans for another run at the White House, Roosevelt died suddenly of a cardiac embolism on Jan. 6, 1919. "No president has ever enjoyed himself as much as I have," he once said.

27. William Howard Taft (1909–13)

By far the largest president at over 330 pounds, William Howard Taft was born in Cincinnati, Ohio, on Sept. 15, 1857. He graduated from Yale in 1878, then followed his father into law and Republican politics: "I always had my plate right side up when offices were falling," Taft wrote. William McKinley sent him to govern the Philippines in 1900, and Theodore Roosevelt appointed him secretary of war in 1904. Taft traveled around the world as Roo-

sevelt's personal emissary, becoming T.R.'s chosen successor in 1908. As president, Taft tried to carry on Roosevelt's policies, but he wrecked the Republican party by alienating progressives from conservative "Stand-Patters" over tariff and conservation issues. Taft initiated the income tax and pursued antitrust suits against big business—but generally he sided with wealthy interests. An infuriated Roosevelt challenged Taft unsuccessfully for the Republican nomination in 1912, then outpolled him in the election, giving Woodrow Wilson the victory. With eight electoral votes, Taft suffered the worst-ever defeat for an incumbent president. But the better part of his career lay ahead: Taft, always more comfortable as a jurist, taught law at Yale until he was appointed chief justice of the United States in 1921. He served with distinction, alternating a liberal nationalism in economic affairs with political and social conservatism. Taft died on Mar. 8, 1930. Never nostalgic for the White House, Taft once said, "I don't remember that I ever was president."

28. Woodrow Wilson (1913–21)

Born on Dec. 28, 1856, in Staunton, Virginia, the son of a Presbyterian minister, Thomas Woodrow Wilson grew up in Virginia, Georgia, South Carolina, and North Carolina—the first southern president since Andrew Jackson. Probably dyslexic, Wilson was slow to read; yet he became the most highly educated president. Graduated from Princeton in 1879, Wilson studied law before taking a Ph.D. in political science at Johns Hopkins in 1886. He taught at Bryn Mawr and Wesleyan University before Princeton appointed him professor in 1890. Wilson attracted the attention of Democratic bosses after he was elected Princeton's president in 1902, and they persuaded him to run for New Jersey governor in 1910. A strong progressive, Wilson won easily—and then turned on party bosses by sponsoring anti-machine reforms. In 1912 the Democrats nominated Wilson for president on the 46th ballot, and he won, with Theodore Roosevelt and William Howard Taft splitting the Republican vote.

Wilson's expert knowledge of government and strong party leadership pushed the Underwood Tariff, the Federal Reserve Act, the Federal Trade Commission, and the Clayton Antitrust Act through Congress by 1914. Restoring competition to the monopoly-plagued economy was the goal of Wilson's "New Freedom," until war in Europe made neutrality his top priority. German attacks on Allied ships carrying Americans strained Wilson's commitment, but he was narrowly reelected in 1916 on the slogan "He Kept Us Out of the War." After Germany spurned Wilson's mediation and resumed attacks on Allied shipping, Congress declared war at Wilson's behest in April 1917. World War I would "make the world safe for democracy," Wilson vowed, and he issued "Fourteen Points" for a just peace. After the armistice in November 1918, Wilson became the first president to visit Europe, when he attended the Paris peace conference that produced the Versailles Treaty. Wilson's dream of "peace without vengeance" was frustrated at Versailles, where he compromised away his Fourteen Points to obtain the League of Nations for collective security. In July 1919, Wilson returned home to face hostile Republicans in the Senate, where his treaty languished. On a nationwide speaking tour, Wilson collapsed from exhaustion in Colorado and suffered a paralytic stroke in October 1919. Wilson, all but incapacitated, refused to compromise as the Senate rejected the Versailles Treaty. Wilson's second wife, Edith Bolling Galt, whom he married in 1915, shielded the disabled president from the press and politicians until the end of his term in

1921. Woodrow Wilson died in his sleep on Feb. 3, 1924, frustrated by his own country's refusal to join the League of Nations.

29. Warren G. Harding (1921–23)

The first president born after the Civil War, Warren Gamaliel Harding was born in Blooming Grove, Ohio, which earlier had been named Corsica, on Nov. 2, 1865. He taught, studied law, and sold insurance before following his father into the newspaper business. Marriage to Florence DeWolfe, a wealthy widow, in 1891 helped finance Harding's paper, the Marion Star. A staunch Republican, Harding's probusiness editorials got him elected state senator and lieutenant governor. Although defeated for governor in 1910, Harding was elected senator four years later. Republicans turned to him in 1920 as a compromise candidate for president, the "best of the second-raters"; his good looks were expected to win over women first-time voters. Elected by an unprecedented 61 percent majority, Harding promised a return to "normalcy" for Americans tired of war and Woodrow Wilson. Harding's administration featured higher tariffs, lower taxes, and immigration restriction—but perhaps most notably, pervasive corruption and incompetence by Harding's crooked appointees. Harding was disturbed by the dishonesty of "my God-damn friends," two of whom committed suicide to avoid prosecution. While visiting San Francisco, Harding died suddenly of an embolism on Aug. 2, 1923. Scandals involving secret love affairs, official graft, and the vast Teapot Dome swindle erupted soon thereafter. Mrs. Harding zealously tracked down Harding's letters and destroyed them, leaving him the most enigmatic president, and certainly one of the worst.

30. Calvin Coolidge (1923–29)

The only president to share the nation's birthday, John Calvin Coolidge was born in Plymouth, Vermont, on July 4, 1872. Descended from a long line of New Englanders, he graduated from Amherst in 1895, practiced law in Massachusetts, and entered Republican politics in 1899. Coolidge rose slowly through a succession of state offices until he was elected governor of Massachusetts in 1918. Acclaimed for crushing the Boston police strike in 1919, Coolidge became the unexpected Republican vice-presidential nominee in 1920. After Warren G. Harding's death while still in office, Coolidge's own father swore him in as the new president. "Silent Cal" was the butt of jokes for his laconic utterances, but his minimalist approach to government fit the public mood, and he restored respectability to the White House, tainted by Harding's corrupt appointees and all-night poker parties. Instead of the whiskey that once flowed freely there, ice water in paper cups was served to visitors. Coolidge, untouched by leftover scandals, won the election in his own right in 1924. Pronouncing that the "business of America is business," he ushered in the heady years of Coolidge Prosperity, as the stock market soared higher and higher. Coolidge ignored foreign affairs and made frugality his trademark, slashing the budget at the expense of farmers and veterans, even driving out a White House cook who could not abide Coolidge's cost cutting. "It's a pretty good idea to get out when they still want you," Coolidge said, surprising the nation at the peak of his success by declining to run again in 1928. A popular president, Coolidge was safely out of politics when the Great Depression arrived. He died on Jan. 5, 1933, on the eve of the New Deal.

31. Herbert Hoover (1929–33)

Born in West Branch, Iowa, on Aug. 10, 1874, Herbert Clark Hoover was the first president from west of the Mississippi. Orphaned at eight and raised by Quaker relatives in Iowa and Oregon, Hoover joined the first graduating class of Stanford University in 1895. He became a world-famous mining engineer and a multimillionaire by age 40. In World War I, Hoover helped rescue Americans stranded in Europe, distributed food supplies to occupied Belgium, and convinced the nation to save food ("Hooverize") for the war effort. Hoover was Woodrow Wilson's economic adviser at Versailles, and he organized relief for famine-struck Russia during the revolution. Joining the Republicans in 1919, Hoover earned prominence as the secretary of commerce in the 1920s and was elected president in 1928—the only electoral victory of his life. He promised a "chicken in every pot," but a few months later, the Wall Street crash brought on the Great Depression. Paralyzed by his conservative instincts, Hoover could not halt the spread of bank failures, bankruptcy, unemployment, and despair. Government should not get involved, he believed, and public relief would ruin American morals—so Hoover called for a balanced budget while promising the return of prosperity. He sent tanks to disperse veterans begging for pensions, and shantytowns across the country were dubbed Hoovervilles. Massively defeated by Franklin D. Roosevelt in 1932, Hoover called the New Deal "socialistic, collectivistic, fascistic and communistic." For decades Americans blamed Hoover for the depression and criticized his hard-hearted refusal to help the needy. Hoover lived another 31 years, the longest postpresidential lifespan, and he salvaged his reputation with more relief work after World War II. In retirement Hoover chaired two bipartisan commissions on government reorganization, issuing many important recommendations for Federal reform. Boulder Dam on the Colorado River was renamed to honor Hoover before he died, at age 90, on Oct. 20, 1964.

32. Franklin D. Roosevelt (1933–45)

The only president elected more than twice, Franklin Delano Roosevelt was born to a wealthy Hyde Park, New York, family on Jan. 30, 1882. He followed his cousin, Theodore Roosevelt, into Harvard and Columbia Law School—but not into the Republican party. F.D.R. was a Democratic state senator, assistant secretary of the navy, and nominee for vice president in 1920. Paralyzed by polio in 1921, Roosevelt learned to walk with braces and canes. As governor of New York after 1928, he pioneered unemployment relief in the Great Depression, earning him the Democratic nomination for president in 1932. Herbert Hoover, brooding and baffled by the depression, posed little challenge to the beaming, magnetic Roosevelt, who won the election by 23 million to 16 million votes. F.D.R. promised vague but bold experimentation ("above all, try something"), and as he took office in the worst inaugural crisis since Abraham Lincoln's, he assured Americans they had "nothing to fear but fear itself." F.D.R.'s first 100 days set a breakneck pace as compliant congressmen approved his New Deal for relief and recovery. Major landmarks were the National Industrial Recovery Act, the Agricultural Adjustment Act, the Tennessee Valley Authority, the Works Progress Administration, the National Labor Relations Act (Wagner Act), and the Social Security Act (1933–35). Though often contradictory and ineffective, the New Deal established the Federal government's responsibility for protecting farmers, workers, and the unemployed while actively regulating the economy to prevent another crash. F.D.R.'s high-profile "fireside chats," public works projects, and Social Security programs overcame despair and restored public confidence in the economy and government.

Reelected by a huge margin in 1936, Roosevelt proved incapable of ending the depression, as he ran afoul of the "nine old men" on the Supreme Court. Many well-to-do Americans criticized Roosevelt for rescuing the common man. Despite alienating many voters with his court-packing plan and "soak the rich" taxes, F.D.R. won an unprecedented third term in 1940. As war loomed in Europe, F.D.R. used his mastery of public opinion to lead Americans away from isolation, helping Britain with the destroyers-for-bases deal (1940) and Lend-Lease Act (1941) even before Pearl Harbor. World War II then occupied F.D.R.'s full attention as he shelved the New Deal and orchestrated the mammoth war effort. Roosevelt crisscrossed the globe to meet with Allied leaders and kept close personal control of diplomacy and grand strategy. He rallied a powerful sense of national purpose in the war, winning his fourth election in 1944. Together with Winston Churchill and Josef Stalin, F.D.R. planned a postwar peace of UN cooperation. Just after the Yalta Conference, Roosevelt died suddenly of a cerebral hemorrhage on Apr. 12, 1945, only four months before the war's end. His wife of 40 years, Eleanor Roosevelt, easily the most influential first lady, led her husband's campaign on behalf of disadvantaged Americans and continued it long after his death.

33. Harry S. Truman (1945–53)

A plain midwestern farmer and World War I artilleryman, Harry S. Truman (the S does not stand for a middle name) was born on May 8, 1884, in Lamar, Missouri. After his Kansas City haberdashery failed, Truman entered politics as a Democrat in the 1920s, and the local Pendergast machine arranged his election to the Senate as a New Dealer in 1934. National attention came to Truman when he headed a congressional committee investigating government waste during World War II. When Franklin D. Roosevelt needed a new vice president in 1944, he chose Truman. After only a few weeks in office, Truman had the presidency thrust upon him by Roosevelt's sudden death in April 1945. "Pray for me, boys," he told his first press conference. Utterly unprepared, Truman did not even know about the atomic bomb project, but he vowed to carry on Roosevelt's policies. Truman proved a remarkably capable chief executive. In his first four months, Truman approved the United Nations, accepted the German surrender, met with Allied leaders at Potsdam, and ordered atomic bombs dropped on Japan. As the Cold War commenced, Truman talked tough with the Soviets, accusing them of breaking agreements and intimidating helpless neighbors. In 1947 he proclaimed the Truman Doctrine, promising U.S. aid to threatened countries, and the Marshall Plan to aid European recovery and contain communism. The next year Truman ordered the Berlin airlift when the Soviets cut off West Berlin, and he promised to help Third World countries with the Point Four program. No less assertive at home, Truman made progress on civil rights, subdued restive unions, and prevented the Republican-controlled Congress from dismantling the New Deal—a specter that he effectively raised to win surprise election in 1948. Truman committed the country to the NATO alliance in 1949 and sent troops to South Korea when Communist armies invaded in 1950. But as Congress rejected Truman's ambitious Fair Deal domestic program and the Korean War bogged down, Truman's last years were barren. He had more vetoes overridden than all presidents but Andrew Johnson, and his poll ratings were lower than all but Jimmy Carter's. Truman, who initially raised fears of subversion with his loyalty program, could not quell the Red Scare

that swept his party from power in 1952, as Republicans hammered away on the theme that Democrats were "soft on communism." Truman was convinced that he saved the world from communism, prevented World War III, and could have won another term if he chose to run in 1952. "He did his damndest" was the only eulogy Harry Truman desired on his death, on Dec. 26, 1972. Out of favor when he left office, Truman gained rising respect after his death.

34. Dwight D. Eisenhower (1953–61)

The last war hero president, Dwight David Eisenhower was born in Denison, Texas, on Oct. 14, 1890, and grew up poor in Kansas. A military history buff, Eisenhower graduated with the 1915 class of West Point that produced 59 generals. He married Mamie Doud, his wife of 52 years, and spent World War I as a tank-training instructor. Eisenhower, only a major at age 40, rose rapidly during World War II, promoted past 350 senior officers to become commander of U.S. forces in Europe in 1942. By the end of 1944, he was made five-star general and Supreme Allied Commander, taking the German surrender in May 1945. By that point a global celebrity, Eisenhower was army chief of staff until 1948, when he resigned to become president of Columbia University. Pres. Truman named him to command NATO forces in 1950, but two years later, Eisenhower retired again to take the Republican nomination and run for president against Adlai E. Stevenson.

"Ike" became perhaps the most popular president in U.S. history, though many questioned his lax work habits, detached management style, and baffling speeches. Prominent millionaires in Eisenhower's cabinet and archconservatives such as Sec. of State John Foster Dulles seemed to have free rein, and Eisenhower acquiesced in Sen. Joe McCarthy's wild charges of subversion. His administration stockpiled atomic weapons and promised "massive retaliation" against Soviet aggression—yet did nothing when the Red Army rolled into Hungary in 1956. Eisenhower did end the Korean War, concluded several alliance agreements, and cut the defense budget. The "Eisenhower Doctrine" promised U.S. aid to Middle Eastern countries fighting communism. When Britain, France, and Israel invaded the Suez Canal region in 1956, Eisenhower led UN condemnation and forced them to withdraw, though he sent U.S. Marines into Lebanon two years later. He began heavy U.S. involvement in Vietnam by backing the French and then the puppet Diem regime. At home Eisenhower promised to scale back the government—yet he expanded Social Security; created the Department of Health, Education, and Welfare; and spent billions on public housing and freeways. He pointedly stressed religious devotion. The Supreme Court's *Brown* decision, which Eisenhower deeply regretted, inaugurated the civil rights movement. Eisenhower defeated Stevenson again in 1956, but Soviet domination of space, revolution in Cuba, embarrassment over the Soviets' shooting down of a U.S. spy plane, and his own ill health marred his second term. Eisenhower reluctantly sent paratroopers to enforce desegregation in Little Rock, Ark., in 1957. Democrats controlled Congress for all but two years of Eisenhower's presidency. In retirement Eisenhower approved of U.S. intervention in Vietnam and counseled presidents until his death on Mar. 28, 1969.

35. John F. Kennedy (1961–63)

The youngest man elected president (though Theodore Roosevelt was younger when he assumed the office following McKinley's death), the only Roman Catholic, and the first born in the 20th century, John Fitzgerald Kennedy was born in Brookline, Massachusetts, on May 29, 1917, to a family of Irish politicos. His father, Joseph P. Kennedy, was ambassador to England and one of the richest men in America. Kennedy attended Dexter and Choate Academies, the London School of Economics, and Princeton before graduating from Harvard in 1940. A patrol boat commander in World War II, Kennedy was decorated for bravery in saving the lives of wounded crew members. Kennedy's father arranged his election to Congress, where he served three undistinguished terms before entering the Senate in 1952. In 1953, he married wealthy socialite Jacqueline Bouvier, and in 1957, he won the Pulitzer Prize for *Profiles in Courage*, a study of principled politicians. In 1960, running on a platform that lambasted Republicans for insufficient anticommunism and "vigor," Kennedy became the first candidate to utilize the presidential primary system to defeat three prominent opponents for the Democratic nomination. In the general election, Kennedy edged sitting vice president Richard M. Nixon by the narrowest of margins: 118,000 votes out of 69 million cast. The campaign was the first to feature televised presidential debates, in which Kennedy's poise, polish, and charisma were an invaluable asset.

During the campaign, Kennedy had pledged a New Frontier, but his social programs languished in Congress. Undaunted, he plunged into foreign affairs, his primary interest. Just after taking office, he approved the disastrous Bay of Pigs invasion, and a year later, he terrified the world by confronting the Soviets over the presence of their missiles in Cuba. He visited the Berlin Wall and expressed solidarity with Germans under the Russian gun. But he also set up the Washington-Moscow hotline, and signed the Nuclear Test Ban Treaty (1963).

Thousands of U.S. troops went to Vietnam as Kennedy escalated the commitment to containing communism. Kennedy vastly increased spending for defense and space programs, vowing to put a man on the Moon. He also engineered a $10 billion tax cut that eventually brought prosperity and increased revenues. As racial unrest spread, Kennedy cautiously supported the civil rights movement, introducing sweeping legislation that would not pass in his lifetime—nor would his plans for aid to education and medical care for the elderly reach fruition before his death. In a Dallas, Tex., motorcade on Nov. 22, 1963, he was fatally shot. Kennedy's alleged assassin, Lee Harvey Oswald, a left-wing ex-marine, was in turn murdered by Jack Ruby two days later. While doubts persisted that Oswald acted alone, Kennedy's martyrdom helped realize his legislative legacy, and subsequent revelation of his many peccadilloes have not tarnished the "Kennedy myth."

36. Lyndon B. Johnson (1963–69)

The eighth vice president to succeed by death of a president, Lyndon Baines Johnson was born on his father's Texas ranch near Stonewall on Aug. 27, 1908. He worked his way through Southwest Texas State Teachers College, taught briefly, then took a job in Washington—where he would live for all but two years until he left the White House. Government fascinated Johnson, and he reveled in making connections, marrying heiress Claudia Alta "Lady Bird" Taylor after a two-month courtship in 1934. An ardent New Dealer, Johnson won election to Congress as a Democrat in 1937. Reelected three times without opposition, Johnson became the first congressman to volunteer for combat in World War II, winning a Silver Star before returning to Washington. In 1948, on his second try, "Landslide Lyndon" was elected to the Senate by just 87 votes. Hard work and Texas oil money made Johnson the youngest Senate majority leader by 1955. A huge man, Johnson's powers of persuasion were legendary, but he failed in his bid for the Democratic nomination for president in 1960. Johnson accepted John F. Kennedy's offer of the vice presidency and campaigned hard in the South to aid their narrow victory. Made president a thousand days later by the tragedy in Dallas, Johnson vowed to continue Kennedy's programs, pushing them through Congress with surprising ease. Notable were the Civil Rights Act outlawing segregation and the Equal Opportunity Act, which declared "war on poverty." After less than a year in office, Johnson defeated Barry Goldwater by the biggest plurality in history.

Now president in his own right, Johnson unveiled plans for a Great Society free from poverty and discrimination and passed the Education Act, Medical Care Act, and the Voting Rights Act in 1965. But Johnson came to grief in Vietnam, where he broke his 1964 campaign promise not to send "American boys to fight Asian wars." Earlier administrations committed the U.S. to defending South Vietnam, but Johnson intervened massively to prove American credibility to allies and enemies alike. Following the Tonkin Gulf incident (1964), Johnson steadily expended American power and lives in Vietnam, but victory, or a means to achieve it, never came within reach—despite the presence of over half a million U.S. troops by 1968. Johnson's presidency unraveled as American losses mounted, antiwar protests grew strident, race riots exploded in inner cities across the nation, and the government developed a credibility gap. Virtually a prisoner of the White House, Johnson faced a war he could neither win nor leave behind and a nation more deeply divided than at any time since the Civil War. In March 1968 Johnson effectively resigned by announcing he would not seek another term. He retired to his sprawling Texas ranch and stayed out of politics until his death, on Jan. 22, 1973.

37. Richard M. Nixon (1969–74)

The only president to resign from office, Richard Milhous Nixon was born in Yorba Linda, California, to a poor Quaker family on Jan. 9, 1913. A graduate of Whittier College and Duke University Law School, Nixon married Thelma "Pat" Ryan in 1940, saw noncombat service in World War II, and rode into Congress on the Republican wave of 1946. He gained fame in the anti-Communist trial of Alger Hiss before entering the Senate in 1950. Dwight D. Eisenhower made Nixon his running mate in 1952, but Nixon was nearly forced to resign for accepting questionable contributions. He appealed for national exoneration in the televised "Checkers" speech. A well-traveled vice president, Nixon almost lost his life to hostile Latin American mobs in 1958, and he waged an impromptu debate in Moscow with Soviet premier Nikita Khrushchev in 1959. Eisenhower's obvious successor in 1960, Nixon narrowly lost the election to John F. Kennedy, and when he lost a California gubernatorial race in 1962, his career seemed over. Yet he practiced law in New York until the Republicans nominated him again in 1968. To a nation riven by the Vietnam War, Nixon promised "law and order," appealing to calm and unity against a background of riots, assassinations, and protest. Nixon defeated Hubert H. Humphrey with the smallest victor's share of the vote since 1912.

Vowing to "bring us together," Nixon tried to thwart the bureaucracy and Democrats in Congress by centralizing executive power. To control inflation, he ordered wage-price controls and devalued the dollar for the first time since the depression. Seeking "peace with honor" in Vietnam, Nixon built up the South Vietnamese army and withdrew U.S. troops—while massively escalating bombing of North Vietnam. Antiwar protests reached fever pitch when the United States invaded Cambodia in 1970. Nixon responded with appeals to the "silent majority," attacks on press freedom, and clandestine harassment of administration critics. High points of his first administration were the Apollo moon landing in 1969, Nixon's path-breaking visit to China in 1972, and the first Strategic Arms Limitation Treaty with the Soviet Union. Twelve days after announcing "peace is at hand" in Vietnam, Nixon was reelected by a landslide, carrying an unprecedented 49 states. During the campaign five burglars were arrested in the Democratic party headquarters, and by early 1973, they were linked to the White House. The ensuing "Watergate" scandal exposed the Nixon administration's rampant corruption, illegality, and deceit. Nixon himself downplayed the scandal as mere politics, but when his aides resigned in disgrace, Nixon's role in ordering an illegal cover-up came to light in the press, courts, and congressional investigations. Nixon evaded taxes, accepted illicit campaign contributions, ordered secret bombings, and harassed opponents with executive agencies, wiretaps, and break-ins. Vice Pres. Spiro T. Agnew resigned in October 1973 for accepting bribes, but Nixon hung on to power, claiming, "I am not a crook," as the House began impeachment proceedings. Subpoenas and Supreme Court orders forced Nixon to release tapes of his White House conversations authorizing the Watergate cover-up. Ultimately, he resigned to avoid impeachment for obstruction of justice, abuse of power, and contempt of Congress. Claiming to have lost his "political base," Nixon announced his resignation on national television on Aug. 9, 1974. He never admitted wrongdoing, though he later conceded errors of judgment. Saved by a blanket pardon from Gerald R. Ford, his second vice president, Nixon retired to California, later moving to New Jersey. He dedicated the remainder of his life to unsullying his name, while becoming a foreign policy adviser to presidents until his death at the age of 81 in 1994.

38. Gerald R. Ford (1974–77)

The only vice president and president never elected to either office, Gerald Rudolph Ford was born in Omaha, Nebraska, on July 14, 1913. An Eagle Scout, he grew up in Michigan and attended the University of Michigan on a football scholarship, playing on the national championship teams of 1932 and 1933. After graduating in 1935, Ford coached football and boxing at Yale while attending law school. In the navy he earned 10 battle stars in the Pacific during World War II. Ford was elected to Congress in 1948 as a Republican. He would be reelected 12 times, never by less than 60 percent. His solid conservative record elevated him to House Republican minority leader by 1965. For supporting Richard M. Nixon, Ford was rewarded with the vice presidency in December 1973, replacing Spiro T. Agnew under the 25th Amendment. Nixon's resignation made Ford the new president on Aug. 9, 1974. When asked at his confirmation hearings if he would ever pardon Nixon, Ford said, "I do not think the public would stand for it." After his inauguration, Ford announced "our long national nightmare is over," but a month later he shocked the nation by giving Nixon a blanket pardon. Ford denied that a deal had been made, but his public standing never recovered. He struggled with huge Democratic ma-

jorities in Congress to stem soaring inflation and unemployment, casting 66 vetoes in all. Ford oversaw the final withdrawal from Vietnam and, in the Mayaguez incident, he sent the marines to rescue 39 Americans captured by Cambodia.

Breaking a 1973 pledge, Ford decided to seek reelection, and while campaigning, he survived two assassination attempts by California women. Ford carried four more states than Jimmy Carter in the election but lost by 57 electoral votes. After his defeat, Ford remained involved with Republican politics and advocated for public policy issues including gay rights almost until his death on Dec. 26, 2006 at the age of 93.

39. Jimmy Carter (1977–81)

James Earl Carter, the first deep-southerner elected president in 128 years, was born in Plains, Georgia, on Oct. 1, 1924. He grew up on a farm with no plumbing or electricity but realized his dream of attending the U.S. Naval Academy. Carter graduated in 1946 and married Rosalynn Smith. He joined the submarine fleet and studied nuclear physics, leaving the Navy in 1953 to run the family peanut business. He was elected to the Georgia state senate in 1962. Defeated for governor in 1966, Carter campaigned constantly for the next four years, winning on his second try in 1970. Carter reorganized the government and hired more blacks, declaring that the "time for racial discrimination is over." A month before leaving office in 1974, Carter was the first Democrat to announce his candidacy for president in 1976, again campaigning constantly. "Jimmy Who?" burst into headlines by winning narrow pluralities over nine rivals in early primaries. Carter's grinning, homespun style and earnest vows of honesty ("I will never lie to you") struck a chord with voters after Watergate. Carter won the nomination and defeated incumbent Gerald R. Ford by 2 percent of the vote. Lack of Washington connections helped his candidacy but not his presidency, for Carter never shook his image as the provincial amateur. Democratic majorities in Congress ignored Carter's pleas for tax reform and a long-range energy policy. Transportation deregulation, environmental protection, and new departments of energy and education were Carter's main domestic achievements.

But as federal spending mounted and oil prices doubled, most Americans blamed Carter for runaway inflation. His 20 percent approval rating in August 1979 was the lowest ever recorded. In foreign affairs Carter obtained a Panama Canal treaty, normalized relations with China, and mediated the Camp David peace accords between Israel and Egypt. He moved toward closer relations with the Soviet Union, signing the SALT II treaty in 1979, but the Soviet invasion of Afghanistan led Carter to embargo grain sales to the U.S.S.R. and to order a boycott of the 1980 Moscow Olympics. The Carter Doctrine announced the United States would defend the Persian Gulf, where ironically, Carter soon met his downfall in the Iran hostage crisis. Early public support for Carter's restraint gradually withered under the glare of relentless media coverage. Carter himself became a hostage of Iran, trapped in the White House as Edward Kennedy nearly deprived him of the Democratic nomination. In April 1980, Carter approved a military rescue mission whose tragic failure reinforced his image of incompetence and weakness, which Republican candidate Ronald Reagan exploited, winning the election in a landslide. Carter left the White House discredited, his informal style ridiculed as inappropriate. However, in later years he won recognition as a trustworthy international negotiator and he was awarded the Nobel Peace Prize in 2002 and continued to be a presence in many international crisis negotiations.

40. Ronald Reagan (1981–89)

Ronald Wilson Reagan was born in Tampico, Illinois, on Feb. 6, 1911. Reagan was a radio sports announcer when he made his first movie in 1937. Over 50 more films would follow in Reagan's prolific Hollywood career. In 1940 he married actress Jane Wyman, who divorced him in 1948. During World War II, Reagan made propaganda films for the U.S. Army, and after the war he became president of the Screen Actors Guild. Then a Democrat, Reagan assailed Communists in Hollywood. He married Nancy Davis, another actress, in 1952. As his movie career waned, Reagan espoused conservative causes, switching to the Republican party in 1960. Reagan made a dramatic speech at the end of the 1964 campaign, and despite his total lack of experience he was elected governor of California in 1966. As governor, Reagan broke all promises by raising taxes, increasing spending, and expanding the state government—yet he easily won reelection in 1970. He made unsuccessful runs for the Republican presidential nomination in 1968 and 1976 before winning it in 1980. He swept past Jimmy Carter in the "Reagan Revolution" of 1980, carrying 44 states and making huge Republican gains in Congress.

"Reaganomics" promised to cut taxes and social spending while vastly increasing the defense budget and somehow balancing the budget. Congress was unmoved until Mar. 30, 1981, when a crazed youth named John Hinckley shot Reagan twice in the chest. Reagan's good humor and rapid recovery charmed Americans—especially the press, which had questioned his age and health. Reagan then prevailed over Congress to pass mammoth tax cuts. The national debt began its meteoric rise under Reagan as increases in defense spending outweighed cuts in social programs. By 1986 the U.S. had become a net borrower for the first time since World War I, but falling oil prices slowed inflation and rekindled economic growth, for which Reagan took credit. Calling the Soviet Union an "evil empire," Reagan built up the armed forces, deployed U.S. nuclear missiles in Europe, and began the Strategic Defense Initiative. He sent U.S. Marines to Lebanon, where 240 of them died in a terrorist attack. To halt the spread of communism, Reagan ordered the invasion of Grenada and isolated the Sandinista government of Nicaragua. Reelected in 1984, with the economy booming and his public esteem high, Reagan seemed headed for an even more successful second term. He ordered bombing raids on Libya and met with Soviet leader Mikhail Gorbachev, eventually producing historic arms control agreements. But in 1987 Reagan's invincible popularity finally succumbed to the Iran-Contra scandal: White House staff had secretly sold arms to Iran in hopes of freeing American hostages held in Lebanon, using the profits illegally to fund Contra fighters in Nicaragua. Many top Reagan aides had to resign, but more damaging was the president's apparent loss of control over his own administration.

As the Iran-Contra trials continued in 1990, Reagan was ordered to testify under oath about his role in the scandal; he responded 130 times with "I don't recall" or "I don't remember." In 1995, he revealed he was suffering from Alzheimer's disease, to which he succumbed in 2004.

41. George H. W. Bush (1989–93)

The first sitting vice president elected president in over 150 years, George Herbert Walker Bush was born in Milton, Massachusetts, on June 12, 1924.

His father was former U.S. Senator Prescott Sheldon Bush (R-Conn., 1952-63) As a Navy pilot during World War II, Bush was shot down over the Pacific and rescued at sea. He married Barbara Pierce, a Smith College student, on Jan. 6, 1945, and graduated Phi Beta Kappa in economics from Yale in 1948. Bush spurned an offer from his millionaire father's Wall Street firm to pursue a career in the Texas oil fields that eventually made him a millionaire in his own right.

Running on a conservative anti-Communist and anti-civil rights platform, Bush won the Republican nomination for Senate in 1964 and again in 1970, but lost the general election both times. In between, he was elected to Congress from a wealthy suburban Houston district. Presidents Richard Nixon and Gerald Ford rewarded the Republican party loyalist with appointed offices, including U.S. ambassador to the United Nations (1971), chairman of the Republican National Committee (1973), and director of the C.I.A. (1976). After losing the Republican presidential nomination to Ronald Reagan in 1980, Bush accepted Reagan's offer to join him on the winning ticket.

One of the few members of Reagan's staff to emerge unscathed by the Iran-Contra affair, Bush bested Bob Dole for the Republican nomination in 1988. Bush defeated Massachusetts governor Michael S. Dukakis, renewing the Reagan pledge of "no new taxes" and vowing to uphold the Reagan legacy of less government, strong defense, and family values. He declared war on "this scourge" of drugs by creating an office of National Drug Control Policy within the White House. Bush's first official act was to proclaim January 20 as the "National Day of Prayer."

Bush suffered early criticism for lack of leadership, but struck back with major initiatives, including major arms control proposals and two summit meetings with Soviet premier Mikhail Gorbachev. In December 1989, Bush ordered the invasion of Panama, he said, to protect U.S. citizens and overthrow the regime of Gen. Manuel Noriega.

As one eastern bloc country after another opted for democracy in 1989 and 1990, Bush enjoyed the highest public approval rating of any postwar president. This popularity gave him the political leverage to renege on his campaign pledge of "no new taxes." His popularity rose to record levels when he ordered Operation Desert Storm to liberate Kuwait from Iraqi occupation. But it later became apparent that Bush had ordered a cease-fire much too early, allowing Saddam Hussein to retain power.

Throughout 1991, as the Soviet Union was crumbling, Bush acted quickly and decisively to support those republics seeking independence and to provide food and medical supplies where needed. He and Gorbachev declared an end to the arms race by signing the first nuclear arms reduction pact in July.

Bush had less success on the domestic front. In spring of 1992, his approval rating dipped below 40 percent, reflecting the deepening economic recession that drove unemployment levels to their highest level in a decade. Bush was challenged first in the primaries and then in the general election by opponents who made the economy the central issue of their campaigns. But unable to get the economy on course, Bush lost to Bill Clinton in a three-way race that saw independent candidate Ross Perot capture nearly 20 percent of the vote.

42. Bill Clinton (1993–2001)

William Jefferson Clinton was born in tiny Hope, Arkansas, on Aug. 19, 1946. His father, William Jefferson Blythe III, was killed before his son was born, leaving his wife, Virginia, to raise their son alone. Four years later, she married Roger Clinton; Bill assumed his stepfather's surname. After graduating from Georgetown University, Bill Clinton went to Oxford University on a Rhodes scholarship and then to Yale Law School, where he met Hillary Rodham, whom he married in 1973.

Clinton was elected Arkansas attorney general in 1976, and two years later became the nation's youngest governor. In 1980 he lost, a victim of the Reagan Republican landslide. But in 1982, Clinton won his old job back, and over the next decade helped Arkansas to transform its economy. He became a leading figure among the so-called New Democrats, who called for welfare reform, smaller government, and other Reagan-like ideas.

In 1992, Clinton emerged as a shaky frontrunner among six Democratic hopefuls for the presidential nomination. Allegations that he had extramarital affairs, dodged the draft during the Vietnam War, and smoked marijuana threatened to derail his campaign. But as the candidate with the most money and the best-articulated campaign strategy—creating more jobs—Clinton was able to stay in the race the longest, fending off all rivals long before the Democratic convention.

In a three-way race against the incumbent George Bush and the billionaire populist Ross Perot, who ran as an independent, Clinton garnered 366 of the 538 electoral votes, despite winning only 43 percent of the popular vote.

Clinton entered office hoping that a Democratic president and a Democratic Congress could untangle the gridlock that had paralyzed Washington for 12 years. But his first act as president, a pledge to end the ban on lesbians and gay men in the armed forces, met with heavy resistance from top military leaders. And his economic stimulus package fell to defeat in the face of a remarkable Republican filibuster in the Senate.

During his second 100 days, he signed the family leave bill, lifted restrictions on abortion counseling at federally funded clinics, and laid the groundwork for the North American Free Trade Agreement. The passage of his first budget—with Vice Pres. Al Gore casting the deciding vote in the Senate—started the nation on the road to recovery from the burden of the enormous deficits created by the Reagan and Bush administrations. In the ensuing economic prosperity, the 5 to 8 percent increase on the tax rates of the wealthiest Americans as well as a surge in capital gains taxes from the booming stock markets generated so much income for the Treasury that deficits turned to surpluses by 1998.

Clinton had several early successes on the foreign policy front, assuring the stability of Russia's government, and negotiating a peace treaty between Israel and the P.L.O. that recognized Palestinian self-rule in Gaza and part of the West Bank. On the domestic front, however, Clinton found little support for his programs. A complex plan (devised by a committee headed by First Lady Hillary Rodham Clinton) called for guaranteed health coverage to all Americans. But it also promised a huge government bureaucracy and the plan was never adopted.

In the 1994 midterm elections, the G.O.P. captured both Houses of Congress for the first time in more than 40 years. New House Speaker Newt Gingrich proclaimed a Republican revolution. In 1995 Republicans in Congress also opened hearings on the Clintons' controversial investment in a land deal known as Whitewater.

As he prepared for a second term, Clinton's approval ratings rebounded. He took centrist positions on issues like abortion and affirmative action, and signed the Republican welfare bill that ended 60-year-old guarantees for poor people. With the stock market soaring, unemployment falling, and inflation firmly in check, Clinton won re-election in 1996 almost effortlessly against Senator Bob Dole.

During Clinton's second term, the Whitewater scandal came back to haunt him in an unexpected way. Failing to uncover anything directly implicating the President or Mrs. Clinton in connection with the land deal, independent counsel Kenneth Starr expanded his inquiry far beyond its original scope and unearthed evidence of an affair between Clinton and a young White House intern, Monica Lewinsky. Clinton emphatically denied the allegation, and then, as the first sitting president ever subpoenaed to testify before a federal grand jury, he lied under oath about the affair.

The Republican-controlled House approved two articles of impeachment against Clinton, making him the first president impeached since Andrew Johnson in 1868. The month-long Senate trial was filled with legal wrangling on all sides, but in the end, not even a simple majority could be mustered for either impeachment article.

The day after his acquittal, Clinton sent 4,000 troops to Kosovo as part of a NATO peacekeeping force. After 72 days of air strikes, Serbian Pres. Slobodan Milosevic agreed to withdraw all military forces from Kosovo. On the domestic front, Clinton and the Republican Congress battled over how to spend the first budget surplus since 1969, resulting in a stalemate although some of the money went to paying down the national debt.

Clinton spent much of his final year on a global "farewell tour" trying to shore up his legacy. He successfully shepherded a bill through Congress granting China permanent trade status, but was unable to broker a lasting peace in the Middle East.

43. George W. Bush (2001–2009)

The election of George Walker Bush in 2000 was unusual in several ways. Like John Quincy Adams, the only other son of a president to win the White House, Bush also lost the popular vote. In an unprecedented ruling, the U.S. Supreme Court intervened in the election process, effectively giving him the presidency.

Bush was born on July 6, 1946 in New Haven, Connecticut. His family moved to Texas when he was nearly 2, but in the family tradition, he went back east for prep school (at the exclusive Phillips Andover), and then to Yale University, where he had an undistinguished academic career.

In 1968, at the height of the Vietnam War, Bush entered the Texas National Guard and spent two years learning to fly. His sudden departure from that unit has never been fully explained. In 1973 he attended Harvard Business School, received an M.B.A. in 1975, and returned to Texas to enter the oil business.

After marrying Laura Welch in 1977, he made his first bid for public office, a 1978 campaign for a Congressional seat, which ended in defeat. After the campaign, Bush returned to his oil business, amassing a great personal fortune even though his business steadily lost money. Meanwhile Bush's parents set up a 1985 meeting with evangelist Billy Graham, which ultimately led the younger Bush to give up alcohol and devote himself to a more serious practice of Christianity.

In 1994, Bush challenged Ann Richards, the popular incumbent governor of Texas. Despite his lack of political experience, Bush's down-home style won him the office. Four years later, he became the first Texas governor elected to a second consecutive four-year term.

Advisers convinced him that 2000 was the right time to run for president. Before he had even committed to the race, he was the clear favorite in the polls and huge sums of money flowed into his campaign treasury from corporations and wealthy Republicans. Bush lost the New Hampshire primary in a bitter fight with Senator John McCain of Arizona, but he rebounded to capture 9 of 13 Super Tuesday states, effectively clinching the nomination.

In the general election Bush and Vice Pres. Al Gore both tried to appeal to moderate voters, Bush calling himself a "compassionate conservative," and although Gore unquestionably won the national popular vote, Florida (with its 25 votes in the Electoral College) held the key to the election. After two recounts and the counting of absentee ballots, Bush led in Florida by fewer than 1,000 votes out of six million cast, but allegations of confusing ballots, defective voting machines, faulty absentee ballots from the military, and illegal barring of many voters threw the process into chaos. The race ended on December 12, when the U.S. Supreme Court ordered an end to the recounts, delivering Florida and the White House to Bush.

On his first day in office, Bush moved to block federal aid to foreign groups that offered counseling or any other assistance to women in obtaining abortions. Days later, he announced his commitment to channeling more federal aid to faith-based service organizations. He angered environmentalists, first reneging on a campaign pledge to regulate carbon dioxide emissions by U.S. power plants, then refusing to join the Kyoto accord to prevent global warming, and finally pursuing an energy policy short on conservation and long on drilling for oil and gas.

The terrorist attacks of September 11th, 2001 transformed the Bush presidency. Bush persuaded Congress to give him "all necessary and appropriate force" to respond to the terrorist attacks. He vowed a U.S. military response that would demolish terrorist networks worldwide, and promised to "end" nations that harbored terrorists. Since Afghanistan was known to be bin Laden's chief sponsor, in late October of 2001 the U.S. mounted an invasion. The attack routed the Taliban in less than three months. Bush's popularity ratings rose above 80 percent.

After initially opposing a separate Dept. of Homeland Security as proposed by the Democrats, Bush eventually approved it, creating an enormous new government agency with more than 170,000 employees. Bush also approved the Patriot Act amid overwhelming congressional approval, though civil libertarians strongly criticized it for giving the Justice Dept. unprecedented powers in conducting investigations.

In his Jan. 2002 State of the Union address, Bush shocked the international community by identifying Iran, Iraq and North Korea as "an axis of evil" that threatened the world, even though he offered no evidence that they were involved in the Sept. 11th attacks. Over the next year the administration redefined two centuries of official U.S. policy by declaring it had the right to preemptively attack any nation that posed a threat to its security. Iraq became the first target of that doctrine and by the summer of 2002 Bush was urging the U.N. Security Council to approve military action to remove Saddam Hussein because he was building weapons of mass destruction.

Over the next six months U.N. weapons inspectors sought out these weapons but found none and the U.N. proposed a continuation of inspections. Bush refused and on March 20, 2003 he ordered the world's most powerful military machine to launch a devastating attack. After only three weeks the U.S., with some help from Great Britain, toppled the regime but was now left to rebuild a devastated country.

Within months, Bush's approval ratings began to plummet. No weapons of mass destruction were found, evidence showed that the intelligence data had been grossly exaggerated, and U.S. casualties continued to mount even though major combat operations were completed in April of 2003. In spring, 2004, support for the war dropped even more as graphic photos were released showing U.S. soldiers torturing Iraqi detainees at Abu Ghraib prison. Added to this blow of America's deteriorating image was the outcry against the more than 700 Muslim detainees being held at Guantanamo Bay in Cuba, most of them never charged and many subjected to interrogation under harsh conditions.

Domestically, Bush continued to press for deep tax cuts at the highest income levels as a way to stimulate a sluggish economy. As a result, after four years of record budget surpluses under Bill Clinton, the Bush administration ran unprecedented deficits of more than $300 billion annually.

Despite these liabilities Bush was able to win the 2004 election by a small but unchallengeable margin against John Kerry, the Democratic candidate and senator from Massachusetts. Kerry was a decorated hero in the Vietnam War while Bush used his family's influence to stay in Texas in the Air National Guard, but polls showed that the president had convinced the people he and his administration would be better able to protect the nation from another terrorist attack. Within a few months of the election, however, as a vicious insurgency in Iraq took an increasing number of U.S. lives (over 1,800 dead, 12,000 seriously wounded) Bush's poll numbers slid below 50 percent by the spring of 2005, and headed toward 40 percent by the summer. Several prominent Republicans in congress began to speak out publicly against the way the war was being managed. On the domestic side Bush's ideas for radically reforming Social Security found few supporters while pork-laden energy and transportation bills gave the lie to stated Republican ideals of fiscal responsibility and small government.

The president suffered another serious blow when a powerful category 5 hurricane called Katrina slammed into the Gulf Coast region, wreaking havoc on parts of Mississippi, Alabama and Louisiana on August 28, 2005. New Orleans was nearly destroyed when two levees on Lake Pontchartrain collapsed, flooding large areas of the city. Hundreds died, tens of thousands were left homeless, and the city's infrastructure was destroyed. The federal government's response was slow and abysmally inefficient. Bush seemed unconcerned but Americans could not fail to notice that hundreds of billions of dollars were going to rebuild Iraq while New Orleans was left to struggle.

But it was the war in Iraq that continued to gnaw away at Bush's standing as he continued throughout 2005–06 to insist the war would be won. Even after huge numbers of Iraqis voted in elections and a constitution was approved, nearly 60 percent of Americans thought the war was a mistake. As congressional elections approached in Nov. 2006 many Republicans were distancing themselves from Bush's position as a vicious insurgency threatened to lead Iraq into civil war. U.S. casualties rose to over 3,000 dead and 20,000 seriously wounded and little or no progress was evident.

The Democrats took control of both houses of Congress in Jan. 2006 and immediately demanded that U.S. troops start to withdraw from Iraq. Bush refused to accept this idea, instead ordering tens of thousands of more troops to quell the growing violence. In 2008, the death toll reached 4,000 with 30,000 wounded. The so-called surge in the number of U.S. troops had a positive effect, as did the enlisting of Sunni militias who were paid goodly sums to fight and to reduce sectarian violence. Near the end of his term, Bush's approval ratings remained below 30 percent and seemed likely to fall further as the financial system seized up, the economy slowed significantly and required dramatic action by the federal government to stave off a complete financial collapse.

44. Barack Obama (2009–)

Barack Hussein Obama, the son of a white woman from Kansas and a black man from Kenya, became the first African-American president in the history of the United States when he was inaugurated on January 21, 2009.

Obama was born in Hawaii in 1961 as the only child of Stanley Ann Dunham and Barack Obama Sr., who had married in 1960 despite concern from both families over the racial differences. The couple divorced after Obama Sr. left to study at Harvard; he later returned to Kenya. Ann Dunham married an Indonesian student, Lolo Soetoro, and the family moved to Jakarta. Barack attended an Indonesian school but Ann also enrolled him in a correspondence course to keep up his English and played recordings of black American leaders for him. Dunham and Soetero divorced a few years later and with his grandparents' help, Barack attended a private prep school in Hawaii. He started college at Occidental College in California, but two years later transferred to Columbia University in New York City.

Obama worked for three years as a community organizer on the South Side of Chicago. In 1988, he was accepted into Harvard Law School and then became the first black president of *Harvard Law Review*. Obama married Michelle Robinson, a Chicago native and graduate of Harvard Law, in 1992. Obama then joined a law firm specializing in civil rights cases and began teaching at the University of Chicago Law School. He wrote a memoir about racial identity, *Dreams from my Father*, which was published in 1995.

Obama led a successful voter registration drive in Chicago, and then decided to get into politics himself as a progressive Democrat. He ran for the Illinois Senate and served from 1997 until 2004. In 2000, he challenged the incumbent U.S. Representative, Bobby Rush, and lost badly in the primary election. However, Obama gained national attention in 2002 with a bold speech against the impending war in Iraq and in 2004 he ran for Illinois's open U.S. Senate seat. That year, he gave the keynote speech at the Democratic convention and his eloquent and fiery address affirmed his status as a rising star of the party. After his first Republican opponent, Jack Ryan, withdrew from the race, Obama beat Alan Keyes with 70 percent of the vote.

In the Senate, Obama gained a seat on the powerful Foreign Relations Committee but disappointed liberals with a 2006 vote opposing a withdrawal date for troops in Iraq. His 2006 book, *The Audacity of Hope*, was a political manifesto that raised his public profile even higher.

In late 2007, just two years into his first Senate term, Obama announced his candidacy for president. At first Obama struggled against the better-established Senator Hillary Rodham Clinton of New York and other Democratic contenders. However, an energetic grassroots effort and a dynamic speech in Des Moines helped him to win the Iowa caucus in early 2008 and mobilize a wildly successful fundraising campaign. He clinched the nomination on June 3, 2008 and turned to the battle against the Republican nominee, Senator John McCain of Arizona.

As the U.S. economy deteriorated and insurgencies gained strength in Iraq and Afghanistan, Obama convinced anxious voters that he offered a new and better approach to the nation's foreign and domestic problems than McCain, who was more experienced but was also affiliated with George W. Bush. Despite an early promise to abide by federal campaign spending limits, Obama opted to forgo $84 million in federal election funds and went on to raise a record $750 million, the majority of it from small donations. Obama's youthful energy gave him an electoral-college victory of 365 to 173, representing 53 percent of the popular vote.

In the early months of Obama's presidency, his agenda to revive the economy, create jobs, reform health care, attend to wars in Iraq and Afghanistan and deal with foreign policy concerns in Pakistan and the Middle East drove him at a hectic pace. Obama quickly began to overturn key components of the Bush legacy. He ordered the military to close Guantánamo Bay prison by 2010, close secret overseas prisons, and end harsh interrogation techniques for detainees. He released memos from the Bush Justice Department that had provided the legal justification for the C.I.A. to use torture but reneged on a promise to declassify photos of such activity. He directed the E.P.A. to reconsider a Bush-era decision to deny states the right to set stricter auto emissions standards, and reversed Bush's ban on federal funds for stem cell research. The first bill Obama signed into law was the Lilly Ledbetter Fair Pay Act of 2009, which relaxed the statute of limitation for equal-pay lawsuits.

Obama's first major legislative triumph came in February 2009, when Congress passed a $787 billion version of his economic stimulus package, which included the largest middle-class tax cut in history. Obama followed that with a $75 billion plan to keep homeowners out of foreclosure, and oversaw bankruptcy filings for GM and Chrysler intended to save the two automakers from collapse. Obama nominated Sonia Sotomayor, a U.S. District Court judge of Puerto Rican descent, to the Supreme Court. When Sotomayor was confirmed by the Senate on August 6, 2009, she became the third woman and first Hispanic to sit on the nation's highest court.

In Feb. 2009, Obama announced that he would send an additional 30,000 troops to Afghanistan, even while sticking to his committment to withdraw combat troops from Iraq in Aug. 2010. His administration sought to initiate a "new era" of diplomatic relations with Russia throughout 2009, and in Dec. Obama accepted the Nobel Peace Prize "for his extraordinary efforts to strengthen international diplomacy and cooperation between peoples." In 2010, he nominated Elena Kagan to the Supreme Court and she was easily confirmed. For the first time where were three women on the highest court. He also managed to pass both health care and financial reform bills, the most sweeping of their kind in several decades; though as the federal deficit continued to grow and the unemployment rate remained at 9.5 percent, Obama's approval ratings declined dramatically, hovering below 50 percent in September 2010.

Presidential Elections, 1796–2008

George Washington of Virginia ran unopposed for president in 1789 and 1792. He received 69 and 132 electoral votes in those years, respectively. John Adams of Massachusetts was elected vice president in both years, receiving 34 and 77 electoral votes.

1796

Party	Candidate	Popular vote	Percent	Electoral vote
Federalist	John Adams (Mass.)	N.A.	N.A.	71
and Thomas Pinckney (S.C.)		N.A.	N.A.	59
Democratic-	Thomas Jefferson (Va.)	N.A.	N.A.	68
Republican	and Aaron Burr (N.Y.)	N.A.	N.A.	30

Key Issues Washington set a precedent by refusing to run for a third term. Though the Founders hoped to avoid parties, factions developed around Hamilton and Jefferson during Washington's first term. Hamilton's Federalists supported a strong central government that would play a major role in the national economy and represent the commercial interests of the north. Jefferson's Republicans advocated states' rights and the agrarian interests of the south. **Regional Influences** Though led by Hamilton, the Federalists nominated the more moderate Adams. Jefferson's strength in the south was balanced by Adams's power in the north. Eleven Federalist electors in New Hampshire failed to vote for Pinckney, their party's vice-presidential nominee, giving the position to Jefferson.

1800

Party	Candidate	Popular vote	Percent	Electoral vote
Democratic-	Thomas Jefferson (Va.)	N.A.	N.A.	73
Republican	and Aaron Burr (N.Y.)	N.A.	N.A.	73
Federalist	John Adams (Mass.)	N.A.	N.A.	65
and Charles C. Pinckney (S.C.)		N.A.	N.A.	64
Federalist	John Jay (N.Y.)	N.A.	N.A.	1

Key Issues Adams divided the Federalists by keeping the U.S. out of war with France over seizures of American ships by the French. In the meantime the Republicans under Jefferson organized nationally. They accused the Federalists of aristocratic and monarchical leanings, citing large taxes levied to maintain a standing army and navy, the Alien and Sedition Acts seeking to silence the administration's critics, and suppression of the Whiskey Rebellion. **Regional Influences** The Republicans again carried the South, but also won New York through the efforts of vice-presidential nominee Burr. The election was thrown into the House when Jefferson and Burr received an equal number of electoral votes. With Hamilton's support, Jefferson won the election in the Federalist-dominated House.

1804

Party	Candidate	Popular vote	Percent	Electoral vote
Democratic-	Thomas Jefferson (Va.)	N.A.	N.A.	162
Republican	and George Clinton (N.Y.)	N.A.	N.A.	162
Federalist	Charles C. Pinckney (S.C.)	N.A.	N.A.	14
and Rufus King (N.Y.)		N.A.	N.A.	14

Key Issues In 1804 Vice President Burr, a northern Republican, joined with a group of northeastern Federalists in a plot to unite New York and New England in a separate nation. The plot was exposed, discrediting the Federalists. Jefferson, already popular for his personal qualities as well as the Louisiana Purchase, swept to an easy victory. **Regional Influences** Jefferson lost only three states, and even swept all of New England with the exception of Connecticut.

1808

Party	Candidate	Popular vote	Percent	Electoral vote[1]
Democratic-	James Madison (Va.)	N.A.	N.A.	122
Republican	and George Clinton (N.Y.)	N.A.	N.A.	113

Federalist	Charles C. Pinckney (S.C.)	N.A.	N.A.	47
and Rufus King (N.Y.)		N.A.	N.A.	47

Key Issues Jefferson reinforced the two-term precedent by refusing to run for a third term. Madison, his chosen successor, easily won the Republican nomination and the presidency. **Regional Influences** Pinckney and the Federalists regained most of the New England votes lost four years earlier and increased their strength in Congress due to commercial opposition to the embargo imposed by Jefferson on the export of American goods to warring European nations.

[1]Clinton received six electoral votes for president. Madison and James Monroe of Virginia both received three electoral votes for vice-president.

1812

Party	Candidate	Popular vote	Percent	Electoral vote
Democratic-	James Madison (Va.)	N.A.	N.A.	128
Republican	and Elbridge Gerry (Mass.)	N.A.	N.A.	131
Federalist	DeWitt Clinton (N.Y.)	N.A.	N.A.	89
and Jared Ingersoll (Pa.)		N.A.	N.A.	86

Key Issues The election was a referendum on Madison's bid for a declaration of war against Great Britain in response to Britain's attempts to block the sale of southern raw materials in European markets. A vote for Madison was a vote for war, a vote for Clinton a vote for peace. **Regional Influences** Commercial interests in the northeast opposed war with Great Britain. The original 13 states were evenly split in the election, favoring Madison 90-89. New England, except Vermont, voted for Clinton, as did a majority of the Middle Atlantic states. The South voted unanimously for Madison. But all of the western states voted for Madison and thus for war.

1816

Party	Candidate	Popular vote	Percent	Electoral vote
Democratic-	James Monroe (Va.)	N.A.	N.A.	183
Republican	and D. D. Tompkins (N.Y.)	N.A.	N.A.	183
Federalist	Rufus King (N.Y.)	N.A.	N.A.	34
and John E. Howard (Md.)		N.A.	N.A.	22

Key Issues Nationalism triumphed after the war with Britain, a time of national and economic growth that saw establishment of an expanded standing army, central bank, Federal tariff and large internal improvements despite opposition from northeastern Federalists. Monroe, Madison's chosen successor, won a landslide victory that seemed to validate Madison's nationalistic program, which called for a stronger standing army, a protective tariff, uniform currency and a nationwide system of roads and canals, including the Cumberland Road. The Federalists won only three states, all in New England.

1820

Party	Candidate	Popular vote	Percent	Electoral vote
Democratic-	James Monroe (Va.)	N.A.	N.A.	231
Republican	and D.D. Tompkins (N.Y.)	N.A.	N.A.	218
Democratic-	John Q. Adams (Mass.)	N.A.	N.A.	1
Republican				

Key Issues The election was held at the height of the "Era of Good Feelings," though sectional differences over slavery earlier in the year led to the Missouri Compromise, which in its final version resulted in the admittance of Missouri as a slave state with the provision that it allow free Negroes of other states to retain their freedom while in Missouri. The Federalists ceased to exist as a functioning party by the time of the election and failed to run a candidate against Monroe. **Regional Influences** Monroe ran unopposed for reelection. One elector from New Hampshire voted for Adams so that only Washington would hold the honor of being elected to the presidency by a unanimous vote.

1824

Party	Popular Candidate	Popular vote	Per- cent	Electoral vote
Democratic- Republican	John Q. Adams (Mass.)	113,122	30.92	84
Democratic- Republican	Andrew Jackson (Tenn.)	151,271	41.34	99
Democratic- Republican	William H. Crawford (Ga.)	40,876	11.17	41
Democratic- Republican	Henry Clay (Ky.)	47,531	12.99	37
Other		13,053	3.57	N.A.

Total Vote 365,833
Jackson Plurality 38,149

Key Issues Personalities dominated an election in which all four candidates ran as Democratic-Republicans. Crawford, Monroe's treasury secretary, won the nomination of the party's congressional caucus. But few attended the caucus and most electors were chosen by state legislatures. Crawford later suffered a stroke and was not a serious candidate. John C. Calhoun of South Carolina ran unopposed for vice president. **Regional Influences** Each candidate represented his region: Adams the commercial northeast, Crawford the cotton south, Clay and Jackson the agrarian west. Jackson, a hero of the War of 1812 and battles against Indians, won a clear plurality of the popular vote and was the only candidate with support outside his home region. But no candidate won a majority of the electoral vote and the election was decided in the House, where Speaker Clay's support gave the victory to Adams.

1828

Party	Popular Candidate	Popular vote	Per- cent	Electoral vote
Democratic- Republican	Andrew Jackson (Tenn.) and John C. Calhoun (S.C.)	642,553	55.97	178 / 171
National- Republican	John Q. Adams (Mass.) and Richard Rush (Pa.)	500,987	43.63	83 / 83
Other		4,568	0.40	N.A.

Total Vote 1,148,018
Jackson Plurality 141,656

Key Issues Personalities again overshadowed issues. The Jackson campaign catered to popular prejudices, portraying the contest as one between democracy and aristocracy. The Jackson coalition was a forerunner of the modern Democratic Party and reestablished two-party politics in the U.S. **Regional Influences** Jackson won the south and west easily, and appealed to discontented laborers in the north. Adams carried only New England, New Jersey, Maryland and Delaware.

1832

Party	Candidate	Popular vote	Per- cent	Electoral vote
Democrat	Andrew Jackson (Tenn.) and Martin Van Buren (N.Y.)	701,780	54.23	219 / 189
National- Republican	Henry Clay (Ky.) and John Sergeant (Pa.)	484,205	37.42	49 / 49
Anti- Masonic	William Wirt (Md.) and Amos Ellmaker (Pa.)	100,715	7.78	7 / 7
Independent	John Floyd (Va.) and Henry Lee (Mass.)	N.A.	N.A.	11 / 11
Other		7,273	0.56	N.A.

Total Vote 1,293,973
Jackson Plurality 217,575

Key Issues The Anti-Masons, the first third-party in American politics, began in opposition to secret societies in particular and privileged groups in general, but were at heart an anti-Jackson party. The two established parties followed the Anti-Masons lead by holding national nominating conventions to select a presidential nominee. While Jackson's opposition to the Bank of the United States was made an issue by the two major parties, the election was more a referendum on Jackson himself. **Regional Influences** Anti-Masonic strength was concentrated in rural sections of New England and the Middle Atlantic states. In those states National-Republicans and Anti-Masons supported the same ticket. With the forces against him divided, Jackson won easily. Clay won only half of the New England states, Wirt won only Vermont. Jackson captured Maine and New

Hampshire. In South Carolina, where electors still were chosen by the legislature, nullificationists cast their ballots for Floyd.

1836

Party	Candidate	Popular vote	Per- cent	Electoral vote
Democrat	Martin Van Buren (N.Y.) and Richard M. Johnson (Ky.)	764,716 / 147	50.83	170
Whig	William Henry Harrison (Ohio)	550,816	36.63	73
Whig	Hugh L. White (Tenn.)	146,107	9.72	26
Whig	Daniel Webster (Mass.)	41,201	2.74	14
Whig	Willie P. Mangum (N.C.)	N.A.	N.A.	11
Other		1,234	0.08	N.A.

Total Vote 1,503,534
Van Buren Plurality 213, 360

Key Issues Jackson's heavy-handed tactics, especially in his successful battle against the national bank, led the National-Republicans to rename themselves Whigs, after the 18th-century British party that tried to lessen the power of the crown. But lacking effective national leadership and divided along sectional lines, the anti-Jackson forces could not agree on a single candidate or platform and instead ran three regional candidates. **Regional Influences** Whig strategy was to throw the election into the House, where they could unite around a single candidate. Webster was to win New England, Harrison the west and Lawson the south. Van Buren, forced on the Democrats by Jackson, foiled the plan by picking up enough states throughout the nation to win by a slim majority. Johnson fell one electoral vote short of a majority for vice president and was selected by the Senate. The South Carolina legislature cast its votes for Mangum.

1840

Party	Candidate	Popular vote	Per- cent	Electoral vote
Whig	William Henry Harrison (Ohio) and John Tyler (Va.)	1,275,390	52.88	234
Democrat	Martin Van Buren (N.Y.)	1,128,854	46.81	60
Liberty	James G. Birney (N.Y.)	6,797	0.28	N.A.
Other		767	0.03	N.A.

Total Vote 2,411,808
Harrison Plurality 146,536

Key Issues With the country still reeling from the Panic of 1837, the Democrats were on the defensive. Though differences prevented them from writing a platform, the Whigs rallied around Harrison. In a campaign notable for its absence of issues, the Whigs turned the tables on Jackson's party. Harrison, despite his wealthy origins, was portrayed as the "log-cabin, hard-cider candidate" opposing the allegedly aristocratic Van Buren. The Democrats left the selection of a vice-presidential candidate to each state. **Regional Influences** Van Buren won only seven states, just one outside of the south or west. Harrison was long associated with the west and Tyler was a conservative Southerner and friend of Henry Clay. For the first time, active two-party politics was established across the nation. The 68-year-old Harrison caught a severe cold after delivering a lengthy Inaugural Address in the rain and died one month into his term.

1844

Party	Candidate	Popular vote	Per- cent	Electoral vote
Democrat	James K. Polk (Tenn.) and George M. Dallas (Pa.)	1,339,494	49.54	170
Whig	Henry Clay (Ky.) and Theodore Frelinghuysen (N.J.)	1,300,004	48.08	105
Abolitionist	James G. Birney (N.Y.)	62,103	2.30	N.A.
Other		2,058	0.08	N.A.

Total Vote 2,703,659
Polk Plurality 39,490

Key Issues Manifest Destiny, the goal of a U.S. stretching from the Atlantic to the Pacific, was the central issue because of the question of the annexation of Texas. With the election approaching, opponents of slavery lead the Senate to reject a treaty between Texas and the Tyler Administration that would have preserved Texan slavery and made it a U.S. territory. The two leading presidential candidates, Clay and Van Buren, sought to smother the Texas issue by ignoring it. But Polk snatched the Democratic nomination with his clear and vocal advocacy of annexation of Texas and general territorial expansion. **Regional Influences** Expansionism was immensely popular, especially in the south and west, where memories of the depression following 1837 added to the attraction of new, vast, and open public lands. Support for manifest destiny more than made up for anti-slavery sentiment elsewhere and Polk won a narrow plurality but a clear victory.

1848

Party	Candidate	Popular vote	Per- cent	Elec- toral vote
Whig	Zachary Taylor (La.) and Millard Fillmore (N.Y.)	1,361,393	47.28	163
Democrat	Lewis Cass (Mich.) and William O. Butler (Ky.)	1,223,460	42.49	127
Free Soil	Martin Van Buren (N.Y.) and Charles Francis Adams (Mass.)	291,501	10.12	N.A.
Other		2,830	0.10	N.A.

Total Vote 2,879,184
Taylor Plurality 137,933

Key Issues The Wilmot Proviso, calling for a ban on extension of slavery into territories acquired in the Mexican War, dominated the election. But both major parties evaded the issue. Slavery foes banded together to form the Free Soil Party, which won no electoral votes but drew enough popular support away from the Democrats to throw the election to "Old Rough and Ready," Zachary Taylor, a slave-holder. Taylor died in July 1850. **Regional Influences** Both major parties balanced their tickets with a Northerner and Southerner. Free Soilers were mostly Northern Democrats, anti-slavery Whigs and abolitionists. There was no distinct pattern in the Electoral College following a lackluster campaign. Free Soil strength in New York gave the state and the election to the Whigs.

1852

Party	Candidate	Popular vote	Per- cent	Elec- toral vote
Democrat	Franklin Pierce (N.H.) and William R. D. King (Ala.)	1,607,510	50.84	254
Whig	Winfield Scott (Va.) and William A. Graham (N.C.)	1,386,942	43.87	42
Free Soil	John P. Hale (N.H.) and George Washington Julian (Ind.)	155,210	4.91	N.A.
Other		12,168	0.38	N.A.

Total Vote 3,161,830
Pierce Plurality 220,568

Key Issues The election was a referendum on the Compromise of 1850, in which Congress voted to admit California as a free state, create the territories of New Mexico and Utah with no restriction on slavery, abolish the slave trade in the District of Columbia, purchase disputed land from Texas on behalf of New Mexico, and toughen the Fugitive Slave Act. The Democrats strongly endorsed the Compromise, but the bitterly divided Whigs only vaguely accepted it. **Regional Influences** The Democrats won a resounding electoral victory, capturing 27 states to the four taken by the Whigs: Massachusetts, Vermont, Kentucky and Tennessee. Free Soilers returned to the Democrats and the Whigs never again were a political force in a nation which believed the slave question was behind it.

1856

Party	Candidate	Popular vote	Per- cent	Elec- toral vote
Democrat	James Buchanan (Pa.) and John C. Breckinridge (Ky.)	1,836,072	45.28	174
Republican	John C. Fremont (Calif.) and William L. Dayton (N.J.)	1,342,345	33.11	114
Whig	Millard Fillmore (N.Y.) and Andrew J. Donelson (Tenn.)	873,053	21.53	8
Other		3,177	0.08	N.A.

Total Vote 4,054,647
Buchanan Plurality 493,727

Key Issues The Democrats firmly endorsed "popular sovereignty" even though it led to great turmoil in the territory of Kansas. But they chose as their nominee Buchanan, largely because he had been out of the country and was untainted by "Bleeding Kansas" battle, which pitted supporters and foes of slavery trying to organize the territory into a slave or free state. The Republicans, a new party of northern Whigs and Democrats committed to the containment of slavery ran Fremont, a popular general and explorer. **Regional Influences** Fremont carried all but five of the free states. But Buchanan won all of the south in addition to the five northern states and was elected. Fillmore, supported by the Know-Nothings and Whig remnants, only won Maryland but strongly challenged the Democrats in the south.

1860

Party	Candidate	Popular vote	Per- cent	Elec- toral vote
Republican	Abraham Lincoln (Ill.) and Hannibal Hamlin (Maine)	1,865,908	39.82	180
Democrat	Stephen A. Douglas (Ill.) and Herschel V. Johnson (Ga.)	1,380,202	29.46	12
Democrat	John C. Breckinridge (Ky.) and Joseph Lane (Oreg.)	848,019	18.09	72
Constitutional	John Bell (Tenn.)	590,901	12.61	39
Union and Other	Edward Everett (Mass.)	531	0.01	N.A.

Total Vote 4,685,561
Lincoln Plurality 485,706

Key Issues Sectional differences over slavery came to a head in 1860. The Democrats could not agree on a candidate and split into northern and southern factions. The Northerners backed Douglas and popular sovereignty, the Southerners Breckinridge and Federal protection of slavery in the territories. The Republicans, virtually all Northerners, were a pro-tariff, nationalistic party that opposed the extension of slavery but did not seek to overturn it where it already existed. Bell, the candidate of Whigs and Know-Nothings who backed Fillmore in 1856, was a compromise candidate expressing support for preservation of the Union. **Regional Influences** In effect there were two separate contests in 1860 Lincoln versus Douglas in the north, Breckinridge versus Bell in the south. Free states outnumbered slave states and cast half again as many electoral votes. Lincoln won every northern state except New Jersey and, though not even on the ballot in 10 southern states, was elected president. Breckinridge captured 11 of the 15 southern states. The four southern states won by Douglas and Bell were in the upper south.

1864

Party	Candidate	Popular vote	Per- cent	Elec- toral vote
Republican	Abraham Lincoln (Ill.) and Andrew Johnson (Tenn.)	2,218,388	55.02	212
Democrat	George B. McClellan (N.Y.) and George H. Pendleton (Ohio)	1,812,807	44.96	21

Total Vote 4,031,887
Lincoln Plurality 405,581

Key Issues Lincoln's renomination was not assured. Radical Republicans thought he was not aggressive enough in his conduct of the war or plans for the eventual peace, but moderation ultimately prevailed. The Republicans ran as the Union Party and nominated Johnson, a pro-Union Democrat, for vice president. The Democrats ran a racist campaign, calling the war a failure. But McClellan, a popular general, broke with his party's platform and denied the war was a failure, denouncing members of his party who seemed to advocate peace at any price. He opposed emancipation as a goal of the war. **Regional Influences** Military victories around election time helped the embattled incumbent. Lincoln won a convincing popular and electoral victory with the support of middle-class professionals, farmers, laborers and the strongly pro-Union voters who voted for Bell four years earlier. McClellan was strongest in areas carried by Breckinridge four years before. Eleven Confederate states did not participate in the election.

1868

Party	Candidate	Popular vote	Per- cent	Elec- toral vote
Republican	Ulysses S. Grant (Ohio) and Schuyler Colfax (Ind.)	3,013,650	52.66	214
Democrat	Horatio S. Seymour (N.Y.) and Francis P. Blair (Mo.)	2,708,744	47.34	80
Other		46	N.A.	N.A.
	Total Vote 5,722,440			
	Grant Plurality 304,906			

Key Issues The Republicans waved the "bloody shirt" of the war and ran on their program of Radical Reconstruction. While calling for Negro suffrage in the south, the Republicans asserted it was a matter for individual northern states to decide for themselves. Democrats ran against Reconstruction, declaring that the question of Negro suffrage should be decided by individual southern states as well. **Regional Influences** Despite Grant's popularity, the Republicans were just able to win the election. Seymour carried only eight states, though he did well in the states won by Grant. Without black votes in the South, Grant would not have received a majority of the popular vote. The votes of the "unreconstructed" states of Mississippi, Texas and Virginia were not counted.

1872

Party	Candidate	Popular vote	Per- cent	Elec- toral vote
Republican	Ulysses S. Grant (Ohio) and Henry Wilson (Mass.)	3,598,235	55.63	286
Liberal Republican/ Democrat	Horace Greeley (N.Y.) and Benjamin Gratz Brown (Mo.)	2,834,761	43.83	N.A.
Straight Democrat	Charles O'Conor (N.Y.)	18,602	N.A.	
	Other	16,081	0.25	163
	Total Vote	6,467,679		
	Grant Plurality 763,474			

Key Issues Liberal Republicans broke with Grant over corruption in his administration, high tariffs and continued Radical Reconstruction. They nominated Greeley, editor of the *New York Tribune*. The Democrats endorsed Greeley and the Liberal platform. But the great scandals of the Grant administration were not yet revealed and the Republicans again waved the bloody shirt to victory. **Regional Influences** Greeley carried only two states in the lower South and four border states. He died shortly after the election (Nov. 29, 1872) and his electoral votes went to other candidates: Thomas Hendricks, Indiana, 42; Benjamin Gratz Brown, Missouri, 18; Charles J. Jenkins, Georgia, 2; and David Davis, Illinois, 1.

1876

Party	Candidate	Popular vote	Per- cent	Elec- toral vote
Republican	Rutherford B. Hayes (Ohio) and William A. Wheeler (N.Y.)	4,034,311	47.95	185
Democrat	Samuel J. Tilden (N.Y.) and Thomas A. Hendricks (Ind.)	4,288,546	50.97	184
Greenback	Peter Cooper (N.Y.)	75,973	0.90	N.A.
Other		14,271	0.17	
	Total Vote 8,413,101			
	Tilden Plurality 254,235			

Key Issues The Republicans were in trouble as 1876 approached due to rampant corruption in the Grant administration and the economic depression that followed the Panic of 1873. Hayes, a three-term Ohio governor known for his unassailable integrity, was nominated to run against the favored Democrat, Tilden, a New York reform governor whose reputation was made in opposition to the Tweed political machine. Both men espoused conservative economics. Cooper and the Greenbacks advocated currency expansion. **Regional Influences** As Election Day approached, Tilden could count on winning all of the south except for the three states still controlled by Republican carpetbaggers: South Carolina, Louisiana, and Florida. But Republicans claimed South Carolina, Louisiana and Florida for Hayes, arguing that thousands of blacks who would have voted for Hayes were barred from voting there. Election boards in those Republican-controlled states gave Hayes the needed majority, and thus the election. In the uproar that followed Congress set up an Election Commission to validate the returns. The commission voted strictly along party lines, eight to seven, to give the election to Hayes. Despite charges that Republicans stole the election, Hayes later was inaugurated peaceably.

1880

Party	Candidate	Popular vote	Per- cent	Elec- toral vote
Republican	James A. Garfield (Ohio) and Chester A. Arthur (N.Y.)	4,461,158	48.27	214
Democrat	Winfield S. Hancock (Pa.) and William H. English (Ind.)	4,444,260	48.25	155
Greenback	James B. Weaver (Iowa) and Benjamin J. Chambers (Tex.)	305,997	3.32	N.A.
Other		14,005	0.15	N.A.
	Total Vote 9,210,420			
	Garfield Plurality 1,898			

Key Issues With the war and Reconstruction behind, no major issues arose over which the major parties disagreed. The Democrats, the party of secession 20 year earlier, nominated General Hancock to help combat the stigma of treason. Garfield made a protectionist tariff central to his campaign. **Regional Influences** The balance between Republican strength in the Midwest and west and Democratic strength in the south resulted in a plurality of less than 2,000 for Garfield out of more than 9 million votes cast. Four months into his term Garfield was shot by a disappointed office-seeker.

1884

Party	Candidate	Popular vote	Per- cent	Elec- toral vote
Democrat	Grover Cleveland (N.Y.) and Thomas A. Hendricks (Ind.)	4,874,621	48.50	219
Republican	James G. Blaine (Maine) and John A. Logan (Ill.)	4,848,936	48.25	182
Greenback	Benjamin F. Butler (Mass.)	175,096	1.74	N.A.
Prohibition	John P. St. John (Kans.)	147,482	1.47	N.A.
Other		3,619	0.04	N.A.
	Total Votes 10,049,754			
	Cleveland Plurality 25,685			

Key Issues The private lives and morals of the candidates were the focus of a campaign notable for mudslinging. Blaine was accused of accepting bribes from a railroad company for whom he obtained a federal grant and Republicans taunted Cleveland for fathering a son out of wedlock. Still, Cleveland, known for his independence and integrity in public life, attracted the votes of many idealistic Republicans and reformers unable to stomach Blaine, a Radical Republican leader. **Regional Influences** Cleveland carried all of the southern states as well as the key swing states of Indiana, New Jersey, Connecticut and New York, becoming the first Democrat elected president since the Civil War. Cleveland carried his home state of New York and its 36 electoral votes by less than 1,200 votes.

1888

Party	Candidate	Popular vote	Percent	Electoral vote
Republican	Benjamin Harrison (Ind.) and Levi P. Morton (N.Y.)	5,443,892	47.82	233
Democrat	Grover Cleveland (N.Y.) and Allen G. Thurman (Ohio)	5,534,488	48.62	168
Prohibition	Clinton B. Fisk (N.J.)	249,813	2.19	N.A.
Union Labor	Alson J. Streeter (Ill.)	146,602	1.29	N.A.
Other		8,519	0.07	N.A.

Total Votes 11,383,320
Cleveland Plurality 90,596

Key Issues Cleveland made tariff reform central to his administration, seeking to lower existing high tariffs. The Republicans campaigned on the need to maintain high wages by keeping a high tariff on imported goods. **Regional Influences** Despite the emphasis on the tariff, Cleveland still carried such manufacturing states as New Jersey and Connecticut as well as most of the south. But though Cleveland won 90,000 more popular votes than Harrison, the Republican carried the pro-tariff swing states of Indiana and New York by slight margins to win the election in the electoral college in one of the most corrupt campaigns in history.

1892

Party	Candidate	Popular vote	Percent	Electoral vote
Democrat	Grover Cleveland (N.Y.) and Adlai E. Stevenson (Ill.)	5,551,883	46.05	277
Republican	Benjamin Harrison (Indiana) and Whitelaw Reid (N.Y.)	5,179,244	42.96	145
Populist	James B. Weaver (Iowa) and James G. Field (Virginia)	1,024,280	8.50	22
Prohibition	John Bidwell (California)	270,770	2.25	N.A.
Other		29,920	0.25	

Total Votes 12,056,097
Cleveland Plurality 372,639

Key Issues Cleveland and Harrison again fought a battle over the tariff, which the Republicans drastically raised in 1890. Both men were out of touch with the growing agrarian and populist discontent. Weaver, campaigning for free silver, became the first third-party candidate to gain electoral votes since the war. **Regional Influences** Cleveland improved upon his 1884 and 1888 showings to win the most decisive presidential victory in 20 years. This time he carried the swing states of New York, New Jersey, Connecticut and Indiana as well as the traditionally Republican states of Illinois, California and Wisconsin.

1896

Party	Candidate	Popular vote	Percent	Electoral vote
Republican	William McKinley (Ohio) and Garret A. Hobart (N.J.)	7,108,480	51.01	271
Democrat/ Populist	William J. Bryan (Nebr.) and Democrat Arthur Sewall (Me.) and Populist Thomas E. Watson (Ga.)	6,511,495	46.73	176 149
National Democrat	John M. Palmer (Ill.)	133,435	0.96	N.A.
Prohibition	Joshua Levering (Md.)	125,072	0.90	N.A.
Other		57,256	0.41	N.A.

Total Votes 13,935,738
McKinley Plurality 596,985

Key Issues The Democrats absorbed Populist energies and abandoned the conservatism of Cleveland by nominating Bryan and adopting key elements of the Populist program, especially the call for free silver. The pro-tariff and pro-gold Republicans led by McKinley and Mark Hanna outspent the Democrats by almost 12 to 1. In losing, Bryan amassed more votes than any victorious candidate before him. **Regional Influences** Bryan did not carry a single state north of Virginia or east of Missouri. His hold on the agricultural south and west was broken by Republican victories in Maryland, Delaware, West Virginia, Kentucky, California and Oregon. Bryan, failing to appeal to labor, carried no industrial or urban states.

1900

Party	Candidate	Popular vote	Percent	Electoral vote
Republican	William McKinley (Ohio) and Theodore Roosevelt (N.Y.)	7,218,039	51.67	292
Democrat	William J. Bryan (Nebr.) and Adlai E. Stevenson (Ill.)	6,358,345	45.51	155
Prohibition	John C. Woolley (Ill.)	209,004	1.50	N.A.
Social Democrat	Eugene V. Debs (Ind.)	86,935	0.62	N.A.
Other		98,147	0.70	N.A.

Total Vote 13,970,470
McKinley Plurality 859,694

Key Issues Imperialism in the Philippines joined free silver and the tariff as the key issues in a replay of the 1896 election. Bryan tried to unite the silver interests in the west and south with supporters of the gold standard in a coalition against imperialism, which the Democratic platform called the "paramount issue" of the campaign. But voters did not desert McKinley in a time of prosperity. **Regional Influences** Bryan carried only the Solid South and four silver states in the west, and was defeated in the silver states of Kansas, South Dakota, Utah and Wyoming as well as his home state of Nebraska. Both houses of Congress were led by significant Republican majorities.

1904

Party	Candidate	Popular vote	Percent	Electoral vote
Republican	Theodore Roosevelt (N.Y.) and Charles W. Fairbanks (Ind.)	7,626,593	56.41	336
Democrat	Alton B. Parker (N.Y.) and Henry G. Davis (W. Va.)	5,082,898	37.60	140
Socialist	Eugene V. Debs (Ind.)	402,489	2.98	N.A.
Prohibition	Silas C. Swallow (Pa.)	258,596	1.91	N.A.
Other		148,388	1.10	N.A.

Total Votes 13,518,964
Roosevelt Plurality 2,543,695

Key Issues Roosevelt stole the mantle of reform from the Democrats with his campaigns against the "malefactors of great wealth." The Democrats turned to the right by nominating the lackluster Parker, a judge with close ties to Wall Street. Parker turned his back on Bryan Democrats by renouncing free silver. **Regional Influences** Roosevelt won a landslide victory based largely on his own personality and popularity. The Democrats won only 13 states, none outside the south.

1908

Party	Candidate	Popular vote	Percent	Electoral vote
Republican	William H. Taft (Ohio) and James S. Sherman (N.Y.)	7,662,258	51.58	321
Democrat	William J. Bryan (Nebr.) and John W. Kern (Ind.)	6,406,801	43.05	162
Socialist	Eugene V. Debs (Ind.)	420,380	2.82	N.A.
Prohibition	Eugene W. Chafin (Ill.)	252,821	1.70	N.A.
Other		126,474	0.85	N.A.

Total Vote 14,882,734
Taft Plurality 1,269,457

Key Issues The immensely popular Roosevelt declined to run. Taft, his secretary of war and handpicked successor, debated Bryan over who was better qualified to complete Roosevelt's progressive program. Bryan abandoned silver and courted labor but ran a lackluster losing campaign. **Regional Influences** Bryan again carried the South. But the appeal of Roosevelt's reform programs helped the Republicans to do well in the west and Taft's background as a Yale graduate and Federal jurist enabled him to carry the east as well.

1912

Party	Candidate	Popular vote	Percent	Electoral vote
Democrat	Woodrow Wilson (N.J.) and Thomas Marshall (Ind.)	6,293,152	41.84	435
Progressive	Theodore Roosevelt (N.Y.) and Hiram Johnson (Calif.)	4,119,207	27.39	88
Republican	William H. Taft (Ohio) and James S. Sherman (N.Y.)	3,486,333	23.18	8
Socialist	Eugene V. Debs (Ind.)	900,369	5.99	N.A.
Other		241,902	1.61	N.A.

Total Vote 15,040,963
Wilson Plurality 2,173,945

Key Issues Taft's conservatism and political ineptitude led Roosevelt to challenge him within the party from the left. Unable to wrest the nomination from Taft, Roosevelt ran a third-party campaign. The election boiled down to a contest between Roosevelt and Wilson and their respective conceptions of progressivism. Roosevelt's "New Nationalism" called for strong Federal regulations to control the trusts and big businesses. The Progressives advocated a broad array of social reforms to be implemented by the Federal government while the Democrats emphasized the primacy of the states in such matters. **Regional Influences** Though he amassed fewer votes than did Bryan in 1908, Wilson took advantage of the split in the Republican ranks to win a decisive plurality of the vote. He did best in traditional Democratic states, but was able to win most traditionally Republican states as well. Roosevelt won only 6 states, including California, which he carried by fewer than 200 votes. Taft carried Utah and Vermont. The Democrats also won control of both houses of Congress, their best overall performance since the Civil War.

1916

Party	Candidate	Popular vote	Percent	Electoral vote
Democrat	Woodrow Wilson (N.J.) and Thomas Marshall (Ind.)	9,126,300	49.24	277
Republican	Charles Evans Hughes (N.Y.) and Charles W. Fairbanks (Ind.)	8,546,789	46.11	254
Socialist	Allen L. Benson (N.Y.)	589,924	3.18	N.A.
Prohibition	James F. Hanly (Ind.)	221,030	1.19	N.A.
Other		50,979	0.28	N.A.

Total Vote 18,535,022
Wilson Plurality 579,511

Key Issues The campaign was a referendum on Wilson's first term, his program of domestic reform, and his policy toward the war in Europe. He ran a peace campaign with the slogan "He kept us out of war" and attracted the votes of many Bull Moosers. Voters who felt Wilson was either too harsh or too lenient toward Germany tended to vote Republican. Irish-American and German-American extremists, virulently opposed to aiding Great Britain, embarrassed Hughes with their vocal support. A coalition of labor, farmers, reformers, and intellectuals won the election for Wilson. **Regional Influences** Hughes, a former reform governor of New York who left the Supreme Court to challenge Wilson, carried all of the east except New Hampshire and all of the Old Northwest except Ohio. But the South was again solid for the Democrats and so was every state west of the Mississippi except Minnesota, Iowa, South Dakota and Oregon, which Wilson lost by close margins.

1920

Party	Candidate	Popular vote	Percent	Electoral vote
Republican	Warren G. Harding (Ohio) and Calvin Coolidge (Mass.)	16,133,314	60.30	404
Democrat	James M. Cox (Ohio) and Franklin D. Roosevelt (N.Y.)	9,140,884	34.17	127
Socialist	Eugene V. Debs (Ind.)	913,664	3.42	N.A.
Farmer-Labor	Parley P. Christensen (Utah)	264,540	0.99	N.A.
Other		301,384	1.13	N.A.

Total Vote 26,753,786

Harding Plurality 6,992,430

Key Issues The voters turned against Wilsonian progressivism and internationalism by electing Harding, a vacuous party hack who promised a "return to normalcy" after the turbulent years of domestic reform and world war. The undistinguished Cox ran in support of the League of Nations and little else. **Regional Influences** Harding carried every state outside of the south, except Tennessee. The Republicans added to their majorities in both houses of Congress, regained in 1918.

1924

Party	Candidate	Popular vote	Percent	Electoral vote
Republican	Calvin Coolidge (Mass.) and Charles G. Dawes (Ohio)	15,717,553	54.00	382
Democrat	John W. Davis (N.Y.) and Charles W. Bryan (Nebr.)	8,386,169	28.84	136
Progressive Socialist	Robert M. LaFollette (Wis.) and Burton K. Wheeler (Mont.)	4,814,050	16.56	13
Other		158,187	0.55	N.A.

Total Vote 29,075,959
Coolidge Plurality 7,331,384

Key Issues The country "kept cool with Coolidge" as the Democrats could not overcome prosperity or themselves. Davis, a conservative Wall Street lawyer, was a compromise nominee selected by a bitterly divided party after 103 ballots. Reformers, labor and farmers flocked to the LaFollette candidacy. **Regional Influences** All 12 of the Democratic states were from the south. LaFollette's 13 electoral votes came from his home of Wisconsin.

1928

Party	Candidate	Popular vote	Percent	Electoral vote
Republican	Herbert C. Hoover (Calif.) and Charles E. Curtis (Kans.)	21,411,911	58.20	444
Democrat	Alfred E. Smith (N.Y.) and Joseph T. Robinson (Ark.)	15,000,185	40.77	87
Socialist	Norman Thomas (N.Y.)	266,453	0.72	N.A.
Worker's	William Z. Foster (Ill.)	48,170	0.13	N.A.
Other		63,565	0.17	N.A.

Total Vote 36,790,364
Hoover Plurality 6,411,806

Key Issues Booze, bigotry, Tammany and prosperity did in the Democrats. Rural America would not vote for an anti-Prohibition, big-city, Catholic machine politician, despite Smith's success as governor of New York, especially while the Republicans could convincingly cite the success of their economic leadership. **Regional Influences** The solid south was shattered as Hoover Democrats gave Republicans the states of Virginia, North Carolina, Tennessee, Florida and Texas for the first time since Reconstruction. Smith lost his own state and every western and border state. But Smith set the stage for the New Deal coalition with the votes of urban ethnics; he carried the nation's 12 largest cities, all of which had been won by the Republicans four years earlier. The Democrats also won votes in the traditionally Republican west among farmers unsure about prosperity.

1932

Party	Candidate	Popular vote	Percent	Electoral vote
Democrat	Franklin D. Roosevelt (N.Y.) and John Nance Garner (Tex.)	22,825,016	57.42	472
Republican	Herbert C. Hoover (Calif.) and Charles E. Curtis (Kans.)	15,758,397	39.64	59
Socialist	Norman Thomas (N.Y.)	883,990	2.22	N.A.
Communist	William Z. Foster (Ill.)	102,221	0.26	N.A.
Other		179,758	0.45	N.A.

Total Vote 39,749,382

Roosevelt Plurality 7,066,619

Key Issues The Democrats won by blaming the Republicans for the Great Depression. Roosevelt was the first presidential nominee of a major party to address his nominating convention, pledging to help "the forgotten man at the bottom of the economic pyramid." In a vague and contradictory platform, the Democrats promised to balance the Federal budget by drastically reducing expenses and vowed to spend Federal dollars to attack the nation's economic woes. **Regional Influences** Roosevelt lost only six states, Maine, New Hampshire, Vermont, Connecticut, Delaware and Pennsylvania, carrying all of the agricultural West and South.

1936

Party	Candidate	Popular vote	Per-cent	Electoral vote
Democrat	Franklin D. Roosevelt (N.Y.) and John Nance Garner (Tex.)	27,747,636	60.79	523
Republican	Alfred M. Landon (Kans.) and Frank Knox (Ill.)	16,679,543	36.54	8
Union	William Lemke (N.Dak.)	892,492	1.96	N.A.
Socialist	Norman Thomas (N.Y.)	187,785	0.41	N.A.
Other		134,847	0.30	N.A.

Total Vote 45,642,303
Roosevelt Plurality 11,068,093

Key Issues Despite intense opposition to the New Deal, its great public appeal was confirmed in the most one-sided election since 1820 and sweeping victories for the Democrats in Congress. The populist forces of the late Huey Long coalesced around Lemke but failed to gather widespread support. **Regional Influences** Roosevelt carried every state except Maine and Vermont. The New Deal coalition was at its height as every large city voted overwhelmingly for F.D.R. The middle-class, farmers in the west and south, big-city ethnics, labor and reform intellectuals flocked to the Democrats. Northern Blacks also began to vote heavily Democratic for the first time.

1940

Party	Candidate	Popular vote	Per-cent	Electoral vote
Democrat	Franklin D. Roosevelt (N.Y.) and Henry A. Wallace (Iowa)	27,263,448	54.70	449
Republican	Wendell L. Willkie (Ind.) and Charles L. McNary (Oreg.)	22,336,260	44.82	82
Socialist	Norman Thomas (N.Y.)	116,827	0.23	N.A.
Prohibition	Roger W. Babson (Mass.)	58,685	0.12	N.A.
Other		65,223	0.13	N.A.

Total Vote 49,840,443
Roosevelt Plurality 4,927,188

Key Issues With war raging in Europe the electorate turned its attention from domestic to foreign affairs. The international scene led the Democrats to break with tradition and renominate F.D.R. for a third term. The Republicans turned to businessman and political neophyte Willkie, a charismatic former Democrat. Willkie's internationalism and the pledge of both candidates to keep the U.S. out of the war minimized the role of foreign policy in the campaign. **Regional Influences** Willkie carried only 10 states, mostly in the Midwest. But Roosevelt's percentage of the popular vote was markedly down from 1936.

1944

Party	Candidate	Popular vote	Per-cent	Electoral vote
Democrat	Franklin D. Roosevelt (N.Y.) and Harry S Truman (Mo.)	25,611,936	53.39	432
Republican	Thomas E. Dewey (N.Y.) and John W. Bricker (Ohio)	22,013,372	45.89	99
Socialist	Norman Thomas (N.Y.)	79,100	0.16	N.A.
Prohibition	Claude A. Watson (Calif.)	74,733	0.16	N.A.
Other		195,778	0.41	N.A.

Total Vote 47,974,819
Roosevelt Plurality 3,598,564

Key Issues With both candidates supporting New Deal social legislation and an international organization to maintain the peace after the war, the nation chose to let F.D.R. lead America into the post-war era. Big-city bosses and southern conservatives, with F.D.R.'s private support, ousted Wallace from the ticket in favor of Truman. **Regional Influences** Roosevelt won 36 states and the Democrats improved their control over Congress and the nation's statehouses. The Republicans only won a handful of western and New England states.

1948

Party	Candidate	Popular vote	Per-cent	Electoral vote
Democrat	Harry S Truman (Mo.) and Alben W. Barkley (Ky.)	24,105,587	49.51	303
Republican	Thomas E. Dewey (N.Y.) and Earl Warren (Calif.)	21,970,017	45.12	189
States' Rights	Strom Thurmond (S.C.) and Fielding L. Wright (Miss.)	1,169,134	2.40	39
Progressive	Henry A. Wallace (Iowa) and Glen H. Taylor (Idaho)	1,157,057	2.38	N.A.
Other		290,647	0.60	N.A.

Total Vote 48,692,442
Truman Plurality 2,135,570

Key Issues The Republicans were sure of victory after 16 years of Democratic rule and the desertion of the Democrats by conservative Southern Dixiecrats and the ultra-liberal Wallace faction. But Dewey's dour personality and Truman's intense whistle-stop campaign against the "do-nothing, good-for-nothing" Republican 80th Congress resulted in one of the biggest upsets in presidential history. **Regional Influences** Dewey captured all of the Middle Atlantic and New England states, except Massachusetts and Connecticut, along with the Dakotas, Nebraska and Kansas in the Midwest and Oregon in the northwest. Thurmond won South Carolina, Mississippi, Alabama and Louisiana in the Deep South.

1952

Party	Candidate	Popular vote	Per-cent	Electoral vote
Republican	Dwight D. Eisenhower (Kans.) and Richard M. Nixon (Calif.)	33,936,137	55.13	442
Democrat	Adlai E. Stevenson (Ill.) and John J. Sparkman (Ala.)	27,314,649	44.38	89
Progressive	Vincent W. Hallinan (Calif.)	140,416	0.23	N.A.
Prohibition	Stuart Hamblen (Calif.)	73,413	0.12	N.A.
Other		86,503	0.14	N.A.

Total Vote 61,551,118
Eisenhower Plurality 6,621,485

Key Issues Popular war hero Eisenhower swept to victory after uniting the internationalist and isolationist factions of the Republican party. He routed the Democrats by promising to kick out alleged crooks and communists in Washington, wage a more aggressive fight against communists worldwide and "go to Korea," implying that he had a plan to end the war there. **Regional Influences** Stevenson, who appealed to northern liberals as well as southern states' rights Democrats, carried only nine states in the south.

1956

Party	Candidate	Popular vote	Per-cent	Electoral vote
Republican	Dwight D. Eisenhower (Kans.) and Richard M. Nixon (Calif.)	35,585,247	57.37	457
Democrat	Adlai E. Stevenson (Ill.) and Estes Kefauver (Tenn.)	26,030,172	41.97	73
Constitution/ States' Rights	T. Coleman Andrews (Va.)	108,055	0.17	N.A.

Socialist-Labor	Eric Hass (New York)	44,300	0.07	N.A.
Other		257,600	0.42	N.A.

Total Vote 62,025,372
Eisenhower Plurality 9,555,073

Key Issues Eisenhower won an easy victory in a rematch of the 1952 election. His popularity did not translate into victories for his party elsewhere, as Democrats increased their control of Congress, regained in 1954, and their hold on the nation's governorships. **Regional Influences** Winning even more handsomely than he did in 1952, Eisenhower lost only seven southern states.

1960

Party	Candidate	Popular vote	Percent	Electoral vote
Democrat	John F. Kennedy (Mass.) and Lyndon B. Johnson (Tex.)	34,221,344	49.72	303
Republican	Richard M. Nixon (Calif.) and Henry Cabot Lodge (Mass.)	34,106,671	49.55	219
Socialist-Labor	Eric Hass (N.Y.)	47,522	0.07	N.A.
Other		337,175	0.48	15
Unpledged		116,248	0.17	N.A.

Total Vote 68,828,960
Kennedy Plurality 114,673

Key Issues Kennedy called for the government to play a larger role in stimulating the national economy in order to fund domestic social programs as well as to sustain a defense build-up and keep ahead militarily of the Soviet Union. The election was the first in which there were nationally televised debates between the two candidates. Kennedy's slick television performance played a role in his narrow triumph. **Regional Influences** The Democrats won a thin victory by narrowly defeating the Republicans in the Middle Atlantic states, the Deep South, Illinois and Texas. Nixon carried most of the Midwest, border and western states. Conservative Democratic Senator Harry F. Byrd of Virginia received 15 electoral votes: all eight of Mississippi's, six of Alabama's 11, and one of Oklahoma's eight.

1964

Party	Candidate	Popular vote	Percent	Electoral vote
Democrat	Lyndon B. Johnson (Tex.) and Hubert H. Humphrey (Minn.)	43,126,584	61.05	486
Republican	Barry M. Goldwater (Ariz.) and William E. Miller (N.Y.)	27,177,838	38.47	52
Socialist-Labor	Eric Hass (N.Y.)	45,187	0.06	N.A.
Socialist Workers	Clifton DeBerry (N.Y.)	32,701	0.05	N.A.
Other		258,794	0.37	N.A.

Total Vote 70,641,104
Johnson Plurality 15,948,746

Key Issues Johnson ran for election in his own right on the basis of his Great Society domestic programs. The reactionary Goldwater campaigned against the New Deal and for the bombing of North Vietnam. **Regional Influences** Johnson won all but six states—Goldwater's home state of Arizona and five states in the Deep South—in the biggest popular and electoral landslide since 1936. Forty new Northern Democrats were elected to the House on L.B.J.'s coattails.

1968

Party	Candidate	Popular vote	Percent	Electoral vote
Republican	Richard M. Nixon (Calif.) and Spiro T. Agnew (Md.)	31,785,148	43.42	301
Democrat	Hubert H. Humphrey (Minn.) and Edmund S. Muskie (Maine)	31,274,503	42.72	191

American Independent	George C. Wallace (Ala.) and Curtis LeMay (Ohio)	901,151	13.53	46
Socialist-Labor	Henning A. Blomen (Mass.)	52,591	0.07	N.A.
Other		189,977	0.20	N.A.

Total Vote 73,203,370
Nixon Plurality 510,645

Key Issues With the country divided over Vietnam, Humphrey failed to emerge from the shadow of the unpopular Johnson, while the previously hawkish Nixon pledged to end the war and hinted that he had a secret plan to do so. Wallace attacked Federal encroachment on states' rights, desegregation, "pointy-headed" intellectuals and the administration's timidity in Vietnam, in an effort to capture blue-collar votes. **Regional Influences** Barely more than 500,000 votes separated Nixon and Humphrey, but the Republican edge in the Electoral College was comfortable and the combined anti-Democratic vote amounted to a repudiation of the Johnson-Humphrey Administration. Humphrey's strength was in the eastern seaboard states. Wallace won five states in the Deep South.

1972

Party	Candidate	Popular vote	Percent	Electoral vote
Republican	Richard M. Nixon (Calif.) and Spiro T. Agnew (Md.)	47,170,179	60.69	520
Democrat	George S. McGovern (S.Dak.) and R. Sargent Shriver (Md.)	29,171,791	37.53	17
American Independent	John G. Schmitz (Calif.)	1,090,673	1.40	N.A.
People's	Benjamin Spock	78,751	0.10	N.A.
Other		216,196	0.28	(1)[1]

Total Vote 77,727,590
Nixon Plurality 17,998,388

Key Issues Seeking to create a Republican majority by converting Wallace Democrats, Nixon pursued a "Southern strategy" of denouncing busing, the welfare state, the media and intellectuals. McGovern was unable to overcome an image of radicalism furthered by Republican charges that he was the candidate of "acid, abortion, and amnesty." **Regional Influences** The GOP's Southern strategy was aided by an assassination attempt on Wallace that knocked him out of the race. Nixon lost only Massachusetts and the District of Columbia, but Democrats added to their majority in the Senate and maintained control of the House.

1. The Libertarian slate of John Hospers and Theodora Nathan received 1 electoral vote from a Republican elector in Virginia.

1976

Party	Candidate	Popular vote	Percent	Electoral vote
Democrat	Jimmy Carter (Ga.) and Walter F. Mondale (Minn.)	40,830,763	50.06	297
Republican	Gerald R. Ford (Mich.) and Robert Dole (Kans.)	39,147,793	48.00	240[1]
Independent	Eugene J. McCarthy (Minn.)	756,691	0.93	N.A.
Libertarian	Roger MacBride (Va.)	173,011	0.21	N.A.
Other		647,631	0.79	N.A.

Total Vote 81,555,889
Carter Plurality 1,682,970

Key Issues In the wake of Watergate, Carter ran a moralistic campaign as a political outsider. Vague on issues, he railed against the Washington bureaucracy and vowed to lead "a government that is as good and honest and decent . . . as filled with love as are the American people." He also promised Americans that he would never lie to them. **Regional Influences** Ford nearly overcame a huge early deficit in the polls. But Carter's background as a southern moderate enabled him to eke out a victory through wins in northern, southern and border states.

1. Ronald Reagan received one electoral vote from an elector in Washington.

1980

Party	Candidate	Popular vote	Percent	Electoral vote
Republican	Ronald Reagan (Calif.) and George Bush (Tex.)	43,901,812	50.75	489
Democrat	Jimmy Carter (Ga.) and Walter F. Mondale (Minn.)	35,483,820	41.02	49
Independent	John B. Anderson (Ill.) and Patrick J. Lucey (Wis.)	5,719,722	6.61	N.A.
Libertarian	Edward E. Clark (Calif.)	921,188	1.06	N.A.
Other		486,754	0.56	N.A.

Total Vote 86,513,296
Reagan Plurality 8,417,992

Key Issues Inflation, an energy shortage, the taking of American hostages by Iran and a strong primary challenge from Edward Kennedy of Massachusetts weakened Carter. Reagan, promising to get government "off the backs to the American people," pledged to cut taxes, increase defense spending, and balance the federal budget. Anderson, a Republican, ran as an independent to the left of both Carter and Reagan. **Regional Influences** Reagan swept to a landslide win in the Electoral College as Carter carried only six states and Washington, D.C.

1984

Party	Candidate	Popular vote	Percent	Electoral vote
Republican	Ronald Reagan (Calif.) and George Bush (Tex.)	54,450,603	58.78	525
Democrat	Walter F. Mondale (Minn.) and Geraldine Ferraro (N.Y.)	37,573,671	40.56	13
Libertarian	David Bergland (Calif.)	227,949	0.25	N.A.
Other		570,343	0.61	

Total Vote 92,628,458
Reagan Plurality 16,876,932

Key Issues The economy was flying after emerging in late 1983 from the worst economic downturn since the Great Depression. Reagan, whose commercials proclaimed it was "morning in America," ridiculed Mondale as an old-fashioned "tax-and-spend, gloom-and-doom" Democrat. Controversy over her husband's finances blunted Ferraro's appeal as the first woman on a major party ticket. **Regional Influences** Mondale carried only his home state of Minnesota and the District of Columbia as Reagan won the greatest electoral victory in American history and the fifth highest share of the popular vote.

1988

Party	Candidate	Popular vote	Percent	Electoral vote
Republican	George Bush (Tex.) and J. Danforth Quayle (Ind.)	48,881,011	53.37	426
Democrat	Michael S. Dukakis (Mass.) and Lloyd Bentsen (Tex.)	41,828,350	45.67	111[1]
Libertarian	Ron Paul (Texas)	431,499	0.47	N.A.
New Alliance	Lenora Fulani (New York)	218,159	0.24	N.A.
Other		226,852	0.25	N.A.

Total Vote 91,585,871
Bush Plurality 7,052,661

Key Issues Trailing Dukakis by 17 points in early summer, Bush made an issue of his opponent's "liberalism," depicting the Massachusetts governor as soft on crime. Bush made a household name out of Willie Horton, a black Mass. prison inmate who raped a woman while on a furlough. Dukakis' failure to respond to those charges and to shed the "liberal" label until late in the campaign ultimately doomed his candidacy, despite Bush's links to the Iran-Contra scandal and to Panama's drug-running leader, Gen. Mañuel Noriega. **Regional Influences** Dukakis won the District of Columbia and only 10 states including his home state of Massachusetts. Bush easily captured the formerly Democratic "solid South."

[1]Bentsen received one electoral vote for President.

1992

Party	Candidate	Popular vote	Percent	Electoral vote
Democrat	Bill Clinton (Ark.) and Al Gore (Tenn.)	44,908,233	42.95	370
Republican	George Bush (Tex.) and J. Danforth Quayle (Ind.)	39,102,282	37.40	168
Independent	H. Ross Perot (Tex.) and James H. Stockdale (Calif.)	19,721,433	18.86	N.A.
Other		820,788	0.79	

Total Vote 104,552,736
Clinton Plurality 5,805,951

Key Issues Bush's approval ratings were sky high as little as 13 months before the election, but a flagging economy and a national debt that wouldn't go away spelled his downfall in a three-way race that saw billionaire Ross Perot capture more votes than any third-party candidate since Theodore Roosevelt in 1912. Excitement for Perot, who entered the race in March, quit in July, and re-entered the campaign in October, brought a record 102 million people to the polls. Clinton ran especially strong among women, who supported his stances in favor of abortion rights and a strong defense of the environment. **Regional Influences** Perot's presence prevented either major party candidate from capturing an outright majority in every state except New York, Maryland, Arkansas (all of which went for Clinton) and Mississippi (which supported Bush). But Clinton won pluralities in 13 states, including delegate-rich California, Pennsylvania and Ohio.

1996

Party	Candidate	Popular vote	Percent	Electoral vote
Democrat	Bill Clinton (Ark.) and Al Gore (Tenn.)	47,402,357	49.24	379
Republican	Bob Dole (Kans.) and Jack Kemp (N.Y.)	39,198,755	40.71	159
Reform	H. Ross Perot and Patrick Choate	8,085,402	8.40	N.A.
Green	Ralph Nader	684,902	0.71	N.A.
Libertarian	Harry Browne	485,798	0.50	N.A.
Other		420,009	0.44	N.A.

Total Vote 96,277,223
Clinton Plurality 8,203,602

Key Issues Clinton easily won re-election, campaigning on the strong economy and declining crime rates. Less than half of the voting age population went to the polls, the lowest number since 1924. Among those who did vote, Clinton ran strong with women, Asian-Americans, and Hispanics, and captured about half of the voters who described themselves as Independents. Dole's refusal to contravene his own party's strict stand against abortion hurt him dearly among women, who overwhelmingly chose Clinton. Perot's presence in the race prevented Clinton from winning an outright majority, but was not nearly as influential as it had been four years earlier.

2000

Party	Candidate	Popular vote	Percent	Electoral vote
Republican	George W. Bush (Tex.) and Dick Cheney (Wyo.)	50,455,156	47.87	271
Democrat	Al Gore (Tenn.) and Joe Lieberman (Conn.)	50,992,335	48.38	266[1]
Green	Ralph Nader and Winona LaDuke	2,882,897	2.74	N.A.
Reform	Pat Buchanan and Ezola Foster	448,892	0.42	N.A.
Libertarian	Harry Browne	384,429	0.36	N.A.
Other		232,932	0.23	N.A.

Total Vote 105,396,641
Gore Plurality 537,179

1. One elector from the District of Columbia abstained.
Key Issues Gore campaigned on the strong economy and budget surplus of the Clinton years, but struggled to distance him-

self from Clinton's scandals. In debates that centered on social security and health-care, Bush dubbed himself a "compassionate conservative" while Gore was seen as wooden and unapproachable. Ralph Nader drew less than 3 percent of the vote, but Democrats viewed him as a spoiler in a tight race. Gore won the popular vote but the Electoral College results were delayed for a month by a recount in Florida, where Bush appeared to win by fewer than 1,000 votes. On Dec. 12, the U.S. Supreme Court, ruling on a lawsuit by Bush, halted the recount and effectively awarded the presidency to Bush. **Regional Influences** Bush won 30 states, including Texas and the South and all of the Rocky Mountain States except New Mexico. Gore carried 20 states, including most of the Northeast and the West Coast, but lost his home state of Tennessee.

2004

Party	Candidate	Popular vote	Per- cent	Electoral vote
Republican	George W. Bush (Tex.) and Dick Cheney (Wyo.)	62,040,610	50.73	286
Democrat	John Kerry (Mass.) and John Edwards (N.C.)	59,028,444	48.27	252
Independent	Ralph Nader and Peter Miguel Camejo	465,650	0.38	N.A.
Libertarian	Michael Badnarik and Richard Campagna	397,265	0.12	N.A.
	Total Vote	122,352,575		
	Bush Plurality	3,012,166		

Key Issues Despite the lack of military progress in Iraq and Afghanistan, a rising national debt, and a falling approval rating, Bush presented himself as more qualified to manage the "War on Terror" than his opponent, Vietnam War veteran Kerry. Both major parties registered millions of new voters and drove turnout with help from non-profit organizations who sponsored aggressive advertising to appeal to interest groups like Christian conservatives. **Regional Influences** The vote was close across the country but Bush carried a wide swath of 30 states and was especially popular in the South although Ohio proved to be the crucial state for him. Kerry won 20 states including the West Coast, most of the Great Lakes region and the entire Northeast.

2008

Party	Candidate	Popular vote	Per- cent	Electoral vote
Democratic	Barack Obama (Ill.) and Joseph Biden (Del.)	69,456,897	52.9	365
Republican	John McCain (Ariz.) and Sarah Palin (Alaska)	59,934,814	45.7	173
Independent	Ralph Nader and Matt Gonzalez	738,475	0.56	N.A.
Libertarian	Bob Barr and Wayne Root	523,686	0.40	N.A.
Other		603,456		
	Total Vote	131,257,328		
	Obama Plurality	9,522,083		

Key Issues Obama and McCain differed over the wars in Iraq and Afghanistan, health care reform, and the proper role of government, but the collapse of the U.S. economy dominated the campaign. Racial tensions also surfaced as the nation considered the possibility of a black president. McCain had bipartisan support, but was tainted by his ties to the Iraq war and to the unpopular incumbent, George W. Bush. In contrast, Obama's dynamic public image, inspiring personal story, and prescription for change resonated with voters across party lines. **Regional Influences** Obama won many of the most populous states, giving him a decisive electoral-college victory. Obama carried 28 states including the entire Northeast, West Coast and Great Lakes regions, plus Florida, Virginia and North Carolina. McCain won 22 states, including rural areas across the Great Plains and the South, but the candidates split the Southwest.

▶ THE ELECTORAL COLLEGE

The Electoral College is the body of electors, chosen by all of the states, that ultimately is responsible for selecting the president of the United States. The Framers did not want the nation's Chief Executive chosen by either the national legislature or the people directly. Instead they set up the Electoral College, under Article II of the Constitution, to provide for indirect election of the president: "Each State shall appoint, in such manner as the legislature thereof may direct, a number of Electors, equal to the whole number of Senators and Representatives to which the State may be entitled in the Congress; but no Senator or Representative, or person holding an office of trust or profit under the United States, shall be appointed an Elector."

Electors were supposed to be distinguished, enlightened citizens who would cast a disinterested vote for president. From the start, however, electors have been instruments of partisan passions. At first, most state legislatures were responsible for choosing electors. By 1828, however, all states except South Carolina allowed electors to be chosen by direct popular election. (In South Carolina, the legislature continued to select electors until the Civil War.) When electors began to be selected by popular vote, parties presented slates of candidates for presidential electors who were tacitly pledged to support the party's nominees for president and vice president. This is how the practice began of states voting as a unit. Subsequently, many states passed laws requiring their electors to vote as a bloc. Where it is not required by law, it is customary for all of a state's electors to vote for the candidate receiving a plurality of the popular vote in that state. The names of the candidates for electors may or may not appear on the ballot alongside the names of the candidates to whom they are pledged. Voters really vote for presidential electors, though, even when they seem to be casting a ballot for a presidential candidate.

The presidential electors chosen by the voters in November meet in their state capitals on the first Monday after the second Wednesday in December to cast their vote for president and vice president. The results of this balloting are sent to the president of the U.S. Senate, the directors of the U.S. General Services Administration, the state's secretary of state, and to the judge of the Federal District Court of the district in which the electors gathered. Sealed state ballots are opened and counted at a joint session of Congress on January 6 following the election year.

Originally electors voted for two individuals for president on a single ballot. The winner of a majority of the vote was elected president, the runner-up vice president. The Framers fully expected there to be many elections in which no candidate would gain a majority of the vote and the president would have to be selected by the House of Representatives, where each state delegation would cast a single vote. But in 1789 and 1792 every elector voted for George Washington. In both years John Adams was the runner-up and, thus, vice president.

Problems inherent in this system became apparent once Washington was no longer a candidate. In 1796, Adams and Thomas Jefferson finished first and second in the balloting and were elected president and vice president, respectively, despite being fierce foes. By 1800, two formal parties had evolved which nominated a single candidate for both president and vice president. A Federalist elector purposely failed to vote for the party's vice presidential nominee, Thomas Pinckney, in order to assure a potential majority for Adams. But overzealous Republican electors all voted for both Jefferson and the party's vice presidential nominee, Aaron Burr. Both men received the same majority of the electoral vote and the election had to be decided by the House, where Jefferson won. This led to adoption of the Twelfth Amendment to the Constitution, implemented in 1804, which requires electors to cast separate ballots for president and vice president. If no candidate achieves a majority of the electoral vote for vice president, the position is filled by the Senate with each senator casting a single ballot. This has happened only once, when the Senate selected Richard M. Johnson after he fell one electoral vote short of a majority for vice president in 1836.

Today, 270 votes are required to reach a majority in the Electoral College. There have been two elections in which no candidate received a majority of the electoral vote. In 1824, no candidate achieved a majority of the vote, and in 1876, disputed results in several states prevented either Rutherford B. Hayes or Samuel J. Tilden from achieving a majority. John Quincy Adams and Hayes won those contests, respectively. A candidate also can be elected president despite losing the popular vote. This occurred, again in 1824 and 1876, when the House selected Adams and Hayes, though they lost the popular vote to Andrew Jackson and Tilden, respectively; in 1888, when Benjamin Harrison was elected over Grover Cleveland despite receiving a minority of the popular vote; and in 2000, when George W. Bush lost the popular vote by more than 500,000 votes to Al Gore, but won enough states for an Electoral College victory.

►THE FEDERAL ELECTION CAMPAIGN ACT

In 1971 Congress passed the Federal Election Campaign Act to deal with various aspects of campaign financing. The law was amended and strengthened in 1974 and 1976, and the Federal Election Commission (FEC) was established to administer the law, which affects candidates for the U.S. House of Representatives, the U.S. Senate, and the presidency. The act requires disclosure of sources and uses of funds for federal elections, provides public financing for presidential elections, and sets limits on campaign contributions.

Campaign Contribution Limits, 2009–10

Type of Contribution	To each candidate[1]	To national party[2]	To state, district, and local party[2]	To any other political committee[2]
Individual[3]	$2,400	$30,400	$10,000[4]	$5,000
National Party	5,000	Unlimited	Unlimited	5,000[6]
State, district, and local party	5,000[4]	Unlimited	Unlimited	5,000
Multi-candidate PAC	5,000	15,000	5,000[4]	5,000
Not multi-candidate PAC	2,400[4]	30,400[5]	10,000[4]	5,000
Authorized campaign committee	2,000	Unlimited	Unlimited	5,000

Notes: 1. Per election. 2. Per calendar year. 3. Up to a biennial limit of $115,5004, including $45,6004 to all candidates and $69,9004 to all PACs and parties. 4. Combined limit. 5. Indexed for inflation. 6. Combined with national Senate campaign committee, may give up to $42,6004 to each Senate candidate per campaign. **Source:** Federal Election Commission.

Voter Turnout in Presidential Elections, 1928–2008

Year	Total Vote	Voting Age Population		Registered Voters	
		Number	Percent Voting	Number[1]	Percent Voting
1928	36,879,414	71,185,000	51.8%	N.A.	N.A.
1932	39,816,522	75,768,000	52.6	N.A.	N.A.
1936	45,646,817	80,354,000	56.8	N.A.	N.A.
1940	49,815,312	84,728,000	58.8	N.A.	N.A.
1944	48,025,684	95,573,000	56.1	N.A.	N.A.
1948	48,833,680	95,573,000	51.1	N.A.	N.A.
1952	61,551,919	99,929,000	61.6	N.A.	N.A.
1956	62,033,908	104,515,000	59.4	N.A.	N.A.
1960	68,838,204	109,159,000	63.06	N.A.	N.A.
1964	70,644,592	114,090,000	61.92	73,715,818	95.83%
1968	73,211,875	120,328,186	60.84	81,658,180	89.65
1972	77,718,554	140,776,000	55.21	97,328,541	79.85
1976	81,555,789	152,309,190	53.55	105,037,986	77.64
1980	86,515,221	164,597,000	52.56	113,043,734	76.53
1984	92,652,680	174,466,000	53.11	124,150,614	74.63
1988	91,594,693	182,778,000	50.11	126,379,628	72.48
1992	104,405,155	189,529,000	55.09	133,821,178	78.01
1996	96,456,345	196,511,000	49.08	146,211,960	65.97
2000	105,586,274	205,815,000	51.30	156,421,311	67.50
2004	122,295,345	215,694,000	56.70	177,265,030	68.99
2008	131,257,328	232,589,000	56.40	189,844,867	69.10

Source: Federal Election Commission. www.fec.gov

Public disclosure Candidates for federal office and the political committees that support them must register and file periodic disclosures of their campaign finance activities with the clerk of the House, the secretary of the Senate, or the FEC. These reports are available to the public within 48 hours of their disclosure. A political committee, also known as a Political Action Committee (PAC) is defined as a club, committee, association, or organization that receives contributions or makes expenditures of more than $1,000 to a federal candidate in any calendar year. PACs are subject to different contirbution limits than are individuals.

Public financing Public financing is provided for eligible presidential candidates in primary and

Speakers of the U.S. House of Representatives

Name	Party	State	Dates in Office
Frederick A.C. Muhlenberg	D-R	Pa.	1789–91
Jonathan Trumbull	Fed.	Conn.	1791–93
Frederick A. C. Muhlenberg	D-R	Pa.	1793–95
Jonathan Dayton	Fed.	N.J.	1795–99
Theodore Sedgwick	Fed.	Mass.	1799–1801
Nathaniel Macon	D-R	N.C.	1801–07
Joseph B. Varnum	D-R	Mass.	1807–11
Henry Clay	D-R	Ky.	1811–14
Langdon Cheves	D-R	S.C.	1814–15
Henry Clay	D-R	Ky.	1815–20
John W. Taylor	D-R	N.Y.	1820–21
Philip Barbour	D-R	Va.	1821–23
Henry Clay	D-R	Ky.	1823-25
John W. Taylor	D-R	N.Y.	1825–27
Andrew Stevenson	D	Va.	1827–34
John Bell	D	Tenn.	1834–35
James K. Polk	D	Tenn.	1835–39
Robert M.T. Hunter	NP	Va.	1839–41
John White	Whig	Ky.	1841–43
John W. Jones	D	Va.	1843–45
John W. Davis	D	Ind.	1845–47
Robert C. Winthrop	Whig	Mass.	1847–49
Howell Cobb	D	Ga.	1849–51
Linn Boyd	D	Ky.	1851–55
Nathaniel Banks	R	Mass.	1855–57
James L. Orr	D	S.C.	1857–59
William Pennington	Whig	N.J.	1859–61
Galusha A. Grow	R	Pa.	1861–63
Schuyler Colfax	R	Ind.	1863–69
James G. Blaine	R	Maine	1869–75
Michael C. Kerr	D	Ind.	1875–76
Samuel J. Randall	D	Pa.	1876–81
J. Warren Keifer	R	Ohio	1881–83
John G. Carlisle	D	Ky.	1883–89
Thomas B. Reed	R	Maine	1889–91
Charles F. Crisp	D	Ga.	1891–95
Thomas B. Reed	R	Maine	1895–99
David B. Henderson	R	Iowa	1899–1903
Joseph G. Cannon	R	Ill.	1903–11
Champ Clark	D	Mo.	1911–19
Frederick H. Gillett	R	Mass.	1919–25
Nicholas Longworth	R	Ohio	1925–31
John Nance Garner	D	Tex.	1931–33
Henry T. Rainey	D	Ill.	1933–34
Joseph W. Byrns	D	Tenn.	1935–36
William B. Bankhead	D	Ala.	1936–39
Sam Rayburn	D	Tex.	1940–46
Joseph W. Martin Jr.	R	Mass.	1947–49
Sam Rayburn	D	Tex.	1949–52
Joseph W. Martin Jr.	R	Mass.	1953–54
Sam Rayburn	D	Tex.	1955–61
John W. McCormack	D	Mass.	1962–71
Carl B. Albert	D	Okla.	1971–76
Thomas P. O'Neill Jr.	D	Mass.	1977–87
James C. Wright Jr.	D	Tex.	1987–89
Thomas S. Foley	D	Wash.	1989–95
Newt Gingrich	R	Ga.	1995–99
J. Dennis Hastert	R	Ill.	1999–2006
Nancy Pelosi	D	Calif.	2006–

Notes: D = Democrat. Fed. = Federalist. R = Republican.

Vice Presidents of the United States

Name	Party	Tenure	State, birth-death
1. John Adams	Fed.	1789–97	Mass., 1735–1826
2. Thomas Jefferson	D-R	1797–1801	Va., 1743–1826
3. Aaron Burr	D-R	1801–05	N.Y., 1756–1836
4. George Clinton	D-R	1805–13†	N.Y., 1739–1812
5. Elbridge Gerry	D-R	1813–17†	Mass., 1744–1814
6. Daniel D. Tompkins	D-R	1817–25	N.Y., 1774–1825
7. John C. Calhoun	D-R	1825–33[1]	S.C., 1782–1850
8. Martin Van Buren	D	1833–37	N.Y., 1782–1862
9. Richard M. Johnson	D	1837–41[2]	Ky., 1780–1850
10. John Tyler	Whig	1841[3]	Va., 1790–1862
11. George M. Dallas	D	1845–49	Pa., 1792–1864
12. Millard Fillmore	Whig	1849–50[4]	N.Y., 1800–74
13. William R. King	D	1853–57†	Ala., 1786–1853
14. John C. Breckenridge	D	1857–61	Ky., 1821–75
15. Hannibal Hamlin	R	1861–65	Maine, 1809–91
16. Andrew Johnson	R	1865[5]	Tenn., 1808–75
17. Schuyler Colfax	R	1869–73	Ind., 1823–85
18. Henry Wilson	R	1873–77†	Mass., 1812–75
19. William A. Wheeler	R	1877–81	N.Y., 1819–87
20. Chester A. Arthur	R	1881[6]	N.Y., 1829–86
21. Thomas A. Hendricks	D	1885†	Ind., 1819–85
22. Levi P. Morton	R	1889–93	N.Y., 1824–1920
23. Adlai E. Stevenson	D	1893–97	Ill., 1835–1914
24. Garret A. Hobart	R	1897–1901†N.J., 1844–99
25. Theodore Roosevelt	R	1901[7]	N.Y., 1858–1919
26. Charles W. Fairbanks	R	1905–09	Ind., 1852–1918
27. James S. Sherman	R	1909–13†	N.Y., 1855–1912
28. Thomas R. Marshall	D	1913–21	Ind., 1854–1925
29. Calvin Coolidge	R	1921–23[8]	Mass., 1872–1933
30. Charles G. Dawes	R	1925–29	Ill., 1865–1951
31. Charles Curtis	R	1929–33	Kans., 1860–1936
32. John Nance Garner	D	1933–41	Tex., 1868–1967
33. Henry A. Wallace	D	1941–45	Iowa, 1888–1965
34. Harry S Truman	D	1945[9]	Mo., 1884–1972
35. Alben W. Barkley	D	1949–53	Ky., 1877–1956
36. Richard M. Nixon	R	1953–61	Calif., 1913–95
37. Lyndon B. Johnson	D	1961–63[10]	Tex., 1908–73
38. Hubert H. Humphrey	D	1965–69	Minn., 1911–78
39. Spiro T. Agnew	R	1969–73[11]	Md., 1918–96
40. Gerald R. Ford	R	1973–74[12]	Mich., 1913–2006
41. Nelson A. Rockefeller	R	1974–77[13]	N.Y., 1908–79
42. Walter F. Mondale	D	1977–81	Minn., 1928–
43. George H.W. Bush	R	1981–89	Tex., 1924–
44. J. Danforth Quayle	R	1989–93	Ind., 1947–
45. Albert Gore	D	1993–2001	Tenn., 1948–
46. Richard Cheney	R	2001–2009	Wyo., 1941–
47. Joseph R. Biden Jr.	D	2009–	Del., 1942–

Notes: Fed. = Federalist. D = Democrat. D-R = Democratic-Republican. R = Republican. † = Died in office. 1. Resigned to become senator from South Carolina (1832-43). 2. Voted in by senate after no candidate for vice president gained a majority in the electoral college. 3. Became president after William Henry Harrison's death. 4. Became president after Zachary Taylor's death. 5. Nominated by Republicans to run with Abraham Lincoln on the Union ticket; became president after Lincoln's assassination. 6. Became president after James Garfield's assassination. 7. Became president after William McKinley's assassination. 8. Became president after Warren Harding's death. 9. Became president after Franklin D. Roosevelt's death. 10. Became president after John F. Kennedy's assassination. 11. Resigned while under investigation for receiving kickbacks as governor of Maryland. 12. First vice president named under terms of the 25th amendment; assumed presidency after Richard Nixon resigned. 13. Named vice president by Ford.

general elections, and for national party committees for the nominating conventions. Financing is given in the form of matching payments to primary candidates, public grants to nominees in the general election, and public grants to the national party committees for the conventions. The money for public financing is raised by the Presidential Election Campaign Fund, which collects three dollars from the tax payment of every taxpayer who checks off this box on his or her federal income tax return.

Contribution limits and prohibitions The Federal Election Campaign Act capped contributions to individual candidates at $1,000 per two-year election cycle, and donations to national political party committees to $20,000 per year. But a 1978 FEC ruling opened a loophole that allowed national political parties to accept unlimited "soft money" contributions from corporations, unions, and individuals, which did not count against the $20,000 limit. In theory, soft money contributions were supposedly limited to general party-building activities, but in practice, these monies were almost always spent in support of specific candidates for office.

After years of failed attempts, Congress in 2002 finally passed a campaign finance reform bill that closed the soft money loophole. The legislation, which took effect after the 2002 elections (subject to review by the Supreme Court) doubled the contribution limit to $2,000 per candidate per election cycle, raised the cap on hard money contributions to national political parties to $25,000 per year, and increased the limit on contributions to state and local political parties (for get-out-the-vote and voter registration efforts) from $5,000 to $10,000 per year. In addition, the law prohibits unions, corporations, and nonprofit groups from paying for so-called "issue ads" advocating the election or defeat of specific candidates within 60 days of a general election and 30 days of a primary. These ads must now be paid for only with regulated hard money.

In 2010 the Supreme Court rule that corporations and unions may spend freely in candidate elections, striking down a central part of the 2002 McCain–Feingold campaign finance law, and overturning two important precedents.

POLITICAL OFFICE HOLDERS

▶THE VICE PRESIDENCY

Until adoption of the 25th Amendment to the Constitution in 1967, there was no provision to fill a vacancy in the vice presidency. Under the amendment, the president must name a vice president when the office is vacant, and the nominee must pass a majority vote of approval in both houses of Congress. Gerald Ford, Richard Nixon's choice to replace Spiro Agnew after the latter's resignation in 1973, was the first vice president to gain the office under the amendment. While the 25th Amendment does not supersede the presidential order of succession, it decreases the likelihood of the office's ever falling to the speaker of the House or a sitting cabinet member.

▶PRESIDENTIAL ORDER OF SUCCESSION

Article II of the Constitution gives to Congress the power to determine the presidential order of succession should both the president and vice president die, become incapacitated or be disqualified from office. The present law, passed in 1947, puts the Speaker of the House first in line to the presidency, followed by the president pro tempore of the Senate. The order of succession then goes through the members of the Cabinet, in the order in which the executive departments were established:

(1) Secretary of State, (2) Secretary of the Treasury, (3) Secretary of Defense, (4) Attorney General, (5) Secretary of the Interior, (6) Secretary of Agriculture, (7) Secretary of Commerce, (8) Secretary of Labor, (9) Secretary of Health and Human Services, (10) Secretary of Housing and Urban Development, (11) Secretary of Transportation, (12) Secretary of Energy, (13) Secretary of Education, (14) Secretary of Veterans' Affairs (15) Secretary of Homeland Security. A Cabinet member must be a natural-born U.S. citizen and at least 35 years old in order to become acting president. If a Cabinet member next-in-line to fill a presidential vacancy were not yet 35, the presidency would pass to the next Cabinet member in the order of succession who had attained that age.

Cabinet Members

Washington Administration (1789-97)

Secretary of State	Thomas Jefferson	1789–93
	Edmund Randolph	1794–95
	Timothy Pickering	1795–97
Secretary of Treasury	Alexander Hamilton	1789–95
	Oliver Wolcott	1795–97
Secretary of War	Henry Knox	1789–94
	Timothy Pickering	1795
	James McHenry	1796–97
Attorney General	Edmund Randolph	1789–93
	William Bradford	1794–95
	Charles Lee	1795–97
Postmaster General	Samuel Osgood	1789–91
	Timothy Pickering	1791–94
	Joseph Habersham	1795–97

John Adams Administration (1797–1801)

Secretary of State	Timothy Pickering	1797–1800
	John Marshall	1800–1801

Secretary of Treasury	Oliver Wolcott	1797–1800
	Samuel Dexter	1800–1801
Secretary of War	James McHenry	1797–1800
	Samuel Dexter	1800–1801
Attorney General	Charles Lee	1797–1801
Postmaster General	Joseph Habersham	1797–1801
Secretary of Navy	Benjamin Stoddert	1798–1801

Jefferson Administration (1801–09)

Secretary of State	James Madison	1801–09
Secretary of Treasury	Samuel Dexter	1801
	Albert Gallatin	1801–09
Secretary of War	Henry Dearborn	1801–09
Attorney General	Levi Lincoln	1801–05
	Robert Smith	1805
	John Breckinridge	1805–06
	Caesar Rodney	1807–09
Postmaster General	Joseph Habersham	1801
	Gideon Granger	1801–09

| Secretary of Navy | Robert Smith | 1801–09 |

Madison Administration (1809–17)

Secretary of State	Robert Smith	1809–11
	James Monroe	1811–17
Secretary of Treasury	Albert Gallatin	1809–13
	George Campbell	1814
	Alexander Dallas	1814–16
	William Crawford	1816–17
Secretary of War	William Eustis	1809–13
	John Armstrong	1813–14
	James Monroe	1814–15
	William Crawford	1815–17
Attorney General	Caesar Rodney	1809–11
	William Pinkney	1811–14
	Richard Rush	1814–17
Postmaster General	Gideon Granger	1809–14
	Return Meigs	1814–17
Secretary of Navy	Paul Hamilton	1809–13
	William Jones	1813–14
	Benjamin Crowninshield	1814–17

Monroe Administration (1817–25)

Secretary of State	John Quincy Adams	1817–25
Secretary of Treasury	William Crawford	1817–25
Secretary of War	George Graham	1817
	John C. Calhoun	1817–25
Attorney General	Richard Rush	1817
	William Wirt	1817–25
Postmaster General	Return Meigs	1817–23
	John McLean	1823–25
Secretary of Navy	Benjamin Crowninshield	1817–18
	Smith Thompson	1818–23
	Samuel Southard	1823–25

John Quincy Adams Administration (1825–29)

Secretary of State	Henry Clay	1825–25
Secretary of Treasury	Richard Rush	1825–25
Secretary of War	James Barbour	1825–29
	Peter Porter	1828–29
Attorney General	William Wirt	1825–29
Postmaster General	John McLean	1825–29
Secretary of Navy	Samuel Southard	1825–29

Jackson Administration (1829–37)

Secretary of State	Martin Van Buren	1829–33
	Edward Livingston	1831–33
	Louis McLane	1833–34
	John Forsyth	1834–37
Secretary of Treasury	Samuel Ingham	1829–31
	Louis McLane	1831–33
	William Duane	1833
	Roger B. Taney	1833–34
	Levi Woodbury	1834–37
Secretary of War	John H. Eaton	1829–31
	Lewis Cass	1831–37
	Benjamin Butler	1837
Attorney General	John M. Berrien	1829–31
	Roger B. Taney	1831–33
	Benjamin Butler	1833–37
Postmaster General	William Barry	1829–35
	Amos Kendall	1835–37
Secretary of Navy	John Branch	1829–31
	Levi Woodbury	1831–34
	Mahlon Dickerson	1834–37

Van Buren Administration (1837–41)

Secretary of State	John Forsyth	1837–41
Secretary of Treasury	Levi Woodbury	1837–41
Secretary of War	Joel Poinsett	1837–41
Attorney General	Benjamin Butler	1837–38
	Felix Grundy	1838–40
	Henry D. Gilpin	1840–41
Postmaster General	Amos Kendall	1837–40
	John M. Niles	1840–41
Secretary of Navy	Mahlon Dickerson	1837–38
	James Paulding	1838–41

William Harrison Administration (1841)

Secretary of State	Daniel Webster	1841
Secretary of Treasury	Thomas Ewing	1841
Secretary of War	John Bell	1841
Attorney General	John J. Crittenden	1841
Postmaster General	Francis Granger	1841
Secretary of Navy	George Badger	1841

Tyler Administration (1841–45)

Secretary of State	Daniel Webster	1841–43
	Hugh S. Legaré	1843
	Abel P. Upshur	1843–44
	John C. Calhoun	1844–45
Secretary of Treasury	Thomas Ewing	1841
	Walter Forward	1841–43
	John C. Spencer	1843–44
	George Bibb	1844–45
Secretary of War	John Bell	1841
	John C. Spencer	1841–43
	James M. Porter	1843–44
	William Wilkins	1844–45
Attorney General	John J. Crittenden	1841
	Hugh S. Legaré	1841–43
	John Nelson	1843–45
Postmaster General	Francis Granger	1841
	Charles Wickliffe	1841
Secretary of Navy	George Badger	1841
	Abel P. Upshur	1841
	David Henshaw	1843–44
	Thomas Gilmer	1844
	John Y. Mason	1844–45

Polk Administration (1845–49)

Secretary of State	James Buchanan	1845–49
Secretary of Treasury	Robert J. Walker	1845–49
Secretary of War	William L. Marcy	1845–49
Attorney General	John Y. Mason	1845–46
	Nathan Clifford	1846–48
	Isaac Toucey	1848–49
Postmaster General	Cave Johnson	1845–49
Secretary of Navy	George Bancroft	1845–46
	John Y. Mason	1846–49

Taylor Administration (1849–50)

Secretary of State	John M. Clayton	1849–50
Secretary of Treasury	William Meredith	1849–50
Secretary of War	George Crawford	1849–50
Attorney General	Reverdy Johnson	1849–50
Postmaster General	Jacob Collamer	1849–50
Secretary of Navy	William Preston	1849–50
Secretary of Interior	Thomas Ewing	1849–50

Fillmore Administration (1850–53)

Secretary of State	Daniel Webster	1850–52
	Edward Everett	1852–53
Secretary of Treasury	Thomas Corwin	1850–53
Secretary of War	Charles Conrad	1850–53
Attorney General	John J. Crittenden	1850–53
Postmaster General	Nathan Hall	1850–52
	Sam D. Hubbard	1852–53
Secretary of Navy	William A. Graham	1852–53
	John P. Kennedy	1852–53
Secretary of Interior	Thomas McKennan	1850
	Alexander Stuart	1850–53

Pierce Administration (1853–57)

Secretary of State	William L. Marcy	1853–57
Secretary of Treasury	James Guthrie	1853–57
Secretary of War	Jefferson Davis	1853–57
Attorney General	Caleb Cushing	1853–57
Postmaster General	James Campbell	1853–57
Secretary of Navy	James C. Dobbin	1853–57
Secretary of Interior	Robert McClelland	1853–57

Buchanan Administration (1857–61)

Secretary of State	Lewis Cass	1857–60
	Jeremiah S. Black	1860–61
Secretary of Treasury	Howell Cobb	1857–60
	Philip Thomas	1860–61
	John A. Dix	1861
Secretary of War	John B. Floyd	1857–61
	Joseph Holt	1861
Attorney General	Jeremiah S. Black	1857–60
	Edwin M. Stanton	1860–61
Postmaster General	Aaron W. Brown	1857–59
	Joseph Holt	1859–61
	Horatio King	1861
Secretary of Navy	Isaac Toucey	1857–61
Secretary of Interior	Jacob Thompson	1857–61

Lincoln Administration (1861–65)

Secretary of State	William H. Seward	1861–65
Secretary of Treasury	Salmon P. Chase	1861–65
	William P. Fessenden	1864–65
	Hugh McCulloch	1865
Secretary of War	Simon Cameron	1861–62
	Edwin M. Stanton	1862–65
Attorney General	Edward Bates	1861–64
	James Speed	1864–65
Postmaster General	Horatio King	1861
	Montgomery Blair	1861–64
	William Dennison	1864–65
Secretary of Navy	Gideon Welles	1861–65
Secretary of Interior	Caleb B. Smith	1861–63
	John P. Usher	1863–65

Andrew Johnson Administration (1865–69)

Secretary of State	William H. Seward	1865–69
Secretary of Treasury	Hugh McCulloch	1865–69
Secretary of War	Edwin M. Stanton	1865–67
	Ulysses S. Grant	1867–68
	Lorenzo Thomas	1868
	John M. Schofield	1868–69
Attorney General	James Speed	1865–66
	Henry Stanbery	1866–68
	William M. Evarts	1868–69
Postmaster General	William Dennison	1865–66
	Alexander Randall	1866–69
Secretary of Navy	Gideon Welles	1865–69
Secretary of Interior	John P. Usher	1865
	James Harlan	1865–66
	Orville H. Browning	1866–69

Grant Administration (1869–77)

Secretary of State	Elihu B. Washburne	1869
	Hamilton Fish	1869–77
Secretary of Treasury	George S. Boutwell	1869–73
	William Richardson	1873–74
	Benjamin Bristow	1874–76
	Lot M. Morrill	1876–77
Secretary of War	John A. Rawlins	1869
	William T. Sherman	1869
	William W. Belknap	1869–76
	Alphonso Taft	1876
	James D. Cameron	1876–77
Attorney General	Ebenezer Hoar	1869–70
	Amos T. Ackerman	1870–71
	G. H. Williams	1871–75

	Edwards Pierrepont	1875–76
	Alphonso Taft	1876–77
Postmaster General	John A. J. Creswell	1869–74
	James W. Marshall	1874
	Marshall Jewell	1874–76
	James N. Tyner	1876–77
Secretary of Navy	Adolph E. Borie	1869
	George M. Robeson	1869–77
Secretary of Interior	Jacob D. Cox	1869–70
	Columbus Delano	1870–75
	Zachariah Chandler	1875–77

Hayes Administration (1877–81)

Secretary of State	William M. Evarts	1877–81
Secretary of Treasury	John Sherman	1877–81
Secretary of War	George W. McCrary	1877–79
	Alex Ramsey	1879–81
Attorney General	Charles Devens	1877–81
Postmaster General	David M. Key	1877–80
	Horace Maynard	1880–81
Secretary of Navy	Richard W. Thompson	1877–80
	Nathan Goff, Jr.	1881
Secretary of Interior	Carl Schurz	1877–81

Garfield Administration (1881)

Secretary of State	James G. Blaine	1881
Secretary of Treasury	William Windom	1881
Secretary of War	Robert T. Lincoln	1881
Attorney General	Wayne MacVeagh	1881
Postmaster General	Thomas L. James	1881
Secretary of Navy	William H. Hunt	1881
Secretary of Interior	Samuel J. Kirkwood	1881

Arthur Administration (1881–85)

Secretary of State	F. T. Frelinghuysen	1881–85
Secretary of Treasury	Charles J. Folger	1881–84
	Walter Q. Gresham	1884
	Hugh McCulloch	1884–85
Secretary of War	Robert T. Lincoln	1881–85
Attorney General	Benjamin H. Brewster	1881–85
Postmaster General	Timothy O. Howe	1881–83
	Walter Q. Gresham	1883–84
	Frank Hatton	1884–85
Secretary of Navy	William H. Hunt	1881–82
	William E. Chandler	1882–85
Secretary of Interior	Samuel J. Kirkwood	1881–82
	Henry M. Teller	1882–85

Cleveland Administration (1885–89)

Secretary of State	Thomas F. Bayard	1885–89
Secretary of Treasury	Daniel Manning	1885–87
	Charles S. Fairchild	1887–89
Secretary of War	William C. Endicott	1885–89
Attorney General	Augustus H. Garland	1885–89
Postmaster General	William F. Vilas	1885–88
	Don M. Dickinson	1888–89
Secretary of Navy	William C. Whitney	1885–89
Secretary of Interior	Lucius Q. C. Lamar	1885–88
	William F. Vilas	1888–89
Secretary of Agriculture	Norman J. Colman	1889

Benjamin Harrison Administration (1889–93)

Secretary of State	James G. Blaine	1889–92
	John W. Foster	1892–93
Secretary of Treasury	William Windom	1889–91
	Charles Foster	1891–93
Secretary of War	Redfield Proctor	1889–91
	Stephen B. Elkins	1891–93
Attorney General	William H. H. Miller	1889–91
Postmaster General	John Wanamaker	1889–93
Secretary of Navy	Benjamin F. Tracy	1889–93
Secretary of Interior	John W. Noble	1889–93
Secretary of Agriculture	Jeremiah M. Rusk	1889–93

Cleveland Administration (1893–97)

Secretary of State	Walter Q. Gresham	1893–95
	Richard Olney	1895–97
Secretary of Treasury	John G. Carlisle	1893–97
Secretary of War	Daniel S. Lamont	1893–97
Attorney General	Richard Olney	1893–95
	James Harmon	1895–97
Postmaster General	Wilson S. Bissell	1893–95
	William L. Wilson	1895–95
Secretary of Navy	Hilary A. Herbert	1893–97
Secretary of Interior	Hoke Smith	1893–96
	David R. Francis	1896–97
Secretary of Agriculture	Julius S. Morton	1893–97

McKinley Administration (1897–1901)

Secretary of State	John Sherman	1897–98
	William R. Day	1898
	John Hay	1898–1901
Secretary of Treasury	Lyman J. Gage	1897–1901
Secretary of War	Russell A. Alger	1897–99
	Elihu Root	1899–1901
Attorney General	Joseph McKenna	1897–98
	John W. Griggs	1898–1901
	Philander C. Knox	1901
Postmaster General	James A. Gary	1897–98
	Charles E. Smith	1898–1901
Secretary of Navy	John D. Long	1897–1901
Secretary of Interior	Cornelius N. Bliss	1897–99
	Ethan A. Hitchcock	1899–1901
Secretary of Agriculture	James Wilson	1897–1901

Theodore Roosevelt Administration (1901–09)

Secretary of State	John Hay	1901–05
	Elihu Root	1905–09
	Robert Bacon	1909
Secretary of Treasury	Lyman J. Gage	1901–02
	Leslie M. Shaw	1902–07
	George B. Cortelyou	1907–09
Secretary of War	Elihu Root	1901–04
	William H. Taft	1904–08
	Luke E. Wright	1908–09
Attorney General	Philander C. Knox	1901–04
	William H. Moody	1904–06
	Charles J. Bonaparte	1906–09
Postmaster General	Charles E. Smith	1901–02
	Henry C. Payne	1902–04
	Robert J. Wynne	1904–05
	George B. Cortelyou	1905–07
	George von L. Meyer	1907–09
Secretary of Navy	John D. Long	1901–02
	William H. Moody	1902–04
	Paul Morton	1904–05
	Charles J. Bonaparte	1905–06
	Victor H. Metcalf	1906–08
	Truman H. Newberry	1908–09
Secretary of Interior	Ethan A. Hitchcock	1901–07
	James R. Garfield	1907–09
Secretary of Agriculture	James Wilson	1901–09
Secretary of Labor and Commerce	George B. Cortelyou	1903–04
	Victor H. Metcalf	1904–06
	Oscar S. Straus	1906–09
	Charles Nagel	1909

Taft Administration (1909–13)

Secretary of State	Philander C. Knox	1909–13
Secretary of Treasury	Franklin MacVeagh	1909–13
Secretary of War	Jacob M. Dickinson	1909–11
	Henry L. Stimson	1911–13
Attorney General	George W. Wickersham	1909–13
Postmaster General	Frank H. Hitchcock	1909–13
Secretary of Navy	George von L. Meyer	1909–13
Secretary of Interior	Richard A. Ballinger	1909–11
	Walter Fisher	1911–13

Secretary of Agriculture	James Wilson	1909–13
Secretary of Labor and Commerce	Charles Nagel	1909–13

Wilson Administration (1913–21)

Secretary of State	William J. Bryan	1913–15
	Robert Lansing	1915–20
	Bainbridge Colby	1920–21
Secretary of Treasury	William G. McAdoo	1913–18
	Carter Glass	1918–20
	David F. Houston	1920–21
Secretary of War	Lindley M. Garrison	1913–16
	Newton D. Baker	1916–21
Attorney General	James C. McReynolds	1913–14
	Thomas W. Gregory	1914–19
	A. Mitchell Palmer	1919–21
Postmaster General	Albert S. Burleson	1913–21
Secretary of Navy	Josephus Daniels	1913–21
Secretary of Interior	Franklin K. Lane	1913–20
	John B. Payne	1920–21
Secretary of Agriculture	David F. Houston	1913–20
	Edwin T. Meredith	1920–21
Secretary of Commerce	William C. Redfield	1913–19
Secretary of Labor	William B. Wilson	1913–21

Harding Administration (1921–23)

Secretary of State	Charles E. Hughes	1921–23
Secretary of Treasury	Andrew Mellon	1921–23
Secretary of War	John W. Weeks	1921–23
Attorney General	Harry M. Daugherty	1921–23
Postmaster General	Will H. Hays	1921–22
	Hubert Work	1922–23
	Harry S. New	1923
Secretary of Navy	Edwin Denby	1921–23
Secretary of Interior	Albert B. Fall	1921–23
	Hubert Work	1923
Secretary of Agriculture	Henry C. Wallace	1921–23
Secretary of Commerce	Herbert C. Hoover	1921–23
Secretary of Labor	James J. Davis	1921–23

Coolidge Administration (1923–29)

Secretary of State	Charles E. Hughes	1923–25
	Frank B. Kellogg	1925–29
Secretary of Treasury	Andrew W. Mellon	1923–29
Secretary of War	John W. Weeks	1923–25
	Dwight F. Davis	1925–29
Attorney General	Henry M. Daugherty	1923–24
	Harlan F. Stone	1923–25
	John G. Sargent	1925–29
Postmaster General	Harry S. New	1923–29
Secretary of Navy	Edwin Denby	1923–24
	Curtis D. Wilbur	1924–29
Secretary of Interior	Hubert Work	1923–28
	Roy O. West	1928–29
Secretary of Agriculture	Henry C. Wallace	1923–24
	Howard M. Gore	1924–25
	William M. Jardine	1925–29
Secretary of Commerce	Herbert C. Hoover	1923–28
	William F. Whiting	1928–29
Secretary of Labor	James J. Davis	1923–29

Hoover Administration (1929–33)

Secretary of State	Henry L. Stimson	1929–33
Secretary of Treasury	Andrew Mellon	1929–32
	Ogden L. Mills	1932–33
Secretary of War	James W. Good	1929
	Patrick J. Hurley	1929–33
Attorney General	William D. Mitchell	1929–33
Postmaster General	Walter F. Brown	1929–33
Secretary of Navy	Charles F. Adams	1929–33
Secretary of Interior	Ray L. Wilbur	1929–33
Secretary of Agriculture	Arthur M. Hyde	1929–33
Secretary of Commerce	Robert P. Lamont	1929–32

	Roy D. Chapin	1932–33
Secretary of Labor	James J. Davis	1929–30
	William N. Doak	1930–33

Franklin D. Roosevelt Administration (1933–45)

Secretary of State	Cordell Hull	1933–44
	Edward R. Stettinius, Jr.	1944–45
Secretary of Treasury	William H. Woodin	1933–34
	Henry Morgenthau, Jr.	1934–45
Secretary of War	George H. Dern	1933–36
	Henry A. Woodring	1936–40
	Henry L. Stimson	1940–45
Attorney General	Homer S. Cummings	1933–39
	Frank Murphy	1939–40
	Robert H. Jackson	1940–41
	Francis Biddle	1941–45
Postmaster General	James A. Farley	1933–40
	Frank C. Walker	1940–45
Secretary of Navy	Claude A. Swanson	1933–40
	Charles Edison	1940
	Frank Knox	1940–44
	James V. Forrestal	1944–45
Secretary of Interior	Harold L. Ickes	1933–45
Secretary of Agriculture	Henry A. Wallace	1933–40
	Claude R. Wickard	1940–45
Secretary of Commerce	Daniel C. Roper	1933–39
	Harry L. Hopkins	1939–40
	Jesse Jones	1940–45
	Henry A. Wallace	1945
Secretary of Labor	Frances Perkins	1933–45

Truman Administration (1945–53)

Secretary of State	Edward R. Stettinius, Jr.	1945
	James F. Byrnes	1945–47
	George C. Marshall	1947–49
	Dean G. Acheson	1949–53
Secretary of Treasury	Fred M. Vinson	1945–46
	John W. Snyder	1946–53
Secretary of War	Robert P. Patterson	1945–47
	Kenneth C. Royall	1947
Attorney General	Tom C. Clark	1945–49
	J. Howard McGrath	1949–52
	James P. McGranery	1952–53
Postmaster General	Frank C. Walker	1945
	Robert E. Hannegan	1945–47
	Jesse M. Donaldson	1947–53
Secretary of Navy	James V. Forrestal	1945–47
Secretary of Interior	Harold L. Ickes	1945–46
	Julius A. Krug	1946–49
	Oscar L. Chapman	1949–53
Secretary of Agriculture	Clinton P. Anderson	1945–48
	Charles F. Brannan	1948–53
Secretary of Commerce	Henry A. Wallace	1945–46
	W. Averell Harriman	1946–48
	Charles W. Sawyer	1948–53
Secretary of Labor	Lewis B. Schwellenbach	1945–48
	Maurice J. Tobin	1948–53
Secretary of Defense	James V. Forrestal	1947–49
	Louis A. Johnson	1949–50
	George C. Marshall	1950–51
	Robert A. Lovett	1951–53

Eisenhower Administration (1953–61)

Secretary of State	John Foster Dulles	1953–59
	Christian A. Herter	1959–61
Secretary of Treasury	George M. Humphrey	1953–57
	Robert B. Anderson	1957–61
Attorney General	Herbert Brownell, Jr.	1953–58
	William P. Rogers	1958–61
Postmaster General	Arthur E. Summerfield	1953–61
Secretary of Interior	Douglas McKay	1953–56
	Fred A. Seaton	1956–61
Secretary of Agriculture	Ezra T. Benson	1953–61
Secretary of Commerce	Sinclair Weeks	1953–58
	Lewis L. Strauss	1958–59

	Frederick H. Mueller	1959–61
Secretary of Labor	Martin P. Durkin	1953
	James P. Mitchell	1953–61
Secretary of Defense	Charles E. Wilson	1953–57
	Neil H. McElroy	1957–59
	Thomas S. Gates, Jr.	1959–61
Secretary of Health, Education, and Welfare	Oveta Culp Hobby	1953–55
	Marion B. Folsom	1955–58
	Arthur S. Flemming	1958–61

Kennedy Administration (1961–63)

Secretary of State	Dean Rusk	1961–63
Secretary of Treasury	C. Douglas Dillon	1961–63
Attorney General	Robert F. Kennedy	1961–63
Postmaster General	J. Edward Day	1961–63
	John A. Gronouski	1963
Secretary of Interior	Stewart L. Udall	1961–63
Secretary of Agriculture	Orville L. Freeman	1961–63
Secretary of Commerce	Luther H. Hodges	1961–63
Secretary of Labor	Arthur J. Goldberg	1961–62
	W. Willard Wirtz	1962–63
Secretary of Defense	Robert S. McNamara	1961–63
Secretary of Health, Education, and Welfare	Abraham A. Ribicoff	1961–62
	Anthony J. Celebrezze	1962–63

Lyndon Johnson Administration (1963–69)

Secretary of State	Dean Rusk	1963–69
Secretary of Treasury	C. Douglas Dillon	1963–65
	Henry H. Fowler	1965–69
Attorney General	Robert F. Kennedy	1963–64
	Nicholas Katzenbach	1965–66
	Ramsey Clark	1967–69
Postmaster General	John A. Gronouski	1963–65
	Lawrence F. O'Brien	1965–68
	Marvin Watson	1968–69
Secretary of Interior	Stewart L. Udall	1963–69
Secretary of Agriculture	Orville L. Freeman	1963–69
Secretary of Commerce	Luther H. Hodges	1963–64
	John T. Connor	1964–67
	Alexander B. Trowbridge	1967–68
	Cyrus R. Smith	1968–69
Secretary of Labor	W. Willard Wirtz	1963–69
Secretary of Defense	Robert F. McNamara	1963–68
	Clark Clifford	1968–69
Secretary of Health, Education, and Welfare	Anthony J. Celebrezze	1963–65
	John W. Gardner	1965–68
	Wilbur J. Cohen	1968–69
Secretary of Housing & Urban Development	Robert C. Weaver	1966–69
	Robert C. Wood	1969
Secretary of Transportation	Alan S. Boyd	1967–69

Nixon Administration (1969–74)

Secretary of State	William P. Rogers	1969–73
	Henry A. Kissinger	1973–74
Secretary of Treasury	David M. Kennedy	1969–70
	John B. Connally	1971–72
	George P. Shultz	1972–74
	William E. Simon	1974
Attorney General	John N. Mitchell	1969–72
	Richard G. Kleindienst	1973–73
	Elliot L. Richardson	1973
	William B. Saxbe	1973–74
Postmaster General	Winton M. Blount	1969–71
Secretary of Interior	Walter J. Hickel	1969–70
	Rogers Morton	1971–74
Secretary of Agriculture	Clifford M. Hardin	1969–71
	Earl L. Butz	1971–74
Secretary of Commerce	Maurice H. Stans	1969–72
	Peter G. Peterson	1972–73
	Frederick B. Dent	1973–74
Secretary of Labor	George P. Shultz	1969–70
	James D. Hodgson	1970–73
	Peter J. Brennan	1973–74
Secretary of Defense	Melvin R. Laird	1969–73
	Elliot L. Richardson	1973

	James R. Schlesinger	1973–74
Secretary of Health, Education, and Welfare	Robert H. Finch	1969–70
	Elliot L. Richardson	1970–73
	Caspar W. Weinberger	1973–74
Secretary of Housing & Urban Development	George Romney	1969–73
	James T. Lyon	1973–74
Secretary of Transportation	John A. Volpe	1969–73
	Claude S. Brinegar	1973–74

Ford Administration (1974–77)

Secretary of State	Henry A. Kissinger	1974–77
Secretary of Treasury	William E. Simon	1974–77
Attorney General	William Saxbe	1974–75
	Edward Levi	1975–77
Secretary of Interior	Rogers Morton	1974–75
	Stanley K. Hathaway	1975
	Thomas Kleppe	1975–77
Secretary of Agriculture	Earl L. Butz	1974–76
	John A. Knebel	1976–77
Secretary of Commerce	Frederick B. Dent	1974–75
	Rogers Morton	1975–76
	Elliot L. Richardson	1976–77
Secretary of Labor	Peter J. Brennan	1974–75
	John T. Dunlop	1975–76
	W. J. Usery	1976–77
Secretary of Defense	James R. Schlesinger	1974–75
	Donald Rumsfeld	1975–77
Secretary of Health, Education, and Welfare	Caspar Weinberger	1974–75
	Forrest D. Mathews	1975–77
Secretary of Housing & Urban Development	James T. Lynn	1974–75
	Carla A. Hills	1975–77
Secretary of Transportation	William T. Coleman	1975–77

Carter Administration (1977–81)

Secretary of State	Cyrus R. Vance	1977–80
	Edmund Muskie	1980–81
Secretary of Treasury	W. Michael Blumenthal	1977–79
	G. William Miller	1979–81
Attorney General	Griffin Bell	1977–79
	Benjamin R. Civiletti	1979–81
Secretary of Interior	Cecil D. Andrus	1977–81
Secretary of Agriculture	Robert Bergland	1977–81
Secretary of Commerce	Juanita M. Kreps	1977–79
	Philip M. Klutznick	1979–81
Secretary of Labor	F. Ray Marshall	1977–81
Secretary of Defense	Harold Brown	1977–81
Secretary of Health, Education, and Welfare	Joseph A. Califano	1977–81
	Patricia R. Harris	1979–80
Secretary of Health & Human Services[1]	Patricia R. Harris	1980–81
Secretary of Housing & Urban Development	Patricia R. Harris	1977–79
	Moon Landrieu	1979–81
Secretary of Transportation	Brock Adams	1977–79
	Neil E. Goldschmidt	1979–81
Secretary of Energy	James R. Schlesinger	1977–79
	Charles W. Duncan	1979–81
Secretary of Education[1]	Shirley M. Hufstedler	1980–81

1. The Dept. of Health, Education, and Welfare was split into the Dept. of Education and the Dept. of Health and Human Services on May 4, 1980.

Reagan Administration (1981–89)

Secretary of State	Alexander M. Haig	1981–82
	George P. Shultz	1982–89
Secretary of Treasury	Donald Regan	1981–85
	James A. Baker, III	1985–89
Secretary of Defense	Caspar Weinberger	1981–87
	Frank Carlucci	1987–89
Attorney General	William F. Smith	1981–85
	Edwin A. Meese, III	1985–88
	Richard L. Thornburgh	1988–89
Secretary of Interior	James Watt	1981–83

	William P. Clark, Jr.	1983–85
	Donald P. Hodel	1985–89
Secretary of Agriculture	John Block	1981–86
	Richard E. Lyng	1986–89
Secretary of Commerce	Malcolm Baldrige	1981–87
	C. William Verity Jr	1987-89
Secretary of Labor	Raymond Donovan	1981–85
	William E. Brock	1985–89
Secretary of Health & Human Services	Richard Schweiker	1981–83
	Margaret Heckler	1983–85
	Otis R. Bowen	1985–89
Secretary of Housing & Urban Development	Samuel Pierce	1981–89
Secretary of Transportation	Drew Lewis	1981–83
	Elizabeth Dole	1983–89
Secretary of Energy	James Edwards	1981–82
	Donald P. Hodel	1982–85
	John S. Herrington	1985–89
Secretary of Education	Terrel H. Bell	1981–85
	William J. Bennett	1985–89

George Bush Administration (1989–93)

Secretary of State	James A. Baker III	1989–92
	Lawrence Eagleburger	1992–93
Secretary of Treasury	Nicholas F. Brady	1989–93
Secretary of Defense	Dick Cheney	1989–93
Attorney General	Richard L. Thornburgh	1989–91
	William P. Barr	1991–93
Secretary of Interior	Manuel Lujan	1989–93
Secretary of Agriculture	Clayton K. Yeutter	1989–91
	Edward Madigan	1991–93
Secretary of Commerce	Robert A. Mosbacher	1989–91
	Barbara Franklin	1991–93
Secretary of Labor	Elizabeth Hanford Dole	1989–90
	Lynn Martin	1990–93
Secretary of Health & Human Services	Louis Sullivan	1989–93
Secretary of Housing & Urban Development	Jack F. Kemp	1989–93
Secretary of Transportation	Samuel K. Skinner	1989–91
	Andrew Card	1991–93
Secretary of Energy	James D. Watkins	1989–93
Secretary of Education	Lauro D. Cavazos	1989–90
	Lamar Alexander	1990–93
Secretary of Veterans' Affairs	Edward J. Derwinski	1989–92
	Anthony J. Principi	1992–93

Clinton Administration (1993–2001)

Secretary of State	Warren M. Christopher	1993–97
	Madeleine K. Albright	1997–2001
Secretary of Treasury	Lloyd Bentsen	1993–94
	Robert E. Rubin	1994–99
	Lawrence H. Summers	1999–2001
Secretary of Defense	Les Aspin	1993–94
	William Perry	1994–97
	William S. Cohen	1997–2001
Attorney General	Janet Reno	1993–2001
Secretary of Interior	Bruce Babbitt	1993–2001
Secretary of Agriculture	Mike Espy	1993–94
	Dan Glickman	1995–2001
Secretary of Commerce	Ronald H. Brown	1993–96
	Mickey Kantor	1996–97
	William M. Daley	1997–2000
	Norman Y. Mineta	2000–2001
Secretary of Labor	Robert B. Reich	1993–97
	Alexis M. Herman	1997–2001
Secretary of Health & Human Services	Donna E. Shalala	1993–2001
Secretary of Housing & Urban Development	Henry G. Cisneros	1993–97
	Andrew M. Cuomo	1997–2001
Secretary of Transportation	Federico F. Peña	1993–97
	Rodney E. Slater	1997–2001
Secretary of Energy	Hazel O'Leary	1993–97
	Federico F. Peña	1997–98
	Bill Richardson	1998–2001
Secretary of Education	Richard W. Riley	1993–2001

Secretary of Veterans' Affairs	Jesse Brown	1993–97
	Hershel Gober, acting	1997–98
	Togo D. West Jr.	1998–99
	Hershel Gober, acting	1999–2001

George W. Bush Administration (2001–2009)

Secretary of State	Colin Powell	2001–05
	Condoleezza Rice	2005–09
Secretary of Treasury	Paul O'Neill	2001–02
	John Snow	2003-06
	Henry M. Paulson, Jr.	2006–09
Secretary of Defense	Donald Rumsfeld	2001-06
	Robert M. Gates	2006–09
Attorney General	John Ashcroft	2001–05
	Alberto Gonzales	2005-07
	Michael Mukasey	2007–09
Secretary of Interior	Gale Norton	2001–06
	Dirk Kempthorne	2006–09
Secretary of Agriculture	Ann Veneman	2001–05
	Michael Johanns	2005–07
	Ed Schafer	2008–09
Secretary of Commerce	Donald Evans	2001–05
	Carlos Gutierrez	2005–09
Secretary of Labor	Elaine Chao	2001–09
Secretary of Health & Human Services	Tommy Thompson	2001–05
	Michael Leavitt	2005–09
Secretary of Housing & Urban Development	Mel Martinez	2001–04
	Alphonso Jackson	2004–08
	Steve Preston	2008–09
Secretary of Transportation	Norman Mineta	2001–06
	Mary Peters	2006–09

Secretary of Energy	Spencer Abraham	2001–05
	Samuel Bodman	2005–09
Secretary of Education	Rod Paige	2001–05
	Margaret Spellings	2005–09
Secretary of Veterans' Affairs	Anthony Principi	2001–05
	Jim Nicholson	2005–07
	James Peake	2007–09
Secretary of Homeland Security	Tom Ridge	2002–05
	Michael Chertoff	2005–09

Obama Administration (2009–)

Secretary of State	Hillary Rodham Clinton	2009–
Secretary of the Treasury	Timothy F. Geithner	2009–
Secretary of Defense	Robert M. Gates	2009–
Attorney General	Eric H. Holder Jr.	2009–
Secretary of Interior	Kenneth L. Salazar	2009–
Secretary of Agriculture	Thomas J. Vilsack	2009–
Secretary of Commerce	Gary F. Locke	2009–
Secretary of Labor	Hilda L. Solis	2009–
Secretary of Health & Human Services	Kathleen Sebelius	2009–
Secretary of Housing & Urban Development	Shaun L.S. Donovan	2009–
Secretary of Transportation	Raymond L. LaHood	2009–
Secretary of Energy	Steven Chu	2009–
Secretary of Education	Arne Duncan	2009–
Secretary of Veterans Affairs	Eric K. Shinseki	2009–
Secretary of Homeland Security	Janet A. Napolitano	2009–

THE U.S. SUPREME COURT

▶IMPORTANT SUPREME COURT DECISIONS

Marbury v. Madison (1803) The Court struck down a law "repugnant to the constitution" for the first time and set the precedent for judicial review of acts of Congress. In a politically ingenious ruling on the Judiciary Act of 1789, Chief Justice John Marshall asserted the Supreme Court's power "to say what the law is," while avoiding a confrontation with President Thomas Jefferson. Not until the *Dred Scott* case of 1857 would another Federal law be ruled unconstitutional.

Fletcher v. Peck (1810) The Court ruled that Georgia could not deprive land speculators of their title, even though the previous owners had obtained the land from the state through fraud and bribery. Arising from the infamous Yazoo land frauds of 1795, this decision followed the Constitution's obligation of contracts clause and was the first time the Court invalidated a state law.

Dartmouth College v. Woodward (1819) The Court encouraged business investment with this decision by treating corporate charters as fully protected contracts. Not even the state legislatures that originally granted them could tamper with charters to private corporations, unless they retained the power to do so. Dartmouth College remained a private institution despite New Hampshire's attempt to take it over. This decision, which opened the way for abuse of corporate privileges, would later be modified in the *Charles River Bridge* (1837) and *Munn v. Illinois* (1877) cases.

McCulloch v. Maryland (1819) "Broad," as opposed to "strict," construction of the Constitution received high court approval in Chief Justice John Marshall's opinion upholding the constitutionality of the national bank against a Maryland challenge. This ruling enhanced Federal governmental authority by liberally interpreting the power of Congress to make laws "nec-essary and proper" for its specified powers. At a time when states were trying to tax the Bank of the United States out of existence, this decision also forbade such state interference with the Federal government. "The power to tax," Marshall wrote, "involves the power to destroy."

Cohens v. Virginia (1821) With this ruling, the Court reiterated its power to hear appeals from state courts, and affirmed the national supremacy of Federal judicial power. Virginia's conviction of the Cohens for selling lottery tickets in violation of state law was upheld, but so too was the Cohens' right to appeal to the Court, which Virginia had challenged. Critics of judicial "consolidationism" were reminded of the Court's comprehensive powers as the ultimate appellate court for all Americans.

Gibbons v. Ogden (1824) In a dispute arising from a New York ferry monopoly, the Court ruled that states could not restrain interstate commerce in any way, and that congressional power to regulate interstate commerce "does not stop at the jurisdictional lines of the several states." The decision helped prevent interstate trade wars, quite common under the Articles of Confederation, from breaking out under the Constitution. Chief Justice Marshall's opinion also confirmed the broad potential power of the Constitution's commerce clause.

Charles River Bridge v. Warren Bridge (1837) A key decision for economic development, this case arose when state-chartered proprietors of a Boston toll bridge objected that a new state-chartered bridge across the Charles River would put them out of business. Chief Justice Roger B. Taney, in his first constitutional ruling, held that state charters implied no vested rights and that ambiguities must be construed in favor of the public, which would benefit from the new toll-free bridge. This decision balanced private property rights against the public welfare.

Dred Scott v. Sanford (1857) Dred Scott, a Missouri slave, sued for his liberty after his owner took him into free territory. The Court ruled that Congress could not bar slavery in the territories. Scott remained a slave because the Missouri Compromise of 1820, prohibiting slavery from part of the Louisiana Purchase, violated the Fifth Amendment by depriving slave owners of their right to enjoy property without due process of law. Scott himself could not even sue, for he was held to be property, not a citizen. This decision sharpened sectional conflict by sweeping away legal barriers to the expansion of slavery.

Ex Parte Milligan (1866) President Abraham Lincoln's suspension of some civil liberties during the Civil War was attacked in this decision, which upheld the right of *habeas corpus*. The Court ruled that the president could not hold military tribunals in areas remote from battle and where civil courts were open and functioning. Milligan's conviction by such a Civil War tribunal in Indianapolis, was overturned. The Constitution, admonished the Court, applies "at all times, and under all circumstances."

Slaughter-House Cases (1873) In its first ruling on the Fourteenth Amendment, the Court held that Louisiana's grant of a butcher monopoly did not violate the privileges and immunities of competitors, nor deny them equal protection of the laws, nor deprive them of property without due process. Only a few rights deriving from "Federal citizenship" were subject to Federal protection, while states still protected most civil and property rights. Federal protection of civil rights, even for former slaves, was very narrowly interpreted in this ruling. But this decision broadly upheld business regulation by states until *Santa Clara Co. v. Southern Pacific Railroad Co.* (1886) applied the Fourteenth Amendment to defense of corporate property rights.

Munn v. Illinois (1877) This decision, in one of the "Granger Cases," enabled states to regulate private property in the public interest when the public had an interest in that property. The Court held that Illinois laws setting maximum rates for grain storage did not violate the Fourteenth Amendment's ban on deprivation of property without due process of law, and did not restrain interstate commerce. But for the next half century, the Court imposed the burden of proof on the states for their regulatory laws.

Civil Rights Cases (1883) Racial equality was postponed 80 years by this decision, which struck down the Civil Rights Act of 1875 and allowed for private segregation. The Fourteenth Amendment's guarantee of equal protection, the Court ruled, applied against state action—but not against private individuals, whose discrimination unaided by the states was beyond Federal control. Segregation of public facilities was approved soon afterward in *Plessy v. Ferguson* (1896).

United States v. E.C. Knight Co. (1895) The first ruling on the Sherman Antitrust Act of 1890, this decision curtailed Federal regulation of monopolies by placing national manufacturers beyond the reach of the Constitution's commerce clause. Only the actual interstate commerce of monopolies, not their production activities, was subject to Federal control. The Court's distinction between production and commerce impeded Federal regulation of manufacturing until *National Labor Relations Board v. Jones & Laughlin Steel Corp.* (1937).

Plessy v. Ferguson (1896) The "separate but equal" doctrine supporting public segregation by law received the Court's approval in this ruling, which originated with segregated railroad cars in Louisiana. The Court held that as long as equal accommodations were provided, segregation was not discrimination and did not deprive blacks of equal protection of the laws under the Fourteenth Amendment. This decision was overturned in *Brown v. Board of Education* (1954).

Lochner v. New York (1905) This decision struck down a New York law placing limits on maximum

working hours for bakers. The law violated the Fourteenth Amendment by restricting individual "freedom of contract" to buy and sell labor, and was an excessive use of state police power, the Court held. The ruling was soon modified in *Muller v. Oregon* (1908), which approved state-regulated limits on women's labor after the Court used sociological and economic data to consider the health and morals of women workers.

Standard Oil Co. of New Jersey v. United States (1911) Federal efforts to break up monopolies under the Sherman Antitrust Act had to follow the "rule of reason," according to this ruling. Only those combinations in restraint of trade which were contrary to the public interest, and therefore unreasonable, were illegal. Although the Taft administration's prosecution of Standard Oil was upheld, breaking up one of the nation's leading monopolies, further antitrust suits were impaired by this decision, which facilitated the 1920s merger movement.

Schenk v. United States (1919) The Court unanimously held that World War I limits on freedom of speech did not violate the First Amendment—if the speech in question represented a "clear and present danger." That famous doctrine of Justice Oliver Wendell Holmes, which approved the arrest of a draft resister for handing out pamphlets to soldiers in wartime, became an important standard for interpreting the First Amendment. But in subsequent cases of this period, the Court added that the mere "bad tendency" of speech to cause danger could be grounds for censorship.

Schechter Poultry Corp. v. United States (1935) At the height of its assault on the New Deal, the Court struck down the National Industrial Recovery Act in the famous "Sick Chicken Case." The NIRA was found to delegate excessive legislative regulatory powers to the executive without constitutional authority, and to regulate commerce within states in violation of the commerce clause. Schechter's kosher chicken supply house in New York did not have to abide by the NIRA's rigid industry codes, the Court ruled.

National Labor Relations Board v. Jones & Laughlin Steel Corp. (1937) Under pressure from the public and President Franklin D. Roosevelt, the Court abruptly reversed itself and began approving New Deal legislation. In this case, laws protecting unions

Chief Justices of the United States

Chief Justice	Tenure[1]	Appointed by
John Jay	1789–95	George Washington
John Rutledge[3]	1795	George Washington
Oliver Ellsworth	1796–1800	George Washington
John Marshall[4]	1801–35	John Adams
Roger B. Taney	1836–64	Andrew Jackson
Salmon P. Chase	1864–73	Abraham Lincoln
Morrison R. Waite	1874–88	Ulysses S. Grant
Melville W. Fuller	1888–1910	Grover Cleveland
Edward D. White	1910–21	William Howard Taft
William Howard Taft[5]	1921–30	Warren G. Harding
Charles Evans Hughes[2]	1930–41	Herbert Hoover
Harlan F. Stone[2]	1941–46	Franklin D. Roosevelt
Fred M. Vinson	1946–53	Harry S Truman
Earl Warren	1953–69	Dwight D. Eisenhower
Warren E. Burger	1969–86	Richard M. Nixon
William H. Rehnquist[2]	1986–2005	Ronald Reagan
John G. Roberts, Jr.	2005–	George W. Bush

Notes: 1. Dates are for tenure as Chief Justice. For complete tenure on Supreme Court, see "Supreme Court Justices." 2. Served as Associate Justice prior to appointment as Chief Justice. 3. Served one term, but appointment not confirmed by Senate. 4. Longest tenure as Chief Justice. 5. Formerly served as 27th president of the United States.

Justices of the Supreme Court of the United States, 1789–2010

Name	Tenure	Appointed by	Name	Tenure	Appointed by
Alito, Samuel A., Jr.	2006–	George W. Bush	Livingston, H. Brockholst	1806–23	Thomas Jefferson
Baldwin, Henry	1830–44	Andrew Jackson	Lurton, Horace H.	1910–14	William Howard Taft
Barbour, Philip P.	1836–41	Andrew Jackson	Marshall, John[1]	1801–35	John Adams
Black, Hugo L.	1937–71	Franklin D. Roosevelt	Marshall, Thurgood	1967–92	Lyndon B. Johnson
Blackmun, Harry A.	1970–94	Richard M. Nixon	Matthews, Stanley	1881–89	James A. Garfield
Blair, John	1789–96	George Washington	McKenna, Joseph	1898–1925	William McKinley
Blatchford, Samuel	1882–93	Chester A. Arthur	McKinley, John	1837–52	Martin Van Buren
Bradley, Joseph P.	1870–92	Ulysses S. Grant	McLean, John	1829–61	Andrew Jackson
Brandeis, Louis D.	1916–39	Woodrow Wilson	McReynolds, James C.	1914–41	Woodrow Wilson
Brennan, William J., Jr.	1956–90	Dwight D. Eisenhower	Miller, Samuel F.	1862–90	Abraham Lincoln
Brewer, David J.	1889–1910	Benjamin Harrison	Minton, Sherman	1949–56	Harry S Truman
Breyer, Stephen G.	1994–	Bill Clinton	Moody, William H.	1906–10	Theodore Roosevelt
Brown, Henry B.	1890–1906	Benjamin Harrison	Moore, Alfred	1799–1804	John Adams
Burger, Warren E.[1]	1969–87	Richard M. Nixon	Murphy, Frank	1940–49	Franklin D. Roosevelt
Burton, Harold H.	1945–58	Harry S Truman	Nelson, Samuel	1845–72	John Tyler
Butler, Pierce	1922–39	Warren G. Harding	O'Connor, Sandra Day	1981–2005	Ronald Reagan
Byrnes, James F.	1941–42	Franklin D. Roosevelt	Paterson, William	1793–1806	George Washington
Campbell, John A.	1853–61	Franklin Pierce	Peckham, Rufus W.	1895–1910	Grover Cleveland
Cardozo, Benjamin N.	1932–38	Herbert Hoover	Pitney, Mahlon	1912–22	William Howard Taft
Catron, John	1837–65	Martin Van Buren	Powell, Lewis F., Jr.	1972–87	Richard M. Nixon
Chase, Salmon P.[1]	1864–73	Abraham Lincoln	Reed, Stanley F.	1938–57	Franklin D. Roosevelt
Chase, Samuel	1796–1811	George Washington	Rehnquist, William H.[1]	1972–2005	Richard M. Nixon
Clark, Tom C.	1949–67	Harry S Truman	Roberts, John G., Jr.	2005–	George W. Bush
Clarke, John H.	1916–22	Woodrow Wilson	Roberts, Owen J.	1930–45	Herbert Hoover
Clifford, Nathan	1858–81	James J. Buchanan	Rutledge, John[1]	1789–91	George Washington
Curtis, Benjamin R.	1851–57	Millard Fillmore		1795	George Washington
Cushing, William	1789–1810	George Washington	Rutledge, Wiley B.	1943–49	Franklin D. Roosevelt
Daniel, Peter V.	1841–60	Martin Van Buren	Sanford, Edward T.	1923–30	Warren G. Harding
Davis, David	1862–77	Abraham Lincoln	Scalia, Antonin	1986–	Ronald Reagan
Day, William R.	1903–22	Theodore Roosevelt	Shiras, George	1892–1903	Benjamin Harrison
Douglas, William O.[2]	1939–75	Franklin D. Roosevelt	Sotomayor, Sonia	2009–	Barack Obama
Duval, Gabriel	1811–36	James Madison	Souter, David H.	1990–2009	George Bush
Ellsworth, Oliver[1]	1796–1800	George Washington	Stevens, John Paul	1975–2010	Gerald R. Ford
Field, Stephen J.	1863–97	Abraham Lincoln	Stewart, Potter	1959–81	Dwight D. Eisenhower
Fortas, Abe	1965–69	Lyndon B. Johnson	Stone, Harlan F.[1]	1925–46	Calvin Coolidge
Frankfurter, Felix	1939–62	Franklin D. Roosevelt	Story, Joseph	1811–45	James Madison
Fuller, Melville W.[1]	1888–1910	Grover Cleveland	Strong, William	1870–80	Ulysses S. Grant
Ginsburg, Ruth Bader	1993–	Bill Clinton	Sutherland, George	1922–38	Warren G. Harding
Goldberg, Arthur J.	1962–65	John F. Kennedy	Swayne, Noah H.	1862–81	Abraham Lincoln
Gray, Horace	1881–1902	Chester A. Arthur	Taft, William Howard[1,5]	1921–30	Warren G. Harding
Grier, Robert C.	1846–70	James K. Polk	Taney, Roger B.[1]	1836–64	Andrew Jackson
Harlan, John Marshall	1877–1911	Rutherford B. Hayes	Thomas, Clarence	1991–	George Bush
Harlan, John Marshall[3]	1955–71	Dwight D. Eisenhower	Thompson, Smith	1823–43	James Monroe
Harrison, Robert H.	1789–90	George Washington	Todd, Thomas	1807–26	Thomas Jefferson
Holmes, Oliver Wendell	1902–32	Theodore Roosevelt	Trimble, Robert	1826–28	John Quincy Adams
Hughes, Charles Evans[1,4]	1910–16	William Howard Taft	Van Devanter, Willis	1910–37	William Howard Taft
	1930–41	Herbert Hoover	Vinson, Fred M.[1]	1946–53	Harry S Truman
Hunt, Ward	1872–82	Ulysses S. Grant	Waite, Morrison R.[1]	1874–88	Ulysses S. Grant
Iredell, James	1790–99	George Washington	Warren, Earl[1]	1953–69	Dwight D. Eisenhower
Jackson, Howell E.	1893–95	Benjamin Harrison	Washington, Bushrod	1798–1829	John Adams
Jackson, Robert H.	1941–54	Franklin D. Roosevelt	Wayne, James M.	1835–67	Andrew Jackson
Jay, John[1]	1789–95	George Washington	White, Byron R.	1962–93	John F. Kennedy
Johnson, Thomas	1791–93	George Washington	White, Edward D.[1]	1894–1921	Grover Cleveland
Johnson, William	1804–34	Thomas Jefferson	Whittaker, Charles E.	1957–62	Dwight D. Eisenhower
Kagan, Elena	2010–	Barack Obama	Wilson, James	1789–98	George Washington
Kennedy, Anthony M.	1987–	Ronald Reagan	Woodbury, Levi	1845–51	James K. Polk
Lamar, Joseph R.	1911–16	William Howard Taft	Woods, William B.	1880–87	Rutherford B. Hayes
Lamar, Lucius Q. C.	1888–93	Grover Cleveland			

Notes: Dates reflect complete tenure on the Supreme Court, including tenure as Chief Justice. 1. See "Chief Justices of the United States" for dates of tenure and appointment as Chief Justice. 2. Longest-serving justice. 3. The two Harlans were grandfather and grandson. 4. Stepped down as Associate Justice to run for president in 1916; later appointed Chief Justice. 5. Formerly served as 27th U.S. president.

and barring "unfair labor practices" were upheld by the "stream of commerce" doctrine that employers who sold their goods and obtained their raw materials through interstate commerce were subject to Federal regulation. This ruling overturned *U.S. v. E.C. Knight Co.* (1895) and became the basis for the expansive understanding of the commerce power.

West Virginia Board of Education v. Barnette (1943)
The Court reversed its earlier ruling in *Minersville School District v. Gobitis* (1940), which had required Jehovah's Witnesses to salute the flag in school. In this case, also brought against a Jehovah's Witness, the Court recognized that refusing to salute the flag did not violate anyone's rights, and that the First Amendment protected the "right of silence" as well as freedom of speech.

Korematsu v. United States (1944)   President Franklin D. Roosevelt's Executive Order No. 9066, which approved the West Coast evacuation and internment of 120,000 Japanese-Americans during World War II, was upheld on the grounds of "military necessity" in this ruling. The Court was reluctant to interfere with executive authority in time of national emergency. But in *Ex parte Endo* (1944), the Court held that persons of proven loyalty should not be interned. In August 1988, Congress made a formal apology to former internees and appropriated $1.25 billion in compensation for the 60,000 survivors.

Dennis v. United States (1951)   At the height of the postwar "Red Scare," the Court upheld the conviction of 11 American Communist leaders under the Smith Act of 1940, which made it a crime to belong to organizations teaching or advocating the violent overthrow of the government. The "clear and present danger" doctrine could be disregarded, the Court held, if "the gravity of the 'evil,' discounted by its improbability, justifies such invasion of free speech as is necessary to avoid the evil." Over 100 Communists were indicted as a result, effectively destroying the Communist Party as a political force.

Youngstown Sheet and Tube Co. v. Sawyer (1952)
During the Korean War, when President Harry S Truman seized steel plants to keep them operating despite a strike, the Court held that his action was an unconstitutional usurpation of legislative authority. Only an act of Congress, not the president's inherent executive powers or military powers as commander-in-chief, could justify such a sizeable confiscation of property, even in wartime.

Brown v. Board of Education of Topeka (1954)   Chief Justice Earl Warren led the Court unanimously to decide that segregated schools violated the equal protection clause of the Fourteenth Amendment. The "separate but equal" doctrine of *Plessy v. Ferguson* (1896) was overruled after a series of cases dating back to *Missouri ex. rel. Gaines v. Canada* (1938) had already limited it. "Separate educational facilities are inherently unequal," held the Court. Efforts to desegregate southern schools after the *Brown* decision met with massive resistance for many years.

Baker v. Carr (1962)   Overrepresentation of rural districts in state legislatures, which effectively disfranchised millions of voters, led the Court to abandon its traditional non-interference in drawing legislative boundaries. Tennessee citizens deprived of full representation by "arbitrary and capricious" malapportionment were denied equal protection under the Fourteenth Amendment, ruled the Court. All states eventually reapportioned their legislatures in conformance with the "one man, one vote" doctrine of *Reynolds v. Sims* (1964).

Gideon v. Wainwright (1963)   Reversing an earlier ruling in *Betts v. Brady* (1942), the Court held that the Sixth Amendment guaranteed access to qualified counsel, which was "fundamental to a fair trial." Gideon was entitled to a retrial because Florida failed to provide him with an attorney. After this decision,

states were required to furnish public defenders for indigent defendants in felony cases. In *Argersinger v. Hamlin* (1972), the ruling was extended to all cases that might result in imprisonment.

Heart of Atlanta Motel, Inc. v. United States (1964)
The Court upheld Title II of the Civil Rights Act of 1964, outlawing private discrimination in public accommodations, as a legitimate exertion of Federal power over interstate commerce. Congress had "ample power" to forbid racial discrimination in facilities that affected commerce by serving interstate travelers. The Heart of Atlanta Motel was located on two interstate highways, so the Court could sidestep the *Civil Rights Cases* (1883) protection of private discrimination to overrule it.

Griswold v. Connecticut (1965)   In striking down an 1879 Connecticut law against the use of contraceptives, the Court established a "right to privacy" that was implied by, though not specifically enumerated in, the First, Third, Fourth, Fifth, Ninth, and Fourteenth Amendments. The case is most notable for laying the groundwork for other legal challenges invoking this newfound right to privacy. Foremost among them is the 1973 *Roe v. Wade* decision allowing women to choose abortion.

South Carolina v. Katzenbach (1966)   Federal intervention on behalf of voting rights was upheld in this decision. South Carolina sued the Attorney General, contending that the 1965 Voting Rights Act encroached on the reserved powers of the states, treated the states unequally, and violated separation of powers. Chief Justice Warren ruled that the Fifteenth Amendment gave Congress broad powers to "use any rational means to effectuate the constitutional prohibition of racial discrimination in voting." After this decision, blacks registered and voted in massive numbers in the South.

Miranda v. Arizona (1966)   Expanding upon *Gideon v. Wainwright* (1963) and *Escobedo v. Illinois* (1964), the Court set forth stringent interrogation procedures for criminal suspects to protect their Fifth Amendment freedom from self-incrimination. Miranda's confession to kidnapping and rape was obtained without counsel and without his having been advised of his right to silence, so it was ruled inadmissible as evidence. This decision obliged police to advise suspects of their rights upon taking them into custody.

New York Times Co. v. United States (1971)   When the *New York Times* and the *Washington Post* published the top-secret "Pentagon Papers" in 1971, revealing government duplicity in the Vietnam War, the Nixon administration obtained an injunction against the *Times* on grounds of national security. But in a brief *per curiam* opinion, the Court observed that in this case, the government had not met the "heavy burden of showing justification" for "prior restraint" on freedom of the press.

Roe v. Wade (1973)   In a controversial ruling, the Court held that state laws restricting abortion were an unconstitutional invasion of a woman's right to privacy. Only in the last trimester of pregnancy, when the fetus achieved viability outside the womb, might states regulate abortion—except when the life or health of the mother was at stake. In *Planned Parenthood of Central Missouri v. Danforth* (1976), the Court added that wives did not need their husbands' consent to obtain abortions. However, in *Gonzales v. Carhart* (2007), a more conservative Court for the first time upheld a prohibition on a specific form of abortion when it reversed lower court rulings that had found the 2003 federal Partial-Birth Abortion Ban Act to be unconstitutional because it did not provide a broad exception for the health of the mother.

United States v. Nixon (1974)   In a unanimous ruling, the Court held that the secret White House recordings of President Richard M. Nixon's conversations with aides were subject to subpoena in the Watergate coverup trial. Nixon's claim to "executive privilege" was rejected as invalid because military and national security issues were not at stake, and Chief Justice Warren Burger cited *Marbury v. Madison* (1803) to assert the Court's primacy in constitutional issues. Once the tapes were released, documenting Nixon's obstruction of justice, the president resigned to avoid impeachment.

University of California Regents v. Bakke (1978)

Twice refused admission to medical school, Bakke sued the University of California for giving "affirmative action" preference to less-qualified black applicants. In an ambiguous 5–4 ruling, the Court agreed that Bakke's right to equal protection had been denied, that he should be admitted, and that affirmative action quotas should be discarded. But at the same time, the Court recognized race as "a factor" in admissions and hiring decisions. Affirmative action could continue as long as rigid quotas did not constitute, in effect, "reverse discrimination."

Immigration and Naturalization Service v. Chadha (1983)

The legislative veto, contained in hundreds of Federal statutes since 1932, was disallowed in this decision. Congress exceeded its constitutional powers when it blocked the Attorney General's suspension of a deportation order for Jagdish Rai Chadha, a Kenyan student who overstayed his visa. The Court held that the Immigration and Nationality Act's legislative veto provision violated the constitutional separation of powers. Chief Justice Warren Burger recognized that Congress would prefer to delegate authority to the executive branch and reserve the right to veto administrative regulations, but "we have not found a better way to preserve freedom" than the separation of powers.

Bush v. Gore (2000)

For the first time ever, the Court decided a presidential election. With Florida's decisive 25 electoral votes in the balance, Vice Pres. Al Gore filed suit in state court to begin a recount of ballots in several counties where machines were unable to determine the voter's selection. Texas Gov. George W. Bush appealed the decision to the Supreme Court, which ruled that because there were no uniform standards for how to conduct a recount, doing so would violate the Fourteenth Amendment's guarantee of equal protection. The highly controversial 5-4 decision ended the recount 36 days after Election Day, and with it, Gore's chance of winning the presidency.

Lawrence v. Texas (2003)

In overturning a Texas law against sodomy, the Court explicitly reversed *Bowers v. Hardwick* (1986). The majority opinion in Lawrence echoed Justice John Paul Stevens' dissent in *Bowers*, with its broad interpretation of due process rights. "The liberty protected by the Constitution allows homosexual persons the right to choose to enter upon relationships in the confines of their homes and their own private lives." The fact that 12 states repealed sodomy laws after Bowers was further evidence that "Bowers was not correct when it was decided, is not correct today, and is hereby overruled."

Hamdi v. Rumsfeld (2004)

In a case that maintained judicial authority over a wartime executive, the Court ruled that the president could not deny defendants access to American courts simply by labeling them "enemy combatants." Declaring that "a state of war is not a blank check for the president," the Court said the government had deprived Yaser Esam Hamdi, an American citizen seized in Afghanistan, of his due process rights. In two companion cases, the Court ruled that non-citizens seized during military operations could not be held without access to U.S. courts.

Kelo v. City of New London (2005)

This eminent domain case was brought against New London, Connecticut by its residents. The city planned to turn a faded residential neighborhood into a multi-use complex, but the owners of 15 of the houses scheduled for demolition rejected the city's compensation offer and filed suit. Taking private property for "public use" traditionally referred to highway projects and utility right-of-ways, but the Court ruled that "public use" should be understood as "public purpose," and that the city's plan for economic rejuvenation fell under that heading. The 5–4 decision upholding the plan was met with strenuous objections from politicians and the public.

Hamdan v. Rumsfeld (2006)

In a 5-3 decision, the Court blocked President Bush's plan to try Guantanamo Bay detainees before the military commission he established without Congressional approval in 2001. Salim Ahmed Hamdan, a Yemini detainee captured in Afghanistan in 2001, brought to Guantanamo in 2002, and charged with conspiracy to commit terrorism in 2004, would have been the first tried before the commission. The Court ruled that the commission's procedures violated the Uniform Code of Military Justice and the Geneva Conventions by permitting a defendant to be barred from his trial and denied access to evidence presented against him.

Massachusetts v. Environmental Protection Agency (2007)

Twelve states, two cities and several interest groups filed suit against the Environmental Protection Agency (E.P.A.) in an attempt to force the agency to regulate carbon dioxide emissions, which the Bush Administration had declined to do, citing a lack of regulatory authority. This 5–4 decision found that the Clean Air Act gives the agency that authority and obligation and the court ordered the E.P.A. to either implement such regulations or justify its refusal to do so. The most significant aspect of the decision may be the court's conclusion that sovereign states have "standing to sue" the federal government.

Parents Involved in Community Schools v. Seattle School District No. 1 (2007)

Combining two affirmative action cases, the court invalidated school integration plans adopted by Seattle and Louisville, Ky. school systems, finding that they violated the 14th Amendment guarantee of equal protection. While the plans differed, both were similar to those in hundreds of school districts around the country that seek to maintain school diversity by using race as a deciding factor in granting school assignment or transfer requests. Although the minority found that such plans were consistent with *Brown v. Board of Education*, Chief Justice Roberts, writing for the 5–4 majority, said, "The way to stop discrimination on the basis of race is to stop discriminating on the basis of race."

Boumediene v. Bush (2008)

In 2004, the Court ruled (*Rasul v. Bush*) that foreign detainees who were being held without charges outside U.S. territory were entitled to challenge their detentions through habeas corpus. Lakhdar Boumediene, an Algerian held since 2001 on suspicion of planning an attack on the U.S. embassy in Bosnia, and 36 other Guantanamo Bay detainees then filed a joint habeas corpus petition. But, in 2005, Congress passed the Detainee Treatment Act, which stripped federal courts of the power to hear such cases, and instead gave the D.C. Court of Appeals sole jurisdiction to review decisions of the military tribunals overseeing such detainees. In a 5–4 decision that brought strong words from the minority and politicians, the court majority declared these provisions unconstitutional, holding that habeas corpus does apply to aliens imprisoned at Guantanamo and that a military tribunal with only a limited appeal is not an adequate substitution for a writ in a federal court.

Citizens United v. Federal Election Commission (2010)

In a 5–4 decision, the Court ruled that the federal government may not limit political spending by corporations and unions in elections. While the majority held that the decision upheld the First Amendment freedom of speech clause, the dissenters warned that corporate money would corrupt the political process. The decision overturned two recent decisions that restricted corporate and union election spending.

The Federal Government

To ensure a system of "checks and balances" in the federal government, the Founding Fathers divided power into three distinct branches: the legislative, the judicial, and the executive. They set down the purpose, organization, and workings of these branches in the Constitution and, beneath the large bureaucracy that has developed since 1787, that structure remains essentially unchanged. Generally, Congress makes laws, imposes taxes and pays debts, can declare war, and regulates the government, military, commerce, and immigration. The President commands the military, oversees federal executive agencies, makes foreign treaties, and appoints ambassadors, judges, and other officials. The judiciary rules on the application of the Constitution and the laws and treaties of the United States, and on controversies involving at least one state and another entity.

The following list describes the major bodies within the Federal Government, including contact information. (The primary source of this information is the National Archives and Records Administration *U.S. Government Manual*.)

THE JUDICIAL BRANCH

►THE SUPREME COURT
United States Supreme Court Building, 1 First St. NE, Washington, D.C. 20543. (202) 479-3000. *www.supremecourtus.gov.* Created by the Judiciary Act of September 24, 1789 in accordance with Article III, section 1 of the Constitution. Composed of the chief justice and a number of associate justices to be fixed by Congress. Justices are chosen by the president with the advice and consent of the Senate and have lifetime tenure. Court terms begin the first Monday of October and end on the preceding day of the following year. Approximately 8,000 cases are filed with the Court each term, but it hears only a small fraction of these cases.

►LOWER COURTS
U.S. Courts of Appeals
These intermediate appellate courts were created by an act on March 3, 1891, to relieve the Supreme Court of having to reconsider all trials originally decided by federal courts. Decisions of these courts are final except when law provides for direct review by the Supreme Court. Every U.S. state, territory, and district is assigned to one of 11 appellate court circuits. The Federal Appellate Court has nationwide jurisdiction defined by subject matter.

District of Columbia Circuit: Washington, D.C.
First Circuit: Maine, Massachusetts, New Hampshire, Rhode Island, Puerto Rico
Second Circuit: Connecticut, New York, Vermont
Third Circuit: Delaware, New Jersey, Pennsylvania, Virgin Islands

The Supreme Court, 2010–11

Name	Appointed by	Born	Law school
John G. Roberts, Jr. Chief Justice	Bush, 2005	1955	Harvard
Antonin Scalia	Reagan, 1986	1936	Harvard
Anthony M. Kennedy	Reagan, 1987	1936	Harvard
Clarence Thomas	Bush, 1991	1948	Yale
Ruth Bader Ginsburg	Clinton, 1993	1933	Columbia
Stephen G. Breyer	Clinton, 1994	1938	Harvard
Samuel A. Alito, Jr.	Bush, 2006	1950	Yale
Sonia Sotomayor	Obama, 2009	1954	Yale
Elena Kagan[1]	Obama, 2010	1960	Harvard

Note: 1. Justice John Paul Stevens retired effective summer 2010. Justice Kagan was sworn in for the fall 2010 term.

Cases Before U.S. Supreme Court, U.S. Courts of Appeals, and U.S. District Courts, 1970–2009

Status	1970	1980	1990	1995	2000	2005	2009
U.S. Supreme Court							
Total cases on docket	4,212	5,144	6,316	7,565	8,445	8,588	8,966
Cases argued	151	154	125	90	83	87	87
Number of signed opinions	109	123	112	75	79	85	83
U.S. Courts of Appeals							
Cases commenced	11,662	23,200	40,898	49,671	54,967	68,473	57,740
Cases terminated	10,699	20,887	38,520	50,085	56,512	61,975	60,508
Cases disposed of[1]	6,139	10,607	21,006	28,187	27,516	29,913	30,160
Median months to final disposition[2]	8.2	8.9	10.1	10.5	11.6	11.8	12.2
U.S. District Courts							
Civil cases commenced[3]	87,300	168,800	217,900	239,013	259,517	253,273	276,397
Trials[3, 4]	8,000	10,100	9,200	7,700	5,780	5,294	5,309
Percent reaching trial	10.0%	6.5%	4.3%	3.4%	2.2%	2.0%	1.9%
Criminal cases commenced[3,5]	38,100	28,000	46,500	44,200	62,745	69,575	76,655
Defendants disposed of	36,400	36,600	56,500	55,300	75,071	86,000	95,206
Not convicted	8,200	8,000	9,800	9,000	8,035	8,661	8,892
Convicted	28,200	28,600	46,700	46,300	67,036	73,616	86,314

Notes: Data are for the 12 months ending on September 30 of year shown, except Supreme Court 2009, as of year ending Dec. 2008. 1. Terminated on the merits after hearing or submission. Data prior to 1980 not comparable due to change in criteria. 2. Prior to 1985, measured from filing of complete record to final disposition; beginning 1985, measured from filing notice of appeal to final disposition. 3. Figures rounded in source. 4. A trial is defined as a contested proceeding (other than a hearing on a motion) before either court or jury in which evidence is introduced and final judgment sought. 5. Prior to 2009, excludes transfers; beginning 2009, includes transfers. **Source:** Administrative Office of the U.S. Courts. *Judicial Business of the United States Courts,* 2010.

Fourth Circuit: Maryland, North Carolina, South Carolina, Virginia, West Virginia
Fifth Circuit: Louisiana, Mississippi, Texas
Sixth Circuit: Kentucky, Michigan, Ohio, Tennessee
Seventh Circuit: Illinois, Indiana, Wisconsin
Eighth Circuit: Arkansas, Iowa, Minnesota, Missouri, Nebraska, North Dakota, South Dakota
Ninth Circuit: Alaska, Arizona, California, Guam, Hawaii, Idaho, Montana, Nevada, Northern Mariana Islands, Oregon, Washington
Tenth Circuit: Colorado, Kansas, New Mexico, Oklahoma, Utah, Wyoming
Eleventh Circuit: Alabama, Florida, Georgia
Federal Circuit: nationwide

U.S. District Courts These are trial courts of general federal jurisdiction and their decisions are reviewable by the courts of appeals. There are 89 district courts—including at least one in each state—plus one in the District of Columbia and one in Puerto Rico. Each court has from two to 28 judgeships, depending on the amount of work within the district. Usually only one judge is required to hear a case, but some limited instances require three judges to comprise the court. There are 667 permanent district judges and additional temporary judgeships may be created as necessary.

THE LEGISLATIVE BRANCH

Architect of the Capitol U.S. Capitol, Washington, D.C. 20515. (202) 228-1793. *www.aoc.gov*. First Architect appointed in 1793 by President Washington. Permanent authority for care of Capitol established by Act of August 15, 1876. Responsible for care, operation, and maintenance of Capitol buildings and grounds, Library of Congress buildings, U.S. Supreme Court building, Thurgood Marshall Federal Judiciary Building, U.S. Botanic Garden, and House and Senate office buldings. Plans future construction, renovation, reconstruction, and alterations to existing buildings and landscaping. Maintains, operates, and cares for House and Senate office buildings. Plans future construction, renovation, reconstruction, and alterations to existing buildings.

U.S. Botanic Garden Director's Office: 245 First Street SW, Washington, D.C. 20024. (202) 225-6670. *www.usbg.gov*. Conservatory: Maryland Avenue-First to Second Streets SW; Washington, D.C. 20001. Horticultural Hotline: (202) 226-4785. Created in 1820. Collects, cultivates, and grows vegetable and plant matter of this and other countries for exhibition and display. Provides study materials on vegetable and plant matter for students, botanists, horticulturists, floriculturists, and garden clubs.

Government Accountability Office (GAO) 441 G Street NW Washington, D.C. 20548. (202) 512-3000. *www.gao.gov*. Created in 1921 by Budget and Accounting Act. Investigative arm of the Congress. Audits Federal agencies and disbursement of public funds, evaluates Government policies and programs, and issues legal opinions.

Government Printing Office (GPO) 732 North Capitol Street NW, Washington, D.C. 20401. (202) 512-0000. *www.gpo.gov*. Created June 23, 1860 by Congressional Joint Resolution 25. Produces, procures and disseminates printed and electronic publications for all three branches of the Federal Government through GPO facilities and through contracts with private vendors.

Administrative Office of the U.S. Courts One Columbus Circle NE, Washington, D.C. 20544. (202) 502-2600. *www.uscourts.gov*. Created by act of Aug. 7, 1939 as a support agency for federal courts except the Supreme Court. Administers courts, supervises probation office, and oversees administration of bankruptcy courts, magistrate offices, and public defender's offices.

Federal Judicial Center Thurgood Marshall Federal Judiciary Building, One Columbus Circle NE, Washington, D.C. 20002-8003. (202) 502-4000. *www.fjc.gov*. Created by act of Dec. 20, 1967. Its mission is to further the development and adoption of improved judicial administration in U.S. courts. The Chief Justice of the Supreme Court is the permanent chairman of the center's Board of Directors.

United States Sentencing Commission Suite 2-500, South Lobby, One Columbus Circle NE, Washington, D.C. 20002-8002. (202) 502-4500. *www.ussc.gov*. Created by the Sentencing Reform Act of 1984. Establishes sentencing guidelines (including forms and severity of punishment) for offenders convicted of federal crimes.

Library of Congress 101 Independence Ave. SE Washington, D.C. 20540. (202) 707-5000. *www.loc.gov*. Created by act of April 24, 1800. National library of the United States. Librarian appointed by President. Buys books necessary for use by Congress and other governmental agencies. Develops and promotes cataloging systems and bibliographical guides. Provides research and reference services to Congress, Federal agencies and the general public. Copyright Office serves as national registry for creative works.

Congressional Budget Office (CBO) Ford House Office Building, Fourth Floor, Second and D Streets SW, Washington, D.C. 20515. (202) 226-2600. *www.cbo.gov*. Created by Congressional Budget Act of 1974. Provides basic budget data to Congress. Analyzes and evaluates fiscal and budgetary policy options to Congress. Publishes annual report on the budget.

How A Bill Becomes Law

Usually bills are raised in any of the various committees of the Senate or House of Representatives. If the bill is supported by a majority of the committee, it is brought to the floor of the house in which it originated, and voted upon. If it gains majority support in the full Senate or House, the other house of Congress votes on it. If the bill is passed in both the Senate and House, it is sent to the President, who may either sign it, veto it, or not act on it.

If the president signs it or refuses to act within 10 days and the Congress is still in session, the bill becomes law. If the president vetoes it, it is returned to the Senate and the House for another vote; a two-thirds majority in each house is then required to overturn the presidential veto. However, if the president refuses to act on a bill and Congress adjourns before the end of the 10-day period, the legislation is dead. This is known as a *pocket veto*.

Occasionally, bills are raised on the floor of the Senate or the House, in which case the first step of committee voting is avoided and the legislation process begins with the full Senate or House Vote. All other processes remain the same.

How to Contact Your Senator or Representative

To contact any senator, call (202) 224-3121. More information about the Senate is available on the Internet at *www.senate.gov*. To reach a Representative, call (202) 225-3121. More information about the House is available on the Internet at *www.house.gov*.

The 112th Congress of the United States

The upper house of the U.S. Congress, the Senate, is composed of 100 members: two from each state. Senators are elected to six-year terms and one-third of the Senate faces re-election every two years. Senators must have been U.S. citizens for at least nine years and must be at least 30 years old.

The lower house of government, the House of Representatives, is composed of 435 members. The number of representatives from each state is determined by population every 10 years; every state is entitled to at least one representative. The entire House faces re-election every two years. Representatives must have been U.S. citizens for at least seven years and must be at least 25 years old.

In addition to state representatives, there are delegates from the District of Columbia, American Samoa, Guam, and the Virgin Islands, and a resident commissioner from Puerto Rico. They may take part in floor debates, but they may not vote.

SENATE OFFICES

President	Joseph R. Biden Jr. (D–Delaware)	**Majority Whip**	Richard Durbin (D–Illinois)
President Pro Tem	Daniel K. Inouye (D–Hawaii)	**Minority Leader**	Mitch McConnell (R–Kentucky)
Majority Leader	Harry Reid (D–Nevada)	**Minority Whip**	John Kyl (R–Arizona)

U.S. SENATORS

Alabama
*Richard C. Shelby (R)
Jeff Sessions (R)

Alaska
*Lisa Murkowski (R)[2]
Mark Begich (D)

Arizona
*John McCain (R)
Jon Kyl (R)

Arkansas
*Blanche Lincoln (D)
Mark Pryor (D)

California
Dianne Feinstein (D)
*Barbara Boxer (D)

Colorado
*Michael Bennet (D)
Mark Udall (D)

Connecticut
*Christopher Dodd (D)[1]
Joseph I. Lieberman (I)

Delaware
Thomas R. Carper (D)
Edward Kaufman (D)

Florida
Bill Nelson (D)
*George LeMieux (R)

Georgia
Saxby Chambliss (R)
*Johnny Isakson (R)

Hawaii
*Daniel K. Inouye (D)
Daniel K. Akaka (D)

Idaho
*Mike Crapo (R)
James Risch (R)

Illinois
Richard J. Durbin (D)
*Roland Burris (D)

Indiana
Richard G. Lugar (R)
*Evan Bayh (D)[1]

Iowa
*Chuck Grassley (R)
Tom Harkin (D)

Kansas
Pat Roberts (R)
*Sam Brownback (R)

Kentucky
Mitch McConnell (R)
*Jim Bunning (R)[1]

Louisiana
Mary Landrieu (D)
*David Vitter (R)

Maine
Olympia J. Snowe (R)
Susan Collins (R)

Maryland
*Barbara A. Mikulski (D)
Benjamin L. Cardin (D

Massachusetts
Scott Brown (R)
John F. Kerry (D)

Michigan
Carl Levin (D)
Debbie Stabenow (D)

Minnesota
Amy Klobuchar (D)
Al Franken (D)

Mississippi
Thad Cochran (R)
Roger Wicker (R)

Missouri
*Christopher S. Bond (R)
Claire McCaskill (D)

Montana
Max Baucus (D)
Jon Tester (D)

Nebraska
Benjamin E. Nelson (D)
Mike Johanns (R)

Nevada
*Harry Reid (D)
John Ensign (R)

New Hampshire
*Judd Gregg (R)[1]
Jeanne Shaheen (D)

New Jersey
Frank Lautenberg (D)
Robert Menendez (D)

New Mexico
Jeff Bingaman (D)
Tom Udall (D)

New York
*Charles Schumer (D)
Kirsten Gillibrand (D)

North Carolina
Richard Burr (R)
Kay Hagan (D)

North Dakota
Kent Conrad (D)
*Byron L. Dorgan (D)

Ohio
*George Voinovich (R)
Sherrod Brown (D)

Oklahoma
James Inhofe (R)
*Tom Coburn (R)

Oregon
*Ron Wyden (D)
Jeff Merkley (D)

Pennsylvania
*Arlen Specter (D)[2]
Robert P. Casey Jr. (D)

Rhode Island
Jack Reed (D)
Sheldon Whitehouse (D)

South Carolina
Lindsey Graham (R)
*Jim DeMint (R)

South Dakota
Tim Johnson (D)
*John Thune (R)

Tennessee
Lamar Alexander (R)
Bob Corker (R)

Texas
Kay Bailey
   Hutchison (R)
John Cornyn (R)

Utah
Orrin G. Hatch (R)
*Robert F. Bennett (R)[2]

Vermont
*Patrick J. Leahy (D)
Bernard Sanders (I)

Virginia
Jim Webb (D)
Mark Warner (D)

Washington
*Patty Murray (D)
Maria Cantwell (D)

West Virginia
Robert C. Byrd (D)[3]
John D.
   Rockefeller IV (D)

Wisconsin
Herb Kohl (D)
*Russell D. Feingold (D)

Wyoming
Michael Enzi (R)
John Barrasso (R)

Note: The senior senator is listed first. * = Seat up for re-election in Nov. 2010. 1. Retiring. 2. Lost 2010 primary. 3. Deceased July 2010, special election to be held November, 2010.

HOUSE OFFICES

Speaker	Nancy Pelosi (D–California)	**Minority Leader**	John Boehner (R–Ohio)
Majority Leader	Steny Hoyer (D–Maryland)	**Minority Whip**	Eric Cantor (R–Virginia)
Majority Whip	James E. Clyburn (D–S. Carolina)		

U.S. REPRESENTATIVES
(as of November 2010)

District	Representative	Place of Residence	District	Representative	Place of Residence
Alabama			35	Maxine Waters (D)	Los Angeles
1	Jo Bonner (R)	Mobile	36	Jane Harman (D)	Venice
2	Bobby Bright (D)	Montgomery	37	Laura Richardson (D)	Long Beach
3	Mike Rogers (R)	Anniston	38	Grace Napolitano (D)	Norwalk
4	Robert Aderholt (R)	Haleyville	39	Linda Sanchez (D)	Lakewood
5	Parker Griffith (D)	Huntsville	40	Ed Royce (R)	Fullerton
6	Spencer Bachus (R)	Vestavia Hills	41	Jerry Lewis (R)	Redlands
7	Artur Davis (D)	Birmingham	42	Gary Miller (R)	Diamond Bar
			43	Joe Baca (D)	Rialto
Alaska			44	Ken Calvert (R)	Corona
At-Large	Don Young (R)	Fort Yukon	45	Mary Bono Mack (R)	Palm Springs
			46	Dana Rohrabacher (R)	Huntington Beach
Arizona			47	Loretta Sanchez (D)	Anaheim
1	Ann Kirkpatrick (D)	Flagstaff	48	John Campbell (R)	Irvine
2	Trent Franks (R)	Glendale	49	Darrell Issa (R)	Vista
3	John Shadegg (R)	Phoenix	50	Brian Bilbray (R)	Carlsbad
4	Ed Pastor (D)	Phoenix	51	Bob Filner (D)	San Diego
5	Harry Mitchell (D)	Tempe	52	Duncan D. Hunter (R)	Lakeside
6	Jeff Flake (R)	Mesa	53	Susan Davis (D)	San Diego
7	Raul Grijalva (D)	Tucson			
8	Gabrielle Giffords (D)	Tucson	**Colorado**		
			1	Diana DeGette (D)	Denver
			2	Jared Polis (D)	Boulder
Arkansas			3	John Salazar (D)	Manassa
1	Marion Berry (D)	Gillett	4	Betsy Markey (D)	Fort Collins
2	Vic Snyder (D)	Little Rock	5	Doug Lamborn (R)	Colorado Springs
3	John Boozman (R)	Rogers	6	Mike Coffman (R)	Aurora
4	Mike Ross (D)	Prescott	7	Ed Perlmutter (D)	Golden
California			**Connecticut**		
1	Mike Thompson (D)	St. Helena	1	John Larson (D)	East Hartford
2	Wally Herger (R)	Chico	2	Joe Courtney (D)	Vernon
3	Dan Lungren (R)	Gold River	3	Rosa DeLauro (D)	New Haven
4	Tom McClintock (R)	Roseville	4	Jim Himes (D)	Cos Cob
5	Doris Matsui (D)	Sacramento	5	Chris Murphy (D)	Cheshire
6	Lynn Woolsey (D)	Petaluma			
7	George Miller (D)	Martinez	**Delaware**		
8	Nancy Pelosi (D)	San Francisco	At-Large	Mike Castle (R)	Wilmington
9	Barbara Lee (D)	Oakland			
10	John Garamendi (D)	Walnut Grove	**Florida**		
11	Jerry McNerney (D)	Pleasanton	1	Jeff Miller (R)	Chumuckla
12	Jackie Speier (D)	Hillsborough	2	Allen Boyd (D)	Monticello
13	Fortney Pete Stark (D)	Fremont	3	Corrine Brown (D)	Jacksonville
14	Anna Eshoo (D)	Atherton	4	Ander Crenshaw (R)	Jacksonville
15	Mike Honda (D)	San Jose	5	Ginny Brown-Waite (R)	Brooksville
16	Zoe Lofgren (D)	San Jose	6	Cliff Stearns (R)	Ocala
17	Sam Farr (D)	Carmel	7	John Mica (R)	Winter Park
18	Dennis Cardoza (D)	Atwater	8	Alan Grayson (D)	Orlando
19	George Radanovich (R)	Mariposa	9	Gus Bilirakis (R)	Palm Harbor
20	Jim Costa (D)	Fresno	10	Bill Young (R)	Indian Shores
21	Devin Nunes (R)	Tulare	11	Kathy Castor (D)	Tampa
22	Kevin McCarthy (R)	Bakersfield	12	Adam Putnam (R)	Bartow
23	Lois Capps (D)	Santa Barbara	13	Vern Buchanan (R)	Sarasota
24	Elton Gallegly (R)	Simi Valley	14	Connie Mack (R)	Fort Myers
25	Buck McKeon (R)	Santa Clarita	15	Bill Posey (R)	Rockledge
26	David Dreier (R)	San Dimas	16	Tom Rooney (R)	Tequesta
27	Brad Sherman (D)	Sherman Oaks	17	Kendrick Meek (D)	Miami
28	Howard Berman (D)	North Hollywood	18	Ileana Ros-Lehtinen (R)	Miami
29	Adam Schiff (D)	Burbank	19	Robert Wexler (D)	Boca Raton
30	Henry Waxman (D)	Los Angeles	20	Debbie Wasserman Schultz (D)	Weston
31	Xavier Becerra (D)	Los Angeles	21	Lincoln Diaz-Balart (R)	Miami
32	Judy Chu (D)	Baldwin Park	22	Ron Klein (D)	Boca Raton
33	Diane Watson (D)	Los Angeles	23	Alcee Hastings (D)	Miramar
34	Lucille Roybal-Allard (D)	Los Angeles	24	Suzanne Kosmas (D)	New Smyrna Beach

District	Representative	Place of Residence
25	Mario Diaz-Balart (R)	Miami

Georgia

District	Representative	Place of Residence
1	Jack Kingston (R)	Savannah
2	Sanford Bishop (D)	Albany
3	Lynn Westmoreland (R)	Grantville
4	Hank Johnson (D)	Lithonia
5	John Lewis (D)	Atlanta
6	Tom Price (R)	Roswell
7	John Linder (R)	Duluth
8	Jim Marshall (D)	Macon
9	Nathan Deal (R)	Gainesville
10	Paul Broun (R)	Athens
11	Phil Gingrey (R)	Marietta
12	John Barrow (D)	Savannah
13	David Scott (D)	Atlanta

Hawaii

1	Neil Abercrombie (D)	Honolulu
2	Mazie Hirono (D)	Honolulu

Idaho

1	Walt Minnick (D)	Boise
2	Mike Simpson (R)	Idaho Falls

Illinois

1	Bobby Rush (D)	Chicago
2	Jesse Jackson, Jr. (D)	Chicago
3	Daniel Lipinski (D)	Western Springs
4	Luis Gutierrez (D)	Chicago
5	Mike Quigley (D)	Chicago
6	Peter Roskam (R)	Wheaton
7	Danny Davis (D)	Chicago
8	Melissa Bean (D)	Barrington
9	Jan Schakowsky (D)	Evanston
10	Mark Kirk (R)	Highland Park
11	Debbie Halvorson (D)	Crete
12	Jerry Costello (D)	Belleville
13	Judy Biggert (R)	Hinsdale
14	Bill Foster (D)	Batavia
15	Tim Johnson (R)	Urbana
16	Donald Manzullo (R)	Egan
17	Phil Hare (D)	Rock Island
18	Aaron Schock (R)	Peoria
19	John Shimkus (R)	Collinsville

Indiana

1	Peter Visclosky (D)	Merrillville
2	Joe Donnelly (D)	Granger
3	Mark Souder (R)	Fort Wayne
4	Steve Buyer (R)	Monticello
5	Dan Burton (R)	Indianapolis
6	Mike Pence (R)	Columbus
7	André Carson (D)	Indianapolis
8	Brad Ellsworth (D)	Evansville
9	Baron Hill (D)	Seymour

Iowa

1	Bruce Braley (D)	Waterloo
2	Dave Loebsack (D)	Mt. Vernon
3	Leonard Boswell (D)	Des Moines
4	Tom Latham (R)	Ames
5	Steve King (R)	Kiron

Kansas

1	Jerry Moran (R)	Hays
2	Lynn Jenkins (R)	Topeka
3	Dennis Moore (D)	Lenexa
4	Todd Tiahrt (R)	Goddard

Kentucky

1	Ed Whitfield (R)	Hopkinsville
2	Brett Guthrie (R)	Bowling Green

District	Representative	Place of Residence
3	John Yarmuth (D)	Louisville
4	Geoff Davis (R)	Hebron
5	Hal Rogers (R)	Somerset
6	Ben Chandler (D)	Versailles

Louisiana

1	Steve Scalise (R)	Jefferson
2	Joseph Cao (R)	New Orleans
3	Charlie Melancon (D)	Napoleonville
4	John Fleming (R)	Minden
5	Rodney Alexander (R)	Quitman
6	Bill Cassidy (R)	Baton Rouge
7	Charles Boustany (R)	Lafayette

Maine

1	Chellie Pingree (D)	North Haven
2	Mike Michaud (D)	East Millinocket

Maryland

1	Frank Kratovil (D)	Stevensville
2	Dutch Ruppersberger (D)	Cockeysville
3	John Sarbanes (D)	Baltimore
4	Donna Edwards (D)	Fort Washington
5	Steny Hoyer (D)	Mechanicsville
6	Roscoe Bartlett (R)	Frederick
7	Elijah Cummings (D)	Baltimore
8	Chris Van Hollen (D)	Kensington

Massachusetts

1	John Olver (D)	Amherst
2	Richard Neal (D)	Springfield
3	James McGovern (D)	Worcester
4	Barney Frank (D)	Newton
5	Niki Tsongas (D)	Lowell
6	John Tierney (D)	Salem
7	Edward Markey (D)	Malden
8	Michael Capuano (D)	Somerville
9	Stephen Lynch (D)	South Boston
10	Bill Delahunt (D)	Quincy

Michigan

1	Bart Stupak (D)	Menominee
2	Pete Hoekstra (R)	Holland
3	Vernon Ehlers (R)	Grand Rapids
4	Dave Camp (R)	Midland
5	Dale Kildee (D)	Flint
6	Fred Upton (R)	St. Joseph
7	Mark Schauer (D)	Battle Creek
8	Mike Rogers (R)	Brighton
9	Gary Peters (D)	Bloomfield Township
10	Candice Miller (R)	Harrison Township
11	Thad McCotter (R)	Livonia
12	Sander Levin (D)	Royal Oak
13	Carolyn Cheeks Kilpatrick (D)	Detroit
14	John Conyers (D)	Detroit
15	John Dingell (D)	Dearborn

Minnesota

1	Tim Walz (D)	Mankato
2	John Kline (R)	Lakeville
3	Erik Paulsen (R)	Eden Prairie
4	Betty McCollum (D)	St. Paul
5	Keith Ellison (D)	Minneapolis
6	Michele Bachmann (R)	Stillwater
7	Collin Peterson (D)	Detroit Lakes
8	James Oberstar (D)	Chisholm

Mississippi

1	Travis Childers (D)	Booneville
2	Bennie Thompson (D)	Bolton
3	Gregg Harper (R)	Pearl
4	Gene Taylor (D)	Bay St. Louis

District	Representative	Place of Residence
Missouri		
1	Lacy Clay (D)	St. Louis
2	Todd Akin (R)	St. Louis
3	Russ Carnahan (D)	St. Louis
4	Ike Skelton (D)	Lexington
5	Emanuel Cleaver (D)	Kansas City
6	Sam Graves (R)	Tarkio
7	Roy Blunt (R)	Springfield
8	Jo Ann Emerson (R)	Cape Girardeau
9	Blaine Luetkemeyer (R)	St. Elizabeth
Montana		
At-Large	Denny Rehberg (R)	Billings
Nebraska		
1	Jeff Fortenberry (R)	Lincoln
2	Lee Terry (R)	Omaha
3	Adrian Smith (R)	Gering
Nevada		
1	Shelley Berkley (D)	Las Vegas
2	Dean Heller (R)	Carson City
3	Dina Titus (D)	Las Vegas
New Hampshire		
1	Carol Shea-Porter (D)	Rochester
2	Paul Hodes (D)	Concord
New Jersey		
1	Robert Andrews (D)	Haddon Heights
2	Frank LoBiondo (R)	Ventnor
3	John Adler (D)	Cherry Hill
4	Chris Smith (R)	Hamilton
5	Scott Garrett (R)	Wantage
6	Frank Pallone (D)	Long Branch
7	Leonard Lance (R)	Clinton Township
8	Bill Pascrell (D)	Paterson
9	Steve Rothman (D)	Fair Lawn
10	Donald Payne (D)	Newark
11	Rodney Frelinghuysen (R)	Morristown
12	Rush Holt (D)	Hopewell Township
13	Albio Sires (D)	West New York
New Mexico		
1	Martin Heinrich (D)	Albuquerque
2	Harry Teague (D)	Hobbs
3	Ben R. Luján (D)	Nambé
New York		
1	Timothy Bishop (D)	Southampton
2	Steve Israel (D)	Huntington
3	Peter King (R)	Seaford
4	Carolyn McCarthy (D)	Mineola
5	Gary Ackerman (D)	Roslyn Heights
6	Gregory Meeks (D)	Queens
7	Joseph Crowley (D)	Queens/Bronx
8	Jerrold Nadler (D)	New York
9	Anthony Weiner (D)	Queens
10	Edolphus Towns (D)	Brooklyn
11	Yvette Clarke (D)	Brooklyn
12	Nydia Velázquez (D)	Brooklyn
13	Michael McMahon (D)	Staten Island
14	Carolyn Maloney (D)	New York
15	Charles Rangel (D)	New York
16	Jose E. Serrano (D)	Bronx
17	Eliot Engel (D)	Bronx
18	Nita Lowey (D)	Harrison
19	John Hall (D)	Dover Plains
20	Scott Murphy (D)	Glens Falls
21	Paul Tonko (D)	Amsterdam
22	Maurice Hinchey (D)	Saugerties
23	John McHugh (R)	Pierrepont Manor
24	Michael Arcuri (D)	Utica
25	Daniel Maffei (D)	DeWitt

District	Representative	Place of Residence
26	Christopher Lee (R)	Clarence
27	Brian Higgins (D)	Buffalo
28	Louise Slaughter (D)	Fairpoint
29	Eric Massa (D)	Coming
North Carolina		
1	G.K. Butterfield (D)	Wilson
2	Bob Etheridge (D)	Lillington
3	Walter Jones (R)	Farmville
4	David Price (D)	Chapel Hill
5	Virginia Foxx (R)	Grandfather Community
6	Howard Coble (R)	Greensboro
7	Mike McIntyre (D)	Lumberton
8	Larry Kissell (D)	Biscoe
9	Sue Myrick (R)	Charlotte
10	Patrick McHenry (R)	Cherryville
11	Heath Shuler (D)	Waynesville
12	Mel Watt (D)	Charlotte
13	Brad Miller (D)	Raleigh
North Dakota		
At-Large	Earl Pomeroy (D)	Valley City
Ohio		
1	Steve Driehaus (D)	Cincinnati
2	Jean Schmidt (R)	Miami Township
3	Mike Turner (R)	Dayton
4	Jim Jordan (R)	Urbana
5	Bob Latta (R)	Bowling Green
6	Charlie Wilson (D)	St. Clairsville
7	Steve Austria (R)	Beavercreek
8	John Boehner (R)	West Chester
9	Marcy Kaptur (D)	Toledo
10	Dennis Kucinich (D)	Cleveland
11	Marcia Fudge (D)	Warrensville Heights
12	Pat Tiberi (R)	Galena
13	Betty Sutton (D)	Copley
14	Steven LaTourette (R)	Bainbridge Township
15	Steve Stivers (R)	Columbus
16	John Boccieri (D)	Alliance
17	Tim Ryan (D)	Niles
18	Zack Space (D)	Dover
Oklahoma		
1	John Sullivan (R)	Tulsa
2	Dan Boren (D)	Muskogee
3	Frank Lucas (R)	Cheyenne
4	Tom Cole (R)	Moore
5	Mary Fallin (R)	Oklahoma City
Oregon		
1	David Wu (D)	Portland
2	Greg Walden (R)	Hood River
3	Earl Blumenauer (D)	Portland
4	Peter DeFazio (D)	Springfield
5	Kurt Schrader (D)	Canby
Pennsylvania		
1	Robert Brady (D)	Philadelphia
2	Chaka Fattah (D)	Philadelphia
3	Kathy Dahlkemper (D)	Erie
4	Jason Altmire (D)	McCandless
5	Glenn Thompson (R)	Howard
6	Jim Gerlach (R)	Chester Springs
7	Joe Sestak (D)	Edgmont
8	Patrick Murphy (D)	Bristol
9	Bill Shuster (R)	Hollidaysburg
10	Christopher Carney (D)	Dimock
11	Paul Kanjorski (D)	Nanticoke
12	John Murtha (D)	Johnstown
13	Allyson Schwartz (D)	Jenkintown
14	Mike Doyle (D)	Forest Hills
15	Charles Dent (R)	Allentown
16	Joseph Pitts (R)	Kennett Square

District	Representative	Place of Residence
17	Tim Holden (D)	St. Clair
18	Tim Murphy (R)	Pittsburgh
19	Todd Platts (R)	York

Rhode Island

1	Patrick Kennedy (D)	Portsmouth
2	Jim Langevin (D)	Warwick

South Carolina

1	Henry Brown (R)	Hanahan
2	Joe Wilson (R)	Springdale
3	Gresham Barrett (R)	Westminster
4	Bob Inglis (R)	Travelers Rest
5	John Spratt (D)	York
6	Jim Clyburn (D)	Columbia

South Dakota

At-Large	Stephanie Herseth Sandlin (D)	Brookings

Tennessee

1	Phil Roe (R)	Johnson City
2	John Duncan (R)	Knoxville
3	Zach Wamp (R)	Chattanooga
4	Lincoln Davis (D)	Pall Mall
5	Jim Cooper (D)	Nashville
6	Bart Gordon (D)	Murfreesboro
7	Marsha Blackburn (R)	Brentwood
8	John Tanner (D)	Union City
9	Steve Cohen (D)	Memphis

Texas

1	Louie Gohmert (R)	Tyler
2	Ted Poe (R)	Humble
3	Sam Johnson (R)	Plano
4	Ralph Hall (R)	Rockwall
5	Jeb Hensarling (R)	Dallas
6	Joe Barton (R)	Ennis
7	John Culberson (R)	Houston
8	Kevin Brady (R)	The Woodlands
9	Al Green (D)	Houston
10	Michael McCaul (R)	Austin
11	Mike Conaway (R)	Midland
12	Kay Granger (R)	Fort Worth
13	Mac Thornberry (R)	Clarendon
14	Ron Paul (R)	Lake Jackson
15	Rubén Hinojosa (D)	Mercedes
16	Silvestre Reyes (D)	El Paso
17	Chet Edwards (D)	Waco
18	Sheila Jackson Lee (D)	Houston
19	Randy Neugebauer (R)	Lubbock
20	Charlie Gonzalez (D)	San Antonio
21	Lamar Smith (R)	San Antonio
22	Pete Olson (R)	Sugar Land
23	Ciro Rodriguez (D)	San Antonio
24	Kenny Marchant (R)	Coppell
25	Lloyd Doggett (D)	Austin
26	Michael Burgess (R)	Lewisville
27	Solomon Ortiz (D)	Corpus Christi
28	Henry Cuellar (D)	Laredo
29	Gene Green (D)	Houston
30	Eddie Bernice Johnson (D)	Dallas
31	John Carter (R)	Round Rock
32	Pete Sessions (R)	Dallas

District	Representative	Place of Residence
Utah		
1	Rob Bishop (R)	Brigham City
2	Jim Matheson (D)	Salt Lake City
3	Jason Chaffetz (R)	Alpine

Vermont

At-large	Peter Welch (D)	Hartland

Virginia

1	Rob Wittman (R)	Montross
2	Glenn Nye (D)	Norfolk
3	Bobby Scott (D)	Newport News
4	Randy Forbes (R)	Chesapeake
5	Tom Perriello (D)	Charlottesville
6	Bob Goodlatte (R)	Roanoke
7	Eric Cantor (R)	Richmond
8	Jim Moran (D)	Arlington
9	Rick Boucher (D)	Abdingdon
10	Frank Wolf (R)	Vienna
11	Gerry Connolly (D)	Fairfax

Washington

1	Jay Inslee (D)	Bainbridge Island
2	Rick Larsen (D)	Everett
3	Brian Baird (D)	Vancouver
4	Doc Hastings (R)	Pasco
5	Cathy McMorris Rodgers (R)	Spokane
6	Norm Dicks (D)	Belfair
7	Jim McDermott (D)	Seattle
8	Dave Reichert (R)	Auburn
9	Adam Smith (D)	Tacoma

West Virginia

1	Alan Mollohan (D)	Fairmont
2	Shelley Moore Capito (R)	Charleston
3	Nick Rahall (D)	Beckley

Wisconsin

1	Paul Ryan (R)	Janesville
2	Tammy Baldwin (D)	Madison
3	Ron Kind (D)	La Crosse
4	Gwen Moore (D)	Milwaukee
5	Jim Sensenbrenner (R)	Menomonee Falls
6	Tom Petri (R)	Fond du Lac
7	David Obey (D)	Wausau
8	Steven Kagen (D)	Appleton

Wyoming

At-Large	Cynthia Lummis (R)	Cheyenne

NON-VOTING REPRESENTATIVES

American Samoa	Eni F. H. Faleomavaega (D)
District of Columbia	Eleanor Holmes Norton (D)
Guam	Madeliene Bordallo (D)
Northern Mariana Islands	Gregorio Kilili Camacho Sabian (D)
Puerto Rico	Pedro Pierluisi (D)
U.S. Virgin Islands	Donna Christensen (D)

Note: D = Democrat; I = Independent; R = Republican. **Source:** Clerk of the U.S. House of Representatives.

Congressional Reapportionment

The Constitution mandates a decennial census of the population in order to distribute the 435 seats in the House of Representatives proportionally among the states according to population. Each state is guaranteed at least one seat regardless of population size, and based on the 2000 Census, each House member represents an average of 646,952 citizens. As a result of populations shifts reported in the 2000 Census, eight states gained representatives (Arizona, Florida, Georgia, and Texas each gained two; California, Colorado, Nevada, and North Carolina each gained one), while 10 states lost representatives (New York and Pennsylvania each lost two; Connecticut, Illinois, Indiana, Michigan, Mississippi, Ohio, Oklahoma, and Wisconsin each lost one). Any congressional reapportionment resulting from the 2010 Census will likely take effect prior to the 2012 elections.

THE EXECUTIVE BRANCH

▶**EXECUTIVE OFFICE OF THE PRESIDENT**
White House Office 1600 Pennsylvania Ave. NW, Washington, D.C. 20500 (202) 456-1414. *www.whitehouse.gov*. Created Dec. 12, 1977 by Executive Order. Serves president in performance of duties incident to his office. Maintains communication with Congress, individual members of Congress, heads of executive agencies, media, and public.

Office of the Vice President of the United States Eisenhower Executive Office Building, Washington, D.C. 20501. (202) 456-2326. *www.whitehouse.gov/vicepresident*. Vice president participates in cabinet meetings, serves as president of Senate, and is, by statute, a member of National Security Council and board of regents of the Smithsonian Institution; empowered to succeed to presidency pursuant to Article II and the 20th and 25th amendments to the Constitution.

Council of Economic Advisers 1800 G St. NW; Washington, D.C. 20502. (202) 395-5084. *www.whitehouse.gov/cea*. Created by Employment Act of 1946. Council's three members—appointed by president—analyze the various segments of the economy, appraise and assess existing economic programs, recommend new economic programs, and assist in preparation President's economic reports to Congress.

Council on Environmental Quality 722 Jackson Place NW, Washington D.C. 20503. (202) 395-5750. *www.whitehouse.gov/ceq*. Created by National Environmental Policy Act of 1969. Coordinates Federal environmental efforts. Recommends national policies to improve quality of environment. Analyzes environmental changes and trends. Evaluates existing environmental programs. Assists president in compiling annual environmental quality report to Congress. Chair serves as environmental advisor to president.

National Security Council (N.S.C.) Eisenhower Executive Office Building, Washington D.C. 20504. (202) 456-1414. *www.whitehouse.gov/nsc*. Created by National Security Act of 1947. Chaired by president. Members include vice president and secretaries of state and defense. Chairman of Joint Chiefs of Staff is statutory military adviser; Director of National Intelligence is statutory intelligence adviser. Advises president on integration of domestic, foreign, and military policies relating to national security.

Office of Administration Eisenhower Executive Office Building, 1650 Pennsylvania Ave. NW, Washington, D.C. 20503. (202) 456-2861. *www.whitehouse.gov/oa*. Created Dec. 12, 1977 by Reorganization Plan No. 1. Provides administrative services to all units within executive office including, upon request, those in direct support of president.

Office of Management and Budget (O.M.B.) 725 17th St. NW, Washington, D.C. 20503. (202) 395-3080. *www.whitehouse.gov/omb*. Created by Reorganization Plan No. 1 in 1939. Assists president in overseeing the preparation of the federal budget and supervises its administration in executive branch agencies. Evaluates the effectiveness of agency programs, policies, and procedures, assesses funding demands, and sets funding priorities. Ensures that agency reports, rules, testimony, and proposed legislation are consistent with budget and administration policies. Oversees and coordinates the administration's procurement, financial management, information, and regulatory policies.

Office of National Drug Control Policy 750 17th St. NW, Washington, D.C., 20503. (202) 395-6700. Drug Policy Information Clearinghouse: 800-666-3332. *www.ondcp.gov*. Created by National Narcotics Leadership Act of 1988. Produces national drug control strategy and coordinates Federal, state, and local efforts to control illegal drug use, manufacturing, trafficking and related crime.

Office of Policy Development Eisenhower Executive Office Building, Washington, D.C. 20502. *www.whitehouse.gov/administration/eop*. Created by Executive Order in 1970, reorganized in 1993. Composed of the **Domestic Policy Council** (202) 456-5594 and the **National Economic Council** (202) 456-2800, which are responsible for advising and assisting the president in the formulation, coordination, and implementation of domestic and economic policy. Includes **Office of National AIDS Policy, Office of Faith-Based and Neighborhood Partnerships**, and other policy advisors.

Office of Science and Technology Policy 725 17th St., Washington, D.C. 20502. (202) 456-7116. *www.ostp.gov*. Created May 11, 1976. Serves as source of scientific, engineering, and technological analysis and expertise for president with respect to public policy in areas of economy, national security, health, foreign relations, and environment. Appraises sale, quality and effectiveness of U.S. efforts in science and technology.

Office of the U.S. Trade Representative 600 17th St. NW, Washington, D.C. 20508. (202) 395-3230. *www.ustr.gov*. Created as Office of the Special Representative for Trade Negotiations, Jan. 15, 1963. Congress made it agency of executive office under Trade Act of 1974. Sets and administers overall trade policy. Representative is chief U.S. representative for all activities of the General Agreement on Tariffs and Trade (GATT) and at discussions, meetings, and negotiations in most conferences in which trade and commodity are issues.

▶DEPARTMENT OF AGRICULTURE (U.S.D.A.)

1400 Independence Ave. SW, Washington, D.C. 20250. (202) 720-4623. *www.usda.gov*. Created May 15, 1862; incorporated into cabinet, Feb. 8, 1889. Maintains and improves farm income, develops agricultural markets for U.S. crops, curbs poverty, hunger and malnutrition. Sets and safeguards standards of quality in the nation's food supply. Provides loans, grants, technical assistance and research funding to support rural and agricultural businesses. U.S.D.A. was reorganized in 1994 into seven program areas: Rural Develop-

The Cabinet

The president is the administrative head of the executive branch of the Federal Government. A creation of custom and tradition dating back to George Washington's administration, the cabinet functions at the pleasure of the president. Its purpose is to advise the president on any subject on which he requests information. The cabinet is composed of the heads of the 15 executive departments and certain other executive officials to whom the president accords cabinet rank. In the Obama Administration, cabinet-level rank has been accorded to the officials listed below (as of September, 2010).

President Barack H. Obama
Vice President Joseph R. Biden Jr.

Office	Officer
Secretary of State	Hillary Rodham Clinton
Secretary of the Treasury	Timothy F. Geithner
Secretary of Defense	Robert M. Gates
Attorney General (Department of Justice)	Eric H. Holder Jr.
Secretary of the Interior	Kenneth L. Salazar
Secretary of Agriculture	Thomas J. Vilsack
Secretary of Commerce	Gary F. Locke
Secretary of Labor	Hilda L. Solis
Secretary of Health and Human Services	Kathleen Sebelius
Secretary of Housing and Urban Development	Shaun L.S. Donovan
Secretary of Transportation	Raymond L. LaHood
Secretary of Energy	Steven Chu
Secretary of Education	Arne Duncan
Secretary of Veterans Affairs	Eric K. Shinseki
Secretary of Homeland Security	Janet A. Napolitano
Chair, Council of Economic Advisers	Austan Goolsbee
Administrator, Environmental Protection Agency	Lisa P. Jackson
Director, Office of Management & Budget	Jeffrey Zients[1]
U.S. Trade Representative	Ronald Kirk
U.S. Ambassador to the United Nations	Susan Rice
White House Chief of Staff	Rahm I. Emanuel

Note: 1. Acting Director as of Sept. 2010. **Source:** White House Press Office

ment; Marketing & Regulatory Programs; Food Safety; Food Nutrition & Consumer Services; Farm & Foreign Agriculture Services; Research Education & Economics; and Natural Resources & Environment. Each program area may be further divided into more specific agencies, such as the Rural Housing Service or the Food Safety and Inspection Service.

▶DEPARTMENT OF COMMERCE

1401 Constitution Ave. NW, Washington, D.C. 20230. (202) 482-2000. *www.commerce.gov*. Created Feb. 14, 1903 as part of Dept. of Commerce and Labor. Redesignated Dept. of Commerce Mar. 4, 1913. Promotes international trade, economic growth, and technological advancement through encouragement of competitive free-enterprise system, prevention of unfair trade, granting of patents, promotion of tourism and assistance in the growth of minority businesses. The department is divided into 12 operating units; only the major agencies are described in detail below.

Bureau of the Census *www.census.gov*. Collects, tabulates, and publishes statistics about America, its people, and its economy. Conducts decennial census for Congressional reapportionment. Information collected must be kept confidential and used only for statistical purposes. Statistics are used by Congress, the president, and the public to develop and evaluate public policy. Performs population and housing censuses every 10 years. Performs censuses of agriculture, state and local governments, manufacturers, mineral industries, distributive trades, and construction and transportation industries every five years. Performs special censuses on request from state and local governments.

Economic Development Administration (E.D.A.) *www.eda.gov*. Created by Public Works and Economic Development Act of 1965. Promotes new jobs, protects existing jobs, and stimulates job growth in areas where unemployment is high or incomes are low.

International Trade Administration (I.T.A.) *www.trade.gov*. Created Jan. 2, 1980. Promotes world trade and strengthens U.S. position in relation to world trade and investment.

Minority Business Development Agency (M.B.D.A.) *www.mbda.gov*. Created Mar. 5, 1969; reorganized 1979. Promotes minority business. Ensures effective, equitable, and competitive participation by minority business in free enterprise system.

National Oceanic and Atmospheric Administration (N.O.A.A.) *www.noaa.gov*. Created Oct. 3, 1970 from merger of existing agencies. Investigates and maps world oceans. Discovers, utilizes and conserves living resources of oceans. Monitors and predicts conditions of atmosphere, sun, and oceans, and effects of man-made events and circumstances. Provides weather reports and forecasts. Forecasts floods, hurricanes, and other weather-related natural disturbances.

National Institute of Standards and Technology (N.I.S.T.) *www.nist.gov*. Created by Congress in 1901 and expanded in 2007 by America COMPETES Act. Promotes U.S. innovation and industrial competitiveness by conducting research, advising on standards and advancing technology.

►DEPARTMENT OF DEFENSE (D.O.D.)

The Pentagon, Washington, D.C. 20301-1151. (703) 545-6700. *www.defenselink.mil.* Created by National Security Act Amendments of 1949. Provides necessary military forces to deter war and protect security of the country. The three armed forces departments and the Organization of the Joint Chiefs of Staff make up the military side of the Defense Dept. (Additional information can be found in "National Defense.")

Organization of the Joint Chiefs of Staff

Consists of Chairman of Joint Chiefs of Staff, the chiefs of staff of the three armed forces departments, and the Commandant of the Marine Corps. Advises and assists president and secretary of defense on most military issues. Assists president and secretary of defense in planning, direction, and allocation of strategic resources. Compares strengths and capabilities of American forces with those of potential adversaries.

Department of the Air Force *www.af.mil.*

Created Sept. 18, 1947 by National Security Act of 1947. Works in conjunction with other armed forces to protect peace and security of the U.S. Focuses on air missions and protecting American interests from invasion by air.

Department of the Army *www.army.mil.* U.S.

Army created June 14, 1775 by Continental Congress. Dept. of the Army created by National Security Act of 1947. Organizes, trains, and equips active and reserve forces to protect peace, security, welfare, and defense of the U.S. Mission focuses on land operations and maneuvers.

Department of the Navy *www.navy.mil.* U.S.

Navy created Oct. 13, 1775, by Continental Congress. Dept. of the Navy created Apr. 30, 1798. Encompasses Marine Corps. Protects U.S. from attack by sea and maintains freedom of the seas.

►DEPARTMENT OF EDUCATION

400 Maryland Ave. SW, Washington, D.C. 20202. (800) USA-LEARN. *www.ed.gov.* Created Oct. 17, 1979, by Dept. of Education Organization Act. Establishes policy for, administers, and coordinates almost all federal assistance to education.

►DEPARTMENT OF ENERGY (D.O.E.)

1000 Independence Ave. SW, Washington, D.C. 20585. (202) 586-5000. *www.energy.gov.* Created Oct. 1, 1977, by Dept. of Energy Organization Act. Coordinates and administrates energy functions of Federal Government, including research and development of energy technology, marketing federal power, energy conservation, nuclear weapons and energy regulation.

►DEPARTMENT OF HEALTH AND HUMAN SERVICES (H.H.S.)

200 Independence Ave. SW, Washington, D.C. 20201. (202) 619-0257. *www.hhs.gov.* Created Apr. 11, 1953, as Dept. of Health, Education, and Welfare. Re-designated Dept. of Health and Human Services Oct. 17, 1979, by Dept. of Education Organization Act. Advises president in formulation of public policy regarding health, welfare, and income and security programs. The department is divided in 12 major administrations and agencies; only the major agencies are described in detail below.

Administration for Children and Families (A.C.F.) *www.acf.hhs.gov.* Created April 15, 1991. Administers child welfare services, foster care and child care programs, the Head Start Pro-

gram, and other family preservation and support services.

Centers for Disease Control and Prevention (C.D.C.) *www.cdc.gov.* Reorganized, Nov. 9, 1995. Responsible for protecting the public health by preventing and controlling diseases. Compiles data and statistics on health and wellness.

Centers for Medicare and Medicaid Services (C.M.S.) *www.cms.gov.* Formerly Health Care Financing Administration; reorganized June 14, 2001. Oversees Medicare and Medicaid Health Insurance and grant programs. (See "Social Insurance Programs" for additional information).

Food and Drug Administration (F.D.A.) *www.fda.gov.* Created by Agricultural Appropriation Act of 1931; reorganized into H.H.S. in Nov., 1995. It protects the health of the nation against impure and unsafe foods, drugs, cosmetics and other hazards.

National Institutes of Health (N.I.H.) *www.nih.gov.* Reorganized, Nov. 1995. The principal biomedical research agency of the Federal Government, its mission is to employ science in the pursuit of knowledge to improve human health conditions.

Substance Abuse and Mental Health Services Administration *www.samhsa.gov.* Disseminates accurate and up-to-date information on and provides leadership in the prevention and treatment of addictive and mental disorders.

►DEPARTMENT OF HOMELAND SECURITY

Washington, D.C. 20528. (202) 282-8000. *www.dhs.gov.* Created Jan. 24, 2003 by the Homeland Security Act of 2002. Aims to protect the nation against terrorist attacks while allowing for the free flow of people, goods, and commerce. Provides public services such as natural disaster assistance and citizenship services.

Federal Emergency Management Agency (F.E.M.A.) 500 C St. SW, Washington, D.C. 20472. (800) 621-FEMA. *www.fema.gov.* Created Mar. 31, 1979. Transferred to Dept. of Homeland Security Jan. 24, 2003. Provides single point of accountability for all federal emergency preparedness, mitigation, and response activities. Facilitates most efficient use of resources in cases of natural or man-made emergencies.

U.S. Citizenship and Immigration Services (U.S.C.I.S.) *www.uscis.gov.* Created Mar. 3, 1891. Transferred to Dept. of Homeland Security March 1, 2003. Controls immigration into U.S. by facilitating entry to qualified persons and denying admission to unqualified aliens. Deports illegal aliens already in U.S. encourages and facilitates naturalization and citizenship.

United States Coast Guard *www.uscg.mil.* Created Jan. 28, 1915 as a merger of Revenue Cutter Service and U.S. Lifesaving Service. Moved to Dept. of Transportation Apr. 1, 1967. Transferred to Dept. of Homeland Security in 2003. The Coast Guard is at all times a branch of armed forces and a service within Dept. of Homeland Security except when operating as part of Navy during war. Primary maritime law enforcement agency for U.S. Suppresses drug smuggling and trafficking. Licenses marine vessels. Administers and inspects violations of safety standards for design, construction, equipment and maintenance of commercial marine vessels and offshore structures in U.S. waters. Provides

search and rescue functions for saving lives and property in U.S. waters. Operates ice-breaking vessels to facilitate marine transportation.

United States Customs and Border Protection
www.cbp.gov. Created Mar. 3, 1927 as Bureau of Customs. Re-designated Customs Service Apr. 4, 1973. Renamed and transferred to Dept. of Homeland Security, Jan. 24, 2003. Priority mission of keeping terrorists and weapons out of the U.S. Responsible for securing and facilitating trade and travel, enforcing customs treaties, collecting customs duties, excise taxes, fees and penalties on imports. Supresses illegal trade; quarantines animals, plants and food. Enforces U.S. regulations including immigration, copyright, trademark, patent and drug laws. Includes border patrol.

United States Secret Service
www.secretservice.gov. Protects president and vice president (and president-elect and vice president) of U.S. and their families. Protects former presidents and their spouses until their death. Protects distinguished foreign visitors and U.S. officials abroad at direction of president. Detects and apprehends counterfeiters. Suppresses forgery of government securities and documents.

Transportation Security Administration
www.tsa.gov. Formed by the Aviation and Transportation Security Act on Nov. 19, 2001. Transferred to Dept. of Homeland Security in 2003. Protects U.S. transportation systems, screens cargo and passengers for weapons and provides transportation law enforcement.

▶DEPARTMENT OF HOUSING AND URBAN DEVELOPMENT (H.U.D.)
451 Seventh St. SW, Washington, D.C. 20410. (202) 708-1112. *www.hud.gov.* Created Nov. 9, 1965, by Dept. of Housing and Urban Development Act. Administers mortgage programs for aspiring homeowners. Fosters construction of new housing and renovation of existing rental housing. Provides rental aid for low-income families. Enacts programs to prevent housing discrimination and encourages strong private sector housing industry.

▶DEPARTMENT OF THE INTERIOR
1849 C St. NW, Washington, D.C. 20240. (202) 208-3100. *www.doi.gov.* Created Mar. 3, 1849. Principal U.S. conservation agency. Directs use and conservation of public lands and natural resources; administers over 500 million acres of Federal land and has trust responsibilities for approximately 70 million acres, mostly Indian reservations. Prescribes use of land and water resources, fish and wildlife, national parks and historic places, and mineral resources; aids in preservation of American Indian reservation communities. Major bureaus are described below.

United States Fish and Wildlife Service
www.fws.gov. Conserves and protects fish and wildlife and their habitats. Assesses environmental impact of pesticides, thermal pollution, hydroelectric dams and nuclear power sites.

National Park Service
www.nps.gov. Created Aug. 25, 1916. Administers, protects, and maintains diverse system of national parks, monuments, historic areas and recreation areas; encourages understanding of the historic value of these sites through lectures, tours, and exhibits.

U.S. Geological Survey
www.usgs.gov. Created Mar. 3, 1879. Identifies and classifies land, water, energy, and mineral resources. Investigates potential hazards such as earthquakes and volcanoes. Conducts topographic mapping.

Bureau of Indian Affairs
www.bia.gov. Created 1824 as part of Dept. of War. Transferred to Dept. of Interior in 1849. Provides services to American Indian and Alaska native peoples who manage their own affairs under trust relationship with the Federal Government. Manages 66 million acres of land held in trust and facilitates public and private aid to advancement of these peoples.

Bureau of Land Management (B.L.M.)
www.blm.gov. Created July 16, 1946, by consolidation of the General Land Office and the Grazing Service. Manages 270 million acres of public lands primarily in Far West and in Alaska and an additional 300 million acres of underground mineral estate. Responsible for managing and conserving resources in these lands, including timber, oil, gas, hard minerals and wildlife habitats.

▶DEPARTMENT OF JUSTICE
950 Pennsylvania Ave. NW, Washington, D.C. 20530. (202) 514-2000. *www.usdoj.gov.* Created June 22, 1870. Enforces the law in the public interest. Ensures fair competition in free enterprise system; enforces drug, immigration, and naturalization laws; conducts all Supreme Court suits in which U.S. is party or is concerned. Advises president on legal matters. Major bureaus described below.

Federal Bureau of Investigation (F.B.I.)
www.fbi.gov. Created 1908. Principal investigative bureau of Justice Dept. Investigates violations of Federal law. Areas of primary concern are organized crime (including drug trafficking), terrorism, white-collar crime, cybercrime, federal civil rights violations, and foreign counterintelligence.

Bureau of Alcohol, Tobacco, Firearms, and Explosives
www.atf.gov. Created July 1, 1972. Transferred to Dept. of Justice in 2003. Enforces and administers laws regulating production, use, distribution, and sale of alcohol and tobacco products, firearms, and explosives. A principal law enforcement agency within the Dept. of Justice.

Bureau of Prisons
www.bop.gov. Created 1930. Imprisons and rehabilitates criminals convicted of Federal crimes and sentenced to federal prison.

United States Marshals Service
www.usmarshals.gov. Provides security and support to federal court system. Apprehends federal fugitives. Ensures safety of federal witnesses. Executes court orders and arrest warrants. Maintains custody, manages, and sells property seized from criminals.

Drug Enforcement Administration (D.E.A.)
www.dea.gov. Created July 1973. Investigates interstate drug-trafficking. Enforces Government regulations regarding manufacture, distribution, sale and dispensing of controlled substances.

▶DEPARTMENT OF LABOR
200 Constitution Ave NW, Washington, D.C. 20210. (202) 693-5000. *www.dol.gov.* Created Mar. 4, 1913. Improves welfare and working conditions of wage earners. Guarantees minimum wages and overtime pay as well as unemployment insurance

and workers' compensation. Prevents employment discrimination. Protects pension rights. Provides for job training programs. Pays special attention to labor-related needs of minority workers, old and young, women and disabled people. Major bureaus described below.

Employee Benefits Security Administration (E.B.S.A.)
www.dol.gov/ebsa. (Formerly Pension and Welfare Benefits Administration.) Created Sept. 2, 1974, by Employment Retirement Income Security Act of 1974 (ERISA). Requires private pension and welfare plan administrators to give participants summaries of pension and welfare plans. Keeps summaries on file. Regulates financial operations of pension and welfare plans.

Employment and Training Administration (E.T.A.)
www.doleta.gov. Provides employment security through unemployment insurance, worker dislocation programs and federal-state employment service system. Trains or retrains and finds employment for disadvantaged workers through Job Training Partnership Act (JTPA).

Occupational Safety and Health Administration (O.S.H.A.)
www.osha.gov. Created 1970 by Occupational Safety and Health Act. Promotes safety and health standards in workplace. Issues regulations, conducts investigations, issues citations, and proposes penalties for violations of health standards and regulations.

Bureau of Labor Statistics (B.L.S.)
www.bls.gov. Data-gathering agency. Collects, processes, interprets, and distributes data involving employment, unemployment, wages, family income and expenditures, worker's compensation, industrial relations, productivity and technological change.

Veterans' Employment and Training Service (V.E.T.S.)
www.dol.gov/vets. Maximizes training and employment opportunities for veterans and disabled. Ensures that legislation involving veterans is carried out by local public employment services and by private enterprise.

▶DEPARTMENT OF STATE
2201 C Street NW; Washington, D.C. 20520. (202) 647-4000. *www.state.gov.* Created July 27, 1789, as Dept. of Foreign Affairs. Renamed Dept. of State Sept. 15, 1789. Advises president on foreign policy. Formulates and executes policy to protect and defend American interests overseas. Negotiates treaties and agreements with foreign countries. Consulates provide protection and assistance to U.S. citizens abroad. (*www.travel.state.gov*) Oversees and administers overseas information and cultural programs, including Voice of America and Fulbright scholarship program.

United States Mission to the United Nations
Represents U.S. at U.N.. Carries out U.S. foreign policy as it relates to U.N.

Foreign Service
Maintains relations with more than 140 nations around world. Reports to State Dept. on developments relating to safety and welfare of U.S., its citizens, and their interests. Ambassadors to each country are personal representatives of the president and have full responsibility for carrying out U.S. foreign policy within the country. Ambassadors negotiate agreements between host country and U.S., explain and administer U.S. foreign policy, and maintain relations with government and public of host country.

▶DEPARTMENT OF TRANSPORTATION
1200 New Jersey Ave. SW, Washington, D.C. 20590. (202) 366-4000. *www.dot.gov.* Created Oct. 15, 1966. Establishes nation's comprehensive transportation policy. Major administrations are responsible for highway planning, development, and construction; urban mass transit; railroads; aviation; and the safety of waterways, ports, highways, and oil and gas pipelines.

Federal Aviation Administration (F.A.A.)
www.faa.gov. Created 1958 by Federal Aviation Act. Included in Dept. of Transportation in 1967. Regulates air commerce in effort to promote safety and secure national defense interests. Directs use of navigable U.S. airspace. Develops and operates system of air traffic control for both civil and military aircraft. Regulates aircraft noise.

Federal Highway Administration (F.H.W.A.)
www.fhwa.dot.gov. Included in Dept. of Transportation in 1967 by Dept. of Transportation Act. Promotes highway safety. Provides aid for construction and maintenance of state and Federal highway systems.

Federal Railroad Administration (F.R.A.)
www.fra.dot.gov. Created by Dept. of Transportation Act of 1966. Administers and enforces railroad safety regulations such as track maintenance, inspection and equipment standards, and operating practices. Administers federal grants to Amtrak.

National Highway Traffic Safety Administration
www.nhtsa.gov. Created by Highway Safety Act of 1970. Research and development programs are aimed at reducing number of highway collisions, reducing severity of injuries and economic loss involved in highway accidents, and reducing fatalities resulting from highway crashes.

Federal Transit Administration
www.fta.dot.gov. Created July 1, 1968. Improves equipment and methods used in urban mass transit. Encourages planning of cost-effective mass transit systems. Provides economic and technical assistance for mass transit programs.

Maritime Administration (M.A.R.A.D.)
www.marad.dot.gov. Created May 24, 1950. Included in Dept. of Transportation Aug. 6, 1981, by Maritime Act of 1981. Promotes water-based transportation and the viability of the U.S. merchant marine. Constructs or supervises construction and maintenance of U.S. flag merchant ships for federal government. Generates business for U.S. ships. Develops ports and facilities for maritime transport.

Saint Lawrence Seaway Development Corporation
www.seaway.dot.gov. Created May 13, 1954. Owns, develops, maintains, and operates St. Lawrence Seaway between Montreal and Lake Erie within territorial limits of U.S. Provides safe and efficient waterway for maritime commerce.

Research and Innovative Technology Administration
www.rita.dot.gov. Created Nov. 30, 2004. Conducts research on innovative technologies, including intelligent transportation, provides education and training in education fields. Bureau of Transportation Statistics (*www.bts.gov*) compiles statistics and other information on U.S. transportation systems.

▶DEPARTMENT OF THE TREASURY

1500 Pennsylvania Ave. NW, Washington, D.C. 20220. (202) 622-2000. *www.treas.gov.* Created Sept. 2, 1789. Formulates and recommends economic, financial, tax, and fiscal policies. Acts as financial agent for U.S. Government. Manufactures coins and currency.

Alcohol and Tobacco Tax and Trade Bureau

www.ttb.gov. Created Jan, 24, 2003. Collects alcohol, tobacco, firearms and ammunition excise taxes. Ensures that regulated products comply with federal requirements for labeling, advertising and marketing.

Bureau of Engraving and Printing

www.moneyfactory.gov. Created July 11, 1862. Designs, prints, and finishes Federal Reserve notes, U.S. postage stamps, identification cards, and Treasury securities. Inhibits counterfeiting of these documents.

Internal Revenue Service (I.R.S.)

www.irs.gov. Created July 1, 1862. Administers and enforces internal revenue laws except those relating to alcohol, tobacco, firearms and explosives. Determines, assesses, and collects federal tax revenues from public. Encourages, assesses, and enforces compliance with tax laws.

United States Mint

www.usmint.gov. Mint of the United States created Apr. 2, 1792. Bureau of the Mint created Feb. 12, 1873. Renamed United States Mint Jan. 9, 1984. Manufactures and distributes coins for circulation through Federal Reserve Banks. Mints foreign coins. Processes gold and silver bullion. Manufactures national medals, proof coin sets, and commemorative coins for sale to public.

Bureau of the Public Debt

www.publicdebt.treas.gov. Created June 30, 1940. Manages public debt. Offers public debt securities. Audits retired securities and interest coupons. Maintains accounting control over public debt receipts and expenditures, securities, and interest costs. Adjudicates claims of lost, stolen or destroyed securities.

Office of Thrift Supervision (O.T.S.)

www.ots.treas.gov. Created by the Financial Institutions Reform, Recovery and Enforcement Act, Aug. 9, 1989. Established by Congress as part of a reorganization of the thrift regulatory structure, the OTS has authority to charter federal thrift institutions, and to serve as the primary regulator of federal- and state-chartered thrifts belonging to the Savings Association Insurance Fund (SAIF).

▶DEPARTMENT OF VETERANS AFFAIRS

810 Vermont Ave. NW, Washington, D.C. 20420. (202) 273-4800. *www.va.gov.* Created by Dept. of Veterans Affairs Act of 1988; predecessor Veterans Administration created 1930. Administers benefit programs for veterans and their families, including military-related death or disability compensation, pensions, education and rehabilitation, home loan guaranty, medical care programs, and the National Cemetery System.

Veterans Health Administration

877-222-8387 *www.va.gov/health* Provides hospital, nursing home and outpatient care to eligible veterans. Operates over 150 medical centers, nearly 800 outpatient clinics, over 130 nursing home care units and 232 veteran outreach centers.

Veterans Benefits Administration

800-827-1000 *www.vba.va.gov* Has responsibility for claims for disability compensation and pension, specially adapted housing and automobiles, special clothing allowances, and emergency officers' retirement pay, survivors' claims for death compensation, dependency and indemnity compensation, burial and plot allowance claims, and reimbursement for headstones.

▶INDEPENDENT ESTABLISHMENTS & GOVERNMENT CORPORATIONS

African Development Foundation 1400 Eye St. NW, Suite 1000, Washington, D.C. 20005. (202) 673-3916. *www.asadf.gov.* Created in 1984 by African Development Foundation Act. Nonprofit Government corporation. Through grants, loans, and loan guarantees, aids self-help efforts by poor people in African countries.

AMTRAK (National Railroad Passenger Corporation) 60 Massachusetts Ave. NE, Washington, D.C. 20002. (202) 906-3000. *www.amtrak.com.* Created by Rail Passenger Service Act of 1970 as a for-profit corporation. Develops, operates, and improves inter-city rail passenger service to create national rail transportation system.

Central Intelligence Agency (C.I.A.) Washington, D.C. 20505. (703) 482-0623. *www.cia.gov.* Created by National Security Act of 1947. Under direction of president and National Security Council. Advises NSC on intelligence matters of national security. Collects, evaluates, and disseminates intelligence information relating to national security and to drug production and trafficking. Collects, produces and disseminates counterintelligence and foreign intelligence here (in conjunction with FBI) and abroad. Conducts special activities as directed by president. Protects security of its activities, information, and personnel by necessary and appropriate means.

Money Men

The first U.S. paper money was printed in 1862. Until then, state banks printed their own notes, but there were no federal bills. The Secretary of the Treasury selects the designs shown on United States currency and coinage. In 1862, Treasury Secretary Salmon Chase put his face on the first U.S. notes in an attempt to further his political ambitions. To this day, he remains on the front of the $10,000 bill, though it is no longer in circulation.

Federal law now prohibits portraits of living persons from appearing on government securities. Therefore, the portraits on our currency notes and coins are of deceased persons whose places in history are well-known.

Note	Portrait, Importance
$ 1	George Washington, 1st President
$ 2	Thomas Jefferson, 3rd-President
$ 5	Abraham Lincoln, 16th President
$ 10	Alexander Hamilton, 1st Sec. of Treasury
$ 20	Andrew Jackson, 7th President
$ 50	Ulysses Grant, 18th President
$100	Ben Franklin, Statesman
$500[1]	William McKinley, 25th President
$1,000[1]	Grover Cleveland, 22nd/24th President
$5,000[1]	James Madison, 4th President
$10,000[1]	Salmon Chase, Sec. of Treasury in 1862
$100,000[2]	Woodrow Wilson, 28th President

Notes: 1. No longer in circulation. 2. This note never appeared in general circulation, and was only used in transactions between Federal Reserve Banks. **Source:** U.S. Bureau of Engraving and Printing, www.moneyfactory.com.

Commodity Futures Trading Commission (C.F.T.C.) 1155 21st St. NW, Washington, D.C. 20581. (202) 418-5000. *www.cftc.gov.* Created May 14, 1973 by Commodity Futures Act of 1973. Regulates trading on the 11 U.S. futures exchanges. Regulates activities of commodity exchange members, public brokerage houses, commodity trading advisers and other related employees.

Consumer Product Safety Commission (C.P.S.C.) East-West Towers, 4330 East-West Highway, Bethesda, Md. 20814. *www.cpsc.gov.* (301) 504-7923. Created May 14, 1973 by Consumer Product Safety Act. Protects public from unreasonable risk of injury from consumer products. Develops, enforces, and evaluates safety standards for consumer products.

Corporation for National Community Service 1201 New York Ave. NW, Washington, D.C. 20525. (202) 606-5000. *www.nationalservice.gov.* Created by National and Community Service Act of 1993. Incorporates programs previously administered by ACTION. Administers agencies such as SeniorCorps, AmeriCorps and AmeriCorps VISTA, which encourage and provide national and community service by volunteers, schools, and retired and senior volunteers.

Defense Nuclear Facilities Safety Board 625 Indiana Ave. NW, Suite 700, Washington, D.C. 20004. (202) 694-7000. *www.dnfsb.gov.* Created by Atomic Energy Act of 1954; established as independent agency Sept. 29, 1988. Reviews and evaluates standards for defense nuclear facilities of the Department of Energy. Investigates practices that may imperil public health and safety.

Environmental Protection Agency (E.P.A.) 1200 Pennsylvania Avenue NW., Washington, D.C. 20460-0001. (202) 272-0167. *www.epa.gov.* Created Dec. 2, 1970. Protects and enhances environment. Controls and reduces pollution of air and water. Regulates solid-waste disposal and use of pesticides, radiation and toxic substances.

Equal Employment Opportunity Commission (E.E.O.C.) 1801 L Street NW, Washington, D.C. 20507. (202) 663-4900. *www.eeoc.gov.* Created July 2, 1965, by Title VII of Civil Rights Act of 1964. Protects against discrimination based on race, color, handicap, religion, sex, age and national origin in hiring, promoting, firing, wages, testing, training, apprenticeship and all other terms and conditions of employment.

Export-Import Bank of the United States 811 Vermont Ave. NW, Washington, D.C. 20571. (800) 565-EXIM. *www.exim.gov.* Created Feb. 2, 1934. Facilitates and aids exports of U.S. goods and services through loans, loan guarantees and insurance to exporters and private banks.

Farm Credit Administration 1501 Farm Credit Drive, McLean, VA 22102-5090. (703) 883-4056. *www.fca.gov.* Created by Farm Credit Act of 1971. Regulates and examines programs, banks, associations, and organizations of the Farm Credit System, which provides credit to farmers, ranchers, producers of farm products, rural home owners, and associations and organizations of farmers, ranchers, and farm-equipment producers.

Federal Communications Commission (F.C.C.) 445 12th St. SW, Washington, D.C. 20554. (888) 225-5322. *www.fcc.gov.* Created by Communications Act of 1934. Regulates interstate and foreign communications by radio, television, wire, satellite, and cable. Oversees development of broadcast services and the rapid, efficient provision of telephone and telegraph services at reasonable rates.

Federal Deposit Insurance Corporation (F.D.I.C.) 550 17th St. NW, Washington, D.C. 20429. (877) 275-3342. *www.fdic.gov.* Created June 16, 1933, by Federal Reserve Act. Protects money supply by insuring deposits in and reviewing operations of state-chartered banks that are not members of the Federal Reserve System. Assumed responsibility for insuring savings and loan institutions formerly insured by defunct Federal Savings and Loan Insurance Corp. (FSLIC) in 1989.

Federal Election Commission (F.E.C.) 999 E St. NW, Washington, D.C. 20463. (800) 424-9530. *www.fec.gov.* Created by Federal Election Campaign Act of 1971. Provides public funding for presidential elections. Ensures public disclosure of campaign finance activities. Administers and enforces contribution and spending limits for Federal elections. (See also "U.S. Presidential Elections.")

Federal Housing and Finance Agency 1700 G Street NW, Washington, DC 20552. (866) 796-5595. *www.fhfa.gov.* Created by Federal Housing Finance Regulatory Reform Act of 2008, which merged Federal Housing Finance Board and other functions and added regulatory powers. Ensures the security and supervision of Fannie Mae, Freddie Mac, Federal Home Loan Banks, and the Office of Finance, to further affordable housing and community investment goals.

Federal Labor Relations Authority (F.L.R.A.) 1400 K St. NW, Washington, D.C. 20005. (202) 218-7770. *www.flra.gov.* Created Jan. 1, 1979. Protects rights of federal employees to organize, bargain collectively, and participate in labor organizations. Oversees rights and obligations of federal employees and the labor organizations that represent them.

Federal Maritime Commission 800 North Capitol St. NW, Washington, D.C. 20573-0001. (202) 523-5707. *www.fmc.gov.* Created August 12, 1961. Regulates waterborne foreign commerce, insures that U.S. international trade is open to all nations on fair and equitable terms, and protects against unauthorized, concerted activity in U.S. waterborne commerce.

Federal Mediation and Conciliation Service 2100 K. St. NW, Washington, D.C. 20427. (202) 606-8100. *www.fmcs.gov.* Created in 1947 by Labor Management Relations Act. Promotes development of stable labor management relations. Prevents or minimizes work stoppages by helping to settle disputes and by advocating collective bargaining, mediation, and arbitration.

Federal Reserve System 20th St. and Constitution Ave. NW, Washington, D.C. 20551. (202) 452-3000. *www.federalreserve.gov.* Created Dec. 23, 1913, by Federal Reserve Act. Central Bank of U.S. Administers and creates national credit and monetary policy. Regulates money supply. Maintains soundness of banking industry. (See also the section on "The U.S. Economy".)

Federal Trade Commission (F.T.C.) 600 Pennsylvania Ave. NW, Washington, D.C. 20580. (202) 326-2222. *www.ftc.gov.* Created in 1914 by Federal Trade Commission Act and Clayton Act. Maintains free and fair competition in free enterprise system. Breaks up monopolies. Seeks to prevent corruption, restraints on trade, unfair trade practices and identity theft.

General Services Administration (G.S.A.) 1800 F St. NW, Washington, D.C. 20405. (202) 501-

5082. *www.gsa.gov.* Created July 1, 1949, by Federal Property and Administrative Services Act of 1949. Establishes policy for and manages Government property and records, construction of buildings, distribution of supplies, and other government services.

Inter-American Foundation 901 North Stuart St., 10th Fl., Arlington, VA 22203. (703) 306-4301. *www.iaf.gov.* Created by Congress in 1969. Supports social and economic development in Latin America and Caribbean. Makes grants to self-help organizations for the poor.

National Aeronautics and Space Administration (N.A.S.A.) 300 E Street SW, Washington, D.C. 20546. (202) 358-0000. *www.nasa.gov.* Created by National Aeronautics and Space Act of 1958. Develops, constructs, tests, and operates vehicles for in-flight research within and outside Earth's atmosphere. Disseminates information about space exploration and agency's activities.

National Archives and Records Administration (N.A.R.A.) 8601 Adelphi Rd., College Park, MD 20740-6001. (866) 272-6272. *www.archives.gov.* Created Oct. 19, 1984. Establishes policy for managing records of U.S. government and making them available to public. Maintains 14 regional archives and 17 federal records centers, as well as 13 presidential libraries. Publishes the daily *Federal Register.*

National Capital Planning Commission Suite 500, 401 Ninth St. NW, Washington, D.C. 20004. (202) 482-7200. *www.ncpc.gov.* Created as a park planning agency by act of June 6, 1924. Serves as the central planning agency for development activities for federal lands in the National Capital region in and around Washington.

National Credit Union Administration (N.C.U.A.) 1775 Duke St., Alexandria, VA 22314-3428. (703) 518-6300. *www.ncua.gov.* Created Mar. 10, 1970. Charters, insures, supervises and examines federal credit unions. Administers National Credit Union Share Insurance Fund. Supplies emergency loans to credit unions through Central Liquidity Facility.

National Foundation on the Arts and the Humanities 1100 Pennsylvania Ave. NW, Washington, D.C. 20506. Created in 1965. Its three divisions encourage and support national progress in humanities and arts. The *National Endowment for the Arts (NEA)* (202-682-5400; *www.arts.gov*) fosters professional excellence in arts. The *National Endowment for the Humanities (NEH)* (202-606-8400; *www.neh.gov*) is an independent grant-making agency that supports research, education, and public programs in the humanities. The *Institute of Museum and Library Services* (1800 M St, 9th Fl, Washington DC 20036; *www.imls.gov*; 202-653-4657) assists museums and libraries in maintaining, increasing, and improving services to the public.

National Labor Relations Board (N.L.R.B.) 1099 14th Street NW, Washington, D.C. 20570. (202) 273-1000. *www.nlrb.gov.* Created by National Labor Relations Act of 1935 (also known as Wagner Act). Administers Federal labor law. Safeguards employees' right to organize, conducts elections to determine whether workers want unions as their bargaining representative, and prevents or remedies unfair labor practices.

National Mediation Board 1301 K Street NW, Suite 250 East, Washington, D.C. 20005-7011. (202) 692-5050. *www.nmb.gov.* Created June 21, 1934, by amendment to Railway Labor Act. Resolves and investigates representation disputes in railroad and airline industries that could interrupt flow of commerce and endanger national economy.

National Science Foundation (N.S.F.) 4201 Wilson Blvd., Arlington, VA 22230. (703) 292-5111; *www.nsf.gov.* Created by National Science Foundation Act of 1950. Promotes progress of science and engineering through support of research and education programs.

National Transportation Safety Board (N.T.S.B.) 490 L'Enfant Plaza SW, Washington, D.C. 20594. (202) 314-6000. *www.ntsb.gov.* Created Apr. 1, 1975, by Independent Safety Board Act of 1974. Ensures safe operation of all types of transportation in U.S. Investigates accidents, conducts studies, and makes policy recommendations to government agencies, transportation industry and others.

Nuclear Regulatory Commission (N.R.C.) Washington, D.C. 20555-0001. (301) 415-7000. *www.nrc.gov.* Regulates uses of civilian nuclear energy to protect public health and environment. Sets licensing regulations, issues licenses for, and inspects construction, ownership, and operation of nuclear reactors and nuclear materials.

Office of Personnel Management (O.P.M.) 1900 E St. NW, Washington, D.C. 20415. (202) 606-1800. *www.opm.gov.* Created Jan. 1, 1979. Recruits, examines, trains, and promotes people for Government jobs, regardless of race, religion, sex, political influence and other nonmerit factors. Provides direct benefits, including health and life insurance, to employees and to retired employees and their survivors.

Office of Special Counsel Suite 218, 1730 M Street NW., Washington, D.C. 20036-4505. (202) 254-3600. *www.osc.gov.* Created Jan. 1, 1979. Investigates allegations of certain activities prohibited by civil service laws, rules, or regulations before the Merit Sysems Protection Board. Protects whistleblowers from reprisals by their employers or former employers.

Overseas Private Investment Corporation (O.P.I.C.) 1100 New York Ave. NW, Washington, D.C. 20527. (202) 336-8400. *www.opic.gov.* Established as an independent agency in 1998. Promotes economic growth in developing countries by encouraging U.S. private investment in those nations.

Peace Corps 1111 20th St. NW, Washington, D.C. 20526. (800) 424-8580. *www.peacecorps.gov.* Created by Peace Corps Act of 1961. Promotes world friendship. Helps people of other countries develop infrastructure by bringing U.S. volunteers abroad to participate in public works programs in poorest areas of countries served.

Pension Benefit Guaranty Corporation (P.B.G.C.) 1200 K St. NW, Washington, D.C. 20005. (800) 400-4272. *www.pbgc.gov.* Created Sept. 2, 1974, by Title IV of Employee Retirement Income Security Act of 1974. Guarantees payment of non-forfeitable pension benefits in covered private sector defined benefit pension plans.

Postal Regulatory Commission 901 New York Avenue SW, Washington, D.C. 20268-0001. (202) 789-6800. *www.prc.gov.* Created Aug. 12, 1970, by Postal Reorganization Act. Recommends changes in postal rates, fees, services, programs, studies and mail classification schedules. Hears complaints about postal rates, services, and fees.

Securities and Exchange Commission (S.E.C.) 100 F Street NE, Washington, D.C. 20549. (202) 551-7500. *www.sec.gov.* Created July 2, 1934 by Securities Exchange Act of 1934. Provides fullest possible disclosure to the public of securities sales, operations, and registrations. Protects public against malpractice in securities and financial markets.

Selective Service System National Headquarters, Arlington, VA 22209-2425. (703) 605-4100. *www.sss.gov.* Created June 24, 1948, by Military Selective Service Act. Requires registration, and maintains list of males age 18 to 26 eligible to serve in armed forces in case of national security emergency.

Small Business Administration (S.B.A.) 409 Third St. SW, Washington, D.C. 20416. (202) 205-6600. *www.sba.gov.* Created by Small Business Act of 1953. Aids, counsels, makes loans to and protects interests of small businesses; ensures that they receive a fair amount of government purchases and contracts.

Social Security Administration 6401 Security Blvd., Baltimore, MD 21235. (800) 772-1213. *www.ssa.gov.* Created July 16, 1946; made independent agency by Social Security Independence Act of 1994. Manages the nation's social insurance program, consisting of retirement, survivors, and disability insurance programs, commonly known as Social Security. Administers Supplemental Security Income program for the aged, blind, and disabled. Studies poverty and recommends solutions. Assigns Social Security numbers to all U.S. workers.

Tennessee Valley Authority (T.V.A.) 400 West Summit Hill Dr., Knoxville, TN 37902. (865) 632-2101. *www.tva.gov.* Created May 18, 1933. Government-owned corporation. Conducts resource development programs for advancement of growth in Tennessee Valley region. Controls floods, develops navigation, produces electric power, develops fertilizer, improves recreation, and develops forestry and wildlife.

United States Agency for International Development (A.I.D.) Ronald Reagan Bldg., Washington, DC 20523-1000. (202) 712-4810. *www.usaid.gov.* Established as independent agency in 1998. Administers foreign economic and humanitarian assistance programs in the developing world, Central and Eastern Europe, and the countries of the former Soviet Union.

United States Commission on Civil Rights 624 Ninth St. NW, Washington, D.C. 20425. (202) 376-7700. *www.usccr.gov.* Created by Civil Rights Act of 1957. Collects and studies information on discrimination based on race, color, religion, age, sex, handicap or national origin. Assures equal protection in voting rights and enforcement of civil rights laws. Promotes equal opportunity in education, employment, and housing.

United States International Trade Commission 500 E St. SW, Washington, D.C. 20436. (202) 205-2000. *www.usitc.gov.* Created Sept. 8, 1916. Furnishes studies, reports, and recommendations regarding international trade and tariffs to president, Congress, and other government agencies.

United States Postal Service 475 L'Enfant Plaza SW, Washington, D.C. 20260-0010. (202) 268-2000. *www.usps.gov.* Created Aug. 12, 1970, by Postal Reorganization Act. Provides mail processing and delivery service to individuals and businesses in U.S. Protects mail from loss or theft and apprehends violators of postal laws.

FEDERAL EMPLOYEES AND BUDGET

▶ **FEDERAL JOBS AND SALARIES**
As of March 31, 2009, there were 1,815,380 permanent full-time non-postal civilian employees of the U.S. government. Nearly 97 percent of federal employees worked in the United States; 18,242 (less than one percent) worked in U.S. Territories; and 70,069 (2.5 percent) worked in foreign countries. The majority of these employees worked in metropolitan areas, with 345,501 (12.3 percent) in the Washington, D.C. area.

More than 68 percent of the federal civilian non-postal workforce was employed in one of five executive departments in 2009. The Department of Defense employed 703,000 civilians (35.5 percent of the total), Veterans Affairs employed 272,000 (13.7 percent), Homeland Security 170,000 (8.5 percent), and the Justice and Treasury Departments each employed 109,000 (5.5).

Most federal government civilian employees are paid according to one of the standardized wage systems such as the General Schedule (GS) or the Federal Wage Systems, but locality-based adjustments and other administrative determinations also regulate salaries. In 2009, the average salary for full-time civilian government employees was $74,219. Employees under the General Schedule earned more on average than those on Federal Wage Systems ($71,239 to $51,237), but not as much as employees covered by other acts and determinations, who averaged $86,238. Average salaries also vary by major geographic area: United States averages $74,435; Washington, D.C. area $100,518; foreign countries $67,933; and U.S. territories $55,001.

White-Collar Employees General Schedule
White-collar employees paid under the General Schedule make up two-thirds of the federal civilian

Federal Employees and Budget, 1901–2010

| Year | Number of employees[1] | Budget (millions) | | |
		Receipts	Outlays	Surplus or deficit (–)
1901	239,476	$588	$525	$63
1910	388,708	676	694	–18
1920	655,265	6,649	6,358	291
1930	601,319	4,058	3,320	738
1940	1,042,420	6,548	9,468	–2,920
1945	3,816,310	45,159	92,712	–47,553
1950	1,960,708	39,443	42,562	–3,119
1960	2,398,704	92,492	92,191	301
1970	2,984,574	192,807	195,649	–2,842
1980	2,875,866	517,112	590,941	–73,830
1990	3,128,267	1,031,969	1,253,165	–221,195
2000	2,702,258	2,025,457	1,789,216	236,241
2005	2,701,920	2,153,859	2,472,205	–318,346
2007	2,698,989	2,568,239	2,730,241	–162,002
2009	2,719,010	2,104,995	3,517,681	–1,412,686
2010[2]	2,892,217	2,165,119	3,720,701	–1,555,582

Notes: 1. Paid civilians only. 2. Projected. **Source:** Office of Management and Budget, *Budget of the United States Government, FY 2011.*

workforce. The number of full-time General Schedule employees declined from 1,283,663 in 2004 to 1,162,408 in 2008 then rose to 1,204,966 by December 2009. The General Schedule consists of 15 grades broadly defined in terms of responsibility, difficulty and qualifications. Each grade is sub-divided into 10 steps and within-grade advancement occurs on a fixed schedule, although employees demonstrating "high-quality performance" can receive "quality step increases."

Veterans Affairs   The Department of Veterans Affairs has its own wage system, which covered 258,157 full-time workers in 2009, including 11,523 physicians with an average salary of $194,141; 5,403 pharmacists ($112,895); and 1,177 physical therapists ($76,932).

Executive Schedule and Senior Executive Service   The very top executive branch employees are paid under the Executive Schedule (EX). In 2009, the Executive Schedule covered 399

employees with an average salary of $160,478. The five Executive Schedule levels include most political appointees: level I—cabinet members; level II—deputy secretaries of major departments; level III—presidential advisors, chief administrators of major independent agencies, and under secretaries; level IV—assistant secretaries, deputy under secretaries, and general counsels in executive departments; and level V—deputy assistant secretaries, administrators, commissioners, and directors. The Senior Executive Service (SES) comprises most of the managerial and policy positions in the executive branch that do not require Senate confirmation. The SES covered 7,801 employees in 2009, with an average salary of $163,106. Since SES employees do not necessarily leave their posts

Salaries of Federal Officials, 2010

The Ethics Reform Act of 1989 provided an automatic annual cost of living increase for Congress unless legislators actively vote against it, as they did in 2009 and 2010, when they declined pay raises for themselves for 2010 and 2011. Salaries in the judicial branch are pegged to those in Congress, so whenever legislators get a raise, so does the judiciary. The President's salary, however, is raised only by Congressional vote and has been at the same level since 2001.

Branch/Official	2010 Salary
Executive Branch	
President	$400,000
Vice President	230,700
Legislative Branch	
Senate	
President pro tempore	$193,400
Majority and minority leaders	193,400
Senators	174,000
House of Representatives	
Speaker of the House	$223,500
Minority and majority leaders	193,400
Representatives	174,000
Judicial Branch	
Chief Justice	$223,500
Associate justices	213,900
Circuit judges	184,500
District judges	174,000

Source: Federal Register, *Vol. 74*, Dec. 30, 2009.

Federal Government Pay Systems, 2010

Grade	Employees[1]	Salary Range[2]
General Schedule		
GS-1	3,437	$17,803–22,269
GS-2	4,808	20,017–25,191
GS-3	14,661	21,840–28,392
GS-4	45,015	24,518–31,871
GS-5	93,809	27,431–35,657
GS-6	77,513	30,577–39,748
GS-7	124,879	33,979–44,176
GS-8	44,749	37,631–47,663
GS-9	117,815	41,563–54,028
GS-10	12,416	45,771–59,505
GS-11	184,031	50,287–65,371
GS-12	192,595	60,274–78,355
GS-13	167,541	71,674–93,175
GS-14	80,885	84,697–110,104
GS-15	42,265	99,628–129,517
Senior Level (SL)		
Total	694	$119,554–179,700
Executive Schedule (EX)		
Level I	19	$199,700
Level II	41	179,700
Level III	88	165,300
Level IV	233	155,500
Level V	17	145,700
Total	399	
Senior Executive Service (SES)		
Total	7,801	$119,554–179,700

Note: 1. As of December, 2009. 2. Effective January 2010.
Source: U.S. Office of Personnel Management, 2010.

U.S. Federal Employment, 1992–2009

Description	1992	2000	2005	2009
Executive branch civilian employment[1]	**2,226,778**	**1,778,138**	**1,872,200**	**1,977,774**
U.S. Postal Service[2]	792,049	860,777	764,210	674,844
Military personnel on active duty[3]	1,847,600	1,426,338	1,430,104	1,590,754
Department of Defense	1,808,131	1,384,338	1,389,394	1,541,235
Department of Homeland Security (Coast Guard)	39,469	36,157	40,710	42,939
Total executive branch employment	**4,866,427**	**4,065,253**	**4,066,514**	**4,243,372**
Legislative branch	38,509	31,157	30,816	32,104
Judicial branch	27,987	32,186	34,064	34,288
Total federal employment	**4,932,923**	**4,128,596**	**4,131,394**	**4,309,764**

Notes: 1.Excludes Postal Service employees. 2. Includes Postal Rate Commission. 3. Excludes reserve components. 4. Data for Senate includes only positions filled. **Source:** Office of Management and Budget, *Budget of the United States Government, FY 2011.*

Government Employment and Population, 1962–2008

	Government employment					
Fiscal year	Federal executive branch[1] ('000s)	Total Federal personnel ('000s)	State and local governments ('000s)	All governmental units ('000s)	Executive branch employment as a percent of all governmental units[1]	Executive branch employment per 1,000 population[1]
1962	2,485	5,354	6,549	11,903	20.9%	13.3
1965	2,496	5,215	7,696	12,911	19.3	12.8
1970[2]	2,944	6,085	9,822	15,907	18.5	14.4
1975	2,848	5,061	11,937	16,998	16.8	13.2
1980[2]	2,821	4,965	13,375	18,340	15.4	12.4
1985	3,008	5,256	13,519	18,775	16.0	12.6
1990[2]	3,067	5,234	15,219	20,453	15.0	12.3
1995	2,858	4,475	16,484	20,959	13.6	10.7
2000[2]	2,639	4,129	17,925	22,054	12.0	9.4
2005	2,636	4,138	19,078	23,216	11.4	8.9
2007	2,636	4,127	19,538	23,665	11.1	8.7
2008	2,650	4,258	N.A.	N.A.	N.A.	6.5

Notes: 1. Civilian employment only, including full-time permanent, temporary, part-time, and intermittent employees in the executive branch, including the Postal Service, and beginning in 1970, includes various disadvantaged worker-trainee programs. 2. Includes temporary employees in the decennial census. **Source:** Office of Management and Budget, *Budget of the United States Government, FY 2009.*

Federal Government Employment and Outlays, by Branch and Agency, 1990–2010

Agency	Employment 2009	Outlays (millions of dollars)			
		1990	2000	2009	2010[2]
Legislative branch	32,104	$2,241	$2,911	$4,702	$5,423
Judicial branch	34,288	1,646	4,086	6,645	7,159
Executive branch[3]					
Executive Office of the President	N.A.	158	283	743	715
Department of Agriculture	94,200	46,012	75,663	114,440	142,016
Department of Commerce	56,000	3,734	7,807	10,718	16,714
Department of Defense[4] (military functions)	702,700	289,755	281,223	636,775	692,031
Department of Defense (civil functions)	22,200	21,692	32,864	64,118	64,853
Department of Education	4,000	22,972	33,900	53,389	106,944
Department of Energy	15,500	12,084	15,010	23,683	38,278
Department of Health and Human Services	63,000	175,531	382,626	796,267	868,762
Department of Homeland Security	169,600	N.A.	N.A.	51,725	52,903
Dept. of Housing and Urban Development	9,500	20,167	30,828	61,019	62,518
Department of the Interior	68,600	5,825	8,029	11,775	12,042
Department of Justice	109,100	6,507	20,064	27,711	30,333
Department of Labor	16,000	25,215	31,876	138,157	209,265
Department of State	30,400	4,802	6,850	21,427	25,726
Department of Transportation	56,400	28,650	45,965	73,004	90,944
Department of the Treasury	108,700	255,172	390,677	701,775	502,980
Department of Veterans Affairs	272,000	28,998	47,087	95,457	124,565
Environmental Protection Agency	17,000	5,108	7,238	8,070	11,301
General Services Administration	12,000	−93	28	319	1,782
National Aeronautics & Space Administration (NASA)	18,300	12,429	13,442	19,168	19,123
Office of Personnel Management	4,700	31,949	48,660	72,302	71,603
Small Business Administration	3,900	692	−421	2,246	5,978
Social Security Administration (off-budget)	64,100	244,998	396,169	648,892	683,867
Totals[5, 6]	**2,044,166**	**$1,253,198**	**$1,788,773**	**$3,517,681**	**$3,720,701**

Notes: Outlays are the measure of Government spending—payments to liquidate obligations (other than the repayment of debt), net of cash, and offsetting collections. Outlays are generally recorded on a cash basis, but also include many cash-equivalent transactions and interest accrued on public issues of the public debt. 1. Employment figures exclude developmental positions under the Worker-Trainee Opportunity Program; participants in the Cooperative Education Program; disadvantaged summer and part-time workers under such Office of Personnel Management programs as Summer Aides, stay-in-school, and junior fellowship; and certain statutory exemptions. Figures for executive branch rounded at source. 2. Estimate. 3. Civilian employment. 4. By law (10 U.S.C. Chapter 4, section 140b) the Department of Defense is exempt from full-time equivalent employment controls. Data shown are estimated. 5. Employment totals do not include FDIC or U.S. Postal Service. 6. Outlay totals do not account for undistributed offsetting receipts. **Source:** Office of Management and Budget, *The Budget of the United States Government, FY 2011.*

when a new president enters office, the average SES tenure is almost 23 years, compared to just over eight years for Executive Schedule employees.

Special rates   If the government has difficulty recruiting and retaining qualified personnel in occupations with higher competitive market rates, it can establish special salary rates for such occupations.   The number of white-collar employees receiving special-rate salaries varies from year to year. As locality pay amounts have increased and some agencies have established banded pay systems, the number of Federal employees receiving special rates has declined.   In 2007, about 74,000 employees were on special rates.

Blue-Collar Employees   The federal government employed 181,081 full-time workers in blue-collar (trades and labor) occupations in 2009—ten percent of the civilian government workforce.

The Congressional Budget Process

On or before	Action to be completed
First Monday in February	President submits his budget. Congressional committees have six weeks to submit views and estimates to Budget Committees.
February 15	Congressional Budget Office submits report to budget committees.
April 1	Senate budget committee reports concurrent resolution on the budget.
April 15	Congress completes action on concurrent resolution on the budget.
May 15	Annual appropriation bills may be considered in the House.
June 10	House Appropriations Committee reports last annual appropriations bill.
June 15	Congress completes action on reconciliation legislation.
June 30	House completes action on annual appropriation bills.
October 1	Fiscal year begins.

Note: 1. A concurrent resolution sets levels for new budget authority and outlays, direct loan obligations, primary loan guarantee commitments, the amount by which Federal revenues should be increased or decreased, the budget surplus or deficit, the public debt, and so on. **Source:** Committee on Ways and Means, U.S. House of Representatives, *Overview of Entitlement Programs*, (annual).

Nearly three-quarters of these employees (130,447) worked for the Defense Department, while the Department of Veterans Affairs employed another 26,221 (14.5 percent). Pay rates for trade and labor workers are governed by Federal Wage Systems and determined on a prevailing rate basis by pay locality. The vast majority of blue-collar federal employees (178,707) work in the U.S., where their average salary is $51,857. Average wages are highest in Alaska ($65,681), but much lower in foreign countries ($45,300) and U.S. territories ($39,066).

▶DEFICITS AND THE FEDERAL DEBT

After 30 years of annual budget deficits, the federal government recorded four consecutive years of surpluses from 1998–2001, a feat not seen since before the Depression. Yet even these surpluses did little to dent the immense federal debt incurred over the past 40 years; they didn't even equal the net interest payments on this huge debt. Since 2002, the government has returned to running annual budget deficits, sending the gross federal debt spiraling to $11.9 trillion in 2009—more than twice what it was in 2001. (See "U.S. Economy" for an explanation of the difference between deficits and the debt.)

▶GLOSSARY OF FEDERAL BUDGET TERMS

Budget authority   The term budget authority means the authority provided by law to incur financial obligations that result in immediate or future outlays involving government funds or to collect offsetting receipts.

Budget deficit/surplus   A budget deficit occurs when government outlays exceed government receipts; a surplus occurs when receipts exceed outlays. The record budget surplus was $236.4 billion in 2000; the record deficit is the $1,412.7 billion recorded in 2009—more than three times the previous record of $458.6 billion set one year earlier in 2008.

Fiscal year   The federal government's fiscal year (FY) begins Oct. 1 and ends Sept. 30 of the next calendar year. So FY 2011 began Oct. 1, 2010 and ends Sept. 30, 2011.

Intergovernmental expenditure/revenue   Amounts paid to or received from other governments either in the form of shared revenues and grants-in-aid, as reimbursements for performance of general government activities or for specific services such

Federal Government Receipts by Source, 1934–2010 (billions of dollars)

Year	Individual income taxes	Corporation income taxes[1]	Social insurance & retirement receipts	Excise taxes	Other[2]	Total
1934	$ 0.4	$ 0.3	[3]	$ 1.4	$ .8	$ 3.0
1940	0.9	1.2	$ 1.8	2.0	0.7	6.5
1950	15.8	10.4	4.3	7.6	1.4	39.4
1960	40.7	21.5	14.7	11.7	3.9	92.5
1970	90.4	32.8	44.3	15.7	9.5	192.8
1980	244.1	64.6	157.8	24.3	26.3	517.1
1990	466.9	93.5	380.0	35.3	56.2	1,032.0
2000	1,004.5	207.3	652.9	68.9	92.0	2,025.5
2005	927.2	278.3	794.1	73.1	81.1	2,153.9
2009	915.3	138.2	890.9	62.5	98.1	2,105.0
2010[4]	935.1	156.7	875.8	73.2	123.6	2,165.1

Notes: 1. Beginning in 1990 includes trust fund receipts for the hazardous substance Superfund. 2. Includes estate and gift taxes, customs duties and fees, federal reserve deposits, and other. 3. Less than $100 million. 4. Estimate.
Source: Office of Management and Budget, *Budget of the United States Government, FY 2011.*

as care of prisoners for the paying government, or in lieu of taxes.

Off-budget/on-budget Some presentations in the federal budget distinguish on-budget totals from off-budget totals. On-budget totals reflect the transactions of all federal government entities except those excluded from the budget totals by law, the two Social Security trust funds (old-age and survivors insurance and the federal disability insurance trust funds), and the Postal Service fund. Off-budget totals reflect the transactions of

government entities excluded from the on-budget totals by law.

Offsetting collections Offsetting collections are collections from the public that result from business-type or market-oriented activities and collections; examples include proceeds from the sale of electric power by the Tennessee Valley Authority, voluntary medical insurance premiums paid to the supplementary medical insurance trust fund, and the sale of postage stamps.

Outlays by Budget Enforcement Act Category, 1970–2010 (billions)

Category	1970	1980	1990	2000	2005	2009	2010[1]
Total Outlays	**$195.6**	**$590.9**	**$1,253.2**	**$1,789.18**	**$2,472.2**	**$3,517.7**	**$3,720.7**
Discretionary outlays	120.3	276.3	500.6	614.8	968.5	1,237.7	1,408.2
National defense	81.9	134.6	300.1	295.0	493.6	656.8	714.1
Non-defense	38.3	141.7	200.4	319.9	474.8	581.0	694.1
Mandatory outlays	61.0	262.1	568.2	951.4	1,319.8	2,093.0	2,123.5
Social Security	29.6	117.1	246.5	406.0	518.7	677.7	715.3
Deposit Insurance	-0.5	-0.4	57.9	-3.1	-1.4	22.5	-26.7
Means-tested entitlements[2]	10.1	45.0	94.1	232.6	350.9	487.9	585.8
Other	30.4	120.4	206.4	358.4	516.7	997.5	928.7
Undistributed offsetting receipts[3]	-8.6	-19.9	-36.7	-42.6	-65.2	-92.6	-79.7
Net interest	14.4	52.5	184.4	222.9	184.0	186.9	187.8

Notes: 1. Estimate. 2. Includes Medicaid, food stamps, family support assistance (AFDC), supplemental security income (SSI), child nutrition programs, earned income tax credits, and veterans' pensions. 3. Includes asset sales. **Source:** Office of Management and Budget, *Budget of the United States Government, FY 2011.*

Budget Outlays and Percent Distribution, by Function, 1970–2010, (millions of dollars)

Function	1970	1980	1990	2000	2009	2010[1]
National defense	**$81,692**	**$133,995**	**$299,331**	**$294,394**	**$661,049**	**$719,179**
Human resources	**75,349**	**313,374**	**619,329**	**1,115,665**	**2,155,782**	**2,504,037**
Education, training, employment & social services	8,634	31,843	38,755	53,789	79,746	142,521
Health	5,907	23,169	57,716	154,533	334,327	372,336
Medicare	6,213	32,090	98,102	197,113	430,093	457,159
Income Security	15,655	86,540	147,076	253,724	533,224	685,870
Social Security	30,270	118,547	248,623	409,423	682,963	721,496
Veterans benefits & services	8,669	21,185	29,058	47,083	95,429	124,655
Physical resources	**15,574**	**65,985**	**126,039**	**84,954**	**443,797**	**175,599**
Energy	997	10,156	3,341	-761	4,749	18,952
Natural resources & environment	3,065	13,858	17,080	25,031	35,574	47,039
Commerce and housing credit	2,112	9,390	67,600	3,208	291,535	-25,319
Transportation	7,008	21,329	29,485	46,853	84,289	106,458
Community and regional development	2,392	11,252	8,498	10,623	27,650	28,469
Net interest	**14,380**	**52,538**	**184,380**	**222,949**	**186,902**	**187,772**
Other functions	**17,286**	**44,996**	**60,734**	**113,835**	**162,790**	**213,845**
International affairs	4,330	12,714	13,764	17,216	37,529	51,138
General science, space, & technology	4,511	5,832	14,444	18,633	29,449	33,032
Agriculture	5,166	8,839	11,958	36,459	22,237	26,610
Administration of justice	959	4,584	9,993	28,499	51,549	55,025
General government	2,320	13,028	10,575	13,028	22,026	29,290
Total[2]	**$195,649**	**$590,947**	**$1,253,198**	**$1,789,216**	**$3,517,681**	**$3,720,701**
As Percentage Of Total						
National defense	41.8%	22.7%	23.9%	16.5%	18.8%	19.3%
Human resources	38.5	53.0	49.4	62.4	61.3	67.3
Physical resources	8.0	11.2	10.1	4.7	12.6	4.7
Net interest	7.4	8.9	14.7	12.5	5.3	5.0
Other functions	8.8	7.6	4.8	6.4	4.6	5.7

Notes: 1.Estimate. 2. Includes undistributed offsetting receipts not shown separately. **Source:** Office of Management and Budget, *Budget of the United States Government, FY 2011.*

Outlays Budget outlays are expenditures and net lending of funds under budget authority during the fiscal year. They constitute the spending side of the budget and are compared to receipts in calculating the budget surplus or deficit.

Receipts Budget receipts constitute the income side of the budget and are composed almost entirely of taxes or other compulsory payments to the government. They are compared to outlays in calculating the budget surplus or deficit.

Trust fund In the federal budget, a trust fund means only that the law requires that funds must be accounted for separately and used only for specified purposes. The largest trust funds are those for civil service and military retirement, Social Security, Medicare and unemployment insurance. These are financed largely by Social Security taxes and contributions and payments from the general fund. There are also major trust funds for transportation and bank deposit insurance which are financed by user charges.

User charges These are charges for services rendered, collected in the form of taxes, such as highway excise taxes to fund the highway trust fund.

Federal Government Finances, 1990–2010 (in millions of dollars)

Category	1990	2000	2009	2010[1]
RECEIPTS, TOTAL	**$1,031,969**	**$2,025,218**	**$2,104,995**	**$2,165,119**
Individual income taxes, total	**466,884**	**1,004,462**	**915,308**	**935,771**
Corporation income taxes, total	**93,507**	**207,289**	**138,229**	**156,741**
Social insurance and retirement receipts, total	**380,047**	**652,852**	**890,917**	**875,756**
Employment and general retirement:	**353,891**	**620,451**	**848,885**	**819,820**
Old-age and survivors insurance (Off-budget)	255,031	411,677	559,067	542,993
Disability insurance (Off-budget)	26,625	68,907	94,942	92,190
Hospital insurance	68,556	135,529	190,663	180,474
Railroad retirement:	2,292	4,338	2,301	2,266
Unemployment insurance:	21,635	27,640	37,889	51,496
Other retirement:	4,522	4,761	4,143	4,440
Federal employees' retirement—employee share	4,405	4,691	4,105	4,413
Non-Federal employees retirement[2]	117	70	38	27
Excise taxes, total	**35,345**	**68,865**	**62,483**	**73,204**
Federal funds, total	15,591	22,692	13,854	21,988
Alcohol taxes	5,695	8,140	9,903	9,917
Tobacco taxes	4,081	7,221	12,841	17,391
Telephone taxes	2,995	5,670	1,115	879
Transportation fuels taxes	N.A.	819	−10,324	−8,372
Other Federal fund excise taxes	2,460	717	319	2,173
Trust funds, total	19,754	46,173	48,629	51,216
Highway	13,867	34,972	34,961	36,237
Airport and airway	3,700	9,739	10,569	11,798
Aquatic resources	218	342	576	573
Black lung disability insurance	665	518	645	638
Inland waterway	63	101	76	84
Vaccine injury compensation	159	133	235	295
Leaking underground storage tank	122	184	169	182
Estate and gift taxes, total	**11,500**	**29,010**	**23,482**	**17,011**
Customs duties, total	**16,707**	**19,914**	**22,453**	**23,787**
Miscellaneous receipts, total	**27,978**	**42,826**	**52,123**	**82,849**
OUTLAYS, TOTAL	**$1,253,116**	**$1,789,067**	**$3,517,681**	**$3,720,701**
National defense, total	**299,331**	**294,495**	**661,049**	**719,179**
Department of Defense—Military, total	289,704	281,161	636,742	692,032
Military Personnel	75,622	75,950	147,348	155,006
Operation and Maintenance	88,294	105,812	259,312	279,424
Procurement	80,972	51,696	129,218	147,234
Research, Development, Test, and Evaluation	37,454	37,602	79,030	79,322
Military Construction	5,080	5,109	17,614	23,758
Family Housing	3,501	3,413	2,721	3,977
Other	−1,218	1,579	1,499	3,311
Atomic energy defense activities	8,988	12,138	17,552	19,975
Defense-related activities	639	1,196	6,755	7,172
International affairs, total	**13,764**	**17,216**	**37,529**	**51,138**
International development and humanitarian assistance	5,498	6,518	22,095	26,527
International security assistance	8,652	6,387	6,247	9,896
Conduct of foreign affairs	3,050	4,709	12,152	13,249
Foreign information and exchange activities	1,103	817	1,330	1,356
International financial programs	−4,539	−1,215	−4,295	110
General science, space and technology, total	**14,443**	**18,633**	**29,449**	**33,032**
General science and basic research	2,834	6,206	11,052	14,480
Space flight, research, and supporting activities	11,609	12,427	18,397	18,552
Energy, total	**3,341**	**−761**	**4,749**	**18,952**
Energy supply	1,976	−1,818	2,045	8,779

Category	1990	2000	2009	2010[1]
Energy conservation	$365	$666	$1,432	$9,192
Emergency energy preparedness	442	162	754	243
Energy information, policy, and regulation	558	229	518	738
Natural resources and environment, total	**17,080**	**25,031**	**35,574**	**47,039**
Water resources	4,401	5,081	8,063	12,390
Conservation and land management	4,030	6,762	9,813	12,538
Recreational resources	1,400	2,558	3,550	4,034
Pollution control and abatement	5,170	7,402	8,276	11,486
Other natural resources	2,080	3,228	5,872	6,591
Agriculture, total	**11,806**	**36,459**	**22,237**	**26,610**
Farm income stabilization	9,717	33,446	17,635	21,272
Agricultural research and services	2,089	3,013	4,602	5,338
Commerce and housing credit, total	**67,600**	**3,208**	**291,535**	**−25,319**
Mortgage credit	3,845	−3,335	99,760	55,739
Postal Service	2,116	2,129	−978	1,038
Deposit insurance	57,891	−3,053	22,573	−26,627
Other advancement of commerce	3,748	7,467	170,180	−55,469
Transportation, total	**29,485**	**46,853**	**84,289**	**106,458**
Ground transportation	18,954	31,697	54,103	72,668
Air transportation	7,234	10,571	20,799	22,721
Water transportation	3,151	4,394	9,093	10,373
Other transportation	146	191	294	696
Community and regional development, total	**8,531**	**10,623**	**27,650**	**28,469**
Community development	3,530	5,480	7,719	9,810
Area and regional development	2,902	2,538	3,221	2,119
Disaster relief and insurance	2,098	2,605	16,710	16,540
Education, training, employment, and social services, total	**37,176**	**53,754**	**79,746**	**142,521**
Elementary, secondary, and vocational education	9,918	20,578	53,206	84,087
Higher education	11,107	10,116	−3,258	20,448
Research and general education aids	1,577	2,532	3,456	3,802
Training and employment	5,619	6,772	7,652	10,893
Other labor services	810	1,199	1,646	1,860
Social services	8,145	12,557	17,044	21,431
Health, total	**57,716**	**154,533**	**334,327**	**372,336**
Health care services	47,642	136,230	300,010	335,241
Health research and training	8,611	15,979	30,565	32,697
Consumer and occupational health and safety	1,462	2,324	3,752	4,398
Medicare, total	**98,102**	**197,113**	**430,093**	**457,159**
Income security, total	**148,655**	**253,575**	**533,224**	**685,870**
General retirement and disability insurance (excluding social security)	5,148	5,189	8,218	7,953
Federal employee retirement and disability	52,037	77,152	118,119	120,628
Unemployment compensation	18,889	23,012	122,537	194,270
Housing assistance	15,891	28,800	50,913	76,969
Food and nutrition assistance	23,964	32,483	79,080	99,258
Other income security	32,725	86,939	154,357	186,792
Social security, total	**248,623**	**409,423**	**682,963**	**721,496**
Veterans benefits and services, total	**29,058**	**47,083**	**95,429**	**124,655**
Income security for veterans	15,566	25,461	45,952	63,143
Veterans education, training and rehabilitation	395	1,430	3,495	8,978
Hospital and medical care for veterans	12,107	19,477	41,882	46,240
Veterans housing	633	364	−578	559
Other veterans benefits and services	356	351	4,678	5,735
Administration of justice, total	**10,185**	**28,501**	**51,549**	**55,025**
Federal law enforcement activities	4,840	12,123	27,552	28,845
Federal litigative and judicial activities	3,577	7,762	12,083	12,855
Federal correctional activities	1,291	3,707	7,298	7,746
Criminal justice assistance	477	4,909	4,616	5,579
General government, total	**10,490**	**12,960**	**22,026**	**29,290**
Legislative functions	1,759	2,223	3,813	4,306
Executive direction and management	160	456	535	569
Central fiscal operations	5,826	8,285	10,752	11,293
General property and records management	−32	−29	554	2,148
Central personnel management	184	184	102	176
General purpose fiscal assistance	2,161	2,084	4,097	7,009
Other general government	792	2,241	3,174	5,147
Deductions for offsetting receipts	−361	−2,484	−1,001	−1,358
Net interest, total	**$184,347**	**$222,949**	**$186,902**	**$187,772**

Notes: 1. Estimate. 2. Represents employer and employee contributions to the civil service retirement and disability fund for covered employees of Government-sponsored, privately owned enterprises and the District of Columbia municipal government.
Source: Office of Management and Budget, *Budget of the United States Government, FY 2010.*

Federal Government Revenues and Outlays, Fiscal Year 2010

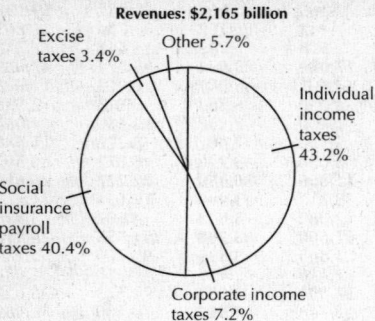

Revenues: $2,165 billion

Excise taxes 3.4%
Other 5.7%
Individual income taxes 43.2%
Social insurance payroll taxes 40.4%
Corporate income taxes 7.2%

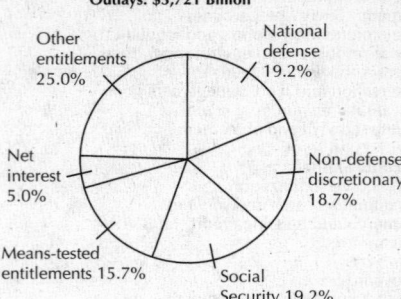

Outlays: $3,721 Billion

Other entitlements 25.0%
National defense 19.2%
Net interest 5.0%
Non-defense discretionary 18.7%
Means-tested entitlements 15.7%
Social Security 19.2%

Federal Budget Outlays for National Defense Functions, 1962–2010 (millions of dollars)

Function	1962	1970	1980	1990	2000	2009	2010[1]
Military personnel	$16,331	$29,032	$40,897	$75,622	$75,950	$147,348	$155,006
Percent of defense budget	31.2%	35.4%	30.5%	25.2%	25.8%	22.3%	21.6%
Operations & maintenance	$11,594	$21,609	$44,788	$88,294	$105,812	$259,312	$279,424
Procurement	14,532	21,584	29,021	80,972	51,696	129,218	147,234
Research, development, test and evaluation	6,319	7,166	13,127	37,454	37,602	79,030	79,322
Military construction	1,347	1,168	2,450	5,080	5,109	17,614	23,758
Family housing	259	614	1,680	3,501	3,413	2,721	3,977
Other	−271	−1,050	−1,050	−1,218	1,478	1,499	3,311
Total outlays[2]	$52,345	$81,692	$133,995	$299,331	$294,394	$661,049	$719,179

Notes: 1. Estimate. 2. Includes atomic energy defense activities and other defense-related activities not shown separately.
Source: Office of Management and Budget, *Budget of the United States Government, FY 2011.*

NATIONAL DEFENSE

In 2010, the United States spent over $700 billion dollars to keep 1.4 million people in active military service and to build and maintain the largest arsenal of weapons ever known.

Since the end of World War II, a large percentage of people and material have been committed to regions around the world that the government has determined are vital to U.S. interests. Between 1961 and 1980, the defense budget averaged around $200 billion annually (in 1982 constant dollars)—even during the Vietnam War. In 1981, however, the Reagan administration began a massive defense buildup that swelled successive defense budgets to unprecedented peacetime levels and in the process helped to quadruple the annual federal deficit in less than five years.

When the cold war ended, the defense budget started to recede from its previous high of $303 billion in 1989. But since 1998, the amount spent on the military has been increasing steadily every year, to its present all-time high. The operations in Afghanistan (2001–) and Iraq (2003–) have caused the defense budget to double since 2000. In the 2010 budget, one-fifth of all Federal Outlays were slated for National Defense.

The defense establishment The earliest precursor to the Department of Defense was the War Department, established by Congress in 1789; a separate Navy Department was created in 1798. These were merged under the National Security Act of 1947 and subsequent amendments. By 1949 the secretary of defense was established as the principal assistant to the president on defense matters in charge of the Defense Department.

The Department of Defense (DoD) is a cabinet-level organization responsible for providing the military forces needed to deter war and protect the security of the United States. The major elements of these forces are the Army, Navy, Air Force, and Marine Corps. Under the president, who is also the commander-in-chief, the secretary of defense exercises direction, authority and control over the Department of Defense, which includes the three military departments, the Joint Chiefs of Staff and Joint Staff, nine unified commands, 15 defense agencies, and seven DoD field activities.

The four armed services are subordinate to the military departments, which are responsible for recruiting, training and equipping their forces. The Marine Corps is the second armed service in the Department of the Navy. (A fifth armed service, the U.S. Coast Guard, joined the Department of Homeland Security in 2003.)

Chain of command Operational command of U.S. combat forces is assigned to the nation's unified and specified commands. The chain of command runs from the president to the secretary of defense, through the Joint Chiefs of Staff, to the commanders-in-chief of the unified and specified commands. The four service secretaries are not part of this chain of command. A *unified command* is composed of forces from two or more services, has a broad and continuing mission and is normally organized on a geographical basis.

▶**U.S. ARMY**
In peacetime, the primary mission of the continental U.S. armies is to train reserves and national guard, plan for mobilization, and coordinate domestic emergency relief efforts. The largest unit is a numbered *army*, such as the Fifth Army. (In time of war, two or three armies may be brought under a single command in an *army group*.) An *army* is made up of two or more corps plus a headquarters (HQ) unit; a *corps* is made up of two to five divisions and an HQ.

There are 10 active and eight reserve divisions in the U.S. Army combat forces. The *division* is a self-sufficient force, typically consisting of three *brigades* (each comprising three to five battalions) and various combat support elements. A *brigade* is made up of two or more regiments or battalions; a *regiment*, of subordinate units such as battalions, companies or squadrons; a *battalion*, of four or more companies; a *company* of several platoons; and a *platoon* of four squads. A *squad* consists of about 10 soldiers.

▶**U.S. MARINE CORPS**
Marine Corps organization emphasizes the close integration of air-ground operations for service

Chairmen of the Joint Chiefs of Staff, 1949–2010

Gen. Omar N. Bradley, USA	1949–53
Adm. Arthur W. Radford, USN	1953–57
Gen. Nathan F. Twining, USAF	1957–60
Gen. Lyman L. Lemnitzer, USA	1960–62
Gen. Maxwell D. Taylor, USA	1962–64
Gen. Earle G. Wheeler, USA	1964–70
Adm. Thomas H. Moorer, USN	1970–74
Gen. George S. Brown, USAF	1974–78
Gen. David C. Jones, USAF	1978–82
Gen. John W. Vessey Jr., USA	1982–85
Adm. William J. Crowe, USN	1985–89
Gen. Colin L. Powell, USA	1989–93
Gen. John Shalikashvili, USA	1993–97
Gen. H. Hugh Shelton, USA	1997–2001
Gen. Richard B. Myers, USAF	2001–05
Gen. Peter Pace, USMC	2005–07
Adm. Michael Mullen, USN	2007–

Defense Establishment Employees, 2010

	Active Duty[1]			Civilian
Branch	Officers	Enlisted	Total	employees[2]
Army	92,063	464,321	560,873	287,870
Navy	51,700	273,642	329,788	192,777
Marine Corps	21,461	180,848	202,309	N.A.
Air Force	65,354	266,437	336,245	164,137
Total DoD	230,578	1,185,248	1,429,215	748,026

Notes: 1. As of April 30, 2010. Includes Academy Cadets and Midshipmen, not shown separately. 2. As of December 31, 2009. Marine Corps Civilian personnel are included under Navy. Total civilian employees includes other Defense Dept. organizations not shown separately. **Source:** U.S. Department of Defense, *DoD Personnel and Military Casualty Statistics.*

Military Personnel on Active Duty, 1789–2010

Year/War	Total	Year/War	Total	Year/War	Total	Year/War	Total
1789	718	*1862*	*673,124*	*1942*	*3,858,791*	**1980**	2,050,627
1795	5,296	*1863*	*960,061*	*1943*	*9,044,745*	**1985**	2,151,032
1801	7,108	*1864*	*1,031,724*	*1944*	*11,451,719*		
1810	11,554	*1865*	*1,062,848*	*1945*	*12,123,455*	**Operation Desert Storm**	
		1870	*50,348*	*1946*	*3,030,088*	**(1990–91)**	
War of 1812 (1812–15)		*1880*	*37,894*			*1990*	*2,043,705*
1812	*12,631*	*1890*	*38,666*	**Korean Conflict**		*1991*	*1,985,555*
1813	*25,152*			**(1950–53)**			
1814	*46,858*	**Spanish–American War**		*1950*	*1,460,261*	**1995**	1,518,224
1815	*40,885*	**(1898)**		*1951*	*3,249,455*	**2000**	1,384,338
		1898	*235,785*	*1952*	*3,635,912*		
1820	15,113			*1953*	*3,555,067*	**Operation Enduring**	
1830	11,942	**1900**	139,344			**Freedom (2001–)**	
1840	21,616	**1915**	174,112	**1960**	2,476,435	*2001*	*1,385,116*
						2002	*1,411,600*
Mexican War (1846–48)		**World War I (1917–18)**		**Vietnam Conflict**			
1846	*39,165*	*1917*	*643,833*	**(1964–73)**		**Operation Iraqi Freedom**	
1847	*57,761*	*1918*	*2,897,167*	*1964*	*2,687,409*	**(2003–)**	
1848	*60,308*			*1965*	*2,655,389*	*2003*	*1,434,377*
		1919	*1,172,602*	*1966*	*3,094,058*	*2004*	*1,426,836*
1850	20,824	**1920**	343,302	*1967*	*3,376,880*	*2005*	*1,389,394*
1860	27,958	**1930**	255,648	*1968*	*3,547,902*	*2006*	*1,384,960*
		1940	458,365	*1969*	*3,460,162*	*2007*	*1,367,426*
				1970	*3,066,294*	*2008*	*1,402,227*
Civil War (1861–65)		**World War II (1941–46)**				*2009*	*1,421,668*
1861	*217,112*	*1941*	*1,801,101*	**1975**	2,128,120	*2010[1]*	*1,429,215*

Note: Figures in italics are wartime years. Totals exclude Coast Guard. 1. As of April 30, 2010. **Source:** U.S. Census Bureau, *Statistical History of the U.S.* (1976) and U.S. Dept. of Defense, unpublished statistics.

with the U.S. fleet and for the conduct of land operations essential to the prosecution of a naval campaign. All Marines serve "at the pleasure of the president," and the Corps's mission includes "performing such other duties as the President may direct."

The smallest tactical unit of Marine Corps infantry is the *fire team*, which consists of four Marines. A *squad* is made up of three fire teams, and there are three squads to a *platoon*, three platoons to a *company*, three companies to a *battalion*, three battalions to a *regiment*, three regiments to a *brigade*, and three brigades to a *division*.

These components are organized into three basic organizational structures called *Marine airground task forces*, or MAGTFs. The largest—about 47,500 personnel—is the *Marine Expeditionary Force* (MEF), which consists of a Marine air wing (330 planes), a Marine division, and a force service support group. The *Marine Expeditionary Brigade* (MEB) consists of a Marine air group (150 planes), a regimental landing group and a brigade service support group—about 15,000 personnel. The smallest and most responsive Marine force, the *Marine Expeditionary Unit* (MEU), consists of

about 2,500 personnel and is made up of a helicopter squadron, a battalion landing team, and a unit service support group. MEUs are sea-based, can be airlifted and they are equipped and trained to be self-sustaining in the field for up to 15 days.

▶U.S. NAVY

The ships of the U.S. Navy are organized into the Pacific Fleet, the Atlantic Fleet, and U.S. Naval Forces Europe. These are composed of numbered fleets which consist of *carrier battle groups*, *battleship surface action groups* and one or more *underway replenishment groups*. Smaller subdivisions of naval forces are the *flotilla* consisting of two or more squadrons; a *squadron*, of two or more divisions; and a *division*, normally made up of four ships.

A naval *task force* designates a collection of ships under a single command designed to accomplish a particular tactical or strategic purpose. An *amphibious squadron* consists of amphibious assault ships, amphibious transport docks, dock landing ships and tank landing ships, and transports troops, and equipment necessary for an assault landing from the sea.

U.S. Service and Casualties in Major Wars and Conflicts

War or conflict	Number serving	Battle deaths	Other deaths	Wounds not mortal	War or conflict	Number serving	Battle deaths	Other deaths	Wounds not mortal
Revolutionary War (1775–83)					**World War II (1941– 46)**				
Army	N.A.	4,044	N.A.	6,004	Army	11,260,000	234,874	83,400	565,861
Navy	N.A.	342	N.A.	114	Navy	4,183,466	36,950	25,664	37,778
Marines	N.A.	49	N.A.	70	Marines	669,100	19,733	4,778	67,207
Total	N.A.	4,435	N.A.	6,188	Total	16,112,566	291,557	113,842	670,846
War of 1812 (1812–15)					**Korean Conflict (1950–53)**				
Army	N.A.	1,950	N.A.	4,000	Army	2,834,000	27,709	806	77,596
Navy	N.A.	265	N.A.	439	Navy	1,177,000	468	939	1,576
Marines	N.A.	45	N.A.	66	Marines	424,000	4,267	1,261	23,744
Total	286,730	2,260	N.A.	4,505	Air Force	1,285,000	1,302	243	368
Mexican War (1846–48)					Total	5,720,000	33,746	3,249	103,284
Army	N.A.	1,721	11,550	4,102	**Vietnam Conflict (1964–73)**				
Navy	N.A.	1	N.A.	3	Army	4,368,000	30,905	7,275	96,802
Marines	N.A.	11	N.A.	47	Navy	1,842,000	1,631	925	4,178
Total	78,718	1,733	11,550	4,152	Marines	794,000	13,081	1,754	51,392
Civil War (1861–65)[1]					Air Force	1,740,000	1,738	842	931
Army	2,128,948	138,154	221,374	280,040	Total	8,744,000	47,355	10,796	153,303
Navy	84,415[2]	2,112	2,411	1,710	**Operation Desert Storm (1990–91)[3]**				
Marines	N.A.	148	312	131	Army	782,000	98	126	354
Total	2,213,363	140,414	224,097	281,881	Navy	669,000	5	50	12
Spanish-American War (1898)					Marines	213,000	24	44	92
Army	280,564	369	2,061	1,594	Air Force	561,000	20	15	9
Navy	22,875	10	0	47	Total	2,225,000	147	235	467
Marines	3,321	6	0	21	**Operation Enduring Freedom (Oct. 2001–)[4]**				
Total	306,760	385	2,061	1,662	Army	46,400	586	193	4,443
World War I (1917–1918)					Navy[5]	3,500	36	21	125
Army	4,057,101	50,510	55,868	193,663	Marines	13,000	150	44	1,509
Navy	599,051	431	6,856	819	Air Force	8,100	23	26	155
Marines	78,839	2,461	390	9,520	Total	71,000	795	284	6,232
Total	4,734,991	53,402	63,114	204,002	**Operation Iraqi Freedom (March 2003–)[4]**				
					Army	108,300	2,532	686	22,138
					Navy[5]	18,300	65	38	636
					Marines	6,800	851	171	8,624
					Air Force	17,600	29	22	446
					Total	151,000	3,477	917	31,844

Note: Prior to World War I, dates are approximate. Actual period covered for World War I: Apr. 6, 1917–Nov. 11, 1918; World War II: Dec. 7, 1941–Dec. 31, 1946; Korea: June 25, 1950–July 27, 1953; Vietnam: Aug. 4, 1964–Jan. 27, 1973. 1. Union forces only; authoritative statistics for Confederate forces not available. Estimates of the number who served range from 600,000 to 1.5 million. The Final Report of the Provost Marshal General, 1863–1866 indicated 133,821 Confederate deaths (74,524 battle and 59,297 other) based upon incomplete returns. In addition, an estimated 26,000–31,000 Confederate prisoners died in prisons. 2. Includes Navy and Marines. 3. DMDC, Sept. 9, 1991. Deployment figures changed continuously throughout the operation and have since, and have depended on, among other things, the timely reporting and posting of data. 4. Number serving as of Dec. 31, 2009. Casualties as of June 5, 2010. 5. Navy figures include Coast Guard. **Source:** U.S. Dept. of Defense, *Personnel and Military Statistics*.

▶ U.S. COAST GUARD

A successor to the Revenue Marine established in 1790, the primary function of the Coast Guard is to enforce federal maritime law. For most of its history, the Coast Guard served as part of the Department of Transportation during peacetime and as part of the Navy during wartime. On January 24, 2003, the Coast Guard became part of the newly created Department of Homeland Security, though it may still operate as an element of the Defense Department in the event of war or at the President's direction.

▶ U.S. AIR FORCE

The Air Force is organized into a number of commands. Within commands concerned with the strategic or tactical operation of aircraft, the primary subdivisions are indicated by the term air force prefaced by a number, as the Eighth Air Force. Such an *air force* is comprised of wings; a *wing* consists of two or more groups or

U.S. Armed Forces Worldwide, 2010

Region/Area	Total	Army	Navy	Marine Corps	Air Force
United States and Territories[1]	**1,137,568**	**486,310**	**208,291**	**164,578**	**278,389**
Continental United States	941,629	441,143	108,755	132,551	259,180
Alaska	20,450	12,684	76	24	7,666
Hawaii	37,245	21,116	5,468	6,132	4,529
Guam	2,972	43	962	11	1,956
Puerto Rico	179	85	47	23	24
Transients	50,625	11,239	8,522	25,834	5,030
Afloat	84,461	0	84,461	0	0
Europe[1]	**77,917**	**42,087**	**4,570**	**837**	**30,423**
Belgium[2]	1,253	673	108	26	446
Germany[2]	52,440	37,302	248	333	14,557
Greece[2]	370	11	291	11	57
Greenland[2]	138	0	0	0	138
Italy[2]	9,660	3,244	2,323	54	4,039
Netherlands[2]	505	244	23	16	222
Portugal[2]	700	26	29	10	635
Spain[2]	1,262	93	705	93	371
Turkey[2]	1,592	58	8	29	1,497
United Kingdom[2]	9,015	334	295	89	8,297
Afloat	511	0	511	0	0
Former Soviet Union[1]	**141**	**38**	**4**	**87**	**12**
East Asia and Pacific[1]	**47,236**	**2,695**	**10,673**	**21,344**	**12,524**
Australia	134	33	20	22	59
China (includes Hong Kong)	73	10	10	44	9
Japan	35,688	2,541	3,740	17,009	12,398
Korea, Republic of[7]	N.A.	N.A.	N.A.	N.A.	N.A.
Philippines	453	10	5	429	9
Singapore	118	7	83	15	13
Thailand	110	42	9	35	24
Afloat	10,541	0	6,796	3,745	0
North Africa, Near East, South Asia[1]	**3,362**	**659**	**1,900**	**295**	**508**
Bahrain	1,337	19	1,230	64	24
Diego Garcia	245	0	209	0	36
Egypt	269	206	6	27	30
Qatar	466	233	4	37	192
Saudi Arabia	270	138	24	30	78
United Arab Emirates	103	3	1	19	80
Afloat	412	0	412	0	0
Sub-Saharan Africa[1]	**1,355**	**105**	**692**	**270**	**288**
Djibouti	1,055	40	660	84	271
Western Hemisphere[1]	**1,941**	**678**	**595**	**329**	**339**
Canada	130	6	28	9	87
Colombia	78	45	4	19	10
Cuba (Guantanamo)	880	294	457	129	0
Honduras	415	223	2	7	183
Afloat	11	0	11	0	0
Total–Foreign Countries	**284,100**	**67,016**	**121,227**	**39,575**	**56,282**
Total–Worldwide	**1,421,668**	**553,326**	**329,518**	**204,153**	**334,671**
Ashore	1,319,559	553,326	231,154	200,408	334,671
Afloat	102,109	0	98,364	3,745	0
DEPLOYMENTS					
Operation Enduring Freedom[3,5]	71,000	46,400	3,500	13,000	8,100
Operation Iraqi Freedom[4,5]	151,000	108,300	18,300	6,800	17,600

Notes: As of Dec. 31, 2009. 1. Includes other countries not shown separately. 2. Member of NATO Europe. 3. Total personnel (including Reserve/National Guard) deployed in and around Afghanistan. 4. Total personnel (including Reserve/National Guard) deployed in and around Iraq. 5. Number rounded in source. 6. As. of Dec. 31, 2009. 7. Figures not available.
Source: U.S. Dept. of Defense. *Military Personnel Statistics.*

squadrons; a *group* consists of two or more squadrons; and a *squadron* is made up of two or more flights. A *flight* is the basic tactical unit and consists of four or more planes.

▶ SPECIAL OPERATIONS FORCES (SOF)

A unified command whose elements are drawn from the four major services, the special operations forces are designated to achieve military objectives of a limited and specific nature. Among the various elements of the SOF are: *Army* special forces; Rangers; psychological operations, civil affairs, and special operations aviation units; *Navy* SEAL and SEAL delivery vehicle teams; and *Air Force* Twenty-third Air Force special operations force.

Top Defense Contractors, 2008–09

2009 Rank, Company (2008 rank)	Awards (billions) 2008	2009
1. Lockheed Martin Corp. (1)	$28.5	$31.1
2. Boeing Company (2)	22.1	20.4
3. General Dynamics Corp. (5)	15.1	15.8
4. Northrop Grumman Corp. (3)	17.1	15.4
5. Raytheon Company (6)	13.9	15.3
6. L-3 Comm. Holding Inc. (8)	6.8	6.9
7. United Technologies Corp. (7)	8.3	6.9
8. BAE Systems PLC (4)	15.9	6.7

Source: Federal Procurement Data System, www.USAspending.gov

Military and Civilian Personnel, by State, 2006

State	Total[1]	Army	Navy/ Marine[2]	Air Force	Reserve & Ntl. Guard
Alabama	9,742	6,022	419	3,301	30,012
Alaska	20,363	11,183	101	9,079	5,845
Arizona	21,997	5,267	5,456	11,274	18,496
Arkansas	4,905	88	59	4,758	17,798
California	149,481	7,004	122,707	19,770	84,352
Colorado	29,932	15,593	808	13,531	16,112
Connecticut	6,594	23	6,465	106	8,175
Delaware	3,297	7	24	3,266	5,390
District of Columbia	12,351	4,740	4,634	2,977	8,022
Florida	58,100	2,419	30,569	25,112	49,726
Georgia	68,928	52,107	6,907	9,914	36,150
Hawaii	45,366	18,687	21,561	5,118	11,337
Idaho	4,042	20	41	3,981	7,095
Illinois	24,536	504	18,652	5,380	32,779
Indiana	805	420	275	110	22,628
Iowa	390	190	141	59	14,342
Kansas	17,645	14,725	197	2,723	15,446
Kentucky	38,799	38,335	266	198	15,555
Louisiana	15,069	7,999	1,303	5,767	22,081
Maine	2,096	224	1,853	19	5,592
Maryland	29,626	7,552	15,021	7,053	21,587
Massachusetts	2,175	208	576	1,391	18,916
Michigan	1,073	379	562	132	22,874
Minnesota	729	25	389	85	24,637
Mississippi	10,158	401	3,729	6,028	19,136
Missouri	16,241	11,053	1,537	3,651	25,726
Montana	3,589	15	28	3,546	5,761
Nebraska	6,784	136	469	6,179	8,553
Nevada	9,127	97	1,003	8,027	7,394
New Hampshire	912	3	861	48	4,550
New Jersey	6,293	888	6,964	4,741	20,060
New Mexico	10,834	444	158	10,232	7,342
New York	26,240	23,464	2,376	400	39,353
North Carolina	102,845	43,384	49,775	9,686	30,031
North Dakota	7,013	23	11	6,979	5,640
Ohio	6,745	539	608	5,698	35,074
Oklahoma	25,064	14,297	1,953	8,814	18,399
Oregon	558	190	306	62	13,421
Pennsylvania	2,979	1,075	1,655	249	43,478
Rhode Island	2,403	109	2,214	80	5,112
South Carolina	38,090	12,372	16,695	9,023	21,677
South Dakota	3,150	23	4	3,123	5,668
Tennessee	2,441	302	1,918	221	23,695
Texas	119,176	73,654	6,986	38,536	72,955
Utah	5,188	291	163	4,734	13,770
Vermont	70	16	31	23	4,130
Virginia	128,515	24,084	90,758	13,673	35,668
Washington	49,887	22,787	20,285	6,815	25,925
West Virginia	373	30	308	35	10,068
Wisconsin	449	193	176	80	20,270
Wyoming	3,043	4	1	3,038	3,739

Notes: 1. Includes other defense activities not shown. 2. Personnel who are in afloat duty status at the time of the report are included in their homeport locations. Source: U.S. Dept. of Defense, DoD Personnel and Procurement Statistics.

▶RESERVE FORCES

The U.S. has always relied on reserve forces that can be called to active duty or mobilized to deal with emergencies beyond the capacities of active forces. The reserve forces constitute the initial and primary augmentation of active forces in any emergency requiring rapid expansion of those forces.

There are seven reserve components: Army National Guard, Army Reserve, Naval Reserve, Marine Corps Reserve, Air National Guard, Air Force Reserve, and Coast Guard Reserve. All National Guard and Reserve personnel are assigned to one of three categories: the Ready Reserve, the

Standby Reserve, or the Retired Reserve. All National Guard members are in the Ready Reserve. The Ready Reserve consists of the Selected Reserve, the Individual Ready Reserve, and the Inactive National Guard. All are subject to orders for active duty in time of war or national emergency.

In addition, members of the Selected Reserve may be ordered to active duty under implementation of the presidential call-up authority, under which the president can activate up to 200,000 members of the Selected Reserve involuntarily, for operational missions, for not more than 90 days, without declaring a national emergency.

Minorities in Uniform, 2008

Service	Black Americans		Hispanic Americans		Other[1]		DoD Total	
	Number	Percent	Number	Percent	Number	Percent	Number	Percent
Officers, Total	**18,126**	**8.5%**	**10,804**	**5.1%**	**11,059**	**5.2%**	**212,313**	**15.1%**
Army	9,135	12.5	3,989	5.5	3,413	4.7	72,928	5.2
Navy	3,903	7.8	2,860	5.8	3,072	6.2	49,735	3.5
Air Force	3,838	5.9	2,379	3.7	3,076	4.8	64,805	4.6
Marines	954	5.2	1,182	6.5	833	4.6	18,297	1.3
Coast Guard	296	4.5	394	6.0	665	10.2	6,548	0.5
Enlisted, Total	**219,012**	**18.3%**	**138,876**	**11.6%**	**90,916**	**7.5%**	**1,196,897**	**84.9%**
Army	97,239	21.5	53,571	11.9	19,483	4.4	452,065	32.1
Navy	56,994	20.7	43,964	16.0	42,643	15.5	275,296	19.5
Air Force	43,566	16.9	14,137	5.5	16,156	6.3	258,095	18.3
Marines	19,208	10.8	23,358	13.1	8,718	4.9	178,213	12.6
Coast Guard	2,005	6.0	3,846	11.6	3,916	11.7	33,228	2.4
Active Duty, Total	**237,138**	**16.8%**	**149,680**	**10.6%**	**101,975**	**7.3%**	**1,409,210**	**100%**

Note: As of September, 2008. 1. Includes Native Americans, Alaskan Natives, Pacific Islanders, Asian Americans and Multi-Race. Source: U.S. Dept. of Defense, *Annual Demographic Profile of the Department of Defense and Coast Guard*, 2008.

Guard and Reserve Forces, 2010

Status	Army National Guard	Army Reserve	Naval Reserve	Marine Corps Reserve	Air National Guard	Air Force Reserve	Total DoD	Coast Guard Reserve
Selected Reserve								
Officers	40,964	36,475	14,224	3,769	14,416	14,653	124,501	1,349
Enlisted	321,978	171,497	51,269	35,690	94,102	54,620	729,156	6,189
Total	362,942	207,972	65,493	39,459	108,518	69,273	853,657	7,538
Individual Ready Reserve/Inactive National Guard								
Officers	166	6,845	9,407	2,045	N.A.	11,858	30,321	120
Enlisted	4,145	70,735	28,052	51,435	N.A.	29,282	183,649	1,367
Total	4,311	77,580	37,459	53,480	N.A.	41,140	213,970	1,487
Total Ready Reserve								
Officers	41,130	43,320	23,631	5,814	14,416	26,511	154,822	1,469
Enlisted	326,123	242,232	79,321	87,125	94,102	83,902	912,805	7,556
Total	367,253	285,552	102,952	92,939	108,518	110,413	1,067,627	9,025

Note: As of April 2010. Source: U.S. Dept. of Defense, *Guard and Reserve Summary Strength Report, April 2010*.

Women in Uniform: Female Active Duty Military Personnel 1945–2009

Year	Total DoD[1]	Army		Navy		Marine Corps.		Air Force	
		Officers	Enlisted	Officers	Enlisted	Officers	Enlisted	Officers	Enlisted
1945	266,256	62,775	93,095	19,188	72,833	809	17,556	N.A.	N.A.
1950	22,069	4,431	6,551	2,447	2,746	45	535	1,532	3,782
1960	31,550	4,263	8,279	2,711	5,360	123	1,488	3,675	5,651
1970	41,479	5,248	11,476	2,888	5,795	299	2,119	4,667	8,987
1980	171,418	7,609	61,729	4,877	30,103	487	6,219	8,493	51,901
1990	227,018	12,404	71,217	7,808	52,099	677	8,679	13,331	60,803
2000	202,601	10,814	62,889	7,846	43,760	932	9,530	11,819	55,011
2009	203,375	14,322	59,401	7,884	42,225	1,202	11,749	12,097	51,965

Note: 1. Includes Academy Cadets and Midshipmen not shown separately. Source: U.S. Dept. of Defense, *Military Personnel Statistics*, (Sept. 2009).

►NUCLEAR FORCES

Nuclear forces are classified as either strategic or nonstrategic. The strategic triad—a cornerstone of post–World War II U.S. defense—is composed of land-based missile forces, including intercontinental ballistic missiles (ICBMs); submarine-launched ballistic missiles (SLBMs); and manned aircraft of the strategic bomber force. Nonstrategic nuclear weapons are shorter-range weapons that can be deployed on the battlefield and include sea-launched cruise missiles, artillery-fired atomic projectiles, and dual-capable (conventional and nuclear) aircraft.

Department of Defense Contract Awards, Payroll, and Civilian and Military Personnel by State, Fiscal 2009

State	Payroll[1] ('000s)	Contract awards[2] ('000s)	Personnel Military[3]	Personnel Civilian	Personnel Total
Alabama	$ 4,723,956	$ 9,501,617	$ 33,995	$24,794	$ 58,789
Alaska	2,659,561	2,180,004	27,925	5,356	33,281
Arizona	3,137,634	12,064,904	35,071	9,591	44,662
Arkansas	1,621,707	985,545	19,768	4,168	23,936
California	14,568,458	41,697,621	175,598	61,365	236,963
Colorado	5,125,122	5,544,160	47,895	11,585	59,480
Connecticut	720,299	11,817,700	8,283	2,625	10,908
Delaware	536,758	315,358	8,751	1,622	10,373
District of Columbia	3,599,245	4,740,563	19,802	16,088	35,890
Florida	9,417,919	13,188,889	77,295	28,429	105,724
Georgia	11,494,647	7,039,045	103,346	37,012	140,358
Hawaii	6,344,467	2,377,271	50,150	18,400	68,550
Idaho	709,220	166,118	10,859	1,716	12,575
Illinois	3,128,538	5,936,547	35,195	15,770	50,965
Indiana	2,338,121	6,795,168	24,181	10,932	35,113
Iowa	747,256	1,285,344	13,686	1,733	15,419
Kansas	3,667,675	3,158,303	36,961	7,800	44,761
Kentucky	5,680,752	6,534,291	56,264	8,962	65,226
Louisiana	2,688,149	6,407,579	35,409	6,647	42,056
Maine	846,681	1,407,038	4,883	6,946	11,829
Maryland	6,537,841	12,911,613	45,160	34,966	80,126
Massachusetts	1,490,630	13,347,134	18,540	6,918	25,458
Michigan	1,826,987	5,331,864	20,476	8,972	29,448
Minnesota	1,208,062	1,529,964	21,153	2,752	23,905
Mississippi	2,224,346	3,447,072	27,227	9,124	36,351
Missouri	3,786,836	10,453,949	41,694	9,982	51,676
Montana	540,644	288,759	8,371	1,596	9,967
Nebraska	1,151,981	931,306	14,343	3,785	18,128
Nevada	1,414,606	1,818,505	16,121	2,319	18,440
New Hampshire	410,882	1,567,821	4,926	1,047	5,973
New Jersey	2,671,220	8,226,697	23,985	15,217	39,202
New Mexico	1,626,461	1,604,488	16,237	7,029	23,266
New York	4,818,679	8,544,864	59,915	12,318	72,233
North Carolina	10,558,150	3,994,861	138,615	20,426	159,041
North Dakota	630,939	437,227	11,878	1,910	13,788
Ohio	3,834,470	6,249,462	36,784	25,001	61,785
Oklahoma	4,099,633	2,880,203	37,313	22,115	59,428
Oregon	1,051,047	1,545,991	12,085	3,561	15,646
Pennsylvania	4,210,386	12,362,728	37,512	27,107	64,619
Rhode Island	743,035	661,794	5,928	4,372	10,300
South Carolina	3,682,987	5,298,645	51,620	10,406	62,026
South Dakota	513,643	444,618	8,892	1,388	10,280
Tennessee	2,235,302	3,083,056	24,117	7,967	32,084
Texas	19,298,889	22,483,566	187,915	48,057	235,972
Utah	2,115,968	2,206,025	18,236	14,818	33,054
Vermont	261,505	549,931	4,517	729	5,246
Virginia	18,071,415	38,731,568	88,269	89,713	177,982
Washington	8,223,735	5,173,959	65,631	27,980	93,611
West Virginia	616,823	396,440	10,502	2,146	12,648
Wisconsin	1,151,891	7,673,970	17,879	2,810	20,689
Wyoming	405,020	140,406	6,625	1,193	7,818
Total U.S.	$195,170,178	$327,461,911	$1,907,783	$709,265	$2,617,048

Notes: 1. Payroll estimates cover active duty military and direct hire civilian personnel, including Army Corps of Engineers. 2. Military awards for supplies, services and construction; expenditures relating to awards may extend over several years. Net value of contracts of over $25,000 for work in each state; the state in which the prime contractor is located is not necessarily the state in which the subcontracted work is done. 3. Military personnel includes active duty, reserve and National Guard.
Source: U.S. Dept. of Defense, *DoD Personnel and Procurement Statistics.*

Military Active Duty Monthly Basic Pay Table, 2010

Pay Grade	Army Rank	Two	Ten	Twenty	Thirty
		Years of Service			
	Commissioned Officers				
O–10	General, Admiral	N.A.	N.A.	$14,975	$14,975
O–9	Lieut. General, Vice-Admiral	N.A.	N.A.	13,284	14,946
O–8	Maj. General, Rear Admiral	$9,707	$10,748	12,586	13,219
O–7	Brig. General, Commodore	8,173	9,230	11,381	11,668
O–6	Colonel, Captain	6,359	7,133	9,096	10,248
O–5	Lt. Colonel, Commander	5,436	6,568	7,959	8,198
O–4	Major, Lt. Commander	4,820	6,230	6,952	6,952
O–3	Captain, Lieutenant	4,150	5,540	5,956	5,956
O–2	1st Lieutenant, Lieut. (J.G.)	3,602	4,377	4,377	4,377
O–1	2nd Lieutenant, Ensign	2,858	3,454	3,454	3,454
	Warrant Officers				
W–5	Chief Warrant Officer	N.A.	N.A.	$6,727	$7,984
W–4	Chief Warrant Officer	$4,070	$4,893	6,104	7,047
W–3	Chief Warrant Officer	3,599	4,571	5,607	6,060
W–2	Chief Warrant Officer	3,346	4,155	4,919	5,103
W–1	Warrant Officer	2,972	3,828	4,637	4,637
	Enlisted Personnel				
E–9	Sgt. Major, Master C.P.O.	N.A.	$4,571	$5,362	$6,436
E–8	Master Sgt., Senior C.P.O.	N.A.	3,907	4,627	5,336
E–7	Sgt.1st Class, Chief Petty Officer	$2,839	3,506	4,131	4,675
E–6	Staff Sgt., Petty Officer 1st Class	2,475	3,148	3,485	3,485
E–5	Sergeant, Petty Officer 2d Class	2,199	2,907	2,925	2,925
E–4	Corporal, Petty Officer 3d Class	1,986	2,294	2,294	2,294
E–3	Private First Class, Seaman	1,813	1,923	1,923	1,923
E–2	Private, Seaman	1,622	1,622	1,622	1,622
E–1	Recruit, Seaman Recruit[1]	1,447	1,447	1,447	1,447

Note: Effective Jan. 1, 2010. Numbers rounded to nearest dollar. 1. Applicable to E–1 with 4 or more months of active duty. Basic pay for an E–1 with less than 4 months of active duty is $1,339. **Source:** U.S. Department of Defense.

SOCIAL INSURANCE PROGRAMS

In order to provide a "safety net" for the disadvantaged, the elderly, and the disabled, the federal government administers a range of social insurance and social assistance programs. Many of these programs are administered by the Social Security Administration, which became an independent government agency in 1995. But many cabinet-level departments, other independent government agencies, and state government human services agencies also run programs such as food assistance (Dept. of Agriculture), public housing (Dept. of Housing and Urban Development), and programs for veterans (Dept. of Veterans Affairs).

Social insurance programs were not developed all at once to fulfill a specific agenda of national need. Rather they are a hodgepodge of legislation passed (and often altered) over the years to meet the needs of particular groups of citizens at particular times. In what the government calls "social insurance programs," certain risks—injury, disability, unemployment, old age, and death—are lumped together. "Premiums," usually in the form of a payroll tax, are paid by employees and/or their employers. The benefit is paid, regardless of other financial resources (other than earnings), when one of those "risks" occurs.

►SOCIAL SECURITY

The Depression proved that the traditional support systems—the family, private charities, and local government—failed in nationwide economic hard times. Many old people had exhausted their savings and were destitute; in fact, during the Depression less than 10 percent of the aged left estates large enough to be probated. This led to the enactment of one of the most comprehensive pieces of legislation ever passed by Congress, the Social Security Act.

Signed into law by Pres. Franklin Roosevelt on August 14, 1935, the Social Security Act established two social insurance programs: a federal system of old-age benefits for retired workers in commerce and industry and a federal-state system of unemployment insurance. The law also provided for federal matching grants-in-aid to states to help them assist the needy aged, the blind, and children. Today, in the words of former Social Security Commissioner Dorcas R. Hardy, it is "the most complex government program that God and Congress ever created."

The first payments of monthly benefits were made in 1940. Major changes in the scope of Social Security were made in 1956, when the program was broadened through the addition of disability insurance; in 1965, through the addition of Medicare and Medicaid; in 1970, when the black lung program was developed to provide benefits to coal miners (and their survivors) who suffer from pneumoconiosis (black lung disease); in 1972, when Congress authorized provisions for cost-of-living increases; and in 1974, when Social Security insurance was taken over by the Social Security Administration. In 1983, amendments provided for the taxing of up to one-half of benefits for certain upper-income beneficiaries.

Workers and their employers each contribute an equal amount to the Social Security program to pay for retirement, disability, and Medicare benefits. This is sometimes referred to as the "payroll tax." The tax money collected is placed in a trust fund, which can be used only to pay Social Security benefits and expenses

Since 1990, the Federal Insurance Contributions Act (FICA) has mandated that 15.3 percent be deducted from each worker's paycheck. Half of that amount (7.65 percent) is paid by the employer; the other half is paid by the employee. Self-employed workers, who are both employee and employer, pay both shares, or a total of 15.3 percent. Earnings above a certain amount ($106,800 in 2010) are not subject to the deduction for Social Security, but they are subject to

---

SOCIAL SERVICE PROGRAMS INFORMATION

Information about social service programs can be obtained from the following government agencies:

Black lung program Office of Workers Compensation Programs, U.S. Dept. of Labor. (800) 638-7072. *www.dol.gov*

Head Start Administration for Children and Families, U.S. Dept. of Health and Human Services. (866) 763-6481. *www.acf.hhs.gov*

Making Home Affordable Housing and Urban Development. (888) 995-4673. *www.makinghomeaffordable.gov*

Medicaid Centers for Medicare & Medicaid Services, U.S. Dept. of Health and Human Services. (877) 267-2323. *www.cms.gov*

Medicare (HI) Health Care Financing Administration, U.S. Dept. of Health and Human Services. (800) 633-4227. *www.medicare.gov*

Social Security (OASDI) Social Security Administration. (800) 772-1213. *www.ssa.gov*

Special nutrition programs Food and Nutrition Service, U.S. Dept. of Agriculture. (703) 305-2052. *www.fns.usda.gov*

Supplemental Nutrition Assistance Program Food and Nutrition Service, U.S. Dept. of Agriculture. (800) 221-5689. *www.fns.usda.gov/snap*

Supplemental Security Income (SSI) Social Security Administration. (800) 772-1213. *www.ssa.gov*

Temporary Assistance to Needy Families (TANF) Administration for Children and Families, U.S. Dept. of Health and Human Services. (202) 401-5150. *www.acf.hhs.gov*

Temporary disability insurance Office of Workers Compensation Programs, U.S. Dept. of Labor. (866) 487-2365. *www.dol.gov/owcp*

Unemployment insurance Office of Workers Compensation Programs, U.S. Dept. of Labor. (866) 487-2365. *www.dol.gov/owcp*

Veterans' benefits U.S. Dept. of Veterans Affairs. (800) 827-1000. *www.va.gov*

Medicare taxes (1.45 percent each for employer and employee; 2.9 percent for the self-employed).

Old Age, Survivors and Disability Insurance (OASDI)

This is the program most people mean when they refer to "social security." It has three basic principles: 1) benefits are related to earnings from covered work; 2) benefits are paid regardless of additional income from savings, pensions, and other retirement accounts; and 3) universal compulsory coverage assures a base of economic security. In 2010, about 150 million people worked in OASDI-covered employment.

The addition of disability insurance in 1956 broadened the program's scope, and in 1972 Congress authorized provisions for cost-of-living increases. The 1983 amendments improved the program's financial footing by raising the self-employment tax rate, and by taxing up to one-half of benefits for certain upper-income beneficiaries.

Old Age At the program's inception, workers became eligible for full benefits at the age of 65. But in 2003, the retirement age started increasing. People born between 1943 and 1954 are eligible for full benefits at age 66, while the minimum retirement age for people born after January 1, 1960 is 67. Anybody can still retire as early as age 62, but doing so brings a reduction of as much as 30 percent in annual benefits.

To receive Social Security benefits, you must have worked for at least 10 years during which you contributed to the fund. Your Social Security benefit is based on your average earnings over your working years, not directly on the number of years that you worked. The average recipient receives benefits equal to 42 percent of an average working year's earnings. But because Social Security is designed to especially assist low-income workers,

The Retirement Age Is Going Up

For many years, workers became eligible for Social Security benefits upon turning 65. But in 2003, the retirement age started increasing by two months each year. You should still apply for Medicare benefits upon turning 65, regardless of when you were born.

Year of birth	Full retirement age	Year of birth	Full retirement age
1937 or earlier	65 years	**1943–54**	66 years
		1956	66 & 4 months
1938	65 & 2 months	**1957**	66 & 6 months
1939	65 & 4 months	**1958**	66 & 8 months
1940	65 & 6 months	**1959**	66 & 10 months
1941	65 & 8 months	**1960 or later**	67 years
1942	65 & 10 months		

Source: Social Security Administration.

OASDI Beneficiaries and Benefit Payments, 2010

Type of Beneficiaries	Number ('000s)	Monthly rate (millions)	Average monthly benefit
Retired workers	33,513	$39,020	$1,164
Dependents of retired workers	2,904	1,665	573
Survivors of deceased workers[1]	6,410	6,329	987
Disabled workers	7,789	8,290	1,064
Dependents of disabled workers[1]	1,908	602	315
Total monthly beneficiaries	**52,523**	**$55,906**	**N.A.**

Note: OASDI = old-age, survivors and disability insurance. 1. Benefits vary depending on relationship to beneficiary. Range of benefits shown. **Source:** Social Security Administration, *Fact Sheet on OASDI,* (Dec.31, 2009).

people with high average lifetime earnings generally receive a lower percentage of their average working year earnings. The maximum Social Security benefit in 2010 is $2,346 per month. The average monthly retirement benefit in January 2010 was $1,164.

You can still work and earn money while collecting Social Security. In 2010, recipients under full retirement age may earn up to $14,160 ($1,180 per month) before their benefits are reduced; after that amount, $1 is withheld for every $2 earned. In the year that a worker reaches full retirement age, the earning limit is raised to $37,680, after which benefits are reduced by $1 for each $3 earned. After recipients reach their full retirement age, there is no limit to the amount of money that they may earn while collecting Social Security benefits.

Disability   If you become disabled, you are eligible for additional benefits after six months. Disabled is defined as having a physical or mental impairment that permanently prevents you from doing any substantial work. For 2010, "substantial" work was defined as earning more than $1,000 a month ($1,640 for blind workers).

Survivors   Additional benefits are also paid to the survivors of workers who would have been eligible for Social Security. Widows and widowers over the age of 50, children under the age of 18 (or 19 if they're still in high school), and certain other survivors each receive amounts ranging from 71.5 to 100 percent of what the deceased worker would have received from Social Security. There is, however, a per-family benefit limit, usually equal to 150 to 180 percent of the worker's benefit rate.

Approximate Annual Retirement, Disability, and Survivor Benefits

Worker's age, 2009	Beneficiaries	Worker's lifetime average annual earnings level			
		$20,000	$40,000	$60,000	Maximum[1]
Retirement Benefits[2]					
25	Retired worker only	$11,724	$18,132	$23,760	$30,060
35	Retired worker only	11,724	18,132	23,760	30,108
45	Retired worker only	11,724	18,132	23,760	30,132
55	Retired worker only	11,724	18,132	23,760	30,000
65	Retired worker only	11,232	17,376	22,752	28,140
Disability Benefits[3]					
25	Disabled worker only	$ 8,220	$11,280	$14,340	$29,220
35	Disabled worker only	10,248	15,324	20,412	29,196
45	Disabled worker only	11,136	17,100	22,704	29,196
55	Disabled worker only	11,496	17,832	23,220	28,932
Survivor Benefits[4]					
25	1 child only	$ 6,396	$ 8,904	$11,424	$22,008
	Spouse and 1 child	12,792	17,808	22,848	44,016
	Spouse and 2 children	12,792	18,420	27,540	51,384
35	1 child only	7,992	12,120	16,236	22,008
	Spouse and 1 child	15,984	24,240	32,472	44,016
	Spouse and 2 children	15,996	30,048	37,896	51,360
45	1 child only	8,412	12,948	17,112	21,912
	Spouse and 1 child	16,824	25,896	34,224	43,824
	Spouse and 2 children	16,836	31,956	39,960	51,156
60	Spouse only	8,184	12,672	16,548	20,292
	1 child only	8,592	13,296	17,364	21,288
	Spouse and 2 children	17,244	32,568	40,524	49,692

Notes: Earnings level reflects the average of the highest 35 years of wage-indexed earnings. Scaled earnings patterns starting at age 21 are assumed for all but the maximum earnings levels. 1. For 2008, maximum annual earnings level was $102,000 or more. 2. If worker retires at normal retirement age. 3. For workers who died in 2009; benefits are based on 2008 earnings. 4. Spouse is assumed to be the same age as worker.
Source: Social Security Administration, *Illustrative Benefits for Retired Workers, Disabled Workers, and Survivors, 2009*.

Medicare: Recipients and Benefits, 1966–2009

	Enrollment (in thousands)									
	Hospital Insurance (Part A)			Supplemental Medical Insurance				Average Yearly Benefit		
						Part B		Part D		
Year	Total	Aged	Disabled	Total	Aged	Disabled	Part D Total	Part A	Part B	Part D
1966	19,082	19,082	N.A.	17,736	17,736	N.A.	N.A.	N.A.	N.A.	N.A.
1970	20,104	20,361	N.A.	19,496	19,584	N.A.	N.A.	$255	$101	N.A.
1975	24,481	22,472	2,168	23,744	21,945	1,959	N.A.	462	180	N.A.
1980	28,002	25,104	2,963	27,278	24,680	2,719	N.A.	895	390	N.A.
1985	30,621	27,683	2,907	29,869	27,311	2,678	N.A.	1,554	768	N.A.
1990	33,747	30,464	3,255	32,567	29,686	2,943	N.A.	1,963	1,304	N.A.
1995	37,175	32,742	4,393	35,641	31,742	3,942	N.A.	3,130	1,823	N.A.
2000	39,257	33,833	5,367	37,335	32,590	4,770	N.A.	3,272	2,381	N.A.
2005	42,181	35,400	6,700	39,968	33,700	5,900	1,841	4,268	3,759	N.A.
2009	45,970	N.A.	N.A.	42,846	N.A.	N.A.	33,401	5,205	4,728	$1,810

Source: Centers for Medicare and Medicaid Services, *2010 Medicare Trustees Report*.

Medicare

The Social Security Amendments of 1965 established two contributory health insurance programs designed to provide assistance for medical expenses for the aged and disabled. The first is a compulsory program of hospital insurance (HI), which provides basic protection against the costs of inpatient hospital services and related post-hospital care, including home health services, part-time nursing care, and physical therapy. This is commonly referred to as Part A.

As with OASDI, hospital insurance is financed by part of the 7.65 percent tax on earnings (FICA) deducted from employee paychecks: 6.2 percent is for OASDI and 1.45 percent is for Medicare. States may Persons reaching full retirement age without enough work-based contributions to qualify for HI may enroll by paying a monthly premium. In 2010, the premium was $254 per month for people who had contributed to Medicare for 30-39 quarters (7.5-10 years), or $461 for those who had worked fewer than 30 quarters.

For beneficiaries, HI pays all hospital bills for the first 60 days except for a deductible ($1,100 in 2010). After 60 days, the patient is also responsible for a daily co-payment of $275 for days 61-90. After 90 days, a beneficiary may draw from a nonrenewable "lifetime reserve" of 60 additional hospital days, which require co-payments of $550 per day. For nursing home stays, the first 20 days have no deductible, but days 21-100 require a co-payment of $137.50. Home heath care requires no deductible or co-payment.

The second health program is supplemental medical insurance (SMI), a voluntary program in which enrolled individuals pay a monthly premium for subsidized coverage. SMI coverage includes physicians' and surgeons' services, emergency and ambulance services, laboratory tests, home health services and equipment, most organ transplants and comprehensive outpatient services. In 2010, the standard monthly premium was $110.50, although premiums vary with income levels. SMI pays for 80 percent of most covered services after a $150 deductible.

SMI was originally known as Medicare Part B, but beginning in 2004 an additional program known as Part D was added to SMI to allow anyone eligible for Medicare to obtain subsidized discount cards for prescription drugs by paying a monthly premium. The base premium paid by Plan D enrollees was $31.94 in 2010, but state subsidies and other factors may greatly reduce these premiums. The standard Part D coverage requires an initial deductible ($310 in 2010), then covers 75 percent of drug costs up to an initial limit of $2,830. The beneficiary then pays all costs between the initial limit and an out-of-pocket threshold of $4,550. Catastrophic coverage applies above that threshold. Although together they now make up the SMI program, Part B and Part D have separate funding and accounting systems.

In 1997, the original fee-for-service Medicare program was expanded to include Part C or Medicare Advantage plans. These alternative insurance plans are offered by private health-care companies under contract with Medicare and are open to most people eligible for Medicare. These plans include both managed care and private fee-for-service options and may offer additional benefits (prescription drugs, vision or hearing coverage, more hospital days) or may reduce co-payments or premiums, but doctor choice is usually limited in comparison to Medicare.

Supplemental Security Insurance Beneficiaries and Benefits, 1975-2008

| | Beneficiaries | | | | Benefits (millions) | | |
| | | | State Supplement | | | | State |
Year	Total[1]	Federal SSI	Federally administered	State supplement	Total	Federal SSI	supplement[2]
Total							
1975	4,314,275	3,893,419	1,684,018	420,856	$5,716.1	$4,313.5	$1,402.5
1990	4,817,127	4,412,131	2,058,273	404,996	16,133.0	12,893.8	3,239.2
2000	6,601,686	6,319,907	2,480,637	281,779	30,671.7	27,290.2	3,381.5
2005	7,113,879	6,818,944	2,242,112	294,935	37,235.8	33,058.1	4,177.8
2008	7,520,501	7,219,012	2,343,599	301,489	43,040.5	38,655.8	4,384.7
Aged							
1975	2,307,105	2,024,765	843,917	282,340	$2,526.5	$1,843.0	$673.5
1990	1,454,041	1,256,623	649,530	197,418	3,559.4	2,521.4	1,038.0
2000	1,289,339	1,186,309	622,668	103,030	4,540.0	3,597.5	942.5
2005	1,214,296	1,112,779	584,787	101,517	4,964.6	3,836.6	1,128.0
2008	1,203,256	1,100,188	600,909	103,068	5,378.9	4,180.8	1,198.1
Blind							
1975	74,489	68,375	31,376	6,114	$127.2	$92.4	$34.8
1990	83,686	74,781	40,334	8,905	328.9	238.4	90.5
2000	78,511	72,931	35,940	5,580	385.9	312.2	73.7
2005	75,039	69,637	31,346	5,402	414.1	330.6	83.6
2008	70,325	65,330	29,535	4,995	416.0	335.2	80.8
Disabled							
1975	1,932,681	1,800,279	808,725	132,402	$3,072.3	$2,378.1	$694.2
1990	3,279,400	3,080,727	1,368,409	198,673	12,244.6	10,134.0	2,110.6
2000	5,233,836	5,060,667	1,822,029	173,169	25,745.7	23,380.5	2,365.2
2005	5,824,544	5,636,528	1,625,979	188,016	31,857.1	28,890.8	2,966.2
2008	6,246,920	6,053,494	1,713,155	193,426	37,245.5	34,139.8	3,105.7

Notes: 1. Total beneficiaries includes some people who receive both Federal SSI and a state supplement. 2. Federally administered only.
Source: Social Security Administration, *Annual Statistical Supplement to the Social Security Bulletin, 2009.*

Supplemental Security Income (SSI)

In 1974, Congress replaced the federal-state programs for needy aged (over 65 years old), blind, and disabled people with a single Federal Supplementary Security Income program. SSI eligibility depends on whether you work, and in what state you live. In addition, SSI recipients may have no more than $2,000 in assets ($3,000 for married couples), though houses and cars are not usually counted as assets in this equation. The qualifying standards for disability benefits are the same as those used for the Social Security disability insurance program. More than 7.5 million people received SSI benefits in 2009. The basic monthly federal benefit is the same in all states; in 2010 it was $674 for one person and $1,011 for a couple. However, many states supplement Federal SSI under their own programs. In 2009, more than 2.3 million people received state supplemented SSI.

Black Lung Program

Established by the Federal Coal Mine Health and Safety Act of 1969, this program provides monthly payments and medical treatment to coal miners who are totally disabled because of "black lung" disease (pneumoconiosis) and to survivors of miners who die from this disease. Benefits are paid mostly out of a trust fund which coal mine operators are required to finance. The monthly benefit in 2010 ranged from $625 for a single recipient to $1,251 for a recipient with three or more dependents. The number of beneficiaries has declined significantly in recent decades as older beneficiaries are dying in greater numbers than new claimants are entering the program. In 2009, $255 million in annual benefits was paid to 30,826 claimants, of whom approximately 25,000 were widows of miners.

Social Security Information

While Social Security benefits are calculated automatically for all people who hold a Social Security card and who are eligible for programs, the Social Security Administration (SSA) advises workers to check their official earnings for accuracy. If the SSA records are not correct—the SSA says that 1 percent of eligible wages are not credited to workers' records—then retirement benefits may be lower than they should be. The SSA mails an annual Social Security Statement to each eligible person, but statements are also available at any local Social Security office, or by calling 1-800-772-1213, or online at *www.ssa.gov*.

▶OTHER INCOME SUPPORT PROGRAMS
Welfare

The Social Security Act of 1935 included a provision authorizing Aid to Families with Dependent Children (AFDC), commonly known as "welfare." Benefits were limited to families with children under 18. But in the much-ballyhooed 1996 welfare reform effort, the federal government ended more than 60 years of guaranteed assistance to the needy, and replaced it with a system of block grants to the states, who could use the money to enact their own welfare programs. The Temporary Assistance to Needy Families (TANF) Block Grant replaced AFDC on July 1, 1997. TANF gives states broad discretion to determine eligibility and benefit levels. However, families may not receive benefits for longer than 60 months, unwed teenage parents must stay in school and live at home, and people convicted of drug-related felonies are banned from receiving TANF or Food Stamp benefits. In addition, non-working adults must participate in community service within two months of receiving benefits, and must find work within two years. Parents with children under age one are exempt from the work requirements (under age six if child care is not available).

Following welfare reform, the number of Americans receiving government assistance dropped steadily from an all-time high of 14.4 million in March 1994 to 3.7 million in July 2008, but then rose to 4.4 million by December 2009. The characteristics of welfare recipients have also changed in that time. The average number of children in families on welfare declined from 2 children in 1997 to an average of 1.8 in 2008, when more than 50 percent of recipient families had only one child. However, the percentage of married recipients also declined from 16 percent in 1997 to 13.3 percent in 2008. Meanwhile, the percentage of adult recipients with at least a high school education rose from 42.8 percent in 1997 to 56.5 percent in 2008. The employment rate among welfare recipients increased from 11 percent in 1996 to 32.5 percent in 2006, but it dropped to 25.9 percent in 2008.

Medicaid

Enacted jointly with Medicare in 1965, Medicaid provides federal matching funds to help states pay the cost of medical care and services for many low-income residents, with an emphasis on dependent children and their mothers. Eligibility is determined by each state but to receive matching funds, state Medicaid programs must include certain basic services and must cover all persons who receive TANF assistance. Most SSI recipients are also covered. Eligible Medicare recipients may use Medicaid to pay for supplementary medical insurance premiums, the deductible and co-insurance costs of hospital insurance, and for some medical services that Medicare does not cover. In 2008, Medicaid provided $356.3 billion in medical care for more than 60 million poor, aged, blind or disabled persons. Medicaid now covers approximately 41 percent of all births in the U.S., as well as 40 percent of all nursing facility care. Visit www.cms.gov for more information.

Welfare Beneficiaries and Benefits, 1970–2009

Year	Average monthly beneficiaries ('000s)			Average monthly benefit per family
	Total	Families	Children	
1970	7,429	1,909	5,494	$178
1975	11,067	3,269	7,821	208
1980	10,597	3,574	7,220	269
1985	10,813	3,692	7,165	329
1990	11,460	3,974	7,755	389
1995	13,652	4,876	9,274	377
2000	5,943	2,216	4,370	388
2005	4,471	1,895	3,405	370
2007	3,964	1,692	3,045	N.A.
2009	4,155	1,769	3,157	N.A.

Note: "Welfare" refers to the Aid to Families with Dependent Children (AFDC) program through 1996; in 1997, AFDC was renamed Temporary Assistance to Needy Families (TANF), and many more restrictions were added. **Source:** Administration for Children and Families, Office of Family Assistance, *Caseload Data, Total Number of Recipients 2009.*

Supplemental Nutrition Assistance Program

This program, formerly known as "food stamps," enables eligible families to purchase a nutritionally adequate diet by providing funds to buy healthy food. The federal government finances the program through the U.S.D.A.'s Food and Nutrition Service, but states administer the funds and set specific eligibility criteria. In general, a household is eligible if all members are receiving public assistance, if it has less than $2,000 in liquid assets ($3,000 if one person in the home is 60 or over), or if 30 percent of its countable income is less than the U.S.D.A.'s monthly food costs allotment. Use of the program fluctuates with the economy, but recent reforms have increased participation by broadening eligibility requirements and streamlining use. In 2004, paper food stamp coupons were replaced by Electronic Benefit Transfer (EBT) cards, which act like a bank debit card. The EBT cards have reduced the stigma associated with food stamps, lowered the administrative burden for states and merchants, and may reduce fraud. In March 2010, SNAP reached an all-time high of 40.2 million participants (18.5 million households) at a monthly cost of $6.2 billion. Visit www.fns.usda.gov/snap for more information.

Special nutrition programs

The U.S.D.A. administers a number of programs intended to help states safeguard the health of the

Federal Food Assistance Programs, 1970–2009

Program	1970	1980	1990	2000	2005	2008	2009
Participants (millions)							
Supplemental Nutrition Assistance[1]	4.3	21.1	20.0	17.2	25.7	28.4	33.7
National school lunch program[2]	22.4	26.6	24.1	27.3	29.6	31.0	31.3
School breakfast[2]	0.5	3.6	4.1	7.6	9.4	10.6	11.1
Women-infants-children (WIC)[3]	N.A.	1.9	4.5	7.2	8.0	8.7	9.1
Child and adult care[4]	0.1	0.7	1.5	2.7	3.1	3.3	3.3
Federal cost (millions)							
Supplemental Nutrition Assistance[1]	$550	$8,721	$14,186	$14,983	$28,566	$34,608	$50,360
National school lunch program[2]	300	2,279	3,214	5,494	7,055	9,318	8,873
School breakfast[2]	11	288	596	1,393	1,927	2,366	2,582
Women-infants-children[3]	N.A.	584	1,637	2,853	3,603	4,534	4,642
Child and adult care[4]	6	207	719	1,500	1,904	2,169	2,289

Notes: 1. Known as food stamps prior to 2008. 2. Average monthly participation during school year. Covers public and private elementary and secondary schools and residential child care institutions. 3. Costs do not include the value of U.S.D.A. donated commodities. 4. WIC serves pregnant and postpartum women, infants and children up to age five. 5. Provides year-round subsidies to feed preschool children in child care centers and family day care programs. Certain care centers serving disabled or elderly adults also receive meal subsidies. **Source:** U.S. Department of Agriculture, *Annual Summary of Food and Nutrition Service Programs, 2005–2009.*

Medicaid Recipients and Vendor Payments 1975–2007

Year	Aged	Blind/Disabled[1]	Dependent children under 21	Adults in families with dependent children	Other/ Unknown	Total
Recipients (thousands)						
1975	3,615	2,464	9,598	4,529	1,800	22,007
1980	3,440	2,911	9,333	4,877	1,499	21,605
1985	3,061	3,017	9,757	5,518	1,214	21,814
1990	3,202	3,718	11,220	6,010	1,105	25,255
1995	4,119	5,859	17,164	7,604	1,537	36,282
2000	4,289	7,479	21,086	10,543	862	42,886
2005[2]	4,396	8,210	26,337	12,529	6,171	57,643
2007[2,3]	4,043	8,424	26,584	12,371	5,402	56,825
Payments (millions of dollars)						
1975	$4,358	$3,145	$2,186	$2,062	$492	$12,242
1980	8,739	7,621	3,123	3,231	596	23,311
1985	14,096	13,452	4,414	4,746	798	37,508
1990	21,508	24,403	9,100	8,590	1,257	64,859
1995	36,527	49,418	17,976	13,511	2,708	120,141
2000	44,560	72,772	23,490	17,671	9,948	168,442
2005[2]	63,358	119,647	42,012	32,385	18,167	275,569
2007[2,3]	57,362	119,621	47,763	33,764	18,029	276,539
Average payment (dollars)						
1975	$1,205	$1,296	$228	$455	$273	$556
1980	2,540	2,659	335	663	398	1,079
1985	4,605	4,496	452	860	658	1,719
1990	6,717	6,595	811	1,429	1,138	2,568
1995	8,868	8,422	1,047	1,777	1,762	3,311
2000	10,388	9,729	1,114	1,676	11,536	3,928
2005[2]	14,413	14,574	1,595	2,585	2,944	4,781
2007[2,3]	14,187	14,200	1,797	2,729	3,337	4,867

Notes: Figures are in current dollars. A small number of recipients are in more than one category. 1. Figures for blind were combined with those for the disabled in 1997. 2. 2004 data used for Maine. 3. 2006 data used for Hawaii.
Source: Social Security Administration, *Annual Statistical Supplement, 2009.*

nation's children and elderly by providing adequate meals at a moderate cost. The programs include the National School Lunch Program, the School Breakfast Program, the Summer Food Service Program, the Child Care Food Program, the Special Milk Program, and the Special Supplemental Food Program for Women, Infants, and Children (WIC) Program. The nutrition program for the elderly requires no income test, but preference is given to those with the greatest need.

Head Start

Head Start provides grants to local service agencies that boost the school readiness of low-income children. Its goals are to promote long-term educational success by improving the health and nutrition, social competence, and learning skills of economically disadvantaged children up to the age of five. Agencies offer educational, medical (including screenings, immunizations, dental, and mental health), nutritional, social and other services to enrolled children and families. The program stresses parental involvement through workshops, volunteer participation—especially as aides in classrooms, and employment as Head Start staff.

At least 90 percent of Head Start children come from families with incomes at or below the poverty line, and at least 10 percent of enrollment slots in each state must be available to disabled children (in 2009, 11.5 percent of enrollees were children with disabilities). Head Start enrolled 904,153 children in 2009, at a total federal cost of $7.1 billion, or an average of $7,600 per child. The program has served more than 27 million children since it began in 1965. In recent decades, the demographic make-up of Head Start children has become younger and more Hispanic. In 1980, five-year olds made up 21 percent of the Head Start population; in 2009, they constituted only 3 percent. The percentage of three-year-olds increased from 24 to 36 percent over the same period. Meanwhile, the percentage of Head Start children who were black decreased from 42 percent to 30 percent, and the percentage who were Hispanic increased from 19 percent to 36 percent.

Housing subsidies

The federal government has traditionally provided housing aid to lower-income households in the form of rental and mortgage-interest subsidies. Housing assistance is intended to improve housing quality, promote residential construction, expand housing opportunities for disadvantaged groups and groups with special housing needs, preserve and revitalize neighborhoods, and increase homeownership, especially among the poor. In 2009, an additional set of programs was initiated to help homeowners avoid foreclosure by offering federal support in refinancing mortgages.

Most housing aid is managed by the Department of Housing and Urban Development (HUD) and administered by local public housing agencies through two major types of assistance programs. Project-based aid is tied to specific rental housing that is either contracted from existing housing stock or produced through new construction or renovations as public housing for low-income families, the elderly, and persons with disabilities. In 2009, approximately 1.1 million households lived in public housing and an additional 1.3 million received project-based rental assistance in contracted housing.

Tenant-based aid, the Section 8 Housing Choice Voucher Program, allows low-income participants to choose from privately owned housing units. The vouchers generally reduce tenants' rent payments to 30 percent of their income, with the government paying the balance up to the Fair Market Rent. Recent revisions to Section 8 allow local housing authorities to permit the use of vouchers to pay mortgage payments for certain homebuyers. Nearly 2.1 million families received housing vouchers in 2009.

The federal government also promotes homeownership through the Federal Housing Administration's mortgage insurance, which lowers the mortgage interest rates for some lower- and moderate-income homebuyers, thereby reducing their mortgage payments to a fixed percentage of income. Additional housing subsidies are managed by the U.S.D.A.'s Rural Development program and the Veteran's Administration.

Housing for the homeless

HUD funding to help the homeless is allocated to state and local governments, Indian tribes, and nonprofit organizations through several pro-

Head Start Participation and Funding, 1966–2009		
Year	Enrollment	Appropriations
1966	733,000	$198,900,000
1970	477,400	325,700,000
1980	376,300	735,000,000
1990	540,930	1,552,000,000
1995	750,696	3,534,128,000
2000	857,664	5,267,000,000
2004	905,851	6,773,909,000
2008	906,153	6,877,975,000
2009	904,153	7,112,786,000

Source: U.S. Dept of Health and Human Services, Administration for Children and Families. www.acf.hhs.gov.

U.S. Weighted Average Poverty Thresholds by Family Size, 1960–2009							
	Maximum yearly family income						
Year	1 person	2 people	3 people	4 people	5 people	6 people	7 people
1960	$1,490	$1,924	$2,359	$3,022	$3,560	$4,002	$4,921[1]
1970	1,954	2,525	3,099	3,968	4,680	5,260	6,468[1]
1980	4,190	5,363	6,565	8,414	9,966	11,269	12,761
1990	6,652	8,509	10,419	13,359	15,792	17,839	20,241
2000	8,791	11,235	13,740	17,604	20,815	23,533	26,750
2005	9,973	12,755	15,577	19,971	23,613	26,683	30,249
2008	11,201	14,417	16,841	22,207	26,781	30,803	35,442
2009[2]	10,952	14,001	17,102	21,947	25,956	29,351	33,410

Note: 1. Seven or more people. 2. Preliminary estimates. Source: U.S. Census Bureau, data as of February, 2010.

grams: the Supportive Housing Program, the Shelter Plus Care Program, the Single Room Occupancy Program, Emergency Shelter Grant Programs, and the Title V and Base Relocation and Closure programs to redistribute surplus federal and military property.

Poverty income guidelines

The poverty income guidelines are used to determine whether a person or family is eligible for assistance under a particular federal program. The poverty threshold is established each year by increasing the previous year's threshold by the change in the Consumer Price Index. The original poverty threshold was devised in 1960 and was equal to three times the amount of money to buy the cheapest "nutritionally adequate" diet as dictated by the Department of Agriculture.

Unemployment Compensation

The Social Security Act provided an inducement to states to enact unemployment insurance laws, and by 1937 all 48 states, the territories of Alaska and Hawaii, and the District of Columbia had passed such laws. All contributions collected under state laws are deposited in the unemployment trust fund of the U.S. Treasury, but each state maintains a separate account. A state may withdraw money from its account only to pay benefits. Each state has major responsibility for the content and development of its unemployment insurance law. Nationwide, unemployment insurance covered about 127 million workers in 2008, out of a civilian labor force totaling 153 million.

Workers must be ready, able and willing to work and must be registered for work at a state public employment office. A worker's benefit is based on his or her employment in covered work over a prior performance period. No state can deny benefit to a claimant if he or she refuses to accept a new job under substandard labor conditions or where he or she would be required to join a company union. Generally, workers may collect benefits for up to 26 weeks but additional weeks may be available during times of high unemployment.

In 2009, a record 29.5 million people made initial unemployment claims and 7.3 million exhausted their compensation. The average weekly benefit was $309.58, and the average duration of benefits was 18.8 weeks. The average total benefit was $5,613. Weekly benefits vary by state, but generally compensate for between 50 percent and 70 percent of average weekly pre-tax wages.

Workers' compensation

Social insurance began in the United States with worker's compensation. A law covering federal civilian employees was passed in 1908; the first state compensation law to be held constitutional was enacted in 1911. These laws made industry responsible for the compensation of workers (or their survivors) injured or killed while on the job. A worker incurring an occupational injury is compensated regardless of fault or blame in the accident. A separate federal program enacted in 1969 protects coal miners (See "Black lung program").

Workers' compensation is almost exclusively financed by employers on the principle that the cost of work-related accidents is part of the expense of production. Every state except Texas mandates coverage under workers' compensation for private employees. Certain categories of workers, usually domestic, agricultural, and casual laborers, are often exempted from this requirement. Employers can use private insurance companies or can qualify as self-insurers. Workers' compensation covered nearly 132 million U.S. workers in 2007; total payments on workers' behalf was $0.95 per $100 of covered wages, at a cost to employers of $1.45 per $100 of covered wages. The cash benefit for temporary total disability, permanent, total or partial disability, or death of a breadwinner is usually about two-thirds of weekly earnings at the time of the accident. Most state laws pay temporary disability benefits for as long as the disability lasts and the condition has not been stabilized to the point where no further improvement can result from medical treatment. Total benefit payments under workers' compensation programs in 2007 were $55.4 billion, a 2 percent increase from $54.3 billion in 2006.

Permanent partial disability compensation for specific, or "schedule" injuries (for clearly measurable matters) is generally subject to different (usually lower) dollar maximums and is determined without regard to loss of earning power. Compensation for "nonschedule" injuries (injuries to head, back, nervous system) is the difference between wages before and after impairment. Death benefits are related to earnings and graduated by the number of dependents. Medical benefits are furnished without limit as to time or amount for accidental injuries. Temporary Disability Insurance provides coverage against the risk of lost wages due to short-term nonoccupational disability. The Federal Unemployment Tax Act permits states where employees make contributions under the unemployment insurance program to use some or all of those contributions for disability benefits. It is estimated that about two-thirds of the nation's wage and salary earners in private employment have some protection through various voluntary and governmental group arrangements. In general the benefit amount for a week is intended to replace at least half the weekly wage loss for a maximum of 26 to 39 weeks per year.

▶ VETERANS' BENEFITS

The tradition of veterans' benefits dates to the 18th century, when the Continental Congress provided disability pensions for veterans of the Revolutionary War. Today, the Department of Veterans Affairs (V.A.) offers a range of services and benefits to eligible veterans, their dependents, and their survivors.

The total number of living veterans has been decreasing in recent years, from about 29.5 mil-

Unemployment Insurance Compensation, 1975–2009

Year	Total initial claims ('000s)	Total exhaustions ('000s)	Average weekly benefit per recipient	Average duration of benefits (in weeks)	Average total benefit per recipient
1975	24,843	4,195	$70.23	15.7	$1,103
1980	25,370	3,072	99.59	14.9	1,485
1985	20,634	2,572	128.11	14.3	1,827
1990	20,183	2,323	161.20	13.5	2,171
1995	18,553	2,662	187.04	14.8	2,759
2000	15,633	2,144	221.01	13.7	3,028
2004	17,958	3,532	262.50	16.1	4,226
2005	17,053	2,856	266.62	15.3	4,079
2008	22,136	3,424	297.09	14.9	4,282
2009	29,451	7,330	309.58	18.8	5,613

Source: U.S. Dept. of Labor, www.workforcesecurity.doleta.gov

lion in 1975 to 23.1 million in 2010. (An estimated 850 veterans of WWII died each day in 2009.) Nearly 40 percent of veterans are age 65 or older and the use and cost of medical care for these aging veterans is expected to grow more rapidly in the near future than other benefits and services. The number of beneficiaries receiving compensation and pensions is decreasing due to deaths, terminations for excess incomes, and age limitations for dependents. However, the number of trainees under the expanded GI Bill is likely to increase as more veterans become eligible.

Veterans who have incurred injuries or illness while in service are entitled to service-connected compensation. The amounts are determined by disability ratings. Death compensation or dependency and indemnity compensation is paid to survivors of veterans who died as a result of service-connected causes. War veterans who have become permanently and totally disabled from non-service-connected causes, and to survivors of war veterans may receive means-tested veterans' pensions. Benefits are based on family size, and the pensions provide a floor of income.

Medical programs The V.A. operates 153 hospital centers, 134 nursing homes, 50 residential rehabilitation centers, and 788 community-based outpatient clinics. In 2009, the V.A. treated 5.6 million people. The V.A. extends free priority care to service-connected disabled veterans, to veterans in special categories, and to needy non-service-connected veterans. As facilities and other resources permit, the V.A. provides care to non-service-connected veterans with incomes that exceed the mandatory care income limits. Since 1979, the V.A. has also operated Vet Centers, which provide psychological counseling for war-related trauma and other social services to more than 2 million veterans and their families. There were 232 such centers in 2009; they served more than 130,000 veterans, who made over 1 million visits.

Housing and loan programs Since 1944, when the GI bill began helping veterans buy homes, the V.A. has guaranteed more than 18.7 million loans worth nearly $1 trillion. In fiscal 2009, the V.A. guaranteed 325,700 loans, bringing the total number of current V.A. backed loans to 1.37 million. The V.A. also provides grants for specially adapted housing for disabled veterans. During 2009, the V.A. distributed 1,270 such grants, worth up to $63,780 each.

Other veterans' programs The GI Bill has provided education and training programs to more than 21.8 million veterans and family members since 1944, at a total cost of more than $83.6 billion. The Montgomery GI Bill requires contributions and offers veterans a basic educational benefit of up to $1,368 per month for 36 months while in an educational program. The post-9/11 GI Bill, effective August 2008, expanded the number of people who qualify for educational support and provides from 40 to 100 percent of the highest in-state undergraduate tuition, a monthly housing allowance, and a yearly stipend of up to $1,000 for supplies. In 2009, the GI Bills helped fund education or training for 376,400 veterans and active duty personnel, 106,400 National Guard and reserve members, and 81,300 survivors.

The Veterans Job Training Act program provides payments to defray training costs of employers who hire certain veterans of the Korean conflict or Vietnam era who have been unemployed for long periods of time.

Veterans Benefits and Services: Outlays and Recipients, 1975–2009

Fiscal year	Compensation and pensions	Readjustment, education, job training	Medical programs	Housing
Outlays (millions)				
1975	$ 7,860	$4,593	$3,665	N.A.
1980	11,688	2,342	6,515	N.A.
1985	14,714	1,059	9,547	N.A.
1990	15,241	278	12,134	N.A.
1995	18,966	1,124	15,981	N.A.
2000	21,500	N.A.	19,326	N.A.
2005	30,800	N.A.	N.A.	N.A.
2009	45,917	4,468	45,504	$480
Recipients ('000s)				
1975	4,855	2,804	1,985	290
1980	4,646	1,232	2,671	297
1985	4,005	491	2,963	179
1990	3,614	329	3,018	196
1995	3,332	476	2,859	263
2000	2,700	279	3,817	200
2005	3,500	336	5,300	166
2009	3,919	670	5,626	327

Source: Departent of Veterans Affairs, *Facts About the Department of Veterans Affairs* and *2009 Performance and Accountability Report.*

THE INTERNAL REVENUE SERVICE

Founded in 1862, the Internal Revenue Service (I.R.S.) is the office of the Department of the Treasury charged with collecting federal taxes. The Constitution empowers Congress to levy excise taxes and—in emergencies—to raise direct taxes. Congress's right to levy taxes on the income of individuals and corporations was contested throughout the 19th century, but that authority was written into the Constitution with the passage of the 16th Amendment in 1913. Today, the source of most of the federal government's revenues are the individual income tax, corporate income tax, excise taxes, estate taxes, and gift taxes. The I.R.S. is responsible for these taxes as well as for collecting employee and employer payments for social insurance and retirement insurance (See "Social Insurance Programs").

In 1998, Congress enacted a major overhaul of the I.R.S. in hopes of transforming the agency from a menacing symbol of government authority into a resource for taxpayers trying to cope with the increasingly bewildering tax code. The legislation established an outside board with broad authority to supervise the I.R.S.'s operations, and perhaps more important, shifted the burden of proof in tax dispute cases to the I.R.S. (previously, taxpayers had to prove their innocence). Initial reaction to the legislation was overwhelmingly favorable, but tax experts correctly predicted the law would give scofflaws greater incentive to cheat on their taxes. Property seizures dropped by 98 percent between 1997 and 1999, garnishments of bank accounts and paychecks were a quarter of their level two years earlier, and tax liens, which insure that back taxes are paid when properties are sold, were down by 67 percent.

The most damaging change was the anti-harassment section of the legislation, which tax collectors say has thwarted them from collecting taxes from delinquent filers. Several I.R.S. agents said they no longer pursued outstanding tax bills vigorously because they feared losing their jobs under the anti-harassment policy. In 1998, the I.R.S. gave up on collecting back taxes from just 98 taxpayers; in 2000, the agency wrote off $2.5 billion in back taxes owed by more than 650,000 delinquent taxpayers.

In 2009, the agency examined just 1.6 million of the 184 returns filed, a rate of 0.9 percent. The I.R.S. audited just under 2 million individual returns in 1996; that number was down to 1.4 million in 2009. The agency also eased up on corporate tax filings. It audited 69,650 corporate returns (2.7 percent) in 1996; but fewer than half as many (28,188 or 1.3 percent) in 2009.

Tax Returns Processed, 1990–2009

Type of return	Number of returns ('000s)				
	1990	1995	2000	2005	2009
Income Taxes					
Individual income tax (Form 1040 series)	112,492	116,298	127,590	132,845	171,985
Individual estimated tax (Form 1040ES)	38,188	35,475	39,230	28,669	24,197
Fiduciary estate and trust (Form 1041 series)	2,702	3,187	3,530	3,684	3,143
Fiduciary estate and trust estimated tax	651	583	892	503	542
Partnership (Form 1065)	1,741	1,572	2,048	2,665	3,565
Corporation (Forms 1120 series, 1066)	4,311	4,781	5,458	6,128	6,972
Estate tax (Forms 706, 706NA)	59	83	121	66	47
Gift tax (Form 709)	146	215	305	277	245
Employment taxes (Forms 94X series, CT-1, 1042)	28,914	29,006	28,911	30,872	30,223
Tax-exempt organizations (Forms 990 series, 4720, 5227)	484	560	707	815	1,132
Excise taxes (Forms 720, 730, 2290, 11C)	840	787	916	1,064	809
Supplemental documents (1040X, 2688, 4868, 7004, 1041A)	10,170	11,937	15,260	19,090	21,525
Total tax returns	**201,715**	**205,747**	**226,130**	**226,677**	**236,503**

Source: Internal Revenue Service, *2009 Data Book* (2010).

Tax Rate Schedules, 2010

Taxable income	What you pay
Single Individual	
Not over $8,375	10% of the taxable income
Over $8,375 but not over $34,000	$837.50 plus 15% of the excess over $8,375
Over $34,000 but not over $82,400	$4,681.25 plus 25% of the excess over $34,000
Over $82,400 but not over $171,850	$16,781.25 plus 28% of the excess over $82,400
Over $171,850 but not over $373,650	$41,827.25 plus 33% of the excess over $171,850
Over $373,650	$108,421.25 plus 35% of the excess over $373,650
Married individuals filing jointly, or qualifying widow(er)	
Not over $16,750	10% of the taxable income
Over $16,750 but not over $68,000	$1,675 plus 15% of the excess over $16,750
Over $68,000 but not over $137,300	$9,362.50 plus 25% of the excess over $68,000
Over $137,300 but not over $209,250	$26,687.50 plus 28% of the excess over $137,300
Over $209,250 but not over $373,650	$46,833.50 plus 33% of the excess over $209,250
Over $373,650	$101,085.50 plus 35% of the excess over $373,650
Married, Filing Separate Return	
Not over $8,375	10% of the taxable income
Over $8,375 but not over $34,000	$837.50 plus 15% of the excess over $8,375
Over $34,000 but not over $68,650	$4,681.25 plus 25% of the excess over $34,000
Over $68,650 but not over $104,625	$13,343.75 plus 28% of the excess over $68,650
Over $104,625 but not over $186,825	$23,416.75 plus 33% of the excess over $104,625
Over $186,825	$50,542.75 plus 35% of the excess over $186,825
Heads of Households	
Not over $11,950	10% of the taxable income
Over $11,950 but not over $45,550	$1,195 plus 15% of the excess over $11,950
Over $45,550 but not over $117,650	$6,235 plus 25% of the excess over $45,550
Over $117,650 but not over $190,550	$24,260 plus 28% of the excess over $117,650
Over $190,550 but not over $373,650	$44,672 plus 33% of the excess over $190,550
Over $373,650	$105,095 plus 35% of the excess over $373,650

Source: Internal Revenue Service, *Internal Revenue Bulletin*, Rev. Proc. 2009–50.

The shift is partly related to a decline in the number of I.R.S. employees, which was reduced from an all-time-high of 115,628 in 1996 to just 90,647 in 2008 before rebounding slightly to 92,577 in 2009. The number of returns filed has increased in that time, but the agency has gotten leaner primarily by focusing its auditors on the taxpayers with the highest incomes. In 2009, it examined 26 percent of the 14,683 returns filed by corporations with total revenues of $250 million or more, resulting in an additional $28.6 billion in additional taxes, or an average of $7.8 million per audit. The other closely monitored group of tax returns is from estates valued at $5 million or more. There were 9,495 such returns filed in 2009; the I.R.S. examined 21.6 percent of them, resulting in $1.34 billion in additional taxes.

▶TAX CHANGES 2009
The American Recovery and Reinvestment Act of 2009 included several temporary tax changes including a refundable tax credit of up to $400 for working individuals and $800 for working families that would phase out for taxpayers with adjusted gross income above $75,000 ($150,000 for married couples filing jointly). It increased the standard deduction for most taxpayers; increased the earned income credit for families with three or more children and raised the phase-out limits of the credit for all married couples; raised the health coverage tax credit; and added new tax credits for education, energy efficiency and renewable energy purchases. An expanded first-time homebuyer credit of up to $8,000 applied to homes purchased through April 30, 2010. In 2009, nearly half a million homebuyers claimed the credit, totaling $3.6 million in tax breaks.

▶PRINCIPAL DEDUCTIONS
Taxes: Taxpayers who pay a state and/or local tax may deduct this amount from their federal tax payment. In addition, in Alabama, Iowa, Louisiana, Missouri, Oklahoma, Oregon and Utah, taxpayers may deduct their federal income tax before calculating their state tax payments.

Personal exemptions: Taxpayers are allowed to claim personal exemptions for the taxpayer and each dependent claimed in filing income tax.

Returns Filed and Examined, and Additional Taxes and Penalties, 2008

Type of return	Total returns filed, 2008[1]	Total returns examined	Percent examined	Recommended additional taxes Total (000's)	Average per return[2]
All returns, total	**183,052,945**	**1,540,771**	**0.8%**	**$43,437,364**	**$85,306**
Individual, total[4]	**137,849,635**	**1,391,581**	**1.0**	**12,462,770**	**19,150**
Nonbusiness, income under $200,000	78,608,856	342,958	0.4	1,189,047	9,299
Schedule E, income under $200,000	15,409,542	205,432	1.3	893,908	7,927
with EIC, receipts under $25,000	21,028,686	410,889	2.0	1,642,114	4,493
with EIC, receipts over $25,000	1,470,688	51,368	3.5	304,239	8,838
Business, receipts under $25,000	10,496,414	122,321	1.2	502,902	6,233
Business, receipts $25,000–$100,000	3,228,160	59,739	1.9	531,263	8,717
Business, receipts $100,000–$200,000	943,174	36,131	3.8	846,166	21,672
Business, receipts over $200,000	730,815	22,869	3.1	379,659	18,628
Farm returns	1,366,833	7,542	0.6	89,282	21,355
Nonbusiness, income $200,000–$1 mil.	2,741,555	72,006	2.6	1,502,421	23,148
Business, income $200,000–$1 mil.	1,307,825	36,871	2.8	839,476	21,888
Income over $1 mil.	392,776	21,874	5.6	3,736,403	197,791
International returns	124,311	1,581	1.3	5,890	27,918
Corporation, total except Form 1120S	**2,255,443**	**30,417**	**1.3%**	**$26,817,682**	**$942,780**
No balance sheet	448,117	1,924	0.4	86,149	46,563
Under $250,000	1,137,067	9,073	0.8	149,272	19,523
$250,000–$1 mil.	366,845	5,030	1.4	132,983	26,941
$1 mil–$ 5 mil.	182,734	3,585	2.0	151,527	43,325
$5 mil–$10 mil.	31,434	968	3.1	81,586	86,793
$10 mil–$50 mil.	32,697	3,833	15.3	612,758	154,098
$50 mil–$100 mil.	7,629	893	11.7	152,612	146,614
$100 mil–$250 mil.	7,999	1,026	11.7	347,963	345,723
$250 mil. and over[4]	13,316	3,654	27.4	24,308,572	N.A.
Form 1120F	27,605	431	1.6	794,260	2,063,013
Fiduciary	3,729,793	4,582	0.1	113,920	114,723
Estate, total	**47,298**	**3,852**	**8.1%**	**$834,285**	**$216,697**
Gross estate under $5 mil.	38,696	2,182	5.6	202,009	92,665
Gross estate $5 mil. and over	8,602	1,670	19.4	632,276	378,608
Gift	**255,123**	**1,071**	**0.4%**	**$223,537**	**$208,718**
Employment	**30,717,441**	**60,346**	**0.2**	**2,765,036**	**60,738**
Excise	**895,388**	**16,134**	**1.8**	**120,004**	**8,768**
Miscellaneous taxable[3]	**N.A.**	**1,943**	**N.A.**	**89,806**	**50,928**
Partnerships	**3,136,994**	**13,203**	**0.4**	**N.A.**	**N.A.**
S–Corporations (Form 1120S)	**4,155,830**	**16,634**	**0.4**	**N.A.**	**N.A.**

Notes: Totals may not add due to rounding. 1. Calendar year. 2. Includes only returns reviewed by revenue agents. Additional taxes and penalties were recovered through reviews of individual returns by tax auditors and service centers. 3. Includes returns examined for taxpayers claiming an Earned Income Tax Credit and for those with total positive income of $1 million or more. 4. Estimated average per return. **Source:** Internal Revenue Service, *2008 Data Book* (2009).

Congress determines the amount (since 1990, pegged to the inflation rate) allowable for deductions on personal and other exemptions. Prior to 2004, the personal exemption was the same for a married couple as for a single person but married couples can now claim the full exemption for each spouse. In 2009, this was $3,650 per person.

Interest expenses: The most common interest deduction is on home mortgage, thus making the cost of owning a home more affordable to most Americans. Although politically very popular, the mortgage deduction is what experts call an "upside-down" subsidy because the more a taxpayer earns, the greater the tax cut yielded. In recent years, 20 percent of the tax savings from home mortgage interest has gone to taxpayers earning more than $200,000.

Medical expenses: Although almost all medical expenses are deductible, your unreimbursed expenses for the year must total 7.5 percent of your adjusted gross income in order to deduct them.

▶ELECTRONIC FILING
The number of people filing their tax returns electronically has jumped dramatically since the program was introduced in 1990. Just over 4 million individuals filed electronically in 1990; by 1993, that number had tripled to 12.3 million; in 2009, 101 million returns (including two-thirds of all individual returns) were filed electronically.

▶CHECK BOXES
More than 15 million people check the little box authorizing the I.R.S. to send $3 from their tax to the Presidential Election Campaign Fund. A total of $45.2 million went to that fund in fiscal 2009, down from $49.5 million in 2008.

Checking the box does not increase the amount of tax owed or reduce the size of any refund.

Internal Revenue Collections, Costs, and Tax Per Capita, 1960–2009

Fiscal year	Collections ('000s)	Cost of collecting $100	Tax per capita
1960	$ 91,774,803	$ 0.40	$ 508
1965	114,434,634	0.52	589
1970	195,722,096	0.45	955
1975	293,822,726	0.54	1,376
1980	519,375,273	0.44	2,276
1985	742,871,541	0.48	3,099
1990	1,056,365,652	0.52	4,208
1995	1,375,731,835	0.54	5,144
2000	2,096,916,925	0.39	7,404
2004	2,018,502,103	0.48	6,849
2005	2,268,895,122	0.46	7,620
2006	2,518,680,230	0.42	8,379
2007	2,691,537,557	0.40	8,871
2008	2,745,035,410	0.41	8,979
2009	2,345,337,000	0.50	7,614

Note: In current dollars. **Source:** Internal Revenue Service, *2009 Data Book* (2010).

Internal Revenue Collections, 2009

Type of return	Gross collections ('000s)	Refunds[1] ('000s)	Net collections Amount ('000s)	Net collections Percent of total
Corporation income taxes	$ 225,481,588	$ 95,200,297	$130,281,291	6.8%
Individual income taxes[2]	1,190,382,757	336,344,148[3]	854,038,609	44.8
Employment taxes, total	858,163,864	3,395,775	854,768,089	44.8
Estate and gift taxes, total	24,677,322	1,248,550	23,428,772	1.2
Excise taxes	46,631,646	1,496,864	45,134,782	2.4
Grand total	**$2,345,337,177**	**437,685,634**	**1,907,651,543**	**100.0%**

Note: Excludes excise taxes paid to the Alcohol and Tobacco Tax and Trade Bureau. 1. Includes interest payments and $77.9 billion in refundable tax credits. 2. Collections include $45.2 million in Presidential Election Campaign Funds contributions. 3. Includes $11.5 billion in Economic Stimulus Payments. **Source:** Internal Revenue Service, *2009 Data Book* (2010).

I.R.S. Collections by Principal Sources, 1961–2009 (thousands of dollars)

Year	Total Internal Revenue collections	Corporate income & profits tax	Individual income tax	Employment taxes	Estate and gift taxes	Excise taxes
1961	$ 94,401,086	$ 21,764,940	$ 46,153,001	$ 12,502,451	$ 1,916,392	$12,064,302
1970	195,722,096	35,036,983	103,651,585	37,449,188	3,680,076	15,904,264
1980	519,375,273	72,379,610	287,547,782	128,330,480	6,498,381	24,619,021
1990	1,056,365,652	110,016,539	540,228,408	367,219,321	11,761,939	27,139,445
1995	1,375,731,835	174,422,173	675,779,337	465,405,305	15,144,394	44,980,627
1998	1,769,408,739	213,270,011	928,065,856	557,799,193	24,630,962	45,642,716
1999	1,904,151,888	216,324,889	1,002,185,765	598,669,865	28,385,607	58,585,763
2000	2,096,916,925	235,654,894	1,137,077,702	639,651,814	29,721,620	54,810,895
2004	2,018,502,103	230,619,359	990,248,760	717,247,296	25,579,462	54,807,225
2005	2,268,895,122	307,094,837	1,107,500,994	771,441,662	25,605,531	57,252,098
2006	2,518,680,230	380,924,573	1,236,259,371	814,819,218	28,687,525	57,989,543
2007	2,691,537,557	395,535,825	1,366,241,437	849,732,729	26,977,953	53,049,612
2008	2,745,035,410	354,315,825	1,425,990,183	883,197,626	29,823,935	51,707,840
2009	2,345,337,177	225,481,588	1,175,421,788	858,163,864	39,638,291[1]	46,631,646

Note: In current dollars. 1. Includes Estate and Trust income tax. **Source:** Internal Revenue Service, *2009 Data Book* (2010).

THE U.S. POSTAL SERVICE

With 712,000 employees securely moving an average 584 million pieces of mail per day to more than 150 million delivery points, the U.S. Postal Service provides one of the most vital government services. It does this with no tax dollars and at a cost to the customer much lower than in any other industrial nation. In 2009, first class postage in the U.S. cost $0.44, compared to the equivalent of $0.64 in Great Britain, $0.83 in Japan, and $1.25 in Norway—despite the much smaller size of those countries.

First established by the Continental Congress in 1775, the Postal Service was made part of the federal system in the Constitution and the office of postmaster general established in George Washington's very first cabinet. In 1969, however, in response to vociferous complaints of mismanagement, waste, unreliable service and staggering financial losses, the Nixon administration reorganized the service as an independent establishment within the executive branch. The Postal Service Act of 1969 removed the postmaster general from the cabinet and created a self-supporting postal corporation owned by the federal government and vested power in an 11-member Board of Governors, nine of whom are appointed by the president with the consent of the Senate; these in turn appoint the postmaster general who serves as the C.E.O. of the postal service; the 11th member of the board is chosen by the other 10 and serves as deputy postmaster general.

Finally, the 1969 law established an independent Postal Rate Commission of five members, appointed by the president, to recommend postal rates and classification for adoption by the Board of Governors. Since then, the Postal Service has fluctuated between profitability and loss, earning a record profit of $3.9 billion in 2003, but losing $3.8 billion in 2009. To cut costs, the Postal Service eliminated the equivalent of 65,000 jobs, closed six district offices and 227 post offices, and reduced hours. However, while mail volume dropped 14.5 percent from 2008 to 2009, the number of delivery addresses grew by 923,595. In 2010, projecting a $7 billion loss, the Postal Service asked Congress to consider reducing delivery from six days per week to five.

In 2009, the Postal Service delivered 176 billion pieces of mail, operated 218,684 vehicles, and owned or leased 33,264 facilities ranging from 60 square feet to 34 acres in size. If the Postal Service were privately held, its $68 billion in 2009 revenues would have ranked it as one of the 100 largest companies in the world.

Domestic Postage Rates

Type of Mail	Rate
Postcards	$0.28
Letters	
up to 1 ounce	$0.44
1–2 ounces	0.61
2–3 ounces	0.78
3–3.5 ounces	0.95
over 3.5 ounces	**Use flat rate sizes**
Flats	
up to 1 ounce	$0.88
1–2 ounces	1.05
2–3 ounces	1.22
3–4 ounces	1.39
4–5 ounces	1.56
5–6 ounces	1.73
6–7 ounces	1.90
7–8 ounces	2.07
8–9 ounces	2.24
9–10 ounces	2.41
10–11 ounces	2.58
11–12 ounces	2.75
over 13 ounces	**Use Priority Mail**

Priority mail provides two-day delivery to all major parts of the U.S. Items are priced by flat rate packages or by weight and distance. For packages over one pound, rates depend on the zone; the greater the distance, the greater the cost.

up to 1 pound	$4.95
1–2 pounds	4.95–8.70
2–3 pounds	5.50–11.95
3–4 pounds	6.10–14.70
4–5 pounds	6.85–17.15
5–10 pounds	7.55–29.95
10–20 pounds	10.55–43.55
21–70 pounds	14.70–108.25

Express mail is an overnight and second-day delivery service. A flat rate of $17.50 is charged, regardless of weight, for matter sent in a USPS flat-rate envelope. Cheaper rates apply for Express Mail sent from one post office to another.

up to 1/2 pound	$13.05–21.20
1/2 pound–1 pound	15.00–25.15
1–2 pounds	16.30–27.65
4–5 pounds	18.60–35.60
9–10 pounds	28.75–55.60
11–70 pounds	32.35–259.80

Parcel Post is a zone-based class of mail for sending books, circulars, catalogs, other printed matter, and merchandise-weighing not more than 70 pounds. The cheapest rate, for a machine-sorted package up to one pound, is $4.90; the maximum rate is $38.61 for a 35-pound package sent to zone 8. Oversized parcels (more than 35 pounds or 108 inches in combined length and girth) are charged additional fees and priced by weight and distance.

Pickups Mail carriers pick up mail and packages on their regular routes for free, but the post office will also pick up properly posted priority mail and express mail packages on demand for a fee of $15.30 per pickup. Call 1-800-222-1811.

Note: As of Oct. 1, 2010.
Source: U.S. Postal Service. www.usps.gov

International Postage Rates

Weight up to	Canada	Mexico	Other countries[1]
Airmail letters			
up to 1.0 ounces	$0.75	$0.75	$0.98
1–2 ounces	1.00	1.34	1.82
2–3 ounces	1.25	1.89	2.66
3.5 ounces	1.50	2.44	3.50
Postcards	$0.75	$0.79	$0.98

Note: As of Oct. 1, 2010. 1. Rates for weights not shown maybe higher in some countries, but lower in Micronesia and the Marshall Islands. **Source:** U.S. Postal Service.

Postage online   If you know the weight of a package, you can determine the amount of postage you will need, purchase postage, and print shipping labels online at *www.usps.gov.*

Forever Stamps   Because the price of stamps tends to rise with the rate of inflation, the Post Office in 2007 introduced the Forever Stamp. It costs whatever the current rate is for first class postage, but is valid forever.   No additional postage is required even if the price of stamps goes up.

ZIP Codes   There are about 42,000 separate ZIP codes in the U.S.; the number is constantly changing. The lowest ZIP code number is 00501 for the IRS center in Holtsville, NY; the highest is 99950 in Ketchikan, AK. A national ZIP code directory is available in every post office. Directory assistance telephone operators can provide ZIP code information, and there is also a ZIP code lookup at www.usps.gov.

Volume and Revenue of Mail by Type, 1990–2009

Type of Service	Millions of pieces				Revenues (millions)	
	1990	2000	2005	2009	2000	2009
First-class	89,269	103,526	98,071	83,770	$35,516	$35,873
Standard mail	63,725	90,057	100,942	82,706	15,193	17,364
Priority mail	518	1,222	888	790	4,837	5,362
Package services	663	1,128	1,166	730	1,912	1,683
Periodicals	10,682	10,365	9,070	7,954	2,171	2,038
Express mail	59	71	56	47	996	885
International air	632	1,021	829	302[1]	1,477	1,345[1]
International economy	166	79	22	N.A.	180	N.A.
Mailgrams	14	4	0.8	N.A.	1	N.A.
U.S. Postal Service	538	363	621	455	N.A.	N.A.
Free for the blind	35	47	76	62	N.A.	N.A.
Total mail	166,301	207,882	211,743	177,058	$62,284	$68,116[2]

Notes: 1. Includes all international mail. 2. Includes services, investment income and other revenue not listed separately.
Source: U.S. Postal Service, *Final Revenue, Pieces, and Weight 2009.*

Postal Abbreviations for States and Territories

State	Abb.	State	Abb.
Alabama	AL	Nevada	NV
Alaska	AK	New Hampshire	NH
Arizona	AZ	New Jersey	NJ
Arkansas	AR	New Mexico	NM
California	CA	New York	NY
Colorado	CO	North Carolina	NC
Connecticut	CT	North Dakota	ND
Delaware	DE	Ohio	OH
District of	DC	Oklahoma	OK
Columbia		Oregon	OR
Florida	FL	Pennsylvania	PA
Georgia	GA	Rhode Island	RI
Hawaii	HI	South Carolina	SC
Idaho	ID	South Dakota	SD
Illinois	IL	Tennessee	TN
Indiana	IN	Texas	TX
Iowa	IA	Utah	UT
Kansas	KS	Vermont	VT
Kentucky	KY	Virginia	VA
Louisiana	LA	Washington	WA
Maine	ME	West Virginia	WV
Maryland	MD	Wisconsin	WI
Massachusetts	MA	Wyoming	WY
Michigan	MI	American Samoa	AS
Minnesota	MN	Guam	GU
Mississippi	MS	Northern Mariana	CM
Missouri	MO	Islands	
Montana	MT	Puerto Rico	PR
Nebraska	NE	Virgin Islands	VI

Postal Service Employees and Offices, 1990–2009

Category	1990	2009
Employees		
Headquarters (Washington, D.C.)	2,291	2,811
Field support units	5,691	4,455
Inspection services (field)	4,259	2,617
Inspector General	N.A.	1,155
Area offices	N.A.	1,047
Postmasters	26,995	23,672
Supervisors, managers	43,458	28,812
Professional, administrative, and technical personnel	9,793	6,460
Clerks	290,380	177,842
Nurses	286	0
Mail Handlers	51,123	52,954
City delivery carriers	236,081	200,658
Motor vehicle operators	7,308	8,113
Rural delivery carriers (full-time)	42,252	67,749
Building and equipment maintenance personnel	33,323	39,531
Vehicle maintenance personnel	4,874	5,252
Total career employees	**760,668**	**623,128**
Non-career employees (casuals)	26,829	4,271
Offices, stations and branches	**40,067**	**N.A.**
Post offices	28,959	27,161
Classified stations and branches	5,008	5,501
Contract stations and branches	4,397	3,037
Community post offices	1,703	797

Source: U.S. Postal Service, *2009 Annual Report.*

States, Territories, and Possessions

This section, a compilation of history and statistics about the 50 United States, the District of Columbia, and U.S. territories and possessions, includes a brief history of each state and territory; its official motto and other emblems; a summary of geographic, demographic, and economic facts; and a list of prominent natives, places, and dates.

Statistical sources include the U.S. Census Bureau's 2000 decennial census and *The Statistical Abstract* (annual); the Council of State Government's *Book of the States* and *State Elective Officials and the Legislatures*; and the Bureau of Economic Analysis' *Survey of Current Business*. Data results from the 2010 census were not available at the time that this book went to print.

The headings for demographic statistics in the paragraphs on People and Language conform to U.S. Census Bureau usage, except that "Black" is used as short for Black or African American, "Indian" is used for American Indian and Alaska Native, and "Pacific Islander" is used for Native Hawaiian and other Pacific Islander. Note that Hispanics may be of any race.

U.S. Resident Population, by State, 1990–2000

| State | Population ('000s) | | Change 1990 to 2000 | |
	2000 Census	1990 Census	Number	Percent
United States	281,422	248,710	32,712	13.2%
Alabama	4,447	4,041	407	10.1
Alaska	627	550	77	14.0
Arizona	5,131	3,665	1,465	40.0
Arkansas	2,673	2,351	323	13.7
California	33,872	29,760	4,112	13.8
Colorado	4,301	3,294	1,007	30.6
Connecticut	3,406	3,287	118	3.6
Delaware	784	666	117	17.6
Dist. of Columbia	572	607	-35	-5.7
Florida	15,982	12,938	3,044	23.5
Georgia	8,186	6,478	1,708	26.4
Hawaii	1,212	1,108	103	9.3
Idaho	1,294	1,007	287	28.5
Illinois	12,419	11,431	989	8.6
Indiana	6,080	5,544	536	9.7
Iowa	2,926	2,777	150	5.4
Kansas	2,688	2,478	211	8.5
Kentucky	4,042	3,685	356	9.7
Louisiana	4,469	4,220	249	5.9
Maine	1,275	1,228	47	3.8
Maryland	5,296	4,781	515	10.8
Massachusetts	6,349	6,016	333	5.5
Michigan	9,938	9,295	643	6.9
Minnesota	4,919	4,375	544	12.4
Mississippi	2,845	2,573	271	10.5
Missouri	5,595	5,117	478	9.3
Montana	902	799	103	12.9
Nebraska	1,711	1,578	133	8.4
Nevada	1,998	1,202	796	66.3
New Hampshire	1,236	1,109	127	11.4
New Jersey	8,414	7,730	684	8.9
New Mexico	1,819	1,515	304	20.1
New York	18,976	17,990	986	5.5
North Carolina	8,049	6,629	1,421	21.4
North Dakota	642	639	3	0.5
Ohio	11,353	10,847	506	4.7
Oklahoma	3,451	3,146	305	9.7
Oregon	3,421	2,842	579	20.4
Pennsylvania	12,281	11,882	399	3.4
Rhode Island	1,048	1,003	45	4.5
South Carolina	4,012	3,487	525	15.1
South Dakota	755	696	59	8.5
Tennessee	5,689	4,877	812	16.7
Texas	20,852	16,987	3,865	22.8
Utah	2,233	1,723	510	29.6
Vermont	609	563	46	8.2
Virginia	7,079	6,187	891	14.4
Washington	5,894	4,867	1,027	21.1
West Virginia	1,808	1,793	15	0.8
Wisconsin	5,364	4,892	472	9.6
Wyoming	494	454	40	8.9

Note: Includes armed forces residing in each state. **Source:** U.S. Census Bureau, *Statistical Abstract of the United States, 2009* (2009).

▶ ALABAMA

The memory of the Native American presence is particularly strong in Alabama. Trade with the Northeast via the Ohio River valley began during the Burial Mound Period (1000 B.C.–A.D. 700) and continued until European contact. Meso-American influence is evident in the agrarian Mississippian culture that followed. Pressured by white settlers in the early 19th century, the Creeks warred against the U.S. government until defeated by General Andrew Jackson.

The cradle of the Confederacy during the Civil War, Alabama was at center stage in the civil rights movement of the 1950s and 1960s. Although cotton is still a major crop, the northern part of the state around Birmingham is a major industrial area with abundant coal, iron ore, limestone, and electricity from the TVA. Increasingly urban—70 percent of the population lived in rural areas 50 years ago, compared with roughly 30 percent today—Alabama's economy is progressing slowly, although it still ranks near last in taxes and in money spent on education.

Name Probably after Alabama tribe. **Nickname** Yellowhammer State, Heart of Dixie. **Capital** Montgomery. **Entered union** Dec. 14, 1819 (22nd). **Motto** "We dare defend our rights." **Emblems** **Bird** Yellowhammer. **Dance** Square dance. **Game bird** Wild turkey. **Fish** Tarpon. **Fossil** *Basilosaurus oetoides*. **Mineral** Hematite. **Nut** Pecan. **Song** "Alabama." **Stone** Marble. **Tree** Southern (longleaf) pine.

Land **Total area** 52,419 sq. mi. (30th), incl. 1,675 sq. mi. inland water. **Borders** Tenn., Ga., Fla., Gulf of Mexico, Miss. **Rivers** Alabama, Chattahoochee, Mobile, Tennessee, Tennessee-Tombigbee Waterway, Tensaw, Tombigbee. **Lakes** Guntersville, Pickwick, Wheeler, Wilson (all formed by Tennessee Valley Authority [TVA]); Dannelly Res., Martin, Lewis Smith, Weiss. **Mountains** Cumberland, Lookout, Raccoon, Sand.

Elected officials Gov. Bob Riley (R, term exp. 2010). Lt. Gov. Jim Folsom Jr. (D). Sec. State Beth Chapman (R). Atty. Gen. Troy King (R).

People (July 2009 est.) 4,708,708 (23rd). Race/Hispanic Origin: White 71.0%. Black 26.4%. Indian 0.5%. Asian 1.0%. Two or more races 1.1%. Hispanic 2.7%.

Cities (2006) Birmingham 229,424. Montgomery 201,998. Mobile 192,830. Huntsville 168,132. Tuscaloosa 83,052. Hoover 68,707.

Dothan 64,053. Decatur 55,778. Auburn 51,906. Gadsden 37,291.

Business　Gross State Product, 2008: $137.1 **Leading Sectors of GSP:** Services 18.10%; Manufacturing 17.80%; Government 15.8%. *Fortune 500* **Companies (2009):** 1.

Famous natives　Hank Aaron, baseball player. Tallulah Bankhead, actress. William B. Bankhead, politician. Charles Barkley, basketball player. Hugo L. Black, jurist. Wernher von Braun (b. Germany), rocket scientist. Nat "King" Cole, singer. Red Eagle (William Weatherfield), Creek leader. W.C. Handy, musician. Frank M. Johnson, Jr., jurist. Helen Keller, author. Coretta Scott King, reformer. Harper Lee, author. Joe Louis, boxer. Jesse Owens, runner. Condoleeza Rice, secretary of state. Leroy Robert "Satchell" Paige, baseball player. Walker Percy, author. George Wallace, politician. Hank Williams, singer. Tammy Wynette, singer.

Noteworthy places　Alabama Deep Sea Fishing Rodeo, Dauphin Island. Alabama Space and Rocket Center, U.S. Space Camp, Huntsville. Battleship USS *Alabama*, Mobile. Birmingham Museum of Art. First White House of the Confederacy, Montgomery. Horseshoe Bend Natl. Military Park. Mound State Monument Archaeological Museum, Moundville. Museum of Natural History, Univ. Alabama, Tuscaloosa. Point Clear (resort). Russell Cave Natl. Monument. Tuskegee Institute.

Memorable events　Humans first inhabit Russell Cave c. 6000 B.C. Temple Mound culture flourishes around Moundville, A.D. 1200–1500. First Europeans in Mobile Bay 1519. Hernando de Soto's battle with Tuscaloosa possibly bloodiest encounter ever between Europeans and Native Americans in U.S. 1540. Spanish at Mobile Bay 1599. Pierre Le Moyne, sieur d'Iberville, establishes first permanent colony at Mobile 1711. Treaty of Paris gives Mobile to Britain 1763. U.S. control recognized 1783. Chickasaws, Choctaws, and Cherokees cede lands to U.S. 1805. First Baptist Church established 1808. Gen. Andrew Jackson defeats Creek Indian Confederacy at Horseshoe Bend 1814. Cotton principal cash crop 1820s. Beginning of coal and iron mining and steel manufacturing 1850s. Alabama secedes from Union; first capital of Confederate States of America at Montgomery 1861. Battle of Mobile Bay 1864. Readmitted to Union 1868. Booker T. Washington founds Tuskegee Institute 1881. Destruction of cotton crops by boll weevils leads to diversification of rural economy 1915. Tennessee Valley Authority enacted by Congress 1933. Montgomery bus boycott 1955. Freedom march from Selma to Montgomery 1965.

Tourist information　(800) ALABAMA **www.800alabama.com**

▶ **ALASKA**
One-fifth the size of the entire lower 48 states, Alaska is a vast, geographically varied wilderness. The coast from the Bering Sea to the Arctic was originally inhabited by Eskimos and Aleuts, while inland and to the south were Athapascans and people of the Northwest Indian culture. Russian fur traders in the 1740s were the first Europeans to recognize the region's commercial potential, and the Russian Orthodox faith is still found in the old territorial capital of Sitka (New Archangel).

Russia sold Alaska to the United States in 1867 for $7.2 million—2 cents an acre—and Alaska experienced successive booms in furs, fishing and whaling, and gold. Discovery of oil on the North

Population Density of U.S. States, 1980–2000

State	Population per square mile 1980	1990	2000
U.S. Total	**64.1**	**70.4**	**79.6**
Alabama	76.7	79.6	87.6
Alaska	0.7	1.0	1.1
Arizona	23.9	32.3	45.2
Arkansas	43.9	45.1	51.3
California	151.7	191.0	217.2
Colorado	27.9	31.8	41.5
Connecticut	641.4	678.5	702.9
Delaware	304.0	340.8	401.1
Dist. of Columbia	10,397.9	9,884.4	9,316.4
Florida	180.7	239.9	296.4
Georgia	94.3	111.8	141.4
Hawaii	150.2	172.5	188.6
Idaho	11.4	12.2	15.6
Illinois	205.6	205.6	223.4
Indiana	153.1	154.6	169.5
Iowa	52.1	49.7	52.4
Kansas	28.9	30.3	32.9
Kentucky	92.1	92.8	101.7
Louisiana	96.5	96.9	102.6
Maine	36.5	39.8	41.3
Maryland	431.4	489.1	541.9
Massachusetts	732.0	767.6	809.8
Michigan	163.0	163.6	175.0
Minnesota	51.2	55.0	61.8
Mississippi	53.7	54.9	60.6
Missouri	71.4	74.3	81.2
Montana	5.4	5.5	6.2
Nebraska	20.4	20.5	22.3
Nevada	7.3	10.9	18.2
New Hampshire	102.6	123.7	137.8
New Jersey	992.7	1,044.3	1,134.4
New Mexico	10.7	12.5	15.0
New York	371.8	381.0	401.9
North Carolina	120.7	136.1	165.2
North Dakota	9.5	9.3	9.3
Ohio	263.7	264.9	277.3
Oklahoma	44.1	45.8	50.3
Oregon	27.4	29.6	35.6
Pennsylvania	264.7	265.1	274.0
Rhode Island	906.4	960.3	1,003.2
South Carolina	103.6	115.8	133.2
South Dakota	9.1	9.2	9.9
Tennessee	111.4	118.3	138.0
Texas	54.3	64.9	79.6
Utah	17.8	21.0	27.2
Vermont	55.3	60.8	65.8
Virginia	135.0	156.3	178.8
Washington	62.1	73.1	88.6
West Virginia	81.0	74.5	75.1
Wisconsin	86.6	90.1	98.8
Wyoming	4.8	4.7	5.1

Note: Persons per square mile for all years calculated on the basis of land area data from the 1990 census. **Source:** U.S. Census Bureau, *Statisical Abstract of the United States, 2009* (2009).

Slope near Prudhoe Bay in 1968 and completion of an 800-mile trans-Alaska pipeline a decade later made oil production the centerpiece of the state's economy in the 1980s. Although the population grew by more than 20 percent since the 1990s, the number of people per square mile remains below 1.5. In recent years, tourism based on the state's extraordinary beauty has grown substantially and now many Alaskans oppose proposed oil exploration at the Arctic National Wildlife Refuge. The memory of the *Exxon Valdez* oil spill into Prince William Sound in 1989 has had a powerful effect.

Name From Aleut *alaska* and Eskimo *alakshak,* both meaning "mainland." **Nickname** "The Last Frontier." **Capital** Juneau. **Entered union** Jan. 3, 1959 (49th). **Motto** "North to the future."

Emblems **Bird** Willow ptarmigan. **Fish** King salmon. **Flower** Forget-me-not. **Gem** Jade. **Marine mammal** Bowhead whale. **Mineral** Gold. **Song** "Alaska's Flag." **Sport** Mushing (dog-team racing). **Tree** Sitka spruce.

Land **Total area** 663,267 sq. mi (1st), incl. 91,316 sq. mi. inland water. **Borders** Arctic Ocean (Chukchi Sea, Beaufort Sea), Yukon, British Columbia, Pacific Ocean, Bering Strait. **Rivers** Colville, Porcupine, Noatak, Yukon, Susitna, Copper, Kobuk, Koyukuk, Kuskokwim, Tanana. **Mountains** Alaska Range (Mt. McKinley 20,320 ft., highest in North America), Aleutian Range, Brooks Range, Kuskokwim, St. Elias. **Other notable features** Aleutian Islands, Alexander Archipelago, Kodiak Island, Nunivak Island, Point Barrow (71°23'N), Pribilof Islands, Seward Peninsula, St. Lawrence Island.

Elected officials Gov. Sean Parnell (R, term exp. 2010). Lt. Gov. Craig E. Campbell (R). Atty. Gen. Daniel S. Sullivan (R).

People (July 2009 est.) 698,473 (47th). Race/Hispanic Origin: White 70.6%. Black 4.3%. Indian 15.3%. Asian 4.5%. Pacific Islander 0.7%. Two or more races 4.6%. Hispanic 6.1%.

Cities (2006) Anchorage 278,700. Fairbanks 31,142. Juneau 30,737. Wasilla 9,236. Sitka 8,920. Kenai 7,533. Ketchikan 7,446. Bethel 6,356. Kodiak 6,259.

Business **Gross State Product, 2008:** $30.0 bil. **Leading Sectors of GSP:** Mining 19.56%; Government 19.50%; Oil and gas extraction 17.12%. *Fortune 500* Companies (2009): 0.

Famous natives Aleksandr Baranov (b. Russia), first governor of Russian America. Vitus Bering (b. Denmark), explorer. Ernest Gruening (b. N.Y.), governor. Carl Ben Eielson, bush pilot. Walter Hickel (b. Kans.), governor.

Noteworthy places Aniakchak Natl. Monument. Bering Land Bridge Natl. Preserve. Cape Krusenstern Natl. Monument. Denali Natl. Park (formerly Mt. McKinley Natl. Park). Gates of the Arctic Natl. Park. Glacier Bay Natl. Park. Katmai Natl. Park (Valley of Ten Thousand Smokes). Kenai Fjords Natl. Park. Klondike Gold Rush Natl. Hist. Park. Kobuk Valley Natl. Park. Lake Clark Natl. Park. Little Diomede Island—2.5 mi. from Big Diomede Island (Russia). Sitka Natl. Hist. Park. St. Michael's Cathedral, Sitka. Wrangell–St. Elias Natl. Park.

Memorable events Earliest migration from Asia to Americas across Bering Sea land bridge, c. 15,000 years ago. Alaska inhabited by Tlingits, Tinnehs, Aleuts, and Eskimos. Peter the Great sponsors expedition to find land opposite Siberia 1728. Bering expedition lands near Mt. Elias; begins Pacific Northwest fur trade with Europe and Asia 1741. Russians establish first European settlement at Three Saints Bay 1784. Russian-American Company chartered 1799. Baranov's massacre of Tlingits at Sitka 1802. Gold discovered at Stikine Creek (1861), Juneau (1880), Fortymile Creek (1886), Nome (1898), Fairbanks (1903). Russians sell Alaska to U.S. for $7.2 million 1867. First salmon cannery established 1878. First oil well drilled at Cook's Inlet 1896. Japanese occupy Agattu, Attu, and Kiska islands 1942–43. Alaskans vote for statehood 1946. Statehood 1959. Earthquake destroys Anchorage, Northwest Pan-

handle, and Cook Inlet; tsunami wipes out Valdez; coast sinks 32 ft. at Kodiak and Seward and rises 16 ft. at Cordova 1964. Oil discovered on North Slope 1968. Alaska Native Claims Settlement Act gives Alaska's Native Americans 44 million acres for native landholdings 1971. Completion of 789-mi. pipeline to Valdez 1977. Population growth of 32.8% highest in U.S. 1980–86. *Exxon Valdez* spills 10 million gallons of oil into Prince William Sound off Valdez — worst oil spill in U.S. history 1989.

Tourist information (907) 929-2200
www.travelalaska.com

▶ARIZONA

The Hopi village of Oraibi is the oldest continuously inhabited town in the United States, and today vast tracts of Arizona are reserved for Apaches, Hopis, Navajos, Papagos and other Native Americans. Last of the 48 conterminous states admitted to the union, Arizona was sparsely settled until the advent of air conditioning in the postwar years made it habitable and a popular destination for retirees. More recently, there has been a boom in manufacturing and light industry, and in the last decade, population growth has been among the highest in the nation. Mexican-Americans are an important political force.

As in most southwestern states, water scarcity is a major problem. Arizona draws 2.8 million acre-feet of water from the Colorado River, whose water it shares with five other states and Mexico.

Name Probably from the Pima or Papago for "place of small springs." **Nickname** Grand Canyon State. **Capital** Phoenix. **Entered union** Feb. 14, 1912 (48th). **Motto** *Ditat deus* (God enriches).

Emblems **Bird** Cactus wren. **Flower** Blossom of the saguaro cactus. **Gemstone** Turquoise. **Official neck wear** Bolo tie. **Songs** "Arizona March Song," "Arizona." **Tree** Palo verde.

Land **Total area** 113,998 sq. mi. (6th), incl. 364 sq. mi. inland water. **Borders** Utah, Colo., N.Mex., Sonora, Baja California Norte, Calif., Nev. **Rivers** Colorado, Gila, Little Colorado, Salt, Zuni. **Lakes** Havasu, Mead, Mohave, Powell, Roosevelt, San Carlos. **Mountains** Black, Gila, Hualpai, Mohawk, San Francisco Peaks (Humphreys Peak 12,633 ft.). **Other notable features** Grand Canyon, Kaibab Plateau, Painted and Sonoran Deserts, Petrified Forest.

Elected officials Gov. Jan Brewer (R, term exp. 2010). Atty. Gen. Terry Goddard (D). Sec. State Ken Bennett (R).

People (July 2009 est.) 6,595,778 (14th). Race/Hispanic Origin: White 86.5%. Black 4.2%. Indian 4.9%. Asian 2.5%. Pacific Islander 0.2%. Two or more races 1.8%. Hispanic 30.1%.

Cities (2006) Phoenix 1,512,986. Tucson 518,956. Mesa 447,541. Glendale 246,531. Chandler 240,595. Scottsdale 231,127. Gilbert 191,517. Tempe 169,712. Peoria 142,024. Yuma 87,423.

Business **Gross State Product, 2008:** $210.2 bil. **Leading Sectors of GSP:** Services 21.46%; Finance, insurance, and real estate 19.53%; Manufacturing 13.51%. *Fortune 500* Companies (2009): 5.

Famous natives Bruce Babbitt, politician. Cesar Chavez, labor leader. Cochise, Apache chief. Andrew Ellicott Douglass (b. Vt.), dendrochronologist. Wyatt Earp (b. Ill.), lawman. Barry Goldwater, politician. Goyathlay (Geronimo), Apache chieftain. Carl Hayden, congressman. Eusebio Kino (b. Italy), missionary. Sandra Day O'Connor, jurist. Marty Robbins, singer. Linda Ronstadt, singer. Kerri Strug, gymnast. Morris Udall, politician.

Noteworthy Places Canyon de Chelly Natl. Monument. Casa Grande Ruins Natl. Monument. Chiricahua Natl. Monument. Ft. Bowie. Grand Canyon Natl. Park. Heard Museum, Phoenix. London Bridge, Lake Havasu City. Montezuma Castle Natl. Monument. Navajo Natl. Monument. Organ Pipe Cactus Natl. Monument. Painted Desert. Petrified Forest Natl. Park. Pipe Spring Natl. Monument. Saguaro Natl. Monument. Slot canyons, Upper and Lower Antelope Canyons, near Page. Sunset Crater Natl. Monument. Taliesin West, near Scottsdale. Tonto Natl. Monument. Tumacacori Natl. Monument. Tuzigoot Natl. Monument. Walnut Canyon Natl. Monument. Wupatki Natl. Monument.

Memorable events Apaches and Navajos absorb Pueblos c. A.D. 1000. Alvar Núñez Cabeza de Vaca, first Spanish explorer 1536. Marcos de Niza 1539. Ruled as part of New Spain 1598–1821. First missionaries among Hopis 1638. Tubac first European settlement 1752. Tucson founded 1776. Apaches wipe out settlements under Mexican control, except Tucson 1821. Northern part ceded to U.S. following Mexican War 1848. Area south of Gila River to U.S. after Gadsden Purchase 1853. Territory 1863. Southern Pacific Railroad reaches Tucson 1880. Apaches subjugated 1886. Congress refuses to grant statehood 1906. Roosevelt Dam and Reservoir built on Salt River 1911. Native Americans given right to vote 1948. Glen Canyon Dam built on Colorado River 1964. Population growth of 24.3 percent is second highest in U.S., 1990–97.

Tourist information (866) 275-5816
www.azot.gov

▶ARKANSAS

First inhabited by bluff dwellers 10,000 years ago, the Boston and Ouachita mountains of western Arkansas are the only mountains between the Appalachians and the Rockies. By the time of the Hernando De Soto expedition of 1541, Arkansas was inhabited by a variety of peoples: the agrarian Quapaws to the south, the Caddo to the west and south, the Osage to the north, and the Chickasaw and Choctaw in the northeast. The Arkansas Post, the first permanent settlement in the Mississippi Valley, became the pillar of the French claim to the region that became the Louisiana Purchase.

Not fully part of the deep south, and cut off geographically from the Midwest, Arkansas has developed slowly. Although cotton was a mainstay of the economy and Arkansas joined the Confederacy during the Civil War, it was the first southern state to have integrated public colleges after World War II, a fact overshadowed by Gov. Orville Faubus's resistance to the integration of the Little Rock public schools. In recent years, Arkansas has attracted manufacturing and industry, but has one of the highest rural populations and ranks low in services, income, and education attainment.

Name From term for Quapaw tribe given by other Indians. **Nickname** Land of Opportunity. **Capital** Little Rock. **Entered union** June 15, 1836 (25th). **Motto** *Regnat populus* (Let the people rule). **Emblems** **Bird** Mockingbird. **Flower** Apple blossom. **Gem** Diamond. **Song** "Arkansas." **Tree** Pine. **Land** **Total area** 53,179 sq. mi (29th), incl. 1,110 sq. mi. inland water. **Borders** Mo., Tenn, Miss., La., Tex., Okla. **Rivers** Arkansas, Mississippi, Ouachita, Red, St. Francis, White. **Lakes** Beaver, Bull Shoals, Chicot, Dardanelle, Greers Ferry, Greeson, Norfolk, Ouachita. **Mountains** Ozark Mts.

Elected officials Gov. Mike Beebe (D). Lt. Gov. Bill Halter (R). Sec. State Charlie Daniels (D). Atty. Gen. Dustin McDaniel (D).
People (July 2009 est.) 2,889,450 (32nd). Race/Hispanic Origin: White 80.8%. Black 15.8%. Indian 0.9%. Asian 1.1%. Pacific Islander 0.1%. Two or more races 1.4%. Hispanic 5.6%.
Cities (2006) Little Rock 184,422. Fort Smith 83,461. Fayetteville 68,726. Springdale 63,082. Jonesboro 60,489. North Little Rock 58,896. Conway 55,334. Rogers 52,181. Pine Bluff 51,758. Hot Springs 38,468.
Business **Gross State Product, 2008:** $79.2 bil. **Leading Sectors of GSP:** Manufacturing 19.34%; Services 16.95%; Government 13.07%. *Fortune 500* **Companies (2009): 4.**
Famous natives Maya Angelou, author. Linda Bloodworth-Thomason, television writer. Glen Campbell, singer. Hattie W. Caraway, first woman senator. Johnny Cash, singer. Eldridge Cleaver, author. Bill Clinton, U.S. president. William Fulbright (b. Mo.), politician. John Grisham, author. Alan Ladd, actor. Douglas MacArthur, general. Brooks Robinson, baseball player. Winthrop Rockefeller (b. N.Y.), politician/philanthropist. Edward Durrell Stone, architect. Billy Bob Thornton, actor. C. Vann Woodward, historian.
Noteworthy places Arkansas Post Natl. Monument (first permanent French settlement in lower Mississippi Valley). Buffalo Natl. River. Clinton Presidential Library. Crater of Diamonds State Park, Murfreesboro. Eureka Springs. Ft. Smith Natl. Hist. Site. Hot Springs Natl. Park. Pea Ridge Natl. Military Park.
Memorable Events Bluff-dwellers present by c. A.D. 500, followed by mound-building cultures. Hernando de Soto explores for Spain 1541. Jacques Marquette and Louis Jolliet explore for France 1673. René-Robert de La Salle meets Quapaws 1682. Henri de Tonti founds Arkansas Post on Arkansas River 1686. Ceded from France to Spain 1782; to France 1800; to U.S. 1803. Territory 1819. Admitted to Union as slave state, under terms of 1820 Missouri Compromise, 1836. Secedes from Union 1861. Fall of Little Rock to Union army 1863. Readmitted to Union 1868. Bauxite discovered 1887. Oil production begins 1920s. Federal troops called to Little Rock to ensure high school desegregation 1957. Winthrop Rockefeller (b. N.Y.) first Republican governor since Reconstruction 1966. McClellan-Kerr Arkansas River Navigation System links Arkansas and Oklahoma to Mississippi River system 1971. Governor Bill Clinton Elected U.S. President 1992.
Tourist information (800) NATURAL
www.arkansas.com.

▶CALIFORNIA

Before the arrival of Europeans, no area of comparable size in North America was home to a greater variety of languages and cultures than what is now California, and today the state's population is more diverse than that of any other. In 2001, non-Hispanic whites became a minority of California's population and demographers project that the majority of Californians will be Hispanic by 2040.

The largest state by population since the 1960s, California gained seven Congressional representatives in the 1990 Census redistricting, and one more in 2000. By some estimates, California is the sixth largest economic power in the world.

Despite its allure of rugged terrain and dramatic vistas, by the end of the first decade of the 21st century, California had increasing economic worries and the state's position as a leader in agriculture masks an alarming lack of water. It draws 4.5 to over 5 million acre-feet annually from the Colorado River, mostly for irrigating the Imperial Valley—a desert when settlers crossed it 150 years ago. Almost the entire flow of the San Joaquin River is similarly diverted for the Central Valley. This leaves less and less water for citizens, whose numbers have leaped from 15 million in 1960 to over 36 million today. In 2008, the governor declared official drought conditions in the state, and 2010 may mark the fourth year of serious drought.

The threat of earthquakes is a constant concern for California, which has suffered eight major earthquakes and dozens of smaller ones since 1900. The 1906 quake destroyed San Francisco, and the Loma Prieta earthquake in 1989 killed 67 people and left 48,000 homeless. The 1994 Northridge quake killed 60 people, injured 7,000 and left 20,000 more homeless, destroyed freeway overpasses and caused over $13 billion in damages.

Name Probably from mythical island in García Ordoñez de Montalvo's 16th-century romance, *The Deeds of Esplandián.* **Nickname** Golden State. **Capital** Sacramento. **Entered union** Sept. 9, 1850 (31st). **Motto** *"Eureka"* (I have found it). **Emblems** **Animal** California grizzly bear (extinct). **Bird** California valley quail. **Fish** California golden trout. **Flower** Golden poppy. **Fossil** California saber-toothed cat. **Gemstone** Benitoite. **Insect** California dog-face butterfly. **Marine mammal** California gray whale. **Mineral** Gold. **Reptile** California desert tortoise. **Rock** Serpentine. **Song** "I Love You, California." **Tree** California redwood. **Land** **Total area** 163,696 sq. mi (3rd), incl. 7,736 sq. mi. inland water. **Borders** Oreg., Nev., Ariz., Baja California Norte, Pacific Ocean. **Rivers** American, Colorado, Colorado River Aqueduct, Eel, Friant-Kern Canal, Klamath, Russian, Sacramento, Salinas, San Joaquin. **Lakes** Clear, Goose, Honey, Mono, Owens, Salton Sea, Shasta, Tahoe. **Mountains** Coast Ranges, Klamath, Lassen Peak, Sierra Nevada (Mt. Whitney 14,494 ft.). **Other notable features** Catalina Islands, Death Valley (282 ft. below sea level), San Francisco Bay, San Joaquin Valley.

Elected officials Gov. Arnold Schwarzenegger (R). Lt. Gov. John Garamendi (D). Sec. State Debra Bowen (D). Atty. Gen. Edmund G. Brown, Jr. (D). **People** (July 2009 est.) 36,961,664 (1st). Race/Hispanic Origin: White 76.6%. Black 6.7%. Indian 1.2%. Asian 12.5%. Pacific Islander 0.4%. Two or more races 2.6%. Hispanic 36.6%.

Cities (2006) Los Angeles 3,849,378. San Diego 1,256,951. San Jose 929,936. San Francisco 744,041. Long Beach 472,494. Fresno 466,714. Sacramento 453,781. Oakland 397,067. Santa Ana 340,024. Anaheim 334,425.

Business **Gross State Product, 2008**: $1,546.1 bil. **Leading Sectors of GSP**: Services 23.99%; Finance, insurance, and real estate 23.36%; Real estate 16.21%. *Fortune 500* **Companies (2009)**: 51.

Famous natives Ansel Adams, photographer. Dave Brubeck, musician. Luther Burbank (b. Mass.), horticulturist. John Cage, composer. Joe DiMaggio, baseball player. Robert Frost, poet. Ernest and Julio Gallo (b. Italy), vintners. Pancho Gonzales, tennis player. Samuel Ichiye Hayakawa, politician/educator. William Randolph Hearst, publisher. Steve Jobs, computer scientist. Billie Jean King, tennis player. Allen Lockheed, aviator. Jack London, author. Paul Masson (b. France), vintner. Marilyn Monroe, actress. John Muir (b. Scotland), naturalist. Richard M. Nixon, U.S. president. John Northrop, aviator. Adlai Stevenson, politician. John Steinbeck, author. Levi Strauss (b. Germany), clothier. Edward Teller (b. Hungary), nuclear physicist. Shirley Temple, actress. Earl Warren, politician/jurist.

Noteworthy places Big Sur, Monterey. Cabrillo Natl. Monument. California Academy of Sciences, San Francisco. California Palace of the Legion of Honor, San Francisco. Channel Islands Natl. Park. Devils Postpile Natl. Monument. Death Valley Natl. Monument. Disneyland. Fine Arts Museum of San Francisco. Fishermen's Wharf, San Francisco. Hollywood. Huntington Library and Botanical Gardens, San Marino. J. Paul Getty Museum, Malibu. Joshua Tree Natl. Monument. Kings Canyon Natl. Park. Lassen Volcanic Natl. Park. Lava Beds Natl. Monument. Los Angeles Co. Museum of Art. Muir Woods Natl. Monument. Mt. Palomar Observatory. Natl. Maritime Museum, San Francisco. Natural History Museum, Los Angeles. Natural History Museum of San Diego. Norton Simon Museum of Art at Pasadena. Pinnacles Natl. Monument. Redwood Natl. Park. Rosicrucian Egyptian Museum, San José. San Diego Museum of Art. San Diego Museum of Man. San Diego Zoo. San Francisco Museum of Modern Art. Sequoia Natl. Park. Southwest Museum (Casa de Adobe), Los Angeles. Yosemite Natl. Park.

Memorable events João Rodrigues Cabrilho lands at San Diego Bay 1542. Francis Drake lands north of San Francisco Bay 1579. Junípero Serra founds missions at San Diego (1769), Monterey (1770), San Luis Obispo (1772), and San Juan Capistrano (1776). California declares allegiance to independent Mexico 1821. First wagon train from Missouri 1841. Gold discovered north of Los Angeles 1842. California declares itself independent republic 1846. Gold found at John Sutter's mill; nine days later, by Treaty of Guadalupe Hidalgo, Mexico cedes California to U.S. 1848. Announcement of gold discovery brings 80,000 "Forty-niners." Gold rush peaks 1852. Transcontinental railroad completed 1869. Chinese excusion act effectively halts immigration of Chinese laborers 1882, 1892, and 1902; Act repealed 1943. San Francisco earthquake kills 452, destroys 28,000 buildings 1906. Webb Alien Land Law prohibits Japanese from holding land 1913. Los Angeles has one car for every three people, twice national average, 1925. Dust Bowl immigrants 1930. Hollywood produces bulk of movies for U.S. theaters, which number more than banks 1940. Most populous state 1963. Proposition 13 limits property tax 1978. Loma Prieta earthquake registers 7.1 on Richter scale — second most powerful in U.S. history; 67 dead, 48,000 homeless, and $10 billion in property damage 1989. Riots in Los Angeles kill 60 and cause $1 billion in damage 1992.

Tourist information (877) 225-4367
www.visitcalifornia.com

▶ COLORADO

The native peoples of Colorado were the Plains Indians (Arapahoe and Cheyenne) to the east and Great Basin Indians (Utes) to the west. This pre-Columbian division of the land is reflected today in Colorado's economy, which is a mix of agriculture and technology in the east and mining and ski tourism in the mountains. During the oil price shocks of the 1970s, shale-oil production on the Western Slope created a boom comparable to Colorado's silver and lead boom in the late 19th century. Strong job growth and an outdoor lifestyle has attracted many young people since the early 1990s: while the population has increased, the percentage of people over 65 has fallen to one of the lowest in the nation. While a state of great natural beauty, Colorado's high altitude almost doubles the effect of auto emissions. Economic development largely means resource extraction and requires more and more water, whose limited supply poses a great challenge.

Name From Spanish for the color red. **Nickname** Centennial State. **Capital** Denver. **Entered union** Aug. 1, 1876 (38th). **Motto** *Nil sine numine* (Nothing without providence).
Emblems **Animal** Rocky Mountain bighorn sheep. **Bird** Lark bunting. **Flower** Rocky Mountain Columbine. **Gem** Aquamarine. **Song** "Where the Columbines Grow." **Tree** Colorado blue spruce.
Land **Total area** 104,094 sq. mi (8th), incl. 376 sq. mi. inland water. **Borders** Wyo., Nebr., Kans., N.Mex., Ariz., Utah. **Rivers** Arkansas, Colorado, Green, Platte, Rio Grande. **Lakes** Blue Mesa, Dillon, Granby. **Mountains** Front Range, Laramie, Sangre de Cristo, San Juan, Sawatch Range (Mt. Elbert 14,443 ft.).
Elected officials Gov. Bill Ritter (D). Lt. Gov. Barbara O'Brien (D). Sec. State Bernie Buescher (D). Atty. Gen. John Suthers (R).
People (July 2009 est.) 5,024,748 (22nd). Race/Hispanic Origin: White 89.7%. Black 4.3%. Indian 1.2%. Asian 2.7%. Pacific Islander 0.2%. Two or more races 2.0%. Hispanic 20.2%.
Cities (2006) Denver 566,974. Colorado Springs 372,437. Aurora 303,582. Lakewood 140,024. Fort Collins 129,467. Thornton 109,155. Westminster 105,753. Arvada 104,830. Pueblo 103,730. Centennial 98,270.
Business **Gross State Product, 2008:** $203.0 bil. **Leading Sectors of GSP:** Services 24.09%; Finance, insurance, and real estate 18.31%; Government 11.82%. *Fortune 500* **Companies (2009):** 11.
Famous natives Charlie Bent (b. Va.), trapper. "Unsinkable" Molly Brown, *Titanic* survivor. Scott Carpenter, astronaut. Lon Chaney, actor. Jack Dempsey, boxer. Mamie Eisenhower, first lady. Douglas Fairbanks, actor. Horace Greeley, journalist. Scott Hamilton, ice skater. Anne Parrish, novelist. Lowell Thomas, journalist. Byron R. White, jurist.
Noteworthy places Black Canyon of the Gunnison National Park. Buffalo Bill grave site, Evergreen. Central City Opera House. Colorado Springs Fine Arts Center. Denver Art Museum. Denver Mint. Denver Museum of Natural History. Dinosaur Natl. Monument. Florissant Fossil Beds Natl. Monument. Garden of the Gods, Colorado Springs. Great Sand Dunes Natl. Monument. Hovenweep Natl. Monument. Mesa Verde Natl. Park. Molly Brown House, Denver. Pikes Peak. Red Rocks Amphitheater. Rocky Mountain Natl. Park, Aspen. Rocky Mountain Natl. Park. U.S. Air Force Academy, Colorado Springs. U.S. Olympic Headquarters, Colorado Springs. Yucca House Natl. Monument.
Memorable events Anasazi build cliff dwellings near Mesa Verde through 1200s. Arapahos and Cheyennes settle area after 13th century. France abandons claims 1763. Juan de Uribarri explores area 1786. Spain restores area to France 1801. To United States as part of Louisiana Purchase 1803. Zebulon Pike explores for United States 1806. Kit Carson and other scouts explore and trade with Native Americans 1810s–20s. Native Americans form alliance at Brent's Fork 1840. John Frémont's explorations 1842–53. Present territorial limits after Mexican War 1848. First permanent settlement at San Luis 1851. Gold found west of Denver—"Pikes Peak or Bust"—1858.

Mineral springs bring first tourists 1861. Homestead Act encourages farming 1862. U.S. Army kills 400 Cheyenne at Sand Creek Massacre 1864. Utes and Cheyennes fight white settlement through 1870s. John Wesley Powell and nine others navigate Colorado River from the Green River branch in Wyoming to the end of Grand Canyon in Arizona 1869. Railroad link to Denver 1870. Silver and lead discoveries 1875. Uranium discovered near Grand Junction 1946. U.S. Air Force Academy founded Denver 1954; to Colorado Springs 1958. Shale oil boom on Western Slope 1974 and 1979. Accumulation of nuclear waste threatens suspension of operations at Rocky Flats 1988.
Tourist information (800) COLORADO **www.colorado.gov**

▶CONNECTICUT

Called the "arsenal of the nation" during the Revolution, Connecticut remained in modern times the leader among the 50 states in defense-contract dollars per capita. In the late 20th century, this caused a serious dislocation in the economy as the nation downsized its military capabilities. Still, with eleven *Fortune* 500 companies (including major insurance companies), and easy access to New York City, Connecticut remains the state with the country's highest per capita income.

Severe budget deficits in 1991 forced passage of a state income tax and helped to reveal the disparities in wealth between the very rich suburbs and the decaying industrial cities such as Bridgeport. As the economy was retooled, population growth slowed and the state has recently lost population.

Name From Mahican word meaning "beside the long tidal river." **Nicknames** Constitution State, Nutmeg State. **Capital** Hartford. **Entered union** Jan. 9, 1788 (5th). **Motto** *Qui transtulit sustinet* (He who transplanted still sustains).
Emblems **Animal** Sperm whale. **Bird** American robin. **Flower** Mountain laurel. **Hero** Nathan Hale. **Insect** European praying mantis. **Mineral** Garnet. **Ship** USS *Nautilus*. **Song** "Yankee Doodle." **Tree** White oak.
Land **Total area** 5,543 sq. mi (48th), incl. 699 sq. mi. inland water. **Borders** Mass., R.I., Long Island Sound, N.Y. **Rivers** Connecticut, Housatonic, Mianus, Naugatuck, Thames. **Lakes** Bantam, Barkhamstead, Candlewood, Waramaug. **Other notable features** Berkshire Hills, Long Island Sound.
Elected officials Gov. M. Jodi Rell (R, term exp. 2010). Lt. Gov. Michael Fedele (R). Sec. State Susan Bysiewicz (D). Atty. Gen. Richard Blumenthal (D).
People (July 2009 est.) 3,518,288 (29th). Race/Hispanic Origin: White 84.3%. Black 10.3%. Indian 0.4%. Asian 3.5%. Pacific Islander 0.1%. Two or more races 1.5%. Hispanic 12.0%.
Cities (2006) Bridgeport 137,912. Hartford 124,512. New Haven 124,001. Stamford 119,261. Waterbury 107,251. Norwalk 84,187. Danbury 79,285. New Britain 70,746. Bristol 61,161. Meriden 59,439.
Business **Gross State Product, 2008:** $640.7 bil. **Leading Sectors of GSP:** Finance, insurance, and real estate 30.97%; Services 21.46%; Real estate 15.82%. *Fortune 500* **Companies (2009):** 11.
Famous natives Benedict Arnold, traitor. P.T. Barnum, showman. Lyman Beecher, theologian. John Brown, abolitionist. Samuel Colt, inventor. Jonathan Edwards, theologian. Charles Goodyear, inventor. Nathan Hale, patriot. Katharine Hepburn, actress. Charles Ives, composer. J.P. Mor-

gan, financier. Ralph Nader, consumer advocate. Frederick Law Olmsted, landscape architect. Harriet Beecher Stowe, author. John Trumbell, artist. Noah Webster, lexicographer. Eli Whitney, inventor. **Noteworthy places** Charles Ives Center, Danbury. Eugene O'Neill Memorial Theater Center, Waterford. Gilette Castle. Housatonic State Park. Mark Twain House, Hartford. Mystic Marinelife Aquarium. Mystic Seaport. Norwalk Maritime Center. U.S. Coast Guard Academy. USS *Nautilus*, New London. Wadsworth Atheneum, Hartford. Whitney Museum of Modern Art, Stamford. Yale Center for British Art, New Haven. Yale University, New Haven.
Memorable events Adriaen Block claims for Dutch 1614. First English settlement in Windsor 1633. Royal charter of 1662 hidden in Charter Oak 1687. *Hartford Courant*, oldest continuously published newspaper in U.S., first published 1764. Samuel Colt develops six-shooter 1835. Horace Wells uses first anesthesia 1844. Elias Howe invents sewing machine 1845. U.S. Coast Guard Academy founded New London 1876. First woman governor elected in her own right, Ella T. Grasso, 1974.
Tourist information (888) CTVISIT
www.ctvisit.com

▶DELAWARE

The du Pont family has enjoyed a political and economic prominence in Delaware unmatched in the history of the other 49 states. Seven generations ago E.I. du Pont de Nemours and Co. was founded as a gunpowder mill, then grew into a monopoly, and in the wake of World War I, diversified into today's giant, with interests in banking, media, and real estate. Only half the size of Los Angeles County, Delaware was called the Company State by Ralph Nader's "raiders" in 1973. Its liberal incorporation laws has led more than half the Fortune 500 companies to incorporate there. (A total of more than 170,000 corporations are incorporated in Delaware). It was one of the few states to prosper even during the recessions of the early 1980s and early 1990s, though the state wasn't as fortunate in the first decade of the 2000s.
Name For Thomas West, Lord De La Warre, colonial governor of Virginia. **Nicknames** First State, Diamond State. **Capital** Dover. **Entered union** Dec. 7, 1787 (1st). **Motto** "Liberty and Independence."
Emblems **Bird** Blue hen chicken. **Fish** Weakfish. **Flower** Peach blossom. **Insect** Ladybug. **Rock** Sillimanite. **Song** "Our Delaware." **Tree** American holly.
Land Total area 2,489 sq. mi. (49th), incl. 536 sq. mi. inland water. **Borders** Pa., N.J., Atlantic Ocean, Md. **Rivers** Chesapeake & Delaware Canal, Delaware, Nanticoke.
Elected officials Gov. Jack A. Markell (D). Lt. Gov. Matt Denn (D). Sec. State Jeffrey W. Bullock (D). Atty. Gen. Beau Biden (D).
People (July 2009 est.) 885,122 (45th). Race/Hispanic Origin: White 74.3%. Black 20.9%. Indian 0.4%. Asian 2.9%. Pacific Islander 0.1%. Two or more races 1.4%. Hispanic 6.8%.
Cities (2006) Wilmington 72,664. Dover 32,135. Newark 28,547. Milford 6,732. Seaford 6,699. Middletown 6,161. Elsmere 5,800. Smyrna 5,679. New Castle 4,862. Georgetown 4,643.
Business Gross State Product, 2008: $49.2 bil. **Leading Sectors of GSP:** Finance, insurance, and real estate 43.14%; Depository and nondepository institutions 30.64%. *Fortune 500* **Companies (2009): 1.**

Famous natives Valerie Bertinelli, actress. John Dickinson (b. Md.), Penman of the Revolution. Eleuthère I. du Pont, manufacturer. Pierre S. ("Pete") du Pont, politician. Morgan Edwards, founder of Brown University (R.I.). Thomas Macdonough, navy officer. Howard Pyle, illustrator. Edward R. Squibb, physician/manufacturer. Christopher Ward, historian.
Noteworthy places Brandywine Zoo, Wilmington. Delaware Art Museum, Wilmington. Delaware State Museum, Dover. Dover Downs International Speedway. Grand Opera House, Wilmington. Hagley Museum, Wilmington. Kalmar Nykel Sailing Ship, Cape May. Rehoboth Beach.
Memorable events Dutch arrive 1631. Swedes establish first permanent settlement at Wilmington 1638. Captured by Dutch 1655. To England 1664. Part of territory granted to William Penn 1682. Breaks off from Pennsylvania; first to ratify Constitution 1787. E.I. du Pont de Nemours Co. founded 1802. Railroad connects Wilmington to Philadelphia and Baltimore 1838. Though slave state, sides with Union during Civil War 1861–65. Delaware last state to abolish whipping post (last used 1952) 1972.
Tourist information (866) 284-7483
www.visitdelaware.com

▶DISTRICT OF COLUMBIA

Chosen as the site for the nation's capital by George Washington, Washington, D.C., was built on land ceded by Maryland and Virginia. Although under Federal jurisdiction, the District has petitioned for statehood as New Columbia. In 1961, the 23rd Amendment granted citizens of D.C. the right to vote in Presidential elections for the first time, and 10 years later Congress gave the District one nonvoting delegate to the House of Representatives. In recent years, the District has protested its lack of full representation and issues license plates tagged with the unofficial motto "Taxation Without Representation." D.C.'s largest employer is the federal government, and printing is the largest industry. Pres. John F. Kennedy called it a city of "Southern efficiency and Northern charm," but the city has become a leading patron of the arts. However, the problems of any large city are exacerbated by the transience of D.C.'s government workers. As the seat of the U.S. Government, D.C. attracts more than 17 million visitors annually.
Name After Christopher Columbus; Columbia was commonly used for the United States before 1800. **Nickname** None. **Capital** Washington. **Became capital** Dec. 1, 1800. **Motto** *Justitia omnibus* (Justice for all).
Emblems **Bird** Wood thrush. **Flower** American beauty rose. **Tree** Scarlet oak.
Land Total area 68 sq. mi., incl. 7 sq. mi. inland water. **Borders** Md., Va. **Rivers** Anacostia, Potomac.
Elected officials Mayor Adrian Fenty (D, term exp. 2010).
People (July 2009 est.) 599,657 (N.A.) Race/Hispanic Origin: White 40.1%. Black 54.4%. Indian 0.4%. Asian 3.4%. Pacific Islander 0.1%. Two or more races 1.6%. Hispanic 8.6%.
Business Gross State Product, 2008: $74.8 bil. **Leading Sectors of GSP:** Services 37.65%; Government 35.18%; Federal civilian employment 30.07%. *Fortune 500* **Companies (2009): 3.**
Famous natives Edward Albee, playwright. Carl Bernstein, journalist. John Foster Dulles, politician. Duke Ellington, composer. J. Edgar Hoover, FBI director. Marjorie Kinnan Rawlings, novelist. John Philip Sousa, composer.

Noteworthy places The Capitol. Chesapeake & Ohio Canal Natl. Hist. Park. Corcoran Gallery of Art. Dumbarton Oaks. FDR Memorial. Folger Shakespeare Library. Freer Gallery of Art. Hirshhorn Museum. Jefferson Memorial. Kennedy Center. Korean War Veterans Memorial. Library of Congress. Lincoln Memorial. Natl. Air and Space Museum. Natl. Gallery of Art. Natl. Museum of African Art. Natl. Museum of American Art. Natl. Museum of American History. Natl. Museum of American Indian. Natl. Museum of Natural History. Natl. Portrait Gallery. Naval Observatory. Navy Memorial Museum. Renwick Gallery. Smithsonian Institution. Vietnam Veterans Memorial. Washington Monument. Washington Zoo. White House. Woodrow Wilson House.

Memorable events Originally part of Maryland. Congress approves plan to secure land for seat of Federal Government, no more than 10 miles square, on land in Virginia and Maryland 1787. George Washington commissions Pierre Charles l'Enfant to lay out city 1791. Government moves 1800. British sail up the Potomac and burn capital 1814. Virginia reclaims its half of District 1846. President Abraham Lincoln assassinated 1865. Coxey's Army marches on Washington 1894. The Bonus Army—17,000 veterans—marches on Washington 1932. Led by Martin Luther King, Jr., 200,000 march for Civil Rights 1963. 100,000 protest Vietnam War 1971. Democratic party headquarters at Watergate burglarized by men linked to President Richard M. Nixon's reelection effort 1972. Congress grants limited self-rule; mayor and city council elected 1975.

Tourist information   (202) 789-7000
www.washington.org

▶ **FLORIDA**

A vast network of swamps, rivers, and lakes, much of Florida is barely above sea level. Florida is home to Disney World, Cypress Gardens, the wealth-laden resort of Palm Beach, the *National Enquirer*, and the Okefenokee Swamp. The pleasant climate and proximity to Latin America and the Caribbean have attracted tourists, retirees (over 17 percent of the population is over 65) and immigrants. Over the last two decades, it has been one of the fastest-growing states, but growth has brought attendant increases in drug trafficking, racial disturbances, and environmental damage to such wildlife as the crocodile, alligator, and the Florida panther.

Name By Juan Ponce de León for Pascua Florida (Easter festival of the flowers). **Nickname** Sunshine State. **Capital** Tallahassee. **Entered union** Mar. 3, 1845 (27th). **Motto** "In God We Trust." **Poet laureate** Dr. Edmund Skellings.

Emblems **Animal** Florida panther. **Beverage** Orange juice. **Bird** Mockingbird. **Flower** Orange blossom. **Freshwater fish** Florida largemouth bass. **Gem** Moonstone. **Marine mammals** Dolphin, manatee. **Saltwater fish** Atlantic sailfish. **Shell** Horse conch. **Song** "Old Folks at Home" ("Swanee River"). **Stone** Agatized coral. **Tree** Sabal palmetto palm.

Land **Total area** 65,755 sq. mi (22nd), incl. 11,828 sq. mi. inland water. **Borders** Ga., Atlantic Ocean, Gulf of Mexico, Ala. **Rivers** Apalachicola, Caloosahatchee, Indian, Kissimmee, Perdido, St. Johns, St. Mary's, Suwanee, Withlacoochee. **Lakes** Apopka, George, Okeechobee, Seminole. **Other notable features** Everglades, Florida Keys, Okefenokee Swamp.

Elected officials Gov. Charlie Crist (R, term exp. 2011). Lt. Gov. Jeff Kottkamp (R). Sec. State Kurt Browning (D). Atty. Gen. Bill McCollum (R).

People (July 2009 est.) 18,537,969 (4th). Race/Hispanic Origin: White 79.8%. Black 15.9%. Indian 0.5%. Asian 2.3%. Pacific Islander 0.1%. Two or more races 1.4%. Hispanic 21.0%.

Cities (2006) Jacksonville 794,555. Miami 404,048. Tampa 332,888. St. Petersburg 248,098. Orlando 220,186. Hialeah 217,141. Fort Lauderdale 185,804. Tallahassee 159,012. Cape Coral 151,389. Pembroke Pines 150,064.

Business **Gross State Product, 2008:** $603.5 bil. **Leading Sectors of GSP:** Services 25.62%; Finance, insurance, and real estate 22.08%; Real estate 14.52%. *Fortune 500* **Companies (2009):** 14.

Famous natives Mary Bethune, educator/reformer. Faye Dunaway, actress. Chris Evert, tennis player. Zora Neale Hurston, writer. James Weldon Johnson, lawyer/novelist. Osceola, Seminole chief. Sidney Poitier, actor. A. Philip Randolph, labor leader. Edmund Kirby Smith, Confederate general. Joseph Warren "Vinegar Joe" Stillwell, army officer. Ben Vereen, actor/singer.

Noteworthy places Biscayne Natl. Park. Castillo de San Marcos, St. Augustine. Everglades Natl. Park. Florida State Museum, Gainesville. Ft. Jefferson Natl. Monument. Ft. Matanzas Natl. Monument. Kennedy Space Center, Cape Canaveral. Ringling Museum, Sarasota. St. Augustine. Walt Disney World/EPCOT Center, Orlando.

Memorable events Juan Ponce de León claims Florida for Spain 1513. French stake claim for Florida 1562; build Ft. Caroline 1564. Pedro Menéndez de Avilés founds St. Augustine, first permanent European settlement in U.S. 1565. Spain cedes Florida to United States 1819. Seminole War 1835–42. State secedes from Union 1861. Readmitted 1868. Carl Fisher begins to develop Miami Beach as resort 1912. Florida's first paper mill opens expanding forest industry 1931. More than 100,000 Cuban refugees enter United States, most through Florida, during Mariel boat lift 1980. Army Corps of Engineers announce plans to let Kissimmee River, canalized in 1971, return to natural course to Lake Okeechobee; the largest back-to-nature project ever undertaken in U.S. 1990. Hurricane Andrew causes $10 billion in damage to South Florida 1992. Voting irregularities in Florida during the Presidential election lead to U.S. Supreme Court intervention in 2000.

Tourist information   (888) 735-2872
www.visitflorida.com

▶ **GEORGIA**

Georgia is diverse in its terrain, embracing the woods of the Blue Ridge Mountains to the north and the alligators of the Okefenokee Swamp in the south. Though two-thirds of the population are urban dwellers, Georgia's farms rank at or near the top in poultry production and are leading producers of pecans, cattle, hogs, and peanuts. Atlanta, the largest city in the South, elected Andrew Young the first black member of the U.S. Congress and Maynard Jackson the first black mayor from the South since Reconstruction. Today divisions linger in Georgia, the cities favoring a progressive stance and the rural areas clinging to some of the ways of the Old South. Some of those divisions came to a peaceful resolution in early 2001, when the state redesigned its flag to reduce the size and prominence of the Confederate cross.

Name For King George II of England 1732. **Nicknames** Empire State of the South, Peach State. **Capital** Atlanta. **Entered union** Jan. 2, 1788 (4th). **Motto** "Wisdom, justice, moderation."

Emblems **Bird** Brown thrasher. **Fish** Largemouth bass. **Flower** Cherokee rose. **Fossil** Shark tooth. **Gem** Quartz. **Insect** Honeybee. **Songs** "Georgia," "Georgia on My Mind." **Tree** Live oak. **Wildflower** Azalea.

Land   Total area 59,425 sq. mi (24th), incl. 1,519 sq. mi. inland water. **Borders** Tenn., N.C., S.C., Atlantic Ocean, Fla., Ala. **Rivers** Altamaha, Apalachicola, Chattahoochee, Flint, Ocmulgee, Oconee, Savannah, Suwanee. **Lakes** Clark Hill, Harding, Hartwell, Seminole, Sidney Lanier, Sinclair, Walter F. George, West Point Lake. **Other notable features** Blue Ridge Mountains (Mount Enotah 4,784 ft.), Okefenokee Swamp.

Elected officials   Gov. Sonny Perdue (R, term exp. 2011). Lt. Gov. Casey Cagle (R). Sec. State Brian P. Kemp (R). Atty. Gen. Thurbert E. Baker (D).

People   (July 2009 est.) 9,829,211 (9th). Race/Hispanic Origin: White 65.4%. Black 30.0%. Indian 0.4%. Asian 2.9%. Pacific Islander 0.1%. Two or more races 1.3%. Hispanic 8.0%.

Cities   (2006) Atlanta 486,411. Augusta 189,366. Columbus 188,660. Savannah 127,889. Athens 111,580. Macon 93,665. Roswell 87,802. Sandy Springs 85,771. Albany 75,335. Marietta 63,152.

Business   Gross State Product, 2008: $329.5 bil. **Leading Sectors of GSP:** Services 20.38%; Finance, insurance, and real estate 16.33%; Manufacturing 14.50%. *Fortune 500* **Companies (2009):** 13.

Famous natives   James Brown, singer. Erskine Caldwell, author. James Earl ("Jimmy") Carter, U.S. president. Ray Charles, musician. Ty Cobb, baseball player. James Dickey, poet. Martin Luther King, Jr., minister/reformer. Sidney Lanier, author. Little Richard, musician. Carson McCullers, author. Alexander McGillivray, Creek chief. Margaret Mitchell, author. Elijah Muhammad, religious leader. Flannery O'Connor, author. Burt Reynolds, actor. Jackie Robinson, baseball player. Tomochichi, Yamacraw chief. Ted Turner (b. Ohio), businessman. Joanne Woodward, actress.

Noteworthy places   Chickamauga and Chattanooga Natl. Military Park. Confederate Memorial, Stone Mountain. Ft. Frederica Natl. Monument. Ft. Pulaski Natl. Monument. High Museum of Art, Atlanta. Martin Luther King Natl. Hist. Site., Atlanta. Ocmulgee Natl. Monument. Okefenokee Swamp. Savannah Historic District.

Memorable events   Hernando de Soto explores region 1540. Cotton gin invented 1793. Georgia expels Cherokee Indian tribes on Trail of Tears 1832–38. Secedes from Union 1860. Gen. William T. Sherman's 60,000 troops cut 60-mi. swath and burn Atlanta to the ground in their "march to the sea" 1864. Formula for Coca-Cola developed by chemist in search of hangover cure 1886. Cyclone kills 1,000 in Charleston, S.C., and Savannah 1893. Franklin D. Roosevelt dies at the Little White House, Warm Springs 1945. First state to give vote to 18-year-olds 1948. Emory University designated to receive $100-million gift from Robert W. Woodruff 1979. Dept. of Justice rules that state's process for electing superior court judges violates 1965 Voting Rights Act 1990. Summer Olympics held in Atlanta 1996.

Tourist information   (800) VISIT-GA
www.exploregeorgia.org

▶**HAWAII**
What the air conditioner did for the Sunbelt, the jetliner has done for Hawaii. Affordable air travel has made Hawaii one of the country's most popular vacation and honeymoon spots in the five decades since it entered the Union. Tourism is Hawaii's key industry, attracting more than 6.5 million visitors to the state each year. Recent economic problems in Japan have had a negative ef-

fect on Hawaii's tourism numbers, and the state economy has suffered greatly as a result. Thousands of miles from both California and mainland Asia, Hawaii was originally peopled by Polynesian seafarers around A.D. 500 and has the richest ethnic mix of any state, with the lowest percentage of whites and highest percentages of Asians. It was partly fear of this diversity that stalled its statehood. A link between the United States and Asia, Hawaii is the center of U.S. defense in the Pacific and is home to 100,000 veterans, three-quarters of them veterans of Vietnam. Hawaii produces large quantities of pineapples and sugar cane, and efforts are under way to harness thermal electric power from Mauna Loa volcano.

Name Of unknown origin, perhaps from Hawaii Loa, traditional discoverer of islands, or from Hawaiki, the traditional Polynesian homeland. **Nicknames** Aloha State, Paradise of the Pacific. **Capital** Honolulu. **Entered union** Aug. 21, 1959 (50th). **Motto** *Ua mau ke ea o ka aina i ke pono* (The life of the land is perpetuated in righteousness).

Emblems   Bird Nene (Hawaiian goose). **Fish** Humuhumunukunukuapuaa (reef triggerfish). **Flower** Pua aloalo (hibiscus). **Song** "Hawaii Ponoi." **Tree** Kukui (candlenut).

Land   Total area 10,931 sq. mi (43rd), incl. 4,508 sq. mi. inland water. Surrounded by Pacific Ocean. **Rivers** Kaukonahua Stream, Wailuku Stream. **Lakes** Halulu, Kolekole, Salt Lake, Waiia Res. **Other notable features** Pearl Harbor. Hualalai, Kilauea, Mauna Kea (13,796 ft.), and Mauna Loa volcanoes. **Main islands** Hawaii, Kauai, Lanai, Maui, Molokai, Oahu.

Elected officials   Gov. Linda Lingle (R). Lt. Gov/Sec. State, James Aiona, Jr. (R). Atty. Gen. Mark Bennett (R).

People   (July 2009 est.) 1,295,178 (42nd). Race/Hispanic Origin: White 29.7%. Black 3.1%. Indian 0.6%. Asian 39.3%. Pacific Islander 9.1%. Two or more races 18.3%. Hispanic 8.7%.

Cities   (2006) Honolulu 377,357. (2000) Hilo 40,759. Kailua 36,513. Kaneohe 34,970. Waipahu 33,108. Pearl City 30,976. Waimalu 29,371. Mililani Town 28,608. Kahului 20,146. Kihei 16,749. (The Census Bureau does not update counts for Hawaiian cities other than Honolulu between decennial censuses because most are not incorporated.)

Business   Gross State Product, 2008: $49.8 bil. **Leading Sectors of GSP:** Finance, insurance, and real estate 23.01%; Services 22.92%; Government 21.51%. *Fortune 500* **Companies (2009):** 0.

Famous natives   Bernice P. Bishop, philanthropist. Sanford B. Dole, statehood advocate. Charlotte (b. Ohio) and Luther Halsey Gulick, Camp Fire Girls founders. Don Ho, singer. Daniel J. Inouye, politician. Duke Kahanamoku, swimmer. Victoria Kaiulani, last heiress presumptive to Hawaiian throne. Kamehameha I, king. Kamehameha III, king. Liliuokalani, queen. Bette Midler, singer. Barack Obama, U.S. President.

Noteworthy places   Bernice P. Bishop Museum, Honolulu. Diamond Head. Haleakala Natl. Park, Maui. Hawaii Volcanoes Natl. Park (Kilauea and Mauna Loa), Hawaii. Iolani Palace, Honolulu. Kaloko-Honokohau Natl. Hist. Park, Molokai. Natl. Cemetery of the Pacific and USS *Arizona* Memorial. Polynesian Cultural Center, Laiea. Pu'uhonua o Honaunau Natl. Hist. Park, Hawaii.

Memorable events   Polynesians first arrive 6th century. Second wave of Polynesians arrive 10th century. Captain James Cook first European to visit islands 1778; killed on Hawaii 1779. Sugar production begins 1835. Land reform ends feudal

system 1848. Monarchy rule ends in revolution 1893. Becomes U.S. Territory 1900. Japanese attack Pearl Harbor 1941. Statehood 1959.
Tourist information (800) GOHAWAII
www.gohawaii.com

▶IDAHO

Home to some of the most isolated and rugged country in the United States, Idaho's diversified economy has traditionally been based on lumber and potatoes (more than 13 billion pounds in 1993). In the 1980s these were augmented by a number of small high-tech industries fleeing the high cost of business in California. During the 1990s the population grew rapidly and continued through the first years of the 2000s, slowing only in 2009 when it dropped to the 12th-growing state nationally.

Name Means "gem of the mountains." **Nickname** Gem State. **Capital** Boise. **Entered union** July 3, 1890 (43rd). **Motto** *Esto perpetua* (May it last forever).
Emblems **Bird** Mountain bluebird. **Flower** Syringa. **Gem** Star garnet. **Horse** Appaloosa. **Song** "Here We Have Idaho." **Tree** Western white pine.
Land **Total area** 83,570 sq. mi (14th), incl. 823 sq. mi. inland water. **Borders** British Columbia, Mont., Wyo., Utah, Nev., Oreg., Wash. **Rivers** Bear, Clearwater, Payette, Salmon, Snake. **Lakes** American Falls Res., Coeur d'Alene, Pend Oreille. **Mountains** Bitterroot Range, Centennial, Clearwater, Salmon River, Sawtooth Range (Castle Peak 11,820 ft.), Wasatch Range. **Other notable features** Grand Canyon of the Snake River.
Elected officials Gov. Butch Otter (R). Lt. Gov. Brad Little (R). Sec. State Ben Ysursa (R). Atty. Gen. Lawrence Wasden (R).
People (July 2009 est.) 1,545,801 (39th). Race/ Hispanic Origin: White 94.6%. Black 0.9%. Indian 1.5%. Asian 1.1%. Pacific Islander 0.1%. Two or more races 1.7%. Hispanic 10.2%.
Cities (2006) Boise City 198,638. Nampa 76,587. Meridian 59,832. Pocatello 53,932. Idaho Falls 52,786. Coeur d'Alene 41,328. Twin Falls 40,380. Caldwell 37,056. Lewiston 31,293. Rexburg 26,657.
Business **Gross State Product, 2008:** $45.5 bil. **Leading Sectors of GSP:** Services 17.98%; Manufacturing 17.80%; Government 14.08%. *Fortune 500* **Companies (2009):** 1.
Famous natives Joseph, Nez Percé chief. Ezra Taft Benson, politician. Gutzon Borglum, sculptor. Frank Church, politician. Ezra Pound, poet. Harmon Killebrew, baseball player. Jerry Kramer, football player. Sacagawea (Bird Woman), Shoshone interpreter. Lana Turner, actress.
Noteworthy places Craters of the Moons Natl. Monument. Hell's Canyon Natl. Recreation Area. Nez Percé Natl. Hist. Park. Sawtooth Natl. Recreation Area. Sun Valley ski resort. Yellowstone Natl. Park.
Memorable events Lewis and Clark expedition 1805. Becomes part of U.S. when Idaho Treaty concluded with Britain 1846. Gold Rush 1860. Nez Percé War 1877. Statehood 1890. World's first breeder reactor built at Idaho Falls, 1951. Snake River opened to navigation, linking Lewiston to Pacific Ocean at Astoria, Oregon 1975. New Teton River Dam collapses as it is being filled for first time; 10 dead, $400 million in damage 1976.
Tourist information (800) VISITID
www.visitidaho.org

▶ILLINOIS

The Illinois economy is enormously productive and diverse. While Chicago is a leader in world finance and trade, the southern part of the state has rich farmlands (the state is second to Iowa in corn and soybean exports) and mineral deposits (both coal and gas—there are especially rich coal deposits in the southeast region around Cairo, known as Little Egypt). Manufacturing centers on Chicago, Rockford—the state's second-largest city—and Springfield, the capital. Chicago is also a major transportation hub with extensive rail networks, an international port serving ships from both the Atlantic and Gulf of Mexico, and the second busiest airport in the country in 2007.

Name Corruption of *iliniwek* ("tribe of the superior men"), natives of region at time of earliest French explorations. **Nickname** Prairie State. **Capital** Springfield. **Entered union** Dec. 3, 1818 (21st). **Motto** "State sovereignty—national unity." **Slogan** "Land of Lincoln."
Emblems **Animal** White-tailed deer. **Bird** Cardinal. **Flower** Violet. **Insect** Monarch butterfly. **Mineral** Fluorite. **Song** "Illinois." **Tree** White oak.
Land **Total area** 57,914 sq. mi (25th), incl. 2,331 sq. mi. inland water. **Borders** Wis., Lake Michigan, Ind., Ky., Mo., Iowa. **Rivers** Fox, Illinois, Illinois Waterway, Kankakee, Kaskaskia, Mississippi, Ohio, Rock, Vermillion, Wabash. **Lakes** Carlyle, Crab Orchard. **Other notable features** Charles Mound (1,235 ft.), Little Egypt.
Elected officials Gov. Pat Quinn (D). Lt. Gov. (vacant until 2011 elections). Sec. State Jesse White (D). Atty. Gen. Lisa Madigan (D).
People (July 2009 est.) 12,910,409 (5th). Race/ Hispanic Origin: White 79.1%. Black 14.9%. Indian 0.3%. Asian 4.3%. Pacific Islander 0.1%. Two or more races 1.2%. Hispanic 15.2%.
Cities (2006) Chicago 2,833,321. Aurora 170,617. Rockford 155,138. Naperville 142,901. Joliet 142,702. Springfield 116,482. Peoria 113,107. Elgin 101,903. Waukegan 92,066. Cicero 81,823.
Business **Gross State Product, 2008:** $516.1 bil. **Leading Sectors of GSP:** Services 22.73%; Finance, insurance, and real estate 22.10%; Manufacturing 14.37%. *Fortune 500* **Companies (2009):** 32.
Famous natives Jane Addams, reformer (Nobel Peace Prize, 1930). Ernie Banks, baseball player. Saul Bellow, author (Nobel Prize, 1976). Harry A. Blackmun, jurist. Ray Bradbury, author. Gwendolyn Brooks, poet. William Jennings Bryan, politician. Edgar Rice Burroughs, novelist. St. Frances Xavier Cabrini (b. Italy). Clarence Darrow, lawyer. Miles Davis, musician. John Dos Passos, novelist. Enrico Fermi (b. Italy), nuclear physicist (Nobel Prize, 1938). Robert Louis ("Bob") Fosse, choreographer. Milton Friedman, economist (Nobel Prize, 1976). Benny Goodman, musician. Ernest Hemingway, novelist. Charlton Heston, actor. William Holden, actor. Abraham Lincoln, U.S. President (b. Kentucky). Vachel Lindsay, poet. Archibald MacLeish, poet. Ludwig Mies van der Rohe (b. Germany), architect. Charles W. Post, cereal manufacturer. Ronald Reagan, U.S. president. Carl Sandburg, poet. Albert G. Spalding, merchant. John Paul Stevens, jurist. Gloria Swanson, actress.
Noteworthy places Art Institute of Chicago. Crab Orchard Wildlife Refuge. Dickson Mounds Museum, Lewistown. Field Museum of Natural History, Chicago. Ft. Chartres. Ft. Kaskaskia. Ft. Massac. Frank Lloyd Wright Historic District, Oak Park. Illinois State Museum, Springfield. Lincoln

Home Natl. Hist. Park, Springfield. Mormon Settlement, Nauvoo. Morton Arboretum, Lisle. Museum of Science and Industry, Chicago. Shawnee Natl. Forest. Starved Rock State Park.

Memorable events French missionaries Jacques Marquette and Louis Jolliet explore Illinois 1673. Cahokia first European settlement 1699. Territory to England after French and Indian War 1763. Chicago founded by Jean-Baptiste Point du Sable 1779. Illinois and Michigan Canal links Lake Michigan and Mississippi River 1848. Lincoln-Douglas Debates at Springfield 1860. Half of Chicago destroyed by great fire 1871. Terrorist bombing kills nine and wounds 130 in Haymarket affair, Chicago 1886. Columbia Exposition, Chicago 1893. First successful nuclear chain reaction created at University of Chicago 1942. Argonne National Lab develops first nuclear power generating system in U.S. 1957. Riots at Democratic National Convention in Chicago 1968. Sears Tower, world's tallest building at time (1,454 ft.), completed in Chicago 1973. Mississippi and Illinois rivers flood causing $1.5 billion in damage 1993. In 2009, Governor Rod Blagojevich was impeached after allegations of attempting to sell Barack Obama's vacated senatorial seat.

Tourist information   (800) 2-CONNECT
www.enjoyillinois.com

▶ INDIANA

Indiana is strong in both farms and manufacturing. Its southern half has large coal deposits and produces most of the limestone quarried in the United States. To the north the fertile land helps make Indiana one of the primary farm-belt states. Indiana is also very much a part of the industrial Midwest, where unemployment is always a threat, especially in the heavily industrial areas of Gary and Indianapolis (the latter of which developed into a center for high-tech industries through the 1980s and 1990s). These geographic divisions have parallels in the political history of the state, which during the Civil War was Union in the north and Confederate in the south.

Name For the land of Indians by early settlers, who found many distinct tribes living in region. **Nickname** Hoosier State. **Capital** Indianapolis. **Entered union** Dec. 11, 1816 (19th). **Motto** "The Crossroads of America."

Emblems **Bird** Cardinal. **Flower** Peony. **Poem** "Indiana." **Song** "On the Banks of the Wabash, Far Away." **Stone** Indiana limestone. **Tree** Tulip tree.

Land **Total area** 36,418 sq. mi (38th), incl. 551 sq. mi. inland water. **Borders** Lake Michigan, Mich., Ohio, Ky., Ill. **Rivers** Kankakee, Ohio, Tippecanoe, Wabash, White, Whitewater. **Lakes** Freeman, Shafer.

Elected officials Gov. Mitch Daniels (R). Lt. Gov. Becky Skillman (R). Sec. State Todd Rokita (R). Atty. Gen. Greg Zoeller (R).

People (July 2009 est.) 6,423,113 (16th). Race/Hispanic Origin: White 88.0%. Black 9.1%. Indian 0.3%. Asian 1.4%. Two or more races 1.2%. Hispanic 5.2%.

Cities (2006) Indianapolis 785,597. Fort Wayne 248,637. Evansville 115,738. South Bend 104,905. Gary 97,715. Hammond 78,292. Bloomington 69,247. Muncie 65,287. Fishers 61,840. Lafayette 61,244.

Business **Gross State Product, 2008:** $209.9 bil. **Leading Sectors of GSP:** Manufacturing 27.19%; Durable Goods 18.94%; Services 18.06%. *Fortune* 500 **Companies (2009):** 6.

Famous natives Larry Bird, basketball player. Hoagy Carmichael, composer. Eugene V. Debs, politician/organizer. Theodore Dreiser, author. Benjamin Harrison, U.S. president. Jimmy Hoffa, union leader. Michael Jackson, singer. David Letterman, comedian. Carole Lombard, actress. Cole Porter, composer. Ernie Pyle, journalist. Knute Rockne (b. Norway), football coach. Paul Samuelson, economist (Nobel Prize, 1960). Booth Tarkington, author. Kurt Vonnegut, author. Wendell L. Willkie, politician. Wilbur Wright, aviator.

Noteworthy places Ernie Pyle birthplace, Dana. George Rogers Clark Natl. Hist. Park, Vincennes. Benjamin Harrison home, Indianapolis. Hoosier Natl. Forest. Indiana Dunes Natl. Lakeshore. Indianapolis Motor Speedway and Museum. Indianapolis Museum of Art. New Harmony village. Notre Dame Univ., South Bend. Old state capital, Corydon. Wilbur Wright State Memorial, Millville. Wyandotte Cave. Tippecanoe sites.

Memorable events Mound Builders present c. A.D. 1000. René-Robert Cavelier de La Salle explores for French 1679–87. French near Vincennes from c. 1700. French cede territory to British 1763. Gen. Ambrose Clark captures Ft. Vincennes 1779. Territory ceded to U.S. 1783; included in Northwest Territory 1787. Miamis defeat U.S. twice in 1790. Gen. Anthony Wayne defeats Miamis at Battle of Fallen Timbers 1794. Territory included in Indiana Territory 1800. Gen. William Henry Harrison defeats Tecumseh's Indian Confederation at Tippecanoe 1811. Statehood 1816. Studebaker wagon company founded in South Bend 1852. U.S. Steel establishes mill at company-built town of Gary 1906. First Indianapolis 500 run 1911. Only a dozen companies producing cars, down from a pre-World War I peak of 375, 1920. Studebaker, last Indiana-based car maker, closes 1963.

Tourist information (800) 677-9800
www.in.gov/visitindiana

▶ IOWA

Iowa lies between the two great rivers of the central United States, the Mississippi and the Missouri, with a quarter of the nation's richest and deepest topsoil. Iowa's farmers lead the country in the production of corn, and Iowa is also a big producer of hogs, cattle, and other livestock. With about 75 percent of Iowans employed in agriculture-related industries and 90 percent of the land farmed, Iowa can be deeply affected by natural disasters such as droughts and floods. Yet more than 100 *Fortune 500* Companies have production facilities in this farm state. Industrial production has risen since World War II. Iowans send abroad a quarter of the food they produce.

Name For Iowa tribe. **Nickname** Hawkeye State. **Capital** Des Moines. **Entered union** Dec. 28, 1846 (29th). **Motto** "Our liberties we prize and our rights we will maintain."

Emblems **Bird** Eastern goldfinch. **Flower** Wild rose. **Song** "The Song of Iowa." **Stone** Geode. **Tree** Oak.

Land **Total area** 56,272 sq. mi (26th), incl. 402 sq. mi. inland water. **Borders** Minn., Wis., Ill., Mo., Nebr., S.Dak. **Rivers** Big Sioux, Des Moines, Mississippi, Missouri. **Lakes** Okoboji, Rathbun Res., Red Rock, Saylorville Res., Spirit, Storm. **Other notable features** Ocheyedan Mound (1,675 ft.).

Elected officials Gov. Chet Culver (D, term exp. 2011). Lt. Gov. Patty Judge (D). Sec. State Michael Mauro (D). Atty. Gen. Thomas J. Miller (D).

People (July 2009 est.) 3,007,856 (30th). Race/Hispanic Origin: White 94.2%. Black 2.7%. Indian 0.4%. Asian 1.6%. Two or more races 1.1%. Hispanic 4.2%.

Cities (2006) Des Moines 193,886. Cedar Rapids 124,417. Davenport 99,514. Sioux City 83,262. Waterloo 65,998. Iowa City 62,649. Council Bluffs 60,271. Dubuque 57,696. West Des Moines 53,945. Ames 51,557.
Business Gross State Product, 2008: $110.4 bil. **Leading Sectors of GSP:** Manufacturing 21.02%; Services 17.82%; Finance, insurance, and real estate 16.05%. *Fortune 500* **Companies (2009):** 2.
Famous natives Norman E. Borlaug, agronomist (Nobel Peace Prize, 1970). William F. "Buffalo Bill" Cody, scout/showman. George Gallup, pollster. Josiah B. Grinnell (b. Vt.), abolitionist. Herbert Hoover, U.S. president. Harry L. Hopkins, politician. John L. Lewis, labor leader. John R. Mott, religious leader. Billy Sunday, baseball player/evangelist. John Wayne, actor. Meredith Wilson, composer. Grant Wood, painter.
Noteworthy places Amana Colonies. Davenport Art Gallery. Des Moines Art Center. Effigy Mounds Natl. Monument, Marquette. Ft. Dodge Hist. Museum. Herbert Hoover birthplace and library, West Branch. Natl. Rivers Hall of Fame, Dubuque. Putnam Museum, Davenport.
Memorable events Mound Builders present c. A.D. 1000. Jacques Marquette and Louis Jolliet claim land for France 1673. Part of Louisiana Purchase 1803. Part of Missouri Territory 1812–21. Black Hawk Wars 1832, 1834–37. First permanent settlement at Dubuque 1833. Organized as Iowa Territory (incl. parts of Minnesota, North Dakota, and South Dakota) 1838. Statehood 1846. Capital moved from Iowa City to Des Moines 1857. Fifty percent of Iowa's farms foreclosed during depression 1929–35. Iowa's urban population exceeds rural for first time 1960. Population loss of 7.9 percent in the 1980s. Floods cause $2.2 billion in damage 1993 and struck again in 2008. State recognizes gay marriage, 2009.
Tourist information (888) 472-6035
www.traveliowa.com

▶**KANSAS**

Kansas burst on the American scene as the territory called Bleeding Kansas, seething with conflict over the spread of slavery. Victorious New England abolitionists imprinted the state with the Puritan ethic. They were early supporters of prohibition, partly to discourage foreign newcomers. Kansas suffered enormously during the Great Depression and "Dust Bowl" days of the 1930s but rebounded strongly during the war. Wichita's aircraft industries, vital to the war effort, helped the Kansas economy to remain strong in the postwar years as family farming declined dramatically. Today Kansas remains a primary producer
of wheat, cattle, and other agricultural products. Its manufacturing base still includes extensive aircraft industries, and it leads the states in the production of helium. The geographic center of the lower 48 U.S. states is near Lebanon.
Name For Kansa or Kaw, "people of the south wind." **Nickname** Sunflower State. **Capital** Topeka. **Entered union** Jan. 29, 1861 (34th). **Motto** *Ad astra per aspera* (To the stars through adversity).
Emblems Animal American buffalo. **Bird** Western meadowlark. **Flower** Wild native sunflower. **March** "The Kansas March." **Song** "Home on the Range." **Tree** Cottonwood.
Land Total area 82,277 sq. mi (15th), incl. 462 sq. mi. inland water. **Borders** Nebr., Mo., Okla., Colo. **Rivers** Arkansas, Kansas, Missouri, Republican, Saline, Smoky Hill, Solomon. **Lakes**
Kanapolis, Malvern, Perry, Pomona, Tuttle Creek, Waconda. **Other notable features** Flint Hills.
Elected officials Gov. Mark Parkinson (D, term exp. 2010). Lt. Gov. Troy Findley (D). Sec. State Ron Thornburgh (R). Atty. Gen. Stephen Six (D).
People (July 2009 est.) 2,818,747 (33rd). Race/Hispanic Origin: White 88.7%. Black 6.2%. Indian 1.0%. Asian 2.2%. Pacific Islander 0.1%. Two or more races 1.8%. Hispanic 9.1%.
Cities (2006) Wichita 357,698. Overland Park 166,722. Kansas City 143,801. Topeka 122,113. Olathe 114,662. Lawrence 88,605. Shawnee 59,252. Manhattan 50,737. Salina 46,140. Lenexa 44,520.
Business Gross State Product, 2008: $98.1 bil. **Leading Sectors of GSP:** Services 17.81%; Manufacturing 16.12%; Government 13.77%. *Fortune 500* **Companies (2009):** 3.
Famous natives "Buffalo Bill" Cody. Walter Chrysler, carmaker. Robert Dole, politician. Amelia Earhart, aviator. Dwight David Eisenhower (b. Tex.), general/U.S. president. Dennis Hopper, actor. William Inge, playwright. Nancy Landon Kassebaum, politician. Alf Landon, politician. Edgar Lee Masters, poet. James Naismith, inventor of basketball. Carrie Nation (b. Ky.), prohibitionist. Charlie "Bird" Parker, musician. Damon Runyon, writer. Gale Sayers, football player. William Allen White, the Sage of Emporia, editor.
Noteworthy places Agricultural Hall of Fame, Kansas City. Dodge City. Eisenhower Center, Abilene. Ft. Larned. Ft. Leavenworth. Ft. Riley. Ft. Scott. John Brown's Cabin, Osawatomie. Kansas Cosmosphere and Space Discovery Center, Hutchinson. Kansas State Historical Society Museum, Topeka. Wichita Art Museum.
Memorable events First major expedition to region under Francisco Vásquez de Coronado 1540–41. La Salle claims territory including Kansas for France 1682. Part of Louisiana Purchase 1803. Area visited by Meriwether Lewis and George Rogers Clark (1803), Zebulon Pike (1806), and Stephen H. Long (1819). Santa Fe Trail crosses Kansas 1821. Fts. Leavenworth (1827), Scott (1842), and Riley (1853) established to protect pioneers on Santa Fe and Oregon trails. Organized as Territory by Kansas-Nebraska Act 1854, which repealed Missouri Compromise of 1820. "Bleeding Kansas" scene of free vs. slave rivalry 1854–56. Statehood 1861. Introduction of winter wheat makes Kansas leading U.S. wheat producer 1870. Airplane manufacturing starts in Wichita 1919. World-famous Menninger Foundation for mental health founded 1919. "Dust Bowl" drought drives thousands of farmers off the land, especially in western Kansas, 1934–35. Murder of Clutter family by Richard E. Hickock and Perry E. Smith at Holcomb (later the subject of Truman Capote's *In Cold Blood*) 1959.
Tourist information (785) 296-2009
www.travelks.com

▶**KENTUCKY, COMMONWEALTH OF**

First pioneered by English immigrants in the mid-17th century, Kentucky's golden age as a choice frontier destination in the early 1800s was brought to an end by the Civil War. During the Civil War, the Bluegrass gentry supported the Confederacy, while the Appalachian backwoods men enlisted in the Union Army. Many took advantage of their uniforms to settle old accounts, and the social order was often threatened before the turn of the century. Though the state is known today for its bourbon and horse breeding, many Kentuckians make their living from the land as tobacco farmers or coal miners. The Appalachian part of the state in the east delivers about 20 percent of the nation's coal, but its economic problems remain acute, despite vast expenditures during the "war on poverty."

Name Corruption of the Iroquois *kenta-ke* (meadow land) or Wyandot *kah-ten-tah-teh* (land of tomorrow). **Nickname** Bluegrass State. **Capital** Frankfort. **Entered union** June 1, 1792 (15th). **Motto** "United we stand, divided we fall." **Emblems** **Bird** Cardinal. **Colors** Blue and gold. **Fish** Bass. **Flower** Goldenrod. **Song** "My Old Kentucky Home." **Tree** Tulip poplar. **Wild animal** Gray squirrel.

Land Total area 40,409 sq. mi (37th), incl. 681 sq. mi. inland water. **Borders** Ind., Ohio, W.Va., Va., Tenn., Mo., Ill. **Rivers** Cumberland, Kentucky, Licking, Ohio, Tennessee. **Lakes** Barkley, Barren River Res., Dewey, Grayson Res., Laurel Res., Nolin Res., Rough Res. **Mountains** Appalachian (Black Mt. 4,145 ft.), Cumberland. **Other notable features** Tennessee Valley.

Elected officials Gov. Steve Beshear (D, term exp. 2011). Lt. Gov. Daniel Mongiardo (D). Sec. State Trey Grayson (R). Atty. Gen. Jack Conway (D). **People** (July 2009 est.) 4,314,113 (26th). Race/Hispanic Origin: White 89.9%. Black 7.7%. Indian 0.3%. Asian 1.0%. Two or more races 1.1%. Hispanic 2.4%.

Cities (2006) Louisville 554,496. Lexington 270,789. Owensboro 55,525. Bowling Green 53,176. Covington 42,797. Richmond 31,431. Hopkinsville 27,415. Henderson 27,915. Frankfort 27,077. Florence 26,929.

Business Gross State Product, 2008: $127.0 bil. **Leading Sectors of GSP:** Manufacturing 25.19%; Services 16.70%; Durable Goods 15.79%. *Fortune 500* Companies (2009): 5.

Famous natives Muhammad Ali, boxer. Alben W. Barkley, politician. Daniel Boone (b. Pa.), frontiersman. Louis D. Brandeis, jurist. Kit Carson, frontiersman. Henry Clay, politician. Jefferson Davis, president of Confederate States of America. D.W. Griffith, director. John Marshall Harlan, jurist. Abraham Lincoln, U.S. president. Col. Harland Sanders, entrepreneur. Frederick M. Vinson, jurist. Robert Penn Warren, author.

Noteworthy places Abraham Lincoln birthplace, Hodgenville. Churchill Downs, Louisville. George S. Patton, Jr. Military Museum, Fort Knox. J.B. Speed Art Museum, Louisville. Land Between the Lakes Natl. Rec. Area. Mammoth Cave Natl. Park. My Old Kentucky Home, Bardstown. Old Ft. Harrod State Park.

Memorable events English enter territory through Cumberland Gap 1750. Territory included in area ceded by French 1763. Daniel Boone leads expeditions into region 1769. First settlement Harrodsburg 1774. Daniel Boone blazes Wilderness Trail through Cumberland Gap, establishes Ft. Boonesborough 1775. Organized as a county of Virginia 1776. British support Indian resistance ("Dark and Bloody Wars") until George Rogers Clark captures British forts in Indiana and Illinois 1778. Included as part of United States after Revolution 1783. Virginia approves separate statehood, achieved 1792. First steamboat reaches Louisville from New Orleans 1815. Invaded by Confederate armies 1862. Kentucky Derby first run at Louisville 1875. State has highest per capita income of southern states 1900; ranks last among all 48 states in per capita income 1940. Farm population decreases by 76 percent, and total number of farms by 53 percent,

1945–80. The number of farms continued decrease from 102,000 in 1980 to 83,000 in 2007.
Tourist information (800) 225-8747
www.kentuckytourism.com

▶**LOUISIANA**

European influences and ethnic diversity distinguish Louisiana from the rest of the nation. When Louisiana entered the Union in 1812, it brought with it a French legal system and a bilingualism that still survive. African-Americans, Cajuns and Creoles have contributed to its distinctive music and cuisine. The state has rich farmland, more oil and gas reserves than any other state but Texas, and in New Orleans an international port that serves the most extensive river system in North America.

The "devil's bargain" with the petrochemical industry struck by charismatic populist governor Huey Long (assassinated in 1935) brought needed jobs to the state. But the environmental impact of 100 loosely regulated petrochemical plants on the Mississippi River between New Orleans and Baton Rouge is only now being assessed. The state's reliance on the petroleum industry led to massive unemployment after a drop in oil prices in the 1980s. Tourism, especially in New Orleans, helped to diversify the economy, but the devastating hurricanes of 2005 and the oil spill of 2010 created new challenges.

Name For King Louis XIV. **Nickname** Pelican State. **Capital** Baton Rouge. **Entered union** Apr. 30, 1812 (18th). **Motto** "Union, justice, confidence." **Emblems** **Bird** Eastern brown pelican. **Colors** Gold, white, and blue. **Crustacean** Crawfish. **Dog** Catahoula leopard. **Flower** Magnolia. **Fossil** Petrified palmwood. **Gem** Agate. **Insect** Honeybee. **Songs** "Give Me Louisiana," "You Are My Sunshine." **Tree** Bald cypress.

Land Total area 51,840 sq. mi (31st), incl. 8,278 sq. mi. inland water. **Borders** Ark., Miss., Gulf of Mexico, Tex. **Rivers** Atchafalaya, Mississippi, Ouachita, Pearl, Red, Sabine. **Lakes** Bistineau, Borgne, Caddo, Catahoula, Grand, Maurepas, Pontchartrain, Salvador, White. **Other notable features** Bayou Barataria, Bayou Bodcau, Bayou D'Arbonne, Driskill Mt. (535 ft.).

Elected officials Gov. Bobby Jindal (R, term exp. 2012). Lt. Gov. Scott Angelle (D) . Sec. State Jay Dardenne (R). Atty. Gen. Buddy Caldwell (D). **People** (July 2009 est.) 4,492,076 (25th). Race/Hispanic Origin: White 64.8%. Black 32.0%. Indian 0.6%. Asian 1.4%. Two or more races 1.1%. Hispanic 3.4%.

Cities (2006) Baton Rouge 229,553. New Orleans 223,388. Shreveport 200,199. Metairie 130,000. Lafayette 114,214. Lake Charles 70,224. Kenner 66,592. Bossier City 61,306. Monroe 51,555. Alexandria 45,836.

Business Gross State Product, 2008: $144.9 bil. **Leading Sectors of GSP:** Mining 28.11%; Oil and gas extraction 18.77%; Services 16.82%. *Fortune 500* Companies (2009): 2.

Famous natives Louis "Satchmo" Armstrong, jazz musician. Pierre Beauregard, Confederate general. Terry Bradshaw, football player. Braxton Bragg, Confederate general. Truman Capote, author. Clyde Cessna, aviator. Michael DeBakey, surgeon. Fats Domino, singer. Lillian Hellman, author. Mahalia Jackson, singer. Jean Baptiste Le Moyne, sieur de Bienville (b. Canada), founded New Orleans. Jerry Lee Lewis, singer. Huey P. Long, senator. Ferdinand Joseph La Menthe "Jelly Roll" Morton, musician. Leonidas K. Polk, clergyman/Confederate general. Henry Miller Shreve (b. NJ), riverboat captain. Edward D. White, Jr., jurist.

Noteworthy places Avery Island. Cabildo, New Orleans. French Quarter, New Orleans. Garden District, New Orleans. Hodges Gardens, Natchitoches. Jean Lafitte Natl. Hist. Park, Chalmette. Kent House Museum, Alexandria. Longfellow-Evangeline State Commemorative Area, St. Martinsville. Louisiana Maritime Museum, Baton Rouge. New Orleans Museum of Art.

Memorable events Area first visited by Alonso Alvarez de Piñeda 1519. Claimed by René-Robert Cavelier de La Salle for France 1682. New Orleans founded 1718. French crown colony 1731. Four thousand Acadians (Cajuns) from Nova Scotia forcibly transported by British to Louisiana and settled in Bayou Teche 1755. Lands west of Mississippi given to Spain for help in French and Indian War 1763. Lands east of Mississippi ceded to Britain 1763. Same lands retroceded to France 1800. Jefferson negotiates Louisiana Purchase; U.S. acquires 885,000 sq. mi. for $15 million 1803. Statehood 1812. Andrew Jackson beats British at Battle of New Orleans 1815. State secedes 1861. Surrenders to Union forces 1862. Readmitted to Union 1868. Petroleum discovered 1901. Huey "The Kingfish" Long elected to Senate 1928; assassinated 1935. Racial designation law of 1970 repealed 1983. New Orleans flooded by Hurricane Katrina 2005.

Tourist information (800) 33-GUMBO
www.louisianatravel.com

▶**MAINE**
Down-Easters—the original Puritans and the later French Canadians—are distinct from the New Englanders of Maine's economically stronger sister states. Their land, especially the coast, is rugged, and the living everywhere is hard. The first state to see the sunrise, Maine borders only one other state, and it preserves much of its historic isolation. More than half of the state is still unincorporated territory. Lumbering, fishing, shipbuilding and potato farming are still practiced as traditional occupations. The 18th century brought canneries, textile and shoe factories but most of those jobs have gone abroad. Maine's economy now combines light industry with tourism and the modern Maine entrepreneur—sometimes an out-of-stater—develops small businesses in keeping with Maine's independent spirit.

Name Either for Maine in France or to distinguish mainland from islands in the Gulf of Maine. **Nickname** Pine Tree State. **Capital** Augusta. **Entered union** Mar. 15, 1820 (23rd). **Motto** *Dirigo* (I lead). **Emblems Animal** Moose. **Bird** Chickadee. **Fish** Landlocked salmon. **Flower** White pinecone and tassel. **Insect** Honeybee. **Mineral** Tourmaline. **Song** "State of Maine Song." **Tree** Eastern white pine.

Land Total area 35,385 sq. mi (39th), incl. 4,523 sq. mi. inland water. **Borders** Quebec, New Brunswick, Atlantic Ocean, N.H. **Rivers** Allagash, Androscoggin, Aroostock, Kennebec, Machias, Penobscot, Piscataqua, Salmon Falls, St. John. **Lakes** Chamberlain, Chesuncook, Grand, Moosehead, Rangeley, Sebago. **Other notable features** Mt. Katahadin (5,268 ft.), Mt. Desert Island, Penobscot Bay.

Elected officials Gov. John Baldacci (D, term exp. 2010). Sec. State Matthew Dunlap (D). Atty. Gen. Janet T. Mills (D).

People (July 2009 est.) 1,318,301 (40th). Race/ Hispanic Origin: White 96.4%. Black 1.0%. Indian 0.6%. Asian 0.9%. Two or more races 1.1%. Hispanic 1.3%. **Cities** (2006) Portland 63,011. Lewiston 35,734. Bangor 31,008. South Portland 23,784. Auburn

23,156. Biddeford 21,898. Augusta 18,560. Saco 18,289. Westbrook 16,201. Waterville 15,639.

Business Gross State Product, 2008: $40.3 bil. **Leading Sectors of GSP:** Services 21.28%; Finance, insurance, and real estate 19.21%; Government 14.41%. **Fortune 500 Companies (2009):** 0.

Famous natives L.L. Bean, entrepreneur. Cyrus H.K. Curtis, publisher. Hannibal Hamlin, politician. Sarah Orne Jewett, novelist. Henry Wadsworth Longfellow, poet. Stephen King, novelist. Sir Hiram and Hudson Maxim, inventors. Edna St. Vincent Millay, poet. Edmund S. Muskie, politician. John Knowles Paine, composer. Kenneth Roberts, novelist. Edward Arlington Robinson, poet. Nelson Rockefeller, politician. Marguerite Yourcenar (b. France), author.

Noteworthy places Acadia National Park, Mt. Desert Island. Allagash National Wilderness Waterway. Boothbay Railway Museum. Campobello-Longfellow House, Portland. Maine Maritime Museum, Bath. Portland Art Museum Roosevelt-Campobello Intl. Park, Campobello Island. St. Croix Island Natl. Monument.

Memorable events Vikings explore coast c. A.D.1000. Bartholomew Gosnold sails along coast 1602. French settlers at St. Croix River 1604. Included in grant to Plymouth Company 1606. Monhegan Island and Saco settled 1622. Annexed to Massachusetts Colony 1652. French attack northern territory intermittently through 1713. Statehood 1820. Border with Canada settled 1842. First state prohibition law enacted 1851. Penobscot and Passamaquoddy tribes file claim against state for $300 million compensation for land seized in violation of 1790 Indian Non-Intercourse Act, 1972; settled for $81.5 million 1980.

Tourist information (888) 624-6345
www.visitmaine.com

▶**MARYLAND**
Maryland wraps like a fishhook from the Atlantic Ocean around the fish-rich Chesapeake Bay and into the Cumberland Mountains in the northwest. Baltimore—full of urban problems but newly redeveloped with urban homesteading and shopsteading—holds the center. The suburbs of Baltimore and Washington seem far removed from the Delmarva (Delaware, Maryland, Virginia) peninsula with its watermen hanging on to an older way of life. Terrain, cultures, and history are a border state's mix of North and South. Founded as a haven for Catholics, Maryland's population is still 20 percent Catholic.

Name For Henrietta Maria, queen consort of Charles I. **Nicknames** Old Line State, Free State. **Capital** Annapolis. **Entered union** Apr. 28, 1788 (7th). **Motto** *Fatti maschii, parole femine* (Manly deeds, womanly words).

Emblems Bird Baltimore oriole. **Dog** Chesapeake Bay retriever. **Fish** Rockfish. **Flower** Black-eyed Susan. **Fossil** *Ecphora quadricostata* (extinct snail). **Insect** Baltimore checkerspot butterfly. **Song** "Maryland, My Maryland." **Sport** Jousting. **Tree** White oak.

Land Total area 12,407 sq. mi (42nd), incl. 2,633 sq. mi. inland water. **Borders** Pa., Del., Atlantic Ocean, Va., D.C., W.Va. **Rivers** Chester, Choptank, Nanticoke, Patapsco, Patuxent, Pocomoke, Potomac, Susquehanna. **Other notable features** Allegheny Mts., Blue Ridge Mts., Chesapeake Bay.

Elected officials Gov. Martin O'Malley (D, term exp. 2011). Lt. Gov. Anthony G. Brown (D).

Sec. State John McDonough (D). Atty. Gen. Douglas F. Gansler (D).

People (July 2009 est.) 5,699,478 (19th). Race/Hispanic Origin: White 63.4%. Black 29.4%. Indian 0.4%. Asian 5.1%. Pacific Islander 0.1%. Two or more races 1.6%. Hispanic 6.7%.

Cities (2006) Baltimore 651,154. Columbia 88,254. Silver Spring 76,540. Dundalk 62,306. Wheaton-Glenmont 60,500. Ellicott City 56,397. Germantown 55,419. Bethesda 55,277. Frederick 52,816. Gaithersburg 52,455.

Business **Gross State Product, 2008:** $220.9 bil. **Leading Sectors of GSP:** Services 24.89%; Finance, insurance, and real estate 21.55%; Government 17.58%. *Fortune 500* **Companies (2009):** 7.

Famous natives Russell Baker, journalist. Benjamin Banneker, surveyor. Eubie Blake, pianist. Rachel Carson, biologist/author. Stephen Decatur, navy officer. Frederick Douglass, abolitionist. Billie Holiday, singer. Johns Hopkins, financier/philanthropist. Francis Scott Key, lawyer/poet. Thurgood Marshall, jurist. H.L. Mencken, writer. Charles Willson Peale, artist. William Pinckney, statesman. James Rouse, urban planner. Babe Ruth, baseball player. Upton Sinclair, author. Roger B. Taney, jurist. Harriet Tubman, abolitionist. John Waters, filmmaker.

Noteworthy places Aberdeen Proving Ground. Antietam Natl. Battlefield, Sharpsburg. Assateague Island Natl. Seashore. Natl. Aquarium in Baltimore. Baltimore Museum of Art. Baltimore Museum of Industry. Calvert Marine Museum, Solomons. Chesapeake & Ohio Canal Natl. Hist. Park. Chesapeake Bay Maritime Museum, St. Michaels. Ft. McHenry Natl. Monument, Baltimore. Harpers Ferry Natl. Hist. Park. Liberty ship *John W. Brown*, Baltimore. Peabody Institute, Baltimore. St. Marys City. State House, Annapolis. U.S. Naval Academy, Annapolis. USS *Constellation*, Baltimore. Walters Art Gallery, Baltimore.

Memorable events John Smith explores area 1608. William Claiborne sets up trading post on Kent Island 1631. Land granted to Cecilius Calvert, Lord Baltimore, 1632. Leonard Calvert and 200 Roman Catholic settlers land on Blakistone Island 1634. Mason Dixon Line establishes northern boundary of state 1763–67; later identified as boundary between slave and nonslave states. Francis Scott Key composes "The Star Spangled Banner" after British fail to take Ft. McHenry 1814. U.S. Naval Academy founded Annapolis 1845. State under federal military control during Civil War 1861–65. First state to adopt income tax 1938. Alabama Gov. George C. Wallace shot while campaigning in Democratic presidential primary 1972.

Tourist Information (866) MD-WELCOME www.visitmaryland.org

▶**MASSACHUSETTS, COMMONWEALTH OF**

Massachusetts is central to the history of the early American republic. The Boston Tea Party, the "shot heard round the world" from Lexington and Concord, and the Battle of Bunker Hill are American folklore. So is the feast of Thanksgiving, first celebrated by the Puritans at Plymouth. Fishing, trade, textiles and leather industries were the backbone of Massachusetts's 19th-century economy. In the 1980s, Boston's Route 128 became the East Coast counterpart to California's Silicon Valley, with some of the nation's most advanced computer and electronic research and manufacturing. The state's "economic miracle" of the 1980s ended abruptly, and Massachusetts endured a severe downturn during the recession of the early 1990s. It recently rebounded, along with most of the nation.

A staple of the Massachusetts scene is higher education, in which the state is a national leader. Boston alone boasts such institutions as Harvard University (founded 1636), M.I.T., Northeastern, Brandeis, Boston University, Boston College, Wellesley and Tufts. To the west are the University of Massachusetts, Amherst, Williams, Smith and Mt. Holyoke.

Name For Massachuset tribe, whose name means "at or about the great hill." **Nickname** Bay State. **Capital** Boston. **Entered union** Feb. 6, 1788 (6th). **Motto** *Ense petit placidam sub libertate quietem* (By the sword we seek peace, but peace only under liberty).

Emblems **Beverage** Cranberry juice. **Bird** Chickadee. **Dog** Boston terrier. **Fish** Cod. **Flower** Mayflower. **Gem** Rhodonite. **Insect** Ladybug. **Mineral** Babingtonite. **Song** "All Hail to Massachusetts." **Tree** American elm.

Land **Total area** 10,555 sq. mi (44th), incl. 2,715 sq. mi. inland water. **Borders** Vt., N.H., Atlantic Ocean, R.I., Conn., N.Y. **Rivers** Cape Cod Canal, Connecticut, Merrimack, Taunton. **Other notable features** Buzzard's Bay, Cape Ann, Cape Cod, Cape Cod Bay, Connecticut Valley, Elizabeth Islands, Martha's Vineyard, Monomoy Island, Nantucket Island.

Elected officials Gov. Deval Patrick (D). Lt. Gov. Timothy P. Murray (D). Sec. of Commonwealth William Francis Galvin (D). Atty. Gen. Martha Coakley (D).

People (July 2009 est.) 6,593,587 (15th). Race/Hispanic Origin: White 86.2%. Black 7.0%. Indian 0.3%. Asian 4.9%. Pacific Islander 0.1%. Two or more races 1.4%. Hispanic 8.6%.

Cities (2006) Boston 590,763. Worcester 175,454. Springfield 151,176. Lowell 103,229. Cambridge 101,365. Brockton 94,191. New Bedford 92,538. Fall River 91,474. Quincy 91,058. Lynn 87,991.

Business **Gross State Product, 2008:** $312.5 bil. **Leading Sectors of GSP:** Services 27.76%; Finance, insurance, and real estate 25.67%; Real estate 14.48%. *Fortune 500* **Companies (2009):** 12.

Famous natives John Adams, U.S. president. John Quincy Adams, U.S. president. Samuel Adams, patriot. Horatio Alger, clergyman/author. Susan B. Anthony, suffragette. Clara Barton, nurse. Leonard Bernstein, composer. George Herbert Walker Bush, U.S. president. John ("Johnny Appleseed") Chapman, pioneer. Richard Cardinal Cushing, prelate. Bette Davis, actress. Emily Dickinson, poet. Ralph Waldo Emerson, author. Marshall Field, merchant. R. Buckminster Fuller, inventor/engineer. John Hancock, patriot. Oliver Wendell Holmes, jurist. Winslow Homer, painter. John F. Kennedy, U.S. president. Jack Kerouac, author. Cotton Mather, theologian. Samuel Eliot Morison, historian. Samuel Morse, inventor. Thomas P. "Tip" O'Neill, congressman. Edgar Allan Poe, poet/author. Paul Revere patriot/silversmith. Louis Sullivan, architect. Henry David Thoreau, author.

Noteworthy places Addison Gallery of American Art, Andover. Arnold Arboretum, Boston. Arthur M. Sackler Museum, Cambridge. Berkshires Museum, Pittsfield. Boston Museum of Fine Arts. Boston Natl. Hist. Park (incl. Bunker Hill, Charlestown Navy Yard, Old North Church). Busch-Reisinger Museum, Cambridge. Cape Cod Natl. Seashore. Clark Art Institute, Williamsburg. Fogg Art Museum, Boston. Gardner Art Museum, Boston. Hancock Shaker Village. Kennedy Presidential Library, Boston. Lowell Natl. Hist. Park.

Minute Man Natl. Hist. Park, Lexington and Concord. Nantucket Hist. Society. Old Sturbridge Village. Peabody Museum, Salem. Plimoth Plantation, Plymouth. Tanglewood Music Festival, Lenox. *U.S.S. Constitution* ("Old Ironsides"), Charlestown. Walden Pond. Woods Hole Oceanographic Institute. Worcester Art Museum.

Memorable events Pilgrims land at Plymouth 1620. First Thanksgiving celebrated 1621. Harvard College founded 1636. Region acquires province of Maine 1652. Colonists battle Wampanoags in King Philip's War 1655–56. Boston Massacre 1770. Boston Tea Party protests taxation 1773. Battles at Lexington, Concord, and Bunker Hill 1775. Shays's Rebellion 1785–86. Maine becomes a separate state 1820. Massachusetts receives influx of Irish immigrants fleeing famine 1845. Textile workers' strike at Lawrence brings International Workers of the World (IWW) to prominence in East 1912. Cape Cod Canal completed 1914. International protest follows trial and execution of anarchists Nicola Sacco and Bartolomeo Vanzetti for robbery and murder 1920; names cleared by governor's proclamation 1970. Eleven robbers steal $2.7 million from Brink's North Terminal Garage 1950. Martha's Vineyard and Nantucket symbolically vote to secede from state 1973. State votes in favor of same-sex marriage 2004.

Tourist information　(800) 227-MASS
www.massvacation.com

▶ MICHIGAN

The automobile is the commodity with which Michigan is identified, and it is the home of General Motors and Ford, the nation's two largest automakers. More than 50 percent of Michiganders live in the southeastern corner of the state, where the car industry flourishes. In the Upper Peninsula, across the Straits of Mackinac, lumber and copper have been the principal commodities from the 19th century, and the northern part of the Lower Peninsula boasts rich farmland. Michigan includes parts of four of the five Great Lakes, and it has more coastline than any state except Alaska. Michigan has an outstanding reputation in higher education, and the University of Michigan at Ann Arbor and Michigan State are helping to foster the state's high-tech industries. But Michigan's reliance on auto manufacturing makes it vulnerable to economic downturns, as well as the general contraction of the American industry, as what happened in 2008, when the federal government "bailed out" the automotive industry.

Name From the Fox *mesikami*, "large lake."
Nicknames Wolverine State, Lake State. **Capital** Lansing. **Entered union** Jan. 26, 1837 (26th). **Motto** *Si quaeris peninsulam amoenam circumspice* (If you are looking for a beautiful peninsula, look around you).

Emblems **Bird** Robin. **Fish** Trout. **Flower** Apple blossom. **Gem** Chlorastrolite. **Insect** Dragonfly. **Song** "Michigan, My Michigan." **Stone** Petoskey stone. **Tree** White pine.

Land **Total area** 96,716 sq. mi (11th), incl. 39,912 sq. mi. inland water. **Borders** Lake Superior, Ontario, Lake Huron, Lake Erie, Ohio, Ind., Lake Michigan, Wisc. **Rivers** Brule, Detroit, Kalamazoo, Menominee, Montreal, Muskegon, St. Joseph, St. Mary's. **Lakes** Burt, Higgins, Houghton, Huron, Manistique, Michigan, Mullett, St. Clair, Superior. **Other notable features** Isle Royale, Mt. Curwood (1,980 ft.), Saginaw Bay, Traverse Bay, Whitefish Bay.

Elected officials　Gov. Jennifer Granholm (D, term exp. 2011). Lt. Gov. John D. Cherry (D). Sec. State Terri Lynn Land (R). Atty. Gen. Mike Cox (R).
People (July 2009 est.) 9,969,727 (8th). Race/Hispanic Origin: White 81.2%. Black 14.2%. Indian 0.6%. Asian 2.4%. Two or more races 1.5%. Hispanic 4.1%.
Cities (2006) Detroit 871,121. Grand Rapids 193,083. Warren 134,589. Sterling Heights 127,991. Flint 117,068. Lansing 114,276. Ann Arbor 113,206. Clinton 93,781. Livonia 96,736. Dearborn 92,382.
Business **Gross State Product, 2008:** $326.1 bil. **Leading Sectors of GSP:** Manufacturing 23.07%; Services 20.72%; Durable goods 17.40%. *Fortune 500* **Companies (2009):** 21.
Famous natives Ralph J. Bunche, statesman (Nobel Peace Prize, 1950). Paul de Kruif, bacteriologist. Thomas Dewey, politician. Herbert H. Dow (b. Canada), chemical manufacturer. Edna Ferber, author. Gerald Ford (b. Neb.) U.S. president. Francis Ford Coppola, moviemaker. Henry Ford, industrialist. Edgar Guest, journalist/poet. Robert Ingersoll, industrialist. Earvin "Magic" Johnson, basketball player. Will Kellogg, businessman/philanthropist. Charles A. Lindbergh, aviator. Madonna, singer. Antoine de La Mothe, sieur de Cadillac (b. France), founded Detroit. Pontiac, Ottawa chief. Theodore Roethke, poet. Diana Ross, singer. Tom Selleck, actor. William Upjohn, drug manufacturer. Stevie Wonder, musician.
Noteworthy places Air Zoo, Kalamazoo. Detroit Historical Society. Detroit Institute of Arts. Dossin Great Lakes Museum, Detroit. Gerald Ford Museum, Grand Rapids. Great Lakes Indian Interpretive Museum, Detroit. Greenfield Village, Dearborn. Historic Ft. Wayne, Detroit. Isle Royale Natl. Park. Mackinac Island. Pictured Rocks Natl. Lakeshore, Lake Superior. Sleeping Bear Dunes Natl. Lakeshore, Lake Superior.
Memorable events French explorers in region 1634. Jacques Marquette settles Sault Ste. Marie 1668. Detroit founded as French military post 1701. Region ceded to England 1763; to United States 1783. Included in Northwest Territory but British maintain control until 1796. Michigan Territory 1805. First steamboat on Great Lakes reaches Detroit 1818. Statehood 1837. First state to outlaw capital punishment 1846. Republican party organized at Jackson 1854. Canals at Sault Ste. Marie link Lakes Superior and Huron 1855. Ransom E. Olds and Henry Ford, working independently, develop gasoline-powered car 1896. United Auto Workers first to use sit-down strike successfully in contract negotiations 1935. Race riot, one of the worst in U.S. history, leaves 43 dead and $200 million in damages in Detroit 1967. Congress authorizes $1.5 billion in federal loan guarantees to bail out Chrysler Corp. 1979; $4 billion 2009. Congress authorizes $9.4 billion in federal loan to bail out General Motors, 2009.
Tourist information　(888) 784-7328
www.michigan.org

▶ MINNESOTA

A land of at least 10,000 lakes, Minnesota is a magnet for those who love the outdoors. It is also home to the largest Scandinavian population in the United States. Originally exploited for its wealth of lumber and iron—the Mesabi Range still produces much of the nation's iron ore—Minnesota also has highly developed agribusinesses (especially dairy products), manufacturing and transportation industries. Minneapolis and St. Paul are at the north end of the Mississippi River system, and Duluth at the westernmost point of

Lake Superior is the largest U.S. inland port. Minnesota has one of the best state school systems. **Name** From the Sioux *minisota*, "sky-tinted waters." **Nicknames** North Star State, Gopher State, Land of 10,000 Lakes. **Capital** St. Paul. **Entered union** May 11, 1858 (32rd). **Motto** *L'étoile du nord* (Star of the north).
Emblems **Bird** Common loon. **Beverage** Milk. **Fish** Walleye. **Flower** Pink and white lady's slipper. **Gem** Lake Superior agate. **Grain** Wild rice. **Mushroom** Morel, or sponge mushroom. **Song** "Hail, Minnesota!." **Tree** Red pine.
Land **Total area** 86,939 sq. mi (12th), incl. 7,329 sq. mi. inland water. **Borders** Manitoba, Ontario, Lake Superior, Wisc., Iowa, S.Dak., N.Dak. **Rivers** Minnesota, Mississippi, Red River of the North, St. Croix. **Lakes** Itasca, Lake of the Woods, Leech, Mille Lacs, Red, Winnibigoshish. **Other notable features** Mesabi Range.
Elected officials Gov. Tim Pawlenty (R, term exp. 2011). Lt. Gov. Carol Molnau (R). Sec. State Mark Ritchie (D). Atty. Gen. Lori Swanson (D).
People (July 2009 est.) 5,266,214 (21st). Race/Hispanic Origin: White 89.0%. Black 4.6%. Indian 1.2%. Asian 3.5%. Pacific Islander 0.1%. Two or more races 1.5%. Hispanic 4.1%.
Cities (2006) Minneapolis 372,833. St. Paul 273,535. Rochester 96,975. Duluth 84,167. Bloomington 80,869. Plymouth 70,102. Brooklyn Park 69,942. Eagan 66,228. Coon Rapids 63,736. Burnsville 62,207.
Business **Gross State Product, 2008:** $217.0 bil. **Leading Sectors of GSP:** Services 21.58%; Finance, insurance, and real estate 19.33%; Manufacturing 15.85%. *Fortune 500* **Companies (2009):** 19.
Famous natives Warren Burger, jurist. Bob Dylan, musician. F. Scott Fitzgerald, novelist. Judy Garland, actress. J. Paul Getty, businessman. Garrison Keillor, humorist. Sinclair Lewis, author (Nobel Prize, 1930). Paul Manship, sculptor. William and Charles Mayo, surgeons. Eugene McCarthy, politician. Walter F. Mondale, politician. Charles Schulz, cartoonist. Richard W. Sears, merchant.
Noteworthy places Boundary Waters Canoe Area. Grand Portage Natl. Monument. International Falls. Lake Itasca State Park (headwaters of Mississippi). Mall of America. Mayo Clinic, Rochester. Minneapolis Institute of Arts. Minnehaha Falls, Minneapolis. Minnesota Zoo, Apple Valley. Paul Bunyanland, Brainerd. Pipestone Natl. Monument. Tyrone Guthrie Theater, Minneapolis. Voyageurs Natl. Park. Walker Art Center, Minneapolis.
Memorable events Pierre Esprit Radisson and Médard Chouart des Grosselliers visit area 1654–60. René-Robert de La Salle and Louis Hennepin explore upper Mississippi 1680. Daniel Greysolon, sieur de Duluth, claims region for France 1679. Area east of Mississippi to Britain 1763; to United States 1783. Western region of state as part of Louisiana Purchase 1803. Britain cedes northern strip to United States 1818. Ft. Snelling built 1820. Northern border settled by Ashburton Treaty 1842. Minnesota Territory created 1849. Statehood 1858. Sioux driven from state after uprising led by Chief Little Crow 1862. Iron ore deposits discovered in Mesabi Range 1890. Democratic party merges with Farmer-Labor party 1944. Interstate bridge collapses, killing 13 and injuring 145 in Minneapolis, 2007.
Tourist information (888) TOURISM
www.exploreminnesota.com

▶ **MISSISSIPPI**
Mississippi's rank as one of the poorest states in the nation can be traced to the Civil War. Before the Civil War, Mississippi was the fifth-wealthiest state in the nation but the war cost the state 30,000 men. Plantation owners who survived the war were virtually bankrupted by the emancipation of the slaves, and Union troops under Sherman and others left widespread destruction in their wake. The increasingly harsh race-laws passed around 1900 also cost the state in the emigration of almost half a million (75 percent blacks, 25 percent whites) by the 1940s. Compounding all this was the fact that until World War II, Mississippi had virtually no urban center such as Jackson to attract or sustain major industry. In race relations particularly, Mississippi has made vast improvements, and there have been substantial gains in education and the attraction of out-of-state companies, especially light industry.
Name From the Ojibwa *misi sipi*, "great river." **Nickname** Magnolia State. **Capital** Jackson. **Entered union** Dec. 10, 1817 (20th). **Motto** *Virtute et armis* (By virtue and arms).
Emblems **Beverage** Milk. **Bird** Mockingbird. **Fish** Largemouth or black bass. **Flower** Magnolia. **Fossil** Prehistoric whale. **Insect** Honeybee. **Mammal** White-tailed deer. **Song** "Go, Mississippi." **Stone** Petrified wood. **Tree** Magnolia. **Waterfowl** Wood duck. **Water mammal** Porpoise.
Land **Total area** 48,430 sq. mi (32nd), incl. 1,523 sq. mi. inland water. **Borders** Tenn., Ala., Gulf of Mexico, La., Ark. **Rivers** Big Black, Mississippi, Pearl, Tennessee, Yazoo. **Lakes** Arkabutla, Grenada, Ross Barnett Res., Sardis. **Other notable features** Pontotoc Ridge.
Elected officials Gov. Haley Barbour (R, term exp. 2012). Lt. Gov. Phil Bryant (R). Sec. State Delbert Hosemann (R). Atty. Gen. Jim Hood (D).
People (July 2009 est.) 2,951,996 (31st). Race/Hispanic Origin: White 60.6%. Black 37.2%. Indian 0.5%. Asian 0.8%. Two or more races 0.9%. Hispanic 2.2%.
Cities (2006) Jackson 176,614. Gulfport 64,316. Hattiesburg 48,012. Biloxi 44,342. Southaven 41,295. Meridian 38,200. Greenville 37,801. Tupelo 35,930. Olive Branch 29,861. Clinton 26,212.
Business **Gross State Product, 2008:** $71.7 bil. **Leading Sectors of GSP:** Services 17.95%; Manufacturing 17.94%; Government 17.15%. *Fortune 500* **Companies (2009):** 0.
Famous natives Medgar Evers, civil rights leader. William Faulkner, novelist. Shelby Foote, historian. Jim Henson, puppeteer. B.B. King, musician. Elvis Presley, singer. Leontyne Price, opera singer. Jerry Rice, football player. John C. Stennis, politician. Conway Twitty, singer. Muddy Waters, musician. Eudora Welty, novelist. Ben Ames Williams, novelist. Tennessee Williams, playwright. Richard Wright, author.
Noteworthy places Delta Blues Museum, Clarksdale. Natchez Trace Natl. Parkway. Seafood Industry Museum, Biloxi. Tupelo Natl. Battlefield. Vicksburg Natl. Military Park.
Memorable events Hernando de Soto's expedition travels through Mississippi 1540–41. René-Robert Cavelier de La Salle claims Mississippi valley for France 1682. Pierre Le Moyne, sieur d'Iberville builds Ft. Maurepas on Biloxi Bay 1699. Natchez (Ft. Rosalie) established 1716. France cedes territory to Britain 1763. Mississippi Territory (including presentday Alabama) created 1798. Statehood (Natchez first capital) 1817. Secedes from Union; Jefferson Davis becomes president of Confederacy 1861. Siege of Vicksburg

1863. Petroleum discovered 1939. Gov. Ross R. Barnett found guilty of contempt in preventing desegregation of University of Mississippi; James H. Meredith first black enrolled at University of Mississippi 1962. Civil rights leader Medgar Evers assassinated in Jackson and buried in Arlington National Cemetery 1963. White civil rights workers James Cheney, Andrew Goodman, and Michael Schwerner killed, 1964.

Tourist information   (866) SEE-MISS
www.visitmississippi.org

▶MISSOURI

Missouri is remarkable for the number and variety of its neighbors—southern states (Arkansas, Kentucky, and Tennessee), midwestern states (Illinois and Iowa), and Plains states (Oklahoma, Nebraska, and Kansas). For Missouri, geography was destiny. Still one of the country's most important inland ports, St. Louis was founded at the confluence of the Missouri and Mississippi rivers and became the gateway to the West; and Independence (now part of metropolitan Kansas City) got its start provisioning wagons for the Oregon and Santa Fe trails. The Pony Express from St. Joseph to Sacramento began in 1860, and the first attempt at airmail service was tried in St. Louis in 1911. While farming and livestock are still important to the state's economy, manufacturing, and services are now the biggest sectors.

Name From the Iliniwek *missouri*, "owner of big canoes." **Nickname** Show Me State. **Capital** Jefferson City. **Entered union** Aug. 10, 1821 (24th). **Motto** *Salus populi suprema lex esto* (The welfare of the people shall be the supreme law).
Emblems   Bird Bluebird. **Flower** Hawthorne. **Insect** Honeybee. **Mineral** Galena. **Rock** Mozarkite. **Song** "Missouri Waltz." **Tree** Dogwood.
Land   Total area 69,704 sq. mi. (21st), incl. 818 sq. mi. inland water. **Borders** Iowa, Ill., Ky., Tenn., Ark., Okla., Kans., Nebr. **Rivers** Des Moines, Mississippi, Missouri, Osage, St. Francis. **Lakes** Bull Shoals, Clearwater, Lake of the Ozarks, Lake of the Woods, Table, Wappapella. **Other notable features** Ozark Mts. (Taum Sauk Mt. 1,772 ft.).
Elected officials   Gov. Jay Nixon (D). Lt. Gov. Peter Kinder (R). Sec. State Robin Carnahan (D). Atty. Gen. Chris Koster (D).
People   (July 2009 est.) 5,987,580 (18th). Race/Hispanic Origin: White 85.0%. Black 11.5%. Indian 0.5%. Asian 1.5%. Pacific Islander 0.1%. Two or more races 1.4%. Hispanic 3.2%.
Cities   (2006) Kansas City 447,306. St. Louis 347,181. Springfield 150,797. Independence 109,400. Columbia 94,428. Lee's Summit 81,913. St. Joseph 72,651. O'Fallon 72,477. St. Charles 63,009. St. Peters 54,839.
Business   Gross State Product, 2008: $193.8 bil. **Leading Sectors of GSP:** Services 21.29%; Manufacturing 16.77%; Finance, insurance, and real estate 16.34%. *Fortune 500* **Companies (2009):** 8.
Famous natives   Thomas Hart Benton, painter. Yogi Berra, baseball player. George Caleb Bingham (b. Va.), painter. Omar Bradley, general. Adophus Busch (b. Germany), brewer. George Washington Carver, botanist. Walter Cronkite, journalist. Walt Disney, film producer. T.S. Eliot, poet. Walker Evans, photographer. Langston Hughes, poet. Jesse James, outlaw. Marianne Moore, poet. Reinhold Niebuhr, theologian. J.C. Penny, businessman. John J. "Black Jack" Pershing, soldier. Joseph Pulitzer (b. Hungary), publisher. Ginger Rogers, dancer. Casey Stengel, baseball player.

Virgil Thompson, composer. Harry S Truman, U.S. president. Mark Twain, writer. Tom Watson, golfer. Shelley Winters, actress.
Noteworthy places   Churchill Memorial, Gateway Arch, St. Louis. George Washington Carver Natl. Monument, Diamond. Harry S Truman Library, Independence. Mark Twain Area, Hannibal. Nelson-Atkins Museum of Art, Kansas City. Pony Express Museum, St. Joseph. St. Louis Art Museum. Wilson's Creek Natl. Battlefield. Cahokia Mounds State Historic Site, near St. Louis.
Memorable events   French miners and hunters settle at Ste. Genevieve 1735. Pierre Laclade settles St. Louis 1765. New Madrid earthquakes (8.6 on Richter scale) rock buildings as far away as Baltimore 1811-12. Statehood 1821. Missouri legislature split over secesssion: minority party adopts secession ordinance; Missouri admitted to Confederacy; majority party remains loyal to Union 1861. Jesse James killed by fellow gang member at St. Joseph 1882. Lake of the Ozarks formed after completion of Bagnell Dam on Missouri River 1931. Winston Churchill delivers "iron curtain" speech at Fulton 1952. Gateway Arch, 630 ft. high, opens at St. Louis 1964. St. Louis population declines 53 percent 1950–90. Floods cause $3 billion in damage 1993.

Tourist information   (800) 519-2100
www.visitmo.com

▶MONTANA

Mountains account for only the western two-fifths of "Big Sky Country," where copper mining, lumber and tourism are the chief industries. The eastern portion of the state is part of the Great Plains, devoted to agriculture and ranching. For many years Montana was in the grip of the Anaconda Copper Mining Company, which virtually owned the state government and took most of its profits out of the state. After Anaconda's demise in the 1970s, Montana developed some of the most stringent environmental laws in the West. In recent years, many famous Hollywood stars, as well as media mogul Ted Turner, have bought large tracts of land in western Montana.

Name From Spanish *montaña*, "mountainous." **Nicknames** Treasure State, Big Sky Country. **Capital** Helena. **Entered union** Nov. 8, 1889 (41st). **Motto** *Oro y plata* (Gold and silver).
Emblems   Bird Western meadowlark. **Fish** Blackspotted cutthroat trout. **Flower** Bitterroot. **Gems** Yogo sapphire, Montana agate. **Grass** Bluebunch wheatgrass. **Song** "Montana." **State ballad** "Montana Melody." **Tree** Ponderosa pine.
Land   Total area 147,042 sq. mi (4th), incl. 1,490 sq. mi. inland water. **Borders** British Columbia, Alberta, Saskatchewan, N.Dak., S.Dak., Wyo., Idaho. **Rivers** Kootenai, Milk, Missouri, Musselshell, Powder, Yellowstone. **Lakes** Bighorn, Canyon Ferry, Elwell, Flathead, Ft. Peck. **Mountains** Absaroka Range, Beartooth Range (Granite Peak 12,799 ft.), Big Belt, Bitterroot Range, Centennial, Crazy, Lewis Range, Little Belt. **Other notable features** Continental Divide, Missoula Valley.
Elected officials   Gov. Brian Schweitzer (D). Lt. Gov. John Bohlinger (D). Sec. State Linda McCulloch (D). Atty. Gen. Steve Bullock (D).
People   (July 2009 est.) 974,989 (44th). Race/Hispanic Origin: White 90.5%. Black 0.7%. Indian 6.4%. Asian 0.6%. Pacific Islander 0.1%. Two or more races 1.7%. Hispanic 3.0%.
Cities   (2006) Billings 100,148. Missoula 64,081. Great Falls 56,215. Bozeman 35,061. Butte-Silver Bow 32,110. Helena 27,885.

Business Gross State Product, 2008: $27.3 bil. **Leading Sectors of GSP:** Services 21.22%; Government 17.12%; Finance, insurance, and real estate 14.14%. *Fortune 500* **Companies (2009):** 0.

Famous natives Gary Cooper, actor. Marcus Daly (b. Ireland), mine owner. Chet Huntley, journalist. Myrna Loy, actress. Mike Mansfield (b. N.Y.), politician/diplomat. Jeanette Rankin, politician/reformer. Charles M. Russell, artist.

Noteworthy places Big Hole Natl. Battlefield. Bob Marshall Wilderness. Charles M. Russell Museum, Great Falls. Custer Battlefield Natl. Monument. Ft. Union Trading Post Natl. Hist. Site. Lewis and Clark Caverns State Park. Museum of the Plains Indian, Browning. Natl. Bison Range. Waterton-Glacier International Peace Park. World Museum of Mining, Butte. Yellowstone Natl. Park.

Memorable events French explorers and trappers visit region 1740s. Large part of state in Louisiana Purchase 1803. Lewis and Clark expedition 1805–6. Ft. Benton first permanent settlement 1846. Western part of state included in Washington Territory 1853 and 1859; eastern part in Nebraska (1854) and Dakota (1861) territories. Gold discovered at Bannack (1862) and Alder Gulch (1863). Organized as Montana Territory 1864. Dakota and Cheyenne defeat U.S. troops under Gen. William Armstrong Custer at Battle of Little Bighorn 1876. Under Chief Joseph, Nez Percé beat U.S. Army at Big Hole Basin 1877. Marcus Daly discovers copper near Butte 1880s. Statehood 1889. Homesteaders enter state 1909. Ft. Peck Dam completed 1940. Anaconda Copper Mining, dominant in Montana industry and politics since 1915, closes mining operations at Butte 1983. Elizabeth Prophet (Guru Ma) convinces 3,000 disciples of the Church Universal and Triumphant to await nuclear cataclysm in underground shelters in Paradise Valley while state bureaucrats worried over sewage facilities 1990.

Tourist information (800) 847-4868 www.visitmt.com

▶ NEBRASKA

Although set aside as Indian territory in 1834 and made off-limits to white settlement, thousands of whites crossed the region along the Independence, Mormon and Oregon trails. Eventually Congress opened the land to settlement, which accelerated after the Homestead Act of 1862 and the coming of the railroads. The newcomers took up ranching and farming under hard conditions. The winter of 1886–87 killed thousands of cattle and drove many large-scale ranchers into bankruptcy, while the dust bowl of the 1930s spurred a mass exodus. Significant industry did not develop until World War II, when many war-related industries and army airfields moved to the center of the country. Nebraska is among the leading agricultural states, especially in the production of corn for grain and livestock. A state constitutional amendment passed in 1982 prevents the sale of farmlands and ranch lands from being sold to anyone other than a Nebraska family farm corporation.

Name From the Oto *nebrathka*, "flat water." **Nickname** Cornhusker State. **Capital** Lincoln. **Entered union** Mar. 1, 1867 (37th). **Motto** "Equality before the law."

Emblems Bird Western meadowlark. **Flower** Goldenrod. **Fossil** Mammoth. **Gem** Blue agate. **Grass** Little blue stem. **Insect** Honeybee. **Mammal** White-tailed deer. **Rock** Prairie agate. **Soil** Soils of the Holdrege series. **Song** "Beautiful Nebraska." **Tree** Western cottonwood.

Land Total area 77,354 sq. mi (16th), incl. 481 sq. mi. inland water. **Borders** S.Dak., Iowa, Mo., Kans., Colo., Wyo. **Rivers** Missouri, North Platte, Republican, South Platte. **Lakes** Harlan Co. Res., Lewis and Clark Lake. **Other notable features** Pine Ridge, Sand Hills.

Elected officials Gov. Dave Heineman (R, term exp. 2010). Lt. Gov. Rick Sheehy (R). Sec. State John A. Gale (R). Atty. Gen. Jon Bruning (R).

People (July 2009 est.) 1,796,619 (38th). Race/Hispanic Origin: White 91.4%. Black 4.5%. Indian 1.1%. Asian 1.7%. Pacific Islander 0.1%. Two or more races 1.3%. Hispanic 7.9%.

Cities (2006) Omaha 419,545. Lincoln 241,167. Bellevue 47,594. Grand Island 44,632. Kearney 29,385. Fremont 25,417. Hastings 25,144. North Platte 24,386. Norfolk 23,896. Columbus 21,414.

Business Gross State Product, 2008: $66.6 bil. **Leading Sectors of GSP:** Services 20.25%; Finance, insurance, and real estate 15.77%; Government 14.40%. *Fortune 500* **Companies (2009):** 4.

Famous natives Fred Astaire, dancer. Marlon Brando, actor. William Jennings Bryan, politician. Johnny Carson (b. Iowa), comedian. Willa Cather (b. Va.), author. Loren Eiseley, anthropologist. The Rev. Edward J. Flanagan (b. Ireland), reformer. Henry Fonda, actor. Rollin Kirby, cartoonist. Melvin Laird, politician. Harold Lloyd, actor. Mahpiua Luta (Red Cloud), Oglala Sioux chief. Malcolm X, religious leader. Roscoe Pound, educator.

Noteworthy places Agate Fossil Beds Natl. Monument. Arbor Lodge State Park, Nebraska City. Boys Town, Omaha. Buffalo Bill Ranch State Hist. Park. Chimney Rock Hist. Site. Homestead Natl. Monument, Beatrice. Oregon Trail. Pioneer Village, Minden. Scotts Bluff Natl. Monument. Strategic Air and Space Museum, Ashland. Stuhr Museum of the Prairie Pioneer, Grand Island.

Memorable events Acquired as part of Louisiana Purchase 1803. Separate territory created by Kansas-Nebraska Act 1854. Size reduced after creation of Colorado and Dakota territories 1861. Statehood 1867. To encourage tree planting, becomes first state to observe Arbor Day 1872. Adopts unicameral legislature 1937. Oil discovered 1939. Population peaks at 1,605,000 1984–85.

Tourist information (877) NEBRASKA www.visitnebraska.org

▶ NEVADA

Set in the Great Basin desert, Nevada is one of the most barren places in North America, and the state receives less rainfall than any other. First explored by Europeans in 1776, it was 75 years before anyone thought of establishing a town in the area, and it did not last a decade. Miners came to Nevada early, but the discovery of the Comstock Lode in 1859 brought thousands. To add free-state Congressional votes, Nevada was hustled into the Union in 1864, three years before its boundaries were settled. That boom was over by the 1870s, and it took more gold and silver strikes in the early 1900s, as well as the discovery of copper, to get the economy rolling again. The mainstay of the economy since World War II has been the gambling industry, which generates virtually half of all tax revenues. Since the 1990s, Nevada has on and off been the fastest growing state in the union, with skyrocketing tourism fueling much of the growth.

Name From Spanish, meaning "snow-covered sierra." **Nicknames** Sagebrush State, Silver State. **Capital** Carson City. **Entered union** Oct. 31, 1864 (36th). **Motto** "All for our country."

Emblems Animal Desert bighorn sheep. **Bird** Mountain bluebird. **Flower** Sagebrush. **Fossil** Icthyosaur. **Grass** Indian ricegrass. **Metal** Silver. **Song** "Home Means Nevada." **Tree** Single-leaf piñon. **Land Total area** 110,561 sq. mi (7th), incl. 735 sq. mi. inland water. **Borders** Oreg., Idaho, Utah, Ariz., Calif. **Rivers** Colorado, Humboldt. **Lakes** Pyramid, Walker, Winnemucca. **Other notable features** Black Rock Desert, Carson Sink, Humboldt Salt Marsh, Mojave Desert.
Elected officials Gov. Jim Gibbons (R, term exp. 2011). Lt. Gov. Brian Krolicki (R). Sec. State Ross Miller (D). Atty. Gen. Catherine Cortez Masto (D).
People (July 2009 est.) 2,643,085 (35th). Race/ Hispanic Origin: White 80.9%. Black 8.1%. Indian 1.5%. Asian 6.2%. Pacific Islander 0.5%. Two or more races 2.8%. Hispanic 25.7%.
Cities (2006) Las Vegas 552,539. Henderson 240,614. Reno 210,255. North Las Vegas 197,567. Sunrise Manor 191,858. Paradise 186,370. Spring Valley 172,110. Enterprise 119,100. Sparks 83,959. Carson City 55,289.
Business Gross State Product, 2008: $103.2 bil. **Leading Sectors of GSP:** Services 31.82%; Finance, insurance, and real estate 18.76%; Hotels and other lodging places 14.31%. *Fortune 500* **Companies (2009):** 2.
Famous natives Andre Agassi, tennis player. Walter Van Tilburg Clark (b. Me.), author. Sarah Winnemucca Hopkins, interpeter/teacher. John William MacKay, miner. William Morris Stewart (b. N.Y.), lawyer/senator.
Noteworthy places Death Valley Natl. Monument. Las Vegas. Lehman Caves Natl. Monument. Valley of the Fire State Park, Overton.
Memorable events Francisco Tomás Garcés explores area 1775–76. Jedediah Smith, trader, crosses region 1826–27. Old Spanish Trail (1830) and California Trail (1833) cross region. John Frémont explores area 1843–45. To United States after Mexican War 1846. Genoa, first settlement in Nevada, founded as Mormon Station 1849. Gold of Comstock Lode discovered 1859. Organized as separate territory 1861. Statehood 1864. Nevada legalizes gambling 1931. Hoover Dam built on Colorado River 1935. Nuclear tests begun at Yucca Flats 1951. In 1991 the annual Burning Man art festival and week-long experimental society moves to the Black Rock Desert near the California border. Population grows more than 550 percent 1950–88, and 25 percent in 1990s, but slowed as the housing bubble burst at the end of the first decade of the 2000s.
Tourist information (800) NEVADA8
www.travelnevada.com

▶**NEW HAMPSHIRE**
New Hampshire has a disproportionate influence on presidential elections because by state law its primary must fall at least one week before any other state's (though Iowa's caucuses can come earlier). Through the Colonial era, mainstays of the economy were fishing, trade and farming, but eventually Boston proved more suitable for trade and New Hampshire's stubborn land was outproduced by the more fertile valleys to the south and west. The state's economy receded until the beginning of the Industrial Revolution, when there was tremendous growth in textile-producing mill towns in the Merrimack River Valley. The mills began to close after World War I, and the state's economy faltered again. Improvement came as high-tech firms from Boston sought refuge in New Hampshire's favorable tax climate. The state's economy was pummeled by the severe New England recession in the early 1990s, but has rebounded since.
Name For English county of Hampshire. **Nickname** Granite State. **Capital** Concord. **Entered union** June 21, 1788 (9th). **Motto** "Live free or die." **Emblems Amphibian** Spotted newt. **Bird** Purple finch. **Flower** Purple lilac. **Gem** Smoke quartz. **Insect** Ladybug. **Mineral** Beryl. **Song** "Old New Hampshire." **Tree** White birch.
Land Total area 9,350 sq. mi (46th), incl. 382 sq. mi. inland water. **Borders** Quebec, Maine, Atlantic Ocean, Mass., Vt. **Rivers** Connecticut, Merrimack, Piscataqua, Saco, Salmon Falls. **Lakes** First Connecticut, Francis, Newfound, Ossipee, Sunapee, Winnipesaukee. **Other notable features** Isles of Shoals, White Mts. (Mt. Washington 6,288 ft., highest peak in Northeast).
Elected officials Gov. John Lynch (D). Sec. State William Gardner (D). Atty. Gen. Kelly A. Ayotte (R).
People (July 2009 est.) 1,324,575 (41st). Race/ Hispanic Origin: White 95.5%. Black 1.2%. Indian 0.3%. Asian 1.9%. Two or more races 1.1%. Hispanic 2.6%.
Cities (2006) Manchester 109,497. Nashua 87,157. Concord 42,378. Derry 34,103. Rochester 30,117. Salem 29,580. Dover 28,422. Merrimack 26,613. Londonderry 24,879. Hudson 24,729.
Business Gross State Product, 2008: $50.5 bil. **Leading Sectors of GSP:** Finance, insurance, and real estate 24.99%; Services 21.57%; Manufacturing 16.13%. *Fortune 500* **Companies (2009):** 0.
Famous natives Salmon P. Chase, jurist. Ralph Adams Cram, architect. Mary Baker Eddy, founder, Church of Christ, Scientist. Daniel Chester French, sculptor. Horace Greeley, journalist. Sarah Buell Hale, author. Franklin Pierce, U.S. president. Augustus Saint-Gaudens (b. Ireland), sculptor. Alan Shepard, astronaut. Daniel Webster, politician. Eleazar Wheelock (b. Conn.), Dartmouth founder.
Noteworthy places Currier Gallery of Art, Manchester. The Flume (gorge). Franconia Notch. Isles of Shoals. Lake Winnipesaukee. Mt. Washington. Shaker Village, Canterbury. St. Gaudens Natl. Hist. Site. Strawbery Bank. White Mountains Natl. Forest.
Memorable events Martin Pring sails along coast 1603. Champlain explores area 1604. John Smith visits Isles of Shoals 1614. Included in king's grant to John Mason and Sir Ferdinando Gorges 1622. First settlers at Little Harbor, near Portsmouth 1623. Made separate royal province 1679, though under Massachusetts governor 1699–1741. Rogers's Rangers halt Indian raids 1759. New Hampshire patriots seize British fort at Portsmouth and drive out Royal governor 1775. Province relinquishes claims to New Connecticut (Vermont) 1782. First textile mill built 1803. Treaty of Portsmouth ends Russo-Japanese War 1905. Bretton Woods conference leads to establishment of International Monetary Fund 1944. First state to adopt lottery to support public education 1963. Passes legislation to allow same-sex marriage, 2009.
Tourist information (603) 271-2665
www.visitnh.gov

▶**NEW JERSEY**
With the entire state population classified as living in metro areas, New Jersey is the most densely populated state, 15 times the national average, and its public schools are among the very best in the nation. Pharmaceuticals and chemicals are

New Jersey's leading products, but the next most important industry is tourism, because of its beautiful ocean beaches, many lovely lakes, and because of the money tourists spend at the gaming tables of Atlantic City. What earns New Jersey its nick-name, the Garden State, is its extensive small-scale agriculture, which produces tomatoes, dairy products, asparagus, blueberries, corn and poultry.

New Jersey lies on a plain between Philadelphia and New York City, two larger neighbors that have overshadowed New Jersey on the national scene since colonial days. Yet during the Revolution, more than 100 battles were fought on New Jersey soil, and today the overwhelming majority of containerized shipping in the Port of New York and New Jersey is shipped from New Jersey terminals. Per capita income is always among the top five in the nation.

Name After English Channel Island of Jersey. **Nickname** Garden State. **Capital** Trenton. **Entered union** Dec. 18, 1787 (3rd). **Motto** "Liberty and prosperity."

Emblems **Animal** Horse. **Bird** Eastern goldfinch. **Flower** Violet. **Insect** Honeybee. **Memorial tree** Dogwood. **Tree** Red oak.

Land **Total area** 8,721 sq. mi (47th), incl. 1,304 sq. mi. inland water. **Borders** N.Y., Atlantic Ocean, Del., Pa. **Rivers** Delaware, Hackensack, Hudson, Passaic. **Lakes** Greenwood, Hopatcong, Round Valley Res., Spruce Run. **Other notable features** Delaware Water Gap, Kittatinny Mts., Palisades, Pine Barrens, Ramapo Mts.

Elected officials Gov. Chris Christie (R). Sec. State Kim Guadagno (R). Atty. Gen. Paula T. Dow (D).

People (July 2009 est.) 8,707,739 (11th). Race/Hispanic Origin: White 76.0%. Black 14.5%. Indian 0.3%. Asian 7.7%. Pacific Islander 0.1%. Two or more races 1.4%. Hispanic 16.3%.

Cities (2006) Newark 281,402. Jersey City 241,789. Paterson 148,708. Elizabeth 126,179. Edison 99,523. Toms River 93,500. Trenton 83,923. Clifton 79,606. Camden 79,318. Brick Township 78,232.

Business **Gross State Product, 2008:** $390.4 bil. **Leading Sectors of GSP:** Finance, insurance, and real estate 24.66%; Services 22.85%; Real estate 15.71%. *Fortune 500* **Companies (2009):** 21.

Famous natives Buzz Aldrin, astronaut. Count Basie, jazz musician. William J. Brennan, jurist. Aaron Burr, politician. Grover Cleveland, U.S. president. James Fenimore Cooper, novelist/historian. Stephen Crane, author. Thomas Edison, inventor. Albert Einstein (b. Germany), nuclear physicist. Waldo Frank, author. Joyce Kilmer, poet. Jerry Lewis, actor. Jack Nicholson, actor. Zebulon Pike, explorer. Molly Pitcher, Revolutionary War heroine. Paul Robeson, actor/singer. Walter Schirra, astronaut. Frank Sinatra, singer. Bruce Springsteen, the boss. Alfred Stieglitz, photographer. Meryl Streep, actress. Aaron Montgomery Ward, merchant. William Carlos Williams, poet. Woodrow Wilson (b. Va.), U.S. president.

Noteworthy places Atlantic City. Cape May Historic District. Edison Natl. Hist. Site, West Orange. Lakehurst Naval Air Station. Liberty State Park, Jersey City. Morristown Natl. Hist. Park. Newark Museum. Palisades Interstate Park. Pine Barrens wilderness area. Princeton University. Walt Whitman House, Camden.

Memorable events Giovanni de Verrazano explores 1524. Hudson explores up Hudson River 1609. Dutch settlers establish Ft. Nassau 1623. New Jersey taken over by British and organized as colony under Sir George Carteret 1665. Major battles of Revolution at Trenton (1776), Princeton (1777), and Monmouth (1778). Women given vote at Elizabethtown 1800. Voting rights restricted to men 1807. Adopts state constitution 1844. Passenger ship *Morro Castle* burns off Asbury Park; 134 die 1934. Dirigible *Hindenburg* explodes while mooring at Lakehurst; 36 die 1937. New Jersey Turnpike linking New York City and Philadelphia opens 1952. Five days of race riots in Newark leave 26 dead 1967. Gambling legalized in Atlantic City 1978. State enacts strictest gun legislation in U.S. 1990. In 2007 Gov. Corzine signs into law legislation to eliminate the death penalty, making New Jersey the first state to do so since 1965.

Tourist information (800) VISITNJ www.visitnj.org

▶ NEW MEXICO

The development problem of the western states is shared by New Mexico, which of all states has the smallest percentage of its area covered by water. While also rich in other resources, it is the uranium capital of the world. The state mineral tax brings in a large percentage of state revenues, some of which g into permanent endowments. Distribution of wealth in New Mexico remains uneven, but Hispanics, who tend to register as Democrats, vote in roughly the same ways as Anglos. A higher percentage of Native Americans live in New Mexico than in any other state.

Today, mining's influence on the state economy has waned in favor of service industry jobs. Despite the enormous governmental investment in research at Los Alamos, where the atom bomb was born, the highly classified nature of this work limits the development of related industry.

Name By Spanish explorers after Mexico. **Nickname** Land of Enchantment. **Capital** Santa Fe. **Entered union** Jan. 6, 1912 (47th). **Motto** *Crescit eundo* (It grows as it goes).

Emblems **Animal** Black bear. **Bird** Roadrunner (chaparral bird). **Fish** Cutthroat trout. **Flower** Yucca. **Fossil** *Coelphysis* dinosaur. **Gem** Turquoise. **Songs** "O, Fair New Mexico," "Así es Nuevo Mejico." **Tree** Piñon. **Vegetables** Frijole, chili.

Land **Total area** 121,589 sq. mi (5th), incl. 234 sq. mi. inland water. **Borders** Colo., Okla., Tex., Chihuahua, Ariz. **Rivers** Gila, Pecos, Rio Grande, Zuni. **Lakes** Conchas Res., Eagle Nest, Elephant Butte Res., Navajo Res., Ute Res. **Mountains** Chuska, Guadalupe, Sacramento, San Andres, Sangre de Cristo. **Other notable features** Carlsbad Caverns, Continental Divide, Staked Plain.

Elected officials Gov. Bill Richardson (D, term exp. 2010). Lt. Gov. Diane Denish (D). Sec. State Mary Herrera (D). Atty. Gen. Gary King (D).

People (July 2009 est.) 2,009,671 (36th). Race/Hispanic Origin: White 84.0%. Black 3.0%. Indian 9.7%. Asian 1.4%. Pacific Islander 0.1%. Two or more races 1.8%. Hispanic 44.9%.

Cities (2006) Albuquerque 504,949. Las Cruces 86,268. Santa Fe 72,056. Rio Rancho 71,607. Roswell 45,582. Farmington 43,573. South Valley 40,500. Alamogordo 36,069. Clovis 33,258. Hobbs 29,292.

Business **Gross State Product, 2008:** $61.4 bil. **Leading Sectors of GSP:** Services 18.30%; Government 18.05%; Manufacturing 13.61%. *Fortune 500* **Companies (2009):** 0.

Famous natives William "Billy the Kid" Bonney (b. N.Y.), outlaw. Peter Hurd, artist. Archbishop Jean Baptiste Lamy (b. France), missionary. Georgia O'Keeffe (b. Wis.), artist. Popé, Tewa Pueblo chief. Harrison Schmitt, astronaut.

Noteworthy places Aztec Ruins Natl. Monument. Bandelier Natl. Monument. Capulin Mt. Natl. Monument. Carlsbad Caverns Natl. Park. Chaco Culture Natl. Hist. Park. El Morro Natl. Monument. Ft. Union Natl. Monument. Gila Cliff Dwellings Natl. Monument. Museum of New Mexico, Santa Fe. Pecos Mission. Salinas Mission. Santa Fe Opera. Wheelwright Museum of the American Indian, Santa Fe. White Sands Natl. Monument.

Memorable events Marcos de Niza enters Zuni country 1539. Juan de Oñate establishes first Spanish settlement on Rio Grande near Espanola 1598. Santa Fe founded; becomes capital of New Mexico 1710. Santa Fe Trail from Independence, Missouri, completed; Mexico secedes from Spain 1821. Manuel Armijo suppresses revolt against Mexican rule (1837); defeats invasion from Republic of Texas (1841). Land annexed by United States after Mexican-American War 1848. Organized as territory with Arizona and part of Colorado 1850. Lincoln County War pits cattlemen against merchants 1878–81. Statehood; 17 killed in raid by Pancho Villa 1912. Los Alamos selected as first research and development facility for nuclear weapons 1942. First atom bomb exploded at Alamagordo Air Base 1945.

Tourist information (505) 827-7400
www.newmexico.org

▶ NEW YORK

New York's greatest and most inviting asset has always been its strategic location and long arteries into the hinterland. New York Bay is one of the great natural harbors of the world, and the broad Hudson River is one of the most fortunately placed. After the opening of the Erie Canal between the Hudson and Lake Erie in 1825, New York City became the trading center for the Midwest as well as the Hudson Valley and the Atlantic Coast. Buffalo also experienced a boom, becoming a major Great Lakes industrial port. New York is still the first state in number of manufacturing establishments and employees. Wall Street alone employs half a million people.

Although New York's population grew by nearly half a million people between 1980 and 1990, its relatively slow rate of growth resulted in a loss of three Congressional seats—an indication of the change in the state's political clout. As its place among the 50 states has fallen by some measures, New York City's worldwide importance in business, culture and communications has risen.

Name For Duke of York, later James II, of England. **Nickname** Empire State. **Capital** Albany. **Entered union** July 26, 1788 (11th). **Motto** *Excelsior* (Higher).

Emblems **Animal** Beaver. **Beverage** Milk. **Bird** Bluebird. **Fish** Brook or speckled trout. **Flower** Rose. **Fossil** Prehistoric crab (*Eurypterus remipes*). **Fruit** Apple. **Gem** Garnet. **Song** "I Love New York." **Tree** Sugar maple.

Land **Total area** 54,556 sq. mi (27th), incl. 7,342 sq. mi. inland water. **Borders** Lake Ontario, Ontario, Quebec, Vt., Mass., Conn., Atlantic Ocean, N.J., Pa., Lake Erie. **Rivers** Allegheny, Delaware, Genesee, Hudson, Mohawk, New York State Barge Canal, Niagara, St. Lawrence, Susquehanna. **Lakes** Cayuga, Champlain, Chautauqua, Erie, George, Oneida, Ontario, Seneca. **Mountains** Adirondack (Mt. Marcy 5,344 ft.), Allegheny, Berkshire Hills, Catskill, Kittatinny, Ramapo. **Other notable features** Hudson Valley, Mohawk Valley, Niagara Falls, Palisades, Thousand Islands.

Elected officials Gov. David Paterson (D, term exp. 2010). Lt. Gov. Richard Ravitch (D). Sec. State Lorriane Cortes-Vazquez (D). Atty. Gen. Andrew M. Cuomo (D).

People (July 2009 est.) 19,541,453 (3rd). Race/Hispanic Origin: White 73.4%. Black, 17.3%. Indian 0.6%. Asian 7.0%. Pacific Islander 0.1%. Two or more races 1.6%. Hispanic 16.7%.

Cities (2006) New York 8,214,426. Buffalo 276,059. Rochester 208,123. Yonkers 197,852. Syracuse 140,658. Albany 93,963. Cheektowaga 80,700. New Rochelle 73,446. Mount Vernon 68,395. Schenectady 61,560.

Business **Gross State Product, 2008:** $964.8 bil. **Leading Sectors of GSP:** Finance, insurance, and real estate 34.23%; Services 23.01%; Real Estate 14.10%. *Fortune 500* **Companies (2009):** 56.

Famous natives Woody Allen, director. John Jacob Astor (b. Germany), merchant. Humphrey Bogart, actor. George Burns, actor. Aaron Copland, composer. Agnes de Mille, choreographer. George Eastman, camera inventor. Millard Fillmore, U.S. president. Lou Gehrig, baseball player. George Gershwin, composer. Julia Ward Howe, reformer. Washington Irving, author. Henry James, author. Vince Lombardi, football coach. Groucho Marx, comedian. Herman Melville, author. Ogden Nash, poet/humorist. Eugene O'Neill, playwright. Otetiani "Red Jacket", Seneca chief. Channing E. Phillips, minister/reformer. John D. Rockefeller, industrialist. Norman Rockwell, illustrator. Richard Rodgers, composer. Franklin Delano Roosevelt, U.S. president. Theodore Roosevelt, U.S. president. Jonas Salk, physician. Elizabeth Ann Seton, first American saint. Elizabeth Cady Stanton, suffragette. James Johnson Sweeney, art critic. Martin Van Buren, U.S. president. Mae West, actress. E.B. White, author. Walt Whitman, poet.

Noteworthy places Albright-Knox Gallery of American Art, Buffalo. American Merchant Marine Museum, Kings Point. Baseball Hall of Fame, Cooperstown. Bear Mt. State Park. Buffalo Museum of Science. Corning Glass Center, Corning. Erie Canal Museum, Syracuse. Farmers' Museum, Cooperstown. Fenimore House, Cooperstown. Franklin D. Roosevelt Natl. Hist. Site, Hyde Park. Ft. Stanwix Natl. Monument, Rome. Ft. Ticonderoga. Hudson Valley. Mohawk Valley. Niagara Falls. Palisades Interstate Park. Saratoga Natl. Hist. Park. Vanderbilt Museum, Hyde Park. U.S. Military Academy, West Point. Women's Rights Natl. Hist. Park, Seneca Falls. **New York City** American Academy of Arts & Sciences. American Museum of Natural History. Bronx Zoo. Brooklyn Botanical Garden. Brooklyn Museum. Cathedral of St. John the Divine. Cooper-Hewitt Museum. Federal Hall. Fraunces Tavern. Frick Collection. Guggenheim Museum. Hispanic Society of America. Jewish Museum. Lincoln Center for the Performing Arts. Metropolitan Museum of Art. Museum of Modern Art. Museum of the American Indian. N.Y. Public Library. Coney Island. N.Y. Stock Exchange. Rockefeller Center. South Street Seaport Museum. Statue of Liberty. United Nations.

Memorable events Giovanni de Verrazano sails into New York Bay 1524. Samuel de Champlain sails down the St. Lawrence River 1603. Henry Hudson sails up Hudson River 1609. Dutch establish Ft. Orange (Albany) 1614. Peter Minuit buys Manhattan Island and founds colony of New Amsterdam 1625. British take New Amsterdam and name it New York 1664. Ethan Allen takes Ft. Ticonderoga 1775. George Washington inaugurated president New York City 1789. U.S. Military Academy founded West

Point 1802. Erie Canal opened 1825. Statue of Liberty dedicated 1886. New York City includes Manhattan, Bronx, Queens, Brooklyn, and Staten Island 1898. President William McKinley assassinated in Buffalo 1901. UN headquarters established at New York City 1945. St. Lawrence Seaway opened 1959. One-fourth of New York City below poverty level, 1984. Terrorist attack destroys World Trade Center in New York City, killing 3,000 people 2001. Governor Eliot Spitzer resigns after federal investigation 2008.
Tourist information (800) CALL-NYS www.iloveny.com

▶NORTH CAROLINA

At the time of the Revolution, tobacco and rice plantations dominated the economy of the eastern part of the state, which in turn dominated the legislature. Next to last to ratify the Constitution, North Carolina was the last Southern state to secede from the Union. The Civil War cost North Carolina dearly; reconstruction was short-lived, and blacks were effectively disenfranchised again by the turn of the century. Since World War II, the state has grown increasingly prosperous, especially in the "academic triangle" that encloses the University of North Carolina at Chapel Hill, Duke, and North Carolina State. The traditional industries of textiles, furniture, and tobacco still lead, partly because of diversification within them. North Carolina benefits from the general Sunbelt boom and from an influx of foreign capital; it maintains a healthy manufacturing sector.

Name For King Charles I (*Carolus* is Latin for Charles). **Nicknames** Tarheel State, Old North State. **Capital** Raleigh. **Entered union** Nov. 21, 1789 (12th). **Motto** *Esse quam videri* (To be rather than to seem).
Emblems **Bird** Cardinal. **Fish** Channel bass. **Flower** Dogwood. **Insect** Honeybee. **Precious stone** Emerald. **Reptile** Eastern box turtle. **Rock** Granite. **Shell** Scotch bonnet. **Song** "The Old North State." **Tree** Pine.
Land **Total area** 53,819 sq. mi (28th), incl. 5,108 sq. mi. inland water. **Borders** Va., Atlantic Ocean, S.C., Tenn., Georgia. **Rivers** Pee Dee, Roanoke, Yadkin. **Lakes** Buggs Island, High Rock, Mattamuskeet, Norman, Waccamaw. **Mountains** Black, Blue Ridge, Great Smoky, Unaka. **Other notable features** Great Dismal Swamp, Mount Mitchell, Outer Banks, Pamlico Sound.
Elected officials Gov. Bev Purdue (D). Lt. Gov. Walter Dalton (D). Sec. State Elaine F. Marshall (D). Atty. Gen. Roy Cooper (D).
People (July 2009 est.) 9,380,884 (10th). Race/Hispanic Origin: White 73.9%. Black 21.6%. Indian 1.3%. Asian 1.9%. Pacific Islander 0.1%. Two or more races 1.2%. Hispanic 7.4%.
Cities (2006) Charlotte 630,478. Raleigh 356,321. Greensboro 236,865. Durham 209,009. Winston-Salem 196,990. Fayetteville 168,033. Cary 112,414. High Point 97,796. Wilmington 95,944. Asheville 72,789.
Business **Gross State Product, 2008:** $329.4 bil. **Leading Sectors of GSP:** Manufacturing 21.38%; Finance, insurance, and real estate 18.98%; Services 17.41%. *Fortune 500* **Companies (2009):** 13.
Famous natives Benjamin Newton Duke and James Buchanan Duke, industrialists/philanthropists. Richard J. Gatling, inventor. Billy Graham, minister. Andy Griffith, actor. O. Henry, writer. Andrew Johnson, U.S. president. William Rufus King, politician. Charles Kuralt, journalist. Meadowlark Lemon, athlete. Dolley

Madison, First Lady. Thelonius Monk, musician. Edward R. Murrow, journalist. James Knox Polk, U.S. president. Moses Waddell, Confederate general. Thomas Wolfe, author.
Noteworthy places Bennett Place. Blue Ridge Natl. Parkway. Cape Hatteras and Cape Lookout Natl. Seashore. Carl Sandburg home, Hendersonville. Ft. Raleigh. Great Smoky Mountains Natl. Park. Great Smoky Mountains Natl. Hist. Park. Guilford Courthouse Natl. Military Park. Mint Museum, Charlotte. Moores Creek Natl. Battlefield. North Carolina Maritime Museum, Beaufort. North Carolina Museum of Art, Raleigh. Roanoke Island. Wright Brothers Natl. Memorial, Kitty Hawk.
Memorable events Part of Carolina grant given to eight noblemen by Charles II 1663. Culpepper's Rebellion in reaction to unfair tax collection policies 1677. Tuscarora lose war against European immigrants 1713. Proprietors sell rights to Crown; becomes royal province 1729. Mecklenburg Declaration (1775), forerunner of Declaration of Independence. Becomes first colony to sanction explicitly declaration of independence from Britain in Apr. 1776. Gen. Charles Cornwallis wins Battle of Guilford Courthouse, but British lose control of colony 1781. Ratifies Constitution 1789. Gives up claims to western territories, now part of Tennessee 1790. Establishes first state university system in United States 1829. Cherokees driven out of North Carolina to Oklahoma 1838. Secedes 1861. Readmitted to Union 1868. American Tobacco Company founded 1890. Wright brothers launch first successful airplane at Kitty Hawk 1903. Confrontation between Ku Klux Klan and anti-Klan demonstrators leaves five dead; 12 Klansmen charged with first-degree murder 1979.
Tourist information (800) VISIT-NC www.visitnc.com

▶NORTH DAKOTA

The first permanent settlers in North Dakota were Scots-Canadians who settled at Pembina on the Red River near the Canadian border, and who traded primarily with Winnipeg and St. Paul. The arrival of the Northern Pacific Railway in 1872 created a surge of huge farms, many of which were wiped out by drought and harsh winters in the 1880s. There followed a huge influx of Norwegians and Germans whose influence is still very apparent today. North Dakota's economy is heavily agricultural and leads the nation in production of wheat. Farming is centered in the fertile Red River of the North Valley, with livestock throughout the rest of the state.

Name For northern section of Dakota territory; *dakota* is Sioux word for "allies." **Nicknames** Sioux State, Peace Garden State, Flickertail State. **Capital** Bismarck. **Entered union** Nov. 2, 1889 (39th). **Motto** "Liberty and union, now and forever, one and inseparable."
Emblems **Beverage** Milk. **Bird** Western meadowlark. **Fish** Northern pike. **Flower** Wild prairie rose. **Fossil** Teredo petrified wood. **Grass** Western wheatgrass. **March** "Spirit of North Dakota." **Song** "North Dakota Hymn." **Tree** American elm.
Land **Total area** 70,700 sq. mi (19th), incl. 1,724 sq. mi. inland water. **Borders** Saskatchewan, Manitoba, Minn., S.Dak., Mont. **Rivers** Missouri, Red River of the North. **Lakes** Ashtabula, Devils, Oahe, Sakakawea. **Other notable features** Geographical center of North America, Missouri Plateau, Red River Valley, Rolling Drift Prairie.

Elected officials   Gov. John Hoeven (R, term exp. 2010). Lt. Gov. John Dalrymple (R). Sec. State Alvin A. Jaeger (R). Atty. Gen. Wayne Stenehjem (R).
People   (July 2009 est.) 646,844 (48th). Race/ Hispanic Origin: White 91.4%. Black 1.1%. Indian 5.6%. Asian 0.7%. Pacific Islander 0.1%. Two or more races 1.2%. Hispanic 2.1%.
Cities   (2006) Fargo 90,056. Bismarck 58,333. Grand Forks 50,372. Minot 34,745. West Fargo 21,508. Jamestown 14,680. Mandan 17,449. Dickinson 15,636. Williston 12,303. Wahpeton 7,907.
Business   Gross State Product, 2008: $24.3 bil. **Leading Sectors of GSP:** Services 19.27%; Government 15.60%; Finance, insurance, and real estate 14.58%. **Fortune 500 Companies (2009):** 1.
Famous natives   Angie Dickinson, actress. John Bernard Flannagan, sculptor. Louis L'Amour, novelist. Peggy Lee, singer. Roger Maris, baseball player. Eric Sevareid, broadcaster. Vihjalmur Stefansson (b. Canada), ethnologist. Lawrence Welk, entertainer.
Noteworthy places   Arrowwood Natl. Wildlife Refuge. Dinosaur Museum, Dickinson. Ft. Abraham Lincoln State Park. Ft. Union Trading Post Natl. Hist. Site. International Peace Garden. Knife River Indian Villages Natl. Hist. Site. Theodore Roosevelt Natl. Park, the Badlands.
Memorable events   Pierre Gaultier de Varennes, sieur de Vérendrye first European to visit area 1738. United States acquires half of territory in Louisiana Purchase 1803. Meriwether Lewis and William Clark expedition builds Ft. Mandan 1804–5. First permanent settlement at Pembina 1812. Britain cedes western half of state to United States 1818. Missouri River steamboats reach territory 1838. First railroad arrives 1873. Statehood 1889. First state to hold presidential primary 1912. Garrison Dam completed forming Lake Sakakawea; gambling (blackjack) legalized 1981. Red River floods, devastating agriculture, 1997.
Tourist information   (800) HELLO-ND
www.ndtourism.com

▶**OHIO**
The first settlements in Ohio were Marietta, in 1788, and Cincinnati in 1789, on the Ohio River, but significant migration into the state didn't occur until after the War of 1812. Shipping flourished in the 1820s and 1830s thanks to a network of canals connecting the Ohio and Lake Erie. Since 1959 the St. Lawrence Seaway has helped keep Ohio among the top five exporting states. Heavy industry also flourished in the northern cities that had access to coal and iron ore from the Lake Superior region. The 1870s saw the development of a manufacturing base that later became an integral part of the automotive industry. Although Ohio's economy has traditionally been well balanced between agriculture, industry, mining, and trade, the recession of the early 1980s weakened manufacturing, triggered flight from the industrial cities, and saw a dramatic shift to a service economy and to high-tech industry.
Name From the Iroquois *oheo*, "beautiful."
Nickname Buckeye State. **Capital** Columbus. **Entered union** Mar. 1, 1803 (17th). **Motto** "With God, all things are possible."
Emblems   Beverage Tomato juice. **Bird** Cardinal. **Flower** Scarlet carnation. **Gem** Ohio flint. **Insect** Ladybug. **Song** "Beautiful Ohio." **Tree** Buckeye.
Land   Total area 44,825 sq. mi (34th), incl. 3,877 sq. mi. inland water. **Borders** Mich., Lake Erie, Pa., W.Va., Ky., Ind. **Rivers** Cuyahoga, Maumee, Miami, Muskingum, Ohio, Sandusky, Scioto. **Lakes** Berlin Res., Dillon Res., Erie, Mosquito Res., St. Mary's.

Elected officials   Gov. Ted Strickland (D, term exp. 2011). Lt. Gov. Lee Fisher (D). Sec. State. Jennifer Brunner (D). Atty. Gen. Richard Cordray (D).
People   (July 2009 est.) 11,542,645 (7th). Race/ Hispanic Origin: White 84.8%. Black 12.0%. Indian 0.3%. Asian 1.6%. Two or more races 1.3%. Hispanic 2.6%.
Cities   (2006) Columbus 733,203. Cleveland 444,313. Cincinnati 332,252. Toledo 298,446. Akron 209,704. Dayton 156,771. Youngstown 81,520. Parma 80,009. Canton 78,924. Lorain 70,592.
Business   Gross State Product, 2008: $385.6 bil. **Leading Sectors of GSP:** Manufacturing 21.30%; Services 19.61%; Finance, insurance, and real estate 17.78%. **Fortune 500 Companies (2009):** 27.
Famous natives   Sherwood Anderson, writer. Neil Armstrong, astronaut. George Bellows, artist. Ambrose Bierce, author. George Armstrong Custer, army officer. Paul Laurence Dunbar, poet. Thomas A. Edison, inventor. James A. Garfield, U.S. president. John Glenn, astronaut/politician. Ulysses S. Grant, U.S. president/general. Zane Grey, author. Warren G. Harding, U.S. president. Benjamin Harrison, U.S. president. Rutherford B. Hayes, U.S. president. Bob Hope, entertainer. William McKinley, U.S. president. Annie Oakley, markswoman. Ransom Eli Olds, carmaker. Eddie Rickenbacker, pilot. William Sherman, army officer. William Howard Taft, U.S. president/chief justice. Art Tatum, pianist. Tecumseh, Shawnee chief. James Thurber, humorist. Orville Wright, airplane inventor.
Noteworthy places   Air Force Museum, Dayton. National Underground Railroad Freedom Center, Cincinnati. Cleveland Museum of Art. Cleveland Museum of Natural History. Columbus Museum of Art. Great Lakes Historical Society Museum, Vermilion. Cincinnati Museum of Natural History. Mound City Group Natl. Monument, Chillicothe. Neil Armstrong Air and Space Museum, Wapakoneta. Ohio River Museum, Marietta. Pro Football Hall of Fame, Canton. Rock and Roll Hall of Fame, Cleveland. Toledo Museum of Art.
Memorable events   Hopewell Mound-Builders present throughout state prior to arrival of Miamis, Shawnees, Wyandots, and Delawares. Conflicting claims by France, Virginia, Connecticut, and New York 1609–1786. René-Roger Cavelier de La Salle visits region 1669–70. Becomes part of Northwest Territory 1787. First settlement at Marietta 1788. Gen. "Mad" Anthony Wayne beats Tecumseh at Battle of Fallen Timbers 1794. Enters Union 1803. Harrison beats Tecumseh at Battle of Tippecanoe 1811. Oliver Hazard Perry beats British fleet at Battle of Put-in-Bay 1813. Ohio and Erie Canal completed 1832. First game of Cincinnati Red Stockings, first professional baseball team, 1869. Dayton flood kills 400 in Miami River Valley; damage put at $100 million 1913. Carl B. Stokes elected mayor of Cleveland, first black mayor of major U.S. city 1967. Four students protesting Vietnam War killed by National Guard at Kent State University 1970.
Tourist information   (800) BUCKEYE
www.discoverohio.com

▶**OKLAHOMA**
French trappers entered the region of Oklahoma in the 1700s. In 1830 the land was designated the Indian Country, set aside for members of the Cherokees, Chickasaw, Choctaw, Creek, and Seminole deported from the southeast by the Indian Removal Act of 1830. These "Five Civilized Tribes," among others, fared well until the Civil War. They supported the Confederacy (some were actually

slave-holders), and in 1868 Col. George Armstrong Custer led a massacre of Cheyenne at the Battle of the Washita. Twenty years later the government abrogated its treaty commitments and opened the territory to settlement. Today the state has a distinctly southern character. The region bordering the Red River is known as "Little Dixie," and as many as two-thirds of all Oklahomans consider themselves born-again Christians.

Oklahoma has a diversified economy. The state led the country in oil and gas production through the 1920s. Agriculture was hit heavily by the dust bowl of the 1930s, and thousands of "Okies" fled west. While agriculture and petroleum are still vital to the economy, manufacturing is increasingly important. The state is crossed by two of the country's longest rivers. The Arkansas links Catoosa (near Tulsa) to the Gulf of Mexico and the Mississippi River system; but the Red River is not navigable in Oklahoma, and dissolved salts make it useless for agriculture, industry or residential purposes.

Name From the Choctaw *okla humma*, "land of the red people." **Nickname** Sooner State. **Capital** Oklahoma City. **Entered union** Nov. 16, 1907 (46th). **Motto** *Labor omnia vincit* (Work overcomes all obstacles).

Emblems **Animal** American buffalo. **Bird** Scissor-tailed flycatcher. **Colors** Green and white. **Fish** White bass. **Floral emblem** Mistletoe. **Grass** Indian grass. **Poem** "Howdy Folks." **Reptile** Collared lizard (mountain boomer). **Song** "Oklahoma!" **Stone** Barite rose (rose rock). **Tree** Redbud. **Waltz** "Oklahoma Wind."

Land Total area 69,898 sq. mi (20th), incl. 1,231 sq. mi. inland water. **Borders** Kans., Mo., Ark., Tex., N.Mex., Colo. **Rivers** Arkansas, Canadian, Cimarron, Red. **Lakes** Canton, Lake o' the Cherokees, Oologah, Texoma. **Other notable features** Ouachita Mts., Ozark Plateau, Staked Plain, Wichita Mts.

Elected officials Gov. Brad Henry (D, term exp. 2010). Lt. Gov. Jari Askins (D). Sec. State Susan Savage (D). Atty. Gen. Drew Edmondson (D).

People (July 2009 est.) 3,687,050 (28th). Race/Hispanic Origin: White 78.1%. Black 8.0%. Indian 8.0%. Asian 1.7%. Pacific Islander 0.1%. Two or more races 4.1%. Hispanic 7.6%.

Cities (2006) Oklahoma City 537,734. Tulsa 382,872. Norman 102,827. Broken Arrow 88,314. Lawton 87,540. Edmond 76,644. Midwest City 55,161. Moore 49,277. Enid 46,514. Stillwater 44,818.

Business **Gross State Product, 2008:** $106.9 bil. **Leading Sectors of GSP:** Services 18.73%; Government 16.81%; Manufacturing 13.89%. *Fortune 500* **Companies (2009):** 4.

Famous natives Ralph Ellison, author. Woody Guthrie, reformer/musician. Patrick J. Hurley, diplomat. Karl Jansky, electrical engineer. Mickey Mantle, baseball player. Wiley Post, aviator. Tony Randall, actor. Oral Roberts, evangelist. Will Rogers, humorist. Maria Tallchief, ballerina. Jim Thorpe, athlete.

Noteworthy places American Indian Hall of Fame, Anadarko. Chisholm Trail Museum, Kingfisher. Ft. Gibson Stockade, Muskogee. Natl. Cowboy Hall of Fame, Oklahoma City. Ouachita Natl. Forest. Pioneer Woman Museum, Ponca City. Wildlife Heritage Center Museum, Antlers. Will Rogers Memorial, Claremore.

Memorable events Francisco Vásquez de Coronado expedition in territory 1541. Except for panhandle, becomes part of Louisiana purchase 1803. Region made Indian Territory (not organized) in 1830 and becomes home of "Five Civilized Tribes"—Cherokee, Choctaw, Chickasaw, Creek, and Seminole—after they left the southeast on Trail of Tears 1828–46. United States acquires panhandle with annexation of Texas 1845. Territory opened to homesteaders 1889. Commercial oil well at Bartlesville 1897. Indian Territory and Oklahoma Territory merged and granted statehood 1907. Gov. John C. Walton impeached after declaring martial law to quell violence 1923. McClellan-Kerr Arkansas River Navigation system links Oklahoma to Mississippi, making Catoosa (Tulsa) major inland port 1971. Timothy McVeigh blows up Federal Building in Oklahoma City, killing 168 people 1995.

Tourist information (800) 652-6552
www.travelok.com

▶ OREGON

Although the Lewis and Clark expedition reached the mouth of the Columbia River in 1805, interest in the area was kindled by the Hudson's Bay Company and later by Jason Lee, a Methodist minister who settled near Salem in 1834. After the decline of the fur trade, lumbering became the most important industry in Oregon. Though lumbering and related industries are still leading employers—the state is the leading grower of Christmas trees—Oregon has benefited from the arrival of smaller computer and electronics firms leaving California in search of a more favorable business climate. Traditionally progressive, it is one of most active states in the environmental protection movement. Only one-third of the population is affiliated with an organized religion.

Name Unknown origin, first applied to Columbia River. **Nickname** Beaver State. **Capital** Salem. **Entered union** Feb. 14, 1859 (33rd). **Motto** "She flies with her own wings." **Poet laureate** William E. Stafford.

Emblems **Animal** Beaver. **Bird** Western meadowlark. **Dance** Square dance. **Fish** Chinook salmon. **Flower** Oregon grape. **Insect** Swallowtail butterfly. **Song** "Oregon, My Oregon." **Stone** Thunderegg. **Tree** Douglas fir.

Land Total area 98,381 sq. mi (9th), incl. 2,384 sq. mi. inland water. **Borders** Wash., Idaho, Nev., Calif., Pacific Ocean. **Rivers** Columbia, Snake, Willamette. **Mountains** Cascade Range, Coast Range, Klamath. **Other notable features** Willamette Valley.

Elected officials Gov. Ted Kulongoski (D, term exp. 2011). Sec. State Kate Brown (D). Atty. Gen. John Kroger (D).

People (July 2009 est.) 3,825,657 (27th). Race/Hispanic Origin: White 90.1%. Black 2.0%. Indian 1.4%. Asian 3.6%. Pacific Islander 0.3%. Two or more races 2.4%. Hispanic 11.0%.

Cities (2006) Portland 537,081. Salem 152,239. Eugene 146,356. Gresham 97,105. Beaverton 89,643. Hillsboro 87,732. Bend 71,892. Medford 71,138. Springfield 55,848. Corvallis 49,807.

Business **Gross State Product, 2008:** $147.1 bil. **Leading Sectors of GSP:** Manufacturing 25.50%; Durable Goods 22.00%; Services 18.20%. *Fortune 500* **Companies (2009):** 2.

Famous natives Beverly Cleary, author. In-mut-too-yah-lat-lat (Joseph), Nez Percé chief. Matt Groening, cartoonist. Ursula LeGuin (b. Calif.), author. Edwin Markham, poet. Dr. John McLoughlin, fur trader, "Father of Oregon". Linus Pauling, chemist. John Reed, author. William Simon U'Ren (b. Wis.), lawyer/reformer.

Noteworthy places Bonneville Dam, Columbia River. Columbia River Gorge. Columbia River Museum, Astoria. Crater Lake Natl. Park. Ft. Clatsop Natl. Monument. Hells Canyon. High Desert

Museum, Bend. John Day Fossil Beds Natl. Monument. Mt. Hood. Oregon Caves Natl. Monument. Oregon Dunes Natl. Recreation Area. Point Perpetua. Timberline Lodge.

Memorable events Sir Francis Drake turns away from fogbound coast of Pacific Northwest 1578. Capt. James Cook visits 1778. Mouth of Columbia River explored by Capt. Robert Gray, who claims region for U.S. 1792. Meriwether Lewis and George Rogers Clark expedition arrives at mouth of Columbia 1805. Claims to Oregon Territory, from California border to Alaska and east to Montana and Wyoming, relinquished by Spain (1819), Russia (1825), and Britain (1846). First settlers arrive Willamette Valley 1843. Organized as territory 1848. Statehood 1859. Railroad arrives 1883. Bonneville Dam completed 1937. Following severe rain and snow that claim 40 lives, Oregon declared disaster area 1964. First state to enact "bottle law" 1972. Snake River opened to navigation, linking Astoria to Lewiston, Idaho 1975.

Tourist information (800) 547-7842
www.traveloregon.com

▶PENNSYLVANIA, COMMONWEALTH OF

William Penn and his Quakers encouraged settlement and religious tolerance, and Pennsylvania was the first state to abolish slavery. In the late colonial period, Philadelphia was the cultural capital of the colonies. The first Continental Congress convened there in 1774, and it was the U.S. capital for a decade. With access to both the Great Lakes and to the Atlantic, Pennsylvanians took a lead in opening up the Midwest. Its resources include large coal deposits—which contribute to its iron-making capabilities—lumber, textiles, and leather. Leadership in these sectors lasted well into the 20th century, when Pennsylvania lost ground to Sunbelt states. As in many states, there has been growth in tourist and service industries, though machinery production and trade continue to expand significantly.

Name For Adm. William Penn, father of William Penn, founder of commonwealth. **Nickname** Keystone State. **Capital** Harrisburg. **Entered union** Dec. 12, 1787 (2nd). **Motto** "Virtue, liberty and independence."

Emblems **Animal** White-tailed deer. **Beautification and conservation plant** Penngift crown vetch. **Beverage** Milk. **Bird** Ruffed grouse. **Dog** Great Dane. **Fish** Brook trout. **Flower** Mountain laurel. **Insect** Firefly. **Tree** Hemlock.

Land Total area 46,055 sq. mi. (33rd), incl. 1,239 sq. mi. inland water. **Borders** N.Y., N.J., Del., Md., W.Va., Ohio, Lake Erie. **Rivers** Allegheny, Delaware, Juniata, Monongahela, Ohio, Schuylkill, Susquehanna. **Lakes** Allegheny Res., Erie, Pymatuning Res., Shenango Res. **Mountains** Allegheny, Kittatinny, Laurel Hills, Pocono.

Elected officials Gov. Edward Rendell (D, term exp. 2011). Lt. Gov. Joe Scarnati (R). Sec. Commonwealth Pedro Cortes (D). Atty. Gen. Tom Corbett (R).

People (July 2009 est.) 12,604,767 (6th). Race/Hispanic Origin: White 85.4%. Black 10.8%. Indian 0.2%. Asian 2.4%. Two or more races 1.1%. Hispanic 4.8%.

Cities (2006) Philadelphia 1,448,394. Pittsburgh 312,819. Allentown 107,294. Erie 102,036. Reading 81,183. Scranton 72,861. Bethlehem 72,704. Lancaster 54,779. Levittown 53,500. Harrisburg 47,164.

Business Gross State Product, 2008: $443.7 bil. Leading Sectors of GSP: Services 23.65%; Finance, insurance, and real estate 19.42%; Manu-

facturing 16.72%. *Fortune 500* **Companies (2009):** 24.

Famous natives Louisa May Alcott, author. Maxwell Anderson, playwright. James Buchanan, U.S. president. Alexander Calder, sculptor. Andrew Carnegie (b. Scotland), industrialist/philanthropist. Mary Cassatt, painter. Wilt Chamberlain, basketball player. Bill Cosby, comedian/philanthropist. Stephen Foster, songwriter. Benjamin Franklin (b. Mass.), inventor/statesman. Robert Fulton, inventor. Milton S. Hershey, chocolatier. George C. Marshall, statesman. Andrew W. Mellon, financier/philanthropist. Robert E. Peary, explorer. Betsy Ross, patriot. Andy Warhol, artist. Johnny Weissmuller, swimmer/actor. Benjamin West, painter.

Noteworthy places Academy of Natural Sciences, Philadelphia. Carnegie Institute, Pittsburgh. Delaware Water Gap Natl. Recreation Area. Ft. Necessity Natl. Battlefield. Franklin Institute, Philadelphia. Gettysburg Battlefield. Hugh Moore Hist. Park and Museums, Easton. Independence Natl. Hist. Park, Philadelphia. Liberty Bell, Carpenters Hall, Philadelphia. Pennsylvania Academy of Fine Arts, Philadelphia. Pennsylvania Dutch Country. Hershey Park and Factory, Hershey. Philadelphia Museum of Art. Pine Creek Gorge. Rodin Museum, Philadelphia. Valley Forge Natl. Hist. Park.

Memorable events Cornelis Jacobssen sails into Delaware Bay 1614. Swedes settle at Tinicum Island 1643. Charles II grants proprietary charter to William Penn 1681. First U.S. hospital established, in Philadelphia, 1751. Mason-Dixon Line establishes southern boundary of state 1763–67—later boundary between slave and nonslave states. Declaration of Independence (1776) and Constitution (1787) signed in Philadelphia. Becomes first state to abolish slavery 1780. Bank of North America becomes first bank chartered in United States 1781. Philadelphia capital of United States 1790–1800. First iron furnace in U.S. 1792. First oil well in the world driven near Titusville 1859. Battle of Gettysburg turning point in Civil War; Lincoln's Gettysburg Address 1863. Centennial Exhibition at Philadelphia 1876. Johnstown flood—worst in U.S. history—kills 2,200 people 1889. Pinkerton detectives kill 12 strikers at Homestead steel works near Pittsburgh 1892. Twenty coal miners killed during strike for eight-hour day and other concessions 1897. More than 500 injured during three-day race riot in Philadelphia 1964. Partial meltdown at Three Mile Island forces closure of nuclear reactor 1979. Storage tank spills 713,000 gallons diesel fuel into Monongahela River, disrupting water supplies in Pennsylvania, West Virginia, and Ohio 1988. Casino gambling is legalized 2010.

Tourist information (800) VISIT-PA
www.visitpa.com

▶RHODE ISLAND AND PROVIDENCE PLANTATIONS

Giovanni de Verrazano was the first European to record visiting the area of Narragansett Bay, the prominent inlet that almost splits the eastern third of the state from the rest. The first settlers were followers of Roger Williams, who left the restrictive religious atmosphere of the Puritan Massachusetts Bay Colony to found Providence in 1636. Rhode Island is the site of the first U.S. Baptist church, at Providence, and at Newport the first Quaker meetinghouse and the first synagogue. It was the last of the 13 original colonies to ratify the

Constitution, the centralized federalism of which many Rhode Islanders objected to. The development of 19th-century Rhode Island was influenced by immigration and the Industrial Revolution; the state's leading manufacturers are still silver, jewelry and textiles. Although it ranks 43rd in population, Rhode Island is second in population density (behind New Jersey) at 948 people per square mile.

Name For Rhode Island in Narragansett Bay, named in turn for Mediterranean island of Rhodes. **Nicknames** Ocean State, Little Rhody. **Capital** Providence. **Entered union** May 29, 1790 (13th). **Motto** "Hope."

Emblems **Bird** Rhode Island red. **Flower** Violet. **Mineral** Bowenite. **Rock** Cumberlandite. **Song** "Rhode Island's It for Me." **Tree** Red maple. **Land** Total area 1,545 sq. mi (50th), incl. 500 sq. mi. inland water. **Borders** Mass., Atlantic Ocean, Conn. **Rivers** Blackstone, Pawcatuck, Providence, Sakonnet. **Other notable features** Block Island, Narragansett Bay, Aquidneck Island.

Elected officials Gov. Donald Carcieri (R, term exp. 2011). Lt. Gov. Elizabeth Roberts (D). Sec. State A. Ralph Mollis (D). Atty. Gen. Patrick Lynch (D).

People (July 2009 est.) 1,053,209 (43rd). Race/Hispanic Origin: White 88.5%. Black 6.4%. Indian 0.6%. Asian 2.8%. Pacific Islander 0.1%. Two or more races 1.6%. Hispanic 11.6%.

Cities (2006) Providence 175,255. Warwick 85,925. Cranston 81,479. Pawtucket 72,998. East Providence 49,123. Woonsocket 43,940. North Providence 32,993. West Warwick 29,564. Bristol 24,498. Newport 24,409.

Business **Gross State Product, 2008:** $38.1 bil. **Leading Sectors of GSP:** Finance, insurance, and real estate 29.60%; Services 21.52%; Real estate 14.35%. *Fortune 500* **Companies (2009):** 2.

Famous natives George M. Cohan, actor/producer. Nathanael Greene, army officer. Galway Kinell, poet. Metacomet (King Philip), Wampanoag chief. Oliver H. Perry and Matthew C. Perry, naval officers. Gilbert Stuart, portraitist.

Noteworthy places Brown University, Providence. First Baptist Church in North America (1638), Providence. Hoffenreffer Museum of Anthropology, Bristol. John Carter Brown Library, Providence. Rhode Island School of Design, Providence. Nathanael Greene homestead, Coventry. Museum of Yachting, Newport. Newport mansions. Tennis Hall of Fame, Newport. Touro Synagogue (oldest extant in North America), Newport.

Memorable events Roger Williams, expelled from Massachusetts Bay Colony, settles in Providence 1636. Other religious exiles settle in Portsmouth (1638), Newport (1639), and Warwick (1642). King Philip's War 1675–76. First Quaker meetinghouse in North America founded 1699. First colony to renounce allegiance to Britain 1776. Last colony to ratify Constitution 1790. Dorr's Rebellion achieves liberalization of state constitution, which had remained unchanged since 1663, 1842. America's Cup Race held in Newport for first time 1930. Newport Bridge across Narragansett Bay completed 1969. *Australia II* first non-U.S. boat to win America's Cup in 132 years 1983. Nightclub fire kills 100 in West Warwick 2003

Tourist information (800) 250-7384
www.visitrhodeisland.com

▶SOUTH CAROLINA

South Carolina's early economy was based on rice—its plantations worked by slaves—though tobacco later played a major role. As was true in North Carolina, many settlers made their way into the back country where they eked out a living as tenant farmers. During the Revolution, Ft. Charlotte was the first British installation to fall to Colonial troops, and at the outbreak of the Civil War, Ft. Sumter was the first Union installation to fall to Confederate forces. While agriculture remained a staple of the state's economy through the close of the 19th century, textile manufacture took over in the early 20th century. The postwar era has seen the rapid expansion of the chemical and paper industries, as well as large-scale development of the Atlantic Coast ports of Charleston, Georgetown, and Port Royal.

Name For King Charles II (Carolus is Latin for Charles). **Nickname** Palmetto State. **Capital** Columbia. **Entered union** May 23, 1788 (8th). **Motto** *Animis opibusque parati* (Prepared in mind and deed); *Dum spiro spero* (While I breathe I hope). **Poet laureate** Helen von Kolnitz Hyer.

Emblems **Animal** White-tailed deer. **Beverage** Milk. **Bird** Carolina wren. **Dance** Shag. **Dog** Boykin spaniel. **Fish** Striped bass. **Flower** Yellow jessamine. **Fruit** Peach. **Shell** Lettered olive. **Song** "Carolina." **Stone** Blue granite. **Tree** Palmetto. **Wild game bird** Wild turkey.

Land Total area 32,020 sq. mi (40th), incl. 1,911 sq. mi. inland water. **Borders** N.C., Atlantic Ocean, Ga. **Rivers** Catawba, Congaree, Edisto, Pee Dee, Savannah, Tugalos, Wateree. **Lakes** Greenwood, Hartwell, Keowee, Marion, Murray, Santee Res., Wylie. **Other notable features** Blue Ridge Mts., Congaree Swamp, Sea Islands.

Elected officials Gov. Mark Sanford (R, term exp. 2011). Lt. Gov. Andre Bauer (R). Sec. State J. Mark Hammond (R). Atty. Gen. Henry McMaster (R).

People (July 2009 est.) 4,561,242 (24th). Race/Hispanic Origin: White 68.7%. Black 28.5%. Indian 0.4%. Asian 1.2%. Pacific Islander 0.1%. Two or more races 1.1%. Hispanic 4.1%.

Cities (2006) Columbia 119,961. Charleston 107,845. North Charleston 87,482. Rock Hill 61,620. Mount Pleasant 59,113. Greenville 57,428. Summerville 41,575. Sumter 39,159. Spartanburg 38,561. Hilton Head Island 33,838.

Business **Gross State Product, 2008:** $127.1 bil. **Leading Sectors of GSP:** Manufacturing 20.07%; Services 17.00%; Government 15.54%. *Fortune 500* **Companies (2009):** 2.

Famous natives James Brown, singer. James F. Byrnes, politician/jurist. John C. Calhoun, politician. Joe Frazier, boxer. Dizzy Gillespie, musician. Althea Gibson, athlete. DuBose Heyward, author. Andrew Jackson, U.S. president. Jasper Johns, artist. Eartha Kitt, singer. James Longstreet, army officer. Francis Marion, army officer/politician. Charles C. Pinckney and Thomas Pinckney, diplomats. Edward Rutledge and John Rutledge, politicians. Strom Thurmond, politician.

Noteworthy places Charleston Museum (1773, oldest in United States). Congaree Swamp Natl. Monument. Cowpens Natl. Battlefield. Ft. Moultrie, Ft. Johnson, and Ft. Sumter Natl. Monument, Charleston. Hilton Head Island. Kings Mountain Natl. Military Park. Ninety-Six Natl. Hist. Site, Greenwood. Patriots Point Maritime Museum, Charleston. Sea Islands. Spoleto Music Festival, Charleston.

Memorable events Spanish visit 1521. French Huguenots at Port Royal 1562. Included in Carolina grant by Charles II 1663. Charleston founded 1680. Becomes royal province 1729. Ratifies Constitution 1787. *Best Friend of Charleston,* first American steam locomotive built for passenger use 1833. First state to secede from Union Dec. 20, 1860. Confederate forces attack Ft. Sumter

Apr. 12, 1861. Secession repealed 1865. Readmitted to Union 1868. Cyclone kills 1,000 in Savannah, Georgia, and Charleston 1893. Savannah River nuclear plant begins production near Aiken 1951; closed for safety reasons 1988. Hurricane Hugo kills 24 and causes $700 million in damages 1989. BMW opens plant in Spartanburg 1994. Governor Mark Sanford embroiled in affair scandal, 2009.
Tourist information (866) 224-9339 www.discoversouthcarolina.com

▶SOUTH DAKOTA
The United States did not organize the Dakota Territory until 1861, and even then interest in the region was scant until gold was discovered in 1874. The majority of those who remained after the gold rush turned to cattle ranching, which was a mainstay of the economy through the first half of the 20th century. The manufacturing base was developed after four major dams were built on the Missouri River in the 1930s. They provided hydroelectric power and increased irrigation along the Missouri, which cuts the state in half. Concerned especially over the abrogation of 19th-century treaties, the American Indian Movement (AIM) took over the courthouse at Wounded Knee for 10 weeks in 1973. While U.S. courts have found in favor of the Sioux in several cases concerning the earlier treaties, many maintain that the settlements were insufficient.

Name For southern section of Dakota territory; *dakota* is Sioux word for "allies." **Nicknames** Coyote State, Sunshine State. **Capital** Pierre. **Entered union** Nov. 2, 1889 (40th). **Motto** "Under God the people rule."
Emblems Animal Coyote. **Bird** Chinese ring-necked pheasant. **Fish** Walleye. **Flower** Pasque .
Land Total area 77,116 sq. mi (17th), incl. 1,232 sq. mi. inland water. **Borders** N.Dak., Minn., Iowa, Nebr., Wyo., Mont. **Rivers** Cheyenne, James, Missouri, Moreau, White. **Lakes** Belle Fourche Res., Big Stone, Traverse. **Other notable features** Badlands, Black Hills (Harney Peak 7,242 ft.).
Elected officials Gov. M. Michael Rounds (R, term exp. 2011). Lt. Gov. Dennis Daugaard (R). Sec. State Chris Nelson (R). Atty. Gen. Marty J. Jackley (R).
People (July 2009 est.) 812,383 (46th). Race/Hispanic Origin: White 88.2%. Black 1.1%. Indian 8.5%. Asian 0.7%. Pacific Islander 0.1%. Two or more races 1.4%. Hispanic 2.6%.
Cities (2006) Sioux Falls 142,396. Rapid City 62,715. Aberdeen 24,071. Watertown 20,526. Brookings 18,802. Mitchell 14,887. Pierre 14,095. Yankton 13,767. Huron 10,909. Vermillion 9,862.
Business Gross State Product, 2008: $30.3 bil. **Leading Sectors of GSP:** Finance, insurance, and real estate 22.07%; Services 17.32%; Depository and nondepository 13.94%. *Fortune 500* **Companies (2009):** 0.
Famous natives Tom Brokaw, journalist. Martha "Calamity" Jane Burk (b. Mo.), frontierswoman. Alvin Hansen, economist. Hubert H. Humphrey, politician. Ernest O. Lawrence, physicist (Nobel Prize, 1939). George McGovern, politician. Ta-sunko-witko (Crazy Horse), Oglala Sioux chief. Tatanka Iyotake (Sitting Bull), Sioux chief.
Noteworthy places Badlands Natl. Park. Crazy Horse State Memorial, Custer. Custer State Park. Ft. Sisseton. Geographical center of the United States. Jewel Cave Natl. Monument. Mount Rushmore. Natl. Memorial. Wind Cave Natl. Park.

Memorable events French visit region 1742–43. To United States in Louisiana Purchase 1803. Ft. Pierre first permanent settlement 1817. Part of Dakota Territory 1861. Gold discovered in Black Hills 1874. Divided from North Dakota; statehood 1889. U.S. troops massacre Sioux at Battle of Wounded Knee 1890.
Tourist information (800) SDAKOTA www.travelsd.com

▶TENNESSEE
First claimed by Virginia and later by North Carolina, Tennessee had its first great pioneer in Daniel Boone, who traversed the region in the 1760s. Political attitudes in the 18th century were shaped by the land, with the cotton and tobacco growers in the fertile western part of the state favoring slavery and the backwoods people of the eastern hills opposed to it. The Cherokees were removed to Oklahoma by the federal government in the 1830s. The state was captured by Union troops in 1862 and put under the governorship of Andrew Johnson, later a U.S. president.

Its economy was radically altered in the 1930s and 1940s by the creation of the Tennessee Valley Authority, which provided abundant energy for industry, and to a lesser extent by the location of the government's first uranium enrichment facility at Oak Ridge during World War II. The state's leading industries are textiles, food processing, and chemicals, and there is considerable lead and coal mining in the east.

Name For Tenase, principal village of Cherokees. **Nickname** Volunteer State. **Capital** Nashville. **Entered union** June 1, 1796 (16th). **Motto** "Agriculture and commerce." **Slogan** "Tennessee—America at its best." **Poet laureate** Margaret Britton Vaughn.
Emblems Animal Raccoon. **Bird** Mockingbird. **Folk dance** Square dance. **Cultivated flower** Iris. **Gem** Tennessee pearl. **Insects** Ladybug, firefly. **Poem** "Oh Tennessee, My Tennessee." **Public school song** "My Tennessee." **Rock** Limestone agate. **Songs** "When It's Iris Time in Tennessee," "The Tennessee Waltz," "My Homeland, Tennessee," "Rocky Top." **Tree** Tulip poplar. **Wildflower** Passion flower.
Land Total area 42,143 sq. mi (36th), incl. 926 sq. mi. inland water. **Borders** Ky., Va., N.C., Ga., Ala., Miss., Ark., Mo. **Rivers** Clinch, Cumberland, Mississippi, Tennessee. **Lakes** Boone, Center Hill, Cherokee, Dale Hollow, Douglass, J. Percy Priest, Watauga. **Other notable features** Cumberland Mts., Great Smoky Mts., Tennessee Valley, Unaka Mts.
Elected officials Gov. Phil Bredesen (D, term exp. 2011). Lt. Gov. Ron Ramsey (R). Sec. State Tre Hargett (R). Atty. Gen. Robert E. Cooper (D).
People (July 2009 est.) 6,296,254 (17th). Race/Hispanic Origin: White 80.4%. Black 16.8%. Indian 0.3%. Asian 1.3%. Pacific Islander 0.1%. Two or more races 1.1%. Hispanic 3.7%.
Cities (2006) Memphis 670,902. Nashville 552,120. Knoxville 182,337. Chattanooga 155,190. Clarksville 113,175. Murfreesboro 92,559. Jackson 62,711. Johnson City 59,866. Franklin 55,870. Bartlett 46,932.
Business Gross State Product, 2008: $210.2 bil. (18th). **Leading Sectors of GSP (2001):** Services 21.73%; Manufacturing 18.72%; Finance, insurance, and real estate 15.09%. *Fortune 500* **Companies (2009):** 8.
Famous natives James Agee, author. Davy Crockett, frontiersman. David Farragut, naval officer. Aretha Franklin, singer. Morgan Freeman,

actor. Al Gore, (b. Washington, D.C.), politician. Cordell Hull, statesman (Nobel Peace Prize, 1945). Dolly Parton, singer. Sikawyi (Sequoya), Cherokee scholar. Alvin York, soldier.

Noteworthy places American Museum of Science and Energy, Oak Ridge. Andrew Johnson Natl. Hist. Site, Greenville. Chickamauga and Chattanooga Natl. Military Park. Cumberland Natl. Hist. Park. Ft. Donelson Natl. Military Park. Graceland, Memphis. Grand Old Opry, Nashville. Great Smoky Mountains Natl. Park. The Hermitage (Andrew Jackson home), Nashville. Lookout Mountain, Chattanooga. Dollywood, Gatlinburg. The Parthenon, Nashville. Shiloh Natl. Mil. Park, Pittsburgh Landing. Stones River Natl. Battlefield, Murfreesboro.

Memorable events De Soto expedition passes through region 1540. French claim territory as part of Louisiana; English claim territory as part of Carolina grant 1663. French claim given up after French and Indian War 1763. State of Franklin established in what is now eastern Tennessee 1784–87. Organized as Territory South of the Ohio 1790. Statehood 1796. Secedes from Union 1861. Battles of Shiloh (1862), Chattanooga (1863), Stones River (1863), and Nashville (1864). Readmitted to Union 1866. Clarence Darrow defends John T. Scopes for violating ban on teaching evolution in public schools; loses case 1925. Congress creates Tennessee Valley Authority 1933. First operational nuclear reactor at Oak Ridge 1943. Martin Luther King assassinated at Memphis 1968. World's Fair held in Knoxville 1982.

Tourist information (800) 462-8366
www.tnvacation.com

▶ TEXAS

The land that is Texas today was originally part of Spain's holdings in Mexico. After Mexico won independence, the new government invited U.S. citizens to settle there. After many clashes between the Mexican and Anglo cultures, Texas broke away and for 10 years was an independent country before becoming a state in 1845. Modern Texas was made by oil, discovered at Spindletop in 1901, and the state's economy has been tied to the oil market ever since. After World War II, the Texas economy soared, bringing both prosperity and an unprecedented population boom. With the oil glut of the early 1980s, growth came to a halt, causing a drastic realignment of economic priorities. Unemployment jumped more than 20 percent during the 1980s, and remained higher than the national average in 1990, a year that saw many bank failures. The economy has been forced to diversify; currently the petroleum industry accounts for only 7 percent of state revenues, down from 25 percent a decade before. Texas has enormous resources ranging from cotton, cattle and timber to aerospace, computers and electronics. The largest of the 48 conterminous states, Texas's image as a state of wide-open spaces is understandable, but fully 80 percent of its people live in metropolitan areas, and Dallas, Houston and San Antonio are among the nation's 10 largest cities. Thirty-six percent of the population is Hispanic; the majority of those are Mexican-American.

Name From the Caddo *tavshas*, "friends." **Nickname** Lone Star State. **Capital** Austin. **Entered union** Dec. 29, 1845 (28th). **Motto** "Friendship." **Emblems Bird** Mockingbird. **Dish** Chili. **Flower** Bluebonnet. **Gem** Topaz. **Grass** Sideoats grama. **Songs** "Texas, Our Texas," "The Eyes of Texas." **Stone** Palmwood. **Tree** Pecan.

Land Total area 268,581 sq. mi (2nd), incl. 6,784 sq. mi. inland water. **Borders** Okla., Ark., La., Gulf of Mexico, Tamaulipas, Coahuila, Chihuahua, N.Mex. **Rivers** Brazos, Colorado, Natchez, Red, Rio Grande, Sabine, Trinity. **Lakes** Sam Rayburn Res., Texoma, Toledo Bend Res. **Other notable features** Balcones Escarpment, Diablo Sierra, Edwards Plateau, Guadalupe Mts., Staked Plain, Stockton Plateau.

Elected officials Gov. Rick Perry (R, term exp. 2011). Lt. Gov. David Dewhurst (R). Sec. State Hope Andrade (R). Atty. Gen. Greg Abbott (R).

People (July 2009 est.) 24,782,302 (2nd). Race/Hispanic Origin: White 82.4%. Black 11.9%. Indian 0.8%. Asian 3.5%. Pacific Islander 0.1%. Two or more races 1.3%. Hispanic 36.5%.

Cities (2006) Houston 2,144,491. San Antonio 1,296,682. Dallas 1,232,940. Austin 709,893. Fort Worth 653,320. El Paso 609,415. Arlington 367,197. Corpus Christi 285,267. Plano 255,009. Garland 217,963.

Business Gross State Product, 2008: $925.5 bil. **Leading Sectors of GSP:** Services 20.48%; Finance, insurance, and real estate 15.48%; Manufacturing 12.27%. **Fortune 500 Companies (2009):** 64.

Famous natives Lance Armstrong, cyclist. Stephen Austin (b. Va.), pioneer. James "Jim" Bowie (b. Ky.), army officer. Carol Burnett, comedian. J. Frank Dobie, folklorist. Dwight D. Eisenhower, U.S. president/general. Samuel Houston (b. Va.), president Republic of Texas/governor State of Texas. Howard Hughes, industrialist/aviator. Lyndon Baines Johnson, U.S. president. Janis Joplin, singer. Barbara Jordan, politician. Audie Murphy, soldier/actor. Chester Nimitz, navy officer. Katherine Anne Porter, author. Samuel T. Rayburn, politician. Mildred "Babe" Didrikson Zaharias, athlete.

Noteworthy places The Alamo, San Antonio. Alibates Flint Quarries Natl. Monument. Big Bend Natl. Park. Ft. Davis. Galveston Historical Foundation. Guadalupe Mountains Natl. Park. Houston Museum of Fine Arts. Lyndon B. Johnson Natl. Hist. Park, Johnson City. Lyndon B. Johnson Space Center, Houston. Old Stone Ft., Nacogdoches. Padre Island Natl. Seashore. San Antonio Missions Natl. Hist. Park. Texas Ranger Museum, Waco.

Memorable events Alonzo Alvarez de Piñeda sails along coast 1519. Estevanico blazes trail through West Texas 1539. Spanish establish settlement at Ysleta near El Paso 1682. René-Robert Cavalier de La Salle attempts to found colony on Matagorda Bay, establishing claim to region for France 1685. Effective Spanish occupation 1715. United States acquires French claim to region with Louisiana Purchase 1803. United States relinquishes claim to Spain 1819. Americans move into region in early 19th century. Mexico, of which Texas is a province, wins independence from Spain 1821. Declaration of Independence from Mexico; Santa Anna victor at Battle of the Alamo; Sam Houston victor at Battle of San Jacinto; founding of Republic of Texas 1836. Texas granted statehood by United States 1845. Secedes from Union 1861; readmitted 1870. Hurricane kills 6,000 at Galveston 1900. NASA Space Center opens at Houston 1962. Pres. Kennedy assassinated at Dallas 1963. Price of oil plunges during 1980s, crippling state economy. In 2010 a collision between two vessels in a Port Arthur waterway spills 450,000 gallons of oil.

Tourist information (800) 888-8TEX
www.traveltex.com

▶UTAH

In the middle of the Great Basin between the Rocky Mountains and the Sierra Nevada, Utah was an arid and uninviting region. After Joseph Smith, the founder of the Church of Jesus Christ of Latter-day Saints (Mormons), was shot in Illinois, Brigham Young led his people west, ultimately to the Salt Lake Valley in 1847. The chief obstacle to statehood was polygamy, which the church eventually renounced. There was an influx of non-Mormons after the discovery of silver in 1863, but Mormons still comprise two-thirds of the state's population, and the state remains conservative in outlook. Although the federal government is a major employer, government policy has lately been challenged by increased concern over the issues of chemical weapons testing, the MX missile, and disposal of nuclear waste from the Rocky Mountain Arsenal in neighboring Colorado.

Name For Ute Indians. **Nicknames** Beehive State, Mormon State. **Capital** Salt Lake City. **Entered Union** Jan. 4, 1896 (45th). **Motto:** "Industry."
Emblems Animal Elk. **Bird** California Gull. **Emblem** Beehive **Fish** Rainbow Trout **Flower** Sego Lily. **Gem** Topaz. **Song** "Utah, We Love Thee." **Tree** Blue spruce.
Land Total area 84,899 sq. mi (13th), incl. 2,755 sq. mi. inland water. **Borders** Idaho, Wyo., Colo., Ariz., Nev. **Rivers** Bear, Colorado, Green, Sevier. **Lakes** Bear, Great Salt, Utah. **Mountains** La Sal, Uinta (Kings Peak 13,528 ft.) Wasatch Range. **Other notable features** Great Salt Lake Desert (Bonneville Salt Flats), Kaibab Plateau.
Elected officials Gov. Gary R. Herbert (R). Lt. Gov. Greg Bell (R). Atty. Gen. Mark Shurtleff (R).
People (July 2009 est.) 2,784,572 (34th). Race/Hispanic Origin: White 92.9%. Black 1.3%. Indian 1.4%. Asian 2.0%. Pacific Islander 0.8%. Two or more races 1.7%. Hispanic 12.0%.
Cities (2006) Salt Lake City 178,858. West Valley City 119,841. Provo 113,984. West Jordan 94,309. Sandy 94,203. Orem 90,857. Ogden 78,086. St. George 67,614. Layton 62,716. Taylorsville 58,048.
Business Gross State Product, 2008: $87.7 bil. **Leading Sectors of GSP:** Services 20.59%; Finance, insurance, and real estate 20.08%; Government 14.65%. *Fortune 500* **Companies (2009):** 1.
Famous natives Maud Adams, actress. John Moses Browning, inventor. Philo Farnsworth, engineer. Merlin Olsen, football player/actor. Ivy Baker Priest, U.S. treasurer. Brigham Young (b. Vt.), religious leader. Loretta Young, actress.
Noteworthy places Arches Natl. Park. Bryce Canyon Natl. Park. Canyonlands Natl. Park. Capitol Reef Natl. Park. Cedar Breaks Natl. Monument. Dinosaur Natl. Monument. Flaming Gorge Dam Natl. Monument. Grand Staircase-Escalante Natl. Monument. Great Salt Lake. Lake Powell Natl. Monument. Monument Valley. Mormon Tabernacle, Salt Lake City. Natural Bridges Natl. Monument. Promontory Point. Rainbow Bridge Natl. Monument. Temple Square, Salt Lake City. Timpanogas Cave Natl. Monument. Zion Natl. Park.
Memorable events Probably first visited by explorers from Coronado expedition 1540. Silvestre Vélez de Escalante and Francisco Atanasio Dominguez explore for Spain 1776. James Bridger discovers Great Salt Lake 1824. Led by Brigham Young, Mormons reach Great Salt Lake 1847. United States acquires Utah region from Mexico 1848. Mormons organize state of Deseret 1849; Congress refuses to recognize and instead organizes Territory of Utah 1850. Silver discovered at Little Cottonwood Canyon 1868. First transcontinental railroad completed with driving of golden spike at Promontory Point 1869. Mormon church renounces polygamy 1890, paving way to statehood 1896. Uranium discovered near Moab 1952. Winter Olympics held in Salt Lake City 2002.
Tourist Information (800) 200-1160
www.utah.com

▶VERMONT

Originally claimed by both New Hampshire and New York, Vermont's independence was asserted by Ethan Allen. His Green Mountain Boys rid the state of New Yorkers in 1770, fought well against the British in the Revolution, and declared the independent republic of New Connecticut in 1777. Allen was eventually overthrown, and Vermont joined the Union in 1791.

Vermont traditionally has strong ties to Canada, and there was an influx of French-Canadians as Vermont began to develop its manufacturing base in the mid-19th century. Vermont's politics have always been characterized by tolerance and progressivism. As New Connecticut, it abolished slavery and allowed universal male suffrage. Vermont's environmental concerns focus on acid rain and the degree to which development (especially by the tourist industry) should infringe on the state's remaining unspoiled land.

Name From French *vert mont*, "green mountain." **Nickname** Green Mountain State. **Capital** Montpelier. **Entered Union** Mar. 4, 1791 (14th). **Motto** "Freedom and unity."
Emblems Animal Morgan horse. **Beverage** Milk. **Bird** Hermit thrush. **Cold-Water Fish** Brook trout. **Flower** Red Clover. **Insect** Honeybee. **Song** "These Green Mountains" **Tree** Sugar Maple. **Warm-Water Fish** Walleye pike.
Land Total Area 9,614 sq. mi (45th), incl. 365 sq. mi. inland water. **Borders** Quebec, N.H., Mass., N.Y. **Rivers** Connecticut, Lamoille, Otter Creek, Poultney, White, Winooski. **Lakes** Bomoseen, Champlain, Memphremagog, Willoughby. **Other Notable Features** Grand Isle, Green Mts. (Mt. Mansfield 4,393 ft.), Taconic Mts.
Elected officials Gov. James H. Douglas (R). Lt. Gov. Brian Dubie (R). Sec. State Deborah L. Markowitz (D). Atty. Gen. William H. Sorrell (D).
People (July 2009 est.) 621,760 (49th). Race/Hispanic Origin: White 96.4%. Black 0.9%. Indian 0.4%. Asian 1.1%. Two or more races 1.2%. Hispanic 1.4%.
Cities (2006) Burlington 38,358. Essex 19,264. Colchester 17,180. South Burlington 17,014. Rutland 16,964. Bennington 15,349. Brattleboro 11,741. Hartford 10,829. Milton 10,347. Barre 9,078.
Business Gross State Product, 2008: $21.7 bil. **Leading Sectors of GSP:** Services 22.88%; Finance, insurance, and real estate 18.41%; Manufacturing 15.66%. *Fortune 500* **Companies (2009):** 0.
Famous natives Ethan Allen (b. Conn.), army officer. Chester A. Arthur, U.S. President. Calvin Coolidge, U.S. president. John Deere, industrialist. George Dewey, naval officer. John Dewey, philosopher. Stephen Douglas, politician. James Fisk, financier. Robert Frost (b. Calif.), poet. Rudy Vallee, singer.
Noteworthy places Bennington Battleground/Monument. Billings Farm and Museum, Woodstock. Calvin Coolidge Homestead, Plymouth. Maple Grove Maple Museum, Rock of Ages Tourist Center, Graniteville. Shelburne Museum. St. Johnsbury. Vermont Marble Exhibit, Proctor.

Memorable events Samuel de Champlain explores for France 1609. First French settlement at Ste. Anne 1666. First English settlers build Ft. Drummer near Brattleboro 1724. Bennington settled 1761. Ethan Allen organizes Green Mountain Boys 1764. Green Mountain Boys capture Ft. Ticonderoga and Ft. Crown Point 1775. Gen. John Stark defeats British general John Burgoyne near Bennington; constitution abolishes slavery and grants universal male suffrage 1777. Claims to area relinquished by Massachusetts (1781), New Hampshire (1782), and New York (1790). First state admitted after original 13 1791. MacDonough defeats British Lake Champlain fleet 1814. Canal between Hudson River and Lake Champlain gives Vermont direct access to port of New York 1823. Confederate soldiers steal $400,000 from St. Albans bank 1864. State recognizes same-sex marriage in some jurisdictions, 2009.

Tourist Information   (800) VERMONT
www.travel-vermont.com

▶ VIRGINIA, COMMONWEALTH OF

The first successful English settlement in America was at Jamestown in 1607. The differences between the Virginia colonists and those of Massachusetts were pronounced, and the commercial southern planter class shared little of their New England counterparts' religious zeal. Virginia bred its own strain of independence, and it was the fiery Patrick Henry who heralded the American Revolution with the cry "Give me liberty or give me death." Seven of the first 12 presidents were from Virginia. With an economy very dependent on labor-intensive tobacco in the mid-19th century, Virginia seceded from the Union over the slavery issue, despite the misgivings of many, including Robert E. Lee. After the war Virginia developed an increasingly diversified industrial and manufacturing base that survives today, with food products, tobacco, and chemicals leading the way. Despite the dramatic decline of the American merchant marine, Virginia's shipbuilding industry in Newport News flourished in the 1980s, thanks to the Pentagon's commitment to a 600-ship navy. Norfolk is also one of the country's leading commercial ports.

Name For Elizabeth I, called Virgin Queen. **Nicknames** Old Dominion, Mother of Presidents, Mother of States. **Capital** Richmond. **Entered union** June 25, 1788 (10th). **Motto** Sic semper tyrannis (Thus always to tyrants).

Emblems **Beverage** Milk. **Bird** Cardinal. **Dog** Foxhound. **Flower** Dogwood. **Shell** Oyster. **Song** "Carry Me Back to Old Virginia." **Tree** Dogwood. **Land** **Total area** 42,774 sq. mi (35th), incl. 3,180 sq. mi. inland water. **Borders** Md., D.C., Atlantic Ocean, N.C., Tenn., Ky., W.Va. **Rivers** James, Potomac, Rappahannock, Roanoke, Shenandoah, York. **Lakes** Buggs Island, Claytor, Gaston, Leesville. **Mountains** Allegheny, Blue Ridge, Cumberland, Unaka. **Other notable features** Great Dismal Swamp, Shenandoah Valley.

Elected officials   Gov. Tim Kaine (D, term exp. 2011). Lt. Gov. William Bolling (R). Sec. Commonwealth Janet Polarek (R). Atty. Gen. Kenneth T. Cuccinelli, II (R).

People   (July 2009 est.) 7,882,590 (12th). Race/Hispanic Origin: White 73.0%. Black 19.9%. Indian 0.4%. Asian 4.9%. Pacific Islander 0.1%. Two or more races 1.7%. Hispanic 6.8%.

Cities   (2006) Virginia Beach 435,619. Norfolk 229,112. Chesapeake 220,560. Arlington 199,776. Richmond 192,913.   Newport News 178,281.

Hampton   145,017.   Alexandria   136,974. Portsmouth 101,377. Roanoke 91,552.

Business   **Gross State Product, 2008:** $324.5 bil.   **Leading Sectors of GSP:** Services 23.63%; Finance, insurance, and real estate 18.97%; Government 17.67%. *Fortune 500* **Companies (2009):** 18.

Famous natives   Arthur Ashe, tennis player. Richard E. Byrd, explorer/aviator. William Clark, explorer. Jerry Falwell, evangelist. William Henry Harrison, U.S. president. Patrick Henry, Revolutionary patriot. Thomas Jefferson, U.S. president. Joseph E. Johnston, Confederate general. John Paul Jones (b. Scotland), navy officer. Robert E. Lee, Confederate general. Meriwether Lewis, explorer. James Madison, U.S. president. John Marshall, jurist. Cyrus Hall McCormick, inventor. James Monroe, U.S. president. Walter Reed, doctor. Pat Robertson, evangelist/politician. Bill "Bojangles" Robinson, dancer. George C. Scott, actor. Thomas Sumter, army officer. Zachary Taylor, U.S. president. John Tyler, U.S. president. Booker T. Washington, educator. George Washington, U.S. president. Woodrow Wilson, U.S. president.

Noteworthy places   Appomattox Courthouse Natl. Hist Park. Arlington Natl. Cemetery. Booker T. Washington Natl. Monument, Roanoke. Colonial Natl. Hist. Park (incl. Jamestown, Yorktown & Williamsburg). Fredericksburg and Spotsylvania Natl. Military Park. George Washington birthplace, Frederick Co. Harpers Ferry Natl. Hist. Site. The Mariners' Museum, Newport News. Monticello, Charlottesville. Mount Vernon. Petersburg Natl. Battlefield. Robert E. Lee Memorial, Lexington. Shenandoah Natl. Park. Virginia Beach. Virginia Museum of Fine Arts. Wolf Trap Farm for the Performing Arts, Reston.

Memorable events   John Smith founds Jamestown, first permanent settlement in North America, 1607. John Rolfe marries Pocahontas, daughter of Powhatan, leader of so-called Powhatan Confederacy 1614. First English women arrive at Jamestown; House of Burgesses established 1619. Northampton Declaration first resistance to taxation without representation 1653. College of William and Mary founded 1693. First state to establish Committee of Correspondence 1773. American Revolution ends with Charles Cornwallis's surrender to George Washington at Yorktown 1781. Nat Turner's slave revolt 1831. State secedes from Union 1861. Civil War ends with Robert E. Lee's surrender to Ulysses S. Grant at Appomattox Courthouse 1865. Readmitted to Union 1870. Norfolk Naval Base founded 1917. John D. Rockefeller, Jr. restores Colonial Williamsburg 1926. E. Claiborne Robins donates $50 million to University of Richmond 1969. Douglas Wilder becomes nation's first black governor 1989.

Tourist information   (800) VISIT-VA
www.virginia.org

▶ WASHINGTON

The northwest corner of the continental U.S. was originally the locus of a rich Native American culture noted today primarily for its ornately carved canoes and totem poles. In 1792, Boston merchant Capt. Robert Gray began a trade in sea otter pelts; but the first permanent settlers in the region did not establish themselves for almost 50 years. Agriculture and lumbering were, and remain, mainstays of the state's economy—the farming regions in the east, rich in dairy products, fruit and wheat, and the lumber industry in the western part of the state rely heavily on exports to the Far East. This geographic split reflects the weather patterns: eastern Washington rarely gets more than 10 inches of rain in a year, while on the Pacific coast almost 40 inches is the average.

Since World War I, Puget Sound has been a center of heavy industry and shipbuilding, and 60 percent of the population is concentrated in the region. Boeing maintains one of the country's largest airplane-manufacturing plants in the Seattle-Tacoma area, and Microsoft, the world's leading software company, is located in Redmond. The industrial work force was open to progressive and sometimes radical unionism, and the International Workers of the World (Wobblies) had their national headquarters at Seattle. Before statehood the territorial government pioneered women's suffrage, but Congress declared the women's right to vote unconstitutional.

Name For George Washington. **Nickname** Evergreen State. **Capital** Olympia. **Entered union** Nov. 11, 1889 (42nd). **Motto** *Alki* (By and by).
Emblems Bird Willow goldfinch. **Fish** Steelhead trout. **Flower** Coast rhododendron. **Gem** Petrified wood. **Song** "Washington, My Home." **Tree** Western hemlock.
Land   **Total area** 71,300 sq. mi (18th), incl. 4,756 sq. mi. inland water. **Borders** British Columbia, Idaho, Oreg., Pacific Ocean. **Rivers** Chehalis, Columbia, Pend Oreille, Snake, Yakima. **Lakes** Baker, Bank, Chelan, Franklin D. Roosevelt, Ross, Rufus Woods. **Mountains** Cascade Range, Coast Range, Kettle River Range, Olympic. **Other notable features** Puget Sound, San Juan Islands, Strait of Juan de Fuca.
Elected officials   Gov. Christine Gregoire (D). Lt. Gov. Brad Owen (D). Sec. State Sam Reed (D). Atty. Gen. Rob McKenna (R).
People   (July 2009 est.) 6,664,195 (13th). Race/Hispanic Origin: White 84.3%. Black 3.7%. Indian 1.7%. Asian 6.7%. Pacific Islander 0.5%. Two or more races 3.1%. Hispanic 9.8%.
Cities   (2006) Seattle 582,454. Spokane 198,081. Tacoma 196,532. Vancouver 158,855. Bellevue 118,186. Everett 98,514. Federal Way 84,166. Kent 83,501. Yakima 82,805. Bellingham 75,150.
Business   **Gross State Product, 2008:** $264.6 bil. **Leading Sectors of GSP:** Services 23.38%; Finance, insurance, and real estate 18.41%; Government 13.82%. *Fortune 500* **Companies (2009):** 8.
Famous natives   Harry L. "Bing" Crosby, singer. Merce Cunningham, choreographer. Bill Gates, businessman. Jimi Hendrix, guitarist. Henry M. "Scoop" Jackson, politician. Robert Joffrey, choreographer. Gary Larson, cartoonist. Edward R. Murrow, reporter (b. North Carolina). Theodore Roethke (b. Mich.), poet. Marcus Whitman (b. N.Y.), missionary/pioneer.
Noteworthy places   Grand Coulee Dam. Klondike Gold Rush Natl. Hist. Park, Seattle. Mount Rainier Natl. Park. Mount Saint Helens Natl. Monument. North Cascades Natl. Park. Olympic Natl. Park. San Juan Islands Natl. Hist. Park. Seattle Art Museum. Space Needle, Seattle.
Memorable events   Sir Francis Drake skirts coast of Pacific Northwest 1579. Juan de Fuca sails into straits now bearing his name. Bruno de Heceta lands at Hoh River 1775. Capt. James Cook arrives 1778. Capt. Robert Gray discovers mouth of Columbia River, which he names for his ship; George Vancouver explores Puget Sound 1792. Lewis and Clark expedition winters at Columbia River 1805. Marcus Whitman, Protestant Mission Board, settles near Walla Walla 1836. Territorial status 1853. Northern Pacific railroad reaches Puget Sound 1883. Alaska-Yukon-Pacific Exposition

at Seattle 1909. Grand Coulee Dam, largest concrete hydroelectric dam in United States, completed 1941. Hanford works atomic energy plant opens 1943. Upholding treaty provisions from Washinton's days as a territory, a decision awards Native Americans half the catch of Northwest salmon and steelhead 1974. Mt. Saint Helens erupts, killing 61, 1980. Washington Public Power Supply System (known as "whoops") defaults on $8.25 billion bond issue 1983.
Tourist information   (800) 544-1800
www.experiencewa.com

▶ WEST VIRGINIA

When Virginia seceded in 1861, its western counties reorganized and in 1863 were admitted to the Union as a separate state. Despite the rugged terrain, through which transportation has always been difficult, farming remained the backbone of the economy until the close of the 19th century, when coal mining and other extractive industries developed. After World War II, the manufacturing base developed to include steel and chemical manufacturing. Even with vast natural resources, West Virginia has long been one of the poorest states in the union. Population losses since the 1950s have been pronounced, and the 8 percent loss between 1980 and 1990 was the highest in the country. There is low participation in the workforce by women and educational achievement is well below the national average.

Name for western part of Virginia. **Nickname** Mountain State. **Capital** Charleston. **Entered union** June 20, 1863 (35th). **Motto** *Montani semper liberi* (Mountaineers are always free).
Emblems Animal Black bear. **Bird** Cardinal. **Colors** Old gold and blue. **Fish** Brook trout. **Flower** *Rhododendron maximum* (big laurel). **Fruit** Apple. **Songs** "The West Virginia Hills," "West Virginia, My Home Sweet Home," "This Is My West Virginia." **Tree** Sugar maple.
Land   **Total area** 24,230 sq. mi (41st), incl. 152 sq. mi. inland water. **Borders** Ohio, Pa., Md., Va., Ky. **Rivers** Big Sandy, Guayandotte, Kanawha, Little Kanawha, Monongahela, Ohio, Potomac. **Lakes** Summersville Dam. **Mountains** Allegheny, Blue Ridge, Cumberland.
Elected officials   Gov. Joe Manchin III (D). Lt. Gov. Earl Ray Tomblin (D). Sec. State Natalie E. Tennant (D). Atty. Gen. Darrell V. McGraw (D).
People   (July 2009 est.) 1,819,777 (37th). Race/Hispanic Origin: White 94.5%. Black 3.6%. Indian 0.2%. Asian 0.7%. Two or more races 1.0%. Hispanic 1.1%.
Cities   (2006) Charleston 50,846. Huntington 49,007. Parkersburg 31,755. Wheeling 29,330. Morgantown 28,654. Weirton 19,250. Fairmont 19,145. Beckley 16,828. Clarksburg 16,459. Martinsburg 16,392.
Business   **Gross State Product, 2008:** $46.3 bil. **Leading Sectors of GSP:** Services 18.26%; Government 16.07%; Manufacturing 15.99%. *Fortune 500* **Companies (2009):** 0.
Famous natives   Newton D. Baker, politician. Pearl Buck, novelist (Nobel Prize, 1938). John W. Davis, politician. Dwight Whitney Morrow, lawyer/diplomat. Michael Owens, manufacturer. Walter Reuther, labor leader. Cyrus Vance, statesman. Jerry West, basketball player. Charles "Chuck" Yeager, pilot.
Noteworthy places   Cass Scenic Railroad. Harpers Ferry Natl. Hist. Park. Monongahela Natl. Forest. New River Gorge Bridge. Science and Cultural Center, Charleston.

Memorable events First permanent settlement by Morgan Morgan at Mill Creek 1731. Coal discovered on Coal River 1742. Wheeling Convention repudiates act of secession; forms new state of Kanawha 1861. Enters Union as West Virginia 1863. Population peaks at 2.5 million 1950. Unemployment jumps to 18 percent, highest in nation, 1980–83. Coal mine explosion at Sago Mine in 2006 traps 13 miners for two days, killing 12.

Tourist information   (800) CALL-WVA
www.wvtourism.com

▶ **WISCONSIN**

The indigenous people of the region had a largely agricultural economy, but the fur trade drew Europeans into the region. Native resistance to white settlement was strong and not overcome until the Black Hawk Wars of 1832. In the early 19th century, German, Scandinavian, and Dutch farmers migrated to the region in large numbers. Many social welfare policies now common to the nation as a whole—including aid to dependent children, workmen's compensation, and old-age assistance—were pioneered in Wisconsin. Although manufacturing accounts for the lion's share of Wisconsin's profits, agriculture is extremely important, and the state is the nation's leading producer of dairy products. There are major shipping facilities at Superior, Green Bay, and Milwaukee.

Name From the Ojibwa *wishkonsing*, "place of the bearer." **Nickname** Badger State. **Capital** Madison. **Entered union** May 29, 1848 (30th). **Motto** "Forward."

Emblems **Animal** Badger. **Bird** Robin. **Domestic animal** Dairy cow. **Fish** Muskellunge. **Flower** Wood violet. **Insect** Honeybee. **Mineral** Galena. **Rock** Red granite. **Soil** Antigo silt loam. **Song** "On, Wisconsin!" **Symbol of peace** Mourning dove. **Tree** Sugar maple. **Wildlife animal** White-tailed deer.

Land Total area 65,498 sq. mi (23rd), incl. 11,188 sq. mi. inland water. **Borders** Minn., Lake Superior, Mich., Lake Michigan, Ill., Iowa. **Rivers** Black, Chippewa, Menominee, Mississippi, St. Croix, Wisconsin. **Lakes** Chippewa, Du Bay, Mendota, Michigan, Superior, Winnebago. **Other notable features** Apostle Islands, Door Peninsula, Green Bay.

Elected officials Gov. Jim Doyle (D, term exp. 2011). Lt. Gov. Barbara Lawton (D). Sec. State Douglas La Follette (D). Atty. Gen. J.B. Van Hollen (R).

People (July 2009 est.) 5,654,7747 (20th). Race/Hispanic Origin: White 89.7%. Black 6.1%. Indian 1.0%. Asian 2.0%. Two or more races 1.2%. Hispanic 5.1%.

Cities (2006) Milwaukee 578,887. Madison 221,551. Green Bay 101,203. Kenosha 95,240. Racine 79,392. Appleton 70,217. Waukesha 67,658. Oshkosh 63,485. Eau Claire 62,570. Janesville 61,962.

Business Gross State Product, 2008: $198.3 bil. **Leading Sectors of GSP:** Manufacturing 25.38%; Services 18.21%; Finance, insurance, and real estate 15.81%. *Fortune 500* **Companies (2009):** 10.

Famous natives King Camp Gillette, inventor/businessman. Eric Heiden, speed skater. Harry Houdini (b. Hungary), magician. Robert La Follette, politician. Liberace (Wladziu Valentino), pianist. Alfred Lunt, actor. Joseph R. McCarthy, politician. Spencer Tracy, actor. Thorstein Veblen, economist. Orson Welles, director. Laura Ingalls Wilder, novelist. Thornton Wilder, author. Frank Lloyd Wright, architect.

Noteworthy places Apostle Island Natl. Lakeshore. Chequamegon Natl. Forest. Circus World Museum, Baraboo. Door County Peninsula.

Ice Age Natl. Scientific Reserve. Little House Wayside, Pepin. Manitowoc Maritime Museum. Milwaukee Art Museum. Milwaukee Public Museum. Nicolet Natl. Forest. Old Wade House and Carriage Museum, Greenbush. Old World Wisconsin, Eagle. Villa Louis, Prairie du Chien. Wisconsin Dells.

Memorable events Jean Nicolet lands at Green Bay 1634. French establish mission and trading post near Ashland 1634. British take control of region 1763. Land ceded to United States 1787, but U.S. control not established until after War of 1812. Becomes independent Territory 1836. Statehood 1848. More than 800 die in forest fire near Peshtigo 1871. First hydroelectric plant completed at Appleton 1882. Ringling Brothers circus formed at Baraboo 1884. First state to enact income tax 1911. Milwaukee transfers more than 11,000 students between city and surburban schools 1986.

Tourist information   (800) 432-8747
www.tourism.state.wi.us

▶ **WYOMING**

Tens of thousands of migrants traveled through the region along the Oregon Trail, but few settled the land until Ft. Laramie was built in 1834. Territorial status came in 1869. Wyoming was the first state to give the vote to women, and in 1925 Nellie Tayloe Ross became the first woman governor following the death of her husband. Cattle ranching is the traditional mainstay of the economy. The state ranks second in uranium output, petroleum and coal production have become increasingly important. Wyoming is best known for its natural wonders. Yellowstone National Park—the site of Old Faithful—is the oldest and largest national park in the country. Following a decade-long mining boom in the 1970s and 1980s, Wyoming's population declined, and it has fallen behind even Alaska in total population. Although the population has increased in the 1990s, there are still no more than five people per square mile.

Name From the Delaware *maugh-wau-wa-ma*, "large plains" or "mountains and valleys alternating." **Nickname** Equality State. **Capital** Cheyenne. **Entered union** July 10, 1890 (44th). **Motto** "Equal rights."

Emblems **Bird** Meadowlark. **Flower** Indian paintbrush. **Gem** Jade. **Song** "Wyoming." **Tree** Cottonwood.

Land Total area 97,814 sq. mi (10th), incl. 713 sq. mi. inland water. **Borders** Mont., S.Dak., Nebr., Colo., Utah, Idaho. **Rivers** Bighorn, Green, North Platte, Powder, Snake, Yellowstone. **Lakes** Bighorn, Yellowstone. **Mountains** Absaroka, Bighorn, Black Hills, Laramie, Owl Creek, Teton Range, Wind River Range, Wyoming Range.

Elected officials Gov. Dave Freudenthal (D). Sec. State Max Maxfield (R). Atty. Gen. Bruce A. Salzburg (D).

People (July 2009 est.) 544,270 (50th). Race/Hispanic Origin: White 93.9%. Black 1.3%. Indian 2.5%. Asian 0.7%. Pacific Islander 0.1%. Two or more races 1.5%. Hispanic 7.3%.

Cities (2006) Cheyenne 55,314. Casper 52,089. Laramie 25,688. Gillette 23,899. Rock Springs 19,324. Sheridan 16,429. Green River 11,933. Evanston 11,567. Riverton 9,728. Cody 9,217.

Business Gross State Product, 2008: $21.8 bil. **Leading Sectors of GSP:** Mining 24.35%; Transportation & utilities 13.61%; Government 13.42%. *Fortune 500* **Companies (2009):** 0.

Famous natives James Bridger (b. Va.), pioneer. J.C. Penney, businessman. Jackson Pollock, painter. Nellie Tayloe Ross (b. Mo.), politician.

Noteworthy places Bighorn Canyon Natl. Rec. Area. Buffalo Bill Museum, Cody. Devil's Tower Natl. Monument. Ft. Bridger State Park. Ft. Laramie Natl. Hist. Site. Fossil Butte Natl. Monument. Grand Teton Natl. Park. Medicine Wheel Natl. Hist. Landmark, near Lovell. Natl. Elk Refuge. Yellowstone Natl. Park (Old Faithful).

Memorable events Part of Louisiana Territory claimed for France 1682. Pierre Gaultier de Varennes, sieur de Vérendrye explores region for France 1743. Region to United States with Louisiana Purchase 1803. John Colter crosses area of Yellowstone 1807–08. Indian Wars follow massacre of army detachments 1854 and 1866. Wyoming Territory organized 1868. Women's suffrage adopted permanently (first instance in United States); Union Pacific railroad crosses state 1869. Yellowstone, world's first national park, opens 1872. White mob kills 28 Chinese miners and burns Chinatown in Rock Springs 1885. Statehood 1890. Nellie Tayloe Ross first woman governor 1925. First Intercontinental Ballistic Missile (ICBM) base opens near Cheyenne 1951. Fires consume 1.6 million acres of forest in and around Yellowstone Park 1988. Matthew Shephard is murdered, sparking a national discussion and eventual legislation of hate crimes against homosexuality, 1998.

Tourist information (800) CALL-WYO
www.wyomingtourism.org

State Rankings, 2010

2010 Rank/State	2009 Rank	Change
1. Minnesota	4	3
2. Iowa	2	0
3. Nebraska	5	2
4. New Hampshire	3	−1
5. North Dakota	6	1
6. Wyoming	1	−5
7. South Dakota	11	4
8. Utah	9	1
9. Vermont	7	−2
10. Kansas	10	0
11. Massachusetts	12	1
12. Colorado	14	2
13. Virginia	15	2
14. Connecticut	8	−6
15. New Jersey	13	−2
16. Maine	19	3
17. Hawaii	20	3
18. Alaska	21	3
19. Maryland	17	−2
20. Montana	22	2
21. Wisconsin	23	2
22. Washington	18	−4
23. Idaho	16	−7
24. New York	24	0
25. Oregon	25	0
26. Missouri	32	6
27. Pennsylvania	28	1
28. Rhode Island	27	−1
29. Delaware	31	2
30. Illinois[1]	26	−4
30. Texas[1]	34	4
32. Oklahoma	30	−2
33. Indiana[1]	37	4
33. California[1]	29	−5
35. Michigan	33	−2
36. Louisiana	44	8
37. West Virginia	40	3
38. Nevada	35	−3
39. New Mexico	38	−1
40. Ohio	36	−4
41. North Carolina	42	1
42. Arkansas	43	1
43. Georgia	44	1
44. Florida	41	−3
45. Arizona	39	−6
46. Alabama	46	0
47. Tennessee	47	0
48. Kentucky	48	0
49. Mississippi	50	1
50. South Carolina	49	−1

Note: Ratings based on average of several statistics, including crime, education, and access to health care. 1. Both California and Indiana had a ranking of 23.48. Both Illinois and Texas had a ranking of 23.43 **Source:** CQ Press (formerly Morgan Quitno Press), *State & City Ranking Publications*, 2010.

Health Care State Rankings, 2010

2010 Rank/State	2009 Rank	Change
1. Vermont	6	5
2. Minnesota	1	−1
3. Massachusetts	2	−1
4. Hawaii	3	−1
5. New Hampshire	5	0
6. Utah	7	1
7. Maine	8	1
8. Iowa	4	−4
9. Rhode Island	11	2
10. Nebraksa	10	0
11. Washington	12	1
12. Connecticut	9	−3
13. North Dakota	13	0
14. New Jersey	14	0
15. Wisconsin	15	0
16. California	17	1
17. Oregon	19	2
18. Kansas	16	2
19. Idaho	23	4
20. Virginia	24	4
21. Ohio	26	5
22. West Virginia	18	−4
23. Michigan	20	−3
24. Pennsylvania	21	−3
25. South Dakota	22	−3
26. New York	31	5
27. Colorado	27	0
28. Indiana	25	3
29. Maryland	33	4
30. Arkansas	28	−3
31. Montana	32	1
32. North Carolina	34	2
33. Wyoming	30	−3
34. Missouri	36	2
35. Kentucky	29	−6
36. Tennessee	39	3
37. Delaware	35	−2
38. Arkansas	38	0
39. Georgia	40	1
40. Alabama	42	2
41. Texas	43	2
42. Alaska	37	−5
43. Arizona	41	−2
44. Oklahoma	44	0
45. Florida	45	0
46. South Carolina	46	0
47. New Mexico	48	1
48. Nevada	47	−1
49. Louisiana	49	0
50. Mississippi	50	0

Note: Ratings based on compilation of several health care statistics, including teenage birth rates, access to doctors, infant mortality, smoking, cancer cases, and more. **Source:** CQ Press (formerly Morgan Quitno Press), *State & City Ranking Publications*, 2008.

Composition of State Legislatures, 2010

State	Senate Total	Dem.	Rep.	House Total	Dem.	Rep.
Alabama	35	**20**	15	105	**60**	45
Alaska	20	10	10	40	18	**22**
Arizona	30	12	**18**	60	25	**35**
Arkansas	35	**27**	8	100	**72**	28
California	40	**25**	14	80	**49**	29
Colorado	35	**21**	14	165	**37**	27
Connecticut	36	**24**	12	151	**114**	36
Delaware	21	**15**	6	41	**24**	17
Florida	40	14	**26**	120	43	**76**
Georgia	56	21	**35**	180	74	**105**
Hawaii	25	**23**	2	51	**45**	6
Idaho	35	7	**28**	70	18	**52**
Illinois	59	**37**	22	118	**70**	48
Indiana	50	17	**33**	100	**52**	48
Iowa	50	**32**	18	100	**56**	44
Kansas	40	9	**21**	125	49	**76**
Kentucky	38	17	**20**	100	**64**	35
Louisiana	39	**23**	16	105	**52**	50
Maine	35	**20**	15	151	**95**	55
Maryland	47	**33**	14	141	**104**	36
Massachusetts	40	**34**	6	160	**144**	16
Michigan	38	16	**22**	110	**66**	43
Minnesota	67	**46**	21	134	**87**	47
Mississippi	52	**27**	25	122	**72**	50
Missouri	34	11	**23**	163	73	**89**
Montana	50	23	**27**	100	50	50
Nebraska	49	Nonpartisan		Unicameral		
Nevada	21	**12**	8	42	**28**	14
New Hampshire	24	**14**	10	400	**222**	176
New Jersey	40	**23**	17	80	**47**	33
New Mexico	42	**27**	15	70	**45**	25
New York	62	**32**	30	150	**107**	43
North Carolina	50	**30**	20	120	**68**	52
North Dakota	47	21	**26**	94	36	**58**
Ohio	33	12	**21**	99	**53**	46
Oklahoma	48	22	**26**	101	40	**61**
Oregon	30	**18**	12	60	**36**	24
Pennsylvania	50	20	**30**	203	**103**	97
Rhode Island	38	**33**	4	75	**69**	6
South Carolina	46	19	**27**	124	51	**73**
South Dakota	35	14	**21**	70	24	**46**
Tennessee	33	14	**19**	99	48	**50**
Texas	31	12	**19**	150	73	**77**
Utah	29	8	**21**	75	22	**53**
Vermont	30	**22**	7	150	**95**	48
Virginia	40	**22**	18	100	39	**59**
Washington	49	**31**	18	98	**62**	36
West Virginia	34	**26**	8	100	**71**	29
Wisconsin	33	**18**	15	99	**52**	46
Wyoming	30	7	**23**	60	19	**41**
TOTALS	**1,971**	**1,020**	**894**	**5,411**	**3,023**	**2,356**

Notes: Data is as of May 30, 2010. Numbers in **bold** indicate the party in the majority. **Source:** National Conference of State Legislatures, 2010. www.ncsl.org

Tax Collections in 2009 by region (in millions)

State	Sales Tax	Income Tax Personal	Corporate
U.S. Totals	**$169,534**	**$192,133**	**$30,026**
Eastern Region	**31,205**	**74,416**	**10,981**
Connecticut	3,319	6,386	616
Delaware	N.A.	913	134
Maine	975	1,243	143
Maryland	3,611	6,782	582
Massachusetts	3,869	10,584	1,549
New Hampshire	N.A.	N.A.	250
New Jersey[1]	1	1	1
New York	10,274	36,840	5,556
Pennsylvania	8,136	10,199	1,980
Rhode Island	808	941	104
Vermont	214	530	66
Midwestern Region	**41,572**	**48,445**	**7,525**
Illinois	6,773	9,223	1,710
Indiana[2]	6,153	4,314	839
Iowa	2,327	3,331	417
Kansas	1,925	2,682	240
Michigan[1]	6,212	6,058	2,160
Minnesota	4,378	7,012	710
Nebraska	1,326	1,600	199
North Dakota	622	375	99
Ohio	7,113	7,628	521
South Dakota	659	N.A.	N.A.
Wisconsin	4,084	6,223	630
Southern Region	**75,908**	**50,594**	**8,865**
Alabama	1,796	2,661	427
Arkansas	2,081	2,239	334
Florida	16,531	N.A.	1,833
Georgia	5,343	7,815	695
Kentucky	2,858	3,315	268
Louisiana	2,841	2,831	881
Mississippi	1,922	1,475	422
Missouri	1,813	4,876	358
North Carolina	4,678	9,470	836
Oklahoma	1,647	2,014	266
South Carolina	2,248	2,327	207
Tennessee[3]	6,331	221	1,369
Texas	21,700	N.A.	N.A.
Virginia	2,961	9,697	685
West Virginia	1,159	1,653	285
Western Region	**20,849**	**18,678**	**2,655**
Alaska	N.A.	N.A.	685
Arizona	3,756	2,568	592
California	N.A.	N.A.	N.A.
Colorado	1,931	4,333	293
Hawaii	2,418	1,338	54
Idaho	1,022	1,168	141
Montana	15	815	166
Nevada	N.A.	N.A.	N.A.
New Mexico	2,310	1,015	200
Oregon	N.A.	5,117	244
Utah	1,544	2,323	281
Washington	7,330	N.A.	N.A.
Wyoming	522	N.A.	N.A.

Notes: 1. These numbers are still being developed and researched. 2. Sales tax revenues include revenue from the one penny increase in the sales tax rate effective April 1, 2008. The increase was part of the property tax reform plan that shifted over $1 billion of expenses from local units to state government. 3. Corporate income tax includes excise tax and franchise tax. Sales tax, personal income tax, and corporate excise tax are shared with local governments. **Source:** National Association of State Budget Officers, The Fiscal Survey of the States (December 2009).

State Taxes There are three major sources of state tax revenue—sales taxes, personal income taxes, and corporate income taxes. (There are nine states without a personal income tax). Revenues are used for projects ranging from the education sector to road construction. In 2009, states faced unprecedented challenges as state tax revenues steeply declined, though state tax collections showed signs of stabilization in the first two months of 2010. Combined revenues in 45 states fell only 2.2 percent and a report released by the National Conference of State Legislatures shows that 42 states project that their revenue will grow in the fiscal year that ends in June 2011.

Summary of State Government Finances, 2003–2007

Item	Amount (millions) 2003	2007	Item	Amount (millions) 2003	2007
TOTAL REVENUES	**$1,295,658**	**$1,992,826**	Exhibit: Salaries and wages	183,385	215,876
General revenue	1,112,349	1,450,636	General expenditure	$1,163,968	$1,423,311
Intergovernmental revenue	361,617	430,202	Intergovernmental expenditure	382,196	457,377
Taxes	548,990	749,785	Direct expenditure	781,772	965,935
General sales	184,596	235,867	**General expenditures, by function:**		
Individual income tax	181,932	266,356	Education	411,094	514,924
Corporate income tax	28,384	52,978	Public welfare	314,406	393,142
Other taxes	38,382	38,289	Hospitals	38,395	48,285
Current charges	106,356	140,765	Health	50,221	57,814
Miscellaneous general revenue	95,384	129,884	Highways	85,726	103,167
Utility revenue	12,517	16,765	Police protection	11,144	12,876
Liquor store revenue	4,517	5,799	Correction	39,188	46,490
Insurance trust revenue	166,273	519,661	Natural resources	18,577	21,981
			Parks and recreation	5,844	6,024
TOTAL EXPENDITURES	**$1,359,048**	**$1,634,801**	Government administration	43,909	50,882
Intergovernmental expenditure	382,196	457,377	Interest on general debt	31,294	40,812
Direct expenditure	976,851	965,935	Other and unallocable	14,170	126,915
Current operation	656,989	810,498	Utility expenditure	22,404	24,367
Capital outlay	91,942	110,302	Liquor store expenditure	3,696	4,664
Insurance benefits and repayments	168,978	182,459	Insurance trust expenditure	168,978	182,459
Assistance and subsidies	25,900	31,363	**Debt at end of fiscal year**	**$697,929**	**$937,799**
Interest on debt	33,039	42,803	**Cash and security holdings**	**$2,594,215**	**$3,917,961**

Source: U.S. Bureau of the Census, Governments Division, *State Government Finances* (2008).**Source:** U.S. Bureau of the Census, Governments Division, *State Government Finances* (2008).

State Government Individual Income Taxes, 2009

State	Taxable income rate range (%)	Taxable income brackets Lowest: amount under	Highest: amount over	State	Taxable income rate range (%)	Taxable income brackets Lowest: amount under	Highest: amount over
Alabama[1]	2.0–5.0	$ 500	$ 3,000	Mississippi	3.0–5.0	$ 5,000	$10,000
Arizona	2.59–4.54	10,000	150,000	Missouri[6]	1.5–6.0	1,000	9,000
Arkansas	1.0–7.0	3,799	31,700	Montana	1.0–6.9	2,600	15,600
California	1.0–9.3	7,168	47,055	Nebraska	2.56–6.84	2,000	25,000
Colorado	4.63 percent[2]			New Hampshire	5.0 percent[7]		
Connecticut[3]	3.0–5.0	10,000	10,000	New Jersey	1.4–8.97	20,000	500,000
Delaware	2.2–5.95	5,000	60,000	New Mexico	1.7–5.3	4,000	20,000
District of Columbia	4.0–8.5	10,000	40,000	New York	4.0–6.85	8,000	20,000
Georgia	1.0–6.0	500	5,000	North Carolina[8]	6.0–8.0	10,625	100,000
Hawaii	1.4–8.25	2,400	48,000	North Dakota	1.84–4.86	28,375	186,475
Idaho[4]	1.6–7.8	1,272	25,441	Ohio[6]	5.87–5.925	5,000	200,001
Illinois	3.0 percent[5]			Oklahoma	0.5–5.65	1,000	10,500
Indiana[1]	3.4[6]			Oregon[6]	5.0–9.0	3,050	7,600
Iowa	0.36–8.98	1,407	63,315	Pennsylvania[6]	3.07 percent[9]		
Kansas	3.5–6.45	15,000	30,000	Rhode Island	3.75–9.9	36,000	374,250
Kentucky	2.0–6.0	3,000	75,000	South Carolina	3.0–7.0	2,670	13,350
Louisiana	2.0–6.0	12,500	25,000	Tennessee	6.0 percent[10]		
Maine	2.0–8.5	4,850	19,450	Utah	2.3–6.98	1,000	5,500
Maryland[6]	2.0–4.75	1,000	3,000	Vermont	3.6–9.5	30,650	336,550
Massachusetts	5.3 percent[5]			Virginia	2.0–5.75	3,000	17,000
Michigan[6]	4.35 percent[5]			West Virginia	3.0–6.5	5,000	30,000
Minnesota	5.35–7.85	16,160	65,990	Wisconsin	4.6–6.75	6,810	102,190

Note: Rates and brackets shown are for single taxpayers as of January 1, 2009. Brackets for married taxpayers filing jointly are usually double those shown. Alaska, Florida, Nevada, South Dakota, Texas, Washington, and Wyoming have no state income tax. 1. Does not include various local income taxes. 2. Of federal income with certain modifications. 3. Head of Household personal exemption is $19,000. 4. Does not include filing fee of $10. 5. Of taxable net income. 6. Does not include various local income taxes. 7. On dividend and interest income over personal exemption. 8. A taxpayer whose Federal AGI is >=50 percent of the amounts shown in the "maximum over" column is allowed a personal exemption of $2,000 and $2,000 for each dependent. 9. Of specified classes of taxable income. 10. On interest and dividend income. **Source:** Government of the District of Columbia, Dept. of Finance and Revenue, *Tax Rates and Tax Burdens in the District of Columbia: A Nationwide Comparison* (August 2009).

U.S. TERRITORIES AND POSSESSIONS

The United States administers a number of overseas territories and commonwealth states under a variety of circumstances. The provisions of the Northwest Ordinance of 1787 established the system under which territories of the United States can achieve statehood. In order to elect a territorial legislature and send a nonvoting delegate to Congress, a territory must contain 5,000 inhabitants of voting age; it is eligible for statehood when the population numbers 60,000.

▶ AMERICAN SAMOA
Territory of American Samoa
Geography Location: seven islands (Tutuila, Ta'u, Olosega, Ofu, Aunun, Rose, Swain's) in southern central Pacific Ocean. **Boundaries:** Hawaii about 2,300 mi. (3,700 km) to NNE, Cook Islands to E, Tonga to SW, Western Samoa to W. **Total area:** 76.1 sq. mi. (199 sq km). **Coastline:** 72 mi. (116 km). **Comparative area:** slightly larger than Washington, D.C. **Land use:** 10% arable land; 15% permanent crops; 75% other. **Major cities:** (2000 census) Nu'uuli 5,154. Pago Pago (capital) 4,278. Leone 3,568.
People Population: 65,628 (July 2009 est.) **Nationality:** noun—American Samoan(s); adjective—American Samoan. **Ethnic groups:** Pacific Islander 91.6%. Asian 2.8%. White 1.1%. Two or more races 4.2%. Other 0.3%. **Languages:** Samoan (closely related to Hawaiian and other Polynesian languages) and English; most people are bilingual. **Religions:** 50% Christian Congregationalist, 20% Roman Catholic, 30% mostly Protestant denominations and other.
Government Type: unincorporated and unorganized territory of U.S. **Constitution:** ratified 1966, in effect 1967. **National holiday:** Flag Day, Apr. 17 (1900). **Heads of Government:** Togiola T.A. Tulafono, Governor (since April, 2003). **Structure:** executive—governor is popularly elected to four-year term and exercises authority under direction of U.S. Secretary of Interior; legislative—bicameral legislature (Fono) with 18 member Senate chosen by county councils to serve four-year terms and House of Representatives with 20 members popularly elected to serve two-year terms, plus a nonvoting delegate from Swain's Island; judicial—High Court with chief justice and associate justices appointed by U.S. Secretary of Interior.
Economy Monetary unit: U.S. dollar. **Budget:** (2007 est.) income: $155.4 mil.; expend.: 183.6 mil. **GDP:** $575.3 mil.; $8,000 per capita (2007). **Chief crops:** bananas, coconuts, vegetables, taro, breadfruit, yams, copra, pineapples, papayas. **Natural resources:** pumice and pumicite. **Major industries:** tuna canneries, handicrafts. **Labor force:** 17,630 (2005) 34% agriculture, 33% industry, 33% services. 29.8% unemployment rate (2004 est.). **Exports:** $415.6 mil. (2004); 93% canned tuna. **Imports:** $308.8 mil. (2004); 56% material for canneries, 8% food, 7% petroleum products, 6% machinery and parts. **Major trading partners:** (2006) *exports:* Indonesia 28.2%, India 22.3 %, Australia 15.3%, Japan 11.2%, New Zealand 7.1%. *imports:* Australia 66%, Samoa 13.8%, New Zealand 10.8%.

American Samoa consists of seven islands between 14° and 15°S, and 168° and 171°W. It was first peopled by Polynesians in the first millennium B.C. The first European to visit the islands was Louis Antoine de Bougainville, who came in 1768 and called them "The Islands of the Navigators," in recognition of the islanders' seamanship. American whalers and missionaries began visiting the islands in the 1830s, and the United States secured trading privileges by treaty in 1878. In 1889, the United States, Britain, and Germany established tripartite control of the islands. The High Chiefs of Tutuila ceded the islands of Tutuila and Aunun to the United States in 1900, and the High Chiefs of the Manu'a islands ceded those of Tau, Ofu, Olosega, and Rose in 1904. Swain's Island became part of American Samoa in 1925. The islands have been administered by Department of Interior since 1951.

▶ BAKER AND HOWLAND ISLANDS
About 1,600 mi. (2,575 km) southwest of Hawaii and 1,000 miles west of Jarvis Island are Baker Island (0°14'N, 176°28'W) and Howland Island (0°48'N, 176°38'W, 40 miles north of Baker). Discovered in 1842, the two coral atolls were worked for guano until about 1890. Great Britain claimed them in 1889, but the U.S. made them territories in 1935 and sent colonists to them. With an area about of about 1 sq. mi. each, neither is inhabited today. Both are unincorporated territories administered by the U.S. Fish and Wildlife Service as part of the Pacific/Remote Islands National Wildlife Refuge.

▶ GUAM
Territory of Guam
Geography Location: southernmost and largest of Mariana Islands in western North Pacific Ocean; Agaña 13°28'N, 144°47'E. **Boundaries:** Tokyo, Japan about 1,350 mi. (2,170 km) to N, Honolulu, Hawaii 3,300 mi. (5,955 km) to ENE; Federated States of Micronesia to S, Philippines to W across Philippine Sea. **Total area:** 209 sq. mi. (541 sq km). **Coastline:** 78 mi. (125.5 km). **Comparative area:** Three times size of Washington, D.C. **Land use:** 3.64% arable land; 18.18% permanent crops; 78.18% other. **Major cities:** (2000 census) Tamunig 10,833; Mangilao 7,794; Yigo 6,391; Astumbo 5,207; Hagatna (or Agaña) (capital) 1,112.
People Population: 178,430 (July 2009 est.) **Nationality:** noun—Guamanian(s); adjective—Guamanian. **Ethnic groups:** Chamorro 37.1% Filipino 26.3%. Other Pacific Islander 11.3%. White 6.9%. Other Asian 6.3%. Other or mixed 12.1%. **Languages:** English, Chamorro, Philippine, other Asian. **Religions:** 85% Roman Catholic, 15% other.
Government Type: organized, unincorporated territory of U.S. **Constitution:** Organic Act of Aug. 1, 1950. **National holiday:** Guam Discovery Day, first Monday in Mar. (1521) **Heads of Government:** Felix Camacho, governor (since January 2003). **Structure:** executive—governor elected to 4-year term; legislative—unicameral; Senate has 15 members elected for 2-year terms; judicial—U.S. District Court, Guam Superior Court.
Economy Monetary unit: U.S. dollar. **Budget:** (2002) revenues: $319.6 mil.; expend.: $427.8 mil. **GDP:** $2.5 bil., $15,000 per capita (2005 est.). **Chief crops:** fruits, copra, vegetables, eggs; relatively undeveloped with most food imported.

Livestock: poultry, pigs, cows. **Natural resources:** fishing (largely undeveloped), tourism (especially from Japan). **Major industries:** U.S. military, tourism, construction, transshipment services, concrete products, printing and publishing, food processing, textiles. **Labor force:** 62,050 (2002 est.); 26% agriculture, 10% industry, 64% service. (2004) **Exports:** $45 mil. (f.o.b., 2004) mostly transshipments of refined petroleum products, construction materials, fish, food and beverage products. **Imports:** $701 mil. (f.o.b. 2004); petroleum and petroleum products; food, manufactured goods. **Major trading partners:** (2006) *exports:* Japan 67.2%, Singapore 11.6%, U.K. 4.8%; *imports:* Singapore 50%, South Korea 21.4%, Japan 14%, Hong Kong 4.6%.

Guam was inhabited by Chamorros from the Malay Peninsula as early as 1500 B.C. The first European to stop at Guam was Ferdinand Magellan in 1521. Spanish colonization began with the arrival of Jesuit missionaries in 1668. By 1700 pestilence and insurrection had reduced the Chamorro population from 50,000 to about 2,000. Guam was ceded to the United States in 1899. In 1941 it was occupied by Japan—the only inhabited territory of the U.S. to be seized by enemy forces during World War II. It was retaken by the Americans in 1944. Though unincorporated, the Congressionally approved Guam Organic Act provides for a republican form of government with executive, legislative, and judicial branches.

Guam receives major financial assistance from the U.S. federal government and Guamanians pay no federal income or excise taxes.

The U.S. plans to shift 8,000 marines to Guam from Okinawa over the next decade, though the plan, anticipated to be complete in 2014, has faced popular opposition in Guam.

▶ JARVIS ISLAND, KINGMAN REEF, AND PALMYRA ATOLL

Jarvis Island (0°23'S, 160°02'W, about 1,510 mi. S of Hawaii), Kingman Reef (6°24'N, 162°22'W, about 1,070 mi. SSW of Hawaii), and Palmyra Atoll (5°52'N, 162°05'W, about 1,100 mi. SSW of Hawaii) in the Line Island group.

Discovered in 1798, Kingman Reef (0.4 sq. mi.; 1 sq km) was annexed by the U.S. in 1922, and used as an aviation station during the 1930s. Discovered in 1802, Palmyra Atoll consists of about 50 islets with a combined area of four square miles. It was annexed by the Kingdom of Hawaii in 1862, by Great Britain in 1889, and claimed by the U.S. in 1912. Privately owned, it is administered by the Department of the Navy, as is Kingman Reef. Jarvis Island was claimed by the U.S. in 1857, annexed by Great Britain in 1889, and reclaimed by the U.S. in 1935. Its rich guano deposits were worked by U.S. and British companies in the late 19th century.

▶ JOHNSTON ATOLL

Geography Location: Johnston Island and Sand Island (uninhabited) in central Pacific Ocean. **Boundaries:** Honolulu, Hawaii about 825 mi. (1,330 km) to ENE, Marshall Islands to SW. **Total area:** 1.1 sq. mi. (2.8 sq km). **Coastline:** 6.21 mi. (10 km). **Comparative area:** about 4.7 times size of The Mall in Washington, D.C. **Land use:** 0% arable land; 0% permanent crops; 0% meadows and pastures; 0% forest and woodland; 100% other. **Major cities:** none.

People Population: 1,000 (May 2005), all U.S. government personnel and contractors.

Government Type: unincorporated territory of U.S.

Johnston Atoll (16°45N, 169°32'W) , 820 miles SW of Hawaii) includes Johnston, Hikina, and Akan Islands, with a total area of 1.1 square miles. Claimed by the U.S. in 1858, Johnston Atoll is manned and administered by the U.S. Defense Special Weapons Agency and managed jointly as a National Wildlife Refuge by the DSWA and the Fish and Wildlife Service.

▶ MIDWAY ISLANDS

Geography Location: Sand Island and Eastern Island in northern Pacific Ocean; 28°15'N, 177°22'W. **Boundaries:** Honolulu, Hawaii about 1,460 mi. (2,350 km) to SE, Marshall Islands to SW. **Total area:** 2.0 sq. mi. (5.2 sq km). **Coastline:** 9.3 mi. (15.0 km). **Comparative area:** about nine times size of The Mall in Washington, D.C. **Land use:** 0% arable land; 0% permanent crops; 100% other. **Major cities:** none.

People Population: 40 U.S. Fish and Wildlife Service personnel and contractors (July 2008 est.). No indigenous population. **Nationality:** noun—Midway Islander(s); adjective—Midway Island. **Languages:** English.

Government Type: unincorporated territory of U.S.

Economy Monetary unit: U.S. dollar. **Major industries:** support of National Wildlife Refuge activities.

Midway Atoll consists of Eastern Island and Sand Island. Although they are part of the Leeward Islands—the westernmost islands of the Hawaiian chain—they are not part of the state of Hawaii. They were the site of the Battle of Midway, June 1942, a turning point in the Pacific theater of World War II. The islands continued to serve as a naval station until 1993; since 1996, they have been managed by the U.S. Fish and Wildlife Service as a National Wildlife Refuge open to the public for snorkeling, scuba diving, and sportfishing.

▶ NAVASSA

Located in the Caribbean between the islands of Jamaica and Haiti and 100 mi. (160km) south of the U.S. Naval Base at Guantánamo, Cuba, Navassa was claimed by the U.S. in 1857. It is uninhabited. A lighthouse built in 1917 was shut down by the U.S. Coast Guard in 1996. The island, which is about 2 sq. mi. (5.2 sq km), was designated a National Wildlife Refuge in 1999 and is administered by the Fish and Wildlife Service.

▶ NORTHERN MARIANA ISLANDS
Commonwealth of the Northern Mariana Islands (CNMI)

Geography Location: Fourteen major islands (including Saipan, Rota, and Tinian) in western central Pacific Ocean. Saipan 15°12'N, 145°44'E. **Boundaries:** Japan to N; Honolulu, Hawaii about 3,500 mi. (5,635 km) to E; Guam to SW; Philippines to W across Philippine Sea. **Total area:** 184 sq. mi. (477 sq km). **Coastline:** 921 mi. (1482 km). **Comparative area:** slightly more than 2.5 times size of Washington, D.C. **Land use:** 13% arable land, 4.35% permanent crops, 82.61% other. **Major cities:** (2000 census) Saipan (capital) 61,502.

People Population: 88,662 (July 2009 est.). **Nationality:** U.S. citizens. **Ethnic groups:** Asian 56.3%. Pacific Islander 36.3%. White 1.8%. Other and mixed 5.6%. **Languages:** Philippine languages, Chinese, Chamorro, English. 86 percent speak a language other than English at home. **Re-**

ligions: Christian (Roman Catholic majority); some traditional beliefs and taboos.

Government Type: Self-governing commonwealth associated with U.S. **Constitution:** Covenant Agreement effective Nov. 3, 1986. **National holiday:** Commonwealth Day, Jan. 8. **Heads of Government:** Benigno Fitial, governor (since January, 2006). **Structure:** executive—governor elected by popular vote; legislative—bicameral legislature (nine-member Senate elected for four-year term, 20-member House of Representatives elected for two-year term; judiciary—U.S. District Court, Commonwealth Supreme Court, Superior Court.

Economy Monetary unit: U.S. dollar. **Budget:** (FY 2001/02) *revenues:* $193 mil. *expend:* 223 mil. **GDP:** $900 mil., $12,500 per capita (2000). **Chief crops:** coconuts, fruits, vegetables. **Livestock:** cattle. **Natural resources:** arable land, fish. **Major industries:** tourism, construction, light industry, handicrafts. **Labor force:** 44,470 total indigenous labor force, 2,699 unemployed, 28,717 foreign workers (2000). **Exports:** $N.A. garments. **Imports:** $214.4 (2001) food, construction equipment and materials, petroleum products. **Major trading partners:** U.S., Japan.

Running north from the island of Guam across a 600-mile-long archipelago in the Pacific Island group known as Micronesia, the islands of the Northern Marianas (CNMI) were originally settled by Pacific argonauts as early as 1500 B.C. Ferdinand Magellan landed at Saipan in 1521, introducing Western culture to the region. The Spanish took control of the archipelago in 1565 and ruled until 1898, when Germany took over the islands. After World War I, the League of Nations mandated the Marianas to Japan, who developed extensive sugar processing works on Saipan. Allied forces took the Marianas in 1944.

In 1947, the islands were included in the United Nations Trust Territory of the Pacific and placed under U.S. administration. In 1976, the CNMI adopted its own constitution. A mutually approved Covenant to Establish a Commonwealth was implemented by the Marianas and the United States in 1986. The Northern Marianas are subject to provisions of U.S. law, except regarding customs, minimum wages, immigration, and taxation. The people are, as a rule, U.S. citizens. The CNMI benefits from substantially from United States assistance and from duty and quota exemptions for garments produced by 17,500 workers—most of whom are Chinese.

▶ **PUERTO RICO**
Commonwealth of Puerto Rico
GEOGRAPHY Location: Large island of Puerto Rico, together with Vieques, Culebra, and many smaller islands, in northeastern Caribbean Sea. 18° 15'N, 66° 30'W **Boundaries:** Atlantic Ocean to N, Virgin Islands to E, Caribbean Sea to S, Dominican Republic 50 mi. (80 km) to W. **Total land area:** 3,459 sq. mi. (8,959 sq km). **Coastline:** 311 mi. (501 km). **Comparative area:** slightly less than three times size of Rhode Island. **Land use:** 3.69% arable land, 5.59% permanent crops, 90.72% other. **Major cities:** (2000 Census) San Juan (capital) 421,958, Bayamón 203,499, Carolina 168,164, Ponce 155,038, Caguas 88,680.

People Population: 3,971,020 (July 2009 est.). **Nationality:** noun—Puerto Rican(s); adjective—Puerto Rican. **Ethnic groups:** White (mostly Hispanic) 80.5%. Black 8%. Native American 0.4%. Asian 0.2%. Other and mixed 10.9%. **Languages:**

Spanish (official), English. **Religions:** 85% Roman Catholic, 15% Protestant denominations and other.

Government Type: commonwealth associated with U.S. **Constitution:** effective July 25, 1952. **National holiday:** U.S. Independence Day, July 4. Puerto Rico Constitution Day, July 25. **Heads of Government:** Gov. Luis Fortuno (since January 2009). **Structure:** executive—governor elected by direct vote to four-year term; legislative—bicameral legislature (Senate with 29 members, House of Representatives with 51 members, all elected by popular vote to four-year terms); judiciary—Supreme Court appointed by governor.

Economy Monetary unit: U.S. dollar. **Budget:** (2007 est.) *income:* $6.7 bil.; *expend.:* $9.6 bil. **GDP:** $70.6 bil., $17,800 per capita (2008 est.). **Chief crops:** sugarcane, coffee, pineapples, plantains, bananas (imports a large share of food needs). **Livestock:** cattle, chickens. **Natural resources:** copper, nickel; potential for crude oil. **Major industries:** manufacturing of pharmaceuticals, electronics, apparel, food products, instruments, tourism. **Labor force:** 1.3 mil. (2000); agriculture 3%, industry 20%, services 77%. Unemployment rate 12%. **Exports:** $46.9 bil. (f.o.b. 2001); pharmaceuticals, electronics, apparel, canned tuna, rum, beverage concentrates, medical equipment, tourism. **Imports:** $29.1 bil. (c.i.f. 2001); chemicals, machinery and equipment, clothing, food, fish, petroleum products. **Major trading partners:** (2006) *exports:* U.S. 90.3%, U.K. 1.6%, Dominican Republic 1.4%, Netherlands 1.4%; *imports:* U.S. 55%, Ireland 23.7%, Japan 5.4%.

Puerto Rico was initially peopled by the Igneri and Taíno tribes. The island's first European visitor was Christopher Columbus, who landed on the island in 1493. In 1508, Juan Ponce de Léon led the first settlers to San Juan, and by 1514 the Taíno population had dropped from an estimated 30,000 to 4,000. In the 17th and 18th centuries, Puerto Rico was invaded by both English and Danish forces, and though San Juan was captured or burned several times, the Spanish maintained control.

The Spanish constitution granted Puerto Ricans citizenship in 1812, but a revolution was put down in 1868. Spain granted Puerto Rico self-government in 1897 but this was repealed when sovereignty was transferred to the U.S. after the Spanish-American War. Despite early attempts to Americanize Puerto Rico, including an effort to make English the official language and granting citizenship in 1917, the Popular Democratic Party, founded in 1938, brought about a change in political status from that of a U.S. colony to an autonomous commonwealth in 1952.

Governed under the Puerto Rican Federal Relations Act and a constitution modeled on that of the U.S., Puerto Rico is nonetheless an autonomous political entity in voluntary association with the U.S. Despite dramatic increases in industrial development since the 1950s, Puerto Rico suffered from net outward migration until 1988.

Puerto Ricans remain almost equally divided between those who favor statehood and those who favor maintaining commonwealth status, with those seeking independence constituting a vocal but small minority. The statehood-minded argue that limited citizenship is disadvantageous since it allows them to be drafted into the U.S. military but they cannot vote in national elections. The other side fears the burden of full U.S. taxes. In the most recent balloting on the issue, held December 13, 1998, 50.2 percent of Puerto Ricans voted for "none of the above," an option that maintained Puerto Rico's commonwealth status; 46.5 percent voted for statehood, while 2.5 percent preferred independence.

▶ VIRGIN ISLANDS
Virgin Islands of the United States
GEOGRAPHY Location: three main inhabited islands (St. Croix, St. Thomas and St. John) and about 50 smaller islands, mostly uninhabited, in northeastern Caribbean Sea. 18°20'N, 64°50'W. **Boundaries:** British Virgin Islands to N, Netherlands Antilles to E, Caribbean Sea to S, Puerto Rico about 40 mi. (64 km) to W. **Total area:** 136 sq. mi. (352 sq km). **Coastline:** 117 mi. (188 km). **Comparative area:** twice the size of Washington, D.C. **Land use:** 5.71% arable land. 2.86% permanent crops. 91.43% other. **Major cities:** (2000 census) Charlotte Amalie (capital) 11,004; Christiansted 2,637.
  People Population: 109,825 (July 2009 est.) **Nationality:** noun—Virgin Islander(s); adjective—Virgin Islander. **Ethnic groups:** 74% West Indian (45% born in Virgin Islands, 29% born elsewhere in West Indies), 13% U.S. mainland, 5% Puerto Rican, 8% other; Black 76.2%. White 13.1%. Asian 1.1% Other and mixed 9.6%. **Languages:** English (official), Spanish, Creole. **Religions:** 42% Baptist, 34% Roman Catholic, 17% Episcopalian, 7% other.
  Government Type: organized, unincorporated territory of U.S. **Constitution:** Revised Organic Act of July 22, 1954 serves as constitution. **National holiday:** Transfer Day (from Denmark to U.S.), Mar. 27 (1917) **Heads of Government:** John DeJohngh, governor (since January 2007). **Structure:** executive—governor elected to four-year term; unicameral legislature—senate with 15 members elected to two-year terms; judiciary—U.S. district court under Third Circuit jurisdiction, Superior Court of the Virgin Islands—judges appointed by governor for 10-year terms.
  Economy Monetary unit: U.S. dollar. **Budget:** (2008) *income:* $837 mil.; *expend.:* $837 mil. **GDP:** $1.6 bil., $14,500 per capita (2004). **Chief crops:** fruit, vegetables, sorghum. **Livestock:** Senepol cattle. **Natural resources:** sun, sand, sea, surf. **Major industries:** tourism, petroleum refining, watch assembly, rum distilling, construction, pharmaceuticals, textiles, electronics. **Labor force:** 43,980 (2004); 1% agriculture. 19% industry. 80% services. 6.2% unemployment rate. (2004) **Exports:** $4.23 bil; refined petroleum products to

U.S. **Imports:** $4.6 bil.; 82% crude petroleum, foodstuffs. **Major trading partners:** *exports:* U.S., Puerto Rico; *imports:* U.S., Puerto Rico.
  The Virgin Islands of the United States (USVI) consists of more than 50 islands located about 40 miles east of Puerto Rico, and about 1,730 east-southeast of Miami. Excavations have revealed evidence of human habitation in the Virgin Islands from as early as A.D. 100. By 1493, when Christopher Columbus landed in the islands—which he named for the virgin martyr St. Ursula—they were inhabited by Carib Indians who were driven out by the Spanish in 1555.
  In 1672, St. Thomas was settled by the Danish West India Company. The Danes laid claim to St. John in 1683 and purchased St. Croix from the French in 1773. The United States purchased the Virgin Islands from Denmark for $25 million in 1917, and they were made a territory under the jurisdiction of the Navy. U.S. citizenship was granted in 1927, and the Department of the Interior assumed administration of the islands in 1931. The first governor elected by popular vote was installed in 1970, and an independent constitution was voted down by the electorate 1979.
  The primary industry is tourism, which accounts for 70 percent of GDP and employs 70 percent of the work force. International business and financial services are increasingly important.

▶ WAKE ISLANDS
GEOGRAPHY Location: three islands (Wake, Wilkes, and Peale) in North Pacific Ocean; Wake 19°17'N, 166°39'E. **Boundaries:** Honolulu, Hawaii 2,3000 mi. (3,700 km) to E, Marshall Islands to S, Guam about 1,280 mi. (2,060 km) to W. **Total area:** 2.5 sq. mi. (6.5 sq km). **Coastline:** 12 mi. (19.3 km) **Comparative area:** about 11 times size of the Mall in Washington, D.C. **Land use:** 0% arable land; 0% permanent crops; 100% other. **Major cities:** none.
  People Population: no indigenous inhabitants; temporary population of military personnel and 75 civilian contractors (July 2008).
  Government Type: territory of U.S., administered by Dept. of the Interior with U.S. Air Force.
  The Wake Island group was first discovered by British captain William Wake in 1796. It was chartered by Capt. Charles Wilkes' surveying expedition, which was accompanied by a naturalist named Peale. Annexed by the United States in 1898, Wake became a civil aviation station in the 1930s, and was captured by the Japanese in December 1941. It was retaken in 1944. Formerly an important commercial aviation base, it is now

Resident Population of U.S. Territories, 1960–2020 (in thousands)							
Territory	1960	1970	1980	1990	2000	2010[1]	2020[1]
Puerto Rico	2,358	2,7122	3,210	3,537	3,916	4,088	4,196
Guam	67	86	107	134	155	184	211
Virgin Islands	33	63	100	104	121	133	144
American Samoa	20	27	32	47	65	81	95
Northern Mariana Islands	9	12	17	44	72	99	123

1. Projected. **Source:** U.S. Census Bureau, International Data Base.

Cities and Counties in the U.S.

Included here is basic information about population change, cost of living, and government finances in major U.S. cities, metropolitan statistical areas and counties. In addition, there are brief descriptions of the 50 largest cities—from Albuquerque to Virginia Beach. Statistical sources include the U.S. Census Bureau's decennial census, *City Government Finances, County Government Finances,* and the *Statistical Abstract of the United States* (all annual publications).

▶ FORMS OF LOCAL GOVERNMENT

In addition to the one federal and 50 state governments, the Bureau of the Census recognizes five basic types of organized local government. In addition to these, which are authorized in state constitutions and statutes, some local governments operate under a "home-rule charter" the form and organization of which are specified by locally approved charters rather than by general or special state law. The number of local governments and officials continues to climb even as the size of the federal bureaucracy shrinks. In 2007, there were a total of 89,527 state and local governments compared with 87,453 just 10 years earlier.

Counties

County governments are established to provide general government; and include those governments designated as boroughs in Alaska, parishes in Louisiana, and counties in the other states. In 2007, there were 3,033 county governments; the most common forms are:

Council–commission A county government without a chief executive but with an elected governing body that shares administrative responsibility with officials elected or appointed to specific positions.

Council–administrator A county government with an elected governing body responsible for overall policy, and an appointed administrator (sometimes called a county manager, county commissioner, or county judge) responsible for administration. The powers of the administrator under this form of government may vary widely.

Council–elected executive A county government with an elected governing body and an elected chief executive—sometimes called a president or a chairperson of the board. The powers of the executive under this form of government may vary widely.

Municipalities

Municipal governments are established to provide general government for a specific concentration of population in a defined area and include those governments designated as cities, villages, boroughs (except in Alaska), and towns (except in the six New England states, Minnesota, New York and Wisconsin). In 2007, there were 19,492 municipal governments; the most common forms are:

Mayor–council A municipal government with an elected mayor and an elected council or other governing body. In some mayor-council municipalities, the mayor is the chief executive, with broad powers. In some other mayor-council cities, the mayor has limited powers.

Council–manager A municipal government with an elected council or other governing body responsible for overall policy, and an appointed manager responsible for administration. The council may select a chairperson from among their own number who may be designated as the mayor.

Commission A municipal government with an elected board of commissioners responsible for overall policy. Each commissioner is responsible for administration of one or more departments of the municipal government. The board may select a chairperson from among their own number who may be designated as the mayor.

Towns

Township governments are established to provide general government for areas defined without regard to population concentration and include those governments designated as towns in Connecticut, Maine (including organized plantations), Massachusetts, Minnesota, New Hampshire (including organized locations), New York, Rhode Island, Vermont, and Wisconsin, and townships in other states. In 2007, there were 16,519 township governments; the most common forms are:

Town meeting A township government in which an annual town meeting of resident voters makes basic policy. An elected board (often called "a board of selectmen" or "township supervisors") is responsible for day-to-day administration of the township.

Representative town meeting A township government in which a town meeting composed of elected representatives of the resident voters makes basic policy. This form of government is usually found in more populous towns or townships. An elected board (often called "a board of selectmen" or "township supervisors") is responsible for day-to-day administration of the township.

School districts

School district governments are organized local entities providing public elementary, secondary and/or higher education which, under state law, have sufficient administrative and fiscal autonomy to qualify as separate governments. Excludes "dependent public school systems" of county, township or state governments. In 2007, there were 13,051 school district governments.

Special district governments

All organized local entities other than the four categories listed above, authorized by state law to provide only one or a limited number of designated functions, and with sufficient administrative and fiscal autonomy to qualify as separate governments; known by a variety of titles, including districts, authorities, boards, commissions, etc., as specified in the state legislation. In 2007, there were 37,381 special district governments.

Source: U.S. Bureau of the Census.

THE 50 LARGEST CITIES, 2009

Between 1990 and 2000, the westward movement of the U.S. population again revealed its strength as four cities in the so-called Rust Belt (Buffalo, Cincinnati, Pittsburgh and Toledo) fell from the list of the 50 largest cities in the U.S. They were replaced by Colorado Springs, Las Vegas, Mesa, Ariz. and Wichita, Kansas. By 2006, Witchita had been replaced by Arlington, Texas, and St. Louis had been bumped by Louisville.

Among the largest cities in the U.S., however, no city came close to Las Vegas in terms of population growth. Between 1990 and 2000, its population increased from 258,295 to 478,434, leapfrogging more than 30 cities in going from the 63rd largest city to the 32nd.

Following are brief descriptions of the 50 largest cities in the U.S. according to the most recent data available from the Census Bureau. They are set forth in alphabetical order. Several tables showing the growth of major cities in America follow this section. See also the section on Metropolitan Statistical Areas (MSAs) later in this chapter.

▶ ALBUQUERQUE, NEW MEXICO

Seventy million years ago, earthquakes and volcanoes pushed the land that is now Albuquerque above the sea, forming the Rio Grande Valley and a ring of mountain ranges. Even today, the 10,000-foot-high Sandia Mountains are rising slowly and the Rio Grande Valley continues gradually to deepen. During the Ice Age, Sandia Man roamed the area hunting mastodon and buffalo, and some 3,000 years ago, the Anasazi built stone and adobe cities which still stand. The 1530s marked the arrival of Spanish conquistadors and missionaries.

Founded as a Spanish Villa in 1706, when 35 families moved to the land along the Rio Grande, Albuquerque was named by Don Francisco Cuervo y Valdez in honor of the Duke of Albuquerque, King Phillip's Viceroy of New Spain.

Indian raids arrested the villa's expansion, and 100 years after its founding, its population numbered a mere 2,200. Benefitting from their proximity to the Santa Fe Trail, the people farmed, raised cattle, marketed wool and adobe for building, and ran trading posts, military supply depots, saloons, hotels, and mercantile businesses. The introduction of the railroad in 1880 spurred Albuquerque's growth, and the 1940 population of 35,000 has since grown more than tenfold.

Today, Albuquerque occupies a central position along the Rio Grande Research Corridor, which stretches from Los Alamos to Las Cruces, and is home to the University of New Mexico and such major high-tech installments as Honeywell, GE, and Sandia National Laboratories. Albuquerque's cultural and historical attractions include the Albuquerque Museum, the Indian Pueblo Culture Center, the Maxwell Museum of Anthropology, the National Museum of Nuclear Science & History, and Petroglyph National Monument.

Population   528,497 (2009). Rank: 34th. Race/Hispanic Origin (2006–2008): White 67.5%. Black 3.5%. Indian 5.1%. Asian 2.6%. Other 18%. Two or more races 3.3%. Hispanic 15.1%.

Location: 35°05'N, 106°47'W. County: Bernalillo.

Terrain and climate   Elev.: 5,300 ft. Area: 127.2 sq. mi. (329.4 sq km). Avg. daily min. temp.: Jan.: 22.3°F/-5.3°C; avg. daily max. July: 92.8°F/33.7°C. Avg. annual: rainfall, 8.12"; snowfall, 11"; clear days, 71; precipitation days, 135.

Government   Form: mayor and council. Mayor: Richard J. Berry. (505) 768-3000

www.cabq.gov

Visitor info: (505) 842-9918 or (800) 284-2282

www.itsatrip.org

▶ ARLINGTON, TEXAS

Nestled squarely between Dallas and Fort Worth, Arlington traces its roots back a century and a half to a small frontier outpost set up in the 1840s at Marrow Bone Spring near Johnson Station. Authorized by Texas Republic President Sam Houston, it served as a dividing line between white settlers and a collection of Native American tribes driven to the area by American westward expansion. In 1877 it was named Arlington after the Virginia estate of Confederate commander Robert E. Lee.

Arlington developed into an agricultural center where Old West mentalities took shootouts to the streets. The city had as many as five working cotton gins at one time and became a major distribution point for cotton as well as hay, oats, and corn. The town was also famed for its mineral water, which was bottled and sold and from which medicinal crystals were produced.

Population increased steadily throughout the 19th century, and until pari-mutuel betting was made illegal in Texas in 1937, racetrack Arlington Downs drew thousands of visitors every year. By the mid-20th century, industrialization had taken over the city and with the construction of a General Motors Assembly plant in 1951, the population skyrocketed again. To accommodate the recreational needs of the booming population, Lake Arlington was developed in 1957, and Six Flags Over Texas opened in 1961. In 1972, the city became home to the Texas Rangers who play at Rangers Ballpark in Arlington. There are two universities (University of Texas at Arlington and Tarrant County College Southeast Campus), and the public is served by four independent school districts. Cowboys Stadium, the retractable-domed home of the Dallas Cowboys, opened in 2009. Super Bowl XLV in 2011 is expected to be held at the new stadium.

Population   380,084 (2009). Rank: 49th. Race/Hispanic Origin (2006–2008): White 63.2%. Black 17.4%. Indian 0.5%. Asian 6.4%. Other 10.1%. Two or more races 2.3%. Hispanic 26.0%.

Location: 32°43'N, 97°8'W. County: Tarrant.

Terrain and climate   Elev.: 598 ft. Area: 99.5 sq. mi. (257.7 sq km). Avg. daily min. temp.: Jan.: 43.5°F/6.39°C; avg. daily mix. July: 84.5°F/29.2°C. Avg. annual: rainfall, 34.73"; clear days, 135; precipitation days, 77.

Government   Form: mayor   and   council. Mayor: Robert Cluck. (817) 459-6122

www.arlingtontx.gov

Visitor info: (800) 433-5374

www.arlington.org

▶ ATLANTA, GEORGIA

Atlanta, the capital and largest city of Georgia, lies at the base of the Blue Ridge Mountains, near the Chattahoochee River. First settled in 1836, the area became the terminus for the Georgia Railroad in 1845 and took the name Atlanta. The population grew to 15,000 by 1861, and during the Civil War, Atlanta became a strategic Confederate depot and collection point for recruits, establishing it as one of the most important cities of the Confederacy and making it a vital objective during Gen. William Tecumseh Sherman's infamous "March to the Sea" in 1864. After two months of bitter battle, Sherman took the city on Sept. 1 and burned most of it to the ground. After the war, the ravaged city was rebuilt; it became the state capital in 1868.

The leading city of the "New South," Atlanta is a chief commercial hub of the southeastern United States. Atlanta is nicknamed the "City Without Limits" because there are no major rivers, mountains, or coastlines to retard its burgeoning growth into the ever-expanding suburbs. Several *Fortune* 500 Companies have their headquarters in Atlanta (including Coca-Cola and United Parcel Service) as do CNN and the U.S. Centers for Disease Control. Hartsfield-Jackson Atlanta International (the major hub for Delta Airlines) is the world's busiest airport, giving rise to the saying, "whether you're going to heaven or hell, you still have to change planes in Atlanta."

The city is also an important educational and cultural center, home to more than 30 institutions of higher learning, including Georgia Tech, Emory University, and Morehouse and Spelman Colleges. The Jimmy Carter Presidential Library is here, as is the grave of the Rev. Martin Luther King Jr.

The 1996 Summer Olympics thrust Atlanta into the international spotlight, and helped fuel the city's economic future. The Olympiad added hundreds of thousands of jobs (most of them permanent) and an estimated $500 million in construction to Atlanta's economy. It also brought Centennial Olympic Park and Turner Field to the downtown landscape.

Population 540,921 (2009). Rank: 33rd. Race/Hispanic Origin (2006–2008): White 38.4%. Black 55.8%. Indian 0.2%. Asian 1.9%. Other 2.6%. Two or more races 1.1%. Hispanic 4.9%.
Location: 33°50'N, 84°24'W. County: Fulton.
Terrain and climate Elev.: 1,034 ft. Area: 131.2 sq. mi. (339.80 sq km). Avg. daily min. temp.: Jan.: 32.6°F/0.3°C; avg. daily max. July: 87.9°F/31°C. Avg. annual: rainfall, 48.61"; snowfall, 2"; clear days, 108; precipitation days, 116.
Government Form: mayor and council. Mayor: Kasim Reed. (404) 330-6100
www.atlantaga.gov
Visitor info: (800) ATLANTA
www.atlanta.net

▶ **AUSTIN, TEXAS**

Austin, the capital of Texas, lies about 80 miles northeast of San Antonio on the banks of the Colorado River. First inhabited by nomadic Indian tribes, the area had as its first permanent European settler Jacob Harrell, in 1835, who established the town of Waterloo. In 1839, it was chosen as the site of the Texas Republic's capital and was renamed after Stephen F. Austin, who brought the first Anglo settlers to Texas in the 1820s. After 1845, when Texas gained admission into the Union, Austin began to flourish, and by 1930 it had grown into a major regional center with a population of 75,000.

Originally a business and distribution center serving the farmers of the Blackland Prairies to the east, Austin's farmers produce cotton, maize, corn, livestock, and poultry. Traditional industries such as meat packing, canning, and furniture manufacturing have been outstripped by the high-tech companies that have helped to nearly double the population since 1970. The city's economic landscape has for decades been defined by the state government (responsible for 131,000 jobs, or one-fourth of Austin's workforce). The University of Texas, founded in 1881 in Austin, boasts the highest endowment of any U.S. university—a legacy of the Texas oil fields. As the University developed into a first-class institution (with 50,000 students) feeding the city's cultural and economic life, and with the influx of electronics and computer companies, Austin has prospered into a metropolis of national, even worldwide, scope.

In recent years, the university's academic excellence and Austin's reputation for liberalism and progressivism (coffeehouses are more common here than cowboy hats) have attracted both the arts and high-tech companies such as Dell Computer, Motorola, 3M, IBM, and Texas Instruments.
Population 786,382 (2009). Rank: 15th. Race/Hispanic Origin (2006–2008): White 63.7%. Black 8.2%. Indian 0.4%. Asian 5.5%. Other 19.8%. Two or more races 2.3%. Hispanic 35.0%.
Location: 30°20'N, 97°45'W. Counties: Travis, Williamson
Terrain and climate Elev.: 570 ft. Area: 232 sq. mi. (600.9 sq km). Avg. daily min. temp.: Jan.: 38.8°F/3.8°C; avg. daily max. July: 95.4°F/35.2°C. Avg. annual: rainfall, 31.50"; snowfall, 1"; clear days, 115; precipitation days, 82.
Government Form: council and manager. Mayor: Lee Leffingwell. (512) 974-2250
www.ci.austin.tx.us
Visitor info: (800) 926-ACVB
www.austintexas.org

▶ **BALTIMORE, MARYLAND**

One of America's most active seaports since Colonial days and chartered in 1729 as a major conduit of tobacco exportation, Baltimore was named after the founder of the colony of Maryland, George Calvert, Lord Baltimore. By the time of the Revolutionary War, it earned fame as an important commercial and maritime center, and ships sailing from Baltimore plied their trade with northern Europe, the Mediterranean and the Caribbean. Chartered as a city in 1797, Baltimore's commercial activity began to surge, spurred by its burgeoning iron and copper industries, its proximity to the nation's capital, and the arrival of the Baltimore and Ohio Railroad, which developed links to the Midwest. However, the deep, divisive passions of the Civil War stunted growth and it would take years before the city recovered.

A fire in 1904 destroyed almost every building in the downtown area, providing impetus for needed revitalization. The two world wars renewed demands for Baltimore's port facilities and fostered development of a solid heavy industrial base. As the population peaked in the decade after World War II, however, the city's infrastructure aged and decayed. Baltimore remains a significant port and industrial city although jobs in higher education and health care have proved more durable in recent years. Much of the city has been rebuilt through urban renewal efforts, including the nationally acclaimed Inner Harbor Project, and Oriole Park at Camden Yards. The population continues to drop, although at much smaller levels than past decades.

Among the city's historic sites is Fort McHenry, where Francis Scott Key wrote "The Star-Spangled Banner." Baltimore is home to St. Mary's Seminary and University (1791), Johns Hopkins University (1876), and the University of Baltimore (1925), among other noted institutions of higher learning.
Population 637,418 (2009). Rank: 21st. Race/Hispanic Origin (2006–2008): White 31.9%. Black 63.4%. Indian 0.2%. Asian 1.9%. Other 0.9%. Two or more races 1.6%. Hispanic 2.6%.
Location: 39°18'N, 76°37'W. County: independent city within Baltimore County.

Terrain and climate   Elev.: 155 ft. Area: 80.3 sq. mi. (208 sq km). Avg. daily min. temp.: Jan.: 24.3°F/-4.2°C; avg. daily max. July: 87.1°F/30.6°C. Avg. annual: rainfall, 43.39"; snowfall, 22"; clear days, 106; precipitation days, 112.
Government   Form: mayor and council. Mayor: Stephanie Rawlings-Blake. (410) 396-3835
www.baltimorecity.gov
Visitor info: (877) BALTIMORE
www.baltimore.org

▶BOSTON, MASSACHUSETTS

Named for the English port from which many Puritan immigrants to America came, Boston was first settled in 1630 under the leadership of John Winthrop. As the capital of the Massachusetts Bay Colony, it quickly became the cultural and mercantile capital of the New England colonies. Bostonians never wholly embraced British authority, and they provided the earliest challenges to British rule in their reaction to the Stamp Act (1765) and the Boston Tea Party (1773). The colonists killed in the Boston Massacre (1770) were the first to fall in the years immediately preceding the American Revolution.

With the end of the Revolution, Boston merchants found themselves shut out of English ports by prohibitive tariffs, and in their quest for new markets for American goods opened American trade to the Orient and India. In the 19th century, Boston benefitted early from the industrial revolution, and from several waves of immigration, particularly blacks from the southern states, and Irish and Italians from Europe.

Although Boston's preeminence in trade and industry did not survive the 19th century, it continues to be a major center for banking and financial services. Since World War II, its suburbs have flourished as a center of research and development and of the computer industry—Route 128 was the East Coast's answer to California's Silicon Valley during the 1980s—spurring investment in downtown Boston. As the gateway to New England and the birthplace of the Revolution, Boston is also a center for tourism.

Perhaps most important to its identity is Boston's wealth of educational, cultural, and religious tolerance. Harvard University (across the Charles River in Cambridge, 1636) is the country's oldest, and Roxbury Latin (1645) the country's oldest privately endowed secondary school. Today Boston is home to more than 30 colleges and universities, as well as to some of the finest cultural institutions in the country, including the American Academy of Arts and Sciences (1780), the Massachusetts Historical Society (1791), the Boston Athenaeum (1807), the Boston Public Library (the nation's first, 1854), the Boston Museum of Fine Arts (1870), and the Boston Symphony (1881). Boston is also home to three major medical schools and 27 hospitals including the world famous Massachusetts General and Brigham and Women's.
Population   645,169 (2009). Rank: 20th. Race/Hispanic Origin (2006–2008): White 56.3%. Black 23.5%. Indian 0.4%. Asian 8.2%. Other 8.5%. Two or more races 3.1%. Hispanic 16.1%.
Location: 42°20'N, 71°05'W. County: Suffolk.
Terrain and climate   Elev.: 10 ft. Area: 47.2 sq. mi. (122.2 sq km). Avg. daily min. temp.: Jan.: 22.8°F/-5.1°C; avg. daily max. July: 81.8°F/27.6°C. Avg. annual: rainfall, 43.81"; snowfall, 42"; clear days, 99; precipitation days, 128.
Government   Form: mayor and council. Mayor: Thomas M. Menino. (617) 635-4500
www.cityofboston.gov

Visitor info: (888) SEE-BOSTON
www.bostonusa.com

▶CHARLOTTE, NORTH CAROLINA

An area of lush green foothills lying at the southernmost tip of the Carolina Piedmont, Charlotte has long been a crossroads city and an important distribution point for the surrounding farmlands. About 250 years ago, Scotch-Irish settlers retracing old Catawba Indian trading routes established a settlement where the paths crossed, and in 1762 it was named Charlotte, after the new bride of King George III. Remembering Gen. Cornwallis's reference to Charlotte as a "hornet's nest" while his army briefly occupied it during the American Revolution, the city adopted the symbol as its emblem.

The discovery of a 17-pound gold nugget in 1799 triggered a gold rush, and although the mines dotting the landscape boosted business, the California gold rush in the mid-1800s lured away prospectors, putting Charlotte on its future course as a top cotton producer. A leading city of the Confederacy in the Civil War, Charlotte hosted the last full meeting of the Confederate cabinet in 1865. The Queen City's second population surge has occurred over the past 20 years. Charlotte is one of the country's largest banking centers, with Bank of America making its headquarters there. Charlotte is also the home of Duke Energy, one of the largest electric utilities in the United States, and the teachers pension fund TIAA-CREF.

Recently, the city's economic base has diversified beyond the production of chemicals, foodstuffs, machinery, metals, and textiles, and matured into a major center of world trade and technology, with more than 160 multinational companies engaging in such businesses as microelectronics, insurance, machining and biomedical supplies. North Carolina's status as a right-to-work state has given Charlotte the country's second-lowest unionization rate (less than 4 percent). Located at the intersection of Interstates I-77 and I-85, Charlotte is a key distribution hub, equidistant from the northwestern, midwestern, and southern Florida markets. The Carolina Panthers and the Charlotte Motor Speedway, are both sources of the city's legendary civic pride and boosterism.
Population   709,441 (2009). Rank: 18th. Race/Hispanic Origin (2006–2008): White 55.5%. Black 33.5%. Indian 0.4%. Asian 4.1%. Other 4.6%. Two or more races 1.8%. Hispanic 11.2%.
Location: 35°16'N, 80°46'W. County: Mecklenburg.
Terrain and climate   Elev.: 665 ft. Area: 152.1 sq. mi. (393.9 sq km). Avg. daily min. temp.: Jan.: 30.7°F/-0.7°C; avg. daily max. July: 88.3°F/31.2°C. Avg. annual: rainfall, 43.16"; snowfall, 6"; clear days, 111; precipitation days, 111.
Government   Form: council and manager. Mayor: Anthony Foxx. (704) 336-2241
www.charmeck.org
Visitor Info: (800) 231-4636
www.charlottesgotalot.com

▶CHICAGO, ILLINOIS

Chicago extends roughly 26 miles along the southwestern shoreline of Lake Michigan. The city has historically been a major transportation hub and gateway to the Great Plains, and continues to be one today with major air, rail, and highway hubs. Chicago remains a major railroad hub, linked with every major U.S. and Canadian city. The city has three major airports, including O'Hare, the second-busiest in the nation. It is also the terminus for major interstate highways running east-west and north-south.

Historically, Chicago's rise parallels the growth of the American republic to the west. Chicago was first settled in 1779, when Jean Baptiste Point de Sable built a house on the site. In 1803, federal troops built a stockade named Fort Dearborn, but by 1830 only 12 families had settled in the area. In the 1830s, however, the population grew rapidly as Americans spread westward, and the city of Chicago was incorporated in 1837 with a population of 4,170. Chicago then began to grow into a bustling Great Lakes port, connected to the Mississippi via a system of rivers and canals.

Chicago has maintained its strategic importance despite changes in transportation technology and remains today a prosperous city. Over the years, Chicago has been noted as a hotbed of labor reform, the center of violent organized crime gang wars during the prohibition era, and a prime example of the good and the bad of American city machine politics. But despite its checkered past, it has grown into the wealthiest and most vibrant city in the Midwest with hardly a sign of the rust belt malaise plaguing many of its sister cities. Chicago has grown into a financial center with three of the nation's four largest futures exchanges and the world's largest listed stock options exchange.

Chicago also far outstrips other midwestern cities in cultural, entertainment, recreational and commercial facilities. Major attractions include the Museum of Science and Industry, the Field Museum of Natural History, the Chicago Historical Society, the Lincoln Park Zoo, the Chicago Lyric Opera Company, the Chicago Symphony Orchestra and the Chicago Art Institute. Downtown Chicago currently has four of the tallest manmade structures in the world—the Willis Tower (formerly the Sears Tower) (1,454 ft. high), the Trump International Hotel and Tower (1,362 ft), the John Hancock Building (1,127 ft.) and the AON Center (1,136 ft.). It is also home to the 70-story Lake Point Tower apartment complex and the Merchandise Mart, formerly the world's largest commercial building.

Population   2,851,268 (2009). Rank: 3rd. Race/ Hispanic Origin (2006–2008): White 39.9%. Black 34.6%. Indian 0.2%. Asian 4.9%. Other 18.6%. Two or more races 1.7%. Hispanic 27.8%.
Location: 41°53'N, 87°40'W. County: Cook.
Terrain and climate   Elev.: 623 ft. Area: 228.1 sq. mi. (590.8 sq km). Avg. daily min. temp.: Jan.: 13.6°F/-10.2°C; avg. daily max. July: 83.3°F/28.5°C. Avg. annual: rainfall, 33.34"; snowfall, 40"; clear days, 94; precipitation days, 123.
Government Form: mayor and council. Mayor: Richard M. Daley. (312) 744-3300
www.cityofchicago.org
Visitor Info: (312) 567-8500
www.choosechicago.com

▶ CLEVELAND, OHIO

The heart of the largest metropolitan area in Ohio, Cleveland was founded in 1796 and named after Moses Cleaveland, a surveyor with the Connecticut Land Company, which administered the state of Connecticut's lingering claim on 3.5 million acres of what is now Ohio (the Western Reserve). A frontier village at the mouth of the Cuyahoga River on Lake Erie, Cleveland was transformed into the business and manufacturing center of northern Ohio by the opening of the Erie Canal in 1825, and the Ohio and Erie Canal, which linked Cleveland with Portsmouth on the Ohio River. When the Soo Locks opened Lake Superior to trade with the Lower Lakes in 1855, Cleveland became a major shipping center for ore, lumber, copper, coal and farm produce.

During the Civil War, the city's iron ore and coal deposits were mined for steel production and commercial activity increased to meet the Union's increased demands for heavy machinery, railroad equipment and ships. In the postwar years, Cleveland's mills and factories expanded even further to satisfy the increased needs of the new cities and farms springing up in the wake of westward migration.

Although manufacturing still employs about 13 percent of the region's workforce, the national trend toward a service economy had a severe impact on the local economy, and the population of the Cleveland metropolitan area declined from a high of 2.8 million in 1970 to 2.1 million today. Nonetheless, Cleveland is still home to many large industrial companies. There are also many medical and industrial research firms, most notably the world-famous Cleveland Clinic and NASA's Lewis Research Center.

Cleveland's industrial strength manifests itself in its flourishing cultural institutions, including the Cleveland Play House, the oldest repertory house in the nation, the world-famous Cleveland Orchestra, the Cleveland Institute of Art, the Cleveland Museum of Natural History, Western Reserve Historical Society, the Allen Memorial Medical Library and the Cleveland Metroparks Zoo.

Population   431,363 (2009). Rank: 43rd. Race/ Hispanic Origin (2006–2008): White 40.4%. Black 52.5%. Indian 0.3%. Asian 1.5%. Other 3.0%. Two or more races 2.2%. Hispanic 9.0%.
Location: 41°28'N, 81°43'W. County: Cuyahoga.
Terrain and climate   Elev.: 805 ft. Area: 79 sq. mi. (204.6 sq km). Avg. daily min. temp.: Jan.: 18.5°F/-7.5°C; avg. daily max. July: 81.7°F/27.6°C. Avg. annual: rainfall, 35.40"; snowfall, 52"; clear days, 70; precipitation days, 156.
Government Form: mayor and council. Mayor: Frank G. Jackson. (216) 664-3990
www.city.cleveland.oh.us
Visitor Info: (800) 321-1004 or (216) 875-6600
www.positivelycleveland.com

▶ COLORADO SPRINGS, COLORADO

Colorado's second-largest city lies on the eastern edge of the Rocky Mountains, some 60 miles south of Denver. Most of Colorado Springs is nestled among rolling hills with views of the 14,110–foot Pikes Peak to the west. General William Jackson Palmer was the first to recognize the area's natural beauty when he founded the city in 1871. In its early years, it was popular with Europeans, especially Britons, and the city acquired the nickname Little London.

The city's first big boom came during the 1890s, after gold was discovered in nearby Cripple Creek in 1891. The gold rush ended in 1917, when the U.S. began coining money with silver. Since the beginning of World War II, the military has been a major presence in Colorado Springs, beginning with the establishment of Fort Carson in 1942 and continuing with the location of the Air Force Academy, several Air Force bases and the North American Aerospace Defense Command (NORAD) over the years since then.

The city's manufacturing base experienced record growth during the 1960s and 70s due to Colorado Springs' low cost of living and sunny weather patterns (the city has 127 clear days a year and receives less snow than Denver or Minneapolis). Semiconductors, electronic equipment, computers and plastics are among the major manufacturing industries.

Leading an expansion of the service industry in the Pikes Peak region, the United States Olympic Committee has its headquarters in Colorado Springs, as well as its Olympic Training Center, the world's premier multi-sport training facility.

Colorado Springs also prides itself on its extremely clean air. According to local officials, the city's pollen counts are among the lowest in the country, providing relief to people suffering from asthma, nasal allergies, and other respiratory ailments.

Population 399,827 (2009). Rank: 46th. Race/ Hispanic Origin (2006–2008): White 79.3%. Black 6.6%. Indian 0.8%. Asian 2.9%. Other 5.6%. Two or more races 4.6%. Hispanic 14.6%.

Location: 38°48′N, 104°42′W. County: El Paso.

Terrain and climate Elev. 6,145 ft. Area 183.2 sq. mi. (474.5 sq km). Avg. daily min. temp.: Jan.: 16.1°F/–8.8°C; avg. daily max. July: 86.5°F/30.3°C. Avg. annual: rainfall, 16.24″; snowfall, 51″; clear days, 129; precipitation days, 98.

Government Form: council and manager. Mayor: Lionel Rivera. (719) 385-5986
www.springsgov.com
Visitor info: (800) DO-VISIT or (719) 635-7506
www.experiencecoloradosprings.com

▶COLUMBUS, OHIO

The Ohio legislature designated a site along the banks of the Scioto River in the center of the state as the capital in 1812, and named it Columbus in honor of the famous explorer of the New World. From the first, the city exploited its status as the seat of government and its prime location in the middle of the nation's growing network of roads, canals and highways. Incorporated in 1834, Columbus became a thriving hub of agricultural trade.

Between 1850 and 1900, its population grew from 17,800 to over 100,000. Because of the many carriage factories, in the 19th century Columbus was known as the "Buggy Capital of the World." Five railroads passed through the city, so banks soon began to spring up, making Columbus a financial center for the surrounding farm counties.

As in the 19th century, Columbus's modern economy is built on government, agriculture, local finance, and education. In 1950, to counter the trend of suburbanization, the city developed a policy of annexation of surrounding communities. Because it is less reliant on heavy industry than other midwestern cities, it has weathered the decline of the rust belt better than most and it remains a bustling metropolis. In the 1980s, the city realized the creation of more than $780 million in new development and about 100,000 new jobs.

The Ohio State University, one of the nation's largest universities, opened as the Ohio Agricultural and Mechanical College in 1870, and the city today has a rich academic community that includes the Ohio Dominican College (whose origins date to 1868), the Columbus College of Art and Design and the Ohio Institute of Technology. Business leaders and politicians have joined in an effort to make the city a center for the arts, refurbishing three theaters and building a complex of three more.

Population 769,360 (2009). Rank: 16th. Race/ Hispanic Origin (2006–2008): White 65.4%. Black 26.4%. Indian 0.2%. Asian 4.1%. Other 1.4%. Two or more races 2.4%. Hispanic 4.5%.

Location: 39°57′N, 83°01′W. Counties: Fairfield, Franklin.

Terrain and climate Elev.: 833 ft. Area: 186.8 sq. mi. (483.8 sq km). Avg. daily min. temp.: Jan.: 19.4°F/–7°C; avg. daily max. July: 84.4°F/29.1°C. Avg. annual: rainfall, 36.97″; snowfall, 28″; clear days, 75; precipitation days, 136.

Government Form: mayor and council. Mayor: Michael B. Coleman. (614) 645-7671
www.cityofcolumbus.org
Visitor info: (866) EXP-COLS or (614) 221-6623
www.experiencecolumbus.com

▶DALLAS, TEXAS

First settled in 1841 by John Neely Bryan, a Tennessee trader and lawyer, Dallas stretches about 30 miles east of Forth Worth on the Trinity River. Named in 1846 after James K. Polk's vice president, George Mifflin Dallas, it was chartered as a city in 1871. Though it grew substantially with the arrival of railroads in 1872, the population numbered a mere 92,000 in 1910.

Located in the heart of the northern Texas oil belt, Dallas today thrives on a diverse economic base, which, in addition to oil and natural gas, includes production of brick clay and the raw materials for Portland cement, and cotton, grains, fruits, beef, dairy cattle, hogs, sheep and poultry from the farms that surround the city. One of the largest inland cotton markets, and a leading distributor of farm goods and machinery, Dallas also serves as the southwest's banking center with major banks, insurance companies, and the Federal Reserve Bank for the Eleventh District. Key manufacturing industries include aerospace, electronics, transportation equipment, machinery, food and related products, and apparel. Among its leading high-tech employers are Texas Instruments and Electronic Data Systems.

Some of Dallas' distinguished universities are Southern Methodist, Southwestern Medical School of the University of Texas, the Dallas Theological Seminary and Graduate School of Theology, and the Baylor University Schools of Dentistry and Nursing. The Dallas Symphony Orchestra, the Dallas Theater Center, the Dallas Civic Opera, the Dallas Historical Society Museum in the Texas Hall of State, and the Dallas Garden Center, contribute to the city's rich cultural life. Fair Park, the site of the annual State Fair of Texas, remains the most widely attended state fair in the country.

Population 1,299,543 (2009). Rank: 9th. Race/ Hispanic Origin (2006–2008): White 56.6%. Black 23.2%. Indian 0.4%. Asian 2.5%. Other 15.9%. Two or more races 1.3%. Hispanic 43.1%.

Location: 32°50′N, 96°50′W. Counties: Collin, Dallas, Denton, Kaufman, Rockwall.

Terrain and climate Elev.: 596 ft. Area: 331.4 sq. mi. (858.3 sq km). Avg. daily min. temp.: Jan.: 33.9°F/1°C; avg. daily max. July: 97.8°F/36.5°C. Avg. annual: rainfall, 34.16″; snowfall, 3″; clear days, 138; precipitation days, 79.

Government Form: council and manager. Mayor: Tom Leppert. (214) 670-4054
www.dallascityhall.com.
Visitor info: (800) CDALLAS or (214) 571-1000
www.visitdallas.com

▶DENVER, COLORADO

Denver was born during the great "Pikes Peak or Bust" gold rush of 1859 when small flakes of placer gold were found where the South Platte River meets Cherry Creek. In its first few years, the city survived a flood, several major fires, attacks from native Americans, and an invasion by Confederate soldiers during the Civil War. With the discovery of more gold in the Rocky Mountains, Denver became a boom town. Saloons, gambling halls, and wagon trains lined the mud-filled streets and just about every outlaw, desperado, and lawman in the West made at least one visit to the city. The turn of the century brought respectability and the wealth of the mountains was poured into parks, fountains, tree-lined streets, and elaborate mansions.

During the oil crisis of the late 1970s and early 80s, Denver experienced a second boom when it became a corporate center for oil-from-shale companies working the Western Slope of the Rockies. Then one of the fastest-growing cities in the United States, in 1983, it doubled its office space as part of a five-year building campaign that added 16 skyscrapers, a $76 million pedestrian mall, and an $80 million performing arts center. Expansion was slowed by the energy glut of the mid-1980s, but it has rebounded dramatically in the 1990s and the population grew by close to 10,000 per year in the first few years of the 1990s.

In 1993, the Colorado Rockies baseball team drew more than four million fans to a converted football stadium. And in 1995, after countless setbacks stemming from problems with its automated baggage system, the much-heralded Denver International Airport finally opened its doors, thus completing the final chapter of a vastly overbudget boondoggle.

Denver's population is among the youngest in the nation, and the youthful flavor of the city is very evident. Denver leads the nation in movie attendance and has more sporting goods stores per resident than any city in the world. The city's 205 parks are so active that a speed limit was instituted—for bicycles.

Population   610,345 (2009). Rank: 24th. Race/Hispanic Origin (2006–2008): White 74.1%. Black 9.6%. Indian 1.1%. Asian 3.3%. Other 9.2%. Two or more races 2.5%. Hispanic 34.1%.
Location: 39°45'N, 105°00'W. County: Denver.
Terrain and climate Elev.: 5,280 ft. Area: 106.8 sq. mi. (276.6 sq km). Avg. daily min. temp.: Jan.: 15.9°F/-8.9°C; avg. daily max. July: 88°F/31°C. Avg. annual: rainfall, 15.31"; snowfall, 60"; clear days, 115; precipitation days, 88.
Government Form: mayor and council. Mayor: John Hickenlooper. (720) 865-9000
www.denvergov.org
Visitor info: (303) 892-1112
www.denver.org

▶ DETROIT, MICHIGAN

Founded in 1701 by Antoine de La Mothe, sieur de Cadillac, Detroit lies on the Detroit River between Lake Erie and Lake Huron. Named Fort Pontchartrain-du-Détroit (of the strait), the oldest permanent settlement on the Great Lakes flourished as a trading post for trappers, under French control (to 1760), then British (to 1796) and then American.

The first steamboat reached Detroit from Buffalo in 1818, but it was the easy access to eastern markets via the Erie Canal in 1825 that allowed Detroit to exploit the abundant natural resources in the Michigan peninsula and fostered its emergence as a modern industrial giant in the post-Civil War years. Tenth among cities in the value of its manufactures by 1899, Detroit's main exports included iron ore, copper, lead, salt, and fish. The development of the automotive industry, which eventually became centered in Detroit, propelled Detroit to number three by the 1920s. While Detroit is the home of General Motors, Chrysler, and Ford, recently the automotive industry has been as much a curse as a blessing, for every setback to any of the "Big Three" is felt throughout the Motor City. This proved exceptionally true in 2009 when the auto-

motive industry suffered such serious setbacks that the federal government stepped in.

Despite the fact that it still ranks high in industrial manufacturing, Detroit has been plagued by urban decline. The relatively low standard of living among the predominantly black inhabitants ignited riots in the 1940s and 1960s, and the city's crime rate is today among the highest in the nation. However, it was Detroit blacks who gave rise to one of the most sensational expressions of popular culture in the 1960s. Founded in 1960, the Tamla Motown label propelled the Jackson 5, the Supremes, and Stevie Wonder—among others—to world renown, and in the process created one of the largest black-owned businesses in the country.

The city's rich and diverse cultural institutions include the Detroit Institute of Arts (which contains one of the largest collections of American art in the world in addition to extensive European holdings), the Detroit Symphony, the Cranbrook Academy of Art, and the 1,000-acre Belle Isle Park, situated on an island in the Detroit River and featuring beaches, a yacht basin, a zoo, an aquarium, and a botanical gardens. In 2000, Detroit became the first U.S. city that had had 1 million residents see its population drop below 1 million.

Population   910,920 (2009). Rank: 11th. Race/Hispanic Origin (2006–2008): White 10.5%. Black 83.0%. Indian 0.3%. Asian 1.0%. Other 3.8%. Two or more races 1.4%. Hispanic 6.4%.
Location: 42°23'N, 83°05'W. County: Wayne.
Terrain and climate Elev.: 581 ft. Area: 135.6 sq. mi. (351.2 sq km). Avg. daily min. temp.: Jan.: 16.1°F/-8.8°C; avg. daily max. July: 83.1°F/28.3°C. Avg. annual: rainfall, 30.97"; snowfall, 39"; clear days, 75; precipitation days, 133.
Government Form: mayor and council. Mayor: Dave Bing (313) 224-3400
www.detroitmi.gov
Visitor info: (800) DETROIT
www.visitdetroit.com

▶ EL PASO, TEXAS

The largest Texas city bordering Mexico, El Paso sits in the western part of the state on the northern bank of the Rio Grande across from Juarez. A major port of entry, with the biggest commercial and manufacturing base in the area, the city encompasses a region of mines, oil fields, livestock ranches, and farms (principal crops: pecans, fruit, cotton, alfalfa, onions, lettuce, chiles). Important industries include metals smelting and refining, oil and gas refining, textiles, meat packing, and food processing. The city is also home to the University of Texas, at El Paso.

In 1536, Alvar Núñez Cabeza de Vaca crossed the Rio Grande, becoming the first European to set foot in the area, but settlement did not follow until 1659, with the establishment of both El Paso del Norte on the southern bank of the Rio Grande, and the Mission of Guadalupe. In 1682, settlers from New Mexico founded Ysleta, an area within the current city limits of El Paso, but permanent settlement did not begin until the arrival of Juan Maria Ponce de Leon in 1827. Incorporated as a city in 1873, El Paso grew into a major industrial center with the introduction of the railroads in 1881.

El Paso's access to sources of cheap labor complemented its mining, refining, and agricultural activities and helped build the city's manufacturing base. In recent years, however, the movement of manufacturing back to Mexico, where labor costs are far less, has created some concern for that portion of the economy. El Paso's proximity to Juarez, Mexico, makes it a vibrant tourist haven, and its pleasant climate, combined with its posi-

tion on the immigration route from Latin America, have made El Paso one of the fastest-growing cities in the U.S. El Paso also has the highest percentage of citizens with Hispanic ancestry of any American city, more than 3 out of 4.
Population 620,447 (2009). Rank: 22nd. Race/Hispanic Origin (2006–2008): White 77.8%. Black 3.1%. Indian 0.5%. Asian 1.2%. Other 15.1%. Two or more races 2.2%. Hispanic 80.0%.
Location: 31°50'N, 106°30'W. County: El Paso.
Terrain and climate Elev.: 3,700 ft. Area: 239.7 sq. mi. (620.8 sq km). Avg. daily min. temp.: Jan.: 30.4°F/-0.8°C; avg. daily max. July: 95.3°F/35.1°C. Avg. annual: rainfall, 7.82"; snowfall, 5"; clear days, 194; precipitation days, 45.
Government Form: council and manager. Mayor: John Cook. (915) 541-4145
www.elpasotexas.gov
Visitor info: (800) 351-6024 or (915) 534-0601
www.visitelpaso.com

▶**FORT WORTH, TEXAS**
Named in 1849 after Gen. William J. Worth, commander of the U.S. Army in Texas, Forth Worth originally served to protect settlers from Indian attacks. It grew slowly mainly as a stopover on the cattle drives along the Chisholm Trail until the Texas and Pacific Railroad reached the city in 1871. Stockyards sprang up, making Fort Worth a conduit of cattle shipping, and with the building of a grain elevator, it developed into a milling center as well. By the turn of the century, it had also emerged as a flourishing meat packing market. Oil was discovered in 1917, bringing prosperity and transforming the city into a major refining center with a dozen operating facilities. The two world wars introduced military installations (particularly airfields) to the area. Fort Worth is the sixth largest city in Texas, boasting the state's three finest art museums and a network of parks with total acreage second only to Chicago's.
Population 727,575 (2009). Rank: 17th. Race/Hispanic Origin (2006–2008): White 63.0%. Black 18.0%. Indian 0.5%. Asian 3.5%. Other 13.2%. Two or more races 1.8%. Hispanic 33.8%.
Location 32°45'N, 97°25'W. County: Tarrant.
Terrain and climate Elev.: 670 ft. Area: 258.5 sq. mi. (670.3 sq km). Avg. daily min. temp.: Jan.: 33.9°F/1°C; avg. daily max. July: 97.8°F/36.5°C. Avg. annual: rainfall, 29.45"; snowfall, 1.4"; clear days, 137; precipitation days, 78.
Government Form: council and manager. Mayor: Michael J. Moncrief. (817) 392-6118
www.fortworthgov.org
Visitor info: (800) 433-5747
www.fortworth.com

▶**FRESNO, CALIFORNIA**
Fresno grew up around a train station established in 1872 for what became the Southern Pacific Railway. The city was incorporated in 1874. With the introduction of irrigation to the fertile San Joaquin Valley in the 1880s, the small city thrived at the center of a healthy agricultural economy. Today Fresno County is the number one producer of agricultural products in the nation—and the world—and averages more than $2 billion a year in the production and processing of 200 commercial crops, including grapes (for raisins and wine), melon, cotton, alfalfa, barley, grains, cattle, sheep, and poultry.

Fresno's population grew 63 percent between 1980 and 1990, and in the 1980s it was the ninth fastest growing city in the United States and by far the fastest growing of the nation's 50 largest cities.

Located in central California, Fresno—the name is Spanish for ash tree—is a gateway to the Sierra Nevadas, and it is less than 90 minutes from three national parks—Kings Canyon (55 miles), Sequoia (85 miles) and Yosemite (92 miles). Among the attractions to be found within the city limits are the Fresno Art Museum, the Fresno Zoo, the Kearney Mansion Museum (restored home of Theo Kearney, "Raisin King of California"), the Fresno Metropolitan Museum, and the Discovery Center. There are also 10 colleges and universities including a campus of California State University and Fresno City College.
Population 479,921 (2009). Rank: 36th. Race/Hispanic Origin (2006–2008): White 53.3%. Black 8.0%. Indian 1.1%. Asian 11.6%. Other 21.8%. Two or more races 4.1%. Hispanic 44.6%.
Location 36°47'N, 119°50'W. County: Fresno.
Terrain and climate Elev. 328 ft.; Area: 99.4 sq. mi. (257 sq. km). Avg. daily min. temp. Jan.: 37.4°/3°C; avg. daily max. July: 98°.7F/37°C. Avg. annual rainfall: 10"; snowfall 0"; clear days: 200; precipitation days: 44.
Government Form: council and manager. Mayor: Ashley Swearengin. (559) 621-8000
www.fresno.gov
Visitor info: (800) 788-0836 or (559) 445-8300
www.playfresno.org

▶**HONOLULU, HAWAII**
First visited by Europeans in 1794, Honolulu, meaning "sheltered harbor," has attracted droves of visitors ever since. Situated on Oahu Island, it benefits from a large bay fully protected by coral reefs and its large port facilities. Because of its hospitable climate, the beaches of Waikiki, its majestic mountains, and exotic locale, tourism is Honolulu's major industry; several million visitors come annually, mainly from the U.S. mainland and the Far East, particularly from Japan.

The defense industry is the second mainstay of Honolulu's economy, as the U.S. has long maintained major installations around the island, including the naval base at Pearl Harbor, Hickam Air Force Base, and the U.S. Army's Schofield Barracks and Fort Shafter. Honolulu also serves as the center for Hawaii's export crops—sugar, pineapple, and molasses—and is the principal port for the import of much of the island state's necessities.
Population 374,701 (2009). Rank: 50th. Race/Hispanic Origin (2006–2008): White 21.4%. Black 1.9%. Indian 0.2%. Asian 54.6%. Pacific Islander 6.2%. Other 0.8%. Two or more races 14.9%. Hispanic 3.8%.
Location: 21°19'N, 157°52'W. County: Honolulu.
Terrain and climate Elev.: 15 ft. Area: 25.3 sq. mi. (65.52 sq km). Avg. daily min. temp.: Jan.: 65.3°F/18.5°C; avg. daily max. July: 87.1°F/30.6°C. Avg. annual rainfall: 23.47"; snowfall: 0"; clear days: 90; precipitation days: 102.
Government Form: mayor and council. Mayor: Mufi Hannemann. (808) 768-4141
www.co.honolulu.hi.us
Visitor info: (877) 525-OAHU
www.visit-oahu.com

▶**HOUSTON, TEXAS**
On August 30, 1836, brothers August C. and John K. Allen founded this city and named it after Sam Houston, the first president of the Republic of Texas. The Allens paid just over $1.40 per share for 6,642 acres of land near the headwaters of Buffalo Bayou about 50 miles inland from the Gulf of Mexico. Houston's proximity to Stephen Austin's central Texas colonies gave it great potential as a

marketing and distribution site. Incorporated in 1837, the city served as capital of the Republic of Texas until 1840. When the first railroad in Texas began operating out of Houston in 1853, the city developed into a major agricultural center while the discovery of oil in southeast Texas at Spindletop in 1901, and the opening of the man-made Houston Ship Channel in 1914, stimulated petroleum refining and metal fabricating. During World War II, petrochemical production began on a large scale, and with the building of NASA's $761 million complex in the early 1960s (now known as the Johnson Space Center), Houston took center stage as the main player in manned spacecraft.

A major corporate and international business center—more than a dozen Fortune 500 companies are based here—present-day Houston has successfully limited its dependence on the energy economy. The Port of Houston is one of the largest in the world in terms of tonnage handled (16th in the world); the city is also home to four of the nation's 10 major liquid gas pipelines. The presence of the Texas Medical Center also makes Houston a vital U.S. center for the practice and progress of modern high-tech medicine. The Center's many institutions occupy in excess of 550 acres and employ more than 50,000 workers. Houston's total health employment exceeds 100,000.

Population 2,257,926 (2009). Rank: 4th. Race/Hispanic Origin (2006–2008): White 53.8%. Black 24.1%. Indian 0.4%. Asian 5.3%. Other 15.2%. Two or more races 1.1%. Hispanic 41.9%.
Location: 29°50'N, 95°20'W. Counties: Fort Bend, Harris, Montgomery.
Terrain and climate Elev.: 49 ft. Area: 572.7 sq. mi. (1,483.3 sq km). Avg. daily min. temp.: Jan.: 40.8°F/4.8°C; avg. daily max. July: 93.6°F/34.2°C. Avg. annual rainfall: 44.77"; snowfall: 0"; clear days: 94; precipitation days: 107.
Government Form: mayor and council. Mayor: Annise D. Parker. (713) 837-0311
www.houstontx.gov
Visitor info: (800) 4HOUSTON or (713) 437-5200
www.visithoustontexas.com

▶ **INDIANAPOLIS, INDIANA**
Indianapolis, the capital of Indiana and a major commercial center in the country's heartland, is intersected by more highways than any other in the nation, earning it the name, the "Crossroads of America." Fifty percent of America's population is within a day's drive of the city, a geographic asset that makes it a focal point of transportation and manufacturing.

The first European-American settlement, established in 1820 where Fall Creek meets the White River, was chosen as the location of Indiana's capital in 1825. The state government created jobs triggering an expanding population that further swelled with the routing of the National Road (U.S. 40) in 1830. Development mushroomed in 1839 with the building of the Central Canal on the White River, providing a vital transportation link and the necessary water power to run factories, sawmills, and paper mills. Maintenance of the canal, however, proved impossible, and the town declined until the introduction of the railroad. By 1853, railroad lines fed into Indianapolis from every corner of the nation and at one point, nearly 200 trains passed through daily. At the turn of the century, Indianapolis had emerged as a sophisticated city with sidewalks and streetcars. The city's economy prospered during the early stages of the automotive industry, producing more than 50 types of car—including

the Duesenberg, the Marmon, and the Stutz—before Detroit gained ascendancy.

Having survived the decline in heavy industry and the flight of the affluent to the suburbs, Indianapolis remains a hub of manufacturing and transportation, with a bustling wheat, soybean, and livestock market. Key industries include electronics, metal fabrication, pharmaceuticals, and transportation equipment. Downtown Indianapolis has enjoyed a renaissance with the construction of a convention center, the RCA Dome, Lucas Oil Stadium, Conseco Fieldhouse, and the refurbishment of Union Station. But the city's premier attraction remains the Indianapolis 500, the annual Memorial Day weekend auto race, first held in 1911.

Population 807,584 (2009). Rank: 14th. Race/Hispanic Origin (2006–2008): White 66.6%. Black 25.9%. Indian 0.2%. Asian 1.7%. Other 3.4%. Two or more races 2.1%. Hispanic 7.0%.
Location 39°42'N, 86°10'W. County: Marion.
Terrain and climate Elev.: 808 ft. Area: 352 sq. mi. (911.7 sq km). Avg. daily min. temp.: Jan.: 17.8°F/-7.8°C; avg. daily max. July: 85.2°F/29.5°C. Avg. annual rainfall: 39.12"; snowfall: 21"; clear days: 90; precipitation days: 122.
Government Form: mayor and council. Mayor: Gregory A. Ballard. (317) 327-3601
www.indygov.org
Visitor info: (317) 639-4282
www.indy.org

▶ **JACKSONVILLE, FLORIDA**
The first Europeans to visit the area were French Huguenots who in 1564 established a colony at Fort Caroline on the Saint Johns River in northeast Florida. The Spanish destroyed the fort in the following year. Permanent settlement began in 1816, and in 1822 Jacksonville was laid out and named for then Maj. Gen. Andrew Jackson, who had led the U.S. campaign to take Florida from the Spanish. Growth was slow until after the Civil War. After World War II, several large naval bases were located here and by 1960 the population was over 200,000. In 1968, the population jumped to more than 500,000 when it was consolidated with Duval County, and Jacksonville became one of the largest cities by area in the U.S.

Florida's largest city, Jacksonville is a major regional center for commerce, industry, finance, and medicine. After years of improvements on its harbor, 25 miles west from the mouth of the Saint Johns, it has grown into a major port of entry and it is the primary distribution center for the region. Jacksonville has also emerged as a leading resort with extensive recreational and convention facilities. Among its amenities are the Cummer Gallery of Art, the Museum of Contemporary Art Jacksonville, the Jacksonville Zoological Gardens, the Saint Johns River Park, and Fort Caroline National Memorial, site of the first European colony in Florida. Among its leading educational institutions are Jacksonville University and the University of Northern Florida.
Population 813,518 (2009). Rank: 13th. Race/Hispanic Origin (2006–2008): White 62.3%. Black 30.1%. Indian 0.3%. Asian 3.5%. Other 1.8%. Two or more races 1.9%. Hispanic 6.2%.
Location: 30°15'N, 81°38'W. County: Duval.
Terrain and climate Elev.: 31 ft. Area: 840 sq. mi. (1,967.6 sq km). Avg. daily min. temp.: Jan.: 41.7°F/ 5.4°C; avg. daily max. July: 90.7°F/29.5°C. Avg. annual rainfall: 52.77"; snowfall: 0"; clear days: 98; precipitation days: 116.
Government Form: mayor and council. Mayor: John Peyton. (904) 630-1776

www.coj.net
Visitor info: (800) 733-2668 or (904) 798-9111
www.visitjacksonville.com

▶KANSAS CITY, MISSOURI

Kansas City was begun as a trading outpost by the French fur trader François Chouteau in 1821. In 1833, the town of Westport was founded nearby, and in 1850 the City of Kansas received its first charter. (Its name was changed to Kansas City in 1889.)

Situated at the confluence of the Kansas and Missouri rivers, Kansas City prospered early on as a river port and as the terminus of the Santa Fe and Oregon trails. With the arrival of the railroad in 1866, Kansas City's status as a major commercial hub was assured. Thanks to its central location and the development of excellent and diversified transportation and storage facilities, Kansas City is one of the nation's key markets for agricultural and livestock products, as well as for the distribution of heavy agricultural machinery. The Kansas City Board of Trade is one of the largest grain and commodities trading markets in the world. Other major industries are greeting card publishing, telecommunications, and high-tech manufacturing, especially instrument landing systems for airplanes. Kansas City is also home to the 10th Federal Reserve Bank.

An early oasis of culture in the midst of an un-settled, untamed prairie (the city once boasted two opera houses), Kansas City remains a mecca of the arts, with cultural offerings like the Kansas City Art Institute, the Nelson-Atkins Museum of Art, the Kansas City Symphony, the Lyric Opera, and the Kansas City Repertory Theatre. The Power & Light District, a downtown entertainment center, opened in 2007. The city's beginnings are pre-served in the Lone Jack Civil War Museum and Missouri Town 1855, and it is the site of the annual American Royal Livestock, Horse Show, and Rodeo, held as part of the annual convention of the Future Farmers of America. Among its institutes of higher learning are Rockhurst College (1916) and the University of Missouri-Kansas City.
Population 482,299 (2009). Rank: 35th. Race/ Hispanic Origin (2006–2008): White 62.8%. Black 28.6%. Indian 0.4%. Asian 2.0%. Other 3.2%. Two or more races 2.7%. Hispanic 9.2%.
Location: 39°07'N, 94°38'W. Counties: Cass, Clay, Jackson, and Platte.
Terrain and climate Elev.: 744 ft. Area: 316.4 sq. mi. (819.5 sq km). Avg. daily min. temp.: Jan.: 17.2°F/-8.2°C; avg. daily max. July: 88.5°F/31.3°C. Avg. annual rainfall: 29.27"; snowfall: 5.9"; clear days: 132; precipitation days: 97.
Government Form: council and manager. Mayor: Mark Funkhouser. (816) 513-3500.
www.kcmo.org
Visitor info: (800) 767-7700 or (816) 221-5242
www.visitkc.com

▶LAS VEGAS, NEVADA

Las Vegas was originally settled by Mormons in 1855, but its modern history began in 1931, when Nevada legalized gambling and liberalized marriage and divorce laws. From then until 1978 (when Atlantic City re-opened its casinos), Las Vegas prospered while it enjoyed a monopoly on casino gambling in the U.S. Since 1980, it has been one of America's fastest-growing cities, more than doubling in size between 1980 and 1996. There were 164,674 people living in Las Vegas in 1980; by 1996 the city's population had climbed to 376,906. Population growth continued through the 2000s, until mid-decade when it dramatically

reversed—there was a loss of 10,000 residents between 2007 and 2008 alone.

To be sure, gambling helped to fuel this growth—commercial racetrack and casino revenues topped $36 billion in 2008—but the city's expansion has come even as dozens of other cities across the country have legalized casino gambling on riverboats, at Native American reservations, or even in the French Quarter of New Orleans. Las Vegas has thrived because of a mix of gambling, nightlife, shopping, and an unequivocal commitment to excess. The nation's 10 largest hotels (including the 5,000-room MGM Grand) are all here. The city has built hotels replicating New York City, Paris, Venice (complete with canals), and the pyramids of Egypt.

More than 35 million visitors (including 5 million conventioneers) travel to Las Vegas each year. With all this tourism came tens of thousands of new jobs and new housing. Yet the unemployment rate tripled from 4 percent in May 2007 to over 12.3 percent in July 2009. Existing home sales prices fell by 20 percent between 2008 and 2009. Because the city is laid out in a desert, there are few geographical barriers to limit urban expansion, except the availability of drinking water. The city is confronting problems of urban sprawl such as traffic, air pollution, and distribution of resources such as schools and water.
Population 567,641 (2009). Rank: 28th. Race/ Hispanic Origin (2006–2008): White 70.8%. Black 10.3%. Indian 0.6%. Asian 5.5%. Other 8.8%. Two or more races 3.6%. Hispanic 30.0%.
Location: 36° 05'N, 115°10'W. County: Clark.
Terrain and climate Elev.: 2,162 ft. Area: 83.3 sq. mi. (215.7 sq km). Avg. daily min. temp.: Jan.: 33.6°F/0.9°C; avg. daily max. July: 105.9°F/41.1°C. Avg. annual rainfall: 4"; snowfall: 1"; clear days: 211; precipitation days: 26.
Government Form: council and manager. Mayor: Oscar B. Goodman. (702) 229-6241
www.lasvegasnevada.gov
Visitor info: (877) VISIT-LV or (702) 892-7575
www.visitlasvegas.com

▶LONG BEACH, CALIFORNIA

Originally the site of a native American trading camp, by the end of the 18th century the area of what is now Long Beach was part of the Spanish Ranchos Los Alamitos and Cerritos. In 1881, William E. Willmore began development of the land as a resort (which he named for himself). When first incorporated in 1888, the town was named Long Beach after its 8.5 miles of Pacific beachfront. Content to remain a resort community, Long Beach saw its fortunes rewritten in 1921 when extensive petroleum deposits were discovered at Signal Hill. Today, industry is a major presence in Long Beach—especially ship repair, transportation, oil refining, and marine research.

Among the cultural and recreational attractions Long Beach boasts are its own Museum of Art, the Terrace Theater, home of the Long Beach Symphony Orchestra, and the Long Beach Community Playhouse. Popular tourist attractions include Los Cerritos (a Spanish adobe house which dates to 1844), the Aquarium of the Pacific, and the magnificent ocean liner Queen Mary which today serves as a floating maritime museum, convention center, and hotel. Long Beach is also the site of a Formula 1 Grand Prix every spring. Disneyland is in nearby Anaheim.
Population: 462,604 (2009). Rank: 38th. Race/ Hispanic Origin (2006–2008): White 44.0%. Black 13.4%. Indian 0.4%. Asian 13.2%. Other 24.1%. Two or more races 4.0%. Hispanic 40.2%.

Location: 33°46'N, 118°10'W. County: Los Angeles.
Terrain and climate   Elev.: 35 ft. Area: 49.8 sq. mi. (129 sq km). Avg. daily min. temp.: Jan.: 44.3°F/6.8°C; avg. daily max. July: 83°F/28.3°C. Avg. annual rainfall: 12"; snowfall: 0"; clear days: 143; precipitation days: 35.
Government   Form: council and manager.
Mayor: Bob Foster. (562) 570-6801
www.longbeach.gov
Visitor info: (800) 452-7829 or (562) 436-3645
www.visitlongbeach.com

▶ LOS ANGELES, CALIFORNIA

In pre-Spanish days, the area of Los Angeles was inhabited by approximately 4,000 Indians representing some 30 tribes. The village of Yang-na, with a population of 300, was located in what is now downtown Los Angeles, in the vicinity of Alameda and Commercial Streets. In October of 1542, João Rodrigues Cabrilho, a Portuguese explorer in the employ of Spain, became the first European to set foot on Los Angeles soil, but 200 years passed before a land expedition under the command of Gaspar de Portola crossed the territory on the way from Monterey to San Diego, in 1769.

The establishment of the Mission of San Gabriel (destined to become the largest of the Franciscan Missions) followed and in 1781, the Spanish Governor Felipe Neve founded the city of El Pueblo de Nuestra Señora de los Angeles de Porciuncula ("The Village of Our Lady of the Angels") as part of a plan to colonize California. Spanish rule continued until 1822 when Spain relinquished her holdings in western America, prompting California to pledge her allegiance to the Mexican empire. With the Treaty of Guadalupe Hidalgo (1848) the U.S. acquired all of California from Mexico and in 1850 Los Angeles was incorporated as a city. Introduction of the Southern Pacific Railroad in 1876 sparked a 12-year land boom, promoting the city's growth. By 1892, Los Angeles thrived as a center of oil production and in 1899 work began on the largest man-made deep-water facility in the world. Emerging as the motion picture capital of the world by 1910, industry accelerated in the 1920s and today L.A. ranks as one of the three great industrial cities in the country.

A thriving metropolis, Los Angeles boasts one of the finest highway systems in the world, handling about 6 million cars registered in its five-county area—a car for every two people, the highest ratio in the world. Three transcontinental railway systems terminate in L.A., about 40 certified air carriers fly to all parts of the world, its harbors have 46 miles of waterfront, and the city has the largest trucking center in the west. L.A. remains the world's movie mecca, teeming with studios, stars, and the starstruck.

Los Angelenos live with daily problems of smog, traffic jams, spectacular traffic accidents, and the ever-present threats of mud slides, fires, floods, high winds, and earthquakes. But the year-round sunshine, and the number of beaches and mountain areas, all within an easy drive, tend to ameliorate one's anxiety.
Population   3,831,868 (2009). Rank: 2nd. Race/Hispanic Origin (2006–2008): White 49.5%. Black 9.9%. Indian 0.6%. Asian 10.4%. Other 26.5%. Two or more races 2.9%. Hispanic 48.4%.
Location: 34°00'N, 118°10'W. County: Los Angeles.
Terrain and climate   Elev.: 104 ft. Area: 465.9 sq. mi. (1206.7 sq km). Avg. daily min. temp.: Jan.: 47.3°F/8.5°C; avg. daily max. July: 75.3°F/24°C. Avg. annual rainfall: 14.85"; snowfall: 0"; clear days: 143; precipitation days: 35.

Government   Form: mayor and council.
Mayor: Antonio Villaraigosa. (213) 978-0600
www.lacity.org
Visitor info: (800) 228-2452 or (213) 624-7300
www.discoverlosangeles.com

▶ LOUISVILLE, KENTUCKY

Known as "the Gateway to the South," Louisville lies mainly on a long low flood plain along a bend of the Ohio River across from the towns of New Albany and Jeffersonville, Indiana, at a series of rapids known as the Falls of the Ohio. The first permanent settlement on the site of present-day Louisville was established in June 1778. In 1780 the Commonwealth of Virginia, of which Kentucky was then still a part, approved the town charter of Louisville, named after Louis XVI of France in gratitude for his support of the American Revolution. Louisville was established as the seat of Jefferson County and became an incorporated city in 1828. The completion of a canal in 1830 greatly increased the importance of Louisville as a center of commercial shipping.

Despite being a slave state, Kentucky stayed in the Union throughout the Civil War, and Louisville was the base from which major operations in the west were carried out. The first Kentucky Derby was run in 1875 at the Louisville Jockey Club, officially renamed Churchill Downs in 1937.

Louisville has twice been hit by major tornadoes. On March 27, 1890, an F4 twister took about 100 lives and destroyed much of downtown. Another F4 tornado struck in 1974, destroying hundreds of houses, but this time there were only two fatalities. In late winter, 1937, a great flood submerged 70 percent of the city and forced the evacuation of 175,000 people.

The Ohio River is less important commercially than it used to be, but Louisville remains a major shipping center. Louisville became one of the 50 largest cities when it merged with Jefferson County in 2003. Three Interstate highways pass through the city, and its airport is an international hub for United Parcel Service (UPS). Louisville's major industries include tobacco and motor vehicles, and it is the home of the Louisville "Slugger" and to several leading producers of bourbon. The city is also home to the University of Louisville which enrolls 22,000 students and houses one of the most prestigious medical research facilities in the country which developed the first self-contained artificial heart transplant in 2001, and the first cervical cancer vaccine in 2006.
Population   566,503 (2009). Rank: 29th. Race/Hispanic Origin (2000): White 62.9%. Black 33.0%. Indian 0.2%. Asian 1.4%. Pacific Islander N.A. Other 0.7%. Two or more races 1.7%. Hispanic 1.9%.
Location: 38°13'N, 85°44'W. County: Jefferson.
Terrain and climate   Elev.: 462 ft. Area: 385 sq. mi. (997 sq km). Avg. daily min. temp.: Jan.: 33°F/-0.5°C; avg. daily max. July: 78.4°F/25.8°C. Avg. annual rainfall: 44.53"; snowfall: 16.4"; clear days: 95; precipitation days: 125.
Government   Form: mayor and council.
Mayor: Jerry Abramson. (502) 574-2003
www.louisvilleky.gov
Visitor info: (800) 626-5646 or (502) 584-2121
www.gotolouisville.com

▶ MEMPHIS, TENNESSEE

The first settlers in the area of Memphis arrived on the bluffs overlooking the Mississippi River more than 1,000 years ago. The Chickasaw forcibly displaced these people and then lived there for eight centuries until 1838, when the U.S. government scattered the entire tribe to

Oklahoma and parts further west so its citizens could develop the land. The Spanish explorer Hernando de Soto first set eyes on the bluffs in 1541. Other explorers passed through over the next century and in 1739 the French built Fort Assumption. The French, Spanish, and the Chickasaw fought over the land for the balance of the 18th century until it became a part of the U.S. in 1797. The area's original American owners, Gen. James Winchester, Judge John Overton, and Gen. Andrew Jackson (who later sold his share and went on to become President), established the town in 1819, and named it Memphis, after the ancient Egyptian city on the Nile.

Riverboatmen gave young Memphis a reputation for brawls and bawdiness, while mosquitoes gave it a history of yellow fever epidemics, which in the 1880s claimed more than half the city's population and jeopardized its charter. A sewage system, the first of its kind, helped finally conquer the epidemic. Between the river traffic and cotton crops, the city prospered, attracting Irish and German immigrants, and by the 20th century was on its way to becoming the unofficial capital of the mid-south. Elvis Presley, who expanded the city's rhythm and blues tradition to become the world's first rock-and-roll idol, remains the city's most enduring contribution to popular culture. In 1991, the Lorraine Motel, where civil rights leader Dr. Martin Luther King Jr. was assassinated in 1968, was opened as the National Civil Rights Museum. In recent years the city's central location has helped it to attract major corporations, most notably FedEx and Northwest Airlines.
Population   676,640 (2009). Rank: 19th. Race/Hispanic Origin (2006–2008): White 31.7%. Black 62.6%. Indian 0.2%. Asian 1.7%. Other 2.7%. Two or more races 1.2%. Hispanic 5.0%.
Location: 35°07'N, 90°00'W. County: Shelby.
Terrain and climate   Elev.: 307 ft. Area: 264.1 sq. mi. (684 sq km). Avg. daily min. temp.: Jan.: 30.9°F/-0.6°C; avg. daily max. July: 91.5°F/33°C. Avg. annual rainfall: 51.57"; snowfall: 6"; clear days: 118; precipitation days: 106.
Government   Form: mayor and council. Mayor: A. C. Wharton, Jr. (901) 576-6007
www.cityofmemphis.org
Visitor Info: (901) 543-5300
www.memphistravel.com

▶**MESA, ARIZONA**
Just 15 miles east of Phoenix is Mesa, a one-time suburb that has quickly climbed onto the list of the nation's largest cities. Arizona's third largest city grew by 37.6 percent between 1990 and 2000. There are solid reasons for Mesa's growth: low costs of doing business; a reasonable tax structure; a skilled and well-educated workforce; low crime rate; superior schools; affordable housing; and an abundant water supply. Founded in 1878 and incorporated in 1883, Mesa is the Spanish word for "table top," describing a flat-topped, raised area. The first settlers built homes and farms on a mesa above the surrounding area.
Population   462,604 (2009). Rank: 39th. Race/Hispanic Origin (2006–2008): White 84.9%. Black 2.7%. Indian 2.1%. Asian 1.8%. Other 5.8%. Two or more races 2.5%. Hispanic 26.5%.
Location: 33°N, 112°W. County: Maricopa.
Terrain and climate   Elev.: 1,241 ft. Area: 124.62 sq. mi. Avg. daily min temp.: Jan.: 35.6°F/2°C; avg. daily max. July: 104.3°F/40.16°C. Avg. annual: rainfall, 7.52"; snowfall, 0"; clear days, 320; precipitation days, 45.
Government   Form: council and manager. Mayor: Scott Smith. (480) 644-2388

www.mesaaz.gov
Visitor info: (800) 283-6372 or (480) 827-4700
www.visitmesa.com

▶**MIAMI, FLORIDA**
Miami, the most southerly major city in the continental U.S., sits about two degrees north of the Tropic of Cancer, a location that has made it a long-standing resort haven. Miami in the 1980s also thrived as a major hub of commerce and as a population center for Latin American immigrants, particularly those arriving from Cuba, whose ambition and business acumen contributed to the city's prosperity. While tourists still generate more than 60 percent of the area's economic activity, many other areas of enterprise, such as construction, light industry, and agriculture (limes, tomatoes, avocados, mangoes, and beans) have flourished.

Miami (whose name is thought to derive from the Indian *mayami*, meaning "big water"), dates back to the 16th century when Native Americans occupied the southern part of Florida. Fort Dallas, built near the mouth of the Miami River in 1836 as a base of war against the Seminoles, became the first permanent European-American settlement. The building of the Florida East Coast Railroad, coinciding with Miami's incorporation as a city in 1896 (population 343), offered ready access to the area. Resort hotels quickly cropped up and Miami, along with the rest of Florida, enjoyed great success. In 1926, a severe hurricane submerged much of its land under water, abruptly ending Miami's prosperity, but the city managed to steadily grow by draining and developing swampland. After World War II, new resorts rose up, and Miami thrived both as a haven for older retirees and a refuge for a substantial number of Cubans fleeing Castro's repressive regime. A skyscraper boom has transformed the skyline, with more than 20 buildings higher than 500 feet added since 2000.

As the U.S. city closest to Central and South America, Miami bills itself as the "Gateway of the Americas." Foreign banking has expanded rapidly.
Population   433,136 (2009). Rank: 42nd. Race/Hispanic Origin (2006–2008): White 72.7%. Black 22.0%. Indian 0.1%. Asian 0.8%. Other 3.1%. Two or more races 1.2%. Hispanic 69.4%.
Location: 25°45'N, 80°15'W. County: Dade.
Terrain and climate   Elev.: 12 ft. Area: 34.3 sq. mi. (88.8 sq km). Avg. daily min. temp.: Jan.: 59.2°F/15.1°C; avg. daily max. July: 88.7°F/31.5°C. Avg. annual rainfall: 57.55"; snowfall: 0"; clear days: 76; precipitation days: 129.
Government   Form: council and manager. Mayor: Tomas P. Regalado. (305) 250-5300
www.miamigov.com
Visitor info: (800) 933-8448 or (305) 539-3000
www.miamiandbeaches.com

▶**MILWAUKEE, WISCONSIN**
During the 1670s the French explorers Jacques Marquette and Louis Joliet were the first Europeans to visit the site of present-day Milwaukee, an area on the western shore of Lake Michigan at the confluence of the Menomonee and Kinnickinnic Rivers. In 1795, Jacques Vieau of the North West Company established a trading post and in 1818, Solomon Laurent Juneau, the first permanent settler, founded Milwaukee (from the Indian term *millioke*, meaning "beautiful land"). From the 1840s on, large numbers of German immigrants came to the city, making up over 60 percent of the 1850 population; today, an estimated one-third of the city's residents are of German descent.

A flourishing agricultural center, Milwaukee

had by the Civil War become the largest wheat market in the world. Its industrial base expanded after the war and by 1940 the city ranked fourth in manufacturing among U.S. cities. Still one of the most vigorous producers of durable goods, especially automotive parts, construction and road building equipment, diesel and gasoline engines, tractors, and outboard motors, Milwaukee also emerged as a major meat-packing center. Reflecting its German heritage, the city developed a thriving brewing industry with several of the largest beer-producing companies in the U.S. (though almost all have since disappeared). A major Great Lakes and international port, Milwaukee handles several international steamship lines.

Population 604,133 (2009). Rank: 26th. Race/Hispanic Origin (2006–2008): White 46.8%. Black 38.3%. Indian 0.8%. Asian 3.2%. Other 8.5%. Two or more races 2.3%. Hispanic 15.7%.

Location: 43°09'N, 87°58'W. County: Milwaukee.

Terrain and climate Elev.: 581 ft. Area: 95.8 sq. mi. (248.1 sq km). Avg. daily min. temp.: Jan.: 11.3°F/-11.5°C; avg. daily max. July: 79.8°F/26.5°C. Avg. annual rainfall: 30.94"; snowfall: 45"; clear days: 96; precipitation days: 122.

Government Form: mayor and council. Mayor: Tom Barrett. (414) 286-2200

www.ci.mil.wi.us

Visitor info: (800) 554-1448 or (414) 273-7222

www.milwaukee.org

▶ MINNEAPOLIS, MINNESOTA

With an average annual temperature of 45° F, Minneapolis is the second coldest city in the U.S. But despite its arctic winters, it is one of the most desirable cities in the U.S. It sits astride the Mississippi River, near the headwaters of the Minnesota River, about 350 miles northwest of Chicago. While it is the largest commercial metropolis in the north between Milwaukee and Seattle, no single industry dominates, although many large computer and electronics companies make Minneapolis their home. A regional banking center and the site of the Federal Reserve Bank for the Ninth District, Minneapolis has the world's largest cash grain exchange, the world's four largest wheat-flour-milling companies, and provides the upper Midwest with truck, barge, and air transport.

In 1682 Father Louis Hennepin, the French priest who explored the Mississippi, was the first European to set eyes on the Falls of St. Anthony, the future site of Minneapolis. Unsettled until Fort Snelling was built in 1819 to protect the fur traders from the Sioux and Chippewa, the town of St. Anthony began growing up on one side of the Mississippi and a second settlement sprang up on the other. The two were consolidated in 1872; the new name was a hybrid of the Indian word *minne*, meaning "water," and the Greek word for "city," polis. Minneapolis blossomed on the basis of its flour and lumber milling. By century's end, the forests to the north had been depleted, but flour milling continues as a thriving industry to this day.

Long considered a center of progressive political and social thinking, it is a mecca of education and culture. Minneapolis contains the main campus of the University of Minnesota, and boasts the Minnesota Orchestra and the Minneapolis Institute of the Arts. A haven for outdoor enthusiasts, there are more than 150 parks covering more than 6,000 acres. With 12 lakes within its city limits, Minneapolis has 10 percent of its surface covered by water. Despite all this, the city lost one fifth of its population to suburban areas in the last half of the 20th century.

Population 385,542 (2009). Rank: 48th. Race/Hispanic Origin (2006–2008): White 70.2%. Black 17.4%. Indian 1.7%. Asian 4.9%. Other 2.8%. Two or more races 3.0%. Hispanic 9.2%.

Location: 44°58'N, 93°20'W. County: Hennepin.

Terrain and climate Elev.: 828 ft. Area: 55.1 sq. mi. (142.7 sq km). Avg. daily min. temp.: Jan.: 2.4°F/-16.4°C; avg. daily max. July: 83.4°F/28.5°C. Avg. annual rainfall: 26.36"; snowfall: 46"; clear days: 100; precipitation days: 113.

Government Form: mayor and council. Mayor: R.T. Rybak. (612) 673-2100

www.ci.minneapolis.mn.us

Visitor info: (888) 676-MPLS

www.minneapolis.org

▶ NASHVILLE, TENNESSEE

In the winter of 1779–80, settlers from North Carolina, led by James Robertson, arrived at a place on the Cumberland River called Big Salt Lick, and built forts on both sides of the river, one of which they named Nashborough, after Gen. Francis Nash of the Revolutionary Army. Adopting the name Nashville in 1784, the settlement was chartered as a city in 1806, became state capital in 1843, and prospered until the Civil War as the northern terminus of the Natchez Trace, a 500-mile road to Natchez, Mississippi. The site of one of the war's last major battles in December 1864, the city underwent a long period of rebuilding and by the end of the century, the population reached 81,000. The city continued to grow, doubling in population by World War II, and has experienced even greater expansion since that time.

While best known as a major center of both the recording and music-publishing industries, Nashville enjoys a widely diversified economic foundation and serves as a distribution and marketing point for the upper southern region of the U.S. Several religious organizations and their publishing operations are headquartered here, and the city is home to more than a dozen institutions of higher learning, including Vanderbilt University, Fisk University, and Tennessee State University. With a growing base of manufacturing, especially in the automotive sector, and with the insurance and banking industries firmly entrenched, Nashville leaders project a prosperous future. As home of the Grand Ole Opry, Nashville has also developed into a regional tourist and convention attraction. A full-scale replica of the Greek temple the Parthenon is a noted site.

Population 605,473 (2009). Rank: 25th. Race/Hispanic Origin (2006–2008): White 64.9%. Black 27.9%. Indian 0.4%. Asian 3.1%. Other 2.4%. Two or more races 1.2%. Hispanic 7.8%.

Location: 36°12'N, 86°46'W. County: Davidson.

Terrain and climate Elev.: 605 ft. Area: 479.5 sq. mi. (1241.9 sq km). Avg. daily min. temp.: Jan.: 27.8°F/-2.3°C; avg. daily max. July: 89.8°F/32.1°C. Avg. annual rainfall: 48.49"; snowfall: 10.7"; clear days: 103; precipitation days: 119.

Government Form: mayor and council. Mayor: Karl Dean. (615) 862-6000

www.nashville.gov

Visitor info: (800) 657-6910

www.visitmusiccity.com

▶ NEW YORK CITY, NEW YORK

Even before the arrival of Europeans in North America, the waters that today make New York one of the world's foremost ports—and the foremost city in the United States—were the scene of lively trade between the predominant Algonquian tribes in the region. The city's modern history dates to 1524 when the Florentine explorer, Giovanni de Verrazano, sailed into New York Bay. In 1609, Henry Hudson, an English navigator sailing for the Dutch East India Company, explored the river that bears his name today. In 1625, the Dutch West India Company purchased Manhattan and established Nieuw Amsterdam, which quickly became a profitable trading post. Dutch settlers soon expanded beyond the original colony settling Breukelen, Nieuw Harlem, Bronck, and Staaten Eylandt. Taken by the British in 1664 (the Dutch briefly regained control in 1673–74), and renamed for the Duke of York, the town continued to prosper.

As resentment of British authority grew, New York became a seat of colonial discontent, participating in actions against the Stamp Act (1763) and tea tax (1773). But after the Battle of Long Island and Washington's retreat in August 1776, the British held New York through the end of the war. Yet Washington was inaugurated president at Federal Hall (today the site of the second Federal Reserve Bank) on Wall Street, and from 1789–90 New York was the nation's capital.

Industry and trade expanded dramatically after the opening of the Erie Canal from Troy (150 miles up the Hudson River) and Buffalo (350 miles west of Troy) gave New York direct access to the raw materials and the markets of the Great Lakes states. In the mid-19th century, New York became the primary port of immigration to the U.S. and many of the millions of immigrants who came to America carved out distinctly ethnic neighborhoods throughout the city in a patchwork that survives to the present.

In 1898, an act of the state legislature created "Greater New York," and today New York's population is greater than that of Los Angeles and Chicago (the second and third largest cities in the country) combined. Even if they were separate cities, four of New York's five boroughs would rank in the top 10—Brooklyn third (2.5 million), Queens fourth (2.3 million), Manhattan sixth (1.6 million), and the Bronx ninth (1.4 million).

New York's attractions are seemingly innumerable—enough to draw more than 17 million visitors annually—but they include 150 museums, 400 art galleries, dozens of Broadway theaters, and scores of concert halls, clubs, and dance halls. In addition, there are close to 1,000 landmark buildings, more than 50 landmark interiors, and more than 50 historic districts. (A list of attractions can be found under "New York State.") The city leads the nation in the arts, fashion, advertising, banking and financial services, publishing, broadcasting, and certain service industries; it is also the home of the General Assembly of the United Nations. There are more than 80 colleges and universities here, including Columbia University, New York University, Long Island University, Brooklyn College, Fordham University, the Pratt Institute of Technology, the Juilliard School, and the School of Visual Arts. Manufactured goods include apparel, chemicals, metal products, and printing.

New York City was the site of the worst terrorist attack in U.S. history on Sept. 11, 2001, when two hijacked commercial jets crashed into the twin towers of the World Trade Center, causing the complete collapse of both buildings and killing more than 2,800 people.

Population 8,391,881 (2009). Rank: 1st. Race/Hispanic Origin (2006–2008): White 44.6%. Black 25.1%. Indian 0.4%. Asian 11.8%. Other 16.0%. Two or more races 2.1%. Hispanic 27.5%.
Location: 40°45'N, 74°00'W. Counties: Bronx, Kings, New York, Queens, and Richmond.
Terrain and climate Elev.: 87 ft. Area: 301.5 sq. mi. (780.9 sq km). Avg. daily min. temp.: Jan.: 25.6°F/-3.5°C; avg. daily max. July: 85.3°F/29.6°C. Avg. annual rainfall: 44.12"; snowfall: 29"; clear days: 107; precipitation days: 121.
Government Form: mayor and council. Mayor: Michael R. Bloomberg. (212) 639-9675
www.nyc.gov
Visitor info: (212) 484-1200
www.nycgo.com

▶OAKLAND, CALIFORNIA

The first European-American to settle present-day Oakland was Dom Luis Maria Peralta, who established the 44,000-acre settlement called Rancho San Antonio in 1820. Its first real growth began with the establishment of ferry service to San Francisco in 1852, though the ferry's importance was overshadowed by Oakland's selection as the western terminus of the first transcontinental railroad in 1869. The city remained in the economic shadow of its more sophisticated neighbor across the Bay until the San Francisco earthquake of 1906 drove 100,000–150,000 people to Oakland for shelter. An estimated 65,000 of these are thought to have settled there permanently, providing an impetus for a long period of growth as an international port and industrial center.

A major commercial and cultural center with one of the top container ports in the world, Oakland is also the major northern hub of the California freeway system, which is integrated into the Bay Area Rapid Transit (BART) system. It has also become the premier biotechnology center in the region, and it is home to regional and international headquarters for firms in finance, medicine, telecommunications, international trade, and heavy industry.

Long a primarily industrial urban center, Oakland has pumped hundreds of millions of dollars into development of its downtown area and the Jack London waterfront—named for the author who spent his youth on the Oakland docks. Oakland embraces a racially and culturally diverse populace. Oakland sustained heavy damage in the 1989 Loma Prieta earthquake. Two years later, almost to the day, the second worst fire in California history leveled more than 1,000 buildings in the Oakland Hills neighborhood, killing 14 people and inflicting more than $1.5 billion in damage.
Population 409,184 (2009). Rank: 44th. Race/Hispanic Origin (2006–2008): White 36.9%. Black 29.8%. Indian 0.6%. Asian 15.6%. Other 12.9%. Two or more races 3.7%. Hispanic 25.2%.
Location: 37°50'N, 122°18'W. County: Alameda.
Terrain and climate Elev.: 42 ft. Area: 53.9 sq. mi. (139.6 sq km). Avg. daily min. temp.: Jan.: 43.4°F/6.3°C; avg. daily max. July: 70.6°F/29.6°C. Avg. annual rainfall: 18.03"; snowfall: N.A.; clear days: N.A; precipitation days: N.A.
Government Form: council and manager. Mayor: Ron Dellums. (510) 238-3141
www.oaklandnet.com
Visitor info: (510) 839-9000
www2.oaklandcvb.com

▶OKLAHOMA CITY, OKLAHOMA

Oklahoma City quite literally sprang up during the Great Land Rush of 1889 and, by presidential proclamation, opened for European-American settlement officially on April 22 of that year. At day's end, approximately 10,000 settlers had moved in— the greatest one-day non-annexation population increase in the history of cities. Oklahoma became a state in 1907 and Oklahoma City its capital in 1910, by which time the population had swelled to about 64,000. Since then, it has become Oklahoma's largest city, its leading commercial center, and home to the National Cowboy Hall of Fame.

Oklahoma City's economy, based on oil and livestock, thrives on petroleum production, meat processing, and the breeding of stocker and feeder cattle. The city hosts a flourishing printing and publishing industry and manufactures a diversity of products including automobiles, electronic equipment, computers, communications switches, and oil well supplies. As a vital banking center serving the central and western regions of the state, Oklahoma City boasts a Federal Reserve branch bank. However, Oklahoma City reportedly sparked the "go-go" banking syndrome that characterized the 1970s oil boom, when Penn Square Bank's ill-advised oil patch loans nearly devastated the U.S. banking system.

Oklahoma City was the site of one of the deadliest terrorist bombings in U.S. history on April 19, 1995, when a 5,000-pound car bomb ripped a huge hole in the Alfred Murrah Federal Building, killing 169 people, including 15 children in a day care center within the building.

Population 560,332 (2009). Rank: 31st. Race/Hispanic Origin (2006–2008): White 67.7%. Black 14.1%. Indian 2.9%. Asian 4.0%. Other 5.1%. Two or more races 6.3%. Hispanic 14.6%.

Location: 35°25'N, 97°30'W. Counties: Canadian, Cleveland, McClain, Oklahoma.

Terrain and climate Elev.: 1,304 ft. Area: 604 sq. mi. (1,564.4 sq km). Avg. daily min. temp.: Jan.: 25.2°F/-3.7°C; avg. daily max. July: 93.5°F/34.1°C. Avg. annual: rainfall, 30.89"; snowfall, 9"; clear days, 141; precipitation days, 81.

Government Form: council and manager. Mayor: Mick Cornett. (405) 297-2424
www.okc.gov
Visitor info: (800) 225-5652 or (405) 297-8912
www.okccvb.org

▶ OMAHA, NEBRASKA

Permanent settlement in what is now Omaha began with a fur-trading post established shortly after the Lewis and Clark expedition passed through the area in 1804. In 1820, the government built Ft. Atkinson, and the surrounding community became a major stop on both the Mormon and the Lewis and Clark trails, and was incorporated as a city in 1854. After strong lobbying by citizens of Council Bluffs, Iowa, just across the Missouri River to the east, Omaha (the name means "above all others on the stream") became the eastern terminus of the Union-Pacific transcontinental railroad, the country's first, in 1869. Within six years, the population grew to 39,000 and by the turn of the century, it had passed the 100,000 mark.

As a major transportation hub of the Midwest—Omaha today boasts seven major railroads and the recently expanded Port of Omaha services a dozen barge lines—the city became a major distribution center for meat and grain, living up to its motto "We feed the world" (ConAgra is based here). Its major food products include pasta, potato chips, coffee, pancake mixes, frozen dinners, and Omaha steaks. With many of *Fortune* 500 manufacturing operations, and a healthy publishing industry (roughly one out of every four manufacturers is either a publisher or printer) located here, Omaha's diversified economy also has strong roots in insurance (Mutual of Omaha), communications, direct mail/telemarketing, and sophisticated medical facilities are centered at the medical schools of

Creighton University and the University of Nebraska.

Among its performing arts institutions are the Omaha Symphony, Opera/Omaha, the Omaha Ballet, the Orpheum Theater, and the Omaha Community Playhouse. Museums and historic sites include the Boys Town Hall of Fame, the Henry Doorly Zoo and Aquarium, the Great Plains Black Museum, the historic ships *U.S.S. Hazard* and *U.S.S. Marlin*, and the Old Market, a mixed-use National Historic District on the Missouri River.

Population 454,731 (2009). Rank: 40th. Race/Hispanic Origin (2006–2008): White 76.7%. Black 12.8%. Indian 0.4%. Asian 2.1%. Other 5.1%. Two or more races 2.8%. Hispanic 11.4%.

Location: 41°15'N, 95°55'W. County: Douglas.

Terrain and climate Elev.: 982 ft. Area: 99.3 sq. mi. (257.2 sq km). Avg. daily min. temp.: Jan.: 10.2°F/-12.1°C; avg. daily max. July: 88.5°F/31.3°C. Avg. annual rainfall: 30.34"; snowfall: 32"; clear days: 113; precipitation days: 99.

Government Form: mayor and council. Mayor: Jim Suttle. (402) 444-5000
www.cityofomaha.org
Visitor info: (866) 937-6624 or (402) 444-4660
www.visitomaha.com

▶ PHILADELPHIA, PENNSYLVANIA

In 1632, a small contingent of Swedes and Finns came to the land where the Schuylkill River meets the Delaware and founded New Sweden. In 1655, Peter Stuyvesant seized New Sweden for the Dutch, inciting conflict with the British until the Dutch relinquished their rights to the territory in 1673. Nine years later, William Penn established a town between the Schuylkill and the Delaware Rivers, named it Philadelphia, "the city of brotherly love," and in two years it evolved into an active settlement of about 2,500 people, most of them Quakers.

In the mid-1700s, Benjamin Franklin began shaping the destiny of Philadelphia by presiding over the founding of the University of Pennsylvania, the Pennsylvania Hospital, and a fire insurance company (the last two were firsts for the young nation). Under his guidance, Philadelphia became the premier colonial city for the arts and the home of many famous educators, scientists, mathematicians, authors, and painters. In addition, a total of 17 libraries were founded at this time. The meeting place of the Continental Congress and the site of the signing of the Declaration of Independence, Philadelphia was the nation's capital from 1790 to 1800, when the federal government moved permanently to Washington, D.C.

Throughout the 19th century, the influx first of Irish and German, then Jewish, Italian, Polish, and Slavic immigrants from Europe, and blacks from the South, helped build the city's industrial base. Today, Philadelphia ranks high among U.S. cities in oil refining; other principal industries are electrical machinery, automobile and truck bodies, petrochemicals, metalworking, and scientific instruments. But many other businesses have left the city and unemployment and poverty have taken a heavy toll in recent years. Since 1990, the city has lost nearly 9 percent of its population.

Population 1,547,297 (2009). Rank: 6th. Race/Hispanic Origin (2006–2008): White 42.5%. Black 43.5%. Indian 0.3%. Asian 5.5%. Other 6.4%. Two or more races 1.8%. Hispanic 11.0%.

Location: 40°00'N, 75°10'W. County: Philadelphia.

Terrain and climate Elev.: 28 ft. Area: 136 sq. mi. (352.2 sq km). Avg. daily min. temp.: Jan.: 23.8°F/-4.5°C; avg. daily max. July: 86.1°F/30°C. Avg. annual rainfall: 41.42"; snowfall: 20"; clear

days: 92; precipitation days: 116.
Government Form: mayor and council.
Mayor: Michael A. Nutter. (215) 686-2181
www.phila.gov
Visitor info: (800) 537-7676 or (215) 636-3300
www.visitphilly.com

▶PHOENIX, ARIZONA

Arizona's capital and its largest city sits in the Salt River Valley in a former desert that has become a prosperous agricultural area because of a network of irrigated dams located northeast of the city. Long a resort area owing to its mild climate, Phoenix has recently emerged as a lively commercial and agricultural center as well. A flourishing high-tech haven attracting businesses engaged in electronics, communications, and research and development, the city also has a strong manufacturing base that includes airplane parts, electronic equipment, agricultural chemicals, radios, air conditioners, and leather goods. Among its agricultural products are lettuce, melons, vegetables, grapefruit, oranges, lemons, and olives.

While Phoenix benefits from modern irrigation efforts, the Hohokam Indian people dug the area's first irrigation ditches in the 3rd century, B.C. and developed an extensive network of canals that lasted until their culture's decline in A.D. 1400. The area was not resettled until 1864, when a hay camp was established to supply Camp McDowell 30 miles away. Jack Swilling and "Lord Darrell" Dupa rebuilt the old Indian irrigation ditches in 1867, and named the site Phoenix, after the mythical bird that rose from its own ashes. The settlement grew as a trading post, was incorporated as a city in 1881, became capital of the territory in 1889 and the state capital when Arizona was admitted to the Union in 1912.

With the westward exodus from the snowbelt states, and the perfecting of air conditioning to make the summer heat bearable, the small 1950s resort city of 106,818 people has since swelled to be the fifth largest city in the U.S. In the 1980s, Phoenix's population grew 24.5 percent from 789,704 to just under a million. Growth between 1990 and 2000 was even faster (34 percent).
Population 1,601,587 (2009). Rank: 5th. Race/Hispanic Origin (2006–2008): White 77.2%. Black 5.4%. Indian 1.9%. Asian 2.5%. Other 10.9%. Two or more races 1.9%. Hispanic 42.1%.
Location: 33°30'N, 112°04'W. County: Maricopa.
Terrain and climate Elev.: 1,117 ft. Area: 375 sq. mi. (971.3 sq km). Avg. daily min. temp.: Jan.: 44.4°F/6.8°C; avg. daily max. July: 107.5°F/41°C. Avg. annual rainfall: 7.11"; snowfall: 0"; clear days: 214; precipitation days: 34.
Government Form: council and manager. Mayor: Phil Gordon. (602) 262-7111
www.phoenix.gov
Visitor info: (877) CALL-PHX or (602) 254-6500
www.visitphoenix.com

▶PORTLAND, OREGON

Portland's renowned beauty is a result of its unique natural setting, which offers a view of the Cascade Mountains and Mt. Hood to the east, Mt. Adams to the northeast, and Mt. St. Helens and Mt. Rainier to the north. Eleven bridges span the Willamette River, which divides the city into east and west sections.

Indian traders traveling between Oregon City and Vancouver carved out an acre of land by the Willamette River 12 miles north of Oregon City, which became known as The Clearing. In 1884 William Overton claimed the 640 acres surrounding the area, which he then sold to Asa Lovejoy and Francis W. Pettygrove, who set out to build a city. Winning a coin toss, Pettygrove named the city-to-be after his hometown in Maine.

As a vital port of entry (the coast's only freshwater port) with a large inland harbor, Portland is a leader in the shipping of lumber, flour, and grain, and has blossomed into Oregon's largest city. Main industries also include paper and pulp, mining, high-technology equipment, and aerospace. Portland enjoys a flourishing arts community and its residents partake of the beaches and ski slopes within easy driving distance.
Population 566,141 (2009). Rank: 30th. Race/Hispanic Origin (2006–2008): White 78.6%. Black 6.4%. Indian 1.4%. Asian 6.5%. Other 2.9%. Two or more races 3.7%. Hispanic 8.8%.
Location: 45°35'N, 122°40'W. Counties: Clackamas, Multnomah, Washington.
Terrain and climate Elev.: 39 ft. Area: 113.9 sq. mi. (295 sq km). Avg. daily min. temp.: Jan.: 33.5°F/0.8°C; avg. daily max. July: 79.5°F/26.3°C. Avg. annual rainfall: 37.39"; snowfall: 7"; clear days: 69; precipitation days: 152.
Government Form: commission. Mayor: Sam Adams. (503) 823-4120
www.portlandonline.com
Visitor info: (800) 962-3700 or (503) 275-9750
www.travelportland.com

▶RALEIGH, NORTH CAROLINA

An early planned community, Raleigh was created as North Carolina's capital and is now the second largest city in the state. Never a major manufacturing area, Raleigh has instead become a retail, educational and cultural center, with well-regarded public schools, the land-grant North Carolina State University, two women's colleges and two historically black colleges.

In the 1760s, tavernkeeper Isaac Hunter began serving travelers along North Carolina's main north-south road in an area of the Piedmont region that became known as Wake Crossroads. Nearby landowner Joel Lane convinced the colony to form a new county in 1770, with the crossroads as the seat. After the American Revolution, the State of North Carolina chose centrally-located Wake County as the site for a legislative capital and purchased 1,000 acres from Lane in 1792, naming the new city in honor of the explorer Sir Walter Raleigh.

During the Civil War, a training camp outside Raleigh held more than 5,000 Confederate soldiers. However, Raleigh survived the war with little harm and was quietly surrendered to Union General William T. Sherman in 1865.

In recent decades, Raleigh's mild four-season climate, excellent educational systems, and the Research Triangle Park, located between Raleigh and Durham, have drawn high-tech and biotech businesses and research organizations. While it has become a popular retirement area, the city's gracious old architecture, natural beauty, and good jobs also attract many young workers and population has grown dramatically from 207,951 in 1990 to nearly 400,000 today.
Population 405,791 (2009). Rank 45th. Race/Hispanic Origin (2006–2008): White 60.2%. Black 28.4%. Indian 0.3%. Asian 3.8%. Other 6.0%. Two or more races 1.2%. Hispanic 9.7%.
Location: 35°77'N, 78°65'W. County: Wake, Durham.
Terrain and climate Elev.: 298 ft. Area: 114.6 sq. mi. (296.8 sq km). Avg. daily min. temp.: Jan.: 29.6°F/1.3°C; avg. daily max. July: 89.1°F/31.7°C. Avg. annual rainfall: 43.05"; snowfall: 7.6"; clear days: 215; precipitation days: 113.

Government Form: council and manager.
Mayor: Charles Meeker. (919) 996-3050
www.raleigh-nc.org
Visitor info: (800) 849-8499 or (919) 834-5900
www.visitraleigh.com

▶**SACRAMENTO, CALIFORNIA**
The capital of California and its seventh largest
city, Sacramento sits 75 miles northeast of San
Francisco at the confluence of the American and
Sacramento rivers. A wholesale and retail center
for the surrounding rich farmland, the city includes among its main commercial enterprises
food processing and canning, and one of the
world's largest almond-shelling plants.

Receiving a land grant from the Mexican government in 1839, Swiss-American John Augustus
Sutter founded a colony called New Helvetia, and
when Fort Sutter was constructed in 1844, it became one of California's chief trading posts. Established soon after the discovery of gold in 1848,
Sacramento grew to 7,000 residents by 1850, became state capital in 1854, and in 1863 was incorporated as a city.

The "Gateway to the Goldfields," "Old Sacramento" became a pivotal point of commerce in
the 1860s, connected to the mining towns by the
American River, and transporting produce from
the farms and orchards lining the banks of the
Sacramento River. Sailors stopping in San Francisco visited Sacramento to replenish their stocks
of fresh produce and to entertain themselves in
the saloons and gambling halls. The wealthy lived
in great mansions by the river and the cobble-
stone streets, gaslights, and wood sidewalks imbued the town with a touch of civility. Today's
Sacramento, appreciated for its subtle, quiet
charms, boasts 120 parks, hiking and biking trails
along the American River Parkway, a large collection of art galleries, two symphony orchestras,
ballet, theater and opera companies, and a number of jazz clubs and coffee houses.
Population 466,687 (2009). Rank: 37th. Race/
Hispanic Origin (2006–2008): White 51.1%. Black
14.0%. Indian 1.2%. Asian 17.5%. Other 10.0%.
Two or more races 5.0%. Hispanic 24.6%.
Location: 38°33'N, 121°30'W. County: Sacramento.
Terrain and climate Elev.: 25 ft. Area: 97.3 sq.
mi. (252 sq km). Avg. daily min. temp.: Jan.:
37.9°F/3.2°C; avg. daily max. July: 93.3°F/34°C.
Avg. annual rainfall: 17.87"; snowfall: 0.1"; clear
days: 193; precipitation days: 57.
Government Form: council and manager.
Mayor: Kevin Johnson. (916) 808-5300
www.cityofsacramento.org
Visitor info: (800) 292-2334
www.discovergold.org

▶**SAN ANTONIO, TEXAS**
San Antonio, the third-largest city in Texas, lies in
the state's south-central region at the edge of the
Gulf Coastal Plain 140 miles from the Gulf of
Mexico. Its economy thrives on agriculture, livestock, and the activity of the wholesale traders
who dominate the commerce of southwestern
Texas and northern Mexico. It is also a regional
leader in biotechnology. Adding further stimulus
to the economy are five major military installations—Fort Sam Houston, Randolph Air Force
Base, Kelly Air Force Base, Lackland Air Force
Base, and Brooks Air Force Base. The military contributes approximately $3 billion annually to the
area economy.

The founding of the mission of San Antonio de
Valero (later known as the Alamo) and the Pre-
sidio of San Antonio in 1718 represented the area's

first permanent settlement. When 56 settlers from
the Canary Islands joined the original coterie
of ranchmen, missionaries, and soldiers, they
formed the first municipal organization in Texas,
called the villa of San Fernando de Bexar, which
became a city in 1809, and suffered under Mexican rule until the battle of San Jacinto in 1836.
With the influx of American pioneers and German
immigrants (following Texas's statehood in 1845),
the population grew to over 96,000 by 1910, and
has since increased nearly tenfold. By 2000 it had
reached 1.1 million, up 22 percent since 1990.

Today San Antonio is a popular haven for vaca-
tioners, with over 10 million visitors per year. San
Antonio's attractions include the Alamo and its
four sister missions, the Riverwalk along the San
Antonio River, Breckenridge Park (home of one of
America's largest zoos), Sea World San Antonio; La
Villita, the Tower of the Americas, and the Spanish
Governor's Palace.
Population 1,373,668 (2009). Rank: 7th. Race/
Hispanic Origin (2006–2008): White 68.9%. Black
6.6%. Indian 0.6%. Asian 2.0%. Other 19.4%. Two
or more races 2.4%. Hispanic 61.2%.
Location: 29°30'N, 98°30'W. County: Bexar.
Terrain and climate Elev.: 701 ft. Area: 304.5
sq. mi. (788.7 sq km). Avg. daily min. temp.: Jan.:
39°F/3.8°C; avg. daily max. July: 96.3°F/35.7°C.
Avg. annual rainfall: 29.13"; snowfall: 0.5"; clear
days: 110; precipitation days: 81.
Government Form: council and manager.
Mayor: Julián Castro. (210) 207-7060
www.sanantonio.gov
Visitor info: (800) 447-3372 or (210) 207-6700
www.sanantoniovisit.com

▶**SAN DIEGO, CALIFORNIA**
Sixty years after João Rodrigues Cabrilho first
sailed into San Diego Bay, Sebastian Vizcaino embarked from Spain with three ships to explore the
coast of California, and in November 1602 an-
chored on the lee of what is now known as Point
Loma. When he finished charting the bay two
days later, he changed its original name, San
Miguel, to San Diego, in honor of the saint San
Diego de Alcalal de Henares, In 1769, Father Junipero Serra established California's first mission,
the Mission San Diego de Alcala.

Compared to its sister cities to the north—Los
Angeles and San Francisco—San Diego developed
slowly, despite its large and hospitable harbor. In
1887, the city became the southern terminus for
the Santa Fe Railroad, but floods soon washed out
the tracks and trackbeds, and the railroad was rebuilt to terminate in L.A. which had a new man-
made harbor. This put San Diego at an almost
insurmountable disadvantage. With its industrial
development stunted, San Diego welcomed the
establishment of a U.S. Navy base during World
War I; since then, about a quarter of the Navy's
seagoing vessels and roughly 20 percent of the
Marine Corps' forces have been located there.
Jonas Salk's work on polio and the emergence of
the University of California at San Diego have
earned the city the reputation as a premier biomedical research center, luring billions of dollars
in development and research grants.

San Diego, a picturesque city with many tourist
attractions, enjoys an average of 150 days of sunshine, enticing both residents and visitors to its 70
beaches and the parks, resorts, and health spas
lining its great bay. Coronado Island is a popular
attraction. Balboa Park, host to international ex-
positions in 1915 and 1935, contains the San
Diego Zoo, one of the finest in the nation. The
pleasure boats berthed at the city's numerous

yacht clubs offer a curious contrast to the naval warships moored nearby. San Diego was the site of the 1992 America's Cup yacht races.

Population 1,306,301 (2009). Rank: 8th. Race/Hispanic Origin (2006–2008): White 67.4%. Black 6.7%. Indian 0.7%. Asian 14.7%. Other 6.5%. Two or more races 3.6%. Hispanic 27.3%.

Location: 32°43'N, 117°10'W. County: San Diego.

Terrain and climate Elev.: 13 ft. Area: 329 sq. mi. (852.1 sq km). Avg. daily min. temp.: Jan.: 48.4°F/9.1°C; avg. daily max. July: 75.6°F/24.2°C. Avg. annual rainfall: 9.32"; snowfall: 0"; clear days: 150; precipitation days: 41.

Government Form: council and manager. Mayor: Jerry Sanders. (619) 236-6330
www.sandiego.gov
Visitor info: (619) 232-3101
www.sandiego.org

▶ SAN FRANCISCO, CALIFORNIA

Located near the Golden Gate, the strait between San Francisco Bay and the Pacific Ocean, fog-bound San Francisco hid from some of the greatest European navigators to explore the West Coast. João Rodrigues Cabrilho discovered the Farallon Islands just off the coast in 1542 and Sir Francis Drake landed a few miles north of the Golden Gate in 1579. Yet it was another 200 years before Don Gasper de Portola sailed into the Bay, followed six years later by Don Juan Manuel Ayala who established a town and mission.

Neither the Spanish nor (after 1821) the Mexican governments were very keen on capitalizing on San Francisco's temperate and strategic location, and when Captain John Montgomery raised the American flag there on July 9, 1846, the community consisted of only 840 people. The discovery of gold at Sutter's mill in 1848, and the gold rush of 1849—which brought 40,000 of the hopeful to California, most by ship—catapulted San Francisco onto the world map, and the following year it was incorporated as a city.

San Francisco continued to prosper as a major transportation and industrial center, but in 1906 an earthquake registering 8.6 on the Richter scale claimed 452 lives, 28,000 buildings, and losses totalling approximately $350 million. San Francisco rose from the ashes to become a thriving, multi-faceted, cosmopolitan city and one of the country's leaders in world trade. Another major earthquake, measuring 7.1 on the Richter scale, struck on Oct. 17, 1989, causing extensive damage and 67 deaths in the region, but did not devastate the city as thoroughly as the 1906 tremor.

San Francisco today is a port of call for more than 40 steamship lines which import approximately $25 billion worth of goods from more than 300 ports around the world. A major international financial center, it is the headquarters of two of the nation's largest banks and the 12th Federal Reserve District. There are also many insurance companies, and the city is a haven for venture capitalists and entrepreneurs: more than 90 percent of its businesses have fewer than 25 employees. There are also several U.S. military installations in the area.

Well known for its spirit of individualism, San Francisco was a haven for the beat movement of the 1950s, and the capital of the hippie movement of the 1960s was the Haight-Ashbury district. Its more traditional arts institutions include the San Francisco Ballet, the San Francisco Opera, the San Francisco Symphony, and the American Conservatory Theater. Among its leading educational institutions are the University of San Francisco, the Heald College, the University of California San Francisco, the San Francisco Art Institute, and the San Francisco Conservatory of Music. Among its many museums are the National Maritime Historic Park, the de Young, and the California Palace of the Legion of Honor. Other attractions include its historic cable cars (first used in 1873), Chinatown, and Fisherman's Wharf.

Population 815,358 (2009). Rank: 12th. Race/Hispanic Origin (2006–2008): White 54.5%. Black 6.5%. Indian 0.4%. Asian 31.3%. Other 3.9%. Two or more races 3.0%. Hispanic 14.0%.

Location: 37°47'N, 122°30'W. County: San Francisco.

Terrain and climate Elev.: 155 ft. Area: 46.4 sq. mi. (120.2 sq km). Avg. daily min. temp.: Jan.: 41.5°F/5.2°C; avg. daily max. July: 71°F/21°C. Avg. annual rainfall: 19.71"; snowfall: 0"; clear days: 162; precipitation days: 67.

Government Form: mayor and council. Mayor: Gavin Newsom. (415) 554-6141
www.sfgov.org
Visitor info: (415) 391-2000
www.onlyinsanfrancisco.com

▶ SAN JOSE, CALIFORNIA

Located at the southern end of San Francisco Bay, about 45 miles south of San Francisco, San Jose was the first non-religious European community founded in California. Pueblo de San Jose de Guadalupe was settled in 1777 by enterprising farmers who sought to make themselves and the region independent of Mexico and the Spanish mission network for their supplies. Fruit and olive trees, hides, tallow, livestock, grain, and lively retail activity all contributed to San Jose's early prosperity, and it was the first state capital (1849–52).

San Jose remained an agricultural center until World War II, when industry and technology began to expand. The rapid growth of innovative industry over the last 20 years, taking its lead from research and development begun at nearby Stanford University in the 1930s, changed the area dramatically. With the revolution in high technology, Santa Clara County became known as Silicon Valley, excelling in the production of information systems, personal computers, peripherals, and fostering a burgeoning semi-conductor industry. At the same time, financial services, real estate, construction, and retail industries all flourished.

More than 4,000 high-tech companies employing 182,000 people are located in San Jose, and one-fifth of the labor force works in manufacturing. Santa Clara County has one of the highest median family income in California, and median housing prices in San Jose are perennially among the highest in the nation. San Jose is also the safest large city in the country. These could be reasons for the population explosion—San Jose grew 61 percent from 598,541 in 2008 to almost a million in 2009.

Population 964,695 (2009). Rank: 10th. Race/Hispanic Origin (2006–2008): White 48.6%. Black 3.0%. Indian 0.6%. Asian 31.2%. Other 12.8%. Two or more races 3.4%. Hispanic 31.5%.

Location: 37°20'N, 121°53'W. County: Santa Clara.

Terrain and climate Elev.: 65 ft. Area: 169.2 sq. mi. (438.2 sq km). Avg. daily min. temp.: Jan.: 41.1°F/5°C; avg. daily max. July: 81.5°F/27.5°C. Avg. annual rainfall: 13.86"; snowfall: 0"; clear days: N.A.; precipitation days: N.A.

Government Form: council and manager. Mayor: Chuck Reed. (408) 535-4800
www.sanjoseca.gov
Visitor info: (800) SAN JOSE
www.sanjose.org

▶**SEATTLE, WASHINGTON**

Located on the protected waters of Puget Sound, Seattle was the first European-American settlement established in the Pacific Northwest north of the Columbia River. Starting out at Alki Point in 1851, the settlers moved to what is now known as Pioneer Square. Befriended by the Suquamish Chief Sealth (Seattle is a loose approximation of his name), the people turned to lumber harvesting and log milling, which formed the backbone of the city's economy.

With the completion of the Great Northern Railway in 1893 and the Alaska gold rush of 1897, when Seattle became "the Gateway to the Klondike," the city was transformed into a metropolis of merchants and entrepreneurs. Even as gold fever abated, and despite a devastating fire in 1899, the city prospered as a major port to the Orient and as an industrial center. In 1909 Seattle was the site of the Alaska-Yukon-Pacific Exposition. The completion of the Panama Canal in 1914 brought even more business to the already bustling port. Two years later, a small company began building two-seater biplanes; in time the little company became Boeing, the world's largest producer of commercial planes, and the largest employer (more than 80,000 people) in the Seattle area. In 2001, the company stunned the Emerald City by announcing that it was moving its corporate headquarters (and 500 jobs) to Chicago.

Endowed with spectacular natural beauty, with the broad expanse of Puget Sound before it, and the snow-capped peaks of the Cascade Mountains and Mt. Rainier visible to the south and east, the Seattle area offers a wide variety of outdoor activities, from skiing and hiking to fishing and boating. A second international exposition, the Seattle World's Fair in 1962, helped establish the city's reputation as a center of technology, trade, industry, and tourism. In 1974 Bill Gates and Paul Allen founded Microsoft and Seattle has since been seen as the hub of the computer world. The leading cultural programs are put on by the Seattle Symphony Orchestra, the Seattle Opera Association, and the Seattle Repertory Theater. Other attractions include the Seattle Art Museum, Pioneer Square, Pike Place Market, the historic ships on Lake Union, and Woodland Park and Zoo, as well as the many events at the 74-acre Seattle Convention Center, whose buildings (including the famed Space Needle), and park-like grounds and fountains are legacies of the World's Fair. Among the 20 universities and colleges in the area are the University of Washington and Seattle Pacific University.

Population 617,334 (2009). Rank: 23rd. Race/Hispanic Origin (2006–2008): White 71.3%. Black 8.0%. Indian 0.9%. Asian 13.2%. Other 2.2%. Two or more races 4.0%. Hispanic 5.6%.
Location: 47°41'N, 122°15'W. County: King.
Terrain and climate Elev.: 450 ft. Area: 83.6 sq. mi. (216.5 sq km). Avg. daily min. temp.: Jan.: 34.3°F/1.2°C; avg. daily max.: July: 75.2°F/24°C. Avg. annual rainfall: 38.85"; snowfall: 15"; clear days: 57; precipitation days: 160.
Government Form: mayor and council. Mayor: Mike McGinn. (206) 684-4000
www.seattle.gov
Visitor info: (206) 461-5840
www.visitseattle.org

▶**TUCSON, ARIZONA**

The first European to travel through the area that is now Tucson was the Jesuit missionary Eusebio Kino, in 1692. In 1700 the mission of San Xavier del Bac was established among the Papago Indians nearby. It was not until 1776, however, that the Spanish established a permanent settlement, taking its name from the Papago Stjukshon (or Chuk Shon), meaning "village of the dark spring at the foot of the mountain." Tucson remained under Spanish and Mexican control until acquired by the U.S. government as part of the Gadsden Purchase in 1853. During the Civil War it was under Confederate control, but from 1867 to 1877 it was the territorial capital.

Despite the arrival of the Southern Pacific railroad in 1880 and the discovery of extensive copper deposits in southern Arizona, neither the city's location nor its natural resources much stimulated its economy. It was best known as a winter and health resort, and as a commercial hub for the surrounding agricultural and mining industries. In 1950, the population was only 45,500.

The last half-century has seen a dramatic change. One of the many beneficiaries of the exodus from the industrial states to the Sunbelt, Tucson's population has grown almost tenfold in that period, and in the 1990s Tucson added 20,000 manufacturing jobs. Surrounded by a wealth of natural beauty, the city is still appealing to retirees and tourists, as is reflected in the many golf courses, ranches, and resorts in and around Tucson. It is ringed by four mountain ranges: the Rincon, Santa Catalina, Tucson, and Santa Rita. Other natural wonders include Sabino Canyon (which has the only year-round stream in the region), the Saguaro National Monument (a preserve for Saguaro cacti), and Tucson Mountain Park, home of the Arizona-Sonora Desert Museum. The University of Arizona is located in Tucson, and the Davis-Monthan Air Force Base and Kitts Peak Observatory are nearby.

Population 548,555 (2009). Rank: 32nd. Race/Hispanic Origin (2006–2008): White 68.8%. Black 4.4%. Indian 2.8%. Asian 2.7%. Other 17.8%. Two or more races 3.4%. Hispanic 39.5%.
Location: 32°14'N, 110°59'W. County: Pima.
Terrain and climate   Elev.: 2,584 ft. Area: 125 sq. mi. (324.8 sq km). Avg. daily min. temp.: Jan.: 38.1°F/3.3°C; avg. daily max. July: 98.5°F/3.3°C. Avg. annual rainfall: 11.14"; snowfall: 2"; clear days: 198; precipitation days: 50.
Government Form: council and manager. Mayor: Bob Walkup. (520) 791-4201
www.tucsonaz.gov
Visitor info: (888) 2TUCSON
www.visittucson.org

▶**TULSA, OKLAHOMA**

Tulsa was first settled by Indian nations forced out of the South Atlantic States by the Indian Removal Act of 1830. The name they chose for their new home was Tulsey Town, a corruption of Tullahassee, meaning "old town." The name Tulsa was made official with the establishment of a post office in 1879. In 1900, Tulsa's population numbered less than 2,000, but the discovery of extensive oil fields at the turn of the century, beginning with the Glenn Pool and Red Fork strikes, started Tulsa on the way from a small Indian settlement to a sizable metropolis. By 1907, its population had increased to 7,298, and by 1920 it was 10 times that. Soon Tulsa was "the Oil Capital of the World."

While still heavily involved in the oil and gas industry—it remains the home of about 500 oil-related companies—modern Tulsa is a far more diverse city than its oil patch origins. Among Tulsa's top employers are regional, national and international firms involved in aviation and aerospace, energy, computer technology, insurance, telecommunications, health care, and electronic equipment. The Port of Catoosa, which opened in 1972 after the completion of the 445-mile Arkansas-Mississippi Waterway, is a major inland port which provides Tulsa with a direct link to the Mississippi River system and the Gulf of Mexico.

While growing in business, Tulsa has preserved the cultural heritage of its early oil barons and workers as well as that of its original Indian settlers. Thomas Gilcrease, a Creek Indian, became a millionaire with the Glenn Pool oil strike, and founded the Thomas Gilcrease Institute of American History and Art, devoted to the American Indian. The Tulsa Opera Company was founded in the early 1900s, and along with the city's symphony orchestra, ballet, and theaters, it gives Tulsa just cause to lay claim to being the cultural capital of Oklahoma. Tulsans also honor their roots through rodeos and regional music festivals. In addition, representatives of the state's 65 Indian tribes gather in Tulsa each summer for their annual powwow. Among Tulsa's universities are the University of Tulsa and Oral Roberts University.

Population 389,625 (2009). Rank: 47th. Race/Hispanic Origin (2006–2008): White 68.5%. Black 15.9%. Indian 3.6%. Asian 2.0%. Other 4.3%. Two or more races 5.7%. Hispanic 12.1%.
Location: 36°10'N, 96°00'W. Counties: Osage, Tulsa.
Terrain and climate   Elev.: 676 ft. Area: 186.1 sq. mi. (482 sq km). Avg. daily min. temp.; Jan.: 24.8°F/-4°C; avg. daily max. July: 93.9°F/34.3°C. Avg. annual rainfall: 38.77"; snowfall: 9"; clear days: 127; precipitation days: 90.
Government Form: mayor and council. Mayor: Dewey Bartlett. (918) 596-2100
www.cityoftulsa.org
Visitor info: (800) 558-3311
www.visittulsa.com

▶ VIRGINIA BEACH, VIRGINIA

Throughout much of its history—from the landing of the Jamestown colonists at Point Henry in 1607—Virginia Beach was overshadowed by its northern neighbor, Norfolk, which was long the home of many shipping and naval enterprises at the mouth of Chesapeake Bay. But Virginia Beach has seen remarkable change in the last two decades.

In 1970, Virginia Beach's population was 172,000, only slightly more than half that of Norfolk. By 1990, it had grown 128 percent, to 393,000, and surpassing Norfolk as the state's largest city, a distinction it still holds today, though growth cooled to 8.2 percent between 1990 and 2000. Local initiative accounts for most of this growth: in the same period Norfolk's population fell 10 percent. A dominant presence is the U.S. Navy, which has three bases—Oceana Naval Air Station, Little Creek Naval Amphibious Base, and the Dam Neck Fleet Training

Center—and which together with the U.S. Army's Fort Story employs 36,000 military and civilian personnel.

With 38 miles of Atlantic shoreline, 28 miles of public beaches, and the Seashore State Park—2,700 acres of shady upland woods, cypress swamps, and Spanish moss—the city continues to depend on tourism as a major factor in its economy, attracting millions of visitors a year. The city's main industries, which include marine and engineering services, construction, communications, and electronics, occupy 10 industrial/business parks, including four built by the Virginia Beach Development Authority.

Among Virginia Beach's outstanding historic and recreational attractions are the Virginia Aquarium, the Adam Thoroughgood House (c. 1680, one of the oldest brick houses in North America), the Old Cape Henry Lighthouse, authorized by the first Congress in 1790, and the statue of Admiral Compte de Grasse whose defeat of the British at the Battle of the Virginia Capes brought about the defeat of Gen. Cornwallis at Yorktown and the end of the American Revolution in 1781.

Population 433,575 (2009). Rank: 41st Race/Hispanic Origin (2006–2008): White 70.1%. Black 19.4%. Indian 0.2%. Asian 5.5%. Other 1.3%. Two or more races 3.3%. Hispanic 5.8%.
Location: 36°54'N, 75°58'W. County: independent city.
Terrain and climate   Elev.: 12 ft. Area: 225.9 sq. mi. (585.1 sq km). Avg. daily min. temp.: Jan.: 31.7°F/-0.1°C; avg. daily max. July: 86.9°F/30.5°C. Avg. annual rainfall: 45.22"; snowfall: 7"; clear days: 110; precipitation days: 115.
Government Form: council and manager. Mayor: William D. Sessoms, Jr. (757) 385-4581
www.vbgov.com
Visitor info: (800) VA-BEACH
www.vbfun.com

▶ WASHINGTON, D.C.

[For description, see District of Columbia entry in "States, Territories, and Possessions."]
Population 599,657 (2009). Rank: 27th. Race/Hispanic Origin (2000): White 30.8%. Black 60.0%. Indian 0.3%. Asian 2.7%. Pacific Islander 0.1%. Other 3.8%. Two or more races 2.4%. Hispanic 7.9%.
Location: 38°52'N, 77°00'W. County: independent city.
Terrain and climate   Elev.: 30 ft. Area: 62.7 sq. mi. (162.4 sq km). Avg. daily min. temp.: Jan.: 27.5°F/-2.5°C; avg. daily max. July: 87.9°F/31°C. Avg. annual rainfall: 39"; snowfall: 16"; clear days: 101; precipitation days: 111.
Government Form: mayor and council. Mayor: Adrian Fenty. (202) 727-6263.
www.dc.gov
Visitor info: (202) 789-7000.
www.washington.org

Most Popular U.S. Cities for Overseas Travelers, 2000–2008 (numbers in thousands)

2008 Rank, City	Overseas Travelers Visiting			2008 Rank, City	Overseas Travelers Visiting		
	2000	2005	2008		2000	2005	2008
1. New York, NY	5,714	5,810	8,211	6. Las Vegas, NV	2,260	1,778	2,027
2. Los Angeles, CA	3,533	2,580	2,788	7. Honolulu, HI	2,234	1,821	1,495
3. San Francisco, CA	2,831	2,124	2,610	8. Washington D.C.	1,481	1,106	1,470
4. Miami, FL	2,935	2,081	2,585	9. Chicago, IL	1,351	1,084	1,368
5. Orlando, FL	3,013	2,016	2,433	10. Boston, MA	1,325	802	1,115

Source: U.S. Census Bureau, *Statistical Abstract of the United States, 2010.*

CITIES IN AMERICA

The number of large U.S. cities continues to grow. The 2000 Census recorded 243 cities with populations over 100,000, up from 199 such places in 1990.

The number of very large cities also continues to grow. In 1990, the only cities with more than a million residents were New York, Los Angeles, Chicago, Houston, Philadelphia, Detroit, Dallas and San Diego. In the 2000 Census, Detroit's population dropped below a million (mostly from flight to the suburbs), but Phoenix, and San Antonio topped a million.

New York, the nation's largest city, grew by 685,000 people between censuses, with most of that growth coming in the latter half of the decade. Meanwhile, Los Angeles, which declined in population early in the decade, grew by an overall 479,000 people.

Major U.S. Cities: Population, Population Change, Population Density, and Land Area, 1970–2000

City (Rank, 2000)	Population ('000s)				Percent change	Population per sq. mi.	Land area (sq. mi.)
	1970	1980	1990	2000	1990-2000	1990	1990
Abilene, Texas (197)	90	98	107	116	8.7%	1,035	103.1
Akron, Ohio (82)	275	237	223	217	-2.7	3,586	62.2
Albuquerque, N.Mex. (35)	245	332	385	449	16.6	2,909	132.2
Alexandria, Va. (170)	111	103	111	128	15.4	7,267	15.3
Allentown, Pa. (219)	110	104	105	107	1.5	5,949	17.7
Amarillo, Texas (120)	127	149	158	174	10.2	1,793	87.9
Anaheim, Calif. (56)	166	219	266	328	23.1	6,014	44.3
Anchorage, Alaska[1] (66)	48	174	226	260	15.0	133	1,697.7
Ann Arbor, Mich. (199)	100	108	110	114	4.0	4,231	25.9
Arlington, Texas (54)	90	160	262	333	27.2	2,814	93.0
Arvada, Colo. (235)	N.A.	N.A.	89	102	14.5	N.A.	N.A.
Athens–Clarke County, Ga.[1] (237)	N.A.	N.A.	46	101	121.9	N.A.	N.A.
Atlanta, Ga. (40)	495	425	394	416	5.7	2,990	131.8
Augusta–Richmond County, Ga.[1] (91)	N.A.	N.A.	45	200	347.5	N.A.	N.A.
Aurora, Colo. (62)	75	159	222	276	24.4	1,676	132.5
Aurora, Ill. (151)	N.A.	N.A.	100	143	43.6	N.A.	N.A.
Austin, Texas (16)	254	346	466	657	41.0	2,138	217.8
Bakersfield, Calif. (70)	70	106	175	247	41.3	1,904	91.8
Baltimore, Md. (17)	905	787	736	651	-11.5	9,108	80.8
Baton Rouge, La. (75)	166	220	220	228	3.8	2,969	74.0
Bayamon, Puerto Rico (86)	N.A.	N.A.	202	203	0.7	N.A.	N.A.
Beaumont, Texas (200)	118	118	114	114	-0.4	1,427	80.1
Bellevue, Wash. (210)	N.A.	N.A.	87	110	26.1	N.A.	N.A.
Berkeley, Calif. (231)	114	103	103	103	0.0	9,783	10.5
Birmingham, Ala. (72)	301	284	266	243	-8.7	1,791	148.5
Boise City, Idaho (108)	75	102	126	186	47.8	2,726	46.1
Boston, Mass. (20)	641	563	574	589	2.6	11,860	48.4
Bridgeport, Conn. (156)	157	143	142	140	-1.5	8,855	16.0
Brownsville, Texas (155)	N.A.	N.A.	99	140	41.2	N.A.	N.A.
Buffalo, N.Y. (59)	463	358	328	293	-10.8	8,083	40.6
Burbank, Calif. (243)	N.A.	N.A.	94	100	7.1	N.A.	N.A.
Cambridge, Mass. (238)	N.A.	N.A.	96	101	5.8	N.A.	N.A.
Cape Coral, Fla. (234)	N.A.	N.A.	75	102	36.4	N.A.	N.A.
Carolina, Puerto Rico (125)	N.A.	N.A.	162	168	3.5	N.A.	N.A.
Carrollton, Texas (209)	N.A.	N.A.	82	110	33.4	N.A.	N.A.
Cedar Rapids, Iowa (185)	111	110	109	121	11.0	2,033	53.5
Chandler, Ariz. (116)	N.A.	N.A.	91	177	95.0	N.A.	N.A.
Charlotte, N.C. (26)	241	315	396	541	36.6	2,272	174.3
Chattanooga, Tenn. (132)	120	170	152	156	2.0	1,288	118.4
Chesapeake, Va. (93)	90	114	152	199	31.1	446	340.7
Chicago, Ill. (3)	3,369	3,005	2,784	2,896	4.0	12,251	227.2
Chula Vista, Calif. (122)	68	84	135	174	28.4	4,661	29.0
Cincinnati, Ohio (55)	454	385	364	331	-9.0	4,717	77.2
Clarksville, Tenn. (228)	N.A.	N.A.	75	103	37.0	N.A.	N.A.
Clearwater, Fla. (212)	N.A.	N.A.	99	109	10.1	N.A.	N.A.
Cleveland, Ohio (33)	751	574	506	478	-5.4	6,565	77.0
Colorado Springs, Colo. (49)	136	215	281	361	28.4	1,535	183.2
Columbia, S.C. (195)	114	101	98	116	18.6	884	117.1
Columbus, Ga.[1] (106)	155	169	179	186	3.9	827	216.1
Columbus, Ohio (15)	540	565	633	711	12.4	3,315	190.9
Concord, Calif. (181)	85	104	111	122	9.4	3,773	29.5
Coral Springs, Fla. (190)	N.A.	N.A.	79	118	48.0	N.A.	N.A.
Corona, Calif. (174)	N.A.	N.A.	76	125	64.2	N.A.	N.A.
Corpus Christi, Texas (61)	205	232	257	277	7.8	1,907	135.0

City (Rank, 2000)	Population ('000s)				Percent change 1990-2000	Population per sq. mi. 1990	Land area (sq. mi.) 1990
	1970	1980	1990	2000			
Costa Mesa, Calif. (213)	N.A.	N.A.	96	109	12.8%	N.A.	N.A.
Dallas, Texas (8)	844	905	1,007	1,189	18.0	2,943	342.4
Daly City, Calif. (227)	N.A.	N.A.	92	104	12.3	N.A.	N.A.
Dayton, Ohio (126)	243	194	182	166	–8.7	3,310	55.0
Denver, Colo.[1] (25)	515	493	468	555	18.6	3,051	153.3
Des Moines, Iowa (95)	201	191	193	199	2.8	2,567	75.3
Detroit, Mich. (10)	1,514	1,203	1,028	951	–7.5	7,410	138.7
Downey, Calif. (216)	N.A.	N.A.	91	107	17.4	N.A.	N.A.
Durham, N.C. (105)	95	101	137	187	36.9	1,972	69.3
El Monte, Calif. (196)	70	79	106	116	9.2	11,175	9.5
El Paso, Texas (23)	322	425	515	564	9.4	2,100	245.4
Elizabeth, N.J. (186)	113	106	110	121	9.6	8,929	12.3
Erie, Pa. (226)	129	119	109	104	–4.6	4,944	22.0
Escondido, Calif. (164)	37	64	109	134	22.9	3,048	35.6
Eugene, Oreg. (160)	79	106	113	138	22.4	2,962	38.0
Evansville, Ind. (182)	139	130	126	122	–3.7	3,102	40.7
Fayetteville, N.C. (184)	N.A.	N.A.	76	121	59.9	N.A.	N.A.
Flint, Mich. (175)	193	160	141	125	–11.2	4,161	33.8
Fontana, Calif. (167)	N.A.	N.A.	88	129	47.3	N.A.	N.A.
Fort Collins, Colo. (189)	N.A.	N.A.	88	119	35.2	N.A.	N.A.
Fort Lauderdale, Fla. (134)	140	153	149	152	2.0	4,753	31.4
Fort Wayne, Ind. (85)	178	172	173	206	18.9	2,762	62.7
Fort Worth, Texas (27)	393	385	448	535	19.5	1,592	281.1
Fremont, Calif. (87)	101	132	173	203	17.3	2,250	77.0
Fresno, Calif. (37)	166	217	354	428	20.7	3,573	99.1
Fullerton, Calif. (173)	86	102	114	126	10.4	5,160	22.1
Garden Grove, Calif. (127)	121	123	143	165	15.5	7,974	17.9
Garland, Texas (83)	81	139	181	216	19.4	3,150	57.4
Gary, Ind. (230)	175	152	117	103	–11.9	2,322	50.2
Gilbert town, Ariz. (208)	N.A.	N.A.	29	110	275.8	N.A.	N.A.
Glendale, Ariz. (81)	36	97	148	219	47.7	2,837	52.2
Glendale, Calif. (100)	133	139	180	195	8.3	5,882	30.6
Grand Prairie, Texas (172)	N.A.	N.A.	100	127	27.9	N.A.	N.A.
Grand Rapids, Mich. (96)	198	182	189	198	4.6	4,273	44.3
Green Bay, Wisc. (233)	N.A.	N.A.	96	102	6.1	N.A.	N.A.
Greensboro, N.C. (78)	144	156	184	224	22.0	2,304	79.8
Hampton, Va. (147)	121	123	134	146	9.5	2,583	51.8
Hartford, Conn. (183)	158	136	140	122	–13.0	8,077	17.3
Hayward, Calif. (154)	93	94	111	140	25.6	2,560	43.5
Henderson, Nevada (118)	N.A.	N.A.	65	175	170.1	N.A.	N.A.
Hialeah, Fla. (76)	102	145	188	226	20.4	9,772	19.2
Hollywood, Fla. (157)	107	121	122	139	14.5	4,464	27.3
Honolulu, Hawaii[2] (47)	325	365	365	372	1.7	4,400	85.7
Houston, Texas (4)	1,234	1,595	1,631	1,954	19.8	3,021	539.9
Huntington Beach, Calif. (103)	116	171	182	190	4.4	6,871	26.4
Huntsville, Ala. (130)	139	143	160	158	–1.0	973	164.4
Independence, Mo. (202)	112	112	112	113	0.9	1,436	78.2
Indianapolis , Ind. (12)	737	701	742	792	6.7	2,022	361.7
Inglewood, Calif. (204)	90	94	110	113	2.7	11,952	9.2
Irvine, Calif. (150)	[3]	62	110	143	29.7	2,607	42.3
Irving, Texas (102)	97	110	155	192	23.6	2,293	67.6
Jackson, Miss. (111)	154	203	197	184	–6.3	1,804	109.0
Jacksonville, Fla. (14)	504	541	635	736	15.8	837	758.7
Jersey City, N.J. (73)	260	224	229	240	5.0	15,337	14.9
Joliet, Ill. (221)	N.A.	N.A.	77	106	38.2	N.A.	N.A.
Kansas City, Kans. (146)	168	161	150	147	–1.9	1,390	107.8
Kansas City, Mo. (36)	507	448	435	442	1.5	1,397	311.5
Knoxville, Tenn. (119)	175	175	165	174	5.3	2,135	77.2
Lafayette, La. (207)	N.A.	N.A.	94	110	16.7	N.A.	N.A.
Lakewood, Colo. (148)	93	114	126	144	14.0	3,100	40.8
Lancaster, Calif. (188)	N.A.	N.A.	97	119	22.0	N.A.	N.A.
Lansing, Mich. (187)	131	130	127	119	–6.4	3,755	33.9
Laredo, Texas (117)	69	91	123	177	43.7	3,739	32.9
Las Vegas, Nevada (32)	126	165	258	478	85.2	3,100	83.3
Lexington–Fayette, Ky. (65)	108	204	225	261	15.6	792	284.5
Lincoln, Neb. (77)	150	172	192	226	17.5	3,033	63.3
Little Rock, Ark. (112)	132	159	176	183	4.2	1,709	102.9
Livonia, Mich. (242)	110	105	101	101	–0.3	2,823	35.7
Long Beach, Calif. (34)	359	361	429	462	7.5	8,586	50.0
Los Angeles, Calif. (2)	2,812	2,969	3,485	3,695	6.0	7,426	469.3
Louisville, Ky. (67)	362	299	269	256	–4.8	4,341	62.1
Lowell, Mass. (222)	94	92	103	105	1.7	7,506	13.8

City (Rank, 2000)	Population ('000s)				Percent change 1990-2000	Population per sq. mi. 1990	Land area (sq. mi.) 1990
	1970	1980	1990	2000			
Lubbock, Texas (92)	149	174	186	200	7.2%	1,789	104.1
Madison, Wisc. (84)	172	171	191	208	8.8	3,300	57.8
Manchester, N.H. (218)	N.A.	N.A.	100	107	7.5	N.A.	N.A.
McAllen, Texas (220)	N.A.	N.A.	84	106	26.7	N.A.	N.A.
Memphis, Tenn. (18)	624	646	610	650	6.5	2,384	256.0
Mesa, Ariz. (43)	63	152	288	396	37.6	2,653	108.6
Mesquite, Texas (176)	55	67	101	125	22.7	2,369	42.8
Miami, Fla. (48)	335	347	359	362	1.1	10,074	35.6
Milwaukee, Wisc. (19)	717	636	628	597	-5.0	6,537	96.1
Minneapolis, Minn. (46)	434	371	368	383	3.9	6,706	54.9
Mobile, Ala. (94)	190	200	196	199	1.3	1,663	118.0
Modesto, Calif. (104)	62	107	165	189	14.6	5,458	30.2
Montgomery, Ala. (89)	133	178	187	202	7.7	1,389	135.0
Moreno Valley, Calif. (152)	3	3	119	142	19.9	2,418	49.1
Naperville, Ill. (169)	N.A.	N.A.	85	128	50.4	N.A.	N.A.
Nashville–Davidson, Tenn.[1] (22)	426	456	511	570	11.6	1,032	473.3
New Haven, Conn. (179)	138	126	130	124	-5.2	6,922	18.9
New Orleans, La. (31)	593	558	497	485	-2.5	2,751	180.7
New York, N.Y. (1)	7,896	7,072	7,323	8,008	9.4	23,701	309.0
Newark, N.J. (64)	382	329	275	274	-0.6	11,554	23.8
Newport News, Va. (115)	138	145	170	180	5.9	2,510	68.3
Norfolk, Va. (74)	308	267	261	234	-10.3	4,856	53.8
North Las Vegas, Nevada (198)	N.A.	N.A.	48	115	142.1	N.A.	N.A.
Norwalk, Calif. (229)	N.A.	N.A.	94	103	9.6	N.A.	N.A.
Oakland, Calif. (42)	362	339	372	399	7.3	6,640	56.1
Oceanside, Calif. (128)	40	77	128	161	25.4	3,164	40.5
Oklahoma City, Okla. (29)	368	404	445	506	13.8	731	608.2
Omaha, Neb. (45)	347	314	336	390	16.1	3,336	100.7
Ontario, Calif. (131)	64	89	133	158	18.6	3,624	36.8
Orange, Calif. (168)	77	91	111	129	16.4	4,741	23.3
Orlando, Fla. (107)	99	128	165	186	12.9	2,448	67.3
Overland Park, Kans. (143)	78	82	112	149	33.4	2,007	55.7
Oxnard, Calif. (124)	71	108	142	170	19.8	5,843	24.4
Palmdale, Calif. (194)	N.A.	N.A.	69	117	69.5	N.A.	N.A.
Pasadena, Calif. (163)	113	118	132	134	1.8	5,724	23.0
Pasadena, Texas (153)	90	113	119	142	18.7	2,726	43.8
Paterson, N.J. (142)	145	138	141	149	5.9	16,693	8.4
Pembroke Pines, Fla. (161)	N.A.	N.A.	65	137	110.0	N.A.	N.A.
Peoria, Ariz. (214)	N.A.	N.A.	51	108	114.1	N.A.	N.A.
Peoria, Ill. (203)	127	124	114	113	-0.5	2,776	40.9
Philadelphia, Pa.[1] (5)	1,949	1,688	1,586	1,518	-4.3	11,734	135.1
Phoenix, Ariz. (6)	584	790	983	1,321	34.3	2,342	419.9
Pittsburgh, Pa. (53)	520	424	370	335	-9.5	6,649	55.6
Plano, Texas (79)	18	72	129	222	72.5	1,929	66.3
Pomona, Calif. (141)	87	93	132	149	13.5	5,770	22.8
Ponce, Puerto Rico (133)	N.A.	N.A.	159	155	-2.6	N.A.	N.A.
Portland, Oreg. (28)	380	368	437	529	21.0	3,508	124.7
Portsmouth, Va. (241)	111	105	104	101	-3.2	3,139	33.1
Providence, R.I. (121)	179	157	161	174	8.0	8,707	18.5
Provo, Utah (223)	N.A.	N.A.	87	105	21.1	N.A.	N.A.
Pueblo, Colo. (236)	N.A.	N.A.	99	102	3.5	N.A.	N.A.
Raleigh, N.C. (63)	123	150	208	276	32.8	2,395	88.1
Rancho Cucamonga, Calif. (171)	3	55	101	128	26.0	2,682	37.8
Reno, Nevada (114)	73	101	134	180	34.8	2,328	57.5
Richmond, Va. (97)	249	219	203	198	-2.6	3,374	60.1
Riverside, Calif. (68)	140	171	227	255	12.7	2,916	77.7
Rochester, N.Y. (80)	295	242	232	220	-5.1	6,435	35.8
Rockford, Ill. (140)	147	140	139	150	7.7	3,110	45.0
Sacramento, Calif. (41)	257	276	369	407	10.2	3,836	96.3
Salem, Oreg. (162)	69	89	108	137	27.0	2,595	41.5
Salinas, Calif. (138)	59	80	109	151	38.9	5,839	18.6
Salt Lake City, Utah (113)	176	163	160	182	13.6	1,467	109.0
San Antonio, Texas (9)	654	786	936	1,145	22.3	2,810	333.0
San Bernardino, Calif. (110)	107	119	164	185	12.9	2,980	55.1
San Diego, Calif. (7)	697	876	1,111	1,223	10.2	3,428	324.0
San Francisco, Calif.[1] (13)	716	679	724	777	7.3	15,502	46.7
San Jose, Calif. (11)	460	629	782	895	14.4	4,568	171.3
San Juan , Puerto Rico (39)	N.A.	N.A.	427	422	-1.1	N.A.	N.A.
Santa Ana, Calif. (52)	156	204	294	338	15.1	10,842	27.1
Santa Clara, Calif. (232)	N.A.	N.A.	94	102	9.3	N.A.	N.A.
Santa Clarita, Calif. (137)	3	3	111	151	36.6	2,733	40.5
Santa Rosa, Calif. (144)	50	83	113	148	30.3	3,362	33.7

| City (Rank, 2000) | Population ('000s) | | | | Percent change | Population per sq. mi. | Land area (sq. mi.) |
	1970	1980	1990	2000	1990-2000	1990	1990
Savannah, Ga. (166)	118	142	138	132	−4.4%	2,204	62.6
Scottsdale, Ariz. (88)	68	89	130	203	55.8	706	184.4
Seattle, Wash. (24)	531	494	516	563	9.1	6,154	83.9
Shreveport, La. (90)	182	206	199	200	0.8	2,013	98.6
Simi Valley, Calif. (206)	60	78	100	111	11.1	3,034	33.0
Sioux Falls, S.D. (178)	72	81	101	124	23.0	2,236	45.1
South Bend, Ind. (215)	126	110	106	108	2.2	2,897	36.4
Spokane, Wash. (99)	171	171	177	196	10.4	3,169	55.9
Springfield, Ill. (205)	92	100	105	111	5.9	2,474	42.5
Springfield, Mass. (135)	164	152	157	152	−3.1	4,890	32.1
Springfield, Mo. (136)	120	133	140	152	7.9	2,068	68.0
St. Louis, Mo. (50)	622	453	397	348	−12.2	6,405	61.9
St. Paul, Minn. (60)	310	270	272	287	5.5	5,157	52.8
St. Petersburg, Fla. (69)	216	239	239	248	4.0	4,059	59.2
Stamford, Conn. (191)	109	102	108	117	8.4	2,865	37.7
Sterling Heights, Mich. (177)	61	109	118	124	5.7	3,215	36.6
Stockton, Calif. (71)	110	150	211	244	15.6	4,013	52.6
Sunnyvale, Calif. (165)	96	107	117	132	12.4	5,353	21.9
Syracuse, N.Y. (145)	197	170	164	147	−10.1	6,528	25.1
Tacoma, Wash. (101)	154	159	177	194	9.6	3,677	48.1
Tallahassee, Fla. (139)	73	82	125	151	20.7	1,972	63.3
Tampa, Fla. (58)	278	272	280	303	8.4	2,577	108.7
Tempe, Ariz. (129)	64	107	142	159	11.8	3,590	39.5
Thousand Oaks, Calif. (192)	36	77	104	117	12.1	2,104	49.6
Toledo, Ohio (57)	383	355	333	314	−5.8	4,132	80.6
Topeka, Kans. (180)	125	119	120	122	2.1	2,173	55.2
Torrance, Calif. (159)	135	130	133	138	3.6	6,487	20.5
Tucson, Ariz. (30)	263	331	405	487	20.1	2,594	156.3
Tulsa, Okla. (44)	330	361	367	393	7.0	2,001	183.5
Vallejo, Calif. (193)	72	80	109	117	6.9	3,613	30.2
Vancouver, Wash. (149)	N.A.	N.A.	46	144	209.5	N.A.	N.A.
Ventura, Calif. (240)	N.A.	N.A.	93	101	9.0	N.A.	N.A.
Virginia Beach, Va. (38)	172	262	393	425	8.2	1,583	248.3
Waco, Texas (201)	95	101	104	114	9.8	1,367	75.8
Warren, Mich. (158)	179	161	145	138	−4.6	4,226	34.3
Washington, D.C. (21)	757	638	607	572	−5.7	9,883	61.4
Waterbury, Conn. (217)	108	103	109	107	−1.6	3,815	28.6
West Covina, Calif. (224)	N.A.	N.A.	96	105	9.4	N.A.	N.A.
West Valley City, Utah (211)	N.A.	N.A.	87	109	25.2	N.A.	N.A.
Westminster, Colo. (239)	N.A.	N.A.	75	101	35.3	N.A.	N.A.
Wichita Falls, Texas (225)	N.A.	N.A.	96	104	8.2	N.A.	N.A.
Wichita, Kans. (51)	277	280	304	344	13.2	2,640	115.1
Winston-Salem, N.C. (109)	134	132	143	186	29.5	2,018	71.1
Worcester, Mass. (123)	177	162	170	173	1.7	4,520	37.6
Yonkers, N.Y. (98)	204	195	188	196	4.3	10,403	18.1

Notes: Cities over 100,000 population. 1. Represents the portion of a consolidated city not within one or more separately incorporated areas. 2. Data represent the census designated place of Honolulu, as delineated by the State of Hawaii. **Source:** U.S. Census Bureau, *Statistical Abstract of the United States 1990 and 2000, and Release (2001).*

Historical Rankings, Top 10 Cities

1910		1960		2009	
City	Population	City	Population	City	Population
New York	4,766,883	New York	7,781,984	New York	8,391,881
Chicago	2,185,283	Chicago	3,550,404	Los Angeles	3,831,868
Philadelphia	1,549,008	Los Angeles	2,479,015	Chicago	2,851,268
St. Louis	687,029	Philadelphia	2,002,512	Houston	2,257,926
Boston	670,585	Detroit	1,670,144	Phoenix	1,601,587
Cleveland	560,663	Baltimore	939,024	Philadelphia	1,547,297
Baltimore	558,485	Houston	938,219	San Antonio	1,373,668
Pittsburgh	533,905	Cleveland	876,050	San Diego	1,306,301
Detroit	465,766	Washington, D.C.	763,956	Dallas	1,299,543
Buffalo, N.Y.	423,715	St. Louis	750,026	San Jose, Calif.	964,695

Source: U.S. Census Bureau, Public Information Office Press Release (July 1, 2010).

Resident Population of Major U.S Cities by Race and Hispanic Origin, 2000

Geographic area	Total population	Black	American Indian	Asian	Native Hawaiian	Some other race	Two or more races	Hispanic or Latino (any race)
Abilene, Texas	115,930	8.8%	0.6%	1.3%	0.1%	8.7%	2.4%	19.4%
Akron, Ohio	217,074	28.5	0.3	1.5	N.A.	0.4	2.1	1.2
Albuquerque, N. Mex.	448,607	3.1	3.9	2.2	0.1	14.8	4.3	39.9
Alexandria, Va.	128,283	22.5	0.3	5.7	0.1	7.4	4.3	14.7
Allentown, Pa.	106,632	7.8	0.3	2.3	0.1	13.4	3.6	24.4
Amarillo, Texas	173,627	6.0	0.8	2.1	N.A.	11.3	2.3	21.9
Anaheim, Calif.	328,014	2.7	0.9	12.0	0.4	24.2	5.0	46.8
Anchorage, Alaska	260,283	5.8	7.3	5.5	0.9	2.2	6.0	5.7
Ann Arbor, Mich.	114,024	8.8	0.3	11.9	N.A.	1.2	3.1	3.3
Arlington, Texas	332,969	13.7	0.5	6.0	0.1	8.9	2.9	18.3
Arlington, Va.	189,453	9.3	0.3	8.6	0.1	8.3	4.3	18.6
Arvada, Colo.	102,153	0.7	0.7	2.2	0.1	3.1	2.3	9.8
Athens, Ga.	101,489	27.3	0.2	3.1	N.A.	3.1	1.4	6.3
Atlanta, Ga.	416,474	61.4	0.2	1.9	N.A.	2.0	1.2	4.5
Augusta, Ga.	199,775	49.8	0.3	1.5	0.1	1.0	1.8	2.8
Aurora, Colo.	276,393	13.4	0.8	4.4	0.2	8.1	4.2	19.8
Aurora, Ill.	142,990	11.1	0.4	3.1	N.A.	14.5	2.9	32.6
Austin, Texas	656,562	10.0	0.6	4.7	0.1	16.2	3.0	30.5
Bakersfield, Calif.	247,057	9.2	1.4	4.3	0.1	18.7	4.4	32.5
Baltimore, Md.	651,154	64.3	0.3	1.5	N.A.	0.7	1.5	1.7
Baton Rouge, La.	227,818	50.0	0.2	2.6	N.A.	0.5	1.0	1.7
Beaumont, Texas	113,866	45.8	0.2	2.5	N.A.	3.5	1.5	7.9
Bellevue, Wash.	109,569	2.0	0.3	17.4	0.2	2.5	3.2	5.3
Berkeley, Calif.	102,743	13.6	0.5	16.4	0.1	4.6	5.6	9.7
Birmingham, Ala.	242,820	73.5	0.2	0.8	N.A.	0.6	0.8	1.6
Boise City, Idaho	185,787	0.8	0.7	2.1	0.2	1.7	2.4	4.5
Boston, Mass.	589,141	25.3	0.4	7.5	0.1	7.8	4.4	14.4
Bridgeport, Conn.	139,529	30.8	0.5	3.3	0.1	14.8	5.6	31.9
Brownsville, Texas	139,722	0.4	0.4	0.5	N.A.	14.7	2.3	91.3
Buffalo, N.Y.	292,648	37.2	0.8	1.4	N.A.	3.7	2.5	7.5
Burbank, Calif.	100,316	2.1	0.5	9.2	0.1	9.9	6.0	24.9
Cambridge, Mass.	101,355	11.9	0.3	11.9	0.1	3.2	4.6	7.4
Cape Coral, Fla.	102,286	2.0	0.3	0.9	0.1	2.2	1.6	8.3
Carrollton, Texas	109,576	6.3	0.5	10.9	0.1	7.7	2.7	19.5
Cedar Rapids, Iowa	120,758	3.7	0.3	1.8	0.1	0.6	1.8	1.7
Chandler, Ariz.	176,581	3.5	1.2	4.2	0.1	10.8	3.0	21.0
Charlotte, N.C.	540,828	32.7	0.3	3.4	0.1	3.6	1.7	7.4
Chattanooga, Tenn.	155,554	36.1	0.3	1.5	0.1	1.0	1.3	2.1
Chesapeake, Va.	199,184	28.5	0.4	1.8	0.1	0.7	1.6	2.0
Chicago, Ill.	2,896,016	36.8	0.4	4.3	0.1	13.6	2.9	26.0
Chula Vista, Calif.	173,556	4.6	0.8	11.0	0.6	22.1	5.8	49.6
Cincinnati, Ohio	331,285	42.9	0.2	1.5	N.A.	0.6	1.7	1.3
Clarksville, Tenn.	103,455	23.2	0.5	2.2	0.3	2.6	3.3	6.0
Clearwater, Fla.	108,787	9.8	0.3	1.6	0.1	2.5	1.8	9.0
Cleveland, Ohio	478,403	51.0	0.3	1.3	N.A.	3.6	2.2	7.3
Colorado Springs, Colo.	360,890	6.6	0.9	2.8	0.2	5.0	3.9	12.0
Columbia, S.C.	116,278	46.0	0.3	1.7	0.1	1.4	1.4	3.0
Columbus, Ga.	186,291	43.7	0.4	1.5	0.1	1.9	1.9	4.5
Columbus, Ohio	711,470	24.5	0.3	3.4	0.1	1.2	2.6	2.5
Concord, Calif.	121,780	3.0	0.8	9.4	0.5	9.7	5.9	21.8
Coral Springs, Fla.	117,549	9.2	0.2	3.5	0.1	3.0	2.5	15.5
Corona, Calif.	124,966	6.4	0.9	7.5	0.3	17.5	5.3	35.7
Corpus Christi, Texas	277,454	4.7	0.6	1.3	0.1	18.6	3.1	54.3
Costa Mesa, Calif.	108,724	1.4	0.8	6.9	0.6	16.6	4.3	31.8
Dallas, Texas	1,188,580	25.9	0.5	2.7	N.A.	17.2	2.7	35.6
Daly City, Calif.	103,621	4.6	0.4	50.7	0.9	11.3	6.2	22.3
Dayton, Ohio	166,179	43.1	0.3	0.6	N.A.	0.7	1.8	1.6
Denver, Colo.	554,636	11.1	1.3	2.8	0.1	15.6	3.7	31.7
Des Moines, Iowa	198,682	8.1	0.4	3.5	N.A.	3.5	2.2	6.6
Detroit, Mich.	951,270	81.6	0.3	1.0	N.A.	2.5	2.3	5.0
Downey, Calif.	107,323	3.8	0.9	7.7	0.2	29.1	4.9	57.9
Durham, N.C.	187,035	43.8	0.3	3.6	N.A.	4.7	1.9	8.6
East Los Angeles, Calif.	124,283	0.4	1.3	0.8	0.1	54.0	4.2	96.8
El Monte, Calif.	115,965	0.8	1.4	18.5	0.1	39.3	4.3	72.4
El Paso, Texas	563,662	3.1	0.8	1.1	0.1	18.2	3.4	76.6
Elizabeth, N.J.	120,568	20.0	0.5	2.3	N.A.	15.5	5.9	49.5
Erie, Pa.	103,717	14.2	0.2	0.7	N.A.	1.9	2.3	4.4
Escondido, Calif.	133,559	2.3	1.2	4.5	0.2	19.2	4.8	38.7

Geographic area	Total population	Black	American Indian	Asian	Native Hawaiian	Some other race	Two or more races	Hispanic or Latino (any race)
Eugene, Oreg.	137,893	1.3%	0.9%	3.6%	0.2%	2.2%	3.7%	5.0%
Evansville, Ind.	121,582	10.9	0.2	0.7	N.A.	0.5	1.4	1.1
Fayetteville, N.C.	121,015	42.4	1.1	2.2	0.2	2.5	2.8	5.7
Flint, Mich.	124,943	53.3	0.6	0.4	N.A.	1.1	3.1	3.0
Fontana, Calif.	128,929	11.8	1.1	4.4	0.3	31.9	5.4	57.7
Fort Collins, Colo.	118,652	1.0	0.6	2.5	0.1	3.6	2.5	8.8
Fort Lauderdale, Fla.	152,397	28.9	0.2	1.0	N.A.	1.8	3.8	9.5
Fort Wayne, Ind.	205,727	17.4	0.4	1.6	N.A.	2.9	2.3	5.8
Fort Worth, Texas	534,694	20.3	0.6	2.6	0.1	14.0	2.7	29.8
Fremont, Calif.	203,413	3.1	0.5	37.0	0.4	5.5	5.8	13.5
Fresno, Calif.	427,652	8.4	1.6	11.2	0.1	23.4	5.2	39.9
Fullerton, Calif.	126,003	2.3	0.7	16.1	0.2	14.8	4.0	30.2
Garden Grove, Calif.	165,196	1.3	0.8	30.9	0.7	15.4	4.1	32.5
Garland, Texas	215,768	11.9	0.6	7.3	0.1	12.0	2.9	25.6
Gary, Ind.	102,746	84.0	0.2	0.1	N.A.	2.0	1.7	4.9
Gilbert, Ariz.	109,697	2.4	0.6	3.6	0.1	4.8	2.8	11.9
Glendale, Ariz.	218,812	4.7	1.5	2.7	0.1	12.0	3.5	24.8
Glendale, Calif.	194,973	1.3	0.3	16.1	0.1	8.6	10.1	19.7
Grand Prairie, Texas	127,427	13.5	0.8	4.4	0.1	15.9	3.3	33.0
Grand Rapids, Mich.	197,800	20.4	0.7	1.6	0.1	6.6	3.2	13.1
Green Bay, Wisc.	102,313	1.4	3.3	3.8	N.A.	3.7	2.0	7.1
Greensboro, N.C.	223,891	37.4	0.4	2.8	N.A.	2.1	1.7	4.4
Hampton, Va.	146,437	44.7	0.4	1.8	0.1	1.0	2.4	2.8
Hartford, Conn.	121,578	38.1	0.5	1.6	0.1	26.5	5.4	40.5
Hayward, Calif.	140,030	11.0	0.8	19.0	1.9	16.8	7.5	34.2
Henderson, Nevada	175,381	3.8	0.7	4.0	0.4	3.2	3.5	10.7
Hialeah, Fla.	226,419	2.4	0.1	0.4	N.A.	5.5	3.6	90.3
Hollywood, Fla.	139,357	12.1	0.3	2.0	0.1	4.0	3.3	22.5
Honolulu, Hawaii	371,657	1.6	0.2	55.9	6.8	0.9	14.9	4.4
Houston, Texas	1,953,631	25.3	0.4	5.3	0.1	16.5	3.1	37.4
Huntington Beach, Calif.	189,594	0.8	0.6	9.3	0.2	5.8	3.9	14.7
Huntsville, Ala.	158,216	30.2	0.5	2.2	0.1	0.7	1.8	2.0
Independence, Mo.	113,288	2.6	0.6	0.7	0.5	1.4	2.3	3.7
Indianapolis, Ind.	791,926	25.3	0.3	1.4	N.A.	2.0	1.6	3.9
Inglewood, Calif.	112,580	47.1	0.7	1.1	0.4	27.4	4.2	46.0
Irvine, Calif.	143,072	1.4	0.2	29.8	0.1	2.5	4.8	7.4
Irving, Texas	191,615	10.2	0.6	8.2	0.1	13.4	3.2	31.2
Jackson, Miss.	184,256	70.6	0.1	0.6	N.A.	0.2	0.7	0.8
Jacksonville, Fla.	735,617	29.0	0.3	2.8	0.1	1.3	2.0	4.2
Jersey City, N.J.	240,055	28.3	0.4	16.2	0.1	15.1	5.8	28.3
Joliet, Ill.	106,221	18.2	0.3	1.1	N.A.	9.0	2.1	18.4
Kansas City, Kans.	146,866	30.1	0.8	1.7	N.A.	8.6	3.0	16.8
Kansas City, Mo.	441,545	31.2	0.5	1.9	0.1	3.2	2.4	6.9
Knoxville, Tenn.	173,890	16.2	0.3	1.5	N.A.	0.7	1.6	1.6
Lafayette, La.	110,257	28.5	0.2	1.4	N.A.	0.6	1.0	1.9
Lakewood, Colo.	144,126	1.5	1.1	2.7	0.1	4.9	2.6	14.5
Lancaster, Calif.	118,718	16.0	1.0	3.8	0.2	11.1	5.0	24.1
Lansing, Mich.	119,128	21.9	0.8	2.8	0.1	4.5	4.6	10.0
Laredo, Texas	176,576	0.4	0.4	0.5	N.A.	13.9	2.5	94.1
Las Vegas, Nevada	478,434	10.4	0.7	4.8	0.4	9.7	4.1	23.6
Lexington–Fayette, Ky.	260,512	13.5	0.2	2.5	N.A.	1.2	1.6	3.3
Lincoln, Neb.	225,581	3.1	0.7	3.1	0.1	1.8	2.0	3.6
Little Rock, Ark.	183,133	40.4	0.3	1.7	N.A.	1.3	1.3	2.7
Livonia, Mich.	100,545	0.9	0.2	1.9	N.A.	0.3	1.1	1.7
Long Beach, Calif.	461,522	14.9	0.8	12.0	1.2	20.6	5.3	35.8
Los Angeles, Calif.	3,694,820	11.2	0.8	10.0	0.2	25.7	5.2	46.5
Louisville, Ky.	256,231	33.0	0.2	1.4	N.A.	0.7	1.7	1.9
Lowell, Mass.	105,167	4.2	0.2	16.5	N.A.	6.5	3.9	14.0
Lubbock, Texas	199,564	8.7	0.6	1.5	N.A.	14.3	2.0	27.5
Madison, Wisc.	208,054	5.8	0.4	5.8	N.A.	1.7	2.3	4.1
Manchester, N.H.	107,006	2.1	0.3	2.3	N.A.	1.8	1.7	4.6
McAllen, Texas	106,414	0.6	0.4	1.9	N.A.	15.8	2.7	80.3
Memphis, Tenn.	650,100	61.4	0.2	1.5	N.A.	1.5	1.0	3.0
Mesa, Ariz.	396,375	2.5	1.7	1.5	0.2	9.7	2.8	19.7
Mesquite, Texas	124,523	13.3	0.6	3.7	0.1	6.4	2.3	15.7
Metairie, La.	146,136	6.8	0.3	2.8	N.A.	1.9	1.7	7.3
Miami, Fla.	362,470	22.3	0.2	0.7	N.A.	5.4	4.7	65.8
Milwaukee, Wisc.	596,974	37.3	0.9	2.9	0.1	6.1	2.7	12.0
Minneapolis, Minn.	382,618	18.0	2.2	6.1	0.1	4.1	4.4	7.6
Mobile, Ala.	198,915	46.3	0.2	1.5	N.A.	0.5	1.0	1.4
Modesto, Calif.	188,856	4.0	1.2	6.0	0.5	12.7	5.9	25.6

Geographic area	Total population	Black	American Indian	Asian	Native Hawaiian	Some other race	Two or more races	Hispanic or Latino (any race)
Montgomery, Ala.	201,568	49.6%	0.2%	1.1%	N.A.%	0.4%	1.0%	1.2%
Moreno Valley, Calif.	142,381	19.9	0.9	5.9	0.5	20.1	5.8	38.4
Naperville, Ill.	128,358	3.0	0.1	9.6	N.A.	0.8	1.2	3.2
Nashville–Davidson, Tenn..	569,891	25.9	0.3	2.3	0.1	2.4	2.0	4.6
New Haven, Conn.	123,626	37.4	0.4	3.9	0.1	10.9	3.9	21.4
New Orleans, La.	484,674	67.3	0.2	2.3	N.A.	0.9	1.3	3.1
New York, N.Y.	8,008,278	26.6	0.5	9.8	0.1	13.4	4.9	27.0
Bronx borough	1,332,650	35.6	0.9	3.0	0.1	24.7	5.8	48.4
Brooklyn borough	2,465,326	36.4	0.4	7.5	0.1	10.1	4.3	19.8
Manhattan borough	1,537,195	17.4	0.5	9.4	0.1	14.1	4.1	27.2
Queens borough	2,229,379	20.0	0.5	17.6	0.1	11.7	6.1	25.0
Staten Island borough	443,728	9.7	0.2	5.7	N.A.	4.1	2.7	12.1
Newark, N.J.	273,546	53.5	0.4	1.2	N.A.	14.0	4.4	29.5
Newport News, Va.	180,150	39.1	0.4	2.3	0.1	1.8	2.8	4.2
Norfolk, Va.	234,403	44.1	0.5	2.8	0.1	1.7	2.5	3.8
North Las Vegas, Nevada	115,488	19.0	0.8	3.2	0.5	15.8	4.7	37.6
Norwalk, Calif.	103,298	4.6	1.2	11.5	0.4	32.7	4.7	62.9
Oakland, Calif.	399,484	35.7	0.7	15.2	0.5	11.7	5.0	21.9
Oceanside, Calif.	161,029	6.3	0.9	5.5	1.3	14.5	5.2	30.2
Oklahoma City, Okla.	506,132	15.4	3.5	3.5	0.1	5.3	3.9	10.1
Omaha, Neb.	390,007	13.3	0.7	1.7	0.1	3.9	1.9	7.5
Ontario, Calif.	158,007	7.5	1.1	3.9	0.4	34.1	5.3	59.9
Orange, Calif.	128,821	1.6	0.8	9.3	0.2	13.8	3.8	32.2
Orlando, Fla.	185,951	26.9	0.3	2.7	0.1	5.4	3.5	17.5
Overland Park, Kans.	149,080	2.5	0.3	3.8	N.A.	1.2	1.4	3.8
Oxnard, Calif.	170,358	3.8	1.3	7.4	0.4	40.4	4.7	66.2
Palmdale, Calif.	116,670	14.5	1.0	3.8	0.2	20.4	5.2	37.7
Paradise, Nevada	186,070	6.6	0.8	6.5	0.6	8.4	4.7	23.5
Pasadena, Calif.	133,936	14.4	0.7	10.0	0.1	16.0	5.4	33.4
Pasadena, Texas	141,674	1.6	0.7	1.8	N.A.	21.3	3.1	48.2
Paterson, N.J.	149,222	32.9	0.6	1.9	0.1	27.6	6.2	50.1
Pembroke Pines, Fla.	137,427	13.3	0.2	3.8	N.A.	3.7	3.5	28.2
Peoria, Ariz.	108,364	2.8	0.7	1.9	0.1	7.1	2.5	15.4
Peoria, Ill.	112,936	24.8	0.2	2.3	N.A.	1.2	2.2	2.5
Philadelphia, Pa.	1,517,550	43.2	0.3	4.5	N.A.	4.8	2.2	8.5
Phoenix, Ariz.	1,321,045	5.1	2.0	2.0	0.1	16.4	3.3	34.1
Pittsburgh, Pa.	334,563	27.1	0.2	2.7	N.A.	0.7	1.6	1.3
Plano, Texas	222,030	5.0	0.4	10.2	N.A.	3.9	2.3	10.1
Pomona, Calif.	149,473	9.6	1.3	7.2	0.2	34.9	5.0	64.5
Portland, Oreg.	529,121	6.6	1.1	6.3	0.4	3.5	4.1	6.8
Portsmouth, Va.	100,565	50.6	0.5	0.8	0.1	0.6	1.6	1.7
Providence, R.I.	173,618	14.5	1.1	6.0	0.2	17.6	6.1	30.0
Provo, Utah	105,166	0.5	0.8	1.8	0.8	5.1	2.4	10.5
Pueblo, Colo.	102,121	2.4	1.7	0.7	0.1	15.2	3.7	44.1
Raleigh, N.C.	276,093	27.8	0.4	3.4	N.A.	3.2	1.9	7.0
Rancho Cucamonga, Calif.	127,743	7.9	0.7	6.0	0.3	13.3	5.4	27.8
Reno, Nevada	180,480	2.6	1.3	5.3	0.6	9.3	3.6	19.2
Richmond, Va.	197,790	57.2	0.2	1.2	0.1	1.5	1.5	2.6
Riverside, Calif.	255,166	7.4	1.1	5.7	0.4	21.0	5.1	38.1
Rochester, N.Y.	219,773	38.5	0.5	2.2	N.A.	6.6	3.8	12.8
Rockford, Ill.	150,115	17.4	0.3	2.2	N.A.	4.8	2.5	10.2
Sacramento, Calif.	407,018	15.5	1.3	16.6	0.9	11.0	6.4	21.6
Salem, Oreg.	136,924	1.3	1.5	2.4	0.5	7.9	3.4	14.6
Salinas, Calif.	151,060	3.3	1.3	6.2	0.3	38.7	5.1	64.1
Salt Lake City, Utah	181,743	1.9	1.3	3.6	1.9	8.5	3.5	18.8
San Antonio, Texas	1,144,646	6.8	0.8	1.6	0.1	19.3	3.7	58.7
San Bernardino, Calif.	185,401	16.4	1.4	4.2	0.4	27.1	5.3	47.5
San Diego, Calif.	1,223,400	7.9	0.6	13.6	0.5	12.4	4.8	25.4
San Francisco, Calif.	776,733	7.8	0.4	30.8	0.5	6.5	4.3	14.1
San Jose, Calif.	894,943	3.5	0.8	26.9	0.4	15.9	5.0	30.2
Santa Ana, Calif.	337,977	1.7	1.2	8.8	0.3	40.6	4.6	76.1
Santa Clara, Calif.	102,361	2.3	0.5	29.3	0.4	6.9	5.0	16.0
Santa Clarita, Calif.	151,088	2.1	0.6	5.2	0.1	8.5	3.9	20.5
Santa Rosa, Calif.	147,595	2.2	1.4	3.8	0.3	10.3	4.4	19.2
Savannah, Ga.	131,510	57.1	0.2	1.5	0.1	0.9	1.3	2.2
Scottsdale, Ariz.	202,705	1.2	0.6	2.0	0.1	2.3	1.7	7.0
Seattle, Wash.	563,374	8.4	1.0	13.1	0.5	2.4	4.5	5.3
Shreveport, La.	200,145	50.8	0.3	0.8	N.A.	0.4	1.0	1.6
Simi Valley, Calif.	111,351	1.3	0.7	6.3	0.1	6.5	3.7	16.8
Sioux Falls, S. Dak.	123,975	1.8	2.1	1.2	0.1	1.2	1.7	2.5
South Bend, Ind.	107,789	24.6	0.4	1.2	0.1	4.9	2.8	8.5

Geographic area	Total population	Black	American Indian	Asian	Native Hawaiian	Some other race	Two or more races	Hispanic or Latino (any race)
Spokane, Wash.	195,629	2.1%	1.8%	2.2%	0.2%	0.9%	3.4%	3.0%
Spring Valley, Nevada	117,390	5.3	0.6	11.2	0.5	5.1	4.7	13.8
Springfield, Ill.	111,454	15.3	0.2	1.5	N.A.	0.5	1.5	1.2
Springfield, Mass.	152,082	21.0	0.4	1.9	0.1	16.4	4.0	27.2
Springfield, Mo.	151,580	3.3	0.8	1.4	0.1	0.9	2.0	2.3
St. Louis, Mo.	348,189	51.2	0.3	2.0	N.A.	0.8	1.9	2.0
St. Paul, Minn.	287,151	11.7	1.1	12.4	0.1	3.8	3.9	7.9
St. Petersburg, Fla.	248,232	22.4	0.3	2.7	0.1	1.1	2.2	4.2
Stamford, Conn.	117,083	15.4	0.2	5.0	N.A.	6.5	3.1	16.8
Sterling Heights, Mich.	124,471	1.3	0.2	4.9	N.A.	0.3	2.5	1.3
Stockton, Calif.	243,771	11.2	1.1	19.9	0.4	17.3	6.8	32.5
Sunnyvale, Calif.	131,760	2.2	0.5	32.3	0.3	7.2	4.3	15.5
Sunrise Manor, Nevada	156,120	12.9	1.0	5.4	0.5	10.1	4.7	26.0
Syracuse, N.Y.	147,306	25.3	1.1	3.4	N.A.	2.2	3.6	5.3
Tacoma, Wash.	193,556	11.2	2.0	7.6	0.9	2.9	6.3	6.9
Tallahassee, Fla.	150,624	34.2	0.2	2.4	0.1	1.0	1.7	4.2
Tampa, Fla.	303,447	26.1	0.4	2.2	0.1	4.2	2.9	19.3
Tempe, Ariz.	158,625	3.7	2.0	4.7	0.3	8.5	3.3	17.9
Thousand Oaks, Calif.	117,005	1.1	0.5	5.9	0.1	4.5	2.8	13.1
Toledo, Ohio	313,619	23.5	0.3	1.0	N.A.	2.3	2.6	5.5
Topeka, Kans.	122,377	11.7	1.3	1.1	N.A.	4.1	3.3	8.9
Torrance, Calif.	137,946	2.2	0.4	28.6	0.3	4.6	4.7	12.8
Tucson, Ariz.	486,699	4.3	2.3	2.5	0.2	16.8	3.8	35.7
Tulsa, Okla.	393,049	15.5	4.7	1.8	0.1	3.5	4.4	7.2
Vallejo, Calif.	116,760	23.7	0.7	24.2	1.1	7.9	6.6	15.9
Vancouver, Wash.	143,560	2.5	1.0	4.5	0.5	2.9	3.8	6.3
Ventura, Calif.	100,916	1.4	1.2	3.0	0.2	11.1	4.3	24.3
Virginia Beach, Va.	425,257	19.0	0.4	4.9	0.1	1.5	2.7	4.2
Waco, Texas	113,726	22.6	0.5	1.4	0.1	12.4	2.3	23.6
Warren, Mich.	138,247	2.7	0.4	3.1	N.A.	0.3	2.2	1.4
Washington, D.C.	572,059	60.0	0.3	2.7	0.1	3.8	2.4	7.9
Waterbury, Conn.	107,271	16.3	0.4	1.5	0.1	10.9	3.7	21.8
West Covina, Calif.	105,080	6.4	0.8	22.7	0.2	21.2	4.9	45.7
West Valley City, Utah	108,896	1.1	1.2	4.3	2.9	8.7	3.5	18.5
Westminster, Colo.	100,940	1.2	0.7	5.5	0.1	5.5	2.8	15.2
Wichita Falls, Texas	104,197	12.4	0.9	2.2	0.1	6.4	3.0	14.0
Wichita, Kans.	344,284	11.4	1.2	4.0	0.1	5.1	3.1	9.6
Winston-Salem, N.C.	185,776	37.1	0.3	1.1	N.A.	4.3	1.6	8.6
Worcester, Mass.	172,648	6.9	0.4	4.9	0.1	7.2	3.4	15.1
Yonkers, N.Y	196,086	16.6	0.4	4.9	N.A.	13.4	4.4	25.9

Note: Black includes African-American. Native American includes Alaska Native. Native Hawaiian Includes other Pacific Islander. Cities with populations over 100,000 as of April 1, 2000. **Source:** U.S. Bureau of the Census, 2000.

Population Change in the 75 Largest U.S. Cities, 1980–2000

City (2000 Rank)	Population			Percent change, 1980–2000	Change, 1990–2000	
	1980	1990	2000		Number	Percent
Albuquerque, N. Mex (35)	332,920	384,736	448,607	15.6%	63,871	16.6%
Anaheim, Calif. (56)	219,494	266,406	328,014	21.4	61,608	23.1
Anchorage, Alaska (66)	174,731	226,338	260,283	29.5	33,945	15.0
Arlington, Texas (54)	160,113	261,721	332,969	63.5	71,248	27.2
Atlanta, Ga. (40)	425,022	394,017	416,474	–7.3	22,457	5.7
Aurora, Colo. (62)	158,588	222,103	276,393	40.1	54,290	24.4
Austin, Texas (16)	345,890	465,622	656,562	34.6	190,940	41.0
Bakersfield, Calif. (70)	N.A.	174,820	247,057	N.A.	72,237	41.3
Baltimore, Md. (17)	786,741	736,014	651,154	–6.4	–84,860	–11.5
Baton Rouge, La. (75)	220,394	219,531	227,818	–0.4	8,287	3.8
Birmingham, Ala. (72)	284,413	265,968	242,820	–6.5	–23,148	–8.7
Boston, Mass. (20)	562,994	574,283	589,141	2.0	14,858	2.6
Buffalo, N.Y (59)	357,870	328,123	292,648	–8.3	–35,475	–10.8
Charlotte, N.C (26)	315,474	395,934	540,828	25.5	144,894	36.6
Chicago, Ill. (3)	3,005,072	2,783,726	2,896,016	–7.4	112,290	4.0
Cincinnati, Ohio (55)	385,409	364,040	331,285	–5.5	–32,755	–9.0
Cleveland, Ohio (33)	573,822	505,616	478,403	–11.9	–27,213	–5.4
Colorado Springs, Colo. (49)	215,105	281,140	360,890	30.7	79,750	28.4
Columbus, Ohio (15)	565,021	632,910	711,470	12.0	78,560	12.4

City (2000 Rank)	Population			Percent change,	Change, 1990–2000	
	1980	1990	2000	1980–2000	Number	Percent
Corpus Christi, Texas (61)	232,134	257,453	277,454	10.9%	20,001	7.8%
Dallas, Texas (8)	904,599	1,006,877	1,188,580	11.3	181,703	18.0
Denver, Colo. (25)	492,686	467,610	554,636	–5.1	87,026	18.6
Detroit, Mich. (10)	1,203,368	1,027,974	951,270	–14.6	–76,704	–7.5
El Paso, Texas (23)	425,259	515,342	563,662	21.2	48,320	9.4
Fort Worth, Texas (27)	385,164	447,619	534,694	16.2	87,075	19.5
Fresno, Calif. (37)	217,491	354,202	427,652	62.9	73,450	20.7
Honolulu, Hawaii. (47)	365,048	365,272	371,657	0.1	6,385	1.7
Houston, Texas (4)	1,595,138	1,630,553	1,953,631	2.2	323,078	19.8
Indianapolis, Ind. (12)	711,539	741,952	791,926	4.3	49,974	6.7
Jacksonville, Fla. (14)	571,003	635,230	735,617	17.9	100,387	15.8
Jersey City, N.J. (73)	223,532	228,537	240,055	2.2	11,518	5.0
Kansas City, Mo. (36)	448,028	435,146	441,545	–2.9	6,399	1.5
Las Vegas, Nev. (32)	164,674	258,295	478,434	56.9	220,139	85.2
Lexington–Fayette, Ky. (65)	204,165	225,366	260,512	10.4	35,146	15.6
Long Beach, Calif. (34)	361,498	429,433	461,522	18.8	32,089	7.5
Los Angeles, Calif. (2)	2,968,528	3,485,557	3,694,820	17.4	209,422	6.0
Louisville, Ky. (67)	298,694	269,063	256,231	–9.9	–12,832	–4.8
Memphis, Tenn. (18)	646,174	610,337	650,100	–5.5	39,763	6.5
Mesa, Ariz. (43)	152,404	288,091	396,375	89.0	108,284	37.6
Miami, Fla. (48)	346,681	358,548	362,470	3.4	3,922	1.1
Milwaukee, Wis. (19)	636,297	628,088	596,974	–1.3	–31,114	–5.0
Minneapolis, Minn. (46)	370,951	368,383	382,618	–0.7	14,235	3.9
Nashville, Tenn. (22)	477,811	510,784	569,891	6.9	59,107	11.6
New Orleans, La. (31)	557,927	496,938	484,674	–10.9	–12,264	–2.5
New York, N.Y. (1)	7,071,639	7,322,564	8,008,278	3.5	685,714	9.4
Newark, N.J. (64)	329,248	275,221	273,546	–16.4	–1,675	–0.6
Norfolk, Va. (74)	266,979	261,229	234,403	–2.2	–26,826	–10.3
Oakland, Calif. (42)	339,337	372,242	399,484	9.7	27,242	7.3
Oklahoma City, Okla. (29)	404,014	444,719	506,132	10.1	61,413	13.8
Omaha, Nebr. (45)	313,939	335,795	390,007	7.0	54,212	16.1
Philadelphia, Pa. (5)	1,688,210	1,585,577	1,517,550	–6.1	–68,027	–4.3
Phoenix, Ariz. (6)	789,704	983,403	1,321,045	24.5	337,642	34.3
Pittsburgh, Pa. (53)	423,959	369,879	334,563	–12.8	–35,316	–9.5
Portland, Oreg. (28)	368,148	437,319	529,121	18.8	91,802	21.0
Raleigh, N.C. (63)	150,255	207,951	276,093	38.4	68,142	32.8
Riverside, Calif. (68)	170,591	226,505	255,166	32.8	28,661	12.7
Sacramento, Calif. (41)	275,741	369,365	407,018	34.0	37,653	10.2
San Antonio, Texas (9)	785,940	935,933	1,144,646	19.1	208,713	22.3
San Diego, Calif. (7)	875,538	1,110,549	1,223,400	26.8	112,851	10.2
San Francisco, Calif. (13)	678,974	723,959	776,733	6.6	52,774	7.3
San Jose, Calif. (11)	629,400	782,248	894,943	24.3	112,695	14.4
San Juan, Puerto Rico (39)	N.A.	426,832	421,958	N.A.	–4,874	–1.1
Santa Ana, Calif. (52)	204,023	293,742	337,977	44.0	44,235	15.1
Seattle, Wash. (24)	493,846	516,259	563,374	4.5	47,115	9.1
St. Louis, Mo. (50)	452,801	396,685	348,189	–12.4	–48,496	–12.2
St. Paul, Minn. (60)	270,320	272,235	287,151	0.7	14,916	5.5
St. Petersburg, Fla. (69)	238,647	238,629	248,232	–0.0	9,603	4.0
Stockton, Calif. (71)	148,283	210,943	243,771	42.3	32,828	15.6
Tampa, Fla. (58)	271,577	280,015	303,447	3.1	23,432	8.4
Toledo, Ohio (57)	354,635	332,943	313,619	–6.1	–19,324	–5.8
Tucson, Ariz. (30)	330,537	405,390	486,699	22.6	81,309	20.1
Tulsa, Okla. (44)	360,919	367,302	393,049	1.8	25,747	7.0
Virginia Beach, Va. (38)	262,199	393,069	425,257	49.9	32,188	8.2
Washington, D.C. (21)	638,432	606,900	572,059	–4.9	–34,841	–5.7
Wichita, Kans. (51)	279,838	304,011	344,284	8.6	40,273	13.2

Source: U.S. Census Bureau, 2000.

Population of the 50 Largest Cities, 1950–2000

2000 Rank, City	1950	1960	1970[1]	1980[1]	1990	2000	Population change, 1990–2000
1. New York, N.Y.	7,891,957	7,781,984	7,896,000	7,072,000	7,322,564	8,008,278	685,714
2. Los Angeles, Calif.	1,970,358	2,479,015	2,812,000	2,969,000	3,485,557	3,694,820	209,422
3. Chicago, Ill.	3,620,962	3,550,404	3,369,000	3,005,000	2,783,726	2,896,016	112,290
4. Houston, Texas	596,163	938,219	1,234,000	1,595,000	1,630,864	1,953,631	323,078
5. Philadelphia, Pa.	2,071,605	2,002,512	1,949,000	1,688,000	1,585,577	1,517,550	–68,027
6. Phoenix, Ariz.	[2]	439,170	584,000	790,000	984,309	1,321,045	337,642
7. San Diego, Calif.	334,387	573,224	697,000	876,000	1,110,623	1,223,400	112,851
8. Dallas, Texas	434,462	679,684	844,000	905,000	1,007,618	1,188,580	181,703
9. San Antonio, Texas	408,442	587,718	654,000	786,000	935,393	1,144,646	208,713
10. Detroit, Mich.	1,849,568	1,670,144	1,514,000	1,203,000	1,027,974	951,270	–76,704
11. San Jose, Calif.	[2]	[2]	460,000	629,000	782,224	894,943	112,695
12. Indianapolis, Ind.[3]	427,173	476,258	737,000	701,000	731,278	791,926	49,974
13. San Francisco, Calif.	775,357	742,855	716,000	679,000	723,959	776,733	52,774
14. Jacksonville, Fla.[3]	204,517	[2]	504,000	541,000	635,230	735,617	100,387
15. Columbus, Ohio	375,901	471,316	540,000	565,000	632,945	711,470	78,560
16. Austin, Texas	[2]	[2]	254,000	346,000	472,020	656,562	190,940
17. Baltimore, Md.	949,708	939,024	905,000	787,000	736,014	651,154	–84,860
18. Memphis, Tenn.	396,000	497,524	624,000	646,000	618,652	650,100	39,763
19. Milwaukee, Wisc.	637,392	741,324	717,000	636,000	628,088	596,974	–31,114
20. Boston, Mass.	801,444	697,197	641,000	563,000	574,283	589,141	14,858
21. Washington, D.C.	802,178	763,956	757,000	638,000	606,900	572,059	–34,841
22. Nashville, Tenn.[3]	[2]	[2]	426,000	456,000	488,366	569,891	59,107
23. El Paso, Texas	[2]	276,687	322,000	425,000	515,342	563,662	48,320
24. Seattle, Wash.	467,591	557,087	531,000	494,000	516,259	563,374	47,115
25. Denver, Colo.	415,786	493,887	515,000	493,000	467,610	554,636	87,026
26. Charlotte, N.C.	[2]	[2]	241,000	315,000	419,558	540,828	144,894
27. Fort Worth, Texas	278,778	356,268	393,000	385,000	447,619	534,694	87,075
28. Portland, Oreg.	373,628	372,676	380,000	368,000	485,975	529,121	91,802
29. Oklahoma City, Okla.	243,504	324,253	368,000	404,000	444,724	506,132	61,413
30. Tucson, Ariz.	[2]	[2]	263,000	331,000	415,444	486,699	81,309
31. New Orleans, La.	570,445	627,525	593,000	558,000	496,938	484,674	–12,264
32. Las Vegas, Nev.	[2]	[2]	[2]	[2]	258,295	478,434	220,139
33. Cleveland, Ohio	914,808	876,050	751,000	574,000	505,616	478,403	–27,213
34. Long Beach, Calif.	250,767	344,168	359,000	361,000	429,321	461,522	32,089
35. Albuquerque, N. Mex.	[2]	[2]	245,000	332,000	384,619	448,607	63,871
36. Kansas City, Mo.	456,622	475,539	507,000	448,000	434,829	441,545	6,399
37. Fresno, Calif.	[2]	[2]	166,000	217,000	354,091	427,652	73,450
38. Virginia Beach, Va.	[2]	[2]	172,000	262,000	393,089	425,257	32,188
39. Atlanta, Ga.	332,314	487,455	495,000	425,000	394,017	416,474	22,457
40. Sacramento, Calif.	[2]	[2]	257,000	276,000	369,365	407,018	37,653
41. Oakland, Calif.	384,575	367,548	362,000	339,000	372,242	399,484	27,472
42. Mesa, Ariz.	[2]	[2]	[2]	[2]	288,091	396,375	108,284
43. Tulsa, Okla.	[2]	261,685	330,000	361,000	367,302	393,049	25,747
44. Omaha, Neb.	251,117	301,598	347,000	314,000	335,795	390,007	54,212
45. Minneapolis, Minn.	521,718	482,872	434,000	371,000	368,383	382,618	14,235
46. Honolulu, Hawaii[4]	248,034	294,194	325,000	365,000	365,272	371,657	6,385
47. Miami, Fla.	249,276	291,688	335,000	347,000	358,548	362,470	3,922
48. Colorado Springs, Colo.	[2]	[2]	[2]	[2]	281,140	360,890	79,750
49. St. Louis, Mo.	856,796	750,026	622,000	453,000	396,685	348,189	–48,496
50. Wichita, Kans.	[2]	[2]	[2]	279,838	304,011	344,284	40,273

Notes: 1. Figure rounded in source. 2. City was not one of the 50 largest that year. 3. City is part of a consolidated city-county government; populations of the other incorporated places in the county have been excluded from the population totals shown here. 4. Not incorporated as a city, but recognized for census purposes as large urban places. Honolulu CDP is coextensive with Honolulu Judicial District within the City and County of Honolulu. **Source:** U.S. Census Bureau, 2001

25 Fastest-Growing Major Cities in the U.S., 1990–2000

2000 Rank, City	Population 1990	Population 2000	Change, 1990–2000 Number	Change, 1990–2000 Percent	Overall rank, 2000
1. Augusta, Ga.	44,639	199,775	155,136	347.5%	91
2. Gilbert, Ariz.	29,188	109,697	80,509	275.8	208
3. Vancouver, Wash.	46,380	143,560	97,180	209.5	149
4. Henderson, Nev.	64,942	175,381	110,439	170.1	118
5. North Las Vegas, Nev.	47,707	115,488	67,781	142.1	198
6. Athens, Ga.	45,734	101,489	55,755	121.9	237
7. Peoria, Ariz.	50,618	108,364	57,746	114.1	214
8. Pembroke Pines, Fla.	65,452	137,427	71,975	110.0	161
9. Chandler, Ariz.	90,533	176,581	86,048	95.0	116
10. Las Vegas, Nevada	258,295	478,434	220,139	85.2	32
11. Plano, Texas	128,713	222,030	93,317	72.5	79
12. Palmdale, Calif.	68,842	116,670	47,828	69.5	194
13. Corona, Calif.	76,095	124,966	48,871	64.2	174
14. Fayetteville, N.C.	75,695	121,015	45,320	59.9	184
15. Scottsdale, Ariz.	130,069	202,705	72,636	55.8	88
16. Naperville, Ill.	85,351	128,358	43,007	50.4	169
17. Coral Springs, Fla.	79,443	117,549	38,106	48.0	190
18. Boise City, Idaho	125,738	185,787	60,049	47.8	108
19. Glendale, Ariz.	148,134	218,812	70,678	47.7	81
20. Fontana, Calif.	87,535	128,929	41,394	47.3	167
21. Laredo, Texas	122,899	176,576	53,677	43.7	117
22. Aurora, Ill.	99,581	142,990	43,409	43.6	151
23. Bakersfield, Calif.	174,820	247,057	72,237	41.3	70
24. Brownsville, Texas	98,962	139,722	40,760	41.2	155
25. Austin, Texas	465,622	656,562	190,940	41.0	16

Note: Cities over 100,000 population.   Source: U.S. Census Bureau, 2000.

25 Fastest-Declining Major U.S. Cities, 1990–2000

2000 Rank, City	Population 1990	Population 2000	Change, 1990–2000 Number	Change, 1990–2000 Percent	Overall rank, 2000
1. Hartford, Conn.	139,739	121,578	−18,161	−13.0%	183
2. St. Louis, Miss.	396,685	348,189	−48,496	−12.2	50
3. Gary, Ind.	116,646	102,746	−13,900	−11.9	230
4. Baltimore, Md.	736,014	651,154	−84,860	−11.5	17
5. Flint, Mich.	140,761	124,943	−15,818	−11.2	175
6. Buffalo, N.Y.	328,123	292,648	−35,475	−10.8	59
7. Norfolk, Va.	261,229	234,403	−26,826	−10.3	74
8. Syracuse, N.Y.	163,860	147,306	−16,554	−10.1	145
9. Pittsburgh, Penn.	369,879	334,563	−35,316	−9.5	53
10. Cincinnati, Ohio	364,040	331,285	−32,755	−9.0	55
11. Dayton, Ohio	182,044	166,179	−15,865	−8.7	126
12. Birmingham, Ala.	265,968	242,820	−23,148	−8.7	72
13. Detroit, Mich.	1,027,974	951,270	−76,704	−7.5	10
14. Lansing, Mich.	127,321	119,128	−8,193	−6.4	187
15. Jackson, Miss.	196,637	184,256	−12,381	−6.3	111
16. Toledo, Ohio	332,943	313,619	−19,324	−5.8	57
17. Washington, D.C.	606,900	572,059	−34,841	−5.7	21
18. Cleveland, Ohio	505,616	478,403	−27,213	−5.4	33
19. New Haven, Conn.	130,474	123,626	−6,848	−5.2	179
20. Rochester, N.Y.	231,636	219,773	−11,863	−5.1	80
21. Milwaukee, Wis.	628,088	596,974	−31,114	−5.0	19
22. Louisville, Ky.	269,063	256,231	−12,832	−4.8	67
23. Erie, Penn.	108,718	103,717	−5,001	−4.6	226
24. Warren, Mich.	144,864	138,247	−6,617	−4.6	158
25. Savannah, Ga.	137,560	131,510	−6,050	−4.4	166

Note: Cities over 100,000 population in 1990.   Source: U.S. Census Bureau, 2000.

CITY FINANCES

► **TAX BURDENS AND PROGRESSIVITY IN MAJOR U.S. CITIES**

Tax rates differ widely not only from state to state and city to city, but also from one income level to another. Any tax system in which the percentage

of taxes paid rises with the income level is said to be *progressive*. A system where the percentage tax burden is the same at all income levels is said to be *proportional*. And a system in which the percentage of taxes paid decreases as income rises is said to be *regressive*. Because progressivity is measured as the ratio of one tax rate to another, progressivity does not necessarily reflect the actual tax burden.

Several factors contribute to the progressivity of a tax system. A graduated individual income tax

Estimated Burden of State & Local Taxes by Income Level in Selected Cities, 2008

City	$25,000[3] Percent[1]	Amount	$50,000[3] Percent[1]	Amount	$75,000[3] Percent[1]	Amount	$100,000[3] Percent[1]	Amount
Albuquerque, N. Mex.	9.9	2,478	7.7	3,849	7.7	5,787	7.9	7,895
Anchorage, Alaska	8.9	2,229	5.3	2,654	4.3	3,200	3.6	3,610
Atlanta, Ga.	13.0	3,241	8.8	4,423	9.2	6,929	9.7	9,666
Baltimore, Md.	8.7	2,183	9.5	4,749	9.7	7,293	10.1	10,087
Billings, Mont.	7.5	1,878	4.4	2,190	5.6	4,218	6.1	6,136
Birmingham, Ala.	14.6	3,642	7.7	3,872	7.7	5,802	8.0	8,004
Boise City, Idaho	9.0	2,248	6.2	3,096	7.2	5,424	8.0	7,987
Boston, Mass.	12.5	3,113	9.8	4,897	9.0	6,757	8.8	8,787
Bridgeport, Conn.	11.9	2,975	20.1	10,069	18.1	13,583	16.9	16,943
Burlington, Vt.	9.3	2,317	8.4	4,214	8.0	5,973	8.2	8,194
Charleston, W. Va.	11.5	2,886	7.6	3,818	8.1	6,105	8.5	8,545
Charlotte, N.C.	12.7	3,170	8.5	4,245	9.1	6,799	9.6	9,604
Cheyenne, Wyo.	9.4	2,347	4.4	2,223	3.9	2,949	4.0	4,032
Chicago, Ill.	13.1	3,274	12.5	6,226	10.8	8,093	10.0	10,037
Columbia, S.C.	10.2	2,553	7.1	3,564	8.1	6,066	8.7	8,707
Columbus, Ohio	12.1	3,017	10.4	5,183	10.0	7,516	10.2	10,196
Denver, Colo.	11.3	2,828	6.6	3,277	6.7	5,055	7.3	7,324
Des Moines, Iowa	11.4	2,846	9.7	4,846	9.8	7,326	9.9	9,942
Detroit, Mich.	11.5	2,871	11.5	5,769	11.2	8,385	11.1	11,069
Fargo, N. Dak.	7.8	1,954	5.9	2,969	5.7	4,247	5.9	5,894
Honolulu, Hawaii	12.9	3,213	5.1	2,545	5.9	4,441	6.7	6,701
Houston, Tex.	9.9	2,479	6.1	3,047	5.6	4,228	5.4	5,357
Indianapolis, Ind.	12.7	3,184	10.1	5,044	9.6	7,189	9.6	9,611
Jackson, Miss.	10.8	2,703	8.6	4,315	8.8	6,593	9.2	9,225
Jacksonville, Fla.	10.4	2,594	4.6	2,323	4.1	3,096	4.0	4,000
Kansas City, Mo.	12.1	3,021	8.4	4,181	8.6	6,477	8.9	8,908
Las Vegas, Nev.	9.8	2,455	6.5	3,243	5.4	4,046	5.0	4,988
Little Rock, Ark.	12.4	3,090	7.5	3,734	8.2	6,121	8.8	8,796
Los Angeles, Calif.	10.7	2,665	10.0	4,993	8.6	6,417	8.5	8,508
Louisville, Ky.	13.6	3,401	9.6	4,800	9.8	7,333	10.2	10,195
Manchester, N.H.	8.5	2,120	7.4	3,719	5.7	4,298	4.9	4,850
Memphis, Tenn.	11.0	2,738	6.0	3,005	5.5	4,155	5.2	5,194
Milwaukee, Wis.	9.3	2,316	10.1	5,058	9.6	7,224	9.9	9,898
Minneapolis, Minn.	10.9	2,724	8.5	4,226	8.4	6,290	8.7	8,663
New Orleans, La.	10.9	2,713	6.4	3,198	6.9	5,207	7.5	7,469
New York, N.Y.	11.6	2,890	9.1	4,542	9.8	7,337	10.7	10,689
Newark, N.J.	10.1	2,536	10.8	5,386	9.1	6,838	8.2	8,207
Oklahoma City, Okla.	10.9	2,719	7.3	3,627	7.9	5,901	8.2	8,180
Omaha, Nebr.	9.6	2,406	8.5	4,227	8.5	6,412	9.3	9,348
Philadelphia, Penn.	16.4	4,103	13.7	6,864	12.4	9,293	11.8	11,839
Phoenix, Ariz.	11.6	2,911	5.9	2,962	5.8	4,327	6.3	6,290
Portland, Maine	9.5	2,379	8.5	4,264	9.1	6,847	9.9	9,935
Portland, Oreg.	10.8	2,695	7.3	3,672	7.8	5,886	8.0	8,042
Providence, R.I.	10.0	2,503	9.2	4,621	8.3	6,255	9.0	9,041
Salt Lake City, Utah	11.4	2,856	7.2	3,599	7.7	5,778	8.0	8,022
Seattle, Wash.	11.3	2,831	7.6	3,790	6.5	4,865	5.6	5,636
Sioux Falls, S. Dak.	9.6	2,398	5.2	2,623	4.8	3,573	4.5	4,490
Virginia Beach, Va.	10.4	2,600	7.4	3,682	7.6	5,734	7.9	7,936
Washington, D.C.	10.3	2,564	6.6	3,311	7.5	5,620	7.9	7,938
Wichita, Kans.	10.0	2,503	7.0	3,522	8.0	5,995	8.6	8,862
Wilmington Del.	9.4	2,343	8.0	4,017	7.9	5,948	7.9	7,933
51 city avg.[2]	10.9%	$2,720	8.2%	$4,084	8.0%	$6,024	8.2%	$8,179

Notes: Tax burdens computed for a family of three. The four major taxes compared are the individual income tax, real property taxes on residential property, general sales and use taxes, and various automobile taxes, including the gasoline tax, registration fees, excise taxes, and personal property taxes. 1. Percentage of income. 2. Average of the largest city in each state plus the District of Columbia. 3. Income level. **Source:** Government of the District of Columbia, Dept. of Finance and Revenue, *Tax Rates and Tax Burdens in the District of Columbia: A Nationwide Comparison* (2009).

rate combined with exemptions and credits to lessen the regressiveness of the property tax will increase the progressivity of a tax system. Progressivity can be lessened by a lack of an individual income tax as well as by reliance on regressive taxes such as the sales tax and certain automobile taxes. The upper and lower income levels chosen for comparison also affect progressiveness.

The Cost of Living Index in Selected U.S. Cities, 2010

Urban area	Composite index (100%)	Grocery items (13%)	Housing (30%)	Utilities (10%)	Transportation (12%)	Health care (4%)	Misc. goods & services (32%)
Atlanta, Ga.	96.2	98.4	91.0	88.9	96.6	100.9	101.7
Austin, Texas	91.7	83.4	81.3	108.6	90.4	97.5	99.1
Baltimore, Md.	119.1	108.9	156.3	115.0	105.5	98.5	98.6
Birmingham, Ala.	90.9	95.1	71.0	107.0	92.8	88.2	101.8
Boston, Mass.	131.1	116.7	152.4	135.8	103.0	124.8	127.5
Charleston, S.C.	98.3	106.8	91.2	97.3	94.0	102.6	102.8
Charlotte, N.C.	93.5	96.1	79.9	89.7	99.4	111.1	101.6
Chicago, Ill.	118.3	113.2	134.3	126.3	119.7	108.5	104.2
Cincinnati, Ohio	93.7	96.0	83.3	106.6	102.8	91.2	95.2
Dallas, Texas	90.4	95.9	71.9	105.4	97.9	103.4	97.1
Denver, Colo.	102.0	98.8	104.9	106.3	93.6	106.6	102.0
Detroit, Mich.	102.6	91.7	99.6	132.4	102.9	96.8	100.9
Honolulu, Hawaii	163.0	154.0	244.3	147.1	125.1	121.0	117.4
Kansas City, Mo.-Ks.	97.6	95.6	88.1	97.9	99.8	96.0	106.1
Little Rock, Ark.	86.8	96.6	77.7	90.3	96.6	90.3	85.8
Los Angeles-Long Beach, Calif.	136.2	105.0	206.7	103.3	115.6	108.1	106.5
Memphis, Tenn.	90.2	94.8	77.7	86.7	91.2	100.1	99.1
Miami/Dade County, Fla.	104.7	109.1	104.3	88.5	108.3	104.6	106.9
Milwaukee, Wisc.	103.5	96.0	114.6	105.3	99.2	111.0	96.5
Minneapolis, Minn.	109.7	110.6	115.9	104.1	101.8	105.4	109.2
Newark, N.J.	128.8	116.1	166.1	132.4	103.8	103.2	111.6
New Orleans, La.	97.7	96.0	101.8	77.3	97.8	96.0	101.4
New York, N.Y.[1]	218.0	161.0	388.9	171.0	119.9	132.2	148.6
Omaha, Neb.	87.9	90.5	78.6	91.3	100.2	96.6	88.6
Orlando, Fla.	97.4	99.7	86.5	109.0	103.6	92.3	101.1
Philadelphia, Pa.	126.5	127.2	141.1	137.2	104.2	110.9	119.8
Portland, Maine	119.2	101.6	146.8	109.3	110.3	106.6	109.3
Portland, Oreg.	109.5	104.9	131.6	87.2	101.2	110.9	101.3
Providence, R.I.	121.7	110.6	125.4	127.6	102.9	115.2	129.0
Reno, Nev.	101.4	108.4	102.0	94.3	104.5	103.0	99.0
San Diego, Calif.	132.3	105.1	194.3	104.7	114.7	111.3	105.0
San Francisco, Calif.	162.1	115.9	273.9	94.1	108.8	119.1	126.2
Seattle, Wash.	123.3	119.6	145.5	84.2	117.5	118.7	119.6
South Bend, Ind.	91.6	92.6	81.6	97.1	97.4	95.0	96.0
St. Louis, Mo.	90.1	96.7	74.0	91.2	96.6	101.5	97.7
Tampa, Fla.	92.6	94.3	85.5	94.3	102.4	96.9	93.5
Tucson, Ariz.	96.8	97.0	94.0	87.6	101.9	99.7	99.9
Virginia Beach, Va.	112.6	102.1	123.0	109.4	100.3	112.5	113.2
Washington, D.C.	137.9	109.5	219.1	98.9	109.2	103.4	103.3

Note: Percentage figures in parentheses show relative weight of component indexes used in calculating composite index. Percentages are rounded, and so do not add exactly to 100. Figures are from first quarter 2010. 1. Figures are for Manhattan only. Source: The Council for Community and Economic Research (C2ER) ACCRA Cost of Living Index (2010).

Cities, by Population Size, 1960–2008

Population size	Number of Cities				Population (mil.)				Percent of Total			
	1960	1980	2000	2008	1960	1980	2000	2008	1960	1980	2000	2008
Total	18,088	19,097	19,496	19,496	115.9	140.3	177.1	190.0	100%	100%	100%	100%
1 million +	5	6	9	9	17.5	17.5	23.0	24.2	15.1	12.5	13.0	12.7
499,999–1 million	16	16	21	25	11.1	10.9	13.5	16.5	9.6	7.8	7.6	8.7
249,999–500,000	30	33	38	41	10.8	11.8	13.7	14.1	9.3	8.4	7.8	7.4
99,999–250,000	79	114	176	198	11.4	16.6	26.1	29.4	9.8	11.8	14.7	15.5
49,999–100,000	180	250	374	424	12.5	17.6	25.7	29.1	10.8	12.3	14.5	15.3
24,999–50,000	366	526	657	686	12.7	18.4	23.0	23.9	11.0	13.1	13.0	12.6
10,000–25,000	978	1,260	1,466	1,521	15.1	19.8	23.1	24.1	13.1	14.1	13.0	12.7
<10,000	16,434	16,892	16,755	16,592	24.9	28.0	29.0	28.7	21.5	20.0	16.3	15.1

Source: U.S. Census Bureau, Statistical Abstract of the United States (annual).

METROPOLITAN STATISTICAL AREAS (MSAs)

Because population patterns don't conform strictly to city boundaries, statisticians have devised a way of measuring city populations to include people who live around an urban area but whose address is outside the city limits. Known as Metropolitan Statistical Areas (or MSAs), these measures give a much more accurate reflection of how many people actually live in the area than do city population figures. For example, the city of Boston is relatively small: just 589,000 people lived in Boston proper, according to the 2000 Census, making it the 20th-largest city in America. But the Boston metropolitan area, which includes suburbs ranging from Rhode Island to New Hampshire, is the seventh-largest in the country, with a total population of 7.4 million within an hour's commute of the Hub. On the other hand, the population of San Diego proper was more than 1.2 million in 2000, making it the seventh-largest city in the U.S., but the entire San Diego metro area was only 2.8 million, or 17th-largest in the country.

The United States Office of Management and Budget (OMB) first defined metropolitan areas in 1949, subsequently changed the designation to "standard metropolitan area," "standard metropolitan statistical area," and finally "metropolitan statistical area" in 1983.

▶ DEFINING MSAS, CMSAS, AND PMSAS

Currently, the OMB distinguishes between MSAs, consolidated metropolitan statistical areas (CMSAs), and primary metropolitan statistical areas (PMSAs).

Metropolitan Statistical Areas (MSAs) are defined as an area that includes at least one city with 50,000 or more inhabitants, or a Census Bureau-defined urbanized area (of at least 50,000 inhabitants) and a total metropolitan population of at least 100,000. An MSA includes the county in which the central city is located plus any adjacent counties in which at least 50 percent of the population lives in the urbanized area. Additional "outlying counties" are included in

the MSA if they meet specified requirements of commuting to the central counties and other selected requirements of metropolitan character (such as population density and percent urban). In New England, MSAs are defined in terms of cities and towns rather than counties.

Consolidated Metropolitan Statistical Areas (CMSAs) are defined as MSAs with populations of one million or more that also contain separate component areas that can each be identified as smaller urban areas, or *Primary Metropolitan Statistical Areas (PMSAs)*. For example, the New York CMSA includes the Primary MSAs of Nassau and Suffolk Counties on Long Island, Bergen and Passaic Counties in Northern New Jersey, and Bridgeport and Milford Counties in Connecticut. PMSAs, like the CMSAs that contain them, are composed of entire counties, except in New England where they are composed of cities and towns.

The 2000 Census counted 280 MSAs in the U.S (down from 284 in 1990), including 20 CMSAs. The number had risen to 363 in 2008. Although MSAs take up only about 16 percent of the country's land area, they are home to more than 75 percent of all Americans.

According to the 2000 Census, the U.S. population living in all metropolitan areas totaled 229,192,836, an increase of more than 36 million people (19.3 percent) since 1990. That's a significant increase over the previous decade, when MSAs grew by only 11.6 percent. The 1950 Census indicated that there were 14 metropolitan areas of at least one million population; these areas had a combined population of about 45 million people, or less than 30 percent of the national total. By the 1990 Census, the number of MSAs with a million people had grown to 39, with a combined population of 124.8 million people, or 50.2 percent of the U.S. total. By 2000, there were an even 50 MSAs with more than a million people, with a total population of 164.0 million people, or 58.2 percent of the national total.

Population of Metropolitan Statistical Areas, 2000–08

Metropolitan Statistical Area	Population 2000	Population 2008	Change 2000–08 Number	Change 2000–08 Percent	Rank 2000	Rank 2008
Abilene, TX	160,241	159,521	–720	–0.4%	230	244
Akron, OH	694,962	698,553	3,591	0.5	67	72
Albany, GA	157,868	164,919	7,051	4.5	233	235
Albany–Schenectady–Troy, NY	825,873	853,919	28,046	3.4	56	57
Albuquerque, NM	729,648	845,913	116,265	15.9	65	59
Alexandria, LA	145,035	153,105	8,070	5.6	252	252
Allentown–Bethlehem–Easton, PA–NJ	740,402	808,210	67,808	9.2	64	62
Altoona, PA	129,144	125,174	–3,970	–3.1	276	297
Amarillo, TX	226,522	243,838	17,316	7.6	179	182
Ames, IA	79,981	86,754	6,773	8.5	355	354
Anchorage, AK	319,606	364,701	45,095	14.1	143	137
Anderson, IN	133,358	131,501	–1,857	–1.4	268	289
Anderson, SC	165,738	182,825	17,087	10.3	224	223
Ann Arbor, MI	322,770	347,376	24,606	7.6	140	143
Anniston–Oxford, AL	112,243	113,419	1,176	1.0	305	318
Appleton, WI	201,720	219,720	18,000	8.9	191	195
Asheville, NC	369,170	408,436	39,266	10.6	124	118
Athens–Clarke County, GA	166,075	189,264	23,189	14.0	223	218
Atlanta–Sandy Springs–Marietta, GA	4,248,014	5,376,285	1,128,271	26.6	11	8
Atlantic City–Hammonton, NJ	252,552	270,681	18,129	7.2	165	165
Auburn–Opelika, AL	115,124	133,010	17,886	15.5	297	285
Augusta–Richmond County, GA–SC	499,656	534,218	34,562	6.9	89	95

Metropolitan Statistical Area	Population 2000	Population 2008	Change 2000–08 Number	Change 2000–08 Percent	Rank 2000	Rank 2008
Austin–Round Rock, TX	1,249,747	1,652,602	402,855	32.2%	40	36
Bakersfield, CA	661,653	800,458	138,805	21.0	70	63
Baltimore–Towson, MD	2,553,000	2,667,117	114,117	4.5	19	20
Bangor, ME	144,919	148,651	3,732	2.6	253	260
Barnstable Town, MA	222,232	221,049	−1,183	−0.5	184	193
Baton Rouge, LA	705,902	774,327	68,425	9.7	66	67
Battle Creek, MI	137,985	135,861	−2,124	−1.5	265	279
Bay City, MI	110,157	107,495	−2,662	−2.4	310	329
Beaumont–Port Arthur, TX	385,090	378,255	−6,835	−1.8	117	132
Bellingham, WA	166,828	196,529	29,701	17.8	222	210
Bend, OR	115,367	158,456	43,089	37.3	296	247
Billings, MT	138,902	152,005	13,103	9.4	264	255
Binghamton, NY	252,323	245,189	−7,134	−2.8	166	180
Birmingham–Hoover, AL	1,051,301	1,117,608	66,307	6.3	48	48
Bismarck, ND	94,733	104,944	10,211	10.8	342	334
Blacksburg–Christiansburg–Radford, VA	151,324	158,328	7,004	4.6	242	248
Bloomington, IN	175,507	183,944	8,437	4.8	211	221
Bloomington–Normal, IL	150,433	165,298	14,865	9.9	244	233
Boise City–Nampa, ID	464,840	599,753	134,913	29.0	97	85
Boston–Cambridge–Quincy, MA–NH	4,392,345	4,522,858	130,513	3.0	10	10
Boulder, CO	269,773	293,161	23,388	8.7	159	157
Bowling Green, KY	104,168	117,947	13,779	13.2	324	310
Bradenton–Sarasota–Venice, FL	589,966	687,823	97,857	16.6	79	74
Bremerton–Silverdale, WA	231,966	239,769	7,803	3.4	177	183
Bridgeport–Stamford–Norwalk, CT	882,567	895,030	12,463	1.4	51	56
Brownsville–Harlingen, TX	335,227	392,736	57,509	17.2	137	128
Brunswick, GA	93,044	102,850	9,806	10.5	343	337
Buffalo–Niagara Falls, NY	1,170,109	1,124,309	−45,800	−3.9	42	47
Burlington, NC	130,800	148,053	17,253	13.2	272	262
Burlington–South Burlington, VT	198,892	208,460	9,568	4.8	193	197
Canton–Massillon, OH	406,968	407,653	685	0.2	110	120
Cape Coral–Fort Myers, FL	440,888	593,136	152,248	34.5	103	86
Carson City, NV	52,457	54,867	2,410	4.6	362	363
Casper, WY	66,533	73,129	6,596	9.9	360	360
Cedar Rapids, IA	237,230	255,452	18,222	7.7	174	175
Champaign–Urbana, IL	210,279	224,191	13,912	6.6	187	192
Charleston, WV	309,635	303,944	−5,691	−1.8	147	152
Charleston–Summerville, SC	548,972	644,506	95,534	17.4	85	80
Charlotte–Gastonia–Concord, NC–SC	1,330,525	1,701,799	371,274	27.9	37	34
Charlottesville, VA	174,021	194,391	20,370	11.7	215	214
Chattanooga, TN–GA	476,512	518,441	41,929	8.8	94	98
Cheyenne, WY	81,607	87,542	5,935	7.3	353	353
Chicago–Naperville–Joliet, IL–IN–WI	9,098,624	9,569,624	470,995	5.2	3	3
Chico, CA	203,171	220,337	17,166	8.4	190	194
Cincinnati–Middletown, OH–KY–IN	2,009,654	2,155,137	145,483	7.2	24	24
Clarksville, TN–KY	232,045	261,220	29,175	12.6	176	170
Cleveland, TN	104,003	112,143	8,140	7.8	325	323
Cleveland–Elyria–Mentor, OH	2,148,017	2,088,291	−59,726	−2.8	23	26
Coeur d'Alene, ID	108,685	137,475	28,790	26.5	315	277
College Station–Bryan, TX	184,885	207,425	22,540	12.2	204	198
Colorado Springs, CO	537,488	617,714	80,226	14.9	86	83
Columbia, MO	145,666	164,283	18,617	12.8	251	236
Columbia, SC	647,248	728,063	80,815	12.5	73	69
Columbus, GA–AL	281,736	287,653	5,917	2.1	154	160
Columbus, IN	71,435	75,360	3,925	5.5	359	359
Columbus, OH	1,612,844	1,773,120	160,276	9.9	31	32
Corpus Christi, TX	403,282	415,376	12,094	3.0	111	115
Corvallis, OR	78,139	81,859	3,720	4.8	357	356
Cumberland, MD–WV	102,008	99,033	−2,975	−2.9	333	343
Dallas–Fort Worth–Arlington, TX	5,161,530	6,300,006	1,138,476	22.1	5	4
Dalton, GA	120,061	134,139	14,078	11.7	289	281
Danville, IL	83,924	80,680	−3,244	−3.9	350	357
Danville, VA	110,156	105,783	−4,373	−4.0	311	332
Davenport–Moline–Rock Island, IA–IL	376,052	377,626	1,574	0.4	121	133
Dayton, OH	848,155	836,544	−11,611	−1.4	54	61
Decatur, AL	145,873	150,125	4,252	2.9	250	256
Decatur, IL	114,706	108,328	−6,378	−5.6	299	327
Deltona–Daytona Beach–Ormond Beach, FL	443,341	498,036	54,695	12.3	101	102
Denver–Aurora, CO	2,179,338	2,506,626	327,288	15.0	22	21

Metropolitan Statistical Area	Population		Change 2000–08		Rank	
	2000	2008	Number	Percent	2000	2008
Des Moines–West Des Moines, IA	481,394	556,230	74,836	15.5%	93	90
Detroit–Warren–Livonia, MI	4,452,558	4,425,110	−27,448	−0.6	9	11
Dothan, AL	130,859	140,961	10,102	7.7	271	273
Dover, DE	126,702	155,415	28,713	22.7	279	251
Dubuque, IA	89,156	92,724	3,568	4.0	348	349
Duluth, MN–WI	275,485	274,571	−914	−0.3	156	164
Durham, NC	423,796	489,762	65,966	15.6	105	103
Eau Claire, WI	148,337	158,742	10,405	7.0	246	246
El Centro, CA	142,361	163,972	21,611	15.2	258	238
Elizabethtown, KY	107,550	112,268	4,718	4.4	319	322
Elkhart–Goshen, IN	182,791	199,137	16,346	8.9	205	209
Elmira, NY	91,070	87,813	−3,257	−3.6	345	352
El Paso, TX	679,622	742,062	62,440	9.2	69	68
Erie, PA	280,845	279,175	−1,670	−0.6	155	163
Eugene–Springfield, OR	322,979	346,560	23,581	7.3	139	145
Evansville, IN–KY	342,816	350,261	7,445	2.2	133	142
Fairbanks, AK	82,840	97,970	15,130	18.3	352	344
Fargo, ND–MN	174,367	195,685	21,318	12.2	214	213
Farmington, NM	113,801	122,500	8,699	7.6	300	302
Fayetteville, NC	336,608	356,105	19,497	5.8	136	140
Fayetteville–Springdale–Rogers, AR–MO	347,036	443,976	96,940	27.9	130	110
Flagstaff, AZ	116,318	128,558	12,240	10.5	294	295
Flint, MI	436,148	428,790	−7,358	−1.7	104	111
Florence, SC	193,155	199,831	6,676	3.5	198	207
Florence–Muscle Shoals, AL	142,944	143,791	847	0.6	257	270
Fond du Lac, WI	97,296	99,453	2,157	2.2	339	341
Fort Collins–Loveland, CO	251,494	292,825	41,331	16.4	167	158
Fort Smith, AR–OK	273,177	290,977	17,800	6.5	158	159
Fort Walton Beach–Crestview–Destin, FL	170,497	179,693	9,196	5.4	217	226
Fort Wayne, IN	390,156	411,154	20,998	5.4	116	117
Fresno, CA	799,407	909,153	109,746	13.7	58	54
Gadsden, AL	103,459	103,303	−156	−0.2	328	336
Gainesville, FL	232,396	258,555	26,159	11.3	175	173
Gainesville, GA	139,315	184,814	45,499	32.7	262	220
Glens Falls, NY	124,345	128,775	4,430	3.6	281	294
Goldsboro, NC	113,329	113,671	342	0.3	301	317
Grand Forks, ND–MN	97,478	97,279	−199	−0.2	338	346
Grand Junction, CO	116,935	143,171	26,236	22.4	293	271
Grand Rapids–Wyoming, MI	740,490	776,833	36,343	4.9	63	66
Great Falls, MT	80,357	82,026	1,669	2.1	354	355
Greeley, CO	180,857	249,775	68,918	38.1	208	177
Green Bay, WI	282,499	302,935	20,436	7.2	153	153
Greensboro–High Point, NC	643,449	705,684	62,235	9.7	74	71
Greenville, NC	152,693	176,758	24,065	15.8	238	227
Greenville–Mauldin–Easley, SC	559,922	624,715	64,793	11.6	84	82
Gulfport–Biloxi, MS	246,197	234,625	−11,572	−4.7	171	186
Hagerstown–Martinsburg, MD–WV	222,771	263,753	40,982	18.4	181	169
Hanford–Corcoran, CA	129,461	149,518	20,057	15.5	274	258
Harrisburg–Carlisle, PA	509,084	531,108	22,024	4.3	87	97
Harrisonburg, VA	108,169	118,409	10,240	9.5	317	308
Hartford–West–East, CT	1,148,620	1,190,512	41,892	3.6	44	45
Hattiesburg, MS	123,812	140,781	16,969	13.7	284	274
Hickory–Lenoir–Morganton, NC	341,820	363,036	21,216	6.2	135	138
Hinesville–Fort Stewart, GA	71,914	69,943	−1,971	−2.7	358	361
Holland–Grand Haven, MI	238,314	260,364	22,050	9.3	173	171
Honolulu, HI	876,158	905,034	28,876	3.3	52	55
Hot Springs, AR	88,068	97,465	9,397	10.7	349	345
Houma–Bayou Cane–Thibodaux, LA	194,477	201,148	6,671	3.4	195	204
Houston–Sugar Land–Baytown, TX	4,715,417	5,728,143	1,012,726	21.5	8	6
Huntington–Ashland, WV–KY–OH	288,651	284,234	−4,417	−1.5	151	161
Huntsville, AL	342,628	395,645	53,017	15.5	134	127
Idaho Falls, ID	101,677	122,995	21,318	21.0	334	300
Indianapolis–Carmel, IN	1,525,103	1,715,459	190,356	12.5	34	33
Iowa City, IA	131,676	149,437	17,761	13.5	270	259
Ithaca, NY	96,502	101,136	4,634	4.8	340	339
Jackson, MI	158,422	160,180	1,758	1.1	232	243
Jackson, MS	497,200	537,285	40,085	8.1	90	93
Jackson, TN	107,365	112,685	5,320	5.0	320	320
Jacksonville, FL	1,122,750	1,313,228	190,478	17.0	45	40

Metropolitan Statistical Area	Population 2000	Population 2008	Change 2000–08 Number	Change 2000–08 Percent	Rank 2000	Rank 2008
Jacksonville, NC	150,355	165,938	15,583	10.4%	245	232
Janesville, WI	152,307	160,213	7,906	5.2	240	242
Jefferson City, MO	140,053	146,363	6,310	4.5	261	264
Johnson City, TN	181,605	195,849	14,244	7.8	206	212
Johnstown, PA	152,598	144,319	–8,279	–5.4	239	268
Jonesboro, AR	107,762	117,361	9,599	8.9	318	311
Joplin, MO	157,322	172,933	15,611	9.9	234	229
Kalamazoo–Portage, MI	314,866	323,713	8,847	2.8	146	148
Kankakee–Bradley, IL	103,833	112,524	8,691	8.4	326	321
Kansas City, MO–KS	1,836,425	2,002,047	165,622	9.0	26	29
Kennewick–Pasco–Richland, WA	191,825	235,841	44,016	22.9	201	185
Killeen–Temple–Fort Hood, TX	330,712	378,935	48,223	14.6	138	131
Kingsport–Bristol–Bristol, TN–VA	298,486	304,689	6,203	2.1	149	151
Kingston, NY	177,749	181,670	3,921	2.2	210	224
Knoxville, TN	616,076	691,152	75,076	12.2	76	73
Kokomo, IN	101,541	99,304	–2,237	–2.2	335	342
La Crosse, WI–MN	126,838	131,872	5,034	4.0	278	288
Lafayette, IN	178,541	192,870	14,329	8.0	209	216
Lafayette, LA	238,906	259,073	20,167	8.4	172	172
Lake Charles, LA	193,565	192,856	–709	–0.4	197	217
Lake Havasu City–Kingman, AZ	155,032	196,281	41,249	26.6	236	211
Lakeland–Winter Haven, FL	483,924	580,594	96,670	20.0	92	87
Lancaster, PA	470,658	502,370	31,712	6.7	96	101
Lansing–East Lansing, MI	447,821	454,035	6,214	1.4	99	107
Laredo, TX	193,117	236,941	43,824	22.7	199	184
Las Cruces, NM	174,682	201,603	26,921	15.4	213	202
Las Vegas–Paradise, NV	1,375,535	1,865,746	490,211	35.6	36	30
Lawrence, KS	99,962	114,748	14,786	14.8	336	313
Lawton, OK	114,998	111,772	–3,226	–2.8	298	324
Lebanon, PA	120,326	128,934	8,608	7.2	288	293
Lewiston, ID–WA	57,961	60,395	2,434	4.2	361	362
Lewiston–Auburn, ME	103,793	106,877	3,084	3.0	327	331
Lexington–Fayette, KY	408,326	453,424	45,098	11.0	109	108
Lima, OH	108,473	105,168	–3,305	–3.0	316	333
Lincoln, NE	266,787	295,486	28,699	10.8	160	155
Little Rock–North Little Rock–Conway, AR	610,514	675,069	64,555	10.6	77	76
Logan, UT–ID	102,720	125,070	22,350	21.8	331	298
Longview, TX	194,042	204,746	10,704	5.5	196	201
Longview, WA	92,948	101,254	8,306	8.9	344	338
Los Angeles–Long Beach–Santa Ana, CA	12,365,624	12,872,808	507,184	4.1	2	2
Louisville/Jefferson County, KY–IN	1,162,414	1,244,696	82,282	7.1	43	42
Lubbock, TX	249,700	270,610	20,910	8.4	169	166
Lynchburg, VA	228,616	245,809	17,193	7.5	178	179
Macon, GA	222,385	230,777	8,392	3.8	183	189
Madera, CA	123,109	148,333	25,224	20.5	285	261
Madison, WI	501,773	561,505	59,732	11.9	88	89
Manchester–Nashua, NH	380,843	402,042	21,199	5.6	119	126
Mansfield, OH	128,852	124,999	–3,853	–3.0	277	299
McAllen–Edinburg–Mission, TX	569,463	726,604	157,141	27.6	81	70
Medford, OR	181,275	201,138	19,863	11.0	207	205
Memphis, TN–MS–AR	1,205,196	1,285,732	80,536	6.7	41	41
Merced, CA	210,546	246,117	35,571	16.9	186	178
Miami–Ft. Lauderdale–Pompano Beach, FL	5,007,992	5,414,772	406,780	8.1	6	7
Michigan City–La Porte, IN	110,106	110,888	782	0.7	312	325
Midland, TX	116,009	129,494	13,485	11.6	295	291
Milwaukee–Waukesha–West Allis, WI	1,500,743	1,549,308	48,565	3.2	35	39
Minneapolis–St. Paul, MN–WI	2,968,818	3,229,878	261,060	8.8	16	16
Missoula, MT	95,799	107,320	11,521	12.0	341	330
Mobile, AL	399,843	406,309	6,466	1.6	113	122
Modesto, CA	446,998	510,694	63,696	14.2	100	100
Monroe, LA	170,053	172,743	2,690	1.6	219	230
Monroe, MI	145,945	152,949	7,004	4.8	249	254
Montgomery, AL	346,522	365,924	19,402	5.6	131	135
Morgantown, WV	111,201	118,506	7,305	6.6	307	307
Morristown, TN	123,081	135,914	12,833	10.4	286	278
Mount Vernon–Anacortes, WA	102,975	118,000	15,025	14.6	330	309
Muncie, IN	118,769	114,685	–4,084	–3.4	292	314
Muskegon–Norton Shores, MI	170,200	174,344	4,144	2.4	218	228
Myrtle Beach–Conway, SC	196,660	257,380	60,720	30.9	194	174

Metropolitan Statistical Area	Population		Change 2000–08		Rank	
	2000	2008	Number	Percent	2000	2008
Napa, CA	124,279	133,433	9,154	7.4%	282	282
Naples–Marco Island, FL	251,377	315,258	63,881	25.4	168	150
Nashville–Davidson–Murfreesboro –Franklin, TN	1,311,789	1,550,733	238,944	18.2	39	38
New Haven–Milford, CT	824,008	846,101	22,093	2.7	57	58
New Orleans–Metairie–Kenner, LA	1,316,512	1,134,029	-182,483	-13.9	38	46
New York–Northern New Jersey– Long Island, NY–NJ	18,323,391	19,006,798	683,407	3.7	1	1
Niles–Benton Harbor, MI	162,455	159,481	-2,974	-1.8	229	245
Norwich–New London, CT	259,106	264,519	5,413	2.1	161	168
Ocala, FL	258,914	329,628	70,714	27.3	162	147
Ocean City, NJ	102,326	95,838	-6,488	-6.3	332	348
Odessa, TX	121,123	131,941	10,818	8.9	287	287
Ogden–Clearfield, UT	442,656	531,488	88,832	20.1	102	96
Oklahoma City, OK	1,095,422	1,206,142	110,720	10.1	47	44
Olympia, WA	207,353	245,181	37,828	18.2	189	181
Omaha–Council Bluffs, NE–IA	767,144	837,925	70,781	9.2	60	60
Orlando–Kissimmee, FL	1,644,547	2,054,574	410,027	24.9	30	27
Oshkosh–Neenah, WI	156,763	162,111	5,348	3.4	235	240
Owensboro, KY	109,875	112,762	2,887	2.6	313	319
Oxnard–Thousand Oaks–Ventura, CA	753,186	797,740	44,554	5.9	61	64
Palm Bay–Melbourne–Titusville, FL	476,230	536,521	60,291	12.7	95	94
Palm Coast, FL	49,832	91,247	41,415	83.1	363	350
Panama City–Lynn Haven, FL	148,218	163,946	15,728	10.6	247	239
Parkersburg–Marietta–Vienna, WV–OH	164,620	160,678	-3,942	-2.4	225	241
Pascagoula, MS	150,564	153,100	2,536	1.7	243	253
Pensacola–Ferry Pass–Brent, FL	412,153	452,992	40,839	9.9	108	109
Peoria, IL	366,878	372,487	5,609	1.5	127	134
Philadelphia–Camden–Wilmington, PA–NJ–DE–MD	5,687,150	5,838,471	151,321	2.7	4	5
Phoenix–Mesa–Scottsdale, AZ	3,251,887	4,281,899	1,030,012	31.7	14	12
Pine Bluff, AR	107,344	100,647	-6,699	-6.2	321	340
Pittsburgh, PA	2,431,088	2,351,192	-79,896	-3.3	20	22
Pittsfield, MA	134,953	129,395	-5,558	-4.1	267	292
Pocatello, ID	83,103	88,495	5,392	6.5	351	351
Portland–South Portland–Biddeford, ME	487,566	514,065	26,499	5.4	91	99
Portland–Vancouver–Beaverton, OR–WA	1,927,883	2,207,462	279,579	14.5	25	23
Port St. Lucie, FL	319,426	403,768	84,342	26.4	144	124
Poughkeepsie–Newburgh–Middletown, NY	621,515	672,525	51,010	8.2	75	77
Prescott, AZ	167,517	215,503	47,986	28.6	220	196
Providence–New Bedford–Fall River, MA	1,582,997	1,596,611	13,614	0.9	32	37
Provo–Orem, UT	376,778	540,820	164,042	43.5	120	92
Pueblo, CO	141,472	156,737	15,265	10.8	260	250
Punta Gorda, FL	141,627	150,060	8,433	6.0	259	257
Racine, WI	188,833	199,510	10,677	5.7	202	208
Raleigh–Cary, NC	797,065	1,088,765	291,700	36.6	59	50
Rapid City, SD	112,818	122,522	9,704	8.6	303	301
Reading, PA	373,638	403,595	29,957	8.0	123	125
Redding, CA	163,256	180,214	16,958	10.4	228	225
Reno–Sparks, NV	342,885	414,784	71,899	21.0	132	116
Richmond, VA	1,096,947	1,225,626	128,679	11.7	46	43
Riverside–San Bernardino–Ontario, CA	3,254,817	4,115,871	861,054	26.5	13	14
Roanoke, VA	288,249	298,108	9,859	3.4	152	154
Rochester, MN	163,617	182,924	19,307	11.8	227	222
Rochester, NY	1,037,836	1,034,090	-3,746	-0.4	49	51
Rockford, IL	320,206	354,394	34,188	10.7	142	141
Rocky Mount, NC	142,991	146,356	3,365	2.4	256	265
Rome, GA	90,565	95,980	5,415	6.0	346	347
Sacramento–Arden–Arcade–Roseville, CA	1,796,852	2,109,832	312,980	17.4	27	25
Saginaw–Saginaw Township North, MI	210,042	200,745	-9,297	-4.4	188	206
St. Cloud, MN	167,391	186,954	19,563	11.7	221	219
St. George, UT	90,354	137,589	47,235	52.3	347	276
St. Joseph, MO–KS	123,820	126,359	2,539	2.1	283	296
St. Louis, MO–IL	2,698,664	2,816,710	118,046	4.4	18	18
Salem, OR	347,217	391,680	44,463	12.8	129	129
Salinas, CA	401,761	408,238	6,477	1.6	112	119
Salisbury, MD	109,391	120,165	10,774	9.8	314	305
Salt Lake City, UT	968,883	1,115,692	146,809	15.2	50	49
San Angelo, TX	105,781	109,563	3,782	3.6	322	326

Metropolitan Statistical Area	Population 2000	Population 2008	Change 2000–08 Number	Change 2000–08 Percent	Rank 2000	Rank 2008
San Antonio, TX	1,711,717	2,031,445	319,728	18.7%	29	28
San Diego–Carlsbad–San Marcos, CA	2,813,834	3,001,072	187,238	6.7	17	17
Sandusky, OH	79,551	77,062	–2,489	–3.1	356	358
San Francisco–Oakland–Fremont, CA	4,123,747	4,274,531	150,784	3.7	12	13
San Jose–Sunnyvale–Santa Clara, CA	1,735,818	1,819,198	83,380	4.8	28	31
San Luis Obispo–Paso Robles, CA	246,681	265,297	18,616	7.5	170	167
Santa Barbara–Santa Maria–Goleta, CA	399,356	405,396	6,040	1.5	114	123
Santa Cruz–Watsonville, CA	255,600	253,137	–2,463	–1.0	163	176
Santa Fe, NM	129,295	143,937	14,642	11.3	275	269
Santa Rosa–Petaluma, CA	458,616	466,741	8,125	1.8	98	105
Savannah, GA	293,302	334,353	41,051	14.0	150	146
Scranton–Wilkes-Barre, PA	560,631	549,150	–11,481	–2.0	83	91
Seattle–Tacoma–Bellevue, WA	3,043,897	3,344,813	300,916	9.9	15	15
Sebastian–Vero Beach, FL	112,943	132,315	19,372	17.2	302	286
Sheboygan, WI	112,656	114,561	1,905	1.7	304	315
Sherman–Denison, TX	110,595	118,804	8,209	7.4	309	306
Shreveport–Bossier City, LA	375,971	389,533	13,562	3.6	122	130
Sioux City, IA–NE–SD	143,053	143,157	104	0.1	255	272
Sioux Falls, SD	187,095	232,930	45,835	24.5	203	188
South Bend–Mishawaka, IN–MI	316,661	316,865	204	0.1	145	149
Spartanburg, SC	253,782	280,738	26,956	10.6	164	162
Spokane, WA	417,939	462,677	44,738	10.7	107	106
Springfield, IL	201,444	207,389	5,945	3.0	192	199
Springfield, MA	680,016	687,558	7,542	1.1	68	75
Springfield, MO	368,375	426,144	57,769	15.7	125	113
Springfield, OH	144,738	139,859	–4,879	–3.4	254	275
State College, PA	135,760	144,779	9,019	6.6	266	267
Stockton, CA	563,603	672,388	108,785	19.3	82	78
Sumter, SC	104,636	104,148	–488	–0.5	323	335
Syracuse, NY	650,154	643,794	–6,360	–1.0	72	81
Tallahassee, FL	320,309	357,259	36,950	11.5	141	139
Tampa–St. Petersburg–Clearwater, FL	2,396,011	2,733,761	337,750	14.1	21	19
Terre Haute, IN	170,954	170,233	–721	–0.4	216	231
Texarkana, TX–Texarkana, AR	129,749	135,509	5,760	4.4	273	280
Toledo, OH	659,185	649,104	–10,081	–1.5	71	79
Topeka, KS	224,549	229,619	5,070	2.3	180	191
Trenton–Ewing, NJ	350,761	364,883	14,122	4.0	128	136
Tucson, AZ	843,742	1,012,018	168,276	19.9	55	52
Tulsa, OK	859,533	916,079	56,546	6.6	53	53
Tuscaloosa, AL	193,105	206,765	13,660	7.1	200	200
Tyler, TX	174,706	201,277	26,571	15.2	212	203
Utica–Rome, NY	299,896	293,790	–6,106	–2.0	148	156
Valdosta, GA	119,566	133,348	13,782	11.5	291	283
Vallejo–Fairfield, CA	394,545	407,515	12,970	3.3	115	121
Victoria, TX	111,668	114,313	2,645	2.4	306	316
Vineland–Millville–Bridgeton, NJ	146,434	156,830	10,396	7.1	248	249
Virg. Beach–Norfolk–Newport News, VA	1,576,916	1,658,292	81,376	5.2	33	35
Visalia–Porterville, CA	368,021	426,276	58,255	15.8	126	112
Waco, TX	213,519	230,213	16,694	7.8	185	190
Warner Robins, GA	110,765	133,161	22,396	20.2	308	284
Washington–Arlington–Alexandria, DC–VA–MD–WV	4,796,065	5,358,130	562,065	11.7	7	9
Waterloo–Cedar Falls, IA	163,707	164,220	513	0.3	226	237
Wausau, WI	125,836	130,962	5,126	4.1	280	290
Weirton–Steubenville, WV–OH	132,008	122,054	–9,954	–7.5	269	304
Wenatchee, WA	99,216	108,193	8,977	9.0	337	328
Wheeling, WV–OH	153,178	144,847	–8,331	–5.4	237	266
Wichita, KS	571,171	603,716	32,545	5.7	80	84
Wichita Falls, TX	151,524	147,328	–4,196	–2.8	241	263
Williamsport, PA	120,048	116,670	–3,378	–2.8	290	312
Wilmington, NC	274,552	347,012	72,460	26.4	157	144
Winchester, VA–WV	102,996	122,369	19,373	18.8	329	303
Winston–Salem, NC	421,963	468,124	46,161	10.9	106	104
Worcester, MA	749,973	783,806	33,833	4.5	62	65
Yakima, WA	222,579	234,564	11,985	5.4	182	187
York–Hanover, PA	381,753	424,583	42,830	11.2	118	114
Youngstown–Warren–Boardman, OH–PA	602,963	565,947	–37,016	–6.1	78	88
Yuba City, CA	139,149	165,274	26,125	18.8	263	234
Yuma, AZ	160,026	194,322	34,296	21.4	231	215

Source: U.S. Census Bureau, *Cumulative Estimates of Population Change for Micropolitan Statistical Areas and Rankings: April 1, 2000 to July 1, 2009.*

Population of U.S. Metropolitan Areas by Race and Hispanic Origin, 2000

Metropolitan area	Total	White	Black	Indian/ Alaska Native	Asian	Pacific Islander	Other	Two or more races	Hispanic[1]
Abilene, Texas MSA	126,555	80.6%	6.7%	0.6%	1.2%	0.1%	8.3%	2.4%	17.6%
Albany, Ga. MSA	120,822	46.9	51.0	0.2	0.6	0.0	0.5	0.7	1.3
Albany–Schenectady–Troy, N.Y. MSA	875,583	89.4	6.1	0.2	1.8	0.0	0.9	1.5	2.7
Albuquerque, N.Mex. MSA	712,738	69.6	2.5	5.6	1.7	0.1	16.3	4.2	41.6
Alexandria, La. MSA	126,337	66.5	30.4	0.7	0.9	0.0	0.4	1.0	1.4
Allentown–Bethlehem– Easton, Pa. MSA	637,958	89.8	3.0	0.2	1.6	0.0	3.9	1.5	7.9
Altoona, Pa. MSA	129,144	97.6	1.2	0.1	0.4	0.0	0.1	0.6	0.5
Amarillo, Texas MSA	217,858	79.1	5.9	0.8	1.8	0.0	10.3	2.1	19.6
Anchorage, Alaska MSA	260,283	72.2	5.8	7.3	5.5	0.9	2.2	6.0	5.7
Anniston, Ala. MSA	112,249	78.9	18.5	0.4	0.6	0.1	0.6	1.0	1.6
Appleton–Oshkosh– Neenah, Wis. MSA	358,365	94.6	0.8	0.9	2.0	0.0	0.7	0.9	1.9
Asheville, N.C. MSA	225,965	89.8	6.9	0.4	0.6	0.0	1.1	1.2	2.7
Athens, Ga. MSA	153,444	73.2	20.5	0.2	2.4	0.0	2.5	1.2	5.1
Atlanta, Ga. MSA	4,112,198	63.0	28.9	0.3	3.3	0.0	2.8	1.7	6.5
Auburn–Opelika, Ala. MSA	115,092	74.1	22.7	0.2	1.6	0.0	0.5	0.9	1.4
Augusta–Aiken, Ga.–S.C. MSA	477,441	61.5	34.4	0.3	1.5	0.1	0.9	1.5	2.4
Austin–San Marcos, Texas MSA	1,249,763	72.5	8.0	0.6	3.5	0.1	12.8	2.6	26.2
Bakersfield, Calif. MSA	661,645	61.6	6.0	1.5	3.4	0.1	23.2	4.1	38.4
Bangor, Maine MSA	90,864	95.6	0.7	1.3	1.0	0.0	0.3	1.1	0.7
Barnstable–Yarmouth, Mass. MSA	162,582	94.4	1.7	0.6	0.6	0.0	1.1	1.6	1.3
Baton Rouge, La. MSA	602,894	64.9	31.9	0.2	1.5	0.0	0.5	0.9	1.8
Beaumont–Port Arthur, Texas MSA	385,090	68.2	24.8	0.4	2.1	0.0	3.1	1.4	8.0
Bellingham, Wash. MSA	166,814	88.4	0.7	2.8	2.8	0.1	2.5	2.7	5.2
Benton Harbor, Mich. MSA	162,453	79.7	15.9	0.4	1.1	0.0	1.1	1.6	3.0
Billings, Mont. MSA	129,352	92.8	0.4	3.1	0.5	0.0	1.3	1.9	3.7
Biloxi–Gulfport– Pascagoula, Miss.MSA	363,988	76.0	19.3	0.4	2.0	0.1	0.8	1.4	2.3
Binghamton, N.Y. MSA	252,320	92.6	2.7	0.2	2.3	0.0	0.7	1.5	1.8
Birmingham, Ala. MSA	921,106	67.3	30.1	0.3	0.8	0.0	0.7	0.8	1.8
Bismarck, N.Dak. MSA	94,719	95.2	0.2	3.0	0.4	0.0	0.2	0.9	0.7
Bloomington, Ind. MSA	120,563	90.8	3.0	0.3	3.4	0.0	0.9	1.6	1.9
Bloomington–Normal, Ill. MSA	150,433	89.2	6.2	0.2	2.1	0.0	1.0	1.4	2.5
Boise City, Idaho MSA	432,345	89.9	0.5	0.7	1.5	0.1	4.9	2.4	8.8
Boston–Worcester–Lawrence, Mass.–N.H.–Maine–Conn. CMSA	5,819,100	85.1	5.1	0.2	4.0	0.0	3.3	2.2	6.2
Boston, MA–NH PMSA	3,406,829	82.5	7.0	0.2	4.9	0.0	3.0	2.4	5.9
Brockton, MA PMSA	255,459	82.4	7.6	0.2	1.3	0.0	5.0	3.5	3.7
Fitchburg–Leominster, MA PMSA	142,284	89.5	2.6	0.2	2.3	0.0	3.4	2.0	8.3
Lawrence, MA–NH PMSA	396,230	85.6	1.7	0.3	2.1	0.0	8.1	2.1	14.0
Lowell, MA–NH PMSA	301,686	85.9	1.9	0.2	7.6	0.0	2.5	2.0	5.7
Manchester, NH PMSA	198,378	94.4	1.3	0.3	1.7	0.0	1.1	1.3	3.0
Nashua, NH PMSA	190,949	93.4	1.3	0.2	2.4	0.0	1.5	1.1	3.4
New Bedford, MA PMSA	175,198	85.9	2.7	0.4	0.7	0.0	6.4	3.8	5.9
Portsmouth–Rochester, NH–ME PMSA	240,698	96.5	0.7	0.2	1.3	0.0	0.3	1.0	1.0
Worcester, MA–CT PMSA	511,389	88.7	3.0	0.3	3.0	0.0	3.2	1.9	7.1
Brownsville–Harlingen– San Benito, Texas MSA	335,227	80.3	0.5	0.4	0.5	0.0	16.0	2.3	84.3
Bryan–College Station, Texas MSA	152,415	74.5	10.7	0.4	4.0	0.1	8.4	2.0	17.9
Buffalo–Niagara Falls, N.Y. MSA	1,170,111	83.8	11.7	0.7	1.3	0.0	1.2	1.3	2.9
Burlington, Vt. MSA	169,391	95.2	0.8	0.5	1.8	0.0	0.3	1.4	1.0
Canton–Massillon, Ohio MSA	406,934	90.8	6.7	0.2	0.5	0.0	0.3	1.4	0.9
Casper, Wyo. MSA	66,533	94.2	0.8	1.0	0.4	0.0	1.9	1.7	4.9
Cedar Rapids, Iowa MSA	191,701	93.9	2.6	0.2	1.4	0.0	0.5	1.4	1.4
Champaign–Urbana, Ill. MSA	179,669	78.8	11.2	0.2	6.5	0.0	1.3	2.0	2.9
Charleston–North Charleston, S.C. MSA	549,033	65.1	30.8	0.4	1.3	0.1	1.0	1.3	2.4
Charleston, W.Va. MSA	251,662	92.0	5.7	0.2	0.8	0.0	0.2	1.1	0.6
Charlotte–Gastonia–Rock Hill, N.C.–S.C. MSA	1,499,293	73.6	20.5	0.4	1.9	0.0	2.3	1.2	5.1
Charlottesville, Va. MSA	159,576	80.6	14.0	0.2	2.9	0.0	0.8	1.5	2.2
Chattanooga, Tenn.–Ga. MSA	465,161	82.8	14.2	0.3	1.0	0.0	0.6	1.0	1.5
Cheyenne, Wyo. MSA	81,607	88.9	2.6	0.8	1.0	0.1	4.0	2.6	10.9
Chicago–Gary–Kenosha, Ill.–Ind.–Wis. CMSA	9,157,540	66.8	18.6	0.3	4.2	0.0	7.7	2.2	16.4
Chicago, IL PMSA	8,272,768	65.8	18.9	0.3	4.6	0.0	8.2	2.3	17.1
Gary, IN PMSA	631,362	73.4	19.7	0.3	0.8	0.0	4.1	1.7	10.5

Metropolitan area	Total	White	Black	Indian/ Alaska Native	Asian	Pacific Islander	Other	Two or more races	Hispanic[1]
Kankakee, IL PMSA	103,833	79.9%	15.5%	0.2%	0.7%	0.0%	2.4%	1.4%	4.8%
Kenosha, WI PMSA	149,577	88.4	5.1	0.4	0.9	0.0	3.3	1.9	7.2
Chico–Paradise, Calif. MSA	203,171	84.5	1.4	1.9	3.3	0.1	4.8	3.9	10.5
Cincinnati–Hamilton, Ohio–Ky.– Ind. CMSA	1,979,202	85.3	11.7	0.2	1.2	0.0	0.5	1.1	1.1
Cincinnati, OH–KY–IN PMSA	1,646,395	84.1	13.0	0.2	1.2	0.0	0.4	1.1	1.1
Hamilton–Middletown, OH PMSA	332,807	91.2	5.3	0.2	1.5	0.0	0.6	1.1	1.4
Clarksville–Hopkinsville, Tenn.–Ky. MSA	207,033	72.0	20.8	0.5	1.5	0.2	2.2	2.7	5.0
Cleveland–Akron, Ohio CMSA	2,945,831	79.0	16.8	0.2	1.3	0.0	1.2	1.5	2.7
Akron, OH PMSA	694,960	85.9	11.0	0.2	1.3	0.0	0.3	1.3	0.8
Cleveland–Lorain– Elyria, OH PMSA	2,250,871	76.9	18.5	0.2	1.4	0.0	1.4	1.6	3.3
Colorado Springs, Colo. MSA	516,929	81.2	6.5	0.9	2.5	0.2	4.7	3.9	11.3
Columbia, Mo. MSA	135,454	85.4	8.5	0.4	3.0	0.0	0.7	1.9	1.8
Columbia, S.C. MSA	536,691	63.9	32.1	0.3	1.4	0.1	1.0	1.2	2.4
Columbus, Ga.–Ala. MSA	274,624	54.4	40.4	0.4	1.3	0.1	1.7	1.7	4.0
Columbus, Ohio MSA	1,540,157	81.3	13.4	0.3	2.4	0.0	0.8	1.9	1.8
Corpus Christi, Texas MSA	380,783	72.9	4.0	0.6	1.1	0.1	18.2	3.1	54.7
Corvallis, Oreg. MSA	78,153	89.2	0.8	0.8	4.5	0.2	1.9	2.6	4.7
Cumberland, Md.–W.Va. MSA	102,008	93.9	4.6	0.1	0.4	0.0	0.2	0.8	0.7
Dallas–Fort Worth, Texas CMSA	5,221,801	69.5	13.8	0.6	3.7	0.1	9.9	2.4	21.5
Dallas, TX PMSA	3,519,176	67.2	15.1	0.6	4.0	0.1	10.7	2.4	23.0
Fort Worth–Arlington, TX PMSA	1,702,625	74.3	11.2	0.6	3.2	0.1	8.3	2.4	18.2
Danville, Va. MSA	110,156	65.7	32.6	0.2	0.4	0.0	0.4	0.7	1.2
Davenport–Moline–Rock Island, Iowa–Ill. MSA	359,062	88.4	6.0	0.3	1.2	0.0	2.5	1.7	5.8
Dayton–Springfield, Ohio MSA	950,558	82.3	14.2	0.2	1.2	0.0	0.5	1.5	1.2
Daytona Beach, Fla. MSA	493,175	86.2	9.2	0.3	1.0	0.0	1.7	1.4	6.4
Decatur, Ala. MSA	145,867	83.3	11.7	1.8	0.4	0.1	1.0	1.7	2.8
Decatur, Ill. MSA	114,706	83.5	14.1	0.2	0.6	0.0	0.3	1.4	1.0
Denver–Boulder–Greeley, Colo. CMSA	2,581,506	80.6	4.6	0.9	2.8	0.1	8.1	2.9	18.5
Boulder–Longmont, CO PMSA	291,288	88.5	0.9	0.6	3.1	0.1	4.7	2.2	10.5
Denver, CO PMSA	2,109,282	79.4	5.5	0.9	3.0	0.1	8.1	3.0	18.8
Greeley, CO PMSA	180,936	81.7	0.6	0.9	0.8	0.1	13.3	2.7	27.0
Des Moines, Iowa MSA	456,022	89.8	4.1	0.2	2.3	0.1	2.1	1.5	4.2
Detroit–Ann Arbor–Flint, Mich. CMSA	5,456,428	73.1	21.1	0.4	2.4	0.0	1.1	2.1	2.9
Ann Arbor, MI PMSA	578,736	85.3	7.3	0.4	3.7	0.0	1.2	2.0	3.1
Detroit, MI PMSA	4,441,551	71.2	22.9	0.3	2.3	0.0	1.1	2.1	2.9
Flint, MI PMSA	436,141	75.3	20.4	0.6	0.8	0.0	0.8	2.2	2.3
Dothan, Ala. MSA	137,916	73.5	23.1	0.5	0.8	0.1	0.7	1.4	2.0
Dover, Del. MSA	126,697	73.5	20.7	0.6	1.7	0.0	1.3	2.2	3.2
Dubuque, Iowa MSA	89,143	97.1	0.9	0.1	0.6	0.1	0.5	0.8	1.2
Duluth–Superior, Minn.–Wis. MSA	243,815	94.9	0.8	2.0	0.7	0.0	0.2	1.4	0.8
Eau Claire, Wis. MSA	148,337	96.0	0.4	0.5	1.9	0.0	0.3	0.9	0.8
El Paso, Texas MSA	679,622	73.9	3.1	0.8	1.0	0.1	17.9	3.2	78.2
Elkhart–Goshen, Ind. MSA	182,791	86.4	5.2	0.3	0.9	0.0	5.4	1.8	8.9
Elmira, N.Y. MSA	91,070	91.0	5.8	0.2	0.8	0.0	0.7	1.4	1.8
Enid, Okla. MSA	57,813	88.7	3.3	2.1	0.8	0.5	2.0	2.6	4.1
Erie, Pa. MSA	280,843	90.9	6.1	0.2	0.7	0.0	0.9	1.2	2.2
Eugene–Springfield, Oreg. MSA	322,959	90.6	0.8	1.1	2.0	0.2	1.9	3.3	4.6
Evansville–Henderson, Ind.–Ky. MSA	296,195	91.8	6.1	0.2	0.6	0.0	0.3	0.9	0.9
Fargo–Moorhead, N.Dak.– Minn. MSA	174,367	94.8	0.7	1.2	1.1	0.0	0.8	1.3	1.9
Fayetteville, N.C. MSA	302,963	55.2	34.9	1.5	1.9	0.3	3.1	3.1	6.9
Fayetteville–Springdale–Rogers, Ark. MSA	311,121	89.4	1.3	1.4	1.3	0.3	4.2	2.0	8.5
Flagstaff, Ariz.–Utah MSA	122,366	64.7	1.0	27.2	0.8	0.1	4.0	2.3	10.5
Florence, Ala. MSA	142,950	85.7	12.5	0.3	0.3	0.0	0.4	0.8	1.1
Florence, S.C. MSA	125,761	58.7	39.3	0.2	0.7	0.0	0.4	0.7	1.1
Fort Collins–Loveland, Colo. MSA	251,494	91.4	0.7	0.7	1.6	0.1	3.4	2.2	8.3
Fort Myers–Cape Coral, Fla. MSA	440,888	87.7	6.6	0.3	0.8	0.0	3.1	1.6	9.5
Fort Pierce–Port St. Lucie, Fla. MSA	319,426	83.4	11.4	0.3	0.8	0.1	2.5	1.5	7.9
Fort Smith, Ark.–Okla. MSA	207,290	82.2	4.0	5.1	2.3	0.0	2.6	3.8	4.9
Fort Walton Beach, Fla. MSA	170,498	83.4	9.1	0.6	2.5	0.1	1.3	3.0	4.3
Fort Wayne, Ind. MSA	502,141	88.1	7.5	0.3	1.0	0.0	1.6	1.4	3.3
Fresno, Calif. MSA	922,516	55.4	5.1	1.7	7.1	0.1	25.7	4.8	44.0
Gadsden, Ala. MSA	103,459	82.9	14.7	0.3	0.4	0.0	0.7	0.9	1.7
Gainesville, Fla. MSA	217,955	73.5	19.3	0.2	3.5	0.0	1.4	2.0	5.7

Metropolitan area	Total	White	Black	Indian/ Alaska Native	Asian	Pacific Islander	Other	Two or more races	Hispanic[1]
Glens Falls, N.Y. MSA	124,345	96.2%	1.8%	0.2%	0.4%	0.0%	0.5%	0.8%	1.5%
Goldsboro, N.C. MSA	113,329	61.3	33.0	0.4	1.0	0.0	3.1	1.3	4.9
Grand Forks, N.Dak.–Minn. MSA	97,478	93.4	1.0	2.0	0.8	0.1	1.3	1.5	2.9
Grand Junction, Colo. MSA	116,255	92.3	0.5	0.9	0.5	0.1	3.7	2.0	10.0
Grand Rapids–Muskegon– Holland, Mich. MSA	1,088,514	85.7	7.3	0.5	1.6	0.0	3.0	1.9	6.3
Great Falls, Mont. MSA	80,357	90.7	1.1	4.2	0.8	0.1	0.7	2.4	2.4
Green Bay, Wis. MSA	226,778	91.1	1.2	2.3	2.2	0.0	1.9	1.3	3.8
Greensboro–Winston-Salem– High Point, N.C. MSA	1,251,509	74.4	20.2	0.4	1.4	0.0	2.4	1.2	5.0
Greenville, N.C. MSA	133,798	62.1	33.6	0.3	1.1	0.0	1.8	1.1	3.2
Greenville–Spartanburg– Anderson, S.C. MSA	962,441	79.0	17.5	0.2	1.2	0.0	1.1	1.0	2.7
Harrisburg–Lebanon– Carlisle, Pa. MSA	629,401	87.8	7.8	0.1	1.5	0.0	1.4	1.3	3.1
Hartford, Conn. MSA	1,183,110	80.7	9.5	0.2	2.2	0.0	5.2	2.1	9.6
Hattiesburg, Miss.MSA	111,674	71.7	26.3	0.2	0.7	0.0	0.4	0.7	1.2
Hickory–Morganton–Lenoir, N.C. MSA	341,851	87.5	6.9	0.2	2.3	0.1	2.0	1.0	4.0
Honolulu, Hawaii MSA	876,156	21.3	2.4	0.2	46.0	8.9	1.3	19.9	6.7
Houma, La. MSA	194,477	78.1	15.4	3.9	0.7	0.0	0.6	1.2	1.5
Houston–Galveston–Brazoria, Texas CMSA	4,669,571	62.6	16.9	0.4	4.9	0.1	12.4	2.7	28.9
Brazoria, TX PMSA	241,767	77.1	8.5	0.5	2.0	0.0	9.6	2.2	22.8
Galveston–Texas City, TX PMSA	250,158	72.7	15.4	0.5	2.1	0.0	7.2	2.1	18.0
Houston, TX PMSA	4,177,646	61.1	17.5	0.4	5.2	0.1	12.9	2.8	29.9
Huntington–Ashland, W.Va.– Ky.–Ohio MSA	315,538	96.2	2.2	0.2	0.4	0.0	0.1	0.8	0.7
Huntsville, Ala. MSA	342,376	74.3	21.0	0.7	1.6	0.1	0.7	1.7	2.0
Indianapolis, Ind. MSA	1,607,486	82.1	13.9	0.2	1.2	0.0	1.3	1.3	2.7
Iowa City, Iowa MSA	111,006	90.1	2.9	0.3	4.1	0.0	1.0	1.5	2.5
Jackson, Mich. MSA	158,422	88.5	7.9	0.4	0.5	0.0	0.8	1.7	2.2
Jackson, Miss.MSA	440,801	52.6	45.6	0.1	0.7	0.0	0.3	0.6	1.0
Jackson, Tenn. MSA	107,377	68.5	29.2	0.2	0.6	0.0	0.6	0.9	1.6
Jacksonville, Fla. MSA	1,100,491	72.6	21.7	0.3	2.3	0.1	1.2	1.8	3.8
Jacksonville, N.C. MSA	150,355	72.1	18.5	0.7	1.7	0.2	3.6	3.2	7.2
Jamestown, N.Y. MSA	139,750	94.0	2.2	0.4	0.4	0.0	1.7	1.2	4.2
Janesville–Beloit, Wis. MSA	152,307	91.0	4.6	0.3	0.8	0.0	1.8	1.5	3.9
Johnson City–Kingsport–Bristol, Tenn.–Va. MSA	480,091	96.2	2.1	0.2	0.4	0.0	0.3	0.7	0.9
Johnstown, Pa. MSA	232,621	96.3	2.4	0.1	0.3	0.0	0.3	0.6	0.8
Jonesboro, Ark. MSA	82,148	89.3	7.8	0.3	0.6	0.0	0.9	1.1	2.1
Joplin, Mo. MSA	157,322	92.8	1.2	1.6	0.6	0.1	1.4	2.2	3.0
Kalamazoo–Battle Creek, Mich. MSA	452,851	84.9	9.3	0.6	1.4	0.0	1.6	2.1	3.6
Kansas City, Mo.–Kans. MSA	1,776,062	80.8	12.8	0.5	1.6	0.1	2.3	2.0	5.2
Killeen–Temple, Texas MSA	312,952	63.9	20.8	0.8	2.4	0.5	8.0	3.8	15.7
Knoxville, Tenn. MSA	687,249	91.3	5.8	0.3	1.0	0.0	0.5	1.1	1.3
Kokomo, Ind. MSA	101,541	91.1	5.5	0.3	0.9	0.0	0.8	1.4	1.9
La Crosse, Wis.–Minn. MSA	126,838	94.8	0.8	0.4	2.7	0.0	0.2	0.9	0.9
Lafayette, La. MSA	385,647	69.7	28.2	0.2	0.7	0.0	0.4	0.8	1.3
Lafayette, Ind. MSA	182,821	89.9	2.1	0.3	3.7	0.0	2.8	1.3	5.6
Lake Charles, La. MSA	183,577	73.6	24.0	0.3	0.6	0.0	0.4	1.0	1.3
Lakeland–Winter Haven, Fla. MSA	483,924	79.6	13.5	0.4	0.9	0.0	3.8	1.7	9.5
Lancaster, Pa. MSA	470,658	91.5	2.8	0.1	1.4	0.0	2.9	1.3	5.7
Lansing–East Lansing, Mich. MSA	447,728	84.4	8.1	0.5	2.6	0.0	1.9	2.4	4.7
Laredo, Texas MSA	193,117	82.2	0.4	0.5	0.4	0.0	14.0	2.5	94.3
Las Cruces, N.Mex. MSA	174,682	67.8	1.6	1.5	0.8	0.1	24.7	3.6	63.4
Las Vegas, Nev.–Ariz. MSA	1,563,282	73.8	8.1	1.0	4.7	0.4	8.0	4.0	20.6
Lawrence, Kans. MSA	99,962	86.1	4.2	2.6	3.1	0.1	1.2	2.7	3.3
Lawton, Okla. MSA	114,996	65.2	19.0	5.1	2.1	0.4	3.5	4.7	8.4
Lewiston–Auburn, Maine MSA	90,830	96.8	0.7	0.3	0.6	0.0	0.3	1.3	1.0
Lexington, Ky. MSA	479,198	86.4	9.5	0.2	1.6	0.0	1.0	1.3	2.5
Lima, Ohio MSA	155,084	88.9	8.6	0.2	0.5	0.0	0.5	1.3	1.2
Lincoln, Nebr. MSA	250,291	90.1	2.8	0.6	2.9	0.1	1.7	1.9	3.4
Little Rock–North Little Rock, Ark. MSA	583,845	74.5	21.9	0.4	1.0	0.0	0.9	1.3	2.1
Longview–Marshall, Texas MSA	208,780	74.6	19.5	0.5	0.5	0.0	3.6	1.3	7.1
Los Angeles–Riverside–Orange County, Calif. CMSA	16,373,645	55.1	7.6	0.9	10.4	0.3	21.0	4.7	40.3
Los Angeles–Long Beach, Calif. PMSA	9,519,338	48.7	9.8	0.8	11.9	0.3	23.5	4.9	44.6

Metropolitan area	Total	White	Black	Indian/ Alaska Native	Asian	Pacific Islander	Other	Two or more races	Hispanic[1]
Orange County, Calif. PMSA	2,846,289	64.8%	1.7%	0.7%	13.6%	0.3%	14.8%	4.1%	30.8%
Riverside–San Bernardino, Calif. PMSA	3,254,821	62.1	7.7	1.2	4.2	0.3	19.8	4.7	37.8
Ventura, CA PMSA	753,197	69.9	1.9	0.9	5.3	0.2	17.7	3.9	33.4
Louisville, Ky.–Ind. MSA	1,025,598	82.8	13.9	0.2	1.1	0.0	0.6	1.3	1.6
Lubbock, Texas MSA	242,628	74.3	7.7	0.6	1.3	0.0	14.1	2.0	27.5
Lynchburg, Va. MSA	214,911	79.6	17.9	0.3	0.7	0.0	0.4	1.0	1.0
Macon, Ga. MSA	322,549	59.2	37.5	0.2	1.1	0.0	0.7	1.1	2.1
Madison, Wis. MSA	426,526	89.0	4.0	0.3	3.5	0.0	1.4	1.8	3.4
Mansfield, Ohio MSA	175,818	90.8	7.1	0.2	0.5	0.0	0.3	1.1	0.9
McAllen–Edinburg–Mission, Texas MSA	569,463	77.7	0.5	0.4	0.6	0.0	18.6	2.1	88.3
Medford–Ashland, Oreg. MSA	181,269	91.6	0.4	1.1	0.9	0.2	2.9	2.9	6.7
Melbourne–Titusville–Palm Bay, Fla. MSA	476,230	86.8	8.4	0.4	1.5	0.1	1.1	1.8	4.6
Memphis, Tenn.–Ark.–Miss.MSA	1,135,614	52.9	43.4	0.2	1.4	0.0	1.1	1.0	2.4
Merced, Calif. MSA	210,554	56.2	3.8	1.2	6.8	0.2	26.1	5.7	45.3
Miami–Fort Lauderdale, Fla. CMSA	3,876,380	70.1	20.4	0.2	1.8	0.0	3.9	3.6	40.3
Fort Lauderdale, FL PMSA	1,623,018	70.6	20.5	0.2	2.3	0.1	3.0	3.4	16.7
Miami, FL PMSA	2,253,362	69.7	20.3	0.2	1.4	0.0	4.6	3.8	57.3
Milwaukee–Racine, Wis. CMSA	1,689,572	77.8	15.1	0.5	1.9	0.0	3.0	1.7	6.5
Milwaukee–Waukesha, WI PMSA	1,500,741	77.1	15.7	0.5	2.1	0.0	2.9	1.7	6.3
Racine, WI PMSA	188,831	83.0	10.5	0.4	0.7	0.0	3.7	1.7	7.9
Minneapolis–St. Paul, Minn.– Wis. MSA	2,968,806	86.1	5.3	0.7	4.1	0.0	1.6	2.1	3.3
Missoula, Mont. MSA	95,802	94.0	0.3	2.3	1.0	0.1	0.4	1.9	1.6
Mobile, Ala. MSA	540,258	69.3	27.4	0.6	1.1	0.0	0.4	1.0	1.4
Modesto, Calif. MSA	446,997	69.3	2.6	1.3	4.2	0.3	16.8	5.4	31.7
Monroe, La. MSA	147,250	64.5	33.6	0.2	0.6	0.0	0.3	0.7	1.2
Montgomery, Ala. MSA	333,055	58.6	38.9	0.3	0.8	0.0	0.4	1.0	1.2
Muncie, Ind. MSA	118,769	90.7	6.7	0.2	0.7	0.1	0.5	1.1	1.1
Myrtle Beach, S.C. MSA	196,629	81.0	15.5	0.4	0.8	0.1	1.2	1.1	2.6
Naples, Fla. MSA	251,377	86.1	4.5	0.3	0.6	0.1	6.2	2.2	19.6
Nashville, Tenn. MSA	1,231,311	79.4	15.6	0.3	1.6	0.0	1.6	1.4	3.3
New London–Norwich, Conn.–R.I. MSA	293,566	88.0	4.7	0.9	1.9	0.1	1.8	2.5	4.7
New Orleans, La. MSA	1,337,726	57.3	37.5	0.4	2.1	0.0	1.2	1.4	4.4
New York–Northern New Jersey– Long Island, N.Y.–N.J.– Conn.–Pa. CMSA	21,199,865	64.1	17.2	0.3	6.8	0.0	8.2	3.4	18.2
Bergen–Passaic, NJ PMSA	1,373,167	72.7	8.1	0.3	8.2	0.0	7.9	2.9	17.3
Bridgeport, CT PMSA	459,479	78.1	11.5	0.2	2.3	0.0	5.3	2.5	12.4
Danbury, CT PMSA	217,980	88.6	3.0	0.2	3.2	0.0	3.0	2.0	7.0
Dutchess County, NY PMSA	280,150	83.7	9.3	0.2	2.5	0.0	2.4	1.9	6.4
Jersey City, NJ PMSA	608,975	55.6	13.5	0.4	9.4	0.1	15.5	5.6	39.8
Middlesex–Somerset– Hunterdon, NJ PMSA	1,169,641	73.9	8.0	0.2	11.2	0.0	4.4	2.2	11.2
Monmouth–Ocean, NJ PMSA	1,126,217	88.3	5.8	0.1	2.7	0.0	1.5	1.5	5.7
Nassau–Suffolk, NY PMSA	2,753,913	82.0	8.5	0.2	3.6	0.0	3.6	2.1	10.3
New Haven–Meriden, CT PMSA	542,149	77.4	13.1	0.2	2.7	0.0	4.3	2.1	9.8
New York, NY PMSA	9,314,235	48.8	24.6	0.5	9.1	0.1	12.3	4.6	25.1
Newark, NJ PMSA	2,032,989	65.9	22.3	0.2	4.0	0.0	4.9	2.7	13.3
Newburgh, NY–PA PMSA	387,669	84.8	7.5	0.3	1.4	0.0	3.8	2.1	10.8
Stamford–Norwalk, CT PMSA	353,556	81.0	9.2	0.1	3.9	0.0	3.5	2.2	10.8
Trenton, NJ PMSA	350,761	68.5	19.8	0.2	4.9	0.1	4.3	2.2	9.7
Waterbury, CT PMSA	228,984	82.2	8.3	0.3	1.3	0.0	5.5	2.3	11.5
Norfolk–Virginia Beach– Newport News, Va.–N.C. MSA	1,569,541	62.5	30.9	0.4	2.7	0.1	1.2	2.2	3.1
Ocala, Fla. MSA	258,916	84.2	11.5	0.4	0.7	0.0	1.7	1.4	6.0
Odessa–Midland, Texas MSA	237,132	75.5	5.8	0.7	0.8	0.0	14.8	2.4	35.8
Oklahoma City, Okla. MSA	1,083,346	75.7	10.6	4.2	2.5	0.1	3.2	3.9	6.7
Omaha, Nebr.–Iowa MSA	716,998	85.2	8.3	0.5	1.5	0.1	2.7	1.7	5.5
Orlando, Fla. MSA	1,644,561	75.0	13.9	0.3	2.7	0.1	5.1	2.9	16.5
Owensboro, Ky. MSA	91,545	93.7	4.3	0.1	0.4	0.0	0.4	0.9	0.9
Panama City, Fla. MSA	148,217	84.2	10.6	0.8	1.7	0.1	0.7	1.9	2.4
Parkersburg–Marietta, W.Va.– Ohio MSA	151,237	97.3	1.0	0.2	0.5	0.0	0.1	0.8	0.6
Pensacola, Fla. MSA	412,153	77.6	16.5	0.9	2.0	0.1	0.8	2.1	2.6
Peoria–Pekin, Ill. MSA	347,387	88.0	8.9	0.2	1.1	0.0	0.6	1.2	1.6

Metropolitan area	Total	White	Black	Indian/ Alaska Native	Asian	Pacific Islander	Other	Two or more races	Hispanic[1]
Philadelphia–Wilmington– Atlantic City, Pa.–N.J.–Del.– Md. CMSA	6,188,463	72.5%	19.6%	0.2%	3.2%	0.0%	2.7%	1.7%	5.6%
Atlantic–Cape May, NJ PMSA	354,878	75.0	14.0	0.2	3.8	0.0	4.7	2.2	9.6
Philadelphia, PA–NJ PMSA	5,100,931	72.1	20.1	0.2	3.4	0.0	2.5	1.6	5.1
Vineland–Millville–Bridgeton, NJ PMSA	146,438	65.9	20.2	1.0	1.0	0.1	9.1	2.9	19.0
Wilmington–Newark, DE–MD PMSA	586,216	76.1	17.8	0.2	2.3	0.0	2.0	1.6	4.7
Phoenix–Mesa, Ariz. MSA	3,251,876	77.0	3.7	2.2	2.1	0.1	12.1	2.9	25.1
Pine Bluff, Ark. MSA	84,278	48.5	49.6	0.2	0.7	0.0	0.3	0.8	1.0
Pittsburgh, Pa. MSA	2,358,695	89.5	8.1	0.1	1.1	0.0	0.3	0.9	0.7
Pittsfield, Mass. MSA	84,699	94.8	2.3	0.1	0.9	0.0	0.6	1.2	1.7
Pocatello, Idaho MSA	75,565	91.3	0.6	2.9	1.0	0.2	2.1	2.0	4.7
Portland, Maine MSA	243,537	95.8	1.0	0.3	1.4	0.0	0.3	1.1	0.9
Portland–Salem, Oreg.– Wash. CMSA	2,265,223	84.3	2.4	1.0	4.1	0.3	4.6	3.3	8.7
Portland–Vancouver, OR– WA PMSA	1,918,009	84.5	2.7	0.9	4.6	0.3	3.8	3.3	7.4
Salem, OR PMSA	347,214	83.0	0.8	1.5	1.6	0.3	9.5	3.2	15.6
Providence–Fall River–Warwick, R.I.–Mass. MSA	1,188,613	86.2	4.0	0.4	2.2	0.0	4.5	2.6	7.9
Provo–Orem, Utah MSA	368,536	92.4	0.3	0.6	1.1	0.6	3.2	1.9	7.0
Pueblo, Colo. MSA	141,472	79.5	1.9	1.6	0.7	0.1	12.9	3.4	38.0
Punta Gorda, Fla. MSA	141,627	92.6	4.4	0.2	0.9	0.0	0.8	1.1	3.3
Raleigh–Durham–Chapel Hill, N.C. MSA	1,187,941	69.4	22.7	0.4	2.9	0.0	3.1	1.6	6.1
Rapid City, S.Dak. MSA	88,565	86.7	0.9	8.1	0.9	0.1	0.7	2.7	2.6
Reading, Pa. MSA	373,638	88.2	3.7	0.2	1.0	0.0	5.4	1.5	9.7
Redding, Calif. MSA	163,256	89.3	0.8	2.8	1.9	0.1	1.7	3.5	5.5
Reno, Nev. MSA	339,486	80.4	2.1	1.8	4.3	0.5	7.7	3.3	16.6
Richland–Kennewick–Pasco, Wash. MSA	191,822	80.0	1.3	0.8	2.1	0.1	12.7	3.1	21.3
Richmond–Petersburg, Va. MSA	996,512	64.9	30.2	0.4	2.1	0.0	1.1	1.3	2.3
Roanoke, Va. MSA	235,932	83.9	13.0	0.2	1.2	0.0	0.5	1.2	1.1
Rochester, Minn. MSA	124,277	90.3	2.7	0.3	4.3	0.0	0.9	1.5	2.4
Rochester, N.Y. MSA	1,098,201	84.0	10.3	0.3	1.8	0.0	1.9	1.7	4.3
Rockford, Ill. MSA	371,236	85.1	8.1	0.3	1.4	0.0	3.4	1.7	7.4
Rocky Mount, N.C. MSA	143,026	53.4	43.1	0.4	0.4	0.0	1.9	0.8	3.1
Sacramento–Yolo, Calif. CMSA	1,796,857	70.0	7.1	1.1	9.0	0.5	7.2	5.2	15.5
Sacramento, CA PMSA	1,628,197	70.2	7.7	1.1	8.9	0.5	6.5	5.2	14.4
Yolo, CA PMSA	168,660	67.7	2.0	1.2	9.9	0.3	13.8	5.2	25.9
Saginaw–Bay City–Midland, Mich. MSA	403,070	84.8	10.3	0.4	0.9	0.0	1.9	1.7	4.9
St. Cloud, Minn. MSA	167,392	96.0	0.8	0.3	1.5	0.0	0.4	0.8	1.3
St. Joseph, Mo. MSA	102,490	93.6	3.7	0.4	0.4	0.0	0.6	1.2	2.2
St. Louis, Mo.–Ill. MSA	2,603,607	78.3	18.3	0.2	1.4	0.0	0.5	1.2	1.5
Salinas, Calif. MSA	401,762	55.9	3.7	1.0	6.0	0.4	27.8	5.0	46.8
Salt Lake City–Ogden, Utah MSA	1,333,914	87.6	1.1	0.8	2.2	0.9	5.0	2.4	10.8
San Angelo, Texas MSA	104,010	79.1	4.1	0.7	0.9	0.1	12.8	2.4	30.7
San Antonio, Texas MSA	1,592,383	70.6	6.6	0.8	1.5	0.1	16.9	3.5	51.2
San Diego, Calif. MSA	2,813,833	66.5	5.7	0.9	8.9	0.5	12.8	4.7	26.7
San Francisco–Oakland– San Jose, Calif. CMSA	7,039,362	58.7	7.3	0.7	18.4	0.5	9.5	4.9	19.7*
Oakland, CA PMSA	2,392,557	55.4	12.7	0.6	16.7	0.5	8.6	5.4	18.5
San Francisco, CA PMSA	1,731,183	58.6	5.3	0.4	22.7	0.8	7.7	4.5	16.8
San Jose, CA PMSA	1,682,585	53.8	2.8	0.7	25.6	0.3	12.1	4.7	24.0
Santa Cruz–Watsonville, CA PMSA	255,602	75.1	1.0	1.0	3.4	0.1	15.0	4.4	26.8
Santa Rosa, CA PMSA	458,614	81.6	1.4	1.2	3.1	0.2	8.4	4.1	17.3
Vallejo–Fairfield–Napa, CA PMSA	518,821	62.0	11.7	0.8	10.4	0.6	8.7	5.8	19.1
San Luis Obispo–Atascadero– Paso Robles, Calif. MSA	246,681	84.6	2.0	0.9	2.7	0.1	6.2	3.4	16.3
Santa Barbara–Santa Maria– Lompoc, Calif. MSA	399,347	72.7	2.3	1.2	4.1	0.2	15.2	4.3	34.2
Santa Fe, N.Mex. MSA	147,635	75.6	0.6	2.8	1.2	0.1	15.9	3.9	44.4
Sarasota–Bradenton, Fla. MSA	589,959	89.8	6.0	0.2	0.8	0.0	1.9	1.2	6.6
Savannah, Ga. MSA	293,000	61.2	34.9	0.3	1.5	0.1	0.8	1.3	2.2
Scranton–Wilkes-Barre– Hazleton, Pa. MSA	624,776	96.8	1.4	0.1	0.6	0.0	0.4	0.6	1.2
Seattle–Tacoma–Bremerton, Wash. CMSA	3,554,760	79.3	4.7	1.2	7.9	0.6	2.2	4.2	5.2

Metropolitan area	Total	White	Black	Indian/ Alaska Native	Asian	Pacific Islander	Other	Two or more races	Hispanic[1]
Bremerton, WA PMSA	231,969	84.3%	2.9%	1.6%	4.4%	0.8%	1.4%	4.6%	4.1%
Olympia, WA PMSA	207,355	85.7	2.4	1.5	4.4	0.5	1.7	3.9	4.5
Seattle–Bellevue–Everett, WA PMSA	2,414,616	78.6	4.4	1.0	9.4	0.5	2.4	3.9	5.2
Tacoma, WA PMSA	700,820	78.4	7.0	1.4	5.1	0.8	2.2	5.1	5.5
Sharon, Pa. MSA	120,293	93.1	5.3	0.1	0.4	0.0	0.2	0.9	0.7
Sheboygan, Wis. MSA	112,646	92.7	1.1	0.4	3.3	0.0	1.5	1.1	3.4
Sherman–Denison, Texas MSA	110,595	87.2	5.9	1.3	0.6	0.0	2.9	2.1	6.8
Shreveport–Bossier City, La. MSA	392,302	59.7	37.4	0.4	0.8	0.0	0.5	1.1	1.8
Sioux City, Iowa–Nebr. MSA	124,130	86.1	1.8	1.7	2.5	0.0	5.8	2.1	11.3
Sioux Falls, S.Dak. MSA	172,412	93.7	1.4	1.7	0.9	0.0	0.9	1.4	1.9
South Bend, Ind. MSA	265,559	82.4	11.5	0.4	1.3	0.1	2.5	2.0	4.7
Spokane, Wash. MSA	417,939	91.4	1.6	1.4	1.9	0.2	0.8	2.8	2.8
Springfield, Ill. MSA	201,437	88.1	9.1	0.2	1.0	0.0	0.4	1.2	1.0
Springfield, Mo. MSA	325,721	94.4	1.8	0.6	0.9	0.1	0.6	1.6	1.7
Springfield, Mass. MSA	591,932	81.6	6.7	0.2	1.9	0.1	7.2	2.2	12.5
State College, Pa. MSA	135,758	91.4	2.6	0.1	4.0	0.1	0.7	1.1	1.7
Steubenville–Weirton, Ohio– W.Va. MSA	132,008	94.5	3.9	0.2	0.3	0.0	0.2	0.9	0.6
Stockton–Lodi, Calif. MSA	563,598	58.1	6.7	1.1	11.4	0.3	16.3	6.0	30.5
Sumter, S.C. MSA	104,646	50.1	46.7	0.3	0.9	0.1	0.8	1.2	1.8
Syracuse, N.Y. MSA	732,117	88.9	6.5	0.7	1.5	0.0	0.8	1.6	2.1
Tallahassee, Fla. MSA	284,539	62.0	33.6	0.3	1.6	0.0	1.1	1.4	3.9
Tampa–St. Petersburg– Clearwater, Fla. MSA	2,395,997	82.9	10.2	0.3	1.9	0.1	2.7	2.0	10.4
Terre Haute, Ind. MSA	149,192	92.9	4.4	0.3	0.9	0.0	0.3	1.2	1.0
Texarkana, Texas–Texarkana, Ark. MSA	129,749	73.5	23.3	0.6	0.4	0.0	0.9	1.2	3.6
Toledo, Ohio MSA	618,203	82.1	12.8	0.3	1.1	0.0	1.8	1.9	4.4
Topeka, Kans. MSA	169,871	82.9	9.0	1.2	1.0	0.0	3.2	2.7	7.3
Tucson, Ariz. MSA	843,746	75.1	3.0	3.2	2.0	0.1	13.3	3.2	29.3
Tulsa, Okla. MSA	803,235	76.0	8.8	6.9	1.2	0.0	2.1	4.8	4.8
Tuscaloosa, Ala. MSA	164,875	68.1	29.3	0.2	0.9	0.0	0.6	0.8	1.3
Tyler, Texas MSA	174,706	72.6	19.1	0.4	0.7	0.0	5.7	1.4	11.2
Utica–Rome, N.Y. MSA	299,896	91.8	4.6	0.2	1.0	0.0	0.9	1.4	2.7
Victoria, Texas MSA	84,088	74.2	6.3	0.5	0.8	0.0	15.9	2.2	39.2
Visalia–Tulare–Porterville, Calif. MSA	368,021	58.1	1.6	1.6	3.3	0.1	30.8	4.6	50.8
Waco, Texas MSA	213,517	72.2	15.2	0.5	1.1	0.0	9.2	1.8	17.9
Washington–Baltimore, D.C.– Md.–Va.–W.Va. CMSA	7,608,070	63.0	26.2	0.3	5.3	0.1	2.7	2.4	6.4
Baltimore, MD PMSA	2,552,994	67.3	27.4	0.3	2.7	0.0	0.7	1.5	2.0
Hagerstown, MD PMSA	131,923	89.7	7.8	0.2	0.8	0.0	0.5	1.0	1.2
Washington, DC–MD–VA– WV PMSA	4,923,153	60.1	26.0	0.3	6.7	0.1	3.9	2.9	8.8
Waterloo–Cedar Falls, Iowa MSA	128,012	88.4	8.0	0.2	1.0	0.0	0.9	1.5	1.8
Wausau, Wis. MSA	125,834	93.8	0.3	0.3	4.5	0.0	0.3	0.7	0.8
West Palm Beach–Boca Raton, Fla. MSA	1,131,184	79.1	13.8	0.2	1.5	0.1	3.0	2.4	12.4
Wheeling, W.Va.–Ohio MSA	153,172	95.6	2.9	0.1	0.4	0.0	0.1	0.8	0.5
Wichita, Kans. MSA	545,220	81.8	7.8	1.1	2.9	0.1	3.8	2.6	7.4
Wichita Falls, Texas MSA	140,518	79.8	9.6	0.9	1.7	0.1	5.3	2.6	11.8
Williamsport, Pa. MSA	120,044	93.9	4.3	0.2	0.4	0.0	0.3	0.9	0.7
Wilmington, N.C. MSA	233,450	80.7	16.2	0.5	0.7	0.1	1.0	1.0	2.2
Yakima, Wash. MSA	222,581	65.6	1.0	4.5	1.0	0.1	24.4	3.5	35.9
York, Pa. MSA	381,751	92.8	3.7	0.2	0.9	0.0	1.4	1.1	3.0
Youngstown–Warren, Ohio MSA	594,746	87.4	10.3	0.2	0.4	0.0	0.6	1.2	1.8
Yuba City, Calif. MSA	139,149	68.9	2.5	2.0	9.6	0.2	11.7	5.2	20.1
Yuma, Ariz. MSA	160,026	68.3	2.2	1.6	0.9	0.1	23.6	3.2	50.5
Aguadilla, PR MSA	146,424	87.1	3.9	0.2	0.1	0.0	5.8	2.8	98.8
Mayag.ez, PR MSA	253,347	85.7	4.4	0.3	0.2	0.0	4.9	4.6	99.1
Ponce, PR MSA	361,094	83.4	5.4	0.3	0.1	0.0	5.8	4.9	99.2
San Juan–Caguas–Arecibo, PR CMSA	2,450,292	78.2	9.5	0.4	0.3	0.0	7.3	4.4	98.6
Arecibo, PR PMSA	174,300	89.9	3.4	0.2	0.1	0.0	3.8	2.7	99.2
Caguas, PR PMSA	308,365	83.5	5.8	0.3	0.1	0.0	7.3	2.9	99.2
San Juan–Bayamon, PR PMSA	1,967,627	76.3	10.6	0.4	0.3	0.0	7.6	4.7	98.5

Notes: MSA= metropolitan statistical area. CMSA= consolidated metropolitan statistical area. 1. Hispanic persons may be of any race.
Source: U.S Census Bureau, Press Release CB91-229 (2001).

Population Change in the Top 100 Metropolitan Statistical Areas, 1990–2000

Since the 1990 Census, the Census Bureau has changed the boundaries of several dozen metropolitan statistical areas (MSAs), merging some areas and separating others. As a result, population statistics before and after 1990 are not directly comparable for more than 75 MSAs.

Rank, Metropolitan Statistical Area	Population		Change, 1990–2000	
	1990	2000	Number	Percent
1. New York–Northern New Jersey–Long Island, N.Y.–N.J.–Conn.–Pa. CMSA	19,549,649	21,199,865	1,650,216	8.4%
2. Los Angeles–Riverside–Orange County, Calif. CMSA	14,531,529	16,373,645	1,842,116	12.7
3. Chicago–Gary–Kenosha, Ill.–Ind.–Wisc. CMSA	8,239,820	9,157,540	917,720	11.1
4. Washington–Baltimore, D.C.–Md.–Va.–WV CMSA	6,727,050	7,608,070	881,020	13.1
5. San Francisco–Oakland–San Jose, Calif. CMSA	6,253,311	7,039,362	786,051	12.6
6. Philadelphia–Wilmington–Atlantic City, Pa.–N.J.–Del.–Md. CMSA	5,892,937	6,188,463	295,526	5.0
7. Boston–Worcester–Lawrence, Mass.–N.H.–Maine–Conn. CMSA	5,455,403	5,819,100	363,697	6.7
8. Detroit–Ann Arbor–Flint, Mich. CMSA	5,187,171	5,456,428	269,257	5.2
9. Dallas–Fort Worth, Texas CMSA	4,037,282	5,221,801	1,184,519	29.3
10. Houston–Galveston–Brazoria, Texas CMSA	3,731,131	4,669,571	938,440	25.2
11. Atlanta, Ga. MSA	2,959,950	4,112,198	1,152,248	38.9
12. Miami–Fort Lauderdale, Fla. CMSA	3,192,582	3,876,380	683,798	21.4
13. Seattle–Tacoma–Bremerton, Wash. CMSA	2,970,328	3,554,760	584,432	19.7
14. Phoenix–Mesa, Ariz. MSA	2,238,480	3,251,876	1,013,396	45.3
15. Minneapolis–St. Paul, Minn.–Wisc. MSA	2,538,834	2,968,806	429,972	16.9
16. Cleveland–Akron, Ohio CMSA	2,859,644	2,945,831	86,187	3.0
17. San Diego, Calif. MSA	2,498,016	2,813,833	315,817	12.6
18. St. Louis, Mo.–Ill. MSA	2,492,525	2,603,607	111,082	4.5
19. Denver–Boulder–Greeley, Colo. CMSA	1,980,140	2,581,506	601,366	30.4
20. San Juan–Caguas–Arecibo, Puerto Rico CMSA	2,270,808	2,450,292	179,484	7.9
21. Tampa–St. Petersburg–Clearwater, Fla. MSA	2,067,959	2,395,997	328,038	15.9
22. Pittsburgh, Pa. MSA	2,394,811	2,358,695	–36,116	–1.5
23. Portland–Salem, Oreg.–Wash. CMSA	1,793,476	2,265,223	471,747	26.3
24. Cincinnati–Hamilton, Ohio–KY–Ind. CMSA	1,817,571	1,979,202	161,631	8.9
25. Sacramento–Yolo, Calif. CMSA	1,481,102	1,796,857	315,755	21.3
26. Kansas City, Mo.–Kans. MSA	1,582,875	1,776,062	193,187	12.2
27. Milwaukee–Racine, Wisc. CMSA	1,607,183	1,689,572	82,389	5.1
28. Orlando, Fla. MSA	1,224,852	1,644,561	419,709	34.3
29. Indianapolis, Ind. MSA	1,380,491	1,607,486	226,995	16.4
30. San Antonio, Texas MSA	1,324,749	1,592,383	267,634	20.2
31. Norfolk–Virginia Beach–Newport News, Va.–N.C. MSA	1,443,244	1,569,541	126,297	8.8
32. Las Vegas, Nev.–Ariz. MSA	852,737	1,563,282	710,545	83.3
33. Columbus, Ohio MSA	1,345,450	1,540,157	194,707	14.5
34. Charlotte–Gastonia–Rock Hill, N.C.–S.C. MSA	1,162,093	1,499,293	337,200	29.0
35. New Orleans, La. MSA	1,285,270	1,337,726	52,456	4.1
36. Salt Lake City–Ogden, Utah MSA	1,072,227	1,333,914	261,687	24.4
37. Greensboro–Winston-Salem–High Point, N.C. MSA	1,050,304	1,251,509	201,205	19.2
38. Austin–San Marcos, Texas MSA	846,227	1,249,763	403,536	47.7
39. Nashville, Tenn. MSA	985,026	1,231,311	246,285	25.0
40. Providence–Fall River–Warwick, R.I.–Mass. MSA	1,134,350	1,188,613	54,263	4.8
41. Raleigh–Durham–Chapel Hill, N.C. MSA	855,545	1,187,941	332,396	38.9
42. Hartford, Conn. MSA	1,157,585	1,183,110	25,525	2.2
43. Buffalo–Niagara Falls, N.Y. MSA	1,189,288	1,170,111	–19,177	–1.6
44. Memphis, Tenn.–Ark.–Miss. MSA	1,007,306	1,135,614	128,308	12.7
45. West Palm Beach–Boca Raton, Fla. MSA	863,518	1,131,184	267,666	31.0
46. Jacksonville, Fla. MSA	906,727	1,100,491	193,764	21.4
47. Rochester, N.Y. MSA	1,062,470	1,098,201	35,731	3.4
48. Grand Rapids–Muskegon–Holland, Mich. MSA	937,891	1,088,514	150,623	16.1
49. Oklahoma City, Okla. MSA	958,839	1,083,346	124,507	13.0
50. Louisville, Ky.–Ind. MSA	948,829	1,025,598	76,769	8.1
51. Richmond–Petersburg, Va. MSA	865,640	996,512	130,872	15.1
52. Greenville–Spartanburg–Anderson, S.C. MSA	830,563	962,441	131,878	15.9
53. Dayton–Springfield, Ohio MSA	951,270	950,558	–712	–0.1
54. Fresno, Calif. MSA	755,580	922,516	166,936	22.1
55. Birmingham, Ala. MSA	840,140	921,106	80,966	9.6
56. Honolulu, Hawaii MSA	836,231	876,156	39,925	4.8
57. Albany–Schenectady–Troy, N.Y. MSA	861,424	875,583	14,159	1.6
58. Tucson, Ariz. MSA	666,880	843,746	176,866	26.5
59. Tulsa, Okla. MSA	708,954	803,235	94,281	13.3
60. Syracuse, N.Y. MSA	742,177	732,117	–10,060	–1.4
61. Omaha, Neb.–Iowa MSA	639,580	716,998	77,418	12.1
62. Albuquerque, New Mex. MSA	589,131	712,738	123,607	21.0
63. Knoxville, Tenn. MSA	585,960	687,249	101,289	17.3

Rank, Metropolitan Statistical Area	Population		Change, 1990–2000	
	1990	2000	Number	Percent
64. El Paso, Texas MSA	591,610	679,622	88,012	14.9%
65. Bakersfield, Calif. MSA	543,477	661,645	118,168	21.7
66. Allentown–Bethlehem–Easton, Pa. MSA	595,081	637,958	42,877	7.2
67. Harrisburg–Lebanon–Carlisle, Pa. MSA	587,986	629,401	41,415	7.0
68. Scranton–Wilkes-Barre–Hazleton, Pa. MSA	638,466	624,776	–13,690	–2.1
69. Toledo, Ohio MSA	614,128	618,203	4,075	0.7
70. Baton Rouge, LA MSA	528,264	602,894	74,630	14.1
71. Youngstown–Warren, Ohio MSA	600,895	594,746	–6,149	–1.0
72. Springfield, Mass. MSA	587,884	591,932	4,048	0.7
73. Sarasota–Bradenton, Fla. MSA	489,483	589,959	100,476	20.5
74. Little Rock–North Little Rock, Ark. MSA	513,117	583,845	70,728	13.8
75. McAllen–Edinburg–Mission, Texas MSA	383,545	569,463	185,918	48.5
76. Stockton–Lodi, Calif. MSA	480,628	563,598	82,970	17.3
77. Charleston–North Charleston, S.C. MSA	506,875	549,033	42,158	8.3
78. Wichita, Kans. MSA	485,270	545,220	59,950	12.4
79. Mobile, Ala. MSA	476,923	540,258	63,335	13.3
80. Columbia, S.C. MSA	453,331	536,691	83,360	18.4
81. Colorado Springs, Colo. MSA	397,014	516,929	119,915	30.2
82. Fort Wayne, Ind. MSA	456,281	502,141	45,860	10.1
83. Daytona Beach, Fla. MSA	399,413	493,175	93,762	23.5
84. Lakeland–Winter Haven, Fla. MSA	405,382	483,924	78,542	19.4
85. Johnson City–Kingsport–Bristol, Tenn.–Va. MSA	436,047	480,091	44,044	10.1
86. Lexington, Ky. MSA	405,936	479,198	73,262	18.0
87. Augusta–Aiken, Ga.–S.C. MSA	415,184	477,441	62,257	15.0
88. Melbourne–Titusville–Palm Bay, Fla. MSA	398,978	476,230	77,252	19.4
89. Lancaster, Pa. MSA	422,822	470,658	47,836	11.3
90. Chattanooga, Tenn.–Ga. MSA	424,347	465,161	40,814	9.6
91. Des Moines, Iowa MSA	392,928	456,022	63,094	16.1
92. Kalamazoo–Battle Creek, Mich. MSA	429,453	452,851	23,398	5.4
93. Lansing–East Lansing, Mich. MSA	432,674	447,728	15,054	3.5
94. Modesto, Calif. MSA	370,522	446,997	76,475	20.6
95. Fort Myers–Cape Coral, Fla. MSA	335,113	440,888	105,775	31.6
96. Jackson, Miss. MSA	395,396	440,801	45,405	11.5
97. Boise City, Idaho MSA	295,851	432,345	136,494	46.1
98. Madison, Wisc. MSA	367,085	426,526	59,441	16.2
99. Spokane, Wash. MSA	361,364	417,939	56,575	15.7
100. Pensacola, Fla. MSA	344,406	412,153	67,747	19.7

Note: CMSA = consolidated metropolitan statistical area; MSA = metropolitan statistical area. For component areas see "Population of Metropolitan Statistical Areas, 1990–2000." **Source:** U.S. Census Bureau (2001).

Fastest Growing and Declining Metropolitan Statistical Areas, 1990–2000

Rank, Metropolitan Statistical Area	Population		Change, 1990–2000	
	1990	2000	Number	Percent
FASTEST GROWING				
1. Las Vegas, Nev.–Ariz. MSA	852,737	1,563,282	710,545	83.3%
2. Naples, Fla. MSA	152,099	251,377	99,278	65.3
3. Yuma, Ariz. MSA	106,895	160,026	53,131	49.7
4. McAllen–Edinburg–Mission, Texas MSA	383,545	569,463	185,918	48.5
5. Austin–San Marcos, Texas MSA	846,227	1,249,763	403,536	47.7
6. Fayetteville–Springdale–Rogers, Ark. MSA	210,908	311,121	100,213	47.5
7. Boise City, Idaho MSA	295,851	432,345	136,494	46.1
8. Phoenix–Mesa, Ariz. MSA	2,238,480	3,251,876	1,013,396	45.3
9. Laredo, Texas MSA	133,239	193,117	59,878	44.9
10. Provo–Orem, Utah MSA	263,590	368,536	104,946	39.8
FASTEST DECLINING				
1. Steubenville–Weirton, Ohio–W.Va. MSA	142,523	132,008	–10,515	–7.4%
2. Grand Forks, N.Dak.–Minn. MSA	103,181	97,478	–5,703	–5.5
3. Utica–Rome, N.Y. MSA	316,633	299,896	–16,737	–5.3
4. Binghamton, N.Y. MSA	264,497	252,320	–12,177	–4.6
5. Pittsfield, Mass. MSA	88,695	84,699	–3,996	–4.5
6. Elmira, N.Y. MSA	95,195	91,070	–4,125	–4.3
7. Alexandria, La. MSA	131,556	126,337	–5,219	–4.0
8. Wheeling, W.Va.–Ohio MSA	159,301	153,172	–6,129	–3.8
9. Johnstown, Pa. MSA	241,247	232,621	–8,626	–3.6
10. Anniston, Ala. MSA	116,034	112,249	–3,785	–3.3

Note: For component areas see "Population of Metropolitan Statistical Areas, 1990–2000." **Source:** U.S. Census Bureau (2001).

COUNTIES IN AMERICA

In 2007 there were 3,033 counties in the United States. While only 50 percent of Americans live in cities, almost every American lives in a county. Counties were originally the creation of state governments, which saw them as the local arm of state authority, with special responsibility for rural areas. Counties were intended more for the administrative convenience of the state than to meet the immediate needs of county residents and were not designed to have the intimate relationship with, or understanding of, the needs of localities theoretically characteristic of municipalities. But most states have loosened the reins on county governments in recent years, giving them more authority to meet the needs of population centers that have pushed beyond municipal limits. (Note that in Louisiana, counties are called parishes, and in Alaska and New York City, they are known as boroughs.)

Like cities and metropolitan areas, the fastest-growing counties are in the southern and western United States. Seven of the 10 fastest-growing counties in 2000 were in Colorado or Georgia; the other three were in Virginia, Utah and Idaho.

The counties with the largest numerical increase in population between 1990 and 2000 are all in the western U.S.: Maricopa County, Ariz. (950,048), Los Angeles County, Calif. (656,174), Clark County, Nevada (634,306), Harris County, Texas (582,379), and Orange County, Calif. (435,733).

In addition, most of the counties with greatest growth are those in or around major metropolitan areas. Colorado's Douglas and Elbert Counties, which border both the Denver and Colorado Springs metropolitan areas, ranked 1 and 3 in population growth between 1990 and 2000. Both more than doubled over that period. Forsyth County, Ga. (within the Atlanta metropolitan area) was the second-fastest-growing county, increasing by 123.2 percent.

The 50 Largest Counties, 1990–2000

Rank, 2000/County	Population, 1990	Population, 2000	Change, 1990–2000	Percent Change
1. Los Angeles County, Calif.	8,863,164	9,519,338	656,174	7.4%
2. Cook County, Ill.	5,105,067	5,376,741	271,674	5.3
3. Harris County, Texas	2,818,199	3,400,578	582,379	20.7
4. Maricopa County, Ariz.	2,122,101	3,072,149	950,048	44.8
5. Orange County, Calif.	2,410,556	2,846,289	435,733	18.1
6. San Diego County, Calif.	2,498,016	2,813,833	315,817	12.6
7. Kings County, N.Y.	2,300,664	2,465,326	164,662	7.2
8. Miami-Dade County, Fla.	1,937,094	2,253,362	316,268	16.3
9. Queens County, N.Y.	1,951,598	2,229,379	277,781	14.2
10. Dallas County, Texas	1,852,810	2,218,899	366,089	19.8
11. Wayne County, Mich.	2,111,687	2,061,162	−50,525	−2.4
12. King County, Wash.	1,507,319	1,737,034	229,715	15.2
13. San Bernardino County, Calif.	1,418,380	1,709,434	291,054	20.5
14. Santa Clara County, Calif.	1,497,577	1,682,585	185,008	12.4
15. Broward County, Fla.	1,255,488	1,623,018	367,530	29.3
16. Riverside County, Calif.	1,170,413	1,545,387	374,974	32.0
17. New York County, N.Y.	1,487,536	1,537,195	49,659	3.3
18. Philadelphia County, Pa.	1,585,577	1,517,550	−68,027	−4.3
19. Middlesex County, Mass.	1,398,468	1,465,396	66,928	4.8
20. Tarrant County, Texas	1,170,103	1,446,219	276,116	23.6
21. Alameda County, Calif.	1,279,182	1,443,741	164,559	12.9
22. Suffolk County, N.Y.	1,321,864	1,419,369	97,505	7.4
23. Cuyahoga County, Ohio	1,412,140	1,393,978	−18,162	−1.3
24. Bexar County, Texas	1,185,394	1,392,931	207,537	17.5
25. Clark County, Nev.	741,459	1,375,765	634,306	85.5
26. Nassau County, N.Y.	1,287,348	1,334,544	47,196	3.7
27. Bronx County, N.Y.	1,203,789	1,332,650	128,861	10.7
28. Allegheny County, Pa.	1,336,449	1,281,666	−54,783	−4.1
29. Sacramento County, Calif.	1,041,219	1,223,499	182,280	17.5
30. Oakland County, Mich.	1,083,592	1,194,156	110,564	10.2
31. Palm Beach County, Fla.	863,518	1,131,184	267,666	31.0
32. Hennepin County, Minn.	1,032,431	1,116,200	83,769	8.1
33. Franklin County, Ohio	961,437	1,068,978	107,541	11.2
34. St. Louis County, Mo.	993,529	1,016,315	22,786	2.3
35. Hillsborough County, Fla.	834,054	998,948	164,894	19.8
36. Fairfax County, Va.	818,584	969,749	151,165	18.5
37. Erie County, N.Y.	968,532	950,265	−18,267	−1.9
38. Contra Costa County, Calif.	803,732	948,816	145,084	18.1
39. Milwaukee County, Wis.	959,275	940,164	−19,111	−2.0
40. Westchester County, N.Y.	874,866	923,459	48,593	5.6
41. Pinellas County, Fla.	851,659	921,482	69,823	8.2
42. DuPage County, Ill.	781,666	904,161	122,495	15.7
43. Salt Lake County, Utah	725,956	898,387	172,431	23.8
44. Shelby County, Tenn.	826,330	897,472	71,142	8.6
45. Orange County, Fla.	677,491	896,344	218,853	32.3
46. Bergen County, N.J.	825,380	884,118	58,738	7.1
47. Fairfield County, Conn.	827,645	882,567	54,922	6.6
48. Honolulu County, Hawaii	836,231	876,156	39,925	4.8
49. Montgomery County, Md.	757,027	873,341	116,314	15.4
50. Marion County, Ind.	797,159	860,454	63,295	7.9

Source: U.S. Census Bureau (2001).

The 75 Largest Counties, 2000–08

Rank, 2008/County	April 1, 2000	July 1, 2008	Change 2000–08	Percent change
1. Los Angeles County, CA	9,519,331	9,862,049	342,718	3.6%
2. Cook County, IL	5,376,834	5,294,664	–82,170	–1.5
3. Harris County, TX	3,400,590	3,984,349	583,759	17.2
4. Maricopa County, AZ	3,072,172	3,954,598	882,426	28.7
5. Orange County, CA	2,846,293	3,010,759	164,466	5.8
6. San Diego County, CA	2,813,834	3,001,072	187,238	6.7
7. Kings County, NY	2,465,525	2,556,598	91,073	3.7
8. Dallas County, TX	2,218,792	2,412,827	194,035	8.7
9. Miami-Dade County, FL	2,253,786	2,398,145	144,459	6.4
10. Queens County, NY	2,229,379	2,293,007	63,628	2.9
11. Riverside County, CA	1,545,374	2,100,516	555,142	35.9
12. San Bernardino County, CA	1,709,443	2,015,355	305,912	17.9
13. Wayne County, MI	2,061,161	1,949,929	–111,232	–5.4
14. King County, WA	1,737,047	1,875,519	138,472	8.0
15. Clark County, NV	1,375,535	1,865,746	490,211	35.6
16. Santa Clara County, CA	1,682,584	1,764,499	81,915	4.9
17. Broward County, FL	1,623,016	1,751,234	128,218	7.9
18. Tarrant County, TX	1,446,224	1,750,091	303,867	21.0
19. New York County, NY	1,537,372	1,634,795	97,423	6.3
20. Bexar County, TX	1,392,936	1,622,899	229,963	16.5
21. Suffolk County, NY	1,419,371	1,512,224	92,853	6.5
22. Middlesex County, MA	1,466,396	1,482,478	16,082	1.1
23. Alameda County, CA	1,443,744	1,474,368	30,624	2.1
24. Philadelphia County, PA	1,517,550	1,447,395	–70,155	–4.6
25. Sacramento County, CA	1,223,497	1,394,154	170,657	13.9
26. Bronx County, NY	1,332,650	1,391,903	59,253	4.4
27. Nassau County, NY	1,334,542	1,351,625	17,083	1.3
28. Cuyahoga County, OH	1,393,848	1,283,925	–109,923	–7.9
29. Palm Beach County, FL	1,131,190	1,265,293	134,103	11.9
30. Allegheny County, PA	1,281,666	1,215,103	–66,563	–5.2
31. Oakland County, MI	1,194,156	1,202,174	8,018	0.7
32. Hillsborough County, FL	998,943	1,180,784	181,841	18.2
33. Hennepin County, MN	1,116,037	1,140,988	24,951	2.2
34. Franklin County, OH	1,068,869	1,129,067	60,198	5.6
35. Orange County, FL	896,346	1,072,801	176,455	19.7
36. Contra Costa County, CA	948,817	1,029,703	80,886	8.5
37. Salt Lake County, UT	898,412	1,022,651	124,239	13.8
38. Fairfax County, VA	969,682	1,015,302	45,620	4.7
39. Fulton County, GA	815,844	1,014,932	199,088	24.4
40. Pima County, AZ	843,742	1,012,018	168,276	19.9
41. Travis County, TX	812,282	998,543	186,261	22.9
42. St. Louis County, MO	1,016,301	991,830	–24,471	–2.4
43. Westchester County, NY	923,459	953,943	30,484	3.3
44. Milwaukee County, WI	940,165	953,328	13,163	1.4
45. Montgomery County, MD	873,341	950,680	77,339	8.9
44. DuPage County, IL	904,152	930,528	26,376	2.9
46. Pinellas County, FL	921,497	910,260	–11,237	–1.2
47. Erie County, NY	950,265	909,845	–40,420	–4.3
49. Fresno County, CA	799,407	909,153	109,746	13.7
50. Shelby County, TN	897,472	906,825	9,353	1.0
51. Honolulu County, HI	876,158	905,034	28,876	3.3
52. Fairfield County, CT	882,567	895,030	12,463	1.4
53. Bergen County, NJ	884,118	894,840	10,722	1.2
54. Mecklenburg County, NC	695,370	890,515	195,145	28.1
55. Marion County, IN	860,457	880,380	19,923	2.3
56. Hartford County, CT	857,183	877,312	20,129	2.3
57. Wake County, NC	627,850	866,410	238,560	38.0
58. Hamilton County, OH	845,302	851,494	6,192	0.7
59. Duval County, FL	778,866	850,962	72,096	9.3
60. New Haven County, CT	824,008	846,101	22,093	2.7
61. Macomb County, MI	788,149	830,663	42,514	5.4
62. Prince George's County, MD	801,515	820,852	19,337	2.4
63. Kern County, CA	661,653	800,458	138,805	21.0
64. Ventura County, CA	753,186	797,740	44,554	5.9
65. Gwinnett County, GA	588,450	789,499	201,049	34.2
66. Middlesex County, NJ	750,172	789,102	38,930	5.2
67. Pierce County, WA	700,819	785,639	84,820	12.1
68. Baltimore County, MD	754,292	785,618	31,326	4.2
69. Worcester County, MA	749,973	783,806	33,833	4.5
70. Montgomery County, PA	748,987	778,048	29,061	3.9
71. Essex County, NJ	792,311	770,675	–21,636	–2.7
72. Collin County, TX	491,776	762,010	270,234	55.0
73. El Paso County, TX	679,622	742,062	62,440	9.2
74. DeKalb County, GA	666,036	739,956	73,920	11.1
75. Essex County, MA	723,421	736,457	13,036	1.8

Source: U.S. Census Bureau, *Cumulative Estimates of Population Change and County Rankings: April 1, 2000 to July 1, 2008* (2009).

The American People Today

The United States is the third most populous nation in the world, ranking behind only China and India. The population increased 9.1 percent from 2000 to 2009; it was estimated at 307,006,550 in 2009 and by May 2010 at 309,314,342. There were just under 250 million in 1990; the U.S. population has increased by more than 100 million since 1960, and has more than doubled since 1950.

The single most noteworthy characteristic of the U.S. population continues to be the "baby boom generation," the 75 million people born between 1946 and 1964. During these years the crude birth rate soared to as high as 24 live births per 1,000 population (compared to 20 or so in the years before World War II). Fertility rates, too, which had stood at about 75 live births per 1,000 women aged 15–44, jumped to a high of 121. As a result the population grew at an annual rate of between 1.4 percent and 1.8 percent.

The baby boom produced a generation of Americans much larger than any other; the result has been that this generation attracts a great deal of attention as it passes through statistical age categories. Demographers sometimes refer to baby boomers, somewhat inelegantly perhaps, as the "pig in the python" in order to explain how this group has continued to distort the normal contours of the general body of the population. During the 1950s, their numbers required great capital outlays for new schools, and in the 1960s, for expanding colleges and universities. In the 1970s, they jammed the labor market causing higher unemployment rates, but helped the economy by increasing consumption and expanding the housing market.

The most troubling aspect of the 2000 Census is its stark revelation that the American population is very rapidly growing older. In 1970, 9.8 percent of the population was 65 or over; by 2000, 12.6 percent were. In 2030, the Census Bureau projects that fully 20 percent of Americans will be 65 or over.

The impact of this change on the Social Security system cannot be taken seriously enough. In 2013, the first baby boomers turn 67 (the aging of the population has forced a deferral of the traditional retirement age from 65), and will begin collecting Social Security instead of paying into the fund. Ordinarily, this wouldn't be a remarkable fact. But the generation that followed the baby boom—the so-called baby bust generation, also known as Generation X—was unusually small. By 1968 the population growth rate had sunk to 1.0 percent; the birth rate to fewer than 18 live births per 1,000 population, and fertility rates to about 85 live births per woman aged 15–44. As a result, the ratio of people working and paying into Social Security to those receiving payments will shrink dramatically. Today, that ratio is only 3.5–1, but by 2030 it will be closer to 2–1.

In the pages that follow, we have attempted to create a statistical portrait of the population. Note that the Census Bureau updates some information more often than every 10 years with annual population estimates.

THE CENSUS

Article I, section 2 of the U.S. Constitution requires Congress to undertake a census of the population every 10 years for the purpose of apportioning seats in the House of Representatives. Today the decennial census is also used to apportion federal and state funds totalling as much as $400 billion a year, so it is vitally important to local governments and individuals throughout the country. City and county planners, health care administrators, as well as the entire marketing and advertising industries are all strongly dependent on census data for their day-to-day operations. It's not surprising that the 2000 census was the largest undertaking of its kind in our history, and that the 2010 count promises to be even larger. Preliminary canvassing officially began April 1, 2009. By May 2010 more than 72 percent of households had mailed back their census forms. A major change in the 2010 census is the elimination of the long form census, which had in previous years asked for detailed social and economic information.

▶HIGHLIGHTS OF THE 2000 CENSUS
Population growth The resident U.S. population grew from 248.7 million people in 1990 to 281.4 million in 2000. For the first time in the 20th century, every state gained population. The total increase (32.7 million) is the largest numerical increase ever between censuses, though by percentage of total population (13.1), it still ranks below the 28 million person jump caused by the baby boom between 1950 and 1960 (an 18.5 percent increase), and far below the 35.1 percent increase between 1790 and 1800.

State and regional growth The greatest growth occurred in the West and South. The five fastest-growing states were all in the West: Nevada (which grew an astounding 66.3 percent since 1990), Arizona (40 percent), Colorado (30.6 percent), Utah (29.6 percent), and Idaho (28.5 percent). Overall, the West grew by 10.4 million people to a total of 63.2 million, or an increase of 19.7 percent. The South increased by 14.8 million, or 17.3 percent. Georgia was the fastest-growing state in the South, increasing by 26.4 percent.

The Midwest grew by 7.9 percent, while the Northeast experienced 5.5 percent growth. Minnesota, up 12.4 percent, was the fastest-growing state in the Midwest, while New Hampshire, which also grew by 12.4 percent, led the Northeast. The state with the lowest population growth was North Dakota, which increased only 0.5 percent.

The center of U.S. population—the exact spot where an imaginary map of the U.S. would balance perfectly if all 281 million residents were of equal weight—was approximately 2.8 miles east of a town called Edgar Springs, Mo.

U.S. Resident Population and Population Change by State, 1990–2000

State	1990 Population	Rank	2000 Population	Rank	Change, 1990–2000 Number	Percent
United States	248,709,873	N.A.	281,421,906	N.A.	32,712,033	13.2%
Alabama	4,040,587	22	4,447,100	23	406,513	10.1
Alaska	550,043	49	626,932	48	76,889	14.0
Arizona	3,665,228	24	5,130,632	20	1,465,404	40.0
Arkansas	2,350,725	33	2,673,400	33	322,675	13.7
California	29,760,021	1	33,871,648	1	4,111,627	13.8
Colorado	3,294,394	26	4,301,261	24	1,006,867	30.6
Connecticut	3,287,116	27	3,405,565	29	118,449	3.6
Delaware	666,168	46	783,600	45	117,432	17.6
District of Columbia[1]	606,900	N.A.	572,059	N.A.	-34,841	-5.7
Florida	12,937,926	4	15,982,378	4	3,044,452	23.5
Georgia	6,478,216	11	8,186,453	10	1,708,237	26.4
Hawaii	1,108,229	41	1,211,537	42	103,308	9.3
Idaho	1,006,749	42	1,293,953	39	287,204	28.5
Illinois	11,430,602	6	12,419,293	5	988,691	8.6
Indiana	5,544,159	14	6,080,485	14	536,326	9.7
Iowa	2,776,755	30	2,926,324	30	149,569	5.4
Kansas	2,477,574	32	2,688,418	32	210,844	8.5
Kentucky	3,685,296	23	4,041,769	25	356,473	9.7
Louisiana	4,219,973	21	4,468,976	22	249,003	5.9
Maine	1,227,928	38	1,274,923	40	46,995	3.8
Maryland	4,781,468	19	5,296,486	19	515,018	10.8
Massachusetts	6,016,425	13	6,349,097	13	332,672	5.5
Michigan	9,295,297	8	9,938,444	8	643,147	6.9
Minnesota	4,375,099	20	4,919,479	21	544,380	12.4
Mississippi	2,573,216	31	2,844,658	31	271,442	10.5
Missouri	5,117,073	15	5,595,211	17	478,138	9.3
Montana	799,065	44	902,195	44	103,130	12.9
Nebraska	1,578,385	36	1,711,263	38	132,878	8.4
Nevada	1,201,833	39	1,998,257	35	796,424	66.3
New Hampshire	1,109,252	40	1,235,786	41	126,534	11.4
New Jersey	7,730,188	9	8,414,350	9	684,162	8.9
New Mexico	1,515,069	37	1,819,046	36	303,977	20.1
New York	17,990,455	2	18,976,457	3	986,002	5.5
North Carolina	6,628,637	10	8,049,313	11	1,420,676	21.4
North Dakota	638,800	47	642,200	47	3,400	0.5
Ohio	10,847,115	7	11,353,140	7	506,025	4.7
Oklahoma	3,145,585	28	3,450,654	27	305,069	9.7
Oregon	2,842,321	29	3,421,399	28	579,078	20.4
Pennsylvania	11,881,643	5	12,281,054	6	399,411	3.4
Rhode Island	1,003,464	43	1,048,319	43	44,855	4.5
South Carolina	3,486,703	25	4,012,012	26	525,309	15.1
South Dakota	696,004	45	754,844	46	58,840	8.5
Tennessee	4,877,185	17	5,689,283	16	812,098	16.7
Texas	16,986,510	3	20,851,820	2	3,865,310	22.8
Utah	1,722,850	35	2,233,169	34	510,319	29.6
Vermont	562,758	48	608,827	49	46,069	8.2
Virginia	6,187,358	12	7,078,515	12	891,157	14.4
Washington	4,866,692	18	5,894,121	15	1,027,429	21.1
West Virginia	1,793,477	34	1,808,344	37	14,867	0.8
Wisconsin	4,891,769	16	5,363,675	18	471,906	9.6
Wyoming	453,588	50	493,782	50	40,194	8.9

Note: 1. If the District of Columbia were included with the states, it would have ranked 48th in 1990 and 49th in 2000. Source: U.S. Census Bureau, 2001.

Congressional representation Because each state's number of representatives in Congress is based on its population, the population shift to the South and West brought with it a corresponding shift in representation. A total of eight states gained representatives (four of them gained two), while 10 states lost representatives (two states lost two each). States cannot have fewer than one representative, so even though North Dakota experienced a much lower growth rate than New York, it did not lose its sole member of Congress, whereas New York lost two representatives.

Gainers		Losers	
Arizona	+2	New York	-2
Florida	+2	Pennsylvania	-2
Georgia	+2	Connecticut	-1
Texas	+2	Illinois	-1
California	+1	Indiana	-1
Colorado	+1	Michigan	-1
Nevada	+1	Mississippi	-1
North Carolina	+1	Ohio	-1
		Oklahoma	-1
		Wisconsin	-1

State, Urban, and Rural Percentage of Land Area and Population, 1990–2000

State	Sq. miles	Land area, 2000 Urban	Rural	Population 1990 Urban	Rural	2000 Urban	Rural
U.S. total	3,620,501	2.5%	97.5%	75.2%	24.8%	79.0%	21.0%
Alabama	50,753	6.3	93.7	60.4	39.6	55.4	44.5
Alaska	570,374	0.2	99.8	67.5	32.5	65.6	34.4
Arizona	113,609	2.5	97.5	87.5	12.5	88.2	11.8
Arkansas	52,079	2.2	97.8	53.5	46.5	52.5	47.5
California	156,062	6.0	94.0	92.6	7.4	94.4	5.6
Colorado	103,729	1.7	98.3	82.4	17.6	84.5	15.5
Connecticut	4,844	32.1	67.9	79.1	20.9	87.7	12.3
Delaware	1,978	14.1	85.9	73.0	27.0	80.1	19.9
District of Columbia	61.4	100.0	0.0	100.0	0.0	100.0	0.0
Florida	59,120	21.8	78.2	84.8	15.2	89.3	10.7
Georgia	58,051	6.3	93.7	63.2	36.8	71.6	28.4
Hawaii	6,425	4.1	95.9	89.0	11.0	91.5	8.5
Idaho	82,752	2.8	97.2	57.4	42.6	66.4	33.5
Illinois	55,588	7.4	92.6	84.6	15.4	87.8	12.2
Indiana	36,097	5.8	94.2	64.9	35.1	70.8	29.2
Iowa	57,853	1.9	98.1	60.6	39.4	61.1	38.9
Kansas	81,822	1.4	98.6	69.1	30.9	71.4	28.6
Kentucky	39,733	3.5	98.1	51.8	48.2	55.8	44.2
Louisiana	43,026	3.7	96.3	68.1	31.9	72.6	27.4
Maine	30,685	1.6	98.4	44.6	55.4	40.2	59.8
Maryland	9,833	17.5	82.5	81.3	18.7	86.1	13.9
Massachusetts	7,839	38.9	61.1	84.3	15.7	91.4	8.6
Michigan	56,804	6.3	93.7	70.5	29.5	74.7	25.3
Minnesota	79,617	2.3	97.7	69.9	30.1	70.9	29.1
Mississippi	46,918	2.5	97.5	47.1	52.9	48.8	51.2
Missouri	68,898	3.2	96.8	68.7	31.3	69.4	30.6
Montana	145,556	0.2	99.8	52.5	47.5	54.1	45.9
Nebraska	76,878	0.6	99.4	66.1	33.9	69.8	30.3
Nevada	109,806	0.8	99.2	88.3	11.7	91.5	8.5
New Hampshire	8,970	5.2	94.8	51.0	49.0	59.3	40.7
New Jersey	7,419	32.1	67.9	89.4	10.6	94.4	5.6
New Mexico	121,577	0.4	99.6	73.0	27.0	75.0	25.1
New York	47,224	11.6	88.4	84.3	15.7	87.5	12.5
North Carolina	48,715	6.6	93.4	50.4	49.6	60.2	39.8
North Dakota	68,994	0.3	99.7	53.3	46.7	55.9	44.1
Ohio	40,953	10.9	89.1	74.1	25.9	77.4	22.6
Oklahoma	68,680	2.7	97.3	67.7	32.3	65.3	34.7
Oregon	95,997	1.0	99.0	70.5	29.5	78.7	21.3
Pennsylvania	44,820	8.7	91.3	68.9	31.1	77.1	22.9
Rhode Island	1,045	50.5	49.5	86.0	14.0	90.9	9.1
South Carolina	30,111	4.7	93.4	54.6	45.4	60.5	39.5
South Dakota	75,898	0.3	99.7	50.0	50.0	51.9	48.1
Tennessee	41,219	6.6	93.4	60.9	39.1	63.6	36.4
Texas	261,914	3.4	96.6	80.3	19.7	82.5	17.5
Utah	82,168	1.1	98.9	87.0	13.0	88.2	11.8
Vermont	1,149	2.5	97.5	32.2	67.8	38.2	61.7
Virginia	39,598	6.3	93.7	69.4	30.6	73.0	27.0
Washington	66,581	3.3	96.7	76.4	23.6	82.0	18.0
West Virginia	24,664	1.8	98.2	36.1	63.9	46.1	54.0
Wisconsin	54,464	1.5	98.5	65.7	34.3	68.3	31.7
Wyoming	97,105	0.5	99.5	65.0	35.0	65.1	34.8

Source: U.S. Census Bureau, 2002.

Since 1960, California's representatives have increased from 38 to 53, Florida's have more than doubled from 12 to 25, and Texas's have grown from 23 to 32. Over the same period, New York lost a total of 12 representatives while Illinois has lost 5.

Urban and rural population growth Since the 1920 census, more than one half of all Americans have lived in an urban area, which can be loosely defined as a place of 2,500 or more inhabitants. During the 1990s, the population of urban areas grew by 35 million people, from 187.1 to 222.3 million people, an increase of 19 percent. By 2000, the proportion of the U.S. population living in urban areas reached 79.0 percent, up from 75.2 percent in 1990. California and New Jersey had the highest proportion of urban population, at 94.4 percent each. In comparison, the country's rural population shrank by 2.6 percent, from 61.7 million in 1990 to 59.1 million in 2000. Vermont had the highest rural percentage of population: 61.7 percent, down from 67.8 percent in 1990.

U.S. Population by State, 1800–2000

State	1800	1810	1820	1830	1840	1850	1860
Total U.S.	5,308,483	7,239,881	9,638,453	12,860,702	17,063,353	23,191,876	31,443,321
Alabama	1,250	9,046	127,901	309,527	590,756	771,623	964,201
Alaska	N.A.	N.A.	N.A.	N.A.	N.A.	N.A.	N.A.
Arizona	N.A.	N.A.	N.A.	N.A.	N.A.	N.A.	N.A.
Arkansas	N.A.	1,062	14,273	30,388	97,574	209,897	435,450
California	N.A.	N.A.	N.A.	N.A.	N.A.	92,597	379,994
Colorado	N.A.	N.A.	N.A.	N.A.	N.A.	N.A.	34,277
Connecticut	251,002	261,942	275,248	297,675	309,978	370,792	460,147
Delaware	64,273	72,674	72,749	76,748	78,085	91,532	112,216
District of Columbia	8,144	15,471	23,336	30,261	33,745	51,687	75,080
Florida	N.A.	N.A.	N.A.	34,730	54,477	87,445	140,424
Georgia	162,686	252,433	340,989	516,823	691,392	906,185	1,057,286
Hawaii	N.A.	N.A.	N.A.	N.A.	N.A.	N.A.	N.A.
Idaho	N.A.	N.A.	N.A.	N.A.	N.A.	N.A.	N.A.
Illinois	N.A.	12,282	55,211	157,445	476,183	851,470	1,711,951
Indiana	5,641	24,520	147,178	343,031	685,866	988,416	1,350,428
Iowa	N.A.	N.A.	N.A.	N.A.	43,112	192,214	674,913
Kansas	N.A.	N.A.	N.A.	N.A.	N.A.	N.A.	107,206
Kentucky	220,955	406,511	564,317	687,917	779,828	982,405	1,155,684
Louisiana	N.A.	76,556	153,407	215,739	352,411	517,762	708,002
Maine	151,719	228,705	298,335	399,455	501,793	583,169	628,279
Maryland	341,548	380,546	407,350	447,040	470,019	583,034	687,049
Massachusetts	422,845	472,040	523,287	610,408	737,699	994,514	1,231,066
Michigan	N.A.	4,762	8,896	31,369	212,267	397,654	749,113
Minnesota	N.A.	N.A.	N.A.	N.A.	N.A.	6,077	172,023
Mississippi	7,600	31,306	75,448	136,621	375,651	606,526	791,305
Missouri	N.A.	19,783	66,586	140,455	383,702	682,044	1,182,012
Montana	N.A.	N.A.	N.A.	N.A.	N.A.	N.A.	N.A.
Nebraska	N.A.	N.A.	N.A.	N.A.	N.A.	N.A.	28,841
Nevada	N.A.	N.A.	N.A.	N.A.	N.A.	N.A.	6,857
New Hampshire	183,858	214,460	244,161	269,328	284,574	317,976	326,073
New Jersey	211,149	245,562	277,575	320,823	373,306	489,555	672,035
New Mexico	N.A.	N.A.	N.A.	N.A.	N.A.	61,547	93,516
New York	589,051	959,049	1,372,812	1,918,608	2,428,921	3,097,394	3,880,735
North Carolina	478,103	555,500	638,829	737,987	753,419	869,039	992,622
North Dakota	N.A.	N.A.	N.A.	N.A.	N.A.	N.A.	N.A.
Ohio	45,365	230,760	581,434	937,903	1,519,467	1,980,329	2,339,511
Oklahoma	N.A.	N.A.	N.A.	N.A.	N.A.	N.A.	N.A.
Oregon	N.A.	N.A.	N.A.	N.A.	N.A.	12,093	52,465
Pennsylvania	602,365	810,091	1,049,458	1,348,233	1,724,033	2,311,786	2,906,215
Rhode Island	69,122	76,931	83,059	97,199	108,830	147,545	174,620
South Carolina	345,591	415,115	502,741	581,185	594,398	668,507	703,708
South Dakota	N.A.	N.A.	N.A.	N.A.	N.A.	N.A.	4,837
Tennessee	105,602	261,727	422,832	681,904	829,210	1,002,717	1,109,801
Texas	N.A.	N.A.	N.A.	N.A.	N.A.	212,592	604,215
Utah	N.A.	N.A.	N.A.	N.A.	N.A.	11,380	40,273
Vermont	154,465	217,895	235,981	280,652	291,948	314,120	315,098
Virginia[2]	880,200	974,600	1,065,366	1,211,405	1,239,797	1,421,661	1,596,318
Washington	N.A.	N.A.	N.A.	N.A.	N.A.	1,201	11,594
West Virginia	N.A.	N.A.	N.A.	N.A.	N.A.	N.A.	N.A.
Wisconsin	N.A.	N.A.	N.A.	N.A.	30,945	305,391	775,881
Wyoming	N.A.	N.A.	N.A.	N.A.	N.A.	N.A.	N.A.

Population growth in metropolitan areas

The 2000 census revealed that more than 80 percent of all U.S. residents (226.0 million) lived in metropolitan areas, while just under 30 percent (84.1 million) lived in metro areas of 5 million people or more. Areas with populations between 2.0 million and 5.0 million grew the fastest: they increased by a total of 20 percent. Metro areas with more than 1 million but fewer than 2 million people grew by 17.7 percent. Nonmetropolitan areas grew slowest: a total of 10.2 percent between 1990 and 2000. That's better than the previous decade, however, when nonmetropolitan areas grew by only 3.9 percent.

The 10 fastest-growing metropolitan areas were all in the South or the West. Las Vegas, which leaped from 852,737 to 1.5 million, grew by an astounding 83.3 percent. Naples, Fla. was second, with 65.3 percent growth. Yuma, Ariz. (49.7), McAllen-Edinburg Mission, Texas (48.5) and Austin-San Marcos, Texas (47.7) rounded out the top five.

Race and Hispanic origin

Since 1960, each Census has approached the issue of race in slightly different ways. The most important change for the 2000 Census was the ability of respondents to classify themselves as members of more than one race. In previous censuses, someone who was part black and part white had to choose one race or the other on Census forms. For the 2000 Census, however, people with more than

State	1870	1880	1890	1900	1910	1920	1930
Total U.S.	38,558,371	50,189,209	62,979,766	76,212,168	92,228,496	106,021,537	123,202,624
Alabama	996,992	1,262,505	1,513,401	1,828,697	2,138,093	2,348,174	2,646,248
Alaska	N.A.	33,426	32,052	63,592	64,356	55,036	59,278
Arizona	9,658	40,440	88,243	122,931	204,354	334,162	435,573
Arkansas	484,471	802,525	1,128,211	1,311,564	1,574,449	1,752,204	1,854,482
California	560,247	864,694	1,213,396	1,485,053	2,377,549	3,426,861	5,677,251
Colorado	39,864	194,327	413,249	539,700	799,024	939,629	1,035,791
Connecticut	537,454	622,700	746,258	908,420	1,114,756	1,380,631	1,606,903
Delaware	125,015	146,608	168,493	184,735	202,322	223,003	238,380
District of Columbia	131,700	177,624	230,392	278,718	331,069	437,571	486,869
Florida	187,748	269,493	391,422	528,542	752,619	968,470	1,468,211
Georgia	1,184,109	1,542,180	1,837,353	2,216,331	2,609,121	2,895,832	2,908,506
Hawaii	N.A.	N.A.	N.A.	154,001	191,874	255,881	368,300
Idaho	14,999	32,610	88,548	161,772	325,594	431,866	445,032
Illinois	2,539,891	3,077,871	3,826,352	4,821,550	5,638,591	6,485,280	7,630,654
Indiana	1,680,637	1,978,301	2,192,404	2,516,462	2,700,876	2,930,390	3,238,503
Iowa	1,194,020	1,624,615	1,912,297	2,231,853	2,224,771	2,404,021	2,470,939
Kansas	364,399	996,096	1,428,108	1,470,495	1,690,949	1,769,257	1,880,999
Kentucky	1,321,011	1,648,690	1,858,635	2,147,174	2,289,905	2,416,630	2,614,589
Louisiana	726,915	939,946	1,118,588	1,381,625	1,656,388	1,798,509	2,101,593
Maine	626,915	648,936	661,086	694,466	742,371	768,014	797,423
Maryland	780,894	934,943	1,042,390	1,188,044	1,295,346	1,449,661	1,631,526
Massachusetts	1,457,351	1,783,085	2,238,947	2,805,346	3,366,416	3,852,356	4,249,614
Michigan	1,184,059	1,636,937	2,093,890	2,420,982	2,810,173	3,668,412	4,842,325
Minnesota	439,706	780,773	1,310,283	1,751,394	2,075,708	2,387,125	2,563,953
Mississippi	827,922	1,131,597	1,289,600	1,551,270	1,797,114	1,790,618	2,009,821
Missouri	1,721,295	2,168,380	2,679,185	3,106,665	3,293,335	3,404,055	3,629,367
Montana	20,595	39,159	142,924	243,329	376,053	548,889	537,606
Nebraska	122,993	452,402	1,062,656	1,066,300	1,192,214	1,296,372	1,377,963
Nevada	42,491	62,266	47,355	42,335	81,875	77,407	91,058
New Hampshire	318,300	346,991	376,530	411,588	430,572	443,083	465,293
New Jersey	906,096	1,131,116	1,444,933	1,883,669	2,537,167	3,155,900	4,041,334
New Mexico	91,874	119,565	160,282	195,310	327,301	360,350	423,317
New York	4,382,759	5,082,871	6,003,174	7,268,894	9,113,614	10,385,227	12,588,066
North Carolina	1,071,361	1,399,750	1,617,949	1,893,810	2,206,287	2,559,123	3,170,276
North Dakota	2,405	36,909	190,983	319,146	577,056	646,872	680,845
Ohio	2,665,260	3,198,062	3,672,329	4,157,545	4,767,121	5,759,394	6,646,697
Oklahoma	N.A.	N.A.	258,657	790,371	1,657,155	2,028,283	2,396,040
Oregon	90,923	174,768	317,704	413,536	672,765	783,389	953,786
Pennsylvania	3,521,951	4,282,891	5,258,113	6,302,115	7,665,111	8,720,017	9,631,350
Rhode Island	217,353	276,531	345,506	428,556	542,610	604,397	687,497
South Carolina	705,606	995,577	1,151,149	1,340,316	1,515,400	1,683,724	1,738,765
South Dakota	11,776	98,268	348,600	401,570	583,888	636,547	692,849
Tennessee	1,258,520	1,542,359	1,767,518	2,020,616	2,184,789	2,337,885	2,616,556
Texas	818,579	1,591,749	2,235,527	3,048,710	3,896,542	4,663,228	5,824,715
Utah	86,786	143,963	210,779	276,749	373,351	449,396	507,847
Vermont	330,551	332,286	332,422	343,641	355,956	352,428	359,611
Virginia[2]	1,225,163	1,512,565	1,655,980	1,854,184	2,061,612	2,309,187	2,421,851
Washington	23,955	75,116	357,232	518,103	1,141,990	1,356,621	1,563,396
West Virginia	442,014	618,457	762,794	958,800	1,221,119	1,463,701	1,729,205
Wisconsin	1,054,670	1,315,497	1,693,330	2,069,042	2,333,860	2,632,067	2,939,006
Wyoming	9,118	20,789	62,555	92,531	145,965	194,402	225,565

one race in their heritage were permitted to identify all their racial backgrounds. More than 6.8 million people identified themselves as being of more than one race. Because it is impossible to know how people of more than one race identified themselves in the past, racial data from the 2000 Census is not strictly comparable with those from previous censuses.

The United States remains overwhelmingly white, though less so than in the past. There were 211 million white people in the U.S. in 2000, and 5 million more who were white and at least one other race. The white-only population was 75.1 percent of the total U.S. population in 2000, down from 80.3 percent 10 years earlier. In 1970, the white population of the U.S. was 87.5 percent of the total.

The black-only population was 34.7 million in 2000, up from just under 30 million in 1990. An-

other 1.8 million people were black and at least one other race. The black-only population is 12.3 percent of the total, up slightly from 12.1 in 1990 and 11.1 percent in 1970.

The Asian population increased from 6.9 million in 1990 to 10.2 million (Asian-only) in 2000. Another 1.6 million people considered themselves Asian and at least one other race. The Asian-only population represented 3.6 percent of the total, up from 2.8 in 1990. For 2000, the Census Bureau separated out Native Hawaiian and other Pacific Islander from the Asian population for the first time.

People of Hispanic origin may be of any race. Hispanics or Latinos continue to be the fastest-growing segment of the population, primarily because of immigration and high birth rates. The Hispanic or Latino population grew 53 percent between 1980 and 1990 and another 58 percent

State	1940	1950	1960	1970	1980	1990	2000
Total U.S.	132,164,569	151,325,798	179,323,175	203,302,031	226,542,203	248,709,873	281,421,906
Alabama	2,832,961	3,061,743	3,266,740	3,444,354	3,894,025	4,040,587	4,447,100
Alaska	72,524	128,643	226,167	302,583	401,851	550,043	626,932
Arizona	499.261	749,587	1,302,161	1,775,399	2,716,546	3,665,228	5,130,632
Arkansas	1,949,387	1,909,511	1,786,272	1,923,322	2,286,357	2,350,725	2,673,400
California	6,907,387	10,586,223	15,717,204	19,971,069	23,667,764	29,760,021	33,871,648
Colorado	1,123,296	1,325,089	1,753,947	2,209,596	2,889,735	3,294,394	4,301,261
Connecticut	1,709,242	2,007,280	2,535,234	3,032,217	3,107,564	3,287,116	3,405,565
Delaware	266,505	318,085	446,292	548,104	594,338	666,168	783,600
District of Columbia	663,091	802,178	763,956	756,668	638,432	606,900	572,059
Florida	1,897,414	2,771,305	4,951,560	6,791,418	9,746,961	12,937,926	15,982,378
Georgia	3,123,723	3,444,578	3,943,116	4,587,930	5,462,982	6,478,216	8,186,453
Hawaii	422,770	499,794	632,772	769,913	964,691	1,108,229	1,211,537
Idaho	524,873	588,637	667,191	713,015	944,127	1,006,749	1,293,953
Illinois	7,897,241	8,712,176	10,081,158	11,110,285	11,427,409	11,430,602	12,419,293
Indiana	3,427,796	3,934,224	4,662,498	5,195,392	5,490,214	5,544,159	6,080,485
Iowa	2,538,268	2,621,073	2,757,537	2,825,368	2,913,808	2,776,755	2,926,324
Kansas	1,801,028	1,905,299	2,178,611	2,249,071	2,364,236	2,477,574	2,688,418
Kentucky	2,845,627	2,944,806	3,038,156	3,220,711	3,660,324	3,685,296	4,041,769
Louisiana	2,363,880	2,683,516	3,257,022	3,644,637	4,206,116	4,219,973	4,468,976
Maine	847,226	913,774	969,265	993,722	1,125,043	1,227,928	1,274,923
Maryland	1,821,244	2,343,001	3,100,689	3,923,897	4,216,933	4,781,468	5,296,486
Massachusetts	4,316,721	4,690,514	5,148,578	5,689,170	5,737,093	6,016,425	6,349,097
Michigan	5,256,106	6,371,766	7,823,194	8,881,826	9,262,044	9,295,297	9,938,444
Minnesota	2,792,300	2,982,483	3,413,864	3,806,103	4,075,970	4,375,099	4,919,479
Mississippi	2,183,796	2,178,914	2,178,141	2,216,994	2,520,770	2,573,216	2,844,658
Missouri	3,784,664	3,954,653	4,319,813	4,677,623	4,916,762	5,117,073	5,595,211
Montana	559,456	591,024	674,767	694,409	786,690	799,065	902,195
Nebraska	1,315,834	1,325,510	1,411,330	1,485,333	1,569,825	1,578,385	1,711,263
Nevada	110,247	160,083	285,278	488,738	800,508	1,201,833	1,998,257
New Hampshire	491,524	533,242	606,921	737,681	920,610	1,109,252	1,235,786
New Jersey	4,160,165	4,835,329	6,066,782	7,171,112	7,365,011	7,730,188	8,414,350
New Mexico	531,818	681,187	951,023	1,017,055	1,303,302	1,515,069	1,819,046
New York	13,479,142	14,830,192	16,782,304	18,241,391	17,558,165	17,990,455	18,976,457
North Carolina	3,571,623	4,061,929	4,556,155	5,084,411	5,880,095	6,628,637	8,049,313
North Dakota	641,935	619,636	632,446	617,792	652,717	638,800	642,200
Ohio	6,907,612	7,946,627	9,706,397	10,657,423	10,797,603	10,847,115	11,353,140
Oklahoma	2,336,434	2,233,351	2,328,284	2,559,463	3,025,487	3,145,585	3,450,654
Oregon	1,089,684	1,521,341	1,768,687	2,091,533	2,633,156	2,842,321	3,421,399
Pennsylvania	9,900,180	10,498,012	11,319,366	11,800,766	11,864,720	11,881,643	12,281,054
Rhode Island	713,346	791,896	859,488	949,723	947,154	1,003,464	1,048,319
South Carolina	1,899,804	2,117,027	2,382,594	2,590,713	3,120,729	3,486,703	4,012,012
South Dakota	642,961	652,740	680,514	666,257	690,768	696,004	754,844
Tennessee	2,915,841	3,291,718	3,567,089	3,926,018	4,591,023	4,877,185	5,689,283
Texas	6,414,824	7,711,194	9,579,677	11,198,655	14,225,513	16,986,510	20,851,820
Utah	550,310	688,862	890,627	1,059,273	1,461,037	1,722,850	2,233,169
Vermont	359,231	377,747	389,881	444,732	511,456	562,758	608,827
Virginia[2]	2,677,773	3,318,680	3,966,949	4,651,448	5,346,797	6,187,358	7,078,515
Washington	1,736,191	2,378,963	2,853,214	3,413,244	4,132,353	4,866,692	5,894,121
West Virginia	1,901,974	2,005,552	1,860,421	1,744,237	1,950,186	1,793,477	1,808,344
Wisconsin	3,137,587	3,434,575	3,951,777	4,417,821	4,705,642	4,891,769	5,363,675
Wyoming	250,742	290,529	330,066	332,416	469,557	453,588	493,782

Notes: Excludes military and overseas population. Wherever possible, 1980 state boundaries are used in calculating populations of regions, areas, and territories prior to their statehoods. 1. 1980 figures are revised estimates issued by the Census Bureau in 1987. 2. The figures for Virginia through 1860 are from the 1960 census; in the 1980 summary, the Census Bureau gave separate figures for West Virginia between 1790 and 1860, even though it did not become a state until 1863. Since the result diminishes Virginia's population by over 300,000 in 1850 and 1860, a crucial period, we decided to keep the earlier breakdowns. **Sources:** U.S. Census Bureau, 2000 Census of Population: U.S. Summary.

between 1990 and 2000. Hispanics now make up 12.5 percent of the U.S. population, up from 9.0 percent in 1990 and 6.4 percent in 1980.

Undercounting the U.S. population in the 1990 and 2000 Censuses

The Census Bureau estimates it undercounted the original 1990 Census by about 1.6 percent nationwide. The Bureau concluded that it failed to enumerate 8 million people, and double-counted about 4 million others. That's a net difference of just over 4 million people, or a little more than the population within the Los Angeles city limits.

To prevent this problem in the 2000 Census, the Bureau planned to use statistical sampling methods to enumerate the hardest-to-count 10 percent of the population, and to conduct a follow-up survey of 750,000 households, which would point out inaccuracies in the initial count. But because census numbers are used to apportion Congressional districts and because blacks and Hispanics (who tend to vote Democratic) made up a significant

Portrait of the U.S. Population, April 1, 2000

Characteristic	Number	Percent
Total population	**281,421,906**	**100.0%**
SEX		
Male	138,053,563	49.1
Female	143,368,343	50.9
AGE		
Under 18 years	6,042,435	2.1
18 years and over	209,128,094	74.3
21 years and over	196,899,193	70.0
65 years and over	34,991,753	12.4
Median age	35.3	N.A.
RACE		
One race, total	274,595,678	97.6
White only	211,460,626	75.1
Black only	34,658,190	12.3
American Indian and Alaska Native only	2,475,956	0.9
Asian only	10,242,998	3.6
Native Hawaiian and other Pacific Islander only	398,835	0.1
Other race	15,359,073	5.5
Two or more races, total	6,826,228	2.4
Hispanic or Latino (of any race)	35,305,818	12.5
HOUSEHOLD TYPE		
Total households	**105,480,101**	**100.0%**
Family households (families)	71,787,347	68.1
With own children under 18 years	34,588,368	32.8
Married-couple family	54,493,232	51.7
With own children under 18 years	24,835,505	23.5
Female householder[1]	12,900,103	12.2
With own children under 18 years	7,561,874	7.2
Nonfamily households	33,692,754	31.9
Householder living alone	27,230,075	25.8
65 years and over	9,722,857	9.2
Average household size (people)	2.59	N.A.
Average family size (people)	3.14	N.A.
HOUSING OCCUPANCY		
Total housing units	**115,904,641**	**100.0%**
Occupied housing units	105,480,101	91.0
Vacant housing units	10,424,540	9.0
For seasonal, recreational or occasional use	3,578,718	3.1
Homeowner vacancy rate (percent)		1.7
Rental vacancy rate (percent)		6.8
HOUSING TENURE		
Occupied housing units	**105,480,101**	**100.0%**
Owner-occupied	69,815,753	66.2
Renter-occupied	35,664,348	33.8

Note: 1. No husband present. **Source:** U.S. Census Bureau, 2001.

U.S. Population by Region, 1990–2000

Region	1990 Census	2000 Census
United States	**248,790,925**	**281,421,906**
Northeast	**50,828,313**	**53,594,378**
New England	13,206,943	13,922,517
Middle Atlantic	37,621,370	39,671,861
Midwest	**59,669,320**	**64,392,776**
East North Central	42,009,114	45,155,037
West North Central	17,660,206	19,237,739
South	**85,455,793**	**100,236,820**
South Atlantic	43,571,473	51,769,160
East South Central	15,179,959	17,022,810
West South Central	26,704,361	31,444,850
West	**52,837,499**	**63,197,932**
Mountain	13,658,794	18,172,295
Pacific	39,178,705	45,025,637

Source: U.S. Census Bureau.

Population Growth by Region, 1790–2000 (in thousands)

Year	Northeast	Midwest[1]	South[2]	West
1790	1,968	N.A.	1,961	N.A.
1800	2,636	51	2,622	N.A.
1810	3,487	292	3,461	N.A.
1820	4,360	859	4,419	N.A.
1830	5,542	1,610	5,708	N.A.
1840	6,761	3,352	6,951	N.A.
1850	8,627	5,404	8,983	179
1860	10,594	9,097	11,133	619
1870	12,299	12,981	12,288	991
1880	14,507	17,364	16,517	1,801
1890	17,407	22,410	20,028	3,134
1900	21,047	26,333	24,524	4,309
1910	25,869	29,889	29,389	7,082
1920	29,662	34,020	33,126	9,214
1930	34,427	38,594	37,858	12,324
1940	35,977	40,143	41,666	14,379
1950	39,478	44,461	47,197	20,190
1960	44,678	51,619	54,973	28,053
1970	49,041	56,572	62,795	34,804
1980	49,135	58,866	75,372	43,172
1990	50,809	59,669	85,446	52,786
2000	53,594	64,393	100,237	63,198

Notes: 1. Called North Central prior to 1980. 2. Includes black slave population through 1860. **Source:** U.S. Census Bureau, *The Statistical History of the U.S.* (1976) and 2000 Census of the U.S.

jected the Clinton administration's appeal of the decision.

As a result, the Census Bureau had to spend an additional $1.7 billion (over the $5 billion budgeted) to count each and every person in 2000, even those who didn't want to cooperate with pollsters; because of this additional cost, the size of the follow-up survey had to be cut to 314,000 interviews. By comparing this survey with results from traditional census-taking methods, the Census Bureau estimated in early 2001 that at least 6.4 million people were not counted in the 2000 census and at least 3.1 million were counted twice. The undercount rate of aproximately 1.2 percent was better than the 1.6 percent undercount in 1990, but controversy over the uncounted millions continued throughout 2001. In March 2001, the Census Bureau announced that it would recommend the use of unadjusted numbers for re-

portion of the 1990 undercount, Republicans in Congress challenged the plan, fearing that an accurate count of the country's minorities would erode G.O.P. numbers. In August 1998, a federal court struck down the use of sampling, saying it violated 1957 and 1976 federal laws governing the census, and in July 1999 the Supreme Court re-

U.S. Population, Population Density, and Area of Residence, 1790–2000

Year	Total population	Percent increase	Population per square mile	Percent urban	Percent rural
1790	3,929,214	N.A.	4.5	5.1%	94.9%
1800	5,308,483	35.1%	6.1	6.1	93.9
1810	7,239,881	36.4	4.3	7.3	92.7
1820	9,638,453	33.1	5.5	7.2	92.8
1830	12,866,020	33.5	7.4	8.8	91.2
1840	17,069,453	32.7	9.8	10.8	89.2
1850	23,191,876	35.9	7.9	15.3	84.7
1860	31,443,321	35.6	10.6	19.8	80.2
1870	39,818,449	26.6	13.4	25.7	74.3
1880	50,155,783	26.0	16.9	28.2	71.8
1890	62,947,714	25.5	21.2	35.1	64.9
1900	75,994,575	20.7	25.6	39.6	60.4
1910	91,972,266	21.0	31.0	45.6	54.4
1920	105,710,620	14.9	35.6	51.2	48.8
1930	122,775,046	16.1	41.2	56.1	43.9
1940	131,669,275	7.2	44.2	56.5	43.5
1950	150,697,361	14.5	50.7	64.0	36.0
1960	179,323,175	18.5	50.6	69.9	30.1
1970	203,302,031	13.4	57.4	73.5	26.5
1980	226,542,199	11.4	64.0	73.7	26.3
1990	248,718,302	9.8	70.3	75.2	24.8
2000	281,421,906	13.1	79.6	79.0	21.0

Note: Figures for 1980, 1990, and 2000 Censuses have been revised since publication. **Source**: U.S. Census Bureau, *The Statistical History of the U.S.* (1976); *The Statistical Abstract of the United States* (annual).

drawing Congressional districts; several large cities planned to sue for the release of detailed data about regional and local undercounts, and debates over the use of adjusted census figures for allocation of other federal and state resources continued throughout the year.
Source: U.S. Bureau of the Census Executive Steering Committee for Accuracy and Coverage Evaluation Policy; www.census.gov.

U.S. POPULATION BY RACE AND HISPANIC ORIGIN

It is important to note that the Census Bureau's classification of the population by race, in its words, "reflects self-identification by people according to the race or races with which they most closely identify. These categories are sociopolitical constructs and should not be interpreted as being scientific or anthropological in nature." Only since 1960, however, have the Census Bureau's race figures been based on self-identification, and only since 1980 has the Bureau reported statistics on Native Americans, Asians and persons of Hispanic origin.

The people of the United States are predominantly white, accounting for an estimated 79.8 percent of the total population in 2008—continuing a downward trend from 84.1 percent in the 1990 census and 81.1 in 2000. This dominance has been true since colonial days, although even then the indigenous peoples and the African slaves were significant racial minorities. In fact as slave labor became essential to the Southern economy so many slaves were brought here that just before the Civil War blacks constituted 15 percent of the U.S. population.

After the war, the proportion of whites rapidly increased as millions of immigrants from northern Europe settled throughout the country. The relentless movement of the population westward deprived the Native Americans of their lands and—with the assistance of several bloody wars—helped to reduce their numbers to a small fraction of what they were estimated to have been only a century before.

The black population, which represented between nine and 13 percent of the total for many decades, remained the only significant minority group until the 1960s, when a surge of new immigrants from Puerto Rico, Mexico and Cuba made the Hispanic presence felt. So rapid and strong an impression did these groups make that the Census Bureau created a new population category, "Hispanic Origin". Since some Hispanics are black, some white, and still others Indian, this designation has nothing to do with race.

During the 1970s and 1980s, the arrival of several million Asians again caused a noticeable change in the composition of the population. The 1990 census was the first one to include a separate category for Asians and Pacific Islanders; in previous years, they had been included together with American Indians, Aleuts and Eskimos in the "other races" grouping.

The 2000 Census took an even more expansive approach. For the first time, it allowed people to identify themselves by more than one race. Although the vast majority of Americans (97.6 percent) still consider themselves of one race, a total of 6.8 million people said they were members of two or more races (2.4 percent). The most common mix was white and American Indian or Alaska Native; just over a million people identified themselves as such. Another 868,395 said they were a mix of white and Asian, and 784,764 said they were white and black or African-American. Another 2.2 million people said they were white and some other race. A total of 410,285 people identified themselves as members of three races, 38,408 said they were of four races, 8,637 were of five races, and 823 people were of six races.

The 2000 Census was also the first to separate out "Native Hawaiian and Other Pacific Islander" from the Asian category. This new category includes people who indicated their races as Guamanian, Chamorro, Samoan, Tahitian, Mariana Islander or Chuukese. The 2000 Census also included an "Other race" category, which includes people who did not identify their race, or who wrote in races such as Moroccan, South African or Belizean. This category also includes people who wrote in a Hispanic origin (e.g. Mexican, Cuban) instead of a race.

As a result of the expanded race categories, data from the 2000 Census is not directly comparable with information from previous censuses. Wherever possible, we have tried to provide two sets of race statistics for 2000: a) those who consider themselves members only of the race (i.e. white only or black only) and b) the aforementioned members of the race plus those who consider themselves members of the race and at least one other race as well

(i.e. white and Asian, or black and Native American). We have also tried to provide more recent population estimates where they are available.

▶THE BLACK POPULATION

Ever since the Founding Fathers reached their famous "compromise" declaring a slave the equivalent of three-fifths of a person, the black population has had a less-than-equal standing in relation to the majority of Americans. Over the last two centuries, the struggle for equality, even in a nation pledged to that ideal, has proven long, hard, and in many cases, intractable, as so many contemporary facts and figures in this book make all too evident. From higher infant mortality rates and poverty rates to lower life expectancy and family income levels, the black population continues to suffer the effects of two centuries of slavery and one of institutionalized segregation.

Resident Population of the U.S., by Race and Hispanic Origin, 1990–2000

The 2000 Census was the first to allow people to identify themselves as of more than one race. In the table below, the fourth and fifth columns include people who described themselves only as the race shown. The last two columns includes all of those people, as well as people who described themselves as the race indicated, in addition to at

least one other race. For example, 10.2 million Americans described themeselves as Asian alone, but an additional 1.7 million described themselves as part Asian and part some other race. Thus, a total of 11.9 million people may be considered at least partly Asian. Note that persons of Hispanic origin may be of any race.

Race/ Hispanic origin	1990 Number	1990 Percent	2000 Race shown only	2000 Percent	2000 Race shown alone or in combination with other race(s)	2000 Percent
Total population	**248,709,873**	**100.0%**	**281,421,906**	**100.0%**	**281,421,906**	**100.0%**
White	199,686,070	80.3	211,460,626	75.1	216,930,975	77.1
Black (African-American)	29,986,060	12.1	34,658,190	12.3	36,419,434	12.9
American Indian and Alaska Native	1,959,234	0.8	2,475,956	0.9	4,119,301	1.5
Asian	6,908,638	2.8	10,242,998	3.6	11,898,828	4.2
Native Hawaiian and other Pacific Islander	365,024	0.1	398,835	0.1	874,414	0.3
Other race	9,804,847	3.9	15,359,073	5.5	18,521,486	6.6
Two or more races	N.A.	N.A.	6,826,228	2.4	N.A.	N.A.
Hispanic origin[1]	22,354,059	9.0	35,305,818	12.5	35,305,818	12.5

Note: 1. Persons of Hispanic origin may be of any race. **Source:** U.S. Census Bureau.

Change in the Resident Population, by Race and Hispanic Origin, 1980–2000

Race/ Hispanic origin	Change, 1980–90 Number	Change, 1980–90 Percent change	Change, 1990–2000 Number (race only)	Change, 1990–2000 Percent change	Change, 1990–2000 Race alone or in combination with other race(s)	Change, 1990–2000 Percent change
Total population	**22,164,068**	**9.8%**	**32,713,033**	**13.2%**	**32,713,033**	**13.2%**
White	11,314,448	6.0	11,774,556	5.9	17,244,905	8.6
Black (African-American)	3,491,035	13.2	4,672,130	15.6	6,433,374	21.5
American Indian and Alaska Native	538,834	37.9	516,722	26.4	2,160,067	110.3
Asian	3,773,223	107.8	3,334,360	18.3	4,990,190	72.2
Native Hawaiian and other Pacific Islander	1	1	33,811	9.3	509,390	139.5
Other race	N.A.	N.A.	5,554,226	56.6	8,716,639	88.9
Hispanic origin[2]	7,745,386	53.0	12,951,759	57.9	12,951,759	57.9

Notes: 1. Native Hawaiian and other Pacific Islander included with Asian from 1980–90. 2. Persons of Hispanic origin may be of any race. **Source:** U.S. Census Bureau.

According to 2008 population estimates, 39,058,834 Americans identify themselves as black only. They represented 12.8 percent of all Americans. An additional 5,167,029 consider themselves black and at least one other race (most often white), making a total of 44,225,863 people (14.5 percent of the population) at least partly black. The black-only population grew by 15.6 percent between the censuses of 1990 and 2000, significantly faster than the overall population, which increased only by 13.2

percent. The number of people who are black or partly black increased even faster: 6.4 million, or 21.5 percent from 1990–2000.

Most black Americans (51.8 percent of the black-only population) continue to live in the South, where they made up 18.1 percent of the population in 2008. Blacks constituted 12.5 percent of the population in the Midwest, 10.8 percent in the Northeast, and just 5.3 percent in the West (up from 4.9 in 2000). The black population of the U.S.

Resident Population of States by Race and Hispanic Origin, 2008

State	Total population	White	Black or African American	American Indian & Alaska Native	Asian	Native Hawaiian	Two or more races	Hispanic or Latino origin
United States	304,059,724	79.8%	12.8%	1.0%	4.5%	0.2%	0.2%	15.4%
Alabama	4,661,900	71.0	26.4	0.5	1.0	0.0	1.1	2.9
Alaska	686,293	70.6	4.3	15.3	4.5	0.7	4.6	6.1
Arizona	6,500,180	86.5	4.2	4.9	2.5	0.2	2.0	30.1
Arkansas	2,855,390	80.1	15.7	0.9	1.1	0.1	1.4	5.6
California	36,756,666	76.6	6.7	1.2	12.5	0.4	2.6	36.6
Colorado	4,939,456	89.7	4.3	1.2	2.7	0.2	2.0	20.2
Connecticut	3,501,252	84.3	10.3	0.4	3.5	0.1	1.5	12.0
Delaware	873,092	74.3	21.0	0.4	2.9	0.1	1.4	6.8
District of Columbia	591,833	40.1	54.4	0.4	3.4	0.1	1.6	8.6
Florida	18,328,340	79.8	15.9	0.5	2.3	0.1	1.4	21.0
Georgia	9,685,744	65.4	30.0	0.4	2.9	0.1	1.3	8.0
Hawaii	1,288,198	29.7	3.1	0.6	39.3	9.1	18.3	8.7
Idaho	1,523,816	94.6	1.0	1.5	1.1	0.1	1.7	10.2
Illinois	12,901,563	79.1	14.9	0.3	4.3	0.1	1.2	15.2
Indiana	6,376,792	88.0	9.1	0.3	1.4	0.0	1.2	5.2
Iowa	3,002,555	94.2	2.7	0.4	1.6	0.0	1.1	4.2
Kansas	2,802,134	88.7	6.2	1.0	2.2	0.1	1.8	9.1
Kentucky	4,269,245	89.9	7.7	0.3	1.0	0.0	1.1	2.4
Louisiana	4,410,796	64.8	32.0	0.6	1.4	0.0	1.1	3.4
Maine	1,316,456	96.4	1.0	0.6	0.9	0.0	1.1	1.3
Maryland	5,633,597	63.4	29.4	0.4	5.1	0.0	1.6	6.7
Massachusetts	6,497,967	86.2	7.0	0.3	4.9	0.1	1.4	8.6
Michigan	10,003,422	81.2	14.2	0.6	2.4	0.0	1.5	4.1
Minnesota	5,220,393	89.0	4.6	1.2	3.5	0.1	1.5	4.1
Mississippi	2,938,618	60.1	37.2	0.5	0.8	0.0	0.9	2.2
Missouri	5,911,605	85.0	11.5	0.5	1.5	0.1	1.4	3.2
Montana	967,440	90.5	0.7	6.4	0.6	0.0	1.7	3.0
Nebraska	1,783,432	91.4	4.5	1.1	1.7	0.1	1.3	7.9
Nevada	2,600,167	80.9	8.1	1.5	6.2	0.5	2.8	25.7
New Hampshire	1,315,809	95.5	1.2	0.3	1.9	0.0	1.1	2.6
New Jersey	8,682,661	76.0	14.5	0.3	7.7	0.1	1.4	16.3
New Mexico	1,984,356	84.0	3.0	9.7	1.4	0.1	1.8	44.9
New York	19,490,297	73.4	17.3	0.6	7.0	0.1	1.6	16.7
North Carolina	9,222,414	73.9	21.6	1.3	1.9	0.1	1.2	7.4
North Dakota	641,481	91.4	1.1	5.6	0.7	0.1	1.2	2.1
Ohio	11,485,910	84.8	12.0	0.3	1.6	0.0	1.3	2.6
Oklahoma	3,642,361	78.1	8.0	8.0	1.7	0.1	4.1	7.6
Oregon	3,790,060	90.1	2.0	1.4	3.6	0.3	2.5	11.0
Pennsylvania	12,448,279	85.4	10.8	0.2	2.4	0.0	1.1	4.8
Rhode Island	1,050,788	88.5	6.4	0.6	2.8	0.1	1.6	11.6
South Carolina	4,479,800	68.7	28.5	0.4	1.2	0.1	1.1	4.1
South Dakota	804,194	88.2	1.1	8.5	0.7	0.1	1.4	2.6
Tennessee	6,214,888	80.4	16.8	0.3	1.3	0.1	1.1	3.7
Texas	24,326,974	82.4	11.9	0.8	3.5	0.1	1.3	36.5
Utah	2,736,424	92.9	1.3	1.4	2.0	0.8	1.7	12.0
Vermont	621,270	96.4	0.9	0.4	1.1	0.0	1.2	1.4
Virginia	7,769,089	73.0	19.9	0.4	4.9	0.1	1.7	6.8
Washington	6,549,224	84.3	3.7	1.7	6.7	0.5	3.1	9.8
West Virginia	1,814,468	94.5	3.6	0.2	0.7	0.0	1.0	1.1
Wisconsin	5,627,967	89.7	6.1	1.0	2.0	0.0	1.2	5.1
Wyoming	532,668	93.9	1.3	2.5	0.7	0.1	1.5	7.7

Note: Persons of Hispanic origin may be of any race. Source: U.S. Census Bureau.

remains highly concentrated. The 10 states with the largest number of blacks (see the accompanying table) had 59 percent of all blacks in America (but only 51 percent of the total U.S. population). Blacks constituted more than 50 percent of the population in 90 counties; all of these counties were in the South and all of them were nonmetropolitan counties (with the exceptions of Baltimore City and Prince George's County, Md.; Orleans Parish, La.; Shelby County, Tenn.; and Clayton and DeKalb Counties, Ga.). New York and Chicago alone accounted for 8 percent of the total black population. Among places with 100,000 or more in population, Gary, Ind. had the highest percentage of blacks, with 84 percent, followed by Detroit, Mich., which was 83 percent black.

Significant differences between the races also exist in other demographic categories, most notably in the high rates of divorce and single-motherhood for blacks. Of the total number of American families with children, 18.5 percent are headed by women without a spouse present, compared to 54 percent of black families with children headed by a woman without a spouse present. Over 12 percent of the black population 18 and over is divorced, compared to 10.4 percent of the total 18 and over population.

(See also "The U.S. Economy" for information about black employment, income, wealth and poverty.)

▶THE HISPANIC POPULATION

The term Hispanic refers to people of Spanish or Latin American origin. American Hispanics are of diverse backgrounds. The vast majority trace their roots to Mexico (64 percent), and then Puerto Rico (9 percent), Cuba, Dominican Republic, and El Salvador with roughly 3 percent each. A mere 0.3 percent of Hispanic-Americans are from Spain. Roughly half of the nation's Dominicans live in New York City, while about half the nation's Cubans live in Miami-Dade County, Florida. In addition to Hispanics living in the U.S., there are approximately 4 million residents of Puerto Rico, a U.S. territory. (In recent years, the flow of Puerto Ricans to U.S. cities has been reversed, with more Puerto Ricans emigrating from the mainland than the island than the other way around.)

Contrary to popular opinion, Spanish-speaking countries are not culturally homogeneous, but varied and complex. They incorporate Spanish and other European influences, as well as Indian and African traits. In the Caribbean area, Panama, and the coasts of Venezuela, Colombia, Ecuador and sections of Peru, African culture has left a strong legacy. In Mexico, most of Central America and the Andean countries, diverse Indian cultures have had a major impact. Latin-American society varies greatly according to social class and vast differences exist between urban and rural areas. Since American Hispanics come from different countries and social backgrounds, they do not compose a uniform, cohesive population group.

U.S. Hispanics are of many races. In some areas, intermingling has made it impossible to distinguish one race from another, but in others, races are clearly defined. In Argentina, for example, there is a

Ten States With Largest Black Populations, 2008

	Black only		Black only or in combination with other race(s)[1]	
Rank, State	Number	Percent	Number	Percent
1. New York	3,362,736	17.3%	3,520,002	18.2%
2. Florida	2,916,174	15.9	3,009,773	16.5
3. Georgia	2,907,944	30.0	2,923,725	30.6
4. Texas	2,898,143	11.9	2,971,494	12.4
5. California	2,451,453	6.7	2,718,070	7.4
6. North Carolina	1,991,654	21.6	2,021,579	22.3
7. Illinois	1,919,701	14.9	1,999,258	15.6
8. Maryland	1,658,422	29.4	1,705,996	30.4
9. Virginia	1,546,444	19.9	1,599,430	20.7
10. Louisiana	1,410,457	32.0	1,517,854	15.1

Note: States ranked by Black-only population. 1. Data is for 2007. **Source:** U.S. Census Bureau.

Ten States with Highest Percentage of Black Population, 2008

	Total	Black only		Black only or in combination with other race(s)[1]	
Rank, State[2]	Population	Number	Percent	Number	Percent
1. Mississippi	2,938,618	1,092,588	37.2%	1,098,181	37.6%
2. Louisiana	4,410,796	1,410,457	32.0	1,388,217	32.7
3. Georgia	9,685,744	2,907,944	30.0	2,923,725	30.6
4. Maryland	5,633,597	1,658,422	29.4	1,705,996	30.4
5. South Carolina	4,479,800	1,275,815	28.5	1,289,010	29.2
6. Alabama	4,661,900	1,229,787	26.4	1,242,344	26.8
7. North Carolina	9,222,414	1,991,654	21.7	2,021,579	22.3
8. Delaware	873,092	182,890	21.0	187,929	21.7
9. Virginia	7,769,089	1,546,444	19.9	1,599,430	20.7
10. New York	19,490,297	3,362,736	17.3	3,520,002	18.2

Notes: States ranked by Black-only population. 1. Data is for 2007. 2. Washington D.C. is 54.4 percent black. (Black population: 322,021; Total population: 591,833). **Source:** U.S. Census Bureau.

Black Population of the U.S., 1790–2008

Year	Number ('000s)	Percent of total population	Year	Number ('000s)	Percent of total population	Year	Number ('000s)	Percent of total population
1790	757	19.3%	1920	10,463	9.9%	1995	33,116	12.6%
1800	1,002	18.9	1930	11,891	9.7	1998	34,427	12.7
1850	3,639	15.7	1940	12,866	9.8	2000[2]	36,419	12.9
1860	4,442	14.1	1950	15,042	10.0	2002[2]	38,248	13.3
1870	4,880	12.7	1960[1]	18,872	10.5	2004[2]	39,204	13.4
1880	6,581	13.1	1970	22,581	11.1	2005[2]	39,718	13.4
1890	7,489	11.9	1980	26,683	11.8	2006[2]	40,241	13.4
1900	8,834	11.6	1985	28,994	12.1	2007[2]	40,744	13.5
1910	9,828	10.7	1990	30,517	12.3	2008[2]	39,059	12.8

Notes: Decennial census figures are as of April 1. Figures for 1998 & 2001–06 are as of July 1. 1. Includes Alaska and Hawaii for first time. 2. Figures are only for "Black only or in combination of other race" after 2000.   **Source:** U.S. Census Bureau, *The Black Population 2000.* (2001); Annual Population Estimates (2009).

Black Population in the Largest U.S. Cities, 2000

City	Total Population		Black-only population			Black only or in combination with other race(s) population		
	Rank	Number	Rank	Number	Percent black	Rank	Number	Percent black
New York, N.Y.	1	8,008,278	1	2,129,762	26.6%	1	2,274,049	28.4%
Los Angeles, Calif.	2	3,694,820	7	415,195	11.2	6	444,635	12.0
Chicago, Ill.	3	2,896,016	2	1,065,009	36.8	2	1,084,221	37.4
Houston, Texas	4	1,953,631	5	494,496	25.3	5	505,101	25.9
Philadelphia, Pa.	5	1,517,550	4	655,824	43.2	4	672,162	44.3
Phoenix, Ariz.	6	1,321,045	60	67,416	5.1	53	76,065	5.8
San Diego, Calif.	7	1,223,400	36	96,216	7.9	32	109,470	8.9
Dallas, Texas	8	1,188,580	11	307,957	25.9	11	314,678	26.5
San Antonio, Texas	9	1,144,646	48	78,120	6.8	45	84,250	7.4
Detroit, Mich.	10	951,270	3	775,772	81.6	3	787,687	82.8
Baltimore, Md.	17	651,154	6	418,951	64.3	7	424,449	65.2
Memphis, Tenn.	18	650,100	8	399,208	61.4	8	402,367	61.9
Washington, D.C.	21	572,059	9	343,312	60.0	9	350,455	61.3
New Orleans, La.	31	484,674	10	325,947	67.3	10	329,171	67.9

Source: U.S. Census Bureau, *The Black Population 2000* (2001).

Black Population of Metropolitan Areas, 2000

Metropolitan Areas with Largest Black Population	Percent	Number
1. New York–Northern New Jersey–Long Island, NY–NJ–CT–PA CMSA	17.2%	3,646,377
2. Washington–Baltimore, DC–MD–VA–WV CMSA	26.2	1,993,314
3. Chicago–Gary–Kenosha, IL–IN–WI CMSA	18.6	1,703,302
4. Los Angeles–Riverside–Orange County, CA CMSA	7.6	1,244,397
5. Philadelphia–Wilmington–Atlantic City, PA–NJ–DE–MD CMSA	19.6	1,212,939
6. Atlanta, GA MSA	28.9	1,188,425
7. Detroit–Ann Arbor–Flint, MI CMSA	21.1	1,151,306
8. Miami–Fort Lauderdale, FL CMSA	20.4	790,782
9. Houston–Galveston–Brazoria, TX CMSA	16.9	789,158
10. Dallas–Fort Worth, TX CMSA	13.8	720,609

Metropolitan Areas with Highest Percentage Black Population	Percent	Number
1. Albany, GA MSA	51.0%	61,619
2. Pine Bluff, AR MSA	49.6	41,802
3. Sumter, SC MSA	46.7	48,870
4. Jackson, MS MSA	45.6	201,005
5. Memphis, TN–AR–MS MSA	43.4	492,856
6. Rocky Mount, NC MSA	43.1	61,644
7. Columbus, GA–AL MSA	40.4	110,948
8. Florence, SC MSA	39.3	49,424
9. Montgomery, AL MSA	38.9	129,558
10. New Orleans, LA MSA	37.5	501,647

Note: Figures are for people identifying their race as black only; data on people identifying themselves as black and one or more other races is not available. **Source:** U.S. Census Bureau.

white majority of 97 percent—mostly of Italian, German, Spanish, or English extraction. Cuba, the Dominican Republic, Panama, Venezuela, and areas of Colombia, Ecuador and Peru all have significant black populations. In Bolivia, about one-half of the population is Indian and a third is mestizo (of mixed white and Indian ancestry). Both Peru and Cuba have concentrations of persons of Chinese ancestry, and Peru has a growing Japanese population. In Mexico, birthplace of the majority of Hispanic-Americans, about 60 percent of the population is mestizo, 30 percent is Indian, and 9 percent is white.

Despite their diversity, the Hispanic peoples are united by many factors, among them language, religion, customs, and attitudes toward self, family and society. In the United States, these factors vary in importance according to the degree to which an individual has assimilated into the mainstream. For example, although language has traditionally been an important unifying factor, large numbers of second-generation Hispanics are English-dominant. About 90 percent of U.S. Hispanics speak English, but 78 percent of American Hispanics five years old and older spoke Spanish at home in 2006. Nearly 35 million U.S. residents speak Spanish at home.

Growth of the Hispanic population

The Hispanic population is the fastest-growing segment of the U.S. population. Between 1980 and 2008, the number of Hispanics more than tripled, from 14.6 million to 46.9 million, according to the Census Bureau. According to numbers from the 2000 Census, the Hispanic population for the first time outnumbered the black-alone population (35.3 million to 34.7 million), although blacks alone or in combination with other races outnumbered Hispanics by just over one million. By July 2005, however, the total number of Hispanics of any race had increased to 42.7 million, finally exceeding the number of blacks alone or in combination with other races,

and officially becoming the largest minority population in the United States. Hispanics currently represent over 15 percent of the U.S. population.

The Hispanic population increased by 57.9 percent overall between 1990 and 2000. Mexicans increased by 52.9 percent, Puerto Ricans increased by 24.9 percent, and Cubans increased by 18.9 percent. The "other Hispanic" category, which includes people from Spain, people from all other Spanish-speaking countries in Latin America, and people who did not specify a detailed origin beyond "Hispanic," was the fastest-growing group of Hispanics, increasing by 96.9 percent.

The rapid growth of the Hispanic population is due primarily to immigration. For example, the number of people of Mexican background living in the U.S. more than doubled between 1980 and 1990, due in large part to the Immigration and Reform Control Act of 1986, which allowed immigrants living illegally in the United States to obtain legal U.S. citizenship. In 2008, 38 percent of the Hispanic population in the United States was foreign born. (See "Immigration" for more information about the foreign born.) Hispanics also have higher fertility rates than do the non-Hispanic population. In 2007, the overall fertility rate per 100,000 women aged 15–44 was 69.5, but for Hispanic women it was 102. The birth rate per 1,000 women for Hispanic teenagers was also almost twice that of all American teenagers in 2007.

Nearly half of all Hispanics lived in one of two states in 2008: California and Texas. Hispanics represented 28.4 percent of the population in the West; they constituted more than 30 percent of the populations of Arizona, California, New Mexico and Texas. Mexicans were the biggest component of Hispanic populations in the South and West, but there were fewer than half a million Mexicans in the Northeast. The majority of Hispanics in the Northeast were of Puerto Rican origin. Over a million Puerto Ricans lived in New York alone; another half million lived in New Jersey and Connecticut.

Hispanic Population of Metropolitan Areas, 2000

Metropolitan Areas with Largest Hispanic Population	Percent	Number
1. Los Angeles–Riverside–Orange County, CA CMSA	40.3%	6,598,578
2. New York–Northern New Jersey–Long Island, NY–NJ–CT–PA CMSA	18.2	3,858,375
3. Miami–Fort Lauderdale, FL CMSA	40.3	1,562,181
4. Chicago–Gary–Kenosha, IL–IN–WI CMSA	16.4	1,501,836
5. San Francisco–Oakland–San Jose, CA CMSA	19.7	1,386,754
6. Houston–Galveston–Brazoria, TX CMSA	28.9	1,349,506
7. Dallas–Fort Worth, TX CMSA	21.5	1,122,687
8. Phoenix–Mesa, AZ MSA	25.1	816,220
9. San Antonio, TX MSA	51.2	815,300
10. San Diego, CA MSA	26.7	751,293

Metropolitan Areas with Highest Percentage Hispanic Population	Percent	Number
1. Laredo, TX MSA	94.3%	182,109
2. McAllen–Edinburg–Mission, TX MSA	88.3	502,835
3. Brownsville–Harlingen–San Benito, TX MSA	84.3	282,596
4. El Paso, TX MSA	78.2	531,464
5. Las Cruces, NM MSA	63.4	110,748
6. Corpus Christi, TX MSA	54.7	208,288
7. San Antonio, TX MSA	51.2	815,300
8. Visalia–Tulare–Porterville, CA MSA	50.8	186,954
9. Yuma, AZ MSA	50.5	80,813
10. Salinas, CA MSA	46.8	188,024

Source: U.S. Census Bureau.

Hispanic Population in the Largest U.S. Cities, 2000

City	Total population		Hispanic population		
	Rank	Number	Rank	Number	Percent Hispanic
New York, N.Y.	1	8,008,278	1	2,160,554	27.0%
Los Angeles, Calif.	2	3,694,820	2	1,719,073	46.5
Chicago, Ill.	3	2,896,016	3	753,644	26.0
Houston, Texas	4	1,953,631	4	730,865	37.4
Philadelphia, Pa.	5	1,517,550	24	128,928	8.5
Phoenix, Ariz.	6	1,321,045	6	449,972	34.1
San Diego, Calif.	7	1,223,400	9	310,752	25.4
Dallas, Texas	8	1,188,580	8	422,587	35.6
San Antonio, Texas	9	1,144,646	5	671,394	58.7
Detroit, Mich.	10	951,270	72	47,167	5.0
El Paso, Texas	23	563,662	7	431,875	76.6
San Jose, Calif.	11	894,943	10	269,989	30.2

Source: U.S. Census Bureau, *The Hispanic Population 2000* (2001).

Resident Hispanic Population by Region and Origin, 2000

	Total, U.S.	Northeast		Midwest		South		West	
	Number	Number	Percent	Number	Percent	Number	Percent	Number	Percent
All Hispanics	35,305,818	5,254,087	14.9%	3,124,532	8.8%	11,586,696	32.8%	15,340,503	43.4%
Mexican	20,640,711	479,169	2.3	2,200,196	10.7	6,548,081	31.7	11,413,265	55.3
Puerto Rican	3,406,178	2,074,574	60.9	325,363	9.6	759,305	22.3	246,936	7.2
Cuban	1,241,685	168,959	13.6	45,305	3.6	921,427	74.2	105,994	8.5
Other Hispanic	10,017,244	2,531,385	25.3	553,668	5.5	3,357,883	33.5	3,574,308	35.7

Source: U.S. Census Bureau, *The Hispanic Population 2000* (2001).

The vast majority of Cubans (67 percent) lived in Florida, where they represented 5.2 percent of the entire state population. The heaviest concentration of Hispanics in the U.S. is the area of East Los Angeles, Calif., where 120,307 of the 124,283 residents (96.8 percent) are Hispanic. Laredo, Texas, is close behind, with a population that is 94.1 percent Hispanic.

►**THE ASIAN AND NATIVE HAWAIIAN/ PACIFIC ISLANDER POPULATION**

In 1970 the Census Bureau counted about 1.5 million Asians and Pacific Islanders living in the U.S. By the 1980 census that figure had more than doubled to 3.4 million, thanks in large part to the more than 400,000 Southeast Asian refugees who came to America between 1975–80 under the Refugee Resettlement Program. By the 1990 Census, their numbers had doubled yet again, with Koreans and Vietnamese responsible for the majority of the increase.

The 2000 Census was the first to consider Native Hawaiians and Other Pacific Islanders (Guamanians, Chamorros and Samoans) separately from Asians. In 2008, a total of 562,121 people identified themselves as Native Hawaiian and Other Pacific Islander alone. In 2008, surprisingly, California had the highest Hawaiian Native and other Pacific Islander population (157,112) followed by Hawaii (117,004), and Washington (31,822). Hawaii, however, had the highest percent of population who identified as Native Hawaiian or Pacific Islander alone (not in addition to any other race) at 9.1 percent, followed by Utah and 0.8 percent and Alaska at 0.7 percent.

States With Largest Hispanic Population, 2008

State	Hispanic population	Total population	Percentage Hispanic
1. California	13,457,397	36,756,666	36.6%
2. Texas	8,870,475	24,326,974	36.5
3. Florida	3,845,069	18,328,346	21.0
4. New York	3,250,038	19,490,297	8.0
5. Illinois	1,967,121	12,901,563	15.2
6. Arizona	1,955,630	6,500,180	30.1
7. New Jersey	1,418,545	8,682,661	16.3
9. Colorado	997,062	4,939,456	20.2
8. New Mexico	891,013	1,984,356	44.9
10. Georgia	777,244	9,685,744	8.0

Note: Ranked by number of Hispanics. Nevada, which is 25.7 percent Hispanic, is ranked fifth by percentage with 668,527 Hispanics. **Source:** U.S. Census Bureau

Contrast that with the Asian population: 13,549,064 people said they were Asian in 2008. The Asian population grew 3.0 percent between 2006 and 2008 (389,721). Chinese are still the largest group of Asians in the U.S., followed closely by Filipinos and Japanese.

►**THE AMERICAN INDIAN AND ALASKA NATIVE POPULATION**

This race was known as the American Indian, Eskimo, and Aleut population for the 1990 Census, which reported a total of 1,959,234 American Indians living in the United States (of these, 85,698 were Eskimos and Aleuts, a.k.a. Alaska Natives). After the 2000 Census, the definition was changed to encompass anyone having origins in any of the native peoples of North and South America, and who maintain community or tribal attachment. According to population estimates for 2008, 3,083,434 people identify themselves as American Indian or Alaska Native. In the 2000 census, the division was broken into tribe affiliation as well—the most populous being Cherokee (729,533), followed by Navajo (298,197) and Latin American Indian (180,940).

Not surprisingly, in 2008 the state with the greatest percentage of American Indians and Alaska natives is Alaska, where people of this race constitute 15.3 percent of the population. New Mexico is second, with 9.7 percent, followed by South Dakota (8.5 percent) and Oklahoma (8.0 percent). The state with the most American Indians and Alaska Natives is California (443,719). Arizona is second, with 315,727, Oklahoma is third, with 291,390, and New Mexico is fourth, with 192,235. Washington, which had 102,940 Native Americans and Alaska Natives in 1990, saw this population drop to 93,301 for the 2000 Census, but because of the revised defintion, the number climbed to 112,965 in 2008. Meanwhile, the American Indian and Alaska Native population of Texas grew from 118,362 in 2000 to 184,649 in 2008. In 2000, almost half of all American Indians

States With Largest American Indian or Alaska Native Population, 2008

Rank, State	Total Population	American Indian or Alaska Native only		American Indian or Alaska Native only or in combination with other race(s)[1]	
		Number	Percent	Number	Percent
1. California	36,756,666	443,719	1.2%	689,120	1.9%
2. Arizona	6,500,180	315,727	4.9	335,381	5.3
3. Oklahoma	3,642,361	291,390	8.0	393,500	10.9
4. New Mexico	1,984,356	192,235	9.7	203,047	10.3
5. Texas	24,326,974	184,649	0.8	277,368	1.2
6. North Carolina	9,222,414	115,635	1.3	146,108	1.6
7. Washington	6,549,224	112,965	1.7	166,026	2.6
8. New York	19,490,297	111,337	0.6	189,601	1.0
9. Alaska	686,293	104,990	15.3	121,560	17.8
10. Florida	18,328,340	91,412	0.5	157,302	0.9

Note: Ranked by American Indian or Alaska Native only population. 1. Data is for 2007. **Source:** U.S. Census Bureau.

Ten Cities With Largest Asian Population, 2000

Rank, State	Total Population	Asian only		Asian only or in combination with other race(s)	
		Number	Percent	Number	Percent
1. New York City	8,008,278	787,047	9.8%	872,777	10.9%
2. Los Angeles	3,694,820	369,254	10.0	407,444	11.0
3. San Jose	894,943	240,375	26.9	257,571	28.8
4. San Francisco	776,733	239,565	30.8	253,477	32.6
5. Honolulu	371,657	207,588	55.9	251,686	67.7
6. San Diego	1,223,400	166,968	13.6	189,413	15.5
7. Chicago	2,896,016	125,974	4.3	140,517	4.9
8. Houston	1,953,631	103,694	5.3	114,140	5.8
9. Fremont, Ca.	203,413	75,165	37.0	80,979	39.8
10. Seattle	563,374	73,910	13.1	84,649	15.0

Note: Ranked by number of Asian only population. Seattle ranks 9th when states are ranked by number of Asians only or Asians in combination with other races. **Source:** U.S. Census Bureau.

Ten States With Largest Asian Population, 2008

Rank, State	Total Population	Asian only		Asian only or in combination with other race(s)[1]	
		Number	Percent	Number	Percent
1. California	36,756,666	4,581,890	12.5%	5,008,379	13.7%
2. New York	19,490,297	1,368,585	7.0	1,443,367	7.5
3. Texas	24,326,974	841,016	3.5	915,201	3.8
4. New Jersey	8,682,661	664,251	7.7	695,118	8.0
5. Illinois	12,901,563	558,933	4.3	602,374	4.7
6. Hawaii	1,288,198	506,159	39.3	705,106	54.9
7. Washington	6,549,224	437,783	6.7	517,057	8.0
8. Florida	18,328,340	416,318	2.3	494,925	2.7
9. Virginia	7,769,089	378,226	4.9	422,802	5.5
10. Massachusetts	6,497,967	321,130	4.9	341,781	5.3

Note: Ranked by number of Asian only population. 1. Data is for 2007. **Source:** U.S. Census Bureau.

and Alaska Natives (1.2 million) reported living in the West, while only 162,558 American Indians and Alaska Natives lived in the Northeast.

There are 564 federally recognized Indian tribes in the U.S. and 326 federally identified areas associated with them, including reservations, which the federal government recognizes as territory in which American Indian tribes have jurisdiction, and "trust lands," which are held in trust by the federal government but consist of property associated with a particular tribe or reservation. Approximately 56.2 million acres are held in trust by the U.S. for various Indian tribes and individuals. The largest is the 16

million acre Navajo Nation Reservation in Arizona, New Mexico, and Utah. The Bureau of Indian Affairs counted approximately 310 reservations in 2008, up from 304 in 2006. Of the 2.4 million people who identified their race as American Indian or Alaska Native alone in the 2000 Census, the two tribes with the largest populations by far were the Cherokee (281,069) and the Navajo (269,202), followed at some distance by Canadian and Latin American Indians (108,802) and the Sioux (108,272) and Chippewa (105,907) tribes. 103,174 people identified themselves as American Indian alone without specifying a tribe.

U.S. POPULATION BY AGE AND SEX

▶ THE POPULATION BY AGE

With birth rates and fertility rates declining rapidly since 1965 it should come as no surprise that the average age of the U.S. population has been increasing almost as quickly. It will continue to rise for the foreseeable future in part because of the aging members of the baby boom generation.

During the Baby Boom years of the 1950s and 1960s, the median age of the population actually declined, the only time it has done so. Since then, however, the steady decline in the percentage of young people, especially those under 18 years of age, (from 34.1 percent in 1970 to 24.3 percent in 2008) combined with the increase of those between 25 and 44 (they were 23.6 percent of the population in 1970, but 27.4 percent in 2008) has driven the median age from 28.0 in 1970 to an estimated 34.1 percent in 2000. A five-year increase in 20 years is unprecedented in U.S. history, but what is more revealing is that we will most likely duplicate that feat over the next 20 years. The estimated median age of the U.S. population had already increased to 36.8 in 2010.

The other major factor in the so-called "graying of America" is the increased life expectancy for older

people. In 1950, the over-65 population totaled 7 percent of all Americans and numbered 9 million. In 2008, 38.9 million Americans (12.8 percent of the population) were over 65; this represents a 332 percent increase since 1958 and a more than 1,000 percent increase since 1900.

As the population ages, 65 no longer seems old to most people, especially when millions more people are living past the age of 80. There were 7 million people 80 or older in 1990, 3 million age 85 or older, nearly a million 90 years or older, and 36,000 people over the age of 100. By 2008, there were 5.7 million age 85 or more.

Over the first decade of the 21st century, the over-65 population will grow another 13–14 percent—but between 2010 and 2030 the over-65 population will nearly double as the baby boom generation finally becomes senior citizens. In the year 2030, an estimated 20 percent of the population, or 70 million Americans, will be 65 years old or older.

Florida, and to a lesser degree, Pennsylvania, have long had the highest concentrations of retirees, but in the 1990s, several states saw dramatic growth in their over-65 population. Nevada's senior population grew by 55 percent between 1990 and 2000, while Alaska's increased 49 percent and Arizona's jumped 29 percent. Hawaii experienced 27 percent growth, Utah saw a 22 percent increase, and Colorado and New Mexico both had increases of 21 percent.

Number of Persons and Percent of Total Population, by Age Group, 1960–2050 (numbers in thousands)

Age in Years	1960	1970	1980	1990	2000	2010	2050
Under 5	20,341	17,166	16,458	18,765	19,176	20,099	26,914
percent	11.3%	8.4%	7.2%	7.5%	6.8%	6.7%	6.7%
5–13	32,965	36,672	31,095	31,839	37,025	35,321	47,582
percent	18.2	17.9	13.7	12.8	13.2	11.8	11.8
14–17	11,219	15,924	16,142	13,345	16,093	16,681	21,252
percent	6.2	7.8	7.1	5.4	5.7	5.6	5.3
18–24	16,128	24,712	30,350	26,961	27,143	30,163	36,804
percent	8.9	12.1	13.3	10.8	9.6	10.1	9.1
25–34	22,919	25,323	37,626	43,174	39,891	38,851	50,458
percent	12.7	12.3	16.5	17.4	14.2	13.0	12.5
35–44	24,221	23,150	25,868	37,444	45,149	39,443	49,588
percent	13.4	11.3	11.4	15.1	16.0	13.2	12.3
45–64	36,203	41,999	44,515	46,178	61,902	81,590	89,089
percent	20.0	20.5	19.5	18.6	22.0	27.2	22.1
65 & over	16,675	20,107	25,704	31,084	34,992	39,715	81,999
percent	9.2	9.8	11.3	12.5	12.4	13.2	20.3
85 & over	940	1,430	2,269	3,022	4,240	5,786	19,352
percent	0.5	0.7	1.0	1.2	1.5	1.9	4.8
100 & over	3	5	15	N.A.	N.A.	129	1,095
percent	N.A.	N.A.	N.A.	N.A.	N.A.	N.A.	0.3
Total U.S. population	**180,671**	**205,052**	**227,757**	**248,791**	**281,422**	**299,862**	**403,687**
Median age	**29.4**	**27.9**	**30.0**	**32.8**	**35.3**	**37.4**	**38.8**

Note: Figures for 2010 and after are the projections the Census Bureau calls the "middle" or "most likely" series.   **Source:** U.S. Census Bureau, *Projections of the Population of the U.S., by Age, Sex, and Race: 1995 to 2050* (2002).

Resident Population of States, by Age, 2010 (in thousands)

State	Total	Under 18 Years	18–44 Years	45–64 Years	65–74 Years	75 Years+
Alabama	4,596	1,092	1,605	1,251	354	295
Alaska	694	184	270	184	35	21
Arizona	6,637	1,688	2,349	1,678	516	406
Arkansas	2,875	703	996	765	227	185
California	38,067	9,497	14,787	9,391	2,333	2,060
Colorado	4,832	1,189	1,863	1,263	282	235
Connecticut	3,577	814	1,257	990	253	262
Delaware	884	202	309	249	68	57
D.C.	530	114	237	118	32	29
Florida	19,252	4,086	6,315	5,431	1,773	1,646
Georgia	9,589	2,502	3,274	2,382	564	417
Hawaii	1,341	316	477	357	101	90
Idaho	1,517	400	554	381	99	82
Illinois	12,917	3,197	4,842	3,277	826	774
Indiana	6,392	1,596	2,328	1,656	425	386
Iowa	3,010	711	1,049	800	217	233
Kansas	2,805	699	1,004	727	185	190
Kentucky	4,265	1,002	1,540	1,165	309	249
Louisiana	4,613	1,172	1,665	1,194	313	270
Maine	1,357	269	462	413	110	102
Maryland	5,905	1,406	2,212	1,568	386	332
Massachusetts	6,649	1,484	2,440	1,817	454	454
Michigan	10,429	2,487	3,822	2,785	699	635
Minnesota	5,421	1,290	2,027	1,433	343	327
Mississippi	2,971	759	1,052	781	209	170
Missouri	5,922	1,411	2,111	1,578	432	390
Montana	969	212	324	287	77	68
Nebraska	1,769	446	619	460	119	125
Nevada	2,691	665	961	735	199	131
New Hampshire	1,386	304	494	408	97	82
New Jersey	9,018	2,088	3,252	2,446	632	600
New Mexico	1,980	479	669	553	153	126
New York	19,444	4,421	7,227	5,144	1,346	1,306
North Carolina	9,346	2,269	3,471	2,445	641	520
North Dakota	637	142	223	174	46	51
Ohio	11,576	2,744	4,123	3,121	816	771
Oklahoma	3,592	895	1,264	938	266	229
Oregon	3,791	863	1,412	1,022	263	231
Pennsylvania	12,584	2,748	4,385	3,496	960	997
Rhode Island	1,117	249	410	300	76	82
South Carolina	4,447	1,036	1,579	1,226	343	263
South Dakota	786	194	269	209	55	60
Tennessee	6,231	1,479	2,249	1,673	461	368
Texas	24,649	6,785	9,417	5,859	1,426	1,162
Utah	2,595	819	1,021	520	127	108
Vermont	653	132	232	195	50	43
Virginia	8,010	1,880	2,997	2,139	554	441
Washington	6,542	1,488	2,481	1,777	429	367
West Virginia	1,829	382	618	536	156	136
Wisconsin	5,727	1,319	2,076	1,561	392	380
Wyoming	520	116	177	154	40	33

Note: Data is projected. Source: Population Division, U.S. Census Bureau, (as of May 14, 2010).

►THE POPULATION BY SEX

The Census Bureau estimates that in 2008, there were 44.7 million men and 51.2 million women 15 years and over who had never married or who were currently widowed, separated, or divorced—a ratio of 87.3 unmarried men per 100 unmarried women. The popular interpretation of these figures—that there is a shortage of eligible men—fails to consider that women are more likely to live longer (and so be counted among the widowed) and less likely to remarry after a divorce. In fact, the surplus of women can be entirely attributed to the fact that there are over 2 million more widows than widowers over the age of 65. But during the peak marrying ages, never-married men actually outnumber never-married women: among persons between the ages of 18 and 24 there were 111.4 never-married men for every 100 never-married women; in the 25-to-34 age group, there were 132.9 men for every 100 women. In fact, in 2008, there were more never-married men than never-married women in all age categories until the 65-to-74 years old delineation, when there were 89.9 men for every 100 women.

Growth of the Over-65 Population, 1900–2050

| Year | Population 65 and over | | Population 85 and over | |
	Number ('000s)	Percent of total population	Number ('000s)	Percent of total population
1900	3,099	4.1%	N.A.	N.A.
1910	3,986	4.3	N.A.	N.A.
1920	4,929	4.7	N.A.	N.A.
1930	6,705	5.5	N.A.	N.A.
1940	9,031	6.9	N.A.	N.A.
1950	12,397	8.1	N.A.	N.A.
1960	16,675	9.2	940	0.5%
1970	20,107	9.8	1,430	0.7
1980	25,549	11.3	2,269	1.0
1990	31,242	12.5	3,080	1.2
2000	34,992	12.4	4,240	1.5
2010	40,244	13.0	6,123	2.0
2020	54,632	16.3	7,269	2.2
2030	71,453	19.7	9,603	2.6
2040	80,050	20.4	15,409	3.9
2050	86,706	20.7	20,861	5.0

Note: Prior to 1960, the Census Bureau did not count persons over 85 separately. Figures for 2010 through 2050 are Census Bureau projections based on their "most likely" series of estimates. **Source:** U.S. Census Bureau, *Resident Population Projections by Sex and Age: 2005 to 2050.*

VITAL STATISTICS

The National Center for Health Statistics does a month-by-month tracking of four sets of numbers, which both it and the Census Bureau refer to as "vital": births, deaths, marriages, and divorces.

Births An estimated 4.3 million babies were born in the U.S. in 2008, up from 4.06 million in 2000. The crude birth rate (the number of live births per 1,000 total population) increased slightly to 14.2, and the fertility rate (the number of births per 1,000 women aged 15–44) was 69.3.

Deaths An estimated 2.45 million people died in 2008, only slightly higher than the 2.40 million in 2000. The crude death rate held steady at 8.1 per 1,000 population. In 1910, by comparison, the death rate was 14.7. (For infant mortality figures and for more specific information about death rates by cause see the section, "Health and Medicine.")

In 2008 there were 1.86 million more births than deaths; this figure is called the *natural increase,* meaning the growth in population without immigration (which accounted for over 1,856,000 people in 2008).

Marriages An estimated 2.16 million couples married during 2008, markedly down from 2.35 million in 2001; the marriage rate of 7.1 per 1,000 people was the lowest rate recorded in over 40 years. In addition to getting married in fewer numbers, people are getting married at a later age. In 1960, for example, about 40 percent of all 19-year-old women were married, but by 2008 only 4.7 percent of 18 and 19-year-old women were. Also in 1960, about 92 percent of all women were married before they reached age 30, but by 2008 only 29.9 percent were. In 2008, 26.1 percent of 30 to 34-year-olds were never married, up dramatically from less than 6 percent in 1970.

Characteristics of Persons 65 or Older, 2008

Characteristic	Total	Male	Female
Total (millions)	**36.8**	**15.8**	**21.0**
Percent distribution			
Marital status:			
Never married	4.1%	4.2%	4.0%
Married	57.0	74.5	43.9
Spouse present	54.6	71.9	41.7
Spouse absent	2.4	2.6	2.3
Widowed	29.8	13.8	41.9
Divorced	9.1	7.5	10.2
Educational attainment:			
Less than ninth grade	11.2%	11.3%	11.1%
Completed grades 9–12 but no diploma	11.4	10.8	11.8
High school graduate	36.9	32.0	40.5
Some college/associate deg.	20.1	19.2	20.8
Bachelor's/advanced deg.	20.5	26.7	15.8
Labor force participation:			
Employed	16.1%	20.5%	12.7%
Unemployed	0.7	1.0	0.5
Not in labor force	83.2	78.5	86.7
Percent below poverty level	9.7	6.6	12.0

Note: 1. Excludes those living in unrelated subfamilies. **Source:** U.S. Census Bureau, *Statistical Abstract of the United States* (2010).

Divorces The National Center for Health Statistics stopped publishing cumulative numbers of divorces in 2000 because six states no longer report divorce statistics. The latest available year for which data is available is 1998, when an estimated 1.13 million divorces were granted, down slightly from the previous year. The divorce rate per 1,000 population was 3.6 in 2008, its lowest rate in more than 30 years. The divorce rate peaked in 1979 at 5.3 per 1,000 population. (In that year there were 22.8 divorced women for every 1,000 married women, up from 9.2 in 1960. While the divorce rate has declined,

U.S. Population by Sex: Totals and Ratio of Males to Females, 1920–2008

Year	Male ('000s)	Female ('000s)	Males per 100 females			
			All ages	14-24	25-44	65+
1920	53,900	51,810	104.0	97.3	105.1	101.3
1930	62,137	60,638	102.5	98.4	101.8	100.5
1940	66,062	65,608	100.7	98.9	98.5	95.5
1950	74,833	75,864	98.6	98.2	96.4	89.6
1960	88,331	90,992	97.1	98.7	95.7	82.8
1970	98,926	104,309	94.8	98.7	95.5	72.1
1980	110,053	116,493	94.5	101.9	97.4	67.6
1990	122,049	127,875	95.1	104.6	98.9	67.2
2000	138,054	143,368	96.3	105.1	100.2	70.0
2004	144,537	149,118	96.9	105.8	101.4	71.7
2008	149,925	154,135	97.3	105.7	102.4	73.5

Source: U.S. Census Bureau, *Statistical Abstract of the United States* (2010).

Births and Deaths in the U.S., 1910–2008

Year	Live births ('000s)	Birth rate[1]	Deaths[2] ('000s)	Death rate[1]
1910	2,777	30.1	N.A.	14.7
1920	2,950	27.7	N.A.	13.0
1930	2,618	21.3	N.A.	11.3
1940	2,559	19.4	1,417	10.8
1950	3,632	24.1	1,452	9.6
1955	4,097	25.0	1,529	9.3
1960	4,258	23.7	1,712	9.5
1965	3,760	19.5	1,828	9.4
1970	3,731	18.4	1,921	9.5
1975	3,144	14.6	1,893	8.8
1980	3,612	15.9	1,990	8.8
1985	3,761	15.8	2,086	8.8
1990	4,158	16.7	2,148	8.6
1995	3,892	14.8	2,309	8.8
1998	3,946	14.6	2,331	8.6
1999	3,965	14.5	2,396	8.8
2000	4,059	14.7	2,403	8.7
2001	4,026	14.1	2,418	8.5
2002	4,022	13.9	2,438	8.5
2003	4,093	14.0	2,423	8.3
2004	4,121	14.0	2,393	8.1
2005	4,138	14.0	2,421	8.2
2006	4,269	14.3	2,416	8.1
2008	4,305	14.2	2,449	8.1

Notes: 1. Per 1,000 total population. 2. Excludes fetal deaths.
Source: U.S. National Center for Health Statistics, *Vital Statistics of the United States* (2009).

Marriages and Divorces in the U.S., 1920–2008

Year	Marriages ('000s)	Rate per 1,000 population	Divorces ('000s)	Rate per 1,000 population
1920	1,274	12.0	171	1.6
1930	1,127	9.2	196	1.6
1940	1,596	12.1	264	2.0
1950	1,667	11.1	385	2.6
1955	1,531	9.3	377	2.3
1960	1,523	8.5	393	2.2
1965	1,800	9.3	479	2.5
1970	2,163	10.6	708	3.5
1975	2,153	10.0	1,036	4.8
1980	2,390	10.0	1,036	4.8
1985	2,413	10.1	1,190	5.0
1990	2,448	9.8	1,175	4.7
1995	2,336	8.9	1,169	4.4
1997	2,384	8.9	1,163	4.3
1998	2,244	8.4	1,135	4.2
1999	2,358	8.6	N.A.	4.1[1]
2000	2,329	8.5	N.A.	4.2[1]
2001	2,327	8.4	N.A.	4.0[1]
2002	2,254	7.8	N.A.	4.0[2]
2003	2,187	7.5	N.A.	3.8[2]
2004	2,178	7.4	N.A.	3.7[3]
2005	2,203	7.7	N.A.	3.6[4]
2006	2,160	7.3[5]	N.A.	3.6[4]
2008	2,140	7.1[5]	N.A.	3.5[4]

Notes: 1. Divorce rates exclude CA, CO, IN, and LA. 2. Divorce rates exclude CA, HI, IN, LA, and OK. 3. Divorce rates exclude CA, GA, HI, IN, and LA. 4. Divorce rates exclude CA, GA, HI, IN, LA, and MN. 5. Marriage rate excludes LA. **Source**: U.S. National Center for Health Statistics, *Vital Statistics of the United States* (2009).

the ratio of divorced persons to married persons (with spouse present) has skyrocketed. Between 1970 and 2008, the proportion nearly quadrupled, from 47 divorced per 1,000 married to 181 per 1,000. For blacks, the rise was even greater, going from 83 per 1,000 to 302 per 1,000 in the same period.

In 2008, there were 23.3 million currently divorced persons in the U.S., more than 10 percent of the total adult population over 18. There are more divorced women (13.6 million) than men (9.8 million) because women are less likely to remarry.

A 2001 study, the most recent data available, by the National Center for Health Statistics revealed that 43 percent of all first marriages end in separation or divorce within 15 years. One in five ends in the first five years, and one in three ends within 10 years. The report also showed a link between the age of the bride and the duration of a marriage. Fifty-

nine percent of first marriages involving women under 18 ended in separation or divorce within 15 years, compared with 36 percent of marriages where the bride was 20 or older.

▶FERTILITY RATES OF AMERICAN WOMEN

Population experts predict future trends by studying many factors including the crude birth rate (see "Vital Statistics") and the all-important fertility rates. The *general fertility rate* measures the ratio of live births to the total number of women aged 15 to 44. (Until 1990, the Census Bureau had reported based on the number of women 18 to 44, thus projecting a higher fertility rate but discounting the high number of teenage pregnancies.) Declining birth rates in 2008 are linked to an economic recession.

The *total fertility rate* is the number of births 1,000 women aged 10 to 50 would have in their lifetimes if, at each year of age, they experienced the birth rates occurring to women of that age in the specified calendar year. The total fertility rate is sometimes defined in the popular media as the number of *likely* births one woman will have in her lifetime; they do this by dividing by 1,000.

The total fertility rate is most helpful in measuring long-term trends, especially in determining whether or not the nation is sustaining a level of reproduction necessary for maintaining current population levels. That level, generally regarded as 2,100 per 1,000 women, was not achieved in the U.S. from 1971 through 1999, but by 2002 the figure had climbed to 2,013 and was almost steady at 2,123 in 2007.

Fertility rates in 2006 were highest among women in their 20s. The fertility rate for women 20–24 was 105.9, for women 25–29 it was 116.8. American Indian women (62.8) had slightly higher fertility rates overall than non-Hispanic white women (59.5), Asian or Pacific Islander women (67.2), or black women (70.6). Women of Hispanic origin had an overall fertility rate of 101.5.

Birth rate refers to general fertility rate.

One clear indication that women are having children much later in life is the increasing fertility rate of women over 35. In 2006, the rate for women 35–39 was 47.3, more than double the rate in 1978.

▶WOMEN AND CHILDBEARING: CURRENT TRENDS

Childless women An increasing number of women are choosing not to have children at all. In 2006, 20 percent of women ages 40–44 had no children—double the level of 30 years ago. For women with advanced degrees, the rate is 27 percent.

Unmarried mothers According to the National Center for Health Statistics, 1.7 million births in 2007 were to unmarried women, which represented nearly 40 percent of all births, and was up significantly from 33.2 percent of all births in 2000. The percentage of births to unmarried women increased for all races and ethnicities, but in 2006 was highest among blacks (70.2 percent) and Native Americans (64.6) and lowest among Asians (16.5). Of these un-

Births and Birth Rates in the U.S., by Age, Race and Hispanic Origin, 2007

	All races	White, Non–Hispanic	Black, Non–Hispanic	American Indian[1]	Asian/Pacific Islander	Hispanic[2]
BIRTHS						
Total, by mothers ages 10–54	4,317,119	2,312,473	627,230	49,284	254,734	1,061,970
10–14	6,218	1,269	2,326	120	92	2,407
15–19	445,045	173,104	106,224	8,925	8,022	148,453
20–24	1,082,837	526,943	200,273	16,759	32,309	305,107
25–29	1,208,504	676,599	157,173	12,420	71,465	287,730
30–34	962,179	566,197	97,332	7,052	86,949	201,212
35–39	499,916	301,666	50,614	3,265	46,379	95,694
40–44	105,571	62,152	12,428	704	8,879	20,273
45–54	7,349	4,544	860	38	639	1,095
BIRTH RATES						
Total, by mothers ages 10–54	69.5	60.1	71.6	64.7	71.4	102.1
10–14	0.6	0.2	1.5	0.9	0.2	1.2
15–19	42.5	27.2	64.3	59.0	17.3	81.7
20–24	106.4	83.3	133.6	116.3	66.2	178.5
25–29	117.5	108.8	107.5	96.4	117.9	155.6
30–34	99.9	99.7	74.4	63.7	125.1	110.8
35–39	47.5	45.8	36.4	29.4	66.3	56.4
40–44	9.5	8.6	8.6	6.1	14.5	13.4
45–54[3]	0.6	0.6	0.6	0.3	1.1	0.8

Notes: Figures are preliminary. 1. Includes births to Aleuts and Eskimos. Also includes origin not stated. 2. Hispanic persons may be of any race. 3. The birth rate is computed by relating the number of births to women aged 45–54 years to women aged 45–49 years; most of the births in this group are to women aged 45–49.
Source: U.S. National Center for Health Statistics, *National Vital Statistics Report* (2009).

Women and Childbearing in the U.S, by Age, 1976–2007

Characteristic	1976	1980	1990	1995	2000	2007
Total number of women, 18–44 years old ('000s)	41,618	45,652	58,381	60,225	60,133	61,920[1]
Births per 1,000 women						
All women 15–44 years old	67.2	68.4	70.9	65.6	67.6	69.5
15–19 years	N.A.	53.0	59.9	56.8	48.7	42.5
20–24 years	93.2	115.1	116.5	109.8	112.5	106.4
25–29 years	104.8	112.9	120.2	112.2	121.7	117.5
30–34 years	56.4	61.9	80.8	82.5	94.2	99.9
35–39 years	22.6	19.8	31.7	34.3	40.3	47.5
40–44 years	6.5	3.9	5.5	6.6	7.9	9.5

Note: 1. Figure is for 2008.
Source: U.S. Census Bureau, U.S. National Center for Health Statistics, *National Vital Statistics Reports* (2009).

Percent of Population Never Married, by Age and Sex, 1960–2008

Age	1960	1970	1980	1990	2000	2008
			MEN			
Total: 15 and over	**23.2%**	**28.1%**	**29.6%**	**29.9%**	**31.3%**	**33.5%**
15–17	98.8	99.4	99.4	99.8	98.7	98.5
18	94.6	95.1	97.4	98.5	98.2	97.7
19	87.1	89.9	90.9	95.3	1	1
20–24	53.1	54.7	68.8	79.3	83.7	87.3
25–29	20.8	19.1	33.1	45.2	51.7	58.8
30–34	11.9	9.4	15.9	27.0	30.1	34.5
35–39	8.8	7.2	7.8	14.7	20.3	23.2
40–44	7.3	6.3	7.1	10.5	15.7	19.7
45–54	7.4	7.5	6.1	6.3	9.4	14.3
55–64	8.0	7.8	5.3	5.8	5.5	7.5
65 and over	7.7	7.5	4.9	4.2	4.2	4.1
			WOMEN			
Total: 15 and over	**17.3%**	**22.1%**	**22.5%**	**22.8%**	**25.1%**	**26.8%**
15–17	93.2	97.3	97.0	98.5	97.9	98.5
18	75.6	82.0	88.0	92.0	93.0	98.2
19	59.7	68.8	77.6	88.7	1	1
20–24	28.4	35.8	50.2	62.8	72.8	94.8
25–29	10.5	10.5	20.9	31.1	38.9	45.5
30–34	6.9	6.2	9.5	16.4	21.9	26.1
35–39	6.1	5.4	6.2	10.4	14.3	16.0
40–44	6.1	4.9	4.8	8.0	11.8	13.5
45–54	7.0	4.9	4.7	5.0	8.6	10.3
55–64	8.0	6.8	4.5	3.9	4.9	6.9
65 and over	8.5	7.7	5.9	4.9	3.6	4.0

Note: 1. Population aged 18–19 included under 18. **Source:** U.S. Census Bureau, *Children's Living Arrangements and Characteristics* (March 2002); *America's Families and Living Arrangements, 2008* (2009).

Marital Status by Race and Hispanic Origin, 1970–2008 (in thousands)

Year and Race	Total Adults	Never married Number	Never married Percent	Married Number	Married Percent	Widowed Number	Widowed Percent	Divorced Number	Divorced Percent	Separated Number	Separated Percent
All Races											
1970	132,507	21,443	16.2%	94,999	71.7%	11,784	8.9%	4,282	3.2%	N.A.	N.A.
1980	159,528	32,342	20.3	104,564	65.5	12,734	8.0	9,886	6.2	N.A.	N.A.
1990	181,849	40,361	22.2	112,552	61.9	13,810	7.6	15,125	8.3	N.A.	N.A.
2000	201,762	48,213	23.9	115,655	57.3	13,655	6.8	19,828	9.8	4,412	2.2%
2008	237,993	71,479	30.0	123,671	51.9	14,314	6.0	23,346	9.8	5,183	2.2
White											
1970	118,179	18,444	15.6	85,784	72.6	10,280	8.7	3,671	3.1	N.A.	N.A.
1980	139,480	26,105	18.9	93,800	67.2	10,938	7.8	8,338	6.0	N.A.	N.A.
1990	155,454	31,633	20.3	99,450	64.0	11,730	7.5	12,640	8.1	N.A.	N.A.
2000	168,140	36,017	21.4	101,159	60.2	11,529	6.9	16,507	9.8	2,928	1.7
2008[1]	195,737	54,205	27.7	106,517	54.5	11,968	6.1	19,426	9.9	3,620	1.8
Black											
1970	12,972	2,668	20.6	8,310	64.1	1,427	11.0	567	4.4	N.A.	N.A.
1980	16,638	5,070	30.5	8,545	51.4	1,627	9.8	1,396	8.4	N.A.	N.A.
1990	20,320	7,141	35.1	9,302	45.8	1,730	8.5	2,146	10.6	N.A.	N.A.
2000	24,016	9,451	39.4	8,818	36.7	1,692	7.0	2,765	11.5	1,290	5.4
2008[1]	29,454	13,547	46.0	9,577	32.5	1,740	5.9	3,253	11.0	1,337	4.5
Hispanic											
1970	5,066	943	18.6	3,637	71.8	286	5.6	200	3.9	N.A.	N.A.
1980	7,888	1,901	24.1	5,176	65.6	350	4.4	460	5.8	N.A.	N.A.
1990	13,560	3,694	27.2	8,365	61.7	548	4.0	952	7.0	N.A.	N.A.
2000	21,109	5,907	28.0	11,864	56.2	881	4.2	1,619	7.7	838	4.0
2008[1,2]	32,677	12,021	36.8	16,111	49.3	1,068	3.3	2,330	7.1	1,147	3.5
Asian and Pacific Islander											
2000	7,859	2,241	28.5	4,792	61.0	332	4.2	360	4.6	135	1.7
2008[1]	11,430	3,518	30.8	6,741	58.9	507	4.4	480	4.2	185	1.6

Notes: Only those people 15 years old and over are included. Hispanic persons may be of any race. 1. Alone or in combination with other races. 2. Hispanic may be of any race. **Source:** U.S. Census Bureau, *Children's Living Arrangements and Characteristics* (March 2004); *America's Families and Living Arrangements, 2008* (2009).

married mothers, 60.8 percent were under 24 years old.

Births to teenagers

Births to teenage mothers, most of whom are unmarried, have generally been declining in recent years. In 2007, there were 445,045 births to mothers under 20, down from 469,000 in 2000 but up from 435,436 in 2006. The birth rate for women aged 15–19 hit a 20-year high of 62.1 in 1991, but has declined almost every year after that, to a record low of 40.5 in 2005, although it was up to 42.5 in 2007.

New mothers in the labor force

Due to economic necessity and career goals, fewer than half of all mothers are stay-at-home parents. In June 2008, 57 percent of women who had a child in the last year were in the labor force. That's up significantly from 38 percent in 1980. Nearly half of the women who are in the labor force and have had a child in the last year are first-time mothers.

▶ADOPTION

Between 1973 and 1994, the percent of never-married women who had ever adopted a child declined from 2.1 percent to 1.3 percent, but climbed to 1.5 in 2002, according to National Surveys of Family Growth. The National Center for Health Statistics attributed the drop to several factors, including the legalization of abortion in 1973 and the new reproductive technologies that have reduced the number of unwanted pregnancies. Almost all of the decrease since 1973 has come in unrelated children; the percent of

women adopting related (by blood or otherwise) children has held steady and 12.6 percent of all women have lived with and cared for a child to whom they did not give birth.

In 2002, nearly twice as many men as women had ever adopted a child—2.1 percent compared to 1.1 percent overall—probably because men are more likely than women to adopt their stepchildren.

Also in 2002, there were 28.3 million currently married women between the ages of 18 and 44. Of these, 35.2 percent had considered adoption, 4.4 percent had taken steps toward adoption, and 566,000 were currently looking to adopt a child. Infertility leads many women to choose adoption: over a quarter of women ages 40–44 who had ever used infertility services had adopted a child.

Perhaps the greatest shifts have come in the number and origin of children available for adoption. Before 1973, never-married women under the age of 45 relinquished 8.7 percent of their children for adoption. In 1995, they gave up less than 1 percent. This drop has resulted in an increase in foreign adoptions.

Of those looking to adopt, 94.6 percent of white women and 92.7 percent of black women said that they would prefer or accept a child of another race. According to a U.S. Census Bureau Special Report, of the 2.1 million adopted children in the U.S. in 2000, 12.5 percent, or 257,792, were foreign-born. Almost half of these foreign-born adopted children were born in Asia, with Korea as the largest single source of foreign-born adoptees —about 57,000 in 2000.

Marital Status of the Population by Sex and Age, 2008 (numbers in thousands)

Sex and Age	Total	Never married		Married		Widowed		Divorced		Separated	
		Number	Percent	Number	Percent	Number	Percent	Number	Percent	Number	Percent
MALE											
Total 15+	115,599	38,685	33.5%	62,073	53.7%	2,916	2.5%	9,782	8.5%	2,144	1.9%
15–17	6,816	6,716	98.5	40	0.6	3	N.A.	10	0.1	47	0.7
18–19	3,998	3,907	97.7	56	1.4	N.A.	N.A.	1	N.A.	34	0.9
20–24	10,380	9,064	87.3	1,130	10.9	9	0.1	78	0.8	99	0.9
25–29	10,711	6,299	58.8	3,883	36.3	15	0.1	318	3.0	195	1.8
30–34	9,471	3,270	34.5	5,351	56.5	17	0.2	603	6.4	230	2.4
35–39	10,283	2,387	23.2	6,716	65.4	24	0.2	935	9.1	222	2.2
40–44	10,585	2,088	19.7	6,903	65.2	54	0.5	1,264	11.9	277	2.6
45–49	11,158	1,822	16.3	7,417	66.5	72	0.6	1,580	14.2	267	2.4
50–54	10,372	1,265	12.2	7,153	69.0	156	1.5	1,556	15.0	242	2.3
55–64	16,072	1,213	6.9	11,878	73.9	398	2.5	2,250	14.0	333	2.1
65–74	8,973	399	7.5	6,957	77.6	619	6.9	851	9.5	147	1.6
75–84	5,302	186	3.5	3,788	71.5	992	18.7	295	5.6	42	0.8
85+	1,479	69	4.7	801	54.2	557	37.7	43	2.9	9	0.6
FEMALE											
Total 15+	122,394	32,794	26.8%	61,599	50.3%	11,398	9.3%	13,564	11.1%	3,039	2.5%
15–17	6,628	6,496	98.0	70	1.0	3	N.A.	14	0.2	47	0.7
18–19	3,856	3,658	94.9	153	4.0	3	0.1	14	0.4	28	0.7
20–24	10,127	7,990	78.9	1,808	17.9	20	0.2	139	1.4	170	1.7
25–29	10,326	4,695	45.5	4,788	46.4	47	0.5	479	4.6	318	3.1
30–34	9,596	2,504	26.1	5,919	61.7	57	0.6	780	8.1	336	3.5
35–39	10,438	1,675	16.0	7,136	67.8	94	0.9	1,193	11.4	400	3.8
40–44	10,806	1,462	13.5	7,437	66.1	165	1.5	1,640	15.2	402	3.7
45–49	11,529	1,290	11.2	7,527	65.3	283	2.5	2,015	17.5	413	3.6
50–54	10,860	1,008	9.3	7,129	65.7	462	4.3	1,915	17.6	346	3.2
55–64	17,215	1,181	6.9	10,991	63.8	1,464	8.5	3,225	18.7	355	2.1
65–74	10,602	444	4.2	5,866	55.3	2,662	25.1	1,472	13.9	157	1.5
75–84	7,605	280	3.7	2,723	35.8	3,996	52.5	544	7.2	62	0.8
85+	2,806	112	4.0	388	14.7	2,141	76.3	134	4.8	5	0.2

Note: Totals may not add up due to independent rounding. **Source:** U.S. Census Bureau.

Fertility Rates of U.S. Women, 1930–2007

Year	General fertility rate	Total fertility rate	Year	General fertility rate	Total fertility rate
1930	89.2	2,600	1995	65.6	1,978
1935	77.2	2,250	1996	65.3	1,976
1940	79.9	2,301	1997	65.0	1,971
1945	85.9	2,491	1998	65.6	1,999
1950	106.2	3,091	1999	65.9	2,007
1955	118.3	3,574	2000	67.5	2,056
1960	118.0	3,654	2001	66.9	2,034
1965	96.6	2,928	2002	64.8	2,013
1970	87.9	2,480	2003	65.8	N.A.
1975	66.0	1,774	2004	66.4	2,045
1980	68.4	1,840	2005	66.7	2,054
1985	66.3	1,840	2006	68.5	2,101
1990	70.9	2,081	2007	69.5	2,123

Source: U.S. National Center for Health Statistics, *National Vital Statistics Reports*.

Median Age at First Marriage, by Sex, 1890–2009

Year	Male	Female	Year	Male	Female
1890	26.1	22.0	1995	26.9	24.5
1900	25.9	21.9	1996	27.1	24.8
1910	25.1	21.6	1998	26.7	25.0
1920	24.6	21.2	1999	26.9	25.1
1930	24.3	21.3	2000	26.8	25.1
1940	24.3	21.5	2001	26.9	25.1
1950	22.8	20.3	2002	26.9	25.3
1960	22.8	20.3	2003	27.1	25.3
1970	23.2	20.8	2004	27.4	25.3
1980	24.7	22.0	2005	27.1	25.3
1990	26.1	23.9	2006	27.5	25.5
1991	26.3	24.1	2008	27.4	25.6
1993	26.5	24.5	2009	27.4	25.6

Source: U.S. Census Bureau, *America's Families and Living Arrangements, 2009* (2010).

Black-White Married Couples in the U.S., 1960–2008 (thousands)

Year	Total married couples	Total black-white couples	Husband black, wife white	Wife black, husband white
1960	40,491	51	25	26
1970	44,598	65	41	24
1980	49,714	167	122	45
1990	53,256	211	150	61
1995	54,937	328	206	122
1998	55,305	330	210	120
1999	55,849	364	240	124
2000	56,497	363	268	95
2002	57,919	395	279	116
2004	59,064	413	287	126
2006	59,528	403	286	117
2008	60,129	481	317	164

Source: U.S. Census Bureau, *America's Families and Living Arrangements 2000* (2001); *Statistical Abstract of the United States, 2008* (2009).

Divorced Persons per 1,000 Married Persons by Sex and Race 1960–2008

Sex/year	All races	White	Black	Hispanic[1]
Both sexes:				
1960	35	33	62	N.A.
1970	47	44	83	61
1980	100	92	203	98
1990	142	133	282	129
2000	175	166	330	145
2003	185	177	339	142
2008[2]	189	181	342	145
Male:				
1960	28	27	45	N.A.
1970	35	32	62	40
1980	79	74	149	64
1990	118	112	208	103
2000	151	145	257	120
2003	153	151	238	122
2008[2]	158	154	252	114
Female:				
1960	42	38	78	N.A.
1970	60	56	104	81
1980	120	110	258	132
1990	166	153	358	155
2000	200	187	406	168
2003	216	204	444	163
2008[2]	220	209	437	177

Notes: Persons 18 years and over. Per 1,000 married persons with spouse present. 1. Persons of Hispanic origin may be of any race. 2. 2008 figures not in combination of other race. Source: U.S. Census Bureau, *Children's Living Arrangements and Characteristics; America's Families and Living Arrangements, 2008* (2009).

Percent of First Marriages Ending in Separation or Divorce, by Length of Marriage and Age of Wife, 2000

Length of Marriage (years)	Percent ending in separation or divorce				
	Total	Wife's age at first marriage			
		Under 18	18–19	20–24	25 and over
1	3%	4%	4%	2%	2%
2	7	10	9	6	5
3	12	17	15	10	8
4	16	23	20	14	11
5	20	29	24	17	15
6	23	34	28	19	17
7	26	39	32	22	19
8	29	42	35	25	20
9	31	45	37	27	22
10	33	48	40	29	24
11	35	49	42	31	26
12	38	52	44	33	29
13	39	54	46	33	30
14	41	57	47	35	31
15+	43	59	49	36	35

Source: National Center for Health Statistics, *Advance Data: First Marriage Dissolution, Divorce, and Remarriage: United States*, May 31, 2001.

HOUSEHOLDS AND FAMILIES

Since the very first census in 1790, the federal government has not only attempted to count every individual, it has also tried to determine where those individuals live and with whom. While the definition of *household* has changed somewhat over the years, it has remained a central element in understanding the basic structure of American society. Since 1970, changes in the size and composition of the household unit have revealed the extent of social change more clearly than any other measure. Note that data on households and families is from the Census Bureau's annual Current Population Survey, not from the decennial census.

▶ HOUSEHOLDS

Virtually all Americans are part of a household. As of March 2000, the Census Bureau determined that 274 million persons belonged to a household, even if that household consisted of only one person. A small number of people in institutions or in unique group living arrangements do not belong to households. According to the official Census Bureau definition, a *household* consists of all persons who occupy a housing unit. A house, an apartment or other group of rooms, or a single room, is regarded as a housing unit when it is occupied or intended for occupancy as separate living quarters; that is when the occupants do not live and eat with any other persons in the structure and there is direct access from the outside or through a common hall.

There are two major categories of households identified by the Census Bureau: family and nonfamily. A *family* or *family household* requires the presence of at least two persons, the householder (i.e. the person in whose name the housing unit is owned or rented) and one or more additional family members related to the householder through birth, adoption or marriage. A *nonfamily household* consists of a householder who either lives alone or exclusively with persons who are not related to the householder. Since 1970 the rapid growth of nonfamily households has led to a continuous increase in the number of households and a fall in the average number of persons in each.

In 2009, there were 117.2 million households in the U.S., the largest number ever, with an average of 2.57 persons in each, up slightly from 2008. The overall trend since the 1970s has been towards larger households; in that decade the number of households increased by more than 20 percent and over 17.3 million units, nearly double the growth of the 1940s and 1950s and over 60 percent more than the relatively explosive 1960s. The most significant change helping to ignite this surge was the unprecedented increase in the number of nonfamily households, which grew by 77.7 percent in the 1970s and 28.4 percent during the 1980s.

Several factors help to account for this change, including the rapid rise in the divorce rate, as well as an increase in the number of young single people living on their own and deciding to postpone marriage. In 2008, 32.2 million people, or more than 28 percent of all households, lived alone—a considerable increase even since the 2000 Census figure of 26.7 million. The number of people living alone grew 59 percent during the 1970s, 21 percent during the 1980s, but only 16 percent from 1990 to 2000.

In 2009, an additional 6.7 million *unmarried-couple households* were another large segment of the nonfamily population. Unmarried couples made up only a small percentage of all U.S. couples, but their numbers have continued to skyrocket since their sudden appearance on the American social landscape during the 1970s. There were only 523,000 unmarried couples living together in 1970, but their numbers had tripled to 1.6 million in 1980. A growing number of unmarried couples (2.6 million in 2009) have children under 18 years old in their households. This doesn't necessarily mean more children are being born out of wedlock, however, since this category includes children from previous marriages living with an un-remarried parent. As currently defined by the Census Bureau, an *unmarried-couple household* is two persons of the opposite sex who share living quarters. Although a close personal relationship is implied, other types—including tenancy—are included. But no more than two unrelated adults are present in an unmarried-couple household although children under age 18 may be present.

In 2008, there were 565,000 *opposite-sex unmarried partner households* in the U.S., down from nearly 780,000 in 2006, but the decrease was likely due to processing procedures due to the number of

U.S. Households, Number and Size, 1940–2009

Year	Number of households ('000s)	Average number per household All ages	Average number per household Under 18 years	Average number per household 18 years and older
1940	34,949	3.67	1.14	2.53
1950	43,544	3.37	1.06	2.31
1960[1]	52,799	3.33	1.21	2.12
1970	63,401	3.14	1.09	2.05
1980	80,776	2.76	0.79	1.97
1990	93,347	2.63	0.69	1.94
1995	98,990	2.65	0.71	1.93
1997	101,018	2.64	0.71	1.93
1999	103,874	2.61	0.69	1.92
2000	104,705	2.62	0.69	1.93
2006	114,384	2.57	0.65	1.92
2008	116,783	2.56	0.64	1.92
2009	117,181	2.57	0.64	1.94

Note: 1. Alaska and Hawaii included for first time. **Source:** U.S. Census Bureau, *The Statistical History of the U.S.* (1976); *America's Families and Living Arrangements, 2009* (2010).

Unmarried Couple Households, 1960–2009

Year	Total	Without children under 15	With children under 15
1960	439,000	242,000	197,000
1970	523,000	327,000	196,000
1980	1,589,000	1,159,000	431,000
1990	2,856,000	1,966,000	891,000
1995	3,668,000	2,349,000	1,319,000
1997	4,130,000	2,660,000	1,470,000
1998	4,236,000	2,716,000	1,520,000
1999	4,486,000	2,981,000	1,505,000
2000	4,736,000	3,061,000	1,675,000
2006	5,012,000	3,041,000[1]	1,971,000[1]
2008	6,799,000	4,217,000[1]	2,581,000[1]
2009	6,661,000	4,103,000[1]	2,558,000[1]

Note: 1. Figures for children under 18. Figures may not add to total due to rounding. **Source:** *America's Families and Living Arrangements, 2009* (2010).

same-sex couples reporting themselves as unmarried couples has steadily increased from 2000 to 2008. In San Francisco same-sex unmarried partners constituted 2.7 percent of all households in 2000. Over 85 percent of same-sex households are in metropolitan areas.

Despite all the attention given to the growth of nonfamily households, the fact remains that the overwhelming majority of Americans live in some kind of family situation. This is not to say that the size and structure of the family hasn't undergone major revamping in recent decades but rather to emphasize its inherent strength as the basic social unit despite the presence of powerful forces for change.

▶ FAMILIES

In 2009 there were 78.9 million family households in the U.S., up from 51.6 million in 1970. But the 21st-century American family bears less and less resemblance to the 20th-century family. Perhaps the greatest change is the drop in the percentage of nuclear families: married couples with their own children. These types of families represented 45 percent of the total in 1960; in 2000, they dropped below 25 percent for the first time (23.5 percent). Market researchers who once assumed the family consisted of four members now base their assumptions on families of three, reflecting a steady, dramatic decline in the average family size, from 3.58 in 1970 to 3.15 in 2009. These numbers indicate a growing number of families opting not to have children. They constituted 44.1 percent of all families in 1970, but since 1990, they have outnumbered families with children. In 2009, 35.6 million families had children under 18, compared to 43.2 million without children under 18.

More important, perhaps, the proportion of married-couple families declined from 86.8 percent of all family households in 1970 to 67.5 percent in 2009, while the number of family households headed by females with no husbands present climbed from 5.5 million, or 10.7 percent of all family households in 1970, to 14.4 million, or 18.3 percent in 2009. (A startling 44.7 percent of black families were headed by single women in 2008, up from 28 percent in 1970, but down from 47.2 percent in 2000).

A related development, recently turned into a political issue by those advocating "family values," has been the rising number of single-parent situations. In 2009, 26.2 percent of families with children were headed by a single parent, up from only 13 percent in 1970. The vast majority of these single-parent families were headed by women. The number of

Households and Families: Growth and Change, 1960–2008

| Type of unit | Number ('000s) | | | | | | % Change |
	1960	1970	1980	1990	2000	2008	2000–2008
All Households	52,799	63,401	80,776	93,347	104,705	116,783	12%
Average size	3.33	3.14	2.76	2.63	2.62	2.56	N.A.
Families	45,111	51,586	59,550	66,090	72,025	77,873	8%
Average size	3.67	3.58	3.29	3.17	3.17	3.15	N.A.
Married couple	39,329	44,755	49,112	52,317	55,311	58,370	6
Male householder[1]	1,275	1,239	1,733	2,884	4,028	5,100	27
Female householder[1]	4,507	5,591	8,705	10,890	12,687	14,404	14
Unrelated subfamilies	207	130	360	534	571	526	9%
Married couple	75	27	20	68	37	95	N.A.[2]
Father–child[1]	47	11	36	45	57	63	N.A.[2]
Mother–child[1]	85	91	304	421	477	368	–23
Related subfamilies	1,514	1,150	1,150	2,403	2,983	3,855	29%
Married couple	871	617	582	871	1,149	1,664	45
Father–child[1]	115	48	54	153	201	335	67
Mother–child[1]	528	484	512	1,378	1,633	1,855	14
Nonfamily households	7,895	11,945	21,226	27,257	32,680	38,910	19%
Male householder	2,716	4,063	8,807	11,606	14,641	17,872	22
Female householder	5,179	7,882	12,419	15,651	18,039	21,038	17
One person	6,896	10,851	18,296	22,999	26,724	32,167	20

Notes: 1. No spouse present. 2. Not shown; base less than 75,000. **Source:** U.S. Census Bureau, *America's Families and Living Arrangements 2009* (2010).

Families: Number, Average Size and Percent Distribution by Number of Children, 1970–2008

| Year | Number of families ('000s) | Average size of family | Percent distribution by number of own children under 18 | | | | |
			None	1	2	3	4 or more
1970	51,586	3.58	44.1%	18.2%	17.4%	10.6%	9.8%
1980	59,550	3.29	47.9	20.9	19.3	7.8	4.1
1985	62,706	3.23	50.4	20.9	18.6	7.2	3.0
1990	66,090	3.17	51.1	20.5	18.5	7.0	2.8
1995	69,305	3.19	50.5	20.3	19.1	7.3	2.8
1997	70,241	3.19	50.6	20.4	18.9	7.3	2.8
1999	71,535	3.18	51.6	20.0	18.3	7.3	2.8
2000	72,025	3.17	50.4	21.5	18.5	6.9	2.8
2005	76,858	3.13	47.1	19.6	17.9	7.0[1]	2.6
2007	78,425	3.13	53.0	20.0	18.0	9.0[1]	N.A.
2008	77,873	3.15	54.1	19.5	16.9	9.5[1]	N.A.

Notes: 1. Represents percentage for 3 or more children. Numbers rounded in source. **Source:** U.S. Census Bureau, *America's Families and Living Arrangements 2009* (2010).

Living Arrangements of Children Under 18, by Race, 1970–2009

Arrangement	1970 Number ('000s)	1970 Percent	1990 Number ('000s)	1990 Percent	2000 Number ('000s)	2000 Percent	2009 Number ('000s)	2009 Percent
All children								
Children under 18	69,162	100.0%	64,137	100.0%	72,012	100.0%	74,230	100.0%
Living with:								
Two parents	58,939	85.2	46,503	72.5	49,795	69.1	51,835	69.8
One Parent	8,199	11.9	15,867	24.7	19,220	26.7	19,415	26.2
Mother only	7,452	10.8	13,874	21.6	16,162	22.4	16,911	22.8
Father only	748	1.1	1,993	3.1	3,058	4.2	2,504	3.4
Other relatives	1,547	2.2	1,421	2.2	2,160	3.0	780[1]	1.1
Nonrelatives only	477	0.7	346	0.5	837	1.2	559	0.8
White children								
Children under 18	58,791	100.0%	51,390	100.0%	56,455	100.0%	56,254	100.0%
Living with:								
Two parents	52,624	89.5	40,593	79.0	42,497	75.3	42,644	75.8
One Parent	5,110	8.7	9,869	19.2	12,192	21.6	11,851	21.1
Mother only	4,581	7.8	8,321	16.2	9,765	17.3	9,930	17.7
Father only	528	0.9	1,549	3.0	2,427	4.3	1,921	3.4
Other relatives	695	1.2	708	1.4	1,132	2.0	433[1]	0.8
Nonrelatives only	362	0.6	220	0.4	634	1.1	380	0.7
Black children								
Children under 18	9,422	100.0%	10,018	100.0%	11,412	100.0%	11,235	100.0%
Living with:								
Two parents	5,508	58.5	3,781	37.7	4,286	37.6	4,281	38.1
One Parent	2,995	31.8	5,484	54.7	6,080	53.3	6,022	53.6
Mother only	2,783	29.5	5,132	51.2	5,596	49.0	5,644	50.2
Father only	213	2.3	353	3.5	484	4.2	378	3.4
Other relatives	822	8.7	655	6.5	879	7.7	257[1]	2.3
Nonrelatives only	97	1.0	98	1.0	167	1.5	141	1.3
Hispanic children								
Children under 18	4,006	100.0%	7,174	100.0%	11,613	100.0%	16,360	100.0%
Living with:								
Two parents	3,111	77.7	4,789	66.8	7,561	65.1	11,242	68.7
One Parent	N.A.	N.A.	2,154	30.0	3,425	29.5	4,481	27.4
Mother only	N.A.	N.A.	1,943	27.1	2,919	25.4	4,070	24.9
Father only	N.A.	N.A.	211	2.9	506	4.4	411	2.5
Other relatives	N.A.	N.A.	177	2.5	431	3.7	223[1]	1.4
Nonrelatives only	N.A.	N.A.	54	0.8	196	1.7	108	0.7

Note: Hispanic children may be of any race. Excludes persons under 18 years who were maintaining households or family groups and spouses. 1. Other relatives only for 2008 data. **Source:** U.S. Census Bureau, *America's Families and Living Arrangements, 2009* (2010).

households headed by never-married women with children continues to grow. There were 248,000 such households in 1970; in 2008, there were 5.1 million, almost the same as the number headed by divorced women with children.

According to the Census Bureau, the period between 1990 and 2000 saw a general stabilizing of these trends; in the past 10 years, the percentage of married-couple families and single-parent families has remained fairly constant. The one startling change was the growth of single-parent homes headed by fathers. In 2008, they numbered 1.8 million, up from 1.7 million in 2007, but down from 2.5 million in 2005.

Another important though less vital sign of change is the growth in the number of so-called *subfamilies*. These are families who live in a household and are either related or not to the householder; the Census Bureau describes a *related subfamily* as a married couple with or without children, or one parent with one or more single (never married) children under 18, living in a household and related to the person who maintains the household. They are not counted in the total number of families. Related subfamilies have more than tripled since 1980 and now stand at 3.9 million.

An *unrelated subfamily* is a group of two persons or more who are related to one another by birth, marriage or adoption, but who are not related to the householder. Unrelated subfamily households numbered 526,000 in 2008.

▶SINGLE PARENTS AND GROWN CHILDREN LIVING AT HOME

Among the social changes that have taken place over the last 20 years, two of the most revealing are where children live, and how soon young people start to live on their own. Since 1970, the percentage of children under 18 living with only one parent has more than doubled. In 2009, 26.2 percent lived with only one parent, as compared to just under 12 percent in 1970 (4.0 percent lived with neither parent in 2009). This increase reflects not only a higher divorce rate, but also an increase in the number of children born to unwed mothers, especially among blacks. The numbers of households headed by unmarried black women and divorced black women were equal in 1970. In 2009, never-married black mother households outnumbered black households headed by divorced or separated black mothers by more than three to one. In 2009, 53.6 percent of black children, 21.1 percent of white children; and 27.4 percent of Hispanic children under the age of 18 lived with one parent only, usually the mother. Older children are living with their parents longer than they used to due in part to delayed marriage and rising housing costs. In 1970, 8 percent of 25–34 year olds lived with their parents, by 1996 that number increased to nearly 12.3 percent. By 2006, a full third of single men ages 22–34 lived in their parents' homes, prompting researchers and social scientists to call this new population "boomerangers." The number of boomerangers has increased drastically because of the 2008 recession—only 46.1 percent of 16 to 24-year-olds were employed in 2009, a smaller share since the Bureau of Labor Statistics began collecting data in 1948. In a 2009 Pew Research Center survey, 10 percent of adults ages 18–34 said that the poor economy forced them to move back in with their parents. About 70 percent of grown children who live with their parents are younger than 30.

▶LIVING WITH GRANDPARENTS

In 2009, the Census Bureau estimated that 4.5 million (6 percent of the nation's 74.2 million) children under age 18 lived in the home of their grandparents. This percentage continues to rise—it was 3.2 in 1970, 3.6 in 1990, and 5.9 in 2008. Of those children, 48.6 percent had at least one parent in the household. Black children were more likely (13.9 percent) to live in a household with a grandparent present, compared with 11.6 percent of Hispanic children, 6.8 percent non-Hispanic white, and 13 percent Asian/Pacific Islanders.

HOUSING

According to the Census Bureau, there were 110.7 million occupied housing units in the U.S. in 2007, the latest year for which data is available. Of these units, 75.6 million (68.3 percent) were occupied by homeowners, while the remaining 35 million (31.7 percent) were occupied by renters.

Housing units The U.S. Department of Housing and Urban Development conducts the American Housing Survey every two years. In 2007, traditional houses were still the vast majority. Nearly two of every three occupied homes (71.4 million) were detached single unit structures. Mobile homes or trailers, numbering 6.9 million, are not included in those totals. Another 6.1 million were attached single-unit structures such as a brownstone or row house. Cooperatives and condominiums, totalling more than 7.1 million, are counted separately since they may include any number of dwellings.

Size of housing units Although the typical American family is growing smaller, the typical American house is growing larger. The median

Characteristics of Occupied Housing Units 1995–2007

Characteristic	1995 Units ('000)	1995 Percent of units	1999 Units ('000)	1999 Percent of units	2003 Units ('000)	2003 Percent of units	2007 Units ('000)	2007 Percent of units
Total occupied units	**97,693**	**100.0%**	**102,803**	**100.0%**	**120,777**	**100.0%**	**110,692**	**100.0%**
Owner occupied	63,544	65	68,796	66.9	72,238	59.8	75,647	68.3
Renter occupied	34,150	35	31,007	30.2	33,604	27.8	35,045	31.7
Units in structure								
Single, detached	60,826	62.30%	64,536	62.80%	74,916	62.0%	71,435	64.5%
Single, attached	5,545	5.7	6,963	6.8	7,227	6.0	6,083	5.5
2 to 4	9,299	9.5	8,572	8.3	9,965	8.3	8,790	7.9
5 to 9	4,803	4.9	4,847	4.7	6,012	5.0	5,258	4.8
10 to 19	4,342	4.4	4,416	4.3	5,433	4.5	4,697	4.2
20 to 49	3,244	3.3	3,343	3.2	3,964	3.3	3,645	3.3
50 or more	3,470	3.6	3,341	3.2	4,289	3.6	3,886	3.5
Mobile home or trailer	6,164	6.3	6,785	6.6	8,971	7.4	6,919	6.3
Median Size								
Size of unit (sq. ft.)	1,732	N.A.	1,730	N.A.	1,708	N.A.	1,807	N.A.
Size of lot (acres)	0.43	N.A.	0.34	N.A.	0.35	N.A.	0.36	N.A.
Number of bedrooms								
One	11,777	12.1%	11,986	11.70%	14,389	11.9%	11,810	10.7%
Two	29,146	29.8	29,166	28.4	34,810	28.8	27,956	25.3
Three	40,302	41.2	43,103	41.9	48,819	40.4	47,521	42.9
Four or more	15,421	15.8	17,689	17.2	21,543	17.8	22,554	20.4
Number of bathrooms								
None	465	0.50%	676	0.70%	642	0.53%	493	0.45%
One	43,777	44.8	42,838	41.7	48,264	40.0	39,771	35.9
One and a half	14,780	15.1	16,189	15.8	17,626	14.6	15,465	14.0
Two or more	38,671	39.6	43,100	41.9	52,625	43.6	54,963	50.0
Median age (years)	**28**	**N.A.**	**31**	**N.A.**	**32**	**N.A.**	**34**	**N.A.**
Mortgage status[1]								
None, owned free and clear	24,518	38.60%	25,604	37.22%	25,020	20.7%	24,885	22.5%
One mortgage	34,730	54.7	28,960	42.1	33,429	27.7	32,963	29.85
Two mortgages	4,244	6.7	6,884	10.0	8,127	6.7	11,741	10.6
Three or more mortgages	52	0.1	415	0.6	855	0.7	847	0.77
Median years remaining	20	N.A.	20	N.A.	22	N.A.	24	N.A.
Median amount outstanding	$48,466	N.A.	$63,939	N.A.	$82,010	N.A.	$100,904	N.A.

Note: 1. In this category, figures are perecentages of owner-occupied units only, which represent approximately two-thirds of all occupied units. Not all homeowners reported their mortgage status. **Source:** U.S. Census Bureau, *American Housing Surveys* 1995, 1999, 2003 and 2007.

size of all single, detached one-family houses (including mobile homes) was 1,807 square feet in 2007, up from 1,737 in 2001 and from 1,795 in 2005. For owner-occupied houses, the figure was 1,876 square feet, also up from 1,798 in 2001 and 1,858 in 2005. About 27 percent of occupied single houses (17 million) had more than 2,500 square feet, and 12.3 percent (7.5 million) had less than 1,000 square feet. The majority of houses in 2007 (75.6 percent) had between 4 and 7 rooms; most houses (63.3 percent) had 3 or more bedrooms, and 49.7 percent had two or more bathrooms.

Homeownership Rates, 1890–2009

Year	Homeownership rate	Year	Homeownership rate
1890	47.8%	1990	64.2%
1900	46.7	1995	64.7
1910	45.9	1997	65.7
1920	45.6	1998	66.3
1930	47.8	1999	66.8
1940	43.6	2000	67.4
1950	55.0	2004	69.0
1960	61.9	2005	68.9
1970	62.9	2007	68.1
1980	64.4	2009	67.4

Note: Figures from 1890-1990 are from the decennial census, which counts every home. Figures from 1995–2009 are from the Census Bureau's annual *Housing Vacancy Survey*, which uses statistical samples. Source: U.S. Census Bureau, *2009 Housing Vacancy Survey* (2010).

Equipment and fuel More houses had a washing machine (82.5 percent) or a clothes dryer (80.2 percent) than air conditioning (68.2 percent) or a dishwasher (64.0 percent). Natural gas was the fuel of choice for most houses: it heated 50.3 percent of houses. Electricity heated 32.6 percent, while 7.9 percent of houses had oil furnaces. Oil is most popular in the Northeast, where it is used to heat 34.2 percent of all houses; outside the Northeast, fewer than 2 percent of houses use oil heat. Gas heats 67.8 percent of the houses in the West and and 79.7 percent of the houses in the Midwest. Electricity heats 56.7 percent of houses in the South. Over 480,000 households reported using alternative energy in 2007, up from 352,000 in 2005.

Growth of housing In 2007, the median age of all housing structures in the U.S. was 34 years (i.e. built in 1973). Only 7.6 million units built before 1919 were still in use. This reflects the extraordinary growth of the housing industry during the 1970s and 80s, when 36.0 million of extant units were built. By comparison, only 16.5 million of the housing units still in use were built between 1920 and 1950.

Home ownership Home ownership rates, while still high, have begun to decline from the record levels earlier in the decade. More than two thirds of householders (67.4 percent) owned their

Homeownership Rates in the U.S. by Age, Race, and Hispanic Origin, 1982–2009

Characteristic	1982	1985	1990	1995	2000	2004	2007	2009
U.S., total	**64.8%**	**63.9%**	**63.9%**	**64.7%**	**67.4%**	**69.0%**	**68.1%**	**67.4%**
By age								
Under 25	19.3	17.2	15.7	15.9	21.7	25.2	24.8%	23.3%
Under 35	41.2	39.9	38.5	38.6	40.8	43.1	41.7	37.8
35 to 44	70.0	68.1	66.3	65.2	67.9	69.2	67.8	66.1
45 to 54	77.4	75.9	75.2	75.2	76.5	77.2	75.4	74.4
55 to 64	80.0	79.5	79.3	79.5	80.3	81.7	80.6	79.6
65 and over	74.4	74.8	76.3	78.1	80.4	81.1	80.4	80.9
By race and origin								
White	N.A.	N.A.	N.A.	68.7	71.1	72.8	72.0%	71.4%
Black	N.A.	N.A.	N.A.	42.7	47.2	49.1	47.2	46.2
Asian or Pacific Islander	N.A.	N.A.	N.A.	50.8	52.8	59.8	60.0	59.3
Hispanic (all races)	N.A.	N.A.	N.A.	42.0	46.3	48.1	49.7	48.4

Source: U.S. Census Bureau, *2001 Housing Vacancy Survey*, 2002; *Housing Vacancies and Homeownership Annual Statistics: 2009* (2010).

Average Sales Prices of New One-Family Houses, by Region, 1965–2009

Year	Northeast	Midwest	South	West	United States Amount	Annual percent change
1965	$ 22,900	$ 22,800	$ 18,900	$ 23,200	$ 21,500	N.A.
1970	32,800	28,000	24,000	26,900	26,600	N.A.
1975	47,000	43,400	39,600	44,300	42,600	N.A.
1980	80,300	74,400	69,100	89,400	76,400	6.4%
1985	121,900	95,400	88,900	111,800	100,800	3.3
1990	190,500	133,000	123,500	180,600	149,800	0.7
1995	216,600	157,200	142,000	169,800	158,700	2.7
1998	240,100	179,200	159,700	200,500	181,900	3.2
2000	274,800	199,300	179,000	238,900	207,000	5.8
2002	301,300	209,800	197,500	276,500	228,700	7.3
2004	366,100	240,800	232,800	340,000	274,500	11.4
2006[1]	428,300	257,100	257,700	405,900	305,900	3.0
2007[1]	437,700	256,800	269,800	403,700	313,600	2.5
2008[1,2]	475,500	250,000	253,400	361,500	292,600	-7.2
2009[1,2]	411,300	227,700	241,200	321,600	216,700	-25.9

Notes: Figures are in current dollars. 1. Starting in 2005, the Sales Price and Price per Square Foot ranges for new one-family homes were updated to better reflect current economic conditions. 2. Price decrease likely due to influx of foreclosed homes on the market. Source: U.S. Census Bureau, *Median and Average Sales Price of New Houses Sold by Region* (2010).

homes in 2009, which was up from 63.9 percent in 1990 but down from the high of 69 percent in 2004. Among those under 25, homeownership dropped from 2006 rates (from 24.8 to 23.3 percent) after climbing from 14.8 percent in 1993. Rates fell from 2006 levels for all other age groups, including those over 65 which fell from 81.5 percent in 2006 to 80.5 percent in 2009. Homeownership rates for the population over 75 was 78.9 percent, down from 79.1 percent in 2006, but well above historical rates, reflecting the relative independence of elderly people today.

The steady decline in homeownership since 2006 is a reversal of an increase that began in the late 1980s. The percentages dropped sharply after the crash of the housing market in 2008.

In 2009, married-couple families had the highest rates of homeownership (82.8 percent) while families with only a female head-of-household had the lowest (49.0 percent). However, among people without families, women were far more likely than men to own their own homes, with the rate for women with no other people present (58.6 percent) well above that for men with no other people present (50.9 percent). Homeownership rates fell across the country but remained highest in the Midwest (71.0 percent) and South (69.6 percent) and lowest in the Northeast (64.0 percent) and West (62.6 percent).

Existing One-Family Houses Sold and Median Sales Price, by Region, 1970–2009

Year	Houses Sold ('000s)					Median Sales Price				
	U.S.	Northeast	Midwest	South	West	U.S.	Northeast	Midwest	South	West
1970	1,612	251	501	568	292	$ 23,000	$ 25,700	$ 20,100	$ 20,100	$ 24,300
1975	2,476	370	701	862	543	35,300	39,300	30,100	30,100	39,600
1980	2,973	403	806	1,092	672	62,200	60,800	51,900	51,900	89,300
1985	3,134	561	806	1,063	704	75,500	88,900	58,900	58,900	95,400
1990	3,219	458	809	1,193	759	92,000	126,400	75,300	75,300	129,600
1995	3,888	547	945	1,433	964	110,500	126,700	94,800	94,800	141,000
1998	4,970	662	1,130	1,868	1,309	128,400	135,900	114,300	114,300	164,800
1999	5,205	656	1,148	2,015	1,386	133,300	139,000	119,600	119,600	173,900
2000	5,152	643	1,119	2,015	1,376	139,000	139,400	123,600	128,300	183,000
2002	5,566	656	1,217	2,203	1,490	158,100	164,300	136,000	147,300	215,400
2005	7,075	1,170	1,587	2,703	1,615	219,600	271,300	170,600	181,700	335,300
2007	5,652	1,006	1,327	2,235	1,084	217,900	288,100	161,400	178,800	342,500
2008	4,913	849	1,129	1,865	1,070	198,100	266,400	154,100	169,200	271,500
2009	5,156	868	1,163	1,914	1,211	172,500	240,500	144,100	153,000	211,100

Source: National Association of Realtors, *Existing Home Sales* (June 2010).

Median Sales Prices of Existing Single-Family Homes for Selected Metropolitan Areas, 1995–2009

Metropolitan area	1995	2000	2005	2007	2009
Atlanta, Ga.	$ 97,500	$131,200	$167,200	$172,000	$123,500
Baltimore, Md.	111,300	153,000	265,300	286,100	251,200
Boston, Mass.	179,000	314,200	413,200	395,600	332,600
Chicago, Ill.	147,900	171,800	264,200	276,600	199,200
Cincinnati, Ohio–Ky.–In.	100,400	126,700	145,900	140,800	125,800
Cleveland, Ohio	104,700	N.A.	138,900	130,000	106,800
Dallas, Tex.	96,400	122,500	147,600	150,900	140,500
Denver, Colo.	127,300	196,800	247,100	245,400	219,900
Detroit, Mich.	98,200	N.A.	134,500	140,300	N.A.
Honolulu, Hawaii	349,000	295,000	590,000	643,500	596,200
Houston, Tex.	79,200	116,100	143,000	152,500	153,100
Kansas City, Mo.–Kans.	91,700	127,400	156,700	153,300	140,700
Las Vegas, Nev.	113,500	137,400	304,700	297,700	142,900
Los Angeles area, Calif.	179,900	215,900	529,000	589,200	333,900
Miami, Fla.	107,100	144,600	370,100	365,500	211,200
Milwaukee, Wis.	114,700	140,700	215,700	223,400	193,400
Minneapolis–St. Paul, Minn.–Wis.	106,800	151,400	234,800	225,200	177,700
New Orleans, La.	87,000	112,000	159,200	160,300	160,100
New York City area, N.Y. – N.J.	169,700	230,200	445,200	469,700	381,400
Philadelphia, Pa–N.J.	118,700	125,200	215,300	234,900	215,900
Phoenix, Ariz.	96,800	134,400	247,400	257,400	137,000
Pittsburgh, Pa.	82,100	93,600	116,100	120,700	118,900
St. Louis, Mo.–Ill.	87,700	108,400	141,000	145,400	127,100
San Diego, Calif.	171,600	269,400	604,300	588,700	359,500
San Francisco Bay Area, Calif.	254,400	454,600	715,700	805,400	493,300
Seattle, Wash.	159,000	230,100	316,800	386,900	306,200
Tampa–St. Petersburg–Clearwater, Fla.	78,300	110,800	205,300	214,900	140,700
Washington, D.C.–Md.–Va.	156,500	182,600	425,800	430,800	308,600
U.S. Average	$112,900	$139,000	$219,600	$217,900	$172,100

Source: National Association of Realtors, *Home Sales* (2010).

Housing costs According to the National Association of Realtors, the median sales price of an existing single-family home in 2009 was $172,500, down 28.1 percent from the 2006 median of $221,000. Prices continued to climb in some areas (such as San Francisco Bay) throughout 2007, but the implosion of the housing bubble in summer 2008 deflated median sales prices of existing homes by the end of the year. The number of existing home sales which fell dramatically throughout 2008, accompanied by massive waves of foreclosures across the country, first began to climb again in 2009. The prices in some MSAs dropped by astounding amounts, such as in Washington D.C., where the median sales price of an existing home decreased 28.4 percent (from $430,800 to $308,600) between 2007 and 2009, or in Phoenix, Ariz., where it decreased 44.6 percent (from $247,400 to $137,000) in the same interim. A growing recession reduced the mean U.S. existing home price 21 percent between 2007 and 2009 (from $217,900 to $172,100). According to the Census Bureau's Department of Manufacturing, Mining, and Construction, the average price per square foot for

Fair Market Monthly Rents for Existing Housing for Selected Metropolitan Areas, 2009 vs. 2010

Metropolitan area	2009			2010		
	1 bedroom	2 bedrooms	3 bedrooms	1 bedroom	2 bedrooms	3 bedrooms
Albuquerque, N.M	$ 596	$ 753	$1,096	$ 619	$ 782	$1,139
Atlanta, Ga.	789	878	1,069	820	812	1,110
Austin-San Marcos, Tex.	749	912	1,228	783	954	1,284
Baltimore, Md.	868	1,037	1,315	1,002	1,203	1,545
Boston, Mass.	1,146	1,345	1,609	1,156	1,357	1,623
Charlotte-Gastonia-Rock Hill, N.C.	682	757	954	726	806	1,016
Chicago, Ill.	894	1,004	1,227	903	1,015	1,240
Cincinnati, Ohio	566	733	981	560	726	972
Cleveland-Lorain-Elyria, Ohio	576	694	890	610	735	942
Colorado Springs, Colo.	630	796	1,136	630	795	1,134
Columbus, Ohio	585	740	931	593	750	944
Dallas, Tex.	746	905	1,201	740	894	1,164
Denver, Colo.	704	891	1,265	728	921	1,308
Detroit, Mich.	676	809	968	665	796	952
El Paso, Tex.	499	595	853	502	598	858
Fort Lauderdale, Fla.	1,092	1,313	1,816	1,130	1,358	1,878
Fort Worth-Arlington, Tex.	689	838	1,120	708	861	1,150
Fresno, Calif.	713	842	1,225	711	840	1,222
Honolulu, Hawaii	1,337	1,631	2,367	1,397	1,704	2,473
Houston, Tex.	714	866	1,154	735	892	1,189
Indianapolis, Ind.	627	745	964	635	754	976
Jacksonville, Fla.	779	907	1,138	776	903	1,133
Kansas City, Mo.	689	791	1,070	726	834	1,128
Las Vegas, Nev.	861	1,013	1,408	904	1,063	1,478
Los Angeles-Long Beach, Calif.	1,090	1,361	1,828	1,137	1,420	1,907
Memphis, Tenn.-Ark.-Miss.	671	746	994	705	783	1,043
Miami, Fla.	953	1,156	1,479	994	1,206	1,542
Milwaukee-Waukeshau, Wis.	702	839	1,057	718	858	1,081
Minneapolis-St. Paul, Minn.	719	873	1,143	741	899	1,177
Nashville, Tenn.	662	761	987	702	807	1,047
New Orleans, La.	811	949	1,219	840	982	1,261
New York, N.Y.[1]	1,180	1,313	1,615	1,222	1,359	1,672
Oakland, Calif.	1,093	1,295	1,756	1,162	1,377	1,867
Oklahoma City, Okla.	565	686	926	545	662	894
Philadelphia, Pa.	842	1,005	1,203	915	1,095	1,339
Phoenix-Mesa, Ariz.	727	877	1,277	762	919	1,338
Pittsburgh, Pa.	594	710	883	610	730	907
Portland-Vancouver, Oreg.-Wash.	700	809	1,178	726	839	1,222
Sacramento, Calif.	838	1,022	1,475	852	1,039	1,499
Saint Louis, Mo.	593	737	949	626	771	993
Salt Lake City, Utah	665	802	1,128	693	836	1,176
San Antonio, Tex.	642	792	1,022	645	796	1,027
San Diego, Calif.	1,168	1,418	2,067	1,082	1,324	1,883
San Francisco, Calif.	1,325	1,658	2,213	1,406	1,760	2,350
San Jose, Calif.	1,113	1,338	1,924	1,196	1,438	2,068
Seattle-Bellevue-Everett, Wash.	820	987	1,395	878	1,056	1,492
Tampa-St. Petersburg, Fla.	782	946	1,199	793	959	1,215
Tucson, Ariz.	579	743	1,070	635	815	1,174
Tulsa, Okla.	578	707	934	582	711	939
Washington, D.C.-Md.-Va.	1,131	1,288	1,647	1,318	1,494	1,927
West Palm Beach-Boca Raton, Fla.	1,096	1,294	1,830	1,066	1,259	1,780

Note: Figures are projections made in the year prior to date shown. 1. Figures include areas outside Manhattan. **Source:** U.S. Dept. of Housing and Urban Development, Office of the Federal Housing Commissioner, *Fair Market Rents*, effective April 1, 2009 and Jan. 1, 2010.

new single-family homes decreased from 2007 to 2008 for the first time since 1999—from $92.51 to $88.31. The price of new single-family homes increased 60 percent (from $181,900 to $292,600) from 1998 to 2008. The size of new homes continues to increase—in 2008 the average single-family house completed had 2,534 square feet, 779 more square feet than in 1978.

Average monthly mortgage payments, including maintenance costs, for all homeowners rose from $1,040 in 2005 to $1,514 in 2008. Most people (34 percent) who own a home pay less than 20 percent of their monthly income in homeowner costs, but 28.8 percent pay 35 percent or more of their monthly income toward owner costs, including mortgage payments. Payments were higher among repeat buyers, but first-time buyers paid a larger percentage of their incomes toward their mortgages. Low interest rates were responsible for the popularity of fixed-rate mortgages, in which the consumer locks into a monthly payment for the life of the loan.

The recent subprime mortgage crisis led to over three million foreclosure filings in 2008, and 3.9 million in 2009, a 120 percent increase in total property foreclosures from 2007. The Housing and Economic Recovery Act was passed in July 2008 to help the 400,000 borrowers in danger of losing their homes refinance into affordable, government-insured mortgages.

A consequence of the housing bubble bursting is the rate of vacancy for all types of homes—both rented and owned. The rental vacancy rate rose from 10.0 in 2008 to 10.6 in 2009. The owned vacancy rate has steadily increased from 2.4 in 2006 to 2.7 in 2007 and 2.8 in 2008 but dropped to 2.6 in 2009. The rates of vacancy are much higher for buildings constructed since 2000, though the number of housing units continues to grow. In 2009 there were 129,060,383 housing units in the U.S., a 0.8 percent decrease from 2008.

The number of vacant units increased 1.5 percent during the same period, from 18,543 in 2008 to 18,815 in 2009. In 2009, the owned vacancy rate for units built since 2000 was 4.7, down from 6.1 in 2008. In 2009, the owned vacancy rate for units built since 2000 was 6.3, down from 7.7 in 2008. The rate was lowest in 2009 (1.6) for structures built from 1970 to 1979; they were lowest in 2008 (1.8) for structures built from 1995 to 2000. The percentage of vacant for-sale units that had been vacant for six months or more increased from 51 to 53 percent from 2008 to 2009. In 2009, the rate of vacancy was the highest in the South (2.9), and lowest in the Northeast (2.0).

Renting In 2008, approximately almost a third of occupied housing was rented, with median rent of $824 per month. Rental vacancies rates in 2009 were the highest in Florida (17.8) and Arizona (17.7), followed by Mississippi and South Carolina.

Moving In 2008, approximately 35 million people, or 12 percent of the population, lived in a different home than they did the year before. The majority of these moves (40.1 percent) were for housing-related reasons; 13.8 percent wanted a new or better house or apartment, while 30.5 percent moved for family reasons.

Housing and the poor The housing problems of the poor have grown worse both in the years leadin up to and then as a consequence of the 2008–09 economic downturn. A shortage of affordable apartments has existed across the nation for several years, forcing 4.4 million poor families to pay more than half their income on rent. In 2008, 15 percent of Americans lived below the poverty line. The major reasons for this development are stagnating wages for the unskilled, rising real estate values, and the government's failure to supply enough subsidized housing. The number of new subsidized units fell to 70,000 a year during the Reagan–Bush years, down from 260,000 during the Carter administration. In 1995, the government stopped expanding the pool of subsidized housing, but in 2008, Pres. George W. Bush signed the National Housing Trust Fund into law, which provided communities with funds to build, rehabilitate, and preserve housing for people with the lowest incomes.

About 15 million households currently qualify for federal housing assistance, but only 4.5 million families get it. Of those, about one-third live in conventional housing projects, while the rest receive subsidies that allow them to live in private housing. In each case, the tenants contribute 30 percent of their income toward the rent and the government provides the rest.

▶ THE HOMELESS

Although homeless people have become a common sight in almost every community, their plight is always surrounded by some kind of controversy, one that is fueled by a wide range of opinions, some based on fact and others on stereotypes. The often shrill debate about just who the homeless are and what can or should be done for them has been hampered by a lack of reliable information on everything from the causes of homelessness to the actual number of people living on the streets or in shelters.

Number of Homeless by Sheltered Status, 2008

Household Type	Number	Percentage
Total	**664,414**	**100.0%**
Sheltered	386,361	58.2
Unsheltered	278,053	41.8
Individuals	**415,202**	**100.0**
Sheltered	204,855	49.3
Unsheltered	210,347	50.7
Persons in Families	**249,212**	**100.0**
Sheltered	181,506	72.8
Unsheltered	67,706	27.2

Note: Data was taken on a single night in January, 2008.
Source: U.S. Department of Housing and Urban Development, 2008 Continuum of Care Applications, *Point-in-Time Homeless Population and Subpopulation Charts.*

States with Highest Percentage of Homeless Population, 2008

Rank, State	Number	Percent of Population
1. Oregon	20,653	0.54%
2. Nevada	12,610	0.48
3. Hawaii	6,061	0.47
4. California	157,277	0.43
5. Washington	21,954	0.34
6. New York	61,125	0.31
7. Colorado	14,747	0.30
8. Michigan	28,248	0.28
9. Florida	50,158	0.27
10. Alaska	1,646	0.24

Notes: 1. District of Columbia is not included, though has 6,044 homeless people, 1.02 percent of the city's population.
Source: U.S. Department of Housing and Urban Development, 2008 Continumm of Care Applications.

The number of homeless Because homelessness is a temporary circumstance, it is nearly impossible to measure the number of homeless. Every year in January, the Department of Housing and Urban Development (HUD) organizes a one-night count. In 2008, there were 664,414 homeless persons, and almost a third of them were families. This number was down from 759,101 in January 2006, but some of the decline may be due to a change in reporting methods. Only 58 percent of these persons were in shelters, the rest were sleeping on the street or in another place not intended for human habitation. Homeless families were more likely to be in a shelter (73 percent) than were individuals (49 percent). Nearly 20 percent of the total were chronically homeless, and about a third of these were individuals.

Not all persons seeking shelter can be accommodated, however. A study by the U.S. Conference of Mayors in 2007 found that 12 of the 23 cities surveyed had to turn people seeking shelter away due to lack of capacity. In addition to emergency shelters, however, the National Coalition for the Homeless describes transitional and permanent supportive housing as well. The average stay for families in an emergency shelter was 70 days in 2008 and 223 days in transitional housing. A 2004 study by the National Law Center on Homelessness and Poverty found that in virtually all 50 cities surveyed, the city's official estimated number of homeless people greatly exceeded the number of emergency shelters and transitional housing spaces.

In 2008 the homeless population was estimated to be 42 percent black, 39 percent white, 13 percent Hispanic, 4 percent American Indian and 2 percent Asian. An estimated 26 percent were considered mentally ill, while 13 percent were physically disabled. Additionally, 19 percent were victims of domestic violence, 13 percent were veterans, and 2 percent were HIV positive. Homelessness among persons in families increased 9 percent between 2007 and 2008.

The vast majority of the homeless are in major cities rather than in suburban or rural areas. In 2008, one in five homeless persons was in Los Angeles, New York, and Detroit. Nearly one in every 66 persons living in a principal U.S. city is homeless, compared to about one in every 450 living in suburban or rural areas.

Federal funding The federal government programs to assist the homeless are grouped under what is now known as the McKinney-Vento Act, which became law in July 1987. The act includes 16 different provisions for emergency shelter, food, health care, mental health care, housing, educational programs, job training and other community services. Federal agencies providing services specifically for the homeless include the Federal Emergency Management Agency, and Departments of Agriculture, Education, Health and Human Services, Housing and Urban Development, Labor and Veterans' Affairs. An additional 34 programs, ranging from Medicaid and the Supplemental Security Income program to the Public and Indian housing program and the Ryan White CARE Act, provide general assistance to low-income people, including the homeless. In 2009, Pres. Obama signed the American Recovery and Reinvestment Act, which allocated an additional $1.5 billion for a Homeless Prevention Fund. Despite HUD's $1.5 billion budget for homeless programs, states and cities still foot the major part of the bill for care of the homeless.

As of 2008, HUD, along with several advocacy groups nationwide, are funding new initiatives that place homeless persons in apartments of their own. Known as the "housing first" approach, the idea was first pioneered in New York during the 1990s. Despite the high costs of living in metropolitan areas where homelessness is most severe, officials of the program have found that they can provide housing and most medical services for $15,000 a year per person. Federal funding has increased more than $1.5 billion for such programs because of their success. Over 200 American cities currently participate in the campaign with ambitious 10-year plans to end chronic homelessness.

IMMIGRATION

Over the last four centuries the mingling of peoples from all parts of the world has been a vital element in the formation of the United States both as a land of opportunity and in its emergence as a world power. In one relatively brief period between 1880 and 1920 the massive influx of more than 20 million European immigrants provided the continuous labor supply necessary to transform the nation from an agricultural society to an industrialized one with extraordinary rapidity.

Over the next 40 years, however, the flow of immigration slowed dramatically as the government decided to close the doors to most foreign groups. Motivated at first by a disconcerting kind of nativism, the nation's anti-immigration sentiments were later bolstered by the Great Depression and the need to provide work for those already living here. World War II and the subsequent national readjustment limited immigration for several decades.

Since 1960 a steadily increasing number of immigrants—both legal and illegal—has had a very

The Statue of Liberty

The Statue of Liberty was conceived and designed by Frédéric-Auguste Bartholdi (with Gustave Eiffel's help) and given to the U.S. by the French government in honor of the centennial of American independence in 1876. Funded by subscriptions from the French people, it was dedicated by President Grover Cleveland in 1886 and became a national monument in 1924.

Measuring 151 feet (46 m) to the top of her torch, Miss Liberty still stands guard over the entrance to New York harbor, the inscription on its base a poignant reminder of the vision Americans once had of their country:

Give me your tired, your poor,
Your huddled masses yearning to breathe free,
The wretched refuse of your teeming shore,
Send these, the homeless, tempest-tost to me:
I lift my lamp beside the golden door.

noticeable impact on both the size and ethnic composition of the American population. The startling upsurge in the number of Asians and Hispanic immigrants during the 1970s, 80s, and 90s has been caused by a variety of factors from wars and political upheaval to the mundane fact of geographical proximity in the case of Mexico. In 2008, 1.11 million persons obtained legal permanent resident status, and well over half are from those two ethnic backgrounds.

In 1998, total immigration hit a 10-year low of 660,477. In 2001 and 2002 legal immigration ex-

U.S. Immigration and Rate by Decade, 1820–2009

Period	Total immigrants	Rate per 1,000 U.S. population
1820–30	151,824	1.2
1831–40	599,125	3.9
1841–50	1,713,251	8.4
1851–60	2,598,214	9.3
1861–70	2,314,824	6.4
1871–80	2,812,191	6.2
1881–90	5,246,613	9.2
1891–1900	3,687,564	5.3
1901–10	8,795,386	10.4
1911–20	5,735,811	5.7
1921–30	4,107,209	3.5
1931–40	528,431	0.4
1941–50	1,035,039	0.7
1951–60	2,515,479	1.5
1961–70	3,321,677	1.7
1971–80	4,493,314	2.1
1981–90	7,338,062	2.9
1991–2000[1]	9,080,500	3.2
2001–2007[2]	7,220,500	3.5
2008–2009[2]	2,237,944	2.7
Total 1820–2007[2]	73,309,431	N.A.

Notes: 1. Includes more than 2 million aliens adjusting under the legalization provisions of the Immigration and Control Act (IRCA) of 1986. 2. Estimate. Source: U.S. Dept. of Homeland Security, 2008 Statistical Yearbook of the Immigration and Naturalization Service (2009).

Immigration as a Percentage of Total Population Growth, 1901–2000

Period	Percent	Period	Percent
1901–10	39.6%	1950–54	10.6%
1911–20	17.7	1955–59	10.7
1921–30	15.0	1960–64	12.5
1931–34	–0.1	1965–69	19.7
1935–39	3.2	1970–80	19.4
1940–44	7.4	1981–90	32.8
1945–49	10.2	1991–2000	27.8

Source: U.S. Dept. of Homeland Security, 2000 Statistical Yearbook of the Immigration and Naturalization Service (2000).

Foreign-Born Population by Region of Birth, 1850–2007

Year	Total population	Foreign-born population	Foreign-born percent	Europe	Asia	Africa	Oceania	Latin America	North America
1850[1]	23,191,876	2,244,602	9.7%	2,031,867	1,135	551	588	20,773	147,711
1860[1]	31,443,321	4,138,697	13.2	3,807,062	36,796	526	2,140	38,315	249,970
1870	38,558,371	5,567,229	14.4	4,941,049	64,565	2,657	4,028	57,871	493,467
1880	50,155,783	6,679,943	13.3	5,751,823	107,630	2,204	6,859	90,073	717,286
1890	62,622,250	9,249,547	14.8	8,030,347	113,383	2,207	9,353	107,307	980,938
1900	75,994,575	10,341,276	13.6	8,881,548	120,248	2,538	8,820	137,458	1,179,922
1910	91,972,266	13,515,886	14.7	11,810,115	191,484	3,992	11,450	279,514	1,209,717
1920	105,710,620	13,920,692	13.2	11,916,048	237,950	16,126	14,626	588,843	1,138,174
1930	122,775,046	14,204,149	11.6	11,784,010	275,665	18,326	17,343	791,840	1,310,369
1940	131,669,275	11,594,896	8.8	N.A.	N.A.	N.A.	N.A.	N.A.	N.A.
1950	150,216,110	10,347,395	6.9	N.A.	N.A.	N.A.	N.A.	N.A.	N.A.
1960	179,325,671	9,738,091	5.4	7,256,311	490,996	35,355	34,730	908,309	952,500
1970	203,210,158	9,619,302	4.7	5,740,891	824,887	80,143	41,258	1,803,970	812,421
1980	226,545,805	14,079,906	6.2	5,149,572	2,539,777	199,723	77,577	4,372,487	853,427
1990	248,709,873	19,767,316	7.9	4,350,403	4,979,037	363,819	104,145	8,407,837	753,917
2000[2]	274,087,000	28,379,000	10.4	4,355,000	7,246,000	N.A.	N.A.	14,407,000	N.A.
2007	299,398,484	38,060,000	12.7	4,990,000	10,185,000	419,000	217,000	20,410,000	839,000

Notes: 1. In 1850 and 1860, information on nativity was not collected for slaves. The data in the table assume, as was done in 1870 census reports, that all slaves in 1850 and 1860 were native, even though 0.2 percent were foreign-born. 2. Numbers for 2000 rounded at source. Source: U.S. Census Bureau, American Community Survey (2008).

Percent of Immigrants Admitted by Region, 1951–2009

Region	Total, 1951–2000	1951–60	1961–70	1971–80	1981–90	1991–2000	2009
Europe	20.0%	52.7%	33.8%	17.8%	10.4%	14.9%	10.2%
Asia	28.8	6.1	12.9	35.3	37.3	30.7	34.9
Africa	2.4	5.6	8.7	1.8	2.4	3.9	10.9
Oceania	N.A.	0.5	0.8	0.9	0.6	0.6	0.5
America[1]	47.8	39.6	51.7	44.1	49.3	49.3	42.4.
Caribbean	11.9	4.9	14.2	16.5	11.9	10.8	12.8
Central America	4.8	1.8	3.1	3.0	6.4	5.8	4.2
Other North America[1]	24.7	26.9	26.1	18.0	24.7	26.8	16.5[2]
South America	6.2	3.6	7.8	6.6	6.3	5.9	9.0

Notes: Data are for fiscal years. 1. Includes more than 2 million illegal immigrants from Mexico granted permanent legal residence under the 1986 Immigration Reform & Control Act. 2. Includes Canada, Newfoundland, and Mexico. Source: U.S. Dept. of Homeland Security, 2009 Yearbook of Immigration Statistics (2010).

Top 20 Countries of Birth for U.S. Immigrants, and Major Categories of Admission, 2009

Country of birth	Total immigrants	Percent of total	Relative preferences	Occupational preferences	Immediate relatives	Refugees and asylees	Other
All countries	1,130,818	100.0%	211,859	144,034	535,554	177,368	62,003
Mexico	164,920	14.6	57,177	8,660	96,187	466	2,430
China, People's Republic	64,238	5.7	11,013	11,295	23,244	18,486	337
Philippines	60,029	5.3	14,286	8,516	37,037	108	82
India	57,304	5.1	12,911	20,264	21,532	2,228	369
Dominican Republic	49,414	4.4	20,611	408	28,212	135	48
Cuba	38,954	3.4	1,022	13	3,385	34,301	233
Vietnam	29,234	2.6	12,748	N.A.	13,038	2,535	498
Colombia	27,849	2.5	3,127	2,850	17,551	4,227	94
South Korea	25,859	2.3	1,660	14,147	9,990	12	50
Haiti	24,280	2.1	7,133	149	11,021	5,402	575
Jamaica	21,783	1.9	4,833	593	16,290	24	43
Pakistan	21,555	1.9	8,654	3,184	8,800	808	69
El Salvador	19,909	1.8	6,823	836	8,628	705	2,917
Iran	18,553	1.6	2,410	1,200	4,054	9,804	1,085
Peru	16,957	1.5	2,714	1,361	11,900	887	95
Bangladesh	16,651	1.5	7,326	957	5,128	232	3,008
Canada	16,140	1.4	635	6,927	8,203	38	337
United Kingdom	15,748	1.4	474	7,044	8,024	14	192
Ethiopia	15,642	1.4	560	169	6,503	4,382	3,848
Nigeria	15,253	1.3	1,394	793	9,086	215	3,765

Source: U.S. Dept of Homeland Security, *2009 Yearbook of Immigration Statistics* (2010).

Top 10 States and Metropolitan Areas of Intended Residence for U.S. Immigrants, 1995–2008

Rank, 2008 and State	1995 Number	1995 Percent of total	2000 Number	2000 Percent of total	2008 Number	2008 Percent of total
1. California	166,482	N.A.	217,753	25.6%	238,444	21.5%
2. New York	128,406	N.A.	106,061	12.5	143,679	13.0
3. Florida	62,023	N.A.	98,391	11.6	133,445	12.1
4. Texas	49,963	N.A.	63,840	7.5	89,811	8.1
5. New Jersey	65,934	N.A.	40,013	4.7	53,997	4.9
6. Illinois	33,898	N.A.	36,180	4.3	42,723	3.9
7. Massachusetts	20,523	N.A.	23,483	2.8	30,369	2.7
8. Virginia	16,319	N.A.	20,087	2.4	30,257	2.7
9. Georgia	N.A.	N.A.	14,707	N.A.	27,769	2.5
10. Maryland	15,055	N.A.	17,705	2.1	27,062	2.4

Rank, 2008 and Metropolitan area	Number	Percent of total	Number	Percent of total	Number	Percent of total
1. New York, N.Y.	111,687	15.5%	85,867	12.3%	179,981	16.3%
2. Los Angeles-Long Beach, Calif.	54,669	7.6	70,644	9.1	96,492	8.7
3. Miami, Fla.	30,935	4.3	47,404	4.4	87,787	7.9
4. Washington D.C.-MD-Va.	25,717	3.6	29,394	3.9	42,827	3.9
5. Chicago, Ill.	31,730	4.4	32,300	4.7	39,826	3.6
6. San Francisco-Oakland, Calif.	N.A.	N.A.	32,236	3.8	36,120	3.3
7. Houston, Tex.	14,379	2.0	17,020	2.0	30,514	2.8
8. Dallas-Ft. Worth, Tex.	N.A.	N.A.	19,643	2.3	26,451	2.4
9. Boston-Lawrence-Lowell, Mass.	16,750	2.3	16,469	2.0	24,691	2.2
10. Atlanta-Marietta, Geo.	N.A.	N.A.	11,660	1.4	22,329	2.0

Source: U.S. Dept. of Homeland Security, *2008 Yearbook of Immigration Statistics* (2009).

Immigration to the U.S. by Country of Last Residence, 1820–2009

Since 1820, Germany has sent more immigrants to the U.S. than has any other country, but Mexico is gaining fast. More than 7 million people immigrated to the U.S. from Mexico between 1820 and 2006, over 5 million since 1980. In 2009, 15 percent of all immigrants came from Mexico, but recent years have also seen a surge in immigrants from Asia, especially from the Philippines, China and India. This table ranks the top 10 nations by the total number of U.S. immigrants from 1820 to 2006.

Country	1820–2006		1991–2000		2009	
	Number	Percent of total	Number	Percent of total	Number	Percent of total
All countries	**72,066,614**	**100.0%**	**9,095,417**	**100.0%**	**1,130,818**	**100.0%**
Germany	7,258,224	10.1	92,606	1.0	8,612	0.8
Mexico	7,144,904	9.9	2,249,421	24.7	164,067	15.0
Italy	5,450,468	7.6	62,722	1.0	3,143	0.3
United Kingdom	5,373,423	7.5	151,866	2.0	17,417	1.5
Ireland	4,790,377	6.6	56,950	1.0	1,708	0.2
Canada	4,643,377	6.4	191,987	2.0	22,508	2.0
Russia[2]	4,190,569	5.8	462,874	5.1	10,362	0.9
Austria[1]	1,856,240	2.6	15,500	0.2	6,260	0.6
Philippines	1,832,691	2.5	503,945	5.5	58,107	5.1
Hungary[1]	1,683,827	2.3	9,382	0.1	1,295	0.1

Notes: 1. Austria and Hungary not counted separately for all years. 2. Includes former Soviet Union. **Source:** U.S. Dept. of Homeland Security, *2009 Yearbook of Immigration Statistics* (2010).

Estimated Number of U.S. Immigrants, by Region and Selected Country of Last Residence, 1820–2009

Region/country	Total 1820–2005	2009	Region/country	Total 1820–2005	2009
EUROPE	**39,176,930**	**114,992**	Philippines	1,761,557	58,107
Austria[1]	1,854,939	6,260	Turkey	468,797	7,943
Belgium	221,955	764	Vietnam	809,704	28,397
Czechoslovakia[2]	162,795	1,649	Other Asia	2,299,171	112,204
Denmark	379,129	606			
France	846,936	4,882	**AMERICAS**	**19,533,562**	**479,845**
Germany	7,247,953	8,612	Canada & Newfoundland	4,619,464	22,508
Greece	735,356	1,076	Mexico	6,974,855	164,067
Hungary[1]	1,682,137	1,295	Caribbean	4,052,572	144,897
Ireland	4,788,339	1,708	Cuba	988,608	38,111
Italy	5,447,062	3,143	Dominican Republic	964,657	49,381
Netherlands	395,935	1,695	Haiti	490,489	23,994
Norway[3]	790,231	429	Jamaica	660,400	21,494
Poland	828,486	8,384	Other Caribbean	948,418	11,917
Portugal	527,065	966	Central America	**1,643,655**	47,013
Romania	275,823	4,557	El Salvador	626,535	19,342
Russia[6]	4,130,809	10,362	Guatemala	317,462	11,881
Spain	312,665	2,118	South America	**2,133,429**	101,359
Sweden[3]	1,304,738	1,297	Argentina	178,214	5,672
Switzerland	377,901	1,015	Colombia	509,096	27,221
United Kingdom	5,353,439	17,417	Ecuador	276,687	12,083
Yugoslavia[4]	290,895	5,992	Other South America	1,169,432	10
Other Europe	1,222,342	27,329	Other America	109,587	1
ASIA	**10,113,486**	**394,874**	**AFRICA**	**963,872**	**122,804**
China[5]	1,252,005	60,896	Egypt	142,839	10,810
Hong Kong	468,045	3,389	Ethiopia	92,858	14,674
India	1,127,109	54,360			
Iran	262,675	8,840	**OCEANIA**	**291,841**	**6,142**
Israel	203,225	6,208			
Japan	573,281	8,218	Not specified	720,659	12,161
Korea	887,917	25,582	**All countries**	**70,800,350**	**1,130,818**

Notes: Because of changes in boundaries and government, figures for many countries, especially those in Asia, are not available for all years or were not reported separately for all years, and are therefore not strictly comparable throughout. Data for many countries are included with countries to which they belonged prior to World War I. 1. Data for Austria and Hungary not reported separately for all years. Total does not include 846,076 immigrants whose country of last residence is listed as Austria-Hungary, including 4,569 in 2005. 2. No data available for Czechoslovakia until 1920. 3. Data for Norway and Sweden not reported separately until 1871. Total does not include 60,255 immigrants whose country of last residence is listed as Norway-Sweden. 4. Since 1922, includes immigrants from the Serb, Croat, and Slovene Kingdom. 5. Beginning in 1957, China includes Taiwan. 6. From 1991- present, the data refer to the Russian Federation: Armenia, Azerbaijan, Belarus, Georgia, Kazakhstan, Kyrgyzstan, Moldova, Russia, Tajikistan, Ukraine, and Uzbekistan.
Source: U.S. Dept. of Homeland Security, *2009 Yearbook of Immigration Statistics* (2010).

ceeded one million. The number rose above one million in 2005 and topped 1.2 million in 2006, but decreased in 2007. It rose again in 2008.

With the dramatic decline in its birth rates and fertility rates, the U.S. might very well begin to experience negative population growth by the year 2030; by 2020 immigration will add more population than natural increase will. According to the Office of Population Research at Princeton University, the U.S. will need 464,000 immigrants each year over the next century just to keep total population in 2100 at the same size as in 1980.

▶ ELIGIBILITY

Prior to 1875 anyone from any foreign country could enter the U.S. freely and take up permanent residence here. Over the next 60 years, however, Congress passed laws restricting immigration on the basis of morality (no prostitutes or convicts), race (the Chinese Exclusion Act of 1882 was the first), and national origin (immigrants from Southern and Central Europe as well as Asia were severely limited during the 1920s). In 1952 Congress passed the Immigration and Nationality Act, which reaffirmed national origin as the central

Foreign-Born Population by State, 2000–2008

	2000			2000–2008[1]		
	Total population	Foreign-born population	Percent foreign-born	Total population	Foreign-born population	Percent foreign-born
United States	281,421,906	31,107,889	11.1%	301,237,703	37,679,592	12.5%
Alabama	4,447,100	87,772	2.0	4,625,354	132,599	2.9
Alaska	626,932	37,170	5.9	681,235	46,470	6.8
Arizona	5,130,632	656,183	12.8	6,343,952	945,226	14.9
Arkansas	2,673,400	73,690	2.8	2,830,047	111,948	4.0
California	33,871,648	8,864,255	26.2	36,418,499	9,855,606	27.1
Colorado	4,301,261	369,903	8.6	4,844,568	489,187	10.1
Connecticut	3,405,565	369,967	10.9	3,493,006	448,034	12.8
Delaware	783,600	44,898	5.7	861,804	66,202	7.7
District of Columbia	572,059	73,561	12.9	588,373	75,416	12.8
Florida	15,982,378	2,670,828	16.7	18,182,321	3,402,391	18.7
Georgia	8,186,453	577,273	7.1	9,509,254	873,670	9.2
Hawaii	1,211,537	212,229	17.5	1,280,273	219,771	17.2
Idaho	1,293,953	64,080	5.0	1,493,713	85,565	5.7
Illinois	12,419,293	1,529,058	12.3	12,829,014	1,763,185	13.7
Indiana	6,080,485	186,534	3.1	6,335,595	261,413	4.1
Iowa	2,926,324	91,085	3.1	2,984,391	115,048	3.9
Kansas	2,688,418	134,735	5.0	2,778,599	167,159	6.0
Kentucky	4,041,769	80,271	2.0	4,234,999	114,115	2.7
Lousiana	4,468,976	115,885	2.6	4,342,582	136,017	3.1
Maine	1,274,923	36,691	2.9	1,315,069	43,077	3.3
Maryland	5,296,486	518,315	9.8	5,618,250	691,341	12.3
Massachussetts	6,349,097	772,983	12.2	6,469,770	919,771	14.2
Michigan	9,938,444	523,589	5.3	10,045,697	594,693	5.9
Minnesota	4,919,479	260,463	5.3	5,181,962	339,680	6.6
Mississippi	2,844,658	39,908	1.4	2,918,790	55,564	1.9
Missouri	5,595,211	151,196	2.7	5,874,327	206,452	3.5
Montana	902,195	16,396	1.8	956,496	18,782	2.0
Nebraska	1,711,263	74,638	4.4	1,770,896	98,639	5.6
Nevada	1,998,257	316,593	15.8	2,546,235	484,537	19.0
New Hampshire	1,235,786	54,154	4.4	1,312,298	67,456	5.1
New Jersey	8,414,350	1,476,327	17.5	8,658,668	1,715,729	19.8
New Mexico	1,819,046	149,606	8.2	1,962,226	191,216	9.7
New York	18,976,457	3,868,133	20.4	19,428,881	4,216,714	21.7
North Carolina	8,049,313	430,000	5.3	9,036,449	623,292	6.9
North Dakota	642,200	12,114	1.9	638,613	14,631	2.3
Ohio	11,353,140	339,279	3.0	11,473,983	420,987	3.7
Oklahoma	3,450,654	131,747	3.8	3,606,200	180,655	5.0
Oregon	3,421,399	289,702	8.5	3,735,524	362,178	9.7
Pennsylvania	12,281,054	508,291	4.1	12,418,756	652,695	5.3
Rhode Island	1,048,319	119,227	11.4	1,054,306	131,969	12.5
South Carolina	4,012,012	115,978	2.9	4,403,175	186,623	4.2
South Dakota	754,844	13,495	1.8	795,757	15,905	2.0
Tennessee	5,689,283	159,004	2.8	6,144,104	246,050	4.0
Texas	20,851,820	2,899,642	13.9	23,845,989	3,787,550	15.9
Utah	2,233,169	158,664	7.1	2,663,500	218,087	8.2
Vermont	608,827	23,245	3.8	620,738	24,074	3.9
Virginia	7,078,515	570,279	8.1	7,698,738	784,015	10.2
Washington	5,894,121	614,457	10.4	6,453,083	792,894	12.3
West Virginia	1,808,344	19,930	1.1	1,810,358	23,056	1.3
Wisconsin	5,363,675	193,751	3.6	5,598,453	247,711	4.4
Wyoming	493,782	11,205	2.3	522,833	14,547	2.8

Note: The estimates represent the average characteristics of the population between January 2006 and December 2008 and do not represent a single point in time. **Source:** U.S. Census Bureau, American FactFinder; *American Community Surveys 2006–2008.*

criterion for eligibility and in 1965, the Hart-Cellar Immigration Act established a preferential system for skilled workers and relatives of U.S. citizens, but restricted the total number of immigrants to 270,000 each year, though the number of exceptions to this limit was far greater. An average of more than 700,000 immigrants legally entered the U.S. each year during the 1980s (not counting ille-

gal aliens naturalized under provisions of the 1986 Immigration Reform and Control Act).

In 1992, the 270,000 limit was replaced with a sliding cap that is even less restrictive than previous immigration laws. The 1990 Immigration Act limited the total number of immigrants to 700,000 from 1992 to 1995, and to 675,000 thereafter. The act increased the number of openings for immi-

Selected Characteristics of Foreign-Born Population, 2008

The foreign-born population of the United States consists of naturalized citizens and more recent immigrants who have not obtained citizenship. As the following table illustrates, the foreign-born population is heavily represented in the West in 2006 (19.1 percent of the population in the West was not born here) and the Northeast (13.7 percent) and lowest in the Midwest (5.9 percent).

		Foreign-born population			
Characteristic	Total U.S. population ('000s)	Total number ('000s)	As percent of U.S. population	Naturalized citizens ('000s)	Not citizens ('000s)
Total Population	299,106	37,264	12.5%	15,050	22,214
Age					
under 5 years	20,902	302	1.4	69	233
5 to 14 years	40,056	1,781	4.4	301	1,480
15 to 24 years	41,843	4,231	10.1	881	3,350
25 to 34 years	40,146	7,986	19.9	1,904	6,082
35 to 44 years	42,132	8,163	19.4	3,018	5,145
45 to 54 years	43,935	6,385	14.5	3,274	3,111
55 to 64 years	33,302	4,023	12.1	2,490	1,533
65 to 74 years	19,580	2,504	12.8	1,716	788
75 to 84 years	12,912	1,450	11.2	1,056	394
85 years and over	4,289	437	10.2	339	98
Sex					
Male	146,856	18,677	12.7	6,900	11,777
Female	152,250	18,587	12.2	8,150	10,437
Educational Attainment					
Not a high school graduate	26,340	9,489	36.0	2,694	6,795
High school graduate or some college	112,117	12,641	11.3	6,337	6,304
Bachelors degree	37,559	5,406	14.4	2,966	2,440
Advanced degree	20,228	3,413	16.9	1,801	1,612
Economic Status[1]					
Blow poverty level	37,276	6,150	16.5	1,426	4,724
At or above poverty level	261,423	31,093	11.9	13,624	17,469
Median earnings (in dollars)	$20,228	31,763	N.A.	41,358	26,701
Region of Residence[2]					
Northeast	54,741	8,202	15.0%	4,086	4,116
Midwest	66,218	4,242	6.4	1,838	2,404
South	109,084	11,375	10.4	4,209	7,167
West	69,356	13,729	19.8	5,635	8,094

Notes: 1. Data from 2007. 2. Data from 2006. **Source:** U.S. Census Bureau, *Statistical Abstract of the United States 2010.*

Estimated Unauthorized Immigrants by Selected States and Country of Birth, 2000 and 2008 (in thousands)

State of Residence	2000	2008	Country of Birth	2000	2008
United States, total	**8,460**	**11,600**	**Total**	**8,460**	**11,600**
California	2,510	2,850	Mexico	4,680	7,030
Texas	1,090	1,680	El Salvador	430	570
Florida	800	840	Guatemala	290	430
New York	540	640	Philippines	200	300
Arizona	330	560	Honduras	160	300
Illinois	440	550	Korea	180	240
Georgia	220	460	China	190	220
New Jersey	350	400	Brazil	100	180
North Carolina	260	380	Ecuador	110	170
Nevada	170	280	India	120	160
Other states	1,760	2,950	Other countries	2,000	2,000

Notes: Unauthorized immigrants refers to foreign-born persons who entered the U.S. without inspection or who were admitted temporarily and stayed past the date they were required to leave. Unauthorized aliens who have applied for but have not yet received approval to lawfully remain in the U.S. are considered to be unauthorized. All of these component populations were resident in the U.S. on January 1, 2008, and entered during the 1980–2007 period. Persons who entered the U.S. prior to 1980 were assumed to be legally resident. **Source:** U.S. Department of Homeland Security, Office of Immigration Statistics, *Estimates of the Unauthorized Immigrant Population Residing in the United States, January 2008* (2009).

grants with valuable employment skills from 54,000 to 140,000 each year, and reserved 55,000 openings each year for immigrants from under-represented countries. In addition, the new law introduced a sliding scale for admitting family-sponsored immigrants. Beginning in 1995, the number of immediate family members admitted in the previous year is subtracted from 480,000 to determine the number of family-sponsored immigrants eligible for admission. The family-sponsored limit may not go below 226,000 in any year,

however. Controversy over illegal immigration continued to swell through the early 2000s. In 2009, the state of Arizona passed a law allowing police to demand papers from anyone, even without due cause.

▶ THE FOREIGN-BORN POPULATION

An increase in the number of immigrants since the 1970s has helped to reshape the makeup of American society. The percentage of the population that was born outside this country continues to in-

Foreign-Born Population by Place of Birth, 2000

Place of Birth	Number	Percent	Place of Birth	Number	Percent
All Foreign-born persons	**28,379,000**	**100.00%**	**North America**	**13,300,000**	**46.87%**
			Canada	678,000	2.39
Europe	**4,355,000**	**15.35%**	Caribbean, total	2,813,000	9.91
Austria	65,000	0.23	Bahamas	13,000	0.05
Belgium	17,000	0.06	Barbados	54,000	0.19
Czechoslovakia	71,000	0.25	Cuba	952,000	3.35
Denmark	8,000	0.03	Dominican Republic	692,000	2.44
Finland	19,000	0.07	Grenada	42,000	0.15
France	127,000	0.45	Haiti	385,000	1.36
Germany	653,000	2.30	Jamaica	411,000	1.45
Greece	136,000	0.48	Trinidad/Tobago	173,000	0.61
Hungary	87,000	0.31	Other Caribbean	91,000	0.32
Ireland	202,000	0.71	Central America, total	9,789,000	34.49
Italy	451,000	1.59	Belize	59,000	0.21
Latvia	11,000	0.04	Costa Rica	77,000	0.27
Lithuania	39,000	0.14	El Salvador	765,000	2.70
Netherlands	93,000	0.33	Guatemala	327,000	1.15
Norway	18,000	0.06	Honduras	250,000	0.88
Poland	445,000	1.57	Mexico	7,841,000	27.63
Portugal	206,000	0.73	Nicaragua	245,000	0.86
Romania	99,000	0.35	Panama	69,000	0.24
Spain	80,000	0.28	Other Central America	157,000	0.55
Sweden	49,000	0.17	Other North America	20,000	0.07
Switzerland	29,000	0.10			
United Kingdom	613,000	2.16			
Yugoslavia	123,000	0.43	**South America**	**1,876,000**	**6.62%**
Other Europe	714,000	2.52	Argentina	89,000	0.31
			Bolivia	44,000	0.16
Soviet Union / Russia	**624,000**	**2.20%**	Brazil	160,000	0.56
			Chile	83,000	0.29
Asia	**7,246,000**	**25.53%**	Colombia	435,000	1.53
Afghanistan	27,000	0.10	Ecuador	281,000	0.99
Cambodia	122,000	0.43	Guyana	202,000	0.71
China	871,000	3.07	Peru	328,000	1.16
Hong Kong	195,000	0.69	Uruguay	73,000	0.26
India	1,007,000	3.55	Venezuela	126,000	0.44
Indonesia	53,000	0.19	Other South America	55,000	0.19
Iran	306,000	1.08			
Iraq	81,000	0.29	**Africa**	**701,000**	**2.47%**
Israel	82,000	0.29	Egypt	126,000	0.44
Japan	274,000	0.97	Ethiopia	68,000	0.24
Jordan	39,000	0.14	Ghana	80,000	0.28
Korea (South)	701,000	2.47	Kenya	28,000	0.10
Laos	74,000	0.26	Morocco	38,000	0.13
Lebanon	127,000	0.45	Nigeria	87,000	0.31
Malaysia	43,000	0.15	South Africa	69,000	0.24
Myanmar	35,000	0.12	Other Africa	205,000	0.72
Pakistan	197,000	0.69			
Philippines	1,222,000	4.31	**Oceania**	**147,000**	**0.52%**
Saudi Arabia	20,000	0.07	Australia	36,000	0.13
Syria	45,000	0.16	Fiji	33,000	0.12
Taiwan	325,000	1.15	New Zealand	20,000	0.07
Thailand	147,000	0.52	Other Oceania	11,682	0.04
Turkey	97,000	0.34			
Vietnam	863,000	3.04			
Other Asia	293,000	1.03	**Not reported**	**916,046**	**3.23%**

Note: The foreign-born population includes 1,864,285 persons who were born abroad of American parents. Numbers are rounded at source. **Source:** U.S. Census Bureau, 2000.

crease. In 2008, according to the Census Bureau, 37.3 million U.S. residents (12.5 percent of the total population) were foreign-born. The last time the figure was significantly higher was in 1920, when 13.2 percent of the population was born in another country. More than half of the foreign-born population in America came from Latin America; of these, the majority listed Mexico as their birthplace. Over 26 percent of the foreign-born population was from Asia. The remainder was divided between Europe and other regions. About 54 percent of the foreign born population was from a Latin American country in 2008.

Many foreign-born residents come to the U.S. and stay. In 2008, naturalized citizens constituted over 40 percent of the foreign-born population. Nearly 80 percent of foreign-born people who arrived before 1980 are now U.S. citizens.

SEX IN AMERICA

Pollsters scrutinize every angle of American life, including what goes on behind closed bedroom doors. The research ranges from the statistical—the survey done by the National Center for Health Statistics—to the anecdotal, such as reader polls taken by popular magazines. Here's a summary of the two most serious studies, one conducted by the federal government, the other by a leading university.

▶ WOMEN AND SEX

The National Survey of Family Growth is conducted periodically by the National Center for Health Statistics, with a national sample of women aged 15 to 44 years old. The most recent comprehensive report, issued in December 2005, used data compiled in 2002. Questions concerned marriage and sexual activity, as well as several other aspects of family life and reproductive health. Some findings from the report:

- 85 percent of all married women had pre-marital intercourse; only 15 percent of women waited until marriage to have sex for the first time.
- 56 percent of women aged 20–44 had their first intercourse by age 18, up from 52 percent in 1997; 75 percent were sexually experienced by age 20.
- Nearly 13 percent of women aged 20–24 had sex before age 15; the median age at first intercourse for these women was 16.6 years old.
- 31 percent of women had ever had an unintended birth; poor women and non-Hispanic black women were most likely to have had an unplanned birth.
- 22.6 percent of women aged 18–44 reported having nonvoluntary intercourse at some time in their lives; more than one-fourth of these women were under 15 when they were forced to have sex.
- 47 percent of unmarried women reported having just one sexual partner in the past year; 10.3 percent had two partners, and 32.5 percent said they had no partners. But over their lifetimes, women of all marital statuses reported many more sexual partners. More than half (55.2 percent) of all women had three or more sexual partners in their lifetimes.

- 61.9 percent of women age 15–44 currently use contraceptives; the remaining 38.1 percent are divided among women who are pregnant, seeking to have children, or abstinent. Only 7.4 percent of women admitted having unprotected sex. Among women using contraceptives, the pill (30.6 percent) was the most popular method, followed by female sterilization (27.0 percent) and the condom (18 percent). Women under the age of 30 were most likely to use the pill.

▶ SEX PARTNERS AND FREQUENCY OF INTERCOURSE

The National Opinion Research Center at the University of Chicago (NORC) periodically conducts a study of the sexual behavior of adults. The Center interviews a nationwide representative sample of about 1,500 adults to collect accurate data on a wide range of topics dealing with sex. Here are some of the survey's primary findings.

Cohabitation As premarital sex becomes more commonplace and the average age at first marriage grows older, the number of couples living together out of wedlock continues to spiral. Just over 1.1 percent of all couples were living together in 1960; in 2002, 9.1 percent of men and women ages 15–44 were living together. In 1988, 23.4 percent of married couples had lived together before marrying; by 1994, 28 percent had. Cohabiting was most popular among younger couples: 11 percent of people 18–29 were cohabiting in 2002, and in 1998, 43.7 percent had cohabited with their current spouse before marriage. The exact same percentage of 30 to 39-year-olds cohabited before marriage in 1998, but only 8.5 percent of the people in this age group were currently cohabiting in 2002.

Extramarital sex Numbers regarding sex out of wedlock are usually unreliable, since most people are reluctant to admit their affairs to interviewers. The percentage of currently married people admitting to extramarital sex within the last year (3.0 percent in 2002) has fluctuated very little since 1988. More people were willing to admit having an affair at one point in their lives. In 1991, 14.6 percent of people who had ever been married admitted having at least one affair while married; in 2002, 17.7 percent said they had had extramarital sex. These figures are much higher than the one-year numbers because they include married people as well as those who are separated and divorced, perhaps as a result of one of these affairs. Men (4.3 percent in the last year, and 21.8 percent ever) were more likely than women (1.9 percent 14.7 respectively) to admit extramarital activity.

Gender of sex partners For the same reasons, many people are also reluctant to admit homosexual behavior. The percentage of sexually active adults admitting to homosexual behavior within the last year has remained steady at between 2 and 3.5 percent since 1988, but the actual number is probably somewhat higher. In 2002, a smaller percentage (1.6 percent of women and 0.4 percent of men) of people claim to have had sex with partners of both genders. Men who attend church regularly (3.2 percent) were as likely to have had a same sex partner than those who attended church occasionally (3.2 percent). Among those who attended church rarely, 3.7 admitted to having a same sex partner.

Number of sex partners The average number of sex partners per person has remained fairly constant over the past few years. A majority of adults have had only one sexual partner in the past five years, and more than two-thirds had only one partner in the past year. Adults in 2006 had an average of 1.18 partners in the last 12 months, and 2.72 partners in the past five years.

Frequency of sexual intercourse Americans had intercourse an average of 56.9 times a year in 2006. That's down from 63.9 times a year in 2002, but not significantly different from data from surveys dating back to 1989. Not surprisingly, married people aged 18-29 had the most sex—96.3 times a year (or almost twice a week); unmarried people over 70 had the least sex: an average of 3.4 times annually in 2006. Just over 19 percent of adults had no sex at all in 2006, 20.9 percent of women and 13.4 percent of men.

Same Sex Couples in the U.S. by Characteristic, 2008

Characteristic	Same-sex married Male	Female	Same-sex unmarried Male	Female
Total	**65,764**	**84,192**	**204,836**	**209,951**
Average age	50.0	54.3	44.6	43.2
Both partners have a college degree	22.0%	21.5%	33.7%	33.9%
Average household income	$98,730	$85,956	$129,607	$96,719
Own home	74.6%	79.2%	71.7%	70.8%
Interracial couple	8.5%	6.0%	14.1%	11.4%
Raising children	33.9%	27.9%	7.4%	25.9%

Source: 2008 American Community Survey

Same Sex Couples per 1,000 households, by State Rank, 2008

Rank	Same-sex spouses	Rate	Same-sex unmarried	Rate	All same-sex couples	Rate
1.	Massachussetts[1]	3.63	District of Columbia[2]	13.22	District of Columbia[2]	14.12
2.	Vermont[2]	2.71	Maine[2]	6.81	Maine[2]	8.23
3.	Hawaii[2]	2.43	Washington[2]	5.84	Massachussetts[1]	7.92
4.	Utah	2.32	Oregon[2]	5.73	Oregon[2]	7.26
5.	Wyoming	2.28	New York[3]	5.15	Washington[2]	6.97
6.	California[1]	1.92	California	5.01	California[1]	6.93
7.	Nevada	1.85	Colorado	4.92	New York[3]	6.41
8.	Connecticut[1]	1.79	Arizona	4.65	Colorado	6.13
9.	New Jersey[2]	1.70	Delaware	4.59	Vermont[2]	6.10
10.	Rhode Island	1.64	Rhode Island	4.41	Delaware	6.09

Notes: 1. State offered marriage to same-sex couples in 2008. 2. State offered non-marital relationship recognition for same-sex couples in 2008. 3. State recognized same-sex marriages in 2008, but they could not be performed there. Source: 2008 American Community Survey.

Frequency of Sexual Intercourse by Age, Race and Marital Status 2002-2008

Mean number of times per year

Marital Status	All Adults	By Race White	Black	By Age 18–29	30–39	40–49	50–59	60–69	70+
2002, Total	**63.9**	**61.2**	**65.6**	N.A.	N.A.	N.A.	N.A.	N.A.	N.A.
Married	N.A.	N.A.	N.A.	110.2	86.2	70.6	54.5	33.4	17.6
Unmarried	N.A.	N.A.	N.A.	74.0	67.8	47.1	31.3	16.3	3.3
2004, Total	**59.6**	**58.2**	**71.2**	N.A.	N.A.	N.A.	N.A.	N.A.	N.A.
Married	N.A.	N.A.	N.A.	102.9	90.6	65.9	38.6	27.4	16.0
Unmarried	N.A.	N.A.	N.A.	77.4	73.3	52.7	21.1	18.1	3.7
2006, Total	**56.9**	**55.8**	**65.1**	N.A.	N.A.	N.A.	N.A.	N.A.	N.A.
Married	N.A.	N.A.	N.A.	96.3	78.9	70.0	45.2	33.6	9.6
Unmarried	N.A.	N.A.	N.A.	77.5	71.9	51.7	29.8	16.7	3.4
2008, Total	**59.6**	**55.8**	**73.9**	N.A.	N.A.	N.A.	N.A.	N.A.	N.A.
Married	N.A.	N.A.	N.A.	102.6	90.6	76.7	60.4	29.0	15.0
Unmarried	N.A.	N.A.	N.A.	74.4	75.1	52.9	21.0	17.9	4.8

Source: National Opinion Research Center (NORC) *General Social Survey,* 2002, 2004, 2006, 2008.

Number of Sexual Partners, 2002-2008

Year	None	1	2	3	4	5–9	10+	Mean
				Last 12 months				
2002	18.8%	67.8%	6.4%	3.1%	1.7%	1.3%	0.7%	1.32
2004	15.7	72.2	5.5	2.8	1.6	1.5	0.6	1.21
2006	19.8	68.3	5.4	2.6	1.5	1.7	0.8	1.18
2008	18.1	69.2	6.5	2.3	1.4	1.5	1.0	1.46
				Last five years				
2002	12.1%	56.5%	9.1%	6.3%	5.0%	7.0%	3.9%	2.81
2004	10.1	61.0	10.4	5.0	4.9	5.3	3.3	2.77
2006	12.0	59.2	9.3	6.2	4.0	5.5	4.0	2.72
2008	11.3	60.9	9.3	6.4	3.3	5.4	3.4	2.87

Source: National Opinion Research Center (NORC) *General Social Surveys,* 2002, 2004, 2006, 2008.

Agriculture

In recent years, U.S. agriculture has become an integral part of the global economy. In 2008, American farmers produced 39.1 percent of the world's corn, 36.8 percent of its soybeans, and 10 percent of its wheat. Much of this is then exported to all parts of the world, but especially to Asia and Latin America. In 1990, U.S. agricultural exports totaled $39.5 billion, and by 2008, exports topped $115 billion. Over 10 percent of this dollar value was for vegetables and preparations; another 10 percent was for grains and feeds.

This is a far cry from the small nation of "embattled farmers" who launched the American Revolution. In the early years of the Republic, agriculture, while vital (involving 95 percent of the population), remained relatively small-scale and in economic terms primitive, with the exception of large plantations in the South devoted to cotton, tobacco and rice. The Civil War brought higher food prices and increased mechanization throughout the farming industry. It also led to federal legislation aimed at encouraging farming; the Homestead Act of 1862 and the Morrill Land Grant College Act were especially important. The decision to build a transcontinental rail system—undertaken by private enterprises abetted by government grants—opened up large areas of the Great Plains to farming, and the railroad companies recruited immigrants to buy and farm the land the government had given the companies.

In the early 20th century, machinery gradually replaced animal power. World War I stimulated agriculture, but the stimulus led to overproduction, which depressed prices and land values. This decline both contributed to and was intensified by the Great Depression. The plight of farmers during the 1930s prompted considerable government remedies, including various forms of credit, price supports, and rural electrification. World War II again gave impetus to agriculture.

After the war, new machinery, new chemicals, and hybrid crops, more resistant to weather and biological enemies, significantly increased crop yields. By the end of the 1940s, the United States had become the world's largest single producer of wheat, corn, and soybeans. One byproduct of this success was the creation of huge surpluses. U.S. agriculture proved a potent force in the world economy and foreign policy, and in 1954, Public Law 480 provided for the export of surplus grains to poorer nations both to prevent starvation and stimulate economic development, and to alleviate the pressures on the domestic agriculture sector caused by the surpluses.

Since 1960, the number of American farms has declined as small units lose out to huge agribusinesses owned by corporations. Between 1980 and 2008, the number of farms fell from 2.44 million to 2.20 million, a decline of 9.8 percent. Overall, the total land area devoted to farming dropped from

Percent of U.S. Agricultural Exports by Region and Selected Nation, 1990–2008

Category	1990	1995	2000	2008
Total agricultural exports (billions)	$39.5	$56.2	$51.2	$115.4
Percent by region and nation				
Asia	40.2%	45.7%	38.8%	38.4%
Japan	20.6	19.8	18.1	11.5
Korea, South	6.7	6.7	5.0	4.8
Taiwan	4.2	4.6	3.9	3.0
China	2.1	4.7	3.3	10.5
Hong Kong	1.8	2.7	2.5	N.A.
Western Europe[1]	20.0	16.4	13.7	11.2
European Union	18.4	15.5	12.7	8.7
Latin America[2]	13.0	14.3	20.8	19.9
Mexico	6.5	6.3	12.5	13.9
Canada	10.7	10.3	14.9	14.1
Africa	4.7	5.0	4.5	5.0

Notes: 1. Data for 2008 include Eurasia. 2. Data for 2008 denote Central America, South America, and Mexico. Source: U.S. Census Bureau, *Statistical Abstract of the United States* (2010).

U.S. Farms, Acreage and Population, 1850–2008

Year	Farms ('000s)	Acreage Total ('000s)	Acreage Avg. per farm	Acreage Percent of U.S.	Farm Population Total ('000s)	Farm Population Percent of U.S.
1850	1,449	293,561	203	15.6%	N.A.	N.A.
1860	2,044	407,213	199	21.4	N.A.	N.A.
1870	2,660	407,735	153	21.4	N.A.	N.A.
1880	4,009	536,082	134	28.2	21,973	43.8%
1890	4,565	623,219	137	32.7	24,771	42.3
1900	5,740	841,202	147	37.0	29,835	41.9
1910	6,406	881,431	139	38.8	32,077	34.9
1920	6,518	958,677	149	42.2	31,974	30.1
1930	6,546	990,112	157	43.6	30,529	24.9
1940	6,350	1,065,114	175	46.8	30,547	23.2
1950	5,648	1,202,019	213	51.1	23,048	15.3
1960	3,963	1,176,646	297	49.5	15,635	8.7
1970	2,949	1,102,371	374	47.0	9,712	4.8
1980	2,440	1,038,885	426	44.8	6,051	2.7
1990	2,146	986,850	460	42.7	4,801	1.9
1995	2,196	962,515	438	N.A.	N.A.	N.A.
2000	2,167	945,080	436	N.A.	N.A.	N.A.
2008	2,200	920,000	418	>1.0	3,282[1]	>1.0

Note: Acreage figures after 1980 rounded in source. 1. Data is for 2007. Source: U.S. Census Bureau, *Statistical History of the United States* (1970); *Statistical Abstract of the United States*; National Agricultural Statistics Service; U.S. Dept. of Agriculture, *2010 Agricultural Statistics*.

1.04 billion acres to 920 million, a decline of 11.5 percent. Meanwhile, improved technology has made farming less labor intensive, so the total farm population has also declined precipitously. In 2008, the number of farm operators—anyone who works on or runs a farm—had fallen to less than 1 percent of the total population, down from 42 percent at the turn of the century, and 15 percent in 1950. Despite the prevalence of agribusiness, the "green revolution" has sparked renewed interest in traditional, organic farming. In 2007, there were over 20,000 organic farms, the vast majority of which (45 percent) were less than 10 acres.

Nevertheless, large farms are far more prevalent and create surpluses of crop, which often required governments to prop up prices, sometimes at the consumer's expense. In 1996, a Republican-led Congress pushed through the "Freedom to Farm" law, which was intended to remove price subsidies on most major crops. But in 2002, just as the program was to become fully effective, President George W. Bush signed legislation that instead raised farm subsidies to $190 billion, an increase of $83 billion. The majority of the subsidy did not go to individual family farms, but to giant agribusinesses, continuing the trend of consolidation in the farming industry. In 2008, Congress passed a controversial farm subsidy bill that increased spending by nearly $20 billion.

Growing concerns about fuel costs and domestic jobs have in some cases hurt farmers who depend upon exporting a large share of their crop. Never-

Number and Acreage of Farms, by State, 1980–2008

State	Number of Farms ('000s)				Acreage (millions)				Acreage per farm			
	1980	1990	2000	2008	1980	1990	2000	2008	1980	1990	2000	2008
U.S. total	2,440	2,146	2,172	2,200	1,039	987	943	920	426	460	434	418
Alabama	59	47	47	49	12	10	9	9	207	215	191	185
Alaska	1	1	1	1	2	1	1	1	3,378	1,707	1,586	1,309
Arizona	8	8	11	16	38	36	27	26	5,080	4,641	3,560	1,673
Arkansas	59	47	48	49	17	16	15	14	280	330	304	278
California	81	85	83	82	34	31	26	25	417	382	318	312
Colorado	27	27	30	37	36	33	32	31	1,358	1,249	1,071	858
Connecticut	4	4	4	5	1	1	1	1	117	108	92	82
Delaware	4	3	3	3	1	1	1	1	186	207	223	200
Florida	39	41	44	48	11	11	10	9	344	266	234	195
Georgia	50	49	48	48	11	11	10	10	260	222	220	218
Hawaii	4	5	6	8	2	2	1	1	458	357	262	148
Idaho	24	22	25	25	15	14	12	11	623	628	486	452
Illinois	107	83	77	76	29	28	28	27	269	342	355	352
Indiana	87	68	63	61	17	16	16	15	193	240	242	243
Iowa	119	104	94	93	34	34	33	31	284	322	345	333
Kansas	75	69	64	66	48	48	48	46	644	694	742	705
Kentucky	102	93	90	85	15	14	14	14	143	152	151	164
Louisiana	37	32	29	30	10	9	8	8	273	278	275	268
Maine	8	7	7	8	2	1	1	1	195	201	187	169
Maryland	18	15	12	13	3	2	2	2	157	148	169	160
Massachusetts	6	6	6	8	1	1	1	1	116	100	93	66
Michigan	65	54	52	55	11	11	10	10	175	200	200	182
Minnesota	104	89	81	81	30	30	29	27	291	337	362	332
Mississippi	55	40	43	42	15	13	11	11	265	325	258	262
Missouri	120	108	109	108	31	30	30	29	261	281	275	269
Montana	24	25	28	30	62	61	57	61	2,601	2,449	2,054	2,061
Nebraska	65	37	54	47	48	47	46	46	734	826	859	962
Nevada	3	3	3	3	9	9	7	6	3,100	3,560	2,267	1,903
New Hampshire	3	3	3	4	1	1	1	1	160	163	135	113
New Jersey	9	8	10	10	1	1	1	1	109	107	86	71
New Mexico	14	14	15	21	47	45	44	43	3,467	3,296	2,895	2,087
New York	47	39	38	37	9	8	8	7	200	218	203	194
North Carolina	93	62	57	53	12	10	9	9	126	156	161	164
North Dakota	40	34	30	32	42	41	39	40	1,043	1,209	1,300	1,238
Ohio	95	83	79	75	16	16	15	14	171	188	186	185
Oklahoma	72	70	85	87	35	33	34	35	481	471	400	405
Oregon	35	37	40	39	18	18	17	16	517	488	430	425
Pennsylvania	53	59	58	63	8	8	8	8	153	131	131	123
Rhode Island	1	1	1	1	1	1	1	1	87	95	86	57
South Carolina	34	25	24	27	6	5	5	5	188	208	200	182
South Dakota	39	35	32	31	45	44	44	44	1,169	1,266	1,354	1,396
Tennessee	96	87	88	79	14	12	12	11	142	139	130	138
Texas	196	196	228	248	138	132	131	130	705	673	575	527
Utah	14	13	16	17	12	11	12	11	919	856	748	673
Vermont	8	7	7	7	2	1	1	1	226	222	200	174
Virginia	58	46	49	47	10	9	9	8	169	193	178	170
Washington	38	37	37	40	16	16	16	15	429	432	393	375
West Virginia	22	21	21	23	4	4	4	4	191	180	176	159
Wisconsin	93	80	78	78	19	16	16	15	200	220	210	195
Wyoming	9	9	9	11	35	35	35	30	3,846	3,899	3,761	2,736

Note: 1. Fewer than 500,000 acres. **Source:** U.S. Census Bureau, *Statistical Abstract of the United States* (2010).

theless, the U.S. continues to export agricultural products worth more than $115 billion a year, the highest percentage of which (38 percent) goes to Asia including the Middle East. Commodity prices rose steadily through the 2000s until dropping suddenly in 2008 and declining nearly 40 percent between July and November alone. The devastating fall renewed famers' worries of the previous decade, knowing they faced a difficult future. Se-

vere drought in the Southwest and part of the Southeast in the first decade of the 2000s also caused hardship. As a result, government subsidies rose from $7.3 billion in 1996 to $23.1 billion in 2000; they fell back to $15.8 billion in 2009. An additional $4.6 billion was spent on agricultural research and services, which includes investigation into shipping practices, disease containment, and the increasing availability of technological tools.

U.S. Agricultural Exports: Principal Commodities by Value and Percentage of Agriculture Exports, 1980–2008

Category	1980 Value (billions)	1980 Percent	1990 Value (billions)	1990 Percent	2000 Value (billions)	2000 Percent	2008 Value (billions)	2008 Percent
Total agricultural exports	$41.2	100.0%	$39.5	100.0%	$50.7	100.0%	$115.4	100%
Commodities								
Grains and feeds	$19.1	46.4%	$14.4	36.5%	$13.8	27.2%	$37.0	32.0%
Oilseeds and products	9.4	22.8	5.7	14.4	8.4	16.6	23.7	20.5
Animals and animal products	3.8	9.2	6.7	16.9	11.5	22.7	21.8	18.9
Cotton	2.9	7.0	2.8	7.0	1.8	3.6	4.8	4.2
Tobacco, unmanufactured	1.3	3.3	1.4	3.6	1.2	2.4	1.2	1.1
Fruits and preparations	1.3	3.3	2.4	6.0	3.4	6.7	4.8	4.2
Vegetables and preparations	1.2	2.9	2.2	5.6	4.4	8.7	5.1[1]	4.4
Nuts and preparations	0.8	1.9	1.0	2.5	1.2	2.4	3.8	3.3
Other	1.5	3.6	2.9	7.3	5.0	9.9	13.1	11.4

Note: Figures might not add up due to independent rounding. 1. Includes pulses. **Source:** U.S. Census Bureau, *Statistical Abstract of the United States* (2010).

U.S. Production of Leading Farm Products as Percent of World Total, 1995–2008

Product	U.S. production (millions of metric tons) 1995	1999	2000	2008	As percent of world total 1995	1999	2000	2008
Total production								
Corn	188.0	240.0	251.9	307	36.5%	39.6%	42.7%	39.1%
Wheat	59.0	63.0	60.6	68	11.0	10.7	10.4	10.0
Soybeans	59.0	72.0	75.1	81	47.4	45.3	42.7	36.8
Cotton[1]	17.9	17.0	17.2	19.2	22.9	16.3	19.4	15.9
Rice, milled	5.6	6.6	5.9	6.5	1.5	1.6	1.5	1.5
Amount exported								
Corn	52.7	49.4	48.3	44.0	72.4%	67.5%	63.2%	57.8%
Wheat	33.7	29.5	28.0	26.5	33.9	26.2	26.9	20.3
Soybeans	23.1	26.5	27.1	32.9	72.4	57.2	50.4	44.5
Cotton[1]	7.7	6.8	6.7	13.7	27.9	24.9	25.5	35.5
Rice, milled	3.1	2.6	2.5	3.4	14.8	10.4	10.2	11.5

Note: 1. Millions of bales. **Source:** U.S. Census Bureau, *Statistical Abstract of the United States* (2010).

Agricultural Imports, Value by Selected Commodity, 1990–2008

Commodity	Value (millions of dollars) 1990	2000	2008	Percent Distribution 1990	2000	2008
Total[1]	$22,918	$38,974	$80,465	100.0%	100.0%	100.0%
Cattle, live	978	1,152	1,761	4.3	3.0	2.2
Beef and veal	1,872	2,399	3,057	8.2	6.2	3.8
Pork	938	997	1,060	4.1	2.6	1.3
Dairy products	891	1,671	3,138	3.9	4.3	3.9
Grains and feeds	1,188	3,075	8,260	5.2	7.9	10.3
Fruits and preparations	2,167	3,851	7,896	9.5	9.9	9.8
Vegetables and preparations[2]	1,979	3,958	8,314	8.6	10.2	10.3
Sugar and related products	1,213	1,555	2,967	5.3	4.0	3.7
Wine	917	2,207	4,635	4.0	5.7	5.8
Malt Beverages	923	2,179	3,668	4.0	5.6	4.6
Coffee and products	1,915	2,700	4,412	8.4	6.9	5.5
Cocoa and products	1,072	1,404	3,299	4.7	3.6	4.1

Notes: 1. Includes other commodities not shown seperately. 2. Includes pulses. **Source:** U.S. Census Bureau, *Statistical Abstract of the United States* (2010).

Crime and Punishment

▶SERIOUS CRIME

Serious crime is the Justice Department's measure of the total number of violent crimes (murder, rape, robbery, and assault) plus property crimes (burglary, larceny/theft, motor vehicle theft, and arson). The number of serious crimes in the U.S. fell from an all-time high of close to 15 million in 1991 to just over 11.6 million in 2000, and has hovered between 11 and 12 million since then.

The number of violent crimes peaked at 1.93 million in 1992 and steadily declined over the next decade. But while the overall number of crimes continues to decline, violent crimes have inched back up since 2004. The number of murders, robberies, and assaults reported to police all increased in 2006 but fell in 2007 and 2008. However, these figures are still far below what they were from 1990–94, when more than 23,000 people were murdered each year. In 2008, there were 16,272 reported murders. Guns remain the weapon of choice, used in about two-thirds of all homicides and in nearly half of robberies; handguns alone account for half of all murders.

Property crime reached its all-time high in 1991, at 12.96 million total offenses reported to police. It has continued to decrease since then, to just under 10 million. The number of burglaries is declining even faster, from close to 4 million in 1980 to just over 2.2 million in 2008.

A strong economy, a thriving job market, and tougher prison sentences were major reasons for the steadily declining number of serious crimes throughout the last 20 years, especially the crimes of robbery, burglary, and motor vehicle theft. Better policing techniques and an aging

population help to explain the decline in the violent crime rate. The recent spike in violent crime has been blamed on everything from video games to methamphetamines, but police say the biggest factor has been easy access to guns by people willing to use them to settle disputes. Aggravated assault with a gun is one of the fastest-growing categories of crime.

The number of forcible rapes is up nearly 70 percent since 1975, though much of this significant jump may be the result of more women reporting this crime to police. The 89,000 rapes reported in 2008 were down from the 1992 high of 109,066, and follow a decline from 90,427 in 2007.

The crime rate   Raw numbers of crime do not necessarily tell the whole story. To account for population growth, criminologists use the crime rate per 100,000 population to compare statistics from different years. Because the population continues to grow, the rate of crime (or the likelihood that you would become a victim of crime) declines if the total number of crimes stays the same or grows slower than the population. While the number of crimes is down slightly, the violent crime rate has dropped 36 percent since 1990, and the overall crime rate has fallen by a third.

The murder rate in 2008 was 5.4 per 100,000 population, the lowest year on record since 1989. The highest year was 1991, with 9.8 reported murders per 1,000 population. Violent crime overall decreased from 466.9 per 1,000 population in 2007 to 454.5 in 2008, down significantly from 506.5 in 2000. The property crime rate continues to fall, from over 5,000 in 1990 to a new low of 3,212.5 per 100,000 residents in 2008.

Serious Crime in the U.S., 1980–2008

Crime	1980	1990	2000	2008	Crime percent change		
Number of Offenses Reported to Police					2yrs	5yrs	10yrs
Violent crime	1,344,520	1,820,127	1,425,486	1,382,012	–1.9%	1.6%	–3.1%
Murder	23,040	23,438	15,586	16,272	–3.9	0.8	4.8
Forcible rape	82,990	102,555	90,178	89,000	–1.6	–6.4	–0.5
Robbery	565,840	639,271	408,016	441,855	–0.7	10.1	7.9
Aggravated assault	672,650	1,054,863	911,706	834,885	–2.5	–1.5	–8.4
Property crime	12,063,700	12,655,486	10,182,584	9,767,915	–0.8	–5.3	–4.3
Burglary	3,795,200	3,073,909	2,050,992	2,222,196	2.0	3.6	5.8
Larceny/theft	7,136,900	7,945,670	6,971,590	6,588,873	0.3	–5.0	–5.3
Motor vehicle theft	1,131,700	1,635,907	1,160,002	956,846	–12.7	–22.7	–16.9
Total serious crimes	13,408,300	14,475,613	11,608,070	11,149,927			
					Rate percent change		
Rate per 100,000 inhabitants					2yrs	5yrs	10yrs
Violent crime	596.6	729.6	506.5	454.5	–2.7%	–1.9%	–13.1%
Murder	10.2	9.4	5.5	5.4	–4.7	–2.7	–6.0
Forcible rape	36.8	41.1	32.0	29.3	–2.4	–9.6	–10.7
Robbery	251.1	256.3	145.0	145.3	–1.5	6.3	–3.2
Aggravated assault	298.5	422.9	324.0	274.6	–3.2	–4.8	–17.9
Property crime	5,353.3	5,073.1	3,618.3	3,212.5	–1.6	–8.6	–14.2
Burglary	1,684.1	1,232.2	728.8	730.8	1.2	0.1	–5.1
Larceny/theft	3,167.0	3,185.1	2,477.3	2,167.0	–0.5	–8.3	–15.0
Motor vehicle theft	502.2	655.8	412.2	314.7	–13.4	–25.3	–25.5
Total serious crimes	5,950.0	5,802.7	4,124.8	N.A.			

Note: Totals may not add up due to independent rounding. **Source:** Federal Bureau of Investigation, *Uniform Crime Reports: Crime in the United States 2007; 2008 Crime in the United States* (2009).

Serious Crime by 100,000 Population by State and Region, 2008

State	All	Murder	Forcible rape	Robbery	Aggravated Assault	All	Burglary	Larceny/ theft	Motor theft
U.S. Total	454.5	5.4	29.3	145.3	274.6	3,212.5	730.8	2,167.0	314.7
Northeast	370.8	4.2	20.0	138.5	208.2	2,248.8	429.5	1,644.9	174.4
Connecticut	297.8	3.5	19.3	111.6	163.5	2,458.7	428.7	8,963	256.0
Maine	117.5	2.4	28.5	25.3	61.4	2,452.4	495.4	1,867.7	89.3
Massachusetts	449.0	2.6	26.7	108.8	310.9	2,400.1	555.5	1,648.6	196.0
New Hampshire	157.2	1.0	29.7	31.8	94.7	2,091.9	325.7	1,660.8	105.4
Rhode Island	249.4	2.8	26.4	83.7	136.7	2,840.6	547.2	1,988.9	304.5
Vermont	135.9	2.7	20.4	14.3	98.3	2,538.5	557.2	1,887.1	94.2
Middle Atlantic	386.4	4.7	18.2	156.0	207.5	2,185.3	405.6	1,612.9	166.8
New Jersey	326.5	4.3	12.9	146.3	163.0	2,293.4	465.3	1,595.7	232.4
New York	398.1	4.3	14.4	163.0	216.4	1,993.5	337.3	1,527.3	128.9
Pennsylvania	410.0	5.6	27.9	151.6	224.8	2,410.2	470.9	1,758.8	180.5
Midwest	400.1	4.8	34.0	126.8	234.5	3,066.5	681.1	2,122.8	262.6
East North Central	419.5	5.1	34.2	147.4	232.8	3,085.7	715.2	2,098.3	272.3
Illinois	525.4	6.1	31.9	186.4	300.9	2,932.6	612.1	2,068.1	252.5
Indiana	333.8	5.1	27.0	118.1	183.5	3,335.8	762.8	2,299.2	273.7
Michigan	501.5	5.4	45.0	129.6	321.5	2,934.8	741.5	1,831.1	362.3
Ohio	348.2	4.7	38.5	163.0	142.1	3,411.7	92.8	2,270.5	248.4
Wisconsin	274.0	2.6	19.9	91.1	160.4	2,756.4	488.3	2,063.4	204.7
West North Central	355.4	4.2	33.4	79.3	238.4	3,022.2	602.9	2,179.1	240.2
Iowa	283.8	2.5	29.6	41.6	210.1	2,420.9	547.9	1,728.8	144.3
Kansas	410.6	4.0	42.5	60.1	304.0	3,377.2	699.9	2,413.4	263.9
Minnesota	262.8	2.1	34.6	80.0	146.1	2,850.6	505.9	2,151.6	193.1
Missouri	504.4	7.7	27.3	125.0	344.4	3,663.7	774.5	2,537.9	351.3
Nebraska	303.7	3.8	32.7	72.8	194.3	2,878.6	492.0	2,151.8	234.8
North Dakota	166.5	0.5	36.2	11.2	118.6	1,894.4	328.3	1,428.6	137.5
South Dakota	201.4	3.2	53.7	14.9	129.6	1,645.6	302.2	1,244.0	99.5
South Atlantic	553.7	6.6	27.2	175.3	344.5	3,788.5	923.2	2,525.7	339.6
Delaware	703.4	6.5	41.9	210.5	444.4	3,585.3	774.3	2,520.0	291.0
D.C.	1,437.7	31.4	31.4	748.5	626.4	5,104.6	640.0	3,372.2	1,092.4
Florida	688.9	6.4	32.6	197.9	452.0	4,140.8	1,028.3	2,766.0	346.5
Georgia	478.9	6.6	22.7	179.2	270.5	4,015.5	1,038.9	2,567.5	409.1
Maryland	628.2	8.8	20.0	234.4	365.1	3,517.6	689.6	2,378.3	449.7
North Carolina	467.3	6.5	24.8	155.4	280.6	4,044.1	1,210.1	2,544.0	290.0
South Carolina	729.7	6.8	36.6	147.3	539.1	4,234.2	1,026.1	2,814.1	394.0
Virginia	255.9	4.7	22.6	95.7	132.8	2,518.1	411.8	1,935.6	170.7
West Virginia	273.8	3.3	20.0	49.0	201.5	2,568.6	609.9	1,782.2	176.6
East South Central	481.2	6.6	33.1	139.2	302.4	3,529.6	941.6	2,329.8	258.2
Alabama	452.8	7.6	34.7	157.6	253.0	4,082.9	1,081.3	2,713.0	288.7
Kentucky	296.2	4.6	33.0	93.8	164.8	2,583.9	675.5	1,728.8	179.6
Mississippi	284.9	8.1	30.3	102.6	143.9	2,940.4	885.6	1,838.7	216.2
Tennessee	722.4	6.6	33.2	173.8	508.9	4,042.6	1,046.0	2,687.3	309.3
West South Central	528.1	6.5	34.4	142.4	344.9	3,896.9	971.2	2,595.1	330.6
Arkansas	503.4	5.7	48.9	95.8	353.1	3,835.1	1,180.0	2,427.1	228.0
Louisiana	656.2	11.9	27.9	135.9	480.4	3,823.1	982.1	2,529.4	311.6
Oklahoma	526.7	5.8	40.2	101.1	379.5	3,442.4	963.1	2,180.5	298.7
Texas	507.9	5.6	32.9	155.2	314.1	3,985.6	946.0	2,688.8	350.8
West	445.4	4.8	30.2	146.4	264.0	3,200.7	679.3	2,063.0	458.3
Arizona	447.0	6.3	25.7	149.2	265.9	4,291.0	868.9	2,849.5	572.6
Colorado	343.1	3.2	42.5	68.1	229.3	2,849.0	572.0	2,003.3	273.7
Idaho	228.6	1.5	36.2	15.8	175.1	2,101.2	439.8	1,552.0	109.5
Montana	258.1	2.4	30.4	17.8	207.6	2,603.0	344.4	2,095.9	162.6
Nevada	724.5	6.3	42.4	248.9	426.9	3,447.5	929.0	1,906.8	611.6
New Mexico	649.9	7.2	57.4	109.5	475.9	3,909.2	1,094.2	2,411.6	403.4
Utah	221.8	1.4	32.6	51.9	135.8	3,357.4	536.5	2,557.9	262.9
Wyoming	232.0	1.9	33.8	16.1	180.2	2,717.3	410.0	2,173.4	133.9
Pacific	457.7	5.0	27.5	163.2	261.9	3,092.3	659.9	1,945.5	487.0
Alaska	651.9	4.1	64.3	94.0	489.6	2,932.3	472.1	2,221.5	238.7
California	503.8	5.8	24.2	188.8	285.0	2,940.3	647.1	1,769.4	523.8
Hawaii	272.6	1.9	28.3	84.3	158.1	3,571.2	728.1	2,444.7	398.5
Oregon	257.2	2.2	30.5	69.7	154.8	3,282.5	550.9	2,432.3	299.0
Washington	331.2	2.9	40.1	96.9	191.2	3,758.4	801.3	2,524.6	432.6

Source: Federal Bureau of Investigation, *2008 Crime in the United States* (2009).

Serious Crime Per 100,000 Population, by Metropolitan Area, 2005

Metropolitan area	All serious crime[1]	Violent crime				Total violent crime[1]	Total property crime[1]
		Murder	Forcible rape	Robbery	Aggravated assault		
25 HIGHEST CRIME RATES							
Hot Springs, Ark.	8,265.1	663.2	8.6	55.9	111.8	486.9	7,601.9
Myrtle Beach-Conway, S.C.	7,722.5	860.5	13.1	52.6	187.2	607.5	6,862.0
Mount Vernon-Anacortes, Wash.	7,683.4	214.1	2.7	53.3	46.2	111.9	7,469.3
Yakima, Wash.	7,346.9	329.5	9.5	56.0	94.7	169.3	7,017.4
Memphis, Tenn.	7,282.6	1,196.8	13.9	45.3	389.8	747.9	6,085.8
Florence, S.C.	7,019.8	1,286.4	8.0	51.0	222.6	1,004.8	5,733.4
Corpus Christi, Texas	6,897.8	601.7	2.9	68.7	129.4	400.7	6,296.1
Macon, Ga.	6,682.3	501.6	11.9	32.8	166.3	290.5	6,180.7
Little Rock-N. Little Rock, Ark.	6,630.7	863.5	8.9	47.6	197.3	609.7	5,767.2
Jackson, Tenn.	6,596.8	989.0	7.2	62.0	174.3	745.5	5,607.8
Fairbanks, Alaska	6,517.5	960.1	6.2	147.7	200.0	606.2	5,557.4
Stockton, Calif.	6,496.8	909.4	8.6	27.7	267.5	605.6	5,587.4
Springfield, Ohio	6,472.0	440.9	6.3	60.3	211.7	162.6	6,031.1
Lubbock, Texas	6,414.2	904.5	5.3	47.7	123.3	728.1	5,509.7
Longview, Wash.	6,403.6	315.9	3.1	67.7	56.4	188.7	6,087.7
Pine Bluff, Ark.	6,318.0	799.9	19.6	49.6	206.8	523.9	5,518.1
Laredo, Texas	6,270.1	502.5	10.3	31.8	113.4	347.0	5,767.6
Miami-Miami Beach, Fla.	6,248.4	989.1	7.1	32.2	305.6	644.3	5,259.3
Wichita Falls, Texas	6,247.3	523.8	5.3	31.9	163.7	322.8	5,723.5
Pueblo, Colo.	6,158.2	483.4	8.5	15.8	110.3	348.8	5,674.8
Fayetteville, N.C.	6,142.2	581.8	6.5	25.5	184.1	365.7	5,560.4
Waco, Texas	6,075.7	552.0	6.2	52.2	128.3	365.3	5,523.7
Modesto, Calif.	6,032.0	614.0	6.0	25.7	132.2	450.1	5,418.0
Seattle-Bellevue-Everett, Wash.	6,025.9	363.0	2.9	37.2	126.2	196.8	5,359.1
Columbus, Ga.	5,890.7	422.1	9.4	13.6	177.2	221.9	5,468.6
25 LOWEST CRIME RATES							
Harrisonburg, Va.	1,676.8	1.8	22.1	33.7	60.2	117.8	1,559.0
Rockingham-Strafford Counties, N.H.	1,717.3	1.2	33.6	19.3	63.8	117.9	1,599.4
Nassau-Suffolk Counties, N.Y.	1,881.9	2.0	7.4	83.7	108.6	201.7	1,680.2
Logan, Utah	1,922.0	1.8	30.0	6.2	29.1	67.1	1,854.9
Fond du Lac, Wisc.	1,950.6	0.0	9.1	11.1	105.9	126.1	1,824.5
Wheeling, W.Va.	2,013.5	0.7	23.4	30.7	121.7	176.5	1,837.0
Elizabethtown, Ky.	2,020.4	0.9	26.3	45.3	88.0	160.5	1,859.9
Wausau, Wisc.	2,029.4	0.0	24.2	22.6	102.1	148.8	1,880.6
Edison, N.J.	2,048.1	1.1	10.6	60.2	100.5	172.4	1,875.7
Holland-Grand Haven, Mich.	2,101.3	0.8	78.8	15.0	99.8	194.4	1,906.9
State College, Pa.	2,108.9	0.7	14.2	12.1	81.0	108.0	2,000.9
Cambridge, Mass.	2,143.8	0.9	14.3	69.3	155.3	239.8	1,904.0
Rochester, Minn.	2,147.8	0.0	35.2	42.6	103.4	181.3	1,966.5
Poughkeepsie-Newburgh-Middletown, N.Y.	2,154.4	2.0	23.0	85.0	164.3	274.3	1,880.1
Manchester-Nashua, N.H.	2,189.8	1.7	30.4	49.8	71.9	153.8	2,036.0
Lynchburg, Va.	2,204.8	4.2	22.5	45.4	130.1	202.2	2,002.6
Appleton, Wisc.	2,254.0	0.9	17.7	9.8	83.1	111.6	2,142.4
Erie, Pa.	2,274.4	2.8	41.4	87.3	129.0	260.5	2,013.9
Kingston, N.Y.	2,287.4	1.6	36.3	59.3	215.9	313.1	1,974.3
Bismarck, N.D.	2,312.8	0.0	19.3	11.2	79.4	109.9	2,202.9
Oshkosh-Neenah, Wisc.	2,313.0	0.6	17.5	13.1	159.6	190.9	2,122.1
Williamsport, Pa.	2,325.6	3.4	24.4	63.1	102.7	193.7	2,131.9
Oxnard-Thousand Oaks-Ventura, Calif.	2,342.5	4.0	18.2	90.8	146.5	259.4	2,083.1
Worcester, Mass.	2,378.8	1.2	40.3	76.4	256.5	374.4	2,004.4
Lancaster, Pa.	2,395.5	1.2	17.4	65.1	88.5	172.2	2,223.3

Note: 1. Serious crimes are violent crimes (offenses of murder, forcible rape, robbery, and aggravated assault) and property crimes (offenses of burglary, larceny-theft, and motor vehicle theft). Data are not included for the property crime of arson. **Source:** Federal Bureau of Investigation, *Uniform Crime Reports: Crime in the United States 2005.*

The largest states, of course, had the most number of crimes. But in 2008, the rate of violent crime was highest in South Carolina (729.7 per 100,000 residents) and Tennessee (722.4), while the property crime rate was highest again in South Carolina (4,234.2 per 100,000 residents) and Florida (4,140.8). The northwestern Midwest had the lowest violent crime rate (355.4) while the southern Atlantic coast had the highest (553.7). The safest state is Maine, with just 117.5 violent crimes per 100,000 residents; the most dangerous place to live remains the nation's capital, with 1,437.7 violent crimes per 100,000 residents, more than double the national average.

In 2005, by metropolitan area, Hot Springs, Ark. (8,265.1), Myrtle Beach, N.C. (7,722.5), and Mount Vernon, Wash. (7,683.4) topped the list of dangerous metro areas. Pine Bluff, Ark. was the murder capital of the United States in 2005, with 19.6 homicides per 100,000 residents. The rate in New York City was 5.0. The safest city in the country was Harrisonburg, Va., where there were just 1,676.8 serious crimes per 100,000 residents.

Violent crime in other nations Although many reports and news stories have emphasized the continuing decline of serious crime, it is helpful to keep in mind that the U.S. remains far and away the most violent industrialized nation. In 1999, the Bureau of Justice Statistics released a detailed comparison of crime rates in the U.S and England. Although violent crime was increasing in England while it was decreasing in the U.S., the rates of murder, rape, and robbery were still significantly higher in this country than in the U.K. The U.S. murder rate was six times as high as England's, the number of rapes per 100,000 population three times as high, and the robbery rate 40 percent higher. It is interesting to note, however, that the rate of assault was 13 percent higher in England, while the rates for burglary and motor vehicle theft were about double U.S. rates.

Homicide, Guns, and Young People Murders by youthful offenders have followed the same downward trend evidenced in the population at

Crimes per 100,000 Population in Select Metropolitan Areas, 1995–2008

Metropolitan area	All serious crimes[1]			Violent crimes[1]			
	1995	2003	2005	1995	2003	2005	2008
Albuquerque, N. Mex.	7,521.9	5,717.8	5,753.3	879.4	815.3	838.9	798.7
Anchorage, Alaska	7,220.9	5,227.2	5,029.8	990.1	678.9	753.7	922.9
Atlanta–Sandy Springs–Marietta, Ga.	N.A.	N.A.	4,607.2	N.A.	N.A.	4,115.2	500.9
Boston–Cambridge–Quincy, Mass.	N.A.	N.A.	2,628.1	N.A.	N.A.	2,229.9	394.7
Charlotte–Gastonia–Concord, N.C.	N.A.	N.A.	6,008.3	N.A.	N.A.	5,170.6	661.0
Cincinnati–Middletown, Ohio	N.A.	N.A.	4,042.8	N.A.	N.A.	3,675.9	376.9
Dallas–Fort Worth–Arlington, Texas	6,571.5	5,668.5	5,278.5	819.2	582.0	550.8	457.5
Denver, Colo.	5,591.3	4,757.8	4,902.0	513.4	390.5	444.3	358.6
El Paso, Texas	6,623.4	4,052.2	3,511.4	802.0	553.4	408.9	437.1
Fresno, Calif.	8,566.2	5,634.4	5,439.8	1,189.0	599.4	638.8	472.2
Honolulu, Hawaii	7,627.8	5,623.8	4,948.0	327.4	287.9	282.9	284.1
Houston–Baytown–Sugar Land, Tex.	5,633.8	5,097.1	4,933.1	856.1	738.5	712.6	688.3
Jacksonville, Fla.	7,557.8	5,318.3	5,253.8	1,168.6	754.8	741.9	820.9
Las Vegas–Paradise, Nev.	7,408.6	5,255.1	5,288.0	1,085.9	694.5	674.9	840.4
Los Angeles–Long Beach, Calif.	6,141.8	3,675.4	3,328.3	1,422.6	721.3	575.5	523.8
Miami, Fla.	12,319.2	5,843.2	5,293.0	1,886.3	813.1	784.5	765.4
Milwaukee–Waukesha–Wisc.	N.A.	N.A.	3,979.4	N.A.	N.A.	457.9	544.7
Minneapolis–St. Paul, Minn.	5,287.2	3,780.1	N.A.	489.9	327.4	N.A.	N.A.
New Orleans, La.	8,210.5	4,981.2	N.A.	1,334.5	660.4	N.A.	622.3
New York, N.Y.	5,669.5	2,651.7	2,429.1	1,392.8	483.3	453.4	398.7
Oklahoma City, Okla.	7,905.8	6,449.4	5,878.1	808.5	563.7	532.7	581.5
Omaha, Nebr.–Iowa	5,602.6	5,256.0	4,606.2	623.7	446.7	430.4	417.3
Orlando, Fla.	7,123.5	5,297.9	5,135.4	1,007.0	758.9	821.4	820.6
Philadelphia–Camden–Wilmington, N.Y.–N.J.–Pa.	N.A.	3,446.0	3,360.4	N.A.	609.4	626.5	628.7
Phoenix–Mesa, Ariz.	8,808.5	6,359.1	5,749.0	765.0	506.5	513.0	455.2
Pittsburgh, Pa.	N.A.	2,767.3	2,794.3	N.A.	359.5	360.5	370.8
Portland–Vancouver, Oreg.	6,738.1	5,321.1	4,734.9	726.9	361.0	327.3	134.7
Riverside–San Bernardino, Calif.	6,409.2	4,234.9	4,165.4	945.5	544.3	481.8	449.2
Salt Lake City–Ogden, Utah	7,200.3	5,940.5	5,619.5	411.4	363.1	332.3	348.4
San Antonio, Texas	6,697.4	6,200.9	5,861.5	484.3	485.0	514.6	570.5
San Diego, Calif.	5,030.5	3,767.0	3,777.2	794.5	476.9	469.3	432.1
San Francisco, Calif.	5,833.8	4,596.1	4,432.3	884.3	537.7	555.6	635.6
San Jose, Calif.	4,244.6	2,785.6	2,964.1	614.5	317.1	316.2	315.9
Seattle–Bellevue–Everett, Wash.	N.A.	5,458.4	5,753.5	N.A.	409.7	405.4	N.A.
Tampa–St. Petersburg, Fla.	7,127.8	5,772.2	4,912.7	1,120.4	863.8	749.7	660.8
Tucson, Ariz.	9,769.5	7,699.9	5,879.5	877.2	639.0	649.7	518.6
Tulsa, Okla.	5,386.7	5,129.2	4,861.9	737.8	633.7	701.4	686.1
Virginia Beach, Va.	N.A.	N.A.	4,153.3	N.A.	N.A.	3,683.0	425.5
Washington D.C.	N.A.	N.A.	3,518.2	N.A.	N.A.	3,036.2	437.8
West Palm Beach–Boca Raton, Fla.	N.A.	N.A.	4,960.1	N.A.	N.A.	4,290.7	N.A.

Note 1. Serious crimes are violent crimes (offenses of murder, forcible rape, robbery, and aggravated assault) and property crimes (offenses of burglary, larceny–theft, and motor vehicle theft). Data are not included for the property crime of arson. **Source:** Federal Bureau of Investigation, *Uniform Crime Reports: Crime in the United States 2005; 2008 Crime in the United States,* Table 6 (2009).

Criminal Victimization Rates, 1992–2008

Crime	Victimizations ('000s)				Victimization rate per 1,000 persons			
	1992	2000	2005	2008	1992	2000	2005	2008
All crimes[1]	42,834	25,893	23,452	21,312	N.A.	N.A.	N.A.	N.A.
Violent crimes[1]	10,249	6,323	5,162	4,857	49.0	27.9	21.2	19.3
Simple assault	6,053	4,038	3,295	3,261	28.9	17.8	13.5	12.9
Aggravated assault	2,317	1,293	1,047	839	11.1	5.7	4.3	3.3
Robbery	1,272	732	630	552	6.1	3.2	2.6	2.2
Rape/sexual assault	607	261	191	204	2.9	1.2	0.8	0.8
Personal theft[2]	369	274	230	137	1.8	1.2	0.9	0.5
Property crime	32,217	19,297	18,060	16,319	325.3	178.1	154.0	134.7
Property thefts	24,579	14,916	13,614	12,335	248.2	137.7	116.2	101.8
Household burglary	5,803	3,444	3,465	3,189	58.6	31.8	29.5	26.3
Motor vehicle theft	1,835	937	982	795	18.5	8.6	8.4	6.6

Note: Rates per 1,000 people ages 12 or older. 1. The National Crime Victimization Survey cannot measure murder because it is impossible to question the victim. 2. Includes pocket picking, purse snatching, and attempted purse snatching. **Source:** Bureau of Justice Statistics Bulletin, *Criminal Victimization 2008* (2009).

Rates of Violent Crime, by Gender, Race, Hispanic Origin, and Age, 2008

Victim	Population	All	Rape/sexual assault	Robbery	Assault		
					All	Aggravated	Simple
Gender							
Male	123,071,020	21.3	0.3[1]	2.7	18.3	3.9	14.5
Female	129,171,510	17.3	1.3	1.7	14.3	2.8	11.5
Race							
White	204,683,500	18.1	0.6	1.6	15.9	3.0	12.8
Black	30,709,860	25.9	1.9[1]	5.5	18.5	5.2	13.3
Other race[2]	13,952,240	15.2	0.9[1]	3.0[1]	11.3	2.8	8.5
Two or more races	2,896,930	51.6	1.9[1]	6.8	42.9	6.8	36.1
Hispanic origin							
Hispanic	34,506,680	16.4	0.6[1]	3.4	12.4	3.5	8.9
Non-Hispanic	217,351,750	19.7	0.8	2.0	16.9	3.3	13.6
Age							
12-15	16,414,550	42.2	1.6[1]	5.5	35.2	6.1	29.0
16-19	17,280,270	37.0	2.2	4.8	30.0	5.6	24.5
20-24	20,547,620	37.8	2.1	5.4	30.3	8.7	21.5
25-34	40,649,500	23.4	0.7	2.3	20.5	4.0	16.5
35-49	65,123,030	16.7	0.8	1.9	14.1	2.7	11.4
50-64	55,116,320	10.7	0.2[1]	0.8	9.7	2.0	7.7
65 or older	37,111,240	3.1	0.2[1]	0.2[1]	2.7	0.4[1]	2.3

Note: The National Crime Victimization Survey includes as violent crime rape, sexual assault, robbery, aggravated assault, and simple assault. Because this survey interviews persons about their victimizations, murder and manslaughter cannot be included. 1. Based upon 10 or fewer sample cases. 2. Includes American Indians, Alaska Natives, Asians, Native Hawaiians, and other Pacific Islanders. **Source:** Bureau of Justice Statistics Bulletin, *Criminal Victimization 2008* (2009).

Property Crime Rates, by Household Income and Household Size, 2008

	Number of households	Victimizations per 1,000 households			
		Total	Burglary	Vehicle theft	Theft
Household income					
Less than $7,500	4,115,470	204.2	56.6	9.4	138.3
$7,500-$14,999	6,361,960	175.0	52.6	7.8	114.6
$15,000-$24,999	9,412,930	161.7	32.3	6.2	123.2
$25,000-$34,999	9,901,970	150.5	33.0	6.0	111.5
$35,000-$49,999	13,497,280	142.7	26.8	7.5	108.5
$50,000-$74,999	14,601,440	125.8	21.1	7.6	97.0
$75,000 or more	24,115,150	133.4	16.3	5.9	111.2
Size of household					
1	34,561,280	100.3	27.4	4.7	68.2
2 or 3	60,022,010	122.2	22.1	6.1	94.0
4 or 5	22,868,210	197.0	33.3	9.1	154.6
6 or more	3,689,560	273.9	41.0	15.7	217.1

Source: Bureau of Justice Statistics Bulletin, *Criminal Victimization 2008* (2009).

Victim and Offender Relationship, 2008

Relationship	Violent crime Number	Percent	Rape/sexual assault Number	Percent	Robbery Number	Percent	Aggravated assault Number	Percent	Simple assault Number	Percent
Male victims										
Total	**2,626,000**	**100%**	**39,590**	**100%**	**328,690**	**100%**	**476,390**	**100%**	**1,781,330**	**100%**
Nonstranger	1,286,170	49	39,590	100[1]	112,230	34	241,900	51	892,440	50
Intimate	88,120	3	8,310	21[1]	0	0[1]	37,430	8[1]	42,380	2
Other relative	83,630	3	0	0[1]	0	0[1]	25,560	5[1]	58,070	3
Acquaintance	1,114,410	42	31,280	79[1]	112,230	34	178,910	38	791,990	44
Stranger	1,163,410	44	0	0[1]	200,150	61	206,300	43	756,970	42
Unknown	176,420	7	0	0[1]	16,310	5[1]	28,190	6[1]	131,920	7
Female victims										
Total	**2,230,500**	**100%**	**164,240**	**100%**	**223,140**	**100%**	**363,550**	**100%**	**1,479,580**	**100%**
Nonstranger	1,556,790	70	102,950	63	118,220	53	250,190	69%	1,085,430	73
Intimate	504,980	23	29,060	18	34,830	16	61,170	17	379,920	26
Other relative	196,070	9	5,220	3[1]	33,210	15[1]	28,150	8[1]	129,490	9
Acquaintance	855,740	38	68,680	42	50,180	22	160,860	44	576,010	39
Stranger	592,570	27	52,890	32	99,450	45	104,410	29	335,810	23
Unknown	81,150	4	8,390	5[1]	5,470	2[1]	8,950	2[1]	58,340	4[1]

Note: Percentages may not total to 100 percent because of rounding. 1. Based on 10 or fewer sample cases. **Source:** Bureau of Justice Statistics Bulletin, *Criminal Victimization 2008* (2009).

Arrests in the U.S., 1984–2008

Offense	Total arrests 1984	1989	2000	2005	2008	Rate per 100,000 in 2008
Violent crime	**400,877**	**619,230**	**415,573**	**445,846**	**457,752**	**198.2**
Murder	15,126	16,701	8,709	10,335	9,888	4.3
Forcible rape	28,565	26,561	17,914	18,733	17,213	7.5
Robbery	115,522	137,811	72,320	85,309	100,738	43.6
Aggravated assault	241,664	438,157	316,630	331,469	329,913	142.9
Property crime	**1,431,812**	**1,620,704**	**1,080,797**	**1,195,560**	**1,305,135**	**565.2**
Burglary	338,737	292,315	189,343	220,391	236,219	107.3
Larceny/theft	981,812	1,164,371	782,082	854,856	982,997	425.7
Motor vehicle theft	96,975	149,053	98,697	108,301	75,137	32.5
Arson	14,288	14,965	10,675	12,012	10,784	4.7
Total arrests	**8,828,447**	**11,407,288**	**9,123,428**	**10,367,072**	**10,708,399**	**4,637.7**

Note: Statistics are based on a survey of more than 10,000 law enforcement agencies representing more than 200 million inhabitants. The number of agencies surveyed and the populations they represent changes from year to year. **Source:** Federal Bureau of Investigation, *2008 Crime in the United States* (2009).

Arrests by Race, 2008

Offense	Total arrests Total	White	Black	Am. Indian	Asian[1]	Percent distribution White	Black	Am. Indian	Asian[1]
All arrests	**10,662,206**	**7,382,063**	**3,015,905**	**142,908**	**121,330**	**69.2%**	**28.3%**	**1.3%**	**1.1%**
Violent crime	**455,967**	**265,754**	**179,636**	**5,431**	**5,146**	**58.3**	**39.4**	**1.2**	**1.1**
Murder	9,859	4,721	4,935	99	104	47.9	50.1	1.0	1.1
Forcible rape	16,847	10,990	5,428	198	231	65.2	32.2	1.2	1.4
Robbery	100,525	41,962	56,948	681	934	41.7	56.7	0.7	0.9
Aggravated assault	328,736	208,081	112,325	4,453	3,877	63.3	34.2	1.4	1.2
Property crime	**1,300,167**	**876,425**	**391,645**	**15,688**	**16,409**	**67.4**	**30.1**	**1.2**	**1.3**
Burglary	235,407	157,252	73,960	2,077	2,118	66.8	31.4	0.9	0.9
Larceny-theft	979,145	666,360	286,844	12,684	13,257	68.1	29.3	1.3	1.4
Motor vehicle theft	74,881	44,674	28,510	795	902	59.7	38.1	1.1	1.2
Arson	10,734	8,139	2,331	132	132	75.8	21.7	1.2	1.2
Embezzlement	**16,314**	**10,517**	**5,455**	**95**	**247**	**64.5**	**33.4**	**0.6**	**1.5**

Note: 1. Data for Asian / Pacfic Islander. **Source:** Federal Breau of Investigation, *2008 Crime in the United States* (2009).

large, but still remain alarmingly high. The rate of homicides by 14- to 17-year-olds dropped from an all-time high of 31.3 per 100,000 in 1993 to about 9.3 murders per 100,000 population in 2005. Similarly, the homicide rate for 18-24-year-olds was 26.5 per 100,000 in 2005, down from highs of more than 40 in 1991 and 1993, but still considerably higher than the 22 in 1985. Over the period 1976–2005, the number of nongun homicides by offenders aged 14–24 has declined slightly, while the number of murders involving guns has increased by nearly 50 percent. By comparison, the number of gun homicides by offenders over the age of 25 has actually declined by more than 2,500 since 1976.

▶CRIME VICTIMS

Crime victimization statistics are a second measure of the so-called crime rate. Unlike reported crime statistics, which are based on reports to law enforcement authorities, crime victimization statistics are based on Bureau of Justice Statistics interviews with a sampling of people about their personal experience with crime. (The BJS does not ask about or keep statistics on homicides because it is impossible to question the victim.) In most years, these different statistical methods have reported similar trends in criminal activity in the U.S.

The victims of most kinds of crime are most likely to be black, young, poor, urban, single, and except for rape and domestic violence, male. In 2007, people with family incomes of less than $7,500 were the most likely to be victimized by crime, especially violent crime. In general, the poorer a person is, the more likely he or she is to be the victim of a crime. And while senior citizens often feel most vulnerable to crime, it is teenagers who are most likely to be victimized by all kinds of crime. Children 16–19 years old are almost 20 times as likely to be the victims of violent crime as people over the age of 65.

▶LAW ENFORCEMENT

In 2008, there were 708,569 sworn police officers in the United States (up from 683,396 the year before) and an additional 315,659 civilians employed in police departments. This translates into 2.3 full-time police officers for every 1,000 residents. In cities with more than 250,000 residents, the ratio averaged 2.8 law enforcement employees per 1,000 residents. In cities with populations between 10,000 and 249,999 the ratio averaged 1.9. In suburban areas (including cities with fewer than 50,000 residents) the average was 2.5.

Overall, civilians made up 30.8 percent of the law enforcement workforce in 2008. In cities, civilians comprised 23.2 percent of the workforce; in suburban and rural areas, they made up approximately 40 percent. Northeastern states have the greatest number of sworn officers (3.4 officers per 1,000 inhabitants); the West has the fewest (1.7). By sex, 88.2 percent of sworn officers nationally and in cities collectively are male, but civilian police employees are overwhelmingly female (61.6 percent on average).

Arrests Nationwide, law enforcement agencies made an estimated 10.7 million arrests in 2008 for all criminal infractions except traffic violations, representing a rate of 4,637.7 arrests per 100,000 population, down slightly from the year before. Among cities, those with populations over 250,000 had the highest rate of arrests, 5,343 per 100,000 population; those with populations from 25,000–49,999 had the lowest rate (4,464.3). The arrest rate was highest in the South (5,120.7 per 100,000) and lowest in the Northeast (3,743.9). The greatest number of arrests were for drug-related offenses (1.7 million), driving under the influence of drugs or alcohol (1.5 million), and larceny or theft (1.27 million).

By age, 4.1 percent of all people arrested nationwide in 2008 were under 15; 15.2 percent were under 18. By sex, 75.5 percent of all those arrested were males. By race, 69.2 percent of all those arrested were white, 28.3 percent were black.

▶ CORRECTIONS

The United States has more people in prison (as well as more people in prison per capita) than any other Western industrialized nation. In 2007, the Bureau of Justice Statistics reported 1.53 million inmates in federal and state prisons. The prison population rose 2.8 percent during 2006. Since 1980 the incarceration rate (the number of sentenced inmates per 100,000 residents) has risen from 139 to 496. Put another way, one of every 136 U.S. residents was behind bars.

The states with the highest incarceration rates were all in the South. In 2007, Louisiana led the way with 865 prisoners per 100,000 residents, followed by Mississippi (734) and Texas (669). The lowest rates were found in Maine (159), Minnesota (181) and North Dakota (221). During 2007, Rhode Island reported the largest increase in its prison population (15.4 percent), followed by Mississippi (11.9 percent) and Kentucky (11.8 percent). The states with the largest declines were Montana (down 3.7 percent), Michigan (down 2.6 percent), and New Mexico (down 2.1 percent).

Prison and race African Americans have made up the majority of the increase in the prison and jail population. Between 1990 (the last year in which white prisoners outnumbered blacks) and 2007, the number of blacks behind bars in prisons or jails jumped from 360,000 to 586,200. Meanwhile, the white prison population grew from 370,900 in 1990 to 607,400 in 2007. Black males have the highest incarceration rates (3,145 per 100,000 residents in 2005) while white females have the lowest (45 per 100,000 residents). Put another way, about 3.5 percent of all black males are in prison. By age, incarceration rates peak between 25 and 35. More than 8 percent of black men aged 25–29 are in prison.

Jails and prisons Although the terms tend to be used synonymously, "jails" and "prisons" differ in the types of inmates they house, their locations, their physical size and their programs. Jails are locally administered facilities that house inmates after arraignment, prisoners serving terms of less than one year, and prisoners who cannot be housed in state prisons due to overcrowding.

Prisons are administered by either state or federal government authority. Typically they hold convicted offenders sentenced to terms of confinement for more than one year. They tend to be located away from dense population centers, and they are usually larger than jails and have more rehabilitation programs.

Costs of prisons According to the Census Bureau's Government Finance Annual, total U.S. expenditures for adult correctional facilities was $65.0 billion in 2005. According to the Bureau of Justice statistics, the average cost in state prisons per inmate was $57.92 per day in 2000.

Total U.S. prison capital costs increased from $538 million in 1980 to $2.8 billion in 2000. Operating costs surged from $3.1 billion in 1980 to $31.4 billion in 2000. In California, where more than 20 new prisons were built during this period, expenditures on prisons rose from $336 million to $4 billion, with capital expenditures increasing by over 1,400 percent (in constant dollars). In Texas, capital expenditures rose over 1,500 percent.

Probation and Parole When an offender is convicted, the primary sentencing alternatives are incarceration or probation. Once imprisoned, the offender may become eligible for parole, a form of conditional release. The explosion in the prison population has understandably led to a corresponding increase in the number of prisoners released on probation or parole. At the end of 2006, according to the Bureau of Justice Statistics, a record 7.2 million people (3.2 percent of all U.S. adult residents, or one in every 32 adults) were under "correctional supervision" in the United States: in jail, in prison, on probation or on parole. More than half this population (4.2 million) were on probation; another 798,202 were on parole.

Recidivism In 2002 the Bureau of Justice Statistics released a study of recidivism among 272,111 inmates (from 15 different states) who were released in 1994. The study found that 67.5 percent were rearrested within three years; 46.9 percent were reconvicted of a new crime; 25.9 percent were resentenced to prison for a new crime; and 51.8 percent were back in prison within three years for either a new prison sentence or a violation of their original release. Prisoners with the highest rates of recidivism included those convicted of possessing or selling stolen property (77.4 percent), car thieves (78.8 percent), and larcenists (74.6 percent); prisoners with the lowest rates included those in prison for homicide (40.7 percent), sexual assault (41.4 percent), and rape (46.0 percent). Overall recidivism was up from 1983, when an earlier study estimated rearrests at 62.5 percent.

Prisoners in the U.S. by System, Sex and Race, 1980–2007

| | By system | | | By sex, race, and Hispanic origin[1] | | | | | |
| | | | | Male | | | Female | | |
Year	Total	Federal	State	White	Black	Hispanic	White	Black	Hispanic
Number									
1980	329,821	24,363	305,458	159,500	140,600	N.A.	5,900	6,300	N.A.
1990	773,919	65,526	708,393	350,700	340,300	N.A.	20,200	19,700	N.A.
1995	1,125,874	100,250	1,025,624	487,400	509,800	N.A.	30,500	31,900	N.A.
2000	1,391,892	145,416	1,245,845	436,500	572,900	206,900	34,500	37,400	10,000
2005	1,525,924	187,618	1,338,306	459,700	547,200	279,000	45,800	29,900	15,900
2006	1,504,700	190,844	1,302,129	478,800	535,100	291,000	49,200	28,600	17,500
2007	1,532,800	197,285	1,315,291	471,400	556,900	301,200	50,500	29,300	17,600
Rate (Prisoners per 100,000 resident population)									
1980	139	9	130	168	1,111	N.A.	6	45	N.A.
1990	292	20	272	338	2,234	N.A.	19	117	N.A.
1995	411	32	379	449	3,095	N.A.	27	176	N.A.
2000	469	44	425	449	3,457	1,220	34	205	60
2005	491	56	435	471	3,145	1,244	45	156	76
2006	501	58	445	487	3,042	1,261	48	148	81
2007	506	59	447	481	3,138	1,259	50	150	79

Note: Prisoners sentenced to more than one year. 1. Prisoners of other races not shown. **Source:** Bureau of Justice Statistics Bulletin, *Prisoners in 2007* (2008).

Jail Population, 1985–2009

Age and sex	1985	1990	1995	2000	2005	2008	2009
Number of inmates at mid-year	256,615	405,320	507,044	621,149	747,529	785,556	767,620
Adults	254,986	403,019	499,300	613,534	740,770	777,852	760,400
Male	235,909	365,821	448,000	543,120	646,807	678,677	667,201
Female	19,077	37,198	51,300	70,414	93,963	99,175	93,199
Juveniles	1,629	2,301	7,800	7,615	6,759	7,703	7,220
Held as adults	N.A.	N.A.	5,900	6,126	5,750	6,410	5,847
Held as juveniles	1,629	2,301	1,800	1,489	1,009	1,294	1,373
Average daily population	265,010	408,075	509,828	618,319	733,442	776,573	767,992

Note: As of June 30 of each year. The average daily population is the sum of the number of inmates in a jail each day for a year, divided by 365. Juveniles are persons defined by state statute as being under a certain age, usually 18, and subject initially to juvenile court authority even if tried as adults. In 1994, the definition was changed to include all persons under age 18. **Source:** Bureau of Justice Statistics, *Prison and Jail Inmates at Midyear 2009* (2010).

Number of Inmates Under Jurisdiction of State or Federal Correctional Authorities, Year-end 2000, 2008, and 2009

	Number of prisoners			Avg. yearly change 2000–08	Percent change 2008–09
	2000	2008	2009		
U.S. total[1]	1,391,261	1,609,759	1,613,656	1.8%	0.2%
Federal	145,416	201,280	208,118	4.1	3.4
State	1,245,845	1,408,479	1,405,538	1.5	−0.2
Northeast	174,826	178,642	177,361	0.3%	−0.7%
Connecticut[1]	18,355	20,661	19,716	1.5	−4.6
Maine	1,679	2,195	2,206	3.4	0.5
Massachusetts	10,722	11,408	11,316	0.8	−0.8
New Hampshire	2,257	2,702	2,731	2.3	1.1
New Jersey	29,784	25,953	25,382	−1.7	−2.2
New York	70,199	60,347	58,687	−1.9	−2.8
Pennsylvania	36,847	49,215	51,429	3.7	4.5
Rhode Island[1]	3,286	4,045	3,674	2.6	−9.2
Vermont[1]	1,697	2,116	2,220	2.8	4.9
Midwest	237,378	264,314	261,603	1.4%	−1.0%
Illinois	45,281	45,474	45,161	0.1	−0.7
Indiana	20,125	28,322	28,808	4.4	1.7
Iowa[2]	7,955	8,766	8,813	1.2	(4)
Kansas	8,344	8,539	8,641	0.3	1.2
Michigan	47,718	48,738	45,478	0.3	−6.7
Minnesota	6,238	9,910	9,986	6.0	0.8
Missouri	27,543	30,186	30,563	1.2	1.2
Nebraska	3,895	4,520	4,474	1.9	−1.0
North Dakota	1,076	1,452	1,486	3.8	2.3
Ohio	45,833	51,686	51,606	1.5	−0.2
South Dakota	2,616	3,342	3,434	3.1	2.8
Wisconsin	20,754	23,379	23,153	1.5	−1.0
South	561,214	647,312	649,451	1.8%	0.3%
Alabama	26,332	30,508	31,790	1.9	4.2
Arkansas	11,915	14,716	15,208	2.7	3.3
Delaware[1]	6,921	7,075	6,794	0.3	−4.0
District of Columbia	7,456	(3)	(3)	(4)	(4)
Florida	71,319	102,388	103,915	4.6	1.5
Georgia[2]	44,232	52,719	53,371	2.2	1.2
Kentucky	14,919	21,706	21,638	4.8	−0.3
Louisiana	35,207	38,381	39,780	1.1	3.6
Maryland	23,538	23,324	22,255	−0.1	−4.6
Mississippi	20,241	22,754	21,482	1.5	−5.6
North Carolina	31,266	39,482	39,860	3.0	1.0
Oklahoma	23,181	25,864	26,397	1.4	2.1
South Carolina	21,778	24,326	24,288	1.4	−0.2
Tennessee	22,166	27,228	26,965	2.6	−1.0
Texas	166,719	172,506	171,249	0.4	−0.7
Virginia	30,168	38,276	38,092	3.0	−0.5
West Virginia	3,856	6,059	6,367	5.8	5.1
West	272,427	318,211	317,123	2.0%	−0.3%
Alaska[1]	4,173	5,014	5,285	2.3	5.4
Arizona[2]	26,510	39,589	40,627	5.1	2.6
California	163,001	173,670	171,275	0.8	−1.4
Colorado	16,833	23,274	22,795	4.1	−2.1
Hawaii[1]	5,053	5,955	5,891	2.1	−1.1
Idaho	5,535	7,290	7,400	3.5	1.5
Montana	3,105	3,545	3,605	1.7	1.7
Nevada	10,063	12,743	12,482	3.0	−2.0
New Mexico	5,342	6,402	6,519	2.3	1.8
Oregon	10,580	14,167	14,403	3.7	1.7
Utah	5,637	6,552	6,533	1.9	−0.3
Washington	14,915	17,926	18,233	2.3	1.7
Wyoming	1,680	2,084	2,075	2.7	−0.4

Notes: 1. Prisons and jails form one integrated system. Data include total jail and prison populations. 2. Prison population based on custody counts. 3. Not applicable. As of December 31, 2001, sentenced felons from the District of Columbia were the responsibility of the Federal Bureau of Prisons. 4. Not calculated. **Source:** Bureau of Justice Statistcs, *Prisoners in 2009* (2010).

Lifetime Likelihood of Going to Prison by Age, Sex, Race and Hispanic Origin

One of every 20 people in the U.S. (5.1 percent) will serve time in a prison during their lifetime, according to a March, 1997, BJS report, if 1991 incarceration rates do not change dramatically. Men (9.0 percent) are much more likely than women (1.1 percent) to be incarcerated in prison at least once during their life, and black men (28.5 percent) are six times as likely as white men (4.4 percent) to be imprisoned. Sixteen percent of Hispanic men are likely to be imprisoned.

Category	Percent expected to go to prison at some time, by age[1]						
	Birth	20	25	30	35	40	45
Total	5.1%	4.5%	3.1%	2.1%	1.4%	0.9%	0.6%
By Sex							
Male	9.0	7.9	5.5	3.7	2.5	1.6	1.0
Female	1.1	1.0	0.8	0.6	0.3	0.2	0.1
By Race/Hispanic origin							
White (non-Hispanic)	2.5%	2.3%	1.7%	1.2%	0.9%	0.6%	0.4%
Male	4.4	4.1	3.0	2.1	1.5	1.1	0.8
Female	0.5	0.5	0.4	0.3	0.2	0.1	0.1
Black (non-Hispanic)	16.2	14.1	9.6	6.0	3.6	2.0	1.2
Male	28.5	25.3	17.3	10.8	6.5	3.6	2.1
Female	3.6	3.5	2.8	1.9	1.1	0.6	0.4
Hispanic	9.4	8.7	6.4	4.9	3.8	2.3	1.6
Male	16.0	14.8	11.1	8.6	6.8	4.3	3.0
Female	1.5	1.5	1.2	0.9	0.6	0.4	0.2

Note: 1. Among those not previously incarcerated. **Source:** Bureau of Justice Statistics *Lifetime Likelihood of Going to State or Federal Prison*, March, 1997.

▶ CAPITAL PUNISHMENT

The United States is the only Western industrialized nation that allows capital punishment. In the period 1930–2005, 4,863 executions were carried out under state or federal authority. The majority of those (3,859) occurred in the years before the Supreme Court ruled capital punishment unconstitutional in 1972. The Court reinstated the death penalty in 1976; since then, an additional 1,044 executions have been carried out; all but nine were males. Another 3,228 prisoners were on death row at the end of 2006 (all of whom had been convicted of murder); 79 prisoners were removed from death row in 2005, while 115 were sentenced to death.

The 53 prisoners executed in 2006 had been on death row an average of 12 years and one month, or twice as long as those executed in 1984. Because capital cases move so deliberately through the court system, it is more expensive to sentence a prisoner to death than to life in prison. A positive aspect of this long delay is that it allows some death row prisoners to prove their innocence before they face the death chamber. According to the Death Penalty Information Center in Washington, D.C., 129 prisoners have been released from death row in 25 states since 1973 because they were improperly convicted or because evidence of their innocence was discovered after they were sentenced to death. The greatest number of exonerations came in 2003, when 12 inmates were released from death row.

Eighteen states have carried out 100 or more executions since 1930. Since the death penalty was reinstated in 1976, Texas has executed far more prisoners (413) than any other state. The Lone Star State executed 26 prisoners in 2007 alone; no other state executed more than three. Fourteen states and the District of Columbia currently do not authorize the death penalty for any crime: Alaska, Hawaii, Iowa, Maine, Massachusetts, Michigan, Minnesota, North Dakota, New Jersey,

Prisoners Executed by Race, 1930–2008

Year	Total	White	Black	Other
1930–39	1,667	827	816	24
1940–49	1,284	490	781	13
1950–59	717	336	376	5
1960–67	191	98	93	0
Total, 1930–67	**3,859**	**1,751**	**2,066**	**42**
1977–79	3	3	0	0
1980–89	117	68	49	0
1990–99	478	303	164	11
2000	85	49	35	1
2001	66	48	17	1
2002	71	53	18	1
2003	65	44	20	0
2004	59	39	19	1
2005	60	41	19	0
2006	53	32	21	0
2007	42	28	14	0
2008	37	20	17	0
Total, 1977–2008	**1,176**	**731**	**393**	**15**

Note: Executions under civil authority only. Does not include 160 executions carried out under military authority since 1930. There were no executions carried out between 1968 and 1977. **Source:** Bureau of Justice Statistics, *Sourcebook of Criminal Justice Statistics,* and *Capital Punishment 2009* (2010).

New York, Rhode Island, Vermont, West Virginia, and Wisconsin. In Maine, Minnesota, and Wisconsin, there has been no death penalty statute in force since 1930, and Alaska and Hawaii have never had death penalty statutes. The death penalty was either abolished or declared unconstitutional in Michigan (1963), Iowa and West Virginia (1965), the District of Columbia (1973), Rhode Island (1979), Massachusetts (1984), New York (2004) and New Jersey (2007). Kansas abolished the death penalty in 1973, but restored it in July, 1994. And South Dakota abolished the death

Prisoners on Death Row, 2008

	Removed from death row, 2008[1]			Executed, 2008			Under sentence of death, 2008		
	Total	White[2]	Black[2]	Total	White[2]	Black[2]	Total	White[2]	Black[2]
U.S. total	82	53	27	37	20	17	3,207	1,798	1,338
Federal[3]	0	0	0	0	0	0	51	23	27
State	82	53	27	37	20	17	3,156	1,775	1,311
Northeast	6	3	2	0	0	0	234	85	140
Connecticut	0	0	0	0	0	0	10	4	6
New Hampshire	0	0	0	0	0	0	1	0	1
New York	0	0	0	0	0	0	0	0	0
Pennsylvania	6	3	2	0	0	0	223	81	133
Midwest	14	8	6	2	1	1	270	143	124
Illinois	1	1	0	0	0	0	15	10	5
Indiana	1	1	0	0	0	0	13	10	3
Kansas	1	1	0	0	0	0	8	4	4
Missouri	1	0	1	0	0	0	50	28	22
Nebraska	0	0	0	0	0	0	9	8	1
Ohio	10	5	5	2	1	1	172	80	89
South Dakota	0	0	0	0	0	0	3	3	0
South	49	32	16	35	19	16	1,706	934	750
Alabama	3	2	1	0	0	0	205	107	98
Arkansas	0	0	0	0	0	0	41	16	25
Delaware	0	0	0	0	0	0	20	10	10
Florida	12	10	2	2	1	1	390	255	135
Georgia	1	1	0	3	2	1	105	57	47
Kentucky	1	0	1	1	1	0	36	30	6
Louisiana	4	4	0	0	0	0	84	28	55
Maryland	0	0	0	0	0	0	5	1	4
Mississippi	3	2	1	2	2	0	60	28	31
North Carolina	6	3	3	0	0	0	161	66	86
Oklahoma	2	0	2	2	2	0	85	45	36
South Carolina	2	1	1	3	1	2	58	25	33
Tennessee	9	7	2	0	0	0	87	49	36
Texas	4	2	1	18	9	9	354	210	140
Virginia	2	0	2	4	1	3	15	7	8
West	13	10	3	0	0	0	946	613	297
Arizona	4	3	1	0	0	0	119	102	13
California	6	4	2	0	0	0	669	397	243
Colorado	0	0	0	0	0	0	2	0	2
Idaho	0	0	0	0	0	0	17	17	0
Montana	0	0	0	0	0	0	2	2	0
Nevada	2	2	0	0	0	0	81	48	32
New Mexico	0	0	0	0	0	0	2	2	0
Oregon	0	0	0	0	0	0	35	31	3
Utah	0	0	0	0	0	0	10	8	1
Washington	0	0	0	0	0	0	8	5	3
Wyoming	1	1	0	0	0	0	1	1	0

Note: 1. Removed from death row includes only prisoners removed for reasons other than execution, and includes 16 deaths from natural causes and 7 deaths from suicides. 2. Includes persons of Hispanic/Latino origin. 3. Excludes persons held under Armed Forces jurisdiction with a military death sentence for murder. **Source:** Bureau of Justice Statistics Bulletin, *Capital Punishment 2008* (2009).

July, 1994. And South Dakota abolished the death penalty in 1915, restored it in 1939, abolished it again in 1977, and restored it again in 1979.

Race and capital punishment Historically, blacks have been more likely to be executed than whites in proportion both to the general population and to the prison population. In the 1940's, for example, blacks made up less than 10 percent of the population, but more than 60 percent of prisoners executed were black. Since 1930, equal numbers of blacks (2,407) and whites (2,399) have been executed, though nearly twice as many whites (609) have been executed since 1977 as blacks (359). But while the race of the defendant has been shown to influence whether he receives a death sentence, the race of the victim plays an even larger role. Murderers of white people were far more likely to be charged with a capital crime than those who killed blacks. Since 1977, nearly four of every five victims of an executed prisoner have been white.

Economy and Business

THE U.S. ECONOMY

▶ **GROSS NATIONAL PRODUCT AND GROSS DOMESTIC PRODUCT**

The goal of an economic system is to transform resources into final products by business enterprises for consumption by society. This includes manufacturing goods such as cars, bread, furniture and so on, and providing services such as health care, education, and motion pictures. The most commonly used measures associated with this goal are Gross National Product (G.N.P.) and Gross Domestic Product (G.D.P.). G.N.P. is the total national output of goods and services valued at market prices. G.N.P. in this broad context measures the output attributable to the factors of production—labor and property—supplied by a country's residents. G.N.P. differs from "national income" mainly in that G.N.P. includes allowances for depreciation and for indirect business taxes (sales and property taxes). G.D.P. is the measure of the output of production attributable to all factors of production (labor and property) physically located within a country. G.D.P., therefore, excludes net property income from abroad (such as the earnings of U.S. nationals working overseas), which is included in the G.N.P.

The word *final* serves to exclude intermediate goods sold to producers and used to make finished products eventually sold to consumers in the market. Auto parts such as batteries and tires are examples of intermediate goods and are included in G.N.P. or G.D.P. only through the price of a car when it is sold. G.N.P. and G.D.P., in terms of expenditure categories, comprise purchases of goods and services by consumers and government, gross private domestic investment (or business purchases), and net exports.

The assessment of G.N.P. and G.D.P. in current dollars is referred to as a nominal measure. Nominal measures may be misleading because G.N.P. and G.D.P. can appear to rise as average prices rise with inflation. An alternative method is to evaluate G.N.P. and G.D.P. by measuring the value of goods and services using constant prices for a given year; the government currently uses 2000 as the base year. Assessments based on constant prices are referred to as real measures because they indicate the change in quantity of output produced by the economy.

▶ **DEFINITIONS OF OUTPUT, INCOME, AND EXPENDITURE TERMS**

Capital consumption adjustment Used for corporations, non-farm sole proprietorships and partnerships, this is the difference between capital consumption claimed on income tax returns

G.D.P. in Current and Constant (2000) Dollars, 1960–2009 (billions)

Item	1960	1970	1980	1990	2000	2007	2009
CURRENT DOLLARS							
Gross domestic product (G.D.P.)	$526.4	$1,038.5	$2,789.5	$5,803.1	$9,817.0	$13,807.5	$14,256.3
Personal consumption expenditures	331.7	648.5	1,757.1	3,839.9	6,739.4	9,710.2	10,089.1
Durable goods	43.3	85.0	214.2	474.2	863.3	1,082.8	1,035.0
Nondurable goods	152.8	272.0	696.1	1,249.9	1,947.2	2,833.0	2,220.2
Services	135.6	291.5	846.9	2,115.9	3,928.8	5,794.4	6,833.9
Gross private domestic investment	78.9	152.4	479.3	861.0	1,735.5	2,130.4	1,628.8
Fixed investment	75.7	150.4	485.6	846.4	1,679.0	2,134.0	1,749.7
Change in private inventories	3.2	2.0	−6.3	14.5	56.5	−3.6	−120.9
Net exports of goods and services	4.2	4.0	−13.1	−78.0	−379.5	−707.8	−392.4
Exports	27.0	59.7	280.8	552.4	1,096.3	1,662.4	1,564.2
Imports	22.8	55.8	293.8	630.3	1,475.8	2,370.2	1,956.6
Government consumption	111.6	233.8	566.2	1,180.2	1,721.6	2,674.8	2,930.7
Federal	64.1	113.5	243.8	508.3	578.8	979.3	1,144.8
National defense	53.4	87.6	168.0	374.0	370.3	662.2	779.0
State and local	47.5	120.3	322.4	671.9	1,142.8	1,695.5	1,785.9
CONSTANT (2000) DOLLARS							
Gross domestic product (G.D.P.)	$2,501.8	$3,771.9	$5,161.7	$7,112.5	$9,817.0	$11,523.9	$12,987.4
Personal consumption expenditures	1,597.4	2,451.9	3,374.1	4,770.3	6,739.4	8,252.8	9,235.1
Gross private domestic investment	266.6	427.1	645.3	895.1	1,735.5	1,809.7	1,527.6
Net exports of goods and services	N.A.	N.A.	N.A.	−54.7	−379.5	−546.5	−355.6
Exports	90.6	161.4	323.5	552.5	1,096.3	1,425.9	1,472.4
Imports	103.3	213.4	310.9	607.1	1,475.8	1,972.4	1,828.0
Government consumption	715.4	1,012.9	1,115.4	1,530.0	1,721.6	2,012.1	2,564.6

Source: U.S. Bureau of Economic Analysis, *National Income and Product Accounts of the United States* (2010).

and capital consumption allowances measured at straight-line depreciation, consistent service lives, and replacement cost. The tax return data are valued at historical costs and reflect changes over time in service lives and depreciation patterns as permitted by tax regulations.

Consumer expenditure Consumer expenditure statistics presented in the accompanying tables are arrived at from the findings of the Consumer Expenditure Survey program, designed to provide a continuous flow of data on the buying habits of American consumers, necessary for future revisions of the Consumer Price Index. One group of 5,000 consumers in 85 urban areas around the country keeps diaries of expenditures on small, frequently purchased items, such as food and beverages, tobacco, housekeeping supplies, nonprescription drugs, and personal care products and services. Another 5,000 consumers are interviewed quarterly for information about large expenditures, such as those for property, automobiles and major appliances, or expenditures occurring on a fairly regular basis, such as rent, utilities and insurance premiums.

Disposable personal income is that income after personal tax and nontax payments; this is the income available to persons for spending and saving. Personal tax and nontax payments are tax payments (except personal contributions for social insurance, net of refunds) by persons that are not chargeable to business expense, and also include certain personal payments to general government that are treated like taxes. Personal taxes include income, estate, gift, and personal property taxes and motor vehicle licenses. Nontax payments include passport fees, fines and penalties, donations, and tuitions and fees paid to schools and hospitals operated mainly by government.

Family income The term *family* refers to a group of two or more persons related by birth, marriage, or adoption who reside together; all such persons are considered as members of one family. Family income refers to the sum of all income of the family members.

Gross state product (G.S.P.) is the gross market value of the goods and services attributable to labor and property located in a state. It is the state counterpart of the nation's G.D.P.

Household income A household includes related family members and all unrelated persons, if any—such as lodgers, foster children, wards or employees—who share a house, an apartment or a single room when it is occupied or intended for occupancy as separate living quarters by that household; that is, when the members of the household do not live and eat with any other persons in the structure and there is direct access from the outside or through a common hall. Household income, therefore, is the sum of all income of household members. The *householder* is the person in whose name the home is owned or rented. In the case of joint ownership, one person in each household is designated as the householder for statistical purposes.

Inventory valuation adjustment This represents the difference between the book value of inventories used in production and the cost of replacing them.

Mean vs. median income Mean (or average) income refers to the sum of all incomes of a group divided by the number of incomes in that group.

National Income by Industry, 1998–2009 (billions)

Industry	1998	2000	2002	2005	2007	2009
National income, Total	$7,661.4	$8,687.4	$11,048.5	$11,875.1	$12,362.4	$12,276.2
Domestic industries	$7,640.1	$8,648.5	$10,955.5	$11,796.9	$12,260.0	12,171.2
Private industries	6,724.6	7,642.8	9,639.0	10,415.7	10,806.5	10,573.8
Agriculture, forestry, fishing, and hunting	78.5	70.1	88.7	82.9	117.4	96.4
Mining	72.6	93.8	158.3	196.7	204.9	189.0
Utilities	138.6	144.3	171.0	204.6	216.3	206.4
Construction	366.6	440.6	601.8	645.1	563.5	553.8
Manufacturing	1,112.1	1,228.5	1,336.5	1,461.8	1,489.6	1,196.4
Durable goods	672.5	744.0	758.7	818.8	839.8	654.9
Nondurable goods	439.5	484.5	577.8	643.1	649.8	541.5
Wholesale trade	505.4	563.8	688.1	739.2	765.2	730.3
Retail trade	591.1	665.3	836.6	884.9	908.0	838.4
Transportation and warehousing	235.3	261.2	319.9	346.4	361.5	313.6
Information	273.7	308.3	417.5	438.0	463.4	423.7
Finance, insurance, real estate, rental, and leasing	1,328.5	1,529.3	1,926.5	2,092.3	2,193.0	2,239.6
Professional and business services[1]	975.1	1,146.6	1,482.5	1,611.2	1,717.3	1,725.6
Educational services, health care, and social assistance	582.7	664.6	941.4	1,001.5	1,060.1	1,225.2
Arts, entertainment, recreation, accommodation, and food services	267.9	310.5	398.8	428.3	449.9	468.1
Other services, except government	196.6	215.8	271.4	282.9	296.4	367.5
Government	$915.5	$1,005.7	$1,316.5	$1,381.2	$1,453.6	$1,597.4

Note: Figures do not include capital consumption adjustment. 1. Professional, scientific, and technical services; management of companies and enterprises; and administrative and waste management services. **Source:** U.S. Bureau of Economic Analysis, *National Income and Product Accounts of the United States* (2010).

Median income is the middle income when they are arranged in order of size—that is, there are the same number of incomes above and below the median. For example, consider incomes of $2,000, $3,000, $4,000, $15,000 and $95,000: the mean income is the sum of these divided by five, or $23,800; the median income is $4,000.

Money income This refers to income received (exclusive of certain money receipts such as capital gains) before payments for such things as personal income taxes, Social Security, union dues, and Medicare deductions. Money income does not include income in the form of noncash benefits such as food stamps, health benefits and subsidized housing; rent-free housing and goods produced and consumed on farms; or the use of business transportation and facilities, full or partial payments by business for retirement programs, medical and educational expenses, and so on. These elements should be considered when comparing income levels. None of the aggregate income concepts (G.N.P., national income, or personal income) is exactly comparable with money income, although personal income is the closest.

National income, the aggregate of labor and property earnings derived from the current production of goods and services, is the sum of employee compensation, proprietors' income, rental income, corporate profits and net interest. It measures the total factor costs of the goods and services produced by the economy. Income is measured before deduction of taxes.

Personal income is the current income received by persons from all sources minus their personal contributions for social insurance. *Persons* include individuals (including owners of unincorporated firms), nonprofit institutions serving individuals, private trust funds and private noninsured welfare funds. Personal income includes transfers (payments not resulting from current production) from government and business, such as Social Security benefits and public assistance, but excludes transfers among persons. Also included are

National Income, by Type of Income, 1960–2009 (billions of current dollars)

Type of Income	1960	1970	1980	1990	2000	2007	2009
National income	**$474.9**	**$930.9**	**$2,439.3**	**$5,089.1**	**$8,795.2**	**$12,270.9**	**$12,288.1**
Compensation of employees	**296.4**	**617.2**	**1,651.8**	**3,338.2**	**5,782.7**	**7,812.3**	**7,791.6**
Wages and salaries	272.9	551.6	1,377.6	2,754.0	4,829.2	6,355.7	6,289.1
Government	49.2	117.2	261.5	517.7	774.7	1,075.2	1,182.4
Other	223.7	434.3	1,116.2	2,236.3	4,054.5	5,280.5	5,106.7
Supplements to wages & salaries	23.6	65.7	274.2	584.2	953.4	1,456.6	1,502.5
Employer contributions to pension and insurance funds	14.3	41.8	185.2	377.8	609.9	991.9	1,043.9
Employer contributions to government social insurance	9.3	23.8	88.9	206.5	343.5	464.7	458.5
Proprietors' income[1, 2]	**50.8**	**78.4**	**174.1**	**380.6**	**728.4**	**1,056.2**	**1,041.0**
Farm	10.5	12.7	11.3	31.9	22.7	44.0	29.3
Nonfarm	40.3	65.7	162.8	348.7	705.7	1,012.2	1,011.7
Rental income of persons[1]	**17.1**	**21.4**	**30.0**	**50.7**	**150.3**	**40.0**	**268.1**
Corporate profits[1,2]	**53.8**	**83.6**	**201.1**	**437.8**	**817.9**	**1,642.4**	**1,308.9**
Taxes on corporate income	22.8	34.8	87.2	145.4	265.2	450.4	314.8
Profits after tax[1,2]	31.0	48.9	113.9	292.4	552.7	1,192.0	994.1
Net dividends	13.4	24.3	64.1	169.1	377.9	788.7	575.8
Undistributed profits[1,2]	17.6	24.6	49.9	123.3	174.8	403.4	418.4
Net interest and miscellaneous	**10.6**	**39.1**	**181.8**	**442.2**	**559.0**	**664.4**	**788.2**
Inventory valuation adjustment	−0.2	−6.6	−42.1	−12.9	−14.1	−51.2	9.1
Capital consumption adjustment	2.3	9.2	−10.2	41.2	58.6	−192.7	−127.8

Notes: 1. With capital consumption adjustment. 2. With inventory valuation adjustment. **Source:** U.S. Bureau of Economic Analysis, *National Income and Product Accounts of the United States* (2010).

Percent Distribution of National Income, by Type, 1960–2009

Type of income	1960	1970	1980	1990	2000	2007	2009
National income, total	**100.0%**	**100.0%**	**100.0%**	**100.0%**	**100.0%**	**100.0%**	**100.0%**
Compensation of employees	**62.4**	**66.3**	**67.7**	**65.6**	**65.8**	**63.7**	**63.4**
Wages and salaries	57.5	59.2	56.5	54.1	54.9	51.8	51.2
Supplements to wages & salaries	5.0	7.1	11.2	11.5	10.8	11.9	12.2
Proprietors' income[1]	**10.7**	**8.4**	**7.1**	**7.5**	**8.3**	**8.6**	**8.5**
Farm	2.2	1.4	0.5	0.6	0.3	0.4	0.2
Non-farm	8.5	7.1	6.7	6.8	8.0	8.2	8.2
Rental income of persons[2]	**3.6**	**2.3**	**1.2**	**1.0**	**1.7**	**0.3**	**2.2**
Corporate profits[1]	**11.3**	**9.0**	**8.2**	**8.6**	**9.3**	**13.4**	**10.7**
Profits before tax	4.8	3.7	3.6	2.9	3.0	6.7	2.6
Profits after tax	6.5	5.2	4.7	5.8	6.3	9.7	8.1
Net interest	**2.2**	**4.2**	**7.4**	**8.7**	**6.4**	**5.4**	**6.4**

Notes: 1. With inventory valuation and capital consumption adjustments (not shown separately). 2. With capital consumption adjustment (not shown separately). **Source:** U.S. Bureau of the Census, based on data from U.S. Bureau of Economic Analysis, *National Income and Product Accounts of the United States* (2010).

certain nonmonetary types of income: estimated net rental value to owner-occupants of their homes, the value of services furnished without payment by financial intermediaries, and food and fuel produced and consumed on farms.

Poverty level is an estimate of the income necessary to purchase what society defines as a minimally acceptable standard of living. Families and unrelated individuals are classified as being above or below the poverty level according to their money income as a group and the number of people in the group (e.g. in 2009, a family of four with income less than $22,050 lived below the poverty level). Classification is based on the poverty index originated by the Social Security Administration in 1964 and revised in 1969 and 1980. The poverty index is based solely on money income and does not reflect the fact that many low-income persons receive noncash benefits such as food stamps, Medicaid, and public housing. The poverty thresholds are updated every year to reflect changes in the Consumer Price Index.

Per Capita Personal Income by State, 1970–2009

State	Personal income (rank)				
	1970	1980	1990	2000	2009
U.S. average	$4,085	$10,114	$19,477	$29,847	$39,138
Alabama	2,957 (49)	7,836 (48)	15,723 (43)	23,768 (45)	33,096 (41)
Alaska	5,263 (1)	14,866 (1)	22,804 (7)	29,870 (16)	42,603 (9)
Arizona	3,835 (27)	9,524 (29)	17,005 (36)	25,656 (38)	32,935 (43)
Arkansas	2,828 (50)	7,524 (50)	14,460 (50)	21,927 (49)	31,946 (45)
California	4,810 (8)	11,951 (4)	21,638 (9)	32,467 (9)	42,325 (10)
Colorado	4,048 (18)	10,746 (14)	19,575 (19)	33,364 (8)	41,344 (15)
Connecticut	5,078 (3)	12,357 (2)	26,504 (1)	41,495 (1)	54,397 (1)
Delaware	4,597 (9)	10,748 (13)	21,422 (10)	30,871 (14)	39,817 (17)
District of Columbia	4,973 (4)	12,291 (3)	26,473 (2)	40,408 (2)	66,000 (N.A.)
Florida	4,004 (20)	9,933 (24)	19,564 (20)	28,512 (21)	37,780 (24)
Georgia	3,378 (39)	8,420 (39)	17,603 (30)	27,990 (27)	33,786 (39)
Hawaii	5,094 (2)	11,443 (8)	22,186 (8)	28,437 (23)	42,009 (11)
Idaho	3,520 (35)	8,648 (36)	15,724 (42)	24,079 (43)	31,632 (48)
Illinois	4,570 (10)	11,005 (11)	20,824 (11)	32,190 (10)	41,411 (14)
Indiana	3,782 (31)	9,374 (31)	17,491 (31)	27,134 (32)	33,725 (40)
Iowa	3,865 (25)	9,585 (28)	17,389 (33)	26,558 (34)	36,751 (27)
Kansas	3,818 (28)	9,953 (23)	18,085 (23)	27,693 (28)	37,916 (23)
Kentucky	3,166 (45)	8,178 (44)	15,437 (45)	24,413 (41)	31,883 (46)
Louisiana	3,090 (47)	8,777 (35)	15,173 (46)	23,082 (46)	35,507 (32)
Maine	3,411 (37)	8,347 (40)	17,376 (34)	25,974 (36)	36,745 (28)
Maryland	4,558 (11)	11,187 (9)	22,852 (6)	34,264 (6)	48,285 (4)
Massachusetts	4,483 (12)	10,602 (15)	23,043 (5)	37,753 (4)	49,875 (3)
Michigan	4,198 (13)	10,314 (16)	18,922 (21)	29,555 (18)	34,025 (37)
Minnesota	4,039 (19)	10,256 (17)	19,891 (16)	32,017 (11)	41,552 (13)
Mississippi	2,617 (51)	7,007 (51)	13,089 (51)	21,008 (51)	30,103 (50)
Missouri	3,850 (26)	9,324 (32)	17,627 (29)	27,243 (31)	35,676 (30)
Montana	3,611 (34)	9,058 (34)	15,448 (44)	22,934 (47)	34,004 (38)
Nebraska	3,792 (29)	9,160 (33)	17,983 (27)	27,626 (30)	38,081 (22)
Nevada	4,936 (5)	11,700 (7)	20,346 (14)	30,436 (15)	38,578 (20)
New Hampshire	3,886 (24)	9,850 (26)	20,512 (12)	33,401 (7)	42,831 (8)
New Jersey	4,821 (7)	11,707 (6)	24,572 (3)	38,377 (3)	50,313 (2)
New Mexico	3,188 (43)	8,346 (41)	14,924 (47)	22,144 (48)	32,992 (42)
New York	4,874 (6)	11,015 (10)	23,523 (4)	34,898 (5)	46,957 (5)
North Carolina	3,267 (40)	8,195 (43)	17,246 (35)	27,067 (33)	34,453 (35)
North Dakota	3,230 (42)	7,907 (47)	15,943 (40)	25,105 (39)	39,530 (19)
Ohio	4,086 (16)	10,046 (22)	18,743 (22)	28,207 (25)	35,381 (33)
Oklahoma	3,475 (36)	9,506 (30)	16,187 (38)	24,410 (42)	35,268 (34)
Oregon	3,924 (22)	10,113 (19)	18,010 (25)	28,099 (26)	35,667 (31)
Pennsylvania	4,071 (17)	10,085 (21)	19,687 (18)	29,698 (17)	39,578 (18)
Rhode Island	4,104 (15)	9,677 (27)	20,006 (15)	29,215 (19)	41,003 (16)
South Carolina	3,051 (48)	7,743 (49)	15,894 (41)	24,425 (40)	31,799 (47)
South Dakota	3,265 (41)	8,073 (46)	16,172 (39)	25,723 (37)	36,935 (25)
Tennessee	3,170 (44)	8,259 (42)	16,692 (37)	26,097 (35)	34,089 (36)
Texas	3,633 (32)	9,880 (25)	17,421 (32)	28,317 (24)	36,484 (29)
Utah	3,389 (38)	8,501 (38)	14,913 (48)	23,866 (44)	30,875 (49)
Vermont	3,617 (33)	8,613 (37)	17,876 (28)	27,683 (29)	38,503 (21)
Virginia	3,789 (30)	10,144 (18)	20,449 (13)	31,086 (13)	43,874 (7)
Washington	4,191 (14)	10,832 (12)	19,865 (17)	31,780 (12)	41,751 (12)
West Virginia	3,108 (46)	8,118 (45)	14,493 (49)	21,905 (50)	32,219 (44)
Wisconsin	3,979 (21)	10,107 (20)	18,072 (24)	28,572 (20)	36,822 (26)
Wyoming	3,904 (23)	11,718 (5)	18,002 (26)	28,470 (22)	45,705 (6)

Note: Current dollars. **Source:** Bureau of Economic Analysis, *Survey of Current Business* (monthly).

Private domestic investment This consists of (1) non-residential fixed investment, i.e., firms' purchases of capital goods such as plants and equipment; (2) residential fixed investment (the building of single- and multi-family housing units); and (3) the change in business inventories, which are stocks on hand of raw materials and finished goods.

►ECONOMIC INDICATORS

All market economies regularly go through cycles of *recession*, a decline of production accompanied by rise of unemployment; and *expansion*, rise of output and employment rise. These "business cycles" are one of the most important factors determining the socioeconomic conditions in any society. Although economists still have very

Per Capita Personal Income by Metropolitan Area, 1970–2008

Metropolitan Statistical Area (ranked by 2008 income)	1970	1980	1990	2000	2008
United States	**$4,085**	**$10,114**	**$19,477**	**$29,847**	**$38,615**
Metropolitan portion	4,306	10,636	20,519	31,468	40,544
Non-metropolitan portion	3,144	7,921	14,670	22,017	28,773
Highest per capita income, 2008					
1. Bridgeport-Stamford-Norwalk, Conn.	$6,085	$15,068	$34,300	$59,006	$81,576
2. Naples-Marco Island, Fla.	5,348	12,239	27,120	39,412	63,276
3. San Francisco-Oakland-Fremont, Calif.	5,562	14,092	27,082	48,338	60,983
4. Sebastian-Vero Beach, Fla.	4,030	11,311	25,207	37,113	59,419
5. San Jose-Sunnyvale-Santa Clara, Calif.	4,969	13,486	25,867	53,419	59,338
6. Washington-Arlington-Alexandria, D.C.-Va-.Md.-W.Va	5,192	12,928	26,839	40,673	54,971
7. Boston-Cambridge-Quincy, Mass.	4,698	11,044	24,702	41,430	53,443
8. Midland, Texas	4,639	14,616	22,610	35,439	52,974
9. New York-Northern New Jersey-Long Island, N.Y.-N.J.-Pa.	5,247	12,040	26,314	39,927	52,855
10. Casper, Wyoming	4,605	14,313	21,732	33,907	52,543
11. Trenton-Ewing, N.J.	4,832	12,066	26,048	39,461	52,255
12. Boulder, Colo.	4,292	11,546	22,072	40,309	51,388
13. Napa, Calif.	4,552	11,549	23,090	37,848	51,218
14. Seattle-Tacoma-Bellevue, Wash.	4,529	11,990	22,595	37,741	49,401
15. Santa Cruz-Watsonville, Calif.	4,379	11,345	21,813	39,142	48,337
16. Hartford-West Hartford-East Hartford, Conn.	4,913	11,955	25,196	36,986	48,330
17. Bradenton- Sarasota-Venice, Fla.	4,412	11,533	24,257	35,481	48,255
18. Barnstable Town, Mass.	4,609	10,875	23,135	35,748	47,640
19. Santa Barbara-Santa Maria-Goleta, Calif.	4,829	12,517	22,656	32,292	47,302
20. Minneapolis-St. Paul-Bloomington, Minn.	4,652	11,768	22,728	36,833	46,752
21. Denver-Aurora-Broomfield, Colo.	4,543	12,019	21,835	37,842	46,682
22. Houston-Sugar Land-Baytown, Texas	4,172	12,219	20,350	34,053	46,471
23. Santa Rosa-Petaluma, Calif.	4,493	11,527	22,419	36,440	46,325
24. Baltimore-Towson, Md.	4,301	11,023	21,798	33,295	45,887
25. Oxnard-Thousand Oaks-Ventura, Calif.	4,202	11,284	22,336	33,532	45,694

Lowest per capita income, 2008	1970	1980	1990	2000	2008
1. McAllen-Edinburg-Mission, Texas	$1,937	$5,297	$9,282	$13,588	$18,316
2. Brownsville-Harlingen, Texas	2,156	5,694	9,853	14,927	19,667
3. Laredo, Texas	2,244	5,418	9,406	15,079	21,423
4. Provo-Orem, Utah	2,716	6,698	12,035	19,566	21,681
5. Yuma, Ariz.	3,445	8,154	13,764	16,513	22,786
6. Logan, Utah	2,745	7,192	12,952	18,721	23,193
7. Hanford-Corcoran, Calif.	3,568	11,016	13,280	16,317	23,418
8. El Centro, Calif.	3,850	9,450	16,018	17,768	23,757
9. Lake Havasu City-Kingman, Ariz.	3,776	8,005	14,859	18,621	23,908
10. St. George, Utah	2,861	6,846	12,532	19,199	24,014
11. Madera-Chowchila, Calif.	3,714	10,575	14,890	18,330	24,359
12. Hinesville-Fort Stewart, Ga.	2,759	6,132	10,094	16,601	24,638
13. Merced, Calif.	3,808	9,493	15,176	19,541	25,012
14. Las Cruces, N.Mex.	2,999	6,864	12,611	17,829	25,106
15. Morristown, Tenn.	2,620	6,499	14,080	21,212	25,757
16. Albany, Ga.	2,761	7,089	14,157	21,370	25,861
17. Visalia-Porterville, Calif.	3,630	9,338	14,785	19,579	25,920
18. Pine Bluff, Ark.	2,697	7,318	13,166	19,075	25,980
19. Greeley, Colo.	3,578	8,428	15,705	25,047	25,668
20. Blacksburg-Christiansburg-Radford, Va.	2,876	7,174	13,629	20,066	26,382
21. Valdosta, Ga.	2,970	6,734	13,888	20,751	26,504
22. El Paso, Texas	2,980	6,498	12,284	18,575	26,585
23. College Station-Bryan, Texas	2,794	7,130	12,963	19,806	26,656
24. Jonesboro, Ark.	2,867	7,173	13,572	20,787	25,732
25. Muskegon-Norton Shores, Mich.	3,687	8,864	15,013	23,130	26,046

Note: Figures in constant 2008 dollars. **Source:** U.S. Bureau of Economic Analysis, *Survey of Current Business* (2010).

little idea what actually causes recessions and what leads the economy to begin expanding again, they have had some success in predicting business cycles. Economic forecasting is the science of making these predictions. It is especially useful to be able to predict recessions sufficiently far in advance so that governments can take actions to stimulate the economy and reduce the severity of these downturns.

Economic indicators track developments in areas of the economy that are thought to be crucial to the future health of the economy, just as a barometer measures changes in air pressure that are crucial to changes in the weather. The development of economic indicators began around World War I, but suffered a setback when the early forecasters failed to predict the Great Depression in 1929. During the depression the government asked a

Per Capita Personal Income by County, 2008

Rank/County	Per capita income 2008	Percent of national average
Highest per capita income		
1. Loving, Texas	$140,275	349.2%
2. Teton, Wyoming	129,956	323.5
3. New York, New York[1]	120,766	300.7
4. Sully, South Dakota	95,764	238.4
5. Marin, California[1]	93,159	231.9
6. Pitkin, Colorado	92,680	230.7
7. Fairfield, Connecticut[1]	79,108	197.0
8. Westchester, New York[1]	77,192	192.2
9. San Mateo, California[1]	73,839	183.3
10. San Francisco, California[1]	72,712	181.0
11. Arlington, Virginia[1]	72,317	180.0
12. Alexandria City, Virginia[1]	72,220	179.8
13. Somerset, New Jersey[1]	72,201	179.8
14. Morris, New Jersey	71,812	178.8
15. Fairfax / Falls Church, Virginia[1]	69,885	174.0
16. Hunterdon, New Jersey[1]	68,785	171.3
17. Bergen, New Jersey[1]	67,696	168.5
18. Montgomery, Maryland[1]	67,531	168.1
19. Cavalier, North Dakota	67,185	167.3
20. North Slope Borough, Alaska	66,664	166.0
21. District of Columbia[1]	66,316	165.1
22. Nantucket, Massachusetts	66,147	164.7
23. Sublette, Wyoming	66,122	164.6
24. Nassau, New York[1]	65,668	163.5
25. Blaine, Idaho	64,875	161.5
Lowest per capita income		
Buffalo, South Dakota	$12,558	31.3%
1. Crowley, Colorado	14,553	36.2
2. Elliott, Kentucky	15,408	38.4
3. Starr, Texas	15,542	38.5
4. Zavala, Texas	16,687	41.5
5. Madison, Idaho	17,010	42.3
6. Shannon, South Dakota	17,603	43.8
7. McPherson, Nebraska	17,926	44.6
8. Jackson, Kentucky	17,936	44.7
9. Todd, South Dakota	18,112	45.1
10. Hancock, Tennessee	18,365	45.7
11. Wheller, Georgia	18,411	45.8
12. Union, Florida	18,535	46.1
13. Lafayette, Florida	18,612	46.3
14. Hamilton, Florida	18,631	46.4
15. Maverick, Texas	18,688	46.5
16. San Juan, Utah	18,705	46.6
17. Slope, North Dakota	18,799	46.8
18. Zapata, Texas	18,849	46.9
19. McCreary, Kentucky	18,884	47.0
20. Menifee, Kentucky	19,255	47.9
21. Saguache, Colorado	19,496	48.5
22. Morgan, Kentucky	19,527	48.6
23. Lewis, Kentucky	19,539	48.6
24. Telfair, Georgia	19,560	48.7

Note: 1. Denotes metropolitan county. **Source:** U.S. Bureau of Economic Analysis, *Survey of Current Business* (2010).

Percent of Persons Below Poverty Level, by State, 1980–2008

State	1980	1990	2000	2008
United States	13.0%	13.5%	11.3%	13.2%
Alabama	21.2	19.2	13.3	15.7
Alaska	9.6	11.4	7.6	8.4
Arizona	12.8	13.7	11.7	14.7
Arkansas	21.5	19.6	16.5	17.3
California	11.0	13.9	12.7	13.3
Colorado	8.6	13.7	9.8	11.4
Connecticut	8.3	6.0	7.7	9.3
Delaware	11.8	6.9	8.4	10.0
District of Columbia	20.9	21.1	15.2	17.2
Florida	16.7	14.4	11.0	13.2
Georgia	13.9	15.8	12.1	14.7
Hawaii	8.5	11.0	8.9	9.1
Idaho	14.7	14.9	12.5	12.6
Illinois	12.3	13.7	10.7	12.2
Indiana	11.8	13.0	8.5	13.1
Iowa	10.8	10.4	8.3	11.5
Kansas	9.4	10.3	8.0	11.3
Kentucky	19.3	17.3	12.6	17.3
Louisiana	20.3	23.6	17.2	17.3
Maine	14.6	13.1	10.1	12.3
Maryland	9.5	9.9	7.4	8.1
Massachusetts	9.5	10.7	9.8	10.0
Michigan	12.9	14.3	9.9	14.4
Minnesota	8.7	12.0	5.7	9.6
Mississippi	24.3	25.7	14.9	21.2
Missouri	13.0	13.4	9.2	13.4
Montana	13.2	16.3	14.1	14.8
Nebraska	13.0	10.3	8.6	10.8
Nevada	8.3	9.8	8.8	11.3
New Hampshire	7.0	6.3	4.5	7.6
New Jersey	9.0	9.2	7.3	8.7
New Mexico	20.6	20.9	17.5	17.1
New York	13.8	14.3	13.9	13.6
North Carolina	15.0	13.0	12.5	14.6
North Dakota	15.5	13.7	10.4	12.0
Ohio	9.8	11.5	10.0	13.4
Oklahoma	13.9	15.6	14.9	15.9
Oregon	11.5	9.2	10.9	13.6
Pennsylvania	9.8	11.0	8.6	12.1
Rhode Island	10.7	7.5	10.2	11.7
South Carolina	16.8	16.2	11.1	15.7
South Dakota	18.8	13.3	10.7	12.5
Tennessee	19.6	16.9	13.5	15.5
Texas	15.7	15.9	15.5	15.8
Utah	10.0	8.2	7.6	9.6
Vermont	12.0	10.9	10.0	10.6
Virginia	12.4	11.1	8.3	10.2
Washington	12.7	8.9	10.8	11.3
West Virginia	15.2	18.1	14.7	17.0
Wisconsin	8.5	9.3	9.3	10.4
Wyoming	10.4	11.0	10.8	9.4

Source: U.S. Census Bureau, *Poverty Status by State* (2009).

Per Capita Money Income, by Race and Hispanic Origin, 1970–2007

Year	Current dollars					Constant (2007) dollars				
	All races	White	Black	Asian	Hispanic	All races	White	Black	Asian	Hispanic
1970	$3,177	$3,354	$1,869	N.A.	N.A.	$15,139	$15,983	$8,906	N.A.	N.A.
1980	7,787	8,23	4,804	N.A.	$4,865	18,656	19,724	11,509	N.A.	$11,655
1990	14,387	15,265	9,017	N.A.	8,424	22,125	23,476	13,867	N.A.	12,955
1995	17,227	18,304	10,982	$16,567	9,300	23,273	24,727	14,836	$22,381	12,564
2000	22,346	23,582	14,796	23,350	12,651	26,905	28,394	17,815	28,114	15,232
2005	25,036	26,496	16,874	27,331	14,483	26,590	28,141	17,922	29,028	15,382
2006	26,352	27,821	17,902	30,474	15,421	27,100	28,610	18,410	31,339	15,858
2007	26,804	28,325	18,428	29,901	15,603	26,804	28,325	18,428	29,901	15,603

Note: Beginning in 2002, figures for each racial category include those who identified themselves as belonging to that race alone. Asian includes Pacific Islander from 1970–2001. Hispanic persons may be of any race. Total includes other races not shown separately.
Source: U.S. Bureau of the Census, *Current Population Survey.*

Median Income of Families by Race and Hispanic Origin, 1980–2007

Year	Current dollars					Constant (2007) dollars				
	All races	White	Black	Asian	Hispanic	All races	White	Black	Asian	Hispanic
1980	$21,023	$21,904	$12,674	N.A.	$14,716	$50,366	$52,477	$30,364	N.A.	$35,256
1990	35,353	36,915	21,423	$42,246	23,431	54,369	56,771	32,946	$64,969	36,034
2000	50,732	53,029	33,676	62,617	34,442	61,083	63,849	40,547	75,393	41,469
2005	56,194	59,317	35,464	68,957	37,867	59,683	63,000	37,666	73,238	40,218
2006	58,407	61,280	38,269	74,612	40,000	60,064	63,018	39,355	76,729	41,135
2007	61,355	64,427	40,143	76,606	40,566	61,355	64,427	40,143	77,133	40,566

Note: Beginning in 2002, figures for each racial category include those who identified themselves as belonging to that race alone. Asian includes Pacific Islander from 1990–2001. Hispanic persons may be of any race. Total includes other races not shown separately. **Source:** U.S. Bureau of the Census, *Current Population Survey.*

Persons Below Poverty Level, by Race, 1960–2007

Year	Number below poverty level (millions)					Percent below poverty level				
	All races	White	Black	Asian	Hispanic	All races	White	Black	Asian	Hispanic
1960	39.9	28.3	N.A.	N.A.	N.A.	22.2%	17.8%	N.A.	N.A.	N.A.
1970	25.4	17.5	7.5	N.A.	N.A.	12.6	9.9	33.5%	N.A.	N.A.
1980	29.3	19.7	8.6	N.A.	3.5	13.0	10.2	32.5	N.A.	25.7%
1990	33.6	22.3	9.8	0.9	6.0	13.5	10.7	31.9	12.2%	28.1
2000	31.6	21.6	8.0	1.3	7.7	11.3	9.5	22.5	9.9	21.5
2005	37.0	24.9	9.2	1.4	9.4	12.6	10.6	24.9	11.1	21.8
2006	36.5	24.4	9.0	1.4	9.2	12.3	10.3	24.3	10.3	20.6
2007	37.3	25.1	9.2	1.3	9.9	12.5	10.5	24.5	10.2	21.5

Note: Beginning in 2002, figures for each racial category include those who identified themselves as belonging to that race alone. Asian includes Pacific Islander from 1960–2001. Hispanic persons may be of any race. Total includes other races not shown separately. **Source:** U.S. Bureau of the Census, *Poverty in the United States 2006* (2007).

private research group, the National Bureau of Economic Research, to develop a set of measures that would help predict changes in business cycles. The group devised a list of measures based on analyses of previous business cycles. Since then, the list has been revised several times to reflect changes in the way the economy is structured.

Leading Indicators

There are currently 10 leading economic indicators, representing a broad spectrum of economic activity. These indicators are said to "lead" because their numbers change months in advance of a change in the general level of economic activity. They are as follows:

1. Average length of workweek of production workers in manufacturing.

2. Average weekly state unemployment insurance claims.

3. New orders for consumer goods and materials (in constant dollars).

4. Vendor performance (percent of companies receiving slower deliveries from suppliers).

5. Contracts and orders for plant and equipment (in constant dollars).

6. Index of new private housing units authorized by local building permits.

7. Index of stock prices, i.e., of 500 common stocks (Standard and Poor's 500).

8. Money supply-M2 in constant dollars. (See "Money and Banking" section.)

9. Interest rate spread.

10. Index of consumer expectations.

This composite of leading economic indicators is published by the U.S. Department of Commerce Bureau of Economic Analysis. The composite has a noteworthy record: since 1948 it has accurately predicted every downturn and upswing in the economy. One major reason for this success is that many of the indicators represent commitments to economic activity in the coming months. The average lead for the index is 9.5

months at business cycle peaks (indicating the end of a business cycle expansion and the beginning of a recession) and 4.5 months at business cycle troughs (indicating the end of a business cycle recession and the beginning of an expansion).

Coincident and Lagging Indicators

In addition to the leading economic indicators, two other sets of measures are used to track business cycles and the state of the economy. One set includes the coincident indicators, which measure how well the economy is doing at that moment (roughly, within three months of the business cycle turning points). These include the number of employees on nonagricultural payrolls; manufacturing and trade sales (in constant dollars); index of industrial production; and personal income less transfer payments (in constant dollars). The second set includes lagging economic indicators. These are the ratio of consumer installment credit outstanding to personal income; commercial and industrial loans outstanding (in constant dollars); the average prime interest rate charged by banks; the ratio of manufacturing and trade inventories to sales (in constant dollars); the average duration of unemployment in weeks (inverted); the change in index of labor cost per unit of output in manufacturing; and the change in the Consumer Price Index for services per unit labor costs. At business cycle peaks, the average lag of the index is 4.5 months, and at business cycle troughs 8.5 months. It seems reasonable to wonder what use there is for an indicator that tells you where you have already been. But in fact that is exactly their use: they provide another way of measuring whether turning points in the business cycle truly have occurred.

The government produces a wide variety of economic indicators in addition to those discussed here for use in tracking more specific aspects of the economy, such as labor or capital markets.

The Employment Cost Index (ECI)

The ECI measures the *rate of change* in total employee compensation (wages, salaries, employer cost for employee benefits) in nonfarm private industry and in state and local governments. Provided quarterly by the Bureau of Labor Statistics,

the ECI has become one of the most closely watched indexes because any significant rise could signal an inflationary trend. The ECI grew annually by 4 to 5 percent in the late 1980s, but fell below 3 percent in the 1990s. The ECI has grown by about 3 percent annually since 2000.

▶ PRICES AND INFLATION
Inflation

Inflation is a sustained rise in the general price level in the economy. It affects the level and timing of spending in the economy since it indicates the extent to which income will cover the purchase of a consumer's basket of goods (food, clothes, entertainment, medical services, housing, gasoline, and so on). For example, if a consumer is considering purchasing a television and inflation is high (that is, prices are rising rapidly), he or she will buy the television as soon as possible since savings may not cover the cost a month or a year from now. Inflation is closely watched to determine wage contracts and Social Security benefits that contain cost-of-living adjustment clauses. If wage contracts cover a long period of time and inflation is rapid, consumers' standard of living will fall in the interim before new contracts can be negotiated. Savings will tend to fall as consumers store their wealth in the form of commodities.

The cause of inflation is often described as "too much money chasing too few goods," brought about by the money supply rising rapidly or production of goods falling behind demand for them. Inflation may be due to (1) cost-push factors—that is, if the cost of inputs such as labor, raw materials, or other intermediate goods rises, the cost of the final product also rises; or (2) demand-pull factors—that is, if the demand for goods and services rises above the full employment level, wages rise as employers compete for labor, and the general price level of goods and services rises.

Consumer Price Index

Often referred to as the "cost of living index," the Consumer Price Index is the most commonly used measure of inflation. The index measures

Composite Index of Economic Indicators, 1960–2010 (2004=100)			
Year	Leading indicators	Coincident indicators	Lagging indicators
1960	30.8	32.9	34.2
1965	39.3	38.1	40.1
1970	40.9	46.4	49.9
1975	39.2	51.0	56.7
1980	47.4	61.3	63.3
1985	53.6	66.3	67.7
1990	61.7	75.6	77.3
1995	72.8	82.8	81.4
2000	86.8	98.0	97.4
2005	101.8	101.5	101.4
2006	104.8	104.2	105.1
2007	104.4	105.9	108.4
2008	102.5	107.0	111.3
2009	98.6	102.5	114.4
2010	107.5	100.0[1]	107.7[1]

Note: As of January of each year. 1. Preliminary. **Source:** The Conference Board. www.conference-board.org (2010).

Employment Cost Index (ECI) 1985–2009 (December 2005=100)			
Year	Civilian workers	Private industry workers	State and local government workers
1985	48.3	48.5	47.1
1990	59.8	59.4	61.4
1995	70.6	70.3	71.9
2000	83.6	83.8	82.7
2001[1]	87.2	87.5	86.1
2003	93.5	93.8	92.7
2004	97.0	97.3	95.9
2005	100.1	100.2	99.8
2006	103.4	103.3	103.9
2007	106.8	106.5	108.2
2008	109.6	109.1	111.5
2009	111.1	110.4	114.7

Note: Figures are as of December of each year and are not seasonally adjusted. Excludes farm, household, and federal government workers 1. Indexes before 2001 are not directly comparable because the BLS switched from the Standard Industrial Classification (SIC) System to the North American Industry Classification System (NAICS). **Source:** U.S. Bureau of Labor Statistics, *Employment Cost Index*, (quarterly).

the average change in prices relative to an arbitrary base year of a common bundle of goods and services bought by the average consumer on a regular basis. The Bureau of Labor Statistics publishes two CPI's: (1) CPI-U for All Urban Consumers, which includes wage earners and clerical workers; professional, managerial, and technical workers; the self-employed; short-term workers; the unemployed; retirees and others not in the labor force—altogether covering 80 percent of the population—and (2) CPI-W for Urban Wage Earners and Clerical Workers, covering 32 percent of the population. Prices (including direct taxes) are collected from over 50,000 housing units and 23,000 establishments in 87 areas across the country. In calculating the index number, based on 100,000 price quotes a month, larger weights are assigned to goods that represent larger proportions of consumer expenditure. The index costs $26 million a year to produce and requires 40 economists and analysts tracking price changes in 365 categories.

Producer Price Index

The Producer Price Index measures average changes in prices received by producers of all commodities, at all stages of processing, pro-

Consumer Price Index (CPI-U) 1915–2009 (1982–84=100)

Year	Consumer Price Index	Year	Consumer Price Index	Year	Consumer Price Index
1915	10.1	1955	26.8	1995	152.4
1920	20.0	1960	29.6	2000	172.2
1925	17.5	1965	31.5	2003	184.0
1930	16.7	1970	38.8	2005	195.3
1935	13.7	1975	53.8	2006	201.6
1940	14.0	1980	82.4	2007	207.3
1945	18.0	1985	107.6	2008	215.3
1950	24.1	1990	130.7	2009	214.5

Source: U.S. Bureau of Labor Statistics, www.bls.gov

Consumer Price Indexes for Selected Metropolitan Statistical Areas, 2008 (1982–84 = 100)

Area	All items	Apparel	Education and communication	Food and beverages	Housing	Medical care	Recreation	Transportation
U.S. City average	214.5	120.1	127.4	218.2	217.1	375.6	114.3	179.3
Anchorage, Alaska	191.7	135.6	110.8	191.8	173.7	397.0	119.3	190.2
Atlanta, Ga.	200.9	122.4	119.6	219.2	200.7	320.7	101.7	168
Boston–Brockton–Nashua, Mass.–N.H.	233.8	136.1	136.9	229.6	233.8	526.2	122.3	169.2
Chicago–Gary–Kenosha Ill.–Ind.–Wisc.	209.9	93.7	136.2	215.3	213.9	385.0	112.0	169.6
Cincinnati–Hamilton, Ohio–Ky.–Ind.	200.6	136.9	123.4	198.2	188.2	383.7	124.2	172.3
Cleveland–Akron, Ohio	200.5	113.9	113.3	219.7	189.4	349.6	114.8	181.8
Dallas–Ft. Worth, Tex.	200.5	125.3	134.8	222.4	182.8	346.4	116.3	181.6
Denver–Boulder–Greeley, Colo.	208.5	102.9	116.7	201.3	192.6	442.9	133.0	217.4
Detroit–Ann Arbor–Flint, Mich.	203.5	109.6	133.5	198.9	190.9	352.9	116.4	205.8
Honolulu, Hawaii	230.0	112.8	122.8	224.3	249.7	321.6	105.2	200.3
Houston–Galveston–Brazoria, Tex.	190.5	144.6	111.7	199.7	183.5	355.2	108.9	156.1
Kansas City, Mo.–Kans.	200.9	109.7	121.1	217.4	193.4	302.6	124.5	174.8
Los Angeles–Riverside– Orange County, Calif.	223.2	107.9	129.8	222.9	244.4	363.4	112.4	178.6
Miami–Ft. Lauderdale, Fla.	221.4	137.7	116.6	225.7	227.5	362.2	118.7	188.7
Milwaukee–Racine, Wisc.	202.9	121.2	130.1	218.7	197.9	368.9	108.8	172.1
Minneapolis–St. Paul, Minn.–Wisc.	207.9	126.9	130.5	237.8	190.6	405.6	117.3	178.8
New York–Northern New Jersey– Long Island, NY–NJ–Conn.–Pa.	236.8	114.5	134.5	227.8	257.1	371.2	116.8	189.9
Philadelphia–Wilmington–Atlantic City Pa.–N.J.–Del.–Md.	223.3	102.9	128.4	206.4	232.6	424.8	122.7	181.1
Phoenix–Mesa, Ariz.	117.6	113.9	118.3	125.6	116.1	138.8	118.3	109.2
Pittsburgh, Pa.	212.1	148.9	136.5	217.9	213.4	372.8	116.5	160.1
Portland–Salem, Oreg.–Wash.	215.6	110.8	110.9	203.2	212.4	428.9	108.1	202.8
San Diego, Calif.	242.3	125.7	125.7	224.0	275.6	377.2	140.3	184.7
San Francisco–Oakland– San Jose, Calif.	224.4	109.1	138.6	228.0	246.2	380.8	106.7	166.7
Seattle–Tacoma–Bremerton, Wash.	226.0	132.3	126.5	229.4	240.2	343.1	97.8	199.5
St. Louis, Mo.–Ill.	198.5	131.6	133.9	210.2	189.9	360.9	115.3	171.4
Tampa–St. Petersburg– Clearwater, Fla.	189.9	154.7	121.1	193.0	187.3	296.4	112.6	169.9
Washington–Baltimore, D.C.– Md.–Va.–W.Va.	139.8	93.7	132.3	139.5	152.1	142.7	116.7	124.5

Note: Figures are not seasonally adjusted. The base period for Education and Communication and for Recreation is December 1997 = 100 in all cities. Except where otherwise indicated, the base period for Phoenix–Mesa is December 2001 = 100; for Tampa–St. Petersburg it is 1987 = 100; and for Washington–Baltimore it is November 1996 = 100. **Source:** U.S. Bureau of Labor Statistics, *Monthly Labor Review* and *CPI Detailed Report* (Jan. 2009).

duced in the United States. Prices used in constructing the index are collected from sellers and generally apply to the first significant large-volume commercial transaction for each commodity—i.e., the manufacturer's or other producer's selling price or the selling price on an organized exchange or at a central market. The weights used in the index represent the total net selling value of commodities produced or processed in the country. Values are f.o.b. (free on board) at the production point and are exclusive of excise taxes.

Implicit Price Deflator

The implicit price deflator (also called the G.D.P. deflator) is derived from the ratio of current-to-constant dollar G.D.P. (multiplied by 100) and measures the value of current production in current prices relative to the value of the same goods and services in prices for the base year. For example, in 2009, GDP in current dollars was $14,256.3 billion and GDP in constant (2000) dollars was $12,987.4 billion. Therefore, the GDP deflator for 2009 was (14,256.3 ÷ 12,987.4) x 100, or 109.8, which is simply a comparison between 2000 and 2009 prices. It is a weighted average of the detailed price indexes used in the deflation of GDP, but the indexes are combined using weights that reflect the composition of GDP in each period. Thus changes in the implicit price deflator reflect not only changes in prices, but also changes in the composition of GDP.

▶ MONEY AND BANKING
Federal Reserve System

The government's interest in monitoring and controlling the banking industry and managing the money supply led to the Federal Reserve Act of 1913. The act created the Federal Reserve System (or the "Fed," as it is popularly known), the nation's central bank. There are 12 regional Fed banks located in major cities throughout the country (Boston, New York, Philadelphia, Cleveland, Richmond, Atlanta, Chicago, St. Louis, Minneapolis, Kansas City, Dallas and San Francisco). Commercial banks within each region select a majority of the directors who run each regional Fed bank. The president of the United States appoints a board of governors for the whole system, and the board is responsible for coordinating

policies across the system. But the regional Feds play an important role in shaping those policies by representing regional interests and decentralizing the decision-making process.

The Fed has three main policy tools for managing the overall economy. First, it controls the *reserve requirements* at all depository institutions. These requirements determine what percentage of a bank's deposits must be held in reserve in the form of either deposits with Federal Reserve banks or vault cash. Raising the reserve requirements reduces the amount of loans available to borrowers and helps slow down the economy.

A more frequently used instrument is *the discount rate*, the interest rate the Federal Reserve banks charge their commercial bank customers to borrow money. The Fed is known as the lender of last resort because of its responsibility to lend to banks in need, and it thus maintains the stability of the banking system. Raising the discount rate generally leads the commercial banks to raise the interest rates they charge their customers. This raises the costs of borrowing in the private sector and slows the economy. (Cutting the discount rate does the reverse and stimulates the economy.)

Most important, the Fed can also control the level of bank reserves through *open market opera-*

Purchasing Power of the Dollar, 1950–2009

| Year | Annual average as measured by: | | Year | Annual average as measured by: | |
	Producer prices	Consumer prices		Producer prices	Consumer Prices
1950	$3.546	$4.151	1990	$0.839	$0.766
1955	3.279	3.732	1995	0.782	0.656
1960	2.994	3.373	2000	0.725	0.581
1965	2.933	3.166	2004	0.673	0.530
1970	2.545	2.574	2005	0.642	0.512
1975	1.718	1.859	2006	0.623	0.496
1980	1.136	1.215	2007	0.600	0.482
1985	0.955	0.928	2009[1]	0.580	0.466

Note: 1. Producer prices data are preliminary. **Source:** U.S. Bureau of Economic Analysis, *Survey of Current Business* (monthly).

Producer Price Indexes for Selected Commodities, 1970–2009 (1982=100)

Commodity group	1970	1980	1990	2000	2005	2007	2008	2009
All commodities	38.1	89.8	116.3	132.7	157.4	172.6	189.6	172.9
Farm products	45.8	102.9	95.1	99.5	118.5	143.4	161.3	134.6
Processed foods and feeds	44.6	95.9	103.5	133.1	153.1	165.1	180.5	176.2
Industrial commodities	35.2	88.0	115.8	134.8	160.2	175.1	192.3	174.8
Textile products and apparel	52.4	89.7	114.9	121.4	122.8	125.8	128.9	129.5
Hides, skins, leather and related products	42.0	94.7	141.7	151.5	165.4	173.6	173.1	157.0
Fuels, related products, power	15.3	82.8	82.2	103.5	156.4	177.6	214.6	158.7
Chemicals and allied products	35.0	89.0	123.6	151.0	192.0	214.8	245.5	229.4
Rubber and plastic products	44.9	90.1	113.6	125.5	143.8	155.0	165.9	165.2
Lumber and wood products	39.9	101.5	129.7	178.2	196.5	192.4	191.3	149.4
Pulp, paper, and allied products	37.5	86.3	141.3	183.7	202.6	216.9	226.8	225.6
Metals and metal products	38.7	95.0	123.0	128.1	160.8	193.5	213.0	186.8
Machinery and equipment	40.0	86.0	120.7	124.0	123.7	127.3	129.7	131.3
Furniture and household durables	51.9	90.7	119.1	132.6	139.4	144.7	148.9	153.1
Nonmetallic mineral products	35.3	88.4	114.7	142.5	164.2	186.2	197.1	202.4
Transportation equipment	41.9	82.9	121.5	143.8	151.0	155.0	158.6	162.2

Source: U.S. Bureau of Labor Statistics, *Producer Price Indexes* (monthly and annual).

tions; that is, the direct sale on purchase of Treasury securities and other government debt instruments. When the Fed sells securities, it takes money from the buyer and holds it in its reserves, reducing the money supply; when it buys these instruments, it pays for them by taking money from its reserves, which then goes into circulation, increasing the money supply.

Controlling the supply of money through open market operations is certainly the most common and, many would argue, the most important function of the Fed. The money supply shapes interest rates, through the supply and demand of money. Because the Fed is constantly involved in these open market operations (in order to keep the size of the money supply in proportion with a growing economy, for example), adjustments can be made subtly.

In addition, the Federal Reserve regulates banks through the Federal Deposit Insurance Corporation, (F.D.I.C.) influences foreign-currency exchange rates through the sale or purchase of foreign currencies, and coordinates international financial policy.

The money supply Money provides a medium of exchange as well as a way to store value. Traditionally, currency (paper money and coins) served that role exclusively. But over time, new financial instruments have developed that serve at least some of the functions of money. Checking accounts serve exactly the same role as currency, and to an extent, so do money market funds and other instruments.

The Fed uses two different measures of the money supply, which include different monetary instruments:

M1 is the original and most commonly reported measure of the money supply, which embraces currency and coins, demand deposits, traveler's checks, and other checkable deposits.

M2 is M1 plus money-market accounts, and savings and small time-deposits.

M3, a measure that included M2 plus money-market mutual-fund balances held by financial institutions, term repurchase agreements and term Eurodollars, and large time-deposits, was discontinued by the Federal Reserve in 2006.

▶ THE U.S. BANKING SYSTEM

Commercial banks are the largest financial institutions in the country and are the principal vehicles for exchanging money. The nation's first commercial bank was the Bank of America (now First Pennsylvania Bank), established in Philadelphia in 1782. Commercial banks hold about two-thirds of the nation's money deposits. Savings and loans, the next-largest source of deposits, hold about half as much.

There are approximately 8,000 commercial banks in the country. They may be chartered either by the federal government or by individual states. While banks themselves may not operate across states, they may be owned by holding companies that can operate interstate, if state laws permit.

Commercial banks can make loans to individuals and to commercial operations, establish

Federal Reserve Bank, Discount Rates, 1914–2010

Year	Range	Year	Range	Year	Range	Year	Range
1914	6.0–5.0%	1941	1.0%	1968	4.5–5.5%	1995	4.75–5.25%
1915	5.0–4.0	1942	1.0–0.5	1969	5.5–6.0	1996	5.00
1916	4.0–3.0	1943	0.5	1970	6.0–5.5	1997	5.00
1917	3.0–3.5	1944	0.5	1971	5.5–4.5	1998	5.0–4.5
1918	3.5–4.0	1945	0.5	1972	4.5	1999	4.5–5.0
1919	4.0–4.75	1946	0.5–1.0	1973	4.5–7.5	2000	5.0–6.0
1920	4.75–7.0	1947	1.0	1974	7.5–8.0–7.75	2001	6.0–1.25
1921	7.0–4.5	1948	1.0–1.5	1975	7.75–6.0	2002	1.25–0.75
1922	4.5–4.0	1949	1.5	1976	6.6–5.25	2003[2]	2.25–2.0
1923	4.0–4.5	1950	1.5–1.75	1977	5.25–6.0	2004	2.0–3.25
1924	4.5–3.0	1951	1.75	1978	6.0–9.5	2005	3.25–5.25
1925	3.0–3.5	1952	1.75	1979	9.5–12.0	Jan. 31, 2006	5.50
1926	3.5–4.0	1953	1.75–2.0	1980[1]	12.0–10.0–13.0	Mar. 28, 2006	5.75
1927	4.0–3.50	1954	2.0–1.5	1981[1]	13.0–14.0–12.0	May 10, 2006	6.00
1928	3.50–5.0	1955	1.5–2.5	1982	12.0–8.5	June 29, 2006	6.25
1929	5.0–6.0–4.5	1956	2.5–3.0	1983	8.5	Aug. 17, 2007	5.75
1930	4.5–2.0	1957	3.0–3.5–3.0	1984	8.5–9.0–8.0	Sept. 18, 2007	5.25
1931	2.0–1.5–3.5	1958	3.0–1.75–2.5	1985	8.0–7.5	Oct. 31, 2007	5.00
1932	3.5–2.5	1959	2.5–4.0	1986	7.5–5.5	Dec. 11, 2007	4.75
1933	2.5–3.2–2.0	1960	4.0–3.0	1987	5.5–6.0	Jan. 22, 2008	4.00
1934	2.0–1.5	1961	3.0	1988	6.0–6.5	Jan. 30, 2008	3.50
1935	1.5	1962	3.0	1989	6.5–7.0	Mar. 18, 2008	2.50
1936	1.5–1.0	1963	3.0–3.5	1990	7.0–6.5	April 30, 2008	2.25
1937	1.0	1964	3.5–4.0	1991	6.5–3.5	Oct. 8, 2008	1.75
1938	1.0	1965	4.0–4.5	1992	3.5–3.0	Oct. 29, 2008	1.25
1939	1.0	1966	4.5	1993	3.00	Dec. 16, 2008	0.50
1940	1.0	1967	4.5–4.0–4.5	1994	3.0–4.75	Feb. 19, 2010	0.75

Notes: 1. The discount rates for 1980 and 1981 do not include the surcharge applied to frequent borrowings by large institutions. The surcharge reached 3% in 1980 and 4% in 1981, and was eliminated in November 1981. 2. The discount rate applied to short term adjustment credit until Jan. 9, 2003, when it was changed to primary credit, in an effort to eliminate the incentive for institutions to borrow for the purpose of exploiting the positive spread of money market rates over the discount rate. **Source:** Board of Governors of the Federal Reserve System, *Federal Reserve Bulletin*, monthly, and *Annual Statistical Digest*.

checking or demand deposits, maintain "trust" departments that make investments for customers, and perform a variety of other functions such as issuing credit cards. Until the deregulation of the 1980s, commercial banks were the only ones permitted to issue checking accounts. Regulations that developed after bank failures in the Great Depression still keep these banks out of the investment business—largely to protect depositors and the solvency of banks from potential effects of bad investments. But deregulation of the banking industry in the 1980s is blurring many of these distinctions. In particular, investment companies are now permitted to issue demand deposits and to compete with banks in other areas as well. (As a result these companies are sometimes referred to as nonbanks.)

Thrifts are depository institutions including savings and loans (S&Ls), savings banks, and credit unions. The largest and most important thrifts are the S&Ls, which were created to provide home mortgages for borrowers and long-term savings deposits for individual investors. Until recently, thrifts were prohibited from engaging in riskier loans—including most commercial loans—and issuing checking deposits, and a ceiling was placed on the rate of interest they could pay depositors. Congress lifted the ceiling on interest payments to depositors in 1980 and in 1982 allowed the S&Ls to issue commercial loans and

to invest directly in real estate developments. Unwise investment in these areas by many thrifts was a major cause of the savings and loan debacle of the late 1980s and early 1990s.

In the wake of that scandal, the Office of Thrift Supervision (O.T.S.) was created in 1989 to oversee federal thrifts and to identify institutions that may be financially distressed or likely to fail. All federally chartered S&Ls are regulated by the system (and must have the word Federal in their name). Less than half the thrifts are federally chartered, however; the rest are chartered by states, although most of these have joined the system as well.

Bank and thrift failures are especially serious problems because of the domino effect they may have on other businesses. Depository institutions ultimately fail when loans go bad and cannot be repaid. But even before that happens, depositors may get nervous about the security of their accounts and withdraw them all at once—a "run on the bank." Because banks loan out deposits and hold in reserve only a small percentage of the value of those deposits, banks experiencing a run would have to call in some of their loans (mainly those already due), putting sudden pressure on many commercial borrowers and causing some to fail. In addition the withdrawal of deposits and loans reduces the money supply sharply. This process was an important cause of

The Money Supply, 1970–2009 (billions of dollars)

Item	1970	1980	1990	2000	2005	2007	2009
M1, total	**$214**	**$408**	**$825**	**$1,088**	**$1,374**	**$1,365**	**$1,696**
Currency[1]	49	115	246	531	724	758	862
Travelers' checks[2]	1	3	8	8	7	6	5
Demand deposits[3]	165	261	277	310	325	293	443
Other checkable deposits[4]	10	28	294	238	319	308	386
M2, total	**$628**	**$1,600**	**$3,278**	**$4,931**	**$6,661**	**$7,417**	**$8,544**
M1	214	408	825	1,088	1,374	1,365	1,696
Non-M1 components in M2	414	1,192	2,453	3,844	5,287	6,053	6,848
Money market funds, retail	10	64	357	921	690	967	829
Savings deposits (including money market deposit accounts)	261	400	923	1,878	3,602	3,869	4,848
Commercial banks	99	186	582	1,424	2,774	3,041	4,007
Thrift institutions	162	215	342	454	828	827	841
Small time deposits[5]	151	729	1,173	1,045	995	1,217	1,171
Commercial banks	79	286	611	700	644	821	852
Thrift institutions	72	442	563	345	351	412	319
M3, total	**$677**	**$1,996**	**$4,153**	**$7,120**	**$10,155**	**N.A.**	**N.A.**
M2	628	1,600	3,278	4,931	6,661	N.A.	N.A.
Non-M1 components in M3	49	396	875	2,186	3,479	N.A.	N.A.
Large time deposits[6]	45	260	480	836	1,354	N.A.	N.A.
Commercial banks[7]	44	215	358	734	1,123	N.A.	N.A.
Thrift institutions	1	45	121	102	231	N.A.	N.A.
Repurchase agreements[8]	4	58	151	364	564	N.A.	N.A.
Eurodollars[8]	9	61	103	195	424	N.A.	N.A.
Money market funds, institution only	9	16	140	788	1,137	N.A.	N.A.

Notes: As of December of year shown. Adjusted seasonally. Figures may not add up because of independent rounding. 1. Currency outside U.S. Treasury, Federal Reserve Banks, and the vaults of depository institutions. 2. Outstanding amount of non-bank issuers. 3. At commercial banks and foreign-related institutions. 4. Consists of negotiable order of withdrawal (NOW) and automatic transfer service (ATS) accounts at all depository institutions, credit union share draft balances and demand deposits at thrift institutions. 5. Issued in amounts of less than $100,000. Includes retail repurchase agreements. Excludes individual retirement accounts (IRAs) and Keogh accounts. 6. Issued in amounts of $100,000 or more. Excludes those booked at international banking facilities. 7. Excludes those held by money market mutual funds, depository institutions, U.S. Government, foreign banks, and official institutions. 8. Excludes those held by depository institutions and money market mutual funds. 9. Less than $500 million. **Source:** Board of Governors of the Federal Reserve System, *Federal Reserve Bulletin*, monthly, and *Money Stock, Liquid Assets, and Debt Measures*, Federal Reserve Statistical Release H.6, weekly.

the Great Depression. Following the banking failures during the depression (2,293 banks failed in 1931, and 4,000 banks failed in 1933), the Federal Deposit Insurance Corporation (FDIC) was created in 1933 to protect the accounts of depositors and, more important, to help prevent bank failures. The FDIC charges banks a premium to pay for this coverage. The corporation is designed to prevent runs on banks by insuring deposits and lending to banks to prevent the need to call in loans.

But banks and thrifts still fail because of bad loans. When an institution fails, the F.D.I.C. pays off each depositor and then sells the bank's assets. Sometimes the F.D.I.C. arranges for another bank's acquisition of the failed bank by subsidizing the sale.

Consumer Credit Outstanding, 1980–2009 (billions of dollars)

Year	Total	Revolving[1]	Other[2]
1980	$ 349.4	$ 55.1	$ 294.3
1985	593.2	124.7	468.5
1990	789.1	238.6	550.5
1995	1,095.8	443.1	652.7
2000	1,704.3	676.9	1,027.4
2003	2,006.6	759.3	1,247.3
2005	2,285.2	824.5	1,460.7
2006	2,387.7	874.6	1,513.1
2007	2,519.0	939.5	1,579.5
2008	2,562.3	960.9	1,601.4
2009	2,448.8	866.1	1,582.7

Notes: 1. Consists mainly of outstanding balances on credit card accounts, but also includes borrowing under check credit and overdraft plans, and unsecured personal lines of credit. 2. Includes automobile loans and all other loans not included in revolving credit, such as loans for mobile homes, trailers or vacations. noninstallment credit. **Source:** Board of Governors of the Federal Reserve System, *Federal Reserve Bulletin* (monthly).

Between 1945 and 1980, U.S. banks failed at the rate of about six per year. Between 1985 and 1992, however, more than 100 banks failed annually, with a whopping 531 shutting their doors in 1989. Most of these failures occurred in agricultural states where the failure of farms led to defaults on loans; more than half of all bank failures during that period were attributed to agriculture loans.

Failures declined dramatically over the next two decades: just 58 banks failed between 1995 and 2007. Compared with the early 1990s, the 70 bank failures between January 2008 and July 2009 may seem small, but the list included some extremely prominent names. California's Indymac Bank, a thrift with $32 billion in assets, collapsed in July 2008; two months later, federal regulators seized Washington Mutual, the nation's largest savings and loan and brokered its sale to JPMorgan Chase for $1.9 billion. Throughout 2008 and early 2009, Citigroup and Bank of America, two of the country's largest banks, teetered on the edge of collapse, leading to calls for their nationalization.

Because so many of the spectacular failures of the latest recession were thrifts, President Barack Obama in June 2009 asked Congress to merge the O.T.S. with the Office of the Comptroller of the Currency, so that a single institution will monitor all the country's largest depository institutions.

Credit unions are employer-sponsored cooperative organizations that provide consumer and mortgage credit to their members. Employers often arrange for payroll-deduction savings plans through the credit union. Perhaps in response to the high rates charged by commercial banks for maintaining checking accounts, the number of people joining credit unions has jumped dramatically in recent years, from 61.4 million members in 1992 to 89 million in 2008.

Assets and Deposits of FDIC/BIF-Insured Banks, 2008–09

	2008			2009		
Charter class	Banks	Assets (millions)	Deposits (millions)	Banks	Assets (millions)	Deposits (millions)
All banks	8,305	$13,743,297	$9,035,732	8,012	$13,107,979	$9,226,794
Commercial banks	7,085	12,310,922	8,082,157	6,839	11,843,784	8,333,158
National banks	1,537	8,478,472	5,370,085	1,461	8,199,032	5,616,139
State banks	5,548	3,832,451	2,712,072	5,378	3,644,751	2,717,018
Savings banks	1,220	1,532,375	953,574	1,173	1,264,195	893,636
Federal charter	743	1,218,132	736,187	701	931,488	650,594
State charter	477	314,243	217,175	472	332,706	243,041

Note: As of Dec. 31 of each year.　**Source:** Federal Deposit Insurance Corp., *Statistics on Banking*. (interactive).

Assets and Deposits of Deposit-Taking Institutions, 2009

Type of institution	Number of institutions	Percent share	Assets (millions)	Percent share	Deposits (millions)	Percent share
Commercial banks	6,839	41.87%	$11,843,784	79.3	$8,333,158	78.4%
Savings banks[1]	1,173	7.18	1,264,195	8.5	893,636	8.4
Savings & Loans (thrifts)[2]	765	4.68	941,705	6.3	653,584	6.14
Credit unions[3]	7,554	46.27	884,757	5.9	752,667	7.06
Total	**16,331**	**100.0%**	**$14,934,441**	**100.0%**	**$10,633,045**	**100.0%**

Note: 1. Includes Federal and State-chartered Savings institutions. 2. Includes only thrifts regulated by the Office of Thrift Supervision. 3. Credit union deposits refer to total savings. **Sources:** Federal Deposit Insurance Corp, *Statistics on Banking* (interactive); Office of Thrift Supervision. *OTS Fact Book;* National Credit Union Association, *2009 Year-End Statistics*.

Top 100 U.S. Banking Companies, 2008

Rank, Bank, City	Assets (millions)
1. JPMorgan Chase & Co., New York	$2,175,052,000
2. Citigroup Inc., New York	1,938,470,000
3. Bank of America Corp., Charlotte	1,822,068,028
4. Wells Fargo & Co., San Francisco	1,309,639,000
5. MetLife Inc., New York	501,678,258
6. PNC Financial Services Group Inc., Pittsburgh	291,092,876
7. U.S. Bancorp, Minneapolis	267,032,000
8. Bank of New York Mellon Corp., New York	237,652,000
9. SunTrust Banks Inc., Atlanta	189,137,961
10. State Street Corp., Boston	176,632,334
11. Capital One Financial Corp., McLean, Va.	165,913,451
12. BB&T Corp., Winston-Salem, N.C.	152,015,025
13. Regions Financial Corp., Birmingham, Ala.	146,253,935
14. Fifth Third Bancorp, Cincinnati	119,763,812
15. KeyCorp, Cleveland	105,231,004
16. Northern Trust Corp., Chicago	82,053,626
17. Comerica Inc., Dallas	67,912,580
18. Marshall & Ilsley Corp., Milwaukee	62,517,618
19. Zions BanCorp., Salt Lake City	55,339,951
20. Huntington Bancshares Inc., Columbus, Ohio	54,355,998
21. *Hudson City Bancorp Inc., Paramus, N.J.	53,906,227
22. *E-Trade Financial Corp., New York	45,070,677
23. Popular Inc., Hato Rey, Puerto Rico	38,883,000
24. Synovus Financial Corp., Columbus, Ga.	35,786,269
25. New York Community Bancorp Inc., Westbury, N.Y.	32,488,105
26. First Horizon National Corp., Memphis	31,022,768
27. Colonial BancGroup Inc., Montgomery, Ala.	25,816,306
28. *Charles Schwab Corp., San Francisco	25,365,108
29. Associated Banc-Corp, Green Bay	24,198,697
30. BOK Financial Corp., Tulsa, Okla.	22,840,287
31. *Astoria Financial Corp., Lake Success, N.Y.	21,977,965
32. First BanCorp., San Juan, Puerto Rico	19,491,268
33. *People's United Financial Inc., Bridgeport, Conn.	19,259,550
34. Webster Financial Corp., Waterbury, Conn.	17,600,122
35. Commerce Bancshares Inc., Kansas City	17,545,887
36. FBOP Corp., Oak Park, Ill.	17,346,706
37. TCF Financial Corp., Wayzata, Minn.	16,782,760
38. First Citizens Bancshares Inc., Raleigh, N.C.	16,745,662
39. City National Corp., Beverly Hills	16,458,765
40. Fulton Financial Corp., Lancaster, Pa.	16,185,106
41. *AmTrust Financial Corp., Cleveland	15,558,190
42. W Holding Co., Inc., Mayaguez, P.R.	15,317,974
43. Cullen/Frost Bankers Inc., San Antonio	15,131,905
44. *Guaranty Financial Group Inc., Austin	15,051,289
45. New York Private Bank and Trust Corp., New York	14,744,507
46. Valley National Bancorp, Wayne, N.J.	14,718,129
47. *Midland Financial Co., Oklahoma City	14,649,039
48. *Flagstar Bancorp Inc., Troy, Mich.	14,157,838
49. *BankUnited Financial Corp., Coral Gables, Fla.	13,733,306
50. Susquehanna Bancshares Inc., Lititz, Pa.	13,682,988

Rank, Bank, City	Assets (millions)
51. South Financial Group Inc., Greenville, S.C.	$13,600,077
52. UCBH Holdings Inc., San Francisco	13,526,809
53. BancorpSouth Inc., Tupelo, Miss.	13,499,414
54. Citizens Republic Bancorp Inc., Flint, Mich.	13,093,861
55. Sterling Financial Corp., Spokane, Wash.	12,793,531
56. Wilmington Trust Corp., Del.	12,586,360
57. *Washington Federal Inc., Seattle	12,516,153
58. International Bancshares Corp., Laredo, Tex.	12,439,341
59. East West Bancorp Inc., Pasadena, Calif.	12,423,491
60. Whitney Holding Corp., New Orleans	12,384,751
61. *Lehman Brothers Holdings Inc., New York	11,987,623
62. Cathay General Bancorp, El Monte, Calif.	11,582,639
63. FirstMerit Corp., Akron, Ohio	11,101,201
64. UMB Financial Corp., Kansas City	10,971,391
65. *Third Federal Savings and Loan MHC, Cleveland	10,833,940
66. First Banks Inc., Clayton, Mo.	10,771,034
67. Bank of Hawaii Corp., Honolulu	10,763,475
68. Wintrust Financial Corp., Lake Forest, Ill.	10,658,326
69. Doral GP Ltd., San Juan, Puerto Rico	10,355,717
70. Arvest Bank Group Inc., Bentonville, Ark.	10,226,011
71. PrivateBancorp Inc., Chicago	10,040,342
72. Trustmark Corp., Jackson, Miss.	9,790,909
73. SVB Financial Group, Santa Clara, Calif.	9,751,359
74. Pacific Capital Bancorp, Santa Barbara, Calif.	9,574,291
75. *Raymond James Financial Inc., St. Petersburg, Fla.	9,457,854
76. National Penn Bancshares Inc., Boyertown, Pa.	9,395,588
77. FirstBank Holding Co., Lakewood, Colo.	9,278,304
78. *First Niagara Financial Group Inc., Lockport, N.Y.	9,239,610
79. Prosperity Bancshares Inc., Houston	9,081,436
80. Central Bancompany Inc., Jefferson City, Mo.	8,962,338
81. Franklin Resources Inc., San Mateo, Calif.	8,962,111
82. MB Financial Inc., Chicago	8,819,763
83. Umpqua Holdings Corp., Portland, Ore.	8,605,203
84. First Midwest Bancorp Inc., Itasca, Ill.	8,530,940
85. United Community Banks Inc., Blairsville, Ga.	8,520,765
86. Corus Bankshares Inc., Chicago	8,409,567
87. F.N.B. Corp., Hermitage, Pa.	8,364,811
88. NewAlliance Bancshares Inc., New Haven, Conn.	8,300,243
89. *Capitol Federal Savings Bank MHC Topeka, Kan.	8,171,795
90. United Bankshares Inc., Charleston, W.Va.	8,102,091
91. Old National Bancorp, Evansville, Ind.	7,874,853
92. Otto Bremer Foundation, St. Paul, Minn.	7,719,803
93. *FirstFed Financial Corp., Los Angeles	7,450,448
94. R&G Financial Corp., Hato Rey, P.R.	7,446,483
95. Boston Private Financial Holdings Inc., Boston	7,339,476
96. Hancock Holding Co., Gulfport, Miss.	7,188,678
97. Investors Bancorp MHC, Short Hills, N.J.	7,186,399
98. Park National Corp., Newark, Ohio	7,070,720
99. *EverBank Financial Corp., Jacksonville, Fla.	7,047,356
100. First Citizens BanCorp., Inc., Columbia, S.C.	7,022,963

Note: Institutions preceded by * are thrifts. **Source:** © 2009 *American Banker*, May 20, 2009. Reprinted by permission.

Mortgage loans Mortgages are loans backed by buildings—either private dwellings or commercial buildings. Until the 1970s, virtually all mortgages had fixed-interest payments and 30-year terms. With the escalation of interest rates beginning in the late 1970s, however, several alternative arrangements have developed. For example, in order to reduce the interest payments, many borrowers repay their loans in 15 years. Others use a *variable* or *adjustable rate mortgage* in which the interest rate varies with market rates. Some mortgages that hold payments down in the first few years and then increase them rapidly for the remaining term of the mortgage are known as balloon mortgages.

Mortgage crisis In the first decade of the 20th century, lenders became ever more creative with mortgages, tempting less-than-ideal buyers with extra-low initial or "teaser" rates that soared in later years, or "interest-only" loans in which the homeowner never paid back the principal. These mortgage products allowed higher-risk (or "subprime") borrowers to get in on the real estate boom that was sweeping the U.S. at the time. They were a sound investment as long as property values continued to increase. But when the housing bubble started to burst in 2006 and 2007, many homeowners found they couldn't keep up with the escalating payments, didn't have any assets that would allow them to refinance, and owed more than the declining value of their homes.

Defaults and foreclosures turned subdivisions into ghost-towns almost overnight. But homeowners weren't the only ones affected. The banks that lent them the money suffered nearly $400 billion in losses on bad loans. And because lenders usually disperse risk by selling their mortgages to third parties, the credit crisis quickly spread to other financial markets.

The first major casualty of the sub-prime mortgage crisis was Bear Stearns, whose heavy investment in mortgage-backed securities caused its stock price to fall from $67 to $2 in just a few weeks. Fearing complete collapse, the government in March 2008, arranged for JP Morgan Chase to buy out Bear Stearns for $10 a share. In July, the Treasury Department created a taxpayer guarantee to bail out Fannie Mae and Freddie Mac, the nation's two largest mortgage finance companies.

Lehman Brothers, a 158-year-old Wall Street banking firm wasn't so lucky. It filed for the largest bankruptcy in U.S. history in September 2008 after the government denied it a similar bailout. Merrill Lynch, which had lost more than $50 billion in mortgage-backed securities, agreed to be acquired by Bank of America.

The crisis quickly spread to insurance companies as well, most notably American International Group, formerly the world's largest insurer. In September 2008, the Federal Reserve Bank saved A.I.G. from bankruptcy with an $85 billion line of credit, and amount it subsequently raised to as much as $185 billion.

►MONEY INSTRUMENTS

Treasury bills, also called T-bills, are securities sold by the U.S. Treasury in denominations of $10,000 that mature at various dates, but all in less than one year. Treasury bills pay an interest rate that is adjusted by the Treasury according to supply and demand. The Treasury bill rate is thought to have the highest risk-free rate of return among all investments.

Federal funds are the reserves the Fed requires depository institutions such as commercial banks to hold on deposit at their regional Federal Reserve Bank as protection against withdrawals. Banks and other depository institutions can loan reserves in excess of those required by the Fed to each other. These Fed Fund loans can provide institutions with large amounts of liquid assets on very short notice, and most loans are for no more than one day.

Money Market Interest Rates and Mortgage Rates, 1970–2009

Type	1970	1980	1990	2000	2005	2007	2009
Federal funds, effective rate	7.18%	13.35%	8.10%	6.24%	3.22%	5.02%	0.16%
Prime rate charged by banks	7.91	15.26	10.01	9.23	6.19	8.05	3.25
Eurodollar deposits, 3-month	8.52	14.03	8.16	6.45	3.51	5.32	1.03
Large negotiable CDs, 3-month, secondary market	7.56	13.07	8.15	6.46	3.51	5.27	0.55
Federal Reserve discount rate[1] (range)	5.50 to 6.00	10.00 to 13.00	6.50 to 7.00	5.00 to 6.00	3.25 to 5.25	4.75 to 6.25	0.5 to 0.75
Taxable money market funds[2,5]	N.A.	12.68	7.82	5.89	2.66	4.70	2.05
Tax-exempt money market funds[2,5]	N.A.	N.A.	5.45	3.54	1.87	3.13	1.77
U.S. Government securities:							
3-month Treasury bill[3]	6.39%	11.39%	7.50%	5.82%	3.15%	4.36%	0.15%
6-month Treasury bill[3]	6.51	11.32	7.46	5.90	3.39	4.44	0.28
1-year Treasury bill[3]	6.48	10.85	7.35	5.78	N.A.	N.A.	0.45
Home mortgages							
New home mortgage yields[4]	N.A.	12.70	10.05%	7.52%	5.94%	6.41%	5.04%
Conventional, 15-year fixed[3]	N.A.	N.A.	9.73	7.76	5.50	6.11	4.57
Conventional, 30-year fixed[3]	N.A.	N.A.	9.97	8.08	5.93	6.40	5.04

Notes: 1. Federal Reserve Bank of New York, low and high. The discount rate for 1980 does not include the 3% surcharge applied to frequent borrowings by large institutions. 2. 12-month return for Dec. 31 of year shown. 3. Annual averages. 4. Effective rate (in the primary market) on conventional mortgages, reflecting fees and charges as well as contract rate and assumed, on the average, repayment after 10 years. 5. Data is from 2008. **Source:** Except as noted, Board of Governors of the Federal Reserve System, *Federal Reserve Bulletin*, monthly.

Certificates of deposit (CDs) Customers who make these deposits at commercial banks or thrift institutions receive a certificate describing the maturity date of the deposit (e.g., a five-year CD). CDs guarantee a rate of return for as long as 10 years into the future. In addition, the fact that they can be purchased at local banks also makes them easy to secure. These factors make them appealing to the general public. The interest paid on CDs is set by the market and is generally the same across large institutions. Smaller institutions often offer higher rates to attract depositors.

Money-market accounts Customers pool their money into a fund that then purchases short-term debt such as Treasury bills and commercial paper in order to earn a high rate of return while maintaining liquidity (i.e., being able to convert assets quickly into cash). Customers typically can write checks on their money-market accounts, which are processed through cooperating banks, but checks generally have to be in large denominations—greater than $250—to prevent customers from using them as demand deposit accounts.

▶ CAPITAL INSTRUMENTS

Stock, or equity, the most important source of capital for firms, represents a claim on the assets or equity of a business as well as on its earnings. (See also "U.S. Business".)

Treasury bonds, or notes, have longer-term dates of maturity, from one to 10 years, than do Treasury bills. They are sold by the Treasury in denominations of $1,000 and are the principal means of funding government borrowing and the national debt. The interest on these bonds is paid out regularly. *Thirty-year Treasury Bonds,* commonly called the Long Bond, are also sold by the Treasury; their yield is watched closely because it forms the basis for all other interest rates, including mortgage-backed securities and fixed rates. Bond prices are determined by the relative number of investors willing to buy and sell them on the open market. Their decisions are in turn based on expectations about inflation. When the Federal Reserve announces that it will not change interest rates, indicating its belief that inflation will remain steady, more investors are willing to buy long-term investments, so bond prices rise, but result in a lower yield. When the economy heats up, however—that is, with increased business activity employing more workers—inflation is expected to rise, resulting in fewer investors willing to buy long-term instruments, and bond prices will fall as yields and other interest rates rise.

Other government securities Some agencies of the government that are involved in lending are permitted to sell securities in order to raise funds. The most important of these is the Federal National Mortgage Association—FNMA, or "Fanny Mae." It buys and sells mortgages insured by the federal government and stabilizes the market for those mortgages in the process.

Municipal bonds are issued by state and local governments to raise funds, usually to provide public works and other facilities. The federal government is prohibited by the Constitution from interfering in the ability of state and local governments to raise revenue, so income from municipal bonds is not subject to federal taxes. So-called revenue bonds are paid for by user fees—for example, tolls collected on a parkway are used to pay for the bonds used to build it. General-obligation bonds are paid for through general taxes. Municipal bonds tend to be very safe, although there have been occasions on which some state and local governments have had to take extraordinary actions to avoid default—most notably, New York City in 1975, which received a federal loan and sold new bonds to its municipal employee unions in order to avoid default.

▶ GOVERNMENT DEBT

One of the most debated economic issues since the 1980s has been the importance of the government's budget deficit. The government raises most of its resources through taxes, but it can also raise money by borrowing. The government borrows by selling bonds (Treasury bonds and savings bonds, for example) which have increasingly been purchased by investors outside the U.S. The bonds raise money now but must be repaid in the future through revenues from taxes. The *budget deficit* in any year indicates the difference between what the government takes in through taxes and other forms of revenues, and the expenditures it makes. The deficit therefore suggests how much the government needed to borrow to fill that gap. The total amount of present and past

Bond Yields, 1970–2009							
Type	1970	1980	1990	2000	2005	2007	2009
U.S. Treasury, constant maturities:[1,2]							
1-year	N.A.	12.00%	7.89%	6.11%	3.62%	4.52%	0.47%
5-year	7.38%	11.45	8.37	6.16	4.05	4.43	2.20
10-year	7.35	11.43	8.55	6.03	4.29	4.63	3.26
State and local govt. bonds, Aaa	6.12	7.86	6.96	5.58	4.28	4.13	4.58[3]
State and local govt. bonds, Baa	6.75	9.02	7.30	6.19	4.86	4.59	5.64[3]
Municipal (Bond Buyer, 20 bonds)	6.35	8.55	7.27	5.71	4.40	4.40	5.44
High-grade municipal bonds (Standard & Poor's)	6.51	8.51	7.25	5.77	4.29	4.42	4.64
Corporate Aaa seasoned	8.04	11.94	9.32	7.62	5.23	5.56	5.31
Corporate Baa seasoned	9.11	13.67	10.36	8.37	6.06	6.48	7.29
Corporate seasoned, all industries	8.51	12.75	9.77	7.98	5.57	6.01	6.44[3]

Note: 1. Yields on the more actively traded issues adjusted to constant maturities by the U.S. Treasury. 2. Through 1990, yields are based on closing bid prices quoted by at least five dealers. Yields since 2000 are based on closing indicative prices quoted by secondary market participants. 3. Data is for 2008. **Sources:** Board of Governors of the Federal Reserve System, *Federal Reserve Bulletin*, monthly; U.S. Council of Economic Advisors, *Economic Indicators*, monthly (high-grade bonds); Moody's Investors Service (corporate bonds).

borrowing, plus interest, constitutes the total *national debt*.

Governments routinely borrow to pay for long-term projects that will give benefits to the community into the future. It can be argued that because much of the benefit from projects such as highways and other public works will be enjoyed by the next generation of taxpayers, they should also bear much of the cost. And they can do that by paying off the government debt (paying the premiums on the government bonds) through taxes in the future. Controversy arises when the government borrows to pay for its more routine expenditures. One justification for such borrowing is that it can be used to manage business cycles in the economy: in other words, during recessions, the government can borrow in order to increase expenditures and expand the economy without raising taxes, which would slow it down.

When the total amount of government debt becomes large, some economists believe that it damages the economy in the following ways. First the fact that the government is selling large amounts of debt means that it is competing for limited investor dollars with private borrowers, driving up the cost of borrowing, and making it harder for private sector businesses to make investments for future growth. Second, the future taxes needed to pay off large amounts of government debt may place a serious drain on the future economy, again diverting resources from investment in the private sector. Politicians are concerned because debt payments must be funded from tax revenues so they must either raise taxes or reduce government spending in other areas (e.g. in defense, or in entitlement programs).

The debate over debt really turns on how much is "too much." Between 1935 and 1981 the only two significant increases in the deficit occurred during World War II and the Vietnam War, when deficits were about $25 billion. Between 1981 and 1989, however, the Reagan administration consistently ran annual deficits averaging $167 billion and more than doubled the nation's total outstanding gross debt.

The Clinton administration posted four straight years of surpluses and wiped out the annual deficit in 1998. But the total national debt never decreased because the interest on the debt were higher even than the record-level surpluses. George W. Bush's 2002 tax cut turned a $126 billion annual surplus into a $158 billion deficit and pushed the total federal debt over the $6 trillion mark.

The deficit set an all time high of $459 billion in 2008, an amount that will likely be dwarfed by the estimated $1.8 trillion for 2009 that resulted in large part from massive government bailouts of the banking industry. The total national debt was likewise expected to skyrocket from $9.9 trillion to $12.9 trillion.

▶ THE LABOR FORCE
Labor Force Participation Rate
The Labor Force Participation Rate (LFPR), often referred to simply as the labor force, is that proportion of the population that is either employed or actively seeking employment. It represents the supply of labor available to the economy. The LFPR is lower for young people because many are in school, and for older people because many have retired. It is highest for married men and for women who are heads of households.

Women in the work force One of the most important developments in the labor force has been the sharp increase in the LFPR of women, which has virtually doubled since the early 1960s.

U.S. Deficits and the Debt, 1940–2009 (billions of dollars)

Year	Total receipts	Total outlays	Surplus or Deficit	Gross Federal Debt	Debt held by the public	Net interest paid[1] Total	Net interest paid[1] As percent of federal outlays
1940	$ 6.5	$ 9.5	$ −2.9	$ 50.7	$ 42.7	$ 1.0	9.5%
1945	45.2	92.7	−47.6	260.1	235.2	3.1	3.4
1950	39.4	42.6	−3.1	256.9	219.0	4.8	11.4
1955	65.5	68.4	−3.0	274.4	226.6	4.9	7.6
1960	92.5	92.2	0.3	290.5	236.8	6.9	8.5
1965	116.8	118.2	−1.4	322.3	260.8	8.6	8.1
1970	192.8	195.6	−2.8	380.9	283.2	14.4	7.9
1975	279.1	332.3	−53.2	541.9	394.7	23.2	7.5
1980	517.1	590.9	−73.8	909.0	711.9	52.5	10.6
1985	734.1	946.4	−212.3	1,817.4	1,507.3	129.5	16.2
1990	1,032.0	1,253.2	−221.2	3,206.3	2,411.6	184.3	16.1
1995	1,351.8	1,515.8	−164.0	4,920.6	3,604.8	232.1	15.8
1998	1,721.8	1,652.6	69.2	5,478.2	3,721.1	241.1	15.1
2000	2,025.5	1,789.2	236.2	5,628.7	3,409.8	223.0	12.0
2001	1,991.4	1,863.2	128.2	5,769.9	3,319.6	206.2	11.1
2002	1,853.4	2,011.2	−157.8	6,198.4	3,540.4	171.0	8.5
2003	1,782.5	2,160.1	−377.6	6,760.0	3,913.4	153.1	7.1
2004	1,880.3	2,293.0	−412.7	7,354.7	4,295.5	160.2	7.0
2005	2,153.9	2,472.2	−318.3	7,905.3	4,592.2	184.0	7.4
2006	2,407.3	2,655.4	−248.2	8,451.4	4,829.0	226.6	8.5
2007	2,568.2	2,730.2	−162.0	8,950.7	5,035.1	237.1	8.5
2008	2,524.3	2,982.9	−458.6	9,985.8	5,802.7	142.7	8.5
2009[2]	2,156.6	3,997.8	−1,841.2	12,867.5	8,531.4	135.9	3.6

Note: For fiscal years ending in year shown. Public debt excludes debt held by Federal Government accounts. 1. Net interest is interest paid on debt held by the public. 2. Estimate. **Source:** *Budget of the United States Government, Fiscal Year 2010* (2009).

With higher levels of education than ever before, most women now opt for careers in the labor force rather than homemaking. Women are having fewer children, and are having them later in life—after they have started to establish their careers—and are returning to work sooner after childbirth. Furthermore, women are continuing to make inroads into professions like law and medicine that have previously been dominated by men.

Women joined the labor force at an astounding rate between 1960 and 1990. Just under 38 percent of women worked in 1960; in 1990, 57 percent did. The percentage of women in the labor force has declined slightly since 2000 and stood at 59.5 percent in 2008. The percentage of men in the labor force continues to drop, from 83.3 percent in 1960 to 73.0 percent in 2008.

Unemployment rate One of the most closely watched labor force statistics is the unemployment rate. Because unemployment is a lagging economic indicator, jobs aren't shed until after the economy starts contracting, and jobless rates remain high even after the economy begins to rebound. In 1997, the unemployment rate fell below 5 percent for the first time in 30 years. It dropped all the way to 3.9 percent in April, 2000, before climbing slowly back over 6 percent in 2003. Unemployment jumped to 5.8 percent for 2008, and continued rising to over 10 percent by the middle of 2009.

The unemployment rate over time for the United States is a measure associated with identifying periods of expansion and recession. It reached a peak of 9.6 percent during the 1982–83 recession. The relatively high periods of unemployment beginning in the mid-1970s are in part due to the expansion of the labor force as the baby boom generation left school and began looking for work. Unemployment rates for women have paralleled those for men since 1990.

Hispanics People of Hispanic origin constitute the fastest-growing population group in the labor force, in large part due to immigration, with Mexicans making up the largest share. The proportion of Hispanic women working—historically, these women were more likely to stay at home—has boosted Hispanic participation in the labor force. But a doubling of the Hispanic population in the U.S. since 1980 has been responsible for most of the growth. In 2008, Hispanic workers made up 14.3 percent of the labor force, up from 1995, when they were only 9.3 percent. Overall, Hispanic workers earn only three-quarters as much as the average for all workers. Hispanics also have a higher unemployment rate, though not as high as the rate for blacks.

Productivity measures how much output an economy or organization can generate from a given amount of input. Higher levels of productivity suggest greater efficiency—i.e. doing more with the same amount of resources, just as an efficient or economical car goes farther on a gallon of gasoline. Increases in productivity, as the result of better tools or improved methods, provide the main mechanism for increasing output in an economy and ultimately for raising standards of living. Productivity is usually measured in terms of labor—such as output per worker or output per

Occupations with Greatest Percentage of Women, Blacks, and Hispanics, 2008

Occupation	Number ('000s)	Percent women
Speech-language pathologists	133	98.1%
Dental hygienists	143	97.7
Preschool and kindergarten teachers	685	97.6
Dental assistants	263	96.3
Secretaries and administrative assistants	3,296	96.1
Occupational therapists	87	95.9
Child care workers	1,314	95.6
Medical records and health information technicians	98	95.0
Receptionists and information clerks	1,413	93.6
Licensed practical and licensed vocational nurses	566	93.3

Occupation	Number ('000s)	Percent black
Nursing, psychiatric, and home health aides	1,889	34.5%
Postal service mail sorters, processors, and processing machine operators	90	34.1
Barbers	87	33.3
Security guards and gaming surveillance officers	867	31.0
Bus drivers	651	30.4
Crossing guards	68	29.9
Residential advisors	70	28.1
Upholsterers	56	27.2
Postal service clerks	167	27.0
Taxi drivers and chauffeurs	373	26.3

Occupation	Number ('000s)	Percent Hispanic
Graders and sorters, agricultural products	63	59.3%
Cement masons, concrete finishers, and terrazzo workers	90	57.7
Drywall installers, ceiling tile installers, and tapers	209	56.9
Miscellaneous agricultural workers	723	45.1
Construction laborers	1,651	44.1
Packers and packagers, hand	391	43.7
Roofers	234	42.9
Carpet, floor, and tile installers and finishers	224	42.7
Packaging and filling machine operators and tenders	261	42.5
Upholsterers	56	42.1

Source: U.S. Department of Labor, Bureau of Labor Statistics, *Employment and Earnings* (January 2009).

Unemployment Rate, 1947–2010

Year	Percent unemployed	Year	Percent unemployed	Year	Percent unemployed
1947	3.9%	1980	7.1%	2004	5.5%
1950	5.3	1985	7.2	2005	5.1
1955	4.4	1990	5.6	2006	4.6
1960	5.5	1995	5.6	2007	4.6
1965	4.5	2000	4.0	2008	5.8
1970	4.9	2002	5.8	2009[1]	9.4
1975	8.5	2003	6.0	2010[2]	9.9

Note: 1. May 2009 only. 2. April 2010 only. Source: U.S. Department of Labor, Bureau of Labor Statistics, *Employment and Earnings* (January 2010).

Employment Status of the Population by Sex, Race, and Hispanic Origin 1960–2009 (numbers in thousands)

Year	Civilian noninstitutional population[1]	Civilian labor force			Employment/ population ratio[2]	Percent unemployed
		Total	Percent of population	Number employed		
Total						
1960	117,245	69,628	59.4%	65,778	56.1%	5.5%
1970	137,085	82,771	60.4	78,678	57.4	4.9
1980	167,745	106,940	63.8	99,303	59.2	7.1
1990	188,049	124,787	66.4	117,914	62.7	5.5
2000[3]	212,577	142,583	67.1	136,891	64.4	4.0
2005	226,082	149,320	66.0	141,730	62.7	5.1
2007	231,867	153,124	66.0	146,047	63.0	4.6
2008	233,788	154,287	66.0	145,632	62.2	5.8
2009	235,801	154,142	65.4	139,877	59.3	9.3
Male						
1960	55,662	46,388	83.3%	43,904	78.9%	5.4%
1970	64,304	51,228	79.7	48,990	76.2	4.4
1980	79,398	61,453	77.4	57,186	72.0	6.9
1990	89,650	68,234	76.1	64,435	71.9	5.6
2000[3]	101,964	76,280	74.8	73,305	71.9	3.9
2005	109,151	80,033	73.3	74,319	69.6	5.1
2007	112,173	82,136	73.2	78,254	69.8	4.7
2008	113,113	82,520	73.0	77,456	68.5	6.1
2009	114,136	82,123	72.0	73,670	64.5	10.3
Female						
1960	61,582	23,240	37.7%	21,874	35.5%	5.9%
1970	72,782	31,543	43.3	29,688	40.8	5.9
1980	88,348	45,487	51.5	42,117	47.7	7.4
1990	98,399	56,554	57.5	53,479	54.3	5.4
2000[3]	110,613	66,303	59.9	63,586	57.5	4.1
2005	116,931	69,288	59.3	65,757	56.2	5.1
2007	119,694	70,988	59.3	67,792	56.6	4.5
2008	120,675	71,767	59.5	67,876	56.2	5.4
2009	121,665	72,019	59.2	66,208	54.4	8.1
White						
1975	134,790	82,831	61.5%	76,411	56.7%	7.8%
1980	146,122	93,600	64.1	87,715	60.0	6.3
1990	160,415	107,177	66.8	102,087	63.6	4.7
2000[3]	176,220	118,545	67.3	114,424	64.9	3.5
2005	184,446	122,299	66.3	116,949	63.4	4.4
2007	188,253	124,935	66.4	119,792	63.6	4.1
2008	189,540	125,635	66.3	11,9126	62.8	5.2
2009	191,628	124,344	64.9	113,416	59.1	8.8
Black						
1975	15,751	9,263	58.8%	7,894	50.1%	14.8%
1980	17,824	10,865	61.0	9,313	52.2	14.3
1990	21,300	13,493	63.3	11,966	56.2	11.3
2000[3]	24,902	16,397	65.8	15,156	60.9	7.6
2005	26,517	17,013	64.2	15,313	57.7	10.0
2007	27,485	17,496	63.7	16,051	58.4	8.3
2008	27,843	17,740	63.7	15,953	57.3	10.1
2009	28,437	17,484	61.5	14,759	51.9	15.6
Hispanic[4]						
1975	N.A.	N.A.	N.A.	N.A.	N.A.	N.A.
1980	9,598	6,146	64.0%	5,527	57.6%	10.1%
1990	14,297	9,576	67.0	8,808	61.6	8.0
2000[3]	23,938	16,689	69.7	15,735	65.7	5.7
2005	29,133	19,824	68.0	18,632	64.0	6.0
2007	31,383	21,602	68.8	20,382	64.9	5.6
2008	32,141	22,024	68.5	20,346	63.3	7.6
2009	33,379	22,481	67.3	19,591	58.7	12.9

Notes: 1. Age 16 and over. 2. Civilians employed as a percent of the civilian noninstitutional population. 3. Data after 1995 are not directly comparable with data for previous years because of a major redesign of the Current Population Survey questionnaire and collection methodology and the introduction of 1990 census-based population controls, adjusted for the estimated undercount. 4. Hispanic persons may be of any race. **Source:** U.S. Bureau of Labor Statistics, *Employment and Earnings* (January 2010).

hour of labor—not only because labor is the most important resource but also because it is one of the easiest to measure.

Wages vary not only among the different professions but also between sexes and regions of the country. For example, women in year-round, full-time executive, administrative, and managerial positions have a median yearly income of only 61 percent of the median income for men in the same occupation group. This percentage is higher in the field of laborers, precision production, craft, and repair; but for all major occupation groups reported by the U.S. Bureau of the Census, women receive only a fraction of that received by their male counterparts. This may be

Average Earnings of Year-Round Full-Time Workers by Age and Educational Attainment, 2007

Age and Sex	All workers	Less than 9th grade	Some high school	High school graduate	Some college	Associate degree	Bachelor's degree or more
Male, total	**$58,373**	**$27,561**	**$32,379**	**$42,042**	**$48,993**	**$52,322**	**$88,641**
18–24 years old	26,260	18,020	22,095	25,153	25,739	29,542	37,429
25–34 years old	46,668	26,624	28,475	35,995	41,551	45,691	66,731
35–44 years old	63,611	25,877	34,094	47,149	55,232	55,394	92,776
45–54 years old	66,285	30,127	35,858	46,677	57,991	56,903	100,260
55–64 years old	68,281	32,337	40,983	46,037	53,532	56,808	97,029
65 years and over	65,586	35,540	40,922	47,557	45,505	54,063	97,614
Female, total	**$42,219**	**$21,320**	**$22,171**	**$30,657**	**$36,836**	**$41,097**	**$58,000**
18–24 years old	24,619	N.A.	18,013	21,389	23,748	25,130	33,639
25–34 years old	40,204	19,341	20,899	30,092	34,561	39,606	49,966
35–44 years old	44,528	23,120	23,344	30,854	38,419	40,762	32,358
45–54 years old	45,878	20,279	23,822	33,079	39,509	45,759	64,429
55–64 years old	43,869	21,428	23,153	31,828	40,648	41,133	61,580
65 years and over	39,668	N.A.	20,480	29,610	50,688	40,408	52,344

Note: High school graduate category includes equivalency. **Source:** U.S. Bureau of the Census, *Current Population Reports* (2010).

Average Hourly and Weekly Earnings in Current and Constant (1982) Dollars, By Private Industry Group, 1970–2009

Average hourly and weekly wages (in current dollars) have increased by about 50 percent since 1990, but as the following table illustrates, when inflation is accounted for, real earnings (in constant dollars) have actually decreased since 1970.

Constant (1982)[1] dollars	1970	1980	1990	2000	2005	2006	2007	2009
Average hourly earnings	$8.46	$8.00	$7.66	$8.04	$8.18	$8.24	$8.33	$8.27
Average weekly earnings	$313	$282	$263	$276	$276	$279	$282	$262

Current dollars	1970	1980	1990	2000	2005	2006	2007	2009
Average hourly earnings	**$3.40**	**$6.84**	**$10.19**	**$14.02**	**$16.13**	**$16.76**	**$17.43**	**$17.99**
Natural resources and mining	3.77	8.97	13.40	16.55	18.72	19.90	20.97	21.79
Construction	4.74	9.37	13.42	17.48	19.46	20.02	20.95	21.72
Manufacturing	3.23	7.15	10.78	14.32	16.56	16.81	17.26	17.68
Trade, transportation, and public utilities	3.65	7.04	9.83	13.31	14.92	15.39	15.78	16.13
Information	5.25	9.47	13.40	19.07	22.06	23.23	23.96	24.71
Financial activities	3.07	5.82	9.99	14.98	17.94	18.80	19.64	20.23
Professional & business services	4.04	7.22	11.14	15.52	18.08	19.13	20.15	20.96
Education and health services	2.88	5.93	10.00	13.95	16.71	17.38	18.11	18.80
Leisure and hospitality	1.78	3.89	5.88	8.32	9.38	9.75	10.41	10.83
Average weekly earnings	**$126**	**$241**	**$349**	**$481**	**$544**	**$568**	**$590**	**$ 753**
Natural resources and mining	166	403	603	735	854	908	963	1,008
Construction	179	351	513	686	751	781	816	853
Manufacturing	129	284	436	591	673	691	712	726
Trade, transportation, utilities	137	246	332	450	498	514	526	542
Information	195	344	480	701	805	850	875	932
Financial activities	112	210	355	537	645	672	705	751
Professional & business services	145	248	381	535	619	662	701	776
Education and health services	97	190	319	449	545	565	590	629
Leisure and hospitality	53	105	152	217	241	250	266	276

Note: Averages include other services not shown separately. 1. Earnings in current dollars divided by the Consumer Price Index on a 1982 base. **Source:** U.S. Bureau of Labor Statistics, *Employment and Earnings* (monthly).

due, in part, to the fact that women enter and leave the work force three times throughout their lives than do men and spend a smaller percentage of their lives economically active.

Another factor influencing the discrepancy between men's and women's wages is the concentration of women in occupations that pay less. As the accompanying table demonstrates, women make up the vast majority of child care workers and receptionists, two poorly paid positions.

Minimum wage in the nation was first enacted by the state of Massachusetts in 1912, covered only women, and was designed to shorten hours and raise pay in the covered industries. The nationwide minimum wage was established in 1938, and has grown in both dollar value and the types of employees it covers since then. Some states may establish minimum wages higher than the federal minimum.

Unions are organizations of workers who engage in collective bargaining with employers for higher wages, better working conditions, and increased benefits. Industrial unions represent workers of a particular firm or industry, such as autoworkers and steelworkers, while craft unions represent employees, such as pilots and musicians, with a specific skill.

In the United States, unions are organized at three levels: (1) local unions, which administer labor contracts, serving individual members, employers, and in some cases, establishments directly; (2) national unions, which coordinate agreements across local unions and conduct collective bargaining negotiations with industry employers; and (3) labor federations or voluntary associations of national unions, which settle disputes between national unions, lobby for favorable labor legislation, and engage in public relations In 1955, the American Federation of Labor merged with the Congress of Industrial Organizations, to form the AFL-CIO, which was for 50 years the only labor federation in the country. But in 2005, several unions, including the Teamsters, Service Employees International Union, the United Food and Commercial Workers, and several others representing a total of more than 6 million workers, disaffiliated from the AFL-CIO to start the rival Change to Win coalition.

Many workers choose not to unionize because of the potential costs involved in membership, such as dues, lost pay during strikes, and possible retribution by employers. Union membership nationwide has declined steadily since 1954, when 25.4 percent of the total labor force was

Federal Minimum Wage Rates, 1938–2009

The Fair Labor Standards Act of 1938 set a minimum wage of 25 cents per hour for employees engaged in interstate commerce or in the production of goods for interstate commerce. Over the years, the government has expanded the numbers of workers covered by the federal minimums (waiters and workers under age 20 in their first three months of work, for example, may be paid less than minimum wage) and has increased the minimum amount. But, as this table shows, the increases have not always kept up with inflation.

Effective date	Hourly minimum (current dollars)	Purchasing power in constant (=1996) dollars
Oct. 24, 1938	$0.25	$2.78
Oct. 24, 1939	0.30	3.39
Oct. 24, 1945	0.40	3.49
Jan. 25, 1950	0.75	4.88
Mar. 1, 1956	1.00	5.77
Sept. 3, 1961	1.15[1]	6.03
Sept. 3, 1961	1.25	6.41
Feb. 1, 1967	1.40[2]	6.58
Feb. 1, 1968	1.60	7.21
May 1, 1974	2.00	6.37
Jan. 1, 1975	2.10	6.12
Jan. 1, 1976	2.30	6.34
Jan. 1, 1978	2.65	6.38
Jan. 1, 1979	2.90	6.27
Jan. 1, 1980	3.10	5.90
Jan. 1, 1981	3.35	5.78
Apr. 1, 1990	3.50	4.56
Apr. 1, 1991	4.25	4.90
Oct. 1, 1996	4.75	4.75
Sept. 1, 1997	5.15	3.90
July 26, 2007	5.85	4.43
July 24, 2008	6.55	4.77
July 24, 2009[3]	7.25	5.27[3]

Notes: Purchasing power is based on the CPI-U Consumer Price Index. 1. A lower rate of $1.00 per hour was extended to employees in large retail and service enterprises as well as to local transit, construction, and gas service station employees. This rate was increased to $1.15 in 1964, and put on par with the higher rate on Sept. 3, 1965. 2. A lower rate of $1.00 was extended to state and local government employees of hospitals, nursing homes, and schools, and to laundries, dry cleaners, and large hotels, motels, restaurants, and farms. This rate continued to lag behind the rate guaranteed other workers until 1977 (1978 for farm workers). 3. As calculated in 2009 using the Consumer Price Index. Source: U.S. Department of Labor (2010).

Work Stoppages, 1947–2009

Year	Number of work stoppages of 1,000 or more workers[1]	Total number of workers involved[2] ('000s)	Days idle Number[3] ('000s)	Days idle Percent of estimated working time[4]
1947	270	1,629	25,720	N.A.
1950	424	1,698	30,390	0.26%
1955	363	2,055	21,180	0.16
1960	222	896	13,260	0.09
1965	268	999	15,140	0.10
1970	381	2,468	52,761	0.29
1975	235	965	17,563	0.09
1980	187	795	20,844	0.09
1985	54	324	7,079	0.03
1990	44	185	5,926	0.02
1995	31	192	5,771	0.02
2000	39	394	20,419	0.06
2005	22	100	1,736	0.01
2006	20	70	2,688	0.01
2007	21	189	1,265	0.01
2008	15	72	1,954	0.01
2009	5	13	124	0.01

Notes: Excludes work stoppages lasting less than 1 day. 1. Beginning in year indicated. 2. Workers counted more than once if involved in more than one stoppage during the year. 3. Resulting from all stoppages in effect in a year, including those that began in an earlier year. 4. Agricultural and government employees are included in the total working time; private household, forestry and fishery employees are excluded. Source: U.S. Bureau of Labor Statistics, Compensation and Conditions, monthly.

unionized. Even as recently as 1983, more than 20 percent of the workforce was unionized. In 2009, only 12.4 percent of the workforce belonged to unions. Notable examples of membership decline are among steelworkers, garment workers, and oil, chemical and atomic workers, which each fell by about 50 percent during 1979-90. Virtually all of these losses are due to the loss of jobs in unionized firms. Several factors may have contributed to this decline, such as changes in technology that displace workers; "downsizing," in which firms lay off large numbers of employees to keep the company's stock prices high; and "outsourcing," in which firms hire cheaper labor overseas to do jobs formerly performed by unionized workers in the United States.

U.S. Membership in AFL-CIO Affiliated Unions, 1979–2009

Labor organization	1979	1985	1995	2000	2009
Total[1]	N.A.	N.A.	12,986,453	12,869,540	8,343,053
Actors and Artists	75,000	100,000	75,893	69,000	76,000
Air Line Pilots	N.A.	N.A.	N.A.	43,633	42,658
Automobile, Aerospace and Agriculture (UAW)	N.A.	974,000	760,038	742,409	427,521
Bakery, Confectionery and Tobacco	131,000	115,000	95,186	108,250	76,972
Boilermakers	129,000	110,000	42,802	39,540	44,084
Bricklayers	106,000	95,000	84,000	63,784	93,761
Carpenters and Joiners	626,000	609,000	354,306	N.A.	N.A.
Communications Workers (CWA)	485,000	524,000	490,482	627,080	576,833
Electrical Workers (IBEW)	825,000	791,000	673,117	663,602	618,740
Electronic, Electrical, and Salaried	243,000	198,000	136,502	N.A.	N.A.
Engineers, Operating	313,000	330,000	295,833	281,167	280,000
Firefighters	150,000	142,000	151,000	175,000	248,000
Flight Attendants	N.A.	N.A.	31,776	40,671	N.A.
Food and Commercial Workers (UFCW)	1,123,000	989,000	1,009,523	1,140,884	N.A.
Garment Workers (ILGWU)	314,000	210,000	N.A.	N.A.	N.A.
Glass, Molders, Pottery, and Plastics	50,000	72,000	69,000	57,466	31,245
Government Employees (AFGE)	236,000	199,000	157,100	191,260	233,591
Graphic Communications	171,000	141,000	95,580	88,772	N.A.
Hotel and Restaurant Employees	373,000	327,000	232,160	234,509	N.A.
Ironworkers	146,000	140,000	80,485	86,294	93,032
Laborers	475,000	383,000	330,694	301,591	N.A.
Letter Carriers (NALC)	151,000	186,000	210,000	210,000	207,333
Longshoreman's Association	63,000	65,000	60,595	61,601	61,306
Machinists and Aerospace (IAM)	688,000	520,000	431,619	458,000	299,107
Mine Workers	N.A.	N.A.	75,021	75,250	65,000
Needletrades, Industrial and Textile Employees	308,000	228,000	244,783	208,232	N.A.
Nurses, United American	N.A.	N.A.	N.A.	N.A.	44,300
Office and Professional Employees	83,000	90,000	82,987	95,760	104,184
Oil, Chemical, Atomic Workers (OCAW)	146,000	108,000	82,080	N.A.	N.A.
Painters	160,000	133,000	90,000	102,044	92,610
Paper, Chemical, and Energy Workers	262,000	232,000	235,302	262,816	N.A.
Plumbing and Pipefitting	228,000	226,000	219,800	219,800	219,800
Postal Workers	245,000	232,000	265,757	275,915	210,894
Retail, Wholesale, Department Store	122,000	106,000	73,133	N.A.	N.A.
Rubber, Cork, Linoleum, Plastic	158,000	106,000	N.A.	N.A.	N.A.
School Employees Assocation, California	N.A.	N.A.	N.A.	N.A.	129,000
Seafarers	84,000	80,000	80,250	80,250	84,245
Service Employees (SEIU)[2]	537,000	688,000	1,077,854	1,261,276	N.A.
Sheet Metal Workers	120,000	108,000	103,042	93,000	95,000
Stage Employees, Moving Picture Machine Operators	50,000	50,000	50,900	55,788	73,375
State, County, Municipal (AFSCME)[2]	889,000	997,000	1,210,949	1,249,306	1,397,879
Steelworkers	964,000	572,000	516,880	450,436	484,190
Teachers (AFT)	423,000	470,000	631,529	822,191	1,129,361
Teamsters	N.A.	N.A.	1,286,371	1,226,300	N.A.
Transit Union	94,000	94,000	96,340	108,117	122,107
Transport Workers	85,000	85,000	75,000	75,000	109,000
Transportation Union, United	121,000	52,000	59,575	90,725	63,256

Note: Membership figures based on average per capita paid membership to the AFL-CIO for the 12 months ending in June of the year shown. Figures reflect all mergers that have occurred since 1999. 1. Includes other AFL-CIO affiliated unions, not shown separately. 2. Figures for 1979 and 1985 exclude Hospital and Health Care Employees which merged with these unions in 1989. 3. As of June 30, 2009. **Source:** American Federation of Labor and Congress of Industrial Organizations, *Report of the AFL-CIO Executive Council* (annual).

Metropolitan Areas with Greatest Projected Job Growth, 2008–30

MOST JOBS ADDED	Number of jobs (000s)		Jobs added
Rank, Metropolitan statistical area	2008	2030	2008–30 (000s)
1. Atlanta–Sandy Springs–Marietta, Ga.	3,262,320	5,829,280	2,566,960
2. Dallas–Fort Worth–Arlington, Texas	3,923,730	6,353,970	2,430,240
3. Phoenix–Mesa–Scottsdale, Ariz.	2,492,140	4,538,020	2,045,880
4. Los Angeles–Long Beach–Santa Ana, Calif.	7,732,930	9,592,200	1,859,270
5. Houston–Baytown–Sugar Land, Texas	3,321,470	5,094,390	1,772,920
6. Las Vegas–Paradise, Nev.	1,252,280	2,959,420	1,707,140
7. Washington D.C.–Arlington–Alexandria, Va.	3,955,540	5,650,980	1,695,440
8. Miami–Ft. Lauderdale–Pompano Beach, Fla.	3,371,940	5,038,330	1,666,390
9. Denver–Aurora, Colo.	1,719,990	2,992,940	1,272,950
10. Orlando–Kissimmee, Fla.	1,387,360	2,604,410	1,217,050
11. Riverside–San Bernardino–Ontario, Calif.	1,810,770	2,872,620	1,061,850
12. Tampa–St. Petersburg–Clearwater, Fla.	1,709,090	2,726,440	1,017,350
13. Austin–Round Rock, Texas	1,038,240	1,989,100	950,860
14. Seattle–Tacoma–Bellevue, Wash.	2,269,840	3,173,160	903,320
15. Minneapolis–St. Paul–Bloomington, Minn.	2,336,290	3,235,330	899,040
16. San Diego–Carlsbad–San Marcos, Calif.	1,924,550	2,767,580	843,030
17. Chicago–Naperville–Joliet, Ill.–Ind.–Wisc.	5,725,050	6,539,300	814,250
18. Sacramento–Arden–Arcade–Roseville, Calif	1,258,400	1,973,940	715,540
19. Portland–Vancouver–Beaverton,Oreg.–Wash.	1,392,900	2,029,060	636,160
20. New York–No. New Jersey–Long Island, N.Y.	10,729,210	11,282,210	553,000
21. Baltimore–Towson, Md.	1,707,170	-2,226,330	519,160
22. Nashville–Davidson–Murfreesbor, Tenn.	1,055,010	1,563,780	508,770
23. San Francisco–Oakland–Fremont, Calif.	2,747,270	3,247,320	500,050
24. Salt Lake City, Utah	811,500	1,262,200	450,700
25. Boston–Cambridge–Quincy, Mass.–N.H.	3,130,670	3,560,790	430,120
26. San Antonio, Texas	1,140,550	1,567,340	426,790
27. Kansas City, Mo.–Kans.	1,322,230	1,742,070	419,840
28. Charlotte–Gastonia–Concord, N.C.–S.C.	1,077,620	1,482,490	404,870
29. Indianapolis, Ind.	1,135,500	1,527,790	392,290
30. Raleigh–Cary, N.C.	663,390	1,044,190	380,800
Total 30 MSA's	**77,404,950**	**108,466,980**	**31,062,030**

FASTEST JOB GROWTH	Number of jobs (000s)		Annual percent
Rank, Metropolitan statistical area	2008	2030	increase, 2008–30
1. St. George, Utah	79,750	227,540	4.88%
2. Palm Coast, Fla.	27,470	72,480	4.51
3. Las Vegas–Paradise, Nev.	1,252,280	2,959,420	3.99
4. Naples–Marco Island, Fla.	215,220	498,490	3.89
5. Lake Havasu City–Kingman, Ariz.	80,120	179,500	3.73
6. Punta Gorda, Fla.	76,270	163,100	3.52
7. Cape Coral–Fort Myers, Fla.	338,200	704,500	3.39
8. Prescott, Ariz.	97,100	194,010	3.20
9. Bend, Oreg.	107,160	212,030	3.15
10. Austin–Round Rock, Texas	1,038,240	1,989,100	3.00
11. Orlando–Kissimmee, Fla.	1,387,360	2,604,410	2.90
12. Phoenix–Mesa–Scottsdale, Ariz.	2,492,140	4,538,020	2.76
13. Port St. Lucie, Fla.	208,420	377,830	2.74
14. Bradenton–Sarasota–Venice, Fla.	438,160	786,390	2.69
15. McAllen–Edinburg–Mission, Texas	295,910	530,840	2.69
16. Atlanta–Sandy Springs–Marietta, Ga.	3,262,320	5,829,280	2.67
17. Ocala, Fla.	153,230	272,280	2.65
18. Coeur D'alene, Idaho	81,550	143,550	2.60
19. Carson City, Nebraska	45,020	79,030	2.59
20. Fort Collins–Loveland, Colo.	202,340	353,530	2.57
21. Denver–Aurora, Colo.	1,719,990	2,992,940	2.55
22. Provo–Orem, Utah	261,250	453,850	2.54
23. Hinesville–Fort Stewart, Ga.	41,270	69,930	2.43
24. Fayetteville–Springdale–Rogers, Ark.–Mo.	278,140	470,490	2.42
25. Myrtle Beach–North Myrtle Beach–Conway, S.C.	158,950	266,680	2.38
26. Flagstaff, Ariz.	85,820	140,930	2.28
27. Reno–Sparks, Nev.	297,640	488,640	2.28
28. Sebastian–Vero Beach, Fla.	74,320	121,810	2.27
29. Boise City–Nampa, Idaho	388,330	634,640	2.26
30. Dallas–Fort Worth–Arlington, Texas	3,923,730	6,353,970	2.22
U.S. Total	**181,595,840**	**237,196,830**	**N.A.**

Source: NPA Data Services, Inc., *Regional Economic Growth in the U.S. Projections for 2008–30* (2009).

U.S. BUSINESS

The Office of Management and Budget (O.M.B.) classifies the entire national economy into industries, based on principal product or activity. There are nine industrial divisions, which are further classified into groups and subgroups. For example, manufacturing includes "food and kindred products" and "meat-packing plants." The nine industrial divisions listed in the O.M.B.'s Standard Industry Classification (SIC) are agriculture, forestry and fishing; mining; construction; manufacturing; transportation and public utilities; finance, insurance and real estate; wholesale trade; retail trade; and services. In 2006, 7.6 million establishments employed 119 million workers with payrolls totaling $4.8 trillion.

Services and Manufacturing

Another way to view the economy is to divide it into manufacturing industries, producing tangible goods such as cars, shoes and furniture, and service industries, whose products are intangible, such as entertainment, tourism and banking. The manufacturing industries are further broken down into those that produce durable goods—that is, goods that are consumed over time, such as cars and houses—and nondurable goods that are consumed in the short run (food and soap).

Services have become an ever-increasing source of jobs in the 21st century economy. That's partly because of a dearth of manufacturing jobs in the U.S. as companies have moved their manufacturing operations to countries where labor is less expensive. It's also because companies that have remained in the U.S. increasingly contract out services such as transportation, accounting, marketing and communications, previously performed in-house.

Financing Business

When an individual or a group of individuals decides to start a new company, they need money to rent or buy office space and equipment and to pay workers. Since there is a time lag between the day a business opens and the day a business sells its first good or service, funds must be borrowed from a bank or other financial institution or from individual investors to meet costs before revenues are generated. Additional funds may be needed throughout the life of the business to finance research and development of a new product or service or for the construction of new factories. Financing can take many forms, from short-term bank loans, commercial paper, or trade credit to long-term stocks and bonds.

Short-term Financing *Trade credit*, the largest category of short-term financing, is an arrangement between a company and its suppliers, whereby materials and supplies are delivered to the company with a promise to pay the invoice, plus interest, usually within a specified number of weeks. *Commercial bank lending* may take the form of a single loan with repayment in a lump sum or in installments over the life of the loan, or it may be a line of credit up to a maximum the bank will allow the company to overdraw on its account. *Commercial paper* is a promissory note of a well-established firm sold primarily to other

Number of Business Establishments with Employees and Payroll, by Major Group, 2006

Major group	Number of establishments	Number of employees	Annual payroll ('000s)
Total	7,601,160	119,917,165	$4,792,429,911
Forestry, fishing, hunting, and agricultural support	23,551	165,661	5,199,819
Forestry & logging	10,723	66,304	2,208,516
Fishing, hunting & trapping	2,372	7,521	347,169
Mining	26,248	554,333	37,489,095
Oil and gas extraction	7,803	92,683	9,566,853
Mining, except oil and gas	7,278	205,349	11,680,859
Support activities for mining	11,167	256,301	16,241,383
Utilities	17,174	614,427	47,692,490
Construction	802,349	7,338,799	322,004,134
Construction of buildings	243,614	1,708,176	82,560,204
Heavy and civil engineering construction	51,122	989,383	52,681,055
Specialty trade contractors	507,613	4,641,240	186,762,875
Manufacturing	331,062	13,631,683	620,223,611
Food	25,382	1,458,738	50,219,339
Beverage & tobacco products	3,684	155,093	7,552,447
Textile mills	3,243	187,766	6,027,949
Textile product mills	6,726	155,586	4,631,794
Apparel	10,967	216,238	5,344,379
Leather & allied products	1,398	38,597	1,174,404
Wood products	16,735	576,506	18,583,842
Paper	5,139	441,430	21,655,684
Printing & related support activities	33,433	641,011	25,335,431
Petroleum & coal products	2,448	102,997	8,151,453
Chemicals	13,247	805,064	51,083,557
Plastics & rubber products	14,592	900,842	34,075,394
Nonmetallic mineral products	17,350	482,459	20,598,480
Primary metals	5,285	449,914	22,783,899
Fabricated metal products	59,064	1,563,713	64,905,442

Major group	Number of establishments	Number of employees	Annual payroll ('000s)
Machinery	26,317	1,126,671	$55,289,135
Computer & electronic products	14,548	1,057,485	69,825,765
Electrical equipment, appliances, & components	6,109	419,691	18,416,031
Transportation equipment	12,707	1,622,527	86,459,228
Furniture & related products	21,449	543,259	17,897,080
Wholesale trade	**429,952**	**6,030,647**	**323,269,989**
Durable goods	244,704	3,430,253	195,012,266
Nondurable goods	130,754	2,267,735	112,445,974
Wholesale electronic markets	54,494	332,659	15,811,749
Retail trade	**1,120,319**	**15,767,866**	**368,277,604**
Motor vehicle & parts dealers	128,403	1,947,516	74,955,029
Furniture & home furnishings stores	65,854	578,075	15,634,515
Electronics & appliance stores	49,323	488,784	12,962,448
Building material and garden equipment stores	87,822	1,366,404	40,689,568
Food & beverage stores	152,375	2,926,489	54,478,171
Health & personal care stores	87,026	1,113,634	29,723,028
Gasoline stations	116,855	913,467	15,025,898
Clothing & clothing accessories stores	152,021	1,631,450	26,491,839
Sporting goods, hobby, book, & music stores	60,515	638,013	10,086,158
General merchandise stores	46,714	2,802,451	53,382,997
Nonstore retailers	48,319	521,738	19,302,742
Transportation & warehousing	**215,117**	**4,306,405**	**166,173,942**
Air transportation	5,610	474,774	24,509,715
Water transportation	1,925	68,438	4,084,113
Truck transportation	120,263	1,532,313	58,934,959
Transit & ground passenger transportation	17,224	418,718	9,079,605
Pipeline transportation	2,653	39,196	3,173,510
Scenic & sightseeing transportation	2,720	26,669	788,754
Support activities for transportation	37,083	579,589	24,128,835
Couriers & messengers	13,790	571,383	19,984,193
Warehousing & storage	13,849	595,325	21,490,258
Information	**141,945**	**3,396,246**	**213,277,018**
Publishing industries (except Internet)	31,821	1,039,739	72,650,853
Motion picture & sound recording industries	23,961	331,231	15,262,640
Broadcasting (except Internet)	10,583	301,983	18,180,043
Internet publishing & broadcasting	2,653	41,588	3,164,339
Telecommunications	47,762	1,161,766	69,821,065
Internet service providers, web search portals	21,002	465,318	32,151,374
Finance & insurance	**494,329**	**6,647,098**	**480,994,365**
Credit intermediation & related activities	224,623	3,281,528	181,333,181
Securities intermediation & related activities	86,554	941,332	148,721,823
Insurance carriers & related activities	180,161	2,377,822	146,418,167
Funds, trusts, & other financial vehicles	2,883	26,397	3,184,590
Real estate & rental & leasing	**382,128**	**2,216,803**	**87,528,338**
Real estate	313,472	1,553,369	64,000,797
Rental & leasing services	66,319	633,948	21,182,061
Professional, scientific, & technical services	846,473	8,054,094	497,406,645
Management of companies & enterprises	48,311	2,915,644	266,267,977
Administrative, support, and waste management	**378,335**	**10,003,626**	**283,240,782**
Administrative and support services	358,416	9,658,292	268,381,213
Waste management and remediation	19,919	345,334	14,859,569
Educational services	**82,647**	**2,979,514**	**88,452,753**
Health care & social assistance	**762,451**	**16,451,361**	**626,586,952**
Ambulatory health care services	530,907	5,683,285	268,146,747
Hospitals	6,843	5,370,540	243,081,913
Nursing & residential care facilities	73,876	2,993,133	69,835,975
Social assistance	150,825	2,404,403	45,522,317
Arts, entertainment, & recreation	**123,048**	**1,973,655**	**56,838,765**
Performing arts and spectator sports	42,430	424,914	26,635,947
Museums and historical sites	7,089	123,177	3,359,875
Amusement, gambling, and recreation industries	73,529	1,425,564	26,842,943
Accommodation and food services	612,254	11,381,226	167,231,246
Accommodation	62,725	1,880,698	43,942,388
Food services and drinking places	549,529	9,500,528	123,288,858
Other services (except public administration)	**736,440**	**5,458,558**	**133,557,722**
Repair & maintenance	225,535	1,307,221	41,206,327
Personal & laundry services	209,772	1,357,791	27,567,742
Religious, grantmaking, civic, and professional organizations	301,133	2,793,546	64,783,653
Unclassified establishments	**27,027**	**29,519**	**716,764**

Note: Excludes most government employees, railroad employees, and self-employed persons. Totals include other categories not shown separately. **Source:** U.S. Census Bureau, *County Business Patterns 2006* (2008).

business firms, with repayments made in two to six months. The only problem with commercial paper is that its resources are limited to the liquidity that corporations have at any given time for lending to other firms.

Intermediate-term financing,

with a time frame of one to 15 years, may take the form of lease financing, whereby a company rents, rather than buys, the assets it uses; conditional sales contracts, by which equipment is bought over a period of time (the seller continues to have title of ownership until payment is completed); or term loans or business credit supplied by commercial banks and life insurance companies, repaid by amortization payments over the life of the loan (one to 15 years).

Long-term financing

The issuance of stocks and bonds constitute the long-term source of finance for firms. *Bonds* are debt instruments (IOUs issued by a company to the bondholder) that obligate the firm to pay interest at specific times. Alternatively firms can raise money by issuing preferred and common stocks. Unlike bonds, *stocks* entitle the holder to share in ownership and profits made by the firm through dividends paid out for the entire period the investor owns the stock. However, if the business has low profits or limited funds, bondholders are paid first, preferred stockholders next, and common stockholders last.

▶ WALL STREET

The U.S. stock market, commonly known as Wall Street, began in the late 18th century as a merchant-organized public auction in stocks and government bonds for the purpose of financing the government and expanding business and trade. At that time, brokers handed over securities to auctioneers who sold securities to the highest bidder. Today, while the form of the stock exchange has changed dramatically, the purpose remains the same.

The most commonly cited index of Wall Street's performance is the Dow Jones Industrial average. (See "Glossary of Financial Terms.") From the Dow's inception in 1896 until the early 1980s, the 1,000 mark was considered the benchmark of a bull market. During that period, the Dow passed the 1,000 mark for the first time in 1972 and re-

mained above that level until 1976. These days, the benchmark of a bull market is closer to 11,000.

The Dow crested 14,000 during the heady summer of 2007; since then it has lost nearly half its value. On September 29, 2008, after the House of Representatives rejected Treasury Secretary Henry Paulson's first plan to bail out the nation's banks, the Dow suffered its greatest single-day loss in history, falling 778 points to 10,371. Although nearly $1.2 trillion in market value evaporated that day, the 7 percent overall decline did not rank among the top 10 percentage declines. It did, however, set off a skid that ultimately pushed the Dow average below 8,000 by November. By August 2010, the Dow average had rebounded to over 10,000.

There are two major stock and bond markets in the U.S., both located in New York City. A third, the American Stock Exchange, was purchased by the New York Stock Exchange in 2004 and completely integrated into the NYSE in 2009. The growth of the U.S. markets has been staggering. A total of 19.7 billion shares were traded on the three exchanges in 1980; today, nearly a trillion shares are traded annually.

New York Stock Exchange (NYSE Euronext)

The oldest exchange in the country was formally founded in 1817, when fewer than 100 shares were traded each day. In 2008, more than 800 billion shares were traded on the NYSE. The growth in the value of those stocks has been equally impressive. The market value of all stocks traded on the NYSE doubled between 1987 and 1993, and then more than doubled again between 1993 and 2000, when it reached a staggering $12.3

NYSE Group Shares Traded, 2004–08

The New York Stock Exchange merged with ARCA in 2004. Figures are not directly comparable with those from before 2004.

Year	Number of trades (millions)	Shares traded (millions)	Dollar volume of shares traded (millions)
2004	728	471,580	$14,402,000
2005	919	516,743	17,857,000
2006	1,288	605,248	22,313,000
2007	2,128	664,019	28,427,880
2008	3,219	802,170	28,080,290

Source: New York Stock Exchange, *Facts and Figures*.

NYSE Listed Stocks, 1924–2009

Year	Shares outstanding (millions)	Market value (millions)	Average price[1]
1924	433	$27,072	$62.45
1945	1,592	73,765	46.33
1950	2,353	93,807	39.86
1960	6,458	306,967	47.53
1970	16,065	636,380	39.61
1980	33,709	1,242,803	36.87
1985	52,427	1,950,332	37.20
1990	90,732	2,819,778	33.40
1995	154,719	6,012,971	38.86
2000	313,937	12,372,304	42.14
2004	382,745	13,562,265	35.43
2008[2]	424,518	15,128,954	35.64
2009[2]	424,028	11,778,833	27.78

Note: 1. This average cannot be used as an index of price trend owing to changes in shares listed caused by new listing, suspensions, stock splits, and stock dividends. 2. Figures are for August of year listed. **Source:** New York Stock Exchange, NYSE *Facts and Figures, 2005;* www.nyxdata.com Factbook.

NYSE: Daily Shares Traded, 1900–2004 (in thousands)

Year	Daily Average	Record High	Record Low
1900	505	1,627	89
1910	601	1,656	111
1920	828	2,008	227
1930	2,959	8,279	1,090
1940	751	3,940	130
1950	1,980	4,859	1,061
1960	3,042	7,077	2,184
1970	11,564	21,345	6,660
1980	44,871	84,297	16,132
1990	156,777	292,364	56,853
2000	1,041,578	1,560,808	403,254
2003	1,398,404	1,886,074	359,769
2004	1,457,000	2,690,200	508,800

Source: New York Stock Exchange, *Facts and Figures*.

trillion. The dollar volume of shares traded nearly doubled again between 2004 ($14.4 billion) and 2008 ($28.0 billion).

NASDAQ The National Association of Securities Dealers Automated Quotations was founded in 1971 and was the first to use computers and high-technology telecommunications to trade—and to monitor the trading of—millions of securities daily. Today, all the major stock markets have followed suit.

Online trading Internet, or online brokerages allow people to trade stocks directly without a broker for commissions as low as $5 per trade. The popularity of online accounts has encouraged investors to make more trades, and to buy and sell more quickly to take advantage of short-term changes in market prices. Online trading has

also sparked the creation of the day trader: an investor who buys and sells thousands of shares in hundreds of different stocks each day.

Mutual funds, in which investors pool their funds to purchase a variety of securities rather than investing in a single stock or bond, date back to 1924 in the U.S., but few Americans were aware of them until their popularity surged in the 1980s. In 2009, according to the Investment Company Institute, 43 percent of all American households owned some kind of mutual funds, up from less than 6 percent in 1980. Total assets of all mutual funds in 2008 dropped 20 percent from the all-time high of $12 trillion reached in 2007, but rose again to 11.12 trillion in 2009. Still, more money is invested in mutual funds today than in any other financial institution except commercial banks, which held a total of $11.3 trillion in assets in 2009, according to the Federal Deposit Insurance Corporation (FDIC).

There are four kinds of mutual funds: stock (or equity), bond, hybrid, and money market. Funds can consist of stocks, bonds, gold, government securities or other assets. The share price of a mutual fund, called the *net asset value (NAV)*, is the market value of all the fund's securities, minus expenses, divided by the total number of shares outstanding, and rises or falls based on the performance of the securities in which the fund is invested. Each fund employs a professional fund manager, who chooses a diverse range of securities, so that a drop in the value of one security will not cause a shock to the entire portfolio. As secu-

Milestones in the Dow Jones Industrial Average

Date	Average	Date	Average
Jan. 12, 1906	100	Feb. 13, 1997	7,000
Sept. 1, 1929	381	July 16, 1997	8,000
March 12, 1956	500	April 6, 1998	9,000
Nov. 14, 1972	1,000	March 16, 1999	10,000
Jan. 8, 1987	2,000	May 3, 1999	11,000
Feb. 23, 1995	4,000	Oct. 18, 2006	12,000
Nov. 21, 1995	5,000	April 25, 2007	13,000
Oct. 14, 1996	6,000	July 17, 2007	14,000

Source: Dow Jones.

Components of the Dow Jones Industrial Average, 2010

The Dow Jones Industrial Average is composed of 30 stocks that collectively reflect the performance of the entire market. There are no rules for admission, but the components of the Dow are typically the largest publicly traded companies in the country. The list is maintained and reviewed by the editors of *The Wall Street Journal*. For the sake of continuity, changes to the roster are infrequent. But the economic downturn of 2008–09 has played havoc with the list. Bank of America and Chevron replaced Altria and Honeywell in February 2008, while American International Group was supplanted by Kraft in September 2008. General Motors and Citigroup, two more casualties of the recession, were dropped in June 2009, in favor of Cisco Systems Inc. and Travelers Cos. The 30 stocks in the Dow are listed in alphabetical order.

3M Co.	Intel Corp.
Alcoa Inc.	I.B.M. Corp.
American Express Co.	Johnson & Johnson
AT&T Inc.	JPMorgan Chase & Co.
Bank of America Corp.	Kraft Foods
Boeing Co.	McDonald's Corp.
Caterpillar Inc.	Merck & Co. Inc.
Chevron Corp.	Microsoft Corp.
Cisco Systems Inc.	Pfizer Inc.
Coca-Cola Co.	Procter & Gamble Co.
E.I. DuPont de Nemours	Travelers Companies
ExxonMobil Corp.	United Technologies Corp.
General Electric Co.	Verizon Communications
Hewlett-Packard Co.	Wal-Mart Stores Inc.
Home Depot Inc.	Walt Disney Co.

Source: Dow Jones (2010).

Top U.S. Mutual Fund Managers, 2008–09, by Assets

Rank, Fund Manager	Assets (billions)	
	2008	2009
1. Fidelity Investments	1,072,084	1,287,713
2. Vanguard Group	987,123	1,257,204
3. Capital Research & Mgmt.	844,671	1,051,841
4. J.P. Morgan Chase & Co.	418,783	443,846
5. BlackRock Funds	357,600	344,744
6. PIMCO Funds	217,469	337,655
7. Franklin Templeton Investments	243,424	319,446
8. Federated Investors	351,307	316,467
9. Bank of New York Mellon/ Dreyfus Co	306,086	286,159
10. Goldman Sachs & Co.	250,513	244,945
11. T. Rowe Price	167,475	236,521
12. Wells Fargo	170,462	235,946
13. Columbia Mgmt. Group	259,456	208,004
14. Schwab Funds	235,749	201,861
15. TIAA-CREF	155,471	198,711
16. OppenheimerFunds/ MassMutual	139,703	169,596
17. Legg Mason	172,491	160,287
18. Morgan Stanley	161,686	152,245
19. Invesco Aim	109,704	117,408
20. Deutsche Asset Mgmt.	106,761	116,825
21. John Hancock Financial Services	86,568	116,247
22. Dodge & Cox	86,694	112,354
23. Prudential Mutual Funds	69,512	106,107
24. Dimensional Fund Advisors	71,591	105,484
25. Northern Trust Mutual Funds	88,535	97,830

Note: Figures are as of Dec. 31 of each year. Source: Investment Company Institute.

rities prices rise or fall, the fund manager may seek to change the composition of the fund's portfolio. Like securities, but unlike investments offered by banks, mutual funds are not insured by the FDIC or any other government agency.

There were 7,691 different mutual funds in 2009, more than twice the number in 1992, representing the full spectrum of investment objectives. *Aggressive growth funds* seek the maximum capital growth but also carry the greatest risk, because the stocks they invest in are very volatile. *Income-equity funds* forgo high growth rates in favor of a constant stream of income from stocks with a history of steady dividends. *Bond funds,* which invest in corporate bonds and government-issued securities, are generally more conservative than stock funds. *Hybrid funds* invest in both stocks and bonds. *Money market funds* are called short-term funds because they invest in securities that mature in a year or less, such as Treasury bills, CDs, and commercial paper. Many money market

funds offer tax-exempt income (though their rate of return is often lower than taxable money market funds). *Special funds* meet the needs of specific investors by investing only in certain segments of financial markets (e.g. biotechnology, telecommunications, small-companies) or by pegging the fund's net asset value to one of several economic indexes (hence the name index fund). *Global equity funds* invest in the stock markets of other countries.

By far the largest segment of the mutual fund industry has been stock or equity funds. Historically, equity funds made up more than half of all mutual fund assets. Assets of equity funds took a tumble in 2008, falling from $6.5 to $3.7 trillion, but rose in 2009 to 4.9 trillion. Bond funds, meanwhile, fell more modestly, from $1.7 to $1.6 trillion in 2008, rising to 2 trillion in 2009. Taxable money market funds saw their net assets increase in 2009, though tax-exempt money market funds saw their net assets decrerase in the same year.

Assets of IRA Plans by Type of Investment, 1990–2009

Year	Total (billions)	Bank and thrift deposits[1]		Life insurance companies		Mutual funds		Securities[2]	
		Amount (billions)	Percent of total	Amount (billions)	Percent of total	Amount (billions)	Percent of total	Amount (billions)	Percent of total
1990	$ 637	$266	41.8%	$ 40	6.3%	$ 139	21.8%	$ 191	30.0%
1995	1,288	261	20.3	81	6.3	470	36.5	477	37.0
2000	2,629	250	9.5	203	7.7	1,249	46.8	928	36.0
2005[3]	3,652	278	7.6	308	8.4	1,700	46.6	1,366	37.4
2007[3]	4,747	340	7.2	325	6.8	2,304	48.5	1,777	37.4
2009[3]	4,230	431	10.2	303[4]	7.2	1,953	46.2	1,544	36.5

Note: 1. Includes Keogh deposits. 2. Stocks, bonds, CDs sold by brokers, and other investments held in brokerage accounts. 3. Estimate. 4. Life insurance company IRA assets are annuities held by IRAs, excluding variable annuity mutual fund IRA assets, which are included in mutual funds. **Source:** Investment Company Institute, *Investment Company Fact Book* (2010).

Number of Funds, Accounts, and Total Assets of Mutual Funds, 1970–2009

	Type of Fund					
				Bond &	Money market	
Year	Total	Equity	Hybrid[1]	Income[1]	Taxable	Tax exempt
Number of Funds						
1970	361	323	N.A.	38	N.A.	N.A.
1980	564	288	N.A.	170	96	10
1990	3,079	1,099	193	1,046	506	235
2000	8,155	4,385	523	2,208	703	336
2005	7,975	4,586	505	2,013	595	276
2007	8,024	4,764	488	1,967	546	259
2009	7,691	4,659	474	1,853	478	227
Number of Accounts (millions)						
1970	10.7	N.A.	N.A.	N.A.	N.A.	N.A.
1980	12.1	5.8	N.A.	1.5	4.8	N.A.
1990	61.9	22.2	3.2	13.6	21.6	1.4
2000	244.7	163.9	13.1	19.6	45.5	2.7
2005	275.5	188.0	21.2	29.4	34.0	2.8
2007	292.6	201.3	22.3	29.8	35.6	3.5
2009	270.9	178.7	21.6	37.1	30.3	3.2
Total Net Assets (billions)						
1970	$ 47.6	$ 45.1	N.A.	$ 2.5	N.A.	N.A.
1980	134.8	44.4	N.A.	14.0	$ 74.5	$ 1.9
1990	1,065.2	239.5	$36.1	291.3	414.7	83.6
2000	6,964.6	3,961.9	346.3	811.2	1,607.2	238.0
2005	8,904.8	4,939.8	567.3	1,357.2	1,706.5	334.0
2007	11,999.5	6,515.9	718.6	1,679.3	2,620.7	465.1
2009	11,120.8	4,957.6	640.8	2,206.2	2,918.8	397.5

Note: 1. Bond and Income Funds were divided into Bond Funds and Hybrid Funds beginning in 1984. Data from before 1984 in all categories is not directly comparable to later years. **Source:** Investment Company Institute, *Investment Company Fact Book* (2010).

Mergers and Acquisitions

Beginning in the 1980s and 1990s, a growing number of companies have sought to increase their power in the new global marketplace by buying rival companies or by merging with one. Because fierce competition tends to drive down prices, making profitability more difficult, and because one company needs fewer employees than two, the reasons for the current merger mania are obviously compelling. An additional incentive is that the CEOs who broker these deals also make huge cash profits on the mergers.

▶ GLOSSARY OF FINANCIAL TERMS

Arbitrage   Simultaneous purchase and sale of a commodity or currency in at least two markets where price discrepancies exist. The arbitrageur makes a profit by buying an asset with a low price in one market and selling it in another market where the asset carries a higher price.

Bear/bull   A bear is a speculator who expects prices to fall and sells stocks or bonds in order to buy them later at a lower price. A bull expects prices to rise and therefore buys now for resale later. Thus, a bearish (bullish) market is one in which prices are generally falling (rising).

Blue chip stock   A stock that is considered a safe investment, with a low yield and a high price per share, issued by companies that are well known and have a history of good management and increasing profit levels.

Bond   A debt obligation that requires the issuer to pay a fixed sum of money annually until maturity (interest payments) and then, at maturity, a fixed sum of money to repay the initial amount borrowed (principal). (See *Corporate Bonds*.)

Capital gain   An increase in the market value of an asset above the price originally paid for it, realized when the asset is sold.

Capital loss   A decrease in the market value of an asset below the price originally paid for it, realized when the asset is sold.

Common stock/equity   A piece of paper that entitles the owner to a share of the firm's profits and a share of the voting power in shareholder elections. In other words, a shareholder is part owner of the firm. If he owns 50 percent of the issued shares of common stock (when no preferred stock is issued), he owns 50 percent of the company, and will receive 50 percent of profits paid out in dividends. Over 40 million Americans invest in common stocks.

Convertible bond   A debt instrument which carries an option for the holder to convert it into a specified amount of company stock.

Corporate bonds   Debt obligations that require the corporation to pay a fixed sum of money annually until maturity (interest payments) and then, at maturity, a fixed sum of money to repay the initial amount borrowed (principal). Bonds carry no claim to ownership and therefore pay no dividends, but payments to bondholders take priority over payments to stockholders.

Debentures   Debt securities issued by a company that pay a fixed interest rate, in order to raise finance for commercial or industrial operations.

Divestiture   The sales by a company of a product line, subsidiary or division. The number of divestitures sold peaked in 1986, with a total of 1,316, for a record total price of $65.2 billion.

Dividends   Payments made to common and preferred stockholders out of a firm's profits either in the form of cash or additional shares.

Mergers and Acquisitions Worldwide, 1990–2009

Year	Number of deals	Total value (millions)
1990	10,002	$ 422,360.2
1995	19,712	927,432.8
2000	38,753	3,406,206.5
2003	28,899	1,379,013.2
2004	31,633	1,912,224.3
2005	33,844	2,745,580.0
2006	38,674	3,614,611.3
2007	31,795	4,029,239.8
2008	31,115	2,838,148.3
2009	38,325	2,072,565.5

Source: ThomsonReuters.

Largest Mergers and Acquisitions in History

Acquiring Company (Country)	Acquired Company (Country)	Date effective	Value (millions)
1. Vodafone AirTouch PLC (U.K.)	Mannesmann (Germany)	June 19, 2000	$202,785
2. America Online Inc. (U.S.)	Time Warner (U.S.)	Jan. 12, 2001	181,569
3. Shareholders (U.S.)	Philip Morris Intl. Inc.(U.S.)	Mar. 28, 2008	112,955
4. RFS Holdings BV (Netherlands)	ABN-AMRO Holding NV (Netherlands)	Nov. 2, 2007	98,189
5. A.T.&T. Inc. (U.S.)	BellSouth Corp. (U.S.)	Dec. 29, 2006	89,432
6. Pfizer Inc. (U.S.)	Warner-Lambert Co. (U.S.)	June 19, 2000	88,771
7. Exxon Corp. (U.S.)	Mobil Corp. (U.S.)	Nov. 30, 1999	85,126
8. Royal Dutch Petroleum Co. (Neth.)	Shell Transport and Trading Co. (U.K.)	Aug. 9, 2005	80,305
9. GlaxoWellcome PLC (U.K)	SmithKline Beecham PLC (U.K.)	Dec. 27, 2000	78,775
10. Gaz de France SA (France)	Suez SA (France)	July 22, 2008	75,242
11. Travelers Group (U.S.)	Citicorp (U.S.)	Oct. 8, 1998	72,558
12. Comcast Corp. (U.S.)	AT&T Broadband & Internet Svcs. (U.S.)	Nov. 18, 2002	72,041
13. Bell Atlantic Corp. (U.S.)	GTE Corp., (U.S.)	June 30, 2000	71,324
14. SBC Communications Inc. (U.S.)	Ameritech Corp., (U.S.)	Oct. 8, 1999	70,395
15. AT&T Corp. (U.S.)	Tele-Communications Inc. (U.S.)	Mar. 9, 1999	69,896
16. Vodafone Group PLC (U.K.)	AirTouch Communications (U.S.)	June 30, 1999	65,763
17. Sanofi-Synthelabo SA (France)	Aventis SA (France)	Aug. 20, 2004	65,657
18. NationsBank Corp., (U.S.)	BankAmerica Corp., (U.S.)	Sept. 30, 1998	61,633
19. Shareholders (U.S.)	Kraft Foods Inc. (U.S.)	Mar. 30, 2007	61,587
20. U.S. Treasury Department (U.S.)	General Motors—Certain Assets (U.S.)	July 10, 2009	61,159

Note: As of August 9, 2009. **Source:** ThomsonReuters.

Securities Industry Revenues and Expenses, 1980–2008 (millions)

Type	1980	1990	1995	2000	2005	2007	2008
Revenues, total	**$19,829**	**$71,356**	**$143,414**	**$349,493**	**$332,501**	**$496,517**	**$178,049.1**
Commissions	6,777	12,032	23,215	54,107	46,803	54,372	58,067
Trading/investment gains	5,091	15,746	28,963	70,778	30,681	4,132	−64,977
Underwriting profits	1,571	3,728	8,865	18,718	19,878	26,503	18,789
Margin interest	2,151	3,179	6,470	24,547	13,270	32,293	18,414
Mutual fund sales	278	3,242	7,434	19,395	20,699	26,228	22,854
Other	3,960	33,428	68,468	161,949	201,170	352,990	59,386
Expenses, total	**$16,668**	**$70,566**	**$132,089**	**$310,390**	**$311,317**	**$491,456**	**$301,508**
Interest expense	3,876	28,093	56,877	131,877	140,240	282,239	124,504
Compensation	7,619	22,931	41,541	95,206	88,813	106,305	96,764
Commissions/clearance paid	1,055	2,959	5,700	15,523	18,645	25,891	25,753
Other	4,119	16,583	27,970	67,784	63,168	74,979	54,488
Net income, pretax	**$3,160**	**$790**	**$11,325**	**$39,103**	**$21,184**	**$5,061**	**$−34,126**

Source: U.S. Securities and Exchange Commission, *2009 Annual Report* (2010).

Dow Jones Industrial Average Dating back to 1893, this index of 30 blue chip stocks in industry traded on the New York Stock Exchange (and determined by the editors of the *Wall Street Journal*) is the most widely cited indicator of how the stock market is doing.

Establishment A physical place of business activity such as a factory, assembly plant, retail store, warehouse, etc. where goods are made, stored or processed, or where services are performed.

Eurocurrency Currency of the major industrial and financial countries held in the banks of major financial and industrial countries for the purpose of lending and borrowing. Most loans are for up to one year and are used for payments of deficits. Eurodollars are U.S. dollars held in foreign banks.

Firm A business organization that owns and/or operates one or more establishments. Also called a company, enterprise or business venture. Firms can be of three types: 1) sole proprietorships—firms owned directly by one person; 2) partnerships—firms whose ownership is shared by a fixed number of proprietors; and 3) corporations—firms created by a government charter, granting them greater accessibility to financial capital through the selling of common or preferred stock, greater accessibility to debt capital through the selling of bonds, and limited liability in the event of bankruptcy.

Futures market/forward market A market in which commodities or securities are bought and sold at prices fixed now, for delivery at specified future date. Futures are traded on the American Stock Exchange; the Chicago Board of Trade; Chicago Board Options Exchange; Chicago Mercantile Exchange; Chicago Rice and Cotton Exchange; Commodity Exchange, New York (COMEX); Kansas City Board of Trade; MidAmerica Commodity Exchange, Chicago; Minneapolis Grain Exchange; New York Coffee, Sugar, and Coca Exchange (including the Citrus Associates); New York Cotton Exchange; New York Futures Exchange; and New York Mercantile Exchange; New York Stock Exchange; Pacific Stock Exchange, Los Angeles and San Francisco; and Philadelphia Stock Exchange.

Greenmail Analogous to blackmail, greenmail is the practice of purchasing enough shares in a firm or trading company to threaten a takeover, thereby forcing the owners to buy them back at a higher rate in order to retain control of the business.

Top 25 Securities Firms by Capital, 2004–07

2007 Rank/Firm	2004	2007
1. Merrill Lynch & Co.[1]	$115,452	$224,251
2. Morgan Stanley[1]	90,467	162,134
3. Goldman Sachs Group,[1,2]	79,114	158,628
4. Lehman Brothers Holdings[1,2]	58,013	113,247
5. Citigroup Global Markets	59,634	78,428
6. Bear Stearns Companies[1,2]	36,901	66,699
7. Credit Suisse (USA), Inc.[1]	33,741	57,902
8. UBS Securities LLC	10,505	15,817
9. Deutsche Bank Securities Inc.	7,068	11,612
10. J.P. Morgan Securities Inc.	5,747	9,972
11. Charles Schwab Corporation[2]	5,233	5,396
12. Wachovia Capital Markets	1,794	4,381
13. UBS Financial Services Inc.	3,057	4,318
14. TD Ameritrade Holding Corp.	2,742	3,456
15. E*TRADE Brokerage Holdings	N.A.	3,029
16. Jefferies Group, Inc.[2]	1,282	3,000
17. RBS Greenwich Capital	1,283	2,977
18. Fidelity Brokerage	1,924	2,611
19. Wachovia Securities, LLC	2,765	2,434
20. Nomura Securities Intl. Inc.	1,656	2,083
21. A.G. Edwards, Inc.	1,738	2,055
22. Pershing LLC	N.A.	1,668
23. Raymond James Financial, Inc.	N.A.	1,644
24. CIBC World Markets Corp.	1,515	1,636
25. ABN-AMRO Incorporated	1,695	1,489

Note: Several of these firms had closed or been absorbed into other firms as of September, 2010. Data as of January 1 of year shown, except as noted. 1. Data as of Nov. 30 of previous year. 2. Firm's capital is the sum of long-term borrowings and ownership equity. Source: Securities Industry Association.

Individual Retirement Account (IRA) An account set up by individual investors to hold and invest funds until retirement. Under a traditional IRA, which was established as an alternative for people not eligible for employee-sponsored pension plans, individuals may contribute up to $2,000 pre-tax per year to a tax-deferred retirement account. In 1997, Congress established the Roth IRA, which allows individuals to contribute $2,000 post-tax to a retirement account on which earnings are tax free forever in most cases.

Inital Public Offfering (IPO) A company's first sale of stock to the public (also known as "going public"). An IPO generates working capital in exchange for equity. A well-publicized IPO can drive up the stock price, making millionaires of company insiders who already own stock or options. For this reason, it is often difficult for outsiders to purchase shares in an IPO at the public offering price.

Insider trading   Illegal trading in the stock market based on information that has not been made public, and which is intended to remain confidential—for example, information that a small company is about to become part of a national corporation. The penalties paid by individuals and corporations for such activities in recent years have reached into the hundreds of millions of dollars. Drexel Burnham Lambert, Inc., was fined $650 million to settle six charges of securities law violations; and investor Ivan Boesky was fined $100 million and imprisoned for his insider trading activities.

Junk bond/high-yield bond   Bonds with a rating below investment grade (at or below Ba1 by Moody's Investors Service, at or below BB+ by Standard & Poor's), or unrated. Issuers of junk bonds are usually small companies that in the past have been limited to borrowing from banks to raise capital for corporate growth. Although the major ratings services consider junk bonds risky (hence their name), they have a historically low default rate—only 1.5 percent between the mid-1970s and mid-1980s. The junk market grew considerably in the 1980s, and by 1987 accounted for over 25 percent of the value of all corporate bonds outstanding.

Leveraged buyout   The purchase of a company by one of its employee groups (usually upper management) or a large shareholder with borrowed funds, usually using the company's assets as security for the loans. Leveraged buy-outs have been used to combat hostile takeover bids.

Mutual fund   A pool of financial assets in which investors may buy shares and get the benefits (or share the losses) depending on the performance of the collective securities. Shares are sold publicly and can be redeemed at any time. Funds can consist of stocks, bonds, gold, government securities or other assets, and their names are descriptive of their primary purpose; for example, bonds funds, equity-fund portfolios, income funds, money market-mutual funds, and municipal funds. (See also "Money Market Accounts" in "Money and Banking.")

Option   A contract to buy or sell commodities or securities within a given time period at a fixed price. For stocks, this period is usually three months. A contract to sell is a *put option* (or put); to buy, a *call option* (or call) and one to buy or sell is a *double option*. A buyer (seller) will gain if the trading price rises (falls) by more than the cost of entering into the contract. Options are traded on the same exchanges as futures contracts (see *Futures market*).

Over-the-counter (OTC) stock   A security not listed on an exchange is traded between two individuals. The name stems from the 18th-century practice of merchants selling stocks over the counter in their own shops directly to investors without the use of stockbrokers or auctioneers.

Pension fund   An arrangement whereby private or public-sector employers, unions, and—as in the case of individual retirement accounts (IRAs) and Keogh plans—individuals contribute to a fund from which money is paid out to the employees, union members, or contributors (or their dependents) upon death, disability or retirement. Contributions can be based on a percentage of salary or corporate profits; in some cases employees may make voluntary or mandatory contributions to the fund. Pension fund assets are usually held in the form of securities or property with a preference for long-term assets.

Ponzi scheme   A fraudulent investment scheme that pays investors returns from their own money or from subsequent investors rather than profit.

Preferred stock   Similar to common stock, except that owners of preferred stock have no voting rights, and preferred stock holders are paid their dividends at a fixed rate, before common stockholders receive any dividends.

Rating   An agency evaluation of the quality of a debt instrument or a company issuing debt. Standard & Poor's and Moody's Investment Service are the two major credit ratings agencies in the U.S. The ratings measure the safety of interest and principal payments of bonds. S&P bond ratings are, from most to least secure: AAA, AA, A, BBB, BB, B, CCC, CC, C. Moody's ratings are: Aaa, Aa, A, Baa, Ba, B, Caa, Ca, C.

Russell Indexes   These measure the performance of the largest U.S.-headquartered companies, based on total market capitalization. The Russell 3,000 Index measures the 3,000 largest U.S.-based companies (their total market capitalization represents approximately 98 percent of the investable U.S. equity market). The Russell 1,000 measures the largest 1,000 of these companies. The Russell 2,000 measures the smallest 2,000 companies in the Russell 3,000.

Securities   Financial assets (usually long-term), such as equities/stocks and debentures/bonds; may also refer to shorter-term assets such as U.S. Treasury bills.

Securities and Exchange Commission (SEC) U.S. government agency that regulates the securities industry by requiring registration of brokers, dealers, and stock exchanges. The SEC also reviews the financial position of companies issuing securities for public sale, and investigates illegal activities such as insider trading.

Standard & Poor's 500 Composite Stock Price Index (S&P 500) A widely used measure of the movement of the U.S. stock market. The S&P 500 was introduced in 1957 and is one of 12 leading economic indicators used by the U.S. Commerce Department. The 500 issues include 400 industrial, 40 utility, 20 transportation and 40 financial companies—primarily those listed on the New York Stock

Venture Capital Investments, 1990–2009		
Year	Total amount invested (millions)	Total number of companies invested in	Average investment per company (millions)
1990	$2,914	1,143	$2.55
1995	7,868	1,483	5.31
1999	53,532	4,347	12.31
2000	105,035	7,905	13.29
2004	22,488	3,082	7.30
2005	23,038	3,146	7.32
2006	26,592	3,647	7.29
2007	30,896	3,914	7.89
2008	28,298	3,808	7.43
2009	17,782	2,868	6.20

Source: Pricewaterhouse Coopers, *MoneyTree Report 2010.*

Exchange (NYSE). The index is considered to be value-weighted because each stock is weighted according to its market value. As of December 31, 1987, the market value of issues tracked by the S&P 500 was equal to approximately 70 percent of the value of all publicly traded U.S. equities. Its value is calculated on a total return basis with dividends reinvested.

Stock exchange A market in which securities (other than bills and similar short-term instruments) issued by central and local government bodies, and public companies are traded (e.g., the New York Stock Exchange, the American Stock Exchange, the London Stock Exchange). Only members of a stock exchange may deal on it, and membership and arrangements for trading are strictly regulated. Stock exchanges in the United States are the American Stock Exchange (New York); Boston Stock Exchange; Cincinnati Stock Exchange; Intermountain Stock Exchange (Salt Lake City); Midwest Stock Exchange (Chicago); New York Stock Exchange; Pacific Stock Exchange (Los Angeles, San Francisco); Philadelphia Stock Exchange; and Spokane Stock Exchange.

Stock market An institution where stocks and shares are traded, existing in all advanced Western countries. Stock markets enable companies to more easily raise equity or loan capital from the public since investors can quickly realize their holdings because of the stock exchange share quotation. In other words, there is a ready market. The principal overseas stock markets are located in Amsterdam, Brussels, Frankfurt, Hong Kong, Johannesburg, London, Milan, Paris, Singapore, Stockholm, Sydney, Tokyo, Toronto and Zurich.

Stockbroker An individual who acts as an adviser and an agent (working on commission), to buy and sell stocks on behalf of a client on a particular stock exchange where the stockbroker is a member.

Venture capital Funds made available to start-up businesses that have excellent growth potential, but are unable to obtain more traditional methods of business financing. Also known as risk capital because these investments have a high risk and a high reward.

Wilshire 5000 Index The broadest measure of the U.S. stock market, containing some 5,000 issues including all publicly traded U.S. stocks for which daily pricing is available (i.e., includes all Amex, NYSE and OTC stocks).

Yield The annual return on a security, as a percentage of its current market price. A stock's divi-

dend yield is the annual dividend divided by its current stock price.

▶ BIG BUSINESS: THE *FORTUNE* 500

The ultimate measure of success in the business world is inclusion on *Fortune* magazine's annual list of the 500 biggest companies in America. In recent years, the global trend toward mega-mergers creating monolithic organizations has raised the bar for admission to this select circle. Since 2005, Wal-Mart and ExxonMobil have each posted more than $300 billion in annual revenues. In 2009, the top 16 companies on the Fortune 500 all had revenues of over $100 billion.

The accompanying tables list the top 100 companies of the *Fortune* 500 by revenues, the top three companies in several performance categories, and the top companies by industry.

▶ SMALL BUSINESS

Small businesses account for 98 percent of the 7 million employer firms in the United States today. Nearly half of the small businesses in America had fewer than four employees. Small businesses create the vast majority of the net new jobs in America every year. Businesses with 100 employees or fewer employed 36 percent of the 114 million employees working for U.S. employer firms, according to the Census Bureau in 2000; 55.2 percent worked in businesses with fewer than 1,000 employees. According to the Small Business Administration, two-thirds of small businesses survive at least two years, and just over half make it four years. About three-quarters of new business owners are still employed in a salaried job when they start their own business; 60 percent of new businesses start at home.

Franchising, a century-old tradition, continues to grow in popularity. The Department of Commerce estimates that franchising accounts for more than half of all sales in the U.S. The benefits to the franchisor are enormous: expansion with little or no risk, royalties and licensing revenue from the franchisee, and an initial franchise fee (usually around $25,000). The benefits to the franchisee are less obvious, but may include name recognition, a national advertising campaign, and training and financial assistance from the parent company. Although tales of self-made millionaires abound in franchising circles, far greater numbers of franchisees go bankrupt.

Fortune 500 Performance Leaders, 2009

Profits	Millions of dollars	Return on Revenues	Percent
1. ExxonMobil (2)	$19,280	1. Liberty Media (227)	62.1%
2. Microsoft (36)	14,569	2. Bristol-Myers Squibb (114)	49.1
3. Wal-Mart Stores (1)	14,335	3. Merck (85)	47.0

Market Value	Millions of dollars	Return to Investors, 1 year	Percent
1. ExxonMobil (2)	$314,154	1. Avis Budget Group (409)	1,774.3%
2. Microsoft (36)	260,132	2. Dana Holding (398)	1,364.9
3. Apple (56)	209,379	3. TRW Automotive Holdings (201)	563.3

Employees	Number	Return to Investors, 10 years	Percent
1. Wal-Mart Stores (1)	2,100,000	1. XTO Energy (258)	43.0%
2. United Parcel Service (43)	408,000	2. Holly (431)	34.2
3. International Business Machines (20)	399,409	3. Precision Castparts (325)	33.0

Note: Numbers in parentheses reflect overall *Fortune* 500 rank. **Source:** *Fortune* magazine (2010).

The Top U.S. Companies, by Industry and *Fortune* 1,000 Rank, 2009

Industry, Company (Rank)	Revenues (millions)
Aerospace and Defense	
Boeing (28)	$68,281.0
United Technologies (37)	52,920.0
Lockheed Martin (44)	45,189.0
Airlines	
Delta Air Lines (84)	28,063.0
AMR (120)	19,917.0
UAL (140)	16,335.0
Apparel	
Nike (124)	19,176.1
VF (310)	7,220.3
Polo Ralph Lauren (417)	5,018.9
Automotive Retailing, Services	
AutoNation (212)	11,015.6
Penske Automotive Group (245)	9,558.1
Hertz Global Holdings (318)	7,101.5
Beverages	
Coca-Cola (72)	30,990.0
Coca-Cola Enterprises (113)	21,645.0
Pepsi Bottling (174)	13,219.0
Chemicals	
Dow Chemical (46)	44,945.0
DuPont (86)	27,328.0
PPG Industries (190)	12,239.0
Commercial Bank	
Bank of America Corp. (5)	150,450.0
J.P. Morgan Chase & Co. (9)	115,632.0
Citigroup (12)	108,785.0
Computer Software	
Microsoft (36)	58,437.0
Oracle (105)	23,252.0
Symantec (353)	6,149.9
Computers, Office Equipment	
Hewlett-Packard (10)	114,552.0
Dell (38)	52,902.0
Apple (56)	36,537.0
Construction & Farm Machinery	
Caterpillar (66)	32,396.0
Deere (107)	23,112.4
Cummins (218)	10,800.0
Diversified Financials	
General Electric (4)	156,779.0
International Assets Holding (49)	43,604.4
Freddie Mac (54)	37,614.0
Diversified Outsourcing	
Aramark (189)	12,297.9
Automatic Data Processing (265)	8,867.1
Electronics	
Emerson Electric (117)	20,915.0
Whirlpool (136)	17,099.0
General Cable (469)	4,385.2
Energy	
Constellation Energy (149)	15,598.8
AES (156)	14,690.0
American Electric Power (172)	13,489.0
Engineering, Construction	
Fluor (111)	21,990.3
KBR (193)	12,105.0
Jacobs Engineering (203)	11,467.4

Industry, Company (Rank)	Revenues (millions)
Entertainment	
Walt Disney (57)	$36,149.0
News Corp. (76)	30,423.0
Time Warner (82)	28,842.0
Food Products (Consumer)	
PepsiCo (50)	43,232.0
Kraft Foods (53)	40,386.0
General Mills (155)	14,691.3
Food & Drug Stores	
CVS Caremark (18)	98,729.0
Kroger (23)	76,733.2
Walgreens (32)	63,335.0
Food Production	
Archer Daniels Midland (27)	69,207.0
Tyson Foods (87)	27,165.0
Smithfield Foods (163)	14,190.5
Food Services	
McDonald's (108)	22,744.7
Yum Brands (216)	10,836.0
Starbucks (241)	9,774.6
Forest & Paper Products	
International Paper (104)	23,366.0
Weyerhaeuser (379)	5,528.0
Domtar (383)	5,465.0
General Merchandisers	
Wal-Mart Stores (1)	408,214.0
Target (30)	65,357.0
Sears Holdings (48)	44,043.0
Health Care	
UnitedHealth Group (21)	87,138.0
WellPoint (31)	65,028.1
Aetna (63)	34,764.1
Home Builders[1]	
Centex (308)	8,406
D.R. Horton (378)	6,646
Pulte Homes (393)	6,290
Home Equipment	
Masco (291)	7,858.0
Fortune Brands (351)	6,205.4
Newell Rubbermaid (373)	5,577.6
Hotels, Casinos & Resorts	
Marriott International (213)	10,908.0
Harrah's Entertainment (264)	8,907.4
MGM Mirage (360)	5,978.6
Household & Personal Products	
Procter & Gamble (22)	79,697.0
Kimberly-Clark (126)	19,115.0
Colgate-Palmolive (151)	15,327.0
Information Technology Services	
IBM (20)	95,758.0
Computer Sciences (138)	16,739.9
SAIC (215)	10,847.0
Insurance	
Berkshire Hathaway (11)	112,493.0
A.I.G. (16)	103,189.0
Allstate (68)	32,013.0
Mail, Package, Freight Delivery	
United Parcel Service (43)	45,297.0
FedEx (60)	35,497.0
Medical Products & Equipment	
Medtronic (160)	14,599.0
Baxter International (185)	12,562.0
Boston Scientific (279)	8,188.0
Metals	
Alcoa (127)	18,745.0
Nucor (206)	11,190.3
United States Steel (211)	11,048.0

Industry, Company (Rank)	Revenues (millions)
Mining, Crude Oil Production	
Occidental Petroleum (150)	$15,531.0
Freeport-McMoRan Copper & Gold (154)	15,040.0
XTO Energy (258)	9,064.0
Motor Vehicles & Parts	
Ford Motor (8)	118,308.0
General Motors (15)	104,589.0
Johnson Controls (83)	28,497.0
Network Communications	
Cisco Systems (58)	36,117.0
Motorola (110)	22,063.0
Qualcomm (225)	10,416.0
Oil and Gas Equipment	
Halliburton (158)	14,675.0
National Oilwell Varco (182)	12,712.0
Baker Hughes (243)	9,664.0
Petroleum Refining	
Exxon Mobil (2)	284,650.0
Chevron (3)	163,527.0
ConocoPhillips (6)	139,515.0
Pharmaceuticals	
Johnson & Johnson (33)	61,897.0
Pfizer (40)	50,009.0
Abbott Laboratories (75)	30,764.7
Pipelines	
Enterprise GP Holdings (92)	25,510.9
Plains All American Pipeline (128)	18,520.0
Oneok (209)	11,111.7
Publishing, Printing	
R.R. Donnelley & Sons (240)	9,857.4
McGraw-Hill (363)	5,951.8
Gannett (370)	5,613.0
Railroads	
Union Pacific (164)	14,143.0
Burlington Nothern Santa Fe (167)	14,016.0
CSX (259)	9,041.0
Real Estate[1]	
ProLogis (426)	5,773
Host Hotels and Resorts (449)	5,294
CB Richard Ellis Grp (464)	5,130
Savings Institutions[1]	
Sovereign Bancorp (674)	3,104
Hudson City Bancorp (740)	2,662
Securities	
BlackRock (441)	4,699.3
NYSE Euronext (444)	4,687.0
Charles Schwab (465)	4,414.0
Semiconductors	
Intel (62)	35,127.0
Jabil Circuit (199)	11,684.5
Texas Instruments (223)	10,427.0
Specialty Retailers	
Costco Wholesale (25)	71,422.0
Home Depot (29)	66,176.0
Lowe's (42)	47,220.0
Telecommunications	
AT&T (7)	123,018.0
Verizon (13)	107,808.0
Comcast (59)	35,756.0

Industry, Company (Rank)	Revenues (millions)	Industry, Company (Rank)	Revenues (millions)	Industry, Company (Rank)	Revenues (millions)
Temporary Help		**Utilities**		**Wholesalers: Food and Grocery**	
Manpower (143)	$16,038.7	Exelon (134)	$17,318.0	Sysco (55)	36,853.3
Kelley Services (479)	4,314.8	Southern (145)	15,743.0	CHS (91)	25,729.9
Tobacco		FPL Group (147)	15,643.0	Nash-Finch (400)	5,212.7
Philip Morris	25,035.0	**Wholesalers Electronics &**		**Wholesalers: Health Care**	
International (94)		**Office Equipment**		McKesson (14)	106,632.0
Altria Group (137)	16,824.0	Ingram Micro (80)	29,515.4	Cardinal Health (17)	99,612.9
Reynolds	8,419.0	Tech Data (109)	22,099.9	AmerisourceBergen (24)	71,789.0
American (272)		Avnet (142)	16,229.9		

Source: *Fortune* magazine (2010). Reprinted by permission.

Fortune 100 Largest U.S. Corporations, 2009

Rank	Company (Rank 2008)	Revenues (millions)	Rank	Company (Rank 2008)	Revenues (millions)
1.	Wal-Mart Stores (2)	408,214.0	51.	MetLife (39)	41,098.0
2.	Exxon Mobil (1)	284,650.0	52.	Safeway (50)	40,850.7
3.	Chevron (3)	163,527.0	53.	Kraft Foods (53)	40,386.0
4.	General Electric (5)	156,779.0	54.	Freddie Mac (220)	37,614.0
5.	Bank of America Corp. (11)	150,450.0	55.	Sysco (62)	36,853.3
6.	ConocoPhillips (4)	139,515.0	56.	Apple (71)	36,537.0
7.	AT&T (8)	123,018.0	57.	Walt Disney (60)	36,149.0
8.	Ford Motor (7)	118,308.0	58.	Cisco Systems (57)	36,117.0
9.	J.P. Morgan Chase & Co. (16)	115,632.0	59.	Comcast (68)	35,756.0
10.	Hewlett-Packard (9)	114,552.0	60.	FedEx (59)	35,497.0
11.	Berkshire Hathaway (13)	112,493.0	61.	Northrop Grumman (69)	35,291.0
12.	Citigroup (12)	108,785.0	62.	Intel (61)	35,127.0
13.	Verizon Communications (17)	107,808.0	63.	Aetna (77)	34,764.1
14.	McKesson (15)	106,632.0	64.	New York Life Insurance (76)	34,014.3
15.	General Motors (6)	104,589.0	65.	Prudential Financial (84)	32,688.0
16.	American International Group (245)	103,189.0	66.	Caterpillar (44)	32,396.0
17.	Cardinal Health (18)	99,612.9	67.	Sprint Nextel (64)	32,260.0
18.	CVS Caremark (19)	98,729.0	68.	Allstate 81)	32,013.0
19.	Wells Fargo (41)	98,636.0	69.	General Dynamics (83)	31,981.0
20.	International Business Machines (14)	95,758.0	70.	Morgan Stanley (30)	31,515.0
21.	UnitedHealth Group (21)	87,138.0	71.	Liberty Mutual Insurance Group (86)	31,094.0
22.	Procter & Gamble (20)	79,697.0	72.	Coca-Cola (73)	30,990.0
23.	Kroger (22)	76,733.2	73.	Humana (85)	30,960.4
24.	AmerisourceBergen (26)	71,789.0	74.	Honeywell International (63)	30,908.0
25.	Costco Wholesale (24)	71,422.0	75.	Abbott Laboratories (80)	30,764.7
26.	Valero Energy (10)	70,035.0	76.	News Corp. (70)	30,423.0
27.	Archer Daniels Midland (27)	69,207.0	77.	HCA (88)	30,052.0
28.	Boeing (34)	68,281.0	78.	Sunoco (41)	29,630.0
29.	Home Depot (25)	66,176.0	79.	Hess (55)	29,569.0
30.	Target (28)	65,357.0	80.	Ingram Micro (67)	29,515.4
31.	WellPoint (32)	65,028.1	81.	Fannie Mae (N.A.)	29,065.0
32.	Walgreen (36)	63,335.0	82.	Time Warner (48)	28,842.0
33.	Johnson & Johnson (29)	61,897.0	83.	Johnson Controls (58)	28,497.0
34.	State Farm Insurance Cos. (31)	61,479.6	84.	Delta Air Lines (111)	28,063.0
35.	Medco Health Solutions (45)	59,804.2	85.	Merck (103)	27,428.3
36.	Microsoft (33)	58,437.0	86.	DuPont (75)	27,328.0
37.	United Technologies (37)	52,920.0	87.	Tyson Foods (89)	27,165.0
38.	Dell (33)	52,902.0	88.	American Express (74)	26,730.0
39.	Goldman Sachs Group (40)	51,673.0	89.	Rite Aid (100)	26,289.5
40.	Pfizer (46)	50,009.0	90.	TIAA-CREF (82)	26,278.0
41.	Marathon Oil (23)	49,403.0	91.	CHS (72)	25,729.9
42.	Lowe's (47)	47,220.0	92.	Enterprise GP Holdings (65)	25,510.9
43.	United Parcel Service (43)	45,297.0	93.	Massachusetts Mutual Insurance (135)	25,423.6
44.	Lockheed Martin (54)	45,189.0	94.	Philip Morris International (93)	25,035.0
45.	Best Buy (56)	45,015.0	95.	Raytheon (108)	24,881.0
46.	Dow Chemical (38)	44,945.0	96.	Express Scripts (115)	24,748.9
47.	Supervalu (51)	44,564.0	97.	Hartford Financial Services (287)	24,701.0
48.	Sears Holdings (49)	44,043.0	98.	Travelers Cos. (99)	24,680.0
49.	International Assets Holding (140)	43,604.4	99.	Publix Super Markets (101)	24,515.0
50.	PepsiCo (52)	43,232.0	100.	Amazon.com (130)	24,509.0

Source: *Fortune* magazine (2009). Reprinted by permission.

Entrepreneur's Top 50 Franchises, 2010

Rank[1], Franchise	Business	Number of franchises	Startup costs[2]	Franchise fees
1. Subway	Sandwiches and salads	31,445	$84,300–258,300	$15,000
2. McDonald's	Burgers, chicken, salads	25,801	995,900–1,842,700	45,000
3. 7-Eleven Inc.	Convenience Store	35,141	40,500–775,300	10,000–. 611,600
4. Hampton Inns (& Suites)	Midprice Hotels	1,636	3,716,000–13,148,800	50,000
5. Supercuts	Hair salon	1,028	111,000–239,700	22,500
6. H & R Block	Tax preparation & filing	4,502	26,427–84,094	0
7. Dunkin' Donuts	Coffee, doughnuts, baked goods	8,924	537,750–1,765,300	40,000– 80,000
8. Jani-King	Commercial cleaning	13,046	11,400–35,050	8,600–16,300
9. Servpro	Insurance/disaster cleaning	1,478	102,250–161,150	40,000
10. ampm Mini Market	Convenience store & gas station	2,956	1,835,823–7,615,065	30,000– 70,000
11. Jan-Pro Franchising Int'l. Inc.	Commercial cleaning	10,099	3,145–50,405	2,520–44,000
12. Kumon Learning Centers	Supplemental education	26,311	32,958–131,070	1,000
13. Stratus Building Solutions	Commercial cleaning	2,148	3,450–57,750	3,000–47,000
14. Miracle-Ear Inc.	Hearing Instruments	1,274	122,500–570,000	30,000– 100,000
15. Pizza Hut Inc.	Pizza, pasta, wings	10,756	316,500–2,974,000	25,000
16. Hardee's	Burgers, chicken, biscuits	1,437	1,182,000–1,583,500	25,000
17. Denny's Inc.	Family restaurant	1,281	1,071,325–2,623,601	40,000
18. Jazzercise Inc.	Dance fitness classes	7,854	2,980–75,500	500–1,000
19. Matco Tools	Tools	1,489	79,926–187,556	0
20. The UPS Store / Mail Boxes Etc.	Postal & business services	4,785	154,947–293,473	29,950
21. Days Inn	Hotels	1,856	406,945–6,704,617	36,000
22. Sonic Drive In Restaurants	Drive-in restaurant	3,055	1,209,300–3,413,800	45,000
23. Midas Int'l.	Auto repair & maintenance	2,370	323,000–418,880	30,000
24. KFC Corp.	Chicken	11,779	1,379,900–2,422,500	45,000
25. Circle K	Convenience Store	4,173	161,000–1,353,000	15,000
26. Papa John's Int'l. Inc.	Pizza	2,814	113,823–528,123	25,000
27. InterContinental Hotels Group	Hotels	4,287	5,136,370–93,855,035	50,000– 150,000
28. Liberty Tax Service	Income tax preparation	2,940	56,800–69,900	40,000
29. Instant Tax Service	Retail tax preparation	1,197	39,000–89,000	34,000
30. Vanguard Cleaning Systems	Commercial cleaning	1,516	8,125–38,100	7,650–37,000
31. ServiceMaster Clean	Comm'l/residential cleaning and disaster restoration	4,940	20,926–132,623	16,900– 61,000
32. Bonus Building Care	Commercial cleaning	2,490	9,000–15,000	7,500
33. Snap-on Tools	Professional tools	4,308	17,619–281,959	5,000–15,000
34. Ace Hardware Corp.	Hardware and home improvement store	4,433	238,500–1,566,250	5,000
35. Cold Stone Creamery	Ice cream, Italian sorbet	1,359	292,375–438,975	42,000
36. Super 8	Motels	2,116	285,445–5,396,983	24,000– 26,500
37. Jiffy Lube Int'l. Inc.	Fast oil change	2,034	229,000–323,000	10,000– 35,000
38. Merry Maids	Residential cleaning	1,408	24,750–59,450	21,000– 31,000
39. Fantastic Sams Hair Salons	Full-service hair salon	1,320	118,000–230,850	30,000
40. Papa Murphy's	Take & bake pizza	2,006	171,655–353,225	25,000
41. The Maids Home Service	Residential cleaning	1,094	106,345–157,095	38,000– 48,000
42. Aaron's Sales & Lease Ownership	Furniture, electronics, computer & appliance leasing & sales	540	233,870–607,580	15,000– 50,000
43. Anytime Fitness	Fitness center	1,111	44,000–300,000	19,999
44. Sylvan Learning	Supplemental education	954	179,069–305,090	42,000– 48,000
45. Taco Bell Corp.	Mexican fast-food	4,502	1,324,300–2,465,500	45,000
46. Results! Travel	Travel services	847	25–10,425	0
47. Baskin–Robbins USA Co.	Ice cream, frozen treats	6,100	41,450–373,595	5,000–35,000
48. Edible Arrangements Int'l. Inc.	Floral-like designs from sculpted fresh fruit	787	154,920–298,005	25,000
49. Anago Cleaning Systems	Commercial cleaning	1,673	8,543–55,306	4,590–32,348
50. Auntie Anne's Hand-Rolled Soft Pretzels	Hand-rolled soft pretzels	1,005	197,875–439,100	30,000

Note: Includes only companies that reported figures to *Entrepreneur*. Does not include franchises owned by the company. 1. Franchises ranked by factors including: financial strength and stability, growth rate, size of system, number of years in business, length of the franchise, start upcosts; etc. 2. Includes franchise fees. **Source:** *Entrepreneur* (Jan. 2010). Reprinted by permission.

ADVERTISING

Few facts and figures reveal the extraordinary growth of the mass-consumption society as vividly as those dealing with the advertising business. In 1950, as the postwar economy began to heat up, American business spent $5.7 billion to advertise its goods and services; by 1960 that figure would double, and then almost double again by 1970. Between 1970 and 1990, as the Baby Boom generation entered the marketplace and the economy expanded, advertising expenditures grew at a spiraling rate, topping $100 billion in 1986. That rate of growth has not been sustained, but advertising spending continued to reach new highs every year until 2000. The industry suffered its worst decline in more than a decade in 2001, when total expenditures fell 6.5 percent, from $243 to $231 billion. Expenditures reached another all-time high of $281 billion in 2006, but the contracting economy caused advertisers to rein in spending in 2007 and 2008.

Nearly 60 percent of all advertising dollars are spent to place ads in newspapers or magazines or to run commercials on radio and television. Meanwhile, although the Internet is the fastest-growing source of advertising dollars, it still represents only a tiny fraction of all advertising dollars spent. Companies continue to spend far more dollars for listings in the Yellow Pages as they do on pop-up ads.

The biggest advertisers are the nation's largest manufacturers of automobiles, food, soft drinks, tobacco, and beer. Most advertising dollars are filtered through about 13,000 advertising agencies, which mainly create the ads and buy the space or time from the media. The agency business has undergone a dramatic restructuring in the last few decades, as many of the largest agencies, most of them with worldwide connections, have merged to form enormous corporations. Today, the industry is dominated by four big agencies, each with more than $6 billion in worldwide revenues: the London-based WPP Group ($13.6 billion), New York's Omnicom Group ($13.4 billion), New York-based Interpublic Group ($7.0 billion), and Paris's Publicis Groupe ($6.9 billion).

Advertising Expenditures in the U.S., 1776-2008 (in millions)

Year	Amount[1]	Year	Amount[1]
1776	$ 0.2	1970	$ 19,550
1800	1	1980	54,780
1820	3	1985	94,750
1840	7	1990	128,640
1850	12	1995	160,930
1860	22	2000	243,680
1867	40	2001	231,300
1880	175	2002	236,875
1890	300	2003	245,477
1900	450	2004	263,766
1909	1,000	2005	271,074
1915	1,100	2006	281,653
1940	2,110	2007	279,612
1950	5,700	2008[2]	142,000
1960	11,960		

Notes: 1. These are estimated figures of the monies spent on placing advertising in all media; the costs of producing the advertising are not included. 2. Preliminary **Source:** *Advertising Age.*

Total U.S. Advertising Measured Spending by Medium, 2007-08

| | 2007 | | 2008 | | Percent change |
	Expenditures (millions)	Share of total	Expenditures (millions)	Share of total	2007-08
Magazines, total	$30,913	20.9%	$28,580	20.1%	−7.5%
Consumer magazine	$25,626	17.3	$23,722	16.7	−7.4
Sunday magazine	2,000	1.4	1,904	1.3	−4.8
B-to-B magazine	3,050	2.1	2,728	1.9	−10.5
Local magazine	237	0.2	226	0.2	−4.6
Newspapers, total	28,134	19.0	25,059	17.7	−10.9
National newspaper	3,347	2.3	2,962	2.1	−11.5
Local newspaper	22,989	15.5	20,266	14.3	−11.8
Free-Standing Inserts	1,798	1.2	1,831	1.3	1.8
Television, total	65,097	44.0	65,137	45.9	0.1
Network TV	26,878	18.2	26,710	18.8	−0.6
Spot TV	15,597	10.5	15,154	10.7	−2.8
Syndicated TV	4,173	2.8	4,445	3.1	6.5
Cable TV networks	18,449	12.5	18,828	13.3	2.1
Radio, total	10,591	7.2	9,501	6.7	−10.3
Network radio	1,002	0.7	975	0.7	−2.7
National spot radio	2,503	1.7	2,223	1.6	−11.2
Local radio	7,086	4.8	6,303	4.4	−11.1
Outdoor	4,033	2.7	3,964	2.8	−1.7
Direct mail	N.A.	N.A.	N.A.	N.A.	N.A.
Internet	9,301	6.3	9,727	6.9	4.6
Total measured spending	$148,068	100%	$141,969	100%	−4.1 %

Note: Total includes miscellaneous other amounts not shown separately. Network TV includes Fox; Syndicated TV includes UPN and WB. **Source:** Prepared for *Advertising Age* by Universal McCann's Robert J. Coen.

Top 25 U.S. Advertising Agencies, by Gross Domestic Income, 2006–07

U.S. Rank /Agency, Headquarters (Parent Company)	U.S. Revenues (millions)		Percent change,	Worldwide revenues (millions)	
	2006	2007	2006–07	2006	2007
1. BBDO Worldwide, New York (Omnicom)	$584.7	$628.0	7.4%	$1,680	$1,899
2. DraftFCB, Chicago/New York (Interpublic)	496.1	518.9	4.6	941	991
3. McCann Erickson Worldwide, New York (Interpublic)	443.4	490.0	10.5	1,479	1,619
4. Epsilon/Purple, Irving, Texas (Alliance Data Systems)	232.0	360.0	55.2	232	370
5. Rapp Collins Worldwide, New York (Omnicom)	306.0	351.9	15.0	517	602
6. Digitas, Boston (Publicis)	257.0	345.0	34.2	257	364
7. OgilvyOne Worldwide, New York (WPP)	297.8	338.5	13.7	604	690
8. JWT, New York (WPP)	303.3	315.5	4.0	1,140	1,237
9. Y&R, New York (WPP)	280.0	307.0	9.6	820	907
10. MindShare Worldwide, New York (WPP)	277.8	302.4	8.9	687	734
11. Avenue A/Razorfish, Seattle (Microsoft Corp.)	235.4	299.3	27.1	268	368
12. Carlson Marketing, Minneapolis (Carlson)	282.0	299.0	6.0	390	413
13. OMD Worldwide, New York (Omnicom)	290.1	298.8	3.0	790	859
14. Wunderman, New York (WPP)	264.0	295.0	11.7	615	720
15. DDB Worldwide, New York (Omnicom)	277.9	290.8	4.6	1,264	1,432
16. Starcom USA, Chicago (Publicis)	227.9	259.0	13.6	228	259
17. Ogilvy & Mather Worldwide, New York (WPP)	250.0	255.0	2.0	770	812
18. Grey, New York (WPP)	235.7	249.8	6.0	605	645
19. Mediaedge:cia, New York (WPP)	196.7	242.9	23.5	539	641
20. Campbell-Ewald, Warren, Mich. (Interpublic)	230.0	239.2	4.0	230	239
21. Zenith Media USA, New York (Publicis)	188.5	215.0	14.1	189	215
22. TBWA Worldwide, New York (Omnicom)	199.0	208.2	4.6	1,135	1,292
23. MediaVest USA, New York (Publicis)	167.1	200.0	19.7	167	200
24. Saatchi & Saatchi, New York (Publicis)	171.7	193.1	12.5	542	603
25. Leo Burnett Worldwide, Chicago (Publicis)	204.8	190.7	–6.9	751	717

Note: Revenues are estimated by Advertising Age and do not include non-advertising specialty and subsidiary shops. **Source:** *Advertising Age* (May 5, 2008); reprinted by permission of Crain Communications, Inc.

The 100 Leading U.S. Advertisers, 1991–2008

2008 Rank, Company (2007 rank)	Total measured spending (millions)				
	1991	1995	2000	2007	2008
1. Procter & Gamble Co. (1)	$1,166.4	$1,507.4	$2,363.5	$5,180.0	$4,838.1
2. Verizon Communications (3)	N.A.	N.A.	1,612.9	3,379.9	3,700.0
3. AT&T (2)	391.7	675.2	1,415.7	3,430.0	3,073.0
4. General Motors Corp. (4)	1,056.5	1,499.6	3,934.8	3,060.2	2,901.1
5. Johnson & Johnson (8)	371.1	601.3	1,601.2	2,408.8	2,529.2
6. Unilever (7)	371.4	442.7	1,453.6	2,417.9	2,422.6
7. Walt Disney Co. (10)	257.3	777.8	1,757.5	1,997.8	2,217.6
8. Time Warner (5)	311.3	543.0	1,770.1	2,754.8	2,207.7
9. General Electric Co. (13)	N.A.	N.A.	1,310.1	1,791.3	2,019.3
10. Sears Holdings Corp. (11)	462.3	557.8	1,455.4	1,956.9	1,864.9
11. Ford Motor Co. (6)	517.7	891.8	2,345.2	2,525.2	1,856.0
12. GlaxoSmithKline (9)	83.3	173.2	1,126.4	2,123.0	1,827.0
13. Toyota Motor Corp. (15)	442.5	513.4	1,273.9	1,757.9	1,690.4
14. L'Oreal (18)	N.A.	N.A.	987.1	1,632.3	1,673.1
15. Walmart Stores (21)	76.7	143.2	497.8	1,432.4	1,659.8
16. Bank of America Corp. (14)	N.A.	N.A	N.A	1,770.9	1,650.0
17. Anheuser-Busch InBev (24)	327.9	320.5	707.6	1,360.0	1,587.3
18. Sprint Nextel Corp. (12)	N.A.	213.9	1,227.3	1,800.0	1,500.0
19. Sony Corp. (17)	262.8	431.0	1,030.0	1,736.8	1,464.9
20. JPMorgan Chase & Co. (19)	N.A.	N.A.	N.A.	1,518.9	1,356.8
21. News Corp. (26)	358.6	275.9	923.2	1,307.5	1,337.8
22. J.C. Penney Co. (25)	105.2	273.9	1,011.2	1,316.0	1,314.0
23. PepsiCo (23)	542.0	730.2	2,100.7	1,362.3	1,293.9
24. Pfizer (27)	N.A.	N.A.	2,265.3	1,291.1	1,292.4
25. Kraft Foods (20)	1,110.4	1,397.7	2,602.9	1,508.0	1,272.1
26. Honda Motor Co. (29)	242.5	388.8	1,035.0	1,234.3	1,254.6
27. Macy's (32)	111.4	407.6	1,127.6	1,194.0	1,239.0
28. Target Corp. (31)	N.A.	N.A.	826.7	1,195.0	1,233.0
29. McDonald's Corp. (34)	87.4	586.4	1,273.9	1,150.1	1,201.0
30. Nissan Motor Co. (22)	212.0	367.7	813.8	1,422.9	1,199.3
31. U.S. Government (37)	123.4	219.9	1,246.3	1,121.9	1,195.6
32. Berkshire Hathaway (38)	N.A.	N.A.	455.8	1,117.7	1,186.1

2008 Rank, Company (2007 rank)	Total measured spending (millions)				
	1991	1995	2000	2007	2008
33. Viacom (33)	N.A.	N.A.	$1,220.9	$1,181.7	$1,178.6
34. General Mills (41)	$419.1	$367.7	639.2	955.2	1,174.3
35. Nestle (28)	307.6	490.1	637.7	1,260.3	1,138.8
36. Chrysler Group (16)	N.A.	N.A.	N.A.	1,739.4	1,129.6
37. American Express Co. (35)	156.2	210.4	538.2	1,146.0	1,056.8
38. Mars Inc. (40)	128.2	210.1	670.8	986.5	1,037.6
39. Home Depot (30)	N.A.	96.6	651.6	1,200.0	1,000.0
40. Citigroup (36)	N.A.	N.A.	N.A.	1,135.3	970.7
41. Yum Brands (39)	N.A.	N.A.	N.A.	1,004.4	960.7
42. Deutsche Telekom (43)	N.A.	N.A.	N.A.	900.0	940.3
43. SABMiller (42)	N.A.	N.A.	N.A.	927.6	934.0
44. Bristol-Myers Squibb Co. (48)	184.0	219.4	1,190.7	810.6	906.2
45. Kohl's Corp. (46)	N.A.	N.A.	231.7	839.0	890.0
46. Eli Lilly & Co. (58)	N.A.	N.A.	N.A.	688.7	847.1
47. Bayer (45)	55.8	160.5	648.9	860.8	840.2
48. Kellogg Co. (44)	381.3	488.2	455.4	871.6	820.3
49. Microsoft Corp. (50)	N.A.	147.7	854.8	764.5	802.3
50. Nike (56)	109.5	146.3	613.5	715.4	790.4
51. Lowe's Cos. (49)	N.A.	N.A.	206.7	788.0	789.0
52. SC Johnson (65)	93.1	115.6	464.8	591.9	774.7
53. Schering-Plough Corp. (47)	95.9	104.0	510.5	831.6	770.1
54. Estee Lauder Cos. (53)	N.A.	N.A.	717.3	751.0	770.0
55. Coca-Cola Co. (55)	218.8	238.2	894.9	726.4	752.1
56. Reckitt Benckiser (64)	N.A.	N.A.	289.2	625.1	725.8
57. Campbell Soup Co. (61)	109.5	169.0	331.2	670.3	711.1
58. LVMH Moet Hennessy Louis Vuitton (62)	N.A.	N.A.	N.A.	667.3	687.3
59. Clorox (59)	127.8	157.8	397.1	683.2	686.3
60. Comcast Corp. (57)	N.A.	N.A.	N.A.	692.6	669.8
61. Capital One Financial Corp. (51)	N.A.	N.A	N.A	757.0	654.1
62. Merck & Co. (52)	129.5	199.0	983.9	751.8	617.7
63. Wyeth (54)	N.A.	N.A.	N.A.	745.0	614.0
64. Best Buy Co. (68)	N.A.	94.0	446.7	569.6	596.0
65. State Farm Mutual Auto Insurance (87)	N.A.	N.A.	N.A.	431.2	576.1
66. AstraZeneca (69)	N.A.	N.A.	N.A.	566.5	576.0
67. Visa (66)	N.A.	N.A.	427.3	581.0	549.1
68. Dell (63)	N.A.	N.A.	429.5	630.8	538.2
69. Diageo (67)	N.A.	N.A.	1,112.1	576.5	536.6
70. Kroger Co. (73)	N.A.	N.A.	551.2	506.0	532.0
71. Allstate Corp. (71)	N.A.	N.A.	N.A.	536.8	526.2
72. Wells Fargo & Co. (70)	N.A.	N.A.	N.A.	548.0	525.0
73. Hyundai Motor Co. (60)	N.A.	N.A.	N.A.	676.1	512.8
74. Limited Brands (72)	N.A.	N.A.	N.A.	507.0	502.0
75. Novartis (84)	N.A.	N.A.	573.9	450.0	494.7
76. FMR Corp. (Fidelity Investments) (75)	N.A.	N.A.	N.A.	499.0	483.8
77. Boehringer Ingelheim (74)	N.A.	N.A.	N.A.	505.3	482.1
78. Abbott Laboratories (107)	N.A.	N.A.	N.A.	329.7	470.9
79. Progressive Corp. (82)	N.A.	N.A.	N.A.	459.7	470.4
80. Wendy's/Arby's Group (85)	61.1	179.4	296.3	445.0	453.4
81. IBM Corp. (83)	387.4	490.6	1,189.0	459.0	445.7
82. DirecTV Group (101)	N.A.	N.A.	N.A.	356.4	442.0
83. MasterCard (77)	N.A.	N.A.	311.1	488.7	437.5
84. Doctor's Associates (Subway) (88)	N.A.	N.A.	N.A.	410.0	432.0
85. eBay (78)	N.A.	N.A.	N.A.	487.8	429.1
86. Sanofi-Aventis (76)	N.A.	N.A.	N.A.	493.1	422.8
87. Safeway (80)	N.A.	N.A.	397.7	473.3	420.2
88. Hewlett-Packard Co. (79)	N.A.	N.A.	791.4	475.0	412.1
89. Qwest Communications Intl. (81)	N.A.	N.A.	N.A.	460.0	411.0
90. Volkswagen (127)	N.A.	N.A.	N.A.	279.0	407.2
91. Circuit City Stores (90)	N.A.	N.A.	N.A.	402.9	404.6
92. Mattel (91)	63.8	184.5	451.4	402.2	403.4
93. Daimler (124)	414.8	954.7	1,984.0	287.3	401.3
94. Coty (JAB Investments) (86)	N.A.	N.A.	N.A.	444.8	394.7
95. Burger King Holdings (97)	N.A.	N.A.	N.A.	364.0	387.8
96. Fortune Brands (92)	N.A.	N.A.	N.A.	395.0	386.0
97. Colgate-Palmolive Co. (96)	N.A.	N.A.	N.A.	372.3	384.3
98. Lions Gate Entertainment Corp. (112)	N.A.	N.A.	N.A.	313.4	375.4
99. ConAgra Foods (89)	N.A.	N.A.	578.5	404.8	352.4
100. Philips Electronics (99)	N.A.	N.A.	N.A.	362.4	351.5

Note: The top 100 companies are not the same each year. **Source:** *Advertising Age*, 100 Leading Advertisers, 2009.

Education

The American people's unwavering commitment to public education dates back more than 150 years. Fueled by a demand for literacy from two different creeds, one described in the Bible, the other in the Declaration of Independence, the American system of education grew to be an essential element in the faith that this nation was uniquely the land of opportunity.

Today that belief has evolved into what is called equality of opportunity, and this vital idea has helped to create a school system whose size, scope and ambitions are unrivaled by any Western democracy. As of fall 2010, nearly 75 million students and 5 million faculty, from elementary to college levels, are directly involved in education. The cost of this undertaking is, of course, staggering: more than half a trillion dollars annually—up to $10,614 per elementary and secondary school

student in 2010—over 7 percent of the gross domestic product (G.D.P. per capita), virtually all of it for public education. The portion of G.D.P. spent on education rose rapidly between 1959 and 1969, declined in the 1970s as enrollment in elementary and secondary schools fell, and began rising steadily again in 1984. Since 1990, it has remained relatively stable. And while some complain bitterly about the quality of the results, or about overt waste, mismanagement and even fraud, there is no doubt as to the essential role of education in American life today.

▶ PUBLIC ELEMENTARY AND SECONDARY SCHOOLS

Expenditures on public elementary and secondary schools have been increasing faster than inflation in almost every year since figures were first recorded in 1900. The exception was the period between 1978 and 1982, when inflation outpaced increases in expenditures. Total expenditures for public elementary and secondary schools topped $601.9 billion in 2008–09, almost double what they were in 1998–99; on the basis of fall enrollment, expenditures per student were approximately $10,259 in 2008–09. In February 2009, Pres. Obama signed the American Recovery and Reinvestment Act, which allocates over $14 billion to elementary and secondary education programs—$10 billion of which is for grants for the education of disadvantaged children. Even after adjusting for inflation, the amount spent to educate each student at public elementary and secondary schools continues to skyrocket.

In 1979, a historic shift occurred in the source of money to operate the American public school system. That was the year the state share of revenues rose above the local share for the first time. The federal share for elementary and secondary schools has always been relatively small.

Enrollment in public elementary schools declined dramatically from 1970 to 1985 (from 32.6 million to 27 million) as the number of young peo-

Revenues for Public Elementary and Secondary Schools, 1920–2007

| School year | Total revenues (thousands) | Percentage | | |
		Federal	State	Local[1]
1919–20	$ 970	0.3%	16.5%	83.2%
1929–30	2,089	0.4	16.9	82.7
1939–40	2,261	1.8	30.3	68.0
1949–50	5,437	2.9	39.8	57.3
1959–60	14,747	4.4	39.1	56.5
1969–70	40,267	8.0	39.9	52.1
1979–80	96,881	9.8	46.8	43.4
1989–90	208,548	6.1	47.3	46.6
1995–96	287,703	6.6	47.5	45.9
1997–98	325,976	6.8	48.4	44.8
1999–2000	372,943	7.3	49.5	43.2
2001–2002	419,502	7.9	49.2	42.9
2003–2004	462,016	9.1	47.1	43.9
2005–2006	520,644	9.1	46.5	44.4
2006–2007	556,900	8.3	47.6	44.1

Notes: 1. Includes a relatively small amount from nongovernmental sources (gifts and tuition and transportation fees from patrons). These sources accounted for 2.5 percent of total revenues in 1997–98. **Source:** U.S. Dept. of Education, National Center for Education Statistics, *Digest of Education Statistics 2009.*

Education Expenditures, 1949–2009

| School year | All educational institutions | | Elementary and Secondary schools | | | Colleges and Universities | |
| | Total expenditures (millions) | As percentage of GDP | Public | | Private (millions) | Public (millions) | Private (millions) |
			Total (millions)	Per pupil (constant dollars)			
1949–50	$ 8,911	3.3%	$ 5,838	$1,738	$ 411	$ 1,430	$ 1,233
1959–60	23,860	4.7	15,613	2,668	1,100	3,904	3,244
1969–70	68,459	6.9	40,683	4,147	2,500	16,234	9,041
1979–80	165,627	6.5	95,962	5,255	7,200	41,434	21,031
1989–90	381,525	7.0	212,770	7,262	18,200	96,387	54,169
1999–2000	649,322	7.0	381,838	9,442	30,700	152,325	84,459
2001–02	752,780	7.4	435,364	10,046	36,700	183,436	97,280
2002–03	795,568	7.6	454,907	10,161	37,900	196,891	105,871
2003–04	829,913	7.6	473,863	10,286	39,300	205,069	111,682
2004–05	878,300	7.5	495,800	N.A.	41,100	218,300	123,100
2005–06	921,800	7.4	515,600	10,692	42,700	229,900	133,600
2006–07	972,000	7.4	553,000	N.A.	46,000	239,000	134,000
2007–08	1,017,000	7.4	577,950	10,615	N.A.	261,000	147,000
2008–09	N.A.	7.4	601,941	10,259	N.A.	271,000	161,000

Source: U.S. Dept. of Education, National Center for Education Statistics, *Digest of Education Statistics 2008*; The National Education Association, *Estimates of School Statistics 2009.*

Number of Schools and Teachers in the U.S., 2007–2008

School type	Schools			Teachers[2]		
	Total	Public	Private	Total	Public	Private
Elementary and secondary[1]	**132,656**	**98,916**	**33,740**	**3,634**	**3,178**	**456**
Elementary	88,902	67,032	21,870	N.A.	N.A.	N.A.
Secondary	27,358	24,426	2,932	N.A.	N.A.	N.A.
Combined	15,160	6,222	8,938	[1]	N.A.	N.A.	N.A.
Other schools	1,236	1,236		N.A.	N.A.	N.A.
Colleges and universities[3]	**6,551**	**2,004**	**4,547**	**1,371**	**877**	**494**
4-year colleges	2,675	653	2,022	N.A.	N.A.	N.A.
2-year colleges	1,677	1,032	645	N.A.	N.A.	N.A.

Notes: Figures are in thousands. 1. Included in other private school categories. 2. Data is for fall 2007. 3. Degree-granting institutions only. **Source:** U.S. Dept. of Education, National Center for Education Statistics, *Digest of Education Statistics 2009.*

School Enrollment, 1970–2009 (millions of students)

	Type of school						
	Elementary (K–8)		Secondary (9–12)		Higher education		
Year	Public	Private	Public	Private	Public	Private	Total
1970	32.6	4.1	13.3	1.3	6.4	2.2	**59.9**
1975	30.5	3.7	14.3	1.3	8.8	2.4	**61.0**
1980	27.6	4.0	13.2	1.3	9.5	2.6	**58.3**
1985	27.0	4.2	12.4	1.4	9.5	2.8	**57.2**
1990	29.9	4.1	11.3	1.2	10.8	3.0	**60.3**
1995	32.3	4.4	12.5	1.3	11.1	3.2	**64.8**
1997	33.1	4.6	13.1	1.2	11.2	3.3	**66.5**
1998	33.3	4.7	13.2	1.2	11.1	3.4	**67.0**
1999	33.5	4.8	13.4	1.3	11.3	3.5	**67.7**
2000	33.7	4.9	13.5	1.3	11.8	3.6	**69.7**
2006	33.9	4.8	15.0	1.4	13.4	4.1	**72.7**
2008	34.9	4.7	14.9	1.4	13.6	4.6	**74.1**
2009	35.0	4.5	14.8	1.4	14.5	5.0	**75.2**

Note: Totals may not add up due to independent rounding. **Source:** U.S. Dept. of Education, National Center for Education Statistics, *Digest of Education Statistics 2009.*

ple decreased. That trend evidenced itself in secondary school populations between 1980 and 1990. Since 1990, however, populations of both elementary and secondary school populations have generally risen. In the fall of 2009, the U.S. Department of Education recorded a public elementary school population of 35 million; public secondary school enrollment reached 14.8 million. These numbers suggest that baby boomers started a baby boom of their own, often called the "boomlet," who started high school in the early 2000s.

Teachers have more than kept pace with the growth in the number of students. There were over 3.7 million public and private elementary and secondary school teachers in 2008, more than double the number in 1955. The number of secondary school teachers has remained relatively constant since 1975, while the number of public elementary school teachers has risen consistently every year since 1982, when they numbered 1.2 million. A more telling statistic, though, is pupil-teacher ratios. Despite constant complaints about overcrowded inner-city classrooms, the average number of pupils supervised by each teacher has declined dramatically in the past 30 years. It was projected that each public school teacher was responsible for 15.7 students in 2008, down from 16.8 in 1997 but up from 15.4 in 2007. Each private school teacher was responsible for 11.1 students in 2008, down from 15.2 in 1997 and from 13.2 in 2007.

According to the National Education Association, during the 2008–09 year the average teacher salary was $53,910, an increase of 3.1 percent over the 2007–08 figure of $52,308. After adjusting for inflation, however, a teacher's average salary is actually 0.7 percent less than it was in 1988 when it was $29,564. Teachers, perhaps because their salaries come from tax revenues, earn significantly less than other college graduates. Employment of elementary, kindergarten, middle, and secondary school teachers is expected to grow by 13 percent between 2008 and 2018. Most job openings will result from the need to replace the large number of retiring baby-boomer teachers. The supply of teachers is expected to rise, and in recent years the total number of Bachelor and Master's degrees in Education has been increasing slowly.

Nursery schools have increased dramatically in popularity since 1965, when 27.1 percent of three to five-year-olds were enrolled in a kindergarten or pre-kindergarten program. That percentage has increased gradually ever since, reaching a high of 65.8 percent in 1999. (In 2006, it was 58.4 percent.) The percentage of youngsters attending full-time nursery school has also risen. In 2006, an additional 31.4 percent of 0–2 year-olds were enrolled in formal care, a surprisingly low number in comparison to some European nations. Most nursery school students were in private schools, while most kindergarten students were enrolled in public schools.

School districts declined drastically between 1930, when there were 119,000 of them, and 1984, when there were a mere 15,695. Numbers since 1985 are not directly comparable with earlier years, but school districts have continued to

How the States Rank in Public Education, 2008–09

State	Enrollment	Rank	Expenditures per pupil[1]	Rank	Average teacher salary[1]	Rank
U.S.	48,960,698	N.A.	$9,963	N.A.	$54,319	N.A.
Alabama	739,198	23	8,875	34	46,879	36
Alaska	130,684	45	10,590	19	58,395	10
Arizona	1,077,873	13	5,346	51	46,358	38
Arkansas	456,795	34	9,591	22	47,472	32
California	6,252,031	1	9,539	26	68,093	2
Colorado	818,443	22	9,335	29	48,487	28
Connecticut	575,287	28	13,533	7	63,152	4
D.C.	57,172	51	17,449	1	62,557	7
Delaware	125,430	46	12,977	8	56,667	13
Florida	2,631,631	4	8,816	36	46,921	35
Georgia	1,655,765	9	9,564	23	52,879	18
Hawaii	179,071	42	11,117	14	55,733	14
Idaho	275,075	39	7,305	47	45,178	41
Illinois	2,112,132	5	10,993	16	61,344	8
Indiana	1,045,551	14	9,432	28	49,569	24
Iowa	487,559	32	8,432	42	48,638	26
Kansas	474,987	33	9,544	25	46,401	37
Kentucky	650,008	26	9,264	32	47,875	31
Louisiana	684,873	25	9,310	30	48,627	27
Maine	194,460	41	12,802	9	44,731	43
Maryland	843,861	20	11,962	10	62,849	6
Massachusetts	958,187	16	13,768	6	66,712	3
Michigan	1,682,738	8	11,082	15	57,327	11
Minnesota	819,207	21	10,560	20	51,938	20
Mississippi	495,665	30	7,175	48	44,498	45
Missouri	892,283	18	8,466	41	44,249	47
Montana	141,969	44	9,029	33	44,426	46
Nebraska	292,043	37	8,752	37	44,957	42
Nevada	437,433	35	7,133	49	50,067	22
New Hampshire	199,305	40	11,447	13	49,872	23
New Jersey	1,377,728	11	15,374	2	63,111	5
New Mexico	327,580	36	9,558	24	45,752	39
New York	2,711,603	3	15,286	3	69,118	1
North Carolina	1,426,729	10	1,615	40	48,648	25
North Dakota	93,396	48	8,638	39	41,654	50
Ohio	1,900,210	6	8,829	35	54,656	15
Oklahoma	644,754	27	7,615	46	43,486	48
Oregon	564,064	29	9,469	27	54,085	17
Pennsylvania	1,806,969	7	11,659	12	57,237	12
Rhode Island	145,342	43	11,905	11	58,407	9
South Carolina	707,739	24	8,721	38	47,421	33
South Dakota	122,997	47	8,250	43	35,070	51
Tennessee	913,500	17	8,022	44	45,549	40
Texas	4,728,204	2	7,978	45	47,157	34
Utah	489,004	31	5,734	50	42,335	49
Vermont	92,908	49	14,336	4	47,884	30
Virginia	1,240,623	12	10,707	17	48,365	29
Washington	1,038,620	15	9,304	31	52,567	19
West Virginia	281,908	38	10,411	21	44,701	44
Wisconsin	873,586	19	10,643	18	51,121	21
Wyoming	86,519	50	13,967	5	54,602	16

Note: 1. Data is for 2007–2008 school year. **Source:** National Education Association, *Rankings and Estimates, 2008–2009* (2010).

decline. There were 15,505 public school districts in 2008–09, up from 15,539 in 2007–08. The greatest number of school districts had between 1,000 and 2,499 students in them, but school districts with 25,000 students or more were responsible for educating nearly one-third of public school students. Recent increases in the number of school districts can largely be attributed to new charter schools designed by states as separate districts.

▶ PRIVATE SCHOOLS

The U.S. Department of Education updates its data on private schools less frequently than it does for public institutions. The 2007–08 school year is the latest year for which data is available for private elementary and secondary schools.

Schools and enrollment   In 2008 there were 28,220 (25 percent of all U.S. schools) private schools engaged in educating 5,165,260 students. Of these schools, 16,370 were elementary schools (responsible for educating 2,462,980 students), 3,040 were secondary schools (850,750 students), and 8,810 offered instruction in all 12 grades (1,851,550 students). Most private schools were religiously affiliated. One-fourth, or 7,378 schools, were affiliated with the Catholic Church; 13,950 were affiliated with other religious groups. Slightly less than 7,000 private schools were nonsectarian, and over 47 percent of these were elementaries only. From 1995 to 2008, the number of Conservative Christian schools has steadily increased.

Tuition   Average tuition for private school students was $8,549 per year in 2007–08, but that average is kept low by the large number of parochial schools offering free or low-cost private education. The average cost of all nonsectarian private schools (elementary and secondary) was $17,316, and roughly half of such schools charge at least $10,000 per year in tuition. Average tuition for nonsectarian secondary schools was $27,302 per year, more than four times what it was in the 1999–2000 school year.

Teachers   There were roughly 459,000 full-time private school teachers in the 2007–08 school year. In 2008, the base teacher salary in private schools was $36,250, a fraction of the $49,630 earned by public school teachers. Male teachers earned substantially more than their female counterparts in both public and private schools, but the difference was most pronounced in private schools, where male compensation ($40,490) was 16 percent greater than female salaries ($34,800).

Race and ethnicity   Private schools are traditionally white enclaves; three-quarters of students were white in the 2007–08 school year. Yet the enrollment of minority students in private

Catholic Schools, Pupils & Teachers, 1960–2009

Year	Schools	Pupils	Total	Religious	Lay
				Teachers	
Elementary schools					
1960	10,501	4,373,000	108,000	79,000	29,000
1970	9,362	3,355,000	112,000	52,000	60,000
1980	8,043	2,269,000	97,000	25,000	72,000
1990	7,291	1,883,906	91,039	10,837	80,202
1995	6,979	1,990,784	116,494	10,564	105,930
2000	6,923	2,013,084	109,404	6,862	102,542
2005	6,574	1,779,638	107,764	4,686	103,078
2007	6,288	1,682,412	107,682	4,097	103,585
2009	6,028	1,588,274	105,518	3,469	102,049
Secondary schools					
1960	2,392	880,000	44,000	33,000	11,000
1970	1,981	1,008,000	55,000	29,000	26,000
1980	1,516	837,000	49,000	14,000	35,000
1990	1,296	591,533	40,159	6,579	33,580
1995	1,238	614,571	46,599	6,193	40,406
2000	1,221	639,954	47,730	4,149	43,581
2005	1,225	640,952	52,389	3,304	49,085
2007	1,210	638,239	51,453	2,967	48,486
2009	1,220	604,257	52,097	2,858	49,239

Source: National Catholic Educational Association (2010).

Average SAT and ACT Scores by Group, 1987–2009

Group	1987	1990	1997	2000	2009[2]	Total test-takers, class of 2009
		Composite scores				
SAT Scores						
American Indian, Alaskan Native	934	934	963	963	1,448	8,974
Asian American, Pacific Islander	1,020	1,029	1,060	1,064	1,623	158,757
Black	839	847	860	860	1,276	187,136
Mexican-American	912	917	913	913	1,362	79,766
Puerto Rican	868	872	899	907	1,345	22,881
Other Hispanic	926	923	927	928	1,364	103,937
White	1,038	1,034	1,054	1,058	1,581	851,054
Men	1,035	1,026	1,040	1,040	1,523	711,368
Women	983	989	998	1,002	1,496	818,760
National average[1]	**1,008**	**1,001**	**1,017**	**1,019**	**1,509**	**1,530,128**
ACT Scores						
American Indian, Alaskan Native	17.5	18.0	19.0	19.0	18.9	15,773
Asian American, Pacific Islander	21.9	21.7	21.8	21.7	23.2	59,093
Black	16.6	17.0	17.1	17.0	16.9	196,149
Mexican-American	18.1	18.3	18.5	18.6	N.A.	N.A.
Other Hispanic	19.3	19.3	19.6	19.5	18.7	133,569
White	21.3	21.2	21.7	21.8	22.2	941,206
Men	21.2	21.0	21.2	21.2	21.3	668,165
Women	20.1	20.3	20.9	20.9	20.9	808,097
National average[1]	**20.6**	**20.6**	**21.0**	**21.0**	**21.1**	**1,480,469**

Notes: 1. Includes students of other ethnicities and students who did not identify their gender or their ethnicity. 2. Composite score includes the 2009 SAT writing section, new to the test in 2006. Scores before 2006 are not directly comparable. **Source:** The College Board, American College Testing Program (2010).

schools continues to rise. In 2007–08, total black enrollment was up to 10 percent, and Hispanic to 10 percent. The racial composition of private schools varied by type of program emphasis. For example, for Asian and Pacific Islander students, enrollment at Montessori schools was 13 percent, greater than Asian and Pacific Islander enrollment in other program types (2 to 7 percent).

Student–teacher ratios Students in private schools continue to get more teacher attention than do students in public schools. The average teacher in public secondary schools was responsible for 16.2 students, compared to 11.9 students for private school teachers in 2007–08.

▶ ENTRANCE EXAMINATION SCORES

SATs (Scholastic Assessment Tests) purportedly measure verbal and mathematical reasoning abilities. These tests are administered by the College Board, a nonprofit organization that provides tests and many other educational services for students, schools and colleges.

The test is scored on a range from 600 to 2400, with average scores usually around 1500. Male students consistently outscore females on the SAT, and whites and Asians typically score about 100 points higher than all other ethnic groups, and about 200 points higher than blacks. In response to criticisms of racial and gender bias, the College Board rewrote the SAT in 1994 to make it a test of aptitude, rather than of knowledge or test-taking techniques. The

Average Cost of 4-Year Colleges in Current and Constant Dollars, 1976–2010 (tuition and fees)

The cost of a college education continues to rise. Tuition and fees in 2009–2010 were nearly five times what they were as recently as 1985–86, and more than ten times what they were in 1976–77.

In constant dollars, the cost of college has more than doubled since 1985–86. That's a departure from the trend during the 1970s, when the real cost of college actually decreased several times, and never reached $8,000. Price increased 6.2 percent for a public 4-year out of state education between 2008–09 and 2009–2010 alone.

Student debt continues to rise astronomically, and a shrinking job market has left 10.6 percent of recent college graduates unemployed by the third quarter of 2009, the highest number on record. The federally-administered National Postsecondary Student Aid Study in 2009 reported that two-thirds of students graduation from 4-year colleges had student loan debt, and that the average amount these students ow has grown about 6 percent per year since 2003–04, reaching $23,200 for the graduating class of 2008.

Tuition and fees

Year	Constant dollars Private	Constant dollars Public	Year	Constant dollars Private	Constant dollars Public
1976–77	$7,940	$1,933	1999–00	$16,876	$3,656
1980–81	7,679	1,707	2000–01	17,050	3,662
1985–86	10,344	2,227	2001–02	17,825	3,844
1990–91	12,826	2,620	2002–03	18,779	4,155
1992–93	13,481	3,012	2003–04	19,710	4,694
1993–94	13,844	3,188	2004–05	20,082	5,132
1994–95	14,328	3,307	2005–06	21,235	5,491
1995–96	14,541	3,346	2006–07	22,218	5,836
1996–97	15,038	3,443	2007–08	23,712	6,185
1997–98	15,674	3,537	2008–09	25,143	6,585
1998–99	16,454	3,632	2009–10	26,273	7,020

Source: The College Board, *Trends in College Pricing* (2010).

Most Popular Majors Among Incoming Freshmen, 1990–2009

Major	Percentage 1990	2000	2009
Accounting	5.6%	2.3%	2.3%
Agriculture	0.8	0.7	0.7
Biological science, total	4.8	6.6	9.7
Business Administration	5.2	4.1	3.0
International Business	0.0	1.5	1.2
Communications (Radio, T.V.)	2.9	2.7	1.9
Data processing and computer programming	0.7	1.5	0.6
Education[1]	N.A.	N.A.	8.2
Elementary Education	5.1	5.6	3.6
Secondary Education	2.2	2.5	2.2
Engineering[1]	9.7	8.7	9.8
Electrical / Electronic	2.3	2.0	1.0
Mechanical	2.1	1.9	2.4
Finance	1.9	1.7	1.4
Fine Arts[1]	4.6	5.3	5.4
Art, fine and applied	2.1	2.5	3.2
Music	1.2	1.5	1.5
Health Professional	9.6	9.3	N.A.
Health Technology	0.7	0.4	0.5
Medical, dental, vet.	3.9	4.4	3.9
Nursing	2.4	2.1	4.7
Pharmacy	1.1	0.8	1.3
Humanities[1]	2.5	3.5	3.6
English	1.8	1.7	1.9
History	1.2	1.1	1.5
Language and Literature[2]	0.4	0.4	0.7
Journalism	1.6	1.7	1.5
Political Science (Government and International relations)	4.0	2.8	3.3
Therapy (Speech, occupational, and physical)	2.3	1.9	2.3

Note: 1. Includes specializations not listed here. 2. Excluding English. **Source:** Higher Education Research Institute, University of California, Los Angeles, *The American Freshman* (2010). Reprinted with permission.

Average Estimated Undergraduate Budgets, 2009–10

Type	Tuition and fees	Room and Board	Books and Supplies	Transportation	Other	Total
Public						
2-year, commuter	$2,544	$7,202	$1,098	$1,445	$1,996	$14,285
4-year, in-state	7,020	8,193	1,122	1,079	1,974	19,388
4-year, out-of-state	18,548	8,193	1,122	1,079	1,974	30,916
Private, not-for-profit						
4-year	$26,273	$9,363	$1,116	$849	$1,427	$39,028

Note: Data is for students living on campus, unless otherwise marked. **Source:** The College Board, *Trends in College Pricing* (2010).

new test had more open-ended questions, which the College Board claimed made the test uncoachable. But scores on the new test suffered from the same gender and ethnicity gaps as the old test.

ACTs are administered by the American College Testing Program, a nonprofit educational organization headquartered in Iowa City, Iowa. Its use is more popular than the SAT in states west of the Mississippi River. The ACT composite score is the average of four tests that measure academic abilities in English, mathematics, social studies and natural sciences. Although similar numbers of students

Educational Attainment by State, 2008

State	Completed high school[1]	Rank	Completed Bachelor's degree	Rank
Alabama	81.9%	46	22.0%	45
Alaska	91.6	2	27.3	22
Arizona	83.8	37	25.1	32
Arkansas	82.0	45	18.8	50
California	80.2	49	29.6	15
Colorado	88.9	17	35.6	3
Connecticut	88.6	19	35.6	3
Delaware	87.2	27	27.5	20
District of Columbia	85.8	32	48.2	1
Florida	85.2	34	25.8	28
Georgia	83.9	36	27.5	20
Hawaii	90.3	8	29.1	17
Idaho	87.9	23	24.0	39
Illinois	85.9	30	29.9	14
Indiana	86.2	29	22.9	42
Iowa	90.3	8	24.3	37
Kansas	89.5	16	29.6	15
Kentucky	81.3	47	19.7	48
Louisiana	81.2	48	20.3	47
Maine	89.7	12	25.4	30
Maryland	88.0	22	35.2	5
Massachusetts	88.7	18	38.1	2
Michigan	88.1	21	24.7	35
Minnesota	91.6	3	31.5	11
Mississippi	79.9	50	19.4	49
Missouri	86.5	28	25.0	34
Montana	90.9	4	27.1	23
Nebraska	90.1	11	27.1	23
Nevada	83.5	40	21.9	46
New Hampshire	90.9	4	33.3	8
New Jersey	87.4	26	34.4	6
Mew Mexico	82.4	43	24.7	35
New York	84.1	35	31.9	10
North Carolina	83.6	39	26.1	27
North Dakota	89.6	13	26.9	25
Ohio	87.6	24	24.1	38
Oklahoma	85.5	33	22.2	44
Oregon	88.6	19	28.1	19
Pennsylvania	87.5	25	26.3	26
Rhode Island	83.7	38	30.0	13
South Carolina	83.2	41	23.7	40
South Dakota	90.3	8	25.1	32
Tennessee	83.0	42	22.9	42
Texas	79.6	51	25.3	31
Utah	90.4	7	29.1	17
Vermont	90.6	6	32.1	9
Virginia	85.9	30	33.7	7
Washington	89.6	13	30.7	12
West Virginia	82.2	44	17.1	51
Wisconsin	89.6	13	25.7	29
Wyoming	91.7	1	23.6	41
United States	**85.0**	N.A.	**27.7**	N.A.

Notes: All data is for persons 25-years=old and older. 1. Includes equivalency. Source: U.S. Census Bureau, *American Community Survey*, 2008 (2009).

take each test, the ACT draws less criticism than the SAT, even though both tests evidence similar racial and gender biases.

▶ HIGHER EDUCATION

The figures on page 374 give a startling picture of just how the coming of age of the baby boom generation transformed U.S. higher education. In just one decade (the 1960s) the number of undergraduate degrees conferred more than doubled, while the number of doctorates actually tripled. These extraordinary changes were matched in kind by dramatic shifts in what students wanted to study: during the late 1960s, for example, the number of degrees in sociology and psychology jumped by more than 15,000 each in just a few years (1966–1970), while interest in business soared during the 1980s. That trend reversed in the 1990s, as the need for social workers and other health and human service professionals has expanded.

College enrollment
Between 1980 and 1992, college enrollment increased about 20 percent, from just over 12 million to a record 14.5 million. Since then, enrollment has increased only to approximately 19.6 million in 2009, even though the traditional college-age population has dropped. This is projected to rise to 21 million by 2018. Much of the growth in college enrollment was fueled by increases in older students, women and minorities on campus. Women have outnumbered men on college campuses since 1979, when there were just under 6 million of each in institutions of higher education. According to a Pew Research Center report cited in *The New York Times*, in 2008 almost 40 percent of the nation's 18- to 24-year-olds were enrolled in college, a record number. The rise, however, was driven almost entirely by a surge in students attending community colleges; 11.8 percent of young adults were enrolled in community college in 2008, up from 10.9 percent in 2007. Overall college enrollment varies by race and ethnicity. Nearly 41 percent of white 18- to 24-year-olds were enrolled in college in 2008, compared with about 32 percent of black young adults and 26 percent of Hispanics in that age group.

▶ EDUCATIONAL ATTAINMENT

In 2008, approximately 86.5 percent of all adults over age 25 had completed high school, and nearly 30 percent of American adults had a bachelor's degree or more. It's not surprising that those numbers were both much lower in 1940, when only 24 percent of adults had graduated from high school and college degrees belonged to fewer than 5 percent of the population. But even as recently as 1980, only 69 percent of adults over 25 had a high school diploma and only 17 percent had graduated from college.

The greatest proof of the importance of education is the correlation between years of schooling and higher salaries. In 2007, the median annual income for men with bachelor's degrees was $56,826 per year and $36,167 for women, compared with $31,337 for men and $18,162 for women with only high school diplomas. At the extreme ends of the spectrum, men with doctorates had a median income of $86,171 ($61,554 for women) while men who failed to graduate from high school measured at only $20,643 (women at $11,982).

Number Of Degrees Conferred in U.S. by Type, 1949–2015

Year	All degrees[1]	Associate's	Bachelor's	First professional	Master's	Doctorate
1949–50	496,661	N.A.	432,058[2]	[2]	58,183	6,420
1959–60	476,704	N.A.	392,440[2]	[2]	74,435	9,829
1969–70	1,065,098	206,023	792,317	34,578	208,291	29,912
1979–80	1,330,244	400,910	929,417	70,131	298,081	32,615
1989–90	1,485,004	455,102	1,051,344	70,988	324,301	38,371
1997–98	1,739,178	558,555	1,184,406	78,598	430,164	46,010
1999–2000	1,819,796	564,933	1,237,875	80,057	457,056	44,808
2002–03	1,987,982	632,912	1,348,503	80,810	512,645	46,024
2004–05	2,850,462	696,660	1,439,264	87,289	574,618	52,631
2006–07	3,007,493	728,114	1,524,092	90,064	604,607	60,616
2008–09	3,138,000	731,000	1,603,000	93,300	649,000	61,700
2010–2011[3]	N.A.	798,000	1,669,000	96,500	659,000	69,600
2012–2013[3]	N.A.	823,000	1,719,000	99,200	684,000	74,800
2014–2015[3]	N.A.	852,000	1,753,000	103,800	717,000	80,000

Notes: 1. Degrees are: medical doctor, law, dentistry, optometry, podiatry, pharmacy, theology, chiropractic, and veterinary medicine. 2. Prior to 1961, bachelor's and first professional degrees were listed together. 3. Projected. Source: U.S. Dept. of Education, National Center for Education Statistics, Digest of Education Statistics 2009 (2010).

Educational Attainment of the Population 25+ Years, 1940–2009

Year	Completed 4 years of high school or more			Completed 4 years of college or more		
	Both Sexes	Male	Female	Both Sexes	Male	Female
1940	24.5%	22.7%	26.3%	4.6%	5.5%	3.8%
1950	34.3	32.6	36.0	6.2	7.3	5.2
1959	43.7	42.2	45.2	8.1	10.3	6.0
1970	55.2	55.0	55.4	11.0	14.1	8.2
1980	68.6	69.1	68.1	17.0	20.8	13.5
1991	78.4	78.5	78.3	21.4	24.3	18.8
1995	81.7	81.7	81.6	23.0	26.0	20.2
2000	84.1	84.2	84.0	25.6	27.8	23.6
2005	85.2	84.8	85.4	27.7	29.4	26.1
2006	85.5	85.0	85.9	28.0	29.2	26.9
2007	87.0	84.9	89.1	29.6	26.3	33.0
2008	86.5	85.9	87.1	29.4	30.0	28.8
2009	86.7	86.2	87.1	29.5	30.1	29.1

Source: U.S. Census Bureau, Current Population Survey: Educational Attainment in the United States, 2009 (2010).

Educational Attainment of the Population, Ages 18 and Over, 2009 (in thousands)

Characteristic	Number of people	None	High school	Some college	Bachelor's degree
			Highest Level of Attainment		
All Persons	226,973	903	70,044	44,241	40,276
Sex:					
Male	110,026	417	34,710	20,954	19,205
Female	116,947	486	35,334	23,287	21,071
Race / Hispanic Origin:					
White	184,396	630	57,072	35,551	33,414
Black	26,794	85	9,421	5,958	3,111
Asian	10,258	147	1,953	1,428	3,060
Hispanic origin[1]	31,028	472	9,229	4,852	2,719
Age Groups:					
25 to 29 years	21,256	27	6,113	4,361	4,927
30 to 34 years	19,264	68	5,239	3,422	4,314
35 to 39 years	20,445	63	5,506	3,472	4,487
40 to 44 years	20,877	63	6,336	3,387	4,367
45 to 49 years	22,712	65	7,348	3,824	4,350
50 to 54 years	21,654	85	6,930	3,705	3,981
55 to 59 years	18,755	90	5,691	3,413	3,466
60 to 64 years	15,534	67	4,681	2,695	2,908
65 to 69 years	11,825	82	4,179	1,904	1,711
70 to 74 years	8,579	76	3,241	1,267	1,134
75 years or older	17,384	159	6,363	2,382	1,990

Note: 1. People of Hispanic origin may be of any race. Source: U.S. Census Bureau, Current Population Survey: Educational Attainment in the United States, 2009 (2010).

U.S. Energy

►ENERGY PRODUCTION AND CONSUMPTION

Energy is usually measured in millions or larger quantities of British thermal units (Btu). One Btu is approximately equal to the energy released in burning a wooden match. An engine burning eight gallons of gasoline releases one million (106) Btu. One quadrillion (1015) Btu is the equivalent of the energy released from an engine burning eight billion gallons of gasoline.

Total U.S. energy production was 72.99 quadrillion Btu in 2009. Natural gas and coal each accounted for more than one-quarter of domestic energy production. Fossil fuels, which also include crude oil, accounted for nearly 78 percent of all energy production, down from 95 percent as recently as 1970. Nuclear energy (11.4 percent) and renewable energy forms like solar energy and wind power (10.6 percent) have made up the difference.

U.S. energy consumption hit an all-time high of 101.6 quadrillion Btu in 2006 and has tapered slightly since. Total consumption in 2009 was 94.6 quadrillion Btu. Since the U.S. consumes more energy than it produces, it must import the difference.

Despite increasing prices for all forms of energy, American consumers continue to be lavish in their use, opting for convenience over energy efficiency at nearly every turn. However, total household consumption in 2005 (10.6 quadrillion Btu) was the same as it had been in 1978. This is largely explained by an increasing efficiency of home appliances that has kept the overall usage stable, even as the population grows. The average household in 1978 used 138 million Btu while in 2005 that number had shrunk to 95 million Btu.

Petroleum continues to be the energy of choice among U.S. consumers. It accounted for more than 37 percent of all U.S. energy consumption in 2009, compared to 25 percent for natural gas and 21 percent for coal. Consumption of nuclear energy has grown steadily from nearly zero in 1960 to 8.35 quadrillion Btu in 2009. Renewable energy consumption grew similarly from 1.66 quadrillion Btu in 1960 to 7.7 quadrillion Btu in 2009.

The relationship between total energy consumption and real gross domestic product (G.D.P.) is a primary indicator of the energy intensity of the economy. In 1949, the country used 17,340 Btu of energy per dollar of G.D.P. (measured in constant 2000 dollars). Since then, energy consumption has more than tripled, but increases in energy efficiency, conservation, and the expansion of the service sector of the economy have propelled G.D.P. sixfold. As a result, energy consumption in 2009 totaled only 7,280 Btu per dollar of G.D.P., or approximately 40 percent of what it was in 1949. In other words, the country is using much more energy, but getting 2.5 times as much bang for its buck.

A second indicator is per capita consumption, which rose from 214 million Btu per capita in 1949 to a record 360 million Btu in 1978. Efforts at conservation persuaded people to decrease their consumption to 312 million Btu in 1983, but per capita use has rebounded since then, to 327 million Btu in 2008, though falling sharply to 308 million Btu in the recession of 2009. Alaska (1.06 billion Btu) and Wyoming (949 million Btu) were the biggest per capita consumers of energy in 2006. Rhode Island (206.6 million Btu) and New York (209.2 million Btu) used the least energy per capita in 2009.

U.S. Energy Overview, 1960–2009

	(Quadrillion Btu)						
Activity and energy source	1960	1970	1980	1990	2000	2008	2009
Production							
Fossil Fuels[2]	39.869	59.186	59.008	58.560	57.366	57.613	56.860
Nuclear Electric Power	.006	.239	2.739	6.104	7.862	8.427	8.349
Renewable Energy[4]	2.929	4.076	5.485	6.208	6.262	7.381	7.761
Total	**42.804**	**63.501**	**67.232**	**70.872**	**71.490**	**73.421**	**72.970**
Trade							
Petroleum Imports[4]	3.999	7.470	14.658	17.117	24.531	27.644	25.160
Total Imports[5]	**4.188**	**8.342**	**15.796**	**18.817**	**28.973**	**32.952**	**2.071**
Coal Exports	1.023	1.936	2.421	2.772	1.528	2.071	1.515
Total Exports[6]	**1.477**	**2.632**	**3.695**	**4.752**	**4.006**	**7.016**	**6.932**
Consumption							
Fossil Fuels[2]	42.137	63.522	69.826	72.333	84.733	83.496	78.368
Nuclear Electric Power	.006	.239	2.739	6.104	7.862	8.427	8.349
Renewable Energy[3]	2.929	4.076	5.485	6.208	6.264	7.366	7.744
Total[7]	**45.087**	**67.844**	**78.122**	**84.654**	**98.975**	**99.402**	**94.578**

Notes: 1. Preliminary. 2. Coal, natural gas (dry), crude oil, and natural gas plant liquids. 3. Includes hydroelectric, geothermal, solar, wind, wood, waste and biofuels. 4. Crude oil and petroleum imports. 5. Also includes imports into the Strategic Petroleum Reserve. 5. Also includes natural gas, coal, coal coke, fuel ethanol, and electricity. 6. Also includes natural gas, petroleum, coal coke, and electricity. 7. Also includes electricity net imports. Source: U.S. Department of Energy, *Annual Energy Review 2009* (2010).

▶ FOSSIL FUELS

Petroleum

Since 1958 the United States has consumed more energy than it produces; the difference has been met with energy imports. Net imports of energy (primarily petroleum) grew rapidly through 1973, when they totaled 13 quadrillion Btu, or 20 percent of consumption.

Despite the Arab oil embargo of 1973–74 and increases in the price of crude oil, petroleum net imports continued to grow, reaching a peak of nearly 19 quadrillion Btu in 1977. That year, U.S. dependence on petroleum net imports peaked at 47 percent of consumption. In 1985, petroleum net imports dropped to 9 quadrillion Btu and U.S.

dependence on foreign oil fell to 27 percent of consumption, its lowest level since 1972.

But a drop in the worldwide price of oil ($12.52 per barrel in 1998, its lowest level in more than two decades) inhibited domestic production and caused U.S. reliance on imports to spring back. Oil prices spiked to $28.26 per barrel in 2000, retreated to $22.95 in 2001, and rebounded to $28.50 in 2003. On August 30, 2005, after Hurricane Katrina hit the Gulf coast, the price of oil skyrocketed to an all-time high of $70.85 a barrel, and continued to rise thereafter, crossing the $100.00 mark in January 2008 and holding near $134.00 a barrel through summer 2008 before falling sharply in the wake of the global financial upheaval late that year. By late 2009, the price per barrel had stabilized at $56.40 per barrel amid the global recession that continued to impact the worldwide oil market. Saudi Arabia, Venezuela, Canada and Mexico are the U.S.'s primary suppliers of foreign oil; each exports more than 1.3 million barrels of oil per day to the U.S.

In June 2006, oil from Canada arrived in Cushing, Okla., a key hub for distribution in the U.S. In 2005, Canada provided 16.1 percent of U.S. oil imports, but this figure is bound to increase as six new pipelines are scheduled to open by 2011, helping to replace oil from less reliable sources.

Natural gas

Once considered a useless byproduct of oil well drilling (it was simply burned off at the site), natural gas is today the primary source of energy for space heating in 52 million U.S. households. U.S. natural gas trade was limited to the border countries of Mexico and Canada until shipping natural gas in liquefied form emerged as an alternative to pipelines. In 1969, the first shipments of liquefied natural gas (LNG) were sent to Japan, and U.S. imports from Algeria began the following year. In 2009, U.S. net imports of natural gas by all routes totaled 3.75 quadrillion Btu (almost all of it from Canada).

U.S. Energy Consumption, Total and Per Capita, 1950–2009

Year	Total energy consumption (billion Btu)	Per capita consumption (billion Btu)
1950	34,616,000	.229
1955	40,208,000	.244
1960	45,087,000	.252
1965	54,017,000	.279
1970	67,844,000	.334
1975	71,999,000	.334
1980	78,122,000	.346
1985	76,493,000	.322
1990	84,654,000	.340
1995	91,174,000	.343
2000	98,975,000	.351
2005	100,485,000	.340
2007	101,527,000	.337
2008	99,402,000	.327
2009	94,578,000	.308

Note: 1. Preliminary. **Source:** U.S. Department of Energy, *Annual Energy Review 2009* (2010).

U.S. Fuel Consumption by Type and End-Use Sector, 1950–2009 (quadrillion Btu)

Year	Residential	Commercial	Industrial	Transportation	Electric utilities	Total
Petroleum						
1950	1.340	0.862	3.951	6.690	0.472	**13.315**
1960	2.265	1.228	5.747	10.126	0.553	**19.919**
1970	2.755	1.551	7.787	15.310	2.117	**29.520**
1980	1.748	1.287	9.525	19.008	2.634	**34.202**
1990	1.407	0.953	8.278	21.625	1.289	**33.553**
2000	1.563	0.756	9.217	25.682	1.144	**38.264**
2009[1]	1.162	0.600	7.775	25.342	0.390	**35.269**
Natural Gas						
1950	1.240	0.401	3.546	0.130	0.651	**5.968**
1960	3.212	1.056	5.973	0.359	1.785	**12.385**
1970	4.987	2.473	9.536	0.745	4.054	**21.795**
1980	4.825	2.651	8.333	0.650	3.778	**20.235**
1990	4.491	2.682	8.451	0.680	3.309	**19.603**
2000	5.105	3.252	9.500	0.672	5.293	**23.824**
2009[1]	4.874	3.187	7.584	0.687	7.039	**23.371**
Coal						
1950	1.261	1.542	5.781	1.564	2.199	**12.347**
1960	0.585	0.407	4.543	0.075	4.228	**9.838**
1970	0.209	0.165	4.656	0.007	7.227	**12.265**
1980	0.031	0.115	3.155	(2)	12.123	**15.423**
1990	0.031	0.124	2.756	(2)	16.261	**19.173**
2000	0.011	0.092	2.256	(2)	20.220	**22.580**
2009[1]	0.007	0.061	1.396	(2)	18.296	**19.760**

Notes: 1. Preliminary. 2. Small quantities consumed by transportation sector are included in industrial column. **Source:** U.S. Department of Energy, *Annual Energy Review 2009* (2010).

Coal

Since World War II coal has been the major U.S. energy export. Throughout most of the 1960's and 1970's, U.S. exports of coal increased, peaking at 112 million short tons in 1981. Exports have dropped steadily since 1991, when they totaled 109 million short tons; in 2006, exports were 49.6 million short tons, less than half the 1991 total. Canada is the largest market for U.S. coal, importing 23 million tons in 2006. Japan, which imported more than 25.8 million short tons as recently as 1982, imported only 1.7 million short tons from the U.S. in 2006.

Electric utilities are the primary domestic consumers of coal. Their consumption grew from 17 percent of the total in 1949 to 94 percent in 2009. Over the same period, consumption in all other sectors declined, most dramatically in the transportation sector, due primarily to railroads switching from coal to petroleum-driven trains. Transportation sector consumption, which topped 1.56 quadrillion Btu in 1950, has totaled fewer than 5 billion Btu every year since 1975. Consumption by the residential and commercial sector has also declined steadily, from a high of 1.26 quadrillion Btu in 1950 to 7 billion Btu in 2009.

▶THE STRATEGIC PETROLEUM RESERVE

In an attempt to minimize the wild fluctuations in prices caused by the Arab oil embargoes of the 1970's, the U.S. in 1977 created the Strategic Petroleum Reserve, which permitted the storage of 580 million barrels of oil. The reserve proved useful in preventing additional oil price hikes during the Iraqi invasion of Kuwait in 1990.

The reserve can also be used as an emergency supply of oil in case of a disaster such as Hurricane Katrina (2005), which shut down production and refining in the Gulf of Mexico for weeks. In 1985, the reserve held enough oil to provide a normal level of petroleum to the U.S. for 115 days in the absence of any other petroleum imports. The reserve, however, had dwindled to 75 days of oil by 2009.

▶ELECTRICITY

Net generation of electricity by electric utilities approached 3.95 trillion megawatthours (kWh) in 2009. Coal continued to fuel nearly half the generation, accounting for 1.76 trillion MWh, while natural gas contributed 920 billion MWh. Petroleum-fired generation was responsible for 38.8 billion MWh, while nuclear-based generation produced 798.7 billion MWh in 2009. Hydroelectric generation rebounded from a decade low of 217 billion MWh in 2001 to 272 billion MWh in 2009.

The weighted average real price (based on 2000 dollars) of electricity to all sectors in 2009 was 9.01 cents per kWh, roughly 10 percent below the price in 1982 (9.7 cents per kWh). Although prices of other major energy sources increased significantly during the same period, electricity remained by far the most expensive source of energy on a Btu basis.

▶NUCLEAR POWER

The number of nuclear power plants in operation in the U.S. skyrocketed from 18 in 1970 to 112 in 1990, and net nuclear generation of electricity jumped from 23.9 billion Btu in 1970 to nearly 8.5 trillion Btu in 2008. Since 1990, three new plants have opened and 10 have closed, but generation nonetheless increased to 787 billion kWh. More than three-quarters of the 104 nuclear power plants in the U.S. are located east of the Mississippi River. The U.S. has the highest number of reactors of any country in the world, but far fewer (104) than the 236 that were in the stages of planning, construction or operation as recently as 1975.

Several factors have contributed to the decline in the number of planned nuclear units, but nuclear plant operators have been able to increase their generation of electricity steadily without increasing the number of reactors. Nuclear plants ran at 91.9 percent of capacity in 2008, up from 66.0 percent in 1990 and 56.3 percent in 1980.

In 2007, an energy bill passed through the Senate at the urging of the nuclear power industry could make builders of new nuclear plants eligible for tens of billions of dollars in government loans. In 2009, the Nuclear Regulatory Commission awarded nearly $20 million in grants to boost proliferation of nuclear energy and education.

A setback for the industry has been the increased public opposition to nuclear power plants because of concerns about their safety and the disposal of spent nuclear fuel. These were heightened in the wake of the 1979 accident at Three Mile Island near Harrisburg, Penn., and the far more devastating one at Chernobyl, Ukraine in 1986.

U.S. Petroleum Prices Per Gallon 1995–2009

| Year | Unleaded Gasoline | | | Consumer Grade | | |
	Regular	Midgrade	Premium	Heating Oil	Diesel Fuel	Propane
1995	$0.72	$0.80	$0.89	$0.87	$0.64	$0.77
1997	0.80	0.88	0.96	0.98	0.71	0.88
1998	0.62	0.71	0.79	0.85	0.56	0.77
1999	0.73	0.81	0.88	0.88	0.65	0.78
2000	1.06	1.15	1.22	1.31	1.01	1.05
2001	1.00	1.09	1.15	1.25	0.91	1.09
2002	0.92	1.00	1.08	1.13	0.84	0.96
2003	1.11	1.20	1.28	1.36	1.01	1.15
2004	1.40	1.48	1.58	1.55	1.32	1.31
2005	1.81	1.88	1.99	2.05	1.89	1.53
2006	2.10	2.18	2.30	2.09	2.17	1.73
2007	2.31	2.41	2.53	2.26	2.35	1.89
2008	2.75	2.85	2.96	3.14	3.80	1.89
2009[1]	1.86	2.00	2.12	1.84	1.83	1.22

Note: Unadjusted prices. Prices reflect price paid at time of transaction. 1. Preliminary. Source: U.S. Department of Energy, Annual Energy Review 2009 (2010).

▶ ENERGY TRADING

Deregulation in the energy industry has led in the past decade to the the development of energy trading companies, large corporations that buy and sell power much like any other commodity. Because of an accounting procedure known as "mark-to-market," energy trading can produce huge paper profits overnight, even though it may take as much as 20 years for the revenues from these trades to appear, and fattens the company's debt load in the meantime. This arcane structure allowed energy traders at Enron to create fictitious trades that boosted profits even more (and triggered performance bonuses for top executives) before they were found out in the summer of 2002.

Primary Energy Production by Source, 1950–2009 (Billion Btu)

Year	Coal	Natural Gas (Dry)	Crude Oil	NGPL	Nuclear electric	Hydro-electric	Geo-thermal	Solar	Wind	Biomass	Total
1950	14,060	6,233	11,447	823	(1)	1,415	N.A.	N.A.	N.A.	1,549	35,540
1955	12,370	9,345	14,410	1,240	(1)	1,360	N.A.	N.A.	N.A.	1,424	40,148
1960	10,817	12,656	14,935	1,461	6	1,608	1	N.A.	N.A.	1,320	42,804
1965	13,055	15,775	16,521	1,883	43	2,059	4	N.A.	N.A.	1,335	50,676
1970	14,607	21,666	20,401	2,512	239	2,634	11	N.A.	N.A.	1,431	63,501
1975	14,989	19,640	17,729	2,374	1,900	3,155	70	N.A.	N.A.	1,499	61,357
1980	18,598	19,908	18,249	2,254	2,739	2,900	110	N.A.	N.A.	2,476	67,232
1985	19,325	16,980	18,992	2,241	4,076	2,970	198	(1)	(1)	3,018	67,801
1990	22,488	18,326	15,571	2,175	6,104	3,046	336	60	29	2,737	70,782
1995	22,130	19,082	13,887	2,442	7,075	3,205	294	70	33	3,103	71,320
2000	22,735	19,662	12,358	2,611	7,862	2,811	317	66	57	3,010	71,490
2005	23,185	18,574	10,963	2,334	8,160	2,703	343	66	178	3,120	69,626
2007	23,493	19,623	10,721	2,409	8,458	2,446	349	81	341	3,583	71,504
2008	23,851	20,834	10,509	2,419	8,427	2,511	360	97	546	3,867	73,421
2009[2]	21,578	21,500	11,241	2,541	8,349	2,682	373	109	697	3,900	72,970

Notes: 1. Less than 0.5 billion Btu. 2. Preliminary estimates. **Source:** U.S. Dept. of Energy, *Annual Energy Review 2009* (2010).

U.S. Commercial Nuclear Plants, 2008

There are 104 operable nuclear reactors in 31 states. The following table lists the states, with the total number of reactors in each, the names of the individual units and their location.

Alabama = 5
Browns Ferry 1, 2 & 3, Decatur
Joseph M. Farley 1 & 2, Dothan
Arizona = 3
Palo Verde 1, 2 & 3, Wintersburg
Arkansas = 2
Arkansas Nuclear 1 & 2, Russellville
California = 4
Diablo Canyon 1 & 2, Avila Beach
San Onofre 2 & 3, San Clemente
Connecticticut = 2
Millstone 2 & 3, Waterford
Florida = 5
Crystal River 3, Red Level
St. Lucie 1 & 2, Ft. Pierce
Turkey Point 3 & 4, Florida City
Georgia = 4
Hatch 1 & 2, Baxley
Vogtle 1 & 2, Waynesboro
Illinois = 11
Braidwood 1 & 2, Braidwood
Byron 1 & 2, Rockfort
Clinton 1, Clinton
Dresden 2 & 3, Morris
La Salle 1 & 2, Seneca
Quad Cities 1 & 2, Cordova
Iowa = 1
Duane Arnold, Cedar Rapids
Kansas = 1
Wolf Creek, Burlington
Louisiana = 2
River Bend 1, St. Francisville
Waterford 3, Taft

Maryland = 2
Calvert Cliffs 1 & 2, Lusby
Massachusetts = 1
Pilgrim 1, Plymouth
Michigan = 3
Donald C. Cook 1 & 2, Benton Harbor
Palisades, South Haven
Minnesota = 3
Monticello, Monticello
Prairie Island 1 & 2, Red Wing
Mississippi = 1
Grand Gulf 1, Port Gibson
Missouri = 1
Callaway 1, Fulton
Nebraska = 2
Cooper, Brownville
Fort Calhoun 1, Fort Calhoun
New Hampshire = 1
Seabrook 1, Seabrook
New Jersey = 4
Hope Creek 1, Hope Creek
Oyster Creek 1, Forked River
Salem 1 & 2, Wilmington
New York = 6
Indian Point 2 & 3, Buchanan
Fitzpatrick 1, Oswego
Nine Mile Point 1 & 2, Oswego
Robert E. Ginna, Rochester
North Carolina = 5
Brunswick 1 & 2, Southport
McGuire 1 & 2, Cowens Ford Dam
Shearon Harris 1, New Hill

Ohio = 3
Davis-Besse 1, Oak Harbor
Fermi 2, Toledo
Perry 1, North Perry
Pennsylvania = 9
Beaver Valley 1 & 2, McCandless
Limerick 1 & 2, Pottstown
Peach Bottom 2 & 3, Lancaster
Susquehanna 1 & 2, Berwick
Three Mile Island 1, Middletown
South Carolina = 7
Catawba 1 & 2, Rock Hill
H.B. Robinson 2, Hartsville
Oconee 1, 2 & 3, Seneca
Summer 1, Jenkinsville
Tennessee = 3
Sequoyah 1 & 2, Daisy
Watts Bar 1, Spring City
Texas = 4
Comanche Peak 1&2, Glen Rose
South Texas 1 & 2, Bay City
Vermont = 1
Vermont Yankee 1, Vernon
Virginia = 4
North Anna 1 & 2, Mineral
Surry 1 & 2, Surry
Washington = 1
Columbia Generative Station, Richland
Wisconsin = 3
Kewaunee, Carlton
Point Beach 1 & 2, Two Creeks

Note: As of Sept. 1, 2010. **Source:** U.S. Nuclear Regulatory Commission, www.nrc.gov

U.S. Health and Medicine

Milestones in the History of Medicine

B.C.
c. 2700   Chinese emperor Shen Nung develops principles of herbal medicine and acupuncture.
c. 1700   The Code of Hammurabi, king of Babylon, comprises regulations concerning physicians, including what they may treat and what their fees should be.
c. 1500   The Ebers Papyrus describes many remedies used in Ancient Egypt to treat dental ailments.
c. 400   Hippocrates of Cos (Greek: c. 460–c. 377), teacher and medical practitioner known as Father of Medicine, writes Hippocratic Oath, which sets ethical standards still followed by physicians throughout the world.
c. 300   Herophilus (Greek: c. 355–280) pioneers dissection of human body and founds first school of anatomy.

A.D.
c. 20   Aulus Cornelius Celsus (Roman: first cent.) writes first-known medical textbook.
c. 100   Romans develop a public medical service and appoint physicians to provide medical help to poor.
c. 180   Galen (Greek: c. 130–c. 201) writes *Methodus Medando*, which summarizes medical knowledge of ancient times. Galen's views on human physiology and disease would influence medical thought for more than 1,500 years.
c. 450   Susruta (Indian) notes relationship of malaria to mosquitoes and of bubonic plague to rats.
c. 900   Rhazes (Persian: c. 865–923/35) is first to describe smallpox and establish criteria for diagnosing and treating it.
1030   Ibn Sina (Avicenna; Persian: 980–1037) publishes *Canon of Medicine*, which becomes leading medical encyclopedia for centuries.
c. 1270–80   Spectacles are introduced by Venetian glassmakers.
1403   Venice imposes world's first quarantine of infected areas as safeguard against Black Death (bubonic plague).
1543   Andreas Vesalius (Flemish: 1514–64) publishes first accurate anatomy text and establishes foundations of modern anatomy.
1597   Gaspare Tagliacozzi (Italian) publishes first textbook of plastic surgery and revives operation of rhinoplasty (nose surgery).
1601   Sir James Lancaster (English: c. 1554–1618) writes that lemon juice helps prevent scurvy.
1628   William Harvey (English: 1578–1657) describes functions of the heart and how blood circulates throughout the body.
1658   Jan Swammerdam (Dutch: 1637–80) discerns red blood cells.
1670   Thomas Willis (English: 1621–75) rediscovers connection between sugar in urine and diabetes (known in antiquity by Greeks, Chinese, and Indians).
1751   Pennsylvania Hospital, first general hospital in U.S., founded in Philadelphia by Quakers.
1761   Leopold Auenbrugger von Auenbrugg (Australian: 1722–1809) discovers that fluid in chest cavity and other health problems can be detected by tapping gently on the chest.
Giovanni B. Morgagni (Italian: 1682–1771) establishes modern pathological anatomy with publication of *On the Seats and Causes of Disease*.

1796   Edward Jenner (English: 1749–1823) develops smallpox vaccine from cowpox serum.
1816   René T.H. Laënnec (French: 1781–1826) invents stethoscope and introduces auscultation (monitoring sounds made by internal organs).
1818   James Blundell (English: 1791–1878) performs first successful human blood transfusion.
1831   Samuel Guthrie (American: 1782–1848) discovers chloroform.
1839   Horace Hayden (American: 1769–1844) and Chapin Harris (1806–60) found world's first dental school, Baltimore College of Dental Surgery.
1842   Crawford Long (American: 1815–78) removes tumor from patient inhaling ether—first known operation under general anesthesia; publishes his findings in 1849, three years after William Morton (American: 1819–68) demonstrates effectiveness of ether as anesthetic.
1850   Hermann Helmholtz (German: 1821–94) invents ophthalmoscope, instrument used to examine interior of the eye.
1855   Manuel Garcia (Spanish: 1805–1906) invents modern laryngoscope, used to inspect the throat, especially the larynx and vocal cords.
1863   International Red Cross established at Geneva, Switzerland.
1865   Joseph Lister (English: 1827–1912) introduces use of disinfectants to reduce infection.
Louis Pasteur (French: 1822–95) shows that spoilage of wine can be prevented by partial heat-sterilization; this process, called pasteurization, soon applied to milk and other foods.
1866   Sir Thomas C. Allbutt (English: 1836–1925) invents clinical thermometer.
1868   Carl Wunderlich (German: 1815–77) establishes that fever is a symptom, not a disease, and introduces use of thermometer for taking body temperature.
1879   Wilhelm Wundt (German: 1832–1920) founds the first laboratory for psychology.
1881   Pasteur produces vaccine that successfully prevents anthrax.
1890   Emil von Behring (German: 1854–1917) and Shibasaburo Kitasato (Japanese: 1852–1931) independently discover antitoxins.
1892   Dmitri Ivanovski (Russian: 1864–1920) discovers filterable viruses (viruses tiny enough to pass through fine filters previously believed to trap all living organisms).
1893   Felix Hoffmann (German: 1868–1946) develops a process for production of acetylsalicylic acid, the form of aspirin used today.
1895   Wilhelm Röntgen (German: 1845–1923) discovers X rays.
1900   Sigmund Freud (Austrian: 1856–1939), founder of psychoanalysis, publishes *The Interpretations of Dreams*.
Karl Landsteiner (Austrian-American: 1868–1943) discovers three blood groups, later named A, B, and O; fourth group, to be named AB, discovered in 1902.
Walter Reed (American: 1851–1902) establishes that yellow fever virus is transmitted by mosquitoes.
1901   Jokichi Takamine (Japanese-American: 1854–1922) isolates adrenaline, first hormone to be isolated.

1902 Eugene Opie (American: 1873–1971) establishes that diabetes results from destruction of specific portions of pancreatic tissue.

1905 Albert Einhorn (Austrian: 1856–1917) synthesizes procaine (novocaine), which becomes the most widely used dental anesthetic.

1906 August von Wassermann (German: 1866–1925) develops blood test for syphilis.

1910 Marie Curie (French: 1867–1934) isolates pure radium metal, which came to be used to treat cancer.

1913 Béla Schick (Hungarian-American: 1877–1967) perfects test for determining susceptibility to diphtheria.

1915 Death certificates come into general use in U.S.

Margaret Sanger (American: 1883–1966) founds the National Birth Control League, which in 1942 becomes Planned Parenthood.

1918 Francis Benedict (American: 1870–1957) devises basal metabolism test for measuring rate at which metabolism (total of all chemical reactions) occurs in the body.

1921 Sir Frederick G. Banting (Canadian: 1891–1941) and Charles H. Best (1899–1978) extract insulin from the pancreas.

1928 Sir Alexander Fleming (Scottish: 1881–1955) discovers penicillin, a substance in the mold *Penicillium notatum* that kills certain bacteria.

1929 Hans Berger (German: 1873–1941) publishes his results of the first electroencephalograms (EEGs) of humans.

1935 Gerhard Domagk (German: 1895–1964) announces discovery of Prontosil (sulfonamide-crysoidin), the first useful sulfa drug.

1937 First blood bank is established, at Cook County Hospital in Chicago.

Alton Ochsner (American: 1896–1981) and Michael De Bakey (1908–2008) suggest that cigarette smoking is cause of lung cancer.

1943 Willem Kolff (Dutch-American: 1911–2009) develops first kidney dialysis machine.

1944 Canadians Oswald Avery (1877–1955), Colin MacLeod (1909–72), and Maclyn McCarty (1911–2005) prove that DNA (deoxyribonucleic acid) is blueprint of heredity that determines how an organism develops.

First eye bank founded in New York.

Albert Schatz (American: 1921–2005) and Selman Waksman (American: 1888–1973) isolate streptomycin, an antibiotic effective against bacterium that causes tuberculosis.

1945 Alfred Blalock (American: 1899–1964) introduces first operation to enable blue, or cyanotic, babies to survive (cyanosis, caused by poor circulatory flow or other problems, results in diminished oxygen in blood, causing bluish discoloration of the skin).

1947 Chloromycetin, developed by Parke-Davis researchers, is used to treat typhus patients; first use of "broadspectrum" antibiotic.

1948 Philip S. Hench (American: 1896–1965) and Edward C. Kendall (1886–1972) synthesize cortisone and use it to treat arthritis victims.

1952 Jonas Salk (American: 1914–95) develops first vaccine against polio.

1953 John H. Gibbon, Jr. (American: 1903–73) uses heart-lung machine he invented in successful open-heart operation.

1954 Surgeons led by Joseph Murray (American: 1919–) perform first successful kidney transplant.

1957 Alick Isaacs (Scottish: 1921–67) and Jean Lindenmann (Swiss) discover interferon, a protein that interferes with viral reproduction.

1958 Wilson Greatbatch (American: 1919–) invents the implantable artificial pacemaker.

1961 Scientists at Bell Laboratories (Americans) announce first continuously operating laser, a tool having many surgical uses.

1963 Thomas Starzl (American: 1926–) performs first human liver transplant operation.

1964 James Hardy (American: 1918–2003) performs first human lung transplant.

1965 Medicare and Medicaid are established, guaranteeing medical insurance coverage for the aged and the poor.

1966 Americans Paul Parkman (1932–) and Harry Meyer (1928–2001) develop vaccine for rubella (German measles).

Insulin synthesized independently by U.S. and Chinese scientists—first hormone to be synthesized.

1967 Christiaan Barnard (South African: 1922–2001) performs world's first heart transplant.

Rene Favaloro (Argentinian: 1923–2000) performs first successful coronary bypass operation.

First modern hospice founded in London.

1969 Denton Cooley (American: 1920–) implants first temporary artificial heart in human being.

1972 Computerized axial tomography (CAT scan) is introduced in Great Britain.

1977 Scientists at Genentech Corporation (Americans) induce bacteria to make human-brain hormone somatostatin—first human chemical produced by recombinant-DNA techniques.

The first known human cases of cyclospora infection are diagnosed.

1978 First "test tube baby" (person conceived outside human body) is born, in England.

1981 Scientists identify acquired immune deficiency syndrome (AIDS) for the first time.

Surgeons at University of California at San Francisco perform first successful operation on a fetus.

1982 A team led by William DeVries (American: 1943–) performs first complete replacement of human heart with artificial heart.

1983 Luc Montagnier (French: 1932–) discovers virus believed to cause AIDS.

1984 First baby produced from frozen embryo is born, in Melbourne, Australia.

1990 R. Michael Blaese, W. French Anderson, and Kenneth W. Culver (Americans) develop procedure to infuse genetically engineered blood cells for treatment of immune system disorder—first gene therapy used in a human.

1993 The U.S. Environmental Protection Agency concludes that environmental tobacco smoke ("secondhand smoke") is a lung carcinogen and causes respiratory problems for infants and young children.

1996 British scientists announce the possibility that a new form of Creutzfeldt-Jakob disease is transmitted to humans through the meat of cattle infected with bovine spongiform encephalopathy ("mad cow disease").

1999 First successful brain surgery on a fetus achieved at Vanderbilt University Medical Center.

2000 Scientists announce they have deciphered most of the human genetic code; by 2003, more than 99 percent is decoded.

2001 U.S. surgeons implant the first self-contained artificial heart.

2006 Gardasil, the first vaccine to target the viruses responsible for most cervical cancers, is approved for sale.

2009 W.H.O. declares that a global pandemic of novel influenza A (HINI) is underway.

2010 Congress passes health care reform bill that will expand health insurance coverage to 32 million currently uninsured Americans.

W.H.O. declares that H1N1 epidemic has ended.

►QUALITY OF HEALTH

Americans are living longer, healthier lives, yet many of the health problems they face could be avoided or alleviated with appropriate prevention or treatment. With this in mind, government health officials have three broad goals: increasing the span of healthy life, reducing health disparities, and achieving access to preventive services for everyone.

Health quality varies significantly by economic level, age group, and geographic region. Among persistent disparities are disease, injury, disability and mortality rates for various racial and ethnic groups. These disparities are especially stark between white and black Americans. For example:

- A white baby can expect to live 78.4 years; a black baby, 73.6 years (2007 data).
- The prevalence of obesity is 51 percent higher among blacks than among whites (2006–08).
- Blacks have almost twice the risk of first strokes than whites (2006).
- The age-adjusted death rate for prostate cancer for black men is more than two times that for white men (2009).
- The prevalence of AIDS cases per 100,000 population is 45.9 among blacks, 6.1 among whites (2007).
- Gonorrhea cases per 100,000 population is 499.4 among blacks, 28.1 among whites (2007).
- The infant mortality rate is 2.4 times greater for black babies than whites (2006).
- Pregnancy-related deaths per 100,000 live births for black women are 3.5 times higher than for white women (2006).
- The average risk of death for blacks is about 30 percent higher than for whites (2007).
- Black adults aged 50 and older have rates of physical limitations similar to white adults a decade older (2001–07).

Evidence indicates that race, discrimination, and economic and cultural factors influence the care that people receive and, consequently, their health. However, other factors, such as gender and genetics, also influence health outcomes.

►HEALTH CARE EXPENDITURES

National health care spending reached $2.3 trillion in 2008. It equaled 16.2 percent of gross domestic product (G.D.P.)—the largest share of G.D.P. on record and leading the rest of the industrialized world by a wide margin. The upward trend is predicted to continue: a 2009 report from the Centers for Medicare & Medicaid Services projected that by 2019 healthcare spending will reach $4.5 trillion and 19.3 percent of G.D.P.

The 2008 health expenditures amounted to $7,681 per person, up from $2,737 in 1990—and only $143 in 1960—yet many Americans are missing out. According to the 2005 National Health Interview Survey, about 7 percent of persons (21.7 million) delayed medical care during the year prior to the survey because of worry about costs; another 5 percent (15.2 million) did not receive needed care because they could not afford it. Persons whose health was assessed as fair or poor were four to five times as likely as persons whose health was assessed as excellent or very good to delay or not receive needed medical care because of costs.

A variety of factors contribute to the high costs of health care, including:

1. Use of sophisticated, expensive medical equipment.

2. New, higher-priced prescription drugs and increased consumer demand induced by advertising.

3. Excessive and arguably unnecessary procedures, including duplication of tests and use of technologies that yield similar results.

4. Increasing elderly population, which use medical care more intensely than younger people.

5. Increasing number of accidents and other incidents that require emergency medical services.

6. Labor intensiveness and earnings growth for health care professionals and executives.

7. Malpractice insurance.

8. Administrative waste.

9. Fraud.

National Expenditures for Health Care, 1960–2008

Category	1960	1970	1980	1990	1997	2000	2005	2008
Total expenditures (billions)	$27.5	$74.9	$253.4	$714.0	$1,125.1	$1,352.9	$1,982.5	$2,338.7
Private[1]	20.7	46.8	147.0	427.4	613.5	756.5	1,082.6	1,232.0
Public	6.8	28.1	106.4	286.8	511.6	596.4	899.8	1,106.7
Federal	2.9	17.7	71.6	193.9	365.3	417.6	641.4	816.9
State and local	3.9	10.4	34.8	92.8	146.3	178.8	258.4	289.8
Total expenditures per capita	$148	$356	$1,100	$2,8143	$4,103	$4,789	$6,701	$7,681
Private[1]	111	222	638	1,684	2,237	2,678	3,660	4,046
Public	36	134	462	1,130	1,866	2,111	3,041	3,635
Federal	15	84	311	764	1,332	1,478	2,168	3,683
State and local	21	49	151	366	533	633	873	952
Total expenditures	100.0%	100.0%	100.0%	100.0%	100.0%	100.0%	100.0%	100.0%
Private[1]	75.3	62.4	58.0	59.8	54.5	55.9	54.6	52.7
Public	24.7	37.6	42.0	40.2	45.5	44.1	45.4	47.3
Federal	10.4	23.7	28.2	27.2	32.5	30.9	32.4	34.9
State and local	14.3	13.9	13.7	13.0	13.0	13.2	13.0	12.4
Health care expenditures as percent of G.D.P.	5.2%	7.2%	9.1%	12.3%	13.5%	13.6%	15.7%	16.2%

Note: Figures may not add to totals because of rounding. 1. Includes out-of-pocket expenses, private health insurance and other funds. **Source:** Centers for Medicare & Medicaid Services, office of the Actuary, National Health Statistics Group; U.S. Dept. of Commerce, Bureau of Economic Analysis; and U.S. Census Bureau (revised 2010).

With U.S. medical costs high, and continuing to climb higher, patients are shopping overseas for less expensive treatments. The Deloitte Center for Health Solutions forecasts that six million people would travel abroad for medical care by 2010. Savings can be significant. Costs in Mexico, a nation with significant medical tourism, are 20 to 25 percent less than those in the United States. At an internationally accredited facility in India the cost of heart bypass surgery is $10,000, versus an average of $130,000 in the United States.

Prescription Drugs   A major component of personal health-care expenditures is prescription drugs, which topped $234 billion in 2008. Diverse reasons account for the rising expenditures. These include the increasing incidence of chronic conditions such as diabetes, arthritis, and elevated cholesterol, due to an aging population but also to factors such as the growing number of overweight Americans. Doctors are treating chronic illnesses more aggressively than in the past. New medicines are typically more expensive than older ones or than generic drugs, and they are heavily marketed to both consumers and doctors. Decision Resources reported in 2009 that European prices of 170 best-selling drugs averaged 40 percent less than U.S. prices in 2008. Japanese drug prices averaged 33 percent less. Many of the drugs with the largest percentage price differentials between the United States and other markets were for older drugs that have lost patent protection in some markets. Manufacturers of branded medicines in Europe typically cut the prices of these drugs when the products lost patent protection, whereas companies in the United States usually maintain brand prices following patent expiration.

The top-selling drug is cholesterol reducer Lipitor (*atorvastatin*), with $13.6 billion in worldwide sales in 2008; the U.S. market accounted for about half of these sales. U.S. spending on outpatient prescription analgesics—commonly known as painkillers and medicines that treat aches and pains—increased from $4.2 billion in 1996 to $13.2 billion in 2006, according to a 2009 government report.

Hospital Care   Spending for hospital care reached $718.4 billion in 2008. Escalating costs reflect several factors, including growing demands for services, new regulatory mandates, and changing technologies. For example, the traditional X-ray machine, which typically costs $175,000, is rapidly being replaced by CAT scan machines that can cost $1 million.

In 2006, an estimated 34.9 million inpatients, excluding newborn infants, were discharged from community hospitals (excluding federal hospitals, psychiatric institutions, and long-term hospitals). The average adult stay was 4.8 days. Average length of stay depended on the procedure; for example: 2.6 days for delivery, 4.4 days for heart disease, 5.1 days for pneumonia, 5.3 days for fractures, and 6.5 days for cancer.

The average age and age distribution of inpatients has also changed dramatically. According to the National Center for Health Statistics, the average age of patients in 1970 was 40.7 years, with 20 percent of all inpatients age 65 or older. By 2006, the average age had increased to 52.5 years with 38 percent of inpatients 65 or older. During the same period, the percent of inpatients under age 15 declined from 13 to 7 percent, and inpatients aged 15 to 44 declined from 43 to 31 percent. Advances in anesthesia and pain relief, the development of minimally invasive procedures, the growing availability of ambulatory surgery, and efforts to contain health-care costs contributed to the shift of care from inpatient to outpatient settings.

Emergency departments (EDs) provide a relatively small portion of outpatient services but they require an intense concentration of resources. Inappropriate emergency department usage is a serious funding challenge; many patients evaluated at EDs have nonemergency conditions that could be treated at a clinic or physician's office, at lesser cost. A 2010 report from the National Center for Health Statistics stated that since 1996 demand for emergency services has been rising; while the number of EDs across the country has decreased, the number of ED visits has increased. The report indicated that one-fifth of the civilian noninstitutionalized population had at least one ED visit in 2007. Uninsured persons under age 65 were more likely to have multiple ED visits in a 12-month period than those with private insurance.

Health Care Spending by Category, 2008

Category	Amount (billions)	Change 2007–08
Hospital care	$718.4	4.5%
Physicians' services	496.2	5.0
Dental services	101.2	5.1
Other professional services	65.7	5.6
Other personal health care	68.1	2.6
Prescription drugs	234.1	3.2
Durable medical equipment	26.6	4.1
Other medical products	39.0	4.2
Nursing-home care	138.4	4.6
Home health care	64.7	9.0
Administration and net cost of private health insurance	159.6	0.8
Government public health activities	69.4	7.1
Research	43.6	2.7
Structure and Equipment	113.9	5.9
Total	**$2,338.8**	**4.4%**

Source: Centers for Medicare & Medicaid Services, Office of the Actuary, National Health Statistics Group (2010).

Health Expenditures as Percent of G.D.P. for Selected Countries, 1970–2007

Nation	1970	1980	1990	2000	2007
United States	6.9%	8.7%	11.9%	13.4%	15.7%
Switzerland	5.6	7.8	8.5	10.2	10.8
Germany	6.2	8.7	8.7	10.3	10.4
Austria	5.3	7.6	7.1	9.9	10.1
Canada	7.0	7.1	9.0	8.8	10.1
Greece	6.1	6.6	7.4	7.9	9.6
Iceland	4.7	6.2	8.0	9.6	9.3
New Zealand	5.1	5.9	6.9	7.7	9.0
Norway	4.4	6.9	7.7	8.4	8.9
Italy	5.1	7.0	8.0	8.1	8.7
Spain	3.6	5.4	6.7	7.2	8.5
United Kingdom	4.5	5.6	6.0	7.0	8.4
Finland	5.6	6.4	7.8	7.2	8.2
Ireland	5.1	8.4	6.1	6.3	7.6

Source: World Health Organization, *World Health Statistics 2010*.

Paying for Health Care

Most medical care is paid for in one of three ways:

1. By patients; according to the U.S. Dept. of Health and Human Services, an estimated 12 percent of the nation's personal health care costs in 2007 were paid directly by patients.
2. By a private insurance plan; employers, employees, and individuals funded 36 percent of all health care spending in 2007.
3. As a public charge, which means that the government—and, ultimately, the taxpayer—pays the bill. In 2007, 45.3 percent ($850.6 billion) of personal health care costs were paid for by federal, state, and local governments. Medicare and Medicaid accounted for 73 percent of public sector expenditures. Workers compensation, Department of Defense and Department of Veterans Affairs programs, and other programs made up the rest.

Public insurance plans   Two government health programs, Medicare and Medicaid, financed $813.5 billion in health care services in 2008, almost one-third of the nation's total health care bill. The remaining federal health spending covers military and veterans' health care.

Medicare is a federal health insurance plan for people age 65 and older, certain disabled people, and people with kidney failure. Medicaid is a health care program for poor people. It is funded jointly by federal and state agencies. (See also Part II: "Social Insurance Programs.")

Private insurance plans   The two main ways to obtain health insurance are by paying into a group plan offered by an employer or by buying an individual plan. There are four major types of health insurance plans: fee-for-service, prepaid (HMO), point-of-service (POS), and preferred provider organization (PPO). Fee-for-service allows people to choose their doctors and other health care providers. These plans involve monthly premiums and a deductible before the insurance company starts playing. The other three plan types—HMO, POS, and PPO—are often referred to as managed care plans because insurance and health care delivery are integrated within one system.   Patients generally must use their group's physicians in order to be reimbursed; using services outside the group generally involve a financial penalty.

Other private plans include disability insurance, which replaces income lost because of a long-term illness or injury, and long-term care insurance, which covers costs of nursing home care.

The uninsured   Some 46.3 million Americans (15.4 percent of the population) did not have health insurance in 2008, with percentages ranging from 5.5 percent in Massachusetts to 25.1 percent in Texas. Among children under 18, about 10 percent were uninsured. Lack of insurance was much more common among people with low incomes. Also, non-citizen immigrants were far more likely to be uninsured than native-born citizens, mainly because they were less likely to be offered health insurance by their employers.

Health care reform   The Patient Protection and Affordable Care Act, along with the Health Care and Education Reconciliation Act of 2010, was signed into law in March 2010. The act's provisions include subsidizing insurance premiums, providing incentives for businesses to provide health care benefits, and establishing health insurance exchanges to facilitate the expansion of insurance coverage to more people. Also, insurance companies will be prohibited from denying coverage based on pre-existing conditions.

Nursing Home Residents Age 65 and Older, 2004

Characteristic	Number	Rate per 1,000 population
Total	**1,317,300**	**36.3**
65–74 years	174,100	9.4
75–84 years	468,700	36.1
85 years and over	674,500	138.8
Male	**336,900**	**22.2**
65–74 years	75,400	8.9
75–84 years	140,900	27.0
85 years and over	120,600	80.0
Female	**980,400**	**46.4**
65–74 years	98,800	9.8
75–84 years	327,800	42.3
85 years and over	553,900	165.2
White	**1,148,900**	**36.2**
65–74 years	134,200	8.5
75–84 years	405,800	35.2
85 years and over	608,900	139.4
Black	**145,400**	**47.7**
65–74 years	34,500	20.2
75–84 years	54,600	55.5
85 years and over	56,300	160.7

Source: Centers for Disease Control and Prevention, National Center for Health Statistics, *National Nursing Home Survey* (2004).

U.S. Hospitals and Their Use, 2007

Characteristic	Number
Registered hospitals	**5,708**
Community hospitals	4,897
Rural community hospitals	1,997
Urban community hospitals	2,900
Federal government hospitals	213
Nonfederal psychiatric hospitals	444
Nonfederal long-term-care hospitals	136
Other	18
Staffed beds in registered hospitals	**945,199**
Staffed beds in community hospitals	800,892
Admissions in registered hospitals	**37,120,387**
Admissions in community hospitals	35,345,986

Source: American Hospital Association, AHA Hospital Statistics (2009).

Ambulatory Surgery, 2006

Characteristic	Number[1]	Percent
Total visits	**34,738**	**100%**
Facility type		
Hospital-based	19,869	57.2
Freestanding	14,869	42.8
Region		
Northeast	5,298	15.3
Midwest	8,047	23.2
South	15,931	45.9
West	5,462	15.7
Metropolitan status		
Metropolitan area	29,715	85.5
Nonmetropolitan area	5,024	14.5

Note: 1. Estimated number in thousands. **Source:** Centers for Disease Control and Prevention, National Center for Health Statistics, *National Health Statistics Reports* (January 28, 2009).

The costs of the law will be offset by a variety of taxes, fees, and cost-saving measures. There also is a tax penalty for people who do not obtain health insurance, unless they are exempt due to low income or other reasons. The Congressional Budget Office estimated that the net effect will be a reduction of $143 billion in the federal deficit over the first decade.

People With and Without Health Insurance Coverage, by State, 2008

State	People with coverage ('000s)	People without coverage ('000s)	Percent of people without coverage
United States	255,143	46,340	15.4%
Alabama	4,159	561	11.9
Alaska	539	133	19.8
Arizona	5,264	1,273	19.5
Arkansas	2,322	505	17.8
California	29,868	6,822	18.6
Colorado	4,136	780	15.9
Connecticut	3,094	343	10.0
Delaware	769	94	10.8
District of Columbia	533	59	10.0
Florida	14,430	3,619	20.0
Georgia	7,850	1,703	17.8
Hawaii	1,159	98	7.8
Idaho	1,282	236	15.6
Illinois	11,065	1,638	12.9
Indiana	5,522	772	12.3
Iowa	2,707	283	9.5
Kansas	2,394	330	12.1
Kentucky	3,574	682	16.0
Louisiana	3,465	869	20.1
Maine	1,182	137	10.4
Maryland	4,870	669	12.1
Massachusetts	6,069	352	5.5
Michigan	8,665	1,151	11.7
Minnesota	4,676	444	8.7
Mississippi	2,388	519	17.9
Missouri	5,132	739	12.6
Montana	819	158	16.1
Nebraska	1,565	211	11.9
Nevada	2,097	487	18.8
New Hampshire	1,168	133	10.2
New Jersey	7,323	1,201	14.1
New Mexico	1,510	468	23.7
New York	16,617	2,720	14.1
North Carolina	7,832	1,421	15.4
North Dakota	552	74	11.8
Ohio	10,088	1,309	11.5
Oklahoma	3,060	498	14.0
Oregon	3,194	621	16.3
Pennsylvania	10,984	1,211	9.9
Rhode Island	921	123	11.8
South Carolina	3,762	707	15.8
South Dakota	698	100	12.5
Tennessee	5,252	931	15.1
Texas	18,110	6,084	25.1
Utah	2,396	364	13.2
Vermont	555	57	9.2
Virginia	6,786	962	12.4
Washington	5,732	808	12.4
West Virginia	1,528	271	15.0
Wisconsin	5,020	535	9.6
Wyoming	458	72	13.6

Note: 1. Base less than 75,000. **Source:** U.S. Census Bureau, *Current Population Survey, 2009 Annual Social and Economic Supplement* (2010).

Nursing-Home Care The approximately 15,800 nursing homes in the United States have some 1.4 million residents, about 91 percent of whom are 65-years-old or older. Typically, residents are white (85 percent), female (72 percent), widowed (57 percent), and 85 or older (46 percent).

Americans spent $800 million on nursing-home care in 1960, $42 billion in 1970, $17.7 billion in 1980, and $52.7 billion in 1990. By 2008, the figure had reached $138.4 billion. State and federal governments pay more than 70 percent of the cost. Out-of-pocket payments, including personal savings and Social Security benefits, cover most of the rest.

According to a 2009 survey from MetLife Mature Market Institute, the average cost of a nursing home stay was $219 per day for a private room, $198 for a semiprivate room. There were large variations from one metropolitan area to another. The costliest metropolitan area surveyed was San Francisco, California at an average of $432 per day for a private room; Baton Rouge and Shreveport, Louisiana, were the lowest at $136 per day. Alaska as a whole was highest, at $584 per day.

Health Care Quality by State

The federal Agency for Healthcare Research and Quality (AHRQ) annually releases *State Snapshots*, which helps people understand the status of health care quality in each of the 50 states plus the District of Columbia. The snapshots are based on

Uninsured Americans, 2008

Category	Number('000s)	Percent of total population
Total	46,340	15.4%
Age		
Under 18	7,348	9.9
18–24	8,200	28.6
25–34	10,754	26.5
35–44	8,035	19.4
45–54	7,054	15.9
55–64	4,301	12.5
65 and older	646	1.7
Citizenship		
Native-born	34,036	12.9
Foreign-born	12,304	33.5
Naturalized citizen	2,792	18.0
Non-citizen	9,511	44.7
Region		
Northeast	6,277	11.6
Midwest	7,588	11.6
South	20,154	18.2
West	12,321	17.2
Education		
No high school diploma	9,921	31.0
High school graduate	14,579	20.8
Some college	7,328	16.6
Associate degree	2,453	12.7
Bachelor's degree or more	4,711	7.7
Annual household income		
Under $25,000	13,673	24.5
$25,000–$49,999	14,908	21.4
$50,000–$74,999	8,034	14.0
$75,000 or more	9,725	8.2

Source: U.S. Census Bureau, *Current Population Survey, 2009 Annual Social and Economic Supplement* (2010).

129 quality measures, each of which evaluates a different segment of health care performance. In a subset of 15 "State Rankings for Selected Measures," specific state strengths are highlighted. In the report released in June 2009, New York, for example, ranked best for its low suicide rate. Oregon ranked first for pneumonia vaccinations for seniors. Utah ranked first for its low colorectal cancer death rate.

For overall health care, the best-performing states in 2008 were Wisconsin (score: 69.20), Minnesota (65.38), Massachusetts (63.91), New Hampshire (63.51), and Michigan (63.18). No state was good at everything, and the report points out areas in which states need improvement. Some shortcomings are widespread. On average, for example, states reported that only about 59 percent of adult surgery patients insured by Medicare received appropriate timing of antibiotics. Only 54 percent of men over 50 reported they ever had a flexible sigmoidoscopy or colonoscopy. Less than 60 percent of adults over 50 reported they ever had a colonoscopy or sigmoidoscopy. Fewer than 32 percent of high-risk

adults ages 18 to 64 received influenza vaccine in the previous 12 months.

▶ SURGERY

Increases in the number of surgical operations during recent years have been accompanied by dramatic changes in the rates of some procedures. An example is the incidence of cesarean sections—surgical incisions through the abdomen and uterus for removal of a baby, performed when normal vaginal delivery is deemed hazardous for the mother or child. Cesareans accounted for 31.8 percent of all live births in 2007—the highest rate ever in the United States and almost six times the rate in 1970 (5.5 percent).

The frequency of certain procedures varies according to age, but, surprisingly, there may also be variations from one geographical region to another. For example, in 2007, when the national rate of cesarean delivery was 31.8 percent, state rates ranged from lows of 22.2 percent in Utah and 22.6 in Alaska to highs of 38.3 in New Jersey and 37.2 in Florida. In 2003, the national rate for heart bypass surgery was 5.2 per 1,000 Medicare enrollees. In

Cardiovascular Procedures in the U.S., 2006

Operation	Sex		Age			
	Male	Female	Under 15	15–44	45–64	65 plus
Totals	4,116	3,119	210	734	2,633	3,658
Cardiac catheterization	666	450	12	87	487	529
Coronary artery angioplasty or atherectomy	429	232	N.A.	33	301	327
Coronary artery stents	425	227	N.A.	33	294	324
Coronary artery bypass	320	123	N.A.	15	191	237
Pacemaker	198	219	N.A.	9	46	361

Note: Numbers in '000s. Does not include outpatient and other nonhospitalized procedures. Source: U.S. Dept. of Health and Human Services, National Center for Health Statistics, 2006 National Hospital Discharge Survey (July 30, 2008).

Common Operations and Procedures, 2006

Type of procedure	Total	Males	Females
All procedures[1]	45,963,000	18,482,000	27,482,000
Transfusion of blood and blood components	1,968,000	851,000	1,117,000
Endoscopy of large or small intestine	1,567,000	669,000	899,000
Repair of lacerations due to giving birth	1,308,000	N.A.	1,308,000
Cesarean section	1,295,000	N.A.	1,295,000
Respiratory therapy	1,088,000	561,000	527,000
Diagnostic ultrasound	888,000	411,000	477,000
CAT scan	740,000	366,000	374,000
Reduction of fracture	672,000	326,000	346,000
Medical induction of labor	653,000	N.A.	653,000
Hemodialysis	645,000	325,000	320,000
Hysterectomy	569,000	N.A.	569,000
Knee replacement (total)	542,000	199,000	344,000
Removal of one or both ovaries	418,000	N.A.	418,000
Gall bladder removal	414,000	134,000	280,000
Removal or wound or burn tissue	402,000	236,000	166,000
Destruction or closing off of fallopian tubes	351,000	N.A.	351,000
Appendectomy	341,000	192,000	150,000
Spinal tap	315,000	158,000	156,000
Nose, mouth, pharynx operations	298,000	183,000	115,000
Bronchoscopy	282,000	152,000	129,000
Spinal disc operation	280,000	135,000	145,000
Hip replacement (total)	231,000	102,000	129,000
Cancer chemotherapy	221,000	130,000	90,000
Prostatectomy	168,000	168,000	N.A.

Note: Discharges of inpatients from non-Federal hospitals. Excludes newborn infants. 1. Includes operations not shown separately. Source: U.S. Dept. of Health and Human Services, National Center for Health Statistics, 2006 National Hospital Discharge Survey (July 30, 2008).

Colorado the rate was 3.0, while in Kentucky it was 6.8.

Organ Transplantation

Transplant surgery is more successful than ever, thanks to improved surgical techniques, a better understanding of the body's immune system, and the development of drugs that combat rejection of implanted organs. Kidney transplants, for instance, enjoy a high rate of success and are much less expensive—and much more convenient—than maintaining a patient on dialysis. Unfortunately, a scarcity of donor organs keeps thousands of patients waiting, sometimes in vain. The number of donors has increased, though have not changed dramatically since 2004, while waiting lists have grown. As of July 9, 2010, 108,130 candidates were on the national patient waiting list for organ transplants. Every 90 minutes someone on the list dies before they can receive the organs they need.

In addition to organs, tissues—cornea, bone, and skin—can be transplanted. In fact, corneal transplants are the most frequently performed transplant surgery. More than 40,000 are performed each year, with a success rate averaging better than 90 percent. As with organs, the need for tissues frequently exceeds the supply.

There are 50 independent and eight hospital organ procurement programs in the United States. According to the United Network for Organ Sharing (UNOS), 258 medical institutions were licensed to operate organ transplant programs as of mid-2004. These can be separated into organ-specific programs, including:

247 kidney transplants
134 heart transplants
140 pancreas transplants
124 liver transplants
59 heart-lung transplants
68 lung transplants
46 intestine transplants
45 pancreas islet cell transplants

Number and Survival Rates of Transplant Operations, 2008

Organ	Year first performed	Number (2008)	Survival rates[1]
Heart	1967	2,163	88.4%
Heart-lung	1982	27	74.7
Intestine	1990	185	82.8
Kidney	1954	16,517	96.6
Cadaver	N.A.	10,551	N.A.
Living donor	N.A.	5,966	N.A.
Kidney-pancreas	1966	836	95.5
Liver	1963	6,318	88.3
Cadaver	N.A.	6,069	N.A.
Living donor	N.A.	249	N.A.
Lung	1963	1,478	81.7
Cadaver[2]	N.A.	1,401	N.A.
Living donor[2]	N.A.	4	N.A.
Pancreas	1966	436	96.8

Notes: 1. One-year adult patient survival rates for operations from January 2006 through June 2008. 2. Figures are for 2006. **Source:** Scientific Registry of Transplant Recipients (2009).

Abortion The deliberate termination of a pregnancy before the fetus is capable of living outside the womb has generally been legal in the United States since 1973, when the Supreme Court ruled (in *Roe v. Wade*) that abortion cannot be prohibited during the first three months of pregnancy. During most years from 1973 through 1984, the ratio of abortions to live births increased, peaking at 364 per 1,000 live births in 1984. Since then the ratio has demonstrated a generally steady decline.

According to a report released by the Centers for Disease Control and Prevention (CDC) in 2009, women who obtained abortions in 2006

Reported Abortions, 1972–2006

Category	1972	1980	1990	1995	2000	2006
NUMBER OF ABORTIONS						
Reported Abortions	586,760	1,297,606	1,429,577	1,210,883	857,475[1]	846,181[1]
Number per 1,000 live births	180	359	345	311	245	236
PERCENT OF TOTAL						
Race						
White	77.0%	69.9%	64.8%	59.5%	56.6%	56.2%
Black[2]	23.0	30.1	31.8	35.0	36.3	36.3
Other	N.A.	N.A.	3.3	5.4	7.1	7.4
Marital Status						
Married	29.7%	23.1%	21.7%	19.7%	18.7%	16.0%
Unmarried	70.3	76.9	78.3	80.3	81.3	84.0
Age						
Under 20	32.6%	29.2%	22.4%	20.1%	18.8%	17.0%
20–24	32.5	35.5	33.2	32.5	32.8	32.6
25 or older	34.9	35.3	44.4	47.4	48.4	50.4
Weeks of gestation						
Up to 8	34.0%	51.7%	51.6%	54.0%	58.1%	62.0%
9–10	30.7	26.2	25.3	23.1	19.8	17.2
11–12	17.5	12.2	11.8	10.9	10.2	9.3
13–15	8.4	5.1	6.4	6.3	6.2	6.4
16–20	8.2	3.9	4.0	4.3	4.3	3.7
21 or more	1.2	0.9	1.0	1.4	1.4	1.3

Notes: 1. Acutal numbers may vary because not all states report data. 2. 1972 and 1980 include other nonwhite groups. **Source:** U.S. Dept of Health and Human Services, Centers for Disease Control and Prevention, *Morbidity and Mortality Weekly Reports*.

were predominantly 29 years of age or younger, white, and unmarried. Over 62 percent of the abortions were performed during the first eight weeks of gestation; 88.5 percent were performed in the first 12 weeks.

▶ DISEASE

Five of the most common categories of disease are:
1. Hereditary diseases—transferred from parent to child by genes. Examples: hemophilia, Down's syndrome, cystic fibrosis, sickle cell anemia, Tay-Sachs disease.
2. Deficiency diseases—caused by lack of vitamins or other essential nutrients. Examples: scurvy, pellagra, rickets, beriberi.
3. Infectious diseases—caused by viruses, bacteria, fungi, and other organisms, and transferred from person to person. Examples: common cold, influenza, chicken pox, measles, tuberculosis, AIDS.

4. Diseases caused by chemical and physical agents such as radiation, smoke, drugs, and poisons. Examples: allergies, asbestosis, bysinosis, lead poisoning.
5. Degenerative diseases—resulting from natural aging processes. In some cases, cancer and high blood pressure are degenerative diseases.

Heart Disease

Cardiovascular diseases (diseases of the heart and blood vessels) are America's number one killer. More than one in three American adults—some 81.1 million people—have one or more types of cardiovascular disease. In 2006, these diseases claimed 831,272 lives, or 34.5 percent of all U.S. deaths—an average of one every 38 seconds.

Death rates vary according to age, sex, race, even geographical location. Rates increase with age and are higher among men than among women. For both sexes, death rates are significantly higher among blacks than among whites.

Reported Cases of Common Infectious Diseases, 1950–2009

Disease	1950	1960	1970	1980	1990	2000	2009
Brucellosis (undulant fever)	3,510	751	213	183	85	63	115
Cholera	N.A.	N.A.	N.A.	9	6	2	10
Legionnellosis	N.A.	N.A.	N.A.	N.A.	1,370	1,127	3,522
Leprosy (Hansen's disease)	44	54	129	223	198	64	103
Malaria	2,184	72	3,051	2,062	1,292	1,560	1,451
Meningococcal infections	3,788	2,259	2,505	2,840	2,451	2,256	980
Mumps	N.A.	N.A.	104,953	8,576	5,292	338	1,991
Pertussis (whooping cough)	120,718	14,809	4,249	1,730	4,570	7,867	16,858
Plague[1]	N.A.	2	13	18	2	6	8
Poliomyelitis	33,300	3,190	33	9	6	0	1
Psittacosis	26	113	35	124	113	11	9
Rabies, in animals	7,901	3,567	3,224	6,421	4,826	6,934	5,343
Rabies, in humans	18	2	3	0	1	2	4
Rubella (German measles)	N.A.	N.A.	56,552	3,904	1,125	176	3
Tetanus	486	368	148	95	64	26	18
Toxic shock syndrome	N.A.	N.A.	N.A.	N.A.	322	125	74
Trichinosis	327	160	109	131	129	15	13
Tuberculosis[2]	121,742	55,494	37,137	27,749	25,701	15,976	11,545
Typhoid fever	2,484	816	346	510	552	317	397
Venereal diseases							
Gonorrhea	286,746	258,933	600,072	1,004,029	690,042	357,570	301,174
Syphilis[3]	23,939	16,145	21,982	27,204	50,578	5,978	13,007

Notes: 1. Plague: disease caused by the bite of fleas infected with the bacterium Yersinia pestis. 2. Data after 1970 not comparable to prior years because of changes in reporting criteria effective in 1975. 3. Primary and secondary syphilis cases. **Sources:** U.S. Dept. of Health and Human Services, Centers for Disease Control and Prevention, *Morbidity and Mortality Weekly Reports* (2010).

Heart Disease Death Rates, 1950–2007 (per 100,000 population)

Age	1950[1]	1960[1]	1970	1980	1990	1995	2000	2007
All ages								
Age adjusted	307.2	286.2	253.6	202.2	152.0	138.3	257.6	190.9
Crude	355.5	369.0	362.0	336.0	289.5	280.7	252.6	204.3
Under 1 year	3.5	6.6	13.1	22.8	20.1	17.1	13.0	10.0
1–4 years	1.3	1.3	1.7	2.6	1.9	1.6	1.2	1.1
5–14 years	2.1	1.3	0.8	0.9	0.9	0.8	0.7	0.6
15–24 years	6.8	4.0	3.0	2.9	2.5	2.9	2.6	2.6
25–34 years	19.4	15.6	11.4	8.3	7.6	8.5	7.4	7.9
35–44 years	86.4	74.6	66.7	44.6	31.4	32.0	29.2	27.4
45–54 years	308.6	271.8	238.4	180.2	120.5	111.0	94.2	85.3
55–64 years	808.1	737.9	652.3	494.1	367.3	322.9	261.2	200.3
65–74 years	1,839.8	1,740.5	1,558.2	1,218.6	894.3	799.9	665.6	462.9
75–84 years	4,310.1	4,089.4	3,683.8	2,993.1	2,295.7	2,064.7	1,780.3	1,315.0
85 and older	9,150.6	9,317.8	7,891.3	7,777.1	6,739.9	6,484.1	5,926.1	4,267.7

Note: Comparability between years is affected by changes in coding of the cause of death. 1. Includes deaths of nonresidents of the U.S. **Source:** U.S. Dept. of Health and Human Services, Center for Health Statistics (2008).

In 2006, Minnesota had the lowest age-adjusted death rate from cardiovascular disease (190.9 per 100,000 population) followed by Hawaii, Utah, Colorado, and Arizona. Mississippi had the highest rate (348.8) followed by Alabama, District of Columbia, Oklahoma, and Arkansas.

The good news is that the death rates from cardiovascular disease have declined dramatically, falling 26.4 percent from 1995 to 2005. This is due in part to improved drug treatments and other medical advancements. For instance, from 1979 to 2001, the number of cardiovascular operations and procedures increased 417 percent. Another factor has been improved personal health habits: people have stopped smoking, lowered dietary fats, and taken other steps that reduce the risks of cardiovascular disease. Evidence suggests that further significant reductions in deaths from heart disease could be achieved through aggressive treatment of high cholesterol. Meanwhile, the estimated direct and indirect costs of cardiovascular disease for 2008 were $475.3 billion.

According to the American Hearth Association, from 1996 to 2006 the total number of inpatient cardiovascular operations and procedures increased 30 percent from 5,444,000 to 7,191,000 annually.

Heart attacks A heart attack, or coronary event, occurs when the blood supply to the heart muscles is blocked. An uncomfortable pressure, fullness, squeezing, or pain in the center of the chest that lasts for two minutes or more may be a sign of a heart attack. Sweating, dizziness, nausea, fainting, or shortness of breath may also occur. Some 935,000 people suffer heart attacks annually. About 610,000 of these are first attacks and 325,000 are recurrent attacks. It is estimated that an additional 195,000 silent heart attacks occur each year. The average age of a person having a first heart attack is 64.5 for men and 70.3 for women. According to the American Heart Association, about every 25 seconds an American will suffer a coronary event and about every minute someone will die from one.

The National Center for Health Statistics estimates that 448,000 bypass operations were performed on 253,000 patients in 2006. In this operation a blood vessel from elsewhere in the body is used to reroute blood around a blocked coronary artery. The purpose is to reduce the person's risk of a heart attack.

Strokes Each year, approximately 795,000 Americans suffer a stroke. The good news is that from 1995 to 2005 the stroke death rate fell 29.7 percent, and the actual number of stroke deaths declined 13.5 percent. However, stroke remains a leading cause of serious long-term disability. A stroke occurs when the blood supply to the brain is blocked, usually by a clot. The primary signal of a stroke is a sudden, temporary weakness or numbness of the face, arm, or leg on one side of the body. Other signals include temporary loss of speech, difficulty in speaking or understanding speech, temporary vision problems (particularly in one eye), unsteadiness, or unexplained dizziness.

Cancer The nation's second leading cause of death is a group of diseases characterized by the unrestrained growth of cells. It afflicts people of all ages and races, although about 78 percent of all cancers are diagnosed at ages 55 and above. Cancers vary greatly in cause, symptoms, response to treatment, and possibility of cure.

A U.S. male has a little less than a one in two risk of developing invasive cancer at some time during his life; a female's risk is a little more than one in three. The incidence of cancer varies from state to state. Between 2002 and 2006, the highest cancer death rates occurred in Kentucky (280.7 deaths per 100,000 males and 178.7 per 100,000 females). The lowest cancer death rates were in Utah (167.0, 118.7) and Hawaii (186.2, 122.4).

Cancer survival rates The National Cancer Institute estimates that approximately 11.4 million Americans alive in 2006 had a history of cancer. Chances of surviving cancer have steadily improved. In the 1930s, about one in four U.S. cancer patients survived at least five years after diagnosis. In contrast, two-thirds of people who get cancer this year will be alive five years after diagnosis.

5-Year Survival Rates for Cancer, by Race and Site, 1975–2005

Cancer Site	Whites			Blacks		
	1975–77	1984–86	1999–2005	1975–77	1984–86	1999–2005
All sites	51%	55%	69%	40%	41%	59%
Brain	23	28	35	27	33	41
Breast (females)	76	80	91	62	65	79
Cervix	71	70	73	65	58	65
Colon	52	60	67	46	50	56
Leukemia	36	43	55	34	34	46
Liver	4	6	13	2	5	10
Lung (and bronchus)	13	14	17	12	11	13
Ovary	37	39	46	43	41	37
Pancreas	3	3	6	2	5	5
Prostate	70	77	100	61	66	98
Rectum	49	58	69	45	46	61
Stomach	15	18	25	16	20	26
Testis	83	93	97	82	87	87
Thyroid	93	94	98	91	90	96
Urinary bladder	75	79	83	51	61	68
Uterus (corpus)	89	85	87	61	58	62

Note: Rates are an average of cases diagnosed in years shown. **Source:** U.S. Dept. of Health and Human Services, National Cancer Institute; published in American Cancer Society, *Cancer Facts and Figures 2010* (2010).

Survival depends on many factors. Two of the most important are the site of the tumor and how much the cancer has spread before treatment is begun. Lifestyle choices are also important. The American Cancer Society estimated that some 171,000 cancer deaths in 2010 would be caused by tobacco use, and that about one-third of all cancer deaths are related to poor nutrition, physical inactivity, and overweight or obesity.

Cancer incidence and death rates   After increasing steadily for most of the 20th century, cancer incidence and death rates declined beginning in 1992. Incidence rates fell by 0.8 percent per year from 1999 to 2005. Death rates declined about 1.8 percent per year from 2002 through 2005, almost double the 1.1 percent per year decrease seen from 1993 through 2002. Improved detection and treatment, coupled with healthier lifestyles, are believed to account for the declining rates.

The American Cancer Society estimated that about 569,490 Americans would die of cancer in 2010—more than 1,500 people a day. Lung cancer is the leading cause of cancer deaths, killing an estimated 86,220 men and 71,080 women in 2010. Among women, breast cancer is the second most common killer, though if detected early and treated properly, it has a very high cure rate. Among men, prostate cancer causes the second greatest number of deaths. It, too, has a high survival rate if discovered while still localized within the general region of the prostate.

Cancer warning signs   Early detection is the key in fighting cancer. See your doctor if one of the following symptoms lasts longer than two weeks.
1. Unusual bleeding or discharge.
2. A sore that does not heal.
3. A change in a wart or mole.
4. A lump or thickening in the breast or elsewhere.
5. A change in bowel or bladder habits.
6. Nagging cough or hoarseness.
7. Indigestion or difficulty in swallowing.

HIV/AIDS   Following the discovery of acquired immune deficiency syndrome (AIDS) in 1981, the disease spread rapidly around the world. In the United States, sharp rises in new infections with human immunodeficiency virus (HIV), which causes AIDS, were recorded throughout the 1980s and into the early 1990s. The number of deaths also jumped annually, reaching almost 50,000 in 1995. The introduction of powerful drugs around that time showed significant success in controlling progression of HIV and AIDS, so that the number of yearly deaths declined to an average of around 17,600 in the years 2001–2005. Still, the rate of HIV infection remained stubbornly high, leveling off at 35,000 to 40,000 new cases a year. Since 1981, AIDS has been diagnosed in more than a million Americans. Of these over 580,000 have died.

HIV is spread through contact with infected body fluids such as blood and semen. Infected

Estimated New Cancer Cases and Deaths by Site and Sex, 2010

Site	New cases			Deaths		
	Total	Male	Female	Total	Male	Female
All Sites[1]	1,529,560	789,620	739,940	569,490	299,200	270,290
Skin[1]	74,010	42,610	31,400	11,790	7,910	3,880
Oral	36,540	25,420	11,120	7,880	5,430	2,450
Lung, bronchus, and other respiratory	222,520	116,750	105,770	157,300	86,220	71,080
Breast	209,060	1,970	207,090	40,230	390	39,840
Esophagus	16,640	13,130	3,510	14,500	11,650	2,850
Stomach	21,000	12,730	8,270	10,570	6,350	4,220
Small intestine	6,960	3,680	3,280	1,100	610	490
Colon, rectum, and anus	147,830	74,090	73,740	52,090	26,860	25,230
Liver, gall bladder, and bile passages	33,880	21,880	12,000	22,230	13,960	8,270
Pancreas	43,140	21,370	21,770	36,800	18,770	18,030
Other digestive organs	4,880	1,660	3,220	2,290	810	1,480
Urinary (bladder, kidney, etc.)	131,260	89,620	41,640	28,550	19,110	9,440
Leukemia	43,050	24,690	18,360	21,840	12,660	9,180
Lymphoma	74,030	40,050	33,980	21,530	11,450	10,080
Myeloma	20,180	11,170	9,010	10,650	5,760	4,890
Bone and joints	2,650	1,530	1,120	1,460	830	630
Endocrine system	46,930	11,890	35,040	2,570	1,140	1,430
Eye	2,480	1,240	1,240	230	120	110
Brain, other nervous system	22,020	11,980	10,040	13,140	7,420	5,720
Ovary	21,880	N.A.	21,880	13,850	N.A.	13,850
Uterus	55,670	N.A.	55,670	12,160	N.A.	12,160
Other genital, female	6,200	N.A.	6,200	1,700	N.A.	1,700
Prostate	217,730	217,730	N.A.	32,050	32,050	N.A.
Testis	8,480	8,480	N.A.	350	350	N.A.
Other genital, male	1,250	1,250	N.A.	310	310	N.A.
All other plus unspecified sites[2]	30,680	15,170	15,510	44,030	23,690	20,340

Notes: Except for urinary bladder, figures for invasive cancer only. Carcinoma in situ of the female breast accounts for about 54,010 new cases annually and melanoma carcinoma in situ accounts for about 46,770 cases annually. 1. Melanoma and other nonepithelial skin cancers only; higher curable basal cell and squamous cell skin cancers account for more than one million new cases annually. 2. More deaths than cases suggest lack of specificity in recording underlying causes of death on death certificate. **Source:** American Cancer Society, *Cancer Facts & Figures* (2010).

people may harbor the virus within their bodies for several years or even longer before developing symptoms of AIDS. Though symptomless, they still can infect others. At the end of 2007, an estimated 455,636 people in the U.S. were living with HIV/AIDS.

No cure for HIV/AIDS is known. Medical experts stress that preventive measures, including sex education, condom distribution, and needle-exchange programs for drug addicts, need to be emphasized. They also fear that the new AIDS drugs are making people complacent and careless about their sexual behavior. In 2004, the first HIV test that uses saliva rather than blood and provides results in 20 minutes was approved. Public health officials hoped the test would result in wider and more frequent testing.

(See "World Health" for information on AIDS worldwide.)

AIDS patients People at highest risk for HIV include men who have sex with men, injecting drug users, persons who received a transfusion or who were tissue transplant recipients before March 1985, heterosexual partners of infected persons, children born to infected mothers, and persons with mucous membrane or through-the-skin exposure to blood or body fluids of infected persons (e.g., health care workers). Men who have sex with men make up the largest group of AIDS cases. The proportion of women with AIDS increased steadily, accounting for 26.6 percent of adult-adolescent cases diagnosed in 2005. Beginning in 1996, blacks outnumbered whites in new AIDS diagnoses. In 2007, there were 17,486 newly diagnosed cases among blacks (59.2 per 100,000 population) and 10,402 among whites (6.1).

AIDS Cases 2007, 2008, and Cumulative

	Diagnoses		Deaths	
	2008	Cumulative[1]	2007	Cumulative[1]
Totals[2]	37,151	1,073,128	17,619	576,384
Age				
Birth to 13	41	9,349	6	4,931
13–19	545	7,905	51	1,449
20–29	5,592	166,490	698	53,739
30–39	10,180	438,665	2,934	218,892
40–49	12,603	308,532	6,842	188,896
50–59	6,188	105,547	4,988	76,671
60–64	1,140	19,669	1,032	15,790
64 or older	862	16,972	1,068	16,015
Race/Ethnicity				
White[3]	10,570	419,905	5,172	249,373
Black[3]	18,328	452,916	9,120	233,364
Hispanic	7,043	180,061	2,736	85,328
Asian / Pac. Islander	576	9,083	97	3,529
Am. Indian/ Alaska Native	199	3,741	90	1,847

Notes: Estimated. 1. From the beginning of the epidemic through 2008 (diagnoses) or 2007 (deaths). 2. Includes persons of unknown race or multiple races and persons whose age at diagnosis is unknown. 3. Not Hispanic. **Source:** U.S. Dept. of Health and Human Services, Centers for Disease Control and Prevention, *HIV/AIDS Surveillance Report*, Vol. 20 (revised June 2010).

Individuals most at risk are those with venereal disease and multiple sex partners. Evidence suggests that sexually transmitted diseases that cause genital ulcers, such as herpes and syphilis, are especially dangerous because they cause breaks in the skin through which HIV can enter. People with these diseases are

Adults and Adolescents With AIDS, 2007

	Males		Females		Total	
Exposure category	Cases	Percent[3]	Cases	Percent[3]	Cases	Percent[3]
Male-to-male sexual contact	487,695	60.0	N.A.	N.A.	487,695	49.0
Intravenous (IV) drug abuse	175,704	22.0	80,155	42.0	255,859	26.0
Male-to-male sexual contact and IV drug abuse	71,242	9.0	N.A.	N.A.	71,242	7.0
Heterosexual contact	63,927	8.0	112,230	58.0	176,157	18.0
Other[1]	12,108	1.0	6,158	<1.0	18,266	2.0
Total[2]	810,676	100.0	192,544	100.0	1,003,220	100.0

Notes: Cases are cumulative since reporting began. Cases with more than one risk factor under the combinations listed are tabulated only in the category listed first. 1. Includes hemophilia/coagulation disorder, receipt of contaminated blood, and patients whose mode of exposure to HIV is unknown. 2. Due to rounding, category totals may not total 100%. 3. Percents rounded at source. **Source:** U.S. Dept. of Health and Human Services, Centers for Disease Control and Prevention, *HIV/AIDS Surveillance Report*, Vol. 19 (revised February 18, 2009).

AIDS in the Cities, 2008

City	Number of cases	City	Number of cases	City	Number of cases
New York, N.Y.	66,426	Ft. Lauderdale, Fla.	7,722	West Palm Beach, Fla.	4,370
Los Angeles, Calif.	24,727	Newark, N.J.	7,297	New Orleans, La.	3,928
Washington, D.C.	15,696	San Diego, Calif.	6,628	Seattle, Wash.	3,793
Chicago, Ill.	14,175	Boston, Mass.	6,548	Santa Anna, Calif.	3,648
Atlanta, Ga.	13,105	Tampa–		Phoenix, Ariz.	3,646
Miami, Fla.	12,732	St. Petersburg, Fla.	5,257	Nassau–Suffolk, N.Y.	3,356
Philadelphia, Pa.	12,469	Riverside–		St. Louis, Mo.	3,233
Houston, Texas	11,277	San Bernardino, Calif.	4,912	Denver, Colo.	3,224
San Francisco, Calif.	11,026	Detroit, Mich.	4,788	Jacksonville, Fla.	2,931
Baltimore, Md.	10,301	Orlando, Fla.	4,554	Edison, N.J.	2,689
Dallas, Texas	9,992	Oakland, Calif.	4,461		

Note: Metropolitan statistical areas. For example, the Atlanta area includes Sandy Springs and Marietta. 1. Living with AIDS, year-end. **Source:** U.S. Dept. of Health and Human Services, Centers for Disease Control and Prevention, *HIV/AIDS Surveillance Report*, Vol. 20 (updated June 2010).

three to five times more likely to get HIV if they have sex with an HIV-infected person.

An encouraging change in the 1990s was the steep reduction in mother-to-fetus transmission of HIV. This resulted from the use of zidovudine (ZDV), taken by the pregnant woman beginning as early as the 14th week of pregnancy and continuing until labor; at birth, the baby takes ZDV for six weeks. In 2007, there were 24 reported cases of AIDS transmission from mothers to newborns, bringing the total to 8,434 since the epidemic began.

The overwhelming majority of AIDS cases are found in large cities and metropolitan areas. Through 2007, metropolitan areas in the U.S. and Puerto Rico with 500,000 or more population accounted for 871,192 of the 1,028,991 reported AIDS cases (84.7 percent).

Sexually Transmitted Diseases The United States has the highest rates of sexually transmitted diseases (STDs) in the industrialized world, some 50 to 100 times higher than in other industrial nations. An estimated 19 million new cases of STDs occur each year in the United States; almost half of these among young people ages 15 to 24. Roughly half of these cases are incurable. STDs are difficult to track, in part because many infected people, though able to infect others, do not have symptoms and remain undiagnosed. Even diagnosed cases frequently remain unreported and uncounted.

The most prevalent STD in the United States, infecting some 45 million people, is genital herpes, caused by a virus. It is followed by human papillomaviruses (HPV), which cause genital warts and cervical cancers; chlamydia, caused by a bacterium; trichomoniasis, caused by a protozoan; gonorrhea, caused by a bacterium; and syphilis, caused by a bacterium. People with these STDs have a significantly increased risk of becoming infected with HIV, in part because they may have open sores that provide the virus with an easy route of entry to the body.

Viral Hepatitis Several viruses are responsible for viral hepatitis, a sometimes-fatal disease that attacks the liver. In the United States almost all cases are accounted for by hepatitis viruses A, B, C, D, and E—particularly the first three.

Hepatitis A is spread primarily by fecal contamination of food and water and through person-to-person contact. Data suggest that one-third of Americans have evidence of past infection (i.e., they demonstrate immunity). Since 1995, vaccines have been available for prevention of infection in people age two and older, and disease incidence has declined dramatically.

Hepatitis B is generally transmitted via contact with the blood of an infected person during sex, during birth, or through contaminated needles and syringes. People at high risk include intravenous drug users who share needles, homosexual men, and heterosexuals with multiple partners.

An estimated 800,000 to 1.4 million Americans are living with chronic hepatitis B infection and are capable of transmitting the virus to others. Approximately half of those infected are Asians or Pacific Islanders, most of whom became infected before arriving in the country. Chronic carriers are at high risk of developing cirrhosis or liver cancer; each year about 3,000 hepatitis B patients die of these illnesses. Vaccines are available for all age groups, and have significantly cut the number of new infections.

Hepatitis C is a major cause of cirrhosis and the leading reason for liver transplants in the United States. It also is believed to be responsible for much of the recent increase in liver cancer. The main risk factors of infection are injecting drugs and having sex with an infected person. An estimated 2.7 to 3.9 million persons are chronically infected, making hepatitis C the most common chronic blood-borne infection in the nation.

Percentage of Overweight Children and Adolescents, 1971–2008

	Years of Surveys					
Age	1971 –74	1976 –80	1988 –94	1999 –2000	2003 –04	2007 –08
2–5	5.0%	5.0%	7.2%	10.3%	13.9%	10.4%
6–11	4.0	6.5	11.3	15.1	18.8	19.6
12–19	6.1	5.0	10.5	14.8	17.4	18.1

Note: Excludes young women who were pregnant.
Source: National Health and Nutrition Examination Surveys.

Death Rates (per 100,000 population) by Sex and Race, 1940–2007

		All races		Whites		Black	
Year	Total	Male	Female	Male	Female	Male	Female
1940	1,076.4	1,197.4	954.6	1,162.2	919.4	N.A.	N.A.
1950	963.8	1,106.1	823.5	1,089.5	803.3	N.A.	N.A.
1960	954.7	1,104.5	809.2	1,098.5	800.9	1,181.7	905.0
1970	945.3	1,090.3	807.8	1,086.7	812.6	1,186.6	829.2
1980	878.3	976.9	785.3	983.3	806.1	1,034.1	733.3
1985	876.9	948.6	809.1	963.6	840.1	989.3	734.2
1990	863.8	918.4	812.0	930.9	846.9	1,008.0	747.9
1995	880.0	914.1	847.3	932.1	891.3	980.7	759.0
2000	854.0	853.0	855.0	887.8	912.3	834.1	733.0
2005	825.9	827.2	824.6	864.5	882.8	799.2	703.9
2007	803.6	809.9	797.4	848.1	854.9	775.6	675.7

Note: Death rates are based on population estimates prepared by the U.S. Census Bureau. Source: U.S. Dept. of Health and Human Services, National Center for Health Statistics. *National Vital Statistics Reports* (2010).

Therapies often are ineffective or cause serious side effects, and no vaccine is available.

Diabetes   Diabetes mellitus is a group of diseases characterized by high blood sugar levels that result from the body's inability to make or use the hormone insulin. Diabetes can lead to debilitating and life-threatening complications including blindness, memory problems, kidney disease, heart disease, nerve damage, and amputations.

The most common type is Type 2 diabetes, which usually develops because the body fails to use insulin properly. It generally occurs in people who are overweight; other risk factors include high cholesterol, high blood pressure, ethnicity, and a family history of diabetes. Treatment includes a healthy diet, weight loss, and regular exercise. Many patients require daily insulin injections.

Two-thirds of American adults are overweight. This has led to increasing numbers of people with Type 2 diabetes. Type 2 was historically referred to as adult-onset diabetes. As recently as 10 years ago it was virtually unknown in people under age 20. Now, in some communities, children and adolescents account for almost 50 percent of new cases. According to the American Diabetes Asso-

Leading Causes of Death, 1970–2007

| Cause of death | Deaths in 2007 | Death rate per 100,000 |||||
		1970	1980	1990	2000	2007
All causes	2,423,712	945.3	878.3	861.9	854.0	803.6
Heart diseases	616,067	362.0	336.0	289.0	240.4	204.3
Cancer	562,875	162.8	183.9	201.7	194.0	186.6
Cerebrovascular diseases	135,952	101.9	75.1	57.9	56.3	45.1
Chronic lower respiratory diseases	127,924	15.2	24.7	35.5	43.7	42.4
Accidents	123,706	56.4	46.7	37.3	35.3	41.0
Alzheimer's disease	74,632	N.A.	N.A.	N.A.	20.2	24.7
Diabetes mellitus	71,382	18.9	15.4	19.5	25.4	23.7
Pneumonia and influenza	52,717	30.9	24.1	31.3	22.7	17.5
Kidney diseases	46,448	4.4	7.4	8.3	14.2	15.4
Septicemia	34,828	1.7	4.2	7.9	11.7	11.5
Suicide	34,598	11.6	11.9	12.3	10.6	11.5
Liver disease and cirrhosis	29,165	15.5	13.5	10.2	9.3	9.7
Hypertension	23,965	N.A.	N.A.	N.A.	7.0	7.9
Parkinson's disease	20,058	N.A.	N.A.	N.A.	N.A.	6.7
Homicide	18,361	8.3	10.7	10.2	6.0	6.2

Note: Causes of death are classified by the International Classification of Diseases, which has been revised periodically, resulting in new cause-of-death titles and breaks in comparability of cause-of-death statistics. **Source:** U.S. Dept. of Health and Human Services, National Center for Health Statistics, *National Vital Statistics Reports* (2010).

Deaths and Death Rates, 2007

| Age | Total deaths | Rate per 100,000 population |||
		Both sexes	Male	Female
All ages	2,423,712	803.6	809.9	797.4
Under 1 year[1]	29,138	684.5	747.8	618.1
1–4 years	4,703	28.6	31.3	25.7
5–9 years	2,711	13.7	15.0	12.3
10–14 years	3,436	16.9	19.9	13.8
15–9 years	13,299	61.9	86.8	35.7
20–24 years	20,683	98.3	145.2	48.4
25–29 years	20,931	99.4	140.2	56.6
30–34 years	21,641	110.8	148.2	72.3
35–39 years	30,881	145.8	185.4	105.7
40–44 years	48,725	221.6	276.8	166.7
45–49 years	77,738	340.0	423.8	258.1
50–54 years	106,948	509.0	646.6	376.8
55–59 years	132,458	726.3	922.2	541.8
60–64 years	154,652	1,068.3	1,328.4	829.7
65–69 years	174,991	1,627.5	2,002.2	1,299.4
70–74 years	214,247	2,491.3	3,046.9	2,037.2
75–79 years	289,029	3,945.9	4,817.2	3,304.0
80–84 years	363,653	6,381.4	7,758.7	5,511.7
85 and older	713,647	12,946.5	14,006.4	12,442.3
Not stated	201	N.A.	N.A.	N.A.

Note: 1. Death rates for "Under 1 year" (based on population estimates) differ from infant mortality rates (based on live births). **Source:** U.S. Dept. of Health and Human Services, National Center for Health Statistics. *National Vital Statistics Reports* (May 2010).

ciation, an estimated 23.6 million Americans—8 percent of the population—have diabetes. In addition, 57 million people have pre-diabetes.

Alzheimer's disease

Alzheimer's disease is a progressive degenerative condition characterized by forgetfulness in early stages and, as the disease progresses, increasingly severe debilitating symptoms that create demanding care-giving needs. An estimated 5 million Americans, most of them elderly, have Alzheimer's disease. It caused 74,632 deaths in 2007, making it the sixth-leading cause of death. Many more women than men die from Alzheimer's, but this mainly reflects the larger number of women alive at older ages. Death rates are much higher for whites than blacks, but the risk of acquiring Alzheimer's is higher for blacks than whites.

▶ DEATH

In 2007, a total of 2,423,712 deaths were registered in the United States, 2,552 fewer than in 2006. The age-adjusted death rate, which takes into account changes and variations in the age composition of the population, reached a record low of 760.2 per 100,000 population, a decrease of 2.1 percent from the 2006 rate and a decline of 26.8 percent since 1980.

Mortality for Hispanics is somewhat understated because of underreporting of Hispanic origin on death certificates, by an estimated 5 percent. However, in 2007, the age-adjusted death rate was 29.7 percent lower for Hispanics than for non-Hispanics. Various hypotheses have been proposed to explain Hispanics' favorable mortality outcomes.

Males experience higher age-adjusted death rates than females, with black males having significantly higher rates than white males. Age-adjusted death rates for 2007 were: white females, 634.8 deaths per 100,000 population; black females, 793.8; white males 890.5; and black males 1,184.4.

Socioeconomic disparities in death rates also exist. A 1998 report from University of Michigan researchers said that adults in the lowest income group (less than $10,000 annual income) were 3.2 times more likely to die compared with those in the highest income bracket ($30,000 or more). Middle income adults ($10,000–$29,999) were 2.3 times as likely to die as those in the high-income group. Possible factors for higher death rates among the poor include depression, social isolation, a lack of optimism, low self-esteem, chronic stress, and inequality in health-care delivery.

Causes of Death

For the purposes of national mortality statistics, every death is attributed to one underlying condition. The 15 leading cases of death in 2007 accounted for 81.4 percent of all deaths in the nation. During the 20th century the leading causes of death changed significantly. In 1900, infectious diseases took many lives; indeed, the leading causes of death were (1) pneumonia and influenza and (2) tuberculosis. Heart disease and cancer have headed the list since the 1940s.

Suicide

Each year, more than 33,000 Americans kill themselves. In addition, over 395,000 people with self-inflicted injuries are treated in emergency rooms each year. Although women report attempting suicide during their lifetime about two to three times as often as men, men are nearly four times more likely to succeed at it. In 2007, 27,269 males and 7,329 females committed suicide. It is the seventh leading cause of death for males and the sixteenth leading cause for females. Among males, firearms are the most commonly used method of suicide (56.0%); among females, poisoning is most common (40.3%).

Suicide is the nation's eleventh-leading cause of death. It is the second leading cause of death among 25–34 year olds and the third leading cause of death among 15 to 24–year olds. Among 15 to 24–year olds, there are approximately 100 to 200 attempts for every completed suicide. Among

Changes in Leading Causes of Death, 1900–2007

Cause of death	Death rate (per 100,000 population)
1900: All causes	**1,719.1**
Pneumonia and influenza	202.2
Tuberculosis	194.4
Diarrhea, enteritis, and ulceration of the intestines	142.7
1920: All causes	**1,298.9**
Pneumonia and influenza	207.3
Heart disease	159.6
Tuberculosis	113.1
1940: All causes	**1,076.4**
Heart disease	291.3
Cancer	120.0
Cerebrovascular disease	90.8
1960: All causes	**954.7**
Heart disease	369.0
Cancer	149.2
Cerebrovascular disease	108.0
1980: All causes	**878.3**
Heart disease	336.0
Cancer	183.9
Cerebrovascular disease	75.1
2000: All causes	**854.0**
Heart disease	252.6
Cancer	196.5
Cerebrovascular disease	59.6
2007: All cases	**803.6**
Heart disease	204.3
Cancer	186.6
Cerebrovascular disease	45.1

Source: U.S. Dept. of Health and Human Services, National Center for Health Statistics.

Suicide in the U.S., 1960–2007

Age	Rate per 100,000 population					
	1960	1970	1980	1990	2000	2007
All ages[1]	**12.5**	**13.1**	**12.2**	**12.5**	**10.4**	**11.1**
0 – 4	N.A.	N.A.	N.A.	N.A.	N.A.	N.A.
5–14	0.3	0.3	0.4	0.8	0.7	0.5
15–24	5.2	8.8	12.3	13.2	10.2	9.7
25–34	10.0	14.1	16.0	15.2	12.0	13.0
35–44	14.2	16.9	15.4	15.3	14.5	15.6
45–54	20.7	20.0	15.9	14.8	14.4	17.7
55–64	23.7	21.4	15.9	16.0	12.1	15.5
65–74	23.0	20.8	16.9	17.9	12.5	12.6
75–84	27.9	21.2	19.1	24.9	17.6	16.3
85 & older	26.0	19.0	19.2	22.2	19.6	15.6

Note: 1. Age-adjusted. Source: U.S. Dept. of Health and Human Services, National Center for Health Statistics. *National Vital Statistics Reports* (2010).

Unintentional Deaths due to Injury, in U.S., 2007

Type	Number of deaths	Age group (years)						
		0–4	5–14	15–24	25–44	45–64	65–74	75+
All accidents	**123,706**	**2,873**	**2,194**	**15,897**	**31,908**	**32,508**	**8,753**	**29,539**
Transport[1]	46,844	708	1,374	10,928	14,281	12,037	3,194	4,309
Poisoning	29,846	53	81	3,159	13,275	12,126	602	547
Falls	22,631	60	32	233	927	3,043	2,594	15,740
Drowning	3,443	515	224	630	798	805	194	272
Fires and burns	3,286	239	211	194	529	980	421	708
Firearms	613	19	46	155	185	139	31	38
All other[2]	17,043	1,279	226	598	1,913	3,378	1,717	7,925

Notes: 1. Motor vehicles, pedestrians, airplanes, etc. 2. Machinery, cuts, overexertion, excessive cold, unspecified, etc. **Source:** U.S. Department of Health and Human Services, *National Vital Statistics Report* (May 2010).

Estimated Number of Injuries in U.S. From Selected Products, 2006

Product group	Estimated injuries
Stairs, ramps, landings, floors	2,329,829
Beds, mattresses, pillows	553,091
Basketball	529,837
Doors, windows, glass panels	496,073
Bicycles, accessories	490,434
Chairs, sofas, sofa beds	473,733
Football	460,210
Bathroom structures and fixtures	331,033
Household containers (cans, bottles, jars)	301,273
ATVs, mopeds, minibikes	275,123
Baseball, softball	274,867
Exercise, exercise equipment	269,249
Ladders, stools	237,030
Clothing	222,007
Playground equipment	221,777
Toys	213,171
Soccer	186,544
Swimming pools, equipment	164,607
Home workshop manual tools	131,742
Carpets, rugs	127,017
Skateboards	125,713
Fences	110,011
Trampolines	109,522
Skiing and snowboarding	96,119
Nursery equipment	86,573
Lawn mowers	78,740
Drug poisoning, children under 5	71,418
Horseback riding	70,915
Television sets and stands	61,356
Hand garden tools	39,827
Razors, shavers, razor blades	38,773
Refrigerators, freezers	38,651

Notes: These national estimates are based on injuries treated in hospital emergency rooms participating in the National Electronic Injury Surveillance System. Patients said their injuries were related to the products; this does not necessarily mean the products caused the injuries. **Source:** Consumer Product Safety Commission, National Electronic Injury Surveillance System, *Consumer Product Safety Review* (Summer 2007).

Accidental Deaths in the U.S., 1910–2007 (per 100,000 population)

Year	Death rate	Year	Death rate	Year	Death rate
1910	84.4	1950	60.3	1990	36.9
1920	71.2	1960	52.1	1995	35.5
1930	80.5	1970	56.2	2000	34.0
1940	73.4	1980	46.5	2007	41.0

Source: U.S. Dept. of Health and Human Services, National Center for Health Statistics.

Life Expectancy in U.S., 1950–2006

Year	All races		Whites		Blacks	
	Male	Female	Male	Female	Male	Female
At birth						
1950[1]	65.6	71.1	66.5	72.2	58.9	62.7
1960[1]	66.6	73.1	67.4	74.1	60.7	65.9
1970	67.1	74.7	68.0	75.6	60.0	68.3
1980	70.0	77.4	70.7	78.1	63.8	72.5
1990	71.8	78.8	72.7	79.4	64.5	73.6
1995	72.5	78.9	73.4	79.6	65.2	73.9
2000	74.3	79.7	74.9	80.1	68.3	75.2
2006	75.1	80.2	75.7	80.6	69.7	76.5
At age 65 (years remaining)						
1950[1]	12.8	15.0	12.8	15.1	12.9	14.9
1960[1]	12.8	15.8	12.9	15.9	12.7	15.1
1970	13.1	17.0	13.1	17.1	12.5	15.7
1980	14.1	18.3	14.2	18.4	13.0	16.8
1990	15.1	18.9	15.2	19.1	13.2	17.2
1995	15.6	18.9	15.7	19.1	13.6	17.1
2000	16.3	19.2	16.3	19.2	14.6	17.5
2006	17.0	19.7	17.1	19.8	15.1	18.6

Note: 1. Includes deaths of persons who were not residents of the 50 states and the District of Columbia. **Source:** U.S. Dept. of Health and Human Services, National Center for Health Statistics, *Health United States 2000, National Vital Statistics Reports.*

adults age 65 and older, there are approximately four attempts for every completed suicide.

Rates are generally higher than the national average in the western states and lower in the eastern and midwestern states. For 2006, the highest rates were reported for Wyoming (22.5 per 100,000 population), Alaska (20.1), Montana (20.0), Nevada (19.5), and New Mexico (18.0). The lowest were for the District of Columbia (5.2), New Jersey (6.7), New York (6.9), Massachusetts (7.0), and Illinois (7.9).

Many experts believe that suicide statistics are grimmer than reported. They contend that numerous suicides are categorized as accidents or other deaths to spare families.

►ACCIDENTS

Every 10 minutes, two people are killed and about 370 suffer a disabling injury in accidents in the United States. Accidents are the nation's fifth most common cause of death. But for people between the ages of 1 and 44, accidents are the leading cause of death.

The accident death rate has declined significantly from the 1912 rate of 82.5 deaths per 100,000 population. In 2000 it reached a low of 34.0. In 2007 the rate was 41.0, or a total of 123,706 accidental deaths, according to the U.S. Department of Health and Human Services. Accident rates vary significantly from one place to another. The highest accidental death rates in 2006 were in New Mexico (66.4), West Virginia (64.7), and Mississippi (63.8). The lowest were in Maryland (25.9), New York (27.1), and Utah (28.0).

Motor Vehicle Deaths   Since the nation's first motor vehicle death (reportedly in New York City on September 13, 1899) some 2.9 million people have died in motor vehicle accidents. Over the years, however, the numbers of deaths per 100,000 population and per 100,000 registered vehicles have declined drastically. For example, there were 3,100 motor vehicle deaths in 1912, when registered vehicles totaled only 950,000. In 2008, there were 37,261 fatalities, but registered vehicles had risen to more than 255 million. The motor vehicle death rate in 2008 fell to a historic low of 1.27 deaths per 100 million vehicle miles. Substantial declines occurred in virtually every

Average Remaining Life Expectancy in U.S. (in years)

Age in 2006	All races M	All races F	White M	White F	Black M	Black F	Age in 2006	All races M	All races F	White M	White F	Black M	Black F
At birth	75.1	80.2	75.7	80.6	69.7	76.5	50	28.8	32.5	29.0	32.6	25.2	30.2
1	74.7	79.7	75.1	80.0	69.7	76.5	51	27.9	31.6	28.2	31.7	24.4	29.4
2	73.7	78.7	74.2	79.0	68.7	75.5	52	27.1	30.7	27.4	30.8	23.7	28.5
3	72.7	77.7	73.2	78.0	67.8	74.6	53	26.3	29.8	26.5	29.9	23.0	27.7
4	71.8	76.8	72.2	77.1	66.8	73.6	54	25.5	28.9	25.7	29.1	22.3	26.9
5	70.8	75.8	71.2	76.1	65.8	72.6	55	24.7	28.0	24.9	28.2	21.6	26.1
6	69.8	74.8	70.2	75.1	64.8	71.6	56	23.9	27.2	24.1	27.3	20.9	25.3
7	68.8	73.8	69.2	74.1	63.9	70.6	57	23.1	26.3	23.2	26.4	20.2	24.5
8	67.8	72.8	68.2	73.1	62.9	69.6	58	22.3	25.5	22.4	25.6	19.5	23.8
9	66.8	71.8	67.3	72.1	61.9	68.6	59	21.5	24.6	21.6	24.7	18.8	23.0
10	65.8	70.8	66.3	71.1	60.9	67.7	60	20.7	23.8	20.9	23.8	18.2	22.2
11	64.8	69.8	65.3	70.1	59.9	66.7	61	19.9	22.9	20.1	23.0	17.5	21.5
12	63.8	68.8	64.3	69.1	58.9	65.7	62	19.2	22.1	19.3	22.2	16.9	20.7
13	62.8	67.8	63.3	68.1	57.9	64.7	63	18.5	21.3	18.6	21.4	16.3	20.0
14	61.9	66.8	62.3	67.1	56.9	63.7	64	17.7	20.5	17.8	20.6	15.7	19.3
15	60.9	65.9	61.3	66.1	56.0	62.7	65	17.0	19.7	17.1	19.8	15.1	18.6
16	59.9	64.9	60.4	65.2	55.0	61.7	66	16.3	18.9	16.4	19.0	14.5	17.9
17	59.0	63.9	59.4	64.2	54.1	60.8	67	15.6	18.1	15.7	18.2	13.9	17.2
18	58.0	62.9	58.4	63.2	53.1	59.8	68	14.9	17.4	15.0	17.4	13.4	16.5
19	57.1	62.0	57.5	62.2	52.2	58.8	69	14.2	16.6	14.3	16.6	12.8	15.8
20	56.1	61.0	56.6	61.3	51.3	57.8	70	13.6	15.9	13.6	15.9	12.3	15.1
21	55.2	60.0	55.6	60.3	50.4	56.9	71	12.9	15.1	12.9	15.1	11.7	14.5
22	54.3	59.0	54.7	59.3	49.5	55.9	72	12.3	14.4	12.3	14.4	11.2	13.8
23	53.4	58.1	53.8	58.3	48.6	54.9	73	11.6	13.7	11.7	13.7	10.7	13.2
24	52.5	57.1	52.9	57.4	47.7	54.0	74	11.0	13.0	11.0	13.0	10.2	12.6
25	51.5	56.1	51.9	56.4	46.8	53.0	75	10.4	12.3	10.5	12.3	9.8	12.9
26	50.6	55.1	51.0	55.4	46.0	52.1	76	9.9	11.7	9.9	11.7	9.3	11.4
27	49.7	54.2	50.1	54.5	45.1	51.1	77	9.3	11.1	9.3	11.0	8.9	10.9
28	48.8	53.2	49.1	53.5	44.2	50.1	78	8.8	10.5	8.8	10.4	8.4	10.3
29	47.8	52.2	48.2	52.5	43.3	49.2	79	8.3	9.9	8.3	9.8	8.0	9.8
30	46.9	51.3	47.3	51.5	42.4	48.2	80	7.8	9.3	7.8	9.3	7.7	9.3
31	46.0	50.3	46.3	50.6	41.5	47.3	81	7.4	8.7	7.3	8.7	7.3	8.8
32	45.0	49.3	45.4	49.6	40.6	46.3	82	6.9	8.2	5.9	8.2	6.9	8.4
33	44.1	48.4	44.5	48.6	39.7	45.7	83	6.5	7.7	6.5	7.7	6.6	7.9
34	43.2	47.4	43.5	47.7	38.8	44.5	84	6.1	7.2	6.0	7.2	6.2	7.5
35	42.2	46.4	42.6	46.7	37.9	43.5	85	5.7	6.8	5.7	6.7	5.9	7.1
36	41.3	45.6	41.6	45.7	37.0	42.6	86	5.3	6.3	5.3	6.3	5.6	6.7
37	40.4	44.5	40.7	44.8	36.1	41.7	87	5.0	5.9	4.9	5.9	5.3	6.3
38	39.4	43.6	39.8	43.8	35.3	40.7	88	4.7	5.5	4.6	5.5	5.1	5.9
39	38.5	42.6	38.9	42.9	34.4	39.8	89	4.4	5.1	4.3	5.1	4.8	5.6
40	37.6	41.7	37.9	41.9	33.5	38.9	90	4.1	4.8	4.0	4.7	4.5	5.3
41	36.7	40.7	37.0	41.0	32.6	38.0	91	3.8	4.4	3.7	4.4	4.3	5.0
42	35.8	39.8	36.1	40.0	31.8	37.1	92	3.5	4.1	3.5	4.1	4.1	4.7
43	34.9	38.9	35.2	39.1	30.9	36.2	93	3.3	3.8	3.2	3.8	3.9	4.4
44	34.0	37.9	34.3	38.2	30.1	35.3	94	3.1	3.6	3.0	3.5	3.6	4.1
45	33.1	37.0	33.4	37.2	29.2	34.5	95	2.9	3.3	2.8	3.3	3.5	3.9
46	32.2	36.1	32.5	36.3	28.4	33.6	96	2.7	3.1	2.6	3.0	3.3	3.6
47	31.4	35.2	31.6	35.4	27.6	32.7	97	2.5	2.8	2.4	2.8	3.1	3.4
48	30.5	34.3	30.8	34.5	26.8	31.9	98	2.3	2.6	2.3	2.6	2.9	3.2
49	29.6	33.4	29.9	33.6	26.0	31.0	99	2.2	2.5	2.1	2.4	2.8	3.0
							100+	2.0	2.3	2.0	2.2	2.6	2.8

Note: Based on an individual's age in 2006. For example, a white male age 26 in 2006 would be expected to live 51 more years, or to 77 years old. A female born in 2006 would be expected to live to about 80 years of age. **Source:** U.S. Dept. Health and Human Services, National Center for Health Statistics, *National Vital Statistics Reports* (June 28, 2010).

major category, led by declines in passenger car occupant fatalities. However, motorcycle deaths increased for the 11th straight year and accounted for 14 percent of all highway fatalities.

Data suggest that safety belts, air bags, bicycle and motorcycle helmets, child safety seats, strict drunk-driving laws, and speed limits save thousands of lives each year. More than 5.8 million police-reported motor vehicle crashes occurred in 2008. About 28 percent of these crashes resulted in an injury, with less than one percent of total crashes (34,017) resulting in a death.

- More than half of the fatal crashes occur on roads with posted speed limits of 55 miles per hour or higher (2005 data).
- 57 percent of fatalities were from single-vehicle crashes (2007 data).

U.S. Infant Mortality Rate, 1940–2007 (per 1,000 live births)

Year	All races	White[1]	Black[1]
1940	47.0	43.2	72.9
1950	29.2	26.8	43.9
1960	26.0	22.9	44.3
1970	20.0	17.8	32.6
1980	12.6	11.0	21.4
1990	9.2	7.6	18.0
1995	7.6	6.3	15.1
2000	6.9	5.7	14.0
2007	6.7	5.6	13.2

Note: 1. Race of mother. **Source:** U.S. Dept. Health and Human Services, National Center for Health Statistics, *Monthly Vital Statistics Reports, National Vital Statistics Reports.*

Child and Adolescent: Recommended Immunization Schedule, 2010

Age	Vaccines
Birth	Hepatitis B
2 months	Hepatitis B, polio, rotavirus, diphtheria, tetanus, pertussis (DTaP), haemophilus B (Hib), pneumonia and other pneumococcal bacteria (PCV)
4 months	Rotavirus, Polio, DTaP, Hib, PCV
6 months	Rotavirus, DTaP, Hib, PCV
6–18 months	Hepatitis B, polio
6 months–18 years	Influenza (yearly)
12–15 months	Hib; measles, mumps, rubella (MMR#1); chicken pox, PCV
12–23 months	Hepatitis A series
15–18 months	DTaP
4–6 years	Polio, DtaP, MMR#2, chicken pox
11–12 years	DTaP, human papillomavirus (HPV, 3 doses, females only), meningococcal (MCV4)

Note: It generally takes several doses of each vaccine for full protection. In some cases, there is a range of acceptable ages for vaccination. For example, the third dose of hepatitis B vaccine may be given between 6 and 18 months of age. Children who have not been vaccinated against Hepatitis B in infancy may begin the series during any childhood visit. For additional information, contact your physician. **Sources:** American Academy of Pediatrics; American Academy of Family Physicians; and U.S. Dept. of Health and Human Services, Centers for Disease Control and Prevention.

- 55 percent of those killed were not wearing seat belts (2008 data).
- 39 percent of fatal crashes involve alcohol; 76 percent of fatal crashes occurring between midnight and 3 A.M. involve alcohol (2005 data).

▶ LIFE EXPECTANCY

Life expectancy figures represent the average number of years that infants are expected to live. Life expectancy has improved steadily over the years, due largely to a decline in deaths during childhood. The development of drugs to combat infectious diseases, plus improved nutrition and better environmental sanitation, have all played major roles in combating early deaths.

In 2007, the average length of life in the U.S. was 77.9 years. Whites were expected to outlive blacks by almost five years: 78.4 years versus 73.6 years. Homicides, killings in police confrontations, auto accidents, AIDS, tuberculosis, and several other diseases have had a disproportionate impact on black people's life expectancy rates in recent years.

▶ INFANT MORTALITY

In 2007, there were 29,138 reported deaths of infants age one year or younger. The most commonly used index for measuring the risk of dying during the first year of life are infant mortality rates, which are calculated by dividing the number of infant deaths by the number of live births registered for the same period. The 2007 rate of 6.7 infant deaths per 1,000 live births was similar to the rate recorded in 2006.

The rate among white infants was less than half that of black infants: 5.6 infant deaths per 1,000 live births for whites in 2007, versus 13.2 per 1,000 for blacks. The reasons for this discrepancy are not clear, although an important factor is believed to be the quality of medical care received by people of different socioeconomic groups. For example, studies have shown that adequate prenatal care is strongly associated with higher infant birth weight and survival. Many black mothers, who are more likely to be poor than white mothers, do not have access to proper prenatal care. Poor nutrition, alcohol and drug abuse, and other social factors also play significant roles.

However, disproportionate poverty among minority groups is not the whole story. Studies have shown that even black infants born to college-educated mothers had nearly twice the mortality rate of comparable white infants.

The leading causes of infant mortality, congenital malformations and chromosomal abnormalities, accounted for 19.9 percent of all infant deaths in 2007. Disorders related to short gestation and low birth weight, the second leading cause of infant deaths, accounted for 16.7 percent.

(See "World Health" for infant mortality rates in other nations.)

▶ SUBSTANCE ABUSE

Illicit Drugs

People abuse drugs, alcohol and tobacco for varied and complicated reasons. The costs, to individuals, families, and society as a whole are enormous. According to the National Institute on Drug Abuse, estimates of the total overall costs of substance abuse in the United States—including health and crime related costs as well as losses in productivity—exceed half a trillion dollars annually.

The Drug Abuse Warning Network (DAWN) of the Substance Abuse and Mental Health Services Administration estimated 2.0 million emergency department (ED) visits for the misuse and abuse of drugs in 2008. Among these visits, half involved illicit drugs such as cocaine and heroin and half involved prescription or over-the-counter drugs used nonmedically.

Prescription drugs An estimated 16.3 million persons age 12 and older used prescription drugs known as psychotherapeutics nonmedically in 2007. Among the most commonly abused of these drugs are opioids, which are often prescribed to treat pain. Medications that fall within this class include morphine, codeine, methadone, oxycodone (e.g. OxyContin, Percodan, Percocet), and hydrocodone (e.g. Vicodin, Hycodan). DAWN showed that the number of ED visits for nonmedical use of opioids increased 111 percent during 2004–2008 (from 144,600 to 305,900 visits).

Another commonly abused class of psychotherapeutics consists of central nervous system depressants, sometimes referred to as sedatives and tranquilizers. These include benzodiazepines such as diazepam (Valium), alprazolam (Zanax), and triazolam (Halcion). According to DAWN, the estimated number of ED visits involving nonmedical use of benzodiazepines increased 89 percent during 2004–2008 (from 143,500 to 271,700 visits).

Marijuana is the most commonly used illegal drug, used by 75 percent of current U.S. drug users; approximately 55 percent of current illicit drug users consume no drugs other than marijuana. It is made from the leaves and flowering tops of the hemp plant, *Cannabis sativa*, which contains psychoactive substances called cannabinoids. The primary psychoactive ingredient in marijuana and hashish (a resin exuded from the flowering tops) is tetrahydrocannabinol, or THC.

Marijuana is typically consumed like tobacco, smoked in hand-rolled cigarettes or in pipes. It typically produces a feeling of well-being, relaxation, and sleepiness. It also interferes with coordination and mental abilities. For instance, it distorts judgment and reaction time, which can be particularly dangerous when a user drives a car. However, there has never been a verified case of someone dying of an overdose.

Possession or sale of marijuana has been illegal in the United States since 1937. Nonetheless, marijuana has legitimate medical uses. A significant body of evidence shows that marijuana combats nausea and weight loss in cancer and AIDS patients. It also helps reduce pressure within the eyes of glaucoma patients.

A study commissioned by the federal government confirmed in 1999 that marijuana has medical uses and that there is no evidence that giving the drug to sick people would increase illicit use in the general population. Since 1996, 14 states have legalized medical marijuana use.

Cocaine is made from the leaves of the coca plant, a shrub native to South America. In the late 1800s and early 1900s, before its dangers were recognized, cocaine was used by doctors as an anesthetic because of its effectiveness in depressing nerve endings. It has since been replaced by less toxic, non-addictive anesthetics.

Cocaine causes a short-lived euphoria. It also suppresses appetite, interferes with sleep, and increases heart rate and blood pressure. Even small doses have been linked to heart attacks and cerebral hemorrhages. Repeated usage is required to maintain a "high." Abusers who try to abstain often experience a tremendous craving for the drug—a hallmark of addiction.

Lifetime Experience With Illicit Drugs, 2008

Age	Used in lifetime	Used in past year	Used in past month
Total[1]	47.0%	14.2%	8.0%
Age			
12–17	26.2	19.0	9.3
18–25	56.6	33.5	19.6
26 and older	48.0	10.3	5.9
Sex			
Male	51.3	16.4	9.9
Female	42.9	12.2	6.3
Race/Ethnicity			
White[2]	50.7	14.4	8.2
Black[2]	46.1	16.9	10.1
Hispanic	36.4	12.3	6.2
Asian	21.2	7.4	3.6

Note: Includes marijuana, cocaine, heroin, hallucinogens, inhalants, or prescription-type psychotherapeutic drugs (stimulants, sedatives, tranquilizers, and analgesics) for nonmedical purposes. 1. Age 12 and older. 2. Non-Hispanic. **Source:** U.S. Dept. of Health and Human Services, Substance Abuse and Mental Health Services Administration, *2008 National Household Survey on Drug Abuse* (Sept. 2009).

Drug Use by U.S. High School Seniors, 1975–2009

Drug	1975	1980	1985	1990	1995	2000	2005	2009
Alcohol	68.2%	72.0%	65.9%	57.1%	51.3%	50.0%	47.0%	43.5%
Cigarettes	36.7	30.5	30.1	29.4	33.5	31.4	23.2	20.1
Marijuana	27.1	33.7	25.7	14.0	21.2	21.6	19.8	20.6
LSD	2.3	2.3	1.6	1.9	4.0	1.6	0.7	0.5
Cocaine	1.9	5.2	6.7	1.9	1.8	2.1	2.3	1.3
Heroin	0.4	0.2	0.3	0.2	0.6	0.7	0.5	0.4
Methamphetamine	N.A.	N.A.	N.A.	N.A.	N.A.	1.9	0.9	0.5

Note: Drug use during the 30 days preceding the survey. **Source:** U.S. Dept. of Health and Human Services, National Institute on Drug Abuse, *Monitoring the Future Study*.

Alcohol Use in U.S., 2007

Characteristic	Total[1]	By Age		26 and older
		12–17	18–25	
Total	51.1%	15.9%	61.2%	54.1%
Race/Ethnicity				
White[2]	56.1	18.2	67.5	58.7
Black[2]	39.3	10.1	50.2	42.4
Hispanic	42.1	15.2	50.7	45.3
Asian	35.2	8.1	50.1	35.9
Sex				
Male	56.6	15.9	65.3	60.8
Female	46.0	16.0	57.1	47.9
Adult Education				
Less than high school	N.A.	N.A.	46.4	34.5
High school graduate	N.A.	N.A.	55.2	49.0
Some college	N.A.	N.A.	68.9	56.5
College graduate	N.A.	N.A.	78.3	67.7
Current Employment				
Full-time	N.A.	N.A.	67.2	62.1
Part-time	N.A.	N.A.	61.1	54.5
Unemployed	N.A.	N.A.	55.4	57.8
Other[3]	N.A.	N.A.	49.3	39.0

Notes: Percentages reporting use of alcohol in the previous month. 1. Age 12 and older. 2. Non-Hispanic. 3. Includes retired, disabled, homemaker, student, etc. **Source:** U.S. Dept. of Health and Human Services, Substance Abuse and Mental Health Services Administration, *2007 National Survey on Drug Use and Health* (Sept. 2008).

U.S. Alcohol Consumption, 1940–2007 (gallons of ethanol, per capita)

	Beer	Wine	Spirits	All beverages
1940	0.73	0.16	0.67	1.56
1950	1.04	0.23	0.77	2.04
1960	0.99	0.22	0.86	2.07
1970	1.14	0.27	1.11	2.52
1980	1.38	0.34	1.04	2.76
1990	1.34	0.33	0.77	2.45
1995	1.23	0.29	0.63	2.15
1998	1.25	0.31	0.63	2.19
2000	1.22	0.31	0.65	2.18
2005	1.18	0.36	0.70	2.23
2007	1.21	0.38	0.73	2.31

Note: Based on population age 15 and older prior to 1970 and on population age 14 and older thereafter. **Source:** U.S. Dept. of Health and Human Services, National Institute on Alcohol Abuse and Alcoholism (updated Oct. 2009).

As of 2007, more than 35.9 million Americans age 12 or older (14.5 percent of that population) had used cocaine at least once in their lifetime. Over 8.6 million (3.5 percent) reported lifetime use of crack, a form of cocaine that can be smoked. However, less than 1 percent had used any form of cocaine within the previous month.

Methamphetamine, popularly called meth, is a powerfully addictive stimulant chemically related to amphetamine but much more potent. It is legally available, via prescriptions that cannot be refilled, for obesity and certain neurological disorders. It is also used illegally to lose weight or maintain alertness, or for recreational purposes. It can be taken orally or by snorting, injection, or smoking. It impairs brain function, increases heart rate and blood pressure, and can lead to convulsions, cardiovascular collapse, and death. The street drug is often referred to as "speed." Methamphetamine hydrochloride, consisting of clear crystals, is popularly referred to as "ice" or "crystal." As of 2007, some 13.1 million Americans age 12 and older had tried methamphetamine at least once in their lifetimes.

Heroin is a synthetic compound derived from morphine, which is extracted from the seed pods of certain varieties of poppy plants. Highly addictive, it comes in various forms, but most illicit heroin comes in powder form in colors ranging from white to dark brown. In 2007, an estimated 153,000 Americans age 12 or older used heroin, including 106,000 who used it for the first time.

Ecstasy, a synthetic drug with both stimulant and hallucinogenic properties, came onto the scene in the 1990s. It is available in pill form, which are often embossed with or in the shape of smiley faces, shamrocks, butterflies, stars, and other enticing designs. A powdered, pure form of ecstasy is known as MDMA, an acronym of its lengthy scientific name, Methylendioxymethamphetamine, which on the streets is known as "Molly". In 2007, some 781,000 people—most of them age 18 or older—used ecstasy for the first time. A growing body of evidence indicates that its use can lead to severe overheating and dehydration, as well as stroke, heart attack, and neurological damage.

Alcohol Consumption of alcohol constitutes the nation's most common drug abuse problem. According to the Centers for Disease Control and Prevention, excessive alcohol use is responsible for more than 75,000 deaths annually. For example, according to the National Highway Traffic Safety Administration, 12,998 people were killed in alcohol-related crashes in 2007. Additionally, alcohol is implicated in the three top causes of teen deaths: accidents, homicide, and suicide.

The 2007 National Survey on Drug Use and Health reported that 51.1 percent of Americans age 12 or older currently used alcohol (defined as any use in the previous month); 23.3 percent engaged in binge drinking (defined as five or more drinks on at least one occasion in the past month). The rate of past month alcohol use was lower in the South (46.8 percent) than in the Northeast (56 percent), Midwest (54.6 percent), or West (50.8 percent).

According to the National Institute of Alcohol Abuse and Alcoholism (NIAAA), men are heavier drinkers than women, and much more likely to be binge drinkers. Younger people drink more than older people. Annual per capita consumption of alcoholic beverages was 2.23 gallons of ethanol in 2004. Consumption was highest in New Hampshire (4.07 gallons), the District of Columbia (3.93), and Nevada (3.66). It was lowest in Utah (1.28), Oklahoma (1.53), and West Virginia (1.75).

Tobacco Smoking is the leading cause of preventable death in the United States, causing approximately 443,000 premature deaths annually and an estimated $157.7 billion in annual health-related economic losses. The good news is that smoking has fallen to its lowest level in recent memory. The decline is attributed to growing appreciation of the link between smoking and health problems; the increased cost of cigarettes, mostly because of tax increases; the growing number of smoking restrictions in public places; and decreasing social acceptability of smoking.

The percentage of adults who smoke decreased dramatically after 1964, the year the U.S. surgeon general first warned about the link between smoking and health problems such as cancer and heart disease. At that time, 40 percent of the adult population were smokers; in 2007, approximately 19.8 percent smoked. The percentage of high school students who reported current cigarette use increased significantly from 1991 to 1997 (27.5 to 36.4 percent), then began to decline, dropping to 19.5 percent in 2009. Surveys indicate that more than 90 percent of adults who are regular smokers began smoking while they were teenagers and that 32 percent of young people who become regular smokers will die of a smoking-related disorder.

Health effects The U.S. surgeon general's report, The Health Consequences of Smoking, released in May 2004, concluded that smoking harms nearly every organ of the body, causing many diseases and reducing the health of smokers in general. Smoking cigarettes with lower machine-measured yields of tar and nicotine provides no clear benefit to health. However, quitting smoking has immediate as well as long-term benefits, reducing risks for diseases caused by smoking and improving health in general.

The effects of smoking include:

- Shortened life span. Each year, some 443,000 Americans—and about six million people worldwide—die prematurely as a result of smoking
- Cancer of the lungs, mouth, esophagus, stomach, bladder, kidney, pancreas, and cervix. Smoking accounts for at least 30 percent of all cancer deaths in the United States each year, including 87 percent of lung cancer deaths.
- Cardiovascular disease, including heart attack, stroke, aneurysm, and the peripheral vascular disease. Smoking weakens the heart's ability to pump blood, promotes clot formation, and damages the inner lining of blood vessels.
- Pulmonary illness, including emphysema, pneumonia, and chronic bronchitis. Annually, more than 80,000 Americans die from non-cancerous chronic lung diseases linked to smoking.
- Fetal and infant mortality. Smoking and secondhand smoke contribute to spontaneous abortions, stillbirths, and sudden infant death syndrome (SIDS). Also, infants of smokers are 74 percent more likely to be of low birth weight than are infants born to mothers who do not smoke.
- Oral health problems. Tobacco, particularly spit tobacco, causes serious oral problems, including cancer of the mouth and gum, periodontitis, and tooth loss.
- Environmental smoking risks. Nonsmokers who are exposed to the tobacco smoke of other people are at increased risk for various diseases. Exposure to secondhand smoke is responsible for approximately 3,000 lung cancer deaths annually among nonsmokers and 150,000 to 300,000 cases of lower respiratory tract infections such as bronchitis and pneumonia in chil-

U.S. Cigarette Consumption, 1900–2006

Year	Cigarettes (billions)	Per capita[1]	Year	Cigarettes (billions)	Per capita[1]
1900	2.5	54	1960	484.4	4,171
1910	8.6	151	1970	536.5	3,985
1920	44.6	665	1980	631.5	3,849
1930	119.3	1,485	1990	525.0	2,817
1940	181.9	1,976	2000	430.0	2,092
1950	369.8	3,552	2006	372.0	1,691[2]

Note: 1. Among persons age 18 and older. 2. Preliminary. **Source:** U.S. Dept. of Health and Human Services, Centers for Disease Control and Prevention; USDA, Economic Research Service.

Teenage Tobacco Use, 1991–2009

Category	1991	1997	2001	2009
Sex				
Male	27.6%	37.7%	29.2%	19.8%
Female	27.3	34.7	27.7	19.1
Race/Ethnicity				
White[1]	30.9	39.7	31.9	22.5
Black[1]	12.6	22.7	14.7	9.5
Hispanic	25.3	34.0	26.6	18.0
High school grade				
9	23.2	33.4	23.0	13.5
10	25.2	35.3	26.9	18.3
11	31.6	36.6	29.8	22.3
12	30.1	39.6	35.2	25.2

Note: Smoked cigarettes within 30 days preceding the survey. 1. Non-Hispanic. **Source:** U.S. Dept. of Health and Human Services, Centers for Disease Control and Prevention, *Morbidity and Mortality Weekly Report*, (July 9, 2010).

Adult Cigarette Smokers in the U.S., 2008

	Men	Women	Total
Total	23.1%	18.3 %	20.6%
Age			
18–24	23.7	19.0	21.4
25–44	26.4	21.1	23.7
45–64	24.8	20.5	22.6
65 and older	10.6	8.4	9.3
Race/Ethnicity			
White[1]	23.5	20.6	22.0
Black[1]	25.6	17.8	21.3
Hispanic	20.7	10.7	15.8
American Indian/ Alaska Native[1]	42.3	22.4	32.4
Asian	15.7	4.7	9.9
Education[2]			
8 years or less[3]	20.4	10.0	15.4
9–11 years	38.1	33.6	35.7
High school graduate	30.0	21.5	25.5
Undergraduate degree	21.8	17.3	19.3
Graduate degree	5.6	5.9	5.7

Notes: 1. Non-Hispanic. 2. Among those age 25 and older. 3. Data is for 2008. **Source:** U.S. Dept. of Health and Human Services, Centers for Disease Control and Prevention, *Morbidity and Mortality Weekly Report*, (Nov. 13, 2009).

The Media

THE PRINT MEDIA

▶ NEWSPAPERS

The first American newspaper was a three-page publication called *Publick Occurrences, Both Foreign and Domestick,* printed in 1690 and immediately suppressed by the Massachussetts government. Despite this setback, a number of newspapers, led by James Franklin's *New England Courant,* slowly emerged, and by 1775, the 2.5 million colonists were served by 48 small weekly newspapers.

In 1783, the *Pennsylvania Evening Post,* which had been the first paper to print the Declaration of Independence, expanded from three printings a week to become the country's first daily newspaper. By 1800 there were 20 dailies and more than 1,000 small-town and frontier weeklies. Most of the dailies, filled with political and business news, were aimed at educated, affluent readers, but rising literacy created an opportunity for cheap, mass-circulation papers. The *New York Sun* started in 1833 and was sold on the street for just one cent. Other "penny presses" copied the *Sun*'s approach and the graphic crime stories, vivid anecdotes and soft features drove their circulations far higher than those of the more staid presses.

During and after the Civil War, innovations like the transatlantic cable, the telephone, electric lights, typewriters, web-fed presses, and typesetting machines made reporting and printing cheaper and easier. In 1900 the number of daily newspapers peaked at 2,326, but readership continued to increase—due in part to the popularity of Sunday editions—to a high of 62,324 in 1990, even as the number of newspapers began to decline.

Newspapers today   The total number of daily newspapers was down to 1,405 in 2009. The continuing decline is partly because of radio, television and the Internet, but also because of newspaper competition and mergers. A century ago, most major cities had at least two newspapers, but today fewer than 50 cities have more than one and, in 12 of those cities, the competing newspapers have actually combined all operations except for the editorial staffs. According to the American Society of News Editors, 5,900 newsroom jobs were lost in 2008 alone—an annual decline of 11.3 percent. The number of newsroom jobs peaked in 2001 at 56,400, but by December 2008, there were only 46,700 people on newspaper staffs.

Newspapers have become volatile business investments, losing nearly 50 percent of their value even before the recession of 2008 and 2009. At the beginning of 2010, the Nieman Journalism Lab projected that newspaper ad revenue would continuously decline, but that newspaper online revenue would increase up to 15 percent by the fourth quarter. Newspaper revenue from print advertising fell to $24.8 million in 2009, a decline of nearly 29 percent from $34.7 million in 2008. Online advertising, which had steadily increased from 2003 to 2007, also continued a downward trend, falling nearly 12 percent from $3.1 million in 2008 to $2.7 million in 2009. Retail advertising had remained relatively constant at around $20 million for the decade since 1998, but fell sharply from $18.8 million in 2008 to $14.2 million in 2009, a decline of 24 percent. Classified advertising also continued to drop—the 2009 figure of $6.2 million is less than half than the 2007 figure of $14.2 million—most likely due to free online classified websites like Craigslist.org.

In 2007, the Federal Communications Commission overturned restrictions that previously prohibited newspaper and TV ownership in the same market. Some family-owned newspapers, like the *Los Angeles Times* and the *Wall Street Journal,* have been sold to conglomerates. Six companies—Gannett, McClatchy Co., Tribune Co., Advance Publications Inc., The New York Times Co., and NewsCorp—now account for almost half of all newspaper circulation. There were no major mergers or acquisitions in 2009, however, most likely because newspaper staffs saw little to gain in the ailing industry by consolidation.

Of the 1,405 daily newspapers published in the U.S. in 2009, most had circulations well under 50,000. Through the 1990s, circulation slid at

Daily Newspapers, Number and Circulation, 1900–2008

Year	Total Number of daily papers	Total Daily circulation ('000s)	Morning Number of papers	Morning Daily circulation ('000s)	Evening Number of papers	Evening Daily circulation ('000s)	Sunday Number of papers	Sunday Daily circulation ('000s)
1900	2,226	15,102	N.A.	N.A.	N.A.	N.A.	N.A.	N.A.
1920	2,042	27,791	437	N.A.	1,605	N.A.	522	17,084
1930	1,942	39,589	388	N.A.	1,554	N.A.	521	26,413
1940	1,878	41,132	380	16,114	1,498	25,008	525	32,371
1950	1,772	53,829	322	21,266	1,450	32,563	549	46,582
1960	1,763	58,882	312	24,029	1,459	34,853	563	47,699
1970	1,748	62,108	334	25,934	1,429	36,174	586	49,217
1980	1,745	62,202	387	29,414	1,388	32,787	735	54,672
1990	1,611	62,324	559	41,308	1,084	21,015	863	62,634
1995	1,533	58,193	656	44,310	891	13,883	888	61,529
2000	1,480	55,773	766	46,772	727	9,000	917	59,421
2004	1,457	54,626	814	46,887	653	7,738	915	57,754
2006	1,437	52,329	833	45,441	614	6,888	907	53,179
2008	1,408	48,597	872	42,757	546	5,840	902	49,115

Note: All-day newspapers are listed in both morning and evening columns, but are counted only once in the total. **Source:** Newspaper Association of America (2009).

Top U.S. Daily and Sunday Newspapers by Circulation, 2009

Rank	Newspaper	Average daily paid circulation	Rank	Newspaper	Average Sunday paid circulation
1.	USA Today[1]	2,113,725	1.	The New York Times	1,451,233
2.	The Wall Street Journal	2,082,189	2.	Los Angeles Times	1,019,388
3.	The New York Times	1,039,031	3.	The Washington Post	868,965
4.	Los Angeles Times	723,181	4.	Chicago Tribune	858,256
5.	The Washington Post	665,383	5.	The Daily News (New York City)	644,766
6.	The Daily News (New York City)	602,857	6.	Detroit Free Press	585,022
7.	The New York Post	558,140	7.	Houston Chronicle	583,364
8.	Chicago Tribune	501,202	8.	Philadelphia Inquirer	550,400
9.	Houston Chronicle	425,138	9.	The Denver Post	526,235
10.	Arizona Republic	389,701	10.	Phoenix Republic	516,562
11.	Denver Post	371,728	11.	Minneapolis Star Tribune	497,678
12.	Newsday (Long Island, NY)	368,194	12.	Dallas Morning News	474,923
13.	Dallas Morning News	331,907	13.	Boston Globe	466,665
14.	Minneapolis Star Tribune	320,076	14.	Atlanta Journal-Constitution	462,011
15.	Chicago Sun-Times	312,141	15.	Newsday (Long Island, NY)	426,510
16.	San Francisco Chronicle	312,118	16.	The St. Louis Post-Dispatch	415,815
17.	Boston Globe	302,638	17.	The St. Petersburg Times	413,929
18.	Cleveland Plain Dealer	291,630	18.	The Star-Ledger (Newark)	404,903
19.	Detroit Free Press	290,730	19.	Cleveland Plain Dealer	393,352
20.	Philadelphia Inquirer	288,270	20.	The Seattle Times	376,515
21.	The Star-Ledger (Newark)	287,082	21.	Milwaukee Journal Sentinel	361,355
22.	St. Petersburg Times	283,093	22.	The New York Post	357,168
23.	The Oregonian (Portland, Ore.)	268,512	23.	San Francisco Chronicle	354,752
24.	Atlanta Journal-Constitution	261,828	24.	Baltimore Sun	351,243
25.	San Diego Union-Tribune	261,253	25.	Kansas City Star	333,006
26.	Sacramento Bee	248,855	26.	Columbus Dispatch	332,052
27.	St. Louis Post-Dispatch	238,400	27.	San Diego Union-Tribune	330,848
28.	Kansas City Star	234,667	28.	The Oregonian (Portland, Ore.)	325,816
29.	Indianapolis Star	232,361	29.	Pittsburgh Post-Gazette	319,987
30.	Orange County (CA) Register	230,877	30.	Orlando Sentinel	315,298
31.	San Jose Mercury News	227,119	31.	Indianapolis Star-Telegram	311,322
32.	The Baltimore Sun	210,098	32.	San Antonio Express-News	303,737
33.	The Pittsburgh Post-Gazette	209,477	33.	The Orange County (CA) Register	300,273
34.	Orlando Sentinel	206,205	34.	The Sacramento Bee	291,115
35.	Milwaukee Journal-Sentinel	203,240	35.	South Florida Sun-Sentinel (Ft. Lauderdale)	285,196
36.	The Seattle Times	203,175	36.	Tampa Tribune & Times	284,583
37.	The Miami Herald	202,122	37.	Fort Worth Star-Telegram	279,190
38.	South Florida Sun-Sentinel (Ft. Lauderdale)	195,522	38.	Cincinnati Enquirer	273,433
39.	The Columbus Dispatch	195,510	39.	The Miami Herald	270,166
40.	The Tampa Tribune	195,277	40.	Arkansas Democrat-Gazette (Little Rock)	269,879
41.	The Courier-Journal (Louisville, KY)	193,992	41.	Chicago Sun-Times	254,379
42.	San Antonio Express-News	192,930	42.	St. Paul Pioneer Press	253,351
43.	Memphis Commercial Appeal	192,631	43.	Buffalo News	252,240
44.	St. Paul Pioneer Press	192,342	44.	The Courier-Journal (Louisville, KY)	250,277
45.	Fort Worth Star Telegram	189,357	45.	San Jose Mercury News	244,661
46.	Cincinnati Enquirer	188,956	46.	The Charlotte Observer	244,494
47.	The Charlotte Observer	187,633	47.	Memphis Commercial Appeal	229,441
48.	Walnut Creek (CA) Contra Costa Times	185,699	48.	Oklahoma City Oklahoman	225,001
49.	Little Rock Democrat Gazette	180,314	49.	Hartford Courant	222,940
50.	Las Vegas Review-Journal	175,439	50.	Des Moines Register	211,668

Note: Average daily and Sunday circulation based on six-month period ending March 31, 2009. 1. The USA Today fell below the Wall Street Journal for the first time in a decade during the first quarter of 2010. Source: Audit Bureau of Circulations (2009).

about one percent a year; in 2005 the rate of decline topped two percent. But in 2009, in the six months ending on September 30, circulation sales fell by 10.6 percent on weekdays and 7.5 percent on Sundays. The USA Today, the most widely-read paper for nearly two decades, dropped 17.1 percent in 2009, below The Wall Street Journal.

About 75 percent of the 100 best-selling newspapers are in Asia. According to the World Association of Newspapers, overall global circulation (including free dailies) rose 1.62 percent in 2008, a slow from a 2.6 percent increase in 2007. The newspaper with the largest circulation is Japan's Yomiuri Shimbun, with more than 14 million readers, and its rival, the Asahi Shimbun, read by more than 12 million people each day.

Circulation figures have steadily declined for several years, and in 2009 the industry sold about 44 million newspaper copies a day—fewer than at any time since the 1940s. Weekday dailies saw a steeper decline than Sunday editions. Among the 25 largest papers, the San Francisco Chronicle suffered the most, losing 22.7 percent of its weekday sales in the first quarter of 2010. There are some signs, however, that circulation may have started to level off. At The New York Times, average weekday circulation in the first quarter of 2010 was slightly up compared to the third quarter numbers of 2009. The Arizona Republic saw an increase in those two periods from 316,000 to 350,000.

Sunday edition readership is traditionally higher, but both daily and Sunday editions have experienced readership decline—31.5 percent and

Weekly Newspapers in the U.S., 1960–2009

Year	Number of newspapers[1]	Average circulation	Total weekly circulation	Year	Number of newspapers[1]	Average circulation	Total weekly circulation
1960	8,174	2,566	20,974,338	1990	7,606	6,958	52,919,846
1965	8,061	3,106	25,036,031	1995[2]	8,453	9,425	79,668,266
1970	7,612	3,660	27,857,332	2000[2]	6,579	7,295	47,990,892
1975	7,612	4,715	35,892,409	2004[2]	6,692	7,444	49,814,806
1980	7,954	5,324	42,347,512	2005[2]	6,659	7,319	49,541,617
1985	7,704	6,359	48,988,801	2009[2]	6,055	7,516	45,506,704

Notes: As of Feb. 2009. 1. Any newspaper published less than four times a week. 2. 1995 and later not comparable to prior years due to change in information collection procedures. **Source:** Newspaper Association of America; 2009 Editor and Publisher International Yearbook.

Top 100 U.S. Magazines by Circulation, 2009

Rank	Magazine	Average paid circulation per issue	Percent change 2008–09	Rank	Magazine	Average paid circulation per issue	Percent change 2008–09
1.	AARP The Magazine	24,463,228	1.4%	51.	Shape	1,674,636	-1.6%
2.	AARP Bulletin	24,174,159	-0.8	52.	American Rifleman	1,643,461	16.1
3.	Reader's Digest	7,629,105	-8.2	53.	Country Living	1,623,411	-0.2
4.	Better Homes And Gardens	7,627,992	-0.4	54.	Fitness	1,539,001	-1.7
5.	Good Housekeeping	4,641,651	-0.8	55.	Self	1,507,499	1.3
6.	National Geographic	4,602,119	-9.1	56.	Field & Stream	1,507,299	-1.5
7.	Woman's Day	3,949,248	1.3	57.	Rolling Stone	1,473,569	0.8
8.	Family Circle	3,874,240	-0.8	58.	Women's Health	1,466,405	25.5
9.	Ladies' Home Journal	3,850,782	0.2	59.	VFW Magazine	1,430,767	-5.4
10.	AAA Westways	3,831,215	0.0	60.	Golf Magazine	1,420,860	0.6
11.	Game Informer Magazine	3,703,120	5.6	61.	Health	1,382,196	0.4
12.	People	3,614,861	-3.5	62.	Bon Appetit	1,347,237	-3.7
13.	Time	3,350,415	-0.7	63.	More	1,347,174	4.8
14.	Taste of Home	3,258,915	1.8	64.	Scholastic Parent & Child	1,344,908	0.5
15.	Sports Illustrated	3,227,409	-0.4	65.	Car and Driver	1,324,892	1.2
16.	Prevention	3,106,409	-6.9	66.	Popular Science	1,311,003	-1.8
17.	Cosmopolitan	2,954,665	0.8	67.	Weight Watchers	1,289,490	-0.3
18.	Southern Living	2,848,107	1.0	68.	Woman's World	1,278,395	-6.0
19.	AAA Via	2,775,449	-1.4	69.	Vogue	1,269,640	0.9
20.	TV Guide Magazine	2,682,799	-17.9	70.	U.S. News & World Report	1,269,260	-26.3
21.	Maxim	2,525,432	-0.1	71.	First	1,261,191	-6.5
22.	AAA Living	2,459,874	0.6	72.	Ebony	1,240,894	-9.6
23.	O, The Oprah Magazine	2,438,710	2.5	73.	Country	1,240,005	5.2
24.	AAA Going Places	2,438,377	-4.5	74.	Sunset	1,228,506	0.8
25.	Glamour	2,419,017	4.1	75.	Home & Away	1,217,833	-2.7
26.	Newsweek	2,316,590	-14.8	76.	Popular Mechanics	1,215,742	-1.6
27.	American Legion Magazine	2,287,971	-7.5	77.	Vanity Fair	1,201,239	2.9
28.	Remedy / Remedy MD	2,275,882	21.4	78.	Food Network Magazine	1,196,835	N.A.
29.	Playboy	2,257,123	-15.1	79.	Reminisce	1,190,374	5.1
30.	Redbook	2,224,448	0.3	80.	Boys' Life	1,169,722	-0.6
31.	Parenting	2,186,320	5.3	81.	Family Handyman	1,157,659	-0.4
32.	FamilyFun	2,175,670	17.1	82.	Motor Trend	1,139,689	2.2
33.	AAA World	2,103,343	-1.1	83.	Lucky	1,127,953	-2.6
34.	Seventeen	2,075,401	2.2	84.	Elle	1,115,552	1.1
35.	ESPN The Magazine	2,070,363	0.8	85.	Star Magazine	1,096,817	-13.9
36.	Parents	2,064,249	-0.5	86.	Allure	1,086,905	-0.6
37.	Martha Stewart Living	2,061,226	1.3	87.	Essence	1,082,319	0.6
38.	Guideposts	2,055,606	-6.8	88.	Everyday Food	1,081,835	9.6
39.	Smithsonian	2,023,786	-0.4	89.	New Yorker	1,044,535	-0.3
40.	Real Simple	1,995,625	-0.4	90.	Teen Vogue	1,030,221	0.9
41.	Money	1,926,070	-0.5	91.	Scouting	1,024,800	-0.6
42.	Us Weekly	1,924,093	1.1	92.	American Hunter	1,013,797	9.7
43.	Men's Health	1,862,937	-0.1	93.	All You	1,007,874	11.1
44.	Endless Vacation	1,838,685	2.0	94.	Marie Claire	981,464	-1.2
45.	Every Day With Rachael Ray	1,801,034	1.9	95.	This Old House	980,461	2.0
46.	Entertainment Weekly	1,788,799	-0.9	96.	Gourmet	978,037	-0.3
47.	Cooking Light	1,772,793	-2.4	97.	Midwest Living	976,154	1.3
48.	In Style	1,763,475	-1.6	98.	Traditional Home	974,015	-0.6
49.	Birds & Blooms	1,747,499	14.9	99.	Travel + Leisure	960,847	-0.7
50.	Golf Digest	1,676,636	1.4	100.	Food & Wine	944,304	0.1
					Total Top 100	**244,141,019**	**-0.3**

Source: Magazine Publishers of America (2010).

Top 50 U.S. Magazines by Advertising Revenues, 2008–09

Rank, Magazine	Advertising revenues	Percent change 2008–09	Rank, Magazine	Advertising revenues	Percent change 2008–09
1. People	933,135,770	3.8	26. Fortune	182,908,879	−33.9
2. Better Homes & Gardens	811,825,109	7.8	27. Harper's Bazaar	171,420,282	−22.2
3. Sports Illustrated	560,365,030	−12.8	28. New York Magazine	169,837,894	−22.5
4. Good Housekeeping	508,230,819	−5.6	29. Car and Driver	168,590,205	−17.7
5. Family Circle	442,686,001	17.9	30. Martha Stewart Living	167,104,881	−13.9
6. Time	404,079,647	−13.3	31. Bride's	166,852,052	−13.5
7. Woman's Day	398,037,552	2.6	32. Self	162,464,364	−17.9
8. Cosmopolitan	344,916,730	−10.1	33. Business Week	162,378,043	−31.2
9. In Style	326,414,678	−10.2	34. Star	161,887,182	−4.4
10. Ladies' Home Journal	321,071,844	6.3	35. GQ	161,579,467	−22.4
11. Us Weekly	310,685,632	0.6	36. Entertainment Weekly	160,003,296	−16.7
12. Glamour	289,543,276	−13.2	37. Maxim	159,579,643	−18.7
13. Vogue	289,137,936	−26.9	38. Rolling Stone	157,852,251	−14.7
14. Elle	273,775,035	−15.9	39. Allure	147,014,262	−25.5
15. Forbes	251,532,222	−25.6	40. New Yorker	145,264,470	−19.0
16. Reader's Digest	245,235,819	−3.8	41. Golf Magazine	144,821,976	−24.3
17. ESPN Magazine	243,405,998	−8.1	42. Men's Health	139,483,047	−16.4
18. Newsweek	241,036,507	−30.4	43. Lucky	137,122,669	−23.0
19. Real Simple	237,104,330	−9.6	44. More	134,211,123	16.2
20. Parents	219,971,716	−5.0	45. Marie Claire	133,616,095	−5.9
21. O, The Oprah Magazine	207,655,975	−24.3	46. Country Living	132,618,560	−7.2
22. Shape Magazine	204,175,950	−4.1	47. Golf Digest	128,436,213	−22.2
23. Vanity Fair	204,063,259	−26.8	48. AARP—The Magazine	127,340,613	−16.2
24. Redbook	203,369,955	−4.5	49. TV Guide	127,033,674	−35.3
25. Southern Living	187,257,684	−2.0	50. Travel + Leisure	121,608,527	−19.4

Source: Magazine Publishers of America, *Publishers Information Bureau Publications Ranked by Revenue, Jan.–Dec. 2009*

27 percent, respectively—from peak totals in the last 25 years. In 2009, 43 percent of Americans reported that they had read any daily newspaper the day before, compared with 48 percent who had read a Sunday paper that week. Respondents in the lowest age brackets, 18 to 24 and 25 to 34, had the lowest readership levels—27 and 28 percent respectively. Older groups also showed declines in readership, though people in the oldest groups were most likely to say they read a newspaper the day before, with 62 percent of those over 65 answering affirmatively. Even this, however, was a decline of two percentage points from 2008.

Newspapers tomorrow   Facing increasing competition from Internet-based news sites for

Top 15 U.S. Newspaper Web sites by Unique Visitors, 2008

Rank, Newspaper	Unique Visitors each month[1]
1. New York Times	19,503,667
2. USA Today	10,845,000
3. The Washington Post	10,260,167
4. Los Angeles Times	7,886,250
5. The Wall Street Journal	7,169,333
6. Boston Globe	5,211,083
7. New York Post	4,335,583
8. Chicago Tribune	4,271,833
9. New York Daily News	4,226,083
10. San Francisco Chronicle	4,158,000
11. Newsday (Long Island, NY)	3,163,000
12. Politico[1]	3,113,000
13. Chicago Sun-Times	2,884,417
14. The Houston Chronicle	2,808,750
15. The Dallas Morning News	2,647,500

Note: Includes only websites of news organizations that also print a newspaper. 1. Only printed when Congress is in session, and Tuesdays when Congress is not. **Source:** Nielsen, *Editor & Publisher's Monthly Reports*; www.niemanlab.org.

readers and advertisers, U.S. newspapers continue to try to establish an online presence. According to a report by the Pew Research Center in 2009, the Internet topped newspapers as the leading news source. Sixty percent of respondents under the age of 30 said they viewed most of their news online. According to Nielsen Online, in January 2009 online readership had reached almost 75 million U.S. readers and 3.7 billion page views. Most newspapers in the U.S. (including the top 100) have Web sites, and some now offer direct electronic transmission to electronic reading devices. At the end of 2009, Amazon's Kindle offered nearly 100 papers, and 2010 saw the advent of more versatile electronic tablets, such as Apple's iPad. Magazine demos suggest that these tablets could eventually offer readers a better product than print editions.

However, news-based Web sites with no print affiliation have been very successful at drawing readers with commentary and other features that traditional newspapers shun. The *Huffington Post* outranks all but six newspaper websites in visitor counts and, in 2007, *Talking Points Memo* became the first Web-only publication to win a major journalism prize, the George Polk Award.

▶MAGAZINES

More than four out of five U.S. adults read magazines. Consumer magazines range from the very specialized (*Fly Fisherman*) and the general interest (*People*) and are sold either by subscription or through retail stores. Some (*Audubon*) published by membership groups are also distributed to members. Trade publications are magazines focused on a particular area of business (e.g. trucking, restaurants, computers). About 2,500 trade publications are sold either by subscription or distributed free. Like newspapers, most major magazines maintain Websites. Magazine presence online increased seven percent from 2007 to 2009, with nearly 76 million unique vistors in the fourth quarter alone of 2009.

Most magazines make money through both circulation sales and advertising. The most financially successful magazines are not necessarily the largest sellers, because they may command high advertising fees. *Vogue*, for example, ranked 13th in advertising revenue for 2009, but was 69th in circulation. Total magazine revenues for 2009 were $21.1 billion, a 17.5 percent decline from 2008.

▶BOOKS

Book sales in the United States declined slightly in 2009 according to figures released by Nielsen BookScan, which tracks about 75 percent of sales. The number of books sold dropped three percent from 2008 to 2009, to 724 million units. The biggest decline in 2009 by category was in adult non-fiction, down seven percent from 2008, but output of

Number and Value of U.S. Books Sold, 2007–2009 (in millions)

Type of publication and market area	Publishers' net units sales			Publishers' net dollar sales		
	2007	2008	2009[T]	2007	2008	2009[T]
Type Of Publication						
Trade	2,282	2,238	2,248	15,048	14,734	14,812
Adult trade	1,381	1,348	1,361	11,392	11,125	11,214
Juvenile trade	901	889	888	3,657	3,609	3,598
Religious	275	247	239	2,575	2,318	2,225
Professional	246	256	265	8,358	8,696	8,961
Scholarly	72	75	76	1,375	1,428	1,446
Elhi	175	182	189	7,056	7,373	7,606
College	78	81	84	5,524	5,772	5,990
All books	3,127	3,079	3,101	39,936	40,321	41,040
Market Area						
Domestic (total)	2,175	2,134	2,144	14,415	14,123	14,198
Wholesalers & Jobbers	584	506	504	3,062	2,642	2,623
Specialty Markets	361	335	332	2,812	2,511	2,509
Internet	N.A.	180	195	N.A.	1,238	1,331
Bookstores	639	559	556	5,138	4,559	4,553
Organizations / Direct	50	47	47	473	441	444
Public Libraries	21	23	23	306	302	304
Educational & Academic	100	100	101	836	790	796
Other	418	385	386	1,789	1,640	1,638
Export	107	103	104	633	611	615
Total	2,282	2,238	2,248	15,048	14,734	14,812

Note: Includes all titles released by publishers in the United States, and imports that appear under the imprint of American publishers. Multi-volume sets are counted as one unit. School libraries included with schools. Does not include standardized tests. Data from 2007 includes sales for small publishers ($50 million and below in annual revenue) and is not directly comparable with previous years.
1. Projected. **Source:** Book Industry Study Group, Inc., *Book Industry TRENDS 2009*, reprinted by permission.

Best Selling Books in America, 1925–2009

Year	Fiction Title, Author	Nonfiction Title, Author
1925	*Soundings*, A. Hamilton Gibbs	*Diet and Health*, Lulu Hunt Peters
1926	*The Private Life of Helen of Troy*, John Erskine	*The Man Nobody Knows*, Bruce Barton
1927	*Elmer Gantry*, Sinclair Lewis	*The Story of Philosophy*, Will Durant
1928	*The Bridge on San Luis Rey*, Thornton Wilder	*Disraeli*, Andre Maurois
1929	*All Quiet on the Western Front*, Erich Maria Remarque	*The Art of Thinking*, Ernest Dimmet
1930	*Cimarron*, Edna Ferber	*The Story of San Michele*, Axel Munthe
1931	*The Good Earth*, Pearl S. Buck	*Education of a Princess*, Grand Duchess Marie
1932	*The Good Earth*, Pearl S. Buck	*The Epic of America*, James Truslow Adams
1933	*Anthony Adverse*, Hervey Allen	*Life Begins at Forty*, Walter Pitkin
1934	*Anthony Adverse*, Hervey Allen	*While Rome Burns*, Alexander Woollcott
1935	*Green Light*, Lloyd C. Douglas	*North to the Orient*, Anne Morrow Lindbergh
1936	*Gone With the Wind*, Margaret Mitchell	*Man the Unknown*, Alexis Carrel
1937	*Gone With the Wind*, Margaret Mitchell	*How to Win Friends and Influence People*, Dale Carnegie
1938	*The Yearling*, Marjorie Kinnan Rawlings	*The Importance of Living*, Lin Yutang
1939	*The Grapes of Wrath*, John Steinbeck	*Days of Our Years*, Piere von Paaseen
1940	*How Green Was My Valley*, Richard Llewellyn	*I Married Adventure*, Osa Johnson
1941	*The Keys of the Kingdom*, A.J. Cronin	*Berlin Diary*, William C. Shirer
1942	*The Song of Bernadette*, Franz Werfel	*See Here, Private Hargrove*, Marion Hargrove
1943	*The Robe*, Lloyd C. Douglas	*Under Cover*, John Roy Carlson
1944	*Strange Fruit*, Lillian Smith	*I Never Left Home* , Bob Hope
1945	*Forever Amber*, Kathleen Winsor	*Brave Men*, Ernie Pyle
1946	*The King's General*, Daphne du Maurier	*The Egg and I*, Betty MacDonald
1947	*The Miracle of the Bells*, Russell Janney	*Peace of Mind*, Joshua L. Liebman
1948	*The Big Fisherman*, Lloyd C. Douglas	*Crusade in Europe*, Dwight D. Eisenhower
1949	*The Egyptian*, Mika Waltari	*White Collar Zoo*, Clare Barnes, Jr.
1950	*The Cardinal*, Henry Morton Robinson	*Betty Crocker's Picture Cookbook*

Year	Fiction Title, Author	Nonfiction Title, Author
1951	*From Here to Eternity*, James Jones	*Look Younger, Live Longer*, Gaylord Hauser
1952	*The Silver Chalice*, Thomas B.Costain	*The Holy Bible: Revised Standard Version*
1953	*The Robe*, Lloyd C. Douglas	*The Holy Bible: Revised Standard Version*
1954	*Not As A Stranger*, Morton Thompson	*The Holy Bible: Revised Standard Version*
1955	*Marjorie Morningstar*, Herman Wouk	*Gift from the Sea*, Anne Morrow Lindbergh
1956	*Don't Go Near the Water*, William Brinkley	*Arthritis and Common Sense*, Dan Dale Alexander
1957	*By Love Possessed*, James Gould Cozzens	*Kids Say the Darndest Things!*, Art Linkletter
1958	*Doctor Zhivago*, Boris Pasternak	*Kids Say the Darndest Things!*, Art Linkletter
1959	*Exodus*, Leon Uris	*'Twixt Twelve and Twenty*, Pat Boone
1960	*Advise and Consent*, Allen Drury	*Folk Medicine*, D.C. Jarvis
1961	*The Agony and the Ecstasy*, Irving Stone	*The New English Bible: The New Testament*
1962	*Ship of Fools*, Katherine Anne Porter	*Calories Don't Count*, Dr. Herman Taller
1963	*The Shoes of the Fisherman*, Morris L. West	*Happiness Is a Warm Puppy*, Charles M. Schulz
1964	*The Spy Who Came in From the Cold*, John le Carré	*Four Days*, American Heritage
1965	*The Source*, James A. Michener	*How To Be a Jewish Mother*, Dan Greenburg
1966	*Valley of the Dolls*, Jacqueline Susann	*How to Avoid Probate*, Norman F. Dacey
1967	*The Arrangement*, Elia Kazan	*Death of a President*, William Manchester
1968	*Airport*, Arthur Hailey	*Better Homes & Gardens New Cook Book*
1969	*Portnoy's Complaint*, Philip Roth	*American Heritage Dictionary of the English Language*, ed. William Morris
1970	*Love Story*, Erich Segal	*Everything You Wanted to Know About Sex but Were Afraid to Ask*, David Reuben, M.D.
1971	*Wheels*, Arthur Hailey	*The Sensuous Man*, "M."
1972	*Jonathan Livingston Seagull*, Richard Bach	*The Living Bible*, Kenneth Taylor
1973	*Jonathan Livingston Seagull*, Richard Bach	*The Living Bible*, Kenneth Taylor
1974	*Centennial*, James A. Michener	*The Total Woman*, Marabel Morgan
1975	*Ragtime*, E. L. Doctorow	*Angels: God's Secret Agents*, Billy Graham
1976	*Trinity*, Leon Uris	*The Final Days*, Bob Woodward, Carl Bernstein
1977	*The Silmarillion*, J.R.R. Tolkien	*Roots*, Alex Haley
1978	*Chesapeake*, James A. Michener	*If Life is a Bowl of Cherries—What Am I Doing in the Pits?* Erma Bombeck
1979	*The Matarese Circle*, Robert Ludlum	*Aunt Erma's Cope Book*, Erma Bombeck
1980	*The Covenant*, James Michener	*Crisis Investing*, Douglas R. Casey
1981	*Noble House*, James Clavell	*The Beverly Hills Diet*, Judy Mazel
1982	*E.T. The Extra-Terrestrial Storybook*	*Jane Fonda's Workout Book*, Jane Fonda with William Kotzwinkle
1983	*Return of the Jedi Storybook*, Joan D. Vinge	*In Search of Excellence*, Thomas J. Peters, Robert H. Waterman Jr.
1984	*The Talisman*, Stephen King, Peter Straub	*Iacocca: An Autobiography*, Lee Iacocca with William Novak
1985	*The Mammoth Hunters*, Jean M.Auel	*Iacocca: An Autobiography*, Lee Iacocca with William Novak
1986	*It*, Stephen King	*Fatherhood*, Bill Cosby
1987	*The Tommyknockers*, Stephen King	*Time Flies*, Bill Cosby
1988	*The Cardinal of the Kremlin*, Tom Clancy	*The Eight-Week Cholesterol Diet*, Robert Kowalski
1989	*Clear and Present Danger*, Tom Clancy	*All I Really Need to Know I Learned in Kindergarten*, Robert Fulghum
1990	*The Plains of Passage*, Jean Auel	*A Life on the Road*, Charles Kuralt
1991	*Scarlett*, Alexandra Ripley	*Me: The Stories of My Life*, Katharine Hepburn
1992	*Dolores Claiborne*, Stephen King	*The Way Things Ought to Be*, Rush Limbaugh
1993	*The Bridges of Madison County*, Robert James Waller	*See, I Told You So*, Rush Limbaugh
1994	*The Chamber*, John Grisham	*In the Kitchen with Rosie*, Rosie Daley
1995	*The Rainmaker*, John Grisham	*Men are From Mars, Women are From Venus*, John Gray
1996	*The Runaway Jury*, John Grisham	*Make the Connection*, Oprah Winfrey & Bob Greene
1997	*The Partner*, John Grisham	*Angela's Ashes*, Frank McCourt
1998	*The Street Lawyer*, John Grisham	*The Nine Steps to Financial Freedom*, Suze Orman
1999	*The Testament*, John Grisham	*Tuesdays with Morrie*, Mitch Albom
2000	*The Brethren*, John Grisham	*Who Moved My Cheese?* Spencer Johnson
2001	*Desecration*, Jerry B. Jenkins and Tim LaHaye	*The Prayer of Jabez*, Bruce Wilkinson
2002	*The Summons*, John Grisham	*Self Matters*, Phillip C. McGraw
2003	*The Da Vinci Code*, Dan Brown	*The Purpose-Driven Life*, Rick Warren
2004	*The Da Vinci Code*, Dan Brown	*The South Beach Diet*, Arthur Agatston
2005	*The Broker*, John Grisham	*Natural Cures "They" Don't Want You to Know About*, Kevin Trudeau
2006	*For One More Day*, Mitch Albom	*The Innocent Man*, John Grisham
2007	*A Thousand Splendid Suns*, Khaled Hosseini	*The Secret*, Rhonda Byrne
2008	*The Appeal*, John Grisham	*The Last Lecture*, Randy Pausch
2009	*The Lost Symbol*, Dan Brown	*Going Rogue*, Sarah Palin

Sources: Alice Payne Hackett, *70 Years of Best Sellers; Publishers Weekly.*

new titles and editions dropped less than half a percent in the same period. Publishers' net revenue in 2008, however, rose 1 percent from 2007 to reach $40.3 billion, indicating that the average price of books increased slightly.

Ironically it is the computer, predicted by many to be the book industry's death knell, which has been responsible for the overall increase in book production since 1990. Computers reduce publishers' production costs, and the use of print-on-demand capabilities for small and major publishers continues to flourish. Bowker projects that 764,448 titles were produced in 2009 that fall outside the definition of "traditional publishing," including both print-on-demand and self-published titles, and electronic editions.

Though still in their infancy, electronic books commanded an estimated three to five percent of the market in 2009. Some estimates state that this share will rise to as much as 25 percent by 2012. The arrival of Apple's iPad in early 2010 revealed the true potential of the e-book market, tapping more than 125 million iTunes customers. According to the

Book Industry Study Group, 25 percent of people who had bought e-books in 2010 said they bought fewer print books than before. Fifteen percent reported they buy no print books.

Number of Libraries in U.S. and Canada by Type, 1980–2000

Type of Library	1980	1990	1999	2000
Public libraries	8,717	9,060	9,837	9,480
Branches	5,936	5,833	6,376	6,957
Special[1]	7,649	9,051	9,691	9,948
Academic	4,591	4,593	4,723	3,491
Government	1,260	1,735	1,874	1,411
Armed forces	485	489	352	341
Total, U.S.[2]		28,638	30,761	33,108	31,628
Total, U.S. and Canada[2]	31,564	34,613	37,039	35,261

Note: 1. Includes medical, religious, and law. 2. Includes categories not listed here. Source: R.R. Bowker Co., *The Bowker Annual: Library and Book Trade Almanac.* (2001). Used with the permission of R.R. Bowker ® a Unit of Cahners Business Information.

The American Library Association's 10 Most Challenged Books of 2009

1. *ttyl, ttfn, l8r, g8r* (series), Lauren Myracle
2. *And Tango Makes Three*, Peter Parnell and Justin Richardson
3. *The Perks of Being A Wallflower*, Stephen Chbosky
4. *To Kill A Mockingbird*, Harper Lee
5. *Twilight* (series), Stephanie Meyer
6. *Catcher in the Rye*, J.D. Salinger
7. *My Sister's Keeper*, Jodi Picoult
8. *The Earth, My Butt, and Other Big, Round Things*, Carolyn Mackler
9. *The Color Purple*, Alice Walker
10. *The Chocolate War*, Robert Cormier

Source: American Library Association

Book Sales by Selected Type, 2003–2009

Type	2003	2005	% change 2003–05	2007	% change 2005–07	2009	% change 2007–09
Trade (all)[1]	$6,872,190	$8,043,471	17.04%	$8,525,932	6.00%	$8,067,524	−5.38%
Book clubs & mail order	775,669	659,290	−15.00	621,605	−5.72	588,461	−5.33
Mass market paperback	1,196,026	1,091,759	−8.72	1,119,140	2.51	1,042,143	−6.88
Audiobooks	161,049	206,299	28.09	218,230	5.78	191,979	−12.03
E-books	19,772	43,832	121.69	67,233	53.39	313,167	365.79

Notes: Dollar amounts in thousands. 1. Includes adult hard- and paperbound and juvenile hard- and paperbound. Source: American Association of Publishers (2010).

New Books and Editions Published, by Subject, 1990–2009

Subject	1990	2000	2009[1]	Subject	1990	2000	2009[1]
Agriculture	514	1,073	1,329	Medicine	3,014	6,234	10,913
Arts	1,262	4,980	9,824	Music	289	1,582	4,397
Biography	1,957	3,899	12,313	Personal Finance	N.A.	N.A.	653
Business	1,191	4,068	8,976	Philosophy, Psychology	1,688	5,556	13,209
Computers	N.A.	N.A.	5,131	Poetry, Drama	874	2,479	11,766
Cookery	N.A.	N.A.	2,647	Religion	2,285	6,206	19,310
Education	1,039	3,378	9,200	Science	2,742	8,464	15,428
Fiction	5,764	14,617	45,181	Sociology, Economics	7,042	14,908	25,992
General works	1,760	1,318	2,563	Sports, Recreation	978	3,483	6,000
History	2,248	7,931	14,291	Technology	2,092	8,582	8,472
Home economics	758	2,513	1,599	Travel	495	3,170	4,868
Juvenile	5,172	8,690	32,348	Non-Traditional	N.A.	N.A.	764,448
Language	649	2,536	5,221	Total[2]	46,748	122,108	1,052,803
Law	896	3,070	5,784				
Literature	2,049	3,371	10,941				

Note: Comprises new books (published for the first time), and new editions. Includes mass-market paperbacks. Excludes government publications, books sold only by subscription, dissertations, periodicals, quarterlies, and pamphlets under 49 pages. 1. Projected. 2. Total numbers before 2009 do not include non-traditionally published titles. Note on Methodology: Beginning in 2006, Bowker changed methodology to include ISBNs without prices, as well as new bindings. The total counts for 2008 cannot be compared directly with previous years. Source: R.R. Bowker Co., *The Bowker Annual Library and Book Trade Almanac*, copyright 2004 Reed Elsevier Inc. Used with the permission of R.R. Bowker, a business unit of Reed Elsevier Inc., and R.R. Bowker *New Book Titles and Editions, 2002–2009*.

THE ELECTRONIC MEDIA

►TELEVISION

There's no doubt as to the pervasiveness of television's influence on America. Once a symbol of luxury, the color television set has found its way into almost every home in America, and a great majority of households have two or more. In 2009, Americans spent over 153 hours per month watching television in their home, a 1.2 percent increase from 2008. The way Americans viewed television

changed drastically in 2009, when in June the Federal Communications Commission (FCC) mandated that all U.S. based TV signals must be transmitted digitally. Most (97.5 percent) of homes were prepared for the analog switch-off, though 2.5 percent of American households were completely unready when the June deadline came. That number dropped to less than 1 percent by October.

Americans are changing the way they watch programming, in more ways than an analog to digital conversion. Monthly time spent watching time-shifted television (i.e. DVR) grew over 40 percent from 2008 to 2009. By 2010, all major networks offered free episodes of their most popular shows to stream from their website. Sites such as

Top 50 Single Shows in TV History, by Rating

Rank, Program	Date	Network	Rating	Share
1. *M*A*S*H* Special (Last episode)	2/28/83	CBS	60.2%	77%
2. *Dallas* (Who Shot J.R.?)	11/21/80	CBS	53.3	76
3. *Roots,* part 8	1/30/77	ABC	51.1	71
4. Super Bowl XVI (San Francisco/Cincinnati)	1/24/82	CBS	49.1	73
5. Super Bowl XVII (Washington/Miami)	1/30/83	NBC	48.6	69
6. XVII Winter Olympics (Figure skating round 1)	2/23/94	CBS	48.5	64
7. Super Bowl XX (Chicago/New England)	1/26/86	NBC	48.3	70
8. *Gone With the Wind,* part 1	11/7/76	NBC	47.7	65
9. *Gone With the Wind,* part 2	11/8/76	NBC	47.4	64
10. Super Bowl XII (Dallas/Denver)	1/15/78	CBS	47.2	67
11. Super Bowl XIII (Pittsburgh/Dallas)	1/21/79	NBC	47.1	74
12. *Bob Hope Christmas Show*	1/15/70	NBC	46.6	64
13. Super Bowl XVIII (L.A. Raiders/Washington)	1/22/84	CBS	46.4	71
14. Super Bowl XLIV (New Orleans/Indianapolis)	2/7/10	CBS	46.4	68
15. Super Bowl XIX (San Francisco/Miami)	1/20/85	ABC	46.4	63
16. Super Bowl XIV (Pittsburgh/L.A. Rams)	1/20/80	CBS	46.3	67
16. Super Bowl XXX (Dallas/Pittsburgh)	1/28/96	NBC	46.0	68
17. *ABC Theater "The Day After"*	1/20/83	ABC	46.0	62
19. *The Fugitive*	8/29/67	ABC	45.9	72
20. *Roots,* part 6	1/28/77	ABC	45.9	66
21. Super Bowl XXI (N.Y. Giants/Denver)	1/25/87	CBS	45.8	66
22. *Roots,* part 5	1/27/77	ABC	45.7	71
23. Super Bowl XXVIII (Dallas/Buffalo)	1/30/94	NBC	45.5	66
24. *Cheers* (Last episode)	5/20/93	NBC	45.5	64
25. *The Ed Sullivan Show*	2/9/64	CBS	45.3	60
26. Super Bowl XXVII (Dallas/Buffalo)	1/31/93	NBC	45.1	66
27. *Bob Hope Christmas Show*	1/14/71	NBC	45.0	61
28. *Roots,* part 3	1/25/77	ABC	44.8	68
29. Super Bowl XXXII (Denver/Green Bay)	1/25/98	NBC	44.5	67
30. Super Bowl XI (Oakland/Minnesota)	1/9/77	NBC	44.4	73
31. Super Bowl XV (Oakland/Philadelphia)	1/25/81	NBC	44.4	63
32. Super Bowl VI (Dallas/Miami)	1/16/72	CBS	44.2	74
33. XVII Winter Olympics (Figure skating finals)	2/25/94	CBS	44.1	64
34. *Roots,* part 2	1/24/77	ABC	44.1	62
35. *The Beverly Hillbillies*	1/8/64	CBS	44.0	65
36. *Roots,* part 4	1/26/77	ABC	43.8	66
37. *The Ed Sullivan Show* (with the Beatles)	2/16/64	CBS	43.8	60
38. Super Bowl XXIII (San Francisco/Cincinnati)	1/22/89	NBC	43.5	68
39. Academy Awards	4/7/70	ABC	43.4	78
40. Super Bowl XXXI (Green Bay/New England)	1/26/97	FOX	43.3	65
41. Super Bowl XXXIV (St. Louis/Tennessee)	1/30/00	ABC	43.3	63
42. *The Thorn Birds,* part 3	3/29/83	ABC	43.2	62
43. *The Thorn Birds,* part 4	3/30/83	ABC	43.1	62
44. NFC Championship game (San Francisco/Dallas)	1/10/82	CBS	42.9	62
45. *The Beverly Hillbillies*	1/15/64	CBS	42.8	62
46. Super Bowl VII (Miami/Washington)	1/14/73	NBC	42.7	72
47. Super Bowl XLI (Indianapolis/Chicago)	2/4/07	CBS	42.6	N.A.
48. *The Thorn Birds,* part 2	3/28/83	ABC	42.5	59
49. Super Bowl IX (Pittsburgh/Minnesota)	1/12/75	NBC	42.4	72
50. *The Beverly Hillbillies*	2/26/64	CBS	42.4	60

Note: As of July 2010. Does not include programs broadcast on more than one network, e.g. the Apollo moon landing or programs under 30 minutes scheduled duration. *Rating* is the number of people watching as a percentage of all television owners. *Share* is the number watching as a percentage of people with their TVs on at that particular time.   **Source:** Nielsen Media Research.

Hulu.com—owned in part by NBC Universal, News Corp., and Disney—offer ad-supported episodes of both traditional television shows and "webisodes" of Made-for-Internet programs. Monthly time spent watching video online (including both user-generated content and already-broadcast programs) grew over 50 percent from 2008 to 2009.

►CABLE TELEVISION

Cable television was originally designed as a means of improving TV reception in some rural areas. In the 1960s, operators realized that viewers were willing to pay for commercial-free programming, but their efforts to capitalize on the idea were hampered by stringent Federal Communications Commission restrictions. Not until 1975, when RCA put its first communications satellite into operation, did the industry really bloom. Under the name Home Box Office, the company started to transmit programming that could be received by independent operators around the country and then relayed to subscribers at minimal cost. When a federal appeals court dismissed most of the FCC's regulations in 1977, the door was opened for the development of what is now a multibillion-dollar industry.

In three decades, cable has changed the television broadcasting landscape, drawing more than

Top 10 TV Shows of 2009

Rank, Program (Network)	Avg. rating
1. American Idol—Wed. (Fox)	14.4
2. American Idol—Tues. (Fox)	13.8
3. Dancing with the Stars (ABC)	12.0
4. NBC Sunday Night Football (NBC)	11.7
5. Dancing with the Stars—Results (ABC)	9.9
6. NCIS: Los Angeles (CBS)	9.8
7. NCIS (CBS)	9.4
8. NFL Regular Season (ESPN)	8.8
8. Sunday Night NFL Pre-kick (NBC)	8.8
10. The Good Wife (CBS)	8.5

Note: From Jan. 1, 2009 – Nov. 29, 2009. Regularly scheduled programs. Includes Live and Same Day timeshifted viewing. *Rating* is the percentage of all television owners watching that program. **Source:** Nielsen Media Research.

Top 5 Single Telecasts of 2009

Rank, Program (Network)	Date	Avg. rating
1. Super Bowl XLIII (NBC)	2/1/09	42.0
2. Super Bowl Pre-Kick (NBC)	2/1/09	35.2
3. Super Bowl Kick-Off (NBC)	2/1/09	29.6
4. Super Bowl Post (NBC)	2/1/09	25.7
5. AFC Championship on CBS (CBS)	1/18/09	22.0

Note: From Jan. 1, 2009 – Nov. 29, 2009. Telecasts over 5 minutes. Includes Live and Same Day timeshifted viewing. **Source:** Nielsen Media Research.

Longest-Running National Network Series of All Time

Program	Seasons	Years[1]
60 Minutes	42	1968–
Walt Disney	33	1954–90
The Ed Sullivan Show	24	1948–71
Gunsmoke	20	1955–75
The Red Skelton Show	20	1951–71
Meet the Press	18	1947–65[2]
What's My Line?	18	1950–67
I've Got a Secret	17	1952–76
Lassie	17	1954–71
The Lawrence Welk Show	17	1955–71

Notes: Includes prime-time (6–11 p.m.) shows only; sports broadcasts and movie series are not included. 1. Dates reflect the first and last broadcasts of each show. Programs did not necessarily run continuously throughout this period. 2. Ceased broadcasting in prime-time in 1965, though still on the air.

Top 10 Cable TV Shows, June 2010

Rank, program (network)	Rating	Viewers (000s)
1. Toy Story 2 (Disney)	3.9	7,479
2. Royal Pains (USA)	3.5	5,599
3. Burn Notice (USA)	3.4	5,674
4. Pawn Stars (History)	3.3	5,287
4. Pawn Stars (History)	3.3	5,354
6. WWE Raw (USA)	3.0	4,954
7. Sprint Cup Racing (TNT)	2.9	4,333
8. WWE Raw (USA)	2.8	4,612
9. Toy Story (Disney)	2.7	5,033
9. True Blood (HBO)	2.7	5,097

Notes: For the week of June 7, 2010. Viewing estimates include Live viewing and DVR playback on the Same Day, defined as 3am–3am. Ratings are the percentage of TV homes in the U.S. tuned into television. **Source:** The Nielsen Company.

Top 15 Cable Programming Networks, 2009

Network	Estimated Subscribers (millions)	Launch date	Content
TBS Superstation	101,900	1976	Movies, sports, and original programming
The Weather Channel	101,700	1982	Weather, news, talk
Discovery	101,500	1985	Nonfiction, nature, science
Nickelodeon	101,400	1979	Programming for kids
USA Network	101,200	1980	Movies, sports, and original programming
TNT (Turner Network Television)	101,100	1988	Movies, sports, and original programming
CNN (Cable News Network)	101,000	1980	24-hour news, special interest reports
Food Network	101,000	1993	Food, travel, and lifestyle programming
HGTV	100,900	1994	Home, garden, and lifestyle programming
Lifetime Television	100,900	1984	Programming aimed at women
TLC The Learning Channel	100,900	1980	Original programming, family entertainment
Spike TV	100,800	2003	Programming aimed at young adult males
ESPN	100,700	1979	Sports events and sports news
Cartoon	100,600	1992	Animated programming
Disney Channel	100,500	1983	Original programming and family entertainment

Source: National Cable & Telecommunications Association, SNL Kagan, *Economics of Basic Cable Networks*, 2009.

one-third of the total television viewing audiences away from broadcast channels. As a result, the fractured total television audience means that no single program will likely ever reach the kind of viewership numbers achieved during the 1960s and 70s, when viewers had only three or four choices. A case in point: the final episode of *Lost* in 2010 was one of the most anticipated shows in a decade, but it didn't even attract as many viewers as regular episodes of *The Beverly Hillbillies*.

The number of basic cable subscribers is currently increasing by about a half million per year (pay cable has grown at a more rapid rate of several million per year). But despite deregulation and increased competition from direct satellite providers, the average basic cable bill has continued to increase, from $7.69 in 1980 to $51.24 in 2009. The number of digital cable subscribers has also increased, from 1.5 million in 1998 to over 40.4 million in 2008, and the number of cable modem subscribers has increased from 500,000 to 35.6 million, including commercial customers. The nation's two largest cable providers in 2009 were Comcast Cable Communications (23.6 million subscribers) and DirecTV (18.6 million subscribers).

Basic Video and Digital Video Customers, 1998–2009

	Basic Video		Digital Video	
Year	Customers (in millions)	Year		Customers (in millions)
1998	65.1	1998		1.4
2000	66.6	2000		8.5
2002	66.1	2002		19.3
2004	65.4	2004		25.4
2006	65.4	2006		32.6
2009	62.1	2009		42.6

Source: National Cable Television Association, *Cable Developments* (2010).

Basic and Pay Cable TV Systems and Subscribers, 1952–2008

Year	Number of systems	Basic cable		Pay cable	
		Subscribers	Percent of U.S. TV households	Subscribers	Percent of households with cable
1952	70	14,000	0.1%	N.A.	N.A.
1955	400	150,000	0.5	N.A.	N.A.
1960	640	650,000	1.4	N.A.	N.A.
1970	2,490	3,900,000	6.7	N.A.	N.A.
1980	4,225	17,671,490	22.6	9,144,000	50.6
1990	9,575	54,871,330	59.0	39,900,000	77.1
2000	10,400	69,297,290	67.8	48,300,000	71.5
2004	9,169	73,575,460	67.1	51,500,000	70.0
2005	8,775	72,965,820	66.8	50,100,000	68.7
2006	8,464	65,500,000	59.2	51,800,000	N.A.
2007	8,174	65,100,000	58.0	53,100,000	N.A.
2008	7,853	63,700,000	N.A.	40,400,000	N.A.

Sources: National Cable & Telecommunications Association (2009); Nielsen Media Research.

Video and Audio: Sales & Penetration in U.S. Homes, 1990–2009

Product	Sales (000s of units)				Percent of U.S. homes			
	1990	2000	2004	2009[1]	1990	2000	2004	2009[1]
Video								
Analog color TV[6]	20,384	24,175	19,934	0	96%	98%	98%	99%
Digital TV set[2]	N.A.	1,117	10,706	35,414	N.A.	N.A.	12	66
TV/VCR combination	424	4,964	1,463	1,995	N.A.	18	30	36
VCR[3]	11,986	35,117	2,267	N.A.	68	93	91	N.A.
TV/DVD combination	N.A.	0	979	N.A.	N.A.	N.A.	N.A.	N.A.
DVD player	N.A.	8,499	19,990	17,258	N.A.	5	70	93
Camcorder[4]	2,962	5,848	5,559	5,669	10	36	54	52
Direct Satellite Receiver	330	4,250	16,250	11,970	2	16	25	31
Audio								
Home Radio	21,585	19,976	14,902	10,694	99%	98%	98%	98%
Home Theater-in-a-Box	N.A.	1,157	4,701	3,291	N.A.	23	32	33
Compact disc player[5]	9,155	54,776	37,470	185	23	74	80	41
Compact audio system	2,447	11,455	6,874	1,433	N.A.	42	44	35
MP3 Players	N.A.	587	7,126	10,543	N.A.	2	11	47

Notes: 1. Estimate. 2. Includes direct-view and projection digital TVs with integrated decoders and stand-alone digital TV displays. Household penetration figures do not include digital projection sets. 3. Includes mono and stereo decks, but not machines that play but do not record. Does not include TV/VCR combinations. As of 2008, no longer tracking sales of VCRs. 4. Includes digital camcorders. 5. Reflects only home CD players, not portable, car, or other devices that play CDs. 6. Analog color TV is no longer on the market. Data reflect both analog and digital TV sets. **Source:** Consumer Electronics Association (2009).

Commercial AM & FM Radio Stations by Primary Format, 2010

Format	2010[1]	Format	2010[1]	Format	2010[1]
Religion[2]	2,365	Classic Hits	629	Pre-Teen	44
News/Talk	2,129	Gospel (Black, Southern)	574	Easy Listening	28
Country	2,006	Top 40	522	Format not available	14
Rock[3]	1,329	Adult Standards	288	Stations off the air	314
Spanish	946	Classical	178		
Variety	694	R&B	153	**Total stations**	**16,749**
Oldies	678	Ethnic	144		
Sports	662	Jazz	121	**Construction permits**	**1,420**
Adult Contemporary	649	R&B Adult/Oldies	51		

Notes: 1. As of May 2010. 2. Includes Contemporary Christian, variety, and teaching. 3. Includes Classic, Modern, Alternative.
Source: M Street Corporation (2010).

▶RADIO

According to the Radio Advertising Bureau, 98 percent of all U.S. households own at least one radio. Of Americans over age 12, 95.3 percent listen to radio for an average of 3 hours and 20 minutes each workday.

Online Radio   Online radio began in 1993 when Carl Malamud launched his Internet Talk Radio, a non-streaming program on which a different computer expert was interviewed each week. In November 1994, the Rolling Stones gave the first "cyber concert," and that same month, WXYC in Chapel Hill, N.C., became the first traditional radio station to announce plans to broadcast online.

Today, online radio enjoys enormous popularity, and most major radio stations offer programs, free of cost, to stream online. Some stations, such as National Public Radio (NPR), offer free podcasts or cheap downloads of popular programs. The real growth of Internet radio, however, has been in Internet music stations. According to AccuStream Research, Internet music audio ads grossed $84 million in 2008, a 212.3 percent increase from $26.9 million in 2006. Listening hours topped 6.6 billion in 2008; and averaged 404.2 million hours per month in 2007, up significantly from 320.5 million hours per month in 2006 (excluding downloads but including subscription sites such as Napster and Rhapsody).

In 2008, AOL's Shoutcast remained the most popular Internet music station, followed by Clear Channel Online, Yahoo Music, AOL Radio Networks, and Pandora.

▶THE RECORDING INDUSTRY

The total U.S. dollar value of all music sold (CDs, vinyl, cassettes, and digital downloads) in 2008 was $9 billion, a 38.4 percent decrease from a high of $14.6 billion in 1999. CD sales continue to drop about 20 percent each year, as digital sales continue to rise. Music video sales rose slightly to $485 million but couldn't offset continuing declines in sales of cassettes, LPs, and Super Audio CDs. Big box stores—such as Wal-Mart—retail more music than music-only stores, and at discounted prices.

Fewer than 100,000 CDs were sold in 1983, the first year they were available, but the format overtook LPs by 1988, and topped cassette sales in 1992. In 2008, CDs accounted for over 77.8 percent of all music sales and revived the entire music industry, which in the late 1970s and early 80s was worried about losing young consumers to movies and videogames.

Internet Music Sales and File-Sharing

Industry concerns surfaced again in the late 1990s, as the popularity of online file-sharing services grew. Napster, the most prominent of these services, was forced to stop the process known as peer-to-peer (P2P) file sharing in 2000 because of a lawsuit brought by the music industry. In 2002 some major record labels responded to ongoing music piracy by making more of their music legally available online, despite fears that such a move would cannibalize more profitable CD sales.

The most successful service has been Apple Computer's iTunes, which sold 10 million song downloads (for an average 99 cents each) in its first four months of operation in 2003, and by 2005 had sold more than 500 million. P2P services remain active, but lawsuits filed by the music industry against hundreds of file sharers (many of them young children), as well as a 2005 Supreme Court decision against two prominent file-sharing software companies, appear to have had a chilling effect on Internet music-sharing. Instead, legal digital downloads have become an important revenue stream for the faltering recording industry, accounting for more than a quarter of all recorded music sales in 2009.

Sales by Category   The sales of different types of music are in almost as constant a flux as the music types themselves. The category defined as rock accounted for nearly half of all music sales

Top-Selling Digital Songs of 2009

Title	Artist
Boom Boom Pow	The Black Eyed Peas
Poker Face	Lady Gaga
Just Dance	Lady Gagy featuring Coby O'Donis
Right Round	Flo Rida
I Gotta Feeling	The Black Eyed Peas
Single Ladies (Put a Ring On It)	Beyonce
Gives You Hell	The All-American Rejects
Love Story	Taylor Swift
Heartless	Kanye West
I'm Yours	Jason Mraz

Note: Data dates Dec. 6, 2008 – Nov. 28, 2009.
Source: Billboard Hot Digital Songs / The Nielsen Company.

Top-Selling Albums of 2009

Title	Artist
Fearless	Taylor Swift
I am... Sasha Fierce	Beyonce
Dark Horse	Nickelback
Twilight	Soundtrack
Hannah Montana: The Movie	Soundtrack
Circus	Britney Spears
808s & Heartbreak	Kayne West
The Fame	Lady Gaga
Relapse	Eminem
The E.N.D.	The Black Eyed Peas

Note: Data dates Dec. 6, 2008 – Nov. 28, 2009.
Source: Billboard 200 / The Nielsen Company.

U.S. Recorded Music Sales by Genre, Format, and Age Group, 1987–2008

Characteristic	1987	1990	1995	2000	2005	2007	2008
Genre							
Rock	45.5%	36.1%	33.5%	24.8%	31.5%	32.4%	31.8%
Pop	13.5	13.7	10.1	11.0	8.1	10.7	9.1
Rap/Hip Hop	3.8	8.5	6.7	12.9	13.3	10.8	10.7
R&B/Urban[1]	9.0	11.6	11.3	9.7	10.2	11.8	10.2
Country	10.6	9.6	16.7	10.7	12.5	11.5	11.9
Religious/Gospel[2]	2.9	2.5	3.1	4.8	5.3	3.9	6.5
Jazz	3.8	4.8	3.0	2.9	1.8	2.6	1.1
Classical	3.9	3.1	2.9	2.7	2.4	2.3	1.9
Other[3]	6.2	8.8	10.1	11.0	8.5	11.5	14.2
Format							
CDs (full length)	11.5%	31.1%	65.0%	89.3%	87.0%	82.6%	77.8%
Cassettes (full length)	62.5	54.7	25.1	4.9	1.1	0.3	0.4
Singles (all types)	5.7	8.7	7.5	2.5	2.7	2.4	3.8
Videos/Video DVDs	N.A.	N.A.	0.9	0.8	0.7	0.4	0.8
DVD Audio	N.A.	N.A.	N.A.	N.A.	0.8	1.2	1.0
Digital Download	N.A.	N.A.	N.A.	N.A.	5.7	11.2	12.8
LPs	20.1	4.7	0.5	0.5	0.7	0.7	1.0
SACD	N.A.	N.A.	N.A.	N.A.	1.2	0.6	1.1
Age group							
10–14	7.3%	7.6%	8.0%	8.9%	8.6%	11.5%	7.3%
15–19	24.2	18.3	17.1	12.9	11.9	12.3	10.9
20–24	19.1	16.5	15.3	12.5	12.7	11.3	10.1
25–29	14.5	14.6	12.3	10.6	12.1	9.2	8.3
30–34	10.8	13.2	12.1	9.8	11.3	11.3	8.9
35–39	8.2	10.2	10.8	10.6	8.8	11.9	9.8
40–44	4.8	7.8	7.5	9.6	9.2	7.9	11.0
45+	10.7	11.1	16.1	23.8	25.5	24.8	33.7

Notes: Figures represent a percentage of that year's total U.S. dollar sales. 1. Includes R&B, blues, dance, disco, funk, fusion, Motown, reggae, soul. 2. Includes Christian, Gospel, Inspirational, Religious, and Spiritual. 3. Includes soundtracks, children's music, and other categories not shown separately. Totals may not add to 100 percent due to "Don't Know/No Answer" Responses. **Source:** Recording Industry Association of America, *Consumer Profile*.

in 1987; in 2008, it was less than a third. Pop, Rap, R & B, and Country have made up the difference. For many years, the single largest group of recorded music consumers (as a percentage of total dollar value) was teenagers (buyers aged 15–19). But the high price of music and Internet music-sharing sites have cut into record sales among younger consumers. In 2008, buyers over 45 accounted for about 34 percent of annual music purchases, compared with just 10.9 percent by 15–19-year-olds. Women made over half of the music purchases in the U.S. in 2008. The recording industry saw promise in online sales of digital downloads of music that accounted for 12.8 percent of 2008 music sales, up from just 0.5 percent in 2002.

A decision in 1996 by Wal-Mart stores to restrict albums with controversial lyrics caused consternation among record executives because of discount stores' increasing influence on the industry's bottom line. In 1989, 71.7 percent of all recorded music was sold in record stores, while 15.6 percent was sold in "other stores," which includes discount and consumer electronic stores. In 2007, record stores accounted for less than one-third of all music purchases (31.1 percent), while "other stores" made up 29.7 percent. Music purchases via the Internet grew from 0.3 percent in 1997 to 10.9 percent in 2007, and by 2008 digital downloads accounted for nearly a quarter of music sales, providing important new outlets.

Individual Record Sales Up until 1958, the term **gold** album simply meant a hit album. But in that year, the Recording Industry Association of America codified the term to mean a record that had reached $1 million in sales. (Separate levels were established for singles, which have since been amended.) The 1943 cast album from *Oklahoma!* was the first gold album. By 1975, inflation had diluted the importance of the award, so the RIAA also required gold records to sell at least 500,000 copies. The following year, it introduced the **platinum** record, awarded to albums that sell at least 1 million copies. The Eagles' *Their Greatest Hits 1971–1975* was the first platinum album, and is to date, the largest-selling album of all time, with 29 million copies sold. **Multi-platinum** awards go to albums selling more than 2 million copies. In 1999, the RIAA introduced the **diamond** award, for singles or records with U.S. sales of 10 million or more. As of December 2008, more than 100 titles had qualified for the award, in genres ranging from pop, R&B, and rock to rap, country, and instrumental. The Beatles have the most diamond records (five).

▶ VIDEO

Video Cassette Recorders (VCRs) In 20 years, the video cassette recorder (VCR) went from a curiosity to a luxury to an appliance found in more than 90 percent of American homes, but it is now losing out to DVDs and VCR ownership is down to 79 percent of homes. As of July 2009, a DVD player could be found in 93 percent of American homes.

DVD (Digital Video Disc) Players are the most common type of home video media, with 2009 sales reaching 17.3 million units, down from 21.2 million in 2007. The average wholesale price for a DVD is $15 to $20; they are more durable than VHS tapes and take up much less space.

DVD sales overtook videocassette sales in 2004, and the steady drop in price for DVD players (an average of $72 in 2007) has increased their presence in American homes (93 percent, up from 25 percent in 2002). In light of this change, video rental and retail stores have shifted to DVDs, much as CDs supplanted vinyl albums and cassette tapes in the 1980s.

Digital Video Recorders (DVRs), also known as Personal Video Recorders (PVRs) have been touted by many as the next big thing in home entertainment: an estimated 3.2 million were sold in 2005, and by 2009, an estimated 28 million were shipped worldwide. This number was projected to hit over 30 million in 2010. Over 75 percent of these were high-definition units. The research group In-Stat predicts that by 2013 there will be roughly 73 million DVR units installed in about 60 million American households.

DVRs perform the same basic function as VCRs—recording television shows—but instead of recording on removable videocassettes, a DVR uses an internal computer hard drive, generally 40 or 80 gigabytes, capable of holding up to 80 hours or more of television programming. Other features, depending on the model of DVR, include the ability to pause and rewind live TV and the ability to automatically record of future programs based on specific criteria (for example, every new episode of a particular sitcom). Tivo Inc. is the most recognized name in the market, but cable companies have moved quickly to capitalize on the growing popularity of DVRs; most cable providers now offer proprietary cable boxes with integrated DVR functionality.

▶ FILM

The motion picture industry grossed more than $10.65 billion in 2009 in ticket sales alone, up seven percent from 2008. The various studios produce about 600 films per year; they submit most of these films to the Motion Picture Association of America for ratings and wide release in theaters. Over half of these movies receive an R rating. Most of the rest receive a PG or PG-13 rating (70 percent of the 20 top-grossing films in 2008). Less than five percent of movies in 2009 were G-rated, and even fewer (less than 1 percent) received an NC-17 or X-rating. Because many theaters refuse to show NC-17 movies, producers are loath to release a film with an NC-17 label. While the number of theaters has fallen recently, the number of movie screens has nearly doubled since 1985. Single-screen theaters made up only four percent of all movie theaters in 2009; miniplexes accounted for 21 percent. There were 1,681 multiplexes (8–15 screens) and 638 megaplexes (16 or more screens). The number of megaplexes grew in 2009, up 1.6 percent from 2008. In 2008, the number of digital movie screens increased to 5,474—up from only 31 in 2000.

Top Rental DVDs, May 2010	
Rank, Title	**Days on top ten**
1. *Sherlock Holmes*	40
1. *Alvin and the Chipmunks: The Squeakquel*	40
2. *Crazy Heart*	19
2. *The Lovely Bones*	19
3. *Avatar*	17
4. *It's Complicated*	12
5. *The Imaginarium of Doctor Parnassus*	12
6. *Tooth Fairy*	5
6. *Leap Year*	5
6. *Nine*	5

Source: The Internet Movie Database (June 2010).

Top Selling DVDs, 2009	
Rank, Title	**Distributor**
1. *Twilight*	Universal
2. *Transformers: Revenge of the Fallen*	Paramount
3. *Up*	Disney / Buena Vista
4. *Madagascar: Escape 2 Africa*	Paramount
5. *Dark Knight*	Warner Home Video
6. *Gran Torino*	Warner Home Video
7. *Star Trek*	Paramount
8. *Bolt*	Disney / Buena Vista
9. *Marley & Me*	20th Century Fox
10. *Quantum of Solace*	20th Century Fox

Note: Data from Jan. 5, 2009–Nov. 29, 2009. Based on Aggregate Disc unit sales (DVD, Blu-Ray, etc.) from Jan. 4, 2009–Nov. 29, 2009. Does not include data from Wal-Mart. Most other sell-through retailers are included. **Source:** The Nielsen Company (2010).

U.S. Film Box-Office Receipts, Screens, Admissions, and Admission Charges, 1926–2009 (in current dollars)

Year	Box office receipts (millions)	Movie Screens			Annual admissions		Average admission charge
		Indoor	Drive-in	Digital	Total	Per person	
1926	$720.0	N.A.	N.A.	N.A.	2,600,000	N.A.	N.A.
1930	732.0	N.A.	N.A.	N.A.	4,680,000	N.A.	N.A.
1935	566.0	N.A.	N.A.	N.A.	3,900,000	N.A.	$0.24
1940	735.0	N.A.	N.A.	N.A.	4,160,000	N.A.	0.24
1950	1,376.0	N.A.	N.A.	N.A.	3,120,000	N.A.	0.53
1960	951.0	N.A.	N.A.	N.A.	2,080,000	N.A.	0.69
1970[1,2]	1,162.0	10,335	3,720	N.A.	920	N.A.	1.55
1980	2,748.5	14,029	3,561	N.A.	1,022	4.5	2.69
1990[3]	5,021.8	22,774	915	N.A.	1,189	4.8	4.23
1995	5,493.5	26,958	847	N.A.	1,263	4.8	4.35
2000	7,661.0	36,679	717	31	1,421	5.2	5.39
2005	8,991.2	37,092	648	324	1,402	5.9	6.41
2009	10,600.0	38,605	628	5,474[3]	1,420	N.A.	$7.50

Notes: 1. Figures are in the millions after 1970. 2. Theater figures are for 1971. 3. Beginning in 1990, admission totals and average prices are supplied by the National Association of Theater Owners and are not strictly comparable with data from previous years, which are based on the U.S. Department of Commerce's Consumer Price Index. 3. Data is for 2008. **Source:** U.S. Dept. of Commerce; *Film Daily Yearbook; Motion Picture Association of America, 2010 U.S. Economic Review, National Association of Theatre Owners.*

20 Top-Grossing Feature Films, 2009

Rank, Film	Distributor	Gross (millions)	Rating
1. Transformers: Revenge of the Fallen	Paramount	$402.1	PG-13
2. Harry Potter and the Half Blood Prince	Warner Bros.	302.0	PG
3. .Up	Disney	293.0	PG
4. The Twilight Saga: New Moon[1]	Summit	284.5	PG-13
5. Avatar[1]	Fox	283.6	PG-13
6. The Hangover	Warner Bros.	277.3	R
7. Star Trek	Paramount	257.7	PG-13
8. Monsters vs. Aliens	Paramount	198.4	PG
9. Ice Age: Dawn of the Dinosaurs	Fox	196.6	PG
10. The Blind Side[1]	Warner Bros.	196.6	PG-13
11. X-Men Origins: Wolverine	Fox	179.9	PG-13
12. Night at the Museum: Battle of the Smithsonian	Fox	177.2	PG
13. The Proposal	Disney	164.0	PG-13
14. 2012[1]	Sony	162.3	PG-13
15. Fast & Furious	Universal	155.2	PG-13
16. G.I. Joe: The Rise of Cobra	Paramount	150.2	PG-13
17. Paul Blart: Mall Cop	Sony	146.3	PG
18. Taken	Fox	145.0	PG-13
19. Gran Torino[2]	Warner Bros.	142.2	R
20. Disney's A Christmas Carol[1]	Disney	136.9	PG

Notes: Totals include both U.S. and Canada box office sales. 1. Film still in theatres in 2010. Box office amount reflects total from Jan. 1, 2009 to Dec. 31, 2009. 2. Film opened in 2008. Box office amount reflects total from Jan. 1, 2009 to Dec. 31, 2009. **Source:** Motion Picture Association of America; Rentak Corporation, CARA.

Most Popular Films, By Decade

Title (Year)	Director	Rental (millions)	Title (Year)	Director	Rental (millions)
Pre-1930			**1970-79**		
The Birth of a Nation (1915)	D.W. Griffith	$10.0	Star Wars (1977)	G. Lucas	$193.8
The Big Parade (1925)	K. Vidor	5.5	Jaws (1975)	S. Spielberg	129.6
The Singing Fool (1928)	L. Bacon	4.0	Grease (1978)	R. Kleiser	96.3
			The Exorcist (1973)	W. Friedkin	89.0
1930-39			The Godfather (1972)	F. F. Coppola	86.3
Gone With the Wind (1939)	V. Fleming	$77.6			
Snow White and the Seven Dwarfs (1937)	(Animated)	62.8	**1980-89**		
			E.T.—The Extra-Terrestrial (1982)	S. Spielberg	$228.2
King Kong (1933)	M. Cooper	5.0	Return of the Jedi (1983)	R. Marquand	168.2
The Wizard of Oz (1939)	V. Fleming	4.5	Batman (1989)	T. Burton	150.5
San Francisco (1936)	W.S. Van Dyke	4.0	The Empire Strikes Back (1980)	J. Kershner	141.7
			Ghostbusters (1984)	I. Reitman	132.7
1940-49[1]			Raiders of the Lost Ark (1981)	S. Spielberg	115.6
Cinderella (1949)	(Animated)	$38.5	Indiana Jones and the Last Crusade (1989)	S. Spielberg	115.5
Pinocchio (1940)	(Animated)	32.9			
Song of the South (1946)	H. Foster/ W. Jackson	29.2	Indiana Jones and the Temple of Doom (1984)	S. Spielberg	109.0
Fantasia (1940)	(Animated)	28.5	Beverly Hills Cop (1984)	M. Brest	108.0
Bambi (1942)	(Animated)	28.4	Back to the Future (1985)	R. Zemeckis	105.5
1950-59			**1990-99**		
The Ten Commandments (1956)	C.B. DeMille	$43.0	Titanic (1997)	J. Cameron	$600.8
Lady and the Tramp (1955)	(Animated)	40.2	Star Wars: Episode One— The Phantom Menace (1999)	G. Lucas	431.1
Ben-Hur (1959)	W. Wyler	36.7	Jurassic Park (1993)	S. Spielberg	357.1
Around the World in 80 Days (1956)	M. Anderson	23.1	Forrest Gump (1994)	R. Zemeckis	329.7
Sleeping Beauty (1959)	(Animated)	21.5	The Lion King (1993)	R. Allers/R. Minkoff	312.9
			Independence Day (1996)	R. Emmerich	306.2
1960-69			The Sixth Sense (1999)	M. Shyamalan	293.5
The Sound of Music (1965)	R. Wise	$80.0	Home Alone (1990)	C. Columbus	285.7
Doctor Zhivago (1965)	D. Lean	61.0	Men in Black (1997)	B. Sonnenfeld	250.7
Butch Cassidy and the Sundance Kid (1969)	G.R. Hill	46.0	Toy Story 2 (1999)	A. Brannon	245.8
Mary Poppins (1964)	R. Stevenson	45.0			
The Graduate (1968)	M. Nichols	44.1			

Note: Films from the 1990's are ranked according to their gross box office receipts. Films for previous decades are ranked according to film rentals, the portion of a film's box-office receipts paid by theater owners to the film's distribution company for renting the film. Figures include the U.S. and Canada. 1. All films listed for this decade were made by Disney studios and have been rereleased on a regular basis ever since. Their dominance on this chart is partly due to the fact that they are continually generating revenue. **Sources:** Variety; Exhibitor Relations Co., Inc.

Top-Grossing Movies of All Time

Because of inflation and periodic re-releases, it is nearly impossible to compare the successes of films from different eras. What is simpler to compare is the number of people who went to see a film, regardless of when it was released, and regardless of how much they paid for their ticket. To arrive at this number, the Exhibitor Relations Co. divides domestic gross receipts by the average ticket prices for the year(s) in which the film was released. The estimated number of admissions is then multiplied by the current average ticket price to give an idea of what each film's domestic gross would be if it were released today. It is admittedly an imperfect measure, but it makes it quite clear that despite its $600 million unadjusted gross, *Titanic* will have to be re-released several times to match the success of *Gone With the Wind*, which has made only $200 million over the years, but has been seen by 70 million more people.

Rank, Film, (Year of Release)	Estimated admissions	Inflation-adjusted domestic gross
1. *Gone With the Wind* (1939)[1]	202,044,600	$1,390,000,000
2. *Star Wars* (1977)[1]	178,119,600	1,225,462,000
3. *The Sound of Music* (1965)[1]	142,415,400[2]	979,817,000
4. *E.T. The Extra-Terrestrial* (1982)[1]	141,854,300	975,957,000
5. *The Ten Commandments* (1956)	131,000,000[2]	901,280,000
6. *Titanic* (1997)	128,345,900	883,019,000
7. *Jaws* (1975)[1]	128,078,800	881,182,000
8. *Doctor Zhivago* (1965)[1]	124,135,500	854,051,000
9. *The Exorcist* (1973)	110,568,700	760,712,000
10. *Snow White and the Seven Dwarfs* (1937)[1]	109,000,000[2]	749,920,000

Notes: As of July 2009. 1. Includes re-issues; ticket price used to calculate admissions is an average of ticket prices charged throughout the film's theatrical runs. 2. Gross estimated from the film rental, which is approximately 50 percent of the gross. **Source:** Exhibitor Relations Co., Inc.

Movie Budgets

The cost of making movies has escalated dramatically in recent years. In 1988, the average price tag of a motion picture was $18.1 million. Today, that's just half of the average marketing budget for a feature film. Rising actors' salaries, increased demand for special effects, and other spiraling costs drove the average cost of making a movie to a whopping $106.6 million in 2007. In addition to production costs, studios spent an average of $35.9 million on advertising and publicity in 2007. The M.P.A.A. no longer cites the average cost of making or marketing a movie, though in 2009 speculation abounded that James Cameron's *Avatar* was the most expensive film ever made, with a budget exceeding $300 million.

▶ COMPUTER AND VIDEO GAMES

The U.S. computer and video game industry showed dramatic growth in recent years, shooting from sales of $2.6 billion in 1996 to $11.7 billion in 2008. Much of the increase has been in video game consoles, which reached $5.12 billion in 2007. Forty-two percent of American homes have a video game console.

The stereotypical computer and video game player is a young male, but in 2008 women constituted 40 percent of the PC and console game-playing population, and the average age of a computer or video game player was 35 years old. Among video game players, the best-selling game genres were action (20 percent), family entertainment (19.3 percent) and sports (15.3 percent); computer gamers spent their money on strategy (34.6 percent) and role-playing games(19.6 percent).

One of the fastest-growing segments of the computer and video game industry is online gaming. Microsoft claims over 10 million subscribers to its Xbox Live service, which allows owners of the Xbox video game console to compete with other gamers over the Internet. Massively Multiplayer Online Role Playing Games (MMORPGs) are also booming in the PC segment; the top-selling *World of Warcraft*, developed by Blizzard Entertainment, boasted 10 million subscribers worldwide (2.5 million of them in North America) as of January 2008.

Top-Selling Computer & Video Games, 2009

COMPUTER GAMES

Rank, Title	Publisher
1. The Sims 3	Electronic Arts
2. World of Warcraft: Wrath of the Lich King	Blizzard Entertainment
3. The Sims 2 Double Deluxe	Electronic Arts
4. World of Warcraft: Battle Chest	Blizzard Entertainment
5. Call of Duty: Modern Warfare 2	Activision
6. World of Warcraft	Blizzard Entertainment
7. The Sims 3: World Adventures Expansion Pack	Electronic Arts
8. Spore	Electronic Arts
9. Dragon Age: Origins	Electronic Arts
10. Empire: Total War	Sega of America

VIDEO GAMES

Rank, Title	Publisher
1. 360 Call of Duty: Modern Warfare 2[1]	Activision Blizzard
2. WII WII Sports Resort w/ WII Motion Plus[1]	Nintendo
3. WII New Super Mario Bros.	Nintendo
4. WII WII Fit w/ Balance Board[1]	Nintendo
5. WII WII Fit Plus[1]	Nintendo
6. WII Mario Kart w/ Wheel	Nintendo
7. WII WII Play w/ Remote[1]	Nintendo
8. PS3 Call of Duty: Modern Warfare 2[1]	Activision Blizzard
9. 360 Halo 3: ODST	Microsoft
10. NDS Pokemon Platinum Version	Nintendo

Note: 1. Includes CE, GOTY editions, etc., but not those bundled with hardware. **Source:** The NPD Group/ Retail Tracking Service.

Religion in America

▶ RELIGIOUS AFFILIATION

The U.S. Census Bureau does not ask questions about religious affiliation, so these numbers can be regarded as educated approximations at best. *The Statistical Abstract*, put out annually by the Census Bureau, includes data about religion taken from the American Religious Identification Survey, put out by the Institute for the Study of Secularism in Society and Culture (ISSSC) based at Trinity College. The numbers that follow are from the 2009 publication, the most recent data available.

In 2008 nearly 80 percent of Americans considered themselves religious. The vast majority of these (76 percent) self-identified as Christian, a decline of 10 percent from 1990. A third of American Christians cited Catholicism as their denomination. The growth of the Latino population in the U.S. from 1990 to 2008 helped the Catholic Church to maintain its position as America's largest religious tradition. The influx of nine million Latino Catholics accounted for most of the 11 million additions to the U.S. Catholic population, and Latinos comprised 32 percent of all U.S. Catholics in 2008.

Just below four percent of American adults considered themselves of a religion other than Christianity. Judaism was the most popular of these, comprising 1.2 percent of the adult population. Judaism is followed by Islam (0.6 percent) and Buddhism (0.5 percent). Overall, about 70 percent of Americans stated that they believed in a personal God, while roughly 12 percent considered themselves Atheist (no God) or Agnostic (unknowable or unsure). Another 12 percent self-identified as deistic (believe in a higher power but no personal God).

The ISSSC surveys reflect subjective rather than objective standards (such as church membership) of religious identification. The following are brief descriptions of each of the Christian denominations and of major non-Christian faiths in the United States. Information is taken from *The Statistical Abstract*, and the 2008 *American Religious Identification Survey*.

(For information about religion internationally, see "Part III: World Religions".)

▶ CHRISTIANITY
Roman Catholic Church

The Roman Catholic Church is the largest single Christian denomination in the United States. It claims over 31 percent of all religiously affiliated people—25 percent of the total adult population. Worldwide, there are over one billion Roman Catholics (See "World Religions").

Many U.S. Catholics—descendants of immigrants from Ireland, Germany, Poland, Italy, and France—are concentrated in the Northeast and the industrial Midwest. Hispanic-Americans in Florida and the Southwest are also predominantly Catholic.

The church is hierarchically organized. Bishops, who administer church affairs in a given region, are appointed by higher authority. The world leader of the Roman church is the pope, who directs the church from Vatican City in Rome.

Priests are male and in most parts of the church must be and remain unmarried. Orders of nuns and monks provide many educational and charitable services. Many local churches operate parochial elementary schools. Regional bodies and religious orders operate high schools and help administer many seminaries and church-related colleges. In recent years the number of applicants for the priesthood and for religious orders has sharply decreased, even as membership in the church has continued to increase. In the last decades of the 20th and first of the 21st century, the Catholic Church has been embroiled in several sex scandals involving clergy and underage church members of both sexes.

Catholic leaders have taken strong stands on many contemporary issues. The National Conference of Catholic Bishops has taken relatively liberal positions on efforts to bring about world peace and economic justice. In areas of personal conduct, the church is more conservative. It leads the campaign to outlaw abortion and opposes artificial means of birth control.

Baptist Churches

The Baptist family of churches is the largest Protestant family in the United States. Baptists trace their theological roots back to radical reformers in Europe in the 1500s, but the number of Baptists in the world was tiny until the 1800s, when Baptist faith and practice became predominant in the American South (both for whites and for blacks). Baptists are still most heavily represented in the southern and border states.

Local Baptist congregations have great independence, determining many of their own policies. At the same time, these churches share many practices. They agree that the rite of baptism should be administered only to those who have reached an age of independent judgment. Consequently, children are baptized no earlier than the age of six or seven, often by total immersion in the baptismal water. A Baptist child is not counted as a member until after baptism.

Most Baptists take a strong stand on the authority of the Bible, and many (though not all) believe that it should be interpreted literally. Baptists have traditionally been strong supporters of separation of church and state. Many Baptist denominations have mounted energetic missionary campaigns to bring the Christian message to people around the world.

The Southern Baptist Convention, a predominantly white church, is the largest Protestant denomination in the United States but has experienced division within its membership in recent years. The split, involving a moderate minority, was sparked by reluctance to accept the increasingly conservative church leadership's insistence that the Bible be interpreted literally and that women submit to their husbands and be barred from serving as pastors. One of these quasi-denominations is the Cooperative Baptist Fellowship, which remains conservative on social issues but allows individuals freedom of conscience and gives autonomy to individual congregations.

The two National Baptist Conventions and the Progressive National Baptist Convention are predominantly black churches. Together they account for the religious affiliation of more blacks than any other family of churches.

Methodist Churches

Methodist churches trace their origins to John Wesley (1703–91), a minister in the Church of England who sought to bring a new sense of warmth and commitment to individuals' religious life. He urged his followers to set aside regular times to study the Bible and pray together. Wesley's opponents laughingly called his followers Methodists because of their discipline and seriousness. Wesley himself remained in the Church of England his whole life, but his followers began to develop independent organizations, both in England and the United States.

On the American frontier, Methodist "circuit riders" traveled from settlement to settlement, preaching and marrying, baptizing, and burying members of pioneer families. Methodism grew with astonishing swiftness. By 1820 it was the largest religious family in the United States, and it remained the largest Protestant family until the 1920s. In 2008, roughly five percent of American adults cited Methodism as their religious affiliation.

The United Methodist Church accounts for nearly two-thirds of the Methodist family's total membership. This denomination is made up of not only traditional Methodists but also several churches of German origin whose beliefs and spirit accorded well with Methodism. The two "African" churches and the Christian Methodist Church are predominantly black churches, and they account for nearly all of the remaining third of the Methodist group.

Lutheran Churches

Lutherans trace their churches back to the German reformer Martin Luther (1483–1546). Luther sought to reform the doctrine and practice of the Roman Christian Church in Europe. He complained about corruption among the clergy and advocated worship in the language of the people rather than in Latin. He also came to favor a married, rather than a celibate, clergy. The Church of Rome considered Luther disloyal and eventually drove him out. He then helped establish independent churches in northern Germany.

Immigrants from Germany and Scandinavia brought the Lutheran faith to North America, concentrating first in Pennsylvania. Later immigrants settled in the upper Midwest. By 1900 scores of small Lutheran church bodies were divided from one another by language, theology, and degree of assimilation into American society. The Evangelical Lutheran Church in America (ELCA) represents a uniting of many of those earlier churches. The Lutheran Church-Missouri Synod, a national church despite its name, is more conservative theologically.

In July 2000, the Evangelical Lutheran Church announced a historic alliance with the Episcopal Church meant to stem declines in church membership. In 2009, the ELCA announced both its acceptance of homosexual clergy and announced the official recognition of the validity of ministers, baptisms, and Eucharistic services of the United Methodist Church, an accord 30 years in the making that had previously been approved by the Methodist Church.

Holiness and Pentecostal Churches

Holiness churches originated when religious revivalists, primarily in Methodist congregations, objected to the excessive bureaucracy of the established denomination. The founders of Holiness congregations sought to refocus religious attention on the need for deep personal change. Around 1900, groups of especially intense Holiness worshippers began experiencing further "gifts of the Spirit," from which grew the first Pentecostal church. In 2008, less than one percent of American adults considered themselves adherents of Holiness teachings, though 2.4 percent call themselves Pentecostal.

Pentecostal churches, initially rejected by Holiness churches for being extremist, share a belief that God grants believers special spiritual gifts—especially the experience called "speaking in tongues," which is a common feature of their worship services. The name is traced to the day of Pentecost, described in the Biblical book of Acts, when early Christians received ecstatic of mystical powers.

Pentecostal congregations tend to be small. They may meet in storefronts or in rented quarters on upper floors. Pentecostal beliefs have had an impact on Roman Catholic, Lutheran, Episcopal, and other denominations. These denominations report a growth among adherents of "charismatic renewal," a movement based on spiritual gifts. The two Churches of God in Christ and the United Pentecostal Church are predominantly black denominations. The Assemblies of God is the largest predominantly white denomination. Many Pentecostal organizations are regional or purely local, and many still today enforce strict dress codes and forbid certain forms of entertainment.

Evangelical and Born-Again Churches

Evangelicalism is one of the fastest-growing Christian denominations in America, with its adherents increasing from 546,000 in 1990 to 2,154,000 in 2008. Evangelical influence was first evident during prohibition, and the National Association of Evangelicals formed in 1942. Evangelicals have been considered pivotal players in American politics at least since the election of President Jimmy Carter. The denomination is widely known for its conservative sociopolitical views, though instead of building Bible schools like its Fundamentalist and conservative Protestant counterparts, the Evangelical movement grew through the construction of liberal arts colleges. Evangelicalism is also critical of Protestantism's identification with militarism and capitalism.

Star preachers, including Billy Graham and Joel Osteen, have perpetuated the Evangelical break with Fundamentalism by welcoming believers of all denominations to share in the Eucharist, and by holding international movements designed to bring Christians of many nations together.

Reformed Churches

Reformed churches trace their descent to the French-Swiss reformer John Calvin (1509–64). These churches were especially significant in the early settlement of the present-day United States. The Pilgrims and Puritans who settled in New England established the Congregational church, which is a main component of today's United Church of Christ. New York was settled by the Dutch, who established the present-day Reformed Church in America. Later, immigrants of Scottish and Scotch-Irish descent established a strong Presbyterian church. Presbyterians differed from Congregationalists in matters of church governance but shared many points of theology and practice.

Reformed church buildings are generally simple and sparsely adorned. Similarly, worship in these churches is austere and simple. Reformed churches generally value a well-educated clergy. In the past they helped found Harvard, Yale, and Princeton, though direct ties to these universities have ended.

The Presbyterian Church (U.S.A.) is the result of several mergers between smaller Presbyterian churches that had been separated by regional and doctrinal differences. The United Church of Christ includes, in addition to Congregational churches, descendants of German Reformed churches and of the Evangelical and Reformed Church (also of German descent). The Reformed Church in America and the Christian Reformed Church are both of Dutch descent.

Orthodox Churches

The first great schism in the Christian church occurred in A.D. 1054 between the Western church, centered at Rome, and the Eastern church, centered at Constantinople (present-day Istanbul). In 1054 Eastern Christianity was predominant in Greece and the Middle East, and missionaries had already introduced the faith in Russia. The Russian church celebrated its 1,000th anniversary in 1988. Immigrants from these countries brought Orthodox churches to the United States.

The two largest Orthodox churches in the U.S. today are Greek and Russian, respectively. The next largest represent Armenians and Syrians. Together these four churches have more than 80 percent of the Orthodox membership.

Orthodox churches are organized hierarchically. Archbishops and bishops possess special spiritual authority and administer church affairs. Religious observances tend to be solemn and elaborate. Ancient liturgies in the ancient languages have been carefully preserved. Orthodox clergy are male, and in most churches they are allowed to marry. Because of differences in calculating feast days, Easter and other movable feasts may occur on different dates in the Orthodox Church than in the Western churches. In the U.S., many Orthodox churches have served as cultural centers for immigrants seeking to preserve their own ethnic heritage.

Latter-day Saints (Mormons)

The Church of Jesus Christ of Latter-day Saints, known popularly as the Mormon church, was "established anew," according to Mormon doctrine, on Apr. 6, 1830, by a 19th-century American prophet named Joseph Smith (1805–44). Smith, who grew up in western New York State, reported direct revelations from God. The Book of Mormon, which Smith said he translated, tells of a visit by the resurrected Jesus Christ to pre-Columbian America.

Smith assembled a community of believers that settled first in western New York and later in Ohio, Missouri, and Illinois. Wherever they went, the Mormons aroused the antagonism of neighboring non-Mormons, in part because Mormons allowed men to take more than one wife. Persecution peaked with the murder of Smith himself in 1844.

The next great leader of the church was Brigham Young (1801–77), who led the majority of Mormons westward to settle in the then-uninhabited basin by the Great Salt Lake. There the church grew and prospered. To this day, the majority of religiously affiliated people in Utah are Mormons. There are also many adherents in surrounding states, especially Colorado and Idaho.

Most of the church's 12 million-plus members live in the United States, but the Mormons' legendary missionary work goes on around the globe. Since about 1900, the church has encouraged converts to stay in their own countries and organize congregations there. The number of American adults who identify as Mormon has continued to grow, increasing nearly 27 percent between 1990 and 2008.

The Reorganized Church is the largest of the groups that did not make the trek to the Great Salt Lake. Its headquarters are in Independence, Missouri, which Smith had designated as the site of a great future temple. Members of the Reorganized Church do not consider themselves Mormons.

Christian Churches and Churches of Christ

This family of churches traces its origins to a great religious awakening in 1800 on the Pennsylvania and Kentucky frontiers. Discouraged by sectarian competition among Methodists, Presbyterians, and others, leaders of the revival did not seek to form a denomination but to reestablish a single nondenominational Christian church. In time they became a denomination themselves.

In the 1870s the Churches of Christ and the Christian Church (Disciples) split over questions of using musical instruments in worship and over the issue of centralizing some church functions. The Churches of Christ opposed both instrumental music and national organization. The Disciples allowed instrumental music and established a central missionary board to coordinate mission work. They are ecumenically minded and have a long history of cooperation and discussion with other denominations.

The third group, the Christian churches and Churches of Christ, split from the Disciples in the 1920s–30s. They allow instrumental music but are theologically more conservative than the Disciples.

Episcopal Family of Churches

The Episcopal churches are descendants of the Church of England, which was established as a separate church by King Henry VIII in 1534. Churches descending from the English church make up the worldwide Anglican Communion. The American church takes its name from the word *bishop*, which suggests its hierarchical organization.

In colonial times the Church of England was established in the southern colonies and had some influence in the middle colonies, but was not welcome in New England, where Reformed churches were predominant. During the American Revolution, most Church of England members and clergy remained loyal to England. Thousands migrated to Canada. Those who remained were under suspicion, and some were persecuted. The church almost ceased to function.

After the Revolution, a small group of Anglicans loyal to the United States gradually revived the church. It never grew as rapidly as the Methodist and Baptist families, but it did gain considerable influence. Especially in eastern cities, many families of wealth and power were Episcopalian.

The Episcopal Church accommodates a wide spectrum of belief and practice. It is usually considered Protestant and shares much with other Protestant denominations, yet its worship services retain much of pre-Reformation Catholic tradition. One wing of the church retains a strong emphasis on the church's Catholic heritage. In July 2000, the Episcopal Church announced an alliance with the Evangelical Lutheran Church.

Jehovah's Witnesses

Jehovah's Witnesses are a remarkably active and dynamic sect, visible to most from street-corner or door-to-door encounters. They were founded by Charles Taze Russell (1852–1916) in western Pennsylvania in the 1870s. The Witnesses preach a slightly unorthodox form of the Christian message and look intently for the end of the present world. In 2008, 1.9 million American adults identified as Jehovah's Witness.

Church of Christ, Scientist

Christian Scientists, as adherents are often known, follow the teaching of Mary Baker Eddy (1821–1910), who founded the church in 1879 in Boston and wrote *Science and Health with a Key to the Scriptures*, which remains a major sourcebook for the church. Christian Science asserts that sickness and other adversities exist only in the mind and that disciplined spiritual thinking can correct them. Thus, Christian Scientists refuse most or all medical treatment. Christian Science practitioners help adherents deal with illness but do not serve as clergy. The church operates many reading rooms open to the public.

The Adventist Family of Churches

Adventist churches sprang up in the U.S. in the 1840s with a wave of concern about prophecies of the end of the world. Adventists anticipate and prepare for the world's end and the second coming of Jesus Christ. The largest Adventist group, the Seventh-Day Adventists, claims nearly one million adult adherents in the U.S. As their name suggests, they worship on Saturday rather than Sunday. They operate parochial schools, colleges, medical schools, and hospitals.

The Salvation Army

The Salvation Army is familiar to outsiders through its work among the homeless and the poor and its fund-raising on the streets, especially before Christmas. The church, which originated in England in 1865, is organized in quasi-military style, and many of its members devote their lives to its service.

Mennonite Churches

Mennonites trace their roots to a small group of Christians after 1530 who sought a reformation

Religious Self-Identification by Percent of Respondents, by State, 1990–2008

State	1990					2008				
	Catholic	Other Christian	Other Religion	None	Unsure/ Refused	Catholic	Other Christian	Other Religion	None	Unsure/ Refused
U.S.	26.2%	60.0%	3.3%	8.2%	2.3%	25.1%	50.9%	3.9%	15.0%	5.2%
Alabama	4	89	1	4	1	6	80	1	11	3
Alaska	N.A.	N.A.	N.A.	N.A.	N.A.	N.A.	N.A.	N.A.	N.A.	N.A.
Arizona	24	57	3	13	3	29	44	5	17	5
Arkansas	5	85	1	6	3	8	79	1	8	3
California	29	49	5	14	3	37	35	5	18	5
Colorado	25	56	4	13	3	21	49	4	21	5
Connecticut	50	36	3	6	4	38	36	8	14	4
Delaware	26	59	1	7	6	26	48	1	23	2
D.C.	16	71	4	7	2	13	59	6	18	4
Florida	23	62	5	8	2	27	49	4	14	6
Georgia	6	86	2	5	1	9	72	4	9	6
Hawaii	N.A.	N.A.	N.A.	N.A.	N.A.	N.A.	N.A.	N.A.	N.A.	N.A.
Idaho	12	72	1	13	3	10	59	3	23	6
Illinois	33	53	3	8	3	32	45	3	13	6
Indiana	19	69	1	8	2	19	59	3	15	4
Iowa	22	69	1	7	1	22	54	4	15	5
Kansas	17	74	1	6	2	21	61	3	11	5
Kentucky	13	77	1	7	2	14	66	1	13	5
Louisiana	47	49	1	3	1	31	57	1	8	3
Maine	31	54	2	11	2	22	47	3	25	4
Maryland	25	61	4	8	2	27	49	6	13	5
Massachussetts	54	29	6	8	3	39	26	5	22	7
Michigan	29	57	3	9	2	20	55	3	16	5
Minnesota	29	61	2	6	2	29	51	4	12	5
Mississippi	7	88	1	3	1	11	80	1	5	3
Missouri	20	69	1	7	2	18	61	3	14	5
Montana	28	58	1	11	3	12	58	4	21	5
Nebraska	29	60	2	7	2	22	53	3	17	6
Nevada	24	56	4	14	2	23	41	4	24	7
New Hampshire	41	44	4	9	2	32	30	2	29	7
New Jersey	46	40	6	6	3	42	30	7	15	6
New Mexico	37	48	2	11	2	33	41	3	16	7
New York	44	36	10	7	3	37	34	8	14	6
North Carolina	6	86	1	5	2	9	73	2	10	4
North Dakota	30	65	0	2	3	28	62	0	7	4
Ohio	24	64	2	8	2	20	56	3	17	4
Oklahoma	8	79	2	7	4	7	73	2	11	6
Oregon	15	62	2	18	2	14	52	3	24	7
Pennsylvania	33	56	3	6	2	31	46	4	15	4
Rhode Island	62	26	3	6	3	46	28	2	19	5
South Carolina	6	88	1	3	2	10	73	2	10	4
South Dakota	26	69	1	4	1	19	59	4	12	5
Tennessee	5	87	1	6	2	7	76	3	9	5
Texas	23	68	2	5	2	32	48	2	12	6
Utah	6	81	1	9	3	7	71	1	14	7
Vermont	37	47	3	13	1	26	29	4	34	6
Virginia	12	76	3	7	2	11	65	4	15	5
Washington	19	60	2	15	3	16	48	5	25	6
West Virginia	6	83	1	8	2	7	70	2	15	5
Wisconsin	39	52	2	6	2	29	47	4	15	5
Wyoming	18	56	9	14	3	13	54	1	28	3

Source: Institute for the Study of Secularism in Society and Culture, Trinity College, *American Religious Identification Survey, 2008* (2010).

even more radical than those advocated by Lutherans and Calvinists. They were called Mennonites after Menno Simons (1469–1561), one of their early leaders. Their most distinctive practice is adult baptism, offered only to those who have made a decision to follow Christ's teachings.

Because they would not swear oaths and would not bear arms in the service of their temporal leaders, Mennonites were severely persecuted. Small bands were scattered to many corners of the world, and began emigrating to the U.S. in the 17th century, first in Pennsylvania. About half a million American adults in 2008 said they were Mennonite.

The Amish are groups with Mennonite beliefs who broke with the Mennonite Church in the 17th century over the idea of excommunication. The Old Order Amish, centered in Pennsylvania, wear "plain" clothing, still drive horses and buggies rather than automobiles, and live agricultural lifestyles without the use of electricity.

Churches of the Brethren

The Brethren, founded as a dissenting group in Germany in the early 1700s, immigrated to Pennsylvania in the 1720s to escape persecution. Brethren share many doctrinal points with the Mennonites; they practice adult baptism, refuse to swear oaths, and will not serve as combatants in war. The various Brethren denominations agree in basic theology but differ on less significant mat-

Composition of Racial and Ethnic Groups by Religious Tradition, 1990–2008

Religion	White[1] 1990	2001	2008	Black[1] 1990	2001	2008	Hispanic[1] 1990	2001	2008	Asian[2] 1990	2001	2008
Catholic	27%	23%	21%	9%	7%	6%	66%	57%	59%	27%	20%	17%
Baptist	15	15	15	50	46	45	7	5	3	9	4	3
Christian generic	17	11	15	9	10	15	8	11	11	13	11	10
Pentecostal / Charismatic	3	3	3	6	7	7	3	4	3	2	1	0
Protestant[3]	2	3	3	4	4	6	2	3	4	2	1	2
Mormon	2	2	2	0	0	0	1	1	0	2	0	0
Jewish	2	2	2	0	0	0	1	1	0	1	0	0
Eastern Religions	0	0	0	0	0	0	0	0	0	8	22	21
Muslim	0	0	0	1	1	1	0	0	0	3	8	8
None	8	15	16	6	11	11	6	13	12	16	22	27
Don't Know / Refused	2	4	4	1	2	2	1	3	5	4	5	5

Notes: Figures in percentage and rounded at source. 1. Non-Hispanic. 2. Asian and other race combined for 1990 data. 3. Includes several denominations. **Source:** Institute for the Study of Secularism in Society and Culture, Trinity College, *American Religious Identification Survey, 2008* (2010).

Self-Described Religious Identification of Adult Population, 1990–2008 (in thousands)

Religious group	1990	2001	2008	Religious group	1990	2001	2008
Total Christian	**151,222**	**159,514**	**173,402**	Nondenominational	194	2,489	8,032
				Disciples of Christ	144	402	263
Catholic	46,004	50,873	57,199	Reformed	161	289	206
Baptist	33,964	33,820	36,148	Apostolic	117	254	970
Protestant[1]	17,214	4,647	5,187	Quaker	67	217	130
Methodist	14,174	14,039	11,366	Christian Reform	40	79	381
Lutheran	9,110	9,580	8,674	Foursquare Gospel	28	70	116
Presbyterian	4,985	5,596	4,723				
Pentecostal	3,116	4,407	5,416	**Total other religions[1]**	**5,853**	**7,740**	**8,796**
Episcopalian	3,043	3,451	2,405	Jewish	3,137	2,837	2,680
Mormon	2,487	2,697	3,158	Muslim	527	1,104	1,349
Churches of Christ	1,769	2,593	1,921	Buddhist	404	1,082	1,189
Jehovah's Witness	1,381	1,331	1,914	Unitarian / Universalist	502	629	586
Seventh-Day Adventist	668	724	938	Hindu	227	766	582
Assemblies of God	617	1,105	810	Native American	47	103	186
Holiness / Holy	610	569	352	Wiccan	8	134	342
Congregational	438	1,378	736	Pagan	N.A.	140	340
Church of the Nazarene	549	544	358	Spiritualist	N.A.	116	426
Church of God	590	943	663	Other unclassified	837	386	735
Orthodox (Eastern)	502	645	824				
Evangelical / Born-Again	546	1,088	2,154	**No religion specified[2]**	**14,331**	**29,481**	**34,169**
Mennonite	235	346	438	Atheist	3	902	1,621
Christian Science	214	194	339	Agnostic	1,186	991	1,985
Churches of the Brethren	206	358	231	No religion	13,116	27,486	30,427
				Refused	4,031	11,246	11,815

Notes: 1. Includes other groups not shown separately. 2. Because of the subjective nature of these questions, they are the most subject to fluctuate over time. 3. Atheist included in Agnostic. **Source:** U.S. Census Bureau, *Statistical Abstract of the United States, 2010.*

basic theology but differ on less significant matters of interpretation.

Unitarian Universalist Association

The Unitarian Universalist Association is not necessarily considered a Christian denomination, primarily because of the belief in the unity of God and the repudiation of the Trinity. They believe that redemption with God is available for anyone, believer or not. Unitarianism was an outgrowth of New England Congregationalism in the late 1700s and early 1800s. They also interpreted other Christian beliefs in a liberal, figurative manner. Universalism was a separate movement emphasizing the availability of God's care to all people, not only to a small chosen group. In 1961 Unitarian and Universalist organizations merged, and by 2008 over a half million American adults were in the association.

Friends (Quaker) Churches

Known popularly as Quakers, the Friends were established by the English religious mystic George Fox (1624–91) in the mid-1600s. Under the protection of William Penn (1644–1718) many settled in Pennsylvania. According to Fox, they were called Quakers because they were admonished to "tremble at the word of the Lord."

The most distinctive doctrine of the Friends is that of the Inner Light, the spark of God in each individual. Friends have avoided setting up formal church structures, and many groups have no clergy. Friends have organized remarkable world relief and peace organizations, by which they are perhaps best known to outsiders.

▶ JUDAISM

Judaism is the largest non-Christian religious family in the United States. According to the American-Israeli Cooperative Enterprise, there are roughly 5.3 million American Jews, over 40 percent of the total world Jewish population. About a million of these consider their Judaism to be more ethnic or cultural than religious.

As descendants of the Jews of biblical times, Jews worship one God and follow the religious precepts in the Hebrew scriptures, the writings called the Old Testament by Christians. Jews recognize Jesus as a religious teacher but do not acknowledge him as the Messiah or Son of God. Jews still await the coming of the Messiah as foretold by the prophets.

A handful of Jews arrived in North America in the 1600s. In the 1800s, Jews from Germany arrived with other immigrants. Then between 1890 and 1920, several million Jews arrived from eastern Europe, fleeing persecution and hard times in Russia and Poland. In the 1930s and 1940s, Jews reached America as refugees from the Nazi extermination campaigns. The slaughter of some 6 million Jews by the Germans, called the Holocaust, is one of two central facts of modern Jewish experience. The second is the establishment of Israel as an independent state in 1948. Today 40.6 percent of the world Jewish population lives in Israel, only 35,000 more than live in the U.S.

There are three main branches of religious Judaism in the U.S. today: Orthodox, Reform, and Conservative. Orthodox Judaism is by far the most rigorous and smallest of the three branches, with an estimated 500,000 adherents. Orthodox Jews may keep entirely separate kitchens for milk and meat, refuse to operate electric and mechanical devices on the Sabbath, and often attend temple services or hold prayer sessions every day. Orthodox services are conducted in Hebrew, and require men and women to pray separately, even when not in temple. Many orthodox communities, especially self-contained communities such as the Hasidic Jews (located mainly in New York), impose strict dress codes. Men usually wear sidelocks called *payots* and married women must keep their hair covered or wear a wig.

Reform Judaism is the least strict branch. It flowered in the U.S. in the late 1800s, especially among immigrants from Germany. Reform Jews do not generally wear yarmulkes, don't usually observe the kosher dietary laws, and conduct their religious services primarily in English (though most of the prayers are recited in Hebrew). About 1.5 million Jews are affiliated with Reform temples, making Reform Judaism the largest branch in North America.

Conservative Judaism rose in response to the Reform movement. It sought to preserve more of the ancient observances of the old orthodoxy, but without losing touch with American culture and behavior. As a middle road between Reform and Orthodox Judaism, Conservative Judaism has gained many adherents. There are 1.5 million Jews in 760 congregations associated with the United Synagogue of Conservative Judaism, which represents the conservative movement in the U.S.

▶ ISLAM

The Islamic faith, whose followers are called Muslims, is one of the three great theistic world religions, along with Judaism and Christianity. The first sizable group of Muslims arrived in the U.S. from Lebanon in the early 1900s. Later waves of immigration have brought Pakistanis, Indians, Arabs, and Iranians, among others.

There are about 1,600 mosques in the U.S. but membership estimates vary greatly, in part because many Muslims are new immigrants or recent converts. Some Muslim groups claim as many as 6 or 7 million American Muslims; but recent surveys by the U.S. Census and the *American Religious Identification Survey* have yielded estimates between 1 and 2 million. Regardless of overall numbers, most Muslims are in cities in the Northeast and industrial Midwest. Observances may vary from one center to another, depending on the nationality of its adherents and their length of residence in the United States. In general, recent immigrants are more conservative and follow Islamic ritual and custom more closely.

▶ BUDDHIST CHURCHES OF AMERICA

The Buddhist Churches of America is the oldest and largest U.S. Buddhist group. It represents the Jodo Shinshu sect of Buddhism, and many of its members are of Japanese descent. There are many other Buddhist organizations in the U.S., and there may be as many as two million additional Americans who subscribe to Buddhist tenets.

▶ NON-BELIEVERS

The number of Americans who describe themselves as not identifying with any organized religion more than doubled between 1990 and 2008—from 14.3 million to 34.2 million. "Non-religion" includes those identifying as Atheist (1.6 million) or Agnostic (2 million). According to the *American Religious Identification Survey*, roughly one in five adults did not identify with a religion of any kind in 2008, compared with one in ten in 1990.

The percentage of people who identify as having no religion is highest in the Northeast (22 percent of respondents) and the Pacific (20 percent) regions, closely followed by the Mountain region, where 19 percent of respondents claimed having no religion. The growth of this group, however, has slowed in the first decade of the present century compared with rapid growth in the 1990s.

Transportation

Americans spend well over $1.5 trillion annually on transportation products and services. Transportation expenditures (which include personal and governmental spending on motor vehicles and parts, gasoline and oil, airfares, and public transportation) accounted for 10.6 percent of gross domestic product in 2007, almost as much as what the country spent on food, and much more than it spent on education. In 2008, the United States recorded over 5.5 trillion passenger miles of travel. More than 254 million vehicles (most of them cars) were involved in domestic transportation in 2007, causing over 40,000 fatalities. The transportation sector consumed 97.4 percent of all U.S. energy consumption in 2008.

The government has traditionally played a leading role in the development of the nation's transportation infrastructure. Technological, economic, and demographic changes all shape the government's priorities. In the 19th and early 20th centuries, for instance, the government made enormous direct and indirect contributions to the development of the nation's railroads. Today, the government spends vastly more on highways and aviation than on mass transit, railroad transportation, or water transportation.

▶ **PASSENGER TRAVEL**
In order to compare the costs of different modes of transportation, statisticians calculate the price for one passenger to travel one mile. For modes of transportation that carry large numbers of passengers at once, these numbers are remarkably similar. It costs about 13 cents for a coach passenger to travel one mile by plane, 18 cents by commuter rail, 31 cents by Amtrak, and 13 by inter-city bus. By comparison, the average cost of operating a car in 2007 (including variable costs for gas and oil, maintenance and tires, and fixed costs for insurance, registration, depreciation and finance charges) was 54.0 cents per mile (up from

49 cents in 2000, largely due to rising gas prices). The average fare in 2007 was $108.36 for an airline seat, $4.32 for commuter rail, and $58.94 for a ride on Amtrak. Most of these fares have tripled since 1980, though airfares have risen just over 50 percent.

▶ **TRANSPORTATION SAFETY**
Because they kill large numbers of people at once, plane crashes attract much more attention than do automobile accidents. But over the course of a year, air travel accounts for only a tiny percentage of transportation fatalities; in a typical year, more people die in boating accidents than in aviation

U.S. Motor Vehicle Factory Sales, 1900–2008

Year	Factory sales		Total
	Passenger cars	Trucks and buses	
1900	4,192	[1]	4,192
1910	181,000	6,000	187,000
1920	1,905,560	321,789	2,227,349
1930	2,787,456	575,364	3,362,820
1940	3,717,385	754,901	4,472,286
1950	6,665,863	1,337,193	8,003,056
1960	6,674,796	1,194,475	7,869,271
1970	6,546,817	1,692,440	8,239,257
1980	6,400,026	1,667,283	8,067,309
1990	6,049,749	3,725,205	9,774,954
1995	6,309,836	5,713,469	12,023,305
2000	5,504,385	7,022,478	12,526,863
2005[2]	8,027,000	7,866,000	15,893,000
2008[2]	8,537,000	7,871,000	16,408,000

Notes: 1. Not measured. 2. Data rounded in source. **Source:** Ward's Communications, *Ward's Motor Vehicle Facts & Figures, 2009,* U.S. Dept. of Transportation, Bureau of Transportation Statistics. Data retrieved 2010.

U.S. Passenger-Miles and Ton-Miles of Freight, by Mode of Transportation, 1960–2008 (in millions)

	1960	1970	1980	1990	2000	2008
Passenger						
Air carrier	31,099	108,442	204,368	345,873	516,129	583,506
Highway, total	1,272,078	2,042,002	2,653,510	3,561,209	4,390,076	4,871,683
Passenger car	1,144,673	1,750,897	2,011,989	2,281,391	2,544,457	2,553,043
Motorcycle	[1]	3,277	12,257	12,424	11,516	18,395
Other 2-axle 4-tire vehicle	[2]	225,613	520,774	999,754	1,467,664	1,921,960
Truck, single-unit	98,551	27,081	39,813	51,901	70,500	83,951
Truck, combination	28,854	35,134	68,678	94,341	135,020	143,507
Bus	N.A.	N.A.	N.A.	121,398	160,919	150,827
Transit, total	N.A.	N.A.	39,854	41,143	47,666	53,712
Rail	17,064	6,179	4,503	6,057	5,498	6,179
Freight						
Air carrier[3]	553	2,709	4,528	9,064	14,983	13,774
Intercity truck[4]	285,000	412,000	555,000	854,000	1,203,000	N.A.
Rail	572,309	764,809	918,958	1,033,969	1,465,960	1,777,236
Water transportation	N.A.	596,195	921,836	833,544	645,799	520,521
Oil pipeline	229,000	431,000	588,200	584,100	577,300	N.A.

Notes: Excludes intraterritorial traffic, for which ton-miles were not compiled. 1. Included in passenger car. 2. Included in other single-unit 2-axle 6-tire or more truck. 3. Includes freight, express, and mail revenue ton-miles. 4. Methodology was changed in 1990 for intercity trucks. Therefore figures prior to 1990 are not comparable to those after 1990. **Source:** U.S. Dept. of Transportation, *National Transportation Statistics 2010* (2010).

mishaps. In 2008, there were 564 avion fatalities, though a major commercial U.S. airline was responsible for only three of these. The vast majority (495) were categorized under general aviation, mostly privately-owned jets and the like. There were over 37,000 highway fatalities in 2008, 66 times as many air carrier deaths in the same year.

Almost 95 percent of transportation fatalities and 99 percent of transportation injuries are a result of automobile accidents. In 2007, there were 6,024,000 automobile accidents, resulting in 2,346,000 injuries (down from 2.5 million in 2007)

and 41,259 fatalities (down from 37,261 in 2007). The number of traffic fatalities in 2008 was the lowest since 1961. Despite safety improvements to the production of automobiles, wider highway lanes, better lighting and lower speed limits, the annual number of automobile accidents, injuries and fatalities did not change much from 1970 to 2000. But over the same period, the number of miles traveled tripled (from one trillion miles in 1970 to nearly 3 trillion in 2007), indicating that

Passenger Vehicle Occupants Killed by Restraint Use, 2007–08

	2007		2008	
Type	Number	Percent	Number	Percent
Fatalities	**29,072**	**100%**	**25,351**	**100%**
Restraint used	13,383	46	11,477	45
Restraint not used	15,689	54	13,874	55
Day	**14,285**	**49**	**12,482**	**49**
Restraint used	7,919	55	6,846	55
Restraint not used	6,366	45	5,636	45
Night	**14,537**	**50**	**12,671**	**50**
Restraint used	5,356	37	4,535	36
Restraint not used	9,181	63	8,136	64

Source: U.S. National Highway Traffic Safety Administration, *2008 Traffic Safety Facts* (2009).

U.S. Roads and Streets, 1904–2008

	Mileage ('000's)			
Year	State control[1]	County & local control	Total[2]	Percent paved
1904	[3]	[3]	2,351	N.A.
1921	203	2,957	3,160	N.A.
1930	324	2,935	3,259	N.A.
1940	551	2,666	3,287	N.A.
1950	609	2,623	3,313	23.5%
1960	694	2,725	3,546	34.7
1970	755	2,762	3,731	44.5
1980	848	2,764	3,860	53.7
1990	798	2,889	3,867	58.4
1995	803	2,937	3,912	60.8
2000	775	3,058	3,950	63.4
2008	783[3]	3,121[3]	4,058	67.4

Notes: Some years contain estimates by the Federal Highway Administration. 1. Reflects state highway agency roadways prior to 1980. Includes state park, state toll, and other state agency roadways beginning in 1980. 2. After 1930, includes mileage in federal parks, forests, and reservations not part of the state and local highway system and not shown separately. 3. Data is for 2007. **Source:** U.S. Department of Transportation, *Highway Statistics Summary to 1995* and *Highway Statistics 2009*.

Number of Vehicles in the U.S., 1970–2007

Mode of Transport	1970	1980	1990	2000	2007
Air, total	**134,422**	**205,305**	**204,083**	**225,588**	**N.A.**
Air carrier, certificated, all services	2,679	3,808	6,083	8,055	N.A.
General aviation	131,743	211,045	198,000	217,533	231,607
Highway, total[1]	**111,242,295**	**161,490,159**	**193,057,376**	**225,821,241**	**254,403,082**
Passenger car & motorcycle	92,067,655	127,294,783	137,959,958	137,967,488	143,071,406
Other 2-axle 4-tire vehicle	14,210,591	27,875,934	48,274,555	79,084,979	101,469,615
Truck, total	4,586,487	5,790,473	6,195,876	8,022,649	9,027,625
Intercity bus	377,562	528,789	626,987	746,125	834,436
Local transit, total[2]	**61,298**	**75,388**	**92,961**	**131,493**	**N.A.**
Motor bus	49,700	59,411	58,714	75,013	65,249
Light rail	1,262	1,013	913	1,577	1,810
Heavy rail	9,286	9,641	10,419	10,591	11,222
Trolley bus	1,050	823	832	951	559
Commuter rail	[6]	4,500	4,415	5,073	6,391
Demand response	[6]	[6]	16,471	33,080	64,865
Other	[6]	[6]	1,197	5,208	13,877
Rail, total[3]	**1,450,998**	**1,198,755**	**679,918**	**582,454**	**N.A.**
Class I Freight cars	1,423,921	1,168,114	658,902	560,154	460,172
Class I Locomotives	27,077	28,094	18,835	20,028	24,143
Amtrak[4]	[6]	2,547	2,181	2,272	1,434
Water transport, total	**5,155,716**	**8,817,509**	**11,036,334**	**12,823,951**	**N.A.**
Non self-propelled vessels	19,337	31,662	31,209	33,152	31,654
Self-propelled vessels	6,455	7,126	8,236	8,202	9,041
Oceangoing ships[5]	1,579	864	636	454	275
Recreational boats	5,128,345	8,777,857	10,996,253	12,782,143	12,875,568

Notes: 1. Registered vehicles. 2. Prior to 1984, excludes most rural and smaller transit systems. 3. Does not include non-Class I freight cars or shippers' freight cars. 4. Includes passenger cars and locomotives. 5. Vessels 1,000 gross tons and over. 6. Not measured. **Source:** U.S. Dept. of Transportation, *National Transportation Statistics 2010* (2010).

Americans are driving many more miles without having any more accidents.

Not only were Americans driving more miles and having fewer accidents, the first decade of the 2000s saw a continuous decline in number of accidents overall. The estimated number of people injured in 2008 was the lowest since the National Highway and Traffic Safety Administration began collecting data in 1988. It marks the ninth consecutive yearly reduction in people injured. The number of motorcyclists injured decreased 6.8 percent, the first time since 1998. The number of people injured only increased for bicyclists (21 percent from 2007 to 2008, to 52,000 injuries), which could be due to a growing number of bicyclists in large cities.

Another change is the number of people killed in accidents involving drunk drivers. In 1985, 43,825 people died in auto collisions and of those, 23,167 died in alcohol-related collisions. In 2007, the total number of fatalities was about the same (41,059), but only 12,998 involved a drunk driver.

U.S. Traffic Fatalities and Fatality Rates, 2007

| | | | | | Fatality Rates per | | | |
State	Traffic Fatalities	Population (thousands)	Licensed Drivers (thousands)	Vehicle Miles Traveled (millions)	100,000 Population	100,000 Licensed Drivers	100,000 Registered Vehicles	100 million Miles Traveled
AL	1,110	4,628	3,692	61,410	23.99	30.07	23.18	1.81
AK	84	683	495	5,153	12.29	16.96	11.90	1.63
AZ	1,066	6,339	4,154	62,963	16.82	25.66	23.70	1.69
AR	650	2,835	2,046	33,171	22.93	31.77	31.33	1.96
CA	3,974	36,553	23,467	328,312	10.87	16.93	11.45	1.21
CO	554	4,862	3,503	48,713	11.40	15.82	30.46	1.14
CT	277	3,502	2,849	32,053	7.91	9.72	8.90	0.86
DE	117	865	624	9,483	13.53	18.74	13.38	1.23
DC	44	588	396	3,609	7.48	11.11	20.09	1.22
FL	3,214	18,251	14,139	206,121	17.61	22.73	18.80	1.56
GA	1,641	9,545	6,134	112,541	17.19	26.75	18.89	1.46
HI	138	1,283	863	10,345	10.75	15.99	13.49	1.33
ID	252	1,499	1,028	15,782	16.81	24.53	19.00	1.60
IL	1,249	12,853	8,190	107,483	9.72	15.25	12.41	1.16
IN	898	6,345	4,309	71,478	14.15	20.84	17.60	1.26
IA	445	2,988	2,094	31,253	14.89	21.25	12.64	1.42
KS	416	2,776	2,018	30,048	14.99	20.61	16.60	1.38
KY	864	4,241	2,933	48,063	20.37	29.46	23.94	1.80
LA	985	4,293	3,034	45,376	22.94	32.47	24.68	2.17
ME	183	1,317	1,010	15,035	13.89	18.12	16.20	1.22
MD	614	5,618	3,738	56,503	10.93	16.43	13.38	1.09
MA	417	6,450	4,699	55,071	6.47	8.87	7.57	0.76
MI	1,088	10,072	7,059	104,614	10.80	15.41	12.86	1.04
MN	504	5,198	3,149	57,233	9.70	16.00	10.11	0.88
MS	884	2,919	1,927	43,337	30.29	45.88	43.43	2.04
MO	992	5,878	4,162	69,151	16.88	23.83	19.80	1.43
MT	277	958	736	11,307	28.92	37.65	28.59	2.45
NE	256	1,775	1,331	19,439	14.43	19.24	14.39	1.32
NV	373	2,565	1,662	22,146	14.54	22.45	25.11	1.68
NH	129	1,316	1,027	13,459	9.80	12.57	10.23	0.96
NJ	724	8,686	5,782	76,152	8.34	12.52	11.29	0.95
NM	413	1,970	1,365	26,850	20.97	30.25	25.09	1.54
NY	1,333	19,298	11,369	136,737	6.91	11.72	11.29	0.97
NC	1,675	9,061	6,384	103,598	18.49	26.24	26.04	1.62
ND	111	640	471	7,844	17.35	23.58	15.04	1.42
OH	1,257	11,467	7,976	110,631	10.96	15.76	11.23	1.14
OK	754	3,617	2,283	47,572	20.84	33.02	22.67	1.58
OR	455	3,747	2,827	34,750	12.14	16.09	14.29	1.31
PA	1,491	12,433	8,601	108,699	11.99	17.34	14.49	1.37
RI	69	1,058	744	8,636	6.52	9.28	8.33	0.80
SC	1,066	4,408	3,127	51,109	24.18	34.09	29.48	2.09
SD	146	796	589	9,005	18.34	24.81	15.81	1.62
TN	1,210	6,157	4,426	71,179	19.65	27.34	22.06	1.70
TX	3,363	23,904	15,184	243,443	14.07	22.15	18.22	1.38
UT	299	2,645	1,652	26,832	11.30	18.10	12.59	1.11
VT	66	621	534	7,694	10.62	12.35	11.17	0.86
VA	1,027	7,712	5,260	82,077	13.32	19.53	15.34	1.25
WA	568	6,468	4,880	56,939	8.78	11.64	9.52	1.00
WV	431	1,812	1,359	20,564	23.79	31.73	29.54	2.10
WI	756	5,602	4,066	59,493	13.50	18.59	14.15	1.27
WY	150	523	398	9,366	28.69	37.66	21.73	1.60
U.S.	41,059	301,621	205,742	3,029,822	13.61	19.96	16.05	1.36

Source: U.S. National Highway Traffic Safety Administration, *Traffic Safety Facts 2007* (2008).

►MOTOR VEHICLES

Although the table on the next page would suggest that the average fuel efficiency of U.S. cars is on the rise, the statistics mask the explosion in the number of light trucks, minivans, and sport utility vehicles favored by so many American drivers of the 1990s. These vehicles get much poorer gas mileage than most cars, but because they are classified as trucks, they are not held to the same fuel efficiency standards as cars. In 1980, over 80 percent of all new vehicles were cars (9.1 million), with an average fuel efficiency of 23 miles per gallon (mpg). In comparison, there were only 2.2 million new trucks, which got 18 miles per gallon. Although gas-guzzling light trucks still commanded 52.8 percent of the market in 2006, sales fell 2.6 percent from 2005 to 16.9 million units. (Light truck sales totaled roughly 9 million in 2001.) On the opposite end of the spectrum, hybrid sales totaled 205,749 in 2005, which, al-

U.S. States by Selected Transportation Characteristic, 2007

State	Motor vehicle registrations (000s)	Gasoline tax rate[1]	Highway mileage	Percent of workers who commute alone, in vehicle	Federal aid from Federal Transit Administration[2]
United States	247,265	N.A.	4,032,126	76.1%	$9,234
Alabama	4,678	18.0	97,323	83.4	64
Alaska	680	8.0	14,438	66.2	53
Arizona	4,372	18.0	60,593	74.8	209
Arkansas	2,010	21.5	99,558	80.8	22
California	33,935	18.0	171,154	73.2	1,290
Colorado	1,707	22.0	88,163	74.5	185
Connecticut	3,047	25.0	21,295	79.6	63
Delaware	851	23.0	6,242	79.9	13
District of Columbia	218	20.0	1,505	38.2	309
Florida	16,474	15.3	121,526	79.6	341
Georgia	8,513	7.5	118,779	78.7	124
Hawaii	993	17.0	4,341	68.0	47
Idaho	1,282	25.0	48,416	76.4	13
Illinois	9,757	19.0	139,157	73.7	546
Indiana	4,956	18.0	95,469	83.1	70
Iowa	3,360	21.0	114,193	78.7	43
Kansas	2,429	24.0	140,271	81.3	27
Kentucky	3,547	21.0	78,587	81.3	54
Louisiana	3,927	20.0	61,008	80.9	75
Maine	1,080	27.6	22,792	79.2	21
Maryland	4,510	23.5	31,300	74.3	181
Massachusetts	5,367	21.0	36,008	73.0	275
Michigan	8,192	19.0	121,593	83.1	154
Minnesota	4,756	20.0	137,693	77.8	110
Mississippi	2,008	18.4	74,622	82.7	17
Missouri	4,917	17.0	129,122	80.7	96
Montana	949	27.8	73,203	73.7	13
Nebraska	1,739	27.0	93,398	79.9	20
Nevada	1,424	24.0	33,872	77.8	52
New Hampshire	1,185	19.6	15,839	81.4	13
New Jersey	6,247	10.5	38,752	71.8	676
New Mexico	1,599	18.9	68,339	77.2	31
New York	11,495	24.7	113,740	54.1	1,647
North Carolina	6,317	29.9	104,412	79.8	168
North Dakota	711	23.0	86,842	78.6	14
Ohio	10,848	28.0	125,160	83.0	183
Oklahoma	3,225	17.0	112,922	80.5	43
Oregon	3,088	24.0	59,758	73.2	205
Pennsylvania	9,938	31.2	121,581	76.7	475
Rhode Island	797	30.0	6,510	80.7	30
South Carolina	3,521	16.0	66,248	81.1	36
South Dakota	865	22.0	83,744	77.3	12
Tennessee	5,340	20.0	91,058	83.4	57
Texas	18,072	20.0	305,855	78.9	450
Utah	2,320	24.5	44,221	74.9	128
Vermont	565	20.0	14,400	74.6	16
Virginia	6,614	17.5	72,662	77.5	122
Washington	5,758	36.0	83,431	73.1	319
West Virginia	1,413	31.5	38,274	81.2	22
Wisconsin	5,018	30.9	114,705	79.8	94
Wyoming	652	14.0	28,052	74.8	9

Notes: 1. State gasoline tax rates in cents per gallon. In effect Dec. 31, 2007. 2. In millions of dollars. Source: U.S. Census Bureau, Statistical Abstract, 2010 (2009).

though it was nearly a 250 percent increase from 2004, still comprised only 1.2 percent of total vehicles sold.

The popularity of larger vehicles, which up until 1999 were allowed to produce up to three times as much pollution per mile as standard cars, has had serious implications for the environment. To remedy that situation, the Clinton administration in 1999 announced that minivans, pickup trucks, and sport utility vehicles would be subject to the same pollution standards as ordinary cars. In 2009, the Obama administration announced new fuel standards that require an average of 39 mpg for cars and 30 mpg for light trucks by 2016. In 2008, SUVs got on average 23.4 mpg.

Traffic According to the Census Bureau, 90 percent of Americans have access to a motor vehicle, and half of the nation's households have two or more vehicles. In 2007, nearly 87 percent of all U.S. workers drove to work: 76 percent drove alone; only 10.4 percent were in car pools, down from 12 percent in 2000. The remaining workers used mass transportation (4.9 percent); walked (2.8), worked at home (4.1), or used bicycles, motorcycles, or some other transportation. The average commute was 25.3 minutes in 2007, down from 25.5 minutes in 2000. Nationally, only 3.4 percent of Americans faced an extreme commute (90 minutes or more) in 2004. New York topped this list for longest average commute for workers by state (31.5 minutes), and North Dakota boasted the shortest (16.1 minutes).

It's no wonder, then, that traffic jams are routine. In 2007, there were nearly 40 million hours spent by people in urban areas in traffic. This cost roughly $840 million in fuel, at an average of 15 gallons per person. In 2007, not surprisingly, delays were longest in Los Angeles, where drivers

Top-Selling Passenger Cars and Trucks in the U.S., 2009

Rank, vehicle	Starting Price	Units Sold
1. Ford F-Series	$22,540	179,632
2. Toyota Camry	20,145	150,242
3. Chevrolet Silverado	20,370	149,949
4. Honda Accord	21,615	131,043
5. Toyota Corolla	16,100	118,459
6. Honda Civic	16,015	118,459
7. Nissan Altima	20,620	96,428
8. Dodge Ram	22,420	94,516
9. Ford Fusion	19,995	85,146
10. Honda CR-V	21,955	78,917

Source: Bankrate, Inc. (2010).

Top High Gas-Mileage Cars in the U.S., 2009

Rank, vehicle	Starting Price	MPG Highway	MPG City
1. Toyota Prius	$22,750	48	51
2. Honda Civic Hybrid	23,650	45	40
3. Honda Civic Insight	20,470	43	40
4. Ford Fusion Hybrid	27,995	36	41
4. Mercury Milan Hybrid	28,225	36	41
6. smart fortwo	12,635	41	33
7. Nissan Altima Hybrid	27,370	33	35
8. Toyota Camry Hybrid	26,900	34	33
9. Volkswagon Jetta TDI	22,970	41	30
10. Mini Cooper	19,200	37	28

Source: Bankrate, Inc. (2010).

Fuel Efficiency of U.S. Passenger Cars and Trucks, 1955–2009

Since 1980, the federal government has required car manufacturers to maintain a corporate average fuel efficiency (CAFE). Since 1985, the CAFE standard for cars has been 27.5 mpg, and 22.5 mpg for light trucks, minivans and sport utility vehicles. These standards, however, are changing. The proposed CAFE standards for model year 2011 vehicles are 30.2 mpg for cars and 24.1 for light trucks.

Model Year	All passenger cars	Average New Vehicle	
		Passenger cars[1]	Light trucks
1955	14.5 mpg	16.0 mpg	[2]
1960	14.3	15.5	[2]
1965	14.3	15.4	[2]
1970	13.5	14.1	[2]
1975	13.5	15.1	[2]
1980	16.0	22.6	18.5 mpg
1985	17.5	26.3	20.7
1990	20.3	26.9	20.8
1995	21.1	27.7	20.5
2000	22.0	28.5	21.2
2005	22.1	30.3	22.1
2009	N.A.	32.6	24.2

Notes: Calculated on the basis of 55% city and 45% highway miles sales weighted average. 1. Domestic vehicles only. 2. Not measured separately. Source: U.S. Dept. of Transportation, National Transportation Statistics 2009 (2010).

Average Cost of Owning and Operating an Automobile[1], 1980–2008

	1980	1990	2000	2005	2006	2008
Gas as a percent of total cost[2]	27.9%	16.4%	14.1%	18.6%	17.1%	18.7%
Average total cost per mile (current $)	$0.212	$0.330	$0.491	$0.522	$0.522	$0.540
Gas[2]	0.059	0.054	0.069	0.095	0.089	0.100
Maintenance[3]	0.011	0.021	0.036	0.049	0.049	0.046
Tires	0.006	0.009	0.017	0.007	0.007	0.008
Average total cost per 15,000 miles	$3,176	$4,954	$7,363	$7,834	$7,823	$8,095
Variable cost	1,143	1,260	1,829	2,265	2,175	2,313
Fixed cost[4]	2,033	3,694	5,534	5,569	5,648	5,783

Notes: 1. All figures reflect the average cost of operating a vehicle 15,000 miles per year in stop and go conditions. 2 Prior to 2004, data include oil cost. 3. Beginning in 2004, data include oil cost. 4. Fixed costs (ownership costs) include insurance, license, registration, taxes, depreciation, and finance charges. Source: U.S. Dept. of Transportation, National Transportation Statistics, 2009 (2010).

lost 38 hours per year to congestion. Dalllas was second, with 32 hours lost annually, followed by Washington D.C. with 31.

▶ AVIATION

U.S. airlines made a modest $186 million profit in 2008, following a steady but slight string of increases since the industry crashed following the September 11, 2001 terrorist attacks, which pushed the already-shaky industry to the edge of financial ruin. A $15 billion bailout by the federal government (a $5 billion giveaway and $10 billion in guaranteed federal loans) prevented an industry collapse, but most airlines remain in dire straits. U.S. Airways received a $900 million federal loan guarantee after emerging from bankruptcy in 2003 and merged with America West Airlines in 2005. The federal government's denial of a $1.8 billion loan guarantee to United Airlines forced the airline to seek bankruptcy protection in 2002, and even American Airlines, the country's largest air carrier, teetered on the verge of bankruptcy in 2003, though by 2010 had recovered and even had reached position 120 on *Fortune 500s* list of companies.

After posting record profits of $5.6 billion in 1999, and $2.6 billion in 2000, the airline industry lost an astonishing $7.7 billion in 2001 and over $11 billion in 2002. By 2008 the industry had stabilized, though airlines had begun adding surcharges, such as a charge for checked baggage, and cutting costs like in-air food service. In 2008, 741.4 million passengers were enplaned, down from 769.4 in 2007, at a revenue of 13.8 cents per passenger mile. Yet overall passenger revenue increased 3.6 percent in the same time.

With the decline in air traffic came a sharp reduction in the number of airport delays. In 2000, 78.9 percent of flights departed on time, and 77 percent arrived on time. In 2008, those numbers declined to 76.7 percent and 73.4 percent respectively. New York's La Guardia, which was the worst airport for delays in 2000 (only 57.1 of flights arrived on-time) boosted its on-time arrival rate to 63.05 percent in 2008.

Some carriers managed to escape much of the recent turmoil. Once regarded as just a regional

On-time Performance and Mishandled Baggage, April 2010, by Major U.S. Airlines		
Airline	Percent of Arrivals on Time	Mishandled bags per 1,000
Airtran Airways	87.7%	1.31
Alaska Airlines	91.7	2.49
American Airlines	83.3	3.08
American Eagle Airlines	82.2	5.95
Atlantic Southeast Airlines	87.4	6.27
Comair	80.5	4.07
Continental Airlines	85.9	2.06
Delta Airlines	84.1	2.78
ExpressJet Airlines	82.3	3.60
Frontier Airlines	85.6	2.05
Hawaiian Airlines	81.9	1.61
JetBlue Airways	85.1	2.13
Mesa Airlines	87.7	2.59
Pinnacle Airlines	86.5	4.93
Skywest Airlines	83.9	4.07
Southwest Airlines	85.1	2.71
United Airlines	88.7	2.94
US Airways	88.9	2.07

Source: Federal Aviation Administration, Office of Aviation Enforcement and Proceedings, *Air Travel Consumer Report* (April 2010).

Top U.S. Airlines, 2008

Rank	Passengers Enplaned (millions)		Rank	Passenger Miles[1] (millions)		Rank	Cargo Ton Miles[2] (millions)	
1.	Delta	120.4	1.	Delta	176.8	1.	FedEx	10,591
2.	Southwest	101.9	2.	American	131.7	2.	UPS	6,866
3.	American	92.8	3.	United	109.8	3.	Atlas	3,187
4.	United	63.1	4.	Continental	80.4	4.	Delta	2,861
5.	US Airways	54.8	5.	Southwest	73.5	5.	American	2,014
6.	Continental	46.9	6.	US Airways	60.5	6.	United	1,921
7.	AirTran	24.6	7.	JetBlue	26.1	7.	Polar	1,435
8.	JetBlue	21.8	8.	AirTran	18.7	8.	Southern	1,400
9.	SkyWest	20.7	9.	Alaska	18.7	9.	Kalitta	1,175
10.	Alaska	16.8	10.	SkyWest	11.2	10.	Continental	951
11.	American Eagle	16.6	11.	Frontier	9.9	11.	World	782
12.	ExpressJet	14.8	12.	ExpressJet	9.1	12.	ABX	614
13.	Atlantic Southeast	12.5	13.	Hawaiian	7.8	13.	Evergreen Int'l	611
14.	Mesa	11.2	14.	American Eagle	7.4	14.	Arrow	433
15.	Frontier	10.6	15.	Spirit	6.6	15.	US Airways	300
16.	Pinnacle	10.3	16.	Atlantic Southeast	5.9	16.	Tradewinds	274
17.	Comair	8.1	17.	Mesa	5.1	17.	Centurion	232
18.	Hawaiian	7.8	18.	Pinnacle	4.8	18.	ASTAR	183
19.	Horizon	7.4	19.	Comair	4.1	19.	Florida West	176
20.	Republic	7.1	20.	Republic	3.6	20.	Air Transport Int'l	162
21.	Spirit	6.8	21.	Allegiant	3.5	21.	Gemini	161
22.	Chautauqua	6.3	22.	Virgin America	3.4	22.	Southwest	138
23.	Air Wisconsin	5.6	23.	Midwest	3.1	23.	Capital Cargo	100
24.	Mesaba	5.3	24.	Chautauqua	2.8	24.	Kalitta Charters II	96
25.	PSA	4.7	25.	Shuttle America	2.7	25.	Hawaiian	77

Notes: 1. One paying passenger traveling one mile generates one revenue passenger mile. 2. One ton of freight traveling one mile generates one freight-ton mile. **Source:** Air Transport Association of America, *2009 Economic Report* (2010).

airline, Southwest flew 101.3 million passengers in 2008, more than any carrier for the third consecutive year. American Airlines is next, with 85.7 million passengers. One reason for Southwest's success is its focus on domestic routes, which produce an average of 13 cents per passenger mile, as compared with 11.85 cents for international flights. Southwest also flies only one kind of aircraft, meaning that all of its mechanics know

how to fix all of its planes. Upstart airline JetBlue has also been a consistently strong performer, and though it suffered from rising fuel costs and bad publicity involving an 11-hour tarmac wait in 2007, in 2008 JetBlue had reached position eight in the ranking of airlines for passengers enplaned.

With more than 43 million people boarding a plane there each year, Hartsfield Atlanta International Airport remained the busiest airport in the

On-time Arrival Rates at Major U.S. Airports, 1995–2010

Airport	Ontime Arrival Rate			Airport	Ontime Arrival Rate		
	1995	2000	2010[1]		1995	2000	2010[1]
Atlanta/Hartsfield Intl.	74.6%	74.9%	86.7%	New York/La Guardia Intl.	80.6%	57.1%	84.1%
Baltimore-Washington Intl.	N.A.	74.9	86.4	Newark Liberty Intl.	75.3	69.2	81.5
Boston/Logan International	74.3	65.5	85.3	Orlando International	77.3	74.0	87.1
Chicago/Midway	N.A.	N.A.	86.4	Oakland International	N.A.	N.A.	85.1
Chicago/O'Hare Intl.	79.0	63.2	81.6	Philadelphia International	79.8	66.7	85.9
Cincinnati/Northern Ky. Intl.	82.3	79.8	88.4	Phoenix/Sky Harbor Intl.	79.1	71.2	87.9
Dallas-Fort Worth Intl.	80.7	78.0	87.1	Pittsburgh International	81.0	76.4	87.8
Denver International[2]	81.2	68.2	85.6	Portland (Oreg.) Intl.	N.A.	71.9	88.4
Detroit Metropolitan	81.5	79.0	85.0	Salt Lake City International	78.1	76.8	86.0
Fort Lauderdale Intl.	N.A.	N.A.	84.3	San Diego/Lindbergh Field	77.8	70.8	85.2
Houston Intercontinental	81.2	79.3	85.3	San Francisco Internationa	71.2	60.8	77.5
Las Vegas/McCarran Intl.	79.2	70.5	85.7	Seattle/Tacoma International	75.0	67.7	89.6
Los Angeles International	70.8	66.6	85.9	St.Louis/Lambert Intl.	75.9	77.6	85.0
Miami International	76.1	73.9	78.2	Tampa International	75.9	73.4	86.7
Minneapolis/St. Paul Intl.	81.7	79.5	84.3	Washington/Dulles Intl.	N.A.	N.A.	87.8
New York/Kennedy Intl.	73.1	71.9	83.5	Washington/Reagan	79.8	76.2	87.0

Notes: 1. Figures for month of April, 2010. 2. Data for 1995 refers to Stapleton Airport. Source: Federal Aviation Administration, Office of Aviation Enforcement and Proceedings, Air Travel Consumer Report (April 2010).

Busiest U.S. Airports, 2008

PASSENGERS[1]		CARGO	
City (Airport Code)	Thousands	City (Airport Code)	Thousands of tons enplaned
1. Atlanta (ATL)	43,612	1. Memphis (MEM)	1,899
2. Chicago O'Hare (ORD)	33,668	2. Louisville (SDF)	1,122
3. Los Angeles (LAX)	28,625	3. Miami (MIA)	938
4. Dallas/Ft. Worth (DFW)	27,149	4. Los Angeles (LAX)	844
5. Denver (DEN)	24,266	5. Anchorage (ANC)	767
6. New York (JFK)	23,592	6. New York (JFK)	756
7. Las Vegas (LAS)	20,882	7. Chicago O'Hare (ORD)	746
8. Houston (IAH)	19,850	8. Indianapolis (IND)	529
9. Phoenix (PHX)	19,432	9. Newark (EWR)	436
10. San Francisco (SFO)	18,099	10. Wilmington (ILN)	375
11. Newark (EWR)	17,605	11. Dallas/Ft. Worth (DFW)	347
12. Orlando (MCO)	17,289	12. Atlanta (ATL)	345
13. Charlotte (CLT)	17,270	13. Oakland (OAK)	319
14. Detroit (DTW)	16,986	14. Philadelphia (PHL)	304
15. Miami (MIA)	16,397	15. San Francisco (SFO)	265
16. Minneapolis/St. Paul (MSP)	16,346	16. Ontario (ONT)	253
17. Seattle (SEA)	15,803	17. Houston (IAH)	234
18. Philadelphia (PHL)	15,576	18. Honolulu (HNL)	225
19. Boston (BOS)	12,784	19. Washington D.C. (IAD)	162
20. New York (LGA)	11,549	20. Seattle (SEA)	159
21. Washington D.C. (IAD)	11,367	21. Boston (BOS)	146
22. Ft. Lauderdale (FLL)	11,018	22. Chicago (RFD)	140
23. Baltimore (BWI)	10,154	23. Phoenix (PHX)	136
24. Salt Lake City (SLC)	9,888	24. Denver (DEN)	127
25. San Diego (SAN)	9,006	25. Minneapolis (MSP)	122
26. Honolulu (HNL)	8,976	26. Toledo (TOL)	114
27. Tampa (TPA)	8,869	27. Portland (PDX)	110
28. Washington D.C. (DCA)	8,692	28. Detroit (DTW)	93
29. Chicago Midway (MDW)	8,014	29. San Juan Luis Munoz Marin (SJU)	92
30. Portland (PDX)	7,074	30. Forth Worth (AFW)	85

Note: 1. All services (scheduled and nonscheduled) by U.S. and non-U.S. airlines. Source: Air Transport Association, 2009 Economic Report.

Top 25 Domestic Airline Routes, 2008

Origin–Destination	Daily Passengers Avg	Each-way Avg Price 2008
1. Fort Lauderdale–New York	4,450	$124.41
2. New York–Orlando	4,126	123.60
3. Chicago–New York	4,044	164.53
4. Los Angeles–New York	3,912	278.73
5. Atlanta–New York	3,409	140.80
6. New York–San Francisco	3,135	277.60
7. Los Angeles–San Francisco	2,421	85.71
8. Las Vegas–New York	2,310	203.76
9. Miami–New York	2,205	144.64
10. New York–West Palm Beach	2,153	134.42
11. Honolulu–Kahului	2,091	53.46
12. New York–Tampa	2,045	125.53
13. Dallas/Fort Worth–Houston	2,002	99.31
14. Boston–New York	1,943	164.29
15. Chicago–Los Angeles	1,879	188.82
16. Chicago–Las Vegas	1,869	152.41
17. Dallas/Fort Worth–New York	1,831	251.37
18. Chicago–Orlando	1,771	125.64
19. Orlando–Philadelphia	1,769	105.41
20. New York–San Juan	1,712	171.45
21. Chicago–Washington	1,705	156.10
22. New York–Washington	1,658	144.72
23. Chicago–Denver	1,624	127.67
24. Chicago–Phoenix	1,621	151.75
25. Boston–Washington	1,603	164.00

Source: Air Transport Association of America, *2009 Economic Report* (2010).

world in 2008. Nationwide, 741.4 million air passengers flew in 2008, suggesting that Americans have recovered from their unwillingness to fly, though the number is down from a record 769.6 million in 2007. Air cargo, however, never suffered such a drop and continues to climb. Tennessee's Memphis International, home of Federal Express, enplaned nearly two million tons of cargo in 2008.

Most Popular U.S. Destinations for Overseas Travelers, 2000 & 2008

2008 Rank/ Destination	Overseas Visitors (000's)	
	2000	2008
1. New York City, NY	5,714	8,211
2. Los Angeles, CA	3,533	2,788
3. San Francisco, CA	2,831	2,610
4. Miami, FL	2,934	2,585
5. Orlando, FL	3,013	2,433
6. Las Vegas, NV	2,260	2,027
7. Honolulu, HI	2,234	1,495
8. Washington, DC	1,481	1,470
9. Chicago, IL	1,351	1,368
10. Boston, MA	1,325	1,115

Note: Excludes visitors from Canada and Mexico. Source: U.S. Department of Commerce, Office of Travel and Tourism Industries, *Overseas Visitation Estimates for U.S. States, Cities, and Census Regions: 2008* (2009).

Tourists in the U.S., by Country of Origin, 2000–2008

Rank/Country	2000	2005	2008
1. Canada	14,667,000	14,862,000	18,925,000
2. Mexico	10,596,000	12,665,000	13,763,000
3. U.K.	4,703,008	4,344,957	4,564,895
4. Japan	5,061,377	3,883,906	3,249,578
5. Germany	1,786,045	1,415,530	1,782,299
6. France	1,087,087	878,648	1,243,942
7. Italy	612,357	545,546	779,463
8. Brazil	737,245	485,373	769,232
9. S. Korea	661,844	705,093	759,394
10. Australia	539,559	581,773	689,927
11. Spain	361,177	385,640	658,333
12. Netherlands	553,297	448,650	607,802
13. India	274,202	344,926	598,971
14. Ireland	285,697	383,400	531,198
15. Venezuela	576,663	340,315	507,153
16. China	249,441	270,272	492,958
17. Colombia	417,065	325,398	419,268
18. Sweden	321,881	290,530	397,017
19. Switzerland	395,031	256,730	341,955
20. Israel	325,199	284,310	332,257
21. Argentina	533,936	188,865	318,144
22. Taiwan	457,302	318,886	294,893
23. Belgium	249,957	191,596	265,383
24. Denmark	149,211	174,581	256,604
25. Dom. Rep.	197,298	221,449	226,184
World Total	51,237,701	49,205,528	58,029,451

Source: U.S. Department of Commerce, International Trade Administration, Office of Travel and Tourism Industries.

Select Destinations for U.S. Tourists, 1997–2007

2007 Rank/ Destination	U.S. tourist arrivals ('000's)		
	1997	2002	2007
1. Mexico	17,909	18,501	19,453
2. Canada	13,401	16,167	13,371
3. U.K.	3,570	3,229	3,777
4. Italy	1,471	1,661	3,123
5. France	2,098	2,223	2,217
6. Germany	1,796	1,591	1,936
7. Japan	1,082	1,287	1,718
8. Bahamas[1]	1,017	796	1,538
9. Jamaica	1,341	983	1,530
10. China	1,147	725	1,374
11. Spain	714	866	1,093
12. India	368	398	999
13. Hong Kong	671	749	968
14. Netherlands	822	866	937
15. Ireland	411	562	749
16. Taiwan	562	632	687
17. Brazil	498	491	687
18. South Korea	649	608	687
19. Switzerland	671	562	656
20. Australia	454	562	593
21. Colombia	325	304	562
22. Greece	433	328	562
23. Israel	303	117	500
24. Thailand	303	398	468
25. Aruba	N.A.	N.A.	422
Total[2]	52,735	58,065	64,052

Notes: Data rounded in source. Includes only countries having a sample size of 400 or more. 1. 2007 figures from 2006. 2. Includes destinations not shown separately. Source: U.S. Department of Commerce, International Trade Adminstration, Office of Travel and Tourism Industries.

Selected U.S. Mass Transit Statistics, 2006

	Heavy Rail	Commuter Rail	Light Rail	Other Rail/ tramway	Motorbus	Ferryboat	Trolleybus
Track Mileage	2,277	7,406	1,464	649	N.A.	N.A.	N.A.
Stations	1,042	1,169	764	68	1,308	68	5
Route Miles	1,623	6,972	1,280	989	222,445	620	424
Passenger Miles (millions)	14,721	10,359	1,866	25	20,390	360	164
Maintenance Facilities	57	62	43	7	526	6	N.A.
Active fleet	11,126	3,520	1,920	N.A.	73,063	N.A.[1]	N.A.[1]

Notes: 1. The number of active fleets in "other regular vehicles," including ferries and trolleys (and others not listed) was 13,143 in 2006.
Source: Federal Transit Administration, *2009 Status of the Nation's Highways, Bridges, and Transit* (2010).

Train Accidents By Railroad, 2005–2008

	2005 Count	2005 Rate	2006 Count	2006 Rate	2007 Count	2007 Rate	2008 Count	2008 Rate
Alton & Southern Rwy [ALS]	18	17.15	11	10.71	13	13.42	10	10.22
Alaska RR Corp. [ARR]	2	1.15	1	0.65	1	0.66	2	1.39
Amtrak [ATK]	112	2.96	104	2.73	84	2.12	92	2.31
BNSF Rwy Co. [BNSF]	676	3.49	656	3.28	619	3.26	571	3.07
Belt Rwy Co. Of Chicago [BRC]	23	44.39	20	39.95	14	28.91	13	27.44
Canadian National–North America [CN]	66	2.98	100	4.65	95	4.65	83	4.19
Canadian Pacific Rwy Co. [CP]	31	2.65	22	1.85	29	2.52	22	1.98
Consolidated Rail Corp. [CRSH]	42	13.62	29	9.76	40	13.29	25	8.32
CSX Transportation [CSX]	489	4.51	389	3.59	332	3.05	296	2.80
Dakota, Minnesota & Eastern RR [DME]	63	19.20	34	10.24	32	9.79	37	11.39
Elgin, Joliet & Eastern Rwy Co. [EJE]	16	22.20	8	10.55	15	20.53	10	12.70
Florida East Coast Rwy Co. [FEC]	15	5.81	12	4.52	11	4.65	2	0.88
Grand Canyon Rwy [GCRX]	362	12.62	392	12.89	366	11.57	309	9.47
Pam Am Rwys/Guilford System [GRS]	6	4.22	10	6.87	3	1.88	3	2.04
Indiana Harbor Belt RR Co. [IHB]	19	12.69	14	9.69	12	8.07	12	8.19
Kansas City Southern Rwy Co. [KCS]	124	14.19	85	7.32	90	7.90	69	6.08
Long Island Rail Road [LI]	12	1.46	9	1.07	5	0.59	13	1.51
MARC Train Service [MACZ]	2	1.66	3	2.51	N.A.	N.A.	3	2.50
Massachusettes Bay Transit Authority [MBTA]	N.A.	N.A.	1	0.25	4	0.99	3	0.71
Montreal, Maine and Atlantic Rwy, Ltd. [MMA]	3	6.09	6	13.95	7	16.32	5	12.99
Metro North Commuter RR Co. [MNCW]	40	4.46	52	5.60	39	4.09	22	2.26
Montana Rail Link [MRL]	15	3.90	22	5.37	11	2.77	27	6.72
Northern Indiana Commuter Transportation District [NICT]	N.A.	N.A.	2	2.65	3	3.92	2	2.61
Northeast IL Regional Commuter Rail Corp. [NIRC]	6	0.65	4	0.42	10	1.04	6	0.63
New Jersey Transit Rail Operations [NJTR]	30	3.17	34	3.57	38	3.80	29	2.71
Norfolk Southern Corp. [NS]	333	3.27	258	2.45	248	2.42	252	2.49
Paducah & Louisville Rwy Co. [PAL]	2	3.47	5	8.52	5	8.21	7	11.22
Port Authority Trans Hudson [PATH]	3	1.38	1	0.47	7	3.45	2	0.99
Peninsular Commuter [PCMZ]	3	2.17	3	2.11	2	1.40	1	0.69
Port Term. RR Association [PTRA]	5	3.91	7	5.47	8	6.25	3	2.34
Southern California Regional Rail Authority [SCAX]	8	4.05	2	0.87	N.A.	N.A.	5	2.04
Southeastern Pennsylvania Transportation Authority	9	1.76	9	1.72	17	3.28	7	1.34
Terminal RR Association of St. Louis [TRRA]	17	23.94	14	20.37	8	12.23	6	9.75
Union Pacific RR Co. [UP]	954	4.79	891	4.38	722	3.72	633	3.48
Union RR Co. [URR]	3	24.46	5	39.31	2	14.73	N.A.	N.A.
Wheeling & Lake Erie Rwy Co. [WE]	14	11.95	16	12.19	12	9.39	14	13.36
Wisconsin & Southern RR Co. [WSOR]	4	13.37	5	15.28	10	27.45	5	12.94

Source: Federal Railroad Administration Office of Safety Analysis (2009) safetydata.fra.dot.gov

Amtrak Operating Statistics, 1985–2009

Category	1985	1990	1995	2000	2009
Passengers (millions)	21	22	21	23	27.2
Passenger miles (millions)	4,582	6,057	5,545	5,498	5,807
Operating fleet (passenger cars)	1,854	1,863	1,722	1,894	N.A.
Average age (years)	14	20	22	19	N.A.
Train-miles operated (millions)	30	33	32	35	N.A.
On-time performance	81%	76%	76%	78%	80%
Short Distance (<400 miles)	82	82	81	81	N.A.
Long Distance (400+ miles)	78	53	57	56	N.A.
Revenues (millions)	$ 825	$1,308	$1,490	$2,111	$2,352.8
Expenses (millions)	1,600	2,012	2,257	2,876	3,507.2

Source: Amtrak FY2007 Annual Report, Monthly Performance Report (June 2008).

▶THE DAWN OF CIVILIZATION (c. 3000–1500 B.C.)

The transition from pre-historic Neolithic culture to civilization seems to have involved in every case two things combined: the establishment of settled agricultural communities instead of nomadic food-gathering communities and, in those settled communities, the development of urban centers with literate religious and social hierarchies in control of irrigation projects. The first condition is found (independently, so far as is now known) in at least four centers: Mexico and Central America; the great bend of the Niger River in Africa; the Yellow River valley in China; and in Mesopotamia (the "land between the waters" of the Tigris and Euphrates Rivers). Priority in time belongs to Mesopotamia. And there also the second condition of civilization, the urban center, first emerged.

Mesopotamia

The 600-mile-long plain of the Tigris and Euphrates valleys stretching to the Persian Gulf is the site of earliest civilization. The city-state of Sumer gives its name to this first flowering which blossomed about 3000 B.C. Each of the cities was a sacred temple city, the realm of a god whose regent on earth was the priest-king. To the Sumerians we owe: the calendar, the invention of writing (cuneiform), the plow, the potter's wheel and wheeled carts, boats using sails, and a host of other "firsts."

The separate and frequently warring city-states such as Lagash, Nippur, and Ur fell under the control of the more northerly *Empire of Akkad* whose greatest king was Sargon (c. 2250 B.C.) which in turn fell under the sway of the *Babylonian Empire* whose king Hammurabi (c. 1750 B.C.) conquered all of Mesopotamia and who is credited with the first known Code of Laws. Shortly before 1500 B.C. this empire fell under the domination of the more barbarous *Kassites* whose advantage lay in the use of horse-and-chariot manned by bowmen.

Egypt

The great valley of the Nile, a thin stream traversing the eastern Sahara desert, had given birth by about 3000 B.C. to no urban centers but to a network of farming villages whose population was of urban density. The legendary founder of Egypt was Menes whose conquest of Lower (i.e., northern) Egypt established the *Old Kingdom* (c. 3000–2200 B.C.). Political unification, quite different from the pattern of Sumer, permitted a rapid assimilation of Sumerian technology while the desert meant relative freedom from invasion. The pharaohs did not rule by permission of the gods, but were divine beings themselves; the building of their colossal tombs, the pyramids, were great religious works directed by the unitary state. The most famous is the Great Pyramid of Cheops at Gizeh (c. 2500 B.C.)

The older diversity of the valley reasserted itself during a century of dissolution and division called the *First Intermediate Period*, after which the traditions of Menes asserted themselves in the *Middle Kingdom* (c. 2100–1800 B.C.). Architecture and sculpture were consciously restorationist, modeled after the Old Kingdom, though temple architecture testifies to the importance of various priesthoods. In literature, it was Egypt's "classical age."

But this age ended with the invasion from Syria-Palestine of the barbarian charioteers known as Hyksos who had become lord during the *Second Intermediate Period* (c. 1800–1600 B.C.). But the Eighteenth Dynasty, with its capital at Thebes, at last managed to drive out the Hyksos and re-establish royal authority throughout the valley, thereby initiating the *New Kingdom* (c. 1600–1100 B.C.).

Other Significant Centers

The *Indus Valley*, stretching from Tibet to the Arabian Sea, had become by about 3000 B.C. another locus of settled agriculture with obvious Sumerian influence. Innumerable small villages but only two cities have been excavated and the ancient Indian script remains a mystery to scholars. This Indian civilization flourished from about 2500 to about 1500 B.C. until it was conquered by Aryan tribesmen also utilizing chariots and arrows.

About the year 2000 B.C. three centers of civilization influenced by Mesopotamia and Egypt began to develop: the *Canaanites* in Syria and Palestine, the *Hittites* in Asia Minor, and the *Minoan civilization* on the island of Crete. It is not clear whether Minos was a name or, like "pharaoh" a title, but it was his palace, the Labyrinth, which dominated the trading city of Knossos, center of an elegant "sea empire" whose ships were in contact with Italy, Egypt, Asia Minor and mainland Greece. Yet by about 1500 B.C. Minoan trade was in decline and not long after a Greek prince was ruling at Knossos.

In China around 1875 B.C., the millet-based agricultural villages of the North China Plain gave rise to the semi-legendary Xia Dynasty, which ushered in the Bronze Age in East Asia. The Xia were overthrown around 1550 B.C. by Tang the Victorious, who established the Shang Dynasty, which endured for five hundred years. The Shang Dynasty is noted for its sophisticated bronze vessels, used in worship of the royal ancestors, and for oracle bones inscribed with an early form of Chinese script asking questions of the gods. Shang culture was enriched after around 1350 B.C. by new technologies from western Eurasia, including the chariot, the cultivation of wheat, and sheep-raising.

▶THE SPREAD OF CIVILIZATION (c. 1500–500 B.C.)

The impact of the chariot warriors from the steppes of Eurasia, a huge stretch of grassland stretching from the Black Sea almost to the Pacific Ocean, altered the earliest civilizations in different ways and to different degrees—least in the Near East, most in India. In the millennium from about 1500 to about 500 B.C., the area of civilized life continued to spread as the civilizations took on their classic form in the "heroic age" of the ancient world.

Egypt

Almost immediately after the hated Hyksos had been expelled from Egypt proper, the pharaohs of the *New Kingdom* (1570–1065 B.C.)—preeminently Thutmose III (c. 1500–1447 B.C.) and his regent queen Hatshepsut (d. 1468 B.C.)—created an empire in Palestine and Syria in which local princes ruled their peoples while Egyptian bureaucrats and garrison commanders oversaw imperial interests, especially the tribute payments. Egyptian control southward along the Nile into the Sudan and Nubia was also reestablished. The empire functioned well until ruled by a pharaoh whose interests lay elsewhere.

The pharaoh Amenhotep IV (ruled c. 1372–1354 B.C.) changed his name to Akhenaton and led a movement after 1370 B.C. to obliterate the name and memory of all the Egyptian gods save for the sun-god Aton (and his incarnation on earth, the pharaoh). This almost-monotheistic revolution absorbed the attention of the monarchy to such an extent that it helped the empire to crumble and the dynasty to be overthrown. A rigid traditionalism accompanied the painful recovery of the empire. Tutankhamen (whose famous tomb was discovered in 1922) was Akhenaton's son-in-law; his name shows the return of the god Amon and the eclipse of Aton. But by 1200 B.C. a series of invasions brought the Egyptians to withdraw from the empire to defend the Nile Valley, a withdrawal complete by about 1100.

The *Post-Empire Period* (1065–525 B.C.) saw Egypt's survival in a cultural and religious sense; but the state grew disunified and finally fell victim to conquests by the Assyrians (671 B.C.) and the Persians (525 B.C.).

Mesopotamia and Persia

The Kassite conquest of the First Babylonian Empire led to no great revolution since the conquerors adopted the culture and political structure of the conquered. To the north, the Assyrians were left under native rulers, then took advantage of a series of barbarian incursions against the Kassites to gain their independence in the *First Assyrian Empire* (c. 1150–728 B.C.). The Assyrians were fierce warriors, and they fell upon the south of Mesopotamia, upon Syria and Palestine, and even, briefly, Egypt, and they established the *Second Assyrian Empire* (728–612 B.C.).

The destruction of the great Assyrian capital of Nineveh (612 B.C.) was the work of the mobile strike force of the cavalry of the Medes who proceeded to conquer the Assyrian territory east of the Tigris as well as Armenia and eastern Iran, forming the short-lived *Median Empire* (625–559 B.C.). Assyria's fall permitted the *Second Babylonian Empire* (625–538 B.C.) to arise in Mesopotamia.

Both fell victim to the *Persian Empire* (559–331 B.C.). Cyrus the Great (550–533 B.C.) overturned his Median overlord (559 B.C.), conquered King Croesus of Lydia in Asia Minor (546 B.C.) and overthrow King Nebuchadnezzar III of Babylon (538 B.C.). It was his son who conquered Egypt and his grandson Darius I (521–485 B.C.)who brought the empire to its greatest extent, expanding eastward beyond the Indus by 519 B.C. Dividing his empire into 20 "satrapies" (administrative offices), Darius improved communications by building good roads and was farsighted enough to commence the construction of a Mediterranean war fleet.

Under this Persian dynasty's patronage, the religious doctrines of Zoroaster (c. 628–c. 551 B.C.) spread through its immense empire. Zoroaster taught a dualist doctrine of a cosmic struggle between the god Ahuramazda, the good god of light, truth and peace, and Ahriman, the evil god of darkness, lies, and discord. It was to prove one of the most profoundly influential teachings in the history of the world.

Israel and Judah

Amidst the ebb and flow of empire emerged the people of Israel. Tracing their origin to the ancient city of Ur in Mesopotamia and the covenant between their patriarch Abraham and their god Yahweh, they migrated to Canaan sometime after 1900 B.C. Entering Egypt, probably in the Hyksos period, they dwelt in the Egyptian delta until about 1280 B.C. when, against strong resistance from the pharaoh, Moses led the Hebrews out of Egypt into the desert of Sinai where, according to the Old Testament, they became Yahweh's chosen people in the Sinai covenant. Shortly before 1200 B.C. they occupied Canaan during the decline of Egyptian power there.

The religious league of clans was transformed into the *Kingdom of Israel* (c. 1020–922 B.C.) which flourished under the kings Saul (1028–1013 B.C.), David (1013–973 B.C.), and Solomon (973–933 B.C.) in the interstices of the great powers. But after the death of Solomon, the kingdom divided into Israel in the north and Judah in the south. The northern kingdom fell to the Assyrians under Sargon II (722–705 B.C.) in 721 B.C. Judah held on until the Second Babylonian Empire under Nebuchadnezzar II (c. 605–562 B.C.)destroyed the capital Jerusalem in 587 B.C.

While ethnic Israel fell, the spiritual Israel was preserved through the work of *the prophets*, especially Isaiah (c. 700 B.C.), Jeremiah (c. 600 B.C.) and the second Isaiah (c. 540) who taught an uncompromising monotheism: Yahweh not the god of the Jews alone, but the one God of mankind.

With the establishment of the Persian Empire, the Jews were permitted (538 B.C.) to return to Palestine and to build the second Temple, there to live under the great code of law, the *Torah*.

Greece

The Minoan culture of Crete had been in contact with the Greek mainland before 1650 B.C. The people of Greece (called Achaeans) had arranged themselves in small principalities of which Mycenae, located on the Greek mainland of the Peloponnesian peninsula, had pre-eminence. Adopting the courtly style of the life of Minoans and the war chariots of the Hyksos, the Achaeans expanded their settlements and with Cretan decline became heirs of Minoan trade with Egypt and Syria. This is the culture pictured for us in the epics of Homer's (c. 800 B.C.), *The Odyssey* and *The Iliad*.

About 1100 B.C., a second wave of Greek-speaking Dorians invaded from the north and the Achaeans were forced to migrate to the islands and the coast of Asia Minor. In defeat they performed their greatest work: the preservation of Mycenaean (and therefore also Minoan) traditions both socially and in the Homeric epics. Through these great poems the enterprise against Troy became the living symbol of the unity of the Greeks, the mythology of Mycenae provided a common religious background for local cults, and the language of the Achaeans became the norm for the whole Greek world.

By about 750 B.C. the Greek world had recovered. Colonies spread westward to Italy and Sicily and eastward to the northern Aegean and the Black Seas. The lyric poetry of Archilochus (c. 700 B.C.) and Sappho (c. 600 B.C.) flourished. The first philosophers (Thales, Heraclitus, Parmenides), later called the pre-Socratics, commenced their speculations on nature and the order of the universe; to this philosophy, the Pythagoreans added mathematical genius. And the characteristic unit of the city-state, the *polis* was created.

The greatest of these city-states were Athens and Sparta. *Sparta* emerged in 716 B.C. as conqueror of about 3,200 square miles of territory; by about 610 B.C. Sparta already had the formidable military organization based on strict education for citizenship to inculcate the "savage valor" that Spartans so esteemed. And by 540 B.C. Sparta had formed the Peloponnesian League, uniting all but two of the city-states of the peninsula.

The polis of *Athens* was, like other Greek cities, dominated by its aristocratic families. The grievous problem of increasing slavery for debt led the Athenian leaders to turn over power to Solon, a wealthy merchant and poet, descended from the old kings. Taking office in 594, he cancelled all debts, abolished debt-slavery, encouraged both agriculture and industry, and opened the assembly to all free men. But Athens remained divided among its landed wealth, its trading class and the poor peasants, the latter led by the nobleman Peisistratus who established a dictatorship in the name of the poor (546–528 B.C.). But its democratic constitution was not in place until it was imposed, in 508 B.C., by the aristocrat Cleisthenes.

India

The charioteers who invaded the civilization of the Indus valley called themselves Aryans, a word meaning "noble" in their Sanskrit language. Those they conquered were called Sudras, "slaves." The Aryans settled in villages along the Indus, organized in tribal principalities about which almost nothing is known. Over the half-millennium from about 800 B.C. to about 300 B.C. they moved south along the coast and east across the peninsula to the delta of the Ganges River. There, once the lush jungle vegetation was cleared (using the new tools of the iron age), rice could be cultivated in the rich soil, a food supply sufficient for a very dense and stable population.

Religiously, this is the classic age of Hinduism. The ancient *Vedas*, hymns to the gods, date back to about 1000 B.C.—though not written down until much later. The *Brahmanas* are a body of instructions for rituals, evidence of the rise of an important priestly body, composed over the years 800–600 B.C. Lastly, about 600 B.C. appeared the *Upanishads* with their stress on asceticism and mysticism.

Embodied in this classic religious literature are the germs of the later "caste" system, for they envision four *varnas* or castes: priests (brahmans), warriors (kshatriyas), peasants and artisans (vaisyas), and slaves (sudras).

China

The late Shang period, known for the extravagance of its royal burials, declined into misrule; the dynasty was overthrown around 1055 B.C. by the ruler of the state of Zhou, which controlled the Wei River Valley in northwestern China. The Duke of Zhou, regent for the third Zhou king, established a sort of feudal system in which the territory of China was parcelled out in small states governed by Zhou clansmen and supporters. These states gradually grew larger at the expense of the Zhou royal domain. The Zhou capital was forcibly moved eastwards from Chang'an (now Xi'an) to Luoyang around 770 B.C. but the Zhou kings continued to lose both territory and political authority. Zhou rule broke down altogether during the Warring States Period (c. 480–221 B.C.), when a handful of large feudal states swallowed up their smaller neighbors.

The principal states of northern China were known collectively as *zhongguo*, the "middle kingdoms"; the Chinese, isolated from the high cultures of western Eurasia and India, imagined their culture to be at the center of the world, surrounded by zones of ever-increasing barbarism. In this view, the Chinese ruler governed "all under heaven" by authority of the Mandate of Heaven (*tian ming*). This theory held that a dynastic founder, because of his own virtue, attracted the cosmic force of heaven itself in his support, bequeathing heaven's mandate to his descendants so long as they cherished the principle of virtuous rule. This poltical theory, which assumed that exhausted and corrupt dynasties would eventually be overthrown by righteous rebellions, was a force for renewal and long-term stability throughout Chinese history.

Confucius (c. 551–479 B.C.), China's first philosopher, sought a remedy for the political turmoil of his time in an attempted revival of the golden age of the Duke of Zhou. Thwarted in his search for a ruler who would put his ideas into practice, Confucius became a teacher whose disciples perpetuated his prescription for good government. Confucius looked to a natural aristocracy of virtue, rather than an hereditary elite, for social leadership; this led centuries later to the Chinese innovation of government by means of a professional civil service recruited through competitive examination. The Taoists, rivals of the Confucian school (and supposedly founded by Laozi, of whose life nothing is known) rejected government altogether in favor of individual self-cultivation.

The Warring States Period was an era of cultural brilliance in philosophy, technology, and the arts, a prelude to China's first great imperial age.

▶THE GROWTH OF WORLD EMPIRES (c. 500 B.C.–A.D. 500)

The millennium after 500 B.C. had as its most characteristic development the conquest of the earliest centers of civilization by certain small nations or tribes—Persians, Macedonians, Romans, Mauryans—on their peripheries. Territories of immense extent (the whole world as they knew it) were organized by these smaller nations, although without any attempt to integrate the conquered peoples into their own cultures. Rarely constructed according to any deliberate plan, these world empires grew up haphazardly.

Significant too was the extraordinary clustering in one generation (at about 500 B.C.) of Pythagoras and Heraclitus, the second Isaiah, Confucius, and the Buddha. And yet more so was the fourth century B.C. eruption of philosophic thought with Plato and Aristotle. Finally, at the middle of the millennium, appeared Jesus Christ.

The Persian Empire and the Greeks

The Persian Wars (499–479 B.C.) began with a failed revolt of the Greek cities of coastal Asia Minor against the Persian Empire (of which they had become a part in 546 B.C.). To punish the mainland Greek allies of the rebels, the city-states of Athens and Eretria, the Persian Empire made war on Greece, but unsuccessfully. From a Persian point of view the Athenian and Spartan victories were only a border issue of minor import; but to the Greeks, the battles of Marathon, Salamis, Plataea and Mycale were inspiring symbols of the superiority of their ideals of liberty and free citizenship over the servitude of Eastern despotism, with the unity of Athens and Sparta embodying what had been prefigured in the united Greek enterprise against Troy. The historian Herodotus first told this story.

Under the leadership of Pericles (d. 429 B.C.) Athens transformed its naval league into an Athenian Empire, thus allowing Sparta to appear the defender of Greek liberties. The former allies, with their leagues, entered their death-struggle, the *Peloponnesian War* (431–404 B.C.) in which the Spartans won a crushing victory. The saga was told by the second great Greek historian, Thucydides (c. 460–400 B.C.) Spartan hegemony in Greece lasted only until 387 B.C. when a league of Greek cities with Persian assistance imposed a settlement which made all Greek poleis autonomous (and therefore weak) except for those in Asia under Persian rule. It was all but the end of the golden age of Greece.

But in just over a century the Greeks had created tragedy (Aeschylus, Sophocles, Euripides), philosophy (Socrates, Plato, Aristotle), history (Herodotus, Thucydides), and the imperishable glory of their monumental architecture (the Parthenon, the Acropolis) and the sculpture of Myron and Phidias.

The Macedonian Empire

Brooding above the disunited Greek city-states lay the small but militarily powerful kingdom of Macedon, militaristic but greatly influenced by Greek civilization. King Philip (356–330 B.C.), having conquered Illyria and Thrace on the northern Aegean, intervened in Greece and forced the formation of a Hellenic League with which Macedon began war against Persia (336 B.C.). No sooner had war began than Philip was assassinated, a death which occasioned the revolt of the Greek cities he dominated. But his son and successor, Alexander the Great (336–323 B.C.) ruthlessly crushed the revolt and plunged on into Asia; after his great victory in the battle of Issus (333 B.C.) over Darius III of Persia, Alexander declared himself successor to the last Persian emperor under the title King of Asia, continuing rule through the satrapies after the final defeat of the Persians in 330 B.C. In the meantime he added Egypt to his conquests (331 B.C.) and founded the great city of Alexandria. He pushed on into Bactria (modern Uzbekistan) and then to the Indus Valley beyond which his soldiers would not go. When he died of a fever in Babylon in 323 B.C. he had assembled in but a dozen years the largest empire the world had known; but his premature death meant the division of the empire among the *Diadochi* (Alexander's generals who claimed the succession) who battled for half a century before stabilizing into fragments, each a formidable military monarchy: descendants of Antigonus ruled Macedonia, those of Ptolemy Egypt, those of Seleucus most of Asia. The fringes, the western Mediterranean and India, were left to their own development.

Rome: From Republic to Empire

About the midpoint of the western side of the 650-mile long peninsula of Italy the primitive, devout, peasant community of Rome overturned their Etruscan rulers and established a republic shortly before the year 500 B.C. as the Greek golden age was just beginning. A century of patient expansion against neighboring tribes in central Italy was undone in 390 B.C. when Celts (or Gauls) from the Po Valley plundered and burnt the city. But the Romans commenced anew and within three generations had brought under their sway all of the peninsula except the Greek cities (Magna Graecia) in the south; and these they added by 272 B.C., just at the time the Diodochi were stabilizing their sectors of Alexander's empire.

The move into southern Italy involved Rome in a struggle with Carthage. Originally a Canaanite colony, the city of Carthage in north Africa had established a necklace of commercial colonies along the Mediterranean coast from Sicily across North Africa and Spain to the mouth of the valley of the Rhone, commanding the western seas. In a prodigious struggle called the *Punic Wars* (264–146 B.C.), during which Rome itself was almost brought to ruin by Hannibal (247–183 B.C.), the Romans utterly vanquished Carthage.

After the Second Punic War (218–201 B.C.) Rome became embroiled in the east as Pergamum, Rhodes and Athens appealed for help against the Diodochi. With the war against Macedon (100–196 B.C.) Rome's eastward expansions began. One by one, Greece, Macedonia, Asia Minor, Syria, Palestine, Egypt, and the whole north African coast came under Roman rule by 62 B.C. making the Mediterranean Sea truly what the Romans called *mare nostrum:* our sea.

But Asia did not beckon; rather the Romans embarked on that extraordinary experiment in the west, the conquest of Gaul by Julius Caesar (100–44 B.C.) in which almost 100 small Celtic principalities were brought into the civilization of the Roman Mediterranean. In time Gaul would lead to Britain (A.D. 43–84), while eastern defense considerations would lead to the annexation of Armenia, Mesopotamia and Assyria (A.D. 114–16). At its greatest extent, the Roman Empire stretched from the North Sea to the Sahara Desert, from the highlands of Scotland to the Persian Gulf.

But in winning their empire, the Romans lost their republic, with its freely elected assemblies and magistrates and its famous "council of elders," the Senate. The tremendous population losses in the Second Punic War, the increase in the slave population with every conquest, the transformation from a peasant agriculture to huge *latifundia* (plantations), the rise of a class of financiers (the *equites*), the rivalry of military commanders, the involvement of the military in politics—all conspired to strangle the old republican institutions. In the century from 298 B.C. to 133 B.C., the rivalry for power among demagogues and generals—the Gracchi brothers, Marius, Sulla, the triumvirate of Pompey, Caesar and Crassus, the dictatorship of Caesar, the second triumvirate of Lepidus, Octavian, and Antony—meant endless civil war leading to the final victory of the revolutionary adventurer Octavian who, renamed Augustus, initiated imperial rule in Rome itself and the *Pax Romana*, 200 years of peace in the Roman imperial orbit (27 B.C.–A.D. 180).

Christianity and the Roman Empire

More impressive than the military aspect of the work of Rome was the spread of the Mediterranean civic tradition into continental Europe: colonies of veterans such as Cologne, legionary headquarters such as York, imitated the old Italian, Greek, Phoenician and Syrian cities as well as the numerous foundations of Alexander. The empire became a network of administrative departments centered on cities with central power at Rome; with the external forms of civic life came economic prosperity and the intellectual culture of the Hellenized Roman civilization.

It was in this world that Christ and Christianity were born. In the reign of Augustus Jesus of Nazareth was born (c. 4 B.C.) and in the reign of Tiberius he died, crucified as a criminal (c. A.D. 30). His closest followers affirmed his resurrection from the dead and his ascent to the one he always called "My Father" and they eagerly preached the "good news" (gospel) that God himself had become man and died for man's sins. This preaching and their communion in their liturgies were the focal points of the early Christians, as the Romans called them. Considering themselves the "second Israel" they nonetheless broke with the synagogue and through missionaries like Paul, Barnabas, and Timothy preached to the Gentiles. While numerically few, they spread through the cities of the Roman world: from Palestine to Syria, Anatolia and Greece, to Africa and Italy; in the second century to Gaul, Germany, Yugoslavia and Spain.

Because they met in secret societies and because they reused to worship the Roman imperial gods, the Christians were persecuted by Roman magistrates; after A.D. 110, adherence to Christianity became a capital offense. Yet the church continued to spread, not only among the poor and outcast but among the nobles and the philosophers (like Justin the Martyr who perished in A.D. 165). These Christians viewed the Pax Romana as providential.

When after the death of the Stoic emperor Marcus Aurelius (A.D. 180) the empire fell into civil war, economic decline, the exhaustion of civic life through excessive taxation and centralized government control, the frontiers became unsafe as well: for after A.D. 226 a revived Persian Empire grew aggressive in the east while great confederations of tribes (Goths, Vandals, Allemani, Franks) arose on the Rhine and Danube Rivers. The emperor Diocletian (284–305) attempted to stem the decline with a political and military reorganization; but it was the emperor Constantine (312–37) who saw that much more was needed.

He attempted to provide a new internal principal of spiritual unity to the Roman Empire through Christianity. His "new Rome" of Constantinople was a Christian city from the start; from persecution to toleration to favored position to state religion—such was the changed estate of the Catholic Church in less than one century. But it had become the religion of a state far gone in decline. Visigothic troops sacked Rome in 410 (for the first time in 800 years) then carved out a realm in southern Gaul and Spain by 450. Vandals tore north Africa away from Rome (429–39). Franks reached the Loire by 486. Saxons, Angles and Jutes

ended the Roman province of Britain. Disintegration in the west seemed complete, under the impact of the so-called *Barbarian Invasions*.

Meanwhile in the Roman east, imperial control remained intact but the subject peoples asserted their nationality in religious, not political, forms, adopting one or another of the heresies that flourished after the formal definition of Christian orthodoxy at the Council of Chalcedon (450); that Christ was truly God and truly man.

India and Southeast Asia

The India that the armies of Alexander entered was a complex welter of tribal principalities and republics, of which a certain primacy attached to the kingdom of Magadha in the Ganges valley ruled by the Nanda dynasty. Resistance to the Macedonians was strongest among the Brahman caste: the Kshatriya princes proved more practical and accommodating. After the last Macedonian satrap left India in 317 B.C. Chandragupta Maurya, who has met Alexander, attacked and conquered Magadha with the aid of northwestern tribes, exterminating the house of Nanda and commencing the *Mauryan Empire* (317–184 B.C.). Married to a Macedonian princess, Chandragupta subdued the Indus valley as well and gained recognition from the Diadochus, Seleucus Nicator. By the reign of his grandson Asoka (269–232 B.C.), central and most of southern India had been added to the empire which extended north to the foothills of the Himalayas and west to the eastern reaches of Afghanistan.

Asoka was known as *the Buddhist Emperor*, personally devout and publicly the protector and propagator of the religion of the *Buddha*. Like Asoka, prince Siddhartha Gautama (563–483 B.C.) was not Brahman but Kshatriya; enlightenment came when he realized that desire is the source of all suffering and that salvation therefore means escape from existence into *nirvana* (or nothingness) through rightful living. (Buddha, in Sanskrit, is a title meaning "the enlightened one.") He founded no church but disciples lived in communities following his "eightfold path" to holiness. It was these communities that Asoka fostered and patronized. The more sternly ascetical *Jainism*, founded by Mahavira (probably a contemporary of the Buddha) had spread without political support amongst an elite; its characteristic doctrines were the eternity of everything that is, even matter, and the attainment of nirvana after nine reincarnations.

After the death of Asoka (233 B.C.) the Mauryan Empire began to crumble into its constituent parts, the last emperor being assassinated by one of his generals in 184 B.C. One of the successor states was the Graeco-Indian kingdom in the north and north-west founded by a general of the Diodoch king of Bactria; another was the Kushan Empire of the first and second centuries A.D., which proved to be the route by which Buddhism expanded into central Asia.

A second Chandragupta was the founder of the last great Indian imperial regime, the *Gupta Empire* (320–535 A.D.) which at its greatest extent stretched across the subcontinent from the mouth of the Indus to the mouth of the Ganges. The source of its unity was a revived Hinduism whose brahmans provided advisors to the emperors and drew up the great codes of Hindu law which articulated the structures of the caste system. It was the age also of the revival of the Sanskrit language both in the drama of Kalidasa (c. 400–55) and in the final composition of the epic poems Mahabharata and Ramayana. The Gupta period was the golden age of Indian science, especially astronomy, and mathematics, to which we owe the decimal system and the invention of the number zero. The sway of the classic Indian civilization was spread far beyond the political borders of the Gupta realm by traders and missionaries to Burma, Thailand, and Indo-China, to the Malay peninsula and beyond into Indonesia. The shores of the Bay of Bengal and of the South China Sea thus became a kind of "greater India", as the Diodoch kingdoms had become a "greater Greece."

The Chinese Empire

In 246 B.C. the cavalry troops of the far western state of Qin, hardened by years of warfare with the barbarian nomads of the steppe, hurtled eastward to conquer and subjugate, one by one, all of the other feudal principalities in a quarter century of war that brought the period of the "warring states" to an abrupt halt. On this territorial basis arose the first *Chinese Empire* under the *Qin Dynasty* (221–206 B.C.) Qin Shihuangdi ("The First Emperor of Qin") proved more than just a conqueror: he oversaw the completion of the Great Wall along the edge of Inner Mongolia and provided a structure of government for the empire by dividing the land into regions of administration and war, governed by deputies responsible to himself alone. The old nobility he destroyed by land confiscations; the Confucian schools he closed, executing many prominent scholars, cowing the rest into submission. And while a weakling successor proved unable to stem rebellion and met his death by assassination (206 B.C.) the structure of imperial rule inaugurated by the Qin would endure for over two thousand years.

A rebel leader named Liu Bang emerged victorious in the confused and bloody uprisings that brought the Qin Dynasty to an end. Liu proclaimed himself emperor of the Han Dynasty, which was to endure (with a brief interregnum under the usurper Wang Mang) for four centuries, from 206 B.C. to A.D. 220. The Han founder retained the imperial structure of Qin rule, while moderating its punitive harshness; he opened the way for renewed Confucian participation in government. The greatest Han ruler, Emperor Wu (r. 140–87 B.C.) instituted the practice of choosing officials on the basis of learning and merit. He brought the rich ricelands of the Yangtze River Valley firmly under imperial control, and also greatly extended the boundaries of the empire, conquering south to the South China Sea, southwest to the borders of Burma and Tibet, northeast to northern Korea, and westward to the deserts of Central Asia. He pacified the northern frontier, defeating the Xiongnu tribes whose descendants the Huns would later invade Europe. In an early arms race, the powerful laminated compound bow and cavalry tactics of the northern nomads were countered by Chinese infantry armed with mass-produced crossbows—a refinement of a weapon of Southeast Asian origin. At this time trade increased along the Silk Route, a network of caravan trails that, through many intermediaries, brought Chinese silk to the Roman Empire and warhorses from Central Asia to China.

The "dynastic cycle" completed its course in the last decades of the Han period, when court corruption, peasant uprisings, and military insurrections led to the overthrow of the last Han emperor in A.D. 220. There followed the Three Kingdoms Period (220–265), when rival states tries without success to reunite the empire, and the period of the Northern and Southern Dynasties (265–589), when northern China was frequently ruled by short-lived dynasties of invaders from the steppes, and southern China was fragmented into equally short-lived and ineffectual kingdoms. During this period of disunion Buddhism, which had entered China via Central Asia in late Han times, began to establish itself as one of China's major religions. Especially successful were sects of Mahayana ("Greater Vehicle") Buddhism, which promised salvation to the faithful through the mediation of saints called *bodhisattvas*.

Japan and Korea

Around 300 B.C., invaders from northeastern Asia had invaded Japan via the Korean Peninsula. These invaders, equipped with horses, bronze weapons, and the wealth produced by rice agriculture, displaced the ancient Jomon culture of the original inhabitants of Japan. This bronze-age Yayoi civilization, which also shows evidence of influence from Austronesian culture via Taiwan and Okinawa, laid the foundations for the subsequent Japanese empire. But for several centuries Japan was fragmented into small states ruled by military clans (*uji*), with those associated with the Shinto shrines at Izumo and Ise claiming some degree of primacy.

In Korea, the decline of the Chinese colony at Lolang led to the establishment of indigenous kingdoms; three of these—Silla, Paekche, and Koguryo—predominated during the period 313–668 A.D. Chinese cultural influence, via Korea, helped to transform the Japanese petty states into a centralized kingdom by the 5th century A.D.

▶ EUROPE'S "DARK AGE" AND THE IMPACT OF ISLAM (A.D. 500–1000)

The seventh-century eruption of Islam with its compact secular-religious civilization and its characteristic institution of the *jihad* (holy war), both rooted in the sacred writings of the Koran, created an empire stretching from the Iberian Peninsula to the Indus Valley but influencing events in far-off Ghana as well. It also provoked in response the formation of eastern and western Christendom.

Untouched by these developments, China underwent another dynastic cycle—one in which Chinese civilization spread to Korea and Japan. And in utter isolation, without iron or even the wheel, civilizations in Central America began.

The Roman Empire and Europe's "Dark Age"

The lapse of direct Roman rule in the west did not imply "the fall of the Roman Empire", for the Germanic barbarians lived in a "greater Rome" whose heir and representative was the Catholic Church while in the east Roman rule continued with enough vigor to experience a great revival under the emperor Justinian (527–65). Maintaining a rough alliance with the Christian Franks in Gaul under their *Merovingian* dynasty, Justinian's armies recovered the western provinces: Vandal Africa, Ostrogothic Italy and the Mediterranean sector of Visigothic Spain. Meanwhile his jurists codified and preserved the whole body of *Roman law* since the days of the republic. And under imperial patronage there grew up a magnificent cluster of churches whose pinnacle was the Hagia Sophia in Constantinople, constructed in 537.

But the cost was very great: the treasury was beggared and the eastern frontiers neglected so that the west might be rewon. After Justinian's death the empire had neither treasure nor troops enough to save Italy from new invaders, the Lombards. The city of Ravenna on its marshes kept its link with Constantinople and Rome itself was saved, principally through the work of the pope, Gregory the Great. In the 14 years of his papacy (590–604) he not only organized the defense of the city but oversaw the work of converting Visigothic Spain and began the restoration of Christianity in faraway Britain through the mission of St. Augustine to Kent. In this evangelizing effort Gregory relied upon the monks who followed the *Rule* of St. Benedict (480–547) who brought moderation and a Roman sense of order to the *monasticism* of the west. In a chaotic world, Benedict's *Rule* provided a uniform way of life for monks living as a community, including vows of poverty, chastity, and obedience, regular and frequent hours of prayer, study of the Bible, and manual work.

The empire, which barely held on in the east against Persia, met catastrophe at the hands of the armies of Islam (see next section). In half a dozen years (636–42) Syria, Egypt and Libya fell away; in a second wave of invasions (696–711) the rest of north Africa and Spain were lost as well; Frankish Gaul was only just saved by the cavalry of Charles Martel in the battle of Tours (732). The Mediterranean seemed on its way toward becoming a Moslem lake.

Two successor states to the old Roman empire emerged. In the east lay the empire proper, but now usually called the *Byzantine Empire* (610–1453). Its wealth and power were based in Asia Minor, its unity dependent upon three factors: Orthodox Christianity (slowly drifting away from Roman Catholicism until the final break with Rome in 1054); Hellenistic culture and the Greek language; and Roman law and administration. Missionary ventures carried Christianity and Byzantine influence to the Serbs and Croats in the Balkans, to the Moravians and Slovaks north of the Danube, and even as far as Kievian Rus, all in the ninth and tenth centuries.

In the west there arose the *Carolingian Empire* (751–888). The son of Charles Martel, Pepin III, cooperated with St. Boniface to reform the Frankish Church in close relation with Rome, deposed (with papal approval) the last Merovingian shadow-king, and was himself anointed king in 751. Before his death in 768 Pepin had made Frankish sovereignty felt southward to the Pyrenees and the Mediterranean. His son Charlemagne (768–814) conquered Lombardy, absorbed Bavaria, expanded into Saxony and beyond the Pyrenees, bringing under his sway an area equal in size to the old Roman Empire in the west. At the same time, to foster missionary endeavors, he ordered the creation of cathedral and monastic schools, drawing heavily for his scholars on Northumbria, the small English kingdom where Celtic and Roman monastic traditions had intermingled. The pinnacle of his work came on Christmas Day in the year 800 when in the city of Rome he was acclaimed and crowned as Roman Emperor, by the pope.

But with his death disintegration began. By 843 his grandsons divided his realm in three parts with a middle kingdom of the emperor Lothair separating the kingdoms of the East and West Franks (the nuclei of Germany and France yet to be). These realms faced deadly peril on all sides: Viking corsairs from the north (who also ravaged the British Isles and established commercial bases between the Baltic and Byzantium), Moslem pirates attacking from the south, and, just as these threats had abated, the fierce horsemen of the Hungarians, about the year 900. The family of the Carolingians proved unable to lead any effective resistance; that arose among the nobles of the empire who, inspired by the example of King Alfred the Great of Wessex (849–901) against the Danes in England, defended their people but demanded in return their obedience and support. This was the origin of that pattern of decentralized authority and allegiance known as *feudalism*. Not that monarchy died, but the medieval kings became "firsts amongst equals": Henry the Fowler (919–36) began the *Saxon Dynasty* of German kings while his son Otto I also assumed (962) the title of Emperor; and Hugh Capet in 987 began the *Capetian Dynasty* of France which ruled into the 19th century.

The aftermath of this terrible dark age was the creation of the new Christian monarchies on the fringe of the older Carolingian world: the restoration of the Empire in 962, replacing Charlemagne's empire, which barbarian tribes had destroyed; the consolidation and conversion of the Scandinavian monarchies about 990; the establishment of an independent and Catholic Poland (966) the already mentioned conversion of Kievian Rus (988) under St. Vladimir; and the founding in 1001 of a Catholic Hungarian kingdom under St. Stephen (997–1038).

The Islamic World

To the Roman Empire, the Arabs were a frontier annoyance, no menace as was Sassanid Persia; yet it was out of the Arabian Desert that the whirlwind of Islam arose. Its founder, Mohammed (or Muhammad) (570–632) was a religious prophet whose revelations came from God; these revelations form the heart of the Moslem sacred book, the *Koran*. Utter simplicity of doctrine (a stern monotheism and a focus on the world to come) and of moral code ("hard against the infidels, merciful among themselves") combine with an elaborate ceremonial (the strict fast of Ramadan, prayer five times daily, the Meccan pilgrimage). Driven out of Mecca to Yathrib (now Medina), Mohammed and his followers formed a religious and political community which, after eight years of desert warfare, returned to capture Mecca (630).

Within two years of Mohammed's death the armies of Islam were marching. From the Romans they wrested Syria, Mesopotamia, Egypt and Libya (636–46); the Persians they conquered outright (637–49). Not until 661 was the vexed question of the succession settled when the old tribal aristocracy triumphed over the family of the prophet and established *Umayyad Dynasty* (661–750) of caliphs ("successors") ruling not from Medina but from Damascus and utilizing the old Persian and Roman bureaucracies. For almost half a century Islam lay quiescent; then, with the conversion of the Berbers, Byzantine Africa was swept away (696) as was Visigothic Spain (711). In the same year a Moslem commander established himself in the lower Indus Valley.

A series of revolts protesting the purely Arabic dominance of the Umayyads led to the establishment of a new dynasty of caliphs, the *Abbasid Dynasty* (750–1258), descended from a cousin of Mohammed. Arab by descent, the Abbasids nonetheless moved the capital to the new city of Baghdad in Mesopotamia where Persian influence came to predominate in politics as in literature while the Islamic scientific and mathematical flowering owed as much to Gupta India and ancient Greece as to archaic Babylonian astral speculations, especially the decimal system of numeration and the use of the zero.

The Umayyads had not been totally overturned; Spain followed their rule when the rest of the empire turned to the house of Abbas; after about 800 there were independent Moslem states in Morocco, Tunis, and eastern Persia; and by about 875 in Egypt and Turkestan. Before the year 1000 the caliphs had lost almost all their political power, becoming largely a focus of religious unity, relying even then on the *ulema*, adepts of Islamic law and lore. To this day, ultimate authority in many Islamic states has remained with the religious leaders.

India and Africa on the Fringe of Islam

After the fall of the Gupta Dynasty in 535, India reverted to its older pattern of a large number of tribal principalities. The White Huns, whose incursion had overturned Gupta power, coexisted with the Hindu princes who knew them as *Rajputs* and established a feudal state across north India east of the Indus valley, the kingdom of Rajputana. The Sind (or lower Indus) was already in Moslem hands after 711. By the ninth century Buddhism had all but disappeared from India, absorbed into Hinduism; one exception was in the state of the Pala kings who ruled Bengal and Magadha into the 12th century. Buddhism remained influential in "greater India": in the small kingdoms of Burma, in the kingdom of Dvaravati in Siam, in Sri Lanka, and in the Sumatran state of Srivishaya under its Sailendra dynasty.

At the other extremity of the caliphate, Moslem traders from Morocco were in contact with the *Kingdom of Ancient Ghana* by about the year 800. Camel caravans crossed the Sahara to the grasslands between the upper Niger and Senegal rivers bearing salt and goods from the Mediterranean basin. There the king of Ghana supplied gold and ivory brought north from the southern reaches of the "shoulder" of Africa. Extracting import and export taxes and monopolizing the gold supply, the kings of Ghana exercised a kind of imperial control over the trading cities of the region, growing wealthy and powerful. Yet by 1076 the caliphs in Morocco were able to conquer the region.

At the opposite side of Africa, Moslem Arabs crossed the Red Sea and annexed the Somali coast (c. 1050) from the ancient Christian kingdom of Ethiopia.

China: Tang and Song Dynasties

Three centuries of disunion in China came to an end with the establishment of the *Sui Dynasty* in 589. Like the Qin, the Sui was a short-lived dynasty that paved the way for a long-enduring one. Extravagant expenditures on construction of the Grand Canal linking Hangzhou and Chang'an (a distance of over 1000 miles), a disastrous attempt to conquer Korea, and a Turkish invasion of northwestern China doomed the Sui. It was replaced in 618 by the *Tang Dynasty*, one of the most glorious eras in all of Chinese history. Buddhism flourished, as did poetry and the fine arts; Tang Chang'an was the largest and most cosmopolitan city in the world by around 700. But in 751 Chinese troops on the westernmost frontier were defeated by an Arab army in the Battle of Talas, and the Tang abandoned much of Central Asia; in 755, China's greatest general, An Lushan, rebelled against the throne. The rebellion was defeated, but the empire never recovered fully. An imperial persecution of Buddhism in the 840's, during which the wealth of many temples was confiscated, signaled the rise of Neo-Confucianism, reinvigorating China's oldest philosophical tradition. But with the imperial house in disarray, the Tang collapsed in 907.

After five decades of inconclusive attempts to restore central rule, the *Song Dynasty* was founded in 960, and endured until 1279. But the Song never had firm control of northern China. The northeast was controlled by the *Liao Dynasty* in the hands of the non-Chinese Khitan people (whose name gives us the world Cathay). They were replaced in the early 12th century by the *Jurchen Jin Dynasty*, which in 1127 conquered all of northern China, sending the Song emperors south to a new capital at Hangzhou. Although the Song were politically weak this was nevertheless a time of cultural brilliance, when Chinese landscape painting was perfected, poetry flourished, and urban life (rich with the wealth of overseas trade) attained new heights of sophistication. With the old northern aristocratic clans destroyed by the downfall of Tang and subsequent centuries of barbarian rule, the Song state was run by a surprisingly modern bureaucratic government recruited from a prosperous and well educated rural gentry.

Japan and Korea

In Korea, the state of Silla in 562 put an and to Japanese attempts to carve out colonial enclaves on the peninsula, and then, with Tang support, turned its attention to defeating its rivals Paekche and Koguryo. This process was completed by 670, and Silla grew prosperous with Tang support and cultural influence. But Silla in turn was defeated in 935 by the small western state of Koryo, which established a dynasty ruling all of Korea until 1392. Relatively isolated from Song influence by the intervening states of Liao, and later Jin, the Koryo state became culturally more independent of China.

In Japan, *the Yamato clan*, which had gradually pressed its claim to recognition as an imperial dynasty on the Chinese model, was firmly established on the throne by the fifth century A.D. Buddhism came to Japan in the following century, along with such continental innovations as the use of Chinese script to write (phonetically) the very different Japanese language. In 589 Prince Shotoku issued a 17-article "constitution" establishing imperial support for Buddhism and enjoining all aristocrats to respect the imperial throne. The throne thereupon came under the influence of the powerful *Soga clan* until 645; a restoration movement emphasized emulation of the Chinese model of government. But the principle of appointment to office on the basis of merit never caught on in Japan, which continued to be ruled by an hereditary aristocracy.

Japan's first permanent capital city was founded at Nara in 710; by 750 the city was wholly dominated by its rich and powerful Buddhist temples. In response the emperors moved the capital to the new city of Heian-kyo (now Kyoto) in 794; the emperors remained there for over a thousand years. Both Nara and Heian-kyo were built on a grid plan, modeled after Tang Chang'an; Heian-kyo especially boasted a glittering cultural life, supported by agrarian wealth from the provinces. The powerful *Fujiwara clan* gained control of the country's political life through the expedient of making sure that every emperor married a Fujiwara daughter, and abdicated the throne for a life of monastic retirement shortly after producing an heir; the head of the Fujiwara clan thus was always the father-in-law of one emperor and the legal guardian of the heir-apparent.

The Classic Age of Mayan Culture
Splendid archaeological remains wrapped in chronological obscurity give tantalizing hints of culture in central America before the year 1000. Sometime around 2500 B.C. (but perhaps a millennium earlier) the hybrid maize (or Indian corn) was developed on present-day Mexico's Gulf coast. Permanent agricultural settlements, stretching from Mexico's central plateau to the Guatemalan highlands, seem to date from about 1500 B.C. But it was not until the period A.D. 300–900 that Central America attained approximately to the cultural level of ancient Mesopotamia. From Guatemala to the Yucatàn the Mayans developed temples, ritual calendars and a system of writing as yet not deciphered. Similarly, in the Mexican Plateau, there grew up a culture associated with the great city of Teotihuacan. Both seem to have been "empires" of city-states, but except for Teotihuacan itself the sites were not really cities, rather religious centers surrounded by agricultural hamlets. The Mexican development seems to have been cut short by invasions about A.D. 900, probably by the Toltecs. The abandonment about the same time of the Mayan temple sites may have been the result of drought, deforestation, and other environmental factors.

▶ THE MUSLIMS, THE TURKS, AND THE RISE OF THE CHRISTIAN WEST (A.D. 1000–1500)
The four major centers of civilization that had been established by the year 1000—European Christendom, the Islamic world, India and China—all underwent tremendous challenges from confederations of warlike Turkish and Mongol tribes in the next 500 years. Of all the developments the most significant for world history proved to be the maturation of western Christendom which had already commenced, before the period closed, its expansion to the Americas, to Africa and to southern Asia as well.

Expansion of the Muslim World: Asia and Africa
The *Abbasid* dynasty of caliphs of Baghdad had long employed Turkish auxiliaries (rather as the Romans had used German tribes) in their Near Eastern armies; one such army, under their chieftain Mohammed of Ghazni, moved out of Afghanistan into the Punjab about the year 1000

and by 1030 established a Muslim dynasty there. Over the next 200 years they spread their conquests over the Rajputs eastward into the plain of the Ganges, establishing their capital at Delhi about the year 1200. The rich Hindu temples were plundered and, as "heathen," destroyed by these Muslim Turks. Under the *sultan* (ruler) Ala-ud-din (1296–1316) most of the subcontinent was brought under one rule for the first time since Asoka.

Unable to break the caste tradition, the ruling Turks became yet another caste, a minority of warrior-aristocrats extracting heavy taxes but relying upon the Hindu princes for administration. Though the Hindu temples had been destroyed, the Turks had to permit a practical tolerance for a now less sacerdotal Hinduism. After the death of Ala-ud-din his empire dissolved into a medley of warring kingdoms ruled by Muslim generals or Hindu princes over whom the sultans of Delhi exercised greater or lesser control.

In the "greater India" of Southeast Asia, Islamic influence expanded through trade and Chinese influence through trade and warfare. In Burma, the Buddhist kingdom founded by Anawrata in 1044 was destroyed by the Mongol armies of Kublai Khan in 1287 and the land was divided into a number of small principalities. Dvaravati Siam (briefly annexed to Cambodia in the 11th century) was overrun by Thai tribesmen from China in the 13th century; by 1350 a Thai kingdom of Siam had established its capital at Ayutthaya, which was to remain its capital until the end of the 18th century. Over the next century, Siam subdued the independent kingdom of Cambodia to the east and expanded against Burma as well. In the archipelago of Indonesia and curving north into the Philippines, Muslim traders and missionaries had established 20 Islamic states by the year 1500. The Hindu aristocracy of Java took refuge on the island of Bali, which still preserves elements of pre-Islamic Indonesian culture.

Muslim expansion occurred in western Africa as well. The conquest of ancient Ghana by Muslim Berbers in 1076 (who had conquered Morocco as well 20 years earlier) led to no new empire but a series of successor states. One of these, Kangaba, had by the 13th century established another trading state of immense size, the *Kingdom of Mali* which stretched, in the 14th century, from the Atlantic coast eastward beyond Gao on the Niger. Under king Mansa Musa (c. 1312–37) Islam spread through the western savanna, the king himself making a pilgrimage to Mecca in 1324. Further east, the king of the Songhay people on the great bend of the Niger had already converted to Islam in the 11th century; thus, when the dominance of Mali was replaced in the 15th century by the *Kingdom of Songhay*, Islam dominated not only the northern coast of Africa but almost the entire belt of savanna south of the Sahara as well.

It was also in this period, but obscurely and beyond the range of Islam, that African tribes (speaking various languages of the Bantu family) continued their long migrations. In the previous period (c. 600-900) they had moved out of the Cameroon highlands east to the Great Lakes; from there they migrated in two streams: southwest to the Congo basin, and south to the savanna of modern Zambia. Now in the period from about 1000 to about 1500, they occupied Kenya and Tanzania on the east and the lands south to the edge of the Kalahari desert.

Transformation of the Muslim World: The Turks

No sooner had Mohammed of Ghazni established Turkish rule in the Punjab than two brothers of the Seljuk clan revolted and took Afghanistan (1037), then expanded into Persia and Mesopotamia (by 1055). After the battle of Manzikert (1071) they took most of Asia Minor from Byzantium. When Syria was added (1084) the *Seljuk Empire* (1037–1243) stretched from Egypt to India. During the 12th century, in the aftermath of the First Crusade (1096–99), their empire became a jumble of small emirates ruled by Seljuk princes or their generals. What brought the Seljuks low was the sudden appearance in the 1240's of the Mongols in the Near East; though menacing to both Muslims and Christians, Mongols power proved ephemeral and the true heirs of the Seljuks proved to be another clan of Turks, the Ottomans. In 1326 they drove Byzantine forces entirely out of Asia Minor, thus beginning the *Ottoman Empire* (1326–1920). By century's end they controlled all of Asia Minor and the Balkans as far north as Bosnia. Half a century later (1453) they took Constantinople, turning Hagia Sophia into a mosque in their re-named capital of Istanbul.

Eastern Christendom Submerged: Mongols and Turks

The 11th century was the apogee of the *Eastern Roman Empire* (Byzantium) as it conquered the Christian kingdom of Bulgaria (1018) and made Serbia a client state in the west, while to the east Armenia and the Crimea were annexed (1022). But by mid-century the Normans, descendants of Vikings who settled in the French province of Normandy, were establishing themselves in Byzantine Italy (and Muslim Sicily), and the battle of Manzikert (1071) proved a catastrophe from which the Empire never recovered, losing both its granary and its military recruiting ground to the Turks in a single blow. Although the first three crusades (1096–1192) were initially successful in wresting the Holy Land from Islam, the subsequent organization of the territory in the French pattern of small squabbling and isolated feudal statelets rendered them impotent and hence of only marginal help to Byzantium. The Fourth Crusade (1202–04) was a disaster, for the crusaders took Constantinople, establishing what is called the *Latin Empire* (1204–61). In 1261, Michael Palaeologus (1261–82) restored a rump Byzantium along the shores of the Aegean and it was against this state that the Ottoman Turks expanded. The doom of Constantinople brought Turkish power right to the borders of Hungary, with the Balkans absorbed into the Ottoman Empire for 450 years.

In the northeast it was not the Turks but the Mongols whose arrival transformed Christendom. Hungary, Poland and Kievian Rus were weakened by dynastic struggles from the 11th century on, yet maintained their independence of the Holy Roman Empire to the west and the Turkish Cumans in the east. But the uniting of the Mongol federation under Genghis Khan (1206-27) created a power great enough to strike at China, the Near East, and Europe at the same time; by his death his realm extended from Korea to the borders of Persia and Rus. A decade later Mongol armies under Genghis Khan's grandson Batu (d. 1255) fell upon Europe (1237–40) attacking beyond Russia into Poland and Hungary and the lands of the German knights on the Baltic; but with the death of the Khan, the Mongols retreated. Still the "Golden Horde," an independent Mongol Khanate organized by Batu on the lower Volga River, ruled all of south Russia and reduced the north Russian principalities to vassal status.

Not until the late 15th century was the prince of Moscow sufficiently established to refuse tribute money to the Empire. His marriage to the niece of the last Byzantine emperor established the claim of Ivan III to imperial succession as he took the title "czar" (= Caesar or emperor) and his conquest of the principality of Novgorod (1478) established a large Russian state northeast of Poland. Poland had attained its status as the largest state in Christendom with the marriage (1386) of its queen Jadwiga (1384–99) to the Grand Duke Jagiello of Lithuania; in the 15th century the Jagellon Dynasty (1386–1572) controlled the entire region between the Baltic and Black Seas. But thereby it was exposed to a four-fold danger: from Ottomans to the south, Germans to the west, Swedes to the north and Russians to the northeast.

The Rise of Western Christendom

For 600 years out of the ruins of the western Roman Empire and the anarchy of barbarian invasions, Western Christendom slowly emerged, the process essentially completed with the conversion to Christianity of the Scandinavians, the Poles and the Magyars (950–1050). It was not a society associated with a great empire (for the Carolingian Empire had fallen in the ninth century) but with the feudal states of France and the tribal duchies of Germany. Its unity, such as it was, was religious and cultural as well as political.

Whether the leadership of this society should fall to the popes or the Holy Roman Emperors was settled in the 11th century in the *Investiture Struggle* in which the papacy emerged victorious. From Pope Gregory VII (1073–85) to Boniface VIII (1294–1303) the papacy gave the lead to western Christendom often in alliance with reforming monastic leaders. In the 12th and 13th centuries the characteristic architecture and sculpture of medieval Europe (*Romanesque* and *Gothic*) spread across Europe under Church patronage while the Leagues of the Peace and the Crusades attempted to limit and channel to constructive use the warrior ethos of the feudal nobles.

Beginning in 11th century Italy and 12th century Netherlands, the commune movement, in which all the inhabitants of a town bound themselves by oath to obey their magistrates, keep the peace, and defend their liberties, revived town life and created the medieval city as a confederation of self-governing guilds. *Guilds* were associations of craftsmen of one trade or merchants bound together for mutual aid. In the west the fairs of Champagne and Burgundy provided ground for the re-establishment of trade while in the Mediterranean, the Italian cities (especially Venice and Genoa) linked the west with Byzantium and the Muslim Near East.

In these towns arose the great universities (Paris, Bologna, Salerno, Oxford) where Greek and Arab learning met with the Christian traditions of the Carolingian schools; the insights of Aristotle re-thought in Christian terms issued into the legal, philosophic, theological and scientific work of *scholasticism*, the work of men like Albertus Magnus, Thomas Aquinas, Bonaventure, Roger Bacon, and Duns Scotus—all members also of the new religious orders, Franciscans (St. Francis, 1182–1226) and Dominicans (St. Dominic, 1170–1221), which arose in the towns of the 13th century. Committed to evangelical poverty and combating heresy, they played a role in university life as well.

Late in the 12th century in Spain and Italy, in the 13th in Germany, England and France, in the 14th and 15th in Hungary, Poland and Scandinavia, the custom arose for monarchs to call the elected representatives of the towns to meet with prelates and nobles to render advice; such was the origin of *parliaments*.

The development of these social and cultural and religious institutions was accompanied by the expansion of western Christendom. One aspect was internal with the clearing of forests and the cultivation of new farmland able to support an increased population. The other was external, not so much the ephemeral Kingdom of Jerusalem (1099–1162) or Latin Empire of Constantinople (1204–61) as the reconquest of Spain from the Muslims (1085–1492), the conquest of Prussia and Livonia by the Teutonic Knights (1229–1466) and the conversion of Lithuania (1386 and after.)

The most significant check to population growth was the *Black Death*, an outbreak of bubonic plague that swept over Europe (1347–51), wiping out perhaps 25 million, a third of the population. The loose unity of western Christendom began to alter in the 14th century in significant ways. First of all, the universality of the papacy seemed compromised when seven popes in succession (1305–78) preferred to reside at Avignon rather than Rome, in too close an association with the kings of France; then, after the return to Rome arose that series of disputed elections to the papacy which is called the *Great Schism* (1378–1417); and third, with the end of the schism, the popes became more and more involved in the politics of Renaissance Italy.

Meanwhile, while theories of sovereignty derived from the study of Roman law exalted the authorities of kings, royal powers disastrously declined due to chronic feudal violence: the "age of princes" in Germany (1273–1493), the Hundred Years' War in England and France (1337–1453), and the dynastic Wars of the Roses in England (1455–85). Out of the turmoil arose the "new monarchies" of more unified states: the Tudors in England (1485), the Valois and in France (1328–1529), and in Spain the Spanish branch of the Habsburgs (1504–1700).

In the Italy of the 14th and 15th centuries, increasingly the plaything of the new monarchies, there began that great cultural transformation known as the *Renaissance*. Humanists like Petrarch (1304–74), and Boccaccio (1313–75) sought a revival of Latin antiquity, both pagan (Cicero, Virgil, Tacitus) and Christian (Augustine and the other Church fathers), in an educational movement that sought to unite the values of Hellenism with Christianity. At the same time artists, studying Roman architecture and Hellenistic sculpture on the one hand and the new sciences of anatomy and perspective on the other, created a new world of beauty. In painting, Botticelli and da Vinci, in architecture Brunelleschi (1377–1446), in sculpture Ghiberti (1378–1455) and Donatello (1386–1466)—these represent the output of the city of Florence alone.

Building on medieval foundations and new navigational discoveries (magnetic compasses, the astolabe, the quadrant), the Portuguese monarchy pioneered the exploration of the African coast; the Gulf of Guinea was reached by 1470, the Cape of Good Hope by 1487, and India itself by 1498. The Spanish monarchs sponsored the western route of Columbus whose four voyages (1492–1504) brought Europeans to the shores of the Caribbean (which he mistook for Japan and the Malay Peninsula). Finally, before the period closed, the new Tudor monarchy of England financed the more northerly westward explorations of the Cabots who reached Newfoundland and New England in 1497 and 1498. Like the humanists, by seeking a very old world, the explorers found something very new as well.

The Americas

The New World which Columbus discovered was dominated by two great empires. In Mexico, the Toltecs established an empire with its capital in the magnificent temple city of Tula; it included most of the old Mayan realm (c. 900–1200). But the 12th and 13th centuries saw a series of incursions of barbarian nomadic hunters from the south known collectively as Chichimecs whose armed might destroyed the Toltec civilization. In time, one of these tribes, the Aztecs, established a capital at Tenochtitlan and over the century from about 1360 to about 1470 conquered neighboring peoples and constructed the sanguinary *Aztec Empire* (c. 1360–1520). The king Montezuma I (died c. 1470) was a ruthless conqueror but a great builder as well, transforming the capital into a magnificent city of stone. By 1500 the Aztecs had reached Guatemala. For the subject peoples war and subjections were evil enough; worse was the Aztec worship of the sun god who required for his nourishment human blood.

Stretching thousands of miles along the west coast of South America lay the empire of the Incas with their capital at Cuzco. Unlike the military Aztec empire of subject states paying tribute including the blood tax, the *Inca Empire* was a centralized bureaucratic state which engaged in social engineering as well as road and bridge building and irrigation projects. Begun about 1200, the empire attained its greatest size under Huayna Capac (c. 1493–1527).

China and East Asia (1200–1500)

Genghis Khan (b. 1162–1227), leader of the Mongol federation, wished to unite all of the nomadic peoples of the Asian steppes under his rule. The Mongol conquest of northern China, ruled by Jurchen tribesmen from Manchuria, was completed by Genghis Khan's successors in 1234. The Mongols then turned their attention to Korea, which they conquered in 1231–36, and to the Chinese Song Dynasty in the Yangtze River Valley. The Song defended their territory vigorously, while the Mongols were slowed down as their horsemen learned to cope with wet ricefields and rivers defended by heavily armed ships; but in 1271 Kubilai Khan (b. 1215–94) proclaimed himself emperor of the *Yuan Dynasty* of China, and in 1279 the last Song emperor capitulated. During his reign Kubilai Khan tried twice to invade Japan; his fleets were stopped by *kamikaze*, "divine winds," i.e. typhoons. An attempt to conquer Java also met with only limited and temporary success.

In China the Mongols were seen as an alien occupying power; their habit of using foreign, Persian-speaking tax-collectors made them especially hated. The successors to Kubilai Khan were mediocre rulers; in 1368 a Chinese nativist rebellion led by a charismatic ex-Buddhist monk named Zhu Yuanzhang succeeded in overthrowing the Mongols and establishing the *Ming Dynasty* (1368–1644). The early Ming emperors were vigorous and forward-looking; they rebuilt the Great Wall, re-routed the Grand Canal to terminate near Beijing, built a new southern capital at Nanjing, and sent maritime expeditions on missions of exploration and diplomacy throughout the South China Sea and the Indian Ocean to the east coast of Africa. These expeditions, under Admiral Zheng He, were however abruptly terminated in 1433, criticized by the conservative Confucian bureaucracy as a waste of money and resources. Thus the Chinese missed by only three decades the chance to confront the Portuguese as rival maritime powers in the Indian Ocean.

In Korea, the *Koryo Dynasty* did not long outlast the rule of their Mongol patrons. The last Koryo king in 1388 sent his best general, Yi Songgye (famous for his victories over Japanese pirates), to invade China to try to overthrow the Ming Dynasty on behalf of the Mongols. General Yi instead turned back at the border, overthrew the Koryo king, and established his own dynasty, the *Kingdom of Choson*, which soon proclaimed its support for the Ming emperors. The third Choson (or Yi Dynasty) ruler, King Sejong (r. 1418–1450) was Korea's greatest sovereign, a patron of art, science and technology during whose reign Korean scholars and craftsmen perfected printing with moveable metal type, invented a syllabic script to write vernacular Korean, and equipped Seoul with what was, for a time, the best astronomical observatory in the world. The Choson monarchs tolerated Buddhism, promoted Confucianism, ruled through a very conservative aristocracy, and remained on the throne until 1910.

In Japan, the Fujiwara-dominated aristocrats of Heian-kyo ignored the rise of a provincial warrior aristocracy in the provinces until it was too late. The Fujiwaras were ousted by the western Taira clan in 1160; they in turn were defeated by Minamoto no Yoritomo at the naval battle of Danno-Ura in 1185. Yoritomo then took the hereditary title of *shogun* ("generalissimo"), and established a military capital at Kamakura, leaving the emperors to reign but not rule in Heian-kyo. The Minamoto were shunted aside by their own hereditary retainers, the *Hojo Clan*, in 1229. A crisis was precipitated in 1331 by Emperor Daigo II, who refused to abdicate on command of the shogun, and attempted to institute direct imperial rule. In 1333 another general, Ashikaga Takauji, helped Daigo II overthrow the Hojo, but Ashikaga then promptly proclaimed himself shogun, moved the military capital to the Muromachi district of Kyoto, and put the emperors firmly in their place once again. The *Muromachi* shogunate endured until 1568, though with little military power; the shoguns were better known as patrons of Zen Buddhism, Noh theater, and the tea ceremony. With the waning of central authority, Japanese merchants were more free to establish domestic and overseas trade routes (and to engage in piracy on the China coast), leading to economic prosperity amidst political instability.

▶ THE EXPANSION OF THE WEST AND THE ENDURANCE OF THE EAST (1500–1650)

During this period, the great empires of Asia—Ottoman Turkey, Safavid Persia, Mogul India and Ming China—remained intact and even expanded, but the dynamic power and movement of this extraordinary age were driven by the emerging nation-states of Europe. Despite severe internal divisions both religious (the Reformation) and national, which led to incessant warfare among all of them, the major powers managed to dominate the sea lanes of the globe and control the coasts and islands of Africa, southern Asia, and the Americas.

The Near East: Ottoman Empire and Safavid Persia

Under their sultans Selim I the Grim (1512–20) and Suleiman I the Magnificent (1520–66) the Ottoman Turks added Syria and Egypt to their domains, then from their fortress at Belgrade launched an invasion of Hungary which climaxed at the battle of Mohacs (1526), where over 20,000 Christian soldiers were slain and three-quarters of the realm fell under Turkish rule either directly or through Ottoman client princes of Transylvania. The Turks moved on to besiege Vienna (1529), halting the campaign because of troubles with Persia. On the seas Turkish fleets added Yemen and Aden on the Persian Gulf and Tripoli, Algeria, and Tunis on the southern shores of the Mediterranean.

But Suleiman's successor was Selim II (the Sot), the first in a series of weak sultans who came to the throne between 1566–1718 as a result of that perennial weakness of Muslim dynasties, harem intrigues of wives and eunuchs, and of the specifically Ottoman problem, the "praetorian guard" of Janissaries. In 1571, the Holy League (the Papacy, Venice, Tuscany and Spain) triumphed over the Turkish navy in the battle of Lepanto, though dissolution of the League after the victory meant that the Ottoman fleet could still raid almost at will through the Mediterranean.

Persia saw the revival of a native Iranian dynasty under the *Safavid Dynasty* (1501–1736). Its founder Shah Ismail seized power from the White Sheep Turks in 1501 and successfully defended Persia from Ottoman expansion into Mesopotamia, a work continued under his son and successor (1514–55). After the reign of the dynasty's greatest representative, Abbas I the Great (1587–1629), there began a period of harem intrigues which greatly weakened the dynasty. The Turks succeeded in taking Baghdad (1638).

Christian trading presence in Persia began with the Portuguese establishment at Hormuz in 1507; by 1622 the Portuguese were turned out by Abbas, English merchants supplanting them.

Mogul India and the Portuguese Spice Trade

In 1526, a descendent of Genghis Khan attacked the sultan at Delhi and established his dominance east of the Indus. Though a Turk, because of the long association of his family with the Mongols, his empire came to be called the *Mogul Empire* (1526–1857). Babur (b. 1483–1530), the founder then expanded east to the borders of Bengal. Although his son lost almost all Babur had conquered, his grandson Akbar (1556–1605), contemporary of Philip II of Spain and Elizabeth of England, restored Babur's realm and expanded it further until it included all of India north of the Deccan Plateau. Vigorous in warfare, gracious in victory, wise in administration, tolerant in religion, Akbar's empire knew peace and prosperity. Most of the Deccan was added in the reign of his grandson Shah Jahan (1628–58), who also built the Taj Mahal.

It seems almost miraculous that Portugal, a tiny state on the edge of the Atlantic, should create a seaborne empire dominating the Indian Ocean, but that is what Portugal did in the 16th century. In 1497, Vasco da Gama (c. 1469–1524) began a journey that took him around Africa's Cape of Good Hope and across the Indian Ocean to Calicut where he encountered the great riches of India's spice trade. After da Gama's second voyage (1502), the Muslim state of Gujerat, allied with Mameluke Egypt, declared a *jihad* against the Portuguese, but at Diu, the Portuguese won a complete victory (1508). The Portuguese viceroy organized the building of a "rosary" of over a dozen forts stretching form Hormuz on the Persian Gulf through Goa to Malacca on the Malay Peninsula. Thus the Portuguese could monopolize the carrying trade in the Indian Ocean as well as divert the spice trade around Africa. And from Malacca they established trading posts in the Spice Islands (Moluccas), China and Japan. This network provided the route for Christian missionaries as well.

But it proved all too much for Portugal. The English and the Dutch had established their East India Companies in 1600 and 1602 and in the 17th century the Dutch, piecemeal, took the place of the Portuguese by war and diplomacy. One portent for the future: by 1639 the English were at Madras.

East Asia: China, Korea, Japan

The late Ming emperors were great patrons of culture, but mediocre rulers. The former Chinese protectorate of Annam, while maintaining its mandarin culture, became independent, the first true monarchy of Vietnam. In 1557 the Portuguese established a trading colony at Macao (due to revert to Chinese rule in 1999). The danger to China from Mongolia, from where Altan Khan (1543–83) raided almost annually across the Great Wall, was kept in check by adroit Ming diplomacy, and further allayed by the Mongol acceptance of Tibetan religious authority; with the spread of Lamaism, monasteries absorbed surplus sons who might otherwise have become warriors. But danger lurked in the lands north of Korea, where descendants of the 12th-century Jurched rulers of the *Jin Dynasty* were forming a new tribal confederation of people who would become known as *Manchus*. Their chieftain Nurhachi took the title of emperor; his son brought all of Mongolia under his rule, overran Korea in 1627, and took the Ming northeastern outpost of Mukden in 1636.

Domestically in China, a combination of rising imperial expenditures and increasing land tax evasion by the rural gentry eventually destabilized even so rich an empire as the Ming. Factionalism and eunuch intrigues in the capital weakened the dynasty further; popular rebellions broke out and were not thoroughly suppressed. In desperation, the last Ming emperor invited a Manchu army to Beijing to expell a rebel band that had seized the city. Having expelled the rebels, the Manchus refused to leave. The Ming emperor hanged himself, and the Manchus proclaimed the founding of the *Qing Dynasty*

(1644–1911). Ming resistance in southern China was quashed by 1661; all Chinese men were required to braid their hair in a queue as a sign of submission.

During the last decades of the Ming, China began to feel the first effects of European influence. The Jesuit missionary Matteo Ricci reached Macao in 1582 and Beijing in 1601. Adapting himself to local custom, he became an accomplished Confucian scholar and used that guise as a means of introducing to China such things as the astrolabe, the weight-driven clock, prisms, and the Mercator map of the world. For a brief time Christianity became a vogue among some members of the mandarin class, but imperial disapproval (exacerbated by factional disputes among the Christian missionary orders) discouraged conversions. Under Qing rule the Jesuits were prohibited from preaching, but allowed to remain in China for their technical skills in astronomy, mathematics, painting, and cannon-founding.

In Korea, the *Choson Dynasty* was badly shaken by a destructive invasion (1592–98) from Japan under the leadership of the shogun Toyotomi Hideyoshi. The invasion was finally repelled with Chinese aid, but Korea suffered long-term economic and social damage. Conquered by the Manchus in 1627, the Koreans had no difficulty in transferring their loyalty from the Ming to the Qing; Choson remained a loyal vassal of China, and isolated from the rest of the world, until the late 19th century.

Japan borrowed the old Chinese term "Warring States Period" to describe the century from 1467 to 1568, when Muromachi rule dissolved in a welter of mutually hostile feudal domains. Order was gradually restored after 1568 by three remarkable generals: Oda Nobunaga, who was the first Japanese general to use firearms extensively in battle; Toyotomi Hideyoshi, a peasant who rose to rule Japan, only to squander his resources in a fruitless invasion of Korea; and Tokugawa Ieyasu, who defeated Hideyoshi's army at the Battle of Sekigahara in 1600 and established the Tokugawa shogunate, military rulers of Japan until 1868. The Tokugawa period is sometimes known as the *Edo Period*, after its capital (now Tokyo).

Japan readily absorbed European influence in the 16th century. The Portuguese arrived as traders in 1543; another Jesuit, Francis Xavier (1506–52) began his mission to the Japanese in 1549. Within three decades the number of Catholic converts, including some members of the high military aristocracy, reached 150,000. Thereafter Hideyoshi began to suppress Christianity as a foreign threat, banishing Portuguese missionaries in 1587. The Tokugawa shoguns persecuted Christianity even more fiercely, executing thousands after 1612 and driving the church underground after the Christian Shimbara Uprising of 1637–38 ended in an appalling slaughter. Thereafter no foreigners were allowed in Japan except for a small number of Dutch traders, who were rigorously confined to an island in Nagasaki harbor.

Africa's Time of Troubles (1500–1650)

The Portuguese sea route to the east diverted attention from the earlier trading contacts with Africa where Portuguese traders brought cotton goods and metal manufactures to exchange for ivory and gold as far as the delta of the Niger river, and where, further south, at the mouth of the Congo, a Bantu-speaking Christian state developed after 1483. And the new world of the Americas, the Spanish Caribbean and Portuguese Brazil, provided a large market for traffic in human beings: the *slave trade* which the Portuguese monopolized until the Dutch drove them out of the Gold Coast in 1642. African slavery, once the result of tribal warfare, now became its cause. First the Portuguese, then the Dutch and, after 1562, the English encouraged tributary states along the west coast to provide them with workers for new world plantations.

The trading *Kingdom of Songhay* which had reached its greatest extent under Askia Mohammed and Askia Dawud in the 16th century was smashed by a Moroccan invasion in 1591. The fall of Songhay brought decline further east to the *Kingdom of Kanem (Bornu)* in the savanna surrounding Lake Chad after 1617. The paradoxical result was the decline of Islamic influence for with the destruction of the Muslim towns the old caravan routes across the Sahara dwindled to a trickle. Further south, the Portuguese established themselves on the west and east coasts in *Angola* (1574) and *Mozambique* (1508) and after 1628 reduced to vassal status the *Kingdom of the Makaranga* which stretched from the Zambesi to the Limpopo with its capital at Great Zimbabwe. At Africa's southern tip the Dutch established themselves, founding Capetown in 1652.

The Americas: Europe's New Provinces

The Treaty of Tordesillas (1494) between Spain and Portugal divided the world by a line 370 leagues west of the Azores, establishing monopolies for Spain westward and Portugal eastward of the line, approximately 45 degrees west longitude. Thus Brazil, not discovered until 1500, accidentally, by Pedro Cabral (c. 1467–c. 1520) on a voyage to India, became Portuguese territory. But the new world seemed a dead end: the shores of the Caribbean were clearly not the islands and coasts of Asia, the Spanish westward route to the Indies bumped up against an apparently interminable barrier, the Americas.

What altered the picture entirely were the events of 1519–22. In 1520, Ferdinand Magellan (c. 1480–1521) sailed around the southern tip of South America, bringing the Spanish to the Philippines and the Moluccas across the Pacific. Then in 1521, the *conquistador* (conqueror) Hernando Cortez's (1485–1547) brutally subdued the Aztec Empire in 1521. When Francisco Pizarro (1476–1541) toppled the Inca Empire in 1534, Spain acquired a stupendous world empire the wealth of whose silver mines dwarfed the riches of the Indies.

Organized into two vice-royalties, the *Spanish Empire* granted *encomiendas* or plantations to the conquerors; although enslavement of the Indians was forbidden, the Spanish reduced them to serflike status and forced them to work for their new lords. Christian missions were immediately established with such success that over 20 bishoprics had been created by the mid-16th century. Five universities were flourishing by the middle of the 17th century.

France also sent exploratory ventures to America led by Giovanni da Verrazano (1524) and Jacques Cartier (1534); but it was not until the 17th century that a permanent settlement was established by Samuel de Champlain (1567–1635) who founded New France (1608)

with a capital at Quebec. Missions began in 1615 but the process of christianizing the Indians met with no such success as did the Spanish endeavor although Jesuits were involved here. Jean de Brébeuf's conversion of the Huron tribe only exposed them the more to the Iroquois savagery who undid his work and that of Isaac Jogues among the Mohawks. The establishment of Montreal made that more westward site the focus of the fur trade on which the economy of New France was based. Earlier the French began colonizing the Lesser Antilles, right on the fringe of the Spanish Empire and by 1656 had colonized a dozen.

England's Queen Elizabeth (1558–1603) limited herself to encouraging courtiers like Sir Humphrey Gilbert and Sir Walter Raleigh in their ill-fated attempts at early settlement (Roanoke I., 1585) and pirates and slave traders like Sir Francis Drake and Sir John Hawkins in their plundering Spanish ships. Not until the Stuart Dynasty (1603–49) did English settlement begin in earnest. Through grants to commercial companies and individual proprietors, the English established colonies from the Chesapeake to Maine broken only by the Swedes on the lower Delaware River and the Dutch in the Hudson Valley. The Chesapeake became the center of a thriving agricultural region based upon tobacco, while New England flourished as a haven for the English Calvinists known as Puritans.

Europe in the Age of the Reformation

The Europe whose sea-borne enterprise established the first truly worldwide empires was a civilization menaced from without by the Ottoman Turks and divided within both by dynastic-national rivalries and the sundering of Christian unity by the *Reformation*. For many years, leading members of the church had cried out for reform of the clergy, who often led scandalous lives amidst great wealth and who sold God's forgiveness (indulgences) for cash. But not even the powerful voices of the Dutch humanist Desiderius Erasmus (1466–1536) or the English statesman Sir Thomas More (1478–1535) had any impact.

In 1517, the call of the Augustinian monk Martin Luther (1483–1546) for a cleansing of the Church on the basis of his doctrine of "salvation by faith alone" (with its implication of the worthlessness of the priesthood and the sacramental system) swept across northern Germany from the Rhine to the Memel; the adherence of the Scandinavian monarchies to the new faith made the Baltic almost a Lutheran lake. The English king Henry VIII (1509–47), while anti-Lutheran, severed his realm from the Catholic Church after 1532. But what secured Protestantism's hold in Europe was the work of John Calvin (1509–64) who, from 1541 until his death, made Geneva a theocratic state and directed the spread of Calvinism to France, the Low Countries and the British Isles.

The attempts of the Holy Roman Emperor Charles V (1519–56) to halt the spread of Lutheranism were hampered by his need to defend the West against the Ottoman Turks (and thus not offend the Lutheran princes) and to maintain his dynastic territories against the kings of France who allied with the Turks against him. For he ruled the Netherlands and Spain in addition to holding the office of Emperor. At his abdication he willed the Empire to his brother Ferdinand along with Habsburg holdings in central Europe; Spain with its empire, both in the new world and Europe (Netherlands, Burgundy, Milan and Naples), he willed to his son Philip II (1556–98).

Philip faced rebellion in the Netherlands, where by the end of his reign the northern provinces had all but won their independence while the southern provinces were held. His Armada (1588) against England met disaster, thereby confirming Queen Elizabeth's rule and the triumph of Protestantism in both England and Scotland. France was given over to the Wars of Religion (1562–98) in which Philip ineffectively intervened on the Catholic side against the Calvinists; the upshot was victory for the Calvinist claimant Henry IV (1589–1610) who, however, turned Catholic but issued the Edict of Nantes (1598) granting French Calvinists ("Huguenots") equal rights, even to the extent of maintaining their own armies.

Philip II considered himself the Catholic champion and it was during his reign that the Catholic *Counter-Reformation* made its greatest strides, not politically but ecclesiastically. Spanish religious leadership came from the new Jesuit Order founded in 1540 by Ignatius Loyola (1491–1556), a fertile source of missionaries, preachers, scholars and schoolmasters, and from the great mystic theologians Theresa of Avila and John of the Cross. Institutionally the *Council of Trent* (1545–63), while not healing the breach with the Protestants, managed to reform the most gratuitous abuses in the Church and provide a clear and authoritative expression of Catholic belief that would last for four centuries.

The uneasy balance between the opposing forces at the start of the 17th century broke down, provoking a time of great crisis. Germany and the Empire were devastated by the Thirty Years' War (1618–48) in which the triumph of the Catholic Habsburgs was prevented by the interventions of Lutheran Sweden and Catholic France personified by King Gustavus Adolphus of Lutheran Sweden and Cardinal Richelieu of France. Britain was shaken by the struggle between Anglicans and Puritans religiously, between the Stuart kings and Parliament politically, the climax coming in the English Civil Wars (1642–49) where the Puritan victory entailed the beheading of King Charles I and the establishment of a military dictatorship under Oliver Cromwell (1649–58).

In eastern Europe there was instability as well. After the long reign of Ivan IV the Terrible (1533–84) in which the entire Volga came under Russian rule and expansion began beyond the Ural Mountains, Russia underwent its "time of troubles." The nobles ("boyars") whose power he thought he had broken rose again to prominence under his weaker son Theodore and confusion as to the succession permitted Polish penetration deep into Russia until the national assembly in 1613 elected Michael Romanov, founder of the *Romanov Dynasty* (1613–1917). In Poland, under Sigismund II (1548–72), the spread of the Reformation was checked and Lithuania was united with Poland into a single state (1569). But Sigismund was the last of the Jagellonian dynasty and at his death the monarchy became in fact what it had always been in theory, elective and thus increasingly the plaything of other great powers. From 1587 to 1648 two members of the Catholic branch of Sweden's royal family, the Vasas, ruled in Poland. Their interventions in Swedish affairs and in Russia during the time of trouble made significant enemies for Poland.

It was a Polish priest, Copernicus (1473–1543) who stands at the beginning of the *Scientific Revolution*, overturning the ancient cosmology of Ptolemy for the heliocentric theory. Expanded by the work of the Dane Tycho Brahe (1546–1601) and his scientific heir, the German Johannes Kepler (1571–1630), the movement reached its first climax in the system of the Italian Galileo (1564–1642), the greatest scientist of the age.

It was also the age of the great flowering of the vernacular literatures of Europe, especially in epic poetry and the drama: in England, Spenser and Shakespeare; in Italy, Ariosto and Tasso; in Spain, Cervantes, Lope de Vega, and Calderon; in Portugal, Camoens. Ironically, this turbulent age also saw the magnificent flowering of painting and sculpture from the universal genius of Michelangelo (1475–1564), the sculptor Bernini (1598–1680), and the painters Raphael, Titian (c. 1490–1576), El Greco (c. 1541–1614), Velasquez (1599–1660), Rubens (1577–1640), and Rembrandt (1606–69).

▶EXPANSION OF THE EUROPEAN WORLD HEGEMONY (1650–1815)

The period in Europe was characterized by the predominance of France, absolutist at the start, revolutionary at the close—a dominance that was as much cultural as it was political. In the western hemisphere, the age saw the maturing of the colonial extensions of western civilization, with the British dominating the north and the Spanish the south. In Africa and the Middle East, western influence grew primarily through trade, principally British controlled. And in the great land mass of Eurasia, two huge empires grew, those of Russia and China.

Europe in Enlightenment and Revolution

The religious wars of the previous period had a double effect: the boundaries of religious division between Catholic and Protestant Europe solidified and there grew up, especially in northwest Europe, men whom the French called *politiques*, seeking peace beyond the reach of religious controversy and division. Parallel with the rise of the politique mentality there had arisen the philosophical movement known as *rationalism*, which sought to reconstruct philosophy on the basis of "clear and distinct ideas" (Rene Descartes, 1596–1650). Then came the climax of the scientific revolution in the achievement of Isaac Newton (1642–1727), whose *Principia Mathematica* (1687) united the key ideas of inertia, gravitation, and centrifugal force.

These three streams flowed together in the movement known as the *Enlightenment*, whose publicists, called "philosophes," skeptical of all things except reason (and reason understood as the application to all matters of the method of Newton), called all authority into question save their own and subjected all traditional institutions, including the Church, to the corrosive solvents of their argument and mockery.

The man who gave his name to the *Age of Louis XIV* (1661–1715) was no philosopher but an absolute monarch whose court at Versailles became the model for sovereigns across Europe, establishing a French cultural dominance more significant than her political power. Not that the latter was insignificant: in a series of four wars the "Sun King" expanded France's frontiers to the Rhine and his Bourbon dynasty to the throne of Spain. It took alliances of almost all Europe to limit him even to this, alliances organized principally by the Dutch stadtholder William of Orange who conspired as well with the Protestant English aristocracy to overturn their Catholic king James II, the second of the Stuarts restored after the Cromwellian dictatorship, and install him as William III of England. This event is known as the "Glorious Revolution" and it turned England essentially into an aristocratic republic dominated by Parliament.

Louis XIV's revocation of the Edict of Nantes (1685) forced the Protestant Huguenots to leave France for Holland, Britain, and Prussia, where they became industrious businessmen and artisans; through their dominance of publishing, they laid the basis for the spread of the Enlightenment.

In eastern Europe the age of Louis XIV was principally the story of the decline of Polish and Ottoman power and the rise to dominance of Prussia and Russia in the Baltic region and the new *Habsburg Empire* in the southeast. With the Spanish Habsburgs sliding toward extinction and the Holy Roman Empire rendered ghostly by the Thirty Years' War, the Austrian Habsburgs drove the Ottomans out of Croatia and Hungary (1699) and added Galicia from helpless Poland (1772). Meanwhile, the War of the Spanish Succession (1702–13) which established the Bourbons on the throne of Spain also detached from Spain its holdings in the Netherlands (roughly modern Belgium) and Italy (Milan and Tuscany), awarding both to the Austrian Habsburgs. This unwieldy dynastic empire, so diverse as to lack even a name, is usually called the *Austrian Empire*, though that title was not taken until 1804. The heart of Catholic Baroque culture in art and architecture and music, Austria became in the reign of Joseph II (1765–80) the seat of an enlightened despotism as well.

More an army than a state, Brandenburg excelled in switching alliances: Frederick William the Great Elector gained sovereignty in the Duchy of Prussia from Poland (1660), and his son a royal title there from the Emperor (1701); thus the *Hohenzollern* dynasty's holdings are usually called *Prussia*. Under Frederick II the Great (1740–86), friend and patron of Voltaire, Prussia snatched Silesia from the Habsburgs (1748). Participating in the partitions of Poland (1772,1793,1795) the Hohenzollerns again doubled the size of their dynastic holdings.

Fought on three continents, the Seven Years' War (1756–63) was the first truly world war. In the European theater the alliances (Great Britain and Prussia against France, Austria and Russia) fought to a draw; the war was won overseas: in North America and in India the British drove out the French and established their hegemony. But in attempting to organize her new and gigantic North American holdings (the "new imperial system") Great Britain provoked into rebellion her old coastal colonies whose independence as the United States of America was recognized in the Peace of Paris (1783). (For North American developments afterward, see Part II: U.S. History.)

The French Revolution

A war for independence rather than, as its common name implies, a revolution, the American experience was an odd model for the tumultuous upheaval known as the *French Revolution*. France

was the most prosperous state in Europe, but the long series of wars since 1660 combined with the clergy's and the aristocracy's exemption from taxation impoverished the monarchy. As a way out of the impasse, Louis XVI resurrected the old medieval Estates General (1789) but the representatives transformed themselves into a constitutional convention called the National Assembly. After abolishing serfdom, setting the peasants free, they remodeled the French state into a constitutional monarchy. But they also confiscated Church lands, dissolved the monasteries, and attempted to make the Church a department of the state, complete with elected bishops. This tore many devout Catholics away from the revolutionary cause.

The universal appeal of the French Revolution to so many people across Europe frightened the monarchs and encouraged the National Assembly to declare war on them all. The new mass armies of the French, fired by ideology and national pride, were a juggernaut against the old-fangled monarchical armies. At home, the war emergency and a revolt in a pro-royalist area (Vendee) against the newly declared republic were used to justify a Committee of Public Safety led by George Danton (1759–94) and Maximilien Robespierre (1758–94) and its *Reign of Terror* (1793–94); it's first victims were the royal family, including Louis XVI and his wife, Marie Antoinette. The rule of the Directory (1795–99) that followed was overturned by its general, the Corsican adventurer and military genius Napoleon Bonaparte (1769–1821), who established a popular and military dictatorship (1799) first disguised as a republic, then under the name *French Empire* (1804–15).

Several coalitions of nations were formed to stop Napoleon, but he defeated all of them. Coalition after coalition broke up in defeat. At its peak, the Empire dominated all of Europe from the English Channel to the Ottoman Empire by incorporation into the Empire, or as satellites, or as allies. But a popular uprising in Spain, supported by Britain, and the failure of Napoleon's invasion of Russia (1812) began the breakup of his Empire. By 1814 the anti-French nationalisms that conquest had evoked and the recovery of the monarchs' courage brought Napoleon down and, when he returned in 1815, produced his final defeat at Waterloo (1815) at the hands of the first Duke of Wellington (1769–1852).

Scarcely noticed, another and perhaps more powerful revolution was already under way before the period ended. Enlightened British landowners were enclosing the commons (the village lands tenant farmers used to graze cattle) and developing new crops while inventors were creating the machinery (the spinning jenny, the waterframe, and the steam engine) which would provide the basis in the following period for the *Industrial Revolution*.

Europe Overseas: The Americas and Africa

Between the crises of the Cromwellian period (1643–60) and the Glorious Revolution (1688) the Stuart kings of England fostered new proprietary grants in the Hudson Valley, in Pennsylvania, and in the Carolinas. Thereafter the North American colonies became habituated to self-government under their elected assemblies in a period of "salutary neglect" by the home government. Legally colonies, they were in fact mature provinces of Britain overseas. When after the Seven Years' War the government attempted to limit settlement beyond the Appalachians, to tax the colonists for the costs of the enlarged British holdings, and to extend toleration to Catholics in Canada, the colonial resistance led to war and to independence.

The Spanish new world colonies, with new viceroyalties of New Granada (1717) (roughly modern Venezuela, Colombia, and Ecuador) and La Plata (1776) (Bolivia, Paraguay, Uruguay, and Argentina) remained essentially Indian states governed paternalistically by *Yo, el rey*—the king, in whose name all regulations were sent to the viceroys. After about 1650 Indian population grew rapidly. While rule remained in the hands of "peninsulares" from the home country and, to a lesser degree, in those of the "creoles," colonists of Spanish descent, in the towns, the Indians' chief contact with Spanish culture was in the Church, whose missionaries and bishops provided a spiritual elite. Of special note were the Jesuit "reductions" on the upper Parana: self-governing, communistic Catholic Indian republics which fell victim to European politics and Brazilian incursions. Brazil by 1800 had a population larger than Portugal's.

To the viceroyalty of New Spain (Mexico) was attached the Philippines. No one was sure where in the Pacific lay the treaty line of 1494 so that while the Philippines were in fact on the Portuguese side, it was Spain that claimed them in 1565, founding Manila in 1571 which became the western terminus of the famous Manila galleons bearing Mexican silver. Through the whole period coasting voyages of English, Dutch and Spanish mariners discovered the islands of the South Pacific: the Carolines, the Marshalls, Tasmania, New Zealand and Australia; but no settlements disturbed the hunting and gathering culture of the Stone Age people who inhabited them.

It was otherwise in Africa where the slave trade continued until the end of the period, peaking in the 1780's but with demand dropping decade by decade thereafter. And in the early years of the 19th century Britain, Denmark and the United States abolished the trade, Britain actively but not always effectively blocking the trade along the African coast. In west Africa, there was an Islamic revival in the savanna as the *Fulbe people*, over the century after 1670, spread eastward toward Lake Chad in a series of *jihads* against *Hausa* cities. In south Africa, the *Zulu* nation, utilizing trained infantry units armed with spears established a small empire in the late 1700's over their neighbors who still relied on the hurling of javelins; while the Dutch at the southern tip, with its Mediterranean climate and its few Khoikhoi (Hottentots), built a Dutch-speaking, Calvinist, multiracial colony which by 1815 had a population of about 80,000. The pioneering "trekboers" beyond the Cape found their expansion limited by the Xhosa people and when the colony passed from the Dutch to the British (1814), British governors attempted to halt the expansion in the name of peace. Finally, on the east coast trade reached inland as far as Lake Victoria, initiated by the Nyamwezi people of Tanzania but falling after 1800 into the hands of the trade network of Oman, an ally of Britain.

Two Eurasian Empires: Russian and Ottoman

In one aspect the development of the Russian Empire was an eastward expansion of Europe, in another it was the creation of a stupendous Oriental state menacing Europe. Russian pioneers had already reached the Pacific by 1637; expansion into Central Asia brought the Russians up against Chinese expansion westward into the same region, peace being established in 1689 by the Treaty of Nerchinsk which set the common boundary along the peaks of the Stanovoi Mountains, the Russians evacuating a fort they had constructed on the Amur. This shifted Russian interests to the northeast, leading eventually to Russian settlements in Canada and California (1805–1912).

A certain important but superficial "westernizing" of Russia took place under Peter the Great (1689–1725) who in a "revolution from above" autocratically imposed upon his land Western modes in manufacturing, in political administration, in military techniques, in court manners and even in dress. Russia had already taken the eastern Ukraine including Kiev from Poland (1667), then the portion (1681) that their allies the Ottomans had won in that war. Peter's attempts to gain Azov—the warm-water port on the Black Sea that would provide access to the Mediterranean— from the Ottoman Empire proved ineffectual. But in the Great Northern War (1700-21) he proved more successful against Sweden, establishing Russia on the Baltic and founding a new capital at St. Petersburg.

Under Catherine II the Great (1762–96), another "enlightened despot" favored by Voltaire, Russia fought a war with the Ottoman Empire. The Treaty of Kuchuk Kainarji (1774) established Russia in the Crimea along the north of the Black Sea, granted navigation rights to Russia in Turkish waters, including the Straits into the Mediterranean, and provided a legal basis for Russia to intervene to protect Orthodox Christians in the provinces of Moldavia and Walachia—i.e. most of what Peter the Great wanted. Catherine also participated in the partitions of Poland (1772, 1793, 1795), which obliterated that ancient Christian state.

In a third stage of expansion Russia took Finland (1809) from Sweden and Bessarabia (1812) from the Ottomans during the Napoleonic Wars. After the invasion of Russia (1812) the czar Alexander I participated in the great coalition that at last brought Napoleon down. In 1815 Russian troops were participating in the occupation of Paris and the Polish Kingdom that emerged from the post-war settlement had Alexander as its king.

The Russian ascendancy was paralleled by Ottoman decline. Of the dozen sultans who ruled between 1648 and 1839 only Selim III (1789–1807) was a man of intelligence and vigor. The period began with misleading signs of strength, as the Turks took Podolia from Poland (1672) and advanced against the Habsburgs, climaxing in the siege of Vienna (1683). The failure of the siege proved a real turning point, the beginning of a long slow sag in Ottoman fortunes that made it by the 19th century "the sick man of Europe." Facing war after war against Austria and Russia (often in tandem) in the west and Persia in the east, the Empire yielded territory, strained its already chaotic finances, and developed a defensive mentality. Its domestic power waned as well as frontier garrisons meant for defense had to be used to suppress rebellions and endemic banditry.

The year after the siege of Vienna was lifted, the Austrians were victorious in the second Battle of Mohacs (1684) which reversed that of 1526, a victory confirmed by the Battle of Zenta (1697): Hungary and Croatia fell away. After the Treaty of Kuchuk Kainarji (1774), the Black Sea was no longer a Turkish lake and Russian ships sailed freely through Ottoman waters. Egypt, temporarily independent in 1769, gained its autonomy in 1805 while Serbia became the first Christian Balkan state to gain autonomy. Even Arabia, the original homeland of Islam, slipped from Ottoman rule as the Saud clan provided the political and economic support necessary for *Wahhabism* which sought a return to the primitive theocracy of the Prophet himself.

The Growth of British Influence in the Middle East and India

With the Portuguese control of the spice route in disarray and the Dutch diverted toward the Spice Islands, British commercial interests grew ascendant in India. Bombay became the headquarters of the *East Indian Company* (1661) from which Calcutta was founded (1690). But not uncontested: the French founded their East India Company in 1664 and established a trading post at Pondichery in 1674.

The Safavid Persian Empire with which the British East India Company had established trade in 1616 entered after 1664 a decline like that which had earlier begun in the Ottoman realm.

In the long reign of Mogul emperor Aurangzeb (1659–1707) the empire had reached its greatest territorial extent, principally through conquests in the Deccan plateau in south-central India. But within the empire his rule was weak as local governors grew increasingly independent. The Maratha people, under their raja Sivadi, established an independent Hindu state against which the emperor waged inconclusive war until his death, and the religious order of Sikhs (blending Hindu and Muslim beliefs) became under Govind Singh a military order.

After Aurangzeb's death Mogul decline became precipitous. Afghanistan became independent in 1709 then invaded Persia (1722) its leader, Mir Mohammed, becoming shah in 1725. With the death of the last Safavid in 1736 the general Nadir Shah reestablished rule over Afghanistan and even invaded India (1738). But all proved ephemeral. With his death Persia came under the rule of the *Zand Dynasty* (1750–94), then the *Kajar Dynasty* (1794–1925) under whom Great Britain gained the right by treaty (1814) to negate any Persian treaty contrary to her interests. The Afghans (1809) became British allies, bound to assist Britain were Persia or France to attack India.

In India during the 18th century the Maratha state became the dominant Indian body, collecting taxes (1720) in Southern India. Nadir Shah's invasion (1738) wrested the north and west from the Moguls. In the turmoil, the European companies began forming private armies of Indian troops ("sepoys") under European officers. After the War of the Austrian Succession (1746–48) French forces ruled virtually the entire south. But in the Indian theater of the Seven Years' War (1756–63) Robert Clive (1725–74) roundly defeated the French; the Treaty of Paris left but a few holdings to the French. In the aftermath, the East India Company gained from the *nawab* (viceroy) of Bengal landowner status over Calcutta, then pensioned off the *nawab* and ruled Bengal directly (1764).

During this struggle the Afghans invaded from the northeast establishing their rule over the Maratha and Sikhs (1761–62). Faced with the two foreign powers most Indian princes gravitated towards the British, a movement not halted by Parliament's India Act (1784) which brought the Company under government control and prohibited it from interfering in Indian affairs or from engaging in war. Still, between 1786 and 1813, the Company's governors-general began a judicial system, gained control over the foreign affairs of most southern principalities in return for British protection, and entered into the treaties with Persia and Afghanistan already mentioned.

In reality, there was no British empire. The Company ruled directly only certain territories whose princes could not secure peace and order and established treaty obligations with other princes. There were no missionaries, no conversions—not even British law: an odd combination of feelings of superiority with respect for Indian culture led to a hands-off policy. And to the Hindus, the British were but another caste.

Chinese Expansion, Japanese Isolation (1650–1800)

The Manchu emperors of China adapted themselves rapidly to the ancient system of empire government, maintaining the examination system for the bureaucracy (though sometimes doubling officials, one Manchu, one Chinese). So serene and sensible (and non-theological) did the Manchu state appear to the European mind that it almost rivaled England in their fantasies.

Taiwan was annexed in 1683, Tibet gradually brought under Chinese control (1705-51) with the emperor controlling succession of the Dalai Lamas. But the great expansion was into central Asia, settled diplomatically with the Russians in 1689 to China's advantage. All this was the work of Kang Xi, the contemporary of Louis XIV.

Under Qian Long, who ruled from 1736-95, Burma had to recognize Chinese overlordship (1769) as did Nepal (1792). Burma had only recently been re-united (1753) and that with British assistance to Alaungpaya, so the relationships became an avenue of British influence. At the same time Annam, largely Chinese in culture and recognizing its overlordship, nonetheless permitted Catholic missions which met with surprising success especially after Gia Long emerged as emperor in 1802.

The whole period was for China one of expansion, not only territorially. In agriculture new crops from the Americas (maize and yams) provided a larger and more diversified food supply, though by the end of the period population was pressing up against its limits. Trade with Europe and with Japan, carried in Portuguese ships, was based upon Chinese exports of tea, silk and porcelain, the latter increasingly produced on a mass basis in imperial and private kilns. But China showed little interest in the outside world. The late 19th-century mission of the British diplomat Lord George MacCartney was met with total indifference. The papacy's finding (1715) that reverence shown toward Confucius or toward one's ancestors was incompatible with Catholic belief led to the ban of Catholic missionaries in 1720.

In Japan the splendid isolation of the Tokugawa period continued. But the internal peace that they enforced left the samurai warriors functionless, increasingly dissolute and in debt to the thriving merchant class. The heyday of the latter in the *Genroku Period* (1688–1704) led to a flourishing of Japanese literature free of Chinese influence: the development of haiku poetry, and of the Kabuki drama. Late in the period there were signs of restiveness against the Tokugawa not only from the great clans excluded from power but from the imperial family as well, both merging patriotic feeling and imperial loyalty with the increasing vogue of the Shinto religion, both worried about the danger of the Westerners to Japan's isolated development.

▶TRIUMPH AND TRAGEDY OF WESTERN CIVILIZATION (1815–1945)

With the defeat of Napoleon in 1815, Europe entered 100 years of peace, the ending of serfdom, the extraordinary development of industrial capitalism, the spread of liberal and democratic institutions, and the apogee of her world-wide imperial influence. But then ensued 30 years of tumultuous upheaval: two world wars, waged with new weapons of mass destruction, flanking the subjection of most of Europe to grim totalitarian domination. At the end Europe lay broken and prostrate, its fate and the fate of the world in the hands of the two atomic superpowers, liberal-democratic America and Communist Russia.

Europe: The Rise of Nationalism

After a quarter-century of exhausting warfare the conservative monarchs and statesmen of Britain, Austria, Prussia and Russia made a generous peace with France, restoring the Bourbon dynasty but hedging her borders with an enlarged Netherlands to the north, the Prussians on the Rhine and the Habsburgs in northern Italy. To maintain the peace they established the Concert of Europe, a series of international conferences (to which France was soon admitted) to regulate European affairs, initiating the longest sustained general European peace since Rome's Antonine emperors in the second century A.D. Fearing revolution as the source of war and so a threat to themselves, they suppressed liberal and nationalist organizations and sent troops into Italy and Spain to prop up their tottering monarchies; but Britain, supporting the U.S. prevented any intervention against the revolts in Latin America. With the devolution of the Ottoman Empire in the Balkans, the powers supported an independent Greece (1829) and autonomy for Serbia, Moldavia and Walachia. Similarly, liberal revolts in Belgium and France (1830) led not to suppression but to independence for the first and a change of dynasty for the second; in the same year, however, Russia crushed a Polish revolt and absorbed that state into her empire. Britain herself, carried out a liberal reform of her constitution (1832) abolishing "rotten" or underpopulated boroughs and expanding the electorate by 50 percent, especially in the new manufacturing centers. Britain was also the first major power to abolish slavery (1833).

The year 1848 saw a remarkable series of liberal and nationalist revolts in virtually all the capitals of the German and Italian principalities and of the Habsburg realms. Yet all proved stillborn, and the armies remained loyal to their sovereigns. Still they had lasting effects, as serfdom was abolished throughout central Europe. The liberal route to national unity, which combined political goals (representative government) with nationalist ones seemed discredited; and the 1848 revolt in Paris led to the establishment of a brief Second Republic, then, in a revival of Bonapartism, a *Second Empire* (1852-70) under Napoleon III (Louis Napoleon Bonaparte, 1808-73).

His assistance was essential in aiding Piedmont's conquests of all the Italian states save Venice and Rome; the *Kingdom of Italy* was proclaimed in 1861 and by 1870 it included Venice and Rome as well. The latter two it gained as an ally of Otto von Bismarck's (1815-98) Prussia, which in a series of three brief wars incorporated all of non-Habsburg Germany into the *German Empire*, proclaimed in 1871. The third of those wars (the Franco-Prussian war), took Alsace and Lorraine from France, toppled Napoleon III, and led to the formation of France's *Third Republic* (1871–1940). The second, which had excluded Austria from German affairs, led that empire to its own reform, the establishment in 1867 of the "Dual Monarchy" of *Austria-Hungary*.

In one decade the map of Europe had been transformed, its most powerful state the new Germany which, with rapid industrialization, became stronger still in the years which led up to the World War I.

Europe: Two World Wars, 1914–45

Bismarck attempted to keep France isolated. He encouraged her colonial expansion to compensate for her diminished status in Europe and in the hope that imperial rivalry with Britain would keep those western states apart. He hoped for similar results from Russian and British rivalry in Persia and Afghanistan. And he formed the Triple Alliance of Germany, Austria-Hungary, and Italy.

But France and Russia allied in 1894 and a decade later, after settling colonial issues that had nearly brought them to war, France and Britain came too a "friendly understanding." The triangle was completed in 1907 when Britain and Russia established spheres of influence in Persia. Bismarck's diplomacy was undone by Kaiser Wilhelm II's (r. 1888–1918) aggressive foreign policy and a naval arms race with Britain.

Not in the colonies but in the Balkans events moved beyond any statesman's ability. In the disintegration of Ottoman power there, Serbia, Romania and Montenegro became independent in 1878 and Bulgaria in 1908. The powers consistently checked Russian advances there while the influence of Austria-Hungary grew. Struggling for territory from the Ottomans and from each other, the Balkan states fought a series of three wars in 1912, 1913 and 1914. It was the third one, which began with the assassination of the Archduke Francis Ferdinand in Sarajevo by a Serbian nationalist that expanded into the catastrophe of World War I.

Outside Europe fighting was slight: German holdings in the Pacific and Africa were taken by British and French imperial forces; Russian and British forces engaged the Ottomans in Mesopotamia and Armenia; and western-backed Arab revolts further weakened Ottoman strength. But in Belgium and northern France developed the horror of four years of trench warfare and on the gigantic eastern front immense armies clashed but without resolution until 1917, when the Bolsheviks, led by Vladimir I. Lenin (1870– 1924), took Russia out of the war after their revolution (Nov. 6, 1917) toppled the Provisional Government that had succeeded the czarist collapse. But Russia's withdrawal in the east was balanced in the west by the American entry that same year, provoked by Germany's resumption of unrestricted submarine warfare in a futile attempt to escape the noose of Britain's naval blockade. The fighting at last ended November 11, 1918.

Besides its immense cost to blood (over eight million died in battle and six million civilians perished) and treasure, the war overturned the old European state system as four empires collapsed and were partitioned. Germany, under the Versailles Treaty (1919) emerged as the Weimar Republic with small territorial losses to France and to a resurrected Poland but burdened with the war guilt clauses and the immense financial reparations they were meant to justify. Russia lost all her western gains since Peter the Great, retreating eastward into the cruel experiment of Communist Revolution. Austria-Hungary disappeared utterly, two republics maintaining the names at least of those once great states. And by 1923 in Asia Minor a one-party Turkish Republic emerged under Mustafa Kemal Ataturk (1818–1938).

The successor states in eastern Europe, readily adopted the parliamentary government of the victorious western Allies which, in the years after 1848, had steadily democratized the franchise. But most contained substantial ethnic minorities whose rivalries poisoned parliamentary life; tariff barriers which arose everywhere fragmented the old common markets of the empires they replaced, protecting inefficient industries.

To the east brooded the reduced but still vast Soviet Union. The death of Lenin in 1924 led to the dictatorship of Joseph Stalin who oversaw the murderous collectivization of agriculture and the forced industrialization of the Five Year Plans, then purged the party and the army and the secret police of all but his own men. Millions died.

Western and central Europe seemed sheltered from these grim developments by the "cordon sanitaire" of the new states of east-central Europe. After a period of post-war adjustment, prosperity returned to the western democracies, especially in Germany whose adherence to the Locarno Treaties (1925) presaged enduring peace. Yet in Italy whose wartime sacrifices seemed unrewarded by territorial gains and whose economy did not recover but rather seemed to dissolve into the chaos of political violence. In 1922 Benito Mussolini came to power as his fascist movement promised a halfway house between liberal individualism and communist class war, stressing a belligerent nationalism with a corporative economy. In fact it was little more than bombast.

But with the collapse of the world economy after 1929, the social and ethnic divisions of the successor states, their boundary grievances, and the real or imagined fear of communist revolution, most of Europe outside the monarchies of the north and west turned to right-wing authoritarian regimes which, though often called "fascist," resembled Italy less than they did Latin America. The very different and very grievous case was Germany where after 1933 Adolf Hitler (1889–1945) established the Nazi dictatorship in the heart of Europe.

The western democracies dithered, deluded themselves, and sought peace through appeasement (not that they had much alternative, unprepared as they were for military action) as Hitler, bent on overturning the Versailles settlement, successfully re-militarized the Rhineland (1936) and absorbed Austria (the Anschluss) and the ethnically German parts of Czechoslovakia (1938) then turned the remainder of Czechoslovakia into a satellite and began demands on Poland (1939). In August 1939, Germany and Russia agreed to partition Poland yet again and with Hitler's invasion in September World War II began.

Until 1941, it was a European war with non-stop totalitarian triumphs; by June of 1940, when France fell, all of Europe outside Britain was neutral or an ally or a satellite of Germany. But in June of 1941 Hitler invaded Russia and in December Hitler's ally, Japan, attacked the U.S. in Hawaii. Japanese dominion reached as far as Burma in 1942, while German armies penetrated as far east as Stalingrad. Nevertheless, the grand alliance of Britain and the U.S. with the U.S.S.R. caused Nazi Germany to fight a two-front war, which ultimately spelled utter defeat in May of 1945—but not before Germany killed six million Jews during the Holocaust. Three months later, atomic bomb attacks on Hiroshima and Nagasaki, by the U.S., hastened Japan's surrender. The United States and the Soviet Union, with Great Britain a very junior partner, bestrode the globe. The European Age in world history was at an end.

The Troubled Independence of Latin America

The impact of the Napoleonic wars upon Europe's trans-Atlantic provinces (and the newly independent United States as well) was profound. For one thing, Haiti's success in maintaining its independence, gained in 1794, against Napoleon's attempt to reconquer it led to his abandonment of any scheme for a New World empire: Louisiana was therefore sold to the United States. For another, placing his brother Joseph on the throne of Spain (1808) threw Spanish America into confusion: which king to obey? Juntas loyal to the Bourbon king Ferdinand VII, led by creoles such as Simon Bolivar (1783–1830) and Jose San Martin (1778–1850), resisted French rule at first, then turned against the absolutism of the restored Ferdinand in whose name they had first risen up. In colony after colony the juntas' armies fought for and won their independence: La Plata (1810), Chile (1818), New Granada (1819), Peru (1821). In separate and more complicated developments, Mexico and Brazil followed in 1822.

The *Monroe Doctrine* (1823) of the United States, instigated and given force by Great Britain, shielded the new states from Spanish repression. But nothing could shield them from the effects of their own inexperience in politics (an effect of Spanish imperial centralization) or from boundary disputes (for New World boundaries too were purely Spanish creations) or from the internal struggles of local leader (*caudillos*) seeking autonomy within the new republics. Thus independence was followed by a long period of wars, civil wars, insurrections and coups.

When the trade links with Spain were cut, the new states found a welcome from Great Britain for their products. British investment fostered mining and industrial development; American investment entered late in the 19th century. The development in the 1880's of adequate methods of refrigeration on steamships meant that beef could join wheat and sugar and coffee as exports. The needs of the Allies in World War I for massive increases in raw materials brought a great increase in trade; large-scale post-war investment from the U.S. both in industry and in plantation agriculture helped economic growth but with serious decline after 1929 in the rate of growth.

This expansion brought social tension through the growth of both a middle class and agricultural and industrial working classes, adding new elements to the older political instability. In the 1930's governments in Mexico and Argentina respectively followed the "popular front" or "corporate state" models of Europe but these were usually but trappings for a new breed of *caudillo*. In the Caribbean, the interests of the United States predominated whether as "policeman" or, as after 1934, "good neighbor."

European Empires in Africa

For 60 years after the Napoleonic wars, Europeans evinced only small interest in Africa. Trading forts dotted the west African coasts while steamboats penetrated only somewhat further inland and missionaries began evangelization on a small scale. "Cash crop" agriculture was no European imposition: the profits from nuts and palm products, especially oil for lighting and machine lubrication, were enough encouragement to African kings and chiefs, especially with the drying up of the trade in slaves. In the south, the expansion of the Zulu after 1818 led to disruptions lasting into the 1850's while amongst the Boers in the south, the British ban on slavery provoked the Great Trek of some 10,000 settlers into the high veld, (or grassy plateau) depopulating the old Cape Colony except for some new British settlers. On the east coast the sultan of Oman moved his capital to Zanzibar the better to control his network of trade in cloves and slaves; the latter brought increasing British estrangement from their protege. Along the Mediterranean coast, the Ottoman Empire was nominally sovereign though rule in fact was exercised by local beys and sultans who gladly countenanced piracy; this provoked the French in 1830 to occupy Algiers and a few coastal cities.

About 1880 a group of French projects—a railways scheme at Dakar, new trading posts on the Ivory Coast and north of the Congo river—alarmed the other powers into the witless "scramble for Africa" which brought Britain and Portugal and eventually even Germany into a contest to annex territory, principally to prevent the others from doing the same and gaining some unknown benefit. The Congress of Berlin (1885) sought to put some order into the competition and in 15 years the entire continent had been divided up, save for the colony of freed American slaves in Liberia and the ancient Christian empire of Ethiopia. Colonial theorists gained the ear of western governments for grand schemes of great belts of territory, the French to stretch from Dakar to the Red Sea, the British from Capetown to Cairo—all just after the construction of the Suez Canal (1859–69) had rendered such imaginings nugatory. Of great interest was the discovery of deposits of gold and diamonds in the republic of Transvaal which led to Britain's conquest of the Boer republics in the Boer War (1889–1901) and her formation (1910) of the Union of South Africa, which through elections Boers soon governed.

There was something illusory about it all: tiny armies setting up the national flag, treaties signed with hundreds of tribal chiefs who lacked authority, boundary lines drawn on maps in European capitals. But European administration did bring some measure of peace, some road and rail construction, some schools and hospitals, some westernizing of tribal leaders. The last would provide a certain leadership class in the independence movements after World War II which dismantled the empires even faster than they had been thrown together before World War I.

Europe's Asian Domination and the Rise of Japan

If Africa experienced European claims of sovereignty with only hints of the reality, Asia underwent the reverse as British rule was established in India, Burma and Malaya, Holland's in Indonesia, America's in the islands of the South Pacific (Hawaii, Samoa, and later the Philippines) and France's in Indochina. Two new provinces of Western civilization grew in Australia and New Zealand. China underwent yet another cycle of imperial decline but with the new element of "southern barbarians" (the Europeans) and the ambitions of a suddenly modernized Japan.

Three 19th-century wars mark the decline of China's power and prestige. Her attempts to maintain Canton as the sole port for western trade and to end Britain's sale of opium led to the Opium War (1841–42) and a thorough British victory. The Treaty of Nanking opened four further cities to trade and ended the "tribute system," Westerners now accepted as China's equals, with a uniform tariff of 5 percent on trade; in addition Hong Kong was ceded to the United Kingdom. In the aftermath of the war, in 1844 and 1845, the United States gained the right of "extraterritoriality" (exemption from Chinese law) for its citizens, soon extended to all the western states, and the French gained toleration for Catholic Christianity, soon extended to Protestant Christians as well.

The social and economic dislocations caused by the Opium War in south China culminated in the *Taiping Rebellion* (1851–64) led by Hong Xiuquan who, having read some Christian missionary pamphlets, imagined himself to be the younger brother of Jesus Christ. A charismatic figure, he raised a huge army and seized much of southern and central China, including the city of Nanjing. To put down the rebellion the Qing emperor resorted to the very dangerous expedient of allowing provincial governors-general to raise their own military units; these were effective but would prove destabilizing in the future.

At the same time China experienced three other major rebellions: Muslim uprisings in the northwest and in Yunnan Province in the southwest, and the millenarian Nian Rebellion in the north-central plains. Total loss of life from these rebellions exceeded 20 million; the dynasty itself barely survived. In 1858, in the midst of this turmoil, the British provoked a small affray called the Arrow War, settled by the Treaty of Tientsin in 1860. The cost was the opening of yet another 11 ports, the legalization of the opium trade, and the collection of China's customs by Great Britain. Sir Robert Hart became, equivalently, China's finance minister through the years 1863–1908.

Japan's attempt to gain concessions like those of the Western powers and to challenge Chinese control over the Manchu tributary state of Korea led to the Sino-Japanese War (1894-95): China had to cede Taiwan and certain mainland territories to Japan and recognize the independence of Korea, a prelude to that kingdom's incorporation into Japan in 1910. Meanwhile in Indochina the French ignored Manchu protests and established protectorates over Annam (1883) and, right on China's border, Tonkin (1893).

After an unsuccessful attempt in 1898 to reform the imperial government, followed by the abortive, anti-Western Boxer Rebellion (1900) discontent with the feebleness of the Manchu government led to the *Chinese Revolution* (1911). The new Chinese Republic's president, General Yuan Shih-k'ai, might have established yet another new dynasty but his death in 1916 permitted the republic to continue, at least in form. But in reality it was the return of feudal anarchy, this time with modern weapons and mass political organizations. Dr. Sun Yat-sen's party, the Kuo Min Tang (KMT), came after his death under the control of his brother-in-law, Chiang Kai-shek, the warlord who controlled south China and whose armies conquered the north in 1927. But the expelling of the Communists from the KMT in 1927 led to a series of failed Communist uprisings and their retreat to the northwest in *The Long March* In their new stronghold of Yan'an, Mao Zedong (1893–1976) emerged as the party leader and Chiang's chief rival. Their struggle was submerged in the 1930's by the need to oppose Japanese dominance; Japan in 1931–32 occupied Manchuria as a protectorate and invaded China in 1937. The great powers, especially America, kept up the illusion that China was a great power with Chiang its ruler, an illusion blown to pieces within four years after the end of World War II.

Japan's rise to great power status was rooted in extraordinary adaptability. After the American Commodore Matthew Perry forced the opening of Japan to western trade in 1853 and 1854 patriotic sentiment, anti-foreign and pro-imperial, grew until in 1867, young patriots at the court of the emperor Mutsuhito felt strong enough to end the shogunate and restore imperial control. From his reigning name, Meiji, we speak of the *Meiji Restoration*. During his long rule until 1912, Japan embarked on a course of furious imitation of western ways, as earlier they had imitated the Chinese; western science, technology, industry and arms became the basis for attaining the goal of "wealthy land, strong army." The imitation reached the extent of inventing (1884) a Japanese peerage so that there might be an upper house on the British model when the Meiji Constitution (1889) established a Diet.

But it was the military (and industrial) aspects, not the political, that showed most rapid advance, providing the basis for triumphs over China (1895) and much more surprisingly Russia (1905), the takeover of some German holdings in the Pacific during World War I, and the incursions against China in the 1930's. The parliamentarianism of the West was repudiated in the reign of Mutsuhito's grandson Hirohito after 1926 as military cliques and gangs came to control the government became the order of the day. The attack on Hawaii in December 1941 was designed to cripple the American Pacific fleet, protection for the invasion of southeast Asia, which brought Japanese forces by mid-1942 to occupy the American Philippines, the Dutch East Indies, British Hong Kong, Malaya, Singapore and Burma while French Indochina and independent Thailand collaborated. By August 1945, however, this whole proud bubble had burst and Japan itself was occupied by American forces.

In India the British kept up the fiction of Mogul rule but proceeded to act more and more like a sovereign power: building roads and irrigation projects; replacing Persian as the language of law courts with English in the higher courts and local tongues in local courts; founding schools whose curriculum was European and whose language of instruction was English; suppressing, in the 1830's, the funerary suicide of widows, banditry, and murder.

In the 1840's warfare in Afghanistan, in the Sind and against the Sikhs made Britain a true imperial power, the ruling authority in India, protecting Indian princes from aggression, annexing territory when princely families died out. After the *Great Mutiny* (1857–58) of the sepoys, Britain banished the last of the Moguls. Twenty years later came the symbolic climax, the proclamation (1877) of Queen Victoria as *Empress of India*.

But at the same time the British were establishing executive and legislative councils with Indians represented and courts with Indian justices sitting on the bench. And between the world wars, in which Indian troops fought loyally and with valor on the British side, the Indian National Congress, first established in 1885, came increasingly under the influence of Mahatma Gandhi. His campaigns of civil disobedience in 1921 and in 1930, presaged the post-war demands that would signal the end of British rule.

More enduring than British India or British rule in Singapore (1819) or Burma (1886) as vehicles of European influence was Australia, a convict colony founded in 1788 which was gradually transformed by generous land grants into the Commonwealth of Australia (1901) and New Zealand where assisted immigration after 1840 and land grants brought dominion status by 1907.

▶THE COLD WAR AND AFTER (1945–PRESENT)

The wartime alliance of Great Britain, France, the United States, and the Soviet Union was one of expediency rather than long-term mutual interest; suspicion and misunderstandings characterized the alliance even during the war. Soon after the war, hostility and divergent interests between the United States and its Western allies, on the one hand, and the Soviet Union, on the other, led to the Cold War, a period of international danger, distrust, and nuclear standoff, during which direct armed conflict was avoided, but wars fought indirectly by proxy nations and movements were endemic.

As the only major power to emerge from World War II with its population, infrastructure, and economy largely intact, the United States saw itself as the leader of the entire postwar world. Its goals, backed by a monopoly on nuclear weapons, included the rapid reconstruction of Western Europe, the fostering of independent and democratic countries in Eastern Europe, rendering Japan harmless in East Asia, encouraging democratic reform in Nationalist China, and promoting peaceful decolonization in Asia and Africa. The United Nations, organized under American leadership in 1945, was to be the vehicle for a postwar *pax Americana*.

The Soviet Union, devastated by the war, its industrial base and agricultural economy in shambles, reeling from military and civilian casualties that probably exceeded 20 million dead, sought on the other hand to insulate itself behind a band of submissive neighbors, vowing never again to suffer the kind of invasion that Germany had mounted during the war. The Soviet Union also determined to make a concerted effort to match the U.S. in production of nuclear weapons and delivery systems; the resulting arms race eventually resulted in the production of enough nuclear weapons by the two powers to obliterate the entire population of the world. (Beginning in the 1960's, a series of agreements between the U.S. and the U.S.S.R. succeeded in limiting the testing and production of nuclear weapons.)

Sharply differing visions of a desirable postwar world set the stage for a prolonged conflict between America and the Soviet Union. In Europe, the Soviet Union's interpretation of the wartime Yalta agreements enabled it to move rapidly to depose fledgling democratic governments in the Eastern European countries under Soviet Occupation; as early as 1946 Winston Churchill warned that an "Iron Curtain" was being drawn around a Soviet zone in Eastern Europe. Soviet power was made credible with the rapid development of atomic weapons. Pro-U.S.S.R. communist governments were in place in Poland, Czechoslovakia, Hungary, Yugoslavia, Bulgaria, and Romania by 1947. Austria and Finland accepted a neutral status highly deferential to the Soviet Union; communist movements in Italy, Greece and Turkey were defeated with American and British support.

The United States moved rapidly, especially after the development of the Marshall Plan aid program in 1948, to rebuild the economic and political stability of Western Europe in part to counter Soviet expansionism. A Soviet attempt to blockade the Western occupied zone of Berlin was met with the Berlin Airlift, which preserved a Western presence in the city; thereafter West and East Germany became for the balance of the Cold War in effect two separate states. The Berlin Wall was built in 1961 to stem a tide of illegal migration from East to West Germany; its fall in 1989 marked the end of the Cold War. Meanwhile the North Atlantic Treaty Organization (NATO) was founded under American leadership in 1949 as a Soviet-containment strategy; it was countered by the organization of the Eastern-bloc Warsaw Pact in 1955. Later popular anti-Soviet uprisings in Hungary (1956), Czechoslovakia (1968), and Poland (1981) were ruthlessly suppressed.

Part of the European price for bowing to American leadership was American acquiescence in the postwar reconstitution of the old colonial empires of Britain, France, the Netherlands, and others. These colonial empires were gradually relinquished during the course of the Cold War, sometimes peacefully, as with the British African colonies, sometimes after bloody nationalist uprisings, as in Portuguese Africa and the French colonies of Algeria and Vietnam. The United States tended to step into the power-vacuum of the post-colonial world, in large part to forestall Soviet influence. The hysteria of McCarthyism in the early 1950's ushered in a long period of reflexive anti-communism that led America to support corrupt, unpopular and repressive—but anti-communist—regimes in various parts of the Third World.

In Asia, the simmering conflict between Communist and Nationalist forces in China broke out into open civil war by 1946, despite American efforts at mediation. With only grudging material support from the U.S.S.R., Chinese Communists under the leadership of Mao Zedong (1893–1976) defeated the far larger and better equipped Nationalists, whose corruption, ineptitude, and bourgeois orientation proved no match for the simple Communist slogan, "Land to the tiller." The Nationalists retreated to Taiwan in 1948–49, and Mao proclaimed the founding of the People's Republic of China in Beijing on October 1, 1949. A break between the U.S.S.R. and the People's Republic of China in the late 1950's, over both geopolitical and ideological issues, did not alter American policy assumptions of a monolithic international communism until the U.S.-Chinese rapprochement of 1973 under the leadership of Pres. Richard M. Nixon.

In Korea, divided after the war into separate occupation zones, a Soviet-backed government led by the veteran communist Kim Il-sung rapidly took control in the north, whereas in the south an ill-prepared American occupation squandered the opportunity for democratic development, and eventually backed the corrupt right-wing movement of Singman Rhee. When North Korean troops invaded the south on June 25, 1950, the United States successfully obtained United Nations backing to rescue the south; the Korean War ensued, fought to a bloody standoff over the next three years.

The "loss" of China and the Korean war transformed American policy in Japan, which was suddenly seen as the anchor of a democratic and capitalist pro-American security zone surrounding communist Asia. India and Pakistan were similarly wooed by Britain and America. Elsewhere in Asia, communist-inspired uprisings in Malaysia and the Philippines were defeated, while an indigenous anti-communist backlash led to the slaughter of tens of thousands of people in Indonesia in 1965. But it was Vietnam that would prove to be the Asian battleground of the Cold War. After the French withdrawal in 1954, America felt impelled to step in to halt what seemed to be a clear case of international communist subversion of a friendly country; the results were devastating to all concerned.

In Latin America, the 1959 triumph of Fidel Castro's Cuban revolution struck the American government as an unacceptable provocation on its own doorstep. The failed Bay of Pigs invasion of anti-Castro partisans trained by the CIA was a humiliation for American policy (1961). In 1954 the Russians had exploded a hydrogen bomb, and in 1957 Sputnik proclaimed the success of Soviet rocketry; the 1960 U.S. presidential election was held in an atmosphere of fear of Russian nuclear missiles. In 1962 the Cuban Missile Crisis was the most potentially deadly confrontation of the entire Cold War. Emboldened by success in that face-off, America intervened militarily to counter what it regarded as communist subversion in Guatemala, El Salvador, Nicaragua, Grenada, and elsewhere in Latin America.

In Africa, both the U.S. and the U.S.S.R. supported client states in the post-colonial period; America had some success in preserving the unity of the Congo (Zaire) and Nigeria, though at the cost of supporting kleptocratic regimes; the Soviet Union maintained an African presence in Angola and Mozambique (both garrisoned with Cuban troops), among other places.

The Middle East was an area of strong Soviet initiatives throughout the Cold War. With Israel seen as a creature of the United States, its Arab neighbors readily accepted Soviet aid and advice. Britain's inept and humiliating loss of the Suez Canal to Egypt in 1956 bolstered Nasser's socialist regime there, already friendly to Russia for aid in building the Aswan High Dam. Iraq, Syria, and Libya became anti-Israeli Soviet clients, while the U.S. sought support among the more conservative Arab monarchies. Further east, the CIA-sponsored overthrow of the democratic Mossadegh regime in 1953 led to the return to power of the shah; in 1979 his unpopular and autocratic government fell to a fundamentalist Islamic revolution. The subsequent Iran-Iraq war led the U.S. into the anomalous position of supporting the former Soviet client, Iraq's Saddam Hussein.

America's strategy throughout the Cold War had been to use its economic power to intimidate the Soviet bloc militarily and tempt the uncommitted nations of the world commercially. In this sense, the dramatic images of Neil Armstrong walking on the moon on July 20, 1969 were a key element in American Cold War propaganda. Conversely, the image of Americans hastily evacuating Saigon at the end of the Vietnam War were devastating to American interests because it seemed to show American impotence in the face of communist-inspired nationalism, even if the reality of the situation was, of course, much more complicated.

The anti-Soviet rhetoric of Pres. Ronald Reagan in the 1980's seemed like a throwback to the Cold War paranoia of the 1950's, but it seems to have hastened the Cold War's end. With a restless population and a crumbling economy, Russia found itself unable to sustain the military expenditures needed to keep pace with the U.S. in Cold War competition around the world. With the domestic softening of policy of Mikahil Gorbachev's *glasnost* and *perestroika* in the mid-80's, people in Poland, East Germany, Czechoslovakia, and elsewhere in Eastern Europe, and also in the Baltic states, rapidly overthrew their governments and threw out Soviet troops. The fall of the Berlin Wall meant in effect the fall of international communism, and the end of the Cold War.

There was fallout, to be sure, in the Persian Gulf War (1990–91), in the turmoil of the ex-Soviet republics, in the struggle of Africa to emerge from the era of Cold War patronage and great-power rivalry. But in the end the Cold War did not seem to amount to much. For all its espionage and paranoia, all the arms races and space races, all the proxy wars in unhappy countries throughout the world, the Cold War passed away with only a whimper. The U.S. emerged as the only superpower both militarily and economically. The challenges for the future were how to maintain peace around the world, helping poorer nations find prosperity, and still remaining faithful to its ideal of self-determination for all peoples of the world.

In the ensuing years, the U.S. response has centered on efforts to strengthen the world economy and to do so on its own terms by maintaining an overwhelming military dominance. Despite the absence of any serious threat from a large power or a coalition of smaller ones, American military budgets continued to exceed $250 billion a year, sufficient to maintain an advanced weaponry program and to keep 1.5 million men and women on active duty. Russia still had nuclear weapons but its military was in disarray and its economy was near collapse. Only China had a larger military force than the U.S., but it lacked anything like America's air, sea, and nuclear power.

Since 1990, China has been the focal point of U.S. foreign policy and economic strategy. Despite the Chinese government's overt acts of repression and manifest evidence of serious human rights abuses, Presidents Bush and Clinton both aggressively pursued an economic alliance that has benefited both countries. Tens of billions of dollars were invested in China in the 1990's and, not surprisingly, China became the chief supplier of low-cost consumer goods and other items to the U.S. In 1997, China sent exports worth $62 billion to the U.S. but imported only $13 billion. By 2003 China's exports to the U.S. ad soared to $152 bil. and China held over $600 bil. in U.S. treasuries (debt).

During the 1990's, the U.S. and its allies promulgated the idea that democracy and economic freedom are inseparable ideals that only market economy rules can bring to fruition. A central element in this creed is free trade, and the U.S. led the fight to end tariffs and other barriers by helping to establish the World Trade Organization to develop international rules and policies for trade. The W.T.O. grew quickly to 148 nations including China. So successful was the U.S. effort to spur free trade that it's imports far exceeded exports creating a trade deficit that made the future worrisome to many economists. In 1994, the North American Free Trade Agreement ended all trade barriers for Canada, Mexico, and the U.S. In Europe, the European Union moved nations closer to economic integration by regulating trade and in 2002 establishing a single currency—the euro—that would quickly rival the dollar. By 2005 the E.U. had grown to embrace 25 nations and over 400 million people.

Politically the early years of the 21st century were driven by the terrorist attacks of Sept. 11, 2001 against New York's World Trade Center, which killed nearly 3,000 people. Symbolically the Arab-led Muslim terrorist group, Al Qaeda had struck a serious blow against the West but in 2002 it was driven underground by a fierce U.S. attack on its headquarters in Afghanistan. The world applauded this response but then strangely President George W. Bush began to link events of 9–11 to Iraq's Saddam Hussein—left in power after his defeat in 1991 by Bush's father—who was falsely accused of possessing weapons of mass destruction capable of attacking the U.S. Despite pleas from around the world the U.S. invaded Iraq in 2003, and quickly subdued the country. Very poor planning by the U.S. Pentagon, an unexpectedly serious insurgency, and increased violence between rival Muslim groups, led to more than 4,000 U.S. deaths and 30,000 seriously wounded by 2008. A military buildup and new counterinsurgency tactics helped bring order, at least temporarily, in 2008–09, although the Iraqi government remained splintered.

As Bush's term was ending a slowly developing financial crisis came to a head in September 2008, when the large, well-established investment bank, Lehman Brothers collapsed, causing a ripple effect that engulfed the world. The central banks of every major country were forced to inject huge amounts of money into their financial systems to avoid a serious depression. The largest U.S. banks had taken on so much bad debt that the federal government, led by a conservative president, had to prop up such financial giants as Citibank, Goldman Sachs, and Morgan Stanley. Within months, stock markets around the world had plummeted, some by 50 percent or more, trade vitrually ceased, and economic activity came to a standstill. In November 2008, Barack Obama was elected as the first African-American president. He first confronted the financial crisis by pouring ever more cash into the stagnant banking system, providing subsidies to U.S. automakers and extending unemployment benefits. The system appeared to stabilize by mid-year but growth remained illusory. In foreign affairs, President Obama disappointed many of his supporters after beginning a withdrawal process in Iraq only to ratchet up the war in Afghanistan and continuing some of Bush's policies, including detention of terrorism suspects without charges and sending detainees to other countries for interrogation.

Rulers of the World

EMPERORS OF ROME 27 B.C.–A.D. 491

Augustus   27 B.C.–14 A.D.
Tiberius   14–37
Caligula   37–41
Claudius   41–54
Nero   54–68
Galba   68–69
Otho   69
Vitellius   69
Vespasian   69–79
Titus   79–81
Domitian   81–96
Nerva   96–98
Trajan   98–117
Hadrian   117–38
Antoninus Pius   138–61
Marcus Aurelius (co-emperor with
  Lucius Verus)   161–69
Marcus Aurelius alone   169–77
Marcus Aurelius (co-emperor with
  Commodus)   177–80
Commodus alone   180–92
Pertinax   193
Didius Julianus   193

Septimius Severus   193–98
Carcalla (co-emperor with Geta)   211–12
Caracalla alone   212–17
Macrinus   217–18
Heliogabalus   218–22
Severus Alexander   222–35
Maximinus   235–38
Gordian I (co-emperor with Gordian II)   238
Pupienus Maximus (co-emperor with
  Balbinus)   238
Gordian III   238–44
Philip ("The Arab")   244–49
Decius   249–51
Hostilianus   251
Gallus   251–53
Aemilianus   253
Valerian (co-emperor with Gallienus)
  253–60
Gallienus alone   253–68
Claudius II ("Gothicus")   268–70
Aurelian   270–75
Tacitus   275–76
Florianus   276
Probus   276–82
Carus   282–83
Carinus (co-emperor with Numerianus)
  283–84
Carinus alone   284–85

Between 270 and 283, there were seven emperors, all chosen by the army. Carus was killed in battle, and Numerianus died on the march. The other five were murdered by their soldiers. In an attempt to end the chaos of the "barracks emperors," Diocletian attempted to establish an orderly succession in the East and West halves of the Empire, the emperor in the East being the senior emperor. Dicocletian and Maximian both abdicated in 305, although Maximian was recalled in 306. Subsequently, the succession became disputed in both East and West, and between 305 and 474 there were 39 claimants to the imperial title, five of whom ruled both the East and the West, most notably Constantine (324–37). With the demise of the last emperor in the West (476), the eastern emperor, Zeno, reunited the imperial office in one person.

East		West
Diocletian 284–305		Maximian 286–308
Galerius 305–11		Constantius I 305–306
Licinius 311–24		Severus 306–307
		Maximin 307–13
	Constantine I *312–37*	
Constantius II 337–61		Constantine II 337–40
		Constans 340–50
	Constantius II *350–61*	
	Julian *361–63*	
	Jovian *363–64*	
Valens 364–78		Valentinian I 364–75
Theodosius I 378–92		Gratian 375–83
		Valentinian II 385–92
	Theodosius I *392–95*	
Arcadius 395–408		Honorius1 395–423
Theodosius II 408–50		Valentinian III 425–55
Marcian 450–57		Petronius Maximus 455
Leo I 457–74		Avitus 455–56
Leo II 474		Marjorian 457–61
Zeno 474–91		Libius Severus 461–65
		Anthemius 467–72
		Olybrius 472–73
		Glycerius 473–74
		Julius Nepos 474–75
		Romulus Augustus 475–76

Note: Names in **bold italics** ruled in both the East and the West. These lists are designed to make history neater than it was, so they do not reflect the turmoil of the fourth and fifth centuries, when usurpers and pretenders were numerous.
1. Stilicho was regent until 408.

DYNASTIES OF EUROPE

▶THE CAROLINGIANS (751-887)

The first Carolingian king of the Franks was Pepin the Short who usurped the title from the Merovingian line in 751. Taking their dynastic name from Pepin's father, Charles (Carolus) Martel, the Carolingians divided their realm among surviving sons. It was in this family that the papacy revived the Roman imperial title in the year 800. The lists below cover only the major figures and ignore brief reigns and minor claimants.

Pepin the Short, King   751-68
Charlemagne and Carloman   768-71
Charlemagne, King   771-814
Charlemagne, Emperor   800-814
Louis the Pious, Emperor   814-40

West Franks
Charles the Bald   843-77 (Emperor 875-77)
Louis II, the Stammerer   877-879
Louis III   879-82
Carloman   879-84

Lotharingia
Lothair, Emperor   840-55
Louis II, Emperor   855-75
Charles, King of Provence   855-63
Lothair II, King of Lorraine   855-69

East Franks
Louis the German   843-76
Carloman   876-80
Louis   876-82
Charles the Fat   882-87, Emperor (881-87)

▶HOLY ROMAN EMPIRE (962-1806)

The Holy Roman Empire refers to the second medieval "revival" of the Roman Empire in the West, in the year 962. Though drained of most of its power after 1250 and virtually all of its power after 1648, the Empire endured until 1806 when it was abolished by the Emperor Francis II (though he had no power to do so) who thereafter ruled as Francis I of the Austrian Empire which had been founded in 1804. Whatever the power of the Emperor, the title was the most prestigious in all of Europe. Normally the king of Germany was emperor once he was crowned by the pope; in 1356 the Golden Bull established a seven-member electoral college to choose the Emperor but from the 15th century on it was traditional for the electors to choose the Habsburg candidate.

Saxon Dynasty

The dukes of Saxony were most able in combatting the Hungarian menace in the 10th century and thus were chosen kings of Germany. The first was Henry the Fowler (919–936). His son Otto was the first Holy Roman Emperor.

Otto I, King   936, Emperor   962–73
Otto II   973–83
Otto III   983–1002
Henry II   1002–24

Franconian (or Salian) Dynasty

When Henry II died without heirs, Conrad of Franconia (a great-great grandson of Otto I) secured the succession. The dynasty intervened in Rome to reform the papacy, perhaps too successfully, for the popes contended with the emperors for the leadership of the Christian world in the Investiture Controversy (1076–1122). Both the imperial office and the kingship of Germany were greatly weakened by the papal victory.

Conrad II   1024–39
Henry III   1039–56
Henry IV   1056–1106
Henry V   1106–25
Lothair II   1125–37

Hohenstaufen Dynasty

The Hohenstaufen of Swabia were nephews of Henry V but the Church tended to support candidates of the Guelph (also known as Welf) family of Saxony and Bavaria. The struggle of these families and the involvement of the papacy fatally weakened the empire ushering in the "Age of the Princes" in Germany and the "Great Interregnum" in the Empire.

Conrad III   1138–52
Frederick I "Barbarossa"   1152–90
Henry VI   1190–97
Philip of Swabia   1198–1208
Otto IV (Guelph) (anti-king)   1198–1208
Otto IV   1208–12
Frederick II   1212–50
Conrad IV   1250–54
Interregnum   1254–73

When kingship and the imperial office were restored in 1273 the princes refused to establish any one dynasty; for a century and a half candidates from four families were elected.

Rudolf I (Habsburg)   1273–91
Adolf (Nassau)   1292–98
Albert I (Habsburg)   1298–1308
Henry VII (Luxemburg)   1308–13
Louis IV (Wittelsbach)   1314–46
Charles IV (Luxemburg)   1346–78
Wenceslas (Luxemburg)   1378–1400
Rupert (Wittelsbach)   1400–1410
Sigismund (Luxemburg)   1410–37

The Habsburgs

The House of Habsburg (the name is a contraction of the name of their castle, Habichtsburg, in Switzerland) was the most illustrious of the European dynasties. From the 15th century they became hereditary rulers of the Empire and through a series of brilliant marriages gained, by inheritance, the Netherlands, the Spanish kingdoms and Spain's empire in the New World, and Hungary and Bohemia. (From the reign of Francis I, the official family name is Habsburg-Lorraine.)

Albert II   1440–93
Frederick III   1440–93
Maximilian I   1493–1519
Charles V   1519–56
Ferdinand I   1556–64
Maximilian II   1564–76
Rudolf II   1576–1612
Matthias   1612–19
Ferdinand II   1619–37
Ferdinand III   1637–57
Leopold I   1658–1705
Joseph I   1705–11
Charles VI   1711–40
Interregnum   1740–42
Charles VII   1742–45
Francis I   1745–65
Joseph II   1765–90
Leopold II   1790–92
Francis II   1792–1806

▶DYNASTIES OF FRANCE (987–1848)

In 987 the West Frankish nobles elected as their king Hugh Capet. His descendants ruled France continuously until the French Revolution and again from 1814 until 1848. The direct line died out in 1328, and the collateral *Valois* branch of the Capetian family succeeded. The Valois ruled with difficulty, as the Hundred Years' War (1337–1453) blighted the beginning and the Wars of Religion (1562–98) the end of their rule. The last three Valois produced no male heirs so the throne passed to the victor in the Wars of Religion, Henry of Navarre (a distant cousin in the male line of Louis IX), who began the reign of the *Bourbon* branch of the Capetians. (After 1700, the Bourbon family became, with many interruptions, kings of Spain.)

Direct Capetians
Hugh Capet   987–96
Robert II the Pious   996–1031
Henry I   1031–60
Philip I   1060–1108
Louis VI   1108–37
Louis VII   1137–80
Philip II Augustus   1180–1223
Louis VIII   1223–26
Louis IX   1226–70
Philip III   1270–85
Philip IV   1285–1314
Louis X   1314–16
John I the Posthumous   1316
Philip V   1316–22
Charles IV   1322–28

Valois Branch
Philip VI   1328–50
John   1350–64
Charles V   1364–80
Charles VI   1380–1422
Charles VII   1422–61
Louis XI   1461–83
Charles VIII   1483–98
Louis XII (Valois-Orléans)   1498–1515
Francis I (Valois-Angoulême)   1515–47
Henry II   1547–59
Francis II   1559–60
Charles IX   1560–74
Henry III   1574–89

Bourbon Branch
Henry IV   1589–1610
Louis XIII   1610–43
Louis XIV   1643–1715
Louis XV   1715–74
Louis XVI   1774–92
French Revolution and Napoleon
   1792–1814

Restored Bourbons
Louis XVIII   1814–24
Charles X   1824–30
Louis Philippe (Bourbon-Orléans)
   1830–48

▶DYNASTIES OF ENGLAND (871–PRESENT)

Saxons
With the end of Roman rule, seven Germanic kingdoms emerged in England. The leader of the resistance to the Vikings was Alfred the Great of Wessex (871–99) who began a reconquest of the island and is considered the first true king of England; his dynasty, with interruptions, continued until the Norman Conquest in 1066.

Alfred the Great   871–99
Edward the Elder   899–924
Aethelstan   924–39
Edmund   939–46
Eadred   946–55
Eadwig   955–59
Edgar   959–75
Edward   975–78
Aethelred "the Unready"   978–1016
Edmund Ironside   1016
Canute   (of   Denmark,   by   conquest)   1016–35
Harold Harefoot   1035–40
Hardicanute (of Denmark)   1040–42
Edward the Confessor   1042–66
Harold Godwinson   1066

Normans
Duke William of Normandy, a cousin of Edward the Confessor, made good his claim to the throne by conquest, bringing with him highly organized Continental feudalism and the French tongue, which so enriched the English language.

William the Conqueror   1066–87
William II   1087–1100
Henry I   1100–1135
Stephen   1135–54

Angevins (Plantagenets)
The grandson of Henry I was Henry of Anjou, who, by marrying the heiress Eleanor of Aquitaine, assembled for his family the greatest feudal state in 12th century Europe. In 1154 he established his family on the throne of England as well; the direct line continued until 1399, when Richard II was deposed and killed by his first cousin, who then ruled as Henry IV and established the *Lancastrian Dynasty*. Another branch of the family, with a stronger claim than the usurping Lancastrians, contested the succession in the War of the Roses and after 1461 ruled briefly as the *Yorkist Dynasty*.

Henry II   1154–89
Richard I   1189–99
John I   1199–1216
Henry III   1216–72
Edward I   1272–1307
Edward II   1307–27
Edward III   1327–77
Richard II   1377–99

Lancastrian Kings
Henry IV   1399–1413
Henry V   1413–22
Henry VI   1422–61

Yorkist Kings
Edward IV   1461–83
Edward V   1483
Richard III   1483–85

Tudors
An obscure Welsh family and adherents of the Lancastrian line, the Tudors became champions of the faction supporting them. Richard III died in battle at Bosworth Field against Henry Tudor, who usurped the throne, ruling as Henry VII and founding the dynasty that brought the Reformation to England.

Henry VII   1485–1509
Henry VIII   1509–47
Edward VI   1547–53
Mary I   1553–58
Elizabeth I   1558–1603

Stuarts

Elizabeth never married and had no heirs, so the Tudor line died with her. Rule passed to Elizabeth's cousin, James VI of Scotland who ruled in England as James I. Serious troubles with the Puritans and Parliament twice turned the Stuarts from the throne: Charles I was beheaded and James II was betrayed by his daughters and the husband of one, William of Orange.

James I   1603–25
Charles I   1625–49
Interregnum—Oliver Cromwell   1649–58
Richard Cromwell   1658–59
Charles II   1660–85
James II   1685–88
William III and Mary II   1689–94
William III alone   1694–1702
Anne   1702–14

Hanoverians and Windsors

Queen Anne had 17 children but died without leaving an heir. Geneological and religious considerations (Anne's brother "James III," the Catholic pretender, was still alive) brought to the throne the German House of Hanover. After the reign of Victoria, the family is Saxe-Coburg-Gotha but in 1917, for political reasons, George V changed the name to Windsor.

George I   1714–27
George II   1727–60
George III   1760–1820
George IV   1820–30
William IV   1830–37
Victoria   1837–1901
Edward VII   1901–10
George V   1910–36
Edward VIII   1936
George VI   1936–52
Elizabeth II   1952–present

▶DYNASTIES OF SPAIN (1506–PRESENT)

Until 1808 there was no kingdom called Spain but a number of separate kingdoms of which Castile and Aragon were only the principal ones. With the deaths of Isabella, then Ferdinand, the crowns passed to their grandson, the Habsburg Charles of Ghent; in the Empire he was Charles V, in the Spanish kingdoms Charles I. His *Habsburg Dynasty* ruled until 1700, when the line died out and was replaced by the *Bourbon Dynasty*, which has ruled with numerous interruptions until the present day.

Habsburgs

Charles I (Holy Roman Emperor as Charles V)   1506–56
Philip II   1556–98
Philip III   1598–1621
Philip IV   1621–65
Charles II   1665–1700

Bourbons

Philip V   1700–1746
Ferdinand VI   1746–59
Charles III   1759–88
Charles IV   1788–1808
Joseph Bonaparte   1808–13

Ferdinand VII   1814–33
Isabella II   1833–68
Interregnum   1868–70
Amadeo   1870–73
Republic   1873–75
Alphonso XII   1875–85
Alphonso XIII   1886–1931
Republic   1931–36
Civil War   1936–39
Franco regime   1939–75
Juan Carlos   1975–present

▶AUSTRIAN HABSBURGS (1792–1918)

When Charles V retired, his worldwide empire was divided into two parts, one Spanish, one Austrian. The Austrian branch always supplied the Holy Roman Emperors except during the reign of Maria Theresa (1740–80) when Charles Albert of Bavaria, then her husband and son held the imperial title. In 1804 Emperor Francis II proclaimed an Austrian Empire, which he ruled as Francis I; two years later he abolished the Holy Roman Empire.

Francis II & I   1792–1835
Ferdinand I   1835–48
Francis Joseph   1848–1916
Charles I   1916–18

▶HOHENZOLLERN DYNASTY (1640–1918)

For centuries the Hohenzollern were electors of Brandenburg in northeastern Germany. In 1701, with permission of the emperor, they took the royal titles King in Prussia. (Prussia was a duchy of Poland, which the family inherited in 1618.) In 1871 they added the title German Emperor. Both titles disappeared with Germany's loss in World War I.

Frederick William, the Great Elector   1640–88
Frederick III, Elector of Brandenburg   1688–1701
Frederick I, King of Prussia   1701–13
Frederick William I   1713–40
Frederick II   1740–86
Frederick William II   1786–97
Frederick William III   1797–1840
Frederick William IV   1840–61
William I (German Emperor after 1871)   1861–88
Frederick III   1888
William II   1888–1918

▶ROMANOV DYNASTY (1613–1917)

At the end of Russia's "time of troubles" early in the 17th century, the national assembly elected Michael Romanov as czar in 1613. The dynasty died out in 1762, when at the death of czarina Elizabeth, her nephew Peter III briefly succeeded. His family ruled until the Russian Revolution. Their name was Holstein-Gottorp but ruled under the name Romanov.

Michael   1613–45
Alexius   1645–76
Theodore III   1676–82
Ivan V and Peter I   1682–89
Peter I, the Great, alone   1689–1725
Catherine I   1725–27
Peter II   1727–30
Anna   1730–40
Ivan VI   1740–41
Elizabeth   1741–62
Peter III   1762
Catherine II the Great   1762–96
Paul   1796–1801
Alexander I   1801–25

Nicholas I   1825–55
Alexander II   1855–81
Alexander III   1881–94
Nicholas II   1894–1917

▶HOUSE OF SAVOY-CARIGNANO (1861–1946)

The dukes of Savoy ruled in a personal union Piedmont, Nice, and Sardinia until 1831, when the line died out and a distant cousin, Charles Albert came to the throne. It was his son, Victor Emmanuel II of Savoy whose armies conquered the rest of Italy over the years 1858–71 and who was proclaimed King of Italy in 1861. The dynasty fell with the end of the Second World War.

Victor Emmanuel II   1861–78
Humbert I   1878–1900
Victor Emmanuel III   1900–46
Humbert II   1946

THE DYNASTIES AND EMPERORS OF CHINA

Dates for the Xia and Shang Dynasties, and for the beginning of the Zhou Dynasty, are uncertain. Rulers of these three dynasties were known as kings (*wang*); only a few notable individuals are listed below. The title "emperor" (*huangdi*) was instituted with the Qin Dynasty. As is customary, names of emperors prior to A.D. 1368 are given in the form of their posthumous "temple names" (*miaohao*); names of emperors for the Ming and Qing Dynasties are given as their reign-title names (*nianhao*).

Xia Dynasty   c. 1875–1550 B.C.
Yü the Great (legendary?)   c. 1875–1850 B.C.
King Jie   c. 1560–1550 B.C.

Shang Dynasty   c. 1550–1055 B.C.
Tang the Victorious   c. 1550–1500 B.C.
King Zhou   c. 1070–1055 B.C.

Zhou Dynasty   c. 1055–256 B.C.
Western Zhou Period   c. 1055–771 B.C.
King Wen (pre-conquest)   c. 1060–1055 B.C.
King Wu   c. 1055–1048 B.C.
Duke of Zhou, regent for
King Cheng   c. 1048–1011 B.C.
Era of the Spring and Autumn Annals 722–481 B.C.
Warring States Period   481–256 B.C.

Qin Dynasty   221–206 B.C.
Shihuangdi   221–209 B.C.
Erhuangdi   209–207 B.C.

Han Dynasty   206 B.C.–A.D. 220
Western or Former Han   206 B.C.–A.D. 9
Gaozu   206–195 B.C.
Huidi   195–188 B.C.
Gaohou (Empress Lü)   188–180 B.C.
Wendi   180–157 B.C.
Jingdi   157–141 B.C.
Wudi   141–87 B.C.
Zhaodi   87–74 B.C.

Xuandi   74–48 B.C.
Yuandi   48–33 B.C.
Chengdi   33–7 B.C.
Aidi   7–1 B.C.
Pingdi   1 B.C. –A.D. 6
Wang Mang (usurper)   A.D. 9–23
Eastern or Latter Han   A.D. 23–220
Guangwudi   25–57
Mingdi   57–75
Zhangdi   75–88
Hedi   88–105
Shangdi   105
Andi   106–25
Shaodi   125
Shundi   125–44
Chongdi   144–45
Zhidi   145–46
Huandi   146–68
Lingdi   168–89
Shaodi   189
Xiandi   189–220

Period of Disunion
The fall of the Han Dynasty ushered in a period of 369 years of disunion during which no dynasty succeeded in bringing all of China under its control This period is divided into the brief Three Kingdoms Period and the longer Period of Northern and Southern Dynasties, of which only the three most important dynasties are listed below.

Three Kingdoms   220–65
Kingdom of Shu Han   220–64
Kingdom of Wei   220–65
Kingdom of Wu   220–65

Period of Northern and Southern Dynasties   265–589
Western Jin Dynasty   265–317
Eastern Jin Dynasty   317–419
Northern Wei Dynasty   424–535

Sui Dynasty   589–618
Wendi   589–604
Yangdi   604–17
Gongdi   617–18

Tang Dynasty   618–907
Gaozu   618–26
Taizong   626–49
Gaozong   649–83
Zhongzong   683–84
Ruizong   684–90
Wuhou   690–705
Zhongzong   705–10
Ruizong   710–12
Xuanzong   712–56
Suzong   756–62
Taizong   762–79
Dezong   779–805
Shunzong   805
Xianzong   805–20
Muzong   820–24
Jingzong   824–26
Wenzong   826–40
Wuzong   840–46
Xuanzong   846–59
Yizong   859–73
Xizong   873–88
Zhaozong   888–904
Jingzong   904–7

Five Dynasties 907–60

Song Dynasty 960–1279
Northern Song 960–1127
Taizu 960–76
Taizong 976–97
Zhenzong 997–1022
Renzong 1022–63
Yingzong 1063–67
Shenzong 1067–85
Zhezong 1085–1100
Huizong 1100–1125
Qinzong 1125–27
Southern Song 1127–1279
Gaozong 1127–62
Xiaozong 1162–89
Guangzong 1189–94
Ningzong 1194–1224
Lizong 1224–64
Duzong 1264–74
Gongzong 1274–76
Duanzong 1276–79

Yuan (Mongol) Dynasty 1279–1368
Shizu (Kubilai Khan) 1260–94
Chengzong (Temür) 1294–1307
Wuzong (Khaishan) 1307–11
Renzong (Buyantu) 1311–20
Yingzong (Sudhipela) 1320–23
Taiding (Yesen-Temür) 1323–28
Mingzong (Asikipa) 1328

Wenzong (Tog-Temür) 1328–33
Xunzong (Toghon-Temür) 1333–68

Ming Dynasty 1368–1644
Hongwu 1368–98
Jianwen 1398–1402
Yongle 1402–24
Hongxi 1424–25
Xuande 1425–35
Zhengtong 1435–49
Jingtai 1449–57
Tianshun 1457–64
Chenghua 1464–87
Hongzhi 1487–1505
Zhengde 1505–21
Jiaqing 1521–66
Wanli 1572–1620
Taichang 1620
Tianzhi 1620–27
Chongzhen 1627–44

Qing Dynasty 1644–1911
Shunzhi 1644–61
Kangxi 1661–1722
Yongzheng 1722–35
Qianlong 1735–96
Jiaqing 1796–1820
Daoguang 1820–50
Xianfeng 1850–61
Tongzhi 1861–75
Guangxu 1875–1908
Puyi 1908–11

CHRONOLOGICAL LISTING OF THE POPES

Peter, Apostle d. c. 64
Linus c.66–c.78
Anacletus c.79–c.91
Clement I c.91–c.101
Evaristus c.100–c.109
Alexander I c.109–c.116
Sixtus I c.116–c.125
Telesphorus c.125–c.136
Hyginus c.138–c.142
Pius I c.142–c.155
Anicetus c.155–c.166
Soter c.166–c.174
Eleutherius, or Eleutherus
    c.174–89
Victor I 189–98
Zephyrinus 198/9–217
Callistus I (often Calixtus)
    217–22
Hippolytus (antipope) 217–35
Urban I 222–30
Pontian 230–35
Anterus 235–36
Fabian 236–50
Cornelius 251–53
Novatian (antipope) 251–58
Lucius I 253–54
Stephen I 254–57
Sixtus II 257–58
Dionysius 260–68
Felix I 269–74
Eutychian 275–83
Gaius, or Caius 283–96
Marcellinus 296–304?
Marcellus I 306–8
Eusebius 310
Miltiades, or Melchiades
    311–31
Silvester I 314–35
Mark 336

Julius I 337–52
Liberius 352–66
Felix II (antipope)[1] 355–65
Damasus I 366–84
Ursinus (antipope) 366–67
Siricius 384–99
Anastasius I 399–401
Innocent I 401–17
Zosimus 417–18
Eulalius (antipope) 418–19
Boniface I 418–22
Celestine I 422–32
Sixtus (Xystus) III 432–40
Leo I 440–61
Hilarus 461–68
Simplicius 468–83
Felix III[1] 483–92
Gelasius I 492–96
Anastasius II 496–98
Symmachus 498–514
Lawrence (antipope) 498–99,
    501–6
Hormisdas 514–23
John I 523–26
Felix III[1] 526–30
Dioscorus (antipope) 530
Boniface II 530–32
John II 533–35
Agapitus I 535–36
Silverius 536–37
Vigilius 537–55
Pelagius I 556–61
John III 561–74
Benedict I 575–79
Pelagius II 579–90
Gregory I 590–604
Sabinian 604–6
Boniface III 607
Boniface IV 608–15

Deusdedit (later Adeodatus I)
    615–18
Boniface V 619–25
Honorius I 625–38
Severinus 640
John IV 640–42
Theodore I 642–49
Martin I 649–53
Eugene I 654–57
Vitalian 657–72
Adeodatus II 672–76
Donus 676–78
Agatho 678–81
Leo II 682–83
Benedict II 684–85
John V 685–86
Conon 686–87
Theodore (antipope) 687
Paschal (antipope) 687
Sergius I 687–701
John VI 701–5
John VII 705–7
Sisinnius 708
Gregory II 715–31
Gregory III 731–41
Zacharias 741–52
Stephen (II)[2] 752
Stephen II (III)[2] 752–57
Paul I 757–67
Constantine (antipope) 767–68
Philip (antipope) 768
Stephen III (IV)[2] 768–72
Hadrian I 772–95
Leo III 795–816
Stephen IV (V)[2] 816–17
Paschal I 817–24
Eugene II 824–27
Valentine 827
Gregory IV 827–44

John (antipope)   844
Sergius II   844–47
Leo IV   847–55
Benedict III   855–58
*Anastasius Bibliothecarius
(antipope)*   855
Nicholas I   858–67
Hadrian II   867–72
John VIII   872–82
Marinus I   882–84
Hadrian III   884–85
Stephen V (VI)[2]   885–91
Formosus   891–96
Boniface VI   896
Stephen VI (VII)[2]   896–97
Romanus   897
Theodore II   897
John IX   898–900
Benedict IV   900–903
Leo V   903
Christopher (antipope)   903–4
Sergius III   904–11
Anastasius III   911–13
Lando   913–14
John X   914–28
Leo VI   928
Stephen VII (VIII)[2]   928–31
John XI   931–36?
Leo VII   936–39
Stephen VIII (IX)[2]   939–42
Marinus II   942–46
Agapitus II   946–55
John XII   955–64
Leo VIII   963–65
Benedict V   964
John XIII   965–72
Benedict VI   973–74
Boniface VII (antipope)   974,
   984–85
Benedict VII   974–83
John XIV   983–84
John XV   985–96
Gregory V   996–99
John XVI (antipope)   997–98
Silvester II   999–1003
John XVII   1003
John XVIII   1003–1009
Sergius IV   1009–12
Benedict VIII   1012–24
Gregory (VI) (antipope)   1012
John XIX   1024–32
Benedict IX   1032–44, 1045,
   1047–48
Silvester III   1045
Gregory VI   1045–46
Clement II   1046–47
Damasus II   1048
Leo IX   1049–54
Victor II   1055–57
Stephen IX (X)[2]   1057–58
Benedict X (antipope)
   1058–59
Nicholas II   1058–61
Alexander II   1061–73
Honorius (II) (antipope)
   1061–64
Gregory VII   1073–85
Clement III (antipope)   1080,
   1084–1100
Victor III   1086–87

Urban II   1088–99
Paschal II   1099–1118
Theoderic (antipope)
   1100–1101
Albert or Adalbert (antipope)
   1101
Silvester IV (antipope)
   1105–11
Gelasius II   1118–19
Gregory (VIII) (antipope)
   1118–21
Callistus II   1119–24
Celestine (II)   1124
Honorius II   1124–30
Innocent II   1130–43
Anacletus II (antipope)
   1130–38
Victor IV (antipope)   1138
Celestine II   1143–44
Lucius II   1144–45
Eugene III   1145–53
Anastasius IV   1153–54
Hadrian IV   1154–59
Alexander III   1159–81
Victor IV (antipope)[3]   1159–64
Paschal III (antipope)   1164–68
Callistus (III) (antipope)
   1168–78
Innocent (III) (antipope)
   1179–80
Lucius III   1181–85
Urban III   1185–87
Gregory VIII   1187
Clement III   1187–91
Celestine III   1191–98
Innocent III   1198–1216
Honorius III   1216–27
Gregory IX   1227–41
Celestine IV   1241
Innocent IV   1243–54
Alexander IV   1254–61
Urban IV   1261–64
Clement IV   1265–68
Gregory X   1271–76
Innocent V   1276
Hadrian V   1276
John XXI   1276–77
Nicholas III   1277–80
Martin IV   1281–85
Honorius IV   1285–87
Nicholas IV   1288–92
Celestine V   1294
Boniface VIII   1294–1303
Benedict XI   1303–4
Clement V   1305–14
John XXII   1316–34
Nicholas (V) (antipope)
   1328–30
Benedict XII   1334–42
Clement VI   1342–52
Innocent VI   1352–62
Urban V   1362–70
Gregory XI   1370–78
Urban VI   1378–89
Clement (VII) (antipope)
   1378–94
Boniface IX   1389–1404
Benedict (XIII) (antipope)
   1394–1417
Innocent VII   1404–6

Gregory XII   1406–15
Alexander V (antipope)
   1409–10
John (XXIII) (antipope)
   1410–15
Martin V   1417–31
Clement (VIII) (antipope)
   1423–29
Benedict (XIV) (antipope)
   1425–?
Eugene IV   1431–47
Felix V (antipope)   1439–49
Nicholas V   1447–55
Callistus III   1455–58
Pius II   1458–64
Paul II   1464–71
Sixtus IV   1471–84
Innocent VIII   1484–92
Alexander VI   1492–1503
Pius III   1503
Julius II   1503–13
Leo X   1513–21
Hadrian VI   1522–23
Clement VII   1523–34
Paul III   1534–49
Julius III   1550–55
Marcellus II   1555
Paul IV   1555–59
Pius IV   1559–65
Pius V   1566–72
Gregory XIII   1572–85
Sixtus V   1585–90
Urban VII   1590
Gregory XIV   1590–91
Innocent IX   1591
Clement VIII   1592–1605
Leo XI   1605
Paul V   1605–21
Gregory XV   1621–23
Urban VIII   1623–44
Innocent X   1644–55
Alexander VII   1655–67
Clement IX   1667–69
Clement X   1670–76
Innocent XI   1676–89
Alexander VIII   1689–91
Innocent XII   1691–1700
Clement XI   1700–21
Innocent XIII   1721–24
Benedict XIII   1724–30
Clement XII   1730–40
Benedict XIV   1740–58
Clement XIII   1758–69
Clement XIV   1769–74
Pius VI   1775–99
Pius VII   1800–23
Leo XII   1823–29
Pius VIII   1829–30
Gregory XVI   1831–46
Pius IX   1846–78
Leo XIII   1878–1903
Pius X   1903–14
Benedict XV   1914–22
Pius XI   1922–39
Pius XII   1939–58
John XXIII   1958–63
Paul VI   1963–78
John Paul I   1978
John Paul II   1978–2005
Benedict XVI   2005–present

Note: Antipopes, listed in italics, were appointed in opposition to the one canonically chosen by the college of cardinals, usually by a prince, king, or emperor. 1. Because Felix II was an antipope, subsequent Felixes were sometimes misnumbered. 2. Although elected and installed as pope, Stephen (II) died before his consecration. Though the Vatican's Annuario Pontificio has excluded him from the official list of popes since 1961, subsequent Stephens have a dual numbering. 3. He should have been Victor V, but he used Victor IV because the previous Victor IV's tenure (1138) as antipope was largely ignored.

World Geography

Geography, in the broadest sense, is the systematic study of the Earth, its physical makeup (oceans, rivers, continents, islands, climate, etc.), and how those elements affect the way humans organize their societies and live productive lives. More specifically geographers examine human populations and population distribution by region and by urban and rural segmentation; political systems; and economic structures such as agriculture, the trade industry , and transportation. The elements that have the greatest impact on human life are: the atmosphere (the air, and in particular climate and weather); the hydrosphere (oceans, lakes, and rivers); the lithosphere (the Earth's crust, the surface of which is the land and the ocean floor); and the biosphere (that part of the atmosphere, lithosphere, and hydrosphere inhabited by living things).

First-order features of the Earth's geography are the continents and the oceans. Second-order continental features include mountain ranges, valleys, plains, and deserts. Third-order features include mountains and valleys. The boundaries of continents and oceans are affected by long-term global changes such as glaciation. During an ice age, much of the globe's water is frozen in ice on land, and sea levels drop accordingly. During the last ice age, which ended about 11,500 years ago, the oceans were about 100 meters (328 ft.) lower than they are today. At that time, the now submerged Bering land bridge connected Asia and North America.

▶ GLOSSARY OF GEOGRAPHICAL WORDS AND TERMS

(See also "Part IV: Science and Technology, Composition of the Earth".)

Altitude The height of a place or thing, usually measured from sea level or the surface of the land.

Archipelago A cluster of islands.

Arctic Circle An imaginary line drawn along approximately latitude 66°30'N. The climate north of the Arctic Circle is very cold, and relatively few people live there.

Atmosphere The mass of air that extends outward from the surface of the earth into space. The atmosphere is divided into four layers: the troposphere, in which temperature decreases as altitude increases; the stratosphere, in which temperature is constant, then increases; the mesosphere, in which it decreases; and the thermosphere, in which it increases again.

Atoll A coral reef that partially or completely surrounds a lagoon.

Basin A portion of land that is lower than the surrounding area. Basins are created when vertical movement causes the earth's crust to warp. Also, the area drained by a river and its tributaries.

Bay Part of an ocean, sea, or other body of water which extends inland. Bays are generally smaller than gulfs.

Bight A bay formed by a bend in the coastline.

Caldera A huge crater formed when the top of a volcano collapses or is exploded away.

Canyon A narrow, deep valley with steep sides. Many canyons have a river on their floor.

Climate General weather conditions over a long period. (See "Climates of the World.")

Continent A large unbroken land mass, distinguished from an island or peninsula. The seven continents are North America, South America, Europe, Asia, Africa, Australia, and Antarctica, though Europe and Asia are a continuous land mass divided along the spine of the Ural Mountains running south from the Arctic Ocean.

Continental drift theory The theory, proposed in 1915 by Alfred Wegener, that all of the continents used to be joined in one supercontinent, Pangaea. Some 200 million years ago Pangaea began to break up, and the continents drifted through the oceans to their present locations. The continental drift theory has now largely been replaced by the plate tectonics theory. (See "Earth Sciences.")

Continental shelf The edge of a continent covered by shallow ocean water, up to about 100 fathoms (600 feet), beyond which is the continental slope, which decends to the deep-sea plain, about 13,000–20,000 feet (4,000–6,000 m).

Cove A small and sheltered bay or inlet. Also, a small valley in a mountain.

Crater The bowl-shaped depression at the top of a volcano. Also, the depression made when a meteorite hits the earth. (See also *Caldera*).

Delta A triangular-shaped piece of land formed by sediment at the mouth of a river.

Desert (See "The Great Deserts.")

Dune A hill or ridge of sand that has been deposited by wind.

Equator An imaginary line circling earth halfway between the poles. The equator is at latitude 0°.

Equinox The two times during the year (on or about March 21 and September 23) when the sun's rays strike the equator vertically. At equinox, day and night are the same length everywhere in the world. (See also *Solstice*.)

Erosion The gradual wearing away of the surface of the land. For example, soil is eroded by wind and water; rock is eroded by freezing and thawing.

Estuary A valley at the mouth of a river where fresh water and sea water mix. Estuaries are created either when the land sinks or when the sea level rises, and are generally shaped like a funnel.

Fjord A long, narrow inlet of the ocean with steeply sloping sides.

Floodplain Flat, low-lying land along either side of a river that is subject to flooding.

Geyser A jet of hot water or steam periodically thrown up by a hot spring.

Glacier A large mass of slowly moving ice. Glaciers are formed on land when snow is compacted and recrystallizes.

Gorge An especially narrow and steep-walled canyon.

Gulf Part of an ocean or sea that extends inland. Gulfs are generally larger than bays.

Hemisphere One half of the Earth's surface, however it is divided. For example, the Northern Hemisphere lies north of the equator; the Southern Hemisphere, south of the equator. By convention, the Eastern Hemisphere consists of the continents of Europe, Asia, and Africa; the Western Hemisphere, of North America and South America.

Inlet   An indentation in the shore of a sea or an ocean or in the bank of a river. Also, a narrow waterway which connects a lagoon to a larger body of water or which passes between two peninsulas.

Island   A land mass completely surrounded by water.

Isthmus   A narrow strip of land that connects two larger land masses.

Lagoon   A shallow pool or pond completely or almost completely separated from the sea.

Lake   A body of water, often of considerable size, surrounded by land.

Latitude and Longitude   Latitude is the angle (measured in degrees, minutes, and seconds) between a point on the Earth's surface north or south of the equator, the center of the Earth, and the equator (0°0'0 latitude). Longitude is the angle between a point on the Earth's surface, the center of the Earth, and the prime meridian (0°0'0 longitude). There are 90° of latitude between the equator and each of the poles (shown on a globe as parallel horizontal lines). There are 360° of longitude (shown as vertical lines) divided into 180° east and west of the prime meridian (180°E and 180°W are thus the same). Since 1884, Greenwich, England (near London), has been universally recognized as the point through which the prime meridien passes. A degree (°) is 1/360 of a circle, a minute (') 1/60 of a degree, and a second (") 1/60 of a minute.

Lava   Magma which reaches the surface of the Earth and from which most of the gases have escaped. (See also *Magma, Volcano*).

Leeward   The direction or side sheltered from the wind. (See also *Windward*).

Magma   Molten rock that lies deep within the earth. In a volcanic eruption, magma bursts through the outer surface of the Earth's crust. (See also *Lava, Volcano*).

Mountain   Land that rises above its surroundings. Mountains are higher than hills. Older mountain ranges, like the Appalachians, are rounded because they are old and worn down; younger ranges, like the Andes and the Himalayas, have jagged peaks because they are still rising.

North Pole   The northernmost point of the Earth's axis, at latitude 90°N. From this point, the only direction is south. It is entirely surrounded by water, and usually covered by ice. The first successful expedition to the North Pole—there is some doubt as to whether they actually reached

the pole—was led by by Adm. Robert E. Peary, Apr. 6, 1909.

Ocean   (See "Oceans of the World.")

Peninsula   A portion of land surrounded by water on three sides.

Plain   A large portion of level or rolling land which is treeless.

Plate tectonics theory   The theory, first proposed in 1968, that Earth's crust is made up of 20 sections or plates, each of which consists of continental and ocean crust. The plates shift, moving continents, changing the size and shape of oceans, causing earthquakes, and creating volcanos and mountains. The plate tectonics theory has largely replaced the continental drift theory.

Plateau   A portion of land, generally large and with a level surface, which is sharply elevated above the surrounding land. Plateaus are created when vertical movement causes the Earth's crust to warp.

Pond   A small body of water surrounded by land.

Prairie   Level or rolling land generally covered with grasses, with few trees.

Rain shadow   An area on the leeward side of a mountain range which receives little rainfall.

River   A large stream.

Sahel   The Arabic word for shore, the Sahel is a dry region separating the Sahara from tropical West Central Africa running from Senegal to Sudan. The meager rainfall (4–8 inches per year) supports limited crops and grazing.

Savanna   A portion of land in the tropics or subtropics with only scattered trees but whose grasses can survive with scant rainfall.

Sea   A large body of saltwater, generally considered smaller than an ocean.

Solstice   The time when the sun's rays strike vertically the Tropic of Cancer or the Tropic of Capricorn. At solstice, the daylight hours reach their maximum or minimum. In the Northern Hemisphere, for example, summer solstice occurs on or about June 22; that is the longest day of the year and signals the beginning of summer. The winter solstice occurs on or about December 22; that is the shortest day of the year and signals the beginning of winter. In the Southern Hemisphere, the longest and shortest days of the year occur on December 22 and June 22, respectively. (See also *Equinox*).

Sound   A body of water that separates an island from the mainland, or that connects two oceans, seas, or other bodies of water. Sounds are generally long and narrow.

World Land Area and Population by Selected Region

	Land Area			Population		
Region	Square miles	Square kilometers	Percent of world total	Total ('000s)	Percent of world total	Per square kilometer
World total[1]	57,308,738	148,429,000	100.0%	6,908,688	100.0%	51
Africa	11,608,156	30,065,000	20.3	1,033,043	15.0	34
Antarctica	5,404,000[3]	14,000,000[3]	9.4	[2]	[2]	[2]
Asia	17,212,041	44,579,000	30.0	4,166,741	60.3	131
Australia	2,967,966	7,687,000	5.2	25,815	0.4	3
Europe	3,837,082	9,938,000	6.7	732,759	10.6	32
North America	9,365,290	24,256,000	16.3	351,659	5.1	16
South America	6,879,952	17,819,000	12.0	393,221	5.7	22

Notes: 1. Land only. Includes small islands not shown separately. 2. Antarctica has no indigenous population. 3. In 2008 and 2009, hundreds of square miles of ice dropped from the Antarctic shelf. **Sources:** *National Geographic Atlas of the World* (1995); U.S. Census Bureau, mid-year 2000 population estimates, United Nations Population Division, Population Database, *World Population Prospects*, 2008 revision.

South Pole The southernmost point of the Earth's axis, at 90°S. First reached by Norwegian explorer Roald Admundsen in 1911, the South Pole lies in the South Polar region.

Steppe A portion of land with little rainfall, extreme temperature variations, and drought-resistant vegetation.

Strait A narrow body of water that connects two large bodies of water.

Stream Any body of running water that flows on or under the surface of the Earth. Brooks and creeks are small streams; rivers are large streams.

Swamp A portion of wet, waterlogged, or flooded land.

Tide The rise and fall of the surface of the ocean and of bays, gulfs, and other bodies of water connected to the ocean. Tides are caused by the gravitational pull of the moon, which passes over the same meridian of the Earth about once every 24 hours and 50 minutes. The length of time between successive high (or low) tides is about 12 hours and 25 minutes.

Tributary A stream or river that flows into a larger stream or river.

Tropic of Cancer Latitude 23½°N, which marks the northernmost limit of the sun's vertical rays. The area between the Tropic of Cancer and the Tropic of Capricorn is known as the tropics.

Tropic of Capricorn Latitude 23½°S, the southernmost limit of the sun's vertical rays.

Tundra An area of treeless plain near or above the Arctic Circle. Tundra subsoil is permanently frozen, but the soil thaws enough to support the growth of mosses, lichens, and some small flowering shrubs.

Valley A long and sometimes narrow depression on the surface of the earth, usually between two mountain ridges or ranges.

Volcano A mountain formed by lava and/or other materials which have burst forth from deep within the Earth. (See also *Caldera*, *Lava*, *Magma*).

Windward The direction or side facing the wind.

►THE OCEANS OF THE WORLD

The water of the world's oceans covers more than 70 percent of the world's surface. While for most of the 20th century the so-called World Ocean was divided into the Pacific, Atlantic, Indian and Arctic Oceans, a decision by the International Hydrographic Organization in 2000 delimited a fifth ocean, the Southern Ocean, extending from 60 degrees south latitude to the coast of Antarctica. Other large bodies of water such as the Caribbean Sea, the Gulf of Mexico, Hudson Bay, the Mediterranean and Black Seas, and the South China Sea are termed marginal seas. The International Hydrographic Organization identifies 66 seas, gulfs, bays, bights, straits, channels, and passages, many of which are

The Oceans of the World

Ocean	Area ('000s sq. km.)	Coastline (km.)	Deepest point	Comparative area
Arctic	14,056	45,389	4,665 m (Fram Basin)	1.5 times size of U.S.
Atlantic	76,762	111,866	8,605 m (Milwaukee Deep, Puerto Rico Trench)	More than 6.5 times size of U.S.
Indian	68,556	66,526	7,258 m (Java Trench)	5.5 times size of U.S.
Pacific	155,557	135,663	10,924 m (Challenger Deep, Mariana Trench)	15 times size of U.S.; approx. 28% of global surface (more than total world land area)
Southern	20,327	17,968	7,235 m (South Sandwich Trench)	More than 2 times size of U.S.

The Continents: Highest and Lowest Elevations

Continent	Highest point	Location	Feet above sea level	Meters above sea level
Africa	Mt. Kilimanjaro	Tanzania	19,340	5,895
Antarctica	Vinson Massif	Ellsworth Mts.	16,066	4,897
Asia	Mt. Everest	Nepal-China	29,028	8,848
Australia	Mt. Kosciusko	New South Wales	7,310	2,228
Europe	Mt. Elbrus	Russia	18,510	5,642
North America	Mt. McKinley	U.S. (Alaska)	20,320	6,194
South America	Mt. Aconcagua	Argentina	22,834	6,960

Continent	Lowest point	Location	Feet below sea level	Meters below sea level
Africa	Lake Assal	Djibouti	512	156
Antarctica	ice covered	N.A.	8,327	2,538
Asia	Dead Sea	Israel-Jordan	1,339	408
Australia	Lake Eyre	South Australia	52	16
Europe	Caspian Sea	Russia, Kazakhstan	92	28
North America	Death Valley	U.S. (California)	282	86
South America	Valdes Peninsula	Argentina	131	40

Source: *National Geographic Atlas of the World* (1995).

Great Deserts of the World

Desert	Location	Approximate size	
		Sq. mi.	Sq. km.
Africa			
Sahara	Northern Africa	3,320,000	8,600,000
Libyan	Libya, Egypt, and The Sudan	N.A.	N.A.
Kalahari	Southwestern Africa	360,000	930,000
Namib	Southwestern Africa	52,000	135,000
North America			
Great Basin	Southwestern U.S.	190,000	492,000
Chihuahuan	Northern Mexico	175,000	450,000
Sonoran	Southwestern U.S. and Baja California	120,000	310,000
Colorado	California, U.S., and northern Mexico	N.A.	N.A.
Yuma	Arizona, U.S., and Sonora, Mexico	N.A.	N.A.
Mojave	Southwestern U.S.	25,000	65,000
South America			
Patagonian	Southern Argentina	260,000	673,000
Atacama	Northern Chile	54,000	140,000
Asia			
Arabia	Southwestern Asia	900,000	2,330,000
Rub'al-Khali	Southern Arabian Peninsula	250,000	650,000
Gobi	Mongolia and northeastern China	500,000	1,300,000
Kyzylkum	Kazakhstan-Uzbekistan	115,000	300,000
Takla Makan	Northern China	105,000	270,000
Karakum	Turkmenistan	135,000	350,000
Kavir	Central Iran	100,000	260,000
Syrian	Saudi Arabia, Jordan, Syria, and Iraq	100,000	260,000
Thar	India and Pakistan	77,000	200,000
Lut	Eastern Iran	20,000	52,000
Negev	Israel	4,700	12,300
Australia			
Great Victoria	Western and South Australia	250,000	647,000
Great Sandy	Northern Western Australia	150,000	400,000
Gibson	Western Australia	N.A.	N.A.
Simpson	Northern Territory	56,000	145,000

Source: Encyclopedia Britannica, "Deserts." Accessed at www.britannica.com, May 2010.

further subdivided. For instance, the Mediterranean Sea is divided into western and eastern basins, and the western basin is subdivided into the Strait of Gibraltar, Aboran Sea, Balearic Sea, Ligurian Sea, Tyrrhenian Sea, Ionian Sea, Adriatic Sea, and Aegean Sea.

►THE GREAT DESERTS OF THE WORLD

To many people, the word *desert* brings to mind images of shifting sand dunes, scorching sun, and occasional lush oases. But there are actually many kinds of deserts, because a desert is simply an area that receives little precipitation and has little plant cover. Thus polar areas can be considered deserts, for their precipitation is locked into ice and snow. So are places like the Taklimakan in China, which lies in a rain shadow on the leeward side of mountain ranges, and the Atacama, which is near cold ocean currents that cool the air and prevent the formation of rain clouds. But most deserts are found in the tropics, where giant high-pressure cells keep rain from forming. Some deserts are indeed flat and sandy, but others are solid rock, loose pebbles, or even mountain plateaus. One of the many fascinating characteristics of deserts is their strangely shaped rock formations, created by wind-whipped sand.

Altogether, arid lands cover about a fifth of the Earth's total land surface—a third if semi-arid areas are also included. About a billion people live in arid and semiarid areas, and more than 100 countries are facing problems associated with expanding deserts.

Desert extremes
- The Sahara is the largest desert, with an area greater than the contiguous United States.
- The driest place on Earth is in the Atacama Desert of Chile, where no rainfall at all was recorded between 1570 and 1971.
- The highest temperature ever recorded—136°F (58°C)—was at Al-Aziziya, in the Libyan Desert, but the Dalol, Denakil Depression in Ethiopia is consistently the hottest place on Earth, with an annual average temperature of 93°F (34 °C).
- The lowest point in the world—1,339 feet (408 m) below sea level—is on the shores of the Dead Sea in the Negev Desert.
- The lowest point in the Western Hemisphere—282 feet (86 meters) below sea level—is in Death Valley, California.

Uses of the desert   Even the hot, sandy tropical deserts are not necessarily, as their name implies, deserted. Traders, herders, and farmers have called the desert home for thousands of years. Settlements have grown up around oases or in irrigated areas, from ancient times to the present. Deserts are important to historians, archaeologists, paleontologists, and other scientists, for the relics of the past that are preserved there. Dinosaur eggs have been found in the Gobi Desert, for instance, and whole cities are said to lie buried beneath the Taklimakan Desert.

Deserts are also important for extractive industries. The Negev was the site of the fabled King Solomon's mines. In the 19th century, borax was mined in Death Valley. Petroleum is found in the Sahara and in the deserts of the Arabian Peninsula. The Atacama is famed for its deposits of nitrate and copper. The Rub al-Khali, or Empty Quarter of Saudi Arabia, is thought to contain deposits of limestone and gravel—but no one is certain because it has never been fully explored.

The World's Highest Mountain Peaks

Mountain peak	Range	Location	Height Feet	Meters
Everest	Himalayas	Nepal-China	29,028	8,848
K2 (Godwin Austen)	Karakoram	Kashmir	28,250	8,611
Kanchenjunga	Himalayas	Nepal-India	28,208	8,598
Lhotse I	Himalayas	Nepal-China	27,923	8,511
Makalu I	Himalayas	Nepal-China	27,824	8,481
Lhotse II	Himalayas	Nepal-China	27,560	8,400
Dhaulagiri	Himalayas	Nepal	26,810	8,172
Manaslu I	Himalayas	Nepal	26,760	8,156
Cho Oyu	Himalayas	Nepal-China	26,750	8,153
Nanga Parbat	Himalayas	Kashmir	26,660	8,126
Annapurna	Himalayas	Nepal	26,504	8,078
Gasherbrum	Karakoram	Kashmir	26,470	8,068
Broad	Karakoram	Kashmir	26,400	8,047
Gosainthan	Himalayas	China	26,287	8,012
Annapurna II	Himalayas	Nepal	26,041	7,937
Gyachung Kang	Himalayas	Nepal-China	25,910	7,897
Disteghil Sar	Himalayas	Kashmir	25,858	7,882
Himalchuli	Himalayas	Nepal	25,801	7,864
Nuptse	Himalayas	Nepal-China	25,726	7,841
Masherbrum	Karakoram	Kashmir	25,660	7,821
Nanda Devi	Himalayas	India	25,645	7,817
Rakaposhi	Karakoram	Kashmir	25,550	7,788
Kanjut Sar	Karakoram	Kashmir	25,461	7,761
Kamet	Himalayas	India-China	25,447	7,756
Namcha Barwa	Himalayas	China	25,445	7,756
Kua-la-man-ta-t'a (Gurla Mandhata)	Himalayas	China	25,355	7,728
Wu-lu-k'o-mu-shih (Ulugh Muztagh)	Kunlun	China	25,340	7,724
Kung-ko-erh (Kungur)	Mu-ssu-t'a-ko-a-t'e (Muztagh Ata)	China	25,325	7,719
Tirich Mir	Hindu Kush	Pakistan	25,230	7,690
Saser Kangri	Karakoram	Kashmir	25,172	7,672
Makalu II	Himalayas	Nepal-China	25,120	7,657
Minya Konka (Gonggashan)	Daxue Shan	China	24,900	7,590
Kula Kangri	Himalayas	Bhutan-China	24,784	7,554
Chang-tzu	Himalayas	Nepal-China	24,780	7,553
Mu-ssu-t'a-ko-a-t'e (Muztagh Ata)	Mu-ssu-t'a-ko-a-t'e (Muztagh Ata)	China	24,757	7,546
Skyang Kangri	Himalayas	Kashmir	24,750	7,544
Communism Peak	Pamirs	Tajikistan	24,590	7,495
Jongsong Peak	Himalayas	Nepal-India	24,472	7,459
Pobeda Peak	Tien Shan	Kyrgyzstan-China	24,406	7,439
Sia Kangri	Himalayas	Kashmir	24,350	7,422
Haramosh Peak	Karakoram	Kashmir	24,270	7,397
Istoro Nal	Hindu Kush	Pakistan	24,240	7,388
Tent Peak	Himalayas	Nepal-India	24,165	7,365
Chomo Lhari	Himalayas	Bhutan-China	24,040	7,327
Chamlang	Himalayas	Nepal	24,012	7,319
Kabru	Himalayas	Nepal-India	24,002	7,316
Alung Gangri	Himalayas	China	24,000	7,315
Baltoro Kangri	Himalayas	Kashmir	23,990	7,312
Muztagh Ata	Kunlun	China	23,890	7,282
Mana	Himalayas	India	23,860	7,273
Baruntse	Himalayas	Nepal	23,688	7,220
Nepal Peak	Himalayas	Nepal-India	23,500	7,163
Amne Machin	Kunlun	China	23,490	7,160

Mountain peak	Range	Location	Height Feet	Meters
Gauri Sankar	Himalayas	Nepal-China	23,440	7,145
Badrinath	Himalayas	India	23,420	7,138
Nunkun	Himalayas	Kashmir	23,410	7,135
Lenin Peak	Pamirs	Tajikistan	23,405	7,134
Pyramid	Himalayas	Nepal-India	23,400	7,132
Api	Himalayas	Nepal	23,399	7,132
Pauhunri	Himalayas	India-China	23,385	7,128
Trisul	Himalayas	India	23,360	7,120
Korzhenevski Peak	Pamirs	Tajikistan	23,310	7,105
Kangto	Himalayas	India-China	23,260	7,090
Nyainqentanglha	Nyainqentanglha Shan	China	23,255	7,088
Trisuli	Himalayas	India	23,210	7,074
Dunagiri	Himalayas	India	23,184	7,066
Revolution Peak	Pamirs	Tajikistan	22,880	6,974
Aconcagua	Andes	Argentina	22,834	6,960
Ojos del Salado	Andes	Argentina-Chile	22,572	6,880
Bonete	Andes	Argentina	22,546	6,872
Tupungato	Andes	Argentina-Chile	22,310	6,800
Moscow Peak	Pamirs	Tajikistan	22,260	6,785
Pissis	Andes	Argentina	22,241	6,779
Mercedario	Andes	Argentina	22,211	6,770
Huascaran	Andes	Peru	22,205	6,768
Llullaillaco	Andes	Argentina-Chile	22,057	6,723
El Libertador	Andes	Argentina	22,047	6,720
Cachi	Andes	Argentina	22,047	6,720
Kailas	Himalayas	China	22,027	6,714
Incahuasi	Andes	Argentina-Chile	21,720	6,620
Yerupaja	Andes	Peru	21,709	6,617
Kurumda	Pamirs	Tajikistan	21,686	6,610
Galan	Andes	Argentina	21,654	6,600
El Muerto	Andes	Argentina-Chile	21,457	6,540
Sajama	Andes	Bolivia	21,391	6,520
Nacimiento	Andes	Argentina	21,302	6,493
Illimani	Andes	Bolivia	21,201	6,462
Coropuna	Andes	Peru	21,083	6,426
Laudo	Andes	Argentina	20,997	6,400
Ancohuma	Andes	Bolivia	20,958	6,388
Ausangate	Andes	Peru	20,945	6,384
Toro	Andes	Argentina-Chile	20,932	6,380
Illampu	Andes	Bolivia	20,873	6,362
Tres Cruces	Andes	Argentina-Chile	20,853	6,356
Huandoy	Andes	Peru	20,852	6,356
Parinacota	Andes	Bolivia-Chile	20,768	6,330
Tortolas	Andes	Argentina-Chile	20,745	6,323
Ampato	Andes	Peru	20,702	6,310
El Condor	Andes	Argentina	20,669	6,300
Salcantay	Andes	Peru	20,574	6,271
Chimborazo	Andes	Ecuador	20,561	6,267
Huancarhuas	Andes	Peru	20,531	6,258
Famatina	Andes	Argentina	20,505	6,250
Pumasillo	Andes	Peru	20,492	6,246
Solo	Andes	Argentina	20,492	6,246
Polleras	Andes	Argentina	20,456	6,235
Pular	Andes	Chile	20,423	6,225
Chani	Andes	Argentina	20,341	6,200
McKinley	Alaska	U.S. (Alaska)	20,320	6,194
Aucanquilcha	Andes	Chile	20,295	6,186
Juncal	Andes	Argentina-Chile	20,276	6,180
Negro	Andes	Argentina	20,184	6,152
Quela	Andes	Argentina	20,128	6,135
Condoriri	Andes	Bolivia	20,095	6,125
Palermo	Andes	Argentina	20,079	6,120
Solimana	Andes	Peru	20,068	6,117
San Juan	Andes	Argentina-Chile	20,049	6,111
(Sierra) Nevada	Andes	Argentina-Chile	20,023	6,103
Antofalla	Andes	Argentina	20,013	6,100
Marmolejo	Andes	Argentina-Chile	20,013	6,100

▶LAKES

A lake is typically defined as a body of water surrounded by land, though the scientific differentiation between lakes, ponds, swamps, and rivers is not well established. Geologically speaking, lakes have transient origins as primary sources are usually melting ice and snow, runoff, precipitation, and ground-springs. Lakes are more common at higher altitudes and in mountainous regions, especially areas that were "recently" covered by glaciers. The North American Great Lakes were formed by glacial movement.

Freshwater lakes make up less than .01 percent of all water in the world but constitute 98 percent of surface water available for human use. The vast majority of these are located in North America, Africa, and Asia, though roughly a quarter of the world's lake water exists in small, scattered, uncounted lakes across the globe.

Lakes have obviously played an important role in the historical development of communities, and modern life is dependent on the purification facilities, agricultural benefits, and cooling effects that lakes provide. As renewable energy becomes increasingly important in the 21st century, so do lakes and the possibilities of hydroelectric power that they present. Economically, lakes play an integral part in the development of major waterways and travel routes, both in the past and today.

Fishing and aquaculture—and the jobs their industry represents—are also principal benefits of living in a lake community.

Very large lakes—or dry lake basins—have been formed by movement of the Earth's crust, known as tectonism. The largest of these basins was formed over five million years ago, and now encompasses the Caspain and Aral Seas, as well as numerous smaller lakes. Faulting (the cracking of the Earth's crust that causes tectonic upheaval) is also the reason for several of the world's larger lakes—the Great Salt Lake in Utah being one of them. Calderas, large surface craters caused by the collapse of magma chambers inside an inactive volcano. A well-known example of this is Crater Lake, in Oregon, but the largest caldera in the world circumscribes Lake Toba in Sumatra. Other lake cavities have been formed by human activity such as damming and mining.

Lake evaporation is nothing new, though the rate of evaporation varies depending on wind speed and thermal convection. Lakes that are currently evaporating at increased levels include Lake Mead, Arizona (some estimate up to seven feet per year); Lake Hefner (4.5 feet per year); Lake Ontario (two to three feet per year); and Lake Mendota, Wisconsin (up to 2.5 feet per year). Decreased water levels obviously pose problems for communities that rely on that body of water.

Major Natural Lakes of the World

Lake	Surface area		Location	Maximum depth		Elevation	
	Sq. mi.	Sq. km.		Feet	Meters	Feet	Meters
Caspian Sea[1]	143,240	370,992	Russia, Kazakhstan, Azerbaijan, Turkmenistan, Iran	3,363	1,025	−92	−28
Superior	31,700	82,103	Ontario, Canada; Mich., Wis., Minn.	1,333	406	600	183
Victoria	26,820	69,464	Uganda, Kenya, Tanzania	279	85	3,720	1,134
Aral Sea[1]	24,904	64,501	Uzbekistan, Kazakhstan	220	67	174	53
Huron	23,000	59,570	Ontario, Can.; Mich.	750	229	576	176
Michigan	22,300	57,757	Mich., Ind., Ill., Wis.	923	281	579	176
Tanganyika	12,350	31,987	Burundi, Tanzania, Zambia, Zaire	4,800	1,463	2,543	775
Baikal	12,160	31,494	Russia	5,315	1,620	1,493	455
Great Bear	12,028	31,153	Northwest Terr., Canada	1,356	413	512	156
Nyasa (Malawi)	11,150	28,879	Tanzania, Mozambique, Malawi	2,280	695	1,550	472
Great Slave	11,030	28,568	Northwest Terr., Canada	2,015	614	513	156
Erie	9,910	25,667	Ontario, Canada; N.Y., Pa., Ohio, Mich.	210	64	570	174
Winnipeg	9,417	24,390	Manitoba, Canada	92	28	713	217
Ontario	7,540	19,529	Ontario, Canada; N.Y.	802	244	245	75
Balkhash[1]	7,115[2]	18,428[2]	Kazakhstan	87	27	1,115	340
Ladoga	6,835	17,703	Russia	755	230	13	4
Chad	6,300	16,317	Chad, Nigeria, Niger	24	7	787	240
Maracaibo[3]	5,200	13,468	Venezuela	197	60	sea level	
Patos[3]	3,920	10,153	Brazil	15	5	[4]	[4]
Onega	3,720	9,635	Russia	394	120	108	33
Titicaca	3,200	8,288	Bolivia, Peru	990	302	12,500	3,810
Nicaragua	3,150	8,159	Nicaragua	230	70	102	31
Mai-Ndombe	3,100	8,029[2]	Zaire	36	11	1,116	340
Athabasca	3,064	7,936	Saskatchewan, Alberta, Canada	407	124	700	213
Eyre[1]	2,970[2]	7,692[2]	Australia	4	1	−52	−16
Reindeer	2,568	6,651	Saskatchewan, Manitoba, Canada	720	219	1,106	337
Tonle Sap	2,500[2]	6,475[2]	Cambodia	39	12	[4]	[4]
Rudolf[1]	2,473	6,405	Kenya, Ethiopia	720	219	1,230	375
Issyk-Kul[1]	2,355	6,099	Kyrghyzstan	2,303	702	5,279	1,609
Torrens[1]	2,230[2]	5,776[2]	Australia	0.5	0.2	92	28

Notes: 1. Saltwater. A lake is a body of water surrounded by land. The Caspian Sea is thus a lake. It was called a sea by the Romans because of its salty water. 2. Subject to large seasonal variation in surface area. 3. Lagoon. 4. No information available.   Source: U.S. Department of Commerce, National Oceanic and Atmospheric Administration, *Principal Rivers and Lakes of the World* (1982).

Major Rivers of the World, by Length

River	Length		Source	Outflow
	Miles	Km		
Nile	4,145	6,673	Tributaries of Lake Victoria, E. Africa	Mediterranean Sea
Amazon	4,000	6,440	Andes Mts., Peru	Atlantic Ocean
Mississippi-Missouri	3,740[1]	6,021[1]	Confluence of Jefferson, Madison, and Galatin R., Montana	Gulf of Mexico
Changjiang (Yangtze)	3,720	5,989	Kunlun Mts., China	China Sea
Yenisei-Angara	3,650[2]	5,877[2]	Lake Baikal, Russia	Kara Sea (Arctic Ocean)
Amur-Argun	3,590[2]	5,780[2]	Khingan Mts., China	Tatar Strait
Ob-Irtysh	3,360[2]	5,410[2]	Altai Mts., China	Gulf of Ob (Arctic Ocean)
Plata-Parana	3,030[2]	4,878[2]	Confluence of the Paranaiba and Grande rivers, Brazil	Atlantic Ocean
Huang He (Yellow)	2,903	4,674	Kunlun Mts., China	Gulf of Chihli (Yellow Sea)
Congo (Zaire)	2,900	4,669	Confluence of the Luapula and Lualaba rivers, Zaire	Atlantic Ocean
Lena	2,730	4,395	Baikal Mts., Russia	Laptev Sea (Arctic Ocean)
MacKenzie	2,635[2]	4,242[2]	Headwaters of Finlay Rivers, British Columbia, Canada	Beaufort Sea (Arctic Ocean)
Mekong	2,600	4,186	T'ang-ku-la Mts., Tibet	South China Sea
Niger	2,600	4,186	Guinea	Gulf of Guinea
Missouri	2,315	3,725	Confluence of Jefferson, Madison, and Montana Galatin rivers, Montana	Mississippi River
Mississippi	2,348[3]	3,780[3]	Lake Itasca, northwestern Minnesota	Gulf of Mexico
Murray-Darling	2,330	3,751	Great Dividing Range, Australia	Indian Ocean
Volga	2,290	3,687	Valdai Hills, Russia	Caspian Sea
Madeira	2,013	3,241	Confluence of the Mamore and Beni rivers, Bolivia/Brazil	Amazon River
Sao Francisco	1,988	3,201	Minas Gerais State, Brazil	Atlantic Ocean
Yukon	1,979	3,186	Confluence of Lewes and Pelly rivers, Yukon Territory, Canada	Bering Sea
Rio Grande	1,885	3,035	San Juan Mts., southwestern Colorado	Gulf of Mexico
Purus	1,860	2,995	Andes Mts., Peru	Amazon River
Tunguska, Lower	1,860	2,995	North of Lake Baikal, Russia	Yenesei River
Indus	1,800	2,898	Himalayas, Tibet	Arabian Sea
Danube	1,776	2,859	Confluence of Breg and Brigach rivers, Germany	Black Sea
Brahmaputra	1,770	2,850	Himalayas, Tibet	Ganges River
Salween	1,750	2,818	Tibetan Plateau, Tibet	Bay of Bengal
Para-Tocantins	1,710[2]	2,753[2]	Goias State, Brazil	Atlantic Ocean
Zambezi	1,700	2,737	Northwestern Zambia	Mozambique Channel
Paraguay	1,610	2,592	Mato Grosso State, Brazil	Parana River
Kolyma	1,320	2,130	Kolyma Mts., Russia	Arctic Ocean
Nelson-Saskatchewan	1,600	2,576	Rocky Mts., Canada	Hudson Bay
Orinoco	1,600	2,576	Sierra Parima Mts., Venezuela	Atlantic Ocean
Amu Darya	1,578	2,541	Pamir Mts., Uzbekistan/ Turkmenistan	Aral Sea
Ural	1,575	2,536	Ural Mountains, Russia	Caspian Sea
Ganges	1,560	2,512	Himalayas, India	Bay of Bengal
Euphrates	1,510	2,431	Confluence of the Murat Nehri and Kara Su rivers, Turkey	Shatt-al-Arab
Arkansas	1,450	2,335	Central Colorado	Mississippi River
Colorado	1,450	2,335	Northern Colorado	Gulf of California
Dneiper	1,420	2,286	Valdai Hills, Russia	Black Sea
Atchafalaya-Red	1,400	2,254	Eastern New Mexico	Gulf of Mexico
Syr Darya	1,370	2,206	Tien Shan, China/Kyrghyzstan	Aral Sea
Kasai	1,338	2,154	Central Angola	Congo (Zaire) River
Irrawaddy	1,300	2,093	Confluence of Mali and Nmai rivers, Myanmar	Bay of Bengal
Ohio-Allegheny	1,300	2,093	Pennsylvania	Mississippi River
Orange	1,300	2,093	Lesotho	Atlantic Ocean
Columbia	1,243	2,001	Columbia Lake, British Columbia, Canada	Pacific Ocean
Tigris	1,180	1,900	Eastern Turkey	Shatt-al-Arab
Rhine	820	1,320	Confluence of Hinterrhein and Vorderrhein rivers, Switzerland	North Sea
St. Lawrence	800	1,288	Lake Ontario	Gulf of St. Lawrence

Notes: 1. From the mouth of the Mississippi, up the Missouri to the Red Rock River in Montana. 2. Includes the length of tributaries that are part of the main trunk stream. 3. From the mouth of the Mississippi, up to its source in Minnesota. **Source:** National Oceanic and Atmospheric Administration, *Principal Rivers and Lakes of the World* (1982).

►DAMS

The International Commission of Large Dams (ICOLD) defines a large dam as any that is higher than 15 meters, higher than 10 meters with a 500 meter crest length, has a storage capacity of at least one million cubic meters, or one with more than a 2,000 cubic meters spilling capacity. Of the 39,000 large dams registered with the Commission across the world, over half were built in the last 35 years. While there is some controversy over the negative environmental effects that dams have on an ecosystem—flooding, interruption for aquatic life in the dam's source, the sometimes necessary resettling of entire communities—there's no doubt as to their necessity. The Commission cites that 75 percent of the world water consumption belongs to the 250 million hectares of land worldwide that are being irrigated; though the world population has increased eightfold in the past 300 years, water withdrawn from freshwater sources has increased by 35.

In addition to agricultural benefits of dams, they also help to prevent devastating droughts, adjust natural runoff with climate variations, and play a role in non-fossil fueled energy production. Hydropower, derived from the force of moving water, generates 2.1 GWh annually, and accounts for roughly seven percent of energy production worldwide. Hydropower generates 20 percent of electricity used worldwide, and in some developing countries is the only natural energy resource available.

World's 10 Largest Volume Dams, 2009

Dam	Location	CU(meters)	CU(yards)	Year
1. Three Gorges	China	39,300,000	51,402,459	UC2008
2. Syncrude Tailings	Canada	540,000	706,320	UC
3. Chapeton	Argentina	296,200	387,410	UC
4. Pati	Argentina	238,180	274,026	UC
5. New Cornelia Tailings	U.S.	209,500	274,026	1973
6. Tarbela	Pakistan	121,720	159,210	1976
7. Kambaratinsk	Kyrgyzstan	112,200	146,758	UC
8. Fort Peck	U.S.	96,049	125,628	1940
9. Lower Usuma	Nigeria	93,000	121,644	1990
10. Cipasang	Indonesia	90,000	117,720	UC

Note: UC denotes dam is under construction. **Source:** International Water Power and Dam Construction.

Highest Dams in the United States, 2009

Dam	River	State	Owner	Feet	Completed
1. Oroville	Feather	California	California DWR	770	1968
2. Hoover	Colorado	Nevada	Bureau of Reclamation	730	1936
3. Dworshak	N. Fork Clearwater	Idaho	Corps of Engineers	717	1973
4. Glen Canyon	Colorado	Arizona	Bureau of Reclamation	710	1964
5. New Bullards Bar	North Yuba	California	Yuba County Water Agency	645	1969
6. Seven Oaks	Santa Ana	California	Corps of Engineers	632	1999
7. New Melones	Stanislaus	California	Bureau of Reclamation	625	1979
8. Mossyrock	Cowlitz	Washington	City of Tacoma	606	1968
9. Shasta	Sacramento	California	Bureau of Reclamation	602	1945
10. Don Pedro	Tuolumne	California	N.A.	585	1971

Source: United States Society on Dams.

Largest Hydroelectric Projects in the United States, 2009

Dam	River	Location	Megawatts
1. Grand Coulee	Columbia	Washington	6180
2. Chief Joseph	Columbia	Washington	2457
3. John Day	Columbia	Oregon	2160
4. Bath County P/S	Little Back Creek	Virginia	2100
5. Robert Moses - Niagara	Niagara	New York	1950
6. The Dalles	Columbia	Oregon	1805
7. Ludington	Lake Michigan	Michigan	1872
8. Raccoon Mountain	Tennessee River	Tennessee	1530
9. Hoover	Colorado	Nevada	1434
10. Pyramid	California Aqueduct	California	1250

Source: United States Society on Dams.

▶MAJOR ISLANDS AND ISLAND GROUPS

Admiralty Is.: see *Bismarck Archipelago*.

Åland Is. (Ahvenanmaa): 60°N, 20°E. Finnish archipelago of more than 6,000 islands between Finland and Sweden.

Aleutian Is.: 51°–°55°N, 163°W–166°E. Chain between Pacific Ocean and Bering Sea stretching 2,700 km: Unimak, Fox Is., Andreanof Is., Rat Is. and Near Is. (Alaska) and Komandorskiye Ostrova (Russia).

Andaman and Nicobar Is.: 12°N, 93°E. Union Territory of India comprising some 300 islands in two major archipelagos stretching 725 km north-south in the Bay of Bengal off the coast of Myanmar.

Anglesey: 53°N, 4°W. Irish Sea island off Wales.

Anticosti: 50°N, 63°W. Canadian island in Gulf of St. Lawrence.

Antigua and Barbuda: 17°N, 62°W. Two-island Caribbean country.

Antilles. Name for the Caribbean islands from Cuba to Trinidad and Tobago, but not including the Bahamas. *Greater Antilles:* Cuba, Jamaica, Hispaniola, and Puerto Rico. *Lesser Antilles:* Leeward Is. Virgin Is., Antigua and Barbuda, and Dominica. *Windward Is.:* Martinique, St. Lucia, St. Vincent, Grenada, Barbados, Trinidad and Tobago, and Aruba.

Aran Is.: 53°N, 10°W. Three islands—Inishmore, Inishmaan and Inisheer—off western Ireland.

Aruba: 12°N, 70°W. Dutch Caribbean island 30 km N of Venezuela.

Ascension: 7°S, 14°W. Island of the British Crown Colony of St. Helena about 1,100 km northwest of St. Helena, 2,250 km east of Brazil and 2,500 km west of Africa

Auckland Is.: 51°S, 166°E. Group about 300 km south of New Zealand.

Azores/Açores: 37°–40°N, 25°–31°W. Portuguese Atlantic group 1,400 km west of Portugal: Faial, Flores, São Miguel; first settled in 1430s.

Baffin: 68°N, 70°W. Largest Canadian Arctic island, on Davis Strait opposite Greenland.

Bahamas: 21°–27°N, 71°–79°W. Chain of 2,700 islands and cays stretching 800 km southeast of Florida; shared by Bahamas, Turks, Caicos (British); Columbus's first American landfall in 1492.

Bahrain: Persian Gulf island 25 km off coast of Saudi Arabia; probable site of ancient Dilmun.

Balearic Is.: 39°N, 3°E. Sixteen Spanish Mediterranean islands: incl. Majorca, Minorca and Ibiza.

Bali: 9°S, 115°E. Predominantly Hindu Indonesian island east of Java.

Banks: 73°N, 121°W. Westernmost large Canadian Arctic island, on Beaufort Sea.

Bear: see *Spitsbergen*.

Barbados: 13°N, 60°W. Island nation about 150 km east of southern Antilles.

Bermuda: 32°N, 65°W. British dependency of 138 coral islands, 20 inhabited, 900 km east of North Carolina.

Bikini: see *Marshall Is*.

Bismarck Archipelago: 5°S, 150°E. Papua New Guinea archipelago: Admiralty Is., New Britain and New Ireland; formerly a German colony.

Block: 41°N, 72°W. Island between Long Island Sound and Atlantic Ocean, 15 km off Rhode Island.

Borneo: 0°N/S, 114°E. Large equatorial Southeast Asian island shared by Indonesia, Malaya and Brunei.

British Isles: Group off Northwest Europe: Great Britain, Ireland, Man, Wight, Hebrides, Shetlands, Orkneys and Anglesey.

Canary Is.: 28°N, 16°W. Spanish archipelago of seven islands 100 km west of Morocco: incl. Tenerife, Gomera, Gran Canaria, Fuertaventura, Lanzarote. Inhabited since antiquity (Latin: *Fortunatae Insulae*); colonized by the Spanish in 1400s.

Cape Verde Is.: 15°–17°N, 23°–25°W. Ten-island nation 500 km west of Senegal: incl. São Tiago, Fogo. Settled by Portuguese in 15th century.

Capri: 41°N, 14°E. Italian island in Bay of Naples.

Caroline Is.: 5°–10°N, 130°–166°E. Micronesian group of more than 600 islands: Belau (Palau), Kusaie, Ponape, Satawal, Truk and Yap.

Cayman Is.: 20°N, 81°W. British dependency of 3 main islands 240 km south of Cuba.

Chagos Archipelago: 6°S, 72°E. Part of the British Indian Ocean Territory 600 km south of the Maldives. Diego Garcia has been a U.K./U.S. military base since the 1970s when its 1,500 inhabitants— the descendents of slaves—were deported.

Channel/Santa Barbara Is.: 34°N, 120°W. Eight-island group off Los Angeles.

Channel Is.: 49°N, 2°W. Group in English Channel near France: Jersey, Guernsey, Alderney and Sark. They are dependent territories of the English Crown, as successor to William the Conqueror, Duke of Normandy, but not part of the U.K.

Chatham Is.: 44°S, 176°W. Polynesian group 860 km east of New Zealand from where they were settled around 1500.

Chincha Is.: 14°S, 76°W. Group of three Peruvian islands; important source of guano before synthetic fertilizers.

Christmas: 10°S, 106°E. Australian dependency 360 km south of Java.

Cocos/Keeling Is.: 12°S, 97°E. Australian archipelago of 27 coral atolls 2,800 km northwest of Perth, settled in 19th century.

Comoros: 12°S, 44°E. Indian Ocean nation of three islands about 325 km east of Mozambique.

Cook Is.: 8°–23°S, 156°–167°W. Group of 15 islands 3,200 km northeast of New Zealand: Rarotonga.

Corsica: 42°N, 9°E. French Mediterranean island; birthplace of Napoleon Bonaparte.

Crete: 41°N, 97°E.

Cuba: 21°N, 80°W. Northernmost Caribbean island, 1,250 km east-west; largest of 1,200 islands in Cuban archipelago.

Cyclades/Kikládhes: 37°N, 25°E. Greek Aegean archipelago of about 220 islands; so-called because they encircle sacred island of Delos.

Cyprus: 35°N, 33°E.

Delos: see *Cyclades*.

Devil's: 5°N, 52°W. Island off French Guiana; used as penal colony until 1938.

Diego Garcia: see *Chagos Archipelago*.

Dodecanese/Sporádhes: 36°N, 27°E. Greek Aegean archipelago of 12 islands, including Samos, Kos and Ródhos.

Dominica: 16°N, 61°W. Caribbean island nation.

Easter Island/Isla de Pascua/Rapa Nui: 27°07′S, 109°22′W. The most remote island on Earth, Rapa Nui is the eastern tip of Polynesia, about 3,700 km west of Chile, which administers it, and 1,600 km east of Pitcairn Island. Settled by Marquesans around the fourth century, it is famous for its thousand carved statues, some 10 meters tall.

Elba: 43°N, 10°E. Italian island where Napoleon was briefly exiled.

The World's Largest Islands

Island	Location	Flags	Area Sq. mi.	Sq. km.
Greenland	N. Atlantic Ocean	Denmark	840,000	2,175,600
New Guinea	S. Pacific Ocean	Indonesia, Papua New Guinea	306,000	792,540
Borneo	Pacific Ocean	Indonesia, Malaysia, Brunei	280,100	725,459
Madagascar	Indian Ocean	Madagascar	226,658	587,044
Baffin	Arctic Ocean	Canada	195,928	507,454
Sumatra	Indian Ocean	Indonesia	165,000	427,350
Honshu	N. Pacific Ocean	Japan	87,805	227,415
Great Britain	N. Atlantic Ocean	United Kingdom	84,200	218,078
Victoria	Arctic Ocean	Canada	83,896	217,291
Ellesmere	Arctic Ocean	Canada	75,767	196,237
Celebes	Pacific Ocean	Indonesia	69,000	178,710
South Island	S. Pacific Ocean	New Zealand	58,305	151,010
Java	S. Pacific Ocean	Indonesia	48,900	126,651
Cuba	Caribbean Sea	Cuba	44,218	114,525
North Island	S. Pacific Ocean	New Zealand	44,035	114,051
Newfoundland	N. Atlantic Ocean	Canada	42,030	108,858
Luzon	N. Pacific Ocean	Philippines	40,880	105,879
Iceland	N. Atlantic Ocean	Iceland	39,769	103,002
Mindanao	N. Pacific Ocean	Philippines	36,775	95,247
Novaya Zemlya	Arctic Ocean	Russia	35,000	90,650
Ireland	N. Atlantic Ocean	Irish Republic, United Kingdom	32,599	84,431
Hokkaido	N. Pacific Ocean	Japan	30,144	78,073
Hispaniola	Caribbean Sea	Haiti, Dominican Republic	29,530	76,483
Sakhalin	N. Pacific Ocean	Russia	29,500	76,405
Banks	Arctic Ocean	Canada	27,033	70,015
Tasmania	S. Pacific Ocean	Australia	26,178	67,801
Sri Lanka	Indian Ocean	Sri Lanka	25,332	65,610
Devon	Arctic Ocean	Canada	21,331	55,247

Ellesmere Island, Nunavut Territory: 79°N, 82°W. Cape Columbia (83°08′N) is the northernmost point in Canada; part of Queen Elizabeth group.

Faeroe Is.: 62°N, 7°W. Group of 18 islands about 118 km north-south, 320 km north of the Shetlands and halfway between Norway and Iceland; settled in 7th century they are an autonomous part of Denmark.

Falkland Is./Islas Malvinas: 51°–53°S, 57°–62°W. British Crown Colony of 340 islands about 600 km east of Argentina. Claimed by French sailors from St. Mâlo (hence Malvinas), contested by Spanish, settled by English. An Argentine invasion in 1982 failed.

Faylakah: 29°N, 48°E. Persian Gulf island off Kuwait.

Fernando de Noronha: 4°S, 32°W. Atlantic island about 500 km east of Brazil.

Fernando Po: 3°S, 9°E. Former name for Bioko, Equatorial Guinea.

Fiji Is.: 16°–19°S, 178°W–177°E. Pacific nation of about 330 islands, a third inhabited, about 1,770 km north of New Zealand.

Florida Keys: 24°–25°N, 80°–82°W. Chain of coral islands running 240 km west from tip of Florida: Key Largo, Islamorada, Key West and Dry Tortugas.

Frisian Is.: 53°–55°N, 5°–8°E. Chain of North Sea islands, 18 inhabited, off The Netherlands, Germany, and Denmark: Rømø, Sylt, Terschelling, Vlieland and Texel.

Galápagos: 1°S, 91°W. Archipelago of 60 volcanic islands about 430 km across and 1,000 km west of Ecuador; known for its diverse flora and fauna and Charles Darwin's research there in 1835.

Gotland: 57°N, 18°E. Swedish Baltic island, thought to be the homeland of the Goths.

Great Britain: 54°N, 3°W. Principal island of British Isles; includes England, Scotland and Wales.

Greenland: 70°N, 40°W. Large North Atlantic island, settled about 2500 B.C.; first visited by Europeans around 1000.

Guadalcanal: see *Solomon Is.*

Guam: see *Mariana Is.*

Guernsey: see *Channel Is.*

Hainan: 19°N, 109°E. Chinese island between South China Sea and Gulf of Tonkin.

Hawaiian Is.: 19°–28°N, 155°–178°W. Polynesian chain comprising eight large and 124 smaller islands stretching 2,400 km from Hawaii to Midway and Kure. Settled in 8th century from the Marquesas. U.S. state: Hawaii, Maui, Lauai, Molokai, Oahu, Kaui and Nihau.

Hebrides/Western Isles: 57°N, 7°W. Islands off the west coast of Scotland. Inner Hebrides: Skye, Mull and Islay; 210-km-long Outer Hebrides: Lewis, North Uist and South Uist.

Hispaniola: 19°N, 71°W. Caribbean island divided between Haiti and Dominican Republic.

Hokkaido: 43°N, 143°E. Northernmost of main Japanese islands.

Hong Kong: 22°N, 114°E. Chinese island at mouth of Pearl River, 145 km southeast of Guangzhou (Canton).

Honshu: 36°N, 136°E. Largest of main Japanese islands; cities include Tokyo.

Ibiza: see *Balearic Is.*

Iceland: 65°N, 18°W. North Atlantic island 900 km west of Norway, settled in 9th century.

Indonesia: From the Greek meaning Indian islands, the name applies to the archipelagic nation of 18,108 islands: Sumatra, Java, Sulawesi, Bali,

Malaku Is., and parts of Borneo, Timor and New Guinea.

Ionian Is.: 39°N, 21°E. Greek Adriatic archipelago of seven islands: Kerkira (Corfu), Kefallinia, Zákinthos and Odysseus's Itháki.

Ireland: 53°N, 8°W. Second largest island in British Isles; divided between Republic of Ireland and Northern Ireland (which is still part of the U.K.).

Iwo Jima: see *Volcano Is.*

Jamaica: 18°N, 75°W. Caribbean island nation about 175 km south of Cuba.

Jan Mayen: 71°N, 8°W. Norwegian island 400 km east of Greenland.

Japanese islands: see *Hokkaido, Honshu, Kyushu, Shikoku, Ryukyu Is., Tsushima* and *Volcano Is.*

Java: 7°S, 110°E. Indonesian island east of Sumatra.

Jersey: see *Channel Is.*

Juan Fernandez Is.: 33°S, 80°W. Three-island group 650 km west of Chile. Alexander Selkirk, model for Daniel Defoe's Robinson Crusoe, was marooned on Más a Tierra 1705–09.

Kerguelen/Desolation Is.: 49°–50°S, 69°–71°E. French Indian Ocean territory of 300 islands and islets, including Crozet Is., about 4,500 km southeast of South Africa.

Komandorskiye Ostrova: 55°N, 167°E. Russian group at western tip of Aleutians.

Krakatoa: 6°S, 105°E. Volcanic Indonesian island west of Java.

Kuril Is.: 44°–51°N, 146°–155°E. Chain of some 56 islands stretching about 1,200 km between Japan and Russia.

Kyushu: 33°N, 131°E. Southernmost of main Japanese islands.

Lakshadweep/Laccadive Is.: 8°–12°N, 71°–74°E. Indian archipelago of 12 atolls, 250 km west of India.

Leeward Is.: see *Antilles.*

Line Is.: 6°N–11°S, 162°–152°W. Group of islands straddling the Equator (Line) south of Hawaii and belonging variously to the U.S., Great Britain and Kiribati.

Lofoten Is.: 69°N, 15°E. Northern Norwegian archipelago.

Long Island: 41°N, 73°W. New York island, 190 km long, between Atlantic Ocean and Long Island Sound.

Luzon: see *Philippines.*

Madagascar: 20°S, 47°E. Indian Ocean island, about 400 km east of Mozambique.

Madeira: 33°N, 17°W. Portuguese Atlantic archipelago of four main islands about 500 km west of Morocco; incl. Madeira, Porto Santo; discovered in 15th century.

Madeleine, Iles de la: 47°N, 61°W. Canadian group in Gulf of St. Lawrence.

Majorca: see *Balearic Is.*

Maldive Is.: 7°N–1°S, 73°E. Country of 26 archipelagos stretching 823 km north-south about 670 km southwest of Sri Lanka; about 750 km southwest of India.

Malta: 36°N, 14°E. Strategic island nation in central Mediterranean south of Sicily.

Maluku (Moluccas)/Spice Is.: 2°N–8°S, 124°–131°E: Indonesian archipelago; in the 16th century, sole source of cloves, nutmeg and mace, and a major goal of European merchants.

Man, Isle of: 54°N, 4°W. Irish Sea crown dependency of Great Britain.

Manhattan: 41°N, 74°W. New York island between the Hudson River and Long Island Sound.

Manitoulin: 46°N, 83°W. Canadian island in Lake Huron.

Mariana Is.: 13°–20°N, 146°E. Micronesian archipelago 2,400 km east of the Philippines comprising Commonwealth of the Northern Mariana Is. (Saipan, 15°N, 146°E), and Guam (13°N, 144°E).

Marquesas Is.: 7°–10°S, 138°–141°W. French Polynesian archipelago of 12 islands about 1,200 km northeast of Tahiti.

Marshall Is.: 5°–15°N, 161°–172°E. Micronesian group of 34 atolls and islands including Ratak and Ralik chains. Bikini was a nuclear test site in the 1940-50s.

Martha's Vineyard: 41°N, 71°W. Massachusetts island south of Cape Cod.

Martinique: 15°N, 61°W. French Caribbean island.

Matsu (26°N, 120°E) and **Quemoy** (24°N, 118°E): Chinese coastal islands about 250 km apart; administered and garrisoned by Taiwan since 1950.

Mauritius: 20°S, 58°E. Indian Ocean island 800 km east of Madagascar. Part of Mascarene Archipelago, with Réunion.

Melanesia: From the Greek meaning black islands; Pacific islands south of Micronesia and west of Polynesia—including New Guinea, the Solomons, New Hebrides and Fiji.

Micronesia: From the Greek meaning small islands; Pacific islands north of the Equator between Hawaii and the Philippines.

Midway: 28°N, 177°W.

Mindanao: see *Philippines.*

Nantucket, Massachusetts: 41°N, 70°W. Massachusetts island south of Cape Cod. Major 19th-century whaling port.

Nauru: 1°S, 167°E. Island nation 2,300 km northeast of Sydney, Australia.

New Caledonia: 18°–22°S, 163°–168°E. Pacific island that forms, with Loyalty Is., French overseas territory.

New Guinea: 5°S, 140°E. Largest island in Melanesia, shared by Indonesia and Papua New Guinea.

Newfoundland: 48°N, 56°W. Large Canadian Atlantic island south of Labrador.

Novaya Zemlya: 74°N, 57°E. New Land; Russian archipelago comprising two main islands, 960 km long, between Barents and Kara Seas.

Novosibirskiye Ostrova: 75°N, 142°E. New Siberian Is.; Russian group between Laptev and East Siberian Seas.

Okinawa: see *Ryukyu Is.*

Orkney Is.: 59°N, 3°W. Group of more than 20 islands, 85 km north-south, 10 km north of Scotland.

Outer Banks, North Carolina: 35°N, 76°W. Barrier islands—Roanoke, Pea, Bodie, Hatteras, Ocracoke and Portsmouth—stretching 145 km north-south off North Carolina between the Atlantic Ocean and Albemarle and Pamlico Sounds.

Ouessant, Ile d' (Ushant): 48°N, 5°W. Atlantic island off northwest France at entrance to English Channel.

Paracel Is.: 17°N, 112°E. South China Sea group about 400 km east of Vietnam; also claimed by China and Taiwan.

Philippines: Southeast Asian nation of more than 7,000 islands: Luzon, Samar, Palawan, Mindanao, Sulu Archipelago, Zamboanga.

Pitcairn: 25°S, 130°W. British colony (with Ducie, Henderson and Oeno Is.) halfway between Tahiti and Easter Island. HMS *Bounty* mutineers arrived in 1790.

Polynesia: From the Greek meaning many islands; Pacific islands within a triangle drawn between Hawaii, New Zealand and Easter Island.

Pribilof Is.: 57°N, 170°W. Alaskan Bering Sea group.

Prince Edward: 46°N, 63°W. Canadian island province in Gulf of St. Lawrence and connected to Nova Scotia by bridge.

Puerto Rico: 18°N, 66°W. Easternmost and fourth largest of Greater Antilles.

Qeshm: 26°N, 56°E. Iranian island in Strait of Hormuz at the mouth of the Persian Gulf.

Queen Charlotte Is.: 51°N, 129°W. Canadian group off British Columbia.

Queen Elizabeth Is.: 74°–82°N, 60°–125°W. Northernmost Canadian Arctic archipelago: Ellesmere Is., Parry Group and Sverdrup Group.

Quemoy: see *Matsu and Quemoy.*

Réunion: 21°S, 56°E. French Indian Ocean island 690 km east of Madagsacar; part of Mascarene Archipelago, with Mauritius.

Ryukyu Is.: 24°–31°N, 123°–131°E. Japanese chain stretching 1,000 km between Taiwan and Kyushu. Okinawa was a major World War II battleground.

Saipan: see *Mariana Is.*

St. Helena: 15°S, 6°W. British Atlantic island where Napoleon was exiled and died.

St. Lawrence Is.: 64°N, 171°W. Alaskan Bering Sea island south of Bering Strait.

St. Lucia: 14°N, 61°W: Second largest of Windward Is.

St. Pierre & Miquelon: 47°N, 56°W. French Atlantic islands southwest of Newfoundland, Canada.

Sakhalin: 51°N, 143°E. Russian island, 950 km long, between Sea of Japan and Sea of Okhostk.

Samoa Is.: 13°–14°S, 168°–173°W. Pacific group divided between Western Samoa and American Samoa.

Sandwich Islands: Former name of the Hawaiian Islands.

Sardinia: 40°N, 9°E. Italian island in western Mediterranean.

Severnaya Zemlya: 80°N, 98°E. Russian group (four main islands) discovered in 1913, between Kara and Laptev Seas.

Seychelles: 4°–5°S, 56°E. Indian Ocean republic of 115 islands extending 1,200 km northeast-southwest about 1,600 km east of Kenya.

Shetland Is.: 61°N, 1°W. British group of about 100 islands 80 km northeast of the Orkneys.

Shikoku: 33°N, 133°E. Smallest of four main Japanese islands.

Sicily: 37°N, 14°E. Italian island in central Mediterranean.

Singapore: 1°N, 104°E. Island nation off tip of Malay Peninsula at east end of Strait of Malacca.

Skye: see *Hebrides/Western Isles.*

Society Is.: 16°–18°S, 148°–154°W. French Polynesian archipelago, 750-km long, including Tahiti; settled around 500 B.C.

Socotra: 13°N, 54°E. Yemeni Indian Ocean island about 250 km northeast of Somalia.

Solomon Is.: 156°–171°E, 5°–13°S. Melanesian archipelago of about 1,000 islands stretching 1,400 km southeast from New Guinea. Guadalcanal was major World War II battleground.

South Georgia Is.: 54°S, 37°W; and South Sandwich Is.: 56°S, 26°W. British dependent territory 1,500 km east of the Falklands.

South Orkney Is.: 61°S, 44°–46°W. British group about 1,440 km southeast of South America.

South Shetland Is.: 61°–64°S, 54°–63°W. Four-group chain, 540-km long, about 120 km north of the Antarctic Peninsula.

Spice Islands: See *Maluku.*

Spitsbergen: 79°N, 20°E: Norwegian Atlantic island; forms, with Bear Island (74°N, 19°E), dependency of Svalbard.

Spratly Is.: 9°N, 112°E. South China Sea archipelago about 500 km southeast of Vietnam; also claimed by China, Taiwan, Malaysia and the Philippines.

Sulawesi (Celebes): 2°S, 121°E. Indonesian island between Borneo and Maluku Is.

Sulu Archipelago: 5°–7°N, 120°–122°E. Philippine archipelago of about 900 islands between Celebes and Sulu Seas.

Sumatra: 0°, 100°E. Largest and westernmost island in Indonesia.

Taiwan: 23°N, 121°E. South China Sea island about 130 km east of mainland China.

Tasmania: 43°S, 17°E. Indian Ocean island 500 km south of southeast Australia; Australian state.

Tierra del Fuego: 54°S, 69°W. Island shared by Chile and Argentina between the Atlantic and Pacific Oceans; separated from South America by Strait of Magellan, and north of Cape Horn (55°59'S, 67°16'W).

Tongan (Friendly) Is.: 15°–23°S, 173°–177°W. Polynesian country of 171 islands (36 inhabited) stretching 1,000 km north-south about 2,000 km northeast of New Zealand.

Trinidad, Isla: 39°S, 62°W. Brazilian island 1,200 east of Brazil.

Trinidad and Tobago: 10°N, 61°W. Caribbean nation group off Venezuela.

Tristan da Cunha: 37°S, 12°W. British Atlantic group about 2,800 km east southeast of South Africa.

Tsushima: 34°N, 129°E. Japanese island in Korean (or Tsushima) Strait.

Tuamotu Archipelago: 14°–23°S, 134°–149°W. French Polynesian chain of 80 islands, 1,700 km long, east of Tahiti.

Vancouver: 50°N, 126°W. Largest island on west coast of Canada; part of British Columbia.

Vanuatu (New Hebrides): 13°–20°S, 166°–170°E. Melanesian island nation, 900 km long.

Victoria: 71°N, 114°W. Canadian Arctic island.

Volcano Is. (Kazan-Retto): 25°N, 141°E. Japanese group of three islands 1,100 km southwest of Tokyo. Iwo Jima was a major World War II battleground.

Wake Is.: 19°N, 177°E. U.S. Pacific atoll, 1,900 km west of Midway: Wilkes, Wake and Peale Islands.

Wight, Isle of: 51°N, 1°W. British English Channel island off Portsmouth and Southampton.

Windward Is.: see *Antilles.*

Wrangel Island (Ostrov Vrangelia): 71°N, 180°E/W. Russian island in East Siberian Sea.

▶THE POLAR REGIONS

Antarctica

• **GEOGRAPHY** **Location:** continent mostly south of Antarctic Circle at 90°S. **Boundaries:** None. Bordered by South Atlantic, Indian and South Pacific oceans. **Total land area:** about 5,404,000 sq. mi. (14,000,000 sq km). **Coastline:** 11,165 mi. (17,968 km). **Comparative area:** twice the size of Australia. **Land use:** 98% continental ice sheet; 2% barren rock. **Natural Resources:** None presently exploited. Iron ore, chromium, copper, gold, nickel, platinum, and other minerals, as well as coal and hydrocarbons have been found in small uncommercial qualities. **Temperature:** Varies with location and altitude. East Antarctica is coldest; Antarctic Peninsula in the west is mildest; mean annual temperature of the interior regions is also −57°C (−71°F); mean temperatures at the coastal McMurdo station range from also −28°C (also −18°F) in August to −3°C (27°F) in January. **Major cities:** none.

● **THE LAND** Some 200 million years ago Antarctica was joined to South America, Africa, India and Australia as one large continent. Geological changes caused the breakup into separate con-

The 50 Tallest Buildings in the World

The two towers of New York City's World Trade Center were, until their destruction by a terrorist plane attack on Sept. 11, 2001, then the fifth- and sixth-tallest buildings in the world, at 1,368 and 1,362 feet. The building being constructed at Ground Zero, One World Trade Center, will be 1,776 feet and is expected to be complete in 2013. On July 16, 2009, Chicago's Sears Tower was renamed the Willis Tower.

Rank, Building	City	Height Meters	Feet	Floors	Year
1. Burj Khalifa	Dubai	828 m	2,716 ft	162	2010
2. Taipei 101	Taipei	509 m	1,671 ft	101	2004
3. Shanghai World Financial Center	Shanghai	492 m	1,614 ft	101	2008
4. International Commerce Center	Hong Kong	484 m	1,588 ft	108	2010
5. Petronas Tower 1	Kuala Lumpur	452 m	1,483 ft	88	1998
6. Petronas Tower 2	Kuala Lumpur	452 m	1,483 ft	88	1998
7. Nanjing Greenland Financial Center	Nanjing	450 m	1,476 ft	66	2010
8. Willis Tower	Chicago	442 m	1,451 ft	108	1974
9. Guangzhou West Tower	Guangzhou	438 m	1,435 ft	103	2010
10. Jin Mao Tower	Shanghai	421 m	1,380 ft	88	1999
11. Two International Finance Center	Hong Kong	415 m	1,362 ft	88	2003
12. Trump International Hotel	Chicago	415 m	1,362 ft	96	2009
13. CITIC Plaza	Guangzhou	391 m	1,283 ft	80	1997
14. Shun Hing Square	Shenzhen	384 m	1,260 ft	69	1996
15. Empire State Building	New York City	381 m	1,250 ft	102	1931
16. Central Plaza	Hong Kong	374 m	1,227 ft	78	1992
17. Bank of China Tower	Hong Kong	367 m	1,205 ft	70	1990
18. Bank of America Tower	New York City	366 m	1,200 ft	54	2009
19. Almas Tower	Dubai	363 m	1,191 ft	68	2009
20. Emirates Office Tower	Dubai	355 m	1,163 ft	54	2000
21. Tuntex Sky Tower	Kaohsiung	348 m	1,140 ft	85	1997
22. Aon Center	Chicago	346 m	1,136 ft	83	1973
23. The Center	Hong Kong	346 m	1,135 ft	73	1998
24. John Hancock Center	Chicago	344 m	1,128 ft	100	1969
25. Wenzhou Trade Center	Wenzhou	333 m	1,094 ft	68	2010
26. Rose Tower	Dubai	333 m	1,093 ft	72	2007
27. Shimao International Plaza	Shanghai	333 m	1,093 ft	60	2006
28. Minsheng Bank Building	Wuhan	331 m	1,087 ft	68	2007
29. Ryugyong Hotel	Pyongyang	330 m	1,083 ft	105	1992
30. China World Trade Center	Beijing	330 m	1,083 ft	74	2009
31. The Index	Dubai	328 m	1,076 ft	80	2010
32. Q1 Tower	Gold Coast City	323 m	1,058 ft	80	2005
33. Burj Al Arab	Dubai	321 m	1,053 ft	60	1999
34. Chrysler Building	New York City	319 m	1,046 ft	77	1930
35. Nina Tower	Hong Kong	319 m	1,046 ft	80	2007
36. New York Times Tower	New York City	319 m	1,046 ft	52	2007
37. HHHR Tower	Dubai	317 m	1,040 ft	72	2010
38. Bank of America Plaza	Atlanta	312 m	1,023 ft	55	1992
39. US Bank Tower	Los Angeles	310 m	1,018 ft	73	1989
40. Menara Telekom	Kuala Lumpur	310 m	1,017 ft	55	2001
41. Ocean Heights	Dubai	310 m	1,017 ft	82	2010
42. Sky Tower	Abu Dhabi	310 m	1,017 ft	74	2010
43. Jumeirah Emirates Towers	Dubai	309 m	1,014 ft	56	2000
44. AT&T Corporate Center	Chicago	307 m	1,007 ft	60	1989
45. The Address Downtown	Dubai	306 m	1,004 ft	63	2008
46. JPMorgan Chase Tower	Houston	305 m	1,002 ft	75	1982
47. Northeast Asia Trade Tower	Incheon	305 m	1,001 ft	70	2010
48. Baiyoke Tower II	Bangkok	304 m	997 ft	85	1997
49. Two Prudential Plaza	Chicago	303 m	995 ft	64	1990
50. Wells Fargo Plaza	Houston	302 m	992 ft	71	1983

Note: Building height measured from sidewalk to structural top, and does not include antennae or poles. **Source:** Emporis © 2010.

tinents. Studies indicate that Antarctica once had a tropical environment, but that its present ice form is at least 20 million years old. Approximately 98 percent of the continent is covered by ice; contains about 90 percent of the world's ice and 70 percent of the fresh water. Elevations average from 6,600 ft. to 13,200 ft. (2,000–4,000 m); mountain ranges up to 16,066 ft. (4,897 m) high. The lowest known land point in Antarctica is in the Bentley Subglacial Trench, which reaches depths as low as –2,540 meters. The Trench at its surface is the deepest ice yet discovered and the world's lowest elevation not under seawater. Ice-free coastal areas include parts of southern Victoria Land, Wilkes Land and Ross Island. The Antarctic ice sheet averages 7,090 ft. (2,160 m) in depth and is 15,670 ft. (4,776 m) deep at its thickest point. Altitude at the South Pole is about 9,800 ft. (3,000 m).

● **LAND/SEA LIFE:** Land life includes bacteria, lichens, mosses, two kinds of flowering plants in the ice-free areas, penguins and some flying birds. Sea life includes several types of seals and whales many of which were hunted to near extinction but are now protected by international conventions.

● **EXPLORATION:** British Captain James Cook circumnavigated the continent without sighting land in 1772–75. U.S. Capt. John Davis made the first known landing on the continent on Feb. 7, 1821. In 1908 the U.K. became the first nation to claim a slice of the continent, subsequently followed by claims from New Zealand (1923), France (1924), Australia (1933), Norway (1939), Chile (1940) and Argentina (1943). The U.S. and Russia have never claimed any Antarctica territory. Claims made by other nations are not recognized by other countries nor by the U.N.

In 1911 Capt. Robert F. Scott and Roald Amundsen of Norway began a race to the pole. Amundsen's party arrived at the South Pole on December 14, 1911 while Scott located the pole on January 18, 1912.

● **SCIENTIFIC RESEARCH:** The greatest scientific study ever conducted in Antarctica occurred in 1957–58 when 67 nations participated in the International Geophysical Year (IGY). Twelve countries established more than 50 stations to study the effects of the continent's huge ice mass on global weather, the oceans, the aurora australis and the ionosphere. During the late 1980s research was focused on the study of the ozone depletion in the stratosphere—called the ozone hole—which allows high levels of potentially harmful ultraviolet radiation to reach the earth's surface.

In 2009, 29 nations, all signatories to the Antarctic Treaty, operated through their National Antarctic program a number of seasonal (summer) and year-round research stations. The countries with the most representation in Antarctica are Argentina, Australia, Russia, Chile, the U.S., and the United Kingdom.

● **PEOPLE Population:** No indigenous inhabitants. Staffing of research stations varies seasonally; Summer (January) population: approx. 4,400; Winter (July) population: approximately 1,000

● **GOVERNMENT Antarctica Treaty:** Signed in 1959 by the 12 IGY nations (in force as of June 23, 1961), it establishes a legal framework for the management of Antarctica. The treaty was re-newed in 1991 in Madrid, where 24 countries, including the United States, signed a protocol to ban mineral and oil exploration for 50 years and to provide wildlife protection. The treaty states that the area is to be used for peaceful purposes only and military activity such as weapons testing is prohibited; calls for freedom of scientific investigation and cooperation and a free exchange of information and personnel; nuclear explosions or disposal of radioactive wastes is forbidden; and, treaty-state observers have free access, including aerial observation, to any area and may inspect all stations, installations and equipment.

In April 2009, more than 400 Antarctic program managers, diplomats, polar scientists, and logistic experts from 47 countries met for the 32nd Antarctic Treaty Consultative Meeting. The main topic of discussion was the limitation of tourist ships; representatives agreed to new regulations that prohibit landings of tourist ships on the continent carrying more than 500 passengers, and a requirement that ships de-board no more than 100 people at a time. They also agreed to support the International Maritime Organization's drive to ensure the safety of polar shipping, and agreed to petition the IMO to extend the boundary of their Antarctic Special Area northward to protect the region's ecosystem. As of 2010, there were 47 signatories to the Treaty, 28 of which have had their activities in Antarctica recognized as "substantial research."

In 2008, New Zealand and the U.S. began building Antarctica's first wind farm, under the shared umbrella of Antarctica New Zealand and the U.S. Antarctic Program. The project is estimated to cut fuel consumption by 122,312 gallons every year, reducing greenhouse gas production by 1,242 tons of carbon dioxide annually.

In October 2009, the journal *Science* reported that ice sheets in Antarctica appeared to be shrinking faster than originally thought. Scientists estimate that if the West Antarctic Ice Sheet were to collapse, sea levels worldwide could rise up to 10 feet.

The Arctic

● **GEOGRAPHY Location:** The Arctic Regions comprise all the lands north of the Arctic Circle—66°30'N—including the northern reaches of Asia, Europe, and North America, the Arctic Ocean, and its islands. In terms of climate, geography, and culture this demarcation is relatively insignificant, but within the Arctic Circle there is at least one 24-hour period during which the sun never sets (summer solstice), and one in which it never rises (winter solstice). The Arctic Ocean is the fourth largest after the Pacific, Atlantic and Indian; its primary marginal seas are Baffin Bay, the Barents Sea, the Beaufort Sea, the Chukchi Sea, the East Siberian Sea, the Greenland Sea, Hudson Bay, Hudson Strait, the Kara Sea, and the Laptev Sea. Some oceanographers consider the Arctic Ocean to be a marginal sea of the Atlantic Ocean. **Boundaries:** None. **Total area:** The Arctic Ocean is 5,440,000 sq. mi. (14,090,000 sq km). The main island groups are the Canadian Arctic Archipelago (550,000 sq. mi.; 1,424,483 sq km), Greenland (840,000 sq. mi.; 2,175,590 sq km), Novaya Zemlya (31,000 sq. mi.; 80,290 sq km), and Svalbard (24,000 sq.

mi.; 62,160 sq km). **Coastline:** 17,525 sq. mi. (45,389 km). **Comparative area:** The Arctic Ocean is about 1.5 times the size of the United States. **Land use:** The central surface is covered by a perennial drifting polar ice cap which averages about 3 meters thick, although pressure ridges may be three times that size. It drifts in a clockwise pattern in the Beaufort Gyral Stream, but exhibits nearly straight-line movement from the New Siberian Islands (Russia) to the Denmark Strait (between Greenland and Iceland). The ice pack is surrounded by open seas during the summer, but more than doubles in size during the winter and extends to the encircling land masses; the ocean floor is about 50 percent continental shelf (the highest percentage of any ocean) with the remainder a central basin interrupted by three submarine ridges (the Alpha Cordillera, Nansen Cordillera, and Lomonsov Ridge). The maximum depth is 17,881 ft. (5,450 m) in the Fram Basin. **Natural resources:** In the Arctic Ocean there are sand and gravel aggregates, placer deposits, polymetallic nodules, oil and gas fields, fish, and marine mammals (seals and whales). **Climate:** The dominant fact of life is the frigid conditions: persistent cold and relatively modest annual temperature ranges; winters characterized by continuous darkness, cold and stable weather conditions and clear skies; summers characterized by continuous daylight, damp and foggy weather, and weak cyclones with rain or snow. Between 60°N and 75°N there is seasonal freezing, while north of 75°N there is permanent ice. In North America, temperatures during the colder months average –25°F (–31°C), while Siberia is somewhat colder at –35°F (–37°C). **Environment:** Endangered marine species include walruses and whales; ice islands occasionally break away from northern Ellesmere Island; icebergs calved from western Greenland and extreme northeastern Canada; maximum snow cover in March or April is about 20–50 cm over the frozen ocean and lasts about 10 months; permafrost in islands; virtually ice-locked from October to June; fragile ecosystem slow to change and slow to recover from disruptions or damage.

● **PEOPLE Population** Ethnologists distinguish three native cultural areas—the Western Arctic, including Eskimo peoples (from the east coast of Greenland to Alaska) and Aleuts; Paleo-Siberian, including the Chukchi and Eskimos of Eastern Asia; and Eurasian Arctic, including some Chukchi, Yakut, Nenets, and Lapps. Today, however, the vast majority of the people living and working within the Arctic Circle are non-native peoples in industry or scientific enterprises.
● **GOVERNMENT** Governments with territory north of the Arctic Circle are Canada, the United States, Russia, Finland, Sweden, Norway, and Denmark (Greenland). Svalbard is the focus of a maritime boundary dispute between Norway and Russia.
● **ECONOMY** While there is a fair amount of economic activity in the continental portions of the Arctic—principally extractive industries in Siberia, northern Canada, and Alaska's North Slope—conditions in the numerous Arctic islands all but prevent significant development there. Norwegian and Russian miners extract about 1 million tons of coal per year from mines on Svalbard, and in Greenland there are large deposits of cryolite, lead, and other minerals, but only lead can be mined economically. Economic activity in the Arctic Ocean is limited to the exploitation of natural resources including crude oil, natural gas, fishing and sealing.
● **COMMUNICATIONS Ports:** Churchill (Canada), Murmansk (Russia), Prudhoe Bay (U.S.). **Telecommunications:** No submarine cables. **Transportation:** There is a sparse network of air, ocean, river, and land routes. The Arctic provides the shortest marine link between the extremes of eastern and western Russia. The two major waterways are the Northwest Passage, in North America, and the Northern Sea Route, in Asia, but ships are subject to superstructure icing from October to May. The U.S. and Russia operate floating research stations. Access to the Arctic Ocean from the Pacific Ocean is through the Bering Strait; from the Atlantic, through the Davis Strait (between Canada and Greenland), the Denmark Strait (between Greenland and Iceland), or the Norwegian Sea (between Iceland and Norway).

Climate and Weather

▶ CLIMATES OF THE WORLD

Knowing the similarities and differences between climates in various parts of the world helps us understand many things about our planet: why people live where they do; how they make their living; the problems and potentials of their land. Climates are very complex, however, and no climatic classification is ideal. The most commonly used classification was developed more than 50 years ago by a German climatologist, Wladimir Köppen. The Köppen system uses temperature and precipitation as the major criteria for grouping climates. Boundaries between climatic zones are determined by the limits of where certain plants grow. The five major climatic zones are known by the capital letters **A**, **B**, **C**, **D**, and **E**; each major zone has subzones. High-altitude areas are sometimes shown with the letter **H** because their climates are so complex that small maps cannot show all the detail.

(Note: In the following chart, **R** stands for the annual rainfall in centimeters; **T** is the average annual temperature in degrees Celsius.)

A: Humid tropical climates. The average temperature of every month is 64° F (18°C) or higher. There is no winter.
Af *Rain forest.* The driest month has at least 2.4 inches (6 cm) of rain. The Amazon Basin is an example of an **Af** climate.
Am *Monsoon.* Similar to **Af** but with a short dry season. The amount of rainfall in the driest month is less than 2.4 inches (6 cm) but equal to or greater than 10 – (R/25). The southwestern coast of India is an example of an **Am** climate.
Aw *Savanna.* There is a well-defined dry season in the winter. The amount of rainfall in the driest month is less than 10 – (R/25). The Brazilian Highlands are a large area with an **Aw** climate.

As (Rare)   There is a well-defined dry season in the summer.

B Dry climates.   Annual rainfall is less than annual potential evaporation. The boundary between dry areas and humid areas is R < 2T + 28 when at least 70 percent of the rainfall occurs in the warmer six months; R < 2T when at least 70 percent of the rainfall occurs in the cooler six months; or R < 2T + 14 when neither half of the year receives at least 70 percent of the total annual rainfall.

BS *Steppe.*   The boundary between steppe and desert is half of the dry/humid boundary. Steppes border many of the world's large deserts.

BSh *Low-latitude steppe.*   The average annual temperature is at least 64° F (18° C).

BSk *Mid-latitude steppe.*   The average annual temperature is less than 64° F (18° C).

BW *Desert.*   The boundary between desert and steppe is half of the dry/humid boundary. The Sahara Desert is the largest area with a **BW** climate.

BWh *Low-latitude desert.*   The average annual temperature is at least 64° F (18° C).

BWk *Mid-latitude desert.*   The average annual temperature is less than 64° F (18° C).

C Subtropical climates.   The average temperature of the coldest month is between 64° F (18° C) and 27° F (–3° C). These are mainly humid mid-latitude areas with mild winters. The principal natural vegetation is broad-leafed forest.

Cw (Rare)   The wettest month occurs in summer and has at least ten times as much rainfall as the driest month in winter. **Cw** zones are mainly areas of evergreen forest in mountainous **Aw** zones.

Cs *Dry summer.*   The wettest month occurs in winter and has at least three times as much rainfall as the driest month in summer. Less than 1.5 inches (4 cm) of rain falls during the driest summer month.

Csa *Warm, dry summer.*   The average temperature of the warmest month is more than 72° F (22° C), and for at least four months the average temperature is more than 50° F (10° C). Italy and other Mediterranean countries have a **Csa** climate.

Csb *Cool, dry summer.*   In no month is the average temperature more than 72° F (22° C), but for at least four months the average temperature is more than 50° F (10° C). **Csb** climates are found near San Francisco, California; on the coast near Santiago, Chile; and in Portugal.

Cf *Humid summer.*   Areas that cannot meet the criteria for **Cw** and **Cs**.

Cfa *Humid, warm summer.*   The average temperature of the warmest month is more than 72° F (22° C), and for at least four months the average temperature is more than 50° F (10° C). Much of the eastern United States has a **Cfa** zone.

Cfb *Marine west coast.*   In no month is the average temperature more than 72° F (22° C), but for at least four months the average temperature is more than 50° F (10° C). Great Britain, New Zealand, and the west coast of Alaska are all examples of **Cfb** climates.

D Continental climates.   The average temperature of the warmest month is more than 50° F (10° C), and the average temperature of the coldest month is 27° F (–3° C) or below. Forests are the principal natural vegetation.

Dfa *Humid, warm summer.*   All seasons have some precipitation. The average temperature of the warmest month is more than 72° F (22° C), and for at least four months the average temperature is more than 50° F (10° C). The northern Great Plains of the United States have a **Dfa** climate.

Dwa *Humid, warm summer.*   The wettest month occurs in summer and has at least ten times as much rainfall as the driest month in winter. The average temperature of the warmest month is more than 72° F (22° C), and for at least four months the average temperature is more than 50° F (10° C). The land around the northern part of the Yellow Sea has a **Dwa** climate.

Dfb *Humid, cool summer.*   All seasons have some precipitation. In no month is the average temperature more than 72° F (22° C), but for at least four months the average temperature is more than 50° F (10° C). A large **Dfb** area stretches from eastern Europe into Asia.

Dwb *Humid, cool summer.*   The wettest month occurs in summer and has at least ten times as much rainfall as the driest month in winter. In no month is the average temperature more than 72° F (22° C), but for at least four months the average temperature is more than 50° F (10° C). Much of the area between Manchuria and the Sea of Okhotsk has a **Dwb** climate.

Dfc *Subpolar.*   All seasons have some precipitation. For one to three months, the average temperature is 50° (10° C) or more. A huge **Dfc** area is in Siberia and adjacent parts of the Soviet Union.

E Polar climates.   The average temperature of the warmest month is less than 50° F (10° C). There is no summer, and no trees grow.

ET *Tundra.* The average temperature of the warmest month is less than 50° F (10° C) but more than 32° F (0° C). Vast areas of northern North America, Europe, and Asia lie in the **ET** climate zone.

EF *Ice cap.*   The average temperature of the warmest 8 month is 32° F (0° C) or less. The **EF** climate is found at the North and South Poles and in interior Greenland.

▶WEATHER EXTREMES

Hottest place: Dallol Danakil Depression, Ethiopia. Average annual temperature: 35°C/95°F.

Hottest temperature ever recorded: 7.8°C/136°F. El Aziza, Libya. Sept. 13, 1922.

Coldest place: Plateau Station, Antarctica. Average annual temperature: –56.7°C/–71.7°F.

Coldest temperature ever recorded: –89.2°C/–128.5°F. Vostok, Antarctica. July 21, 1983.

Wettest place: Mawsynram, Assam, India. Average annual rainfall: 11.873 m/38.925 ft.

Wettest year on record: 26.47 m/86.84 ft. Cherrapunji, India. Aug. 1860–July 1861.

Driest place: Atacama Desert, Chile. Average annual rainfall: too small to measure.

Longest dry period: 173 months. Arica, Chile. Oct. 1903–Jan. 1918.

▶EL NIÑO AND LA NIÑA

The two ends of a natural, very complex climatic balancing act, caused by the interaction between the surface layers of the tropical Pacific Ocean and the atmosphere above it, with winds and planetary-scale ocean waves shipping the changing conditions from one side of the ocean to the other.

The sheer size and breadth of the Pacific allow El Niños and La Niñas time to develop and to have widespread effects. During La Niñas, tropical ocean temperatures become colder in the eastern and central Pacific regions and warmer in the west; tradewinds are stronger and normally wet regions become drier. During El Niños the shift is exactly the opposite: weaker tradewinds, colder tropical water in the west and warmer water in the east off the coast of South America, and much more rain in dry areas—and more frequent and more intense hurricanes in the eastern Pacific. These systemic changes also noticeably affect winters in the continental U.S.: La Niñas bring warmer than normal winters to the Southeast and colder than normal to the Northwest, while El Niños generally cause warmer winters in the North Central states and colder winters in the Southeast and Southwest.

Fishermen off the coasts of Peru, Ecuador and Colombia first noticed and named El Niño for the tendency of its very warm waters to arrive around Christmastime. Before the 1982–83 El Niño, scientists had no ability to forecast these massive weather changes, and, despite great advances in the field, still missed the rapid onset, the great magnitude and sudden demise of the 1997–98 El Niño. Yet once forecasters had some of the data, they were able to predict six months in advance the unusual effects of El Niños and La Niñas, such as increased snowfall, floods, and droughts. La Niñas often (but not always) occur after El Niños. Typically, La Niñas occur less frequently than El Niños, which occur irregularly every 2–7 years and last 12–18 months.

The climate prediction center at the N.O.A.A. reported in May 2010 that, although not a full-blown El Niño effect, since April 2009 the upper-ocean heat content has been above average across the eastern half of the equatorial Pacific Ocean. Sharp increases in heat content during June and October 2009 coincide with the development and subsequent strengthening of El Niño, respectively. Since late February 2010, however, the heat content anamolies have steadily decreased. In August 2009, British journal *The Independent* reported that scientists predict that the current El Niño could make 2010 one of the hottest years on record. In between these extremes is normal weather. Some El Niños are more extreme than others, as are their La Niña counterparts.

So far, researchers have been unable to link El Niños/La Niñas to sunspots or volcanic eruptions. Scientists are studying the compelling question of whether there is a relationship between El Niños/La Niñas and climate change, and though nothing conclusive has yet been discovered, as early as 2000, *Science* reported that the possibilty cannot be excluded. This idea is bolstered by the fact that in the last several decades the number of El Niño events has increased as corresponding La Niñas have decreased. There is, however, still considerable disagreement and contending theories about exactly what constitutes these phenomena, what their effects are, and what role they play in Earth's complex climate and ecology.

▶GLOSSARY OF WEATHER WORDS

Air mass A large body of air that, at a given elevation, has about the same temperature and humidity throughout.

Barometric pressure The weight of a column of air at a particular place is determined by measuring the height of a column of mercury under a vacuum. The instrument for making such a measurement is called a barometer. At sea level, the standard barometric pressure is 29.92 inches (76 cm). In the International System, air pressure is measured in bars or in kiloPascals. A bar is slightly

Determining the Wind-Chill Factor

Sometimes called a wind-chill index, this is a measure of the cooling power of air movement and low temperature on the human body. Because heat passes directly from a warm body to the cooler air surrounding it—a process known as convection—wind produces a continuing source of cooler air and a chilling effect that is equivalent to a lower temperature. The effect on a warm day is pleasant, but as temperatures approach freezing, wind chill is not only unpleasant, but can be dangerous. As the table below shows, a temperature of 5°F combined with a breeze of 20 mph produces a wind-chill temperature of –15°F—a temperature at which frostbite occurs much sooner than at 5°F. Wind speeds above 45 mph have little additional cooling effect.

Actual Temperature	Wind speed								
	5 mph	10 mph	15 mph	20 mph	25 mph	30 mph	35 mph	40 mph	45 mph
35°F	31°F	27°F	25°F	24°F	23°F	22°F	21°F	20°F	19°F
30°F	25	21	19	17	16	15	14	13	12
25°F	19	15	13	11	9	8	7	6	5
20°F	13	9	6	4	3	1	0	–1	–2
15°F	7	3	0	–2	–4	–5	–7	–8	–9
10°F	1	–4	–7	–9	–11	–12	–14	–15	–16
5°F	–5	–10	–13	–15	–17	–19	–21	–22	–23
0°F	–11	–16	–19	–22	–24	–26	–27	–29	–30
–5°F	–16	–22	–26	–29	–31	–33	–34	–36	–37
–10°F	–22	–28	–32	–35	–37	–39	–41	–43	–44
–15°F	–28	–35	–39	–42	–44	–46	–48	–50	–51
–20°F	–34	–41	–45	–48	–51	–53	–55	–57	–58
–25°F	–40	–47	–51	–55	–58	–60	–62	–64	–65
–30°F	–46	–53	–58	–61	–64	–67	–69	–71	–72
–35°F	–52	–59	–64	–68	–71	–73	–76	–78	–79
–40°F	–57	–66	–71	–74	–78	–80	–82	–84	–86
–45°F	–63	–72	–77	–81	–84	–87	–89	–91	–93

Source: National Oceanic and Atmospheric Administration (2000).

less than the standard air pressure at sea level, and a kiloPascal is one-hundredth of a bar. At any location, however, barometric pressure is affected by changes in temperature, humidity, or elevation. When the barometric pressure is falling, the air pressure is decreasing, usually a sign of a storm. When the barometer is rising, fairer weather is on its way.

Climate General weather conditions over a long period of time.

Cold front The place where cold air that is advancing meets warm air that is retreating before it. This kind of weather not only lowers tempera-

ture as it passes but also causes high winds and may cause thunderstorms.

Cyclone A region of low atmospheric pressure (see Depression). Severe cyclones are known as hurricanes, tropical cyclones, and typhoons.

Degree-days A degree-day is one degree of deviation of the daily mean temperature from a given norm, usually 65°F. Cooling degree-days are the number of degrees Fahrenheit by which the mean temperature exceeds 65°F, while heating degree-days are the number of degrees the mean temperature is below 65°F. During a year, keeping track of the total number of degree days for each day is

World Tornado Records

Characteristic	Description	Date	Location
Deadliest Single Tornado	1,300 killed / 12,000 injured	4/26/1989	Manikganj District, Bangladesh
Longest-lasting / greatest distance	352.4km (219 miles) / 3.5 hours duration	3/18/1925	Ellington MO to Princeton IN
Biggest (Numerical) Outbreak	148 Tornadoes	4/3–4/1974	13 central U.S. States
Widest (maximum diameter)	Nearly 4000m (2.5 mi.)	5/22/2004	Hallam, NE
Month with most occurring	543 tornadoes	5/2003	United States
Highest Recorded Wind Speed	135m/s (302 mph)	5/3/1999	Bridge Creek, OK
Longest Tornado Transport	A personal check carried 359 km (223 mi.)	4/11/1991	Stockton, KS to Winnetoon, NE

Source: World Meteorological Organization, Arizona State University, "Global Weather and Climate Extremes."

Worst Hurricanes in U.S. History

The following table ranks hurricanes by the amount of insured losses they caused. Insured losses are the amount claimed by property owners against their insurance policies. It is impossible to calculate the costs incurred by those without insurance. Even after discounting inflation, most of the costliest hurricanes have come within the past 30 years, as more people have built large homes close to shore—and in harm's way. Improved meteorology and organized evacuations, however, have greatly reduced loss of human life. Until Kat-

rina in 2005, the 25 deadliest hurricanes in U.S. history had all occurred before 1975.

The strength of a hurricane is measured in units of atmospheric pressure called Millibars—the strongest storms have the lowest pressure. The most intense hurricane was an unnamed storm that hit the Florida Keys in 1935 with winds greater than 155 mph and minimum pressure of 892 Millibars. By comparison, the two costliest hurricanes—Katrina and Andrew—had minimum pressures of 909 and 920 Millibars, respectively.

COSTLIEST HURRICANES

Rank, Hurricane (year)	Location of primary damage	Insured losses (billions)[1]	Deaths
1. Katrina (2005)	Louisiana, Mississipi	$84.6	1,500
2. Andrew (1992)	Florida, Louisiana	48.1	26
3. Wilma (2005)	Florida	21.5	5
4. Ike (2008)	Texas	19.3	103
5. Charley (2004)	Florida	16.3	10

DEADLIEST HURRICANES

Rank, Hurricane (year)	Deaths[2]
1. Galveston, Texas (1900)	8,000
2. Lake Okeechobee, Fla. (1928)	2,500
3. Katrina—La,. Miss., Ga. (2005)	1,500
4. Cheniere, La. (1893)	1,400
5. Sea Islands, S.C., Ga. (1893)	1,000

Notes: 1. Estimate, adjusted to 2006 dollars. 2. U.S. deaths directly attributable to storm (estimated). **Source:** National Oceanic and Atmospheric Administration, National Hurricane Center. www.nhc.noaa.gov.

Worst Tornadoes in U.S. History

COSTLIEST TORNADOES

Rank, Location	Date	Damages (millions)[1]
1. Topeka, Kansas	June 8, 1966	$1,600
2. Lubbock, Texas	May 11, 1970	1,336
3. Oklahoma City, Okla.	May 3, 1999	1,244
4. Xenia, Ohio	April 3, 1974	1,051
5. Omaha, Neb.	May 6, 1975	966

DEADLIEST TORNADOES

Rank, Location	Date	Deaths
1. Missouri-Illinois-Indiana	Mar. 18, 1925	695
2. Natchez, Miss.	May 6, 1840	317
3. St. Louis, Mo.- E. St. Louis, Ill.	May 27, 1896	255
4. Tupelo, Miss.	April 5, 1936	216
5. Gainesville, Ga.	April 6, 1936	203

Note: 1. In constant (2007) dollars. **Source:** National Oceanic and Atmospheric Administration, National Severe Storms Laboratory, *10 Costliest Tornadoes* (2007), *25 Deadliest Tornadoes* (2007).

used to keep track of cooling or heating needs. For example, oil companies use heating degree-days to estimate how much oil their customers have used and when they might need a refill.

Depression   Any region of low air pressure. In temperate regions over land, the typical depression is a *low*. The often more powerful depression occurring over tropical waters is called a *tropical depression*. If the air pressure in a tropical depression continues to fall, it becomes a tropical storm, or, lower still, a *hurricane*.

Dew point   The temperature at which dew (drops of water) begins to form as air cools. Air can hold only a certain amount of water vapor at a given temperature. When the temperature falls, excess water vapor must turn into a liquid.

El Niño   (See "El Niño and La Niña.")

Front   The boundary between two different air masses.

High   An air mass characterized by higher-than-normal air pressure; usually this is a fair-weather system. Some highs are typically found in the same place each year, such as the one that occurs over Bermuda in most summers.

Hurricane   A huge tropical rainstorm with winds that swirl rapidly around a calm, dry central eye. To be classified a hurricane, a tropical storm must have wind speeds of more than 74 mph (119 km/hr). The average hurricane is 375 miles (600 km) in diameter and extends up 40,000 feet (12,000 m) above the surface of the ocean. The eye averages 12.5 miles (20 km) in diameter. When a hurricane hits land, its fierce winds and floods can do great damage. On average five hurricanes each year threaten the eastern and southern United States.

Jet stream   A strong river or two of high winds in the upper atmosphere (but below the stratosphere) that travels from west to east at between 75 and 150 mph (120–240 km/hr), most often in the middle latitudes. Discovered by American bomber pilots in World War II, it is now known to have significant effects on weather.

La Niña   See "El Niño and La Niña."

Low   An air mass characterized by lower-than-normal air pressure; usually this is the heart of a storm system. Some lows are found in the same region most of the year, such as the low in the Pacific just off the coast of Alaska.

Mean temperature   Technically, this should be the average of all temperatures during the day. Sometimes it is the average of 24 temperatures taken once each hour, but most often the mean temperature is simply the average of the high and low for the day.

Monsoon   A wind system in which the prevailing direction of the wind reverses itself from season to season. Southeast Asia is the most typical monsoon region. The summer (southwest) monsoon, characterized by hot, moist air and heavy rains lasts from April to September. The winter (northeast) monsoon lasts from October to March and is characterized by cool, dry air.

Occluded front   When a cold front overtakes a warm front, the denser cold air flows under the less dense warm air.

Prevailing winds   Throughout the world, winds follow regular patterns. In some places winds are so light and infrequent as to scarcely exist, such as in the doldrums along the equator and in the horse latitudes near latitude 30° north and south. In other places the winds tend to come from a particular direction and are called prevailing winds.

Rain shadow   An area on the leeward side of a mountain range that receives little rainfall.

Relative humidity   The amount of moisture (water vapor) in the air compared with the total amount it can hold expressed as a percent. Warm air can hold more water vapor than cold air, so a relative humidity of 75 percent on a warm summer day is moister than a relative humidity of 75 percent on a cool winter day. However, because evaporation is greater on warm days, the relative humidity is generally higher in summer than in winter.

Secondary cold front   A cold front that sometimes forms behind another cold front and that is often even colder than the first front.

Secondary depression   A low that forms to the south or east of a low that is a storm center.

Squall line   A line of instability that often precedes a cold front, marked by wind gusts and often by heavy rain.

Stationary front   A front that stays in the same place.

Storm surge   The rise in water levels in the ocean or a large lake that comes from a combination of wind and low pressure during a storm, especially pronounced during a hurricane.

Temperature-humidity index   A number derived from a formula relating temperature and humidity to discomfort. When it is 75, many are uncomfortable, while at 80 or above, almost everybody is uncomfortable. Temperatures are less comfortable at high humidities because cooling by sweating is less efficient.

Temperature inversion   A layer of warm air on top of a layer of cooler surface air. Such layering, usually occurring at night, can prevent air pollutants near the surface from rising into the upper air. A long-lasting inversion, especially in industrial areas, can cause an excessive concentration of pollutants to accumulate in the surrounding air.

Tornado   A small and short-lived but very severe windstorm. Tornadoes are whirling columns of air that reach down from a cloud, and they often accompany thunderstorms, rain, and hail. With wind speeds up to 300 mph (480 km/hr), tornadoes can do tremendous damage. The diameter of the average tornado is between 500 and 2,000 feet (150–600 m). The average tornado moves along the ground at 28 mph (45 km/hr) and has a path that is 16 miles (26 km) long. In the United States, some 750 tornadoes are reported every year, most frequently between April and June.

Tropical storm   A storm that forms over the ocean in the tropics and often moves onto land, where it loses strength. Technically, a storm is designated a tropical storm only when winds are between 39 and 73 miles per hour. If winds become greater, a tropical storm becomes a hurricane.

Trough   A low that is long, rather than nearly circular.

Typhoon   A hurricane formed in the western Pacific Ocean.

Warm front   The boundary of a moving warm air mass.

Weather   The condition of the atmosphere—temperature, rain, and wind, for example—in a particular place. A climate is defined by weather conditions over a long period of time.

Wind Any current of air, measured on land in miles per hour, and at sea in knots. The direction of a given wind is determined from the point of the compass from which it blows (e.g., northeast, south). In various regions of the world, names are given to seasonal winds of particular quality. Among these are the *bora*, a cold usually dry north/northeast wind along the eastern Adriatic; *brickfielder*, a hot north wind of southeastern Australia; *buran*, a cold, violent north/northeast wind of Siberia and Central Asia, common in winter; *chinook*, a dry winter or spring wind which blows down the eastern slopes of the Rocky Mountains often warm enough to melt the snow; *harmattan*, a hot, dry north wind in West Africa which cools as it evaporates the moist air of the coast; *mistral*, a cold, strong north/northwest wind of the western Mediterranean with a surface strength of 60 km/hour, frequent in winter; *pampero*, a sudden, cold south or west wind in Argentina and Uruguay frequent in summer; *Santa Ana* a hot, dry wind that blows from the north or east in Southern California; *sirocco*, a hot south wind of North Africa and southern Italy; *southerly burster*, a cold, violent south wind of southeastern Australia; *willi-waw*, a violent squall that blows in the Strait of Magellan (South America); and *zonda*, a hot, dry north wind of Argentina and Uruguay. In 1996 the maximum surface wind gust was recorded at 253 m.p.h. at Barrow Island, Australia (during tropical cyclone Olivia).

Beaufort Wind Scale

In 1806 Adm. Francis Beaufort devised a scale for recording wind force at sea based on the effect of the wind on a full-rigged ship. In 1838, this scale was adopted by the British Admiralty, and in 1874 it was adopted for international use. It is now the chief scale for specifying the force of the wind and is used in all parts of the world, both on land and at sea. Originally, there were no specific wind speeds corresponding to various force numbers on the Beaufort Wind Scale. Since 1946, wind speed has been determined according to measurements made by an anemometer (a device for measuring wind) at 10m (30 ft) above the ground.

Force	Description of wind	Mean wind speed in knots[1]	Specification for use on land and at sea
Force 0	Calm	Less than 1	Calm, smoke rises vertically. Sea like a mirror.
Force 1	Light air	1–3	Direction of wind shown by smoke drift, but not by wind vanes. Ripples with appearance of scales are formed, but without foam crests.
Force 2	Light breeze	4–6	Wind felt on face; leaves rustle; ordinary vane moved by wind. Small wavelets, still short but more pronounced; crests have a glassy appearance and do not break.
Force 3	Gentle breeze	7–10	Leaves and small twigs in constant motion; wind extends light flag. Large wavelets; crests begin to break; foam of glassy appearance; perhaps scattered white horses.
Force 4	Moderate breeze	11–16	Raises dust and loose paper; small branches are moved. Small waves becoming longer; fairly frequent white horses.
Force 5	Fresh breeze	17–21	Small trees in leaf begin to sway; crested wavelets form on inland waters. Moderate waves, taking a more pronounced long form; many white horses are formed (chance of some spray).
Force 6	Strong breeze	22–27	Large branches in motion; whistling heard in telegraph wires; umbrellas used with difficulty. Large waves begin to form; the white foam crests are more extensive everywhere (probably some spray).
Force 7	Moderate gale, near gale	28–33	Whole trees in motion; inconvenience felt when walking against wind. Sea heaps up and white foam from breaking waves begins to be blown in streaks along the direction of the wind.
Force 8	Fresh gale, gale	34–40	Breaks twigs off trees; generally impedes progress. Moderately high waves of greater length; edges of crests begin to break into spindrift; foam is blown in well-marked streaks.
Force 9	Strong gale	41–47	Slight structural damage occurs (chimney pots and slate removed). High waves; dense streaks of foam; crests of waves begin to topple, tumble and roll over.
Force 10	Whole gale, storm	48–55	Seldom experienced inland; trees uprooted; considerable structural damage occurs. Very high waves with long overhanging crests; the resulting foam, in great patches, is blown in dense white streaks; the sea takes a white appearance; the tumbling of the sea becomes heavy and shock like; visibility affected.
Force 11	Storm, violent storm	56–63	Very rarely experienced; accompanied by widespread damage. Exceptionally high waves at sea (medium-sized ships might be lost to view behind the waves); the sea is completely covered with white patches of foam; visibility affected.
Force 12+	Hurricane[2]	64 and above	The air is filled with foam and spray; sea completely white with driving spray; visibility very seriously affected.

Notes: 1. Nautical miles/hour; 1 nautical mile = 1.151 statute miles. 2. Force 13: 72–80 knots; force 14: 81–89; force 15: 90–99; force 16: 100–108; force 17: 109–118. **Sources:** Smithsonian Institution, *Smithsonian Meteorological Tables* (1966); Hydrographer of the Navy (U.K.), *Ocean Passages for the World* (1977).

Average Temperature of U.S. States by Month, 2009

	Jan.	Feb.	Mar.	Apr.	May	June	July	Aug.	Sept.	Oct.	Nov.	Dec.
Alabama	45.2	48.1	57.3	61.2	71.1	79.2	78.0	78.0	75.0	62.6	53.1	45.0
Alaska	N.A.											
Arizona	44.8	46.3	52.8	57.4	71.1	73.4	83.0	79.8	74.4	59.5	52.9	39.5
Arkansas	37.9	47.2	52.4	59.5	67.3	78.8	77.6	76.6	71.0	56.4	54.1	37.9
California	47.6	47.1	51.1	56.5	67.6	68.6	77.7	75.3	73.6	59.5	52.4	43.3
Colorado	27.4	32.4	37.9	42.6	55.8	60.6	67.5	65.2	58.1	40.9	37.8	19.5
Connecticut	20.6	30.1	36.2	48.9	57.3	63.7	68.3	71.3	60.6	48.8	46.0	29.7
Delaware	30.5	38.6	43.2	54.6	63.6	70.6	74.5	77.2	67.1	55.9	50.6	37.1
Florida	57.4	57.2	65.2	69.4	76.5	81.8	81.6	82.0	80.4	75.2	66.0	60.4
Georgia	46.2	47.5	56.3	61.5	71.0	79.6	78.4	78.8	74.3	63.7	55.8	46.2
Hawaii	N.A.											
Idaho	24.4	28.1	33.0	42.8	52.8	59.0	68.2	65.6	61.3	41.1	34.2	20.1
Illinois	20.4	32.3	43.2	51.1	62.5	72.5	70.2	70.6	65.5	49.5	47.1	29.1
Indiana	21.2	32.1	44.0	51.6	61.9	71.5	69.0	70.6	65.2	50.2	46.4	30.4
Iowa	13.3	26.7	36.9	46.8	59.7	68.8	68.0	68.2	63.0	44.4	43.3	19.9
Kansas	31.1	39.6	44.1	51.7	62.7	74.2	75.4	74.1	64.7	48.2	47.4	26.6
Kentucky	29.8	38.1	47.6	55.3	64.6	73.7	71.7	73.4	68.7	53.1	49.1	35.4
Louisiana	50.5	55.8	60.5	65.9	74.5	81.9	82.8	81.2	77.4	66.7	58.6	48.1
Maine	7.6	18.5	25.6	41.8	51.0	58.9	63.2	66.1	54.9	40.9	38.7	22.2
Maryland	28.8	36.7	42.4	54.1	62.7	70.1	72.7	75.6	65.8	54.7	49.4	35.0
Massachussetts	19.7	28.5	35.0	48.1	56.5	62.3	67.3	70.4	59.4	47.4	45.3	28.8
Michigan	12.9	23.0	31.4	42.9	53.2	62.0	63.2	65.1	60.6	44.4	41.3	24.0
Minnesota	2.5	15.3	26.0	42.0	53.3	62.3	64.3	64.4	62.6	39.8	38.1	12.6
Mississippi	45.0	50.6	57.5	62.8	71.8	80.4	79.5	78.9	75.7	62.3	54.6	44.2
Missouri	27.7	38.3	46.5	53.3	63.7	74.6	72.9	72.7	66.4	50.5	50.0	30.7
Montana	20.6	24.9	28.5	40.6	51.4	57.8	65.5	64.1	61.3	37.2	35.4	11.6
Nebraska	25.2	31.8	37.2	45.9	59.0	66.8	70.1	69.1	61.4	41.9	42.2	18.7
Nevada	32.9	35.1	40.5	46.3	60.7	62.7	74.1	69.9	66.5	47.5	40.2	24.7
New Hampshire	12.7	22.2	30.2	44.4	53.3	60.3	64.2	67.0	55.8	43.0	40.7	23.5
New Jersey	27.7	35.6	40.9	52.6	61.5	67.5	72.3	75.3	64.8	53.6	49.7	34.7
New Mexico	37.3	41.2	47.1	51.6	63.7	69.1	75.2	72.5	64.0	52.4	45.0	31.5
New York	15.5	25.0	33.2	46.0	5.4	62.4	65.6	68.2	58.6	45.8	42.2	25.6
North Carolina	39.0	42.7	49.3	58.8	67.5	75.1	75.3	77.4	69.5	58.8	53.1	41.0
North Dakota	4.6	11.3	19.6	39.0	51.3	60.6	64.4	64.2	63.0	37.7	36.4	7.6
Ohio	21.2	31.4	42.3	51.2	61.2	69.1	68.8	71.1	64.6	49.8	46.3	30.8
Oklahoma	37.0	47.0	52.1	58.2	65.7	79.0	80.5	78.7	69.9	54.4	53.3	34.4
Oregon	33.5	36.0	38.6	45.6	54.7	60.6	69.0	66.5	61.8	46.0	39.2	28.7
Pennsylvania	20.5	29.5	38.1	48.9	57.9	64.8	66.7	69.9	61.1	48.1	44.9	28.9
Rhode Island	23.1	31.9	37.4	49.7	58.5	63.8	69.7	73.2	62.0	50.3	47.0	31.5
South Carolina	43.8	46.5	53.7	61.4	70.6	78.9	78.7	79.8	73.4	61.8	55.2	44.6
South Dakota	16.4	23.3	29.5	41.9	55.6	63.1	67.8	67.1	62.7	39.2	39.8	13.8
Tennessee	34.9	42.1	50.2	57.0	66.1	75.6	73.6	74.7	70.3	55.7	50.3	37.7
Texas	47.8	55.3	59.5	64.6	73.3	81.7	84.0	83.1	73.9	63.8	57.3	42.9
Utah	28.1	33.6	40.1	46.4	59.7	63.2	74.3	70.5	65.2	46.2	38.3	20.3
Vermont	10.9	20.7	29.6	43.5	52.9	60.8	64.9	66.6	55.9	42.4	40.0	22.0
Virginia	32.6	38.8	45.0	55.4	63.9	71.7	71.9	75.1	66.3	54.7	49.4	35.8
Washington	30.4	34.4	37.1	46.3	54.7	62.3	69.3	67.1	61.3	45.7	39.5	27.9
West Virginia	27.3	33.8	43.7	51.9	61.0	68.3	67.8	71.1	64.0	50.7	46.8	32.2
Wisconsin	6.4	20.5	30.0	42.9	54.7	63.3	63.7	64.7	61.2	41.9	40.2	18.5
Wyoming	23.0	26.6	31.5	39.2	51.3	56.8	65.0	62.9	58.4	35.6	34.3	13.6

Source: N.O.A.A. Satellite and Information Services, National Climatic Data Center, *Land-Based Data by State*, Jan. 2009–Dec. 2009. Retrieved May, 2010.

Climate of Selected World Cities, 2009

Average low and high temperatures for selected months in degrees Celsius. Average precipitation given in millimeters.

City	January Temp. Max.	Min.	Avg. precip.	April Temp. Max.	Min.	Avg. precip.	July Temp. Max.	Min.	Avg. precip.	October Temp. Max.	Min.	Avg. precip.
Accra, Ghana	23	31	15	24	31	81	23	27	46	23	29	64
Algiers, Algeria	9	15	112	13	20	41	21	28	0	17	23	79
Athens, Greece	6	13	62	11	20	23	23	33	7	15	24	51
Auckland, New Zealand	16	23	79	13	19	97	8	13	145	11	17	102
Baghdad, Iraq	4	16	23	14	29	13	24	43	0	16	33	3
Bangkok, Thailand	20	32	8	25	35	58	24	32	160	24	31	206
Beirut, Lebanon	11	17	191	14	22	56	23	31	0	21	27	51
Berlin, Germany	−3	2	46	4	13	42	14	24	73	6	13	49
Bogota, Colombia	9	19	58	11	19	147	10	18	51	10	19	160
Budapest, Hungary	−4	1	37	7	17	45	16	28	56	7	16	57
Buenos Aires, Argentina	17	29	79	12	22	89	6	14	56	10	21	86
Cairo, Egypt	8	18	5	14	28	3	21	36	0	18	30	0
Calcutta, India	13	27	10	24	36	43	26	32	325	24	32	114
Cape Town, South Africa	16	26	15	12	22	48	7	17	89	11	21	31
Caracas, Venzuela	13	24	23	16	27	33	16	26	109	16	26	109
Castries, St. Lucia	21	28	135	22	31	86	23	31	236	22	31	236
Copenhagen, Denmark	−2	2	49	3	10	38	14	22	71	7	12	59
Dakar, Senegal	18	26	0	18	27	0	24	31	89	24	32	38
Damascus, Syria	2	12	43	9	24	13	18	36	0	12	27	10
Dublin, Ireland	1	8	67	4	13	45	11	20	70	6	14	70
Geneva, Switzerland	−2	4	63	5	15	51	15	25	64	7	14	72
Hanoi, Vietnam	13	20	18	20	28	81	26	33	323	22	29	99
Hong Kong, China	13	18	33	19	24	137	26	31	381	23	27	114
Istanbul, Turkey	3	8	109	7	16	46	18	28	34	13	20	81
Jakarta, Indonesia	23	29	300	24	31	147	23	31	64	23	31	112
Jerusalem, Israel	5	13	132	10	23	28	17	31	0	15	27	13
Kabul, Afghanistan	−8	2	31	6	19	102	16	33	3	6	23	15
Karachi, Pakistan	13	25	13	23	32	3	27	33	81	22	33	0
Kinshasa, Congo, Dem. Rep.	21	31	135	22	32	196	18	27	3	21	31	119
Lagos, Nigeria	23	31	28	25	32	150	23	28	279	23	29	206
Lima, Peru	19	28	3	17	27	0	14	19	8	14	22	3
Lisbon, Portugal	8	14	111	12	20	54	17	27	3	14	22	62
London, England	2	6	54	6	13	37	14	22	57	8	14	57
Madrid, Spain	2	9	39	7	18	48	17	31	11	10	19	53
Manila, Philippines	21	30	23	22	33	18	24	33	254	24	31	356
Melbourne, Australia	14	26	48	11	20	58	6	13	48	9	19	66
Mexico City, Mexico	6	19	13	11	25	20	12	23	152	10	21	51
Mogadishu, Somalia	23	30	0	26	32	58	23	28	48	24	30	23
Moscow, Russia	−16	−9	39	1	10	37	13	23	88	3	9	45
Mumbai, India	19	28	2.5	24	32	0	25	29	617	24	32	64
Nagasaki, Japan	2	9	71	10	19	185	23	29	257	14	22	114
Nairobi, Kenya	12	25	38	14	24	211	11	21	15	13	24	53
Oslo, Norway	−7	−2	49	1	10	43	13	22	82	3	9	74
Ottawa, Canada	−16	−6	74	−1	11	69	14	27	86	3	12	74
Paris, France	1	6	56	6	16	42	15	25	59	8	16	50
Prague, Czech Republic	−5	0	18	3	12	27	13	23	68	5	12	33
Rio de Janeiro, Brazil	23	29	125	21	27	107	17	24	41	19	25	79
Riyadh, Saudi Arabia	8	21	3	18	32	25	26	42	0	16	34	0
Rome, Italy	5	11	71	10	19	51	20	30	15	13	22	99
Santiago, Chile	12	29	3	7	23	13	3	15	76	7	22	15
Santo Domingo, Dominican Republic	19	29	61	21	29	99	22	31	163	22	31	152
Seoul, South Korea	−9	0	31	5	17	76	21	29	376	7	19	41
Shanghai, China	1	8	48	10	19	94	23	32	147	14	23	71
Singapore, Indonesia	23	30	252	24	31	188	24	31	170	23	31	208
Stockholm, Sweden	−5	−1	43	1	8	31	14	22	61	5	9	48
Saint Petersburg, Russia	−13	−7	35	0	8	36	13	21	72	4	9	76
Sydney, Australia	18	26	89	14	22	135	8	16	117	13	22	71
Taipai, Taiwan	12	19	86	17	25	170	24	33	231	19	27	122
Tehran, Iran	−3	7	46	9	22	36	22	37	3	12	24	8
Thessolniki, Greece	2	9	44	10	20	41	21	32	14	13	22	57
Tokyo, Japan	−2	8	48	8	17	135	21	28	142	13	21	208
Toronto, Canada	−9	−1	69	1	10	64	15	26	74	4	13	61
Vienna, Austria	−4	1	39	6	15	45	15	25	84	7	14	56
Warsaw, Poland	−6	0	27	3	12	37	15	24	96	5	13	38

Source: BBC Weather Centre, *World Cities Guide Average Conditions*. Retrieved May 2010.

World Population

The United States Bureau of the Census estimates that in 2010 world population reached 6.853 billion people; 1.2 billion in developed countries and 5.6 billion in the developing regions. Slightly more than half the world population lived in urban areas and this trend towards urbanization is forecast to continue. The Census Bureau estimates that world population will reach 7.2 billion in 2015, 8 billion in 2025 and 9.3 billion in 2050.

World population growth rate has fallen from its peak of two percent per year to around 1.1 percent today. Of the 76 million people added to the world in 2010, some 662,316 were added in the developed countries and 75,567 million were added to the developing areas.

In 2010 the world had two billionaire countries: China at 1.330 billion people and India at 1.173 billion. The United States has the third largest population with 310 million people, followed by Indonesia with 243 million and Brazil with 201 million people.

The Census Bureau estimates that by 2050 India will have a population of 1.656 billion, which will be larger than all the more developed countries combined, that is, all the countries of Europe, including Russia, Australia, New Zealand, Japan, Canada and the United States.

►WORLD POPULATION TRENDS

Four factors are used to determine future world population: birth and death rates, ageing of the population, AIDS and migration. While birth rates continue to decline and couples in developing regions have three children on average, the total population continues to increase with 77 million persons added in 2009. However, population is increasing and decreasing in different regions of the world. Europe has significant population declines and several countries in Africa and the Caribbean are also projected to have fewer people in 2050. European population is estimated at 732.1 million in 2009 and is projected to decline to 691 million by 2050, a loss of 41.1 million people. All European countries have declining population except for Albania, France, Ireland, Netherlands, Norway, and the United Kingdom. In terms of numbers Japan is expected to have the world's largest population decline, losing 25.5 million people or 20 percent of their 2009 population. Russia is calculated to decline by 24.8 million people or 17.6 percent of its population. Germany will lose 11.7 million people or 14 percent and Ukraine will decline by 10.7 million people or 23 percent.

In terms of percent of population loss, Bulgaria is expected to have the world's largest percentage loss, 28.5 percent of its population by 2050 or 2.2 million people from their 2009 population. Belarus is expected to lose 24.5 percent or 2.4 million people and Moldova will decline by 24.1 percent for losing 870,000 people.

In 2009 the world's life expectancy averaged 67.6 years and by 2050 the U.N. estimates that it will reach 75.4 years. However, life expectancy for

Years to Reach Population Milestones

Milestone	Year Reached	Years to Reach	Milestone	Year Reached	Years to Reach
1 billion	1804	N.A.	6 billion	1999	12
2 billion	1927	123	7 billion	2012[1]	13
3 billion	1960	33	8 billion	2026[1]	14
4 billion	1974	14	9 billion	2043[1]	17
5 billion	1987	13			

Note: 1. Projected. **Source:** U.S. Census Bureau, *World Population Profile: 1998* (1999).

World Vital Events per Time Unit, 2010

Time unit	Births	Deaths	Natural Increase
Year	132,397,530	56,167,829	76,229,701
Month	11,033,128	4,680,652	6,352,475
Day	362,733	153,884	208,848
Hour	15,114	6,412	8,702
Minute	252	107	145
Second	4.2	1.8	2.4

Source: U.S. Census Bureau, *International Data Base* (2010).

Distribution of the World's Population, 1950–2050

Area	1950	2000	2050[1]
More developed regions	32.1%	18.1%	13.9%
Less developed regions	67.9	81.9	86.1
Least developed regions	7.9	12.2	18.3
Africa	9.0	14.8	21.8
Asia	55.5	60.3	57.2
Latin America and the Caribbean	6.6	8.5	8.0
Europe	21.6	10.7	7.6
Northern America	6.8	5.1	4.9
Oceania	0.5	0.5	0.6
Total world population (millions)	2,519	6,057	9,322

Source: Population Division of the Department of Economic and Social Affairs of the United Nations Secretariat (2009). *World Population Prospects: The 2008 Revision Highlights* (2009).

World Births, Deaths and Population Growth, 2010

Characteristic	World	Developed	Developing
Population	6,853,019,414	1,231,105,689	5,621,913,725
Births	132,397,533	13,482,444	111,915,090
Deaths	56,167,829	12,820,127	43,347,702
Natural increase	76,229,704	662,316	75,567,388
Births per 1,000 population	19.3	11.0	21.2
Deaths per 1,000 population	8.2	10.4	7.7
Rate of natural increase (percent)	1.1%	0.05%	1.3%

Source: U.S. Bureau of the Census, *International Data Base* (2010).

2005–10 varies from an average of 77.1 years in developed nations to 65.6 years in less developed countries, to 55.9 years in the least developed areas. Longevity, declining birth rates and AIDS are now changing the average median age and the traditional proportion between the old and the young. Median age is the age at which 50 percent of the population is older and 50 percent are younger than that age. The world's median age increased from 24 years in 1950 to 28.1 years in 2009 and is estimated to reach 38.4 years in 2050. The proportion of youth less than 15 years of age was 34 percent of total population in 1950, 27 percent in 2010, and will reduce to 20 percent in 2050. The proportion of people over the age of 60 was 8 percent in 1950, 11 percent in 2010 and is expected to reach 22 percent in 2050.

The world is ageing, and at a rapid rate. It is estimated that global population 65 and over now outnumbers children under five for the first time in human history. Every month the world is adding 870,000 people over 65 and this number is forecast to continue to increase. Europe is the oldest continent, with 23 of the world's 25 oldest countries. By

Countries with Decreasing Population Estimates, 2009–50 (in thousands)

Country	2009	2050	Decrease	Percent
Bulgaria	7,545	5,392	−2,153	−28.5%
Guyana	762	558	−204	−26.8
Belarus	9,634	7,275	−2,359	−24.5
Moldova	3,604	2,734	−8,700	−24.1
Ukraine	45,708	35,026	−10,682	−23.4
Georgia	4,260	3,267	−993	−23.3
Lithuania	3,287	2,579	−708	−21.5
Bosnia & Herzegovina	3,767	3,008	−758	−20.1
Japan	127,000	101,659	−25,498	−20.1
Romania	21,275	17,279	−3,996	−18.8
Russia	140,000	116,097	−24,777	−17.6
Latvia	2,249	1,854	−395	−17.6
Poland	38,074	32,013	−6,060	−15.9
Germany	82,167	70,504	−11,663	−14.2
Croatia	4,416	3,825	−591	−13.4
Cuba	11,204	9,725	−1,479	−13.2
Hungary	9,993	8,934	−1,059	−10.6
Macedonia	2,042	1,857	−186	−9.1
Slovakia	5,406	4,917	−489	−9.0
Estonia	1,340	1,233	−107	−8.0

Source: Population Division of the Department of Economic and Social Affairs of the United Nations Secretariat (2009). *World Population Prospects: The 2008 Revision Highlights* (2009).

Countries with Oldest and Youngest Populations, 2009 and 2050

Country	Median age	Country	Median age
Oldest, 2009		**Oldest, 2050**	
1. Japan	44.4	1. China, Macao	55.8
2. Germany	43.9	2. Japan	55.1
3. Italy	43.0	3. South Korea	53.7
4. Finland	41.8	4. Singapore	53.5
5. Channel Islands	41.7	5. China, Hong Kong	52.7
6. Switzerland	41.6	6. Bosnia & Herzegovina	52.2
7. Bulgaria	41.5	7. Cuba	51.9
8. Austria	41.4	8. Germany	51.7
9. Slovenia	41.4	9. Netherlands Antilles	51.1
10. China, Hong Kong	41.3	10. Poland	51.0
Youngest, 2009		**Youngest, 2050**	
1. Niger	15.1	1. Niger	20.2
2. Uganda	15.5	2. Afghanistan	23.5
3. Congo, Dem. Rep.	16.5	3. Somalia	23.6
4. Burkina Faso	16.7	4. Uganda	24.2
5. Zambia	16.8	5. Chad	24.5
6. Malawi	16.8	6. Zambia	24.7
7. Afghanistan	16.8	7. Tanzania	24.8
8. Chad	17.0	8. Guinea-Bissau	24.8
9. East Timor	17.2	9. East Timor	25.0
10. Angola	17.3	10. Burkina Faso	25.1
World avg, 2009	**28.9**	**World avg, 2050**	**38.4**

Source: Population Division of the Department of Economic and Social Affairs of the United Nations Secretariat (2009). *World Population Prospects: The 2008 Revision Highlights* (2009).

World's Largest Countries, by Population, 2009–20

	2009			2020	
Rank, Country	**Population**	**Percent of Total**	**Rank, Country**	**Population**	**Percent of Total**
1. China	1,345,751,000	19.71%	1. China	1,431,155,000	18.65%
2. India	1,198,003,000	17.54	2. India	1,367,225,000	17.81
3. United States	314,659,000	4.61	3. United States	346,153,000	4.51
4. Indonesia	229,965,000	3.37	4. Indonesia	254,218,000	3.31
5. Brazil	193,734,000	2.84	5. Pakistan	226,187,000	2.95
6. Pakistan	180,808,000	2.65	6. Brazil	209,051,000	2.72
7. Bangladesh	162,221,000	2.38	7. Nigeria	193,252,000	2.52
8. Nigeria	154,729,000	2.27	8. Bangladesh	185,552,000	2.42
9. Russia	140,874,000	2.06	9. Russia	135,406,000	1.76
10. Japan	127,156,000	1.86	10. Japan	123,664,000	1.61
11. Mexico	109,610,000	1.60	11. Mexico	119,682,000	1.56
12. Philippines	91,983,000	1.35	12. Philippines	109,683,000	1.43
13. Vietnam	88,069,000	1.29	13. Ethiopia	107,964,000	1.41
14. Egypt	82,999,000	1.22	14. Egypt	98,638,000	1.29
15. Ethiopia	82,825,000	1.21	15. Vietnam	98,011,000	1.28
16. Germany	82,167,000	1.20	16. Congo, Dem. Rep.	87,640,000	1.14
17. Turkey	74,816,000	1.10	17. Turkey	83,873,000	1.09
18. Iran	74,196,000	1.09	18. Iran	83,740,000	1.09
19. Thailand	68,000,000	0.99	19. Tanzania	59,603,000	0.78
20. Congo, Dem Rep	66,020,000	0.97	20. Uganda	46,319,000	0.60

Source: United Nations, Department of Economic and Social Affairs, Population Division. *World Population Prospects: The 2008 Revision* extract from DEMOBASE, July 2009.

2040, more than one in four Europeans are expected to be at least 65, and one in seven at least 75. Japan is the world's oldest big country, with life expectancy at birth of 82 years, which is the same as Singapore. In Western Europe, France, Sweden and Italy all have life expectancies of more than 80 years. Ageing is also happening in developing countries so that by 2040, they are projected to have more than 1 billion people aged 65 and over—fully 76 percent of the world total.

►URBANIZATION

The United Nations reported that in 2009 slightly more than half the world's population lived in urban areas, 3.42 billion people compared to 3.41 billion in rural areas. It was estimated that 75 percent of people in developed countries lived in urban areas compared to 45 percent in developing regions that were urban dwellers. Globally the level of urbanization is projected to increase from 50 percent urban in 2009 to 69 percent urban in 2050. At this time the world's urban population is expected reach 6.3 billion people and to comprise 86 percent of the more developed areas and 66 percent in less developed countries.

Urban populations are distributed unevenly among cities in different sizes. Over half of the 3.42 billion urban dwellers (51 percent) lived in cities or towns with fewer than 500,000 people. It is projected that between 2009 to 2050 these small cities will account for 45 percent of urban growth.

In 2009, cities with fewer than 100,000 people accounted for one third of the world urban population or 1.5 billion people. Cities with 100,000 to 500,000 people had an additional 629 million people, or 18 percent of the world urban population. All cities having fewer than 500,000 people accounted for 51.9 percent of urban population.

In 2009, there were 21 megacities, each having at least 10 million inhabitants and accounted for 9.4 percent of world urban population. The number of megacities is forecast to increase to 29 by 2025 when they will hold 10.3 percent of world urban dwellers. In 2009 about one in every 20 people on earth lived in a megacity. In 1975 there were just three megacities, New York, Tokyo and Mexico City. Today Asia has 11 megacities, Latin America has four, and Africa, Europe and Northern America have two each.

Today Tokyo is the largest urban agglomeration with 36.5 million people in 2009, which is more people than 196 countries or areas. Tokyo, the megacity, actually comprises Tokyo and 87 surrounding cities and towns. Delhi, India with 22 million is the next largest urban agglomeration, followed by São Paulo and Bombay, each with 20 million, and Mexico City and New York-Newark with 19 million each.

The number of rural dwellers, 3.41 billion in mid-2009, is expected to reach its maximum of 3.5 billion in 2020, and to then slowly decline to 2.9 billion in 2050. Declining populations will also create a decline in urban dwellers in a number of countries, with the largest decreases between 2009 and 2025 projected to be in Russia with a decrease of three million and Ukraine to have a decrease of 700,000 urban dwellers.

►FERTILITY RATES

In 2005–2010 the average number of children a woman had was 2.56. In this period 76 countries or areas, 45 of which were in more developed regions, have fertility rates below 2.1 children per woman, that is, below replacement level.

Replacement level fertility represents the point at which each couple has only the number of births required to replace themselves in the population, 2.1

Population of Areas with 10 Million or more Inhabitants, 1975–2025

1975		2000		2009		2025	
1. Tokyo	26.6	1. Tokyo	34.4	1. Tokyo	36.5	1. Toyko	37.1
2. New York-Newark	15,9	2. Mexico City	18.1	2. Delhi	21.7	2. Delhi	28.6
3. Mexico City	10.7	3. New York-Newark	17.8	3. São Paulo	20.0	3. Mumbai	25.8
		4. São Paulo	17.1	4. Mumbai (Bombay)	19.7	4. São Paulo	21.7
		5. Mumbai	16.1	5. Mexico City	19.3	5. Dhaka	20.9
		6. Shanghai	13.2	6. New York-Newark	19.3	6. Mexico City	20.7
		7. Kolkata (Calcutta)	13.1	7. Shanghai	16.3	7. New York-Newark	20.6
		8. Delhi	12.4	8. Calcutta	15.3	8. Calcutta	20.1
		9. Buenos Aires	11.8	9. Dhaka	14.3	9. Shangshi	20.0
		10. Los Angeles-Long Beach-Santa Ana	11.8	10. Buenos Aires	13.0	10. Karachi	18.7
		11. Osaka-Kobe	11.2	11. Karachi	12.8	11. Lagos	15.8
		12. Jakarta	11.1	12. Los Angeles-Long Beach-Santa Ana	12.7	12. Konshasa	15.0
		13. Rio de Janeiro	10.8	13. Beijing	12.2	13. Beijing	15.9
		14. Cairo	10.4	14. Rio de Janeiro	11.8	14. Manila	14.9
		15. Dhaka	10.2	15. Manila	11.4	15. Buenos	13.7
		16. Moscow	10.1	16. Osaka-Kobe	11.3	16. Los Angeles-Long Beach-Santa Ana	13.7
		17. Karachi	10.0	17. Cairo	10.9	17. Cairo	13.5
		18. Manila	10.0	18. Moscow	10.5	18. Rio de Janeiro	12.7
				19. Paris	10.4	19. Istanbul	12.1
				20. Istanbul	10.4	20. Osaka-Kobe	11.4

Note: An urban area is a central city or central cities, and the surrounding urbanized areas, also called a metropolitan area. **Source:** United Nations Department of Economic and Social Affairs, Population Division, *World Urbanization Prospects: The 2005 Revision* (2006) and *The 2009 Revision* (2010).

births per woman. Women in 120 countries, all in developing areas, have more than 2.1 children per woman and among these countries, 27 have fertility rates at or above five children per woman, 25 of which are in the least developed countries.

Since 1974 fertility rates have declined more than 20 percent in 137 developing countries and by over 50 percent in 57 of them. The fastest reductions were in countries in Asia, including Mongolia, Iran, Maldives, UAE, Vietnam, South Korea, Kuwait and Bangladesh. Women in these countries now average less than 2.34 children per woman.

Seven countries—Afghanistan, East Timor, Somalia, Uganda, Chad, Democratic Republic of the Congo—still have fertility rates of six children or more in 2005–2010 and Niger's fertility rate is more than seven children per woman. In 2009, the majority of people in the developing world live in 76 countries that have total fertility rates ranging from 2.1 to four children per woman.

Fertility rates in the 45 developed countries have been declining since the 1970s to below replacement levels. In 1970–75, 18 countries of the 45 al-

Nations with Highest and Lowest Fertility Rates, 2005–10

HIGHEST RATES		LOWEST RATES	
Country	Fertility rate per woman	Country	Fertility rate per woman
Niger	7.16	China, Macao	0.95
Afghanistan	6.63	China, Hong Kong	1.02
Timor-Leste	6.53	Bosnia & Herzegovina	1.21
Somalia	6.40	South Korea	1.22
Uganda	6.42	Malta	1.26
Chad	6.20	Japan	1.27
Congo, Dem. Rep.	6.07	Poland	1.27
Burkina Faso	5.94	Singapore	1.27
Zambia	5.87	Slovakia	1.28
Angola	5.79	Belarus	1.28

Source: Population Division of the Department of Economic and Social Affairs of the United Nations Secretariat (2009). *World Population Prospects: The 2008 Revision Highlights* (2009).

Population Indicators by Region and Nation

Region/Country	Population estimate ('000s) 2010	Population estimate ('000s) 2050	Population age by percentage 0–14, 2009	Population age by percentage 60+, 2009	Life expectancy, 2005–10	Percent urban, 2009	Fertility rate per woman 2005–10
World Total	**6,853,019**	**9,149,984**	**27.2%**	**10.8%**	**67.6**	**50%**	**2.56%**
More Developed Regions	**1,231,106**	**1,275,000**	**17**	**22**	**77.1**	**75**	**1.6**
Less Developed Regions	**5,621,914**	**7,875,000**	**29**	**9**	**65.6**	**44**	**2.7**
Least Developed Countries	**835,000**	**1,672,000**	**40**	**5**	**55.9**	**28**	**4.4**
Africa	**1,010,000**	**1,998,000**	**40**	**5**	**54.1**	**39**	**4.6**
Arab States	**N.A.**	**N.A.**	**N.A.**	**N.A.**	**N.A.**	**N.A.**	**N.A.**
Asia	**4,121,000**	**5,231,000**	**26**	**10**	**68.9**	**41**	**2.3**
Europe	**732,100**	**691,000**	**15**	**22**	**75.1**	**72**	**1.5**
Latin America and the Caribbean	**591,469**	**729,000**	**28**	**10**	**73.4**	**78**	**2.3**
Northern America	**344,124**	**448,000**	**20**	**18**	**79.3**	**81**	**2.0**
Oceania	**34,982**	**51,000**	**24**	**15**	**76.4**	**71**	**2.4**
Afghanistan	29,121	3,938	46.1	3.8	43.8	24	6.6
Albania	2,987	3,303	23.5	13.4	76.5	47	1.9
Algeria	34,586	49,610	27.3	6.8	72.3	65	2.4
Angola	13,068	42,267	45.0	3.9	46.8	57	5.8
Argentina	41,343	50,943	25.1	14.6	75.2	92	2.3
Armenia	2,967	3,018	20.3	14.4	73.7	64	1.7
Australia	21,516	28,724	19.0	19.1	81.5	89	1.8
Austria	8,214	8,515	14.9	22.9	80.0	67	1.4
Azerbaijan	8,304	10,579	24.2	8.6	70.2	52	2.2
Bahrain	738	1,277	26.4	3.6	75.7	97	2.3
Bangladesh	156,118	222,495	31.5	6.0	65.9	27	2.4
Belarus	9,613	7,275	14.7	18.1	69.1	73	1.3
Belgium	10,423	11,493	16.8	23.0	79.7	97	1.8
Belize	315	506	35.2	5.8	76.2	49	2.9
Benin	9,056	21,982	43.1	5.0	61.3	41	5.5
Bhutan	700	1,013	30.5	7.1	65.8	35	2.7
Bolivia	9,947	14,908	36.2	7.1	65.5	66	3.5
Bosnia and Herzegovina	4,622	3,008	15.4	18.7	75.1	47	1.2
Botswana	2,029	2,758	33.3	5.8	54.9	60	2.9
Brazil	201,103	218,512	25.9	9.9	72.3	86	1.9
Brunei Darussalam	395	658	26.8	5.5	77.1	74	2.1
Bulgaria	7,149	5,392	13.4	24.2	73.2	71	1.4
Burkina Faso	16,242	40,830	46.3	3.3	52.9	20	5.9
Burundi	9,863	14,846	38.4	4.4	50.3	10	4.7
Cambodia	14,454	23,795	33.3	5.7	60.9	22	3.0
Cameroon	19,294	36,736	40.9	5.4	51.0	57	4.7
Canada	33,760	44,414	16.5	19.5	80.7	80	1.6
Central African Republic	4,845	7,603	40.6	5.9	46.9	39	4.9
Chad	10,543	27,776	45.7	4.5	48.7	27	6.2
Chile	16,746	20,657	22.7	12.8	78.5	88	1.9

Region/Country	Population estimate ('000s)		Population age by percentage		Life expec-tancy,	Percent urban,	Fertility rate per woman
	2010	2050	0–14, 2009	60+, 2009	2005–10	2009	2005–10
China	1,330,141	1,417,045	20.2	11.9	73.0	43	1.8
Colombia	44,205	62,877	29.2	8.3	72.8	74	2.5
Congo, Dem. Rep. of	70,916	147,512	46.7	4.2	47.5	34	6.1
Congo, Republic of	4,125	6,863	40.5	5.7	53.6	61	4.4
Costa Rica	4,516	6,373	25.9	9.2	78.8	63	2.0
Croatia	4,487	3,825	15.1	23.1	76.2	57	1.4
Cuba	11,477	9,725	17.7	16.8	78.6	76	1.5
Czech Republic	10,202	10,294	14.1	21.8	76.5	73	1.4
Denmark	5,516	5,551	18.2	23.0	78.3	87	1.8
Djibouti	740	1,469	36.1	5.3	55.3	87	4.0
Dominican Republic	9,824	13,441	31.5	8.6	72.4	69	2.7
Ecuador	14,791	17,989	31.1	9.2	75.0	66	2.6
Egypt	80,472	129,533	32.3	7.3	70.0	43	2.9
El Salvador	6,052	7,882	32.3	10.0	71.4	61	2.4
Eritrea	5,793	10,787	41.5	4.1	59.4	21	4.7
Estonia	1,291	1,233	15.1	22.4	73.1	69	1.6
Ethiopia	88,013	173,811	43.5	5.0	55.0	17	5.4
Fiji	876	910	31.3	7.9	68.8	52	2.8
Finland	5,255	5,445	16.7	24.0	79.6	63	1.8
France	64,768	67,668	18.4	22.7	81.2	77	1.9
Gabon	1,545	2,471	36.1	6.4	60.3	85	3.4
Gambia	1,824	3,763	42.3	4.9	55.8	57	5.1
Georgia	4,600	3,267	16.8	18.8	71.6	53	1.6
Germany	82,283	70,504	13.5	25.7	79.9	74	1.3
Ghana	24,340	45,213	38.4	5.7	56.5	50	4.3
Greece	10,750	10,939	14.2	24.0	79.2	61	1.4
Guatemala	13,550	27,480	41.9	6.4	70.2	49	4.2
Guinea	10,324	23,975	42.8	5.1	57.6	34	5.5
Guinea-Bissau	1,565	3,555	42.6	5.4	47.6	30	5.7
Guyana	748	558	29.7	9.2	66.8	28	2.3
Haiti	9,649	15,485	36.3	6.4	61.2	47	3.6
Honduras	7,989	12,402	37.4	6.1	72.1	48	3.3
Hong Kong SAR, China	7,089	9,000	12.0	17.7	82.2	100	1.0
Hungary	9,993	8,934	14.8	22.1	73.3	68	1.4
Iceland	309	407	20.6	16.3	81.8	93	2.1
India	1,173,108	1,613,800	31.3	7.4	63.5	29	2.8
Indonesia	242,968	288,110	27.0	8.8	70.7	69	2.2
Iran	76,923	96,975	24.1	7.1	71.3	68	1.8
Iraq	29,672	63,995	41.1	4.7	67.4	67	4.1
Ireland	4,623	6,295	20.7	15.9	79.9	61	2.0
Israel	7,354	10,649	27.7	14.2	80.7	92	2.8
Italy	58,091	57,066	14.2	26.4	81.2	68	1.4
Ivory Coast	21,059	34,700	40.6	6.0	57.2	49	4.7
Jamaica	2,719	2,683	29.4	10.6	71.8	53	2.4
Japan	126,804	101,659	13.3	29.7	82.7	66	1.3
Jordan	6,407	10,241	34.5	5.5	72.5	78	3.1
Kazakhstan	15,460	17,848	23.7	10.1	64.9	58	2.3
Kenya	40,047	84,410	42.8	4.1	54.2	22	5.0
Korea, North	22,757	24,700	21.7	14.3	67.3	63	1.9
Korea, South	48,636	44,077	16.8	15.1	79.4	81	1.2
Kuwait	2,789	5,240	23.4	3.8	77.6	98	2.2
Kyrgyzstan	5,509	6,882	29.4	7.2	67.8	36	2.6
Laos	6,368	10,744	37.5	5.5	64.8	31	3.5
Latvia	2,218	1,854	13.8	22.5	72.4	68	1.4
Lebanon	4,125	5,033	25.3	10.3	72.0	87	1.9
Lesotho	1,920	2,491	38.8	7.0	45.3	25	3.4
Liberia	3,685	8,841	42.7	4.9	58.1	60	5.1
Libya	6,461	9,819	30.1	6.5	74.0	78	2.7
Lithuania	3,545	2,579	14.9	21.3	71.7	67	1.3
Luxembourg	498	733	17.8	18.9	79.5	83	1.7
Macedonia	2,072	1,857	18.0	16.5	74.2	67	1.4
Madagascar	21,282	42,693	42.9	4.6	60.1	29	4.8
Malawi	15,448	36,575	46.2	4.8	52.9	19	5.6
Malaysia	28,275	39,664	29.5	7.5	74.2	70	2.6
Maldives	396	455	28.0	6.0	71.3	31	2.1
Mali	13,796	28,260	44.2	3.8	48.3	32	5.5
Malta	407	413	15.6	21.2	79.7	96	1.3
Mauritania	3,205	6,061	39.5	4.4	56.6	41	4.5
Mauritius	1,294	1,426	22.6	11.2	72.1	42	1.8
Mexico	112,469	128,964	28.5	9.1	76.1	77	2.2

Region/Country	Population estimate ('000s) 2010	Population estimate ('000s) 2050	Population age by percentage 0–14, 2009	Population age by percentage 60+, 2009	Life expectancy 2005–10	Percent urban, 2009	Fertility rate per woman 2005–10
Moldova	4,317	2,734	16.9	15.6	68.4	42	1.5
Mongolia	3,087	3,446	26.0	5.9	66.4	57	2.0
Montenegro	667	618	19.4	17.5	74.0	N.A.	1.6
Morocco	31,627	42,583	28.4	7.9	71.2	56	2.4
Mozambique	22,061	44,148	44.0	5.1	47.8	37	5.1
Myanmar	53,414	63,373	26.8	8.0	61.2	33	2.3
Namibia	2,128	3,588	36.9	5.6	61.4	37	3.4
Nepal	28,952	49,028	36.5	6.1	66.6	17	2.9
Netherlands	16,783	17,399	17.8	21.4	80.0	82	1.7
New Zealand	4,252,277	5,349	20.4	17.8	80.2	87	2.0
Nicaragua	5,996	8,143	35.1	6.1	72.9	57	2.8
Niger	15,878	58,216	49.9	3.5	51.1	16	7.2
Nigeria	152,217	289,083	42.5	4.9	47.8	48	5.3
Norway	4,676	5,947	19.0	20.8	80.6	77	1.9
Oman	2,968	4,878	31.5	4.7	75.6	72	3.1
Pakistan	184,401	335,195	36.9	6.1	66.3	36	4.0
Panama	3,411	5,092	29.3	9.5	75.6	73	2.6
Papua New Guinea	6,065	12,871	39.8	4.2	60.8	12	4.1
Paraguay	6,376	9,867	34.0	7.5	71.8	60	3.1
Peru	29,907	39,776	30.3	8.5	73.1	71	2.6
Philippines	99,900	146,156	33.9	6.5	71.7	65	3.1
Poland	38,464	32,013	15.0	18.8	75.6	61	1.3
Portugal	10,736	10,015	15.3	23.3	78.7	59	1.4
Puerto Rico	3,979	4,103	20.3	19.1	78.7	98	1.8
Qatar	841	2,316	16.0	1.9	75.5	96	2.4
Romania	21,959	17,279	15.2	20.0	72.6	54	1.3
Russian Federation	139,390	116,097	14.8	17.8	66.5	73	1.4
Rwanda	11,055	22,082	42.3	3.8	49.9	18	5.4
Saudi Arabia	25,731	43,658	32.4	4.5	72.8	82	3.2
Senegal	12,323	26,102	43.6	4.0	55.4	42	5.1
Serbia	7,344	9,193	17.7	19.4	74.0	52	1.6
Sierra Leone	5,245	12,446	43.4	3.5	47.4	38	5.22
Singapore	4,701	5,221	16.3	15.2	80.3	100	1.3
Slovakia	5,470	4,917	15.4	17.3	74.7	56	1.3
Slovenia	2,003	1,954	13.8	21.9	78.4	48	1.4
Somalia	10,112	23,522	44.9	4.3	49.6	37	6.4
South Africa	49,109	56,802	30.5	7.1	51.6	61	2.6
Spain	46,506	51,260	14.8	22.2	80.9	77	1.4
Sri Lanka	21,514	21,705	24.9	11.8	73.9	15	2.3
Sudan	43,949	75,884	39.1	5.7	58.0	43	4.2
Suriname	487	619	28.9	9.2	68.9	75	2.4
Swaziland	1,354	1,749	39.3	5.2	45.8	25	3.4
Sweden	9,074	10,571	16.6	24.7	80.9	85	1.9
Switzerland	7,623	8,514	15.3	23.0	81.8	73	1.5
Syria	22,198	36,911	35.0	4.8	74.1	54	3.3
Tajikistan	7,487	11,111	36.9	5.0	66.7	26	3.5
Tanzania	41,893	109,450	44.7	4.8	55.4	25	5.6
Thailand	67,090	73,361	21.7	11.2	68.8	33	1.8
Timor-Liste	1,155	3,217	45.0	4.8	60.8	27	6.5
Togo	6,587	13,196	39.9	5.4	62.4	42	4.3
Trinidad and Tobago	1,229	1,278	20.7	10.3	69.4	13	1.6
Tunisia	10,589	12,711	23.2	9.5	73.9	67	1.9
Turkey	77,804	97,389	26.8	8.8	71.8	69	2.1
Turkmenistan	4,941	6,796	29.5	6.0	64.7	49	2.5
Uganda	33,399	91,271	48.9	3.9	52.4	13	6.4
Ukraine	45,416	35,026	13.9	20.8	68.2	68	1.3
United Arab Emirates	4,976	8,253	19.2	1.9	77.4	78	2.0
United Kingdom	62,348	72,365	17.4	22.4	79.4	90	1.8
United States	310,233	403,932	20.3	17.9	79.2	82	2.1
Uruguay	3,510	3,637	22.8	18.3	76.2	92	2.1
Uzbekistan	27,866	36,439	29.3	6.2	67.7	37	2.3
Vanuatu	222	482	38.6	5.3	70.0	24	4.0
Venezuela	27,223	42,042	29.8	8.4	73.8	93	2.6
Vietnam	89,571	111,666	25.7	8.6	74.3	31	2.1
Yemen	23,495	53,689	43.8	3.8	62.7	28	5.3
Zambia	13,460	28,957	46.2	4.8	45.2	35	5.9
Zimbabwe	11,652	22,178	39.9	5.8	44.1	37	3.5

Note: Totals may not add because of rounding numbers. Data for small countries or areas, generally those with population of 200,000 or less in 2007, are not given in this table. Source: U.S. Census Bureau, Population Division, 2010; Population Division of the Department of Economic and Social Affairs of the United Nations Secretariat (2009), *World Population Prospects: The 2008 Revision Highlights* (2009), Department of Economic and Social Affairs of the United Nations Secretariat, *World Urbanization Prospects: The 2007 Executive Summary* (2008).

ready had below-replacement levels. By 2005–10, all developed countries had less than 2.1 children per woman. Six countries have less than 1.3 children per woman, with Bosnia and Herzegovina, Malta, Poland and Japan having the lowest levels in the developed world. China Hong Kong and South Korea had even lower birth rates.

The U.N. projects that at the world level, the fertility rate will be 2.02 children per woman in 2045–2050. Women in developed regions will have 1.80 children per woman and 2.05 children per woman in the less developed areas.

In 2007, 63 percent of women of reproductive age who are married or in union are currently using a contraceptive method for a total of 716 million women. Some 90 percent of women in China have contraceptive access, while 22 percent of women in Sub-Saharan Africa have access. Less than 20 percent of women in Western Africa and the Horn of Africa have access to contraceptive methods.

▶GLOSSARY OF DEMOGRAPHIC TERMS

Birth rate   The average annual number of births during a year per 1,000 population at mid-year; also known as the crude birth rate.

Contraception   Deliberate use of methods to prevent conception or pregnancy. Contraception is an important portion of family planning.

Death rate   The average annual number of deaths during a year per 1,000 population at mid-year; also known as the crude death rate.

Growth rate   The average annual percent change in the population, resulting from a surplus (or deficit) of births over deaths and the balance of migrants entering and leaving a country. The rate may be positive or negative; also known as population growth rate or average annual rate of growth.

Infant mortality rate   The number of deaths to infants under one year of age in a given year per 1,000 live births occurring in the same year.

Least developed countries   Defined by the United Nations as the countries with the poorest living standards. In 2001, the U.N. counted 49 countries, most of them landlocked, among the least developed.

Less developed countries   Defined by the U.N. as countries with poorer people than in more developed countries, with economies based on agricultural production, with low GNPs, and lacking in advanced technologies. Approximately 77 countries, including those in Africa, Latin America, and the Caribbean, Asia (except Japan) and regions of Melanesia, Micronesia and Polynesia, are considered less developed.

More developed countries   The U.N. defines developed countries as industrialized nations with a high gross national product (GNP), high per capita GNP, and advanced science and technology. Approximately 45 countries including those in Europe, North America, Japan, Australia, and New Zealand, are considered developed.

Projections   Data on population and vital rates derived for future years based on statistics from population censuses, vital registration system or sample surveys pertaining to the recent past, and on assumptions about future trends.

Vital rates   Birth rates and death rates.

World Health

The World Health Organization (W.H.O.), a specialized agency of the United Nations, is the global intergovernmental directing and coordinating authority for international health work. Headquartered in Geneva, Switzerland, W.H.O. gathers health statistics, sets international health standards, provides assistance to individual countries when invited, and issues publications. Most of the information here is from the World Health Organization. (See Part II: "Health and Medicine" for information about the U.S.)

The leading causes of death worldwide are high blood pressure (responsible for 13 percent of deaths globally), tobacco use (9 percent), high blood glucose (6 percent), physical inactivity (6 percent), and overweight and obesity (5 percent). These factors also increase the risk of chronic diseases such as heart disease, diabetes and cancers. They affect high income, middle and low income countries.

Five leading risk factors are responsible for one quarter of all deaths in the world: childhood underweight, unsafe sex, alcohol use, unsafe water and sanitation, and high blood pressure. Reducing exposure to these risk factors would increase global life expectancy by nearly five years.

Eight risk factors account for 61 percent of cardiovascular deaths: alcohol use, tobacco use, high blood pressure, high body mass index, high choles¬terol, high blood glucose, low fruit and vegetable intake, and physical inactivity. Combined, these risk factors account for over three quarters of ischaemic heart disease, the leading cause of death worldwide. Reducing exposure to these eight risk factors would increase global life expectancy by almost five years.

W.H.O. estimates that over 17.1 million people died from heart attacks and strokes in 2004, representing 29 percent of all deaths globally. Every six seconds, regardless of age or gender—someone in the world dies from stroke, 5.8 million lives each year. Stroke kills more people each year than AIDS, tuberculosis (TB) and malaria put together. In 2008, AIDS-related deaths totaled two million, 1.8 million people died from TB including 500,000 people with HIV; and, there were 247 million cases of malaria in 2006, causing nearly one million deaths, mostly among African children.

▶THE GLOBAL SITUATION

The World Health Organization reports that compared to the 1990s fewer children today are dying before the age of 5, fewer children are underweight, more women are getting skilled help during childbirth, Tuberculosis treatment is more successful, new HIV infections have declined and more people are receiving treatment, and more people have safe drinking water but not enough have toilets.

While some countries have made health gains, others are falling behind, usually due to high levels of conflict, poor governance, HIV/AIDS, and economic hardship. Annual global deaths of children under five fell to 8.8 million in 2008 which is 30 percent less than in 1990 with diarrhea and pneumonia killing almost three million children annually. In 1990, 25 percent of children under five were underweight and in 2010 it declined to 16 percent. Stunted growth (low height for age) in children under five decreased from 40 percent to 27 percent over the same period, but 104 million children are still undernourished. W.H.O. projects that in Sub-Saharan Africa the number of stunted children will increase from 45 million in 1990 to 60 million in 2010.

The smallest health progress is in maternal health with research indicating that between 1990 to 2008 maternal deaths due to pregnancy and childbirth fell only 1.3 percent. The proportion of women in developing countries who report using contraceptives increased from 50 percent in 1990 to 62 percent in 2005, but many more women report wanting access but are unable to obtain contraceptives.

The percentage of people having access to safe drinking water increased from 77 percent to 87 percent, but there remains a gap between urban and rural areas in many countries. In 2008, 2.6 billion people had no access to a hygienic toilet or latrine. The slowest improvement is in Sub-Saharan Africa where the percentage using toilets or latrines increased from 30 percent in 1990 to 34 percent in 2008.

In 2009 there was a global average of 14 physicians per 10,000 people with Africa averaging two physicians per 10,000, the Americas averaging 23, and Europe having 33 doctors for every 10,000 people. Approximately 16 countries in Africa averaged one physician per 10,000 people, ranging from Angola, Benin, and Eritrea, to Kenya, Uganda, and Zambia. Cuba had the most physicians per 10,000 at 64, many of the former Soviet Republics averaged around 38 with Georgia having 45 and Russia having 43. Netherlands had 39 physicians per 10,000, Iceland had 38, Germany had 35, Italy and Uruguay had 37 each, and the United States averaged 27 physicians per 10,000 people.

In 2007 the world spent an average $802 per capita on health at average exchange rate. Highest per capita total expenditures on health were in Luxembourg at $7,439, followed by Norway at $7,354, then Monaco at $7,338 and the United States at $7,285. Lowest per capita total expenditures on health were in Myanmar at $7, it was $9 each in Eritrea, Ethiopia and the Democratic Republic of the Congo, $14 in Sierra Leone and $16 each in the Central African Republic, Guinea Bissau and Madagascar.

The Global Influenza Surveillance Network (GISN) continues monitoring the global circulation of influenza viruses, including pandemic, seasonal and other influenza viruses infecting, or with the potential to infect, humans including seasonal influenza. As of summer 2010 their research indicates that the 2009 H5N1 flu epidemic is low worldwide with limited virus in parts of the tropics.

Global Health Risk Factors

The World Health Organization estimates health progress for a number of diseases benchmarked to 1990 levels and mostly compared to 2008 statistical reports. Analysis shows that progress in improving health for the world's people cannot be made unless there is progress on food security, gender equality, the empowerment of women, wider access to education and better care of the environment.

There are preventable risk factors for a number of diseases including those caused by unsafe water and lack of sanitation, use of solid fuels in households, low birth weight, poor infant feeding practices, childhood under-nutrition, being overweight or obese, harmful consumption of alcohol, tobacco use, and unsafe sex.

Child growth is the main measurement of nutritional status and includes calculating stunted growth, underweight and overweight. Tobacco smoking is a predictor of future tobacco-related diseases. Harmful alcohol can cause alcohol dependence, hepatic cirrhosis, cancer and injuries. Burning solid fuels—wood, charcoal and crops—in houses creates indoor air pollution and can cause death from pneumonia and other acuter lower respiratory diseases and lung cancer.

Unsafe water and inadequate levels of sanitation and hygiene create the transmission of diarrheal diseases, including cholera; and schistosomiasis, trachoma, and hepatitis. In Somalia 30 percent of the population have good drinking water, 38 percent in Ethiopia, and 47 percent in Mozambique.

The world is seeing success in the implementation of relatively new child-health interventions such as insecticide-treated bed nets to prevent malaria, vaccination against hepatitis B and Haemophilus influence type B pneumonia, supplementing micronutrients, and greater vaccinations against childhood diseases.

The World Health Organization reports that in 2008 there were an estimated 243 million cases of malaria causing 863,000 deaths, mostly in children under five; India reported 95 million cases, Uganda had 11 million cases and five million were reported in the Democratic Republic of the Congo.

W.H.O. estimates that 220 million people worldwide have diabetes with 1.1 million deaths in 2005 which is five percent of all global deaths annually. Some 80 percent of people with diabetes live in low and middle-income countries and are aged 45 to 64, not elderly.

Some one billion people suffer from neglected tropical diseases, including 496 million people treated for lymphatic filariasis in 2008 out of 695 million needing treatment. The same year had 190,130 cholera cases which was up from 177,963 cases in 2007. In 2008, the Democratic Republic of the Congo reported 30,150 cases, Sudan had 17,241 and Mozambique had 9,087.

W.H.O. defines overweight and obesity as abnormal or excessive fat accumulation that may impair health. Approximately 1.6 billion adults (age 15+) were overweight in 2005 and at least 400 million of this number were obese. W.H.O. projects that by 2015, approximately 2.3 billion adults will be overweight and more than 700 million will be obese. Overweight and obesity are major risk factors in chronic diseases including: cardiovascular disease (mainly heart disease and stroke), diabetes, musculoskeletal disorders (especially osteoarthritis) and some cancers (endometrial, breast and colon). Asthma is a chronic disease of the bronchial tubes, the air passages to and from the lungs. Some 300 million people suffer from asthma today,

People Living With Various Health Conditions, 2007

Condition	Number of People
Tuberculosis[1]	2.2 billion
Obesity	1.6 billion
Tropical diseases	1.2 billion
Asthma	300 million
Chronic Obstructive Pulmonary disease[2]	210 million
Diabetes	180 million

Notes: 1. Mainly caused by tobacco smoke, including second-hand smoke. 2. One-third of the world's population is infected with TB bacillus, but 5–10 percent become sick or infectious at some time, not counting those with HIV. **Source:** World Health Organization, various fact sheets, 2007–2009.

Nations with Highest and Lowest Infant Mortality Rates, 2005–10

Country	Infant Mortality Rate[1]	Country	Infant Mortality Rate[1]
Highest rates		**Lowest rates**	
Afghanistan	157.0	Iceland	2.9
Chad	129.9	Sweden	3.1
Angola	117.5	Finland	3.2
Congo, Dem. Rep. of	116.8	Japan	3.2
		Norway	3.5
Guinea Bissau	114.0	Hong Kong, SAR China	3.7
Somalia	109.6		
Nigeria	109.4	Slovenia	3.7
Mali	106.0	Czech Republic	3.8
Sierra Leone	104.3	Greece	3.8
Central African Republic	105.5	France	3.9
		Italy	3.9
		Spain	3.9

Note: 1. Rate per 1,000 live births. **Source:** United Nations Department of Economic and Social Affairs, Population Division (2009), World Population Prospects: The 2008 Revision Highlights, Working Paper No. ESA/P/WP.210.

Top 10 Causes of Death, 2004

Cause / Disease	Number of deaths (in millions)	Percent of deaths
Coronary heart	7.20	12.2
Stroke[1]	5.71	9.7
Lower respiratory infections	4.18	7.1
Chronic obstructive pulmonary	3.02	5.1
Diarrheal	2.16	3.7
HIV/AIDS	2.04	3.5
Tuberculosis	1.46	2.5
Trachea, bronchus, lung cancers	1.32	2.3
Road traffic accidents	1.27	2.2
Prematurity and low birth weight	1.18	2.0

Note: 1. Includes other cerebrovascular diseases. **Source:** World Health Organization, *The Global Burden of Disease: 2004 Update,* Fact Sheet Number 310. Updated October 2008.

Leading Worldwide Causes of Death, 2004

Cause	Estimated deaths (millions)	Percent of total
World total deaths	**58,772**	**100.0%**
Communicable diseases;	17,971	30.6
maternal/perinatal conditions; nutritional deficiencies		
Infectious and parasitic diseases	9,519	16.2
Diarrheal diseases	2,163	3.7
HIV/AIDS	2,040	3.5
Malaria	889	1.5
Childhood cluster diseases	847	1.4
Respiratory diseases	4,259	7.2
Respiratory infections	4,177	7.1
Noncommunicable conditions	35,017	59.6
Cardiovascular diseases	17,073	29.0
Cancers	7,424	12.6
Injuries	5,784	9.8
Intentional	1,642	2.8

Source: World Health Organization, *The Global Burden of Disease: 2004.* Deaths and DALYs 2004: Annex tables.

most being children. The strongest risk factors for asthma are inhaled substances and particles that may create allergic reactions or irritate the airways.

Climate change and weather related disasters claimed 600,000 lives in the 1990s, with 95 percent of these deaths taking place in poor countries. Climate sensitive diseases are among the largest global killers, with diarrhea, malaria and protein-energy malnutrition causing more than 3.3 million deaths in 2002, with 29 percent occurring in Africa. As the earth's temperature rises climate change and weather related disasters are expected to increase.

Tuberculosis The W.H.O. 2005 tuberculosis report states that per capita TB incidence was stable or falling in all six of W.H.O. high risk regions. But, an estimated 1.6 million people died from TB in 2005, and many of these deaths were connected to HIV/AIDS. The slow decline in per capita cases is offset by population growth, so the number of new cases is still rising each year.

Dengue Fever Today some 1.5 billion people are at risk from dengue and dengue haemorrhagic fever and W.H.O. estimates there may be 50 million dengue infections every year. Dengue is a mosquito-borne infection that causes severe flu-like illness but seldom causes death, but it sometimes leads to dengue haemorrhagic fever, which can be deadly. Dengue occurs in tropical and sub-tropical climates worldwide, mostly in urban and semi-urban areas. An estimated 500,000 people with DHF are hospitalized each year, many of whom are children.

Asthma Asthma is a chronic disease of the bronchial tubes, the air passages to and from the lungs. Some 300 million people suffer from asthma today, most being children. The strongest risk factors for asthma are inhaled substances and particles that may create allergic reactions or irritate the airways.

Unsafe Drinking Water The number of people with access to safe drinking water rose from 4.1 billion in 1990 to 5.7 billion in 2006 but 900 million people are still getting their water from unimproved sources. Since 1990, some 1.1 billion people have gained access to improved sanitation, but in 2006, 2.5 billion still did not have access to improved sanitation.

Ageing Populations Globally The United Nations estimated that in 2009 there were 737 million people over the age of 60, with 264 million in developed countries, 473 million in less developed countries and 42,922,000 in the least developed areas. Twelve countries had more than 10 million people aged 60 or over, including China-160 million, India-98 million, United States-56 million, Japan-38 million, Russia-25 million, and Germany with 21 million. In most countries the population over 80 is growing faster than any younger segment. In 2009, there were 102 million people over 80 and their number is expected to reach 395 million by 2050. People over 80 comprised 4 percent of the population in Europe and nearly 4 percent in Northern America, but make up just 1.4 percent of the population in Latin America and the Caribbean, 1.1 percent in Asia and 0.4 percent in Africa.

Currently, 21 percent of the population is over 60 in the developed countries and 8 percent are over 60 in the developing areas. By 2050 almost 33 percent of the population in the developed areas will be over 60, and 26 percent of that number will be over 65, but only 20 percent will be over 60 in the developing world with 15 percent over 65.

In 2009, Japan had 29.1 percent of its population over age 60, Italy had 26.4 percent, Germany had 25.7 percent, Sweden 24.7 percent, Bulgaria had 24.2 percent, and Finland and Greece had 24 percent of their people over 60. The United States had 17.9 percent of its population over age 60. It is estimated that by 2050, Japan and South Korea will have 40 percent of their population over 60.

As the number of older persons is increasing, the number of young persons (under 15) is decreasing from a 1950 global average of 34 percent of the population to 27 percent in 2009.

The median age is the age where half the population is below the median and half the population is above. In 2009 the world median age was 28.1, in developed countries the median was 39.6, it was 25.9 years in less developed countries and 19.6 in least developed areas. Niger and Uganda the world's lowest median age at 15 years and Germany and Japan had the highest median age at 44.

►TOBACCO USE: A GLOBAL HEALTH PROBLEM

The World Health Organization estimates that tobacco is the second major cause of death in the world and is currently responsible for the death of one in 10 adults worldwide (about 5 million deaths each year). If current smoking patterns continue, tobacco will have contributed to 10 million deaths each year by 2020. About one-third of the adult male population smokes and smoking related-diseases kill one in 10 adults globally. About 15 billion cigarettes are sold daily, over 10 million every minute. Approximately 80,000 to 100,000 children start to smoke every day, about half of whom live in Asia.

Smoking is increasing in developing countries and declining in the developed nations. The highest smoking rate is in East Asia and the Pacific, where nearly two-thirds of men smoke. China is the world's largest tobacco producer; about 67 percent of the

Current World Health Indicators, by Nation

Country	Life expectancy at birth (years) 1970	Life expectancy at birth (years) 2005–10	Infant mortality per 1,000 births 2005–10	Population with access to: Improved water, 2008	Population with access to: Improved sanitation, 2008	Physicians per 10,000 population 2000–09	Per capita expenditure on health 2007[1]
Afghanistan	37	44	157	48%	37%	2	$ 42
Albania	67	77	16	97	98	11	244
Algeria	53	72	31	83	95	12	173
Angola	37	47	118	50	57	1	86
Argentina	67	75	13	97	90	32	663
Armenia	N.A.	74	25	96	90	37	133
Australia	71	82	5	100	100	10	3,986
Austria	70	80	4	100	100	38	4,523
Azerbaijan	N.A.	70	43	80	45	38	140
Bahamas	65	73	9	97[2]	100	11[2]	1,535
Bahrain	62	76	10	100[2]	100	30	902
Bangladesh	45	66	45	80	53	3	15
Barbados	69	77	10	100	100	12[2]	932
Belarus	N.A.	69	9	100	93	49	302
Belgium	71	80	4	100	100	42	4,056
Belize	N.A.	76	17	99	90	11	174
Benin	44	61	85	75	12	1	32
Bhutan	42	66	45	92	65	<1	75
Bolivia	46	66	46	86	25	12	89
Bosnia & Herzegovina	N.A.	75	13	99	95	14	397
Botswana	50	55	36	95	60	4	372
Brazil	59	72	23	97	80	17	606
Brunei Darussalam	N.A.	77	6	N.A.	N.A.	11	753
Bulgaria	70	73	12	100	100	37	384
Burkina Faso	40	53	80	76	11	1	29
Burundi	45	50	98	72	46	<1	17
Cambodia	42	61	62	61	29	2	36
Cameroon	49	51	87	74	47	2	54
Canada	73	81	5	100	100	19	4,409
Cape Verde	56	71	26	84	54	6	132
Central African Republic	42	47	106	67	34	1	16
Chad	38	49	130	50	9	<1	32
Chile	62	79	7	96	96	11	615
China	59	73	23	89	55	14	108
Colombia	59	73	19	92	74	14	284
Comoros	48	65	48	95	36	2	23
Congo, Rep. of	51	55	79	71	30	1	52
Congo, Dem. Rep.	N.A.	48	113	46	23	1	9
Costa Rica	67	79	10	97	95	13	488
Croatia	N.A.	76	6	99	99	26	1,009
Cuba	70	79	5	94	91	64	585
Cyprus	71	80	6	100	100	23	1,778
Czech Republic	69	77	4	100	98	36	1,141
Denmark	73	78	4	100	100	32	5,551
Djibouti	40	55	85	92	56	2	71
Dominican Republic	59	72	30	86	83	19	224
East Timor	N.A.	61	67	69	50	1	58
Ecuador	58	75	21	94	92	15	200
Egypt	51	70	35	99	94	24	101
El Salvador	58	71	22	87	87	12	206
Equatorial Guinea	40	50	100	43[2]	51[2]	3	347
Eritrea	N.A.	59	54	61	14	1	9
Estonia	N.A.	73	8	98	95	33	837
Ethiopia	43	55	79	38	12	<1	9
Fiji	64	69	20	47[2]	71[2]	5	157
Finland	70	80	3	100	100	33	3,809
France	72	81	4	100	100	37	4,627
Gabon	44	60	51	87	33	3	373
Gambia	36	56	77	92	67	<1	22
Georgia	N.A.	72	35	98	95	45	191
Germany	71	80	4	100	100	35	4,209
Ghana	49	57	73	82	13	1	54

Country	Life expectancy at birth (years) 1970	Life expectancy at birth (years) 2005–10	Infant mortality per 1,000 births 2005–10	Population with access to: Improved water, 2008	Population with access to: Improved sanitation, 2008	Physicians per 10,000 population 2000–09	Per capita expenditure on health 2007[1]
Greece	72	79	4	100%	98%	54	$2,679
Guatemala	53	70	30	94	81	9[2]	186
Guinea	36	58	98	71	19	1	26
Guinea-Bissau	36	48	114	61	21	<1	16
Guyana	65	67	42	94	81	5	115
Haiti	48	61	62	63	17	3[2]	35
Honduras	53	72	28	86	71	6	107
Hungary	70	73	7	100	100	28	1,019
Iceland	74	82	3	100	100	38	5,971
India	48	64	55	88	31	6	40
Indonesia	47	71	27	80	52	1	42
Iran	55	71	29	94[3]	83[3]	9	253
Iraq	55	67	33	79	73	5	62
Ireland	71	80	5	100	99	31	4,556
Israel	71	81	5	100	100	36	1,893
Italy	72	81	4	100	N.A.	37	3,136
Ivory Coast	N.A.	57	87	80	23	1	35
Jamaica	67	72	23	94	83	9	224
Japan	72	83	3	100	100	21	2,751
Jordan	55	73	19	96	98	26	248
Kazakhstan	N.A.	65	26	95	97	39	253
Kenya	50	54	64	59	31	1	34
Kiribati	N.A.	56[2]	60[2]	65[2]	33[2]	2	191
Korea, South	60	79	4	98	100	17	1,362
Korea, North	N.A.	67	48	100	59[2]	33	N.A.
Kuwait	66	78	9	99	100	18	901
Kyrgyzstan	N.A.	68	37	90	93	23	46
Laos	40	65	50	57	53	3	27
Latvia	N.A.	73	9	99	78	30	784
Lebanon	N.A.	72	22	100	98[2]	33	525
Lesotho	49	45	70	85	29	1	51
Liberia	47	58	95	68	17	<1	22
Libya	52	74	18	71[2]	97	12	299
Lithuania	N.A.	72	9	N.A.	N.A.	40	717
Luxembourg	70	80	4	100	100	29	7,439
Macedonia	N.A.	74	15	100	89	25	277
Madagascar	45	60	65	41	11	2	16
Malawi	40	53	84	80	56	<1	17
Malaysia	62	74	9	100	96	7	307
Maldives	N.A.	71	24	91	98	9	343
Mali	40	48	106	56	36	1	34
Malta	70	80	6	100	100	34	1,362
Mauritania	39	57	73	49	26	1	22
Mauritius	62	72	15	99	91	11	247
Mexico	62	76	17	94	85	29	564
Micronesia	N.A.	69	34	94[2]	25[2]	6	285
Moldova	N.A.	69	18	90	79	27	127
Monaco	N.A.	63[2]	58	100	100	N.A.	7,338
Mongolia	60	66	42	76	50	26	64
Morocco	52	71	31	81	69	6	120
Mozambique	41	48	90	47	17	<1	18
Myanmar	51	61	75	71	81	4	7
Namibia	48	61	35	92	33	3	319
Nepal	42	67	42	88	31	2	20
Netherlands	74	80	5	100	100	39	4,243
New Zealand	72	80	5	100	88[2]	21	2,790
Nicaragua	54	73	22	85	52	4	92
Niger	38	51	88	48	9	<1	16
Nigeria	44	48	109	58	32	4	74
Norway	74	81	4	100	100	39	7,354
Oman	45	76	12	82[2]	88	18	375
Pakistan	48	66	64	90	45	8	23
Panama	66	76	18	93	69	15	396
Papua New Guinea	47	61	51	41	45	1	31
Paraguay	65	72	32	86	70	11	114
Peru	54	73	21	82	68	12[2]	160
Philippines	57	72	23	91	76	12	63

Country	Life expectancy at birth (years) 1970	Life expectancy at birth (years) 2005–10	Infant mortality per 1,000 births 2005–10	Population with access to: Improved water, 2008	Population with access to: Improved sanitation, 2008	Physicians per 10,000 population 2000–09	Per capita expenditure on health 2007[1]
Poland	70	76	7	100%	90%	20	$ 716
Portugal	N.A.	79	4	99	100	34	2,108
Qatar	61	76	8	100	100	28	2,403
Romania	69	73	15	88[2]	72	19	369
Russian Federation	N.A.	67	12	96	87	43	493
Rwanda	48	50	100	65	54	<1	37
Samoa	N.A.	72	22	88	100	3	152
São Tomé & Principe	N.A.	66	72	89[2]	26	5	103
Saudi Arabia	52	73	19	89[2]	100[2]	16	531
Senegal	43	55	58	69	51	1	54
Serbia	N.A.	74	12	99	92	20	408
Seychelles	N.A.	71[2]	12[2]	87[2]	100[2]	15	564
Sierra Leone	34	47	104	49	13	<1	14
Singapore	68	80	3	100	100	15	1,148
Slovakia	N.A.	75	7	100	100	31	1,077
Slovenia	N.A.	78	4	100	100	24	1,836
Solomon Islands	40	66	44	70[2]	32[2]	1	54
Somalia	N.A.	50	110	30	23	<1	N.A.
South Africa	53	52	49	91	77	8	497
Spain	72	81	4	100	100	38	2,712
Sri Lanka	64	74	16	90	91	6	68
St. Kitts & Nevis	N.A.	70[2]	30[2]	99	96	11	623
St. Lucia	62	74	13	98	89[2]	N.A.	361
St. Vincent and The Grenadines	63	72	23	93[2]	96[2]	8	272
Sudan	N.A.	58	69	57	34	3	40
Suriname	64	69	22	93	84	5	361
Swaziland	46	46	66	69	55	2	151
Sweden	75	81	3	100	100	36	4,495
Switzerland	73	82	4	100	100	40	6,108
Syria	56	74	16	89	96	5	68
Tajikistan	N.A.	67	60	70	94	20	29
Tanzania	45	55	65	55	47	<1	22
Thailand	58	69	7	98	96	3	136
Togo	45	62	71	60	12	1	33
Tonga	N.A.	72	22	100	96	3	108
Trinidad and Tobago	66	69	26	94	92	12	785
Tunisia	54	74	20	94	85	13	211
Turkey	57	72	28	99	90	15	465
Turkmenistan	N.A.	65	51	N.A.	98	24	139
Uganda	47	52	74	67	48	1	28
Ukraine	N.A.	68	12	98	95	31	210
United Arab Emirates	61	77	10	100	97	15	1,253
United Kingdom	72	79	5	100	100	21	3,867
United States	71	79	6	99	100	27	7,285
Uruguay	N.A.	76	13	100	100	37	582
Uzbekistan	N.A.	68	48	87	100	26	41
Vanuatu	N.A.	70	28	82	50	1	79
Venezuela	65	74	17	89[2]	83[2]	19	477
Vietnam	N.A.	74	20	94	75	6	58
Yemen	42	63	59	62	52	3	43
Zambia	47	45	95	60	49	1	57
Zimbabwe	51	44	58	82	44	2	79

Notes: 1. Per capita total expenditure on health at average exchange rate in U.S. dollars. 2. 2004 data. 3. 1990 data. **Source:** World Health Organization, *World Health Statistics 2010* (2010); United Nations Department for Economic and Social Affairs, Population Division, *World Population Prospects: The 2008 Revision Highlights* (2009); Chart: World Population, 1996.

men smoke, and four percent of the women. About 3,000 people die each day in China from smoking, and it is estimated that smoking will kill about a third of all Chinese men under 30 today. Half the men in Japan and Malaysia are smokers.

Half of long-term smokers will die from tobacco. Smoking is the single largest preventable cause of disease and premature death. It is a prime factor in heart disease, stroke and chronic lung disease. It can cause cancer of the lungs, larynx, esophagus, mouth, and bladder, and contributes to cancer of the cervix, pancreas and kidneys. Smoking is related to at least a quarter of all deaths from heart disease and about three-quarters of the world's chronic bronchitis.

▶ CIRCULATORY DISEASES

According to the World Health Organization, Cardiovascular diseases (CVDs), a group of disorders of the heart and blood vessels, are the number one cause of death globally. An estimated 17.1 million people died from CVDs in 2004, representing 29 percent of all global deaths. Of these deaths, an estimated 7.2 million were due to coronary heart disease and 5.7 million were due to stroke. Low- and middle-income countries account for 82 percent of

CVD deaths and occur almost equally in men and women. Projections indicate that cardiovascular diseases will continue to be the world's single leading cause of death with 23.6 million deaths estimated for 2030.

Heart attacks and strokes are usually acute events and are mainly caused by a blockage that prevents blood from flowing to the heart or brain. The most common reason for this is a build-up of fatty deposits on the inner walls of the blood vessels that supply the heart or brain. Eighty percent of strokes are caused by a blood clot in the brain, 20 percent of strokes are caused by bleeding inside the brain.

Individuals can reduce their risk of CVDs by engaging in regular physical activity least 30 minutes every day, avoiding tobacco use and second-hand tobacco smoke, choosing a diet rich in fruit and vegetables and avoiding foods that are high in fat, sugar and salt, and maintaining a healthy body weight.

▶ CANCER

The World Health Organization estimates that in 2007 cancer caused 7.9 million deaths or about 13 percent of all deaths. The main types of cancer deaths are: lung (1.4 million deaths/year); stomach (866,000 deaths); liver (653,000 deaths); colon (677,000 deaths); breast (548,000 deaths).

The most frequent types of cancer worldwide (in order of the number of global deaths) differ in men and women. Among men—lung, stomach, liver, colorectal, oesophagus and prostate; Among women—breast, lung, stomach, colorectal and cervical. About 30 percent of cancer deaths can be prevented; tobacco use is the single most important risk factor.

Tobacco use, alcohol use, low fruit and vegetable diet, and infections from hepatitis B, hepatitis C and the human papilloma viruses are leading risk factors for cancer in low- and middle-income countries. Cervical cancer, which is caused by HPV, is a leading cause of cancer death among women in low-income countries. In high-income countries, tobacco use, alcohol use, and being overweight or obese are primary causes of cancer. Other risk factors include low physical activity, unsafe sex, urban air pollution and indoor smoke from household use of solid fuels.

Prevention strategies include increase avoidance of the risk factors listed above, vaccination against human papilloma virus (HPV) and hepatitis B virus (HBV) infection, control of occupational hazards and reduction of exposure to sunlight. Deaths from cancer worldwide are projected to continue rising, with an estimated 12 million deaths in 2030.

▶ MATERNAL DEATHS WORLDWIDE

Approximately 536,000 women die around the world each year from pregnancy-related causes, according to the World Health Organization. In parts of some developing countries, the chance of a woman dying this way is 100 times greater than in the industrialized countries.

The five major causes of maternal death are: hemorrhage (25 percent), indirect causes (19 percent), sepsis or postpartum infection (15 percent), hypertensive disorders of pregnancy and eclampsia (13 percent), and unsafe abortion (13 percent). About 70,000 women die each year from unsafe abortion—600 in developed countries and 69,000 in less developed countries—and an unknown but much larger number suffer infection, injury and trauma. There are an estimated 20 million unsafe abortions each year, 90 percent of them in developing countries.

Women who do not have adequate family planning materials and services more often have unwanted pregnancies and bear too many children, or they have children when they are too young or too old, or have children too close together. Virtually all studies report that most women would prefer using contraceptives and resort to abortion as a last resort.

▶ DEATHS OF CHILDREN

According to 2007 figures, nine million children under the age of 5 die each year, with 70 percent of these deaths preventable. About 4 million babies are still born each year and 4 million die within their first month with about 25 to 50 percent of these deaths occurring in the first 24 hours of life and 75 percent of deaths are in the first week. Safe childbirth and effective neonatal care can prevent most of these deaths. Preterm birth, birth asphyxia (lack of breathing at birth), and infections cause most neonatal deaths which are about 40 percent of child deaths under the age of 5. From the end of the neonatal period and through the first five years of life, the main causes of death are pneumonia, diarrhoea, malaria, measles and HIV/AIDS. Over one third of all child deaths are linked to malnutrition.

About 20 million children worldwide suffer from severe acute malnutrition, which leaves them more vulnerable to serious illness and early death. Malnutrition can be prevented by exclusive breastfeeding for the first six months of life, followed by a combination of breastfeeding and complementary feeding up to age two years or beyond. Children with severe acute malnutrition can be treated successfully with ready-to-use therapeutic foods (RUTF). These highly fortified and energy-rich foods provide the required nutrients for malnourished children starting from age six months to older children, so they can be treated at home.

▶ GLOBAL SEX FACTS

According to the World Health Organization, sexual intercourse occurs more than 100 million times a day around the world, resulting in approximately 910,000 conceptions and 350,000 cases of sexually transmitted diseases. The W.H.O. estimates that 1,440 women die each day (an average of one a minute) because of complications during pregnancy or childbirth. About 150,000 unwanted pregnancies each day end in abortion.

The number of people using contraception in developing countries has increased sharply in recent years, from 31 million in the 1960–65 period to 381 million during 1985–90. Women in developing countries had, on average, 6.1 children in the years 1965–70, but the figure declined to 3.9 in 1985–90.

▶ SEXUALLY TRANSMITTED DISEASES (STDs)

In 2002, some 180,000 people died of sexually transmitted diseases other than HIV, including 152,000 from syphilis, 9,000 from chlamydia and 1,000 from gonorrhea. There are an estimated 333 million new cases of STDs each year. STDs are most frequent in young people aged 15 to 24. Women contract STDs five times more often than men. Almost two-thirds of all cases of infertility are due to STDs. W.H.O. estimates that in 1995, there were 150 million cases of STDs in adults in southern/southeastern Asia, 65 million cases in sub-Saharan Africa, 36 million in Latin America and the Caribbean, and 14 million in North America.

▶ AIDS WORLDWIDE

The Joint United Nations Programme on HIV/AIDS (UNAIDS) and the World Health Organization estimated that at the end of 2007, approximately 33 million adults and children (under age 15) worldwide were living with HIV/AIDS, two-thirds of them in Sub-Saharan Africa. During 2007, an estimated 2.7 million people were newly infected with HIV (370,000 were children) and 2 million people died from AIDS (490,000 were children). Each day during 2007 some 6,800 persons became newly infected with HIV (1,200 were children). Of the 5,800 adults over 15 years of age who became newly infected with HIV each day in 2007 almost 50 percent were women and about 45 percent were young people aged 15 to 24. During 2007 over 5,700 people died from AIDS each day worldwide.

While AIDS appears to be declining overall, the number of women living with HIV increased from 13.8 million in 2001 to 15.4 million in 2007. The number of children living with HIV also rose from 1.5 million in 2001 to two million in 2007. However, the estimated number of new infections declined from 460,000 in 2001 to 370,000 in 2007. Child deaths due to AIDS increased from 330,000 in 2001 to 360,000 in 2005, but have now declined to 330,000 in 2007.

Sub-Saharan African continues to be the region most affected by the AIDS pandemic. Worldwide 67 percent of the adults and nearly 90 percent of children infected with HIV live in this region. At the end of 2007 sub-Saharan Africa had 22 million adults and children infected with HIV or 5 percent of the population, had an estimated 1.9 million new infections during the year and 1.5 million AIDS deaths. More than three in every four (76 percent) AIDS deaths worldwide in 2007 occurred there. Of all the HIV infections in this region, 61 percent are women,

the highest percentage of women living with HIV in the world.

Nine countries in southern Africa remain the global epicenter of HIV infections: 35 percent of all people with HIV live in this sub-region, and 32 percent of all new HIV infections and 38 percent of AIDS deaths occurred there in 2007. South Africa has the world's largest number of people infected with HIV/AIDS, 5.7 million adults while Swaziland has the world's highest percentage of infected people at 26 percent. HIV epidemics in Malawi, South Africa and Zambia appear to have stabilized but the epidemic is growing in Mozambique. Heterosexual intercourse remains the driving force causing HIV infections in sub-Saharan Africa but recent evidence shows that sex work is spreading HIV in West Africa and injecting drug use is a factor in cases in eastern and southern Africa.

In 2007 an estimated five million people in Asia were living with HIV, including 380,000 people who became newly infected; and approximately 380,000 died of AIDS. India's HIV epidemic continues to be large, with 2.6 million infected people in 2006, even though UNAIDS lowered their estimates of the

HIV Estimates By Region, 2007

Region	Adults and children living with HIV[2]	Number of women living with HIV	Adult prevalence[1]	Adults/children newly infected with HIV	Adult and child deaths due to AIDS
Sub-Saharan Africa	22,000,000	1,800,000	5.0%	1,900,000	1,500,000
East Asia	740,000	7,900	0.1	52,000	40,000
South/South-east Asia	4,200,000	140,000	0.3	340,000	340,000
Latin America	1,700,000	36,000	0.5	140,000	63,000
Eastern Europe and Central Asia	1,500,000	9,500	0.8	110,000	58,000
North America	1,200,000	11,000	0.6	54,000	23,000
Western Europe	730,000	3,000	0.3	27,000	8,000
North Africa and Middle East	380,000	26,000	0.3	40,000	27,000
Caribbean	230,000	11,000	1.1	20,000	14,000
Oceania	74,000	1,100	0.4	13,100	1,000
TOTALS	**38,600,000**	**17,587,100**	**1.0**	**4,100,000**	**2,800,700**

Notes: 1. The proportion of adults (15 to 49 years of age) living with HIV/AIDS in 2006, using 2006 population numbers. 2. 2006 figures. **Source:** Joint United Nations Programme on HIV/AIDS (UNAIDS) and World Health Organization, *2008 Report on the Global AIDS Epidemic*, 2005.

Nations with Highest HIV Infected Populations, 2007

Region	Adults and children living with HIV	Adults living with HIV	Number of women living with HIV	Adult prevalence[2]	Orphans age 1–17 due to AIDS	Adult and child deaths due to AIDS
South Africa	5,700,000	5,400,000	3,200,000	18.1	1,400,000	350,000
Nigeria	2,600,000	2,400,000	1,400,000	3.1	1,200,000	170,000
India	2,400,000	2,300,000	880,000	0.3	N.A.	475,000[1]
Mozambique	1,500,000	1,400,000	810,000	12.5	400,000	81,000
Tanzania	1,400,000	1,300,000	760,000	6.2	970,000	96,000
Zimbabwe	1,300,000	1,200,000	680,000	15.3	1,000,000	140,000
Kenya[1]	1,300,000	1,200,000	740,000	6.1	N.A.	140,000
United States	1,200,000	1,100,000	230,000	0.6	N.A.	22,000
Zambia	1,100,000	980,000	560,000	15.2	600,000	56,000
Congo, Dem. Rep.[1]	1,000,000	890,000	520,000	3.2	N.A.	90,000
Ethiopia	980,000	890,000	530,000	2.1	650,000	67,000
Uganda	940,000	810,000	480,000	5.4	1,200,000	77,000
Russia	940,000	940,000	240,000	1.1	N.A.	40,000
Malawi	930,000	840,000	490,000	11.9	550,000	68,000
China	700,000	690,000	200,000	0.1	N.A.	39,000
Brazil	610,000	710,000	240,000	0.6	N.A.	15,000
Thailand	610,000	600,000	250,000	1.4	N.A.	21,000
Cameroon	540,000	500,000	250,000	5.1	300,000	39,000
Ukraine	440,000	430,000	200,000	1.6	N.A.	19,000
Ivory Coast	420,000	680,000	190,000	3.9	420,000	38,000

Notes: Adults are people over age 15. 1. 2005 data. 2. Proportion of adults (15 to 49 years of age) living with HIV/AIDS. **Source:** Joint United Nations Programme on HIV/AIDS (UNAIDS) and World Health Organization, 2008 Report on the Global AIDS Epidemic (August 2008).

number of people living with the virus. HIV infections in China are found mainly among injecting drug users and is expanding among men who have sex with men, now estimated at 7 percent. In some places as many as half of all women who sell sex are infected. Indonesia has one of the fastest growing HIV rates in Asia, mainly due to the use of contaminated injecting equipment, unprotected paid sex and unprotected sex between men.

Total HIV infections in Eastern Europe and Central Asia reached 1.5 million in 2007, including 110,000 new infections. Nearly 90 percent of the reported infections in 2007 were from 2 countries: Russia had 69 percent and the Ukraine 29 percent. Reported infections are also rising in Eurasia. Uzbekistan now has the largest epidemic in Central Asia with nearly two thirds of the 2,205 infections reported in 2006 attributed to injecting drug use and more than one third are due to unprotected heterosexual sex.

Of the 230,000 people living with HIV in the Caribbean, three quarters live in the Dominican Republic and Haiti. An estimated 20,000 became newly infected in 2007 and 14,000 people died of AIDS in the region. The main mode of transmission in this region is unprotected sex between sex workers and clients. Infection seems to have stabilized in both Haiti and the Dominican Republic, due to condom use and a decrease in the number of sex partners.

Latin America had 1.7 million people living with HIV in 2007 with about 140,000 new infections and 63,000 deaths due to AIDS. HIV prevalence continues to be stable. Brazil has 40 percent of the people living with HIV in this region, estimated at 730,000 in 2007, followed by Mexico with 200,000 HIV positive people. The epidemic began among men who have sex with men, then spread to injecting drug users and eventually into the general population, now showing increasing numbers among women.

North America and Western and Central Europe continue to see increases in the number of people living with HIV because of life-prolonging antiretroviral therapy. There were about 2.1 million people living with HIV in 2007, including 81,000 new cases during the year. Due to the widely available drug therapies only about 31,000 people died of AIDS. The HIV rates in Spain, Italy, France and the UK continue to be the largest in the region.

Across the Middle East and North Africa there were an estimated 40,000 new infections in 2007 for a total of 380,000 people living with HIV. Sudan has the most reported HIV cases, which are due to unsafe heterosexual sex. Some 74,000 people were living with HIV in Oceania in 2007, including 13,000 new infections that year. Over 54,000 people in Papua New Guinea have HIV due to unsafe heterosexual sex. Australia had 18,000 HIV infections in 2007, mainly due to unsafe sex between men.

At the end of 2007 nearly 3 million people were receiving antiretroviral treatment in low-and middle-income countries, representing 31 percent of those needing treatment. In Latin America and Caribbean some 390,000 HIV infected people were receiving treatment or 62 percent of the 630,000 who needed it. In sub-Saharan Africa, 30 percent or 2.1 million received treatment out of the 7 million who were infected. In East, South and South-East Asia 420,000 people or 25 percent of the 1.7 people infected with HIV received treatment. In Europe and Central Asia 17 percent, or 54,000 of the 320,000 HIV infected people, received antiretroviral treatment. In the Middle East and North Africa 7,000 or 7 percent of the 100,000 people needing it received treatment. While there is a six-fold increase in global funding of antiretroviral treatment from 2001 to 2007, for every two people on antiretroviral drugs, another five become newly infected.

World Religions

In 2007, 5.7 billion, or an estimated 86 percent of the world's population, identified themselves as adherents of one religion or another. Four religions—Christianity, Islam, Hinduism and Buddhism—claim 4.2 billion adherents, or 73 percent of the world's population. Approximately 14 percent (1.1 billion) of the world's people are atheist or nonreligious.

This section describes the major religions of the world, their basic tenets, scriptures, schools and sects, and their history. (See "Religion in America" in Part II for more information.)

▶JUDAISM

Origins Judaism is the oldest of the world's three major monotheistic religions and a forerunner of Christianity and Islam. The Hebrew Bible recounts the story of the world and mankind from the creation, through the flood, and the work of the patriarch Abraham who brought his people from Mesopotamia to Canaan—the Promised Land. His descendants were enslaved in Egypt until Moses led them out of captivity. During the exodus, Moses received from God the Ten Commandments that form the bedrock of Jewish law. Jewish custom and law further evolved from the 10th century B.C. and the conquest of Canaan to the destruction of Jerusalem by the Romans in A.D. 70.

Scripture The sacred scripture of the Hebrew Bible, or Masorah, consists of 24 books. (The Christian Old Testament divides the same text into 39 books.) The *Torah*, or Law, was composed between the 10th and fifth centuries B.C. These five books—Genesis, Exodus, Leviticus, Numbers and Deuteronomy—are also known by their Greek name, *Pentateuch*. The later history of Israel and the divided kingdom is told in two separate but overlapping traditions known as the Prophets

(13th–sixth centuries B.C.) and the Writings (11th–second centuries B.C.). The Hebrew Bible is also known by the Greek name *Septuagint* (seventy), a reference to the number of authors engaged in its translation from Hebrew to Greek in the third century B.C. In addition to scripture, there is a rich ancient tradition of rabbinical commentary called the *Talmud*, a huge compilation of the Oral Law and the accepted authority for Orthodox Jews. First codified around A.D. 200, the Talmudic tradition continued through the centuries and constitutes not only commentary on the law (*Halakah*), but also stories from the Bible and parables, legends, etc. (*Haggadah*) illustrating religious principles.

Beliefs Central to Jewish belief is the idea of a single God—Yahweh—who made a covenant (i.e. an agreement or contract) with His chosen people that He would protect them and provide for them if they swore Him love and obedience. Yahweh shapes history (the end of which is the kingdom of God) and imposes His will upon mankind; He saves, and He judges. The people of *Israel* have a unique relationship with God affirmed on the one hand by His covenant, and on the other, by His law. While Yahweh the creator guides human destiny, the humanity of mankind is defined by the ability of individuals to make ethical choices in keeping with His law. The failure to act according to His law—that is, to know God—is sin, and a basic tenet of Jewish faith is that sin is a willful act; so, too, is turning, or returning, to God.

The book of Isaiah (eighth century B.C.) brings to the fore a messianic tradition identifying a future Israel under a divine ruler descended from the house of David as a restoration of paradise and the attainment of salvation.

Practice   Jews worship in synagogues in congregations led by a rabbi—a teacher or master. The Sabbath is observed from sunset Friday to sunset Saturday; worship consists of readings from scripture, prayer, and singing. The most important holidays in the Jewish calendar are Rosh Hashanah (New Year), Yom Kippur (Day of Atonement), Hanukah (Festival of Lights), and Pesach (Passover). (See Part I: "Holidays and Holy Days").

Schools and sects   There are three main branches of modern Judaism. Orthodox Jews rigorously observe Jewish law, ritual and custom. Reform Judaism professes a more liberal interpretation of Jewish doctrine and ritual, and is especially prevalent in the United States. Conservative Judaism combines elements of doctrinal reform with more traditional observance. Hasidism is today a branch of Orthodox Judaism with origins in a mystical movement in 18th-century Poland that stressed prayer over studying the Torah. Hasidim are very strict observers of the Jewish religious laws.

History   The Bible recounts the history of the Jewish people from the creation, through the flood and the covenant of the rainbow, the patriarchs Abraham, Isaac and Jacob, and the story of the tribe of Israel in Egypt. The foundation of Jewish faith began with the exodus from Egypt, and the transmission of the Ten Commandments (the Decalogue) from God to his people through Moses, probably sometime between 1450 and 1290 B.C. The people of Israel conquered and settled in Canaan—the promised land—and were ruled by a succession of judges. The monarchical period under Samuel and David dates to the 11th and 10th centuries B.C. Israel and Judah continued under separate rulers until the fall of Israel in 722 B.C. Judah was conquered by Babylonians, and the Temple of David in Jerusalem was destroyed in 586 B.C. at the start of the Babylonian captivity, which also marks the start of the Jewish Diaspora, or dispersal. Exile lasted until 538 B.C., and the Second Temple was dedicated in 516 B.C. Under Seleucid rule the Maccabees successfully resisted efforts to suppress Judaism (168–142 B.C.). Under Roman rule (63 B.C.–A.D. 135), there were several revolts, the first of which resulted in the destruction of the Second Temple (A.D. 70). It was at around this time that Christianity began to diverge sharply from its Jewish sectarian origins.

The early Middle Ages saw the rise of the Talmudic tradition. Following the rise of Islam, Judaism evolved into two distinct strains, the Sephardim, centered in Spain, and the Ashkenazim, found mainly in France and Germany. Organized persecution of European Jewry began with their expulsion from France (1306) and Spain (1492), and culminated in the Nazi regime in Germany's attempt to eradicate all Jews during the Holocaust (1933–45). The Jewish enlightenment (*Haskala*) in 18th-century Germany gave rise to Reform Judaism and Conservative Judaism (1845). The nationalistic Zionist movement, a reaction to extreme anti-Semitism, led eventually to the birth of the State of Israel in 1948. Though Israel is a secular republic, religious parties play an active role in politics.

Geography and numbers   There are an estimated 14 million Jews worldwide, 90 percent of whom live in only six countries. The overwhelming majority of the Jewish population lives in the United States (6.5 million) and Israel (5.6 million). There are an estimated 1.5 million Jews in Europe.

►CHRISTIANITY

Origins   Christianity is based on the acts and sayings of Jesus of Nazareth as related by his followers and apostles. Jesus was born a Jew in Bethlehem in about 4 B.C., but details of his life before about A.D. 26–28 are obscure. In his early 30s, Jesus was baptized by John the Baptist, whose ministry prophesied the coming judgment of God, and who recognized Jesus as the Messiah (Greek for the Christ, or anointed one). Jesus' ministry, chiefly among the poor and dispossessed, lasted only a few years before he was crucified by Roman authorities. According to Christian belief, Jesus rose from the dead three days after his crucifixion, and 40 days later he ascended to heaven to sit at the right hand of God.

Scripture   The Bible consists of the Old Testament (the Hebrew Bible), originally written in Hebrew and Aramaic, and the New Testament (first written in Greek in the first century), which relates the life and teachings of Jesus and his early followers. A 3rd-century translation of the Bible into Latin is called the Vulgate. The central portion of the New Testament consists of the Four Gospels (each attributed to one of Christ's earliest followers: Matthew, Mark, Luke, and John). While each tells the story of Jesus' life and death, they differ in details, with Luke and John providing more stories and greater emphasis on Christ's divinity. The story of the spread of Christianity in the first century is told in the Acts of the Apostles and the epistles (letters) of St. Paul. The Roman Catholic canon also includes 15 books found in the Greek Septuagint but not in the Hebrew Bible. The Orthodox Church accepts four of these Apocryphal books; Protestants accept none.

Beliefs   Christian belief is rooted in three basic ideas: incarnation—Christ was the human embodiment of God; atonement—mankind was reconciled to God through the agency of Christ; and the Trinity—the belief that the one God has three natures, God the Father, God the Son (Jesus), and God the Holy Spirit.

Practice   Central to the practice of most Christians are the seven sacraments: baptism, confirmation, holy matrimony, holy orders, sacrament of the sick, reconciliation (confession), and the Eucharist, (or communion), the sacramental offering and consumption of bread and wine representing the body and blood of Christ. Christians are organized into congregations and worship in churches led by priests or ministers who administer the sacraments. Most denominations designate Sunday as the sabbath and the day for special observance and worship.

Schools and sects   Christianity has three major branches: Eastern Orthodoxy, Roman Catholicism, and Protestantism. The division between Eastern Orthodoxy and Roman Catholicism came in 1054. In the 16th century, reform-minded priests broke with Rome and there emerged a number of distinct denominations known collectively as Protestantism.

The hierarchical authority of the Catholic Church starts with the pope, and includes cardinals, bishops, and priests, all celibate men. In addition there are a number of Catholic lay and priestly orders for men and/or women.

The Eastern Orthodox Church embraces a number of national or regional churches. The laity are invested with more authority than are Catholics, and the bishop of Constantinople, titular head of the eastern church, is regarded as first among equals.

Protestant denominations number in the hundreds. There is no single governing authority for all of them. (See Part II, "Religion in America," for a summary of the major sects.)

History   At the time of his death, Jesus had a small handful of followers among Jews. His teachings were not widely accepted among the larger Jewish community, however, and his disciples preached to non-Jewish gentiles throughout the Roman Empire. Jesus' teachings were gathered in a collection of books known as the Gospel, or New Testament. Christians were widely persecuted until the Emperor Constantine legalized the religion in 313; in 380 Christianity became the official religion of the Roman Empire. Christianity also reached northern Ethiopia.

Disputes over theological issues such as the nature of the Trinity and the person of Christ were resolved at a series of ecumenical councils. In 1054 the Eastern and Western churches split over differences of theology, politics, geography and language. The papacy in Rome acquired the nature of a civil authority and within the Western church ascetic, spiritual traditions competed with secular ones. In the 16th century, papal authority was challenged by such reform-minded priests as Martin Luther and John Calvin, abetted by England's King Henry VIII, who transferred authority over the church in England from the pope to himself. Sectarian wars engulfed Europe for more than a century as Catholics and Protestants vied for temporal and spiritual power.

European explorers and colonists spread Christianity to the Americas, Asia and Africa. The Spanish and Portuguese brought Catholicism to Latin America, while North America became a haven for Protestant denominations from northern Europe. Since the mid-1800s, Protestant and Catholic evangelists have carried out energetic missionary programs to Africa and East Asia.

Geography and numbers Christianity is the most populous and most widespread religion in the world, with over 2 billion adherents in 260 countries. Europe is home to more than 530 million Christians (70 percent of the region's population), but Latin America has proportionally the highest number of Christian adherents—93 percent of the population. While numbers of Christian adherents fluctuate, most all available research points to a declining number of Christians in Europe, even as it continues to grow on other continents. In the year 2000, there were over 350 million Christians in Asia and over 260 million Christians in North America. The fastest growing Christian population is in Africa, increasing 2.4 percent from 380 million in 2000 to 389 million in 2005.

▶ISLAM

Origins The precepts of Islam were revealed through Mohammed, the last of a line of prophets including Abraham, Moses and Jesus. Mohammed was born about 570 at Mecca (in western Saudi Arabia) and died in 632 in the nearby city of Medina.

Scripture The Koran (*recitation*) consists of 114 chapters (*suras*). The text is the infallible word of God as revealed to Mohammed and transcribed by his followers over the course of 23 years.

Beliefs Islam is a monotheistic religion with explicit links to Judaism and Christianity. The Koran's narrative includes stories of Abraham and Isaac, and Moses and the Ten Commandments. Unlike Jews, who trace their descent from Abraham through Isaac, the son of Sarah, Muslims trace their decent through Ishmael, Abraham's son by Hagar. The Koran recounts the virgin birth of Jesus, but does not accept his divinity.

The word Islam comes from the Arabic root *s-l-m*, meaning peace and submission, and a hallmark of Islam is obedience to God.

Practice A Muslim's relations with God are regulated by the Five Pillars of Islam: the Shahadah, or profession of faith—There is no God but God, and Mohammed is his prophet; public and collective prayer five times daily; charity to the poor; fasting during the holy month of Ramadan; and pilgrimage to Mecca, the most holy place in the Muslim world, at least once in one's lifetime.

Islam has strict dietary laws and prohibitions against promiscuity, theft, gambling and lying. Muslims worship in mosques led by imams. The principal weekly worship is on Friday at midday.

Schools and sects The overwhelming majority of Muslims are Sunnites, or traditionalists (85–90 percent, or 1.2 billion people). Shi'ites, or partisans, represent another 10–15 percent (200 million) and smaller sects make up the rest. The Shi'ite/Sunnite schism reflects differences about who should have succeeded Mohammed. Shi'ites follow somewhat different rites than Sunnites, and recognize additional holy days and places.

History Mohammed was born in Arabia in about 570 A.D. Raised by his uncle, at the age of 25 he became a trader, and later married his employer, the widow Khadija. In 610, an angel descended on Mohammed and ordered him to proclaim the word of God. Rebuked in Mecca, in 622 he was invited to Medina to help bring order to the city. He accepted on the condition that the citizens worship Allah—the one God—and accept the precepts of Islam. This move—the *hegira*—is the year from which the Muslim calendar dates. Eight years later Mohammed returned to Mecca, and by the time of his death in 632, most Arabs were Muslims.

Under a succession of secular and theocratic caliphates, Islam swept east and west from Arabia. Muslims reached the Indus River in 713, and their advance in France was only stopped in 733 at the Battle of Tours; Muslims remained in Spain until 1492. Islamic armies captured the Byzantine capital of Constantinople in 1453, and controlled much of southeastern Europe until the 19th century. In the east, Muslims swept through India at the end of the 10th century and reached the East Indies in the 15th century.

The arts, architecture and technology flourished in the golden age of Islam and Islamic learning and culture was responsible for the transmission of much of classical philosophy and science to the West. From the 18th to 20th centuries, traditionally Islamic countries came under Western cultural and political influence. In the 20th century, some traditionally Islamic countries like Turkey opted for a secular state; others such as Saudi Arabia and Iran came under strict fundamentalist rule.

Geography and numbers With 1.6 billion adherents in nearly 200 countries, Islam is the second largest religion in the world and arguably the fastest growing. Though Muslims are found on all five inhabited continents, more than 300 million Muslims (one-fifth of the global Muslim population) live in countries where Islam is not the majority religion. Islam is the dominent religion in the Middle East, and countries here and in North Africa have the highest percentage of Muslim-majority countries by region. Sixty percent of the global Muslim population is in Asia, however; India has the third largest population of Muslims worldwide.

▶HINDUISM

Origins Hinduism is a complex of polytheistic religion and philosophy that evolved from Vedism, an ancient Indian religion of Indo-European origin dating from the second millennium B.C.

Scripture Different Hindu sects rely on different holy texts, but common to the majority are the Vedic texts called the *Upanishads*. The *Svetasvatara Upanishad* describes Siva, the creator, preserver and destroyer of the universe. Sources for Hindu mythology include the *Mahabharata*, *Ramayana* (concerning Rama, the incarnation of the great god Vishnu), and the *Puaranas*. The *Bhagavad Gita* (Lord's song, a part of the *Mahabharata*), is a dialogue between Krishna (another incarnation of the god Vishnu) and Prince Arjuna in which are described the three paths to union with God.

Beliefs Hinduism is rooted in the belief that individuals should connect their selves (Atman) with Brahman, or Godhead, the spiritual source of the tangible universe. Hindus also believe in reincarnation—*samsara*—one's subsequent status being dependent on one's actions (*karma*) and duties (*dharma*) in this life. The cycle of reincarnation is broken when one attains liberation (moksha) from the finite world through self-discovery—the union of self with the Godhead, or *Atman-Brahman*. There are four paths to union with Brahman: *jnana yoga*, based on knowledge; *bhakti yoga*, based on service to God; *karma yoga*, based on work for God (as opposed to oneself); and *raja yoga*, based on psychophysical exercise.

Hinduism has three primary theistic traditions revolving around the cults of anthropomorphic gods. Vishnu is a loving god incarnated as Krishna; Siva is a god at once protective and destructive; and Brahma is creator. Saktism is a form of worship dedicated to the female consorts of Vishnu and Siva.

Hindus have a deep respect for all living things; the most revered animal is the cow.

Practice Hindu worship is largely an individual and family matter. Hindu temples are devoted to a particular god or group of gods. Worship in temples or before domestic shrines includes prayers and offerings to an image of the god. Such rituals are intended to bring the worshipper and the god closer together.

Hindu pilgrimage sites include seven sacred cities, among others, where thousands or even millions of Hindus worship at annual festivals. Some of the most famous temples are on the banks of the Ganges River, which is sacred to Hindus, in northern India. Important festival days include Dipavali, festival of lights, sacred to Lakshmi, goddess of prosperity; holi, a spring festival; and Dashara, a harvest festival.

Individuals follow a code of moral and religious conduct called *dharma*. Traditional Hinduism observes complex societal divisions into four groups (and thousands of subsidiary) castes defined by occupation and social standing: *brahmins:* leaders, philosophers, artists and their families; *kshatriyas:* princes, soldiers and administrators; *vaishyas:* merchants and landowners; and *shudras*, or laborers. Beyond the caste system are untouchables, or outcasts. India's modern constitution outlawed the caste system.

Schools and sects Hinduism comprises myriad religious cults and various schools of philosophy. The principle of religious toleration is reflected in the Hindu belief that Christianity, Islam and other religions offer alternative paths to the same goal. Among the more prominent modes of belief are *yoga* and *tantrism*, both of which evolved in both Hinduism and Buddhism, and *bhakti. Tantrism* emphasizes meditation and ritual involving mystical diagrams (mandalas) and chants (mantras) as a means to enlightenment. *Yoga* emphasizes an eightfold path to enlightenment through physical and mental training. *Bhakti* focuses on the primacy of love for a deity.

History Hinduism is the oldest of the world's great religions. Originating in India, it spread to Nepal and southeast Asia. The oldest Hindu writings are actually Vedic texts brought by Aryan invaders in the second millennium B.C. To the Vedic concept of future life, Hinduism attached the ideas of karma, reincarnation and ultimately release from the cycle of life, death and rebirth. Following the rise of rival religions such as Buddhism and Jainism in the sixth century B.C., ritual sacrifice to Vedic deities overseen by priests gave way to polytheistic worship intended to unite the worshipper with the god worshipped.

The classical period of Hinduism dates from the sixth century B.C. to the 10th century A.D., when the major theistic sects emerged and many of the classic works of Hinduism were composed, including the epic *Mahabharata* and *Ramayana* and a variety of works that discuss the duties of caste, advice to

rulers, the attainment of pleasure and the attainment of liberation, or moksha. Hindu princes successfully resisted Muslim encroachment from the West until the 10th century. The Muslim ascendancy was coupled with the rise of *bhakti*, a devotional Hinduism that stresses love for the deity, and the adoption of vernacular languages for worship rather than Sanskrit.

Since the 18th century there have been several movements to strip Hinduism of its polytheistic practices, and in this century, great emphasis has been laid on Hindu prescriptions for non-violence and social equality, especially as practiced by the founder of modern India, Mahatma Gandhi.

Geography and numbers Hinduism has more than 850 million adherents worldwide. With deep roots in India, and lacking a missionary tradition, it is found almost nowhere outside of India and neighboring countries except in expatriate Indian communities.

▶ BUDDHISM

Origins Buddhism was established by the followers of Siddhartha Gautama (ca. 563–483 B.C.), who was born into a kshatriya caste Hindu family in present-day Nepal. At the age of 29, he left his wife and young son in search of enlightenment. This he attained, according to tradition, while sitting under a bodhi tree near Patna. After 49 days of rapture, and withstanding the temptations of the devil Mara, Buddha—the enlightened one—inspired an order of monks and went forth to preach his philosophy of enlightenment for 45 years before passing into nirvana, in which ideas and consciousness cease to be.

Scripture Of primary importance to all Buddhists is the *Tipitaka* (Three baskets), a record of the Buddha's teachings set down by Buddha's early followers after his death. These tell the story of his life (Buddha), his laws (Dharma) for personal conduct, and the guidelines for the monastic order (Sangha). There is a large body of other writings peculiar to individual sects and schools. The Buddhist canon continued to evolve over many centuries.

Beliefs Buddhists share with Hinduism a belief in the cycle of reincarnation and that this cycle could be broken. Buddha's teachings are predicated on the Four Noble Truths. Life is impermanent and fundamentally produces suffering, or *dukkha*, perpetuated due to the endless cycle of life, death, and rebirth. This suffering results from the pursuit of mortal desires. Desire can be overcome by attaining *nirvana. Nirvana* can be reached by adhering to the Eightfold Path. This path, or Middle Way, consists of right belief, thought, speech, action, livelihood, effort, mindfulness and concentration. These are the backbone of Buddhist ethics.

Practice A hallmark of Buddhist practice is the monastic order, to which monks withdraw from the everyday world and live austere lives of meditation either for a few years or for a lifetime. Mendicants also live on alms contributed by lay Buddhists. In certain sects, adolescents spend time in a monastery as part of a rite of passage into adulthood.

Buddhist temples are primarily for individual meditation, and collective rituals play a smaller part in the life of a Buddhist than in the lives of Jews, Christians and Muslims, or even of Hindus.

Schools and sects There are three main sects in Buddhism. Theravada (or Hinayana) Buddhism, which predominates today in Sri Lanka, Myanmar and Thailand, adheres most closely to the tenets of the early Buddhist sects. In this tradition, attainment of nirvana for oneself is the goal. Mahayana Buddhism, which became the larger sect, spread along the Silk Road from India to China and East Asia. This includes the worship of Buddha and Buddhist saints (*bodhisattvas*). Stressing compassion for others, *boddhisatvas*—literally "wisdom beings"—withhold themselves from attaining nirvana in order to help others attain enlightenment. In Zen Buddhism, a sect of Mahayana, adherents strive for enlightenment through mental conditioning and meditation. The third sect of Tantric Buddhism (Vajrayana), most common in Tibet and Mongolia, attempts to identify the initiate with a visualized deity. The Tantric canon includes esoteric texts, and meditation engages both the mind and the senses with the use of *mantras* (chants), *mudras* (hand gestures) and *mandalas* (visible icons of the universe). The spiritual and temporal leader of Tibetan Buddhists is the Dalai Lama.

History Following Buddha's death, his *sutras* (sermons) and *vinaya* (regulations) were written down by his disciples. Originally, Buddhist mendicants taught for nine months and held retreats during the monsoon. These retreats led to the establishment of monasteries and the rise of differing interpretations of Buddha's teaching. The Mahayana school more easily absorbs (and is absorbed by) different cultures. It received its greatest impetus in India from the Buddhist emperor Ashoka (272–232 B.C.), who sent missionaries to Ceylon, Southeast Asia and China, from where it was carried to Korea and Japan in the sixth century A.D.

The seventh century saw the rise of Zen Buddhism in China and Japan, and of Tantric Buddhism in Tibet. Chinese Buddhism reached its height in the ninth century during the T'ang Dynasty, when it was partially suppressed. Buddhism flourished in Japan until the 19th century, when Shintoism gained imperial favor.

Buddhism lost its influence in India beginning in the eighth century, partly through absorption of its ideas into Hinduism, and partly because of the rise of Islam. By the 13th century, Buddhism was all but extinct there.

Geography and numbers There are an estimated 375 million people in nearly 100 countries who adhere to Buddhist beliefs and practices. Mahayana Buddhists account for about 56 percent (200 million) of all Buddhists, mostly in Japan, Korea and China; Theravada Buddhists account for 38 percent (140 million), in Southeast Asia and Sri Lanka. Lamaist Buddhists account for about six percent (20 million) in Tibet and Mongolia. Buddhist practice in Tibet is under threat from the Chinese government.

▶ OTHER ORGANIZED RELIGIONS

Baha'i Founded by Baha'Ullah (glory of God) in Iran in 1844, Baha'i teaches that the revealed religions of the world are in agreement and that the respective prophet-founders of each revealed the will of God for a particular time and place in history. There are approximately 7 million members of the Baha'i faith; the center of the Baha'i faith is in Haifa, Israel. A major temple in Wilmette, Illinois, attracts many visitors.

Chinese folk religions Chinese folk religions consist of a blend of ancient ancestor worship with elements of Buddhism, Confucianism, and Taoism. Taoism is a philosophy or religion based on the teachings of Lao-tzu, another great teacher of Confucian times. The vast majority of the world's 390 million adherents of Chinese folk religions live in China; the remainder live in scattered Chinese settlements around the world.

Confucianism As much a code of ethical conduct as a religion, Confucianism takes its name from the sixth-century B.C. scholar and civil servant Kung Fu-Tzu (Confucius), whose *Analects* prescribe the proper conduct for life. His impact on China has been enormous, and at times his cult has attained the status of a quasi-official religion. There are about 6 million Confucianists in the world; most of them live in South Korea.

Jainism Jainism is a polytheistic religion established in India by Vardhamana in the sixth century B.C. Its primary features are a belief in the perfection of the soul and in non-injury to living creatures. Almost all of the world's 4.2 million Jainists live in India.

New Religion. This term applies to a variety of more or less organized religious systems that have grown up, primarily in East Asia, since the turn of the century. These religions are characterized by a synthesis of indigenous folk religion with various major Asian traditions (Hinduism, Buddhism, Confucianism and/or Taoism) overlaid with modern Western philosophy. There are more than 105 million people professing adherence to these religions, the majority of them in the Philippines, Indonesia, and Japan.

Parsiism This religion has its roots in Zoroastrianism, an ancient Iranian religion whose central focus is the struggle between good and evil. Its monotheistic tendencies are thought to have influenced the development of Judaism and Christianity. Parsis emigrated to India between the 10th and 15th centuries, and prospered as merchants, especially in Bombay.

Shintoism Evolved from ancient Japanese religious traditions, Shintoism became a state religion under the Meijis in the 19th century. Although some sacred Shinto (literally way of the gods) texts date from the 8th century, none is considered authoritative. There are three strains of Shinto practice: State Shinto, Shrine Shinto, and Folk Shinto.

Sikhism The Sikh religion was founded by Guru Nanak in the early 16th century. A hybrid of Hindu and Islamic beliefs, it advocates a search for eternal truth and, while believing in reincarnation, rejects the notion of divine incarnation. It was led by a succession of ten gurus, the last of whom declared himself the last human guru. Sikhs now follow the sacred text known as Guru Granth Singh, or Collection of Sacred Wisdom. There are over 20 million Sikhs in the world; almost all of them live in the Punjab region of India.

▶ NONRELIGIOUS AND ATHEISTS

An estimated 816 million people (12 percent of the world's population) profess no religion, are agnostic, or are indifferent to religion. Another 156 million people (2.3 percent) are declared atheists who do not believe in God. More than three-quarters of these nonreligious and atheists live in China, where religious observance is sharply curtailed by the government. Vietnam had the highest percentage of people who cited "none" as their religion at 80.8 percent. In 2008, Pew Research released a study that stated that over 40 percent of Americans no longer feel tied to the religion of their upbringing, reflecting an increasing fluidity to religious adherence worldwide.

▶ CHRONOLOGY OF WORLD RELIGION

B.C.
3000 Earliest elements of Hinduism develop in India.
c. 2500 Egyptian pyramids at Giza completed.
c. 1290 Moses leads Israelites out of Egypt.
1010–922 Reigns of Hebrew kings David and Solomon. A great temple built at Jerusalem.
628 Traditional birth date of Zoroaster, religious teacher in Persia. Followers today are Parsees in India.
587 Babylonians destroy Hebrew temple at Jerusalem and take many Hebrews as slaves. Fifty years later, Hebrews are freed and begin to rebuild temple.
560 Birth of Siddartha Gautama in northern India; later known as Buddha. Dies c. 480.
551 Birth of Chinese teacher Confucius. Dies c. 479.
200 Mahayana Buddhism begins to spread in China and Japan.

4 Birth of Jesus Christ. The Western calendar dates from the supposed year of his birth.

A.D.

30 Death and resurrection of Jesus Christ.

66–70 Jewish revolt against Romans ends in destruction of second temple and scattering of Jews.

175 Apostles' Creed, a brief statement of Christian beliefs, formulated.

303–12 In final organized program of persecution, Romans kill estimated 500,000 Christians.

313 The emperor Constantine decrees toleration for Christianity in Roman Empire. In 325, he calls synod of Nicaea, which formulates Nicene Creed.

570 Muhammad, founder of Islam, born in Mecca (now in Saudi Arabia). Dies in 632 in nearby city of Medina.

600+ Tantrism, a Hindu school, grows up, emphasizing special rituals as means of enlightenment; uses mystical diagrams (mandalas) and chants (mantras).

650+ Islam enters India, gains many converts.

700+ Development in China of Zen, a school of Buddhism, which later attracted particular attention in the modern Western world.

711–715 Muslim Arabs settle in Spain.

800 Roman Empire revived in the West with the coronation of Charlemagne as emperor on Christmas Day, in St. Peter's in Rome.

988 Christianity reaches Russia through missionaries from eastern churches.

1054 Eastern (or Orthodox) and Western (or Roman) churches go separate ways after disputes about doctrine and authority.

1096 Christians in Europe go on first Crusade to take Holy Land from Muslims. Seven other major Crusades pursued between 1100 and 1300. Christian warriors temporarily occupy Jerusalem and other cities, but soon lose them again to Muslims.

1216 Pope Innocent III approves formation of Franciscans and Dominicans.

1227 Thomas Aquinas, great Christian theologian, born in Italy.

1300+ Bhakti, a Hindu sect, develops emphasizing primacy of love for a deity and using love between humans as illustration; rejects caste, ritual, and creeds, and emphasizes need for sincerity.

1309 The papacy moves from Rome to Avignon, France, where it remains until 1377 (The Babylonian Captivity of the Church).

1377 English theologian and religious reformer John Wycliffe accused of heresy by Pope Gregory XI for attacks on worldliness of the church.

1378–1417 The Great Western Schism, during which first two, then three, claimants sought recognition as pope.

1415 Excommunication and execution of Czech religious leader Jan Hus, who protested sale of indulgences and other papal excesses, sets off Hussite Wars, which end with Compactata of Prague.

1453 Ottoman Turks (Muslims) conquer capital of Eastern Roman Empire, Constantinople. Turks push westward into Europe.

1454 Johannes Gutenberg prints first Bible with moveable type.

1469 Birth of Nanak, founder of Sikhism, in India.

1492 Muslims overthrown in Spain; Spanish Inquisition begins.

1517 Martin Luther, a German priest, posts 95 theses on cathedral door, questioning church teachings. Luther refuses to recant; is excommunicated from Catholic church and forms new Protestant churches.

1534 King Henry VIII of England denies power of pope over church in England and establishes Church of England responsible to monarch.

1536 John Calvin, a young French scholar, publishes *Institutes of the Christian Religion*, and becomes second major leader of Protestant Christianity.

1540 Ignatius Loyola, a Spaniard, establishes the Jesuits (Society of Jesus) with papal approval.

1545–63 Council of Trent makes major reforms in Catholic church and defines disagreements with Protestants; begins Catholic Reformation.

1598 In the Edict of Nantes, Henry IV proclaims peaceful coexistence of Catholics and Calvinists in France. Revoked in 1685 by Louis XIV.

1618–48 Thirty Years War, caused in part by Protestant-Catholic hatreds, decimates central Europe. Calvinist leaders in England overthrow monarchy and execute king in civil war (1642-49).

1620 Pilgrims, a small group of English Calvinists, establish colony at Plymouth in North America to escape persecution in England.

1683 Muslim Turks defeated near Vienna, Austria, in their last attempt to establish foothold in western Europe.

1734 The Great Awakening, a religious revival, sweeps New England, begun by prominent Massachusetts preacher Jonathan Edwards. English evangelist George Whitefield tours American colonies beginning in 1738, preaching to outdoor gatherings.

1738 Christian conversion experienced by brothers John and Charles Wesley in England. They begin evangelical activities, leading to development of independent Methodist church.

1789 U.S. Constitution guarantees separation of church and state.

1792 Second Awakening sweeps new United States, lasting more than 20 years. Revivals in Kentucky in 1800 result in formation of new denominations, ancestors of Disciples of Christ, Churches of Christ, and Christian churches.

1830 American Joseph Smith has religious visions that lead him to organize the Church of Jesus Christ of the Latter-Day Saints (Mormons).

1844 Baha'i established in Iran.

1869–79 Vatican Council I, convened by Pope Pius IX, declares that teachings of pope in matters of faith and morals are infallible.

1875 Mary Baker Eddy publishes *Science and Health with Key to the Scriptures* in Boston; it becomes basis of Church of Christ, Scientist.

1900 First documented modern Pentecostal experience—worshipers speak in unknown tongues during prayer meeting in Kansas. Within 20 years, Pentecostal churches form major new Christian denomination.

1935–45 Nazi government in Germany carries out destruction of estimated six million European Jews. This event known as the Holocaust.

1945–46 Compulsory adherence to Shintoism ended in Japan; Emperor Hirohito disavows his divinity to Japanese people.

1947 U.N. approves creation of the new state of Israel in Middle East for settlement by Jews.

1948 World Council of Churches established at huge assembly in Amsterdam. This ecumenical organization supported by many Protestant, Anglican, and Orthodox denominations. Headquarters are in Geneva, Switzerland.

1952 L. Ron Rubbard categorizes the belief system of Scientology as a religion.

1962-65 Vatican Council II, convened by Pope John XXIII, announces many liberalizing changes in Roman Catholic liturgy and practice; supports cautious involvement in ecumenical discussions with other Christians.

1978 Karol Josef Wojtyla, archbishop of Krakow, Poland, elected to papacy as John Paul II, the first non-Italian pope since Hadrian VI in 1523.

1988 For the first time, a woman is elected to a bishopric in U.S. Episcopal church.

1991 Religious freedom granted in U.S.S.R.

2006 The Gospel of Judas, the disciple who betrayed Christ, is found, shedding possible new light on the life of Judas Iscariot and his relationship with Jesus.

2008 An estimated 18 people were killed in Tibet during riots directed at Han Chinese migrants.

2010 The first female Orthodox Jewish Rabba was confirmed in New York.

The Books of the Bible

The first five books of the Bible are known as the Torah (to teach in Hebrew) in the Jewish faith. Roman Catholic canon recognizes additional deuterocanonical books, as well as additional parts of other books. Together, they are known as the Apocrypha. They are listed in *italics* following the Old Testament.

Old Testament	Job	Zephaniah	*Second Maccabees*	Philippians
Genesis	Psalms	Haggai	*First Esdras*	Colossians
Exodus	Proverbs	Zechariah	*The Prayer of Manasseh*	First Thessalonians
Leviticus	Ecclesiastes	Malachi	*Psalm 151*	Second
Numbers	Song of Solomon	**The Apocrypha**	*Third Maccabees*	Thessalonians
Deuteronomy	Isaiah	*Tobit*	*Second Esdras*	First Timothy
Joshua	Jeremiah	*Judith*	*Fourth Maccabees*	Second Timothy
Judges	Lamentations	*Additions to Esther*	**New Testament**	Titus
Ruth	Ezekiel	*Wisdom of Solomon*	Matthew	Philemon
First Samuel	Daniel	*Ecclesisasticus (Sirach)*	Mark	Hebrews
Second Samuel	Hosea	*Baruch*	Luke	James
First Kings	Joel	*The Letter of Jeremiah*	John	First Peter
Second Kings	Amos	*The Prayer of Azariah*	Acts	Second Peter
First Chronicles	Obadiah	*and the Song of the*	Romans	First John
Second Chronicles	Jonah	*Three Young Men*	First Corinthians	Second John
Ezra	Micah	*Susanna*	Second Corinthians	Third John
Nehemiah	Nahum	*Bel and the Dragon*	Galatians	Jude
Esther	Habakuk	*First Maccabees*	Ephesians	Revelation

The Koran (*al Kitab*)

God revealed the sacred book of Islam to the prophet Muhammed throughout his life at Mecca and Medina. According to traditional accounts, the stories were written down beginning around the time of the Prophet's death in 632. Several years after the Koran was recorded, the third Caliph, 'Uthman, ordered copies of this Koran to be made and distributed throughout the Islamic world. The 114 written chapters (*suras*) were subsequently collected to form the Koran. Each sura (except Sura 9) begins with the phrase, "In the name of God, the Lord of Mercy, the Giver of Mercy."

Generally speaking, the focus of the Koran is on the life of the Islamic community, with its commitment to justice, equality of believers before God, humility, and piety. Many suras refer to specific instances in the life of Muhammad as he struggled to make his prophesy understood and accepted by his community. Others emphasize the torments of hell that await those who do evil or deny God. In the suras, God provides Muhammad with arguments to use to reassure believers and to persuade disbelievers to change their minds, and Muhammad himself is often counseled to be patient in delivering his message, and not to lose heart. The first sura, or "The Opening," is a brief summary of the entire content of the Koran, memorized in Arabic by Muslims and recited as part of the obligatory daily prayers.

The Koran remains in large part a recited text, and skillful recitation is highly esteemed. All Muslims memorize at least some parts of the Koran for use in daily prayers, and memorization of the entire text is a prerequisite for further training as an Islamic scholar or jurist. The Koran has been translated into many languages, but because the original Arabic version is considered to be the verbatim word of God, no translation can be considered to have religious authority.

Sacred Hindu Texts

There are several texts that comprise the Hindu canon, which differs from the one-text oriented religions of Christianity, Judaism, and Islam. The most important Hindu texts are the Four Vedas, the Sutras, and the Epics. The Vedas are mostly chants or hymns that prescribe specific behavior or address various deities. The most important Veda is the *Rigveda Samhita*, a collection of 1,028 hymns meant to be sung in worship to deities. Each Veda is supplemented by *Brahmanas* (prose discussions describing rules and rituals); *Aranyakas*, or "forest texts" meant to guide adherents who left society in search of secluded enlightenment in nature; and *Upanishads*, philosophic speculation sometimes considered to be a part of the *Aranyakas*. In addition to the Vedas, there are three groups of Sutras—short texts ascribed to particular sages—which date back to the seventh century B.C. The three groups are the *Shrautasutra*, which expounds upon the Vedas, the *Grihyasutra*, which prescribes domestic ceremonies, and the *Dharmasutra*, which develops ideas of correct conduct (dharma). The Epics, the *Mahabharata* and *Ramayana* are perhaps the most well-known Hindu texts, and arguably the most important source of information on the development of Hinduism and an Indian literary tradition. Both, however, are considered less authoritative traditional texts than either the Vedas or the Sutras. Chapters 23 to 40 of the *Mahabharata*—known as the *Bhagavadgita*—is highly influential.

Major Languages of the World

According to UNESCO there were approximately 6,000 living languages in the world in 2010, most of which are spoken only by a small number of people. The eight most common languages—Mandarin Chinese, English, Hindi (with Urdu), Spanish, Russian, Arabic, Bengali, and Portuguese—are spoken by half the world's population. It is estimated that more than 3,000 languages are spoken by less than 10,000 people. These 3,000 are considered "endangered languages," categorized as such when 30 percent of children in the community are no longer taught it. Africa currently has the highest number of languages in danger of extinction; of the continent's 1,400 languages approximately 250 are threatened with imminent disappearance. Languages have had heydays and have disappeared throughout the course of human history due primarily to military or political events and increasing globalization. Some—such as Latin or Sanskrit—are kept alive academically even if no longer spoken.

Chinese This is the mother tongue of more than 1 billion people. Although spoken dialects of Chinese are not mutually intelligible, they share the same writing system—Chinese characters, or *hanzi*. It is possible that two people can speak different dialects and still be able to read each other's writing because *hanzi* characters represent words independently of their pronunciation (just as Arabic numerals can represent the words for numbers in any language), and also because written Chinese has diverged less from a common standard than have the various spoken dialects.

Based on the dialect spoken in northern China around Beijing, Mandarin is an official language in China, Taiwan, and Singapore. The other principal dialects are Cantonese (or *Yue*), spoken in southern China and Hong Kong; *Wu*, spoken in Shanghai and nearby provinces in eastern China; *Min*, found in southeastern China, Taiwan and Malaysia; and *Xiang, Kan,* and *Hakka*, all spoken in southeastern China and Taiwan. Chinese is also an official language of the U.N.

English Although it ranks third in the world's most spoken languages—English is the mother tongue for some 325 million people—it is a secondary language for about 1.4 billion people. From Great Britain, the language spread throughout the British Empire to the Americas, Africa, India, and Oceania. Today, 55 countries as well as the E.U., NAFTA, NATO, the O.A.S., and the U.N. designate English as an official language, though the U.S. is not among them. English is also the most common language used on the Internet; nearly 28 percent of all Internet users in the world.

Hindi Spoken by an estimated 474 million people in India alone, Hindi is the most spoken of that country's 16 official languages, though English is most important politcally. There are significant numbers (relative to the local population) of Hindi speakers in Trinidad, Guyana, South Africa, Mauritius, and other countries with large Indian expatriate communities.

Spanish Carried by Spanish conquistadors from Europe to the Americas and Asia, Spanish is now an official language of 23 nations. In 2009, Spanish was ranked by SIL International as the second most spoken language in the world with 700 million native speakers. By far the greatest number of Spanish speakers live in Mexico (100 million), followed by Colombia (45 million), the United States

(43 million), Spain (42 million), Argentina (39 million), and Venezuela (28 million). Over 15 percent of Americans speak Spanish as a first language.

Arabic Twenty-six countries around the world have adopted Arabic as an official language, more than any other language but English and French. Arabic is also the language of the Koran; and for this reason, it is the second language of many Indians, Indonesians, Iranians and inhabitants of other largely Muslim countries. Most of the world's Muslim population, however, does not speak Arabic aside from recitation of religious texts. There are approximately 280 million native speakers and 250 million non-native speakers across the world, and Arabic is also an official language of the U.N.

Portuguese The transmission of Portuguese paralleled that of Spanish, but today it is used as an official language in only seven countries outside of Portugal: six in Africa, one in Latin America, and in Macau, a special administrative region of China. Of the 210 million native Portuguese speakers worldwide, the vast majority of them live in Brazil. There are roughly 240 million non-native Portuguese speakers.

Russian There are an estimated 164 million people who claim Russian as their mother tongue and four countries where it is an official language: Russia, Belarus, Kazakhstan, and Kyrgyzstan. There are still significant numbers of people claiming Russian as a first language in the former republics of the Soviet Union, and approximately 114 million speak it as a second language. Russian is an official language of the U.N. and the I.A.E.A.

Japanese The official language of only two countries (Japan and Palau), Japanese is spoken by more than 130 million people. The most significant Japanese-speaking minorities outside of Japan are found in Brazil and the United States. Modern Japanese employs four writing systems: *kanji* (adapted from the Chinese *hanzi*), *hiragana, katakana* and *romaji*.

Bengali An official language of Bangladesh and India, more than 180 people worldwide count Bengali as their mother tongue. An estimated 230 million people speak Bengali, making it the sixth most spoken language in the world.

German An official language of six European countries (Germany, Austria, Switzerland, Luxembourg, Liechtenstein, and Belgium) and the E.U., German is spoken natively by more than 120 million and non-natively by 80 million. There are also significant German-speaking minorities in Eastern Europe (Poland and Russia), Brazil and the U.S.

French Although fewer than 150 million people worldwide claim French as a first language, its significance stems from the fact that it is an official language of 29 countries—more than any other language except English—and of the U.N. Most countries in West Africa are among the nations that count French as an official language due to colonization, though in several countries local dialects are spoken more frequently.

Malay Variants and dialects of Malay are used as an official language in Indonesia (where it is known as *Bahasa Indonesia*), Malaysia (*Bahasa Nalaysia*), and Singapore and Brunei (*Bahasa Melayu*). Although these four countries have a combined population of more than 270 million, a mere 40 million people claim Malay as their first language.

World Energy

The world's primary energy sources in 2009 were crude oil, natural gas liquids, natural gas, coal, and electricity from hydroelectric and nuclear power. In order to compare the energy produced by different sources, energy is measured in British thermal units (Btu). Energy production and consumption worldwide increased drastically during the 1980s, but their growth slowed somewhat in the 1990s. Petroleum production and consumption continues to increase, but whereas petroleum once constituted almost half the world's energy, it now accounts for

less than 40 percent. Natural gas and nuclear power have made up most of the difference.

Petroleum World production of petroleum (which includes crude oil and natural gas plant liquids) was 84.4 million barrels per day in 2008. The United States, Russia and Saudi Arabia are the world's largest producers of petroleum; the three countries together account for nearly one-third of the world's petroleum production.

Consumption of petroleum has kept pace with the increase in production. But the United States is

World Primary Energy Production, by Source, 1980–2007 (quadrillion Btu)

Source	1980	1985	1990	1995	2000	2005	2007[1]
Coal	71.17	82.25	90.88	87.99	89.10	123.03	132.73
Dry Natural Gas	54.76	64.12	76.14	80.42	90.96	103.24	108.98
Crude Oil	128.04	115.37	129.35	133.43	146.82	157.63	156.00
NGPL[2]	5.10	5.83	6.87	8.40	9.63	11.47	11.89
Nuclear Electric	7.58	15.30	20.36	23.26	25.65	27.54	27.10
Hydroelectric	17.90	20.39	22.31	25.29	26.73	28.91	29.64
Geothermal and Other	3.03	3.84	4.12	4.71	5.45	7.35	8.80
Total	**287.58**	**307.11**	**350.02**	**363.51**	**394.35**	**459.17**	**475.15**

Note: Totals may not add up due to rounding. 1. Preliminary. 2. Natural gas plant liquids. **Source:** Energy Information Administration, *International Energy Annual, 2007* (2010).

World Energy Production, by Region, 1980–2008

Region	1980	1985	1990	1995	2000	2005	2008[1]
Petroleum[2] (thousand barrels/day)	**63,987**	**59,172**	**66,425**	**70,271**	**77,762**	**84,582**	**N.A.**
North America	14,754	16,068	14,709	14,928	15,267	15,197	N.A.
Central & South America	3,848	3,916	4,703	6,055	7,326	7,244	N.A.
Western Europe	3,047	4,637	4,818	6,872	7,145	6,093	N.A.
Eurasia	11,991	11,935	11,300	7,135	8,191	11,768	N.A.
Middle East	19,024	11,001	17,449	20,420	23,479	25,559	N.A.
Africa	6,229	5,614	6,708	7,357	8,039	10,265	N.A.
Asia & Oceania	5,092	5,999	6,736	7,501	8,313	8,453	N.A.
Dry Natural Gas (trillion cubic feet)	**53.35**	**62.39**	**73.71**	**78.11**	**88.42**	**101.52**	**109.79**
North America	23.06	20.50	22.56	25.16	26.97	26.13	28.26
Central & South America	1.23	1.76	2.01	2.58	3.43	4.86	5.26
Western Europe	9.14	9.19	8.60	9.86	10.98	11.42	11.16
Eurasia	15.37	22.71	28.78	24.88	25.43	28.79	29.94
Middle East	1.42	2.38	3.72	4.99	7.57	11.21	13.51
Africa	0.69	1.86	2.46	3.01	4.44	6.11	7.16
Asia & Oceania	2.49	4.00	5.58	7.64	9.60	13.00	14.51
Coal (million short tons)	**4,188**	**4,896**	**5,354**	**5,105**	**4,950**	**6,492**	**7,271**
North America	874	958	1,113	1,126	1,162	1,218	1,259
Central & South America	12	21	33	40	59	81	104
Western Europe	1,335	1,463	1,332	960	832	806	774
Eurasia	790	801	882	482	443	502	563
Middle East	1	1	1	1	1	2	2
Africa	138	197	201	235	256	276	266
Asia & Oceania	1,039	1,455	1,792	2,262	2,196	3,608	4,303
Electric power[3] (billion kWh)	**8,026.9**	**9,477.1**	**11,322.7**	**12,624.6**	**14,619.2**	**17,350.6**	**N.A.**
North America	2,721.6	3,014.8	3,627.5	4,046.1	4,590.4	4,895.0	N.A.
Central & South America	308.2	405.4	497.2	626.6	781.9	908.7	N.A.
Western Europe	2,154.7	2,448.7	2,696.5	2,873.5	3,211.1	3,494.7	N.A.
Eurasia	1,294.0	1,545.0	1,636.1	1,226.0	1,205.3	1,327.3	N.A.
Middle East	91.4	165.0	225.1	318.8	434.7	602.7	N.A.
Africa	189.0	251.8	307.3	354.2	417.1	533.2	N.A.
Asia & Oceania	1,268.1	1,646.5	2,333.1	3,179.4	3,978.7	5,589.1	N.A.

Notes: 1. Preliminary 2. Includes crude oil and natural gas plant liquids 3. Includes conventional thermal electric, hydroelectric, nuclear, geothermal, solar, and waste electric power **Source:** Energy Information Administration, *International Energy Annual, 2008* (2009).

by far the biggest consumer. In 2007, the U.S. consumed 20.7 million barrels of petroleum per day, more than one-fourth the world's total. That's more than double the amount the U.S. produces each day, forcing America to import more than 13 million barrels of petroleum each day. No other country consumes even half as much oil as the United States. China was second in world consumption with 7.6 million barrels, followed by Japan (5.0 million barrels), Russia (2.9 million), and Germany (2.5 million). Saudi Arabia, the world's largest petroleum producer, consumed 2.3 million barrels per day.

Dry natural gas World production of dry natural gas continued to set all-time highs; in 2008, production was nearly 110 trillion cubic feet. Russia is the world's largest producer of natural gas (23.4 trillion cubic feet, or 23 percent of the world total in 2009), followed by the United States (21.0 trillion cubic feet). The United States consumed 23.1 trillion cubic feet of natural gas in 2007, while Russia consumed 16.7 trillion cubic feet.

Coal World coal production declined during the late 1990s but has increased steadily since 2000 and exceeded 7.2 billion short tons in 2008. China con-

World Net Energy Consumption by Type and Region, 1980–2006 (Quadrillion Btu)

Energy type and region	1980	1985	1990	1995	2000	2005	2006
Crude oil world total	**131.0194**	**123.0553**	**136.4312**	**142.6351**	**155.4490**	**169.8786**	**171.7232**
North America	40.6715	36.9207	40.5177	41.6236	46.3336	49.0707	48.5357
Central & South America	7.5597	6.6526	7.7608	9.1640	10.6356	11.2516	11.6836
Europe	33.9499	28.7387	30.4680	31.8347	32.9220	33.9103	33.9964
Eurasia	18.7335	18.6741	17.5356	9.6973	7.7775	8.5228	8.6089
Middle East	4.3365	5.9404	7.2119	8.5010	9.7693	11.9102	12.4340
Africa	3.0853	3.8004	4.3223	4.6748	5.1394	6.0903	6.1197
Asia & Oceania	22.6831	22.3285	28.6147	37.1396	42.8716	49.1227	50.344
Natural gas world total	**53.806**	**63.456**	**75.304**	**81.175**	**91.007**	**107.048**	**107.998**
North America	22.994	20.948	23.033	26.764	28.346	27.972	27.959
Central & South America	1.390	1.940	2.202	2.802	3.568	4.714	4.814
Europe	10.643	11.669	13.028	15.346	17.820	20.919	20.835
Eurasia	13.861	20.952	25.610	20.916	20.900	24.684	24.740
Middle East	1.373	2.385	3.767	4.960	7.144	10.240	10.765
Africa	0.833	1.208	1.515	1.873	2.202	3.173	3.171
Asia & Oceania	2.712	4.354	6.150	8.514	11.026	15.346	15.715
Coal world total	**70.002**	**82.431**	**89.230**	**88.492**	**93.623**	**121.736**	**127.548**
North America	16.452	18.818	20.585	21.642	24.439	24.739	24.343
Central & South America	0.420	0.592	0.574	0.653	0.764	0.864	0.818
Europe	19.700	21.122	19.534	14.751	14.367	14.245	14.421
Eurasia	11.459	12.070	13.236	7.649	7.374	7.577	7.498
Middle East	0.028	0.119	0.139	0.233	0.330	0.387	0.373
Africa	2.252	2.950	2.960	3.369	3.767	4.217	4.168
Asia & Oceania	19.691	26.760	32.201	40.194	42.581	69.707	75.927
Hydroelectric world total	**17.897**	**20.423**	**22.353**	**25.340**	**26.778**	**28.975**	**29.728**
North America	5.681	6.384	6.345	6.916	6.766	6.576	6.657
Central & South America	2.093	3.003	3.798	4.749	5.576	6.119	6.344
Europe	4.758	4.980	4.935	5.560	5.973	5.413	5.277
Eurasia	1.912	2.142	2.399	2.448	2.323	2.447	2.416
Middle East	0.100	0.112	0.100	0.113	0.081	0.209	0.230
Africa	0.624	0.487	0.571	0.610	0.760	0.896	0.902
Asia & Oceania	2.729	3.314	4.204	4.943	5.300	7.315	7.901
Nuclear electric world total	**7.576**	**15.299**	**20.357**	**23.259**	**25.652**	**27.541**	**27.758**
North America	3.155	4.735	6.928	8.211	8.721	9.249	9.368
Central & South America	0.026	0.094	0.103	0.107	0.121	0.177	0.226
Europe	2.570	6.365	8.059	8.928	9.597	9.984	9.955
Eurasia	0.833	1.949	2.308	1.885	2.234	2.587	2.635
Middle East	0	0	0	0	0	0	0
Africa	0	0.055	0.087	0.113	0.131	0.123	0.101
Asia & Oceania	0.992	2.101	2.873	4.014	4.849	5.422	5.472
Renewables[1] world total	**0.471**	**0.817**	**1.691**	**2.156**	**2.992**	**4.310**	**4.721**
North America	0.146	0.264	1.013	1.115	1.230	1.434	1.523
Central & South America	0.052	0.076	0.090	0.116	0.180	0.267	0.278
Europe	0.173	0.179	0.242	0.440	0.833	1.679	1.908
Eurasia	0	0	0.001	0.016	0.026	0.035	0.038
Middle East	0	0	0.00001	0.00001	0.00003	0.0001	0.001
Africa	0.002	0.009	0.009	0.010	0.017	0.032	0.032
Asia & Oceania	0.098	0.288	0.336	0.459	0.706	0.862	0.939

Note: 1. Includes geothermal, solar, wind, wood, and waste. **Source:** Energy Information Administration, *International Energy Annual, 2006* (2009).

tinues to lead the world in production, with more than 2.8 billion short tons per year. The United States, the world leader until 1987, produced just over 1.1 billion short tons in 2009. Together, the U.S. and China account for half the world's production. They also accounted for the bulk of coal consumption in 2009. China consumed 1.42 billion short tons (27 percent of world consumption) and the U.S. consumed 1.07 million short tons (20 percent).

Hydroelectric power Generation of hydroelectric power worldwide remained mostly constant between 2000 and 2007, at a yearly total of 2.96 trillion kilowatthours (kWh). China (431 billion kWh), Canada (352 billion kWh), and Brazil (345 billion kWh) together produced more than a third of the worldwide total in 2006. U.S. production increased dramatically, from 209 billion kWh in 2001 to 289 billion kWh in 2006.

Nuclear electric power World generation of nuclear electric power more than quadrupled between 1980 and 2006 from 684.4 billion to 3.0 trillion kWh. In 2006, the U.S. produced 806.7 billion kWh. France (419.8 billion kWh) and Japan (241.3 billion kWh) followed the U.S. in total nuclear production in 2007, as well as in the total number of reactors.

Top 10 Producers of Primary Energy, by Source, 2009

Petroleum	Million barrels/day	Natural Gas (2008)	Trillion cubic ft	Coal	Billion short tons
Russia	9.5	Russia	23.4	China	2.85
Saudi Arabia	8.3	United States	21.0	United States	1.17
United States	5.3	Canada	6.0	India	0.57
Iran	4.0	Iran	4.1	Australia	0.44
China	3.8	Norway	3.5	Russia	0.36
Mexico	2.6	Algeria	3.1	Indonesia	0.31
Canada	2.6	Netherlands	3.0	South Africa	0.26
United Arab Emirates	2.4	Saudi Arabia	2.8	Germany	0.21
Iraq	2.4	China	2.7	Poland	0.16
Kuwait	2.4	United Kingdom	2.5	Kazakhstan	0.12

Source: U.S. Dept of Energy, *International Energy Annual, 2009* (2010).

U.S. and World Per Capita Energy Consumption, 1980–2006 (Million Btu)

	1980	1985	1990	1995	2000	2005	2006
United States	343.0	320.8	338.4	342.0	350.6	339.9	334.6
North America	285.4	266.8	277.5	279.6	285.8	279.9	276.2
Central & South America	39.5	38.1	40.7	45.2	49.7	52.2	53.3
Europe	135.5	134.8	137.2	134.5	140.4	146.2	146.2
Eurasia	175.7	200.4	211.4	146.5	141.3	160.3	160.8
Middle East	62.3	75.5	84.1	92.2	104.1	123.8	127.2
Africa	14.4	15.6	15.2	15.0	15.0	16.3	15.9
Asia & Oceania	19.9	21.9	25.2	29.9	31.6	41.0	42.8
World average	**63.8**	**63.7**	**65.9**	**64.3**	**65.6**	**71.7**	**72.4**

Source: Energy Information Administration, *International Energy Annual, 2006* (2009).

World Crude Oil Production, 1960–2009 (million barrels per day)

Country	1960	1970	1980	1990	2000	2005	2009[1]
Organization of Petroleum Exporting Countries (OPEC)[2]	**8.70**	**23.30**	**26.61**	**23.20**	**29.26**	**32.94**	**30.12**
Iran	1.07	3.83	1.66	3.09	3.70	4.14	3.98
Iraq	0.97	1.55	2.51	2.04	2.57	1.88	2.31
Kuwait	1.69	2.99	1.66	1.18	2.08	2.53	2.35
Nigeria	0.02	1.08	2.06	1.81	2.16	2.63	2.11
Saudi Arabia	1.31	3.80	9.90	6.41	8.40	9.55	8.10
United Arab Emirates	0.00	0.78	1.71	2.12	2.37	2.54	2.41
Venezuela	2.85	3.71	2.17	2.14	3.16	2.56	2.17
Non-OPEC countries[2]	**12.29**	**22.59**	**32.99**	**37.37**	**39.10**	**42.36**	**41.81**
Canada	0.52	1.26	1.44	1.55	1.98	2.37	2.64
China	0.10	0.60	2.11	2.77	3.25	3.61	3.74
Mexico	0.27	0.49	1.94	2.55	3.01	3.33	2.67
Norway	0.00	0.00	0.53	1.70	3.20	2.70	2.23
Russia[3]	2.91	6.99	11.71	10.98	6.48	9.04	9.34
United Kingdom	[4]	[4]	1.62	1.82	2.28	1.65	1.44
United States	7.04	9.64	8.60	7.36	5.82	5.18	5.24
Total world	**20.99**	**45.89**	**59.60**	**60.57**	**68.34**	**73.81**	**71.93**

Notes: 1. Three-month average for Jan.–March 2009. 2. Includes other countries not shown separately. In addition to those listed separately, current OPEC members are: Algeria, Angola, Ecuador, Indonesia, Libya, and Qatar. 3. Figures for Russia before 2000 refer to the former Soviet Union. 4. Fewer than 5,000 barrels per day. **Source:** U.S. Dept. of Energy, *Monthly Energy Review* (June 2009).

Leading Suppliers of U.S. Oil, 1990–2009

The United States imports about half of the oil it consumes, or more than 13 million barrels a day. Since 1993, the U.S. has imported more of its oil from non-OPEC countries than from OPEC countries.

Country	U.S. imports, (thousand barrels/day)			
	1990	2000	2008	2009
Canada	934	1,807	2,493	2,429
Saudi Arabia	1,339	1,572	1,529	1,094
Mexico	755	1,373	1,302	1,266
Venezuela	1,025	1,546	1,189	1,407
Nigeria	800	896	988	713
Iraq	518	620	627	479
Algeria	280	225	548	483
Total OPEC countries	4,296	5,203	5,954	4,776
Non-OPEC countries	3,721	6,257	6,961	6,915
Total imports	**8,018**	**11,459**	**12,915**	**11,691**

Source: Energy Information Administration (2009).

World Crude Oil Reserves, 1980–2009

Country	Reserves (billion barrels)			
	1980	2003	2008	2009
1. Saudi Arabia	166.5	261.8	266.8	266.7
2. Canada	N.A.	180.0	178.6	178.1
3. Iran	58.0	89.7	138.4	136.2
4. Iraq	31.0	112.5	115.0	115.0
5. Kuwait	68.5	96.5	104.0	104.0
6. Venezuela	17.9	77.8	87.0	99.4
7. United Arab Emirates	29.4	97.8	97.8	97.8
8. Russia	N.A.	60.0	60.0	60.0
9. Libya	23.5	29.5	41.5	43.7
10. Nigeria	17.4	24.0	36.2	36.2
World Total	**644.9**	**1,213.1**	**1,332.0**	**1,340.0**

Source: Energy Information Administration, *Annual Energy Review, 2009* (2010).

World Nuclear Power Generation, by Region and Country

Region and country	Generation (billion killowatthours)						Operable reactors in 2009
	1980	1990	1995	2000	2005	2006	
North America	**287.00**	**648.89**	**774.38**	**830.86**	**879.69**	**890.61**	**124**
Canada	35.88	69.24	92.95	69.16	87.44	93.07	18
Mexico	0	2.79	8.02	7.81	10.27	10.32	2
United States	251.12	576.86	673.40	753.89	781.99	787.22	104
Central & South America	**2.22**	**8.97**	**9.46**	**10.93**	**16.27**	**20.91**	**4**
Argentina	2.22	7.03	7.07	5.99	6.37	7.15	2
Brazil	0	1.94	2.39	4.94	9.90	13.75	2
Europe	**229.56**	**761.26**	**849.22**	**953.74**	**957.27**	**958.05**	**149**
Belgium	11.91	40.59	39.29	45.75	45.22	44.31	7
Bulgaria	5.81	13.53	16.40	17.27	17.34	18.13	2
Czech Republic	N.A.	N.A.	11.62	12.91	23.59	24.74	6
Finland	6.63	18.26	18.26	21.36	22.10	21.76	4
France	63.42	298.38	358.37	394.40	428.95	427.68	58
Germany[1]	N.A.	N.A.	145.44	161.13	154.85	158.91	17
Hungary	0	13.04	13.32	13.47	13.14	12.79	4
Netherlands	3.95	3.33	3.82	3.73	3.80	3.30	1
Romania	0	0	0	5.23	5.28	5.18	2
Slovakia	N.A.	N.A.	10.87	15.67	16.84	17.11	4
Slovenia	N.A.	N.A.	4.56	4.55	5.61	5.29	1
Spain	5.19	51.56	52.68	59.10	54.66	57.12	8
Sweden	25.33	64.78	66.44	54.45	68.63	63.63	10
Switzerland	12.88	22.42	23.65	25.12	22.17	26.43	5
United Kingdom	32.29	62.46	84.52	80.81	75.17	71.68	19
Eurasia	**83.19**	**251.28**	**224.26**	**268.32**	**235.83**	**240.19**	**48**
Armenia	N.A.	N.A.	0	1.84	2.50	2.42	1
Russia	N.A.	N.A.	94.34	122.46	140.22	144.30	32
Ukraine	N.A.	N.A.	66.98	71.06	83.29	84.89	15
Middle East	**0**	**0**	**0**	**0**	**0**	**0**	**0**
Africa	**0**	**8.45**	**11.30**	**13.01**	**12.24**	**10.07**	**2**
South Africa	0	8.45	11.30	13.01	12.24	10.07	2
Asia & Oceania	**92.73**	**279.93**	**393.64**	**476.80**	**524.27**	**540.03**	**109**
China	0	0	12.38	15.90	50.33	54.85	13
India	3.00	5.61	6.46	14.06	15.73	15.59	19
Japan	78.64	192.16	276.69	305.95	278.39	288.26	54
Korea, South	3.28	50.24	63.68	103.52	139.44	141.31	21
Pakistan	0.002	0.36	0.50	0.38	2.41	2.55	2
Taiwan	7.81	31.55	33.93	37.07	37.97	37.88	6
World Total[2]	**684.38**	**1,908.81**	**2,210.04**	**2,450.31**	**2,625.57**	**2,660.26**	**441**

Notes: Net generation; does not include energy consumed by the generating unit. 1. Data before 1995 includes both the former East Germany and West Germany. 2. Totals include other countries not shown separately. **Sources:** Energy Information Administration, *International Energy Annual, 2005* (2007) and International Atomic Energy Agency, Power Reactor Information System (2009).

The Global Military Situation

According to the Stockholm International Peace Research Institute, global defense spending in 2006 totaled $1.53 trillion—an increase of 49 percent over the $825.7 billion spent in 2000, and a 3 percent decline from the $1.193 trillion spent in 1998.

The ranks of the world's active-duty military personnel have increased yearly since 2001, however the are still below Cold War levels. In mid-2008, according to London-based International Institute for Strategic Studies (IISS), active-duty military personnel totaled 23.9 million worldwide, up 3.5 million from 2001 but down from 28 million in 1985. The largest active-duty military forces are from China (2.1 million), the United States (1.5 million), India (1.3 million), and North Korea (1.1 million).

The latest worldwide totals, however, conceal notable regional differences and shifts in military priorities. Strategic interventions on the part of the United States and NATO allies, concern over the spread of chemical, biological, and nuclear weapons, antiterrorist initiatives, and local conflicts have yielded a major redistribution of military resources—even before the 2003 U.S. invasion of Iraq.

▶NUCLEAR AND CHEMICAL WEAPONS
The demise of the Soviet Union and compliance with disarmament agreements have resulted in large-scale reductions in the global nuclear arsenal. Although the precise size of national nuclear stockpiles and number of deployment vehicles remain official secrets, treaty compliance protocols and estimates from a variety of sources provide some reliable figures for the major nuclear powers. The arsenals of more recent members of the nuclear-weapons "community," such as Israel, India and Pakistan, are less known. By common estimates, the total number of nuclear warheads in the world declined by 100 percent in about 15 years—from approximately 70,000 in the mid-1980s to fewer than 35,000 by 2001–02.

Moreover, less than half of the world's warhead stockpile is operational. The five major nuclear powers—the United States, Russia, China, France and Great Britain—had a combined 13,000 deployed nuclear warheads in 2001. The U.S. accounted for a reported 6,500 of these, and Russia accounted for an estimated 5,600, down 4,600 from three years earlier.

The first years of the new century brought notable progress and changes in the course of global nuclear disarmament. The destruction of stockpiles in Ukraine, Belarus and Kazakhstan, mandated by treaty, was completed by year-end 2001. The United States and Russia, meanwhile, began SALT III talks in 2000, shortly after approval by the Duma (Russian parliament) of SALT II. But the U.S. still had not approved SALT II, which would reduce the deployed missile stockpiles of both nations to 3,500 by 2007, and had rejected the Comprehensive Test Ban Treaty (CTBT), which would prohibit nuclear testing.

The Treaty of Moscow called for a 65 percent cut in each nation's store of strategic warheads over 10 years—from about 6,000 to between 1,700 and 2,200. The U.S. Senate ratified the treaty in March 2003 and the Russian Duma in May.

In August 2003, in compliance with a long-standing international treaty, the United States began destroying its own stockpile of cold-war-era chemical weapons.

Status of World Nuclear Forces, 2010

Country	Strategic	Non-Strategic	Operational	Total
Russia	2,600	2,050	4,650	12,000[1]
United States	1,968	500	2,468	9,600[2]
France	300	N.A.	300[1]	300
China	180	N.A.	180[1]	240
United Kingdom	160	N.A.	<160	225
Israel	80	N.A.	N.A.	80
Pakistan	70–90	N.A.	N.A.	70–90
India	60–80	N.A.	N.A.	60–80
North Korea	<10[3]	N.A.	N.A.	<10[3]
Total	5,400[4]	2,550[4]	7,700[4]	22,600[4]

Notes: 1. Estimated 2. Does not include approx. 4,200 retired warheads, >12,000 plutonium cores (pits) and approx. 5,000 Canned Assemblies (secondaries) in storage. 3. Suspected. 4. Estimated. Numbers may not add up due to rounding and uncertainty. **Source:** Federation of American Scientists, *Status of World Nuclear Forces* (2010).

Terrorist Attacks and Casualties by Region, 2005–09

Region	Attacks				Wounded				Fatalities			
	2006	2007	2008	2009	2006	2007	2008	2009	2006	2007	2008	2009
Africa	422	835	718	853	1,162	2,633	3,918	3,878	1,643	2,187	2,987	3,239
East Asia and Pacific	1,036	1,429	978	821	1,238	1,714	1,573	1,167	854	1,119	762	678
Europe and Eurasia	659	606	774	737	809	742	1,089	1,054	220	227	292	367
Near East[1]	7,755	7,540	4,594	3,297	25,811	30,880	15,820	14,245	13,691	14,010	5,528	4,041
South Asia	3,654	3,607	4,354	4,847	8,506	7,774	11,227	11,502	3,609	4,737	5,826	6,269
Western Hemisphere	826	482	352	444	688	567	497	818	556	405	370	377
Total	**14,352**	**14,499**	**11,770**	**10,999**	**38,214**	**44,310**	**34,124**	**32,664**	**20,573**	**22,685**	**15,765**	**14,971**

Note: 1. In the case of Iraq, only Iraqi civilians wounded or killed by Iraqi militants have been counted as victims of terrorism; otherwise members of militias and fighting forces wounded or killed have been counted as war casualties. **Source:** U.S. Department of State, National Counterterrorism Center, *NCTC Report on Terrorist Incidents* (2007–10).

►CONVENTIONAL ARMS SALES

Yearly worldwide sales of conventional (non-nuclear) arms increased nearly $10 billion between 2000 and 2008. The United States remained the largest arms dealer, with some 68.4 percent of the world total in 2008. The Unites States and Russia have dominated the global arms market in arms transfer agreements from 2005–08. During this period, the United States has totaled $56.3 billion (36.7 percent of all agreements) and Russia has totaled $35.5 billion (22.9 percent of all agreements). Developing nations remained the largest worldwide market for weapons from 2005–08, accounting for about 59.8 percent of all arms transfer agreements. Saudi Arabia is the leading purchaser of conventional arms among developing countries, totaling $36.7 billion in purchases from 2001–08 (16.8 percent of all arms transfer agreements with developing nations from 2005–08). From 2005–08, India ranked second in arms transfer purchase agreements, spending $20.2 billion on conventional arms (13.7 percent of all sales to developing nations during this period).

Arms Transfer Agreements with the World, by Supplier, 2000–08

	2000	2001	2002	2003	2004	2005	2006	2007	2008
United States	$21,273	$13,479	$14,936	$16,260	$13,759	$13,564	$16,703	$24,860	$37,796
Russia	8,157	6,495	6,671	5,287	8,189	7,704	14,647	10,400	3,500
France	4,505	5,196	805	3,150	3,166	8,865	4,609	1,800	2,600
United Kingdom	730	709	805	675	6,551	2,955	4,200	9,800	200
China	730	1,299	460	675	983	3,166	1,434	3,800	800
Germany	1,461	2,362	1,150	1,687	1,856	1,794	2,049	1,500	1,000
Italy	243	1,299	460	675	655	1,583	1,229	900	3,700
All Other European	4,991	3,188	5,060	2,362	6,223	6,755	6,043	4,400	3,200
All Others	2,922	3,070	2,530	1,800	3,385	2,322	3,995	2,500	2,400
Total	45,013	37,097	32,878	32,570	44,767	48,709	54,908	59,960	55,196

Note: In millions of constant 2008 U.S. dollars.
Source: Congressional Research Service, *Conventional Arms Transfers to Developing Nations, 2000–2007* (2008).

Numbers of Weapons Delivered by Suppliers to Developing Nations[1], 2000–08

Weapons Category	U.S.	Russia	China	West European[2]	All Other European	Others
2001–04						
Tanks and Self-Propelled Guns	506	390	240	320	530	70
Artillery	177	40	670	100	1,680	300
APCs and Armored Cars	54	490	390	150	850	740
Major Surface Combatants	10	4	0	11	3	3
Minor Surface Combatants	15	5	54	60	72	114
Guided Missile Boats	0	0	0	5	0	0
Submarines	0	0	0	2	3	0
Supersonic Combat Aircraft	59	300	50	50	30	70
Subsonic Combat Aircraft	15	0	0	20	10	0
Other Aircraft	58	10	110	130	120	160
Helicopters	92	390	0	80	60	60
Surface-to-Air Missiles[3]	2,500	1,920	600	20	670	580
Surface-to-Surface Missiles[3]	0	0	0	0	0	30
Anti-Ship Missiles	342	70	100	80	0	50
2005–08						
Tanks and Self-Propelled Guns	511	360	110	50	370	10
Artillery	240	30	330	10	140	1,090
APCs and Armored Cars	596	2,550	650	130	2,230	390
Major Surface Combatants	0	2	0	14	6	2
Minor Surface Combatants	10	5	36	35	35	72
Guided Missile Boats	0	0	0	7	9	1
Submarines	0	8	0	5	2	0
Supersonic Combat Aircraft	100	100	40	30	60	30
Subsonic Combat Aircraft	2	0	10	50	10	30
Other Aircraft	34	40	170	0	70	40
Helicopters	80	180	0	60	30	30
Surface-to-Air Missiles[3]	909	3,720	1,010	340	790	100
Surface-to-Surface Missiles[3]	0	0	0	0	0	30
Anti-Ship Missiles	209	370	70	120	80	50

Note: 1. Developing nations include all nations except the U.S., Russia, Europe, Canada, Japan, Australia, and New Zealand. 2. Includes France, United Kingdom, Germany, and Italy. 3. 3. Figures given for foreign suppliers are estimates.
Source: Congressional Research Service, *Conventional Arms Transfers to Developing Nations, 2001–2008* (2009).

The Global Economy

(See Part II, "The U.S. Economy" for definitions of G.D.P., G.N.P., etc.)

The unprecedented global economic expansion that marked the late 1990s and first six years of the 21st century started to lose speed in the second half of 2007, especially in the U.S., where the housing and mortgage market crises continued to ripple throughout other industries. By mid-2008 an ever deepening financial crisis reverberated around the world, causing governments to bail out banks and other institutions. By 2010 the global recovery was evolving better than expected, with activity recovering at varying speeds, tepidly in many advanced economies, but solidly in most developing and emerging economies. (See "Major News Stories.")

Calling it the "most severe recession since World War II," in 2009, the I.M.F. projected in 2010 that world output was expected to rise by 4.5 percent, following a half percent contraction in 2009. These projections were bolstered as world trade volume is forecasted to increase 11.2 percent from

2009 to 2010 and real G.D.P. growth forecasted to increase 3.3 percent in the same period.

▶ THE HIERARCHY OF NATIONS
Most contemporary analyses of the global economy begin with the assumption that the nations of the world are divided into two basic categories,

G.N.P. Per Capita, by World Regions, 2006–08

Region	G.N.P. per capita[1]		
	2006	2007	2008
East Asia & Pacific	$1,863	$2,180	$2,515
Eastern Europe & Central Asia	4,796	6,051	7,418
Latin America & Caribbean	4,767	5,540	6,780
Middle East & North Africa	2,481	2,794	3,242
South Asia	766	880	986
Sub-Saharan Africa	842	952	1,082
Western Europe, U.S. Japan, and other high-income areas	36,487	37,566	39,345
World	$7,439	$7,958	$8,579

Note: 1. In U.S. dollars. Source: The World Bank, The World Bank Atlas 2008.

World G.N.P. Per Capita, by Type of Economy, 2008

More than 70 percent of the world's 6.6 billion people live in low-income or lower middle-income economies, according to these World Bank statistics, while only 16 percent of the world's population lives in high-income economies.

Type of Economy	Population (in 000's)	G.N.P. per capita
High-income	1,068,525	$37,141
Upper-middle	948,453	12,297
Lower-middle	3,702,108	4,592
Low-income	972,975	1,407
Total	6,692,062	$10,357

Source: The World Bank, The World Bank Atlas 2009.

Change in World Economic Output, 1992–2010

Category	Annual percent change			
	1992–2001	2002	2009	2010[1]
World Total	3.2%	2.9%	–0.6%	4.2%
Advanced economies	2.8	1.7	–3.2	2.3
United States	3.5	1.8	–2.4	3.1
European Union	2.3	1.4	–4.1	1.0
Japan	0.9	0.3	–5.2	1.9
Other advanced economies	3.7	3.3	–2.3	3.0
Other emerging market and developing economies	3.8%	4.8%	2.4%	6.3%
Central & Eastern Europe	2.6	4.4	–3.7	2.8
Commonwealth of Independent States[2]	N.A.	5.2	–6.6	4.0
Developing Asia	7.3	6.9	6.6	8.7
Middle East & N. Africa	3.4	3.8	2.4	4.5
Sub-Saharan Africa	2.8	7.4	2.1	4.7
Western Hemisphere	3.0	0.5	–1.8	4.0

Note: Output is the value of production minus the cost of inputs by all businesses. 1. Projection. 2. Includes Georgia and Mongolia for reasons of geography. Source: United Nations, UNCTAD, World Investment Report, "Net FDI in Developing Countries", April 2010.

Countries With Highest and Lowest G.N.P. Per Capita, 2008

Country	G.N.P. per capita[1]	Country	G.N.P. per capita[1]
Highest		**Lowest**	
Liechtenstein	[2]	Burundi	$140
Bermuda	[2]	Congo, Dem. Rep.	150
Norway	$87,070	Liberia	170
Luxembourg	84,890	Guinea-Bissau	250
Channel Islands	68,640[2]	Ethiopia	280
Switzerland	65,330	Malawi	290
Denmark	59,130	Eritrea	300
Qatar	[2]	Sierra Leone	320
Sweden	50,940	Niger	330
Netherlands	50,150	Mozambique	370
Ireland	49,590	The Gambia	390
San Marino	46,767[2]	Togo	400
Finland	48,120	Nepal	400
United States	47,580	Rwanda	410
Cayman Islands	[2]	Madagascar	410
Isle of Man	43,710[2]	Guinea	390[2]
Austria	46,260	Central African Rep.	410
United Kingdom	45,390	Uganda	420
Belgium	44,330	Tanzania[4]	430
Kuwait	38,420[2]	Burkina Faso	480
Germany	42,440	Bangladesh	520
France[3]	42,250	Chad	530
Canada	41,730	Mali	580
Australia	40,350	Tajikistan	600
Iceland	40,070	Cambodia	600
Japan	38,210	Haiti	660
Macao, China	35,360[2]	Ghana	670
Italy	35,240	Benin	690
Singapore	34,760	Kyrgyz Rep.	740
Brunei Darussalam	26,740[2]	Lao P.D.R.	750

Note: Rankings based only on countries reporting G.N.P. per capita to The World Bank. 1. Figures in U.S. dollars. 2. 2008 data is unavailable; ranking is appropriate. 3. Includes overseas French territories. 4. Mainland only. Source: The World Bank, The World Bank Atlas 2009.

developed and developing. The developed ones are those with the highest G.N.P. figures, and are characterized by high per capita income, low rates of population growth and illiteracy, as well as having a low proportion of their labor force in agriculture and/or mining.

The wealthiest nations are at the center of the global economy and are responsible for promoting international trade, for helping to finance development in the poorer countries, and for maintaining a stable economic world. They attempt to do this through several organizations including:

Group of Eight (G–8): a loosely knit group of the largest economic powers who meet once a year to discuss policy in what has become a well-publicized media event. **Members:** Canada, France, Germany, Italy, Japan, Russia, U.K., U.S. The European Union also participates in G–8 summits.

Organization of Economic Cooperation and Development (OECD) HQ: 2 rue André Pascal, F-75775 Paris Cedex 16, France. OECD Washington Center, 2001 L St. NW, Washington D.C. 20036. **www.oecdwash.org.** Estab. 1961, . . . to help member countries promote economic growth, employment, and improved standards of living through the coordination of policy (and) . . . to help promote the sound and harmonious development of the world economy and improve the lot of the developing countries, particularly the poorest. **Members (32):** Australia, Austria, Belgium, Canada, Chile,

Net Foreign Direct Investment in Developing Countries, 1990–2008

Region and country	Billions of U.S. dollars					
	1990	1995	2000	2005	2007	2008[1]
All developing countries	**$24.5**	**$104.0**	**$165.5**	**$288.5**	**$470.8**	**$583.0**
By region						
East Asia and the Pacific	$105.1	$50.8	$45.2	$104.2	$115.2	$185.1
Europe and Central Asia	33.3	14.6	24.8	72.2	131.9	170.8
Latin America and the Caribbean	81.2	30.2	79.5	70.4	102.2	124.8
Middle East and North Africa	7.4	0.9	4.8	14.4	30.1	22.5
South Asia	5.4	2.9	4.4	10.0	28.0	47.5
Sub-Saharan Africa	12.1	4.5	6.8	17.3	27.4	32.4
10 leading nations						
China	$ 3.5	$35.8	$38.4	$79.1	$84.0	$108.0
Russia	N.A.	2.1	2.7	12.9	52.5	75.5
Brazil	1.0	4.9	32.8	15.2	34.6	45.1
Mexico	2.6	9.5	17.9	19.9	23.2	23.7
Turkey	N.A.	N.A.	1.0	9.8	22.0	18.1
India	N.A.	N.A.	3.6	6.7	21.0	40.4
Poland	0.1	3.7	9.3	10.4	17.6	14.7
Chile	0.6	3.0	4.9	6.7	14.5	15.2
Ukraine	N.A.	N.A.	0.6	7.8	9.9	10.9
Thailand	N.A.	N.A.	3.4	8.0	9.6	8.5

Note: In 2009, FDI in developing countries is projected to fall by 30 percent to $385 billion due to global financial conditions. 1. Estimate.
Source: The World Bank, *Global Development Finance (2008 & 2009).*

Total External Debt by Region and Nation, 1970–2008 (billions of dollars)

Region and nation	1970	1980	1990	2000	2005	2008
All developing countries	**$70.2**	**$579.6**	**$1,421.6**	**$2,283.9**	**$2,800.4**	**$3,718.5**
By Region						
East Asia and the Pacific	$ 8.6	$ 64.6	$239.0	$498.0	$614.1	$ 771.6
Europe and Central Asia	5.0	75.6	217.9	511.0	822.7	1,399.0
Latin America and the Caribbean	32.6	257.4	475.4	758.7	746.9	894.4
Middle East and North Africa	4.8	83.4	182.9	145.2	148.9	131.5
South Asia	12.3	37.8	129.5	160.0	191.3	326.3
Sub-Saharan Africa	6.9	60.8	176.9	211.0	216.2	195.7
10 most indebted nations						
China	N.A.	N.A.	$ 55.3	$145.7	$281.6	$402.5
Russian Federation	N.A.	N.A.	59.3	160.0	229.1	378.2
Turkey	$2.7	$19.1	49.4	117.3	169.3	277.3
Brazil	5.7	71.5	120.0	239.2	187.3	255.6
Mexico	7.0	57.4	104.4	150.3	167.9	230.6
India	8.4	20.7	83.6	99.1	123.1	218.0
Indonesia	4.5	20.9	69.9	144.4	130.7	204.0
Poland	N.A.	N.A.	49.4	65.8	98.8	150.9
Argentina	5.8	27.2	62.2	147.5	133.0	128.3
Hungary	N.A.	N.A.	N.A.	29.5	66.1	107.6

Source: The World Bank, *Global Development Finance (2010).*

U.S. Merchandise Trade Partners, 2009 (millions of dollars)

Country	U.S. exports to[2]	U.S. imports from	U.S. net balance of trade
Total[1]	$1,570,797	$1,945,705	$–374,908
Belgium	21,608	13,826	7,782
France	26,493	34,236	–7,743
Germany	43,306	71,498	–28,192
Ireland	7,465	28,101	–20,636
Italy	12,268	26,430	–14,162
Netherlands	32,242	16,098	16,144
U.K.	45,704	47,480	–1,776
Canada	204,658	226,248	–21,590
Brazil	26,095	20,070	6,025
Mexico	128,892	176,654	–47,762
Venezuela	9,315	28,059	–18,744
China	69,497	296,374	–226,877
Japan	51,134	95,804	–44,670
Malaysia	10,403	23,283	–12,880
South Korea	28,612	39,216	–10,604
Singapore	22,232	15,705	6,527
Taiwan	18,486	28,362	–9,876
India	16,441	21,166	–4,725

Note: Year-end (final) data. U.S. total trade calculated on a seasonally adjusted Balance of Payments basis; merchandise trade is calculated on a non-seasonally adjusted Census basis. Includes other countries not shown separately. **Source:** U.S. Dept. of Commerce, *U.S. International Transactions.*

Czech Republic, Denmark, Finland, France, Germany, Greece, Hungary, Iceland, Ireland, Italy, Japan, Korea, Luxembourg, Mexico, Netherlands, New Zealand, Norway, Poland, Portugal, Slovakia, South Korea, Spain, Sweden, Switzerland, Turkey, U.K., U.S.

The International Monetary Fund (I.M.F.) and The World Bank Both of these organizations are specialized agencies of the United Nations (see the separate section on the U.N. below) charged with making loans to nations having trouble with debt (I.M.F.) or for long-term growth and development among poorer nations (World Bank).

I.M.F. Classification of Countries
Advanced economies (31): Australia, Austria, Belgium, Canada, Cyprus, Denmark, Finland, France, Germany, Greece, Hong Kong, Iceland, Ireland, Israel, Italy, Japan, Korea, Luxembourg, Malta, Netherlands, New Zealand, Norway, Portugal, Singapore, Slovenia, Spain, Sweden, Switzerland, Taiwan, United Kingdom, the United States.

Other emerging market and developing countries (142): This group includes all other member countries except those non-I.M.F. members (such as Afghanistan) and countries that don't provide data (such as San Marino).

World's Leading Exporters and Importers in Merchandise Trade, 2008

Rank and country	Value 2008 (billions)	Share of world trade	Change in value, 2007–08	Rank and country	Value 2008 (billions)	Share of world trade	Change in value, 2007–08
Exporters				**Importers**			
1. Germany	$1,461.9	9.1%	11%	1. United States	$2,169.5	13.2%	7%
2. China	1,428.3	8.9	17	2. Germany	1,203.8	7.3	14
3. United States	1,287.4	8.0	12	3. China	1,132.5	6.9	8
4. Japan	782.0	4.9	9	4. Japan	762.6	4.6	3
5. Netherlands	633.0	3.9	15	5. France	705.6	4.3	4
6. France	605.4	3.8	10	6. United Kingdom	632.0	3.8	1
7. Italy	538.0	3.3	8	7. Netherlands	573.2	3.5	16
8. Belgium	475.6	3.0	10	8. Italy	554.9	3.4	8
9. Russian Federation	471.6	2.9	33	9. Belgium	469.5	2.9	14
10. United Kingdom	458.6	2.9	4	10. Korea, Republic of	435.3	2.7	22
11. Canada	456.5	2.8	9	11. Canada	418.3	2.5	7
12. Korea, Republic of	422.0	2.6	14	12. Spain	401.4	2.4	3
13. Hong Kong, China[1]	370.2	2.3	6	13. Hong Kong, china	393.0	2.4	6
14. Singapore[1]	338.2	2.1	13	14. Mexico[1]	323.2	2.0	9
15. Saudi Arabia	313.4	2.0	33	15. Singapore	319.8	1.9	22
16. Mexico	291.7	1.8	7	16. India	293.4	1.8	35
17. Spain	268.3	1.7	6	17. Russian Federation[1]	291.9	1.8	31
18. Taipei, Chinese	255.6	1.6	4	18. Taipei, Chinese	240.4	1.5	10
19. United Arab Emirates	231.6	1.4	28	19. Poland	204.3	1.2	23
20. Switzerland	200.3	1.2	16	20. Turkey	202.0	1.2	19
21. Malaysia	199.5	1.2	13	21. Australia	200.3	1.2	21
22. Brazil	197.9	1.2	23	22. Austria	183.4	1.1	13
23. Australia	187.3	1.2	32	23. Switzerland	183.2	1.1	14
24. Sweden	183.4	1.1	9	24. Brazil	182.4	1.1	44
25. Austria	181.0	1.1	11	25. Thailand	178.7	1.1	28
26. Thailand	177.8	1.1	17	26. Sweden	167.2	1.0	10
27. India	177.5	1.1	21	27. United Arab Emirates[3]	165.6	1.0	25
28. Norway	172.5	1.1	27	28. Malaysia	156.9	1.0	7
29. Poland	168.0	1.0	20	29. Czech Republic[1]	141.5	0.9	20
30. Czech Republic	146.3	0.9	19	30. Indonesia	126.2	0.8	36
World Total[1,2]	**$16,070.0**	**100.0%**	**15%**	**World Total**[1,2]	**$16,422.0**	**100.0%**	**15%**

Notes: 1. Includes significant re-exports or imports for re-export. 2. Includes other countries not shown separately. 3. Secondhand estimates. **Source:** World Trade Organization, *International Trade Statistics 2008* (2009).

►INTERNATIONAL FINANCE: BASIC CONCEPTS

Exchange rates Because countries have their own currencies, trade between them also involves exchanging or trading currencies. The *exchange rate* between currencies represents the ratio at which they can be exchanged or the price of one currency in terms of the other. For example, if the exchange rate between the British pound and the U.S. dollar is $1.50, then one British pound can be purchased at that price.

The exchange rate for almost all world currencies is now determined by the market. The exchange rate of a currency rises or appreciates when the demand for it rises and/or the supply falls. This may happen because foreign buyers want to buy more of a nation's goods or because consumers within the country decide to buy fewer imports. It may also happen because the country reduces its money supply. Finally, the central banks of countries can manipulate their exchange rates slightly by buying and selling their own and other currencies (see also Part II: The Federal Reserve).

The gold standard Before World War I, exchange rates for world currencies were fixed, artificially, by tying them to a certain amount of gold—$32, for example, might equal one ounce of gold. Central banks would then buy and sell gold in order to equalize supply and demand for the currencies and maintain the fixed exchange rates. For this reason, the central banks maintained enormous gold stockpiles, like the one the U.S. had at Fort Knox. People therefore referred to currencies as being backed by gold. Long-term changes in trading relationships and in the demand for various currencies eventually made the fixed exchange rates of the gold standard impossible to support. In 1944, the Bretton Woods agreement established the U.S. dollar as the world standard, but the U.S. still backed its dollars with gold and used gold to settle its debts. After 1973, the U.S. abandoned that role, and most of the world's exchange rates were set by the market.

Balance of payments The balance of payments account is the list of transactions between a country and the rest of the world. This account has three parts: *the current account:* a record of exports and imports of goods (e.g. oil, clothing) and services (e.g. tourism); *the capital account:* a record of exports and imports of assets such as bank loans and corporate stock purchases; and *the official-reserves account:* a record of a country's sales and purchases of official reserve assets at the central bank.

Balance of trade When a country imports goods from another country worth more than the value of its exports to it, there is said to be a deficit in the balance of trade between the

Foreign Exchange Rates: Currency Units Per Dollar, 1975–2010

Country/currency	1975	1990	1995	2000	2006	2008	2010[1]
Australia/dollar	$ 0.77	$ 1.28	$ 1.35	$ 1.72	$ 1.33	$ 1.06	$ 0.85
Austria/schilling[2]	17.44	11.33	10.08	N.A.	N.A.	N.A.	N.A.
Belgium/franc[2]	36.80	33.42	29.47	N.A.	N.A.	N.A.	N.A.
Brazil/real	N.A.	N.A.	N.A.	1.83	2.17	1.63	1.80
Canada/dollar	1.02	1.17	1.37	1.49	1.13	1.02	1.04
China/yuan	N.A.	4.79	8.37	8.28	7.97	6.89	6.82
Denmark/krone	5.75	6.19	5.60	8.10	5.94	4.82	6.09
European Community/euro	N.A.	N.A.	0.78	1.08	0.80	0.65	1.22
Finland/markka[2]	3.67	3.83	4.38	N.A.	N.A.	N.A.	N.A.
France/franc[2]	4.29	5.45	4.99	N.A.	N.A.	N.A.	N.A.
Germany/deutsche mark[2]	2.46	1.62	1.43	N.A.	N.A.	N.A.	N.A.
Greece/drachma[2]	32.30	158.59	231.68	365.92	N.A.	N.A.	N.A.
Hong Kong/dollar	4.94	7.79	7.74	7.79	7.77	7.81	7.79
India/rupee	8.40	17.49	32.41	45.00	45.19	42.93	46.50
Ireland/pound[2]	0.45	0.60	0.62	N.A.	N.A.	N.A.	N.A.
Italy/lira[2]	653.10	1,198.27	1,629.45	N.A.	N.A.	N.A.	N.A.
Japan/yen	296.79	145.00	93.96	107.80	116.31	108.19	90.81
Malaysia/ringgit	2.40	2.70	2.51	3.80	3.67	3.27	3.26
Mexico/peso	12.64	2,813.00	6.45	9.46	10.91	10.31	12.71
Netherlands/guilder[2]	2.53	1.82	1.60	N.A.	N.A.	N.A.	N.A.
New Zealand/dollar	0.82	1.68	1.52	2.19	1.54	1.33	0.69
Norway/krone	5.23	6.26	6.34	8.81	6.41	5.18	6.47
Portugal/escudo[2]	25.51	142.70	149.88	N.A.	N.A.	N.A.	N.A.
Singapore/dollar	2.37	1.81	1.42	1.72	1.59	1.37	1.40
South Africa/rand	0.74	2.59	3.63	6.95	6.77	8.10	7.64
South Korea/won	484.00	710.64	772.69	1,130.90	954.32	1,038.50	1,214.11
Spain/peseta[2]	57.43	101.96	124.64	N.A.	N.A.	N.A.	N.A.
Sri Lanka/rupee	6.98	40.08	51.05	76.96	103.94	107.82	113.56
Sweden/krona	4.15	5.92	7.14	9.17	7.37	6.04	7.83
Switzerland/franc	2.58	1.39	1.18	1.69	1.25	1.04	1.13
Taiwan/dollar	38.00	26.92	26.50	31.26	32.50	30.38	32.20
Thailand/baht	N.A.	N.A.	24.92	40.21	37.88	33.24	32.45
United Kingdom/pound	0.45	0.56	0.64	0.65	0.54	0.51	1.48
Venezuela/bolivar	N.A.	N.A.	174.85	680.52	2,144.60	2,144.60	4.29

Note: Averages of certified noon buying rates in New York for cable transfers. 1. Figures are for July, 2010. 2. Country converted its currency to euros as of January 3, 2001. A euro is worth 13.76 Austrian schillings, 40.34 Belgian francs, 5.95 Finnish markkas, 6.56 French francs, 1.96 German marks, 340.75 Greek drachmas, 0.79 Irish pounds, 1,936.27 Italian lire, 2.20 Netherlands guilders, 200.48 Portuguese escudos, or 166.39 Spanish pesetas. **Source:** U.S. Federal Reserve, *Federal Reserve Bulletin*, monthly. (July 1, 2010).

countries. Changes in exchange rates tend to equalize the supply and demand for currencies and the balance of trade; in the above case, the exchange rate for the first country's currency should fall relative to the second country's, reducing imports by making them more expensive and encouraging exports by making them cheaper. But this equalization may take a long time to occur since consumers and producers in the two countries must change their behavior. And central banks may want to slow the pace at which exchange rates adjust to slow the effects on trading sectors within their economies.

The balance of trade is an important issue because it indicates something about how a nation's economy is changing and, ultimately, about its competitiveness vis-à-vis other countries. A rising balance of trade deficit indicates that an economy is not able to sell its goods abroad and that con-

sumers are favoring imports over domestically produced goods.

As the U.S. economy has outsourced manufacturing jobs overseas, the U.S. trade deficit has skyrocketed. In 1980, the deficit was $19.4 billion; by 2000, it had increased to $375 billion, or nearly 20 times that amount. In 2007, the deficit was more 700 billion dollars, yet by 2010 the deficit had fallen to approximately $375 billion. Most of this difference was due to a decrease in the import of foreign goods. The entire U.S. trade deficit is in the manufactured goods sector; the U.S. actually runs a surplus in the services sector. U.S. exports of goods have not kept up with imports in part because the relative strength of the dollar makes U.S. goods more expensive for foreign nations to buy, while people in America have more money to spend on cheap imports.

U.S. International Trade Balance (millions of U.S. dollars) 1960–2009

	Exports		Imports		Balance		
Year	Goods[1]	Services[2]	Goods[1]	Services[2]	Goods[1]	Services[2]	Total
1960	$19,650	$6,290	$14,758	$7,674	$4,892	–$1,385	$3,508
1970	42,469	14,171	39,866	14,520	2,603	–349	2,254
1980	224,250	47,584	249,750	41,491	–25,500	6,093	–19,407
1990	387,401	147,832	498,435	117,659	–111,034	30,173	–80,861
1995	575,204	218,521	749,374	139,420	–174,170	79,101	–95,069
2000	771,994	298,603	1,224,408	223,748	–452,414	74,855	–377,559
2003	713,415	304,342	1,257,121	250,365	–550,892	53,977	–496,915
2005	894,631	389,122	1,681,780	313,540	–787,149	75,582	–711,567
2006	1,023,109	433,905	1,861,380	348,918	–838,270	84,987	–753,283
2007	1,148,481	497,245	1,967,853	378,130	–819,373	119,115	–700,258
2008	1,276,994	549,602	–2,117,245	–405,287	–840,252	144,316	–695,936
2009	1,068,499	502,298	–1,575,443	–370,262	–506,944	132,036	–374,908

Note: The balance is equal to exports minus imports. 1. Adjusted, excluding military. 2. Includes some military goods. **Source** U.S. Bureau of Economic Analysis, Foreign Trade Division, *U.S. International Transactions* (2010).

20 Largest U.S. Merchandise Exports and Imports, 2008–2009

Rank[1], Product	2008	2009[2]	Rank[1], Product	2008	2009[2]
Top 20 Exports			**Top 20 Imports**		
1. Vehicles	$51,031	$27,792	1. Crude Oil	$179,018	$80,441
2. Airplanes, engines, parts[3]	42,316	39,828	2. Vehicles	103,584	51,671
3. Electrical machinery[3]	41,681	29,602	3. TV's, VCR's, etc.	63,167	53,104
4. General industrial machines	27,576	22,469	4. Electrical machinery[3]	56,202	41,552
5. Specialized industrial machines	26,439	18,521	5. ADP equipment and office machines	48,946	38,373
6. Petroleum preparations	25,754	15,217	6. Petroleum preparations	46,512	23,991
7. Scientific instruments[3]	21,397	18,449	7. Clothing	36,246	31,830
8. Chemicals, plastics	21,107	14,753	8. General industrial machines	34,472	25,770
9. Chemicals, organic	18,284	12,281	9. Chemicals, medicinal	29,786	27,446
10. Chemicals, medicinal	17,967	21,723	10. Chemicals, organic	24,652	21,162
11. Power generating[3] machines	16,651	13,895	11. Power generating machines[3]	24,409	17,598
12. Metal ores and scrap	15,144	8,530	12. Natural gas	19,431	8,485
13. ADP equipment and office machines	14,910	10,176	13. Specialized industrial machines	18,744	12,754
14. Chemicals—n.e.s.	12,919	9,674	14. Scientific instruments[3]	18,654	15,019
15. TV's, VCR's, etc.	12,330	9,564	15. Iron / steel mill products	17,081	10,912
16. Gold, non-monetary	10,917	6,515	16. Furniture and bedding	16,274	11,994
17. Metal manufactures	9,424	7,097	17. Metal manufactures	15,017	10,612
18. Iron / steel mill products	8,936	5,620	18. Airplanes, engines, parts[3]	13,730	11,143
19. Soybeans	8,087	6,713	19. Toys, sporting goods, etc.	12,444	10,701
20. Corn	7,545	4,490	20. Textile yarn, fabric	11,054	8,786

Note: In current U.S. dollars. 1. Ranked by 2008 figures. 2. Data for January–June 2009 only. 3. Due to non-disclosure requirements, certain commodity classifications are subject to suppression and require a change in aggregation. **Source:** Bureau of Economic Analysis and U.S. Census Bureau, U.S. Department of Commerce; *News Releases, Exhibit 15.*

▶ GLOBAL CAPITAL MOVEMENT

The current dynamic interaction among these very disparate economies—aided greatly by the technological revolution—has set in motion an unprecedented global movement of capital from the wealthiest nations to developing ones. Because holders of capital always seek greater returns on their investments, they will put their money in economies that show potential growth; if they own or run corporations, they will look for ways to reduce the costs of manufacturing, especially labor costs, so they realize a greater profit. By investing in foreign companies or by establishing their businesses in foreign nations, the power of capital can rapidly transform the economies of poorer nations while rearranging the patterns of daily life for millions.

Foreign Direct Investment (F.D.I) is investment by private companies of one nation in the territory of another nation. The investment can be in an existing enterprise of the host nation or the building of new facilities for the investing foreign company (which would then be known as a multinational enterprise). The amount of money flowing from the wealthy nations to the developing ones in this way has increased from $24.5 billion in 1990 to over $580 billion in 2008.

Portfolio Investment is investing in the stocks and bonds of foreign nations. In March 1994, U.S. holdings of foreign securities totaled $870 billion, according to the U.S. Treasury Dept. That number more than doubled, to $1.76 trillion, by December 1997, and jumped to $2.95 trillion in December 2003. Globalization has caused portfolio investment to double yet again, reaching $5.9 trillion by the end of 2006. Of this amount, $4.3 trillion was invested in equities (stocks) and $1.3 trillion was invested in long-term debt (bonds). By December 2008, U.S. holdings of foreign securities had fallen to an estimated value of $4.3 trillion. Of this, equities were at $2.7 trillion and $1.3 trillion was long-term debt.

▶ INTERNATIONAL TRADE

International trade takes place because some nations have an advantage in producing certain kinds of products either because they have a comparative wealth of resources (capital, labor, natural resources) or more efficient production techniques. Even an economy with the most efficient technology has a limit on its resources, and rather than using them to produce all variety of products, it concentrates its resources on what it makes most efficiently. It then trades that good for other commodities, importing those that it produces least efficiently. As a result, all countries are better off because specialization results in the expansion of the total supply of goods, and the cost of acquiring them then falls.

Just which commodities a country will export and import depends on the relative prices of the factors used in production. A country like India has abundant labor and low wages. It therefore exports labor-intensive products such as garments. A country like Canada, which has abundant natural resources, specializes in agriculture and raw materials. Countries such as Canada and India then import goods for which the factors of production are in relatively short supply.

Of course, there are political reasons why countries do not completely specialize their production. No country, for example, wants to import all of its military equipment for fear that supplies would be cut off in the event of international conflict. Similarly, even inefficient producers, such as farmers in Japan, where land is scarce and expensive, may have political power that forces their governments to subsidize them.

U.S. Exports and Imports in Services, by Type, 1986–2009 (millions)

Category	1986	1990	1995	2000	2006	2009
Services Exports, Total	**$77,545**	**$137,232**	**$203,060**	**$284,027**	**$415,321**	**$483,870**
Travel	20,385	43,007	63,395	82,400	85,720	93,917
Passenger fares	5,582	15,298	18,909	20,687	22,036	26,424
Other transportation	15,438	22,042	26,081	29,803	46,323	35,406
Royalties and license fees	8,113	16,634	30,289	43,233	72,191	89,791
Other private services[1]	**28,027**	**40,251**	**64,386**	**107,904**	**189,050**	**238,332**
Education	3,495	5,126	7,515	10,348	14,645	19,910
Financial	3,301	4,417	7,029	16,026	47,439	55,446
Insurance	1,385	230	588	3,631	10,095	14,651
Telecommunications	1,827	2,735	3,228	3,884	7,278	9,284
Business, professional, & technical	4,813	7,752	16,078	25,319	89,692	116,628
Services Imports, Total	**$64,731**	**$98,210**	**$126,754**	**$207,392**	**$313,865**	**$334,918**
Travel	25,913	37,349	44,916	64,705	72,104	73,230
Passenger fares	6,505	10,531	14,663	24,274	27,501	25,980
Other transportation	17,766	24,966	27,034	41,425	65,262	41,585
Royalties and license fees	1,401	3,135	6,919	16,468	23,777	25,230
Other private services[1]	**13,146**	**22,229**	**33,222**	**60,520**	**125,221**	**168,892**
Education	433	658	1,125	2,032	4,465	5,582
Financial	1,769	2,475	2,472	4,840	14,242	16,454
Insurance	2,200	1,910	3,272	11,284	37,373	55,233
Telecommunications	3,253	5,583	7,305	5,429	6,367	7,048
Business, professional, & technical	1,303	2,093	4,822	9,130	61,068	81,994

Note: 1. Includes other services not shown separately. The dramatic differences in Other Private Services beginning in 2006 result from a change in accounting methods. **Source:** U.S. Bureau of Economic Analysis, Foreign Trade Division, *U.S. International Transactions*, June 17, 2010.

Tariffs and Quotas One way to protect a country's own producers, especially where they are inefficient compared with the international competition, is with import tariffs—taxes on goods that are produced abroad. Import tariffs raise the price of imports relative to domestic alternatives and discourage demand for the former. If one country is the sole importer or even the main importer of another's exports, it is possible that an import tariff will simply force the exporter to cut its selling price (in order to keep the price to consumers—including the tariff—from rising sharply and cutting off demand). In this case, the exporter pays virtually the whole cost of the tariff. If, on the other hand, the importer badly needs the import and there are few substitutes, raising the tariff simply raises the costs to one's own consumers. Critics of U.S. trade policy have pointed out that because Japan has become virtually the sole supplier of many consumer electronic products in the U.S., any tariffs against those products would simply raise their prices and fuel U.S. inflation.

Import quotas attempt to achieve a restriction on imports without the price rises associated with tariffs by setting direct limits on the number of items imported. So-called trade wars start when one country imposes a tariff on imports from a second country, and the latter responds with tariffs of its own against the first country. The arguments presented above about the benefits of trade have led to efforts to restrict the use of tariffs and maintain free trade, i.e. trade without any restrictions. Economists argue that unrestricted trade will always promote economic growth by forcing domestic prices to reflect world prices, thereby encouraging the efficient allocation of resources. Over the last 50 years, i.e. since the end of World War II, many of the leading nations have made a strong and continuous effort to lower or eliminate tariffs, first regionally, then around the world. The most successful regional organization has been the European Union, which has encouraged the formation of many other such alliances in all parts of the world.

Global trade has grown rapidly over the last decade, in large part because of the General Agreement on Tariffs and Trade (GATT) and its successor organization, the World Trade Organization (WTO).

GATT The General Agreement on Tariffs and Trade was first established in 1948. In an attempt to regulate the world's trade, the representatives of 23 leading nations agreed to find ways to lower tariffs, lower quotas, and to make free trade, i.e. trade without restrictions of any kind, their final goal. The United Nations provided headquarters for the group in Geneva, Switzerland. Over a period of almost 50 years the most important trading nations met regularly to discuss specific trade matters and to continue to remove restrictions from trade. Each series of negotiations, called rounds, lasted several years. By 1975 tariffs on manufactured goods had been reduced from 40 percent to 10 percent and world trade more than tripled. By the 1980s, however, the nature of world trade had changed. In 1986 the so-called Uruguay Round of GATT (now with 92 nations represented) addressed these and other issues over a period of eight years. The results—lowering of tariffs of all kind, banning quotas, and protecting copyrights and patents—added an estimated $500 billion annually to the global economy.

World Trade Organization Potentially the most important accomplishment of the 1994 GATT Agreement was the establishment of the World Trade Organization (W.T.O.), a permanent institution with real power to oversee trade agreements, enforce trade rules, and settle disputes. When it was approved by the U.S. Congress (Jan. 1, 1995), the organization became a reality, with 110 members. The basic principles of the W.T.O., derived from the GATT negotiations are the encouragement of fair competition and increased access to markets as well as the development of trade without discrimination (i.e. no nation will be given preferential trading terms). In 2003 the W.T.O. failed to reach agreement on the reduction of farm subsidies from the governments of wealthy nations, but in 2004 the organization succeeded in putting together the framework of an agreement that by 2006 would see the U.S. and other wealthy nations cut subsidies by 20 percent. In 2008 talks collapsed and were broken off without a deal; again subsidies were the key sticking points. Talks have since resumed although little progress has been made. **HQ:** Centre William Rappard, 154 rue de Lausanne, CH-1211 Geneva 21, Switzerland. (41-22) 739 51 11. **Internet Address: www.wto.org Membership:** (153) Albania, Angola, Antigua and Barbuda, Argentina, Armenia, Australia, Austria, Bahrain, Bangladesh, Barbados, Belgium, Belize, Benin, Bolivia, Botswana, Brazil, Brunei Darussalam, Bulgaria, Burkina Faso, Burundi, Cambodia, Cameroon, Canada, Cape Verde, Central African Republic, Chad, Chile, China, Colombia, Congo, Congo (Democratic Rep.), Costa Rica, Croatia, Cuba, Cyprus, Czech Republic, Denmark, Djibouti, Dominica, Dominican Republic, Ecuador, Egypt, El Salvador, Estonia, E.U, Fiji, Finland, France, Gabon, The Gambia, Georgia, Germany, Ghana, Greece, Grenada, Guatemala, Guinea, Guinea Bissau, Guyana, Haiti, Honduras, Hong Kong, Hungary, Iceland, India, Indonesia, Ireland, Israel, Italy, Ivory Coast, Jamaica, Japan, Jordan, Kenya, Kuwait, Kyrgyzstan, Latvia, Lesotho, Liechtenstein, Lithuania, Luxembourg, Macao, Macedonia, Madagascar, Malawi, Malaysia, Maldives, Mali, Malta, Mauritania, Mauritius, Mexico, Moldova, Mongolia, Morocco, Mozambique, Myanmar, Namibia, Nepal, Netherlands, New Zealand, Nicaragua, Niger, Nigeria, Norway, Oman, Pakistan, Panama, Papua New Guinea, Paraguay, Peru, Philippines, Poland, Portugal, Qatar, Romania, Rwanda, Saint Kitts & Nevis, Saint Lucia, Saint Vincent & the Grenadines, Saudi Arabia, Senegal, Sierra Leone, Singapore, Slovak Republic, Slovenia, Solomon Islands, South Africa, South Korea, Spain, Sri Lanka, Suriname, Swaziland, Sweden, Switzerland, Tanzania, Taiwan, Thailand, Togo, Tonga, Trinidad & Tobago, Tunisia, Turkey, Uganda, Ukraine, United Arab Emirates, United Kingdom, United States, Uruguay, Venezuela, Vietnam, Zambia, Zimbabwe. **Observers and applicants:** (32): Afghanistan, Algeria, Andorra, Azerbaijan, Bahamas, Belarus, Bhutan, Bosnia & Herzegovina, Comoros, Equatorial Guinea, Ethiopia, Holy See (Vatican), Iran, Iraq, Kazakhstan, Laos, Lebanon, Liberia, Libya, Montenegro, Russian Federation, Samoa, São Tome & Principe, Serbia, Seychelles, Sudan, Syria, Tajikistan, Uzbekistan, Vanuatu, Yemen. *(With the exception of the Holy See, observers must start accession negotiations within five years of becoming observers.)*

▶EUROPEAN UNION

In 2010, the 53rd year of its founding, the European Union had achieved success beyond the wildest dreams of its founders. It was now an enormous economic superpower, a gigantic market of nearly a half billion people in 27 nations with even more nations eager to join. During the previous decade its leaders had succeeded, despite dire predictions, in introducing almost seamlessly a new common currency called the euro which quickly took root throughout Europe and in world markets. Finally the E.U. had integrated many of the countries of post-Communist east-central Europe.

Origins Out of the wreckage of World War II, with generous American Marshall Plan aid after 1948, western Europe commenced reconstruction; by 1954, several economic miracles occurred. Yet without economic integration, the recoveries of the separate nations involved duplications, inefficiencies, diminished competition, and the threats of local gluts and shortages. A small sign of what might be achieved was Benelux, the customs union between Belgium, the Netherlands and Luxembourg, constructed even before war's end in 1944 and a going concern by 1948 despite the very unequal status of the three economies.

On May 9, 1950, France's foreign minister, Robert Schuman, proposed that German and French coal and steel production (the sinews of war) be placed under a supra-national, not intergovernmental, high authority; the West German chancellor, Konrad Adenauer, responded positively that very evening. By May 1952, ratification of the six-nation European Coal and Steel Community was complete, with Italy and the Benelux countries joining the French and Germans. The dramatic successes of the ECSC led the six toward broader integration, with negotiations culminating in the March 1957 Treaties of Rome which established the European Economic Community (EEC) and the European Atomic Energy Commission (Euratom).

The EEC was designed to reduce and eventually abolish all tariffs among the six; to establish a single external tariff for the Community; and to foster the free movement of not only goods but of labor and capital as well. Euratom was intended for the common peaceful development of nuclear power, though common action proved subsequently difficult to agree on. In 1958 the United Kingdom, which had refused to join the original negotiations, proposed that the EEC be expanded into an Atlantic free-trade area, but France, under her new president, Charles de Gaulle, exercised the veto. The rebuff led Britain with Portugal, Austria, Switzerland and the Scandinavian kingdoms

to form in 1959 the European Free Trade Association. The EFTA's successes were real but no match for the burgeoning EEC. So in 1961 Britain sought EEC membership. But de Gaulle, fearing American influence and objecting to the special terms that Britain sought for Commonwealth countries, again exercised the veto.

At the same time, de Gaulle was pushing for agricultural integration to match the EEC's industrial unity: the huge German market beckoned for France's chronic farm surpluses, yet Germany hesitated to sacrifice her own farmers in return for cheaper food. In fact, a serious crisis impended since each of the Six had its own system of protectionist duties, farm subsidies and crop controls. But the Dutch (Mansholt) proposals met with relatively easy and rapid agreement. The Common Agricultural Policy of 1962 eventually established a highly bureaucratized, centrally financed common market with managed prices, common duties upon imports, and subsidies for exports.

The European Community (E.C.) With agricultural integration, the stage was set for the Brussels treaty of 1965 (often called the The Second Treaty of Rome), which founded the European Community. The earlier three communities (ECSC, EEC and Euratom) were merged into one and were provided with a four-part structure of Commission, Council, Parliament and Court.

It was this refounded E.C. that the United Kingdom was at last permitted to join in 1973 (after another Gaullist veto in 1967). As in its earlier attempts, it was accompanied by Ireland, Denmark and Norway (though Norwegian voters subsequently rejected admission in a referendum). The Nine subsequently became the Twelve with the admission of Greece (1981), Spain and Portugal (1986).

Twenty years after the Brussels Treaty, with the accession of Jacques Delors as president of the European Commission, the E.C. received new impetus toward what the Treaty of Rome had envisioned: a single market free of all barriers to the free movement of goods, services, capital and labor. The first result was the Single European Act of 1987, an unwieldy compendium of almost 300 rules and directives to bring about by 1992 a Europe without frontiers. Even a decade later, its full meaning remains unclear, although both families and giant corporations have been able to hunt for bargains across national borders, tax and interest rates have been leveled, and trans-national regional ties have developed. The abolition of capital controls in 1990 has proven decisive in the movement toward monetary union, the second result of the Delors presidency (and of the strong support given by Helmut Kohl's Germany).

The European Union

Year admitted	Member countries
1957	Belgium, France, Germany, Italy, Luxembourg, Netherlands
1973	Denmark, Ireland, United Kingdom
1981	Greece
1986	Portugal, Spain
1995	Austria, Finland, Sweden
2004	Cyprus, Czech Republic, Estonia, Hungary, Latvia, Lithuania, Malta, Poland, Slovakia, Slovenia
2007	Bulgaria, Romania
Candidates	Croatia, Former Yugoslav Republic of Macedonia, Turkey, Iceland

The European Union (E.U.) In December 1991, the E.C. approved its third foundational treaty, the Treaty of Maastricht. Its three pillars were: monetary union, common foreign and security policies, and cooperation in justice and home affairs. The latter two pillars are intergovernmental, not supranational affairs, and have not been dealt with since 1991, as the E.U.'s clumsy responses to the Bosnian and Albanian crises attest.

Following the simple idea that a single market requires a single currency, the Maastricht Treaty established a three-stage (1991, 1994, 1997) creation of the *European Monetary Union* (EMU). During the first two stages, the E.U. members were to converge according to five criteria: inflation rates, interest rates, currency exchange, rate

stability (variation within 2.25 percent), budget deficits (less than 3 percent of G.D.P.), and public indebtedness (a debt-to-G.D.P. ratio of less than 60 percent). During the second stage would occur the transition from central bank financing of government spending to creation of the European Central Bank. With the third stage, the European Central Bank would propose and carry out the E.U.'s monetary policies and the euro would circulate as bank money—all preparatory to the actual introduction of the monetary union.

A tone of unreality attended attempts to establish the EMU. When Danish voters rejected Maastricht in a June 1992 referendum (unanimous approval being required for the treaty to take force), the E.U., at the time still called the E.C., permitted Denmark a sort of *à la carte* member-

Hourly Compensation Costs in U.S. Dollars For Production Workers, Selected Countries, 1975–2007

Country or Area	1975	1980	1985	1990	1995	2000	2005	2006	2007
Americas									
United States	$6.24	$9.75	$12.87	$15.00	$17.39	$19.88	$23.81	$24.15	$24.59
Brazil	N.A.	N.A.	N.A.	N.A.	N.A.	3.50	4.16	5.01	5.96
Canada	6.40	9.02	11.39	16.62	16.8	16.78	24.4	26.28	28.91
Mexico	1.43	2.15	1.55	1.54	1.70	2.07	2.65	2.77	2.92
Asia and Oceania									
Australia	5.75	8.67	8.41	13.45	15.58	14.51	25.53	26.46	30.17
Hong Kong SAR	0.75	1.50	1.73	3.22	4.81	5.45	5.65	5.78	5.78
Israel	1.99	3.34	3.59	7.56	9.23	11.16	12.13	12.45	13.91
Japan	2.95	5.43	6.24	12.52	23.34	21.69	21.31	19.99	19.75
Korea, Republic of	0.31	0.93	1.20	3.59	7.14	8.08	12.48	14.48	16.02
New Zealand	3.27	5.44	4.55	8.48	10.35	8.38	14.97	14.47	17.27
Philippines	N.A.	N.A.	N.A.	N.A.	0.94	0.73	0.85	0.98	1.10
Singapore	0.85	1.55	2.57	3.81	7.72	7.34	7.34	8.68	8.35
Sri Lanka	0.28	0.22	0.28	0.35	0.48	0.48	0.54	0.57	0.61
Taiwan	0.39	1.05	1.51	3.91	5.99	6.19	6.42	6.56	6.58
Europe									
Austria	4.59	9.03	7.71	18.04	25.67	20.13	30.2	31.3	35.33
Belgium	5.76	11.74	8.21	17.85	25.7	20.15	30.83	31.9	35.45
Czech Republic	N.A.	N.A.	N.A.	N.A.	2.54	2.85	6.08	6.83	8.20
Denmark	6.23	10.83	8.03	18.29	24.87	21.45	34.88	36.67	42.29
Finland	5.09	8.66	8.35	20.97	23.05	17.73	28.69	30.07	34.18
France	5.61	10.06	8.04	16.31	20.06	15.98	24.56	25.47	28.57
Germany	N.A.	N.A.	N.A.	N.A.	30.1	22.66	33.38	34.26	37.66
Greece	1.69	3.73	3.66	6.71	9.04	7.63	15.17	15.96	18.03
Hungary	N.A.	N.A.	N.A.	N.A.	2.98	2.78	6.13	6.30	7.91
Ireland	3.66	6.72	6.49	12.63	14.77	13.66	24.51	25.68	29.04
Italy	4.70	8.21	7.67	17.92	16.69	14.53	24.33	25.17	28.23
Luxembourg	6.23	11.52	7.45	15.94	23.54	17.49	27.36	27.83	30.60
Netherlands	6.58	12.05	8.73	17.98	24.02	18.68	30.02	30.64	34.07
Norway	7.20	12.32	10.93	22.71	25.95	23.5	39.34	41.69	48.56
Poland	N.A.	N.A.	N.A.	N.A.	N.A.	2.81	4.53	5.05	6.17
Portugal	1.50	1.96	1.45	3.55	5.09	4.64	7.42	7.53	8.27
Spain	2.47	5.75	4.55	11.10	12.47	10.46	17.59	18.51	20.98
Sweden	7.12	12.41	9.58	20.75	21.55	20.70	30.50	31.85	36.03
Switzerland	6.09	11.09	9.66	20.85	29.23	21.20	30.86	31.03	32.88
United Kingdom	3.21	7.22	5.97	11.95	13.24	16.31	25.36	26.36	29.73
Trade-Weighted Measures [1]									
All 33 Foreign Economies	4.01	6.69	6.74	12.08	15.11	13.62	19.03	19.77	21.66
OECD [2]	4.32	7.20	7.21	12.86	16.10	14.68	20.80	21.57	23.68
Europe	5.11	9.76	7.85	17.03	21.55	17.83	27.82	28.61	32.12
Euro Area [3]	5.33	10.07	8.01	17.63	23.08	18.10	28.40	29.12	32.71
Eastern Europe [4]	N.A.	N.A.	N.A.	N.A.	N.A.	2.81	5.45	5.93	7.27
East Asia w/o Japan [5]	0.5	1.16	1.44	3.69	6.20	6.56	8.17	9.17	9.65

Notes: 1. Weights based on the relative dollar value of U.S. trade in manufactured commodities (exports plus imports) with each country or area in 2007 2. Organization for Economic Cooperation and Development. 3. European Union member countries that have adopted the Euro as of January 1, 2009. 4. Refers to the Czech Republic, Hungary, and Poland. 5. Includes Hong Kong SAR, the Republic of Korea, the Philippines, Singapore, and Taiwan. **Source:** U.S. Bureau of Labor Statistics, *International Comparisons of Hourly Compensation Costs for Production Workers in Manufacturing,* March 2009.

ship: Denmark could ratify while opting out of the single currency (and other treaty matters). Danish voters in May 1993 thereupon reversed themselves and approved the treaty. German ratification in November 1993 brought the treaty into effect. But between those two votes, the exchange rate variation was altered from 2.25 percent to 15 percent lest the French withdraw from the pact.

It was this oddly flexible E.U. that Austria, Finland and Sweden joined on January 1, 1995. The Norwegian government had sought membership and been approved, but Norwegian voters, as they had in 1973, said no.

The European Monetary Union On Jan. 1, 1999, the E.U. introduced the *euro*. Initially well received in world financial markets, the euro sagged over the next six months, losing almost 20 percent of its value against the dollar. One reason for the flop was the E.U.'s decision to permit Italy's budget deficit to substantially exceed the target 2 percent of GDP; one member's excessive spending was dragging the whole currency down. By September, it had lost about 27 percent of its value against the dollar, prompting voters in Denmark to reject the new currency and instead keep their krone.

On Jan. 1, 2002, 50 billion new euro coins and 14.5 billion euro notes went into circulation in the 12 member countries, and on Feb. 28, 2002, all other currencies were withdrawn from circulation in the member nations. The value of the euro was soon about even with the U.S. dollar. Since then, the euro has continuously outpaced the dollar.

Expansion and Constitution In 2004 the E.U. expanded southward and eastward to include (the Greek part of) Cyprus, the Czech Republic, Estonia, Hungary, Latvia, Lithuania, Malta, Poland, Slovakia and Slovenia. The 10 additional countries made the E.U. truly One Europe, approximately half a billion people with an economy about the size of that of the U.S. While the average G.D.P. of the new states is less that half that of the earlier 15, their rate of growth is noticeably higher, not least because their corporate income tax rates are, on average, one-third lower, which encourages capital flow eastward. But the greatest contrast is in the agricultural sector.

The addition of the new states posed a possible nightmare for E.U. farm subsidies, which already accounted for half of the E.U. budget. By the terms of an Oct. 2002 agreement, the new members received 25 percent of the older states' subsidies until 2007, when the subsidy increased to 40 percent; full parity is achieved in 2013. In June 2003, the E.U.'s agricultural ministers agreed to begin a reform of the Common Agricultural Policy, planning to sever the link between subsidies and production.

On June 17–18, 2004, the Heads of State and Government adopted a treaty establishing a Constitution for Europe, which would have replaced all existing treaties with a single document. Among its notable innovations were: 1) a written bill of rights; 2) a single foreign minister; 3) introduction of majority voting in many policy areas such as energy, agriculture and immigration (while maintaining unanimity in such areas as taxation and foreign policy. However, France and the Netherlands both rejected the Constitution, thus ending its potential for ratification.

The 2007 Treaty of Lisbon did not revisit the idea of a constitution; instead, it focused on making the E.U. more democratic, more efficient, and more transparent. In addition to clearly defining the relationship between the Union and its member states, it explicitly recognized—for the first time—the ability of a member to withdraw from the Union. Ireland rejected it by a large margin in 2008, though in 2009 the treaty passed in a second referendum.

In 2010 the world fiscal crisis caused Spain, Portugal, and especially Greece to encounter severe economic problems mainly about high levels of debt. After much debate the larger members, led by Germany, decided they had to provide a bailout to Greece and to aid others if necessary. (See "Major News Stories.")

Structure of the E.U.
The Commission is composed of 27 commissioners, one appointed by each member country. The Commission supervises implementation of E.U. treaties, initiates and implements E.U. policy, applies E.U. law in member states, transacts negotiations with nonmember states, manages E.U. funds and budgets, and acts as the international mouthpiece of the E.U., enabling the member states to speak with one voice in international forums like the W.T.O.

Unemployment Rates in Leading Developed Nations, 1960–2010

Nation	1960	1970	1980	1990	2000	2005	2007	2008	2010[1]
Australia[2]	1.6%	1.6%	6.1%	6.7%	6.3%	5.1%	4.4%	4.3%	5.3%
Canada	6.5	5.7	7.3	7.7	6.1	6.0	5.3	5.3	7.4
France	1.5	2.5	6.5	8.6	9.1	9.6	8.6	8.1	9.5
Germany[3]	1.1	0.5	2.8	5.0	7.8	11.2	8.7	7.5	7.7
Italy	3.7	3.2	4.4	7.0	10.2	7.8	6.2	6.8	8.7
Japan	1.7	1.2	2.0	2.1	4.8	4.5	3.9	4.0	4.6
Netherlands	N.A.	N.A.	6.0	7.6	3.0	4.8	3.2	2.7	4.1
Sweden[2]	1.7	1.5	2.0	1.8	5.8	7.7	6.1	6.0	8.7
United Kingdom	2.2	3.1	6.9	7.1	5.5	4.9	5.4	5.7	8.0
United States	5.5	4.9	7.1	5.6	5.5	5.1	4.6	5.8	9.7

Notes: 1. First quarter 2010. For previous years, annual mean data is shown; the inclusion of first quarter 2010 data is meant to illustrate the ongoing impact of the global recession, not as direct comparison to previous years. 2. Data for 1960 are estimated. 3. Data for Germany before 1991 refer to the former West Germany. **Source:** U.S. Bureau of Labor Statistics. *International Unemployment Rates and Employment Indexes* (July 1, 2010).

The Council of the European Union consists of one minister from each of the 27 member governments. It is the chief decision-making body of the E.U., passing legislation on the major issues affecting all members. Each country takes the presidency for six months. Voting strength is weighted by population. Germany, France, Italy and the United Kingdom, for example, each have 29 votes, while Malta has 3. The Council meets in Brussels.

The European Parliament The 785 deputies of the European Parliament are elected directly by the citizens of the individual countries. The Parliament oversees the E.U. budget and passes on Commission proposals to the Council of Ministers. The Parliament also passes on new applications to the E.U. Deputies are elected to five-year terms.

The Court of Justice is the court of last resort for the E.U., interpreting E.U. treaties and legislation and hearing complaints about member-government violations. The Court also resolves differences between E.U. legislation and national laws. The 27 justices are appointed by the member governments and serve six-year terms.

The Economic and Social Committee The Economic and Social Committee is composed of 344 members representing labor, farmers and consumer groups, and serves as the bridge between the EU and the general citizenry. No decisions on economic and social policy can be made without consulting the Committee. Voting strength on the Committee is weighted by population, with Germany, France, Italy, and the United Kingdom having the most votes.

Top Bank and Thrift Holding Companies by Assets, 2008

Rank, Institution	Assets Dec. 31, 2008	Assets Dec. 31, 2007	Change
1. JPMorgan Chase & Co. New York	$2,175,052,000	$1,562,147,000	39.2%
2. Citigroup Inc. New York	1,938,470,000	2,187,631,000	−11.4
3. Bank of America Corp. Charlotte	1,822,068,028	1,720,688,423	5.9
4. Wells Fargo & Co. San Francisco	1,309,639,000	575,442,000	127.6
5. MetLife Inc. New York	501,678,258	558,563,489	−10.2
6. HSBC Holdings PLC London	434,715,911	487,754,828	−10.9
7. Deutsche Bank Frankfurt	396,659,000	668,199,000	−40.6
8. PNC Financial Services Group Inc. Pittsburgh	291,092,876	138,976,249	109.5
9. Barclays PLC London	279,777,049	343,735,670	−18.6
10. U.S. Bancorp Minneapolis	267,032,000	237,615,000	12.4
11. Bank of New York Mellon Corp.	237,652,000	197,839,000	20.1
12. SunTrust Banks Inc. Atlanta	189,137,961	179,573,933	5.3
13. State Street Corp. Boston	176,632,334	142,936,851	23.6
14. Capital One Financial Corp. McLean, Va.	165,913,451	150,590,369	10.2
15. Royal Bank of Scotland Group PLC Edinburgh	160,444,183	160,286,202	0.1
16. BB&T Corp. Winston-Salem, N.C.	152,015,025	132,617,601	14.6
17. Regions Financial Corp. Birmingham, Ala.	146,253,935	141,043,932	3.7
18. Toronto-Dominion Bank	122,745,454	60,165,099	104.0
19. Fifth Third Bancorp Cincinnati	119,763,812	110,961,509	7.9
20. KeyCorp Cleveland	105,231,004	99,567,393	5.7
21. Bank of Montreal Toronto	88,258,094	66,320,684	33.1
22. ING Group NV Amsterdam	82,442,966	79,986,341	3.1
23. Northern Trust Corp. Chicago	82,053,626	67,611,226	21.4
24. BNP Paribas Group Paris	79,858,266	74,209,491	7.6
25. Mitsubishi UFJ Financial Group Inc. Tokyo	70,121,446	55,727,748	25.8
26. Comerica Inc. Dallas	67,912,580	62,756,752	8.2
27. Allied Irish Banks PLC Dublin	65,815,757	64,875,639	1.4
28. Marshall & Ilsley Corp. Milwaukee	62,517,618	59,857,466	4.4
29. Banco Bilbao Vizcaya Argentaria SA Spain	62,305,413	58,869,241	5.8
30. Zions Bancorp. Salt Lake City	55,339,951	52,947,444	4.5
31. Huntington Bancshares Inc. Columbus, Ohio	54,355,998	54,629,164	−0.5
32. Hudson City Bancorp Inc. Paramus, N.J.	53,906,227	44,142,119	22.1
33. E-Trade Financial Corp. New York	45,070,677	51,750,910	−12.9
34. Rabobank Nederland Utrecht, Netherlands	40,891,905	62,451,758	−34.5
35. Popular Inc. Hato Rey, Puerto Rico	38,883,000	44,411,000	−12.4
36. Synovus Financial Corp. Columbus, Ga.	35,786,269	33,018,452	8.4
37. New York Community Bancorp Inc. Westbury	32,488,105	30,599,738	6.2
38. Royal Bank of Canada Toronto	32,434,425	25,582,057	26.8
39. First Horizon National Corp. Memphis	31,022,768	37,017,239	−16.2
40. Colonial BancGroup Inc. Montgomery, Ala.	25,816,306	25,971,125	−0.6

Source: *American Banker*, "Bank and Thrift Holding Companies with the Most Assets," May 20, 2009. Reprinted with permission.

The *Fortune* Global 100, 2010

Rank, Company	Revenues ($ millions)	Profits ($ millions)	Rank, Company	Revenues ($ millions)	Profits ($ millions)
1. Wal-Mart Stores	408,214	14,335	51. Honda Motor	92,400	2,891
2. Royal Dutch Shell	285,129	12,518	52. Électricité de France	92,204	5,428
3. Exxon Mobil	284,650	19,280	53. Aviva	92,140	1,692
4. BP	246,138	16,578	54. Petrobras	91,869	15,504
5. Toyota Motor	204,106	2,256	55. Royal Bank of Scotland	91,767	−4,167
6. Japan Post Holdings	202,196	4,849	56. PDVSA	91,182	1,608
7. Sinopec	187,518	5,756	57. Metro	91,152	532
8. State Grid	184,496	−343	58. Tesco	90,234	3,690
9. AXA	175,257	5,012	59. Deutsche Telekom	89,794	491
10. China National Petroleum	165,496	10,272	60. Enel	89,329	7,499
11. Chevron	163,527	10,483	61. UnitedHealth Group	87,138	3,822
12. ING Group	163,204	−1,300	62. Société Générale	84,157	942
13. General Electric	156,779	11,025	63. Nissan Motor	80,963	456
14. Total	155,887	11,741	64. Pemex	80,722	−7,011
15. Bank of America Corp.	150,450	6,276	65. Panasonic	79,893	−1,114
16. Volkswagen	146,205	1,334	66. Procter & Gamble	79,697	13,436
17. ConocoPhillips	139,515	4,858	67. LG	78,892	1,206
18. BNP Paribas	130,708	8,106	68. Telefónica	78,853	10,808
19. Assicurazioni Generali	126,012	1,820	69. Sony	77,696	−439
20. Allianz	125,999	5,973	70. Kroger	76,733	70
21. AT&T	123,018	12,535	71. Groupe BPCE	76,464	746
22. Carrefour	121,452	454	72. Prudential	75,010	1,054
23. Ford Motor	118,308	2,717	73. Munich Re Group	74,764	3,504
24. ENI	117,235	6,070	74. Statoil	74,000	2,912
25. J.P. Morgan Chase & Co.	115,632	11,728	75. Nippon Life Insurance	72,051	2,624
26. Hewlett-Packard	114,552	7,660	76. AmerisourceBergen	71,789	503
27. E.ON	113,849	11,670	77. China Mobile Comm.	71,749	11,656
28. Berkshire Hathaway	112,493	8,055	78. Hyundai Motor	71,678	2,330
29. GDF Suez	111,069	6,223	79. Costco Wholesale	71,422	1,086
30. Daimler	109,700	−3,670	80. Vodafone	70,899	13,782
31. Nippon Telegraph & Telephone	109,656	5,302	81. BASF	70,461	1,960
			82. BMW	70,444	284
32. Samsung Electronics	108,927	7,562	83. Zurich Financial Services	70,272	3,215
33. Citigroup	108,785	−1,606	84. Valero Energy	70,035	−1,982
34. McKesson	108,702	1,263	85. Fiat	69,639	−1,165
35. Verizon Communications	107,808	3,651	86. Deutsche Post	69,427	895
36. Crédit Agricole	106,538	1,564	87. Industrial & Commercial Bank of China	69,295	18,832
37. Banco Santander	106,345	12,430			
38. General Motors	104,589	N.A.	88. Archer Daniels Midland	69,207	1,707
39. HSBC Holdings	103,736	5,834	89. Toshiba	68,731	−213
40. Siemens	103,605	3,097	90. Legal & General Group	68,290	1,346
41. American International Group	103,189	−10,949	91. Boeing	68,281	1,312
			92. U.S. Postal Service	68,090	−3,794
42. Lloyds Banking Group	102,967	4,409	93. Lukoil	68,025	7,011
43. Cardinal Health	99,613	1,152	94. Peugeot	67,297	−1,614
44. Nestlé	99,114	9,604	95. CNP Assurances	66,556	1,396
45. CVS Caremark	98,729	3,696	96. Barclays	66,533	14,648
46. Wells Fargo	98,636	12,275	97. Home Depot	66,176	2,661
47. Hitachi	96,593	−1,152	98. Target	65,357	2,488
48. I.B.M.	95,758	13,425	99. ArcelorMittal	65,110	118
49. Dexia Group	95,144	1,404	100. WellPoint	65,028	4,746
50. Gazprom	94,472	24,556			

Source: *Fortune*, money.cnn.com/magazines/fortune. Retrieved August, 2010.

World Economic Indicators, 2007

Country	G.N.P. (millions of U.S. dollars) 2007	G.N.P. per capita (in U.S. dollars) 2007	Real growth rate 1980–91	Real growth rate 1990–2001	Average inflation rate 2006	Agriculture's share in G.D.P. 1970	Agriculture's share in G.D.P. 2004	Net private capital flows (millions) 2006[1]	Foreign direct investment as percent of G.D.P. 2006
Afghanistan	$10,137	N.A.	N.A.	5%	N.A.	N.A.	N.A.	N.A.	N.A.
Albania	10,456	$3,290	N.A.	N.A.	2%	N.A.	24%	$264	3.13%
Algeria	122,465	3,620	–0.8%	N.A.	4	10%	9	N.A.	1.06
Angola	43,635	2,560	N.A.	5	37	45	9	–256	–3.97
Antigua & Barbuda	977	11,520	3.8	N.A.	N.A.	N.A.	N.A.	112	N.A.
Argentina	238,853	6,050	–1.5	11	4	13	10	289	2.58
Armenia	7,925	2,640	2.1	2	8	N.A.	23	255	5.27
Australia	755,795	35,960	1.2	3	2	6	N.A.	79,383	–4.70
Austria	355,088	42,700	2.1	6	2	7	1	73,435	2.96
Azerbaijan	21,872	2,550	0.4	4	7	N.A.	12	585	13.37
Bahamas	N.A.	N.A.	1.3	12	1	N.A.	N.A.	N.A.	N.A.
Bahrain	14,022	19,350	–3.8	6	N.A.	N.A.	N.A.	9,383	N.A.
Bangladesh	75,047	470	1.9	13	3	55	21	803	1.34
Barbados	N.A.	N.A.	1.3	4	1	11	N.A.	N.A.	N.A.
Belarus	40,897	4,220	3.3	10	18	N.A.	11	266	1.03
Belgium	432,540	40,710	2.1	8	2	, 4	1	44,185	8.62
Belize	1,157	3,800	2.5	3	3	N.A.	N.A.	138	11.41
Benin	5,120	570	–1.1	3	1	49	36	87	0.49
Bhutan	1,166	1,770	6.8	5	5	N.A.	N.A.		0.09
Bolivia	11,964	1,260	–2.0	4	4	17	15	–126	–2.96
Bosnia & Herzegovina	14,051	3,580	N.A.	2	N.A.	N.A.	11	519	3.01
Botswana	10,991	5,840	5.8	7	7	33	2	755	2.70
Brazil	1,133,030	5,910	0.4	4	7	12	10	21,102	1.91
Brunei	10,287	26,930	N.A.	10	N.A.	N.A.	N.A.	N.A.	N.A.
Bulgaria	35,062	4,590	1.7	12	6	N.A.	11	1,226	9.81
Burkina Faso	6,384	430	1.3	4	–0	44	30	N.A.	0.38
Burundi	923	110	1.4	5	13	71	51	N.A.	0.07
Cambodia	7,858	540	N.A.	3	4	N.A.	32	380	6.13
Cameroon	19,447	1,050	–0.9	13	N.A.	31	44	218	0.11
Canada	1,300,025	39,420	2.1	15	2	N.A.	N.A.	49,657	3.07
Cape Verde	1,287	2,430	2.2	10	–2	N.A.	6	54	5.54
Central African Rep.	1,667	380	–1.5	3	–2	35	55	N.A.	0.44
Chad	5,760	540	3.8	N.A.	–5	43	N.A.	N.A.	12.89
Chile	138,630	8,350	1.7	3	1	7	3	9,993	5.78
China	3,120,891	2,360	7.8	2	4	35	13	115,201	3.54
Colombia	149,934	3,250	1.2	2	6	25	11	7,228	8.48
Comoros	425	680	–1.0	3	N.A.	N.A.	41	N.A.	0.26
Congo, Dem. Republic	8,573	140	–0.2	2	4	18	N.A.	N.A.	5.66
Congo Republic	5,797	1,540	–1.6	8	2	16	6	710	14.22
Costa Rica	24,831	5,560	1.0	3	12	23	8	1,920	4.30
Croatia	46,426	10,460	N.A.	7	2	N.A.	8	1,437	4.57
Cuba	N.A.	N.A.	N.A.	7	N.A.	N.A.	N.A.	N.A.	N.A.
Cyprus	19,617	24,940	4.9	5	2	N.A.	N.A.	3,894	7.26
Czech Republic[2]	149,378	14,450	0.4	19	3	N.A.	3	13,289	4.12
Denmark	299,804	54,910	2.1	12	1	N.A.	2	47,997	2.02
Djibouti	908	1,090	N.A.	6	N.A.	N.A.	N.A.	N.A.	3.20
Dominica	310	4,250	4.7	8	2	N.A.	N.A.	25	9.19
Dominican Republic	34,611	3,550	–0.2	5	51	20	11	1,092	3.47
East Timor	1,604	1,510	N.A.	N.A.	N.A.	N.A.	31	N.A.	N.A.
Ecuador	41,148	3,080	–0.3	N.A.	3	24	7	2,240	4.51
Egypt	119,405	1,580	2.0	5	11	29	15	8,871	6.02
El Salvador	19,520	2,850	–0.3	N.A.	4	28	9	292	3.05
Equatorial Guinea	6,527	12,860	3.4	11	N.A.	N.A.	N.A.	N.A.	57.58
Eritrea	1,108	342	N.A.	2	N.A.	N.A.	15	N.A.	1.17
Estonia	17,706	13,200	2.1	3	3	N.A.	4	1,899	22.87
Ethiopia	17,565	220	–1.6	6	3	56	46	265	2.37
Fiji	3,189	3,800	0.0	1.7	3	29	N.A.	N.A.	–0.14
Finland	2,447,090	38,500	1.8	1.5	2	N.A.	2	401,678	3.32
France[3]	8,876	6,670	–4.2	–0.1	8	17%	8	352	3.72
Gabon	544	85	–0.1	0.1	4	33	31	51	11.26
Gambia	9,337	2,120	2.2	–5.5	8	N.A.	17	528	7.03
Georgia	3,197,029	38,860	2.2	1.2	0	3	1	497,423	1.15
Germany[4]	13,905	590	–0.3	1.9	15	47	37	106	0.99
Ghana	234,833	44,400	2.5	2.6	1	N.A.	3	28,912	2.06

Country	G.N.P. (millions of U.S. dollars) 2007	G.N.P. per capita (in U.S. dollars) 2007	Real growth rate 1980–91	Real growth rate 1990–2001	Average inflation rate 2006	Agriculture's share in G.D.P. 1970	Agriculture's share in G.D.P. 2004	Net private capital flows (millions) 2006[1]	Foreign direct investment as percent of G.D.P. 2006
Greece	$331,658	$29,630	1.2%	2.0%	3%	18%	6%	$54,683	0.28%
Grenada	505	4,670	5.3	2.9	3	N.A.	8	34	5.56
Guatemala	32,585	2,440	–1.8	1.4	6	N.A.	22	207	0.66
Guinea	3,722	400	N.A.	1.6	38	N.A.	24	–14	3.10
Guinea-Bissau	331	200	1.3	–1.3	–4	47	62	8	3.32
Guyana	959	1,300	–4.2	1.6	8	19	31	128	9.76
Haiti	5,366	560	–2.4	–2.5	13	N.A.	27	9	0.22
Honduras	11,339	1,600	–0.7	0.3	5	32	N.A.	468	5.60
Hong Kong	218,910	31,610	N.A.	2.1	0	0	N.A.	43,061	20.20
Hungary	116,303	11,570	0.7	2.1	4	18	N.A.	12,027	5.89
Iceland	16,826	54,100	1.3	2.1	9	N.A.	N.A.	16,958	15.63
India	1,069,427	950	3.3	4.0	6	47	21	11,476	0.82
Indonesia	373,125	1,650	3.9	2.3	14	45	15	8,587	1.83
Iran	246,544	3,470	–1.1	2.0	11	19	10	N.A.	0.02
Iraq	N.A.	N.A.	N.A.	N.A.	N.A.	17	N.A.	N.A.	N.A.
Ireland	210,168	48,140	2.2	6.8	3	N.A.	N.A.	318,484	–14.73
Israel	157,065	21,900	1.8	2.0	2	N.A.	N.A.	15,766	4.52
Italy	1,991,284	33,540	2.1	1.4	2	8	2	251,355	1.11
Ivory Coast	17,543	910	–3.4	0.1	6	40	22	344	1.63
Jamaica	9,923	3,710	–0.3	–0.5	6	7	5	3,268	7.13
Japan	4,813,341	37,670	3.7	1.0	–1	6	N.A.	337,301	0.07
Jordan	16,282	2,850	–3.3	0.9	6	10	2	1,519	12.05
Kazakhstan	78,281	5,060	0.9	–1.9	22	N.A.	8	8,502	3.46
Kenya	25,559	680	0.3	–0.6	7	33	26	72	0.11
Kiribati	120	1,170	0.5	0.6	2	N.A.	N.A.	N.A.	N.A.
Korea, South	955,802	19,690	8.8	4.7	0	26	3	27,478	0.55
Kuwait	80,221	31,640	N.A.	–1.0	N.A.	0	N.A.	2,157	0.31
Kyrgyzstan	3,099	590	2.1	–3.9	9	N.A.	36	46	1.74
Laos	3,413	580	1.2	3.9	5	N.A.	46	N.A.	0.96
Latvia	22,595	9,930	2.8	–1.0	11	N.A.	4	1,021	4.61
Lebanon	23,651	5,770	N.A.	3.6	6	9	6	2,910	11.72
Lesotho	2,007	1,000	0.0	2.1	4	35	17	91	6.34
Liberia	554	150	N.A.	3.5	12	24	N.A.	N.A.	35.37
Libya	55,473	9,010	N.A.	N.A.	15	2	N.A.	1,303	N.A.
Lithuania	33,472	9,920	2.5	–1.6	7	N.A.	6	2,008	4.03
Luxembourg	36,420	75,880	3.8	4.2	6	4	0	575,901	301.32
Macedonia	7,052	3,460	N.A.	–0.9	3	N.A.	13	331	1.73
Madagascar	6,331	320	–2.4	–0.6	11	30	28	28	0.57
Malawi	3,506	250	0.1	1.5	19	44	39	5	0.14
Malaysia	173,705	6,540	2.9	3.9	4	29	9	–1,276	3.04
Maldives	977	3,200	6.7	2.5	0	N.A.	N.A.	9	1.24
Mali	6,136	500	0.1	1.6	4	61	35	104	3.00
Malta	6,216	15,310	3.8	3.8	3	7	N.A.	3,211	N.A.
Marshall Islands	204	3,070	N.A.	–3.5	4	N.A.	N.A.	N.A.	N.A.
Mauritania	2,636	840	–1.8	1.2	30	29	18	N.A.	6.22
Mauritius	6,878	5,450	6.1	3.9	4	16	6	59	0.62
Mexico	878,020	8,340	–0.5	1.5	4	12	4	22,486	2.44
Micronesia	274	2,470	N.A.	–1.3	4	N.A.	N.A.	N.A.	N.A.
Moldova	4,323	1,260e	1.8	–8.2	13	N.A.	21	194	6.81
Mongolia	3,362	1,290	N.A.	0.0	23	N.A.	20	45	9.69
Montenegro[5]	3,109	5,180	–1.4	N.A.	3	18	18	N.A.	5.65
Morocco	69,352	2,250	1.6	0.7	2	20	15	1,586	3.01
Mozambique	6,787	320	–3.6	4.3	6	N.A.	21	196	1.63
Myanmar	N.A.	N.A.	N.A.	5.7	N.A.	38	N.A.	213	N.A.
Namibia	6,970	3,360	–1.5	2.2	9	N.A.	9	402	N.A.
Nepal	9,660	340	2.1	2.4	7	67	40	2	0.03
Netherlands	750,526	45,820	1.5	2.3	2	6	2	140,721	6.47
New Zealand	121,708	28,780	0.2	2.0	1	N.A.	N.A.	4,178	1.81
Nicaragua	5,519	980	–4.6	–0.1	11	25	19	233	4.92
Niger	3,992	280	–4.1	–0.9	1	65	N.A.	18	0.35
Nigeria	137,091	930	–1.7	–0.3	8	40	16	–855	2.03
Norway	360,036	76,450	2.2	2.9	7	6	1	55,099	1.11
Oman	27,887	11,120	4.5	0.6	N.A.	16	1	808	0.82
Pakistan	141,009	870	3.2	1.2	9	37	22	2,872	1.97
Palau	167	8,210	N.A.	N.A.	3	N.A.	N.A.	N.A.	N.A.
Panama	18,423	5,510	–1.8	2.1	2	15	7	2,393	6.64

Country	G.N.P. (millions of U.S. dollars) 2007	G.N.P. per capita (in U.S. dollars) 2007	Real growth rate 1980–91	Real growth rate 1990–2001	Average inflation rate 2006	Agriculture's share in G.D.P. 1970	Agriculture's share in G.D.P. 2004	Net private capital flows (millions) 2006[1]	Foreign direct investment as percent of G.D.P. 2006
Papua New Guinea	$5,400	$850	–0.7%	1.0%	10%	37%	N.A.	–$1	0.68%
Paraguay	10,225	1,670	–0.8	–0.6	11	32	27%	57	0.87
Peru	96,241	3,450	–2.6	2.4	7	19	10	5,920	3.17
Philippines	142,623	1,620	–1.2	1.0	5	30	13	6,111	1.14
Poland	374,633	9,840	0.5	4.4	1	N.A.	3	24,202	3.17
Portugal	201,079	18,950	2.7	2.6	3	N.A.	3	38,039	1.75
Qatar	N.A.–	N.A.	–10.9	N.A.	N.A.	N.A.	N.A.	N.A.	N.A.
Romania	132,502	6,150	–0.1	–0.1	10	N.A.	14	7,741	6.73
Russia	1,070,999	7,560	1.3	–3.5	16	N.A.	5	12,063	1.98
Rwanda	3,072	320	–2.6	–1.3	9	62	40	8	0.37
Saint Kitts and Nevis	470	9,630	5.8	3.9	5	N.A.	N.A.	35	10.40
Saint Lucia	929	5,530	2.9	0.7	–2	N.A.	N.A.	114	13.06
Saint Vincent and the Grenadines	507	4,210	5.2	2.5	N.A.	N.A.	8	87	12.93
Samoa	454	2,430	5.1	2.0	5	N.A.	13	–5	–0.90
São Tomé and Príncipe	138	870	–3.5	–0.6	20	37	17	3	9.92
Saudi Arabia	373,490	15,440	–4.2	–1.1	6	6	3	45,662	N.A.
Senegal	10,170	820	0.0	1.1	3	24	16	112	0.66
Serbia[5]	34,969	4,730	–1.4	N.A.	16	18	18	N.A.	5.65
Seychelles	762	8,960	2.5	0.1	2	N.A.	2	75	11.88
Sierra Leone	1,537	260	–1.3	–6.6	14	28	N.A.	66	4.91
Singapore	148,992	32,470	4.9	4.4	0	2	0	37,247	17.19
Slovak Republic	63,324	11,730	N.A.	1.9	3	N.A.	3	1,446	4.11
Slovenia	42,306	20,960	N.A.	3.0	2	N.A.	N.A.	2,113	1.57
Solomon Islands	363	730	3.5	–1.4	7	N.A.	N.A.	N.A.	–0.27
Somalia	N.A.	N.A.	N.A.	N.A.	N.A.	59	N.A.	N.A.	N.A.
South Africa	274,009	5,760	0.9	0.2	7	8	3	11,831	2.61
Spain	1,321,756	29,450	2.9	2.2	4	N.A.	3	272,524	2.03
Sri Lanka	30,785	1,540	2.5	3.6	10	28	17	–257	1.16
Sudan	37,031	960	–2.4	3.2	7	43	39	2,254	8.37
Suriname	2,166	4,730	–4.5	2.6	13	7	N.A.	25	N.A.
Swaziland	2,951	2,580	3.1	0.1	6	33	12	5	–0.59
Sweden	421,342	46,060	1.7	1.7	2	N.A.	1	13,237	2.99
Switzerland	452,121	59,880	1.6	0.3	1	N.A.	N.A.	22,192	4.20
Syria	34,993	1,760	–2.1	1.9	9	20	23	427	1.62
Tajikistan	3,103	460	–0.1	–9.9	20	N.A.	24	54	2.36
Tanzania[6]	16,287	400	–1.1	0.4	6	41	44	475	3.91
Thailand	217,348	3,400	5.9	3.0	5	26	10	13,293	2.56
Togo	2,383	360	–1.7	–0.6	–0	34	41	122	0.12
Tonga	233	2,320	1.5	2.1	7	N.A.	28	N.A.	2.12
Trinidad and Tobago	18,795	14,100	–5.2	2.9	8	5	0	1,813	7.66
Tunisia	32,820	3,200	1.2	3.1	3	20	12	725	2.52
Turkey	592,850	8,020	2.9	1.7	11	30	12	24,630	2.70
Turkmenistan	N.A.	N.A.	0.7	–6.1	N.A.	N.A.	N.A.	N.A.	0.76
Uganda	10,469	340	3.3	3.6	7	54	32	245	2.95
Ukraine	118,445	2,550	2.3	–7.4	14	N.A.	12	10,290	9.42
United Arab Emirates	N.A.	N.A.	–5.8	–1.6	N.A.	N.A.	2	N.A.	N.A.
United Kingdom	2,608,513	42,740	2.6	2.5	2	N.A.	1	576,487	7.22
United States	13,886,472	46,040	2.1	2.1	3	3	N.A.	1,189,353	0.88
Uruguay	21,186	6,380	–0.4	2.1	7	13	11	978	4.23
Uzbekistan	19,721	730	0.8	–1.5	22	N.A.	31	N.A.	0.33
Vanuatu	417	1,840	–0.2	–1.1	0	N.A.	N.A.	13	3.89
Venezuela	201,146	7,320	–1.5	–0.6	17	6	N.A.	5,516	2.11
Vietnam	67,236	790	N.A.	6.0	7	N.A.	21	1,139	3.73
Yemen	19,421	870	N.A.	2.4	13	52	13	–251	–1.76
Zambia	9,479	800	–2.9	–1.7	12	11	20	N.A.	3.56
Zimbabwe	4,466	340	0.2	–0.2	N.A.	15	17	N.A.	3.05

Note: The World Bank reports data on Gross National Income (GNI) rather than Gross National Product (GNP). Some figures are for years other than those specified. 1. Data are shown for low and middle income countries only. 2. Data for years before 1990 refer to Czechoslovakia. 3. Data includes French Guiana, Guadeloupe, Martinique, and Réunion. 4. Data for years before 1990 refer to West Germany. 5. Data before 2006 refer to the former Yugoslavia. 6. Data refers to mainland Tanzania only. **Source:** The World Bank, *The World Bank Atlas* (2008).

Nations of the World

The following section presents major facts about all the nations of the world, including statistics on each nation's geography, people, government, economy, and written text describing highlights of the country's history.

The commonly used name for each country is listed first, followed by the formal name. Geographical descriptions are listed in both miles and kilometers, and the latitude and longitude of most islands are given.

Sources of information include the annual *World Factbook* published by the Central Intelligence Agency of the United States, the United Nations, the U.S. Census Bureau, and the U.S. Department of State. Names of heads of government are from the United Nations official protocol office and are valid as of September 2010.

▶ AFGHANISTAN

• **GEOGRAPHY   Location:** landlocked country in southwestern Asia. **Boundaries:** Turkmenistan to NW, Tajikistan to N, China to NE, Pakistan to E and S, Iran to W. **Total area:** 251,827 sq. mi. (652,230 sq km). **Coastline:** none. **Comparative area:** slightly smaller than Texas. **Land use:** 12% arable land; negl. % permanent crops; 88% other. **Major cities:** Kabul (capital), Qandahar; Herat Mazar-i-Sharif; Jalalabad.

• **PEOPLE   Population:** 29,121,286 (July 2010 est.). **Nationality:** noun—Afghan(s); adjective—Afghan. **Ethnic groups:** 42% Pashtun, 27% Tajik, 9% Hazara, 9% Uzbek. **Languages:** 50% Afghan Persian (Dari), 35% Pashtu, 11% Turkic langs. (primarily Uzbek and Turkmen), 4% minor langs. (30, primarily Balochi and Pashai); much bilingualism. **Religions:** 80% Sunni Muslim, 19% Shi'a Muslim, 1% other.

GOVERNMENT   Type: Islamic Republic. **Independence:** Aug. 19, 1919 (from U.K.). **Constitution:** new constitution drafted 14 December 2003, signed 16 January 2004, ratified 26 January 2004. **National holiday:** Independence Day, Aug.19. **Heads of government:** Hamid• Karzai, president (since December 2004).

• **ECONOMY   Monetary unit:** afghani. **Budget:** (FY 09/10 est.) *income:* 1 bil.; *expend.:* 3.3 bil. note—Afghanistan has also recieved $2.6 bil. from the Reconstruction Trust Fund and $63 mil. from the Law and Order Trust Fund

G.D.P.: $23.35 bil., $800 per capita (2009 est.). **Chief crops:** wheat, opium, fruits, nuts, karakul pelts; wool, mutton. **Natural resources:** natural gas, crude oil, coal, copper, talc. **Major industries:** small-scale production of textiles, soap, furniture, shoes, fertilizer, and cement; hand-woven carpets; natural gas, coal, and copper. **Labor force:** 15 million (2004 est) 78% agriculture and animal husbandry, 16% services, 6% industry (FY 08/09 est.). **Exports:** $547 mil. (2009); opium, fruits and nuts, hand-woven carpets, wool, and cotton. **Imports:** $5.3 bil. (2008); food supplies, petroleum products. **Major trading partners:** (2008) *exports:* 23.5% India, 17.7% Pakistan, 16.5% U.S., 12.8% Tajikistan., 6.9% Netherlands; *imports:* 36% Pakistan, 9.3% U.S., 7.5% Germany, 6.9% India.

Mountainous and landlocked, Afghanistan has been a crossroads of trans-Asian trade and con-

quest since antiquity. A part of the Persian Empire, Bactria was conquered by Alexander the Great, and became independent in the third century B.C. before falling to the Parthians in the next century. In the seventh century A.D., a flourishing Buddhist civilization there fell to Islamic conquests. Genghis Khan overthrew the 11th-century empire of Mahmud of Gazni in the early 13th century, and Afghanistan was the center of Tamerlane's empire in the late 14th century. Thereafter, the region was divided among various tribes and petty kingdoms.

Modern Afghan history began with the establishment of a united emirate by Ahmed Shah Durrani in 1747. In the 19th century, Russia and Great Britain contested domination of Afghanistan. The British Afghan Wars of 1838–42 and 1878–80 left Afghanistan unconquered but within Britain's sphere of influence. Afghanistan achieved full independence from Britain in 1919 under Amanullah Khan, who proclaimed himself king in 1926. Modern reforms were instituted by Amanullah and his successors Mohammed Nadir Shah (1929–33) and Mohammed Zahir Shah (1933–73).

The monarchy fell to a military coup in 1973, and Mohammed Daud Khan established a republic. In 1978 pro-Soviet leftists seized power and, ostensibly at the government's invitation, Soviet troops invaded Afghanistan in Dec. 1979 to put down widespread revolts against Communist rule. In the ensuing civil war, the government's forces and their Soviet allies (with an eventual troop strength of more than 100,000) controlled the cities and main transportation routes but guerrilla forces contested the countryside. In 1988 the Soviet Union began a withdrawal of its troops, completed by February 1989. The rebel factions failed to achieve a united front and the pro-Soviet government held on until Apr. 15, 1992, and rebel troops entered Kabul. A respected religious leader, Sibghatullah Mujaddidi, was named interim president with the backing of a coalition but Gulbaddin Hekmatyar, leader of the fundamentalist Hizbe Islami faction, declined to join, and fighting broke out around Kabul.

On June 28 Mujaddidi turned over his power to the Leadership Council, which then elected Burhanuddin Rabbani as president. Fighting for control of Kabul continued between forces loyal to the Rabbani government and those backing Hekmatyar. Other factions later joined the fighting, and Kabul was subjected to continual rocket attacks in late 1992 and into the spring of 1993. Hekmatyar was named prime minister in an attempt to make peace. Fighting broke out again in early 1994 with Rabbani's followers getting the upper hand after fierce battles in Kabul.

By early 1995, the U.N. had brokered a scheme uniting the nine major factions in a council to which Rabbani would turn over power. But it was quickly undone by the emergence of a fundamentalist Islamic militia called the Taliban, 20,000 strong and composed of students from the Islamic schools. Taliban forces took over most of the country and established a fundamentalist regime based on Islamic law. In Oct. 1996 three remaining groups of opposition forces formed a loose Northern Alliance, but by 1999 the Taliban controlled over 90 percent of Afghanistan's territory.

The Taliban began to enforce a strict Muslim code of behavior. In 2001, the U.N. reported a drop in opium poppies grown in Afghanistan (producer of 75 percent of the world's opium). A second ban, in Feb. 2001, on all statues in the country led to the destruction in March of 1,400-year-old Buddhist cliff carvings in the region of Bamiyan, despite world protest. In Sept. 2001 the U.S. demanded the Taliban turn over the terrorist leaders suspected of plotting the attack on the World Trade Center.

The Anglo-American air strikes that began Oct. 7 led to the fall (Nov. 13) of Kabul to the Northern Alliance. The interim government under Hamid Karzai organized a Grand Council of about 1,600 members which elected Karzai to lead a transitional government until elections in 2004. In Aug. 2003, NATO forces took command of the international peacekeepers. In Jan. 2004 the National Assembly approved a new constitution but renewed attacks by the Taliban made elections impossible until Oct. 2004 when Karzai won over 15 other candidates. Ever-increasing violence continued throughout 2005–06 so that the U.S. asked NATO to take over the fight in the south. By 2007 nearly 50,000 NATO troops were fighting the Taliban resurgence with modest success. In 2009 President Obama sent 30,000 more U.S. troops and in August national elections were held amidst sporadic Taliban attacks. Karzai won easily again, but serious allegations of fraud were rampant.

▶ ALBANIA
Republic of Albania
• **GEOGRAPHY Location:** southeastern Europe. **Boundaries:** Yugoslavia to N, Macedonia to E, Greece to S, and Adriatic and Ionian Seas (parts of Mediterranean Sea) to W. **Total area:** 11,100 sq. mi. (28,750 sq km). **Coastline:** 225 mi. (362 km). **Comparative area:** slightly smaller than Maryland. **Land use:** 21% arable land; 4% permanent crops; 75% other. **Major cities:** Tiranë (Tirana; capital); Durrës (Durazzo); Elbasan; Shkodër (Scutari); Vlorë (Vlonë or Valona).

PEOPLE Population: 3,659,616 (July 2010 est.). **Nationality:** noun—Albanian(s); adjective—Albanian. **Ethnic groups:** 95% Albanian, 3% Greek, 2% Vlach, Gypsy, Serb, and Bulgarian. **Languages:** Albanian (Tosk is official dialect), Greek, Vlach, Romani, Slavic dialects. **Religions:** 70% Muslim, 20% Albanian Orthodox, 10% Roman Catholic (all churches and mosques were closed in 1967 and religious observances prohibited; in November 1990, Albania began allowing private religious practice).

GOVERNMENT Type: republic. **Independence:** Nov. 28, 1912 (from Ottoman Empire). **Constitution:** Nov. 28, 1998. **National holiday:** Independence Day, Nov. 28. **Heads of Government:** Bamir Topi, president (since July 2007); Sali Berisha, prime minister (since Aug. 2005). **Structure:** executive—president, prime minister, Council of Ministers; legislative—unicameral People's Assembly; judicial—Supreme Court.

ECONOMY Monetary unit: lek. **Budget:** (2009 est.) *income:* $3.46 bil.; *expend.:* $4.099 bil. **G.D.P.:** $22.9 bil., $6,300 per capita (2009 est.). **Chief crops:** vegetables, wheat, potatoes, fruits, sugar beets, corn. **Natural resources:** crude oil, natural gas, coal, chromium, copper. **Major industries:** food processing, textiles and clothing, lumber. **Labor force:** 1.103 mil. (2009 est); 58% agriculture,

15% industry, 27% services.(2006 est) **Exports:** $1.194 bil. (2009 est.); textiles, footwear, asphalt, metals and ores, electricity, crude oil, vegetables, fruits, tobacco. **Imports:** $3.602 bil. (2009 est.); machinery, consumer goods, grains. **Major trading partners:** (2008) *exports:* 55.9% Italy, 11.6% Greece, 7.2% China; *imports:* 32.1% Italy, 13.1% Greece, 7.2% Turkey, 6.6% Germany.

The city of Epidamnus (Durrës) was colonized by Greeks from Corinth and Corcyra in 625 B.C. Later the Roman province of Illyricum, Albania was a much-coveted area after the fall of Rome and was in turn ruled by Byzantines, Normans, Venetians, Slavs, and the kings of Naples. Under the leadership of Skanderbeg (1405–68), Albania repelled repeated Turkish invasions. But Albania was part of the Ottoman Empire from 1478 until 1912. Ottoman rule succeeded in converting most of the populace to Islam (with Catholic minorities in the north and Greek Orthodox in the south) but did not destroy the Albanian sense of national identity, based on ties of tribe, clan, and family.

Independence came in 1912 as a result of the First Balkan War, when Austria-Hungary and Italy sponsored the creation of an Albanian state. Albania emerged from the war in a state of near-anarchy. With Yugoslav support, Ahmed Zogu became president of the republic in 1924 and proclaimed himself King Zog I in 1928.

In 1939 Italy invaded and annexed Albania. During World War II, partisan resistance was dominated by Communist forces under the leadership of Enver Hoxha. In 1944 Hoxha seized control of the government. A socialist republic was established in 1946: foreigners were expelled and their assets nationalized; churches were closed; agriculture and industry were collectivized. Albania under Hoxha became one of the world's most thoroughly totalitarian states.

A doctrinaire Stalinist, Hoxha broke with Khruschev's Soviet Union in 1961 and Albania became a client state of China. But with liberalization in China after 1977, Hoxha broke that link as well. Albania became almost totally isolated from world affairs.

Hoxha died in 1985 and was succeeded as president and first secretary of the Albanian Communist party by Ramiz Alia. In 1990, Alia eased restrictions on religion, tourism, and foreign investment, and allowed the formation of an opposition Democratic party. He scheduled elections to the National Assembly for 1991, before awareness had spread of the old regime's faltering power. The Communists carried the rural districts and formed a coalition government with the Democrats, who carried the cities.

In 1992, the Democrats completed the rout of the Communists, winning 92 of the 140 seats in the Assembly, and replacing Alia with Sali Berisha, a heart surgeon. But by the end of the year, factions within the Democratic party were already complaining about Pres. Berisha's "autocratic rule." Meanwhile, anarchy plagued much of the country, with food riots in the cities and armed brigandage in the countryside. E.C. and U.N. grants helped pay for needed imports and Italy provided invaluable assistance to the Albanian police forces. By 1993, zones of law and order were being established, churches were reopening, and 90 percent of farming had been privatized. But in November 1994, voters rejected (54–42) a new constitution proposed by Pres. Berisha.

In 1996 Berisha's Democratic Party won a major electoral victory amidst complaints of fraud, but he and his followers were driven from office in 1997 after a series of pryamid schemes collapsed ruining the finances of tens of thousands of families. Violence and looting occured in many areas and a multi-national force of 7,000 was sent in to help restore order. The Socialists (formerly Communists) returned to power under Fatos Nano. In the spring of 1998, NATO advisors began to train Albania's tiny army as ethnic Albanians in the Kosovo province of Yugoslavia began a violent rebellion. Yugoslavia's suppression of the rebellion drove thousands of ethnic Albanians out of Kosovo into Albania. Amidst this further tumult, internal struggles continued between supporters of the Democratic Party and the Socialists, erupting into serious violence in Sept. 1998. Though Nano resigned as prime minister in late 1998, he returned in 2002 and the economy improved despite widespread corruption. In July 2005, in Albania's first free election, Berisha's Democrats won a small majority but could not take power until protests over election fraud ceased in late August.

▶ ALGERIA
People's Democratic Republic of Algeria
● **GEOGRAPHY Location:** northern coast of Africa. **Boundaries:** Mediterranean Sea to N, Tunisia and Libya to E, Mali and Niger to S, Morocco, Western Sahara, Mauritania to W. **Total area:** 919,595 sq. mi. (2,381,741 sq km). **Coastline:** 620 mi. (998 km). **Comparative area:** slightly less than 3.5 times size of Texas. **Land use:** 3% arable land; negl. % permanent crops; 97% other. **Major cities:** Algiers (capital); Oran; Constantine; Annaba; Blida.
● **PEOPLE Population:** 34,586,184 (July 2010 est.). **Nationality:** noun—Algerian(s); adjective— Algerian. **Ethnic groups:** 99% Arab-Berber, less than 1% European. **Languages:** Arabic (official), French, Berber dialects. **Religions:** 99% Sunni Muslim (state religion), 1% Christian and Jewish.
● **GOVERNMENT Type:** republic. **Independence:** July 5, 1962 (from France). **Constitution:** Nov. 19, 1976, effective Nov. 22, 1976, most recently revised 12 Nov 2008 **National holiday:** Revolution Day, Nov. 1. **Heads of Government:** Abdelaziz Bouteflika, head of state (since Apr. 1999). note— a November 2008 constitutional amendment seperated the position of head of government from that of the prime minister. **Structure:** executive; bicameral legislature; judicial— Supreme Court.
● **ECONOMY Monetary unit:** Algerian dinar. **Budget:** (2009 est.) *income:* $56.24 bil.; *expend.:* $61.34 bil. **G.D.P.:** $239.6 bil., $7,000 per capita (2009 est.). **Chief crops:** wheat, barley, oats, grapes, olives. **Natural resources:** crude oil, natural gas, iron ore, phosphates, uranium. **Major industries:** petroleum, light industries, natural gas, mining. **Labor force:** 9.612 mil. (2009 est.); 32% government, 14% agriculture, 13.4% industry, 10% construction and public works (2003 est.). **Exports:** $52.03 bil. (2009 est.); petroleum and natural gas. **Imports:** $39.51 bil. (2009 est.); capital goods, food, beverages, consumer goods. **Major trading partners:** (2008) *exports:* 23.9% U.S., 15.5% Italy, 11.4% Spain. *imports:* 16.5% France, 11% Italy, 10.3% China, 7.4% Spain.

From around 3000 B.C. nomadic ancestors of the Berbers inhabited Algeria, as the expanding Sahara desert displaced prehistoric grasslands and forests. The Phoenicians established trading centers in the Mediterranean coastal plain around 1200 B.C. Those centers were taken over by the Romans beginning around 200 B.C. With Roman support the Berber chief Masinissa formed the kingdom of Numidia in what is now northern Algeria. From 46 B.C. to about A.D. 640, the area was controlled successively by the Romans, Germanic Vandal tribes, and the Byzantine Empire.

In the eighth century A.D., the Islamic conquests spread Arab culture to Numidia. Most of the Berbers converted to Islam. The blend of Berber and Arab culture in Algeria gave rise to a flourishing and rich Islamic civilization in the coastal plain, while Tuareg and other nomadic peoples controlled the sparsely inhabited interior.

Around 1500 the Christian kingdom of Spain captured Algiers and other coastal cities. In 1518 Barbarossa, a Turkish sea captain, seized Algiers and drove the Spanish out. In so doing, he joined Algeria to the expanding Turkish Ottoman Empire. Piracy became a key source of income for the Ottoman cities of Algeria. In the early 1800s, France, along with England and the U.S., began military operations to suppress piracy in the Mediterranean. In 1830 France invaded Algeria, putting an end to Ottoman rule and establishing their own administration. Algeria was ruled as part of France itself. Many French settlers (*colons*) migrated to Algeria. Both they and the native Algerians were considered citizens of France, but the colons were granted substantial political and economic advantages over the indigenous population.

In 1847 a rebellion led by Abd-al-Qadir, a powerful Muslim leader, was suppressed by the French. In 1848, all of Algeria was conquered by the French and legally confirmed as part of France. During World War II, many Algerians joined the Free French, hoping that their display of loyalty would be rewarded with greater self-rule after the war. Those hopes were disappointed, as French administration was resumed in 1945.

In 1954 the Front de Liberation Nationale (FLN) began a guerrilla war against the French in Algeria. They were opposed by French police and military forces and by the Secret Army Organization (OAS), an underground movement of colons who favored continued French rule. In 1958, French president Charles de Gaulle established a policy designed to prepare Algeria for self-rule.

Algerian independence was proclaimed on July 3, 1962; a million colons fled to France. A power struggle within the new Algerian government was resolved when Ahmed Ben Bella became the country's first premier in 1963. In 1965 Ben Bella was deposed by Col. Houari Boumidienne, who ruled as the head of a military government. In 1967 Algeria declared war on Israel, broke with the West, and established close relations with the U.S.S.R. Since the early 1970s, relations with the West, and particularly with France, have improved (mainly because of oil).

The first free, multiparty elections were held on June 12, 1990. The Islamic Salvation Front, which advocates turning Algeria into an Islamic Republic, won overwhelming control of local assemblies. In 1991 it won 188 seats in Parliament out of 231 up for election and seemed poised to win control of the government when the army interceded to keep the old power structure in place. On June 19, 1992, Pres. Mohammed Boudiaf was assassinated, presumably by Islamic fundamentalists.

The military's High Security Council, knowing the Islamic parties would win any free election, postponed a return to democracy. In January 1994 the High Security Council replaced the collective presidency of the High State Council with Gen. Liamine Zeroual. November 1995 saw the first contested presidential election since 1962, with Gen. Zeroual winning over 60 percent of the vote as major opposition groups boycotted the election. Elections in June 1997 produced Algeria's first mutli-party parliament since 1962, but the ruling military council still remained in control and in August Islamic fundamentalists killed over 300 in one night of terror. These vicious assasinations continued into 1998 with hundreds more killed over several nights. Civil strife and assassinations claimed the lives of over 40,000. In Sept. 1998 Gen. Zeroual announced that elections would be held in Feb. 1999 and he would not be a candidate.

By the time the elections were held in April, all candidates had withdrawn from the race save one, the army-backed Abdelaziz Bouteflika. His new government reached an accord with the rebel Islamic Salvation Front: in return for the end of the uprising, Pres. Bouteflika pledged to release thousands of militant Islamic prisoners on July 5, Algeria's national holiday, and to submit the peace agreement to a referendum. In Sept., 98 percent of voters favored the agreement that gave amnesty to militants who surrendered. When the amnesty period ended (Jan. 2000), the government claimed that 80 percent of the rebels had surrendered then commenced a major army offensive against remaining rebels, now organized as the "Armed Islamic Group" (GIA). While the GIA remained unconquered into 2002, the government was mending fences with the Berber people (who constitute about one third of Algeria's population), recognizing their Tamazight language as a legal language. The FLN won 199 seats in the 389-seat National Assembly and in April 2004, Pres. Bouteflika became Algeria's first democratically reelected president, winning a suspiciously large (84 percent) share of the vote.

Two powerful terrorist attacks in April, 2007, were attributed to a wing of Al Qaeda that wishes to establish an Islamic theocracy, and which has threatened to attack inside France as well. Bouteflika was elected again in 2009 after amending the constitutional limit of two terms.

▶ ANDORRA
Principality of Andorra
• GEOGRAPHY Location: Pyrenees Mountains, southwestern Europe. Boundaries: France to N and E, Spain to S and W. Total area: 174 sq. mi. (468 sq km). Coastline: none. Comparative area: 2.5 times size of Washington, D.C. Land use: 2% arable land; 0% permanent crops; 98% other. Major cities: Andorra la Vella (capital).
• PEOPLE Population: 84,525 (July 2010 est.). Nationality: noun—Andorran(s); adjective—Andorran. Ethnic groups: 43% Spanish, 33% Andorran, 11% Portuguese, 7% French, 6% other. Languages: Catalan (official); many also speak some French and Castilian. Religions: virtually all Roman Catholic.
• GOVERNMENT Type: parliamentary democracy (since March 1993) that retains as head of state a co-principality; the two princes are the president of France and Spanish bishop of Seo de Urgel, who are represented locally by officials called

veguers. Independence: 1278. Constitution: drafted in 1991, approved in March 1993, effective 28 April 1993. National holiday: Mare de Deu de Meritxell, Sept. 8. Heads of Government: French co-prince Nicolas Sarkozy, president of France (since 2007) represented by Christian Fremont(since September 2008) and Spanish co-prince Episcopal Msgr. Joan Enric Vives Sicília (since May 2003) represented by Nemesi Marques Oste (since July 2003); Executive Council President Jaume Bartumeu Cassany (since June 2009) Structure: executive—co-princes, executive council; unicameral legislature; judiciary—Supreme Court at Perpignan, France.
• ECONOMY Monetary unit: euro. Budget: (2008) income: $531.6 mil.; expend.: $531.6 mil. G.D.P.: $4.22 bil., $42,220 per capita (2008 est.). Chief crops: sheep raising; small quantities of tobacco, rye, wheat, barley, oats, and vegetables. Natural resources: hydropower, mineral water, timber, iron ore, lead. Major industries: tourism (particularly skiing), cattle raising, timber, tobacco, banking. Labor force: 42,220. (2008 est.). Exports: $89.5 mil. (2008); tobacco products, furniture. Imports: $1.801 bil. (2008). Major trading partners: (2006) exports: 17% France, 59.5% Spain; imports: 21.1% France, 53.2% Spain.

Set high in the Pyrenees, the tiny state of Andorra has been both a medieval relic and a modern capitalist land. Since 1278 Andorra has owed feudal allegiance to two co-rulers, the bishop of Seo de Urgel in Spain and, now, the president of France. Until 1993, Andorra had no constitution, so the exact rights of the corulers remained vague. Foreign affairs were handled by France.

Andorra's traditional economic mainstay had been the "transshipment of goods" (i.e., smuggling) between France and Spain. Andorra attracts tourists drawn by bargain shopping, and it is a banking center. Spain's 1986 entry into the E.U. led Andorra to seek a customs union with the E.U. The March 1990 treaty was Andorra's first in over 700 years. In the same year, the co-princes introduced Andorra's first penal code and a sales tax, soon followed by the adoption of the E.U.'s external tariff. In March 1993 voters—of whom there are only 9,123—adopted a modern constitution that will reduce the power of the co-princes and establish a government of three branches that will have authority to tax and to make foreign policy. In 1997 Premier Molne's party won a majority of seats in the General Council ending the coalition government. Jaume Bartemeu Cassany, a founder of the Social Democratic Party, was elected prime minister in 2009.

▶ ANGOLA
Republic of Angola
• GEOGRAPHY Location: southwestern Africa. Boundaries: Zaire to N and NE, Zambia to E, Namibia to S, South Atlantic Ocean to W; Cabinda district separated from rest of country by Congo to N, Zaire to S. Total area: 481,354 sq. mi. (1,246,700 sq km). Coastline: 994 mi. (1,600 km). Comparative area: slightly less than twice size of Texas. Land use: 2% arable land; negl. % permanent crops; 97% other. Major cities: Luanda (capital); Huambo (Nova Lisboa); Lobito; Benguela; Lubango (São da Bandeira).
• PEOPLE Population: 13,068,161 (July 2010 est.). Nationality: noun—Angolan(s); adjective—Angolan. Ethnic groups: 37% Ovimbundu, 25% Kimbundu, 13% Bakongo, 2% Mestiço, 1% European, 22% other. Languages: Portuguese

(official), Bantu and other African languages. **Religions:** 47% indigenous beliefs, 38% Roman Catholic, 15% Protestant.
• **Government Type:** republic, multiparty presidential regime. **Independence:** Nov. 11, 1975 (from Portugal). **Constitution:** Adopted by the People's Assembly August 25, 1992. **National holiday:** Independence Day, Nov. 11. **Heads of Government:** José Eduardo dos Santos, president (since Sept. 1979). Antonio Paulo Kassoma, prime minister (Sept. 2008) **Structure:** executive; unicameral legislature; judiciary.
• **Economy Monetary unit:** kwanza. **Budget:** (2009 est.) *income:* $30.82 bil.; *expend.:* $27.91 bil. **G.D.P.:** $114.4 bil., $8,900 per capita (2009 est.). **Chief crops:** bananas, sugarcane, coffee, sisal, corn, cotton, *manioc* (tapioca), vegetables. **Natural resources:** petroleum, diamonds, iron ore, phosphates, copper. **Major industries:** petroleum, mining (diamonds, iron ore, phosphates), food processing. **Labor force:** 7.769 mil. (2009 est.); 85% agriculture, 15% industry and services (2003 est). **Exports:** $40.02 bil. (2009 est.); oil, diamonds, petroleum products, gas, coffee. **Imports:** $12.81 bil. (2009 est.); machinery, electrical equipment, vehicles and spare parts, medicines, food, textiles; substantial military deliveries. **Major trading partners:** (2008) *exports:* 32.9% China, 28.7% U.S., 6% France; *imports:* 17.1% Portugal, 15.2% China, 11% U.S., 10.2% Brazil.

Bantu peoples have occupied Angola for 2,000 years. Portuguese explorers searching for a sea route to India founded Luanda (1575) and Benguela (1617). Portugal, in alliance with the Angolan kingdom of Bakongo, engaged in an extensive trade of slaves to Brazil—3 million in 300 years.

In the late 19th century, Angola was organized as a Portuguese colony, sometimes called Portuguese West Africa. Portuguese settlers dominated local government, and trade, organized plantation-style cultivation of cotton, palm oil, bananas, and coffee. A railroad was built to transport exports of metal from the Katanga region of the Belgian Congo (now Zaire) to the coast.

By the 1950s non-Portuguese Angolans began to agitate for independence. The National Front spearheaded the liberation movement. Guerrilla warfare began in 1961, with several feuding factions fighting the Portuguese. Following the Portuguese revolution of 1974, factional warfare intensified and most Portuguese settlers fled the country. Independence came on Nov. 11, 1975.

Civil war between the National Front, the Popular Movement for the Liberation of Angola (MPLA), and the National Union for the Total Independence of Angola (UNITA) led, in 1976, to the victory of the MPLA, which organized a Marxist state with Soviet backing and Cuban technical support including 37,000 soldiers. Large portions of the country remained in the hands of UNITA, which continued the civil war with Chinese and American support.

Direct clashes between Angolan and South African troops occurred during the 1980s, as Angola gave shelter to SWAPO guerrilla forces seeking independence for Namibia. Cuban troops withdrew from Angola in 1991, and a cease-fire between the government and UNITA was also concluded. While agreeing to recognize the dos

Santos government, UNITA called for elections to be held by Sept. 1992, Angola's first since 1975.

In the elections, MPLA's candidate, José Eduardo dos Santos, decisively defeated UNITA's leader, Jonas Savimbi, but Savimbi's refusal to honor the results led to renewed fighting. The presence of thousands of U.N. peacekeepers from Feb. 1994 until Feb. 1999 made little dent in the continuing struggle which claimed an estimated 100,000 lives. The government succeeded, in 2000, in taking two diamond-mining provinces as well as the town of Cazombo from UNITA, capping the year with an offer of amnesty. But it was not until after Savimbi's death in a gun battle in Feb. 2002 that UNITA could be brought to sign a cease-fire in April. After 27 years of civil war, with one million or more killed and four million displaced, peace finally took hold. Pres. dos Santos pledged elections but they were delayed until Sept. 2008 when the governing party, MPLA, won a landslide victory in a peaceful way. Angola has joined Nigeria as Africa's leading oil producer.

▶ANTIGUA AND BARBUDA

• **Geography Location:** eastern Caribbean Sea approximately 300 mi. (480 km) SE of Puerto Rico. Antigua 17°06'N, 61°50'W; Barbuda 17°38'N, 61°48'W. **Boundaries:** Atlantic Ocean to N and E, Caribbean Sea to S and W. **Total area:** 171 sq. mi. (442 sq km). **Coastline:** 95 mi. (153 km). **Comparative area:** 2.5 times size of Washington, D.C. **Land use:** 18% arable land; 4.55% permanent crops; 77% other. **Major cities:** St. John's (capital).
• **People Population:** 86,754 (July 2010 est.). **Nationality:** noun—Antiguan(s), Barbudan(s); adjective—Antiguan, Barbudan. **Ethnic groups:** almost entirely of black African origin; some of British, Portuguese, Lebanese, and Syrian origin. **Languages:** English (official), local dialects. **Religions:** Anglican (predominant), other Protestant sects, some Roman Catholic.
• **Government Type:** constitutional monarchy with U.K.-style parliament. **Independence:** Nov. 1, 1981 (from U.K.). **Constitution:** Nov. 1, 1981. **National holiday:** Independence Day, Nov. 1. **Heads of Government:** Louisse Lake-Tack, governor-general (since July 2007); Winston Baldwin Spencer, prime minister (since Mar. 2004). **Structure:** executive—governor general, prime minister, and cabinet; bicameral legislature; judiciary—East Caribbean Supreme Court.
• **Economy Monetary unit:** East Caribbean dollar. **Budget:** (2009 est.) *income:* $229.5 mil.; *expend.:* $293.4 mil. **G.D.P.:** $1.55 bil., $18,100 per capita (2009 est.). **Chief crops:** cotton, fruits and vegetables, sugar. **Natural resources:** negl.; pleasant climate fosters tourism. **Major industries:** tourism, construction, light manufacturing (clothing, alcohol, household appliances). **Labor force:** 30,000 (1991); 82% services, 7% agriculture; 11% unemployment (2001 est.). **Exports:** $84.3 mil. (2007); petroleum products, manufactures, machinery and transportation equipment, food and live animals. **Imports:** $522.8 mil. (2007); food and live animals, machinery and transport equipment, manufactures, chemicals, oil. **Major trading partners:** (2006) *exports:* 34% Spain, 21% Germany, 8% Italy, 6% Singapore; *imports:* 21% U.S., 16% China, 13% Germany, 13% Singapore, 6% Spain.

Columbus visited and claimed Antigua for Spain in 1493. It was settled by the British in 1632, who grew tobacco, and later sugar. The island's economy was hobbled by abolition of slavery in 1834, a succession of natural disasters in the 1840s, and the closing of the Royal Dockyard in 1854. Today, tourism is a mainstay of the economy, fostered by the ruling Antigua Labor Party, which won its sixth consecutive parliamentary victory in March 1999. But its second economic mainstay, offshore banking, has been shaken by a U.S. Treasury warning in April 1999 that lax standards make it susceptible to money laundering. In March 2004 the 10-year government of Lester Bird fell to the United Progressive Party.

▶ ARGENTINA
Argentine Republic
• **GEOGRAPHY** **Location:** southern South America. **Boundaries:** Bolivia, Paraguay, Brazil to N.; Uruguay, South Atlantic Ocean to E.; Chile to W. **Total area:** 1,073,518 sq. mi. (2,780,400 sq km) (figures exclude Falkland Islands and Antarctic territory claimed by Argentina). **Coastline:** 3,099 mi. (4,989 km). **Comparative area:** slightly less than three-tenths the size of the United States. **Land use:** 10% arable land; 1% permanent crops; 89% other. **Major cities:** Buenos Aires (capital); Córdoba; La Matanza; Rosario; Morón.
• **PEOPLE** **Population:** 41,343,201 (July 2010 est.). **Nationality:** noun—Argentine(s); adjective— Argentine. **Ethnic groups:** 97% white, 3% mestizo, Indian, and other nonwhite groups. **Languages:** Spanish (official), English, Italian, German, French. **Religions:** 92% Roman Catholic (less than 20% practicing), 2% Protestant, 2% Jewish, 4% other.
• **GOVERNMENT** **Type:** republic. **Independence:** July 9, 1816 (from Spain). **Constitution:** May 1, 1853 (revised Aug. 1994). **National holiday:** Revolution Day, May 25. **Head of Government:** Cristina Fernandez De Kirchner, president (since Dec. 2007). **Structure:** executive; bicameral legislature; judiciary.
• **ECONOMY** **Monetary unit:** argentine peso. **Budget:** (2009 est.) *income:* $84.3 bil.; *expend.:* $86.2 bil. **G.D.P.:** $558 bil., $13,800 per capita (2008 est.) note—data are based on private estimates; official figures lack credibility. **Chief crops:** wheat, corn, soybeans. **Natural resources:** fertile plains of the pampas, lead, zinc, tin, copper, iron ore, petroleum. **Major industries:** food processing (especially meat packing), motor vehicles, consumer durables. **Labor force:** 16.54 mil. *note*—urban areas only (2008 est.); 72% services, 23% industry, 5% agriculture; (2009 est.). **Exports:** $55.7 bil. (2009 est.); edible oils, cereals, feed, motor vehicles. **Imports:** $38.71 bil. (2009 est.); motor vehicles and parts, chemicals, plastics. **Major trading partners:** (2008) *exports:* 18.9% Brazil, 9.1% China, 7.9% U.S., 6.7% Chile; *imports:* 31.3% Brazil, 12.4% China, 12.2% U.S., 4.4% Germany.

The indigenous nomads of the area around the river La Plata resisted Spanish intrusion, which began with the first founding of Buenos Aires by Pedro de Mendoza in 1536. Argentina was part of Spain's Viceroyalty of Peru until reforms in the Bourbon dynasty and a need to defend against Portuguese encroachment from Brazil led to the formation of the Viceroyalty of La Plata, including Argentina, Bolivia, Paraguay, and Uruguay, in 1776. Following the relaxation of trade restrictions two years later, Buenos Aires grew from a small town to a city of 50,000 by 1800. A provisional junta of the Provinces of Río de la Plata was estab-

lished in 1810 after the Napoleonic occupation of Spain, and in 1816 the United Provinces of the Río de la Plata declared their independence.

After independence the question of political relations among the United Provinces was settled by a federalist solution in which the provinces dissolved into a number of practically independent republics. In 1824, a constituent assembly created the office of president, first held by Bernardino Rivadavia. However, the failure to ratify a workable constitution caused Rivadavia to resign.

Juan Manuel de Rosas became governor of Buenos Aires in 1829 and presided over the construction of a federal agreement between the provinces in 1831. Rosas governed Buenos Aires with an iron hand until his expulsion in 1852. The other provinces formed the Argentine Federation, based on a federal constitution of 1853, but Buenos Aires refused to join. Buenos Aires and the Argentine Federation entered into war (1859–61) but reached an agreement on the inclusion of Buenos Aires in the Argentine Republic in 1862.

Argentina joined Brazil and Uruguay in a war (1865–70) against Paraguay. During the latter part of the 1870s, the government took the initiative against the indigenous populations of Patagonia and Tierra del Fuego, which were partitioned with Chile. Immigration from Europe, especially Spain and Italy, resulted in enormous growth. In 1869, there were 2 million inhabitants; by 1914, 8 million; by 1955, 19 million; and by 1990, 32 million.

The Argentine military, led by Lt. Gen. José F. Uriburu, ousted the civilian government of the Radical party in 1930 with the intention of following the European model of politics. In 1946 Juan Domingo Perón won the presidential election and constructed a populist political alliance that included workers, industrialists, and the armed forces. The Perón-inspired populist ideology of *justicialismo* included extension of the franchise to women and redistribution of income to workers and the poor. Perón's charismatic wife, Eva, led the effort to distribute goods to the poor.

Tied in with Perón's populist strategy was his policy of nationalist economic development, whereby state-led development was financed by capital from the old export-agricultural elite. The Perón government incurred great expense to gain control over foreign-owned economic infrastructure, including railway systems, telephone companies, and dock facilities. A number of events led to Perón's downfall in 1955. The market for Argentine goods had deteriorated and Perón shifted his strategy to encourage foreign investment and impose economic austerity, repression against the political opposition grew. The death of Eva Perón in 1952 robbed Perón of an important political resource, and when the government challenged the Catholic church on a number of issues, the military ousted Perón.

After a brief period of military rule, Arturo Frondizi of the "Intransigent" faction of the Radical party won the presidency in 1958. The military repeatedly attempted to keep the Perónistas from returning to power. In 1962 the military forced Frondizi to annul Perónist victories in provincial elections and removed him from office. Pres. Arturo Illia was ousted from office in 1966.

A military regime led by a series of Argentine officers was established during 1966–73. Extreme violence by factions on the Left and Right led the military to accept Perón's return in 1973. Perón died in 1974, and his third wife, Isabel, replaced him but the military removed her in 1976 in the midst of economic and political upheaval.

Determined to deal with what they saw as a leftist threat, the armed forces launched what was later called the "dirty war," during which up to 20,000 people disappeared and were never heard from again. The authoritarian government collapsed after the 1982 Falkland/Malvinas Islands War against Britain led to the resignation of the junta and the holding of elections. Raúl Alfonsín, of the Radical Union party, was elected president in 1983. In 1989, he was succeeded by Carlos Saúl Menem, who agreed to take office early, in the midst of an economic crisis during which inflation reached 3,000 percent and foreign debt $58 billion.

Menem encouraged free enterprise and good relations with the U.S. Government controls on foreign investment and trade were relaxed, and the government sold off many state enterprises. In 1993 Argentina's 11-year debt crisis officially ended, and by 1995 inflation was down to 4 percent. As Argentina's economy began to flourish, Menem was reelected, and his party won majorities in both houses of the legislature and control of half of Argentina's provincial governments.

But in May 1997, violent protests erupted in several major cities, as unemployment rose to nearly 20 percent. The Perónistas lost control of the Chamber of Deputies, for the first time since 1983, to a left-wing coalition known as The Alliance. Presidential elections in 1999 brought the first-ever Perónista defeat, as Alliance's Fernando de la Rúa defeated Eduardo Duhalde.

Throughout 2000, the rather fragile Alliance managed to fight corruption, to reform organized labor, and to balance the federal and state budgets. This was sufficient to gain a pledge from the I.M.F. and other international lenders for a $40 billion bailout, but by the middle of 2001 the recession had grown worse and the government put a severe austerity plan in place. Strikes and rioting at last drove de la Rua to resign in December, and his successor resigned after only a week. A second interim president, but with a two-year term, was chosen by Parliament: Senator Duhalde. His decoupling of the peso from the dollar and its subsequent devaluation brought some relief but no solution.Only a January 2003 roll-over by the I.M.F. prevented a third major default.

In the 2003 presidential election Menem withdrew from the run-off, leaving the presidency to Duhalde's protege, Nestor Kirchner, who presided over the largest default in I.M.F. history. But he was able to negotiate a refinancing of $21 bil. of debt with the I.M.F. and inflation fell quickly and G.D.P. grew for the first time in four years. Over the next two years the economy grew rapidly and inflation fell to 5 percent. By 2007, a full recovery seemed in full swing with unemployment at 10 percent and annual growth at 9 percent. Kirchner's wife, Cristina, was the surprise Peronist candidate for president and in 2007 won an overwhelming majority. But economic setbacks soon ended the Kirchners' appeal and by 2009 their support had declined precipitously.

▶ **ARMENIA**
Republic of Armenia
● **GEOGRAPHY   Location:** southwest Transcaucasia between Europe and Asia. **Boundaries:** Georgia to N, Azerbaijan to E, Iran to S, Turkey to W. Nakhichevan Autonomous Republic, an Azerbaijan territory, is an enclave within Armenian territory. **Total area:** 11,484 sq. mi. (29,743 sq km). **Coastline:** none. **Comparative area:** slightly smaller than Maryland. **Land use:** 17% arable land; 2% permanent crops; 81% other. **Major cities:** Yerevan (capital); Kumayri (formerly Leninakan); Kirovakan.
● **PEOPLE   Population:** 2,966,802 (July 2010 est.). **Nationality:** noun—Armenian(s); adjective— Armenian. **Ethnic groups:** 98% Armenian, 1.3% Yezidi, .8% Russian and other. **Languages:** 98% Armenian, 1% Russian, 1% Yezidi. **Religions:** 95% Armenian Apostolic, 4% other Christian, 1% Yezidi.
● **GOVERNMENT   Type:** republic. **Independence:** Sept. 21, 1991 (from U.S.S.R.). **Constitution:** July 5, 1995, amended Nov. 27, 2005 **National holiday:** Independence Day, Sept. 21. **Heads of Government:** Serzh Sargsian, president (since April 2008); Tigran Sargsian, prime minister (since April 2008). **Structure:** executive; unicameral legislature; judiciary.
● **ECONOMY   Monetary unit:** dram. **Budget:** (2009 est.) *income:* $1.855 bil.; *expend.:*$2.365 bil. **GDP:** $16.18 bil., $5,900 per capita (2009 est.). **Chief crops:** fruit (especially wine grapes), vegetables, livestock. **Natural resources:** small deposits of gold and copper. **Major industries:** Industrial machinery, electrical equipment, tires, textiles (much of industry). **Labor force:** 1.481 mil. (2007 est.). **Exports:** $715 mil. (2009 est.); diamonds, mineral products, foodstuffs. **Imports:** $2.547 bil. (2009 est.); natural gas, petroleum, tobacco products, foodstuffs. **Major trading partners:** (2008) *exports:* 19.7% Russia, 17.4% Germany, 12.4% Netherlands; *imports:* 19.1% Russia, 8.6% China, 7.1% Ukraine, 6% Turkey.

Armenia, a small landlocked country just south of the great Caucasus mountain range, is but a fragment of ancient Armenia, one of the world's oldest civilizations dating back to the sixth century B.C. In about A.D. 300, Armenia adopted Christianity, which continues to be an important component of Armenian national identity. Because Armenia forms part of a land bridge between the Black and the Caspian Seas, and between Turks and Slavs, it has long been overrun and controlled by the Byzantine, Arab, Ottoman, Mongol, and Russian Empires. In 1236 the Tatar and Mongol invasion spelled the end of Armenia as a separate state. In 1639, after the conclusion of a major war between Turkey and Iran, the territory of Armenia was partitioned. By the end of the 17th century, czarist Russia was also involved in Armenia, and in 1828 eastern Armenia was ceded to the Russian empire by the Treaty of Turkmenchai.

During the First World War, those Armenians living in the western part of the country under Ottoman rule were increasingly subjected to persecution by the Turks. In April 1915, the Turks forcibly removed the Armenians from the border area, during which more than a million of them either starved or were killed. In 1918, an Armenian republic emerged as the Russian empire collapsed, but this entity was short-lived, as Turkey, Russia, and later Britain fought for control. Finally, the Soviet Red Army moved into the territory and on Nov. 29, 1920, declared it a Soviet republic. Armenia was made part of the Transcaucasian Soviet Federal Socialist Republic of the U.S.S.R. in 1922, and in 1936, it became one of the Soviet Union's constituent union republics.

Armenian Christians have been subjected to many years of persecution by various invaders, causing a great diaspora of Armenians, especially to the United States and Europe. This large expatriate community has helped Armenia from abroad through difficult times.

Since 1988, Armenia's most pressing issue has been the war over Nagorno-Karabakh, the Armenian Christian enclave of Muslim Azerbaijan. Fighting broke out when 180,000 ethnic Armenians in Azerbaijan demanded that their homeland become part of Armenia. The war continued even as both nations declared their independence from the Soviet Union (Armenia on Sept. 23, 1991; Azerbaijan a month later). In October 1991, Levon Ter-Petrossian was elected president of independent Armenia, and in December, Armenia was one of 11 former Soviet republics to sign the Alma-Ata Declaration, creating the Commonwealth of Independent States. Since independence, Armenia has remained committed to the war over Nagorno-Karabakh, even though it has hindered the functioning of the stagnant Armenian economy.

In 1995, a new "strong president" constitution was approved by 68 percent in a referendum and Pres. Ter-Petrossian's six-party Republic Coalition carried a majority of seats in the first elections for the 190-seat National Assembly. He was reelected in 1996 but resigned in February 1998 in a dispute over policy toward Nagorno-Karabakh with his hard-line premier Robert Kocharian. In March, Kocharian easily won the presidential election over Soviet-era ruler Karen Demirchyan. In October 1999, gunmen entered Parliament, murdering premier Vazgen Sargissian and seven others. President Kocharian named Sargissian's brother, Aram, a political neophyte, as new premier. In March 2003, Kocharian was elected to a second five-year term as president, taking over 60 percent of the disputed vote; in May, his coalition won 70 of 131 parliamentary seats.

▶ **AUSTRALIA**
Commonwealth of Australia
● **GEOGRAPHY Location:** continent of Australia, between Indian and Pacific Oceans. **Boundaries:** nearest neighbor is Papua New Guinea, to N. **Total area:** 2,988,902 sq. mi. (7,741,220 sq km). **Coastline:** 16,010 mi. (25,760 km). **Comparative area:** slightly smaller than U.S. **Land use:** 7% arable land; negl. % permanent crops; 93% other. **Major cities:** Canberra (capital); Sydney; Melbourne; Brisbane; Perth.
● **PEOPLE Population:** 21,515,754 (July 2010 est.). **Nationality:** noun—Australian(s); adjective—Australian. **Ethnic groups:** 92% Caucasian, 7% Asian, 1% aboriginal and other. **Languages:** English, Chinese, Italian, native langs. **Religions:** 25.8% Roman Catholic, 18.7% Anglican, 7.9% other Christian, 2.1% Buddhist, 1.7% Muslim, 18.7% none.
● **GOVERNMENT Type:** federal parliamentary democracy. **Independence:** Jan. 1, 1901 (from federation of U.K. colonies). **Constitution:** July 9, 1900; effective Jan. 1, 1901. **National holiday:** Australia Day, Jan. 26. **Heads of Government:** Quentin Bryce, governor general (since Sept. 2008); Julia Gillard, prime minister (since June 2010). **Structure:** executive—governor general (appointed by the Queen), prime minister, and cabinet; bicameral legislature; independent judiciary.
● **ECONOMY Monetary unit:** Australian dollar. **Budget:** (2009 est.) *income:* $323.6 bil.; *expend.:* $358.4 bil. **G.D.P.:** $824.3 bil.; $38,800 per capita (2009 est.). **Chief crops:** wheat, barley, sugarcane,

fruits; cattle. **Natural resources:** bauxite, coal, iron ore, copper, tin. **Major industries:** mining, industrial and transportation equipment, food processing. **Labor force:** 11.44 mil. (2009); 75% services, 21% industry, 4% agriculture (2009 est.). **Exports:** $161.5 bil. (2009 est.); coal, gold, meat, wool. **Imports:** $160.9 bil. (2009 est.); machinery and transport equipment, computers and office machines, telecommunication equipment and parts. **Major trading partners:** (2008) *exports:* 22.2% Japan, 14.6% China, 8.2% South Korea, 6.1% India, 5.5% U.S.; *imports:* 15.4% China, 12.1% U.S., 9.1% Japan.

The continent-nation of Australia is distinguished by its geographical isolation and by the unique flora and fauna that isolation fostered. The ancestors of today's aborigines arrived from Southeast Asia as much as 40,000 years ago. Thereafter, aborigine culture evolved in isolation except for some contact between the peoples of the northern coast and New Guinea. Australia was first sighted by Europeans at the beginning of the 17th century. In the 18th century, it was visited by the Dutch, who named it New Holland. The eastern coast was systematically explored in 1770 by Capt. James Cook, who claimed it for Great Britain.

British settlement began in 1788, with the landing of about 700 convicts near Sydney. Australia remained a penal colony during the first half of the 19th century, during which time the continent was explored and separate colonies established. Aboriginal populations were displaced and in some areas (most notably the island Tasmania) totally exterminated. Discovery of gold in Victoria in 1851 created a gold rush that greatly accelerated immigration. By 1900, the three mainstays of the Australian economy—livestock, mining, and wheat growing—were firmly established.

In 1901, a commonwealth was established consisting of a confederation of the various states except for the Northern Territory, which was added in 1911. The British Crown was represented by an appointed governor-general; the national government today is a parliamentary system, but much local authority resides in the separate states. Comprehensive social welfare legislation was passed by the state and national governments soon after the commonwealth's formation.

Australian troops fought with distinction in both world wars. A Japanese threat to Australia in 1942 was averted by Allied victory in the Battle of the Coral Sea. Australia and the United States are firm allies, and Australian troops joined U.S. forces in Korea, Vietnam, the Persian Gulf War and the invasion of Iraq. Australia administers several external island groups and claims territory in Antarctica.

The abandonment of discriminatory immigration practices in 1973 led to a new wave of immigration, particularly from Asia. Australian economic ties to Asia and the Pacific Rim have expanded considerably; new exploitation of mineral resources has in many cases been accomplished as a result of Japanese investment.

After 10 years in office, Prime Minister Bob Hawke was ousted by his own Labour party in 1991 and replaced by Paul Keating. Keating's government was reelected in 1993 elections, despite a persistent economic slump. But continued high spending and taxes took their toll, and in 1996, 13 years of Labour rule ended. A coalition of the more conservative Liberal and Nationalist parties captured 94 of 148 seats in the House of Representatives. The popular Liberal party leader John Howard became the new prime minister.

Australia's Constitutional Convention voted (in Feb. 1998) to proclaim Australia a republic, severing its residual ties to the British Crown. But in a 1999 referendum, voters rejected the republic 55 to 45 percent. With respect to aboriginal claims to Australian land, the government carried a Native Title Bill in July 1998, giving Australia's state governments authority to rule on the issue.

Howard gained a third straight term in Nov. 2001 elections, although Labour gained control of every state government. The Howard government's decision to participate in the Iraq war brought a (purely symbolic) vote of "no confidence" in the Senate; the real "no confidence" vote in the House failed. In Nov. 2007, Kevin Rudd led the Labor Party to a convincing victory ending a decade of Conservative rule. In February 2009 wild brushfires killed more than 170 people in Victoria, the largest natural disaster in Australia's history. In early 2010 Rudd's high approval ratings plummeted over his support for a mining tax and his refusal to continue support for attacking climate change. He was replaced by Julia Gillard of the left-center wing of Labor. She is Australia's first woman prime minister. In early September two independent legislators said they would support the Labor Party, thereby allowing Julia Gillard's government to stay in power.

▶ **AUSTRIA**
Republic of Austria
● GEOGRAPHY Location: landlocked country in central Europe. **Boundaries:** Germany and Czech Republic to N, Hungary and Slovak Republic to E, Slovenia and Italy to S, Switzerland and Liechtenstein to W. **Total area:** 32,383 sq. mi. (83,871 sq km). **Coastline:** none. **Comparative area:** slightly smaller than Maine. **Land use:** 17% arable land; 1% permanent crops; 82% other. **Major cities:** Vienna (capital); Graz; Linz; Salzburg; Innsbruck.
● PEOPLE **Population:** 8,214,160 (July 2010 est.). **Nationality:** noun—Austrian(s); adjective—Austrian. **Ethnic groups:** 91% Austrian, 4% former Yugoslavs, 1.6% Turks, 1% German. **Languages:** German, Turkish, Croatian (official in Burgenland). **Religions:** 73% Roman Catholic, 5% Protestant, 4.2% Muslim, 17.5% other or unspecified.
● GOVERNMENT **Type:** federal republic. **Independence:** 976 (Margravate of Austria established) **Constitution:** 1920; revised 1929; reinstated May 1945. **National holiday:** National Day, Oct. 26. **Heads of Government:** Dr. Heinz Fischer, president (since July 2004); Werner Faymann, chancellor (since Dec. 2008). **Structure:** executive; bicameral legislature; directly elected president whose functions are largely representational; independent federal judiciary.
● ECONOMY **Monetary unit:** euro. **Budget:** (2009 est.) *income:* $181.2 bil.; *expend.:* $194.4 bil. **G.D.P.:** $323.1 bil., $39,400 per capita (2009 est.). **Chief crops:** grain, fruits, potatoes, sugar beets. **Natural resources:** iron ore, crude oil, timber, magnesite, lead. **Major industries:** construction machinery, vehicles and parts, food. **Labor force:** 3.68 mil. (2009); 67% services, 27.5% industry, 5.5% agriculture (2007 est.). **Exports:** (2009 est.) $129 bil.; machinery and equipment, paper and cardboard, metal goods. **Imports:** (2009 est.) $136 bil.; vehicles, machinery and equipment, apparel,

metal goods. **Major trading partners:** (2008) *exports:* 28.9% Germany, 8.4% Italy, 4.2% U.S., 4.1% Switzerland; *imports:* 43.6% Germany, 6.9% Italy, 5.1% Switzerland, 4.1% Netherlands.

The Celtic tribes in what is now Austria were conquered by Rome under Emperor Augustus. After the fall of Rome, it was overrun by Huns, Lombards, Ostrogoths, and Bavarians. In 788 it was incorporated into the empire of Charlemagne. From the 9th to the 13th century, its territory was divided among a variety of feudal domains. In the late 13th century, Austria was reunited under Rudolph I of Habsburg, whose dynasty became synonymous with Austrian history for the next seven centuries. Rudolph's successors steadily enlarged their domain by conquest and marital diplomacy until, by the reign of Charles V (1500-58), they ruled not only the Holy Roman Empire (encompassing most of central Europe) but also the Netherlands, Spain, and all of its colonies.

After the reign of Charles V, the Habsburg Empire was split into two branches, one governing Spain, the other the Holy Roman Empire. Habsburg power in Germany declined after the Thirty Years' War (1618-48) but was affirmed in the Danube valley after the defeat of the Turkish siege of Vienna in 1683 and the subsequent reconquest of Hungary from the Turks. The marriage of Maria Teresa to Francis of Lorraine gave rise to the House of Habsburg-Lorraine in 1745. In 1804 the Austrian empire was founded, and two years later, the defunct Holy Roman Empire was abolished. The Ausgleich ("compromise") of 1867 transformed the empire into the Dual Monarchy of Austria-Hungary.

In 1914 the assassination of Archduke Franz Ferdinand, the heir to the Austrian throne, led to the outbreak of World War I, which resulted in a wholesale redrawing of national boundaries in Central Europe. Austria emerged as a small Alpine republic, with about 12 percent of the territory of the old Dual Monarchy. The new republic faced a severe postwar economic crisis, as well as a political stalemate between the Christian Social party and the Social Democratic party, each with the support of about half of the electorate, and each with its own paramilitary organization.

In 1933, as Hitler's National Socialists rose to power in Germany, Austrian Chancellor Engelbert Dollfuss, leader of the Christian Social party, instituted rule by decree and began building a corporate state modeled on Italian fascism. His attempt to disarm the Social Democratic militia led to civil war. The government triumphed, but Dollfuss was assassinated in an attempted coup by Austrian Nazis in July 1934. Hitler finally forced Austrian union with Germany (the Anschluss) in 1938, after which Austria was considered a part of Greater Germany.

Conquered by American and Soviet troops early in 1945, Austria was divided into French, British, American, and Russian zones of occupation after World War II. But the occupying powers permitted the formation of a unified national government, formed in November 1945 and recognized by the Western powers in 1946. The occupation ended in 1955 with the signing of the Austrian State Treaty. The four powers withdrew their forces, and Austria pledged itself to a policy of permanent neutrality, with no foreign military alliances.

The coalition government continued to 1966, when the People's party under Josef Klaus gained a parliamentary majority. In 1970 the Socialist party under Bruno Kreisky came to power. Socialist dominance continued until 1983, when the Socialists had to form a coalition with the right-wing Freedom party in order to stay in power. Kreisky resigned and was succeeded by Fred Sinowatz.

From 1986 to 1997, a "Grand Coalition" of the Socialist and People's Parties governed Austria under Socialist Chancellor Franz Vranitzky. In ten years, the government cautiously privatized state-owned enterprises of the mild Austrian form of socialism, while tourism, a highly developed maunfacturing sector, and substantial petroleum reserves contributed to the country's prosperity. The government dramatically cut taxes and began promoting regional trade with the newly-independent states of East-Central Europe. On Jan. 1, 1995, Austria entered the European Union.

Tensions arising from unemployment and immigration of "economic refugees" from Asia and Africa as well as from Eastern Europe led to the amending of Austria's asylum law, consideration of immigration quotas, and the growing strength of the right-wing Freedom Party. The desire to meet the E.U.'s single currency standards led to welfare spending cuts which provoked further voter dissatisfaction. In Oct. 1996 Austrian voters (participating for the first time in European Parliament elections), gave Freedom Party candidates, who were opposed to Austria's participation in EMU, 27.6 percent of their votes, while Socialists garnered only 29.1 percent and the People's Party took 29.6 percent.

Chancellor Vranitzky resigned in Jan. 1997 and was succeeded by Socialist Finance Minister Viktor Klima. In the Oct. 1999 elections to the National Council, the Social Democrats received only one-third of the votes, while the People's Party and the Freedom Party each took 27 percent. When it proved impossible to reconstruct the "Grand Coalition," the latter two parties, together controlling 104 of 183 seats, formed their own coalition government, with Wolfgang Schuessel of the People's Party as chancellor.

With the Freedom Party entering the Austrian government, the other 14 E.U. governments cut off diplomatic contacts, as did Israel and the U.S. The E.U. lifted the sanctions after their investigative panel reported the superiority of Austria's treatment of immigrants; subsequently, the Freedom Party's share of the vote has shown slippage. In Nov. 2002 parliamentary elections, the party garnered but 10 percent of the vote while Chancellor Schuessel's People's Party won a surprising 43 percent. In Feb. 2003 a new People's-Freedom government was formed which lasted until 2006 when the Social Democrats won a narrow victory and Alfred Gusenbauer became chancellor with immigration still the leading issue. He was succeeded by Werner Faymann in 2008.

►AZERBAIJAN
Azerbaijani Republic
● **GEOGRAPHY** **Location:** southern Transcaucasia between Europe and Asia. **Boundaries:** Georgia to NW, Russian Federation to N, Caspian Sea to E, Iran to S, Armenia to SW. Nakhichevan Autonomous Republic (ASSR) is part of Azerbaijan although it is inside Armenian territory. **Total land area:** 33,436 sq. mi. (86,600 sq km). **Coastline:** 443 mi (713 km) Caspian Sea. **Comparative area:** about the size of Maine. **Land use:** 20.6% arable land; 2.6% permanent crops; 76.77% other. **Major cities:** (1990 est.) Baku

(capital) 1,149,000; Gyanja (formerly Kirovabad) 281,000; Sumgait 235,000.
● **PEOPLE** **Population:** 8,303,512 (July 2010 est.). **Nationality:** noun—Azerbaijani(s) or Azeri(s); adjective—Azerbaijani. **Ethnic groups:** 91% Azeri, 2.2% Dagestani Peoples, 1.8% Russian, 1.5% Armenian, 3.9% other. **Languages:** 90.3% Azeri, 2.2% Lezgi, 1.8% Russian, 1.5% Armenian, 4.3% other. **Religions:** 93.4% Muslim, 2.5% Russian Orthodox, 2.3% Armenian Orthodox, 1.8% other.
● **GOVERNMENT** **Type:** republic. **Independence:** Aug. 30, 1991 (from U.S.S.R.). **Constitution:** Nov. 12, 1995; modified by referendum Aug. 24, 2002 **National holiday:** May 28. **Heads of Government:** Ilham Aliyev, president (since Oct. 2003); Artur Rasizadeh, prime minister (since Nov. 2003). **Structure:** executive; unicameral legislatiure; judiciary.
● **ECONOMY** **Monetary unit:** manat. **Budget:** (2009 est.) *income:* $12.18 bil.; *expend.:* $12.36 bil. **G.D.P.:** $86.03 bil., $10,400 per capita (2009 est.). **Chief crops:** cotton, tea, tobacco, grain, fruit. **Natural resources:** petroleum, natural gas, iron ore. **Major industries:** petroleum and natural gas, construction materials, chemicals. **Labor force:** 4.318 mil. (2008); 60.5% industry, 38% agriculture, 33.7% services. **Exports:** $13.16 bil. (2009 est.); oil, gas, oil field equipment, textiles, cotton. **Imports:** $5.448 bil. (2009 est.); machinery and parts, foodstuffs, metals. **Major trading partners:** (2008) *exports:* 40.2% Italy, 12.6% U.S., 7.6% Israel; *imports:* 18.8% Russia, 11.2% Turkey, 8.3% Germany.

The territory of present-day Azerbaijan has been inhabited since Paleolithic times. The name Azerbaijan is derived (via Arabic and Turkish) from Atropates (a vassal of Alexander III of Macedonia), who founded an independent state here in the fourth century B.C. The population of Azerbaijan is approximately seven million, but nearly seven million additional Azeris with the same language and faith live across the border in Iran.

For much of its history, the territory of Azerbaijan, home to an indigenous nomadic people, has been occupied by Persians, Muslim Arabs, Turkic tribes from Mongolia, Ottoman Turks, Mongols, and in the 18th century, Russians. The capital city of Baku was an important outlet on the Volga River-Caspian Sea route; under Peter the Great, the Russians occupied Baku and Derbent, and for a while controlled the Caspian Sea. Command of this territory shifted between Ottomans, Persians, and Russians in the 18th and 19th centuries, with the Russians ultimately establishing military rule by 1828 with the Treaty of Turkmenchai. This treaty ceded the southern half of the country to Persia and the northern half to Russia.

In 1883 the Russians finished building the Transcaucasian Railway, which linked Baku with the Black Sea coast and central Russia and made Baku one of the most important industrial hubs in the Russian empire. Baku became a revolutionary center around the turn of the century. In 1918 an independent republic was formed, but in 1920 it was overthrown by the Soviet Red Army, and in April 1920 the Azerbaijan Soviet Socialist Republic (SSR) was proclaimed. Two years later, it was joined with the Armenian and Georgian SSRs to form the Transcaucasian Soviet Federal Socialist Republic; in 1936, however, the three again became separate union republics.

While a Soviet republic, Azerbaijan was industrialized, its agriculture collectivized, and religious persecution was severe. It also entered into a war in 1988 with neighboring Armenia over the Nagorno-Karabakh region, which is largely populated with ethnic Armenians but lies within Azerbaijani territory. The local council of Nagorno-Karabakh petitioned the Armenian and Azerbaijani Supreme Soviets to transfer the region to Armenia in 1988, but Azerbaijan refused, spurring a war that has erupted from time to time over the last 20 years.

In Jan. 1990, attacks on Communist party buildings and against Armenians in Azerbaijan precipitated a brutal Soviet Army intervention to restore order. A state of emergency was declared, and the first secretary of the Communist party was replaced by Ayaz Mutalibov. He was elected president in Sept. 1991, and on Oct. 18, 1991, Azerbaijan's Supreme Soviet declared the country's independence. On Dec. 21, 1991, Azerbaijan joined ten other former Soviet republics in forming the Commonwealth of Independent States.

After the dissolution of the U.S.S.R., Azerbaijan had problems consolidating its own future. In 1992, Pres. Mutalibov was forced from office. His successor was in turn driven out of office by armed rebels after the fighting in Nagorno-Karabakh turned decisively in Armenia's favor. He was replaced by Heydar Aliyev, a former Communist party boss, in 1993. Aliyev survived two coup attempts and the country's flagging fortunes in Nagorno-Karabakh to complete a $7.4 billion deal with western companies to develop oil fields in the Caspian Sea in 1994. In parliamentary elections in 1995, Aliyev's New Azerbaijan party won 70 percent of the vote, amidst charges of vote-rigging. And in 1996, Aliyev negotiated an agreement to transport oil from the Caspian Sea via pipeline (through Chechnya) to the Russian port of Novorossiysk. The pipeline opened Nov. 12, 1997, soon after Aliyev met with Pres. Clinton in Washington to sign a treaty.

In Oct. 1998, presidential elections which were boycotted by opposition parties, and which European monitors declared to be seriously irregular, gave Aliyev 76 percent of the vote. In parliamentary elections in Nov. 2000, his New Azerbaijan Party carried 70 percent of the vote, to no one's surprise. The ailing president, in Sept. 2002, oversaw the start of construction on a major oil pipeline from the Caspian through Georgia to Turkey and signed a treaty with Russia regularizing the Caspian border. But he was unable to prevent a presidential election in the secessionist, ethnically Armenian province of Nagorno-Karabakh. In 2003 he appointed his son, Ilham, premier and when illness forced him to withdraw from the presidential race, Ilham was elected with 77 percent of the vote. The new oil pipeline to Turkey was opened helping to spur the economy. In Nov. 2005 Ilham was reelected but international monitors said fraud and abuse were widespread, and this charge was repeated in 2006 parliamentary elections.

▶BAHAMAS
Commonwealth of The Bahamas
● **GEOGRAPHY Location:** nearly 700 islands in an archipelago that extends 590 mi. (950 km) SE-NW between Florida and Haiti. Nassau 25°05'N, 77°20'W. **Boundaries:** western Atlantic Ocean to N, E, S, and W. **Total land area:** 5,359 sq. mi. (13,880 sq km). **Coastline:** 2,200 mi. (3,542 km). **Comparative area:** slightly larger than Connecticut. **Land use:** 0.58% arable land; negl. %

permanent crops; 99% other. **Major cities:** Nassau (capital).
● **PEOPLE Population:** 310,426 (July 2010 est.). **Nationality:** noun—Bahamian(s); adjective—Bahamian. **Ethnic groups:** 85% black, 12% white, 3% Asian & Hispanic. **Languages:** English, some Creole among Haitian immigrants. **Religions:** 35% Baptist, 15% Anglican, 14% Roman Catholic, 8% Pentecostal, 5% Church of God, 4% Methodist, 15% other Christian.
● **GOVERNMENT Type:** constituional parliamentary democracy. **Independence:** July 10, 1973 (from U.K.). **Constitution:** July 10, 1973. **National holiday:** National Day, July 10. **Heads of Government:** Arthur D. Hanna, governor-general (since Feb. 2006); Hubert Ingraham, prime minister (since May 2007). **Structure:** executive—governor general (appointed by queen); bicameral legislature; judiciary.
● **ECONOMY Monetary unit:** Bahamian dollar. **Budget:** (2007 est.) **income:** $1.03 bil.; **expend.:** $1.03 bil. **G.D.P.:** $9.084 bil., $29,800 per capita (2009 est.). **Chief crops:** citrus fruits, vegetables; poultry. **Natural resources:** salt, aragonite, timber. **Major industries:** tourism, banking, cement. **Labor force:** 184,000 (2009); 50% tourism, 40% other services, 5% industry, 5% agriculture (2006 est.). **Exports:** $674 mil. (2006 est.); pharmaceuticals, cement, rum, crawfish. **Imports:** $2.4 bil. (2006 est.); foodstuffs, manufactured goods, crude oil. **Major trading partners:** (2008) **exports:** 21.4% U.S., 18.7% Singapore, 18% Poland, 7.6% Germany; **imports:** 25.7% U.S., 19.3% South Korea, 16.8% Japan, 7.5% Singapore.

Christopher Columbus made his first landfall in the Americas in the Bahamas Oct. 12, 1492. Though the Spanish never settled the islands, they enslaved and removed to Hispaniola 40,000 of the indigenous Arawaks by 1508. Their shallow seas (*baja mar*) made the islands a haven for pirates in the 17th century—as well as during the Civil War, Prohibition, and for drug smugglers today. British colonization of the Bahamas began in 1629 and continued slowly over the next two centuries.

Tourism has been the mainstay of the economy in this century, but high unemployment is a continuing problem. Parliament relaxed restrictions on offshore banking to stem the flight of international capital prompted by allegations of government corruption and involvement in drug trafficking. In 1992 the government of Prime Minister Lynden Pindling was defeated after 25 years in office, largely because of corruption charges. The Progressive Liberal Party remained in power for many years, but was defeated in 2007 by the Free National Movement party.

▶BAHRAIN
Kingdom of Bahrain
● **GEOGRAPHY Location:** group of 35 islands in western Persian Gulf. Manama 26°17'N, 50°33'E. **Boundaries:** Saudi Arabia about 15 mi. (24 km) to W and Qatar about 17 mi. (28 km) to SE. **Total land area:** 286 sq. mi. (741 sq km). **Coastline:** 161 mi. (259 km). **Comparative area:** slightly less than 3.5 times size of Washington, D.C. **Land use:** 2.8% arable land; 5.6% permanent crops; 91.6% other. **Major cities:** Manama (capital); Muharraq Town.
● **PEOPLE Population:** 738,004 note—includes 235,108 non-nationals (July 2010 est.). **Nationality:** noun—Bahraini(s); adjective—Bahraini. **Ethnic groups:** 62.4% Bahraini, 37.6%

non-Bahraini. **Languages:** Arabic, English, Farsi, Urdu. **Religions:** 81.2% Muslim (Shi'a and Sunni), 9% Christian, 9.8% other.
• **GOVERNMENT Type:** constitutional monarchy. **Independence:** Aug. 15, 1971 (from U.K.). **Constitution:** adopted Feb. 14, 2002. **National holiday:** Dec. 16. **Heads of Government:** Hamad Bin Isa Al-Khalifa, amir (since Jan. 2002); Khalifa bin Salman, prime minister (since 1971). **Structure:** executive—amir is traditional arab monarch, appoints cabinet led by prime minister; legislative—amir dissolved National Assembly (Aug. 1975), appointed Advisory Council Dec. 1992; independent judiciary.
• **ECONOMY Monetary unit:** Bahraini dinar. **Budget:** (2009 est.) *income:* $5.809 bil.; *expend.:* $5.86 bil. **G.D.P.:** $27.99 bil., $38,400 per capita (2009 est.). **Chief crops:** not self-sufficient in food production; produces some fruits and vegetables; engages in shrimping and fishing. **Natural resources:** oil, associated and nonassociated natural gas, fish. **Major industries:** petroleum processing and refining, aluminum smelting, offshore banking. **Labor force:** 595,000 (2009 est.); 79% industry, commerce and service (note: 44% of 15-64 age group is non-national). **Exports:** $12.5 bil. (2009 est.); petroleum, aluminum. **Impor ts:** $10.37 bil. (2009). **Major trading partners:** (2008) *exports:* 4% India, 3.4% Saudi Arabia, 2.2% U.A.E. *imports:* 26% Saudi Arabia, 8.7% Japan, 7.6% U.S., 6% China.

Bahrain has been an entrepôt of trade between Arabia and India since the second millenium B.C. The Portuguese fortified Bahrain in the 16th century but were driven out by the Persian shah Abbas I early in the 17th century. At the end of the 18th century, it became an Arab sheikhdom within the Ottoman Empire. Bahrain entered into treaty relations with Great Britain in 1820 and became a British protectorate in 1861. After British forces withdrew from the gulf, the nation became an independent emirate, in August 1971, under Amir Isa bin Sulman al-Khalifa, who had come to the throne in 1961. The U.S. has maintained a large military base here for many years and it is currently home to the Fifth Fleet.

Oil reserves—first discovered in 1932—were depleted by the mid-1970s. The economy diversified to include oil refining, aluminum smelting, international banking, and shipping. Bahrain has close relations with Saudi Arabia.

In June 1995 social and political unrest caused by uneven distribution of wealth, high unemployment, and a repressive government erupted into serious rioting. Protests by the Shiite majority began again in early 1996; a government crackdown led to the arrest of over 600 dissidents. Bahrain's family-run, Sunni Muslim government continued with the March 1999 death of its founding emir and his replacement with his son, Hamad bin Isa al-Khalifa. The new emir, in Feb. 2001, fostered a trio of reform measures: extending amnesty to 400 political prisoners and repatriation to 100 exiles; repealing the State Security Law and abolishing the State Security Court, both of which had been designed to quash Shiite unrest; and sponsoring a referendum which approved (by 98 percent) the restoration of a parliament, the founding of an independent judiciary, and the extension of the right to vote to women. Then, in Feb. 2002, Sheik Hamad declared the state to be a constitutional monarchy, the Kingdom of Bahrain, with himself as king. Municipal elections were

successfully held in May, with elections for the lower house of the legislature in Oct. giving Sunni candidates 19 of 40 seats. In Nov. the King appointed the upper house, including six women and one Jew.

▶ **BANGLADESH**
People's Republic of Bangladesh
• **GEOGRAPHY Location:** southern Asia. **Boundaries:** India to N, E, and W; Myanmar to E, Bay of Bengal to S. **Total land area:** 55,598 sq. mi. (144,000 sq km). **Coastline:** 360 mi. (580 km). **Comparative area:** slightly smaller than Iowa. **Land use:** 55% arable land; 3% permanent crops; 42% other. **Major cities:** Dhaka (formerly Dacca) (capital) ; Chittagong; Khulna; Rajshahi; Barisal.
• **PEOPLE Population:** 158,065,841 (July 2010 est.). **Nationality:** noun—Bangladeshi(s); adjective—Bangladesh. **Ethnic groups:** 98% Bengali, tribal groups, non-Bengali Muslims. **Languages:** Bangla (official); English widely used. **Religions:** 83% Muslim, 16% Hindu, 1% Buddhist, Christian, and other.
• **GOVERNMENT Type:** parliamentary democracy. **Independence:** Dec. 16, 1971 (from Pakistan). **Constitution:** Nov. 4, 1972, effective Dec. 16, 1972, suspended following coup of Mar. 24, 1982, restored Nov. 10, 1986; amended many times. **National holiday:** March 26, Independence Day. **Heads of Government:** Zillur Rahman, president (since Feb. 2009); Sheikh Hasina, Prime Minister (since Jan. 2009). **Structure:** executive—president appoints prime minister and Advisory Council; unicameral legislature dissolved by president following elections on Feb. 15, 1996 and named caretaker prime minister; judiciary.
• **ECONOMY Monetary unit:** taka. **Budget:** (2010 est.) *income:* $11.4 bil.; *expend.:* $16.3 bil. **G.D.P.:** $242.4 bil., $1,600 per capita (2009 est.). **Chief crops:** large-scale subsistence farming, heavily dependent on monsoon rain; main crops are jute, rice, wheat, tea, sugarcane, and potatoes. **Natural resources:** natural gas, arable land, timber. **Major industries:** jute manufactures, cotton textiles, tea processing. **Labor force:** 72.5 mil. (2009 est.); extensive export of labor to Saudi Arabia, UAE, and Oman; 63% agriculture, 26% services, 11% industry and mining. **Exports:** $15.91 bil. (2009 est.); garments, jute, leather, seafood. **Imports:** $20.22 bil. (2009 est); machinery, chemicals, iron and steel, textiles. **Major trading partners:** (2008) *exports:* 24% U.S., 15.3% Germany, 10% U.K., 7.4% France; *imports:* 15.8% China, 15.7% India, 8.1% Kuwait, 7.6% Singapore, 4.4% Japan.

Located on the alluvial plain of the Ganges River northeast of India, Bengal was ruled by Buddhist kings from the eighth to 12th centuries. Conquered by Muslim invaders around 1200, many inhabitants converted to Islam and Bengal became part of the Moghul Empire in the 16th century. The British East India Company established a settlement in 1642, and by 1750 all of Bengal was under British rule. The diverse agricultural economy became dominated by export crops of opium and jute, while rice was grown in the fertile delta.

With Indian independence in 1947, Bengal was partitioned along religious lines, Hindu West Bengal (including Calcutta) remaining with India and Muslim East Bengal becoming the eastern province of Pakistan. In the elections of 1971, the Bengali Awami League gained control of Pakistan's National Assembly. Seating of the new National Assembly was postponed, and riots broke out in East Pakistan. Troops from West Pakistan were sent to quell the riots on May 25; the following day East Pakistan declared its independence as Bangladesh. Civil war followed; 10 million refugees fled to India. Following Indian intervention, Pakistan acknowledged Bangladesh's independence on Dec. 15.

Bangladesh has consistently been one of the world's poorest countries, plagued by violent political instability, military coups, overpopulation, a flagging economy, and frequent catastrophic floods (including one in 1975 that killed half a million people). The first president, Sheik Mujibur Rahman, was assassinated in 1975. Lt. Gen. Hossain Mohammad Ershad, who seized power in a coup in March 1982, was elected president in 1986, but resigned in 1990 in the face of opposition unrest.

In 1991, the Bangladesh Nationalist party (BNP) of Begum Khaleda Zia (widow of former president Ziaur Rahman, who was assassinated in 1981) won 138 of 330 parliamentary seats running on a platform of free enterprise and an Islamic state. In 1991, the constitution was amended to put the prime minister in charge of the government.

In 1994, nearly 150 opposition members of Parliament resigned en masse, eliciting a promise from Prime Minister Zia to hold general elections in June 1996. In those elections, the Awami League, led by Sheik Hasina Wazed, returned to power for the first time since 1975, when the military massacred most of her family, including her father, Pres. Sheik Mujibur Rahman. In 1998, fifteen were convicted and sentenced to death for their role in the assassinations. Zia's call for nation-wide protest strike went unanswered, but her BNP (in Jan. 1999) was one of three parties, with General Ershad's Jatiya and the Moslem Jamaat-e-Islami, to form a bloc seeking to force early elections upon prime minister Hasina. After completing Bangladesh's first-ever five-year term, premier Hasina and her Awami League faced the voters in Oct. 2001 only to be buried in a surprise landslide victory by former premier Khaleda Zia and her Nationalist party coalition. As Zia's term ran out in Oct. 2006, she appointed a caretaker government to run the elections but the opposition protested her choice. By Jan. 2007, as the election approached, cries of fraud and increased violence forced the interim president to declare a state of emergency and the military essentially took power. In April, Sheikh Hasina Wazed and more than 50 people connected to her politically were charged with murder; Zia was under virtual house arrest and her son in jail charged with extortion. The government tried to exile both women and when that failed they accused both of misrule and put them in prison. They were released in time for the December 2008 elections which Sheik Hasina won in a landslide.

▶ BARBADOS

• **Geography** **Location:** easternmost of Caribbean islands, about 200 mi. (320 km) NE of Trinidad. Bridgetown 13°06'N, 59°36'W. **Boundaries:** Atlantic Ocean. **Total land area:** 166 sq. mi. (431 sq km). **Coastline:** 60 mi. (97 km). **Comparative area:** slightly less than 2.5 times size of Washington, D.C. **Land use:** 37% arable land; 2% permanent crops; 61% other. **Major cities:** Bridgetown (capital).

• **People** **Population:** 285,653 (July 2010 est.). **Nationality:** noun—Barbadian(s); adjective—Barbadian. **Ethnic groups:** 90% black, 4% white, 6% Asian and mixed. **Languages:** English. **Religions:** 63.4% Protestant, 4% Roman Catholic, 25% none or other.

• **Government** **Type:** parliamentary democracy recognizing Queen Elizabeth II as chief of state. **Independence:** Nov. 30, 1966 (from U.K.). **Constitution:** Nov. 30, 1966. **National holiday:** Independence Day, Nov. 30. **Heads of Government:** Sir Clifford Husbands, governor general (since June 1996); David Thompson, prime minister (since Jan. 2008). **Structure:** executive—governor general (appointed by the queen) prime minister; bicameral legislature; judiciary.

• **Economy** **Monetary unit:** Barbadian dollar. **Budget:** (2000 est.) *income:* $847 mil.; *expend.:* $886 mil. **G.D.P.:** $5.278 bil., $18,500 per capita (2009 est.). **Chief crops:** sugarcane, vegetables, cotton. **Natural resources:** crude oil, fish, natural gas. **Major industries:** tourism, sugar, light manufacturing. **Labor force:** 175,000 (2007 est.); 75% services, 15% industry, 10% agriculture. **Exports:** $385 mil. (2006 est.); sugar and molasses, rum, other foods and beverages, chemicals. **Imports:** $1.586 bil. (2006 est.); consumer goods, machinery, foodstuffs. **Major trading partners:** (2008) *exports:* 15.6% Trinidad and Tobago, 13.9% Jamaica, 9.9% Brazil. *imports:* 26.9% U.S., 25.4% Trinidad and Tobago, 7% Russia.

Barbados is the only Caribbean island not to have changed hands prior to independence. Although the Spanish removed virtually all the indigenous Arawaks of Barbados by the mid-1500s, the island was not claimed until the British arrived in the 1620s. Tobacco, cotton, and sugarcane—harvested by slaves until 1833—were mainstays of the economy. The 1966 constitution mandates the promotion of economic equality among Barbadians, and the country was fairly prosperous relative to other Caribbean states until the mid-1990s, when declining tourism and record-low sugar production have had serious adverse effects. Still, the Barbados Labor Party retained its popularity, winning 26 of the parliament's 28 seats in Jan. 1999 elections. The economy revived as new hotels and housing complexes created jobs and increased tourism.

▶ BELARUS
Republic of Belarus

• **Geography** **Location:** northeastern Europe. **Boundaries:** Lithuania and Latvia to N, Russian Federation to NE and E, Ukraine to S, Poland to W, Lithuania and Latvia to NW. **Total land area:** 80,154 sq. mi. (207,600 sq km). **Coastline:** none. **Comparative area:** slightly smaller than Kansas. **Land use:** 26.8% arable land; 0.6% permanent crops; 72.6% other. **Major cities:** Minsk (capital); Gomel (Homel); Mahilou (Mogilev); Vitebsk; Grodno.

• **People** **Population:** 9,612,632 (July 2010 est.). **Nationality:** noun—Belarusian(s); adjective—Belarusian. **Ethnic groups:** 81.2% Byelorussian, 11.4% Russian, 7.4% Polish, Ukrainian and other. **Languages:** Byelorusian (official), Russian. **Religions:** 80% Eastern Orthodox.

• **Government** **Type:** republic. **Independence:** Aug. 25, 1991 (from U.S.S.R.). **Constitution:** March 15, 1994, revised in Nov. 1996 and again in Oct. 2004, removing presidential term limits **National holiday:** Independence Day, July 3. **Heads of Government:** Aleksander Lukashenko, president (since July 1994); Sergei Sidorskiy, prime minister (since Dec. 2003). **Structure:** executive—president, prime minister, Council of Ministers; bicameral legislature—most members apointed by the president; judiciary.

• **ECONOMY Monetary unit:** Belarusian ruble. **Budget:** (2009 est.) *income:* $16.15 bil.; *expend.:* $16.9 bil. **G.D.P.:** $116 bil., $11,600 per capita (2009 est.). **Chief crops:** grain, potatoes, vegetables. **Natural resources:** forest, peat, oil, and natural gas. **Major industries:** tractors, metalworking, heavy-duty vehicles. **Labor force:** 5 mil. (2009). **Exports:** $24.8 bil. (2009 est.); machinery, transport equipment, chemicals, metals. **Imports:** $30.4 bil. (2009 est.); mineral products, machinery and equipment, metals, chemicals. **Major trading partners:** (2008) *exports:* 32.3% Russia, 16.5% Netherlands, 8.5% Ukraine, 6.5% Latvia; *imports:* 59.4% Russia, 7.1% Germany, 5.3% Ukraine.

Belarus, also known as White Russia or Byelorussia, has been inhabited since the seventh century. In the 13th and 14th centuries, present-day Belarus became part of the Grand Duchy of Lithuania, which then became part of Poland in the 16th century. Between 1772 and 1795, Poland was partitioned, which resulted in Belarus becoming part of the Russian empire. After the Bolshevik revolution in 1917, Soviet troops came to Minsk, but they were forced to withdraw in the face of approaching German troops. The Treaty of Brest-Litovsk in March 1918 ceded to Germany most of the territory of Belarus. The same year, an independent Belarusian Democratic Republic was founded, but it had little real power. Once the Germans left, the Soviets easily retook Belarus, and on Jan. 1, 1919, the Belarusian Soviet Socialist Republic (SSR) was proclaimed.

This did not end the divisions of the traditional Belarusian lands. In February 1919 they were merged with Lithuania, but the Poles launched an attack in April of the same year and took both Lithuania and Belarus. In 1920 the Belarusian SSR was re-formed, but it included only the eastern portion of historical Belarusian lands. The Treaty of Riga in March 1921 granted the western territories of Belarus to Poland and the eastern portion to the Russian Federation.

After the Soviets invaded Poland in 1939, the lands that Belarus had lost in 1921 were returned to it. Between 1941 and 1945, the Germans occupied the Belarusian lands, and more than a million lost their lives, including most of the large Jewish population. After the war, the Belarusian SSR was restored with all of its historic lands, and Belarus was finally unified.

Under Soviet rule, Belarus turned from a mainly agricultural to an industrial land. Large numbers of Belarusians fiercely fought Stalin's collectivization plan in the 1930s, and thousands were killed or deported. Both Stalin's purges of the 1930s and World War II, which devastated both its agriculture and industry, inflicted great losses on Belarus. After the war, Soviet policy in Belarus concentrated on rebuilding its economy and encouraging Russian immigration (Russian replaced Belarusian as the official language).

The Belarusian SSR was one of the more prosperous and stable of the union republics, so Mikhail Gorbachev's policy of *glasnost*, or openness, in the 1980s was relatively slow to have an impact. In 1987, however, two issues had come to the fore in the Belarusian SSR: the status of the Belarusian language and the ecological dangers of Chernobyl, the famous nuclear reactor that had

exploded in nearby Ukraine in 1986, but which dropped almost three-quarters of its fallout on Belarus. In voicing these concerns, the Belarusians formed several new, non-Communist parties that challenged the authority of the ruling Communist party. On July 27, 1990, Belarus declared its sovereignty from the U.S.S.R.

On Dec. 8, 1991, Belarus, Ukraine, and Russia hosted the talks leading to the Minsk Agreement, which created the Commonwealth of Independent States (CIS). Pres. Aleaksander Lukashenko fostered closer ties with Russia. A 1995 customs union was expanded by the 1996 Union Treaty to include a common currency, joint tax and legal systems, shared energy and transport networks, and common defense and foreign policies. Lukashenko tightened his dictatorial hold on Belarus with a new constitution (Nov. 1996) which allowed presidential rule by decree and gave Lukashenko power to appoint half the members of the Constitutional Court and 20 of the 64 members of the Council of the Republic, the newly-created upper house of the legislature. In 1997, the U.S. announced it was cutting off $4 mil. in aid.

In July 1999, 35 members of the disbanded parliament designated its former speaker, Semyon Sharetsky, as president. Sharetsky promptly fled to Lithuania for safety but claimed the presidency. October saw large demonstrations in Minsk protesting the disappearance of opposition leaders and the proposed reunion with Russia. That reunion was forestalled by a wary Pres. Yeltsin in Dec. 1999, but Pres. Lukashenko was gratified by his party's sweep of all the seats in Oct. 2000 elections for the Chamber of Representatives in what he described as an "absolutely democratic" vote, a stance he took in the presidential election he won overwhelmingly in Sept. 2004. Protests were vigorous but without effect. In March 2006 elections Lukashenko again won by a large margin and again the E.U. and the U.S. protested. Putin and allies of Russia said the vote was legitimate. Later that year Russia doubled the price of oil and gas and threatened to cut off the supply if the government refused to pay. Tensions between the two nations have remained ever since.

▶ **BELGIUM**
Kingdom of Belgium

• **GEOGRAPHY Location:** northwestern Europe. **Boundaries:** Netherlands to N, Luxembourg and Germany to E, France to S, and North Sea to W. **Total land area:** 11,787 sq. mi. (30,528 sq km). **Coastline:** 40 mi. (64 km). **Comparative area:** slightly larger than Maryland. **Land use:** 27.42% arable land; negl. % permanent crops; 72% other. **Major cities:** Bruxelles (Brussels—capital); Antwerpen (Anvers, Antwerp); Gent (Gand, Ghent); Charleroi; Liège (Luik).

• **PEOPLE Population:** 10,423,493 (July 2010 est.). **Nationality:** noun—Belgian(s); adjective—Belgian. **Ethnic groups:** 58% Fleming, 31% Walloon, 11% mixed or other. **Languages:** 60% Dutch, 40% French, less than 1% German (all three official); legally bilingual (Dutch and French). **Religions:** 75% Roman Catholic, remainder Protestant or other.

• **GOVERNMENT Type:** federal parliamentary democracy under a constitutional monarch. **Independence:** Oct. 4, 1830 (from Netherlands). **Constitution:** Feb. 7, 1831; last revised July 14, 1993. **National holiday:** National Day, July 21. **Heads of Government:** Albert II, king (since Aug.

1993); Yves Leterme, prime minister (since Nov. 2009). **Structure:** executive—king, prime minister, and cabinet; bicameral legislature; independent judiciary.

● **ECONOMY Monetary unit:** euro. **Budget:** (2009 est.) *income:* $204.9 bil.; *expend.:* $230.9 bil.. **G.D.P.:** $381 bil., $36,600 per capita (2009 est.). **Chief crops:** sugar beets, vegetables, fruit, grain. **Natural resources:** coal, natural gas. **Major industries:** engineering, metal products, motor vehicle assembly, processed food, beverages, chemicals. **Labor force:** 5.01 mil. (2009); 73% services, 25% industry; 2% agriculture. **Exports:** $296.1 bil. (2009 est.); machinery and equipment, chemicals, diamonds. **Imports:** $315 bil. (2009 est.); machinery and equipment, chemicals, metals. **Major trading partners:** (2008) *exports:* 19.8% Germany, 17.4% France, 12.2% Netherlands; *imports:* 19.4% Netherlands, 17.2% Germany, 11% France.

The country now known as Belgium was, during the Middle Ages, part of the powerful duchy of Burgundy. By marriage and diplomacy, the "Low Countries" became part of the Habsburg Empire in 1482 (see "Austria"). In a struggle lasting from the late 16th century to the Treaty of Westphalia in 1648, the northern part of that region (Netherlands) became independent, but the southern portion remained part of the Habsburg Empire—under the Spanish branch until 1715, then under the Austrian branch until the French Revolution. The Congress of Vienna attached the lands to an enlarged Kingdom of the Netherlands in 1815.

In 1830 the Belgians revolted against the Dutch, and in 1831 the Treaty of London recognized an independent Kingdom of Belgium. Throughout the 19th century, its unity was precarious, as the country was divided politically between Catholic and Liberal parties, and ethnically between Dutch-speaking Flemings and French-speaking Walloons. In 1885 Belgium became a colonial power in Africa with Leopold II's establishment of the Congo Free State (later the Belgian Congo), which gained independence in 1960 as Zaire.

Belgium was a major battleground during World War I, but its boundaries were reestablished in 1919 by the Treaty of Versailles. When German troops overran Belgium in May 1940, King Leopold III quickly signed an armistice, hoping to placate Hitler and avert further fighting. But the Belgian government fled to England, repudiated the armistice, and joined the Allies. The Germans controlled Belgium until Sept. 1944.

Belgium made a swift postwar recovery. But the political atmosphere was poisoned by the issue of what to do about wartime collaborators up to and including the king. A referendum in 1950 narrowly approved Leopold III's return to the throne, but he was persuaded to abdicate in 1951.

Belgium has a flourishing economy with a modernized industrial sector complemented by tourism and agriculture. The issue of language dominates politics; since the 1960s, Belgium has devolved into a de facto confederation of Flemish-, French-, and German-speaking regions, with Brussels a multilingual region unto itself.

In the May 1995 election, the first under the new decentralized constitution of 1993, the Christian Democrat-Socialist coalition government retained a majority in the Chamber of Representatives. In Aug. 1996, the government was shaken by massive demonstrations against inept police and legal handling of a widespread child prostitution and

pornography ring. The "poultry scandal" of early 1999 (the government's tardy reaction to the discovery of dioxin in Belgian meat and dairy products) toppled the coalition of Prime Minister Jean-Luc Dehaene. June 1999 elections to the Chamber of Deputies resulted in a coalition government of Liberals, Socialists and Greens controlling a 19-seat majority under Flemish Liberal premier Guy Verhofstadt. In 2003 Liberals and Socialists formed a coalition government with Verhofstadt still in power. In 2007 he was forced to resign as voters resoundingly voted for a change. The Flemish leader, Yves Leterme, was unable to form a coalition government for more than nine months, but did so in March 2008. Little could be done as the nation seemed on the brink of splitting up along linguistic lines. In June 2010 the separatist Flemish party won a major victory in Flanders but could not form a government.

▶BELIZE

● **GEOGRAPHY Location:** northeastern coast of Central America. **Boundaries:** Mexico to N, Caribbean Sea to E, Guatemala to S and W. **Total land area:** 8,867 sq. mi. (22,966 sq km). **Coastline:** 240 mi. (386 km). **Comparative area:** slightly smaller than Massachusetts. **Land use:** 3% arable land; 1% permanent crops; 96% other. **Major cities:** Belmopan (capital); Belize City; Orange Walk; San Ignacio; Corozal.

● **PEOPLE Population:** 314,522 (July 2010 est.). **Nationality:** noun—Belizean(s); adjective—Belizean. **Ethnic groups:** 49% mestizo, 25% Creole, 11% Maya, 6.1% Garifuna. **Languages:** English (official), Spanish, Mayan, Garifuna (Carib). **Religions:** 50% Roman Catholic, 27% Protestant.

● **GOVERNMENT Type:** parliamentary democracy. **Independence:** Sept. 21, 1981 (from U.K.). **Constitution:** Sept. 21, 1981. **National holiday:** Independence Day, Sept. 21. **Heads of Government:** Sir Colville Norbert Young, governor general (since Nov. 1993); Dean Barrow, prime minister (since Feb. 2008). **Structure:** executive—governor general (appointed by Queen Elizabeth II, who is recognized as the head of state), prime minister, cabinet; bicameral legislature; judiciary.

● **ECONOMY Monetary unit:** Belizean dollar. **Budget:** (2009 est.) *income:* $376.5 mil.; *expend.:* $412.5 mil. **G.D.P.:** $2.49 bil., $8,100 per capita (2009 est.). **Chief crops:** bananas, coca, citrus, sugarcane; cultured shrimp; illegal producer of cannabis for international drug trade. **Natural resources:** arable land potential, timber, fish. **Major industries:** garments, food processing, tourism. **Labor force:** 122,300 (2008 est.); 10.2% agriculture, 18.1% industry, 71.7% services; shortage of skilled labor and all types of technical personnel;(2007 est.). **Exports:** $395 mil. (2009 est.); sugar, citrus, bananas, clothing. **Imports:** $616 mil. (2009 est.); machinery and transportation equipment, manufactured goods, food, fuels, chemicals. **Major trading partners:** (2008) *exports:* 36.9% U.S., 22.3% U.K.; *imports:* 38% U.S., 13.1% Mexico, 7.9% Cuba, 6.2% Guatemala.

During the 1700s, Spain held sovereignty over Belize but never attempted to settle it. The British gradually did settle there, however, and in 1862, British Honduras, as it was called, became a Crown colony. Although Britain granted Belize independence in 1981, Guatemala claimed sovereignty over the area until 1992, when it finally recognized Belize's independence. But as British defense forces withdrew in 1994, Guatemala reasserted its old claims but without consequence.

Dean Barrow's opposition United Democratic Party won election in 2008, unseating Said Musa after 10 years.

▶ BENIN
Republic of Benin

• **GEOGRAPHY Location:** western coast of Africa. **Boundaries:** Burkina Faso and Niger to N, Nigeria to E, Gulf of Guinea to S, Togo to W. **Total land area:** 43,484 sq. mi. (112,622 sq km). **Coastline:** 75 mi. (121 km). **Comparative area:** slightly smaller than Pennsylvania. **Land use:** 23.5% arable land; 2% permanent crops; 74% other. **Major cities:** Porto-Novo (capital); Cotonou.

• **PEOPLE Population:** 9,056,010 (July 2010 est.). **Nationality:** noun—Beninese (sing., pl.); adjective—Beninese. **Ethnic groups:** 98.4% African (predominantly Fon, Adja, Yoruba, Bariba); 1.6% other and European. **Languages:** French (official); Fon and Yoruba in south; at least six major tribal languages in north. **Religions:** 42.8% Christian, 24.4% Muslim, 17.3% Vodoun, 15.5% other.

• **GOVERNMENT Type:** republic. **Independence:** Aug. 1, 1960 (from France). **Constitution:** Dec. 2, 1990. **National holiday:** National Day, Aug. 1. **Head of Government:** Yayi Boni, head of state (since Apr. 2006). **Structure:** executive—president, executive council; unicameral legislature; judiciary.

• **ECONOMY Monetary unit:** Communauté Financiere Africaine franc. **Budget:** (2009 est.) *income:* $1.244 bil.; *expend.:* $1.634 bil. **G.D.P.:** $13.25 bil., $1,500 per capita (2009 est.). **Chief crops:** corn, cotton, cassava, yams. **Natural resources:** small offshore oil deposits, limestone, marble, timber. **Major industries:** textiles, food processing, beverages. **Labor force:** 3.662 mil. (2007 est.); 33.2% agriculture, 14.5% industry, 52.3% services. **Exports:** $1.024 bil. (2009 est.); cotton, crude oil, palm products, cocoa. **Imports:** $1.543 bil. (2009 est.); foodstuffs, beverages, tobacco, petroleum products. **Major trading partners:** (2008) *exports:* China, India, Japan, Niger, U.S.; *imports:* China, France, Thailand, U.S., Malaysia.

Although the early history of Benin is not well-established, a number of kingdoms had appeared in the region by the 11th century, and it was a center of wealth and power by the 1300s. In the 16th century, the Allada kingdom was founded in the south. In 1625, three brothers divided their power between Allada, Adjatché (Porto Novo), and Abomey. Under Ouegbadja (r. 1645–85) the latter, known as Dahomey, predominated. Much of its wealth derived from contact with Europeans, and especially the slave trade, which continued until 1885.

European contact began with the arrival of the Portuguese in 1485. Although traders and missionaries were established at Ouidah and Porto Novo in the 1700s, European influence remained slight. Dahomey expansion continued well into the 19th century. A commercial treaty with the French was signed in 1842, but relations between Dahomeyans and Europeans soon worsened. Outright hostilities began under Behanzin (r. 1858–89), who was defeated by the French, and in 1893 the French assimilated Abomey, Allada, and Porto Novo into the colony of Dahomey.

Independence from French rule came in 1960, followed by several coups until Mathieu Kerekou came to power in 1972. Kerekou established a Marxist regime, nationalizing large private businesses and abolishing opposition parties.

By December 1989, with the economy in a shambles and most trade conducted on the black market, there were demonstrations calling for Kerekou's resignation. A new constitution was approved in a Nov. 1990 referendum, and Nicéphore Soglo, a former World Bank official, was named prime minister. Soglo defeated the Marxist Kerekou in the 1991 presidential election, and appealed to western nations for a "Marshall Plan" for Africa. But in a rematch four years later, Kerekou regained the presidency. Yet, only three years later, in April elections for the National Assembly, it was Soglo's Renaissance of Benin Party that carried the majority. In March 2001 Kerekou won again over Soglo, this time with 84 percent of the vote. In 2006, neither Kerekou nor Soglo were on the ballot because they were over 70 years old. A development banker, Yayi Boni, won the election handily and turned immediately to economic reforms.

▶ BHUTAN
Kingdom of Bhutan

• **GEOGRAPHY Location:** Himalaya Mountains in southern Asia. **Boundaries:** China to N and W, India to S and E. **Total land area:** 14,824 sq. mi. (38,394 sq km). **Coastline:** none. **Comparative area:** about one-half the size of Indiana. **Land use:** 3% arable land; negl. % permanent crops; 97% other. **Major cities:** Timphu (capital).

• **PEOPLE Population:** 699,847 (July 2010 est.). **Nationality:** noun—Bhutanese (sing., pl.); adjective—Bhutanese. **Ethnic groups:** 50% Bhote, 35% ethnic Nepalese, 15% indigenous or migrant tribes. **Languages:** Dzongkha (official), various Tibetan dialects, various Nepalese dialects. **Religions:** 75% Lamaistic Buddhism, 25% Indian-and Nepalese-influenced Hinduism.

• **GOVERNMENT Type:** monarchy; special treaty relationship with India. **Independence:** In 1907 became a unified kingdom; Aug. 8, 1949 (from India). **Constitution:** ratified July 18, 2008 **National holiday:** Dec. 17. **Head of Government:** Jigme Khesar Namgyel Wangchuk, king (since Dec 2006); Lyonchoen J.Y. Thinley, prime minister (since Apr. 2008). **Structure:** executive—king, Royal Advisory Council, Council of Ministers; indirectly elected unicameral National Assembly consisting of 105 village elders, 10 monastic representatives, and 35 designated by the king; judicial—Supreme Court is the king.

• **ECONOMY Monetary unit:** ngultrum, Indian rupee. **Budget:** (FY 09/10 est.) *income:* $302 mil.; *expend.:* $588 mil. note—the government of India finances nearly three-fifths of Bhutan's expenditures. **G.D.P.:** $3.763 bil., $5,400 per capita (2009 est.). **Chief crops:** rice, corn, root crops, citrus. **Livestock:** cattle, poultry, pigs, sheep, yaks. **Natural resources:** timber, hydropower, gypsum, calcium carbide. **Major industries:** cement, wood products, fruits. **Labor force:** 299,900 note—major shortage of skilled labor; (2007) 24.7% agriculture, 38.1% services, 37.2% industry. **Exports:** $513 mil. (2008 est.); cardamom, gypsum, timber, handicrafts. **Imports:** $533 mil. (2008 est.); fuels and lubricants, grain, machinery and parts, vehicles. **Major trading partners:** (2008) *exports:* 86.3% India, 8.1% Bangladesh, 1.5% Italy; *imports:* 63% India, 12.3% Japan, 5.1% China.

A Tibetan-style Lamaistic Buddhist theocracy was established in this Himalayan enclave in the 16th century. The region came under the domination of the British raj in India in 1865, and Britain established a protectorate in 1910. A 1949 treaty with India granted independence to Bhutan. The present Druk Gyalpo, or Precious Ruler of the Dragon People, is the fourth in a dynasty dating from 1907. During the early years of his reign, he introduced reforms into this feudal, medieval country by broadening educational opportunities and compelling Buddhist monks to take up social work outside their monasteries.

From 1998 to 1999, King Wangchuk ruled through a rubber-stamp National Assembly, passing a series of laws aimed at driving out Nepalese and Indian settlers even if their families have resided in Bhutan for decades. More than 70,000 refugees have been registered by the U.N. high commissioner for refugees since 1991, and the numbers continue to grow. A "Gorkha Liberation Movement" has carried out raids in Bhutan from sanctuaries in India and Nepal.

In 1998 King Wangchuk began a second wave of reform, permitting the National Assembly to elect members of the Council of Ministers and even, by two-thirds vote, to call for the King's abdication. 1999 saw a mass amnesty of political prisoners. In late 2007, after 34 years, King Wangchuck announced he was stepping down and that his son, Crown Prince Jigme Kesar Namgyel, would be his successor. In July 2008 a constitution was adopted that established a two-party democracy after nearly a century of absolute monarchy.

▶ BOLIVIA
Republic of Bolivia

● **GEOGRAPHY Location:** landlocked country in central South America. **Boundaries:** Brazil to N and E, Paraguay and Argentina to S, Chile and Peru to W. **Total land area:** 424,164 sq. mi. (1,098,581 sq km). **Coastline:** none. **Comparative area:** slightly less than three times the size of Montana. **Land use:** 3% arable land; negl. % permanent crops; 97% other. **Major cities:** La Paz (administrative capital); Sucre (legal capital and seat of judiciary); Santa Cruz de la Sierra; Cochabamba; Oruro.

● **PEOPLE Population:** 9,947,418 (July 2010 est.). **Nationality:** noun—Bolivian(s); adjective—Bolivian. **Ethnic groups:** 30% Quechua, 25% Aymara, 30% mixed, 15% white. **Languages:** Spanish, Quechua, and Aymara (all official). **Religions:** 95% Roman Catholic; active Protestant minority, especially Methodist.

● **GOVERNMENT Type:** republic. **Independence:** Aug, 6, 1825 (from Spain). **Constitution:** Feb. 2, 1967, revised Aug 1994, new consitution approved Jan. 25, 2009, enacted February 7, 2009. **National holiday:** Independence Day, Aug. 6. **Head of Government:** Evo Morales, president (since Jan. 2006). **Structure:** executive; bicameral legislature; judiciary.

● **ECONOMY Monetary unit:** boliviano. **Budget:** (2009 est.) *income:* $7.946 bil.; *expend.:* $8.319 bil. **G.D.P.:** $45.11 bil., $4,600 per capita (2009 est.). **Chief crops:** soybeans, coffee, coca, cotton, corn, sugarcane, rice, potatoes. **Natural resources:** tin, natural gas, crude oil, zinc, tungsten. **Major industries:** mining, smelting, petroleum. **Labor force:** 4.536 mil.; 40% agriculture, 17% industry, 43% services. (2009) **Exports:** $4.837 bil. (2009 est.); soybeans, natural gas, zinc, gold. **Imports:** $4.166

bil. (2009 est.); capital goods, chemicals, petroleum. **Major trading partners:** (2008) *exports:* 60.1% Brazil, 8.3% U.S., 4.1% Japan; *imports:* 29.4% Brazil, 15.7% Argentina, 10.1% U.S., 9.1% Chile, 6.9% Peru.

The Incan Empire conquered the region that is now Bolivia in the 13th century. The Spanish discovered the fabulous silver deposits of the region and established their presence in the area in the cities of Sucre (1538) and Potosí (1545). From the early colonial period on, Bolivia—then called Upper Peru and part of the Viceroyalty of Peru—depended heavily on the export of minerals. The exploitation of tin and later oil and natural gas has had an important economic and political impact on the country's development.

In 1776, Upper Peru was transferred to the new Viceroyalty of La Plata centered in Buenos Aires. Upper Peru began agitating for independence in 1809, but it was not until liberation by Símon Bolívar (for whom the country was renamed) in 1825 that Bolivia became the last Spanish possession in South America to achieve independence. During 1836-39, Peru formed a brief union with Bolivia, until Chile broke up the confederation.

Bolivia has lost much of its original territory to its neighbors. The dictator Mariano Melgarejo sold large chunks of territory from 1865 to 1871. After the War of the Pacific (1879–84), Bolivia lost its access to the sea. And in the 1932–35 Chaco War with Paraguay, Bolivia lost more territory in the east.

Bolivia has suffered from Indian/non-Indian racial and cultural divisions, and political rivalry between the elites from the Potosí region and those from La Paz and Santa Cruz. Conservatives of the silver-mining southern region of Potosí controlled the government until they were ousted in 1898 by the Liberal tin interests of the La Paz region, who presided over a period of stable republican politics that lasted until the Great Depression and the Chaco War.

One of the results of the Chaco War was the fragmentation of the Bolivian military into competing factions in the struggle for power between conservative landowners and middle-class reformers. In 1941 the National Revolutionary Movement (MNR) was formed with the aim of transferring control of the country from conservative landowning elites to the middle sectors. The leadership of the movement found itself outpaced by revolts sponsored by workers and peasants; the MNR incorporated these elements into its program. When the 1952 revolution brought the MNR to power, its leadership, which included the future four-time president Victor Paz Estenssoro, embarked on a reformist political program. The military overthrew the MNR in 1964, and civilian rule was not restored until 1982. Paz Estenssoro was again elected to the presidency in 1985. Jaime Paz Zamora, leader of the Movement of the Revolutionary Left, gained the presidency in 1989.

In 1993, MNR candidate Gonzalo Sanchez de Lozada won the presidential election. An advocate of free-market economic reform, as planning minister (1986–88) he had reduced the country's hyperinflation rate from 25,000 percent to 15 percent. Opposition to free-market reforms brought a general strike by the leftist Bolivian Workers' Confederation. The government declared a state of siege in April 1995, and suspended civil liberties. Further privatization plans led to another general strike in 1996, with 50,000 demonstrators in the streets of La Paz. Faced with widespread rioting and looting, the government granted large raises to government employees.

Presidential elections in 1997 led to a run-off (settled in Congress) in which retired general Hugo Banzer Suarez, military dictator from 1971 to 1978, was elected president, pledging to continue economic reforms while ensuring that the poor would benefit from the reforms. His government was confronted in April 2000 with nation-wide riots over a planned increase in water rates and a general strike by the Workers Confederation. Timely retreats ended the protests. Banzer's resignation in 2001 for reasons of health brought elections in June 2002, with Congress again having to choose between the top two finishers; ex-president Sánchez de Lozada narrowly topped Socialist Evo Morales, head of the coca workers' union. By 2003, general strikes, mass demostrations, and road blocks (occasioned by the government's coca eradication program and proposal for natural gas project) led to Sanchez's resignation and replacement by vice-president Carlos Mesa Gisbert; he too was forced to resign (June 2005) after weeks of violent protests by workers' groups demanding nationalization of the oil and gas industry. Eduardo Rodríguez was chosen as interim president but national elections in Dec. 2005 brought a decisive victory to leftist Evo Morales, a congressman allied with Hugo Chavez and Fidel Castro. In May 2006, Morales ordered the military to occupy the oil and gas fields and gave foreign countries 180 days to renegotiate all existing contracts, which they did. Morales pushed on with reforms meant to give Indians greater opportunities. Despite violent reactions a new consitution was approved in a split vote in January 2009.

▶BOSNIA AND HERZEGOVINA
Republic of Bosnia and Herzegovina
• **GEOGRAPHY Location:** southeastern Europe. **Boundaries:** Croatia to N, W, Yugoslavia to S, E, and SE, Adriatic Sea to SW. **Total land area:** 19,767 sq. mi. (51,197 sq km). **Coastline:** 13 mi. (20 km). **Comparative area:** slightly smaller than West Virginia. **Land use:** 19.6% arable land; 2% permanent crops; 78.5% other. **Major cities:** Bosnia: Sarajevo (capital) Banja Luka. Herzegovina: Mostar.
• **PEOPLE Population:** 4,621,598 (July 2010 est.) Note: all population data is subject to considerable error due to dislocations caused by military actions and ethnic cleansing. **Nationality:** noun—Bosnian(s); adjective—Bosnian; noun—Herzegovine(s) or Herzegovinian(s); adjective—Herzegovine or Herzegovinian. **Ethnic groups:** 37% Serb, 48% Bozniak, 14% Croat. **Languages:** Croatian, Serbian, Bosnian. **Religions:** 40% Muslim, 31% Orthodox, 15% Catholic, 4% Protestant, 10% other.
• **GOVERNMENT Type:** emerging federal democratic republic. **Independence:** Mar. 1, 1992. **Constitution:** Dayton agreement, signed Dec. 1995, included a new constitution now in force. **National holiday:** National Day, Nov. 25 **Heads of Government:** Haris Silajdzic, president (since Mar. 2010); other members of the three-member presidency: Neboisa Radmanovic and Zeljko Komsic. **Structure:** executive— 3-member rotating presidency, prime minister, cabinet; bicameral legislature; judiciary.

• **ECONOMY Monetary unit:** convertible mark. **Budget:** (2009 est.) *income:* $7.814 bil.; *expend.:* $8.571 bil. **G.D.P.:** $29.07 bil.; $6,300 per capita (2009 est.) note—Bosnia has a large informal sector that may be as much as 50% of official GDP. **Chief crops:** corn, wheat, fruits, vegetables; livestock. **Natural resources:** coal, iron, bauxite, manganese, timber. **Major industries:** steel production, mining, manu-facturing, armaments. **Labor force:** 1.863 mil (2007 est.); 47% services, 32.6% industry. 20.5% agriculture. **Exports:** $3.95 bil. (2009 est.). **Imports:** $8.82 bil. (2009 est.). **Major trading partners:** (2008) *exports:* 20.7% Croatia, 16.7% Slovenia, 16.6% Italy, 13% Germany, 10.3% Austria, 4.8% Hungary; *imports:* 24% Croatia, 12.6% Slovenia, 12.1% Germany, 10.4% Italy, 6.5% Hungary, 6.4% Turkey.

Bosnia-Herzegovina has been in the middle of European power struggles since the 14th century. Its constantly changing boundaries have meant that its population has always been a hodgepodge of races and ethnicities. The name Bosnia comes from the region's geographic location on the Bosna River; Herzegovina was originally an Austrian border duchy (*herzog* means "duke" in German). The two lands were conquered by the Ottoman Empire in the 15th century, Bosnia in 1463, Herzegovina 20 years later. The conquered peoples, united into one administrative district by the Turks, were Roman Catholic Croatians and Orthodox Serbs. Over the centuries, a number of Slavic families, Croatians more than Serbs, gave up their Christianity and adopted the religion of their conquerors: Islam.

A peasant uprising (1875) over Turkish refusal to institute reforms ultimately led to the Russo-Turkish War of 1877–78. In 1878, the Congress of Berlin put Bosnia-Herzegovina under the control of Austria-Hungary. Sarajevo, the capital city, was the birthplace of World War I, where a Serbian nationalist assassinated the Austro-Hungarian archduke Francis Ferdinand in 1914. By 1918, Serbia had annexed Bosnia-Herzegovina and held it until World War II, when Germany incorporated it into the state of Croatia. In 1946, Bosnia-Herzegovina was made one of Yugoslavia's six constituent republics, along with Serbia, Croatia, Slovenia, Montenegro, and Macedonia.

The constant redrawing of Bosnia-Herzegovina's borders has meant that ethnicity in the region came to be based on religion, rather than national origin. Thus a Serb who converted to Roman Catholic Christianity was considered a Croatian, while a Croatian who converted to Eastern Orthodoxy was considered a Serb. And to both groups, converts to Islam appeared to be collaborators with the Ottoman Turks.

Nevertheless, the three ethnic groups coexisted peacefully under the iron hand of president-for-life Marshall Tito (Josip Broz). And even after Tito's death in 1980, his rotating presidency scheme, in which the leaders of each republic took turns serving as "president of the presidency," worked smoothly, as long as Yugoslavia was dominated by communism. At times, the president was a Muslim, the prime minister was a Croatian, and the president of the Assembly was a Serb. But when communism fell in 1989, only Serbia and Montenegro returned Communist governments to power; the other four republics established non- and even anti-Communist governments, and quickly sought to establish political independence from the ultra-Marxist regime of Serbian president Slobodan Milosevic.

Milosevic rigged elections in the provinces of Kosovo and Vojvodina to keep them under Serbian control, but he was unsuccessful in ethnically Serbian areas of Slovenia, Croatia, and Bosnia-Herzegovina. Croatia and Slovenia declared their independence in 1991, forcing Bosnia to choose between independence or a diminished role in a Serb-dominated Yugoslavia.

Bosnia-Herzegovina voted for independence in March 1992. But the mostly Serbian military of the former Yugoslavian army refused to go along with the vote. Led by Radovan Karadzic, they gained control of the region's artillery and proclaimed the existence of the "Serbian Republic of Bosnia-Herzegovina." The siege of Sarajevo began in April, with Serbia waging a ferocious war of "ethnic cleansing," to rid Bosnia of Muslims and Croats. By July 1993, the Serbs had surrounded the city, and despite evidence that the Serbs were raping and torturing Muslims, the Bosnian Parliament in Sept. 1993 rejected a U.N.-sponsored peace plan that would have ended the war.

Several other cease-fire agreements were brokered, but none led to a lasting peace until a 1995 pact brokered by U.S. negotiator Richard Holbrooke, in which the Bosnian Serbs agreed to follow the decisions of Yugoslavia's president Slobodan Milosevic in all peace talks. On Nov. 21, 1995, the presidents of Bosnia-Herzegovina, Croatia, and Serbia met in Dayton, Ohio, to sign a peace accord ending the civil war and dividing Bosnia-Herzegovina into two entities: a Serb republic and a Muslim-Croat federation. The two statelets would be governed by the same legislature and president.

The U.N. sent 60,000 peacekeeping troops in Dec. 1995 to supervise the transition. Elections in Sept. 1996 selected a three-member collective presidency, and a legislature whose 42 members were selected in two separate elections. In Jan. 1997, parliament approved a cabinet with joint (Serb and Muslim) premiers..

Yugoslavia and Bosnia established diplomatic relations in Oct. 1996, with Yugoslavia agreeing to respect Bosnia's boundaries while Bosnia dropped charges of genocide. A new crisis arose when on the same day (March 5, 1999), the West's "High Authority" (under the Dayton Accords) deposed the President of the Serb Republic, who had just been elected. Through 2000 and 2001 incidents of friction continued, provoking interventions by the High Authority and NATO troops, which themselves became sources of tension and even riots. In Oct. 2002, elections of bewildering complexity were held: for the three-man presidency, for the federation's parliament, and for the parliaments of the two member republics, with 57 parties taking part. Where true authority lay was made clear in 2003 as Chairman of the Presidency Mirko Sarovic resigned before he could be sacked by the High Commissioner who, in the same month, transferred control of the armed forces from the republics to the central authority. In Nov. 2005 the leaders of Serbian, Croatian and Muslim factors pledged to work toward a new constitution to create a stronger government, and in Sept. 2006, citizens of all three communities held elections and in Feb. 2007, a new prime minister was chosen. In 2008 Radovan Karadzic, a Bosnian Serb leader accused of war crimes, was found and arrested.

▶ BOTSWANA
Republic of Botswana

• **GEOGRAPHY Location:** landlocked country in southern Africa. **Boundaries:** Namibia to N and W, Zimbabwe to NE, South Africa to SE and S. **Total land area:** 223,607 sq. mi. (581,730 sq km). **Coastline:** none. **Comparative area:** about size of Texas. **Land use:** 1% arable land; negl.% permanent crops; 99% other. **Major cities:** Gaborone (capital); Francistown; Selebi-Phikwe; Molepolole; Serowe.

• **PEOPLE Population:** 2,029,307 (July 2010 est.). **Nationality:** noun and adjective—Motswana (sing.), Batswana (pl.). **Ethnic groups:** 79% Tswana, 11% Kalanga, 3% Basarwa, 7% other. **Languages:** English (official), Setswana. **Religions:** 20.6% none, 71.6% Christian, 6% Badimo, 1.4% other.

• **GOVERNMENT Type:** parliamentary republic. **Independence:** Sept. 30, 1966 (from U.K.). **Constitution:** Mar. 1965, effective Sept. 30, 1966. **National holiday:** Independence Day, Sept. 30. **Head of Government:** Seretse Khama Ian Khama, president (since Apr. 2008). **Structure:** executive; bicameral legislature; judiciary.

• **ECONOMY Monetary unit:** pula. **Budget:** (2009 est.) *income:* $2.675 bil.; *expend.:* $3.868 bil. **G.D.P.:** $26 bil., $13,100 per capita (2009 est.). **Chief crops:** sorghum, maize, millet, peanuts. **Natural resources:** diamonds, copper, nickel, coal, gold, salt, soda ash. **Major industries:** diamonds, copper, nickel, coal, salt, soda ash, potash. **Labor force:** 685,300 (2004) 288,400 formal sector employees; (2004 est.). **Exports:** $2.963 bil. (2009 est.); diamonds, copper and nickel, meat. **Imports:** $3.671 bil. (2009 est.); foodstuffs, vehicles, textiles, petroleum products. **Major trading partners:** (2006) *exports:* 87% European Free Trade Association (EFTA), 7% South African Customs Union (SACU), 3% Zimbabwe; *imports:* 74% SACU, 17% EFTA, 4% Zimbabwe.

Botswana, occupying a high and relatively arid tableland in southern Africa, was traditionally occupied by diverse groups of farmers, pastoralists, and hunter-gatherers. European missionaries arrived from South Africa in the early 19th century. In the late 19th century, native peoples resisted the encroachment of Afrikaners from the Transvaal; in response the British government established a protectorate in what was then called Bechuanaland in 1886. The southern part of the protectorate was organized as a Crown Colony and ultimately passed under the control of South Africa. During the 20th century, the territory remaining in the protectorate saw a steady evolution of local rule.

In 1920 two advisory councils were established to represent the interests of native and European inhabitants. In 1934 British authorities promulgated regulations establishing the powers and jurisdictions of native chiefs and the functions of native councils and courts. In 1951 a joint (native-European) advisory council was set up, and 10 years later an elected legislature met under the provisions of a new constitution.

In 1963–64 the British government accepted Botswanan proposals for self-government. A new capital was established at Gaborone in February 1965; a new constitution came into effect in the following month, and Botswana became fully independent on Sept. 30, 1966. Since independence, Botswana has been a multiparty, multiracial democracy that has remained untouched by the political turmoil affecting most of its neighbors. In National Assembly elections since 1998, voters have given the Botswana Democratic Party and President Festus Mogae strong margins of victory. In 2008 Mogae was succeeded by Seretse Khama Ian Khama, son of Botswana's first president.

Botswana is one of the most prosperous countries in Africa. It is the world's largest producer of diamonds; revenues from diamond exports have been wisely managed, leading to significant budgetary surpluses in recent years. Tourism, bolstered by Botswana's large herds of big game, is the country's major nonmining industry. But the nation's AIDS epidemic (30 percent of the adult population was infected with H.I.V.) had threatened to undermine the gains made over the past three decades, until a very advanced treatment program was introduced in 2005.

▶ **BRAZIL**
Federative Republic of Brazil
• **Geography Location:** central and northeastern South America. **Boundaries:** Colombia, Venezuela, Guyana, Suriname, French Guiana to N; Atlantic Ocean to E; Uruguay, Argentina, Paraguay to S; Peru, Bolivia to W. **Total land area:** 3,287,612 sq. mi. (8,514,877 sq km). **Coastline:** 4,652 mi. (7,491 km). **Comparative area:** slightly smaller than U.S. **Land use:** 6% arable land; 1% permanent crops; 93% other. **Major cities:** Brasília (capital); São Paulo; Rio de Janeiro; Belo Horizonte; Salvador.
• **People Population:** 201,103,330 (July 2010 est.). **Nationality:** noun—Brazilian(s); adjective—Brazilian. **Ethnic groups:** Portuguese, Italian, German, Japanese, black, Amerindian; 53.7% white, 38% mixed, 6% black, 1% other. **Languages:** Portuguese (official), Spanish, English, French. **Religions:** 73.6% Roman Catholic, 15.4% Protestant, 2.6% other, 7.4% none.
• **Government Type:** federative republic. **Independence:** Sept. 7, 1822 (from Portugal). **Constitution:** Oct. 5, 1988. **National holiday:** Independence Day, Sept. 7. **Head of Government:** Luiz Inácio Lula da Silva, president (since Jan. 2003). **Structure:** strong executive with broad powers; bicameral legislature with growing powers; judiciary.
• **Economy Monetary unit:** real. **Budget:** (2007) *income:* $244 bil.; *expend.:* $220 bil. **G.D.P.:** $2.025 tril., $10,200 per capita (2009 est.). **Chief crops:** coffee, soybeans, wheat, rice; beef. **Natural resources:** bauxite, gold, iron ore, manganese, nickel. **Major industries:** textiles and other consumer goods, shoes, chemicals. **Labor force:** 95.21 mil. (2009 est.); 66% services, 20% agriculture, 14% industry (2003 est.); **Exports:** $158.9 bil. (2009 est.); transport equipment, iron ore, soybeans, coffee, footwear. **Imports:** $136 bil. (2009 est.); capital goods, chemical products, oil. **Major trading partners:** (2008) *exports:* 13.7% U.S., 8.7% Argentina, 8.2% China; *imports:* 14.9% U.S., 11.6% China, 7.9% Argentina.

The Portuguese arrived on the coast of what would become Brazil with the expedition of Pedro Alvares Cabral in 1500 and found an indigenous population of semisedentary and nonsedentary cultures. Many of the semisedentary Indians spoke the Tupian language and shared similar cultural features. The Tupians quickly formed economic relationships with the first Europeans, who were interested in the valuable dyewood that was so abundant in Brazil.

The transition of Indian-European economic relations from barter to slavery was given momentum by the introduction of sugar export agriculture, a trend that began in the region in the 1540s. The 1560s saw epidemics of smallpox and measles in the coastal areas, which greatly reduced the indigenous population. Although the European sugar growers initially favored the use of indigenous peoples over imported African slave labor, the shortage of labor resulting from the epidemics led to increasing use of African slave labor by the Portuguese.

The Portuguese vied with other European powers for control of Brazilian territory, and in 1630 the Dutch briefly seized the northeastern sugar-growing area. Brazil's southern regions were underpopulated during the early colonial period, and Portuguese activity was largely limited to cattle raising. With the discovery of gold (1690s) and diamonds (1729), European settlement of the Minas Gerais area in the southeast quickened.

In 1808, the Portuguese royal court escaped Napoleon's armies with the help of the British fleet; the prince regent, Dom João VI, sought refuge in Brazil and made it the seat of the Portuguese empire. Dom João returned to Portugal in 1821, leaving his son Dom Pedro behind as prince regent. In 1822, defying orders to return to Portugal and opposed to the reversion of Brazil to colonial status, Dom Pedro declared Brazil's independence and was crowned emperor. In 1825 an agreement mediated by the British led to Portuguese recognition of Brazil as a separate kingdom.

Dom Pedro became increasingly estranged from his people and began losing control of the Brazilian political situation owing to a continuing series of landowner revolts and to the loss of a war with the United Provinces of Rio de la Plata over what would become Uruguay. In 1831 Dom Pedro abdicated in favor of his five-year-old son, Dom Pedro II; a regency governed Brazil until his accession to the throne in 1840.

The Brazilian empire found itself continually involved in the wars and internal politics of Uruguay, Argentina, and Paraguay in the 1850s and 1860s. The bloody five-year war with Paraguay that began in 1865 resulted in Paraguay's eventual defeat, but the process of the war had important consequences for the future of Brazil: the expansion of military power, the fragmentation of the political party system, and the undermining of the legitimacy of slavery. Slavery was abolished in 1888, and the following year, a military coup overthrew the emperor.

The "Old Republic," which lasted from 1889 to 1930, was a federal system in which much of the political control in Brazilian society was relegated to state-based political networks with local bosses. The presidency was assigned in a de facto rotation system called the "politics of the governors," in which the president's office was controlled by the most important state power networks. The world depression of 1929 hit the Brazilian agricultural export economy hard, and in 1930 the military overthrew the elected president; Getúlio Vargas, a politician from the state of Rio Grande do Sul, took over the presidency.

Vargas centralized power in the presidency. Civil unrest allowed Vargas to declare a state of siege with military backing, and in 1937 established the Estado Novo, a state wherein Vargas had absolute power. The military ousted Vargas in 1945, ushering in the period of the "Second Republic," but Vargas won re-election in 1950; he committed suicide in 1954. Juscelino Kubitschek, elected president in 1955, sought to develop the country and led the way for construction of the new capital of Brasília.

His successor, Jânio da Silva Quadros, resigned in 1961 after only seven months in office, and the presidency passed to populist Vice Pres. João Goulart. The populist mobilization of peasants and workers endorsed by the Goulart government led to his overthrow by the military in 1964.

The Brazilian military governed the country until 1985. Military rule was not maintained in the form of a dictatorship; rather, the military ruled as a more or less cohesive institution. The succession of generals and their technocratic allies attempted to develop the country through a pattern of state-led growth from which civilian politics were excluded. In 1985, Tancredo Neves was elected president, but he died before taking office. José Sarney, the vice presidential candidate, became Brazil's first civilian president since 1964.

Promising to revitalize the economy with a free-market revolution, conservative Fernando Collor de Mello became president in 1990. The military's share of the budget was reduced from 6 to 2.2 percent, and some companies were privatized, but inflation and debt still strained the economy. The 1988 murder of environmental activist Chico Mendes had focused world attention on the rapidly accelerating deforestation of the Amazon River basin. Pres. Collor campaigned actively to halt the destruction and in June 1992 Rio De Janeiro was the site of a U.N.-sponsored conference on development and the environment.

Pres. Collor was forced to resign in Dec. 1992 because of charges he stole or misappropriated over $20 million (after a two-year investigation he was cleared of all charges). His successor, Vice Pres. Itamar Franco, worked to privatize industries and halt inflation, but a new corruption scandal involving at least 18 members of the legislature halted most government activity in 1994.

In presidential elections held in Oct. 1994, former finance minister Fernando Henrique Cardoso ran on an anti-inflation platform and won a landslide victory. The Cardoso government focused on establishing federal control over state banks and supporting land reform for peasants. The rewards were a dramatic drop in both inflation and unemployment and great popularity for Cardoso. In 1997 Congress passed a Constitutional Amendment permitting Cardoso to run for a second term.

In Oct. 1998 Cardoso easily won re-election. Despite an unexpected 1999 devaluation of the Brazilian real, the I.M.F. released the remainder of its 1998 aid package. But Cardoso's popularity plummeted and in 2002 elections leftist Luiz Inacio Lula da Silva swamped Cardoso-backed Jose Serra in the presidential run-off, while his Workers' Party won a plurality in the Chamber of Deputies. The new president surprised everyone by quickly initiating reforms of the social security system and the public workers' pension plan. The economy which had picked up nicely turned tepid in early 2005; then a serious political scandal involving corruption charges brought the government to the brink of dissolution. But Lula survived and won a landslide victory in Oct. 2006 elections. In 2009 the discovery of large pools of oil off the coast was announced, enhancing Brazil's economic prospects. Other parts of the economy was rallied despite financial collapse.

Silva cannot run in the Oct. 2010 election but his party seemed confident of victory.

▶ BRUNEI
Negara Brunei Darussalam
• **GEOGRAPHY Location:** southeastern Asia, Kalimantan (Borneo) island. Bandar Seri Begawan 4°56'N, 114°58'E. **Boundaries:** surrounded on landward side by Sarawak, state, of Malaysia; South China Sea to N. **Total land area:** 2,225 sq. mi. (5,765 sq km). **Coastline:** 100 mi. (161 km). **Comparative area:** slightly larger than Delaware. **Land use:** 1% arable land; 1% permanent crops; 98% other. **Major cities:** Bandar Seri Begawan (formerly Brunei Town) (capital); Seria, Kuala Belait, Tutong.
• **PEOPLE Population:** 395,027 (July 2010 est.). **Nationality:** noun—Bruneian(s); adjective—Bruneian. **Ethnic groups:** 66% Malay, 11.2% Chinese, 3.4% indigenous, 19.1% other. **Languages:** Malay (official), English, Chinese. **Religions:** 67% Muslim (official), 13% Buddhist, 10% Christian, 10% indigenous and other.
• **GOVERNMENT Type:** constitutional sultanate. **Independence:** Jan. 1, 1984 (from U.K.). **Constitution:** Sept. 29, 1959 (some provisions suspended since Dec. 1962, others since independence). **National holiday:** National Day, Feb. 23. **Head of Government:** Sir Hassanal Bolkiah Mu'izzaddin Waddaulah, sultan and prime minister (since Aug. 1968). **Structure:** chief of state is sultan; unicameral legislature; judiciary.
• **ECONOMY Monetary unit:** bruneian dollar. **Budget:** (2008 est.) *income:* $6.889 bil.; *expend.:* $4 bil. **G.D.P.:** $19.43 bil., $50,100 per capita (2009 est.). **Chief crops:** rice, cassava, bananas. **Natural resources:** petroleum, natural gas, timber. **Major industries:** petroleum, petroleum refining, liquefied natural gas, construction. **Labor force:** 188,800 (2008 est.); 4.2% agriculture, 62.8% industry, 33% services (2003 est.). **Exports:** $10.67 bil. (2008 est.); crude oil, natural gas, petroleum products. **Imports:** $2.61 bil. (2008 est.); machinery and transport equipment, manufactured goods, foodstuffs, chemicals. **Major trading partners:** (2008) *exports:* 40.4% Japan, 21.4% Indonesia, 15.3% South Korea, 10% Australia; *imports:* 36.3% Singapore, 18.9% Malaysia, 7.6% Japan, 5.4% China, 5% Thailand, 4.7% U.S..

The Islamic sultanate of Brunei became dominant in northern Borneo in the 16th century but declined in power after the 17th century under pressure from the Dutch and other foreign powers. An Anglo-Dutch agreement of 1824 assigned North Borneo to Great Britain's sphere of influence in Asia. In 1841 a British adventurer, James Brooke, aided the sultan of Brunei in putting down a rebellion and was rewarded by being given the province of Sarawak, comprising more than half of the sultanate's area. Britain established a protectorate over Sabah, the eastern portion of Brunei, in 1881. That left the sultan with a tiny realm on the Brunei River, which was ultimately placed under British protection in 1888. The discovery of Southeast Asia's richest oilfield in Brunei and its offshore waters made the sultanate an enclave of tremendous wealth from the late 1920s onward.

Following Japanese occupation during World War II, British rule resumed in North Borneo. Sarawak and Sabah became part of Malaysia in 1963. Brunei was granted independence from Great Britain on Dec. 1, 1984. The sultan of

Brunei, an absolute monarch, rules from the world's largest royal palace in Bandar Seri Begawan, the nation's capital. The economy is centered almost entirely on petroleum and international banking and investments.

▶BULGARIA
Republic of Bulgaria

• **GEOGRAPHY Location:** southeastern Europe. **Boundaries:** Romania to N, Black Sea to E, Turkey and Greece to S, Macedonia and Yugoslavia to W. **Total land area:** 42,810 sq. mi. (110,879 sq km). **Coastline:** 220 mi. (354 km). **Comparative area:** slightly smaller than Tennessee. **Land use:** 29.9% arable land; 1.9% permanent crops; 68.2% other. **Major cities:** Sofia (capital); Plovdiv; Varna; Burges; Ruse.

• **PEOPLE Population:** 7,148,785 (July 2010 est.). **Nationality:** noun—Bulgarian(s); adjective—Bulgarian. **Ethnic groups:** 83.9% Bulgarian, 9.4% Turk, 4.7% Roma, 2% other. **Languages:** Bulgarian, Turkish, Roma. **Religions:** 82.6% Bulgarian Orthodox, 12.2% Muslim, 1.2% Christian, 4% other.

• **GOVERNMENT Type:** parliamentary democracy. **Independence:** March 3, 1878 (from Ottoman Empire). **Constitution:** July 12, 1991. **National holiday:** Independence Day, Mar. 3. **Heads of Government:** Georgi Parvanov, president (since Jan. 2002); Boyko Borissov, prime minister (since July 2009). **Structure:** executive; unicameral legislature; judiciary.

• **ECONOMY Monetary unit:** lev. **Budget:** (2009 est.) *income:* \$18.4 bil.; *expend:* \$18.9 bil. **G.D.P.:** \$90.51 bil., \$12,600 per capita (2009 est.). **Chief crops:** vegetables, fruits, tobacco; livestock. **Natural resources:** bauxite, copper, lead, zinc, coal. **Major industries:** machine building and metal working, food processing, chemicals. **Labor force:** 3.2 mil. (2009); 35% industry, 7.5% agriculture, 57% services (2008 est.). **Exports:** \$16.23 bil. (2009 est.); machinery and equipment, metals and ores, chemicals and plastics, food, textiles. **Imports:** \$23.27 bil. (2009 est.); fuels, minerals, and raw materials; machinery and equipment; food; textiles and apparel. **Major trading partners:** (2008) *exports:* 9.8% Greece, 9.1% Germany, 8.9% Turkey, 8.5% Italy; *imports:* 14.6% Russia, 11.8% Germany, 7.9% Italy.

Turkic Bulgars arrived at the west shore of the Black Sea in the seventh century, mingling with the indigenous Slavic population. The Bulgars accepted Eastern Orthodox Christianity in the ninth century and were conquered and incorporated into the Byzantine Empire by Basil II in the late 10th century. With the decline of Byzantium, Bulgaria became independent, but it was conquered by the Ottoman Turks in 1396 and remained part of the Ottoman Empire for the next 500 years.

In the Treaty of San Stefano, ending the Russo-Turkish War in 1878, a Bulgarian state was promised that was to stretch from the Adriatic to the Black Sea. But the Great Powers would not permit such a large Russian client state, and instead the Berlin Conference of 1878 sanctioned a much smaller Bulgarian state, under a German dynasty with the Ottoman sultan as nominal overlord. Bulgaria gained full independence in 1908.

The Balkan Wars of 1912 and 1913 led to a reduction of Bulgarian territory, and after World War I, Bulgaria, which had been allied with the Central Powers, lost its Aegean Coastline to Greece. A series of weak parliamentary governments under King Boris III (r. 1918–43) ended when the king established a dictatorship in 1935. Bulgaria joined the Axis powers in 1941 and declared war against the Western powers but not against Russia. Russian troops entered Bulgaria in 1944 and organized a Communist government. The boy-king Simeon II remained on the throne until 1946, when the monarchy was abolished by a popular referendum. The People's Republic of Bulgaria was established in 1947.

Until the end of World War II, Bulgaria was a peasant society, with 80 percent of the population engaged in agriculture; industrial development was rudimentary. The People's Republic established a planned economy on the Soviet model; Russian credits and trade agreements permitted a rapid industrialization focused on machinery and equipment for export.

In 1954 Todor Zhivkov became first secretary of the Bulgarian Communist party. He served as premier in the 1960s and president from 1971 to 1990. In the 1960s Zhivkov promoted decentralization and responsiveness to market forces, but with the 1968 Russian invasion of Czechoslovakia, he returned the economy to central planning and giant state-industrial enterprises. In October 1985 Zhivkov met with Gorbachev and reforms based on Gorbachev's "self-management" policies were instituted.

Democratic reform began with Zhivkov's resignation in Nov. 1989. There followed a year of popular unrest and political turmoil until the election of Zheliu Zhelev of the reform Union of Democratic Forces as president (Bulgaria's first non-Communist leader in 40 years), and the appointment in 1990 of Dimitar Popov as premier of a coalition government dominated by the Socialist (formerly Communist) party.

Elections in October 1991 ended the Socialist grip on power, as the Union of Democratic Forces formed a government under Philip Dimitrov. But within a year the government was bankrupt, inflation at 30 percent and unemployment 40 percent, and Dimitrov's government was ousted by Parliament. Lyuben Berov, an economic adviser to Zhelev, came to power for two years and then he was ousted in elections (Dec. 1994) by the Socialists, led by Zhan Videnov.

Under the Videnov-Zhelev "gridlock," matters only grew worse, with a food crisis developing atop growing unemployment and 300 percent inflation in 1996. Protests and riots marked the latter half of 1996, and in the Nov. presidential elections, the UDF candidate, Peter Stoyanov (who defeated Zhelev in a party primary) won easily. And in 1997 elections to parliament, the UDF coalition took 137 seats to the Socialists' 58. With the promise of economic reform, the I.M.F. and the E.U. provided large new grants.

The new prime minister, Ivan Kostov, commenced some serious reforms of the all-but-insolvent economy, reforms that were on the one hand painful and on the other not radical enough to rid the economy of state control. Bulgaria's last king, Simeon II, founded a political party which in parliamentary elections won about half the seats and transformed the one-time king into the Republic's new prime minister who pushed Bulgaria into NATO and later the E.U. In 2005, his party was forced into a coalition with the socialist party led by Sergei Stanishev. Corruption and the world-wide recession led to serious economic and political problems. In July 2009 voters chose the tough-talking Mayor of Sofia, Boyko Borisov, to change the nation's direction in a larger than expected victory over the socialists.

▶ BURKINA FASO

• **GEOGRAPHY** **Location:** landlocked country in western Africa. **Boundaries:** Mali to N and W, Niger to E, Benin, Togo, Ghana, Ivory Coast to S. **Total land area:** 105,869 sq. mi. (274,200 sq. km). **Coastline:** none. **Comparative area:** slightly larger than Colorado. **Land use:** 17.6% arable land; negl.% permanent crops; 82.1% other. **Major cities:** Ouagadougou (capital); Bobo-Dioulasso; Koudougou; Ouahigouya; Banfora. • **PEOPLE** **Population:** 16,241,811 (July 2010 est.). **Nationality:** noun—Burkinabe (sing., pl.); adjective—Burkinabe. **Ethnic groups:** over 40% Mossi; Gurunsi, Senufo, Lobi, Bobo, Mande, Fulani. **Languages:** French (official); native African languages spoken by 90% of population. **Religions:** 50% Muslim, 40% indigenous beliefs, 10% Christian (mainly Roman Catholic).
• **GOVERNMENT** **Type:** parliamentary republic. **Independence:** Aug. 5, 1960 (from France). **Constitution:** June 2, 1991. **National holiday:** Republic Day, Dec. 11. **Heads of Government:** Blaise Compaore, president (since Dec. 1991); Tertius Zongo, prime minister (since June 2007). **Structure:** executive; bicameral legislature; judiciary.
• **ECONOMY** **Monetary unit:** Communaué Financière Africaine (CFA) franc. **Budget:** (2009 est.) *income:* $1.364 bil.; *expend.:* $1.91 bil. **G.D.P.:** $18.79 bil., $1,200 per capita (2009 est.). **Chief crops:** peanuts, shea nuts, sesame, cotton. **Natural resources:** manganese, limestone, marble; small deposits of gold, antimony, copper, nickel, bauxite. **Major industries:** cotton, beverages, agricultural processing. **Labor force:** 6.67 mil. (2007); 90% agriculture; a large part of male labor force migrates to neighboring countries for seasonal employment. **Exports:** $648 mil. (2009 est.); cotton, gold, animal products. **Imports:** $1.076 bil. (2009 est.); machinery, food products, petroleum. **Major trading partners:** (2008) *exports:* 16.6% Singapore, 12.6% Belgium, 11% China, 8.9% Thailand, 6.8% Ghana; *imports:* 26% Cote D'Ivoire, 20% France, 8% Togo.

The Mossi empire dominated the area of what is now Burkina Faso, a landlocked nation in western Africa with few natural resources and poor agricultural conditions, from as early as the 11th century. They ruled the region, often resisting Muslim invaders, until modern times.

The region was hardly visited by Europeans before the 1880s, but by 1896 the French had captured the Mossi capital city of Ouagadougou and established a protectorate over the area. The French created Upper Volta in 1919, naming it for the upper basin of the Volta River. Upper Volta became a self-governing state with the French Overseas Community in 1958 and gained independence Aug. 5, 1960.

After a brief period of military rule, the nation ratified a new constitution on June 14, 1970, and made a peaceful transition to civilian rule based on the French model. In 1980 the constitution was overthrown and a military government was set up. There was another coup on Aug. 4, 1983, and a government was established patterned after the Libyan government of Muammar al-Qaddafi. On Aug. 14, 1984, Upper Volta officially changed its name to Burkina Faso.

Two attempted coups against the government of Capt. Blaise Compaore, in September and December 1989, were put down and the leaders executed. In 1992, as president, Compaore convened a National Reconciliation Forum followed by legislative elections that resulted in a new prime minister. In 1994 the World Bank reported significant economic progress in this desperately poor country. Compaore won two more elections, the last in 2005.

▶ BURUNDI
Republic of Burundi

• **GEOGRAPHY** **Location:** landlocked country on northeastern shore of Lake Tanganyika in central Africa. **Boundaries:** Rwanda to N, Tanzania to E and S, Zaire to W. **Total land area:** 10,745 sq. mi. (27,830 sq km). **Coastline:** none. **Comparative area:** slightly larger than Maryland. **Land use:** 35.6% arable land; 13% permanent crops; 51.3% other. **Major cities:** Bujumbura (capital); Gitega.
• **PEOPLE** **Population:** 9,863,117 (July 2010 est.). **Nationality:** noun—Burundian(s); adjective—Burundi. **Ethnic groups:** 85% Hutu (Bantu), 14% Tutsi (Hamitic), 1% Twa (Pygmy), 3,000 Europeans, 2,000 South Asians. **Languages:** Kirundi and French (both official), Swahili (along Lake Tanganyika and in Bujumbura area). **Religions:** 67% Christian (62% Roman Catholic, 5% Protestant), 23% indigenous beliefs, 10% Muslim.
• **GOVERNMENT** **Type:** republic. **Independence:** July 1, 1962 (from U.N. trusteeship under Belgian administration). **Constitution:** Ratified by popular referemdum on Feb. 28, 2005 **National holiday:** Independence Day, July 1. **Heads of Government:** Pierre Nkurunziza, president (since June, 2005); **Structure:** executive; unicameral legislature; judiciary. (Note: a miltary government took office during a 1996 coup, but the new leadership has not been officially recognized.)
• **ECONOMY** **Monetary unit:** Burundi franc. **Budget:** (2009 est.) *income:* 342.2 mil; *expend.:* $385.7 mil. **G.D.P.:** $3.247 bil., $300 per capita (2009 est.). **Chief crops:** coffee, cotton, tea, corn, sorghum. **Natural resources:** nickel, uranium, rare earth oxide, peat, cobalt. **Major industries:** light consumer goods such as blankets, shoes, soap; assembly of imported components; public works construction. **Labor force:** (2007 est.) 4.245 mil.; 93% agriculture, 7% other. (2002 est.) **Exports:** $79 mil. (2009 est.); coffee, tea, cotton, hides. **Imports:** $318 mil. (2009 est.); capital goods, petroleum products, foodstuffs. **Major trading partners:** (2008) *exports:* 27.9% Switzerland, 11% UK, 9.5% Pakistan; *imports:* 22.4% Saudi Arabia, 13.6% Belgium, 9.1% Uganda.

Burundi's population is divided between two ethnic groups, the majority Hutu and the minority, but politically powerful, Tutsi. The Hutu were the original settlers of the country and practiced agriculture; the cattle-herding Tutsi arrived several hundred years ago and established a form of feudal overlordship over the Hutu. The traditional government was monarchical, with a king (*mwami*) chosen from among a group of aristocratic families (*ganwa*).

European exploration of Burundi began in 1858, and the territory was incorporated into German

East Africa in 1899. Following World War I, the League of Nations (1923) awarded Burundi, along with neighboring Rwanda, to Belgium as a mandated territory. Belgian rule over the Territory of Ruanda-Urundi, as it was then called, continued under a U.N. trusteeship after World War II.

Burundi became independent on July 1, 1962, as a constitutional monarchy under the traditional mwami. The country rapidly lapsed into political chaos. In 1966 Capt. Michel Micombero overthrew the monarchy and proclaimed a republic. A Hutu rebellion in 1972 against Tutsi political domination left 10,000 Tutsi dead; Tutsi reprisals in 1972–73 resulted in the slaughter of 150,000 Hutu. The Micombero government was overthrown in a bloodless coup, and on Nov. 1, 1976, Lt. Col. Jean-Baptiste Bagaza took control of the government.

Bagaza was overthrown in Sept. 1987, and his successor, Maj. Pierre Buyoya, proclaimed a policy of nonalignment, seeking closer links with the West, while maintaining relations with Libya and the eastern bloc. Domestically, the government pledged to eradicate Bagaza's record of persecution of the Catholic church (62 percent of Burundians are Catholic) and to seek ethnic reconciliation between Hutu and Tutsi, but renewed outbreaks of ethnic violence occurred in 1988. Buyoya led the country to its first free presidential elections in June 1993. Melchior Ndadaye, a Hutu, defeated Buyoya by a wide margin.

But in Oct. 1993 Ndadaye was assassinated, as was his Hutu successor (April 1994). The succeeding regime of Hutu president Ntibantunganya, unsuccesful in forming a stable, ethnically balanced goverment, was overturned in a military coup (July 1996) which dissolved parliament, outlawed all political parties, and named Pierre Buyoya to return as president. Vowing yet another return to democracy after the end of civil war, Buyoya faced economic sanctions by the Organization of African Unity. Meanwhile, the complicated civil war was only worsened by Zaire's attempt to expel almost half a million Tutsi (the Banyamulenge people, settled south on Lake Kivu since the 18th century) in 1996. The Tutsi succesful self defense had the paradoxical effect of driving yet more Hutu (50,000) into Burundi—and almost half a million more into Rwanda.

The civil war continued into 2000, with at least 200,000 dead, with 350,000 Hutu rebels "regrouped" into 50 camps, and with Burundian army involvement (unadmitted) in the Congo conflict. A promising peace accord, brokered by Nelson Mandela in Aug. 2000, collapsed in Feb. 2001 as the capital of Bujumbura fell to Hutu rebels. Government forces re-took it on March 1, and another accord again forged by Mandela was signed by all parties in July 2001. Based on a power-sharing arrangement for three years the new 14 Hutu/12 Tutsi cabinet began ruling Nov. 1. A year later (Dec. 2002) the rebel group "Force for the Defense of Democracy" signed a truce with the government and in April 2003 when (as agreed) Hutu Domitien Ndayizeye was sworn in as president. Yet in July rebels attacked the capital of Bujumbara, while fighting continued in provincial villages as the civil war entered its eleventh year. Sporadic peace talks continued into 2004 but a brutal attack by a rebel group on a Tutsi refugee camp made peace seem a distant reality. Elections were held finally in 2005 and Pierre Nkurunziza, a rebel leader, won the presidency and an uneasy

peace settled in with help from 3,000 U.N. peacekeepers. He ran unopposed in 2010 but opposition parties claimed fraud and intimidation.

▶ CAMBODIA
Kingdom of Cambodia

- **GEOGRAPHY** **Location:** on Indochinese peninsula in Southeast Asia. **Boundaries:** Thailand to W and N, Laos to N, Gulf of Thailand to S, Vietnam to E. **Total land area:** 69,898 sq. mi. (181,035 sq km). **Coastline:** 275 mi. (443 km). **Comparative area:** slightly smaller than Oklahoma. **Land use:** 21% arable land; 1 % permanent crops; 78% other. **Major cities:** Phnom Penh (capital).
- **PEOPLE** **Population:** 14,753,320 (July 2010 est.). **Nationality:** noun—Cambodian(s); adjective—Cambodian. **Ethnic groups:** 90% Khmer (Cambodian), 5% Vietnamese, 1% Chinese, 4% other minorities. **Languages:** Khmer (official), French, English. **Religions:** 95% Theravada Buddhism.
- **GOVERNMENT** **Type:** multiparty liberal democracy under a constitutional monarchy. **Independence:** November 9, 1953 (from France). **Constitution:** promulgated Sept. 21, 1993. **National holiday:** Independence Day, November 9. **Heads of Government:** Norodom Sihamoni, king (since Oct. 2004); Hun Sen, prime minister (since Nov. 1998). **Structure:** executive; bicameral legislature; judiciary.
- **ECONOMY** **Monetary unit:** riel. **Budget:** (2009 est.) income: $1.186 bil.; expend.: $1.748 bil. **G.D.P.:** $28.09 bil., $1,900 per capita (2009 est.). **Chief crops:** rice, rubber, corn, vegetables. **Natural resources:** timber, gemstones, some iron ore, manganese, phosphates, hydropower potential. **Major industries:** garments, rice milling, fishing, wood and wood products. **Labor force:** 8 mil.; 68% agriculture (2009 est.). **Exports:** $4.13 bil. (2009 est.); timber, garments, rubber, soybeans, sesame. **Imports:** $6.004 bil. (2009 est.); cigarettes, gold, construction materials, petroleum products. **Major trading partners:** (2008) exports: 54.5% U.S., 7.7% Germany, 5.9 % Canada, 5.5% U.K. imports: 27.1% Thailand, 19.2% Vietnam, 14.7% China, 8.2% Honk Kong, 7% Singapore, 5.6% Taiwan.

The dominant power in Indochina from the eighth through the 13th centuries, the Khmer Empire encompassed present-day Cambodia and much of western Thailand, southern Laos, and central and southern Vietnam. It built magnificent Buddhist temple cities at Angkor Wat and Angkor Thon. From the 14th century onward, the Khmer Empire came under increasing pressure from the expansionist Vietnamese state of Annam, which absorbed the territories east of the Mekong River. In the 18th century, the kingdom of Siam (Thailand) annexed three western provinces of the Khmer Empire. The remaining Khmer territory became the French protectorate of Cambodia in 1863, and a French colony as part of the Union of Indochina in 1887. In 1907 France forced Siam to return some territory to Cambodia.

Cambodia was occupied by Japan from 1942 to 1945, when French control was restored. After the French defeat in Indochina, Cambodia became independent in 1953 under Prince Norodom Sihanouk, who had ascended the throne in 1941. In 1960 Sihanouk was named head of state under a constitutional monarchy. Shaken by the Vietnam War in the 1960s, Cambodia broke relations with the U.S. in 1965 because of South Vietnamese incursions across the border. In 1969 relations were restored when Sihanouk charged North Vietnam with arming the Khmer Rouge Cambodian Communist rebels. In the same year, American planes began secret bombing raids in Cambodia. In 1970 Sihanouk was ousted by a coup led by pro-U.S. Gen. Lon Nol; the monarchy was abolished, and Prince Sihanouk went into exile.

In April 1975 the Khmer Rouge, led by Pol Pot, captured the capital, Phnom Penh, and established a new government, the Kampuchean People's Republic. In an ensuing reign of terror, an estimated 1.7 million people died and hundreds of thousands more fled to refugee camps in Thailand. In 1978, Vietnamese troops invaded, capturing Phnom Penh on Jan. 7, 1979, and installing a new government led by Heng Samrin. The Kampuchean People's Republic continued to be recognized as the legal government of Cambodia in the United Nations and by most non-Soviet-bloc nations. A coalition dominated by the Khmer Rouge resisted the Vietnamese takeover, but by 1985 almost all of the country was under Vietnamese control with the Communist Party's Hun Sen as Prime Minister.

Most Vietnamese troops withdrew in 1989, and Prince Sihanouk emerged as the leader of a coalition of antigovernment forces. Starting in late 1988 conferences including representatives from all Cambodian factions were held to forge a political settlement to end the 20-year-old civil war. A peace agreement was signed on Oct. 23, 1991, providing for a cease-fire under U.N. supervision, the disarmament of all military factions, the formation of a coalition government, and the scheduling of a national election.

Despite bloody efforts by Khmer Rouge forces to disrupt the planned election, Cambodians went to the polls in large numbers on May 23, 1993. The Royalist party emerged with about 42 percent of the vote, ousting Hun Sen's Cambodian People's party. Hun Sen agreed to take part in a coalition cabinet as "second premier," with Sihanouk's son, Prince Ranariddh, as "first premier." Sihanouk took the title "king." In Jan. 1994, the united government went on the offensive and captured the Khmer Rouge stronghold of Pailin. Sihanouk succesfully negotiated international loans for rebuilding the country.

The coalition government proved ineffective due to the inherent rivalry between the prince and Hun Sen, both of whom built up their security forces. When the Khmer Rouge leadership split in mid-1997, with Pol Pot either assassinated or imprisoned, Hun Sen seized the moment and his forces attacked those of his co-ruler's and drove the prince into exile. New elections were held in July 1998 and Hun Sen emerged victorious but agreed to form a coalition government. Hun Sen became "sole premier" with 12 cabinet posts while Ranariddh became President of the Assembly with 11 cabinet posts. In 1998, the last Khmer Rouge troops surrendered, and by March 1999, most of the remaining Khmer Rouge leaders had surrendered or were captured. In Jan. 2001 the Senate and National Assembly approved Hun Sen's agreement with the U.N. for an international tribunal to try the mass murderers. Elections in July 2003 gave Hun Sen's People's Party almost 50 percent of the vote. In July 2010 the international court convicted the first Khmer Rouge leader of war crimes and crimes against humanity. (See "Major News Stories.")

▶ CAMEROON
Republic of Cameroon

● GEOGRAPHY   Location: western coast of central Africa. Boundaries: Nigeria to NW, Chad to NE, Central African Republic to E, Congo to SE, Gabon, Equatorial Guinea to S, Gulf of Guinea to W. Total land area: 183,568 sq. mi. (475,440 sq km). Coastline: 250 mi. (402 km). Comparative area: slightly larger than California. Land use: 13% arable land; 3% permanent crops; 84% other. Major cities: Yaoundé (capital); Douala; Nkongsamba (and environs); Maroua (and environs).

● PEOPLE   Population: 19,294,149 (July 2010 est.). Nationality: noun—Cameroonian(s); adjective—Cameroonian. Ethnic groups: 31% Cameroon Highlanders, 19% Equatorial Bantu, 11% Kirdi, 10% Fulani, 8% Northwestern Bantu, 7% Eastern Nigritic, 13% other African; less than 1% non-African. Languages: English and French (both official); 24 major African language groups. Religions: 40% indigenous beliefs, 40% Christian, 20% Muslim.

● GOVERNMENT   Type: unitary republic; multiparty presidential regime. Independence: Jan. 1, 1960 (from U.N. trusteeship under French administration). Constitution: May 20, 1972; adopted June 2, 1972; revised Jan. 1996. National holiday: Republic Day, May 20. Heads of Government: Paul Biya, president (since Nov. 1982); Philemon Yang, prime minister (since June 2009). Structure: executive; unicameral legislature; judiciary.

● ECONOMY   Monetary unit: Communauté Financière Africaine franc. Budget: (2009 est.) income: $3.838 bil.; expend.: $3.781 bil. G.D.P.: $42.76 bil., $2,300 per capita (2009 est.). Chief crops: coffee, cocoa, cotton, rubber. Natural resources: crude oil, bauxite, iron ore, timber, hydropower potential. Major industries: crude oil production and refining, food processing. Labor force: 7.313 mil (2009); 70% agriculture, 13% industry and transport, 17% other services. Exports: $3.409 bil. (2009 est.); crude oil and petroleum products, lumber, cocoa beans, aluminum. Imports: $3.739 bil. (2009 est.); machines and electrical equipment, transport equipment, fuel, food. Major trading partners: (2008) exports: 19.4% Spain, 13.2% Italy, 10.4% U.S., 8% France, 7.9% Netherlands; imports: 21.2% France, 13.9% Nigeria, 9.6% China, 6.1% Belgium.

Cameroon was settled by the Sao people about 1,000 years ago. In later times others, including the Bamileke, Bassa, Douala, and Fulani, migrated into the region. Portuguese trading stations were established along the coast beginning in the 15th century. Between 1500 and the early 19th century, the population was severely depleted by the slave trade in the hands of various European nations. European rivalries for domination in Cameroon were settled temporarily in 1884 when Germany established a protectorate.

British and French troops invaded German Cameroon during World War I, and following the war the League of Nations divided the protectorate into two mandated territories—French in the eastern sector and British in the west. French Cameroon rejected the Vichy government in World War II and became an important African base for Charles de Gaulle's Free French. In 1946 British and French rule in Cameroon was reaffirmed under U.N. trusteeships.

In 1958 the French trusteeship was abolished, and the Republic of Cameroon became independent on Jan. 1, 1960. In February 1961 a U.N.-supervised plebiscite was held in British Cameroon, allowing the people of that region to choose between union with Nigeria and union with the Republic of Cameroon. The northern two-thirds of the British territory elected union with Nigeria; the southern portion joined the Republic of Cameroon on Oct. 1, 1961, to form the Federal Republic of Cameroon. In 1972 the federal structure was abolished by a national referendum, and the United Republic of Cameroon was established. In 1984 the nation's name reverted to the Republic of Cameroon.

During the federal period, Cameroon had a multiparty political system, with party divisions coinciding with the old distinctions between west and east Cameroon. In 1966 all political parties were amalgamated to form the Cameroon National Union, which, with various changes in name, has dominated the political life of Cameroon ever since. In 1980 Pres. Ahidjo, the long-time political leader of Cameroon, was elected without opposition to a fifth five-year term in office. He resigned in 1982 and was replaced by Prime Minister Paul Biya, who was reelected in his own right in 1984. He instituted political reforms whereby multiple candidates ran for office within the structure of the country's single-party system. In 1992 he was elected president in the nation's first multiparty elections. His closest rival was put under house arrest.

The economy of Cameroon is based primarily on agriculture; it is self-sufficient in food and exports coffee, cocoa, rubber, cotton, palm oil, and timber. Oil is the principal export, however, accounting for 60 percent of export earnings.

▶ CANADA

• **GEOGRAPHY Location:** northern North America (excluding Alaska and Greenland); second largest country in the world. **Boundaries**: Arctic Ocean to N, Greenland to NE across Baffin Bay, Atlantic Ocean to E, United States to S, Pacific Ocean and Alaska to W. **Total land area:** 3,855,103 sq. mi. (9,984,670 sq km). **Coastline:** 125,566 mi. (202,080 km). **Comparative area:** slightly larger than U.S. **Land use:** 5% arable land; negl.% permanent crops, 95% other. **Major cities:** Ottawa (capital), Toronto; Montréal; Vancouver; Edmonton.

• **PEOPLE Population:** 33,759,742 (July 2010 est.). **Nationality:** noun—Canadian(s); adjective—Canadian. **Ethnic groups:** 28% British Isles origin, 23% French origin, 15% other European, 2% Amerindian, 6% other, mostly Asian, Arab, African. **Languages:** 59.3% English, 23.2% French (both official). **Religions:** 42.6% Roman Catholic, 23.3% Protestant, 14.1% other, 16% none.

• **GOVERNMENT Type:** confederation with parliamentary democracy. **Independence:** July 1, 1867 (from U.K.) recognized by the U.K on Dec. 11, 1931. **Constitution:** amended British North America Act of 1867 transferred power and rights to Canada, Apr. 17, 1982; charter of rights and unwritten customs. **National holiday:** Canada Day, July 1. **Heads of Government:** Stephen Harper, prime minister (since Feb. 2006); Michelle Jean governor-general (since Sept. 2005). **Structure:** executive—cabinet collectively responsible to House of Commons and headed by prime minister; legislative—bicameral Parliament with queen represented by governor general, Senate, and House of Commons; judiciary—judges appointed by governor general with Supreme Court as highest tribunal.

• **ECONOMY Monetary unit:** Canadian dollar. **Budget:** (2009 est.) *income:* $514.5 bil.; *expend.:* $547.2 bil. **G.D.P.:** $1.285 tril., $38,400 per capita (2009 est.). **Chief crops:** grain (principally wheat), oilseeds, tobacco. **Natural resources:** iron ore, nickel, zinc, copper, gold, lead. **Major industries:** processed and unprocessed minerals, food products, wood and paper products. **Labor force:** 18.4 mil.; 2% agriculture, 13% manufacturing, 6% construction, 76% services (2006) . **Exports:** $298.5 bil. (2009 est.); motor vehicles and parts, wood pulp, timber, petroleum. **Imports:** $305.2 bil. (2009 est.); machinery and equipment, petroleum, chemicals, motor vehicles. **Major trading partners:** (2008) *exports:* 77.7% U.S., 2.7% U.K., 2.3% Japan; *imports:* 52.4% U.S., 9.8% China, 4.1% Mexico.

Canada is geographically the second-largest country in the world, but most of its territory is very sparsely settled. The vast majority of the country's 32 million people live in a narrow band along the border with the U.S. Despite a long tradition of national independence, Canada's history has been dominated by relations with Great Britain, the U.S., and, to a lesser extent, France.

Canada's earliest inhabitants arrived via the Bering land bridge from Asia around 15,000 years ago and diversified to form the various Inuit (Eskimo), Northwest Indian, Plains Indian, and forest Indian cultures that still contribute significantly to Canada's national identity. The earliest-known European settlers of Canada were Vikings, who established a short-lived colony in Newfoundland around A.D. 1000. Other European explorers made numerous voyages to Canada during the 16th century, stimulated by Canada's rich resources of fish, forest products, and furs.

The first permanent European settlement in Canada was the French trading station at Quebec, founded by Samuel de Champlain in 1608. Fur traders rapidly spread into the interior along the St. Lawrence River and the Great Lakes; European diseases, particularly smallpox, decimated Native American populations as the explorers advanced. In 1663 New France was organized as a French Crown Colony, and royal governors replaced private commercial interests in governing Quebec.

The Hudson Bay Company was chartered by the British Crown in 1670, inaugurating a long period of commercial and territorial rivalry in Canada between Britain and France. In general, France sought to expand New France northward and westward, while Britain sought to expand its domination southward and westward from Hudson Bay. French and British interests clashed directly along the Atlantic coast, where both British and French settlements were established. Local and regional wars between the French and the British were endemic in Canada throughout the 17th and 18th centuries; each side enlisted Native American allies. These wars were often inconclusive, but in Queen Anne's War (1702–13), Britain gained a significant advantage by winning control of Acadia and Newfoundland, and by driving the French from Hudson Bay.

The French and Indian Wars of 1756–63, a North American extension of Europe's Seven Years' War, proved to be the decisive turning point in the Anglo-French rivalry in Canada. Prior to the outbreak of full-scale war, in 1755 the British deported some 7,000–10,000 French settlers from Acadia, in Nova Scotia, to the West Indies; many later settled in Louisiana. When war broke out in Europe in 1756, Britain employed its superior sea power to cut New France off from Europe and captured Quebec in the Battle of the Plains of Abraham in 1759. Montreal capitulated in 1760, leaving Britain in control of New France.

Faced with the problem of governing New France's large French population (which far outnumbered Canada's English-speaking population), the British in 1774 passed the Quebec Act, which recognized the territory's legal code and system of land tenure, and granted legal status to the Roman Catholic church. The act also extended Canadian territory south to the Ohio River, enraging the 13 American colonies and helping to fuel the American Revolution.

During the American Revolution, nearly 40,000 loyalists fled to Canada from the rebellious colonies, establishing English-speaking settlements in New Brunswick and western Quebec. Friction between English- and French-speaking Canadians led the British in 1791 to divide Canada (west of the Atlantic maritime provinces) into two provinces, Upper Canada and Lower Canada. Each was granted a legislature; Upper Canada's was based on British institutions, Lower Canada's retained the French forms established by the Quebec Act of 1774.

During the War of 1812 between Great Britain and the U.S., Canada became a battleground; Toronto was captured and pillaged by the Americans in 1813. Many Americans hoped to expand the territory of the U.S. at the expense of Canada, or even to entice Canada into a continental American union, but Canadians, whether English- or French-speaking, showed no enthusiasm for joining the U.S. A small British garrison, with the support of Native American irregular forces, kept the Americans at bay. The Convention of 1818 established the border between Canada and the U.S. at latitude 49° N, as far west as the Rocky Mountains, and provided for joint U.S.-British control of Oregon (i.e., the entire Columbia River basin).

Following the War of 1812, British authorities encouraged British immigration to Canada, and between 1815 and 1855, one million Britons answered the call. This immigration radically altered Canada's ethnic balance, making French-speaking Canadians a minority population for the first time. The francophones of Lower Canada, hemmed in on all sides by English speakers, rose in rebellion under the leadership of the Parti Patriote in 1837–38. Lord Durham recommended in 1839 that Canada be united under a single government, and the Union of Canada was enacted in 1841. This move did not, however, quell the growing nationalism of French Canadians.

War with the U.S. threatened in 1844, as the U.S. claimed the entire Columbia River basin north to 54°40' ("fifty-four forty or fight"). But diplomacy triumphed in the end: In 1846 the boundary at 49° was extended westward to the Pacific Ocean. Meanwhile, gold was discovered in British Columbia in 1856, leading to a gold rush and a substantial increase in the population of western Canada.

Growing trade between Canada and the U.S. and the development of a continental system of railroads in both Canada and the U.S. in the 1850s, led to a relative decline in British influence in Canada. The American Civil War had the indirect effect of prompting Canadians to seek self-government in a federal union. Previously, there had been little contact between the Canadas and the maritime provinces, while the vast territories of the west were still privately administered by the Hudson Bay Company. A federal union was forged in a series of conferences beginning in 1864, and the federation of Quebec, Ontario, Nova Scotia, and New Brunswick was recognized by the British North America Act of July 1, 1867.

The Dominion of Canada thus established in 1867 became a self-governing entity within the British Empire; Sir J.A. Macdonald became Canada's first prime minister (1867–73). The dominion rapidly expanded. In 1869 it purchased the western territories of the Hudson Bay Company, and in 1870, in response to a rebellion of French-speaking Métis in Manitoba, Manitoba was granted provincial status within the federation. In 1871 the union of British Columbia with Canada was secured with the promise of a transcontinental railway; the Canadian Pacific Railway was completed in 1885. Prince Edward Island joined the federation in 1873, but neighboring Newfoundland remained a British colony outside the Canadian federation until 1949.

A second francophone rebellion broke out in Saskatchewan in 1885. Its leader, Louis Riel, was executed and became a symbol of French Canadian grievances against the English-speaking majority. Wilfred Laurier became Canada's first francophone prime minister in 1896, but he was unable to solve the problem of the rights of Catholics and French-speakers outside Quebec. Legislation restricting those rights had already been enacted in Manitoba in 1890.

The Klondike Gold Rush of 1897–98 brought Canada worldwide attention and indirectly helped promote the settlement of rich agricultural lands in the Canadian west. Immigrants to the prairie region came not only from eastern Canada, but also from Germany, Scandinavia, and the Ukraine. Japanese farmers and Chinese railroad and mining workers settled west of the Rockies, further increasing Canada's ethnic diversity, though Asian immigrants were denied citizenship. Alberta and Saskatchewan were granted provincial status in 1905; the Yukon Territory and the Northwest Territories continued to be governed by controllers appointed by the federal government and patrolled by the famous Royal Canadian Mounted Police.

Urbanization and industrialization were stimulated in the early 20th century by the exploitation of extensive mineral resources in western Canada and in northern Quebec, and by the development of hydroelectric projects and transportation facilities throughout the country. The long-lived Laurier government fell in 1911, when his proposal for free trade with the U.S. evoked widespread fears that Canada's nascent industries would suffer without protective tariffs.

Laurier's Conservative successor, Robert Borden, sent Canadian troops to fight in World War I in 1914 and bolstered Canada's war efforts in Europe through national conscription in 1917. The distinguished performance of Canada's armed forces in the war bought the country renewed international respect. Borden's wartime English-speaking Conservative-Liberal coalition collapsed in 1921. He was succeeded by the Liberal leader William L. Mackenzie King, who was to be Canada's prime minister for over 20 years

(1921–30, 1935–48). He skillfully managed the economic prosperity of the 1920s, which saw the establishment in Canada of branch plants of many American industrial firms.

The Statute of Westminster, which created the British Commonwealth in 1931, had the effect of granting full self-government to Canada within the Commonwealth. The economic collapse of the 1930s brought both industrial depression and a drought-induced agricultural crisis. Efforts to deal with unemployment, land foreclosures, and other economic ills fell to the provincial governments, which were not up to the task.

Canada's recovery from the Great Depression was stimulated by the advent of World War II, which Canada entered in 1939. Although the war brought price controls, rationing, and other emergency measures, the overall effect of the war was to strengthen all sectors of Canada's economy and to enhance Canada's international status as a leading military and industrial power. A Liberal electoral victory of 1945 gave Mackenzie King a renewed mandate for the postwar era.

The two decades following the war saw the gradual expansion of federal financial responsibility for national welfare measures, including pensions, unemployment insurance, and comprehensive medical care, though the administration of such programs remained a provincial matter. These developments coincided with an increase in urbanization and industrialization in the major centers of Vancouver, Toronto, and Montreal. Formal "equalization payments" were enacted in the 1950s to reduce economic disparities between rich and poor provinces. The early stages of these developments played a part in persuading Newfoundland to join the federation as Canada's 10th province in 1949.

A landslide Conservative victory in 1958 brought John Diefenbaker to the prime ministership, but the Conservatives proved unable to offer a coherent political program and were ousted in the elections of 1963, which returned the Liberals to power. Canadian politics since the 1960s have been marked by increasing regionalization; the Liberal party is based largely in the east, while the New Democratic party, organized in 1961, has little support east of Ontario. The Conservatives offer a broad but insecure national alternative.

The rise of an aggressive Quebecois nationalism in the 1960s led directly to the Liberal prime ministership of Pierre Trudeau, a Quebecois known as a supporter of a strong federal constitution. Trudeau's efforts toward conciliation and for constitutional guarantees for Quebec within a strong federal structure proved unavailing, however. In 1970 he invoked the War Measures Act to send troops to Quebec to put down a wave of separatist terrorism.

The 1976 electoral victory in Quebec of the Parti Québécois under René Lévesque provoked fears that Quebec would secede from Canada. Lévesque's plan for a separate "sovereignty-association" status for Quebec was rejected by a popular referendum in 1980, but only because of Trudeau's pledge to seek full autonomy for Canada in order to secure constitutional protection for Quebec's special interests.

In 1981, Canada's provincial governments reached agreement on proposals for constitutional change. The result was the passage by the British Parliament of the Canada Act, which came into effect on Apr. 17, 1982, granting full independence and constitutional autonomy to Canada and severing its last colonial ties to the British government. Canada's new 1982 Constitution more clearly delineated the powers of the federal and provincial governments, provided for Supreme Court review of legislation, and included a Charter of Rights to protect civil liberties.

A nationwide recession contributed to the defeat of Trudeau's Liberal government and to the election of the Conservative party leader Brian Mulroney (also a native of Quebec) as prime minister in 1984. The Mulroney government encouraged foreign investment and privatization to revitalize Canada's economy. But its most significant achievement was the negotiation and passage, in 1988–89, of a free-trade agreement with the U.S. (that also came to include Mexico).

The Meech Lake Agreement, containing a number of articles clarifying the 1982 Constitution, was worked out between Mulroney and Quebec's Liberal premier Robert Bourassa, along with the leaders of Canada's nine other provinces, and signed on June 23, 1987. Its provisions enhanced the power of the provinces; a key provision gave constitutional protection to Quebec's efforts to remain a "distinct society," linguistically and culturally French. But the aggressive measures of the Quebec government to eradicate the use of English in the public affairs of the province provoked a backlash against bilingualism. The Meech Lake Agreement failed to become law when the legislatures of Newfoundland and Manitoba declined to ratify it by the June 23, 1990, deadline. Canada plunged into the most serious constitutional crisis in its history.

An alternative agreement to restructure the federal government and give more power to the 10 provincial governments was decisively defeated in a national referendum, leaving the nation to deal once again with the awkward status quo.

In 1992, the North American Free Trade Association (NAFTA) with the U.S. and Mexico was finalized, bringing a large increase in trade, especially with the U.S. Mulroney resigned in 1993 and the Progressive Conservative party chose Kim Campbell to lead the government, the first woman to do so. In the 1993 general election, the Conservatives were routed by Jean Chrétien and the Liberals. The new government announced plans in early 1995 to cut the budget deficit through higher taxes and spending cuts on health care and social programs. Although they accomplished this goal, many Canadians were disconcerted because of high unemployment and a decrease in benefits. Chretien was also vulnerable on the problem of Quebec because he and the Liberal Party seemed to favor giving special status to the French province, where in 1995 a separatist referendum was only narrowly defeated. In 1997 elections, the Liberals lost 19 seats, but still held a slim majority. The issue of separatism rose again in Aug. 1998 when the Supreme Court ruled that a referendum on Quebec secession would be invalid without negotiations on the terms with both the provinces and the federation as a whole.

On April 1, 1999 the government officially created a new Arctic territory called Nunavut which is governed solely by the Inuit tribe (called Eskimos in Alaska and Greenland). In Nov. 2000 Chretien's Liberals won their third consecutive victory by a very large margin. The thorny issue of Quebec independence reached a settlement in April 2003 provincial elections in Quebec as the Liberals won

76 of 125 seats, denying another term to the Parti Quebecois, which carried 45 seats.

In 2002 Canada joined with the U.S. to fight the war in Afghanistan, but in 2003, Chretien refused to join the U.S.-led invasion of Iraq. In June elections, 2004 the Liberals fell short of gaining a majority and Paul Martin, Chretien's successor, formed a minority government, the first in Canada since 1980. A serious corruption scandal nearly toppled the government but Martin held on till elections in Jan. 2006 brought the government down and Stephen Harper's Conservative party took power, but also as a minority government.

▶ CAPE VERDE
Republic of Cape Verde
• **Geography** **Location:** archipelago of 15 islands in Atlantic Ocean, off northern Africa. **Boundaries:** Senegal about 300 mi. (500 km) to E. **Total land area:** 1,557 sq. mi. (4,033 sq km). **Coastline:** 600 mi. (965 km). **Comparative area:** slightly larger than Rhode Island. **Land use:** 11% arable land; 1. % permanent crops; 89% other. **Major cities:** Cidade de Praia (capital).
• **People** **Population:** 508,659 (July 2010 est.). **Nationality:** noun—Cape Verdean(s); adjective— Cape Verdean. **Ethnic groups:** 71% Creole (mulatto), 28% African, 1% European. **Languages:** Portuguese and Crioulo (blend of Portuguese and West African). **Religions:** Roman Catholicism fused with indigenous beliefs, Protestantism.
• **Government** **Type:** republic. **Independence:** July 5, 1975 (from Portugal). **Constitution:** Sept. 25, 1992; last revised in 1999 **National holiday:** Independence Day, July 5. **Heads of Government:** Pedro Verona Rodrigues Pires, president (since Mar. 2001); José Maria Neves, prime minister (since Feb. 2001). **Structure:** executive; unicameral legislature; judiciary.
• **Economy** **Monetary unit:** Cape Verdean escudo. **Budget:** (2009 est.) *income:* $480 mil.; *expend.:* $595.9 mil. **G.D.P.:** $1.7 bil., $3,400 per capita (2009 est.). **Chief crops:** bananas, corn, beans. **Natural resources:** salt, basalt rock, pozzolana, limestone, kaolin, fish. **Major industries:** food and beverages, fish processing, salt mining. **Labor force:** 196,100 (2007 est); 9.3% agriculture, 73.9% services, 16.9% industry (1990); 21% unemployment (2000 est.). **Exports:** $97 mil. (2009 est.); shoes, garments, fish, bananas. **Imports:** $767 mil. (2009 est.); foodstuffs, consumer goods, industrial products. **Major trading partners:** (2008) *exports:* 37.6% Japan, 28.5% Spain, 17.5% Portugal, 4.8% Morocco; *imports:* 41.2% Portugal, 12% Netherlands, 6.8% Spain, 6.6% UK, 4.3% Brazil.

In 1462 the Portuguese founded the first European city in the tropics at Ribeira Grande on Santiago, one of the 15 islands that compose the Republic of Cape Verde. Located 385 miles off the west coast of Africa, the Cape Verde Islands prospered during the slave trade in the 16th century and later served as supply stations on sea routes and trading lanes. The rise of whaling in the 19th century led to contact with the U.S., as American ships recruited crews from the islands. The United States set up an American consulate, headquarters for the U.S. Navy African Squadron, and a transatlantic cable station in the islands.

Portugal changed the status of the archipelago from colony to overseas province in 1951; in 1956, citizens of Cape Verde and Portuguese Guinea organized the African Party for the Independence of Guinea-Bissau and Cape Verde (PAIGC) to petition Portugal to improve living conditions. Beginning as a clandestine organization, the PAIGC became an overt political movement on the islands after the 1974 revolution in Portugal. An agreement between the PAIGC and Portugal, providing for a transitional government, paved the way for full independence in 1975.

In 1980 the PAIGC became the PAICV, which remained the "supreme expression" of Cape Verdeans' political will until the opposition party, Movement for Democracy, won a parliamentary majority in the nation's first multiparty elections in Jan. 1991. The new government instituted free market reforms, including privatization of industries. Voters approved of the reforms, giving the Movement for Democracy 50 of the 72 seats in Parliament in Dec. 1995 elections. Ten years of rule by the Movement for Democracy ended in 2001 as the opposition won a majority in the legislature and elected their candidate, Pedro Pires, as president. He won reelection in 2006.

▶ CENTRAL AFRICAN REPUBLIC
• **Geography** **Location:** landlocked country in central Africa. **Boundaries:** Chad to N, Sudan to E, Zaire, Congo to S, Cameroon to W. **Total land area:** 240,535 sq. mi. (622,984 sq km). **Coastline:** none. **Comparative area:** slightly smaller than Texas. **Land use:** 3% arable land; negl.% permanent crops; 97% other. **Major cities:** Bangui (capital); Berbérati; Bouar.
• **People** **Population:** 4,844,927 (July 2010 est.). **Nationality:** noun—Central African(s); adjective— Central African. **Ethnic groups:** 33% Baya, 27% Banda, 13% Mandija, 10% Sara, 7% Mboum, 4% M'Baka; 2% other. **Languages:** French (official), Sangho (lingua franca and national language), tribal languages. **Religions:** 35% indigenous beliefs, 25% Protestant, 25% Roman Catholic, 15% Muslim; indigenous beliefs and practices strongly influence Christian majority.
• **Government** **Type:** republic. **Independence:** Aug. 13, 1960 (from France). **Constitution:** Adopted Jan. 7, 1995; ratified by popular referendum Dec. 5 2004; effective December 27, 2004. **National holiday:** Republic Day, Dec. 1. **Heads of Government:** François Bozize, head of state (since March, 2003); Faustin-Archange Touadera, prime minister (since Jan., 2008). **Structure:** executive; unicameral legislature; judiciary.
• **Economy** **Monetary unit:** Communauté Financière Africaine (CFA) franc. **Budget:** (2009 est.) *income:* $334 mil.; *expend.:* $362 bil. **G.D.P.:** $3.327 bil., $700 per capita (2009 est.). **Chief crops:** cotton, coffee, tobacco. **Natural resources:** diamonds, uranium, timber, gold, oil. **Major industries:** sawmills, breweries, diamond mining. **Labor force:** 1.926 mil (2007 est.); 55% agriculture, 25% services, 20% industry. **Exports:** $146.7 mil. (f.o.b., 2007 est.); diamonds, timber, cotton, coffee, tobacco. **Imports:** $237.3 mil. (f.o.b., 2007); food, textiles, petroleum products, machinery, electrical equipment, motor vehicles. **Major trading partners:** (2008) *exports:* 40.2% Japan, 9.7% Belgium, 8.1% China, 5.9% Morocco, 5.6% Indonesia; *imports:* 20.2% South Korea, 13.6% France, 7.7% Cameroon, 5.7% Netherlands.

A landlocked country in Africa's central region, the Central African Republic is one of the least-developed countries in the world. Most of its people are farmers, and the nation has little manufacturing, few reliable roads, and no railroad. Europeans first came to the area in the early

1800s in their search for slaves, but it was not until 1889 that the French established an outpost as the current capital city of Bangui. The region was organized as the territory of Ubangi-Shari five years later. In 1910 it was incorporated into French Equitorial Africa along with what are now the countries of Chad, the Congo, and Gabon.

The country was granted internal self government by the French under its present name in 1958 and became a member of the French Overseas Community. Independence was achieved on Aug. 13, 1960. The first prime minister, Barthelemy Boganda, was killed in an airplane crash in 1959 and was succeeded by his nephew, David Dacko. Dacko was elected to a seven-year term in January 1964, but an army coup in 1966 overthrew his government. The head of the army, Jean-Bedel Bokassa, was installed as president. Named president for life in 1972, in 1976 Bokassa declared himself emperor and changed the name of the country to the Central African Empire.

Dacko returned to power in 1979, however, and Bokassa went into exile. The name of the country was changed back to the Central African Republic. A multiparty political system was reinstated in 1981, but army officers threw Dacko out of office again six months later and banned all political parties. Opposition parties were legalized in 1991, and Bokassa was released before elections in 1993, elections that made Ange Félix Patassé president. He tried to reduce the army's power but met with rebellions requiring the intervention of peacekeepers from neighboring states. Patassé was overturned in March 2003 by fired army head General Francois Bozize who suspended the constitution and proclaimed himself president. In 2005 Bozize won the presidential election although complaints about the process were numerous. Violence in the north carried out by armed groups has plagued the country for years, displacing tens of thousands. Progress was made in 2008 when two groups agreed to disarm and in 2009 a new unity government was formed.

▶CHAD
Republic of Chad

• **GEOGRAPHY** **Location:** landlocked country in north central Africa. **Boundaries:** Libya to N, Sudan to E, Central African Republic to S, Cameroon, Nigeria to SE, Niger to W. **Total land area:** 495,753 sq. mi. (1,284,000 sq km). **Coastline:** none. **Comparative area:** slightly more than three times the size of California. **Land use:** 3% arable land; negl. % permanent crops; 97% other. **Major cities:** N'Djamena (capital; Sarh; Moundou; Abéché.

• **PEOPLE** **Population:** 10,543,464 (July 2010 est.). **Nationality:** noun—Chadian(s); adjective—Chadian. **Ethnic groups:** Sara, Arab, Mayo-Kebbi, Kanem-Bornou, Ouaddai, Hadjarai, Tandjile, Gorane, Fritri-Batha. **Languages:** French and Arabic (both official); Sara and Sango in south; more than 120 different languages and dialects. **Religions:** 51% Muslim, 35% Christian, 7% Animist, 7% other.

• **GOVERNMENT** **Type:** republic. **Independence:** Aug. 11, 1960 (from France). **Constitution:** Mar. 31, 1996. **National holiday:** Independence Day, Aug. 11. **Heads of Government:** Idriss Deby, president (since Dec. 1990); Emmanuel Nadingar, prime minister (since Mar. 2010). **Structure:** executive; unicameral legislature; judiciary.

• **ECONOMY** **Monetary unit:** Communauté Financière Africaine (CFA) franc. **Budget:** (2009 est.) *income:* $872.5 mil.; *expend.:* $1.454 mil., **G.D.P.:** $16.26 bil., $1,600 per capita (2009 est.). **Chief crops:** cotton, sorghum, millet, peanuts. **Natural resources:** small quantities of crude oil (unexploited but exploitation beginning), uranium, natron (sodium carbonate), kaolin, fish (Lake Chad). **Major industries:** oil, cotton textile mills, slaughterhouses, brewery, natron. **Labor force:** 4.293 mil (2007); 80% agriculture (subsistence farming, herding,fishing), 20% industry and services. **Exports:** $3.164 bil. (2009 est.); cotton, cattle, textiles. **Imports:** $1.454 bil. (2009 est.); machinery and transport equipment, industrial goods, petroleum products, foodstuffs. **Major trading partners:** (2008) *exports:* 90.1% U.S., 2.9% Taiwan, 2.2% Japam; *imports:* 17.6% France, 14.8% Cameroon, 9.9% China.

The Sao and other ancient peoples built centers of civilization near Lake Chad that flourished for many centuries until they were displaced by the medieval kingdoms of Kanem-Bornu, Baguirmi, and Ouaddai. From about A.D. 1400 onward, Chad became a meeting ground between the Muslim cultures of the Sahara and the Sahel and the black African societies of the tropics. Between 1500 and 1800, Arab slave raiders were active around Lake Chad, supplying slaves for European traders on Africa's west coast.

French military forces reached Chad from West Africa in 1891 and fought a series of battles over the next two decades with the Arab rulers of the region. A French governorship of Chad was established in 1905 (based in Brazzaville, the Congo), but the country was not brought entirely under French control until 1914. Chad was incorporated into the federation of French Equatorial Africa in 1910 and was organized as a colony within the federation in 1920.

French Equatorial Africa was dissolved in 1959, and Chad became an autonomous member of the French Community. Full independence followed on Aug. 11, 1960; François Tombalbage became Chad's first president. In 1965 the Muslim northern and eastern parts of the country rebelled against the southern-led government; despite the aid of French troops, the government was unable to suppress the rebellion, and a long civil war ensued.

Tombalbage was overthrown in 1975 in a military coup led by Gen. Felix Malloum. Efforts to broaden the composition of the national government broke down, and in 1979 Prime Minister Hissein Habre broke with the government and led northern forces against the national army. A cease-fire was negotiated under international auspices, and a National Unity Transitional Government (GUNT) was installed in 1979, but civil war broke out again in 1980. Pres. Goukouni Oueddei sought Libyan aid in restoring order; a contingent of 7,000 Libyan troops occupied the country until 1981. They were replaced by an international peacekeeping force organized by the Organization of African Unity.

Civil war broke out again in 1982, and northern forces occupied the capital. A new republican government under the presidency of Hissein Habre was proclaimed on June 7. OAU forces withdrew, and Habre's government soon controlled all of the country except for a few northern areas held by GUNT. In 1983 GUNT launched a counterattack and regained some territory with the aid of Libyan forces. French and Zairian troops were sent to aid Habre's forces. In Sept. 1984 France and Libya agreed to the withdrawal of all foreign forces from Chad, but Libyan forces remained. GUNT forces controlled the country north of the 16th parallel; Libyan forces occupied the Aozou Strip, along the border, with the apparent intention of annexing it to Libya.

Between 1984 and 1986 Habre persuaded most Chadean dissident forces to rejoin the national government, and in Nov. 1986 he launched a campaign to recapture the north. The Chadean forces won a series of victories, and in May 1988 Libya's Col. Qaddafi declared an end to the 20-year war with Chad.

In Nov. 1990, forces led by renegade Gen. Idriss Deby launched attacks from Sudan and ousted Pres. Habre. Deby, who favored multiparty democracy, proclaimed a provisional government and suspended the constitution. A national charter calling for a new constitution and elections to be held within 30 months came into force in March 1991. Deby functioned as president after that, suppressing two attempted coups in 1992, and legalizing opposition parties. Deby's "Higher Transitional Council" remained in command until presidential elections were held in 1996, which Deby won. He was reelected in 2001 and 2006. Fighting between the government and a rebel group has continued since 1998. In 2003, Chad became an oil-producing nation with a pipeline linked to terminals on the Atlantic Ocean. With oil money comes corruption, and Chad succumbed quickly. In 2006 Chad cut ties with Sudan for its support of rebel movements to bring down the Deby government. In 2009 rebels attacked the capital, N'Djamena, but failed to capture it, The U.N. promptly urged support of the government.

▶ CHILE
Republic of Chile

● **GEOGRAPHY** **Location:** South Pacific coast of South America. **Boundaries:** Peru, Bolivia to N, Argentina to E, Pacific Ocean to W. **Total land area:** 281,933 sq. mi. (756,102 sq km). **Coastline:** 3,999 mi. (6,435 km). **Comparative area:** slightly larger than Texas. **Land use:** 3% arable land; negl. % permanent crops; 97% other. **Major cities:** Gran Santiago (capital); Viña del Mar; Concepción; Valparaíso; Temuco.

● **PEOPLE** **Population:** 16,746,491 (July 2010 est.). **Nationality:** noun—Chilean(s); adjective—Chilean. **Ethnic groups:** 95% white and white Amerindian, 3% Amerindian, 2% other. **Languages:** Spanish (official), English, Mapudungun, German. **Religions:** 70% Roman Catholic, 15.1% Evangelical, 1.1% Jehovah Witness, 4.6% other, 8.3% none.

● **GOVERNMENT** **Type:** republic. **Independence:** Sept. 18, 1810 (from Spain). **Constitution:** Sept. 11, 1980, effective Mar. 11, 1981; modified by public referendum on July 30, 1989; most recently amended in 2005. **National holiday:** Independence Day, Sept. 18. **Head of Government:** Sebastian Pinera Echenique, president (since Mar. 2010). **Structure:** executive; bicameral legislature; judiciary.

● **ECONOMY** **Monetary unit:** Chilean peso. **Budget:** (2009 est.) *income:* $31.31 bil.; *expend.:* $37.87 bil. **G.D.P.:** $243.7 bil., $14,700 per capita (2009 est.). **Chief crops:** wheat, corn, grapes, beans, sugar beets. **Natural resources:** copper, timber, iron ore, nitrates, precious metals. **Major industries:** copper, other minerals, foodstuffs,

fish processing. **Labor force:** 7.42 mil. (2009); 63% services, 23.4% industry and commerce, 13.6% agriculture, forestry, fishing (2005); 7% unemployment (2007 est.). **Exports:** $48.85 bil. (2009); copper, fish and fishmeal, other metals and minerals. **Imports:** $40.91 bil. (2009); consumer goods, chemicals, motor vehicles, fuels. **Major trading partners:** (2008) *exports:* 14.1% China, 11.3% U.S., 10.4% Japan; *imports:* 19.1% U.S., 11.9% China, 9.2% Brazil, 8.8% Argentina.

Before the arrival of Europeans in the mid 1530s, indigenous habitation of the territory that would become Chile included the Araucanian population in the south and peoples under the influence of the Inca Empire in the north.

The Spanish founded the cities of Valparaíso in 1536, Santiago in 1541, and Concepción in 1550. Chile was under the authority of the Viceroyalty of Peru, established in 1544. Between 1810 and 1818, fortunes of the Chilean independence movement ebbed and flowed, culminating in the victory of Bernardo O'Higgins and the separatist forces in 1817. Independence was finally achieved in 1818.

From 1818 to 1833, Chile underwent a period of political instability due to power struggles among elite Chilean families. In 1833 a strong presidential-dominant constitution was written under the influence of leading political figure Diego Portales that set the form of government in Chile until 1891. Chile expanded its territory at the expense of Peru and Bolivia, first in a war with the Peruvian-Bolivian Confederation (1836–39) and later as a result of the War of the Pacific (1879–83).

A civil war was fought in 1890–91 between forces of the president, José Balmaceda, and the Chilean Congress over the issue of the limits of presidential authority. The defeat of the presidential forces led to the establishment of a congressional-dominant parliamentary system. The checks on policy initiative resulting from the parliamentary system left government deadlocked in the face of mounting social and political problems arising at the turn of the century. The occurrence of a number of bloody strike actions crystallized political debate around social issues such as better wages and working conditions. The immobilized parliamentary system was unable to respond to these problems. In 1925, when Congress failed to allocate funds for military pay, the forces overthrew the parliamentary government.

A new constitution was drawn up that same year that moved governmental structure toward presidential dominance. Nevertheless, political instability continued until 1933, when the new constitution was implemented. The Chilean balance of political power from 1958 until 1973 remained almost equally divided among parties representing the right, the center, and the left of the political spectrum. In order to prevent an electoral victory for the leftist parties, forces on the right allied themselves with the centrist Christian Democrats in the 1964 election, and this resulted in the victory of Christian Democratic presidential candidate Eduardo Frei Montalva.

The program of the Christian Democrats included agrarian reform and attempts to organize Chile's urban poor. It was believed that these stances would benefit the Christian Democrats at the polls in the 1970 presidential election. As in 1958, the 1970 election fielded three presidential candidates who represented the political right, center, and left. The leftist Popular Unity coalition candidate, Dr. Salvador Allende Gossens, won with

36.3 percent of the vote, but only after bitter debate did Congress recognize Allende's victory.

The Allende government nationalized the foreign-owned copper industry, but an international boycott of Chilean copper imposed in retaliation for this action seriously hurt the country's economy. The government also nationalized the coal and steel industries as well as 60 percent of private banking. The Popular Unity government found itself unable to control peasant seizures of land and factory takeovers by workers. The copper embargo, land and factory seizures, government subsidies to the poor for basic goods, and runaway inflation resulted in a deterioration of the national economy that particularly affected the middle classes. Members of congress from the center and right had hoped to gain enough seats in the 1973 elections to impeach Allende, but instead the Popular Unity made impressive electoral gains.

On Sept. 11, 1973, segments of the military led by commanders of three of Chile's four armed forces took control of the government, killing Allende in the process. Gen. Augusto Pinochet Ugarte emerged as the new president. The junta announced the arrest of some 13,000 persons, many of whom then lost their lives in a wave of brutal repression. (Mass graves were discovered in the desert in 1990, and in 1991 a commission reported that between 1973 and 1990, more than 2,000 people were killed by the government.) In March 1974 the dictatorship published its Declaration of Principles, which included a laissez-faire economic orientation, anti- Marxism, and nationalism.

A new constitution was approved by plebiscite in 1980. The two-phase evolution of Chile's political structure included an authoritarian "transitional period" between 1980 and 1989 and implementation of a new political structure thereafter. The constitution created a presidential system with very extensive executive powers and a "guardian" role for the military. In an Oct. 1988 plebiscite, Chileans rejected continuation of Pinochet rule and called for an end to the dictatorship. On Dec. 14, 1989, Patricio Aylwin Azocar of the Christian Democratic party (one of a 17-party alliance) was elected president with over 55 percent of the vote; he took office in March 1990, ending 17 years of military dictatorship. He was succeeded by Eduardo Frei Ruiz-Tagle in March 1994.

In the following years, Chile's economy expanded, as exports increased, and its large external debt was reduced. Although exports were still dominated by copper, other minerals and manufactures gained in importance. In 1996, Chile joined Mercosur, a free trade agreement among six of the largest South American nations.

In March 1998 Gen. Pinochet resigned as head of the armed forces after 25 years and was sworn in as senator-for-life. In Oct., while in Britain, Pinochet was arrested after Spain sought his extradition for the murder of Spanish citizens. A long legal minuet ended in Jan. 2000 when Britain's Home Secretary declared Pinochet unfit to stand trial. Only days later, in a run-off presidential election, the candidate of the center-left Concertacion Coalition, Ricardo Lagos Escobar, took 51.3 percent of the vote. Though Lagos was the first Socialist president since Allende, he supported a market economy. In 2003 Chile and the U.S. signed a free trade agreement eliminating tariffs on 85 percent of all goods and economic growth rose dramtically.

In 2006, Chile's first woman president, Michelle Bachelet, took office as head of a coalition government headed again by Concertacion. Enormous protests by hundreds of thousands of students over education reform marred her first year in office. But her tenure as president brought peace and prosperity so she became a very popular figure. Legally prohibited from running again, she was succeeded by Sebastián Piñera in March 2010. In February, however, a devastating earthquake brought widespread destruction. (See "Major News Stories.")

▶ CHINA
People's Republic of China

● **GEOGRAPHY   Location:** covers vast area of eastern Asia. **Boundaries:** Russia, Mongolia to N; N. Korea to NE; Pacific Ocean to E; India, Nepal, Bhutan, Myanmar, Laos, and Vietnam to S; Afghanistan and Pakistan to W., Kazakhstan, Kyrgyzstan, and Tajikistan to NW. **Total land area:** 3,705,407 sq. mi. (9,596,961 sq km). **Coastline:** 9,112 mi. (14,500 km). **Comparative area:** between coterminous U.S. and Canada. **Land use:** 14.86% arable land;1% permanent crops, 84% other. **Major cities:** Beijing (capital); Shanghai; Tianjin; Shenyang; Wuhan; Chengdu; Xi'an.

● **PEOPLE   Population:** 1,330,141,295 (July 2010 est.). **Nationality:** noun—Chinese (sing., pl.); adjective—Chinese. **Ethnic groups:** 91.5% Han Chinese; 8.5% Zhuang, Uygur, Hui, Yi, Tibetan, Miao, Manchu, Mongol, Buyi, Korean, and numerous others. **Languages:** Standard Chinese or Mandarin (Putonghua based on the Beijing dialect); Yue (Cantonese), Wu (Shanghainese), Minbei (Fuzhou), Minnan (Hokkien-Taiwanese), Xiang, Gan, Hakka dialects, and minority langs. (see "Ethnic groups" above). **Religions:** officially atheist, but traditionally pragmatic and eclectic; Taoism, Buddhism, 1–2% Muslim, 3–4% Christian.

● **GOVERNMENT   Type:** Communist state. **Constitution:** Dec. 4, 1982; with amendments in 1988 and 1993. **National holiday:** National Day, Oct. 1, (1949) **Heads of Government:** Hu jintao, president (since Mar. 15, 2003); Wen Jiabao, prime minister (since Mar. 16, 2003). **Structure:** executive; unicameral legislature; judiciary.

● **ECONOMY   Monetary unit:** yuan. **Budget:** (2009 est.) *income:* $972.3 bil.; *expend.:* $1.137 tril. **G.D.P.:** $8.789 tril., $6,600 per capita (2009 est.). **Chief crops:** rice, potatoes, sorghum, peanuts. **Natural resources:** coal, iron ore, crude oil, mercury, tin; world's largest hydropower potential. **Major industries:** iron, steel, coal. **Labor force:** 812.7 mil. (2009 est.); 39.5% agriculture, 27.2% industry, 33.2% services. **Exports:** $1.194 tril. (2009); machinery and equipment, textiles, clothing. **Imports:** $921.5 bil. (2009); machinery and equipment, chemicals, plastics, iron and steel. **Major trading partners:** (2008) *exports:* 17.7% U.S., 13.3% Hong Kong, 8.1% Japan; *imports:* 13.3% Japan, 9.9% South Korea, 9.2% Taiwan.

China is one of the world's oldest civilizations. Dynastic rule in the North China Plain began around 2000 B.C. The unifying Qin (221 B.C.) and Han (206 B.C.) dynasties greatly expanded the territory of the empire and established the basic pattern of imperial bureaucratic government that would endure until the beginning of the 20th century. Major dynasties during that period include the Han (206 B.C.–A.D. 220), Tang (618–907), Song

(960–1279), Yuan or Mongol (1279–1368), Ming (1368–1644), and Qing (1644–1911).

By the late 18th century, the Qing dynasty faced increasingly dangerous problems of explosive population growth, bureaucratic stagnation, and trade pressure from the West. Opium—introduced by Great Britain to balance its trade in tea, silk, porcelain, and other goods—created severe social problems. Western demands for free trade resulted in the Opium War (1839–42), in which China was humiliatingly defeated by the British. The treaties of Nanjing (1842) and Tianjin (1858) opened China to Western merchants and missionaries and created foreign-ruled enclaves on Chinese soil. At the same time, the Taiping Rebellion and other popular uprisings led to the deaths of at least 20 million Chinese between 1850 and 1870.

Such reform efforts as the Self-Strengthening Movement (1870s) and the 1898 Reform Movement proved inadequate to the task of strengthening and modernizing China's dynastic government. Japan, modernizing rapidly after the Meiji Restoration of 1868, joined the race for commercial access to China, decisively winning the Sino-Japanese War of 1894–95. The antiforeign Boxer Uprising of 1900 was put down by a joint foreign military force, dealing a mortal blow to Qing rule. On Oct. 10, 1911, the dynasty fell to a coalition of forces led by the veteran revolutionary nationalist Sun Yat-sen.

China's first attempt at republican government, under Pres. Yuan Shikai and subsequent presidents, quickly degenerated into factionalism and warlord control in the provinces. In 1915 Japan successfully demanded further concessions, provoking public outcries. When news reached China on May 4, 1919, that the Treaty of Versailles granted Japan all of Germany's former concessions in China, students rioted throughout the country, demanding reforms and modernization (the May Fourth Movement). Sun Yat-sen's Nationalist party (Kuomintang, or KMT) and the Chinese Communist party (CCP, founded in 1921 by Mao Zedong) joined forces in 1922 in an attempt to create a second republican revolution. Sun Yat-sen died in 1925. His successor, Chiang Kai-shek, consolidated KMT forces in Guangzhou and mounted the Northern Expedition (1927–29) to defeat or co-opt the various provincial warlords and reunify the country. Chiang then turned on his Communist allies. A series of failed Communist uprisings and KMT anti-Communist extermination campaigns between 1927 and 1934 nearly wiped out the CCP. Remnants of the party broke out of encirclement in Jiangxi Province in 1934 and undertook the 6,000-mile Long March to a secure base in Yan'an, Shanxi Province. There, under Mao, Zhou Enlai, and Zhu De, the CCP recovered its strength. In the Xi'an Incident of December 1936, Chiang was kidnapped by mutinous KMT allies and forced at gunpoint to agree to forming a United Front with the CCP against Japan.

Meanwhile Japan continued its penetration of China, with the assassination of Manchurian warlord and KMT ally Jiang Zuolin in 1928, the invasion of Manchuria on Sept. 18, 1931, and the establishment of the puppet state of Manchuguo in 1934. On July 7, 1937, fighting erupted between Japanese and Chinese troops near Beijing. The Japanese rapidly moved south to the Yangtse Valley, bombing and capturing Shanghai. The Nationalist capital at Nanjing fell in November 1937, amid widespread atrocities against civilians. The KMT army and government retreated to a wartime capital at Chongqing. The remainder of World War II in China was largely a stalemate, with Japan occupying most of the country. KMT-held areas opposed the Japanese with conventional forces (supported, after 1941, by the Americans), while the Communists harassed the Japanese with guerrilla tactics.

At the end of World War II, American forces ensured that the KMT would receive Japan's surrender throughout most of China, giving the Nationalists a commanding position while U.S. general George Marshall attempted to mediate the creation of a KMT-CCP coalition government. That effort failed, and civil war broke out. The KMT advantage was dissipated by ruinous inflation, corruption, mismanagement, and military ineffectiveness. At the end of 1947, with the Communist forces making continual advances, the United States pulled out of China. After losing several major battles throughout 1948–49, KMT forces retreated to Taiwan; in Beijing, Mao Zedong proclaimed the establishment of the People's Republic of China (PRC) on Oct. 1, 1949.

With U.S. backing, the Republic of China established a temporary capital at Taipei and continued to claim sovereignty over all of China, retaining China's seat in the U.N. The PRC was quickly granted diplomatic recognition by Soviet bloc nations and some Western nations, notably Great Britain, but was effectively isolated in most international affairs by American support for Nationalist China. Chinese troops entered the Korean War in November 1950. This direct confrontation between China and the United States forestalled any possibility of normal contacts for more than two decades.

Within China the CCP rapidly consolidated its control of the country and began rebuilding the nation after decades of warfare. Land was confiscated from landlords and returned to peasant ownership; landlords and other "class enemies" were tried and condemned by People's Courts set up under party auspices. Under the first five-year plan (1953), peasants were urged to set up rural cooperatives, while industrial recovery began with Soviet assistance. Artists, writers, and intellectuals were ordered to devote themselves to the service of the party and the nation. In 1956 Mao announced a policy of "let a hundred flowers bloom, let a hundred schools of thought contend," inviting criticism of the party and government. He was shocked by the vigor of the criticism; many critics were sent to labor camps in the ensuing Anti-Rightist Campaign of 1957.

Angered by the arrogance of Soviet advisers and by Soviet refusal to share nuclear weapons technology with China, Mao broke with the Soviet Union and expelled all Soviet personnel in 1958. At the same time, he announced the policy of the Great Leap Forward, under which China was to make progress on all fronts without outside aid. Huge rural communes took the place of peasant smallholdings and cooperatives, and agriculture was placed under the direction of centralized planning. In industry, labor and enthusiasm were expected to make up for a shortage of capital and technical expertise. The Great Leap was a catastrophic failure, causing widespread famine and social dislocation, as Mao admitted in a forced self-criticism in 1960. Mao withdrew into the background as a group of party pragmatists led by Liu Shaoqi assumed power in the early 1960s.

In foreign affairs Chinese shelling of the Nationalist-held offshore islands of Quemoy and Matsu in 1958 led to a crisis in the Taiwan Straits, patrolled by the U.S. Seventh Fleet to prevent a recurrence of China's civil war. A rebellion in Tibet in 1959 was suppressed with much bloodshed, and the dalai lama fled to India. Chinese troop movements into Tibet contributed to the outbreak in 1960 of a border war with India. Throughout the 1960s China worried about being drawn into the Vietnam War.

In late 1965 Mao made a bid to return to full power. His vehicle was the Great Proletarian Cultural Revolution, formally launched in 1966. Shock troops of teenage Red Guards were used to attack the entrenched party bureaucracy; Liu Shaoqi was placed under house arrest, and other prominent officials, including Deng Xiaoping, were exiled to rural areas. By 1968 internal disorder was so great that the military intervened to restore control in many areas. Most established organs of power were replaced under the Cultural Revolution by Revolutionary Committees; intellectuals, technical workers, and bureaucrats were severely persecuted. In 1971 Mao's second-in-command, Marshal Lin Biao, staged an abortive coup and died while attempting to flee the country. With Mao increasingly old and ill, most of his power was exercised by his wife, Jiang Qing, and her associates. Her rival, Premier Zhou Enlai, attempted to maintain orderly government functions in the face of this turmoil.

The 1968 Soviet invasion of Czechoslovakia convinced Mao that the U.S.S.R. was a greater threat to China than America was, and he quietly encouraged the growth of better relations with the U.S. With tacit American approval, the PRC replaced the Republic of China (Taiwan) in the U.N. on Oct. 25, 1971. During Feb. 21–28, 1972, U.S. president Richard Nixon visited China. The Shanghai Communiqué, issued at the end of that visit, clarified the positions of both sides and paved the way for the resumption of U.S.–China relations short of formal diplomatic recognition.

Zhou Enlai died in January 1976, and Deng Xiaoping became acting premier. In April 1976 a rally in Beijing commemorating Zhou's birthday was dispersed by police on orders from Jiang Qing, and a riot ensued. Deng was dismissed from office. But when Mao died on Sept. 9, 1976, Deng reemerged as China's paramount leader. Jiang Qing and three associates were arrested along with many of their allies. Labeled the Gang of Four, Jiang Qing's clique was blamed for all the ills of the Cultural Revolution; they were tried and convicted for crimes against the state in 1981.

China's post-Mao transformation took a decisive turn in 1978, with the announcement of the policy of the Four Modernizations (agriculture, industry, science and technology, and defense). Foreign investment and technology transfer were encouraged, and thousands of students were sent to study abroad. In the winter of 1978–79, the authorities tolerated the public posting of written critiques of the government ("Democracy Wall"). Deng consolidated power in his own hands, still acting behind the scenes; Deng's allies Hu Yaobang and Zhao Ziyang were promoted to leadership of the party and government in 1982.

On Jan. 1, 1979, China and the United States entered into formal diplomatic relations; the United States rescinded its recognition of the Republic of China as China's legal government but maintained separate nongovernmental relations with the ROC under the Taiwan Relations Act. A conflict with Great Britain was resolved in 1984 as both sides agreed that Hong Kong would be returned to Chinese sovereignty, but with considerable local autonomy, in 1997. Relations with the Soviet Union remained strained, China insisting that no improvement could come before the U.S.S.R. reduced its troop concentrations on the Sino-Soviet border, withdrew from Afghanistan, and pressured Vietnam into withdrawing from Cambodia.

In the 1980s, China achieved spectacular improvements in agricultural production through dismantling rural communes and returning land to individual peasant holdings under long-term leases. Small-scale private enterprise has been encouraged in both rural and urban areas. Within the overall context of reform, factions of relatively more conservative and reformist leaders have coexisted uneasily. A conservative drive against "spiritual pollution" in 1986 was quickly blunted by Deng, but in January 1987 the reformist party-secretary Hu Yaobang was ousted after student demonstrations calling for more democracy. The CCP 12th Party Congress in Oct. 1987 named the reformist Zhao Ziyang as party secretary, and the conservative pragmatist Li Peng as premier.

In April 1989 student demonstrators in Beijing mourning the death of Hu Yaobang launched a general movement for greater democracy. Demonstrators began a hunger strike and disrupted a summit visit by Soviet president Gorbachev. Martial law was proclaimed in May as demonstrations spread to other cities. Troops opened fire in Tienanmen Square on June 3–4, killing hundreds of demonstrators. In the aftermath, Zhao Ziyang was replaced as party secretary by Jiang Zemin, thousands of protesters and suspected dissidents were arrested (and an unknown number executed), and hard-liners in the government took firm control of the country.

World opinion was outraged by the Tienanmen incident; the United States and many other countries instituted sanctions against China, tourism plummeted, and the economy went into general decline. International trade resumed quickly and the U.S. renewed China's most-favored-nation status in June 1990 after several hundred dissidents were released from prison.

China strove to put Tienanmen Square behind it by holding speedy trials of those charged in connection with demonstrations. The government also made overtures to the former U.S.S.R., and from its permanent seat on the U.N. Security Council supported coalition efforts against Iraq in the Persian Gulf conflict. Economic sanctions were lifted by Western governments in 1991. China continued to pursue its economic reform policies while repressing all signs of political dissent. In 1992–93 runaway growth made China's economy the world's fourth-largest. This resulted in higher wages and increased consumer spending, but also widening income disparities, increased corruption, theft, etc.

Deng's long-expected death, in 1997, produced little immediate effect on the Chinese leadership, except for a new crackdown as leaders competed to seem tough on dissent. But the transition of power to Jiang Zemin, 71, went smoothly.

Domestic affairs in general were overshadowed by national jubilation over the return of Hong Kong to Chinese sovreignty on July 1, 1997.

(Macao would follow, in December 1999, after 442 years as a Portuguese colony.) Pres. Clinton made a long state visit in 1998 and appeared on Chinese TV criticizing China for human rights abuses and urged Mr. Jiang to open Chinese society. Undismayed, the Chinese government proceeded to crush the fledgling China Democracy Party, sentencing three of its leaders to long prison terms for subversion. In Feb. 1999, new missiles menaced Taiwan; tensions grew worse in July when Taiwan's president said publicly that his country was a separate Chinese state.

In the face of not only these issues but also the newer "human rights" issue of China's ban on and persecution of the Falun Gong religious movement, the U.S. reached a trade agreement with China at the end of 1999 (as had Japan in July). In 2001 China signed a 20-year Friendship Treaty with Russia, the first since the end of the Cold War; it pledged peaceful settlement of border disputes and coordination against threats of aggression.

In Nov. 2002 the 16th Communist Party Congress named Hu Jintao as Party Secretary, replacing Jiang Zemin, and the National People's Congress formally ratified the Party decisions. Jiang remains as chairman of the Central Military Commission and unofficial eminence grise.

From 2005–08 China's economy continued its extraordinary expansion through exports of everything from steel to textiles. Free trade agreements with ASEAN nations including Japan and Korea strengthened China's claim to regional leadership. Warnings to Taiwan continued, military spending increased and Russia joined China in military excercises. In 2008 Beijing was host to the Olympic Games in August, but the worldwide acclaim that followed could not disguise the fact that it was a horrendous year for China. In March violent riots in Tibet spread to other regions and in May a major earthquake killed 70,000 people in Sichuan province, including thousands of schoolchildren buried under collapsed buildings deemed by many as unsafe. And finally, the worldwide recession took its toll as economic growth slowed dramatically. But by mid-2009 the economy had revived somewhat although signs of worker unrest made the government uneasy. Trade and travel agreements with Taiwan signalled a possible peaceful way forward until the Obama administration sold billions of dollars of arms to Taiwan. (See "Major News Stories.")

▶ COLOMBIA
Republic of Colombia
● **GEOGRAPHY Location:** northwestern coast of South America. **Boundaries:** Caribbean Sea to N, Venezuela, Brazil to E, Peru, Ecuador to S, Panama, Pacific Ocean to W. **Total land area:** 439,737 sq. mi. (1,138,914 sq km). **Coastline:** 1,992 mi. (3,208 km). **Comparative area:** slightly less than twice the size of Texas. **Land use:** 2% arable land; 2% permanent crops; 96% other. **Major cities:** Bogotá (capital); Cali; Medellín; Cartagena.
● **PEOPLE Population:** 44,205,293 (July 2010 est.). **Nationality:** noun—Colombian(s); adjective—Colombian. **Ethnic groups:** 58% mestizo, 20% white, 14% mulatto, 4% black, 4% other. **Languages:** Spanish. **Religions:** 90% Roman Catholic.
● **GOVERNMENT Type:** republic; executive branch dominates government structure. **Independence:** July 20, 1810 (from Spain). **Constitution:** July 5, 1991; amended many times. **National holiday:** Independence Day, July 20. **Head of Government:**

Juan Manuel Santos, president (since Aug. 2010). **Structure:** executive; bicameral legislature; judiciary.
● **ECONOMY Monetary unit:** Colombian peso. **Budget:** (2009 est.) *income:* $72.55 bil.; *expend.:* $74.6 bil. **G.D.P.:** $401 bil., $9,200 per capita (2009 est.). **Chief crops:** coffee, flowers, bananas, rice; illegal producer of coca and cannabis for international drug trade. **Natural resources:** crude oil, natural gas, coal, iron ore, nickel. **Major industries:** textiles, food processing, oil. **Labor force:** 21.53 mil. (2009 est.); 63.1% services, 18% agriculture, 18.9% industry (2009); 11.8% unemployment (2008 est.). **Exports:** $31.34 bil. (2009 est.); petroleum, coffee, coal, bananas, flowers. **Imports:** $31.67 bil. (2009 est.); industrial equipment, transportation equipment, consumer goods, chemicals. **Major trading partners:** (2008) *exports:* 38% U.S., 16.2% Venezuela, 4% Ecuador; *imports:* 29.2% U.S., 11.5% China, 7.9% Mexico, 5.9% Brazil.

The territory that is now Colombia was home to various cultures prior to the arrival of Europeans. The Chibcha population of the Andean region might have numbered about one million prior to European contact. Portions of the area that make up modern Colombia fell under the authority of the Inca Empire.

In 1538 the colony of New Granada was established with its capital at Bogotá, and for most of the period up until 1740, the area was within the jurisdiction of the Viceroyalty of Peru. In that year a new viceroyalty was established that included modernday Colombia, Ecuador, Panama, and Venezuela. During the wars of independence against Spain, forces under Simón Bolívar were victorious over the royalists at the Battle of Boyacá in 1819, and the region gained independence in 1821.

Colombian territory was a part of the federation of Gran Colombia until its collapse in 1830. Thereafter, the country—called New Granada—remained a separate political entity (which included the area of Panama). By the 1850s a federal system had been adopted but this arrangement rapidly disintegrated, and the practically semisovereign states were involved in a struggle with the central government for autonomy. The effort to define the political structure was largely resolved with the constitution of 1886, which ended federalist regional autonomy and made Colombia a unitary republic.

Colombian political struggle since the 1850s had been characterized by a rivalry between two groups that coalesced into the Liberal and Conservative parties. During much of the 19th century, the Liberal-Conservative ideological battle was influenced to a great extent by the definition of the role of the Roman Catholic church in political and social life. The 1887–88 Concordat gave the church "official protection," while the state was given authority over public education. The settlement left a central position for the church in Colombian society that was not substantially altered by the Concordat of 1942.

The Liberal-Conservative struggle led to at least six civil wars, which often ended in interparty compromise. A struggle in 1854 involved the issue of the future direction of the country's economic development and was followed by a settlement among elites. The Liberal-Conservative war of 1860–63 led to a Liberal victory and a period of Liberal political hegemony that lasted until 1886. The period of Conservative rule from 1886 until

1930 was punctuated by the "War of a Thousand Days" (1899–1902), in which the Conservatives defeated the Liberals. In 1903 the Colombian government rejected a U.S. offer for construction of a canal in Panama. Panama (backed by the U.S.) revolted against the Colombian government, ending in the separation of Panama from Colombia.

The world depression of 1929 disrupted both the economy and the politics of Colombia. The loss of popularity of the ruling Conservatives due to both the economic collapse and their brutal repression of the labor movement led to a Liberal victory in 1930. A new civil war between peasants loyal to the two parties also broke out that year. By 1934 Liberal president Alfonso López Pumarejo had inaugurated his "Revolution on the March" program of socioeconomic reform.

During the 1946 presidential election, Conservatives won the presidency with a minority of the overall vote, defeating a split Liberal party. Armed conflict originally instigated by the two party elites erupted. This marked the beginning of La Violencia (1948–57) during which more than 200,000 people died. In the summer of 1957, leaders of the Liberal and Conservative parties reached an agreement on constitutional reform in an attempt to end the violence. The agreement, known as the National Front, was to be in force for 16 years and included provisions for regular alternation of the presidency between the parties, as well as an accord on equal staffing of all political positions by both parties. The Liberal and Conservative parties agreed they alone would monopolize the arena of legitimate political competition for the 16-year period. The agreement held up until 1968 constitutional revisions allowed for other political groups to be officially recognized.

The emergence of terrorist and paramilitary groups on both the right and left—some with ties to the drug trade—in the 1960s and 1970s weakened the two-party power-sharing monopoly. In March 1990, one of the most notorious left-wing groups, M-19, elected to lay down its arms and enter the political mainstream and immediately captured 19 of 70 seats in a constitutional convention called to rewrite the constitution. Other groups followed suit in 1991.

Throughout the 1980s, narco-terrorists murdered government officials, journalists, and innocent bystanders with impunity. Despite the assassination of four presidential candidates prior to the 1990 election, the Liberal party's César Gaviria Trujillo won the election campaigning against the drug traffickers. In 1994 another Liberal party president (Ernesto Samper Pizano) took office pledging to continue the fight. Samper also promised to invest billions of dollars to improve the infrastructure with money from the newly discovered Cusiana oil field.

In the summer of 1995, the Samper government arrested three of the top seven members of the Cali drug cartel; by Sept. 1996, all seven had been apprehended. Meanwhile, Samper faced accusations that he knew of $6 million contributed by the Cali cartel. Formal charges instituted by Prosecutor General Valdivieso in Feb. 1996 were found groundless by the legislature's Accusations Committee. Still, the United States, which had decertified Colombia as a drug-war partner in March, revoked Samper's visa even as Colombian farmers protested government anti-coca and -poppy programs. In 1997 radical leftist terrorist groups began a wave of murders, kidnappings, and other violence against local government officials, and in 1998 attacked and defeated an army battalion. The election of Conservative Andres Pastrana in June 1998 held out promise of victory in the drug war despite violent outbursts during the remainder of 1998 and early 1999. Government meetings with FARC, the principal rebel group, and National Peace Council meetings with ELN, the second major insurgent group, continued into mid-1999. On Dec. 20, FARC announced a cease-fire (the first since 1984) until January 10. When, on Jan. 11, 2000, FARC forces attacked four towns, the Clinton administration approved a two-year aid package to Colombia of $1.4 billion.

Pastrana's patience gave out in 2002 and he again sent jets and ground troops against FARC, but too late to prevent independent ex-Liberal Álvaro Uribe Vélez from winning the May 2002 presidential election. In 2003 the war entered its 35th year but Uribe's policy of "democratic security"—driving FARC from its strongholds, and pardoning many who wished to leave—had some good effects. In 2005, however, the paramilitaries again went on the attack and peace talks were again started. Uribe won reelection in a landslide in May 2006 and with U.S. aid was able to stifle the violence somewhat. More progress was made over the next four years, and Uribe's defense minister, Juan Manuel Santos, was elected president in 2010.

▶ COMOROS
Union of Comoros Islands

● **GEOGRAPHY Location:** part of archipelago in Mozambique Channel; three main islands, Njazidja, Nzwami, and Mwali (formerly Grande-Comore, Anjouan, and Mohéli). Moroni, Njazidja Is., 11°40s, 43°16'E. **Boundaries:** between Madagascar and southeast Africa. **Total land area:** 863 sq. mi. (2,235 sq km). **Coastline:** 211 mi. (340 km). **Comparative area:** slightly more than 12 times size of Washington, D.C. **Land use:** 35% arable land; 23.32% permanent crops; 40.8% other. **Major cities:** Moroni (capital); Mutsamudu; Fomboni. ● **PEOPLE Population:** 773,407 (July 2010 est.). **Nationality:** noun—Comoran(s); adjective—Comoran. **Ethnic groups:** Antalote, Cafre, Makoa, Oimatsaha, Sakalava. **Languages:** Arabic and French (both official), Shikomoro (a blend of Swahili and Arabic). **Religions:** 98% Sunni Muslim, 2% Roman Catholic.

● **GOVERNMENT Type:** republic. **Independence:** July 6, 1975 (from France). **Constitution:** Dec. 23, 2001 **National holiday:** July 6. **Heads of Government:** Ahmed Abdallah Sambi, head of state (since May 2006). **Structure:** executive; bicameral legislature; judiciary.

● **ECONOMY Monetary unit:** Comoran franc. **Budget:** (2001 est.) *income:* $27.6 mil.; *expend.:* N.A. **G.D.P.:** $761 mil., $1,000 per capita (2009 est.). **Chief crops:** vanilla, cloves, perfume essences. **Natural resources:** negligible. **Major industries:** tourism, perfume distillation. **Labor force:** 268,500 (2007); 80% agriculture; 20% industry and services. **Exports:** $32 mil. (f.o.b., 2006 est.); vanilla, ylang-ylang, cloves, perfume oils. **Imports:** $143 mil. (f.o.b., 2006 est.); rice and other foodstuffs, consumer goods, petroleum products, cement. **Major trading partners:** (2008) *exports:* 29.3% France, 16.4% Turkey, 12.1% Greece, 9.6% Brazil, 7.5% Algeria, 7.4% Singapore; *imports:* 14.4% France, 12.5% China, 10.6% India, 10% U.A.E., 5.7% Italy, 5.7% Pakistan, 4.6% Singapore, 4.5% Kenya.

Comoros is part of an archipelago composed of four prominent islands (the fourth, Mayotte, is a French dependency) and several smaller islands. Numerous groups from Africa, Europe, and Asia invaded the islands over the centuries. Shirazi Arabs introduced Islam to Comoros around the turn of the 16th century, and the French established colonial rule over the archipelago between 1841 and 1912 and developed a plantation-based economy. The islands remained a French territory until 1961 when political autonomy was granted. Comoros gained independence in 1975. Overthrown by foreign mercenaries in 1975, Pres. Ahmed Abdallah Abderemane returned to power in 1978 and helped establish the country's first constitution. In Nov. 1989 he was assassinated by a small group of rebels who quickly dispersed under pressure from the French government. A new constitution was approved in 1992, and the country's first democratic elections were held in Nov. 1992. An attempt, begun in 1997, by the islands of Anjouan and Moheli to gain independence or at least autonomy led to an army coup in April 1999 and Anjouan's claim of independence in Jan. 2000, a claim he soon renounced.

Much of the nation's soil is laden with lava, making it unsuitable for farming, especially on the island of Njazidja (Grand Comore), which is dominated by Mount Kartala, an active volcano. Poor transportation links between the islands and a harsh cyclone season add further to the country's problems. In an effort to end the series of coup attempts (over 20 since 1975), Comoros adopted a new constitution in Dec. 2001, which provides for a rotating presidency among the four islands in four-year terms, as well as a separate president and more autonomy for each of the four islands.

▶ **CONGO**
Democratic Republic of the Congo (formerly Zaire)
● **GEOGRAPHY   Location:** equatorial country in central Africa. **Boundaries:** Central African Republic, Sudan to N, Uganda, Rwanda, Burundi, Tanzania to E, Zambia to S, Angola to SW, Atlantic Ocean, Cabinda district of Angola, Congo to W. **Total land area:** 905,355 sq. mi. (2,344,858 sq km). **Coastline:** 23 mi. (37 km). **Comparative area:** about 1.5 times size of Alaska. **Land use:** 3% arable land; 1 % permanent crops; 96% other. **Major cities:** (Kinshasa (capital); Lubumbashi (Elizabethville); Mbuji-Mayi (Bakwanga); Kananga (Luluabourg); Kisangani (Stanleyville).
● **PEOPLE   Population:** 70,916,439 (July 2010 est.). **Nationality:** noun—Zairian(s);   adjective—Zairian. **Ethnic groups:** 45% of the people belong to one of four largest groups—Mongo, Luba, Kongo (all Bantu), and Mangbetu-Azande; over 200 other ethnic groups. **Languages:** French (official), Lingala, Kingwana, Kikongo, Tshiluba. **Religions:** 50% Roman Catholic, 20% Protestant, 10% Kimbanguist, 10% Muslim, 10% other syncretic sects and traditional beliefs.
● **GOVERNMENT   Type:** republic. **Independence:** June 30, 1960 (from Belgium). **Constitution:** Feb. 18, 2006. **National holiday:** Independence Day, June 30. **Heads of Government:** Joseph Kabila, president (since Jan. 2001); Adolphe Muzito, prime minister (since Oct. 2008);. **Structure:** executive—president elected for five-year term; legislative—500-member National Assembly; judiciary.

● **ECONOMY   Monetary unit:** zaire. **Budget:** (2006 est.) *income:* $700 mil. *expend.:* $2 bil. **G.D.P.:** $21.33 bil., $300 per capita (2009 est.). **Chief crops:** coffee, sugar, palm oil, rubber, tea. **Natural resources:** cobalt, copper, cadmium, crude oil, industrial and gem diamonds. **Major industries:** mining, mineral processing, consumer products (incl. textiles, footwear, cigarettes). **Labor force:** 25.53 mil. (2007 est.); 55% agriculture, 11% industry, 34% services. **Exports:** $6.1 bil. (f.o.b., 2007 est.); diamonds, copper, coffee, cobalt, crude oil. **Imports:** $5.2 bil. (f.o.b., 2007 est.); foodstuffs, mining and other machinery, transport equipment, fuels. **Major trading partners:** (2008) *exports:* 47.3% China, 15.4% Belgium, 9.6% Finland, 8.1% U.S., 4.4% Zambia; *imports:* 28.4% South Africa, 9.9% Belgium, 7.1% Zambia, 6% Zimbabwe.

Pygmies were probably the earliest inhabitants of the Congo region, followed much later by Bantu and Nilotic peoples. By the eighth century A.D., a number of well-established kingdoms and empires occupied the lower reaches of the Congo (now Zaire) River and the coastal plain; these included Kongo (Bakongo), Kuba, Luba, and Lunda.

Portuguese explorers and merchants arrived along the coast in the 1480s and initially traded with these kingdoms on a basis of relative equality; an indigenous Catholic church became established. Soon, however, the Portuguese established a slave trade that brought turmoil and decline to the native states. Europeans did not penetrate the interior of Zaire until the 19th century, but the slave trade (partly in Arab hands, in inland regions) had repercussions everywhere.

Henry Stanley descended the Congo River from east to west in 1876, opening the area for further exploration. In 1878 Stanley was engaged by King Leopold II of Belgium to establish Belgian trading stations along the river. King Leopold established the Congo Free State in 1885, not as a Belgian colony but as a personal possession of which he was king as well as chief stockholder.

The management corporation that ran the Free State abolished slavery but instituted a harsh regime that reduced native peoples to a condition of involuntary servitude. Forced labor and harsh suppression of rebellion resulted in the deaths of unnumbered thousands. Protests against these conditions, led by Great Britain and the U. S., led to the transformation of the Free State into the colony of the Belgian Congo in 1908.

By the 1920s the Belgian Congo had become a major producer of copper, diamonds, gold, rubber, palm oil, and other commodities. Railroads were developed to bring these goods to market. River navigation on the Congo was also developed. All mining, plantation agriculture, industry, and administration was in Belgian hands with no native participation in government.

In the 1950s agitation for increased native participation in government led, in 1957, to elections for local councils. In 1959 rioting against Belgian rule broke out. Elections were held on May 31 in anticipation of independence. Joseph Kasavubu became president, and Patrice Lumumba, head of the Congolese National Movement, became prime minister. On June 30, 1960, Belgium granted independence to the Congo; many Europeans fled the country. On July 4 the army mutinied, and on July 11 the southern province of Katanga (now Shaba), under the leadership of Moise Tshombe, seceded from the Congo and declared its independence. Belgium sent troops to quell the disorder.

On Aug. 9 the U.N. called on Belgium to withdraw its troops. Kasavubu removed Lumumba as prime minister. Lumumba, with the backing of Ghana, fought for control. He fled to Stanleyville (now Kisangani) but was kidnapped in January 1961 and taken to Katanga, where he was murdered, apparently with U.S. and Belgian complicity. Fighting continued in Katanga, where Tshombe's regime was supported by European mercenaries and opposed by U.N. peacekeeping forces. The Katangan rebellion ended in late 1963; rebels fled to Angola, and U.N. forces were withdrawn in June 1964. In a surprising political settlement, Tshombe became president of the Congo on June 30. On Sept. 7 leftist rebels attempted to establish a "people's republic" based in Stanleyville. Tshombe again resorted to the use of mercenaries and many white settlers, as well as Congolese, were killed in fighting and terrorist atrocities. The rebellion ended in July 1965. In Nov. 1965 Tshombe was deposed in a military coup led by Joseph Mobutu, whose government took steps to reduce European influence.

In 1971 Mobutu changed the country's name to Zaire and also changed the name of Leopoldville to Kinshasa. In 1972 he ordered all Zairians with European names to change them to African names; he became Mobutu Sese Seko. Attempts in 1974 to force foreign investors to sell their holdings to Zairians brought economic disruption, and foreign investors were invited back in 1977.

In 1977 rebellion broke out in Katanga; the government put down the rebellion with the aid of France, Egypt, and Morocco. The rebels fled to Angola, but the province's rich mining economy was again disrupted. Although Congo is rich with minerals, forest products, hydroelectric potential, and agriculture, most of these natural resources remain undeveloped and the country was impoverished by the nearly unprecedented corruption of the Mobutu regime.

In June 1991, Mobutu agreed to draft a new constitution and end a 20-year ban on multiparty elections. Étiene Tshisekedi was elected prime minister by a national conference in 1992, but Mobutu fired him in 1993. France and Belgium dispatched troops to protect their nationals and together with the U.S. demanded that Mobutu transfer power to Tshisekedi. Mobutu did not comply, and as his nation's economy sank, he continued to live in luxury, protected by the army and police. In May, 1997, Mobutu was driven from office by the army of Laurent Kabila, who immediately changed the name of the country to Congo.

In the summer of 1998 a new military rebellion began—a rebellion joined by Uganda and Rwanda. By June 1999, a cease-fire seemed near, one that would involve the U.N. and the Organization of African Unity as peacemakers with a mandate to disarm the rebels. The cease-fire came in July 1999, but was not signed by the rebels, only by the six outside states. And an August split in the rebel group brought Rwanda and Uganda to war with each other, each supporting its "own" rebel faction. In 2000 Rwanda proved victorious over Uganda; and by June, the U.N. security council decided that peacekeepers would not be sent.

In Jan. 2001, Pres. Kabila was shot to death by a bodyguard; the (appointed) parliament chose his son, Joseph, as new president. Peace negotiations continued, on and off, through 2003, when Congo reached a series of peace accords with Rwanda, Uganda, and two main rebel groups. A transitional government of President Kabila and four vice presidents ruled until 2006 when elections in July were to bring a new government. Kabila won 45 percent of the vote, thereby forcing a run-off. The U.N. was forced to send troops to stop the violence between rival parties, but in Oct. 2006, Kabila won the presidency. A National Assembly, and local leaders and legislatures were also elected. But incredible violence persisted as rebel forces under General Laurent N'Kunda defeated Congolese forces causing the U.N. to send in the largest peacekeeping force to protect civilians but they failed in large measure. Since 1998 an estimated 4 million have been killed, including many children, while many hundreds of thousands have been driven to refugee camps. In 2009 Rwanda joined with Congo to fight rebels in the east and the U.S. began to send aid and military advisors. In 2010, the Lord's Resistance Army, the largest rebel group, went on a rampage, killing and abducting thousands but were seemingly in retreat.

▶ CONGO, REPUBLIC OF THE

● **GEOGRAPHY** **Location:** equatorial country on western coast of Africa. **Boundaries:** Cameroon to NW, Central African Republic to NE, Zaire to E and S, Angolan district of Cabinda to S, Gulf of Guinea to SW, Gabon to W. **Total land area:** 132,047 sq. mi. (342,000 sq km). **Coastline:** 105 mi. (169 km). **Comparative area:** between New Mexico and Montana. **Land use:** 1 % arable land; negl.% permanent crops; 99% other. **Major cities:** Brazzaville (capital); Pointe-Noire; Pool; Bouenza; Cuvette.

● **PEOPLE** **Population:** 4,125,916 (July 2010 est.). **Nationality:** noun—Congolese (sing., pl.); adjective—Congolese or Congo. **Ethnic groups:** 48% Kongo, 20% Sangha, 17% Teke, 12% M'Bochi; about 8,500 Europeans (may be half that number following 1997 civil war). **Languages:** French (official); many African languages with Lingala and Kikongo most widely used. **Religions:** 50% Christian, 48% Animist, 2% Muslim.

● **GOVERNMENT** **Type:** republic. **Independence:** Aug. 15, 1960 (from France). **Constitution:** Approved by referendum Jan. 2002. **National holiday:** National Day, Aug. 15. **Heads of Government:** Denis Sassou Nguesso, president (since 1997); Isidore Mvouba, prime minister (since 2005). **Structure:** executive; bicameral legislature; judiciary.

● **ECONOMY** **Monetary unit:** Communauté Financière Africaine (CFA) franc. **Budget:** (2009 est.) *income:* $3.431 bil.; *expend.:* $2.723 bil. **G.D.P.:** $16.41 bil., $4,100 per capita (2009 est.). **Chief crops:** cassava, sugar, rice. **Natural resources:** petroleum, timber, potash, lead, zinc. **Major industries:** crude oil, cement, sawmills. **Labor force:** 1.514 mil. (2009); 75% agriculture, 25% commerce, industry, government. **Exports:** $7.542 bil. (2009); petroleum, lumber, plywood. **Imports:** $2.721 bil. (2009); petroleum products, capital equipment, construction materials. **Major trading partners:** (2008) *exports:* 42.1% U.S., 30.1% China, 5.6% Taiwan; *imports:* 22.2% France, 18.7% China, 6% India, 5.6% U.S.

About 1,500 years ago, the lower reaches of the Congo River formed the focus of a number of well-organized states. The Kongo and Ndongo flourished south of the river; north of the river, in what is now the Congo, the Loango, Teke, and

Bobangi were dominant. Some of these states were weakened beginning in the 16th century by the Portuguese slave trade, although the Loango benefited from it through the 19th century.

With the weakening of Portuguese power, the French became the dominant European power in western Africa. In 1883 they established a protectorate over the Teke kingdom, which they renamed Middle Congo. The treaty with the Teke king was concluded by Pierre Savorgnan de Brazza, for whom the capital was named.

In 1910 the French confederated their protectorates of Gabon, Middle Congo, Ubangi-Shari (later the Central African Republic), and Chad to form French Equatorial Africa. The territory became an important base of Free French activity during World War II, in acknowledgment of which Gen. Charles de Gaulle granted French citizenship to the territory's inhabitants in 1946, and local power was devolved upon advisory assemblies. The Republic of the Congo attained full autonomy upon the dissolution of the confederation of French Equatorial Africa in 1959, and the nation gained full independence on Apr. 15, 1960.

In 1963 Pres. Fulbert Youlou was driven from office by violent labor unrest; the military took control and installed a provisional civilian government led by Alphonse Massamba-Debat, who was elected president for a five-year term.

In 1968 Massamba-Debat was overthrown in a military coup and replaced by Capt. Marien Ngouabi, who in 1969 reorganized the Congo as a People's Republic. Despite its Marxist-Leninist stance, Congo remained strongly linked to France, its main source of trade, aid, and foreign investment. Ngouabi was assassinated in 1977 and replaced by a military committee of the Congolese Labor party led by Gen. Joachim Yhomby-Opango, who resigned and was arrested for treason in 1979. He was succeeded by Denis Sassou-Nguesso, who was reelected to a third five-year term in 1989.

In 1990, Congo began a relatively smooth transition to multiparty democracy and opposition parties were legalized as of Jan. 1, 1991. Pascal Lissouba was elected president in Aug. 1992. In June 1997, however, heavy fighting erupted in Brazzaville when Lissouba tried to have his rival, Sassou-Nguesso, arrested just weeks before a new election on the grounds that Sassou-Nguesso was planning a coup. He was and he succeeded, with oil money to buy arms and pay off rivals until by April 2001 a sort of peace and stability ensued, enough to elicit an E.U. loan. But ethnic civil war again broke out in June 2002 and lasted until March 2003. Elections in 2007 seemed odd since the ruling party won 90 percent of the seats in parliament. Sassou-Nguesso secured another seven year term in 2009 when the main opposition candidate was excluded from the election.

▶COSTA RICA
Republic of Costa Rica
● **GEOGRAPHY   Location:** Central American isthmus. **Boundaries:** Nicaragua to N, Caribbean Sea to E, Panama to S, and Pacific Ocean to W. **Total land area:** 19,730 sq. mi. (51,100 sq km). **Coastline:** 801 mi. (1,290 km). **Comparative area:** slightly smaller than West Virginia. **Land use:** 4% arable land; 5% permanent crops; 91% other. **Major cities:** San José (capital); Alajuela; Cartago; Puntarenas; Heredia.
● **PEOPLE   Population:** 4,516,220 (July 2010 est.). **Nationality:** noun—Costa Rican(s); adjective—

Costa Rican. **Ethnic groups:** 94% white (including mestizo), 3% black, 1% Amerindian, 1% Chinese. **Languages:** Spanish (official), Jamaican dialect of English spoken around Puerto Limón. **Religions:** 76.3% Roman Catholic, 13.7% Evangelical Protestant, other Protestant, Jehovah's Witness.
● **GOVERNMENT   Type:** democratic republic. **Independence:** Sept. 15, 1821 (from Spain). **Constitution:** Nov. 7, 1949. **National holiday:** Independence Day, Sept. 15. **Head of Government:** Oscar Arias, president (since May 2006). **Structure:** executive; unicameral legislature; judiciary.
● **ECONOMY   Monetary unit:** Costa Rican colón. **Budget:** (2009 est.) *income:* $3.795 bil.; *expend.:* $4.908 bil. **G.D.P.:** $48.63 bil., $10,900 per capita (2009 est.). **Chief crops:** coffee, bananas, sugarcane, corn, rice, cocoa. **Natural resources:** hydropower potential. **Major industries:** microprocessors, food processing, textiles, clothing, construction materials. **Labor force:** 2.09 mil. note-this official estimate excludes Nicaraguans living in Costa Rica (2009 est.); 22% industry, 14% agriculture, 64% services; 5.5% unemployment (2007 est.). **Exports:** $8.096 bil. (2009 est.); manufactured products, coffee, bananas, textiles, sugar. **Imports:** $10.53 bil. (2009 est.); raw materials, consumer goods, capital equipment. **Major trading partners:** (2008) *exports:* 23.9% U.S., 13.3% Netherlands, 13% China, 5% U.K., 4.9% Mexico; *imports:* 42.7% U.S., 6.9% Mexico, 6.3% Venezuela, 5.4% Japan, 4.6% China, 4.5% Brazil.

Costa Rica was under the jurisdiction of the Spanish colonial kingdom of Guatemala until it broke with Spain in 1821, along with other parts of Central America. With the collapse of the United Provinces of Central America in 1838, Costa Rica became an independent republic, and the country held its first democratic elections in 1889.

An attempt at electoral fraud in 1948 led to a brief civil war, which was won by the National Liberation forces under "Don Pepé" Jose Figueres Ferrer. The Costa Rican army was subsequently abolished. In the 1980s, under Pres. Oscar Arias Sánchez, Costa Rica vigorously promoted the settlement of civil strife in Nicaragua and El Salvador and he was awarded the 1987 Nobel Peace Prize for his Central American peace plan.

Subsequent governments focused on economic matters. In 1994 Jose Maria Figueres Olsen, son of "Don Pepé," was elected president. But out-of-control public spending brought new debt and inflation. In 1998 Miguel Angel Rodriguez captured the presidency, and his Social Christian Unity party carried an absolute majority in the Legislative Assembly. In 2002 the same party's candidate, Abel Pacheco, won the presidency. In 2005 a corruption scandal that revealed three previous presidents had bilked the government and taken bribes from foreign companies rocked the political stability of a nation proud of its standing as a model in the region. In 2006, the people elected a winner of the Nobel Peace Prize, Oscar Arias. A free trade deal with the U.S. was narrowly approved in 2007.

▶COTE D'IVOIRE
(see Ivory Coast)

▶CROATIA
Republic of Croatia
● **GEOGRAPHY   Location:** southeastern Europe. **Boundaries:** Slovenia and Hungary to N, Yugoslavia and Bosnia and Herzegovina to E, Adriatic Sea to S, Slovenia to W. **Total land area:** 21,851 sq.

mi. (56,594 sq km). **Coastline**: 1,105 mi. (1,778 km). **Comparative area**: slightly smaller than West Virginia. **Land use**: 25.82% arable land; 2% permanent crops; 72% other. **Major cities**: Zagreb (capital); Split; Rijeka; Osijek; Zadar.

• **PEOPLE** **Population**: 4,486,881 (July 2010 est.). **Nationality**: noun—Croat(s); adjective—Croatian. **Ethnic groups**: 90% Croat, 5% Serb, 0.5% Bosniak. **Languages**: 96% Croatian. **Religions**: 87.8% Catholic, 4.4% Orthodox, 1.3% Slavic Muslim.

• **GOVERNMENT** **Type**: presidential/parliamentary democracy. **Independence**: June 25, 1991 (from yugoslavia). **Constitution**: Dec. 22, 1990; revised in 2000, 2001. **National holiday**: Statehood Day, May 30. **Heads of Government**: Ivo Josipovic, president (since Feb. 2010); Jadranka Kosor, prime minister (since Jul. 2009). **Structure**: executive; bicameral legislature; judiciary.

• **ECONOMY** **Monetary unit**: Croatian kuna. **Budget**: (2009 est.) *income:* $20.99 bil. *expend.:* $22.35 bil. **G.D.P.**: $79.21 bil.; $17,600 per capita (2009 est.). **Chief crops**: wheat, corn, sugar beets, sunflowers, alfalfa. **Natural resources**: oil, coal, bauxite, low-grade iron ore, calcium. **Major industries**: chemicals and plastics, machine tools, fabricated metal, electronics, pig iron and rolled steel products. **Labor force**: 1.196 mil. (2009 est.); 5% agriculture, 31.3% industry, 63.6% services. **Exports**: $10.57 bil. (2009); textiles, foodstuffs, fuels, chemicals. **Imports**: $22.1 bil. (2009); machinery and transport equipment, chemicals, food and live animals, fuels and lubricants. **Major trading partners**: (2008) *exports:* 19.1% Italy, 15.4% Bosnia and Herzegovina, 10.8% Germany; *imports:* 16.9% Italy, 13.2% Germany, 10.3% Russia.

Croatia is one of Europe's most ancient states, King Tomaslav having created an independent Catholic realm in A.D. 924. In the sixth century the Croats, led by their eponymous chieftain Chrovatos, had migrated to the old Roman province of Illyricum, south of the Danube, where they dwelt in practical independence of the Byzantine Empire. Pope Gregory VII sent a papal crown, and therewith international recognition, to King Zvonimir (1076–89), but the king's death spelt the demise of the native dynasty. In 1102 Hungary's king Kalman was recognized as king of Croatia as well, in a dynastic union in which Croatia retained its own nobility and institutions. From the 14th century, Croatia (along with Hungary and Serbia) formed Europe's bulwark against the Ottoman Empire. After the Turkish victory at Mohacs (1526), the Hungarian and Croatian crowns were added to the Habsburg dynasty. Escaping Turkish sway, Croatia became controlled by Austrian military authorities as the frontier district against the Ottomans.

With the proclamation of the Austrian Empire in 1804, amalgamating the Habsburg possessions into one unified state, the estates of Croatia resisted the royal absolutism, stressing their autonomous status and ties to the Hungarian kingdom, but to slight avail, even after the Croat army of Baron Josip Jellacid proved essential in suppressing the Hungarian revolt of 1848. However, after the 1867 Ausleich ("compromise"), which established a practically independent Hungary within the Dual Monarchy, a further compromise (Nagoda) in the following year recognized Croatian autonomy within the Hungarian realm.

When the Habsburg monarchy collapsed during World War I, Croatia joined the new Yugoslavia, but since that state proved to be no federation but rather a greater Serbia, Croatia resisted Serbian dominance. And after the ferocious ethnic hostility provoked a royal dictatorship in 1929, Ante Pavelic formed the Ustase, a terrorist organization similar to and having ties with the Macedonian IMRO, with the aim of attaining Croatian independence. Just a week before the outbreak of World War II, Croatia was again granted autonomy, but with Hitler's 1941 conquest and dismemberment of Yugoslavia, an "Independent Croat State" was established under Italian protection. While Aimone, Duke of Spoleto was proclaimed king of Croatia under the preposterous name of Tomaslov II, he had the good sense never to enter "his" kingdom, whose governance was left to Pavelic and the Ustase. An "ethnic cleansing" of Croatia commenced, in which perhaps 100,000 Serbs and Jews lost their lives. Since the "chetniks" of Gen. Mihajlovic were Serbs and royalists, anti-Ustase Croats had nowhere to turn but to the Communist "partisans" of Tito (himself a Croat). Postwar vengeance against Tito's enemies, especially the Ustase, was severe but short-lived and Croatia in 1946 became one of the "republics" of the reconstituted Yugoslavia.

With Croatia's June 1991 secession from Yugoslavia, Serbian militias backed by the Yugoslavian army seized about one-third of Croatian territory, but by mid-1995 Croat forces had regained almost all of its land. President Franjo Tudjman also fostered the Muslim-Croat Federation in Bosnia to preserve a sort of Bosnian independence. The Yugoslav-Croat war came to an end in September 1996 with the establishment of diplomatic relations in which Yugoslavia recognized Croatia's boundaries, leaving ethnic Serbs in the lurch. And in Jan. 1998, a U.N. decision returned eastern Slavonia, part of historic Croatia captured by Serb militias in 1991, to Croatia.

Having won a third presidential term in January 1997, despite a stagnant economy, widespread corruption and complaints of autocracy, Tudjman succumbed to stomach cancer in Dec. 1999. Within a month, a six-party opposition coalition had captured 94 of 152 parliamentary seats, with Social Democrat Ivica Racan named premier. In a February 2000 presidential run-off, Stipe Mesic took over 56 percent of the votes, but by 2003 the Croatian Democratic Union returned to power with pledges of leading Croatia into NATO and the E.U. In 2007, changes to the constitution shifted power to the legislature and prime minister Ivo Sanader's conservative HD2 Party won a majority in Nov. 2007.

▶ **CUBA**
Republic of Cuba
• **GEOGRAPHY** **Location**: largest island in Caribbean Sea, about 100 mi. (160 km) S of Florida. **Boundaries**: North Atlantic Ocean to N, Windward Passage to E, Caribbean Sea to S, Yucatan Channel to W. **Total land area**: 42,803 sq. mi. (110,860 sq km). **Coastline**: 2,319 mi. (3,735 km). **Comparative area**: slightly smaller than Pennsylvania. **Land use**: 27.63% arable land; 6.5% permanent crops; 65% other. **Major cities**: Havana (capital); Santiago de Cuba; Camagüey; Holguín; Guantánamo.

• **PEOPLE** **Population**: 11,477,459 (July 2010 est.). **Nationality**: noun—Cuban(s); adjective—Cuban. **Ethnic groups**: 65.1% white, 24.8% mulatto/mestizo, 10.1% black. **Languages**: Spanish. **Religions**: at least 85% Roman Catholic before Castro assumed power.

• **GOVERNMENT** **Type:** Communist state. **Independence:** Dec. 10, 1898 (from Spain; administered by the U.S. from 1898 to 1902). **Constitution:** Feb. 24, 1976; amended July 1992 and June 2002. **National holiday:** January 1 **Head of Government:** Gen. Raul Castro Ruz, president of council of state and president of council of ministers (since Feb. 2008). **Structure:** executive; unicameral legislature; controlled judiciary.

• **ECONOMY** **Monetary unit:** Cuban peso and Convertible peso. **Budget:** (2009 est.) *income:* $39.11 bil.; *expend.:* $42.58 bil. **G.D.P.:** $111.1 bil., $9,700 per capita (2009 est.). **Chief crops:** sugar cane, tobacco, citrus, coffee, rice. **Natural resources:** cobalt, nickel, iron ore, copper, manganese. **Major industries:** sugar, petroleum, food and tobacco processing. **Labor force:** 4.968 mil. (2009); 20% agriculture, 19.4% industry, 60.6% services. **Exports:** $3.253 bil. (2009 est.); sugar, nickel, shellfish, tobacco. **Imports:** $10.86 bil. (2008 est.); petroleum, food, machinery, chemicals. **Major trading partners:** (2008) *exports:* 27.8% Canada, 26.7% China, 6.2% Spain; *imports:* 29.8% Venezuela, 11.8% China, 10% Spain, 6.4% Canada.

At the time of Christopher Columbus's arrival in 1492, Cuba was home to Arawak, Ciboney, and Guanahatabey Indian people. Cuba served as a launching point for Spanish conquests in the Americas, and the 19th-century wars of independence that swept the rest of Spanish America did not overthrow the imposing Spanish garrison there. Slavery was abolished in 1886, but Spanish colonialism lingered until the 1890s.

Spanish control of the island began to deteriorate in the late 1860s with the beginning of the "Ten Years War" (1868-78). Under the terms of the 1898 Treaty of Paris, which ended the Cuban-U.S.-Spanish War, Cuba became a U.S. protectorate. The U.S.-sponsored Platt Amendment (1901) to the new Cuban constitution gave the United States the right to intervene in Cuban affairs.

Corruption and political repression plagued Cuban politics during the first half of the 20th century. Gerardo Machado won election to the presidency in 1925, but quickly turned his administration into a dictatorship that lasted until his ouster by a progressive coalition of students and labor in 1933. The "revolution" of 1933 installed Ramón Grau San Martín as the new head of the government, but the U.S. supported Grau's ouster, and army sergeant Fulgencio Batista replaced him. Batista ruled the country either directly or indirectly for the next quarter century.

In 1953 Fidel Castro Ruz led a failed attack on the Moncada army barracks in Santiago. In Dec. 1956 Fidel and Raúl Castro, Argentine physician Ernesto "Che" Guevara, and 79 others returned to Cuba and waged a guerrilla campaign against the government. Batista's military failed to defeat the guerrillas, and in the wake of increasing demonstrations of public antipathy for his government, the dictator fled the country. The Communist Fidelistas took control Jan. 1, 1959.

By mid-1959, revolutionary tribunals had tried and executed more than 500 political "enemies." The leaders announced an agrarian reform, and by 1960 the nationalization of the economy was in full swing. In 1961 U.S.-Cuban diplomatic relations were severed, and the U.S.-sponsored Bay of Pigs invasion by Cuban exiles failed. In 1962 the Cuban missile crisis brought the world to the brink of nuclear war when U.S. spy planes uncovered Soviet intentions to place nuclear weapons on the island. The Soviets agreed to the withdrawal of missiles in exchange for a U.S. pledge not to invade Cuba.

In its active foreign policy, Cuba provided assistance to a number of left-wing regimes in Africa and Latin America, most notably its military presence in Angola from 1975-91. With the collapse of the Soviet Union in 1991, Cuba lost huge subsidies, forcing its economy into a downward spiral. In 1994, the worsening economy and a growing dissatisfaction with the Castro govenment fueled migration of Cubans to U.S. shores. With thousands of refugees arriving in Florida each day—aboard boats, homemade rafts, ferries—the U.S. and Cuba negotiated an agreement in which the United States would increase annual acceptance levels of Cuban immigrants to 20,000 in return for Cuba's promise to curb illegal migration.

Tensions flared between the U.S. and Cuba on Feb. 24, 1996, when Cuban MiGs shot down two private jets operating out of Miami. The U.S. responded by tightening economic sanctions, with penalties for foreigners investing in Cuba. Castro called for a renewed commitment to Marxism and met with Pope John Paul II who visited Cuba in 1999 and publicly confronted Castro on issues of freedom and religious liberty. But for the regime remains changeless. In January 2003 "elections," 609 candidates ran unopposed for 609 National Assembly seats. In March, 78 dissidents and independent journalists were arrested; in April all 78 were found guilty in closed trials and given sentences of 6 to 28 years. In Aug. 2006 Castro underwent surgery and turned power over to his brother Raul who became the official ruler in 2008. Relations with the U.S. brightened when Pres. Obama signed an order allowing Cuban-Americans to visit Cuba as often as they like.

▶ **CYPRUS**
Republic of Cyprus
• **GEOGRAPHY** **Location:** eastern Mediterranean Sea. Nicosia 35°11'N, 33°23'E. **Boundaries:** 62 mi. (100 km) S of Turkey, Syria to E. **Total land area:** 3,572 sq. mi. (9,251 sq km). **Coastline:** 403 mi. (648 km). **Comparative area:** between Delaware and Connecticut. **Land use:** 11% arable land; 5% permanent crops; 84% other. **Major cities:** Nicosia (capital); Limassol; Larnaca; Famagusta; Phaphos.

• **PEOPLE** **Population:** 1,102,677 (July 2010 est.). **Nationality:** noun—Cypriot(s); adjective—Cypriot. **Ethnic groups:** 77% Greek, 18% Turk, 5% other. **Languages:** Greek, Turkish, English. **Religions:** 78% Greek Orthodox, 18% Muslim.

• **GOVERNMENT** **Type:** republic. **Independence:** Aug. 16, 1960 (from U.K.). **Constitution:** Aug. 16, 1960; negotiations have been held intermittently to create basis for new or revised constitution to govern the island and relations between Greek and Turkish Cypriots. **National holiday:** Independence Day, Oct. 1. **Heads of Government:** Dimitris Christofias, president (since Feb., 2008). **Structure:** republic. *note* - A separation of the Greek and Turkish communities began in 1963. The island was admitted to the EU in 2004, and the election of one Cypriot president in 2008 encouraged the two sides to reopen unification talks.

• **ECONOMY** **Monetary unit:** euro. **Budget:** (2009 est.) *income:* $9.689 bil *expend.:* $10.72 bil **G.D.P.:** $22.97 bil., $21,200 per capita. (2009 est.). **Chief crops:** potatoes, citrus, vegetables, barley, grapes. **Natural resources:** copper, pyrites, asbestos, gypsum, timber. **Major industries:** food, beverages, textiles, chemicals. **Labor force:** (2009) 400,000; 8.5% agriculture, 20.5% industry, 71% services (2006). **Exports:** $1.135 bil. (2009 est.); citrus, potatoes, grapes, textiles. **Imports:** $6.676 bil. (2009 est.); consumer goods, petroleum and lubricants, foodstuffs, minerals, chemicals. **Major trading partners:** (2008) *exports:* 20% Greece, 10.8% U.K., 6% Germany; *imports:* 16.9% Greece, 10.7% Italy, 8.7% U.K., 8.3% Germany, 8.2% Israel.

Recent excavations on Cyprus indicate a human presence at least 10,000 years ago. Mycenean (Greek) culture flourished in the second millenium B.C. Phoenicians colonized the island in the 10th century B.C., and it remained a major entrepôt for eastern Mediterranean trade. Annexed to Rome in 58 B.C. it was later part of the Byzantine Empire until the English Richard I (Lion Hearted) established a crusader state in A.D. 1191. The Lusignan dynasty ruled until 1489, when Cyprus was annexed by Venice. It was subsequently conquered by the Ottoman Empire in 1571.

In 1878 the Congress of Berlin placed Cyprus under British administration. In 1914 it was annexed outright by Great Britain and was made a British colony in 1925. From 1945–48, the British used Cyprus as a detention area for "illegal" Jewish immigrants to Palestine.

After 1947 the Greek Cypriot community continued its long-standing agitation for union (enosis) with Greece, a policy strongly opposed by the Turkish Cypriot community. Communal violence broke out in 1954–55. In 1960 Cyprus was granted full independence under an agreement that forbade either enosis or partition and included guarantees of the rights of both Greeks and Turks. Attempts by the president, Archbishop Makarios, to alter the constitution to favor the Greek majority provoked further communal clashes in 1964, when a U.N. peacekeeping force was sent to the island. On July 15, 1974, a military coup by officers favoring union with Greece deposed the Makarios government. On July 20 Turkey invaded Cyprus and, after the collapse of cease-fire talks in August, occupied the northern two-fifths of the island. In 1975 the Turkish government announced a de facto partition of Cyprus; the northern territory was proclaimed the Turkish Federated State of Cyprus, under Pres. Rauf Denktash.

Makarios returned as president of the Republic of Cyprus, which was thus reduced in size, and remained in office until his death in 1977. He was succeeded by Spyros Kyprianou. Some 200,000 Greek Cypriots were expelled from the Turkish sector to the Republic; many Turks fled from the Republic to the Turkish sector. With a return of political stability, renewed foreign investment, and a customs union negotiated with the EEC, the Republic's economy has prospered, led by agriculture, light manufacturing, and tourism.

The 1998 decision of the E.U. to invite Cyprus to apply for membership and to deny Turkey's application heightened tensions. In June, both Greece and Turkey sent aircraft to Cyprus and the newly-reelected government of Pres. Clerides sought anti-aircraft missiles from Russia. But by December Cyprus had cancelled plans for deployment, at the urging of Greek Premier Simitis. With the peaceful resolution of so serious a crisis, it became possible for Greek-Turkish relations (the key to reunification of Cyprus) to improve, as they did in the January 2000 accords on the Aegean environment, immigration, tourism and the like. Reunifi-

cation talks continued through March 2003 but to no avail. So the E.U.'s treaty with Cyprus, signed in April 2003, concerns only the Greek portion of the island. Turkish Cyprus opened its border in April, while Greek Cyprus dropped its trade sanctions raising hopes for reunification. But a referendum in 2004 saw the Greeks overwhelmingly rejecting the idea while the Turks voted strongly for it. By 2008, however, new leaders in Turkey and Greece began meaningful talks to end the nation's division.

▶ CZECH REPUBLIC

● GEOGRAPHY **Location:** Central Europe. **Boundaries:** Poland to N, Slovakia to E, Austria to S, Germany to W. **Total land area:** 30,451 sq. mi. (78,867 sq km). **Coastline:** none. **Comparative area:** about the size of South Carolina. **Land use:** 40% arable land; 3% permanent crops; 57% other. **Major cities:** Prague (capital); Brno; Ostrava; Pilsen (Plzen); Olomouc.
● PEOPLE **Population:** 10,201,707 (July 2010 est.). **Nationality:** noun—Czech; adjective—Czech. **Ethnic groups:** 90.4% Czech, 3.4% Moravian, 1.9% Slovak. **Languages:** Czech. **Religions:** 59% unaffiliated, 26.8% Roman Catholic, 2.1% Protestant.
● GOVERNMENT **Type:** parliamentary democracy. **Independence:** Oct. 29, 1918 (from Austro-Hungarian Empire); Jan. 1, 1993 (from Czechoslovakia). **Constitution:** Jan. 1, 1993; amended 1997, 2000, 2001 and 2002. **National holiday:** Founding of the Republic, Oct. 28. **Heads of Government:** Václav Klaus, president (since Mar. 7, 2003); Jan Fischer, prime minister (since April 2009). **Structure:** executive; bicameral legislature; judiciary.
● ECONOMY **Monetary unit:** koruna. **Budget:** (2009 est.) *income:* $76.71 bil., *expend.:* $85.65 bil. **G.D.P.:** $256.6 bil., $25,100 per capita (2009 est.). **Chief crops:** wheat, rye, barley, oats, corn, potatoes. **Natural resources:** coal, kaolin, clay, graphite. **Major industries:** fuels, metallurgy, machines. **Labor force:** (2009) 5.38 mil.; 37.6% industry, 58.3% services, 4.1% agriculture. **Exports:** $106.4 bil., (2009); manufactured goods, machinery and equipment, chemicals. **Imports:** $99.97 bil. (2009); machinery and equipment, manufactured goods, chemicals. **Major trading partners:** (2008) *exports:* 28% Germany, 8.5% Taiwan, 8.4% Poland; *imports:* 28.6% Germany, 6.8% Taiwan, 6.2% Slovakia.

A Moravian empire, Christianized by Cyril and Methodius, existed in the ninth century until destroyed by the Magyars. From the 10th through the 14th century, Bohemia and Moravia, "lands of the crown of St. Vaclav," formed an independent kingdom within the Holy Roman Empire under the Czech Premsylid dynasty. In 1526 the crown lands came under Habsburg rule, a rule that lasted until World War I.

They were the richest crown lands of the Austro-Hungarian Empire. Prosperous agriculture in the central plains and mineral wealth in the hill country were supplemented in the 19th century by industrial development led by urban middle classes, who were largely German and Jewish.

With the crumbling of the Habsburg monarchy during the war, a new multinational state of Czechoslovakia emerged, founded by Eduard Beneŝ and Thomas Masaryk, in which the Czechs (only 45 percent of the population) ruled over Germans, Slovaks, Magyars, Poles, and Ukranians, yet it was the most democratic state in Central Europe.

Following the Munich Pact of September 1938, Hitler annexed the German-speaking regions of the "Sudetenland," and in 1939 he established a "protectorate" over the Czech lands, while Slovakia became a self-governing satellite republic. With the collapse of Hitler's Reich, Czechoslovakia was reestablished (except for the Carpatho-Ukraine, which it was compelled to cede to the U.S.S.R.) with Beneš again as president and a socialist government, independent but pro-Soviet. Three million Germans were expelled, with tens of thousands killed either in mob violence or after hasty trials before "Special People's Courts." In 1948 a Communist coup forced Beneš to resign; he was replaced by the Communist leader Klement Gottwald. Jan Masaryk, the foreign minister, committed suicide or was murdered. Purges and persecutions followed.

With Stalin's death in 1953, Gottwald was replaced as party first secretary by Stalinist hardliner Antonin Novotny, who also became president in 1957. In 1968 Novotny was replaced as first secretary by a Slovak liberal, Alexander Dubcek. Czechoslovakia suddenly was in the vanguard of communist reform. The new regime abolished censorship, denounced Stalin, decentralized economic decision-making, and granted real power to the National Assembly.

The brief "Prague Spring" ended in Aug. 1968, when Warsaw Pact troops invaded. In 1969 Dubcek was replaced by Gustáv Husak. The party was purged, censorship restored, dissent repressed, and the centralized economy restored.

The 1970s brought inflation and economic stagnation but produced no change in policy. The rise of the Solidarity movement in Poland in the early 1980s provoked a backlash of preventive repression in Czechoslovakia, aimed especially at Charter 77, a human-rights organization, and at the Catholic church.

The pro-democracy movement began in earnest in October 1989, inspired by a lack of confidence in Communist rule and by reform movements throughout Eastern Europe. The resignation of Communist leaders throughout December culminated in the parliamentary election of Václav Havel, a dissident playwright and head of a loose coalition of opposition groups called Civic Forum, as president, and the vindicated Alexander Dubcek as chairman of Parliament.

Despite severe economic difficulties, revelations of state security abuses, environmental pollution, and other problems inherited from the Communist era, Czechoslovakia's "Velvet Revolution" seemed a resounding political and popular success. In 1990 Soviet troops left and Civic Forum and its Slovakian ally, Public Against Violence, won 47 percent of the vote in parliamentary elections, against 14 percent for the Communists and 12 percent for the Christian Democrats. Vaclav Havel was elected president, and Marian Calfa became prime minister.

But Slovak-Czech resentments and Slovakia's economic distress led to a separation of the two republics, effective Jan. 1, 1993. In June 1996, the first elections in the new Czech Republic gave 99 (out of 200) seats to the three-party center-right coalition (led by Prime Minister Vaclav Klaus and President Havel) which had guided the Czech Republic's successful transition to a market economy. After several years of prosperity, the Republic fell on hard times in 1997, and Klaus introduced austerity mea-

sures. Revelations of campaign finance irregularities brought Klaus' resignation in 1997. In the subsequent 1998 elections, the Social Democrats won a plurality of seats and, with the Civic Democrats' agreement, formed a minority government for the next four years. The budget adopted in 1999 included the republic's first planned deficit as the nagging recession continued, with little economic growth forecast and unemployment rising to 9.5 percent. In the 2002 elections, the Social Democrats won a plurality but no majority in the Chamber of Deputies, necessitating a coalition with the Christian Democratic Union/Freedom Party and Vladimir Spidla remaining prime minister and Vaclav Klaus becoming president. In June, a referendum of Czech voters approved E.U. membership with a 77 percent "yes" vote. Spidla was forced to resign in 2004 when his party did poorly in elections for the E.U. parliament. The government remained fractured through 2007 as coalitions came and went with very little accomplished.

▶DENMARK
Kingdom of Denmark
● **GEOGRAPHY Location:** northern Europe. **Boundaries:** Skagerrak channel to N, Baltic Sea to E, Germany to S, North Sea to W. **Total land area:** 16,639 sq. mi. (43,094 sq km). **Coastline:** 2,100 mi. (3,379 km). **Comparative area:** between Maryland and West Virginia. **Land use:** 56% arable land; negl. % permanent crops; 44% other. **Major cities:** København (Copenhagen—capital); Århus (Aarhus); Odense; Alborg (Aalborg); Esbjerg.
● **PEOPLE Population:** 5,515,575 (July 2010 est.). **Nationality:** noun—Dane(s); adjective—Danish. **Ethnic groups:** Scandinavian, Inuit, Faeroese, German. **Languages:** Danish, Faroese, English, Greenlandic (Eskimo dialect); small German-speaking minority. **Religions:** 95% Evangelical Lutheran, Protestant and Roman Catholic, Muslim.
● **GOVERNMENT Type:** constitutional monarchy. **Constitution:** June 5, 1953. **National holiday:** Constitution Day, June 5. **Heads of Government:** Margrethe II, queen (since Jan. 1972); Lars Lokke Rasmussen, prime minister (since April 2009). **Structure:** executive power vested in Crown, exercised by cabinet responsible to Parliament; unicameral legislature; Supreme Court.
● **ECONOMY Monetary unit:** Danish krone. **Budget:** (2009 est.) *income:* $175.4 bil.; *expend.:* $175.6 bil. **G.D.P.:** $198.6 bil., $36,000 per capita (2009 est.). **Chief crops:** grain, potatoes; meat, dairy; fish. **Natural resources:** crude oil, natural gas, fish, salt, limestone. **Major industries:** food processing, machinery and equipment, textiles, clothing. **Labor force:** 2.94 mil.; 76% services, 21% industry; 3% agriculture (2005) 5.1% unemployment (2002). **Exports:** $91.9 bil. (2009 est.); machinery and instruments, meat and meat products, fuels, dairy products. **Imports:** $84.07 bil. (2009 est.); machinery and equipment, petroleum, chemicals, grain and foodstuffs. **Major trading partners:** (2008) *exports:* 17.8% Germany, 14.5% Sweden, 8% U.K., 6% U.S.; *imports:* 21.6% Germany, 14.4% Sweden, 7% Netherlands, 6% Norway.

Scandinavian by history, not geography, Denmark in the 11th century, under its second Christian king, Canute, ruled a great northern empire including Greenland, Iceland, the Faeroe Islands, Great Britain, and Norway. By 1387 Britain was long independent, but Denmark added Sweden and Finland to its domain. Yet it was never a great power. Its kings never really controlled the nobility, while in foreign affairs it was dominated by the Hansa, the league of German trading cities.

In the 16th century Denmark had to recognize the independence of Sweden and Finland. In the 19th century it lost Norway (to Sweden in 1814) and Schleswig-Holstein (to Prussia in 1864). In the 20th century Denmark sold the Virgin Islands to the United States in 1914 and had to recognize Iceland's independence in 1944.

In the 19th century, Denmark was transformed from a poor peasant society to one of Europe's richest agricultural nations by means of reforms that established agricultural cooperatives and emphasized intensive specialization in the production of dairy products and pork. These products remain a mainstay of the Danish economy.

Denmark remained neutral during World War I. In 1939 Denmark signed a 10-year nonaggression pact with Germany, but Germany nevertheless invaded Denmark in April 1940; the country surrendered without a fight. In 1941 Denmark's ambassador in Washington transferred defense of Greenland to the United States, and much of Denmark's merchant fleet joined the Allied war effort. Denmark was placed under German martial law in August 1943 and was treated as an enemy nation. Danish resistance succeeded in evacuating 7,000 Jews to neutral Sweden. Denmark was liberated by British troops in May 1945.

Denmark became a U.N. member in 1946 and a founding member of NATO in 1949. By the latter year, the postwar recovery was complete, with industrial levels exceeding those of the prewar period. High taxes, unemployment, and inflation remained problems, but the economy was aided by the growth of trade with West Germany.

In 1953 the king assented to a constitutional reform that abolished the upper house of the legislature, leaving the Folketing as the sole legislative body. Proportional representation meant that it was impossible for any party to gain a parliamentary majority, so Denmark is always governed by coalition regimes. In the postwar period, these normally have been led by the Social Democrats.

In the 1950s Denmark adopted a characteristically Scandinavian program of free enterprise, high taxes, and extensive social welfare systems. A high rate of economic growth, spurred by agricultural exports, continued throughout the 1960s. Denmark joined the E.C. in 1972. The 1970s brought economic difficulties, as Danish oil exploration in the North Sea yielded disappointing results, and inflation reached double digits.

The elections of 1982 installed Denmark's first Conservative government since 1905. A Conservative four-party coalition formed in 1984 remained in office until 1993 when Prime Minister Schlüter resigned over charges of misleading the Folketing about restrictions on the immigration of Tamil refugees. Social Democrat Poul Nyrup Rasmussen formed a coalition government with only a one-seat majority.

The general revival of the world economy in the 1980s coupled with government austerity measures led to renewed growth and lowered inflation. In 1986 Danish voters renewed their commitment to the E.C., but in the June 1992 referendum on the Maastricht Treaty—providing for common defense and foreign policy as well as a common currency and central bank—Denmark said "no." The E.U. quickly made concessions that guaranteed Denmark's right to opt out of any common E.U. citizenship, police force, defense policy, or judicial arrangement. In May 1993 Danish voters approved this different version of the treaty. In Sept. 2000 a referendum on the euro was defeated and later the Danes said they would not be part of the E.U.'s army. In Nov. 2001 Folketing elections, the Liberal Party, for the first time since 1920, outpolled the Social Democrats and the Liberal coalition organized a new government of the right under premier Anders Fogh Rasmussen. Within a week they had carried stronger immigration-control measures—the principal issue in the campaign.

In 2006 a Danish publication caused an international incident when it published cartoons belittling Islam, resulting in massive demonstrations around the world. In Nov. 2007 Rasmussen's party was reelected.

▶ DJIBOUTI
Republic of Djibouti

● **GEOGRAPHY Location:** northeastern Africa. **Boundaries:** Red Sea to N, Gulf of Aden to E, Somalia to SE, Ethiopia to S, W, and NW. **Total land area:** 8,494 sq. mi. (23,200 sq km). **Coastline:** 195 mi. (314 km). **Comparative area:** slightly smaller than Massachusetts. **Land use:** 0% arable land; 0% permanent crops; 100% other. **Major cities:** Djibouti (capital); Dikhil, Ali-Sabieh, Tadjourah, Obock.

● **PEOPLE Population:** 740,528 (July 2010 est.). **Nationality:** noun—Djiboutian(s); adjective—Djiboutian. **Ethnic groups:** 60% Somali, 35% Afar, 5% French, Arab, Ethiopian, and Italian. **Languages:** French and Arabic (official); Somali and Afar widely used. **Religions:** 94% Muslim, 6% Christian.

● **GOVERNMENT Type:** republic. **Independence:** June 27, 1977 (from France). **Constitution:** Sep. 4, 1992. **National holiday:** Independence Day, June 27. **Heads of Government:** Ismail Omar Guelleh, president (since May 1999); Deletia Mohamed Deletia, prime minister (since Mar. 2001). **Structure:** executive; unicameral legislature; judiciary.

● **ECONOMY Monetary unit:** Djiboutian franc. **Budget:** (1999 est.) *income:* $135 mil., *expend.:* $182 mil. **G.D.P.:** $2.011 bil., $2,800 per capita (2009 est.). **Chief crops:** limited fruits and vegetables; goats, sheep, camels. **Natural resources:** geothermal areas. **Major industries:** limited to a few small-scale enterprises, such as construction and agricultural processing. **Labor force:** 282,000 (2000 est.); 75% agriculture, 14% services, 11% industry; 59% unemployment urban, 83% unemployment rural (2007 est.). **Exports:** $340 mil. (f.o.b., 2006 est.); hides and skins and transit of coffee. **Imports:** $1.55 bil. (f.o.b., 2006 est.); foods, beverages, transport equipment, chemicals, petroleum. **Major trading partners:** (2006) *exports:* 79.9% Somalia, 4.1% U.A.E., 4.1% Yemen; *imports:* 21.4% Saudi Arabia, 16.8% India, 11.1% China, 6.3% U.S.

This small, arid region on the Horn of Africa near the southern mouth of the Red Sea became the object of British-French rivalry with the opening of the Suez Canal in 1869. The French sphere of influence, called French Somaliland, was affirmed by agreements with Ethiopia in 1897, 1945, and 1954. In the early 20th century, the French constructed a railroad from Addis Ababa to Djibouti, adding to the colony's strategic value.

French and Italian forces clashed at the border of Ethiopia and French Somaliland with the Italian invasion of Ethiopia in the 1930s. During World War

II, the territorial administration at first sided with the Vichy government but in December 1942 established ties with the Free French and the Allies.

The colony was reorganized in 1957 and in 1958 became, by referendum, a French Overseas Territory. In July 1967 its name was changed to the Territory of the Afars and Issas. Growing nationalist sentiment led to a referendum in favor of complete independence. The Republic of Djibouti became independent on June 27, 1977. Hassan Aptidon ruled as president until 1999. Civil war had broken out between the Issas and Afars in the early 1990s that did not end until 2001. But in 1999, multiparty elections were held for the first time and Ismail Omar Guelleh was elected, then reelected in 2005. In 2008 a long-standing border dispute with Eritrea turned violent for a brief time. Djibouti's strategic location has led to the placement of the only U.S. military base in sub-Saharan Africa.

▶ DOMINICA
Commonwealth of Dominica
• **GEOGRAPHY Location:** eastern Caribbean Sea, between Guadeloupe to N and Martinique to S. Roseau 15°18'N, 61°23'W. **Boundaries:** Dominica Passage to N, Atlantic Ocean to E, Martinique Passage to S, Caribbean Sea to W. **Total land area:** 290 sq. mi. (750 sq km). **Coastline:** 92 mi. (148 km). **Comparative area:** slightly more than four times size of Washington, D.C. **Land use:** 6.67% arable land; 21.33% permanent crops; 72% other. **Major cities:** Roseau (capital).
• **PEOPLE Population:** 72,813 (July 2010 est.) **Nationality:** noun—Dominican(s); adjective—Dominican. **Ethnic groups:** black, Carib Amerindians, mixed, European, Syrian. **Languages:** English (official), French patois. **Religions:** 61.4% Roman Catholic, 6% Seventh Day Adventist, 23.4% other Christian, 1.3% Rastafarian, 6.1% none.
• **GOVERNMENT Type:** parliamentary democracy. **Independence:** Nov. 3, 1978 (from U.K.). **Constitution:** Nov. 3, 1978. **National holiday:** Independence Day, Nov. 3. **Heads of Government:** Nicholas Orville Liverpool, president (since Oct. 2003); Roosevelt Skerrit, prime minister (since Jan. 2004). **Structure:** executive; unicameral legislature; judiciary—East Caribbean Supreme Court.
• **ECONOMY Monetary unit:** East Caribbean (EC) dollar. **Budget:** (2001 est.). *income:* $73.9 mil.; *expend.:* $84.4 mil. **G.D.P.:** $743 mil., $10,200 per capita (2009 est.). **Chief crops:** bananas, citrus, mangoes; forestry and fisheries. **Natural resources:** timber, hydropower, arable land. **Major industries:** soap, coconut oil, tourism. **Labor force:** 25,000 (2000); 40% agriculture, 32% industry and commerce, 28% services; 23% unemployment (2000 est.). **Exports:** $94 mil. (2006 est.); bananas, soap, bay oil. **Imports:** $296 mil. (2006 est.); manufactured goods, machinery and equipment, foodstuffs. **Major trading partners:** (2008) *exports:* 33.5% Japan, 17.9% China, 6.8% Antigua & Barbuda, 5.7% Guyana, 4.7% Jamaica; *imports:* 42.9% Japan, 16.8% U.S., 12% China, 8.4% Trinidad and Tobago.

Pre-Columbian Dominica was a stronghold of Carib Indians, who had expelled the Arawaks in the 14th century, and today it is the only island in the Caribbean with a native Carib population. Dominica was visited by Columbus on his second American voyage; but though frequented by Spanish ships, it was not settled until French missionaries arrived in the 1630s. Carib resistance

was so strong that the French and British agreed to consider the island neutral territory, until it passed under British control in 1763.

Later it was administratively joined to the Leeward and then the Windward Islands, and then became part of the West Indies Federation. It entered into political association with the United Kingdom in 1967. In 1978 Dominica gained independence from Britain. Hurricanes in 1979–80 largely destroyed the island's agriculture. The government of Prime Minister Mary Eugenia Charles's Freedom party implemented a program of economic reconstruction and diversification after the disaster. In 1992 it began a controversial policy of granting citizenship to businessmen, Asians in particular, in exchange for investment in Dominica's economy. In 1995, Charles resigned after 15 years in office. The United Workers' party took 11 of 21 seats in parliamentary elections and named its leader, Edison James, the new prime minister. But Jan. 2000 Assembly elections produced a coalition of the Labor and Freedom Parties, as the United Workers went again into opposition. Labor Party leader Roosevelt "Rosie" Douglas was named prime minister, but he died unexpectedly, leaving Pierre Charles to serve as acting prime minister. In 2005 the Labour Party won again with Roosevelt Skerrit as prime minister.

▶ DOMINICAN REPUBLIC
• **GEOGRAPHY Location:** eastern Hispaniola, in Caribbean Sea. Santo Domingo 19°30'N, 70°42'W. **Boundaries:** North Atlantic to N, Mona Passage to E, Caribbean Sea to S, Haiti to W. **Total land area:** 18,792 sq. mi. (48,670 sq km). **Coastline:** 800 mi. (1,288 km). **Comparative area:** slightly more than twice the size of New Hampshire. **Land use:** 22.49% arable land; 10% permanent crops; 67.25% other. **Major cities:** Santo Domingo (capital); Santiago de los Caballeros; La Romana; San Pedro de Macorís; San Francisco de Macorís.
• **PEOPLE Population:** 9,794,487 (July 2010 est.). **Nationality:** noun—Dominican(s); adjective—Dominican. **Ethnic groups:** 73% mixed, 16% white, 11% black. **Languages:** Spanish. **Religions:** 95% Roman Catholic.
• **GOVERNMENT Type:** democratic republic. **Independence:** Feb. 27, 1844 (from Haiti). **Constitution:** Nov. 28, 1966; amended July 25, 2002. **National holiday:** Independence Day, Feb. 27. **Head of Government:** Leonel Fernández Reyna, president (since Aug. 2004). **Structure:** executive; bicameral legislature; judiciary.
• **ECONOMY Monetary unit:** Dominican peso. **Budget:** (2009 est.) *income:* $6.361 bil.; *expend.:* $7.58 bil. **G.D.P.:** $80.53 bil., $8,300 per capita (2009 est.). **Chief crops:** sugarcane, coffee, cotton, cocoa, tobacco; cattle, pigs. **Natural resources:** nickel, bauxite, gold, silver. **Major industries:** tourism, sugar processing, mining. **Labor force:** 4.417 mil. (2009 est.); 58.7% services and government, 24.3% industry, 17% agriculture. **Exports:** $5.37 bil. (2009 est.); ferronickel, sugar, gold, coffee. **Imports:** $12.14 bil. (2009 est.); foodstuffs, petroleum, cotton, fabrics, chemicals. **Major trading partners:** (2008) *exports:* 58.1% U.S., 9.3% Haiti, 2.9% Netherlands; *imports:* 39.2% U.S., 7.7% Venezuela, 5.9% Taiwan, 5.4% Mexico.

The Dominican Republic takes up the eastern two-thirds of the island of Hispaniola, which it shares with Haiti. Christopher Columbus visited the island in 1492, and Santo Domingo is the oldest continually inhabited European settlement in the Americas, with the oldest cathedral, hospital, and monastery in the Western Hemisphere.

Western Hispaniola (Haiti) was ceded to France in 1697, and the eastern part of the island in 1795. Liberated with the Haitian slave revolts of 1801, it fell under Haitian rule from 1804–08 (when it reverted to Spanish rule), and again from 1822 to 1844. It was again occupied by Spain from 1861 to 1865. Under Ulises Heureux (1882–99), the Dominican Republic enjoyed a period of independence and prosperity. The U.S. occupied the Dominican Republic between 1916 and 1924. In 1930 Rafael Trujillo set up a dictatorship lasting 31 years. Dominican political strife triggered another U.S. invasion (1965–66) to end the revolution. Juan Bosch was elected president in 1962 but was deposed in a coup in 1963. Reformist party candidate Joaquín Balaguer, president from 1966 to 1978, regained the presidency in 1986, was reelected in 1990, and again (at age 87) in 1994, but only for two years, a compromise arranged in the face of charges of election fraud.

The 1996 elections resulted in a runoff between Haitian-born Jose Pena Gomez and Leonel Fernandez—both center-left in politics, both committed to economic privatization. Fernandez was the winner. But even the small and halting steps towards economic reform provoked strikes by labor unions and students over low wages, chronic water and electric outages. The death in May 1998 of Pena one week before legislative elections added a sentimental boost to real opposition. His Dominican Revolutionary Party captured large majorities in both the Senate and Chamber of Deputies. And in May 2000, for the first time, the party's candidate for president won, Hipolito Mejia. At 93, Balaguer tried one more time but finished third, defeated in 2004 by former president Fernandez who won again in 2008.

►EAST TIMOR
(see Timor-Leste)

►ECUADOR
Republic of Ecuador

• **Geography** **Location:** northwestern South America. **Boundaries:** Colombia to N, Peru to E and S, Pacific Ocean to W. **Total land area:** 109,484 sq. mi. (283,561 sq km); incl. Galapagos Islands, 0°45'S, 90°19'W. **Coastline:** 1,389 mi. (2,237 km). **Comparative area:** slightly smaller than Nevada. **Land use:** 6% arable land; 5% permanent crops; 89% other. **Major cities:** Quito (capital); Guayaquil; Cuenca; Machala; Portoviejo.
• **People** **Population:** 14,790,608 (July 2010 est.). **Nationality:** noun—Ecuadorian(s); adjective—Ecuadorian. **Ethnic groups:** 65% mestizo, 25% Amerindian, 7% Spanish, 3% black. **Languages:** Spanish (official), Amerindian languages, especially Quechua. **Religions:** 95% Roman Catholic.
• **Government** **Type:** republic. **Independence:** May 24, 1822 (from Spain). **Constitution:** Oct. 20, 2008. **National holiday:** Independence Day, Aug. 10. **Head of Government:** Rafael Correa Delgado, president (since Jan. 2007). **Structure:** executive; unicameral legislature; independent judiciary.
• **Economy** **Monetary unit:** U.S. dollar. **Budget:** (2009 est.) *income:* $15.58 bil.; *expend.:* $17.58 bil. **G.D.P.:** $108.2 bil., $7,400 per capita (2009 est.). **Chief crops:** bananas, coffee, cocoa, rice; cattle, sheep, pigs. **Natural resources:** petroleum, fish, timber. **Major industries:** petroleum, food processing, textiles. **Labor force:** 4.43 mil. (urban)

(2009); 8% agriculture, 70.4% services, 21.2% industry; 9.8% unemployment (2007 est.). **Exports:** $13.76 bil. (2009 est.); petroleum, bananas, shrimp. **Imports:** $14.09 bil. (2009 est.); transport equipment, consumer goods, vehicles, machinery. **Major trading partners:** (2008) *exports:* 33.5% U.S., 6.8% Peru, 6.5% Chile; *imports:* 25.4% U.S., 10.6% Colombia, 6.5% Venezuela, 4.5% Brazil.

The Inca Empire maintained control over the territory that is now Ecuador until the arrival of Spanish conqueror Francisco Pizarro in 1532. The Spanish conquistadores quickly dismantled the indigenous political structure, which had been weakened by a series of wars between the Inca chief Atahualpa and his half brother Huáscar. The Spaniards arrived in the Quito region in 1533 and established the city of Guayaquil shortly thereafter. The administrative center of Spanish rule was originally established through the viceroyalty of Peru in 1544, and an *audiencia* (a regional high court under the nominal authority of the viceroy) was established at Quito in 1563. Administrative control of the region was transferred to Bogotá and the viceroyalty of New Granada in 1718.

The local junta of Quito ousted the audiencia in 1809, but they did not achieve independence for the region until after the military victory of the rebel forces over the royalists at the battle of Pichincha in 1822. Ecuador formed a part of the Confederation of Gran Colombia until the confederation's collapse in 1830. The leader of the forces for independence, Gen. Juan José Flores, removed the country from the Gran Colombian confederation and ruled as dictator until his ouster in 1845. A political rivalry existed between the Liberals of Guayaquil and the Conservatives of Quito, but Conservative dominance of the government lasted until 1895.

During the rule of Conservative president Gabriel García Moreno (1861–75), the Roman Catholic church gained a central place in the political and cultural life of the country. García Moreno tied citizenship requirements to Catholic religious affiliation, brought in the Jesuits to "purify" the country through education, and dedicated the country to the Sacred Heart of Jesus. He was assassinated in 1875.

In 1895 the Radical Liberal (anticlerical) party seized power and held it until 1944. José María Velasco Ibarra, in and out of power until 1972, dominated the political scene. Political stability within the country had much to do with the state of the economy. The traditional reliance on cacao production was superseded in the 1950s by a "banana boom," and the discovery of large oil deposits by U.S. corporations in the 1960s led to a shift toward reliance on oil revenues by the 1970s.

In 1988 Rodrigo Borja, of the Democratic Left party (ID), was elected to the presidency. In 1992 conservative Sixto Durán Ballén, an advocate of free market reforms, won the presidency and immediately moved to eliminate government subsidies and encourage foreign investment.

Duran's successor in 1996 was the bizarre Abdala Bucaram Ortiz, who was removed by Congress in Feb. 1997 for "mental incapacity." Not until July of 1998 was normality restored with the election of Quito mayor Jamil Mahuad Witt. While his austerity measures provoked widespread discontent, Congress passed most of the measures and the 50-year-long border dispute with Peru was peaceably settled in 1998. In Sept. 1999, Ecuador defaulted on part of its international debt, and Witt was overturned in a brief army coup in Jan. 2000; his vice-president, Gustavo Noboa, was installed as president, a change ratified by Congress. In March, Witt's plan to replace the sucre with the U.S. dollar as the national currency was adopted (though it had been the occasion of his overthrow). The 2002 presidential election was won by the somewhat leftist Lucio Gutierrez Borbua, a former army colonel and one of the leaders in the 2002 coup, Ecuador's sixth president in seven years. In April 2005 he was forced to flee the country after dissolving the Supreme Court led to large protests.

Over the next year the vice president tried to lead the country but constant protests by indigenous Indian groups paralyzed the government. National elections in late 2006 brought a U.S.-educated left-wing economist, Rafael Correa, to power and he immediately called for radical changes in the constitution, weakened the power of congress, and set out to strengthen the oil industry. The new constitution was approved by a large margin in 2008. Correa was reelected in 2009 in part because of his willingness to confront Colombia over the drug trade on the border of Ecuador.

▶ **EGYPT**
Arab Republic of Egypt
• **GEOGRAPHY Location:** northeastern Africa and Asia (Sinai peninsula). **Boundaries:** Mediterranean Sea to N, Israel to NE, Red Sea to E, Sudan to S, and Libya to W. **Total land area:** 386,662 sq. mi. (1,001,450 sq km). **Coastline:** 1,523 mi. (2,450 km). **Comparative area:** slightly more than three times the size of New Mexico. **Land use:** 3% arable land; 0% permanent crops; 97% other. **Major cities:** Cairo (capital); El-Iskandriyah (Alexandria); Giza; Shoubra el-kheima; Port Said.
• **PEOPLE Population:** 80,471,869 (July 2010 est.). **Nationality:** noun—Egyptian(s); adjective—Egyptian. **Ethnic groups:** 99% Eastern Hamitic stock. **Languages:** Arabic (official), English and French widely understood by educated classes. **Religions:** 94% Muslim (mostly Sunni), 6% Coptic Christian and other.
• **GOVERNMENT Type:** republic. **Independence:** Feb. 28, 1922 (from U.K.). **Constitution:** Sept. 11, 1971; amended many times, most recently in March 2007. **National holiday:** Anniversary of the Revolution, July 23. **Heads of Government:** Mohammed Hosni Mubarak, president (since 1981); Ahmed Nazif, prime minister (since 2005). **Structure:** executive—president nominated by parliament which is validated by popular referendum; bicameral legislature; judiciary.
• **ECONOMY Monetary unit:** Egyptian pound. **Budget:** (2009 est.) *income:* $48.86 bil.; *expend.:* $61.61 bil. **G.D.P.:** $471.2 bil., $6,000 per capita (2009 est.). **Chief crops:** cotton, rice, corn, wheat, beans, fruit, vegetables; cattle, water buffalo, sheep, goats. **Natural resources:** crude oil, natural gas, iron ore, phosphates, manganese. **Major industries:** textiles, food processing, tourism. **Labor force:** 25.8 mil. (2009 est.); 32% agriculture, 37.7% industry, 49.2% services (2009); 10.1% unemployment (2007 est.). **Exports:** $22.91 bil. (2009 est.); crude oil and petroleum products, cotton yarn, raw cotton, textiles, metal products, chemicals. **Imports:** $43.98 bil. (2009 est.); machinery and equipment, foods, fertilizers, wood products, durable consumer goods, capital goods. **Major trading partners:** (2008) *exports:* 9.5% Italy, 7.1% U.S., 6.2% Spain, 6% India, 4.7% Syria, 4.6% Saudi Ara-

bia; *imports:* 10.2% U.S., 9.9% China, 7.3% Italy, 6.8% Germany, 4.8% Saudi Arabia.

Civilization began in the fertile valley of the Nile River around 5000 B.C. In about 3200 B.C., King Menes established the first of many dynasties of pharaohs that unified the country from the Nile Delta to Upper Egypt, creating a distinctive ancient civilization of great wealth and cultural brilliance.

The last pharaonic dynasty was overthrown by the Persians in 341 B.C. The Persians in turn were replaced by the Alexandrian and Ptolemaic Greek dynasties and then by the Roman Empire. Egypt was part of the Byzantine Empire from the third to the seventh centuries A.D., when it was conquered by the Arab Islamic expansion. Arab rule was ended around 1250 when the Mameluke dynasty, established control. The Mamelukes were defeated by the Turks in 1517, and Egypt was incorporated into the Ottoman Empire.

The Suez Canal was built by a French corporation during 1859–69 but was taken over by the British in 1875. This, together with the expansion of the British Empire in East Africa and the Sudan, led to the establishment of de facto British rule in Egypt in 1882, although Egypt remained nominally part of the Ottoman Empire until 1914. A British protectorate in Egypt was established in that year, replaced by a League of Nations Mandate in 1922. The autonomy of the Egyptian monarchy was strengthened in an Anglo-Egyptian treaty of 1936, but Great Britain continued to maintain military forces in Egypt and controlled the Sudan as an Anglo-Egyptian condominium.

Egypt saw heavy fighting between British and Axis forces during WWII. After the war, a nationalist movement gained strength. The 1936 treaty was abrogated by Egypt in 1951. An uprising of the Society of Free Officers on July 23, 1952, forced King Farouk to abdicate. A republic was proclaimed on June 18, 1953. Lt. Col. Gamal Abdel Nasser became premier in 1954 and president in 1956.

British troops were withdrawn from the Suez Canal zone in June 1956. On July 26, 1956, Egypt announced the nationalization of the canal. Israel invaded the Sinai Peninsula at the end of October 1956. France and Great Britain landed forces and bombed Egyptian positions; a cease-fire went into effect under U.N. supervision on Nov. 17. A U.N. peacekeeping force patrolled the border between Egypt and Israel from 1957–67. Egypt and Syria joined together as the United Arab Republic in 1958. Later joined by Yemen, the union was dissolved in 1961.

Increasing Soviet involvement in Egypt was confirmed with its aid to Egypt in the construction of the Aswan High Dam. The dam, completed in 1971, provides both irrigation and hydropower but at the cost of extensive environmental damage.

A full-scale war with Israel broke out on June 5, 1967. The Six-Day War ended on June 10 with Israel in full control of Gaza and the Sinai peninsula to the banks of the Suez Canal. Sporadic fighting between Egyptian and Israeli forces continued throughout 1969–70. The Suez Canal remained closed to shipping until 1975.

Nasser died in 1970 and was succeeded by Vice Pres. Anwar Sadat, who concluded a treaty of friendship with the U.S.S.R., but expelled all Soviet troops and advisers in 1972. On Oct. 6, 1973, Egyptian troops crossed the Suez Canal and attacked Israeli positions in the Sinai (Syrian forces also attacked Israeli positions in the Golan

Heights). Israel drove back the attackers, and the Yom Kippur War ended in a cease-fire on Oct. 24.

In 1974 Sadat's government became increasingly friendly to the West, welcoming foreign investment and American aid. In 1974 and 1975 disengagement accords were signed with Israel, providing for the return of the Sinai to Egypt in stages. In November 1977 Sadat visited Jerusalem as a gesture of peace, and a peace treaty between Israel and Egypt was signed (after a series of talks mediated by Pres. Jimmy Carter) on Mar. 26, 1979. Formal diplomatic relations were established in 1982. Egypt was suspended from the Arab League—it was readmitted in 1989—and attacked by Libyan forces on several occasions along the Egyptian-Libyan border.

Popular unrest fomented by the Muslim Brotherhood in Sept. 1981 led to a military crackdown. Pres. Sadat was assassinated by members of a military conspiracy on Oct. 6, 1981, and was succeeded by Vice Pres. Mohammed Hosni Mubarak. The government has remained on friendly terms with Israel and the U.S. and has gradually improved relations with the rest of the Arab world. During the Persian Gulf War, it was a staunch member of the anti-Iraq coalition, in return for which the U.S. forgave $7 billion in debt.

Through the 1990s Egypt was troubled by bombings and assassinations by Moslem extremist groups such as Islamic Group and Islamic Jihad (the latter claiming to have killed Sadat). But late in the decade, government crackdowns seem to have been effective; Islamic Group in March 1999 announced a permanent cease-fire. In Sept. 1999 Mubarak ran virtually unopposed, winning a fourth six-year term. In 2005, however, presumably under pressure from the U.S. he allowed opposition candidates although the outcome was never in doubt. Even changes to the constitution in 2007 could not loosen his grip on power.

▶ EL SALVADOR
Republic of El Salvador

● **GEOGRAPHY** **Location:** Pacific coast of Central America. **Boundaries:** Honduras to N and E, Pacific Ocean to S, Guatemala to W. **Total land area:** 8,124 sq. mi. (21,040 sq km). **Coastline:** 191 mi. (307 km). **Comparative area:** about size of Massachusetts. **Land use:** 31.4% arable land; 11.9% permanent crops; 56.8% other. **Major cities:** San Salvador (capital); Soyapango; Santa Ana; San Miguel; Mejicanos.

● **PEOPLE** **Population:** 6,052,064 (July 2010 est.). **Nationality:** noun—Salvadoran(s); adjective—Salvadoran. **Ethnic groups:** 90% mestizo, 1% Amerindian, 9% white. **Languages:** Spanish, Nahua (among some Amerindians). **Religions:** 83% Roman Catholic; extensive activity by Protestant groups throughout country.

● **GOVERNMENT** **Type:** republic. **Independence:** Sept. 15, 1821 (from Spain). **Constitution:** Dec. 20, 1983. **National holiday:** Independence Day, Sept. 15. **Head of Government:** Mauricio Funes Cartagena, president (since June 2009). **Structure:** executive; unicameral legislature; judiciary.

● **ECONOMY** **Monetary unit:** U.S. dollar. **Budget:** (2009 est.) *income:* $3.798 bil.; *expend.:* $4.803 bil. **G.D.P.:** $42.92 bil., $7,100 per capita (2009 est.). **Chief crops:** coffee, sugarcane, corn; beef, dairy; shrimp. **Natural resources:** hydropower and geothermal power, crude oil. **Major industries:** food processing, beverages, petroleum. **Labor force:** 2.917 mil. (2009); 19% agriculture, 58% services,

23% industry. **Exports:** $4.086 bil. (2009 est.); offshore assembly exports, coffee, sugarcane, shrimp. **Imports:** $7.215 bil. (2009 est.); raw materials, consumer goods, foodstuffs, capital goods. **Major trading partners:** (2008) *exports:* 48.1% U.S., 13.6% Guatemala, 13% Honduras, 5.5% Nicaragua; *imports:* 35.4% U.S., 9.2% Mexico, 8.7% Guatemala, 5.1% China.

A number of Indian tribes, of which the Pipil were dominant, originally inhabited the area now called El Salvador. The native population resisted the first attempt at Spanish colonization, begun in 1524, for almost 15 years. In 1821 El Salvador gained its independence from Spain, first as a jurisdiction under the Mexican empire and two years later as a member of the United Provinces of Central America. The Central American Federation collapsed in 1838, and in 1840 El Salvador emerged from a bloody two-year struggle as an independent republic.

The Salvadoran economy was dominated by coffee production from the 1860s onward, and a series of laws in the 1880s allowed for concentration of both land ownership and political power in the hands of a coffee oligarchy. In 1931 a reformist president won election, but the military subsequently dismissed him. A revolt ensued (1932) in which 10,000 to 20,000 Salvadorans—mostly peasants—were killed. The result of the massacre, which was called La Matanza, was a period of relative political stability that lasted until the 1970s.

In 1979 a political coup led by a group of junior military officers overthrew Pres. Gen. Carlos Humberto Romero. Owing to the polarization between conservative and reformist political groups, the first two civilian-military juntas resigned as a result of their failure to have their programs implemented by the military. A third government, which included Christian Democrat José Napoleón Duarte, took over on Mar. 5, 1980, on the basis of an armed forces' pledge to carry out an agrarian reform program. In 1980 the coalition of opposition political organizations became the Democratic Revolutionary Front (FDR), and five revolutionary military organizations consolidated under the banner of the Farabundo Marti Front for National Liberation (FMLN). Six social-democratic political leaders were assassinated in November 1980, further cementing the political opposition around the FMLN-FDR coalition.

A three-part agrarian reform program was initiated in 1980 in El Salvador, but the central part of the program—to redistribute most of the land involved in export agriculture—was dropped as a result of opposition from the agricultural elite. In March 1982 elections for a constituent assembly, a majority of seats went to the rightist ARENA coalition. In December 1983 a new constitution went into effect, and in 1984 Christian Democrat José Napoleón Duarte assumed the presidency.

In 1989, Alfredo Cristiani of the conservative Alliance for National Renovation was elected president. On Nov. 11, 1989, FMLN guerrillas launched a new offensive that lasted for several weeks before fading away. The government's failure to prosecute military officers implicated in the murder of six Jesuit priests shortly thereafter jeopardized U.S. military aid, which totaled $6 billion between 1979 and 1992.

In January 1992, the government signed a peace treaty with the FMLN and the 12-year civil war, in which 70,000 people died, officially ended on December 15. The treaty called for the military to cut its forces by almost half (to 31,000 soldiers), and for the FMLN to lay down its arms and become a political party. A U.N.-sponsored Truth Commission found that 85 percent of all human-rights violations during the war were attributable to the Salvadoran army, security forces, or intelligence-unit death squads. Although the legislature narrowly passed a general amnesty for public officials, military officers, and political party leaders linked to human rights violations in March of 1993, the United States tried to link further military aid to the dismissal of the worst offenders in the military.

In the March 1994 elections, ARENA's candidate Armando Calderon Sol was elected president. ARENA also carried half the seats in the National Assembly. In the 1997 mid-term election, FMLN made a vary strong showing running virtually even with ARENA on the national level. In the March 1999 elections, ARENA and the FMLN carried almost the same number of seats in the National Assembly, but in the presidential election, ARENA easily won for the third straight time, their candidate (Francisco Flores Perez) gaining 51 percent of the vote. In 2004 ARENA again won by a large margin. But in 2009 the nation moved left and elected FMLN's Mauricio Funes.

▶EQUATORIAL GUINEA
Republic of Equatorial Guinea
• **GEOGRAPHY Location:** mainland territory of Río Muni in western Africa and five inhabited islands: Bioko (3°45'N, 8°50'E), Corisco, Great Elobey, Small Elobey, and Pagalu (Annabon). **Boundaries:** Cameroon to N, Gabon to E and S, Gulf of Guinea to W. **Total land area:** 10,831 sq. mi. (28,051 sq km). **Coastline:** 184 mi. (296 km). **Comparative area:** slightly larger than Maryland. **Land use:** 5% arable land; 4% permanent crops; 91% other. **Major cities:** Malabo (capital); Bata.
• **PEOPLE Population:** 650,702 (July 2010 est.). **Nationality:** noun—Equatorial Guinean(s); adjective— Equatorial Guinean. **Ethnic groups:** Fang, Bubi, Mdowe, Annobon, Bujeba. **Languages:** Spanish (official), pidgin English, Fang. **Religions:** Christian, predominantly Roman Catholic; indigenous practices.
• **GOVERNMENT Type:** republic. **Independence:** Oct. 12, 1968 (from Spain). **Constitution:** Nov. 17, 1991; amended January 1995. **National holiday:** Independence Day, Oct. 12. **Heads of Government:** Col. Teodoro Obiang Nguema Mbasogo, president (since Aug. 1979); Ignacio M. Tang, prime minister (since July 2008). **Structure:** executive; unicameral legislature; judiciary.
• **ECONOMY Monetary unit:** Communauté Financière Africaine (CFA) franc. **Budget:** (2009 est.) *income:* $4.481 bil.; *expend.:* $3.551 bil. **G.D.P.:** $23.2 bil., $36,600 per capita (2009 est.). **Chief crops:** coffee, cocoa, rice, yams; livestock; timber. **Natural resources:** timber, crude oil, small unexploited deposits of gold, manganese, uranium. **Major industries:** petroleum, fishing, sawmilling. **Labor force:** N.A.; 30% unemployment. **Exports:** $8.27 bil. (2009 est.); petroleum, timber, cocoa. **Imports:** $2.851 bil. (2009 est.); petroleum, foodstuffs, beverages, clothing, machinery. **Major trading partners:** (2008) *exports:* 22.8% U.S., 18.3% Spain, 14.8% China, 10.8% Taiwan, 8% France; *imports:* 18.2% China, 13.7% Spain, 12.1% U.S., 11.2% France, 7.8% Ivory Coast, 5.7% Italy, 5.3% U.K.

Equatorial Guinea consists of the Mbini River basin on the West African coast, and a number of offshore islands, chiefly Bioko and Pagalu (An-

nobón). Indigenous Pygmies were displaced beginning in the 17th century by migrations of various peoples that now inhabit the coastal region and by the Fang, who comprise 80 percent of the present population.

Bioko was discovered in 1473 by the Portuguese explorer Fernando Po, and until modern times the island bore his name. Portugal controlled the islands and adjacent mainland, exploiting them for the slave trade, until 1778 when the territory was ceded to Spain. Equatorial Guinea remained underdeveloped because of conflicting territorial claims and a lack of Spanish investment. Eventually, however, a plantation system was developed for the cultivation of cocoa, particularly on Bioko, using workers imported from Nigeria.

In 1959 the Spanish territories in the Gulf of Guinea were given status equivalent to a province of Spain. Investment in education, health care facilities, and other social programs, combined with the flourishing plantation economy, made the territory one of the most prosperous and best educated in West Africa. Local autonomy came in 1963, full independence in 1968.

Francisco Macias Nguema was elected Equatorial Guinea's first president in 1968. In 1970 he dissolved all opposition parties and declared a one-party state, and in 1972 proclaimed himself president for life and commenced rule by decree. During the next seven years, a reign of terror resulted in the death or exile of one-third of the country's people. Nigerian workers, along with other foreigners, were expelled from the country in 1976; without their labor and technical skills, the economy was quickly ruined.

Macias Nguema was overthrown in August 1979 in a military coup led by his nephew, Lt. Col. Teodoro Obiang Nguema Mbasogo. Macias Nguema was tried and executed a month later. The new leader moved to reduce Soviet influence and to improve relations with Spain. A new constitution was approved in a referendum in August 1982 and again in 1991, the latter calling for a multiparty political system. Nguema, however, retains firm control. Economic prospects improved with the discovery in the mid-1990s of oil reserves estimated at over 65 million barrels a year.

▶ERITREA
State of Eritrea
• **GEOGRAPHY Location:** Horn of Africa (central-eastern Africa). **Boundaries:** Sudan to N and W, Red Sea to E, Djibouti and Ethiopia to S. **Total land area:** 45,406 sq. mi. (117,600 sq km). **Coastline:** 680 mi. (1,094 km) on Red Sea. **Comparative area:** slightly larger than Pennsylvania. **Land use:** 4% arable land, negl.% permanent crops, 96% other. **Major cities:** Asmara (capital), Asseb, Massawa, Keren.
• **PEOPLE Population:** 5,792,984 (July 2010 est.). **Nationality:** noun—Eritrean(s); adjective—Eritrean. **Ethnic groups:** 50% Tigrinya, 40% Tigre and Kunama, 4% Afar, 3% Saho. **Languages:** Afar, Amharic, Arabic, Tigre and Kunama, Tigrinya, minor ethnic group languages. **Religions:** Muslim, Coptic Christian, Roman Catholic, Protestant.
• **GOVERNMENT Type:** transitional government. **Independence:** May 24, 1993 (from Ethiopia). **Constitution:** promulgated May 1997. **National holiday:** Independence Day, May 24. **Head of Government:** Isaias Afwerki, president (since May 1993). **Structure:** executive; unicameral legislature; judiciary.

• **Economy Monetary unit:** nafka. **Budget :** (2009 est.) *income:* $232.7 mil.; *expend.:* $576.1 mil. **G.D.P.:** $4.198 bil; $700 per capita (2009 est.). **Chief crops:** sorghum, lentils, vegetables; livestock; fish. **Natural resources:** gold, potash, zinc, copper. **Major industries:** food processing, beverages, clothing and textiles. **Labor force:** 1.935 mil.; 80% agriculture, 20% industry and services (2004 est.). **Exports:** $12 mil. (2009); livestock, sorghum, textiles. **Imports:** $590 mil. (2009 est.); processed goods, machinery, petroleum products. **Major trading partners:** (2008) *exports:* 25.3% India, 20.7% Italy, 14.1% Sudan, 12.9% China, 5.5% France, 5.4% Saudi Arabia; *imports:* 20.7% Saudi Arabia, 13.6% India, 12.6% Italy, 9.9% China, 5.1% U.S.

In May 1993, after 30 years of fighting, leaders of the Eritrean People's Liberation Front (EPLF) formally declared this small area of north and northeast Ethiopia to be an independent state. Ethiopia, along with the U.S., the Sudan, and several other states, quickly recognized the authority of the new transitional government led by Issaias Afwerki, former head of the liberation movement.

During the early 20th century, the region of Eritrea was an outpost of the Italian empire, but it came under British rule during World War II. The British made Eritrea part of Ethiopia when independence was granted in 1952. The secessionist movement began immediately, first against Haile Selassie, then in the 1970s–80s against the Marxist Mengistu Haile Mariam, who was finally driven from office by other forces in 1991. The new government quickly made peace with the Eritrean rebels, who promised continued access to the sea after independence became a fact.

Late in 1995 Eritrea began to contest with Yemen control of Greater Hanish Island at the mouth of the Red Sea, a struggle serious enough to elicit U.N. mediation. Further troubles broke out in May 1998 when a small skirmish over the border with Ethiopia escalated into major military clashes in June. The U.S. was attempting to mediate. The bloody border war continued, with much loss of life on both sides, into 2000 until June 18 when Eritrean and Ethiopian foreign ministers signed a cease-fire restoring the borders of May 1998. Both countries in April 2002 accepted the Hague Court of Arbitration's definition of the disputed 620-mile border, but animosity between the two nations never dissipated.

In 2006, Eritrea's government helped to arm Islamic militants in Somalia, forcing Ethiopia to send troops to stop them from seizing power and destabilizing the region. Tensions remained high over the next two years and then Eritrean troops crossed the border of Djibouti causing another serious breach of the peace.

▶ **ESTONIA**
Republic of Estonia
• **Geography Location:** northeastern Europe. **Boundaries:** Gulf of Finland to N and NE, Russian Federation to SE, Latvia to SW, Baltic Sea to NW. **Total land area:** 17,463 sq. mi. (45,228 sq km). **Coastline:** Gulf of Finland. **Comparative area:** about twice the size of New Hampshire. **Land use:** 12% arable land; 0% permanent crops; 88% other. **Major cities:** Tallinn (capital); Tartu; Narva; Kohtla-Järve; Pärnu.
• **People Population:** 1,291,170 (July 2010 est.). **Nationality:** noun—Estonian(s); adjective—Estonian. **Ethnic groups:** 67.9% Estonian, 25.6%

Russian, 2.1% Ukrainian. **Languages:** Estonian (official), Russian, Ukrainian, English, Finnish, other. **Religions:** Lutheran, Orthodox Christian, others.
• **Government Type:** parliamentary republic. **Independence:** Aug. 20, 1991 (from the Soviet Union). **Constitution:** June 28, 1992. **National holiday:** Independence Day, Feb. 24. **Heads of Government:** Toomas Ives, president (since Oct. 2006); Andrus Ansip, prime minister (since Apr. 2007). **Structure:** executive; unicameral legislature; judiciary.
• **Economy Monetary unit:** Estonian kroon. **Budget:** (2009) *income:* $7.29 bil.; *expend.:* $8.04 bil. **G.D.P.:** $24.36 bil., $18,700 per capita (2009 est.). **Chief crops:** potatoes, vegetables, fruit; livestock and dairy products; fish. **Natural resources:** oil shale (world's number two producer), peat, phosphorites. **Major industries:** oil shale processing, shipbuilding, phosphates. **Labor force:** 700,000 (2009 est.); 2.8% agriculture, 22.7% industry, 74.5% services. **Exports:** $9.233 bil. (2009 est.); 29% machinery and equipment, 13% wood and paper, 10% metals, 8% food products. **Imports:** $9.315 bil. (2009 est.); 35% machinery and equipment, 9% chemical products. **Major trading partners:** (2008) *exports:* 18.3% Finland, 13.8% Sweden, 10.3% Russia, 10% Latvia, 5.7% Lithuania, 5% Germany, 4.8% U.S.; *imports:* 14.2% Finland, 13.3% Germany, 10% Sweden, 8.9% Lithuania, 8.9% Latvia, 7.4% Russia, 4.5% Poland.

Ethnic and linguistic "cousins" of the Finns, the Ests acquired their own independent state only in the 20th century. Previously they had been "colonized" by the Danes (who founded the capital, Tallinn), then in the 13th century by the Teutonic Knights, in the 16th century by the Swedes (who brought the Lutheran Reformation), in the 17th century by the Poles, and in the 18th century by the Russians. Through all these regimes the German element predominated, the "Baltic barons" forming a territorial aristocracy with German burghers ruling the towns. The Ests were restricted to farming, normally as serfs, with serfdom not abolished until 1819.

With that abolition there began a cultural revival with the study of folklore, the collecting of folk songs, the compilation of the national epic, *Kalevipoeg*, published between 1857 and 1861, and the circulation of newspapers in the Estonian language. Political expression of this revived national spirit came with the 1918 Treaty of Brest-Litovsk in which the new Soviet Union recognized the independence of Estonia. By 1920 Estonia was fully independent, under its own constitution adopted on June 15 of that year.

A radical land reform dispossessed German landowners of large estates, which were distributed to peasants. Dangers from extremists of Left (Communists) and Right ("liberators") were averted by the strong presidency of Constantice Päts, but the Hitler-Stalin Pact of 1939 spelled the end of Estonian independence. Allotted to Stalin's sphere of influence, Estonia was forced to accept Soviet garrisons larger than its national army in 1939, and 65,000 Germans were "repatriated" (after 700 years) to the Third Reich. Rigged elections in 1940 led to a government that "requested" incorporation into the U.S.S.R., an annexation never recognized by the U.S.

There followed nationalization of private property, amalgamation of Estonia's national forces into the Red Army, and a reign of terror against former political leaders and religious and cultural organizations. During and after the war the Estonian people suffered enormous losses through death in battle, murder, flight, and deportation.

Estonia's return to freedom began Mar. 30, 1990, when a freely elected government declared its intention to secede. Violence provoked by Russian "black berets," mass demonstrations, defiance of Gorbachev's economic sanctions and his January 1991 military crackdown, all marked stages toward the Kremlin's recognition in Sept. 1991 of Estonian independence.

Elections in Sept. 1992 produced a divided Parliament, with the majority a center-right coalition led by the Fatherland Alliance. Parliament chose as president Lennart Meri, a nationalist and devotee of free markets. The effective disenfranchisement of 40 percent of the population, mostly Russians, through laws requiring citizenship since 1940, provoked Russian ire. But by 1994 the law was modified and Russian troops left.

In 1995, parliamentary elections brought into power a far-left alliance of parties led by the Coalition Party (the Communists' new name). In the 1999 parliamentary elections, a coalition of three center-right parties regained control of the legislature. Free-marketeer Mart Laar became Prime Minister for the second time. Interparty squabbling brought the coalition down in 2001 and Parliament elected former Finance Minister Siim Kallas to succeed Laar. In 2003 a new center-right party, Res Publica, led a coalition government under Julian Parts into office. In May 2004 Estonia became a member of the E.U. and was one of the fastest growing economies in Europe until the slowdown of 2008. By 2009 the economy, like in all the Baltic states, was in dire distress.

▶ETHIOPIA
Federal Democratic Republic of Ethiopia
● **Geography** **Location:** Horn of Africa (central eastern Africa). **Boundaries**: Eritrea to N, Djibouti and Somalia to E, Kenya to S, Sudan to W. **Total land area:** 426,373 sq. mi. (1,104,300 sq km). **Coastline**: none. **Comparative area**: somewhat smaller than Alaska. **Land use:** 10% arable land; 1% permanent crops; 89% other. **Major cities:** Addis Ababa (New Flower); Dire Dawa; Harar; Gondar; Nazret.
● **People** **Population:** 88,013,491 (July 2010 est.). **Nationality:** noun—Ethiopian(s); adjective—Ethiopian. **Ethnic groups:** 40% Oromo, 32% Amhara and Tigrean, 9% Sidamo, 6% Shankella. **Languages:** Amharic, Tigrinya, Orominga, Guaraginga, Somali, Arabic, English (major foreign language taught in schools). **Religions:** 61% Christian, 33% Muslim, 4.6% traditional.
● **Government** **Type:** federal republic. **Independence:** oldest independent country in Africa and one of oldest in the world—at least 2,000 years. **Constitution:** Dec. 1994, effective Aug. 22, 1995. **National holiday:** May 28. **Heads of Government:** Girma Wolde Giorgis, president (since Nov. 2001); Meles Zenawi, prime minister (since Aug. 1995). **Structure:** executive; bicameral legislature; judiciary.
● **Economy** **Monetary unit:** birr. **Budget:** (2009 est.) *income:* $4.678 bil.; *expend:* $5.36 bil. **G.D.P.:** $76.74 bil., $900 per capita (2009 est.). **Chief crops:** cereals, pulses, coffee, oilseed; hides, cattle. **Natural resources:** small reserves of gold, platinum, copper, potash. **Major industries:** food processing, beverages, textiles. **Labor force:** 37.9

million (2007); 85% agriculture and animal husbandry, 10% government and services, 5% industry. **Exports:** $1.608 bil. (2009 est.); coffee, leather products, gold, oilseeds. **Imports:** $7.315 bil. (2009 est.); food and live animals, petroleum, chemicals, machinery. **Major trading partners:** (2008) *exports:* 11.8% Germany, 8.7% Saudi Arabia, 8.6% Netherlands.; *imports:* 16.3% China, 12% Saudi Arabia, 8.7% India, 6% Italy.

Ethiopia played an important role in the Red Sea trade of the classical world and was mentioned by the Greek historian Herodotus in the fifth century B.C. According to legend, the Ethiopian monarchy was founded by Melelik I, son of Israel's King Solomon and the Queen of Sheba (Sab'a, i.e., North Yemen). Coptic Christianity became Ethiopia's dominant religion in the fourth century A.D. Ethiopia successfully resisted Islamic invasions in the seventh century except in areas along the Red Sea coast but was cut off from the rest of the Christian world by the Islamic states of North Africa and the Middle East.

Portugal established forts and trading stations on the Red Sea coast beginning in 1493, strengthening their domination of trade in the Indian Ocean. The Portuguese also sponsored Roman Catholic missionaries but with little success. A century of religious strife ended with the expulsion of all foreign missionaries in the 1630s. Ethiopia successfully resisted an attempted Italian invasion in 1880.

Ethiopia began to emerge into the modern world under Melelik II (r. 1889–1913). A period of instability after his death ended with the accession in 1930 of Haile Selassie. Italy invaded again in 1936 and soon conquered the entire country. Protests by the League of Nations had no effect; Haile Selassie fled to exile in England. The Italians were driven out during World War II by British and Ethiopian forces, and Haile Selassie returned to his throne.

Civil unrest broke out in February 1974, and Haile Selassie was deposed on Sept. 13, 1974. A coalition of urban elites and the armed forces took over, abolishing the monarchy in 1975 and curbing the power of the Coptic church. Land reform was instituted, and a socialist state proclaimed. In 1977–78 a period of "red terror" resulted in the arrest and execution of thousands of the regime's opponents. A provisional military council, the Dergue, was confirmed in power under Col. Mengistu Haile-Mariam's leadership.

A military assistance agreement in 1976 between Ethiopia and the U.S.S.R. ended an earlier military relationship with the U.S.; American military advisers were expelled. In 1977 Somalia, taking advantage of Ethiopia's shifting military situation, attacked across the Ogaden desert, aiming to restore certain disputed areas of Ethiopia to Somalia. A massive infusion of Soviet arms and Cuban troops expelled the Somalis in March 1978, but border clashes continued thereafter.

After the expulsion of the Italians during World War II, the province of Eritrea, under a U.N. plan, was to have become autonomous in a federation with Ethiopia. Instead, Eritrea was made a province of the Ethiopian Empire in 1962. A coalition of Marxist and non-Marxist liberation forces—most prominent among them the Eritrean People's Liberation Front (EPLF)—resisted the annexation from the beginning. By the spring of 1991, Eritrean forces had gained control of all of Eritrea, including Ethiopia's outlets to the sea.

Another rebel group, the Ethiopian People's Revolutionary Democratic Front (EPRDF), sought autonomy for Tigre, a northern region between Ethiopia and Eritrea. In February 1991, the EPRDF launched a major offensive, forcing Mengistu Haile Mariam's flight, a week before scheduled cease-fire talks were to start in London. The talks proceeded quickly under the auspices of the United States, and rebel forces under the leadership of the EPRDF entered Addis Ababa virtually unopposed at the end of May.

Years of civil war and devastating famines left Ethiopia in shambles. A transition government was installed to draft a constitution in July 1991, and acknowledged Eritrean independence without incident. But the country's first multiparty elections in June 1992 were so badly handled that the powerful OLF withdrew from the government.

In June 1994, the EPRDF won 484 of the 547 seats in the Constituent Assembly, which by November had drawn up a constitution for a parliamentary government over nine partially autonomous regions. But most opposition parties boycotted the country's first multiparty elections under the new constitution, resulting in decisive victories by the EPRDF, and its leader Meles Zenawi, who became premier.

A small border war with Eritrea in May–June 1998 threatened the fragile political structure. By early 1999, the small war had ballooned into a major conflict with thousands of soldiers on each side struggling for control of some barren borderland near the outpost of Badme. It ended with a cease-fire in June 2000, restoring the May 1998 borders. In May 2002 both countries accepted the Hague Court of Arbitration's delineation of the boundary.

In May 2005 a legislative election was marred by charges of fraud that led to violence and 22 deaths, followed by the arrest and imprisonment of hundreds of opposition leaders. Street protests have been stopped with violence and the government has been strongly criticized by the international community. Meles Zenawi's governing party won every seat in the 2010 parliamentary elections, solidifying his one-party rule and bringing charges of voter intimidation.

▶ FIJI
Republic of Fiji
● **Geography Location:** more than 300 islands (100 inhabited), in South Pacific Ocean. Suva 18°08'S, 178°25'E. **Boundaries:** South Pacific Ocean to N, S, and W; Koro Sea to E; nearest neighbor is Vanuatu, about 600 mi. (1,000 km) to W. **Total area:** 7,056 sq. mi. (18,274 sq km). **Coastline:** 702 mi. (1,129 km). **Comparative area:** slightly smaller than New Jersey. **Land use:** 11% arable land; 5% permanent crops; 84% other. **Major cities:** Suva (capital); Lautoka.
● **People Population:** 957,780 (July 2010 est.). **Nationality:** noun—Fijian(s); adjective—Fijian. **Ethnic groups:** 55% Fijian, 38% Indian, 8% other. **Languages:** English (official), Fijian, Hindustani. **Religions:** 64.5% Christian, 27.9% Hindu, 6.3% Muslim; Fijians are mainly Christian, Indians are Hindu with Muslim minority.
● **Government Type:** republic. **Independence:** Oct. 10, 1970 (from U.K.). **Constitution:** new constitution to allow a non-ethnic Fijian to become prime minister was signed by the president on July 25, 1997 and came into force July 28, 1998. **National holiday:** Independence Day, second Monday in October. **Heads of Government:** Ratu Epeli Nailatikau, head of state (since July 2009); Josai V. Bainimarama, prime minister (since Jan. 2007). **Structure:** executive; bicameral legislature; judiciary.
● **Economy Monetary unit:** Fijian dollar. **Budget:** (2006 est.) **income:** $1.363 bil.; **expend.:** $1.376 bil. **G.D.P.:** $3.704 bil., $3,900 per capita (2009 est.). **Chief crops:** sugar cane, coconuts, cassava; cattle, pigs, horses; fish. **Natural resources:** timber, fish, gold, copper, offshore oil potential. **Major industries:** sugar, tourism, copra. **Labor force:** 335,000 (2007 est.); 70% agriculture, 30% services & industry (2001). **Exports:** $1.202 bil. (f.o.b., 2006); sugar, clothing, gold, processed fish. **Imports:** $3.12 bil. (f.o.b., 2006); machinery and transport equipment, petroleum products, food, chemicals. **Major trading partners:** (2008) **exports:** 15.7% U.S., 12% U.K., 10.6% Australia, 5.4% Samoa, 4.8% Tonga, 4.2% Japan; **imports:** 29.9% Singapore, 20.1% Australia, 15.2% New Zealand, 5.3% China.

First reported to the West by the Dutch navigator Abel Tasman in 1643, the Fiji Islands were annexed as a British Crown Colony in 1874. Between 1879 and 1916, large numbers of Indian indentured laborers were imported to work on sugar plantations; eventually the original Melanesian inhabitants were outnumbered by persons of Indian descent. Fiji became an independent parliamentary democracy on Oct. 10, 1970, with most land ownership and political power vested in the Fijian minority. A parliamentary election in 1987 brought the Indian party to power; the elected government was ousted in a military coup, and Lt. Col. Sitiveni Rabuka assumed control of the government on May 21, 1987. On June 2, 1992, he was sworn in as prime minister under a new constitution that guarantees a majority of seats for ethnic Fijians in the national legislature. He was reelected as the head of a coalition government in Feb. 1994.

Yet another constitution (1997) restored Indian political rights, and elections in May 1999 led to formation of a government with Fiji's first Indian prime minister, Mahendra Chaudhry. But in May 2000 a hostage crisis/coup led to the formation in July of an all-new, all-Fijian government which satisfied no one. Elections in 2001 resolved little: the (ethnic Fijian) Fiji United Party won a narrow victory over the (ethnic Indian) Fiji Labour Party but prime minister Laisenia Qarase appointed only one Indian to his cabinet. Although reelected in 2006, a military coup at the end of the year brought Commodore Josaia V. Bainimarama to power and he became prime minister and ouste the president and Qarase. However, in January 2007 the president was reinstated and he appointed Bainimarama prime minister and granted amnesty to the coup leaders.

▶ FINLAND
Republic of Finland
● **Geography Location:** northern Europe. **Boundaries:** Norway to N, Russian Federation to E, Baltic Sea to S, Gulf of Bothnia, Sweden to W. **Total area:** 130,127 sq. mi. (338,145 sq km). **Coastline:** 700 mi. (1,126 km) excluding islands and coastal indentations. **Comparative area:** slightly smaller than Montana. **Land use:** 7% arable land; 0% permanent crops; 93% other. **Major cities:** Helsinki (capital); Espoo; Tampere; Vantaa; Turku.
● **People Population:** 5,255,068 (July 2010 est.). **Nationality:** noun—Finn(s); adjective—Finnish. **Ethnic groups:** 93% Finn, 6% Swede; Sami, Roma,

Tatar. **Languages:** 91.5% Finnish, 5.5% Swedish (both official); small Sami- and Russian-speaking minorities. **Religions:** 82.5% Lutheran Church of Finland, 1.1% Orthodox, 1.1% other Christian, 15.1% none.

• **GOVERNMENT Type:** republic. **Independence:** Dec. 6, 1917 (from Russia). **Constitution:** Mar. 1, 2000. **National holiday:** Independence Day, Dec. 6. **Heads of Government:** Tarja Halonen, president (since Mar. 2000); Mari Kiviniemi, prime minister (since Jun. 2010). **Structure:** executive; unicameral legislature; judiciary.

• **ECONOMY Monetary unit:** euro. **Budget:** (2009 est.) *income:* $115.7 bil.; *expend.:* $122.6 bil. **G.D.P.:** $182.6 bil., $34,900 per capita (2009 est.). **Chief crops:** cereals, sugar beets, potatoes; dairy, cattle; fish. **Natural resources:** timber, copper, zinc, iron ore, silver. **Major industries:** metal manufacturing, shipbuilding, forestry and wood processing (pulp, paper), copper refining. **Labor force:** 2.68 mil. (2009 est.); 4.5% agriculture and forestry, 18.2% industry, 7.3% construction, 15.9% commerce, 14.5% finance, insurance, and business services, 6.9% transport and communications, 32.7% public services; 6.9% unemployment (2007). **Exports:** $57.88 bil. (2009 est.); machinery, chemicals, paper and pulp. **Imports:** $54.1 bil. (2009 est.); foodstuffs, petroleum and petroleum products, chemicals, transport equipment. **Major trading partners:** (2008) *exports:* 11.6% Russia, 10% Sweden, 10% Germany, 6.4% U.S.; *imports:* 16.2% Russia, 15.6% Germany, 13.5% Sweden, 6.3% Netherlands.

The Finns originated in the Ural Mountains, and their language is akin to Hungarian and closely similar to Estonian. Migrating from western Siberia to what is now Finland in the eighth century, they drove the indigenous Lapps to northernmost Scandinavia. Finland was conquered and Christianized by the Swedes in the 12th century and in the 16th century became a Swedish grand duchy. Ethnic Swedes make up about 7 percent of the present population. Finland was frequently a battleground in wars between Sweden and Russia; about one-third of the population perished in a war-induced famine in 1696. In 1721 Sweden ceded the province of Viborg to Russia, and all of Finland was taken over by Russia in 1809.

Under the Russians the czars became simultaneously grand dukes of Finland and ruled it as a semiautonomous province. Attempts to "Russify" Finland in the later 19th century provoked great popular resistance. When the Russian empire and then the Russian Republic fell in the 1917 Revolution, Finland lapsed into a fierce civil war between Communists and non-Communists. The "whites" under Baron Gustaf Mannerheim were the victors, and Finland became an independent country for the first time in its history.

In 1939 the U.S.S.R. attacked the Finnish Republic; Finland's resistance in the "Winter War" was heroic but unavailing. Defeated, it was forced to cede Western Keralia to the U.S.S.R. After the German invasion of Russia in 1941, fighting between Finland and Russia resumed; England, but not America, declared war on Finland as a cocombatant with Germany. Russia again defeated Finland in 1944 and obliged the Finns to wage war against the German occupying army in northern Finland; much of the country was devastated.

The terms of the 1944 armistice between Finland and the U.S.S.R. were very harsh: Finland ceded the Petsamo region to the Soviet Union, and thus was cut off from the Barents Sea; the Porkkala peninsula was leased to the Soviets for 50 years, and reparations amounting to 80 percent of Finland's exports were paid in kind. Soviet pressure forced Finland to reject Marshall Plan aid after World War II, but Finland benefited indirectly from the rapid postwar recovery of the Scandinavian region. The gross national product returned to prewar levels by 1947.

Finland's economy had traditionally been centered on timber and other forest products, including pulp and paper, and on small-scale, highly productive agriculture. In the postwar period, industrial development was emphasized; the production of heavy machinery became the country's leading industry.

In 1948 the Finns signed a mutual defense pact with the U.S.S.R., renewed in 1955, 1970, and 1983. Finland's presidents, Juho Paasikivi (1946–56), Urho Kekkonen (1956–81), and Mauno Koivisto (1982–94), although conservative and nationalistic, realized that the country's independence required the avoidance of any appearance of anti-Soviet moves in foreign policy. With the establishment of good Soviet-Finnish relations, the Porkkala peninsula was returned to Finland in 1956. Finland joined the Nordic Council and the United Nations in 1955. It became an associate member of the European Free Trade Association in 1961 and a full member in 1985.

With a strong presidency providing stability despite revolving-door coalition governments in the Eduskunta (parliament), and a prudent foreign policy in the shadow of the U.S.S.R., Finland preserved its free economy and civil liberties. The U.S.S.R.'s collapse struck a heavy blow to Finland's economy; through the 1980s 15–25 percent of Finland's exports had gone to the Soviet Union. Unemployment, recession and currency devaluation were constant reminders of these changes.

In politics the U.S.S.R.'s demise brought a rightward shift, with the first nonsocialist coalition government in 25 years being elected in April 1991 under Esko Aho of the Center party as prime minister. 1994 saw Finland's first direct election of a president with Social Democrat Martti Ahtisaari carrying 54 percent of the vote. In March, the E.U. voted to accept Finland as a member in 1995. Prime Minister Aho announced that Finland would join NATO's "partnership for peace" but not as a step to full membership, preferring to maintain Finland's neutrality.

The Finnish electorate and Parliament approved membership in the E.U. in late 1994. But years of recession and high unemployment led to the toppling of the Center party government in 1995 as the Social Democrats emerged as Finland's largest party, with Paavo Lipponen as prime minister. Presidential elections in 2000 gave victory to Social Democrat Tarja Halonen (Finland's first woman president) over ex-premier and Center Party candidate, Esko Aho. In June 2003, newly-installed prime minister Anneli Jaatteenmaki, who had just led her Center Party in March to a slender victory in parliamentary elections, resigned in a scandal in which she was accused of misusing leaked documents during the election campaign, alleging that Social Democrat Prime Minister Lipponen supported the war against Iraq. Defense Minister Matti Vanhanen replaced her. Halonen was reelected in 2006. In 2008 former president Martti Ahtisarri won the Nobel Peace Prize.

▶FRANCE
French Republic

- **GEOGRAPHY Location:** western Europe. **Boundaries:** English Channel to N, Belgium, Luxembourg, Germany, Switzerland, Italy to E, Mediterranean Sea, Spain to S, Atlantic Ocean to W. **Total area:** 248,429 sq. mi. (643,427 sq km). **Coastline:** 2,130 mi. (3,427 km). **Comparative area:** slightly less than the size of Texas. **Land use:** 33% arable land; 2% permanent crops; 65% other. **Major cities:** Paris (capital); Marseille (Marseilles); Lyon (Lyons); Toulouse; Nice.
- **PEOPLE Population:** 64,057,792 (July 2009 est.). **Nationality:** noun—Frenchman (men), Frenchwoman (women); adjective—French. **Ethnic groups:** Celtic and Latin with Teutonic, Slavic, North African, Indochinese, and Basque minorities. **Languages:** French (100% of population); rapidly declining regional dialects (Provençal, Breton, Alsatian, Corsican, Catalan, Basque, Flemish). **Religions:** 83-88% Roman Catholic, 2% Protestant, 1% Jewish, 5-10% Muslim (North African workers), 4% unaffiliated.
- **GOVERNMENT Type:** republic. **Constitution:** Sept. 28, 1958, amended concerning election of president in 1962. **National holiday:** Bastille Day, July 14. **Heads of Government:** Nicolas Sarkozy, president (since May 2007); François Fillon, prime minister (since May 2007). **Structure:** executive; bicameral legislature; judiciary.
- **ECONOMY Monetary unit:** euro. **Budget:** (2009 est.) *income:* $1.229 tril.; *expend.:* $1.445 tril. **G.D.P.:** $2.11 trillion, $32,800 per capita (2009 est.). **Chief crops:** cereals, sugarbeets, potatoes, wine grapes (western Europe's foremost producer); beef, dairy products; fish. **Natural resources:** coal, iron ore, bauxite, fish, timber. **Major industries:** steel, machinery, chemicals, automobiles. **Labor force:** 27.99 mil. (2009); 72% services, 24% industry, 4% agriculture; 8% unemployment (2007 est.). **Exports:** $456.8 bil. (2009 est.); machinery and transport equipment, chemicals, foodstuffs, agricultural products, iron and steel products. **Imports:** $532.2 bil. (2009 est.); crude petroleum, machinery and equipment, vehicles, aircraft, chemicals, iron and steel products. **Major trading partners:** (2008) *exports:* 14.4% Germany, 8.7% Italy, 8.3% Spain, 7.8% U,K.; *imports:* 17.8% Germany, 11.7% Belgium, 8.2% Italy, 6.8% Spain.

Pre-Roman France, known as Gaul, was populated by Celtic tribes. The Mediterranean coast, colonized by Phoenician and Greek traders, was conquered by Rome in the second century B.C. The Roman conquest of all of Gaul was carried out by Julius Caesar between 58 and 51 B.C. Gaul became a prosperous and thoroughly Latinized province of the Roman Empire and Christianity was introduced in the first century A.D.

Barbarian invaders including Visigoths, Franks, and Burgundii swept through France in the fifth century. In 486 Clovis, chief of the Franks, unified the country, accepted Christianity, and established the Merovingian dynasty. France was invaded by Muslim Saracens in the seventh century, but in 732 Charles Martel defeated the Saracens. His son, Pepin the Short, overthrew the last Merovingian ruler in 751 and proclaimed himself king. Pepin's son, Charlemagne, greatly expanded his kingdom and was crowned emperor of the West by the pope in 800.

Ninth-century Viking invasions greatly weakened the power of the Carolingians and France broke up into estates, some of them effectively independent countries, ruled by great aristocrats. Among the most important were the duke- doms of Aquitaine and Burgundy and the counties of Flanders, Blois, and Anjou. In 911 the Vikings, who had repeatedly raided the Atlantic coast of France, established the duchy of Normandy.

In 987 the Carolingian dynasty died out in France (although it survived in the Holy Roman Empire) and was replaced by a new line, the Capetians. Steadily expanding in both territory and power from their base in Paris, the Capetians solidified the foundations of the French monarchy. Paris became a great monastic and university city as well as a center of trade and manufacturing. Under the crusader-king Louis IX (St. Louis), France also became an international power.

During the 14th century, the Black Death, peasant rebellions, and the beginning of the Hundred Years' War (1337–1453) with England further weakened the French monarchy. The Norman conquest of England in 1066 had entwined the fortunes of the French and English monarchies, and with the Capetian line in decline, England pursued its claims in France. Henry V of England defeated the French at Agincourt in 1415, and in 1420 Charles IV made Henry heir to the throne of France. Henry's forces were defeated by French armies inspired by Joan of Arc, and in 1429 his claim to the French throne was overturned. In 1435 Burgundy allied itself with France, and in 1453 the English were driven out of France, except for an enclave at Calais.

Louis XI completed the consolidation of France under the French monarchy. France prospered as a center of commerce, industry, agriculture, learning, and culture throughout the 16th century but was disrupted by religious civil wars stemming from the Reformation. The Protestant Henry of Navarre, heir to the throne, was obliged to accept Catholicism before being crowned in 1594; he became founder of the Bourbon monarchy.

The consolidation of power under a highly centralized monarchy continued under Henry's heirs. With a foreign policy shaped by the powerful prime ministers Cardinal Richelieu and Cardinal Mazarin, France under Louis XIII and Louis XIV enhanced its stature in Europe by defeating the Habsburgs in the Thirty Years' War (1618–48). Louis XIV—the Sun King—moved the court from Paris to his new palace at Versailles and presided over the wealthiest and most powerful monarchy in Europe. His persecution of the Huguenots resulted in a great emigration of Protestants from France. A grand alliance of European states thwarted France's expansionist aims on the continent, but France became a major colonial power in North America, controlling Canada and Louisiana (including most of the Mississippi-Missouri valley), and pursued overseas ventures in Africa and Asia as well.

In the mid-18th century, France was weakened internationally by the expensive and fruitless Wars of the Austrian Succession and the Seven Years' War. Under the Treaty of Paris (1763), France ceded control of Canada to Great Britain. The Enlightenment made France a world center of intellectual activity but also led to the questioning of the political and social bases of the French monarchy. An increasingly wealthy but powerless bourgeoisie chafed under the restrictions of an archaic socioeconomic order.

France under Louis XVI supported the American colonies in the Revolutionary War, incurring a large public debt in the process. Combined with unrestrained extravagance on the part of the court and the aristocracy, poverty increased among the rural peasantry and the urban working class, while the bourgeoisie demanded a greater voice in government. These trends came to a head with the storming of the Bastille on July 14, 1789; soon thereafter, the Estates-General took control of the country, and France was in the throes of revolution.

Revolutionary leaders at first allowed Louis XVI to remain on the throne in a limited monarchy, but the king and Marie Antoinette were subsequently tried for treason and executed in 1793. Thousands died during the Reign of Terror which continued until July 1794, ending with the execution of its primary architects, Augustin Robespierre and Georges Danton. The Directory, with five heads of each division of government (1795–99), failed to maintain public order and suffered military reverses in foreign wars in which successive revolutionary governments had been embroiled since 1792. On Nov. 9, 1799, the Directory was overthrown by the Consulate, with Napoleon Bonaparte named first consul.

Napoleon proclaimed himself emperor of France in 1804. He transformed French law through the Code Napoleon and initially expanded the French empire in Europe and the Middle East. Suffering repeated reverses against British naval forces and disastrous losses in his 1812 invasion of Russia, Napoleon was defeated by the British under Wellington at Waterloo in 1815, and the French empire collapsed.

France restored its monarchy in 1815 but not its monarchical absolutism. Charles X, successor to Louis XVIII, was ousted in a coup d'état in 1830 and replaced by the liberal Louis Philippe. The monarchy came to an end in the wave of popular revolt that swept France, along with most of Europe, in 1848; Louis Napoleon (nephew of Bonaparte) became president of the Second Republic. In 1852 he created the Second Empire, ruling as Napoleon III and presiding over a court that set the standards of fashion for the wealthy bourgeois society of 19th-century Europe.

During the 19th century, France again became a major colonial power, acquiring important possessions in North and West Africa and Indochina. It also became a world leader in art, science, and literature and began its slow transformation into a major industrial power. Politically, however, France suffered from endemic weakness. The Second Empire ended disastrously with defeat in the Franco-Prussian War of 1870–71; the Paris Commune, formed during that war, was overthrown with great bloodshed. The Third Republic (1871–1914), despite the glittering pleasures of the Belle Epoque and France's prestige as a world power, was shaken by the Dreyfus Affair of 1894–1906.

France joined with Great Britain and Russia in forming the Triple Entente of 1907, a defensive agreement against the Triple Alliance of Germany, Italy, and the Austro-Hungarian empire. During World War I—in effect a war between these two alliances—France suffered millions of casualties and severe damage in the north. Although its role as a leader of the victorious alliance was confirmed at the Versailles Conference of 1919, France was seriously weakened by the war and played a diminished role as a world power.

France suffered badly in the world depression of the 1930s and could muster neither political nor military energy to offer effective opposition to the rise of Nazi Germany and fascist Italy. France was a participant in the Munich Agreement of 1938, which sealed the fate of central Europe. When World War II broke out in 1939, Hitler initially held off his attack on France, but when it came in May–June 1940, France was swiftly and ignominiously defeated.

During World War II, northern France was under German occupation, while in the south a collaborationist, semifascistic state was organized, with its capital at Vichy. Meanwhile, in London, Gen. Charles de Gaulle rallied the Free French forces, which fought on the Allied side in various campaigns. After the liberation of Paris a "provisional government" of various Resistance groups combined with de Gaulle's supporters drew up a constitution for the Fourth French Republic.

Although it suffered from inherent political weaknesses and often failed to provide stable cabinets, the Fourth Republic presided over postwar recovery, aided by the Marshall Plan; it promoted a mixed socialist-free enterprise economy and instituted social reforms such as women's suffrage and social security. It also led the way toward a united Europe, playing a leading role in the organization of the EEC in 1957. France became a founding member of NATO in 1949.

The Fourth Republic was unable, however, to withstand the strains of the dismantling of France's empire during the postwar wave of decolonization. France's recovery of Indochina in 1945 set off a war of national liberation there that lasted until France withdrew from the colony in 1954. Morocco and Tunisia won their independence in 1956; in Algeria, regarded as part of France itself, France fought on against Front de Liberation Nationale (FLN) rebels.

The Algerian War seriously polarized French public opinion, and, threatened with an army coup, the National Assembly voted in 1958 to grant Pres. Charles de Gaulle emergency powers for six months. De Gaulle outmaneuvered his army backers and negotiated to turn Algeria over to the FLN, a process completed in 1962. Meanwhile he also restored order at home and presided over the drafting of a new constitution that created the Fifth Republic in 1958.

The new constitution created a strong presidency, with powers to name the premier and the Council of Ministers and to preside over their meetings. The legislature was required to give priority over government initiatives and lacked authority over national defense, education, labor, and local government. Under the governments of premiers Michel Debré and Georges Pompidou, the Gaullist regime further advanced modernization of French industry and greatly benefited French agriculture by expanding the Common Market to include agricultural goods.

De Gaulle followed an independent foreign policy, pursuing European integration as well as closer relations with the Communist bloc and the Third World. He blocked British entry into the Common Market; developed an independent nuclear force, refusing to sign nuclear test-ban and nonproliferation treaties; pursued a historic rapprochement with Germany; recognized the People's Republic of China; established a leading French role in the former French colonies of

Africa; and withdrew French forces from the NATO military command.

Reelected president in 1965, after a runoff election against the Socialist-Communist alliance candidate François Mitterrand, de Gaulle continued his independent policy until student riots in early 1968 provoked police repression, which led to further popular support for the students, especially in Paris. De Gaulle dissolved the National Assembly and, in an emotional campaign on behalf of national stability, won a large electoral majority. In 1969, however, following minor political reverses, de Gaulle resigned as president.

The elections of June 1969 gave the presidency to former premier Georges Pompidou, who died in office in April 1974. He was succeeded by the Independent Republican Valery Giscard d'Estaing, who served until May 1981. During these years the Gaullist heritage was developed and consolidated. In foreign policy the movement toward European unity continued with the development of the European Parliament and, in a reversal of policy in 1973, French support for British membership in the EEC. The economic shock of the OPEC price rises of 1973–74 led to a decision to stress new industrial ventures in high-technology fields, symbolized by the Anglo-French Concorde supersonic transport.

The 1970s were years of social ferment, with a relaxation of divorce laws and the legalization of contraception advertisements and abortion, and a decline in church membership and attendance. In 1978 disillusionment stemming from inflation and social difficulties under Giscard d'Estaing brought about a leftist electoral victory for the first time under the Fifth Republic.

The Gaullist era came to an end in 1981, when Socialist François Mitterrand defeated Giscard in a presidential election. He dissolved the National Assembly and led his party to an absolute majority. Socialist premier Pierre Mauroy formed a government which pursued an aggressive program of nationalization of banks and major industries and reform of local government. Continued economic difficulties led to a loss of popular support for Mitterrand's policies. In the elections of 1986, Jacques Chirac's coalition of Gaullists and Giscardists won an almost absolute majority in the National Assembly, and Chirac became premier—the first time since 1958 that the president and the premier were of opposing parties. An accommodation was worked out in which Mitterrand concentrated on foreign affairs, and Chirac on domestic matters. Mitterrand oversaw a restoration of French military cooperation with NATO.

At home Chirac and his party reversed Mitterrand's policy of nationalization, cut taxes, and brought about a significant reduction in the inflation rate. Chirac ran for president against Mitterrand in 1988 but was defeated. Mitterrand's reelection with over 54 percent of the vote carried his Socialist party to a near majority in the assembly, where they constructed a coalition government. Persistent 9 percent unemployment and the growing appeal of Jean-Marie Le Pen's anti-immigrant National Front brought a cabinet shake-up in May 1991 and the designation of France's first female premier, Edith Cresson.

But the shake-up did nothing to stem voter dissatisfaction with the governing Socialists. Elections to regional councils in 1992 saw the Socialist vote drop to 18 percent, but not to the benefit of the center-right coalition Union for France, which gained only one-third of the vote. The National Front and the two rival "green" parties together gained 28 percent of the vote.

Even the formidable Mitterrand could not prevent the Socialist rout in the March 1993 assembly elections. The Rally for France won the most lopsided victory in the republic's history, carrying 460 (of 577) seats while the left took only 93. Rejecting calls for his resignation, Mitterand vowed to stay on until 1995, when his unprecedented 14-year presidency ended as Jacques Chirac won over Lionel Jospin.

Pledged to tax and spending cuts and continued dismantling of state enterprises, Chirac met with limited success as unemployment reached its highest level ever. A giant truckers' strike blocked French highways without government action, and cutting social welfare spending (to meet the E.U.'s Euro conditions) proved elusive. So, seeking a public mandate for France's participation in the Euro, Chirac dissolved the Assembly a year early. But the result was yet another French "cohabitation": the left coalition took 319 seats and Lionel Jospin became prime minister.

Jospin's run for the presidency ended in embarrassment as he finished third to Pres. Chirac and Jean-Marie LePen, Chirac polling 82 percent in the run-off. Chirac's right wing coalition took 355 of the National Assembly's 577 seats, promising to support "law and order," cut taxes, and privatize the elephantine state pension system. In 2003 Chirac played a leading role in condemning the U.S.-led invasion of Iraq. In 2004 he led the controversial but very popular movement to ban all religious clothing in schools (Muslim head scarves, yarmulkas, large crosses). Chirac's party was humiliated when the E.U. constitution was rejected by a wide margin in 2005, setting the stage for a center-right victory in 2007 led by Nicolas Sarkozy, the new president whose supporters also won a solid majority in the legislature. He immediately sought closer ties with the U.S. and voiced strong support for NATO expansion.

▶ GABON
Gabonese Republic

● **GEOGRAPHY** **Location:** western coast of Africa. **Boundaries:** Equatorial Guinea to NW, Cameroon to N, Congo to E and S, Atlantic Ocean to W. **Total area:** 103,348 sq. mi. (267,670 sq km). **Coastline:** 550 mi. (885 km). **Comparative area:** slightly smaller than Colorado. **Land use:** 1% arable land; 1% permanent crops; 98% other. **Major cities:** Libreville (capital); Port-Gentil; Masuku.

● **PEOPLE** **Population:** 1,514,993 (July 2009 est.). **Nationality:** noun—Gabonese (sing., pl.); adjective—Gabonese. **Ethnic groups:** Bantu tribes, including four major tribal groupings (Fang, Nzebi, Obamba, Bapounou); 154,000 other Africans and Europeans, including 10,700 French and 11,000 of dual nationality. **Languages:** French (official), Fang, Myene, Bateke, Bapounou/Eschira, Bandjabi. **Religions:** 55-75% Christian, less than 1% Muslim; Animist.

● **GOVERNMENT** **Type:** republic; multi-party presidential regime since 1990. **Independence:** Aug. 17, 1960 (from France). **Constitution:** Mar. 14, 1991 **National holidays:** August 17. **Heads of Government:** Ali Ben Bongo Ondimba, president (since Oct. 2009); Paul Biyoghe Mba, prime minister (since Jul. 2009). **Structure:** executive; bicameral legislature; independent judiciary.

• **ECONOMY** **Monetary unit:** Communauté Financière Africaine (CFA) franc. **Budget:** (2008 est.) *income:* $4.463 bil.; *expend.:* $2.746 bil. **G.D.P.:** $21.44 bil., $14,400 per capita (2008 est.). **Chief crops:** coffee, cocoa, sugar; rubber; wood; cattle; fishing. **Natural resources:** crude oil, manganese, uranium, gold, timber, iron ore. **Major industries:** petroleum, manganese, food, beverages. **Labor force:** 592,000; 60% agriculture, 15% industry, 25% services; 21% unemployment (2006). **Exports:** $9.743 bil. (f.o.b., 2008 est.); 77% crude oil, wood, manganese. **Imports:** $2.83 bil. (f.o.b., 2008 est.); machinery and equipment, foodstuffs, chemicals, petroleum products, construction materials. **Major trading partners:** (2006) *exports:* 27.6% U.S., 15.9% China, 7.8% France, 5.4% Trinidad & Tobago, 4.3% Thailand; *imports:* 35.4% France, 7.6% U.S., 5.5% Netherlands, 4.5% Cameroon, 4.3% Belgium.

Gabon, an equatorial nation largely covered by dense rain forest, is inhabited by a highly diverse mixture of people who migrated into the region over the course of the past 700 years; the now-dominant Fang arrived during the 19th century. The first Europeans to reach the area were the Portuguese in the 15th century; they were followed by Dutch, French, and British traders in the 16th century. All engaged in the slave trade.

France established an informal protectorate in 1839–41 and set about suppressing the slave trade. In 1849 a group of freed slaves settled near the American mission station at Baraka and renamed the town Libreville. France established a colonial administration in 1903 and in 1910 made it part of French Equatorial Africa. The territory became an important base of Free French activity during World War II, and in 1946 Gen. Charles de Gaulle granted French citizenship to the territory's inhabitants, and local power was devolved upon advisory assemblies. Gabon became fully independent on Aug. 17, 1960.

Gabon has remained politically stable under its 1961 constitution. Gabon's first president, Leon M'Ba, was briefly deposed by a military coup in 1964 but quickly reinstated with the aid of French troops. He died in 1967 and was succeeded by the vice president, Omar Bongo who combined all political parties into the Gabonese Democratic party in 1968; he was elected president in his own right in 1975 and was reelected in each subsequent election through 1998. Despite initial resistance from the government, Gabon has recently made the transition to multiparty democracy, thereby attracting more foreign investment. Bongo's Gabonese Democratic party remained in power but he died in June 2009 after 42 years in power.

▶ **THE GAMBIA**
Republic of The Gambia
• **GEOGRAPHY** **Location:** narrow territory around Gambia River on northwestern coast of Africa. **Boundaries:** Senegal to N, E, and S, Atlantic Ocean to W. **Total area:** 4,363 sq. mi. (11,300 sq km). **Coastline:** 50 mi. (80 km). **Comparative area:** slightly less than twice the size of Delaware. **Land use:** 20% arable land; 1% permanent crops;79% other. **Major cities:** Banjul (capital); Kombo St. Mary (surrounding urban area).
• **PEOPLE** **Population:** 1,782,893 (July 2009 est.). **Nationality:** noun—Gambian(s); adjective—Gambian. **Ethnic groups:** 42% Mandinka, 18% Fula, 16% Wolof, 10% Jola, 9% Serahuli, 1% non-African. **Languages:** English (official), Mandinka,

Wolof, Fula, and others. **Religions:** 90% Muslim, 9% Christian, 1% indigenous beliefs.
• **GOVERNMENT** **Type:** republic. **Independence:** Feb. 18, 1965 (from U.K.). **Constitution:** Apr. 24, 1970, (suspended July 1994); rewritten, approved and reestablished in Jan. 1997. **National holiday:** Independence Day, Feb. 18. **Head of Government:** Colonel Yahya Jammeh, president (since July 1994). **Structure:** following the coup on July 22, 1994 all elective officers were dissolved; military leaders have promised to return control to a democratically-elected government.
• **ECONOMY** **Monetary unit:** dalasi. **Budget:** (2008 est.) *income:* $194.3 mil.; *expend.:* $228.8 mil. **G.D.P.:** $2.264 bil., $1,300 per capita (2008 est.). **Chief crops:** peanuts, millet, sorghum, rice, maize; cattle, goats, sheep. **Natural resources:** fish. **Major industries:** agricultural processing, tourism, beverages. **Labor force:** 400,000; 75% agriculture, 19% industry, commerce, and services, 6.1% government. **Exports:** $111 mil. (f.o.b., 2008); peanuts and peanut products, fish, cotton. **Imports:** $301 mil. (f.o.b., 2008 est.); foodstuffs, manufacturing, raw materials. **Major trading partners:** (2006) *exports:* 38.6% India, 15.9% U.K., 7.9% Indonesia, 7% France, 4.6% Italy; *imports:* 25.2% China, 11.3% Senegal, 8.1% Cote d'Ivoire, 6.6% Brazil, 4.5% Netherlands, 4% U.K.

Thirty miles across at its widest point, and 295 miles long, the serpentine republic of The Gambia was gerrymandered into being out of competing French and British colonial interests. Once the westernmost part of the kingdom of Mali, The Gambia was visited by the Portuguese in 1455. In 1588, they sold British traders exclusive rights to the Gambia River, and in 1660 British merchants established a trading fort. England and France struggled for 200 years to gain political and economic control over the territory, but in 1783 the French ceded to Great Britain possession of The Gambia. Its present boundaries were established in 1889 when it became a British Crown Colony. Between 1901 and 1906, legislative councils were established to encourage self-government, and slavery was abolished.

After World War II the country moved quickly toward constitutional government, achieving independence as a constitutional monarchy within the British Commonwealth of Nations in 1965. The Gambia became a republic on Apr. 24, 1970, and it had the same president, Sir Dawda K. Jawara, until 1994.

In 1994, Yahya Jammeh, a 29-year-old lieutenant fresh from a military police training course in the United States, led a bloodless coup deposing the government of Pres. Jawara. Jammeh pledged to restore civilian government "as soon as we have set things right." Later that year the United Kingdom, the United States, and the European Union cut off all economic and military aid pending a return to democracy. Pres. Jammeh was reelected Oct. 2001 in a vote deemed fair by outside observers. He granted amnesty to Jawara, who returned from exile in 2002. Jammeh was reelected in 2006.

▶ **GEORGIA**
• **GEOGRAPHY** **Location:** west and central Transcaucasia between Asia and Europe. **Boundaries:** Russian Federation to N and E, Azerbaijan, Armenia to S, Turkey to SW, Black Sea to W. **Total area:** 26,911 sq. mi. (69,700 sq km). **Coastline:** Black Sea. **Comparative area:** slightly smaller than

South Carolina. **Land use:** 11% arable land; 4% permanent crops; 85% other. **Major cities:** Tbilisi (capital); Kutaisi; Rustavi; Batumi; Sukhumi.

• **PEOPLE** **Population:** 4,615,807 (July 2009 est.). **Nationality:** noun—Georgian(s); adjective—Georgian. **Ethnic groups:** 83.8% Georgian, 6.5% Azeri, 5.7% Armenian, 1.5% Russian, 2.5% other. **Languages:** 71% Georgian (official), 9% Russian, 7% Armenian, 6% Azeri; note - Abkhaz is the official language in Abkhazia. **Religions:** 84% Orthodox, 10% Muslim, 4% Armenian Apostolic, 3% other.

• **GOVERNMENT** **Type:** republic. **Independence:** Apr. 9, 1991 (from Soviet Union). **Constitution:** Aug. 24, 1995. **National holiday:** Independence Day, May 26. **Heads of Government:** Mikheil Saakasvili, president (since 2004); Nikoloz Gilauri, prime minister (since Feb. 2009). **Structure:** executive; unicameral legislature; judiciary.

• **ECONOMY** **Monetary unit:** lari. **Budget:** (2008 est.) *income:* $3.778 bil; *expend:* $4.182 bil. **G.D.P.:** $21.6 bil., $4,700 per capita (2008 est.). **Chief crops:** citrus, grapes, tea, vegetables. **Natural resources:** forests, hydropower, manganese. **Major industries:** steel, aircraft, machine tools. **Labor force:** 2.02 mil. (2007); 55.6% agriculture, 35.5% services, 8.9% industry; 13.6% unemployment (2006 est.). **Exports:** $2.761 bil. (2008); citrus fruits, tea, wine. **Imports:** $7.304 bil. (2008); fuel, grain and other foods, machinery and parts. **Major trading partners:** (2006) *exports:* 12.6% Turkey, 10.9% U.S., 7.9% Azerbaijan, 5.9% Armenia, 5.8% U.K., 4.9% Bulgaria, 4.8% Ukraine, 4.7% Russia, 4.4% Turkmenistan; *imports:* 14.1% Turkey, 13.1% Russia, 8.5% Ukraine, 7.4% Azerbaijan, 6.8% Germany, 5% U.S., 4.6% Bulgaria.

Georgia is a land of rugged natural beauty, renowned for its famous war heroes and its hospitality. Georgia's most famous son, Iosif Djugashvili, known as Josef Stalin, was born in the mountain village of Gori in 1879. The name of Georgia derives from the Persian name for the native people, Gorj.

An independent state was founded in the fourth century B.C. following the conquest of the Persian Empire by Alexander III. Christianity became the state religion in the 4th century A.D. Both the Georgian language and the capital city of Tbilisi date from the fifth century A.D. The Georgian people began to develop feudal states in the sixth century. Georgia's later history, however, is one of almost continuous foreign domination. In the 12th century, Georgia gained independence from the Persian Empire, but it came under Mongol rule in 1236. For centuries Georgia was a battleground between Turks and Persians, and the territory was ultimately divided into principalities, some under the control of Persia and some under Turkey. In 1801, the Persian principalities were absorbed into the Russian empire, and by the end of the century the remaining Georgian state under Turkish domination was annexed to Russia.

Once the Russian Empire collapsed in 1917 with the Bolshevik revolution, independent Georgia was proclaimed in May 1918. Although the Soviet Union and Georgia signed a treaty in May 1920 agreeing on their respective borders, the Soviet Red Army came into Georgia and forcibly incorporated it into the Soviet Union as a Socialist republic in early 1921. In 1922 it was made part of the Transcaucasian Soviet Federal Socialist Republic with Armenia and Azerbaijan, and in 1936 it became one of the U.S.S.R.'s union republics.

The Georgians have always been fiercely nationalistic, even in the face of the U.S.S.R.'s "one Soviet people" policy. Georgian pride was evident from the first demonstrations against "russification" in 1956, and again in 1978 when the rewritten U.S.S.R. constitution attempted to weaken the status of Georgian language. In 1988, during Gorbachev's policy of "glasnost," or openness, great numbers of Georgians began to call for sovereignty.

Even as Georgia fought for its independence from the U.S.S.R., the autonomous provinces of Abkhazia, Adzharia, and South Ossetia began fighting for independence from Georgia. Tensions continue to run high in Adzharia, where allegiances to Islam frighten many in Christian Georgia, and in South Ossetia, which is struggling to end its association with Georgia.

But the greatest conflict raged in Abkhazia, the home region of Zviad Gamsakhurdia, who was elected the country's first president in May 1991, but ousted from office seven months later. Fighting between the Georgian army and troops loyal to Gamsakhurdia continued from 1991–93, resulting in more than 2,000 casualties, including Gamsakhurdia, until Pres. Eduard Shevardnadze persuaded Parliament to give him emergency powers to quell the insurgency.

His political power consolidated, Shevardnadze, a former Soviet official, began to renew ties to Russia. In 1994 he agreed to a cooperation pact to increase Russia's military influence and Parliament ratified Georgia's membership in the Commonwealth of Independent States.

In 1995 Parliament overwhelmingly approved a new "strong president" constitution. And in Nov. 1995 Shevardnadze easily won election to a new five-year term, while his two-party coalition captured close to 80 percent of the seats in Parliament. But continued instability in Abkhazia, the presence of Russian troops, and several assasination attempts on Shevardnadze left future development in doubt. Still, Shevardnadze easily won reelection in 2000 and Georgia became the WTO's 137th member. After firing his entire cabinet in Nov. 2001, Shevardnadze announced that U.S. troops (to reach a total of 1,200) were arriving (Apr. 2002) to train Georgian troops in the struggle against Muslim separatists. At the end of 2003, daily non-violent protests against Shevardnadze's autocratic rule led to his resignation. U.S.-educated Mikheil Saakashvili, leader of the National Movement, was overwhelmingly elected president. Constitutional reforms soon followed, but Abkhazia and South Ossetia remained unstable and their defacto governments are supported by Russia. Saakashvili was reelected in Jan. 2008. In August, Georgian troops engaged soldiers from South Ossetia in small arms fire which led to a full-scale Georgian attack. A Russian military strike quickly overwhelmed Georgian forces and the Russian military occupied the disputed territories and parts of Georgia. Western leaders condemned Russia's actions but could do little else.

▶ **GERMANY**
Federal Republic of Germany
• **GEOGRAPHY** **Location:** central Europe. **Boundaries:** Denmark, Baltic Sea to N, Poland, Czech Republic to E, Austria, Switzerland to S, France, Luxembourg, Belgium, Netherlands to W, North Sea to NW. **Total area:** 137,847 sq. mi. (357,022 sq km). **Coastline:** 1,385 mi. (2,389 km). **Comparative area:** slightly smaller than Montana. **Land**

use: 34% arable land; 1% permanent crops; 65% other. **Major cities:** Berlin (capital); Hamburg; München (Munich); Köln (Cologne); Frankfurt. **●People Population:** 82,282,988 (July 2010 est.). **Nationality:** noun—German(s); adjective—German. **Ethnic groups:** 91.5% German, 2.4% Turkish. **Languages:** German. **Religions:** 34% Protestant, 34% Roman Catholic, 3.7% Muslim, 28.3% unaffiliated or other.

● Government Type: federal republic. **Constitution:** May 23, 1949; provisional constitution known as Basic Law became constitution of reunited German state Oct. 3, 1990. **National holiday:** German Unity Day, Oct. 3. **Heads of Government:** Christian Wulff, president (since June 2010); Angela Merkel, chancellor (since Nov. 2005). **Structure:** president (titular head of state); bicameral parliament—Bundesrat (Federal Council, upper house), Bundestag (National Assembly, lower house); independent judiciary.

● Economy Monetary unit: euro. **Budget:** (2009 est.) *income:* $1.398 tril.; *expend.:* $1.54 tril. **G.D.P.:** $2.811 tril., $34,100 per capita (2009 est.). **Chief crops:** wheat, barley, rye, potatoes, sugar beets, fruit; cattle, pigs, poultry. **Natural resources:** iron ore, coal, potash, timber. **Major industries:** among world's largest producers of iron, steel, coal, cement, chemicals, machinery, vehicles, machine tools, electronics, food and beverages; shipbuilding; textiles. **Labor force:** 43.51 mil. (2009 est.); 30% industry, 2.4% agriculture, 67% services. **Exports:** $1.121 tril. (2009 est.); machinery, vehicles, chemicals. **Imports:** $931.3 bil. (2009 est.); machinery, vehicles, chemicals, foodstuffs. **Major trading partners:** (2009) *exports:* 10.2% France, 6.7% U.S., 6.7% Netherlands, 6.6% U.K., 6.3% Italy, 6% Austria, 4.5% China, 4.4% Switzerland; *imports:* 8.5% Netherlands, 8.2% China, 8.2% France, 5.9% U.S., 5.9% Italy, 4.9% U.K., 4.3% Belgium, 4.3% Austria.

The ancient tribes of Germany resisted Roman conquest with mixed success. German federated troops served in the Roman legions, and Germanic invasions contributed to the fall of Rome. Most of Germany was united within the empire of Charlemagne. Divided among his three sons in 843, the empire's eastern regions became the heart of the Germanies. The Holy Roman Empire, founded in 962, gave some unity to the politically fragmented German territories, but its boundaries included more than Germany, and some Germans remained outside it. But that unity was fragile; the Holy Roman emperor was a feudal overlord rather than a ruler, and hundreds of separate political bodies coexisted within the imperial domain. Along the North Sea and Baltic coasts, the Hanseatic League controlled much of the commerce of northern Europe.

With the Reformation in the 16th century, religious divisions added to Germany's existing political fragmentation and local allegiances. The Thirty Years War (1618–48) resulted in the virtual extinction of the Holy Roman Empire and left Germany without even a shadow of unity.

After the Napoleonic Wars, in which much of Germany was conquered by France, the Congress of Vienna (1814–15) sanctioned the creation of a German League to succeed the Holy Roman Empire. The league consisted of 39 states, including five substantial kingdoms and the German parts of the Austrian empire. Prussia, one of the five kingdoms, had already risen to prominence under Frederick the Great in the 18th century. In a series of wars in the mid-19th century, Prussia conquered the other German states; after defeating France in the Franco-Prussian War of 1870–71, Prussia declared the establishment of the German empire. Under its chancellor, Otto von Bismarck, Germany became a major European power in the late 19th century, with a booming industrial economy, flourishing agriculture, a small colonial empire, and growing military might.

The German Empire reached its height under Kaiser Wilhelm II on the eve of World War I. Germany's disastrous defeat in that war was compounded by the harsh terms of the Treaty of Versailles (1919), which stripped Germany of its colonial empire, and returned part of Schleswig to Denmark, Alsace-Lorraine to France, and part of Prussia to Poland.

The Weimar Republic, established in 1919, gradually overcame economic difficulties, including ruinous inflation, to achieve a measure of recovery in the 1920s. The republic was disrupted by labor strife, political fragmentation, and the rise of armed extremist political movements on both left and right. After the onset of the world economic depression in 1929, Adolf Hitler's National Socialist movement gained increasing power, both at the polls and through open thuggery against its opponents. Hitler's appointment as chancellor in 1933 effectively put an end to the Weimar Republic as a functioning democracy.

The onset of World War II in Europe was presaged by Hitler's annexation of Austria and Czechoslovakia in 1938 and precipitated by the German invasion of Poland in 1939. Early military successes gave Germany control of most of Europe, but the eventual victory of the Allied powers in 1945 left the country exhausted and in ruins. Much of the Jewish population of Germany, and of other territories under German control, had been killed during the Holocaust. German cities were reduced to rubble, and a quarter of the country's homes were uninhabitable. Famine and fuel shortages added to the general misery.

Politically, Germany had essentially ceased to exist in 1945. The Allies divided the country into four zones of occupation, with a similar four-part division of Berlin. As the Cold War rift between the Western powers and the U.S.S.R. intensified during the late 1940s, so too the division of Germany hardened. In 1948 the U.S.S.R. imposed a blockade on West Berlin; the city was supplied by a massive airlift from the West for several months. In 1949 two Germanies were created: the German Democratic Republic in the Russian zone in the east, and the Federal Republic of Germany in the Allied zone in the west.

The Federal Republic was largely the creation of one man, Konrad Adenauer. A veteran pre-Hitler politician, he founded the Federation of Christian Democratic Parties (CDU-CSU) in 1945, and as president of the Parliamentary Council formed during the occupation, he virtually wrote the new constitution for West Germany. In the first elections held in the Federal Republic (August 1949), the "bourgeois coalition" led by the CDU-CSU won a parliamentary majority in the Bundestag, and Adenauer became chancellor, a post he held for 14 years. In 1951 the Western powers granted the new state autonomy in foreign affairs, and recognized its full sovereignty in 1954.

Even before the fighting in Germany subsided in 1945, the Soviet Air Force brought Walter Ulbricht, the exiled leader of the German Communist party, back to the U.S.S.R.'s zone of occupation in Germany. Backed by 20 Soviet divisions, Ulbricht and the party commenced the communization of the eastern zone. After local and state elections embarrassed the Communists, Stalin and Ulbricht forced all other parties into the National Front. With no other electoral lists permitted, voters gave a 99.7 percent approval to the National Front in the first elections to East Germany's "People's Chamber" in 1950.

While Ulbricht attempted to collectivize agriculture and plan industrial development in the eastern zone, the Soviet Union extracted heavy reparations payments, bringing on an acute economic crisis. In June 1953, shortly after Stalin's death, strikes and riots erupted. The U.S.S.R. renounced further reparation payments and declared East Germany a sovereign state.

Adenauer relied heavily on friendship with the U.S. and reconciliation with France. He also supported European integration: In 1951 West Germany joined both the Council of Europe and the Coal and Steel Community. West Germany was admitted to NATO in 1955 and in 1957 became one of the six founding members of the EEC.

The political alliance between Adenauer and Ludwig Erhard led to political stability and the creation of a market-driven economy. With a currency reform program and Marshall Plan aid in place by 1948, the stage was set for Germany's "economic miracle" of the 1950s. Between 1949 and 1964, industrial production increased by 60 percent and gross national product tripled, while unemployment fell to one percent, even as millions of refugees from East Germany were integrated into the West German economy.

In 1963 Erhard succeeded Adenauer as chancellor. Economic growth slowed to an annual 3 percent rate, but West Germany was already one of Europe's strongest economic powers, even providing jobs for hundreds of thousands of "guest workers" from southern Europe and Turkey.

By 1963 East Germany had become the second-largest industrial power in Eastern Europe, and in 1968 it surpassed Czechoslovakia in output. A significant shift of labor to industry reduced the farm population to under 20 percent of total population by 1960.

Although East Germany enjoyed prestige within the Eastern bloc as an industrial power, the steady stream of emigrants to West Germany told a different story. After a renewed collectivization policy was implemented in 1960, the stream became a flood, and East Germany responded by building the Berlin Wall. The wall was a visible sign of political failure, but it did slow the stream of emigration to a trickle.

Erhard resigned in 1966 when his coalition fell apart over the issue of a planned tax increase. He was succeeded by Kurt Kiesinger, who presided over a historic "great coalition" of Christian Democrats and Social Democrats. Under Willi Brandt, the Social Democrats had shifted their orientation from a Marxist party to a reformist, market-oriented stance.

Elections in 1969 produced a majority for the coalition headed by the Social Democrats who governed until 1982. Brandt succeeded Kiesinger and pursued an Ostpolitik ("opening to the east"), regularizing relations with East Germany, signing a nonaggression pact with the U.S.S.R., and recognizing the border between East Germany and Poland. But domestically, West Germany suffered

serious dislocations from the OPEC oil price increases of the early 1970s; inflation reached almost 8 percent. Revelations that a Brandt aide was an East German spy led to his replacement as chancellor by Helmut Schmidt in 1974.

Schmidt continued Brandt's eastern policy but economic difficulties persisted, and Schmidt's government fell in 1982. The Christian Democrats returned to power under chancellor Helmut Kohl. The improvement of the world economy in the 1980s led to economic recovery, boosting Kohl's popularity. In East Germany an aging Ulbricht was replaced in May 1971 as party first secretary by Erich Honecker, who also became head of state in 1976. Honecker completed state ownership of all industry in 1972.

After Brandt's Ostpolitik, the two Germanies grew closer, at least economically. East Germany's trade with West Germany gave it access to the EC. However, East Germany resisted Mikhail Gorbachev's reform policies in the 1980s, trying to establish itself as a model of old-style communism in Eastern Europe. In the fall of 1989 tens of thousands of East Germans fled to West Germany through Hungary and Czechoslovakia, triggering a series of dramatic demonstrations and the dismantling of the Berlin Wall in October. Honecker's government collapsed as the momentum for unification became unstoppable. In March 1990 Christian Democrat Lothar de Maizière was elected prime minister on a unification platform.

In July an economic and fiscal union of the Germanies was completed, and in September the victorious wartime allies (the U.S., U.S.S.R., U.K., and France) agreed to a peace treaty that paved the way for political unification. On October 3, six regions of the former East Germany entered the Federal Republic as member states; eleven days later the Christian Democrats won elections in five of them, the Social Democrats winning one.

In December 1990, all-German elections to the Bundestag were held for the first time in 58 years. The CDU-CSU and the Free Democrats won 398 seats, the Social Democrats 239. Helmut Kohl was sworn in as chancellor Jan. 17, 1991. In June Parliament voted to move the capital back to Berlin.

In the years following unification, euphoria gave way to sober realism; economic restructuring would take many years, because the economy of East Germany proved to be in even worse shape than anyone imagined. Related to these economic woes was the wave of violent attacks by radical nationalists and neo-Nazi gangs upon immigrants and asylum seekers (who numbered over two million). In 1993 the government banned several violent groups and amended Germany's liberal asylum law to prevent refugees seeking economic betterment from entering the country.

In the Bundestag elections of 1994, the Kohl coalition (CDU, CSU, and FD) maintained its majority over the opposition, led by the Social Democrats. Kohl was reelected chancellor, for a fourth time, as the economy remained strong. By 1996, however, unemployment was at an all-time postwar high and the Kohl government announced that the budget deficit required sweeping spending cuts, especially in social welfare programs. The economy worsened in 1997 and rebounded in 1998 but not enough to give Kohl another electoral victory as he lost to the Social Democrats and their leader, Gerhard Schröder.

The Bundestag approved new Chancellor Schröder's "red-green" cabinet whose personnel and program appeared further left than Schröder. By March 1999, finance minister LaFontaine, an old-style SD, had been replaced by "moderate" Hans Eichel, financial markets responding positively. The government coalition lost control of the state government of Hesse, thereby losing its majority in the Bundesrat, the upper house whose members are elected by the states, dooming the government's plan to loosen citizenship restrictions. Schröder's attempts to introduce an austerity budget led to further electoral setbacks in state elections in 1999.

The large Christian Democratic advances in state and municipal elections were brought to a halt with the revelations, at the end of 1999, of massive illegal contributions to the CDs over the years 1982–98, leading to heavy fines and the ruin of the reputations of numerous CD politicians, preeminently of former chancellor Helmut Kohl. In return for a fine of 300,000 marks, prosecutors dropped charges against Kohl in 2001. In November the Schröder government narrowly (336–330) survived a vote of confidence over sending 4,000 troops to Afghanistan, but Schröder won re-election in Sept. 2002 in large part because of his opposition to a U.S. strike at Iraq. In 2003, faced with an enduring recession, growing unemployment and budget deficits, Schroeder proposed a reform package to cut unemployment benefits and government pensions, ease job-protection regulations and the Social Democrats grudgingly agreed to back him. The reforms passed in 2004 despite Schröeder's falling approval ratings, but the dye was cast and in the 2005 elections he lost out to Angela Merkel whose integrity was unassailable. In the financial crash of 2008–09, Gemany's leaders were more conservative than the U.S. but a stimulus package did help greatly. Budget cuts and healthcare changes led to a strong drop in the Merkel government's approval ratings. But Germany seemed to regain its economic footing during 2010 more by austerity than stimulus.

▶ GHANA
Republic of Ghana

● GEOGRAPHY Location: western Africa. Boundaries: Burkina Faso to N, Togo to E, Gulf of Guinea to S, Ivory Coast to W. Total area: 92,100 sq. mi. (238,540 sq km). Coastline: 335 mi. (539 km). Comparative area: slightly smaller than Oregon. Land use: 16% arable land; 7% permanent crops; 77% other. Major cities: Accra (capital); Kumasi; Tamale; Tema; Sekondi-Takoradi.
● PEOPLE Population: 23,832,495 (July 2009 est.). Nationality: noun—Ghanaian(s); adjective—Ghanaian. Ethnic groups: 98.5% black African (major groups— Akan, Moshi-Dagomba, Ewe, Ga, Mole-Dagbon), 1.5% European and other. Languages: English (official), Akan, Moshi-Dagomba, Ewe, Ga. Religions: 68.8% Christian, 15.9% Muslim, 8.5% traditional, 6.1% none.
● GOVERNMENT Type: constitutional democracy. Independence: Mar. 6, 1957 (from U.K.). Constitution: Apr. 28, 1992. National holiday: Independence Day, Mar. 6. Head of Government: John Evans Atta Mills, President (since Jan. 2009). Structure: executive; unicameral legislature; judiciary.
● ECONOMY Monetary unit: new cedi. Budget: (2008 est.) income: $4.021 bil.; expend.: $5.521 bil. G.D.P.: $34.04 bil., $1,500 per capita (2008 est.). Chief crops: cocoa, rice, coffee, timber. Natural resources: gold, timber, industrial diamonds,

bauxite, manganese. Major industries: mining, lumbering, light manufacturing. Labor force: 11.52 million (2008); 56% agriculture and fishing, 15% industry, 29% services (2005); 11% unemployed (2000). Exports: $5.439 bil. (f.o.b., 2008); gold, cocoa, timber, tuna. Imports: $9.816 bil. (f.o.b., 2008); capital equipment, petroleum, consumer goods, food. Major trading partners: (2006) exports: 11.3% Netherlands, 8.7% U.K., 6.7% U.S., 5.7% Spain, 5.2% Belgium, 4.4% France; imports: 16.7% Nigeria, 13% China, 5.7% U.K., 4.7% Belgium, 4.7% U.S., 4.1% South Africa, 4.1% France.

The connection between modern Ghana and the 10th century Ghana empire of southern Mali is obscure. In the 13th century, the Akan around the city of Kumasi were trading gold and other commodities with the Mande to the north. The number of competing states in the region grew rapidly after European contact. The Asante empire began in the early 17th century under Osei Tutu. By 1750 it controlled the northern part of Ghana, and by 1820 it had brought the coastal Fante empire under its control.

The Portuguese first explored the area, on Africa's west coast, in 1471, naming it the Gold Coast because of its gold deposits and its reserves of "black gold"—slaves. In the 16th and 17th centuries, the British, Danes, and Dutch established slave trading posts there, which is where most American slaves came from. The slave trade ended in the 1850s, and the British gained control of the Gold Coast, making it a protectorate in 1871 and a colony in 1886. Great Britain gave the colony a new constitution in 1946 under which Africans held a majority of seats in the legislature. Kwame Nkrumah became prime minister of the colony in 1952 and the first prime minister of the nation when it became independent in 1960.

At independence, Ghana boasted Africa's largest man-made deep-water port and the most productive gold mine in the world, and it was the second largest producer of industrial diamonds. Nkrumah began to court Communist bloc nations and exert absolute authority. In January 1964 all opposition parties were outlawed. A military council seized power in February 1966 and ousted Nkrumah.

Civilian governments ran the country briefly, but in 1981, Flt. Lt. Jerry Rawlings took power in a coup and ruled until 2000. Ghana suffered severe economic problems throughout the 1970s and 1980s, and many of Ghana's people left for Nigeria to find work. In 1983 Nigeria returned more than one million of these migrant workers, increasing Ghana's economic woes.

After five years of stagnation, Ghana achieved a 6 percent economic growth rate in 1989 under a World Bank restructuring program. But political unrest remained. A new constitution was approved in an April 1992 referendum, and in November Rawlings received 58 percent of the vote. His National Democratic Congress all but swept the legislative elections due to an opposition boycott. Under the constitution, Rawlings was not permitted to run for a third term and in Dec. 2000 John Kufuor of the opposition New Patriotic Party won the presidency in a run-off election. In June 2007 the government announced the discovery of major offshore oil reserves. In 2009 a Rawlings protege, John Atta Mills, became the nation's third president. In July U.S. President Obama chose Ghana to give his major speech on Africa because of its stability and democracy.

▶GREAT BRITAIN (see United Kingdom)

▶GREECE
Hellenic Republic

● **GEOGRAPHY** **Location:** southeastern Europe. **Boundaries:** Albania, Macedonia, Bulgaria to N, Turkey to NE, Aegean Sea to E, Mediterranean Sea to S, Ionian Sea to W, Albania to NW; numerous islands surround mainland. **Total area:** 50,949 sq. mi. (131,957 sq km). **Coastline:** 8,500 mi. (13,676 km). **Comparative area:** slightly smaller than Alabama. **Land use:** 22% arable land; 8% permanent crops; 70% other. **Major cities:** Athinai (Athens, capital); Thessaloniki; Piraeus; Patras; Iraklion. ●**PEOPLE** **Population:** 10,749,943 (July 2010 est.). **Nationality:** noun—Greek(s); adjective—Greek. **Ethnic groups:** 93% Greek, 7% foreign (note: percentages represent citizenship; Greek government does not collect data on ethnicity). **Languages:** Greek (official); English and French widely understood. **Religions:** 98% Greek Orthodox, 1.3% Muslim, 0.7% other.

● **GOVERNMENT** **Type:** parliamentary republic; monarchy rejected by referendum Dec. 8, 1974. **Independence:** 1829 (from the Ottoman Empire) **Constitution:** June 11, 1975; amended in March 1986 and April 2001. **National holiday:** Independence Day, Mar. 25. **Heads of Government:** Karolos Papoulias, president (since Mar. 2005); Yeoryios (George) Papandreou, prime minister (since Oct. 2009). **Structure:** executive—president elected by unicameral legislature; judiciary.

● **ECONOMY** **Monetary unit:** euro. **Budget:** (2009 est.) *income:* $108.7 bil.; *expend.:* $145.2 bil. **G.D.P.:** $341 bil., $32,100 per capita (2009 est.). **Chief crops:** wheat, corn, barley, sugar beets, olives; meat, dairy products. **Natural resources:** bauxite, lignite, magnesite, crude oil, marble. **Major industries:** tourism, food and tobacco processing, textiles, chemicals. **Labor force:** 5 mil. (2009); 73% services, 4% agriculture, 23% industry (2008); 8% unemployment (2008 est.); **Exports:** $21.37 bil. (2009 est.); manufactured goods, foodstuffs, fuels. **Imports:** $64.27 bil. (2009 est.); manufactured goods, foodstuffs, fuels. **Major trading partners:** (2008) *exports:* 11.5% Italy, 10.5% Germany, 7.1% Bulgaria, 6.2% Cyprus, 5% U.S., 4.7% U.K., 4.4% Romania; *imports:* 12.1% Germany, 11.7% Italy, 7.4% Russia, 5.6% China, 5.1% France, 4.7% Netherlands.

The Bronze Age and Iron Age cultures of Greece evolved to create the most glorious civilization of the ancient world. From the fifth to the third century B.C., the city-states of Greece led the world in art, philosophy, political culture, and science. Greece vied with the Persian Empire for control of Asia Minor and competed with the Phoenicians in maritime commerce in the Mediterranean. Alexander the Great, king of Macedonia, spread Greek civilization widely by conquering much of the Middle East and western Asia, but his empire did not long outlast his death in 323 B.C.

Greece was absorbed into the Roman Empire during the second and first centuries B.C. In the fourth century A.D., with the division of the Roman Empire, Greece became part of the Byzantine (Eastern Roman) Empire. Seven after the Ottoman Turks captured Constantinople in 1453, they overran Greece and ruled it as part of the Ottoman Empire for 350 years.

Under Ottoman rule, much of the administration of Greece was left in local hands, keeping alive a sense of Greek nationhood and a tradition of Greek leadership, particularly through the clergy of the Greek Orthodox church. Inspired by the French Revolution, a romanticized ideal of the classical past, and the tradition of Greek orthodoxy, in 1821 Greece rebelled against Turkish rule. With the support of England, France, and Russia, Greek independence was won in 1827, although the country included only about half of its present territory.

The Western powers sponsored a monarchical government in Greece, ruled by a German prince. Deposed in a revolt, he was succeeded by King George I, a Danish prince who ruled from 1863 until his assassination in 1913. In the three Balkan Wars of 1912, 1913, and 1914, Greece expanded its borders to reach approximately its present size.

In 1923 a Greek Republic was established, but in 1935 King George II returned, placing government control in the hands of the authoritarian Gen. Ioannis Metaxas. In 1940 Metaxas resisted Italy's attempt to conquer Greece, defeating Mussolini's armies so badly that Hitler sent crack troops to his ally's assistance. The German occupation of Greece was complete by June 1941. The Germans pillaged the country and massacred Jews; their Bulgarian allies colonized Macedonia.

During World War II, resistance grew among both Communist and anti-Communist groups. With the German withdrawal in October 1944, resistance groups battled each other; this led to full-scale civil war by 1946. British, and then American assistance (under the Truman Doctrine), enabled the Greek government to defeat the Communist forces when Stalin refused to intervene. King George II died in 1947, succeeded by his brother, King Paul I. Political instability—16 governments during 1946–52—prevailed until, under American pressure, the Greeks adopted a new constitution.

Until the postwar period, Greece's economy had been dominated by agriculture and livestock raising. Industry was limited largely to textiles and food processing; shipping was the major service industry. Under policies instituted in 1952 by the government of Marshall Alexandros Papagos, the industrial sector led a period of vigorous economic growth lasting into the 1960s. A market-oriented economy, tariff protection for Greek industry, tight internal security, and close ties with the West formed the mainstays of Greek policy.

Greece joined NATO in 1951, as did Turkey. Conflict over Cyprus divided the two nominal allies, however. The failure of the government of Constantine Karamanlis to resolve the Cyprus situation eroded his popularity, and he was replaced in 1964 by George Papandreou, who governed at the head of a left-center coalition. King Constantine, who succeeded his father in 1963, forced Papandreou to resign in 1964, after he and members of his government were accused of various improprieties. A military coup, led by Col. George Papadopoulos, toppled the government in 1967. A countercoup by King Constantine failed, and the king fled the country.

A military dictatorship ruled from 1967 to 1974. Its failed attempt to intervene in Cyprus in 1974 provoked a Turkish invasion of the island and led to the military regime's collapse. Karamanlis headed the government once again and a republic was established with the promulgation of a new constitution in 1975. Karamanlis's New Democracy party again won a majority in 1977 elections.

Greece, an associate member of the EC since 1961, became a full member in 1981. Full military membership in NATO was restored in 1980. In 1981 the Panhellenic Socialist Movement under Andreas Papandreou won a parliamentary majority, renewed in 1984. The left-wing Papandreou government was outspokenly anti-NATO, anti-EC, and anti-American, but its policy was more moderate than its rhetoric, extending even to modest cooperation with Turkey in the Aegean. The Papandreou government was shaken by several pro-Palestinian terrorist incidents in Greece, and by a scandal involving the married Papandreou's relationship with a younger woman.

During 1989–90 Greece struggled through three parliamentary elections in less than a year. In the first two, no major party won a clear victory, leading to weak, short-lived coalition governments. The third, in the spring of 1990, resulted in a slim majority for the New Democracy party (headed by Prime Minister Constantine Mitsotakis) and the apparent decline of Papandreou's stature.

But Papandreou strengthened his grip on power in 1993, leading his PASOK party to a landslide victory over the New Democrats, as voters expressed their displeasure with Mitsotakis's deficit-cutting "austerity" policies. Papandreou returned to office promising salary and pension increases and a halt to privatization. But serious illness forced him to resign in January 1996. His successor, Costas Simitas, promised to speed up the stalled privatization program, and his new cabinet removed most Papandreou loyalists.

Greece's economy failed to meet the E.U.'s criteria for participating in the European Monetary Union in 1998. New tensions with Turkey over Cyprus, however, threatened to erupt into serious conflict during mid-year.

In 1999 and 2000 a series of improvements occurred in Greek-Turkish relations: reciprocal earthquake assistance, agreements on sales of electricity (to Turkey) and water (to Cyprus, both Greek and Turkish, from Turkey) and foreign ministers' accords on crime, immigration, commerce, tourism and the Aegean environment. Greece even agreed to support Turkey's admission to the E.U. In April 2000, in Greece's closest parliamentary elections, PASOK became the first Greek party to win three consecutive elections.

The success of the government's austerity program led the E.U. to approve Greece's joining the E.M.U. in early 2001. This led to a $2 bil. aid package but did not prevent the government from losing power in 2004 to the New Democratic party led by Kostas Karamanlis. He was reelected in 2007 and soon engaged in serious talks with Turkey to end the Cyprus dispute. In Dec. 2008, violent youth riots in Athens and other cities over the police shooting of a 15-year-old boy threatened the government's stability for a short period.

Elections in 2009 gave the socialists a convincing victory and made George Papandreou prime minister. The financial crisis of 2008 and 2009 had exposed the Greek economy as so highly leveraged that collapse was imminent. Papandreou pushed through large budget cuts and an end to the welfare system. Aid from the E.U. helped to stabilize the situation. (See "Major News Stories.")

▶ GRENADA
● **GEOGRAPHY** **Location:** southeastern Caribbean Sea, about 100 mi. (160 km) N of Trinidad. St. George's 12°03'N, 61°45'W. **Boundaries:** Atlantic Ocean to NE, E, and SE.; Caribbean Sea to SW, W, and NW. **Total area:** 131 sq. mi. (340 sq km). **Coast-**line: 75 mi. (121 km). **Comparative area:** twice size of Washington, D.C. **Land use:** 6% arable land; 26% permanent crops; 68% other. **Major cities:** St. George's (capital).

● **PEOPLE** **Population:** 90,739 (July 2009 est.). **Nationality:** noun—Grenadian(s); adjective—Grenadian. **Ethnic groups:** 83% black, 13% mixed, 5% European and East Indian. **Languages:** English (official), some French patois. **Religions:** 53% Roman Catholic, 13.8% Anglican, 33.2% other Protestant sects.

● **GOVERNMENT** **Type:** parliamentary democracy and a Commonwealth realm. **Independence:** Feb. 7, 1974 (from U.K.). **Constitution:** Dec. 19, 1973. **National holiday:** Independence Day, Feb. 7. **Heads of Government:** Carlyle Arnold Glean, governor-general (since Nov. 2008); Tillman Thomas, prime minister (since July 2008). **Structure:** executive (cabinet led by prime minister); bicameral legislature; judiciary (West Indies Associate States Supreme Court).

● **ECONOMY** **Monetary unit:** East Caribbean (EC) dollar. **Budget:** (1997 est.) *income:* $85.8 mil.; *expend.:* $102.1 mil. **G.D.P.:** $1.211 bil., $13,400 per capita (2008 est.). **Chief crops:** bananas, cocoa, nutmeg, mace. **Natural resources:** timber, tropical fruit, deep-water harbors. **Major industries:** food and beverages, textiles, light assembly operations. **Labor force:** 42,300 (1996); 62% services, 24% agriculture, 14% industry, 12.5% unemployment. **Exports:** $38 mil. (2006 est.); bananas, cocoa beans, nutmeg. **Imports:** $343 mil. (2006 est.); food, manufactured goods, machinery, chemicals, fuel (1989). **Major trading partners:** (2006) *exports:* 18.8% Santa Lucia, 12.8% Antigua & Barbuda, 11.5% St. Kitts & Nevis, 11.4% Dominica, 11.4% U.S.; *imports:* 33.7% Trinidad & Tobago, 24.2% U.S., 4.3% U.K.

Dominated in the early 1600s by the warlike Carib Indians, Grenada alternated between French and British possession between 1650 and 1783, when British rule was established.

Independence came in 1974. The leftist New Jewel Movement seized power in a 1979 coup, but its leader, Maurice Bishop, was assassinated during a military coup in 1983. Shortly thereafter, the United States invaded and returned power to the governor-general until 1984. Prime Minister Nicholas Braithwaite of the National Democratic Congress party presided over a coalition government from 1990–95, when he was succeeded by George Brizan. In June 1995 the opposition New National party gained an absolute majority in Parliament and designated its leader, Keith Mitchell, as Prime Minister. It won all 18 seats in 1999 and narrowly won again in 2003, but lost in 2008.

▶ GUATEMALA
Republic of Guatemala
● **GEOGRAPHY** **Location:** northern part of Central American isthmus. **Boundaries:** Mexico to N and W, Honduras and Belize to E, El Salvador to S. **Total area:** 42,042 sq. mi. (108,890 sq km). **Coastline:** 248 mi. (400 km). **Comparative area:** slightly smaller than Tennessee. **Land use:** 13% arable land; 5% permanent crops; 82% other. **Major cities:** Guatemala City (capital); Quezaltenango; Escuintla; Mazatenango; Puerto Barrios.

● **PEOPLE** **Population:** 13,276,517 (July 2009 est.) **Nationality:** noun—Guatemalan(s); adjective—Guatemalan. **Ethnic groups:** 59.4% Ladino (mixed Spanish and Amerindian), 9.1% K'iche, 8.4% Kaqchikel, 7.9% Mam, 6.3% Q'eqhi, 8.6%

other Mayan. **Languages:** 60% Spanish, 40% Amerindian languages (23 Amerindian dialects, including Quiche, Cakchiquel, Kekchi). **Religions:** predominantly Roman Catholic, some Protestant and traditional Mayan.

• GOVERNMENT **Type:** constitutional democratic republic. **Independence:** Sept. 15, 1821 (from Spain). **Constitution:** May 31, 1985, effective Jan. 1986; amended in Nov. 1993. **National holiday:** Independence Day, Sept. 15. **Head of Government:** Alvaro Colom Caballeros, president (since Jan. 2008). **Structure:** executive; unicameral legislature (113 seats, elected by popular vote to four-year terms); judiciary.

• ECONOMY **Monetary unit:** quetzal. **Budget:** (2008 est.) *income:* $4.944 bil.; *expend.:* $5.647 bil. **G.D.P.:** $68.02 bil., $5,200 per capita (2008 est.). **Chief crops:** sugarcane, corn, bananas; cattle, sheep, pigs. **Natural resources:** crude oil, nickel, rare woods, fish, chicle. **Major industries:** sugar, textiles and clothing, furniture. **Labor force:** 4.054 mil. (2008 est.); 50% agriculture, 15% industry, 35% services; 7.5% unemployment (1999 est.). **Exports:** $8.028 bil. (f.o.b., 2008); coffee, sugar, bananas. **Imports:** $15.42 bil. (f.o.b., 2008); fuel and petroleum products, machinery, grain, fertilizers, motor vehicles. **Major trading partners:** (2006) *exports:* 44.6% U.S., 11.9% El Salvador, 7.2% Honduras, 5.2% Mexico; *imports:* 33.2% U.S., 8.8% Mexico, 6.5% China, 5.3% El Salvador, 4.9% South Korea.

Modern Guatemala was the heart of the Maya civilization that began early in the Christian era and flourished from the fourth to the 10th centuries. From the 11th century on there were two major powers, the Cakchiquel and the Quiché. They were overthrown by the Spanish who invaded from the north in 1524.

The captaincy general of Guatemala was the seat of Spanish military authority in Central America until the 19th century. After an earthquake destroyed Antiqua in 1773, the capital was moved to Guatemala City. Guatemala was the center of the United Provinces of Central America after independence was gained from Spain (1821) and Mexico (1823). The United Provinces collapsed after an uprising by Rafael Carrera, and Guatemala became a separate country in 1838.

The Liberal party held power from 1851–1944. There was considerable economic development under the repressive regimes of Manuel Estrada Cabrera (1898–1920) and Jorge Ubico (1931–44). Juan José Arévalo was elected president in 1945. He was succeeded, with strong Communist support, by Jacobo Arbenz, who was deposed in 1954 by a U.S.-backed coup led by Col. Carlos Castillo Armas. The military has ruled either directly or indirectly since then, although democratic rule resumed officially in 1986.

A civil war involving the army, right-wing death squads, and the antigovernment guerrilla group, the Guatemalan National Revolutionary Union (URNG) began in 1960 and intensified through the 1980s, resulting in the deaths of 100,000 civilians.

In May 1993, Pres. Jorge Serrano Elias, backed by the military, suspended the constitution in an effort to crack down on labor and student strikes. Eight days later, in the face of overwhelming popular discontent and international protest, the military replaced Serrano with Atty. Gen. for Human Rights Ramiro de Leon Carpio. In March 1994, the URNG and the government reached an agreement to end the 30-year-old civil war, but talks stalled for a year until the two sides could agree on a pact amending the constitution to defend Indian rights. The United States cut off military aid to Guatemala for its failure to prosecute security officers for crimes committed during the civil war.

In January 1996, URNG called a cease-fire during elections, in which Álvaro Arzú Irigoyen won over a candidate backed by the military. The new government purged the military of its corrupt members, and made plans to privatize the economy. The 36-year civil war seemed to end when the last 200 rebels turned in their arms in May 1997.

The April 1998 slaying of a Catholic bishop, a human rights advocate who had authored a report blaming 80 percent of the killings and kidnappings upon the military and right-wing paramilitary forces, remained unsolved a year later, as the lead prosecutor and two successive judges resigned in an atmosphere of threats. In Feb. 1999, an independent report accused the army and paramilitaries of over 90 percent of the civil war abuses.

In May 1999, as the first prosecutions of military and security forces were beginning, Guatemalan voters rejected all the constitutional changes proposed in the 1996 peace. In 1999 elections they gave a majority to the Guatemalan Republican front and overwhelmingly elected its candidate as president. In 2003, however, the more conservative Great National Alliance won both the presidency and a parliamentary majority. A rapid rise in violent crime, much of it caused by the rampant drug trade and police corruption preceded the elections of late 2007, won by businessman Alvaro Colom and his National Unity and Hope Party.

▶ GUINEA
Republic of Guinea

• GEOGRAPHY **Location:** western Africa. **Boundaries:** Guinea-Bissau to NW, Senegal to N, Mali to NE, Ivory Coast to SE, Liberia, Sierra Leone to S, Atlantic Ocean to W. **Total area:** 94,927 sq. mi. (245,860 sq km). **Coastline:** 199 mi. (320 km). **Comparative area:** slightly smaller than Oregon. **Land use:** 4% arable land; 2% permanent crops; 94% other. **Major cities:** Conakry (capital).

• PEOPLE **Population:** 10,057,975 (July 2009 est.). **Nationality:** noun—Guinean(s); adjective—Guinean. **Ethnic groups:** 40% Peuhl, 30% Malinke, 20% Soussou, 10% smaller tribes. **Languages:** French (official), tribal languages. **Religions:** 85% Muslim, 8% Christian, 7% indigenous beliefs.

• GOVERNMENT **Type:** republic. **Independence:** Oct. 2, 1958 (from France). **Constitution:** Dec. 23, 1990. **National holiday:** Independence Day, Oct. 2. **Head of Government:** Gen. Sekouba Konate, interim leader of the National Council for Democracy and Development, who replaced Capt. Camara following an assasination attempt (Dec. 2009); Jean-Marie Dore, Prime Minister of the Transitional Government (since Dec. 2008). **Structure:** executive; unicameral legislature; judiciary.

• ECONOMY **Monetary unit:** Guinean franc. **Budget:** (2008 est.) *income:* $315 mil.; *expend.:* $796.5 mil. **G.D.P.:** $10.44 bil., $1,000 per capita (2008 est.). **Chief crops:** rice, coffee, pineapples; cattle, sheep, goats; timber. **Natural resources:** bauxite, iron ore, diamonds, gold, uranium. **Major industries:** bauxite mining, alumina, diamond mining. **Labor force:** 3.7 mil. (2006); 76% agriculture, 24% industry and services. **Exports:** $1.202 mil. (f.o.b., 2008 est.); bauxite (the world's second largest producer), alumina, diamonds, coffee, fish. **Imports:** $1.392 mil. (f.o.b., 2008 est.); petroleum products, metals, machinery and transport equipment, foodstuffs, textiles. **Major trading partners:** (2006) *exports:* 11.6% Russia, 9.6% Ukraine, 9% Spain, 8.8% South Korea, 7.7% France, 7.7% U.S., 5.4% Germany, 5.1% Ireland; *imports:* 8.6% China, 8% France, 4.8% Netherlands, 4.4% Belgium.

Guinea was formed out of the remains of a series of empires that flourished in West Africa between the 10th and 15th centuries. Situated to the southwest of the Sahara desert on the west coast of Africa, Guinea was a crossroads of West African trade long before Europeans arrived.

French merchants began trading in what is now Guinea in the early 17th century. France began acquiring land in the area in the mid-19th century, and in 1845 the territories were organized as a separate colony. The colony received the name French Guinea in 1893. Most high political posts were held by Europeans until after World War II. In 1946 French Guinea became a territory in the federation of French West Africa. In September 1958 Guinea became the only French colony to reject membership in the Fifth French Republic, resulting in the severance of political ties with France. The territorial assembly proclaimed Guinean independence on Oct. 2, 1958, and a new government headed by Sékou Touré was formed on the same day.

Touré severed ties with France (1960–63) and solicited economic and other assistance from the U.S.S.R., China, and the United States. Touré remained in power until his death in April 1984. Within a week, a military government headed by Gen. Lansana Conte took power and by 1987 had improved relations with France while introducing market mechanisms into the command economy. Conte was elected president in 1993 and in June 1995, in Guinea's first-ever multiparty election, his Unity Progress party took 71 of the 114 legislative seats. He was reelected in 2003, but in 2006 the violent disturbances over corruption and declining economic conditions forced him to make concessions and appoint a prime minister. In December 2008, just hours after Conte's death, a military junta seized power.In June 2010, however, the military permitted a free election that drew 24 candidates for president. A runoff was scheduled for later in the year.

▶ **GUINEA-BISSAU**
Republic of Guinea-Bissau
• **GEOGRAPHY Location:** northwestern coast of Africa. **Boundaries:** Senegal to N, Guinea to E and S, Atlantic Ocean to W. **Total area:** 13,946 sq. mi. (36,120 sq km). **Coastline:** 217 mi. (350 km). **Comparative area:** slightly less than three times the size of Connecticut. **Land use:** 11% arable land; 2% permanent crops; 87%% other. **Major cities:** Bissau (capital); Bafatá; Gabú; Mansoa; Catió.
• **PEOPLE Population:** 1,533,964 (July 2009 est.) **Nationality:** noun—Guinean(s); adjective— Guinean. **Ethnic groups:** about 99% African (30% Balanta, 20% Fula, 14% Manjaca, 13% Mandinga, 7% Papel); less than 1% European and mulatto. **Languages:** Portuguese (official), Crioulo, numerous African languages. **Religions:** 50% indigenous beliefs, 45% Muslim, 5% Christian.
• **GOVERNMENT Type:** republic.**Independence:** Sept. 24, 1973 (unilaterally declared by Guinea-Bissau); Sept. 10, 1974 (recognized by Portugal). **Constitution:** May 16, 1984, amended May 4,

1991, Dec. 4, 1991, Feb. 26, 1993, June 9, 1993, and 1996. **National holiday:** Independence Day, Sept. 24. **Heads of Government:** Malam Bacai Sanha (since Sept. 2009). **Structure:** executive; unicameral legislature; no judiciary (Ministry of Justice).
• **ECONOMY Monetary unit:** Communauté Financière Africaine (CFA) franc. **Budget:** N.A. **G.D.P.:** $857 mil., $600 per capita (2008 est.). **Chief crops:** rice, corn, beans; fishing, forestry. **Natural resources:** fish, timber, phosphates, bauxite, unexploited deposits of petroleum. **Major industries:** agricultural processing, beer, soft drinks. **Labor force:** 480,000; 82% agriculture, 18% industry and services (2000 est.). **Exports:** $133 mil. (f.o.b., 2006 est.); 70% cashews, fish, peanuts. **Imports:** $200 mil. (f.o.b., 2006 est.); foodstuffs, transport equipment, petroleum products. **Major trading partners:** (2006) *exports:* 76.1% India, 18.1% Nigeria, 1.4% Italy; *imports:* 18.7% Portugal, 16.3% Senegal, 13% Italy, 4.5% Pakistan.

The Portuguese began exploring and trading in what is now Guinea-Bissau in the 15th century and in 1630 began to exert administrative control over the territory. The area became the center of the Portuguese slave trade. When the slave trade declined in the 19th century, the coastal port of Bissau became a major commercial center. Later in the 19th century, the Portuguese began to conquer the interior of the territory and in 1879 consolidated the region into a territory called Portuguese Guinea, which in 1952 became an overseas province of Portugal.

A nationalist movement began in 1956 under the leadership of Amilcar Cabral and the African Party for the Independence of Guinea and Cape Verde (PAIGC). Armed insurrection broke out in 1961. By 1972 the PAIGC exerted influence over much of the country. Civilian rule was established in the territory that it controlled, and elections were held for a national assembly. Cabral was assassinated in 1973, but soon after the PAIGC National Assembly declared the independence of Guinea-Bissau from Portugal. Portugal acknowledged the country's new status on Sept. 24, 1973.

The civilian government was overthrown by a military coup in 1980, and the country was run by a Revolutionary Council headed by Brig. Gen. João Bernardo Vieira until a new constitution was adopted in May 1984. Under the new constitution, a new national assembly was selected, and Vieira was elected president in 1984 and 1989. In 1991 the government legalized opposition parties, but presidential elections were postponed.

In June 1998 a former army chief of staff, Ansumane Mane, launched a coup attempt against Vieira who was supported by loyalist troops and the Senegalese army. Hundreds of thousands fled the capital and the surrounding areas as the Senegalese shelled the city. By May 1999, General Mane had driven Vieira to seek asylum with the Portuguese and had installed the leader of the National Popular Assembly, Malan Sanha, as interim president until he was defeated in Jan. 2000 by Kumba Yala (who was overthrown by the army in Sept. 2003). In March 2004 PAIGC won a plurality of seats in the new legislature but failed to capture a majority. In 2005, Vieira was elected president and he brought a modicum of stability, but in March 2009 he was assassinated as was his rival, General Batista Tagme NaWaie. Only three months later two leading politicians were murdered.

▶GUYANA
Co-operative Republic of Guyana
• **GEOGRAPHY Location:** northeastern South America. **Boundaries:** North Atlantic Ocean to N, Suriname to E, Brazil to S, Venezuela to W. **Total area:** 83,000 sq. mi. (214,970 sq km). **Coastline:** 285 mi. (459 km). **Comparative area:** slightly smaller than Idaho. **Land use:** 2% arable land; negl.% permanent crops; 97% other. **Major cities:** Georgetown (capital).
• **PEOPLE Population:** 772, 298 (July 2009 est.). **Nationality:** noun—Guyanese (sing., pl.); adjective—Guyanese. **Ethnic groups:** 50% East Indian, 36% black, 7% Amerindian, 7% white, Chinese and mixed. **Languages:** English, Amerindian dialects. **Religions:** 50% Christian, 35% Hindu, 10% Muslim, 5% other.
• **GOVERNMENT Type:** republic **Independence:** May 26, 1966 (from U.K.). **Constitution:** Oct. 6. 1980. **National holiday:** Republic Day, Feb. 23. **Heads of Government:** Bharrat Jagdeo, executive president (since Aug. 2000); Samuel Hinds, prime minister (since Feb. 1998). **Structure:** executive—president (appoints and heads cabinet); unicameral legislature; judiciary.
• **ECONOMY Monetary unit:** Guyanese dollar. **Budget:** (2008 est.) *income:* $463.7 mil.; *expend.:* $536 mil. **G.D.P.:** $3.01 bil., $3,900 per capita (2008 est.). **Chief crops:** sugarcane, rice, wheat; beef, pork, poultry. **Natural resources:** bauxite, gold, diamonds, hardwood timber, shrimp, fish. **Major industries:** bauxite mining, sugar, rice milling. **Labor force:** 418,000 (2001). **Exports:** $736.9 mil. (f.o.b., 2008); sugar, gold, bauxite/alumina, rice, shrimp, molasses. **Imports:** $1.162 mil. (f.o.b., 2008); manufactures, machinery, food, petroleum. **Major trading partners:** (2006) *exports:* 18.8% U.S., 18.4% Canada, 8.7% U.K., 6.5% Portugal, 4.9% Trinidad & Tobago, 4.3% Netherlands, 4.3% Belgium, 4.1% Japan; *imports:* 23% Trinidad & Tobago, 21.3% U.S., 9.7% China, 6.3% Cuba, 4.5% U.K.

Although the region was visited by Europeans in the 15th century, Guyana was only colonized in the early 1600s by the Dutch. Rule in the area was contested by the French and the British, and it became the colony of British Guiana in 1831. After slavery was abolished, indentured servants from the East Indies were brought to work the land, and their descendants are in the majority today.

The People's National Congress was in power from 1964–92, and socialist policies dominated the political landscape. Most of the country's large companies were nationalized, so despite its having the purest bauxite in the world, some gold, and conditions favorable to agriculture, it remains poor, dependent on foreign aid for much of its revenue.

In 1992 Cheddi Jagan of the People's Progressive party won the presidency, but his attempts to privatize the sugar and bauxite industries have failed. In March 1997 Jagan died and Samuel Hinds, the prime minister became president while Jagan's widow took over as prime minister. In the presidential elections in Dec. 1997, Mrs. Jagan won election in her own right, with 56 percent of the vote, but her appointment of Hinds to be Prime Minister did nothing to stop the rioting and demonstrations by followers of the opposition People's National Congress. The PNC represents, principally, black, while the PPP does the same for East Indians. In Aug. 1999, Jagan resigned for health reasons and was succeeded by Bharrat Jagdeo, a 35-year-old Moscow-educated economist who has been elected twice, in 2001 and 2005.

▶HAITI
Republic of Haiti
• **GEOGRAPHY Location:** western part of Hispaniola in northern Caribbean Sea. Port-au-Prince 18°33′N, 72°20′W. **Boundaries:** North Atlantic Ocean to N, Dominican Republic to E, Caribbean Sea to S, Windward Passage to W. **Total area:** 10,714 sq. mi. (27,750 sq km). **Coastline:** 1,100 mi. (1,771 km). **Comparative area:** slightly smaller than Maryland. **Land use:** 20% arable land; 13% permanent crops; 67% other. **Major cities:** Port-au-Prince (capital).
• **PEOPLE Population:** 9,035,536 (July 2009 est.). **Nationality:** noun—Haitian(s); adjective—Haitian. **Ethnic groups:** 95% black, 5% mulatto and European. **Languages:** French (official, but spoken by only 20% of population); all speak Creole. **Religions:** 80% Roman Catholic, 16% Protestant, 1% none, 3% other; note - roughly half of the population practices voodoo (called vodun).
• **GOVERNMENT Type:** republic. **Independence:** Jan. 1, 1804 (from France). **Constitution:** Mar. 1987, suspended June 1988; return to constitutional rule Oct. 1994. **National Holiday:** Independence Day, Jan. 1. **Heads of Government:** Rene Preval, President (since May 2006); Jean-Max Bellerive, prime minister (since Nov. 2009). **Structure:** executive; bicameral legislature; judiciary.
• **ECONOMY Monetary unit:** gourde. **Budget:** (2008) *income:* $820.6 mil.; *expend.:* $965.2 mil. **G.D.P.:** $11.59 bil., $1,300 per capita (2008 est.). **Chief crops:** coffee, mangoes, sugarcane, rice, corn, sorghum. **Natural resources:** bauxite, copper, calcium carbonate, gold, marble, hydropower. **Major industries:** sugar refining, textiles, flour milling. **Labor force:** 3.6 mil. (1995); 66% agriculture, 25% services, 9% industry; shortage of skilled labor, unskilled labor abundant; widespread unemployment and underemployment. **Exports:** $491 mil. (f.o.b., 2008); light manufactures, coffee, other agriculture. **Imports:** $2.095 bil. (f.o.b., 2008); machines and manufactures, food and beverages, petroleum products. **Major trading partners:** (2006) *exports:* 79.8% U.S., 7.6% Dominican Republic, 3% Canada; *imports:* 46.5% U.S., 11.9% Netherlands, 3.8% Brazil.

The Arawak island of Haiti was discovered by Christopher Columbus, who renamed it Hispaniola, in 1492. In the next century many Arawaks were worked to death or killed by disease. The western third of the island was harassed by French pirates and was ceded to France in 1697. A slave revolt in 1791 led to abolition in 1794, and the island came under French rule the same year. Toussaint Louverture, an ex-slave, became governor-general in 1801, but he was deposed by the French. In 1803 a black army under Jean-Jacques Dessalines (Emperor Jacques I, 1804–06) and Henry Christophe (Henry I, 1806–20) defeated the French in 1803. Independence was declared in 1804. Under Jean-Pierre Boyer (1820–43), Haiti occupied Santo Domingo (which had been restored to Spain in 1808) from 1822 to 1844.

The next century was marked by political instability and an increased U.S. business and military presence in Haitian affairs. From 1905 to 1947, the United States had direct or indirect control of Haitian finances, and from 1915–34 the country was under U.S. military occupation.

François "Papa Doc" Duvalier took power in 1957 and ruled Haiti with a stern hand. In 1971, he transferred power to his son, Jean-Claude (aka "Baby Doc"), whose regime was just as authoritarian. Most of Haiti's wealthy and educated population fled the country, leaving it the poorest and most illiterate nation in the Western Hemisphere.

In 1986, the military ousted Baby Doc, and imposed a succession of short-lived but brutal and incompetent governments. In 1989, Supreme Court Justice Ertha-Pascal Troillot was named interim president, and in 1990, Haiti held its first democratic national elections ever. The winner of those elections was the Rev. Jean-Bertrand Aristide, a 37-year-old Roman Catholic priest. But seven months into his five-year term, Aristide was overthrown in yet another military coup. Aristide fled to the U.S., which refused to recognize the junta and suspended aid to Haiti. But succesive trade embargoes by the U.S., Canada, and Western Europe only served to increase hardship. The junta leaders, propped up by Haiti's wealthy elite and by money from drug trafficking, began a campaign of violence against Aristide supporters, killing more than 3,000 of them.

After months of threats, the U.S. invaded on Oct. 15, 1994, forcing the junta's resignation and reinstating Aristide as president. Aristide disbanded the army, replacing it with a civilian police force. In mid-1995, Aristide's three-party coalition, Lavalas Political Organization, won overwhelming victories; in December, the Lavalas candidate, René Préval, took 88 percent in Haiti's first peaceful presidential election since independence.

By 1997 Lavalas and Pres. Préval had split. From June of that year, Haiti was without a government until Jan. 1999 when Préval announced he would rule by decree, and appointed his own prime minister. The U.S. and the U.N. ended their military mission in early 2000. Senate elections were held in May, giving 16 of 17 contested seats to Lavalas candidates. But in run-off elections held in July, opposition candidates and international observers refused to participate because of irregularities in the earlier election. In November, with the opposition and international monitors boycotting, the presidential election returned Aristide with 92 percent, while in remaining run-offs, Lavalas won all nine Senate races and took 80 percent of the Assembly votes.

In March 2001 Jean-Marie Cherestal was sworn in as prime minister, although the opposition Democratic Convergence coalition had named its own "parallel" president a month earlier. After an attack on the presidential palace by 33 gunmen was thwarted in Dec. 2001, Aristide loyalists meted out savage reprisals to opposition groups. In Feb. 2004 armed groups opposed to Aristide took control of four cities and threatened to kill Aristide (who was taken to Africa by the U.S.). Troops from four nations entered Haiti, disarmed the rebels, and a new government formed under Gerard Latortue. Elections scheduled for Oct. 2005 were cancelled by an upsurge in gang violence. In May of 2006 Rene Preval was elected president in a peaceful election overseen by U.N. troops whose presence has helped end the worst of the violence. In Jan. 2010, Haiti was rocked by a devastating earthquake that nearly destroyed Port-au-Prince and killed over 230,000 people. (See "Major News Stories.")

▶HOLY SEE
The Holy See (State of the Vatican City)

• **GEOGRAPHY Location:** entirely within city of Rome, Italy; outside Vatican City, 13 buildings in Rome and Castel Gandolfo (the pope's summer residence) enjoy extraterritorial rights. **Boundaries:** surrounded by Italian territory. **Total area:** 0.17 sq. mi. (0.44 sq km). **Coastline:** none. **Comparative area:** about seven-tenths size of the Mall in Washington, D.C. **Land use:** 0% arable land; 0% permanent crops; 100% other. **Major cities:** Vatican City (capital).

• **PEOPLE Population:** 826 (July 2009 est.). **Nationality:** N.A. **Ethnic groups:** Italians, Swiss, other. **Languages:** Italian, Latin, various other languages. **Religion:** Roman Catholic.

• **GOVERNMENT Type:** monarchical-sacerdotal state. **Independence:** Feb. 11, 1929 (from Italy). **Constitution:** Apostolic Constitution of 1967 (effective Mar. 1, 1968). **Heads of Government:** Pope Benedict XVI, chief of state (since April 2005); Cardinal Tarcisio Bertone, secretary of state (since Sept. 2006). **Structure:** pope possesses full executive, legislative, and judicial powers; he delegates these powers to president of Pontifical Commission, who is subject to pontifical appointment and recall; Secretariat of State and Council of Public Affairs (which handles Vatican diplomacy) and Prefecture of Economic Affairs; College of Cardinals acts as chief papal adviser.

• **ECONOMY Monetary unit:** euro. **Budget:** (2006 est.) *income:* $310 mil.; *expend.:* $307 mil., supported financially by contributions (known as Peter's Pence) from Roman Catholics throughout world; some income derived from sale of Vatican postage stamps and tourist mementos, fees for admission to museums, and sale of publications. **G.D.P.:** N.A. **Chief crops:** N.A. **Natural resources:** N.A. **Major industries:** consists of printing and production of small amount of mosaics and staff uniforms; worldwide banking and financial activities. **Labor force:** N.A.; dignitaries, priests, nuns, guards, and 3,000 lay workers who live outside the Vatican; Vatican City employees are divided into three categories—executives, office workers, and salaried employees. **Exports:** N.A. **Imports:** N.A. **Major trading partners:** N.A.

The Holy See is the smallest sovereign state in the world both in size and in population. It is a remnant of the "Patrimony of St. Peter," the secular state donated to the popes in the eighth century by Pepin the Short, father of Charlemagne. One of the major political powers on the Italian peninsula throughout the Middle Ages and into modern times, the States of the Church were conquered in 1870 by the new kingdom of Italy, which made Rome its capital.

In 1929 Mussolini's government made peace with the papacy in the Lateran Treaty, which recognized the Holy See as an independent state. The treaty was incorporated into the Italian Constitution of 1947. Under the terms of the treaty, the pope is pledged to perpetual neutrality and may intervene in international affairs as a mediator only upon request.

The pope is the sovereign of the Holy See in his capacity as bishop of Rome, and in that capacity, he accepts the credentials of foreign ambassadors assigned to the Holy See. The United States opened diplomatic relations with the Holy See in 1984, following the repeal of an 1867 law forbidding such relations. Pope John Paul II, a native of Poland, was a source of spiritual leadership especially for Catholics in Eastern Europe. Since the collapse of communism in Eastern Europe, many countries there have renewed diplomatic relations with the Holy See. In a historic breakthrough the Holy See established diplomatic relations with Israel on Dec. 30, 1993.

As sovereign of the Holy See, the pope is an elected absolute monarch who appoints a Pontifical Council to govern the city on his behalf. In recent years the pope and the Vatican have come under withering attacks for their belated response to the child abuse scandals in the U.S. and Europe. (See "Major News Stories.")

▶HONDURAS
Republic of Honduras

● **GEOGRAPHY Location:** Central America. **Boundaries:** Caribbean Sea to N, Nicaragua to E, El Salvador, Nicaragua to S, Guatemala, El Salvador to W. **Total area:** 43,278 sq. mi. (112,090 sq km). **Coastline:** 509 mi. (820 km). **Comparative area:** slightly larger than Tennessee. **Land use:** 15% arable land; 3% permanent crops; 82% other. **Major cities:** Tegucigalpa (capital); San Pedro Sula; El Progreso; Danli; Choluteca.

● **PEOPLE Population:** 7,792,854 (July 2009 est.). **Nationality:** noun—Honduran(s); adjective—Honduran. **Ethnic groups:** 90% mestizo, 7% Amerindian, 2% black, 1% white. **Languages:** Spanish, Amerindian dialects. **Religions:** 97% Roman Catholic, small Protestant minority.

● **GOVERNMENT Type:** democratic constitutional republic. **Independence:** Sept. 15, 1821 (from Spain). **Constitution:** Jan. 11, 1982 (effective Jan. 20, 1982); amended many times. **National holiday:** Independence Day, Sept. 15. **Head of Government:** Porfirio Lobo Sosa, president (since Jan. 2010). **Structure:** executive—elected president; unicameral legislature (128-seat National Congress); elected judicial branch.

● **ECONOMY Monetary unit:** lempira. **Budget:** (2008 est.) *income:* $2.628 bil.; *expend.:* $3.183 bil. **G.D.P.:** $33.63 bil., $4,400 per capita (2008 est.). **Chief crops:** bananas, coffee, citrus; beef; timber; shrimp. **Natural resources:** timber, gold, silver, copper, lead. **Major industries:** agricultural processing (sugar and coffee), textiles, clothing. **Labor force:** 2.892 mil. (2008); 34% agriculture, 45% services, 21% industry; 27.8% unemployment (2007). **Exports:** $6.236 bil. (f.o.b., 2008 est.); bananas, coffee, shrimp, lobster. **Imports:** $10.2 bil. (f.o.b., 2008 est.); machinery and transport equipment, chemicals, basic manufactures. **Major trading partners:** (2007) *exports:* 52% U.S., 4.9% El Salvador, 3.9% Guatemala; *imports:* 53% U.S., 7% Guatemala, 5% El Salvador, 4.5% Mexico.

Early in the Christian era, the Mayan civilization extended south to the pre-Columbian city of Copán in what is now northwestern Honduras. The territory was also home to the Lenca Indians and the indigenous people of the Moskitia area.

A silver strike in the 1570s prompted the first major influx of Spanish. The region was also celebrated for its tropical hardwood forests. Although the British controlled the Caribbean coast in the late 1700s, Honduras was a province of the Spanish captaincy of Guatemala. It became a member of the United Provinces of Central America after independence from Spain and Mexico, and an independent republic after the 1838 collapse of the Central American Federation.

Conservatives dominated Honduran politics until the 1870s, when the Liberals came to power

and adopted a new constitution that reduced the influence of the church. Economic development came especially from a number of U.S. firms whose efforts were regarded as exploitative rather than beneficial; in 1912, U.S. president William Taft sent marines to protect U.S. interests.

Political unrest continued until the presidency of Gen. Tuburcio Carías Andino (1932–49), who was followed by a succession of pro-labor presidents. In 1963, a coup led by Col. Osvaldo López Arellano deposed the civilian president, and the military ruled almost uninterrupted until 1982. In 1969, the expulsion of thousands of Salvadoran peasants who had immigrated during the 1950s and 1960s led to the Soccer War with El Salvador. An armistice was negotiated by the OAS.

During the 1980s, Honduras was threatened by civil wars in El Salvador and Nicaragua. Honduran territory was used by Nicaraguan Contras, for which Honduras received U.S. military and other aid. Demobilization of the Contras alleviated tensions between Left and Right, and in Jan. 1994 the new president, Carlos Roberto Reina Idiaquez, took office with the promise of controlling and reducing the power of the military which was more easily accomplished when the U.S. made severe cuts in military aid. In late 1997 the Liberal Party won reelection, maintaining control of the National Congress, while their candidate, Carlos Roberto Flores, won election as president.

In Oct. 1999, Honduras was devastated by Hurricane Mitch: 7,000 were dead, 600,000 homeless, and 70 percent of its crops destroyed — losses somewhat mitigated by international aid and debt reductions. In Jan. 1999, the legislature unanimously voted to place the autonomous military under civilian control. The Liberal Party was unseated in Nov. 2001 as the National Party elected only its second president since 1981, Ricardo Maduro. In 2006 he was replaced by Manuel Zelaya Rosales. In June 2009 Zelaya was forced from office by the military for attempting to hold a referendum to allow him to stay in office for another term. The OAS and the U.S. intervened saying Zelaya was the duly elected president but the military prevailed and a conservative politician, Porforio Lobo, was installed in Jan. 2010.

▶HUNGARY
Republic of Hungary

● **GEOGRAPHY Location:** landlocked country in eastern Europe. **Boundaries:** Slovakia to N, Ukraine to NE, Romania to E, Yugoslavia to SE, Croatia to SW, Slovenia to W, Austria to NW. **Total area:** 35,919 sq. mi. (93,030 sq km). **Coastline:** none. **Comparative area:** slightly smaller than Indiana. **Land use:** 52% arable land; 3% permanent crops; 45% other. **Major cities:** Budapest (capital); Debrecen; Miskolc; Szeged; Pécs.

● **PEOPLE Population:** 9,880,059 (July 2010 est.). **Nationality:** noun—Hungarian(s); adjective—Hungarian. **Ethnic groups:** 92.3% Hungarian, 1.9% Roma, 5.8% other or unknown. **Languages:** 93.6% Hungarian, 6.4% other. **Religions:** 51.9% Roman Catholic, 15.9% Calvinist, 3% Lutheran, 3.6% other Christian, 14.5% unaffiliated.

● **GOVERNMENT Type:** parliamentary democracy. **Constitution:** Aug. 18, 1949; effective Aug. 20, 1949; revised Oct. 18, 1989; 1997 amendment streamlined judicial system. **National holiday:** St. Stephen's Day, Aug. 20. **Heads of Government:** László Sólyom, president (since Aug 2005); Viktor Orban, prime minister (May 2010). **Structure:** executive—president elected by National Assembly; unicameral legislature—National Assembly (elected by direct suffrage); judicial—elected by Parliament.

• ECONOMY   Monetary unit: forint. **Budget:** (2009 est.) *income:* $44.1 bil.; *expend.:* $44.8 bil. **G.D.P:** $184.9 bil., $18,600 per capita (2009 est.) **Chief crops:** corn, wheat, sunflower seeds, potatoes, sugar beets; chickens, pigs, cattle. **Natural resources:** bauxite, coal, natural gas, fertile soils. **Major industries:** mining, metallurgy, construction materials. **Labor force:** 3.8 mil. (2010); 63% services; 32.4% industry; 5% agriculture; 7.1% unemployment (2008). **Exports:** $83.34 bil. (2009 est.); 57.6% machinery and equipment, 31.0% other manufactures, 7.5% agriculture and food products. **Imports:** $76.89 bil. (2009 est.); 51% machinery and equipment, 35.3% other manufactures, 8.2% fuels and electricity, 2.9% agricultural and food products, 2.0% raw materials. **Major trading partners:** (2008) *exports:* 25.4% Germany, 5.2% Italy, 5.1% Romania, 4.7% Austria, 4.5% Taiwan, 4.5% Slovakia, 4.5% France; *imports:* 24.6% Germany, 8.7% Russia, 7.2% China, 6% Austria, 4.9% Taiwan, 4.4% Netherlands, 4.2% France, 4.1% Italy.

The Magyars, a tribe of Central Asian horsemen, terrorized Europe in the ninth century A.D. and settled in the Hungarian plain where, under their chieftain Arpad, they displaced earlier Germanic and Slavic settlers and organized a kingdom in 896. The Hungarians converted to Christianity late in the 10th century, and King Stephen (later St. Stephen) received a royal crown from Pope Sylvester II in 1001.

After the Battle of Mohacs in 1526, most of Hungary fell under Ottoman rule. The Turks were driven out in a series of battles with the Habsburg Holy Roman emperors at the end of the 17th century. Thereafter Hungary was part of the Habsburg Empire until 1867, when the Dual Monarchy of Austria-Hungary was organized, making Hungary independent of Austria in all but finance, the military, and foreign affairs.

During the 18th and 19th centuries, Hungary experienced extensive immigration of Romanians and Slovaks; by 1900 Magyars formed only a bare majority of the population. The pre-World War I economy was largely agricultural. Agriculture-related industry (beet sugar factories, breweries, tanneries, textile mills) developed in the late 19th century, along with some heavy industry.

In the dismemberment of Austria-Hungary following the defeat of the Central Powers in World War I, Hungary surrendered extensive territories to Romania, Yugoslavia, and Czechoslovakia. With the Treaty of Trianon ("Bloody Trianon") in 1920, the country lost 70 percent of its territory and 60 percent of its population.

Short-lived governments—a republic under Michael Karolyi, and a Bolshevist state under Bela Kun—were replaced in 1920 by a new regime, with Adm. Miklós Horthy serving as regent. The Horthy regime was authoritarian but not fascist; its main objective was the recovery of Hungary's lost territories. Hungary established common cause with Germany in 1938 and 1940, recovering some territory from Czechoslovakia and Romania in the bargain, but at the price of participating in Hitler's war with the Soviet Union. Germany occupied Hungary in 1944 and set up a Hungarian Nazi regime. Late in 1944 the Russian army drove out the Germans and set up their own occupation.

The establishment of a full-scale Soviet-satellite regime was relatively slow. A republic was declared in February 1946, and the non-Communist Zoltan Tildy was elected president. Tildy was forced out in 1947, however, and replaced by the Stalinist dictator, Matias Rakosi. After the death of Stalin in 1953, the moderate Imre Nagy became premier and introduced some economic reforms. Nagy was forced out of office in 1955.

Nikita Khrushchev's denunciation of Stalin in 1956, combined with rising expectations for reforms in Hungary, led to a popular uprising in October 1956. Nagy, backed by the army, formed a coalition government on Oct. 23, proclaimed Hungary's neutrality, ended censorship, opened the borders, and withdrew from the Warsaw Pact. On Nov. 4, Soviet troops launched a massive invasion that crushed the rebellion. The Soviet army installed János Kádár as premier; Nagy was executed. About 200,000 Hungarians fled the country, and many more were imprisoned.

After several years of repressive rule, the Kádár regime announced, in 1963, amnesty for participants in the 1956 rebellion. Stalinists were gradually removed from the government, economic reforms emphasizing profit and productivity were introduced, and trade with the West was expanded. Hungary reluctantly took part in the suppression of Czechoslovakia's "Prague Spring" in 1968. In the same year, it announced the New Economic Mechanism (NEM) policy, ending central economic planning and introducing semifree enterprise under bureaucratic control. In 1982, Hungary joined the World Bank and the I.M.F. Private ownership of subsidiaries of state-owned enterprises was permitted. In 1987 a pro-Gorbachev premier, Karoly Grosz, took office and in 1988 became head of the Communist party as well.

In 1989 the boundary with Austria was opened, making Hungary a key escape point for refugees from East Germany and Czechoslovakia. Nagy's reburial was attended by 300,000. Free elections were held in 1990, and the Democratic Forum, led by Jozsef Antall, won a plurality and formed a coalition government with the Smallholders and Christian Democratic parties. Having already achieved substantial perestroika-style economic reforms under communism, Hungary was well-placed to make a rapid transition to free enterprise and was seeking admission to the E.U.

Hungarian voters signaled just how painful they found the transition in the 1994 parliamentary elections by giving the Socialists an absolute majority in parliament. Privatization moved at a snail's pace, though the new government did appoint a committee to arrange the selling off of about 1,000 state-owned enterprises and soon foreign investment increased faster than anywhere in Central Europe. In 1997 Hungary was one of three eastern European nations invited to apply for admission to NATO and it was admitted in 1999.

Elections in 1998 gave the Socialists only 134 seats (of 386) in Parliament; the new government was formed by Civic Party which won 148 seats of its own, in coalition with the Smallholders and other parties of the right. The 2002 elections returned the Socialists (in coalition with the Free Democrats) to power, toppling the government of Viktor Orban and replacing him with Peter Medgyessy. In a 2003 referendum voters gave 84 percent approval to joining the E.U. In 2004 a business leader, Ferenc Gyurcsány succeeded

Medgyessy and was elected again in 2006. Shortly thereafter, political upheaval followed a tape recording of Gyurcsány saying privately that he and his government had lied about the nation's massive debt (10 percent of G.D.P.). In late 2008 the I.M.F. provided $25 bil. in emergency financing. Gyurcsány resigned in March 2009 and was succeeded by Gordon Majnac, who lost a year later to Viktor Orban.

▶ **ICELAND**
Republic of Iceland
• **GEOGRAPHY Location:** near Arctic Circle in North Atlantic Ocean. Reykjavík 64°09'N, 21°58'W. **Boundaries:** Greenland about 190 mi. (300 km) to NW, Norway about 620 mi. (1,000 km) to E, U.K. 500 mi. (800 km) to S. **Total area:** 39,768 sq. mi. (103,000 sq km). **Coastline:** 3,100 mi. (4,988 km). **Comparative area:** slightly smaller than Kentucky. **Land use:** 1% arable land; 0% permanent crops; 99% other. **Major cities:** Reykjavík (capital). • **PEOPLE Population:** 306,694 (July 2009 est.). **Nationality:** noun—Icelander(s); adjective—Icelandic. **Ethnic groups:** 94% homogeneous mixture of descendants of Norwegians and Celts, 6% of foreign origin. **Languages:** Icelandic (official), English, Nordic languages, German widely spoken. **Religions:** 85.5% Lutheran Church of Iceland, 2.1% Reykjavik Free Church, 2% Roman Catholic, 8% other, 2.4% unaffiliated. • **GOVERNMENT Type:** constitutional republic. **Independence:** June 17, 1944 (from Denmark). **Constitution:** June 16, 1944; effective June 17, 1944. **National holiday:** Anniversary of the Establishment of the Republic, June 17. **Heads of Government:** Ólafur Ragnar Grímsson, president (since Aug. 1996); Johanna Sigurdardottir, prime minister (since Feb. 2009). **Structure:** executive power vested in president but exercised by cabinet responsible to Parliament; unicameral legislature; judiciary (Supreme Court justices appointed for life by president). • **ECONOMY Monetary unit:** Icelandic króna. **Budget:** (2008 est.) *income:* $7.582 bil.; *expend.:* $7.159 bil. **G.D.P.:** $12.15 bil., $39,900 per capita (2008 est.). **Chief crops:** potatoes, turnips; cattle, sheep; fish. **Natural resources:** fish, hydroelectric and geothermal power, diatomite. **Major industries:** fish processing, aluminum smelting, ferrosilicon production. **Labor force:** 166,000 (2008); 71.8% services, 23% industry, 5.1% agriculture (2005); 1% unemployment (2007). **Exports:** $6.846 bil. (f.o.b. 2008); 70% fish and fish products, animal products, aluminum, ferrosilicon, diatomite. **Imports:** $6.543 bil. (f.o.b., 2008); machinery and equipment, petroleum products, foodstuffs, textiles. **Major trading partners:** (2006) *exports:* 16.5% Netherlands, 15.7% U.K., 15% Germany, 10.8% U.S., 6.4% Spain; *imports:* 12.8% U.S., 12.3% Germany, 7.1% Norway, 6.9% Sweden, 61% Denmark, 5.3% U.K., 5.3% China, 4.8% Netherlands, 4.1% Japan.

The volcanic island of Iceland was settled in the ninth century A.D. by Vikings, who established Europe's oldest body of representative government, the Althing, in 930. Christianity was introduced around 1000. In the 13th century, Iceland acknowledged Norwegian rule. In 1380 Denmark, by then in control of all of Scandinavia, conquered Iceland as well. Iceland gained its independence in 1918 but shared a common king, Christian X, with the Danes. During World War II, first British, and then American, troops garrisoned the island; in 1944, with Denmark occupied by the Nazis, Iceland deposed its king and proclaimed itself a republic.

Iceland became a U.N. member in 1946 and a member of NATO in 1949. Lacking its own armed forces, it grudgingly tolerated the presence of an American air base at Keflavik. The republic developed a Scandinavian-style welfare state, with comprehensive social benefits that have produced one of the world's healthiest and best-educated peoples.

Multiparty representation in the Althing has created a trend of government by coalitions or minority cabinets. Politically stable, the republic recently faced economic problems brought on by high taxes, chronic inflation, and a huge national debt. In 1997 and 1998, however, the economy made a strong recovery with G.D.P. growing by 5 percent a year and continuing over a decade.

Iceland maintains close ties with Scandinavia and actively participates in the Nordic Council, but not the E.U., membership in which the government views as harmful to Iceland's all-important fishing industry. In 2006 commercial whaling was resumed. The financial crisis hit Iceland especially hard and its banking system failed in late 2008 leading to a collapse of its currency (the krona) and the fall of its government in January 2009 after a huge demonstration. A center-left government led by Social Democrat Johanna Sigurdardottir, whose party then won the parliamentary elections in April, took power. Although the new government pledged to repay the nation's debts to foreign investors, 92 percent rejected the idea in a 2010 referendum. In April 2010 an ancient volcano under a glacier exploded, spreading ash for thousands of miles and disrupting air traffic in Europe for weeks. (See "Major News Stories.")

▶ **INDIA**
Republic of India
• **GEOGRAPHY Location:** Asian subcontinent, with Himalayan mountain range to N. **Boundaries:** Pakistan to NW; China, Bhutan, Nepal to N; Myanmar to NE; Bangladesh to E (surrounded by Indian territory except for short frontier with Myanmar); Bay of Bengal to E; Sri Lanka to SE across Palk Strait; Arabian Sea to W. **Total area:** 1,269,340 sq. mi. (3,287,590 sq km). **Coastline:** 4,350 mi. (7,000 km). **Comparative area:** slightly more than one-third the size of U.S. **Land use:** 48.8% arable land; 3% permanent crops; 48% other. **Major cities:** New Delhi (capital); Mumbai (Greater Bombay); Calcutta; Madras; Hyderabad. • **PEOPLE Population:** 1,173,108,018 (July 2010 est.). **Nationality:** noun—Indian(s); adjective—Indian. **Ethnic groups:** 72% Indo-Aryan, 25% Dravidian, 3% Mongoloid and other. **Languages:** Hindi, English, and 14 other official languages; 24 languages spoken by a million or more persons each; numerous other languages and dialects; Hindi is national language and primary tongue of 30% of the people; English enjoys associate status but is the most important language for national, political, and commercial communication; Hindustani, a variant of Hindi/Urdu, is spoken throughout northern India. **Religions:** 80.5% Hindu, 13.4% Muslim, 2.3% Christian, 1.9% Sikh. • **GOVERNMENT Type:** federal republic. **Independence:** Aug. 15, 1947 (from U.K.). **Constitution:** Jan. 26, 1950. **National holiday:** Anniversary of the Proclamation of the Republic, Jan. 26. **Heads of Government:** Pratibha Patil, president (since

July 2007); Manmohan Singh, prime minister (since May 2004). **Structure:** executive; bicameral parliament—Council of States, 250 members, up to 12 appointed by pres., remainder chosen by regionally elected officials; judiciary.

• ECONOMY   **Monetary unit:** Indian rupee. **Budget:** (2009 est.) *income:* $129.9 bil.; *expend.:* $237.2 bil. **G.D.P.:** $3.56 trillion, $3,100 per capita (2009 est.). **Chief crops:** rice, wheat, oilseed, cotton; cattle, water, buffalo, sheep; fish. **Natural resources:** coal (4th largest reserves in world), iron ore, manganese, mica, bauxite. **Major industries:** textiles, chemicals, food processing, steel. **Labor force:** 467 mil. (2009 est.); 52% agriculture, 34% services, 14% industry (2009 est.). **Exports:** $165 bil. (2009 est.); clothing, gems and jewelry, engineering goods, chemicals. **Imports:** $253.9 bil. (2009 est.); petroleum, machinery, gems, fertilizer. **Major trading partners:** (2008) *exports:* 12.3% U.A.E.,11.7% U.S., 5.4% China, 4.5% Singapore; *imports:* 10.8% China, 6.9% Saudi Arabia, 6.7% U.S., 6.7% U.A.E.

Indian civilization is one of the oldest in the world. Neolithic agricultural communities had appeared in the Indus River valley by 3000 B.C. and cities at Harappa and Mohenjo-Daro were founded around 2500 B.C. Around 1500 B.C. Indo-Europeans (Aryans) from Central Asia imposed their religion and political system on the indigenous population and generated population movements toward southern India.

Indo-European civilization was characterized by caste; everyone was a member of one of four fundamental divisions of society: Brahmins, hereditary priests responsible for higher learning and rituals; Ksatrias, warriors and administrators; Vaisas, merchants; and Sudras, farmers and subjugated peoples. At the bottom were casteless people, known later as untouchables.

By the mid-first millennium B.C., Brahminism had declined into a state of religious formalism. That situation prompted two reformations around 600 B.C., the first of which produced the Jain religion; the second, Buddhism. Jainism remained confined largely to India, while Buddhism eventually influenced most of the cultures of Asia, though it died out in India itself. Buddhism was adopted as a state religion by Asoka, third and greatest emperor of the Mauryan empire (325–184 b.c) under which much of India was united for the first time. Following the collapse of the Mauryan empire, Hinduism evolved out of Buddhism, Brahminism, and other local cults and became the dominant religion of India.

South India in the post-Mauryan period was divided into numerous states, the most prominent of which was Chola, a Tamil kingdom in the southeast that had extensive trade connections throughout the Indian Ocean.

The Gupta dynasty (c. A.D. 320–544), based in the Ganges River valley, established its rule over most of northern India and created what is generally regarded as a golden age of north Indian culture, with flourishing cities and significant achievements in art, literature, and science.

In the seventh century, King Sri Harsha created a short-lived feudal empire that united most of the petty states in the upper Ganges valley, while the Chalyuka dynasty dominated southern India. In the early eighth century, the Indus River valley was invaded by Arabs who introduced Islam to the region. The empire of Sri Harsha fell apart, replaced by the petty kingdoms of the Rajputs.

The 11th century saw the ascendency of Islam throughout northern India, which came under the shadow of the empire of Mamud of Ghazni, based in Afghanistan. In 1192 the Ghaznavid general Kutb ud-din Aibak defeated a coalition of Rajput states; in 1206 he founded the Sultanate of Delhi, which in the 13th century held off Mongol invasions and brought all of the subcontinent, except for the southernmost states, under its control. While the rulers of the sultanate were Muslims, most of their subjects remained Hindu.

Internal rebellions combined with the sacking of Delhi by Timur Leng (Tamerlane) in 1398 weakened the Sultanate of Delhi. In 1526 Babur, a descendant of Timur Leng, conquered all of northern India and established the Moghul empire. Under Akbar the Great, the empire flourished; Moghul culture gave rise to new styles of architecture, painting, and music.

In the 17th century, the Moghul emperors were threatened by the Hindu Marathas, whose kingdom on the west-central coast rapidly encompassed most of south India. By the late 18th century, Maratha power had spread to the north, and most of the petty kingdoms of the Moghul empire became part of a Maratha confederacy, owing only nominal allegiance to Delhi. By that time all of India was threatened by the expansion of the European powers. Vasco da Gama had landed at Calicut in 1498, and in 1510 the Portuguese founded a colony at Goa. Dutch traders competed with the Portuguese during the 16th century, and British and French merchants followed in the 17th century. British trading stations were established at Surat (1612), Bombay (1661), and Calcutta (1690).

In the mid-18th century, war broke out between British and French forces in India, and the French were confined to a few small enclaves. The growing instability of the Moghul empire in the face of Marathan and Rajput revolts and the expansion of the southern kingdom of Mysore encouraged the British to seek further control of Indian territory. Robert Clive's victory at Plassey in 1757 brought Orissa, Bihar, and Bengal under British control; British rule was extended to the upper Ganges in 1775. Victory over the maharaja of Mysore in 1792 paved the way for British control over the south.

British parliamentary acts of 1773 and 1784 placed these acquisitions firmly under government control, and in 1803 the Moghul emperor accepted the offer of a protectorate, and British suzerainty in India was assured. After a protracted war, 1812–23, Marathan resistance to British control was broken. The first Anglo-Afghan War, 1838–42, was inconclusive in Afghanistan but led to consolidation of British control of the Punjab.

In 1833 Parliament assumed political control of British interests in South Asia, while private merchants had unrestricted access to the economy. Plantation crops, such as opium and cotton, began to displace agriculture, which made India more dependent on imported goods.

In 1857 Indian troops in the British colonial forces staged a mutiny that lasted 14 months. In 1858 the Moghul empire was dissolved, as was the East India Company. The government of India was made directly subject to the British Crown, which exercised control through a viceroy and through the British Colonial Office. Queen Victoria was crowned empress of India in 1877.

British sovereignty in India—the raj—was a patchwork of direct and indirect rule. In general, coastal areas, river valleys, and strategic frontier regions were ruled by British authorities, while interior states continued as British protectorates controlled by British advisers to native princes. In 1861 Indians were appointed to advisory councils of the viceroy and provincial governors.

The Indian National Congress was organized in 1885. In the wake of popular demonstrations in 1905, elections were instituted to choose Indian members of the viceroy's legislative council. Separate electorates were created for the Muslim and Hindu communities, formalizing a divisive force in Indian politics and weakening opposition to British rule. In 1914, with Chinese loss of control in Tibet, India's northern boundary was pushed forward to the McMahon Line, following the highest peaks in the Himalayas. This set the stage for numerous later boundary disputes between China and India, Pakistan, and Burma.

The Government of India Act of 1919 transferred some political power to elected provincial officials but left the appointed British governors firmly in control. In that year Mohandas K. Gandhi organized the first passive-resistance campaigns and was imprisoned. In 1935 the Government of India Act created elected provincial legislatures. In the first elections (1937) the Congress party under Jawaharlal Nehru won control of seven of the 11 provinces. Nehru's goal of a united Indian opposition to British rule was thwarted by Mohammed Ali Jinnah's Muslim League, which demanded the creation of a separate Muslim state.

During World War II, the British military position in South Asia was complicated by calls for Indian independence. An offer of local autonomy, with independence to follow, was spurned by Nehru, and an Indian National army under Subhas Bose fought with the Japanese. Jinnah's call for an independent Pakistan was greatly enhanced by his support of the British.

In 1947, the British raj became two independent nations, predominantly Hindu India and predominantly Muslim Pakistan. Despite its considerable stature in the international community at large, India has been troubled by a number of disputes with its neighbors and separatist movements within its own borders. Following independence, hundreds of semiautonomous princely states were brought under control of the central government. The French ceded their remaining trading colonies in the 1950s, and Portugal gave up Goa in 1961. In 1962, India warred with China in a still unresolved dispute over their border along Kashmir and Assam. The state of Bhutan was granted independence in 1971, and in 1974 Sikkim was annexed and its monarchy abolished.

India's most intractable disputes have been with Pakistan. Immediately after independence, Hindus in Pakistan and Muslims in India were set upon by the majority populations; hundreds of thousands were killed, and at least 12 million refugees fled over the border in both directions. On Jan. 30, 1948, Gandhi was assassinated by a Hindu extremist who blamed him for partition.

In granting independence, Britain had divided states of Bengal and Punjab between the two countries, but fighting erupted over the status of Jammu and Kashmir, and a cease-fire line negotiated by the U.N. in 1949 has never been ratified as a formal national boundary. In 1989, separatists in the Indian part of Kashmir began calling for an end to Indian rule, and relations with Pakistan have worsened as India accused its neighbor of providing support for the guerrillas. In 1971, after 10 million refugees poured across its border, India intervened in the Pakistani civil war in an action that prompted an almost immediate cease-fire and the creation of an independent Bangladesh.

India's main separatist movement involves Sikhs in the Punjab who seek the formation of an independent state of Khalistan, but who are thought to be supported by Pakistan. The government is also contending with separatist movements in the northeastern states of Assam.

The British legacy in India included a sizable national elite, well educated and committed to principles of parliamentary democracy. The English language linked the elites of India's linguistically diverse regions, easing minorities' fears of domination by a Hindi-speaking majority. India's economy had seen some industrial development under the British, but its infrastructure was geared to integration in a colonial empire rather than to independence. Port cities, heavy industry, and plantation agriculture coexisted with widespread rural poverty and the years following independence saw a massive migration of the rural poor into overburdened cities.

Under Prime Minister Jawaharlal Nehru, India assumed a leadership role in the world movement of nonaligned nations and followed a policy of neutrality in international affairs. The development of good relations between the United States and Pakistan led to correspondingly difficult U.S.-India relations. In August 1971 India signed a 20-year friendship treaty with the Soviet Union.

Nehru died on May 27, 1964, and was succeeded by Lal Bahadur Shastri. Nehru's daughter, Mrs. Indira Gandhi, was named prime minister on Jan. 19, 1966. In 1967 the dominant Congress party faced electoral setbacks; in 1969 it split into "Old" and "New" wings. Mrs. Gandhi's New Congress party won control of the legislature.

Faced with protests and strikes after the New Congress party was convicted of voting irregularities in 1975, Mrs. Gandhi declared a state of emergency in June; censorship was imposed, thousands were arrested for political offenses, and various economic-control measures were adopted. An opposition coalition led by the Janata Dal party won a massive victory in parliamentary elections in 1977. Mrs. Gandhi was driven from office, and the state of emergency was annulled. Mrs. Gandhi's party was returned to power in 1980, and she resumed the prime ministership. After an army attack on the Sikhs' Golden Temple in Amritsar, Gandhi was assassinated by Sikh bodyguards in October 1984. She was succeeded in office by her son, Rajiv, who placed the Punjab under direct control of the federal government.

On Dec. 3, 1984, methyl isocyanate gas leaked from a Union Carbide plant in Bhopal, killing over 2,500 people. The accident prompted a broad inquiry into industrial safety standards in India. In 1989, Rajiv Gandhi's Congress party was voted out of office after people close to the government were accused of taking kickbacks in a government purchase scandal. Gandhi was succeeded by V.P. Singh of the Janata Dal party, whose government collapsed after 11 months over a dispute involving Hindu plans to build a temple on the site of a mosque in Ayodhya. (Hindus contend the mosque was built on the site of Rama's birthplace.) Middle-class Hindus also protested an affirmative action policy to set aside federal jobs for members of lower castes.

Singh was followed by Chandra Shekhar, whose minority government served only with the backing of the Congress party. After a parliamentary boycott by the Congress party instigated by Rajiv Gandhi, Shekhar quit the government in March 1991, agreeing to stay on as a caretaker until the May election. The election, postponed two weeks following the assassination of Gandhi, was won by the Congress party, and P.V. Narasimha Rao became prime minister. The Rao government attempted to foster economic growth by relaxing the centralized planning and controls on international trade and investment.

A rise in Hindu extremist feeling, however, strengthened the hand of the opposition Bharatiya Janata party. On Dec. 6, 1992, a Hindu mob demolished the mosque in the city of Ayodhya; in the ensuing turmoil, riots broke out in dozens of cities, most notably Bombay, leading to the deaths of hundreds of Muslims at the hands of Hindu attackers. A series of bomb explosions killed hundreds in Bombay on Mar. 12, 1993, while dozens more were killed by an explosion in Calcutta four days later. Further riots followed, amid unsubstantiated accusations that Muslims, aided by Pakistan, were responsible for the explosions. In 1993 separatist movements in Punjab and Assam waned, but violence in Kashmir and Jammu increased dramatically.

The Rao government's economic policies produced good results, but as India's economy strengthened its political stability weakened. The Congress Party continued to lose power to the Hindu Baratiya Janata Party. Congress was defeated in parliamentary elections in May 1996, ushering in an era of short-lived, weak coalition governments under Pres. K. R. Narayanan. Inder Kumer Gurjal formed a government in April, 1997 that fell in November. The BJP won a plurality of seats in March 1998 elections, but, to govern (under Prime Minister Vajapyee) required a 19-party coalition. Fragile authority need not exclude vigorous policy: it was the BJP coalition that carried out underground tests of five nuclear devices in May, vigorously asserted India's claims in Kashmir, and cut food subsidies as a means of reducing the deficit. It was the latter that dislodged the coalition and in April 1999, Pres. Narayanan dissolved the Lok Sabha, preparatory to India's third election campaign in three years. Perhaps sensing weakness, Muslim insurgents launched attacks against Indian forces in Kashmir. But India retaliated forcefully and peace was restored in July, although India continued to blame Pakistan for the violence. In the election results, the National Democratic Alliance, a 24-party coalition led by the Bharatiya Janata Party, won an absolute majority; so, for the first time in 27 years, an incumbent prime minister won re-election.

On Dec. 13, 2001 an attack on the Parliament in New Delhi by five Pakistan-based terrorists greatly heightened existing tensions between the two countries. While Hindu mobs killed Muslims in Gujarat, Muslim attacks continued, though at a diminished rate in 2002, in Jammu-Kashmir. Upwards of a million troops stood poised on the border with almost daily artillery exchanges. Several terrorist attacks in Kashmir led to U.S. and British diplomatic intervention that eased tensions considerably during 2003. By 2004 serious talks on all issues (including terrorism, nuclear security, and trade) were occuring regularly. In the legislative election a startling victory for the United Progressive Alliance ousted the BJP and brought Manniohan Singh, a Sikh, to the head of the minority government. In 2005 the U.S. formally agreed to provide India with nuclear power expertise despite the presence of nuclear weapons. Singh and the Congress Party won a decisive victory in 2009.

India has enjoyed significant domestic and international achievements in the first half-century after independence. The nation's territory was consolidated, and separatist movements in various provinces successfully resisted. The federal parliamentary system has proved workable, and the federal government has established its constitutional right to intervene in state affairs under some conditions. India's armed forces are large, well trained, and well equipped, with nuclear capability. India has maintained watchful, but generally peaceful, relations with two unfriendly neighbors, Pakistan and China. The Green Revolution of the 1970s made the country self-sufficient in food for the first time since the 19th century. The economy has been growing steadily since 2000 as the computer and Internet revolution has provided a huge number of jobs for India's educated middle class. But poverty remains a persistent and serious problem as does the struggle with Pakistan. In November 2008, 10 terrorists based in Pakistan attacked the city of Mumbai, killing 100 people in the train station, a movie theater, and upscale hotels.

▶INDONESIA
Republic of Indonesia
• **GEOGRAPHY** **Location:** archipelago of about 18,108 islands stretching from Malay peninsula to New Guinea between mainland of Southeast Asia and Australia. Jakarta 6°08'S, 106°45'E. **Boundaries:** land borders with Papua New Guinea, to E of Irian Jaya, and with Malaysian states of Sarawak and Sabah in northern Borneo. **Total area:** 741,097 sq. mi. (1,919,440 sq km). **Coastline:** 34,006 mi. (54,716 km). **Comparative area:** slightly less than three times the size of Texas. **Land use:** 10% arable land; 7% permanent crops; 783% other. **Major cities:** Jakarta (capital); Surabaya; Bandung; Medan; Semarang.
• **PEOPLE** **Population:** 242,968,342 (July 2010 est.). **Nationality:** noun—Indonesian(s); adjective—Indonesian. **Ethnic groups:** 45% Javanese, 14% Sundanese, 7.5% Madurese, 7.5% coastal Malays. **Languages:** Bahasa Indonesia (modified form of Malay; official); English and Dutch, leading foreign languages; local dialects, most widely spoken of which is Javanese. **Religions:** 86.1% Muslim, 5.7% Protestant, 3% Roman Catholic, 1.8% Hindu, 3.4% other and unspecified.
• **GOVERNMENT** **Type:** republic. **Independence:** Aug. 17, 1945 (declared) Dec. 27, 1949 recognized (from Netherlands). **Constitution:** Aug. 1945, abrogated by Federal Constitution of 1949 and Provisional Constitution of 1950, restored July 5, 1959. **National holiday:** Independence Day, Aug. 17. **Head of Government:** Susilo Bambang Yudhoyono, president (since Sept. 2004). **Structure:** executive—headed by president who is chief of state and head of cabinet; cabinet selected by president; unicameral legislature (DPR, or House of Representatives) of 500 members (100 appointed, 400 elected); second body (MPR, or People's Consultative Assembly) of 1,000 members includes legislature and 500 other members (cho-

sen by several processes but not directly elected); judicial—Supreme Court Judges appointed by president.

• **ECONOMY** **Monetary unit:** Indonesian rupiah. **Budget:** (2009 est.) *income:* $83.77 bil.; *expend.:* $97.24 bil. **G.D.P.:** $969.2 bil., $4,000 per capita (2009 est.). **Chief crops:** rice, cassava, peanuts, rubber, cocoa; poultry, pork, beef. **Natural resources:** crude oil, tin, natural gas, nickel, timber. **Major industries:** petroleum and natural gas, textiles, mining. **Labor force:** 113.3 mil. (2009 est.); 42.1% agriculture, 39.3% services, 18.6% industry (2006 est.); 8.4% unemployment (2007 est.). **Exports:** $115.6 bil. (2009 est.); textiles/garments, gas, plywood, rubber. **Imports:** $86.6 bil. (2009 est.); manufactures, chemicals, foodstuffs, fuels. **Major trading partners:** (2008) *exports:* 20.2% Japan, 9.5% U.S., 9.4% Singapore, 8.5% China, 6.7% South Korea, 5.2% India; *imports:* 16.9% Singapore, 11.8% China, 11.7% Japan, 6.9% Malaysia, 6.1% U.S.

The precolonial East Indies consisted of several Islamic and Hindu kingdoms in the western islands and tribal societies in the easterly ones. The Portuguese established trading posts in the 16th century; by the 17th century, control had largely passed to the Dutch East India Company. With the company's bankruptcy in 1799, the Dutch established direct colonial rule. Several 19th-century anticolonial uprisings, though costly to the Dutch, failed to dislodge them. Nationalist sentiment grew in the early 20th century, organized around Islamic groups, the Indonesian Communist party (PKI, founded 1920), and the Indonesian Nationalist party (PNI, founded 1927). Sukarno, founder of the PNI, achieved prominence as a nationalist leader and was jailed by the Dutch.

The Dutch East Indies fell quickly to the Japanese early in 1942. On Aug. 17, 1945, Sukarno proclaimed Indonesia's independence. With British aid, the Dutch returned and tried to reestablish colonial rule; in 1949, threatened with a cutoff of American Marshall Plan aid, they withdrew and acknowledged Indonesia's independent status. Under Sukarno Indonesia took a leading role in international affairs among the nonaligned nations of the Third World.

In 1963 Indonesia gained control of the last Dutch outpost in the Indies, Irian Jaya (western New Guinea). Sukarno's politics moved steadily to the left, and Indonesia became hostile to the West and friendly with China. The influence of the PKI grew steadily. On Sept. 30, 1965, the army crushed an attempted coup by the PKI, setting off a popular reaction in which several hundred thousand people were killed as suspected Communists. Sukarno was shunted aside, and power devolved to Gen. Suharto, who became president in 1968. The PKI was banned, and Indonesian policy swung sharply in favor of the West.

The economy grew rapidly, aided by oil revenue, timber exports to Japan, and the Green Revolution in rice agriculture. A policy of "transmigration" attempted, with mixed success, to move farmers from overcrowded Java and Bali to underdeveloped areas in Sumatra, Borneo, Sulawesi, and Irian Jaya. In 1975 Indonesia invaded the former Portuguese colony of East Timor, which was annexed in 1976. More than 100,000 East Timorese were killed and the annexation was never recognized internationally.

In the early 1990s declining oil revenues were partly offset by the growth of industry and tour-

ism. Pres. Suharto remained in power, at the head of the Golkar united-front party, and was reelected president for a fifth term in 1993. Despite the most violent campaign in Indonesia's history, the ruling Golkar Party was returned to power with nearly 75 percent of the vote in 1997. But Suharto's regime faced serious problems, including continuing unrest in East Timor and rising public dissatisfaction with the alleged corruption of Suharto's family and close associates. The economy boomed but in 1998 the financial crisis that swept through Asia revealed the hollowness of the Indonesian approach. Strikes, protests, and riots forced Suharto to resign in May and his trusted aide, Vice-Pres. Habibie took power promising reforms and new elections in 1999. Habibie began reforming the banking system, initiated inquiries into Suharto family wealth, and agreed with Portugal to hold a referendum on the status of East Timor. Elections were held in June 1999 with Golkar taking about 25 percent of the votes; an anti-Golkar coalition headed by Sukarno's daughter, Megawati Sukarnoputri, held a plurality. The people of East Timor voted overwhelmingly for independence from Indonesia, leading to violent attacks by militia groups and the sending of U.N. troops.

The Assembly approved the East Timor referendum and elected, not Megawati, but ailing Moslem cleric Abdurrahman Wahid as president, with Megawati as vice president. Under attack for his bumbling governance in a time of crisis, Wahid turned over day-to-day management to Megawati in mid-2000. On July 23, 2001 Wahid was formally impeached and replaced by Megawati. In Feb. 2002 a fragile peace was brokered in the Moluccas between Muslims and Christians. On May 20, East Timor became independent for the first time in 500 years.

In August 2002, the People's Consultative Assembly amended the constitution and established direct election of the president and abolished the military's 38 seats in Parliament. In Oct. terrorists linked to Al Qaeda bombed a Bali nightclub killing 180. In Dec. talks in Geneva with the separatist rebels in Aceh province appeared to have reached success; but in May, 2003 Pres. Megawati declared martial law in Aceh and another army offensive began against the rebels who were driven into the mountains. But serious fighting between Christians and Muslims broke out again in April 2004 in the Moluccas. In July elections Megawati finished second to Suseilo Bamband Yudoyono and lost to him in a run off. A devastating tsunami in Dec. 2004 claimed the lives of more than 100,000 Indonesian people and helped bring about a formal peace treaty with Aceh's rebels in Aug. 2005. Unfortunately another tsunami, an earthquake, and flooding followed in 2006–07, setting the economy back severely. In 2009 President Yudoyono was reelected with 16 percent of the vote, just several months after his party had won the legislative election.

▶ **IRAN**
Islamic Republic of Iran
• **GEOGRAPHY** **Location:** western Asia. **Boundaries:** Armenia and Azerbaijan to N, Caspian Sea and Turkmenistan to NE, Pakistan and Afghanistan to E, Persian (Arabian) Gulf and Gulf of Oman to S, and Turkey and Iraq to W. **Total area:** 636,294 sq. mi. (1,648,000 sq km). **Coastline:** 1,516 mi. (2,440 km); Iran also borders the

Caspian Sea (740 km). **Comparative area**: slightly smaller than Alaska. **Land use**: 10% arable land; 1% permanent crops; 89% other. **Major cities**: Tehran (Teheran, capital); Mashad (Meshed); Isfahan (Esfahan); Tabriz; Shiraz.

● **PEOPLE Population**: 67,037,517 (July 2010 est.). **Nationality**: noun—Iranian(s); adjective—Iranian. **Ethnic groups**: 51% Persian, 24% Azerbaijani, 8% Gilaki and Mazandarani, 7% Kurd. **Languages**: 58% Persian, 26% Turkic, 9% Kurdish. **Religions**: 89% Shi'a Muslim; 10% Sunni Muslim; 1% Zoroastrian, Jewish, Christian, and Baha'i.

● **GOVERNMENT Type**: theocratic republic. **Independence**: April 1, 1979 **Constitution**: Dec. 2-3, 1979; revised 1989 to expand powers of the presidency and eliminate the prime minister. **National holiday**: Islamic Republic Day, April 1. **Head of Government**: Ali Hoseini-Khamenei, Supreme Leader (snce June 1989); Mahmoud Ahmadinejad, president (since Aug. 2005). **Structure**: executive; unicameral legislature (Islamic Consultative Assembly); judicial.

● **ECONOMY Monetary unit**: Iranian rial. **Budget**: (2009 est.) *income*: $97.71 bil.; *expend.*: $84.78 bil. **G.D.P.**: $876 bil., $12,900 per capita (2009 est.). **Chief crops**: wheat, rice, sugar beets; dairy, wool; caviar. **Natural resources**: petroleum, natural gas, coal, chromium. **Major industries**: petroleum, petrochemicals, textiles. **Labor force**: 25.02 mil. (2009 est.); 25% agriculture, 31% industry, 45% services (2007); 12.5% unemployment (2008), **Exports**: $70.16 bil. (2009 est.); 80% petroleum; carpets, fruits, nuts, hides. **Imports**: $57.16 bil. (2009 est.); machinery, military supplies, metal works, foodstuffs, pharmaceuticals. **Major trading partners**: (2008) *exports*: 15.2% China, 14.2% Japan, 9.2% India, 6.4% South Korea, 6.4% Turkey, 4.5% Italy; *imports*: 18.8% U.A.E., 12.6% China, 9% Germany, 6.8% South Korea, 5.2% Russia, 5% Italy, 4.1% France.

In 549 B.C. Cyrus the Great established the Persian empire by uniting Persia and conquered Babylonia. Alexander the Great conquered Persia in 333 B.C., but the Persians regained their independence after his death. The Persian Sassanian empire, established in A.D. 226, was the principal eastern rival of the Roman Empire. In 641 the Sassanians were defeated by invading Arabs, and Islam replaced the indigenous Zoroastrian religion. Persia reasserted its national identity—though not its political independence—under Islam and became a major center of Shia Muslim culture. In the early 13th century, Persia was conquered by the Mongols, who ruled the country until 1502.

The brilliant Safavid dynasty (1499–1736) was followed by two centuries of decline. During the 19th century, Persia lost control over Afghanistan and the Caucasus, while internal affairs came increasingly under British and Russian control. In 1907 an Anglo-Russian agreement formally divided Persia into spheres of influence. Following World War I, Persia was recognized as an independent nation, but was virtually a British protectorate. The Soviet Union renounced all claims to Persia in 1921.

In 1921 Reza Khan established a military dictatorship and had himself declared a hereditary monarch, Reza Shah Pahlavi, in 1925. In March 1935, the country's name was formally changed to Iran. In 1941 Great Britain, anxious over access to Iran's rich oil fields, charged Iran with pro-Axis activity, occupied Iran, and forced the abdication of Reza Shah in favor of his son, Mohammad Reza Shah Pahlavi.

Under Mohammed Mossadegh the National Front gained power in 1951. Parliament nationalized the oil industry; Britain responded with an economic blockade. The shah was briefly driven from power, but in August 1953, monarchist elements with clandestine British and American support ousted Mossadegh and restored the shah to the throne. The shah pursued a pro-Western policy of modernization and anticommunism and was rewarded with massive military and economic aid. His combination of secular, authoritarian rule and economic and social modernization was popular with the urban business sector but deeply resented by the rural and urban poor. Unrestrained use of the secret police to suppress dissent led to widespread disaffection.

Religiously inspired protests resulted in widespread violence in late 1978. A military government was installed by the shah on Nov. 6, with Prime Minister Shahpur Bakhtiar given sweeping powers. The shah went into exile on Jan. 16, 1979. On Jan. 31 Iran's dominant religious leader, Ayatollah Ruhollah Khomeini, returned to Iran from his exile in France. Government forces were routed by Khomeini's supporters, and Bakhtiar's government fell on Feb. 11. In 1979 clashes took place between rival religious factions, between religious parties and secular leftists, and between the urban middle class and the disenfranchised poor. Thousands were arrested and executed by the religious militia forces.

On Nov. 4, 1979, militants seized the U.S. embassy in Tehran and held 62 Americans hostage, provoking a long international crisis. An American military raid in April 1980 failed in an attempt to free the hostages. The hostages were finally freed on Jan. 21, 1981, minutes after Ronald Reagan's inauguration. The following day Iran's president, Abolhassan Bani-Sadr, was dismissed and the Ayatollah Khomeini took over executive power. A new wave of executions followed, with political moderates and non-Islamic religious believers among the principal victims.

On Sept. 22, 1980, a dispute between Iran and Iraq over the Shatt al-Arab waterway flared into open warfare. The war severely crippled Iran. Estimates on casualties range from 450,000 to over a million dead on both sides, and the war absorbed nearly all Iran's revenue from oil exports, leaving it nearly bankrupt. The U.S. was also drawn into the conflict. In 1986, Reagan administration officials attempted to secure the release of hostages in Lebanon by trading arms to the Iranians; and on July 3, 1988, an American ship patrolling in the Persian Gulf accidently shot down an Iranian civilian airliner, killing all aboard. In Sept. 1988, a U.N. initiative led to a cease-fire between Iran and Iraq and to the opening of negotiations to find a permanent settlement to the war.

Largely isolated from the world community, Iran's domestic priority was rebuilding the nation's economy. On June 3, 1989, Ayatollah Khomeini died, and Ali-Akbar Rafsanjani assumed the presidency. In elections held Apr. 10, 1992, supporters of Rafsanjani's moderate policies wrested a parliamentary majority from the radical fundamentalist Islamic factions that had controlled the Iranian Parliament for 13 years. But "moderation" proved elusive, as Rafsanjani's party was subjected to pressure from religious extremists.

Although Iran had condemned the presence of Western troops in the Middle East during the Persian Gulf conflict, it abided by U.N. sanctions against Iraq and grounded Iraqi planes that sought refuge from Allied bombing raids. In 1995 the U.S. accused Iran of beginning a strategic military buildup and forbade all trade with Iran.

Iran remained mired in economic and political stagnation with evidence of popular discontent for several years. In the 1997 elections the religious authorities gave the voters a genuine choice of presidential candidates and they shockingly chose (in a landslide) a moderate reformist, Mohammed Khatami. Khatami carefully maneuvered for moderate reforms in the face of Islamic clerical opposition, opening non-governmental dialogue with the American "great Satan", quietly replacing provincial governors with reformers, and reining in secret police agents. In Feb. 1999, the religious leaders permitted the first local elections in twenty years: Khatami's new party, swept all 15 seats in the Tehran city council, winning large victories nationwide.

In July 1999, a militant Islamic group attacked pro-democracy students in Tehran, killing several. Student demonstrations against the government erupted in many cities across the country and in Tehran the police dispersed the crowd with severe violence after students attacked buildings and burned cars. Pres. Khatami condemned the riots, leaving questions about the future of reform.

In Feb. 2000 parliamentary elections, voters gave about two-thirds of the seats in the 290-seat Majlis to reformers. But authorities closed most reform newspapers. In June 2001, Khatami won a landslide victory for re-election but his all his reforms were rejected by the Council of Guardians and all demonstrations violently suppressed. In the wake of the Sept. 11th attacks on the U.S., Pres. Bush included Iran in the "axis of evil" that threatened civilization. In 2003 the U.S. accused Iran of trying to develop nuclear weapons. The U.N.'s International Atomic Energy Agency inspected Iran's nuclear program and found no evidence of weapons development, but in 2004 it accused Iran of providing false information and of making reactor parts that could be used to enrich uranium. The U.S. and Europe continued to pressure Iran about its nuclear plans but no action was taken. In June 2005 Mahmoud Ahmadinejad, the popular mayor of Tehran, was elected president and he immediately began attacking Israel's existence, the U.S. occupation of Iraq, and pressing ahead with Iran's search for nuclear technology leading to weaponization. But a national election revealed that a great many Iranians did not agree with Ahmadinejad's aggressive foreign policy positions or with the continued lack of freedoms imposed by the Islamic order. After Ahmadinejad was declared the winner by a large margin spontaneous protests broke out in Tehran and other cities. Large numbers of people took to the streets only to be violently confronted by government forces who arrested hundreds of people. Unrest went underground but Iran was placed under more U.N. sanctions for its nuclear program. (See "Major News Stories.")

▶ **IRAQ**
Republic of Iraq
● **GEOGRAPHY   Location:** western Asia with narrow outlet to Persian (Arabian) Gulf. **Boundaries:** Turkey to N, Iran to E, Saudi Arabia and Kuwait to S, Syria and Jordan to W. **Total area:** 168,754 sq.

mi. (437,072 sq km). **Coastline:** 36 mi. (58 km). **Comparative area:** slightly more than twice the size of Idaho. **Land use:** 12% arable land; 1% permanent crops; 87% other. **Major cities:** Baghdad (capital); Basra (Basia); Mosul; Kirkuk.
● **PEOPLE   Population:** 29,671,605 (July 2010 est.). **Nationality:** noun—Iraqi(s); adjective—Iraqi. **Ethnic groups:** 75-80% Arab, 15-20% Kurdish, 5% Turkoman, Assyrian, and other. **Languages:** Arabic (official), Kurdish (official in Kurdish areas), Assyrian, Armenian. **Religions:** 97% Muslim (60-65% Shi'a, 32-37% Sunni), 3% Christian and other.
● **GOVERNMENT   Type:** parliamentary democracy. **Independence:** Oct. 3, 1932 (from League of Nations mandate under British administration). **Constitution:** ratified Oct. 15, 2005. **National holiday:** Anniversary of the Revolution, July 17. **Heads of Government:** Jalal Talabani, president (since Apr. 2005); Nuri al-Maliki, prime minister (since May 2006). **Structure:** executive; unicameral legislature (National Assembly)—Kurdish assembly elected in Kurdish areas, but unrecognized by Baghdad.
● **ECONOMY   Monetary unit:** Iraqi dinar. **Budget:** (2009 est.) *income:* $52.8 bil.; *expend.:* $72.4 bil. **G.D.P.:** $112 bil., $3,600 per capita (2009 est.). **Chief crops:** wheat, barley, rice, cotton; cattle, sheep. **Natural resources:** crude oil, natural gas, phosphates, sulphur. **Major industries:** petroleum, chemicals, textiles, construction materials. **Labor force:** 8.175 mil. (2008 est.); 48% services, 30% agriculture, 22% industry; 18-30% unemployment (2006). **Exports:** $38 bil. (2009 est.); crude oil. **Imports:** $55.4 bil. (2009 est.); food, medicine, manufactures. **Major trading partners:** (2008) *exports:* 38.6% U.S., 12.2% India, 9.8% Italy; *imports:* 26.2% Syria, 19.6% Turkey, 10.6% U.S., 6.4% Jordan.

The fertile lands of Mesopotamia, between the Tigris and Euphrates rivers, were the site of one of the world's oldest civilizations. The city-states of Sumer were founded before 3000 B.C. and later became the heart of the Babylonian empire. Babylon became subject to the Assyrian empire after 1350 B.C. and was conquered by the Persians under Cyrus and Darius in the mid-sixth century B.C. Mesopotamia remained under the control of various Persian dynasties for the next 1,000 years.

In the seventh century A.D., the region was rapidly incorporated into the expanding Islamic world. The battle of Basra in 656 decisively established Arab control. In 762 the Caliphate, the center of Islamic rule, was moved from Damascus to the newly founded city of Baghdad, near the ruins of ancient Babylon. Mongol invaders sacked Baghdad in 1258 and destroyed its irrigation works; thereafter the region entered a period of long-term decline. Baghdad fell to the Ottoman Turks in 1534, and Iraq remained a province of the Ottoman Empire until the 20th century.

British troops occupied Iraq in 1915, and Great Britain governed the country under a League of Nations mandate after World War I. A Hashemite monarchy was organized under British protection in 1921. The kingdom of Iraq was granted independence in 1932 but remained closely tied to Great Britain by treaties guaranteeing British interests in petroleum and regional defense. Iraqi oil flowed through British-controlled pipelines traversing Jordan to Haifa (in Israel) and through a French-controlled pipeline traversing Syria.

After 1932 several attempted coups by anti-British factions were put down with the aid of British troops. One such coup in April 1941 sought aid from Italy and Germany; British troops landed at Basra in May and restored the pro-British monarchy. Iraq declared war against the Axis powers in 1943. In 1948 Iraq joined the Arab League and participated in the first Arab-Israeli War. Most of Iraq's 85,000 Jews emigrated to Israel after the war ended. In 1952 a new agreement with Great Britain gave the Iraq Petroleum Company greater control over the country's oil. While remaining part of the Arab League, Iraq in 1955 broke ties with Egypt and expelled the Soviet ambassador and signed a mutual defense treaty with Turkey.

A pan-Arab revolutionary coup overthrew the monarchy in 1958 and established a republic, reversing Iraq's former pro-Western stance in international affairs. Oil resources were nationalized, and large landholdings were broken up. In 1968 a local branch of the international Ba'ath Socialist party came to power and established rule by decree within the republican framework of government. In 1972 the Soviet Union sent arms and advisers to Iraq. In the 1973 Arab-Israeli War, Iraq sent troops to aid Syrian forces.

Iranian aid to a long-standing Kurdish rebellion in Iraq's northern mountains strained relations between the two countries. The Kurds were defeated in a bloody campaign in 1975, though the rebellion continued, leading to Iraq's bombing of Kurdish villages in 1979 and other incidents.

The execution of 21 alleged Communist conspirators in 1978 disrupted relations between Iraq and the U.S.S.R. Trade relations with the West were resumed. On July 16, 1979, Gen. Saddam Hussein at-Takriti assumed control of the government and purged leftist elements in the Ba'ath movement.

Several months of fighting in 1980 between Iraq and Iran for control of the Shatt al-Arab waterway in southern Iraq led to the outbreak of open warfare on Sept. 22, when each country launched bombing attacks on the other's cities. Warfare quickly spread along the entire Iraq-Iran border. The Iran-Iraq War produced eight years of fierce but generally stalemated fighting, with reports of the use of poison gas by both sides. On June 7, 1981, Israeli war planes destroyed a nuclear reactor near Baghdad, claiming it was capable of producing nuclear weapons. The war spread to the gulf in 1984, as both Iran and Iraq attacked tankers using each other's ports.

On May 17, 1987, the *USS Stark*, an American frigate on station in the gulf, was struck by missiles fired by an Iraqi fighter; 37 American sailors were killed. Iraq claimed that the attack was inadvertent and apologized. In Sept. 1988, a U.N. conference led to a cease-fire in the Iran-Iraq War. Refugees in Turkey reported that poison gas had been used against Kurdish villages in northeastern Iraq as the Kurdish rebellion there continued. During 1989–90 Iraq's repressive internal policies and arms buildup provoked international criticism. Iraqi agents were caught attempting to smuggle components of nuclear weapons from the U.S. and Great Britain.

On Aug. 2, 1990, 120,000 Iraqi troops invaded and later annexed neighboring Kuwait. The invasion was met with universal disapproval, led by the U.N. Security Council, and U.S. troops were deployed to Saudi Arabia to defend it against a possible invasion. Coalition forces totaled 500,000 troops from 13 countries. After a six-week air war that destroyed most of Iraq's military capabilities and much of the country's infrastructure, Allied ground forces liberated Kuwait and occupied much of southern Iraq in only four days. Emboldened by the proximity of such overwhelming force, Kurds and Shiites in Iraq began a civil war that was put down with surprising speed and resulted in the displacement of hundreds of thousands of refugees to Turkey and Iran.

During 1992 Saddam Hussein solidified his hold on the military and remained in total control of the nation. However, U.N. inspectors discovered his secret plans to build nuclear weapons, and he was forced to destroy the program.

Throughout 1992–93 American warplanes provided protection for Kurdish areas in the north and Shiite Muslim areas in the southern marshlands. U.N. arms inspectors continued to press for access to Iraqi weapons plants and military research centers. On June 19, 1993, American missiles destroyed the Baghdad headquarters of Iraq's military intelligence service, in retaliation for a 1992 Iraq-backed plot to assassinate Pres. George Bush.

In Nov. 1994 Iraq formally recognized the sovereignty and territorial integrity of Kuwait. Nonetheless, the U.N. retained sanctions against Iraq until two conditions were met: destroying its stockpiles of weapons of mass destruction and improving its treatment of minorities. In May 1996 the U.N. agreed to ease sanctions on Iraq, permitting the sale of $2 billion worth of oil to purchase food and medical supplies. In late 1997 Iraq reneged on its agreement to allow U.N. weapons inspectors free access to all sites causing new tension in the region. Hussein's on-again, off-again cooperation with international inspection teams climaxed in the Dec. 1998 U.S./U.K. air strikes against Iraq. U.S. and U.K. patrols in the "no fly" zones regularly clashed with Iraqi MIGs. After the Security Council decision to review all aspects of U.N.-Iraqi relations in Jan. 1999, U.S. influence was further diminished by revelations that its intelligence agents had infiltrated the U.N. Special Commission and used UNSCOM to spy on Iraq. Three compromise recommendations by U.N. panels now met Iraqi rejection in April.

Iraq continuously rejected U.N. arms-monitoring schemes unless sanctions were lifted first. Yet, "oil-for-food" sales were renewed. British and U.S. airstrikes continued through 2001. Iraqi overtures and invitations to the U.N. to resume arms inspections came with conditions evoking a negative response and a serious threat of war by the U.S. On March 19, 2003 the U.S., Britain, and several smaller nations launched a devastating attack on Baghdad and in only 43 days took over the country. The ensuing occupation proved less manageable. Although nominal authority was turned over to an interim government in June 2004, the U.S. had 130,000 troops battling Muslim insurgents every day in several regions. By Aug. 2005 nearly 2000 Americans had died, 12,000 had been severely wounded and troops complained openly of lack of body armor. The U.S. pushed for elections in early 2005 and Iraqis turned out in large numbers. A draft constitution drawn up with U.S. guidance did not win Sunni approval but was ratified by the people in Oct. 2005. In December, an election was peacefully held and a 275-member Council of Representatives was put in office. In 2006 the insurgency and the growing violence between the Sunnis and the Shiites exploded. By the end of the year, over 3,000 Americans were dead, 20,000 seriously wounded. By mid-2007 over two million Iraqis had left the country and a large percentage were displaced within the country. U.S. casulties passed 4,000 and there seemed no end in sight. Bush and the military then sent in 30,000 additional troops and began to pay large sums of money to Sunni militias and the violence quickly diminished in a meaningful way. The Iraqi government could not take advantage, however, as political infighting intensified and the Kurds in the north remained autonomous and self-governing; they were also making deals for oil development with several nations. Elections in early 2010 produced a stalemate that as of Sept. 2010 had not been solved. (See "Major News Stories.")

▶ IRELAND

● **GEOGRAPHY Location:** 26 of 32 counties comprising island of Ireland, in North Atlantic Ocean. Dublin 53°20'N, 6°15'W. **Boundaries:** Northern Ireland (U.K.) to N, Great Britain 50 mi (80 km) to E. **Total area:** 27,135 sq. mi. (70,280 sq km). **Coastline:** 900 mi. (1,448 km). **Comparative area:** slightly larger than W. Virginia. **Land use:** 20% arable land; negl. % permanent crops; 80% other. **Major cities:** Dublin (capital); Cork; Limerick; Galway; Waterford.

● **PEOPLE Population:** 4,250,163 (July 2010 est.). **Nationality:** noun—Irishman (men), Irishwoman (women), Irish (collective pl.); adjective—Irish. **Ethnic groups:** Celtic, with English minority. **Languages:** Irish (Gaelic) and English (official); English widely spoken. **Religions:** 88.4% Roman Catholic, 3.2% Church of Ireland, 3.2% other, 3.5% none.

● **GOVERNMENT Type:** republic, parliamentary democracy. **Independence:** Dec. 6, 1921 (from U.K.). **Constitution:** Dec. 29, 1937. **National holiday:** St. Patrick's Day, Mar. 17. **Heads of Government:** Mary McAleese, president (since Oct. 1997); Brian Cowen, prime minister (since May 2008). **Structure:** executive; bicameral parliament (Seanad, Dail); judiciary appointed by president on advice of government.

● **ECONOMY Monetary unit:** euro. **Budget:** (2009 est.) *income:* $74.82 bil.; *expend.:* $104.6 bil. **G.D.P.:** $176.9 bil., $42,200 per capita (2009 est.) **Chief crops:** turnips, barley, potatoes, sugar beets, wheat; meat, dairy. **Natural resources:** zinc, lead, natural gas, barite, copper. **Major industries:** food products, brewing, textiles, clothing. **Labor force:** 2.2 mil. (2009 est.); 67% services, 27% industry, 6% agriculture (2006); 6.2% unemployment (2008). **Exports:** $107.3 bil. (2009 est.); chemicals, computers, industrial machinery. **Imports:** $64.9 bil. (2009 est.); data processing equipment, chemicals, petroleum and petroleum products. **Major trading partners:** (2008) *exports:* 18.9% U.S., 18.4% U.K., 14.6% Belgium, 6.9% Germany, 5.8% France, 4.2% Spain; *imports:* 37.6% U.K., 11.6% U.S., 8.6% Germany, 5.6% Netherlands.

Ireland, a collection of warring Celtic chieftainships, was converted to Christianity by St. Patrick in the fifth century. Over the next two centuries, Ireland became a great center of monastic Christianity, sending missionaries to Scotland, England, and the Continent. While the Roman Empire decayed, Ireland was a center of peace, culture, and learning. Viking invasions in the ninth and 10th centuries caused substantial damage and overturned the rule of the great monasteries and their secular allies. By the time an Irish monarchy was reestablished by Brian Boru in 1014 and the surviving invaders were integrated into Irish society, Ireland had become an isolated, poor backwater on the periphery of Europe.

Trade gave rise to English commercial interests in Ireland and to Henry II's claim to overlordship of Ireland in the 12th century. Henry VIII declared himself king of Ireland and introduced the Reformation there. Large-scale Scottish immigration began during the reign of Elizabeth I. Penal laws were applied, banning Catholics from public life and making the Mass an act of treason. A rebellion in 1641 was crushed by Oliver Cromwell, ending with a massacre of thousands of Irish at Drogheda. After William of Orange's "Glorious Revolution" of 1688, the Irish supported James II, who was defeated at the Battle of the Boyne in 1690.

Following these events, British economic sanctions destroyed Ireland's flourishing export trade in wool. "Plantations" were established by British and Scottish Presbyterian landlords and farmers on lands seized from Irish Catholics. Much of the native aristocracy fled into exile, and the Gaelic language declined to near extinction.

A separate Irish Parliament, dominated by the Anglo-Irish establishment, was instituted in 1782, but it had little power. In 1798 a popular uprising led by Wolfe Tone, with inspiration and aid from revolutionary France, was put down with great loss of life. In 1800 Ireland and England were joined by the Act of Union, whereby Ireland was ineffectively represented in the British Parliament. After popular agitation led by Daniel O'-Connell, the Catholic Emancipation Act was enacted by Parliament in 1829, though mandatory tithes continued to support the established Anglican church until 1869.

Under absentee landlords, the Irish population was reduced to a subsistence diet based largely on potatoes. When a potato blight struck the country in the 1840s, disaster ensued. Between 1846 and 1851, one million people starved to death, and 1.6 million emigrated, most to America.

In the late 19th century, a home-rule movement under Charles Stewart Parnell won wide popular support. A Home Rule Act finally was passed by Parliament in 1914, but its effect was postponed for the duration of World War I. The Land Purchase Acts of the early 20th century enabled dispossessed peasants to buy land from absentee landlords, creating a rural economic basis for an independent Ireland. The country's economy, based largely on agriculture and pasturage, began to recover. (Industry, principally shipbuilding and textiles, was largely confined to Northern Ireland.)

The postponement of home rule led to the Easter Rebellion of 1916; brutally suppressed, it was followed by the "Troubles," a period of guerrilla warfare lasting to 1920. In that year the Government of Ireland Act established six of Ulster's nine counties as Northern Ireland, an integral part of the United Kingdom but with its own home-rule Parliament. The south's refusal of similar status led to the passage on Dec. 11, 1922, of the Irish Free State Act, by which Ireland became an independent dominion within the British Commonwealth.

The Fine Gael (People of Ireland) party governed until 1932, when Eamon De Valera, as the head of the Fianna Fail (Soldiers of Destiny) party, was elected president, holding that office until 1948. In 1938 the Constitution was revised to sever all connections with the British government except for an "external association" with the British monarchy. The outlawed Irish Republican Army (I.R.A.) pressed for forcible reunification of Ireland and carried out attacks on British interests in both Ireland and Northern Ireland.

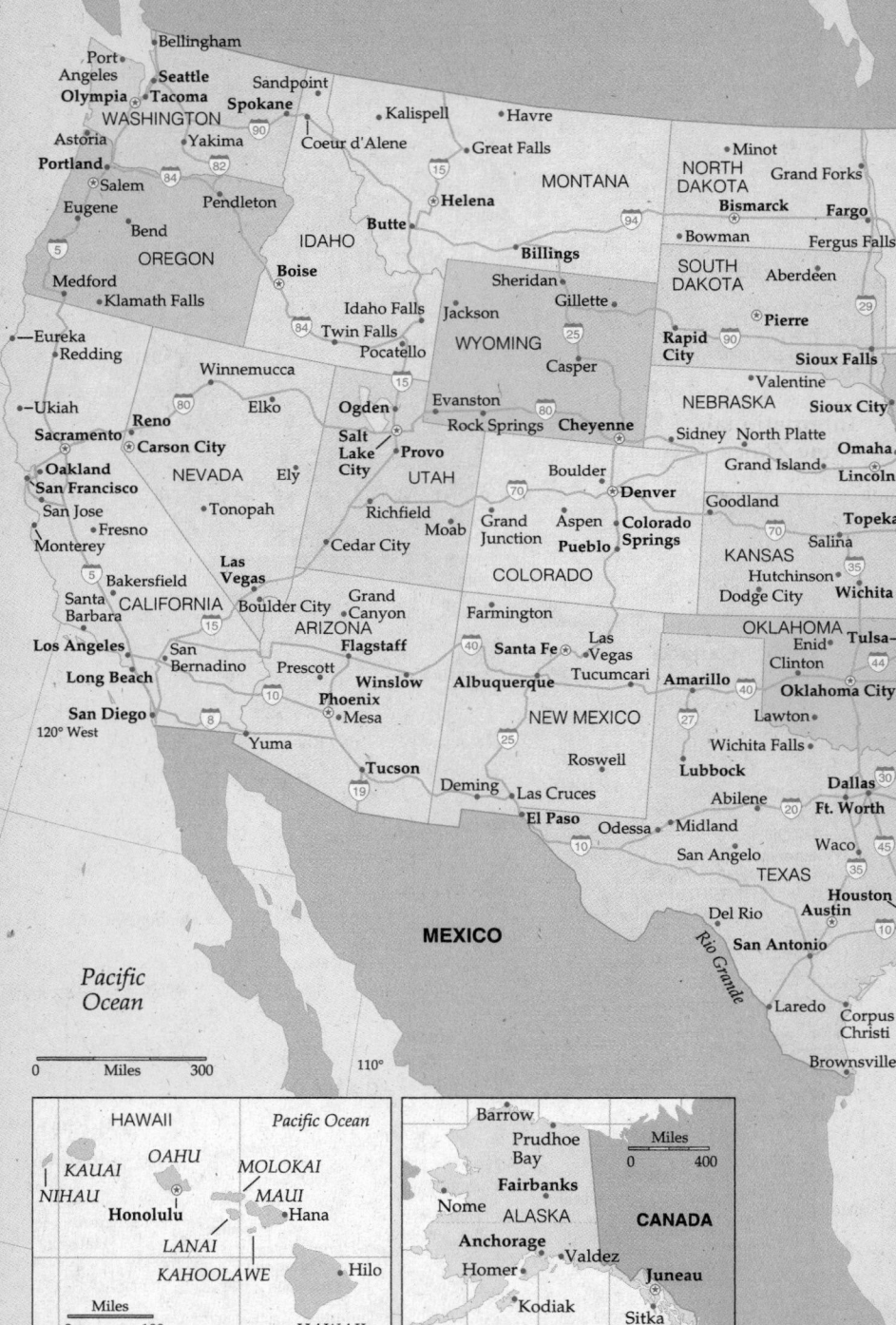

CANADA

Gulf of St. Lawrence

Houlton

MINN.
International Falls
Grand Rapids
Duluth

Lake Superior

Sault Ste. Marie

Marquette

Lake Huron

MAINE
Bangor
Augusta
Brunswick

Montpelier
Burlington

WISCONSIN
MICHIGAN

Minneapolis
Green Bay
Eau Claire
St. Paul
Rochester
La Crosse

Lake Michigan

VT. N.H.

L. Ontario
Syracuse
Rochester

MASS.
CONN.

N.Y.

CAPE COD

40° North

Atlantic Ocean

Milwaukee
Madison
Rockford
Lansing
Grand Rapids
Flint
Detroit

L. Erie
Buffalo
Erie

Waterloo
Des Moines
Dubuque
Cedar Rapids
Chicago
Kalamazoo

IOWA
Burlington
Peoria

Gary
South Bend
Fort Wayne

Cleveland
OHIO
Akron

PENNSYLVANIA
Harrisburg
Pittsburgh

R.I.

N.J.

DEL.

Area of detail

Columbus
Wheeling
Hagerstown

MD.

Springfield
Decatur
Muncie
Dayton
Cincinnati

Washington D.C.

Kansas City
Quincy
Columbia

Indianapolis
INDIANA

Frankfort
Huntington
Lexington

Charleston
Clarksburg

W.VA.

Richmond
Newport News
Norfolk

Joplin
St. Louis
ILLINOIS
Evansville
Louisville

Lynchburg
Roanoke

NORTH CAROLINA

Jefferson City

KENTUCKY
VIRGINIA
Greensboro

MISSOURI
Paducah
Bowling Green

Durham
Raleigh

Springfield
Winston-Salem
Charlotte

Fayetteville
ARKANSAS
TENNESSEE
Nashville
Knoxville
Asheville

Fort Smith
Memphis
Chattanooga
Spartanburg
Fayetteville
Wilmington

Hot Springs
Pine Bluff
Oxford
Huntsville
Greenville
Columbia

Little Rock

Decatur
Atlanta
SOUTH CAROLINA

Texarkana
MISSISSIPPI
Birmingham
Augusta

Monroe
Vicksburg
Tuscaloosa
Macon
Charleston

Shreveport
Jackson
Meridian
ALABAMA
Montgomery
GEORGIA
Savannah

LOUISIANA
Hattiesburg
Dothan
Albany
Brunswick

Baton Rouge
Mobile
Tallahassee
Jacksonville

Lake Charles
Biloxi
Pensacola
Gainesville
Daytona Beach

Lafayette
New Orleans
Panama City
FLORIDA
Orlando

Beaumont

Gulf of Mexico

Tampa
St. Petersburg
Sarasota
West Palm Beach
Fort Myers
Fort Lauderdale
Miami

Key West

CUBA

MEXICO

70°

30°

United States: Political

VERMONT
N.H.
Portland
Rutland
Portsmouth

Glens Falls
Concord

Manchester
Lowell

Schenectady
Brattleboro
Boston

Albany
Pittsfield
MASS.
Worcester

NEW YORK
Springfield
Providence

CONN.

Kingston
Hartford

R.I.

Binghamton

New London
Newport

Newburgh
New Haven

Scranton
Paterson

Newark
New York City

Allentown

Princeton
Trenton

Philadelphia
NEW JERSEY

PA.
Camden

Wilmington
Atlantic City

Baltimore

Dover

DELAWARE

Annapolis
Salisbury

MARYLAND

90° West

80°

20°

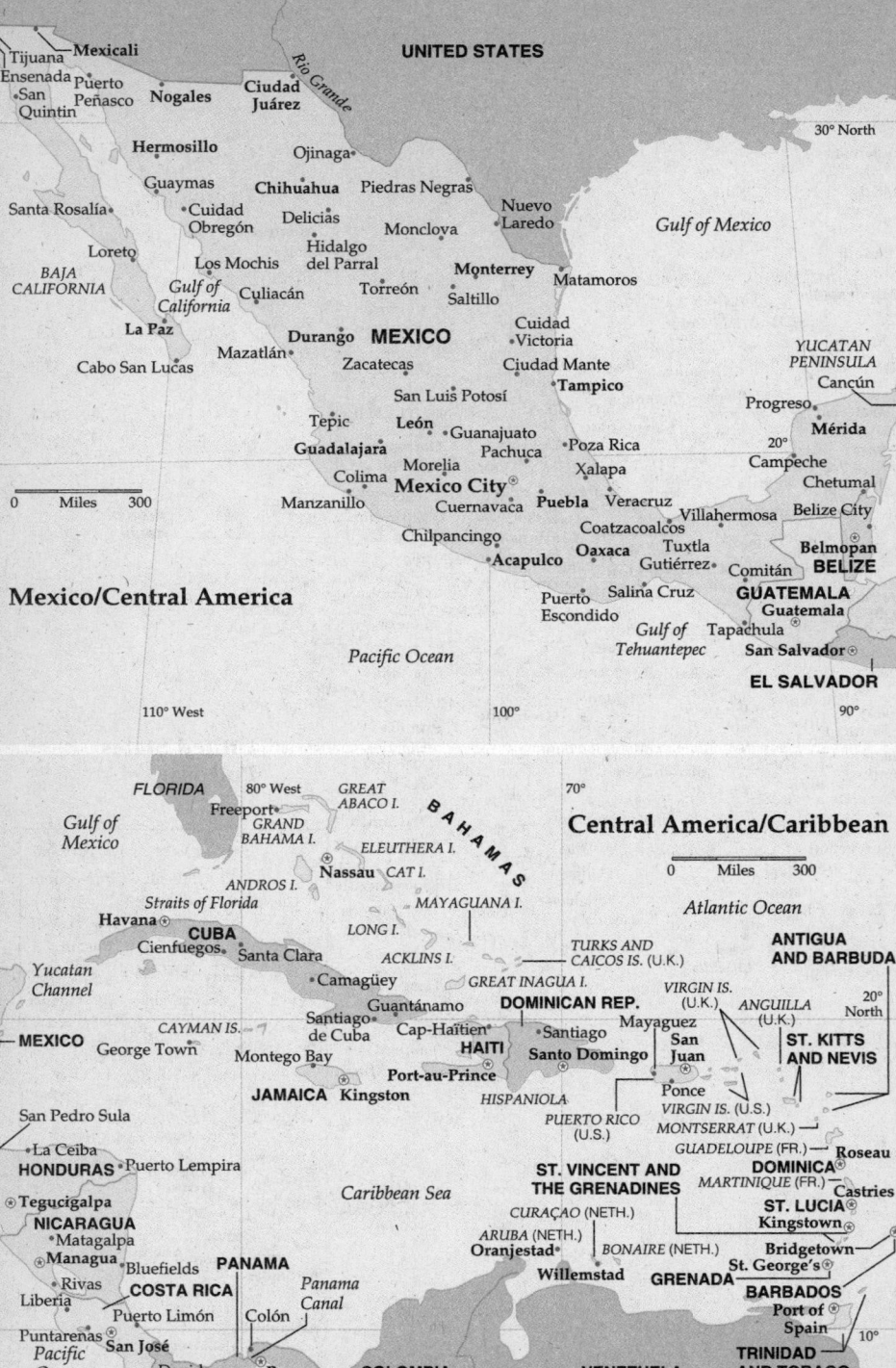

Mexico/Central America

UNITED STATES

Tijuana
Mexicali
Ensenada
San Quintin
Puerto Peñasco
Nogales
Ciudad Juárez
Rio Grande

30° North

Hermosillo
Ojinaga

Guaymas
Chihuahua
Piedras Negras

Santa Rosalía
Cuidad Obregón
Delicias
Nuevo Laredo

Gulf of Mexico

Loreto
Los Mochis
Hidalgo del Parral
Monclova
Matamoros

BAJA CALIFORNIA
Gulf of California
Culiacán
Torreón
Monterrey
Saltillo

La Paz
Durango
MEXICO
Cuidad Victoria

Cabo San Lucas
Mazatlán
Zacatecas
Ciudad Mante
Tampico

YUCATAN PENINSULA
Cancún

San Luis Potosí
Progreso
Mérida

Tepic
León
Guanajuato
Poza Rica
20°
Campeche
Chetumal

Guadalajara
Pachuca
Xalapa

0   Miles   300
Colima
Morelia
Mexico City
Veracruz
Villahermosa
Belize City

Manzanillo
Cuernavaca
Puebla
Coatzacoalcos
Belmopan

Chilpancingo
Oaxaca
Tuxtla Gutiérrez
BELIZE

*Acapulco
Salina Cruz
Comitán
GUATEMALA

Puerto Escondido
Guatemala

Pacific Ocean
Gulf of Tehuantepec
Tapachula
San Salvador

EL SALVADOR

110° West
100°
90°

Central America/Caribbean

FLORIDA
80° West
GREAT ABACO I.
70°

Gulf of Mexico
Freeport
GRAND BAHAMA I.
B A H A M A S

ELEUTHERA I.
0   Miles   300

ANDROS I.
Nassau
CAT I.
Atlantic Ocean

Straits of Florida
LONG I.
MAYAGUANA I.

Havana
CUBA
ACKLINS I.
TURKS AND CAICOS IS. (U.K.)
ANTIGUA AND BARBUDA

Yucatan Channel
Cienfuegos
Santa Clara
GREAT INAGUA I.
20° North

Camagüey
VIRGIN IS. (U.K.)
ANGUILLA (U.K.)

CAYMAN IS.
Santiago de Cuba
Guantánamo
DOMINICAN REP.
Mayaguez
San Juan
ST. KITTS AND NEVIS

MEXICO
George Town
Cap-Haïtien
Santiago
Santo Domingo

Montego Bay
HAITI
Ponce
VIRGIN IS. (U.S.)

San Pedro Sula
JAMAICA
Kingston
Port-au-Prince
HISPANIOLA
PUERTO RICO (U.S.)
MONTSERRAT (U.K.)

La Ceiba
GUADELOUPE (FR.)
Roseau

HONDURAS
Puerto Lempira
Caribbean Sea
ST. VINCENT AND THE GRENADINES
DOMINICA
MARTINIQUE (FR.)

Tegucigalpa
CURAÇAO (NETH.)
ST. LUCIA
Castries

NICARAGUA
ARUBA (NETH.)
Kingstown

Matagalpa
Oranjestad
BONAIRE (NETH.)
Bridgetown

Managua
Bluefields
PANAMA
Willemstad
GRENADA
St. George's
BARBADOS

Rivas
Panama Canal
Port of Spain

COSTA RICA
Colón
10°

Liberia
Puerto Limón
TRINIDAD AND TOBAGO

Puntarenas
San José
David
Panama
COLOMBIA
VENEZUELA

Pacific Ocean

PANAMA

Caribbean Sea

Barranquilla
Cartagena

Valencia Caracas

TRINIDAD
AND TOBAGO

10° North

Maracaibo Maracay
Cucuta VENEZUELA Orinoco R.
Medellín

GUYANA

SURINAME

Atlantic Ocean

Bogotá Puerto
Ayacucho
Cali
Pasto Magadalena R.
Quito Mitú
COLOMBIA
ECUADOR
Guayaquil
Cuenca PERU Iquitos
Talara
Chiclayo Orellana
Trujillo
Huaraz Tarauacá
Huanuco
Cerro de Pasco
Callao Huancayo
Lima Machu Picchu
Ayacucho Cuzco
Ica Puno
Arequipa La Paz
Arica Cochabamba
Sucre
Iquique Tarija
Antofagasta

Georgetown Paramaribo
Cayenne
Camopi
FRENCH
GUIANA (FR.)
Boa Vista
Serro do Navio
Macapá Equator

Negro R.
Belém São Luis
Manaus Santarém Fortaleza
Tefé Amazon R. Imperatriz Teresina
Jacareacanga
Cachimbo São Francisco R. Recife
Pôrto Velho Maceió
Gurupi Aracaju
BRAZIL Barreiras Salvador
Cuiabá Alvorada
Brasília Canavieiras
Goiânia
Campo Grande Belo Horizonte
Vitória 20°
PARAGUAY Campinas Rio De Janeiro
Salta Asunción São Paulo Tropic of
San Miguel Curitiba Capricorn
De Tucumán
Resistencia Florianópolis

Pacific
Ocean

CHILE

Viña del Mar
Valparaíso
Santiago
Concepción

Córdoba

Neuquén

Valdivia

Puerto Montt

San Carlos
de Bariloche

Trelew

ANDES

Paraná R.

Tacuarembó

Rosario
Morón
Buenos Aires

Durazno URUGUAY
Montevideo

Porto Alegre 30°

Atlantic Ocean

ARGENTINA

Bahía Blanca

Mar Del Plata 40°

Comodoro Rivadavia

South America

0   Miles   500

50°

Puerto Santa Cruz

Río Gallegos
Strait of Magellan
Punta Arenas TIERRA DEL FUEGO

Ushuaia

FALKLAND ISLANDS
(U.K.)

SOUTH
GEORGIA
ISLAND
(U.K.)

80° West 70° 60° 50° 40°

Nations of
Former Soviet Union

Tangier
Casablanca • Rabat
MOROCCO
30° North
Marrakesh
Timimoun
~ CANARY ISLANDS (SPAIN)
El Aaiun
WESTERN
SAHARA
(MOROCCO)
Atar
MAURITANIA
Nouakchott

Annaba
Batna
Oran
Algiers
TUNISIA
Ouargla
ALGERIA
Reggane

Tunis
Gafsa • Sfax
Misratah

Mediterranean Sea
Tripoli
LIBYA
Sabhah

Benghazi

SYRIA
LEBANON
ISRAEL
Alexandria
Cairo
Beni Suef
El-Minya
Suez
JORDAN

IRAQ

KUWAIT

Djanet
Marzuq
Al Jawf
EGYPT
Aswan
SAUDI ARABIA

Taoudenni
Tessalit
Araouane
SAHARA
DESERT
Aozou
Bilma
Faya-Largeau
Port Sudan
SUDAN
Atbara
Red
Sea
ERITREA
DJIBOUTI

MALI
GUINEA
BURKINA
FASO
NIGER

NIGERIA

CHAD

Khartoum
El Fasher
White Nile R.—
CENT.
AFRICAN
REP.
Ndele
Wau
Bangassou
Asmara
Mekele
Addis
Ababa
Asela
Goba
Djibouti
Berbera
ETHIOPIA

Blue Nile R.

Area of detail

CAMEROON

Congo R.
Bumba
Mbandaka
Lake
Victoria
Juba UGANDA
Gulu
Kisangani Kampala
KENYA
SOMALIA
Mogadishu

Equator
Port-Gentil • Libreville
GABON
Brazzaville
CONGO
REPUBLIC
Pointe-Noire
Kinshasa
CABINDA
(ANGOLA)
Matadi
Luanda

CONGO
(ZAIRE)
RWANDA
Bujumbura
Lake
Tanganyika
Kananga

Kigali
BURUNDI
Tabora
TANZANIA
Kalemie
Likasi
Lubumbashi

Eldoret
Kisumu
Nairobi
Mombasa
ZANZIBAR
Tanga
Dar es Salaam
Mbeya
Kasama
Kasanga

SEYCHELLES

COMOROS
Moroni
Antsiranana

10°
Malange
Huambo
Luena
ANGOLA
Lubango
Malange

Mongu

Kananga
ZAMBIA
Lusaka
Mbeya
MALAWI
Lilongwe
Zambezi R.
Nampula

Atlantic Ocean

Africa
0 Miles 500

Tsumeb
Windhoek
Walvis Bay
NAMIBIA
Keetmanshoop

Maun
ZIMBABWE
Bulawayo
BOTSWANA
Gaborone
Pietersburg
Pretoria
Johannesburg
Bloemfontein
Kimberley
Oudtshoorn
Cape Town

Harare
Beira
MOZAMBIQUE
Antananarivo
MADAGASCAR
Fianarantsoa
Tuléar
Tolanaro

Maputo
Mbabane
SWAZILAND
LESOTHO
Maseru
Durban
Umtata
Port Elizabeth
East London
Indian Ocean
SOUTH AFRICA

30°

10°   0°   10°   20°   30°   40° East

SENEGAL
Dakar
THE GAMBIA
Banjul
Bissau
GUINEA
Conakry
Freetown
SIERRA
LEONE
GUINEA-
BISSAU

MAURITANIA
Kayes
Niger R.
Bamako
Kankan
Man
Monrovia
LIBERIA

Timbuktu
MALI
Niamey
Ouagadougou
BURKINA FASO
Korhogo
Bouaké
Yamoussoukro
Abidjan
IVORY COAST

Gao
Tahoua
BENIN
Tamale
GHANA
Accra
Lomé
EQUATORIAL
GUINEA

Agadez
NIGER
Zinder
Katsina
Kaduna
Zaria
Abuja
Ibadan
Lagos
Porto-
Novo
TOGO

CHAD
Lake Chad
N'Djamena
Maiduguri
Moundou
Bossangoa
NIGERIA
CAMEROON
Ebolowa
Yaoundé
Malabo
CENT.
AFRICAN
REPUBLIC
Bangui

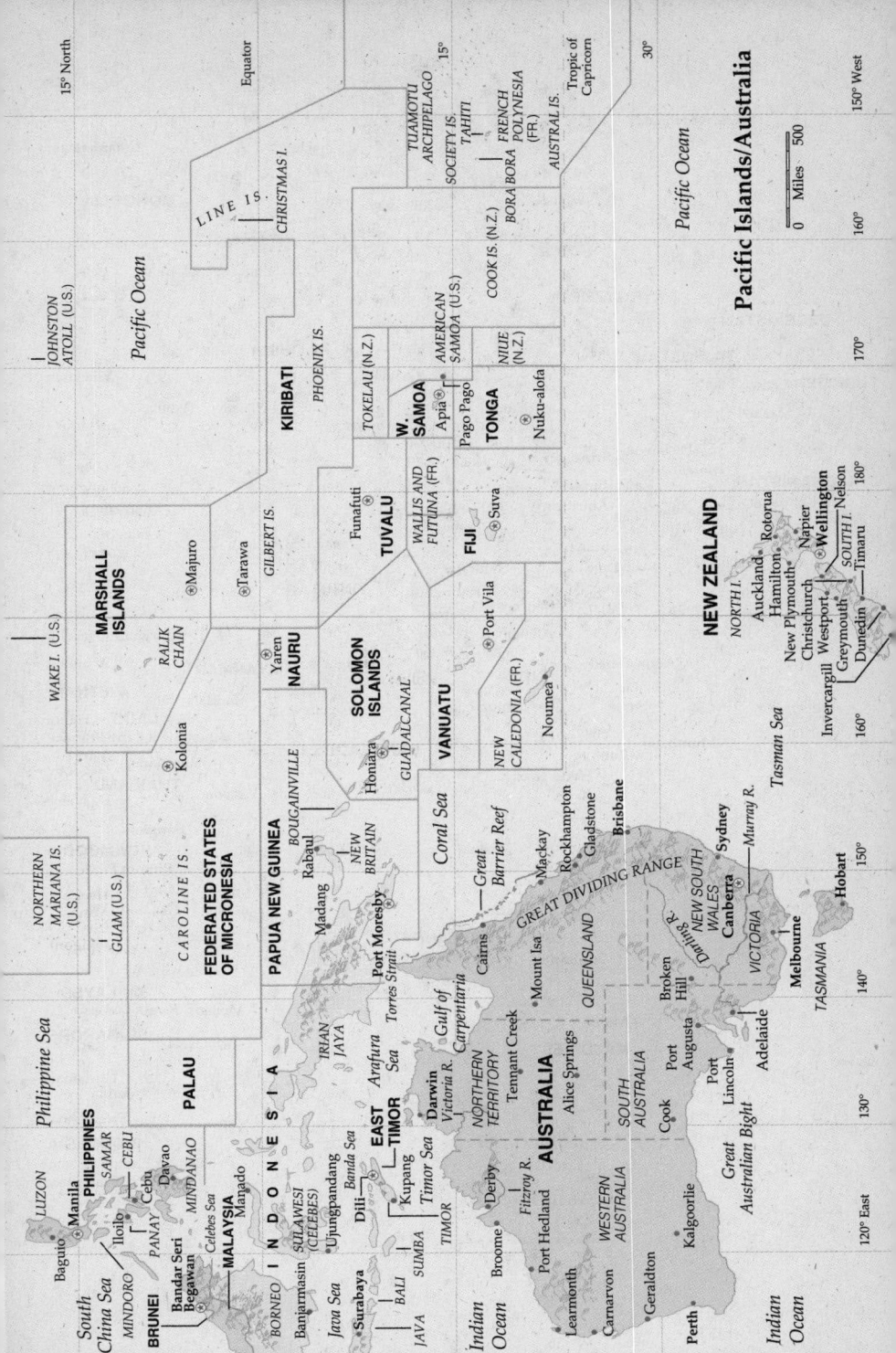

Pacific Islands/Australia

RUSSIA

KAZAKHSTAN

Hovd

Ulaanbaatar

Altay

MONGOLIA

Karamay

Dalandzadagad

L. Balkhash

Aral
Sea

Urumqi

Hami

GOBI
DESERT

KYRGYZSTAN

Korla

Kashi *Yarkant R.*

Tarim R.

Yumen

Yinchuan

UZBEKISTAN

TAJIKISTAN

*TAKLIMAKAN
DESERT*

Qiemo

CHINA

Xining

Lahzhou

TURKMEN.

Hotan

Golmud

Xian

Mazar-i-Sharif

Area claimed by India

*JAMMU AND
KASHMIR*

Chongqing

Herat

Kabul

Peshawar

Srinagar

TIBET

Mianyang

AFGHANISTAN

Islamabad

Rawalpindi

Chengdu

Zigong

Kandahar

Faisalabad

Multan

Amritsar

Lahore

MOUNT
EVEREST

Brahmaputra R.

Mekong R.

Guiyang

Indus R.

Yamuna R.

Ganges R.

HIMALAYAS

Kunming

PAKISTAN

New Delhi

Jaipur

Agra

NEPAL

Katmandu

BHUTAN

Nanning

IRAN

Kanpur

Patna

Hyderabad

*GREAT INDIAN
DESERT*

Allahabad

Ganges R.

Dhaka

MYANMAR

VIETNAM

Karachi

Ahmadabad

INDIA

Kolkata

Chitta-
gong

Mandalay

LAOS

Hanoi

Arabian Sea

Surat

Nagpur

BANGLADESH

Irrawaddy R.

Chang Mai

Luang Prabang

Vinh

Mumbai

Godavari R.

Pune

Hyderabad

Bay of Bengal

Yangon

Vientiane

THAILAND

HAINAN

Da Nang

15° North

Bangalore

Chennai

ANDAMAN IS.
(INDIA)

Dawei

Bangkok

CAMBODIA

Mangalore

Madurai

Jaffna

*Andaman
Sea*

*Gulf of
Thailand*

Phnom Penh

Ho Chi
Minh
City
(Saigon)

SRI LANKA

NICOBAR IS.
(INDIA)

Hat Yai

Colombo

Kotte

Kota Baharu

Male

Medan

Kuala Lumpur

MALAYSIA

MALDIVES

SINGAPORE

Equator

Pontianak

SUMATRA

Jambi

Indian Ocean

Padang

Palembang

INDONESIA

Asia/Pacific

Bandar Lampung

Jakarta

Bandung

JAVA

0   Miles   500

70° East

90°

Arctic Ocean

75° North

Beaufort Sea

Baffin Bay

GREENLAND
(DENMARK)

Norwegian
Sea

Reykjavík

ICELAND

ALASKA

60°

Hudson
Bay

Labrador Sea

UNITED KINGDOM

Bering Sea

Gulf of
Alaska

CANADA

Dublin

IRELAND

45°

Ottawa

Atlantic Ocean

Bay of Biscay

SPAIN

UNITED
STATES

PORTUGAL
Lisbon

Washington, D.C.

Madrid

Rabat

MOROCCO

30°

Gulf of
Mexico

BAHAMAS

Canary Islands

W. SAHARA
(MOROCCO)

ALG.

HAWAII

MEXICO

Havana

CUBA

HAITI

MAURITANIA

15°

Mexico City

BELIZE

DOM. REP.

Nouakchott

MALI

HONDURAS

SENEGAL

Dakar

Bamako

Caribbean Sea

GUYANA

GAMBIA

GUATEMALA

Caracas

SURINAME

GUINEA-BISSAU

EL SALVADOR

GUINEA

NICARAGUA

VENEZUELA

SIERRA LEONE

Monrovia

COSTA RICA

Bogotá

FRENCH GUIANA (FR.)

Equator

PANAMA

COL.

LIBERIA

KIRIBATI

Quito

IVORY
COAST

Pacific Ocean

ECUADOR

PERU

BRAZIL

BURKINA FASO

15°

Lima

Brasília

La Paz

BOLIVIA

Sucre

CHILE

PARAGUAY

Atlantic Ocean

30°

Asunción

Santiago

Buenos
Aires

URUGUAY

Montevideo

ARGENTINA

45°

FALKLAND IS. (U.K.)

165°
West

150°

135°

120°

105°

90°

75°

CAPE
HORN

60°

45°

30°

SOUTH GEORGIA I. (U.K.)

15°

0°

60°

75° South

ANTARCTICA

Barents
Sea
Arctic Ocean
75° North

SWEDEN
NORWAY
FIN.
Helsinki   ESTONIA
Stockholm   LATVIA
DENMARK   LITHUANIA
Berlin   Moscow
POL.   BELA.
1   Kiev
2 GER. 3 4   UKRAINE   KAZAKHSTAN
Paris   6 7   GEORGIA
FR. 5 10 8   ARMENIA   Astana
London 11 12 13   9   AZERBAIJAN
Rome 14 15 16   Black Sea UZBEKISTAN   Ulaanbaatar
ITALY   17   Ankara
Algiers   Athens   TURKEY   TURKMEN.
TUNISIA   SYRIA IRAQ   Teheran
LEBANON   Kabul
Tripoli ISRAEL   Baghdad   IRAN
Cairo   JORDAN KUWAIT   AFGH.   Islamabad
LIBYA   Riyadh   QATAR
EGYPT   SAUDI   UNITED
Red   ARABIA   ARAB
Sea   EMIRATES
NIGER   ERITREA   OMAN
CHAD   Khartoum YEMEN
NIGERIA SUDAN   DJIBOUTI
CENT.   Addis Ababa
AF. REP. ETHIOPIA
CAMEROON UGANDA SOMALIA
GABON   Nairobi KENYA
CONGO   RWANDA
CONGO Kinshasa BURUNDI
REP. Luanda Dar es Salaam
BENIN ANGOLA TANZANIA
TOGO
ZAMBIA
NAMIBIA ZIMBABWE
BOTSWANA MALAWI
Pretoria MOZAMBIQUE
SWAZILAND
LESOTHO
SOUTH AFRICA
CAPE OF
GOOD HOPE

RUSSIA
60°
Sea of
Okhotsk

MONGOLIA
NORTH
KOREA   45°
Beijing
Sea of
Japan   Tokyo
KYRGYZSTAN
TAJIKISTAN CHINA   Seoul   JAPAN
BHUTAN   SOUTH   30°
BANGLADESH KOREA
New   NEPAL   TAIWAN
Delhi   THAILAND South   Pacific Ocean
LAOS   China
MYANMAR Sea
INDIA   Yangon   Philippine Sea   15°
Bay of   Bangkok Manila
Bengal   PHILIPPINES   MARSHALL
SRI LANKA VIETNAM   IS.
CAMBODIA
MALAYSIA PALAU   MICRONESIA
MALDIVES   Equator
INDONESIA
SINGAPORE Java Sea Dili   PAPUA
Jakarta   NEW GUINEA TUVALU
EAST TIMOR Port Moresby
Arabian   Timor Sea   15°
Sea   Coral Sea VANUATU
Indian Ocean   FIJI

AUSTRALIA   30°

Canberra
Tasman Sea
Wellington
NEW ZEALAND 45°

165°
East
0°   15°   30°   45°   60°   75°   90°   105°   120°   135°   150°   60°
Southern Ocean

75° South

ANTARCTICA

1. NETHERLANDS	10. SLOVENIA
2. BELGIUM	11. CROATIA
3. CZECH REPUBLIC	12. BOSNIA AND
4. SLOVAKIA	HERZEGOVINA
5. SWITZERLAND	13. YUGOSLAVIA
6. AUSTRIA	14. ALBANIA
7. HUNGARY	15. MACEDONIA
8. ROMANIA	16. BULGARIA
9. MOLDOVA	17. GREECE

MADAGASCAR
MAURITIUS
SEYCHELLES
COMOROS
ALGERIA

United States: Physical

Mount Olympus
Mount Baker
Mount Rainier
Mount St. Helens
Mount Hood
CASCADE RANGE
Willamette R.
Columbia R.
St. Joe R.
BITTERROOT RANGE
SALMON RIVER MTS.
Snake R.
Mount Shasta
Pyramid Lake
Lake Tahoe
Humboldt R.
Boundary Peak
SIERRA NEVADA
San Joaquin Valley
Sacramento R.
CHANNEL IS.
Pacific Ocean
Mount Whitney
GREAT BASIN
MOJAVE DESERT
Salton Sea
Lake Mead
SONORAN DESERT
Grand Canyon
Lake Powell
Great Salt Lake
Green R.
Kings Peak
Gannett Peak
Grand Teton
ROCKY MOUNTAINS
BIGHORN MTS.
Bighorn R.
BLACK HILLS
Cheyenne R.
Lake Oahe
Yellowstone R.
Fort Peck Lake
Missouri R.
Sheyenne R.
Red R. of the North
Lake of the Woods
Lake Superior
UPPER PENINSULA
Lake Michigan
Grand R.
Lake Huron
Lake Erie
Niagara Falls
Lake Ontario
ADIRONDACK MOUNTAINS
Mount Marcy
APPALACHIAN MOUNTAINS
GREEN MOUNTAINS
WHITE MOUNTAINS
Mount Washington
CAPE COD
LONG I.
Connecticut R.
Hudson R.
Susquehanna R.
CAPE MAY
Potomac R.
Chesapeake Bay
James R.
Roanoke R.
CAPE HATTERAS
OUTER BANKS
Cape Fear R.
Pee Dee R.
Santee R.
Savannah R.
Okefenokee Swamp
Suwannee R.
Lake Okeechobee
The Everglades
FLORIDA KEYS
Straits of Florida
Atlantic Ocean
COASTAL PLAIN
Mount Mitchell
Oconee R.
Chattahoochee R.
Alabama R.
Mobile Bay
Tombigbee R.
Tennessee R.
Cumberland R.
Gulf of Mexico
Red R.
Sabine R.
Brazos R.
Pecos R.
Colorado R.
Rio Grande
SACRAMENTO MTS.
Canadian R.
Arkansas R.
GREAT PLAINS
South Platte R.
Pikes Peak
Longs Peak
FRONT RANGE
North Platte R.
Platte R.
Republican R.
Missouri R.
James R.
Des Moines R.
Minnesota R.
Mississippi R.
CENTRAL LOWLAND
Illinois R.
Wabash R.
Ohio R.
OZARK PLATEAU
Mount Elbert
San Juan R.
Colorado R.
Gila R.
Salt R.

Mount Mitchell

HAWAII
Kauai Channel
Haleakala
Mauna Kea
Mauna Loa
Pacific Ocean
Miles
0   100

ALASKA
Point Barrow
BROOKS RANGE
Yukon R.
ALASKA RANGE
Mount McKinley
Bering Sea
Bristol Bay
ALASKA PEN.
Gulf of Alaska
ALEXANDER ARCHIPELAGO
Miles
0   200

Ireland remained neutral during World War II, and its government objected to British military activities in Northern Ireland. But it was generally sympathetic to the Allied war effort, especially after the United States entered the war in 1941.

In 1949 Ireland severed all ties to the British Crown, becoming a fully independent republic. The Fianna Fail won a majority in the republic's first elections, and De Valera became prime minister. In 1954 a coalition government under John Costello took power. De Valera was elected president of the republic in 1959.

During the 1950s, Ireland developed a moderate welfare state with the support of both the Fianna Fail and Fine Gael. In the 1960s attention turned to industrial development: zinc and lead mining, and export-oriented production of textiles, ceramics, and machinery. Ireland was admitted to the E.C. in 1973.

Beginning in the late 1960s, civil rights demonstrations led frequently to civil disorders and an increase in I.R.A. guerrilla activity in the north. While the 1970s were a boom period for the Irish Republic, sectarian violence and terrorism in the north left over 2,500 dead. The 1980s saw the establishment of an Anglo-Irish Intergovernmental Council (1981) and the Hillsborough accords (1985) between the Thatcher government and the Fine Gael-Labour coalition, which gave Ireland a consultative role in Northern Irish disputes.

The government of Charles Haughey, leader of Fianna Fail, elected in 1987, faced economic problems, forcing Haughey to form a coalition government in 1989. After serious losses in June 1991 local elections, and amid charges of corruption, Haughey resigned in 1992. His successor, Albert Reynolds, faced a deep recession with unemployment rates of about 20 percent. In June 1992, a national vote strongly supported the E.C.'s Maastricht Treaty. Reynolds' coalition fell in Nov. 1992, but he created a new coalition between Fianna Fail and Labour.

In 1993, Reynolds and U.K. prime minister John Major announced the "Downing Street Declaration" that Sinn Fein, the political arm of the I.R.A., would be invited to participate in negotiations on Northern Ireland in return for the I.R.A.'s promise to halt terrorism and violence. In 1994, the I.R.A. announced a cease-fire in its 25-year-old effort to expel British troops from Northern Ireland.

Preliminary talks began optimistically, but bogged down over the British demand that the I.R.A. disarm and the I.R.A. demand that Britain withdraw its forces from Ulster. In 1996, the I.R.A. announced an end to the 17-month-old cease-fire less than an hour before setting off a powerful bomb in East London, injuring 100 people. And in June, an even stronger bomb exploded in Manchester, injuring 200 and casting serious doubt on Sinn Fein leader Gerry Adams's ability to control the more militant members of his party.

Meanwhile, Ireland's governing coalition fell in Nov. 1995, and was replaced by an odd coalition with John Bruton of Fine Gael as prime minister. The new government passed legislation permitting Irish doctors to provide information about foreign abortion providers and sponsored a referendum that overturned the constitutional ban on divorce with remarriage. The Dail elections of 1997 brought a new coalition of Fianna Fail and the Progressive Democrats with Fianna Fail's Bertie Ahern as prime minister.

In April 1998 came the breakthrough agreement (overwhelmingly approved in referendums in Northern Ireland and the Republic in May): extensive home rule in a Northern Ireland remaining part of the U.K. with some Republic of Ireland participation and with all paramilitary groups disarmed. When the deadline of Feb. 1, 2000 came and went without the I.R.A. or any other armed group disarming, Great Britain suspended the government that had been functioning for only 10 weeks (since Dec. 2). But when the I.R.A. in May pledged to put its arms "beyond use" and permit inspections, the Ulster Unionist Party accepted and the new government was functioning again by May 29. On July 26, the inspectors reported to Tony Blair that inspections had begun and that arms dumps were secure against use. Yet the refusal of the I.R.A. and other paramilitary groups to disarm led (on July 1, 2001) to the resignation of Protestant leader David Trimble as first minister, once again jeopardizing the peace accord.

But Trimble and the U.U.P. returned with confirmation that the I.R.A. had decommissioned some weapons although any joy was marred by militia violence in Belfast. In the Republic, Fianna Fail became the first ruling party since 1969 to win reelection. In the spring of 2003 the issue of I.R.A. disarmament again caused Britain to suspend the Northern Assembly yet again. Elections in the North in Nov. 2003 proved divisive as Protestant hard liners took the most seats. Trimble stopped negotiating in March 2004. In July 2005 the I.R.A. vowed to end its military struggle for a united Ireland yet Protestants remained skeptical. Finally in May 2007 Gerry Adams of Sinn Fein and the hardline Protestant leader, the Rev. Ian Paisley agreed to work together in governing the province. Bertie Ahern won reelection yet again as Ireland's economy continued its astonishing growth. In 2008, Ahern chose to resign over a problem with his finances. All political issues, however, soon were overshadowed by the near-collapse of the vaunted Irish economy, made strong by membership in the E.U. In 2008 the booming housing market crashed, banks required government support, and unemployment spiked to over 10 percent. By 2010 it was above 13 percent and the government debt, recently non-existent, soared to 14 percent of G.D.P. Austerity measures made the government very unpopular.

▶ ISRAEL
State of Israel

● **GEOGRAPHY Location:** western Asia, on eastern shore of Mediterranean Sea; has outlet to Red Sea via Gulf of Aqaba. **Boundaries:** Lebanon to N, Syria to NE, Jordan to E, Egypt to SW, Mediterranean Sea to W. **Total area:** 8,522 sq. mi. (22,072 sq km). **Coastline:** 170 mi. (273 km). **Comparative area:** slightly smaller than New Jersey. **Land use:** 17% arable land; 4% permanent crops; 79% other. **Major cities:** Jerusalem (capital); Tel Aviv-Jaffa; Haifa; Holon; Petach-Tikva.

● **PEOPLE Population:** 7,353,985 (July 2010 est.). **Nationality:** noun—Israeli(s); adjective—Israeli. **Ethnic groups:** 76.4% Jewish, 23.6% non-Jewish (mostly Arab). **Languages:** Hebrew (official), Arab (official for Arab minority); English most widely used foreign language. **Religions:** 76.4% Judaism, 16% Islam (mostly Sunni Muslim), 1.7% Arab Christian, 0.4% other Christian, 1.6% Druze, 3.9% unspecified.

• **GOVERNMENT**   Type: parliamentary democracy. **Independence:** May 14, 1948 (from League of Nations Mandate under British administration). **Constitution:** no formal constitution; some functions of constitution are filled by Declaration of Establishment (1948), the basic laws of the Knesset (legislature)— relating to the Knesset, Israeli lands, the president, government—and Israeli citizenship law. **National holiday:** Israel declared independence on May 14, 1948; because Jewish calendar is lunar, however, holiday varies from year to year; all major Jewish religious holidays are also observed as national holidays. **Heads of Government:** Shimon Peres, president (since July 2007); Binjamin Netanyahu, prime minister (since March 2009). **Structure:** executive-president has largely ceremonial functions, except for authority to decide which political leader should try to form ruling coalition following election or fall of previous government, power vested in cabinet; unicameral legislature (Knesset); judiciary-legal system based on combination of English common law, British Mandate regulations, and religious law.

• **ECONOMY**   Monetary unit: new Israeli shekel. **Budget:** (2009 est.) *income:* $45 bil.; *expend.:* $58.6 bil. **G.D.P.:** $206.5 bil., $28,400 per capita (2009 est.). **Chief crops:** citrus and other fruits, vegetables, cotton; beef, poultry, dairy products. **Natural resources:** copper, phosphates, bromide, potash, clay. **Major industries:** food processing, diamond cutting and polishing, high-tech projects. **Labor force:** 3.01 mil. (2009 est.); 82% services, 16% industry, 3% agriculture; 6% unemployment (2007 est.). **Exports:** $44.35 bil. (2009 est.); machinery, software, cut diamonds, chemicals, textiles and clothing. **Imports:** $47.4 bil. (2009 est.); raw materials, military equipment, investment goods, rough diamonds, oil. **Major trading partners:** (2008) *exports:* 32.5% U.S., 7.5% Belgium, 6.7% Hong Kong; *imports:* 12.3% U.S., 6.5% Belgium, 6.5% China, 6.1% Switzerland.

In ancient times called the Land of Canaan, the region between the Jordan River and the Mediterranean Sea was one of the earliest sites of agricultural civilization in the Middle East. Hebrew exiles from Egypt arrived c. 1200 B.C.; their kingdom, Eretz Israel, was well established by 1000 B.C., with its capital at Jerusalem. The kingdom expanded under Kings Saul and David, who extended domination over the Philistines, a local seafaring people, and established the norms of Jewish religious worship at the great temple of Jerusalem.

After the reign of King Solomon, the kingdom split into two parts, Israel and Judah. Israel was conquered by the Assyrians in 722 B.C., and Judah by the Babylonians in 586 B.C. A locally autonomous state was reestablished under the Persian empire in the fifth century B.C. And in the fourth century B.C., Alexander the Great conquered the region, beginning a period of Hellenizing influence.

A new Jewish state was established in 141 B.C. after the revolt of the Maccabees against hellenic rule, the state falling to the Roman Empire around 70 B.C. Roman rule was exerted through the puppet kings of the Herodian dynasty. Christianity, a messianic religion centering on the teachings of Jesus of Nazareth, was suppressed in Israel by both the Herodian kings and the Jewish priesthood but spread widely in the eastern Mediterranean in the early first century A.D.

A Jewish rebellion against Rome in A.D. 66 was forcibly suppressed, and the temple at Jerusalem was destroyed by the Romans in A.D. 70. Large numbers of Jews were expelled from Judea, beginning the Jewish Diaspora throughout the Roman world and beyond. A second rebellion of Jews in Israel was quelled in A.D. 132.

The territory of the kingdoms of Israel and Judah became generally known as Palestine, after the name of its ancient inhabitants, the Philistines. With the official toleration of Christianity in the Roman Empire under Constantine I (early 4th century), Palestine became a major center of Christian pilgrimage. Politically, Palestine was administered as part of the Byzantine Empire.

Expansion of Islam from Arabia brought Palestine under Islamic rule in 636. Thereafter the region was ruled by the Caliphates of Damascus (661–750) and Baghdad (762–1258). Part of Palestine was captured in 1099 by European Crusaders, who established the short-lived Latin Kingdom of Jerusalem. The region was conquered by the Mongols in 1258; defeat of the Mongols in 1260 at the battle of Ain Jalyut, near Nazareth, prevented a Mongol invasion of Egypt. Palestine next became part of the Mamluk empire and was incorporated into the Ottoman Empire in 1516.

The emigration of Jews from Europe to the homeland of Israel began around 1870, under the influence of the Zionist movement. Zionism, traceable in part to the thought of Moses Mendelssohn (1729–86), originally emphasized the need to maintain Jewish identity and religious consciousness as well as to promote Jewish assimilation into European culture. By the time of the First World Zionist Congress, convened in Basel by Theodor Herzl in 1897, emphasis had shifted to the need for a specific Jewish homeland. After 1905, under the leadership of Chaim Weizmann, Jewish emigration to Palestine increased.

With the collapse of the Ottoman Empire during World War I, Palestine came under British rule in 1917. In that year the British government issued the Balfour Declaration, committing Britain to aiding the establishment of a Jewish homeland in Palestine. After Britain received a League of Nations Mandate to govern Palestine (as well as Transjordan) in 1923, Jewish immigration into Palestine increased significantly. Faced with rising Palestinian Arab opposition to a further increase in Jewish immigration, Britain reinterpreted the Balfour Declaration in restricted terms and attempted to limit the number of Jewish arrivals.

The crisis lasted until the outbreak of World War II. During the war the Palestinian Jewish community (then about 500,000) generally supported the British war effort, while some Palestinian Arab leaders translated anti-Zionist sentiments into sympathy for the Axis. Despite the horrible revelations about the Holocaust—the systematic killing of six million Jews during the War—in 1946 British authorities refused a recommendation of the Anglo-American Committee of Inquiry that they permit resettlement of 100,000 European Jews in Palestine and they limited further immigration to 2,000 per month. Jewish leaders pressed their cause at the United Nations, while in Palestine, Zionist terrorist organizations waged covert war against the British authorities.

In 1947 a U.N. Special Committee on Palestine, boycotted by Palestinian Arabs, recommended the partition of Palestine into Jewish and Arab sectors, with Jerusalem to be administered under international control. The U.N. adopted the recommendations on Nov. 29, 1947, and the British began to withdraw their forces, while Palestinian Jews and Arabs prepared for war.

On May 14, 1948, the independent state of Israel was established, with its capital at Tel Aviv. On the same day, troops from the Arab League nations attacked Israel. Fighting and cease-fires alternated throughout 1948; Israel lost control of the Old City of Jerusalem but retained the New City, and elsewhere consolidated its territorial control. Separate armistices between Israel and the Arab nations were concluded in 1949; Jordan retained control of the West Bank, and Egypt occupied Gaza. Large numbers of Palestinian Arab refugees departed for camps in Jordan, Lebanon, and Syria, while equally large numbers of Jews from Arab countries resettled in Israel.

Elections to the Knesset (Parliament) were held in Jan. 1949 and resulted in a coalition government. Chaim Weizmann was elected president, and David Ben-Gurion became prime minister. Laws were enacted to ensure religious control of education and civil law and to affirm the "Right of Return" of all Jews to Israel. The role of labor was protected by law, as was the establishment of agricultural collectives (*kibbutzim*).

Taking advantage of the Suez Crisis involving Great Britain, France, and Egypt, Israel invaded Egypt's Sinai Peninsula on Oct. 29, 1956. Israeli forces withdrew under the terms of a U.N. cease-fire on Nov. 6 but retained control of Gaza.

Throughout this period Israel's population continued to swell with immigrants from Europe, the U.S. and also from the dwindling Jewish communities of the Arab world. Israel's economy, aided by foreign aid and private remittances, grew rapidly, while foreign military aid and the growth of a substantial domestic armaments industry increased its military preparedness.

On May 19, 1967, U.N. peacekeeping forces withdrew from the Egypt-Israel border on the insistence of Egypt's president Gamal Abdel Nasser. Egyptian forces then reoccupied Gaza and closed the Gulf of Aqaba to Israeli shipping. In the Six-Day War, June 5–10, Israel recaptured Gaza, occupied the Sinai Peninsula to the Suez Canal, and captured the West Bank and the Old City of Jerusalem from Jordan and the Golan Heights from Syria. Another U.N.-supervised cease-fire went into effect.

Egypt and Syria, backed by Soviet airlifts, invaded Israel on Yom Kippur, Oct. 6, 1973. Israel, with strong U.S. support, counterattacked, driving back the Syrian forces and crossing the Suez Canal from the Sinai into Egypt. Fighting ceased on Oct. 24, and a disengagement agreement was signed on Jan. 18, 1974. Israeli forces withdrew from the west bank of the Suez Canal and, in stages, from the Sinai Peninsula, completing the withdrawal in 1982.

The government of Prime Minister Golda Meir fell after the Yom Kippur War, and a new coalition took power. A period of domestic and international difficulties followed, with severe inflation in the economy and a marked rise in Palestinian and other terrorist attacks against Israeli targets. Israeli forces repeatedly attacked Palestinian bases in southern Lebanon and aided the Christian militia forces in the Lebanese civil war of 1975-76. On July 3, 1976, Israeli commandos raided the airport at Entebbe, Uganda, to rescue 103 hostages held by Arab and German hijackers.

The 1977 parliamentary elections brought a conservative coalition to power, with Menachem Begin elected prime minister. Egypt's president Anwar Sadat visited Jerusalem in November 1977, and Begin and Sadat met at a conference with U.S. president Jimmy Carter at Camp David in 1979. On Mar. 26, 1979, Egypt and Israel signed a formal peace treaty ending 30 years of war and establishing diplomatic relations between the two nations.

In July 1980 Israel affirmed the transfer of its national capital from Tel Aviv to Jerusalem and the incorporation of the (formerly Jordanian) Old City into Israeli territory. The Israeli government decided in 1980 to promote increased Jewish settlement in the West Bank, provoking protest from Palestinian leaders.

Israeli forces invaded southern Lebanon in March 1978. After a brief occupation, most Israeli forces withdrew and were replaced by a U.N. peacekeeping force, but Israel continued to cooperate with Lebanese Christian militia forces in anti-Palestinian operations.

Israeli and Syrian forces clashed briefly in April 1981. On June 7, 1981, Israeli jets destroyed a nuclear reactor near Baghdad, Iraq, that Israel claimed could have been used to manufacture materials for nuclear weapons. Prime Minister Begin was returned to office in a close election in 1981, and he retired in 1983.

Attacking Palestine Liberation Organization strongholds in Lebanon in May, 1982, Israel mounted a full-scale invasion of Lebanon in June. Israeli and Syrian forces fought in Lebanon's Bekaa Valley but disengaged after a few days. On June 14 Israeli forces surrounded and shelled Beirut, forcing the PLO to evacuate the city. On Sept. 14 Israeli forces occupied West Beirut, following the assassination of the newly elected Lebanese president, Bashir Gemayel. Lebanese Christian militia, with tacit Israeli permission, entered two Palestinian refugee camps at Sabra and Shatila on Sept. 16 and massacred hundreds of civilians, provoking an international outcry against Israel's occupation of Lebanon. Israeli forces withdrew from Lebanon in June 1985, except for a narrow "security zone" along the border.

Parliamentary elections in 1984 resulted in a coalition government, with power shared by Likud leader Yitzhak Shamir and Labor leader Shimon Peres.

In December 1987, Palestinian residents of Gaza and the West Bank launched a series of violent demonstrations against Israeli authorities. The *intifada*, or uprising, continued into 1991 in a cycle of protest and police reaction that led to the deaths of hundreds of demonstrators and a crisis of Israeli control in the occupied territories. Tensions were exacerbated by the immigration of hundreds of thousands of Soviet Jews to Israel.

Parliamentary elections in Nov. 1988 continued the Likud-Labor stalemate and brought increased power to the minor religious parties. A new grand-coalition government announced in Jan. 1989, with Yitzhak Shamir as prime minister and Shimon Peres as minister of finance, collapsed in mid-March because of disagreements over an American-backed plan for peace talks with the Palestinians. This plunged the country into a crisis, resolved in June 1990 with the formation of a coalition government of Likud and several right-wing religious parties. Shamir managed to survive several no-confidence votes, and his alliance with religious party Agudat Israel in Nov. solidified his party's power as the Persian Gulf crisis unfolded.

After months of diplomacy spearheaded by the U.S., direct talks between Israel and a (non-PLO) Jordanian-Palestinian joint delegation opened in Washington in December 1991. The talks broke down in stalemate as Israel refused to compromise over the key issue of new Jewish settlements on the West Bank. In the election of June 1992, the Labor party led by Rabin scored an upset victory over Shamir's Likud coalition government. Rabin disclosed that the Shamir government had pursued a deliberate policy of intransigence in the peace talks in order to allow the accelerated West Bank settlement program to continue.

The Palestinian *intifada* gained renewed momentum in Dec. 1992 when Israel deported 400 Palestinians to Lebanon on the grounds that they were responsible for acts of violence. Israel launched a series of air and land attacks on suspected terrorist bases in Lebanon, resulting in many casualties. The world was stunned only a few weeks later, when on Sept. 13, 1993, Prime Minister Yitzhak Rabin and PLO leader Yasir Arafat signed an agreement in principle for a peace settlement based on Palestinian recognition of Israel's right to exist, and Israel's acceptance of partial self-rule for the Palestinians. Soon, areas in Gaza and the West Bank were under Palestinian control.

By fall of 1995, Israeli troops had begun withdrawing from Palestinian settlements on the West Bank, but a month later an Israeli extremist assassinated Rabin. His successor, Shimon Peres, vowed to continue moves toward peace and moved elections forward from October to May. In early 1996 Israel faced the worst suicide bomber attacks in 20 years: in five days 60 people were dead. Hamas, the Palestinian resistance group, took responsibility for the attacks.

In Israel's first direct election of a prime minister, Likud's hard-line Benjamin Netanyahu narrowly defeated Peres as Israelis chose "security" over "peace." By 1997 the peace process came to a virtual standstill as the Netanyahu government pushed ahead with new settlements in the West Bank and in East Jerusalem. The first sign of a break in the impasse came in June 1998 when Pres. Weizman declared that Netanyahu was undermining peace talks. Negotiations with the Palestinians began anew in July and on Oct. 23, in Washington, Netanyahu and Arafat agreed to the Wye Memorandum by which Israel agreed to surrender about 13 percent of her West Bank holdings. But the Knesset toppled Netanyahu's government and rejected the agreement. Elections in May 1999 brought Ehud Barak, former army chief of staff, to the office of prime minister.

The roller-coaster peace talks between the Barak government and the Palestinians lasted for a year but broke off bitterly (July 25, 2000); what was seen in the Knesset as excessive concessions, especially on Jerusalem, led to the unravelling of Barak's coalition and a call for new elections. In the interim, Israel completed a withdrawal from the security zone it had established in 1978 in Lebanon. In late Sept. renewed violence between Israeli troops and Palestinians forced Barak to resign in December and in Feb. 2001 hard-liner Ariel Sharon won 63 percent of the vote to become prime minister. Nearly 400 people, mainly Palestinians, had died since September and in March began a series of suicide bombings by Palestinians in Israel. The deadly cycle of Palestinian terror-bombings and Israeli reprisals continued without abatement through 2003. Sharon remained firmly in power even after Labor left his coalition forcing new elections in 2003.

In 2004, under pressure from the U.S., Sharon unveiled a plan to remove the settlements from the Gaza Strip while keeping five major ones in the West Bank (to be protected by a 437-mile security wall). In the summer of 2005 all the Gaza settlements were closed down. But at the end of 2005 Sharon suffered a massive stroke and he was replaced by Ehud Olmert. Plans to continue diminishing the number of settlements were put on hold and in July 2006 Israel began a major attack on Hezbollah within Lebanon which ended in a stalemate but with Israel being criticized for the many civilian deaths that resulted. In 2008 a scandal enveloped Olmert and his government lost all support. After Hamas won the 2007 Palestinian parliamentary elections, the Israelis responded to the Hamas rocket attacks with a fierce assault on Gaza that resulted in 1,300 deaths, many of them civilians. In Feb. 2009, elections restored the right-wing Likud to power under Benjamin Netanyahu. (See "Major News Stories.")

Palestinian Territories

As a result of the 1993 peace talks sponsored by the U.S., Israel and the PLO signed the Declaration of Principles on Interim Self-Government Arrangements (known as the DOP) which provided for a transitional period of no more than five years of Palestinian self-government in two areas, the Gaza Strip and the West Bank. Israel agreed to transfer some powers to the Palestinian Authority and a Palestinian Legislative Council was elected in 1996. Israel, however, retained control over security in these areas. Several other minor agreements were readied over the next three years but direct negotiations for a permanent settlement did not begin again until 1999. When the talks failed a new *intifada* broke out in Sept. 2000 and, with the onset of suicide bombings, Israel took stern military measures and ended any talk about a permanent settlement of differences.

Over the next five years periodic violence was the norm. Arafat's death in 2005 led to parliamentary elections and the Islamic party known as Hamas won convincingly. In Feb. 2007 a power sharing agreement was reached with Fatah, the successor to Arafat's PLO, but a violent power struggle continued and in June Hamas fighters routed those of Fatah as over 150 Palestinians were killed. The leader of Fatah, Mahmoud Abbas, ended the coalition agreement and with support from the U.S. began to rebuild his party.

GAZA STRIP This area (totalling 139 sq. mi. or 360 sq. km.) borders the Mediterranean Sea between Egypt and Israel. Approximately 1.5 million people live here. Israeli settlements were removed by the Sharon government in the summer of 2005. In June 2007 Hamas wrestled control of Gaza from Fatah in a bloody battle that killed more than 100, and in 2008 Israel attacked Gaza killing 1,300 and destroying many homes. Major cities include Gaza, Dayr al Balah, Rafah, Khan Yunus, and Abasan.

WEST BANK This area (totalling 2,263 sq. mi. or 5,860 sq. km.) borders Israel and Jordan and includes East Jerusalem and Jerusalem No Man's Land, established after the 1967 war. Approximately 2.6 million people live here including 187,000 Israeli settlers in the West Bank and fewer than 177,000 in East Jerusalem. Major cities include Jericho, Hebron, Bethlehem and Nablus.

▶ ITALY
Italian Republic

• **GEOGRAPHY** **Location:** peninsula, extending from southern Europe into Mediterranean Sea, with a number of adjacent islands, principally Sicily to SW, and Sardinia to W. **Boundaries:** Switzerland and Austria to N, Slovenia to NE, Adriatic Sea to E, Ionian Sea to SE, Mediterranean Sea to W, France to NW. **Total area:** 116,305 sq. mi. (301,230 sq km). **Coastline:** 4,723 mi. (7,600 km). **Comparative area:** slightly larger than Arizona. **Land use:** 28% arable land; 9% permanent crops; 63% other. **Major cities:** Roma (Rome; capital); Milano (Milan); Napoli (Naples); Torino (Turin); Palermo.

• **PEOPLE** **Population:** 58,090,681 (July 2010 est.). **Nationality:** noun—Italian(s); adjective—Italian. **Ethnic groups:** primarily Italian, but includes small clusters of German-, French-, and Slovene-Italians in north and Albanian-Italians in south; Sicilians. **Languages:** Italian; parts of Trentino-Alto Adige region (e.g., Bolzano) are predominantly German-speaking; significant French-speaking minority in Valle d'Aosta region; Slovene-speaking minority in Trieste-Gorizia area. **Religions:** predominantly Roman Catholic.

• **GOVERNMENT** **Type:** republic. **Constitution:** Jan. 1, 1948. **National holiday:** Anniversary of the Republic, June 2. **Heads of Government:** Giorgio Napolitano, president (since May 2006); Silvio Berlusconi, prime minister (since May 2008). **Structure:** executive—president empowered to dissolve Parliament and call national election; commander of armed forces presides over Supreme Defense Council; otherwise, authority to govern invested in Council of Ministers; bicameral legislature—popularly elected Parliament (315-member Senate, 630-member Chamber of Deputies); judiciary—independent.

• **ECONOMY** **Monetary unit:** euro. **Budget:** (2009 est.) *income:* $960.1 bil.; *expend.:* $1.068 tril. **G.D.P.:** $1.76 tril., $30,300 per capita (2009 est.). **Chief crops:** fruits, vegetables, grapes, potatoes, sugar beets, soybeans, grain, olives; meat and dairy products. **Natural resources:** mercury, potash, marble, sulfur, dwindling natural gas and crude oil reserves. **Major industries:** tourism, machinery and transport equipment, iron, steel, chemicals. **Labor force:** 24.95 mil. (2009 est.); 65% services, 31% industry, 4% agriculture (2005); 6.8% unemployment (2007 est.). **Exports:** $369 bil. (2009 est.); engineering products, textiles and clothing, production machinery, motor vehicles. **Imports:** $358.7 bil. (2009 est.); engineering products, chemicals, transport equipment, energy products. **Major trading partners:** (2008) *exports:* 12.7% Germany, 11.2% France, 6.5% Spain; *imports:* 15.9% Germany, 8.5% France, 6.2% China.

Rome became the major power in Italy around 500 B.C., dominating the Etruscans in the north and Greek settlements in the south. The Roman Republic already dominated most of the Mediterranean and western Europe by the time imperial rule was established under Julius Caesar. The empire was divided between Rome and Byzantium in the fourth century A.D. The Roman Empire in the west was severely weakened by Germanic invasions in the fifth century and gradually dissolved, so that Italy became a disunited collection of aristocratic holdings and independent cities.

By the 10th century, the city-states, especially in the north, emerged as major powers, rivaling the Papal States of the central peninsula. Venice and Genoa emerged as major maritime powers during the medieval period, while Florence, Siena, and other cities developed into centers of agricultural and commercial wealth, impelling the successive renaissances of the 12th and 15th centuries. With the rise of the Habsburg empire, the monarchical powers of northern Europe vied for power in Italy, and the peninsula's small states became pawns of France, Spain, and Austria.

At the turn of the 19th century, Napoleon created the short-lived Kingdom of Italy as a French satellite, but after his fall, there was a general return to the old pattern, with Austria dominating the north. Metternich in 1815 called Italy a "geographic expression."

The 19th century saw a growing sense of nationalism. The revolutionary military leader, Giuseppe Garibaldi, and the statesman, Conte Camillo di Cavour, brought about the establishment of the Kingdom of Italy in 1861. The kingdom wrested Venice away from Austria (1866) and absorbed the Papal States in 1870. Although united territorially, the kingdom was divided by conflict between church and state, north and south, modern urban industry versus semifeudal rural poverty. Parliamentary politics under the constitutional monarchy created a regime that was weak and venal, inspiring little popular support.

Italy joined the Allied powers in World War I, but its minor gains in the Peace of Paris scarcely seemed to justify its wartime suffering and one million dead. Postwar economic dislocation, fear of communism, and political disillusionment abetted the rise of fascism. Benito Mussolini took over the Italian government at the invitation of the king in 1922 and soon acquired dictatorial powers. Papal secular authority in Vatican City was reestablished by the Lateran Agreement of 1929. In the late 1920s and early 1930s, Italy appeared to be a major power, defending Austria from Germany, colonizing Ethiopia, supporting Francisco Franco in the Spanish civil war, and joining in an "axis" with Hitler's Germany.

Mussolini was soon eclipsed by Hitler, and Italy was drawn into the disaster of World War II in 1939. Italy annexed Albania and invaded Greece, but that campaign turned into a fiasco from which German troops had to save the Italian army. In 1943 Allied attacks on Italy began; the fascist Grand Council deposed Mussolini, and the king, Victor Emmanuel III, had him arrested. Hitler intervened in September 1943 and began the war in Italy anew, rescuing Mussolini who established another fascist regime in northern Italy, while the legal Italian government in the south switched sides and welcomed Italy's liberation.

The head of the first postwar government was a Christian Democrat, Alcide de Gasperi. The monarchy was abolished by plebiscite in 1946, and the Republic of Italy was established. The north supported the republic, while monarchism retained significant support in the south. This division reflected a roughly accurate generalization that sees Italy as a progressive commercial and industrial north and a backward agricultural/pastoral south. Despite such industrial giants as Fiat and Pirelli, however, Italy's manufacturing has been primarily carried on by medium-size and small firms, while agriculture is characteristic of the whole country. As late as 1956, there were more Italian workers in agriculture than in industry.

In the first elections under the republic, in 1948, the Christian Democrats benefited from American patronage and a split in the ranks of the Left to win a parliamentary majority. Italy accepted Marshall Plan aid and membership in NATO; reintegration into the European mainstream found expression in membership in the Council of Europe and the Coal and Steel Community.

Domestically, reconstruction was the major task, with industrial and agricultural output severely hampered by damage from the war; inflation was rampant and basic social services impaired. The Christian Democrats, normally in Center-Right coalitions in the 1950s and Center-Left coalitions in the 1960s, adopted a policy directed at creating a stable currency, a free market, social welfare programs, and occasional state intervention in the economy. This created an Italian "economic miracle," with industrial production doubling between 1953 and 1961 and an additional 40 percent by 1966, led by steel, automobiles, machinery, and electrical equipment.

In the 1970s the Christian Democrats gradually declined in political influence, normally gaining less than 40 percent of the popular vote while continuing to provide premiers in often short-lived coalition cabinets. Left-wing terrorism became a major national problem. The Christian Democratic leader and former prime minister Aldo Moro was kidnapped and murdered in 1978, and U.S. Brig. Gen./NATO officer James Dozier was kidnapped (and subsequently rescued) in 1981. The government of Bettino Craxi, Italy's first Socialist premier, was severely shaken after it refused to cooperate with the United States in apprehending and trying the hijackers of the Achille Lauro in 1985. Craxi resigned in 1987.

Lacking political unity, Italy's coalition governments—there have been more than 60 since the war—tended to muddle along in the face of slow growth, inflation, and high unemployment. But awareness of Mafia assassinations and revelations of government corruption led to demands for dramatic changes. In April 1993 the electorate overwhelmingly approved reforms that changed the basic elements of Italian political life. The first elections under the reformed system (March 1994) ended half a century of Christian Democrat-led coalition governments. The Christian Democrats, hastily renamed the Italian Popular Party, won only 11 percent of the vote, while the Socialists, normally the second largest party, fell to 2 percent. What replaced the old guard was the right-wing Alliance for Freedom. Wealthy publishing executive Silvio Berlusconi was sworn in as prime minister but his government lasted only five months. Political disputes, union opposition to his austerity budget, and the announcement that magistrates were investigating charges he had bribed tax officials diminished his authority.

Rather than call new elections, Italy's president asked Lamberto Dini to form a new "nonparty" cabinet of businessmen, judges, and professors, a cabinet that won the requisite votes of confidence in the two chambers by Feb. 1, 1995. The new government showed surprising staying power, passing its budget and negotiating reform of Italy's bloated pension system with leading trade unions. It even began the politically touchy process of investigating the anticrime magistrates for possible violations of civil rights.

As corruption trials continued, the Dini government survived successive votes of confidence, the last on condition that he resign with the new year, which he did. New elections were not held until April 1996. The left-wing "Olive Tree Coalition," led by the once-Communist "Democratic Party of the Left," trounced the right-wing "Freedom Alliance." Its new prime minister was Professor Romano Prodi of the Popular party. Prodi concentrated on bringing the economy into line so Italy would be eligible for participation in the EMU which, with much maneuvering, including a stringent austerity budget, and a sudden economic upswing, he did—formal endorsement coming in May 1998. Yet, in October, the Prodi government lost a vote of confidence over budget's cuts in social spending.

The "Olive Tree" government muddled along until the May 2001 elections, convincingly won by the right-wing House of Freedom coalition, spearheaded by Forza Italia, and bringing back Silvio Berlusconi as prime minister. Berlusconi was under indictment for corruption when in June 2003 the legislature granted him immunity until he was out of office but this was later ruled unconstitutional. Prodi returned to power in May 2006 and austerity budgeting became essential as Italy's debt had grown over the past years. But Berlusconi came back in April 2008 to win a solid victory, yet again.

▶ IVORY COAST
Republic of Côte d'Ivoire

• **GEOGRAPHY   Location:** western coast of Africa. **Boundaries:** Mali and Burkina Faso to N, Ghana to E, Gulf of Guinea to S, Liberia and Guinea to W. **Total area:** 124,502 sq. mi. (322,460 sq km). **Coastline:** 320 mi. (515 km). **Comparative area:** slightly larger than New Mexico. **Land use:** 9% arable land; 14% permanent crops; 77% other. **Major cities:** Yamoussoukro (capital—not recognized by U.S., which recognizes Abidjan); Abidjan; Bouaké.
• **PEOPLE   Population:** 20,617,068 (July 2009 est.). **Nationality:** noun—Ivorian(s); adjective—Ivorian. **Ethnic groups:** 41% Akan, 18% Voltaiques or Gur, 17% Northern Mandes, 11% Krous, 10% Southern Mandes, 3% other (including 130,000 Lebanese and 20,000 French). **Languages:** French (official); over 60 African languages and dialects with Dioula most widely spoken. **Religions:** 35-40% Muslim, 20-30%% Christian, 25-40% indigenous beliefs.
• **GOVERNMENT   Type:** republic; multiparty presidential regime established 1960. **Independence:** Aug. 7, 1960 (from France). **Constitution:** Nov. 3, 1960; approved by referendum July 23, 2000. **National holiday:** National Day, Aug. 7. **Heads of Government:** Laurent Gbagbo, president (since Oct. 2000); Guillaume Soro, prime minister (since Apr. 2007). **Structure:** executive—president has broad powers; unicameral legislature—175-member National Assembly; judiciary.
• **ECONOMY   Monetary unit:** Communauté Financière Africaine franc. **Budget:** (2008) income: $4.725 bil.; expend.: $5.082 bil. **G.D.P.:** $34 bil., $1,700 per capita (2008 est.). **Chief crops:** coffee, cocoa, bananas, palm oil; cotton, rubber; timber. **Natural resources:** crude oil, diamonds, manganese, iron ore, cobalt. **Major industries:** foodstuffs, wood processing, oil refinery. **Labor force:** 7.035 mil; 68% agriculture; 40-50% unemployment becuase of civil war. **Exports:** $11.96 bil.

(f.o.b., 2008 est.); cocoa, coffee, tropical woods. **Imports**: $7.948 bil. (f.o.b., 2008 est.); food, consumer goods, capital goods, fuel. **Major trading partners**: (2006) *exports*: 18.3% France, 9.7% Netherlands, 9.1% U.S., 7.2% Nigeria, 4.2% Germany; *imports*: 25.4% France, 27.6% Nigeria, 4.3% China.

The peoples of the Ivory Coast belong to various tribes that had established small and mutually hostile kingdoms prior to the 18th century. The dominant Baule migrated to the Ivory Coast from Ghana about 200 years ago. European contact began with the Portuguese, who established coastal trading stations in the 15th century. They were followed in rapid succession by the Dutch, British, and finally the French, who landed at Assinie in 1637. Dense tropical forests and a lack of good harbors retarded European exploration.

France established a protectorate over the coastal zone in 1842 and during the remainder of the 19th century expanded its control, by conquest and diplomacy, into the interior. In 1893 the Ivory Coast was organized as a French colony, and in 1904 it was made part of French West Africa.

France's Vichy government controlled French West Africa during World War II and harshly suppressed the region's growing nationalist movements. In 1946 a group of West African leaders, inspired by Félix Houphouet-Boigny, formed the African Democratic Assembly, which later cooperated with the French in the implementation of reforms, including, by 1956, universal suffrage and the formation of locally autonomous assemblies. Complete independence for the Ivory Coast came on Aug. 4, 1960 and Félix Houphouet-Boigny was unanimously elected the first president.

His Democratic party was the only one allowed so Houphouet-Boigny easily won reelection. But even after he liberalized the political process in 1990 he retained control, winning a new five-year term in multiparty elections held in 1990. Under his presidency, the Ivory Coast enjoyed both political stability and economic prosperity.

Houphouet-Boigny died in 1993, and was succeeded by Henri Konan Bedie, president of the National Assembly. Bedie won reelection in 1995, and continued the policies of his predecessor. In Sept. 1999, however, after he ordered the arrest of several hundred members of an opposition party, a military coup led by General Robert Gueï overturned the Bedie government on Christmas Eve 1999. But Gueï's attempt to rig the 2000 elections provoked demonstrations that forced him to flee. Laurent Gbagbo became president.

In Sept. 2002, another coup by Gueï, in which he was killed, precipitated a civil war pitting the Gbagbo government against several rebel movements. French troops, sent to protect foreigners, became involved in the fighting and the negotiating. In March 2003 a power-sharing agreement went into effect with Gbagbo appointing a Muslim premier at the head of a 41-member cabinet representing all factions. But civil war continued with the government holding power in the south, the rebels in the north until U.N. peacekeepers arrived in late 2004. In 2007 the leader of the rebel forces, Guillaume Soro, was appointed prime minister by Gbagbo to help bring peace.

▶ **JAMAICA**

• **GEOGRAPHY Location**: northern Caribbean Sea. Kingston 17°58′N, 76°48′W. **Boundaries**: Cuba 87 mi. (145 km) to N. **Total area**: 4,243 sq. mi. (10,990 sq km). **Coastline**: 635 mi. (1,022 km). **Comparative area**: slightly smaller than Connecticut. **Land use**: 16% arable land; 9% permanent crops; 75% other. **Major cities**: Kingston (capital); Spanish Town; Montego Bay.

• **PEOPLE Population**: 2,825,928 (July 2009 est.). **Nationality**: noun—Jamaican(s); adjective—Jamaican. **Ethnic groups**: 91.2% black, 6.2% mixed, 2.6% other, unknown. **Languages**: English, patois English. **Religions**: 62.5% Protestant, 2.6% Roman Catholic, 14.2% other, 20.9% none.

• **GOVERNMENT Type**: constitutional parliamentary democracy. **Independence**: Aug. 6, 1962 (from U.K.). **Constitution**: Aug. 6, 1962. **National holiday**: Independence Day, first Monday in August. **Heads of Government**: Gov. Gen. Dr. Patrick L. Allen, governor-general (since Feb. 2009); Bruce Golding, prime minister (since Sept. 2007). **Structure**: cabinet headed by prime minister; bicameral legislature; judiciary follows British tradition under chief justice.

• **ECONOMY Monetary unit**: Jamaican dollar. **Budget**: (2008 est.) *income*: $4.166 bil.; *expend.*: $4.838 bil. **G.D.P.**: $20.88 bil., $7,400 per capita (2008 est.). **Chief crops**: sugarcane, bananas, coffee, citrus, potatoes, vegetables; poultry, goats, milk. **Natural resources**: bauxite, gypsum, limestone. **Major industries**: tourism, bauxite mining, textiles. **Labor force**: 1.261 bil. (2008); 64% services, 17% agriculture, 19% industry; 10.2% unemployment (2007). **Exports**: $2.569 bil. (f.o.b., 2008 est.); alumina, bauxite, sugar, bananas, rum. **Imports**: $7.191 bil. (f.o.b., 2008 est.); machinery and transport equipment, construction materials, fuel; food; chemicals. **Major trading partners**: (2006) *exports*: 30.2% U.S., 15.6% Canada, 15.2% China, 10.3% U.K., 7% Netherlands, 4.6% Norway; *imports*: 39.3% U.S., 13.6% Trinidad & Tobago, 9.5% Venezuela.

Christopher Columbus visited Jamaica in 1494, and the Spanish ruled the island—exterminating the native Arawaks in the process—until it fell to British control in 1655. A haven for buccaneers, by the 18th century Jamaica was a major sugar producer and the site of one of the busiest slave markets in the world. Emancipation of the slaves in 1833 and abolition of tariff protection in 1846 contributed strongly to the subsequent downfall of the plantation economy.

In 1962 the island gained its independence. The country has been plagued by racial and class division set within the context of an underdeveloped economy. Michael Manley of the People's National party became prime minister in 1972. He nationalized some industry and established closer ties with Cuba. Edward Seaga's Jamaica Labour party came to power in 1980 and encouraged more private-sector involvement in developing the economy. Though Manley was reelected to office in 1989, he did not reverse this general trend; in 1992 he was succeeded by Percival James Patterson, who led the People's National party to a landslide victory in violence-marred elections in March 1993. He was reelected in 1997 despite continuing economic problems. In 2006 he was succeeded by Portia Simpson-Miller of the same party, but in 2007, the center-right Jamaica Labour Party took control for the first time after 18 years of People's National Party rule. In May 2010 violence erupted as the government cracked down on a major drug operation, but nearly 100 were killed.

▶JAPAN

• **GEOGRAPHY Location:** chain of more than 3,000 islands extending 1,300 mi. (2,200 km) NE to SW between Sea of Japan and western Pacific Ocean; southern Japan about 93 mi. (150 km) E of S. Korea; islands of Hokkaido, Honshu, Shikoku, and Kyushu account for 98% of land area. Tokyo 35°40'N, 139°45'E. **Boundaries:** Sea of Okhotsk to N, Pacific Ocean to E, East China Sea to SW, and Sea of Japan to W. **Total area:** 145,882 sq. mi. (377,835 sq km). **Coastline:** 18,487 mi. (29,751 km). **Comparative area:** slightly smaller than California. **Land use:** 12% arable land; 1% permanent crops; 87% other. **Major cities:** Tokyo (capital); Yokohama; Osaka; Nagoya; Sapporo.

• **PEOPLE Population:** 126,804,433 (July 2010 est.). **Nationality:** noun—Japanese (sing., pl.); adjective—Japanese. **Ethnic groups:** 99% Japanese, 1% other (mostly Korean). **Languages:** Japanese. **Religions:** most Japanese observe both Shinto and Buddhist rites; about 16% belong to other faiths, including 0.7% Christian.

• **GOVERNMENT Type:** parliamentary government with a constitutional monarchy. **Constitution:** May 3, 1947. **National holiday:** Birthday of the Emperor, Dec. 23. **Heads of Government:** Akihito, emperor (since Jan. 1989); Naoto Kan, prime minister (since June 2010). **Structure:** executive—emperor is symbolic head of state; power is vested in cabinet appointed by prime minister; bicameral legislature; judiciary.

• **ECONOMY Monetary unit:** yen. **Budget:** (2009 est.) *income:* $1.614 tril.; *expend.:* $1.997 tril. **G.D.P.:** $4.137 tril., $32,600 per capita (2009 est.). **Chief crops:** rice, sugar beets, vegetables, fruits; chickens, pigs, cattle; world's largest fish catch. **Natural resources:** negl. mineral resources, fish. **Major industries:** metallurgical and engineering industries, electrical and electronic industries, motor vehicles. **Labor force:** 66.93 mil. (2009); 67.7% services, 27.8% industry. 4.6% agriculture. **Exports:** $516.3 bil. (2009 est.); semiconductors, office machinery, chemicals, motor vehicles. **Imports:** $490.6 bil. (2009 est.); fuels, foodstuffs, chemicals, textiles, office machinery. **Major trading partners:** (2008) *exports:* 17.8% U.S., 16% China, 7.6% South Korea, 5.9% Taiwan, 5.1% Hong Kong; *imports:* 18.8% China, 10.4% U.S., 6.7% Saudi Arabia, 6.2% Australia.

Japan's ancient Jomon civilization was displaced by proto-Japanese Yayoi migrants from mainland northeast Asia beginning in the fourth century B.C. In the early Yayoi period, a mounted military aristocracy dominated rice-growing commoners. The shamanic religion of the time was ancestral to Japan's later indigenous religion, Shinto. Yayoi society evolved into the Yamato protostate, c. A.D. 250–500. The Yamato kings were buried in large, elaborate tomb mounds together with haniwa clay sculptures. From the third century A.D., contact with the mainland increased. Korean missionaries introduced Buddhism and Chinese writing in the mid-sixth century. A centralized monarchy developed and Prince Shotoku, a great patron of Buddhism, founded the Horyuji and other great temples in the early seventh century.

In 710 the Yamato kings established a permanent capital for the first time, at Nara; the city was modeled on the Chinese capital. In 785 the court, split by factionalism and dominated by Nara's large and wealthy Buddhist temples, abandoned the capital; in 794 the new capital at Heian (Kyoto) was completed. The ensuing Heian period was one of the most brilliant in Japanese history. A small civil aristocracy, dominated by the Fujiwara family, drew great wealth from provincial estates and created a culture of extreme refinement. From the ninth through the 11th centuries, strong Chinese influences were incorporated into Japanese culture.

In the 12th century the power of the Heian court waned as the influence of the provincial military aristocracy (samurai) grew stronger. In 1156 the capital was seized by the Taira family; in 1185 the Taira were overthrown by their rivals, the Minamoto. The Minamoto established a military government under a shogun (generalissimo) at Kamakura; the emperor remained at Kyoto, stripped of all governmental authority. In Kamakura the Minamoto were soon displaced by their former vassals, the Hojo. During the Kamakura period, the Japanese drew away from Chinese influence in art, literature, and religion, creating a more distinctively Japanese culture. In 1274 and again in 1281, Mongol invasions were repulsed with the aid of timely typhoons (*kamikaze*, "divine winds").

In the course of a failed attempt at imperial restoration, the Kamakura shogunate was overthrown in the 1330s by the Ashikaga family, which in 1338 established a new shogunal government at Muromachi, a precinct of Kyoto. The Muromachi period saw the flowering of a warrior culture, marked by military virtues as bravery, loyalty, personal honor, and skill with weapons and by adherence to Zen Buddhism and its associated arts (tea ceremony, calligraphy, etc.). With the Onin Wars of the mid-15th century, the Muromachi shogunate lost most of its power, and the country fell into a century of civil war.

The civil wars were brought to an end during the second half of the 16th century by three successive unifiers, Oda Nobunaga, Hideyoshi, and Tokugawa Ieyasu. At the same time, the Jesuit Francis Xavier and his successors established a short-lived Japanese Christian community. Hideyoshi made several attempts (1592–98) to conquer and annex Korea. In 1601 Tokugawa Ieyasu defeated his rivals in the Battle of Sekigahara. He established a shogunal government at Edo (later Tokyo) in 1603; he and his successors formalized the structure of Japanese feudalism, created a rigid class structure, suppressed Christianity, and enforced the isolation of Japan from virtually all outside influence. Some trade with the mainland and a small Dutch trading station at Nagasaki provided Japan's only windows to the outside world for the next 250 years. The Edo period was marked by urbanization and the development of urban culture (Kabuki theater, wood-block prints, etc.) as the merchant class prospered from internal trade.

The Tokugawa shogun's inability to repel the 1854 visit of American commodore Matthew Perry and subsequently to avoid establishing commercial and diplomatic relations with Western nations deeply shocked the samurai class. Patriotic young samurai from Choshu, Satsuma, and other outlying feudal domains began to call for the abolition of the shogunate and the restoration of imperial rule in order to confront the threat of contact with the West. Quickly realizing that isolationism was doomed, the young radicals' program changed from "respect the emperor, expel the barbarians" to "enrich the state, strengthen the military." With the accession of the Meiji emperor in 1868, shogunal government ended.

Under direct imperial rule, feudalism was abolished and a wide-ranging program of military, industrial, commercial, and social modernization was implemented. The Meiji Constitution of 1889 created a constitutional monarchy and a parliamentary system of government. Having avoided domination by Western nations, Japan itself became an imperialist power. Defeating China in the Sino-Japanese War of 1894–95 and Russia in the Russo-Japanese War of 1904–05, Japan gained a dominant position in Manchuria and in Korea, which became a Japanese colony in 1910.

Under the ineffectual Taisho emperor (reigned 1912–26), parliamentary government flourished. Japan sided with the Allied Powers in World War I, and the Treaty of Versailles advanced Japan's international interests, particularly in China. The prosperity of the 1920s was threatened by the Tokyo earthquake of 1923, by labor strife, and by a stagnant agricultural economy. Militant right-wing nationalism began to play an important role in domestic politics.

During the international economic depression of the early 1930s, right-wing militants gained the upper hand; they assassinated many moderate political figures. Japan invaded Manchuria in 1931 and established the puppet state of Manchuguo in 1934. An attempted military coup in 1936 failed in its immediate objectives but led to the establishment of martial law, under which the Showa emperor (Hirohito; reigned 1926–89) became a pawn of the ultranationalists. An invasion and military takeover of eastern China in 1937 was seen as the first step in the creation of a "Greater East Asian Coprosperity Sphere," designed to unite Asia under Japanese control.

In 1940 Japan entered the Tripartite Alliance with Italy and Nazi Germany. Japan occupied French Indochina in June 1941, provoking increased Allied resistance to Japanese imperial ambitions. Gen. Hideki Tojo became prime minister in Oct. 1941 and ordered simultaneous preemptive strikes against Pearl Harbor, the Philippines, and Malaya on Dec. 7–8. By mid 1942, Japan controlled most of Southeast Asia and the western Pacific, but American victories at the Battle of the Coral Sea in May 1942 and the Battle of Midway in June 1942 halted Japanese expansion. Japanese forces were pushed back in "island-hopping" campaigns in the central Pacific and along the western Pacific rim, and by Allied counterattacks in Burma. Air attacks on Japan itself culminated in the atomic bombing of Hiroshima and Nagasaki in August 1945.

Following Japan's formal surrender on Sept. 2, 1945, an American army in Japan under Gen. Douglas MacArthur took control of the country. A new constitution was promulgated, relegating the emperor to purely symbolic status, renouncing the use of military force, and guaranteeing the civil rights of citizens. The industrial combines that had lent strength to Japan's empire were partially dismantled. An international tribunal tried many wartime leaders as war criminals in 1948. In 1949 considerable authority was returned to the conservative government of Premier Shigeru Yoshida. Japan served as a base for American forces during the Korean War, 1950–53, greatly accelerating Japan's postwar economic recovery. On Apr. 28, 1952, a peace treaty between Japan and the United States ended the Occupation. On Mar. 8, 1954, the two nations signed a mutual defense assistance pact.

Japan was admitted to the United Nations in 1956. The success of Japan's postwar recovery was symbolized by the Tokyo Olympic Games of 1964 and Expo '70 at Osaka. Violent student-protest movements in 1968–69 had no clear political goals and no lasting effect. Politically stable under an unbroken succession of Liberal Democratic party governments, Japan emerged as a major and steadily expanding world industrial power.

Since the mid-1970s, the balance of trade between Japan and the U.S. has weighed heavily in Japan's favor, occasionally leading to strains in U.S.-Japan relations and American charges that Japan engaged in unfair trade practices. Several times during the 1980s and 1990s, especially when the yen was appreciating rapidly against the dollar, Japan pledged to even the trade balance by improving foreign access to Japan's domestic economy.

Domestically, Japan in the 1980s enjoyed a very high standard of living, marred by the extremely high cost and relatively low quality of housing, and by underinvestment in the public infrastructure. A real estate boom led prices of commercial property in downtown Tokyo to increase as much as 200-fold in the span of a decade. This boom extended to the United States, where the rapidly declining dollar made Japanese investment in the U.S. attractive.

For most of its postwar history, Japan has been essentially a one-party state, run by political professionals of the Liberal Democratic party (LDP) according to a system of consensus. But by the end of the 1980s, the system started to crumble as the regime's widespread corruption was revealed. Prime Minister Noburu Takeshita was forced to resign in May 1989 after a bribery scandal. His successor, Sousuke Uno, lasted only two months before resigning in a scandal over his sexual conduct. Public opinion turned sharply against the LDP, which lost control of the upper house of the Diet in July 1989 elections; the Socialist party, led by Takako Doi, posted significant gains.

Uno's successor, Toshiki Kaifu, emerged as an unexpectedly skillful leader who enhanced Japan's international reputation by offering aid to Eastern Europe and the former Soviet Union, and by pledging billions of dollars to support the Persian Gulf War. In Oct. 1991, Kaifu was replaced as LDP chairman by Kiichi Miyazawa, who succeeded in passing legislation authorizing the posting abroad of Japanese troops—for the first time since World War II—for peacekeeping missions in noncombat roles.

An economic slump and political scandals continued to buffet the LDP throughout 1992 and 1993. LDP kingmaker Shin Kanemaru and other party officials resigned after admitting ties to gangsters. The LDP was forced from office in 1993 for the first time in 38 years, and formed coalition governments with the Socialist Party and other parties. The weak coalition governments paved the way for an LDP return to power in 1994 but economic stagnation, scandals involving government and business ties to organized crime, and general malaise continued.

The city of Kobe was hit by a severe earthquake in January, 1995; the government was criticized for ineffective rescue and relief efforts. The country's confidence was further shaken in March, 1995, by a bizarre attack with poison gas in the Tokyo subway, perpetrated by a religious cult, Aum Shinrikyo. Its leader, Shoko Asahara, was eventually arrested and convicted of murder.

Prime Minister Ryutaro Hashimoto, first elected in Jan. 1996, was re-elected leader of the LDP in Sept., 1997. But the Asian economic crisis took a toll on Japan. In the spring of 1998 a plunge in the value of the yen doomed the Hashimoto government; he resigned and was replaced by party stalwart, Keizo Obuchi. In 1999 Japan's economy rebounded slightly as the Obuchi government tried desperately to raise the levels of spending throughout the economy. In April 2000, Premier Obuchi suffered a stroke. His successor Yoshiro Mori led the Liberal Democrats to a near majority in parliamentary elections, forming a coalition government with New Komeito and the Conservatives (a new party, composed of former Liberals). With Mori's resignation in April 2001, the Liberal Democrats selected as their leader, and the lower house named as Prime Minister, Junichiro Koizumi, a man outside the old party "factions" and promising modernizing liberal economic reforms.

Japan's economy grew worse during 2001 and 2002, but rebounded in the following years, and in 2004 foreign direct investment in Japan surged to a record high. Koizumi tried to shake up his party and the nation so when his plan to privatize the post office was defeated in parliament, he called for quick elections in Sept. 2005 which he won in a landslide victory. In 2006, the LDP again won control of the government and elected Shinzo Abe as prime minister. His early popularity faded quickly in light of severe scandals and his aloof manner. After his party suffered a severe defeat in the upper house elections of July, 2007, Abe resigned and was replaced by veteran lawmaker Yasuo Fukuda whose inability to break the political deadlock led to his resignation in Sept. 2008. He was succeeded by Taro Aso, a veteran politician, and the nation's fourth prime minister in two years.

Japan's export-based economy was hit hard in 2008–09 by the worldwide recession as exports fell by five percent. In national elections held in Sept. 2009, the LDP was finally defeated by the Democratic Party of Japan in a landslide victory. But Prime Minister Yukio Hatoyama proved an ineffectual leader who could not deliver on his party's promise to have the U.S. remove or move the marine base in Okinawa. He resigned after only eight months, the fourth prime minister to resign in four years. In Sept. 2010 Prime Minister Kan barely survived a challenge from within his own party by a power broker, Ichiro Ozawa. (See "Major News Stories.")

▶ JORDAN
Hashemite Kingdom of Jordan

● **GEOGRAPHY Location:** western Asia. **Boundaries:** Syria to N, Iraq to NE, Saudi Arabia to SE, Israel to W. **Total area:** 34,445 sq. mi. (89,213 sq km). **Coastline:** 16 mi. (26 km). **Comparative area:** slightly smaller than Indiana. **Land use:** 3% arable land; 2% permanent crops; 95% other. **Major cities:** Amman (capital); Zarqa; Irbid; Russeita.
● **PEOPLE Population:** 6,342,948 (July 2009 est.). **Nationality:** noun—Jordanian(s); adjective—Jordanian. **Ethnic groups:** 98% Arab, 1% Circassian, 1% Armenian. **Languages:** Arabic (official); English widely understood among upper and middle classes. **Religions:** 92% Sunni Muslim, 6% Christian, 2% other.
● **GOVERNMENT Type:** constitutional monarchy. **Independence:** May 25, 1946 (from League of Nations Mandate under British administration). **Constitution:** Jan. 1, 1952. **National holiday:** Independence Day, May 25. **Heads of Government:** Abdullah Bin Al Hussein, king (since Feb. 1999); Samir al-Rifai, prime minister (since Dec. 2009). **Structure:** executive—king is chief of state, prime minister and cabinet are appointed by king; bicameral legislature—House of Representatives has been dissolved by the king several times since 1974; House of Notables appointed by the king; judiciary.

● **ECONOMY Monetary unit:** Jordanian dinar. **Budget:** (2008 est.) *income:* $5.999 bil.; *expend.:* $7.87 bil. **G.D.P.:** $30.76 bil., $5,000 per capita (2008 est.) **Chief crops:** wheat, barley, citrus, tomatoes, melons, olives; poultry, goats, sheep. **Natural resources:** phosphates, potash, shale oil. **Major industries:** phosphate mining, petroleum refining, cement. **Labor force:** 1.615 mil (2008); 82.5% services, 12.5% industry, 5% agriculture; 25-30% unemployment (2001). **Exports:** $6.521 bil. (f.o.b., 2008 est.); phosphates, fertilizers, potash, agricultural products, manufactures. **Imports:** $15.65 bil. (f.o.b., 2008 est.); crude oil, machinery, transport equipment, food, live animals, manufactured goods. **Major trading partners:** (2006) *exports:* 25.2% U.S., 16.9% Iraq, 8% India, 5.8% Saudi Arabia, 4.7% Syria; *imports:* 23.2% Saudi Arabia, 8.3% Germany, 8% China, 5.3% U.S.

The present territory of the Kingdom of Jordan corresponds to the biblical lands of Edom, Gilead, and Moab. The ancient rock city of Petra was the capital of the Edomite and Nabataean kingdoms. The region was incorporated into the Roman Empire, and later the Latin Kingdom of Jerusalem; it was an important early center of Christianity.

In the 630s Jordan became one of the first areas outside Arabia to fall to the expansion of Islam. It became subject to the Caliphate, located at Damascus and later at Baghdad, and in the 11th century became part of the empire of the Seljuk Turks. The Crusades brought European invaders, but with little lasting impact. The Mongols conquered Jordan in the mid-13th century, and it later passed into the control of the Mamluk sultanate. In 1517 Jordan was incorporated into the Ottoman Empire.

Following the post-World War I breakup of the Ottoman Empire, Jordan came under British control as part of a League of Nations Mandate of Palestine. In 1921 Great Britain sponsored the establishment of a monarchy by Abdullah, son of Hussein ibn Ali, ruler of the Hejaz in Arabia. Britain recognized the independence of the Hashemite Kingdom of Transjordan in 1923; a 1928 treaty gave Britain the unrestricted right to station troops in the kingdom.

Transjordan supported the Allies in World War II and was rewarded with full independence in 1946, although strong military ties to Great Britain were maintained. In 1948 the kingdom joined the Arab League, changed its name to Jordan, and joined other Arab states in the first Arab-Israeli War. The war resulted in the occupation by Jordanian troops of the West Bank and the Old City of Jerusalem, which were annexed in 1950. King Hussein I came to the throne on Aug. 11, 1952. All British military forces were withdrawn from the kingdom in 1957.

Israel recaptured the West Bank and the Old City of Jerusalem in the Six-Day War of 1967, and large numbers of Palestinian refugees fled to Jordan. Jordan played no substantial role in the 1974 Arab-Israeli War. In 1974 Jordan accepted the decision of an Arab summit conference designating the Palestine Liberation Organization the sole representative of Palestinians in the West Bank. Jordan's role as a front-line opponent of Israel won it a large annual subvention from Arab oil states; King Hussein's reputation as an Arab moderate led to significant American support.

King Hussein strongly opposed the 1979 Camp David Accords and the Egypt–Israeli peace treaty;

Jordan broke off diplomatic relations with Egypt in March 1979 but resumed full relations in 1984.

In July 1981 King Hussein, charging the Palestine Liberation Organization with subversion, forced the withdrawal of PLO troops and political headquarters from Jordan. While some hoped that Hussein would represent the Palestinians in talks with Israel, in 1988 the king flatly rejected any such role, implied that the PLO should declare an independent state on the West Bank and in the Gaza Strip, and declared that a settlement would require talks between Israel and the PLO.

The Persian Gulf War had a drastic impact on Jordan's economy. King Hussein actively backed Iraq, thus jeopardizing direct aid from Kuwait and Saudi Arabia. But the historic peace treaty signed with Israel in October 1994 restored Hussein's standing while returning some territory taken in the 1967 war. In August 1998, while in the U.S. for medical care, King Hussein made a dramatic visit to the PLO-Israeli talks to appeal for a settlement. Back in Jordan, Hussein deposed his brother Hassan as Crown Prince, swearing in his eldest son Abdullah instead. Twelve days later (Feb. 7), the king died. The new king, Abdullah, pledged to continue his father's policies, asking the current cabinet to stay on. King Abdullah moved cautiously against radical Muslim groups (winning Israeli praise) and restructured the army command. He has maintained a low profile thoughout the turmoil in Israel and Iraq.

▶KAZAKHSTAN
Republic of Kazakhstan
● **GEOGRAPHY   Location:** central Asia. **Boundaries:** Russian Federation to N and NE, China to SE, Kyrgystan, Uzbekistan, and Turkmenistan to S, Caspian Sea to W. **Total area:** 1,049,151 sq. mi. (2,717,300 sq km). **Coastline:** 1,441 mi. (2,320 km) on Caspian Sea. **Comparative area:** slightly less than four times the size of Texas. **Land use:** 11% arable cropland; 1% permanent crops; 88% other. **Major cities:** Astana (capital); Almaty (formerly Alma-Ata); Karaganda.
● **PEOPLE   Population:** 15,399,437 (July 2009 est.). **Nationality:** noun—Kazakhstani(s); adjective—Kazakhstani. **Ethnic groups:** 53.4% Kazakh, 30% Russian, 3.7% Ukrainian, 2.5% Uzbek. **Languages:** 64.4 Kazakh (state language); 95% Russian (official, used in everyday business). **Religions:** 47% Muslim, 44% Russian Orthodox, 2% Protestant.
● **GOVERNMENT   Type:** republic. **Independence:** Dec. 16, 1991 (from the Soviet Union). **Constitution:** Jan 28, 1993; new constitution adopted by national referendum Aug. 30, 1995. **National holiday:** Indepedence Day, Dec. 16. **Heads of Government:** Nursultan A. Nazarbaev, president (since Dec. 1991); Karim Massimov, prime minister (since Jan. 2007). **Structure:** executive—president, prime minister, Council of Ministers; bicameral legislature; judicial.
● **ECONOMY   Monetary unit:** tenge. **Budget:** (2008 est.) **income:** $29.64 bil.; **expend.:** $32.6 bil. **G.D.P.:** $176.9 bil., $11,500 per capita (2008 est.). **Chief crops:** grains, cotton; wool, meat. **Natural resources:** major deposits of petroleum, natural gas, coal, iron ore, manganese. **Major industries:** oil, coal, iron ore, manganese. **Labor force:** 8.358 mil. (2008); 55% services, 6% agriculture, 39% industry (2005); 8.8% unemployment (2002). **Exports:** $66.57 bil. (f.o.b., 2008 est.); oil, ferrous and nonferrous metals, chemicals, grain, wool. **Imports:** $37.53 bil. (f.o.b., 2008 est.); machinery and parts, industrial materials, oil and gas. **Major**

trading partners: (2006) **exports:** 12.4% Germany, 11.6% Russia, 10.9% China, 10.5% Italy, 7.6% France, 4.9% Romania; **imports:** 36.4% Russia, 19.3% China, 7.4% Germany.

Kazakhstan, the largest nation in central Asia, is a land of deserts and plateaus stretching across the rolling tablelands of the Eurasian landmass; approximately 20 percent is mountainous. The Kazakhs are descended from Mongol and Turkic tribes who settled in the area known as Kazakhstan about the first century B.C. In the sixth century A.D. the area formed part of the Turkish Khaganate, a loose federation of nomadic tribes, and in the seventh to ninth centuries Islam became established among the settled population. Although the Mongols ruled the area from 1219 to 1447, the Turkish subjects of the Mongol Horde were to play a decisive role in the future of the region.

In the 15th century, the Kazakhs emerged as a distinct people, but by the 17th century, due to internecine fighting, the Kazakhs split into three nomadic federations, known as the Larger, the Middle, and the Lesser Hordes. In the mid-17th century, the Mongols began to invade the region, and the Kazakhs, not being unified enough to repel them, sought protection from the Russians. By the mid-18th century, the Kazakh lands were completely under Russian control. With the freeing of serfs in 1861 in Russia, Kazakhstan experienced its first major influx of Russian and Ukrainian peasants, who were given Kazakh lands. Resentment over this grew until the Kazakhs rebelled against Russian rule in 1916. The Russians brutally repressed the uprising, but not before thousands of Kazakhs and many Russians were killed.

After the 1917 Communist revolution in Russia, a civil war ensued in Kazakhstan, from which the Bolsheviks emerged victorious. The Kazakh territory was incorporated into Russia in 1920, granted "autonomous" status in 1925, and in 1936 it formally became one of the U.S.S.R.'s union republics. Kazakhstan was industrialized, but it suffered enormously from the U.S.S.R.'s policies. In the 1930s, the traditionally nomadic Kazakh people were forcibly settled on collectivized farms, and more than a million died of starvation. In the 1950s, Khrushchev's failed "Virgin Lands" scheme and the Soviet government's repeated nuclear tests wreaked environmental havoc on Kazakhstan. As a result of years of Soviet economic development programs, the rate of Russian and Ukrainian immigration into Kazakhstan greatly increased. By 1979, 41 percent of Kazakhstan's population was Russian.

Under Mikhail Gorbachev's policy of *glasnost*, or openness, in the 1980s, the corrupt Communist party leader of Kazakhstan and Brezhnev crony Dinmukhamed Kunayev was deposed. He was ultimately replaced by Nursultan Nazarbayev, an ethnic Kazakh, who was elected in April 1990 to the new post of president.

Kazakhstan declared its independence in March 1991 and joined the Commonwealth of Independent States in December. It has pursued closer economic but not political ties with Russia and Belarus. The May 1995 customs union among the three was expanded in March 1996 to include coordination of agricultural and industrial policies and the establishment of joint transport, energy and information systems, with Kyrgystan added as a fourth member. Kazakhstan took part (April 1996) in a five-power non-agression treaty with Russia, China, Kyrgyzstan, and Tajikistan which was extended a year later to include reduction of military forces in border areas. The last remaining Soviet-era nuclear missle was detonated underground in May 1995 and the last ballistic missle silo was torn down in September 1996. In Feb. 1997 the supposedly tame legislature refused to ratify a Russian lease of four nuclear test sites in Kazakhstan.

Independent Kazakhstan's first presidential election was held in December 1991 with Nazarbayev the only candidate. An April 1995 referendum cancelled the 1996 election and extended Nazarbayev's term to 2000 with a gratifying 95 percent "yes" vote; and in August of the year 89 percent approved a new "strong president" constitution, making the president head of the Supreme Court and permitting him to dissolve parliament at will. Nazarbayev had already dissolved parliament in March 1995, a parliament in which his supporters held two-thirds of the seats, but whose pace of economic reform displeased him. He ruled by decree until new elections late in 1995 and early in 1996.

Kazakhstan's economic future is tied to its enormous untapped gas and oil reserves, perhaps 25 billion barrels. In April 1996, Kazakhstan, Russia and Oman established a consortium with eight oil companies to build a 900-mile pipeline linking the Tengiz fields with Russia's Black Sea port of Novorossiyak. And in July of that year, the I.M.F. chipped in with a loan of $446 million.

In 1998 the capital was moved— ostensibly for security reasons—from Almaty to remote Akmola, which was renamed Astana, a word meaning "capital" in Kazakh. In July, Navarbayev signed a pact with Russia, settling the thorny question of dividing the northern Caspian Sea (with its petroleum riches). But with falling world oil prices, the Kazakh economy stalled, bringing Nazarbayev to call for presidential elections 18 months early, elections he not surprisingly won handily, this time with 80 percent of the votes, in 1999. Over the next years he solidified his hold on the government and made several lucrative energy deals. Rising oil prices helped, too, for a while.

▶ **KENYA**
Republic of Kenya
● **GEOGRAPHY Location:** eastern Africa. **Boundaries**: Sudan to NW, Ethiopia to N, Somalia to E, Indian Ocean to SE, Tanzania to SW, Lake Victoria, Uganda to W. **Total area**: 224,962 sq. mi. (582,650 sq km). **Coastline**: 333 mi. (536 km). **Comparative area**: slightly more than twice the size of Nevada. **Land use**: 7% arable land; 1% permanent crops; 92% other. **Major cities**: Nairobi (capital); Mombasa; Nakuru; Kisumu; Thika.
● **PEOPLE Population**: 39,002,772 (July 2009 est.). **Nationality**: noun—Kenyan(s); adjective—Kenyan. **Ethnic groups**: 22% Kikuyu, 14% Luhya, 13% Luo, 12% Kalenjin, 11% Kamba, 6% Kisii, 6% Meru, 15% other African, 1% non-African (Asian, European, and Arab). **Languages**: English and Kiswahili (both official), indigenous languages. **Religions**: 45% Protestant, 35% Roman Catholic, 10% indigenous beliefs, 10% Muslim, 2% other.
● **GOVERNMENT Type**: republic. **Independence**: Dec. 12, 1963 (from U.K.). **Constitution**: Dec. 12, 1963; amended many times, most recently in 2005. **National holiday**: Independence Day, Dec. 12. **Head of Government**: Mwai Kibaki, president (since Jan. 1, 2003); Raila Amolo Odinga, prime minister (since Apr. 2008). **Structure**: executive—president and cabinet; unicameral legislature—

first multiparty election since repeal of one-party state law in 1991; judiciary.
● **ECONOMY Monetary unit:** Kenyan shilling. **Budget:** (2008 est.) *income:* $6.617 bil.; *expend.:* $8.196 bil. **G.D.P.:** $61.83 bil., $1,600 per capita (2008 est.). **Chief crops:** coffee, tea, corn, wheat, sugarcane; cattle, pork, poultry. **Natural resources:** gold, limestone, soda ash, salt barites. **Major industries:** small-scale consumer goods (plastic, furniture, batteries, textiles, soap, cigarettes, flour), agricultural processing, oil refining. **Labor force:** 9.45 mil. (2007); 75-80% agriculture, 20-25% non-agriculture; 40% unemployment (2001). **Exports:** $4.882 bil. (f.o.b., 2008 est.); tea, coffee, petroleum products. **Imports:** $10.77 bil. (f.o.b., 2008 est.); machinery and transport equipment, consumer goods, petroleum and petroleum products **Major trading partners:** (2006) *exports:* 15.9% Uganda, 10% U.K., 8% U.S., 8% Netherlands, 8% Tanzania, 5% Pakistan; *imports:* 12% United Arab Emirates, 9% India, 8% China, 8% Saudi Arabia, 7% U.S., 6% South Africa, 5% U.K., 5% Japan.

Kenya formed part of an ancient network of trade between the Red Sea and the coast of East Africa as early as the fourth century B.C. Persian and Arab trading posts were established on the coast by the eighth century A.D. At about the same time, the indigenous Cushitic people of Kenya had been joined by Bantu and Nilotic immigrants. Swahili, a mixture of Bantu and Arabic, developed as a language of trade throughout the region.

Portuguese explorers reached Kenya in 1498. Portuguese control of the coastal area ended in 1729, when the region came under the control of the sultans of Oman. British adventurers explored Kenya in the late 19th century. In 1885 the Berlin Conference divided East Africa into European spheres of influence. The British East Africa Company established a protectorate over the coastal region in 1890 and extended its control into the interior in 1895. British settlers established farms, mission stations, and towns, and Kenya was given colonial status in 1920.

During World War II, northern Kenya was briefly occupied by troops from the Italian colony of Ethiopia. After the British reasserted control, Africans were granted the right to participate in local government in 1944.

From 1952 to 1959, a state of emergency was declared in Kenya because of the "Mau Mau" rebellion against British colonial rule. In response to local unrest, British authorities widened African participation in government and Africans were elected to the Legislative Council in 1957.

Kenya became independent on Dec. 12, 1963, and in 1964 assumed the status of a republic within the British Commonwealth. Jomo Kenyatta, a member of the dominant Kikuyu population and leader of the main political party, the Kenya African National Union (KANU), was elected Kenya's first president. A leftist party, the Kenya People's Union (KPU) was organized in 1966, led by Oginga Odinga. In 1969 it was implicated in the assassination of Tom Mboya, a prominent political leader; its leaders were imprisoned and the party dissolved. From 1969 to 1992 KANU was Kenya's sole political party.

Kenyatta died on Aug. 22, 1978, and Vice Pres. Daniel arap Moi succeeded him. In 1982 the constitution was amended to make Kenya a one-party state. Moi was reelected president in 1983 and again in 1988, the latter being the first election conducted without secret ballots. Foreign observers accused the Moi government of widespread human rights abuses. Riots broke out in several cities in 1991, and sporadic ethnic violence cost thousands of lives. Odinga formed the opposition Forum for the Restoration of Democracy (FORD), in direct defiance of the government. With Western aid conditioned on economic reform, political pluralism, and improved human rights, Moi allowed presidential elections to be held in Dec. of 1992. The three opposition parties split, and Moi was returned to office for a fourth time.

Kenya had traditionally been viewed as the success story of postcolonial Africa, but by the 1990s, widespread government corruption, and economic inefficiency had taken a heavy toll. Tourism fell due to the rise in violence, and the economy was further strained by the presence of refugees from Ethiopia, Somalia, and Sudan. Early in 1994 the government announced reforms aimed at restoring confidence in the economy, including lifting the restrictions on foreign investment. But Pres. Moi's (April 1995) arrest of two leading opposition figures (bringing the total arrested since 1993 to more than 50) led to frustration among his many political enemies.

In mid-1997, large demonstrations demanding Moi reform the electoral system in time for Dec. presidential elections were broken up by police with a great amount of violence. In the face of international condemnation Moi agreed to the proposed reforms (July 15), but little progress was made in subsequent meetings between the government and the opposition leaders. In Jan. 1998 Moi barely won reelection. (In an unrelated story, the U.S. embassy was attacked by a terrorist truck-bomb August 7, with 250 deaths.)

In 2002 dissensions within Moi's KANU party obliged him not to run for president; his attempt to name his successor (Uhuru Kenyatta, son of Kenya's "founding father") split the party and allowed the opposition National Alliance Party's candidate Mwai Kibaki to win the Dec. 2002 election. A sweeping anti-corruption campaign followed and over 100 judges were suspended. In 2004 allegations were made against Moi himself and his popularity slowly waned. In April 2008 the opposition leader, Raila Odinga, became prime minister in a power-sharing deal after severe violence followed a divided election in Dec. 2007. Over 1,000 were killed and 300,000 displaced. In Aug. 2010 a referendum on a new constitution was held without incident and the measure strongly approved.

▶ **KIRIBATI**
Republic of Kiribati
• **GEOGRAPHY   Location:** 33 atolls, in three main groups (E to W: Line Is., Phoenix Is., Gilbert Is.) in mid-Pacific Ocean; about 2,400 mi. (3,870 km) E to W and 1,275 mi. (2,050 km) N to S. Tarawa (Gilberts) 1°30'N, 173°00'E. **Boundaries:** surrounded by Pacific Ocean; nearest neighbors are Nauru to W, and Tuvalu and Tokelau to S. **Total area:** 277 sq. mi. (811 sq km). **Coastline:** 710 mi. (1,143 km). **Comparative area:** four times the size of Washington, D.C. **Land use:** 0% arable land; 51% permanent crops; 49% other. **Major cities:** Tarawa (capital).
• **PEOPLE   Population:** 112,850 (July 2009 est.). **Nationality:** noun—I-Kiribati (sing., pl.); adjective—I-Kiribati. **Ethnic groups:** Micronesian.

Languages: English (official), Gilbertese. **Religions:** 52% Roman Catholic, 40% Protestant (Congregational), some Seventh-Day Adventist, Church of God, Mormon and Baha'i.
• **GOVERNMENT   Type:** republic. **Independence:** July 12, 1979 (from U.K.). **Constitution:** July 12, 1979. **National holiday:** Independence Day, July 12. **Head of Government:** Anote Tong, president (since July 8, 2003). **Structure:** executive; unicameral legislature; judiciary—all judges appointed by the president.
• **ECONOMY   Monetary unit:** Australian dollar. **Budget:** (2005 est.) *income:* $55.52 mil.; *expend.:* $59.71 mil. **G.D.P.:** $2357.4 mil., $3,200 per capita (2008 est.). **Chief crops:** copra; taro, bread fruit, vegetables; fish. **Natural resources:** phosphate (production discontinued in 1979). **Major industries:** fishing and handicrafts. **Labor force:** 7,870 economically active (2001 est.). **Exports:** $17 mil. (f.o.b., 2004 est.); 62% copra, seaweed, fish. **Imports:** $62 mil. (c.i.f., 2004 est.); foodstuffs, machinery and quipment. **Major trading partners:** (2006) *exports:* 22.8% U.S., 21.5% Belgium, 14.3% Japan, 7.8% Samoa, 7.5% Australia, 6.7% Malaysia, 5.6% Taiwan, 4.6% Denmark; *imports:* 33% Australia, 27.1% Fiji, 18.1% Japan, 6.9% New Zealand.

In 1892 the British established a protectorate over the Gilbert Islands, inhabited principally by Micronesians. In 1915 Britain joined the islands administratively with the Polynesian-speaking Ellice Islands to the south to form a British colony, the Gilbert and Ellice Islands (later expanded to include other islands). The Japanese occupied the Gilberts in 1942; in 1943 the Allied forces recaptured them, and Tarawa was the scene of some of the fiercest combat in the Pacific.

In 1971 Britain granted the colony self-rule. The Ellice Islands broke away in 1975, becoming the independent nation of Tuvalu in 1978. On July 12, 1979, the Gilbert Islands became independent as Kiribati. United States claims to portions of the Line and Phoenix islands were settled by a friendship treaty in 1979.

Kiribati's economy is based on subsistence farming and on fishing. Copra exports and the sale of fishing rights (principally to Japan) are the main earners of hard currency. The islands joined the United Nations in late 1999.

▶ **KOREA, NORTH**
Democratic People's Republic of Korea
• **GEOGRAPHY   Location:** northern part of Korean peninsula in eastern Asia. **Boundaries:** China to NW, Sea of Japan to E, Republic of Korea to S, Yellow Sea to SW. **Total area:** 46,541 sq. mi. (120,540 sq km). **Coastline:** 1,551 mi. (2,495 km). **Comparative area:** slightly smaller than Mississippi. **Land use:** 22% arable land; 2% permanent crops; 76% other. **Major cities:** Pyongyang (capital); Hamhung; Chongjin; Sinuju; Kaesong.
• **PEOPLE   Population:** 22,757,275 (July 2010 est.) **Nationality:** noun—Korean(s); adjective—Korean. **Ethnic groups:** racially homogeneous, with a small Chinese community. **Languages:** Korean. **Religions:** Buddhism and Confucianism; autonomous religious activities now almost nonexistent.
• **GOVERNMENT   Type:** communist state; one-man dictatorship. **Independence:** Aug. 15, 1945 (from Japan). **Constitution:** adopted 1948, revised Apr. 1992 and Sept. 1998. **National holiday:** Foundation Day, Sept. 9. **Heads of Government:** Kim Jong Il, president (since Oct. 1994); Choe Yong Rim,

premier (since June 2010). **Structure:** executive—president is dominant figure in government; Supreme People's Assembly theoretically supervises legislative and judicial functions; State Administration Council (cabinet) oversees ministerial operations.

• ECONOMY **Monetary unit:** North Korean won. **Budget:** (2005 est.) *income:* $2.88 bil.; *expend.*$2.98 bil.; **G.D.P.:** $40 bil., $1,900 per capita (2009 est.). **Chief crops:** corn, rice, vegetables; pigs, cattle. **Natural resources:** coal, lead, tungsten, zinc, graphite. **Major industries:** machine building, military products, electric power, chemicals. **Labor force:** 20 mil. (note - estimates vary widely); 37% agricultural, 63% nonagricultural. **Exports:** $2.062 bil. (2008 est.); minerals, metallurgical products, agricultural and fishery products, manufactures. **Imports:** $3.574 bil. (2008 est.); petroleum, machinery and equipment, coking coal, grain. **Major trading partners:** *exports:* 42% China, 38% South Korea, 5% India; *imports:* 57% China, 25% South Korea, 3% Russia, 3% Singapore.

(For pre-1945 history, see "Republic of Korea.")

The Soviet Union's declaration of war against Japan in the waning days of World War II strengthened its position in northeast Asia, and particularly in Korea. After Japan's surrender, Korea was arbitrarily divided into zones of Soviet and American occupation, north and south of latitude 38° N. The Korean Communist party (KCP), founded in 1922, had functioned in exile in the U.S.S.R. during the Japanese occupation, and KCP workers were quickly moved into the Soviet zone in 1945.

U.S.-Soviet talks aimed at Korean reunification broke down, and in 1948 the establishment of separate regimes in North and South Korea formalized the postwar occupation zones. The Korean Democratic People's Republic was proclaimed on May 1, 1948. It inherited most of the industrial and hydroelectric power infrastructure built during the Japanese colonial period and enjoyed strong Soviet backing.

On June 25, 1950, North Korean troops crossed the 38th parallel in an effort to force the reunification of Korea under a communist regime. U.N. troops under American leadership came to the defense of the South. (For the Korean War, see "South Korea.") The war was fought to a stalemate, and a truce was signed on July 27, 1953.

Until 1994 North Korea had a single leader throughout its national history: Kim Il Sung was the North Korean leader from 1945 to 1994. Under him, North Korea was a typically Stalinist Soviet nation, concentrating its economic energies on heavy industry and imposing a strictly regimented political and social life on its citizens. Economic development was supported by aid from the Soviet Union and China. After an impressive program of postwar reconstruction in the 1950s and 1960s, the country fell into economic stagnation.

Relations between North and South Korea were hostile; the North has made numerous attempts to infiltrate and sabotage the South. In 1983, 17 people, including four South Korean cabinet ministers, were killed in Rangoon by a bomb planted by North Korean agents. In 1990 the leaders of both countries held three cordial but unproductive meetings. Much of the goodwill was harmed by the assertions of the U.S. that North Korea was planning to build nuclear weapons.

In August 1992, China, North Korea's long-term ally established diplomatic relations with South Korea, leaving North Korea completely isolated. High-level contacts between North and South Korea continued, but reconciliation talks stalled in 1993 as the issue of North Korean nuclear weapons came to the fore. North Korean leaders refused to allow international arms inspectors access to some facilities and withdrew from the Nuclear Non-Proliferation Treaty. In June 1994 former U.S. president Jimmy Carter met with Kim Il Sung and arranged for a summit meeting with South Korea and for another with Pres. Clinton to resolve the nuclear weapons issue. Kim Il Sung's sudden death in July prevented immediate progress, but in 1995 an agreement was reached that called for North Korea to dismantle its nuclear facilities in exchange for two new reactors from which weapons-grade plutonium is hard to extract. In 1996 severe floods destroyed most of the rice crop, left half a million homeless, and forced North Korea to accept emergency grants of rice from Japan and South Korea.

Continued severe famine spurred North Korea to pursue reconciliation talks with the South, but those talks were repeatedly disrupted by strife over its nuclear-weapons programs, incidents of clandestine landing of northern commandos in the south, and the defection of senior communist officials. In the fall of 1997 Kim Jung Il assumed his father's old position as general secretary of the Worker's Party. U.S. suspicions, voiced in 1998, of a new underground nuclear plant were proven baseless in May of 1999, the Great Leader permitting an inspection in return for food aid. (Estimates of 2.3 million deaths from the famine must have influenced the decision). Talks with South Korea in Beijing were broken off in June 1999 after South Korea sank a North Korean torpedo boat in the Yellow Sea. But talks in Geneva continued with South Korea, China and the U.S., supplemented in March 2000 with secret talks with South Korea, as diplomatic relations were opened with Italy and Australia. The secret talks led, in June, to a Pyongyang visit by South Korea's president Kim. The two pledged themselves to peace and reunification. Family visits across the border ensued.

In 2002, a naval attack in the Yellow Sea, in which a North Korean vessel sank a South Korean patrol boat, seriously eclipsed the "sunshine policy." In Oct. North Korean officials admitted to the U.S. they had been secretly developing nuclear weapons and in Dec. they expelled U.N. monitors. Named as part of the Bush administration "axis of evil" North Korea went into an aggressive' mode threatening Japan with attack and continuously asserting its right to develop nuclear weapons. The U.S. and China continued to oppose this and a diplomatic surge helped bring North Korea back to the negotiating table, only to see a renewed pattern of launching missiles and then acting peaceably. A stalemate ensued but the sinking of a South Korean warship in March 2010 killing 46 sailors revived tensions, especially after South Korea blamed the North. (See "Major News Stories.")

▶KOREA, SOUTH
Republic of Korea

• GEOGRAPHY **Location:** southern part of Korean peninsula in eastern Asia. **Boundaries:** North Korea to N, separated by frontier roughly following 38th parallel; Sea of Japan to E, East China Sea to S, and Yellow Sea to W. **Total area:** 38,023 sq. mi. (98,480 sq km). **Coastline:** 1,500 mi. (2,413 km). **Comparative area:** slightly larger than Indiana. **Land use:** 17% arable land; 2% permanent crops;

81% other. **Major cities**: Seoul (capital); Pusan; Taegu; Inchon; Kwangju.

• **PEOPLE Population**: 48,636,068 (July 2010 est.) **Nationality**: noun—Korean(s); adjective—Korean. **Ethnic groups**: homogeneous; small Chinese minority (about 20,000). **Languages**: Korean; English widely taught in high school. **Religions**: 26.3% Christianity, 23.2% Buddhism, 49.3% none.

• **GOVERNMENT Type**: republic. **Constitution**: July 17, 1948; amended and rewritten many timess; most current constitution approved on Oct. 29, 1987. **National holiday**: Liberation Day, Aug. 15. **Heads of Government**: Lee Myung-bak, president (since Feb. 2008); Kim Taeho, prime minister (since Sep. 2010). **Structure**: executive; unicameral legislature (National Assembly); judiciary.

• **ECONOMY Monetary unit**: South Korean won. **Budget**: (2009 est.) *income*: $191.5 bil.; *expend.*: $227.2 bil. **G.D.P.**: $1.356 tril., $28,000 per capita (2009 est.). **Chief crops**: rice, root crops, barley, vegetables, fruit; cattle, pigs, chickens, milk, eggs; fish catch of 2.9 mil. metric tons, seventh largest in the world. **Natural resources**: coal, tungsten, graphite, molybdenum. **Major industries**: electronics, automobiles, chemicals, shipbuilding. **Labor force**: 24.37 mil. (2009 est.); 68% services, 25% industry; 7.2% agriculture, fishing, and forestry; 3.2% unemployment (2007). **Exports**: $355.1 bil. (2009 est.); electronic and electrical equipment, electrical machinery, steel, automobiles. **Imports**: $313.4 bil. (2009 est.); machinery, electronics and electronic equipment, oil, steel, transport equipment, textiles. **Major trading partners**: (2008) *exports*: 21.5% China, 10.9% U.S., 6.6% Japan, 4.6% Hong Kong; *imports*: 17.7% China, 14% Japan, 8.9% U.S., 7.8% Saudi Arabia, 4.4% U.A.E.

From ancient times Korea has struggled successfully to preserve its national independence. To the native culture—marked by a warrior aristocracy, shamanic religion, and a subject class of rice cultivators—was added, under continuous Chinese influence, a strong adherence to Buddhism and a system of government modeled on Chinese Confucian bureaucratism. The three rival kingdoms of Silla, Paekche, and Koguryo were united, through Chinese intervention, in the seventh century A.D.; unified dynastic rule was maintained thereafter.

The Yi dynasty (1392–1910), when Korea was known as the Kingdom of Choson, was a staunch tributary ally of China under both the Ming (1368–1644) and Qing (1644–1911) dynasties. A Japanese invasion of Korea in 1592 conquered most of the country but was finally repelled by combined Chinese and Korean forces. From the late 17th century to the 1870s, all non-Chinese foreign influence was rigorously excluded.

Korea's isolation, and its status as a Chinese tributary, ended in 1874, when Japan imposed on it the Treaty of Kangwha, guaranteeing Japanese commercial access and other interests. The Sino-Japanese War of 1894–95 was fought primarily over the status of Korea; following Japan's victory in that war, Korea was made a Japanese protectorate and was annexed as a Japanese colony in 1910. A harsh regime was established with the aim of eradicating Korean culture and incorporating Korea entirely into the Japanese empire.

During the colonial period, Korean resistance to the Japanese regime was violently suppressed, but resistance movements survived in exile—notably the Korean Communist party in the Soviet Union and a republican movement in China. During World War II, tens of thousands of Koreans were conscripted as forced laborers to work in Japan and in Japanese-occupied territories.

Following Japan's surrender, Korea was arbitrarily divided into zones of Soviet and American occupation, north and south of 38° N latitude. The dividing line split Korea economically as well as geographically and politically; Korea's industry and hydroelectric power was concentrated in the north, while the south was primarily agricultural. In contrast to well-laid Soviet plans for installing a Communist government in the north, American attempts to reunify the country under a republican regime were inept. By 1948 it had become clear that plans for reunification were hopeless. In May of that year, the Republic of Korea was organized in the south, with Dr. Syngman Rhee as president. The United States withdrew its occupation forces in June 1949.

On June 25, 1950, North Korean troops invaded the south in an apparent attempt to unify the country forcibly under the communist regime. An emergency session of the U.N. Security Council voted to send troops to Korea; the U.S.S.R., having boycotted the session, was unable to exercise its veto on North Korea's behalf. U.N. troops, dominated by American forces and commanded by Gen. Douglas MacArthur, launched a counterattack in September with a landing at Inchon and swept north, reaching the Chinese border by Nov. 20. On Nov. 26 the tide turned again when Chinese troops entered the war, ostensibly to defend the Chinese border but also to aid their North Korean allies in driving the U.N. forces south again. Seoul fell once more on Jan. 4, 1951. In February and March another U.N. counteroffensive drove the combined Chinese and North Korean forces back to the 38th parallel. The battle lines remained generally stable, although fierce fighting continued for another two years. On Apr. 11, 1951, Gen. MacArthur was relieved of the Korean command for making unauthorized policy statements and was replaced by Gen. Matthew Ridgway.

Armistice talks began in July 1951 but broke down repeatedly. A truce was signed on July 27, 1953, creating a demilitarized zone along the 38th parallel and establishing a framework for talks on a permanent settlement of the war. Negotiations continued fruitlessly at the Panmunjom armistice conference headquarters.

Postwar reconstruction, with significant U.S. aid, was overseen by the government of Syngman Rhee. Pres. Rhee resigned in 1960 after a wave of student demonstrations charging him with corruption and undemocratic practices. On May 16, 1961, Gen. Park Chung Hee seized power in a military coup. The military government was given democratic trappings when in 1972 a referendum was passed allowing Gen. Park to run for an unlimited series of six-year presidential terms. Gen. Park was assassinated on Oct. 26, 1979, by the government's chief of intelligence. Gen. Chun Doo Hwan rose to power, continuing the military rule of Gen. Park. Gen. Chun's regime was marked by widespread violent political protests but the economy made great strides. The agrarian country was transformed into a modernized, urban, industrial nation. In 1986 South Korea achieved a favorable balance-of-payments ratio in foreign trade, and the favorable balance increased rapidly, led by exports of automobiles, textiles and clothing, and consumer electronic goods.

After weeks of widespread demonstrations in mid-1987, Gen. Chun agreed to allow direct presidential elections to choose his successor. In the elections, the government candidate, Roh Tae Woo, achieved a plurality over the sharply divided opposition parties. Under Pres. Roh, the political situation calmed, although student demonstrations continued, calling for greater efforts for Korean reunification and protesting the presence of large numbers of American troops.

High-level talks between North and South began in 1990, and an agreement in principle was reached that reunification would take place in the near future. In 1992, longtime political opposition leader Kim Young Sam won election as South Korea's first postwar civilian president. Although he was initially able to liberalize some aspects of civil rights, the renewed threat of war with North Korea became the overriding preoccupation of the government until late 1994, when an agreement was reached calling for North Korea to dismantle its nuclear facilities in exchange for new reactors.

The ruling Democratic Labor Party was plagued by scandals that hampered its effectiveness. Pres. Kim's predecessor, Pres. Roh, was arrested for bribe-taking, as was his predecessor. Several key businessmen, including Kim's own son, were jailed for corruption. In elections in April 1996 the party lost its parliamentary majority but continued to govern as part of a coalition.

South Korea's economy was battered by the Asian economic crisis of 1997–98, leading to severe hardship for many workers. On Dec. 18, 1997, long-time democracy advocate and dissident Kim Dae Jung was elected. In May 1999 (after promising economic figures suggested a rising G.D.P. and falling unemployment) he was able to reshuffle the cabinet to more closely accord with his "sunshine policy" of reforming the great conglomerate business empires and of improving relations with North Korea. In June talks with the North, held in Beijing, were abbreviated after South Korea sank a North Korean torpedo boat in a fishing grounds dispute in the Yellow Sea. Yet talks in Geneva continued and secret talks began in March 2000, leading to a "summit" in Pyongyang in June between President Kim and Kim Jong Il which promised peace and reunification.

Domestic financial scandals involving Pres. Kim's son and some of his aides led him to distance himself from the Millenium Party, resigning as its head in Nov. 2001 and from the party itself in May. A June 2002 North Korean naval attack called the "sunshine policy" into serious question. In December's presidential election, the Millennium Democrats' candidate, Rho Moo Hyun, defeated Lee Hoi Chang of the Grand National Party. Roh's opponents pushed through a bill impeaching him in March 2004 and removing him from office until the courts ruled in his favor in May. This helped Roh's supporters to win a majority in the National Assembly. In 2008 businessman Lee Myung-bak was elected by a record margin and his party won control of parliament. In March 2010 a South Korean warship was hit with a torpedo killing 46 sailors. In May South Korea produced evidence it claimed proved the attack was launched by North Korea, which rejected the charge. In August the U.S. fleet joined with South Korea in large-scale military exercises.

▶KUWAIT
State of Kuwait

● **Geography** **Location:** northeastern Arabian peninsula. **Boundaries:** Iraq to N, Saudi Arabia to S, Persian Gulf to E. **Total area:** 6,880 sq. mi. (17,820 sq km). **Coastline:** 310 mi. (499 km). **Comparative area:** slightly smaller than New Jersey. **Land use:** negl. % arable land; negl. % permanent crops; 100% other. **Major cities:** Kuwait City (capital); Salmiya; Hawalli; Faranawiya; Abraq Kheetan.

● **People** **Population:** 2,691,158 (July 2009 est.). **Nationality:** noun—Kuwaiti(s); adjective— Kuwaiti. **Ethnic groups:** 45% Kuwaiti, 35% other Arab, 9% South Asian, 4% Iranian, 7% other. **Languages:** Arabic (official), English widely spoken. **Religions:** 85% Muslim (30% Shi'a, 70% Sunni), 15% Christian, Hindu, Parsi, and other.

● **Government** **Type:** constitutional emirate **Independence:** June 19, 1961 (from U.K.). **Constitution:** Nov. 11, 1962 (some provisions suspended since Aug. 29, 1962). **National holiday:** National Day, Feb. 25. **Head of Government:** Sabah al-Ahmad al-Jabir Al-Sabah, emir (since Feb. 7, 2006); Nasser Al-Mohammed Al-Ahmad Al-Sabah, prime minister (since Jan., 2006). **Structure:** executive; unicameral legislature; judiciary.

● **Economy** **Monetary unit:** Kuwaiti dinar. **Budget:** (2008 est.) *income:* $113.3 bil.; *expend.:* $63.55 bil. **G.D.P.:** $149.1 bil., $57,400 per capita (2008 est.). **Chief crops:** virtually none; extensive fishing; about 75% of potable water must be distilled or imported. **Natural resources:** petroleum, fish, shrimp, natural gas. **Major industries:** petroleum, petrochemicals, desalination. **Labor force:** 2.225 mil. (2008 est.); non-Kuwaitis make up 80% of the work force. **Exports:** $95.46 bil. (f.o.b., 2008 est.); oil and refined products, fertilizers. **Imports:** $26.54 bil. (f.o.b., 2008 est.); food, construction materials, vehicles and parts, clothing. **Major trading partners:** (2006) *exports:* 20.4% Japan, 16.2% South Korea, 10.8% Taiwan, 9.7% Singapore, 9% U.S., 5.3% Netherlands, 4.1% China; *imports:* 14.1% U.S., 7.9% Germany, 7.8% Japan, 6.8% Saudi Arabia, 5.7% China, 5.4% U.K., 4.6% Italy.

Kuwait, at the head of the Persian Gulf, was part of the Abbasid empire from the eighth century and was absorbed into the Ottoman Empire in the late 16th century. It was organized as a principality under the al-Sabah dynasty in 1756, but the Ottomans continued to assert sovereignty. Increasing British influence during the 19th century was formalized in 1899, when Kuwait became a British protectorate.

The discovery of oil, first exported from Kuwait after World War II, rapidly made the principality one of the wealthiest in the Middle East. The British protectorate ended in 1961, when Kuwait gained full independence. The great majority of oil field workers in Kuwait are non-Kuwaiti Arabs, including many Palestinians. Oil revenues have made possible a total welfare state for Kuwaiti citizens, who pay no taxes and enjoy a wide range of free social services.

Kuwait allied itself with Iraq in the Iran-Iraq War of 1980–88; Kuwaiti tankers came under heavy attack from Iranian warships in the gulf. In July 1987, Kuwaiti tankers were reflagged with the U.S. flag and placed under escort of American warships in an operation that continued into 1989. Most of Kuwait's territory is barren but with proven crude oil reserves of 94 billion barrels other economic endeavors are not needed.

On Aug. 2, 1990, Kuwait was invaded, and later annexed, by Iraq. In February 1991 it was liberated by a coalition of Arab, non-Arab Muslim, and Western nations led by the United States. Much of the country was destroyed or looted by the Iraqis. After its return to power, the ruling al-Sabah family came under strong pressure to institute democratic reforms. Parliamentary elections were held in 1992, and opposition candidates won 30 of 50 seats. The sultan then announced a new cabinet with more nonroyal members than ever before.

A brief war-scare flared up in October 1994 as 20,000 Iraqi Republican Guards were moved to the Kuwaiti border, only to retreat in the face of U.S. military opposition. In November, Iraq formally recognized Kuwait's sovereignty. In Jan. 2006 the long-reigning emir Sheik jaber al-Ahmad al-Sabah died and was succeeded by the prime minister, Sheik Sabah al-Ahmad al-Sabah.

▶ KYRGYZSTAN
Kyrgyz Republic

• **GEOGRAPHY Location:** eastern central Asia. **Boundaries:** Kazakhstan to N and NE, China to SE and S, Tajikistan to SW, Uzbekistan to W. **Total area:** 76,641 sq. mi. (198,500 sq km). **Coastline:** none. **Comparative area:** slightly smaller than South Dakota. **Land use:** 7% arable land; 0% permanent crops; 93% other. **Major cities:** Bishkek (known as Frunze 1926-91) (capital).
• **PEOPLE Population:** 5,431,747 (July 2009 est.). **Nationality:** noun—Kyrgyzstani(s); adjective—Kyrgyzstani. **Ethnic groups:** 52.4% Kirghiz, 18% Russian, 12.9% Uzbek, 2.5% Ukrainian, 2.4% German, 11.8% other. **Languages:** Kirghiz and Russian (both official), Kirghiz is a member of south Turkic language group written in Cyrillic since 1940. **Religions:** 75% Muslim; 20% Russian Orthodox.
• **GOVERNMENT Type:** republic. **Independence:** Aug. 31, 1991 (from Soviet Union). **Constitution:** adopted May 5, 1993; a new version was approved by referendum in Nov. 2006. **National holiday:** National Day, Dec. 2; Independence Day, Aug. 31. **Heads of Government:** Roza Otunbaeva, president (since May 2010), Otunbaeva became acting president in April 2010 following the riots that overthrew President Bakiev. **Structure:** executive—president, prime ministers, Cabinet of Ministers; bicameral legislature; judiciary.
• **ECONOMY Monetary unit:** som. **Budget:** (2008 est.) *income:* $1.17 bil.; *expend.:* $1.192 bil. **G.D.P.:** $11.41 bil., $2,100 per capita (2008 est.). **Chief crops:** wool, tobacco; cotton; sheep, goats, cattle. **Natural resources:** hydroelectric potential; gold; coal, natural gas, petroleum, lead, zinc. **Major industries:** small machinery, textiles, food processing, cement. **Labor force:** 2.7 mil. (2000); 55% agriculture and forest, 30% services, 15% industry and construction. **Exports:** $1.676 bil. (f.o.b., 2008 est.); cotton, wool, meat, tobacco; ferrous and nonferrous metals. **Imports:** $3.476 mil. (f.o.b., 2008 est.); foodstuffs, fuel, machinery. **Major trading partners:** (2006) *exports:* 26.1% Switzerland, 20.4% Kazakhstan, 19.3% Russia, 9.4% Afghanistan, 4.8% China; *imports:* 38.1% Russia, 14.4% China, 11.7% Kazakhstan, 5.7% U.S.

Kyrgyzstan is largely mountainous, dominated by the massive Tien Shan range in the northeast and the Pamir-Alay range in the southwest. Most of the population lives in one of three major valleys, the Fergana, the Chu, and the Talas, since much of the country is permanently ice-capped and covered with glaciers. The Kyrgyz people are

mentioned in early Turkic inscriptions that date back at least to the eighth century A.D.

They were one of the great nomadic tribes of central Asia, who until the 10th century settled around the Upper Yenisei River. With the Mongol invasions of the 13th century, they migrated to the areas of the Tien Shan range in present-day Kyrgyzstan, a territory that has been controlled variously by Mongols, Kalmyks, Manchus, the large tribal empire of the Kokand khanate, and the Russians. In the mid-17th century, the Kyrgyz began to be converted to Islam, but the Manchus defeated the Mongols and the Kyrgyz people became Chinese subjects. The Chinese did not interfere with their nomadic life, but in the 19th century they were attacked and came under the control of the khanate of Kokand, during which time Islam was strengthened. In 1868 the khanate became a Russian protectorate and in 1876, the area was merged into the Russian empire as Fergana region. A large Russian influx followed, and many Kyrgyz migrated to China and Afghanistan.

The period immediately following the 1917 Bolshevik revolution was one of confusion and fighting between the Kyrgyz, the Reds, the Whites, and foreign interventionists. Soviet power was established in 1919, although fighting continued in some parts until 1922. In 1918, Kyrgyzstan was included in the Russian republic's Turkestan ·Autonomous Soviet Socialist Republic; then, with the National Delimitation of Central Asian Republics in 1924, its name changed to Kara-Kirghiz Autonomous Province. On Dec. 5, 1936, it became a Soviet Socialist Republic (SSR) of the U.S.S.R.

In the 1920s and 1930s, land reform and collectivization ended the traditional nomadic way of life. Kyrgyz nationalists strongly opposed the changes that Soviet rule brought, but the central government won in the end, and the nationalists were repressed. From the 1930s, ethnic Russians held most of the leading Communist party and government positions in the Kyrgyz SSR.

Mikhail Gorbachev's policy of *glasnost*, or openness, was responsible for the first public discussion of corruption in government, the emergence of a more liberal Kyrgyz press by 1988, and the emergence of opposition parties and ethnic conflicts. In 1990 disputes over housing and land in the Osh region of the crowded Fergana Valley led to violent confrontations between the Kyrgyz and the republic's Uzbeks. Osh had been incorporated into Kyrgyzstan in 1924, even though the majority population was Uzbek, and at various times the Uzbeks had lobbied for the establishment of an autonomous Uzbek region in Osh.

In Feb. 1990 traditional Soviet-style elections brought into office many Communist party officials, and in April the Supreme Soviet elected Absamat Masaliyev, who had been the Kyrgyz republic's Communist party First Secretary. In Oct. 1990, however, largely due to the violence in Osh, Masaliyev did not receive enough Supreme Soviet votes, and the reformer Askar Akayev was elected as president. After the failed coup in Moscow in August 1991, Communist party activities were suspended, although most leaders were still party members. In Dec. 1991 Kyrgyzstan signed the Alma-Ata Declaration that founded the Commonwealth of Independent States.

In 1992, with the help of the I.M.F., Akayev embarked on a radical economic program that included lowering wages, raising prices, and abolishing tariffs with Central Asian neighbors

Kazakhstan and Uzbekistan. Although the program initially caused hardship, it proved successful. In 1995, elections, Akayev was elected to a second term with 60 percent of the vote. This came six months after international lenders, led by the World Bank, agreed in June to $680 million in aid.

In 1996 Kyrgyzstan joined the common market among Russia, Belarus, and Kazakhstan as it expanded to include development of common energy, transport and information systems. The government signed a non-aggression pact with Russia, China, Kazakhstan and Tajikistan and in Oct. 2000 Akayev won a third term with 75 percent of the vote and in Feb. 2003 a "Constitutional Referendum" gave him greatly expanded powers. But a popular uprising in March 2005 forced him to flee and Kurmanbek Bakiyev became interim president. In July he won a landslide presidential election and was reelected in 2007, although irregularities were reported everywhere. Since 2001 the U.S. has had a large military base here which the Russians have opposed. In 2009 the U.S. was forced to pay a much higher fee to keep the base. (See "Major News Stories.")

▶ LAOS
Lao People's Democratic Republic

• **GEOGRAPHY Location:** landlocked country in Southeast Asia. **Boundaries:** Myanmar to NW, China to N, Vietnam to E, Cambodia to S, and Thailand to W. **Total area:** 91,429 sq. mi. (236,800 sq km). **Coastline:** none. **Comparative area:** slightly larger than Utah. **Land use:** 3% arable land; negl. % permanent crops; 97% other. **Major cities:** Vientiane (capital); Savannaket; Pakse; Luang Prabang; Saya Bury.
• **PEOPLE Population:** 6,834,942 (July 2009 est.). **Nationality:** noun—Lao or Laotian (sing. and pl.); adjective—Lao or Laotian. **Ethnic groups:** 68% Lao Loum, 22% Lao Theung, 9% Lao Soung including Hmong and Yao. **Languages:** Lao (official), French, English, ethnic languages. **Religions:** 60% Buddhist, 40% animist and other.
• **GOVERNMENT Type:** communist state. **Independence:** July 19, 1949 (from France). **Constitution:** Aug. 14, 1991. **National holiday:** Republic Day, Dec. 2. **Heads of Government:** Choummali Saignason, president (since June 2006); Bouasone Bouphavanh, prime minister (since June 2006). **Structure:** executive; unicameral legislature; independent judiciary.
• **ECONOMY Monetary unit:** new kip. **Budget:** (2008 est.) *income:* $809.6 mil.; *expend.:* $954 mil. **G.D.P.:** $13.99 bil., $2,100 per capita (2008 est.). **Chief crops:** sweet potatoes, vegetables, coffee, sugarcane, cotton; water buffalo, pigs, cattle, poultry; tobacco. **Natural resources:** tin, timber, gypsum, hydropower potential. **Major industries:** timber, hydropower, tin and gypsum. **Labor force:** 2.1 mil. (2006); 80% agriculture; 2.4% unemployment (2005). **Exports:** $1.033 bil. (f.o.b., 2008 est.); electricity, wood products, coffee, tin. **Imports:** $1.278 bil. (f.o.b., 2008 est.); machinery and equipment, vehicles, fuel. **Major trading partners:** (2006) *exports:* 42.1% Thailand, 9.4% Vietnam, 4% China; *imports:* 68.8% Thailand, 11.3% China, 5.6% Vietnam.

Inhabited by the Thai-speaking Lao people in the river valleys and by Hmong and other tribal people in the highlands, Laos historically had little national cohesion and was dominated by its more powerful neighbors, Siam (Thailand) to the west and Vietnam to the east. In 1893 France

forced Siam to recognize Laos as a French protectorate; the country was thereafter incorporated into the French Union of Indochina. Laos was occupied by Japan during World War II but saw little major fighting.

In 1946 Laos was united under the Luang Prabang dynasty and was granted local autonomy as a constitutional monarchy in 1949. During the final phases of the Indochina War against French colonialism in 1953–54, Vietnamese Communist (Vietminh) incursions reinforced the position of the Laotian Communist party (Pathet Lao) in Laotian politics. Following the French withdrawal in December 1954, Laos became an independent nation and was admitted to the United Nations in 1955.

The creation of a coalition government under Prince Souvana Phouma in 1962 temporarily resolved a turbulent political situation; an international agreement signed in Geneva that year guaranteed Laos's neutrality. The Pathet Lao withdrew from the coalition in 1964 and renewed its armed uprising against the government, with North Vietnamese support. American planes bombed Vietnamese supply lines along the Ho Chi Minh trail, and American agents recruited Hmong tribesmen as irregular troops to attack Pathet Lao positions. The Pathet Lao nevertheless made steady gains, especially after 1970. In 1973, Prince Souvana Phouma ordered a cease-fire, and in 1975 the Pathet Lao took control of the capital, Vientiane. The Lao People's Democratic Republic was proclaimed on Dec. 3, 1975. Large numbers of Hmong and other tribal people fled to Thailand.

Subsequently, Laos was strongly dominated by Vietnam, which stationed significant numbers of troops in the country. In 1989, in Laos's first election since the communist takeover, a Supreme People's Assembly was elected specifically to approve a new constitution, which it did in 1991; the constitution confirmed the Lao People's Revolutionary party as the sole legal political party. Single-party elections in 1992 did little to alter the country's political climate, though observers predicted changes as the Communists began to pass from the scene. In 1997, Laos was admitted to the Association of Southeast Asian Nations. Not until 2006, however, was a non-Communist government elected and the National Assembly appointed a prime minister and cabinet.

▶ LATVIA
Republic of Latvia

• **GEOGRAPHY Location:** eastern coast of Baltic Sea in northeastern Europe. **Boundaries:** Baltic Sea to N, Estonia to NE, Russian Federation, Belarus to S, Lithuania to W. **Total area:** 24,749 sq. mi. (64,100 sq km). **Coastline:** Baltic Sea. **Comparative area:** slightly larger than West Virginia. **Land use:** 29% arable land; negl.% permanent crops, 71% other. **Major cities:** Riga (capital); Daugav'pils; Liepāja; Jelgava; Jurmala.
• **PEOPLE Population:** 2,217,969 (July 2010 est.). **Nationality:** noun—Latvian(s); adjective—Latvian. **Ethnic groups:** 57.7% Latvian, 29.6% Russian, 4.1% Belarussian, 2.7% Ukrainian, 2.5% Polish. **Languages:** Latvian (official), Lithuanian, Russian, other. **Religions:** Lutheran, Roman Catholic, Russian Orthodox.
• **GOVERNMENT Type:** parliamentary democracy. **Independence:** Nov. 18, 1918 (from Soviet Russia); Aug. 21, 1991 (from Soviet Union). **Constitution:** the 1991 Constitutional Law supplements the 1922 constitution and provides for basic rights and free-

doms. **National holiday:** Independence Day, Nov. 18. **Heads of Government:** Valdis Zatlers, president (since July 2007); Valdis Dombrovskis, prime minister (since March 2009). **Structure:** executive; unicameral legislature; judiciary.

• **ECONOMY Monetary unit:** lats. **Budget:** (2009 est.) *income:* $9.501 bil.; *expend:* $12.15 bil. **G.D.P.:** $32.4 bil., $14,500 per capita (2009 est.). **Chief crops:** grain, potatoes, sugar beets, vegetables; meat, milk, eggs; fish. **Natural resources:** minimal; amber, peat, limestone, dolomite. **Major industries:** machine building, metalworking, chemical processing. **Labor force:** 1.205 mil. (2009 est.); 21.3% industry, 3.5% agriculture, 75.2% services (2007); 5.9% unemployment (2007). **Exports:** $6.721 bil. (2009 est.); timber, textiles, foodstuffs. **Imports:** $8.849 bil. (2009 est.); fuels, machinery and equipment, chemicals. **Major trading partners:** (2008) *exports:* 15.4% Lithuania, 14.7% Russia, 13.1% Estonia, 7.6% Germany, 6.2% Sweden, 4.3% Denmark; *imports:* 16% Lithuania, 12.8% Germany, 10.6% Russia, 7% Poland, 7% Estonia, 4.3% Sweden, 4.3% Finland.

Though the Letts ethnically and linguistically are quite distinct from their northern neighbors the Ests, Latvia's history parallels that of Estonia. German merchants, knights, and missionaries made Latvia a semi-ecclesiastical German colony in the 13th century; in the 16th century Latvia passed under first Swedish, then Lithuanian rule; in the 18th century Peter the Great's Russian empire absorbed the land.

A 19th-century cultural revival, inspired in part by Johann von Herder, a native of Riga, found expression in folkloric societies, archaeological research and the compilation of the epic poem, Lacplesis. Brest-Litovsk, the Soviet Union's 1918 peace treaty with Germany, granted Latvia's political independence for the first time in its history.

The constitution of 1922 established a one-house legislature. To avoid violence between left and right armed extremists, Prime Minister Karlis Umanlis dissolved the Parliament in May 1934 and ruled as dictator until a new constitution that provided for expanded presidential powers and a second house of the legislature, based on the conception of a corporate state, came into existence in 1938 just before the Hitler-Stalin Pact awarded Latvia to the Russian sphere of interest. Stalin garrisoned troops in Latvia, rigged elections, and incorporated the country as a new union republic of the U.S.S.R. in 1940.

For 50 years, harsh Soviet rule continued. The larger cities were Russianized and the highly educated middle and upper-middle classes were deported throughout Russia. Industrialization brought relative prosperity, but the national consciousness was never eradicated.

Mikhail Gorbachev's policy of glasnost, or openness, led to the creation of dissident groups who staged public demonstrations on the anniversaries of the Stalin-Hitler Pact and of the establishment of Latvian independence. After the head of the Latvian Communist party, Boris Pugo was transferred to Moscow, Latvia's Communist party came under the influence of the newly created Latvian Popular Front. With the new political influence of non-Communists, on Sept. 29, 1988, Latvian replaced Russian as the official language.

In March 1990, following Lithuania's example, Latvia announced its intention to secede, survived Gorbachev's January 1991 military crackdown, and after the failed August 1991 coup in Moscow, declared independence.

In 1995 summer elections revealed deep political divisions as the three major parties took half the seats. It was not until December that Andris Skele was able to become prime minister, heading a cabinet containing members of six of Latvia's nine parties. Skele was forced to resign in July 1997 because of corruption charges and over disappointment that the E.U. would not consider Latvia's application until the "second wave." Parliamentary elections in Oct. 1998 resulted in the same degree of party splintering, but Vilis Kristopans was able to form a government. More significantly, in a referendum voters eased the citizenship laws, making it simpler for ethnic Russians (one-third of the population) to become citizens. Coalition discord brought the end of the Kristopanis government in July 1999; the successor government, under Andris Skele collapsed in April 2000, with Andris Berzins as his successor.

In 2002 a four-party center-right coalition government was founded with Einers Repse as prime minister but another minority government was needed yet again in 2003, this time headed by a prime minister from the Green Party, Indulis Emsis. In 2004 Latvia joined the E.U. and NATO, but government stability remained an issue as ministers continued to change on a regular basis. After the economy contracted in 2008–09 during the worldwide recession, large protests forced the government to resign in 2009.

▶ LEBANON
Lebanese Republic

• **GEOGRAPHY Location:** western Asia. **Boundaries:** Syria to N and E, Israel to S, Mediterranean Sea to W. **Total area:** 4,015 sq. mi. (10,400 sq km). **Coastline:** 140 mi. (225 km). **Comparative area:** about 0.7 times the size of Connecticut. **Land use:** 18% arable land; 13% permanent crops; 69% other. **Major cities:** Beirut (capital); Tarabulus (Tripoli); Zahleh; Saida (Sidon); Sur (Tyre).

• **PEOPLE Population:** 4,017,095 (July 2009 est.). **Nationality:** noun—Lebanese (sing., pl.); adjective—Lebanese. **Ethnic groups:** 95% Arab, 4% Armenian, 1% other. **Languages:** Arabic (official), French, Armenian, English. **Religions:** 59.7% Muslim, 39% Christian, 1.3% other.

• **GOVERNMENT Type:** republic. **Independence:** Nov. 22, 1943 (from League of Nations Mandate under French administration). **Constitution:** May 23, 1926 (amended multiple times). **National holiday:** Independence Day, Nov. 22. **Heads of Government:** Michel Sulayman, president (since May 2008); Saad Hariri, prime minister (since June 2009). **Structure:** executive—by custom, president is Maronite Christian, prime minister is Sunni Muslim, and president of legislature is Shia Muslim; unicameral legislature; judiciary—three courts for civil and commercial cases, one court for civil cases.

• **ECONOMY Monetary unit:** Lebanese pound. **Budget:** (2008 est.) *income:* $7 bil.; *expend.:* $10 bil. **G.D.P.:** $44.07 bil., $11,100 per capita (2008 est.). **Chief crops:** citrus, vegetables, potatoes, olives, tobacco, hemp (hashish); sheep, goats. **Natural resources:** limestone, iron ore, salt; water-surplus state in water-deficit region. **Major industries:** banking, food processing, textiles. **Labor force:** 1.1 mil. plus as many as 1 mil. foreign workers (2007 est.); 20% unemployment (2006 est.). **Exports:** 3.5 bil. (f.o.b., 2008 est.); foodstuffs and tobacco, textiles, chemicals, metals. **Imports:** $16.1 bil. (f.o.b., 2008 est.); foodstuffs, machinery &

transport equipment, consumer goods. **Major trading partners:** (2006) *exports:* 26.8% Syria, 12% United Arab Emirates, 6% Switzerland, 5.7% Saudi Arabia, 4.5% Turkey; *imports:* 11.6% Syria, 9.8% Italy, 9.3% U.S., 7.7% France, 6.1% Germany, 5% China, 4.7% Saudi Arabia.

The ancient history of Lebanon is essentially coextensive with that of Syria, of which it was long a part. The port cities of Tripoli, Tyre, and Sidon were important centers of the Phoenician empire. The parallel ranges of the Lebanon and Anti-Lebanon mountains, crowned with the country's famous cedar trees, enclose the fertile Bekaa Valley. The coastal cities became strongholds of early Christianity, later fragmented into numerous sects, including Maronites (Syrian Catholic), Roman Catholic, Greek Orthodox, Syrian Orthodox, and others. The mountains of the south became the center of the Druze sect of Islam, while orthodox Sunni Islam dominated in the Bekaa Valley.

Lebanon came under French influence in the late 18th century, as France claimed the role of protector of Syria's Christian community. France intervened in Lebanon in 1841 and again in 1860 when fighting between Maronite and Druze communities led to the massacre of many Christians. Under pressure from France, the Ottoman Empire granted some local autonomy to the Maronites.

In the dismemberment of the Ottoman Empire after World War I, France was granted a League of Nations Mandate over the Levant States (Lebanon and Syria), ensuring French control of the Iraq Petroleum Company pipeline from Iraq to Tripoli. In 1926 Lebanon became a self-governing republic under the mandate, but internal unrest and anti-French sentiment continued.

In June 1940 the French administration in Lebanon declared its allegiance to the Vichy government. British and Free French forces occupied Lebanon in June 1941 and declared it an independent republic; but France retained control, and full independence did not come until Jan. 1, 1944.

Under a National Covenant in 1943, political power in the Lebanese parliament was apportioned among the nation's various communities. The president was always to be a Maronite Christian, the prime minister a Sunni Muslim. This provided a workable formula for power sharing but also ensured that the national government would always be hostage to the considerable power of separate communities and clans.

The years from the end of World War II to the early 1970s were a brief golden age for Lebanon. Beirut developed into a wealthy, cosmopolitan city, the center of Middle Eastern banking and trade, while agriculture and small-scale industry flourished in the rest of the country. A Syrian-backed Muslim uprising in 1958 had no significant impact; U.S. Marines landed in May 1958 to protect American interests and remained until October. By the late 1960s, however, Lebanon's stability was threatened by PLO attacks on Israel from refugee camps in southern Lebanon and by a shift in the country's demographic balance. Muslims had become a majority in Lebanon by the late 1960s and demanded a revision of the National Covenant, while Maronite Christians continued to cling to their position of political dominance.

Throughout the 1970s, Palestinian raids from Lebanon into Israel brought Israeli retaliatory strikes in southern Lebanon. Israeli troops occupied southern Lebanon in 1978 and again in 1980. The Palestinian-Israeli conflict polarized opinion within Lebanon, inflaming anti-Western feelings among Lebanon's Sunni Muslims.

Civil war broke out in 1975, with Palestinian and leftist Muslim militias battling militias of the Maronite community, the Christian Phalange party, and other groups. More than 60,000 died, and damage ranged into the billions of dollars. Syrian troops intervened in 1976, battling Palestinian forces in an attempt to restore the status quo. Arab League efforts to negotiate a cease-fire produced an unstable peace at the end of 1976, though Syrian troops remained in Lebanon.

Fighting broke out between Syrian forces and Christian militiamen near Zahle on Apr. 1, 1981. Other groups joined the fighting in a general war of each against all. Israel staged commando raids against Palestinian positions in Tyre and Tulin. Israeli air raids on Beirut caused extensive loss of life and property damage. Israel invaded Lebanon in a full-scale assault on June 6, 1982, in an attempt to drive out the PLO. Israeli forces surrounded Beirut and began a heavy bombardment of the city. On Aug. 1, Palestinian forces withdrew from Beirut under international supervision. On Sept. 14 newly elected Pres. Bashir Gemayel, a Maronite Christian, was assassinated; Israeli troops occupied the Muslim quarters of West Beirut in response. With tacit Israeli approval, Christian militiamen invaded two refugee camps and slaughtered hundreds of Palestinian civilians.

Beirut remained a battle zone in 1983, divided by the "Green Line" into Christian and Muslim sectors. Terrorist bombings were common. The U.S., France, Italy, and other Western nations stationed troops in Beirut in an attempt to enforce a cease-fire. Fifty people were killed when a bomb partly destroyed the U.S. embassy on Apr. 18; separate attacks on military installations on Oct. 23 killed 241 U.S. Marines and 58 French soldiers.

Rashid Karami became premier with Syrian support on Apr. 26, 1984. The civil war continued, with fighting among various groups of Christian, Druze, Sunni, Shiite, and Palestinian militias. War between Shiite and Palestinian forces broke out in May 1985. Israeli forces withdrew from most of Lebanon in June, but maintained a "security zone" in the southern part of the country. Premier Karami was assassinated on June 1, 1987, when a bomb destroyed his helicopter.

At an October 1989 Arab League-sponsored meeting, Christian and Muslim leaders agreed on a new national charter. The Taif accord was condemned by Christian militants, led by Gen. Michel Aoun, and Muslim militia leaders. Newly elected Pres. René Mowad, a Syrian-backed Christian, was assassinated on Nov. 22 and succeeded by Elias Hraoui. In 1990, rival Shiite militias—the Syrian-backed Amal and Iranian-backed Party of God—signed an agreement ending three years of fighting. In February 1991 Lebanese troops moved to defend the area for the first time in 13 years and called for Israel to abandon its "security zone" in southern Lebanon. In addition to leaving 150,000 dead, the civil war severely disrupted the economy.

The government of Christian prime minister Omar Karami collapsed in May 1992, after riots protesting economic hardship. New elections were held under Syrian supervision with Hezbollah and other Islamic fundamentalist parties gaining the most seats, in part because the Christian parties called for a boycott. In 1994, as Israeli-Hezbollah skirmishes continued, the government banned the Christian political party. Lebanese

Forces arrested some of its leaders, and stopped all "political" broadcasts not government-controlled. In 1995, Syria-backed premier Rafik Hariri won a second term together with a 2–1 backing in Parliament. His attempts at reform were hindered by repeated skirmishes between Israel and Hezbollah Shiite guerrillas in Israel's "security zone" in southern Lebanon. In April 1996 the fighting escalated as Israel launched 600 airraids and 24,000 artillery shells some of which hit a U.N. refugee camp near Tyre, killing over 100 and wounding 100 more. The U.N. voted 64–2 (with 65 abstaining) to condemn the attack.

By 1997 order had been restored but no peace agreement reached with Israel. With $3 bil. in U.S. and E.U. aid the government set about to rebuild this ravaged land. Deadly skirmishes still occured in the "security zone." In 1998 Lebanon held its first municipal elections in 35 years; no clear pattern emerged. In Oct., the (pro-Syrian) National Assembly unanimously elected General Emile Lahoud as president. He nominated Selim al-Hoss as prime minister after Hariri declined a fourth consecutive government. In 1999 the Israeli-Hezbollah warfare in south Lebanon intensified until, suddenly, Israel withdrew completely (May 24, 2000), accompanied by about 3,000 Christian militiamen of the South Lebanese Army to whom Israel offered haven. In early Sept. Hariri won a decisive victory in parliamentary elections and he adopted an anti-Syrian approach to politics. By 2005 Lebanese feelings towards Syria's powerful military presence had turned vociferous and when Hariri, now out of office, was assassinated (Feb.) mass protests followed demanding the ouster of Pres. Lahoud who was backed by Syria. U.S. opposition to Syria's presence soon forced a withdrawal. In June elections the anti-Syrian groups won a clear majority in parliament and again an assassination of a prominent anti-Syrian figure followed. In July 2006 Israel launched another major military assault against Hezbollah with great destruction to Lebanon's infrastructure. A U.N.-brokered ceasefire has held but Hezbollah's leaders reject U.N. calls for disarming.

In May 2008 a new president, army chief Michel Suleiman, was chosen by parliament after a six-month deadlock. He quickly moved to ease tensions with Syria. In June 2009 a U.S.-supported coalition defeated the Hezbollah-led parties in an upset many attributed to President Obama's conciliatory speech to the region in the spring. Elections in 2009 resulted in a five-month stalemate but in November a compromise gave 15 seats to the Western-aligned majority and 10 to Hezbollah.

▶ **LESOTHO**
Kingdom of Lesotho
• **GEOGRAPHY** **Location:** landlocked country in southern Africa. **Boundaries:** entirely surrounded by South African territory. **Total area:** 11,718 sq. mi. (30,350 sq km). **Coastline:** none. **Comparative area:** slightly smaller than Maryland. **Land use:** 11% arable land; 0% permanent crops; 89% other. **Major cities:** Maseru (capital).
• **PEOPLE** **Population:** 2,130,819 (July 2009 est.). **Nationality:** noun—Mosotho (sing.), Basotho (pl.); adjective—Basotho. **Ethnic groups:** 99.7% Sotho; 0.3% Europeans, Asians and other. **Languages:** Sesotho (southern Sotho), English (official), Zulu, Xhosa. **Religions:** 80% Christian, 20% indigenous beliefs.

• **GOVERNMENT** **Type:** parliamentary constitutional monarchy. **Independence:** Oct. 4, 1966 (from U.K.). **Constitution:** Apr. 2, 1993. **National holiday:** Independence Day, Oct. 4. **Heads of Government:** Letsie III, king (since Feb. 1996); Pakalitha Bethuel Mosisili, prime minister (since May 1998). **Structure:** executive—king is chief of state but has no power and can be deposed by College of Chiefs; legislature—bicameral legislature; judiciary.
• **ECONOMY** **Monetary unit:** loti. **Budget:** (2008 est.) *income:* $523 mil.; *expend.:* $479.5 mil. **G.D.P.:** $3.37 bil., $1,600 per capita (2008 est.). **Chief crops:** corn, wheat, pulses, sorghum, barley; livestock. **Natural resources:** some diamonds and other minerals, water, agricultural and grazing land. **Major industries:** tourism, food, beverages. **Labor force:** 838,000 economically active; 86% subsistence agriculture; 35% work in South Africa (2002 est.). **Exports:** $1.06 mil. (f.o.b., 2008 est.); 75% manufactures, wool and mohair, food and live animals. **Imports:** $1.339 bil. (f.o.b., 2008 est.); food, building materials, vehicles, machinery. **Major trading partners:** (2006) *exports:* 81.9% U.S., 15% Belgium, 1.9% Canada; *imports:* 33.4% Hong Kong, 31.2% China, 7.7% Germany, 7.3% India.

Lesotho, formerly Basutoland, is an independent kingdom surrounded entirely by the Republic of South Africa. The area was sparsely populated by Bushmen until the 16th century when refugees from tribal wars in surrounding areas began to move in, an influx that continued through the 19th century. These immigrants coalesced into a homogenous cultural group, the Basothos.

Under King Moshoeshoe (1823–70), several Basotho groups were consolidated, but much land was lost in a series of wars with South Africa. Moshoeshoe appealed to Queen Victoria for aid, and in 1868 the nation became a British protectorate. Between 1884 and 1959 all executive and legislative authority was in the hands of a British high commissioner. In 1903 a Basotho consultative body was established, and in 1959 a new constitution gave the council power to legislate on internal affairs.

On Oct. 4, 1966, Basutoland achieved full independence as the Kingdom of Lesotho. The first elections after independence, in 1970, were nullified by the ruling Basutoland National party (BNP) when early returns indicated that the party might lose. A state of emergency was declared, the constitution was suspended, and parliament dissolved.

Elections in 1985 were boycotted by opposition parties. In 1986 the BNP government was ousted in a coup. The nation was run by a military council, which in 1990 stripped King Moshoeshoe II of his powers. Military rule ended in April 1993 when Ntsu Mokhehle was elected prime minister and his Basotholand Congress party (BCP) gained all 243 seats in the legislature. King Moshoeshoe II was restored in Jan. 1995 but died a year later in an auto accident. The Traditional College of Chiefs named his son Letsie III as his successor.

Elections in May 1998 kept the ruling party in power with a new prime minister, Pakalitha Mosisili, but the opposition and some outside observers said the elections were dishonest and when pro-opposition army officers mutinied the government pledged new and free elections. These were held in March 2003 and Mosisili and his party returned to power and remains so in 2008. A severe drought caused much suffering in 2007.

▶ LIBERIA
Republic of Liberia

• **GEOGRAPHY** **Location:** western Africa. **Boundaries:** Sierra Leone, Guinea to N, Ivory Coast to E, Atlantic Ocean to S and W. **Total area:** 43,000 sq. mi. (111,370 sq km). **Coastline:** 360 mi. (579 km). **Comparative area:** slightly larger than Tennessee. **Land use:** 2% arable land; 2% permanent crops; 96% other. **Major cities:** Monrovia (capital).

• **PEOPLE** **Population:** 3,441.790 (July 2009 est.). **Nationality:** noun—Liberian(s); adjective—Liberian. **Ethnic groups:** 95% indigenous peoples, including Kpelle, Bassa, Gio, Kru, Grebo, Mano, Krahn, Gola, Gbandi, Loma, Kissi, Vai, Bella; 2.5% descendants of repatriated slaves from the U.S. known as Americo-Liberians, 2.5% descendents of repatriated slaves from the Carribean known as Congo-people. **Languages:** 20% English (official); more than 20 languages of Niger-Congo language group. **Religions:** 40% indigenous beliefs, 20% Muslim, 40% Christian.

• **GOVERNMENT** **Type:** republic. **Independence:** July 26, 1847. **Constitution:** Jan. 6, 1986. **National holiday:** Independence Day, July 26. **Head of Government:** Ellen Johnson Sirleaf, president (since Jan. 2006). **Structure:** executive—president, appointed cabinet; bicameral legislature; judiciary.

• **ECONOMY** **Monetary unit:** Liberian dollar. **Budget:** N.A. **G.D.P.:** $1.532 bil., $500 per capita (2008 est.). **Chief crops:** rubber, coffee, cocoa, rice, cassava, palm oil, sugarcane; sheep, goats; timber. **Natural resources:** iron ore, timber, diamonds, gold. **Major industries:** rubber processing, palm oil processing, diamonds. **Labor force:** 70% agriculture; 85% unemployment (2000 est.) **Exports:** $1.197 bil. (f.o.b., 2006 est.); diamonds, iron ore, rubber, timber, coffee. **Imports:** $7.143 bil. (f.o.b., 2006 est.); fuels, chemicals, machinery, transportation equipment. **Major trading partners:** (2006) *exports:* 40.1% Germany, 12% South Africa, 11.7% Poland, 8.5% U.S., 8.2% Spain; *imports:* 43.2% South Korea, 15% Singapore, 12.8% Japan, 8.2% China.

Liberia was populated by migrants from the north and east beginning in the 12th century, but it remained relatively isolated from the remainder of West Africa and was not incorporated into any of the region's premodern kingdoms and empires. Portuguese explorers first reached the Liberian coast in 1461 to be followed by other European traders. Until the 19th century, Liberia was largely ignored by the world except for a small-scale coastal trade in slaves and forest products.

In 1816 the U.S. Congress granted a charter to the American Colonization Society, ACS, a private organization dedicated to the African repatriation of freed slaves. The first settlers landed in 1822 at the town that was later to become Monrovia. In 1838 the settlers organized the Commonwealth of Liberia under a governor appointed by the ACS. The commonwealth declared its independence as the Republic of Liberia in 1847 and adopted a constitution modeled after that of the United States. The new government, Africa's first independent republic, was granted diplomatic recognition by Great Britain in 1848, France in 1852, and the United States in 1862.

Bolstered by the moral backing of the U.S., Liberia in its first 100 years of independence succeeded in fending off British and French attempts to encroach on its territory from their neighboring colonies. Although descendants of freed American slaves are a minority in Liberia's ethnically diverse population, they have consistently dominated the country's political life.

William V.S. Tubman was elected president in 1944 and served until his death in 1971, successfully steering Liberia through the post War age of African nationalism and decolonization. He was succeeded by William R. Tolbert, Jr. On Apr. 12, 1980, Tolbert was deposed in a military coup led by Master Sgt. Samuel K. Doe. Doe suspended the constitution and imposed martial law but pledged a new constitution by 1985.

Presidential elections were held on Oct. 15, 1985, under the terms of a provisional constitution that for the first time enacted universal suffrage. Doe was elected and his party won 80 percent of the seats in the legislature. Despite allegations of fraud that led to a violent but unsuccessful coup attempt in November 1985, the Second Republic, under the new constitution, was inaugurated on Jan. 6, 1986.

On Dec. 24, 1989, about 150 antigovernment guerrillas of the National Patriotic Forces of Liberia (NPFL), led by Charles Taylor, crossed the border from the Ivory Coast. The fighting degenerated into ethnic warfare between the Krahn and Mandingo, in support of the government, and the Gio and Mano, who supported the rebels. Prince Johnson split from Taylor's forces and took up fighting both government troops and Taylor. A peacekeeping force of the Economic Community of West African States (ECOWAS) landed at Monrovia on Aug. 24 to mediate a cease-fire and prepare for free elections. On Sept. 10 Pres. Doe was killed by Prince Johnson, but a cease-fire was not agreed upon until Nov. 28, 1990.

From 1990 to 1992 Charles Taylor solidified his hold on the country despite the establishment of a government (under Amos Sawyer) in Monrovia by the West African States. By 1993 the government and ECOWAS forces succeeded in containing Taylor's forces. In 1994 an interim coalition government representing the country's three major factions came into power as peace talks began. Elections were scheduled for Nov. 1995 but extensive fighting broke out continually through the end of 1996. Over 150,000 had died up to then.

In early 1997 ECOWAS, led by a Nigerian, helped to restore order and arrange for elections in July. Charles Taylor won a landslide victory. Doubts arose about domestic peace when Taylor attempted to arrest opposition militia leader Roosevelt Johnson; 50 died in the fighting as Johnson fled to the U.S. Embassy for safety. In early 1999, Taylor faced broad international condemnation for Liberia's aid to rebels in Sierra Leone. But the U.N. agreed to place international monitors along Liberia's border with Sierra Leone. In return for Pres. Taylor's support for the RUF rebels in Sierra Leone, he controlled their illegal diamond trade, skimming as much as 90 percent of the profit.

In Aug. 2003 Taylor was forced into exile by ECOWAS and international pressure. An interim government was set up but riots in Dec. 2003 delayed the international effort to bring needed aid to the nation. But it was not until late 2005 that elections could be held, but they were won by a U.S.-educated economist, Ellen Johnson-Sirleaf, Africa's first elected woman head-of-state. Taylor was arrested in March 2006 and went on trial in 2009.

►LIBYA
Socialist People's Libyan Arab Jamahiriya

● **GEOGRAPHY Location:** along Mediterranean coast of North Africa. **Boundaries:** Mediterranean Sea to N, Egypt to E, Sudan to SE, Niger, Chad to S, Tunisia, Algeria to W. **Total area:** 679,359 sq. mi. (1,759,540 sq km). **Coastline:** 1,100 mi. (1,770 km). **Comparative area:** slightly larger than Alaska. **Land use:** 1% arable land; 0% permanent crops; 99% other. **Major cities:** in Jan. 1987, Col. Qaddafi designated Hun, a town 404 mi. (650 km) SE of Tripoli, as administrative capital of country; Tripoli; Benghazi; Misurata.

● **PEOPLE Population:** 6,310,434 (July 2009 est.). **Nationality:** noun—Libyan(s); adjective—Libyan. **Ethnic groups:** 97% Berber and Arab; some Greeks, Maltese, Italians, Egyptians, Pakistanis, Turks, Indians, Tunisians. **Languages:** Arabic, Italian, and English widely understood in major cities. **Religions:** 97% Sunni Muslim.

● **GOVERNMENT Type:** Jamahiriya (a state of the masses) in theory, governed by populace through local councils; in practice, an authoritarian state. **Independence:** Dec. 24, 1951 (from UN trusteeship). **Constitution:** Dec. 11, 1969, amended Mar. 2, 1977. **National holiday:** Revolution Day, Sept. 1. **Head of Government:** Col. Muammar al-Qaddafi (no official title; runs country and is treated as chief of state) (since Sept. 1969); Al Baghdadi Ali Al-Mahmoudi, prime minister (since Feb. 2007). **Structure:** officially, paramount political power and authority rests with General People's Congress, which theoretically functions as a parliament with a cabinet called General People's Committee; elections are indirect.

● **ECONOMY Monetary unit:** Libyan dinar. **Budget:** (2008 est.) *income:* $56.35 bil.; *expend.:* $29.12 bil. **G.D.P.:** $88.86 bil., $14,400 per capita (2008 est.) **Chief crops:** wheat, barley, olives, dates, citrus fruits; meat, eggs. **Natural resources:** crude oil, natural gas, gypsum. **Major industries:** petroleum, food processing, textiles. **Labor force:** 1.916 mil.; 23% industry, 59% services, 17% agriculture. **Exports:** 66.13 bil. (f.o.b., 2008 est.); petroleum. **Imports:** $20.64 bil. (f.o.b., 2008 est.) machinery and transport equipment, food. **Major trading partners:** (2006) *exports:* 36.7% Italy, 14.3% Germany, 8.7% Spain, 6.1% U.S., 5.6% France, 5.3% Turkey; *imports:* 18.9% Italy, 7.9% Germany, 7.5% China, 6.3% Tunisia, 5.8% France, 5.2% Turkey, 4.7% U.S., 4.3% South Korea, 4% U.K.

The coastal cities of Libya played an important cultural and commercial role in the Mediterranean in antiquity and were prized possessions of numerous empires. The Libyan coast was successively ruled by Phoenicians, Carthaginians, Berbers, Romans, and Vandals before being incorporated into the Byzantine Empire in the fourth century A.D.; nomadic tribes in the interior were beyond the reach of any government. The Islamic conquests of the seventh and eighth centuries brought Libya into the Muslim world.

Libya was incorporated into the Ottoman Empire shortly after the Ottoman conquest of Egypt in 1517 and was ruled by local Ottoman vassals until 1835 when direct Ottoman government was established. In 1911 Libya was invaded and conquered by Italy. After World War I, local resistance to Italian colonial rule was led by King Idris I, Emir of Cyrenaica. British troops drove Italian and German forces from Libya in 1943. King Idris returned from exile in 1944. Following World War II, most of

Libya was ruled as a British protectorate with a smaller portion under French administration.

Libya became an independent constitutional monarchy on Dec. 24, 1951. In 1959 significant oil reserves were discovered, rapidly transforming Libya from one of the poorest states in North Africa to one of the wealthiest.

A military coup on Sept. 1, 1969, led by Col. Muammar al-Qaddafi, deposed the monarchy and declared the establishment of the Libyan Arab Republic. Qaddafi moved rapidly to nationalize foreign assets, expel foreign troops, and close foreign libraries and cultural centers. He also assumed full dictatorial powers under a political system that gives equal weight to Islamic law and his own political philosophy. Popular participation in elections is mandatory, although no government organization outside Qaddafi and his circle of advisers exerts any real authority.

Libya has given strong political and financial aid to various radical Palestinian groups and other enemies of Israel, sponsoring terrorist activities throughout Europe and the Middle East in support of the Palestinian cause. Numerous anti-Qaddafi Libyan exiles were assassinated in Europe. Libya also engaged in sporadic military campaigns against Egypt and the Sudan.

Relations between Libya and the U.S. were very hostile in the 1980s. On May 6, 1981, the U.S. closed the Libyan "People's Bureau" (embassy) in Washington. On Aug. 2, 1981, U.S. jets shot down two attacking Libyan warplanes during U.S. naval exercises in the Gulf of Sidra, which Libya claims as national waters. In 1986 the United States imposed economic sanctions on Libya, ordered all Americans to leave the country, and froze Libyan assets in the U.S. Another clash in March 1986 ended with the loss of two Libyan ships.

On Apr. 5, 1986, Libyan-sponsored terrorists bombed a nightclub in West Berlin, killing two U.S. soldiers; in response, American bombers attacked Tripoli and Benghazi on Apr. 14 in an apparent attempt to kill Col. Qaddafi himself. In 1990, investigators announced they had linked Libyan agents to the bombing of a Pan Am Jet over Lockerbie, Scotland, in 1988.

In January 1989 an international outcry arose when a West German company admitted selling equipment to Libya for a chemical weapons plant. Qaddafi's difficulties with the Western powers continued in 1992, as they demanded he release the suspected terrorists in the Lockerbie bombing. The U.N. imposed sanctions on Libya, including a prohibition on sales of military equipment and a ban on all flights in and out of the country. In Sept. 1995 Qaddafi began the expulsion of the 30,000 Palestinians in Libya, provoking fighting between Libyan security forces and Islamic militants. In 1997 as the Vatican announced that it would establish diplomatic relations, the U.S. listed Libya as one of several nations sponsoring terrorism.

Elaborate diplomatic maneuvers led to President Qaddafi's handing over (April, 1999) two Libyans for trial in the 1988 bombing of Pan Am flight 103. U.N. sanctions were suspended but the U.S. announced that its anti-terrorism sanctions would continue. In Jan. 2001 the Pan Am 103 trial ended with one conviction (with life imprisonment) and one acquittal. Qaddafi denounced the conviction but in 2003 Libya accepted responsibility and agreed to pay victims' families $2.7 bil. In Dec. 2003 Libya suddenly announced its willingness to stop all biological, chemical, and nuclear weapons development and to sign the Nuclear Nonproliferation Treaty. The U.S. soon ended all sanctions, reestablished diplomatic relations and began to purchase Libyan oil.

►LIECHTENSTEIN
Principality of Liechtenstein

• **GEOGRAPHY** **Location:** landlocked country in central Europe. **Boundaries:** Austria to N and E, Switzerland to S and W. **Total area:** 62 sq. mi. (160 sq km). **Coastline:** none. **Comparative area:** about 0.9 times the size of Washington, D.C. **Land use:** 25% arable land; 0% permanent crops; 75% other. **Major cities:** Väduz (capital); Schaan; Balzers; Triesen; Eschen.

• **PEOPLE** **Population:** 34,761 (July 2009 est.). **Nationality:** noun—Liechtensteiner(s); adjective—Liechtenstein. **Ethnic groups:** 86% Alemannic, 14% Italian, Turkish and other. **Languages:** German (official), Alemannic dialect. **Religions:** 76.2% Roman Catholic, 7.0% Protestant.

• **GOVERNMENT** **Type:** hereditary constitutional monarchy. **Independence:** Jan 23, 1719 (Principality of Liechtenstein established); July 12, 1806 (Independence from the Holy Roman Empire). **Constitution:** Oct. 5, 1921; amended Sept. 15, 2003. **National holiday:** Assumption Day, Aug. 15. **Heads of Government:** Hans-Adam II, prince (since Nov. 1989); Klaus Tschutscher, prime minister (since March 2009). **Structure:** executive—hereditary prince; unicameral legislature; judiciary—independent.

• **ECONOMY** **Monetary unit:** Swiss franc. **Budget:** N.A. **G.D.P.:** $4.16 bil., $118,000 per capita (2007 est.). **Chief Crops:** wheat, barley, maize, potatoes; livestock, dairy products. **Natural resources:** hydroelectric potential. **Major industries:** electronics, metal manufacturing, tourism. **Labor force:** 31,000 of which 19,000 are foreign workers (mostly from Switzerland and Austria) (2001 est.); 54% services, 43.9% industry, 2.1% agriculture (2005); 1.3% unemployment (2002). **Exports:** $2.47 bil. (f.o.b., 1996 est.); small specialty machinery, dental products, stamps, hardware, pottery. **Imports:** $917.3 mil. (c.i.f., 1996 est.); machinery, metal goods, textiles, foodstuffs, motor vehicles. **Major trading partners:** (2006) *exports:* 62.6% E.U., 18.9% U.S., 15.7% Switzerland; *imports:* E.U. countries, Switzerland.

The alpine principality of Liechtenstein, bordered by Austria and Switzerland, is a remnant of the Holy Roman Empire, an ancient constitutional monarchy with a modern industrial economy. The current dynasty was established in 1699; Prince Franz Josef II came to the throne in 1938, yielding his executive powers to his heir apparent, Hans Adam, in 1984.

Liechtenstein was tied to the Austro-Hungarian monarchy until 1918. Since then it has remained in a customs union with Switzerland, which also handles its foreign affairs. The single-chamber diet, the Landtag is elected by universal suffrage, women having won the right to vote in 1984. For almost 60 years the government was a coalition of the conservcative Progressive Citizens Party and the liberal Fatherland Union. Since April, 1997 Premier Mario Frick has governed with a cabinet of his own Fatherland Union with the PCP in opposition. Liechtenstein joined the U.N. in 1990.

A referendum in 2003 amended the constitution giving the prince authority to dismiss the government and veto legislation; citizens gained the right to vote "no confidence" in the prince. Liechtenstein is a corporate haven, with some 25,000 corporations maintaining nominal headquarters there. Foreign workers constitute about 40 percent of the work force.

►LITHUANIA
Republic of Lithuania

• **GEOGRAPHY** **Location:** eastern coast of Baltic Sea in northeastern Europe. **Boundaries:** Latvia to N, Belarus to E and SE, Poland to SW, Russian Federation (Kaliningrad) to W, Baltic Sea to NW. **Total area:** 25,174 sq. mi. (65,300 sq km). **Coastline:** Baltic Sea. **Comparative area:** slightly larger than West Virginia. **Land use:** 45% arable land; 1% permanent crops; 54% other. **Major cities:** Vilnius (capital); Kaunas; Klaipeda; Siauliai; Panevezys.

• **PEOPLE** **Population:** 3,545,319 (July 2010 est.). **Nationality:** noun—Lithuanian(s); adjective—Lithuanian. **Ethnic groups:** 83.4% Lithuanian, 6.3% Russian, 6.7% Polish. **Languages:** Lithuanian (official), Russian, Polish. **Religions:** primarily Roman Catholic, also Lutheran, Russian Orthodox, Protestant, evangelical Christian Baptist, Islam, Judaism.

• **GOVERNMENT** **Type:** parliamentary democracy. **Independence:** March 11, 1990 (declared); Sept. 6, 1991 (from Soviet Union). **Constitution:** Oct. 25, 1992; most recently amended July 13, 2004. **National holiday:** Statehood Day, Feb. 16. **Heads of Government:** Dalia Grybauskaite, president (since July 2009); Andrius Kubilius, prime minister (since Nov. 2008). **Structure:** executive; unicameral legislature; judiciary.

• **ECONOMY** **Monetary unit:** litas. **Budget:** (2009 est.). *income:* $13.09 bil.; *expend.:* $16.62 bil. **G.D.P.:** $54.85 bil., $15,400 per capita (2009 est.). **Chief crops:** grain, potatoes, sugar beets, vegetables; meat, milk, eggs; fish; flax fiber. **Natural resources:** peat. **Major industries:** machine building, metalworking, food processing. **Labor force:** 1.656 mil. (2009 est.); 56% services, 29.1% industry, 14% agriculture (2005 est.); 5.7% unemployment (2007 est.). **Exports:** $16.1 bil. (2009 est.); 22% machinery and equipment, 15% mineral products, 12% chemicals. **Imports:** $17.84 bil. (2009 est.); 18% machinery and equipment, 16% mineral products, 10% chemicals. **Major trading partners:** (2008) *exports:* 13.2% Russia, 10% Latvia, 9.6% Germany, 7.1% Poland, 7.1% Estonia, 4.7% Belarus, 4.3% U.K.; *imports:* 30.1% Russia, 11.1% Germany, 9.9% Poland, 6.3% Latvia.

Lithuanians and Latvians are closely related peoples whose languages are quite similar. But their histories, at least until 1795, were radically different. Fierce warriors able to stem the German tide during the Middle Ages, the Lithuanians repeatedly defeated the Teutonic knights, defending their independence and retaining their own religion.

In the 14th century, under Grand Duke Gediminas and his sons, Lithuania conquered White Russia (Belarus) and Ukraine and extended the dynasty from the Baltic almost to the Black Sea. The completion of Gediminas's policies came in 1386 when his grandson Jogaila was baptized, married the Polish heiress Jadwiga, and was crowned king of Poland under the title Wladislaw II, thereby creating the Poland-Lithuania Commonwealth. A condition of the union was that Lithuania had to adopt Christianity, which it did in 1387.

With the Third Partition of Poland in 1795, Lithuania was absorbed into Russia. The upper and educated classes took part in Poland's anti–Russian rebellions in 1830 and 1863. After the latter, the Russians required Lithuanians to use the Russian alphabet instead of the Latin as a move to stop any national renaissance; but after 1883 literature smuggled into the czarist empire from Prussia and secret Lithuanian schools and societies kept alive a national identity based on ethnic, religious, and linguistic grounds.

In Jan. 1921 the victorious allies of World War I acknowledged a new Lithuanian republic in the Soviet-German Treaty of Brest-Litovsk of March 1918. Formal recognition came in 1922. The territory of Memel (Klaipeda in Lithuanian), separated from Germany in the Treaty of Versailles, was seized in Jan. 1923 and organized as an autonomous unit of the new republic. The city itself was largely German, but its countryside was Lithuanian and it was Lithuania's only possible outlet to the sea. With the historic capital Vilnius annexed by the new Polish state, the de facto capital became the university city of Kaunas.

Danger from communists and fascists led the army to dispense with Parliament in Dec. 1926; an authoritarian regime under Pres. Antana Smetona followed. In 1939 Lithuania was doomed by the 1939 Nazi-Soviet Pact. In June 1940 the Soviet Army invaded Lithuania and a Soviet-approved "people's government" was formed. After an election in which only pro-Soviet candidates were permitted to run, the Lithuanian Soviet Socialist Republic was proclaimed on July 21, 1940.

Thousands of Lithuanians fled westward, while other thousands disappeared into Siberia. Stalin returned Vilnius (from Poland) and Klaipeda (which Hitler had taken) to Lithuania and fostered industrialization, which elevated living standards above most of the U.S.S.R. A high Lithuanian birth rate enabled the country to resist "Russification" more easily than Latvia or Estonia.

Mikhail Gorbachev's policy of *glasnost*, or openness, spurred the strong Lithuanian nationalist and dissident movement into action. It began with a public discussion of the "secret protocols" of the 1939 Nazi-Soviet Pact, which had permitted the U.S.S.R. to annex Lithuania and which the Soviet government long had denied existed. In 1987 the Soviet government tolerated demonstrations in Vilnius, but by Feb. 1988, Soviet troops prevented the Lithuanians from celebrating their 70th year of independence. The Soviet stance resulted in the founding of the new Lithuanian Movement for Reconstruction (Sajudis), which became the main political vehicle for Lithuanian independence from the U.S.S.R.

On Mar. 11, 1990, Lithuania declared its independence, and in response the Soviets began an economic blockade. On Jan. 13, 1991, the world watched as Soviet paratroopers and tanks attacked the radio and television centers, beginning a standoff between the Soviets and the Lithuanians that lasted until Sept. 6, 1991, when the U.S.S.R. recognized Lithuanian independence.

After independence, Lithuania struggled to break a political deadlock caused by its lack of a constitution. In November 1992 free elections were held. The Democratic Labor party (the renamed Communists) gained 47 percent of the vote and 77 seats in Parliament, while Sajudis gained only 22 percent of the vote and 28 seats. In February 1993 the Democratic Labor candidate, Algirdas Brazauskas, handily won the presidential election with 61 percent of the vote.

The last Soviet troops left Lithuanian soil Aug. 31, 1993 and the government moved on a path to a free economy and worked for good relations with Russia and the other former Soviet states. In 1996 the Communists were routed and the Homeland Union party took control of the government. Over the next few years Lithuania followed strict fiscal and monetary policies thereby attracting over $1 bil. in foreign investment and strong G.D.P. growth of 6 to 7 percent. In 1997–98 presidential elections, Valdas Adamkus won a close victory. While Oct. 2000 elections brought a center-right coalition to power, led by Rolandas Paksas, squabbles over tax-cutting and privatization of utilities broke the coalition in June. The upshot on July 3 was the return of Lithuania's last Communist dictator, Algirdas Brazauskas, as premier. Paksas became president in 2003 and voters gave 90 percent approval to joining the E.U. But Paksas was impeached in April 2004 for corruption and Adamkus was reelected.

Lithuania was admitted to the E.U. and NATO in 2004, but political instability continued and a new government, the 14th since independence, was elected in 2006 with corruption still the major issue. In 2009, with the economy rapidly shrinking, former finance minister Dalia Grybauskaite won a landslide victory for the presidency.

▶ LUXEMBOURG
Grand Duchy of Luxembourg

● **GEOGRAPHY   Location:** landlocked country in western Europe. **Boundaries:** Belgium to N and W, Germany to E, France to S. **Total area:** 998 sq. mi. (2,586 sq km). **Coastline:** none. **Comparative area:** slightly smaller than Rhode Island. **Land use:** 25% arable land; 0% permanent crops; 75% other. **Major cities:** (Luxembourg-Ville (capital); Esch-sur-Alzette;   Differdange;   Dudelange.
● **PEOPLE   Population:** 491,775 (July 2009 est.). **Nationality:** noun—Luxembourger(s); adjective—Luxembourg. **Ethnic groups:** Celtic base, with French and German blend; also, guest and worker residents from Portugal, Italy, and other European countries. **Languages:** Luxembourgish, German, French (both administrative languages), English. **Religions:** 87% Roman Catholic, 13% Protestant, Jewish, Muslim.
● **GOVERNMENT   Type:** constitutional monarchy. **Independence:** 1839 (from the Netherlands). **Constitution:** Oct. 17, 1868, occasional revisions. **National holiday:** Grand Duke's birthday, National Day, June 23. **Heads of Government:** Henri de Luxembourg, grand duke (since Oct. 2000); Jean-Claude Juncker, prime minister (since Aug. 1999). **Structure:** executive—prime minister appointed by Grand Duke but responsible to parliament; unicameral legislature—Chamber of Deputies, appointed for appointed for five-year term; judiciary.
● **ECONOMY   Monetary unit:** euro. **Budget:** (2008 est.) *income:* $22.25 bil.; *expend.:* $22.08 bil. **G.D.P.:** $39.42 bil., $81,100 per capita (2008 est.). **Chief crops:** barley, oats, potatoes, wheat, fruits, wine grapes; livestock products. **Natural resources:** iron ore (no longer exploited). **Major industries:** banking, iron and steel, food processing. **Labor force:** 207,100 of whom 125,400 are foreign (2008); 81% services, 17% industry, 2% agriculture (2007). **Exports:** $20.78 bil. (f.o.b., 2008); finished steel products, chemicals, rubber products, glass, aluminum. **Imports:** $28.12 bil. (c.i.f., 2008); minerals, metals, foodstuffs, machinery, quality consumer goods. **Major trading partners:** (2006) *exports:* 19% Germany, 16% France, 10% Italy,

10% U.K., 9% Belgium, 5% Spain, 5% Netherlands; *imports:* 26% Belgium, 20% Germany, 17% China, 9% France, 6% U.K., 4% Netherlands.

One of hundreds of small principalities in the Holy Roman Empire, Luxembourg joined the German League when the empire was abolished in 1806. It shared a monarchy with the Netherlands, but the two countries remained distinct under a single sovereign. In 1831 Luxembourg lost its French-speaking territory to Belgium. The Treaty of London granted sovereignty to Luxembourg in 1867. When King William III died in 1890, different rules of succession severed the dual monarchy; Queen Wilhelmina succeeded him in the Netherlands, while Adolf of Nassau became grand duke of Luxembourg. The nation's full independence dates from that event.

During the 19th century, Luxembourg developed a balanced modern economy, with prosperous small farms being complemented by industry, particularly mining and steel production. As late as 1970, steel accounted for over 25 percent of the nation's G.D.P. and five-eighths of export earnings, although rising international competition has led to a decline since then.

Luxembourg was overrun by Germany during World War I and again in May 1940, in the early stages of World War II. Archduchess Charlotte fled to London and returned with the Allied armed forces in 1944. The constitutional monarchy has enjoyed political stability since the war, with the Christian Social party normally the senior partner in a three-way coalition.

Luxembourg formed a customs union with Belgium in 1921 and joined the Benelux (Belgium, Netherlands, Luxembourg) union even before World War II had ended. A founding member of the United Nations in 1945, Luxembourg abandoned its traditional neutrality in 1948 and joined NATO in 1949. It was a founding member of the EEC under the 1956 Treaty of Rome and is now home to numerous European Union institutions. International banking accounts for over half of its gross national product. The country's chief problems are a shrinking and aging citizenry and demands by G-20 nations to know more about the tax haven aspects of the banking system. After 35 years Grand Duke John abdicated in 2000, succeeded by his son Henri.

▶MACEDONIA
The Former Yugoslav Republic of Macedonia

● **GEOGRAPHY Location:** southern part of the Balkan Peninsula. **Boundaries**: Serbia to N, Bulgaria to E, Greece to S, Albania to W, Yugoslavia to NE and N. **Total area**: 9,781 sq. mi. (25,333 sq km.). **Coastline**: none. **Comparative area**: slightly larger than Vermont. **Land use**: 24% arable land; 2% permanent crops; 74% other. **Major cities**: Skopje (Skoplje or, in Turkish, Uskub); Bitola; Kumanovo, Tetovo.

● **PEOPLE Population:** 2,066,718 (July 2009 est.). **Nationality:** noun—Macedonian(s); adj.—Macedonian. **Ethnic groups:** 64.2% Macedonian, 25.1% Albanian, 3.9% Turkish, 1.8% Serb, 7% other (includes gypsies). **Languages:** 66.5% Macedonian (official), 25.1% Albanian, 3% Turkish, 3% Serbo-Croatian, 3% other. **Religions:** 64.7% Macedonian Orthodox, 33.3% Muslim, 3% other.

● **GOVERNMENT Type:** parliamentary democracy. **Independence:** Sept. 8, 1991 (from Yugoslavia). **Constitution:** Nov. 17, 1991; amended Nov. 2001

and 2005. **National holiday:** August 2 (Ilinden Uprising Day). **Heads of Government:** Georgi Ivanov, president (since May 2009); Nikola Gruevski, prime minister (since Aug. 2006). **Structure:** executive; unicameral legislature; judiciary.

● **ECONOMY Monetary unit:** denar. **Budget:** (2008 est.) *income:* $2.889 bil.; *expend.:* $2.985 bil. **G.D.P.:** $18.52 bil.; $9,000 per capita (2008 est.). **Chief crops:** rice, tobacco, wheat, corn, millet; beef, pork, poultry, mutton. **Natural resources:** chrome, lead, marble, zinc. **Major industries:** metallurgy and metal processing, chemicals, textiles, timber. **Labor force:** 900,000 mil. (2008 est.); 50% services, 30% industry, 20% agriculture (2007); 34.5% unemployed (2008 est.). **Exports:** $4.397 bil. (f.o.b., 2008 est.); food, beverage, tobacco, machinery and transport equipment, other manufactured goods. **Imports:** $6.663 bil. (f.o.b., 2008 est.); machinery and transport equipment, chemicals, fuels. **Major trading partners:** (2006) *exports:* 23% Serbia & Montenegro, 15.6% Germany, 15.1% Greece, 10% Italy, 5.4% Bulgaria, 5.2% Croatia; *imports:* 15% Russia, 10% Germany, 9% Greece, 7.5% Serbia & Montenegro, 6.7% Bulgaria, 6% Italy.

Located at the center of the Balkan peninsula, Macedonia is an epitome of the entire region in its history and ethnic complexity as well. While there is a Macedonian language (a Slavic tongue more akin to Bulgarian than to Serbo-Croatian and codified in grammar and orthography only after World War II), the question of whether or not there is a Macedonian nation is contested: to Serbians, Macedonians are "south Serbs"; to Greeks, they are "Slavophone Greeks"; to Bulgars, they are kindred people, ethnic "cousins."

In any case, Macedonians are not related to the classical people of King Philip and Alexander the Great. Their realm had become a Roman province by 146 B.C. and remained part of the Byzantine Empire even after being invaded and settled by Slavic peoples in the sixth and seventh centuries. Contested in the Middle Ages by the Byzantine, Bulgarian, and Serbian empires, Macedonia fell at last to the Ottoman Turks in 1371. Well into the 19th century its population called itself "Christian" or "Slav," while Greek served as the language of culture and business until a literary awakening associated with folk songs and heroic poetry brought a Macedonian consciousness. This found significant political expression with the formation in 1893 of the IMRO (Internal Macedonian Revolutionary Organization) that sought to unify all non-Turks—Bulgars, Greeks, Albanians, Vlacha—in an independent state and which did not shrink from terrorism and revolution.

The peace treaties of Paris concluding World War I divided Macedonia among three states: Greece, Bulgaria, and the newly created Yugoslavia. IMRO turned against Serbian dominance in Yugoslavia and filled the 1930s with violent struggles against "denationalization." Bulgarian claims to Macedonia led that state to ally with Hitler's Germany and to occupy Macedonia in 1941. With the victory of Tito's partisans and the reconstruction of the Yugoslav state as a federation of Communist "republics," a Macedonian People's Republic was established in 1946.

After Tito's death in 1980, Macedonia took part in the "collegial rule" whereby the presidency of Yugoslavia rotated annually among the republics. But as the separate republics declared independence in 1991 and civil war began, Macedonia declared its own independence in Jan. 1992. Greece's opposition to the new nation's name and flag—as menaces to the northern Greek province of the same name—prevented international recognition until a 1995 agreement between the two countries. Under the pact, Macedonia removed an ancient Greek symbol from its flag and changed its constitution so as to remove any suggestion of a claim on Greek Macedonia. With U.N. recognition came both U.N. "peacekeeping forces" to patrol the frontier with rump Yugoslavia and the painful need to comply with the U.N. embargo against Serbia. An April 1996 treaty with Yugoslavia resolved border questions.

Elections in 1998 saw the ruling Social Democrats ousted by the right-wing Coalition for Changes which organized a government under Ljuplo Georgievski. In April, NATO pledged to defend Macedonia from Yugoslav incursions in the latter's struggle again Albanian separatists in Kosovo. Refugees from Kosovo flooded Macedonia, straining its humanitarian capacities. The decision of "founding" president Gligorov not to seek a second term brought presidential elections won by Boris Trajkovski of the governing coalition. In March 2001 ethnic Albanians rose up to fight for equal rights, taking over one-third of the country. A cease-fire in August and NATO intervention led to a peaceful settlement. In Sept. 2002 elections, the ruling party lost to a coalition that included Ali Ahmeti, leader of the guerilla uprising and on the U.S. terrorist list. In Feb. 2004 Pres. Trajkovski was killed in a plane crash and Prime Minister Crvenkovski was elected president in April but tension remained and in Dec. 2004 Parliament chose Vlado Buckovski as Prime Minister who pledged he would bring the country into NATO and eventually the E.U. A center-right party won the 2006 and 2008 elections.

▶MADAGASCAR
Republic of Madagascar
● **GEOGRAPHY** **Location:** off southeast Africa in western Indian Ocean. Antananarivo: 18°52'S, 47°30'E. **Boundaries:** about 300 mi. (500 km) E of Mozambique. **Total area:** 226,656 sq. mi. (587,040 sq km). **Coastline:** 3,000 mi. (4,828 km). **Comparative area:** slightly less than twice the size of Arizona. **Land use:** 4% arable land; 1% permanent crops; 95% other. **Major cities:** Antananarivo (capital); Antsirabé; Toamasina (Tamatave); Fianarantsoa; Mahajanga (Majunga). ● **PEOPLE** **Population:** 20,653,556 (July 2008 est.). **Nationality:** noun—Malagasy (sing., pl.); adjective— Malagasy. **Ethnic groups:** highlanders of predominantly Malayo-Indonesian origin (Merina and related Betsileo); coastal peoples collectively termed Cotiers, with mixed African, Malayo-Indonesian, and Arab ancestry (Betsimisaraka, Tsimihety, Antaisaka, Sakalava); French, Indian, Creole, Comoran. **Languages:** French and Malagasy (both official). **Religions:** 52% indigenous beliefs, 41% Christian, 7% Muslim. ● **GOVERNMENT** **Type:** republic. **Independence:** June 26, 1960 (from France). **Constitution:** Aug. 19, 1992. **National holiday:** Independence Day, June 26. **Heads of Government:** Andry Rajoelina, president (since March 2009); Albert Camille Vital, prime minister (since Dec. 2009). **Structure:** executive; unicameral legislature, scheduled to become bicameral—two-thirds of upper house will be filled from directly elected regional assemblies, rest by presidential appointment; judiciary.

● **ECONOMY** **Monetary unit:** Malagasy ariary. **Budget:** (2008 est.) *income:* $1.688 bil; *expend.:* $2.066 bil. **G.D.P.:** $20.76 bil., $1,000 per capita (2008 est.). **Chief crops:** coffee, vanilla, cloves, sugar; livestock. **Natural resources:** graphite, chromite, coal, bauxite, salt. **Major industries:** agricultural processing (meat canneries, soap factories, brewery, tanneries, sugar refining), light consumer goods industries (textiles, glassware), cement. **Labor force:** (2000) 7.3 mil. **Exports:** $1.316 bil. (f.o.b., 2008 est.); coffee, vanilla, cloves, shellfish, sugar, petroleum products. **Imports:** $2.541 mil. (f.o.b., 2008); 30% intermediate manufactures, capital goods, petroleum, consumer goods, food. **Major trading partners:** (2006) *exports:* 32.1% France, 25.3% U.S., 6.1% Germany, 5% Italy, 4.1% U.K.; *imports:* 14.5% France, 12% China, 9.3% Iran, 5.6% Mauritius, 4.7% Hong Kong.

The largest island nation, and fourth largest island in the world, Madagascar was settled by Malayo-Indonesian migrants some 2,000 years ago. Although later waves of African and Arab migrants were absorbed into the population, to a large extent it is still ethnically and culturally Asian. A Portuguese attempt to colonize the island in the 16th century failed, and during the 18th and 19th centuries, a unified kingdom backed by the British ruled the country. Foreign interests—largely British and French—developed extensive coffee plantations, and the French made Madagascar a protectorate in 1885 and a colony in 1896.

During World War II Madagascar sided with the Free French, and French colonial rule was reestablished after the war. The Malagasy Republic was founded as an independent nation on June 26, 1960. A coup in 1972 brought a repressive anti-French government to power.

A new federal constitution was approved in 1992, and in 1993 elections, Albert Zafy defeated the 17-year incumbent Didier Ratsiraka for the presidency, but the results were reversed in 1997 and Ratsiraka immediately set out to cut inflation, and renegotiate the nation's many foreign loans. The presidential election of 2001 turned into (except for the bloodshed) an opera bouffa, as neither incumbent Didier Ratsiraka nor challenger Marc Ravalomanana would concede defeat and each set up his own government. The military successes of troops loyal to Ravalomanana led to Ratsiraka's July 5 flight to the Seychelles. Corruption was so prevalent that Ratsiraka and others were sent to prison in 2003. In 2007, the I Love Madagascar Party won parliamentary elections, but the turmoil was awakened in early 2009 when President Ravalomanana was ousted from office by Andry Rajoelina, who has the support of the military but may be a frontman for former Presient Ratsiraka. Elections, a constitution, and reform have all been promised, but nothing has been delivered.

Madagascar's wildlife (a mixture of African species and others of domestic evolution) and its isolation make it of unique scientific interest. (In 1990, scientists discovered the smallest mammal known to science: the dwarf lemur.) But some 75 percent of the population live in poverty, which has been worsened by frequent cyclones.

▶MALAWI
Republic of Malawi
● **GEOGRAPHY** **Location:** landlocked country in southern central Africa. **Boundaries:** Tanzania to N, Mozambique to E, S, and SW, Zambia to W;

Lake Malawi forms much of eastern boundary. **Total area:** 45,745 sq. mi. (118,480 sq km). **Coastline:** none. **Comparative area:** slightly smaller than Pennsylvania. **Land use:** 20% arable land; 1% permanent crops; 79% other. **Major cities:** Lilongwe (capital); Blantyre.

• **PEOPLE** **Population:** 14,268,711 (July 2009 est.). **Nationality:** noun—Malawian(s); adjective—Malawian. **Ethnic groups:** Chewa, Nyanja, Tumbuko, Yao, Lomwe, Sena, Tonga, Ngoni, Asian, European. **Languages:** English and Chichewa (both official); Tombuka and other regional languages. **Religions:** 55% Protestant, 20% Roman Catholic, 20% Muslim, 3% indigenous beliefs.

• **GOVERNMENT** **Type:** multiparty democracy. **Independence:** July 6, 1964 (from U.K.). **Constitution:** May 18, 1994. **National holiday:** Republic Day, July 6. **Head of Government:** Bingu Wa Mutharika, president (since May 2004). **Structure:** executive; legislature—National Assembly of 193 members elected to five-year terms; judiciary.

• **ECONOMY** **Monetary unit:** Malawian kwacha. **Budget:** (2008 est.) *income:* $1.227 bil.; *expend.:* $1.337 bil. **G.D.P.:** $11.56 bil., $800 per capita (2008 est.). **Chief crops:** tobacco, tea, sugar, cotton; cattle, goats. **Natural resources:** limestone; hydropower; unexploited deposits of uranium, coal, bauxite. **Major industries:** agricultural processing (tea, tobacco, sugar), sawmilling, cement. **Labor force:** 4.5 mil. (2001 est.); 86% agriculture. **Exports:** $679 mil. (f.o.b., 2008); tobacco, tea, sugar, coffee, wood products. **Imports:** $1.023 mil. (f.o.b., 2008); food, petroleum products, semimanufactures, consumer goods. **Major trading partners:** (2006) *exports:* 12.6% South Africa, 9.7% Germany, 9.6% Egypt, 9.5% U.S, 8.5% Zimbabwe, 5.4% Russia, 4.4% Netherlands; *imports:* 33.9% South Africa, 8% India, 7.6% Zambia, 6.3% U.S., 5.7% Tanzania, 4.5% Germany, 4.2% China.

Malawi derives its name from the Maravi, a Bantu people who settled in the region in the 13th century and whose descendants, the Chewas, make up a significant segment of the current population. In the 1830s, the Ngoni, driven from what is now South Africa by the Zulus, arrived in the area around Lake Nyasa. The arrival of the Scottish missionary David Livingstone in 1859 led to the establishment of the British-controlled Nyasaland Protectorate in 1891. In 1953 Nyasaland formed a federation with Northern and Southern Rhodesia (Zambia and Zimbabwe) and began to organize an independence movement. The fight for independence was led by Dr. H. Kamuzu Banda, an expatriate who assumed the presidency of the Nyasaland African Congress, later the Malawi Congress party, upon his return in 1958. The British granted Nyasaland self-governing status in 1962, and Banda was elected prime minister the following year. Malawi achieved full independence under its present name in 1964.

Banda soon introduced one-party rule and had himself declared president for life in 1971. All dissent was crushed while corruption and nepotism strangled the economy, leaving Malawi's citizens among the poorest in the world. By 1990 internal unrest and the decline of Banda's popularity (he was now in his 90s) rapidly led to change. In 1992 a series of violent strikes by workers in the two largest cities resulted in more than 35 deaths. In June 1993 Malawians voted 2–1 to institute a multiparty system and in May 1994 Banda lost his nation's only free election in 30 years to Bakili Muluzi's United Democratic Front (UDF). Corruption remained the nation's major problem through several successive leaders.

▶ **MALAYSIA**

• **GEOGRAPHY** **Location:** 13 states in Southeast Asia; 11 are in Peninsular Malaysia and two, Sabah and Sarawak, lie about 400 mi. (640 km) across South China Sea on northern coast of island of Borneo (Kalimantan). **Boundaries:** Peninsular Malaysia—Thailand to N, South China Sea to E, Island of Singapore to S across Johor Strait, and Indonesian island of Sumatra to W across Strait of Malacca; Sabah and Sarawak—South China Sea to NW, Sulu Sea to NE, Celebes Sea to E, Indonesia to S; Brunei is enclosed within Sarawak on coast of South China Sea. **Total area:** 127,317 sq. mi. (329,750 sq km). **Coastline:** 2,905 mi. (4,675 km). **Comparative area:** slightly larger than New Mexico. **Land use:** 6% arable land; 18% permanent crops; 76% other. **Major cities:** Kuala Lumpur (capital); Ipoh; Johor Baharu; Melaka (Malacca); Petaling Jaya.

• **PEOPLE** **Population:** 26,160,256 (July 2010 est.) **Nationality:** noun—Malaysian(s); adjective—Malaysian. **Ethnic groups:** 50.4% Malay, 23.7% Chinese, 11% indigenous, 7.1% Indian, 7.8% other. **Languages:** Bahasa Melayu (official); English, Chinese dialects, Tamil, Telugu, Malayalam, Panjabi, Thai; note—in addition, in East Malaysia several indigenous languages are spoken, the largest of which are Iban and Kadazan. **Religions:** Islam, Buddhism, Daoism, Hinduism, Christianity, other traditional Chinese religions.

• **GOVERNMENT** **Type:** constitutional monarchy; Peninsular Malaysian states—hereditary rulers in all but Melaka and Penang, where governors are appointed by Malaysian government, with powers of state governments limited by federal constitution; Sabah—self-governing state, holding 20 seats in House of Representatives, with foreign affairs, defense, internal security, and other powers delegated to federal government; Sarawak—self-governing state, which holds 24 seats in House of Representatives, with foreign affairs, defense, internal security, and other powers delegated to federal government. **Independence:** Aug. 31, 1957 (from U.K.). **Constitution:** Aug. 31, 1957, amended Sept. 16, 1963, when Federation of Malaya became Federation of Malaysia; most recently amended in 2007. **National holiday:** National Day, Aug. 31. **Heads of Government:** Sultan Mizan Zainal Abidin, king (since Dec. 2006); Mohamed Najib bin Abdul Razak, prime minister (since April 2009). **Structure:** executive—paramount ruler chosen by and from the nine state rulers for five-year term; bicameral legislature; judiciary.

• **ECONOMY** **Monetary unit:** Malaysian ringgit. **Budget:** (2009 est.) *income:* $44.6 bil. *expend.:* $60.72 bil. **G.D.P.:** $381.1 bil., $14,800 per capita (2007 est.). **Chief crops:** Peninsular Malaysia—natural rubber, palm oil, rice; Sabah—mainly subsistence, main crops are rubber, timber, coconut, rice; Sarawak—rubber, timber, pepper. **Natural resources:** tin, crude oil, timber, copper, iron ore. **Major industries:** Peninsular Malaysia—rubber and oil-palm processing and manufacturing, light manufacturing industry, electronics; Sabah—logging, petroleum production; Sarawak—agriculture processing, petroleum production and refining, logging. **Labor force:** 11.29 mil. (2009 est.); 51% services, 36% industry, 13% agriculture (2005); 3.1% unemployment (2007).

Exports: $156.4 bil. (2009 est.); electronic equipment, petroleum products, palm oil, wood products, rubber, textiles. **Imports:** $119.5 bil. (2009 est.); machinery and equipment, chemicals, food. **Major trading partners:** (2008) *exports:* 13.9% Singapore, 12.2% China, 10.9% U.S., 9.8% Japan, 5.4% Thailand, 5.2% Hong Kong; *imports:* 13.9% China, 12.5% Japan, 11.2% U.S., 11.1% Singapore, 6% Thailand, 5.3% Indonesia.

From ancient times a group of petty principalities in the southern part of the Malay Peninsula, bordering the Strait of Malacca, maintained extensive ties of maritime commerce throughout Southeast Asia. The early Malay states were Hindu, under Indian influence; with the rise of the Kingdom of Malacca in the 15th century, conversion to Islam was widespread. European influence in the Spice Islands began in the 16th century; the Portuguese, initially dominant, gave way to the Dutch, who seized Malacca in 1641.

British influence grew during the 18th century, with the founding of a trading settlement at Penang in 1789. Singapore was founded in 1819, and the Dutch ceded Malacca to Britain in 1824. By a series of treaties in the late 19th century, the various Malay states became British protectorates; Britain controlled the entire southern peninsula after 1909. Under British rule, commercial tin mining and the establishment of extensive rubber plantations led to the importation of many Indian and Chinese laborers; eventually ethnic Chinese dominated Malaya's domestic economy.

Japan overran Malaya by February 1942. Following World War II, the various Malay states (except Singapore) organized into a federation, which replaced the confusing prewar regime of federated and unfederated protectorates. A Communist rebellion disrupted the country throughout the early 1950s. Following the suppression of the Communist movement, elections were held in mid-1955 for a home-rule government. The elections brought the Alliance party of Tungku Abdul Rahman to power, and the Federation of Malaya became independent in 1957.

The nation expanded on Sept. 16, 1963, with the creation of Malaysia, incorporating the Federation of Malaya as well as Singapore and the former British colonies of North Borneo (thereafter called Sabah) and Sarawak. Singapore seceded in 1965 and became an independent nation.

Malaysia was ruled from 1981–2003 by the coalition government of Mahathir Mohamad, who transformed the country from an agriculture-based economy to one of the fastest-growing economies in Asia. The country sustained annual growth rates of 8 percent through the 1980s. In 1995 Malaysia received $5.8 bil. in foreign direct investment, the most in East Asia. The Asian financial crisis of 1997–98 hit Malaysia very hard as the currency and stockmarkets declined steeply.

Facing Malaysia's first recession in 13 years, Mahathir announced that the free market system had proven a failure and dismissed his finance minister, Anwar Ibrahim in Sept. 1998. Arrested and beaten by police, Anwar faced charges of sodomy and corruption and in 1999 he was found guilty and sentenced to six years in prison. His wife, Azizah Ismail announced a new opposition National Justice Party. But when elections were suddenly called in November, her new party took only five of the 193 seats, as Mahathir's National Front carried 148. Mahathir announced in 2002 he would resign effective Oct. 25; deputy P.M. Abdullah

Badawi had been groomed to succeed and in March 2004 won the election handily. But by 2008 the nation seemed ready for a change from the repressive policies of the National Front. In August, Anwar won a landslide victory for a seat in parliament.

▶**MALDIVES**
Republic of Maldives
● **GEOGRAPHY Location:** chain of more than 1,200 small coral islands (about 220 inhabited), 475 mi. (764 km) from N to S and 80 mi. (207 km) from W to E in Indian Ocean; northernmost atoll about 370 mi. (960 km) southwest of India. Malé 4°00'N, 73°28'E. **Boundaries:** Laccadive Sea to NE, Arabian Sea to N, Indian Ocean to S and W. **Total area:** 116 sq. mi. (300 sq km). **Coastline:** 400 mi. (644 km). **Comparative area:** about 1.7 times size of Washington, D.C. **Land use:** 13% arable land; 30% permanent crops; 57% other. **Major cities:** Malé (capital).
● **PEOPLE Population:** 396,334 (July 2009 est.). **Nationality:** noun—Maldivian(s); adjective—Maldivian. **Ethnic groups:** South Indian, Sinhalese, and Arab. **Languages:** Maldivian Divehi (dialect of Sinhala; script derived from Arabic); English spoken by most government officials. **Religions:** Sunni Muslim.
● **GOVERNMENT Type:** republic. **Independence:** July 26, 1965 (from U.K.). **Constitution:** Adopted Jan. 1998; new constitution ratified Aug. 7, 2008. **National holiday:** Independence Day, July 26. **Head of Government:** Mohamed "Anni" Nasheed, president (since Nov. 2008). **Structure:** executive; unicameral legislature; judiciary.
● **ECONOMY Monetary unit:** rufiyaa. **Budget:** (2008 est.) *income:* $762 mil.; *expend.:* $884 mil. **G.D.P.:** $1.738 bil., $5,000 per capita (2008 est.). **Chief crops:** coconut, corn, sweet potatoes; fishing. **Natural resources:** fish. **Major industries:** fishing, tourism, shipbuilding, some coconut processing. **Labor force:** 128,800 (2006 est.); 77% services, 16% agriculture, 7% industry (2006 est.). **Exports:** $113 mil. (f.o.b., 2008 est.); fish, clothing. **Imports:** $1.276 bil. (f.o.b., 2008 est.); intermediate and capital goods, consumer goods, petroleum products. **Major trading partners:** (2006) *exports:* 33.1% Thailand, 14.3% U.K., 11.9% Sri Lanka, 10.3% Japan, 6.9% France, 6.1% Algeria; *imports:* 23.2% Singapore, 15.8% United Arab Emirates, 11.1% India, 7.9% Malaysia, 6.9% Thailand, 5.6% Sri Lanka.

The small sultanate of the Maldive Islands, with an Islamic population of Sinhalese descent, was made a British protectorate in 1887. The islands' tiny area and poor soil limited development; fishing and fish processing are the main industries, and copra (dried coconut meat for coconut oil) is the only significant crop. The Maldives became an independent nation on July 26, 1965. In 1968 the sultanate was abolished and replaced by a republic. Since independence, tourism has become economically important and now accounts for 18 percent of the G.D.P. Protests over the concentration of development on the island of Malé in recent years have led to political unrest in the other islands, while attempts to address the basic needs of those islands have strained the nation's tiny economic base.

Maumoon Abdul Gayoom was elected president in 1978 and subsequently reelected every time. An attempted coup against the Gayoom government on Nov. 4, 1988, was put down with the intervention of Indian troops. The 2004 tsunami killed hundreds and did severe structural damage. The first multi-party elections for president were held in 2008 and Mohamed Nasheed was elected.

▶ MALI
Republic of Mali

• **GEOGRAPHY Location:** northwestern Africa. **Boundaries:** Algeria to N, Niger to E, Burkina Faso, Ivory Coast, Guinea to S, Senegal and Mauritania to W. **Total area:** 478,765 sq. mi. (1,240,000 sq km). **Coastline:** none. **Comparative area:** slightly less than twice the size of Texas. **Land use:** 4% arable land; negl. % permanent crops; 96% other. **Major cities:** Bamako (capital); Ségou; Mopti; Sikasso; Kayes.

• **PEOPLE Population:** 12,666,987 (July 2009 est.) **Nationality:** noun—Malian(s); adjective— Malian. **Ethnic groups:** 50% Mande (Bambara, Malinke, Soninke), 17% Peul, 12% Voltaic, 6% Songhai, 10% Tuareg and Moor. **Languages:** French (official); Bambara spoken by 80% of population. **Religions:** 90% Muslim, 9% indigenous beliefs, 1% Christian.

• **GOVERNMENT Type:** republic. **Independence:** Sept. 22, 1960 (from France). **Constitution:** Jan. 12, 1992. **National holiday:** Anniversary of the Proclamation of the Republic, Sept. 22. **Heads of Government:** Amadou Toumani Touré, president (since June 2002); Modibo Sidibe, prime minister (since Sept. 2007). **Structure:** executive; unicameral legislature; judiciary.

• **ECONOMY Monetary unit:** Communauté Financière Africaine (CFA) franc. **Budget:** (2006 est.) *income:* $1.5 bil.; *expend.:* $1.8 bil. **G.D.P.:** $14.48 bil., $1,200 per capita (2008 est.). **Chief crops:** cotton, millet, rice, corn; goats, sheep, cattle. **Natural resources:** gold, phosphates, kaolin, salt, limestone, uranium; bauxite, iron ore, manganese, tin, and copper deposits are known but not exploited. **Major industries:** small local consumer goods and food processing, construction, phosphate, gold. **Labor force:** 5.4 mil; 80% agriculture, 19% services. **Exports:** $294 mil. (f.o.b., 2006 est.); cotton, livestock, gold. **Imports:** $2.358 bil. (f.o.b., 2006 est.); machinery and equipment, foodstuffs, construction materials, petroleum. **Major trading partners:** (2006) *exports:* 26.8% China, 24.9% Germany, 7.1% Thailand, 4.9% Taiwan, 4% Bangladesh; *imports:* 12.8% France, 12.2% Senegal, 10.5% Cote d'Ivoire.

Mali has been a center of West African civilization for over 4,000 years. Iron Age civilizations flourished on the middle reaches of the Niger River from about 200 B.C. The kingdom of Ghana arose about A.D. 750 on the strength of the gold trade with North African Berbers. Ghana was overthrown by the Muslim Almoravids, who ruled only 11 years, though Islam remained a major influence from that time. From 1200–1400, the Kingdom of Mali was dominant in the region and was renowned throughout Islam and even in Christian Europe for its wealth and power; when Mansa Musa's retinue stopped in Cairo en route to Mecca, it carried so much gold that the price of gold fell 20 percent. By the end of the 14th century, the Mali empire had been eclipsed by the Songhai (Soyinka) empire, centered on the Niger River cities of Gao and Timbuktu.

The Songhai empire collapsed after Timbuktu was sacked by Moroccans in 1591. It fragmented into a series of smaller states, and power shifted from the desert fringe back to the Niger valley, bringing with it a further spread of Islam.

French exploration of Mali led to conquest in 1896 and the creation of the colony of French Sudan in 1898, governed from Dakar, Senegal. Timbuktu declined in importance, and Bamako became the country's principal urban center.

Malians were granted French citizenship and limited self-rule in 1946. In 1958 the territory became autonomous within the French Overseas Community. In 1959, with French support, the French Sudan and Senegal formed the Federation of Mali, which became independent on June 20, 1960. Senegal seceded from the federation almost immediately, and Mali became an independent republic on Sept. 22, 1960. Modibo Keita was elected the country's first president.

Keita's program of radical control of society and the economy by the central government provoked discontent, and he was overthrown in 1968 by military officers led by Lt. Moussa Traore. Traore's Military Committee of National Liberation ruled until 1979 when it was reorganized under a new constitution as the Malian People's Democratic Union. Traore was ousted in a 1991 coup and a transitional government under a civilian prime minister, Soumana Sacko, set up multiparty elections for June 1992. Alpha Konaré was elected president and his Alliance for Democracy in Mali party won 76 of 116 legislative seats. In 1995, the government reached an agreement in its longstanding dispute with the ethnic Tuareg nomads in the northern part of the country.

Pres. Konaré's government succeeded in reviving the economy (cotton and gold production rank among the top in Africa) and winning praise from the World Bank. Political opposition, though small, turned violent in 1997 and caused a cancellation of the results of elections in April. Opposition parties claimed the government had fixed the elections and boycotted new ones held in May that gave Konare victory. Konare bowed to a constitutional provision barring a third term and voters in May 2002 gave 65 percent of the votes to Amadou Toure, who was reelected in 2007.

▶ MALTA
Republic of Malta

• **GEOGRAPHY Location:** archipelago (largest islands are Malta, Gozo, and Comino) in central Mediterranean. Valletta 35°54'N, 14°32'E. **Boundaries:** Sicily 58 mi. (93 km) to N, Libya 180 mi. (290 km) to S, Tunisia to W. **Total area:** 124 sq. mi. (320 sq km). **Coastline:** 87 mi. (140 km). **Comparative area:** slightly less than twice the size of Washington, D.C. **Land use:** 31% arable land; 3% permanent crops; 66% other. **Major cities:** Valletta (capital), Birkirkara, Qormi, Sliema.

• **PEOPLE Population:** 405,165 (July 2009 est.) **Nationality:** noun—Maltese (sing., pl.); adjective—Maltese. **Ethnic groups:** Maltese (descendants of ancient Carthaginians and Phoenicians, with strong elements of Italian and other Mediterranean stock) **Languages:** Maltese and English (both official). **Religions:** 98% Roman Catholic.

• **GOVERNMENT Type:** republic. **Independence:** Sept. 21, 1964 (from U.K.). **Constitution:** Dec. 13, 1964; amended many times. **National holiday:** Independence Day, Sept. 21. **Heads of Government:** George Abela, president (since Apr. 2009); Lawrence Gonzi, prime minister (since Mar. 2004). **Structure:** executive; unicameral legislature—seats are given to largest popular party to ensure a majority, usually 65; judiciary.

• **ECONOMY Monetary unit:** euro. **Budget:** (2008 est.) *income:* $3.457 bil.; *expend.:* $3.653 bil. **G.D.P.:** $9.801 bil., $24,200 per capita (2008 est.). **Chief crops:** potatoes, cauliflower, grapes, wheat, barley; milk, pork, poultry. **Natural resources:** limestone, salt. **Major industries:** tourism, electronics, ship repair yard, construction. **Labor force:** 173,000 (2008); 22% industry, 75% services, 3% agriculture; 6.8% unemployment (2005). **Exports:** $3.491 bil. (f.o.b., 2008); machinery and transport equipment, manufactures. **Imports:** $4.963 bil. (f.o.b., 2008); machinery and transport equipment, manufactured goods; food, drink and tobacco. **Major trading partners:** (2006) *exports:* 215.3% France, 13.2% Singapore, 13% U.S., 12.5% Germany, 9.5% U.K., 4.9% Japan, 4.2% Hong Kong; *imports:* 28% Italy, 10.5% U.K., 8.7% France, 7.6% Germany, 6.8% Singapore, 5.6% U.S.

Malta, an ancient crossroads of Mediterranean trade, was ruled successively by Phoenicians, Carthaginians, Greeks, Romans, and Byzantines before being conquered by Islamic Saracens from North Africa in the ninth century. In 1090 the Norman kings of Sicily conquered it and made it a way station for the First Crusade. In 1530 Charles V gave the island to the Knights Hospitalers (the Knights of Malta). The island withstood a siege by the Ottoman Turks in 1565 and fell only to Napoleon in 1798.

Malta came under British rule in 1800, and was annexed in 1814. Limited self-rule was granted under the constitutions of 1921 and 1939. During World War II, Malta suffered devastating air raids by German and Italian forces; the entire population was awarded the George Cross for bravery.

In 1964 Malta was granted independence within the British Commonwealth, with Elizabeth II as its sovereign. Abrogating its mutual defense treaty with Great Britain in 1971, the Maltese government severed all ties to the British Crown, becoming a fully independent republic. British forces withdrew from the island in 1979.

Malta was governed by the leftist, anticlerical, and neutralist Labour party from 1971–87, whose leader, the ardent nationalist Dominic Mintoff, was prime minister from 1971 to 1984, succeeded by Mifsud Bonnici. In 1997 the Catholic and pro-Western Nationalist party won a popular electoral majority but not a majority in Parliament. Under a 1987 constitutional amendment, it was granted sufficient extra seats in Parliament to allow it to organize a government under Prime Minister Eddie Fenech Adami.

The Nationalist party ruled for nine years until in 1996 elections the Labour party won a slim majority, but returned to power in Sept. 1998 with Adami returning as prime minister. In 2003 voters approved a move to enter the E.U. which it did in 2004.

▶MARSHALL ISLANDS
Republic of the Marshall Islands

• **GEOGRAPHY Location:** two groups of islands, the Ratak and Ralik chains, comprising 31 atolls in western Pacific. Majuro 7°09′N, 171°12′E. **Boundaries:** Guam about 1,300 mi. (2,100 km) to NW, Hawaii about 2,000 mi. (3,200 km) to NE, Kiribati to S, Federated States of Micronesia to W. **Total area:** 70 sq. mi. (181 sq km). **Coastline:** 230 (370 km). **Comparative area:** about the size of Washington, D.C. **Land use:** 11% arable land; 44% permanent crops; 44% other. **Major cities:** Majuro (capital).

• **PEOPLE Population:** 64,522 (July 2009 est.). **Nationality:** noun—Marshallese; adjective—Marshallese.   **Ethnic   groups:**   Micronesian. **Languages:** English (official), two major Marshallese dialects from Malayo-Polynesian family, Japanese. **Religions:** Christian, mostly Protestant.

• **GOVERNMENT Type:** constitutional government in free association with U.S.; Compact of Free Association entered into force Oct. 21, 1986. **Independence:** Oct. 21, 1986 (from U.S.-administered U.N. trusteeship). **Constitution:** May 1, 1979. **National holiday:** Proclamation of the Republic of the Marshall Islands, May 1. **Head of Government:** Jurelang Zedkaia, president (since Nov. 2009). **Structure:** executive; unicameral legislature; judiciary.

• **ECONOMY Monetary unit:** U.S. dollar. **Budget:** (2008) *income:* $123.3 mil.; *expend:* $1.213 bil. **G.D.P.:** $133.5 mil., $2,500 per capita (2008 est.). **Chief crops:** coconuts, cacao, taro, breadfruit, fruits; pigs, chickens. **Natural resources:** phosphate deposits, marine products, deep seabed minerals. **Major industries:** copra, fish, tourism. **Labor force:** 14,680 (2000). **Exports:** $19.4 mil. (f.o.b., 2008 est.); coconut oil, fish, trochus shells. **Imports:** $79.4 mil. (f.o.b., 2008 est.); foodstuffs, machinery and equipment, fuels, beverages and tobacco. **Major trading partners:** (2006) *exports:* U.S., Japan, Australia, China; *imports:* U.S., Japan, Australia, NZ, Singapore, Fiji, China, Philippines.

The Marshall Islands, part of the geographic region known as Micronesia, are made up of 31 atolls of the Ratak (Sunrise) and Ralik (Sunset) chains located between 4° and 14°N and 160° and 173°E. Although claimed by Spain in 1592, the islands were left undisturbed by the Spanish empire for 300 years. In 1885, Germany took over the administration on the islands of Jaluit and Ebon. At that time copra (dried coconut meat) trade was the primary industry. Japan assumed control of the Marshalls at the beginning of World War I and held them until 1944, when Allied forces occupied the islands. In 1947 the islands were included in the U.N. Trust Territory of the Pacific and placed under U.S. administration. In 1946 the U.S. government resettled the inhabitants of Bikini and Enewetak in order to begin nuclear tests, which continued through 1958. Residents began returning to Enewetak in 1980 and the U.S. granted them sovereignty. The estimated cost of a complete cleanup of Bikini was $100 million but in 2001 a settlement of $563 million was agreed to. Not all of it was paid, however, due to a legal technicality.

▶MAURITANIA
Islamic Republic of Mauritania

• **GEOGRAPHY Location:** northwestern Africa. **Boundaries:** territory of Western Sahara to N, Algeria to NE, Mali to E and S, Senegal to S, Atlantic Ocean to W. **Total area:** 397,954 sq. mi. (1,030,700 sq km). **Coastline:** 469 mi. (754 km). **Comparative area:** slightly larger than three times the size of New Mexico. **Land use:** negl. % arable land; negl. % permanent crops; 99% other. **Major cities:** Nouakchott (capital); Nouadhibou (Port Etienne); Kaédi; Zouérate; Rosso.

• **PEOPLE Population:** 3,129,486 (July 2009 est.). **Nationality:** noun—Mauritanian(s); adjective—Mauritanian.   **Ethnic   groups:**   40%   mixed Maur/black, 30% Maur, 30% black. **Languages:**

Hassaniya Arabic (official), Wolof (official), Pular, Soninke, French. **Religions:** 100% Muslim. ● **GOVERNMENT Type:** military junta. **Independence:** Nov. 28, 1960 (from France). **Constitution:** July 12, 1991. **National holiday:** Independence Day, Nov. 28. **Heads of Government:** Mohamed Ouid Abdel Aziz, president of the High Council of State (since Aug. 2009); Moulaye Ould Mohamed Laghdaf, prime minister (since Aug. 2008). **Structure:** executive; bicameral legislature; judiciary. ● **ECONOMY Monetary unit:** ouguiya. **Budget:** (2007 est.) *income:* $770 mil.; *expend.:* $770 mil. **G.D.P.:** $6.31 bil., $2,100 per capita (2008 est.) **Chief crops:** dates, millet, sorghum; cattle, sheep; fish. **Natural resources:** iron ore, gypsum, fish, copper, phosphate. **Major industries:** fish processing, mining of iron ore and gypsum. **Labor force:** 786,000 (2001 est.); 50% agriculture, 40% services, 10% industry and commerce; 21% unemployment (1999). **Exports:** $1.395 bil. (f.o.b., 2006); fish and fish products, iron ore, gold. **Imports:** $1.475 bil. (f.o.b., 2006); machinery and equipment, foodstuffs, consumer goods, petroleum products, capital goods. **Major trading partners:** (2006) *exports:* 26.1% China, 11.7% Italy, 10.5% France, 6.9% Spain, 6.8% Belgium, 5.4% Japan, 4.6% Cote d'Ivoire; *imports:* 11.9% France, 8.1% China, 6.8% Belgium, 6.7% U.S., 5.9% Italy, 5.7% Spain, 5.5% Brazil.

The population of Mauritania is divided between an Arab and Berber majority in the north and various black African peoples in the south. From the ninth through the 15th centuries, southern Mauritania was part of the kingdoms of, successively, Ghana, Mali, and Sanghay. In the 1050s, a puritanical Muslim sect, the Almoravids conquered Ghana, Morocco, Western Algeria, and Spain; they were eclipsed in the next century.

Portuguese trade on the Mauritania coast began in the early 15th century; the Portuguese remained dominant until about 1600 when their control was contested by the British, French, and Dutch. France established a protectorate in 1903, and the area was made a French colony in 1920.

In 1958 Mauritania became a self-governing republic within the French Overseas Community. In 1959 Mokhtar Ould Daddah was elected prime minister, and the country became fully independent on Nov. 28, 1960. A new constitution was adopted in 1961, establishing a presidential form of government. The four major political parties were combined into a single party in 1965.

Morocco claimed Mauritania as part of its sphere of influence; after talks about unifying the two countries broke down, Morocco recognized Mauritanian independence in 1970. Spain relinquished its claim to the Spanish Sahara in 1976. The southern part of that territory was annexed by Mauritania, while the larger northern section was annexed by Morocco. Rebels of the Polisario Front proclaimed the independent state of Western Sahara, and in 1980 Mauritania relinquished its claims to its portion of the Western Sahara, signed a treaty with Polisario, and resumed relations with Algeria, Polisario's chief backer.

In 1978 Ould Daddah was removed from office in a military coup and was replaced as president by Lt. Col. Haidalla. In turn, he was overthrown on Dec. 12, 1984, by Chief of Staff Maaouya Ould Sid' Ahmed Taya. Taya normalized relations with Morocco and held regional and local elections in 1986 and 1987 in a first step toward the restoration of democracy.

Border incidents erupted between Mauritania and Senegal in 1989 and Mauritania expelled 40,000 black Senegalese workers. Racial and religious strife has severely hampered the country's economy. Taya introduced multiparty elections in 1991 and a new constitution was approved; Taya and his Democratic and Social Republican party won the presidency and control of the legislature in 1992 and again in 1997. In the run-up to the 2003 elections, Taya had several top leaders arrested, but he won two-thirds of the vote in a suspicious election. In 2005, however, a military junta overthrew him and in the first honest elections in 2007 a civilian government was installed under Pres. Ould Abdellahi. But he too was ousted by the military in Aug. 2008 and Gen. Mohamed Ould Aziz declared himself president and a year later won a disputed election by a large margin.

▶MAURITIUS
Republic of Mauritius

● **GEOGRAPHY Location:** southwestern Indian Ocean. Port Louis 20°09'S, 57°29'E. **Boundaries:** nearest neighbor is Réunion to SW. **Total area:** 718 sq. mi. (1,860 sq km). **Coastline:** 110 mi. (177 km). **Comparative area:** almost 11 times the size of Washington D.C.. **Land use:** 49% arable land; 3% permanent crops; 48% other. **Major cities:** Port Louis (capital); Beau Bassin/Rose Hill; Vacoas-Phoenix; Curepipe; Quatre Bornes. ● **PEOPLE Population:** 1,284,264 (July 2009 est.). **Nationality:** noun—Mauritian(s); adjective—Mauritian. **Ethnic groups:** 68% Indo-Mauritian, 27% Creole, 3% Sino-Mauritian, 2% Franco-Mauritian. **Languages:** English (official), Creole, French, Hindi, Urdu, Hakka, Bojpoori. **Religions:** 52% Hindu, 28.3% Christian (mostly Roman Catholic with a few Anglicans), 16.6% Muslim. ● **GOVERNMENT Type:** parliamentary democracy. **Independence:** Mar. 12, 1968 (from U.K.). **Constitution:** Mar. 12, 1968, amended Mar. 12, 1992. **National holiday:** Independence Day, Mar. 12. **Heads of Government:** Anerood Jugnauth, president (since Oct. 2003); Navinchandra Ramgoolam, prime minister (since Mar. 2008). **Structure:** executive; unicameral legislature; judiciary. ● **ECONOMY Monetary unit:** Mauritian rupee. **Budget:** (2008 est.) *income:* $1.866 bil.; *expend.:* $2.243 bil. **G.D.P.:** $15.36 bil., $12,100 per capita (2008 est.). **Chief crops:** sugarcane, tea, corn, potatoes; cattle, goats; fish. **Natural resources:** arable land, fish. **Major industries:** food processing (largely sugar milling), textiles, and wearing apparel. **Labor force:** 584,000 (2008); 51% services, 30% industry, 9% agriculture. **Exports:** $2.36 bil. (f.o.b., 2008); clothing and textiles, sugar. **Imports:** $4.503 bil. (f.o.b., 2008); manufactured goods, capital equipment, foodstuffs, petroleum products, chemicals. **Major trading partners:** (2006) *exports:* 32.5% U.K., 15.1% France, 11.4% United Arab Emirates, 8.3% U.S., 4.8% Madagascar; *imports:* 14.3% France, 13.6% India, 8.6% China, 7.3% South Africa.

The volcanic island of Mauritius and its seven smaller neighbors lie about 500 miles east of Madagascar and 2,400 miles southwest of India. They were uninhabited when discovered by the Dutch in 1507. Following sporadic Dutch settlement in the 17th century, the French took over in 1721, establishing sugarcane plantations worked by slaves imported from Africa. Mauritius was captured by the British in 1810. Following the abolition of slavery in the British Empire (1834), Indian workers were imported to labor in the cane fields. A majority of the population is of Indian descent. On Mar. 12, 1968, Mauritius became an independent parliamentary democracy within the British Commonwealth. In 1992 it became a republic and the National Assembly elected Cassam Uteem as the country's first president.

In December 1995 the opposition party of Navinchandra Ramgoolam won 65.2 percent of the votes, and captured all 60 seats in Parliament defeating Aneerood Jugnauth, PM for 13 years. These results were reversed in Sept. 2000 and in July 2005 Ramgoolam was reelected.

Although sugar remains an important element in the economy, textile manufacturing and tourism have helped to make Mauritius one of the strongest economies in Africa.

▶ MEXICO
United Mexican States

● **GEOGRAPHY Location:** southernmost state in North America. **Boundaries:** U.S. to N, Gulf of Mexico to E, Belize and Guatemala to S, Pacific Ocean to W. **Total area:** 761,603 sq. mi. (1,972,550 sq km). **Coastline:** 5,798 mi. (9,329 km). **Comparative area:** slightly less than three times the size of Texas. **Land use:** 13% arable land; 1% permanent crops;86% other. **Major cities:** Ciudad de México (Mexico City) (capital); Guadalajara; Netzahualcóyotl; Monterrey; Heróica Puebla de Zaragoza (Puebla).

● **PEOPLE Population:** 112,468,855 (July 2010 est.). **Nationality:** noun—Mexican(s); adjective—Mexican. **Ethnic groups:** 60% mestizo, 30% Amerindian or predominantly Amerindian, 9% white, 1% other. **Languages:** Spanish, various Mayan, Nahuatl, and other regional indigenous languages. **Religions:** 76.5% Roman Catholic, 6.3% Protestant, 0.3% other, 13.8% unspecified, 3.1% none.

● **GOVERNMENT Type:** federal republic. **Independence:** Sept. 16, 1810 (declared); Sept. 27, 1821 (recognized by Spain). **Constitution:** Feb. 5, 1917. **National holiday:** Independence Day, Sept. 16. **Head of Government:** Felipe Calderon, president (since 2006). **Structure:** dominant executive; bicameral legislature (National Congress—Senate, Federal Chamber of Deputies); Supreme Court.

● **ECONOMY Monetary unit:** peso. **Budget:** (2009 est.) *income:* $208.6 bil.; *expend.:* $229 bil. **G.D.P.:** $1.482 tril., $13,500 per capita (2009 est.). **Chief crops:** corn, wheat, soybeans, rice, beans, cotton, coffee, fruit, tomatoes; beef, poultry, dairy products; wood products. **Natural resources:** crude oil, silver, copper, gold, lead. **Major industries:** food and beverages, tobacco, chemicals. **Labor force:** 47 mil. (2009); 58% services; 18% agriculture, forestry, hunting, fishing; 24% industry; 3.6% unemployment (2005), plus considerable underemployment. **Exports:** $229.7 bil. (2009 est); crude oil, oil products, coffee, silver, engines, cotton. **Imports:** $234.4 bil. (2009 est.); metal manufactures, agricultural machinery, electrical equipment. **Major trading partners:** (2008) *exports:* 80.5% U.S., 3.6% Canada, 1.4% Germany; *imports:* 48% U.S., 13.5% China, 4.8% Japan, 4.6% South Korea.

The pre-Columbian history of indigenous Mexican cultures is very rich and includes the high civilizations of the Olmecs, Mayas, Toltecs, and Aztecs, in addition to numerous nomadic cultures. In 1519 Hernán Cortés and several hundred Spanish soldiers entered Tenochtitlán (now Mexico City). A two-year campaign against the Aztecs under Montezuma II ended with the Spanish capture of the city. The Viceroyalty of New Spain—with its center at Mexico City—was proclaimed in 1535. At its height it encompassed the lands from California to Panama, Florida, Spain's Caribbean holdings, and the Philippines.

As was the case with the rest of Spanish America, the movement for independence in New Spain coincided with the weakening of the authority of the Spanish Crown as a result of the Napoleonic takeover of Spain in 1808. In 1810 Miguel Hidalgo led a failed uprising and was executed. Following in Hidalgo's footsteps, José María Morelos led another uprising in the south, and he in turn was captured and put to death. Agustín de Iturbide, leader of the royalist forces, defected to the side of those struggling for independence in 1821. Envisioning independent Mexico as a monarchy, military groups proclaimed Iturbide emperor of Mexico in 1822.

The Mexican empire did not last long, and the Central American counties seceded after Iturbide's ouster by Antonio de Santa Anna in 1823. A republic was declared and Guadalupe Victoria was the first president (1824–29). In 1836, Texas seceded from Mexico in a revolution that cost Santa Anna the presidency. Between 1845 and 1848, Mexico fought the United States over U.S. annexation of Texas, and in 1847 U.S. troops occupied Mexico City. Under the Treaty of Guadalupe Hidalgo (1848), Mexico sold about half its territory—including California, Nevada, Utah, most of Arizona, and parts of New Mexico, Colorado, and Wyoming to the United States—for $15 million.

Santa Anna ruled again, as dictator, from 1853 to 1855, before being toppled by the liberal movement, La Reforma. A new constitution was proclaimed in 1857, but Conservatives declared it void. Following the War of Reform (1858–61), France, Britain, and Spain all claimed compensation for destruction of Mexican's property, and in 1862 they landed troops at Veracruz. Britain and Spain withdrew, but Napoleon III attempted to establish a dependent empire in Mexico and installed Archduke Ferdinand Maximilian of Austria on the Mexican throne in 1864. In the face of Mexican resistance and U.S. threats, France ended its Mexican adventure, and in 1867 Maximilian was captured and executed by Liberal forces.

Benito Juárez, who served as provisional president during the War of Reform, was a major force behind the liberal movement called La Reforma, which stressed the promotion of capitalism. Juárez won a third presidential term in 1871 but died in office and was succeeded in office by Sebastián Lerdo de Tejada, who was in turn overthrown by Gen. Porfirio Díaz. During the stable dictatorship known as the Porfiriato (1876–1911), Mexico experienced economic growth, though wealthy landowners and the church benefited at the expense of the poor.

The Mexican Revolution began in 1910 after Porfirio Díaz had his electoral opponent, Francisco I. Madero, jailed. Madero formulated his Plan of San Luis Potosí, calling for armed resistance. Rebellions broke out in the northern state of Chihuahua under the leadership of Pancho Villa and in the southern state of Morelos led by Emiliano Zapata. The two states soon came under rebel control, and in 1911 Díaz left Mexico. Madero was elected president, but his failure to carry through promised reforms resulted in the continuation of the rebellion.

Backed by the U.S., Gen. Victoriano Huerta overthrew Madero in 1913. But the fighting continued, and Huerta lost the support of the U.S. and was forced from office by Zapata, Villa, and Venustiano Carranza, who became president (1914–20). Zapata and Villa continued their resistance, but by 1916 Gen. Alvaro Obregón had driven Villa back to Chihuahua and Zapata's armies had been contained. Carranza called for the election of delegates to a constitutional convention in 1916, and by the following year, the progressive Mexican Constitution of 1917 was in place.

Obregón deposed Carranza in 1920 and served as president until 1924. He was reelected in 1928 but was assassinated before he could take office. In 1929 Calles founded the National Revolutionary party, which became the Institutional Revolutionary party (PRI) in 1946.

Lázaro Cárdenas won the presidency in 1934, sending Calles into exile. This, coupled with Cárdenas's decision to remove himself from politics at the end of his term, greatly stabilized the institutional structure created by the Mexican Revolution. Cárdenas was the last of the "revolutionary" leaders to make good on the promises to labor and the peasantry. He presided over extensive redistribution of land and in 1938 reorganized the ruling party into four constituencies: peasants, labor, the military, and the middle class. Cárdenas also used the national ownership of subsoil rights enshrined in the Mexican constitution to nationalize U.S. oil companies. The political movement of Mexican presidents since Cárdenas has been away from its peasant and labor constituencies toward business and the popular sector, beginning with Miguel Alemán's election in 1946.

The PRI's stability was seriously challenged in the 1980s as a result of the economic crisis stemming from the severe decline in the price of oil. Mexico borrowed heavily from foreign creditors during the 1970s on the expectation that oil prices would remain high. The debt problem led to cutbacks in government spending, a catastrophic drop in the value of the currency, and capital and human flight out of the country. Carlos Salinas de Gortari, the PRI's candidate in the 1988 presidential election, won by one of the narrowest margins ever in a contest widely believed to have been rigged.

Pres. Salinas pursued economic reform and lobbied for passage of the North American Free Trade Agreement with the U.S. and Canada, which promised to bring more jobs and increases in capital investment. But the very day NAFTA went into effect, Jan. 2, 1994, a guerrilla group of poor Indians calling itself the Zapata Army of National Liberation declared war against the government and began fighting government troops in the southern state of Chiapas under the leadership of "Subcomandante Marcos."

The (unrelated) assassination of the PRI presidential candidate at a campaign stop in Tiajuana led Salinas to appoint the campaign manager Ernesto Zedillo, a member of the PRI's reform-minded wing, as the PRI's presidential candidate (over the objections of the "old guard"). With just over 50 percent of the vote (the lowest majority ever for the PRI), Zedillo won the 1994 election. The immediate crisis he faced was the collapse of the peso, which declined by 40 percent in two months. In 1995, in exchange for austere economic measures, the I.M.F. and U.S. offered an enormous bailout aid package with Mexican oil revenues as collateral. By June 1996 Mexico managed the early repayment of $4.7 billion to the U.S. by privately refinancing the debt.

Zedillo was successful with the situation in Chiapas, arranging 1996 peace talks with the rebels to end fighting and increase Indian autonomy. The appearance of a similar group (the Popular Revolutionary army) in the state of Guerrero began troubles which continued into 1997.

The July 1997 elections saw the PRI lose its majority in the Chamber of Deputies, as it carried only 39 percent of the vote. In March 1999, Pres. Zedillo broke with tradition by not nominating a successor. Democracy entered the PRI itself with primary elections won by Francisco Labastida. But in the July 2000 presidential election, it was the National Action Party (PAN) candidate, Vincente Fox, who triumphed. The new president's economic reform agenda stalled in the divided legislature. In 2006 a contentious presidential election resulted in conservative Felipe Calderon defeating leftist Andres Manuel Lopez Obrador, who refused to accept the results, even after an electoral tribunal certified the election.

Calderon's tenure was marked by determination to end the power of the drug lords as violence escalated dramatically. In the spring of 2009 many drug-related murders and arrests put Mexico in a negative light, which did not help the tourism needed to boost the economy in deep recession. In July 2009 Calderon's party lost parliamentary elections to the PRI. Drug-related violence reached new heights in 2010 as police and military made several raids on drug lords and their gangs. Retaliation led to more than 5,000 civilian deaths, including a candidate for governor of Tamaulipas. (See "Major News Stories.")

▶ MICRONESIA
Federated States of Micronesia

● **GEOGRAPHY Location:** forms (with Palau) archipelago of Caroline Islands, Ponape (6°52'N, 158°15'E), Yap (9°32'N, 138°08'E), Kosrae (5°19'N, 162°59'E), and Truk (7°22'N, 151°54'E), in western Pacific Ocean. **Boundaries:** Guam to NW, Marshall Islands to E, Papua New Guinea to S, Philippines about 497 mi. (800 km) to W. **Total area:** 271 sq. mi. (702 sq km). **Coastline:** 3,798 (6,112 km). **Comparative area:** about four times size of Washington, D.C. **Land use:** 6% arable land; 46% permanent crops; 48% other. **Major cities:** Palikir (capital).

● **PEOPLE Population:** 107,434 (July 2009 est.). **Nationality:** noun—Micronesian(s); adjective—Micronesian, Kosrae(s), Pohnpeian(s), Trukese, Yapese. **Ethnic groups:** nine ethnic Micronesian and Polynesian groups. **Languages:** English (official and common language), Trukese, Pohnpeian, Yapese, Kosrean. **Religions:** 50% Roman Catholic, 47% Protestant.

● **GOVERNMENT Type:** constitutional government in free association with U.S.; Compact of Free Association entered into force Nov. 3, 1986. **Independence:** Nov. 3, 1986 (from U.S.-administered U.N. Trusteeship). **Constitution:** May 10, 1979. **National holiday:** Constitution Day, May 10. **Head of Government:** Emanuel Mori, president (since May 2007). **Structure:** executive; unicameral legislature; judiciary.

● **ECONOMY Monetary unit:** U.S. dollar. **Budget:** (FY07 est.) *income:* $166 mil.; *expend.:* $152.7 mil.

G.D.P.: $238.1 mil., $2,200 per capita (2008 est.). **Chief crops:** black pepper, tropical fruits and vegetables, coconuts, cassava, sweet potatoes; pigs, chickens. **Natural resources:** forests, marine products, deep seabed minerals. **Major industries:** tourism, construction, fish processing. **Labor force:** 16,360 (2008) two-thirds are government employees. **Exports:** $14 mil. (f.o.b., 2004 est.); fish, garments, bananas, black pepper. **Imports:** $132.7 mil. (c.i.f., 2004 est.); food, manufactured goods, machinery and equipment, beverages. **Major trading partners:** (2006) *exports:* U.S., Japan, Guam; *imports:* U.S., Japan, Hong Kong.

The Federated States of Micronesia extend 1,800 miles across an archipelago of the Caroline Islands in the larger island group of Micronesia. Ethnically diverse (there are eight primary languages, not including dialects), the islands are thought to be the first in the Pacific settled by argonauts from the Philippines and Indonesia, in about 1500 B.C. Ferdinand Magellan landed in the Marianas in A.D. 1521, and Spain claimed sovereignty from 1565 to 1899, when the Caroline Islands were sold to Germany. After World War I, the League of Nations mandated the islands to Japan, which developed agriculture (especially sugarcane), mining, and fishing. After World War II, the islands were included in the U.N. Trust Territory of the Pacific and placed under U.S. administration. A compact of free association between Micronesia and the United States was signed in 1986, and Micronesia's trust territory status with the U.N. trusteeship council was dissolved in December 1990.

▶ **MOLDOVA**
Republic of Moldova
• **GEOGRAPHY   Location:** southeastern Europe. **Boundaries:** Ukraine to N, E, S, Romania to W. **Total area:** 13,012 sq. mi. (33,700 sq. km). **Coastline:** none. **Comparative area:** slightly more than twice the size of Hawaii. **Land use:** 54% arable land; 12% permanent crops; 34% other. **Major cities:** Kishinev (Chisinău) (capital); Tiraspol; Beltsy (Balti).
• **PEOPLE   Population:** 4,320,748 (July 2009 est.). **Nationality:** noun—Moldovan(s); adjective—Moldovan. **Ethnic groups:** 64.5% Moldovan/Romanian, 13.8% Ukrainian, 13% Russian, 1.5% Jewish, 2% Bulgarian, 5.2% Gaguaz and other. **Languages:** Moldovan (official), based on Romanian, but using a Cyrillic alphabet; Russian, Gagauz. **Religions:** 98% Eastern Orthodox, 1.5% Jewish.
• **GOVERNMENT   Type:** republic. **Independence:** Aug. 27, 1991 (from Soviet Union). **Constitution:** July 28, 1994. **National holiday:** Independence Day, Aug. 27. **Heads of Government:** Vladimir Voronin, president (since Apr. 2001); Vladimir Filat, prime minister (since Sep. 2009). **Structure:** executive; unicameral legislature; judiciary.
• **ECONOMY   Monetary unit:** leu. **Budget:** (2008 est.) *income:* $1.95 bil.; *expend.:* $2.01 bil. **G.D.P.:** $10.63 bil., $2,500 per capita (2008 est.). **Chief crops:** sugar beets, grain, vegetables, wine grapes, other fruit. **Natural resources:** lignites, phosporites, gypsum. **Major industries:** food processing, agricultural machinery, foundry equipment, textiles, chemicals. **Labor force:** 1.327 mil. (2008); 47% services, 41% agriculture, 12% industry (2005 est.); 2.1% unemployment (2007). **Exports:** $1.79 bil. (f.o.b., 2008); foodstuffs, wine, tobacco, textiles, footwear. **Imports:** $5 bil. (f.o.b.,

2008); oil, gas, coal, steel, machinery. **Major trading partners:** (2006) *exports:* 22.8% Russia, 12.2% Germany, 11.1% Italy, 9.7% Romania, 9.6% Ukraine, 5.7% Belarusse; *imports:* 20.8% Russia, 16.9% Ukraine, 13.4% Romania, 8.7% Germany, 6.1% Italy, 4.4% Poland.

Historical Moldavia, of which present-day Moldova is only a small portion, encompassed territories that are now in Romania and Ukraine (including southern Bessarabia and northern Bukovina). Moldova is a hilly, fertile land, bounded by two great rivers, the Dniester and the Prut, that flow into the Black Sea. Its climate is very favorable to agriculture.

Moldavia was part of Scythia in the first millennium B.C. and later came under the Roman Empire. Lying on the gateway to Europe, it was invaded successively, but came under the control of Kievan Rus between the 10th and 12th centuries A.D., and in the 13th century it was invaded by the Mongolian empire. In the 16th century, eastern Moldavia, or Bessarabia, came under Turkish control but in 1812 was ceded to the Russian empire. Southern Bessarabia (now in Ukraine) was controlled variously by the Russian empire and by Romania, and in 1878 it again became part of Russia. After the Bolsheviks came to power in 1917 and created the U.S.S.R., a Moldavian Autonomous Soviet Socialist Republic (ASSR) was formed on the eastern side of the Dniester River, a territory claimed by Romania but populated by Ukrainians. In June 1940, as a result of the Nazi-Soviet Pact of 1939, Romania was forced to cede Bessarabia and northern Bukovina to the Soviet Union. These lands were made part of the Ukrainian Soviet Socialist Republic (SSR), and the remaining Bessarabian sections were merged with the old Moldavian ASSR to create on Aug. 2, 1940, the Moldavian SSR. Between 1941 and 1944, while Romania and the U.S.S.R. were at war, Bessarabia again became part of Romania, but in 1944 the Soviets reestablished it as a union republic.

While under Soviet control, Moldavians in the new republic were officially differentiated from their counterparts across the border in Romania. In 1940, the Cyrillic alphabet was imposed on the Romanian language; this official language was called "Moldavian." Contacts between the two countries were discouraged, and the U.S.S.R. encouraged Russian and Ukrainian immigration to the Moldavian SSR. While a part of the U.S.S.R., Moldavia created a diversified economy, which was based on agriculture and food processing.

Gorbachev's policy of glasnost, or openness, in the late 1980s gave vent to Moldavian complaints about "Russification" and immigration of non-Moldavians. In Sept. 1989, Romanian, now in a Latin script, was restored as the official language. Glasnost also gave birth to new political parties, the largest of which was the Popular Front of Moldavia, which organized protest demonstrations against Soviet power. Disturbances during the 1989 celebration of Soviet Revolution Day in the capital city of Kishinev led to the dismissal of the Slavic Communist party First Secretary, and his replacement by an ethnic Romanian.

The Communist party was banned in Moldova in 1990, and laws to develop the basics of a multi-party system were adopted in September 1991. Moldova officially declared its independence from the U.S.S.R. on Aug. 27, 1991, and in December, United Front-supported Mircea Snegur was elected president with 98.2 percent of the votes cast.

At the time Moldova declared its independence, sentiment was strong for reunification with Romania. So strong, in fact, that ethnic Russians and Ukrainians living in the Trans-Dniester region in eastern Moldova, fearing reunification with Romania, declared an independent Trans-Dniester republic, sparking ethnic violence there. But since then, most activity has focused on reestablishing ties with countries from the former U.S.S.R. In 1991, Moldova singed the Alma-Ata Declaration, joining the other former Soviet republics in the Commonwealth of Independent States. And in the country's first parlimantary elections, held in Feb. of 1994, two nationalist parties captured a combined 15 percent of the vote, while the pro-Russian Socialist party won 25 percent, and the Agrarian Democratic Party, led by former Communists, took 45 percent. Then, in a plebiscite held Mar. 6, 1994, an overwhelming majority (90 percent) of voters rejected reunification with Romania in favor of an independent Moldova. Two-thirds of Moldova's 2.3 million eligible voters cast ballots on the plebiscite. Snegur intended to use the referendum result to entice Trans-Dniester to rejoin Moldova.

In late 1996 Snegur lost the presidency to Petro Lucinschi who quickly recognized Trans-Dniester as autonomous and began a reform program to stimulate the weak economy. A strong Communist showing in 1998 legislative elections made this agenda more difficult to establish. The slow pace of reform led Prime Minister Ion Ciubuc to resign in Feb. 1999 (replaced by Ion Sturza) and Pres. Lucinschi to propose a referendum to increase the constitutional powers of the president.

Elections in Feb. 2001 gave the Communists a majority in parliament which selected Vladimir Voronin as president and Vasile Tarlev as prime minister. They won again in March 2005 but it is hard to know why since 40 percent of the population is forced to look for work abroad. In April 2009 more than 10,000 young people rioted after the Communists won the parliamentary elections. But in July new elections reversed the result and pro-Western parties unseated the Communists for the first time.

▶MONACO
Principality of Monaco
- **GEOGRAPHY Location:** tiny enclave on Mediterranean coast of France. **Boundaries:** France to N, E, and W; Mediterranean Sea to S. **Total area:** 1.21 sq. mi. (1.95 sq km). **Coastline:** 2.6 mi. (4.1 km). **Comparative area:** about three times size of the Mall in Washington, D.C. **Land use:** 0% arable land; 0% permanent crops; 100% other. **Major cities:** Monaco (capital).
- **PEOPLE Population:** 32,965 (2009 est.). **Nationality:** noun—Monacan(s) or Monegasque(s); adjective—Monacan or Monegasque. **Ethnic groups:** 47% French, 16% Monegasque, 16% Italian, 21% other. **Languages:** French (official), English, Italian, Monegasque. **Religions:** 90% Roman Catholic.
- **GOVERNMENT Type:** constitutional monarchy. **Independence:** 1419. **Constitution:** Dec. 17, 1962; modified April 2, 2002. **National holiday:** National Day, Nov. 19. **Head of Government:** Albert II, chief of state (since Apr. 2005); Michel Roger, prime minister (since Mar. 2010). **Structure:** executive—prince, minister of state (senior French civil servant appointed by prince), and Council of

Government as cabinet; unicameral legislature—prince and National Council of 18 members; judiciary—authority delegated by prince to Supreme Tribunal.
- **ECONOMY Monetary unit:** euro. **Budget:** (2005 est.) *income:* $863 mil.; *expend:* $920.6 mil. **G.D.P.:** $870 mil., $30,000 per capita (2006 est.). **Chief crops:** N.A. **Natural resources:** none. **Major industries:** Tourism, construction, small-scale industry and consumer products. **Labor force:** (2005 est.) 44,000; 95.1% services, 4.9% industry. **Exports:** 716.3 mil. (2007 est.) **Imports:** 916.1 mil. (2007 est.) **Major trading partners:** full customs integration with France, which collects and rebates Monacan trade duties; also participates in E.U. market system through customs union with France.

Known to Phoenicians and Greeks from the beginning of the first millenium B.C., the history of the port of Monaco is coextensive with that of southeastern France for much of its history. A western colony of the great trading city-state of Genoa in the 13th century, Monaco in 1368 became an independent principality under the rule of the Matignon-Grimaldi family. At various times a protectorate of Spain, France, and Sardinia, it was restored to independence in 1861 by the Franco-Monegasque treaty.

In 1911 Monaco became a constitutional monarchy under the Matignon-Grimaldi dynasty. In 1918 France required the principality to conform to its national interests in all respects; by an agreement of 1919, should the dynasty fail to produce a male heir, Monaco would be absorbed into France. However, the family is allowed to adopt an heir if they so choose. The marriage of Prince Ranier III to the U.S film star Grace Kelly produced an heir apparent for this generation. The constitutional monarchy under its "Most Serene Prince" was essentially a one-party state in which in every election since 1968 the National and Democratic Union won all the seats in the National Council until February 2003 when the Union for Monaco won 21 of the 24 seats with almost 60 percent of the popular vote. In 1993 Monaco became the smallest member nation of the U.N.

Despite the fame of the Monte Carlo casino, gambling accounts for only 4 percent of the principality's revenues. The principal industry is tourism, followed by light manufacturing. Monaco also supports a prominent institute of oceanography. Land reclamation projects, impelled by a real estate boom, have added about 20 percent to the nation's territory since World War II. Prince Rainer died in 2005 and was succeeded by his son, Albert.

▶MONGOLIA
- **GEOGRAPHY Location:** landlocked country in central Asia. **Boundaries:** Russia to N, China to E, S, and W. **Total area:** 604,247 sq. mi. (1,565,000 sq km). **Coastline:** none. **Comparative area:** slightly larger than Alaska. **Land use:** 1% arable land; 0% permanent crops; 99% other. **Major cities:** Ulan Bator (capital); Darhan; Erdenet.
- **PEOPLE Population:** 3,041,142 (2009 est.). **Nationality:** noun—Mongolian(s) adjective—Mongolian. **Ethnic groups:** 94.9% Mongol, 5% Turkic, 0.1% other. **Languages:** Khalkha Mongol used by over 90% of population; Turkic, Russian, Chinese. **Religions:** predominantly Lamaist Buddhist, 4% Muslim, Shamanism and Christian, 40% none.

• **GOVERNMENT** Type: parliamentary. **Independence:** July 11, 1921 (from China). **Constitution:** Jan. 13, 1992. **National holiday:** National Day, July 11. **Heads of Government:** Tsakhia Elbegdorj, president (since June 2009); Sukhbaatar Batbold, prime minister (since Oct. 2009). **Structure:** executive; unicameral legislature; judiciary.

• **ECONOMY** Monetary unit: tughrik. **Budget:** (2008) *income:* $1.71 bil.; *expend.:* $1.95 bil. **G.D.P.:** $9.557 bil., $3,200 per capita (2008 est.). **Chief crops:** livestock raising predominates; wheat, barley. **Natural resources:** oil, coal, copper, molybdenum, tungsten, phosphates. **Major industries:** copper, processing of animal products, building materials, foods and beverages. **Labor force:** 1.068 mil. (2008); 41% services, 40% industry, 18.8% agriculture. **Exports:** $2.539 bil. (f.o.b., 2008); copper, livestock, animal products, wool, hides, fluorospar, nonferrous metals. **Imports:** $3.615 bil. (c.i.f., 2008); machinery and equipment, fuels, food products, industrial consumer goods, chemicals. **Major trading partners:** (2006) *exports:* 71.7% China, 11.7% Canada, 7.3% U.S.; *imports:* 29.7% Russia, 29.4% China, 11.9% Japan.

Mongols under Genghis Khan conquered most of Eurasia in the early 13th century. The Mongol empire broke up in the mid-14th century, and Mongolia lapsed into tribal disunion and political insignificance. Chinese rule was established thereafter in Inner Mongolia and, in 1691, in Outer Mongolia (a province under local rule). With the 1911 Chinese Revolution, Outer Mongolia unsuccessfully proclaimed its independence from China. The nationalist religious leader, the Bogdo Lama, sought Russian support in 1920. Under the revolutionary leaders Sukhe Bataar and Khorloin Choibalsan, a "provisional people's government" again declared independence in 1921. Sukhe Bataar died in 1923; on Nov. 26, 1924, the Mongolian People's Republic (MPR) was established with Soviet sponsorship. The early years of the republic were marked by repeated Stalinist purges of Mongol revolutionary leaders and by disastrous attempts at centralized planning.

Choibalsan emerged as party leader and was confirmed as premier in 1940. In 1939 Soviet and Mongolian armies prevented a Japanese conquest of Mongolia. In 1945 the Republic of China recognized the MPR; recognition was reaffirmed by the People's Republic of China in 1949. In 1948 the first of a series of five-year plans began to bring industrial and agricultural development to Mongolia, with extensive Soviet aid and support. Choibalsan died in 1952 and was succeeded as premier by Yumjaagiyn Tsedenbal. Following the Sino-Soviet split of 1958, heavy concentrations of Soviet troops and missiles were stationed along the Chinese-Mongolian border. On Oct. 27, 1961, the MPR was admitted to the United Nations and diplomatic relations with various other non-Soviet bloc nations developed gradually. Tsedenbal was ousted in 1984 and replaced by Zhambyn Batmonh as party chairman and by Dumaagiin Sodnom as premier. The MPR established diplomatic relations with the United States in 1987.

Following widespread demonstrations calling for human rights, religious freedom, and an end to special privileges for Communist officials, the Communist party voted to give up its constitutional power in March 1990. In 1992, under the new constitution, elections were held for four-year terms in the new single-chamber Great Hural: the Communists (now calling themselves the Mongolian People's Revolutionary Party) won 70 of the 76 seats but in the first popular elections for president the following year, acting president Punsalmaagiin Ochirbat, a reformist ex-communist trounced the hardline MPRP candidate. The resultant political deadlock only exacerbated the economic crisis brought on by severance of Mongolia's old ties with the Soviet bloc, though international aid kept the state afloat.

A coalition of opposition parties, called the Democratic Alliance, won 50 seats in the 1996 elections for the Great Hural, ending the communist rule that began in 1921. But one year of economic reform brought disillusion with the DA and the triumph in 1997 of MPRP chairman Natsagiin Bagabandi over Ochirbat in the presidential election. This second political deadlock was broken in the 2000 Great Hural elections when the MPRP swept 72 seats. The return of the Communists was confirmed a year later with Bagabandi's re-election in 2001. The MPRP lost half its seats in 2004 legislative elections, with the new opposition alliance, Motherland Democratic Coalition, taking 35 of the 76 seats. This dramatic gain did not end the MPRP control of the Great Hural and in the 2005 presidential election the leader of the MPRP won a convincing victory.

A state of emergency was declared in July 2008 as police subdued protestors marching against vote-rigging after the MPRP won the presidential election. Only a year later the opposition Democratic party won and the new president, Tsakhiagiin Elbegdorg, took office without incident.

▶ MONTENEGRO

• **GEOGRAPHY** Location: southeastern Europe between the Adriatic Sea and Serbia. **Boundaries:** Albania, Bosnia and Herzegovina, Croatia, Serbia. **Total area:** 5,415 sq. mi. (14,026 sq km). **Coastline:** 182 mi. (293.5 km). **Comparative area:** slightly smaller than Connecticut. **Land use:** 13.7% arable land; 1% permanent crops; 85.3% other. **Major cities:** Podgorica (capital); Niksic; Pljevlja; Berane.

• **PEOPLE** Population: 672,180 (July 2009 est.). **Nationality:** noun—Montenegrin(s); adjective—Montenegrin. **Ethnic groups:** Montenegrin 43%, Serbian 32%, Bosniak 8%, Albanian 5%, other 12%. **Languages:** Serbian (official), Ijekavian dialect), Bosnian, Albanian, Croatian. **Religions:** Orthodox, Muslim, Roman Catholic.

• **GOVERNMENT** Type: republic. **Independence:** June 3, 2006 (from Serbia and Montenegro). **Constitution:** Oct. 19, 2007. **National holiday:** National Day, July 13. **Heads of Government:** Filip Vujanovic, president (since May 2003); Milo Djukanovic, prime minister (since Feb. 2008). **Structure:** unicameral assembly; judiciary.

• **ECONOMY** Monetary unit: euro. **Budget:** N.A. **G.D.P.:** $6.6 bil., $9,700 per capita (2008 est.). **Chief crops:** grains, tobacco, potatoes, citrus fruits, olives, grapes. **Natural resources:** bauxite, hydroelectricity. **Major industries:** steelmaking, aluminum, agricultural processing, consumer goods, tourism. **Labor force:** 259,100 (2004 est.); 2% agriculture, 30% industry, 68% services (2004). **Exports:** $171.3 mil. (2003). **Imports:** $601.7 bil. (2003). **Major trading partners:** (2006) *exports:* 84% Switzerland, 6% Italy, 1.3% Bosnia & Herzegovina; *imports:* 10% Greece, 10% Italy, 9.6% Germany, 9.2% Bosnia & Herzegovina.

After existing as an independent monarchy from 1878–1918, Montenegro became a constituent republic of the Socialist Federal Republic of Yugoslavia. When that country dissolved in 1992, Montenegro joined with Serbia to form the Federal Republic of Yugoslavia, and in 2003, became the looser union of Serbia and Montenegro. On May 21, 2006, 55.5 percent of Montenegrins voted to sever ties with Serbia, and independence was declared on June 3. By the end of the month, Montenegro had been incorporated as the 192nd member of the U.N. In the following year, the country joined the World Bank, the IMF, and initiated an agreement with the E.U. In addition, the first steps were taken to join NATO. To the chagrin of many, Prime Minister Milo Djukanovic resigned in October 2006, and appointed Zeljko Sturanovic as his successor but he returned in 2008.

(For ancient and 20th century Montenegrin history, see "Serbia.")

▶MOROCCO
Kingdom of Morocco
● **GEOGRAPHY** Location: northwestern Africa. Boundaries: North Atlantic Ocean to W and NW, Strait of Gibraltar to N, Mediterranean Sea to NE, Algeria to E and SE, Western Sahara to SW. **Total area**: 172,413 sq. mi. (446,550 sq km). **Coastline**: 1,140 mi. (1,835 km). **Comparative area**: slightly larger than California. **Land use:** 20% arable land; 2% permanent crops; 78% other. **Major cities**: Rabat (including Sale; capital); Casablanca; Marrakech (Marrakesh); Fès (Fez); Oujda.
● **PEOPLE** **Population:** 34,859,364 (July 2009 est.). **Nationality:** noun—Moroccan(s); adjective—Moroccan. **Ethnic groups:** 99.1% Arab-Berber, 0.7% non-Moroccan, 0.2% Jewish. **Languages:** Arabic (official), several Berber dialects; French is language of business, government and diplomacy. **Religions:** 98.7% Muslim, 1.1% Christian, 0.2% Jewish.
● **GOVERNMENT** **Type:** constitutional monarchy. **Independence:** Mar. 2, 1956 (from France). **Constitution:** Mar. 10, 1972, revised Sept. 4, 1992, amended to create bicameral legislature Sept. 1996. **National holiday:** National Day, July 30. **Heads of Government:** Mohammed VI, king (since July 1999); Abbas El Fassi, prime minister (since Sept. 2007). **Structure:** executive—king has paramount powers; bicameral legislature—two-thirds of members are directly elected and one-third are indirectly elected; judiciary—independent of other branches.
● **ECONOMY** Monetary unit: dirham. **Budget:** (2008 est.) *income:* $26.09 bil.; *expend.:* $28.41 bil. **G.D.P.:** $137.3 bil., $4,000 per capita (2008 est.). **Chief crops:** cereal farming and livestock raising predominant; barley, wheat, citrus fruit, wine, vegetables; livestock. **Natural resources:** phosphates, iron ore, manganese, lead, zinc, fish, salt. **Major industries:** phosphate rock mining and processing, food processing, leather goods. **Labor force:** 11.5 mil. (2008); 40% agriculture, 45% services, 15% industry (2003); 10% unemployment (2008 est.). **Exports:** $16.14 bil. (f.o.b., 2008 est.); food and beverages, semiprocessed goods, consumer goods. **Imports:** $34.44 bil. (f.o.b., 2008 est.); semiprocessed goods, capital goods, food and beverages, fuel and lubricants. **Major trading partners:** (2006) *exports:* 20.6% Spain, 20.5% France, 4.8% U.K., 4.7% Italy, 4% India; *imports:*

17.5% France, 13.9% Spain, 6.9% Saudi Arabia, 6.9% China, 6.3% Italy, 6% Germany.

Neolithic inhabitants of Morocco were displaced by Berbers around 1000 B.C. Phoenician and Carthaginian settlements were established along the Mediterranean coast. Morocco came under Roman rule around A.D. 40 and was invaded via Spain by Germanic Vandals in the fifth century. The Islamic invasions of the mid-seventh century established Arab rule in Morocco, and most of the indigenous Berbers converted to Islam. Ethnic tension between Berbers and Arabs has been a basic element of Moroccan politics and society ever since.

In the late eighth century, King Idris ibn Adballah united Berbers and Arabs in a monarchy that lasted for 200 years and made the capital city of Fez one of the major religious and cultural centers of the Islamic world. In the 11th century, the Almoravid dynasty from Mauritania conquered Morocco, western Algeria, and Spain. It was ousted by another Muslin sect, the Almohads. After about 1200 the tide of Moorish expansion in the Iberian Peninsula turned; in 1492 Ferdinand and Isabella expelled the last Moors from Grenada.

Naval conflict between Morocco, Spain, and Portugal continued in the western Mediterranean and along the Atlantic coast of Africa for several centuries more. In the mid-17th century, Morocco was reunited under the present Alawid dynasty. In the early 19th century, American and British forces combatted Moroccan piracy in the Mediterranean, and Spain established colonies in Tangier in the north and along the Atlantic coast between Morocco and Mauritania.

The attempts of Sultan Hassan I (r. 1873–94) to implement reforms to strengthen Morocco's independence were thwarted by European interests. By the early 20th century, France, securely established in Algeria, began exerting increasing control in Morocco. A multipower conference at Algeciras in 1906 affirmed Moroccan independence but upheld the special rights claimed by Spain and France. The Treaty of Fez, signed in 1912 between France and Sultan Abd-al-Hafidn, ended Moroccan independence by granting the country to France and reaffirming a Spanish sphere of influence in the southwest.

Nationalist unrest and tribal uprisings disrupted French administration in Morocco throughout the 1920s and 1930s. Morocco became a battleground during World War II between the Axis-supported Vichy French government and the Free French and their Allied backers. In 1943 Churchill and Roosevelt met at Casablanca to discuss wartime strategy; in the same year, the Istiqlal (Independence) party was founded to fight for independence from the French in the postwar era.

In 1947 Moroccan liberation forces began open warfare against the French. The exiled Sultan Mohammad V was allowed to return, and France promised independence by 1955.

With the withdrawal of French forces, Morocco became independent on Mar. 2, 1956. Tangier (under international administration since 1923) was incorporated into the newly independent state in October 1956, and the Spanish enclave of Ifni was ceded to Morocco in 1969.

A period of instability ensued after 1957 as newly formed political parties vied for power. King Mohammad I died in 1961 and was succeeded by his son, Hassan II. In 1962 an elected parliamentary government took power under the constitutional monarchy. Political unrest and economic difficulties led to the declaration of states of emergency in 1965 and 1970 and a new constitution in 1977.

Spain withdrew from its former territory of Spanish (now Western) Sahara, a phosphate-rich desert territory on Morocco's southern border, in Feb. 1976. On Apr. 14, 1976, Morocco annexed the northern two-thirds of the territory, while Mauritania claimed the remainder. The Polisario Spanish Saharan liberation movement, backed by Algeria and Libya, conducted guerrilla operations against Moroccan and Mauritanian forces. In 1979 Mauritania gave up its claims, and Morocco claimed the entire region.

In 1987, Morocco completed construction of a 2,000-mile sand wall completely enclosing Western Sahara. Polisario forces control much of the Western Saharan countryside, while Morocco holds the cities and towns. In May 1987 a Moroccan-Algerian summit was held under the sponsorship of Saudi Arabia, which offered King Hassan $260 million to rebuild Morocco's war-torn economy in return for allowing a self-determination referendum in the Western Sahara. The king refused. By mid-1992 the situation was resolved as Polisario's leaders accepted an offer of amnesty, leaving the Moroccan government in possession of the territory.

The Persian Gulf crisis made an already weak economy weaker, and riots during a general strike protesting low wages and poor job prospects in Fez left 100 dead and hundreds more injured in 1991. Although Morocco was an active member of the Allied coalition against Iraq, Moroccans also staged huge demonstrations in support of Saddam Hussein at the height of the war.

In 1992, demands of Muslim fundamentalist factions for greater political power threatened the stability of King Hassan II's government. In a gesture toward political reform, parliamentary elections were held in June 1993, but the results never posed any immediate challenge to the monarchy.

In March 1998 the king appointed Morocco's first opposition-led government, a coalition of seven political parties. Hassan died in July 1999 and was succeeded by his son Mohammed VI. A government trial balloon on women's rights produced a protest rally of 500,000 in March 2000. In May 2003, five simultaneous suicide bombings rocked Casablanca.

▶ MOZAMBIQUE
Republic of Mozambique
• **GEOGRAPHY Location:** eastern coast of Africa. **Boundaries:** Zambia and Malawi to NW, Tanzania to N, Indian Ocean to E and SE, South Africa and Swaziland to SW, Zimbabwe to W. **Total area:** 309,494 sq. mi. (801,590 sq km). **Coastline:** 1,535 mi. (2,470 km). **Comparative area:** slightly less than twice size of California. **Land use:** 4% arable land; negl. % permanent crops; 96% other. **Major cities:** Maputo (capital).
• **PEOPLE Population:** 21,669,278 (July 2009 est.). **Nationality:** noun—Mozambican(s); adjective—Mozambican. **Ethnic groups:** 99.66% indigenous tribal groups (Shangaan, Chokwe, Manyika, Sena, Makua, and others). **Languages:** Portuguese (official), indigenous languages. **Religions:** 50% indigenous beliefs, 30% Christian, 20% Muslim.
• **GOVERNMENT Type:** republic. **Independence:** June 25, 1975 (from Portugal). **Constitution:** Nov. 30, 1990. **National holiday:** Independence Day,

June 25. **Heads of Government:** Armando Emilio Guebuza, president (since Feb. 2005); Aires Bonifaco Ali, prime minister (since Jan. 2010.). **Structure:** executive; unicameral legislature; judiciary. • **ECONOMY Monetary unit:** metical. **Budget:** (2008 est.) *income:* $2.786 bil.; *expend:* $3.108 bil. **G.D.P.:** $18.95 bil., $900 per capita (2008 est.). **Chief crops:** cotton, cashew nuts, sugar, tea; beef, poultry. **Natural resources:** coal, natural gas, titanium. **Major industries:** food and beverages, chemicals (fertilizer, soap, paints), petroleum. **Labor force:** 10.04 mil. (2008 est.); 23% agriculture, 30% industry, 47% services (2007). **Exports:** $2.693 bil. (f.o.b., 2008 est.); shrimp; cashews, cotton, sugar. **Imports:** $3.292 bil. (f.o.b., 2008 est.); food, clothing, farm equipment, petroleum. **Major trading partners:** (2006) *exports:* 59.7% Netherlands, 15.2% South Africa, 3.2% Zimbabwe; *imports:* 36.3% South Africa, 15.6% Netherlands, 3.3% Portugal.

Mozambique has been inhabited since prehistoric times by a variety of Bantu peoples. Portuguese trading stations were established starting in 1505, and Portugal developed an extensive coastal trade in gold and ivory. Mozambique also served as a way station for Portuguese trade to East Asia.

Despite competition from other European nations, Portugal maintained control of the Mozambique coast. Settlement by sizable numbers of Portuguese immigrants began in the late 19th century. Mozambique was organized as a colony, sometimes called Portuguese East Africa, in 1885; boundaries in the interior were defined in 1891.

Economic development of Mozambique in the 20th century remained almost entirely in Portuguese hands. By the 1950s native peoples began to protest Portuguese rule; a rebellion of the Frelimo (Front for the Liberation of Mozambique) guerrilla movement began in 1961. Rebels controlled most of the northern part of the country by 1964. Fighting continued for another decade.

Following the Portuguese revolution of 1974, Portugal agreed to independence for Mozambique, and many Portuguese settlers returned to Portugal, leaving the country bereft of administrative personnel and infrastructure support. Mozambique became fully independent on June 25, 1975. A Marxist Frelimo government took office, with Samora Michel as the country's first president. The new government formed agricultural collectives and nationalized most private land and industry as well as all social services.

In the late 1970s, fighting broke out between Mozambique and Rhodesia. When Rhodesia achieved independence (and changed its name to Zimbabwe) in 1980, relations between the two governments improved. But a rebel movement, Renamo (Mozambique National Resistance), dedicated to overthrowing the Frelimo government grew stronger during the 1980s.

In 1986, following the death of Samora Michel, Joachím Chissanó became president. His government reintroduced some private agriculture, loosened ties to the Eastern bloc, and appealed to the West for economic assistance. In 1987 a U.N.-led relief effort began. In 1989 Mozambique signed a cooperation agreement with South Africa, which cut off its aid to the Renamo insurgents. But fighting continued into 1990.

In Nov. 1990, Mozambique adopted a new constitution widening individual rights and freedoms, including abolition of the death penalty, freedom of the press and speech, and an independent judiciary, as well as establishing multiparty democracy, a presidential regime, and free-market economy. On Oct. 4, 1992, Pres. Chissanó and Renamo leader Afonso Dhlakama signed a cease-fire; the U.N. dispatched 7,500 military and civilian personnel to oversee the disarmament and organize elections.

Mozambique's first multiparty elections were held in Oct. 1994. Pres. Chissanó was elected with 53 percent of the vote while his Frelimo party took 129 of the Parliament's 250 seats. (Renamo carried all but nine of the remaining seats.) Chissano was re-elected in Dec. 1999 with Frelimo taking 133 seats.

Mozambique is rich in agricultural land and mineral resources. Nevertheless, years of communism, drought, and civil war have left the country poor and dependent on foreign aid. In 1992 the worst drought in memory brought the nation to a virtual standstill, as an estimated 1.8 million people became dependent on donations of food from outsiders for survival. In recent years the I.M.F. has helped enormously with loans and planning advice but Mozambique remains one of the poorest nations. In 2005 Armando Guebuza became president and began serious economic reforms that have proven effective.

▶MYANMAR
Union of Burma

• **GEOGRAPHY** **Location:** NW region of Southeast Asia. **Boundaries:** China and Laos to NE, Bangladesh, India to NW, Thailand to SE, Andaman Sea to S, and Bay of Bengal to SW. **Total area:** 261,969 sq. mi. (678,500 sq km). **Coastline:** 1,200 mi. (1,930 km). **Comparative area:** slightly smaller than Texas. **Land use:** 15% arable land; 1% permanent crops; 84% other. **Major cities:** Nay Pyi Taw (administrative capital); Yangon (formerly Rangoon; capital); Mandalay; Bassein; Moulmein; Akyab.

• **PEOPLE** **Population:** 48,137,741 (July 2009 est.). **Nationality:** noun—Burmese (sing., pl.); adjective—Burmese. **Ethnic groups:** 68% Burman, 9% Shan, 7% Karen, 4% Rakhine, 3% Chinese, 2% Mon, 2% Indian, 5% other. **Languages:** Burmese, minority ethnic languages. **Religions:** 89% Buddhist, 4% Muslim, 4% Christian, 1% animist beliefs.

• **GOVERNMENT** **Type:** military junta. **Independence:** Jan. 4, 1948 (from U.K.). **Constitution:** Jan. 3, 1974; new constitution being drafted. **National holiday:** Independence Day, Jan.4; Union Day, Feb. 12. **Head of Government:** Gen. Than Shwe, chairman State Law and Order Restoration Council (SLORC) (since Apr. 1992); Lt. Gen. Thein Sein, prime minister (since Oct. 2007). **Structure:** executive—military junta controls legislature—last election held in 1990, but never convened; judiciary—not independent, no guarantees.

• **ECONOMY** **Monetary unit:** kyat. **Budget:** (2008 est.) *income:* $983.6 mil.; *expend:* $1.775 bil. **G.D.P.:** $91.13 bil., $1,900 per capita (2007 est.). **Chief crops:** paddy rice, corn, oilseeds; hardwood. **Natural resources:** crude oil, timber, tin, copper, tungsten. **Major industries:** agricultural processing, textiles and footwear, wood and wood products. **Labor force:** 30.04 mil. (2008 est.); 70% agriculture, 7% industry, 23% services (2001 est.). **Exports:** $6.149 bil. (f.o.b., 2008); teak, rice, pulses, beans. **Imports:** $3.589 bil. (f.o.b., 2008); machinery, transport equipment, chemicals, food products. **Major trading partners:** (2006) *exports:* 48.8% Thailand, 12.7% India, 5.2% China, 5.2% Japan; *imports:* 35.1% China, 22.1% Thailand, 16.4% Singapore, 4.8% Malaysia.

(Until the summer of 1989 this country was known as Burma.)

Burma, an independent Buddhist monarchy from the 11th century, fell to the Mongol empire in the 13th century, and after the 14th century was a satellite state of China. Anglo-French rivalry over trade left Burma under French influence in the early 19th century, but in a series of three wars (1824–26, 1852, 1885), Great Britain succeeded in bringing all of Burma into the British raj of India. The country became self-governing under a British protectorate in 1937.

Japanese occupation of Burma in early 1942 made the country a major theater of fighting during World War II. The Burma Road, built by the Allies to connect northeastern India with southwestern China, was a key link in bringing supplies to the Chinese Nationalist army during the war.

Burma achieved independence as the Union of Burma on Jan. 4, 1948. Promises of autonomy for ethnic minority regions such as the Shan and Karen States have not been fulfilled, leading to armed separatist movements in those areas ever since. In 1962 a coup led by Gen. Ne Win overthrew the democratic government and established a one-party state under the Burmese Socialist Program party. The party's "Burmese Path to Socialism" resulted in self-imposed international isolation and economic stagnation at home despite the country's potential wealth in agriculture, timber, minerals, and gems.

In July 1988 Ne Win resigned from office in the face of mounting popular demonstrations. A series of short-lived successor governments were unable to restore public order and normal governmental functions; direct military rule was announced in September 1988 as demonstrations continued. In the general election held on May 27, 1990 (the first multiparty free elections in three decades), the opposition National League for Democracy, led by Aung San Suu Kyi, won a decisive victory, but the results of the election were nullified by the State Law and Order Restoration Council (SLORC), and leaders of the elected government were placed under house arrest.

In 1991 the continued political repression in Myanmar was brought to international attention when Aung San Suu Kyi was awarded the Nobel Peace Prize. A new leader of the ruling military junta, Gen. Than Shwe, began peace talks with the Karen rebels in early 1994, and released Aung San Suu Kyi in July 1995. In 1998, renewed pressure by NLD upon the junta to convene the 1990 parliament brought renewed repression and mass arrests; a committee of NLD delcared itself to be the legal parliament of Myanmar, asserting that all the junta legislation since 1990 was invalid. After releasing Aung from her 14-month arrest in May 2002, the junta "detained" Aung and 19 other NLD members in May 2003. In Sept. 2002 three grandsons of Ne Win and a son-in-law were sentenced to death for treason (an alleged coup attempt); Ne Win himself died shortly after. In 2003 Japan and the U.S. froze aid and banned imports, which led to some NLD leaders being released. Aung has refused freedom until all remaining prisoners are released. Protests were forbidden but in Sept. 2007 Buddhist monks took to the streets for two days. In May 2008 a cyclone killed over 100,000 but the junta refused outside aid. In 2010 a new constitution solidifying the military's power was introduced and elections scheduled for November.

▶ NAMIBIA
Republic of Namibia

• **GEOGRAPHY Location:** southwest Africa. **Boundaries:** Angola to N, Botswana to E, South Africa to S, Atlantic Ocean to W. **Total area:** 318,259 sq. mi. (824,290 sq km). **Coastline:** 976 mi. (1,572 km). **Comparative area:** slightly more than half the size of Alaska. **Land use:** 1% arable land; negl. % permanent crops; 99% other. **Major cities:** Windhoek (capital).

• **PEOPLE Population:** 2,108,665 (2009 est.). **Nationality:** noun—Namibian(s); adjective—Namibian. **Ethnic groups:** 87.5% black, 6% white, 6.5% mixed; 50% of the population belongs to the Ovambo tribe. **Languages:** Afrikaans common language, 32% German, and 7% English (official); several indigenous languages. **Religions:** 80%-90% Christian, 10%-20% indigenous religions.

• **GOVERNMENT Type:** republic. **Independence:** Mar. 21, 1990 (from South Africa). **Constitution:** Feb. 9, 1990; effective March 12, 1990. **National holiday:** Independence Day, Mar. 21. **Heads of Government:** H. Pohamba, president (since Mar. 2005); Nahas Angula, prime minister (since Mar. 2005). **Structure:** executive; bicameral legislature; judiciary.

• **ECONOMY Monetary unit:** Namibian dollar. **Budget:** (2008) *income:* $2.668 bil.; *expend.:* $2.896 bil. **G.D.P.:** $11.23 bil., $5,400 per capita (2008 est.). **Chief crops:** millet, sorghum, peanuts; livestock; fish. **Natural resources:** diamonds, copper, uranium, gold, lead. **Major industries:** meat packing, fish processing, dairy products, mining (copper, lead, zinc, diamonds, and uranium). **Labor force:** 667,000 (2008 est.); 47% agriculture, 20% industry and commerce, 33% services; 35% unemployment (1998 est.). **Exports:** $2.98 bil. (f.o.b., 2008 est.); diamonds, copper, gold, zinc, lead, uranium; meat, processed fish. **Imports:** $3.56 bil. (f.o.b., 2008 est.); foodstuffs, petroleum products, machinery and equipment, chemicals. **Major trading partners:** (2006) *exports:* 33.4% South Africa, 4% U.S.; *imports:* 85.2% South Africa, U.S.

The Kalahari desert, on the Namibian plateau, has been inhabited since ancient times by San hunter-gatherers. Various Nama and Bantu peoples migrated into the area more recently. British and Dutch explorers and traders began to penetrate Namibia in the 18th century.

In 1872 Great Britain occupied the area around Walvis Bay and in 1884 annexed it to the Cape Colony. Also in 1884 Germany claimed most of South-West Africa; negotiations between the two powers resulted in German acceptance of Britain's claim of Walvis Bay and British acceptance of Germany's claim to the rest of the coastal region with a sphere of influence in the interior.

During World War I, British troops from South Africa occupied South-West Africa in 1915. In 1920 South Africa received a League of Nations mandate to administer the area. In 1946 when the United Nations succeeded the League, the United Nations proposed that South Africa continue its administration under a U.N. trusteeship. South Africa refused and annexed South-West Africa.

The proposed U.N. trusteeship was revoked by the United Nations in 1966. At the same time, the South-West Africa People's Organization (SWAPO), operating from bases in Zambia and Angola, began guerrilla actions against South African troops in the region. In 1968 the United Nations formally renamed the territory Namibia and appointed an 11-nation council to supervise its affairs and devise a plan leading to independence.

In 1971 the International Court of Justice upheld the U.N.'s authority over Namibia and ruled that South Africa's continued occupation of the territory was illegal. In 1975 South Africa convened the Turnhalle Conference, which proposed a plan for Namibian independence based on the racial-separation principles of apartheid. This was rejected by the U.N. and in 1978 the U.N. Security Council approved Resolution 435, which called for a general cease-fire to be followed by U.N.-supervised elections.

In response, South Africa unilaterally held elections in Namibia, which were boycotted by SWAPO and other African organizations and rejected by the U.N. In 1982 South Africa declared it would enter into talks about the future of Namibia only after Cuban troops were withdrawn from Angola. In 1983 South Africa launched a major military operation against SWAPO forces in Angola. In October 1984 Angolan president dos Santos agreed to work out a plan for withdrawal of Cuban troops as part of a settlement in Namibia. In June 1985 South Africa granted limited local authority to a Namibian government made up of a coalition of parties, excluding SWAPO. In 1987 South African troops occupied southern Angola (to aid Angolan rebels), and in early 1988, fighting between South African troops and Namibian rebels in northern Namibia and southern Angola intensified.

A new round of talks on the future of Namibia among South Africa, Cuba, and Angola, began in 1988, and the three parties agreed on a plan for Namibian independence and a pullout of Cuban troops from Angola. In Jan. 1989 the Cuban withdrawal from Angola began. On Apr. 1, U.N. Resolution 435 went into effect in Namibia, and a U.N. peacekeeping force arrived to supervise the transition to independence. Elections were held in Nov. 1989: SWAPO leader Sam Nujoma won an overwhelming victory. A Western-style democratic constitution was adopted Feb. 16, 1990, and full independence came on Mar. 21. The first elections under the new constitution were held in Dec. 1994 with SWAPO gaining even stronger control of Parliament. In Dec. 1999 elections, Sam Nujoma won a third term as president with 77 percent of the vote while SWAPO took 76 percent of the votes for the National Assembly. Tourism and mining helped bring a modicum of prosperity in the following years. Nujoma left office in Mar. 2005 and was succeeded by his friend and co-founder of SWAPO in 1965, Hifikepunye Pohamba, who began land reform by confiscating white-owned farms.

▶ NAURU
Republic of Nauru

• **GEOGRAPHY Location:** central Pacific Ocean (0°32'S, 166°56'E), about 2,800 mi. (4,500 km) southwest of Hawaii. **Boundaries:** nearest neighbor is Banaba (Ocean Island), in Kiribati, about 185 mi. (300 km) to E. **Total area:** 8 sq. mi. (21 sq km). **Coastline:** 19 mi. (30 km). **Comparative area:** about one-tenth size of Washington, D.C. **Land use:** 0% arable land; 0% permanent crops; 100% other. **Major cities:** none as such; government offices in Yaren district.

• **People** Population: 14,019 (2009 est.). **Nationality:** noun—Nauruan(s) adjective—Nauruan. **Ethnic groups:** 58% Nauruan, 26% other Pacific Islander, 8% Chinese, 8% European. **Languages:** Nauruan, a distinct Pacific Island language (official); English widely understood and spoken and used for most government and commercial purposes. **Religions:** Christian (two-thirds Protestant, one-third Catholic).

• **Government** Type: republic. **Independence:** Jan. 31, 1968 (from U.N. trusteeship under Australia, New Zealand, and U.K.). **Constitution:** Jan. 29, 1968; amended May 1968. **National holiday:** Independence Day, Jan. 31. **Head of Government:** Marcus Stephen, president (since Dec. 2007). **Structure:** executive—president elected from and by Parliament for unfixed term; unicameral legislature; judiciary.

• **Economy** Monetary unit: Australian dollar. **Budget:** (2005 est.) *income:* $13.5 mil.; *expend.:* $13.5 mil. **G.D.P.:** $60 mil., $5,000 per capita (2005 est.). **Chief crops:** coconuts. **Natural resources:** phosphates. **Major industries:** phosphate mining (about 2 mil. tons per year), financial services, coconuts. **Labor force:** N.A.; 90% unemployment (2004 est.) **Exports:** $64,000 (f.o.b., 2005); phosphates. **Imports:** $20 mil. (c.i.f., 2004); food, fuel, manufactures, building materials, machinery. **Major trading partners:** (2006) *exports:* 63.7% South Africa, 7.6% South Korea, 6.6% Canada; *imports:* 43.8% South Korea, 36.2% Australia, 5.9% U.S., 4.3% Germany.

Nauru, formerly known as Pleasant Island, is an isolated island lying west of the Gilbert Islands. It became a German protectorate in 1888. After World War I, Nauru was administered by Australia under a League of Nations mandate. It was occupied by Japan throughout World War II. In 1947 it became a U.N. Trust Territory administered by Australia, and on Jan. 31, 1968, an independent republic. Nauru has a parliament of 18 members, who elect a prime minister and a cabinet.

Phosphate deposits used to account for almost all of Nauru's revenues, but reserves are now depleted. Trust funds created with phosphate income have also been spent down, leaving the government near bankruptcy and dependent on Australia for assistance. A campaign to encourage registration of offshore banks and corporations has done little to halt rapid deterioration in housing and services throughout Nauru.

▶ **NEPAL**
Kingdom of Nepal
• **Geography** Location: central Asia, in Himalayan mountain range. **Boundaries:** China to N, India to E, S, and W. **Total area:** 54,363 sq. mi. (147,181 sq km). **Coastline:** none. **Comparative area:** slightly larger than Arkansas. **Land use:** 20% arable land; negl. % permanent crops; 79% other. **Major cities:** Kathmandu (capital).

• **People** Population: 28,563,377 (July 2009 est.). **Nationality:** noun—Nepalese (sing. and pl.); adjective—Nepalese. **Ethnic groups:** Chhettri, Newars, Indians, Tibetans, Gurungs, Magars, Tamangs, Bhotias, Rais, Limbus, Sherpas. **Languages:** Nepali (official); 20 other languages divided into numerous dialects. **Religions:** 80.6% Hindu, 11% Buddhist, 4.2% Muslim; only official Hindu kingdom in world, although no sharp distinction between many Hindu and Buddhist groups.

• **Government** Type: federal democratic republic. **Constitution:** Jan. 15, 2007. **National holiday:** Republic Day, May 29; Democracy Day, April 24. **Heads of Government:** Ram Baran Yadav, president (since July 2008) Vacant, prime minister, Madhav Kumar Nepal resigned June 2010 . **Structure:** executive—prime minister appointed by king from leading party in parliament; bicameral legislature—upper house (National Assembly) consists of 60 members, 50 appointed by lower house, 10 by the king; judiciary.

• **Economy** Monetary unit: Nepalese rupee. **Budget:** (2008 est.) *income:* $1.7 bil.; *expend.:* $2.3 bil. **G.D.P.:** $31.09 bil., $1,100 per capita (2008 est.). **Chief crops:** rice, corn, wheat, sugarcane; milk, water buffalo meat. **Natural resources:** quartz, water, timber, hydroelectric potential, scenic beauty. **Major industries:** carpet and textiles, small rice, jute, sugar, and oilseed mills; cigarette and brick factories; tourism. **Labor force:** 14.6 mil. (2008 est.); 76% agriculture, 18% services, 6% industry; 46% unemployment (2008 est.). **Exports:** $868 mil. (f.o.b., 2008) (does not include unrecorded border trade with India); clothing, carpets, leather goods, jute goods, grain. **Imports:** $3.229 bil. (f.o.b., 2008); gold, petroleum products, fertilizer, machinery. **Major trading partners:** (2006) *exports:* 68% India, 12% U.S., 4% Germany; *imports:* 62% India, 4% China, 3% Indonesia.

The birthplace of Gautama Buddha (c. 600 B.C.), Nepal was for centuries a collection of principalities, inhabited by Tibeto-Burman peoples who mostly practiced Lamaistic Buddhism. In 1769 the country's three geographical zones—floodplain, foothills, and high mountains—were united under the Gurkhas, who made Hinduism the country's official religion. Nepal established treaty relations with Great Britain in 1792 and fought a border war with British India in 1814–16, but it was never incorporated into the British Empire.

A revolution in 1950 overthrew a government of heriditary rulers that had overthrown the Shah dynasty in the 19th century. King Tribuhavan (a Shah) was restored and tried to introduce democratic reforms, but his son Mahendra dissolved Parliament and introduced a tiered system of town, district, and national councils. Road and air links to India, Pakistan, and Tibet were improved, and Nepal began to emerge from its customary isolation. The successful climb of Mt. Everest by Sir Edmund Hillary and Tenzing Norgay in 1953 focused international attention on Nepal.

Mahendra was succeeded in 1972 by his son, Birendra. Antigovernment demonstrations in 1990 led to the shooting deaths of 63 civilians, so Birendra lifted a 30-year-old ban on political parties and ordered the constitution rewritten to establish multiparty democracy and human rights as essentials of the political system. The king retains control of the military and is still head of state.

The Nepali Congress Party formed the first government in 1991, but after 1994 a series of brief coalitions governed Nepal until the May 1999 elections permitted the Nepali Congress Party to govern without a coalition. But prime minister Krishna Prasad Bhattarai proved too ill to deal with Nepal's depressed economy and with the Maoist guerrilla force ("People's War") afflicting Nepal since 1996; he resigned in March 2000 to be replaced by Giriji Prasad Koirala.

On June 1, 2001 Crown Prince Dipendra murdered his parents and eight other members of the royal family, after which he shot himself. His uncle became King Gyanendra. In the turmoil, the Maoist rebels increased their depredations. The accession of Sher Bahadur Deuba as prime minister in July 2001 brought a harder line against the Maoist rebels: no negotiations before surrender. In Oct. 2002, King Gyanendra suspended the constitution, appointed Lokendra Chand as interim prime minister to open dialogue with the Maoists. Secret talks and quickly-broken truces led nowhere. Chand resigned in May 2002 with the rebels holding about 40 percent of the country. Surya Bahadur Thapa replaced him, only to resign in May 2004. In Feb. 2005 Gyandera seized power and cracked down on all dissent as he vowed to end the Maoist rebellion, but in April 2006, after weeks of angry pro-democracy protests, the king handed back power to parliament. In June, the Maoist rebels agreed to lay down their arms and joined the government in 2007. In May 2008 the monarchy was abolished and in August parliament elected Maoist leader Prachanda, known as "the fierce one", to be prime minister. In May 2009 he resigned over the refusal of the president to fire the leading general, who had refused to integrate Maoist troops into the military. In June 2010 his successor resigned and a stalemate over who would be the next prime minister lasted for months.

▶ **NETHERLANDS**
Kingdom of The Netherlands
• **GEOGRAPHY Location:** western Europe. **Boundaries:** North Sea to N and W, Germany to E, Belgium to S. **Total area:** 14,413 sq. mi. (37,330 sq km). **Coastline:** 280 mi. (451 km). **Comparative area:** slightly less than twice the size of New Jersey. **Land use:** 22% arable land; 0.7% permanent crops; 77% other. **Major cities:** Amsterdam (capital); Rotterdam; The Hague; Utrecht; Eindhoven. The Hague is the seat of government.
• **PEOPLE Population:** 16,783,092 (July 2010 est.). **Nationality:** noun—Dutchman (men), Dutchwoman (women); adjective—Dutch. **Ethnic groups:** 83% Dutch, 17% other (9% of which are Moroccans, Turks, Antilleans, Surinamese and Indonesians). **Languages:** Dutch, Frisian (official); English widely spoken. **Religions:** 31% Roman Catholic, 21% Protestant, 40% unaffiliated, 3% Muslim.
• **GOVERNMENT Type:** constitutional monarchy. **Independence:** 1579 (from Spain). **Constitution:** 1814; last amended 2002. **National holiday:** Queen's Day, Apr. 30. **Heads of Government:** Beatrix Wilhelmina Armgard, queen (since Apr. 1980); Dr. Jan Peter Balkenende, prime minister (since July 2002). **Structure:** executive—queen is constitutional monarch, prime minister is head of government; bicameral parliament; independent judiciary.
• **ECONOMY Monetary unit:** euro. **Budget:** (2009 est.) *income:* $335.4 bil.; *expend.:* $372.5 bil. **G.D.P.:** $654.9 bil., $39,200 per capita (2009 est.). **Chief crops:** grains, potatoes, sugar beets; livestock. **Natural recources:** natural gas, crude oil, fertile soil. **Major industries:** agro-industries, metal and engineering products, electrical machinery and equipment. **Labor force:** 8.33 mil. (2009 est.); 76% services, 21% industry, 3% agriculture (2005); 4.5% unemployment (2008). **Exports:** $397.6 bil. (2009 est.); machinery and equipment, chemicals, fuels, food and tobacco.

Imports: $358.9 bil. (2009 est.); machinery and transport equipment, chemicals, foodstuffs, fuels, clothing. **Major trading partners:** (2008) *exports:* 25.4% Germany, 13.7% Belgium, 8.9% France, 8.8% U.K., 5.2% Italy; *imports:* 25.4% Germany, 13.7% Belgium, 8.9% France, 8.8% U.K., 5.2% Italy.

Historically, the name Netherlands referred to the low-lying areas of the Holy Roman Empire near the mouths of the Rhine, Meuse, and Scheldt rivers. The Habsburg emperor Charles V willed these territories to his son Philip II of Spain in 1555, but by the end of the 16th century, the northern provinces—the Union of Utrecht, formed in 1579 by William the Silent, of the House of Orange—won their independence in a war that was both religious (Calvinist vs. Catholic) and constitutional (aristocratic/patrician vs. foreign monarchy). The independence of the Netherlands was recognized in the Treaty of Westphalia, which ended the Thirty Years' War in 1648.

Dutch prosperity, founded on the woolen trade with England, grew tremendously through trade and seafaring under the 17th-century republic. The Netherlands amassed a world empire, including the Indonesian archipelago, the island of Sri Lanka (then Ceylon), South Africa, Suriname, parts of the West Indies, and the Hudson valley in New Amsterdam (later New York); in addition to monopolized Western trade with Japan after 1637.

The Netherlands were incorporated into the Napoleonic empire. At the Congress of Vienna in 1815, a Dutch monarchy was established, which included Belgium until 1830. Land drainage and reclamation programs maintained the prosperity of the country's small-scale agriculture, while trade and colonial revenues were increasingly supplemented by industrial development in the 19th century. Dutch prosperity and the country's strategic position gave the Netherlands extraordinary influence and prestige in European affairs into the 20th century, despite the country's small size. It remained neutral in World War I.

Germany invaded the Netherlands in May 1940, taking control of the country after five days of fighting. Preparing to incorporate Holland into the Third Reich, Hitler installed a Nazi civilian government that ruled through totalitarian exploitation and cooperated in the persecution of Jews. But Queen Wilhelmina and the Dutch government escaped to England and maintained a government-in-exile throughout the war.

The final stages of fighting on the western front inflicted severe damage on the country, while in Asia the recovery of Indonesia from Japan led to a declaration of independence under Sukarno. Marshall Plan aid was intended to support a domestic postwar recovery; an equal amount was spent by the Dutch government in an attempt to recapture control of Indonesia before that country's independence was recognized in 1949.

Devastated by World War II and the loss of its empire, the country faced a bleak future. Forced to turn its attention to recovery at home, the Netherlands worked through the Benelux (Belgium, Netherlands, Luxembourg) union (founded in 1944) and the Common Market to create another European "economic miracle" between the early 1950s and the 1970s. The older bases of the economy—commerce, maritime industry, dairy farming, and flower farming—were expanded and modernized; Rotterdam was rebuilt to become an important port. Newer industries, such as chemicals and oil refining, electronics, and steel, relied on the country's highly skilled and productive labor force to turn imported raw materials into finished high-value exports. A huge impoundment project turned the Zuider Zee into a new province, increasing the country's land area by 10 percent.

This postwar prosperity has been based in large part on political stability. A coalition of the Catholic State party and the Labor (formerly Social Democratic) party governed for 10 years under Premier Willem Drees. After 1958 cabinets normally were formed from coalitions headed by three Christian parties (merged in 1980 to form the United Christian Appeal) or by the Liberal party; all pursued essentially the same policies of free enterprise, comprehensive social welfare programs, high taxation, and social liberalism.

From 1982 to 1989 a coalition of Christian Democrats and Liberals provided a cabinet headed by Prime Minister Ruud Lubbers; after 1989 the coalition has been of Christian Democrats and Labor. In 1994 Wim Kok, head of Labor, became prime minister, the first government to exclude the Christian Democrats since 1945.

Just 10 days before the May 15, 2002 elections, radical libertarian and anti-Muslim newcomer Pim Fortuyn was assassinated by an animal-rights activist. The election proved a nightmare for Kok's center-left coalition: the Christian Democrats topped the polls, followed by Fortuyn's party. These two put together an inexperienced coalition under CD prime minister Jan Peter Balkenende, but it lasted only three months. Balkendale cobbled together a new coalition after 2003 elections.

In May 2005, voters rejected the E.U. constitution, and in 2006 the government again collapsed over immigration. A new coalition took office in Feb. 2007 and collapsed again in early 2010. The June election ended in a stalemate leaving the old government to carry on.

▶ **NEW ZEALAND**
● **GEOGRAPHY Location:** South Pacific Ocean about 1,100 mi. (1,750 km) SE of Australia. **Boundaries:** South Pacific Ocean to N, E, and S; Tasman Sea to. W. **Total area:** 103,738 sq. mi. (268,680 sq km). **Coastline:** 9,406 mi. (15,134 km). **Comparative area:** about size of Colorado. **Land use:** 6% arable land; 6% permanent crops; 88% other. **Major cities:** Wellington (capital); Auckland; Christchurch; Hamilton; Napier-Hastings. ● **PEOPLE Population:** 4,252,277 (July 2010 est.). **Nationality:** noun—New Zealander(s); adjective—New Zealand. **Ethnic groups:** 70% New Zealand European, 8% Maori, 8% mixed, 4.4% Pacific Islander, 8% Asian and other. **Languages:** English, Maori, sign language (official). **Religions:** 24% Anglican, 18% Presbyterian, 15% Roman Catholic, 5% Methodist, 2% Baptist, 3% other Protestant, 33% none or unspecified. ● **GOVERNMENT Type:** parliamentary democracy. **Independence:** Sept. 26, 1907 (from U.K.). **Constitution:** no formal, written constitution; consists of various documents, including certain acts of U.K. and New Zealand Parliaments. Constitution Act 1986 was to have come into force Jan. 1, 1987, but has not been enacted. **National holiday:** Waitangi Day, Feb. 6.; ANZAC Day, April 25. **Heads of Government:** Anand Satyanand, governor-general (since Aug. 2006); John Key, prime minister (since Aug. 2008). **Structure:** executive— governor-general represents queen, prime minister is head of government; unicameral legislature; judiciary.

● **ECONOMY Monetary unit:** New Zealand dollar. **Budget:** (2009 est.) *income:* $46.54 bil.; *expend.:* $55.56 bil. **G.D.P.:** $114.9 bil., $27,300 per capita (2008 est.). **Chief crops:** wheat, barley, potatoes, fruits; wool, meat, dairy. **Natural resources:** natural gas, iron ore, sand, coal, timber. **Major industries:** food processing, wood and paper products, textiles, aluminum smelting, tourism. **Labor force:** 2.29 mil. (2009); 74% services, 19% industry, 7% agriculture (2006); 3.5% unemployment (2007). **Exports:** $26.25 bil. (2009 est.); wool, lamb, mutton, beef, fruit, fish. **Imports:** $24.29 bil. (2009 est.); machinery and equipment, vehicles and aircraft, petroleum, consumer goods, plastics. **Major trading partners:** (2008) *exports:* 23.2% Australia, 10.1% U.S., 8.4% Japan, 5.9% China; *imports:* 18.1% Australia, 13.2% China, 9.5% U.S., 8.3% Japan, 4.7% Singapore, 4.4% Malaysia.

New Zealand was settled by Maori voyagers from Polynesia from about the ninth century a.d. The first European to sight it was the Dutch explorer Abel Tasman, in 1642; he named it, but did not take possession. In 1769, Capt. James Cook visited and claimed it for Britain. The first British missionaries arrived in 1814, and New Zealand became a full-fledged British colony in 1841. By the Treaty of Waitangi in 1840, the Maoris recognized Queen Victoria's protection and agreed to admit British settlers; in return, they were guaranteed possession of their lands. But in a series of bloody wars lasting until 1870, the Maoris were displaced from lands devoted to the expanding British settlements.

As a result of their defeat and of introduced diseases, the Maori population dwindled to about 40,000 by the 1890s. Their numbers have since recovered to over 400,000, and in recent decades, the Maoris have become a cohesive culture and significant political force, directly electing several members of Parliament. In 1985, the Waitangi Tribunal was given power to hear Maori claims for repayment for land taken without compensation since the 1840 treaty. Large financial settlements were negotiated by the government.

New Zealand was one of the first nations to introduce universal adult suffrage (1893) and to establish a comprehensive welfare state. Legislation beginning in 1898 regulates labor practices, and mandates universal old-age pensions, public sector medical care, and other social services. Since 1907, the country has been an independent member of the British Commonwealth. The crown is represented by a governor-general; government is drawn from a parliament and headed by a prime minister. Since the 1930s, government has alternated between the National and Labour parties.

New Zealand troops fought on the side of the Allies in both world wars, with U.N. forces in Korea, and with the U.S. in Vietnam. In 1951, New Zealand joined Australia and the U.S. in the ANZUS mutual-defense treaty, but was excluded from it in 1986 after denying port facilities to ships carrying nuclear weapons. New Zealand has also objected strenuously to French testing of nuclear weapons in the South Pacific and pressed for a comprehensive international nuclear test ban treaty.

Upon its election in 1984, the Labour government launched an economic restructuring program to transform the country from a protected agrarian economy to an open free-market economy. This program, continued by the National Party, which regained power in 1990, eliminated government subsidies, cut spending, liberalized imports, deregulated financial markets, reduced tax rates, and deregulated the labor market. The reforms resulted in an expanding and competitive economy with low inflation, and, in 1993–94, the first budget surplus in 18 years. The government responded in 1995 by cutting taxes again. 1996 election results, however, forced the Nationalist Party into coalition with the new populist/zenophobic New Zealand First Party. The new government now had to defer tax cuts, halt sales of state-owned businesses, and increase spending on health and education. The coalition lasted 19 months but the government did not fall as votes of confidence in 1998 and 1999 permitted continuance of a minority government headed by New Zealand's first female prime minister, Jenny Shipley. Nine years of National Party rule ended in 1999 as a coalition government of Labor and Alliance established Helen Clark as prime minister. In June 2001 elections, the Nationalists garnered only 27 seats, their worse showing in their 66-year history. Clark's Labour Party gained 52 seats. Without a formal coalition, an alliance with the Greens yielded exactly 60 of the 120 votes. The Clark government was able to carry out an almost complete severance from the U.K. and Clark remained in power until 2008 when John Key was elected.

▶ NICARAGUA
Republic of Nicaragua
● **GEOGRAPHY Location:** Central American isthmus. **Boundaries:** Honduras to N, Caribbean Sea to E, Costa Rica to S, Pacific Ocean to W. **Total area:** 49,998 sq. mi. (129,494 sq km). **Coastline:** 565 mi. (910 km). **Comparative area:** slightly smaller than New York State. **Land use:** 15% arable land; 2% permanent crops; 83% other. **Major cities:** Managua (capital); León; Granada; Masaya; Chinandega.
● **PEOPLE Population:** 5,891,199 (2009 est.). **Nationality:** noun—Nicaraguan(s); adjective—Nicaraguan. **Ethnic groups:** 69% mestizo, 17% white, 9% black, 5% Amerindian. **Languages:** Spanish (official); English- and Amerindian-speaking minorities on Atlantic coast. **Religions:** 73% Roman Catholic, 16.5% Protestant 2% other, 8.5% none.
● **GOVERNMENT Type:** republic. **Independence:** Sept. 15, 1821 (from Spain). **Constitution:** Jan. 9, 1987 with reforms in 1995, 2000 and 2005. **National holiday:** Independence Day, Sept. 15. **Head of Government:** Daniel Ortega, president (since Jan. 2007). **Structure:** executive branch; unicameral legislature; judiciary.
● **ECONOMY Monetary unit:** córdoba. **Budget:** (2008 est.) **income:** $1.271 bil.; **expend.:** $1.593 bil. **G.D.P.:** $16.83 bil., $2,900 per capita (2008 est.). **Chief crops:** cotton, bananas, coffee, sugarcane, rice, corn, beans. **Natural resources:** gold, silver, copper, tungsten, lead. **Major industries:** food processing, chemicals, metal products. **Labor force:** 2.322 mil. (2008); 52% services, 29% agriculture, 19% industry (2006); 5.6% unemployment (2007). **Exports:** $3.183 bil. (f.o.b., 2008 est.); coffee, seafood, cotton, tobacco, sugar, gold, bananas. **Imports:** $5.279 bil. (f.o.b., 2008 est.); consumer goods, machinery and equipment, petroleum products. **Major trading partners:** (2006) **exports:** 65.2% U.S., 6.9% El Salvador, 3.8% Honduras; **imports:** 20.1% U.S., 14% Mexico, 9.4% Venezuela, 6.9% Costa Rica, 5.4% Guatemala, 4.3% China.

Nicaragua gained independence from Spain in 1821 and formed a constituent part of the United Provinces of Central America in 1823. With the dissolution of the federation in 1838, Nicaragua became an independent republic. Throughout the United Provinces, an intra-elite struggle between Liberal and Conservative factions defined the political arena during the early 19th century. Nicaraguan Liberals invited the adventurer William Walker of Tennessee to take their part against their Conservative rivals in 1855. Walker took control of the country in 1856 but was driven out by a combined Central American force the following year.

The Conservatives held power in Nicaragua until 1893, when a planters' revolt brought Liberal José Santos Zelaya to the presidency. Because of Zelaya's intention to pursue an isthmian canal project, the U.S. government intervened in support of a Conservative uprising. The United States sent marines to Nicaragua in 1909, and Zelaya resigned in 1910. The marines occupied the country during 1909–25 and 1926–33.

Refusing to abide by a political settlement between the U.S. government and Nicaraguan Liberal forces in 1927, Augusto César Sandino, led a guerrilla war against U.S. occupation forces. In 1934, Anastasio Somoza García, head of the Nicaraguan National Guard, had Sandino assassinated and took over the presidency in 1937. Somoza and his sons Luis and Anastasio Somoza Debayle controlled Nicaragua until 1979.

A broad coalition of groups led by the Sandinista National Liberation Front (FSLN) overthrew the Somoza dictatorship in 1979. Elections were held in 1984 for the presidency, vice presidency, and a constituent assembly. The Sandinistas won the election for the presidency, captured a working majority in the National Assembly, and wrote a new constitution in 1987.

Between 1981 and 1990, the United States actively, but covertly supported Contra rebels fighting the Sandinista regime in a civil war that cost the country dearly. In 1989, Pres. Daniel Ortega announced elections for early 1990, which he lost in a stunning upset to Violeta Barrios de Chamorro, who headed a 17-party coalition, the United Nicaragua Opposition. Since then, the transition has been relatively peaceful, highlighted by Gen. Humberto Ortega's uneventful transfer of command of the army in 1995, the first peaceful transfer in Nicaragua's history. In late 1996 presidential elections the Liberal Alliance candidate, Arnoldo Alemán, won a decisive victory over former president Daniel Ortega and voters opted for a return to free enterprise and closer ties with the U.S. Limitations on the Aleman government's free enterprising policies were shown by student protests and transport workers' strikes which forced the government to boost university spending while cutting back fuel taxes. In Nov. 2000 the Sandinistas and Daniel Ortega were again defeated as Liberal Alliance candidate Enrique Bolanos Geyer carried 54 percent of the presidential vote. At the end of 2006, however, Ortega made a comeback, winning the election by promising to make no radical changes in economic policy.

▶ NIGER
Republic of Niger
● **GEOGRAPHY Location:** landlocked country in western Africa. **Boundaries:** Algeria and Libya to N, Chad to E, Nigeria to S, Benin, Burkina Faso to SW, Mali to W. **Total area:** 489,189 sq. mi. (1,267,000 sq km). **Coastline:** none. **Comparative**

area: slighlty less than twice the size of Texas. **Land use:** 11.4% arable land; negl.% permanent crops; 88% other. **Major cities:** Niamey (capital); Zinder; Maradi; Tahoua; Agadez.

• **PEOPLE Population:** 15,306,252 (2009 est.). **Nationality:** noun—Nigerien(s); adjective—Nigerien. **Ethnic groups:** 55.4% Hausa, 21% Djerma, Tuareg, Pechl, Kanouri, Manga. **Languages:** French (official), Hausa, Djerma. **Religions:** 80% Muslim, 20% indigenous beliefs and Christians.

• **GOVERNMENT Type:** republic. **Independence:** Aug. 3, 1960 (from France). **Constitution:** revised May 12, 1996 and July 18, 1999. **National holiday:** Republic Day, Dec. 18. **Heads of Government:** Salou Djibo, chairman of the Supreme Council for the Restoration of Democracy, and a leader of the military coup that deposed President Tandja (since Feb. 2010); Mahamadou Danda, prime minister (since Feb. 2010). **Structure:** executive; unicameral legislature; judiciary.

• **ECONOMY Monetary unit:** Communauté Financière Africaine (CFA) franc. **Budget:** (2002 est.) *income:* $320 mil.; *expend.:* $320 mil. **G.D.P.:** $9.784 bil., $700 per capita (2008 est.). **Chief crops:** cowpeas, cotton, peanuts, millet, sorghum, cassava, rice; goats, sheep, cattle. **Natural resources:** uranium, coal, iron ore, tin, phosphates. **Major industries:** uranium mining, cement, brick, textiles. **Labor force:** 70,000 receive regular wages or salaries; 90% agriculture; 6% industry and commerce, 4% government. **Exports:** $428 mil. (f.o.b., 2006 est.); uranium ore, livestock, cowpeas, onions. **Imports:** $800 mil. (f.o.b., 2006); consumer goods, primary materials, machinery, vehicles and parts, petroleum, cereals. **Major trading partners:** (2006) *exports:* 35% France, 26% U.S., 18% Nigeria, 11.3% Russia; *imports:* 14.1% U.S., 12% France, 7.8% China, 7.7% Nigeria, 7.7% French Polynesia, 4.9% Cote d'Ivoire.

Most of Niger's territory is dominated by the Sahara and the Sahel (the "shore" of the desert), which have spread southward since prehistoric times. Much of the population lives in the narrow fertile belt south of the Niger River. Much of Niger was incorporated during medieval times in large empires centered in neighboring Mali, Chad, and Nigeria.

In the 18th century, Tuaregs migrating from the northern desert began to form tribal confederations in Niger. They united with local Hausa peoples to wage war against the Fulani empire. In the 19th century, British and German explorers explored the region. In the European rivalry that followed, the French, began to dominate Niger by 1900; Niger became a French colony in 1922, administered from Dakar, Senegal.

In 1946 the people of Niger, in common with other peoples in French Africa, were granted French citizenship, and limited self-rule began. This local autonomy was expanded in 1956, and in 1958 Niger became an autonomous state within the French Overseas Community. Full independence followed on Aug. 3, 1960; Niger maintained close ties to France.

Hamani Diori was elected Niger's first president in 1960, reelected in 1965 and 1970. He was overthrown in 1974 in a military coup led by Lt. Col. Seyni Kountche. In 1987, Pres. Kountche died and was succeeded by Col. Ali Saibou, who was elected president by the Supreme Military Council. The country began moving toward democracy again in 1989, and a new constitution was approved in 1992. Mahame Ousmane was elected president in 1993, but he and Prime Minister

Hama Amadou were ousted in a violent military coup in Jan. 1996. The leader of the coup, Lt. Col. Ibrahim Barré, who criticized Ousmane's handling of the Taureg Liberation Front, became the new president. He survived an assasination attempt in Jan. 1998, but fell to another in April 1999. Junior army officers formed a junta, supported by all the civilian opposition parties, maintaining Ibrahim Mayaki in his post as prime minister. The junta promised a "nine-month transition", and presidential elections were held in Nov. 1999 in which Tandja Mamadou defeated former premier Mohamadou Issoufou. In 2004–05 a sustained drought brought famine and many deaths. In 2007 an insurgency began pitting a Taureg ethnic group against the government for control of large amounts of uranium found in the Taureg region. Tándja's government was overthrown in Feb. 2010 by military strongman Salou Djibo.

▶ NIGERIA
Federal Republic of Nigeria

• **GEOGRAPHY Location:** western coast of Africa. **Boundaries:** Niger to N, Cameroon to E, Gulf of Guinea to S, Benin to W. **Total area:** 356,668 sq. mi. (923,770 sq km). **Coastline:** 530 mi. (853 km). **Comparative area:** slightly more than twice the size of California. **Land use:** 31% arable land; 3% permanent crops; 66% other. **Major cities:** Abuja (capital); Lagos; Ibadan; Kano; Ogbomosho.

• **PEOPLE Population:** 152,217,341 (2010 est.). **Nationality:** noun—Nigerian(s); adjective—Nigerian. **Ethnic groups:** over 50 ethnic groups, inlcuding 29% Hausa and Fulani, 21% Yoruba, 18% Ibo, 10% Ijaw, Kanuri, Ibibio, Tiv. **Languages:** English (official); Hausa, Yoruba, Ibo, Fulani. **Religions:** 50% Muslim, 40% Christian, 10% indigenous beliefs.

• **GOVERNMENT Type:** federal republic. **Independence:** Oct. 1, 1960 (from U.K.). **Constitution:** New constitution adopted in 1999. **National holiday:** Independence Day, Oct. 1. **Head of Government:** Goodluck Jonathan, president (since May 2010). **Structure:** executive; bicameral legislature; judiciary.

• **ECONOMY Monetary unit:** naira. **Budget:** (2009 est.) *income:* $10.49 bil.; *expend:* $18.08 bil. **G.D.P.:** $357.2 bil., $2,400 per capita (2009 est.). **Chief crops:** peanuts, cocoa, palm oil, rubber, corn; goats, sheep, cattle, pigs; fish. **Natural resources:** crude oil, tin, columbite, iron ore, coal. **Major industries:** crude oil, coal, tin, columbite; palm oil, peanuts, cotton, rubber; textiles, cement, building materials. **Labor force:** 47.33 mil. (2009 est.); 70% agriculture; 10% industry, 20% services; 5.8% unemployment (2006 est.). **Exports:** $45.43 bil. (2009 est.); 95% petroleum and petroleum products, cocoa, rubber. **Imports:** $42.1 bil. (2009 est.); machinery, chemicals, transportation equipment, manufactured goods, food and animals. **Major trading partners:** (2008) *exports:* 42% U.S., 9.5% Brazil, 9% India, 7.3% Spain; *imports:* 16.1% China, 11.3% Netherlands, 9.8% U.S., 6.2% U.K., 6.1% South Korea, 5.1% France, 4.4% Germany.

The Nok culture of central Nigeria (500–200 B.C.) was one of the richest and most advanced ancient civilizations in western Africa. Around A.D. 1000, the Muslim Kanem civilization expanded into northern Nigeria; by the 14th century, the amalgamated kingdom of Kanem-Bornu took northern Nigeria as its political center, from which it dominated the Sahel and developed trade routes stretching throughout northern Africa and as far as Europe and the Middle East. During the 15th and 16th centuries, the Hausa Songhai empire rose to power. It was overthrown by the Fulani Muslim leader Uthman Dan Fodio, who created the Sokoto caliphate.

Southern Nigeria is dominated by the Yoruba, whose Oyo kingdom, centered at Ife, became a major power by A.D. 1000. Oyo gave rise to the Benin civilization, which flourished from the 15th to the 18th centuries and is famous for its brass, bronze, and ivory sculpture.

The Portuguese established trading stations on the Benin coast in the 15th century; initially, trade relations were cordial, and Benin became well-known in Europe as a powerful and advanced kingdom. With the rise of the slave trade (which began with the cooperation of the Benin kings, who brought slaves from the interior), relations became hostile, and Benin declined under European pressure. The Dutch, British, and other Europeans competed strenuously with Portugal for control of the slave trade, and by the 18th century, most of the coastal region of Nigeria was under British control. By the turn of the 19th century, Britain suppressed the slave trade; slaves captured aboard European ships were transported by the British to Freetown in Sierra Leone.

The British traded with Nigerians for agricultural and forest products and commenced exploration of the Niger River. Lagos came under British control in 1851, and in 1861 Nigeria was made a British colony. Despite native resistance the colony was expanded in 1906 to include territory east of the Niger River, which was called the Protectorate of Southern Nigeria, The two areas were administratively joined in 1914.

During the 1920s Britain began to respond to Nigerian demands for self-rule. In 1946 the colony was divided into three regions, each with an advisory assembly. In 1954 the colony was reorganized as the Nigerian Federation, and the assemblies were given more authority. Sir Akubar Tafawa Balewa became Nigeria's first prime minister.

The 1960s were marked by a struggle for political dominance among the major ethnic groups of Nigeria, including the Ibo (or Igbo), Yoruba, Hausa, and Fulani. Attempts to partition the country on tribal lines for administrative purposes provoked controversy, and charges of corruption and fraud in elections held in 1964 and 1965 led to violence and rioting.

In January 1966 civil war broke out when a group of Ibo army officers overthrew the central government. Prime Minister Balewa was killed, along with many other political leaders. Gen. Johnson Aguiyi-Ironsi, leader of the Ibo forces, took control of the government. Aguiyi-Ironsi abolished the country's federal structure and set up a strong central government, dominated by the Ibo. Anti-Ibo riots broke out in the north, and many Ibo were massacred. In July 1966 Aguiyi-Ironsi was assassinated by a group of northern army officers. Army Chief of Staff Yakubu Gowon became head of a new military government. In 1967 Gowon reapportioned Nigeria into 12 states. The Eastern Region rejected this plan and seceded from Nigeria to form the independent state of Biafra, provoking a civil war that lasted until January 1970, when Biafra was rejoined with Nigeria. An estimated one million Biafrans, mostly Ibos, died in the war.

Gowon tried to rebuild the Eastern Region and create a harmonious multitribal government, but he was overthrown in a coup in 1975. His successor was assassinated in 1976 and succeeded by Lt. Gen. Olusegun Obasanjo who increased the number of states from 12 to 19 and promised a return to civilian rule. Shehu Shagari was elected president in 1979 and reelected in 1983, but in Dec. 1983 the military again intervened.

Nigeria's crude oil resources fueled the economy and made it attractive for foreign investment. During the 1970s, petroleum exports helped Nigeria recover from the Biafran War. But corruption and overspending of projected petroleum revenues led to an economic crisis in the early 1980s as oil prices collapsed worldwide. Inflation, unemployment, and food shortages led to rioting in major population centers in 1986. And in 1987, religious violence broke out between the Christian south and the Muslim north.

The government of Maj. Gen. Ibrahim Babangida responded by announcing plans for a new constitution, various economic austerity measures, and the restoration of civilian rule by 1992. He also limited the number of political parties and dictated both party platforms in National Assembly elections held in 1992, and in 1993 he annulled the results of the presidential election, which international monitors said would have been won by opposition leader Moshood K. Abiola, who was taken prisoner for the "treason" of declaring himself the election winner. Babangida resigned in Aug. 1993, but his self-appointed successor was ousted in a November 1993 coup by Defense Minister Sani Abacha.

Abacha's tyranny survived until his death in June 1998. A "transitional" military government led by army chief of staff, Abdusalem Abubakar, freed political prisoners, held local, state, and national elections, and turned over power, May 29, 1999 to the first popularly-elected president in 16 years, former general and once military ruler, Olusegun Obasanjo. The new government faced formidable problems: increased Muslim-Christian violence as northern states attempted to impose Sharia (Koranic law); civil disorder and rioting in the face of increased fuel prices.

In July 2000, violence and bloodshed over the imposition of Sharia increased. Attempts to meet I.M.F. loan conditions, such as ending subsidies which kept oil prices low or reducing government payrolls, provoked riots and strikes. Amidst religious, ethnic, and economic turmoil, Pres. Obasanjo (the first civilian president after almost 20 years of military rule) won a second term in 2003. But in 2007, a new president, Umaru Yar'Adua, was elected although observers criticized the elections for fraud and corruption.

Nigeria is one of the world's leading suppliers of oil, but the people are among the poorest in Africa. In 2006 rebel forces (MEND) from the oil-producing regions began guerilla attacks on refineries and pipelines. In 2008 they initiated attacks against facilities of the major foreign oil companies. Sectarian violence in the north began again and in the oil regions continued unabated.

▶ NORWAY
Kingdom of Norway

• GEOGRAPHY **Location:** western Scandinavian peninsula, northern Europe. **Boundaries:** Norwegian Sea to N and W, Russian Federation, Finland to NE, Sweden to E, North Sea to S and W. **Total**

area: 125,182 sq. mi. (323,802 sq km). **Coastline**: 13,626 mi. (21,925 km)—2,125 mi. (3,419 km) mainland; 1,500 mi. (2,413 km) large islands; 10,002 mi. (16,093 km) long fjords, numerous small islands, and minor indentations. **Comparative area**: slightly larger than New Mexico. **Land use:** 3% arable land; negl.% permanent crops; n97% other. **Major cities:** Oslo (capital); Bergen; Trondheim; Stavanger; Kristiansand.

• **PEOPLE Population:** 4,676,305 (July 2010 est.). **Nationality:** noun—Norwegian(s); adjective—Norwegian. **Ethnic groups:** Norwegian (Nordic, Alpine, Baltic), 20,000 Lapps (Sami). **Languages:** Norwegian (official), Lapp- and Finnish-speaking minorities. **Religions:** 86% Church of Norway, 1% Pentacostal, 1% Roman Catholic, 2.4% other Christian, 2% Muslim, 8% other.

• **GOVERNMENT Type:** constitutional monarchy. **Independence:** Oct. 26, 1905 (from Sweden). **Constitution:** May 17, 1814, and modified in 1884. **National holiday:** Constitution Day, May 17. **Heads of Government:** Harald V, king (since Jan. 1991); Jens Stoltenberg, prime minister (since Oct. 2005). **Structure:** executive—prime minister heads government; unicameral legislature—for certain purposes, STORTING divides itself into two chambers and elects 25 percent of its members to an upper house; judiciary.

• **ECONOMY Monetary unit:** Norwegian kroner. **Budget:** (2009 est.) *income:* $206.9 bil.; *expend.:* $169 bil. **G.D.P.:** $273.1 bil., $58,600 per capita (2008 est.). **Chief crops:** oats, feed grains; beef, milk; fish (among worlds top ten fishing nations). **Natural resources:** crude oil, copper, natural gas, pyrites, nickel. **Major industries:** petroleum and gas, food processing, shipbuilding. **Labor force:** 2.6 mil. (2009 est.); 74% services, 22% industry, 4% agriculture, forestry and fishing; 3.9% unemployment (1999). **Exports:** $122 bil. (2009 est.); petroleum and petroleum products, metals, chemicals, ships, fish. **Imports:** $64.5 bil. (2009 est.); machinery and equipment, chemicals, metals, foodstuffs. **Major trading partners:** (2008) *exports:* 27% U.K., 12% Germany, 10% Netherlands, 8% France, 6% Sweden, 6% U.S.; *imports:* 15% Sweden, 14% Germany, 7% Denmark, 6% U.K., 6% China, 5% U.S., 4% Netherlands.

The Viking age began in 793 with the sack of Lindisfarne in Ireland. By the 10th century, Norse and Danish Vikings had touched in almost every navigable river of Western Europe from Germany to Spain. In addition to coastal raiding, the Norse were beginning the first open-ocean voyages from Europe, sailing direct to Iceland (800 miles) and even to Greenland (2,200 miles), which they colonized in the 10th century.

At the beginning of the 10th century, Harold I united the petty kingdoms of western Scandinavia and extended his realm as far as the Orkney and Shetland islands. Viking nobles fleeing from his conquests consoled the Norse duchy of Normandy in France. Christianity was established under Olaf II at the beginning of the 11th century.

Under Magnus VI (1263–80), medieval Norway reached the height of its power and prosperity. Norwegian independence ended with the accession in 1319 of Magnus VII, who was king of Sweden as well. Under the Kalmar Union of 1397, the three kingdoms of Scandinavia were merged under Danish control; Norway ceased to exist as a nation-state and was governed by the Danes for the following four centuries.

In 1814 Denmark, which had sided with France in the Napoleonic wars, was forced by the victorious powers to cede Norway to Sweden. Under Sweden's military control Norway attempted to establish its own monarchy. The attempt failed, but in 1815 Sweden acknowledged the independence of Norway in perpetual union with the Swedish Crown.

Relations between Norway and Sweden remained strained throughout the 19th century. In 1905 the Norwegian legislature, the Storting, declared the union void and deposed Swedish King Oscar II as king of Norway. Sweden acquiesced, and Prince Charles of Denmark was enthroned as king of Norway, ruling as Haakon VII for 52 years.

During the 19th century, large numbers of Norwegians emigrated to North America. A rising tide of cultural nationalism was expressed in the flourishing Norwegian literature and art, and in Arctic exploration. In the 20th century, industrialization, aided by the development of hydroelectric power, began to supplement Norway's traditional economic mainstays of fishing and seafaring.

Norway remained neutral during World War I and was relatively unaffected by the postwar upheavals. Norway attempted to remain neutral in World War II as well but was invaded and occupied by German troops in April 1940. The king and government fled to London and established a government-in-exile. The Norwegian merchant marine fleet was largely transferred to Great Britain and contributed to the Allied cause in the North Atlantic. At home, resistance grew to the collaborationist government of the Fascist leader Vidkun Quisling. As the Nazis retreated in 1945, King Haakon and his government returned home.

Elections in 1945 returned a majority Labor government in the Storting. Labor set about establishing a Scandinavian welfare state, emphasizing privately owned, free-market industry, publicly owned utilities, state planning to ensure ample housing as well as full employment through export-oriented industries, a comprehensive social welfare system, and high taxes.

Norway was a founding member of the United Nations and provided that body with its first secretary-general, Trygve Lie. With the hardening of the Cold War, Norway joined the NATO alliance in 1949. In 1959 Norway became one of the original members of the European Free Trade Association. Through the 1960s industrial development and exports continued to fuel an economic boom that led to great national prosperity and stability.

The 1970s were the decade of oil and gas, with extensive development of North Sea fields. As international energy prices rose, the government's petroleum monopoly, Statoil, seemed to provide an endless source of funds. Because Norway's hydroelectric plants made the country self-sufficient in electric power, almost all of the oil and gas was available for export; by 1981 energy exports amounted to one-third, and by 1985 one-half, of Norway's total exports. The government expanded the welfare state and encouraged large wage increases. Public spending swelled and government debt mounted; meanwhile Norway became an economic hostage to OPEC oil prices.

In the 1981 elections, the Conservative party formed a government for the first time since 1928; its austerity policy of holding down government spending while increasing taxes on consumer goods aroused popular opposition, and the government fell in 1986. The new Socialist coalition government faced even greater drops in oil revenues, combined with labor unrest and continued inflation. But in 1987 Norway negotiated the sale of gas to E.U. countries, and the recovery of energy prices brought a partial return to economic stability and prosperity.

In 1993 the government of Prime Minister Brundtland sought admission to the E.U. On Mar. 29, 1994, the E.U. agreed to admit Norway to membership after long and intricate negotiations limiting Spanish and Portuguese fishing rights in Norwegian waters. But Norweigian voters in a Nov. 1994 referendum rejected E.U. membership. Brundtland resigned in Oct. 1996 and was replaced by Thorbjoern Jagland, but he remained prime minister less than a year. After 1997 elections to the Storting, a right-wing three-party coalition, which controlled only 24 of the 165 seats, formed a government under Christian Democrat Kjell Magne Bondevik. Even Bondevik's three-week leave of absence (to treat depression) in Sept. 1998 failed to shake the stability of Norway's politics. But a March 2000 no-confidence vote toppled the government, replacing it with a Labor-Conservative coalition under Labor's Jens Stoltenberg as prime minister.

Storting elections in Sept. 2001 brought another of western Europe's right-wing victories as Labor made its worst showing since 1924, losing 22 seats. Conservative Kjell Bondevik became Norway's new prime minister. In 2005 Labor rebounded strongly even though Norway's economy was booming because of rising oil prices. Stoltenberg was able to form the first majority government in two decades. Norway's thriftiness paid off during the worldwide recession when the economy actually grew by three percent.

▶ **OMAN**
Sultanate of Oman
• **GEOGRAPHY Location:** southeastern Arabian peninsula. **Boundaries:** Gulf of Oman to N, Arabian Sea to E and S, Yemen to SW, Saudi Arabia to W, United Arab Emirates to NW; detached portion of Oman lies at tip of Musandam peninsula, on Strait of Hormuz. **Total area:** 82,031 sq. mi. (212,460 sq km). **Coastline:** 1,299 mi. (2,092 km). **Comparative area:** slightly smaller than Kansas. **Land use:** 0% arable land; negl. % permanent crops; 100% other. **Major cities:** Muscat (capital); Al-Batinah; Al-Sharquia.
• **PEOPLE Population:** 3,418,085 (July 2009 est.). **Nationality:** noun—Omani(s); adjective—Omani. **Ethnic groups:** Arab, Baluchi, South Asian, African. **Languages:** Arabic (official), English, Baluchi, Urdu, Indian dialects. **Religions:** 75% Ibadhi Muslim, Sunni Muslim, Shi'a Muslim, Hindu.
• **GOVERNMENT Type:** monarchy. **Constitution:** none. **National holiday:** Birthday of the Sultan, Nov. 18. **Head of Government:** Qaboos bin Said, sultan and prime minister (since July 1970). **Structure:** executive—sultan is hereditary monarch; bicameral legislature-advisory powers only; judiciary—traditional Islamic judges in nascent civil court system; supreme court with non-Islamic judges.
• **ECONOMY Monetary unit:** Omani rial. **Budget:** (2009 est.) *income:* $14.6 bil.; *expend.:* $16.7 bil. **G.D.P.:** $67 bil., $20,000 per capita (2008 est.). **Chief crops:** dates, limes, bananas, alfalfa, vegetables, cattle, camels; annual fish catch averages 100,000 metric tons. **Natural resources:** crude oil, copper, asbestos, some marble, limestone. **Major**

industries: crude oil production and refining, natural gas production, construction. **Labor force:** 920,000 (2002 est.). **Exports:** $33.9 bil. (f.o.b., 2008 est.); petroleum, reexports, fish, metals, textiles. **Imports:** $13.32 bil. (f.o.b., 2008 est.); machinery, transportation equipment, manufactured goods, food, livestock, lubricants. **Major trading partners:** (2006) *exports:* 23.6% China, 11% Japan, 17.9% South Korea, 10.7% Thailand, 7.7% South Africa, 6.3% United Arab Emirates; *imports:* 22.4% UAE, 16.4% Japan, 8.1% U.S., 5.5% Germany, 4.3% India.

Oman occupies the southeastern corner of Arabia. From ancient times an important center of trade in the Persian Gulf and the Indian Ocean, Oman was dominated by Persia prior to 1750. The principal port, Muscat, was captured by the Portuguese in 1508 and held by them until 1659, when the Ottoman Turks took possession. They were driven out in 1741 by Ahmed ibn Said of Yemen, who consolidated the sultanate of Oman in 1744 and founded the present royal line.

In the early 19th century, Oman was the most powerful state in Arabia, controlling Zanzibar, the southern coast of Iran, and much of Baluchistan (between Pakistan and Iran). Zanzibar was separated from Oman in 1856, and the Persian coast and much of Baluchistan was detached from Oman during the latter half of the 19th century. In 1958 Oman's sole remaining Baluchi possession, the city-state of Gwadar, was ceded to Pakistan in return for a monetary settlement.

Growing British influence was consolidated by the formation of a British protectorate in 1891, reconfirmed in 1951. In the 1950s Britain aided the sultanate in putting down rebellions in the desert interior. The British protectorate ended with Britain's withdrawal from the gulf in 1971. On July 23, 1970, Sultan Said ibn Taimur was overthrown by his son, Sultan Qaboos bin Said, who instituted a national development program and in 1975 defeated a leftist uprising in the western desert.

Petroleum makes up 95 percent of exports. Banking and shipping services are also important. The country is generally barren, with scattered flocks of sheep and camels. In April 1996 Oman joined with Russia and Kazakhstan to establish a consortium with eight oil companies to build a 900 mile pipeline to move oil to Russia's port in the Black Sea. In 2006 a free trade deal with the U.S. was also concluded.

▶ **PAKISTAN**
Islamic Republic of Pakistan
• **GEOGRAPHY Location:** southern Asia. **Boundaries:** Afghanistan to N, China to far NE, India to E, Arabian Sea to S, and Iran to W. **Total area:** 310,402 sq. mi. (803,940 sq km). **Coastline:** 650 mi. (1,046 km). **Comparative area:** slightly less than twice the size of California. **Land use:** 24% arable land; .8% permanent crops; 75% other. **Major cities:** Islamabad (capital); Karachi; Lahore; Faisalabad (Lyallpur); Rawalpindi.
• **PEOPLE Population:** 177,276,594 (July 2010 est.). **Nationality:** noun—Pakistani(s); adjective—Pakistani. **Ethnic groups:** Punjabi, Sindhi, Pashtun (Pathan), Baloch, Muhajir (immigrants from India and their descendants). **Languages:** 48% Punjabi, 12% Sindhi, 10% Siraiki, 8% Pashtu, 8% Urdu (official), 3% Balochi, 2% Hindko, 1% Brahui, English (official and lingua franca of Pakistani elite and most government ministries), 8% Burushaski and other. **Religions:** 97% Muslim

(77% Sunni, 20% Shi'a); 3% Christian, Hindu, and other.

• **GOVERNMENT** **Type:** federal republic. **Independence:** Aug. 14, 1947 (from U.K.). **Constitution:** Apr. 12, 1973; suspended July 5, 1977; restored Dec. 30, 1985; suspended Oct. 15, 1999, restored Dec. 31, 2002; suspended Nov. 2007, restored Dec. 2007. **National holiday:** Republic Day, Mar. 23. **Heads of Government:** Asif Ali Zardari, president (since Sept. 2008); Syed Yousuf Raza Gilani, prime minister (since Mar. 2008). **Structure:** executive—prime minister is head of government; bicameral legislature—dissolved after military takeover; judiciary.

• **ECONOMY** **Monetary unit:** Pakistani rupee. **Budget:** (2009 est.) *income:* $23.21 bil.; *expend.:* $30.05 bil. **G.D.P.:** $449.3 bil., $2,600 per capita (2009 est.). **Chief crops:** wheat, rice, sugarcane, cotton; beef, milk, mutton, eggs. · **Natural resources:** land, extensive natural gas reserves, limited petroleum, poor quality coal, iron ore. **Major industries:** cotton textiles, food processing. **Labor force:** 55.88 mil.; 42% agriculture, 20% industry, 38% services (2004 est.); 7.5% unemployment (2007 est.); extensive export of labor, mostly to the Middle East, and use of child labor. **Exports:** $17.87 bil. (2009 est.); cotton, textiles, clothing, rice, leather, carpets. **Imports:** $28.31 bil. (2009 est.); petroleum, petroleum products, machinery, transportation equipment, cooking oils. **Major trading partners:** (2008) *exports:* 16.1% U.S., 11.7% U.A.E., 8.6% Afghanistan, 4.5% U.K., 4.2% China; *imports:* 14.3% China, 12.2% Saudi Arabia, 11.3% U.A.E., 5.5% Kuwait, 4.8% U.S.

Pakistan occupies the heartland of ancient South Asian civilization, in the Indus River valley. Agricultural settlements in that area arose by 3000 B.C., and the great cities at Harappa and Mohenjo-Daro were founded some 500 years later. Indo-European (Aryan) invaders from Central Asia overthrew the ancient civilization around 1500 B.C. and established a new culture that spread throughout Pakistan and northern India. Brahmanism, the religious culture of the early Indo-European invaders, gave rise to Buddhism and Jainism around the sixth century B.C., and evolved into Hinduism in the early centuries A.D. The Indus valley was incorporated into the empire of Alexander the Great, c. 350 B.C., and then into the Mauryan empire of Asoka, which by the third century B.C. controlled all of South Asia except for the southernmost portion of India.

Under various rulers the Indus Valley and the areas to its northwest were a great center of Buddhist culture until the beginning of the eighth century, when the area fell to Muslim Arab invaders. Thereafter, Islam was firmly established throughout the region. But Baluchistan and the Northwest Frontier region became culturally allied to the Persian civilization of Iran and Afghanistan, while Sind and the Punjab were more closely akin to the culture of northern India.

Northern Pakistan was incorporated into the empire of Mahmud of Gazni in the 11th century, and fell to the Mongols in the 13th century. The Indus River became the boundary between the Mongol Inkhanate of Persia and the sultanate of Delhi. The region was conquered by Timur Leng at the end of the 14th century, and after the fall of the Timurid empire was divided between the kingdoms of Sind and Multan, in southern and central Pakistan, and the sultanate of Delhi, in the Punjab. All of Pakistan and northern India was re-united after 1526, when the conquests of Babur established the Mogul empire.

The expansion of British power in India during the 18th century left Pakistan largely untouched; the area was divided among various states, including Sind, the Punjab, Kashmir, and the western reaches of Rajputana. In the first half of the 19th century, British rule extended to the northwest; after the defeat of the Indian Mutiny of 1857, the entire Indus valley came under British rule. Sind and the Punjab were ruled directly by the British, while the native states were ruled as British protectorates.

From the beginning of the 20th century, various nationalist movements arose throughout British India. The Muslim League, under the leadership of Mohammad Ali Jinnah after 1916, advocated greater popular political participation, dominion status for India, and a strong Muslim voice in Indian administration. Muslims and Hindus were allied in the Non-Cooperation movement of the 1920s, but the alliance soon broke down and degenerated into communal frictions. With growing power of the Congress party in Hindu areas and Gandhi's civil disobedience movement in the 1930s, Jinnah's Muslim League charted an increasingly separate course and called for the creation of a separate Muslim state in 1940.

With the British withdrawal from India in 1947, Hindus in the Muslim majority areas of the Indus valley and in East Bengal fled to Hindu India, while Muslims in Hindu areas fled toward the Punjab. These massive population movements were accompanied by widespread violence leading to the loss of hundreds of thousands of lives. Jinnah died in 1948. Pakistan, encompassing Sind, the Punjab, Baluchistan, the Northwest Frontier Territories, part of Jammu and Kashmir, and adjacent areas in the west and East Bengal in the east, was granted dominion status within the British Commonwealth in 1947, becoming an independent republic in 1956.

Pakistan joined the Central Treaty Organization and became allied with the West, in contrast to the Soviet-leaning nonalignment of India. In 1958 Gen. Mohammad Ayub Khan seized power in a coup; he was elected president in 1960 and re-elected in 1965. Following border clashes with India in 1962, Pakistan entered into friendly relations with China, which also had engaged in border warfare with India. Ayub Khan resigned as president in early 1969 after failing to put down widespread demonstrations in East Pakistan. A new government was formed under Gen. Yahya Khan, and martial law was declared. A parliamentary victory by the East Pakistani Awami League in December 1970 led to civil war and the secession of East Pakistan in 1971 (see "Bangladesh").

India's intervention on behalf of East Bengal had led to war on a western front with Pakistan. On July 3, 1972, India and Pakistan agreed to a mutual withdrawal of troops and entered into negotiations. Diplomatic relations between India and Pakistan were resumed in 1976.

The elections of 1970 that had precipitated the civil war also brought Zulfikar Ali Bhutto to the presidency. He remained in office until July 1977, when he was overthrown in a military coup led by Gen. Mohammad Zia ul-Haq. He was convicted of complicity in a 1974 political murder and hanged in April 1979. Under Pres. Zia, Pakistan moved toward the implementation of Islamic law in parallel with the constitutional law of Pakistan's parliamentary system. In 1986 Bhutto's daughter, Benazir Bhutto, returned to Pakistan from exile in Europe to organize opposition parties against Pres. Zia, leading to widespread rioting.

On Aug. 17, 1988, Pres. Zia was killed in an airplane crash. From 1988 to 1999 the position of prime minister alternated between Benazir Bhutto as head of the Pakistan People's Party and Nawaz Sharif as leader of the Muslim League, each accusing the other in turn of tyranny and corruption, amidst endless tension with India over Jammu-Kashmir. The latter struggle lay at the root of the nuclear-test rivalry in May 1998, after which the prime ministers, Vajpayee and Sharif, attempted to lower the political temperature while not appearing to "cave in" to the other. Sharif's July 1999 agreement in Washington D.C. to withdraw support for Muslims in Kashmir made it appear that he was the one to blink first.

Sharif's dismissal of Gen. Pervez Musharraf over the army's support of Kashmir rebels led to a military coup and Sharif's trial on corruption charges which ended with a guilty verdict and life imprisonment. Musharraf pledged a return to civilian rule, but in June 2001 appointed himself president. Musharraf had to walk a delicate line after the Sept. 11th attacks on the U.S. Backing the U.S. in Afghanistan, he fired his three top generals for their ties to the Taliban and arrested leaders of demonstrations against the war in Afghanistan. He denounced a murderous Pakistani Muslim attack on the Indian Parliament. In Oct. 2002, Pakistan held its first elections since 1997, with Musharraf's party gaining a plurality. In the same month both India and Pakistan announced troop withdrawals from their borders (though not the Kashmir border). And in May 2003 Musharraf reciprocated India's decision to restore diplomatic and rail links between the two countries. By Feb. 2004, both agreed to a "road map" for comprehensive peace negotiations. Musharraf survived a Dec. 2003 assassination attempt and then agreed to step down as army chief and to remain as president until 2007 elections. But those elections were not scheduled and his popularity continued to wane dramatically, leading to the possibility of an alliance with Benazir Bhutto who returned from exile in Oct. 2007 to run for office. She was assasinated in December, and her husband was later elected after Musharraf resigned. Asif Ali Zardari's government tried both to confront the Taliban occupying some of its territories and also to work with the U.S. military. The worst floods in 80 years devastated Pakistan in the summer of 2010, as millions were left homeless. (See "Major News Stories.")

▶ **PALAU**
Republic of Palau
● **GEOGRAPHY Location:** more than 200 islands, in a chain about 400 mi. (650 km) long, in western central Pacific Ocean; Koror 71°21'N, 134°31'vE. **Boundaries:** Guam 720 mi. (1,160 km) to NE, Federated States of Micronesia to E, island of New Guinea to S, Philippines 530 mi. (850 km) to NW. **Total area:** 177 sq. mi. (458 sq km). **Coastline:** 944 mi. (1,519 km). **Comparative area:** slightly more than 2.5 times size of Washington, D.C. **Land use:** 8.7% arable land; 4% permanent crops; 87% other. **Major cities:** Melekeok (capital), Koror, Babelthuap.
● **PEOPLE Population:** 20,796 (2009 est.). **Nationality:** noun—Palauan(s); adjective—Palauan. **Eth-**nic groups: composite of Polynesian, Malayan, and Melanesian races. **Languages:** English (official) in all 16 states; Palauan (official) in 13 states; Sonsorolese, Angaur, Japanese, Tobi in one state each. **Religions:** 65% Christian (49% Roman Catholic, Seventh-Day Adventist, Jehovah's Witness, the Assembly of God, the Liebenzell Mission, and Latter-Day Saints), 8.8% Modekngei (indigenous faith).
● **GOVERNMENT Type:** constitutional government in free association with the U.S.; the Compact of Free Association entered into force Oct. 1, 1994. **Independence:** Oct. 1, 1994 (from U.S.-administered U.N. Trusteeship). **Constitution:** Jan. 1, 1981. **National holiday:** Constitution Day, July 9. **Heads of Government:** Johnson Toribiong, president (since Jan. 2009); Kerai Mariur, vice president (since Jan. 2009). **Structure:** executive—president and vice president popularly elected; legislative—bicameral legislature; judicial—Supreme Court headed by chief justice.
● **ECONOMY Monetary unit:** U.S. dollar. **Budget:** (2008 est.) *income:* $114.8 mil.; *expend.:* $99.5 mil. **G.D.P.:** $164 mil., $8,100 per capita (2008 est.). **Chief crops:** coconuts, copra, cassava, sweet potatoes. **Livestock:** N.A. **Natural resources:** forests, minerals (especially gold), marine products, deepseabed minerals. **Major industries:** tourism, craft items (shell, wood, pearl), some commercial fishing and agriculture. **Labor force:** 9,777 (2005). **Exports:** $5.882 mil. (f.o.b., 2004); trochus, tuna, copra, handicrafts. **Imports:** $107.3 mil. (f.o.b., 2004). **Major trading partners:** (2006) *exports:* U.S., Japan, Singapore; *imports:* U.S., Singapore, Japan, South Korea.

The first inhabitants of Palau (or Belau) probably arrived from Indonesia and the Philippines about 1500 B.C. The first European to visit the area was Ferdinand Magellan, in 1521. However, it was the British who dominated trade to Palau until 1885, when Pope Leo XIII acknowledged Spain's claims to the Carolines. Spain controlled Palau from 1885 to 1899, when it sold the territory to Germany. The Germans introduced coconut planting and phosphate mining, and introduced sanitary measures that arrested the deadly epidemics of dysentery and influenza, which over 120 years had reduced the population from 40,000 to 4,000.

Japan occupied Palau in 1914, and over the next 30 years increased the mining, agriculture, and fishing industries. In 1938, Palau became a closed military area, and it was the site of heavy fighting during World War II. On July 18, 1947, the United Nations Trusteeship Council placed the Trust Territory of the Pacific Islands, including Palau, under U.S. authority. This trusteeship ended on Oct. 1, 1994, when the Compact of Free Association with the United States (approved by the voters of Palau) went into effect, making Palau an independent country in association with the United States. The United States continues to provide for Palau's defense and to provide aid. In return, the United States has the right to dock military vessels (including nuclear-powered vessels) in the islands for 50 years, and continues to consult closely on economic and environmental matters.

▶ **PANAMA**
Republic of Panama
● **GEOGRAPHY Location:** southern Central America. **Boundaries:** Caribbean Sea to N, Colombia to E, Pacific Ocean to S, Costa Rica to W. **Total area:** 30,193 sq. mi. (78,200 sq km). **Coastline:** 1,546 mi.

(2,490 km). **Comparative area**: slightly smaller than South Carolina. **Land use:** 7% arable land; 2% permanent crops; 91% other. **Major cities:** Panamá (Panama City—capital); Colón; David.
• **PEOPLE Population:** 3,360,474 (2009 est.). **Nationality:** noun—Panamanian(s); adjective—Panamanian. **Ethnic groups:** 70% mestizo, 14% Amerindian and mixed (West Indian), 10% white, 6% Amerindian. **Languages:** Spanish (official), 14% speak English as native tongue; many Panamanians are bilingual. **Religions:** 85% Roman Catholic, 15% Protestant.
• **GOVERNMENT Type:** constitutional democracy. **Independence:** Nov. 3, 1903 (from Colombia); became independent from Spain Nov. 28, 1821. **Constitution:** Oct. 11, 1972, with major reforms adopted in Apr. 1983, 1994 and in 2004. **National holiday:** Independence Day, Nov. 3. **Head of Government:** Ricardo Martinelli, president (since Sept. 2009). **Structure:** executive—president, two vice presidents, cabinet; unicameral legislature; judiciary.
• **ECONOMY Monetary unit:** balboa. **Budget:** (2008) *income:* $6.09 bil.; *expend.:* $6 bil. **G.D.P.:** $38.49 bil., $11,600 per capita (2008 est.). **Chief crops:** bananas, rice, sugarcane, coffee, corn; livestock, fishing. **Natural resources:** copper, mahogany forests, shrimp. **Major industries:** manufacturing and construction, petroleum refining, brewing, cement and other construction material. **Labor force:** 1.392 mil. (2008 est.); 15% agriculture, 18% industry, 67% services (2006 est.). **Exports:** $10.37 bil. (f.o.b., 2008 est.); bananas, shrimp, clothing, sugar, coffee. **Imports:** $15.18 bil. (f.o.b., 2008 est.); capital goods, crude oil, foodstuffs. **Major trading partners:** (2006) *exports:* 39.8% U.S., 8.1% Spain, 6.7% Netherlands, 6.5% Sweden, 4.5% Costa Rica; *imports:* 27% U.S., 10% Netherlands, 5.1% Costa Rica, 4.7% Japan.

The Spanish first arrived in what is now Panama in 1501. Vasco Nuñez de Balboa returned in 1510, and Pedro Arias Dávila founded the City of Panama in 1519. Panama became attached to the viceroyalty of New Granada after 1739 and left the Spanish empire with the rest of New Granada in 1821, becoming a part of Gran Colombia. The first canal company proposing the construction of a transisthmian passageway was formed in 1825–26. The completion of a U.S.-financed railway from Colón to Panama City by 1855 enhanced Panama's importance as a transoceanic passage.

Panamanian nationalists waged a "War of a Thousand Days" against the Bogotá government between 1899 and 1902. In 1903 Panama gained independence from Colombia with U.S. complicity. Within a month Panamanian officials accepted an agreement with the United States that created a canal zone under the control of the U.S. government "in perpetuity," and the Panama Canal was completed and opened in 1914.

Panama experienced protectorate status under U.S. control after independence insofar as the United States "guaranteed the independence" of Panama. The United States explicitly upheld its right of unilateral military intervention in Panama when in 1918 it sent troops there without the permission of the Panamanian government. The 1936 Hull-Alvaro Treaty eliminated protectorate status, and the U.S. dropped its claim to a right of intervention in the cities of Panama and Colón.

In 1968 a power struggle between Pres. Arnulfo Arias and the Panamanian National Guard led to the ouster of the president. A National Guard junta took control of the government, and Col. (later Gen.) Omar Torrijos Herrera became the ruler of the country the following year. In 1972 a new assembly under Torrijos's control offered him the title of Jefe Maximo (chief executive) in addition to drafting a new constitution for the country. Torrijos constructed a populist following through the creation of housing projects, a new labor code, an agrarian reform, and an increase in tax rates imposed on foreign banana-interests.

The Panamanian government and the U.S. concluded a new canal treaty in 1977, the key provisions of which included integration of the Canal Zone with the rest of Panamanian territory and full Panamanian control of the canal in 2000. In 1981 Omar Torrijos died in an air accident.

In 1988 the head of the military and de facto ruler of the country, Gen. Mañuel Noriega, was indicted in the U.S. on narcotics charges. But Noriega refused to submit to demands by the U.S. and by Panamanian president Eric Arturo Delvalle for his resignation. Delvalle was forced to go into hiding. The U.S. responded by freezing Panamanian assets.

In May 1989 Gen. Noriega annulled election results that showed him losing to Guillermo Endara and assumed the role of dictator. After an unsuccessful coup attempt, the United States invaded Panama on December 20, captured Noriega, and brought him to Miami, where he was convicted on narcotics charges. Endara was restored to the presidency and in December 1990 U.S. forces helped put down a rebellion led by Noriega's former chief of the national police.

Endara's government was often accused of corruption but he left power peacefully in 1994. He helped to arrange honest elections that saw U.S.-educated businessman Ernesto Perez Balladares come to power with promises of improving the economy as Panama prepared to take over control of the canal. His free market reforms and a loosening of trade barriers have brought strong growth in G.D.P. An August 1998 referendum turned down (by 64 percent) Perez' seeking a second term. Voters in May 1999 chose Mireya Moscoso de Grubar, widow of three-time president Arnulfo Arias, over Martin Torrijos, son of the dictator who negotiated the 1977 Canal Treaty with the U.S., as Panama's new president. But Torrijos won in May 2004. A free trade deal with the U.S. was signed in 2006. In 2009 fear of the worldwide recession led the voters to choose Ricardo Martinelli, a multi-millionaire businessman, as president, defying the leftist trend in Latin American politics.

▶ PAPUA NEW GUINEA
Independent State of Papua New Guinea
• **GEOGRAPHY Location:** eastern section of island of New Guinea and about 600 smaller islands in Bismarck Archipelago (New Britain, New Ireland, and Manus) and northern part of Solomon Islands. Port Moresby 9°30s, 147°07'E. **Boundaries:** Bismarck Sea to N, Solomon Sea to E, Australia to S, and Indonesia to W. **Total area:** 178,259 sq. mi. (462,840 sq km). **Coastline:** 3,202 mi. (5,152 km). **Comparative area:** slightly larger than California. **Land use:** negl.% arable land; 1% permanent crops; 99% other. **Major cities:** Port Moresby (administrative capital).
• **PEOPLE Population:** 6,057,263 (July 2009 est.). **Nationality:** noun—Papua New Guinean(s); adjective—Papua New Guinean. **Ethnic groups:** predominantly Melanesian and Papuan; some Negrito, Micronesian, and Polynesian. **Lan-

guages: 820 indigenous languages; English spoken by 1%-2%, pidgin English widespread, Motu spoken in Papua region. **Religions:** 27% Roman Catholic, 20% Lutheran, 50% other Christian, 3% indigenous beliefs.
• **Government Type:** parliamentary democracy. **Independence:** Sept. 16, 1975 (from U.N. trusteeship under Australian administration). **Constitution:** Sept. 16, 1975. **National holiday:** Independence Day, Sept. 16. **Heads of Government:** Paulius Matane, governor-general (since June 2004); Sir Michael T. Somare, prime minister (since Aug. 2002). **Structure:** executive—British monarch (represented by governor general), chief of state, prime minister; unicameral legislature; judiciary.
• **Economy Monetary unit:** kina. **Budget:** (2008 est.) *income:* $3.098 bil.; *expend.:* $2.949 bil. **G.D.P.:** $13.29 bil., $2,200 per capita (2007 est.). **Chief crops:** cocoa, coffee, coconuts, rubber, palm kernels; pigs, chickens. **Natural resources:** gold, copper, silver, natural gas, timber. **Major industries:** copra crushing, palmoil processing, plywood processing. **Labor force:** 3.639 mil., 85% agriculture. **Exports:** $5.658 bil. (f.o.b., 2008 est.): gold, copper ore, oil, logs, coffee, palm oil, cocoa, lobster. **Imports:** $3.013 bil. (f.o.b, 2008 est.); machinery and transport equipment, manufactured goods, food, fuels, chemicals. **Major trading partners:** (2006) *exports:* 30.2% Australia, 8.2% Japan, 5.7% China; *imports:* 52% Australia, 12.6% Singapore, 5.9% China, 4.3% Japan.

The island of New Guinea, the world's second-largest, was settled thousands of years ago by waves of Papuan and Melanesian migrants who developed large numbers of linguistically diverse and mutually hostile tribes of hunters and small cultivators. In the 19th century, the island was divided between the Dutch (to the west, in what is now the Indonesian province of Irian Jaya), Germany, and the British. The German sector was occupied by Australia in 1914 and administered under a League of Nations mandate after WWI.

Japanese attempts to occupy New Guinea in 1942 met with only partial success. In a series of counteroffensives, the Allies regained control over the entire island by mid-1944.

Beginning in 1949 the former German and British colonies were administered by Australia under a U.N. mandate. The territories were made self-governing in 1973 and achieved full independence as Papua New Guinea on Sept. 16, 1975. The nation maintains close ties with Australia. In 1989 a rebellion on the mineral-rich island of Bougainville closed a large Australian-run copper mine, led to the deaths of many people and frightened away foreign investors.

An inexplicable decision to recognize Taiwan rather than mainland China, made in 1999 by prime minister Bill Skate, brought domestic (as well as Chinese) opposition, Skate's resignation, and the designation of Sir Mekere Morauta as the new prime minister. He immediately reversed the Taiwan agreement. In Feb. 2000 the government began a program of privatizing all state-owned enterprise within three years. In 2002 elections, violence kept the country without a government for three months until three-time prime minister Michael Somare was able to form a government. In recent years Australia has increased aid significantly and is providing police protection to halt continuing violence caused by extreme poverty among 85 percent of the population. Somare won

another term in 2007, vowing to fight rampant crime and corruption, and to fight the spread of AIDS.

▶ **PARAGUAY**
Republic of Paraguay
• **Geography Location:** landlocked country in central South America. **Boundaries:** Bolivia to N, Brazil to E, Argentina to S and W. **Total area:** 157,046 sq. mi. (406,750 sq km). **Coastline:** none. **Comparative area:** slightly smaller than California. **Land use:** 6% arable land; 0% permanent crops; 94% other. **Major cities:** Asunción (capital); Ciudad del Este (formerly Presidente Stroessner); Pedro Juan Caballero; Encarnación; Villarrica.
• **People Population:** 6,995,655 (July 2009 est.). **Nationality:** noun—Paraguayan(s); adjective— Paraguayan. **Ethnic groups:** 95% mestizo (mixed white and Amerindian). **Languages:** Spanish (official), Guaraní. **Religions:** 90% Roman Catholic, Mennonite and other Protestant denominations.
• **Government Type:** constitutional republic. **Independence:** May 14, 1811 (from Spain). **Constitution:** June 20, 1992. **National holiday:** Independence Day, May 14. **Head of Government:** Fernando Lugo, president (since Aug., 2008). **Structure:** president heads executive; bicameral legislature (Senate, Chamber of Deputies); judiciary.
• **Economy Monetary unit:** guarani. **Budget:** (2008 est.) *income:* $2.939 bil.; *expend.:* $2.866 bil. **G.D.P.:** $28.71 bil., $4,200 per capita (2008 est.). **Chief crops:** sugarcane, soybeans, cotton, wheat; beef, pork; timber. **Natural resources:** iron ore, manganese, limestone, hydropower, timber. **Major industries:** sugar, cement, textiles, beverages. **Labor force:** 2.839 mil. (2008 est.); 31% agriculture, 17% industry, 52% services (2007); 11.4% unemployment (2007 est.). **Exports:** $6.901 bil. (f.o.b., 2008 est.); cotton, soybeans, timber, vegetable oils, feed, tung oil. **Imports:** $7.351 bil. (f.o.b., 2008 est.); consumer goods, tobacco, raw materials, fuels. **Major trading partners:** (2006) *exports:* 22% Uruguay, 17.2% Brazil, 11.9% Russia, 8.8% Argentina, 6.9% Chile; *imports:* 27% China, 20% Brazil, 13.6% Argentina, 8.3% Japan, 6.4% U.S.

When Europeans arrived in what is now Paraguay in the early 16th century, they encountered various groups of indigenous peoples. The Spanish entered into alliances with the Tupian semisedentary Guaraní against the nomadic Guaycuru Indians in the west of the region. Asunción, founded in 1537, was little more than a Spanish defense outpost against the Portuguese and a trading stopover between the silver mines of Potosí and Buenos Aires.

From early in the 17th century, the Jesuits established an extensive network of missions in the southern portion of the colony, and a rivalry grew between the Jesuits and the elites of Asunción over who would determine the colony's social and economic structure. The isolation of the settlers from the mainstream of Spanish colonial society combined with the lack of valuable resources led to the evolution of a relatively egalitarian social structure. The political elite of Asunción deposed Spanish authority in 1811, and Paraguayan independence was declared in 1813.

Authoritarian rule marked the period from independence until 1870. José Gaspar Rodríguez de Francia was declared ruler for life in 1816 and remained in power until his death in 1840. A period of political turmoil followed but was resolved in the election of Carlos Antonio López in 1844; in 1857 he was named president for life. López chose his son Francisco Solano López to succeed him in office in 1862. He intervened in a Brazilian attempt to control the fate of Uruguay, beginning the Paraguayan War, or the War of the Triple Alliance (Brazil, Argentina, Uruguay) from 1865 to 1870. The war was catastrophic for Paraguay, reducing the population from 450,000 to 220,000; and Paraguay lost 60,000 square miles of territory while being saddled with a war debt of 19 million gold pesos ($200,000,000), later dropped as unrealistic.

After the war the Colorado and Liberal parties developed, although the real political distinctions were dependent more on individuals and families than political ideology. Colorado-party general Bernardino Caballero, backed by Brazil, was the power behind the scenes of frequent changes in government personnel between 1874 and 1904. The Liberals, backed by Argentina, were in power from 1904 until 1936.

Gen. Alfredo Stroessner, with the backing of Colorado party factions, began his iron-fisted authoritarian rule in 1954. Stroessner held power until 1989, when Gen. Andrés Rodríguez overthrew him. Nevertheless, the Colorados maintained their hold on the presidency in hotly contested elections in 1993, when Juan Carlos Wasmosy gained 40 percent of the vote. However, a strong showing by the opposition Authentic Radical Liberal Party (PLRA) and National Encounter prevented a Colorado majority in Congress. A complex political struggle between Pres. Wasmosy and Lino Oviedo, one of the generals who overthrew Stroessner, led to Oviedo's imprisonment. His ally, Raul Cubas Grau, won the 1998 election by vowing to have Oviedo share power even from prison. Three days after taking office in August, however, Cubas released the popular general.

In March 1999, the vice president was assassinated, Congress accusing Cubas and Oviedo. Impeached the next day, Cubas remanded Oviedo to state custody but refused to appear at his own trial in the Senate. Oviedo fled to Argentina, Cubas to Brazil. Congress named the president of the Senate, Luis Gonzalez Macchi, as president. Gonzalez appointed a cabinet with four opposition members among the 10, the first coalition since 1946. A coup attempt by Oviedo allies was foiled in May 2000. Three weeks later, Oviedo was arrested in Brazil.

In Feb. 2003 the senate tried, but failed, to impeach Gonzalez on corruption charges. Still the Colorado party candidate Nicanor Duarte Frutos won the presidential election and won high marks for his crackdown on corruption, although crime remains a serious problem, especially a sudden increase in high-profile kidnapping. The presidential election of April 2008 brought down the Colorado party for the first time in decades. The winner, Fernando Lugo, was formerly a priest and a bishop who promised land reform. Lugo was unable to move the legislature toward acceptance of his policies. He rejected calls for his resignation in 2009 when it was revealed he had fathered an illegitimate child while he was a bishop.

► PERU
Republic of Peru
● GEOGRAPHY   Location: western coast of South America. Boundaries: Ecuador, Colombia to N, Brazil, Bolivia to E, Chile to S, Pacific Ocean to W. Total area: 496,224 sq. mi. (1,285,220 sq km).

Coastline: 1,546 mi. (2,414 km). Comparative area: slightly smaller than Alaska. Land use: 3% arable land; negl. % permanent crops; 97% other. Major cities: Lima (capital); Arequipa; Trujillo; Chiclayo; Callao
● PEOPLE   Population: 29,907,003 (July 2010 est.). Nationality: noun—Peruvian(s); adjective—Peruvian. Ethnic groups: 45% Amerindian, 37% mestizo, 15% white, 3% black, Japanese, Chinese, and other. Languages: Spanish and Quechua (official), Aymara. Religions: 81% Roman Catholic, 13% Evangelical, 7% none or other.
● GOVERNMENT   Type: constitutional republic. Independence: July 28, 1821 (from Spain). Constitution: Dec. 29, 1993. National holiday: Independence Day, July 28. Heads of Government: Alan García Pérez, president (since July 2006); Javier Velasquez Quesquen, prime minister (since July 2009). Structure: executive; unicameral legislature; judiciary.
● ECONOMY   Monetary unit: nuevo sol. Budget: (2009 est.) income: $33.55 bil.; expend.: $37.97 bil. G.D.P.: $253 bil., $8,600 per capita (2009 est.). Chief crops: coffee, cotton, sugarcane, rice, poultry, meat, wool; fish. Natural resources: copper, silver, gold, petroleum, timber. Major industries: mining of metals, petroleum, fishing. Labor force: 10.26 mil. (2009); 1% agriculture, 23.8% industry, 75.5% services (2005); 9.4% unemployment (2002 est.). Exports: $23.07 bil. (2009 est.); copper, zinc, gold, petroleum. Imports: $20.3 bil. (2009 est.); machinery, transport equipment, foodstuffs, petroleum. Major trading partners: exports: 20.2% U.S., 15.2% China, 8.3% Canada, 7% Japan, 5.8% Chile, 4.2% Brazil; imports: 23.4% U.S., 10.5% China, 8.7% Brazil, 6.4% Ecuador, 5% Chile.

Peru was the site of the Inca empire. The Incas had extended their control over most of the Andean region by the late 15th century. The civilization was advanced in terms of its ability to provide for the welfare of its subjects and was in possession of sophisticated knowledge in a number of fields, including medicine. By the time of the arrival of the Spanish conqueror Francisco Pizarro in 1532, the empire was already in decline, and a combination of plague and civil war in the decade prior to the appearance of Europeans no doubt made the empire more vulnerable to Spanish conquest. Inca resistance to Spanish domination was not quelled until the execution of Tupac Amarú in 1571. European-borne diseases such as smallpox and measles devastated the Indian population.

Because of the great wealth of precious metals discovered by the Spanish and the adaptability of a sedentary indigenous civilization to the imposition of Spanish imperial control, Peru quickly became a major focal point of Spanish colonialism; they founded Lima in 1535. The viceroyalty of Peru, established in 1544, originally served as the political and administrative nerve center of Spanish colonization of South America. For nearly two centuries, Lima was the seat of power and wealth for the whole region. Peru was "liberated" by Simón Bolívar and José de San Martín in 1821 when Bolívar's army defeated the royalist forces at the battles of Junín and Ayacucho.

In the 40 years after independence, the presidency changed hands 35 times, and the country generated at least 15 different constitutions. Only four of the presidents of the period were constitutionally chosen, and the vast majority were military figures. In 1829 Peru tried and failed to annex Ecuador; in the 1830s an attempt at political federation between Peru and Bolivia collapsed with the Chilean invasion of 1839.

A political movement in favor of civilian rule, the Civilistas, began to organize by the 1860s. Chile defeated Peru in the War of the Pacific (1879–83), and Chileans occupied Lima and its port city of Callao for two years. The Peruvian government was deeply in debt after the war, resulting in the loss of ownership of much of Peru's infrastructure and natural resources to foreigners.

Peru experienced a period of civilian leadership between 1895 and 1930. Pres. Augusto B. Leguía (1908–12, 1919–30) extended his rule in an extra-constitutional manner until 1930, when Col. Luis Sánchez Cerro seized power; he ruled until his assassination in 1933. Gen. Oscar Benavides succeeded Cerro and managed to restore confidence in the economy. In 1939 civilian banker Manuel Prado was elected to the presidency, and the military allowed him to complete his term in office, which expired in 1945. During Prado's administration, Peru went to war with Ecuador and was victorious, seizing a great deal of territory.

Víctor Raúl Haya de la Torre founded Peru's most prominent political party, the American Popular Revolutionary Alliance (APRA), in 1924. As initiated, the party put forward an "anti-imperialist" platform aiming at nationalization of land and reconstruction of society in favor of oppressed people. Haya de la Torre was apparently fraudulently deprived of a presidential electoral victory in 1931. The following year Apristas (APRA supporters) seized Trujillo and killed some military personnel. By way of revenge, the army massacred 6,000 Apristas. The result was a continuing enmity between the Peruvian armed forces and the APRA party lasting until the 1980s. Although APRA clearly had majority support, the party was not allowed to take power until 1985.

The Peruvian military, led by Gen. Juan Velasco Alvarado, seized power in 1968 and embarked upon a course of reform that included the nationalization of Standard Oil's holdings. The Peruvian military took steps to restructure economic and political power by joining the Andean Pact and undermining the power of the traditional agricultural elite in the country by sponsoring an agrarian reform that mobilized the peasants.

The presidency of Peru returned to civilian leadership under Fernando Belaúnde Terry (1980–85). In 1985, the military allowed the APRA presidential candidate, Alan García Pérez, to take office. García promised to spend no more than 10 percent of the country's export earnings on payment of Peru's huge outstanding foreign debt and he was popular during his first years in office. But his public support was undermined by a growing insurgency sponsored by the Sendero Luminoso ("Shining Path") Maoist guerrillas and by runaway inflation.

On June 10, 1990, political outsider Alberto Fujimori, the son of Japanese immigrants, defeated the well-known writer Mario Vargas Llosa for the presidency. Throughout 1991 and 1992, Shining Path's influence spread, demoralizing and almost paralyzing the government, and at a cost of 25,000 lives. But in April 1992, Fujimori implemented a "zero tolerance" policy toward terrorism, dissolving the legislature and proclaiming martial law. The capture of Abimael Guzmán Reynoso, Path's founder-leader, broke the back of the insurgency.

Fujimori pursued free-market reforms, taming runaway inflation and privatizing state-run dinosaurs, so that by 1994 the Peruvian economy was growing at a rate of 12 percent, fastest in the world. In April of that year, Fujimori was elected to a second term with 64 percent of the vote.

The dramatic liberation in April 1997 of 600 prisoners held for ransom in the Japanese ambassador's compound by another radical terrorist group maintained the president's repute. In Oct. 1998, Peru completed a treaty with Ecuador ending a 50-year old border conflict. But all these achievements were accompanied by a rather ham-handed authoritarian streak which cost Fujimori much esteem. In elections for Congress, held in April 2000, his Peru 2000 party carried a plurality of seats but he himself just failed of a majority in the presidential race. A week before the May 28 run-off, his remaining opponent withdrew, claiming the election was a fraud; the final tally brought Fujimori only 51 percent. His inauguration was marred by rioting, with six dead and many public buildings in Lima burnt. While in Japan, Fujimori resigned, but Congress refused to accept, so it could remove him for abandoning office and dereliction of duty.

In June 2001, in a close run-off against former president Alan García, Alejandro Toledo was elected president, the first Indian elected president in Peru's history. He was able to decentralize the government in 2002 and sucessfully prosecute Fujimori's right-hand man, but strikes by teachers and farmers in 2003 led to a state of emergency and the use of troops to bring order. In 2003 Peru joined the free trade group Mercosur, the last Shining Path leader, "Marcelo," was captured, and the Truth and Reconciliation Commission published its report documenting the killings in the 1980s. In a surprising comeback, Alan García won the election of 2006 and began an economic program that helped grow the economy and tame inflation. But his popularity declined as protests in the poorer sections of the country grew in size. Drug trafficking and organized crime remained serious concerns that García tried to attack.

In 2009 protests erupted when the Peruvian government opened the rain forest to foreign investments without involving the indigenous people who lived there. The protests have disrupted oil production and pipelines, blocked commerce on roads and waterways, and halted flights at remote airports. The government agreed to negotiate after several people were killed.

▶ PHILIPPINES
Republic of the Philippines
● **GEOGRAPHY   Location:** archipelago of some 7,100 islands about 500 mi. (800 km) off southeastern Asia; about 1,100 mi. (2,800 km) from N to S and 650 mi. (1,684 km) from W to E; Luzon in N and Mindanao in S account for 66% of land area. Manila 14°36′N, 120°59′E. **Boundaries:** Luzon Strait to N, Philippine Sea to E, Celebes Sea to S, Sulu Sea to SW, and South China Sea to W. **Total area:** 115,830 sq. mi. (300,000 sq km). **Coastline:** 22,554 mi. (36,289 km). **Comparative area:** slightly larger than Arizona. **Land use:** 18% arable land; 15% permanent crops; 67% other. **Major cities:** Manila (capital); Quezon City; Davao City; Caloocan City; Cebu City.
● **PEOPLE   Population:** 99,900,177 (July 2010 est.). **Nationality:** noun—Filipino(s); adjective—Philippine. **Ethnic groups:** 91.5% Christian Malay, 4% Muslim Malay, 1.5% Chinese, 3% other. **Languages:** Pilipino (based on Tagalog) and English (both official). **Religions:** 83% Roman Catholic, 8%

other Christian, 5% Muslim, 3% Buddhist and other.

• **GOVERNMENT Type:** republic. **Independence:** June 12, 1898 (from Spain); July 4, 1946 (from U.S.). **Constitution:** Feb. 2, 1987, effective Feb. 11, 1987. **National holiday:** Independence Day, June 12. **Head of Government:** Benigno Aquino, president (since Jun. 2010). **Structure:** executive; bicameral legislature; judiciary.

• **ECONOMY Monetary unit:** Philippine peso. **Budget:** (2009 est.) *income:* $23.29 bil.; *expend.:* $29.23 bil. **G.D.P.:** $324.8 bil., $3,300 per capita (2009 est.). **Chief crops:** rice, corn, coconut, sugarcane, bananas; pork, eggs, beef; fish. **Natural resources:** timber, crude oil, nickel, cobalt, silver. **Major industries:** textiles, pharmaceuticals, chemicals. **Labor force:** 37.89 mil. (2009 est.); 34% agriculture, 51% services, 15% industry (2007 est.); 7.3% unemployment (2007). **Exports:** $37.2 bil. (2009 est.); electronics and telecommunications, machinery and transport, garments. **Imports:** $45.8 bil. (2009 est.); raw materials and intermediate goods, capital goods, consumer goods, fuels. **Major trading partners:** (2008) *exports:* 17.6% U.S., 16.2% Japan, 9.8% Netherlands, 8.6% Hong Kong, 7.7% China; *imports:* 12.5% Japan, 12% U.S., 8.8% China, 8.7% Singapore, 7.9% South Korea, 7.1% Taiwan, 5.7% Thailand.

The Philippines were anciently settled by various Malayan peoples in several waves of migration from Southeast Asia. Tribal societies coexisted with petty principalities that had trade links to China, the East Indies, and countries in the Indian Ocean. The Philippines were visited by Magellan (who was killed there) in 1521, and Spanish conquest of the islands began in 1564. The Spanish colonial capital at Manila was founded in 1571 and became a key transit point for trade between Mexico and the Far East. Under Spanish rule a majority of Filipinos became Christian except in the southwestern islands, which remained Muslim. The Spanish period was marked by a torpid colonial administration and a rise in the power and wealth of the Catholic church.

In the late 19th century, a nationalist movement led by José Rizal gained a wide following. In 1896 an armed uprising began, led by Emilio Aguinaldo. The 1898 victory of Adm. George Dewey at the Battle of Manila Bay during the Spanish-American War led Spain to cede the Philippines to the U.S. in return for a payment of $20 million. Expecting immediate independence with U.S. support, Aguinaldo declared the islands a republic. When this was not recognized by the U.S., Aguinaldo led a new war for independence, which was bloodily suppressed by American troops in a six-year campaign, 1899–1905.

American policy in the Philippines combined military control with a desire to encourage home rule leading to independence. In 1935 the Commonwealth of the Philippines was established, with Manuel Quezon as its first president, beginning what was conceived of as a 10-year period of controlled autonomy leading to full independence on July 4, 1946. In November 1941, Quezon was reelected to the presidency. On Dec. 8, 1941, Japan attacked Manila and destroyed the American bases there. American and Filipino troops, after weeks of fierce fighting, evacuated the islands in March 1942. The battle to recapture the Philippines began with the Battle of Leyte Gulf in October 1944 and was completed by July 1945.

In April 1946, Manuel Roxas was elected president of the Commonwealth. Independence came as scheduled on July 4 of that year, with the United States retaining military bases by treaty and establishing a special economic relationship with the Philippines. The leftist Hukbalahap Rebellion, originally a partisan campaign against the Japanese, caused severe difficulties for the new nation until it was finally defeated in military campaigns led by Ramon Magsaysay who was elected to the presidency in November 1953.

The early years of independence were marked by some economic development, but also great economic inequality. Most land was held by huge estates, and the economy depended primarily on plantation crops (sugar, copra), mining, and timber. Villagers fleeing the rural subsistence economy poured into the cities, leading to huge slums and a climate of urban poverty and violence.

In 1966 Ferdinand Marcos was elected president on a reform platform. Overwhelmed in the early 1970s by demonstrations, a new leftist guerrilla movement, and a separatist rebellion by Islamic Moros in Mindinao, Marcos declared martial law on Sept. 21, 1972. On Jan. 17, 1973, Marcos promulgated a new constitution giving unprecedented power to the presidency. His wife, Imelda, began to wield considerable influence, and the climate of unrest, poverty, and corruption worsened throughout the 1970s. Martial law was lifted, however, on Jan. 17, 1981, and Marcos was reelected to a new six-year term as president.

The airport assassination of opposition leader Benigno Aquino on his return to the Philippines on Aug. 21, 1983, led to a new phase in opposition to Marcos's rule. In a bitterly contested presidential election in February 1986, Marcos was officially declared the winner over Aquino's widow, Corazon. Mrs. Aquino also declared herself the winner, and her supporters took to the streets in massive anti-Marcos demonstrations. Deserted by key supporters in the military, church, and middle class, Marcos fled the country on Feb. 25, 1986. Mrs. Aquino took office pledging land reform, a new constitution, and a commission to recover the wealth Marcos had plundered.

Under Pres. Aquino the Philippines remained unsettled. Her former ally, Vice Pres. Salvadore Laurel, formed an opposition party. Military and political measures aimed at putting down the Communist insurrection yielded mixed results. The economy of the Philippines continued to be dependent on U.S. and international assistance, and sentiment against the continued presence of U.S. military bases was strong. An eruption of Mount Pinatubo in June 1991 caused massive devastation in Luzon and destroyed Clark Air Base. In September, the national legislature voted not to renew the leases on U.S. military bases.

Aquino declined to run for re-election in 1992. Fidel Ramos won the presidency in a field of strong contenders, including Imelda Marcos. Lifted by a coalition that gave him a controlling majority in both houses of Congress after the 1994 elections, Ramos made "national reconciliation" his priority. In 1994 he proclaimed a cease-fire and amnesty for various insurgencies.

The Philippines' robust economic growth was slowed but not crippled by the Asian economic crisis of 1997–98. Pres. Ramos decided not to seek reelection in 1998; in a crowded field of candidates, Joseph Estrada, a popular actor, won the presidential election of May 1998, but the ruling LAKAS party elected the vice-president and took control of the lower house. A series of hostage crises with Muslim rebels on Mindanao punctuated the year 2000 but became overshadowed by serious bribery charges against Pres. Estrada. When the Senate in Jan. 2001 suspended the president's trial, the protests expanded to a general strike; and when the heads of the armed forces joined the protests, Estrada's days were through. Vice-president Gloria Macagapal Arroyo was sworn in as Estrada resigned. By May the anti-Estrada coalition controlled the Congress and Estrada was under arrest.

The U.S. war on terrorism arrived here in 2001–02 as 4,000 troops landed in Mindanao to train Phillipine soldiers for the fight against the Abu Sayyaf Muslim insurgency. But the insurgency, along with the Moro Islamic Liberation Front and the (Indonesia-based) Jemaah Islamica, did not abate. Pres. Arroyo's re-election campaign against an action-movie star was confirmed in June 2004 by a Congressional Committee.

In July 2005 a tape of Pres. Arroyo talking about ballot tampering with an election official during the last campaign caused her popularity to plummet and led to many calls for her resignation. She survived but her government was severely weakened. In February 2006 her declaration of a state of emergency because of an alleged coup attempt was viewed by many as a means to silencing opposition critics. In 2010 the son of Corazon Aquino and her murdered husband was elected president.

▶ POLAND
Republic of Poland

• **GEOGRAPHY Location:** eastern Europe. **Boundaries:** Baltic Sea to N, Russia and Lithuania to NE, Belarus and Ukraine to E, Czech Republic and Slovakia to S, Germany to W. **Total area:** 120,728 sq. mi. (312,685 sq km). **Coastline:** 305 mi. (491 km). **Comparative area:** slightly smaller than New Mexico. **Land use:** 40.25% arable land; 1% permanent crops; 58.75% other. **Major cities:** Warszawa (Warsaw, capital); Lodz; Krakow (Cracow); Wroclaw; Poznan.
• **PEOPLE Population:** 38,463,689 (July 2010 est.). **Nationality:** noun—Pole(s); adjective—Polish. **Ethnic groups:** 96.7% Polish, 1.3% German, 0.6% Ukrainian, 0.5% Byelorussian. **Languages:** Polish. **Religions:** 89.8% Roman Catholic (about 75% practicing), 5% Eastern Orthodox, Protestant, and other.
• **GOVERNMENT Type:** republic. **Independence:** Nov. 11, 1918 (independent republic proclaimed) **Constitution:** Oct. 16, 1997; adopted by the National Assembly on Apr. 2, 1997; passed by national referendum May 25, 1997. **National holiday:** Constitution Day, May 3. **Heads of Government:** Grzegorz Schetyna, elected president in special election following the death of President Lech Kaczynski in an airplane crash (since Aug. 2010); Donald Tusk, prime minister (since Nov. 2007). **Structure:** executive—prime minister is head of government; bicameral legislature—2 seats in lower house are constitutionally assigned to ethnic German parties; judiciary.
• **ECONOMY Monetary unit:** zloty. **Budget:** (2009 est.) *income:* $83.68 bil.; *expend.:* $93.47 bil. **G.D.P.:** $690.1 bil., $17,900 per capita (2009 est.). **Chief crops:** potatoes, milk, cheese, fruits, vegetables, wheat; poultry and eggs; pork, beef. **Natural resources:** coal, sulfur, copper, natural gas, silver. **Major industries:** machine building, iron and steel, extractive industries. **Labor force:** 16.99

mil. (2009 est.); 22.1% industry and construction, 27.5% agriculture, 50.4% services. **Exports:** $134.7 bil. (2009 est.); manufactured goods, chemicals; machinery and equipment; food and live animals. **Imports:** 141.7 bil. (2009 est.); manufactured goods, chemicals; machinery and equipment; mineral fuels. **Major trading partners:** (2008) *exports:* 24.4% Germany, 6% France, 5.9% Italy, 5.6% U.K., 5.5% Czech Republic, 5.2% Russia; *imports:* 28% Germany, 9.7% Russia, 6.1% Italy, 5.3% Netherlands, 4.7% France.

The Slavic people known as Polonians accepted Christianity in the second half of the 10th century, during the reign of Duke Mieszko, whose close relationship with the papacy prevented the Holy Roman Empire from absorbing Poland. A strong and united Polish kingdom existed under the Piast dynasty until 1370, when the Anjou king of Hungary succeeded to the throne, followed by his daughter Jadwiga, who in 1386 married the grand duke of Lithuania, thus forming the great Commonwealth of Poland-Lithuania.

With the end of the Jagellonian line in 1572, the monarchy became elective. With a large nobility, equaling about 10 percent of the population, the monarchy grew weak, and Poland increasingly was subject to foreign intervention. The rise of the expansionist powers of Sweden, Prussia, Russia, and Austria came in part at the expense of the Poles. Jan Sobieski (1624–96), who ruled Poland as John III, saved Vienna from the Turks and briefly revived the Polish monarchy, but Polish royal power ended with his death. In a series of partitions in 1772, 1793, and 1795, Poland was dismembered and finally obliterated as a state.

Napoleon revived a Polish national entity with the Grand Duchy of Warsaw; with Napoleon's fall, the Congress of Vienna re-created a Kingdom of Poland in 1815, under the rule of the czar of Russia. After 1830 Poland was subjected to systematic Russification. The fall of Russia in World War I led to Poland's revival. The Lithuanian Socialist Jósef Pilsudski led Poland in war against the new Bolshevik government of Russia until, in the 1921 Treaty of Riga, Poland emerged with its boundaries restored to those after the partition of 1793. It was ethnically about 70 percent Polish, a triumph for Polish nationalism but the end of Pilsudski's dream of a federation of northeastern Europe. Poland also had the largest Jewish population of any country in Europe.

With a strong legislature and a weak president, the new state seemed to Pilsudski too weak for its own defense. He became a virtual dictator in 1926 and ruled until his death in 1935. After his death a weak parliamentary government was controlled by military officers; the tentative revival of republicanism was halted by Hitler's and Stalin's aggression in 1939, yet another partition of Poland.

Poland was primarily an agricultural country, and the postwar republic attempted land reform, with some success; about 750,000 new private farm holdings were created by 1938. Mining—of coal and copper—was the principal traditional industrial activity in the 20th century, supplemented by extraction of natural gas. In the mid-1930s shipbuilding and railroad construction led the way toward a modern economy.

World War II commenced in September 1939, with attacks on Poland by Germany and the Soviet Union. The war brought severe destruction to Poland and the extermination of virtually its entire Jewish population. A government-in-exile was established in London, but the Soviet Union broke relations with it in 1943 when it requested a Red Cross investigation into the murder of 14,000 Polish officers whose bodies were discovered in Katyn Forest. (The Soviet government acknowledged responsibility for the massacre in 1990.) The Soviets established a puppet government in Lublin in 1944. In August the Red Army paused in its western advance on the outskirts of Warsaw, permitting the Nazis to obliterate the Polish Home Army. On Jan. 1, 1945, the U.S.S.R. recognized the Lublin regime as Poland's government.

By the time of the Allied Powers Conference in Yalta in February 1945, the Red Army was only 40 miles from Berlin and had total control of Poland. The Allies agreed to Stalin's proposal, allowing Russia to incorporate the eastern half of the country, and agreed that the government should be constituted from an enlargement of the Lublin regime. At Potsdam in Aug. 1945, Poland's borders were shifted approximately 200 miles westward from the prewar configuration. The German population was expelled.

The free elections promised in the Yalta Agreement were postponed until 1947, by which time a Communist victory could be assured. In 1948 the Socialists were forcibly merged into the Communist party; in 1949 Premier Boleslaw Bierut requested that Soviet general Konstantin Rokossovski be appointed minister of defense and commander in chief of the Polish army. All cultural periodicals and all writers' and artists' associations were taken over by the Communist party.

But there was little collectivization of agriculture or forced industrialization on the Stalinist model. Intellectuals, bolstered by the Catholic church, questioned the regime with some boldness. In 1956 both Bierut and Party Secretary Minc died, and Wladislaw Gomulka was elected party chairman in Oct. 1956. As Soviet warships sailed toward Poland, Nikita Khrushchev flew to Poland with a delegation of Soviet generals, where Gomulka assured them that Poland would follow the Soviet lead. Distracted by the crisis in Hungary, the Russians left Gomulka in power and even canceled Poland's debt.

For a short time Gomulka permitted cultural and educational freedom, but by 1958 he had reverted to Stalinist form, imposing controls and pursuing a somewhat anti-Semitic Polish nationalism. Gomulka ruled until 1971, when he was replaced as party secretary by Edward Gierek. But moral leadership within Poland had clearly passed to Stefan Cardinal Wyszynski, leader of the increasingly vocal Catholic church; Gierek was forced to improve relations with the church in order to maintain his own credibility as a national leader.

Gierek presided over a decade of increasing unrest and growing discontent. Polish exports of ham and furniture to the West earned some hard currency but could not curb the rising national debt. The most significant event in Poland in the 1970s was the election of Karol Wojtyla, bishop of Krakow, as Pope John Paul II in October 1978. His visit to Poland in 1979 set the stage for the extraordinary events of the 1980s.

Gierek's austerity program of 1980 sent meat prices soaring. Strikes for wage adjustments, especially at the Lenin Shipyards in Gdansk, thrust Lech Walesa, a shipyard worker, into a position of national leadership. Walesa was elected chairman of the national coordinating committee of independent labor unions, Solidarity. Solidarity's demands went far beyond lower prices and higher wages; they included independent labor unions with the right to strike, freedom for political prisoners, and an end to censorship. In September Gierek resigned as party secretary and was replaced by Stanislaw Kania. By December, 40 independent trade unions had been formed, and a "rural Solidarity" movement was growing. In Feb. 1981 Soviet Army general Wojciech Jaruzelski was named prime minister. When in December Solidarity announced plans to hold a referendum on the Jaruzelski regime, martial law was declared; Solidarity leaders were arrested, all its activities banned, and the right to strike was abolished.

But the government was never able to suppress Solidarity as a popular force, and it was legalized in 1989. In 1989 elections Solidarity won 99 of 100 Senate seats and 299 of 460 seats in the lower house, although 65 percent had been reserved for the Communist party. Jaruzelski was elected president by Parliament and Solidarity leader Tadeusz Mazowiecki became prime minister.

The Communist party voted to disband on Jan. 28, 1990, and the Mazowiecki government announced a program of economic reform, winning promises of foreign aid and increased investment from the West. In June 1990, a commission was appointed to draft a new constitution, and in presidential elections, Walesa, at the head of Solidarity's labor/Catholic faction, defeated Mazowiecki, representing Solidarity's political/technocrat faction.

The new prime minister, Krzysztof Bielecki, continued the reformist policies of curbing inflation and government spending, fostering foreign investment, and privatizing state enterprises. But the shock therapy, with its higher prices and unemployment (even while creating more than a million new jobs), led to disillusionment. In the first fully free parliamentary elections, held in Oct. 1991, only 42 percent of the voters participated, electing a fragmented 29-party Parliament. Reluctantly, Pres. Walesa named Jan Olszewski as prime minister of a coalition government. The Olszewski coalition collapsed in June 1992, replaced by an equally fragile seven-party coalition led by Hanna Suchocka, Poland's first female prime minister.

Despite high inflation (40 percent) and high unemployment (13 percent), under Poland's "iron lady" the private sector expanded and even the remaining state-owned enterprises responded to market demand, pushing exports from $8 bil. in 1988 to $14 bil. in 1992. And in May 1993, Parliament passed a bill privatizing 600 companies.

Still, at the end of May 1993, the Suchocka government fell, by one vote, to a Solidarity-sponsored no-confidence measure, in protest against her austerity budget. In new elections held in Oct. 1993, the Communist party (now called the Democratic Left Alliance) formed a coalition with the Peasants party to forge a return to power. The Communist prime minister, Josef Oleksy, was joined by his party-mate Aleksander Kwasniewski, who defeated Walesa in presidential elections held in Nov. 1995. A month after the election Oleksy was accused of spying for Russia, and although he protested his innocence, he resigned.

Poland's economy was among the fastest growing in Europe (a 7 percent rise in G.D.P. and billions in direct foreign investment) although inflation ran high. In 1997, a new constitution and invitations to join NATO and eventually the E.U. gave the Poles a reason to believe the future looked very positive. The first elections under the new constitution produced a center-right coalition government. In 1999 Poland joined NATO, finally achieving security against the Russian expansion it always feared.

Bucking western Europe's right-wing electoral tide, Poland's Democratic Left Alliance captured control of the Sjem, garnering a near majority of the 460 seats. Leszek Miller became premier in coalition with the Polish Peasants' Party. In June 2003 voters gave overwhelming approval (77 percent) to joining the E.U. Miller's government fell in May 2004. A new, center right coalition government headed by Lech Kaczynski took power at the end of 2005. He appointed his twin brother, Jaroslaw, to be prime minister (July 2006) to raised eyebrows at home and abroad.

Poland's entry into the E.U. proved a boon to the economy but rejection of the constitution by France and the Netherlands in 2005 was viewed as a sign of fear that cheap labor from Poland, etc. was causing a backlash. About two million Poles had gone to work in other E.U. nations. In 2007, the Kaczynski government began to fall apart as it concentrated on social issues such as abortion and its demand to examine the past records of 700,000 people for ties to the communist regime, soon overruled by the courts. In Aug. 2007, its coalition dissolved and a snap election resulted in a victory for a liberal, pro-E.U. party. In Aug. 2008 an agreement was reached with the U.S. to put a missile defense system in Poland despite strong Russian protests. The Obama administration backed off the plan in Sept. 2009. In April 2010 Pres. Kaczynski and dozens of high-ranking officials were killed in a plane crash in western Russia.

▶ **PORTUGAL**
Portuguese Republic
● **GEOGRAPHY Location:** Iberian Peninsula in southwest Europe; also two archipelagos in Atlantic Ocean: Azores (37°29'N, 25°40'W) and Madeira Islands (32°40'N, 16°55'W). **Boundaries:** Spain to N and E, Atlantic Ocean to S and W. **Total area:** 35,552 sq. mi. (92,080 sq km). **Coastline:** 1,114 mi. (1,793 km). **Comparative area:** slightly smaller than Indiana. **Land use:** 21% arable land; 8% permanent crops; 71% other. **Major cities:** Lisboa (Lisbon, capital); Porto (Oporto); Amadora; Setubal; Coimbra.
● **PEOPLE Population:** 10,735,765 (2010 est.). **Nationality:** noun—Portuguese (sing., pl.); adjective—Portuguese. **Ethnic groups:** homogeneous Mediterranean stock; citizens of African descent who immigrated during decolonization number less than 100,000. **Languages:** Portuguese. **Religions:** 85% Roman Catholic, Protestant, 2% other Christian, 4% none.
● **GOVERNMENT Type:** parliamentary democracy, republic. **Independence:** Oct. 5, 1910. **Constitution:** Apr. 25, 1976, revised Oct. 1982 and June 1989, Nov. 1992, Sept. 1997. **National holiday:** Day of Portugal, June 10. **Heads of Government:** Anibal Cavaco Silva, president (since March 2006); José Socrates, prime minister (since March 2005). **Structure:** executive—president and prime minister; unicameral legislature-(popularly elected 230-seat Assembly of the Republic); judiciary.
● **ECONOMY Monetary unit:** euro. **Budget:** (2009 est.) *income:* $91.89 bil.; *expend.:* $106.8 bil. **G.D.P.:** $233.4 bil.; $21,800 per capita (2009 est.). **Chief crops:** grains, potatoes, olives, grapes for wine; livestock. **Natural resources:** fish, forests

(cork), tungsten, iron ore, uranium ore. **Major industries:** textiles, footwear, wood pulp, paper, cork. **Labor force:** 5.58 mil. (2009); 60% services, 30% industry, 10% agriculture (2007); 4.7% unemployment (2001 est.). **Exports:** $41.43 bil. (2009 est.); clothing and footwear, machinery, chemicals, cork and paper products, hides. **Imports:** $58.79 bil. (2009 est.); machinery and transport equipment, chemicals, petroleum, textiles, agricultural products. **Major trading partners:** (2008) *exports:* 25.6% Spain, 12.6% Germany, 11.1% France, 5.9% Angola, 5.3% U.K.; *imports:* 28.9% Spain, 11.6% Germany, 8% France, 4.9% Italy, 4.4% Netherlands.

Portugal traces its origins back to the warlike Lusitanian tribes of Roman times. The nation-state originated as a county of the kingdom of Leon-Castile, reconquered from the Moors in the 11th century. Portugal won recognition as an independent kingdom in 1143, and conquered Lisbon four years later. In 1267 the Algarve was conquered, and by then Portugal had expanded to its modern boundaries. Except for the period 1580–1640, when it was ruled by the Spanish Habsburgs, the Portuguese dynasty maintained its independence into the 20th century.

Portuguese fishermen had probably frequented the Grand Banks from before the time of Columbus, and the nation's tradition of seafaring gave rise to a world empire in the 15th and 16th centuries. Prince Henry the Navigator (1394–1460) colonized the Azores and the Madeiras and sponsored voyages of exploration along the west coast of Africa. Under his successors, Portugal controlled the west African coast, the shores of the Indian Ocean, and large stretches of southern Asia, as well as, in the Western Hemisphere, Brazil. Yet the rise of the empires of Spain and the Netherlands quickly reduced the Portuguese to second-rank status, leaving only Macao, Goa, and Timor in Asia; Portuguese Guinea (Guinea Bissau), Mozambique, and Angola in Africa; and the great territory of Brazil in Latin America.

In the 19th century, a series of dynastic civil wars weakened the monarchy, allowing Britain to gain control of the country's foreign policy (in addition to the wine trade of Oporto, long in British hands). Brazil declared its independence in 1822.

In 1910 Portugal became the first kingdom in the 20th century to be transformed into a republic. But in the next 15 years, chaos ensued: eight presidents, 44 governments, and a nearcollapse of the economy. Finally, the military established a dictatorship, lasting until recent times. In 1928 the military installed a civilian dictator, a professor of economics, Antonio Salazar. A firm believer in law and order, he managed to control the turbulence of political life and made the escudo one of Europe's most stable currencies, yet he could do nothing to alter Portugal's fundamental poverty. Although he ruled through civilian governments, his essential support always came from the army.

World War II affected Portugal very little. Salazar deftly managed to remain Britain's ally while keeping his country out of the war as a neutral state. In the postwar period, Portugal accepted Marshall Plan aid and became a member of NATO in 1949. Portugal was a founding member of the European Free Trade Association in 1959 and negotiated a special relationship with the EC in 1972 (when its trading partner and ally, Great Britain, joined that body).

Portugal joined the United Nations in 1955, just in time to become embroiled in the worldwide movement for decolonization. Protesting that Portugal had, not colonies, but "overseas provinces," Salazar refused to bow to the pressure of world opinion. In 1961 India forcibly annexed Goa and other Portuguese enclaves on the subcontinent. In the same year, nationalist revolts broke out in Angola, Guinea and Mozambique.

The colonial wars of the 1960s placed a terrible strain on Portugal's economy. Salazar, gravely ill, retired in 1968 and was replaced by Marcelo Caetano who was deposed in a bloodless coup staged by the Armed Forces in 1974. The coup's leader, Antonio de Spinola, after reaching agreements on the independence of most of Portugal's old colonies, resigned as head of government in September 1974. Costa Gomes replaced Spinola, as a Revolutionary Council was instituted. The council survived two coup attempts, one by right-wing soldiers, the other by Communists, and it promulgated a Socialist constitution in 1976. Through a series of unstable governments, the old agrarian estates were expropriated, and banking, insurance, and large industrial concerns were nationalized. The shock of this economic transformation, along with the OPEC price rises, created a recession in the 1970s. In addition Portugal had to absorb a million Portuguese refugees from the former colonies.

Attempts by center-right coalitions in the 1980s to undo the nationalizations of the 1970s were thwarted by vetoes of the Constitutional Tribunal, even when the free-market Social Democratic party held an absolute majority in the assembly. Portugal entered the EC on Jan. 1, 1986, pledging to reduce tariffs and end agricultural subsidies over a 10-year transitional period.

In 1987 the Social Democrats, running on a platform of spending cuts, privatization of state-owned firms, and reversal of agricultural collectivism, became the first party since 1974 to win an absolute majority in the legislative assembly. Per capita income tripled over the years 1985-92, so that Portugal was no longer the poorest country in the E.U. The 1992 sale of the huge state-owned Petrogal oil company was a harbinger of a return to free enterprise. In Oct. 1995, Antonio Guterres of the Socialist party displaced the Social Democrats. And in January 1996, Jorge Sampaio won the presidential election, giving Portugal both a Socialist president and prime minister for the first time since democracy was restored.

Portugal's economic stability was ratified in 1998 by the E.U. when the latter approved Portugal's membership in the Monetary Union. G.D.P. growth averaged 3.5 percent through the late 1990s. In Dec. 1999 the colony of Macao was returned to Chinese rule after 442 years. In 2001 Sampaio was easily reelected. March elections brought another center-right coalition as the Social Democrats took 102 (of 230) seats, selecting Manual Durao Barroso as prime minister. In 2005 the Socialists won a landslide victory as the economy hit a stalling pattern, and José Socrates became prime minister. His budget cuts aimed at stimulating the economy did not enhance his popularity, and the 2008–09 recession sank the economy badly. By 2010 fears that Portugal's debt would lead to a default on its obligations forced the government to begin an austerity plan that led to strikes and protests.

▶ QATAR
State of Qatar

• **GEOGRAPHY Location:** occupies a peninsula projecting northward from Arabian mainland into western part of Persian (Arabian) Gulf. **Boundaries:** Persian Gulf to N, E, and W; Saudi Arabia and United Arab Emirates to S. **Total area:** 4,247 sq. mi. (11,000 sq km). **Coastline:** 350 mi. (563 km). **Comparative area:** slightly smaller than Connecticut. **Land use:** 1% arable land; 0% permanent crops; 99% other. **Major cities:** Doha (capital); Al Rayyan; Al Wakrah.

• **PEOPLE Population:** 833,285 (July 2009 est.). **Nationality:** noun—Qatari(s); adjective—Qatari. **Ethnic groups:** 40% Arab, 18% Pakistani, 18% Indian, 10% Iranian, 14% other. **Languages:** Arabic (official), English commonly used as second language. **Religions:** 77% Muslim, 9% Christian, 14% Other.

• **GOVERNMENT Type:** emirate. **Independence:** Sept. 3, 1971 (from U.K.). **Constitution:** provisional constitution enacted Apr. 19, 1972; permanent constitution approved by referendum Apr. 29, 2003; effective June 2005. **National holiday:** Independence Day, Sept. 3. **Head of Government:** Sheikh Hamad bin Jassim bin Jabr Al-Thani (since Apr. 2007). **Structure:** executive—amir is head of government and chief of state; unicameral legislature—consultative, no elections since 1970, members terms extended every four years; judiciary.

• **ECONOMY Monetary unit:** Qatari riyal. **Budget:** (2008 est.) *income:* $40.36 bil.; *expend.:* $28.08 bil. **G.D.P.:** $85.35 bil., $103,500 per capita (2008 est.). **Chief crops:** fruits, vegetables; poultry, dairy products, beef; fish. **Natural resources:** crude oil, natural gas, fish. **Major industries:** crude oil production and refining, fertilizers, petrochemicals. **Labor force:** 1.124 mil. (2008 est.); less than 1% unemployment (2007). **Exports:** $62.44 bil. (f.o.b., 2008 est.); 80% petroleum products, steel, fertilizers. **Imports:** $24.96 bil. (f.o.b., 2008 est.); machinery, consumer goods, food, chemicals. **Major trading partners:** (2006) *exports:* 40% Japan, 16% South Korea, 7% Singapore, 4% Thailand; *imports:* 13% France, 10% Japan, 9% Italy, 9% U.S., 8% Germany, 6% U.K., 6% South Africa, 5% South Korea.

The Qatar peninsula was ruled as part of the sheikhdom of Bahrain from the late 18th century until the mid-19th century. An informal British protectorate was established in 1868; the Ottoman Empire also asserted authority over the sheikhs of Qatar from 1872 to 1916. The Ottomans ceded authority to the British in that year, and a formal British protectorate was organized. When British forces withdrew from the Persian Gulf region in 1971, Qatar entered into negotiations with the emirates of the Trucial Coast to join the federation of the United Arab Emirates. When those negotiations broke down, Qatar declared its independence on Sept. 3, 1971. For over 30 years it has been politically stable under one ruler, Sheik Hamad bin Khalifa al-Thani, although he was deposed by his son in a bloodless coup in June 1995. He has claimed he wants to move the country toward democracy and has called for a free press, limited elections, and allowing women to vote. Much of this was accomplished by 1999, and in 2005 a constitution came into force with elections for some members of parliament scheduled for 2007. These were rescheduled for 2008, but had not happened as of September 2010.

▶ ROMANIA

• **GEOGRAPHY Location:** southeastern Europe. **Boundaries:** Ukraine to N, Moldova to NE, Black Sea to E, Bulgaria to S, Yugoslavia (Serbia) to SW, Hungary to NW. **Total area:** 91,699 sq. mi. (237,500 sq km). **Coastline:** 140 mi. (225 km). **Comparative area:** slightly smaller than Oregon. **Land use:** 41% arable land; 3% permanent crops; 21% meadows and pastures; 29% forest and woodland; 6% other; includes 11% irrigated. **Major cities:** Bucharesti (Bucharest, capital); Constanta; Iasi; Timisoara; Cluj-Napoca.

• **PEOPLE Population:** 22,215,421 (July 2009 est.). **Nationality:** noun—Romanian(s); adjective—Romanian. **Ethnic groups:** 89.5% Romanian, 6.6% Hungarian, 2.5% Roma, German, Ukrainian, Russian, Turk, other. **Languages:** Romanian, Hungarian, German. **Religions:** 87% Eastern Orthodox, 6% Roman Catholic, 7% Protestant.

• **GOVERNMENT Type:** republic. **Independence:** 1881 (from Turkey); republic proclaimed Dec. 30, 1947. **Constitution:** Dec. 8, 1991; revised Oct.29, 2003. **National holiday:** Unification Day, Dec. 1. **Heads of Government:** Traian Basescu, president (since Dec. 2004); Emil Boc, prime minister (since Dec. 2008). **Structure:** executive; bicameral legislature; judiciary.

• **ECONOMY Monetary unit:** leu. **Budget:** (2008 est.): *income:* $64.44 bil.; *expend.:* $71.16 bil. **G.D.P.:** $271.2 bil., $12,200 per capita (2008 est.). **Chief crops:** corn, wheat; milk, eggs, meat. **Natural resources:** crude oil (reserves declining); timber, natural gas, coal, iron ore. **Major industries:** mining, timber, construction materials. **Labor force:** 9.32 mil. (2008 est.); 4.1% unemployment (2007). **Exports:** $59.75 bil. (f.o.b., 2008 est.); textiles and footwear, metals and metal products, machinery and equipment. **Imports:** $92.09 bil. (f.o.b., 2008 est.); machinery and equipment, fuels and minerals, chemicals. **Major trading partners:** (2006) *exports:* 18% Italy, 16% Germany, 8% Turkey, 8% France, 5% Hungary, 4% U.K.; *imports:* 15% Germany, 14% Italy, 8% Russia, 6% France, 5% turkey, 4% China.

The Roman province of Dacia was sufficiently Latinized to retain the name of Rome long after the legions withdrew in A.D. 27. Overrun by invading Bulgars in the eighth century, the Romanians retained their Latinate language and orthodox Christianity; Romania remained beyond the borders of the Byzantine Empire but was in close contact with it. The area was conquered by the Mongols in the 13th century and formed the independent principalities of Moldavia and Walachia after the Mongols withdrew.

By the 15th century, Moldavia and Walachia had become vassal states of the Ottoman Empire, though with some local autonomy that permitted retention of orthodox Christianity and the creation of a rich local culture. Attempts at national unity against Ottoman rule in 1601 and 1711 failed; in 1861 the provinces united as an autonomous state under the name Romania, within the Ottoman Empire, under Greek administration. Independence came in 1878.

Romania was for centuries the poorest country in Europe. Thoroughly agricultural, it was a land of unfree peasants working the great estates of landowners who were generally wealthy, usually absentee, and often Greek. The peasants not only paid taxes but also were required to perform feudal labor services for the estate owners.

After enlarging itself at Bulgaria's expense in the Second Balkan War (1913), Romania switched sides three times in World War I, joining the Allies just before the war's end. Its reward was a huge expansion, doubling its territory with lands taken from Austria, Hungary, Russia, and Bulgaria.

The interwar period was one of political turbulence, marked by violence and assassinations. Twice King Carol II went into exile, leaving his throne to his son Prince Michael; the second time was in 1940, when Russia (in accordance with the Hitler-Stalin pact) reclaimed the territories of Bessarabia and northern Bukovina it had lost to Romania in 1920; Hitler required Romania to return about half of Transylvania to Hungary.

During World War II, the pro-Hitler dictator Marshall Ion Antonescu took power, supported by a semifascist "Iron Guard," but when the latter attempted a coup, the military crushed the uprising. Romanian troops participated in Hitler's invasion of Russia in 1941, and the country paid the price in 1944 when Russian troops "liberated" the country, with devastating results.

The country was quickly transformed into a Soviet satellite through rigged elections in which the communist National Democratic Front replaced the Peasant Alliance in power; a People's Republic was proclaimed on Dec. 30, 1947, and King Michael was forced to abdicate. A peace treaty in 1947 confirmed the loss of Bessarabia to Russia but returned Transylvania to Romania.

Under Russian occupation Romania was a virtual Soviet colony. The occupying armies did not leave until after reparation payments were completed in 1958, leaving the dictator Gheorghe Gheorghiu-Dej in power. Despite Council of Mutual Economic Assistance (COMECON) plans for Romania to become a major food supplier to the Soviet bloc, Gheorghiu-Dej pursued industrialization on the Stalinist model, in the process ruining Romanian agriculture while creating large, labor-intensive, and highly inefficient factories. The result was an economic depression; politically, however, it produced a de facto independence for Romania within the Soviet bloc. Russian troops were forbidden on Romanian soil, and Romania declined to participate in COMECON policies.

With the death of Gheorghiu-Dej in 1965, power passed to Nicolae Ceauşescu. He promulgated a new constitution and instituted a series of purges; he became party leader in 1965, prime minister in 1967, and president of the republic in 1974. Ceauşescu continued his predecessor's economic policy, deepening the country's misery; he also pursued a policy of "independence" from the U.S.S.R., refusing to go along with Soviet policies of de-Stalinization and liberalization. Romania's "national communism" was expressed in militant nationalism, coupled with severe repression of ethnic minorities. Ceauşescu's ambitions included the creation of a family dynasty in the Romanian leadership. In 1979 his wife Elena was named first deputy premier and elevated to the Council of Ministers. Her brothers were given important government positions; Ceauşescu's son, despite his reputation as a playboy, was groomed to replace his father.

Romania's transition from Communist rule was sudden and violent. On Dec. 16–18, 1989, demonstrations in Timisoara calling for Ceauşescu's ouster were put down with brute force by the Securitate (secret police), but they spread and citizens and regular army troops fought pitched battles with Securitate forces in Bucharest. Ceaușescu and his wife fled Bucharest but were captured, tried, and executed. The newly organized Council of National Salvation established a provisional government, consisting primarily of anti-Ceaușescu Communists in league with the Romanian army, with former Communist party official Ion Iliescu as president.

The Communist party was outlawed on Jan. 12, 1990. Despite the Council's domination by former Communists, no effective opposition movement emerged, and in hastily called and rigged elections on May 20, Iliescu was elected president and the Council won 233 of 296 seats in the house.

In June 1990, many anti-Communist demonstrators were beaten and several killed by troops and armed miners brought to Bucharest by the government. Calls for Iliescu's resignation and a purge of Communists from government grew. Tensions were aggravated when the government's abrupt move to a market economy resulted in food shortages and price increases. Continued rioting in 1991 led to the appointment of the non-Communist Theodor Stolojan at the head of a "caretaker" coalition. Elections in 1992 gave the National Salvation Front 28 percent of the seats in Parliament while the opposition Democratic Convention gained 20 percent; Iliescu defeated the Democratic Convention candidate in the presidential election. Iliescu pledged to slow the transition to a market economy but by 1994 with inflation at over 250 percent (leading to a massive workers' strike in Feb.) the government agreed to I.M.F.'s demand for increased privatization and fiscal austerity in order to receive a $700 mil. loan. Iliescu's presidency ended in Nov. 1996 with a coalition government headed by Emil Constantinescu forging links to the Romanian Orthodox Church ending decades of official atheism and taking action against corrupt banking officials, businessmen, and politicians. The economy remained in dire straits but in early 1997 loans were secured from the I.M.F. and the World Bank.

Elections in Nov. 1997 were won by Constantinescu who became president and Victor Ciorbea the prime minister. Inflation and unemployment were falling but G.D.P. growth was lagging and, international default looked likely. I.M.F. demands for restructuring as a condition of further loans produced government plans which included the closing of mines but that in turn produced, in early 1999, widespread protest marches and violence by mine workers. Parliamentary elections in Nov. 2000 gave a preponderance to the parties of the left, but the presidential election drew greater interest: Ion Iliescu, claiming now to be a reformer and a pro-westerner, carried two-thirds of the vote in the run-off.

The nation moved toward closer ties with the West, joining NATO in 2004 and the E.U. in 2007. Corruption in government remained a major problem and led to the election of an outsider, Traian Basecu, as president in 2004, and again in 2007 after attempts to impeach him failed in a public referendum. His reforms to the justice system and of public services were severe but needed for entry into the E.U. But the financial collapse of 2009 put the nation's economy in jeopardy, requiring a $24 bil. aid package from the I.M.F. and the E.U.

▶ **RUSSIA**
Russian Federation

● **GEOGRAPHY** **Location:** northeastern Europe and northern Asia. **Boundaries:** Baltic Sea, Barents Sea, Kara Sea, East Siberian Sea to N, Bering Sea, Sea of Okhotsk, Sea of Japan to E, China, North Korea, Mongolia, Kazakhstan, Caspian Sea, Azerbaijan, Georgia, Black Sea to S, Ukraine, Belarus to W, Latvia, Estonia, Finland, Norway to NW. **Total area:** 6,592,745 sq. mi. (17,075,200 sq. km). **Coastline:** 23,402 mi. (37,653 km). **Comparative area:** slightly less than 1.8 times the size of the United States. **Land use:** 7% arable land, 0% permanent crops, 93% other. **Major cities:** Moscow (capital); St. Petersburg; Nizhnyi Novgorod; Novosibirsk.

● **PEOPLE** **Population:** 139,390,205 (July 2010 est.). **Nationality:** noun—Russian(s); adjective—Russian. **Ethnic groups:** Russian, Tatar, Ukrainian, Chuvash. **Languages:** Russian, other. **Religions:** Russian Orthodox, Muslim, other.

● **GOVERNMENT** **Type:** federation. **Independence:** Aug. 24, 1991 (from Soviet Union). **Constitution:** Dec. 12, 1993. **National holiday:** Russia Day, June 12, celebrating first presidential election. **Heads of Government:** Dmitriy Medvedev, president (since May 2008); Vladimir V. Putin, prime minister (since May 2008). **Structure:** executive—president, premier, various advisory bodies; bicameral legislature; judiciary.

● **ECONOMY** **Monetary unit:** ruble. **Budget:** (2009 est.) *income:* $205.3 bil..; *expend.:* $306.6 bil. **G.D.P.:** $2.116 tril., $15,100 per capita (2009 est.). **Chief crops:** grain, sugar beets, vegetables, sunflower seed; meat, milk. **Natural resources:** oil, natural gas, coal, timber. **Major industries:** extraction and processing raw materials, machine building from rolling mills to high-performance aircraft. **Labor force:** 75.81 mil. (2009). **Exports:** $295.6 bil. (2009 est.); petroleum and petroleum products, natural gas, wood and wood products, coal, metals, chemicals. **Imports:** $196.8 bil. (2009 est.); machinery and equipment, consumer goods, medicines, meat, grain, sugar, semifinished metal products. **Major trading partners:** (2008) *exports:* 12.2% Netherlands, 9% Italy, 6.9% Germany, 5.9% Turkey, 5% Ukraine, 4.5% China, 4.3% Poland; *imports:* 12.9% China, 12.6% Germany, 6.9% Japan, 6% Ukraine, 5.1% U.S., 4.1% Italy.

Russia is the largest and most powerful of the states to emerge from the former Soviet Union. As the seat of the Soviet empire that existed for over 70 years, the Russians wielded tremendous power both within the U.S.S.R. and in the international sphere. Almost from their emergence as a separate people, the Russians have extended the boundaries of their country to include a wide variety of non-Russian people. Both the Russian Czars and the Bolsheviks who came to power in 1917 have a long history of expansionist policies, which explains why, even today, an important part of the Russian national identity is that of leader of a large empire.

In the ninth century A.D., Viking traders organized a state, which they called Rus, in the river valleys between the Baltic and the Black Seas, centered on the cities of Kiev and Novgorod. In time the Vikings were absorbed into the native Slavic population; in 998 a Ruthenian prince of Kiev accepted Christianity from Constantinople. In the 13th century, Mongols under Genghis Khan and his descendants conquered most of Russia, and the Mongol Golden Horde maintained its power through the 14th century, exercising loose control over Novgorod and Moscow.

From the mid-19th century, Moscow grew to become the center of a new state that gathered in other cities and territories as Mongol power waned. Ivan III (Ivan the Great, 1440–1505) consolidated the power of Moscow; his marriage to a Byzantine princess led him to regard his empire as a third Rome, heir to the religious tradition of Constantinople. His grandson, Ivan IV (Ivan the Terrible, 1530–84), adopted the title czar (from the Latin caesar). He broke the power of the aristocratic boyar class and greatly extended the power of Moscow through military conquest.

Over the next two centuries, Russia carried out a steady program of expansion eastward into Siberia and across the Bering Strait to Alaska, until the empire covered one-sixth of the land surface of the globe. Peter the Great (1672–1725) made Russia a Baltic and Black Sea naval power, brought Russia into the European state system, and instituted a sweeping, if superficial, Westernization of his realm. His new capital at St. Petersburg became one of the most splendid cities in Europe. At the end of the 18th century, Catherine the Great (1729–96) participated with Prussia and Austria in the partitions of Poland, and Russia thereby became a major power in central Europe.

Catherine's grandson Alexander I (1777–1825), member of the grand coalition that defeated Napoleon, was not only czar of Russia but also king of Poland and grand duke of Finland. His troops occupied Paris in 1815. The Russian aristocracy became ardent Francophiles in the 19th century, ignoring growing problems at home. After losing the Crimean War in 1856, Russia began to develop Siberia and the southern territories near the border of Persia. Alaska was sold to the United States in 1867. In a major reform of the agricultural system, serfdom was abolished under Alexander II in 1861, though the newly independent peasantry, organized into agricultural cooperatives, only slowly derived benefits from its freedom. The late 19th century also marked the beginning of modern industrialization in Russia and of extensive development in Siberia, aided by state investment in railroads and mining.

Under the last czar, Nicholas II (1868–1918), Russia was defeated by Japan in a war over Manchuria in 1905. The defeat sparked a naval mutiny and an abortive revolution, which led to the establishment of a constitutional monarchy and other limited political reforms. Further military losses in World War I set the stage for the monarchy's downfall in the revolution of 1917.

The initial revolution of March 1917 brought a relatively moderate socialist (Menshevik) group to power. Its principal leader, Aleksandr Kerensky, organized a republican government and tried to maintain the Russian war effort but failed to gain control of the many contending revolutionary factions of the time. The Germans allowed the radical Bolshevik leader, Vladimir I. Lenin, to return to Russia, where he and his followers organized workers' soviets (councils) hostile to the Menshevik republic. Bolshevik forces occupied Petrograd (St. Petersburg was renamed in 1914) on Nov. 7, 1917 (October in the old Byzantine calendar, hence the name October Revolution), arrested the cabinet, and put in place a Council of People's Commissars, under Lenin's chairmanship. There followed four years of civil war between Bolshevik, Menshevik, and czarist forces, in the course of which Nicholas II and his family were executed by the Bolsheviks in 1918.

Decreeing land to the peasants, worker management in industry, and repudiation of czarist debts, the Bolsheviks won the survival of their regime by withdrawing from World War I. The 1918 Treaty of Brest-Litovsk, which gained peace with Germany, granted freedom to Finland, the Baltic republics, Poland, Ukraine, and Bessarabia. At the conclusion of the civil war in 1921, the Soviet state was established, with Ukraine reabsorbed into the Soviet Union. The Bolshevik victory also resulted in the creation in 1921 of the Mongolian People's Republic as a close Soviet ally.

The early 1920s are now remembered as a "golden age" of Soviet history. Lenin's New Economic Policy (NEP) allowed some role for market forces and private ownership and led to a brief burst of economic growth. Art, literature, and science flourished in an atmosphere of revolutionary enthusiasm and little censorship.

Lenin died on Jan. 21, 1924, and after a power struggle, was succeeded by Josef Stalin. Stalin supported communist revolutions in China and elsewhere through the Communist International (Comintern) but generally withdrew from foreign engagements in order to concentrate on domestic affairs. Under Lenin, and even more under Stalin, the Communist party established a police state, condemning millions of people to internal exile in the 1920s and consolidating all power in the hands of the state. In 1929 agriculture was forcibly collectivized, leading to the starvation or execution of millions of peasants, while forced industrialization was carried out under a series of five-year plans. Under the guise of socialist revolution, the Russians continued in much the same manner as their czarist heirs. The Bolsheviks forcibly incorporated most of the territories of the old empire, and once in charge, insisted that Russian be the state language and that Russian Communist party officials run the republics.

On the national level, Stalin's chief rival, Leon Trotsky, was expelled from the U.S.S.R. in 1929 (and assassinated by Stalinist agents in Mexico in 1940). Stalin's obsession with eliminating all possible rivals for power led to a series of purges which saw the summary execution of an estimated seven million of presumed "enemies of the state" and the imprisonment in concentration camps of an estimated 12 million more.

Russia's reemergence as a world power was signaled by the signing in Aug. 1939 of the Hitler-Stalin Pact, a nonaggression treaty through which Stalin aimed to recover territories lost in 1918. Poland was partitioned, Bessarabia annexed (as the Moldavian republic), Finland conquered and partitioned, and the Baltic republics absorbed.

When in June 1941 Hitler turned against his ally and invaded Russia, unprepared Russian armies retreated. But Stalin emerged as a national leader in the "Great Patriotic War," restructuring the army and enlisting the support of the Orthodox church and relying on calls to Russian patriotism in rallying the population. In the early winter of 1942, the war changed course as Russia broke the German siege of Stalingrad, and Russian armies began their westward push that would carry them to the Elbe River by April 1945.

By the end of World War II, Stalin had reestablished the old czarist boundaries of Russia, and he had a ring of occupied states along his western boundary and a divided Germany beyond. Over the years 1945–48, he engineered a thorough communization of those occupied states, turning them into Russian satellites.

Stalin died in March 1953. He was succeeded by a collegial form of party and government leadership, from which Nikita Khrushchev, the party chairman, emerged as the paramount figure. In a secret speech to the party leadership in 1956, Khrushchev denounced Stalin for crimes against the party. He announced a set of new policies designed to bring about rapid modernization and consolidated his power when he became premier in 1958. The Khrushchev years brought a small but steady rise in living standards and a "thaw" in police state methods, the KGB (state security police) being brought under party control.

In foreign policy there was a thaw as well. In 1953 the Soviets agreed to an armistice in Korea and tolerated the formation of a more liberal government in Hungary. In 1955 Russia returned the Porkkala peninsula to Finland and agreed to the Austrian State Treaty, which created an independent and neutral Austria. But the limits of disengagement became clear in 1956 with the ruthless Soviet suppression of the Hungarian uprising. A summit conference between Khrushchev and Eisenhower in 1960 led to a propaganda victory for Russia when an American U-2 spy plane was shot down over Russian territory on May 1. And in 1962 Khrushchev tried to install Soviet missiles in Cuba, a reckless adventure from which he had to back down during the Cuban missile crisis.

While on vacation in 1964, Khrushchev was removed from office and replaced as party secretary by Leonid Brezhnev and as premier by Aleksei Kosygin. His failure to deliver on promises for domestic economic growth and his recklessness in foreign affairs seem to have been responsible for his downfall. The new leaders embarked on an ambitious program of military (especially naval) expansion and pressed ahead vigorously with a space program that had begun with the triumphant launching of Sputnik I in 1957.

Under Brezhnev and Kosygin the U.S.S.R. became more aggressive in foreign policy. The severe suppression of Czechoslovakia's "Prague Spring" in 1968 occasioned development of the Brezhnev Doctrine, whereby Russia claimed the right to intervene militarily in any socialist state. Soviet involvement in the Third World grew, with Russia supporting Vietnam against China; Syria and the PLO against Israel; leftist regimes in Angola, Ethiopia, and elsewhere in Africa; and the Sandinistas in Nicaragua. Cuba emerged as the principal Soviet proxy in supplying troops for leftist causes in the Third World. In 1979 Soviet troops moved into Afghanistan, allegedly at the invitation of its Marxist government, and remained bogged down there for a decade. Under American pressure, Brezhnev permitted the emigration of about 130,000 Jews and 40,000 ethnic Germans.

Domestically, the regime grew more oppressive; censorship was tightened and dissidents sentenced to terms in penal mental institutions. Elitism and nepotism created a self-perpetuating and interlocking network of power at the top, while the nation as a whole stagnated. Brezhnev's death in 1982 brought about a rapid series of leadership transfers. Yuri Andropov, head of the KGB, succeeded Brezhnev as party secretary but died after only 15 months. He was succeeded by Konstantin Chernenko, who died 13 months later. In March 1985 Mikhail Gorbachev became party secretary, ushering in a new era.

Gorbachev first instituted a cautious shake-up of state and party bureaucrats, promoting younger men who were technocrats rather than party professionals. Under the slogan *glasnost* (openness, candor), censorship was relaxed and policy was openly debated in the press. Jamming of broadcasts from the West was ended. By the end of 1990, freedom of the press and of religion had been approved, and private citizens were given limited rights to own small businesses.

Gorbachev's other slogan, *perestroika* (restructuring), addressed his aim to boost morale and increase economic efficiency by devolving responsibility for economic decisions away from the party and government and toward industrial and agricultural managers. Perestroika raised expectations but not output; the system remained sluggish, inefficient, and burdened with the vested interests of state planners. The nuclear power plant disaster of Chernobyl in April 1986 and a gas pipeline fire that killed hundreds of passengers in passing railroad trains in June 1989 exemplified the industrial mismanagement against which Gorbachev's policies were aimed. During 1989–91 there were strikes by coal miners, and shortages of food and consumer goods worsened.

In foreign policy Gorbachev pursued arms reduction agreements with the United States and withdrew Soviet forces from Afghanistan. His international stature exceeded that of any previous Soviet leader; but his problems at home made him increasingly unpopular. Foremost among his problems at home concerned the U.S.S.R.'s various ethnic nationalities. The southern Muslim regions of the U.S.S.R. were the scene of turmoil since the anti-Russian riots in Kazakhstan in 1986; in 1988 riots broke out in the Christian republic of Armenia over the status of ethnic Armenians in the neighboring Muslim republic of Azerbaijan. Fighting in Armenia and Azerbaijan worsened in 1989–90, leading to a breakdown of government control in some areas. Ethnic warfare between Uzbeks and Turks in Uzbekistan led to numerous deaths, and sporadic violence in other central Asian republics broke out in 1990.

The Baltic republics of Estonia, Latvia, and Lithuania raised their old national flags, enacted laws giving their native languages priority over Russian, and proclaimed the superiority of local republican law over the laws of the Soviet Union. Lithuania proclaimed its independence from the U.S.S.R. in Dec. 1989, provoking a confrontation with international ramifications; Lithuania finally agreed to postpone its independence in 1990 pending negotiations with the Soviet government. Within the U.S.S.R. itself, the Russian republic elected maverick Boris Yeltsin as president and pressed for greater autonomy; Yeltsin resigned from the Communist party in July 1990.

The total collapse of communist governments in Eastern Europe in 1989–90 added to Gorbachev's problems and led to the dissolution of the Warsaw Pact; the Berlin Wall fell in Nov. 1989; and the Council of Mutual Economic Assistance (COMECON) was dissolved in July 1990. Gorbachev responded by assuming the presidency of the U.S.S.R. and increasing the powers of that office, and he held off challenges to his leadership in 1990–91. Yet defections from the party by both right- and left-wing groups threw the party's future role in the U.S.S.R. itself in doubt. Demonstrations against Gorbachev and the Communist party took place in Moscow and elsewhere as the economy worsened and food supplies dwindled.

In June of 1991, Boris Yeltsin was elected president of the Russian republic in the first direct elections for the post. His stature soared when he rallied opposition to an unsuccessful coup to topple Gorbachev in August. In December 1991 Gorbachev and Yeltsin agreed that the U.S.S.R. would cease to exist as of Jan. 1, 1992.

In early December 1991, Ukraine, Belarus, and the Russian Federation signed the Minsk Agreement that created the Commonwealth of Independent States, and on Dec. 21, Ukraine and 11 other former union republics officially committed themselves to the union by signing the Alma-Ata Declaration. In Feb. 1992 Russian president Yeltsin agreed to begin dismantling the vast arsenal of Russian nuclear weapons, 80 percent of which were on Russia's territory, the rest being scattered across Ukraine, Belarus, and Kazkhstan. While Belarus agreed to allow Russia to control the weapons, Kazakhstan and Ukraine used their weapons as bargaining chips.

Throughout 1992, Pres. Yeltsin took center stage, first signing the historic second Strategic Arms Reduction Treaty (START II) with the U.S. in January, then in April rallying the people to support a referendum on government elections and to approve his policies, and finally in June calling together a Constitutional Assembly to write a new constitution. As the Russian economy continued to founder, however, Yeltsin became the target of attacks by former Communists. In Dec. 1992, Yeltsin barely survived a series of votes in Parliament that would have severely limited his control.

This struggle came to a violent head on Sept. 21, 1993, when Yeltsin declared Parliament dissolved and called for new elections to be held in December; Parliament then voted to impeach Yeltsin and appointed Vice Pres. Aleksandr V. Rutskoi to replace him. Anti-Yeltsin forces called for a national strike and barricaded themselves inside the Parliament building for two weeks. Anti-Yeltsin rallies escalated into serious violence when 10,000 protesters overwhelmed riot police and broke through government barricades, causing Yeltsin to summon military police. The leaders of the revolt surrendered after tanks fired directly on the Parliament building, and were immediately sent to prison. At least 100 people were killed.

In the aftermath, Yeltsin moved quickly to parlay his victory into even greater political power, by banning several opposition parties, firing powerful opponents, and calling for new parliamentary elections. In Nov. 1993 he unveiled the country's first post-Soviet constitution, which centralized power in the executive presidency and limited the powers of the constituent regions. One of these regions, Chechnya, had long threatened secession from Russia and in 1994 its leaders took that action. In Dec. Yeltsin ordered the army to restore government control, but it took months of fighting before Grozny, the rebel capital, fell.

In 1996, unrest by Russia's nationalist faction eroded much of Yeltsin's support, forcing him into a runoff election against the Communist candidate Gennadi Zyuganov in May 1996. But in the runoff, Yeltsin decisively beat back the Communist challenger. In August, Yeltsin formed a cabinet of pro-business technocrats; in the Fall he agreed to the final withdrawl of Russia's Chechnya brigades.

Yeltsin met Pres. Clinton in Helsinki in March 1997 subsequently agreeing to NATO's eastward expansion in return for NATO's agreement neither to deploy nor to store nuclear weapons there. Economic difficulties reached serious proportions in 1998 and the I.M.F. and the U.S. pledged huge amounts to keep the economy from crumbling. In the spring, Yeltsin replaced many of his ministers with reform-minded bureaucrats. But in the summer, the economy turned down again, and Yeltsin was forced to devalue the ruble. As the economy worsened day-by-day and international lenders refused aid, Russia stood on the brink of collapse.

Even with Mr. Yeltsin's illnesses, personal volatility, and political capriciousness, the I.M.F. and various western investment "Clubs" managed to keep rescheduling Russian debt, so Russia was able to stumble on despite essentially defaulting on loan repayments. The August 1999 appointment of Vladimir Putin as prime minister made him the fifth in 18 months, the third in a row drawn from the secret police. One day after Putin's appointment, insurgents in the Federal Republic of Dagestan, operating out of Chechnya, proclaimed an independent Islamic state; hence, Putin's determination to have it out with Chechnya. Vigorously pursued and very popular, the war went well for Russia and Putin's popularity soared as Grozny fell. Putin triumphed in the March presidential election occasioned by Yeltsin's resignation. Putin consolidated his power and took a leading role in opposing U.S. plans to build a missile shield but cooperating with U.S. determination to end terrorism.

As 2001 drew to a close, three-pronged Russian American talks continued: American would support closer Russian ties with NATO; both would reduce by two-thirds their nuclear arms; and the U.S. would withdraw from the 1972 ABM pact. In July 2002 Russia and China signed a 20-year Friendship Treaty. The war in Chechnya took a particularly nasty turn, from the Oct. 2002 Moscow theater hostage crisis to the eight suicide bombings of May–August 2003 which killed over 150. At the end of 2003 Putin's United Russia party won about half of the seats in the Duma and in March 2004 he was reelected president with 71 percent of the vote.

The Chechen insurgency grew far worse culminating in a horrific slaughter of hundreds, including schoolchildren, in Sept. 2004. Putin never wavered, however, and the insurgency was checked. Putin doggedly pursued the build-up of Russia's vast energy supplies, bringing income and influence in the region and the world. In 2008 Putin's handpicked successor, Dmitri Medvedev, was easily elected president with Putin becoming prime minister. Russia used an attack by Georgia on Russia's client state of South Ossetia to show its military strength by easily routing Georgia's forces and then occupying the area for months. The financial crisis of 2008–09 hit Russia hard as oil and gas prices declined. After Pres. Obama took office a serious dialogue began about nuclear weapons which both governments agreed to reduce significantly. The U.S. also agreed to change the nature of the defensive missiles to be put in central Europe. (See "Major News Stories.")

▶ RWANDA
Rwandese Republic
- **GEOGRAPHY** **Location:** landlocked country in central Africa. **Boundaries:** Uganda to N, Tanza-

nia to E, Burundi to S, Zaire to W. **Total area**: 10,170 sq. mi. (26,340 sq km). **Coastline**: none. **Comparative area**: slightly smaller than Maryland. **Land use**: 45.5% arable land; 10% permanent crops; 44% other. **Major cities**: Kigali (capital); Butare; Ruhengeri; Gisenyi.
● **PEOPLE   Population**: 10,473,282 (July 2009 est.). **Nationality**: noun—Rwandan(s); adjective—Rwandan. **Ethnic groups**: 84% Hutu, 15% Tutsi, 1% Twa (Pygmoid). **Languages**: Kinyarwanda (official) universal Bantu vernacular, French and English (both official), Kiswahili (Swahili) used in commercial centers. **Religions**: 57% Catholic, 26% Protestant, 11% Adventist, 5% Muslim.
● **GOVERNMENT   Type**: republic; presidential system; multiparty system. **Independence**: July 1, 1962 (from U.N. trusteeship under Belgian administration). **Constitution**: May 5, 1995, the Transitional National Assembly adopted a new constitution passed by referndum May 26, 2003. **National holiday**: Independence Day, July 1. **Heads of Government**: Paul Kagame, president (since April 2000); Bernard Makuza, prime minister (since March 2000). **Structure**: executive—president; unicameral legislature; judiciary.
● **ECONOMY   Monetary unit**: Rwandan franc. **Budget**: (2008 est.) *income*: $902.2 mil.; *expend.*: $1.032 bil. **G.D.P.**: $9.061 bil., $900 per capita (2008 est.). **Chief crops**: coffee, tea, pyrethrum, bananas, beans, sorghum, potatoes; livestock. **Natural resources**: gold, cassiterite (tin ore), wolframite (tungsten ore), natural gas, hydropower. **Major industries**: agricultural products, small-scale beverage, soap, furniture industries, cement. **Labor force**: 4.6 mil. (2000); 90% agriculture. **Exports**: $219 mil. (f.o.b., 2008 est.); coffee, tea, hides, tin ore. **Imports**: $759 mil. (f.o.b., 2008 est.); foodstuffs, machines and equipment, petroleum products, cement and construction material. **Major trading partners**: (2006) *exports*: 10.3% China, 9.7% Germany, 4.3% U.S.; *imports*: 19.6% Kenya, 7.9% Germany, 6.8% Uganda, 5.1% Belgium.

Tutsi cattle-breeders came to Rwanda, in the late 15th century and slowly conquered the native Hutu farmers. The Tutsi established a monarchy, forcing the Hutus into serfdom. Germans were the first Europeans to arrive in Rwanda and declared it a protectorate in 1899. After World War I Belgium was given a League of Nations mandate over the territory, which became a U.N. trusteeship after World War II.

Tutsi traditionalists resisted Belgian attempts in the 1950s to institute democratic institutions. In 1959 the Hutus revolted against the monarchy in a bloody conflict which led to a mass exodus of Tutsis. Two years later the Hutus won a U.N.-supervised referendum and were granted internal autonomy by Belgium on Jan. 1, 1962. Full independence came on July 1, 1962. Political unrest led to the overthrow of the government in 1973. Maj. Gen. Juvénal Habyarimana dissolved the National Assembly and banned all political activity.

In 1990 Tutsi refugees in Uganda fought with the army, and by 1993 as many as one million people were displaced. A cease-fire and amnesty paved the way for political reform, and a new constitution allowing for multi-party democracy, separation of powers, and presidential term limits went into effect in June 1992. Proposals to merge the armies of the government (Hutu) and the Tutsi Rwandan Patriotic Front were signed in 1993.

But in April 1994, the Hutu presidents of Rwanda and Burundi were both killed when rocket fire (perhaps launched by Hutu dissidents) shot down their plane as it returned from a peace conference in Tanzania. In renewed civil war, the Hutu dominated army of Rwanda and the Hutu militias were driven by the Tutsi-led Patriotic Front into Zaire, Tanzania, Uganda and Burundi; the Hutus reportedly slaughtered over 500,000 Tutsi and countless Hutu moderates as they went. The result was threefold: a million dead, three million refugees, and a Tutsi-dominated but multi-ethnic "government of national unity".

As the Mobutu regime collapsed in neighboring Zaire, the Zaire military attempted to expel a Tutsi community of 400,000 (the Banyamulenge people) who had been settled south of Lake Kivu since the 18th century. The Tutsi resistance gained support from the Rwandan government (Oct. 1996); thus commenced a de facto war between Rwanda and Zaire. The 500,000 Hutu militiamen and other refugees who, as a result, fled Zaire back to Rwanda joined another half million driven from Tanzania by the Tanzanian army. Yet another wave of killings by Hutu militants had begun in Rwanda. By 1999 the Hutu rebellion was petering out in small but vicious skirmishes and the government of Rwanda was continuing its military aid to insurgents in Congo while attacking Hutu bases in the eastern parts of that country, despite the July cease-fire. In April 2000, Paul Kagame was elected the first Tutsi president of Rwanda, and re-elected in 2003 and 2010.

▶ **SAINT KITTS AND NEVIS**
Federation of Saint Kitts and Nevis
● **GEOGRAPHY   Location**: two islands in eastern Caribbean Sea, about 45 mi. (72 km) NW of Antigua. Nevis 17°08'N, 62°37'W; St. Kitts 17°17'N, 62°43'W. **Boundaries**: Caribbean Sea to N, E, S, and W. **Total area**: 104 sq. mi. (269 sq km). **Coastline**: 84 mi. (135 km). **Comparative area**: 1.5 times the size of Washington, D.C. **Land use**: 17% arable land; 3% permanent crops; 80% other. **Major cities**: Basseterre (capital).
● **PEOPLE   Population**: 40,131 (July 2009 est.). **Nationality**: noun—Kittitian(s), Nevisian(s); adjective—Kittitian, Nevisian. **Ethnic groups**: mainly of black African descent. **Languages**: English. **Religions**: Anglican, other Protestant sects, Roman Catholic.
● **GOVERNMENT   Type**: parliamentary democracy. **Independence**: Sept. 19, 1983 (from U.K.). **Constitution**: Sept. 19, 1983. **National holiday**: Independence Day, Sept 19. **Heads of Government**: Cuthbert Sebastian, governor-general (since Jan. 1996); Denzil Douglas, prime minister (since July 1995). **Structure**: executive—cabinet headed by prime minister; unicameral legislature; judiciary—East Caribbean Supreme Court, based on Saint Lucia.
● **ECONOMY   Monetary unit**: East Caribbean (EC) dollar. **Budget**: (2003 est.) *income*: $89.7 mil.; *expend.*: $128.2 mil. **G.D.P.**: $784.9 mil., $19,700 per capita (2008 est.). **Chief crops**: sugarcane, rice, yams, vegetables, bananas. **Natural resources**: negl. **Major industries**: sugar processing, tourism, cotton. **Labor force**: 18,170 (1995); 69% services, 31% manufacturing. **Exports**: $84 mil. (2006 est.); machinery, food, electronics, beverages, tobacco. **Imports**: $383 mil. (2006 est.); machinery, manufactures, food, fuel. **Major trading partners**: (2006) *exports*: 62% U.S., 9.4% Canada,

6.6% Netherlands, 5% Azerbaijan; *imports:* 48.9% U.S., 13.1% Trinidad & Tobago, 4.6% Spain, 4.5% U.K.

The French settled St. Kitts in 1627; the English settled Nevis in 1628. In 1783 both became British possessions, and the two islands were united in 1882. Britain granted them independence in 1983. The country's economy is almost entirely based on sugar exports, so when Hurricane Hugo devastated sugar crops in 1990, the welfare of the entire population was affected. The reign of Kennedy Alphonse Simmonds, the only prime minister St. Kitts and Nevis had ever known, ended in July 1995, when Denzil Douglas's opposition Labour party defeated Kennedy's People's Action Movement. March 2000 elections confirmed the change: Labour took eight of the 11 seats, PAN took none. The continued fall of world sugar prices hurt the economy and in 1997 some leaders in Nevis started a movement to separate from St. Kitts because of high taxes. In 1998 a referendum on separation resulted in a majority yes-vote but not the two-thirds necessary.

▶ **SAINT LUCIA**
• **GEOGRAPHY   Location:** southeastern Caribbean Sea, between Martinique to N and St. Vincent to SW. Castries 14°01'N, 60°59'W. **Boundaries:** St. Lucia Channel to N, Atlantic Ocean to E, St. Vincent Passage to S, Caribbean Sea to W. **Total area:** 239 sq. mi. (620 sq km). **Coastline:** 98 mi. (158 km). **Comparative area:** 3.5 times size of Washington, D.C. **Land use:** 5% arable land; 23% permanent crops; 72% other. **Major cities:** Castries (capital).
• **PEOPLE   Population:** 160,267 (July 2009 est.). **Nationality:** noun—St. Lucian(s); adjective—St. Lucian. **Ethnic groups:** 82.5% black African descent, 11.9% mixed, 2.4% East Indian, 3.1% unspecified. **Languages:** English (official), French patois. **Religions:** 67.5% Roman Catholic, 20% Protestant, 2% Anglican, 2.1% Rastafarian, 4.5% none.
• **GOVERNMENT   Type:** parliamentary democracy. **Independence:** Feb. 22, 1979 (from U.K.). **Constitution:** Feb. 22, 1979. **National holiday:** Independence Day, Feb. 22. **Heads of Government:** Perlette Louisy, governor-general (since Sept. 1997); Stephenson King, prime minister (since Sept. 2007). **Structure:** executive—cabinet headed by prime minister; bicameral legislature—Senate, House of Representatives; judiciary—East Caribbean Supreme Court.
• **ECONOMY   Monetary unit:** East Caribbean (EC) dollar. **Budget:** (2000 est.) *income:* $141.2 mil.; *expend.:* $146.7 mil. **G.D.P.:** $1.801 bil., $11,300 per capita (2008 est.). **Chief crops:** bananas, coconuts, vegetables, root crops, citrus, cocoa. **Natural resources:** forests, sandy beaches, minerals (pumice), mineral springs, geothermal potential. **Major industries:** clothing, assembly of electronic components, beverages. **Labor force:** 43,800 (2001 est.); 21.7% agriculture, 53.6% services, 24.7% industry and commerce; 16.7% unemployment (2002). **Exports:** $288 mil. (2006 est.); 41% bananas, clothing, cocoa, vegetables, fruits, coconut oil. **Imports:** $791 mil. (2006 est.); 23% food, 21% manufactured goods, 19% machinery and transport equipment, chemicals, fuels. **Major trading partners:** (2006) *exports:* 69.7% France, 10.2% U.S., 8.8% U.K.; *imports:* 21.1% U.S., 14.9% Trinidad & Tobago, 12.3% Italy, 11.8% France, 7.2% Venezuela, 6.9% U.K., 5.8% Netherlands.

In 1650 the French settled St. Lucia, which was ceded to Britain in 1783. A member of the Federation of the West Indies from 1958 to 1962, St. Lucia became internally self-governing in 1967 but was still under Great Britain's protection. In 1979 St. Lucia gained full independence and since then has enjoyed stable competitive politics. Hurricane Allen destroyed many of the country's banana plantations in 1980, and the economy took years to recover from the disaster. The government of Prime Minister John Compton of the United Workers party worked for agrarian reform and proposed legalizing gambling to stimulate tourism but after 15 years in power lost the 1997 elections to the Labour Party led by Kenny B. Anthony. In 2006, however, Compton won back the prime minister's title but he died in Sept. 2007 and was replaced by Stephenson King.

▶ **SAINT VINCENT AND THE GRENADINES**
• **GEOGRAPHY   Location:** large island of St. Vincent (13°12'N, 61°14'W) and about 50 smaller islands in southeastern Caribbean Sea about 21 mi. (34 km) SW of St. Lucia and 100 mi. (160 km) W of Barbados. **Boundaries:** St. Vincent Passage to N, Atlantic Ocean to E and SE, Caribbean Sea to SW and W. **Total area:** 131 sq. mi. (340 sq km). **Coastline:** 52 mi. (84 km). **Comparative area:** twice size of Washington, D.C. **Land use:** 18% arable land; 18% permanent crops; 64% other. **Major cities:** Kingstown (capital).
• **PEOPLE   Population:** 104,574 (2009 est.). **Nationality:** noun—St. Vincentian(s) or Vincentian(s); adjective—St. Vincentian or Vincentian. **Ethnic groups:** mainly of black African descent, remainder mixed, with some white, East Indian, and Carib Amerindian. **Languages:** English, French patois. **Religions:** Anglican, Methodist, Roman Catholic, Seventh-Day Adventist.
• **GOVERNMENT   Type:** parliamentary monarchy. **Independence:** Oct. 27, 1979 (from U.K.). **Constitution:** Oct. 27, 1979. **National holiday:** Independence Day, Oct. 27. **Heads of Government:** Frederick Nathaniel Ballantyne, governor-general (since Sept. 2, 2002); Ralph E. Gonsalves, prime minister (since Mar. 2001). **Structure:** executive—prime minister is head of government; bicameral legislature—15-member elected House of Representatives and 6-member appointed Senate; judiciary—East Caribbean Supreme Court.
• **ECONOMY   Monetary unit:** East Caribbean (EC) dollar. **Budget:** (2000 est.) *income:* $94.6 mil.; *expend.:* $85.8 mil. **G.D.P.:** $1.103 bil., $10,500 per capita (2008 est.). **Chief crops:** bananas, coconuts, sweet potatoes, spices; small numbers of cattle, sheep, pigs, goats; small fish catch used locally. **Natural resources:** negl. **Major industries:** food processing (sugar, flour), cement, furniture. **Labor force:** 41,680 (1991 est.); 26% agriculture, 17% industry, 57% services; 22% unemployed (1997). **Exports:** $193 mil. (2006 est.); 39% bananas, eddoes and dasheen (taro), arrowroot starch, tennis racquets. **Imports:** $578 mil. (2006 est.); foodstuffs, machinery and equipment, chemicals and fertilizers, minerals and fuels. **Major trading partners:** (2006) *exports:* 26.2% France, 21.3% Germany, 18.9% Italy, 7.2% Russia, 6.8% U.K.; *imports:* 17.3% Singapore, 12.1% Trinidad & Tobago, 11.1% U.S., 11% Italy, 9.5% Spain, 4.6% Turkey, 4.4% Germany.

Although ceded to Britain in 1763, St. Vincent was inhabited by the fierce Carib Indians, who continued fighting for control of the island until 1796, when they had all been either killed or deported. Just prior to its independence in 1979, St. Vincent and the Grenadines was a self-governing state in association with Great Britain. It is one of the poorest countries in the West Indies. Several natural disasters have plagued the economy, including a 1979 volcanic eruption and two destructive hurricanes in 1980 and 1986. Prime Minister James Mitchell of the New Democratic party currently governs the country, winning his fourth term after June 1997 elections gave his New Democratic Party a slender one-vote majority in the 15-seat legislature. But March 2001 elections overturned N.D.P. rule as united Labor won 12 of 15 parliamentary seats. The new left-wing government of Ralph Gonsalves has been seeking international accords with Libya and Cuba. He was reelected in 2005.

▶ SAMOA
Formerly Western Samoa
Independent State of Samoa
• **GEOGRAPHY Location:** two large and seven small islands (five inhabited) in South Pacific Ocean, about 1,500 mi. (2,400 km) NE of New Zealand. Apia 13°49'S, 171°45'W. **Boundaries:** surrounded by Pacific Ocean; nearest neighbor is American Samoa to E. **Total area:** 1,104 sq. mi. (2,860 sq km). **Coastline:** 250 mi. (403 km). **Comparative area:** slightly smaller than Rhode Island. **Land use:** 19% arable land; 24% permanent crops; 57% other. **Major cities:** Apia (capital).
• **PEOPLE Population:** 219,998 (July 2008 est.). **Nationality:** noun—Samoan(s); adjective—Samoan. **Ethnic groups:** 92.6% Samoan; about 7% Euronesians (persons of European and Polynesian blood), 0.4% Europeans. **Languages:** Samoan (Polynesian), English. **Religions:** 99.7% Christian (about half of population associated with London Missionary Society; includes Congregational, Roman Catholic, Methodist, Latter-Day Saints, Seventh-Day Adventist).
• **GOVERNMENT Type:** parliamentary democracy. **Independence:** Jan. 1, 1962 (from U.N. trusteeship administered by New Zealand). **Constitution:** Jan. 1, 1962. **National holiday:** Independence Day, Jun. 1. **Heads of Government:** Tuiatua Tupua Tamasese Efi, head of state (since June 2007); Tuilaepa Sailele Malielegaoi, prime minister (since Nov. 1998). **Structure:** executive—chief of state appoints prime minister; unicameral legislature (47-member Legislative Assembly); judiciary.
• **ECONOMY Monetary unit:** tala. **Budget:** (2005 est.) *income:* $171.3 mil.; *expend.:* $78.1 mil. **G.D.P.:** $1.057 bil., $4,900 per capita (2008 est.). **Chief crops:** coconuts, bananas, taro, yams. **Natural resources:** hardwood forests, fish. **Major industries:** timber, tourism, food processing. **Labor force:** 90,000 (2000 est.); 65% agriculture, 30% services. **Exports:** $131 mil. (f.o.b.; 2006); coconut oil and cream, copra, fish, beer. **Imports:** $324 mil. (f.o.b., 2006); intermediate goods, food, capital goods. **Major trading partners:** (2006) *exports:* 44.1% Australia, 29.9% American Samoa, 11.3% Taiwan; *imports:* 21.5% New Zealand, 14.8% Fiji, 13.2% Singapore, 8.6% Australia, 8.6% Japan, 6.2% U.S., 5% Indonesia, 4.4% China.

The Polynesian island group of Samoa (Navigator's Islands) was partitioned in 1899 between the United States, which had established a naval base at Pago Pago on Tutuila in 1878, and Germany, which organized the westerly islands into a colony

in 1894. In 1914 New Zealand troops occupied the German-held islands. New Zealand administered Western Samoa under a League of Nations mandate beginning in 1920 and continued to control the islands as a U.N. Trust Territory after 1945. In 1959 home rule was established under an elected local government. Western Samoa became an independent nation on Jan. 1, 1962. The constitution blends Western parliamentary government and traditional Samoan forms of rule. The parliamentary electorate is limited to the *matai*, heads of extended families; the malai are wholly responsible for local affairs. The local culture is similarly a blend of Samoan tradition with Christianity. The economy is based on subsistence agriculture, forestry, fishing, and tourism.

In November 1998, after 16 years of stable and peaceful rule, Prime Minister Tofilau Eti Alesana resigned for health reasons and was replaced by his deputy, Tuilaepa Sailele Malielegaoi whose Human Rights Protection Party won the next two elections (2001 and 2006). After 45 years on the throne, King Malietoa Tanumafili II died in May 2007, and was succeeded as head of state by Tuiatua Tupua Tamasese Efi in June.

▶ SAN MARINO
Republic of San Marino
• **GEOGRAPHY Location:** on slopes of Mt. Titano, in the Apennines, within central Italian region of Emilia-Romagna. **Boundaries:** surrounded by Italian territory. **Total area:** 23 sq. mi. (60 sq km). **Coastline:** none. **Comparative area:** about three-tenths the size of Washington, D.C. **Land use:** 17% arable land; 0% permanent crops; 83% other. **Major cities:** San Marino (capital).
• **PEOPLE Population:** 30,324 (July 2009 est.). **Nationality:** noun—Sammarinese (sing., pl.); adjective—Sammarinese. **Ethnic groups:** Sammarinese, Italian. **Languages:** Italian. **Religions:** Roman Catholic.
• **GOVERNMENT Type:** republic. **Independence:** 301 A.D. **Constitution:** Oct. 8, 1600; electoral law of 1926 serves some of functions of constitution. **National holiday:** Anniversary of the Foundation of the Republic, Sept. 3. **Heads of Government:** Two co-presidents who rule for six months, Captain Regent Marco Conti and Captain Regent Glauco Sansovini (April–Oct. 2010). **Structure:** executive—two captain-regents with six-month terms elected by and from the legislature, actual power wielded by secretary of state for foreign affairs; unicameral legislature—Great and General Council elected by popular vote for five-year terms; judicial—Council of Twelve is supreme judicial body.
• **ECONOMY Monetary unit:** Euro. **Budget:** (2006 est.) *income:* $690.6 mil.; *expend:* $652.9 mil. **G.D.P.:** $1.662 bil., $41,900 per capita (2007 est.). **Chief crops:** wheat, grapes, maize, olives; cattle, pigs, horses, meat, cheese, hides. **Natural resources:** building stones. **Major industries:** tourism, textiles, electronics. **Labor force:** 22,660 (2008); 60% services, 40% industry, less than 1% agriculture. **Exports:** $4.628 bil (2007 est.) trade data included with Italian statistics; commodity trade consisting primarily of exchanging building stone, lime, wood, chestnuts, wheat, and wine for a wide variety of consumer manufactures. **Imports:** $3.744 bil (2007 est.) see exports. **Major trading partners:** N.A.

The "Most Serene Republic" of San Marino, entirely surrounded by Italy near the city of Rimini, is the oldest republic in the world, with communitarian roots dating to the fourth century a.d. While Piedmont-Sardinia was conquering all of the rest of the Italian peninsula during the period 1860–70, it left San Marino independent; the new kingdom of Italy signed a treaty of friendship and cooperation with the republic in 1862.

Leftist coalitions governed from 1978 through 1986, giving San Marino the only Communist government west of the Soviet bloc. Since 1986 the government has been controlled by a coalition of Communists and Christian Democrats. In 1992 San Marino joined the United Nations.

The economy is balanced between small-scale agriculture (primarily wine grapes and livestock) and industry, including textiles, ceramics, and furniture. Philatelic sales and tourism are important sources of revenue. Lacking extremes of wealth and poverty and with low unemployment, the republic enjoys general prosperity.

▶ SÃO TOMÉ AND PRÍNCIPE
Democratic Republic of Saõ Tomé and Príncipe

• **GEOGRAPHY   Location:** two main islands, São Tomé (0°19'N, 6°43'E) and Príncipe, and Caroço, Pedras, Tinhosas (off Príncipe), and Rolas (off São Tomé), off west coast of Africa. **Boundaries:** west of Gabon in Gulf of Guinea. **Total area:** 371 sq. mi. (960 sq km). **Coastline:** 130 mi. (209 km). **Comparative area:** more than 5.5 times size of Washington, D.C. **Land use:** 8% arable land; 49% permanent crops; 43% other. **Major cities:** São Tomé (capital).
• **PEOPLE   Population:** 212,679 (July 2009 est.). **Nationality:** noun—São Toméan(s); adjective— São Toméan. **Ethnic groups:** mestiço, angolares (descendants of Angolan slaves), forros (descendents of freed slaves), servicais (contract laborers from Angola, Mozambique, and Cape Verde), tongas (children of servicais born on the islands), and Europeans (primarily Portuguese). **Languages:** Portuguese (official). **Religions:** Roman Catholic, Evangelical Protestant, Seventh-Day Adventist, New Apostolic, 20% none.
• **GOVERNMENT   Type:** republic. **Independence:** July 12, 1975 (from Portugal). **Constitution:** Sept. 10, 1990. **National holiday:** Independence Day, July 12. **Heads of Government:** Fradique Bandeira Melo de Menezes, president (since Sept. 2001); Joaquim Branco, prime minister (since June 2008). **Structure:** executive—president assisted by cabinet of ministers; unicameral legislature; judiciary.
• **ECONOMY   Monetary unit:** dobra. **Budget:** (2008 est.) *income:* $47.65 mil.; *expend.:* $51.48 mil. **G.D.P.:** $276.6 mil., $1,300 per capita (2008 est.). **Chief crops:** cocoa, copra, coconuts, coffee, palm kernels, bananas, cinnamon, pepper, papaya, beans; poultry, fish. **Natural resources:** fish. **Major industries:** light construction, textiles, soap, beer; fish processing. **Labor force:** most of population engaged in subsistence agriculture and fishing; labor shortages of skilled workers. **Exports:** $9 mil. (f.o.b., 2008 est.); 90% cocoa, copra, coffee, palm oil. **Imports:** $91 mil. (f.o.b., 2008 est.); machinery and electrical equipment, food products, fuels. **Major trading partners:** (2006) *exports:* 48% Netherlands, 19% Belgium, 9% Portugal; *imports:* 49% Portugal, 20% France, 5% Belgium, 5% U.S.

The islands of São Tomé and Príncipe, located in the Atlantic Ocean 275 and 125 miles, respectively, off the northern coast of Gabon, make up the smallest nation in Africa. They were uninhabited when first discovered by the Portuguese in 1470 but by the mid-1500s became Africa's foremost exporter of sugar. As the sugar market declined, the islands became a major slave-trading center and producer of coffee and cocoa. By 1908 São Tomé was the world's largest cocoa producer.

Portugal did not abolish slavery until 1876, and abusive labor practices continued until well into the 20th century. In 1953 hundreds of workers were killed in clashes with the Portuguese. Soon after, a small number of São Toméans formed the Movement for the Liberation of São Tomé and Príncipe (MLSTP) with its base in Gabon. But the islands did not gain independence until July 12, 1975.

The MLSTP took over after independence and became the country's only official party. By 1986 the country relied on foreign aid for 41 percent of its G.N.P. Although in the past it received military advisers from the former Soviet Union and economic advisers from Cuba, São Tomé and Príncipe has announced a foreign policy based upon nonalignment. Multi-party democracy was introduced in 1991. At the beginning of the new century oil was discovered and shortly later (July 2002) a military junta seized power. Nigeria agreed to build the port and refinery and bids for exploration were taken in 2003. The junta agreed to the return of the president who pledged equitable distribution of oil revenues. Fradique de Menezes was elected president in 2001 and 2006.

▶ SAUDI ARABIA
Kingdom of Saudi Arabia

• **GEOGRAPHY   Location:** occupies four-fifths of Arabian peninsula in southwestern Asia. **Boundaries:** Jordan, Iraq, and Kuwait to N, Persian Gulf, Qatar, and United Arab Emirates to E, Oman to SE, Yemen to S and SE, Red Sea to W. **Total area:** 756,982 sq. mi. (1,960,582 sq km). **Coastline:** 1,641 mi. (2,640 km). **Comparative area:** slightly more than one-fifth the size of the U.S. **Land use:** 2% arable land; negl. % permanent crops; 98% other. **Major cities:** Riyadh (capital); Jid'dah; Mecca; Taif; Medina.
• **PEOPLE   Population:** 29,207,277 (July 2010 est.). **Nationality:** noun—Saudi(s); adjective—Saudi or Saudi Arabian. **Ethnic groups:** 90% Arab, 10% Afro-Asian. **Languages:** Arabic. **Religions:** 100% Muslim.
• **GOVERNMENT   Type:** monarchy. **Constitution:** none; governed according to Shari'a or Islamic law. **National holiday:** Unification of the Kingdom, Sept. 23. **Head of Government:** Abdullah Bin Abdulaziz al-Saud, king (since Aug. 2005). **Structure:** king rules in consultation with royal family and Council of Ministers; no elected legislature; Supreme Council of Justice.
• **ECONOMY   Monetary unit:** Saudi riyal. **Budget:** (2009 est.) *income:* $167.7 bil.; *expend.:* $164.3 bil. **G.D.P.:** $585.8 bil., $20,400 per capita (2009 est.). **Chief crops:** wheat, barley, tomatoes, melons, dates, citrus; mutton, chickens, eggs, milk. **Natural resources:** crude oil, natural gas, iron ore, gold, copper. **Major industries:** crude oil production, petroleum refining, basic petrochemicals. **Labor force:** 6.922 mil. (2009); 25% industry, 63% services, 12% agriculture. **Exports:** $180.5 bil. (2009 est.); 90% petroleum and petroleum products. **Imports:** $86.61 bil. (2009 est.); machinery and equipment, foodstuffs, chemicals, motor vehicles, textiles. **Major trading partners:** (2008) *exports:* 17.2% U.S., 15.3% Japan, 10.2% South Korea,

9.4% China, 5.9% India; *imports:* 12% U.S., 10.4% China, 7.6% Japan, 7.3% Germany, 5.1% South Korea.

In ancient times various cultures flourished in the Arabian peninsula, particularly along the western rim, in cities devoted to trade between the Gulf of Aden and the eastern Mediterranean, and in such agricultural and trading centers as Yemen and Oman. Political unity was lacking, however, until the rise of Mohammed, the prophet of Islam. In A.D. 622 Mohammed fled from Mecca, the center of Arabian paganism, to the nearby city of Medina; the Islamic era dates from that year. Preaching from Medina, Mohammed gained converts to Islam throughout Arabia. His army captured Mecca in 630, converting its sacred shrine, the Kaaba, to an Islamic place of worship. By 632, when Mohammed died, all of Arabia was unified under Islamic rule.

In 661 the Caliphate, the ruling body of early Islam, moved from Medina to Damascus. Thereafter Arabia was nominally unified under Islamic rule—but in practice was usually divided among various principalities in the arable areas and trading centers, and under tribal rule in the arid interior. Mecca fell to the Ottoman Empire in 1517, but Ottoman control of Arabia was never complete. The rise of the Wahabi sect of Islam in the 18th century posed a challenge to Ottoman rule. In the 19th century, the Saud family rose to leadership in the Wahabi movement and established a kingdom in Nejd, the central region of Arabia, with a capital at Riyadh. In 1902 Ibn Saud (1880–1953) consolidated his family's control at Riyadh and in 1912–13 led a new Wahabi revolt against the Ottoman Turks.

During World War I, the British aided Ibn Saud's rebellion in the Nejd, along with that of Ibn Saud's rival Hussein ibn Ali in the Hejaz, in the mountains of western Arabia along the coast of the Red Sea. A British protectorate was established in both regions in 1915, and Great Britain maintained a dominant position in Arabia after World War I.

In 1924 Ibn Saud captured Hussein ibn Ali's capital at Mecca, and he proclaimed himself king of Hejaz in 1926 and of Nejd in 1927. Ibn Saud consolidated his control over the following two years, and his kingdom was formally recognized by Great Britain in 1927. The country was renamed Saudi Arabia in 1932.

Saudi Arabia is an absolute monarchy based on Islamic law; it has no written constitution and no parliament. The king exercises sole authority and rules in consultation with a Council of Ministers. Islamic law is enforced; alcohol is prohibited and the public activities of women severely restricted. The Saudi kings have great power within the Islamic world through their control over the holy cities of Mecca and Medina and their administration of the annual Muslim pilgrimages to those cities.

The discovery of oil in eastern Arabia in the early 1930s rapidly transformed Saudi Arabia from an impoverished nation to a center of great wealth. In 1933 an exclusive concession for the exploitation of Saudi Arabian oil was granted to an American-chartered corporation, the Arabian-American Oil Company (Aramco). For many years wealth remained concentrated in the hands of the Saudi clan, and little change was felt in the desert interior, where Bedouin nomads continued to raise sheep and camels. Large numbers of Yemenis, Palestinians, Pakistanis, and other foreign workers are employed in the oil fields.

Saudi Arabia remained neutral during most of World War II but declared war on the Axis powers in March 1945; in the same year, it became a founding member of both the United Nations and the Arab League.

Ibn Saud became a leader of Arab anti-Zionism and contributed a small contingent of troops to the 1948 Arab-Israeli War. That policy was maintained by Ibn Saud's second son and successor, King Faisal, who instituted a policy of providing large annual subsidies to Egypt and other Arab League states following the 1967 Arab-Israeli War. In 1973 King Faisal sent Saudi units to fight in the Arab-Israeli War of that year. He played a leading role in organizing the 1973–74 Arab oil embargo in an effort to force the United States and its allies to take a harder line with Israel.

King Faisal was assassinated by his nephew, Prince Faisal, on Mar. 25, 1975, and was succeeded by King Khalid. Little change in policy resulted. In 1979 Saudi Arabia denounced the Camp David talks and the Egyptian-Israeli peace treaty and led the Arab League effort to ostracize Egypt within the Arab world. Saudi Arabia has consistently opposed leftist and radical movements in the Arab world, sending troops to help put down leftist rebellions in North Yemen and Oman in the 1970s. Saudi kings have taken a moderate approach toward relations with the West. Following the transfer of Aramco assets to full Saudi Arabian ownership during 1973–76, Saudi Arabia used its leading position within the Organization of Petroleum Exporting Countries (OPEC) to argue for a policy of stable production and prices.

This moderate policy has been rewarded by the willingness of the U.S., Great Britain, France, and other Western nations to sell arms—including jet fighters, tanks, and other sophisticated weapons— to Saudi Arabia despite Israeli protests.

Saudi Arabia experienced repeated disturbances in the 1980s. Muslim fundamentalist terrorists seized the Grand Mosque at Mecca on Nov. 20, 1979, provoking a crisis for the Saudi monarchy. On July 31, 1987, Iranian pilgrims rioted in Mecca and were fired upon by Saudi security forces; 402 persons died, including 275 Iranians. Iran's Ayatollah Khomeini denounced the Saudi government and said it was unworthy of being the guardian of Islam's sacred shrines.

A longtime supporter of the Palestine Liberation Organization, the Saudi government gave the PLO $850 million during the 1980s, but ceased when the PLO backed Saddam Hussein's invasion of Kuwait in 1990. During the Persian Gulf War, King Fahd granted permission to station U.S. troops in Saudi Arabia to guard against a possible Iraqi attack. The Saudis promised the United States $16.8 billion and Egypt $1.5 billion to defray the costs of the war.

In 1996 King Fahd, ailing from a 1995 stroke, temporarily ceded power to his legal successor, Crown Prince Abdullah. In June, terrorists bombed an apartment complex in Dhahran, killing 19 American soldiers stationed there and wounding more than 300 people.

U.S.–Saudi relations were strained when the 9/11 attacks were revealed to have been perpetrated by Saudi citizens. In May 2003 terrorist attacks in the form of four suicide bombings occurred in Riyad. In Aug. a U.S. Congressional report on the 9/11 attacks appeared with 28 pages deleted by the White House, pages reportedly describing support provided by Saudi government officials to the hijacker-terrorists.

In 2005 King Fahd died and Prince Abdullah ascended the throne. In April 2007, however, the Saudi government uncovered a serious terrorist plot on its own territory, a plot it claimed derived from the war in Iraq. In 2009 Amnesty International accused the government of human rights abuses saying thousands had been arrested and detained under the guise of fighting terrorism.

▶ SENEGAL
Republic of Senegal
• **GEOGRAPHY** **Location:** northwestern coast of Africa. **Boundaries:** Mauritania to N, Mali to E, Guinea and Guinea-Bissau to S, Atlantic Ocean to W; The Gambia forms narrow enclave extending 200 mi. (320 km) inland from Atlantic coast. **Total area:** 75,749 sq. mi. (196,190 sq km). **Coastline:** 330 mi. (531 km). **Comparative area:** slightly smaller than South Dakota. **Land use:** 12% arable land; negl.% permanent crops; 88% other. **Major cities:** Dakar (capital); Thies; Kaolack.
• **PEOPLE** **Population:** 13,711,597 (July 2009 est.). **Nationality:** noun—Senegalese (sing., pl.); adjective—Senegalese. **Ethnic groups:** 43.3% Wolof, 23.8% Pular, 14.7% Serer, 3.7% Diola, 3% Mandink, 1.1% Soninke, 1% European and Lebanese. **Languages:** French (official), Wolof, Pulaar, Diola, Mandingo. **Religions:** 94% Muslim, 1% indigenous beliefs, 5% Christian (mostly Roman Catholic).
• **GOVERNMENT** **Type:** republic under multi-party democratic rule. **Independence:** Apr. 4, 1960 (from France). **Constitution:** a new constitution was adopted Jan. 7, 2001. **National holiday:** Independence Day, Apr. 4. **Heads of Government:** Abdoulaye Wade, president (since Apr. 2000); Soulayemane Ndene Ndiaye, prime minister (since May 2009). **Structure:** executive—president; unicameral legislature; judiciary—Constitutional Court, Council of State, Court of Final Appeals, Court of Appeals.
• **ECONOMY** **Monetary unit:** Communauté Financière Africaine (CFA) franc. **Budget:** (2008 est.) **income:** $3.141 bil.; **expend.:** $3.799 bil. **G.D.P.:** $21.9 bil., $1,600 per capita (2008 est.). **Chief crops:** peanuts, millet, corn, sorghum, rice, cotton, tomotoes, green vegetables; cattle, poultry, pigs; fish. **Natural resources:** fish, phosphates, iron ore. **Major industries:** fishing, agricultural processing, phosphate mining. **Labor force:** 4.973 mil (2008 est.), 77.5% agriculture, 22.5% industry and services; 48% unemployment (2007 est.). **Exports:** $1.904 bil. (f.o.b., 2008); fish, peanuts, petroleum products, phosphates, cotton. **Imports:** $4.654 bil. (f.o.b., 2008); foods and beverages, consumer goods, capital goods, petroleum products. **Major trading partners:** (2006) **exports:** 19.2% Mali, 8.3% France, 5.8% India, 5.3% The Gambia, 5.1% Spain, 4.9% Italy; **imports:** 25.1% France, 5.2% U.K., 4.8% Thailand, 4.5% China, 4% Spain.

Inhabited since ancient times, Senegal was dominated in the 13th and 14th centuries by the Mandingo and Jolof empires. Portuguese traders and explorers arrived in Senegal in the early 15th century and later competed with the British, Dutch, and French for domination in Senegal. The French established a trading station at Saint-Louis in 1659 and maintained possession thereafter, except for the British enclave along the Gambia River.

In the early 19th century, the French began a series of campaigns to bring the entire country under their control; the last independent sultanate surrendered in 1893. Senegal became a French colony in 1920, and Dakar became the capital of French West Africa. Senegal became a major contributor of African troops to the French armed forces.

In 1946 a territorial assembly was established, with a limited electorate and advisory powers, which were gradually expanded in subsequent years. With the creation of the French Community of Nations in 1958, Senegal achieved local self-rule within the community.

In 1959, with the encouragement of France, Senegal and French Sudan (now Mali) formed the Federation of Mali, which became fully independent on June 20, 1960. Senegal seceded from the federation on Aug. 20 and declared itself the Republic of Senegal. Leopold Sedar Senghor became Senegal's first president.

In 1962 Prime Minister Mamdou Dia attempted a coup against the Senghor government; it failed, and Dia was imprisoned. A new constitution was subsequently adopted, strengthening the power of the presidency. Senghor retired from office in 1981 and was succeeded by Adbou Diouf. He encouraged political pluralism and presided over a generally stable government. Diouf was elected in his own right in 1983 and reelected in 1988. Following the 1988 elections, riots broke out over charges of electoral fraud, and a state of emergency was declared.

Diouf was reelected for the third time in 1993, and he consolidated his power so well that in 1998 Parliament passed a law allowing him to become President for life. His involvement in the civil war in Guinea-Bissau, however, caused dissension in the army. His creation of a Senate as "upper house" to the National Assembly meant little for democracy since, with all opposition parties boycotting the election, his Socialist Party carried all 45 seats up for election. So the March 2000 presidential election was a surprise: Abdoulaye Wade of the Democratic Party (who had run four times since 1978) took 60 percent of the vote to become Senegal's third, and first non-Socialist, president. At the end of 2004 he was able to end a small but destructive insurgency demanding autonomy for a small piece of land (Casamance) that has befuddled the nation since the early 1980s.

Although now over 80 years old, Wade ran again in March 2007, and was reelected, though some judged the election unfair. Legislative elections in June were boycotted by groups opposed to Wade.

▶ SERBIA
• **GEOGRAPHY** **Location:** Southern central Europe. **Boundaries:** Hungary to N, Romania to NE, Bulgaria to E, Macedonia and Albania to S, Adriatic Sea, Bosnia and Herzegovina to W., Croatia to NW. **Total area:** 39,517 sq. mi. (102,350 sq km). **Coastline:** 124 mi. (199 km). **Comparative area:** Slightly smaller than Kentucky. **Land use:** 36% arable; 3% permanent crops; 61% other. **Major cities:** Belgrade (capital); Nis; Kragujevac; Novi Sad; Podoricj.
• **PEOPLE** **Population:** 7,344,847 (July 2010 est.). **Nationality:** noun—Serb(s) and Montenegrin(s); adjective—Serbian and Montenegrin. **Ethnic groups:** 82.9% Serbian, 1% Montenegrin, 4% Hungarian, 13.4% other. **Languages:** 95% Serbian, 5% Albanian. **Religions:** 65% Orthodox, 19% Mus-

lim, 4% Roman Catholic, 1% Protestant, 11% other.

● **GOVERNMENT Type:** republic. **Independence:** Proclaimed itself successor to former Socialist Federal Republic of Yugoslavia Apr. 11, 1992; became the Republic of Serbia on June 5th, 2006. **Constitution:** Nov. 2006. **National holiday:** Feb. 15. **Heads of Government:** Boris Tadić, president (since June 2004); Mirko Cvetković, prime minister (since June 2006); **Structure:** executive—president; bicameral legislature; judiciary—judges elected by legislature.

● **ECONOMY Monetary unit:** Yugoslav new dinar. **Budget:** (2010 est.) *income:* $9.7 bil., *expend:* $11.3 bil. **G.D.P.:** $78.36 bil., $10,400 per capita (2009 est.). **Chief crops:** cereal, fruits, vegetables, tobacco, olives; cattle, sheep, goats. **Natural resources:** oil, gas, coal, antimony, copper. **Major industries:** machine building, metallurgy, mining, consumer goods, electronics, petroleum products, chemicals, pharmaceuticals. **Labor force:** 3.107 mil. (2009 est.); 18.8% unemployment (2007 est.). **Exports:** $8.34 bil. (2009); manufactured goods, food and live animals, raw materials. **Imports:** $15.85 bil. (2009); machinery and transport equipment, fuels and lubricants, manufactured goods, chemicals, food and live animals, raw materials. **Major trading partners:** Bosnia and Herzegovnia, Italy, Russia.

The lands that composed Yugoslavia until 1991 were incorporated into the Roman Empire as the province of Illyricum in the first century A.D. Christianity became dominant by A.D. 600. Its nucleus was Serbia, settled in the seventh century by South Slav migrants from the Over and Vistula, and converted to Christianity, in its Eastern Orthodox form, in the ninth century. Twice (in 1077 and again in 1202), the Vatican sent royal crowns to Serbian kings, emphasizing their independence, despite the religious differences. Serbia's medieval zenith came during the reign of Stephen Dushan (1331–55), who subjected Albania, Macedonia, Thessaly, and Epirus to his rule, and who gained the vassalage of Bulgaria in addition. But within 30 years of his death, the Ottoman Turks had overrun his realm, a dominance sealed by the Serbian catastrophe at the Battle of Kosovo (1389). Not until 1878 did Serbia regain independence.

The complexities of Balkan politics occupied European statesmen throughout the late 19th century, and the Balkan Wars of 1912 and 1913 led directly to the outbreak of World War I. After the collapse of the Austro-Hungarian Empire during the war, the multiethnic and multinational state of Yugoslavia was patched together in 1918–19. To Serbia were annexed the old Austro-Hungarian lands of Slovenia and Croatia, as well as the ethnically Croatian and Serbian lands of Bosnia and Herzegovina and Montenegro, Macedonia and Kosovo. The last three were Serbian, Bulgarian, and Albanian in nationality, respectively.

The nationalities coexisted in a state of mutual hostility, provoking a royal dictatorship, instituted by King Alexander in 1929 and enduring after his assassination in 1934. Hitler invaded Yugoslavia in 1941; German troops were welcomed in Croatia as liberators from the Serbs. Resistance began almost immediately, split into two mutually hostile groups: Draza Mihajlovic's Serbian royalist Chetniks, and the Partisans, a group of pan-Yugoslav Communists and non-Serbian anti-German forces led by Tito (a.k.a. Josip Broz). By the end of the war, over two million Yugoslavs had died, and

3.5 million were homeless. Backed by both Churchill and Stalin, Tito ruled over a ruined land: the new Federal People's Republic of Yugoslavia.

Tito imposed agricultural collectivization on the Stalinist model, and pushed for the development of industry under state ownership. Politically, harsh repression fell on members of the Chetnik resistance as well as on the Slovene Home Guard and the Croatian Ustasa. But the postwar period of tyranny was short-lived. Tito refused to permit Yugoslavia to become a Soviet satellite; in 1948 he expelled Russian military advisers, and was himself expelled from the Comintern.

In the face of economic pressure and military threats, Tito turned westward. Stalinism yielded to decentralized communism. The 1953 Agrarian Reform Law permitted private agricultural holdings, and 80 percent of the land returned to private ownership; "self-management" rather than central control was encouraged in the industrial sector. Economic growth averaged 7 percent per year for three decades, lifting Yugoslavia into the ranks of the semideveloped countries.

Despite a reconciliation with Khruschev's Soviet Union in 1955–56, Tito continued to chart an independent course, taking a leading role in the Third World Non-Aligned Movement and providing a political and economic alternative model for Eastern Europe. But Yugoslavian nationalism masked the development of separate nationalisms within the Yugoslavian federation.

The country's major ethnic groups (Serbs, Croats, and Muslims) coexisted under Tito's iron hand, and even after Tito's death in 1980, his rotating presidency scheme, in which the leaders of each republic took turns serving as "president of the presidency," worked smoothly. But when communism fell in 1989, only Serbia and Montenegro voted for Communist governments, while the republics of Croatia, Slovenia, Macedonia, and Bosnia-Herzegovina sought independence.

A vicious civil war ensued in which Yugoslavia's Serbian president Slobodan Milosevic sought to keep all ethnically Serbian areas under Serbian control. While Serb militias captured about one-third of Croatia in 1991, the Croatian army won back most of the region in 1995. And Yugoslavia's attempt to keep Bosnia-Herzegovina within a "greater Serbia" failed as well, the failure ratified in the November 1995 "Dayton Accords," which brought NATO peacekeepers to the region. The year 1996 saw the formal end of the civil wars, as Milosevic endorsed treaties guaranteeing the boundaries of Macedonia, Croatia and Bosnia; additionally, a pact with the Albanians of Serbia's Kosovo province permitted Albanian as the language of instruction in Kosovo's schools.

Though Milosevic and his political allies won 84 of 138 seats in Yugoslavia's parliament in Nov. 1996, the political opposition, called Zajedno ("Together"), won control of 14 large cities. The annulments of these results by Yugoslav courts and electoral commissions provoked 11 weeks of popular protests until Milosevic conceded in Feb. 1997. In July, however, Milosevic maneuvered to take back the presidency by receiving a majority of votes in Parliament.

In 1998 ethnic Albanians in the Kosovo province of Serbia launched a terrorist campaign to secede from Serbia and join Albania. The Serbs put down the rebellion with unexpected ferocity. In the winter of 1999 Serbia launched a full-scale attack against Kosovo that drove 700,000 ethnic

Albanians from their homes. Despite NATO warnings, Pres. Milosevic continued his ethnic cleansing of Serbia's province and at the end of March NATO began a bombing campaign that lasted 72 days. In June Serbia surrendered and Milosevic agreed to 50,000 NATO troops in Kosovo and the withdrawal of all Yugoslav troops. The U.N. supervised peace was slow to form and soon Serbs were being driven from Kosovo. In 2000 Milosevic managed to maintain his power but his attempt to rig elections in the summer led to mass protests that forced the Milosevic regime to take police-state measures. A coalition of 15 parties backed Vojislav Kostunica against Milosevic in the Sept. presidential elections. Hundreds of thousands protested the Milosevic attempts to force a run-off and Kostunica was sworn in Oct. 7. Milosevic was turned over to the U.N. for trial on war-crimes charges. In March 2002 the presidents of Serbia and Montenegro agreed to maintain foreign affairs and defense as the sole bonds in a loose federation. The very name "Yugoslavia" was dropped in favor of "Serbia and Montenegro."

In the 2003 elections in Montenegro, former president Milo Djukanovic became prime minister of a government favoring independence. In Serbia, ex-president Koštunica became prime minister after the assassination of Djindjic. Boris Tadic was elected president in June 2004. In May 2006, 55.5 percent of Montenegro's voters chose independence from Serbia for their future. The process of separation began immediately, and Montenegro and Serbia became independent states. In Oct. 2006, the Serbian parliament unanimously confirmed a new constitution.

In 2007, Kosovo's bid to become independent was stopped by Russia's refusal to accept that idea but in Feb. 2008, Kosovo declared its independence. Tadic was reelected, and Radovan Karadzic was accused of war crimes, arrested, and sent to the Hague. By 2009, 60 nations had recognized Kosovo but Serbia did not and asked the U.N. to provide a ruling. In 2010, the International Court of Justice ruled in favor of Kosovo.

▶ **SEYCHELLES**
Republic of Seychelles
• **GEOGRAPHY** **Location:** more than 90 widely scattered islands in western Indian Ocean about 1,000 mi. (1,600 km) E of Kenya and Tanzania. Victoria (Mahé Is.) 4°37'S, 55°28'E. **Boundaries:** surrounded by Indian Ocean; nearest neighbor is Madagascar about 130 mi. (210 km) S of southernmost island group. **Total area:** 176 sq. mi. (455 sq km). **Coastline:** 305 mi. (491 km). **Comparative area:** 2.5 times the size of Washington, D.C. **Land use:** 2% arable land; 13% permanent crops; 85% other. **Major cities:** Victoria (capital).
• **PEOPLE** **Population:** 87,476 (July 2009 est.). **Nationality:** noun—Seychellois (sing., pl.); adjective—Seychelles. **Ethnic groups:** Seychellois (mixture of Asians, Africans, Europeans, Arab, Chinese). **Languages:** English, French (both official); Creole. **Religions:** 82% Roman Catholic, 6% Anglican, 6% other, 1% Muslim, 2% Hindu.
• **GOVERNMENT** **Type:** republic. **Independence:** June 29, 1976 (from U.K.). **Constitution:** June 18, 1993. **National holiday:** National Day, June 18. **Head of Government:** James A. Michel, president (since Apr. 2004). **Structure:** executive—president; unicameral legislature; judiciary.
• **ECONOMY** **Monetary unit:** Seychelles rupee. **Budget:** (2008 est.) *income:* $318.1 mil.; *expend.:*

$324.6 mil. **G.D.P.:** $1.473 bil., $17,000 per capita (2008 est.). **Chief crops:** coconuts, cinnamon, vanilla, sweet potatoes, cassava, bananas; broiler chickens; tuna fishing (expansion under way). **Natural resources:** fish, copra, cinnamon trees. **Major industries:** tourism is largest industry; processing of coconut and vanilla; fishing. **Labor force:** 39,560 (2006); 23% industry, 74% services, 3% agriculture, forestry, and fishing. **Exports:** $425 mil. (f.o.b., 2008); fish, cinnamon bark, copra, petroleum products (reexports). **Imports:** $952 mil. (f.o.b., 2008); food, petroleum products, machinery, transportation equipment. **Major trading partners:** (2006) *exports:* 25.5% U.K., 17.5% France, 12% Italy, 8.5% Mauritius, 8.3% Japan, 8.2% Spain, 4.3% Netherlands; *imports:* 17.7% Saudi Arabia, 9.7% South Africa, 8.1% Spain, 7.8% France, 7.2% Singapore, 4.8% Italy, 4% U.K.

The Seychelles Islands were occupied by France in the 18th century and seized by Great Britain in 1794. They were administered along with Mauritius until 1903, when the Seychelles became a separate British colony. African and Indian workers were brought in to work in coconut and spice plantations and in guano mining. The present population is of mixed African, Indian, and European descent.

In the post-World War II period, a home-rule government rejected independence as impracticable. At the urging of the Organization of African Unity and the United Nations, the Seychelles declared independence on June 29, 1976. Its first president was ousted in a socialist coup in 1977 led by Prime Minister France Albert René. A new constitution, promulgated in March 1979, formalized one-party Socialist rule. In July 1992 a commission was elected to rewrite the constitution before the end of the year, but the delegates defeated the first results. Rene retired in 2004 and his vice president James Michel took over and was elected in 2006 for five years.

Since independence, the economy of the Seychelles has become heavily dependent on the tourist industry, which accounts for 90 percent of the country's foreign exchange earnings. Fishing accounts for 40 percent of exports.

▶ **SIERRA LEONE**
Republic of Sierra Leone
• **GEOGRAPHY** **Location:** west central Africa. **Boundaries:** Guinea to N and E, Liberia to S, Atlantic Ocean to W. **Total area:** 27,699 sq. mi. (71,740 sq km). **Coastline:** 250 mi. (402 km). **Comparative area:** slightly smaller than South Carolina. **Land use:** 7% arable land; 1% permanent crops; 92% other. **Major cities:** Freetown (capital); Koindu; Bo; Kenema; Makeni.
• **PEOPLE** **Population:** 6,440,053 (July 2009 est.). **Nationality:** noun—Sierra Leonean(s); adjective—Sierra Leonean. **Ethnic groups:** over 90% African (30% Temne, 30% Mende), 10% creole. **Languages:** English (official); regular use limited to literate minority; principal languages are Mende in south and Temne in north; Krio is language of resettled ex-slave population of Freetown area and is lingua franca. **Religions:** 60% Muslim, 30% indigenous beliefs, 10% Christian.
• **GOVERNMENT** **Type:** constitutional democracy. **Independence:** Apr. 27, 1961 (from U.K.). **Constitution:** Oct. 1, 1991. **National holiday:** Independence Day, Apr. 27. **Heads of Government:** Ernest Bai Koroma, president (since Sept. 2007). **Structure:** executive—president; unicameral legisla-

ture—68 elected seats, 12 filled by paramount chiefs; judiciary.
• ECONOMY **Monetary unit:** leone. **Budget:** (2000 est.) *income:* $96 mil.; *expend.:* $351 mil. **G.D.P.:** $4.307 bil., $700 per capita (2008 est.). **Chief crops:** palm kernels, coffee, cocoa, rice, palm oil, peanuts; poultry, cattle, sheep, pigs; fish. **Natural resources:** diamonds, titanium ore, bauxite, iron ore, gold. **Major industries:** mining (diamonds, iron ore, bauxite, rutile), small-scale manufacturing (beverages, textiles, cigarettes, footwear), petroleum refinery. **Labor force:** 1.369 mil. (1981); 65% agriculture, 19% industry, 16% services; only small minority, some 65,000, earn wages. **Exports:** $216 mil. (f.o.b., 2006); diamonds, rutile, cocoa, coffee, fish. **Imports:** $560 mil. (f.o.b., 2006); foodstuffs, machinery and equipment, fuels and lubricants. **Major trading partners:** (2006) *exports:* 52% Belgium, 19% U.S., 7% Netherlands; *imports:* 9.3% Cote d'Ivoire, 7.7% U.S., 7% Brazil, 6.7% U.K., 5.5% Netherlands, 4.5% South Africa, 4.3% India, 4.2% France.

Portuguese domination of the Sierra Leone coast began in 1462. English explorers, including Francis Drake, arrived in the late 16th century. Europeans traded for slaves in Sierra Leone, but in 1787 Freetown was founded by the British Sierra Leone Co. as a haven for freed slaves. The settlement was populated by former slaves from Great Britain, North America, and the Caribbean, and later by slaves liberated from slave trading ships by the British navy.

Sierra Leone was reorganized as a British colony in 1808. The ex-slave population, from diverse tribal and national backgrounds, developed an English-speaking Creole culture unique in Africa. Freetown became the center of British colonial administration and trade in West Africa and was the focus of missionary-supported projects in health care and economic development.

The native peoples of Sierra Leone staged numerous rebellions against the British and the Creole elite; resentment focused on the tax system and on the privileges of the English-speaking descendents of ex-slaves. During the 20th century, home rule developed through an elected advisory legislature. In 1951 a constitutional framework had been developed as the basis of decolonization. Sir Milton Margei became chief minister in 1953, and prime minister in 1961. The last ties with the British Crown were cut on Apr. 27, 1961, when Sierra Leone became a republic. A referendum in 1978 created a one-party state. In 1984 and 1985 student and public employee protests against the government led to riots and the restoration of multi-party elections.

In April 1992, Momoh was ousted in a coup by Capt. Valentine Strasser. Despite the country's wealth of natural resources, Strasser's corruption and mismanagement threatened to derail the economy. Strasser was overthrown in Jan. 1996 by army officers who pledged to continue his plan for multi-party elections. Ahmad Tejan Kabbah of the People's party captured close to 60 percent of the votes.

In 1991 Sierra Leone was attacked by a murderous gang led by "rebel" Fodaj Sankoh, calling itself the Revolutionary United Front. By July 1999 it controlled perhaps half of the country, including diamond mines which they looted, then marketed through Liberia's president, Charles Taylor. In May 1997 regular army troops loyal to Major Johnny Paul Koroma briefly overthrew Pres. Kabbah until

Nigerian-led west African troops restored Kabbah and assisted against the RUF gang. A July 1999 cease-fire brought four RUF killers into the government and an amnesty for Sankoh. But the RUF did not disarm, and continued the struggle into 2000. Sankoh was captured late in May. In 2001 Parliament, with U.N. and British approval, postponed the scheduled March elections and extended President Kabbah's term for six months. With Sankoh captured, more U.N. troops in the country, and, most importantly, diminished support from Pres. Taylor, RUF began in May to disarm and to release hundreds of its boy-soldiers. But fighting continued in the diamond-rich east.

The July 18, 2001 agreement of the U.N., Sierra Leone, and the RUF rebels was strong enough for the government to declare (Jan. 18, 2002) the 11-year civil war over. On March 4, Foday Sankah was charged with murder; and on May 19 elections brought overwhelming approval to both Pres. Kabbah and his Sierra Leone's People's Party (which gained 83 of the 112 parliamentary seats); 17,000 U.N. troops remained in Sierra Leone until 2005. In 2007, opposition leader Ernest Bai Koroma was elected in a presidential run-off, defeating the Sierra Leone People's Party.

▶ **SINGAPORE**
Republic of Singapore
• GEOGRAPHY **Location:** Singapore Island and some 57 islets off southern Malay peninsula (linked by a causeway). **Boundaries:** Johor Strait to N; Pacific Ocean to E; Strait of Malacca to SW, separating Singapore from Indonesian island of Sumatra; and Indian Ocean to W. **Total area:** 244 sq. mi. (633 sq km). **Coastline:** 120 mi. (193 km). **Comparative area:** slightly more than 3.5 times size of Washington, D.C. **Land use:** 2% arable land; 0% permanent crops; 98% other. **Major cities:** Singapore (capital).
• PEOPLE **Population:** 4,701,069 (July 2010 est.). **Nationality:** noun—Singaporean(s); adjective—Singapore. **Ethnic groups:** 77% Chinese, 14% Malay, 7.9% Indian, 1.4% other. **Languages:** Chinese, Malay, Tamil, and English (all official); Malay (national). **Religions:** majority of Chinese are Buddhists or atheists; Malays nearly all Muslim; minorities include Christians, Hindus, Sikhs, Taoists, Confucianists.
• GOVERNMENT **Type:** parliamentary republic. **Independence:** Aug. 9, 1965 (from Malaysia). **Constitution:** June 3, 1959, amended 1965; based on preindependence State of Singapore constitution. **National holiday:** Aug. 9. **Heads of Government:** S.R. Nathan, president (since Sept. 1999); Lee Hsien Loong, prime minister (since Aug. 2004). **Structure:** executive—ceremonial president, power exercised by prime minister and cabinet; unicameral legislature; judiciary.
• ECONOMY **Monetary unit:** Singapore dollar. **Budget:** (2009 est.) *income:* $21.29 bil.; *expend.:* $24.14 bil. **G.D.P.:** $235.7 bil., $50,300 per capita (2009 est.). **Chief crops:** rubber, copra, fruits, vegetables; poultry. **Natural resources:** fish, deep-water ports. **Major industries:** financial services, petroleum refining, electronics, oil drilling equipment. **Labor force:** 3.03 mil. (2009 est.); 42% services, 26% industry, 25% other (2006). **Exports:** $268.9 bil. (2009 est.); computer equipment, petroleum products, telecommunications equipment. **Imports:** $245 bil. (2009 est.); machinery and equipment, petroleum, chemicals, foodstuffs. **Major trading partners:** (2008) *exports:*

11.6% Hong Kong, 11.5% Malaysia, 11.2% U.S., 9.7% Indonesia, 9.7% China, 4.6% Japan; *imports:* 14.7% U.S., 11.6% Malaysia, 10.5% China, 7.6% Japan, 5.8% Indonesia, 5.7% South Korea.

Singapore was founded in 1819 by Sir Thomas Stamford Raffles on land ceded to the East India Company by the sultanate of Johore (see "Malaysia"). An Anglo-Dutch treaty turned Singapore over to the British Crown in 1824, and eventually it was administered as part of the Straits Settlements. With its excellent harbor, Singapore eclipsed Penang and Malacca as the dominant port for trade through the Straits of Malacca.

Fortified as a bastion of British defense in Southeast Asia, Singapore was overrun by Japanese troops in Feb. 1942. The British reoccupied the city in Sept. 1945 and reorganized it as a British colony in 1946. On June 5, 1959, Singapore became a self-governing parliamentary democracy within the British Commonwealth. Lee Kwan Yew became prime minister. On Sept. 16, 1963, Singapore, along with Malaya, Sarawak, and Sabah, formed the Malaysian Federation. Singapore, ethnically Chinese, was uncomfortable within the Malay-dominated federation and seceded after two years, becoming an independent nation on Aug. 9, 1965.

Independent Singapore has enjoyed stable, if authoritarian, government, economic growth, and a high standard of living. Still a major port, its economy now encompasses international banking, finance, communications, high-technology manufacturing, and tourism. On Nov. 26, 1990, Lee Kuan Yew, Singapore's only prime minister since independence and the longest serving prime minister in the world, resigned. He was succeeded by Goh Chok Tong, but he continued to be a force in Singapore's political life.

Measures in 2000 opened up segments of the economy to foreign firms, especially telecommunications and law, while the government ended its monopoly on broadcasting and newspapers. In 2004 Lee Kwan Yew's son, Lee Hsien Loong, chairman of the central bank and deputy prime minister, became prime minister.

▶ SLOVAKIA
Slovak Republic
● GEOGRAPHY **Location:** Central Europe. **Boundaries:** Czech Republic and Poland to N, Ukraine to E, Hungary to S, Austria to W. **Total area:** 18,859 sq. mi. (48,845 sq km). **Coastline:** none. **Comparative area:** about twice the size of New Hampshire. **Land use:** 31% arable, 3% permanent crops, 66% other. **Major cities:** Bratislava (capital); Kosice; Nitra; Presov; Banská Bystrica.
● PEOPLE **Population:** 5,470,306 (July 2010 est.). **Nationality:** noun—Slovak(s); adjective—Slovak. **Ethnic groups:** 85.7% Slovak, 10.6% Hungarian, 1.6% Roma. **Languages:** Slovak (official), Hungarian. **Religions:** 60.3% Roman Catholic, 9.7% atheist, 8.4% Protestant, 4.1% Orthodox.
● GOVERNMENT **Type:** parliamentary democracy. **Independence:** Jan. 1, 1993 (from Czechoslovakia). **Constitution:** Jan. 1, 1993; changed Sept. 1996 to allow direct election of president; amended Feb. 2001. **National holiday:** Slovak Constitution Day, Sept. 1. **Heads of Government:** Ivan Gasparovic, president (since June 2004); Iveta Radicova, prime minister (since July 2010). **Structure:** executive—president, prime minister, Council of Ministers; legislature—unicameral (National Council); judicial—Supreme Court.

● ECONOMY **Monetary unit:** euro. **Budget:** (2009 est.) *income:* $29.08 bil.; *expend.:* $34.68 bil. **G.D.P.:** $115.7 bil., $21,200 per capita (2009 est.). **Chief crops:** grains, potatoes, sugar beets, hops, fruit; hogs, cattle, poultry; forest products. **Natural resources:** brown coal and lignite; small amounts of iron ore, copper and manganese ore, salt. **Major industries:** metal working, food, beverages, fuels, chemicals. **Labor force:** 2.365 mil.; 27% industry, 3.5% agriculture, 69.4% services (2009 est.); 8.6% unemployment (2007). **Exports:** $55.4 bil. (2009 est.); 39% machinery and transport equipment; 18% intermediate manufactured goods, 10% miscellaneous manufactured goods. **Imports:** $53.74 bil. (2009 est.); 38% machinery and transport equipment; 18% intermediate manufactured goods, 13% fuels. **Major trading partners:** (2009) *exports:* 20.1% Germany, 12.9% Czech Republic, 7.8% France, 7.2% Poland, 6.3% Hungary, 6.1% Italy; *imports:* 16.8% Germany, 12.3% Czech Republic, 9% Russia, 6.8% South Korea, 5.8% China, 5.3% Hungary.

Though the Czech and Slovak languages are similar, the two peoples have always been far apart culturally and historically (much like the Letts and Lithuanians). The ninth-century Moravian Empire has been claimed as heritage by both peoples; but with the Magyar invasion of the Pannonian Plain in the 10th century, the Slovaks passed under Hungarian rule for 1,000 years. When in the 19th century a romantic-nationalist revival occurred, the Slovaks, under the leadership of Ludovit Štur, decided to use their own language in literature (though some of the most prominent writers in the Czech tongue were of Slovak origin, such as the poet Jan Kollár and the historian P.J. Šafarik). Unlike the Czechs, the Slovaks took no part in the revolutions of 1848. They lacked a native aristocracy; their national leadership came from wealthy peasants, small-town shopkeepers and, above all, their priests.

In the peacemaking at the end of World War I, as the Austro-Hungarian Empire collapsed, the Czech politicians Beneš and Masaryk claimed to speak for the (nonexistent) Czechoslovak nation. They carried the day despite apparent Slovak loyalty to Hungary and even the opposition of Fr. Hlinka's Slovak Populist party to union with the Czechs. The synthetic "nation" of Czechoslovakia was created, governed by a sort of benevolent democratic dictatorship of the Czechs over the other nations. With the Munich crisis of October 1939, Hitler imposed a federal structure giving Slovakia almost complete autonomy in the renamed Czecho-Slovakia; in the following March, when Hitler obliterated Czech independence, an "independent" Slovakia was formed with Hlinka's successor, Magr Tiso, as president.

But under the circumstances independence was illusory. German protection (against Hungarian revisionism) required complete Slovak accord with Reich foreign policy, including declarations of war on Poland (1939) and on the U.S.S.R., the United States, and Great Britain (1941). Domestically, Msgr. Tiso organized a one-party state with anti-Jewish legislation, half unwilling and half unable to resist the expulsion (and eventual extermination) of 60,000 Jews.

The cement for a restored Czechoslovakia after the war was the Communist tyranny imposed in 1948. But the "Velvet Revolution" in 1989 overturned Yalta and brought victory over the Communists. As the Czech premier Václav Klaus pushed for free-market "shock therapy," the Slovak premier Vladimír Meciar defended a slower "Slovak way" to capitalism. Economic differences inflamed by ancient Slovak resentment of the Czech majority led to a much-diminished federal government by the spring of 1992. In the summer the split became the "Velvet Divorce."

In July 1992 Slovak deputies to the federal Parliament blocked the reelection of Václav Havel to the presidency, and the Slovak National Council approved, by a vote of 113 to 24, a declaration of sovereignty. In September the two parliaments agreed to the terms. In accord with a two-to-one ratio of the republics' populations, the military and financial assets of Czechoslovakia were divided. By February only a customs union linked the two parts of the old state.

On Feb. 15, 1993, the Slovak Parliament elected its first president, Michal Kovác, with Meciar, as prime minister. Inflation and high unemployment coupled with a corruption scandal toppled the Meciar government in 1994, but a coalition government including many former Communists restored him as prime minister. In Sept. 1998, a four-party opposition coalition toppled Meciar's regime. Mikuláš Dzurinda became prime minister, heading a government whose principal focus was NATO and E.U. membership.

On May 29, 1999, in Slovakia's first popular election of a president, Rudolf Schuster defeated Meciar in a run-off; but in July 2000, the cabinet, with Schuster incapacitated by illness, transferred presidential powers to the prime minister and parliament's speaker. Meciar was arrested on charges of fraud and abuse of power. Dzurinda put together a four-party coalition to stay in office and in May 2003, 93 percent of voters approved, joining the E.U. But in 2004 elections, Ivan Gasparovic defeated Meciar and a center-left government took office. Gasparovic was reelected in 2010.

▶ **SLOVENIA**
Republic of Slovenia
● **GEOGRAPHY Location:** southeastern Europe. **Boundaries:** Austria to N, Hungary to NE, Croatia to E and S, Adriatic Sea and Italy to W. **Total area:** 7,836 sq. mi. (20,296 sq km). **Coastline:** 20 mi. (32 km). **Comparative area:** Slightly smaller than New Jersey. **Land use:** 11% arable land, 3% permanent crops, 86% other. **Major cities:** Ljubljana (capital); Maribor; Celje; Kranj.
● **PEOPLE Population:** 2,003,136 (July 2010 est.). **Nationality:** noun—Slovene(s); adjective—Slovenian. **Ethnic groups:** 83.1% Slovene, 1.8% Croat, 2% Serb, 1% Bosniak. **Languages:** 91% Slovenian, 6% Serbo-Croatian. **Religions:** 58% Catholic, 1% Muslim, 27.4% other, 10% none.
● **GOVERNMENT Type:** parliamentary democratic republic. **Independence:** June 25, 1991 (from Yugoslavia). **Constitution:** Dec. 23, 1991; amended July 1997 and July 2000. **National holiday:** National Statehood Day, June 25. **Heads of Government:** Danilo Turk, president of the presidency (four other members) (since Dec., 2007); Borut Pahor, prime minister (since Nov. 2008). **Structure:** executive—president, prime minister, cabinet; legislative—unicameral parliament-second chamber has only advisory powers; judicial—Supreme Court, Constitutional Court.
● **ECONOMY Monetary unit:** euro. **Budget:** (2009 est.) *income:* $20.58 bil.; *expend.:* $23.54 bil. **G.D.P.:** $55.84 bil., $27,900 per capita (2009 est.). **Chief crops:** potatoes, hops, wheat, sugar beets,

corn, grapes; cattle, sheep, poultry. **Natural resources:** lignite coal, lead, zinc, mercury, uranium. **Major industries:** ferrous metallurgy and rolling mill products, aluminum reduction and rolled products, lead and zinc smelting, electronics, trucks, electric power equipment, wood products, textiles. **Labor force:** 914,000; 62.8% services, 35% industry, 2.2% agriculture (2009). **Exports:** $24.3 bil. (2009 est.); manufactured goods, machinery and transport equipment, chemicals. **Imports:** $22.9 bil. (2009 est.); machinery and transport equipment, other manufactured goods, chemicals. **Major trading partners:** (2008) *exports:* 18.2% Germany, 11.4% Italy, 8.1% Croatia, 7.3% Austria, 5.5% France, 4.7% Russia; *imports:* 17% Germany, 16.4% Italy, 11.1% Austria, 4.6% France, 4.1% Croatia.

In the sixth century, as part of the great Slavic migrations out of the Vistula and Oder basins, the Slovene people crossed the Carpathians into the Danube plain, penetrating as far as the eastern Alps. In the eighth and ninth centuries the lands they inhabited were subject to Bavarian colonization as part of the Ostmark (Eastern March) of the Carolingian Empire. For 1,000 years, Slovene history was Austrian history. Thus, like the Croats, Christianity came in its western (Roman Catholic) form.

Lacking their own nobility and even a burgher class for most of their history, the Slovenes tended to look to their priests for leadership, regularly electing them as their representatives to the Reichstag in Vienna (as they did later to the Skupstina in Belgrade after Slovenia became part of Yugoslavia). The 19th-century rise of a national consciousness, associated with literary collections of legend and folklore, took a special turn in the Slovene case because of Napoleon's conquests. His "province of Illyria" was the first association of the Slovenes with Croats and Serbs and his minister of education there was the Slovene Franciscan Valentin Vodnik, so that Slovene "nationalism" had from a start a "Yugoslav" tinge.

In 1815 the Slovenes were again part of the Austrian Empire and were confirmed in the Ausgleich of 1867 as part of the Austrian, not Hungarian, part of the dual Monarchy. As that monarchy collapsed in World War I, it was the Slovene monsignor Anton Korosec who served as president of "The National Council of the Serbs, Croats, and Slovenes" out of which the new state of Yugoslavia emerged. Though the new Yugoslavia was a highly centralized, unitary state, circumstances brought a kind of privileged position to Slovenia. Their distinct language made Serbian administration a practical impossibility and Serbian struggles against Croat separatism led them to favor the Slovenes to Croatia's north. Moreoover, as a part of the long Austrian connection, the Slovenes were better educated and more industrially advanced than any other part of Yugoslavia.

After the interlude of Hitler's break-up of Yugoslavia (in which Slovenia itself was partitioned between Germany and Italy) Slovenia became a constituent "republic" in Tito's reconstructed Yugoslavia and, despite the enduring enmity provoked by the Communist slaughter of the Slovene Domobranci (Home Guard), again assumed a kind of privileged status in Yugoslavia. After the dictator's death in 1980, the Slovene Socialist Republic took part in the "collegial rule" of Yugoslavia, but with the end of Communist rule in 1990, Slovenia became the first of the republics to secede, in June 1991. After the Slovene militia inflicted a humiliating defeat on the Yugoslav army in July and with E.U. recognition in December, Slovenia became independent for the first time in its history. Forging economic ties with Austria, Hungary, and Italy, it remained prosperously apart from the debacle to its south.

In Nov. 1996 elections, the center-right coalition calling itself Slovenian Spring captured 45 (of 90) seats in the Parliament with the Liberal Democrats and its allies controlling the other 45. After months of deadlock LD leader Janos Drnovsek was confirmed as prime minister. In 2002 he was elected president and Anton Rop became prime minister. In 2003 voters approved joining both the E.U. and NATO which they did in 2004. A left-leaning president, Danilo Turk, was elected at the end of 2007. Border disputes with Croatia dating back to 1980 remained bitter and Slovenia did all it could to keep Croatia out of NATO and the E.U. In 2009 the borders were agreed to.

▶ SOLOMON ISLANDS
• **Geography Location**: archipelago in South Pacific E of Papua New Guinea. Honiara (Guadalcanal Is.) 9°28′S, 159°57′E. **Boundaries**: South Pacific Ocean to N, E, and S, Solomon Sea to W; nearest neighbor is Santa Cruz Islands to SE. **Total area**: 10,985 sq. mi. (28,450 sq km). **Coastline**: 3,302 mi. (5,313 km). **Comparative area**: slightly smaller than Maryland. **Land use**: 6% arable land; 2% permanent crops; 92% other. **Major cities**: Honiara (capital).
• **People Population**: 595,613 (July 2009 est.). **Nationality**: noun—Solomon Islander(s); adjective—Solomon Islander. **Ethnic groups**: 93% Melanesian, 4% Polynesian, 1.5% Micronesian, 0.8% European, 0.3% Chinese. **Languages**: 120 indigenous languages; Melanesian pidgin in much of country is lingua franca; English spoken by 1-2% of population. **Religions**: 34% Anglican, 19% Roman Catholic, 17% Baptist, 11% United (Methodist/Presbyterian), 11% Seventh-Day Adventist, 5% other Protestant, 4% traditional beliefs.
• **Government Type**: parliamentary democracy. **Independence**: July 7, 1978 (from U.K.). **Constitution**: July 7, 1978. **National holiday**: Independence Day, July 7. **Heads of Government**: Frank Kabui, governor-general (since July 2009); Derek Sikua, prime minister (since Dec. 2007). **Structure**: executive—authority in governor-general; unicameral legislature; judiciary.
• **Economy Monetary unit**: Solomon Islands dollar. **Budget**: (2003 est.) *income*: $49.7 mil.; *expend*.: 75.1 mil. **G.D.P.**: $1.078 bil., $1,900 per capita (2008 est.). **Chief crops**: cocoa, beans, coconuts, palm kernels, rice, potatoes, vegetables, fruits; cattle, pigs; timber; fish. **Natural resources**: fish, forests, gold, bauxite, phosphates. **Major industries**: fish (tuna), mining, timber. **Labor force**: 249,200 (1999 est.); 20% services, 75% agriculture, forestry, and fishing, 5% industry. **Exports**: $237 mil. (f.o.b., 2006 est.); timber, fish, palm oil, cocoa, copra. **Imports**: $256 mil. (f.o.b., 2006 est.); plant and equipment, manufactured goods, food and live animals, fuel. **Major trading partners**: (2006) *exports*: 48% China, 10% South Korea, 9% Japan, 5% Thailand, 4% Italy, 4% Philippines; *imports*: 26% Australia, 24% Singapore, 8% Japan, 5% New Zealand, 4% Fiji, 4% Papua New Guinea.

In 1893 Britain established a protectorate over the South Solomon Islands, including the large islands of Guadalcanal, San Cristobal, and Malata; the protectorate was extended to the smaller easterly islands of the chain in 1898. In 1900 Germany relinquished to Great Britain its claim to the North Solomons, including Choiseul and Santa Isabel; Bougainville Island was retained by Germany (see "Papua New Guinea"). The major islands were occupied by Japan in 1942 and retaken by the Allies in a series of battles in 1943.

The Solomon Islands were made self-governing in January 1976 and became an independent nation on July 7, 1978. The economy is based on subsistence agriculture and fishing. The sale of tuna fishing rights in the surrounding waters gave the nation a favorable balance of payments.

In June 1999 ethnic violence erupted on Guadalcanal against settlers from the island of Malaita. Then, in June 2000, gunmen from the Malaita Eagle Force (MEF) placed the prime minister under house arrest and captured Honiara airport. On the eve of a parliamentary no-confidence vote, prime minister Ulufa'alu resigned June 14. On July 1 parliament elected opposition leader Mannasseh Sogavare to be prime minister. In 2001, a truce between militias brought no disarmament, but Sogavare used foreign aid to buy off the Eagle Force. With Dec. 2001 elections, his rule was overturned, Sir Allen Kamekeza becoming prime minister after his People's Alliance won a majority in the legislature. But continued ethnic violence through 2003 led the Pacific Islands Forum to approve a regional force led by Australia to restore law and order. The Australian presence brought peace and a bit of prosperity, but in 2006 serious riots against government corruption forced the prime minister to resign and parliament elected Sogavare again. His tenure was short-lived and Derek Sikua succeded him in Dec. 2007.

▶ SOMALIA
• **Geography Location**: eastern coast of Africa. **Boundaries**: short frontier with Djibouti to NW, Gulf of Aden to N, long coastline on Indian Ocean to E, Kenya to SW, Ethiopia to W. **Total area**: 246,201 sq. mi. (637,660 sq km). **Coastline**: 1,880 mi. (3,025 km). **Comparative area**: slightly smaller than Texas. **Land use**: 2% arable land; negl. % permanent crops; 98% other. **Major cities**: Mogadishu (capital); Hargeysa; Kismayo; Merca.
• **People Population**: 10,112,453 (July 2010 est.). **Nationality**: adjective—Somali. **Ethnic groups**: 85% Somali, rest mainly Bantu; 30,000 Arabs. **Languages**: Somali (official), Arabic, Italian, English. **Religions**: almost entirely Sunni Muslim.
• **Government Type**: none. **Independence**: July 1, 1960 (from a merger of British Somaliland, which became independent from U.K. June 26, 1960, and Italian Somaliland, which became independent from Italian-administered U.N. trusteeship July 1, 1960, to form the Somali Republic). **Constitution**: Aug. 25, 1979, presidential approval Sept. 23, 1979. **National holiday**: N.A. **Heads of Government**: Sheikh Sharif Ahmed, president (since Jan. 2009); Omar Abdirashid Ali Sharmarke, prime minister (since Feb. 2009).
• **Economy Monetary unit**: Somali shilling. **Budget**: N.A. **G.D.P.**: $5.731 bil., $600 per capita (2009 est.). **Chief crops**: bananas, sorghum, corn, mangoes, sugarcane, sesame seeds, beans; cattle, sheep, goats; fishing potential largely unexploited. **Natural resources**: uranium, largely unexploited reserves of iron ore, tin, gypsum, bauxite. **Major industries**: a few small industries, including sugar refining, textiles, petroleum refining. **Labor force**: about 3.447 mil. (1993 est.); very few are skilled laborers; 71% agriculture (pastoral

nomadism), 29% industry and services. **Exports:** $300 mil. (f.o.b., 2006 est.); livestock, bananas, hides, fish. **Imports:** $798 mil. (f.o.b., 2006 est.); manufactures, petroleum products, foodstuffs, construction materials. **Major trading partners:** (2008) *exports:* 56.8% U.A.E., 21.2% Yemen, 3.7% Saudi Arabia; *imports:* 30.3% Djibouti, 7.9% Kenya, 7.7% India, 6.2% U.S., 5.8% Oman, 5.7% U.A.E, 4.9% Yemen.

Arab trading settlements in Somalia were established in the seventh century and gradually evolved into independent sultanates. Portuguese traders established settlements and forts along the coast during the 15th and 16th centuries.

In the early 19th century, Great Britain arranged through local treaties to use harbors along the Somali coast and gained control over the northern part of the country by 1840. The border between Somalia and Ethiopia was demarcated by a treaty between Great Britain and Ethiopia in 1897. In 1885 the sultan of Zanzibar granted commercial advantages to Italy, and in 1897 and 1908 Italy gained control over southern Somalia.

During the early 20th century, an uprising against British rule was led by Mohamed Abdullah. Abdullah was defeated by the British with help from his local rivals but is now regarded as the father of Somali nationalism.

The Italian invasion of Ethiopia in 1936 gave Italy a dominant position in the Horn of Africa. In the early phases of World War II, Italian troops drove the British from British Somaliland, but a 1940 counterattack led to British occupation of all of Somalia by 1941. After World War II, Britain handed over the Ogaden and neighboring territories to Ethiopia.

A U.N. pact of 1949 created an Italian trusteeship in the former Italian Somaliland. Italy terminated its trusteeship and British Somaliland, a U.K. protectorate, achieved independence on June 26, 1960. On July 1 the two entities joined to become Somalia. The new country was plagued by clan-based rivalries, with the Somali Youth League emerging as a unifying national force. In 1969 Maj. Gen. Mohamed Siad Barre took control, and established both a socialist regime and relations with the U.S.S.R.

In 1972 Somali forces began border raids into Ethiopia's Ogaden region, peopled largely by ethnic Somalis. The Somali army invaded the Ogaden in 1977. The Soviet Union switched its support to Ethiopia, and with Soviet aid and Cuban troops, Ethiopia drove back the Somali invasion. Over a million refugees fled from Ethiopia into Somalia. The United States was Somalia's principal source of military and economic aid after 1978.

In May 1988, the Somali National Movement captured a number of cities in the northwest and held them. In the summer of 1990, the United Somali Congress began a peaceful antigovernment movement around Mogadishu. In Dec. 1990, this flared into a brief but bloody civil war that resulted in the ouster of Pres. Barre on Jan. 26. The Somali National Congress proclaimed a provisional government, but it was not recognized either by the United Somali Movement, which threatened secession, or the Somali Patriotic Movement, which controlled much of central and southern Somalia. The continued unrest left an estimated 50,000 people killed between 1988–90.

Despite U.N. attempts to initiate peace talks, widespread clan and tribal warfare led to a complete breakdown of government authority in 1991–92. A severe drought helped to create over two million refugees, and widespread starvation gripped the nation. Relief workers were prevented by warring armed factions from distributing emergency food supplies. An estimated 300,000 people died in 1991–92.

In Dec. 1992, the United States began Operation Restore Hope, sending 28,000 troops to secure distribution of food and aid. The U.S. presence deterred the factions from further open hostilities and brought warring leaders to the peace table. The U.N. took over the operation but led by the followers of Gen. Mohammed Farah Aidid, Somali renegades ambushed U.S. troops and shot down a helicopter leading to a U.S. withdrawal in March 1994. U.N. troops left Mogadishu in 1995.

Clan warfare reignited in March 1995, and in June, Aidid declared himself president for life. However, no country recognized any Somali government and in Aug. 1996 Aidid was shot and killed. His son, a former U.S. Marine, replaced him but brutal clan violence continued. In Dec. 1997 a tentative peace agreement was reached among the major factions. Peace settled in during 1998, helped by flooding that killed 2,000. During the summer of 2000, however, a group of leaders met in Djibouti and formed a new government with Abdikassim Salad Hassan as president. But by March 2001 many warlords met in Ethiopia to form an opposition group and by May new clan warfare erupted. In 2004 a National Assembly was cobbled together and in Oct. elected Abdullahi Yusuf, a career soldier, to be president. But chaos returned in Feb. 2006 as Islamists tried to seize power from the ruling warlords. In Dec., Ethiopia sent in troops to fight with the government and capture Mogadishu. In Feb., the U.N. authorized a peacekeeping mission by the African Union, but they encountered the worst violence in years as a pitched battle between government forces backed by Ethiopian soldiers and Islamist insurgents killed over 1,000 in the capital city. In June, a U.S. warship shelled Al-Qaeda targets but also killed a number of civilians.

A provisional government faced more attacks from Islamists who took over the southern region in late 2008. The lack of authority (and of economic stability) led to Somali pirates causing havoc on international sea lanes.

▶ SOUTH AFRICA
Republic of South Africa

● **GEOGRAPHY Location:** southern Africa. **Boundaries:** Namibia to NW, Botswana, Zimbabwe to N, Mozambique to NE, Swaziland, Indian Ocean to E, Atlantic Ocean to W; Lesotho entirely surrounded by South African territory. **Total area:** 471,444 sq. mi. (1,221,040 sq km). **Coastline:** 1,739 mi. (2,798 km). **Comparative area:** slighlty less than twice the size of Texas. **Land use:** 12% arable land; 1% permanent crops;87% other. **Major cities:** Cape Town (legislative capital); Pretoria (administrative capital); Johannesburg; Durban; Port Elizabeth.

● **PEOPLE Population:** 49,109,107 (July 2010 est.). **Nationality:** noun—South African(s); adjective—South African. **Ethnic groups:** 79% black, 9.6% white, 2.6% Indian; 8.6% other. **Languages:** Afrikaans, English, Zulu, Xhosa, Sotho, Ndebele, Pedi, Swazi, Tsonga, Venda, Tswana (all official). **Religions:** 68% Christian (most whites and about 60% of blacks), 2% Muslim, 1.5% Hindu (60% of Indians), 28.5% traditional and animistic beliefs.

● **GOVERNMENT Type:** republic. **Independence:** May 31, 1910 (from U.K.). **Constitution:** signed Dec. 10, 1996 by then-President Mandela—being implemented in phases. **National holiday:** Freedom Day, Apr. 27. **Head of Government:** Jacob Zuma, president (since May 2009). **Structure:** executive—president is head of govt. and chairman of cabinet; bicameral legislature—National Assembly, National Council of Provinces; judiciary—courts maintain substantial independence from government influence.

● **ECONOMY**   **Monetary unit:** South African rand. **Budget:** (2009 est.) *income:* $74.92 bil.; *expend.:* $86.26 bil. **G.D.P.:** $495.1 bil., $10,100 per capita (2009 est.). **Chief crops:** corn, wheat, sugarcane, fruits, vegetables; beef, poultry, mutton, wool, dairy products. **Natural resources:** gold, chromium, antimony, coal, iron ore. **Major industries:** mining (world's largest producer of platinum, gold, chromium), automobile assembly, metalworking. **Labor force:** 17.32 mil. economically active (2009); 65% services, 26% industry, 9% agriculture; 21.7% unemployment (2008 est.). **Exports:** $67.93 bil. (2009 est.); gold, minerals and metals, food, chemicals. **Imports:** $70.24 bil. (2009 est.); machinery, chemicals, transport equipment. **Major trading partners:** (2008) *exports:* 11.1% Japan, 11.1% U.S., 8% Germany, 6.8% U.K., 6% China, 5.2% Netherlands; *imports:* 11.2% Germany, 11% China, 7.8% U.S., 6.2% Saudi Arabia, 5.5% Japan.

South Africa was originally inhabited by San and related peoples. Bantu peoples, including the Zulu and Xhosa, migrated to the region beginning around the 15th century and established large native kingdoms.

The Portuguese explorer Bartholomew Diaz discovered and named the Cape of Good Hope in 1488. The Dutch East India Company established a permanent settlement at Cape Town in 1652, which served as a supply and transshipment point for Dutch trade to the East Indies. It attracted Protestant settlers from throughout Western Europe. In a series of wars, the Xhosa people were expelled from the area under Dutch rule.

Great Britain began to dispute Dutch control of the Cape of Good Hope region in the late 18th century. To escape increasing British hegemony, in 1836 many Dutch farmers undertook the Great Trek, a northward migration to lands not under the control of any European power. These Afrikaner pioneers later became known as Boers (farmers). They came into conflict with the Zulu kingdom that, under King Shaka, had recently widened its dominion in the South African interior. The Zulus were defeated at the Battle of Blood River in 1838, but they retained substantial power and territory for another 40 years.

Great Britain formally took control of the Cape Colony in 1841 and annexed Natal in 1843. The other two Afrikaner provinces, the Orange Free State and the Transvaal, remained free of British control. But when diamonds were discovered in the Orange Free State in 1867 and gold in the Transvaal in 1886, an influx of British miners and entrepreneurs provoked tensions between the British and the Boer.

In 1878 the Zulu Kingdom under its last great king, Cetewayo, rebelled against British rule in Natal. British troops attacked Zululand in 1878 and crushed the rebellion in 1879.

The first Anglo-Boer War of 1881–82 led to total British victory. A renewed uprising led to the Boer War of 1899–1902, which was fought with great ferocity between British regular troops and Afrikaner guerrilla forces. The eventual British victory led to the establishment of British rule in all of South Africa and to the formation of the Union of South Africa in 1910. The union became a self-governing state within the British Empire in 1934.

South African politics became dominated by friction between British and Afrikaner whites; no effective black participation in government was permitted. The United South African party, led by Jan C. Smuts, advocated cooperation between the two groups and led South Africa to join World War II on the Allied side, over the opposition of the pro-Afrikaner Nationalist party.

After the war the Nationalists prevailed and won control of the government in 1948. Racial politics became the country's paramount concern, and the Nationalists introduced the policy of "apartheid" (separateness), under which racial groups were rigidly defined as white, black, Asian (primarily Indian), and colored (mixed ancestry). Each group was to be kept physically separate and develop its own political institutions within defined areas of residence; mixed neighborhoods, intermarriage, and other relations were prohibited. Blacks, in particular, were restricted by "pass laws" that allowed them only temporary access to white areas for employment.

International condemnation of these policies began almost immediately, as India broke relations with South Africa in 1946 over discrimination against Asians, and South Africa became the focus of mounting protest, U.N. resolutions, and international sanctions beginning in the 1960s. On May 31, 1961, South Africa gave up its dominion status and became a republic; its application for membership in the British Commonwealth was withdrawn in the face of strong opposition. The African National Congress (ANC), organized in 1912, was banned by South African authorities. The imprisonment of its leader, Nelson Mandela, provided a focus for black political protest and nationalist aspirations.

Homelands were established under the Promotion of Bantu Self-Government Act of 1959 to further the policy of apartheid by creating separate, but dependent, states for South Africa's blacks. Their form of government was set up in the Black Constitution Act of 1971. The South African government intended that the homelands be regarded as separate nations, but none was ever internationally recognized. The scattered homeland territories comprised only a tiny portion of the total area of South Africa, and tended to include marginal and underdeveloped lands. Residents of the homelands were not considered citizens of South Africa, but rather citizens only of their homeland. As such, they could be considered temporary migrant workers and were therefore ineligible for unemployment and other benefits.

An uprising in Soweto in 1976 was put down by South African armed forces with the loss of hundreds of lives. Pieter Willem Botha was elected president in 1978, pledging to uphold apartheid while seeking solutions to racial problems. In 1983, a majority of white voters approved a new constitution that provided for limited power sharing by coloreds and Asians. Blacks, however, continued to be excluded.

In the early 1980s, South African troops intervened in civil wars in Angola and Mozambique and were deployed to counteract growing proindependence rebellions in Namibia. Within South Africa, terrorism and uprisings led by the African National Union grew in intensity in 1983–84. A state of emergency was declared in 1985, accompanied by renewed political and economic pressure from abroad. In 1986, Bishop Desmond Tutu, a leading black nationalist, addressed the United Nations and called for renewed sanctions. The Botha government announced an end to the pass laws and promised limited black participation in government. Fighting among black groups in 1986–87 further increased domestic tension.

On May 19, 1986, South African troops conducted raids against ANC bases in Zambia, Zimbabwe, and Botswana. A new national state of emergency was declared as strikes and riots marked the 10th anniversary of the Soweto uprising. The U.S. announced measures designed to end American investment in South Africa.

In early 1989, in anticipation of elections to be held in September, various proposals were put forward for constitutional reform. Most called for expanded power sharing but still within the context of defined racial groups. In July 1989 Pres. Botha had an unprecedented meeting with Nelson Mandela, amid strong suggestions that the white government was seeking an accommodation with the antiapartheid leadership. Botha's successor, F.W. de Klerk, continued that policy.

A series of measures in 1989–90 resulted in the partial dismantling of apartheid, against the vehement opposition of the white right wing, but violence between supporters of the ANC and the Zulu Inkatha movement in Natal led to the declaration of a state of emergency in the province.

Mandela was released from prison in the spring of 1990 and received a rapturous welcome from South Africa's blacks, and later made a triumphant tour of Western Europe and North America. His glory was short-lived, however, as the struggle for supremacy again erupted in murder and violence between Mandela's ANC and Mangosuthu Buthelezi's Inkatha Freedom party throughout the latter part of 1990 and 1991.

At the same time, Pres. de Klerk and Parliament continued to move the nation toward the ending of apartheid by repealing 60 years of segregation in hospitals, libraries, schools, and other public institutions. The government also released other political prisoners and completely repealed the legal foundations of apartheid: the Land Acts of 1913 and 1936, the Group Areas Act, and the Population Registration Act. The United States and other countries began lifting trade sanctions against South Africa in the summer of 1991.

In 1991, de Klerk, Mandela, and Buthelezi, together with 20 antiapartheid groups, signed an accord to end violence. De Klerk proposed a new constitution that would provide universal suffrage and create a two-chamber parliament open to all races. The new constitution abolished the black homelands, consolidating them into one large, multiracial South Africa. In March 1992 a referendum of white voters overwhelmingly approved a government proposal to dismantle all forms of apartheid and to conduct talks with black leaders designed to end white-only rule.

The new constitution was approved on Nov. 17, 1993, by all of the country's major political parties, except for Chief Mangosuthu Buthelezi's Zulu-based Inkatha Freedom party, which withheld its support until a week before the country's first-ever multiracial elections in April. More than 22 million voters cast ballots. An overwhelming majority chose the 75-year-old Mandela to lead a coalition government that included de Klerk's National party and Buthelezi's Inkatha Freedom party.

In May 1996 South Africa completed the transition to democracy when it approved a permanent constitution. It created a strong central government, an independent judiciary, and a bill of rights with one of the broadest guarantees of liberty in the world. In addition to freedom of speech, movement, and political activity, the South African Bill of Rights protects rights to adequate food, housing, water, education, and health care. The day after the new constitution was approved, de Klerk and his colleagues in the National party quit their cabinet posts, saying that the government was strong enough to handle "robust opposition."

In 1997 there were riots in Johannesburg suburbs by coloreds against discrimination in favor of blacks, and in March, a mass rally (which turned violent) in Johannesburg by Zulus. Bitter feelings between the Inkatha Freedom Party and Mandela's ANC surfaced again when the Truth and Reconciliation Committee reported testimony linking Inkatha leaders to assassination squads during the apartheid era.

On June 2, 1999, South Africa held its second post-apartheid elections: the ANC won a gigantic victory, taking 266 seats in the 400-seat Assembly. An "alliance" with the one member of the (Indian) Minority Front gave ANC the 2/3 majority that permits it to amend the Constitution. Thabo Mbeki, who replaced Nelson Mandela as party chief in December, was elected unopposed to be his successor as South Africa's president as well. In Dec. 2000 local elections the ANC took only 59 percent and a serious bribery scandal developed over a 1999 $3.5 billion arms deal. And the government's own report of March 2001 highlighted the gravity of South Africa's AIDS crisis. But it took until late 2003 before the government agreed to spend $1.8 bil. to provide free drugs to AIDS sufferers. Elections in 2004 gave the ANC its third landslide win (70 percent of the vote). In early 2008, Mbeki lost his power in the ANC and was replaced by Jacob Zuma who faced corruption charges during the summer. Mbeki resigned the presidency in September 2008, and was replaced by former trade unionist and freedom fighter Kgalema Motlanthe, but Zuma won the presidency in 2009.

South Africa has the continent's most highly developed economy; it is a fully-developed, capitalist industrial-commercial society with manufacturing, mining, agricultural, service, and other sectors. It remains the world's largest producer of gold, a key source of chromium and other strategic metals, and of gem-quality diamonds. But even these assets could not prevent the serious economic setback caused by the worldwide recession in 2009. The 2010 World Cup helped South Africa gain prestige throughout the world. (See "Major News Stories.")

▶ SPAIN
Kingdom of Spain

● **GEOGRAPHY Location:** Iberian Peninsula in southwest Europe; Canary Is. off West Africa (28°07'N, 15°26'W). **Boundaries:** Bay of Biscay and France to N; Mediterranean Sea to E; Morocco 19 mi. (30 km) to S, across Strait of Gibraltar; Portugal to W. **Total area:** 194,884 sq. mi. (504,750 sq km). **Coastline:** 3,085 mi. (4,964 km). **Comparative area:** slightly more than twice the size of Oregon. **Land use:** 29% arable land; 10% permanent crops; 261% other. **Major cities:** Madrid (capital); Barcelona; València; Sevilla (Seville); Zaragoza (Saragossa).

● **PEOPLE Population:** 40,548,753 (July 2010 est.). **Nationality:** noun—Spaniard(s); adjective—Spanish. **Ethnic groups:** composite of Mediterranean and Nordic types. **Languages:** 74% Castilian Spanish (official); 17% Catalán, 7% Galician, 2% Basque. **Religions:** 94% Roman Catholic, 6% other.

• **GOVERNMENT** **Type:** parliamentary monarchy. **Independence:** 1492 (expulsion of Moors and unification). **Constitution:** Dec. 6, 1978, effective Dec. 29, 1978. **National holiday:** Oct. 12. **Heads of Government:** Juan Carlos I, king (since Nov. 1975); José Luis Rodriguez Zapatero, prime minister (since Apr. 2004). **Structure:** executive—king is chief of state, prime minister is head of government; bicameral legislature; judiciary— independent.

• **ECONOMY** **Monetary unit:** euro. **Budget:** (2009 est.) *income:* $420.4 bil.; *expend.:* $536.3 bil. **G.D.P.:** $1.368 tril., $33,700 per capita (2009 est). **Chief crops:** grains, vegetables, olives, wine grapes, sugar beets, citrus; beef, pork, poultry, dairy prodcts; fish. **Natural resources:** coal, lignite, iron ore, uranium, mercury. **Major industries:** textiles, apparel (including footwear), food and beverages, metals and metal manufacturing. **Labor force:** 22.97 mil. (2009 est.); 64.6% services, 30.1% industry, 5.3% agriculture. **Exports:** $215.7 bil. (2009 est.); cars and trucks, manufactured goods, foodstuffs, other consumer goods. **Imports:** $293.2 bil. (2009 est.); machinery, transport equipment, fuels, semifinished goods, foodstuffs, consumer goods, chemicals. **Major trading partners:** (2008) *exports:* 18.3% France, 10.6% Germany, 8.7% Portugal, 8% Italy, 6.7% U.K., 4.2% U.S.; *imports:* 14.5% Germany, 11.1% France, 7.4% Italy, 6.2% China, 4.5% U.K., 4.4% Netherlands.

Prehistoric Spain was populated by Iberians, Basques, and Celts. Its Mediterranean ports were frequented by Phoenician traders, and part of the country was incorporated into the empire of Carthage. Spain fell under the Roman Empire around 200 B.C.; Roman rule ended when the Visigoths invaded and took control of the Iberian Peninsula in the fifth century. The Visigoths adopted Christianity but were in turn conquered by Moors from northwest Africa in A.D. 711. The Berber/Arab civilization of the Moors produced the most elegant and cultivated culture in medieval Europe, and was an important conduit for the reintroduction of Greek science into Europe in the 12th century.

The Christian reconquest of the Iberian Peninsula began almost immediately after the Moors had established themselves and proceeded slowly but steadily over a period of 750 years. The consolidation of the region's small, contentious Christian kingdoms came with the marital alliance of Ferdinand of Aragon and Isabella of Castile in 1469. Granada, the last Moorish outpost in Spain, fell to the forces of Ferdinand and Isabella in 1492, just as Columbus, with Isabella's sponsorship, was discovering the lands that were to become Spain's New World empire. Under the Inquisition, begun in 1478, Jews were expelled from Spain in 1492, and Muslims in 1502.

Under the Habsburg dynasty (1516–1700), Spain reached the zenith of its power and prestige around the year 1600 (despite the 1588 defeat of the Spanish Armada by England), controlling an empire that embraced nearly all of South America (except Brazil), Central America, Mexico, western North America, the Philippines, and smaller territories in Africa and Asia. But Spain's loss of the Netherlands, endless struggles with the French in Europe and the Turks in the Mediterranean, and relentless inflation caused by imports of New World silver—all took their toll. During the 18th century, the Bourbons ruled a declining but still powerful Spain, until Napoleon installed his brother as king in 1808.

After Napoleon's defeat, the Bourbons returned in 1814, but the loss of the South American colonies, three dynastic wars, and a brief republican interlude after 1868 were all signs of progressive weakness. The crowning blow to Spanish power and prestige was the loss of the Spanish-American War to the United States in 1898, leading to the independence of Cuba and the American takeover of Puerto Rico and the Philippines.

Spain remained neutral in World War I. In 1923 Primo de Rivera established a dictatorship; he was forced out of office by King Alfonso XIII in 1930, but in 1931 the king was forced to abdicate. A republic replaced the monarchy. Its volatile mixture of socialism, anticlericalism, and decentralization provoked a right-wing reaction. The government moved to the Right, and in 1934 a miner's strike in Asturia was put down with great bloodshed. A left-wing government was elected in 1936 and deposed in a coup, which led to the terrible Civil War of 1936–39, in which Spain became a battleground for competing world ideologies. The Nationalists, aided by Hitler and Mussolini, defeated the Republicans, aided by Stalin and by leftist volunteers from many countries. Out of the wreckage emerged the dictatorship of the intensely patriotic and Catholic general Francisco Franco.

At the time of the Civil War, Spain was still an agricultural country, with small holdings in the north and great estates in the south. In the Basque country, the mining of iron, copper, and lead provided both exports and a domestic iron and steel industry, which had been the case since the 19th century. In the 20th century, shipbuilding and chemicals were added to the traditional textile industries of the Mediterranean coastal cities. The war largely destroyed this industrial base, which was not rebuilt until the 1950s.

Except for a contingent of troops sent to fight with the German invaders of the Soviet Union, Spain remained precariously neutral during World War II; Franco declined to repay Hitler for his support in the Civil War. But wartime Spain, despite its neutrality, could not muster the resources to undertake national reconstruction.

In postwar Europe, the Franco regime seemed like a remnant of the fascism of the 1930s; Stalin's active hostility led the United Nations to treat Spain as an international pariah. At home Franco represented peace and stability; few Spaniards were willing to risk a return to civil strife by opposing him. Over time the military and Catholic aspects of the regime grew more pronounced, while fascist elements were downplayed. In 1947 the Law of Succession made Spain a monarchy without a king, awaiting the restoration of the throne in the post-Franco era.

The Cold War led to friendlier American relations with Spain and the establishment of American military bases in 1953. U.N. membership followed in 1955. Despite some resultant growth in international trade, Spain's economy lagged, with industrialization barely beginning.

In 1958 Franco turned the direction of the economy over to a group of technocrats, mostly neoliberal members of the Opus Dei lay Catholic order. With U.S. economic and military aid, a growing tourist industry, increased foreign investment, and, especially, freer markets, the economy revived. Older industries like iron, steel, and textiles were rejuvenated, while newer ones, such as chemicals, plastics, automobile assembly, and power plants, were created. Agriculture was increasingly mechanized, and it shifted to export-oriented ranching and horticulture.

In 1967 Franco proclaimed the Organic Law, which, while confirming him as head of state, granted some independence to the Cortes (legislature) and permitted heads of families to vote for some of its delegates. This, along with a relaxation of censorship, softened the growing opposition to the regime among students, labor unions, and regional separatists. In 1969 Prince Juan Carlos was named heir apparent to the Spanish throne.

Franco died in 1975 and was duly succeeded by Juan Carlos. With the new prime minister, Adolfo Suarez, the king worked to liberalize the Franco inheritance: Political parties were legalized; the Cortes was transformed into a bicameral legislature, with both houses elected by universal suffrage; the first elections since 1936 were held; and a new constitution was promulgated—all by 1978.

In 1980, Catalonia and the Basque country were granted home rule, following overwhelming plebiscite victories. In the Basque lands, however, violent terrorist agitation for complete independence continues sporadically.

Under the new monarchy, Spain became a full participant in the affairs of Europe. It joined the Council of Europe in 1977, NATO in 1982, and the E.U. in 1986. The Socialist Workers' party controlled both houses of the Cortes from 1982 to 1996, but the party abandoned both Marxism and labor radicalism. Under Prime Minister Felipe Gonzalez Marquéz, G.D.P. grew by an average of almost 5 percent between 1986 and 1990, and business investment jumped by over 10 percent a year. In 1992, the Summer Olympics in Barcelona and the Universal Exposition in Seville focused world attention on Spain.

Economic growth slowed in 1992, and unemployment reached 22 percent. In 1994, Gonzalez's power eroded when members of his government were indicted for their involvement with an antiterrorist death squad accused of assassinating 27 Basque separatists during the 1980s. After 10 years of Gonzalez and the Socialists, the May 1996 elections brought the Popular Party and its leader Jose Maria Aznar to power. In July 1998, 12 officials of the Gonzalez government were sentenced to jail for crimes in the anti-Basque "dirty war," although Gonzalez himself was not implicated.

Spain's economy quickly reversed itself and annual growth surpassed three percent, so that Spain was able to meet the criteria for membership in the European Monetary Union.

Somewhat unexpectedly the ETA, the Basque terrorist organization, declared on September 16, 1998, a "total and indefinite" cease-fire. But despite talks with the Aznar government and the release of "political prisoners," the ETA, in late 1999, resumed its war with car-bombings and assassinations. In March 2000, the Popular Party won an unexpected majority in the Congreso. In Sept. 2002, two important leaders of ETA were captured in France and government officials believed the group, responsible for over 800 deaths, would be crippled.

On the eve of the March 2004 election, 10 bombs exploded on four Madrid commuter trains killing over 200 with 1400 wounded. The Aznar government immediately blamed ETA but it quickly became clear that it was the work of Islamist terrorists. The elections brought the Socialists to power and the removal of Spanish troops from Iraq. In 2006, ETA declared a cease-fire and Prime Minister Zapatero agreed to peace talks, which were suspended after a car bomb attack at a Madrid airport. In 2008 Zapatero's party won re-election handily. The worldwide fiscal crisis hit Spain especially hard and austerity measures were put in place to control the nation's spiraling debt.

▶ **SRI LANKA**
Democratic Socialist Republic of Sri Lanka

• **GEOGRAPHY Location:** Indian Ocean about 50 mi. (80 km) SE of India. Colombo 6°55'N, 79°52'E. **Boundaries:** Palk Strait to N, Bay of Bengal to E, Indian Ocean to S and SW, and Gulf of Mannar to NW. **Total area:** 25,332 sq. mi. (65,610 sq km). **Coastline:** 833 mi. (1,340 km). **Comparative area:** slightly larger than West Virginia. **Land use:** 13% arable land; 16% permanent crops; 71% other. **Major cities:** Colombo (capital); Dehiwala-Mount Lavinia; Moratuwa.

• **PEOPLE Population:** 21,324,791 (July 2009 est.). **Nationality:** noun—Sri Lankan(s); adjective—Sri Lankan. **Ethnic groups:** 74% Sinhalese; 18% Tamil; 7% Moor; 1% Burgher, Malay, and Veddah. **Languages:** Sinhala (official); Sinhala and Tamil listed as national languages; Sinhala spoken by about 74% of population, Tamil spoken by about 18%; English commonly used in government and spoken by about 10% of population. **Religions:** 70% Buddhist, 15% Hindu, 8% Christian, 7% Muslim.

• **GOVERNMENT Type:** republic. **Independence:** Feb. 4, 1948 (from U.K.). **Constitution:** Aug. 16, 1978; amended Dec. 2000. **National holiday:** Independence Day, Feb. 4. **Heads of Government:** Mahinda Rajapaksa, president (since Nov. 2005). **Structure:** executive—president is head of government and chief of state; unicameral legislature; judiciary—Supreme Court, Court of Appeals.

• **ECONOMY Monetary unit:** Sri Lankan rupee. **Budget:** (2009 est.) *income:* $7.8 bil.; *expend.:* $11 bil. **G.D.P.:** $91.9 bil., $4,300 per capita (2008 est.). **Chief crops:** rice, sugarcane, grains, pulses, oilseed, roots, spices, coconuts, tea, rubber; milk, eggs, hides, meat. **Natural resources:** limestone, graphite, mineral sands, gems, phosphates. **Major industries:** processing of rubber, tea, coconuts, and other agricultural commodities; cement, petroleum refining. **Labor force:** 7.588 mil. (2008 est.); 40.4% services, 34.3% agriculture, 25.3% industry. **Exports:** $8.1 bil. (f.o.b., 2008); tea, textiles and garments, petroleum products, gems, rubber. **Imports:** $14.05 bil. (f.o.b., 2008 est.); machinery and equipment, textiles, petroleum. **Major trading partners:** (2006) *exports:* 27.6% U.S., 11.3% U.K., 9.3% India, 4.7% Belgium, 4.3% Germany; *imports:* 19.5% India, 10.4% China, 8.7% Singapore, 5.6% Iran, 5% Malaysia, 4.2% Hong Kong, 4% Japan.

The ancient Veddah inhabitants of Sri Lanka were conquered by Sinhalese migrants from northern India in the sixth century B.C. The island's spices and precious stones and its position on the trans-Indian Ocean trade routes made it well known in ancient times. From the third century A.D., Sri Lanka became a major center of Buddhist culture. Despite numerous invasions from India, the island was usually ruled by native kingdoms, but the invasions added a Tamil community to the premodern population.

The Portuguese conquered the coastal areas after 1505 and also introduced Roman Catholicism. The Dutch displaced the Portugese in 1648; the British expelled the Dutch in 1795. Great Britain was the first foreign power to extend its rule over the entire island, with the defeat of the central kingdom of Kandy in 1833. In that year all of Sri Lanka was incorporated into the British Crown colony of Ceylon. Under British rule, tea and rubber plantations were established in the island's interior, and coconut plantations in coastal areas were consolidated under foreign control.

Ceylon became an independent member of the British Commonwealth on Feb. 4, 1948; the Republic of Sri Lanka was proclaimed on May 22, 1972.

Prime Minister W.R.D. Bandaranaike was assassinated on Sept. 25, 1959. His widow, Sirimavo Bandaranaike, leader of the Freedom party, was elected as his successor. In 1962 her government expropriated the property of foreign oil companies. The conservative United National party won a majority in Parliament in 1965 and agreed to pay compensation for the expropriated assets. In May 1970 Mrs. Bandaranaike was again elected prime minister. Leftists secured the nationalization of foreign plantations in the mid-1970s. Mrs. Bandaranaike's party was ousted by the United National party in 1977. Constitutional reform in 1978 aimed at increasing stability by establishing a presidential form of government. Pres. J.R. Jayawardene was elected on Feb. 4, 1978.

But stability has eluded Sri Lanka because of the long struggle between Tamils and the Sinhalese. The political power acquired by the Tamil (mostly Hindu) middle class under the British was deeply resented by the Sinhalese (Buddhist) majority, which after independence slowly eroded Tamil rights. In 1957 the government proposed a Tamil state in a federal union and gave Tamil the status of a national (but not official) language. The pact was not fully implemented, and in the 1970s extremists began agitating for an independent Tamil state. The Tamils' minority status was reaffirmed in the constitution of 1972, the year the oldest insurgent group, the Liberation Tigers or Tamil Tigers, was founded.

In July 1987 Pres. Jayawardene accepted an offer from India's Prime Minister Rajiv Gandhi to supervise a truce in the Jaffna region under which the government pledged to hold a referendum aimed at granting self-rule to Tamil majority areas in the north. The plan failed and Indian troops became bogged down in battling the rebels, while the planned referendum was disrupted by fighting between separatists who demanded total independence for Tamil areas.

At the Sri Lankan government's request, India withdrew its forces in March 1989, and the Tamil Tigers agreed to a cease-fire but this cease-fire broke down with the assassination of both the opposition political leader in April 1993 and Pres. Ranasinghe Pemadasa a month later. In parliamentary elections held in 1994, the People's Alliance ended the United National party's 17-year rule. Prime Minister Chandrika Bandaranaike Kumaratunga won a landslide victory in presidential elections, and appointed her 78-year-old mother, Sirimavo Bandaranaike, as prime minister.

Hours after the new president's inauguration, the Tamil Tigers announced a cease-fire. The truce was formalized in Jan. 1995, but when the government offered a peace plan to divide Sri Lanka into autonomous regions, the Tamil rebels renewed the civil war. Pres. Kumaratunga handily won re-election in Dec. 1999 but on the battlefield the Tamils grew more successful in 2000. A series of failed offensives against the Tigers in 2001 brought government to a halt and the loss of its majority. In Oct. 2001, elections brought a three-party United Front to power. A Norway-negotiated truce in Feb. 2002 led to renewed peace talks in Thailand between the new government and the Tigers, but talks went nowhere. In Nov. 2003 troops were deployed in Colombo. But the peace held and the tragedy of the Dec. 2004 tsunami (which took 30,000 lives in Sri Lanka) seemed to ease political tensions. In Nov. 2005 Mahinda Rajapaksa, a hardliner who opposes power sharing with the Tigers, narrowly won the presidential elections. By Aug. 2006 fierce fighting had begun anew, and continued until a final bloody battle in May 2009 killed hundreds of rebels including their leader. After 26 years of bloodshed that took 60,000 lives and displaced a million Tamils, the war was ended. Rajapaksa was challenged in the 2010 election by General Sarath Fonseka, who claimed fraud after he lost. Fonseka was soon arrested and faced a court martial.

▶ SUDAN
Republic of the Sudan
• **GEOGRAPHY Location:** northeastern Africa. **Boundaries:** Egypt to N, Red Sea, Eritrea, and Ethiopia to E, Kenya, Uganda, and Zaire to S, Central African Republic, Chad and Libya to W. **Total area:** 967,495 sq. mi. (2,505,810 sq km). **Coastline:** 530 mi. (853 km). **Comparative area:** slightly more than one-quarter the size of the U.S. **Land use:** 7% arable land; negl. % permanent crops; 93% other. **Major cities:** Khartoum (capital); Nyala; Shargen-Nil; Port Sudan; Omdurman.
• **PEOPLE Population:** 41,980,182 (July 2010 est.). **Nationality:** noun—Sudanese (sing., pl.); adjective—Sudanese. **Ethnic groups:** 52% black, 39% Arab, 6% Beja, 2% foreigners. **Languages:** Arabic (official), Nubian, Ta Bedawie, diverse dialects of Nilotic, Nilo-Hamitic, and Sudanic languages, English; program of Arabization in progress. **Religions:** 70% Sunni Muslim (in north), 25% indigenous beliefs, 5% Christian (mostly in south).
• **GOVERNMENT Type:** transitional, with plans for national elections in 2010. **Independence:** Jan. 1, 1956 (from Egypt and U.K.). **Constitution:** Apr. 12, 1973, suspended following coup of Apr. 6, 1985; new constitution implemented June 1998, partially suspended Dec. 12 1999 by President Bashir;; interim National Constitution ratified July 5, 2005. **National holiday:** Independence Day, Jan. 1. **Head of Government:** Lt. Gen. Omer Hassan Ahmed Al Bashir, president (since Jan. 1993). **Structure:** executive—president is head of government and chief of state; unicameral legislature; judiciary.
• **ECONOMY Monetary unit:** Sudanese pound. **Budget:** (2009 est.) *income:* $9.046 bil.; *expend.:* $10.83 bil. **G.D.P.:** $92.81 bil., $2,300 per capita (2009 est.). **Chief crops:** cotton, peanuts,sorghum, millet, wheat, gum arabic, sesame; sheep. **Natural resources:** petroleum, reserves of iron oil, copper, chromium ore, zinc. **Major industries:** cotton ginning, textiles, cement. **Labor force:** 11.92 mil. (2007 est.); 80% agriculture, 7% industry and commerce, 13% government; labor shortages for almost all categories of skilled employment. **Exports:** $8.464 bil. (2009 est.); cotton, sesame, livestock/meat. **Imports:** $6.823 bil. (2009 est.); foodstuffs, petroleum products, manufactured goods, machinery and equipment, medicines and chemicals, textiles. **Major trading partners:** (2008) *exports:* 48% China, 32.2% Japan, 5.3% Indonesia; *imports:* 20.3% China, 8.5% Saudi Arabia, 6.3% U.A.E., 5.6% Egypt, 5.1% India, 4.1% Italy.

The northern Sudan, the ancient land of Nubia, was loosely controlled by Egypt in antiquity and incorporated into the Arab world by the Islamic expansion of the seventh century. The southern Sudan was part of tribal black Africa, under no external control but subject to continual raids by slave traders from the north.

Ottoman Egypt conquered the northern Sudan in 1820–21; British influence in Egypt in the 19th century extended into the Sudan as well. In 1881 Muhammed Ahmed ibn Abdalla, a religious leader known as the Mahdi, united northern and north-central Sudan and led a resistance movement against Anglo-Egyptian control. Khartoum, defended by British general Charles George Gordon, fell in 1885, but the Mahdi died soon thereafter, and his revolt came to an end. An Anglo-Egyptian force under Kitchener regained control in 1898; Anglo-Egyptian joint rule was established in the Sudan in 1899.

Great Britain and Egypt granted self-government and self-determination to the Sudan in 1953, and a Sudanese parliament was seated in 1954. Full independence came in 1956. Gen. Ibrahim Abboud took power in a bloodless coup in 1958 but was forced to resign after riots in 1964. In 1969 a new military coup installed a ruling Revolutionary Command Council and instituted a socialist regime. The council's leader, Gen. Muhammed Nimeiri, became prime minister. Disputes between Marxists and non-Marxists, and between arabized northerners and black southerners, led to continual difficulties. In 1972 Sudan's three black southern provinces were granted local autonomy. Another attempted coup in 1976 was put down by the Nimeiri government, and hundreds of prominent citizens were executed.

In 1983 attempts by the Nimeiri government to institute Islamic law led to riots in the south and the imposition of a state of emergency in 1984. Popular unrest was exacerbated by drought and famine in 1985. On Apr. 6, 1985, Nimeiri was overthrown in a coup by Gen. Suwar El Dahab. After a brief period of rule by a transitional military council, a civilian cabinet was installed, and free parliamentary elections were held in 1986.

In June 1989 the government was overthrown in a coup led by Lt. Gen. Omar Ahmed al-Bashir. The Bashir government renewed the fight against the southern rebels, and supported the imposition of Islamic law throughout the nation. Within three years the civil service, the military, the judiciary, and the educational system were under the control of Muslims and their political organization, the National Islamic Front headed by Hassan al-Turabi who was also the leader of parliament and the most powerful figure in Sudan. All opposition parties, newspapers, and unions were banned and a stepped up military campaign against christians in the South was launched.

In Oct. 1990, the U.S. government stopped aid to the Sudan, which openly supported Iraq during the Persian Gulf War. In 1991, the U.N. suspended relief efforts to help the estimated 7.1 million Sudanese threatened by famine. In 1993, the U.S. added Sudan to its list of states that sponsor terrorism, and in 1995, the U.N. endorsed an accusation that Sudan was sheltering the Islamic militants who attempted to assassinate Egyptian Pres. Hosni Mubarak. In 1997 the government made peace with some rebel factions, promising a referendum on self determination. The main force of the Sudan People's Liberation Army (SPLA), led by John Garang, continued to fight.

Another famine in 1998 brought a ceasefire as aid workers transported huge amounts of food to over 300,000 in the south. In Aug. 1998 the U.S. launched cruise missiles at Khartoum to retaliate for the bombing of its embassies in Kenya and Tanzania and to destroy what it said was a chemical weapons plant. Since July 1998, both the SPLA and the Sudanese government have declared a series of cease-fires to permit international food relief. The rebels lost some international support as Uganda, Ethiopia and Eritrea became embroiled in wars of their own.

The Sudanese government's "restoration" of a multi-party system at the start of 1999 was met with skepticism by the opposition. In 1999 Pres. Bashir sought some sort of reconciliation with opposition parties and with the southern rebels. In December he struck against Turabi, declaring a state of emergency, dissolving parliament dismissing the entire government, and replacing it with his supporters. In Jan. 2002 a cease-fire and in July a peace accord signed in Nairobi brought hope at last that the war might end.

In early 2004 SPLA signed a deal with the government splitting oil wealth 50-50 and the civil war seemed to come to an end. But a war between the Sudan Liberation Army and the Justice and Equity Movement in Darfur led to 70,000 deaths and two million people fled their homes. Over 200,000 refugees settled in Chad.

International outrage helped both sides to a peace agreement in Jan. 2005 and in July Pres. Bashir made rebel leader John Garang his vice president. Garang died in a plane crash shortly thereafter and the peace held, but only for a few months. A peace brokered by the African Union in 2006 also fell apart, but in 2007 the government finally accepted 26,000 U.N. peacekeepers in Darfur. The U.N. reported that over 200,000 had been killed and two million displaced. In July 2008 the International Criminal Court requested an arrest warrant for President Omar Hassan al-Bashir on charges of genocide and war crimes. He was formally charged a year later and he then ordered all aid workers in Darfur to leave.

▶ SURINAME
Republic of Suriname

• **GEOGRAPHY   Location:** northeastern coast of South America. **Boundaries:** North Atlantic Ocean to N, French Guiana to E, Brazil to S, Guyana to W. **Total area:** 63,039 sq. mi. (163,270 sq km). **Coastline:** 240 mi. (386 km). **Comparative area:** slightly larger than Georgia. **Land use:** negl. % arable land; negl. % permanent crops; 100% other. **Major cities:** Paramaribo (capital).

• **PEOPLE   Population:** 481,267 (July 2009 est.). **Nationality:** noun—Surinamer(s); adjective—Surinamese. **Ethnic groups:** 31% Hindustani (East Indian), 31% Creole (black and mixed), 15% Javanese, 10% black. **Languages:** Dutch (official), English widely spoken, Sranang Tongo (Surinamese, sometimes called Taki-Taki, the native language of Creoles and much of younger population and lingua franca among others), Hindustani, Javanese. **Religions:** 27.4% Hindu, 25.2% Protestant (predominantly Moravian), 22.8% Roman Catholic, 19.6% Muslim.

• **GOVERNMENT   Type:** constitutional democracy. **Constitution:** Sept. 30, 1987. **Independence:** Nov. 25, 1975 (from Netherlands). **National holiday:** Independence Day, Nov. 25. **Heads of Government:** Desire Bouterse, president (since Aug. 2010); **Structure:** executive—president is chief of state and head of government, Commander in Chief of the National Army maintains significant power; unicameral legislature; judiciary.

• **ECONOMY   Monetary unit:** Surinamese guilder. **Budget:** (2004 est.) *income:* $392.6 mil.; *expend.:* $425.9 mil. **G.D.P.:** $4.256 bil., $8,900 per capita (2008 est.). **Chief crops:** rice, bananas, palm oil, timber. **Natural resources:** timber, hydropower potential, fish, shrimp, bauxite. **Major industries:**

bauxite mining, alumina and aluminum production, lumbering. **Labor force:** 156,700; 8% agriculture, 14% industry, 78% services (2004); 17% unemployment (2000). **Exports:** $1.391 bil. (f.o.b., 2006); alumina, aluminum, crude oil, lumber, shrimp and fish, rice, bananas. **Imports:** $1.297 bil. (f.o.b., 2006); capital equipment, petroleum, foodstuffs, cotton, consumer goods. **Major trading partners:** (2006) *exports:* 23% Norway, 16% Canada, 12% U.S., 10% Belgium, 9% France, 7% United Arab Emirates, 4% Iceland; *imports:* 29% U.S., 19% Netherlands, 15% Trinidad & Tobago, 5% Japan, 5% China.

In the early 17th century, the Dutch and English settled Suriname, which became a Dutch colony in 1667. Except for brief episodes of British rule, Suriname remained under Dutch control until its independence in 1975, shifting toward authoritarian military rule in 1980. The military created its own political party (the February 25 movement) and banned opposition organizations. The 1988 National Assembly election of Pres. Ramsewak Shankar ended direct military rule, but the restriction of civil liberties continued.

The Shankar government was overthrown in a bloodless coup led by Cmdr. Ivan Graanoogst in 1990, and civilian rule was restored in 1991 although the former military ruler, Col. Desi Bouterse, who led the coup and remains "Advisor of the State," is apparently still the defacto ruler. In June 1999, after the National Assembly voted "no confidence," President Jules Wijdenbosch agreed to resign—but to remain in office until after the May 2000 National Assembly elections, elections in which Ronald Venetiaan became president. Economic problems plagued the country before and since, but Venetiaan was reelected in 2005. In 2010, however, he lost to political strongman Desire Bouterse, who pledged to revive the economy.

▶ SWAZILAND
Kingdom of Swaziland
● **GEOGRAPHY Location:** landlocked country in southern Africa. **Boundaries:** South Africa to N, SE, S, and W; Mozambique to E. **Total area:** 6,703 sq. mi. (17,360 sq km). **Coastline:** none. **Comparative area:** slightly smaller than New Jersey. **Land use:** 11% arable land; negl. % permanent crops; 89% other. **Major cities:** Mbabane (capital); Manzini.
● **PEOPLE Population:** 1,123,913 (July 2009 est.). **Nationality:** noun—Swazi(s); adjective—Swazi. **Ethnic groups:** 97% African, 3% European. **Languages:** English and siSwati (both official); government business conducted in English. **Religions:** 40% Zionist (mixture of Christianity and indigenous beliefs), 20% Roman Catholic, 10% Muslim, 10% other.
● **GOVERNMENT Type:** monarchy; independent member of Commonwealth. **Independence:** Sept. 6, 1968 (from U.K.). **Constitution:** suspended Apr. 12, 1973; new constitution promulgated Oct. 13, 1978; signed by the King in July 2005, went into effect on Feb. 8, 2006. **National holiday:** Somhlolo (Independence) Day, Sept. 6. **Heads of Government:** Mswati III, king (since Apr. 1986); Sibusiso Barnabas Dlamini, prime minister (since Aug. 1996). **Structure:** executive—king is hereditary monarch, appoints prime minister; bicameral legislature (lower house-10 members appointed by king, 55 elected; upper house-20 members appointed by king, 10 elected by lower house); judiciary—judges appointed by king.

● **ECONOMY Monetary unit:** lilangeni. **Budget:** (2008 est.) *income:* $1.215 bil.; *expend.:* $1.155 bil. **G.D.P.:** $5.703 bil., $5,100 per capita (2008 est.). **Chief crops:** sugarcane, maize, cotton, maize, tobacco, rice, citrus fruits; cattle, goats, sheep. **Natural resources:** asbestos, coal, clay, cassiterite, hydropower. **Major industries:** mining (coal and asbestos), wood pulp, sugar. **Labor force:** 300,000; 40% unemployment (2006). **Exports:** $1.83 bil. (f.o.b., 2008); soft drink concentrates, sugar, wood pulp, cotton yarn. **Imports:** $1.978 bil. (f.o.b., 2008); motor vehicles, machinery, transport equipment, foodstuffs, chemicals, petroleum products. **Major trading partners:** (2006) *exports:* 60% South Africa, 9% E.U., 9% U.S., 6% Mozambique; *imports:* 96% South Africa, 1% E.U., 1% Japan.

The Kingdom of Swaziland, a landlocked African country, is surrounded on three sides by South Africa and on the fourth by Mozambique. The Swazi are of Bantu origin. They are believed to have migrated in the late 1700s, under their chief Ngwane II, into what is now southeastern Swaziland, finding several different peoples there. Ngwane II and his successors united these tribal clans by the beginning of the 19th century.

Although British and Boer traders began exploring the area in the 1830s, it was not until gold was discovered in the 1880s that settlers began coming in large numbers. They hoodwinked the illiterate Swazi leadership into signing away their rights to the land. The British and Boer governments agreed in 1894 that the Boers would control Swaziland, but power reverted to Great Britain after they defeated the Boers in the Boer War, which ended in 1902. Not until the 1967 did they give Swaziland authority over its internal affairs. Under the Britishauthored constitution, Swaziland gained its independence in September 1968 as a constitutional monarchy led by King Sobhuza II. He set aside the constitution in 1973 and disbanded the legislature. He ruled the country with the aid of a council of conservative ministers and named a committee to write a new constitution that was supposed to be more in keeping with Swazi traditions. A new legislature was created in 1979. The king died in 1982 and was replaced by his 18-year-old son, who took the name King Mswati III, in 1986, and has ruled autocratically ever since. His lavish lifestyle and many wives (13 at last count, with two fiances) have caused protests, but no violence or uprisings.

▶ SWEDEN
Kingdom of Sweden
● **GEOGRAPHY Location:** Scandinavian peninsula, northwest Europe. **Boundaries:** Norway to NE and W, Finland to NE, Gulf of Bothnia to E, Baltic Sea to E and S, Skagerrak channel to SW. **Total area:** 173,731 sq. mi. (449,964 sq km). **Coastline:** 2,000 mi. (3,218 km). **Comparative area:** slightly larger than California. **Land use:** 7% arable land; 0% permanent crops; 93% other. **Major cities:** Stockholm (capital); Göteburg (Gothenburg); Malmö; Uppsala; Linköping.
● **PEOPLE Population:** 9,074,055 (July 2010 est.). **Nationality:** noun—Swede(s); adjective—Swedish. **Ethnic groups:** homogeneous white population; small Lappish minority; about 12% foreign-born or first-generation immigrants (Finns, Yugoslavs, Danes, Norwegians, Greeks, Turks). **Languages:** Swedish, small Lapp- and Finnish-speaking minorities. **Religions:** 87% Lutheran, Roman Catholic, Orthodox, Baptist, other.

• **GOVERNMENT** Type: constitutional monarchy. **Constitution:** Jan. 1, 1975. **National holiday:** Day of the Swedish Flag, June 6. **Head of Government:** Carl XVI Gustaf, king (since Nov. 1973); Fredrick Reinfeldt, prime minister (since Sept. 2006). **Structure:** executive—prime minister is head of government; unicameral legislature; judiciary. • **ECONOMY Monetary unit:** Swedish krona. **Budget:** (2009 est.) *income:* $196.9 bil.; *expend.:* $211.4 bil. **G.D.P.:** $333.5 bil., $36,800 per capita (2009 est.). **Chief crops:** grain, sugar beets, potatoes; meat, milk. **Natural resources:** zinc, iron ore, lead, copper, silver. **Major industries:** iron and steel, precision equipment (bearings, radio and telephone parts, armaments), wood pulp. **Labor force:** 4.93 mil. (2009 est.); 74% services, 24% industry, 2% agriculture. **Exports:** $132.8 bil. (2009 est.); 35% machinery, motor vehicles, paper products, pulp and wood, iron and steel products. **Imports:** $121.1 bil. (2009 est.); machinery, petroleum and petroleum products, chemicals, motor vehicles, foodstuffs. **Major trading partners:** (2008) *exports:* 10.4% Germany, 9.5% Norway, 7.4% Denmark, 7.3% U.K., 6.6% U.S.; *imports:* 17.5% Germany, 9.4% Denmark, 8.5% Norway, 6.2% U.K., 5.7% Finland, 5.6% Netherlands, 5% France, 4.4% Russia.

The earliest Swedes, the Svear, conquered and merged with their southern neighbors, the Gotar, by the sixth century. Organized into petty kingdoms, Swedes joined with other Norsemen in the Viking raids of the seventh through 11th centuries; in the 10th century, they began to dominate a trading empire that stretched through Russia to the Black Sea. Christianity was introduced by St. Ansgar in 829 but became fully established only in the 12th century, during the reign of Eric IX, who also conquered Finland. For centuries Sweden warred with its neighbors, Norway and Denmark, for control in the north, and it competed with the German Hanseatic League for control of the Baltic trade.

The Swedish and Norwegian monarchies were merged in 1319 by Magnus VII, and in 1397 Queen Margaret effected the Kalmar Union, which united Sweden, Denmark, and Norway under a single monarchy. Sweden resisted Danish rule, and in 1520 King Christian II responded with the massacre of the Swedish nobility at Stockholm. Sweden then rose against the Danish throne and in 1523 enthroned Gustavus Wasa as Gustavus I, founder of the Swedish monarchy. The Wasa dynasty slowly introduced Lutheran Christianity and in 1604 banned Catholicism.

Sweden became a European champion of Protestantism in the 17th century, intervening against the Habsburgs in the Thirty Years' War. Emerging among the victors after 1648, Sweden successfully waged wars with Denmark and Poland, built a great northern empire, and made the Baltic Sea virtually a Swedish lake. But in the late 17th century and into the 18th, the Russians deprived Sweden of the Baltic's eastern shore and, in 1808, of Finland, while the Prussians drove Sweden from the southern Baltic coast.

The kings of Sweden during the 18th century pursued a pointless despotism that weakened the country politically and socially. Sweden joined the European powers against Napoleon in 1813 and was rewarded with Norway in 1814. In 1905 Norway gained its independence, and Sweden took on its modern boundaries.

Sweden's natural resources—timber, iron ore, and hydroelectric power—were exploited by traditional industries, which supplemented other economic activities (fishing, maritime trade). All provided the basis for industrialization in the 19th and 20th centuries, leading to an economic prosperity that was enhanced by political neutrality.

Sweden's neutrality was largely respected by Hitler during World War II. Through the war Sweden continued to be ruled, under King Gustavus V, by a national coalition government lasting until 1945. Sweden's gross national product (GNP) rose by 20 percent during the war years.

The Social Democratic party dominated the Swedish government after 1936, and again after 1945, lasting until 1976 under the leadership of Tage Erlander. Sweden, like its Scandinavian neighbors, constructed an economy based on free enterprise, public ownership of utilities, exports, social welfare, and high taxes.

A U.N. charter member, Sweden accepted Marshall Plan aid and joined the Council of Europe in 1948. Sweden's plan for a Nordic Defense Alliance failed when Norway and Denmark joined NATO (Sweden refused to join), but the political and economic Nordic Council (Sweden, Norway, Denmark, Iceland, and, after 1956, Finland) was formed in 1952–53. This consultative body backed the establishment of SAS as the joint national airline of the first three members; coordination of the welfare programs of member states; and abolition of passport controls and controls on the migration of labor within Scandinavia.

Erlander retired in 1969 and was succeeded by Olaf Palme, who pursued a more rigid socialist program. Advocating legislation to make incomes more equal, provoking some labor unrest. When King Gustav VI Adolf died in 1973 the Palme government passed the 1974 Instrument of Government Act, divesting the king of his role as commander in chief and of his right to appoint prime ministers.

Economic growth came to a virtual halt in the 1970s; Sweden's oil import costs rose 700 percent between 1972 and 1979. Consumer prices rose sharply, and labor unrest grew. The Social Democrats were turned out by a conservative coalition in 1976 but returned with a minority cabinet in 1982.

Palme was assassinated in 1986, and he was succeeded by Ingvar Carlsson, whose Social Democratic program focused on a scheme whereby business profits are taxed to fund labor union purchases of sufficient stock to gain labor ownership of private enterprise. Elections (Sept. 1991) unseated Carlsson and the Social Democrats, who had ruled for 53 of the last 59 years. A coalition government of four conservative parties pledged to cut taxes and phase out some welfare programs. But in elections held in Sept. 1994, Carlsson returned to power as voters expressed dissatisfaction with inflation, unemployment, and an enormous public debt, all of which spiraled under the conservative coalition. The Social Democrats fell 13 votes short of a majority in Parliament, however, forcing them to seek the support of the right-centrist Liberal party in a coalition government.

On Jan. 1, 1995, Sweden entered the European Union. In March 1996, Finance Minister Göran Persson succeeded Carlsson as prime minister. In 1998 Sweden announced it would not join the European Monetary Union, and in Sept. elections Persson's Government won enough votes to keep power by pledging more money for social welfare services. More significant for Sweden's future was the 1999 completion of the 10-mile, $2.6 billion bridge over (and under) the Baltic, linking Copenhagen with Malmö (Sweden's third largest city).

On Dec. 17, 1999, after almost 500 years, the Lutheran Church was disestablished. Persson and the Social Democrats won the Sept. 2002 elections. In Sept. 2003 Foreign Minister Anna Lindh was assassinated days before voters rejected participation in the European Monetary Union. In Sept. 2006 Persson was badly defeated in large part over welfare and labor issues. The Moderate party under new prime minister Fredrik Reinfeldt pledged to revitalize the economy.

▶ SWITZERLAND
Swiss Confederation

● **GEOGRAPHY   Location:** landlocked country in central Europe. **Boundaries:** Germany to N, Austria to E, Italy to S, and France to W. **Total area:** 15,942 sq. mi. (41,290 sq km). **Coastline:** none. **Comparative area:** slightly less than twice the size of New Jersey. **Land use:** 11% arable land; 1% permanent crops; 88% other. **Major cities:** Berne (Bern, capital); Zürich; Basel; Genève (Geneva or Genf); Lausanne.

● **PEOPLE   Population:** 7,623,438 (July 2010 est.). **Nationality:** noun—Swiss (sing., pl.); adjective—Swiss. **Ethnic groups:** 65% German, 18% French, 10% Italian, 1% Romansch, 6% other. **Languages:** 63.7% German, 19.2% French, 7.6% Italian (all official); 0.6% Romansch, 8.9% other. **Religions:** 41.8% Catholic, 35.3% Protestant, 4% Muslim.

● **GOVERNMENT   Type:** federal republic. **Independence:** Aug. 1, 1291. **Constitution:** May 29, 1874; revised in 1998, officially approved Jan. 2000. **National holiday:** Anniversary of the Founding of the Swiss Confederation, Aug. 1. **Head of Government:** Doris Leuthard, president (since Jan. 2010). **Structure:** executive—president is head of government and chief of state; bicameral legislature—National Council, Council of States; judiciary left chiefly to cantons.

● **ECONOMY   Monetary unit:** Swiss franc. **Budget:** (2009 est.) *income:* $151.5 bil.; *expend.:* $150 bil. **G.D.P.:** $317 bil., $41,700 per capita (2009 est.). **Chief crops:** grains, fruits, vegetables; meat, eggs. **Natural resources:** hydropower potential, timber, salt. **Major industries:** machinery, chemicals, watches. **Labor force:** 4.28 mil.; 72.5% services, 23.7% industry, 3.8% agriculture (2009). **Exports:** $190.1 bil. (2009 est.); machinery, chemicals, metals, watches, agricultural products. **Imports:** $177.2 bil. (2009 est.); machinery, chemicals, vehicles, metals, agricultural products. **Major trading partners:** (2008) *exports:* 19.7% Germany, 9.6% U.S., 8.7% Italy, 8.6% France, 5.2% U.K.; *imports:* 33.3% Germany, 11% Italy, 9.4% France, 5.8% U.S., 4.5% Netherlands.

Switzerland, the Roman province of Helvetia, began to assume its modern form in A.D. 1291, when three independent cantons formed a defensive league against the expansion of Habsburg power. The Swiss League grew to eight cantons in 1353, 13 in 1513, 22 in 1815. The league continues to evolve; it reached its present size of 20 cantons and six half-cantons with the creation of the Canton of Jura in 1979.

The Treaty of Westphalia, which ended the Thirty Years' War in 1648, gave international recognition to the independence of Switzerland from the Holy Roman Empire. Switzerland became a client state of France in the Napoleonic period; the European powers guaranteed Swiss independence and neutrality at the Congress of Vienna in 1815. Constitutional changes in 1848 and 1874 somewhat increased the power of the central government, but the individual cantons

cling stubbornly to their independence, helping to ensure stability within a multilingual nation.

The Swiss government consists of an upper house, representing the cantons, and a lower house that is directly elected. No executive can veto, nor court disallow, a bill of the Swiss legislature. Executive power is vested in a seven-member committee chosen by the legislature, with a rotating presidency.

Swiss neutrality is defended by more than simply international guarantees. Switzerland is a highly militarized society; every male is required to serve in the citizen's militia until age 47, keeping an assault rifle and other equipment ready at home. The armed forces are equipped with modern weapons, and military spending amounts to 30 percent of the Swiss federal budget.

Landlocked, with little fertile farmland and lacking both natural resources and a colonial empire, Switzerland was traditionally one of Europe's poorest countries. Until the 19th century, its principal export was mercenaries who supplied military services to any European sovereign who could pay for them. (The pope's Swiss Guard is a remnant of this tradition.) With the spread in the late 18th century of the Romantic movement, Europeans learned to appreciate the Alpine scenery, and a tourist industry was born. It was expanded in the 20th century with the development of Alpine skiing. Tourism remains a conspicuous, though minor, part of the Swiss economy.

Swiss prosperity came in the 20th century with specialized manufacturing and free trade within the world economy. By 1940 half of the population was engaged in manufacturing, producing products requiring high degrees of skill: processed foods, watches, electrical machinery, engines, fine textiles, and the like.

Neutral in both world wars, Switzerland required no postwar recovery in the 1940s. It capitalized on the restructuring of European politics and economics to expand into the service sector, which now employs half of the work force. Tourism, banking, insurance, and clerical/bureaucratic services to the many international organizations with headquarters in Switzerland help give the nation one of Europe's highest standards of living. Under pressure from the E.C. and the United States, Switzerland agreed to phase out its famous "Form B" (i.e., secret bank accounts).

Referenda at this time brought overwhelming rejection of U.N. membership, and support for restrictive immigration legislation. The most significant political changes were the gradual extension of women's right to vote and the 1993 approval of casino gambling to fund social security.

In 1996 and 1997 the Swiss government, responding to international pressures, appointed a panel to examine what funds in Swiss banks the Nazis might have stolen or that Holocaust victims (or their families) might have deposited and were unable to retrieve. A less than rigorous accounting, however, resulted in several lawsuits which were settled in 1998 with the Swiss banks agreeing to pay $1.2 bil. On Dec. 9, 1998, Social Democrat Ruth Dreifuss became Switzerland's first female and first Jewish president. A June 1999 referendum (carried 70 percent–30 percent) to restrict refugee asylum prefigured a very strong showing in the October National Council elections by the nativist Swiss People's Party which had the largest total vote and won the second largest number of seats. Recent referenda reflect divisions in Swiss minds over the country's identity and her role in the new Europe. In 2000, 64 percent refused to set a limit (18 percent) on the number of foreigners residing in Switzerland, and 74 percent refused to begin negotiations for E.U. membership. Yet in July, by a slender margin (50.9 percent), voters approved the arming of Swiss troops serving under international auspices as well as joint training of Swiss soldiers with foreign armies, and in 2002 Switzerland entered the U.N. In 2005, voters approved closer ties with the E.U. In 2008 voters rejected a referendum to limit naturalization of foreigners.

▶ SYRIA
Syrian Arab Republic

● **GEOGRAPHY Location:** western Asia. **Boundaries:** Turkey to N, Iraq to E, Jordan to S, Lebanon and Israel to SW, Mediterranean Sea to W. **Total area:** 71,498 sq. mi. (185,180 sq km). **Coastline:** 193 mi. (193 km). **Comparative area:** slightly larger than North Dakota. **Land use:** 26% arable land; 4% permanent crops; 70% other. **Major cities:** Damascus (capital); Aleppo; Homs; Latakia; Hama.
● **PEOPLE Population:** 22,198,110 (July 2010 est.). **Nationality:** noun—Syrian(s); adjective—Syrian. **Ethnic groups:** 90.3% Arab, 9.7% Kurds, Armenians, and other. **Languages:** Arabic (official), Kurdish, Armenian, Aramaic, Circassian, French. **Religions:** 74% Sunni Muslim; 16% Alawite, Druze, and other Muslim sects; 10% Christian.
● **GOVERNMENT Type:** republic under military regime since Mar. 1963. **Independence:** Apr. 17, 1946 (from League of Nations Mandate under French administration). **Constitution:** Mar. 13, 1973. **National holiday:** National Day, Apr. 17. **Heads of Government:** Dr. Bashar Al-Assad, president (since July 2000); Naji Al-Utri, prime minister (since Sept. 2003). **Structure:** executive powers vested in president and Council of Ministers; unicameral legislature (People's Council); judiciary.
● **ECONOMY Monetary unit:** Syrian pound. **Budget:** (2009 est.) *income:* 9.02 bil.; *expend.:* $13.14 bil. **G.D.P.:** $100.7 bil., $4,600 per capita (2009 est.). **Chief crops:** cotton, wheat, barley, lentils; beef, lamb, eggs, poultry, milk. **Natural resources:** crude oil, phosphates, chrome and manganese ores, asphalt, iron ore. **Major industries:** petroleum, textiles, food processing, beverages. **Labor force:** 5.772 mil. (2009 est.); 66% services, 19% agriculture, 15% industry. **Exports:** $11.76 bil. (2009 est.); 65% petroleum, 10% textiles, 9% food and live animals. **Imports:** $13.34 bil. (2009 est.); 21% machinery, 18% foodstuffs/animals, 15% metal and metal products, 10% chemicals. **Major trading partners:** (2008) *exports:* 30.7% Iraq, 9.8% Germany, 9.6% Lebanon, 6.4% Italy, 5.5% France, 5.4% Egypt; *imports:* 11.7% Saudi Arabia, 8.7% China, 7.5% Russia, 5.9% Italy, 5.8% Egypt, 5.7% U.A.E., 4.3% Turkey, 4.2% Iran.

The home of some of the world's most ancient centers of civilization, Syria was successively part of the Hittite, Assyrian, and Persian empires. At various times it was conquered by the Babylonians and the Egyptians. From about 1250 B.C., the coastal cities came under Phoenician rule. Alexander the Great brought Syria into the Hellenic world with his conquests in 332 B.C. After the fall of the Alexandrian empire, Syria came under the domain of the Seleucid empire but was constantly threatened by the Hellenic kingdom of Egypt, based in Alexandria.

In the classical period, Syria embraced a much larger territory than that of the present Syrian nation; it included the entire Levant and parts of present-day Turkey, Iraq, Iran, and Jordan. Greater Syria was conquered by Rome in 63 B.C. Under Roman rule the oasis region of Palmyra grew into a powerful semiautonomous kingdom. With the division of the Roman Empire in the fourth century A.D., Syria became part of the Eastern Roman (Byzantine) Empire. Throughout the Roman and Byzantine periods, the country was an important center of Christianity.

Syria was one of the first areas conquered when Islam began expansion from Arabia; Islamic rule was established by 636. From 661 to 751, Damascus was the center of the Caliphate, the ruling body of the Islamic world. By the late 11th century, the Seljuk Turks had conquered Syria. The large Syrian Christian population welcomed the European Crusaders as liberators from the Turks, but both Christians and Turks were defeated by the Arab general Saladin in the late 12th century. Saladin's rule was followed by that of the Mamluk empire of Egypt. During the Mamluk period, Mongol armies twice invaded Syria, in the mid-13th century and at the turn of the 15th century.

An Ottoman army defeated the Mamluks in Syria in 1516, making Syria part of the Ottoman Empire. In the 18th century, France declared itself the protector of Syria's Christian community against Ottoman abuses. Napoleon invaded Syria in 1799 but withdrew after a brief occupation. In the 1830s Egyptian troops occupied Syria but were forced to withdraw by the European powers.

Syrian nationalist aspirations emerged as the Ottoman Empire began to crumble before World War I. During the war the British encouraged Syrians to rebel against Turkish rule. After World War I, France governed both Syria and Lebanon under a League of Nations mandate. Under French rule, the region was divided into small territorial states along communal lines; Lebanon became independent in 1926. After prolonged negotiations much of Syria was organized into a semiautonomous state in 1930–32.

In June 1940 the French administration in Syria declared its loyalty to the Vichy government. British and Free French forces invaded in June 1941, and an independent Syrian republic was established in September 1941. Separately administered territories were consolidated with the republic over the next two years, and full independence was declared on Jan. 1, 1944; foreign troops did not withdraw, however, until April 1946.

Syria became a founding member of the Arab League and participated in the first Arab-Israeli War in 1948. An armistice with Israel was signed in July 1949. Severe political instability marked the early years of Syrian independence; the government was overthrown by military coups three times in 1949 alone.

Most of Syria's Jews emigrated to Israel before or during 1948, and much of its once-substantial Christian population has emigrated also. Syrian politics remain dominated by communal concerns, however; the Arab majority is divided into Sunni, Shiite, Alawite, and Druze communities.

Syria and Egypt merged as the United Arab Republic in February 1958; Syria seceded from the federation on Sept. 30, 1961. In Mar. 1963 a military coup established the pan-Arab Socialist Baath party in power; all other political parties were abolished. The Baath party leadership is dominated by the minority Alawite community. Pres. Hafez al-Assad took power on Feb. 22, 1971.

In the 1967 Arab-Israeli War (the Six Day War), Israel seized and held the Golan Heights region of Syria, from which Syria had long shelled Israeli communities and military installations. The Golan Heights were incorporated into Israeli territory. Syrian troops aided Palestinian forces fighting government troops in Jordan in September 1970. After the expulsion of Palestinian forces from Jordan in July 1971, Syria broke off relations with Jordan; relations were restored in 1975.

On Oct. 6, 1973, Syrian and Egyptian forces attacked Israel, touching off the the Yom Kippur War. A cease-fire took effect on Oct. 24; Syria failed to regain territory lost to Israel in 1967. Following the 1973 war, Syria became a major recipient of economic aid from the Arab oil states and of military equipment from the Soviet Union.

In 1976 Syrian troops entered Lebanon in an attempt to mediate a civil war there and became enmeshed in that conflict. Major fighting between Syrian troops and Lebanese Christian militiamen broke out in April 1981. On June 6, 1982, Israeli troops invaded Lebanon and engaged Syrian troops in a five-day war in the Bekaa Valley. Following serious losses of aircraft and troops, Syria agreed to a cease-fire with Israel on June 11. Syrian troops continue to occupy parts of Lebanon.

An attempted coup, in February 1982, by the Muslim Brotherhood, led to serious fighting within Syria, but the rebellion was put down; casualties topped 5,000 on both sides.

From the time of the 1973 Arab-Israeli War, Syria adopted a radical stance in Middle Eastern politics, rejecting the 1979 Egyptian-Israeli accord and all other attempts at Arab-Israeli reconciliation. Supporting radical movements within the Palestine Liberation Organization, Syria aided Palestinian militants in driving Yasir Arafat's centrist faction of the PLO from its headquarters in Tripoli in 1983. The government was implicated in various acts of international terrorism in support of Palestinian, Libyan, and Iranian causes.

Syria played a major role in the Lebanese peace process and accommodating a peace settlement between rival Shiite militias. Syria also took part in the anti-Iraq coalition in 1990–91, sending 20,000 troops to Saudi Arabia. Syria in 1994 made serious efforts toward achieving peace in the Middle East, including an offer to normalize relations in exchange for a return of the Golan Heights. But talks were suspended after bombings by the militant Islamic group Hamas.

In Oct. 1998, Syria reached an accord with Turkey; with 10,000 Turkish troops massed on Syria's border, Syria agreed to cease supporting Kurdish rebels. In Feb. 1999, Assad won, with 99.95 percent approval in his sole candidacy, election to a fifth seven-year term as president. A cabinet shake-up in March 2000 produced 22 new members among the 36 under new premier Mohammed Mustafa Zubi just three months before the death of Assad. After his 30 years of rule, the government backed his son (and armed forces commander) Bashar al-Assad, 34. In 2005 Syria was forced to remove all of its security forces from Lebanon after mass demonstrations followed the assassination of a popular Lebanese politcian. In 2007 Israel destroyed a nuclear reactor site in Syria.

▶ TAIWAN

• GEOGRAPHY Location: one large and several smaller islands about 100 mi. (160 km) off SE coast of mainland China. Taipei 25°03'N, 121°30'E. Boundaries: East China Sea to N, Pacific Ocean to E, Bashi Channel to S, and Formosa Strait to W; separated from mainland by Formosa Strait. Total area: 13,892 sq. mi. (35,980 sq km).

Coastline: 900 mi. (1,448 km). Comparative area: slightly smaller than Maryland. Land use: 24% arable land; 1% permanent crops;75% other. Major cities: Taipei (capital); Kaohsiung; Taichung; Tainan; Panchiao.

• PEOPLE Population: 23,024,956 (July 2009 est.). Nationality: noun—Chinese (sing., pl.); adjective—Chinese. Ethnic groups: 84% Taiwanese, 14% mainland Chinese, 2% aborigine. Languages: Mandarin Chinese (official); Taiwanese and Hakka dialects also used. Religions: 93% mixture of Buddhist, Confucian, and Taoist; 4.5% Christian, 2.5% other.

• GOVERNMENT Type: multi-party democratic regime headed by popularly elected president. Constitution: Jan. 1, 1947, amended 1992, 1994, and 1997. National holiday: National Day, Oct. 10. Heads of Government: Ma Ying-jeou, president (since May 2008); Wu Den-yih, premier (since Sep. 2009). Structure: executive—president appoints premier; two-chamber legislature—Legislative Yuan, National Assembly; judiciary—Judicial Yuan.

• ECONOMY Monetary unit: New Taiwan dollar. Budget: (2009 est.) income: $53.3 bil.; expend.: $57.2 bil. G.D.P.: $717.7 bil., $29,800 per capita (2009 est.). Chief crops: rice, wheat, corn, soybeans, vegetables, fruit, tea; pigs, poultry, beef, milk; fish. Natural resources: small deposits of coal, natural gas, limestone, marble, and asbestos. Major industries: electronics, petroleum refining, textiles, clothing, chemicals. Labor force: 10.92 mil. (2009 est.); 37% industry, 58% services, 5% agriculture. Exports: $203.7 bil. (2009 est.); 54% electrical equipment and machinery, metals, textiles, plastics, chemicals, electronic products. Imports: $174.7 bil. (2009 est.); 44.5% machinery and electrical equipment, electronic products, minerals, precision instruments. Major trading partners: (2009 est.) exports: 26.6% China, 14.4% Hong Kong, 11.6% U.S., 7.2% Japan; imports: 20.7% Japan, 14% China, 10.3% U.S., 6% South Korea, 4.8% Saudi Arabia.

Nominally part of the Chinese empire since the Song dynasty (960–1279), Taiwan was inhabited only by non-Chinese aboriginals before the 17th century. Around 1600 the Portuguese established a trading station on Taiwan; they named the island Ilha Formosa. In 1620 the Dutch built Fort Zeelandia near present-day Tainan, controlling the island until they were driven out by the Chinese pirate-patriot Koxinga (Zheng Chenggong). Remnants of the overthrown Ming dynasty (1368–1644) held out on the island until 1683, when it came under the sway of the Qing dynasty (1644–1911). Thereafter, substantial numbers of farmers from Fujian Province migrated to the fertile western lowlands of the island, driving the aboriginals into the central mountains. The Qing dynasty administered Taiwan as a semiautonomous subprovince of Fujian Province.

Following China's defeat by Japan in the Sino-Japanese War of 1894–95, Taiwan was ceded to Japan as a colony. The Japanese built roads and railroads to exploit Taiwan's resources of rice, timber, and minerals. In 1945, after Japan's defeat in World War II, Taiwan was returned to China.

As the Chinese civil war turned against the Nationalist party of Chiang Kai-shek (see "China"), Nationalist troops began to prepare Taiwan as a base for a retreat from the mainland.

In 1947 Nationalist agents executed several thousand students and others suspected of favoring Taiwan's independence from China. In 1949 approximately two million Nationalist soldiers, government officials, and civilian sympathizers retreated to Taiwan. The relocated Republic of China (ROC) continued to claim to be the legitimate government of all of China, now under Communist control. In addition to Taiwan proper, the Nationalists occupied the P'eng-hu Islands in the Taiwan Straits and the small islands of Quemoy and Matsu just off the coast of Fujian. Recovery of the mainland became a cornerstone of ROC policy, but no serious attempt was made to do so. U.S. policy in the Taiwan Straits was to defend Taiwan against Communist attack but also to keep the two rival governments of China separated.

A successful program of land reform in the early 1950s led to the creation of surplus capital, which fueled the development of an industrial base on the island. Foreign investment from Japan and the United States, and American military and economic aid, also enhanced economic development. By the early 1970s, the island had developed an export-oriented economy, producing textiles, cement, plastics, assembled electronic appliances, and other manufactured goods.

Chiang Kai-shek, president of the Republic of China since 1928, died in 1975 and was succeeded by his son, Chiang Ching-kuo. Under both the Nationalist party (Kuomintang, or KMT) controlled both the ROC and the Taiwan Provincial governments; mainland refugees and their descendants (15 percent of the population) dominated senior government posts and the military officer corps. Native Taiwanese played the leading role in agriculture, industry, and in local governments.

In 1971 China's seat in the United Nations was taken away from the ROC and awarded to the People's Republic of China, leaving Taiwan in international diplomatic limbo. On Jan. 1, 1979, the United States withdrew its recognition of the ROC and inaugurated mutual diplomatic relations with the People's Republic. Under the Taiwan Relations Act of 1979, nominally nongovernmental relations were maintained between the U.S. and Taiwan. Taiwan enjoys a substantial favorable balance of trade with the U.S.

In 1987 Pres. Chiang Ching-kuo began a policy of liberalization when he abolished martial law and allowed non-KMT political parties to function legally. Some barriers to travel and communication with the mainland by ROC citizens were eased, but Taiwan's government continued to rebuff all calls from the mainland for discussions of reunification. Chiang Ching-kuo died in Jan. 1988 and was succeeded by his vice president, Lee Teng-hui. The ruling KMT maintained its hold on power in legislative elections in 1992, but the opposition Democratic Progressive party scored a stunning success, tripling its number of legislative seats and bringing the issue of Taiwanese independence to the forefront. Factional rivalry deepened in the KMT, with Pres. Lee's Wisdom Coalition challenged by the New Kuomintang Alliance of Prime Minister (and former general) Hau Pei-tsun. Hau resigned on Feb. 3, 1993, but his faction, with military backing, continued to pose a threat to Pres. Lee's power.

During the campaign for Taiwan's presidential election in March, 1996, China held aggressive military exercises off the coast of Taiwan in an effort to influence the voting; the U.S. sent two aircraft carriers to the area. In a rebuke to Beijing, President Lee, who had campaigned for a more visible international role for Taiwan, was resoundingly re-elected; he was also re-elected as the head of the KMT in August, 1997. The ruling KMT saw its power eroded in local elections as voters protested corruption and economic stagnation related to the Asia-wide economic crises of 1997–98. The KMT rebounded strongly in 1998 elections but tensions rose in 1999 with mainland China, when Pres. Lee's expressed interest in Taiwan's being included in a proposed anti-missile defense of its Asian allies (the "last straw" to Beijing). Later, Lee announced that Taiwan would conduct its relations with China on a "state-to-state" basis, meaning Taiwan was an independent state—to Beijing, an "extremely dangerous step".

In March 2000, the KMT was peacefully voted out of power after 50 years. Chen Shui-Bian of the Democratic-Progressive Party was elected president but political rivalries prevented Chen's party from gaining a significant majority and he barely won reelection in 2004. In 2005 his government met with China and these talks ended in a pledge to seek an end to hostilities, but charges of corruption resulted in falling popularity and in 2008 a Nationalist Party president was elected, Ma Ying-jeou, who immediately began the first formal talks with China since 1999. Trade with the mainland increased and direct air routes between the two parties were established. In 2010 China and Taiwan signed an historic trade pact. The U.S., however, continued to sell arms to Taiwan.

▶ TAJIKISTAN
Republic of Tajikistan

● **GEOGRAPHY** **Location:** southeast central Asia. **Boundaries:** Kyrgyzstan to NE, China to E, Afghanistan to S and SW, Uzbekistan to NW and N. **Total area:** 55,251 sq. mi. (143,100 sq km). **Coastline:** none. **Comparative area:** slightly smaller than Wisconsin. **Land use:** 6% arable land; 1% permanent crops; 93% other. **Major cities:** Dushanbe (Stalinabad 1929-61) (capital); Khodzhent (formerly Leninabad).
● **PEOPLE** **Population:** 7,349,145 (July 2009 est.). **Nationality:** noun—Tajikistani(s); adjective—Tajikistani. **Ethnic groups:** 64.9% Tajik, 25% Uzbek, 3.5% Russian, 6.6% other. **Languages:** Tajik (official) is closely related to Farsi (Persian) and was written in Cyrillic script since 1940; Russian widely used in government and business. **Religions:** 85% Sunni Muslim, 5% Shi'a Muslim.
● **GOVERNMENT** **Type:** republic. **Independence:** Sept. 9, 1991 (from Soviet Union). **Constitution:** Nov. 6, 1994. **National holiday:** National Day, Sept. 9. **Heads of Government:** Emomali Rahmon; head of state (since Nov. 1994); Oqil Oqilov, prime minister (since Nov. 2006). **Structure:** executive—popularly-elected president appoints prime minister and cabinet; bicameral legislature; judiciary.
● **ECONOMY** **Monetary unit:** Tajikistani ruble. **Budget:** (2008 est.) *income:* $1.28 bil.; *expend.:* $1.3 bil. **G.D.P.:** $15.4 bil., $2,100 per capita (2008 est.). **Chief crops:** cotton, vegetables, fruit, grain, grapes; cattle, sheep, goats. **Natural resources:** significant hydropower potential, some petroleum, uranium, mercury, brown coal. **Major industries:** mineral processing, chemicals, fertilizers, cement. **Labor force:** 2.1 mil. (2008); 67% agriculture, 8% industry, 25% services. **Exports:** $1.4 bil. (f.o.b., 2008 est.); cotton, aluminum, electricity, fruits, vegetable oil, textiles. **Imports:** $3.2 bil. (f.o.b., 2008 est.); fuel, electricity, chemicals, machinery and transport equipment, foodstuffs. **Major trading partners:** (2006) *exports:* 40.7% Netherlands, 31.7% Turkey, 5.4% Iran, 4.8% Uzbekistan, 4.7% Russia; *imports:* 24.6% Russia, 10.8% Kazakhstan, 10.2% Uzbekistan, 8.6% China, 8% Azerbaijan.

Tajikistan is a mountainous country, with over half of its territory above 10,000 feet. Its mountain ranges are the northern and southern Tian Shan and the Pamirs, where the former Soviet Union's highest points of Lenin Peak and Communism Peak are found. The dense river system and the many fertile valleys make habitation possible in such a mountainous country, although the entire territory is prone to earthquakes.

Tajikistan exemplifies the complexities of central Asia, since, unlike other ethnic groups on the region, the Tajiks were not nomadic but sedentary, and their language was Persian, not Turkic. They are a population that somehow escaped the waves of Turkish influence that swept through central Asia. As early as the eighth century a.d., the Tajiks probably formed a distinctive ethnic group, although they have never been a completely independent people. Despite the formation of several semi-independent states in their history, they have always been a small part of the larger Uzbek lands. In the mid-19th century, the Russian empire expanded southward, and the northern Tajik territories came under Russian rule. At the same time, the tribal state known as the Khanate of Bukhara controlled the southern Tajik territories.

In April 1918 northern Tajikistan came under Soviet control and was included in the Turkestan Autonomous Soviet Socialist Republic (ASSR). Three years later, the Red Army took the other regions that had been ruled by Bukhara. There was local opposition to Soviet rule, and the fighting meant that full Soviet authority over all of the area was not established until 1925. When the U.S.S.R. created the National Delimitation of the Central Asian Republics in 1924, it founded the Tajik ASSR as part of the Uzbek Soviet Socialist Republic (SSR); on Oct. 16, 1929, it became the Tajik SSR.

The Tajiks were fiercely opposed to the policies of land reform and collectivization, and during the ensuing Soviet repression of the 1930s, almost all native Tajiks were replaced by Russians in leading government and party positions. There have been reports of rising Islamic influence and increasing anti-Russian sentiment and even riots during the 1970s, evidence that the animosity toward the Russians that stemmed with its forced incorporation into the U.S.S.R. had not abated since the 1920s. Under Soviet rule, there was some economic and social progress.

However, living standards in Tajikistan are still among the lowest in the former union. Most people continue to live in rural qishlaqs, or settlements, consisting of 200–700 one-family houses built along an irrigation ditch or a river. The country is a major producer of cotton, and its industries are nonferrous metallurgy, cotton processing, fruit canning, and wine making.

Mikhail Gorbachev's glasnost, or openness, policy resulted in a campaign against corruption, a relaxation of censorship in the press, and increased ethnic tensions over alleged discrimination against Tajiks living in Uzbekistan. In June 1989 there were violent clashes between the two groups on the border between the two republics. There were also riots in February 1990 in Dushanbe, when the suggestion that Armenian refugees would be resettled there spurred the local Tajiks into action. Increased freedom of the press has given rise to a growing interest in Iran and Iranian culture, for even though they are closely related, contact between Iran and the Tajiks was severely limited during the Soviet period.

In large part due to the riots, opposition candidates were barred from the March 1990 elections and the Communist party won 94 percent of the seats. After the failed Aug. 1991 coup in Moscow, the Communist party was banned, and the president was forced to resign over his support of the coup. Since then, there have been several Communist party coups, and the party has been banned and reinstated several times. In the presidential elections, former Communist party leader Rakhmon Nabiyev won with 58 percent of the vote. But after a relatively tranquil six months, Islamic fundamentalists, armed allegedly by Iran and Afghanistan, rose up against the Nabiyev regime. Vicious fighting for almost four months led to Nabiyev's resignation at gunpoint and the launching of a fundamentalist government.

In 1992 the pro-Communist forces launched a successful counterattack in which thousands were killed and perhaps 300,000 displaced. Voters in Nov. 1994 approved by referendum a new (highly presidential) constitution with 90 percent of the vote, and elected as president Emomali Rakhmonov with 60 percent. But the civil war of the current, ex-Communist and Russian-backed government against Islamic rebels continued, despite U.N.-mediated cease-fires signed in Sept. 1994 and May 1995. Sporadic fighting between government troops and several rebel groups continued throughout 1997, and while the government appeared to be taking control, flareups continued into 2000. In Sept. 1999 voters amended the constitution to allow opposition Moslem parties and to extend the presidential term from five to seven years. In November President Rakhmanov won a new term with 96 percent of the vote. He won again in 2006. Russia's president, Vladmir Putin, established a military presence there in 2003.

▶TANZANIA
United Republic of Tanzania

● GEOGRAPHY **Location:** Tanganyika, on eastern coast of Africa, and islands of Zanzibar and Pemba, about 25 mi. (40 km) off Tanganyika coast in Indian Ocean. **Boundaries:** Burundi, Rwanda to NW, Uganda, Kenya to N, Indian Ocean to E, Mozambique, Malawi to S, Zambia to SW, Zaire to W. **Total area:** 364,900 sq. mi. (945,090 sq km). **Coastline:** 885 mi. (1,424 km). **Comparative area:** slightly larger than twice size of California. **Land use:** 4% arable land; 1% permanent crops; 95% other. **Major cities:** Dar es Salaam (capital); Mwanza; Tabora; Mbeya; Tanga.

● PEOPLE **Population:** 41,048,532 (July 2009 est.). **Nationality:** noun—Tanzanian(s); adjective—Tanzanian. **Ethnic groups:** mainland—99% native Africans of over 130 groups; 1% Asian, European, and Arab; Zanzibar—Arab, native African, mixed Arab and native African. **Languages:** Kiswahili and Swahili and English (all official); English primary language of commerce, administration, higher education; Swahili widely understood, generally used for communication between ethnic groups; first language of most people is one of local languages; primary education generally in Swahili. **Religions:** mainland—30% Christian, 35% Muslim, 35% indigenous beliefs; Zanzibar—almost all Muslim.

● GOVERNMENT **Type:** republic. **Independence:** Tanganyika became independent Dec. 9, 1961 (from U.N. trusteeship under British administration); Zanzibar became independent Dec. 19, 1963 (from U.K.); Tanganyika united with Zanzibar Apr. 26, 1964. **Constitution:** Apr. 25, 1977, revised Oct. 1984 (Zanzibar has own constitution but remains subject to provisions of union constitution). **National holiday:** Union Day, Apr. 26.

Heads of Government: Jakaya Kikwete, president (since Dec. 2005); **Structure:** executive—president is head of government and chief of state; unicameral legislature (Zanzibar has its own House of Representatives to make laws especially for Zanzibar; judiciary.

• ECONOMY   **Monetary unit:** Tanzanian shilling. **Budget:** (2008 est.) *income:* $4.216 bil.; *expend.:* $4.658 bil. **G.D.P.:** $54.26 bil., $1,300 per capita (2008 est.). **Chief crops:** cotton, coffee, sisal, vegetables, fruits, grain on mainland; cloves and coconuts on Zanzibar; cattle, sheep, goats. **Natural resources:** hydropower potential, tin, phosphates, iron ore and coal, gemstones. **Major industries:** agricultural processing (sugar, beer, cigarettes, sisal twine), diamond mining, oil refining. **Labor force:** 20.38 mil. (2008 est.); 80% agriculture, 20% industry and commerce. **Exports:** $2.49 bil. (f.o.b., 2008 est.); coffee, manufactured goods, cotton, sisal, cashew nuts, tobacco, cloves. **Imports:** $5.901 bil. (f.o.b., 2008 est.); consumer goods, machinery and transport equipment, crude oil. **Major trading partners:** (2006) *exports:* 8.8% China, 8.8% India, 6.2% Netherlands, 5.3% Japan, 4.2% United Arab Emirates, 4.2% Germany; *imports:* 9.8% South Africa, 9.4% China, 7.8% Kenya, 6.7% India, 5.9% United Arab Emirates, 5.7% Zambia.

Formerly known as Tanganyika, Tanzania's indigenous population includes people of diverse ethnic background, including San, Bantu, and Nilotic peoples. It has been the site of a number of relatively advanced and well-organized societies.

Zanzibar and the neighboring island of Pemba have been a crossroads of trade in East Africa since ancient times. Trade via Zanzibar between the Tanganyika coast and the Middle East, primarily ivory, gold, and iron, dates to the late Roman Empire. The coast was dominated by various Arab and Persian powers, usually based in Zanzibar, from about the eighth century. Zanzibar and Tanganyika were visited by Vasco da Gama in 1498, and Portugal claimed Zanzibar in 1503 and the entire Tanganyika coast in 1506. The Portuguese established coastal trading stations but did not colonize the interior.

The Portuguese were driven from Zanzibar in 1652 by the sultanate of Oman, which soon expelled them from the mainland as well. Under Omani rule, trade in gold, ivory, and gems was supplemented by a sizable slave trade, and the clove plantations of Zanzibar became commercially important. Under Sultan Seyyid Said, the capital of the sultanate of Oman was transferred to Zanzibar in 1824, and Zanzibar became independent of Oman upon his death in 1856.

Both Germany and Great Britain became active in the region in the 19th century. Tanganyika was organized as the colony of German East Africa in 1884, while Zanzibar became a British protectorate in 1890. Tanganyika became a secondary battlefield of World War I, with frequent clashes between German and British troops.

Britain assumed control of Tanganyika in 1920 under a League of Nations Mandate and maintained control under a U.N. trusteeship after 1946. The temperate southern highlands were extensively colonized by British immigrants, and railroads and mines were developed by the British.

Elections for a local legislature were held in Zanzibar in July 1957. The island's politics were dominated by a split between Arab and African residents. Zanzibar became independent on Dec. 19, 1963. In January 1964 an African revolt overthrew the sultan of Zanzibar and resulted in the deaths of thousands of Arab residents and the emigration of many more. Political control shifted to the African party and Abeid Karume became president.

Tanganyika became independent in 1961. Julius K. Nyerere was Tanganyika's dominant political figure. Tanzania was formed from the union of Tanganyika and Zanzibar on April 26, 1964, with Zanzibar retaining local autonomy.

Nyerere advocated an "African socialist" form of development and formed close ties with China. The Tan-Zan Railroad between Dar es Salaam and Lusaka, Zambia was built with Chinese aid between 1970 and 1975. The ruling parties of Tanganyika and Zanzibar were united in 1977 under Nyerere's leadership. Political tensions eased and Tanzania adopted a more open political structure in the 1980s. Pres. Ali Hassan Mwinyi encouraged free-market economic reforms, including encouragement of foreign investment and strengthened ties with Kenya and Uganda (Tanzania invaded the latter in 1979 in an effort to depose Idi Amin). Tanzania's economy has great potential because of the country's extensive natural resources and one of Africa's best educational systems; literacy in both English and Swahili is relatively high.

In 1992, the Revolutionary party of Tanzania voted in favor of a secular multiparty system, that is one based on neither ethnic nor regional lines. It won the country's first-ever multiparty elections in 1995. Benjamin Mkapa succeeded Mwinyi, who was barred by law from seeking a third term as president.

The elections of Oct. 2000 returned Mkapa to the presidency with 72 percent of the vote while the ruling party carried 167 of the National Assembly's 181 seats; similar results were reported from semiautonomous Zanzibar. The obviously rigged elections provoked demands for new elections from the opposition's Civic United Front and demonstrations in which over 40 were killed. In 2005, Mkapa was succeeded by a member of the ruling party, Jakaya Kikwete, whose leadership has helped to boost the economy significantly.

▶ THAILAND
Kingdom of Thailand

• GEOGRAPHY   **Location:** extends southward, along isthmus of Kra, to Malay peninsula, in Southeast Asia. **Boundaries:** Myanmar to W and N, Laos to NE, Cambodia and Gulf of Thailand to E, Malaysia to S, Andaman Sea to SW. **Total area:** 198,456 sq. mi. (514,000 sq km). **Coastline:** 2,001 mi. (3,219 km). **Comparative area:** slightly more than twice the size of Wyoming. **Land use:** 33% arable land; 7% permanent crops; 70% other. **Major cities:** Bangkok (capital); Songkhla; Chon Buri; Nakhon Si Thammarat; Chiang Mai.

• PEOPLE   **Population:** 66,404,688 (July 2010 est.). **Nationality:** noun—Thai (sing., pl.); adjective—Thai. **Ethnic groups:** 75% Thai, 14% Chinese, 11% other. **Languages:** Thai; English is secondary language of elite; ethnic and regional dialects. **Religions:** 94.6% Buddhist, 4.6% Muslim, 0.7% Christianity, 0.1% other.

• GOVERNMENT   **Type:** constitutional monarchy. **Constitution:** new constitution signed by King Phumiphon Oct. 11, 1997; amended Aug. 24, 2007. **National holiday:** Birthday of His Majesty the King, Dec. 5. **Heads of Government:** Bhumibol Adulyadej, king (since June 1946); Abhisit Vejjajiva , prime minister (since Dec. 2008). **Structure:** executive—king is head of state with nominal powers, prime minister is head of government; bicameral legislature (National Assembly—Senate appointed by king, to be phased into an elected body starting in 2000; elected House of Representatives); judiciary relatively independent except in important political subversion cases. ● ECONOMY   Monetary unit: baht. Budget: (FY 10 est.) *income:* $40.9 bil. *expend.:* $51.5 bil. G.D.P.: $538.6 bil., $8,100 per capita (2009 est.). Chief crops: rice, cassava, sugar, corn, rubber, manioc, coconuts, soybean. Natural resources: tin, rubber, natural gas, tungsten, tantalum. Major industries: tourism, textiles and garments, agricultural processing, beverages; world's second-largest tungsten producer and third-largest tin producer. Labor force: 38.24 mil. (2009 est.); 42.4% agriculture, 19.7% industry, 37.9% services including government; 1.7% unemployment (2007). Exports: $150.9 bil. (2009 est.); computers and parts, textiles, rice. Imports: $131.5 bil. (2009 est.); capital goods, intermediate goods, consumer goods, fuels. Major trading partners: (2009) *exports:* 10.9% U.S., 10.6% China, 10.3% Japan, 6.2% Hong Kong, 5.6% Australia, 5% Malaysia; *imports:* 18.7% Japan, 12.7% China, 6.4% Malaysia, 6.3% U.S., 5% United Arab Emirates, 4.3% Singapore.

Ethnic Thai migrating south from China after about A.D. 1000 created a number of petty states in the region, most notably the kingdom of Sukhothai. These came under the influence of Indian civilization from the adjacent states of Burma and the Khmer empire, and Buddhism became established as the dominant religion of the Thai. A unified kingdom of Siam was established c. 1350, with its capital at Ayutthaya. Portuguese and other European traders and missionaries were active in Siam after 1511.

In 1767 Ayutthaya was destroyed in a war with Burma. In 1782 the Chakkri dynasty was established at Bangkok and restored the power of the Thai monarchy. By skillfully playing off the European powers against one another, Kings Mongkut (r. 1851–68) and Chulalongkorn (r. 1868–1910) enabled Siam to be the only Southeast Asian nation to escape European colonization or political domination. In a series of treaties with Great Britain and France, however, King Chulalongkorn was forced to renounce Siam's claims to portions of Malaya, Laos, and Cambodia.

Absolute monarchy ended in 1932, when a military coup forced the granting of a constitution. Japanese troops occupied Siam in Dec. 1941. Siam concluded a nominal alliance with Japan in 1942 and declared war on Great Britain and the U.S, while the monarchy secretly supported a strong anti-Japanese resistance movement. A period of postwar political turmoil ended with the accession in 1950 of King Phumiphon, who instituted a reformist and pro-Western policy.

Thai politics since World War II have been democratic but dominated by an oligarchy of military officers and civilians with strong military ties. During the Vietnam War, Thailand was an important staging area for American forces. Since then, U.S. and other foreign investment contributed to significant economic growth.

On Dec. 8, 1990, Prime Minister Chatichai Choonhavan resigned amid charges of corruption. Reappointed by the king the next day, Chatichai was overthrown on Feb. 23 by military forces, who invited former diplomat Anand Panyarachun to serve as interim prime minister. After parliamentary elections in March 1992, Gen. Suchinda Kraprayoon, was named prime minister in a government dominated by the military. Mass demonstrations against the Suchinda government, led by former Bangkok governor Chamlong Srimuang, culminated on May 17–18, when troops fired on demonstrators, causing hundreds of fatalities. The king intervened and Suchinda resigned. Chamlong agreed to call off the demonstrations and Anand Panyarachun was invited to head another transitional government, and Parliament agreed in principle to a new constitution with a provision that the prime minister must be an elected member of Parliament.

Parliamentary elections in 1992 gained a majority for a five-party coalition headed by Chuan Leekpai that managed to govern for almost three years, liberalizing financial arrangements, spending heavily on infrastructure, and bringing Thailand to an 8 percent growth rate in 1994. In elections held in 1995, the Thai Nation party captured the largest number of seats; its leader, Banharn Silpa-Archa, became prime minister but the party lost the 1996 elections and a coalition government led by General Chavalit took over. Only six months later the Thai economy began a steep decline and the currency was devalued in June 1997. The U.S. and the I.M.F. agreed to provide loans to stabalize the economy. Chuan Leekpai returned as prime minister in Nov. 1997.

Elections in Jan. 2001 brought a near majority to the Thai Rak Thai party of computer and telecommunications billionaire Thaksin Shinawatra, who was named prime minister but who faced serious legal charges of tax evasion. The Constitutional Court acquitted Thaksin by a vote of 8–7 and with no written opinion issued. In early 2005, shortly after the tsunami devastated parts of Thailand he won a convincing electoral victory. In July he signed an emergency decree that allowed him broad powers to ban public gatherings, detain suspects, etc. all to help fight a growing insurgency. But by 2006 Thaksin was under pressure to resign and in Sept., while he was at the U.N. in New York, the military removed him in a bloodless coup and installed a retired general, Surayud Chulanont, as prime minister, promising a new constitution and election. Thaksin and his party were banned from politics for five years.

In Aug., 2007, voters strongly approved the new constitution and elections in December Thaksin's party prevailed but Thaksin himself remained in exile. Samak Sundaravej, a Thaksin protege, was elected prime minister. Thaksin returned to face corruption charges but when his wife was convicted of tax evasion (Aug.) they both fled the country. Massive protests against the government began in August and in September a new prime minister was chosen, Thaksin's brother-in-law, Somchai Wongsawat. In December 2008 the Thaksin forces lost power to the opposition Democratic Party with the young Abhisit Vejjajiva becoming prime minister. But now Thaksin's supporters continued daily protests, blocking streets for months until in April government troops used extreme force to disperse them. (See "Major News Stories.")

▶ **TIMOR-LESTE**
Democratic Republic of Timor-Leste
● **GEOGRAPHY**   Location: eastern half of island of Timor. Boundaries: Banda Sea to N, Timor Sea to S, Indonesia to W. Coastline: 706 km. Comparative area: slightly larger than Connecticut. Land use: 8% arable; 5% permanent crop; 87% other. Total land area: 7,336 sq. mi. (19,000 sq km). Major cities: Dili (capital).
● **PEOPLE**   Population: 1, 131, 612 (July 2009 est.). Nationality: noun—Timorese; adjective—Timorese. Ethnic Groups: Austronesian (Malayo-Polynesian), Papuan, small Chinese minority. Languages: Tetum and Portuguese (official); Eng-

lish, Indonesian. **Religions:** 90% Roman Catholic, 4% Muslim, 3% Protestant.

● **GOVERNMENT** **Type:** Republic. **Independence:** May 20, 2002 (from Indonesia; Nov. 28, 1975 from Portugal). **Constitution:** March 22, 2002. **National Holiday:** Independence Day: Nov. 28. **Head of Government:** José Ramos-Horta, president (since May 2007); Kay Rala X. Gusmão, prime minister (since Aug. 2007).

● **ECONOMY** Monetary unit: Indonesian Rupiah. **Budget:** (2007) *income:* $733 mil., *expend.:* $309 mil. **G.D.P.:** $2.713 bil., $2,400 per capita (2008 est.). **Chief crops:** coffee, rice, maize, cassava. **Natural resources:** gold, petroleum, natural gas, manganese, marble. **Major industries:** printing, soap manufacturing, handicrafts, woven cloth. **Labor force:** N.A., 50% unemployment. **Exports:** $10 mil. note - excludes oil. (2005 est.); oil, coffee, sandalwood, marble. **Imports:** $202 mil (2004 est.); mainly food. **Major trading partners:** (2006) *exports:* U.S., Germany, Portugal, Australia, Indonesia; *imports:* N.A.

Early in the 16th century, Portuguese traders settled on some of the islands of the Malayan Archipelago, including Timor, and established trading posts there. In 1613 rival traders from the Netherlands settled in western Timor and began the slow process of pushing the Portuguese eastward. (The actual boundary on Timor was no settled by treaty until 1859.) As Dutch, and then British, power waxed through the 17th century, that of Portugal waned, leaving but a handful of fragments, like Goa and Macao and East Timor, of the Portuguese eastern sea empire.

But unlike the Dutch or English, the Portuguese sought to maintain close bonds among economic, political, and religious expansion. A missionary effort made East Timor something of a Catholic enclave amidst the predominantly Muslim Dutch East Indies (and, after 1949, Indonesia). Still, as late as 1975 only about one-third were Catholic; it was the independence struggle that brought the Catholic presence to its current 90 percent.

The leftist coup in Portugal in April 1974, with its socialist, democratic, but above all anti-imperialist ideology, led to the abandonment of East Timor; in Dec. 1975 Indonesia began its brutal conquest and annexation which led to an enduring guerilla warfare and eventually independence. The 1998 fall of Indonesia's dictator Suharto gave space for the 1999 U.N.-sponsored referendum on independence: 78 percent voted "yes." While Muslim militias, aided by segments of the Indonesian armed forces, ravaged the country, a U.N. trusteeship, run principally by Australia and Portugal, readied the new state for independence, finally celebrated May 20, 2002 under its first president, resistance leader José Gusmao. In 2006, a military mutiny toppled the government and Nobel Peace Prize recipient, José Ramos-Horta became prime minister. A 3,000-member U.N. international peacekeeping force was deployed and in 2007 Ramos-Horta was elected president, bringing hope the violence could be stopped. But an assasination attempt against Ramos-Horta disspelled that idea and the U.N. considered extending its mandate.

▶**TOGO**
Togolese Republic
● **GEOGRAPHY** **Location:** western coast of Africa. **Boundaries:** Burkina Faso to N, Benin to E, Gulf of Guinea to S, Ghana to W. **Total area:** 21,927 sq. mi. (56,790 sq km). **Coastline:** 35 mi. (56 km). Com-

parative area: slightly smaller than West Virginia. **Land use:** 41% arable land; 2% permanent crops; 57% other. **Major cities:** Lomé (capital); Sokodé; Kpalimé; Atakpamé; Tsevie.

● **PEOPLE** **Population:** 6,019,877 (July 2009 est.). **Nationality:** noun—Togolese (sing., pl.); adjective—Togolese. **Ethnic groups:** 37 groups; largest are Ewe, Mina, and Kabre; under 1% European and Syrian-Lebanese. **Languages:** French (both official and language of commerce); Ewe and Mina in south, Dagomba and Kabyè in north. **Religions:** about 51% indigenous beliefs, 29% Christian, 20% Muslim.

● **GOVERNMENT** **Type:** republic under transition to multiparty democratic rule; **Independence:** Apr. 27, 1960 (from U.N. trusteeship under French administration). **Constitution:** Sept. 27, 1992. **National holiday:** Independence Day, Apr. 27. **Heads of Government:** Faure E. Gnassingbé, president (since May 2005); Gilbert Houngbo, prime minister (since Sept. 2008). **Structure:** executive—president appoints prime minister; unicameral legislature—National Assembly; judiciary.

● **ECONOMY** Monetary unit: Communauté Financière Africaine (CFA) franc. **Budget:** (2008 est.) *income:* $551.5 mil.; *expend.:* $620.1 mil. **G.D.P.:** $5.105 bil., $900 per capita (2008 est.). **Chief crops:** coffee, cocoa, cotton, yams, cassava, corn, beans, rice; meat, fish. **Natural resources:** phosphates, limestone, marble. **Major industries:** phosphate mining, agricultural processing, cement, handicrafts, textiles, beverages. **Labor force:** 1.302 mil. (1998 est.); 65% agriculture, 30% services, 5% industry. **Exports:** $1.001 bil. (f.o.b., 2008); cotton, phosphates, coffee, cocoa. **Imports:** $1.725 bil. (f.o.b., 2008); machinery and equipment, consumer goods, petroleum products. **Major trading partners:** (2006) *exports:* 16.7% Ghana 14.4% Burkina Faso, 9.1% Benin, 6.1% Belgium, 5.8% Mali, 5.4% Germany, 4.6% India, 4.6% Netherlands; *imports:* 29.8% China, 10.9% U.K., 8.9% France, 6% Netherlands, 5.8% Belgium, 4.6% U.S., 4.2% Estonia.

Ewe-speaking peoples began to migrate into what is now Togo, located on Africa's west coast, early in the 14th century. Portuguese explorers arrived in the late 15th century, turning the coast into a point of departure for slaves captured from nearby villages, and between the 1600s and 1800s, the region became known as the "Slave Coast." Germans started to explore and trade in the region in the mid-19th century and declared a protectorate over the area in 1884. After World War I, however, Britain and France divided the nation between them, Britain receiving the western third, France the eastern two-thirds. The League of Nations confirmed this arrangement, giving mandates to British Togoland (later a part of Ghana) and French Togoland.

In 1956 France made French Togo an autonomous republic but retained control of its foreign affairs, defense, and currency; Nicholas Grunitzky was prime minister. The United Nations rejected this plan and in elections in 1958 advocates of complete independence won control of the legislature. On Apr. 27, 1960, French Togo cut its ties with France and became the fully independent Republic of Togo. Sylvanus Olympio became the new nation's first prime minister. Grunitzsky went into exile but returned when Olympio was assassinated in January 1963. He led the new government and oversaw the writing of a new constitution allowing more political freedoms.

In 1967 army officers led by Lt. Col. Gnassingbé Eyadema overthrew Grunitzsky, suspended the constitution, and named Eyadema president. In 1990, Eyadema was forced out by democratic reformers, and Kokou J. Koffigoh was elected prime minister by a national conference in 1991. Eyadema resumed the presidency in 1992, but his refusal to embrace multiparty democracy and Koffigoh's weak leadership led to violence and public calls for the ouster of both men. Under a new constitution, ratified in 1992, General Eyadema's party, Rally of the Togolese People, dominated, with prime ministers coming and going at his pleasure. In 2002, parliament amended the constitution, removing the two-term limit on the presidency and in 2003 Eyadema was elected again. Upon his death on Feb. 5, 2005 the army pushed to have one of his sons, Faure Gnassingbé, proclaimed president and the legislature agreed. But pressure from the African Union and weeks of violent street protests led to elections in April. Gnassingbé was declared the winner and again protests erupted and in 2007 free and fair elections were finally held and the government was reelected so E.U. economic cooperation was restored.

▶ TONGA
Kingdom of Tonga
• **GEOGRAPHY Location:** 172 islands in South Pacific Ocean, 36 permanently inhabited. Nuku'alofa 21°09'S, 175°14'W. **Boundaries:** surrounded by South Pacific Ocean; Fiji is about 400 mi. (650 km) to NW and Western Samoa lies N. **Total area:** 289 sq. mi. (748 sq km). **Coastline:** 260 mi. (419 km). **Comparative area:** four times the size of Washington, D.C. **Land use:** 20% arable land; 15% permanent crops; 65% other. **Major cities:** Nuku'alofa (capital); Tongatapu; Vava'u; Ha'apai; Eua.
• **PEOPLE Population:** 120,898 (July 2009 est.). **Nationality:** noun—Tongan(s); adjective—Tongan. **Ethnic groups:** Polynesian; about 300 Europeans. **Languages:** Tongan, English. **Religions:** Christian (Free Wesleyan Church claims over 30,000 adherents).
• **GOVERNMENT Type:** hereditary constitutional monarchy. **Independence:** June 4, 1970 (from U.K.). **Constitution:** Nov. 4, 1875; revised Jan. 1, 1967. **National holiday:** Independence Day, June 4. **Heads of Government:** King George Tupou V (since Sept. 2006); Feleti Sevele, premier (since Feb. 2006). **Structure:** executive—king, prime minister, cabinet; unicameral legislature—30-seat Legislative Assembly, 9 elected by popular vote, 12 are for cabinet ministers, 9 reserved for nobles; judiciary—appointed by king.
• **ECONOMY Monetary unit:** pa'anga. **Budget:** (2007 est.) *income:* $80.48 mil.; *expend.:* $109.8 mil. **G.D.P.:** $549.1 mil. , $4,600 per capita (2008 est.). **Chief crops:** squash, coconut, copra, bananas, vanilla beans, cocoa, coffee, ginger, black pepper, fish. **Natural resources:** fish, fertile soil. **Major industries:** tourism, fishing. **Labor force:** 33,910 (2003 est.); 65% engaged in agriculture. **Exports:** $22 mil. (f.o.b., 2006); squash, fish, vanilla. **Imports:** $139 mil. (f.o.b., 2006); food products, machinery and transport equipment, fuels, chemicals. **Major trading partners:** (2006) *exports:* 39.7% U.S., 27.8% Japan, 8.2% New Zealand, 7.6% South Korea; *imports:* 30.3% Fiji, 27.7% New Zealand, 8.2% U.S., 7.5% Australia, 5.7% France, 4.7% U.K.

The Polynesian islands that now compose Tonga were settled some 3,000 years ago. A highly stratified society whose the kings of Tonga dominated much of Polynesia by the 13th century. The islands were visited in 1643 by Abel Tasman, and in 1773 by Capt. James Cook, who named them the Friendly Islands. English missionaries arrived in 1797, and the islands came under British political influence. A code of laws was promulgated in 1862, and a constitutional monarchy established in 1875. A series of treaties with Western powers recognized Tonga's independence, but the kingdom became a British protectorate in 1900.

The islands were outside the Japanese perimeter in the Pacific theater of World War II. On June 4, 1970, the British dissolved their protectorate and the Kingdom of Tonga became independent as a member of the British Commonwealth. King Taufa'ahau Tupou IV came to the throne in 1965 and survived until 2006.

Tonga joined the U.N. in late 1999 and a movement for democratic reform soon followed. In 2006 rioting helped bring changes and elections in 2008 brought a pro-democracy government.

▶ TRINIDAD AND TOBAGO
Republic of Trinidad and Tobago
• **GEOGRAPHY Location:** two islands (Port of Spain, Trinidad Is., 10°38'N, 61°31'W; Tobago Is., 11°11'N, 60°45'W) in southeastern Caribbean Sea, off northeastern South America. **Boundaries:** Caribbean Sea to N and W, Atlantic Ocean to E and S. **Total area:** 1,981 sq. mi. (5,130 sq km). **Coastline:** 225 mi. (362 km). **Comparative area:** slightly smaller than Delaware. **Land use:** 15% arable land; 9% permanent crops; 26% other. **Major cities:** Port of Spain (capital); San Fernando; Arima (borough).
• **PEOPLE Population:** 1,229,953 (July 2008 est.). **Nationality:** noun—Trinidadian(s), Tobagonian(s); adjective—Trinidadian, Tobagonian. **Ethnic groups:** 40% Indian, 37.5% African, 20.5% mixed, 2% other. **Languages:** English (official), Hindi, French, Spanish, Chinese. **Religions:** 26% Roman Catholic, 22.5% Hindu, 7.8% Anglican, 14% other Protestant, 5.8% Muslim.
• **GOVERNMENT Type:** parliamentary democracy. **Independence:** Aug. 31, 1962 (from U.K.). **Constitution:** Aug. 1, 1976. **National holiday:** Independence Day, Aug. 31. **Heads of Government:** George Maxwell Richards, president (since Mar. 2003); Kamla Persad-Bissessar, prime minister (since May 2010). **Structure:** executive—is cabinet led by prime minister; bicameral legislature (elected House of Representatives and appointed Senate); judiciary headed by chief justice and includes court of appeal, high court, and lower courts.
• **ECONOMY Monetary unit:** Trinidad and Tobago dollar. **Budget:** (2008 est.) *income:* $7.421 bil.; *expend.:* $7.141 bil. **G.D.P.:** $24.19 bil., $18,600 per capita (2008 est.). **Chief crops:** sugar, cocoa, coffee, rice, citrus, bananas; poultry. **Natural resources:** crude oil, natural gas, asphalt. **Major industries:** petroleum, chemicals, tourism. **Labor force:** 615,400 (2007 est.); 66% services, 30% industry, 4% agriculture. **Exports:** $15.9 bil. (f.o.b., 2008); petroleum and petroleum products, chemicals, steel products, fertilizer, sugar, cocoa, coffee, citrus, flowers. **Imports:** $9.843 bil. (f.o.b., 2008 est.); machinery, transport equipment, manufactured goods, food, live animals. **Major trading partners:** (2006) *exports:* 50% U.S., 5% Spain, 5% Jamaica; *imports:* 31% U.S., 12% Brazil, 7% Venezuela, 5% Gabon, 4% Colombia.

Trinidad was a possession of Spain from 1498 to 1797, when it was surrendered to the British. England took control of Tobago in 1802. Together the two islands achieved independence from the U.K. in 1962. Prime Minister Arthur Robinson's National Alliance for Reconstruction currently governs the country. Civil and political rights are well respected, and political party competition tends to divide along ethnic (black, East Indian) lines. Agrarian reform designed to create tenable landholdings is a central political issue.

In 1990, militant Muslims seized Prime Minister A.N.R. Robinson and dozens of others in Parliament, paralyzing the government for five days. Peace was restored when the government promised reforms. People's National Movement candidate Carson Charles was elected prime minister in 1991, and in the interest of preserving the peace, he granted the Muslim militants amnesty in 1992. Robinson won the presidential election in 1997 in a landslide. Dec. 2001 elections produced an 18–18 tie between the (Indian-descent) United National Congress and the (African-descent) People's National Movement. Both parties agreed to allow Pres. Robinson to choose. His choice: Patrick Manning of the P.N.M. Under his direction the nation has prospered mainly from sales of natural gas to the U.S., and methanol and ammonia to the rest of world. He was succeeded by Maxwell Richards who continued to strengthen the island's commitment to natural gas exports.

▶ TUNISIA
Republic of Tunisia
• **GEOGRAPHY Location:** northern coast of Africa. **Boundaries:** Mediterranean to N and E, Libya to SE, Algeria to W. **Total area:** 63,170 sq. mi. (163,610 sq km); includes land and inland waters. **Coastline:** 714 mi. (1,148 km). **Comparative area:** slightly larger than Georgia. **Land use:** 19% arable land; 13% permanent crops; 68% other. **Major cities:** Tunis (capital); Sfax (Safaqis); Ariana; Ehadhamen; Sousse.
• **PEOPLE Population:** 10,486,339 (July 2009 est.). **Nationality:** noun—Tunisian(s); adjective—Tunisian. **Ethnic groups:** 98% Arab, 1% European, 1% Jewish and other. **Languages:** Arabic (official), Arabic and French (commerce). **Religions:** 98% Muslim, 1% Christian, 1% Jewish and other.
• **GOVERNMENT Type:** republic. **Independence:** Mar. 20, 1956 (from France). **Constitution:** June 1, 1959, amended July 12, 1988. **National holiday:** Independence Day, Mar. 20. **Heads of Government:** Zine el-Abidine Ben Ali, president (since Nov. 1987); Mohamed Ghannouchi, prime minister (since Nov. 1999). **Structure:** executive dominant; unicameral legislature (Chamber of Deputies) largely advisory; judiciary patterned on French and Koranic systems.
• **ECONOMY Monetary unit:** Tunisian dinar. **Budget:** (2008 est.) *income:* $9.843 bil.; *expend.:* $11.3 bil. **G.D.P.:** $81.88 bil., $7,900 per capita (2008 est.). **Chief crops:** olives, dates, oranges, almonds, grain, sugar beets, grapes; poultry, beef, dairy products. **Natural resources:** crude oil, phosphates, iron ore, lead, zinc. **Major industries:** petroleum, mining (particularly phosphates and iron ore), tourism, textiles. **Labor force:** 3.676 mil.; 55% services, 23% industry, 22% agriculture; 13.9% unemployment (2007 est.); shortage of skilled labor. **Exports:** $19.22 bil. (f.o.b., 2008 est.); hydrocarbons, textiles, agricultural products, phosphates and chemicals. **Imports:** $23.23 bil. (f.o.b., 2007 est.); industrial goods, hydrocarbons, food. **Major trading partners:** (2006) *exports:* 29% France, 20% Italy, 9% Germany, 6% Spain, 5% Libya, 4% U.S.; *imports:* 25% France, 22% Italy, 10% Germany, 5% Spain.

The Phoenicians, an ancient seafaring people from the eastern Mediterranean, founded settlements in Tunisia dating back to 1000 B.C. The most important of these was Carthage, which dominated trade in the central Mediterranean until it was conquered and destroyed by Rome in 146 B.C. Tunisia remained part of the Roman Empire until it was conquered by the Vandals in the mid-fifth century A.D. The Byzantine Empire reconquered Tunisia in the sixth century. Tunisia became part of the Arab world with the expansion of Islam in the seventh century and soon emerged as a principal center of Islamic culture in North Africa. Tunisia was incorporated into the Ottoman Empire in 1574 and was ruled from Constantinople by Turkish governors, or beys.

With the waning of Ottoman power in the 19th century, Tunisia became a French protectorate in 1881. Nationalist movements began in the early 20th century. During World War II Tunisia was under Vichy French rule and was the scene of fighting between the Axis and Allies in 1942–43. Nationalist unrest resumed when France reestablished its rule in the postwar period. Widespread popular unrest in the early 1950s led to a French grant of self-rule in 1954. Full independence was proclaimed on Mar. 20, 1956; large numbers of French settlers returned to France. The French-sponsored monarchy was abolished in 1957, and the Neo-Destour (New Constitution) party under the leadership of Habib Bourguiba took power. Bourguiba was elected president in 1959 without opposition and was named president for life. Under his rule, political parties flourished, leading to both democratic politics and the granting of legal status of women.

Relations with France were strained in 1964 when Tunisia nationalized foreign assets but have since improved. The basic thrust of Tunisian government was socialist, with state ownership of principal industries and heavy subsidies of basic commodities. In foreign affairs Tunisia has been closely tied to France and has been a moderate voice within the Arab League.

Popular unrest and labor strife characterized Tunisia's internal situation in the 1980s, as political maneuvering began in anticipation of the end of the Bourguiba era, which came in 1987 when the aged leader was overthrown by Ben Ali. In 1989 new elections were planned as part of a political and economic restructuring. Ben Ali was elected president, twice winning 99 percent of the vote, while his party won virtually all the seats in the National Assembly. In 1994 and 1995, however, the political stability was threatened by radical Muslim groups both from within and from Algeria. Rumors of brutal repression were rife. In Oct. 1999, in Tunisia's first "multiparty" elections, Ben Ali was re-elected president, again with 99.42 percent of the vote while his Constitutional Union Party carried 148 of the 182 parliamentary seats.

Tunisia's economy has developed rapidly, led by textiles, food processing and other light industry, tourism, phosphate mining, and other mineral processing. The large agricultural sector includes grain, olives, dates, and winter fruits and vegetables for export to Europe. In 1998 the government reached an accord with the E.U. to lower trade barriers, and with other African nations in 2004. Fundamentalist Muslims have periodically resorted to violence since then and have been brutally repressed.

▶ TURKEY
Republic of Turkey
• **GEOGRAPHY Location:** partly in southeastern Europe and partly in western Asia. **Boundaries:** Black Sea to N; Georgia and Armenia to NE; Iran

to E; Iraq, Syria, Mediterranean Sea to S; Aegean Sea, Greece to W; and Bulgaria to NW. **Total area:** 301,382 sq. mi. (780,580 sq km). **Coastline:** 4,471 mi. (7,200 km). **Comparative area:** slightly larger than Texas. **Land use:** 35% arable land; 3% permanent crops; 62% other. **Major cities:** Ankara (capital); Istanbul; Izmir; Adana; Bursa.
• **PEOPLE Population:** 77,804,122 (July 2010 est.). **Nationality:** noun—Turk(s); adjective—Turkish. **Ethnic groups:** 80% Turkish, 20% Kurdish. **Languages:** Turkish (official), Kurdish, Arabic. **Religions:** 99.8% Muslim (mostly Sunni), 0.2% other (mostly Christian and Jewish).
• **GOVERNMENT Type:** republican parliamentary democracy. **Independence:** Oct. 29, 1923 (from Ottoman Empire). **Constitution:** Nov. 7, 1982. **National holiday:** Independence Day. **Heads of Government:** Abdullah Gul, president (since Aug. 2007); Recep Tayyip Erdogan, prime minister (since Mar. 14, 2003). **Structure:** executive—president empowered to call new elections, promulgate laws (elected for seven-year term); unicameral legislature; independent judiciary.
• **ECONOMY Monetary unit:** Turkish lira. **Budget:** (2009) *income:* $145.3 bil.; *expend.:* $180.6 bil. **G.D.P.:** $863.3 bil., $11,200 per capita (2009 est.). **Chief crops:** cotton, tobacco, grain, olives, sugar beets, pulses, citrus; livestock. **Natural resources:** antimony, coal, chromium, mercury, copper. **Major industries:** textiles, food processing, mining (coal, chromite, copper, boron minerals). **Labor force:** 25.3 mil. (2009 est.); 35.9% agriculture, 41.2% services, 22.8% industry; about 1.2 million Turks work abroad (2004 est.); 9.7% unemployment (2007 est.). **Exports:** $102.2 bil. (2009 est.); 28% textiles and apparel, 17% foodstuffs, 9% iron and steel products. **Imports:** $140.8 bil. (2009 est.); 29% machinery, fuels, minerals, foodstuffs. **Major trading partners:** (2009) *exports:* 9.6% Germany, 6.1% France, 5.8%, U.K., 5.8% Italy, 5% Iraq *imports:* 14% Russia, 10% Germany, 9% China, 6.1% U.S., 5.4% Italy, 5% France.

The Hittites, an Indo-European people, created an empire in Anatolia before 2000 B.C. and controlled most of what is modern-day Turkey for nearly 1,000 years. The rise of Troy and other Hellenic city-states on the coast of Asia Minor and the expansion of the Assyrian empire led to the collapse of Hittite power by around 900 B.C. Except for some Hellenic enclaves on the Aegean Coast (Ionia), all of Turkey was incorporated into the Persian empire of Cyrus and Darius in the sixth century B.C. Alexander the Great conquered Turkey, but it returned to Persian rule following the collapse of his empire, c. 300 B.C.

All of Turkey, comprising Thracia, Galatia, Cappadocia, Cilicia, and other provinces, was incorporated into the Roman Empire by the end of the first century A.D. Constantine the Great founded the city of Constantinople on the site of ancient Byzantium in 330 as the empire's eastern capital. Following the decline of the western Roman Empire, Constantinople became the capital of the Eastern Roman (Byzantine) Empire. The Byzantine Empire fought off repeated attacks by Arab Islamic forces in the seventh and eighth centuries but lost control of central Anatolia to the Seljuk Turkish rulers of Persia after 1038.

The 13th-century Mongol invasions left Turkey largely untouched but weakened both Byzantine and Seljuk power. At the end of the 13th century, the Ottomans, a small Turkish tribe, expanded from their stronghold in western Anatolia and within a century captured most of Turkey, Bulgaria, and Serbia. Constantinople fell to the Ottomans in 1453. By the middle of the 16th century, the Ottoman Empire extended from southeastern Europe into the Crimea and Iran and included most of the Middle East, Egypt, and Arabia.

At its height the Ottoman Empire was a great world power and a substantial participant in European international relations. But in the 18th century, the empire lost much of its autonomy through unequal treaties with European powers, and throughout the 19th century, parts of the empire were detached and either granted independence or placed under European protection. The Ottoman Empire became the "Sick Man of Europe." A liberal constitution was adopted in 1876 but largely ignored until the Young Turk Rebellion of 1908 forced the sultan to accept its provisions.

Siding with the Central Powers in World War I, the Ottoman Empire lost most of its non-Turkish possessions to the Allies. The Treaty of Sèvres (1920) reduced the Ottoman state to a small part of northern Anatolia. Before the treaty was ratified, however, Kemal Ataturk seized power and regained much territory in a series of campaigns with Soviet assistance. The Treaty of Lausanne (1923) established the present boundaries of Turkey, which was proclaimed a republic. The Caliphate was renounced in 1924, ending the Ottoman claim of leadership in the Islamic world.

The Turkish Republic became officially a secular and multiethnic state. Large numbers of Armenians had been killed or driven from the country in widespread campaigns of persecution in the late 19th and early 20th centuries; after 1923 most Greek and Bulgarian residents were forcibly repatriated. The large minority of Kurds in southeastern Turkey were pressured to abandon their ethnic identity. Today more than 85 percent of the population is Turkish. Islam is widely practiced, but the veil and other Islamic dress were prohibited, as were religious political parties. In 1928 the Latin alphabet was adopted in place of Arabic script for writing Turkish. In 1930 Constantinople was officially renamed Istanbul.

Turkey joined the League of Nations in 1932. A series of treaties in the 1930s made small adjustments to Turkey's borders and confirmed Turkey's status as a European nation. Under Ismet Inonu, who became president upon Ataturk's death in 1938, Turkey remained neutral throughout most of World War II but declared war against Germany in Jan. 1945 and became a founding member of the United Nations. Following World War II, Turkey became a major recipient of American aid under the Truman Doctrine. Turkish troops joined U.N. forces in the Korean War. Continuing the Europe-oriented policy, Turkey joined NATO.

In 1974, long-standing discord with Greece erupted over the status of Cyprus, an independent nation with strong ties to Greece. On July 20, 1974, Turkish troops invaded Cyprus, occupying the northeastern 40 percent of the island. The United States cut off military aid to Turkey in 1975. Turkey forced resettlement of Greek and Turkish Cypriot residents; the Turkish sector seceded from Cyprus and became a Turkish federated state on July 8, 1975. American aid was restored in 1978.

Politically, postwar Turkey has alternated between civil and military governments. In the wake of mounting violence, martial law was imposed in 1978, and a military takeover of the government occurred on Sept. 12, 1980. Civil government was restored in 1983, and martial law lifted in 1984.

Turkey tried to remain aloof from the political turmoil of the Middle East, but it was a crucial member of the anti-Iraq coalition in the Persian

Gulf War. It supported the U.N. trade embargo and allowed the Allies to use Turkish bases. The Kurdish problem was aggravated after the war as Turkey tried to offer humanitarian assistance to Kurdish refugees from Iraq without encouraging Kurdish nationalists at home. A continuing insurgency in the southeast led to sporadic but serious violence in 1992-93. Muslim fundamentalists became more active and several violent episodes resulted in deaths and destruction.

Pres. Turgut Özal died in Apr. 1993. He was succeeded as president by Prime Minister Suleyman Demirel. On June 14 the ruling True Path party elected as the new prime minister, Mrs. Tansu Ciller, Turkey's first-ever woman prime minister. While the economy was her first concern (inflation hit 70 percent in 1994), military operations against the Kurdish rebels intensified with the launching of an attack into Iraq by 50,000 Turkish troops who aimed to end guerrilla raids.

The Ciller government collapsed in a corruption scandal, and elections held in Dec. 1995 gave Refah (Welfare), a pro-Islamic political party, its first national victory. The other parties, committed to the long tradition of secularism, refused to form a government with the Welfare party. After months of successive coalition governments, in June 1996 the Welfare party leader, Necmettim Erbakan, became prime minister of Turkey's first openly pro-Islamic government. A year later, he was forced from office by pressure from Turkey's military. In the wake of this de facto military coup, the new prime minister, Mesut Yilmaz, put together a fragile coalition government in July 1997 that closed some Islamic schools and banned traditional Muslim garb while the Supreme Court banned Erbakan from politics for five years.

Violence in Cyprus flared up in 1998 but the E.U.'s rejection of Turkey's application was the most serious event of the year. In 1999 Turkey finally wrung an accord from Syria not to aid Kurd rebels (with 10,000 Turkish troops poised on Syria's border), but the Yilmaz government still lost a vote of confidence on corruption charges. Pres. Demirel asked Bulent Ecevit to form a minority, interim government. The results were splintered, and the president asked Ecevit to stay on as head of a coalition government. Kurdish leader Ocalan was apprehended in Nairobi and, after trial, sentenced to death by hanging. From his cell, Ocalan renounced Kurdish independence and called upon his band to stop fighting.

In Aug. 1999 an earthquake brought great devastation and the loss of thousands of lives. It also brought aid from both the E.U. and Greece; Turkey reciprocated in the September earthquake in Greece. In Feb. 2000 the Kurd leadership renounced all violence. In May, Parliament elected chief justice Ahmet Necdet Sezer president to succeed Demirel. Faced with a mass hunger strike by political prisoners in Dec. 2000, Pres. Sezer announced an amnesty plan to release 72,000. A personal argument between Sezer and Ecevit in 2001 provoked fears of government instability which led to a serious economic crisis as foreign investors pulled out of Turkey and the currency lost one-third of its value. While the I.M.F. signalled its approval of Ecevits's economic reforms in a series of loans, parliament voted to hold new elections in Nov. 2002, 18 months early. Justice and Development (an offshoot of the Islamic Welfare Party) gained 363 of the 550 seats, the first majority government in 15 years. None of the cabinet formed by Abdullah Gul had any public association with Islam. In December, President Sezer first vetoed,

then signed a constitutional amendment to allow the party's leader, Recip Erdogan, to run for Parliament. He carried a March 2003 by-election with 85 percent of the vote and was named prime minister. Parliament refused to allow U.S. troops to deploy in preparation for the Iraq invasion.

In June 2003 Parliament, in an attempt to apease E.U. sentiment, voted certain civil rights for Kurds. The military budget was brought under parliamentary control and members of the Kurdish Workers Party (PKK) granted amnesty. In June 2004, however, PKK ended a defacto cease-fire and began sporadic attacks on government troops. In Aug. 2006 two terrorist attacks on tourist areas by Kurdish seperatists revived tensions, and in June 2007, Turkish troops massed on the border of Iraq threatening to invade Kurdistan to halt terrorist attacks but withdrew suddenly.

Turkish politics were roiled in April 2007 elections when the military as well as hundreds of thousands of protesters objected to the election of Abdullah Gul, a religious Muslim as president. Prime Minister Erdogan quickly scheduled elections for July and his party won a very strong victory. Parliament elected Gul president in Aug. 2007. In 2008 parliament approved a measure that could lead to women being allowed to wear head scarves in universities. A case to ban the Islamic Party failed in court. On the world stage, Turkey has emerged as a key player politically and economically because of its location. In 2009 Turkey made separate agreements with both Russia and four European nations to facilitate the flow of natural gas. In Sept. 2010 voters gave strong support to constitutional reforms that will revamp the one the military imposed 30 years ago.

▶ TURKMENISTAN

- **GEOGRAPHY Location:** southwestern central Asia. **Boundaries:** Kazakhstan to N, Uzbekistan to N and E, Iran to S, Afghanistan to SE, Caspian Sea to W. **Total area:** 188,456 sq. mi. (488,100 sq km). **Coastline:** Caspian Sea. **Comparative size:** slightly larger than California. **Land use:** 4% arable land; 0% permanent crops; 96% other. **Major cities:** Ashkhabad (capital); Chardzou (Carzou).
- **PEOPLE Population:** 4,884,887 (July 2009 est.). **Nationality:** noun—Turkmen; adjective—Turkmen. **Ethnic groups:** 85% Turkmen, 5% Uzbek, 4% Russian, 6% other. **Languages:** 72% Turkmen (official), member of southern Turkic language group written in Cyrillic script since 1940; 12% Russian, 9% Uzbek, ethnic languages. **Religions:** 89% Muslim, 9% Eastern Orthodox, 2% unknown.
- **GOVERNMENT Type:** republic. **Independence:** Oct. 27, 1991 (from Soviet Union). **Constitution:** May 18, 1992. **National holiday:** Independence Day, Oct. 27. **Head of Government:** Gurbanguly Berdymukhammedov, president (since Feb. 2007). **Structure:** executive—president, Council of Ministers; bicameral legislature; judicial—Supreme Court.
- **ECONOMY Monetary unit:** Turkmen manat. **Budget:** (2008 est.) *income:* $1.667 bil; *expend.:* $1.407 bil. **G.D.P.:** $29.65 bil., $6,100 per capita (2008 est.). **Chief crops:** cotton, grain; livestock. **Natural resources:** petroleum, natural gas, coal, sulfur, sodium chloride. **Major industries:** natural gas, oil, petroleum products, textiles. **Labor force:** 13.51 mil. (2004). **Exports:** $11.92 bil. (f.o.b., 2008 est.); 63% oil and gas, 18% cotton. **Imports:** $5.66bil. (c.i.f., 2008 est.); chemicals, foodstuffs, machinery and parts. **Major trading partners:** (2006) *exports:* 47.7% Ukraine, 16.4% Iran, 5.3% Azerbaijan; *imports:* 15.5% United Arab Emirates,

11.1% Turkey, 9.1% Ukraine, 9% Russia, 7.8% Germany, 7.6% Iran, 6.4% China, 4.5% U.S.

Turkmenistan, long a battleground for warring Asian empires, is bordered on the north by Uzbekistan and Kazakhstan, and on the west by the Caspian Sea. It also has a long international border with Iran and Afghanistan. About 90 percent of Turkmenistan is covered by the Kara Kum (Black Sand) desert, one of the largest in the world, and the southern areas are mountainous and prone to serious earthquakes.

A very remote and sparsely populated country, Turkmenistan has been inhabited since prehistoric times, first by Iranian-speaking people, then by Turkic tribes. In the 10th century A.D., Oghuz tribes (from Mongolia) arrived, bringing Islam with them. Although the Turkmen had emerged as a distinct ethnic group by the 15th century, they were ruled by the Persians in the south and the Uzbek khanates in the north for about 200 years. In the 19th century, Russian expansionism into Turkmen territory had begun, culminating in the Russian victory in the famous 1881 battle of Gok Tepe that killed 150,000 Turkmen.

In 1917 the Bolsheviks unsuccessfully attempted to seize power in Turkmen territory. By Apr. 30, 1918, the Soviets succeeded in creating the Turkestan Autonomous Soviet Socialist Republic (ASSR) as part of the Russian republic, but in July the ASSR was overthrown by nationalist elements with the help of the British. Once the British withdrew, however, the territory of Turkmen fell to the Soviets, and in 1924 the National Delimitation of Central Asian Republics took place. This created several central Asian republics, including the Turkmen Soviet Socialist Republic, which came into being on Oct. 27, 1924.

The nomadic Turkmen people suffered enormously under forced collectivization and the many bloody antireligious campaigns. The purges of Turkmen intelligentsia in the 1930s were widespread. The Soviets undertook a small-scale industrialization campaign in Turkmenistan, but aside from the extraction of natural gas and petroleum, the majority of the population continued to work in agriculture.

Under Gorbachev, the environment became the main issue for Turkmenistan. Large-scale cotton planting had led to serious environmental and health hazards. The Kara Kum Canal, which carries water from the Amu-Dar'ya to Turkmenistan's arid regions, is one of the main factors leading to the desiccation of the Aral Sea. Turkmenistan's main cultural issue was the status of the Turkmen language, for until May 1990 the official language had been listed as Russian (although only 25 percent of Turkmen people claimed to speak Russian). Due to its remoteness, Turkmenistan did not become involved in the democratic changes that engaged the other former union republics. Its Communist party dominated and still dominates Turkmen politics, although the Turkmen president, Saparmurat A. Niyazov (1990–2006), stood for popular election and was elected by direct ballot in Oct. 1990 by 98.3 percent of the population. However, the Turkmen government has banned demonstrations, picketing, and strikes, and it censors its media.

Turkmenistan was one of the early supporters of Gorbachev's proposal to form a new Union Treaty. When that led to the 1991 coup in Moscow, the Turkmen Supreme Soviet claimed independence on Oct. 27, 1991. Since then, Turkmenistan has begun to develop political and economic relations with Iran and Turkey. With vast oil and gas reserves Turkmenistan faces a brighter future than it ever expected.

Niyazov was overwhelmingly endorsed in a referendum, held Jan. 15, 1994 extending his mandate until 2002, bypassing a constitutional requirement for the reelection of a president every five years. In 1998 Niyazov visited the U.S., conferring with Pres. Clinton and concluding agreements with several U.S. energy firms to study the possibility of a cross-Caucasian gas pipeline to Turkey and the west (bypassing Iran). In Dec. 1999 the 50-member parliament elected (unanimously) Niyazov president-for-life (as recommended by the People's Council, headed by Niyazov). The cult of personality grew to an incredible state as the Council renamed the month of January after him in 2002. His iron-fisted rule has led the U.S. State Dept. to say he governs in a "Soviet-era authoritarian style." Niyazov was suspected of embezzling huge sums from the gas revenues, as he cuts pensions and benefits. In Dec. 2006, he died suddenly of heart disease at age 66. A special election, heavily influenced by the government, in Feb. 2007, gave 90 percent of the vote to a former aide to Niyazov, Gurbanguly Berdymakhammedov. In July he made a deal with Russia to build a pipeline north of the Caspian Sea to guarantee Russian access to natural gas. In 2009 he also made pipeline deals with Iran and China.

▶ TUVALU

• **GEOGRAPHY** **Location:** group of nine small atolls, about 350 mi. (560 km) from N to S, in South Pacific Ocean. Funafuti 8°30s, 179°12'E. **Boundaries:** surrounded by South Pacific Ocean; Kiribati to N, Fiji to S, Solomon Islands to W. **Total area:** 10 sq. mi. (26 sq km). **Coastline:** 15 mi. (24 km). **Comparative area:** one-tenth size of Washington, D.C. **Land use:** 0% arable land; 0% permanent crops; 100% other. **Major cities:** Funafuti (capital); Vaitupu; Niutao; Nanumea; Nukufetau.
• **PEOPLE** **Population:** 12,373 (July 2009 est.). **Nationality:** noun—Tuvaluan(s); adjective—Tuvaluan. **Ethnic groups:** 96% Polynesian. **Languages:** Tuvaluan, English. **Religions:** 97% Church of Tuvalu (Congregationalist), 1.4% Seventh-Day Adventists, 1% Baha'i.
• **GOVERNMENT** **Type:** parliamentary democracy. **Independence:** Oct. 1, 1978 (from U.K.). **Constitution:** Oct. 1, 1978. **National holiday:** Independence Day, Oct. 1. **Heads of Government:** Filoimea Telito, governor-general; Apisai Ielemia, prime minister (since Aug. 2006). **Structure:** executive—prime minister and cabinet; unicameral legislature—12-member House of Assembly; judicial—high court, chief justice presides over sessions twice a year.
• **ECONOMY** **Monetary unit:** Tuvaluan dollar or Australian dollar. **Budget:** (2006) *income:* $21.54 mil.; *expend.:* $23.05 mil. **G.D.P.:** $12.2 mil., $1,100 per capita (2002 est.). **Chief crops:** coconuts; fish. **Natural resources:** fish. **Major industries:** fishing, tourism, copra. **Labor force:** 3,615 (2004 est.). **Exports:** $1 mil. (f.o.b., 2004); copra. **Imports:** $12.91 mil. (c.i.f., 2005); food, animals, mineral fuels, machinery, manufactured goods. **Major trading partners:** (2006) *exports:* 60.5% Germany, 20.1% Italy, 6.9% Fiji; *imports:* 46.1% Fiji, 18.9% Japan, 18.2% China, 7.7% Australia, 4.1% New Zealand.

A British protectorate was established in 1892, and the islands were incorporated into the British colony of the Gilbert and Ellice Islands in 1915. The nine principal islands that make up the Ellice group escaped Japanese occupation in World War II and were used as Allied bases in the campaign to recapture the Pacific.

The Gilbert and Ellice Islands colony was granted self-rule in 1971. In 1975 the Ellice Islands, inhabited mainly by Polynesians, seceded from the other (mainly Micronesian) islands of the colony and became independent as Tuvalu on Oct. 1, 1978. (See also "Kiribati.") In a 1979 U.S.-Tuvalu friendship treaty, the United States relinquished claims, based on 19th-century guano mining, to the four southernmost islands, in return for access to World War II military airfields and veto power over other nations' use of the islands for military purposes.

The economy is based on subsistence farming and fishing. Exports include copra and woven palm-leaf products, and hydroponic agriculture and offshore fisheries are being developed. Tuvalu remains heavily dependent on foreign aid, principally from Australia, New Zealand, and the United Kingdom. In 2000, Tuvalu was admitted to the U.N.

▶ **UGANDA**
Republic of Uganda
• **GEOGRAPHY Location:** landlocked equatorial country in eastern Africa. **Boundaries:** Sudan to N, Kenya to E, Tanzania to S, Rwanda to SW, Zaire to W. **Total area:** 91,135 sq. mi. (236,040 sq km). **Coastline:** none. **Comparative area:** slightly smaller than Oregon. **Land use:** 25% arable land; 9% permanent crops; 9% meadows and pastures; 56% other. **Major cities:** Kampala (capital); Jinja; Mbale; Masaka; Gulu.
• **PEOPLE Population:** 32,369,558 (July 2009 est.). **Nationality:** noun—Ugandan(s); adjective—Ugandan. **Ethnic groups:** 17% Baganda, 8% Basogo, 8% Iteso, 7% Bakiga, 6% Langi, 6% Rwanda, 5% Bagisu, 4% Acholi, 4% Lugbara, 3% Bunyoro, 2% Karamojong. **Languages:** English (official), Luganda, Swahili, Arabic and other Niger-Congo languages. **Religions:** 33% Roman Catholic, 33% Protestant, 16% Muslim, 18% indigenous beliefs.
• **GOVERNMENT Type:** republic. **Independence:** Oct. 9, 1962 (from UK). **Constitution:** Oct. 8, 1995, amended in 2005. **National holiday:** Independence Day, Oct. 9. **Heads of Government:** Yoweri Kaguta Museveni, president (since Jan. 1986); Prof. Apolo Nsibambi, prime minister (since Apr. 1999). **Structure:** executive—president is head of government and state; unicameral legislature; judiciary.
• **ECONOMY Monetary unit:** Ugandan shilling. **Budget:** (2008 est.) *income:* $2.621 bil.; *expend.:* $2.939 bil. **G.D.P.:** $35.88 bil., $1,100 per capita (2008 est.). **Chief crops:** coffee, cotton, tobacco; beef, milk, poultry. **Natural resources:** copper, cobalt, limestone, salt. **Major industries:** sugar, brewing, tobacco. **Labor force:** 14.54 mil. (2007 est.); 82% agriculture, 13% services, 5% industry. **Exports:** $2.017 bil. (f.o.b., 2008); coffee, gold, fish. **Imports:** $3.594 bil. (f.o.b., 2008); transportation equipment, petroleum, medical supplies, cereals. **Major trading partners:** (2006) *exports:* 10% Belgium, 9% Netherlands, 8% France, 8% Germany, 6% Rwanda, 5% Sudan; *imports:* 34% Kenya, 9% United Arab Emirates, 7% China, 6% India, 5% South Africa, 4% Japan.

Prior to 1800 Uganda was the site of several important kingdoms, notably Buganda, centered on Kampala on the northern shore of Lake Victoria. After 1830, Arabs from the sultanate of Oman, based in Zanzibar, asserted loose control over the region and dominated its trade. British explorers, seeking the source of the Nile, reached the Lake Victoria region in the mid-19th century. Mission stations were established in 1877; a Muslim rebel-lion destroyed the missions and occupied Kampala in 1888.

Uganda was brought under the control of the British East Africa Company in 1890, and Britain established a protectorate in 1894 that was expanded to include neighboring territories in 1896. In 1902 some of the protectorate's territory was transferred to Kenya. British immigrants extensively developed the agricultural potential of Uganda's fertile and temperate highlands, establishing large and prosperous farms. Lake Victoria was the scene of naval battles between Great Britain and Germany during World War I.

In 1955 the British administration created a local parliamentary government in which both whites and Africans held ministerial office. Talks on the terms for independence began in 1961 and after some difficulty arrived at a formula for a national structure in which Buganda and other traditional kingdoms would retain local autonomy. Several political parties competed for power; the Uganda People's Congress led by Milton Obote became dominant. Uganda became independent within the British Commonwealth on Oct. 9, 1962. Several constitutional changes in the early 1960s led to an end to the autonomy of the kingdoms and the effective concentration of all power in Obote's presidency. In 1967 a new constitution proclaimed Uganda an independent republic.

Obote was overthrown on Jan. 25, 1971, by Idi Amin Dada, commander of Uganda's armed forces. Amin declared himself president, dissolved the Parliament, and assumed absolute powers. In 1972 he expelled Uganda's Asians (primarily people of Indian and Pakistani descent), who controlled most of the country's small-scale commerce. The U.S. broke off diplomatic relations in 1973. In 1976 Amin declared himself president for life. His eight-year reign was marked by extreme violence and persecution of political and tribal opponents; as many as 300,000 may have been killed between 1971 and 1979. The country's prosperous economy was devastated, and its infrastructure, including a good road and rail network and Makerere University, fell into ruins.

On July 3, 1976, Israeli airborne troops landed at Entebbe and rescued 103 hostages who had been captured in a skyjacking carried out by Palestinian and German terrorists. In 1978 Amin, with the aid of Libyan troops, invaded Tanzania. Tanzanian troops countered by invading Uganda; they captured Kampala on Apr. 11, 1979, and drove Amin into exile. Diplomatic relations with the U.S. resumed. Elections in 1981 returned Obote to power. Obote's new regime was marked by repression of opponents and by rebellion in the northern part of the country by the National Resistance Army (NRA) under Yoweri Museveni.

Obote fled into exile in 1985 and was succeeded by Lt. Gen. Basilio Olara-Okello, but the NRA rebellion continued. Kenyan president Daniel arap Moi mediated peace talks between Olara-Okello and the NRA in late 1985; in Jan. 1986 Olara-Okello fled, and Museveni organized a new government. Despite continued insurgencies by rival military factions and a rebellion led by the charismatic religious leader, Alice Lakwena, the Museveni government restored order and, with aid from the World Bank and the I.M.F., began to rebuild Uganda's shattered society.

A constituent assembly was elected in 1994. In 1995, it enacted a new constitution, which extended for five years a ban on political parties, and scheduled presidential elections for 1996, elections Museveni won easily. By 1997 Uganda had the fastest growing economy in Africa and in 1998 Pres. Clinton's visit helped to create interest among foreign investors. Museveni won re-election as president in 2001 and announced in April that Uganda was withdrawing from the Congo peace accord and its troops were withdrawing also since they had accomplished their aim of defeating the Hutu extremists who threatened Uganda's borders.

In 2002 fighting within Uganda intensified against the Lord's Resistance Army (LRA), a militia largely of the Acholi tribe, led by Joseph Kony, seeking to establish a theocracy based upon the Ten Commandments through mass kidnapping, rape, and murder both in northern Uganda and in the Sudan. In 2008 the LRA agreed to a ceasefire, but in December a U.S.-backed plan to attack the rebels went badly and the initiative was shelved. In 2010 violence returned with Somali Islamic terrorists bombing a large gathering of World Cup fans watching a game on an outdoor TV. More than 20 were killed.

▶**UKRAINE**
• **GEOGRAPHY Location:** east-central Europe. **Boundaries:** Belarus to N, Russian Federation to NE and E, Sea of Azov and Black Sea to S, Moldova and Romania to SW, Hungary, Slovakia, Poland to W. **Total area:** 233,089 sq. mi. (603,700 sq km). **Coastline:** Black Sea. **Comparative area:** slightly smaller than Texas. **Land use:** 57% arable land; 2% permanent crops, 41% other. **Major cities:** Kiev (capital); Kharkov (Kharkiv); Dnepropetrovsk; Donetsk (Donetske); Odessa (Odesa).
• **PEOPLE Population:** 45,415,596 (July 2010 est.). **Nationality:** noun—Ukrainian(s); adjective—Ukrainian. **Ethnic groups:** 78% Ukrainian, 17% Russian, 5% other. **Languages:** Ukrainian, Russian, Romanian, Polish, Hungarian. **Religions:** Ukrainian Orthodox—Moscow Patriarchate, Ukrainian Orthodox—Kiev Patriarchate, Ukrainian Autocephalous Orthodox, Ukrainian Catholic, Protestant; Jewish.
• **GOVERNMENT Type:** republic. **Independence:** Aug. 24, 1991 (from Soviet Union). **Constitution:** June 28, 1996. **National holiday:** Independence Day, Aug. 24. **Heads of Government:** Viktor Yanukovych, president (since Feb. 2010); Mykola Azarov, prime minister (since Mar. 2010). **Structure:** executive—president, Cabinet of Ministers; legislative—Supreme Council (450 deputies); judicial—Supreme Court.
• **ECONOMY Monetary unit:** hryvnia. **Budget:** (2009) **income:** $26.35 bil.; **expend.:** $34.37 bil. **G.D.P.:** $294.3 bil., $6,400 per capita (2009 est.). **Chief crops:** grain, sugar beets, sunflower seeds, vegetables; meat, milk. **Natural resources:** coal, iron ore, manganese, natural gas, oil. **Major industries:** coal, electric power, metals, machinery and transport, chemicals. **Labor force:** 20.4 mil. (2009 est.); 32% industry and construction, 24% agriculture and forestry, 44% services, 32% industry. **Exports:** $41.49 bil. (2009 est.); energy, chemicals, machinery and transport equipment. **Imports:** $45.58 bil. (2009 est.); energy, machinery and parts, transportation equipment, chemicals. **Major trading partners:** (2008) **exports:** 21.1% Russia, 5.3% Turkey, 3.8% China; **imports:** 28% Russia, 8.6% Germany, 6.1% China, 4.9% Kazakhstan.

Ukraine is the center of the original Russian state, known as Kievan Rus, which came into existence in the ninth century A.D. In the 13th and 14th centuries, during the Mongol invasion, Ukraine was controlled by Lithuania and Poland, and in 1654 it first entered the Russian empire. In the latter half of the 17th century, Ukraine was di-

vided, with the eastern regions becoming part of Russia and the western part annexed by Poland; when Poland was subsequently partitioned, the western sections were ceded to Austria.

Until 1917 eastern Ukraine was a province of Russia called "Little Russia," and for two centuries the dominant country tried to Russianize the Ukrainian clergy and upper classes, and ban the Ukrainian language. Nevertheless, secret societies for the study of Ukrainian history, language, and culture formed, and when in the 19th century the Russians exiled Ukrainians to Siberia, modern Ukrainian nationalism was born.

In 1917, when the Russian empire collapsed, Ukrainian nationalists demanded Ukraine's autonomy by establishing a Ukrainian People's Republic, but within a few months, Red Army troops had occupied Ukraine. For the next few years, however, Ukraine was in the middle of the civil war and was even ceded to Germany under the Brest-Litovsk treaty of 1918, but in December 1920 a Ukrainian Soviet Socialist Republic (SSR) was established. Ukraine again was divided under the 1921 Treaty of Riga, which gave western Ukraine to Poland, Czechoslovakia, and Romania, while eastern Ukraine formed the Ukrainian SSR. Ukraine became one of the original members of the U.S.S.R. in December 1922.

The Ukrainians strongly opposed Stalin's policy of forced collectivization of agriculture in the 1930s, and the resulting chaos, famine, and deportation resulted in the deaths of millions of Ukrainians. Likewise, Stalin's great terror of the 1930s hit Ukraine hard, with the first victims being Ukrainian nationalists. World War II largely devastated Ukraine and killed millions of Ukrainians, but as a result of the war, Ukraine regained its old territories from Romania and Poland and was enlarged by the addition of historical Tatar lands in 1954. (The native Tatar inhabitants were forcibly deported to central Asia in the 1940s.)

Mikhail Gorbachev's policy of glasnost was slow to take root in Ukraine, largely because the head of the Communist party in Ukraine was a loyal Brezhnev crony, Vladimir Shcherbitsky. Outwardly, he appeared to agree with Gorbachev's policies, but Ukraine dissidents were still being arrested and cultural groups harassed by secret police. In 1986 a deadly nuclear power explosion at Chernobyl—and Soviet attempts at covering it up—turned international attention to Ukraine and gave rise to a number of new, powerful opposition movements. Rukh (the Ukrainian People's Movement for Restructuring), the most important of these, was founded in Kiev by a prominent group of intellectuals. By 1989 branches of Rukh had been organized in most parts of Ukraine. At the same time, Ukrainian miners became active in strikes, and the Ukrainian Catholic church and the Ukrainian Orthodox church became politically active. Shcherbitsky's failure to contain these groups led to his dismissal in 1989.

On July 16, 1990, the Ukrainian Supreme Soviet adopted a declaration of sovereignty, and Communist party Secretary Leonid Kravchuk became chairman of the Supreme Soviet. In March 1991 Ukraine participated in the negotiations to form a new union treaty, despite more radical demands by Rukh for complete independence. The Ukrainian Communist party's failure to denounce the attempted coup in Moscow in August 1991 led to significant changes in Ukraine's political situation. After the coup collapsed, the Communist party was banned, and on Aug. 24, 1991, Ukraine adopted a declaration of total independence and Kravchuk was elected president.

Ukraine, Belarus, and the Russian Federation signed the Minsk Agreement that created the Commonwealth of Independent States, and on Dec. 21, Ukraine and 10 other former union republics officially committed themselves to the union by signing the Alma-Ata Declaration.

Potentially dangerous conflicts with Russia remained, however, including control of the powerful Black Sea fleet. Soon after the fall of the Soviet government armed conflict erupted in April 1994, when Russia removed a ship from Odessa laden with marine-research and navigational equipment valued at more than $10 million. A compromise was reached in 1995 that divided the 635-vessel fleet equally, with Russia then buying 32 percent of the ships from the Ukraine and paying rent for use of the naval base at Sevastopol.

The other conflict involved 2,000 nuclear warheads present in Ukraine. In Jan. 1994, Kravchuk, Boris Yeltsin, and Bill Clinton negotiated an agreement to dismantle Ukraine's 175 long-range missiles and more than 1,800 warheads. But Ukraine's Parliament refused, even after Clinton made a $350 million U.S. aid package conditional on total disarmament. Kravchuk in July 1994 lost the presidential election to reformer Leonid Kuchma. In Nov. Parliament overwhelmingly approved the Nuclear Nonproliferation Treaty and loans from the U.S. and the I.M.F. ensued. The U.S. also pledged $400 million to help dismantle the missiles.

In July 1996 the Rada approved a new "strong president" Constitution which guaranteed rights to own property and to engage in business, abolished local councils ("soviets"), and made Ukrainian the only legal language. The May 1997 Friendship Treaty with Russia settled the Black Sea fleet division, guaranteed Russia's right to rent part of the port facilities of Sevastopol to service the fleet, and confirmed Ukrainian sovereignty over all of Crimea.

In Aug. 1998 the I.M.F. agreed to loans totalling $2.2 bil. to assist the government despite its inability to make reforms. Kuchma easily won re-election in Nov. 1999. Kuchma's authority began to unravel in November when charges, backed by tape recordings, surfaced that he had connived in the murder of an opposition journalist; the tapes also held evidence of election tampering and bribery. Although Kuchma's future seemed shaky, a coalition government emerged that supported him. Large public protests arose and by late 2004 grew to such an extent that Kuchma tried to rig the presidential elections. An "Orange Revolution" for a new vote and Victor Yuschenko emerged as the solid winner but by Aug. 2006 he was forced to cede power to Viktor Yanukovych, a man he once called "a bandit." New elections in Sept. 2007 gave a bit more power to pro-Russian parties, but Yuschenko returned to power with the support of Prime Minister Yulia Tymoshenko. Their government collapsed in Sept. 2008 and the next year a paralysis set in that had kept the government ineffective and vulnerable to Russian threats involving the cutoff of gas supplies during the winter. In Feb. 2010 Yanukovych won a run-off election over Ms. Tymoshenko and immediately made waves by making a 25-year deal for Russia to continue its lease for the Black Sea Fleet. The downturn in the world economy hit Ukraine hard forcing it to ask for a loan from the I.M.F.

▶ UNITED ARAB EMIRATES

● **GEOGRAPHY** **Location:** eastern Arabian peninsula. **Boundaries:** Persian Gulf to N, Gulf of Oman to NE, Oman to E, Saudi Arabia to S and W, short frontier with Qatar to NW. **Total area:** 31,969 sq. mi. (82,880 sq km). **Coastline:** 819 mi. (1,318 km). **Comparative area:** slightly smaller than Maine. **Land use:** negl.% arable land; negl.% permanent crops; 99% other. **Major cities:** Abu Dhabi (capital); Dubai; Sharjah.

● **PEOPLE** **Population:** 4,975,593 (July 2010 est.). **Nationality:** noun—Emirati(s); adjective—Emirati. **Ethnic groups:** 19% Emirati, 23% other Arab and Iranian, 50% South Asian, 8% other expatriates (includes Westerners and East Asians); less than 20% of population are UAE citizens (1982). **Languages:** Arabic (official), Persian, English, Hindi, Urdu. **Religions:** 96% Muslim (16% Shia), 4% Christian, Hindu, and other.

● **GOVERNMENT** **Type:** federation with specified powers delegated to UAE central government and other powers reserved to member emirates. **Independence:** Dec. 2, 1971 (from UK). **Constitution::** Dec. 2, 1971; made permanent 1996. **National holiday:** National Day, Dec. 2. **Heads of Government:** Sheikh Khalifa Bin Zayed Al-Nahyan, president (since Nov. 2004); Muhammad Bin Rashid al-Maktum, prime minister (since Jan. 2006). **Structure:** executive—Supreme Council of Rulers (seven members), from which president and vice president are elected; prime minister and Council of Ministers; unicameral legislature—Federal National Council; judicial—Union Supreme Court.

● **ECONOMY** **Monetary unit:** Emirian dirham. **Budget:** (2009 est.) *income:* $54.05 bil.; *expend.:* $54.68 bil. **G.D.P.:** $201.4 bil., $42,000 per capita (2009 est.). **Chief crops:** dates, vegetables, watermelons; poultry, eggs, dairy products; fish. **Natural resources:** crude oil, natural gas. **Major industries:** petroleum, petrochemicals. **Labor force:** 3.168 mil. (2009 est.); 78% services, 15% industry and commerce, 7% agriculture. **Exports:** $174 bil. (2009 est.); 45% crude oil, natural gas, re-exports, dried fish, dates. **Imports:** $141 bil. (2009 est.); manufactured goods, machinery and transport equipment, chemicals, food. **Major trading partners:** (2008) *exports:* 26.5% Japan, 10.9% South Korea, 10.7% India, 7.5% Iran; *imports:* 12.9% China, 12% India, 8.6% U.S., 6.4% Germany.

In the 1820s Great Britain established protectorates over seven small sheikhdoms along the gulf coast between Qatar and Oman—Abu Dhabi, Dubai, Sharjah, Ajmar, Fujairah, and Umm al-Qaiwain. The region, which had been known as the Pirate Coast, then was generally referred to as the Trucial Coast or Trucial Oman. Under terms of a treaty in 1892, the sheikhdoms agreed not to enter into relations with any other country.

After Great Britain announced that it would withdraw its forces from the gulf in 1971, the seven sheikhdoms formed a federation and became independent as the United Arab Emirates on Dec. 2, 1971.

Just prior to his invasion of Kuwait in August 1990, Saddam Hussein threatened both the UAE and Kuwait for overproduction of petroleum, and the UAE was an integral part of the Allied coalition against Iraq. In 1995 the government signed a defensive alliance with France, who supplies the army with most of its weapons.

The economy is almost entirely dominated by petroleum. Citizens of the UAE receive extensive social services and enjoy one of the world's highest per capita incomes. The government has embarked on an enormous building program to create modern cities in the desert and has created plans to expand the economy beyond oil.

▶ UNITED KINGDOM
United Kingdom of Great Britain and Northern Ireland

• **GEOGRAPHY** **Location:** northwestern Europe, occupying major portion of British Isles. **Boundaries:** Atlantic Ocean to NW and W, North Sea to E; separated from France by English Channel to S; Republic of Ireland to W. **Total area:** 94,525 sq. mi. (244,820 sq km). **Coastline:** 7,723 mi. (12,429 km). **Comparative area:** slightly smaller than Oregon. **Land use:** 26% arable land; negl. % permanent crops; 473% other. **Major cities:** London (capital); Birmingham; Leeds; Glasgow; Sheffield.

• **PEOPLE** **Population:** 61,284,806 (July 2010 est.). **Nationality:** noun—Briton(s), British (collective pl.); adjective—British. **Ethnic groups:** 83.6% English, 8.6% Scottish, 2.9% Irish, 4.9% Welsh, 1.8% Ulster, 2.8% West Indian, Indian, Pakistani, and other. **Languages:** English, Welsh (about 26% of population of Wales), Scottish form of Gaelic (about 60,000 in Scotland). **Religions:** 71.6% Christian, 2.7% Muslim, 1% Hindu, 1.6% other, 23.1% unspecified and none.

• **GOVERNMENT** **Type:** constitutional monarchy. **Independence:** N.A. **Constitution:** unwritten; partly statutes, partly common law and practice. **National holiday:** Celebration of the Birthday of the Queen, second Saturday in June. **Heads of Government:** Elizabeth II, queen (since Feb. 1952); David Cameron, prime minister (since May 2010). **Structure:** executive authority lies with collectively responsible cabinet led by prime minister; legislative authority rests with Parliament (House of Lords, House of Commons); House of Lords is supreme judicial authority and highest court of appeals.

• **ECONOMY** **Monetary unit:** British pound. **Budget:** (2009 est.) *income:* $819.9 bil.; *expend.:* $1.132 tril. **G.D.P.:** $2.149 tril., $35,200 per capita (2009 est.). **Chief crops:** cereals, oilseed, potatoes, vegetables; cattle, sheep, poultry; fish. **Natural resources:** coal, crude oil, natural gas, tin, limestone. **Major industries:** machinery and transportation equipment, metals, food processing. **Labor force:** 31.25 mil. (2009); 80.4% services, 18.2% industry, 1.4% agriculture (2006 est.), 4.7% unemployment (2005 est.). **Exports:** $351.3 bil. (2009 est.); manufactured goods, machinery, fuels, chemicals. **Imports:** $473.6 bil. (2009 est.); manufactured goods, machinery, fuels, foodstuffs. **Major trading partners:** (2008) *exports:* 13.8% U.S., 11.5% Germany, 7.8% Netherlands, 7.6% France, 7.5% Ireland, 5.3% Belgium; *imports:* 13% Germany, 8.7% U.S., 7.5% China, 7.4% Netherlands, 6.8% France.

Early megalithic and Iron Age peoples of Britain, primarily Celtic, developed tribal states that were conquered by Roman invaders in A.D. 43. After Roman legions withdrew from Britain in 410, invasions of Jutes, Angles, and Saxons conquered much of England, while Celtic peoples flourished in Wales, Scotland, and especially Ireland. Viking invaders established settlements in the eighth century. A united Saxon kingdom fell to the Norman invasion of William the Conqueror in 1066.

An aristocratic rebellion against the royal absolutism of King John in 1215 led to the royal acceptance of the Magna Carta, guaranteeing legal rights and laying the foundations of parliamentary government. From the 12th to the 15th century, the Plantagenet dynasty ruled England and claimed overlordship over Ireland; Wales was con-

quered in 1283. The Plantagenets also controlled sizable territories in France.

The Hundred Years' War (1337–1453) cost England its French possessions; the War of the Roses, (1455–85) ended the Plantagenet dynasty and brought Henry Tudor (Henry VII) to the throne. The Tudors gradually centralized royal control by bringing pressure against both the church and the nobility. Henry VIII broke with Rome in 1534 and established the Church of England. Under Elizabeth I, the last of the Tudors, England defeated Spain at sea and laid the foundations of later worldwide English sea power. The English Renaissance began under Elizabeth I (1533–1603) with the works of Shakespeare and continued into the 17th century with Milton and Newton.

The Stuart dynasty was founded by James I (1566–1625), uniting the crowns of England and Scotland in 1603. The English Civil War (1642–49) culminated in the execution of Charles I and the proclamation of the Commonwealth (later the Protectorate) under Oliver Cromwell. The monarchy was restored with Charles II in 1660. In the bloodless Glorious Revolution (1688), James II fled before a Protestant army under the Dutch William of Orange, who married and ruled jointly with James's daughter Mary II. The English Bill of Rights established the supremacy of Parliament and made the government a model of constitutional monarchy.

In the last gasp of the Stuart claimants to the throne, Irish supporters of James II were defeated at the Battle of the Boyne (1690), which temporarily crushed Irish resistance to annexation by England. The United Kingdom was created when Scotland was joined with England in a common Parliament by the Act of Union in 1707. A Scottish uprising led by the Young Pretender, Charles Edward Stuart, was crushed at Culloden Moor in 1745. Ireland was made part of the United Kingdom in 1801.

In the 1700s the United Kingdom became the greatest sea power in the world, controlling an empire that included much of North America and India. Agrarian "enclosures" of the 18th century ruined the peasantry but created an entrepreneurial revolution in agriculture that ultimately led to greatly increased agricultural productivity. The capital created in the process contributed to the success of the Industrial Revolution, which over the next century made England the wealthiest land on earth.

Despite the loss of the 13 colonies after the American Revolution (1775–83), England consolidated its holdings in the Indian subcontinent, Australia and New Zealand, Malaya, Hong Kong, much of eastern Africa from "Cape to Cairo," and elsewhere. Britain's prosperity and moral purpose were embodied in the person of Victoria, Queen of Great Britain and Ireland (1836–1901) and Empress of India (from 1836).

The repeal of the protectionist Corn Laws in 1846 led to an agricultural depression and hastened the migration of labor from the countryside to the industrial cities. The rise of labor activism led in 1906 to laws granting privileged status to trade unions, which organized the Labour party to promote their interests.

Britain's involvement in the Triple Entente with France and Russia ensured its participation in World War I (1914–18) against Germany, Italy, and Austria-Hungary. Victory came at the cost of an entire generation of British youth, but Britain emerged from the war with its empire at a high point, adding Tanganyika, Jordan, Palestine, and Iraq as part of the postwar division of spoils. Most of Ireland became independent in 1921, however, leaving only Northern Ireland as part of the United Kingdom.

Between the two world wars, Britain's navy and air force were the largest in the world, its army the third largest. Yet its industry was aging, the Great Depression hit especially hard in the British Isles, strikes and labor unrest weakened the social fabric, and colonial ties began to weaken in the 1930s. Economic retrenchment led to a failure to rearm in the face of the rising threat of Hitler's Germany and Mussolini's Italy.

The Munich Pact of 1938 gave Hitler a license for war; his invasion of Poland in 1939 forced Britain into the conflict. When Winston Churchill became prime minister in 1940, Britain was under daily air attack and in danger of an invasion by sea, and the country was dependent on American friendship and lend-lease war materials. But 1941 brought alliance with the United States and the Soviet Union, and a slowly turning tide of war leading to victory in 1945. Still, postwar Britain dropped to the second rank of superpowers.

The coalition between the Conservative and Labour parties that had governed Great Britain during the war seemed no longer necessary in 1945 as the war wound down. Labour won a landslide victory in the 1945 elections; Churchill was recalled in the midst of the Potsdam Conference, and Clement Atlee became prime minister. A brief Labour flirtation with the U.S.S.R. quickly ended in the postwar 1940s; England became a founding member of the United Nations and also, in 1949, of NATO. As the Cold War took shape, Britain developed its own nuclear arsenal.

The Labour party nationalized the Bank of England along with railroads, public utilities, and heavy industry. A comprehensive welfare state apparatus was created, including a national health service, unemployment and retirement benefits, and free education at all levels. But Britain was in many respects too poor to afford such changes; in order to cut expenditures, the government hastened the process of withdrawal from colonies and military bases around the world. India was granted independence in 1947, and Palestine, Burma, and Ceylon in 1948–49.

The elections of 1951 brought Churchill back to the prime ministership at the head of a Conservative majority that would last for 13 years. The Conservatives returned steel and trucking to the private sector but in general refrained from undoing the social policies of their Labour predecessors. Economic growth began in the 1950s and held steady at about 2.5 percent per year, a significantly lower rate than in continental Europe; obsolescence, excessive wage and benefit settlements, and a low savings rate all took their toll. The coronation of Elizabeth II in 1953 added a much-needed element of national celebration.

Churchill retired in 1955 and was succeeded by Anthony Eden. Eden's government fell in 1956 over the failed Anglo-French invasion of Suez. Eden's fall in 1957 brought to power Harold Macmillan, who pursued close relations with the United States. Most important, he presided over the transformation of an empire to a commonwealth; in the early 1960s, Ghana, Nigeria, Malaya, Singapore, and numerous other colonies were granted independence and Commonwealth status. Immigrants from the Commonwealth promptly flocked to England, straining housing, social services, and the labor market and creating problems of assimilation that remain unsolved.

Britain under Macmillan was the moving force behind the European Free Trade Association in 1960. In 1961 Britain applied for membership in the EEC, but that application was humiliatingly vetoed by France's Charles de Gaulle in 1963. Macmillan's government fell with the Profumo Scandal of 1963, and Douglas Home became a caretaker prime minister pending new elections.

The 1964 elections brought the Labour party to power under Harold Wilson, whose moderate positions made him unpopular with his own party, especially when he sponsored legislation to ban wildcat strikes. Strikes, wage inflation, the steady growth of the public sector (including renationalization of the steel industry), and the rise of turmoil in Northern Ireland in 1968–69 combined to make public support for Labour evaporate.

The Conservative victory in the 1970 elections brought Edward Heath to the office of prime minister. Heath's government imposed ineffective wage controls in an attempt to slow inflation and passed the 1971 Industrial Relations Act to regulate unions. When unions defied that act, the government fell. Heath's major achievement was the United Kingdom's admission to the EC in 1973. Continued turmoil in Northern Ireland was met with the abolition of Ulster's Stourmount Parliament in 1972 and the imposition of direct British rule.

Wilson returned to the prime ministership in 1974 and retired in 1976, passing on the office to James Callaghan, who governed until 1979 at the head of a Labour-Liberal coalition. The continued power of trade unions was seen in the repeal of the Industrial Relations Act and the extension of union privileges. The left wing of the Labour party brought increasing pressure against defense spending, membership in NATO, and also loudly criticized American involvement in Vietnam.

The OPEC oil price rises of 1972–74 hurt Great Britain in the short run but also encouraged development of oil and gas fields in the North Sea, which made the nation a major petroleum exporter and helped revitalize its economy. Oil exploration in the North Sea also encouraged Scottish nationalism, with some damage to national unity, although in both Scotland and Wales, proposals in 1979 for separate parliaments were soundly defeated by plebiscites.

The 1979 elections brought the Conservatives to power again, behind Margaret Thatcher, Great Britain's (and Europe's) first female prime minister. She proved to be the only British prime minister in modern times to lead her party successfully in three elections. Thatcher's agenda involved undoing much of the course of postwar British history. The first target was inflation, attacked through a freeze on expenditures and reduction of government borrowing. The policy was a success; inflation fell from 18 percent in 1980 to 3 percent in 1989. But the austerity program had a high cost in unemployment, which remained at 14 percent in the mid-1980s. In 1982 national attention turned abruptly to overseas concerns, as Argentina invaded the Falkland ("Malvinas") Islands (only 300 miles east of Argentina), which it had long claimed as Argentine national territory, on Apr. 2. On May 21 British forces launched a counteroffensive, and the invading Argentine forces surrendered on June 14. The nation's success provoked an upsurge of patriotism that swept Thatcher's party into a second term in 1983.

After the election the government turned to denationalization of industry. Over $30 billion in state property—from industrial giants, such as Britoil and British Gas, to individual apartments in municipal housing projects—was sold to private interests. In 1986 the top income-tax rate dropped from 98 percent to 40 percent. Britain agreed in 1985 to return Hong Kong to Chinese sovereignty in 1997.

The 1987 elections pitted the Conservatives against a weak Labour party that opposed NATO missile deployment in Great Britain, advocating unilateral disarmament and calling for renationalization of industry and a return to higher taxes for the wealthy. The Conservatives easily won their third straight election. By 1989 the "Thatcher Revolution" had produced a decisive long-term economic recovery, but one that was unevenly distributed: the southern part of the country enjoyed an economic boom, while the older industrial cities of the north remained stagnant. In 1990 an economic slowdown and rising inflation led to a strong decline in support for Mrs. Thatcher and her government. She resigned in November 1990.

Thatcher was replaced by Chancellor of the Exchequer John Major, whose greatest challenge has been Britain's role in a united Europe, to which Britain now has a land link via the 31-mile Channel Tunnel (Chunnel), completed in 1994. In the April 1992 elections, the Conservatives, led by Major, won a comfortable 21-seat margin in Parliament despite a recession. Not since the Napoleonic Wars had a British political party been able to form four consecutive governments. Yet only 13 months later Major's ratings in the polls had fallen to 21 percent as the economy stalled and the Conservatives themselves split badly over the E.C.'s Maastricht Treaty. The Conservatives were further beset in 1994 with a series of tabloid scandals and allegations of political corruption concerning arms sales to Iraq and Malaysia. In 1994 the government clumsily handled the news that scientists had concluded that eating English beef could cause the fatal "mad-cow" disease. After insisting that there was no cause for alarm the government was forced to deal with an E.U. boycott.

The parliamentary election of May 1997 ended 18 years of Tory government with Labour winning its largest majority since 1935, 419 seats to the Conservatives 165. The new Prime Minister Tony Blair appointed a cabinet of political moderates. In 1997 Hong Kong was returned to China and in April 1998 the Blair government succeeded in negotiating a settlement in Northern Ireland.

In May 1999 the first elections to the Scottish Parliament and the Welsh Assembly were held. Labour won a plurality in both (over nationalist parties). The two bodies have authority over education, environment, health care, housing, and law enforcement. The Scottish Parliament also possesses authority to tax. In the 2001 elections Blair's Labour Party won a huge victory, taking 413 of 659 seats, the first time Labour had won two consecutive victories. The vote on invading Iraq in 2003 carried overwhelmingly (412–143); yet in the aftermath of victory serious troubles arose for the Blair government over the intelligence accounts used to justify British participation. Blair still won a decisive victory in the 2005 elections but his standing had declined. A terrorist attack in London in July 2005 killed 56 people and wounded hundreds. A year later the authorities arrested and charged 14 Muslim men in a plot to blow up planes headed to the U.S., and in 2007 a car loaded with explosives was crashed into a terminal at Glasgow airport, but with little damage. Tony Blair resigned in July 2007, replaced by Gordon Brown who quickly planned Britain's exit from Iraq. But the economy turned sour in 2008

and the Labor Party suffered its worst local election results in 40 years. With finance having become a central element in the economy, the great recession would force the government to take on huge amounts of debt to salvage failing banks and unemployment. In the 2010 election the nation proved so divided that the Conservatives could not win a majority and were forced to accept a deal with the much smaller Liberal Party to form a government. (See "Major News Stories.")

▶ **UNITED STATES OF AMERICA**
● **GEOGRAPHY** **Location:** 48 conterminous states in North America, between Atlantic and Pacific Oceans; Alaska in northwest North America; Hawaiian Islands in Pacific Ocean about 3,000 miles W of California. **Boundaries:** Canada to N; Atlantic Ocean to E; Gulf of Mexico, Mexico to S; Pacific Ocean to W. Alaska bounded on E by Canada, on S and W by Pacific Ocean, on W and N by Arctic Ocean. **Total area:** 3,717,797 sq. mi. (9,629,091 sq km). **Coastline:** 11,954 mi. (19,924 km). **Comparative area:** slightly larger than Brazil; fourth-largest country. **Land use:** 19% arable land; negl. % permanent crops; 80% other. **Major cities:** Washington, D.C. (capital); New York; Los Angeles; Chicago; Houston; Philadelphia; Miami.
● **PEOPLE** **Population:** 310,232,863 (July 2010 est.). **Nationality:** noun—American(s); adjective—American. **Ethnic groups:** 81.7% white, 12.9% black, 4.2% Asian, 1% Amerindian or Alaska native, .2% Hawaiian and other Pacific islander. **Languages:** predominantly English; sizable Spanish-speaking minority. **Religions:** 51.3% Protestant, 23.9% Roman Catholic, 4% none, 1% Jewish, 1.7% Mormon, 1.7% Muslim, 10% other.
● **GOVERNMENT** **Type:** federal republic; strong democratic tradition. **Independence:** July 4, 1776 (from U.K.). **Constitution:** Sept. 17, 1787, effective March 4,1789. **National holiday:** Independence Day, July 4. **Heads of Government:** Barack Obama, president (since Jan. 2009); Joseph Biden, vice president (since Jan. 2009). **Structure:** executive—president, vice president, cabinet; legislative—bicameral Congress (House of Representatives and Senate); judicial—Supreme Court; branches, in principle, independent and maintain balance of power.
● **ECONOMY** **Monetary unit:** United States dollar **Budget:** (2009) *income:* $1.914 tril.; *expend:* $3.615 tril. **G.D.P.:** $14.26 tril., $46,400 per capita (2009). **Chief crops:** wheat, other grains, corn, fruits, vegetables, cotton; beef, pork, poultry, dairy products; forest products; fish. **Natural resources:** coal, copper, lead, molybdenum, phosphates. **Major industries:** leading industrial power in the world, highly diversified; petroleum, steel, motor vehicles, aerospace, telecommunications, chemicals, electronics, food processing, consumer goods, fishing, lumber, mining. **Labor force:** 154.1 mil. (2009); 76.8% services, 22.6% industry, 0.6% agriculture; 4.6% unemployment (2007). **Exports:** $994.7 bil. (2009 est.); capital goods, automobiles, industrial supplies and raw materials, consumer goods, agricultural products. **Imports:** $1.445 tril. (2009 est.); crude oil and refined petroleum, machinery, automobiles, consumer goods, industrial raw materials, food and beverages. **Major trading partners:** (2008) *exports:* 20.1% Canada, 11.7% Mexico, 5.5% China, 5.1% Japan, 4.2% Germany; *imports:* 16.4% China, 15.7% Canada, 10.1% Mexico, 6.6% Japan, 4.6% Germany.

(For current events and history see Part I: "Major News Stories of the Year," and Part II: "Chronology of American History.")

▶ URUGUAY
Oriental Republic of Uruguay

• **GEOGRAPHY Location:** southeastern coast of South America. **Boundaries:** Brazil to N, Atlantic Ocean to E and S, Argentina to W. **Total area:** 68,039 sq. mi. (176,220 sq km). **Coastline:** 410 mi. (660 km). **Comparative area:** slightly smaller than Washington State. **Land use:** 7% arable land; negl. % permanent crops; 93% other. **Major cities:** Montevideo (capital); Salto; Paysandú; Las Piedras; Rivera.

• **PEOPLE Population:** 3,510,386 (July 2010 est.). **Nationality:** noun—Uruguayan(s); adjective—Uruguayan. **Ethnic groups:** 88% white, 8% mestizo, 4% black. **Languages:** Spanish, Portunol, or Brazilero; Portuguese-Spanish mix on the Brazilian frontier. **Religions:** 66% Roman Catholic, 2% Protestant, 1% Jewish, 30% nonprofessing or other (less than half of the adult population attends church regularly).

• **GOVERNMENT Type:** republic. **Independence:** Aug. 25, 1825 (from Brazil). **Constitution:** Nov. 27, 1966; effective Feb. 1967; suspended June 27, 1973; constitutional reforms approved Jan. 7, 1997. **National holiday:** Independence Day, Aug. 25. **Head of Government:** Jose Mujica Cordano, president (since Mar. 2010). **Structure:** executive—headed by president; bicameral legislature (Senate and House of Deputies); national judiciary headed by Supreme Court.

• **ECONOMY Monetary unit:** Uruguayan peso. **Budget:** (2009 est.) *income:* $8.841 bil.; *expend.:* $9.666 bil. **G.D.P.:** $44.52 bil., $12,700 per capita (2009 est.). **Chief crops:** wheat, rice, corn, sorghum; livestock; fishing. **Natural resources:** fertile soil, hydropower potential, minor minerals, fisheries. **Major industries:** meat processing, wool and hides, sugar. **Labor force:** 1.636 mil. (2009 est.); 76% services, 9% agriculture, 15% industry; 9.2% unemployment (2007). **Exports:** $6.32 bil. (2009 est.); wool and textile manufactures, beef and other animal products, rice, fish. **Imports:** $6.576 bil. (2009 est.); machinery and equipment, vehicles, chemicals, minerals, plastics, oil. **Major trading partners:** (2008) *exports:* 18.7% Brazil, 8.5% China, 7.3% Argentina, 6.5% Germany, 4.9% Mexico; *imports:* 19.6% Argentina, 17.9% Brazil, 11% China, 9.7% U.S., 6.5% Paraguay, 4.5% Nigeria.

Uruguay was known as the Banda Oriental del Uruguay (Eastern Shore of the Uruguay River) during the colonial period. Although the Spanish first explored the area in 1516, they did not immediately settle there. Instead, the Portuguese founded the Colonia de Sacramento, near Buenos Aires, in 1680. They did not permanently establish the settlement of Montevideo until 1726. Under the leadership of José Gervasio Artigas, Uruguayans fought against both the Portuguese and the junta of Buenos Aires between 1811 and 1814 in an effort to establish their independence; in 1815 they proclaimed the Autonomous Government of the Eastern Provinces.

In 1817 the Portuguese again took control of the region, but Uruguayan nationals ousted them in 1828. A new constitution for the country was promulgated in 1830; however, domestic rivalry among elites soon led to civil war. The two contending factions, Liberals (Colorados) and Conservatives (Blancos), wore red and white armbands, respectively. Civil war continued through the 1840s and 1850s, until the victory of the Colorados in 1865. In the War of the Triple Alliance (1865–70), Uruguay allied itself with Argentina and Brazil against Paraguay. The consequence of the war for Uruguay was independence from the other regional powers.

The Colorado party dominated Uruguayan government from 1865 until 1958. Waves of European immigrants transformed Uruguayan society during the latter half of the 19th century, and by 1880 immigrants made up almost half of the population. The last civil war between the Blancos and the Colorados took place in 1904; the Colorados won victory under Pres. José Batlle y Ordóñez, one of Uruguay's political legends.

Batlle inaugurated a labor and social-welfare reform program that created Latin America's first eight-hour working day as well as progressive legislation on women's rights. Impressed with the Swiss plural executive Federal Council during his stay in Switzerland, Batlle believed such a structure could help Uruguay avoid the Latin American hazard of *caudillismo* (authoritarian rule). He proposed the idea of a plural executive, and a version of the idea became part of the constitution in 1919. The new constitution provided for both a president and a collegial National Council, both of which would make up the executive structure.

In 1933 a military coup by Pres. Gabriel Terra sought to dissolve both the legislature and the National Council and to reestablish the single executive presidential system. He managed this by sponsoring a constituent assembly that drew up a new constitution in 1934. In a 1951 plebiscite, Uruguayan voters approved a return to the plural executive system, and a new constitutional order reflecting this went into effect the following year. The debate over the form of the executive was not over, however; in 1966 the public voted for yet another constitution, which once again established the single president as the executive power.

Uruguay's economy began to falter during the 1950s. This, combined with the expansion of governmental bureaucracy tied to the country's social welfare programs, led to increasing popular discontent. In 1958 the Blancos won two successive victories. A candidate from the conservative wing of the Colorado party, Jorge Pacheco Areco, regained the presidency in 1967, but neither the Blancos nor the Colorados were able to deal with Uruguay's deteriorating economy or with its growing political unrest.

Uruguay's politics became increasingly polarized during the 1960s and into the 1970s. The leftist National Liberation Movement (MLN or Tupamaros), formed in 1967, began urban guerrilla activity that included robbery and kidnapping. The Tupamaros, many of whom were young and middle class, embarrassed government officials and were largely successful in eroding the public image of the civilian government. Tupamaro activity generated violence from the military and police, and as the political situation deteriorated in the early seventies, the government granted the military increasing authority.

By 1973 the military was in control of the country, and they dissolved the Congress. The military allowed Pres. Juan María Bordaberry to remain in office until 1976, at which time they installed Aparicio Méndez in the presidency. It was Bordaberry, however, who proposed the dismantling of the political parties in 1976. Uruguayan military rule was brutally repressive, and the armed forces perpetrated many human rights abuses. By some estimates, the Uruguayan military regime had the world's largest number of political prisoners in proportion to the population.

In 1980, Uruguayans rejected in a plebiscite the army's constitution, which would have amounted to continued de facto military control. Finally, in 1984, Colorado party candidate Julio María Sanguinetti won a civilian presidential election. Sanguinetti approved a general amnesty for the leaders of the military regime, but also had success in attracting foreign investment and righting the Uruguayan economy. He was unseated five years later by National party candidate Luis Alberto Lacalle, who further liberalized trade. But his austerity on social problems led voters to overturn some of his reforms by referendum. In 1994 elections, Sanguinetti won back the presidency. In Nov. 1999 the Colorado candidate, Jorge Batlle, pledged to continue the pro-market reforms of Sanguinetti, defeated in a run-off the (left-wing) Broad Front candidate, Tabaré Vázquez, who had led in the first round. But in 2005 Vásquez won the election on a more centrist platform. Over the next five years Vázquez's government stabilized the economy and reduced poverty and unemployment. In Nov. 2009, the Broad Front Party won again with José Mujica, a former guerrilla fighter, becoming president.

▶UZBEKISTAN
Republic of Uzbekistan
● **GEOGRAPHY Location:** central Asia. **Boundaries:** Kazakhstan to N, NE, and NW, Kyrgyzstan to E, Tajikistan to SE, Afghanistan to S, Turkmenistan to SW and W. **Total area:** 172,741 sq. mi. (447,400 sq km). **Coastline:** Aral Sea. **Comparative area:** slightly larger than California. **Land use:** 11% arable land; 1% permanent crops; 88% other. **Major cities:** Tashkent (capital); Samarkand; Namangan; Andizhan; Bukhara.
● **PEOPLE Population:** 27,865,738 (July 2010 est.). **Nationality:** noun—Uzbekistani(s); adjective— Uzbekistani. **Ethnic groups:** 80% Uzbek, 5.5% Russian, 5% Tajik, 3% Kazakh, 2.5% Karakalpak, 1.5% Tatar. **Languages:** 74.3% Uzbek (official), member of Eastern Turk language group written in Cyrillic script since 1940; 14.2% Russian, 4.4% Tajik, 7.1% other languages. **Religions:** 88% Muslim (mostly Sunnis), 9% Eastern Orthodox, 3% other.
● **GOVERNMENT Type:** republic. **Independence:** Sept. 1, 1991 (from Soviet Union). **Constitution:** Dec. 8, 1992. **National holiday:** Independence Day, Sept. 1. **Heads of Government:** Islam A. Karimov, president (since Dec. 1991); Shavkat Mirziyoyev, prime minister (since Dec. 2003). **Structure:** executive—president, Cabinet of Ministers; legislative— Supreme Assembly; judicial—Supreme Court.
● **ECONOMY Monetary unit:** som. **Budget:** (2009 est.) *income:* $8.826 bil.; *expend:* $9.209 bil. **G.D.P.:** $77.55 bil., $2,800 per capita (2009 est.). **Chief crops:** cotton, vegetables, fruits, grain; livestock. **Natural resources:** natural gas, coal, petroleum, gold, uranium. **Major industries:** textiles, food processing, machine building, metallurgy, natural gas. **Labor force:** 15.65 mil. (2009). **Exports:** $9.47 bil. (2009 est.); cotton, gold, natural gas, mineral fertilizers, ferrous metals, textiles, food products, autos. **Imports:** $6.51 bil. (2009 est.); machinery and parts, foodstuffs, chemicals, metals. **Major trading partners:** (2008) *exports:* 27.4% Ukraine, 16.9% Russia, 7.5% Turkey, 5.9% Kazakhstan, 5% Bangladesh; *imports:* 25.1% Russia, 15.3% China, 13.5% South Korea, 7.1% Ukraine, 5.4% Germany.

Uzbekistan, a land of deserts and steppe, lies in the heart of central Asia. Although the territory has been inhabited since prehistoric times, today's Uzbeks are actually descendants of nomadic Mongol, Iranian, and Turkic tribes who mixed with the populations there beginning in the 13th century A.D. The Uzbeks take their name from Khan Uzbek (1282–1342), the ruler responsible for converting the Mongol Golden Horde (the westernmost part of the Mongolian empire) to Islam. In the 18th and 19th centuries, the tribal states known as the Uzbek khanates of Bukhara, Samarkand, and Kokand were formed. Russian conquest of the Uzbek lands began in the 18th century and was completed in 1876 with the conquering of the khanate of Kokand. The Russian empire quickly built the Transcaucasian Railway to connect it with the region's major cities, thus sealing its hold on the area.

As with Kazakhstan, there was a large influx of Russians into Uzbekistan. Uzbek resentment of Russian immigrants precipitated a riot in 1898 in Andidzhan and again in 1916, when a decree that drafted central Asians into the Army was promulgated. Soviet power was established in 1917 in the city of Tashkent, and after some fighting, the region of Uzbekistan was incorporated as the Turkestan Autonomous Soviet Socialist Republic (ASSR) in April 1918. In October 1924, the Uzbek Soviet Socialist Republic (SSR) came into being. During 1924–25, the Soviet government initiated the National Delimitation of the Central Asian Republics to create Uzbek national symbols, to develop a new literary language, and to increase literacy among Uzbeks. It also conducted a brutal campaign against Islam and its believers. The Soviets modernized agriculture and industrialized the territory, although the native Uzbek population for the most part continued to live in rural areas and worked harvesting cotton, while the Russian population worked in industry. During World War II, Uzbekistan's industrial base expanded as major factories were moved there to keep them safe from enemy attack.

Mikhail Gorbachev's policy of glasnost, or openness, did not immediately result in political changes in Uzbekistan. In time, Uzbeks became politically active over many of the same issues that affected their Kazakh neighbors, such as the environmental problems causing the drying up of its rivers, the desiccation of the Aral Sea, and the salinization of the soil. They also demanded that Uzbek (and not Russian) be the official language.

In March 1990 the Supreme Soviet elected Islam Karimov as president, and on Aug. 31, 1991, Uzbekistan declared its independence, and joined the Commonwealth of Independent States (CIS).

In Dec. 1991 Karimov won the presidential election, and he moved to reduce Uzbekistan's dependence on Russia. In 1994 he signed a free-trade agreement with Kazakhstan and Kyrgyzstan and he banned use of the ruble in order to strengthen the som, Uzbekistan's monetary unit. In Dec. 1994 Karimov's supporters won an overwhelming majority in Uzbekistan's first parliamentary elections. The country made a slow but steady economic recovery as Karimov ruled with an iron hand. His human rights abuses were ignored after the 9/11 attacks when the U.S. military set up a large base of operations for the war on terror. In May 2005, however, Karimov's government violently supressed a demonstration killing perhaps 1,000 people. When the U.N. helped the fleeing refugees Karimov ordered the U.S. to leave. The E.U. imposed sanctions and the World Bank ended its loan program. Relations with the West improved in 2008 as Europe searched for new energy supplies and the U.S. sought help for the war in Afghanistan.

▶ VANUATU
Republic of Vanuatu
• **GEOGRAPHY** **Location:** chain of 12 principal and some 60 smaller islands in Pacific Ocean, about 500 mi. (800 km) W of Fiji and 1,100 mi. (2,800 km) E of Australia. Port Vila 17°45'S, 168°18'E. **Boundaries:** surrounded by South Pacific Ocean; nearest neighbor is Santa Cruz Islands to N. **Total area:** 5,699 sq. mi. (14,760 sq km). **Coastline:** 1,571 mi. (2,528 km). **Comparative area:** slightly larger than Connecticut. **Land use:** 3% arable land; 7% permanent crops; 90% other. **Major cities:** Port Vila (capital).
• **PEOPLE** **Population:** 218,519 (July 2009 est.). **Nationality:** noun—Ni-Vanuatu (sing. and pl.); adjective—Ni-Vanuatu. **Ethnic groups:** 98.5% Ni-Vanuatu, 1.5% other. **Languages:** English and French (official); pidgin (known as Bislama or Bichelama). **Religions:** 36.7% Presbyterian, 15% Anglican, 15% Catholic, 7.6% indigenous beliefs, 6.2% Seventh-Day Adventist, 3.8% Church of Christ, 15.7% other.
• **GOVERNMENT** **Type:** parliamentary republic. **Independence:** July 30, 1980 (from France and U.K.). **Constitution:** July 30, 1980. **National holiday:** Independence Day, July 30. **Heads of Government:** Iolu Johnson Abbil, president (since Sept. 2009); Edward Natapei, prime minister (since Sept. 2008). **Structure:** executive—president, prime minister, council of ministers; unicameral legislature; judiciary.
• **ECONOMY** **Monetary unit:** vatu. **Budget:** (2005 est.) *income:* $78.7 mil. *expend.:* $72.23 mil. **G.D.P.:** $983.2 mil. (2008 est.), $4,600 per capita (2008 est.). **Chief crops:** copra, coconuts, cocoa, coffee, taro, yams, fruits, vegetables; fish, beef. **Natural resources:** manganese, hardwood forests, fish. **Major industries:** food and fish freezing, forestry processing, meat canning. **Labor force:** 76,410; 65% agriculture, 30% services, 5% industry (2000 est.). **Exports:** $40 mil. (f.o.b., 2006); copra, beef, cocoa, timber, coffee. **Imports:** $156 mil. (c.i.f., 2006); machines and vehicles, food and beverages, fuels. **Major trading partners:** (2006) *exports:* 59.6% Thailand, 16.8% India, 11.5% Japan; *imports:* 20.6% Australia, 19.7% Japan, 12.1% Singapore, 8.8% New Zealand, 7.7% Fiji, 7.4% China, 4.3% New Caledonia.

Formerly known as the New Hebrides, Vanuatu is a rugged, volcanic island chain with heavily forested mountains; peaks rise to over 6,000 feet (on Espiritu Santo, the largest island). The people are Melanesians. In 1887 the islands were placed under the administration of an Anglo-French naval commission, becoming a joint Anglo-French colony (condominium) in 1906. The islands escaped Japanese occupation during World War II; they sided with the Free French and were used as bases for Allied campaigns in the Pacific. The New Hebrides were granted independence as Vanuatu on July 30, 1980, with membership in the British Commonwealth. The government is a parliamentary system, complemented by a National Council of Chiefs to decide matters of tradition and customary law.

The economy is based on subsistence agriculture, cattle raising, and fishing. Tourism is developing rapidly, and the sale of long-term tuna-fishing rights, principally to Japan, Australia, and the United States, is an important earner of foreign exchange.

▶ VENEZUELA
Republic of Venezuela
• **GEOGRAPHY** **Location:** northern coast of South America. **Boundaries:** Caribbean Sea to N, Guyana to E, Brazil to S, Colombia to W. **Total area:** 352,144 sq. mi. (912,050 sq km). **Coastline:** 1,739 mi. (2,800 km). **Comparative area:** slightly more than twice the size of California. **Land use:** 3% arable land; 1% permanent crops; 96% other. **Major cities:** Caracas (capital); Maracaibo; Valencia; Maracay; Barquisimeto.
• **PEOPLE** **Population:** 27,223,228 (July 2010 est.). **Nationality:** noun—Venezuelan(s); adjective—Venezuelan. **Ethnic groups:** Spanish, Italian, Portuguese, Arab, German, African, indigenous people. **Languages:** Spanish (official), native dialects (spoken by about 200,000 Amerindians in remote interior). **Religions:** 96% nominally Roman Catholic, 2% Protestant.
• **GOVERNMENT** **Type:** federal republic. **Independence:** July 5, 1811 (from Spain). **Constitution:** Dec. 30, 1999. **National holiday:** Independence Day, July 5. **Head of Government:** Hugo Chávez Frías, president (since Feb. 1999). **Structure:** executive (president); bicameral legislature (National Congress—Senate, Chamber of Deputies); judiciary.
• **ECONOMY** **Monetary unit:** bolívar. **Budget:** (2009 est.) *income:* $65.14 bil.; *expend.:* $92.04 bil. **G.D.P.:** $350.1 bil., $13,100 per capita (2009 est.). **Chief crops:** corn, sorghum, sugarcane, rice, bananas, vegetables, coffee; beef, pork, milk, eggs; fish. **Natural resources:** crude oil, natural gas, iron ore, gold, bauxite. **Major industries:** petroleum, iron ore mining, construction materials. **Labor force:** 12.67 mil. (2009); 64% services, 23% industry, 13% agriculture; 17% unemployment (2002). **Exports:** $51.99 bil. (2009 est.); petroleum, bauxite, aluminum, steel, chemicals, agricultural products, basic manufactures. **Imports:** $41.04 bil. (2009 est.); raw materials, construction materials, machinery and transport equipment. **Major trading partners:** (2008) *exports:* 39.8% U.S., 7.6% Netherlands Antilles, 4.6% China; *imports:* 26.1% U.S., 12.6% Colombia, 10.7% Brazil, 6.9% China, 4.8% Mexico.

At the time of European contact in the early 16th century, coastal Venezuela was home to nearly 50,000 semisedentary Indians. Although the region was "discovered" by Christopher Columbus in 1498, European settlement of the area was slow in comparison with the neighboring region of New Granada. The Spaniards explored and exploited Venezuela in the 1520s, searching for gold and pearls.

Early attempts at agriculture by the Spaniards failed until they discovered that the area around Caracas (founded in 1567) could sustain the production of both wheat and cocoa. African slave labor was an important part of the economic structure, and as markets for cocoa expanded, Caracas grew in importance. Venezuela became a captaincy general (an administrative region below the level of viceroyalty) with an audiencia (high court) established at Caracas in 1777–78.

As early as 1797, Venezuelan society was in rebellion against the Spanish empire. A major hindrance to the revolutionary leadership of Simón Bolívar was the need to accommodate both conservative landowners and the pardos, lower class citizens of mixed African and European ancestry. The wars of independence were particularly destructive in Venezuela, but in 1821 the region achieved independence and became part of the federation of Gran Colombia, which also included

New Granada and Ecuador. By 1830 Gran Colombia was in a state of political collapse, and Venezuela became an independent republic.

The military caudillo (leader) José Antonio Páez controlled the country for three decades. With the demise of Páez and his conservative allies in the 1860s, the forces of liberalism under Antonio Guzmán Blanco took over. The Guzmán Blanco era ended during a brief civil war in 1889, won by Gen. Cipriano Castro, who proceeded to establish his own rule. In 1908 Gen. Juan Vicente Gómez occupied the presidency, and he controlled the politics of Venezuela until his death in 1935.

The shift from dictatorship to democracy began with the Generation of 28, a student movement that organized urban workers and peasants into a viable political opposition. The Generation of 28 later became the modern Democratic Action party. In 1945 a group of young military officers overthrew the conservative dictatorship and supported the Democratic Action group in writing a new democratic constitution. Democratic Action won the elections of 1947, but military elements overthrew the new government the following year. The coup brought Col. Marcos Pérez Jiménez to power until his ouster in 1958.

The election of Democratic Action candidate Romulo Betancourt as president marked the beginning of multiparty democratic politics in Venezuela. The stability of the system owed much to political possibilities provided by the country's petroleum revenues. Venezuela nationalized foreign-owned oil and iron firms in 1975 and 1976, but dependence on petroleum revenues precipitated economic problems for the country in the 1980s. The downturn of the global oil market caused Venezuela's economic base to shrink.

The Christian Democrats defeated Democratic Action in 1968 and again in 1978. Pres. Luis Herrera Campíns's administration took the country in a more conservative direction but Democratic Action regained the presidency in 1983 under Jaime Lusinchi.

Venezuela's huge foreign debt in the 1980s led to tight economic controls and a reduction in social spending. The administration of Pres. Carlos Andrés Perez, elected in 1989, began with antigovernment riots in which hundreds died. In Feb. 1992, Latin America's oldest civilian government thwarted an attempted coup by soldiers angered over connections between high-ranking officers and drug traffickers; a second coup in November also failed. But in early 1993, Pres. Perez was suspended after the Senate ordered impeachment proceedings against him on charges he embezzled $17 million from the government; the Congress overwhelmingly elected Sen. Ramon Jose Valasquez Mujica to serve as interim president.

In early 1994 Rafael Caldera became president and immediately faced severe economic problems as the currency depreciated by more than 80 percent. Caldera imposed price and currency controls and suspended several constitutional guarantees. In July 1995, he restored those rights, except along Venezuela's borders with Colombia and Brazil, where crime and economic crises were most severe. Violent anti-government demonstrations continued into 1996 but Caldera persisted in austerity plans that resulted in a $1.4 bil. loan from I.M.F. By early 1997 inflation seemed to be in check and the economy stabilizing although the continuing fall in worldwide oil prices added more pressure for budget cuts. By 1998 Venezuela's economy was caught in the world-wide financial crisis and spinning toward chaos as the presidential election approached.

In the December elections, the two old parties (Christian Democrats and Democratic Action) which had dominated for 40 years all but disappeared. The Patriotic Pole Coalition candidate, Hugo Chavez Frias (who had led the unsuccessful coup in 1992 against Perez) easily triumphed over Henrique Salas Romer. Two days later stock shares rose 22 percent despite Chavez' calls for redistribution of wealth, privatization of the government oil company and abolition of Congress. Chavez called for a Constitutional Assembly to rewrite the constitution (88 percent voted their approval in April 1999). In elections for the Assembly Chavez's supporters won all but seven of 128 seats. In December the Assembly adopted a new constitution (Venezuela's 26th) whose major features are a unicameral National Assembly and a six-year renewable presidential term.

Elections in Aug. 2000 confirmed Chavez for a new term and "Chavista" dominance of the Assembly. Chavez demanded OPEC cut production and he agreed to sell oil to Castro's Cuba at bargain prices. In Nov. the new National Assembly gave him authority to rule by decree in 37 legislative areas. But Chavez's excesses (such as decreeing 49 new laws in one day) provoked resistance by both business and labor, both of whom backed an army coup attempt on April 12, 2002. Within 48 hours, however, Chavez was back, the coup undercut by divisions in the armed forces. A general strike, called in Oct. by business and labor groups, became a crisis for the regime when 30,000 oil workers joined. The OAS brokered an agreement that both sides would disarm and recognize a constitutional right to a recall referendum. In Sept. 2003 the National Electoral Council rejected the petition signed by 3.2 million people demanding a recall referendum. After surmounting every legal hurdle, the recall referendum was held on August 16, 2004 and Chavez easily triumphed over a stunned opposition. Since then Chavez has grown more popular by using the nation's oil wealth to improve social services, education, and infrastructure, and by openly challenging U.S. dominance in the region. As he continues to assume more and more power through legal changes, several nations in South America have begun to distance themselves from him. In December 2007 a referendum to expand his powers under the constitution was narrowly defeated, Chavez's first electoral setback in nine years.

▶ VIETNAM
Socialist Republic of Viet Nam

● **GEOGRAPHY   Location:** Southeast Asia. **Boundaries:** China to N, Gulf of Tonkin to NE, South China Sea to E, Laos and Cambodia to W. **Total area:** 127,243 sq. mi. (329,560 sq km). **Coastline:** 2,140 mi. (3,444 km) excluding islands. **Comparative area:** slightly larger than New Mexico. **Land use:** 17% arable land; 5% permanent crops; 78% other. **Major cities:** Hanoi (capital); Ho Chi Minh City (formerly Saigon); Haiphong; Da Nang; Long Xuyen.

● **PEOPLE   Population:** 89,571,130 (July 2010 est.). **Nationality:** noun—Vietnamese (sing., pl.); adjective—Vietnamese. **Ethnic groups:** 86.2% Kinh, 2% Tay, 1.7% Thai; Muong, Khome, Hoa, Nun, Hmong. **Languages:** Vietnamese (official); French, Chinese, English, Khmer, ethnic langs. (Mon-Khmer and Malayo-Polynesian). **Religions:** Buddhist, Taoist, Roman Catholic, indigenous beliefs, Islam, Protestant, Cao Dai, Hoa Hao.

• **GOVERNMENT** Type: Communist state. **Independence:** Sept. 2, 1945 (from France). **Constitution:** Apr. 15, 1992. **National holiday:** Independence Day, Sept. 2. **Heads of Government:** Nguyen Minh Triet, president, (since June 2006); Nguyen Tan Dung, prime minister (since June 2006). **Structure:** executive—president, prime minister, cabinet; unicameral legislature; judiciary—elected by legislature.

• **ECONOMY** Monetary unit: new dong. **Budget:** (2009 est.) *income:* $21.89 bil.; *expend.:* $30.42 bil. **G.D.P.:** $258.1 bil., $2,900 per capita (2009 est.). **Chief crops:** paddy rice, corn, potatoes, rubber, soybeans, coffee, tea, bananas; poultry, pigs; fish. **Natural resources:** phosphates, coal, manganese, bauxite, chromate. **Major industries:** food processing, textiles, machine building. **Labor force:** 43.87 mil. (2009 est.); 56.8% agriculture, 37% industry. 6.2% services, 2.4% unemployment (2005 est.). **Exports:** 56.55 bil. (2009 est.); crude oil, marine products, rice, coffee, rubber, tea, garments, shoes. **Imports:** $68.8 bil. (2009 est.); machinery and equipment, petroleum products, fertilizer, steel products, raw cotton, grain, cement, motorcycles. **Major trading partners:** (2008) *exports:* 18.9% U.S., 13.6% Japan, 7.2% China, 6.7% Australia, 4.2% Singapore; *imports:* 22.4% China, 13.4% Singapore, 12% Taiwan, 10.1% South Korea, 7% Thailand.

The southward expansion of the Chinese empire in the first millennium B.C. drove the Vietnamese peoples southward into northern Vietnam (Tonkin). The area came under direct Chinese rule in 111 B.C. Chinese rule endured, with some interruptions, until A.D. 948; thereafter, Vietnam was independent under strong Chinese influence.

The Hindu-Buddhist kingdom of Annam, in central Vietnam, gradually increased in size and power at the expense of Tonkin and the Khmer empire and Champa, to the west and south. In 1558 the kingdom of Annam split, with independent courts established at Hanoi, controlling Tonkin and the Red River valley, and Hue, in central Vietnam. A remnant of the old Champa state remained independent in the Mekong delta in the south. In 1802 the monarchy was reunited, with the court at Hue controlling all of Vietnam and exercising hegemony over Cambodia.

European penetration of the region began in the 16th century; by the early 19th century, France was the dominant foreign power in Indochina. Efforts to establish French military control began in 1858–59 with the establishment of a colony in Cochin China, in southern Vietnam. Campaigns in the Red River valley in 1873 and 1882 were complicated by Chinese intervention and the determined resistance of the Vietnamese court. In 1884 separate protectorates were established in Tonkin and Annam; in 1887 those, along with Cochin China and Cambodia, were combined into the Union of Indochina under French colonial rule. Rubber plantations were established, and rice and timber exports were under French control. A nationalist rebellion under Phan Boi Chau was suppressed in the early 20th century.

Nationalist resistance to French colonialism continued, resulting in the creation in 1939 of the Vietminh, or Independence League. In 1940 Japanese troops occupied French Indochina, with the collaboration of colonial administrators loyal to the Vichy regime. The Vietminh spearheaded anti-Japanese guerrilla resistance and in 1945 forced the abdication of King Bao Dai, head of a pro-Japanese puppet state. In 1945 France reoccupied Indochina; in 1946 the leader of the Vietminh, Ho Chi Minh, became president of a separatist government at Hanoi. France ceded local autonomy to Tonkin and Annam but sought to retain Cochin China as a colony. Fighting between the French and the Vietminh resumed. On July 1, 1949, the French reinstalled Bao Dai as king of Vietnam, and in February 1950 recognized the independence of Vietnam within the French Union. Ho Chi Minh's republican government also claimed control of all of Vietnam.

Fighting between the two rivals culminated in the French defeat at Dienbienphu on May 7, 1954. An armistice was concluded and the country was partitioned at a demilitarized zone at latitude 17° north, the northern part going to the Communist-controlled Vietminh government, the southern to Bao Dai. Nearly one million refugees, fled from the north to the south. An international conference in Geneva agreed that elections would be held throughout Vietnam in 1956. In June 1954 Ngo Dinh Diem became premier of South Vietnam; full sovereignty in the south was transferred by France to the Vietnamese government in Dec. 1954. In October 1955 Diem held elections in the south that resulted in the dismissal of Bao Dai as king and the proclamation of an independent Republic of Vietnam.

The scheduled elections of 1956 were never held. French troops withdrew from South Vietnam in that year. Fighting continued in the south, as the Vietminh-backed National Liberation Front (Vietcong) sought to overthrow the Diem government. On Dec. 31, 1959, the Democratic Republic of Vietnam in the north adopted a new constitution calling for the reunification of the country; northern aid to the Vietcong increased significantly, as did American aid to the south. After 1962 American military advisers increased in number and combat exposure.

In 1963 widespead demonstrations, under Buddhist leadership, led to a coup on Nov. 1–2 in which Diem was deposed and assassinated. A series of short-lived military regimes followed until Sept. 1967, when Nguyen Van Thieu was elected president. U.S. air strikes against North Vietnam began in 1964. In the same year, the flow of troops and supplies from north to south increased. American combat troops entered the war in 1965. Despite U.S.-South Vietnamese superiority in arms and troops, and total control of the air, Vietcong control over the countryside increased. Both Operation Phoenix, in which antigovernment rural leaders were assassinated, and the establishment of fortified strategic hamlets to control the rural population, failed to reverse the tide.

The combined Vietcong-North Vietnamese Tet Offensive in early 1968 resulted in serious losses for South Vietnamese and American forces. The war spread to Laos and to Cambodia, the latter bombed in 1969. American air strikes in North Vietnam were stepped up, and U.S. troop strength reached a maximum of 543,000 in 1969. In July 1969 a series of U.S. troop withdrawals began, and secret talks were initiated in search of a negotiated settlement of the war. Following heavy U.S. bombardment of the north in 1972, a cease-fire agreement was signed in Paris by South Vietnam, North Vietnam, the Vietcong, and the United States on Jan. 27, 1973. It was never implemented, but the American withdrawal continued. In early 1975 South Vietnamese forces collapsed in the face of a series of North Vietnamese-Vietcong offensives. Remaining U.S. personnel were evacuated, and Saigon fell on Apr. 30, 1975. Hundreds of thousands of refugees ("boat people") fled the country over the next decade.

Following the fall of Saigon, the country was occupied by northern troops and administrators. Businesses were nationalized, agriculture collectivized, and tens of thousands of people sent to labor camps for "reeducation." A unified National Assembly met in 1976, and the country was officially reunified on July 2, 1976, under the existing government of the north. Saigon was renamed Ho Chi Minh City. A Soviet naval base was established at the former U.S. base at Cam Ranh Bay.

In 1978 Vietnamese troops occupied Cambodia ousting the government of Pol Pot. In Feb.1979 China launched an unsuccessful attack over its border with Vietnam to display displeasure with the invasion of Cambodia and with the treatment of ethnic Chinese in Vietnam. In 1988 Vietnam pledged to withdraw its troops from Cambodia and completed the withdrawal in Sept. 1989.

Vietnam's communist government ruled through the party's powerful Central Committee; no strong personalities emerged to replace the leaders of the wartime generation. The economy was functioning only at a basic level, with the infrastructure in disrepair and agriculture hampered by excessive collectivization. The collapse of the Soviet Union brought about a drastic reduction of the Soviet aid that had kept the Vietnamese economy afloat. Facing economic ruin, Vietnam's leadership eventually turned a blind eye to individual private enterprise. By 1992 the government was encouraging foreign investment.

Resumption of contacts with the U.S. had been precluded by American insistence that Vietnam account more fully for American prisoners of war and troops missing in action. But high-level talks on the normalization of relations and the Cambodian question opened in 1990, and the success of those negotiations helped to open diplomatic channels between Vietnam and the U.S.

In 1994, Pres. Clinton, satisfied with Vietnam's efforts to account for POWs and MIAs, ended the 19-year U.S. trade embargo; the following day, American firms were operating in Ho Chi Minh City. In July 1995, full diplomatic relations were established and in October Vietnam's National Assembly adopted its first-ever national civil code under the Communist government. The document spelled out rights to land, personal property, inheritances, and raising capital. Close to 90 percent of the Assembly members voted in favor of the code.

In July 2000 the U.S. and Vietnam signed a far-reaching trade agreement. In April 2001, the Central Committee of the Communist Party appointed a new Secretary General, Nong Duc Manh, with the aim of modernizing the economy and ending corruption. By rumor, Nong an illegitimate son of Ho Chi Minh. In Dec. 2001 Vietnam took two steps toward its goal of joining the W.T.O.: a trade agreement with the U.S. and the granting to private investors equal access to bank credit with the public sector. The Communists had no intention of easing their political control, however, was made clear by the May 2002 "elections" to the National Assembly in which the Communists carried 447 of 498 seats. In June 2005 Prime Minister Phan Van Khai became the first Vietnamese leader to be received by the White House.

The government leadership changed in 2006 and the economy began to expand rapidly. Economic liberalization continued and Vietnam joined the W.T.O. in 2007. By then it was second in economic growth only to China among Asian nations.

▶ **WESTERN SAMOA**
see "Samoa"

▶ **YEMEN**
Republic of Yemen
● **GEOGRAPHY Location:** southern shore of Arabian peninsula and southwest corner of Arabian peninsula. **Boundaries:** Saudi Arabia to N, Oman to E, Gulf of Aden to S, Red Sea to W. **Total area:** 203,850 sq. mi. (527,970 sq km). **Coastline:** 1,184 mi. (1,906 km). **Comparative area:** slightly larger than twice the size of Wyoming. **Land use:** 3% arable land; negl. % permanent crops; 97% other. **Major cities:** Sana'a (capital); Aden; Hodeida; Mukalla; Taiz.
● **PEOPLE Population:** 23,495,361 (July 2010 est.). **Nationality:** noun—Yemini(s); adjective—Yemeni. **Ethnic groups:** predominantly Arab; Afro-Arab concentrations in western coastal locations; South Asians in southern regions; small European communities in major metropolitan areas. **Languages:** Arabic. **Religions:** Muslim including Shaf'i (Sunni) and Zaydi (Shia), small numbers of Jewish, Christian, and Hindu.
● **GOVERNMENT Type:** republic. **Independence:** May 22, 1990 (merger of North and South Yemen). **Constitution:** May 16, 1991: amended Sept. 29, 1994 and Feb. 2001. **National holiday:** Proclamation of the Republic, May 22. **Heads of Government:** Ali Abdullah Saleh, president (since May 1994); Ali Mujawar, prime minister (since Apr. 2007). **Structure:** executive—president and cabinet; unicameral legislature; judicial—Supreme Court and lesser courts.
● **ECONOMY Monetary unit:** Yemeni rial. **Budget:** (2009 est.) *income:* $6.202 bil.; *expend:* $9.355 bil. **G.D.P.:** $58.19 bil., $2,500 per capita (2009 est.). **Chief crops:** grain, fruits, vegetables, qat, coffee, cotton; dairy products, poultry, meat; fish. **Natural resources:** petroleum, fish, rocksalt, marble, small deposits of coal. **Major industries:** crude oil, petroleum refining, cotton textiles and leather goods, food processing, handicrafts, aluminum products, cement. **Labor force:** 6.641 mil. (2009 est.) mostly agriculture and herding; also services, construction, industry, commerce. **Exports:** $5.55 bil. (2009 est.); crude oil, cotton, coffee, dried and salted fish. **Imports:** $7.12 bil., (2009 est.); food and live animals, machinery and equipment, manufactured goods. **Major trading partners:** (2008) *exports:* 30.9% China, 25.7% Thailand, 14.6% South Africa, 8.8% India, 5.1% Japan; *imports:* 15.5% U.A.E. 11.8% China, 8.4% India, 7.3% Saudi Arabia, 5.4% Kuwait, 4.1% U.S.

Yemen—in ancient times Sheba or Saba—is strategically located in the southwestern corner of the Arabian peninsula, near the southern end of the Red Sea. In biblical times and for many centuries thereafter, Yemen dominated the caravan trade in spices, gold, and other luxury goods from India and Africa to the Middle East.

The Islamic unification of Arabia in 628 resulted in the incorporation of Yemen into Arabia as a whole, but many local uprisings broke out over the course of the following three centuries. In the 10th century, control passed to a line of Yemeni kings who were simultaneously imams of the Zaidi sect of Islam; the Zaidi imams ruled until 1962.

Aden was the most important port of the ancient kingdom of Sheba and retained that status under the Zaidi imams of Yemen. Portuguese activity around Aden began in the 15th century; from the mid-16th century, control of the port was disputed by the Portuguese, the Yemeni kings, the Ottoman Turks, and, later, the British.

In 1839, Aden was made a British Crown Colony; the Hadramaut region of southern Arabia, north and east of Aden, became the British Protectorate of Aden. The colony and protectorate were both administered as part of British India.

Yemen came under the control of the Ottoman Empire from the mid-16th to the mid-17th centuries, and again from 1849 to 1918. The Turks were expelled at the end of World War I, and Yemen became an independent kingdom in 1918. The kingdom's independence was threatened by a Saudi invasion in 1934 and by a 1954 dispute with Great Britain over the status of Aden, which was the key to British military power in the western Indian Ocean and Persian Gulf after India's independence in 1947.

Imam Ahmed came to the throne of Yemen in 1948, following the assassination of his predecessor. Most of Yemen's large Jewish population was evacuated to Israel in 1949–50. A palace coup against the imam in 1955 failed, but after his death in 1962, his successor was quickly ousted and the country was proclaimed the Yemen Arab Republic (North Yemen) under the leadership of Brig. Gen. Abdullah al-Salal.

A struggle for independence began in Aden and the protectorate in 1963, with two rival groups competing for power. The National Liberation Front (NLF) gained the upper hand over the Egyptian-backed Front for the Liberation of Occupied South Yemen, as both groups waged guerrilla war against the British. British forces withdrew in 1967, and South Yemen became independent. The nation's territory included Socotra and adjacent islands off the Horn of Africa, which had been British possessions since 1876.

In 1969 a leftist faction of the NLF seized power, nationalized key industries, and instituted a socialist regime. In the mid-1970s, South Yemeni troops aided leftist guerrillas in Oman, and fought in Ethiopia against Eritrean rebels. Subsequently Pres. Salem Robaye Ali took a more moderate stance and improved relations with Oman and Saudi Arabia. He was overthrown in a coup in June 1978 and executed. The succeeding government was overthrown on Jan. 13, 1986; on Feb. 8, Hasin Said Numan became prime minister.

In North Yemen, civil war between royalist and republican factions lasted until April 1970, when a coalition republican government was formed with the aid of Saudi mediation. Col. Ibrahim al-Hamidi came to power in a military coup in 1974; he was assassinated in 1977. Pres. Ali Abdullah Saleh assumed office in 1978, after the assassination of Pres. al-Gashmi.

Border skirmishes between North Yemen and South Yemen broke out during 1972–73. After several years of uneasy peace, South Yemen launched a full-scale war against the north on Feb. 24, 1979. Arab League pressure quickly led to a truce. Relations improved during the 1980s and North Yemen and South Yemen merged as the Republic of Yemen on May 22, 1990. Ali Abdullah Saleh, president of North Yemen, became the new country's president. San'a was proclaimed the capital of the United Yemen, though Aden remained its most important economic center.

The Gulf War forced the repatriation of tens of thousands of Yemeni workers from Kuwait and other Gulf states; later Saudi Arabia expelled 850,000 more to express its displeasure with Yemen's unenthusiastic stance toward the Gulf War. These repatriations deprived Yemen of a most important source of foreign exchange, and severely damaged the economy.

Yemen held its first general election since unification on Apr. 27, 1993, and a coalition government was formed. In Feb. 1994, fighting began and a full-scale civil war broke out in May. But in July the capture of Aden by government troops ended the conflict. The first direct presidential election was held in Sept. 1999 but the Socialist Party was not allowed to field a candidate so Saleh won easily.

On Oct. 10, 2000, over 50,000 protested in Aden against U.S. support for Israel; two days later, the U.S. destroyer *Cole*, refueling in Aden, was attacked, leaving 17 dead and 39 wounded. The Saleh government permitted F.B.I. attendance at the questioning of witnesses; but the F.B.I. (and Navy) investigators became a new object of attack, by the terrorist "Islamic Army of Aden."

A sporadic insurgency threatens the Saleh government as it tries to cooperate with the huge U.S. military presence in the region. Al Qaeda's growing presence and the separatist movement in the north made Yemen a focus of U.S. military activity in 2010. (See "Major News Stories.")

▶ YUGOSLAVIA (SEE SERBIA AND MONTENEGRO)

▶ ZAIRE (SEE CONGO, DEMOCRATIC REPUBLIC)

▶ ZAMBIA
Republic of Zambia
● GEOGRAPHY **Location:** landlocked country in southern central Africa. **Boundaries:** Zaire to N, Tanzania to NE, Malawi to E, Mozambique to SE, Zimbabwe to S, Namibia to SW, Angola to W. **Total area:** 290,583 sq. mi. (752,610 sq km). **Coastline:** none. **Comparative area:** slightly larger than Texas. **Land use:** 7% arable land; negl. % permanent crops; 93% other. **Major cities:** Lusaka (capital); Kitwe; Ndola; Kabwe.

● PEOPLE **Population:** 11,862,740 (July 2009 est.). **Nationality:** noun—Zambian(s); adjective—Zambian. **Ethnic groups:** 98.7% African, 1.1% European, 0.2% other. **Languages:** English (official), major vernaculars—Bemba, Kaonda, Lozi, Lunda, Luvale, Nyanja, Tonga, and about 70 indigenous languages. **Religions:** 50-75% Christian, 24-49% Muslim and Hindu, 1% indigenous beliefs.

Government **Type:** republic. **Independence:** Oct. 24, 1964 (from U.K.). **Constitution:** Aug. 2, 1991; amended 1996. **National holiday:** Independence Day, Oct. 24. **Heads of Government:** Rupiah Banda, president (since Aug. 2008). **Structure:** executive—modified presidential system; legislative—unicameral National Assembly; judiciary.

● ECONOMY **Monetary unit:** kwacha. **Budget:** (2008 est.) *income:* $3.291 bil.; *expend.:* $3.578 bil. **G.D.P.:** $17.39 bil., $1,500 per capita (2008 est.). **Chief crops:** corn, sorghum, rice, peanuts, sunflower seed, tobacco, cotton, sugarcane, cassava; cattle, goats, pigs, poultry, beef, pork, milk, eggs, hides. **Natural resources:** copper, cobalt, zinc, lead, coal. **Major industries:** copper mining and processing, foodstuffs, construction. **Labor force:** 5.235 mil. (2008 est.) ; 85% agriculture, 9% services, 6% industry. **Exports:** $4.818 bil. (f.o.b., 2008 est.); copper, cobalt, zinc, lead, tobacco. **Imports:** $4.694 bil. (f.o.b., 2008 est.); machinery, transport equipment, foodstuffs, fuels, petroleum products, electricity. **Major trading partners:** (2006) *exports:* 38.4% Switzerland, 21.6% South Africa, 10.3% China, 7.6% U.K., 6.4% Tanzania; *imports:* 47.3% South Africa, 10.4% United Arab Emirates, 5.7% Zimbabwe, 4% Norway.

Bantu peoples—including Luba, Lunda, Ngoni, and others—moved into what is now Zambia between the 15th and the 19th centuries, displacing or absorbing aboriginal populations. Occasional Portuguese explorers from Angola and Mozambique entered the region, and Angolan slave-raiders were active in the late 18th and early 19th centuries, but serious European influence did not begin until the mid-19th century. At that time British missionaries and merchants arrived, most notably David Livingstone and Cecil Rhodes.

Local rulers granted mineral concessions to Rhodes in both Northern and Southern Rhodesia (now Zambia and Zimbabwe). Rhodesia was declared a British sphere of influence in 1888; a British protectorate was established in 1891 and enlarged in 1894–95. The borders of Northern Rhodesia were established in 1911. The country was administered by the British South Africa Co. until 1924, when direct colonial rule began. Large numbers of British settlers arrived and developed farms and ranches and mined the region's substantial copper deposits. A railroad was built linking Northern Rhodesia with Elizabethville in the Belgian Congo (now Lubumbashi, Zaire).

In 1953 Northern and Southern Rhodesia (Zimbabwe) were joined with Nyasaland (now Malawi) to form the Federation of Rhodesia and Nyasaland. The country entered a period of unrest as native peoples demanding greater participation in government, while white settlers clung to their privileged positions.

As the result of an election in 1962, the federation was dissolved. A National Assembly was created on the basis of a broader, multiracial electorate. Northern Rhodesia became independent as the Republic of Zambia on Oct. 24, 1964. Relations between Zambia and white-ruled Rhodesia became strained in 1965 in a dispute over ownership and administration of the railway that spanned both countries. A new constitution was promulgated in 1973, creating a stronger presidency and a unicameral legislature; the United National Independence party was made the sole legal political party. Opposition parties were allowed to form again starting in Dec. 1990.

Pres. Kenneth Kaunda, in office after Zambia's independence, led a moderate government that won the support of both whites and blacks. Zambia's economy did not fare well as the price of copper, the nation's main earner of foreign exchange, declined around the world causing massive foreign debt and labor unrest. The I.M.F. demanded reforms as a condition for future aid, and in 1987 Pres. Kaunda announced a program of economic restructuring. In 1990 his government survived an attempted coup precipitated by a doubling in the price of the staple food, maize meal.

At the end of 1991, Kaunda was defeated by Frederick Chiluba, head of the new Labor party.

Chiluba's economic reforms helped Zambia repay more than $1.2 billion in outstanding debt, prompting the I.M.F. to restore its eligibility for international loans. But political problems resurfaced when Chiluba's government found a way to block Kaunda from winning in the 1996 presidential election. Kaunda was shot and wounded by a sniper in Aug. 1997 as he continued to criticize the government. In Oct. 1997 a failed coup attempt by army officers was blamed on Kaunda who was arrested in Dec. and put on trial. He was freed in June and all charges dropped on condition that he leave politics. In March 1999 Zambia's High Court declared him not a citizen. Pres. Chiluba honored his pledge not to run for re-election and the Dec. 2001 election was won by Levy Mwanawasa. The new president began a serious investigation into official corruption and Parliament stripped Chiluba of his immunity and he was arrested in Feb. 2003 on charges of stealing millions of dollars.

Mwanawasa was reelected in 2006 based on the economic stability he established. Foreign investment, especially from China, has helped the economy upward. Mwanawasa's death in June 2008 led to elections in November, which were won by the ruling party but called a fraud by the opposition.

▶ ZIMBABWE
Republic of Zimbabwe
• **GEOGRAPHY Location:** landlocked country in southern Africa. **Boundaries:** Zambia to NW, Mozambique to E, South Africa to S, Botswana to SW. **Total area:** 150,803 sq. mi. (390,580 sq km). **Coastline:** none. **Comparative area:** slightly larger than Montana. **Land use:** 8% arable land; negl. % permanent crops; 91% other. **Major cities:** Harare (capital); Bulawayo; Chitungwiza; Mutare; Gweru.
• **PEOPLE Population:** 11,392,629 (July 2009 est.). **Nationality:** noun—Zimbabwean(s); adjective—Zimbabwean. **Ethnic groups:** 98% African (82% Shona, 14% Ndebele, 2% other), 1% white, 1% mixed and Asian. **Languages:** English (official), Shona, Sindebele. **Religions:** 50% syncretic (part Christian, part indigenous beliefs), 25% Christian, 24% indigenous beliefs, 1% Muslim.
• **GOVERNMENT Type:** parliamentary democracy. **Independence:** Apr. 18, 1980 (from U.K.). **Constitution:** Dec. 21, 1979. **National holiday:** Independence Day, Apr. 18. **Head of Government:** Robert Gabriel Mugabe, president (since Dec. 1987), prime minister Margan Tsvangirai (since Feb. 2009). **Structure:** executive—cabinet led by president; unicameral legislature—120 of 150 members are popularly elected, others appointed; judiciary.
• **ECONOMY Monetary unit:** Zimbabwean dollar. **Budget:** (2008 est.) *income:* $1.092 bil.; *expend.:* $0.941 bil. **G.D.P.:** $1.959 bil., $200 per capita (2008 est.). **Chief crops:** tobacco, corn, tea, sugarcane, cotton, wheat, coffee, peanuts; cattle, sheep, goats, pigs. **Natural resources:** coal, chromium ore, asbestos, gold, nickel. **Major industries:** mining, steel, clothing and footwear. **Labor force:** 4.039 mil. (2008 est.); 80% unemployment (2005 est.). **Exports:** $1.321 bil. (f.o.b., 2008 est.); 23% tobacco, 14% gold, ferroalloys, cotton. **Imports:** $1.915 bil. (f.o.b., 2008 est.); 39% machinery and transport equipment, 18% manufactures, 15% chemicals, 10% fuels. **Major trading partners:** (2006) *exports:* 24.8% South Africa, 17.6% Democratic Republic of the Congo, 15.7% Botswana, 10.4% U.S.; *imports:* 40.8% South Africa, 29.6% Zambia, 4.9% U.S.

Massive stone structures at Great Zimbabwe give evidence of a sizable urban society that flourished from the ninth to the 13th centuries and dominated Iron Age trade in southeastern Africa. Bantu peoples migrated into the region in the 15th century; the Mashona dominated until the 19th century, when they were displaced by the Matebele.

Portuguese slave traders from Mozambique were active in Zimbabwe from the 16th to the mid-19th centuries. Mineral concessions were granted to Cecil Rhodes by local rulers in the late 19th century, and the region became a British protectorate in 1888. Salisbury (now Harare) was founded in 1890, and the territory comprising Zimbabwe and Zambia was named Rhodesia in 1895. Rhodesia was governed by the British South Africa Co. until 1923, when it was partitioned into Northern and Southern Rhodesia. Northern Rhodesia became a British colony; Southern Rhodesia, rejecting union with South Africa, became a self-governing (and white-ruled) state within the British Empire.

Southern Rhodesia had been heavily settled by whites from Great Britain, South Africa, and elsewhere, who developed extensive farms and ranches, forest products industries, and rich mines. The country prospered but with little native participation in government. In 1953 Northern Rhodesia, Southern Rhodesia, and Nyasaland were joined in the Federation of Rhodesia and Nyasaland. Increasing agitation for black participation in government, especially in the north and in Nyasaland, led to the dissolution of the federation in 1963; Northern Rhodesia subsequently became independent as Zambia, Nyasaland as Malawi. In 1961 Southern Rhodesia adopted a constitution that guaranteed the continuation of white rule. White resistance to black political demands led to the rise of the Rhodesian Front party, whose leader, Ian D. Smith, became prime minister of Rhodesia (formerly Southern Rhodesia). After British-led negotiations for a biracial political compromise broke down, the Smith government on Nov. 11, 1965, issued a unilateral declaration of independence, which was declared illegal and invalid by the British government. The U.N. condemned the Smith government and imposed economic sanctions, and in May 1968 voted to impose a trade embargo on Rhodesia.

In 1970 a new constitution effectively barred black participation in national politics. By 1974 mounting pressure from other African countries led the Smith government to enter into serious negotiations. Guerrilla warfare pitting black nationalist groups against white settlers and mercenaries raged sporadically, and many white settlers emigrated. A 1977 British-American proposal for majority rule provided the basis for a settlement. An "internal settlement" was announced in April 1978 by Smith and three major nationalist leaders: Bishop Abel Muzorewa, leader of the United African National Congress, the Rev. Ndabaningi Sithole, former leader of the Zimbabwe African National Union (ZANU), and Chief Jeremiah Chirau. The settlement was rejected by the Patriotic Front that united ZANU (now led by Robert Mugabe) and Joshua Nkomo's Zimbabwe African People's Union (ZAPU).

Elections were held in April 1979 and Bishop Muzorewa assumed office on June 1 as prime minister of "Zimbabwe-Rhodesia," but the Patriotic Front continued to oppose the government.

On Dec. 10 the "Zimbabwe-Rhodesia" Parliament dissolved itself, and the country reverted briefly to British colonial rule. On Dec. 21 all parties agreed to a cease-fire and to a period of transitional British rule leading to independence.

Elections held in 1980 resulted in a clear majority for Mugabe's ZANU party. Zimbabwe became independent, with Mugabe as prime minister, on April 18. As Mugabe embarked on an ambitious program of national reconstruction, Nkomo became leader of the opposition. Guerrillas linked to ZAPU, with Nkomo's tacit leadership, continued to engage in sporadic warfare against Mugabe's government, and banditry disrupted the countryside.

The elections of 1985 increased ZANU's majority in Parliament. In 1987 the constitution was amended to strengthen the presidency and to end the separate role of blacks and whites in government; new elections were held for black members of Parliament to fill seats formerly reserved for whites. Guerrillas renewed attacks on white-owned farms.

In Dec. 1987 Mugabe and Nkomo agreed to merge ZANU and ZAPU (ZANU-PF), creating a de facto one-party state under Mugabe. A presidential election was scheduled for 1996, but in 1995, the Rev. Ndonga Sithole, leader of the opposition Zimbabwe African National Union, was arrested and charged with plotting to kill Mugabe.

Amidst a fuel crisis, 60 percent inflation and 50 percent unemployment, Zimbabwe voters in Feb. 2000 rejected a new constitution granting Mugabe 12 more years and power to seize white farmlands without compensation. But, with government approval, squatters began seizing white farms and preventing the tobacco harvest (30 percent of Zimbabwe's export earnings). June elections gave 57 of 120 seats contested to the opposition, sufficient to block any plan for a new constitution. But throughout 2001 Mugabe continued his plan to seize white-owned farms and began to arrest his political opponents. Court-packing, press controls, prohibition of assemblages, banning of non-governmental election-monitors, arrests of opponents—all preceded March 2002 presidential elections in which Mugabe claimed 1.7 million votes to 1.3 million for his principal opponent, Morgan Tsuangirai. Torture and rape by the army drove tens of thousands of Tsuangirai's supporters to flight. Mugabe seized further white farms amidst the worst famine in 60 years. A wave of arrests - over 300 members of opposition Movement for Democratic Change, including Tsuangirai, six members of Parliament—followed a weak attempt at a general strike in June 2003.

Unsurprisingly Mugabe easily won reelection in April 2005 and began a violent crackdown against thousands of poor urban dwellers, destroying their shanty-homes and sending them back to rural areas. Economic collapse seemed inevitable by mid-2007 with unemployment over 60 percent and the economy shrunk by half. Not surprisingly then the opposition party won the parliamentary elections in 2008, and their leader, Morgan Tsvangirai won the first round of presidential elections. As a runoff election was being set, violence increased, causing Tsvangirai to boycott the election in June 2008. Mugabe finally agreed to a power-sharing deal. In February 2009 Mugabe himself swore in his rival as prime minister. But Mugabe's control of the military and the police meant little change could be effected.

Selected Territories of the World

The community of nations has long recognized the existence of territories that do not have the status of independent states and that are subordinate in some degree to another power. The United Nations refers to these as "non-self-governing territories." Except for mandates and trusteeships specified by the League of Nations and the U.N., the relationships between more and less powerful states have tended to evolve outside any rigid legal framework, and none of the following terms has an absolutely fixed meaning.

Colonies are dependent possessions whose inhabitants are not constitutionally under the dominant state's system of government but whose inhabitants are nationals of that state.

Commonwealths are autonomous states equal in status, united in their allegiance to a central power but not subordinate either to it or to one another in internal or external affairs.

Dependencies are states, provinces, or other places subject to the control of another power of which they do not form an integral part. The best known is Hong Kong, which China ceded to the United Kingdom in perpetuity in 1842, but which reverted to Chinese rule in 1997. The governor is appointed by the British monarch and foreign relations and defense are the responsibility of the U.K., but Hong Kong has substantial autonomy in commercial relations.

Mandates were territories surrendered by Turkey and Germany after World War I and, according to the League of Nations, "inhabited by peoples not yet able to stand by themselves" and therefore placed under the "tutelage" of different members of the League as "mandatories on behalf of the League." The last mandate to gain independence was South West Africa, now Namibia.

Protectorates *(associated states)* are states or territories partly under the control of another state but autonomous in domestic and certain external affairs. Protectorates are established by treaties.

Territories are regions (especially of Australia, Canada, and the United States) administered by a federal government and having some degree of self-government but not organized as a province or a state.

▶ AUSTRALIA
CHRISTMAS ISLAND
Location: eastern Indian Ocean;10°25'S, 105°39'E. **Total area:** 52 sq. mi. (135 sq km), about seven-tenths size of Washington, D.C. **Population:** 1,042 (July 2010 est.). **Type:** territory of Australia.
COCOS (KEELING) ISLANDS
Location: 27 islands in eastern Indian Ocean.West Island 12°05'S, 96°53'E. **Total area:** 5.4 sq. mi. (14.0 sq km), about 24 times size of the Mall in Washington, D.C. **Population:** 596 (July 2010 est.). **Type:** territory of Australia.
NORFOLK ISLAND
Location: island in western Pacific Ocean; 29°04'S, 167°57'E. **Total area:** 13.3 sq. mi. (34.6 sq km), about one-fifth size ofWashington, D.C. **Population:** 2,155 (July 2010 est.). **Type:** territory of Australia.
UNINHABITED TERRITORIES OF AUSTRALIA
Ashmore Is. (12°15'S, 123°05'E); Cartier Is. (12°30s, 123°30'E); Coral Sea Is. (18°00s, 158°00'E); Heard Is. (53°00s, 73°35'E); McDonald Is. (52°29'S, 72°50'E).

▶ DENMARK
FAEROE ISLANDS
Location: group of 18 islands (17 inhabited) in Atlantic Ocean SE of Iceland. Tórshavn 62°02'N, 6°47'W. **Total area:** 541 sq. mi. (1,399 sq km), eight times size of Washington, D.C. **Population:** 49,057 (July 2010 est.).**Type:** self-governing
GREENLAND
Location: North Atlantic Ocean, largely within Arctic Circle. Godthåb 64°11'N, 51°44'W. **Total area:** 840,000 sq.mi. (2,175,600 sq km); land area 131,931 sq. mi. (341,700 sq km) ice free, slightly more than three times size of Texas. **Population:** 57,637 (July 2010 est.). **Type:** parliamentary democracy with constitutional monarch.

▶ FRANCE
FRENCH GUIANA
Location: NE coast of South America. **Total area:** 35,135 sq. mi. (91,000 sq km), slightly smaller than Indiana. **Population:** 221,500 (2008 est.). **Type:** overseas department of France.
FRENCH POLYNESIA
Location: five island groups or archipelagoes—Gambier, Marquesas, Society (includes Tahiti and Bora Bora),Tuamotu, and Tubuai (Austral Islands)—in South Pacific Ocean about halfway between South America and Australia. Papeete (Society Is.) 17°32'S, 149°34'W. **Total area:** 2,589 sq. mi. (4,167 sq km), slightly less than one third size of Connecticut. **Population:** 291,000 (July 2010 est.). **Type:** overseas territory of France.
GUADELOUPE
Location: eastern Caribbean Sea: Guadeloupe 16°00'N, 61°42'W; St. Barthélemy 17°55'N, 63°50'W; Marie Galante 15°57'N, 61°20'W. **Total area:** 687 sq.mi. (1,780 sq km),10 times size of Washington, D.C. **Population:** 405,500 (2008 est.). **Type:** overseas department of France.
NEW CALEDONIA
Location: one large and several smaller islands in western South Pacific. Nouméa 22°16'S, 166°26'E. **Total area:** 7,359 sq. mi. (19,060 sq km), slightly smaller than New Jersey. **Population:** 229,993 (July 2010 est.). **Type:** overseas territory of France.
MARTINIQUE
Location: eastern Caribbean Sea (14°36'N, 61°05'W). **Total area:** 425 sq.mi. (1,100 sq km), slightly more than six times size of Washington, D.C. **Population:** 402,000 (2008 est.). **Type:** overseas department of France.
MAYOTTE
Location: Comoros archipelago in eastern Indian Ocean (12°47'S, 45°12'E).**Total area:** 145 sq. mi. (375 sq km), slightly more than twice size ofWashington, D.C. **Population:** 231,139 (July 2010 est.). **Type:** territorial collectivity of France.
ST. PIERRE AND MIQUELON
Location: North Atlantic off east coast of Canada. St. Pierre 46°46'N, 56°12'W. **Total area:** 93 sq.mi. (242 sq km),1.5 times size of Washington, D.C. **Population:** 6,010 (July 2010 est.). **Type:** territorial collectivity of France.
WALLIS AND FUTUNA
Location: two island groups (Wallis to NE, Hooru, incl. Futuna Is., to SW) in South Pacific. Mata-Utu (Wallis group) 13°22'S, 176°12'W. **Total area:** 106 sq.mi. (274 sq km). **Population:** 15,343 (July 2010 est.). **Type:** overseas territory of France.

UNINHABITED TERRITORIES OF FRANCE
Bassas da India (21°25'S, 39°42'E); Clipperton Is. (10°21'N, 109°13'W); Europa Is. (22°20s, 40°22'E); French Southern and Antarctic Lands (Kerguelen Is. 49°20s, 69°30'E); Glorioso Is. (11°30s, 47°20'E); Tromelin Is. (15°52'S, 54°25'E).

▶ **MOROCCO**
WESTERN SAHARA
Location: northwestern coast of Africa. **Total area:** 102,703 sq. mi. (266,000 sq km), about the size of Colorado. **Population:** 491,519 (July 2010 est.). **Type:** legal status and sovereignty still unresolved.

▶ **NETHERLANDS**
ARUBA
Location: southern Caribbean Sea (12°32'N, 70°02'W), off NW Venezuela. **Total area:** 75 sq. mi. (193 sq km), slightly larger than Washington, D.C. **Population:** 104,589 (July 2010 est.). **Type:** Part of the Netherlands, but full autonomy in internal affairs obtained in 1986 upon separation from Netherlands Antilles; parliamentary democracy.
NETHERLANDS ANTILLES
Location: two island groups in Caribbean Sea, about 500 mi. (800 km) apart. **Total area:** 371 sq. mi. (960 sq km), more than 5 times size ofWashington, D.C. **Population:** 228,693 (July 2010 est.). **Type:** autonomous part of Netherlands; parliamentary.

▶ **NEW ZEALAND**
COOK ISLANDS
Location: 15 islands (13 inhabited) in South Pacific. Avarua 21°12'S, 159° 46'W. **Total area:** 93 sq. mi. (240 sq km). **Population:** 11,488 (July 2010 est.). **Type:** self-governing parliamentary democracy in free association with New Zealand; Cook Islands government is fully responsible for internal affairs and has right at any time to move to full independence by unilateral action; New Zealand responsible for external affairs, in consultation with Cook Islands government.
NIUE
Location: coral island in western South Pacific (19°02'S, 169°55'W). **Total area:** 100 sq.mi. (260 sq km), 1.5 times size of Washington, D.C. **Population:** 1,354 (July 2010 est.). **Type:** self-governing parliamentary democracy territory in free association with New Zealand.
TOKELAU
Location: three atolls (Atafu, Nukunonu, Fakaofo) in South Pacific. Atafu 8°33'S, 172°30'W. **Total area:** 4 sq. mi. (10 sq km), about 17 times size of the Mall in Washington, D.C. **Population:** 1,400 (July 2010 est.). **Type:** territory of New Zealand.

▶ **NORWAY**
SVALBARD
Location: nine large and numerous smaller islands in Arctic Ocean. **Total area:** 38,557 sq. mi. (62,049 sq km), slightly smaller than West Virginia. **Population:** 2,067 (July 2010 est.). **Type:** territory of Norway.
UNINHABITED TERRITORIES OF NORWAY
Bouvet Is. (54°26'S, 3°24'E); Jan Mayen Is. (71°00'N, 8°30'W).

▶ **UNITED KINGDOM**
ANGUILLA
Location: island in northeastern Caribbean (18°03'N, 63°04'W). **Total area:** 35 sq.mi. (91 sq km), about one-half size of Washington,D.C. **Population:** 14,764 (July 2010 est.). **Type:** dependent territory of U.K.

BERMUDA
Location: archipelago of about 150 islands, in southernNorth Atlantic Ocean (32° 18'N, 64°47'W). **Total area:** 19 sq. mi. (50 sq km), about three-tenths size of Washington, D.C. **Population:** 68,268 (July 2010 est.). **Type:** British dependent territory.
BRITISH VIRGIN ISLANDS
Location: more than 40 mountainous islands (15 inhabited) in northeastern Caribbean. City of Road Town (on Tortola Is.), 18°26'N, 64°32'W. **Total area:** 58 sq.mi. (150 sq km), 0.9 times size of Washington, D.C. **Population:** 24,939 (July 2010 est.). **Type:** dependent territory of U.K.
GIBRALTAR
Location: narrow peninsula running southward from southwest coast of Spain, to which it is connected by an isthmus. **Total area:** 3 sq.mi. (6.5 sq km), about 11 times size of the Mall in Washington, D.C. **Population:** 28,877 (July 2010 est.). **Type:** colony of UK.
MONTSERRAT
(Two years of volcanic eruptions have left the southern half of this small island covered with ash and rock. More than half of its population had fled by mid-1997) **Location:** eastern Caribbean Sea (16°44'N, 62°14'W). **Total area:** 39 sq. mi. (100 sq km), about three-fifths size of Washington, D.C. **Population:** 5,118 (July 2010 est.); an estimated 8,000 refugees left the island following volcanic activity in 1995; some have returned. **Type:** colony of U.K.
CAYMAN ISLANDS
Location: three main and numerous smaller islands in western Caribbean. George Town (Grand Cayman Is.) 19°20'N, 81°23'W. **Total area:** 100 sq. mi. (260 sq km), 1.5 times size of Washington, D.C. **Population:** 50,209 (July 2010 est.). **Type:** British dependent territory.
FALKLAND ISLANDS
Location: two large and about 2,000 smaller islands in southwestern Atlantic Ocean. Stanley (East Falkland) 51°45'S, 57° 56'W. **Total area:** 4,699 sq. mi. (12,173 sq km), slightly smaller than Connecticut. **Population:** 3,140 (July 2010 est.). **Type:** colony of U.K.
PITCAIRN ISLANDS
Location: group of islands (one inhabited) in South Pacific. Pitcairn 25°04'S 130°04'W. **Total area:** 18 sq. mi. (47 sq km), three-tenths size of Washington, D.C. **Population:** 48 (July 2010 est.). **Type:** colony of U.K.
ST. HELENA
Location: eastern South Atlantic (15°56'S, 5°43'W). Dependencies are Ascension Is. (7°56'S, 14°25'W) 700 mi. to NW, and Tristan da Cunha (37°05'S, 12°17'W) 1,500 mi to SSW. **Total area:** 158 sq. mi. (410 sq km), slightly more than two times size of Washington, D.C. **Population:** 7,670 (July 2010 est.). **Type:** dependent territory of U.K.
TURKS AND CAICOS ISLANDS
Location: more than 30 islands forming southeastern end of Bahamas Islands in Caribbean Sea. **Total area:** 166 sq.mi. (430 sq km), 2.5 times size of Washington, D.C. **Population:** 23,528 (July 2010 est.). **Type:** colony of U.K.
UNINHABITED TERRITORIES
OF THE UNITED KINGDOM
British Indian Ocean Territory (Diego Garcia 6°34'S, 72°12'E); South Georgia Is. (54°15'S, 36°45'W); South Orkney Is. (60°35'S, 45°30'W); South Sandwich Is. (56°00s, 26°30'W); South Shetland Is. (62°00s, 58°00'W).

The United Nations

▶STRUCTURE

Establishment Pres. Franklin D. Roosevelt coined the name "United Nations," which was first used in the "Declaration by United Nations" of Jan. 1, 1942, during World War II, when representatives of 26 countries pledged their governments to continue fighting together against the Axis Powers. From August to October 1944, representatives of China, the Soviet Union, the United Kingdom and the United States met at Dumbarton Oaks, a mansion in Washington, D.C., to discuss creating an international peacekeeping organization. Out of these meetings came a general outline for the United Nations.

At the United Nations Conference on International Organization, which met at San Francisco from Apr. 25 to June 26, 1945, representatives from 50 countries drew up the United Nations Charter and signed it on June 26, 1945. Poland, not present at the Conference, signed on October 15, 1945, and is considered one of the founding member states.

The United Nations officially came into existence on October 24, 1945, when the charter was ratified by China, France, the Soviet Union, the United Kingdom, and the United States and by a majority of the other signatories.

U.N. Charter Full text of the Charter may be purchased for $3.00 from the United Nations, Sales Section, New York, NY 10017 U.S. The Preamble to the Charter sets forth the hopes for the United Nations: WE THE PEOPLES OF THE UNITED NATIONS DETERMINED

- to save succeeding generations from the scourge of war . . .
- to reaffirm faith in fundamental human rights, in the dignity and worth of the human person, in the equal rights of men and women and of nations large and small . . .
- to establish conditions under which justice and respect for the obligations arising from treaties and other sources of international law can be maintained . . .
- to promote social progress and better standards of life in larger freedom.

AND FOR THESE ENDS

- to practice tolerance and live together in peace with one another as good neighbors
- to unite our strength to maintain international peace and security
- to ensure, by the acceptance of principles and the institution of methods, that armed force shall not be used, save in the common interest
- to employ international machinery for the promotion of the economic and social advancement of all peoples

HAVE RESOLVED TO COMBINE OUR EFFORTS TO ACCOMPLISH THESE AIMS. Accordingly, our respective Governments, through representatives assembled in the city of San Francisco, who have exhibited their full powers found to be in good and due form, have agreed to the present Charter of the United Nations and do hereby establish an international organization to be known as the United Nations.

Purposes The purposes of the United Nations are set forth in Article 1 of the Charter. They are: 1. To maintain international peace and security. 2. To develop friendly relations among nations based on respect for the principle of equal rights and self-determination of peoples. 3. To cooperate in solving international problems of an economic, social, cultural or humanitarian character, and in promoting respect for human rights and fundamental freedoms for all. 4. To be a center for harmonizing the actions of nations in the attainment of these common ends.

Official languages Originally, there were five official languages of the United Nations: Chinese, English, French, Russian and Spanish. Arabic was added to the General Assembly in 1973, to the Security Council in 1982 and to the Economic and Social Council in 1983. Major United Nations documents and all meetings of the General Assembly, the Security Council and the Economic and Social Council are translated into the six working languages.

United Nations headquarters United Nations, New York, NY 10017 U.S. U.N. headquarters covers a 16-acre site in New York City along the East River from 42nd to 48th Streets. It consists of the interconnected General Assembly, Secretariat and Dag Hammarskjöld Library buildings. Acquisition of the site was made possible by a gift of $8.5 million from John D. Rockefeller, Jr., and one-third of that amount from New York City. In 1951, the 39-story Secretariat building was completed and began functioning as the official home of the United Nations.

Permanent observers to the U.N. at New York headquarters cannot vote and do not have diplomatic privileges or immunities unless connected to the member nation's consulate. They do have free access to the public meetings and distribution of relevant documentation.

Non-member observer the Holy See.

Intergovernmental and observer organizations: More than 25 organizations have observer status at the U.N. Following is a representative sample: Caribbean Community, Commonwealth of Independent States; Council of Europe; International Federation of Red Cross and Red Crescent Societies; League of Arab States; Organization of African Unity; Organization of American States; Organization of Islamic Conference; Palestine.

PRINCIPAL ORGANS

General Assembly

The Assembly is the world's forum for discussing major issues facing the international community including world peace and security, human rights, global environment, disarmament, health issues including AIDS, and the rights of women and children.

The Assembly consists of all 192 member states, each having one vote. On important issues a two-thirds majority of those present and voting is required; other questions require a simple majority vote. It holds its annual session from September to December, and may call for extra sessions as needed. Its agenda of more than 150 matters for discussion is first dealt with in six main committees: Its agenda of more than 150 matters for discussion is first dealt with in six main committees: First Committee: Disarmament and International Security; Second Committee: Economic and Financial; Third Committee: Social, Humanitarian and Cultural; Fourth Committee: Special Political and De-colonization; Fifth Committee: Administrative and Budgetary; Sixth Committee: Legal. After discussing issues facing the world, it adopts recommendations (called resolutions) but has no power to enforce its decisions (resolutions), except the power of world opinion.

The Assembly considers and approves U.N. budget and assesses member states according to their ability to pay.

Security Council
The Council may investigate any dispute or situation that might lead to international friction, and may recommend methods for adjusting such disputes or terms for their settlement. While other organs of the U.N. make recommendations to governments, the Security Council alone has the power to take decisions that member states are obligated under the Charter to carry out.

The Security Council has 15 members: five permanent members, and the General Assembly elects 10 other members for two-year terms. They are not eligible for immediate re-election. The Council may be called into session at any time, and a representative of each member state must be present at U.N. headquarters at all times.

The five permanent members are China, France, Russia, the United Kingdom and the United States.

The terms of office of each non-permanent member ends on December 31 of the year indicated in parentheses: Austria (2010), Bosnia and Herzegovina (2011), Brazil (2011), Gabon (2011), Japan (2010), Lebanon (2011), Mexico (2010), Nigeria (2011), Turkey (2010), Uganda (2010).

Decisions on matters of procedure require the approval of at least nine of the 15 members. Decisions on all other matters also require nine votes, including the concurring votes of all five permanent members. A negative vote by any permanent member on a non-procedural matter is often referred to as the "veto," which results in the rejection of the proposal. A state that is involved in a dispute may not vote.

Economic and Social Council (ECOSOC)
The Council is the principal organ to co-ordinate the economic and social work of the U.N. and its specialized agencies. It makes recommendations and initiates activities relating to world trade, industrialization, natural resources, human rights, the status of women, population, social welfare, education, health and related matters, science and technology and many other economic and social questions.

ECOSOC has 54 members elected for three-year terms by the General Assembly.

International Court of Justice (World Court)
The Court is the judicial organ of the U.N. and sits in The Hague, Netherlands. All U.N. member states are automatically members of the Court. One country that is not a member of the U.N. is party to the Court–Switzerland. The Court is not open to individuals. It issues judgments on all questions that states refer to it and all matters provided for in the U.N. Charter or in treaties or conventions in force. Both the General Assembly and the Security Council can ask the Court for an advisory opinion on any legal question as can other organs of the U.N. or specialized agencies, when authorized to do so by the Assembly.

The Court has dealt with a wide variety of subjects, including territorial rights, the delimitation of territorial waters and continental shelves, fishing jurisdiction, questions of nationality and the right of individuals to asylum, territorial sovereignty, and the right of passage through foreign territory.

The judgment of the Court is final and without appeal. However, a revision may be applied for within ten years from the date of the judgment on the ground of a new decisive factor. If a party rejects the judgment, the other party may take the issue to the Security Council.

Judges: The ICJ has 15 independent judges, of different nationalities, elected by both the General Assembly and the Security Council. Judges hold nine-year terms and may be re-elected. All questions are decided by a majority of the judges present; the president votes only in case of a tie.

Secretariat
The Secretariat services the other organs of the U.N. and administers the programs and policies they develop. Headed by the Secretary-General, it consists of an international staff of more than 25,000 men and women from over 150 countries.

Secretaries-General: The General Assembly elects the Secretary-General to terms of office of five years (they may be re-elected). The Secretary-General, by tradition, does not come from one of the permanent member states of the Security Council–China, France, Russia, UK or the U.S. Those who have served in this post are:

Trygve Lie, Norway, Feb. 1, 1946, to Nov. 10, 1952;
Dag Hammarskjöld, Sweden, Apr. 11, 1953, to Sept. 17, 1961;
U Thant, Burma, Nov. 3, 1961, to Dec. 31, 1971;
Kurt Waldheim, Austria, Jan. 1, 1972, to Dec. 31, 1981;
Javier Perez de Cuellar, Peru Jan. 1, 1982 to Dec. 31,1991;
Boutros Boutros-Ghali, Egypt, Jan. 1, 1992, to Dec. 31, 1996;
Kofi Annan, Ghana, Jan. 1, 1997 to Dec. 31, 2006.
Ban Ki-Moon, South Korea, Jan. 1, 2007 to present.

►UNITED NATIONS PROGRAMS
Each U.N. program was created by the General Assembly and reports to it through the Economic and Social Council (ECOSOC). Each member of the U.N. is a member of each Program.

International Research and Training Institute for the Advancement of Women (INSTRAW) Estab.: 1979 (made U.N. program in 1985); **HQ:** Calle Cesar Nicolas Penson, 102-A, Santo Domingo, Dominican Republic. Carries out research, training and information activities worldwide to show and increase women's key role in development.

United Nations Centre for Human Settlements (Habitat) Estab.: 1978; **HQ:** P.O. Box 30030, Nairobi, Kenya. Works to provide models and tools so people can improve their housing. Major concerns are planning, financing and management of human settlements—especially in developing countries.

United Nations Children's Fund (UNICEF) Estab.: 1946; **HQ:** UNICEF House, Three United Nations Plaza, New York, NY 10017, U.S. Provides care for children in developing countries by providing low-cost community-based services in maternal and child health, immunization, breast-feeding, growth monitoring, nutrition, clean water and sanitation, and education.

United Nations Conference on Trade and Development (UNCTAD) Estab.: 1964; **HQ:** Place des Nations, 8-14, Av. de la Paix, 1211 Geneva 10, Switzerland. Works to bring developing countries into global trade by formulating international trade policies, mediating multilateral trade agreements and providing assistance to governments.

United Nations Development Programme (UNDP) Estab.: 1965; **HQ:** One United Nations Plaza, New

U.S. Representatives to the U.N.

The U.S. representative to the U.N. holds the title of Ambassador Extraordinary and Plenipotentiary Permanent Representative and heads the U.S. Mission to the U.N.

Year	Ambassador
1946	Edward R. Stettinius Jr.
1946–47	Herschel V. Johnson (acting)
1947–53	Warren R. Austin
1953–60	Henry Cabot Lodge Jr.
1960–61	James J. Wadsworth
1961–65	Adlai E. Stevenson
1965–68	Arthur J. Goldberg
1968	George W. Ball
1968–69	James Russell Wiggins
1969–71	Charles W. Yost
1971–73	George H.W. Bush
1973–75	John A. Scali
1975–76	Daniel P. Moynihan
1976–77	William W. Scranton
1977–79	Andrew Young
1979–81	Donald McHenry
1981–85	Jeane J. Kirkpatrick
1985–89	Vernon A. Walters
1989–92	Thomas J. Pickering
1992–93	Edward J. Perkins
1993–96	Madeleine K. Albright
1997–98	Bill Richardson
1999–2001	Richard C. Holbrooke
2001–2004	John D. Negroponte
2004–2005	John C. Danforth
2005–2007	John R. Bolton
2007–2009	Dr. Zalmay Khalilzad
2009–present	Susan E. Rice

York, NY 10017, U.S. Coordinates development activities within the U.N. Operates more than 5,000 projects in 150 countries and territories to facilitate development in economic and social sectors, including: farming, fishing, forestry, mining, manufacturing, power, transport, communications, housing, trade, health and environmental sanitation, economic planning and public administration.

United Nations Environment Programme (UNEP) Estab.: 1972; **HQ:** United Nations Avenue, Gigiri,P.O. Box 30552, Nairobi, Kenya. Coordinates international environment issues, including international environment conventions, monitors significant changes in environment and coordinates sound environmental practices.

United Nations Fund for Population Activities (UNFPA) Estab.: 1969; **HQ:** 220 E. 42nd Street, New York, NY 10017, U.S. Provides assistance to population programs in developing countries; promotes understanding of key population factors: population growth, fertility, mortality, spatial distribution and migration.

Office of the United Nations High Commissioner for Refugees (UNHCR) Estab.: 1950; **HQ:** Case Postale 2500, CH-1211 Geneve 2 Depot, Switzerland. Provides food, clothing and shelter for refugees and works with governments to establish safe conditions whereby refugees may return home and, when that is not possible, seeks to ensure that refugees receive asylum.

United Nations Institute for Training and Research (UNITAR) Estab: 1965; **HQ:** Palais des Nations, CH1211 Geneva 10, Switzerland. Provides training for members of U.N.'s permanent missions, including courses on international economics, workshops on drafting and negotiating international legal instruments, dispute settlement,

and training on peace, security, human rights and humanitarian assistance.

United Nations University (UNU) Estab.: 1973; **HQ:** 53-70 Jingumae 5-chome, Shibuya-ku, Tokyo 150, Japan. UNU has no students of its own, no campus and no faculty. It is an international community of scholars engaged in research operating through worldwide networks of academic research institutions.

World Food Council (WFC) Estab.: 1974; **HQ:** Via delle Terme di Caracalla, 00100 Rome, Italy. Encourages developing countries to adopt a national food strategy whereby they assess their food situation needs, supply, potential for increasing production, storage, processing, transportation and distribution.

World Food Programme (WFP) (Joint program operated by U.N. and Food and Agriculture Organization (FAO) **Estab.:** 1963; **HQ:** Via C.G.Viola 68/70, Parco dei Medici, 00148 Rome, Italy. Provides food to support development activities and in times of emergencies. Operates projects in forestry, soil erosion control, irrigation, land rehabilitation and rural settlements.

▶SPECIALIZED AGENCIES OF THE U.N.

The specialized agencies associated with the United Nations are self-governing, independent organizations that work with the U.N. system and each other through the coordination machinery of the Economic and Social Council (ECOSOC). Each country affiliates with each agency on an individual basis. Membership in an agency is separate from U.N. membership. Nongovernmental organizations (NGOs) having expertise in the area may affiliate with each agency on a separate basis.

Food and Agriculture Organization of the United Nations (FAO) Member States: 189; **Estab.:** Oct. 16, 1945; **HQ:** Via delle Terme di Caracalla, 00100 Rome, Italy. Works to increase output of farmlands, forests and fisheries and to raise nutritional levels. Co-sponsors World Food Programme, which uses food, cash and services donated by member states for emergency situations.

International Atomic Energy Agency (IAEA) Member States: 144; **Estab.:** July 29, 1957; **HQ:** Vienna International Centre, P.O. Box 100, A-1400 Vienna, Austria. (Not regular specialized agency in that it does not report through ECOSOC but directly to General Assembly.) Fosters and guides development of peaceful uses of atomic energy, establishes standards for nuclear safety and environmental protection, aids member countries through technical cooperation, and fosters exchange of information on nuclear energy.

International Civil Aviation Organization (ICAO) Member States: 190; **Estab.:** Apr. 4, 1947; **HQ:** 999 University Street, Montreal, Quebec H3C 5H7, Canada. Works for safer air travel conditions worldwide. Establishes visual and instrument flight rules for pilots and crews; develops aeronautical charts for navigation; co-ordinates aircraft radio frequencies and works with customs procedures.

International Fund for Agricultural Development (IFAD) Member States: 164; **Estab.:** Nov. 30, 1977; **HQ:** Via del Serafico 107, 00142 Rome, Italy. Lends money to peoples in developing countries for agricultural development projects, including livestock, fisheries, processing and storage, irrigation, research and training.

International Labor Organization (ILO) Member States: 175; **Estab.:** 1919, under the Treaty of Versailles; (became U.N. specialized agency Dec. 14, 1946);. **HQ:** 4, route des Morillons, CH-1211 Geneva

22, Switzerland. Promotes social justice for working people everywhere by formulating international policies and programs to help improve working and living conditions; creates international labor standards as guidelines for governments and assists in vocational training, management techniques, occupational safety and health.

International Maritime Organization (IMO) Member States: 167; **Estab.:** Mar. 17, 1958; **HQ:** 4 Albert Embankment, London SE1 SR, England. Works to improve international shipping procedures and encourages highest standards in maritime safety; seeks to prevent and control marine pollution from ships and sets standards for training and certification of seafarers.

International Telecommunication Union (ITU) Member States: 191; **Estab.:** 1865, it became a U.N. specialized agency in Jan. 1949; **HQ:** Place des Nations, 1211 Geneva 20, Switzerland. Coordinates use of radio frequencies, tracks positions assigned by countries to geostationary satellites; coordinates modem and Internet standards.

United Nations Educational, Scientific and Cultural Organization (UNESCO) Member States: 192; **Estab.:** Nov. 4, 1946; **HQ:** 7, Place de Fontenoy, 75007 Paris, France. Promotes literacy through teacher training, building schools, and developing textbooks. Natural science programs include Man and the Biosphere and Intergovernmental Oceanographic Commission. Undertakes study and development of cultures, and conservation of world's inheritance of books, art and monuments.

United Nations Industrial Development Organization (UNIDO) Member States: 172; **Estab.:** 1966 (became U.N. specialized agency Jan. 1, 1986); **HQ:** P.O. Box 300, A-1400 Vienna, Austria. Promotes and accelerates industrialization of developing countries by providing technical assistance, training programs and advisory services.

Universal Postal Union (UPU) Member States: 191; **Estab.:** July 1, 1875 (became U.N. specialized agency July 1, 1948); **HQ:** International Bureau, Case postale 13, 3000 Berne 15, Switzerland. Establishes regulations for smooth exchange of mail worldwide.

World Bank Group Group of five closely related institutions. **HQ:** 1818 H Street, N.W., Washington, D.C. 20433 *International Bank for Reconstruction and Development (IBRD)* **Member States:** 185; **Estab.:** Dec. 27, 1945, to provide loans and technical assistance to developing countries to assist in their reconstruction and development. *International Finance Corporation (IFC)* **Member States:** 179 (Membership is open only to World Bank members.); **Estab.:** July 20, 1956, to stimulate flow of private capital into productive investment in member countries. While closely associated with Bank, IFC is separate legal entity and its funds are distinct from those of Bank. *International Development Association (IDA)* **Member States:** 166; **Estab.:** Sept. 24, 1960. (Affiliate of the Bank, IDA has same directors and staff as Bank.) Lends money to poor countries with interest-free credits. Financial resources are from contributions by donor governments. *Multilateral Investment Guarantee Agency (MIGA)* **Member States:** 171; **Estab.:** 1988. Augments capacity of other insurers through coinsurance or reinsurance, thereby insuring investment in countries restricted or excluded by policies of other insurers.

International Monetary Fund (IMF) Member States: 185; Estab.: Dec. 27, 1945; HQ: 700 19th Street, N.W., Washington, D.C. 20431. Makes financing available to members in balance-of-payments difficulties and provides technical assistance and training to improve their economic management.

World Health Organization (WHO) Member States: 193; **Estab.:** April 7, 1948; **HQ:** 20, avenue Appia, 1211 Geneva 27, Switzerland. Coordinates programs aimed at solving health problems by working with governments, other U.N. agencies and non-governmental organizations. (See "World Health" section.)

World Intellectual Property Organization (WIPO) Member States: 184; **Estab.:** 1883, (became U.N. specialized agency Dec. 17, 1974); **HQ:** 34, chemin des Colombettes, 121 Geneva 20, Switzerland. Promotes protection of intellectual property and cooperation in enforcement of agreements on matters such as copyrights, trademarks, industrial designs and patents.

World Meteorological Organization (WMO) Member States: 182; **Estab.:** 1873. (became U.N. specialized agency Mar. 23, 1950); **HQ:** 7 bis Avenue de la Paix, CP 2300, 1211 Geneva 2, Switzerland. Facilitates exchange of weather reports among countries; "World Weather Watch" tracks global weather conditions.

World Tourism Group (WTO) Member States: 150. **Estab.:** 1970; **HQ:** Capitan Haya 42, 28020 Madrid, Spain. Serves as a global forum for tourism policy issues and a practical source of tourism know-how.

▶PEACEKEEPING OPERATIONS

United Nations peacekeeping is the use of multinational forces, under U.N. command, to keep disputing countries or communities from fighting while efforts are made to help them negotiate a solution. It is undertaken only with the agreement of both hostile parties. United Nations Peacekeeping Forces received the Nobel Peace Prize in 1988. As of mid 2010, the U.N. had almost 124,000 personnel in 16 peacekeeping operations from 115 countries. More than 88,000 are troops and military observers, about 13,000 are police personnel, more than 5,800 are international civilian personnel, nearly 14,000 are local civilian staff and some 2,400 are U.N. Volunteers. Approximately 30 percent of civilians are women who are needed to interview victims of sexual and gender-based violence, work with women in prisons, assist female ex-combatants in the process of demobilizing and reintegration into civilian life, and mentor female cadets at police academies. The approved budget for July 1, 2009 to June 30, 2010 is approximately U.S. $7.9 billion. Following peacekeeping operations are administered by U.N. Department of Peacekeeping Operations (DPKO). Strength of the following operations is as of April 30, 2010.

Africa

African Union/United Nations Hybrid operation in Darfur (UNAMID). Since July 2007. Works in Darfur to support implementation of Darfur Peace Agreement. **Strength:** 21,993 total uniformed personnel, including 16,883 troops, 253 military observers, 4,797 police officers, supported by 1076 international civilian personnel, 1,557 local civilian staff and 419 U.N. Volunteers.

Chad, United Nations Mission in the Central African Republic and Chad (MINURCAT). Since September 2007. In concert with European Union to help create security conditions conducive to a voluntary, secure and sustainable return of refugees and displaced persons. **Strength:** 3,425 total uniformed personnel, including 3,425 troops, 29 military observers and 224 police officers, supported by 421 international civilian personnel, 567 local civilian staff and 146 U.N. Volunteers.

Democratic Republic of the Congo—MONUSCO —U.N. Organization Stabilization Mission in the Democratic Republic of the Congo (replaces U.N. Organization Mission in the Democratic Republic of the Congo MONUC). Since 1 July 2010. Authorized to have maximum of 19,815 military personnel, 760 military observers, 391 police personnel and 1,050 personnel of formed police units.

Ivory Coast, U.N. Operation in Ivory Coast (UNOCI). Since April 2004. A political mission to facilitate implementation by the Ivorian parties of the peace agreement signed by them in Jan. 2003. **Strength:** 8,503 total uniformed personnel, including 7,195 troops, 180 military observers; 1,128 police; supported by 401 international civilian personnel, 697 local staff and 294 U.N. Volunteers.

Liberia, U.N. Mission in Liberia (UNMIL). Since September 2003. Supports implementation of ceasefire agreement and peace process. **Strength:** 9,644 total uniformed personnel, including 8,226 troops and 124 military observers; 1,294 police; supported by 441 international civilian personnel, 989 local staff and 207 U.N. Volunteers.

Sudan, U.N. Mission in the Sudan (UNMIS). Since March 2005. Supports implementation of the Comprehensive Peace Agreement signed by the Government of Sudan and the Sudan People's Liberation Movement/Army on 9 January 2005; **Strength:** 10,571 total uniformed personnel, including 9,428 troops, 475 military observers, and 668 police; supported by 862 international civilian personnel, 2,631 local civilian and 371 U.N. Volunteers.

Western Sahara, U.N. Mission for the Referendum in Western Sahara (MINURSO). Since April 1991. Monitors cease-fire and is to organize and conduct a referendum which would allow people of Western Sahara to decide Territory's future status. **Strength:** 222 total uniformed personnel, including 20 troops, 6 police officers, 196 military observers; supported by 93 international civilian personnel, 161 local civilian staff and 20 U.N. Volunteers.

Americas

Haiti, U.N. Stabilization Mission in Haiti (MINUSTAH). Since June 2004. Supports Transitional Government to ensure secure and stable environment within which constitutional and political processes in Haiti can take place. **Strength:** 10,565 total uniformed personnel, including 8,304 troops and 2,261 police, supported by 471 international civilian personnel, 1,235 local civilian staff and 207 U.N. Volunteers.

Asia and the Pacific

East Timor—United Nations Integrated Mission in Timor-Leste—(UNMIT). Since August 2006. Supports Government in consolidating stability, enhancing a culture of democratic governance, and facilitating political dialogue. **Strength:** 1,565 total uniformed personnel, including 1,530 police and 35 military liaison officers; 362 international civilian staff; 902 local civilian personnel; and 173 U.N. Volunteers.

India–Pakistan, U.N. Military Observer Group in India and Pakistan (UNMOGIP). Since 1971. Stationed on both sides of Line of Control to observe cease-fire agreed upon by India and Pakistan under Simla Agreement of July 1972. **Strength:** 44 military observers, supported by 23 international civilian personnel and 47 local civilian staff.

Europe

Cyprus, U.N. Peacekeeping Force in Cyprus (UNFICYP). Since March 1964. Supervises cease-fire lines, maintains buffer zone, undertakes humanitarian activities. **Strength:** 925 total unifomed personnel, including 857 troops and 68 police; supported by 40 international civilian personnel and 114 local civilian staff.

Kosovo, U.N. Interim Administration Mission in Kosova (UNMIK). Since June 1999. Interim civilian administration supported by European Union and Organization for Security and Cooperation in Europe. **Authorized strength:** 225—in process of drawdown.

Middle East

Golan Heights, U.N. Disengagement Observer Force (UNDOF). Since June 1974. Maintains "area of separation" on Golan Heights between Israel and Syria and verifies arms limitation on both sides. **Strength:** 1,043 troops, assisted by some 76 military observers of UNTSO's Observer Group Golan; and supported by 39 international civilian personnel and 105 local civilian staff.

Lebanon, U.N. Interim Force in Lebanon (UNIFIL). Since March 1978. To confirm Israeli withdrawal from Lebanon, restore peace and security, help Lebanese government restore its authority. **Strength:** 11,871 military personnel, supported by some 319 international civilian and 657 local civilian staff. UNIFIL is also supported by around 50 UNTSO military observers of the Observer Group Lebanon.

Middle East, U.N. Truce Supervision Organization (UNTSO). Since May 1948. First U.N. peacekeeping operation. Monitors cease-fire, supervises armistice agreements, prevents isolated incidents from escalating and assists other U.N. peacekeeping operations in the region. **Strength:** 152 military observers; supported by 88 international civilian personnel and 121 local civilian staff.

▶FURTHER U.N. INFORMATION

www.un.org

United Nations Bookstore Room GA-32, New York, NY, 10017; 212-963-7680; 1-800-553-3210; Fax: 212-963-4910.

▶KEY EVENTS IN U.N. HISTORY

1946 (Jan. 10) First session of General Assembly begins at London with 51 member states.

1947 (Nov. 29) General Assembly passes Plan of Partition with Economic Union concerning future government of Palestine.

1948 (Dec. 10) Universal Declaration of Human Rights adopted by General Assembly.

U.N. pioneers concept of peacekeeping observer missions and peacekeeping forces (1956).

1949 Mediates cease-fire between India and Pakistan, ending two years of fighting over Kashmir.

1950 Security Council calls member states to help South Korea repel invasion by North Korea.

Economic and Social Council adopts Standard International Trade Classification as basis for gathering world trade statistics.

1953 U.N. coordinates first global-census effort to establish Earth's population for first time in history–2.4 billion people.

1955 First of ongoing congresses of criminologists and police officials draws up international principles and standards of criminal justice.

1959 U.N. General Assembly adopts Declaration on the Rights of the Child.

1960 Under de-colonization program, 17 territories become independent states; 16 in Africa join U.N.

1962 Secretary-General plays key role in resolving U.S.-Soviet confrontation over issue of nuclear missiles in Cuba.

1963 Security Council calls for arms embargo against South Africa. (Made mandatory in 1972.)

1967 After war erupts in Middle East, Security Council adopts Resolution 242, calling for withdrawal of forces from occupied territories, and recognizes right of all states in area to security.

Mediates settlement of Six-Day Arab-Israeli War.

1970 General Assembly adopts first international agreed-upon set of principles on seabed and ocean floor beyond national jurisdiction. Declares area "common heritage" of humanity.

1972 Security Council orders cease-fire in 17-day-old Middle East War and sends peacekeeping force to prevent further fighting between Israel and Arab states.

1975 U.N. conference at Mexico City launches Decade for Women to begin major effort toward women's equality worldwide.

1979 World Health Organization announces smallpox eradicated from all peoples on earth.

1988 Mediates ending of Iran-Iraq War. Mediates Soviet withdrawal from Afghanistan.

1990 Upon invitation, U.N. monitors demobilization of Nicaraguan rebel forces, and for first time monitors a presidential campaign and election in an independent nation.

Security Council Resolution 678 calls upon member states to restore peace and security in Kuwait by "all necessary means."

Responding to request by Haiti, U.N. supervises election of Haiti's first freely elected president.

1991 Security Council Resolution 687 sets terms of cease-fire in Gulf War and gives U.N. variety of duties to ensure peace.

Secretary-general negotiates release of last six hostages held in Lebanon.

General Assembly rescinds Resolution 3379 of Nov. 10, 1975, equating Zionism with racism.

1992 Secretary-general completes peace negotiations between government of El Salvador and rebel Farabundo Marti National Liberation Front.

1993 145 nations co-sponsor Convention on Prohibition of the Development, Production, Stockpiling and Use of Chemical Weapons.

Human Rights Commission adopts Resolution 1993/8, first formal statement that declares rape, conducted during war, an international war crime under Geneva Convention.

General Assembly creates post of High Commissioner for Human Rights with power to intervene wherever basic freedoms are suppressed.

1994 Security Council removes South Africa from its agenda, declaring end of apartheid.

Security Council establishes International Tribunal for Rwanda to prosecute persons responsible for genocide and other violations of international humanitarian law.

1995 Secretary-general launches 50th anniversary commemoration. International Tribunal for Former Yugoslavia, established in 1993 to prosecute persons responsible for serious violations of international humanitarian law in former Yugoslavia since 1991, schedules first trials for September with 15 judges from 15 countries.

1996 Upon request of the government, U.N. supervises free and fair elections in Sierra Leone that changes rule from military regime to democracy.

Hague-based International Criminal Tribunal for the former Yugoslavia begins trial for first war crimes in 50 years. Dusan Tadic, Bosnian Serb charged with torturing and murdering Bosnian Muslims and Croats at Omarska prison camp in Prijedor, Bosnia, in 1992. He is convicted in 1997 and sentenced to 20 years in prison.

1997 U.N. launches CyberSchoolBus to reach tens of thousands of students worldwide; provides lesson plans, global trends, quizzes; on-line Model U.N. discussion is first of its kind to reach 60,000 high schools and college students.

Thirteen nations ask for and receive U.N. assistance in holding their elections, including Algeria, Cambodia, Gambia, Guyana, Haiti, Honduras, Liberia, Mali and Yemen.

1998 1998 U.N. Conference on Rome adopts statute to create Permanent International Criminal Court to try individuals for genocide, war crimes, and crimes against humanity.

1999 Secretary-General issues Global Compact — enlisting businesses to advance universally agreed principles on human rights, labor and environment.

Security Council invests U.N. peacekeeping mission authority over Kosovo territory and people, including all legislative, executive, and judicial administration. First ever cooperation with non-U.N. organizations, including the E.U. and the Organization for Security in Europe.

Economic and Social Council holds first live broadcast of its high-level meeting over the Internet allowing global viewing.

2000 Millennium Summit, the largest single gathering of Heads of State and/or Government, brings 180 presidents, prime ministers and monarchs to the U.N. They issue the Millennium Declaration, which intends to solve humanity's most pressing problems, send every child to school, and deliver millions from poverty by 2015.

2001 (Sept. 28, 2001) Security Council establishes Counter Terrorism Committee and calls on all member states to cooperate in various measures to fight terrorism.

2002 (Jan.) Global Fund to fight AIDS, tuberculosis and malaria is launched.

(July 1) Statute of International Criminal Court enters into force. Anyone who commits any crimes under the Statute after this date will be liable for prosecution by the Court.

(July 1) Statute of International Criminal Court enters into force. Anyone who commits any crimes under the Statute after this date will be liable ffor prosecution by the Court.

2003 (Sept. 8, 9, 10) U.N. conducts first webcast of annual conference for nongovernmental organizations allowing people around the world to view and participate via e-mail. Daily live and on-demand webcasts of many U.N. meetings.

2004 (Aug. 12) Security Council unanimously renews for one more year the U.N. Assistance Mission for Iraq (UNAMI) whose tasks include coordinating various humanitarian operations and helping to organize elections by end of Jan. 2005 and draft a new constitution.

2005 (June 23–24) First General Assembly Hearing: 200 nongovernmental organizations present their ideas to Member States.

(Sept. 14–16) U.N. holds 5-year evaluation of Millennium Development Goals.

2007 (May 4) Intergovernmental Panel on Climate Change (IPCC) releases 4th Assesment Report, produced by 600 authors from 40 countries.

2010 General Assembly adopts Resolution Toward Global Partnerships to encourage U.N. system to develop common and systemic approach to partnerships with private sector with emphasis on impact, transparency, accountability and sustainability.

United Nations Member States (192)

Country	Joined U.N.	Country	Joined U.N.	Country	Joined U.N.
Afghanistan	1946	Ghana	1957	Pakistan	1947
Albania	1955	Greece	1945	Palau	1994
Algeria	1962	Grenada	1974	Panama	1945
Andorra	1993	Guatemala	1945	Papua New Guinea	1975
Angola	1976	Guinea	1958	Paraguay	1945
Antigua and Barbuda	1981	Guinea-Bissau	1974	Peru	1945
Argentina	1945	Guyana	1966	Philippines	1945
Armenia	1992	Haiti	1945	Poland	1945
Australia	1945	Honduras	1945	Portugal	1955
Austria	1955	Hungary	1955	Qatar	1971
Azerbaijan	1992	Iceland	1946	Moldova	1992
Bahamas	1973	India	1945	Romania	1955
Bahrain	1971	Indonesia	1950	Russian Federation	1945
Bangladesh	1974	Iran	1945	Rwanda	1962
Barbados	1966	Iraq	1945	Saint Kitts and Nevis	1983
Belarus	1945	Ireland	1955	Saint Lucia	1979
Belgium	1945	Israel	1949	Saint Vincent and the	1980
Belize	1981	Italy	1955	Grenadines	
Benin	1960	Ivory Coast	1960	Samoa	1976
Bhutan	1971	Jamaica	1962	San Marino	1992
Bolivia	1945	Japan	1956	São Tome and Principe	1975
Bosnia and Herzegovina	1992	Jordan	1955	Saudi Arabia	1945
Botswana	1966	Kazakhstan	1992	Senegal	1960
Brazil	1945	Kenya	1963	Serbia	2000
Brunei Darussalam	1984	Kiribati	1999	Seychelles	1976
Bulgaria	1955	Kuwait	1963	Sierra Leone	1961
Burkina Faso	1960	Kyrgyzstan	1992	Singapore	1965
Burundi	1962	Laos	1955	Slovakia[2]	1993
Cambodia	1955	Latvia	1991	Slovenia	1992
Cameroon	1960	Lebanon	1945	Solomon Islands	1978
Canada	1945	Lesotho	1966	Somalia	1960
Cape Verde	1975	Liberia	1945	South Africa	1945
Central African Republic	1960	Libya	1955	South Korea	1991
Chad	1960	Liechtenstein	1990	Spain	1955
Chile	1945	Lithuania	1991	Sri Lanka	1955
China	1945	Luxembourg	1945	Sudan	1956
Colombia	1945	Macedonia[3]	1993	Suriname	1975
Comoros	1975	Madagascar	1960	Swaziland	1968
Congo	1960	Malawi	1964	Sweden	1946
Congo, Democratic	1960	Malaysia	1957	Switzerland	2002
Republic of[1]		Maldives	1965	Syria	1945
Costa Rica	1945	Mali	1960	Tanzania	1961
Croatia	1992	Malta	1964	Tajikistan	1992
Cuba	1945	Marshall Islands	1991	Thailand	1946
Cyprus	1960	Mauritania	1961	Togo	1960
Czech Republic[2]	1993	Mauritius	1968	Tonga	1999
Denmark	1945	Mexico	1945	Trinidad and Tobago	1962
Djibouti	1977	Micronesia	1991	Tunisia	1956
Dominica	1978	Monaco	1993	Turkey	1945
Dominican Republic	1945	Mongolia	1961	Turkmenistan	1992
East Timor	2002	Montenegro	2006	Tuvalu	2000
Ecuador	1945	Morocco	1956	Uganda	1962
Egypt	1945	Mozambique	1975	Ukraine	1945
El Salvador	1945	Myanmar	1948	United Arab Emirates	1971
Equatorial Guinea	1968	Namibia	1990	United Kingdom	1945
Eritrea	1993	Nauru	1999	United States	1945
Estonia	1991	Nepal	1955	Uruguay	1945
Ethiopia	1945	Netherlands	1945	Uzbekistan	1992
Fiji	1970	New Zealand	1945	Vanuatu	1981
Finland	1955	Nicaragua	1945	Venezuela	1945
France	1945	Niger	1960	Vietnam	1977
Gabon	1960	Nigeria	1960	Yemen[4]	1947
Gambia	1965	North Korea	1991	Zambia	1964
Georgia	1992	Norway	1945	Zimbabwe	1980
Germany	1973	Oman	1971		

Notes: 1. Formerly Zaire. 2. Czechoslovakia was an original member of the U.N.; when the nation split into separate Czech and Slovak Republics, both new republics were admitted as member states on Jan. 19, 1993. 3. Provisionally referred to for all purposes within the U.N. as "The former Yugoslav Republic of Macedonia" pending settlement of a difference with Greek Macedonia over the name. 4. Includes the former Democratic Yemen (admitted as a separate member in 1967), which merged with Yemen in 1990. **Source:** United Nations.

Major International Organizations

African Union (AU) *[successor to the Organization of African Unity (OAU)]* HQ: P.O. Box 3243, Roosvelt Street, W21K19, Addis Ababa, Ethiopia. **Estab.:** By Constitutive Act at Lone, Togo, July 11, 2000 to achieve greater unity and solidarity between African countries and the peoples of Africa; accelerate political and socio-economic integration of the continent; promote democratic principles and institutions, popular participation and good governance. **Members** (53): Algeria, Angola, Benin, Burkina Faso, Burundi, Cameroon, Cape Verde, Central African Republic, Chad, Comoros, Congo, Congo, Dem. Rep, Côte d´Ivoire, Djibouti, Egypt, Equatorial Guinea, Eritrea, Ethiopia, Gabon, Gambia, Ghana, Guinea Bissau, Guinea Conakry, Kenya, Lesotho, Liberia, Libya, Madagascar, Malawi, Mali, Mauritania, Mauritius, Mozambique, Namibia, Niger, Nigeria, Rwanda, Saharawi Arab Democratic Republic, São Tomé & Príncipe, Senegal, Seychelles, Somalia, South Africa, Sudan, Swaziland, Tanzania, Togo, Tunisia, Uganda, Zambia, Zimbabwe.

Commonwealth HQ: Marlborough House, Pall Mall, London, SW1Y 5HX, UK. **Estab.:** By some members of British Empire through evolutionary process formalized by Statute of Westminster on Dec. 13, 1931. As voluntary association of independent states, Commonwealth has no written constitution and no rigid contractual obligations. Emphasis is on consultation and exchange of views for cooperation, especially in economic affairs, drug trafficking, international terrorism and technical assistance to less developed states. Some countries that were part of British Empire are not part of Commonwealth. **Members** (53): Antigua and Barbuda, Australia, Bahamas, Bangladesh, Barbados, Belize, Botswana, Brunei, Cameroon, Canada, Cyprus, Dominica, Fiji, Gambia, Ghana, Grenada, Guyana, India, Jamaica, Kenya, Kiribati, Lesotho, Malawi, Malaysia, Maldives, Malta, Mauritius, Mozambique, Namibia, Nauru, New Zealand, Nigeria, Pakistan, Papua New Guinea, Saint Kitts and Nevis, Saint Lucia, Saint Vincent and the Grenadines, Samoa, Seychelles, Sierra Leone, Singapore, Solomon Islands, South Africa, Sri Lanka, Swaziland, Tanzania, Tong, Trinidad and Tobago, Tuvalu, Uganda, United Kingdom, Vanuatu, Zambia.

Commonwealth of Independent States (CIS) HQ: Uliza Kirowa 17, Minsk 220000. **Estab.:** Dec. 8, 1991, by Byelorussia (Belarus), Russia, and Ukraine, which dissolved USSR and created CIS. Members agree to broad cooperation, including to cooperate in political, economic, ecological, humanitarian, and cultural fields. **Members** (12): Armenia, Azerbaijan, Belarus, Georgia, Kazakhstan, Kyrgyzstan, Moldova, Russia, Tajikistan, Turkmenistan, Ukraine, Uzbekistan.

European Union (EU, the Common Market), (See Part III: "The Global Economy.")

League of Arab States (LAS, the Arab League) HQ: Tahrir Square, Cairo, Egypt. **Estab.:** By treaty signed on Mar. 22, 1945 at Cairo, Egypt, to strengthen relations among members in financial, communications, cultural, health, social, nationality and social areas. **Members** (22): Algeria, Bahrain, Comoros, Djibouti, Egypt, Iraq, Jordan, Kuwait, Lebanon, Libya, Mauritania, Morocco, Oman, Palestine Liberation Organization, Qatar, Saudi Arabia, Somalia, Sudan, Syria, Tunisia, United Arab Emirates, Yemen.

North Atlantic Treaty Organization (NATO) HQ: B-1110 Brussels, Belgium. **Estab.:** By North Atlantic Treaty on Aug. 24, 1949, to maintain security among member states. NATO attempted to maintain military balance with countries of the Warsaw Pact: Bulgaria, Czechoslovakia, East Germany, Hungary, Poland, Romania, USSR. Since 1989 security challenges have shifted to possible adverse consequences from serious economic, social, and political difficulties, including ethnic rivalries and territorial disputes, arms proliferation, and terrorism. In 1997, leaders of NATO voted to admit Czech Republic, Hungary and Poland, and their official membership received final approval in 1999. In May 2002, Russia became a participant (but not a full-fledged member) of the organization. Russia is not bound by NATO's collective defense pact, nor will it have a veto over NATO decisions. **Members** (28): Albania, Belgium, Bulgaria, Canada, Croatia, Czech Republic, Denmark, Estonia, France, Germany, Greece, Hungary, Iceland, Italy, Latvia, Lithuania, Luxembourg, Netherlands, Norway, Poland, Portugal, Romania, Slovakia, Slovenia, Spain, Turkey, United Kingdom, U.S.

Organization of American States (OAS) HQ: 1889 F St., NW, Washington, DC 20006-4499, U.S. **Estab.:** By charter signed at Bogotá, Columbia, effective Dec. 13, 1951, to strengthen peace and security on continent, promote cooperation in human rights, education, economic and social development and scientific exchanges, and to seek solutions to political, juridical and economic problems. **Members** (35): Antigua and Barbuda, Argentina, Bahamas, Barbados, Belize, Bolivia, Brazil, Canada, Chile, Colombia, Costa Rica, Cuba (suspended from OAS activities but not membership in 1962), Dominica, Dominican Republic, Ecuador, El Salvador, Grenada, Guatemala, Guyana, Haiti, Honduras, Jamaica, Mexico, Nicaragua, Panama, Paraguay, Peru, Saint Kitts and Nevis, Saint Lucia, Saint Vincent and the Grenadines, Suriname, Trinidad and Tobago, U.S., Uruguay, Venezuela.

Organization of Petroleum Exporting Countries (OPEC) HQ: Obere Donaustrasse 93, A-1020 Vienna, Austria. **Estab.:** Nov. 14, 1960 by resolution adopted at Baghdad Conference, to coordinate and unify petroleum policies and to stabilize international oil prices to prevent harmful fluctuations. **Members** (13): Algeria, Angola, Ecuador, Indonesia, Iran, Iraq, Kuwait, Libya, Nigeria, Qatar, Saudi Arabia, United Arab Emirates, Venezuela.

Organization for Security and Cooperation in Europe (OSCE) HQ: Kärtnerring 5-7, A-1010 Vienna, Austria. **Estab.:** by Final Act of Conference on Security and Cooperation in Europe in 1975. In 1990, CSCE members declared end of "era of confrontation and division of Europe" and beginning of "a new era of democracy, peace and unity." Serves as forum for dialogue, negotiation, cooperation, and direction in shaping new Europe. **Members** (56): Albania, Andorra, Armenia, Austria, Azerbaijan, Belarus, Belgium, Bosnia and Herzegovina, Bulgaria, Canada, Croatia, Cyprus, Czech Republic, Denmark, Estonia, Finland, France, Georgia, Germany, Greece, Holy See, Hungary, Iceland, Ireland, Italy, Kazakhstan, Kyrgyzstan, Latvia, Liechtenstein, Lithuania, Luxembourg, Macedonia, Malta, Moldova, Monaco, Montenegro, Netherlands, Norway, Poland, Portugal, Romania, Russia, San Marino, Serbia, Slovakia, Slovenia, Spain, Sweden, Switzerland, Tajikistan, Turkmenistan, Turkey, Ukraine, UK, U.S., Uzbekistan.

ASTRONOMY

Astronomy is the oldest science, but it continues to be at the forefront of scientific thought. The ancients of the Northern Hemisphere knew the skies, probably better than most of us do. They recognized that most stars appear to rise in the east at night and travel in circular paths across the sky, and that a few are wanderers—planets—that move among the other stars. They named the groups of stars that we call constellations and recognized that constellations visible in winter are different from those visible in summer (although some are visible all year). They learned how to find the extremities of the sunrise and built giant stone structures, such as Stonehenge, probably to locate certain positions of the Sun or other stars.

In 1609 Galileo introduced the first artificial device for exploring the universe—the astronomical telescope. Even in that first year, he saw wonders the ancients never knew. Since then, we have built larger and better telescopes, devices for detecting radio waves, microwaves, X-rays, infrared waves, and gamma rays from space, and have even traveled to our own Moon. We have sent space probes to many of the nearby bodies in space, and these have transmitted television close-ups to Earth.

►THE SOLAR SYSTEM

All bodies under the gravitational influence of our local star, the Sun, together with the Sun, form the solar system. The largest bodies, including Earth, are called planets. There have been nine bodies recognized as planets by the International Astronomical Union for over 65 years. In August 2006, however, the Union voted to reduce the status of Pluto to a "dwarf planet," of which there are three. Often smaller cool bodies, called satellites or moons, orbit a planet. Bodies smaller than planets that orbit the Sun are classed as asteroids if they are rocky or metallic, comets if they are mostly ice and dust, and meteoroids if they are very small. Most comets release gases as they near the heat of the Sun, producing a luminous cloud called a coma and often a long tail. A meteoroid that burns in Earth's atmosphere is a meteor, while one that reaches Earth without burning completely becomes a meteorite.

It is currently believed that the solar system formed when a cloud of gas condensed to form the Sun. Parts of the cloud formed small bodies similar to today's asteroids, comets, and meteoroids. Collectively, these small bodies are called planetesimals or planetoids. Early in the history of the solar system, about 4.6 billion years ago, the planetoids frequently

---

Major Events in Astronomy and Space

B.C.
585 Thales of Miletus (Greek: c. 625–c. 547) predicts solar eclipse in Asia Minor.
c. 480 Astronomer Oenopides of Chios (Greek: 5th cent.) discovers that Earth is tilted with respect to Sun.
352 Chinese report "guest star," or supernova, the earliest known sighting.
c. 340 Astronomer Kidinnu (Kidenas; Babylon: c. 379) discovers precession of equinoxes, the apparent change in position of stars caused by Earth's wobbling on its orbit.
c. 300 Chinese astronomers compile star maps.
c. 240 Chinese astronomers observe Halley's comet. Eratosthenes of Cyrene (Greek: c.276–c.194) correctly calculates Earth's size.
165 Chinese astronomers notice sunspots.
c. 130 Astronomer Hipparchus of Nicea (Greek: 147–127) correctly determines distance to Moon and rediscovers precession of equinoxes (see 340 B.C.).

A.D.
c. 140 *Almagest* of Ptolemy (Greek: c. 90–168) develops astronomy of solar system in form based on Sun and planets revolving about Earth.
1543 *De Revolutionibus* by Nicholas Copernicus (Polish: 1473–1543) presents convincing arguments that Earth and other planets orbit Sun.
1577 Tycho Brahe (Danish: 1546–1601) proves that comets are visitors from space, not weather phenomena as previously believed.
1592 David Fabricius (German: 1564–1617) discovers star, later named Mira, that gradually disappears; in studying it in 1638, Phocyclides Ho-

lawarda recognizes that it appears and reappears on regular basis—the first-known variable star.
1609 Johannes Kepler (German: 1571–1630) discovers that the planets move in elliptical orbits.
1610 Galileo observes Jupiter's moons, phases of Venus, and (although he does not recognize what they are) rings of Saturn.
1611 Several astronomers simultaneously discover sunspots for first time in West.
1671 Giovanni Domenico Cassini (Italian-French: 1625-1712) correctly determines distances of the planets from Sun.
1682 Edmond Halley (English: 1656–1742) describes comet now known by his name and in 1705 correctly predicts its return in 1758.
1718 Halley discovers that stars move with respect to each other.
1755 Immanuel Kant (German: 1724–1804) proposes that many nebulas are actually composed of millions of stars and that solar system formed when giant cloud of dust condensed.
1781 William Herschel (German-English: 1738–1822) discovers planet Uranus.
1785 Herschel demonstrates that Milky Way is disk- or lens-shaped group of many stars, one of which is the Sun.
1801 Guiseppe Piazzi (Italian: 1746–1826) discovers first-known asteroid, Ceres.
1838 Friedrich W. Bessel (German: 1784–1846) determines distance to star other than the Sun.
1846 Johann G. Galle (German: 1812–1910) discovers planet Neptune using predictions of Urbain J.J. Leverrier (French: 1811–77) and John Couch Adams (English: 1819–92).

1924   Edwin Hubble (American: 1889–1953) shows that galaxies are "island universes"—giant aggregations of stars as large as Milky Way.

1929   Hubble finds that universe is expanding.

1930   Clyde Tombaugh (American: 1906–97) discovers planet Pluto.

1931   Karl Jansky (American: 1905–50) discovers that radio waves are coming from space, leading to founding of radio astronomy.

1948   George Gamow (Russian-American: 1904–68), Ralph Alpher (American: 1921–), and Robert Herman (American: 1914–97) develop Big Bang theory of origin of universe.

Jan Hendrik Oort (Dutch: 1900–1992) proposes that comets come from a vast cloud of material orbiting far beyond Pluto; the material is now known as the Oort Cloud.

1957   USSR launches *Sputnik 1,* the first man-made satellite.

1961   Soviet cosmonaut Yuri A. Gagarin (Russian: 1934–68) is first human to orbit Earth.

1962   U.S. space probe *Mariner 2* is first to reach neighborhood of another planet, Venus.

1963   Maarten Schmidt (Dutch-American: 1929–) is first astronomer to recognize a quasar.

1964   Arno Penzias (German-American: 1933–) and Robert Wilson (American: 1936–) find radio waves pervading space, proving to most astronomers that Big Bang actually occurred.

1967   Jocelyn Bell-Burnell (English: 1943–) discovers first-known pulsar while working for Antony Hewish (English: 1924–); Hewish later gets Nobel Prize for discovery.

1969   Neil Armstrong (American: 1930–) and Edwin E. "Buzz" Aldrin (American: 1930–) walk on Moon.

1971   American spacecraft, *Mariner 9,* is first to orbit another planet, Mars.

1975   Soviet space probe transmits pictures from surface of Venus.

1976   U.S. Viking space probes begin transmitting pictures of surface of Mars—unsuccessful in detecting life on planet.

1977   Rings of Uranus are discovered.

1979   U.S. space probe *Voyager 1* discovers that, like Saturn and Uranus, Jupiter has rings.

1980   Alan Guth (American: 1947–) develops theory of inflationary universe, an explanation of how Big Bang occurred.

1981   U.S. introduces reusable spacecraft, the space shuttle.

1987   The explosion of Supernova 1987A, the nearest supernova that has been visible from Earth since 1604, is observed.

1989   U.S. space probe *Voyager 2* flies by Neptune, farthest planet from the Sun at that time, imaging the planet, its rings, and its moons.

1990   The Hubble Space Telescope is launched.

1992   The Magellan Venus orbiter completes mapping 95 percent of the planet's surface with radar.

Observations from the *Cosmic Background Explorer Satellite (COBE)* confirm the Big Bang theory.

1993   Members of the crew of the Space Shuttle *Endeavour* successfully repair the main lens of the Hubble Space Telescope.

1994   Comet Shoemaker-Levy 9, broken into 21 fragments, some nearly half a kilometer in diameter, slams into the far side of Jupiter in July.

1995   Astronomers Michel Mayor (Swiss:) and Didier Queloz (Swiss: 1966–) announce the first planet to orbit an ordinary star other than the Sun.

The Hubble Space Telescope focuses on a single patch of the northern sky long enough to reveal previously unknown objects at great distances from Earth. The experiment, called the Hubble Deep Field, is repeated for the sky's southern hemisphere in 1998.

1996   Firm evidence is found for a massive black hole at the center of the Milky Way galaxy.

1997   Jupiter's moon Europa is found to have a sea of liquid water beneath a surface of ice crossed by giant fissures; astronomers conclude that it is possible that living organisms could exist in Europa's ocean.

The space probe *Pathfinder* lands safely on Mars on July 4. Pathfinder's rover, Sojourner, leaves the craft and sends to Earth reports of its close-up observation of Martian rocks in what appears to be an ancient flood plain.

1998   Astronomers conclude that there isn't enough matter in the universe to stop expansion; expansion may be accelerated by a small antigravity force.

1999   Two independent teams of astronomers determine that a system of at least three planets orbits the star Upsilon Andromedae.

2000   Studies using the Chandra X-Ray Observatory, a satellite launched in 1999, reveal that the pervasive X-ray background of the universe is caused by black holes that lurk in the hearts of most galaxies.

Permanent occupation of the International Space Station begins on May 19.

Calculations based on the U.S. BOOMERANG (Balloon Observations of Millimetric Extragalactic Radiation and Geophysics) experiment, a balloon-borne study of the cosmic background radiation conducted in 1998, reveal that the universe is flat, not curved.

2001   Timothy Beers (American: 1957–) of Michigan State University and coworkers use uranium-238 to date the oldest stars in the universe at 12.5 billion years (with an uncertainty of 3 billion years), giving the minimum age for the universe.

In February the space probe *NEAR-Shoemaker* lands softly on asteroid 433 Eros, after orbiting it for a year.

The orbit of comet 200 CR-105 is calculated to be distorted as if by the presence of a planet larger than Pluto orbiting far beyond Neptune, now or at some time in the distant past.

2002   Kenneth R. Sembach and coworkers report studies based on *FUSE (Far Ultraviolet Spectroscopic Explorer)* satellite observations show that the Milky Way is enveloped in a huge cloud of hot gas that extends almost to the nearest galaxies.

The Martian *Odyssey* space probe determined that a large amount of water, frozen into ice, is just below the surface of both poles of Mars.

NASA Scientists propose that an unusual astronomical object named RXJ1856.6-3754 is a "quark star."

A dozen unusual radio sources that appear as X patterns formed by giant jets of hot matter and radiation are recognized as the results of pairs of black holes colliding and merging.

2003   Images obtained with NASA's *Wilkinson Microwave Anisotropy Probe* (WMAP) confirm Hubble observations for the age of the universe—13,700,000,000 years—with an accuracy of 1 percent.

2004   The robot Mars rover Opportunity shows that rocks on Mars could only have been formed in the presence of liquid water.

2005   Michael Brown, Chad Trujillo, and David Rabinowitz announce the discovery of a body in the outer solar system later named Eris that is larger than Pluto.

2006   Pluto is reduced to "dwarf planet" status.

2008   NASA's Phoenix Mars mission sends report of ice and water on the planet, supporting views that the planet was once, and might be again, capable of supporting life.

2010   An international team of astronomers using gravitational lensing observations from the Hubble Space Telescope begin to probe "dark energy," a phenomenon which appears to power the universe's accelerating expansion.

Basic Facts About the Planets

Characteristic	Terrestrial Planets				Gas Giants			
	Mercury	Venus	Earth	Mars	Jupiter	Saturn	Uranus	Neptune
Distance from Sun								
Miles (millions)	36.0	67.2	93.0	141.6	483.78	890.75	1,784.86	2,793.0
Kilometers (millions)	57.9	108.2	149.6	227.9	778.57	1,433.53	2,872.46	4,495.1
Rotation period	59 days	243 days[1]	23.9 hrs	24.6 hrs	9.925 hrs	10.656 hrs	17.24 hrs	16.1 hrs
Orbital period (days)	88	224.7	365.256	686.98	4,331	10,747	30,589	59,800
Orbital velocity (miles/second)	29.74	21.76	18.51	14.99	8.12	6.02	4.23	3.37
Inclination of axis	0.01	3.39	23.45	25.19	3.13	26.73	97.77	28.32
Equatorial diameter								
Miles	3,032	7,521	7,926	4,222	88,846	74,897	31,763	30,775
Kilometers	4,879	12,104	12,756	6,794	142,984	120,536	51,118	49,528
In relation to Earth:								
Diameter	38.3%	94.9%	100%	53.3%	1,121%	945%	401%	388%
Mass	5.53%	81.5%	100%	10.7%	31,783%	9,516.2%	1,453.6%	1,714.7%
Gravity	37.8%	90.7%	100%	37.7%	236.4%	91.6%	88.90%	112%
Escape velocity								
Miles/second	2.7	6.4	7.0	3.1	37.0	22.1	13.2	14.6
Kilometers/second	4.3	10.36	11.186	5.03	59.5	35.5	21.3	23.5
Average surface temperature	332.4°F	867.0°F	59°F	−85°F	−166°F	−220°F	−320°F	−330°F
	166.9°C	463.9°C	15°C	−65°C	−110°C	−140°C	−195°C	−200°C
Planetary satellites	0	0	1	2	63	47	27	13

Note: 1. Venus's rotation is retrograde, or opposite the direction of other planets. **Source:** NASA: National Space Science Data Center (NSSDC).

crashed into one another. While this sometimes resulted in one or more of the planetoids breaking up, often a small planetoid would stick to a larger one, making it larger still. The end products of this process, it is proposed, are the nine solar-system planets and their moons, along with the existing asteroids, comets, and meteoroids.

The solar system is located in a large system of stars called the Milky Way galaxy. The solar system is 28,000 light-years (defined below) from the center of the Milky Way and 67 light-years from the plane defined by the galactic spiral.

The Terrestrial Planets

In terms of distance from the Sun, these are the first four planets of the solar system—Mercury, Venus, Earth and Mars. Terrestrial planets all have a comparatively high density, a concentration of metallic elements, and hard, rocky surfaces. Earth is the largest of the terrestrial planets but is dwarfed by the enormous sizes of the outer "gas giant" planets (Jupiter, Saturn, Uranus and Neptune). Mercury, Earth and Mars have magnetic fields; Venus does not have a detectable magnetic field. Earth and Venus have thick atmospheres, Mars has a thin atmosphere, and Mercury's atmosphere is almost nonexistent.

Mercury

Main components of atmosphere: 98 percent helium, 2 percent hydrogen. Mercury is the planet closest to the Sun and in keeping with its namesake—Mercury, the winged messenger—moves the fastest in its orbit. Usually obscured from view from Earth by the Sun's glare, it is sometimes visible on Earth's horizon just after sunset, when it is called the Evening Star, or just before dawn, when it is called the Morning Star. About 14 times in each 100 years, Mercury can also be seen crossing directly in front of the Sun's disk.

Mercury is the smallest planet. The U.S. *Mariner 10* space probe provided the first detailed pictures of Mercury's surface during flybys in 1974 and 1975.

Glossary of Planetary Terms

Escape velocity   The speed needed for an object to be propelled from the surface of a planet and not fall back. The escape velocity for Earth is 6.96 miles (11.2 km) per second, thus an object must travel at least that fast, or approximately 7 miles per second, to leave Earth's gravitational influence.

Inclination of axis   The angle that the axis about which a planet rotates makes with the plane defined by its path around the Sun.

Orbital period   The time it takes for a planet to orbit the Sun.

Orbital velocity   The speed of a planet in its path around the Sun.

Rotation period   The time it takes for a planet to rotate once about itself.

Mariner 10 mapped about 35 percent of the planet's heavily cratered, moonlike surface. In 2004 the *Messenger* space probe to Mercury was launched, expected to orbit the planet starting in 2011. As of October 2008, *Messenger* had recorded photos of about 95 percent of the planet's surface.

Mercury is a waterless, airless world that alternately bakes and freezes as it orbits the Sun. Its tenuous atmosphere is thought to be one-trillionth the density of Earth's atmosphere and largely composed of helium. On Mercury's sunlit side temperatures reach 850°F (450°C) and plummet to −300°F (−180°C) on the dark side. These extremes are largely due to Mercury's slow rate of rotation: one single rotation is two-thirds of a Mercury year, or 59 days for a rotation compared to 88 days for a revolution. Mercury's axis is almost perpendicular to its plane of rotation, so any single place on the planet sees dawn only once every 176 days—the planet must rotate three times and go through two of its "years" before a new day dawns.

Mercury's surface is scarred with hundreds of thousands of meteor craters. Many such craters were probably formed during the planetoid showers believed to have occurred soon after the formation of the solar system. Many areas have had the craters smoothed over by ancient lava flows, however. This indicates extensive volcanic activity on Mercury during and after the time of the planetoid showers. The surface is also crisscrossed by huge cliffs, or scarps. These probably formed as Mercury's surface cooled and shrank. Some of the scarps are up to 1.2 miles (1.9 km) high and 932 miles (1,500 km) long.

Mercury is so dense for its size that astronomers think that its rocky outer crust is very thin and that the planet is mostly iron. It probably was once larger. During the early bombardment, it is conjectured that one of the larger planetoids (about a sixth of the size of the early planet) hit Mercury so hard that it blasted most of the rocky crust away.

Venus

Main components of atmosphere: 96.5 percent carbon dioxide, 3.5 percent nitrogen. As seen in the night sky from Earth, Venus is second only to the Moon in brightness. Venus, named for the Roman goddess of love, is the planet that passes closest to Earth (24,000,000 mi., or 39,000,000 km). Since it is between Earth and the Sun, Venus, like Mercury, is seen either as the Morning Star or the Evening Star.

Because of its proximity to Earth and its position between Earth and the Sun, Venus became (in 1962) the first planet beyond Earth to be scanned by a space probe in its neighborhood (*Mariner 2*). The pull of the Sun's gravity makes Venus and Mercury "downhill" from the Earth; one must travel against the Sun's gravity to reach other planets. Since 1962 Venus has been visited by numerous U.S. and Soviet spacecraft. Soviet space probes *Venera 13* and *Venera 14* were the first to make a soft landing and send back pictures from the Venusian surface.

The Venusian atmosphere is thick with clouds that have shrouded the planet's surface from view, making the planet somewhat mysterious. The Venusian clouds range from about 28 to 37 miles (45 to 60 km) above the planet's surface and are differentiated into three layers. Droplets of sulfuric acid and water have been identified in the clouds.

The clouds and high level of carbon dioxide in the atmosphere have combined to trap heat in the lower atmosphere of Venus. This is an extreme form of the greenhouse effect and is responsible for high temperatures in the lower atmosphere, 870°F (460°C)—hot enough to melt lead. The atmospheric pressure at the surface is 92 times that of Earth. Radiation of heat from the lower atmosphere is so inefficient that there is little variation of temperature between night and day.

One feature of the Venusian upper atmosphere is markedly different from that of Earth. The atmosphere super-rotates on Venus—that is, the atmosphere above the clouds moves 60 times faster than the planet rotates—whereas the Earth and its atmosphere rotate at the same speed. So, high winds and steady upper-atmosphere winds—100 mph (160 km/hr) or faster—are a dominant factor in Venusian weather. But at ground level, winds are calmer, with an average closer to 2 miles per hour (3.6 km/hr).

Soviet space probes that soft-landed on Venus have provided photographs of the planet's surface. Radar maps of 99 percent of the Venusian surface, completed by the U.S. Pioneer spacecraft (from 1978 to 1993), and *Magellan* (from 1989 to 1994), now give a detailed picture of features as small as 350 ft. (100 m) in diameter. More than a thousand Venusian mountains, volcanoes, rifts, basins, impact craters, and other features have been identified.

About 10 percent of the surface is highland terrain, 70 percent rolling uplands, and 20 percent lowland plains. There are two major highland areas: one about half the size of Africa and located in the equatorial region and the other, about the size of Australia, located to the north. The highest mountain on Venus—Maxwell Montes—is in the northern highlands and is higher than Earth's Mt. Everest. Volcanic activity dominates Venus; the planet is covered with volcanic domes and lava channels.

Like Earth, Venus is thought to have an internal structure. The crust, however, is much thicker than that of Earth, perhaps twice as deep on the average, making the crust of Venus about 60 mi. (100 km) thick. Below the crust is a large layer called the mantle; below the mantle is a core thought to be molten nickel-iron, similar to Earth's outer core.

Earth

Main components of atmosphere: 78 percent nitrogen, 21 percent oxygen, 1 percent water, 0.93 percent argon. Earth is the third planet from the Sun and the only one in the solar system known to harbor life. From space, our planet appears as a bright, blue-and-white sphere—blue because some 70 percent of the surface is covered by water, and white because clouds cover about half the planet's surface.

Earth's atmosphere and composition are discussed in "Earth Sciences" below. Earth's mass is 6.583×10^{21} tons. (5.972×10^{21} metric tons).

The Moon is Earth's only natural satellite. It is over one-quarter the size of Earth in diameter (2,160 mi. or 3,476 km). At an average distance of 238,000 mi. (380,000 km), it is the brightest object in Earth's nighttime sky. The Moon regularly changes in appearance as seen from Earth. See the discussion of these changes, called "Phases of the Moon," in Part I.

The Moon is slightly egg-shaped, and the same side of the satellite always faces Earth—this side being the elongated small end. As a result, the Moon rotates once during each revolution. The side we do not see is called the far side (not the dark side—all parts of the moon undergo 14 Earth days of light, followed by 14 days of darkness).

Over a decade of exploration of the Moon by space probes was capped by the landing of two U.S. astronauts on the Moon on July 20, 1969. A total of six two-man crews of American astronauts eventually landed on the Moon between 1969 and 1972, and they brought back some 842 pounds (382 kg) of samples of Moon rocks. The world these astronauts found was airless and devoid of life. Temperatures on the Moon range from up to 273°F (134°C) on the bright side to –274°F (–170°C) on the unlighted side.

A mixture of fine powder and broken rock blankets the Moon's surface. The near side also has large regions (called maria, or seas) of solidified lava. The lunar surface is pockmarked with craters up to 56 miles (90 km) across and is broken by huge mountain ranges. Some craters at the poles may contain frozen water in their depths.

Mars

Main components of atmosphere: 95 percent carbon dioxide, 3 percent nitrogen, 2 percent argon. Mars is the outermost of the four terrestrial planets and has a distinctive reddish coloring, coming from iron oxide in the Martian soil. The Romans named the planet after their god of war, and the two irregularly shaped satellites of Mars have been named after the horses—Deimos (terror) and Phobos (fear)—that pulled the war god's chariot. Mars is usually visible in Earth's nighttime sky and is lined up with Earth between it and the Sun once every 780 days, though its closest approach to Earth (33,800,000 mi., or 54,500,000 km) comes at 15- or 17-year intervals; 2003 was the closest approach since 1986.

The so-called canals on Mars—later found to be optical illusions—were first observed by 19th-century astronomers and led to the widespread belief that there was life on Mars. (In 1900 the French Academy offered a prize to the first person to find life on any planet except Mars, presumably because everyone knew that there was life on that planet). The planet thus became the target of numerous space probes, both U.S. and Soviet, from the early years of interplanetary exploration.

The first successful flyby of Mars was achieved by the U.S. spacecraft *Mariner 4* in 1965. The Soviets became the first to land a probe successfully on the surface of Mars in 1971, but the probe malfunctioned and stopped transmitting after only 20 seconds. It was not until 1976, when the U.S. *Viking 1* and *Viking 2* landers touched down on Mars, that extensive study of the planet from its surface became possible. The *Viking 1* lander continued to function until 1983. *Pathfinder* landed on Mars on July 4, 1997. Using a remote-controlled robot called *Sojourner,* whose travels to Martian rocks were televised, the *Pathfinder* mission reported the details of the weather and geology of Mars.

The big question of whether there is (or was) life on Mars has yet to be answered with certainty. The *Viking* landers conducted three experiments on Martian soil to check for biological processes. Some of the tests yielded positive results, but these could also be explained by the soil chemistry. The lack of other evidence of organic molecules adds to the case against life on Mars.

Orbiting satellites have mapped the entire planet down to a resolution of 500–1,000 ft. (150–300 m). The planet's surface is heavily cratered, and there is extensive evidence of once-active volcanoes. There are also such spectacular features as Olympus Mons (an extinct volcano three times as high as Earth's Mt. Everest); mammoth canyons, one of which is four times deeper than the Grand Canyon; and a gigantic basin (larger than Alaska) in the southern hemisphere that was probably created by a single, huge asteroid. The planet has ice caps at both poles (water ice with some frozen carbon dioxide), and the ice caps advance and recede with changes in the seasons.

But the most intriguing aspect of the Martian surface is that water once flowed there in great quantities. Parts of the terrain apparently have sedimentary origins, and there are many long channels, complete with smaller tributary channels and islands, that extend for hundreds of kilometers. Scientists speculate that Mars once had a much thicker atmosphere, made up of gases vented during volcanic eruptions, which would have made it possible for water in its liquid state to exist on the surface. Martian atmospheric pressure is now so low, however, that surface water would immediately vaporize. It is conjectured that in the past, water flowed through the channels to lowland areas and then sank into the Martian regolith, or upper soil layer, since there is no geologic evidence that standing bodies of water ever existed. In 2002 the orbiting Mars *Odyssey* detected signs of a large amount of water ice just below soil level in the south polar region.

Mars is too small to sustain continual volcanic activity. Its atmosphere apparently thinned out after volcanic activity ceased. Atmospheric pressure is now just seven one-thousandths of that on Earth at sea level, and the predominant gas is carbon dioxide, which is relatively heavy. A small amount of water vapor in the atmosphere is enough to form some clouds, small patches of fog in some valleys, and occasionally even patches of frost. Surface temperatures vary from a high of about 70°F (20°C) during summer at the equator to a low of about -220°F (-140°C) during winter at the poles.

By far the most pronounced feature of Martian weather is dust storms, which regularly engulf the entire planet for a period of several months.

Jupiter

Main components of atmosphere: 90 percent hydrogen, 10 percent helium. Jupiter is the largest planet in the solar system. It has 2.5 times more mass than all the other planets of the solar system together and is 11 times as large as Earth in diameter. Jupiter is so large that scientists believe it almost became a star: as the gases and dust contracted to form the planet, gravitational forces created tremendous pressure and temperature inside the core—perhaps as high as tens of thousands of degrees. But there was not enough mass available to create the temperatures needed to start a fusion reaction such as that of the Sun (above 27,000,000°F, or 15,000,000°C, at the Sun's core); thus Jupiter has been slowly cooling down ever since. Even so, Jupiter still radiates about 2.5 times as much heat as it receives from the Sun.

The first object to reach Jupiter from Earth was *Pioneer 10.* It returned the first close-up pictures of the giant planet in 1973. Subsequently, the more sophisticated space probes *Voyager 1* and *Voyager 2* passed by Jupiter in 1979 and sent back images and more data on the planet. One of the most exciting discoveries by *Voyager 1* was that Jupiter has a faint but extensive ring system that extends almost 186,000 miles (300,000 km) out from the planet's surface. *Galileo* found another faint ring at 1 million miles (1.6 million km) in 1998. A probe from *Galileo* arrived at Jupiter on December 7, 1995, finding winds of 435 mph (700 km/hr) and much less water vapor than expected. Scientists later determined that the probe had arrived in what amounts to a Jovian desert. In September 2003, *Galileo's* mission ended with a final plunge into Jupiter's atmosphere.

Jupiter's thick atmosphere, which may extend above the planetary surface as much as 600 miles (1,000 km), is primarily made up of hydrogen, with some helium and traces of other gases. Because the planet spins so fast (one rotation in just under 10 hours), its clouds tend to form bands that give the planet a striped appearance. Darker bands are called belts, while light ones are zones. Clouds at higher altitudes are carried eastward by jet streams, while those at lower levels are blown westward.

There are numerous eddies and swirls in Jupiter's atmosphere, but none can compare with the Great Red Spot, apparently a massive hurricane (rotating counterclockwise) located in the southern hemisphere near the equator. The Great Red Spot was first observed some 300 years ago, and this storm continues unabated today. Since 1938 three smaller white ovals have been observed to the south of the Great Red Spot.

Jupiter's cloud tops are extremely cold (about -202°F, or -130°C), but temperatures increase deeper inside the atmosphere. Pressure also increases, and at about 600 miles (1,000 km) below the outermost atmospheric layers, great oceans of liquid hydrogen form Jupiter's surface. These may be some 12,000 miles (20,000 km) deep. Beneath them the hydrogen is so densely compacted it is thought to be in a metallic state. Within this is the core, thought to be an iron and silicate rock ball about the size of Earth.

Jupiter is now known to have 63 moons, many of them quite small (less than 6 miles in diameter). The four largest are the Galilean moons, so called because they were first observed by Galileo. The Galilean moons are Ganymede, Callisto, Europa, and Io—after the Roman god Jupiter's cupbearer (Ganymede) and three of Jupiter's inamorata. Ganymede is the largest moon in the solar system and is larger even than the planets Pluto and Mercury. It is a huge, cratered ball of ice and may have a core of solid silicate rock with liquid water between the thick ice covering and the core. Callisto, with an orbit outside that of Ganymede, is also covered with ice and is riddled with thousands of craters. Europa, which orbits inside Ganymede, is about the size of our Moon and has a smooth surface marked by networks of cracks. The most interesting of Jupiter's moons are Io, which orbits closest to Jupiter, and Europa.

Io undergoes the most intense volcanic activity known; thought to be heated by its orbit's proximity to Jupiter. One giant volcano may have been erupting for the past 19 years. Orange-red patches on Io's mottled surface are apparently molten sulfur beds, but most other parts of Io's surface are cold (about −229°F, or −145°C).

Europa, on the other hand, is covered in ice, but some have speculated that a liquid ocean beneath the ice could contain life. The liquid, which probably contains salts like oceans on Earth, could be heated by the same tidal forces that propel Io's volcanoes.

Saturn

Main components of atmosphere: 90 percent hydrogen, 3 percent helium. Saturn is the sixth planet of the solar system and the second largest, after Jupiter. The outermost of the planets that can be identified easily in Earth's nighttime sky with the unaided eye, Saturn has a pale yellowish color and is not nearly so bright as Mars. Saturn's spectacular ring system, which makes it one of the most interesting of the planets, is visible only through a telescope. Its rings are more extensive than those of any other planet.

Like Jupiter, Saturn is composed of densely compacted hydrogen, helium, and other gases. Liquid or metallic hydrogen probably exists underneath the planet's thick atmosphere, and scientists believe there is a solid core of rock about two times the size of Earth at its center. Saturn's high rotational speed (once every 10 hours, 12 minutes) makes it the most oblate (flattened) of all the planets; it is almost 6,800 miles (11,000 km) wider at the equator than on a line through the poles.

Exploration of Saturn began in 1979 with the first fly-by (*Pioneer 11*), but the *Voyager 1* (1980) and *Voyager 2* (1981) missions provided the first detailed look at the planet. Scientists have spent years sifting through the data gathered. The *Cassini–Huygens* probe, which arrived in 2004, revealed two previously unidentified rings. The first *Cassini* mission was completed in 2008, but was then extended through September 2010. The extension was primarily to explore moons Titan and Enceladus.

The *Voyagers* found a huge storm thousands of miles across on Saturn, along with a wide band of extremely high winds—up to 1,000 miles (1,600 km) per hour—at the equator. Winds in this band all travel in the direction of the planet's rotation (unlike bands of wind on Jupiter). The *Voyagers* also discovered a vast hydrogen cloud circling the planet above the equator.

The *Voyagers'* most exciting discoveries concern the planetary rings. Previously, about six different rings had been identified within the ring system, but *Voyager 1* pictures show as many as 1,000 separate rings. Narrow rings can even be seen within the Cassini Division, once thought to be an empty gap between the two major parts of the ring system. Some rings are not circular, and at least two rings are intertwined, or "braided." A strange new phenomenon was also discovered in the rings. *Voyager 1* pictures clearly show dark, radial fingers or "spokes" moving inside the rings in the direction of rotation. Scientists speculate that they are made of ice crystals.

Voyager 2 pictures show that Saturn has far more than 1,000 rings—perhaps as many as a hundred thousand or more. One of the brightest rings is under 152 meters (500 ft.) thick. *Voyager 2* also found seasonal differences between the planet's two hemispheres and photographed a storm 4,000 miles (6,500 km) wide.

Twelve of Saturn's moons were known before the arrival of the *Voyagers*, and instruments aboard the space probe helped locate five new ones in the 1980s. In 1990 an 18th moon, later named Pan, was located in images made by *Voyager 2*. The discovery of 12 small moons of Saturn, found with ground-based telescopes, was reported in 2002 and another in 2003. Astronomers and *Cassini* observed more since then, bringing the total to 47. Most of Saturn's moons are relatively small and composed of rock and ice. All but one of the small moons are pock-marked by meteor craters, and in some cases the moons appear to have been cracked by collisions with especially large meteors. But *Voyager* pictures show that one moon, Enceladus, is smooth in large regions apparently unmarked by collisions with meteors. Scientists believe that Enceladus is being pulled and stretched by the combined gravities of a nearby moon and Saturn itself. Tidal forces have apparently heated the core of Enceladus and made its surface soft enough to smooth over any craters formed by meteor impacts.

Titan, Saturn's largest moon (3,000 mi., or 4,800 km in diameter) is one of the few moons in the solar system known to have an atmosphere of any substance. Scientists suspect that at least some precursors of life may have formed there. For this reason *Voyager 1* was guided to within about 2,500 miles (4,000 km) of Titan during the Saturn flyby. Though Titan's surface was obscured by dense clouds, Voyager's sensors nevertheless returned a considerable amount of information about the moon and its atmosphere. Titan's atmosphere is composed mostly of nitrogen, like that of Earth, with only a small percentage of methane and carbon monoxide. Atmospheric pressure is at least 1.5 times that on Earth and temperatures range around −294°F (−181°C). Titan in fact appears to be a frozen version of Earth before life evolved.

The possibility of oceans of liquid methane (or of nitrogen or methane rain) on Titan was a matter of considerable controversy for some time after *Voyager 1* investigated the moon. But Titan is "dry," at least in the regions investigated. Pools of liquid methane might still exist in other low-lying regions, but it is unlikely that either methane or nitrogen condenses to liquid form on Titan.

Uranus

Main components of atmosphere: 82 percent hydrogen, 15 percent helium, 2 percent methane. Uranus is the seventh planet in the solar system and the third of the gas giants. The planet is barely visible in

Earth's nighttime sky (it looks like a faint star) and for that reason, it went undiscovered until 1781.

Nearly the same size as Neptune and only about 5 percent of Jupiter's mass, Uranus is a faintly greenish color, perhaps because its atmosphere contains methane. The planet's axis of rotation is tipped over on its side. Astronomers discovered a system of nine faint rings in 1977, and *Voyager* found two more rings in 1986. There are thought to be 27 moons of Uranus. Among these, Caliban and Sycorax were found in 1997; a still-unnamed moon was noticed in 1999 by a researcher studying a 1986 photograph taken by *Voyager 2*. Three more discovered later in 1999 have been named Prospero, Setebos, and Stephano.

Uranus's atmosphere is very cold (–355°F, or –215°C). No clouds have been observed. Scientists speculate that, as on Jupiter and Saturn, temperatures and pressures increase dramatically down through the outer layer of atmosphere. At some point the hydrogen and helium would be sufficiently compressed to form a liquid or slushy surface "crust." Underneath this crust they believe is a mantle of solidified methane, ammonia, and water; and inside this mantle, a rocky core of silicon and iron about 15 times as massive as Earth. The core is thought to be hot, probably about 12,000°F (7,000°C).

Neptune

Main components of atmosphere: 80 percent hydrogen, 19 percent helium, 1 percent methane. The last of the gas giants, Neptune is the eighth planet in the solar system. It was discovered in 1846 after mathematical calculations based on irregularities in the orbit of Uranus provided astronomers with the correct location of the planet. Neptune, like Uranus, has been surrounded by considerable uncertainty because of its enormous distance from Earth. The 1989 visit by *Voyager 2* contributed greatly to improved understanding of the planet.

Neptune is a pale bluish color, but it has a clear atmosphere, and is very cold at the cloud tops (about –365°F or –220°C).

Scientists believe Neptune has a three-layered structure similar to that of Uranus: a crust of solidified or liquid hydrogen and helium that gradually thins outward into an atmosphere; a mantle of solidified gases and water; and a hot, rocky core (about 12,000°F or 7,000°C) some 15 times as massive as Earth. But one aspect of Neptune remains a mystery. Despite similarities with Uranus, Neptune has been found to radiate 2.7 times as much heat as it receives from the Sun (at a rate of 0.03 microwatts per ton of mass). Uranus, on the other hand, does not emit as much excess heat.

Neptune has 13 known moons, Triton and Nereid, discovered from Earth, six others discovered by *Voyager 2*, three more newly spotted in 2002. Triton is the largest moon and has an atmosphere. Triton is unusual in that it travels in a direction opposite that of Neptune's rotation, suggesting that it has a different origin from the planet. Triton also has volcanic activity: geysers of nitrogen rising as high as five miles (8 km).

Dwarf Planets

From 1930 through the end of the 20th century, the solar system was thought to contain nine planets, the ninth planet being Pluto. In recent years, however, several objects similar to Pluto were discovered in the outer solar system. This caused a rethinking of what makes a planet a planet.

On August 24, 2006, the International Astronomical Union (I.A.U.) for the first time defined the term "planet." In this new definition, a planet is a celestial body that is in orbit around a star, has sufficient mass so that it assumes a nearly round shape, and has cleared its orbit of planetesimals and similar debris. The first eight planets (Mercury through Neptune) meet all three criteria, but Pluto meets only the first two.

Pluto was thus removed from the rank of major planets and reclassified as a dwarf planet. The I.A.U. classifies a dwarf planet as a celestial body that is in orbit around the sun, has sufficient mass so that it assumes a nearly round shape, has not cleared its orbit of planetesimals, and is not a satellite of another similar object. Today there are three recognized dwarf planets: Pluto, Eris, and Ceres.

Pluto

Average distance from Sun: 39.5 AU. *Mass:* 0.002 Earth masses. *Diameter:* 0.18 Earth diameters. *Orbit time:* 248 years. *Rotation time:* 6.4 days. *Main components of atmosphere:* methane and nitrogen (quantities unknown). A ball of frozen gases probably only about the size of Earth's moon, Pluto was discovered in 1930 as a result of an extensive search by Clyde Tombaugh. It was originally thought to be a planet, until that term was redefined by the I.A.U. in 2006. Pluto resides in the Kuiper Belt outside the orbit of Neptune; it's chaotic orbit causes it at times to cross inside Neptune's orbit.

Today Pluto is about as close to the Sun as it ever gets and possesses a thin atmosphere, but it is expected to freeze solid as the planet moves away from the sun. Pluto has one known moon, Charon, discovered in 1978. Charon is about half the size of Pluto. Pluto and Charon rotate and revolve synchronously like a double planet system.

Eris

Average distance from Sun: 67.7 AU. *Mass:* .0027 Earth masses. *Diameter:* 0.19 Earth diameters. *Orbit time:* 557 years. *Rotation time:* not yet known. *Main components of atmosphere:* methane and nitrogen (quantities unknown). Similar in composition to Pluto, Eris is the largest dwarf planet in the solar system and the ninth largest body orbiting the Sun. It was discovered in 2005 by a Mount Palomar-based team of astronomers, led by Michael Brown. Eris has one known moon, Dysnomia. Eris resides in the Kuiper Belt, and is at this time the most distant known body in the solar system; its orbit is more eccentric and tilted than that of its neighbor Pluto.

Ceres

Average distance from Sun: 2.767 AU. *Mass:* 0.00016 Earth masses. *Diameter:* .075 Earth diameters. *Orbit time:* 4.6 years. *Rotation time:* 9 hours. Discovered in 1801 by Giuseppe Piazzi, Ceres is the largest and most massive body in the asteroid belt between Mars and Jupiter. First thought to be a comet, then a large asteroid, Ceres has most recently been classified as a dwarf planet. Unlike other objects in the asteroid belt, Ceres is spherical; it has no discernable atmosphere.

The Asteroids

Also called minor planets, the asteroids are very small bodies ranging from less than 1 to 600 miles in diameter. The name asteroid means "starlike" and was given to asteroids because they are so small they appear as points of light (as do stars) even in powerful telescopes. Otherwise, asteroids are not like stars at all.

The first four asteroids were discovered between 1801 and 1807. Today several hundred thousand asteroids are known and a million may exist in all. But the total mass of all known asteroids is less than that of Earth's Moon; only 26 asteroids are more than 130 miles (200 km) in diameter. Many asteroids occur in pairs that orbit each other. Some are thought to be solid bodies, while others may be collections of rocks held together by slight gravitational interactions.

Asteroids are found in several locations. The main belt is between Mars and Jupiter, but many inside the orbit of Mars are known as near-Earth asteroids. Asteroids that are thought to be larger than about 500 feet (150 m) in diameter that may travel as close as about 5 million miles (7.5 million km) to Earth are called potentially hazardous objects (PHOs). There are about 300 known PHOs, but none are expected to impact Earth in the foreseeable future. Two groups in the same orbit as Jupiter are called the Trojans because the larger ones are named for characters from Homer's *Iliad*.

The Outer Planets

Beyond Mars and the asteroid belt lie the five known outer planets of our solar system. Four of these planets—Jupiter, Saturn, Uranus, and Neptune—are the so-called gas giants. Many times larger than the terrestrial planets, these planets are huge, dense balls of hydrogen and other gases. Orbiting beyond them (most of the time) lies the Kuiper belt, a group of large bodies that includes Pluto and that have been called planets, asteroids, and even giant comets. The largest of these Eris, followed in size by Pluto and several known bodies that are nearly as big as Pluto, including 2003 EL612, 2005 FY9, and Sedna.

The Sun

Virtually all of the energy used by living things comes from the Sun. The Sun's light causes photosynthesis in green plants, and its heat causes winds. Fossil fuels, such as coal, oil, and natural gas, got their energy originally from photosynthesis, as did wood. Animals derive their energy from plants that photosynthesize, either directly or indirectly. The only natural nonsolar energy sources are nuclear reactions (which also produce geothermal energy), some bacteria that metabolize sulfur, and the tides, which on Earth are produced largely by the Moon, but in part by the Sun.

Because the Sun is a ball of gases, it does not rotate as a whole. The equator rotates in about 25 days, while gas near the poles rotates in about 30 days. The period of rotation at each latitude can be found by observing sunspots, which are magnetic storms. Sunspots appear and disappear in a mysterious 11-year cycle that many think influences weather on Earth, although convincing proof is lacking. Sometimes sunspots disappear for tens of years at a time,

as during the period from 1645 to 1715. It may or may not be a coincidence that those years coincided with the "Little Ice Age" in Europe, when temperatures were far below average.

Like Earth, the Sun is composed of various layers. The part we see is called the photosphere. In the Sun's interior, energy is generated when hydrogen in the core fuses to become helium. Above the photosphere is a region of pinkish gases, the chromosphere. Above that is a large halo, visible only in eclipses, called the corona. Particles from the Sun, the solar wind, stream through the solar system, creating among other things auroras on Earth. Strong increases in solar wind during solar flares can interfere with radio communication.

▶PLANETS OUTSIDE THE SOLAR SYSTEM

A detectable wobble or periodic dimming, observed in about 140 nearby stars, indicated that each such star is orbited by one or more planets, known as "extrasolar planets." The star 55 Cancri is known to have at least four extrasolar planets, and 12 other stars have two or three for a total of about 165 planets. At least two pulsars have planets, and several stars are surrounded by dusty regions that may indicate planet formation.

In 1995 the first planet that orbits an ordinary star other than the Sun was established on the basis of regular changes in the position of the Sun-like star 51 Pegasi, which is nearly 50 light-years from the solar system. This discovery by Swiss astronomers Michel Mayor and Didier Queloz was soon followed by detection of many other ordinary stars that move back and forth in space. Such small movements indicate one or more large planets in orbit around each star. This method works for relatively nearby stars orbited by very large planets—planets about half the size of Saturn to eleven times the size of Jupiter. The planets found generally orbit closer to their stars than the orbit of Mercury about the Sun, although one system discovered in 2001 has two planets in orbits about as far from the star as Mars and Jupiter are from the Sun. Some planets have also been detected as they reduce visible light from their stars by passing between the stars and Earth. By 2010, astronomers had identified 479 extrasolar planets using astrometry, microlensing, imaging, and timing. The most recent of these was found in August 2010 using the Spitzer telescope, an extrasolar planet being formed 430 light years away.

Changes in the pulses from a pulsar are easier to observe than the exact position of an ordinary star, so the first known extrasolar planet was found at a pulsar. In 1991, American astronomer Aleksander Wolszczan observed that the pulsar PSR 1257+12

Characteristics of the Sun

Position in solar system	Center
Mean distance from Earth	92,960,000 mi. (149,600,000 km)
Distance from center of Milky Way galaxy	27,710 light-years
Period of rotation	25.45 days at 16° longitude
Inclination (relative to Earth's orbit)	7.25°
Equatorial diameter	865,000 mi. (1,392,000 km)
Diameter relative to Earth	109.2 times
Mass	2.192×10^{27} tons (1.9891×10^{30} kg)
Mass converted to energy each second	9,500 million pounds (4,300 million kg)
Surface gravity relative to Earth's	28 times
Temperature at core	28,280,000°F (15,710,000°C)
Temperature at bottom of photosphere	12,400°F (6,900°C)
Main components	Hydrogen and helium
Present age	4.6 billion years
Expected future life of hydrogen fuel supply	6.4 billion years

The Constellations

Name	Genitive	Abbr.	Translation	Remarks
Andromeda	Andromedae	And	Andromeda	Character in Greek myth
Antlia	Antliae	Ant	Air pump	Named by Nicolas Lacaille in 1750
Apus	Apodis	Aps	Swift, or Bird of Paradise	Named by Johann Bayer in 1603
Aquarius	Aquarii	Aqr	Water Bearer	In zodiac
Aquila	Aquilae	Aql	Eagle	Contains Altair
Ara	Arae	Ara	Altar	Part of the Centaurus group
Aries	Arietis	Ari	Ram	In zodiac
Auriga	Aurigae	Aur	Charioteer	Contains Capella
Boötes	Boötis	Boo	Herdsman	Contains Arcturus
Caelum	Caeli	Cae	Chisel, or graving tool	Lacaille, 1750
Camelopardalis	Camelopardalis	Cam	Giraffe	Named by Jakob Bartsch in 1661
Cancer	Cancri	Cnc	Crab	In zodiac
Canes Venatici	Canum Venaticorum	CVn	Hunting dogs	Named by Johannes Hevelius in 1687
Canis Major	Canis Majoris	CMa	Big Dog	Contains Sirius and Adhara
Canis Minor	Canis Minoris	CMi	Little Dog	Contains Procyon
Capricornus	Capricorni	Cap	Goat	In zodiac
Carina	Carinae	Car	Ship's Keel[1]	Lacaille, 1750; contains Canopus
Cassiopeia	Cassiopeiae	Cas	Cassiopeia	Character in Greek myth
Centaurus	Centauri	Cen	Centaur	Character in Greek myth; contains Rigil Kentaurus and Hadar/Agena
Cepheus	Cephei	Cep	Cepheus	Character in Greek myth
Cetus	Ceti	Cet	Whale	Sea monster slain by Perseus
Chamaeleon	Chamaeleontis	Cha	Chameleon	Bayer, 1603
Circinus	Circini	Cir	Compass	Lacaille, 1750
Columba	Columbae	Col	Dove	Bayer, 1603
Coma Berenices	Comae Berenices	Com	Berenice's Hair	Third Century B.C. Egyptian Queen
Corona Australis	Coronae Australis	CrA	Southern Crown	Also Sagittarius' crown
Corona Borealis	Coronae Borealis	CrB	Northern Crown	Also Ariadne's crown
Corvus	Corvi	Crv	Crow	Companion of Orpheus
Crater	Crateris	Crt	Cup	N.A.
Crux[2]	Crucis	Cru	Southern Cross	Named by Augustine Royer in 1679; Contains Beta Crucis and Acrux
Cygnus	Cygni	Cyg	Swan	Contains Deneb
Delphinus	Delphini	Del	Dolphin	N.A.
Dorado	Doradus	Dor	Goldfish	Bayer, 1603
Draco	Draconis	Dra	Dragon	Dragon slain by Hercules
Equuleus	Equulei	Equ	Little Horse	N.A.
Eridanus	Eridani	Eri	River Eridanus	Contains Achernar
Fornax	Fornacis	For	Furnace	Lacaille, 1750
Gemini	Geminorum	Gem	Twins	In zodiac; contains Pollux
Grus	Gruis	Gru	Crane	Bayer, 1603
Hercules	Herculis	Her	Hercules	Character from Greek myth
Horologium	Horologii	Hor	Clock	Lacaille, 1750.
Hydra[3]	Hydrae	Hya	Hydra	Monster from Greek myth
Hydrus	Hydri	Hyi	Sea serpent	Bayer, 1603
Indus	Indi	Ind	Indian	Bayer, 1603
Lacerta	Lacertae	Lac	Lizard	Hevelius, 1687
Leo	Leonis	Leo	Lion	In zodiac; contains Regulus
Leo Minor	Leonis Minoris	LMi	Little Lion	Hevelius, 1687
Lepus	Leporis	Lep	Hare	Prey of Orion
Libra	Librae	Lib	Scales	In zodiac
Lupus	Lupi	Lup	Wolf	Part of Centaurus group
Lynx	Lyncis	Lyn	Lynx	Hevelius, 1687
Lyra	Lyrae	Lyr	Harp	Contains Vega
Mensa	Mensae	Men	Table (mountain)	Lacaille, 1750
Microscopium	Microscopii	Mic	Microscope	Lacaille, 1750
Monoceros	Monocerotis	Mon	Unicorn	Royer, 1679
Musca	Muscae	Mus	Fly	Bayer, 1603
Norma	Normae	Nor	Carpenter's Square	Lacaille, 1750
Octans	Octantis	Oct	Octant	Lacaille, 1750
Ophiuchus	Ophiuchi	Oph	Serpent Bearer	Character in Greek myth
Orion	Orionis	Ori	The Hunter	Character in Greek myth; contains Rigel, Betelgeuse, and Bellatrix
Pavo	Pavonis	Pav	Peacock	Bayer, 1603
Pegasus	Pegasi	Peg	Pegasus	Winged horse in Greek myth

Name	Genitive	Abbr.	Translation	Remarks
Perseus	Persei	Per	Perseus	Character in Greek myth
Phoenix	Phoenicis	Phe	Phoenix	Bayer, 1603
Pictor	Pictoris	Pic	Easel	Lacaille, 1750
Pisces	Piscium	Psc	Fish	In zodiac
Piscis Austrinus	Piscis Austrin	PsA	Southern Fish	Contains Fomalhaut
Puppis	Puppis	Pup	Ship's Stern[1]	Lacaille, 1750
Pyxis	Pyxidis	Pyx	Ship's Compass[1]	Lacaille, 1750
Reticulum	Reticuli	Ret	Net	Lacaille, 1750
Sagitta	Sagittae	Sge	Arrow	N.A.
Sagittarius	Sagittarii	Sgr	Archer	In zodiac
Scorpius	Scorpii	Sco	Scorpion	In zodiac; contains Antares and Shaula
Sculptor	Sculptoris	Scl	Sculptor	Lacaille, 1750
Scutum	Scuti	Sct	Shield	Hevelius, 1687
Serpens	Serpentis	Ser	Serpent	Snake held by giant Ophiuchus
Sextans	Sextantis	Sex	Sextant	Hevelius, 1687
Taurus	Tauri	Tau	Bull	In zodiac; contains Aldebran and El nath
Telescopium	Telescopii	Tel	Telescope	Lacaille, 1750
Triangulum	Trianguli	Tri	Triangle	Contains spiral galaxy M33
Triangulum Australe	Trianguli Australis	TrA	Southern Triangle	Bayer, 1603
Tucana	Tucanae	Tuc	Toucan	Bayer, 1603
Ursa Major	Ursae Majoria	UMa	Big Bear	Big Dipper
Ursa Minor	Ursae Minoris	UMi	Little Bear	Little Dipper
Vela	Velorum	Vel	Ship's Sails[1]	Lacaille, 1750
Virgo	Virginis	Vir	Virgin	In zodiac; contains Spica
Volans	Volantis	Vol	Flying Fish	Bayer, 1603
Vulpecula	Vulpeculae	Vul	Little Fox	Hevelius, 1687

Notes: 1. Formerly part of the constellation Argo Navis, the Argonauts' ship. 2. Smallest constellation. 3. Largest constellation.

regularly changed the timing of its pulses as if being pulled back and forth in space by several bodies in orbit. Calculations since then show that two of the bodies, each about the size of Earth, move in small, swift orbits about the pulsar. A third planet is about the size of Earth's Moon and orbits inside the other two.

As early as 1983, infrared studies from space revealed dust clouds that might be the seeds of planets around such nearby stars as Vega and Fomalhaut. In 2001, astronomers studying a young star in the Orion nebula observed what appear to be larger clumps of dust, the predicted next step in planet building. In 2001 even larger clumps about the star Zeta Leopris were observed, and by 2009, this dust had been identified as coming from a massive asteroid belt—the first extrasolar asteroid belt to be discovered.

▶ STARS AND THE UNIVERSE
Astronomical Distances
The very large distances between stars and the even larger ones between the vast groups of stars called galaxies are usually expressed in terms of units of length that are peculiar to astronomy. The most familiar is the **light-year,** defined as the distance light travels through a vacuum in a year (approximately 365¼ days). Light travels through a vacuum at the rate of about 186,250 miles per second (exactly 299,792,458 m/s—exact because the meter is defined in terms of the speed of light in a vacuum). A light-year is approximately 5,880 trillion miles (9,460 trillion km).

Astronomers also use a measure even larger than the light-year, the **parsec,** equal to about 3.26 light-years, or about 19,170 trillion miles (30,840 trillion km).

A smaller unit, for measurements within the solar system, is the **astronomical unit,** which is the average distance between the Earth and the Sun, or about 93 million miles (150 million km).

Big Bang   The accepted theory of how the universe began is known as the Big Bang theory, since it proposes that the universe began as something like an explosion, which has caused all parts of the universe to rush away from one another (the expansion of the universe). Evidence for the Big Bang theory includes the discovery of cosmic background radiation, a radiation that seems to come equally from all directions. Cosmic background radiation has the characteristics expected if the universe resulted from a small, dense region exploding.

Binary stars   Almost half the stars in the visible universe are actually pairs of stars that orbit each other. Astronomers can sometimes see both stars, but more commonly they recognize that a star is part of a binary because of the influence of the dimmer star's gravitational pull on the other star.

Black holes   When a body becomes so dense for its size that not even light can escape the powerful gravitational pull it exerts, it is called a black hole. Black holes were predicted as early as 1784 (by John Michell) and invoked later by various astronomers and physicists to explain many strange astronomical phenomena. Black holes have been observed at the center of many galaxies, including our own Milky Way. Several smaller black holes, thought to be remains of supernova explosions, have also been located.

Brown dwarfs   are bodies too small to be stars, but too large to be planets. They glow dimly as a result of energy released by gravitational contraction. A brown dwarf must be between 13 and 80 times the mass of Jupiter. The first brown dwarf to be definitely established orbits the star Gliese 229. Although about 50 times Jupiter's mass, its diameter is about the same as Jupiter's. Since then, a number of brown dwarfs have been located, including some not in orbit about other stars.

The Constellations

Constellations consist of several bright stars that are treated as a group. Long ago, before recorded history, people began naming these groups. By Sumerian times (3000–2500 B.C.), stories were already being told about how particular constellations were formed. Most of our present knowledge of such stories, however, comes from the ancient Greeks.

One group of constellations has exerted a special influence on human thought, at least since 1500 B.C. As the Sun, Moon, and planets move through the sky, they pass through a group of 12 constellations, called the constellations of the zodiac. The ancient belief that the presence of the Sun in one of these constellations at a person's birth influences happenings on Earth is called astrology.

Today astronomers use constellations for mapping the sky. Each part of the sky is named by a particular constellation. These constellations, especially in the southern hemisphere, may not be traditional ones, but rather, groups of stars astronomers have named so that for reference purposes all of the sky is labeled.

Dwarfs Dwarfs are small stars—the brightest are blue dwarfs, the dimmest red dwarfs. The Sun is a yellow dwarf; there are also white and brown dwarfs.

Expanding universe When Albert Einstein developed his general theory of relativity, he found it predicted that the universe would either expand as if it were exploding, or else collapse. He tried to correct this prediction by inserting a term in his equations to counteract the prediction, but in the 1920s, Edwin Hubble discovered that the universe actually is expanding. It is easier to measure the speed of recession than the distance, so astronomers commonly use the speed at which something is moving away as the measure of its distance from us. Of course, it is not just moving away from us. In the expanding universe, everything is moving away from everything else. NASA purports that the universe's accelerating and continuous expansion is due to the force of dark energy. In 2010, using observations from the Hubble Space Telescope, astronomers began to observe this previously unexplained dark energy.

Galaxies are systems of very many stars separated from one another by largely empty space (sometimes galaxies are called island universes). In the 18th century, William Herschel concluded that many cloudy patches of light seen among the stars were actually giant systems of billions of stars, but so far away from Earth as to look like clouds. Better telescopes proved him right in the early 20th century, and these far-off, great masses of stars became known as galaxies, after our own Milky Way, the galaxy that includes the Sun. Observation with large telescopes in the 20th century has revealed two main types of galaxies—spiral and elliptical—although some galaxies are neither (irregular).

Magnitude The brightness of a star is designated by a number called its magnitude, although the relationship between size and brightness is complicated. When the magnitude system was first developed, by the early Greek astronomers Hipparchus (c. 190–c. 120 B.C.) and Ptolemy (c. 100–c. 170), astronomers did not know the actual distances to stars, so magnitude always referred to brightness as seen from Earth. They classed the brightest stars as the first magnitude and the dimmest they could see as the sixth. These numbers were somewhat arbitrary until 1856, when George Phillips Bond (American: 1825–65) determined that photographs of stars show magnitude in a way that is directly measurable—bright stars appear as larger spots than dim stars in photographs even though all stars appear as points to the naked eye. Astronomers could use accurate measures to compare two stars and thus measure magnitude with mathematical

25 Brightest Stars: Magnitudes and Distances From Earth

The stars we see in the evening sky differ in how bright they appear because of a combination of two factors: 1) their total energy output, or **luminosity** (directly related to their absolute magnitude) and 2) their distance from Earth. Astronomers refer to this combination of effects as the **apparent magnitude** of a star, a measure of how bright the star appears in the nighttime sky. To separate the two effects, astronomers define **absolute magnitude** as the brightness of a star as measured from a fixed distance. Most of the stars we see in the sky have a large absolute magnitude but are relatively far away. If all the stars were placed the same distance from Earth, Deneb would be the brightest and the Sun would be the faintest (about 250,000 times fainter than Deneb). Note that negative magnitudes are higher than positive magnitudes.

Rank/ Common name	Star name	Apparent magnitude	Absolute magnitude	Distance from Earth (light-years)
1. Sirius	α CMa	−1.44	1.45	8.6
2. Canopus[1]	α Car	−0.62	−5.53	312.6
3. Rigil Kentaurus[2]	α Cen A	−0.28	4.07	4.4
4. Arcturus	α Boo	−0.05	−0.31	36.7
5. Vega	α Lyr	0.03	0.58	25.3
6. Capella	α Aur A	0.08	−0.48	42.2
7. Rigel[1]	β Ori	0.18	−6.69	772.5
8. Procyon	β CMi	0.40	2.68	11.4
9. Achernar	α Eri	0.45	−2.77	143.7
10. Betelgeuse[1]	α Ori	0.45	−5.14	427.3
11. Hadar[1]	β Cen	0.61	−5.42	525.0
12. Altair	α Aql	0.76	2.20	16.8
13. Acrux[1,3]	α Cru	0.77	3	320.6
14. Aldebaran	α Tau	0.87	−0.63	65.1
15. Spica	α Vir	0.98	−3.55	262.1
16. Antares[1]	α Sco	1.06	−5.28	603.7
17. Pollux	β Gem	1.16	1.09	33.7
18. Fomalhaut	α PsA	1.17	1.74	25.1
19. Mimosa	β Cru	1.25	−3.92	352.4
20. Deneb[1]	α Cyg	1.25	−8.73	3,227.7
21. Regulus	α Leo	1.36	−0.52	77.5
22. Adhara[1]	ε CMa	1.50	−4.10	430.6
23. Castor[1]	α Gem	1.58	0.59	51.5
24. Gacrux	γ Cru	1.59	−0.56	87.9
25. Shaula[1]	λ Sco	1.62	−5.05	702.6

Note: The magnitudes of many stars on this list vary slightly over time, although for most stars, the variation is quite small. Betelgeuse and Antares have the largest variations (about 1 magnitude). For consistency, median magnitudes are shown for all stars. 1. Stars more than 300 light-years away have an uncertainty of about 20 percent or more in their distances (and therefore in their absolute magnitudes as well). The distance of Deneb, in particular, may be wrong by half (i.e. only 1,600 light-years away). That would reduce Deneb's absolute magnitude to -7.22, still higher than any other star on this list. 2. A binary star, with both stars orbiting around each other. They appear to the naked eye to be the same star, with a combined apparent and absolute magnitude. 3. Acrux appears to the naked eye to be a single star, but in fact, it is the combined light of two stars, each at different distances from Earth. Its absolute magnitude, therefore, is impossible to define. **Source:** NASA.

precision. Under Bond's system, stars with a magnitude of 1.00 are exactly 100 times as bright as those with a magnitude of 6.00. On this scale, the very brightest stars have negative magnitudes.

· Roughly, each whole number difference in magnitude corresponds to 2.5 times the brightness.

By the time this system was introduced, astronomers already were able to determine the distances of some stars from Earth. Friedrich Wilhelm Bessel was the first to make such a measurement, which he announced in 1838. A closer star appears brighter than a similar star that is farther away. To better understand the relative brightness of stars as they actually are, astronomers imagine viewing all stars from the same distance away. A star's brightness from this distance, which is 10 parsecs or 32.6 light-years, is called its absolute magnitude.

If we could see it clearly, the star Cygnus OB2 #12 would be the brightest star in the Milky Way galaxy (absolute magnitude –9.9), but it is not only far from Earth but also is obscured by dust. The brightest single object known is not a star, but a quasar (See also "The Universe"), BR 1202-07, with an absolute magnitude of about –33. The Sun has the brightest apparent magnitude of any star, –26.8, but its absolute magnitude is only 4.75.

Milky Way This is the galaxy to which the Sun and Earth belong; it contains about 100 billion stars. If you are in a place unafflicted with much light pollution, when you look at the night sky, you can see a faint band crossing it. The ancient Greeks named this the Milky Way (galaxy in Greek). Early in the 19th century, William Herschel determined that our Sun was a star in a vast lens-shaped star system, and that the Milky Way was the part of the star system we see from our vantage point inside it. Today, recognizing there are very many other such star systems, scientists often call it the Milky Way galaxy.

Missing mass and dark energy are thought to be the main part of the universe, with ordinary matter forming only 5 percent of the universe by mass. The evidence is that galaxies rotate in a way that indicates they must be embedded in a gravitational field caused by undetectable matter (*missing mass*) while all galaxies are flying apart with increasing speed caused by some unknown force that opposes gravity (*dark energy*). There are a number of competing theories as to the nature of these entities. The missing mass may consist of slow-moving unknown subatomic particles, while dark energy might be a cosmological constant inherent in the vacuum of empty space.

Nebulae are patches of gas and dust observable in telescopes. Before Herschel discovered that some cloudy patches seen through telescopes were vast collections of stars, all such patches were called nebulae (meaning clouds). Some "clouds" turned out to be galaxies, but many did not. The patches of gas emit light, often by the same mechanism that a fluorescent light does; energy from stars ionizes the gas, which gives off visible light. Some patches of dust also glow, usually reflecting the light of nearby stars. Other patches of dust are opaque or nearly so, blocking out part of the sky. Some of the most striking nebulae consist of glowing gas surrounded by opaque dust or vice versa, which gives the nebula a definite shape, such as the North America Nebula or the Horsehead Nebula. Herschel also studied a class of nebulae that looked to be giant spheres. He correctly concluded that these planetary nebulae were balls of gas produced when a star exploded.

Neutron stars are stars that have collapsed in a violent explosion, such as a supernova, so that the force keeping electrons apart is overcome. All the neutrons and protons can touch, forming the equivalent of a giant atomic nucleus. The star is electrically neutral because of the charge of the collapsed electrons. Such a star may be only a dozen miles in diameter but may have a mass twice that of the Sun.

Novae are stars that seem to appear out of nowhere. Later, they disappear. Early peoples were surprised from time to time by the appearance of a new (nova) star in the sky. Ancient Chinese astronomers called them guest stars. It is now clear that a truly new star does not appear; instead, a dim, existing star suddenly brightens. In early days, before the telescope, the dim stars could not be seen at all, so it looked as if a star came from nowhere. Today we know that there are two different types of "guest stars," and we reserve the name nova for one type and call the other a supernova (see below). The type referred to today as novae are less bright than supernovae and may appear more than once. It is thought that they occur when material from one star in a binary pair falls on the other star, causing it suddenly to flare up.

Pulsars are neutron stars that emit electromagnetic signals from their magnetic poles in a direction that reaches Earth. All neutron stars emit signals and rotate very rapidly (at least when they are first formed; they gradually slow down). These signals form a tight beam. If the beam intersects Earth, a radio telescope observes a fast pulsing on and off. The pulses are so regular that when they were first discovered, they were thought to be the work of extraterrestrial beings.

Quasars are distant sources of great energy. The name quasar is short for Quasi-Stellar Object, and the objects are so called because they seem to be about the size and general appearance of stars, but produce far too much energy to be stars. No one knows for sure what they are, but there is some evidence that quasars are caused by black holes in the central part of distant galaxies. The stars in the galaxies cannot be seen because of the great distance, so we see only the central part, which is the quasar.

Red giants are stars that have used their hydrogen fuel and expanded as a result. Young stars "burn" hydrogen in a nuclear fusion process that leads to helium. When a star has consumed the hydrogen in its core, new fusion reactions that start with helium begin, leading to carbon. The new reactions are hotter than the fusion of hydrogen to helium. This added energy causes the hydrogen and helium outside the core to expand. The star is red because the outer layers are relatively cool. When the Sun becomes a red giant in the distant future, it will expand almost to the orbit of Earth, completely engulfing Mercury and Venus, and charring Earth to a cinder.

Star Names
While astronomers often use the traditional names of stars, most of which come to us from Latin or Arabic sources, they also use another system for naming objects in the sky that is based on constellations. Generally, the brightest star in a particular astronomical constellation is called alpha ($\propto$), the next brightest beta (ß), and so on through several letters of the Greek alphabet; then numbers are used. All astronomers' constellations are named in Latin. When astronomers refer to a star within its constellation, they use the genitive case, meaning "of the

thing." Thus the constellation Big Dog is officially Canis Major, and Sirius is alpha Canis Majoris, or "alpha of Big Dog," usually abbreviated to ∝CMa. This means it is the brightest star in the constellation Big Dog (Sirius has long been known as the dog star). Since Sirius is a binary star (see "Binary stars"), the much brighter main star is officially ∝CMa A. Numbered stars in the news in the 1990s included 51 Pegasi and 71 Virginis.

Superclusters and clusters of galaxies
are groups of galaxies associated in space. There may be just a few members of a cluster or as many as thousands. About two dozen galaxies near us form, with the Milky Way, our Local Group. The members of the Local Group also include the Andromeda galaxy and the Large and Small Magellanic Clouds. All are traveling through the universe together. The Local Group is a member of a supercluster of galaxies, called the Local Supercluster, that contains about 100 clusters. Clusters and superclusters are recognized because the average distance within a cluster or a supercluster from one galaxy or cluster to another is much less than the distance to other galaxies or clusters.

Supernovae
are explosions of large stars. A supernova explosion is much more dramatic than the brightening of a nova. A supernova reported by Chinese astronomers from A.D. 1054 was visible in the daytime. The remnants of this explosion are known today as the Crab Nebula. At its heart the Crab Nebula has a pulsar, all that is left of the star that exploded.

The Universe
Most of the universe was greatly misunderstood until the 20th century. The most common notion from the time of the ancient Greek philosophers until the end of the Middle Ages was that a number of crystal spheres revolved about Earth, and that each of the planets, the Sun, and Earth's Moon occupied one of these spheres. All the stars occupied the farthest sphere. There were only about 6,000 stars known, those visible to the naked eye (and about half of these were south of the equator, so few Europeans had ever seen them).

In 1609 Galileo of Italy turned the first astronomical telescope on the heavens. Galileo's early telescopes were good enough to show that the Milky Way was not merely a whitish band across the sky but consisted of a vast number of stars, far more than the few thousand visible with the naked eye. His observations also disproved the old idea of crystal spheres. People began to speculate about astronomical entities beyond a simple sphere of stars. Not until 1924 were telescopes sufficiently powerful to show that many cloudy patches in the sky consisted of millions of stars far away from the Milky Way. This discovery led to the recognition of the enormous complexity and diversity of the universe.

White dwarfs
are stars whose cores have collapsed until all the atoms are pressed very close together. A single teaspoonful of the matter in a white dwarf weighs about five tons. The core collapses because a red giant has used all its helium for fuel.

Major Accomplishments of Satellites and Space Probes, 1957–2010

While much attention is focused on human beings in space, most of the serious scientific progress has been made by satellites or probes—the general name for space vehicles that neither carry humans nor orbit Earth—that are directed internally or from Earth.

10/4/57 *Sputnik 1* First satellite to orbit Earth (USSR).
11/3/57 *Sputnik 2* Carries Laika, first dog in space; burns in atmosphere 4/14/58.
1/31/58 *Explorer 1* First satellite to detect Van Allen radiation belts; first U.S. satellite.
3/17/58 *Vanguard* Demonstrates Earth is pear-shaped with a bulge in Southern Hemisphere (U.S.).
1/2/59 *Mechta* First space probe to go into orbit around Sun, passing 5,000 mi. from Moon (at which it was aimed) (USSR).
3/3/59 *Pioneer 4* First American probe aimed at Moon; misses and goes into orbit about Sun.
9/12/59 *Lunik 2* First space probe to reach Moon, where it crash-lands (USSR).
10/4/59 *Lunik 3* First space probe to return photographs of far side of Moon (USSR).
4/1/60 *Tiros 1* First weather satellite (U.S.).
6/22/60 *Transit 1-B* First navigational satellite (U.S.).
8/12/60 *Echo 1* First communications satellite—actually a large balloon off which radio signals could be bounced (U.S.).
8/18/60 *Corona* First U.S. spy satellite.
8/19/60 *Sputnik 5* Carries dogs Belka and Streika. Successfully returns them to Earth; 18 orbits.
12/12/61 *Venera 1* First space probe intended to reach another planet—Venus (USSR).
3/7/62 *OSO 1* Orbiting Solar Observatory—first major astronomical satellite (U.S.).
4/23/62 *Ranger 4* First U.S. probe to reach Moon.
4/26/62 *Cosmos 4* First Soviet spy satellite.
7/10/62 *Telstar* First active communications satellite, allowing direct television between Europe and U.S. (U.S.).
8/27/62 *Mariner 2* First space probe to reach vicinity of another planet (Venus) and return scientific information (U.S.).

11/1/62 *Mars 1* First space probe aimed at Mars; contact lost about 66 million mi. from Earth (USSR).
6/26/63 *Syncom 2* First communications satellite to go into synchronous orbit with Earth (U.S.).
8/28/64 *Nimbus 1* First weather satellite stabilized so that cameras always point toward Earth (U.S.).
11/28/64 *Mariner 4* Flies by Mars and takes 21 pictures of its surface, successfully transmitting them back to Earth; its closest approach is 6,118 mi. (U.S.).
4/6/65 *Early Bird* First commercial satellite (U.S.).
7/16/65 *Proton 1* At 26,896 lbs., it is largest Earth satellite to this date (USSR).
11/16/65 *Venera 3* Crash-lands on Venus; first space probe to make physical contact with another planet; radio contact lost before it reaches immediate vicinity of planet (USSR).
12/16/65 *Pioneer 6* Launched into solar orbit; still partially functions today (U.S.).
1/31/66 *Luna 9* Although main vehicle crash-lands, ejected capsule lands safely on Moon and transmits photographs to Earth (USSR).
5/30/66 *Surveyor 1* First soft landing of complete vehicle on Moon (U.S.).
3/31/66 *Luna 10* First space vehicle to go into orbit about Moon (USSR).
8/10/66 *Lunar Orbiter 1* First American space vehicle to go into orbit about Moon.
8/17/70 *Venera 7* First Venus probe to return signals from planet's surface (USSR).
9/12/70 *Luna 16* First space probe to land on Moon without humans aboard, scoop up samples, and return them to Earth (USSR).
11/10/70 *Luna 17* Carries roving vehicle to Moon's surface; vehicle roams for 2 weeks at a time (during day-

light), then "sleeps"; as it roams, it returns photos and other data to Earth (USSR).

12/12/70 *Uhuru* First X-ray satellite telescope (U.S.).

5/28/71 *Mars 3* First space probe to soft-land on Mars; it quickly ceases functioning (USSR).

5/30/71 *Mariner 9* First space probe to orbit another planet (Mars); returns 7,329 photographs of planet (U.S.).

3/2/72 *Pioneer 10* First space probe to study Jupiter and, on June 13, 1983, first to leave solar system (U.S.); contact still maintained as of July 14, 2002.

11/3/73 *Mariner 10* First space probe to observe 2 planets, Venus and Mercury, and only probe ever to observe Mercury (U.S.).

6/8/75 *Venera 9* Returns first photographs from surface of Venus (USSR).

8/20/75 *Viking 1* First American space probe to soft-land on Mars; returns data until Nov., 1982.

8/20/77 *Voyager 2* After studying Jupiter and Saturn, it becomes first space probe to reach vicinities of Uranus and Neptune (U.S.).

9/5/77 *Voyager 1* Studies Jupiter; becomes first probe to reach vicinity of Saturn, then furthest probe from Sun on Feb. 17, 1998; by 2004 is more than 8.4 billion miles (13.5 billion km) from Earth (U.S.).

5/20/78 *Pioneer 12 (Venus 1)* First space probe to go into orbit about Venus. (U.S.).

6/26/78 *Seasat* Analyzes ocean currents and ice flow (U.S.).

12/13/78 *HEAO-2* High-Energy Astronomy Observatory (or Einstein Observatory); makes high-resolution X-ray images of the universe (U.S.).

1/25/83 *IRAS* Infrared Astronomical Satellite studies galactic and extragalactic infrared sources and discovers new planets forming (U.S.).

12/15/84 *Vega 1* First Soviet mission to study Halley's comet; along the way it drops balloon probe into atmosphere of Venus.

7/2/85 *Giotto* Joint European mission to Halley's comet; passes closest to the comet—375 mi. (600 km)— and later is redirected to comet Grigg-Skjellerup, which it passes 7/10/92 at a distance of 125 mi. (200 km).

5/4/89 *Magellan* American probe orbits Venus and maps it in detail with radar.

10/18/89 *Galileo* After passing near Venus and Earth (twice), it reports on Jupiter's moons before crashing into Jupiter in Sept. 2003. (U.S.).

11/18/89 *Cosmic Background Explorer (COBE)* Studied cosmic background radiation in hopes of learning cause of galaxy formation.

4/24/90 *Hubble Space Telescope* Flawed optical telescope placed in orbit about Earth by U.S.; successfully repaired 12/10/93.

10/6/90 *Ulysses* Studying previously unobserved north and south poles of the Sun (U.S.-ESA).

8/31/91 *Yohkoh* Japanese satellite that reports on X-rays and gamma rays from the Sun.

6/7/92 *Extreme Ultraviolet Explorer (EUVE)* American satellite studies high range of ultraviolet radiation in universe.

7/3/92 *Solar Anomalous and Magnetospheric Particle Explorer (SAMPEX)* American satellite that reports on particles in space, including space dust and the solar wind.

7/24/92 *Geotail* Japanese satellite launched by NASA to study Earth's magnetosphere.

1/25/94 *Clementine* Joint U.S. military-science mission; maps the moon from lunar orbit and later visits the asteroid Geographos.

11/1/94 *WIND* Goes into a figure-8 orbit around the Earth and Moon, studying the solar wind.

3/18/95 *Infrared Telescope in Space (IRTS)* Japan's infrared space telescope surveys 7 percent of the sky over a period of 28 days.

11/17/95 *Infrared Space Observatory (ISO)* A European Space Agency satellite that extends the work of the earlier IRAS. Nicknamed "Europe's Hubble" (ESA).

12/2/95 *Solar and Heliospheric Observatory (SOHO)* Studies the sun from an orbit of about 930,000 miles (1.5 million km) from Earth (ESA/U.S.).

12/30/95 *Rossi X-Ray Timing Explorer (XTE)* First U.S. X-ray telescope since 1978; studies X-ray sources in Milky Way including stars, pulsars, and possible black holes.

2/17/96 *Shoemaker Near Earth Asteroid Rendezvous (NEAR-Shoemaker)* First of the new, less-expensive Discovery series of space probes. *NEAR* orbits asteroid 433 Eros starting in February 2000, and lands on asteroid on February 12, 2001 (U.S.).

4/30/96 *BeppoSAX (Satellite per Astronimica a Raggi X)* This small orbiting observatory studies X-ray-emitting events from outer space. Pinpoints the location of a gamma-ray burster for the first time. (Italy/Netherlands/ESA).

8/21/96 *FAST (Fast Auroral Snapshot)* Smaller, cheaper satellite of the Small-Class Explorer series studies auroras from low-Earth orbit (U.S.).

11/7/96 *Mars Global Surveyor* A probe to Mars orbits the planet and surveys it from space for one Mars year (687 Earth days) starting in March, 1999, after delays caused by a defective solar panel. (U.S.).

12/4/96 *Mars Pathfinder* Bounces to the surface of Mars in the Ares Vallis region on 7/4/97, where it releases a rover named *Sojourner* to report on Martian geology. (U.S.).

8/25/97 *Advanced Composition Explorer (ACE)* Studies solar wind and particles from interstellar space (cosmic rays) as it orbits a stable point where the gravity from the Earth and Sun are in balance (U.S.)

10/15/97 *Cassini-Huygens* Mission to orbit Saturn and study its satellites; *Cassini* is the orbiter that began orbiting Saturn on July 1, 2004, while *Huygens* is a probe that sent close-ups of Titan, Saturn's largest moon, as it parachuted through the atmosphere on January 14, 2005. *Huygens* broadcast additional images for 2.5 hours after landing (U.S./ESA).

4/2/98 *Transition Region and Coronal Explorer (TRACE)* Uses ultraviolet telescope to study magnetism in the Sun's corona from a polar orbit about Earth. (U.S.).

10/24/98 *Deep Space 1* Tests new technologies for space use including ion-propulsion system. (U.S.).

12/5/98 *Submillimeter Wave Astronomy Satellite (SWAS)* Space-based radio telescopes analyze microwaves to study chemical composition of interstellar gas clouds, the homes of new star formation. (U.S)

2/7/99 *Stardust* First mission intended to return material from a comet; flew within 149 miles (214 km) of comet Wild 2 on January 2, 2004, and gathered samples of particles streaming from the comet. Will radio data and images to Earth in 2004, then return in January 2006 and parachute comet samples and interstellar dust back to Earth. (U.S.)

6/24/99 *Far Ultraviolet Spectroscopic Explorer (FUSE)* Exploring the universe at wavelengths slightly longer than X-rays, FUSE fills a significant gap in coverage of the electromagnetic spectrum (U.S./Canada/France).

7/23/99 *Chandra X-Ray Observatory* Its X-ray telescopes reveal previously unknown details of black holes, white dwarfs, neutron stars, and the X-ray background radiation. (U.S.).

12/10/99 *XXM-Newton* The most powerful X-ray detector ever, XXM-Newton has 3 X-ray telescopes using 58 mirrors each as well as 2 X-ray spectrographs and an optical telescope. Its orbit takes it 1/3 the way to the Moon (ESA).

10/9/00 *High Energy Transient Explorer (HETE II)* Observes, reports, and locates gamma-ray bursts for follow up by astronomers and surveys X-ray sources across the universe. (U.S., France, Japan, Italy).

4/7/01 *Mars Odyssey* Entered Mars orbit on October 23, 2001; primary mission from Feb. 2002 to Aug. 2004 is to search for water using instruments that recognize certain minerals and that detect hydrogen and also study the amount of radiation present; it will also be a communication relay for other Mars probes to be launched starting in 2003.

6/30/01 *Wilkinson Microwave Anisotropy Probe (MAP)* Mission to measure temperature fluctuations in the cosmic microwave background. From its solar orbit at the L2 Lagrange point, 1 million miles (1.6 million km) from Earth, it has made the first full-sky map of the oldest light in the universe, improving understanding of how and when galaxies formed. (U.S.)

8/8/01 *Genesis* A mission designed to spend three years in solar orbit, collecting particles from the solar wind, and then returning the material to Earth. Although its parachute failed to deploy on 9/8/04, usable data was recovered from the crash site. (U.S.)

12/7/01 *Thermosphere-Ionosphere-Mesosphere-Energetics and Dynamics (TIMED)* Studies influence of Sun and humans on the upper atmosphere. (U.S.)

2/5/02 *Reuven Ramaty High Energy Solar Spectroscopic Imager (RHESSI)* Explores the basic physics of particle acceleration and energy release by solar flares. (U.S.)

3/17/02 *Gravity Recovery and Climate Experiment (GRACE)* Two spacecraft flying in tandem make extremely precise measurements of Earth's gravitational field. (U.S.-Germany)

10/17/2002 *International Gamma-Ray Astrophysics Laboratory (INTEGRAL)* The elongated orbit and sensitive detectors of *INTEGRAL* enable it to study gamma rays from the far reaches of the universe. (ESA/Russia/U.S.)

1/12/2003 *Cosmic Hot Interstellar Plasma Spectrometer (CHIPS)* Studying a poorly monitored wavelength region of the electromagnetic spectrum, *CHIPS* will report on hot gas, dissociated into electrons and nuclei, that occupies our region of space. (U.S.)

4/28/2003 *Galaxy Evolution Explorer (GALEX)* A small satellite studying ultraviolet emissions of nearby galaxies in an effort to uncover the origin and evolution of the universe and how stars are formed. (U.S.)

6/2/2003 *Mars Express* This Mars orbiter launched a small lander toward the Red Planet, but the lander, *Beagle 2*, lost contact after its December 19, 2003, separa-

tion from the orbiter. The orbiter is using photography and radar to explore the planet. (ESA/U.S.)

6/10/03 and **7/7/03** *Mars Exploration Rovers Mission* Both rovers—*Spirit* and *Opportunity*—successfully landed on Mars and have been transmitting images and data from their two landing sites. A major discovery is the confirmation that liquid water once existed on Mars' surface. (U.S.)

8/25/03 *Spitzer Space Telescope* One of NASA's "four great observatories" (with Hubble, Chandra, and Compton Gamma-Ray Observatory); a sensitive infrared observatory orbiting Earth. (U.S.)

3/2/04 *Rosetta* A mission to Comet 67 P/Churyumov-Gerasimenko ("67/P" for short) that will take a ten-year journey, using three gravity assists from Earth and one from Mars, before entering orbit about the 67/P. In November 2014 it will release a probe (named *Philae*) intended to land on the comet. (ESA)

4/20/04 *Gravity Probe – B* A satellite using precise gyroscopes to test Einstein's general relativity prediction of how Earth's presence and rotation warp nearby spacetime. (U.S.)

8/3/04 *MESSENGER* The first space probe intended to orbit the planet Mercury. *MESSENGER* will fly by Earth once, Venus twice, and Mercury three times before settling into orbit about Mercury in March 2011. (U.S.)

1/12/05 *Deep Impact* Successfully blasts a crater in the comet Tempel 1 on July 4, 2005. (U.S.)

8/12/05 *Mars Reconnaissance Orbiter* Entered a low Mars orbit in March 2006; the *MRO* will examine the surface of Mars in great detail. (U.S.)

1/19/06 *New Horizons* First space probe sent to study Pluto and objects in the Kuiper Belt. Scheduled to reach Pluto in 2016 and Kuiper belt in 2018. (U.S.)

12/18/07 *Dawn* First space probe sent to study Ceres, Vesta, and other objects in the belt between Mars and Jupiter. Scheduled to reach Ceres in 2011 and Vesta in 2015. (U.S.)

10/22/08 *Chandrayaan–1* India's first unmanned lunar probe.

5/21/10 *Ikaros* India's World's first spacecraft to use solar sailing as the main propulsion. Scheduled to reach Venus in September 2010 and the Sun in 2013.

Selected Spaceflights Carrying People, 1965–May 2010

The space programs of the former Soviet Union and the United States both had dramatic flights by human pilots as an important component, although many scientists felt that most goals of the space program could be achieved without risking lives. The *Vostok, Voskhod* and *Soyuz* missions were part of the Soviet program; *Mercury, Gemini, Apollo, Skylab* and the shuttle are part of the U.S. program. The first spaceflight by a human was the Vostok 1 in 1961, manned by Yuri A. Gagarin, but until 1965, missions were primarily to prove that people can venture into space.

Planning for Operations in Space

3/18/65 *Voskhod 2* (26 hrs.) A. Leonov, P. Belyayev. First extravehicular activity (EVA) by Leonov (20 min.); 17 orbits.

3/23/65 *Gemini 3* (4 hrs. 53 min.) Virgil "Gus" Grissom, John Young. First American multi-person crew; 3 orbits.

6/3/65 *Gemini 4* (97 hrs. 56 min.) James McDivitt, Edward White II. 62 orbits; first American EVA; first use of personal propulsion unit.

8/21/65 *Gemini 5* (190 hrs. 56 min.) Gordon Cooper, Charles Conrad 120 orbits; demonstrates feasibility of lunar mission; simulated rendezvous.

12/4/65 *Gemini 7* (330 hrs. 35 min.) Frank Borman, James Lovell. 206 orbits; extensions of testing and performance; target for first rendezvous.

12/16/65 *Gemini 6A* (25 hrs. 51 min.) Walter Schirra, Thomas Stafford. 15 orbits; rendezvous with *Gemini 7.*

3/16/66 *Gemini 8* (10 hrs. 42 min.) Neil Armstrong, David Scott. 6.5 orbits; first dual launch and docking; first Pacific landing.

6/3/66 *Gemini 9A* (72 hrs. 21 min. Thomas Stafford, Eugene Cernan. 44 orbits; unable to dock with target vehicle; 2 hrs. 7 min. of EVA.

7/18/66 *Gemini 10* (70 hrs. 47 min.) John Young, Michael Collins. 43 orbits; first dual rendezvous; docking maneuvers, umbilical EVA.

9/12/66 *Gemini 11* (71 hrs. 17 min.) Charles Conrad Jr., Richard Gordon Jr. 44 orbits; rendezvous and docking.

11/11/66 *Gemini 12* (94 hrs. 34 min.) James Lovell, Edwin "Buzz" Aldrin Jr. 59 orbits; final *Gemini* mission; 5 hours of EVA.

To the Moon and Beyond

4/23/67 *Soyuz 1* (26 hrs. 48 min.) Vladimir M. Komarov, 18 orbits; Komarov is killed when parachute fails; first fatality of space program.

10/11/68 *Apollo 7* (260 hrs. 8 min.) Walter Schirra, Donn Eisele, Walter Cunningham. 8 service propulsion firings; 7 live TV sessions with crew; rendezvous with S-IVB stage performed.

10/26/68 *Soyuz 3* (94 hrs. 51 min.) G. Beregovoi. 64 orbits; approaches unpiloted *Soyuz 2* to distance of 650 ft. (198 m).

12/21/68 *Apollo 8* (147 hrs.) Frank Borman, James Lovell, William Anders. First *Saturn-V* propelled flight; first lunar orbital mission (10 orbits); returns lunar photography.

1/14/69 *Soyuz 4* (71 hrs. 14 min.) V. Shatalov, 48 orbits; docks with *Soyuz 5* in first linkup of 2 space vehicles both carrying people.

1/15/69 *Soyuz 5* (72 hrs. 46 min.) B. Volynov, A. Yeliseyev, Y. Khrunov. 3 cosmonauts perform EVA, transferred to *Soyuz 4* in rescue rehearsal.

3/3/69 *Apollo 9* (241 hrs. 1 min.) James McDivitt, David Scott, Russell Schweickart. First flight of all lunar hardware in Earth orbit, incl. lunar module.

5/18/69 *Apollo 10* (192 hrs. 3 min.) Eugene Cernan, John Young, Thomas Stafford. Lunar mission development flight to evaluate lunar module performance in lunar environment; descent to within 50,000 ft. of Moon.

7/16/69 *Apollo 11* (165 hrs. 18 min.) Neil Armstrong, Michael Collins, Edwin "Buzz" Aldrin Jr. First lunar landing (July 20); limited inspection, photography, evaluation, and sampling of lunar soil.

10/11/69 *Soyuz 6* (118 hrs. 42 min.) G. Shonin, V. Kubasov. First triple launch (with *Soyuz 7* and *8*).

10/12/69 *Soyuz 7* (118 hrs. 41 min.) A. Filipchenko, V. Volkov, V. Gorbatko. With *Soyuz 6* and *8*, conducts experiments in navigation and photography.

10/13/69 *Soyuz 8* (118 hrs. 59 min.) V. Shatalov, A. Yeliseyev. 80 orbits.

11/14/69 *Apollo 12* (244 hrs. 36 min.) Charles Conrad Jr., Richard Gordon Jr., Alan Bean. Second lunar landing; demonstrates point landing capability; samples more area.

4/11/70 *Apollo 13* (142 hrs. 55 min.) James Lovell, Fred Haise Jr., John Swigert Jr. Third lunar landing attempt aborted owing to loss of pressure in liquid oxygen in service module and fuel cell failure.

6/2/70 *Soyuz 9* (424 hrs. 59 min. [17 days 16 hrs.]) A. Nikolayev, V. Sevastianov. Longest spaceflight to this time.

1/31/71 *Apollo 14* (9 days 42 min.) Alan Shepard, Stuart Roosa, Edgar Mitchell. Third lunar landing, returns 98 lbs. of material.

4/23/71 *Soyuz 10* (47 hrs. 46 min.) V. Shatalov, A. Yeliseyev, N. Rukavishnikov. Docks with *Salyut 1*, the first space station.

6/6/71 *Soyuz 11* (23 days 18 hrs. 22 min.) G. Dobrovolsky, V. Patsayev, V. Volkov. All 3 cosmonauts killed during reentry.

7/26/71 *Apollo 15* (12 days 7 hrs. 12 min.) David Scott, Alfred Worden, James Irwin. Fourth lunar landing; first to carry Lunar Roving Vehicle (LRV).

4/16/72 *Apollo 16* (11 days 14 hrs. 51 min.) John Young, Ken Mattingly, Charles Duke Jr. Fifth lunar landing; second to carry LRV. Returns 213 lbs. of material.

12/7/72 *Apollo 17* (12 days 13 hrs. 52 min.) Eugene Cernan, Ronald Evans, Harrison Schmitt. Last manned lunar landing; third with LRV; total EVA time: 44 hrs. 8 min.; returns 243 lbs. of material.

First Stations in Space

5/25/73 *Skylab 2* (28 days 49 min.) Charles. Conrad Jr., Joseph Kerwin, Paul Weitz. First *Skylab* launch; establishes *Skylab Orbital Assembly* in earth orbit; conducts medical and other experiments.

7/29/73 *Skylab 3* (59 days 11 hrs. 9 min.) Alan Bean, Owen Garriott, Jack Lousma. Second *Skylab*; crew performs systems and operational tests and thermal shield deployment.

9/27/73 *Soyuz 12* (47 hrs. 16 min.) V. Lazarev, O. Makarov. First Soviet spaceflight to carry humans since *Soyuz 11* tragedy.

11/16/73 *Skylab 4* (84 days 1 hr. 7 min.) Gerald P. Carr, Edward G. Gibson, William R. Pogue. Services unmanned Saturn workshop; obtains medical data for extending spaceflights.

12/2/74 *Soyuz 16* (5 days 22 hrs. 24 min.) A. Filipchenko, N. Rukavishnikov. Taken to check modifications to *Salyut* system.

1/10/75 *Soyuz 17* (29 days 13 hrs. 20 min.) A. Gubarev, G. Grechko. Docks with *Salyut 4*; sets Soviet endurance record.

5/24/75 *Soyuz 18B* (63 days) P. Klimuk, V. Sevastyanov. Docks with *Salyut 4*.

7/15/75 *ASTP* (9 days 1 hr. 30 min.) Thomas Stafford, Vance Brand, Donald Slayton. *Apollo-Soyuz Test Project*, cooperative U.S.-Soviet mission.

7/15/75 *Soyuz 19* (5 days 23 hrs. 31 min.) A. Leonov, V. Kubasov. Docks with *ASTP*, the U.S. *Apollo* capsule.

The Soviet Study of Human Biology in Space

11/17/75 *Soyuz 20* (90 days) No crew. Biological mission; docks with *Salyut 4*.

10/14/76 *Soyuz 23* (2 days) V. Zudov, V. Rozhdestvensky. Unsuccessful attempt to dock with *Salyut 5*; first landing in water (unplanned) for Soviet program (crew survives).

2/7/77 *Soyuz 24* (7 days) V. Gorbatko, Y. Glazkov. Docks with *Salyut 5* for 18 days of experiments.

10/9/77 *Soyuz 25* (2 days) V. Kovalyonok, V. Ryumin. Unsuccessful attempt to dock with *Salyut 6*.

12/10/77 *Soyuz 26* (96 days) Y. Romanenko, G. Grechko. Docks with *Salyut 6*; crew sets endurance record.

1/10/78 *Soyuz 27* (6 days) V. Dzhanibekov, O. Makarov. Carries second crew to dock with *Salyut 6* space station.

3/2/78 *Soyuz 28* (8 days) V. Remek, A. Gubarev. Carries third crew to board *Salyut 6*; Remek first non-Russian, non-American in space (Czech).

6/15/78 *Soyuz 29* (140 days) V. Kovalyonok, A. Ivanchenkov. Docks with *Salyut 6*; crew sets new endurance record.

2/25/79 *Soyuz 32* (175 days) V. Lyakhov, V. Ryumin. Carries crew to *Salyut 6*; sets new endurance record.

7/23/80 *Soyuz 37* (8 days) V. Gorbatko, P. Tuan (first Vietnamese in space). Exchanges cosmonauts in *Salyut 6*; returns *Soyuz 35* crew after 185 days in orbit.

9/18/80 *Soyuz 38* (8 days) Y. Romanenko, A. Tamayo-Mendez (first Cuban). Ferries to *Salyut 6*.

11/27/80 *Soyuz T-3* (13 days) L. Kizim, O. Makarov, G. Strekalov. Ferries to *Salyut 6*; first 3-person crew since *Soyuz 11*.

3/12/81 *Soyuz T-4* (75 days) V. Kovalyonok, V. Savinykh. Mission to *Salyut 6*.

3/22/81 *Soyuz 39* (8 days) V. Dzhanibekov, J. Gurragcha (first Mongolian). Docks with *Salyut 6*.

The Space Shuttle: U.S. Reentry in Space

4/12/81 *Columbia* (2 days 6 hrs.) John Young, Robert Crippen. First flight of reusable space shuttle; first landing of U.S. spacecraft on land.

11/12/81 *Columbia* (2 days 6 hrs.) Joe Engle, Richard Truly. First reuse of space shuttle; ends early due to loss of fuel cell.

3/22/82 *Columbia* (8 days) Jack Lousma, Gordon Fullerton. Third shuttle flight; payload includes space science experiments.

6/27/82 *Columbia* (7 days 1 hr.) Ken. Mattingly Henry Hartsfield Jr. Fourth shuttle mission; first landing on hard surface.

11/11/82 *Columbia* (5 days 2 hrs.) Vance Brand, Robert Overmyer, Joseph Allen, William Lenoir. First operational mission; first 4-man crew; first deployment of satellites from shuttle.

4/4/83 *Challenger* (5 days) Paul Weitz, Karol Bobko, Donald Peterson, Story Musgrave. Second shuttle joins fleet; deploys TDRS tracking satellite; first shuttle EVA.

6/18/83 *Challenger* (6 days) Robert Crippen, Frederick Hauck, John Fabian, Sally Ride, Norman Thagard. First 5-person crew; Ride is first U.S. woman in space; first use of Remote Manipulator Structure ("Arm") to deploy and retrieve satellite.

8/30/83 *Challenger* (6 days) Richard Truly, Daniel Brandenstein, William Thornton, Guion Bluford (first black American), Dale Gardner. First night launch. Launches weather/communications satellite for India.

11/28/83 *Columbia* (10 days) John Young, Brewster Shaw Robert Parker, Owen Garriott, Byron Lichtenberg, Ulf Merbold. Launches *Spacelab*; crew performs experiments in astronomy and medicine.

2/3/84 *Challenger* (8 days) Vance Brand, Bruce McCandless, Robert Stewart, Ronald McNair, Robert Gibson. Jet-propelled backpacks carry 2 astronauts on first untethered space walks; 2 satellites lost; first landing at Kennedy Space Center.

4/6/84 *Challenger* (7 days) Robert Crippen, Richard Scobee, Terry Hart, George Nelson, James van Hoften. Deploys Long Duration Exposure Facility for experiments in space durability; snares Solar Max satellite; repairs altitude-control system.

8/30/84 *Discovery* (7 days) Henry Hartsfield Jr., Michael Coats, Steven Hawley, Judith Resnik, Richard Mullane, Charles Walker. Third shuttle in fleet; deploys 3 satellites and tests a solar sail.

10/5/84 *Challenger* (8 days) Robert Crippen, Jon McBride, Kathryn Sullivan, Sally Ride, Marc Garneau, David Leestma, Paul Scully-Power. First Canadian astronaut, Garneau; deploys Earth Radiation Budget Satellite and uses Sir-B radar system to see beneath surface of sand.

11/8/84 *Discovery* (8 days) Frederick Hauck, David Walker, Anna Fisher, Joseph Allen, Dale Gardner. Salvages two inoperative satellites.

1/24/85 *Discovery* (4 days) Ken Mattingly, Loren Schriver, James Buchli, Ellison Onizuka, Gary Payton. Secret military mission.

4/12/85 *Discovery* (7 days) Karol Bobko, Donald Williams, Jake Garn, Charles Walker, Jeffrey Hoffman, David Griggs, Margaret Rhea Seddon. First U.S. senator in space, Garn.

4/29/85 *Challenger* (7 days) Robert Overmyer, Frederick Gregory, Don Lind, Taylor Wang, Lodewijk van den Berg, Norman Thagard, William Thornton. Carries European Spacelab module.

6/17/85 *Discovery* (7 days) John Creighton, Shannon Lucid, Steven Nagel, Daniel Brandenstein, John Fabian, Prince Salman al-Saud, Patrick Baudry. First Arabian in space, al-Saud; successfully launches 4 satellites.

7/29/85 *Challenger* (8 days) Roy Bridges, Anthony England, Karl Henize, Story Musgrave, Gordon Fullerton, Loren Acton, John-David Bartoe. Carries *Spacelab* 2, a group of scientific experiments.

8/27/85 *Discovery* (7 days) John Lounge, James van Hoften, William Fisher, Joe Engle, Richard Covey. Repairs satellite Syncom 3.

10/3/85 *Atlantis* (4 days) Karol Bobko, Ronald Grabe, David Hilmers, William Pailes, Robert Stewart. Fourth shuttle.

10/30/85 *Challenger* (7 days) Henry Hartsfield Jr., Steven Nagel, Bonnie Dunbar, Guion Bluford, Ernst Messerschmid, Reinhard Furrer, Wubbo Ockels. Carries Spacelab 1-D; scientific experiments conducted by Germans.

11/26/85 *Atlantis* (7 days) Brewster Shaw, Bryan O'Conner, Charles Walker, Rudolfo Neri Vela, Jerry L.

Ross, Sherwood C. Spring, Mary Cleave. First Mexican in space, Vela.

1/12/86 *Columbia* (5 days) Robert Gibson, Charles Bolden Jr., George Nelson, Franklin Chang-Diaz, Steven Hawley, Robert Cenker. First U.S. congressman in space, Nelson.

1/28/86 *Challenger* (73 seconds) Richard Scobee, Michael Smith, Robert McNair, Ellison Onizuka, Judith Resnik, Gregory Jarvis, Christa McAuliffe. O-rings in solid-fuel boosters wear through, and fuel supply explodes, killing all 6 regular astronauts and schoolteacher McAuliffe.

The First Space Station (Soyuz flight durations N.A.)

2/20/86 *Mir* Soviet space station, No crew.

9/29/88 *Discovery* (4 days) John Lounge, David Hilmers, Frederick Hauck, George Nelson, Richard Covey. Redesigned shuttle makes first flight since the *Challenger* disaster.

11/26/88 *Soyuz TM-7* A. Volkov, S. Krikalev, J. Chrétien. *Mir* temporarily abandoned for first time.

12/2/88 *Atlantis* (4 days) Robert Gibson, Jerry Ross, William Shepherd, Guy Gardner, Richard Mullane. Secret military mission known to have deployed radar spy satellite.

3/13/89 *Discovery* (5 days) Michael Coats, John Blaha, James Buchli, James Bagian, Robert Springer. Deploys NASA's third relay satellite and tests thermal control system for proposed U.S. space station.

5/4/89 *Atlantis* (4 days) David Walker, Ronald Grabe, Mary Cleave, Norman Thagard, Mark Lee. Launches probe *Magellan* to map Venus with radar.

8/9/89 *Columbia* (5 days) Brewster Shaw, Richard Richards, David Leestma, James Adamson, Mark Brown. Secret military mission to launch spy satellite.

10/18/89 *Atlantis* (5 days) Donald Williams, Michael McCulley, Shannon Lucid, Franklin Chang-Diaz, Ellen Baker. Launches *Galileo* probe.

11/22/89 *Discovery* (5 days) Frederick Gregory, John Blaha, Story Musgrave, Kathryn Thornton, Manley Lanier Carter Jr. Secret military mission.

1/9/90 *Columbia* (11 days) Daniel Brandenstein, Bonnie Dunbar, Marsha Ivens, David Low, James Wetherbee. Launches communication satellite Syncom IV and retrieves the *Long Duration Exposure Facility* (see 4/6/84).

2/28/90 *Atlantis* (4 days) John Creighton, John Caspar, David Hilmers, Richard Mullane, Pierre Thuot. Secret military mission.

4/24/90 *Discovery* (5 days) Loren Shriver, Charles Bolden Jr., Bruce McCandless, Steven Hawley, Kathryn Sullivan. Launches Hubble Space Telescope.

10/6/90 *Discovery* (4 days) Richard Richards, Robert Cabana, Bruce Melnick, William Shepherd, Thomas Akers. Launches *Ulysses* space probe into solar orbit.

11/15/90 *Atlantis* (5 days) Richard Covey, Frank Culberston Jr., Charles Gemar, Carl Meade, Robert Springer. NASA announces this as last secret military mission.

12/2/90 *Columbia* (9 days) Vance Brand, Guy Gardner, Jeffrey Hoffman, John Lounge, Robert Parker, Samuel Durrance, Ronald Parise. Carries 3 UV and 1 X-ray telescope.

4/5/91 *Atlantis* (6 days) Steven Nagel, Kenneth Cameron, Linda Godwin, Jerry Ross, Jerome Apt. Launches 17-ton *Gamma Ray Observatory*; unscheduled spacewalk required to open satellite's antenna properly.

4/28/91 *Discovery* (8 days) Michael Coats, Blaine Hammond Jr., Gregory Harbaugh, Charles Lacy Veach, Guion Bluford Jr., Richard Hieb, Donald McMonagle. Tests detection devices and recovers Star Wars satellite.

6/5/91 *Columbia* (9 days) Bryan D. O'Connor, Sidney M. Gutierrez, James P. Bagian, Margaret Rhea Seddon, Francis A. Gaffney, Millie Hughes-Fulford, Tamara E. Jernigan. Performs human and animal space-adaptation experiments.

8/21/91 *Atlantis* (9 days) John Blaha, Michael Baker, Shannon Lucid, David Low, James Adamson. Performs 22 experiments and launches communications satellite.

9/12/91 *Discovery* (5 days) John Creighton, Kenneth Reightler Jr., Mark Brown, James Buchlim, Charles Gemar. Launches upper-atmosphere research satellite.

11/24/91 *Atlantis* (7 days) Frederick Gregory, Tom Henricks, James Voss, Mario Runco Jr., Story Musgrave, Thomas Hennen. First completely nonsecret military flight; studies how well military installations can be seen from space.

1/22/92 *Discovery* (8 days) Ronald Grabe, Stephen Oswald, Norman Thagard, William Readdy, David Hilmers, Roberta Bondar, Ulf Merbold. Performs experiments as the First International Microgravity Lab.

3/24/92 *Atlantis* (9 days) Charles Bolden Jr., Brian Duffy, Kathryn Sullivan, David Leestma, Michael Foale, Byron Lichtenberg, Dirk Frimout. Inaugural flight of Mission to Planet Earth studies Earth's atmosphere and auroras.

5/7/92 *Endeavour* (9 days) Daniel Brandenstein, Kevin Chilton, Thomas Akers, Richard Hieb, Bruce Melnick, Kathryn Thornton, Pierre Thout. The first flight of the replacement for *Challenger* succeeds relaunching an erring communications satellite; first ever 3-person EVA.

6/25/92 *Columbia* (14 days) Richard Richards, Kenneth Bowersox, Bonnie Dunbar, Lawrence DeLucas, Ellen Baker, Eugene Trinh, Carl Meade. Sets record for duration of shuttle mission; carries U.S. Microgravity Laboratory.

7/31/92 *Atlantis* (8 days) Loren Shriver, Andrew Allen, Marsha Ivins, Jeffrey Hoffman, Franklin Chang-Diaz, Claude Nicollier, Franco Mallerba. Launches European Retrievable Carrier (Eureca) satellite. First Swiss astronaut (Nicollier); first Italian (Mallerba).

9/12/92 *Endeavour* (8 days) Robert Gibson, Curtis Brown Jr., Jay Apt, Jan Davis, Mae Carol Jemison, Mark Lee, Mamoru Mohri. First professional Japanese astronaut in space (Mohri); first married couple in space (Lee and Davis); first black female astronaut (Jemison). Japanese-sponsored mission to study biology in space.

10/22/92 *Columbia* (10 days) James Wetherbee, Michael Baker, Glenwood MacLean, Tamara Jernigan, William Shepherd, Charles Lacy Veach. Launches the Italian-made satellite *LAGEOS-2*, to provide information about Earth's gravitational field.

12/2/92 *Discovery* (7 days) Daniel Walker, Robert Cabana, Guion Bluford Jr., James Voss, Michael Clifford. Last scheduled military flight for the space shuttle; future military flights to use disposable rockets. Launches secret military satellite.

1/13/93 *Endeavour* (6 days) John Caspar, Gregory Harbaugh, Donald McMonagle, Susan Helms, Mario Runco Jr.. Observes X-rays and launches a TDRS (Tracking and Data Relay Satellite).

4/8/93 *Discovery* (9 days) Kenneth Cameron, Stephen Oswald, Kenneth Cockrell, Michael Foale, Ellen Ochoa. Launches and retrieves the *Spartan* Sun probe, used to study the solar corona, and observes Earth's ozone layer.

4/26/93 *Columbia* (10 days) Steven Nagel, Tom Henricks, Jerry Ross, Charles Precourt, Bernard Harris Jr., Ulrich Walter, Hans Schlegel. The European Spacelab with two German scientists (Walter and Schlegel) conducts experiments on weightlessness.

6/21/93 *Endeavour* (10 days) Ronald Grabe, Brian Duffy, Donald Low, Peter Wisoff, Nancy Jane Sherlock, Janice Voss. Recovers Europe's *Eureca* satellite; and conducts experiments using a pressurized laboratory called Spacehab.

9/12/93 *Discovery* (10 days) Frank Culbertson Jr., William Readdy, James Newman, Daniel Bursch, Carl Walz. Tests equipment and procedures to be used in repairing Hubble Space Telescope; first night landing at Kennedy.

10/18/93 *Columbia* (14 days) John Blaha, Richard Searfoss, William McArthur Jr., Shannon Lucid, Martin Fettman, Margaret Rhea Seddon, David Wolf. Conducts biological experiments on humans and rats; first dissection of animal in space.

12/2/93 *Endeavour* (11 days) Richard Covey, Kenneth Bowersox, Claude Nicollier, Story Musgrave, Thomas Akers, Kathryn Thornton, Jeffrey Hoffman. Repairs defective lens on Hubble Space Telescope.

The U.S. and Russia Work Together in Space

2/3/94 *Discovery* (8 days) Charles Bolden Jr., Sergei Krikalev, Kenneth Reightler Jr., Jan Davis, Franklin Chang-Diaz, Ronald Sega. Krikalev first Russian on U.S. space shuttle mission.

3/4/94 *Columbia* (14 days) John Caspar, Andrew Allen, Charles Gemar, Marsha Ivins, Pierre Thuot. Develops techniques for use in space-station construction.

4/9/94 *Endeavour* (11 days) Sidney Gutierrez, Kevin Chilton, Michael Clifford, Linda Godwin, Jay Apt, Thomas Jones. Uses radar to map details of Earth in 3-D.

7/1/94 *Soyuz TM-19* Y. Malenchenko, T. Musabayev. Relieves Afanasyev and Usachyov on *Mir*.

7/8/94 *Columbia* (15 days) Robert Cabana, Leroy Chiao, James Halsell Jr., Richard Hieb, Chiaki Naito-Mukai, Donald Thomas, Carl Walz. Orbits Earth 236 times, a new record. First Japanese woman in space (heart surgeon Naito-Mukai).

9/9/94 *Discovery* (11 days) Richard Richards, Blaine Hammond Jr., Susan Helms, Mark Lee, J.M. Lineger, Carl Meade. Conducts laser experiments to measure pollution in atmosphere. Releases and recaptures satellite that collects data on solar wind; Meade and Lee use jet pack for untethered spacewalk.

9/30/94 *Endeavour* (11 days) Michael Baker, Daniel Bursch, Thomas Jones, Steven Smith, Jeff Wisoff, Terrence Wukcytt. The *Space Radar Laboratory* 2 mission is follow-up of nearly identical mission flown in the spring to detect seasonal changes.

10/4/94 *Soyuz TM-20* A. Viktorenko, Y. Kondakova, U. Merbold. Merbold, from the European Space Agency, studies space biology aboard *Mir* and returns to Earth on 11/4/94. Viktorenko and Kondakova relieve Malenchenko and Musabaye on *Mir*.

11/3/94 *Atlantis* (11 days) Curtis Brown, Donald McMonagle, Jean-François Clervoy (from ESA), Scott Parazynski, Joseph Tanner. Third shuttle flight since 1992 to carry the *Atlas* lab (Atmospheric Laboratory for Applications and Science).

2/3/95 *Discovery* (8 days) James Wetherbee, Eileen Collins, Michael Foale, Bernard Harris Jr., Vladimir Titov, Janice Voss. Carries Russian Titov to within 1 m (37 ft.) of *Mir*.

3/2/95 *Endeavour* (17 days) Stephen Oswald, Samuel Durrance, Tamara Jernigan, William Gregory, John Grunsfeld, Wendy Lawrence, Ronald Parise. Carries the lab *Astro 2*, used to study volcanic eruptions on Jupiter's moon Io.

3/14/95 *Soyuz TM-21* N. Thagard, V. Dezhurov, G. Strekalov. Thagard becomes the first U.S. astronaut to live aboard *Mir*; he studies the body's reaction to weightlessness; Polyakov, who returns on 3/22/95, with Kondakova and Viktorenko, sets endurance record of 14.5 months in space.

6/27/95 *Atlantis* (10 days) Robert Gibson, Charles Precourt, Ellen Baker, Gregory Harbaugh, Bonnie Dunbar, Anatoly Solovyev, Nikolai Budarin.

Docks with *Mir* for 5 days. Spacelab on Atlantis and Spekter module of *Mir* used for biomedical research. Solovyev and Budarin relieve Thagard, Dezhurov, and Strekalov as crew of *Mir*.

7/13/95 *Discovery* (9 days) Tom Henricks, Kevin Kregel, Nancy Currie, Donald Thomas, Mary Ellen Weber. Launches Tracking and Data Relay Satellite (TDRS) to replace one lost when *Challenger* blew up.

9/3/95 *Soyuz TM-22* T. Reiter (Germany), Y. Gidzenko, S. Avdeyev. Replaces Solovyev and Budarin, who return to Earth 9/11/88.

9/7/95 *Endeavour* (11 days) Michael Gernhart, David Walker, Kenneth Cockrell, James Newman, James Voss. Uses an orbiting shield to produce a vacuum in its wake 10,000 times greater than any found on Earth.

10/20/95 *Columbia* (16 days) Ken Bowersox, Kent Rominger, Kathryn Thornton, Cady Coleman, Michael Lopez-Alegria, Fred Leslie, Albert Sacco Conducts microgravity experiments in Spacelab.

11/12/95 *Atlantis* (8 days) Kenneth Cameron, James Halsell Jr., Jerry Ross, William McArthur Jr., Chris Hadfield (Canada). Changes configuration of *Mir* to make docking easier in future missions.

1/11/96 *Endeavour* (9 days) Brian Duffy, Brent Jett Jr., Leroy Chiao, Winston Scott, Daniel Barry, Koichi Wakata (Japan). Recovers Japanese science-experiment orbiting platform, which had been launched by a Japanese H-2 rocket in March 1995.

2/21/96 *Soyuz TM-23* Y. Onufrienko, Y. Usachev. Relieves *Mir* crew.

2/22/96 *Columbia* (15 days) Nobie Stone, Jeffrey Hoffman, Andrew Allen, Doc Horowitz, Franklin Chang-Diaz, Claude Nicollier (ESA), Maurizio Cheli (ESA), Umberto Guidoni (Italian Space Agency).. Tethered satellite experiment partly successful, but satellite is mysteriously lost from end of tether.

3/22/96 *Atlantis* (9 days) Kevin Childon, Richard Seafoss, Ronald Sega, Michael Clifford, Shannon Lucid, Linda Godwin. Docks with *Mir*. Lucid stays behind on the space station.

5/19/96 *Endeavour* (10 days) John Caspar, Curtis Brown Jr., Daniel Bursch, Mario Runco Jr., Marc Garneau (Canadian), Andrew Thomas. Deploys first inflatable antenna from Spartan satellite. Conducts rendezvous studies of the *PAMS* satellite, a test of a system in which a satellite stabilizes itself without expending rocket fuel.

6/20/96 *Columbia* (17 days) Tom Henricks, Kevin Kregel, Rick Linnehan, Susan Helms, Charles Brady, Jean-Jacques Favier (Canada), Robert Thirsk. Carries the Life/Microgravity Spacelab, to study the effects of space flight on the human body, on rats, and on fish embryos; and SAREX-II.

8/17/96 *Soyuz TM-24* V. Korzun, A. Kaleri, C. Andre-Deshays (France). Korzun and Kaleri relieve Onufrienko and Usachev on *Mir*.

9/16/96 *Atlantis* (10 days) William Readdy, Terrence Wilcutt, Tom Akers, Jay Apt, Carl Walz, John Blaha, Shannon Lucid. Blaha relieves Lucid on *Mir*.

11/19/96 *Columbia* (18 days) Kenneth Cockrell, Kent Rominger, Story Musgrave, Thomas Jones, Tamara Jernigan. Deploys and retrieves *ORFEUS-SPAS*, a satellite gathering data about matter in space between the stars and the WSF-3/Wake Shield Facility, a satellite used in testing a method of producing a high vacuum to be used in manufacturing ultra pure semiconductor devices.

1/12/97 *Atlantis* (10 days) Mike Baker, Brent Jett, Jeff Wisoff, John Grunsfeld, Marsha Ivins, J.M. Linenger, John Blaha. Linenger relieves Blaha on *Mir*.

2/10/97 *Soyuz TM-25* V. Tsbliyev, A. Lazutkin, R. Ewald (Germany), V. Korzun, A. Kaleri. Tsbliyev and Lazutkin relieve Korzun and Kaleri on *Mir*.

2/11/97 *Discovery* (10 days) Ken Bowersox, Scott Horowitz, Joe Tanner, Steve Hawley, Greg Harbaugh, Mark Lee, Steve Smith. Replaces eight instruments in the Hubble Space Telescope and adds two new ones, greatly improving its abilities.

4/4/97 *Columbia* (4 days) Jim Halsell, Susan Still, Janice Voss, Mike Gernhardt, Don Thomas, Roger Crouch, Greg Linteris. Carries the Microgravity Science Lab, but 85 percent of the experiments are canceled because of a problem with the fuel cells.

5/15/97 *Atlantis* (9 days) Charlie Precourt, Eileen Collins, Jean-François Clervoy, Carlos Noriega, Ed Lu, Elena Kondakova (Russia), Mike Foale, Jerry Linenger. Docks with Mir, taking Linenger back to Earth and leaving Foale. Brings needed supplies and replacement equipment to aging *Mir*, which has had problems with fires and failures.

7/1/97 *Columbia* (16 days) James Halsell, Susan Still, Janice Voss, Michael Gernhardt, Donald Thomas, Roger Crouch, Gregory Linteris. Replacement for flight of 4/4/97.

8/7/97 *Discovery* (11 days) Curt Brown, Kent Rominger, Jan Davis, Robert Curbeam, Steve Robinson, Bjarni Tryggvason. In the fourth cooperative German-American scientific mission, various experiments using infrared imagining, lasers, and cryogenic devices are conducted.

9/25/97 *Atlantis* (11 days) James Wetherbee, Mike Bloomfield, Vladimir Titov, Scott Parazynski, Jean-Loup Chrétien, Wendy Lawrence, David Wolf, Michael Foale. Takes Wolf to *Mir*, returns with Foale.

11/19/97 *Columbia* (16 days) Kevin Kregel, Steve Lindsey, Kalpana Chawla, Winston Scott, Takao Doi, Leonid Kadenyuk (first Ukranian to fly aboard a shuttle). Conducts microgravity experiments and attempts to launch *SPARTAN* solar research satellite; when *SPARTAN* malfunctions, astronauts retrieve it for a future attempt on a later flight.

1/22/98 *Endeavour* (9 days) Terrence Wilcutt, Joe Edwards, James Reilly, Michael Anderson, Bonnie Dunbar, Salizhan Sharipov, Andrew Thomas, David Wolf. Thomas relieves Wolf on *Mir*. Performs microgravity experiments with plants and crystals.

4/17/98 *Columbia* (16 days) Richard Searfoss, Scott Altman, Kathryn Hire, Richard Linnehan, Dave Williams, Jay Buckey, James Pawelczyk. Carries the *Neurolab* into space where the effects of space flight on the brains and reproduction of various species of animals and plants are studied.

6/2/98 *Discovery* (10 days) Charles Precourt, Dominic Gorie, Wendy Lawrence, Franklin Chang-Diaz, Janet Kavandi, Andrew Thomas, Valery Victorovitch Ryumin. Final U.S. astronaut mission on *Mir* completed as Thomas is returned to Earth.

11/20/98 *Discovery* (9 days) Curtis Brown Jr., Steven Lindsey, Scott Parazynski, Stephen Robinson, Pedro Duque, Chiaki Mukai, John Glenn. Glenn, first American to orbit Earth in 1962, becomes oldest astronaut; studies effects of weightlessness on older humans.

Era of the International Space Station (ISS)

12/04/98 *Endeavour* (12 days) Robert Cabana, Frederick Sturckow, James Newman, Nancy Currie, Jerry Ross, Sergei Konstantinovich Krikalev (Russia). Crew docks with the Russian-built Functional Energy Block Zarya and adds Node-1 (Unity) to begin assembly of the International Space Station.

5/27/99 *Discovery* (10 days) Kent Rominger, Rick Husband, Tamara Jernigan, Ellen Ochoa, Daniel Barry, Julie Payette (Canada), Valery Ivanovich Tokarev (Russia). Brings cargo for outfitting (ISS), including Russian cargo crane to be mounted on exterior of Functional Energy Block.

7/22/99 *Columbia* (5 days) Eileen Collins, Jeffrey Ashby, Steven Hawley, Catherine Coleman, Michael Tognini (France). Collins first female commander. Launches Chandra X-ray Observatory.

12/19/99 *Discovery* (8 days) Curtis Brown Jr., Scott Kelly, John Grunsfeld, Michael Foales, Steven Smith, Jean-François Clervoy (France), Claude Nicollier (Switzerland). Captures, services, and re-launches Hubble Space Telescope.

2/11/00 *Endeavour* (11 days) Kevin Kregel, Dominic Gorie, Janet Kavandi, Janice Voss, Gerhard Thiele (German-ESA), Mamoru Mohri (Japan). The Shuttle Radar Topography Mission obtain the most detailed topographical map of the Earth to date.

5/19/00 *Atlantis* (10 days) James Halsell Jr., Scott Horowitz, Susan Helms, Mary Ellen Weber, Jeffrey Williams, James Voss, Yury Usachev (Russian). Carries supplies to ISS. Helms and Usachev remain on ISS as part of first crew.

9/8/00 *Atlantis* (12 days) Terry Wilcutt, Scott Altman, Dan Burbank, Ed Lu, Rick Mastracchio, Yuri Malenchenko (Russia), and Boris Morukov (Russia). Brings supplies to ISS and conducts space walk to perform station maintenance.

10/11/00 *Discovery* (13 days) Brian Duffy, Pamela Melroy, Leroy Chiao, Jeff Wisoff, Michael Lopez-Alegria, William McArthur, Jr., Koichi Wakata (Japan). Brings and installs parts needed for solar arrays, communications, and attitude control for ISS.

10/31/00 *Soyuz TM-31* (139 days) Bill Shepherd, Y. Gidzenko, S. Krikalev. This is Expedition 1, beginning the permanent occupation of ISS.

11/30/00 *Endeavour* (12 days) Brent Jett, Michael Bloomfield, Joseph Tanner, Carlos Noriega, Marc Garneau (Canada). Adds photovoltaic modules to the ISS's solar arrays; brings radiators for cooling photovoltaic cells; activates the S-band communications system.

2/7/01 *Atlantis* (13 days) Kenneth Cockrell, Mark Polansky, Robert Curbeam, Thomas Jones, Marsha Ivins. Installs ISS's "Destiny" laboratory module.

3/8/01 *Discovery* (13 days) Jim Wetherbee, Jim Kelly, Andy Thomas, Paul Richards. Brings Expedition 2 crew (Yury Usachev, James Voss, and Susan Helms) to ISS. Returns Expedition 1 crew (see 10/31/00). Brings additional laboratory equipment.

4/19/01 *Endeavour* (12 days) Kent Rominger , Jeffrey Ashby, Scott Umberto Guidoni (ESA), Scott Parazynski, Chris Hadfield (Canada), Yuri Lonchakov (Russia), John Phillips. Delivers the Italian "Raffaello" module and the Canadian mechanical arm to the ISS.

7/12/01 *Atlantis* (11 days) Steven Lindsey, Charles Hobaugh, Michael Gernhardt, Janet Kavandi, James Reilly. Delivers the Joint Airlock; resolves problems with the Canadian robotic arm.

8/10/01 *Discovery* (12 days) Scott Horowitz, Rick Sturckow, Daniel Barry, Patrick Forrester. Installs the Leonardo Multi-Purpose Module; launches Simplesat, a demonstration satellite built with "off-the-shelf" commercial hardware. Brings Expedition 3 crew (Frank Culbertson, Vladimir Dezhurov, and Mikhail Tyurin). Returns Expedition 2 crew (see 3/8/01).

10/21/01 *Soyuz TM-33* (165 days) Viktor Afanasyev (Russia), Konstantin Kozeev (Russia), Claudie Haignere (ESA). Conducts experiments in materials research, life sciences, meteorological phenomena. Emergency vehicle exchanged; crew returns on *Soyuz TM-32*.

12/5/01 *Endeavour* (12 days) Linda Godwin, Dominic Gorie, Mark Kelly, Daniel Tani. Brings Expedition 4 crew (Yury Onufrienko, Carl Walz, Daniel Bursh) and 3 tons (2.7 metric tons) of equipment and supplies. Returns Expedition 3 crew (see 8/10/01).

3/1/02 *Columbia* (11 days) Scott Altman, Duane Carey, Nancy Currie, John Grunsfeld, Richard Linnehan, Michael Massimino, James Newman. Fourth Hubble Space Telescope servicing mission; during five EVAs installs a new power control unit, new camera, new solar arrays.

4/8/02 *Atlantis* (11 days) Crew: Michael Bloomfield, Stephen Frick, Lee Morin, Ellen Ochoa, Jerry Ross, Steven Smith, Rex Walheim. Delivered and installed central truss segment to ISS, the first of nine parts of the space station's external frame.

4/25/02 *Soyuz TM-34* (11 days) Yuri Gidzenko (Russia), Roberto Vittori (ESA), Mark Shuttleworth (a paying tourist from South Africa). Exchange of *Soyuz* emergency vehicles; crew returned on *Soyuz TM-33*.

6/5/02 *Endeavour* (14 days) Franklin Chang-Diaz, Kenneth Cockrell, Paul Lockhart, Philippe Perrin (France). Delivers Microgravity Science Glovebox, enabling crew to work safely with experiments involving fluids, flames, fumes, etc. Delivers Expedition 5 crew (Peggy Whitson, Valery Korzun, Sergei Treschev), returns Expedition 4 crew (see 12/5/01).

10/7/02 *Atlantis* (11 days) Jeffrey Ashby, Pamela Melroy, David Wolf, Piers Sellers, Sandra Magnus, Fyodor Yurchikhin. Delivers S1 Truss.

10/30/02 *Soyuz TMA-1* (9 days) S. Zaletin, F. De Winne (Belgium), Y. Lonchakov, A. Lazutkin. Test flight of new *Soyuz TMA*. Conducts experiments with Microgravity Science Glovebox. Returns *Soyuz TM-34*.

11/23/02 *Endeavour* (14 days) Jim Wetherbee, Paul Lockhart, Michael Lopez-Alegria, John Herrington. Delivers Expedition 6 crew (Peggy Whitson, Valery Korzun, Sergei Treschev) and parts to improve space station's thermal control system. Returns Expedition 5 crew (see 6/5/02).

1/16/03 *Columbia* (16 days) Rick Husband, Willie McCool, Michael Anderson, Kalpana Chawla, David Brown, Laurel Clark, Ilan Ramon. Shuttle explodes on re-entry, killing all aboard.

4/26/03 *Soyuz TMA-2* Yuri Milanchenko (Russia), Edward Lu. Retrieves Expedition 6 crew (see 11/23/02) trapped aboard ISS as Space Shuttle Program is grounded in wake of *Columbia* disaster.

10/18/03 *Soyuz TMA-3* Alexander Kaleri (Russia), Mike Foale (U.S.), and Pedro Duque (Spain). Foale and Kaleri stay on ISS until Expedition 9 arrives, while Duque, after 8 days of research in space for ESA, returns along with *Expedition 7* crew (see 4/26/03).

10/4/04 *SpaceShipOne* Brian Binnie. In the first non-governmental spaceflight, *SpaceShipOne* wins privately funded $10M X Prize competition to reach outer space twice in two weeks using same reusable craft.

7/26/05 *Discovery* (14 days) Steve Robinson, Jim Kelly, Andy Thomas, Wendy Lawrence, Charlie Camarda, Eileen Collins and Soichi Noguchi. First return to space after *Columbia* disaster is dogged with falling debris from booster and other problems, but inspection resolves most concerns and a space walk repair corrects others. Astronauts also replace failed main gyroscope on International Space Station.

7/4/06 *Discovery* (12 days) Stephanie Wilson, Michael Fossum, Steven Lindsey, Piers Sellers, Mark Kelly, Thomas Reiter and Lisa Nowak. Performs three spacewalks and services the International Space Station.

9/9/06 *Atlantis* (11 days) Brent Jett, Jr., Christopher Ferguson, Heidemarie Stefanyshyn-Piper, Joe Tanner, Daniel Burbank, and Steven MacLean. Resumes assembly of the International Space Station, and performs three spacewalks

12/9/06 *Discovery* (13 days) Mark Polansky, William Oefelein, Robert Curbeam, Joan Higginbotham, Nicholas Patrick, Christer Fuglesang, and Sunita Williams. Delivers Williams to the International Space Station to replace Thomas Reiter, who had been there since July 2006.

7/8/07 *Atlantis* (14 days) Frederick Sturckow, Lee Archambault, James Reilly II, Patrick Forrester, Steven Swanson, John Olivas. Retrieves Sunita Williams from the International Space Station and continues assembly and repairs to the station.

8/8/07 *Endeavor* (12 days) Alvin Drew, Barbara Morgan, Scott Kelly, Charlie Hobaugh, Tracy Caldwell, Rick Martracchio, and Dave WIlliams. Continues construction of the International Space Station.

10/23/2007 *Discovery* (15 days) Pam Melroy, George Zamka, Scott Parazynski, Doug Wheelock, Stephanie Wilson, Paolo Nespoli, Daniel Tani, and

Clay Anderson. Continues construction of the I.S.S.

2/7/2008 *Atlantis* (12 days) Steve Frick, Alan Poindexter, Rex Walheim, Stanley Love, Leland Melvin, Hans Schlegel, Leopold Eyharts, and Daniel Tani. Delivers and installs European Columbus laboratory for International Space Station.

3/11/2008 *Endeavor* (16 days) Dominic Gorie, Gregory Johnson, Richard Linnehan, Garrett Reismann, Robert Behnken, Michael Foreman, and Takao Doi. Delivers Garrett Reismann to the International Space Station, continues construction and ferries Leopold Eyharts back to Earth.

5/31/2008 *Discovery* (15 days) Mark Kelly, Ken Ham, Karen Nyberg, Ronald Garan, Michael Fossum, Akihiko Hoshide, and Gregory Chamitoff. Continues construction of the International Space Station and delivers Gregory Chamitoff to station in exchange for Garrett Reismann.

3/15/2009 *Discovery* (12 days) Lee Archambault, Tony Antonelli, Joseph Acaba, John Phillips, Steve Swanson, Richard Arnold, Koichi Wakata. Delivers Koichi Wakata to International Space Station in exchange for Sandra Magnus. Installed solar arrays

5/11/2009 *Atlantis* (12 Days) Michael Massimino, Michael T. Good, Gregory C. Johnson, Scott D. Altman, K. Megan McArthur, John M. Grunsfeld, Andrew J. Feustel. Repaired and upgraded the Hubble.

7/15/2009 *Endeavour* (16 days) Mark L. Polansky, Doug Hurley, Christopher Cassidy, Tom Marsburn, Dave Wolf, Julie Payette, Tim Kopra. Delivers Tom Kopra to I.S.S. in exchange for Koichi Wakata. When Endeavour astronauts joined the six resident members aboard the space station, a record 13 people were aboard the orbiting laboratory.

8/28/2009 *Discovery* (13 Days) Rick Sturckow, Kevin Ford, Jose Hernandez, John Olivas, Nicole Scott, Christer Fuglesang, Patrick Forrester. Delivers Nicole Stott to International Space Station in exchange for Timothy Kopra. Delivered Leonardo Multi-Purpose Logistics Module to I.S.S.

11/16/2009 *Atlantis* (10 Days) Charles Hobaugh, Mike Foreman, Leland Melvin, Robert Satcher Jr., Randy Bresnik, Barry Wilmore, Nicole Stott. Delivered parts to International Space Station and returned Nicole Stott to Earth

2/8/2010 *Endeavour* (13 Days) Nicholas Patrick, Terry Virts, Robert Behnken, Kathryn Hire, George Zamka, Stephen Robinson. Delivered a third connecting module, the Tranquility node, to the International Space Station

4/5/2010 *Discovery* (15 Days) Alan Poindexter, James P. Dutton Jr., Dorothy Metcalf-Lindenburger, Rick Mastracchio, Naoko Yamazaki, Clayton Anderson, Stephanie Wilson. Delivered a multi-purpose logistics module filled with science racks and replaced an ammonia tank assembly on the International Space Station

5/14/2010 *Atlantis* (11 Days) Ken Ham, Garrett Reisman, Michael Good, Tony Antonelli, Piers Sellers, Steve Bowen. In Atlantis' final mission, the crew delivered an Integrated Cargo Carrier and a Russian-built Mini Research Module to the I.S.S.

EARTH SCIENCES

Earth sciences include geology (the study of Earth's rocks and interior), oceanography (the study of ocean water, currents, and the ocean floor), paleontology (the study of fossils and ancient life-forms), parts of astronomy, and meteorology (the study of the atmosphere, including weather). Except for astronomy and weather, which are covered elsewhere, this section deals with all of these studies.

▶ THE EARTH'S COMPOSITION

In their study of the Earth, scientists distinguish a number of distinct layers from the inner core—the center of which is 6,371 km (roughly 4,000 mi.) below the surface—to the farthest limit of the atmosphere, about 1,000 km (600 mi.) above the surface. This section describes these layers, from the innermost to the outermost.

Core The core consists of two parts—one solid, the other liquid—both thought to be a mixture of iron and a lighter element, probably sulfur or oxygen. The solid inner core begins about 5,150 km (3,200 mi.) from the surface, and the liquid outer core at 2,891 km (about 1,800 mi.) from the surface.

Mantle The bulk of the Earth—roughly two-thirds of its mass—is composed of the mantle, which extends from the outer core to within about 80 km (50 mi.) of the Earth's surface below the higher mountains, and to within only 5 to 8 km (3 to 5 mi.) of the Earth's surface below some areas of the oceans. Silicon dioxide constitutes almost half of the mantle, and there is an abundance of magnesium oxide, some iron oxide, and smaller amounts of oxides of other metals. (Although silicon dioxide is known as quartz when found in the Earth's crust, under the heat and pressure of the mantle it may have very different properties from the form we know.) Part of the upper mantle is somewhat fluid and is known as the asthenosphere.

Crust The crust is the outermost solid layer of the Earth. Under the continents, the crust varies from 30 to 80 km (19 to 50 mi.) in thickness, while under the oceans it is generally only 5 to 8 km (3 to 5 mi.) thick. Continental and oceanic crust differ from each other in thickness and composition. Continental crust consists of granite and other relatively light rocks, while oceanic crust is made up chiefly of basalt. The crust is separated from the mantle by the Mohorovičić discontinuity, or Moho. The crust that is accessible to accurate measurements contains the following principal elements:

Element	Percent	Element	Percent
Oxygen	45.6%	Magnesium	2.8%
Silicon	27.3	Sodium	2.3
Aluminum	8.4	Potassium	1.8
Iron	6.2	Hydrogen	1.5
Calcium	4.7	Titanium	0.6

Note: Adds to more than 100% due to independent rounding.

Hydrosphere Water—virtually all of it sea water—covers about 71 percent of the Earth's surface and thereby constitutes a distinct layer of the Earth. Sea water varies in composition from place to place, but on average it is about 3.5 percent salts—that is, evaporating 100 lb. of sea water would yield 3.5 lb. of salt. Sodium chloride (ordinary table salt) constitutes 2.7 percent of sea water, or 77.8 percent of total solids in sea water. The typical composition of solids in sea water is as follows:

Compound	Percent
Sodium chloride	77.8%
Magnesium chloride	10.9
Magnesium sulfide	4.7
Calcium sulfate	3.6
Potassium sulfate	2.5
Calcium carbonate	0.3
Magnesium bromide	0.2
Other compounds	trace

Atmosphere The atmosphere is the gaseous layer that envelopes the Earth. The lower atmosphere consists of the troposphere and the stratosphere. The *troposphere* has an average thickness of about 11 km (7 mi.), although it is only 8 km (5 mi.) at the poles and as much as 16 km (10 mi.) around the equator. Most clouds and weather phenomena occur in this region. The composition of dry air at sea level is: nitrogen, 78.08 percent; oxygen, 20.05 percent; argon, 0.93 percent; and carbon dioxide, 0.03 percent. There are also lesser amounts of neon, helium, krypton, and xenon. These proportions change with altitude, lighter gases being more common at higher altitudes, but they are approximately the same everywhere on Earth at the same altitude. There are also variable quantities of water vapor, dust particles, and other compounds whose proportions change from place to place at the same altitude—fewer dust particles being found over oceans, and less water vapor over deserts. Temperature decreases with altitude in the troposphere.

Geologic Time Scale

The history of the planet has been divided by geologists and other earth scientists into periods of varying length based on the fossils found in rock strata. Geologists often speak of the period before 545 million years ago as Precambrian Time. The eras after 545 million years ago are grouped into the Phanerozoic Eon.

Mass extinctions—brief periods when large numbers of species become extinct—often mark the boundaries between geologic time periods. In the greatest such extinction, known as the Final Permian (250 million years ago), perhaps as many as 80 to 90 percent of all species became extinct in less than a million years. No one knows what causes most mass extinctions, but the Final Cretaceous of 65 million years ago (also called the K-T extinction) and the Final Permian were almost certainly caused by impacts of asteroids. The most recent extinction, at the end of the last ice age (11,000 years ago), may have been caused by human hunting. Some biologists believe that human activities are causing a new mass extinction today as well.

Era or Eon, Period, Epoch	Organisms	Beginning of Interval (millions of years ago)
HADEAN EON	No evidence of life	4,600
ARCHEAN EON	Monerans (bacteria and blue-green algae); Archaea	3,800
PROTEROZOIC EON	Protists, algae, and soft-bodied creatures similar to jellyfish and worms	2,500
PHANEROZOIC EON		
Cambrian period	Tiny fossils with skeletons followed by animals with shells, notably trilobites	542.0
Ordovician period	Brachiopods (shellfish similar to clams), corals, starfish, and some organisms that have no modern counterparts, called sea scorpions and conodonts	488.3
Silurian period	Snails, clams and mussels, ammonoids (similar to the nautilus), jawless fish, sea scorpions, land plants and animals (club mosses, land scorpions); modern groups of algae and fungi	443.7
Devonian period	Spiders, amphibians, jawed fish, lobe-finned fish, sharks, lungfish, and ferns	416.0
Carboniferous period	Insects, land snails, amphibians, early reptiles, sea lilies, giant club mosses, and seed ferns	359.2
Permian period	Mammal-like reptiles and fin-backed reptiles, cycads, ginkgoes, and conifers	289.0
MEZOZOIC ERA		
Triassic period	Marine reptiles (plesiosaurs and ichthyosaurs), crocodiles, frogs, turtles, early mammals, and early dinosaurs	251.0
Jurassic period	Dinosaurs (such as stegosaurs), pterosaurs (such as pterodactyl), early birds, dinoflagellates, diatoms, early flowering plants	199.6
Cretaceous period	Dinosaurs (such as tyrannosaurs, triceratops, and apatosaurs), salamanders, modern bony fishes, mosasaurs (marine lizards), flowering plants, placental and marsupial mammals	145.5
CENOZOIC ERA		
Palaeogene period		
Paleocene epoch	Early primates, early horses, rodents, sycamores	65.8
Eocene epoch	Whales, penguins, roses, bats, camels, early elephants, dogs, cats, weasels	57.8
Oligocene epoch	Deer, pigs, saber-toothed cats, monkeys	36.6
Neogene period		
Miocene epoch	Seals, dolphins, grasses, daisies, asters, sunflowers, lettuce, giraffes, bears, hyenas, early apes	23.03
Pliocene epoch	Apes, *Ardipithecus* and australopithecines (early hominids), *Homo habilis* and *rudolfensis* (first human species), mammoths, giant sloths and armadillos	5.2
Pleistocene epoch	*Homo erectus* and other early human species, modern humans; large mammals such as giant bison and beavers; many kinds of hoofed animals	1.6
Holocene epoch	Modern humans and flora and fauna of today	0.01 (11,000 years)

The *stratosphere* is found between 11 km and 50 km (7–30 miles) out from the Earth's surface. Temperatures in this region rise slightly as altitude increases, to a maximum of about 0°C (32°F). Virtually coextensive with the stratosphere is the *ozonosphere*, or ozone layer, the region in which most of the atmosphere's ozone is found. Because ozone absorbs most of the sun's ultraviolet radiation, it is vital to the continued existence of life on the planet.

Beyond the stratosphere is the upper atmosphere, or *ionosphere*, so called because it is the layer in which atmospheric gases have been ionized by solar radiation. The ionosphere reflects certain wavelengths back to the surface, making it possible to transmit radio waves around the curve of the Earth. The ionosphere is further divided into the *mesosphere*, between 50 km and 80 km (30–50 miles), in which the temperature decreases with altitude to –90°C (–130°F); and the *thermosphere*, from about 80 km to 450 km (50–280 mi.), in which the molecular temperature increases to as much as 1,475°C (2,690°F). To spacecraft traveling in the atmosphere, as the space shuttle does, however, the temperature seems cold because the molecules are so widely spaced. Beyond the thermosphere is the *exosphere*, extending to about 1,000 km (600 miles). In this layer, temperature no longer has the customary meaning. (See also "Global Warming" and "The Ozone Layer").

Major Discoveries in Earth Sciences

B.C.

c.300 Dicaearchus (Greek: c. 320) develops map of Earth on a sphere using lines of latitude.

A.D.

132 Zhang Heng (Chinese: 78–139) develops first crude seismograph.

1600 William Gilbert (English: 1544–1603) suggests that Earth is giant magnet, which is why magnetic compasses indicate north.

1669 Nicolaus Steno (Niels Stensen; Danish: 1638–86) correctly explains origin of fossils.

1777 Nicolas Desmarest (French: 1725–1815) proposes that the rock basalt starts as lava.

1785 James Hutton (Scottish: 1726–97) explains features of Earth on basis of tiny changes taking place over long periods of time (uniformitarianism).

1795 Baron Georges Cuvier (French: 1769–1832) shows that giant bones found in Meuse River are remains of extinct giant reptile.

1797 Sir James Hall (Scottish: 1761–1832) shows that melted rocks form crystals upon cooling.

1822 Gideon A. Mantell (English: 1790–1852) and his wife, Mary Ann, discover and recognize dinosaur bones as those of a giant, extinct reptile.

1830 Sir Charles Lyell (Scottish: 1797–1875) begins to publish *Principles of Geology,* the work that convinced geologists that Earth is at least several hundred million years old.

1880 John Milne (English: 1850–1913) invents modern seismograph.

1896 Svante A. Arrhenius (Swedish: 1859–1927) calculates that global temperatures will rise with higher levels of carbon dioxide in atmosphere.

1902 Léon-Philippe Teisserenc de Bort (French: 1855–1913) discovers the stratosphere.

1906 Richard D. Oldham (English: 1858–1936) establishes existence of Earth's core.

1907 Bertram B. Boltwood (American: 1870–1927) shows that age of rocks containing uranium can be determined by measuring ratio of uranium to lead.

1909 Andrija Mohorovičić (Croatia: 1857–1936) discovers boundary between Earth's crust and mantle, now known as Mohorovičić discontinuity, or "Moho."

1912 Alfred L. Wegener (German: 1880–1930) proposes theory of continental drift, idea that a single continent—Pangaea—split into present-day continents, which have drifted away from each other.

1925 The German *Meteor* expedition discovers Mid-Atlantic Ridge, a mountain range in the Atlantic Ocean.

1929 Motonori Matuyama (Japanese: 1884–1958) shows that Earth's magnetic field reverses every few hundred million years.

1958 James A. Van Allen (American: 1914–2006) discovers belts of radiation that surround Earth in space, now known as Van Allen belts.

1979 American oceanographers discover hot vents in oceans, surrounded by exotic forms of life based on sulfur, not oxygen.

1980 Walter Alvarez (American: 1940–) and coworkers discover geologic layer of iridium in region identified with the demise of the dinosaurs; he attributes both iridium and extinction to a large comet or meteorite striking Earth.

1993 Ice cores from Greenland and Antarctica reveal the Earth's climate for the past 250,000 years.

Weather scientists discover unexpected displays of electromagnetism in Earth's upper atmosphere; the displays are named Sprites, ELVES, and blue jets.

1996 A farmer in Liaoning Province in China discovers a dinosaur whose skin is covered with a feathery down, the first major find at what proves to be an important fossil site that also includes dinosaurs with more highly developed feathers.

Scientists from the Scripps Institution of Oceanography at San Diego find evidence that life has existed on Earth for at least 3.85 billion years.

1998 Paul F. Hoffman (Canadian: 1941–) of Harvard University proposes that some 200 million years ago the surface of Earth was completely frozen from the poles to the equator, a condition known as "snowball Earth;" computer studies in 2000, indicate that a narrow band at the equator remained unfrozen.

2002 Laboratory studies reveal that Earth's mantle (the layer between the crust and core) could hold five times as much water as is in all the oceans.

2003 Marcelo R. Sánchez-Villagra, Orangel Aguilera, and Inés Horovitz discover in Venezuela the first nearly complete fossil of the rodent *Phoberomys pattersoni,* a guinea-pig relative that at 700 kg (1500 lb) was the largest known rodent, about the size of a bison.

2004 Researchers in China find fossil of the oldest known primate, dated from 55 million years ago.

Geologists from the Univ. of Utah in Salt Lake City establish that a powerful earthquake can alter the periods of geyser eruptions 2,000 miles (3,100 km) away.

2008 Scientists at the Carnegie Institution of Washington and McGill Univ. in Montreal used geochemical methods to obtain an age of 4.28 billion years for samples of Canadian bedrock, making it 250 million years more ancient than any previously discovered rocks.

2009 Ardipithecus ramidus, or "Ardi", a fossilized skeleton discovered in Ethiopia in 1974 is identified as the oldest fossil skeleton of a human ancestor ever discovered by a team at U.C. Berkeley

2010 Princeton professor Adam Maloof and graduate student Catherine Rose discover fossils in Australia that indicate animal life on Earth began at least 650 million years ago, about 70 million years earlier than previous estimates

▶ THE CHANGING EARTH

Despite its apparent solidity, the crust and interior of the Earth are constantly changing.

Plate tectonics   The earth's outer crust is composed of about 20 lithospheric (or tectonic) plates that move from a few millimeters to several centimeters per year. Hundreds of millions of years ago, these plates formed a continuous landmass known as Pangaea, surrounded by ocean. Eventually the plates separated, until they reached the positions they occupy today.

As plates move away from each other, molten rock emerges from the mantle to form oceanic crust. Where they come together, one plate is usually forced under the other, forming either oceanic trenches or mountain ranges (such as the Himalayas) or both. In a few places, one plate slips by the other along a giant crack called a fault, such as the San Andreas Fault in California. These areas are also the site of greatest volcanic and earthquake activity.

Earthquakes and tsunamis   Most earthquakes are caused when rock on one side of a fault (or crack) in the Earth's crust moves with respect to the rock on the other side of the fault. The motion causes vibrations in the crust that travel through the rock as shock waves. When these reach the surface, they cause it to move in various ways, which is called seismic motion. Small earthquakes that accompany volcanic eruptions are caused by the motion of liquid rock, or magma.

More than 800,000 earthquakes are registered by seismographs each year, but the overwhelming majority go unnoticed. However, large earthquakes are of great concern to many people living in regions of significant seismic activity. Although research on earthquake prediction has yielded no breakthroughs, death and destruction have been reduced somewhat by improvements in construction codes and techniques.

One common side effect of undersea earthquakes is tsunamis—or (incorrectly) tidal waves—against which there is little protection. Tsunamis are caused when an earthquake raises or lowers a section of seabed, thereby producing a wave that, while not generally noticeable at sea, can reach great heights as it approaches land. Similar to and as destructive as tsunamis, harbor waves are generated when a landslide falls into a bay, strait, or other confined body of water causing almost immediate flooding. High waves are also caused by volcanic explosions or collapses, such as the explosion and collapse of Krakatau in 1883.

Volcanoes   are openings in the Earth's crust that emit molten or partially molten rock (lava), various hot gases, and ash. (A volcano is also the mountain formed by solidified lava or ash ejected from the opening.) If the opening is like a crack, it is called a vent. If it is larger and fairly circular, it is called a crater. A caldera is a basin formed by the settling of the top of a volcanic mountain, and it may have several vents or craters on its floor.

Most volcanoes are found where two tectonic plates meet, such as along the famous "Ring of Fire" around the Pacific Ocean. A few, such as the volcanoes of the Hawaiian Islands, appear to be over "hot spots" in the Earth's crust where liquid rock flows upward with sufficient force to burn through the crust.

Although volcanoes are associated with destruction, they have many positive effects. Minerals from deep within the Earth make the land around many volcanoes extremely fertile; volcanoes can create new landforms in the sea; and the study of volcanoes contributes enormously to our understanding of the Earth's interior.

Although geologists consider a volcano active if it has shown signs of activity in historic times, it is not usually clear whether a volcano is extinct or only dormant and could be active again. (Thus Tambora, which has not erupted since 1815, is considered active.) Some volcanoes once thought to be extinct have become active, and there are now about 600 volcanoes that are considered active. The accompanying list contains about a fourth of all volcanoes known to have been active in recent years, with special emphasis on volcanoes in the United States and volcanoes that have had famous eruptions.

Richter Scale and Effects Near the Epicenter

Note: The epicenter is the point on Earth's surface above the center of the quake

Below 2.5   Not felt except by a very few under specially favorable circumstances.

2.5 to 3.5   Felt only by a few persons at rest, especially on upper floors of buildings.

3.5 to 4.5   At lower levels or further from the quake, it is felt by many people, sometimes quite noticeably indoors, especially on upper floors of buildings, but many people do not recognize as an earthquake. At somewhat higher levels or nearer to the epicenter, during the day the quake is felt indoors by many; outdoors by few. Sensation is like heavy truck striking building. At the highest level, the earth movement is felt by nearly everyone; with many awakened if during the night. Disturbances of trees, telephone poles, and other tall objects sometimes can be noticed.

4.5 to 6.0   Felt by all; many frightened and run outdoors. Some heavy furniture moved; there will be a few instances of fallen plaster or damaged chimneys. Other slight local damage may occur. At higher level, however, everybody runs outdoors. At the upper level, while damage is still negligible in buildings of good design and construction, there can be moderate damage even to well-built ordinary structures; there will be considerable damage to poorly built or badly designed structures.

6.0 to 7.0   A destructive earthquake. Damage may still be slight in specially designed structures, but will be considerable in ordinary substantial buildings, often with partial collapse. Damage will be great in poorly built structures, including collapse of chimneys, factory stacks, columns, monuments, and walls. At the upper level, damage is likely to be considerable even in specially designed structures. Most ordinary buildings will be shifted off foundations. Even the ground will be cracked conspicuously.

7.0 to 8.0   A major earthquake. Worldwide, about 10 of these occur each year. Some well-built wooden structures will be destroyed. Most masonry and frame structures will be destroyed along with their foundations. Ground becomes badly cracked.

8.0 and above   Great earthquakes. These occur once every five to 10 years. Few, if any masonry structures remain standing. Bridges are destroyed. Broad fissures appear in ground. At the highest levels and near the epicenter, damage total. Waves seen on solid ground. Heavy objects thrown upward into air.

The destruction caused by volcanoes is usually localized, but their effects can be felt around the world and take many forms. At their worst, volcanoes can blow themselves to pieces, as the island of Thera did about 1650 B.C. More often, volcanic ash blankets an area (as Mt. Vesuvius did at Pompeii), or clouds of hot gases and dust sweep down the side of the volcano poisoning the air. Lava generally moves too slowly to be a menace to people. Even more unpredictable, heat from a volcano can melt glaciers or snowcaps, triggering massive mud slides (as happened in Colombia in 1985) or releasing lakes of boiling water.

►MEASURING EARTHQUAKES

The size of an earthquake is generally reported in the United States using the Richter scale, a system developed by seismologist Charles Richter (American: 1900–85) in 1935. The Richter scale measures the magnitude of an earthquake, that is, the size of ground waves generated by an earthquake as shown on a measuring device called a seismograph. Each whole number on the scale represents a tenfold increase (or decrease) in magnitude: a magnitude 6 earthquake produces a ground wave 10 times greater than a magnitude 5.

This does not mean, however, that a magnitude 6 earthquake has 10 times the energy as one of magnitude 5. Measuring the actual energy requires instruments placed at the site of the earthquake. Various methods have been developed for inferring energy from magnitude and these suggest that one change in magnitude corresponds to a thirty- to sixtyfold change in energy. Using these proportions, the energy of a magnitude 8 earthquake, a very serious event, can be as much as 1 million to 10 million times as much as that of a magnitude 4 earthquake, one that can be felt but causes almost no damage.

Major Earthquakes, 856–2010

Date	Location and remarks	Estimated deaths	Richter magnitude	Date	Location and remarks	Estimated deaths	Richter magnitude
856	Corinth, Greece	45,000	N.A.	Aug. 17, 1906	Santiago, Chile	20,000	8.6
Dec. 22, 856	Iran	200,000	N.A.	1907	Tajikistan	40,000	N.A.
Mar. 23, 893	Iran	150,000	N.A.	Dec. 28, 1908	Messina, Sicily	75,000	7.5
1036	Shansi	23,000	N.A.	Jan. 13, 1916	Avezzano, Italy	29,980	7.5
1057	Chihli (Hopeh), China	25,000	N.A.	Dec. 16, 1920	Gansu, China	200,000	8.5
Aug. 9, 1138	Aleppo, Syria	230,000	N.A.	Sept. 1, 1923	Tokyo/Yokohama, Japan	143,000	8.3
1170	Sicily	15,000	N.A.	Mar. 7, 1927	Tango, Japan	3,020	7.9
1268	Silicia (Turkey)	60,000	N.A.	May 22, 1927	Nan-Shan, China	200,000	8.3
Sept. 1290	Chihli, China	100,000	N.A.	Dec. 25, 1932	Gansu, China	70,000	7.6
May 20, 1293	Kamakura, Japan	30,000	N.A.	Mar. 2, 1933	Sanriku, Japan (tsunami)	2,990	8.9
Jan. 26, 1531	Lisbon, Portugal	30,000	N.A.	Mar. 11, 1933	Long Beach, California	115	6.3
Jan. 23, 1556	Shansi, China	830,000	N.A.	Jan. 15, 1934	Bihar, India and Nepal	10,700	8.4
Nov. 1667	Shemakha, Azerbaijan	80,000	N.A.	May 30, 1935	Quetta, India (Pakistan)	50,000	7.5
June 7, 1692	Port Royal, Jamaica	30,000	N.A.	Jan. 25, 1939	Chillan, Chile	30,000	8.3
Jan. 11, 1693	Catania province, Sicily	60,000	N.A.	Dec. 27, 1939	Erzincan, Turkey	30,000	8.0
1693	Naples, Italy	93,000	N.A.	Apr. 1, 1946	Earthquake at Unimak Island, Alaska, causes tsunami striking Hilo, Hawaii	165	7.3
1707	Tsunami hits Japan	30,000	N.A.				
Nov. 18, 1727	Tabriz, Iran	77,000	N.A.				
Dec. 30, 1730	Hokkaido Island, Japan	137,000	N.A.	Dec. 20, 1946	Tonankai, Japan	1,330	8.4
1731	Beijing, China	100,000	N.A.	June 28, 1948	Fukui, Japan	5,390	7.3
Oct. 11, 1737	Calcutta, India	300,000	N.A.	Oct. 5, 1948	Ashkabad, Turkmenistan	110,000	7.3
June 7, 1755	Northern Iran	40,000	N.A.	Aug. 5, 1949	Pelileo, Ecuador	6,000	6.8
Nov. 1, 1755	Lisbon, Portugal (earthquake, tsunami)	60,000	8.6	Aug. 15, 1950	Assam State, India	1,530	8.7
				July 21, 1952	Kern County, California	12	7.5
Feb. 4, 1783	Calabria, Italy	50,000	N.A.	June 10-17, 1956	Northern Afghanistan	2,000	7.7
Feb. 4, 1797	Quito, Ecuador and Cuzco, Peru	41,000	N.A.				
				July 2, 1957	Northern Iran	1,200	7.4
Dec. 16, 1811	New Madrid, Missouri	<10	7.7	Dec. 13, 1957	Western Iran	1,130	7.3
Feb. 7, 1812	New Madrid, Missouri	0	7.9	Aug. 17, 1959	Hebgen Lake, Montana	28	7.3
Sept. 5, 1822	Aleppo (Syria)	22,000	N.A.	Feb. 29, 1960	Agadir, Morocco	12,000	5.9
Dec. 28, 1828	Echigo, Japan	30,000	N.A.	May 21-30, 1960	Southern Chile; tsunami strikes various Pacific islands, killing 61 in Hawaii; greatest earthquake ever recorded	5,700	9.5
Dec. 24, 1854	Tokai, Japan	3,000	8.4				
Oct. 1855	Tokyo, Japan	2,000+	N.A.				
Jan. 9, 1857	Fort Tejon, California	1	7.9				
1857	East of Naples, Italy	10,000+	N.A.	Sept. 1, 1962	Northwestern Iran	12,230	7.3
Aug. 13-15, 1868	Peru and Ecuador	40,000	N.A.	Mar. 28, 1964	Southern Alaska	125	9.2
				Aug. 19, 1966	Eastern Turkey	2,520	7.1
May 16, 1875	Venezuela and Colombia	16,000	N.A.	Aug. 31, 1968	Khurasan, Iran	12,000	7.3
Aug. 31, 1886	Charleston, South Carolina	60	7.6	July 25, 1969	Eastern China	3,000	5.9
Oct. 28, 1891	Central Japan	7,300	N.A.	Jan. 5, 1970	Yunnan Province, China	10,000	7.5
June 15, 1896	Sanriku and Kamaishi, Japan (tsunami)	26,000	N.A.	May 31, 1970	Yungay, Ranrahirca, and Huarás, Peru	66,000	7.8
Apr. 4, 1905	Kangra, India	19,000	8.6	Feb. 9, 1971	San Fernando Valley Calif.	65	6.6
Apr. 18, 1906	San Francisco, California	3,000	7.7	Apr. 10, 1972	Ghir, Iran	5,054	7.1

Date	Location and remarks	Estimated deaths	Richter magnitude	Date	Location and remarks	Estimated deaths	Richter magnitude
Dec. 23, 1972	Managua, Nicaragua	5,000	6.2	Jan. 26, 2001	Southern India	20,005	7.7
Dec. 28, 1974	North Pakistan	5,300	6.2	Feb. 13, 2001	El Salvador	315	6.6
Feb. 4, 1975	Liaoning Province, China (predicted)	10,000	7.4	June 23, 2001	Coast of Peru	74	8.4
				Jan. 10, 2002	Near north coast of New Guinea	1	6.7
Sept. 6, 1975	Lice, Turkey	2,300	6.7	Mar. 3, 2002	Hindu Kush, Afghanistan	163	7.4
Feb. 4, 1976	Guatemala City,	23,000	7.5	Mar. 25, 2002	Hindu Kush, Afghanistan	1,000	6.1
June 25, 1976	New Guinea and Irian Jaya, Indonesia	8,000+	7.1	June 22, 2002	Western Iran	227	6.5
				Oct. 31, 2002	Southern Italy	29	5.9
July 27, 1976	Tangshan, China	655,000	8.0	Nov. 1, 2002	Kashmir, India/Pakistan	11	5.4
Aug. 16, 1976	Mindanao, Philippines (earthquake and tsunami)	8,000	7.9	Nov. 20, 2002	Kashmir, India/Pakistan	19	6.3
				Jan. 22, 2003	Colima, Mexico	29	7.6
Nov. 24, 1976	Eastern Turkey	5,000	7.3	Feb. 24, 2003	Xingjiang, China	261	6.3
Sept. 16, 1978	Northeast Iran	15,000	7.8	May 1, 2003	Turkey	177	6.4
Oct. 10, 1980	Northwestern Algeria	3,500	7.7	May 21, 2003	Algeria	2,266	6.8
Nov. 23, 1980	Southern Italy	3,000	7.2*	July 21, 2003	Yunnan, China	16	6.0
July 28, 1981	Kerman province, Iran	2,500	7.3	Dec. 1. 2003	Kazakhstan-China border	11	6.0
Dec. 13, 1982	Yemen	2,800	6.0	Dec. 22, 2003	Paso Robles, California	2	6.5
Sept. 19, 1985	Mexico City	9,500	8.1	Dec. 26, 2003	Iran	43,200	6.6
Oct. 10, 1986	San Salvador, El Salvador	1,000+	5.5	Jan. 1, 2004	Bali, Indonesia	1	5.8
Mar. 6, 1987	Ecuador	1,000+	7.0	Feb. 14, 2004	Pakistan	24	5.5
Dec. 7, 1988	Armenia	25,000	7.0	Feb. 16, 2004	Sumatra, Indonesia	5	6.0
Oct. 18, 1989	Loma Prieta, California (Santa Cruz Mountains), destructive in San Francisco and Oakland	63	7.2	Feb. 24, 2004	Burundi	3	4.7
				Feb. 24, 2004	Morocco and Spain	628	6.4
				Mar. 25, 2004	Turkey	10	5.6
				Apr. 5, 2004	Afghanistan	3	6.6
June 20, 1990	Caspian Sea, Iran	50,000	7.7	May 28, 2004	Iran	35	6.3
July 16, 1990	Cabanatuan (Luzon I.), Philippines	1,621	7.8	July 1, 2004	Turkey	18	5.4
				Dec. 26, 2004	Centered off west coast of Sumatra, tsunamis strike Sumatra, Sri Lanka, Thailand, and other coastal nations	297,200	9.0
Oct. 21, 1991	India and Nepal	2,000	7.0				
Dec. 12, 1992	Flores Island, Indonesia (tsunami)	2,500	7.5				
Sept. 29, 1993	Bombay, India	9,748	6.3	Feb. 22, 2005	Central Iran	612	6.4
Jan. 17, 1994	Northridge, California	61	6.8	Mar. 28, 2005	Nias Island, N. Sumatra	1,203	8.7
Jan. 16, 1995	Near Kobe, Japan	5,502	6.9	Oct. 8, 2005	Islamabad, Pakistan	86,000	7.6
May 27, 1995	Sakhalin Island, Russia	1,989	7.5	May 26, 2006	Java, Indonesia	5,749	6.3
Feb. 28, 1997	Northwestern Iran	1,000+	6.1	July 17, 2006	South of Java, Indonesia	730	7.7
May 10, 1997	Northeastern Iran	1,560	7.5	Mar. 6, 2006	Southern Sumatra, Indonesia	70	6.4
Feb. 4, 1998	Afghanistan	2,323	6.1	Apr. 1, 2007	Solomon Islands	54	8.1
May 30, 1998	Afghanistan-Tajikistan border	4,000	6.9	Aug. 15, 2007	Near Coast of Peru	514	8.0
July 17, 1998	Tsunamis strike Papua, New Guinea	2,183	7.1	May 12, 2008	Eastern Sichuan, China	69,185	7.9
				Apr. 6, 2009	L'Aquila, Italy	308	6.3
Jan. 25, 1999	Armenia, Colombia	1,885	6.4	Sep. 30, 2009	Off west coast of Sumatra, Indonesia	1,100	7.6
Aug. 17, 1999	Northwestern Turkey	17,118	7.4				
Sept. 20, 1999	Nantou, Taiwan	2,101	7.6	Jan. 12, 2010	Haiti	230,000	7.0
Nov. 12, 1999	Turkey ·	843	7.5	Feb. 27, 2010	Chile	521	8.9
Jan 13, 2001	El Salvador	844	7.7				

Volcano Eruptions and Landslides, 1628 B.C.–A.D. 2010

Date	Event	Deaths	Date	Event	Deaths
B.C.			1782	Eruption of Mt. Unzen in Japan causes tidal wave.	15,000
1628 or 1645	Mediterranean volcanic island of Thera (Santorini) explodes.	N.A.	June 1783– Feb. 1784	Laki fissure on Mt. Skaptar, Iceland erupts; poisonous gases kill crops and livestock, and thick haze interrupts fishing on oceans.	9,800
A.D.					
Aug. 24–26, 79	Mt. Vesuvius, near Naples, Italy, erupts, destroying towns of Pompeii and Herculaneum.	2,000+			
			Sept. 2, 1806	Rossberg Peak collapses, causing landslides in Goldau Valley, Switzerland.	500
260	Mt. Ilopango in El Salvador erupts, apparently destroying the early Maya civilization.	N.A.	Apr. 5, 1815	Mt. Tambora on Sumbawa in East Indies begins series of eruptions that kill about 10,000 people; another 50,000 die of famine and disease locally	162,000
Sept. 4, 1618	Landslides hit Chiavenna Valley, Italy.	2,420			
Dec. 16, 1631	Mt. Vesuvius erupts.	4,000+	Oct. 8 and 12, 1822	Mt. Galunggung on Java erupts, causing slides of mud and boiling water.	4,000
Mar. 25, 1669	Mt. Etna at Catania, Sicily, erupts.	20,000			
Jan. 11, 1683	Mt. Etna erupts, accompanied by earthquakes.	60,000	1845	Eruption of Nevada del Ruiz in northern Colombia causes mud slides from melting snow.	1,000
Aug. 11–12, 1772	Mt. Papandayan on Java explodes.	3,000+			

Date	Event	Deaths	Date	Event	Deaths
July 28, 1883	Epomeo volcano on Italian Isle of Ischia erupts, causing destructive earthquakes.	2,000+	May 18, 1980	Mt. St. Helens volcano erupts in Washington.	61
Aug. 26, 1883	Krakatau volcano in East Indies erupts, producing giant waves that strike nearby islands.	36,000	May 20, 1981	Landslides caused by eruption of Semeru in Java, Indonesia.	252
May 7, 1902	La Soufriére on St. Vincent in West Indies erupts.	1,500–2,000	Mar. 28 and Apr. 3-4, 1982	El Chichón in Chiapas, Mexico, erupts, sending cloud of volcanic ash around world.	2,000
May 8, 1902	Pelée volcano on neighboring Martinique erupts, pouring cloud of flaming gas on city of St. Pierre.	29,000	Aug. 16, 1984	Carbon dioxide emitted by Lake Monoun, Cameroon, spreads in region around lake.	37
Aug. 30, 1902	Mt. Pelée erupts.	2,000	Nov. 13, 1985	Eruption of Nevada del Ruiz in northern Colombia causes massive mud slide covering town of Armero.	25,000
Apr. 18, 1906	Mt. Vesuvius near Naples erupts.	150+			
1911	Taal volcano, near Manila, Philippines, erupts.	1,300	Aug. 21, 1986	Carbon dioxide from Lake Nyos, Cameroon, spreads through region.	1,700+
May 1919	Crater lake of Mt. Kelut in Indonesia, boiling from volcanic activity, breaks through side of the mountain.	5,000+	July 13, 1990	Earthquake triggers landslide in Pamir Mts., Tajikistan, USSR.	40+
1937	Eruption of Rabaul caldera on New Britain, Papua New Guinea.	500+	Oct. 13, 1990	Geyserlike explosion in the Ahuachapán Geothermal Field, El Salvador, releases wave of carbon dioxide and water.	26
Jan. 15, 1951	Mt. Lamington on New Guinea produces cloud of hot gas and dust, similar to that at Mt. Pelée in 1902 and Mt. St. Helens in 1980.	3,000–5,000	June 3, 1991	Eruption of Mt. Unzen, Kyushu, Japan.	43
			June 9, 1991	Mount Pinatubo erupts, as predicted, in Luzon, Philippines; 358 killed by disease in evacuation camps.	754
Dec. 4, 1951	Mt. Catarman (Hibokhibok) in Philippines releases cloud of hot gas.	500	Jan. 14, 1993	Galeras in Colombia unexpectedly erupts during a scientific workshop, killing six volcanologists who had been on the rim studying the volcano.	9
Sept. 24, 1952	Japanese research ship investigating undersea volcano is destroyed in eruptive event.	29			
Dec. 25, 1953	Dam, created by 1945 eruption of Ruapehu volcano on New Zealand, gives way; avalanche of mud and snow strikes passenger train.	150	Feb. 2, 1993	An unexpected eruption of Mayon on Luzon, Philippines produces a cloud of hot gas and dust that rolls down the slope.	70
Jan. 10, 1962	Landslide on Mt. Huascarán, Peru.	3,000	June 6, 1994	An earthquake at the Volcano Nevada de Huila in Colombia causes mud slides that destroy a dozen villages on its slopes.	650+
Mar. 14, 1962	Two landslides near Paucartambno Hydroelectric Station in Peru.	204			
Mar. 17-21, 1963	Mt. Agung volcano in Bali, Indonesia, erupts.	1,584			
Aug. 10, 1963	Landslide in Nepal sweeps villages into Trisuli River.	200	Nov. 22, 1994	Various flows of hot ash and gases down the slope of Merapi volcano on Java in Indonesia kill workers at a water-treatment plant and sweep through villages where superstitious villagers ignored a call to evacuate.	64
Oct. 9, 1963	Flood occurs when Valont Dam near Langarone, Italy, overflows as result of landslide into its reservoir.	2,200			
1965	Taal volcano near Manila in the Philippines erupts.	150	Feb. 18, 1997	Mudslide caused by heavy rains destroys two Peruvian villages	300
Aug. 30, 1965	Avalanche near Saas-Fee, Switzerland, from Allalin glacier strikes workers building dam.	40-100	May 5-6, 1998	Mudslides caused by heavy rains pour down Mount Sarno, east of Naples, Italy.	135
1968	Eruption of Arenal in Costa Rica.	78	Oct. 30, 1998	Hurricane Mitch causes landslide on San Cristobal volcano in Nicaragua.	1600
July 22, 1970	Landslide diverts Alaknanda River in India, causing sudden flood.	600			
Mar. 18, 1971	Landslide into Lake Yanahuani, creates 60-foot wave that sweeps over Chungar, Peru.	200	Dec., 1999	Heavy rains cause floods and landslides in northern Venezuela.	20,000
July 29, 1971	Landslide into high lake in Hindu Kush mountains of Afghanistan causes instant flood.	1,000+	Jan. 13, 2001	Landslides triggered by an earthquake near Santa Tecla, El Salvador bury villages,	585
			Jan. 17, 2002	Lava flows from eruption of Nyirangongo volcano in the Congo.	45
June 28, 1974	Landslides along Quebrada Blanca Canyon in Eastern Colombia.	200	Mar. 3, 2002	Landslide caused by earthquake in the Hindu Kush region of Afghanistan dams and floods Surkundara Valley.	150
Jan. 10, 1977	Fast-moving stream of lava from volcano near Goma, Zaire, overtakes fleeing residents.	70			
			Aug. 14, 2002	Landslides from heavy rains bury villages in Yunnan Province, China.	52
Feb. 21, 1979	Sinila volcano in Java, Indonesia	175+	Feb. 17, 2006	Landslides from heavy rains wipe out villages in the Philippine province of Southern Leyte	1,126
Apr. 30, 1979	Landslide covers side of Marapi volcano in Sumatra, Indonesia.	82+			
July 18, 1979	Landslide on Mt. Werung causes wave to strike beach areas on Lomblen Island, Indonesia.	539	Apr. 14, 2010	The eruption of Eyjafjallajökull in Iceland sent massive plumes of ash into the atmosphere, disrupting European air travel for months	0

Major Active Volcanoes

Volcano	Location	Height (feet above sea level)	Last reported eruption
Africa and the Indian Ocean			
Cameroon	Cameroon	13,435	2000
Fogo	Cape Verde Islands	9,281	1995
Karthala	Comoros	7,746	1991
Ol Donyo Lengai	Tanzania	9,482	2002
Piton de la Fournaise	Réunion Island	8,632	2004
Nyamuragira	Zaire	10,033	2004
Nyirangongo	Zaire	11,384	2004
Asia			
Agung	Bali, Indonesia	10,308	1964
Akan	Hokkaido, Japan	4,918	1998
Alaid	Kuril Isl. Russia	7,674	1996
Asama	Honshu, Japan	8,339	2004
Aso	Kyushu, Japan	5,223	1995
Batur	Bali, Indonesia	5,633	2000
Bezymianny	Kamchatka, Russia	9,455	2004
Bulusan	Luzon, Philippines	5,134	1995
Chokai	Honshu, Japan	7,339	1974
Dieng Volc	Java, Indonesia	8,415	1996
Dukono	Halmahera, Indonesia	3,888	2004
Fuji	Honshu, Japan	12,388	1708
Galunggung	Java, Indonesia	7,113	1984
Gamalama	Ternate, Indonesia	5,627	2003
Karangetang	Siau Island, Indonesia	5,853	2003
Karymsky	Kamchatka, Russia	5,039	2004
Kelut	Java, Indonesia	5,679	1990
Kerenci	Sumatra, Indonesia	12,467	2004
Kliuchevskoi	Kamchatka, Russia	15,863	2004
Komaga-take	Hokkaido, Japan	3,740	2000
Koryaksky	Kamchatka, Russia	11,338	1957
Krakatau	Indonesia	2,667	2004
Lewotobi	Flores Isl., Indonesia	5,587	2003
Lokon-Empung	Sulawesi, Indonesia	5,184	2003
Mayon	Luzon, Philippines	8,077	2001
Merapi	Java, Indonesia	9,669	2002
Miyake-jima	Izu Islands, Japan	2,674	2002
Nasu	Honshu, Japan	6,289	1963
Nigata Yake-yama	Honshu, Japan	7,874	1989
On-take	Honshu, Japan	10,049	1980
Peuet Sague	Sumatra, Indonesia	9,190	2000
Pinatubo	Luzon, Philippines	4,875	1993
Raung	Java, Indonesia	10,932	2000
Rinjani	Lombok Island, Indonesia	12,224	1994
Sakura-jima	Kyushu, Japan	3,665	2004
Sangeang Api	Lesser Sunda, Indonesia	6,394	1988
Sarychev Peak	Kuril Islands, Russia	4,908	1989
Semeru	Java, Indonesia	12,060	2004
Shiveluch	Kamchatka, Russia	10,771	2002
Slamet	Java, Indonesia	11,260	1999
Suwanose-jima	Ryukyu Islands, Japan	2,621	2001
Taal	Luzon, Philippines	1,342	1977
Tambora	Sumbawa, Indonesia	9,350	1967
Tengger Caldera	Java, Indonesia	7,641	2001
Tiatia	Kuril Isl., Russia	5,968	1981
Unzen	Kyushu, Japan	4,921	1996
Usu	Hokkaido, Japan	2,398	2001
Europe and the Atlantic Ocean			
Askja	Iceland	4,974	1961
Beerenberg	Jan Mayen Island, Norway	7,470	1985
Etna	Italy	10,991	2002
Fogo	Cape Verde Islands	9,281	1995

Volcano	Location	Height (feet above sea level)	Last reported eruption
Grímsvötn	Iceland	5,659	1998
Hekla	Iceland	4,892	2000
Krafla	Iceland	2,133	1984
Stromboli	Italy	3,058	2002
Tristan da Cunha	Tristan da Cunha, U.K.	6,758	2004
Vesuvius	Italy	4,203	1944
North America			
Akutan	Alaska	4,275	1992
Amukta	Alaska	3,497	1997
Atka	Alaska	5,029	1998
Augustine	Alaska	4,108	1986
Baker	Washington	10,777	1880
Carlisle	Alaska	5,315	1828
Cerberus	Alaska	2,539	1987
Cleveland	Alaska	5,676	2001
Colima	Mexico	12,631	2004
Crater Lake	Oregon	8,159 c.	2290 B.C.
El Chichon	Mexico	3,773	1982
Fisher	Alaska	3,648	1830
Gareloi	Alaska	5,161	1989
Great Sitkin	Alaska	5,709	1974
Hood	Oregon	11,240	1866
Iliamna	Alaska	10,016	1876
Kagamil	Alaska	2,930	1929
Kanaga	Alaska	4,288	1995
Katmai	Alaska	6,716	1912
Kiska	Alaska	4,003	1990
Lassen Peak	California	10,456	1917
Little Sitkin	Alaska	3,852	1830
Makushin	Alaska	5,905	1995
Martin	Alaska	6,112	1953
Novarupta	Alaska	2,759	1912
Okmok	Alaska	3,520	1997
Parícutin	Mexico	1,500	1952
Pavlof	Alaska	8,264	1997
Pavlof Sister	Alaska	7,027	1786
Popocatépetl	Mexico	17,802	2004
Rainier	Washington	14,409	1825
Redoubt	Alaska	10,197	1990
St. Helens	Washington	8,363	1991
Seguam	Alaska	3,458	1993
Shasta	California	14,163	1786
Shishaldin	Alaska	9,373	1999
South Sister	Oregon	10,357	c. 50 B.C.
Spurr	Alaska	11,069	2004
Tanaga	Alaska	5,925	1914
Trident	Alaska	6,115	1975
Veniaminof	Alaska	8,225	1994
Westdahl	Alaska	5,426	1992
Yunaska	Alaska	1,804	1937
Central America and the Caribbean			
Acatenango	Guatemala	13,044	1972
Arenal	Costa Rica	5,436	2004
Cerro Negro	Nicaragua	2,388	1999
Concepción	Nicaragua	5,577	1999
Fuego	Guatemala	12,346	2004
Irazú	Costa Rica	11,260	1994
Izalco	El Salvador	6,398	1966
Masaya	Nicaragua	2,083	2001
Pacaya	Guatemala	8,373	2003
Pelée	Martinique	4,583	1932
Poás	Costa Rica	8,884	1996
Rincón de la Vieja	Costa Rica	6,286	1998
San Cristóbal	Nicaragua	5,725	2002
San Miguel	El Salvador	6,988	1997
Santa María	Guatemala	12,375	2004

Volcano	Location	Height (feet above sea level)	Last reported eruption
Soufrière Hills	Montserrat	3,002	2004
Soufriere St. Vincent	St Vincent and the Grenadines	4,003	1979
Tacaná	Mexico/Guatemala	13,320	1986
Telica	Nicaragua	3,481	2000
South America			
Alcedo	Galápagos Islands, Ecuador	3,707	1993
Azul, Cerro	Galápagos Islands, Ecuador	5,381	1998
Copahué	Chile/Argentina	9,728	2000
Cotopaxi	Ecuador	19,393	1940
Galeras	Colombia	14,029	2004
Guagua Pichincha	Ecuador	15,695	2001
Guallatiri	Chile	19,918	1960
Hudson, Cerro	Chile	6,250	1991
Lascar	Chile	18,346	2003
Llaima	Chile	10,253	1998
Lonquimay	Chile	9,399	1990
Puracé	Colombia	15,256	1977
Reventador	Ecuador	11,686	1976
Ruiz, Nevado del	Colombia	17,457	1991
Sangay	Ecuador	17,159	2002
Tungurahua	Ecuador	16,479	2002
Villarrica	Chile	9,340	2000

Volcano	Location	Height (feet above sea level)	Last reported eruption
Oceania—Australia, New Zealand, and the Pacific Islands			
Ambrym	Vanuatu	4,377	2004
Bagana	Bougainville Island, Papua New Guinea	5,741	2004
Haleakala	Hawaii	10,023	c.1790
Hualalai	Hawaii	8,277	1801
Karkar	Papua New Guinea	6,033	1979
Kilauea	Hawaii	4,009	2004
Langila	New Britain, Papua New Guinea	4,363	2002
Lopevei	Vanuatu	4.636	2001
Mauna Loa	Hawaii	13,681	1984
Manam	Papua New Guinea	5,928	2000
Ngauruhoe	North Island, New Zealand	6,489	1977
Pagan	Mariana Islands	1,870	1993
Rabaul	New Britain, Papua New Guinea	2,257	2004
Ruapehu	North Island, New Zealand	9,176	1997
Ulawun	New Britain, Papua New Guinea	7,657	2004
White Island	North Island, New Zealand	1,053	2001
Antarctica			
Big Ben	Heard Island	9,007	1993
Mount Erebus	Ross Island	13,444	2001

CHEMISTRY

Chemistry is concerned with the way substances interact with one another. These interactions are chiefly the result of outer electrons of an atom interacting with the outer electrons of another atom. It has increasingly become clear that the shapes of the various combinations of atoms (called molecules) also affect chemical reactions, and physical chemistry is one of the most vital parts of chemistry today. Another vital branch is biochemistry, the study of the chemistry of molecules in living organisms. Organic chemistry generally deals with chemicals formed by living organisms and other chemicals containing carbon, but it treats them as chemicals outside the organism. Inorganic chemistry is concerned with chemicals that do not contain carbon.

▶ THE PERIODIC TABLE

In the 19th century, chemists began to determine how much one atom of an element weighed with respect to another—the atomic weight (also known as the atomic mass and measured in atomic mass units, or amu; in modern chemistry, one amu is equal to one-twelfth the weight of the most common form of carbon atom). The first comprehensive list of atomic weights was prepared by Jöns Jakob Berzelius in 1828. When chemists made lists of elements in the order of atomic weights, they noticed that every seven or eight elements in the list had similar properties. In

1869 Dmitri Mendeleyev boldly interchanged some elements in the list and left blanks for others to make sure the properties matched for every "period" of eight elements. This was the first periodic table. Mendeleyev had only 63 elements to work with, but he correctly predicted three more that would make his list more complete. Today the elements up to 116, with the exceptions of 113 and 115, have been identified. Claims for elements 116 and 118 were made in 1999 by Lawrence Berkeley National Laboratory in California and withdrawn in 2002, but element 116 was produced by the Joint Institute for Nuclear Research, Dubna, Russia, in 2000. The International Union of Pure and Applied Chemistry (IUPAC) officially recommended the name Darmstadtium for recently-discovered element 110 in 2003, and Roentgenium for element 111 in 2004. As of 2009, element 112 was temporarily called Ununbium and element 116 was temporarily called Ununhexium. There was no temporary name for Element 114.

Early in the 20th century, atoms were discovered to consist of protons and electrons (in 1932 it was discovered that neutrons also are found in atoms). The number of protons is the atomic number, which is a different number for every element from hydrogen (atomic number 1) to the unnamed element 116 (elements 113 and 115 have yet to be synthesized). The periodic table was improved by arranging the elements in order of atomic number instead of atomic weight. This clearly showed where the blanks were.

Each column of the periodic table includes elements with similar properties, although hydrogen in the first column is less typical in this respect.

Major Discoveries in Chemistry

B.C.

c. 450 Leucippus of Miletus (Greek: 5th cent.) introduces concept of atom, later expanded upon by his pupil Democritus of Abdera (c. 460–c. 370).

A.D.

1662 Robert Boyle (Anglo-Irish: 1627–91) announces what becomes known as Boyle's law: For gas kept at constant temperature, pressure and volume vary inversely.

1755 Joseph Black (Scottish: 1728–99) discovers carbon dioxide.

1778 Antoine-Laurent Lavoisier (French: 1743–94) discovers that air is mostly mixture of nitrogen and oxygen.

1784 Henry Cavendish (English: 1731–1810) announces water is compound of hydrogen and oxygen.

1789 Lavoisier explicitly states law of conservation of matter: In chemical change, matter is neither created nor destroyed.

1791 Jeremias Benjamin Richter (German: 1762–1807) shows that acids and bases always neutralize each other in same proportion.

1803 John Dalton (English: 1766–1844) establishes atomic theory of matter.

1811 Amedeo Avogadro (Italian: 1776–1856) proposes that equal volumes of gas at same temperature and pressure contain same number of molecules (Avogadro's law).

1824 Joseph-Louis Gay-Lussac (French: 1778–1850) discovers chemical isomers, chemicals with same formula but different structures.

1828 Friedrich Wöhler (German: 1800–1882) prepares organic compound from inorganic chemicals, showing that life is basically same as other matter.

1859 Gustav Robert Kirchhoff (German: 1824–87) and Robert Wilhelm Bunsen (German: 1811–99) introduce use of spectroscope to identify elements from light they give off when heated.

1869 Dmitry Ivanovich Mendeleyev (Russian: 1834–1907) publishes his first version of periodic table of elements.

1906 Mikhail Tsvett (Russian: 1872–1919) develops paper chromatography, the beginning of modern methods of chemical analysis.

1908 Fritz Haber (German: 1868–1934) develops cheap process for making ammonia from nitrogen in the air.

1962 Neil Bartlett (English: 1932–) creates a compound of xenon, platinum, and fluorine, showing that the noble gases can form compounds.

1984 Dany Schechtman (American) and coworkers discover first quasicrystal, a "crystal" that violates the symmetry rules of all other crystals.

1985 Richard E. Smalley (American: 1943–) and Harry Kroto (English: 1939–) discover buckminsterfullerene, a carbon molecule containing 60 carbon atoms arranged in a geodesic sphere (nicknamed "the bucky ball").

1991 Sumio Iijima (Japanese: 1939–) of NEC Corp. discovers that carbon forms tiny hollow cylinders called nanotubes.

1998 Research on carbon nanotubes shows that they conduct electricity with almost no resistance at room temperature (although they are not superconductors), emit light when carrying an electric current, and can behave either as semiconductors or metals depending on the alignment of atoms in the tube.

2001 Researchers discover that the common mineral calcite (calcium carbonate) tends to segregate left-handed amino acids on one face and right-handed ones on another, suggesting a possible origin for all amino acids in living organisms being left-handed; similarly the handedness of amino acids affects crystal formation in calcite.

2002 Researchers at the University of California, Davis, discover that distributing molecules of gadolinium nitrate through porous silicon creates a form of silicon that explodes like gunpowder when scratched or when exposed to a spark from a low-power battery.

Scientists in Rome create molecules consisting of four nitrogen atoms (molecules of nitrogen in air contain two atoms only.)

2003 Takashi Saito of Toyota Central Research and Development Laboratories in Nagukute, Japan, and coworkers produce alloys of titanium that have a low and constant coefficient of expansion and that can be formed easily into desired shapes at room temperature.

2004 Chemists at Cornell University discover a new chemical reaction for splitting nitrogen molecules of the kind found in air, one that operates at the temperature of boiling water at one atmosphere of pressure. Then hydrogen can be added to form ammonia.

But the other elements in the first column are all soft metals that are highly reactive. Similarly, the last column of the table contains the gases that react only minimally. In general, elements are metals on the left side of the table (hydrogen is a metal only under great pressure), becoming mostly nonmetals in the last six columns. These last columns include some elements that are metals, such as aluminum. (A broken, heavy line separates the metals from the nonmetals.)

The row of rare earth elements beginning with lanthanum and the row of actinide elements beginning with actinium do not fit neatly into the rest of the table. Elements from atomic number 57 to 71 are all similar to lanthanum, while elements from atomic number 89 to 103 are similar to actinium. The rare earths are not generally rare, nor do they resemble soil. They are moderately common metals that, because of atomic structure, are very similar chemically. The actinide elements are radioactive metals.

The periodic table as shown here also includes the atomic mass as well as the atomic number. The atomic mass is a relative number; it shows the weight of an element as compared to the weight of an atom of carbon-12, which is assigned a weight of exactly 12. Most elements occur with several different atomic weights (in addition to carbon-12, for example, there are both carbon-13 and carbon-14; carbon-14 has 6 protons and 8 neutrons and is radioactive). These different forms are called isotopes. In the periodic table, the atomic mass given for most elements is the one that would be found by averaging the different isotopes in the amounts they naturally occur. Carbon is given an atomic mass of 12.01 because there is so much more carbon-12 than there is carbon-13 or carbon-14 in an ordinary sample of carbon. For some radioactive elements, natural abundance is meaningless, since there is no stable form. For these, the atomic mass of the most stable form is given, indicated by putting the atomic mass in parentheses.

THE PERIODIC TABLE OF THE ELEMENTS

Legend:

6	— atomic number
C	— chemical number
12.01	— atomic mass
Carbon	— name of element

Period	alkali metals I A	alkaline earth metals II A	III B	IV B	V B	VI B	VII B	← transition metals	VIII	→	I B	II B	III A	IV A	V A	VI A	VII A	noble gases O
1	1 **H** 1.01 Hydrogen																	2 **He** 4.00 Helium
2	3 **Li** 6.94 Lithium	4 **Be** 9.01 Beryllium											5 **B** 10.81 Boron	6 **C** 12.01 Carbon	7 **N** 14.01 Nitrogen	8 **O** 16.00 Oxygen	9 **F** 19.00 Fluorine	10 **Ne** 20.18 Neon
3	11 **Na** 22.99 Sodium	12 **Mg** 24.31 Magnesium											13 **Al** 26.98 Aluminum	14 **Si** 28.09 Silicon	15 **P** 30.97 Phosphorus	16 **S** 32.07 Sulfur	17 **Cl** 35.45 Chlorine	18 **Ar** 39.95 Argon
4	19 **K** 39.10 Potassium	20 **Ca** 40.08 Calcium	21 **Sc** 44.96 Scandium	22 **Ti** 47.88 Titanium	23 **V** 50.94 Vanadium	24 **Cr** 52.00 Chromium	25 **Mn** 54.95 Manganese	26 **Fe** 55.85 Iron	27 **Co** 58.93 Cobalt	28 **Ni** 58.70 Nickel	29 **Cu** 63.55 Copper	30 **Zn** 65.39 Zinc	31 **Ga** 69.72 Gallium	32 **Ge** 72.61 Germanium	33 **As** 74.92 Arsenic	34 **Se** 78.96 Selenium	35 **Br** 79.90 Bromine	36 **Kr** 83.80 Krypton
5	37 **Rb** 85.47 Rubidium	38 **Sr** 87.62 Strontium	39 **Y** 88.91 Yttrium	40 **Zr** 91.22 Zirconium	41 **Nb** 92.91 Niobium	42 **Mo** 95.94 Molybdenum	43 **Tc** (98) Technetium	44 **Ru** 101.07 Ruthenium	45 **Rh** 102.91 Rhodium	46 **Pd** 106.4 Palladium	47 **Ag** 107.87 Silver	48 **Cd** 112.41 Cadmium	49 **In** 114.82 Indium	50 **Sn** 118.71 Tin	51 **Sb** 121.74 Antimony	52 **Te** 127.60 Tellurium	53 **I** 126.90 Iodine	54 **Xe** 131.29 Xenon
6	55 **Cs** 132.91 Cesium	56 **Ba** 137.33 Barium	57 **La** 138.91 Lanthanum (Lanthanide series see below)	72 **Hf** 178.49 Hafnium	73 **Ta** 180.95 Tantalum	74 **W** 183.85 Tungsten	75 **Re** 186.21 Rhenium	76 **Os** 190.23 Osmium	77 **Ir** 192.22 Iridium	78 **Pt** 195.08 Platinum	79 **Au** 196.97 Gold	80 **Hg** 200.59 Mercury	81 **Tl** 204.38 Thallium	82 **Pb** 207.2 Lead	83 **Bi** 208.98 Bismuth	84 **Po** (209) Polonium	85 **At** (210) Astatine	86 **Rn** (222) Radon
7	87 **Fr** (223) Francium	88 **Ra** 226.03 Radium	89 **Ac** 227.03 Actinium (Actinide series see below)	104 **Rf** (261) Rutherfordium	105 **Db** (262) Dubnium	106 **Sg** (263) Seaborgium	107 **Bh** (262) Bohrium	108 **Hs** (265) Hassium	109 **Mt** (266) Meitnerium	110 **Ds** (269) Darmstadtium	111 **Rg** (272) Roentgenium	112 (277)	113 (287)	114 (281)	115 (291)	116 (292)		

nonmetals

rare earth elements — Lanthanide series

58 **Ce** 140.12 Cerium	59 **Pr** 140.91 Praseodymium	60 **Nd** 144.24 Neodymium	61 **Pm** (145) Promethium	62 **Sm** 150.4 Samarium	63 **Eu** 151.96 Europium	64 **Gd** 157.25 Gadolinium	65 **Tb** 158.93 Terbium	66 **Dy** 162.50 Dysprosium	67 **Ho** 164.93 Holmium	68 **Er** 167.26 Erbium	69 **Tm** 168.93 Thulium	70 **Yb** 173.04 Ytterbium	71 **Lu** 174.97 Lutetium

Actinide series

90 **Th** 232.04 Thorium	91 **Pa** 231.04 Protactinium	92 **U** 238.03 Uranium	93 **Np** 237.05 Neptunium	94 **Pu** (244) Plutonium	95 **Am** (243) Americium	96 **Cm** (247) Curium	97 **Bk** (247) Berkelium	98 **Cf** (251) Californium	99 **Es** (252) Einsteinium	100 **Fm** (257) Fermium	101 **Md** (258) Mendelevium	102 **No** (259) Nobelium	103 **Lr** (260) Lawrencium

Properties and Discovery of the Elements

All **ordinary matter is** made from one or more substances called elements (because they cannot be changed by chemical means). Ninety elements are found in nature, and people have created others, for a current total of 114. In this table each of the elements is listed in alphabetical order. The chemical symbol and the atomic number can be used to locate other information about the elements in the periodic table reprinted below. Many elements, known from ancient times, are labeled "prehistoric." Others are given with their first discovery—many elements having been independently rediscovered by others. In the following table, elements 112, 114, and 116, as yet unnamed, are listed as "Element 112" and so forth.

Element/Type[1]	Symbol/ (Atomic number)	Melting point F/(C)[1]	Boiling point F/(C)[1]	Derivation of name (Discoverer, Year)
Actinium Radioactive metal	Ac (89)	1924°F (1051°C)	5788°F (3198°C)	Greek aktis, a ray. (André-Louis Debierne, 1899)
Aluminum Metal	Al (13)	1220°F (660°C)	4566°F (2519°C)	Latin alumen, a substance with astringent taste (Hans Christian Oersted, 1825)
Americium Radioactive metal	Am (95)	2149°F (1176°C)	3652°F (2011°C)	Named for America (Glenn T. Seaborg & coworkers,1944)
Antimony Metal	Sb (51)	1168°F (631°C)	2889°F (1587°C)	Greek antimonos, opposed to solitude; symbol Sb from Latin stibium. (Rhazes, c. 900)
Argon Gas	Ar (18)	–308°F (–189°C)	–303°F (–186°C)	Greek argus, neutral inactive. (Sir William Ramsay, 1894)
Arsenic[2] Nonmetal	As (33)	N.A.	1117°F (603°C)	Latin arsenicum; folk etymology connects with yellow and maleness. (Albertus Magnus, 1250)
Astatine Radioactive nonmetal	At (85)	576°F (302°C)	unk.	Greek astatos, unstable. (Emilio Segrè, D.R. Corson, & K.R. MacKenzie, 1940)
Barium Metal	Ba (56)	1341°F (727°C)	3447°F (1897°C)	Greek baros, heavy, because of its dense compounds. (Humphry Davy, 1808)
Berkelium Radioactive metal	Bk (97)	1922°F (1050°C)	unk.	First made at Univ. of California. (Glenn T. Seaborg & coworkers,1949)
Beryllium Metal	Be (4)	2349°F (1287°C)	4480°F (2471°C)	Latin beryllus, Greek beryllos, gem. (Louis-Nicolas Vauquelin,1798)
Bismuth Metal	Bi (83)	520°F (271°C)	2847°F (1564°C)	German weisse masse, white mass; changed to bismat. (Claude J. Geoffrey, 1753
Bohrium Radioactive metal	Bh (107)	unk.	unk.	Named for Danish physicist Niels Bohr. (Russian scientists at Dubna, 1977)
Boron Nonmetal	B (5)	3767°F (2075°C)	7232°F (4000°C)	Arabic borak (borax); BORax + carbON. (Joseph-Louis Gay-Lussac & Louis-Jacques Thénard, 1808)
Bromine Liquid nonmetal	Br (35)	19°F (–7°C)	138°F (59°C)	Greek bromos, a stench; because of odor of its vapors. (Antoine-Jérôme Balard, 1826)
Cadmium Metal	Cd (48)	610°F (321°C)	1413°F (767°C)	Greek cadmia, earthy. (Friedrich Strohmeyer, 1817)
Calcium Metal	Ca (20)	1548°F (842°C)	2703°F (1484°C)	Latin calx, calcis, lime. (Humphry Davy, 1808)
Californium Radioactive metal	Cf (98)	1652°F (900°C)	unk.	First made at Univ. of California. (Glenn T. Seaborg & coworkers, 1949)
Carbon[2] Nonmetal	C (6)	N.A. N.A.	6917°F (3825°C)	Latin carbo, coal. (Prehistoric)
Cerium Rare earth	Ce (58)	1468°F (798°C)	6229°F (3443°C)	Named for asteroid Ceres, discovered in 1801. (Martin Klaproth, 1803)
Cesium Metal	Cs (55)	84°F (29°C)	1240°F (671°C)	Latin caesius, bluish gray. (Gustav Kirchhoff & Robert Bunsen, 1860)
Chlorine Gas	Cl (17)	–152°F (–102°C)	–29°F (–34°C)	Greek chloros, grass-green; from color of gas. (Humphry Davy, 1810)
Chromium Metal	Cr (24)	3465°F (1907°C)	4840°F (2671°C)	Greek chroma, color; because many of its compounds are colored. (Louis-Nicolas Vauquelin, 1797)
Cobalt Metal	Co (27)	2723°F (1495°C)	5301°F (2927°C)	German Kobalt, a goblin. (Georg Brandt, 1735)
Copper Metal	Cu (29)	1985°F (1085°C)	4644°F (2562°C)	Latin cuprum; for island of Cyprus. (Prehistoric)
Curium Radioactive metal	Cm (96)	2453°F (1345°C)	5612°F (3100°C)	Named after Pierre and Marie Curie. (Glenn T. Seaborg & coworkers, 1944)
Darmstadtium Radioactive metal	Ds (110)	unk.	unk.	Named for city, Darmstadt, near place of discovery, 2003. (Created at Society for Heavy Ion Research, Germany, 1994)
Dubnium Radioactive metal	Db (105)	unk.	unk.	Named for the Joint Institute for Nuclear Research at Dubna,Russia. (Russian scientists at Dubna, 1967)
Dysprosium Rare earth	Dy (66)	2574°F (1412°C)	4653°F (2567°C)	Greek dysprositos, difficult of access. (Paul-Emile Lecoq deBoisbaudran, 1886)

Element/Type[1]	Symbol/ (Atomic number)	Melting point F/(C)[1]	Boiling point F/(C)[1]	Derivation of name (Discoverer, Year)
Einsteinium Radioactive metal	Es (99)	1580°F (860°C)	unk.	Named after Albert Einstein. (Albert Ghiorso & coworkers, 1952)
Element 112[4] Radioactive metal	N.A. (112)	unk.	unk.	(Society for Heavy Ion Research, Darmstadt, Germany, 1996)
Element 113 Radioactive metal	N.A. (113)	unk.	unk.	(Scientists at Dubna, 2004)
Element 114 Radioactive metal	N.A. (114)	unk.	unk.	(Dubna and Lawrence Livermore, 1998)
Element 115 Radioactive metal	N.A. (115)	unk.	unk.	(Scientists at Dubna, 2004)
Element 116[5] Radioactive metal	N.A. (116)	unk.	unk.	(Scientists at Dubna, 2000)
Erbium Rare earth	Er (68)	2784°F (1529°C)	5194°F (2868°C)	Named for Ytterby, village in Sweden. (Carl Gustav Mosander, 1843)
Europium Rare earth	Eu (63)	1512°F (822°C)	2784°F (1529°C)	Named for Europe. (Eugène-Anatole Demarçay, 1896)
Fermium Radioactive metal	Fm (100)	2781°F (1527°C)	unk.	Named after Italian physicist Enrico Fermi. (Albert Ghiorso & coworkers, 1952)
Fluorine Gas	F (9)	−364°F (−220°C)	−306°F (−188°C)	Latin *fluere*, to flow. (Ferdinand-Frédéric-Henri Moissan, 1886)
Francium Radioactive metal	Fr (87)	81°F (27°C)	unk.	Named for France. (Marguerite Perey, 1939)
Gadolinium Rare earth	Gd (64)	2395°F (1313°C)	5923°F (3273°C)	Named after gadolinite, mineral named for Johan Gadolin, Finnish chemist. (Jean-Charles Marignac, 1880)
Gallium Metal	Ga (31)	86°F (30°C)	3999°F (2204°C)	Latin *Gallia*, France; also Latin *gallus*, a cock—a pun on Lecoq. (Paul-Emile Lecoq de Boisbaudran, 1875)
Germanium Metal	Ge (32)	1721°F (938°C)	5131°F (2833°C)	Named for Germany. (Clemens Winkler, 1886)
Gold Metal	Au (79)	1948°F (1064°C)	5173°F (2856°C)	Anglo-Saxon *gold*; Sanskrit *juel*, to shine; symbol from Latin *aurum*, shining dawn. (Prehistoric)
Hafnium Metal	Hf (72)	4051°F (2233°C)	8317°F (4603°C)	From *Hafnia*, ancient name of Copenhagen. (Dirk Coster & György Hevesy, 1923)
Hassium Radioactive metal	Hs (108)	unk.	unk.	Named for the German province of Hesse, where Darmstadt is located. (Society for Heavy Ion Research, Darmstadt, Germany, 1984)
Helium Gas	He (2)	N.A.	−452°F (−269°C)	Greek *helios*, the Sun; first observed in Sun's atmosphere. (Pierre-Jules-César Janssen & Sir Joseph Norman Lockyer, 1868)
Holmium Rare earth	Ho (67)	2685°F (1474°C)	4892°F (2700°C)	From *Holmia*, Latinized form of Stockholm. (Per Teodor Cleve, 1879)
Hydrogen Gas	H (1)	−435°F (−259°C)	−423°F (−253°C)	Greek *hydor*, water, plus *gen*, forming. (Henry Cavendish, 1766)
Indium Metal	In (49)	314°F (157°C)	3762°F (2072°C)	Latin *indicum*, indigo. (Ferdinand Reich & Hieronymus Theodor Richter, 1863)
Iodine[2] Nonmetal	I (53)	237°F (114°C)	364°F (184°C)	Greek *iodes*, violet; from color of its vapor. (Bernard Courtois, 1811)
Iridium Metal	Ir (77)	4435°F (2446°C)	8002°F (4428°C)	Greek *iris*, a rainbow, from changing color of its salts. (Smithson Tennant, 1803)
Iron Metal	Fe (26)	2800°F (1538°C)	5182°F (2861°C)	Anglo-Saxon *iren*; symbol from Latin *ferrum*. (Prehistoric)
Krypton[3] Gas	Kr (36)	−251°F (−157°C)	−244°F (−153°C)	Greek *kryptos*, hidden. (Alexander Ramsay & Morris William Travers, 1898)
Lanthanum Rare earth	La (57)	1684°F (918°C)	6267°F (3464°C)	Greek *lanthanein*, to be concealed. (Carl Gustav Mosander, 1839)
Lawrencium Radioactive metal	Lr (103)	2961°F (1627°C)	unk.	Named after American physicist Ernest Lawrence. (Albert Ghiorso & coworkers, 1961)
Lead Metal	Pb (82)	621°F (327°C)	3180°F (1749°C)	Anglo-Saxon *lead*; symbol from Latin *plumbum*. (Prehistoric)
Lithium Metal	Li (3)	351°F (181°C)	2448°F (1342°C)	Greek *lithos*, stony. (Johann A. Arfvedson, 1817)
Lutetium Rare earth	Lu (71)	3025°F (1663°C)	6159°F (3404°C)	Latin *Lutetia*, ancient name for Paris. (Georges Urbain, 1907)
Magnesium Metal	Mg (12)	1202°F (650°C)	1994°F (1090°C)	Latin *Magnesia*, a district in Asia Minor. (Humphry Davy, 1808)
Manganese Metal	Mn (25)	2275°F (1246°C)	3742°F (2061°C)	Latin *magnes*, magnet; because of confusion with magnetic iron ores. (Johann Gottlieb Gahn, 1774)
Meitnerium Radioactive metal	Mt (109)	unk.	unk.	Named for the Austrian-Swedish physicist Lise Meitner. (Society for Heavy Ion Research, Darmstadt, Germany, 1982)

Element/Type[1]	Symbol/ (Atomic number)	Melting point F/(C)[1]	Boiling point F/(C)[1]	Derivation of name (Discoverer, Year)
Mendelevium Radioactive metal	Md (101)	1521°F (827°C)	unk.	Named after Russian chemist Dmitri Mendeléev. (Albert Ghiorso & coworkers, 1955)
Mercury Liquid metal	Hg (80)	−38°F (−39°C)	674°F (357°C)	Named for Roman god Mercurius; symbol from Latin *hydrargyrum*. (Prehistoric)
Molybdenum Metal	Mo (42)	4753°F (2623°C)	8382°F (4639°C)	Greek *molybdos*, lead. (Karl Wilhelm Scheele, 1778)
Neodymium Rare earth	Nd (60)	1870°F (1021°C)	5565°F (3074°C)	Greek *neo*, new, plus *didymon*, twin (with the element praseodymium). (Karl Auer (Baron von Welsbach), 1885)
Neon Gas	Ne (10)	−415°F (−249°C)	−411°F (−246°C)	Greek *neo*, new. (Alexander Ramsay & Morris William Travers, 1898)
Neptunium Radioactive metal	Np (93)	1191°F (644°C)	unk.	Named for planet Neptune. (Edwin McMillan & Philip Abelson,1940)
Nickel Metal	Ni (28)	2651°F (1455°C)	5308°F (2931°C)	German *Nickel*, Satan (Old Nick). (Axel Cronstedt, 1751)
Niobium Metal	Nb (41)	4491°F (2477°C)	8571°F (4744°C)	Latin *Niobe*, daughter of Tantalus. (Charles Hachett, 1801)
Nitrogen Gas	N (7)	−346°F (−210°C)	−320°F (−196°C)	Latin, forming *niter*, a compound of nitrogen. (Daniel Rutherford, 1772)
Nobelium Radioactive metal	No (102)	1521°F (827°C)	unk.	Named after Alfred Nobel; made at Nobel Institute. (Albert Ghiorso & coworkers, 1958)
Osmium Metal	Os (76)	5491°F (3033°C)	9054°F (5012°C)	Greek *osme*, smell; for malodorousness. (Smithson Tennant, 1803)
Oxygen Gas	O (8)	−362°F (−219°C)	−297°F (−183°C)	Greek *oxys*, sharp, plus *gen*, forming; from incorrect belief that oxygen forms acids. (Joseph Priestley, 1774)
Palladium Metal	Pd (46)	2831°F (1555°C)	5365°F (2963°C)	Named for Greek goddess Pallas; from asteroid Pallas. (William Hyde Wollaston, 1803)
Phosphorus Nonmetal	P (15)	111°F (44°C)	537°F (281°C)	Greek *phosphoros*, light-bringer; glows because of rapid oxidation(Hennig Brand, 1669)
Platinum Metal	Pt (78)	3215°F (1768°C)	6917°F (3825°C)	Diminutive of Spanish *plata*, silver, *platina*. (Antonio de Ulloa, 1735)
Plutonium Radioactive metal	Pu (94)	1184°F (640°C)	5842°F (3228°C)	Named for planet Pluto. (Glenn T. Seaborg & coworkers, 1940)
Polonium Radioactive metal	Po (84)	489°F (254°C)	1764°F (962°C)	Named by Marie Curie for her native Poland. (Marie & Pierre Curie, 1898)
Potassium Metal	K (19)	146°F (64°C)	1398°F (759°C)	Named for potash, a compound of potassium; symbol from Latin *kalium*. (Humphry Davy, 1807)
Praseodymium Rare earth	Pr (59)	1708°F (931°C)	6368°F (3520°C)	Greek *prasios*, green, plus *didymos*, twin (with neodymium). (Karl Auer (Baron von Welsbach), 1885)
Promethium Radioactive	Pm (61)	1908°F (1042°C)	5432°F (3000°C)	Named for Greek god Prometheus, who stole fire from heaven. (J.A. Marinsky, L.E. Glendenin, & C.D.Coryell, 1945)
Protactinium Radioactive metal	Pa (91)	2862°F (1572°C)	unk.	Latin *proto*, first, plus actinium, one of the elements. (Otto Hahn & Lise Meitner, 1918)
Radium Radioactive metal	Ra (88)	1292°F (700°C)	unk.	Latin *radius*, ray. (Marie Curie & Pierre Curie, 1898)
Radon Radioactive gas	Rn (86)	−96°F (−71°C)	−79°F (−62°C)	*Radium* plus *on*, as in *neon*. (Friedrich Ernst Dorn, 1900)
Rhenium Metal	Re (75)	5767°F (3186°C)	10105°F (5596°C)	Latin *Rhenus*, Rhine. (Walter Noddack, Ida Tacke, & Otto Berg, 1925)
Rhodium Metal	Rh (45)	3567°F (1964°C)	6683°F (3695°C)	Greek *rhodon*, rose; for red color of its salts. (William Hyde Wollaston, 1803)
Roentgenium Radioactive metal	Rg (111)	unk.	unk.	Named for Wilhelm Conrad Röntgen, 2004. (Created at Society for Heavy Ion Research, Germany, 1994).
Rubidium Metal	Rb (37)	103°F (39°C)	1270°F (688°C)	Latin *rubidus*, red; from red lines in its spectrum. (Gustav Kirchhoff & Robert Bunsen, 1861)
Ruthenium Metal	Ru (44)	4233°F (2334°C)	7502°F (4150°C)	Named for Ruthenia in Urals, where ore was first found. (Carl Claus, 1844)
Rutherfordium Radioactive metal	Rf (104)	unk.	unk.	Named for the New Zealand-born English physicist Ernest Rutherford. (Russian scientists at Dubna, 1964)
Samarium Rare earth	Sm (62)	1965°F (1074°C)	3261°F (1794°C)	Named for Scandinavian mineral samarskite. (Paul-Emile Lecoq de Boisbaudran, 1879)
Scandium Metal	Sc (21)	2806°F (1541°C)	5137°F (2836°C)	Named for Scandinavia. (Lars Fredrik Nilson, 1879)
Seaborgium Radioactive metal	Sg (106)	unk.	unk.	Named for American physicist Glenn T. Seaborg. (Russian scientists at Dubna and U.S. team from Berkeley and Lawrence Livermore Laboratories, 1974)
Selenium Nonmetal	Se (34)	429°F (221°C)	1265°F (685°C)	Greek *selene*, the Moon. (Jöns Jakob Berzelius, 1818)

Element/Type[1]	Symbol/ (Atomic number)	Melting point F/(C)[1]	Boiling point F/(C)[1]	Derivation of name (Discoverer, Year))
Silicon Nonmetal	Si (14)	2577°F (1414°C)	5909°F (3265°C)	Latin *silex*, flint. (Jöns Jakob Berzelius, 1824)
Silver Metal	Ag (47)	1763°F (962°C)	3924°F (2162°C)	Anglo-Saxon *sealfor*; symbol is from Latin *argentum* (Prehistoric)
Sodium Metal	Na (11)	208°F (98°C)	1621°F (883°C)	English *soda*, a sodium compound; symbol from Latin *natrium* (Humphry Davy, 1807)
Strontium Metal	Sr (38)	1431°F (777°C)	2520°F (1382°C)	For Strontian, a town in Scotland. (Humphry Davy, 1808)
Sulfur Nonmetal	S (16)	247°F (120°C)	832°F (445°C)	Sanskrit *solvere*, Latin *sulphur*. (Prehistoric)
Tantalum Metal	Ta (73)	5463°F (3017°C)	9856°F (5458°C)	For mythical king Tantalus, condemned to thirst; because of its insolubility. (Anders Ekeberg, 1802)
Technetium Radioactive metal	Tc (43)	3915°F (2157°C)	7709°F (4265°C)	Greek *technetos*, artificial; first artificial element. (Emilio Segrè, 1937)
Tellurium Metal	Te (52)	841°F (450°C)	1810°F (988°C)	Latin *tellus*, the Earth. (Franz Joseph Müller, 1782)
Terbium Rare earth	Tb (65)	2473°F (1356°C)	5846°F (3230°C)	For Ytterby, village in Sweden. (Carl Gustav Mosander, 1843)
Thallium Metal	Tl (81)	579°F (304°C)	2683°F (1473°C)	Greek *thallos*, a green twig; after color of its spectrum (William Crookes, 1861)
Thorium Radioactive metal	Th (90)	3182°F (1750°C)	8650°F (4788°C)	For Norse god Thor. (Jöns Jakob Berzelius, 1829)
Thulium Rare earth	Tm (69)	2813°F (1545°C)	3542°F (1950°C)	Greek *Thule*, Greek name for land north of Britain. (Per Teodor Cleve, 1879)
Tin Metal	Sn (50)	449°F (232°C)	4716°F (2602°C)	Anglo-Saxon *tin*; symbol from Latin *stannum*. (Prehistoric)
Titanium Metal	Ti (22)	3034°F (1668°C)	5949°F (3287°C)	For Titans of classical mythology. (William Gregor, 1791)
Tungsten Metal	W (74)	6192°F (3422°C)	10,031°F (5555°C)	Swedish *tung sten*, heavy stone; symbol from German *Wolfram*. (Fausto and Juan José d'Elhuyar, 1783)
Uranium Radioactive metal	U (92)	2075°F (1135°C)	7468°F (4131°C)	For planet Uranus. (Martin Klaproth, 1789)
Vanadium Metal	V (23)	3470°F (1910°C)	6165°F (3407°C)	For Scandinavian goddess Vanadis. (Andrès del Rio, 1801)
Xenon[3] Gas	Xe (54)	−169°F (−112°C)	−163°F (−108°C)	Greek *xenon*, stranger. (Alexander Ramsay & Morris William Travers, 1898)
Ytterbium Rare earth	Yb (70)	1506°F (819°C)	2185°F (1196°C)	For Ytterby, a village in Sweden. (George Urbain, 1907)
Yttrium Rare earth	Y (39)	2772°F (1522°C)	6053°F (3345°C)	For Ytterby, a village in Sweden. (Carl Gustav Mosander, 1843)
Zinc Metal	Zn (30)	787°F (420°C)	1665°F (907°C)	German *zink*. (Prehistoric)
Zirconium Metal	Zr (40)	3371°F (1855°C)	7968°F (4409°C)	Arabic *zargun*, gold color. (Martin Klaproth, 1789)

Notes: 1. At a pressure of one atmosphere and, for type, at room temperature. 2. This element sublimes (goes directly from a solid to a gas). 3. Liquefaction also requires great pressure. 4. Temporarily named Ununbium. 5. Temporarily named Ununhexium.

PHYSICS

Physics is the basis of the other sciences because it is concerned with the fundamental interactions of matter and energy. The first physicists studied how ordinary objects and very large objects (Moon, planets and stars) moved in response to forces. Their study was extremely successful. Near the end of the 19th century, physicists began to investigate radiation in detail, leading to the discovery of various forms of electromagnetic radiation (of which only forms of light, including infrared and ultraviolet, were known previously) and particles smaller than the atom (subatomic particles, such as the electron and proton). In the 20th century, the study of subatomic particles, called particle physics, became a major branch of the science. Many particle physicists limit their work to the particles in the nucleus of atoms and to the behavior of nuclei. Another major branch, condensed-matter physics, is concerned with the physical behavior of materials—for example, their electrical and magnetic properties. Major successes in condensed-matter physics include development of the transistor and related devices (chips) and superconductivity, a state in which electric currents can be transmitted with no resistance. Today many physicists are also cosmologists, who study how the universe began and is constructed, or astrophysicists, who study processes in stars.

Major Discoveries in Physics

1586 Simon Stevinus (Belgian-Dutch: 1548–1620) shows that two different weights dropped at same time from same height will reach ground at same time.

1604 Galileo (Italian: 1564–1642) announces his discovery that a body falling freely will increase its distance as the square of time.

1663 Blaise Pascal (French: 1623–62) proposes what becomes known as Pascal's law: pressure in fluid is transmitted equally in all directions

1675 Ole Rømer (Danish: 1644–1710) becomes first to measure speed of light, although his value is somewhat too slow by today's standards.

1676 Robert Hooke (English: 1635–1703) discovers what becomes known as Hooke's law: The amount a spring stretches varies directly with its tension.

1678 Christiaan Huygens (Dutch: 1629–95) introduces wave theory of light.

1687 Sir Isaac Newton's (English: 1642–1727) *Principia* is published, containing his laws of motion and theory of gravity.

1746 At least two experimenters in Leyden, the Netherlands, invent method for storing static electricity, which becomes known as Leyden jar.

1752 Benjamin Franklin (American: 1706–90) performs kite experiment, demonstrating that lightning is form of electricity.

1787 Jacques A.C. Charles (French: 1746–1823) discovers what is later known as Charles's law: All gases expand same amount with given rise in temperature; e.g., same rise in temperature that will cause hydrogen to double in volume will also cause air to double in volume.

1791 Luigi Galvani (Italian: 1737–98) announces his discovery that when two different metals touch in frog's muscle, they produce electric current.

1798 Benjamin Thompson, Count von Rumford (American-German: 1753–1814) shows that heat is form of motion.

Henry Cavendish (English: 1731–1810) determines gravitational constant and mass of Earth.

1800 William Herschel (German-English: 1738–1822) announces his discovery of infrared light.

1801 Johann W. Ritter (German: 1776–1810) discovers ultraviolet light.

1802 Thomas Young (English: 1773–1829) develops his wave theory of light.

1820 Hans Christian Oersted (Danish: 1777–1851) discovers that magnetism and electricity are two different manifestations of same force.

André-Marie Ampère (French: 1775–1836) formulates first laws of electromagnetism.

1831 Michael Faraday (English: 1791–1867) in England and Joseph Henry (American: 1797–1878) in U.S. (in 1830) independently discover principle of dynamo.

1842 Julius Robert von Mayer (German: 1814–78) is first scientist to state law of conservation of energy.

1848 William Thompson, Baron Kelvin (Scottish: 1824–1907), proposes concept of absolute zero, the lowest possible temperature (−460°F, or −273°C).

1850 Rudolf J.E. Clausius (German: 1822–88) makes first clear statement of second law of thermodynamics: Energy in closed system tends to degrade into heat.

1873 James Clerk Maxwell (Scottish: 1831–79) publishes complete theory of electromagnetism.

1888 Heinrich P. Hertz (German: 1857–94) produces and detects radio waves.

1895 Wilhelm Konrad Röntgen (German: 1845–1923) discovers X rays.

1896 Henri Becquerel (French: 1852–1908) discovers natural radioactivity.

1897 Sir Joseph John Thomson (English: 1856–1940) discovers electron.

1900 Max K.E.L. Planck (German: 1858–1947) explains behavior of electromagnetic radiation by proposing that there is smallest step a physical process can take, which he names quantum.

1905 Albert Einstein (German-American: 1879–1955) shows that photoelectric effect—ejection of electrons from metal by action of light—can be explained if light has particle nature as well as wave nature.

Einstein shows that motion of small particles in liquid ("Brownian motion") can be explained by assuming that the liquid is made of molecules.

Einstein develops his special theory of relativity and the law $E = mc^2$ (energy equals mass times square of speed of light).

1911 Heike Kamerlingh Onnes (Dutch: 1853–1926) discovers superconductivity.

Ernest Rutherford (British: 1871–1937) discovers the proton.

1915 Einstein completes his general theory of relativity, a theory of gravity more accurate than that of Sir Isaac Newton, and publishes it the following year.

1924 Louis-Victor de Broglie (French: 1892–1987) publishes his theory that particles, such as electrons, also have wave nature.

1925 Wolfgang Pauli (Austrian-American: 1900–1958) discovers exclusion principal: Two electrons or protons described by same numbers (called quantum numbers) cannot exist in same atom.

Werner Karl Heisenberg (German: 1901–76) develops matrix version of quantum mechanics, a mathematical treatment that explains behavior of electrons and protons.

1926 Erwin Schrödinger (Austrian: 1887–1961) develops wave version of quantum mechanics, a different mathematical treatment producing same results as Heisenberg's matrix mechanics.

1927 Heisenberg develops his uncertainty principle: It is impossible to measure accurately position and momentum of electron or proton at same time.

1932 Sir James Chadwick (British: 1891–1974) discovers neutron, a neutral particle about same mass as proton.

Carl D. Anderson (American: 1905–91) discovers positron, a positively charged analog of electron.

Sir John G. Cockcroft (English: 1897–1967) and Ernest Walton (Irish: 1903–95) develop first particle accelerator (often still known as "atom smasher").

1937 Carl Anderson, with other physicists, performs the work that culminates in the discovery of the muon.

1938 Otto Hahn (German: 1870–1968), in experiments interpreted by Lise Meitner (Austrian-Swedish: 1878–1968), splits uranium atom, opening way for nuclear bombs and nuclear power.

1945 Scientists funded by U.S. government and led by J. Robert Oppenheimer (American: 1904–67) detonate first nuclear-fission explosion (atomic bomb).

1947 Cecil Frank Powell (English: 1903–69) and coworkers discover pion, first-known meson, a subatomic particle involved in holding nucleus of atom together.

1955 Owen Chamberlain (American: 1920–) and Emilio Segrè (Italian-American: 1905–89) produce antiprotons, negatively charged analogs of proton.

1956 Clyde Cowan Jr. (American: 1919–74) and Frederick Reines (American: 1918–98) are first to observe a neutrino, a subatomic particle with no mass or charge produced in certain forms of radioactive decay.

1957 Experiments by group led by Chien-Shiung Wu (Chinese-American: 1912–97) and quickly confirmed by others show that right and left are distinguished by behavior of electrons emitted in certain forms of radioactivity.

John Bardeen (American: 1908–91), Leon Cooper (American: 1930–), and Bob Schrieffer (American: 1931–) develop a theory explaining superconductivity.

1961 Murray Gell-Mann (American: 1929–) and, independently, Yu'val Ne'eman (Israeli: 1925–) and others develop method of classifying heavy sub-atomic particles that comes to be known as "eight-fold way."

1964 Murray Gell-Mann introduces concept of quarks as components of heavy subatomic particles, such as protons and mesons.

1967 Steven Weinberg (American: 1933–), Abdus Salam (Pakistani-British: 1926–96), and Sheldon Lee Glashow (American: 1932–) independently develop theory that combines electromagnetic force with weak force.

1980 Heinrich Rohrer (Swiss: 1933–) and Gerd Binnig (German: 1947–) invent the scanning tunneling microscope, with which it is possible to produce images of individual atoms on crystal surfaces.

1986 Karl Alexander Müller (Swiss: 1927–) and Johannes Georg Bednorz (German: 1950–) discover first "high-temperature" superconductor.

1995 Physicists at Fermilab in Batavia, Ill., announce the first observations of the sixth and last expected quark, known as top.

Eric Cornell of the U.S. National Institute of Standards and Technology and coworkers produce the first sample of the fifth state of matter, known as a Bose-Einstein Condensate (BEC), in which atoms huddle together in essentially the same place and condition.

Physicists at CERN (the European Laboratory for Particle Physics) produce the first few atoms of antihydrogen, with a positron orbiting an antiproton.

1997 Two groups of physicists, one in Austria and one in Rome, show that it is possible to entangle two particles so that measuring an exact quantum state of one of them will instantly determine the corresponding state of the other across any distance, a phenomenon known as "quantum teleportation."

1998 Scientists working with the Super-Kamiokande neutrino telescope in Japan establish indirectly that the neutrinos must have a nonzero, although small, mass.

2000 An experiment at Fermilab creates and detects the tau neutrino, predicted in 1975.

2001 Physicists at Harvard University and the Harvard-Smithsonian Center for Astrophysics, both in Cambridge, MA, independently stop light completely for brief intervals as it travels through ultracold gases.

The SPring-8 synchrotron particle accelerator in Japan produces the first examples of particles that contain five quarks, termed pentaquarks.

2002 Researchers produce the first antimatter hydrogen gas at CERN in Geneva, trapping positrons and antiprotons which combine to form about 50,000 antihydrogen atoms.

Two independent teams of physicists discover a new form of radioactivity, the simultaneous emission of two protons from iron-45 nuclei.

2003 A thermonuclear device called Z at Sandia National Laboratories in Albuquerque, New Mexico, achieves fusion by using a sudden blast of X rays aimed at a tiny capsule of deuterium to fuse it into tritium and helium, producing 10,000,000,000 neutrons with each blast of X rays.

Two groups independently succeed in creating Bose-Einstein Condensates (BECs) from ultracold molecules.

2004 German material scientists discover a form of supercooled liquid water, high-density liquid water (HDL), which is 17 percent denser than ordinary liquid water at the same pressure and temperature.

Two different groups of researchers succeed in using triplets of entangled ions to transmit characteristics from one atom to another via quantum teleportation.

A type of subatomic particle known as DsJ(2632), a meson containing a strange quark and a charm antiquark, is observed to decay in a manner contrary to the standard model of particle physics.

2008 Tokyo-based researchers test a mercury-based clock expected to be the world's most accurate timepiece, which would improve measurements and Global Positioning System (GPS) signals.

▶ THE BASIC LAWS OF PHYSICS

Key Terms

Mass is a measure of the amount of matter; it is proportional to weight. Near the surface of Earth it is roughly equivalent to weight.

Velocity measures how an object changes position with time.

Acceleration is how an object changes velocity with time.

Momentum is the product of mass and velocity.

Energy is the ability to do work.

Law of Gravity

The gravitational force between any two objects is proportional to the product of their masses and inversely proportional to the square of the distance between them. If F is the force, G is the number that represents the ratio (the gravitational constant), m and M are the two masses, and r is the distance between the objects:

$$F = \frac{GmM}{r^2}$$

In metric measure, the gravitational constant is 0.0000000000667390 (6.67390 x 10^{-11}) newton m^2/kg^2, so another way of writing the basic law of gravity is

$$F = \frac{0.0000000000667390\, mM}{r^2}$$

This law implies that objects falling near the surface of Earth will fall with the same rate of acceleration (ignoring drag caused by air). This rate is 32.174 feet per second per second (ft./sec²), or 9.8 m/sec², and is conventionally labeled g. Applying this rate to falling objects gives the velocity, v, and distance, d, after any amount of time, t, in seconds. If the object starts at rest and 32 ft./sec² is used as an approximation for g,

$$v = 32t$$
$$d = 16t^2$$

For example, after 3 seconds, a dropped object that is still falling will have a velocity of 32 x 3 = 96 feet per second and will have fallen a distance of 16 x 3² = 144 feet.

If the object has an initial velocity v_0 and an initial height above the ground of a, the equations describing the velocity and the distance, d, above the ground (a positive velocity is up and a negative velocity is down) become

$$v = v_0 - 32t$$

and

$$d = -16t^2 + v_0 t + a.$$

After 3 seconds, an object tossed in the air from a height of 6 feet with a velocity of 88 feet per second will reach a speed of 88 - 96 = -8 feet per second, meaning that it has begun to descend, and will have a height of (-16 x 9) + (88 x 3) + 6 = -144 + 264 + 6 = 126 feet above the ground.

The maximum height, H, reached by the object with an initial velocity v_0 and initial height a is

$$H = a + \frac{v_0^2}{64}$$

For the object tossed upward at 88 feet per second from a height of 6 feet, the maximum height reached would be 6 + 88²/64 = 6 + 121 = 127 feet. Therefore, after 3 seconds, the object has just reached its peak and has fallen back only 1 foot.

Albert Einstein's general theory of relativity introduced laws of gravity more accurate than those just given, which were discovered by Sir Isaac Newton. Newton's gravitational theory is extremely accurate for most practical situations, however. For example, Newton's theory is used to determine how to launch satellites into proper orbits.

Newton's Laws of Motion

Newton's Laws of Motion apply to objects in a vacuum and are not easily observed in the real world, where forces such as friction tend to overwhelm the natural motion of objects. To obtain realistic solutions to problems, however, physicists and engineers begin with Newton's laws and then add in the various forces that also affect motion.

1. *Any object at rest tends to stay at rest. A body in motion moves at the same velocity in a straight line unless acted upon by a force.* This is also known as the law of inertia. Note that this law implies that an object will travel in a curved path only so long as a force is acting on it. When the force is released, the object will travel in a straight line. A weight on a string swung in a circle will travel in a straight line when the string is released, for the string was supplying the force that caused circular motion.

2. *The acceleration of an object is directly proportional to the force acting on it and inversely proportional to the mass of the object.* This law, for an acceleration a, a force F, and a mass m, is more commonly expressed in terms of finding the force when you know the mass and the acceleration. In this form it is written as

$$F = ma.$$

The implication of this law is that a constant force will produce acceleration, which is an increase in velocity. Thus, a rocket, which is propelled by a constant force as long as its fuel is burning, constantly increases in velocity. Even with an infinite supply of fuel, the rocket would eventually cease to increase in velocity, however, because Einstein's other relativity theory, the special theory of relativity, states that no object can

exceed the speed of light in a vacuum (see "Conservation of mass-energy" below). Nevertheless, even a small force, constantly applied, can cause a large mass to reach velocities near the speed of light if enough time is allowed.

3. *For every action there is an equal and opposite reaction.* (See Conservation of momentum below.)

Conservation Laws

Many results in physics come from various conservation laws. A conservation law is a rule that a certain entity must not change in amount during a certain class of operations. All such conservation laws treat closed systems. Anything added from outside the system could affect the amount of the entity being conserved.

Conservation of momentum In a closed system, momentum stays the same. This law is equivalent to Newton's third law. Since momentum is the product of mass and velocity, if the mass of a system changes, then the velocity must change. For example, consider a person holding a heavy anchor in a stationary rowboat in the water. The momentum of the system is 0, since the masses have no velocity. Now the person in the rowboat tosses the anchor toward the shore. The momentum of the anchor is now a positive number if velocity toward the shore is measured as positive. To conserve momentum, the rowboat is accelerated in the opposite direction, away from the shore. The positive momentum of the anchor is balanced by the negative momentum of the rowboat and its cargo. In terms of two masses, m and M, and matching velocities v and V,

$$mv = MV$$

Conservation of angular momentum

An object moving in a circle has a special kind of momentum, called angular momentum. As noted above, motion in a circle requires some force. Angular momentum combines mass, velocity, and acceleration (produced by the force). For a body moving in a circle, the acceleration depends on both the speed of the body in its path and the square of the radius of the circle. The product of this speed, the mass, and the square of the radius is the angular momentum of the mass.

In a closed system, angular momentum is conserved. This effect is used by skaters to change their velocity of spinning. Angular momentum is partly determined by the masses of a skater's arms combined with the rate of rotation and the square of the radius to the center of mass of each arm (the point that can represent the total mass of the arm). When skaters bring their arms close to their body, this would tend to reduce the angular momentum, because the center of mass is closer to the body. But, since angular momentum is conserved, the rate of rotation has to increase to compensate for the decreased radius. Because the rate depends on the square of the radius, the rate increases dramatically.

Conservation of mass *In a closed system, the total amount of mass appears to be conserved in all but nuclear reactions and other extreme conditions.*

Conservation of energy *In a closed system, energy appears to be conserved in all but nuclear reactions and other extreme conditions.* Energy comes in very many forms: mechanical, chemical, electrical, heat, and so forth. As one form is changed into another (excepting nuclear reactions and extreme conditions), this law guarantees that the total amount remains the same. Thus, when you change the chemical energy of a dry cell into electrical energy and use that to turn a motor, the total amount of energy does not change (although some becomes heat energy—see "Laws of Thermodynamics" below).

Conservation of mass-energy   Einstein discovered that his special theory of relativity implies that energy and mass are related. Consequently, mass and energy by themselves are not conserved, since one can be converted into the other. Mass and energy appear to be conserved in ordinary situations because the effect of Einstein's discovery is very small most of the time. The more general law, then, is the law of conservation of mass-energy: *The total amount of mass and energy must be conserved*. Einstein found the following equation that links mass and energy:

$$E = mc^2$$

In this equation, E is the amount of energy, m is the mass, and c is the speed of light in a vacuum.

One instance of energy changing to mass occurs in Einstein's equation for how the mass increases with velocity. If m_0 is the mass of the object when it is not moving, v is the velocity of the object in relation to an observer who is considered to be at rest, and c is the speed of light in a vacuum, then the mass, m, is given by the equation

$$m = \frac{m_0}{\sqrt{1 - \frac{v^2}{c^2}}}$$

This accounts for the rule that no object can exceed the speed of light in a vacuum. As the object approaches this speed, so much of the energy is converted to mass that it cannot continue to accelerate.

In both nuclear fission (splitting of the atomic nucleus) and nuclear fusion (the joining of atomic nuclei, producing the energy of a hydrogen bomb), mass is converted into energy.

Conservation for particles   Many properties associated with atoms and subatomic particles are also conserved. Among them are charge, spin, isospin, and a combination known as CPT for *charge conjugation, parity,* and *time*.

First and Second Laws of Thermodynamics

First law   This is the same as the law of conservation of energy. It is a law of thermodynamics, or the movement of heat, because heat must be treated as a form of energy to keep the total amount of energy constant. All bodies contain heat as energy no matter how cold they are, although there is not much heat at temperatures close to absolute zero.

Second law   *Heat in a closed system can never travel from a low temperature region to one of higher temperature in a self-sustaining process*. Self-sustaining in this case means a process that does not need energy from outside the system to keep it going. In a refrigerator, heat from the cold inside of the refrigerator is transferred to a warmer room, but energy from outside is required to make the transfer happen, so the process is not self-sustaining.

The second law has many implications. One of them is that no perpetual motion machine can be constructed. Another is that all energy in a closed system eventually becomes heat that is diffused equally throughout the system, so that one can no longer obtain work from the system.

The equations that describe the behavior of heat also can be applied to order and therefore to information. The word *entropy* refers to diffuse heat, disorder, or lack of information. Another form of the second law of thermodynamics is that in a closed system, entropy always increases.

Laws of Current Electricity

Key terms   When electrons flow in a conductor, the result is electric current. The amount of current is based on an amount of electric charge called the *coulomb*, which is the charge of about 6.25 quintillion (6.25 x 10^{18}) electrons. When 1 coulomb of charge moves past a point in 1 second, it creates a current of 1 ampere. Just as a stream can carry the same amount of water swiftly through a narrow channel or slowly through a broad channel, the energy of an electric current varies depending on the difference in charge between places along the conductor. This is called *potential difference* and is measured in volts. The voltage is affected by the nature of the conductors. Some substances conduct an electric current much more easily than others. This resistance to the current is measured in ohms. *Electric power* is the rate at which electricity is used.

Ohm's law   *Electric current is directly proportional to the potential difference and inversely proportional to resistance*. If you measure current, I, in amperes, potential difference, V, in volts, and resistance, R, in ohms, then the current is equal to the potential difference divided by the resistance.

$$I = \frac{V}{R}$$

Law of electric power   If electric power, P, is measured in watts, then the power is equal to the product of the current measured in amperes and the potential difference measured in volts.

$$P = IV$$

Laws of Light and Electromagnetic Radiation

Key terms   Light is a part of a general form of radiation known as *electromagnetic waves*, or, when thought of as particles, *photons*. Here, electromagnetic radiation is considered as a wave phenomenon for the most part. The velocity of a wave is how fast the wave travels as a whole. The *wavelength* is the distance between one crest of the wave and the next crest. The *frequency* is how many crests pass a particular location in a unit of time. One crest passing each second is called a hertz.

Law of electromagnetic energy   The energy of an electromagnetic wave depends on a small number known as Planck's constant. Measured in joules per hertz (energy per frequency), Planck's constant is 6.67259 x 10^{-34}. *The energy is equal to the product of Planck's constant and the* *frequency.* Using E for energy, h for Planck's constant, and f for frequency,

$$E = hf$$

When thought of in terms of the particles called photons, the energy of a photon obeys the same law. The law of wave motion and the law of electromagnetic energy can be combined with the speed of light in a vacuum (c) to give

$$E = \frac{hc}{l}$$

The energy of a photon is the product of Planck's constant and the speed of light, divided by the wavelength (l) of the photon.

Inverse-square law
All radiation obeys an inverse-square law, which is similar to the law of gravity. *The intensity of the radiation decreases as the inverse of the square of the distance from a point source of radiation.*

Two Basic Laws of Quantum Physics
When one considers effects on very small masses and at very small distances, it is necessary to recognize that objects behave differently from their action at sizes and distances one can observe directly. Since these effects occur in discrete steps based upon Planck's constant times the frequency, called the quantum—which is the size by which energy changes in steps (instead of continuously)—the science of such effects is called quantum physics. Small masses act sometimes like particles and sometimes like waves. Two laws in particular that describe the behavior of small masses are basic and easily stated.

Heisenberg's uncertainty principle
It is impossible to specify completely the position and momentum of a particle, such as an electron, at the same time.

Pauli's exclusion principle
Two particles of matter cannot be in the same exact state. Particles of matter include the electron, neutron, and proton. Bosons, particles of force, do not obey Pauli's exclusion principle. (See "Subatomic Particles").

▶ SUBATOMIC PARTICLES
The idea of an atom goes back to the ancient Greek philosophers, who thought that matter was composed of tiny indivisible particles. The concept was put on a scientific basis by John Dalton (English: 1766–1844) in 1803 and became the foundation of chemistry. Nearly a hundred years later, experiments by J.J. Thomson (English: 1856–1940) in 1899 were the first to show that atoms are not indivisible after all. In the past hundred years, physics at almost all levels has been completely revolutionized by the study of the particles that make up atoms or that are smaller than atoms. In the last decades of the 20th century physicists developed the standard model of elementary particles. This model incorporates three of the four fundamental forces in nature, the strong and weak nuclear forces and electromagnetic forces (the other force is gravity). In the model, bosons mediate the forces: gluons, for the strong nuclear force; the photon for electromagnetism, and W and Z particles for the weak nuclear force. Within this model, the weak and electromagnetic forces have been combined into electroweak theory. The standard model has thus far met all experimental challenges, but it has some gaps in addition to the omission of gravity:

in particular, the strong and electroweak forces are not completely unified. Theories that attempt to unify the strong and electroweak forces are called Grand Unified Theories (GUTs). Beyond Grand Unified Theories, a great challenge for physicists is a Theory of Everything (TOE) that would account for all of the fundamental forces in nature. Below is a list of all the most important subatomic particles given in the chronological order of their discovery.

1897 Electron   The first subatomic particle to be identified, also by J.J. Thomson, was the electron, a low-mass particle that can be found in the outer reaches of the atom. One property of the electron is charge, the response to electric or magnetic fields. The charge of a single electron is always the same, which is identified as –1 (negative one). Each atom consists of a cloud of electrons around a center of positive charge, which is called the nucleus.

1905 Photon   The photon is the particle that carries the electromagnetic force. This concept began with Albert Einstein (German-American: 1879–1955) in 1905, when he established that light acts sometimes as a particle instead of as waves. Although we usually think of the photon as the particle of light, it is also the particle form of radio waves, X-rays, or gamma rays. The mass of the photon is 0.

1911 Proton   At least one proton is always found in the nucleus of every atom. The proton has a charge that is the same in size as that of the electron, but responds in the opposite direction to an electric or magnetic field. This charge is +1 (positive one). Each proton is almost 2,000 times as heavy as an electron, or about the same as the mass of a single hydrogen atom.

1924 Bosons   While matter is made from subatomic particles, the forces that act on matter are also produced by subatomic particles. The particles that create these forces are collectively called bosons because the mathematics of the behavior of this type of particle was worked out originally by Satyendranath Bose (Indian: 1894–1974) in 1924, although put into final form by Einstein. The observed bosons are the photon, pions, gluons, W particles, and Z particles. Bosons that are predicted, but that have not been observed, include the Higgs particle and the graviton.

1925–26 Quantum Mechanics   The basic theory of subatomic particles, called quantum mechanics, was developed in two different forms, in 1925 by Werner Heisenberg (German: 1901–76) and in 1926 by Erwin Schrödinger (Austrian: 1887–1961). Although the two forms appear very different, they produce the same results.

1926 Fermions   All the particles that make up matter are called fermions, as opposed to the bosons that create forces. The fermions include all the leptons and quarks as well as the particles made from quarks (see below). Fermions are named for Enrico Fermi (Italian-American: 1901–54), who first worked out the mathematics of their interactions in 1926. Fermions all obey the *Pauli exclusion principle* (see the section on *Basic Laws of Physics*, earlier in this chapter), which means that they occupy a definite space. Two fermions cannot be in the same place at the same time.

1930 Antiparticles   When Paul A.M. Dirac (English-American: 1902–84) completed his mathematical version of the theory of the electron in 1930, he observed that one solution to his equations predicted a particle that would be a mirror image of the electron, exactly the same as the electron but with a positive charge instead of negative. The particle, discovered two years later in 1932, was named the positron. The same equations predicted mirror images for all subatomic particles. These particles are called the antiparticles, so another name for positron is antielectron.

1932 Neutron The neutron is very much like a neutral proton, with just slightly more mass. Neutrons are stable when they are found in atoms, but decay into other particles when left to themselves.

1935 Muon The muon is now recognized as a high energy analog to the electron with a mass about 200 times that of the electron.

1947 Pion A pion carries the strong force that holds the nucleus of atoms together, but since each pion appears and disappears almost instantly, the pions are not usually counted as part of the nucleus. (Predicted in 1935.) In the same year that the pion was found, theoreticians were able to work out a comprehensive theory of the electron, called quantum electrodynamics (QED).

1950 Strange particles Starting in 1950 experimenters observed a number of previously undetected particles that did not behave as particles were expected to do. Because these particles have masses greater than that of the proton and neutron, they were called hyperons. Other unexpected particles, about the size of the pion, were classed as mesons. A classification scheme for the hyperons developed in 1961 helped physicists understand them better, but their essential difference was already labeled "strangeness."

1955 Neutrinos Neutrinos are thought to be among the most common particles in the universe, but they interact with ordinary matter so weakly that they are very difficult to observe. Predicted in 1930, neutrinos were thought to have no rest mass, but Canadian experiments in 2001 indicate that they have a very small mass equal to less than about 10^{-7} of the mass of an electron. Different neutrinos are associated with electrons, muons, and tauons.

1964–95 Quarks Murray Gell-Mann (American: 1928–) and several other physicists determined that a way to explain the properties of protons, neutrons, mesons, and hyperons, is to think of the heavy particles as made from combinations of light ones, just as the atom is made from combinations of electrons, protons, and neutrons. The smaller particles are quarks; there are six of them in all. Two quarks, known as up and down, form protons and neutrons. The top quark is the most massive—about as heavy as an atom of gold—and the last to be detected. (First version of theory in 1964, evidence for top quark in 1995.)

1965–73 Gluons The eight different bosons that produce a force between quarks known as the color force are called gluons. The color force is also the basis of the strong force that holds the nucleus together. Because of the color force, the study of quarks and gluons is today called quantum chromodynamics (QCD).

1974 J/psi particle Like the strange hyperons, the J/psi particle is a heavy particle that appears at high energies. It also is produced by a different kind of quark, the charm quark. The odd name J/psi comes from the particle having been discovered independently by two investigators, one of whom called it J and the other of whom named it psi.

1983 W and Z particles The particles that produce the weak force are called W and Z. At high energies, however, the weak force merges with the electromagnetic force, so the W and Z are to some extent analogs to the photon, although they could not be more different, since the photon has a 0 rest mass and both W particles and the single Z particle are very massive.

1995 Antiatoms Since antiparticles have all the properties of ordinary particles except for being mirror images, it is possible to create an antiatom by combining subatomic antiparticles. This was accomplished in 1995 with the production of a few antiatoms of antihydrogen made by causing an antielectron (positron) to orbit an antiproton.

(Not yet observed) Graviton and Higgs particle A particle that produces gravitational force by its exchange between all kinds of particles is known as the graviton, but so far it is only known in theory. The Laser Interferometer Gravitational Wave Observatory (LIGO) that began operations in 2000 seeks to observe gravity waves, the wave version of the graviton. The Higgs particle is the main undetected particle of the standard model of subatomic particles. Physicists believe that the Higgs, named after English physicist Peter Higgs who predicted it in 1964, confers mass to all other particles.

LIFE SCIENCES

While the scientific study of living creatures seems to have begun with Aristotle, there was considerable practical experimentation with living things much earlier, going back to the domestication of a species, the dog, perhaps as early as 14,000 B.C. In the years that followed the Scientific Revolution of the 17th century, the science of biology came to include most of the then-known life sciences: zoology (the study of animals), botany (the study of plants), and taxonomy (the classification of living things). In the 19th century, biology began to fragment into other studies: microbiology (the study of creatures visible only through the microscope), genetics (the study of how traits are inherited), biochemistry (the study of molecules in living things), and so forth. At the same time, different ways of studying living organisms were developed, among them anthropology (the study of human beings), ecology (the study of interactions between different living things and their environment), and ethology (the study of animal behavior).

▶ MAJOR GROUPS OF LIVING ORGANISMS

Biologists classify all living things (organisms) according to a system first introduced by Carolus Linnaeus in 1735. At that time Linnaeus and other scientists divided all life forms into two kingdoms: plants and animals. Since then, biologists have learned that there are fundamental differences among organisms that go beyond the differences between plants and animals and have added four kingdoms. The six kingdoms commonly recognized today are: Monera, Archaea, Protists, Fungi, Plants, and Animals.

Following Linnaeus, all classification terms are usually given in Latin. In the following list, English terms are substituted when they are an exact translation—for example, animals instead of Animalia and birds instead of Aves. If there is no exact translation, the Latin form is kept.

Each kingdom is divided into two or more phyla (singular: phylum). Organisms within one phylum are more closely related to one another than to members of other phyla.

The phyla are also divided into parts, which are then further divided, each time on the basis of closer and closer relationships. In descending order of size, the main divisions are as follows:

Kingdom
    Phylum
        Class
            Order
                Family
                    Genus
                        Species

Many biologists add to this list by classifying groups of species with sub- or super-, as in subphylum or superfamily.

By convention, Latin names except for genus and species are given in Roman type; genus and species are italicized.

Kingdom: Monera   One-celled organisms with simple cells that lack a membrane around the genetic material. Bacteria do not produce their own food; blue-green algae do.
Phylum: Bacteria (also called Eubacteria)
Phylum: Blue-green algae, also called blue-green bacteria or cyanobacteria

Kingdom: Archaea   One-celled organisms, sometimes called Archaeobacteria, that are genetically more like the other kingdoms than they are like the Monera. The Archaea were first discovered as creatures living in hot springs and other high-temperature situations. They were later observed among the one-celled creatures that metabolize chemicals such as methane or sulfur instead of using oxygen. They also have been found in great abundance in the oceans and deep in the Earth's crust.

Kingdom: Protists   One-celled or colonial; complex cells that have a membrane around their genetic material; protozoans and slime molds do not produce their own food; all other phyla in this kingdom can.

Kingdom: Fungi   One-celled or multicelled; cells have nuclei, which stream between cells, giving the appearance that cells have many nuclei; fungi do not produce their own food.
Phylum: Zygomycetes (e.g., black bread mold)
Phylum: Ascomycetes (includes Penicillium, truffles, yeasts)
Phylum: Basidiomycetes (includes mushrooms)

Kingdom: Plants   Multicellular organisms that carry out photosynthesis; cells have nuclei and cell walls.
Phylum: Mosses and liverworts
Phylum: Club mosses
Phylum: Horsetails
Phylum: Ferns
Phylum: Conifers
Phylum: Cone-bearing desert plants
Phylum: Cycads
Phylum: The ginkgo
Phylum: Flowering plants
  Subphylum: Dicots (plants with two seed leaves—e.g., most fruits and vegetables, common flowers, and trees)
  Subphylum: Monocots (plants with a single seed leaf—e.g., onions, lilies, and grasses)

Kingdom: Animals   Multicellular organisms that get their food by ingestion; most are able to move from place to place; cells have nuclei but not cell walls.
Phylum: Porifera (sponges)
Phylum: Cnidaria (jellyfish, anemones, corals)
Phylum: Platyhelminthes (flatworms)
Phylum: Nematodes (roundworms)
Phylum: Rotifers (microscopic wormlike or spherical animals)
Phylum: Bryozoa (moss animals)
Phylum: Brachiopods (lampshells)
Phylum: Phoronida (tube worms)
Phylum: Annelids (segmented worms, such as earthworms, leeches)
Phylum: Mollusks (soft-bodied animals with a mantle and foot)
  Class: Chitons
  Class: Bivalves (clams, oysters, mussels)
  Class: Scaphopoda (tooth or tusk shells)
  Class: Gastropods (slugs and snails)
  Class: Cephalopods (octopus, squid)
Phylum: Arthropods (segmented animals with an external skeleton)
  Class: Horseshoe crabs
  Class: Crustaceans (lobsters, crabs, shrimp)
  Class: Arachnids (scorpions, spiders, mites, ticks)
  Class: Insects
  Class: Millipedes and centipedes
Phylum: Cycliophora (known only as a tiny species growing in the mouths of lobsters)
Phylum: Echinoderms (starfish, brittle stars)
Phylum: Hemichordata (acorn worms)
Phylum: Chordates
  Subphylum: Tunicates
  Subphylum: Lancelets
  Subphylum: Vertebrates (animals with backbones)
  Class: Agnatha (lampreys, hagfish)
  Class: Sharks and rays
  Class: Bony fish
  Class: Amphibians
  Class: Reptiles
  Class: Birds
  Class: Mammals
    Subclass: Monotremes (egg-laying mammals)
    Subclass: Marsupials
    Subclass: Placentals
    Order: Insectivores (shrews, moles, hedgehogs)
    Order: Flying lemurs
    Order: Bats
    Order: Primates (lemurs, monkeys, apes, humans)
    Order: Edentates (anteaters, sloths, armadillos)
    Order: Pangolins
    Order: Lagomorphs (rabbits, hares)
    Order: Rodents (squirrels, rats, mice, porcupines)
    Order: Cetaceans (whales, dolphins)
    Order: Carnivores (wolves, cats, bears, raccoons, weasels, badgers, skunks, otters, hyenas)
    Order: Seals
    Order: The aardvark
    Order: Elephants
    Order: Hyraxes
    Order: Sirenians (dugongs, manatees)
    Order: Odd-toed ungulates (horses, tapirs, rhinoceroses)
    Order: Even-toed ungulates (pigs, hippopotamuses, camels, deer, giraffes, pronghorns, cattle, goats, sheep)

►CLASSIFYING HUMANS

KINGDOM: Animals Organisms that use other organisms for food and that sometimes move rapidly.

PHYLUM: Chordates Animals that are partially supported by a rod of cartilage or bone vertebrae and an internal skeleton.

SUBPHYLUM: Vertebrates Chordates that have vertebrae, such as fish, amphibians, reptiles, birds, and mammals.

CLASS: Mammals Vertebrates that have hair and suckle their young.

ORDER: Primates Mammals that use sight more than scent, have nails instead of claws on grasping hands and feet, are mostly active in daylight, and have relatively large brains.

SUPERFAMILY: Hominoids Primates that are tailless, generally large in size, can climb trees, and have relatively flat faces, such as *Sahelanthropus, Ardipithecus, Kenyapithecus,* australopithecines, and human beings.

FAMILY: Hominids Hominoids that walk upright, have small canines, and large brains; specifically, the australopithecines and human beings.

GENUS: *Homo* Hominids, with especially large brains, that speak and show other signs of culture; specifically, *Homo habilis, Homo erectus* and related species, and *Homo sapiens.*

SPECIES: *Homo sapiens* Modern human beings.

►THE HUMAN GENOME PROJECT

On June 25, 2000, President Clinton, British Prime Minister Tony Blair, and Craig Venter of Celera Genomics jointly announced the completion of decoding all the bases that make up the genes in a human. Many assumed it meant that the Human Genome Project had succeeded in deciphering all human genes. In 2003, however, scientists from the International Human Genome Sequencing Consortium and from Celera completed the original goals of the Human Genome Project: to identify all the approximately 20,000–25,000 genes in human DNA, and to determine the sequence of the three billion base pairs that make up human DNA.

Every organism is almost completely described by its own genes, combinations of triplets of four chemical building blocks, called bases, carried on long molecules of a chemical named deoxyribonucleic acid (DNA). Several different DNA molecules are found in every cell. Most human cells have 46 such molecules as the working parts of the chromosomes and additional DNA in small, energy-producing bodies called mitochondria. The total group of all the DNA for an organism is called its genome. The DNA bases are usually known by their abbreviations, T, G, C, and A.

The National Center for Human Genome Research was instituted on January 3, 1989, and with the participation of both the U.S. Department of Energy and National Institutes for Health, became the Human Genome Project in 1990. Scientists from the European Union, Japan and China also participate, forming together the International Human Genome Sequencing Consortium. Another group has developed out of this effort that plans to concentrate on the genomes of disease-causing organisms, primarily bacteria.

Along the way, the genomes of organisms other than human have been sequenced. Celera achieved the first, the small bacterium *Haemophilus influenzae*, in 1995. Since then, bacteria that cause syphilis, chlamydia, tuberculosis, cholera and staph infections, among many others, have had their genomes sequenced. The small genomes of several viruses have also been sequenced, and the much larger genomes of three higher organisms have been completed as well—baker's yeast, the roundworm, and the fruit fly.

Scientists then targeted commonly used experimental organisms. Teams from the U.S. and Britain completed the genome of the first animal, *Caenorhabditis elegans,* a nematode worm, at the end of 1998. Celera concentrated on the fruit fly, *Drosophila melanogaster,* and established its sequence of 1.8 billion bases by September 9, 1999. In plants, the first success came at the end of 2000 with the mustard *Arabidopsis thaliana,* the common laboratory plant for botanists. In October, 2001, sequencing of the genome of the Japanese puffer fish was finished, the first fish. Scientists have proceeded to sequence the genomes of common laboratory animals, such as the mouse, rat, and chimpanzee, as well as the genomes of species important in agriculture, such as rice and the honeybee. By 2009, the number of species sequenced had reached nearly 200. Mammals chosen for sequencing in the next few years are intended to reflect genetic diversity: an elephant, the domestic cat, a rabbit, the hedgehog, the guinea pig, the common shrew, an armadillo, and a tenrec, the last a hedgehog-like creature from Madagascar, which may be more closely related to elephants than to European hedgehogs.

During 2009 and 2010 there was a pointed shift toward the commercialization of genetics with a dramatic increase in the number of companies offering personal genome sequencing services, with prices ranging from $100 per genome up to $30,000 for a full genome sequence.

►THE FOSSIL RECORD

Much of what we know about the history of life on Earth is because of *fossils,* the remains or imprints of organisms preserved in layers of sedimentary rock. A preserved remnant of an organism is deemed a fossil if it dates back to roughly 10,000 years ago, and the totality of these is known as the *fossil record.* Fossils can range in size from a mere singular-cell imprint in a rock to full hominid skeletons. In addition to being supportive (though not integral) evidence for evolution, fossils also show us how major crises, like mass extinctions, occurred and how life recovered.

The major constituents of the fossil record for the first 3.5 billion years of life on Earth are *stromatolites,* layered deposits of mostly limestone formed by the growth of algae. Fossils older than 70,000 years, like these, cannot be dated by carbon-14 dating (the most common method used by archaeologists) and are instead pinpointed in history through radiometric dating, which can be employed for fossils up to 48.6 billion years. Evidence in the fossil record has convinced most scientists that the age of the Earth is 4.6 billion years.

Interpretation of the fossil record has been underway since well before modern times. Aristotle noted that seashells preserved in rocks were similar to living animals, and Persian doctor and geologist Avicenna attempted to explain "stoniness of fossils" in *The Book of Healing* in 1027. The discovery of new fossils unlocks mysteries pertaining to evolution. In 2010 fossils were discovered in Gabon, Africa, that revealed a multicellular organism dating back to 2.1 billion years ago, the earliest on record, and seemingly every year another fossil is found that illustrates the evolution of the human story. (See "The Human Family Tree.")

Major Discoveries in Life Sciences

B.C.

c.9000 Agricultural Revolution starts in Near East with domestication of sheep and goats in Persia (Iran) and Afghanistan and of pigs in Anatolia (Turkey); and cultivation of wheat in Canaan (Israel and Jordan).

c.8000 Agricultural Revolution starts independently in what are now Peru, Central America, and Indochina.

c.350 Aristotle (Greek: 384–322 B.C.) classifies known animals in system that will continue to be used until 1735.

A.D.

1648 Jan Baptista van Helmont (Flemish: 1580–1644) shows that plants do not obtain large amounts of material for their growth from soil.

1665 Robert Hooke (English: 1635–1703) observes and names the cell.

1668 Francesco Redi (Italian: 1626–97) shows that maggots in meat do not arise spontaneously but are hatched from flies' eggs.

1669 Anton van Leeuwenhoek (Dutch: 1632–1723) discovers microorganisms—creatures too small to see with naked eye—and recognizes that sperm are part of reproduction.

1683 Leeuwenhoek is first to observe bacteria.

1735 Carolus Linnaeus (Carl Linné; Swedish: 1707–78) introduces system in use today for classifying plants and animals.

1779 Jan Ingenhousz (Dutch: 1730–99) discovers that plants release oxygen when exposed to sunlight and they consume carbon dioxide; this is first step in understanding photosynthesis.

1839 Theodor A.H. Schwann (German: 1810–82), building on work of Matthias Jakob Schleiden (German: 1804–81) in 1838, develops cell theory of life.

1856 First skeleton of what we now call Neandertals is found in cave in Neander Valley, near Düsseldorf (Germany).

Louis Pasteur (French: 1822–95) discovers that fermentation is caused by microorganisms.

1858 Charles R. Darwin (English: 1809–82) and Alfred R. Wallace (English: 1823–1913) announce their theory of evolution by natural selection to the Linnean Society.

1859 Darwin publishes *On the Origin of Species*.

1865 Gregor Johann Mendel's (Austrian: 1822–84) theory of dominant and recessive genes is published in obscure local journal.

1868 Workers building road in France discover skeletons of first-known Cro-Magnons in cave.

1894 Eugène Dubois (Dutch: 1858–1940) announces discovery of "Java ape-man," now known to be first specimen of *Homo erectus*.

1898 Mosaic disease of tobacco plants is recognized as being caused by virus, the first identification of a virus.

1900 Three different biologists rediscover laws of genetics originally found by Mendel.

1924 Raymond A. Dart (Australian-South African: 1893–1988) identifies first fossil of an australopithecine, a close relative of early humans.

1953 James D. Watson (American: 1928–) and Francis Crick (English: 1916–) determine structure of DNA, the basis of heredity.

1961 Louis S.B. Leakey (English: 1903–72) and Mary D. Leakey (English: 1913–96) discover a previously unknown ancestor of humans, *Homo habilis*, in the Olduvai Gorge of northern Tanzania.

Marshall W. Nirenberg (American: 1927–) learns to read one of the "letters" of genetic code.

1973 Stanley Cohen (American: 1922–) and Herbert Boyer (American: 1936–) put specific gene into bacterium, the first instance of true genetic engineering.

1974 Donald C. Johanson (American: 1943–) and coworkers discover Lucy in Afar region of Ethiopia, the nearly complete skeleton—but not the skull—of *Australopithecus afarensis*, an early relative of humans (more than 3 million years old).

1995 César Milstein (Argentine-English: 1927–) announces discovery of how to produce monoclonal antibodies, highly specific chemicals that can be made to react with particular proteins or other chemicals in the body.

1980 Martin Cline (American: 1934–) and coworkers succeed in transferring functioning gene from one mouse to another.

1983 Kary B. Mullis (American: 1945–) invents the use of the polymerase chain reaction to make copies of DNA sequences, a vital tool in finding specific genes.

1988 The complete developmental history of every cell in the nematode *Caenorhabditis elegans* published.

1994 Gen Suwa (Japanese), discovers the first fossil of *Ardipithecus ramidus*, the oldest known hominid, in Ethiopia.

1995 Craig Venter (American: 1946–) of the Institute for Genomic Research publishes the complete base sequences for all the genes of a free-living organism, the bacterium *Haemophilus influenzae*.

1997 Ian Wilmut (English: 1944–) succeeds in cloning a sheep from a cell from an adult ewe.

Svante Pääbo of the University of Munich, Germany, and coworkers clone DNA from the first discovered Neandertal fossil and compare the DNA to that of modern humans. They conclude that the Neandertal is a different species from our own.

1998 Elizabeth Gould and co-workers at Princeton University demonstrate that adult monkeys continue to grow new brain cells, a feat previously thought impossible for adult primates.

1999 Berhane Asfaw (Ethiopian: 1954-) and coworkers announce the discovery in Ethiopia of fossils of a new hominid species, *Australopithecus garhi* ("surprising southern ape").

2000 Tools are found at a Cactus Hill site in Virginia from 15,000 years ago, tending to disprove the theory that early Americans reached the continent through Alaska about 12,000 years ago.

The Human Genome Project and Celera Genomics announce jointly that they have developed a rough draft of the entire human genetic sequence.

2001 Meave G. Leakey (English-Kenyan: 1942-) of the National Museums of Kenya in Nairobi discovers the skull of a 3.5-million-year-old human ancestor, which she names *Kenyanthropus platyops* ("flat-faced man from Kenya").

2002 For the first time in 87 years, a new order of insects is recognized (similar to Lepidoptera for butterflies and moths). Mantophasmatodea includes two genera and three species, popularly named gladiators, each somewhat like a cross between a mantis and a grasshopper.

Michel Brunet and Martin Pickford discover in Chad the oldest hominid fossil found so far, the skull of *Sahelanthropus tchadensis*, who lived 6 to 7 million years ago in a setting of woods broken with patches of savanna.

2003 Tim White and coworkers in Ethiopia announce they have found skulls of the earliest modern humans known, dating from between 154,000 and 160,000 years ago, which they term the subspecies *H. sapiens idaltu* ("elder wise man").

2004 Teams led by Peter Brown and Michael J. Morwood discover a new species of human, *Homo floresiensis*, which lived on Flores Island (Indonesia) from at least 36,000 B.C. until 10,000 B.C, making it contemporary with modern *H. sapiens*. It appears to be a dwarfed form of *H. erectus*, reduced in size by its island habitat. Scientists nicknamed the species "the hobbit," after the small creatures in *The Lord of the Rings*. Hobbits are thought to have preyed on the small elephants. This claim has been called into question recently.

2010 J. Craig Venter Institute successfully creates the first self-replicating synthetic bacteria cell, the largest piece of DNA synthesized to date

The Human Family Tree

EVOLUTION OF THE HUMAN FAMILY

New fossil finds since the start of 2000 have extended our knowledge of the ancestry of humans deep into the past. Anthropologists continue to argue as to the meaning of specific fossils; and new tools, such as DNA analysis, provide another framework for primate evolution. Several indicators now point to the first primate developing some 85 million years ago, long before the first fossil identified as a primate. The higher primates (monkeys, apes and humans), long thought to have evolved in Africa, may instead have split from the tarsier group in Asia.

Eosimis *c. 45 million years ago. Central and eastern China.* Evidence from fossils announced in 2000 strongly suggests that *Eosimis*, a small creature thought previously to be a tarsier, walked on all fours on tops of branches as monkeys do, which implies that it was a higher primate, the earliest known.

Catopithecus *c. 40 million years ago. Egypt.* For those anthropologists who think higher primates arose in Africa and that *Eosimis* is a tarsier ancestor, *Catopithecus* is the earliest representative of the higher primates.

Aegyptopithecus *c. 35 million years ago. Egypt.* A small, monkey-like, fruit-eating creature about the size of a house cat, *Aegyptopithecus* is sometimes called the "dawn ape" and may be the earliest known ancestor of the hominoids.

Afropithecus and Proconsul *c. 15 to 20 million years ago. East Africa.* Several different early apes lived in Africa and Asia about this time. Opinion is divided on whether *Afropithecus* or *Proconsul* is the ancestor to the hominids.

Sahelanthropus tchadensis *c. 6 to 7 million years ago. Chad.* Discovered in 2001, this is the earliest known hominid, combining a flat human-looking face with a brain the size of a chimpanzee's. It lived in a mixed region of woods and savanna near a large lake.

Orrorin tugenensis *c. 6 million years ago. Kenya (Tugen Hills).* Twelve fossils, including fragments of limb bone and jawbones, were found in 2000. The name means "original man of Tugen," for the discoverers claim that this is the ancestor to the human line.

Ardipithecus ramidus kadabba *c. 5.5 million year ago. Ethiopia (Middle Awash River Valley).* Announced in 2001, these fossils include a jawbone with teeth, hand and foot bones, and fragments of other bones. The team was led by Ethiopians Yohannes Haile-Selassie and Giday WoldeGabriel. The discoverers label this as a subspecies of *Ardipithecus* (see below), but are not sure whether *Ardipithecus* is ancestral to australopithecines and humans or to chimpanzees.

Ardipithecus ramidus *c. 4.4 million years ago. Ethiopia.* Discovered in 1994 at Aramis, Ethiopia, *A. ramidus* lived in woodlands with patches of savanna, rather than in the true savanna, previously thought to have been the home of ancestors to humans.

Australopithecus anamensis *c. 4.2 to 3.9 million years ago. Northern Kenya (Lake Turkana region)* These fossils, discovered in 1993 by Meave G. Leakey and Alan Walker, indicate that *A. anamensis* could walk upright on two legs.

Kenyapithecus platyops *c. 3.5 to 3.3 million years ago. Kenya.* Skull found in 2001 identified as a new genus. Leakey also thinks that some fossils previously identified as *Homo rudolfensis* may belong to *Kenyapithecus* genus.

Australopithecus afarensis *"Lucy" and "The First Family" c. 3.6 to 2.9 million years ago. Ethiopia and East Africa.* Many think *A. afarensis* is on the direct line to modern humans. A trail of footprints in volcanic ash at Laetoli, Tanzania, made by *A. afarensis* demonstrates that it walked upright.

Australopithecus africanus. *c. 3 to 2 million years ago. South Africa* First nonhuman hominid to be discovered, in 1924, although few anthropologists accepted it until the 1950's. Walked upright and, while large brained for a primate, had a brain that was much smaller than early *Homo* species. Thought to be on direct line to *Homo*.

Paranthropus (Australopithecus) aethiopicus *c. 2.7 to 2.3 million years ago. East Africa.* Thought to be the link between *A. africanus* and three "robust" species that many assign to the genus *Paranthropus* while others consider them australopithecines.

Australopithecus garhi *c. 2.5 million years ago. Ethiopia.* Fossils are found at same site as butchered animals and primitive stone tools, raising possibility that australopithecines used tools found at various early sites.

Australopithecus sediba *c 1.95 to 1.78 million years ago. South Africa.* Discovered in 2008 by a nine year old boy, *A. sediba* was originally thought to be a transitional species between *A. africanus* and *H. habilis*. Many scientists now believe *A. sediba* is a late southern African branch of Australopithecus, co-existing with members of the Homo genus.

Homo habilis *c. 2.5 to 1.5 million years ago. Tanzania and South Africa—possibly Central Eurasia (Georgia).* Earliest known species of our own genus. *H. habilis* ("Handy Man") named for tools found at sites near fossil sites, although tools also could have been made by australopithecines whose contemporaneous fossils are also found nearby.

Homo rudolfensis *c. 2.4 to 1.5 million years ago. Kenya.* A different member of genus *Homo* that lived in the same general region at the same time as *H. habilis*.

Paranthropus (Australopithecus) robustus and P. bosei *c. 2.3 to 1.4 million years ago.* Although the *Paranthropus* line is now extinct, these robust hominids were successful contemporaries of *Homo* for about a million years.

Homo ergaster *c. 1.8 to 1.4 million years ago. Africa and Central Eurasia (Georgia).* Fossils once classed as African *H. erectus* are now often called *H. ergaster* ("Work Man"). Probable ancestor of *H. sapiens*.

Homo erectus *"Java Ape Man" and "Peking Man" c. 1.6 million to 40,000 years ago. Africa, Asia and Europe.* This maker of hand axes and user of fire has often been thought to be the immediate ancestor of *H. sapiens*, but the last groups of *H. erectus* ("Upright Man") were contemporaries to our species.

Homo heidelbergensis *c. 600,000 years ago to 120,000 years ago. Europe and North Africa.* Some early members of this group, perhaps those in Spain or North Africa sometimes called *Homo antecessor*, appear to be ancestor to the Neanderthals.

Homo neanderthalensis *c. 200,000 years ago to 30,000 years ago. Europe and the Near East.* This species was successful in the Ice Age, but became extinct shortly after *H. sapiens* spread across Europe. Although DNA studies indicate that *H. neanderthalis* and *H. sapiens* are different species, a few fossils have mixed characteristics that many think implies breeding across species lines.

Homo florsiensis *"the hobbit" c. 38,000 years ago to 12,000 years ago—perhaps until recent times. Flores Island, Indonesia.* At 3 feet tall, *H. florsiensis* was smaller than a modern pygmy, but made sophisticated stone tools and may have used fire.

Homo sapiens *c. 160,000 years ago to present. Worldwide.* The earliest, *H. sapiens idaltu* and other "archaic" humans, lived in Africa. DNA evidence suggests that about 100,000 years ago they spread into Asia and Europe. By 30,000 years ago they were the only remaining hominid (although some authorities include chimpanzees, and perhaps the gorilla, in the hominids).

Elements in a 150-Pound Person

Element/ Weight	Use by the body	Element/ Weight	Use by the body
Oxygen 97.5 lbs	Part of all major nutrients, which make up tissues of the body, but also vital to production of energy in the form of elemental oxygen obtained from air.	**Chlorine** 0.3 lbs	Used in form of chloride ions to transport messages from the body to cells; helps regulate electrical activity.
Carbon 27.0 lbs	Essential element for life—most compounds based on carbon are called organic, meaning "from life." An essential part of proteins, carbohydrates, and fats, the building blocks of human cells	**Sodium** 0.165 lbs	Required by vertebrates to control fluid pressure in cells.
		Magnesium 0.06 lbs	Required by both plants (it is in chlorophyll) and animals. In humans, works with enzymes to speed chemical reactions, is involved in transmission of messages between nerves, and has a role in bone structure.
Hydrogen 15.0 lbs	Part of each of major nutrients, and thus a building block of every cell. Unlike oxygen, has no part in respiration.		
Nitrogen 4.5 lbs	Essential part of proteins, DNA, and RNA, the compounds most active in controlling cells; most of the body's functions depend on nitrogen compounds at one stage or another.	**Iron** 0.006 lbs	Essential for carrying oxygen to cells and carbon dioxide waste away. Lack of iron causes anemia.
Calcium 3.0 lbs	Mostly locked into hard compounds that form nonliving parts of bone. One of principal messengers between cells, telling them when to act and when to stay quiet.	**Cobalt** 0.00024 lbs	Part of vitamin B12, found in meats and dairy products; its exact role in the body is not well understood.
		Copper 0.00023 lbs	Helps form red blood cells, maintain nervous system, and regulate cholesterol levels.
Phosphorus 1.8 lbs	Important element in bone building, but, like calcium, has another role: it is essential in producing energy in cell.	**Manganese** 0.00020 lbs	Aids in bone formation, helps regulate nervous system, and is part of sex hormones.
Potassium 0.3 lbs	Regulates contraction of muscle cells (and some other cell functions) along with sodium. Potassium is involved with muscle contractions and general maintenance of pressure a cell exerts on its covering membrane.	**Iodine** 0.00006 lbs	Part of thyroid hormone that controls rate at which food is burned for energy.
		Zinc trace	Needed for some enzymes, for proper sex development, in healing wounds, for sense of taste, and for normal sperm count.
Sulfur 0.3 lbs	Essential to most forms of life. An important constituent of proteins.	**Fluorine** trace	Strengthens teeth and bones.
		Chromium trace	Used in metabolism of sugar and the regulation of fats.
		Selenium trace	In small amounts, may reduce cell damage and promote growth.

Note: In addition, the body contains trace amounts of boron, aluminum, vanadium, molybdenum, and silicon. Their roles, however, are not fully understood.

MATHEMATICS

Strictly speaking, mathematics is not considered a science but a separate branch of learning on its own. Because the use of mathematics has been so important to science, however, it is generally treated along with sciences.

Mathematics consists of a set of abstract symbols and of rules for manipulating them, along with the results of that manipulation. Because of this, some have classified mathematics as a kind of language, while others view it as a kind of game. Many mathematicians believe there is a much deeper reality than those classifications, but it is one that is very difficult to explain. Even when mathematics is treated as a game, the results seem to be strongly connected to the real world.

The 20th century was an era of impressive progress in many fields of mathematics and statistics (see the discoveries listed in Milestones), and this progress continues today. Applied methods of statistical inference ("confidence intervals" and other techniques) based on the work of Sir R.A. Fisher (British, 1890–1962) and others have been highly developed and widely applied, through computer programs, in the sciences, engineering, and social sciences. There have also been dramatic advances in the ancient science of geometry, such as the development of fractal geometry (Benoit Mandelbrot, French-American, b. Poland, 1924–), in which patterns of smaller parts (such as a coastline seen very close up) relate in complex ways to the same coastline seen from a distance. Encryption methods have developed rapidly, spurred by the need to protect information sent by the Internet. An important class of such methods is based on the use of prime numbers (numbers divisible only by 1 and themselves). The largest prime identified as of August 2009 is $(2^{43,112,609})-1$, a number with more than 4 million digits. Another area in which important advances have been made is in computerizing numerical techniques for solving the equations in weather forecasting models, a use of mathematics that affects everyone's life. These and many other modern developments in mathematics and statistics mean that, while students today study some math that is thousands of years old—Greek geometry; and some that is hundreds of years old—the calculus of Leibniz and Newton; they also study, and their lives are affected by, up-to-date mathematical techniques embodied in powerful computational packages.

Milestones in the History of Mathematics

B.C.

c. 30,000 People in Europe begin using scratches or notches to record numbers.

c. 3500 Egyptians develop numeration system that can record very large numbers, with different symbols for ones, tens, hundreds, etc.

c. 2400 A numeration system based on place value (similar to Hindu-Arabic system) is introduced in Mesopotamia.

c. 2000 Mesopotamian mathematicians learn how to solve quadratic equations.

c. 1900 Mesopotamian mathematicians discover what we now call the Pythagorean theorem: The sum of the squares of the legs of a right triangle equals the square of the hypotenuse.

c. 470 Mathematician Hippasus of Metapontum (Greek: c. 500) discovers dodecahedron, a regular solid with 12 faces.

c. 450 Pythagoreans show that some lengths, such as the diagonal of a 1 x 1 square ($\sqrt{2}$), cannot be measured exactly using a side as a unit.

c. 300 Euclid's (Greek: c. 300) *Elements* shows that virtually all parts of mathematics known at the time can be proved from short list of assumptions.

c. 260 In Central America, Maya develop numeration system based on place value.

c. 250 Archimedes (Greek: c. 287–212) establishes important theorems about volumes of solids, calculates an excellent approximation of π, and develops a system for representing very large whole numbers.

c. 230 Apollonius of Perga (Greek: c. 262–190) writes *Conics*, an analysis of such curves as parabola, ellipse, and hyperbola.

A.D.

876 The first-known use of a symbol for zero as a number occurs in India.

c. 1100 Poet, mathematician, and astronomer Omar Khayyám (Persian: 1048-c. 1131) develops geometric methods for solving cubic equations.

1321 Levi ben Gershom (Gersonides; French: 1288–1344) is first to use mathematical induction.

c. 1515 Scipione del Ferro (Italian: 1465–1526) discovers algebraic method for solving one form of cubic equations.

1536 Niccolò Tartaglia (Italian: 1499–1557) solves two types of cubic equations.

1545 Girolamo Cardano's (Italian: 1501–76) *Ars Magna* contains Lodovico Ferrari's (Italian: 1522–65) complete solution of the quartic, and a complete solution of the cubic based on Tartaglia's work.

1572 Rafael Bombelli (Italian: 1526–c. 1573) uses complex numbers to solve equations.

1614 John Napier (Scottish: 1550–1617) describes logarithms.

1637 René Descartes (French: 1596–1650) publishes first account of analytic geometry; also discovered by Pierre de Fermat (French: 1601–65).

1639 Gérard Desargues (French: 1591–1661) introduces projective geometry.

1654 Blaise Pascal (French: 1623–62) and Pierre de Fermat develop basic laws of probability.

1666 Sir Isaac Newton (English: 1642–1727) describes his invention of the calculus but does not have it published at this time.

1684 Gottfried Wilhelm Leibniz (German: 1646–1716) publishes first account of his independent discovery of the calculus.

1799 Karl Friedrich Gauss (German: 1777–1855) proves fundamental theorem of algebra, which is that every polynomial equation has solution.

Paolo Ruffini (Italian: 1765–1822) offers first proof that not all polynomial equations of fifth degree can be solved by algebraic methods.

1826 Nikolai Ivanovich Lobachevski (Russian: 1793–1856) gives first public address concerning non-Euclidean geometry.

1877 Georg F.L.P. Cantor (German: 1845–1918) shows that number of points in a line segment is same as number in interior of a square.

1882 Ferdinand von Lindemann (German: 1852–1939) proves that the circle cannot be squared with straightedge and compass.

1892 Cantor proves there are at least two types of infinities—specifically, that infinity of real numbers (including all infinite decimals) is bigger than infinity of counting numbers (1, 2, 3, . . .).

1900 David Hilbert (German: 1862–1943) proposes his famous list of 23 unsolved problems.

1931 Kurt Gödel (Austrian-American: 1906–78) shows that mathematical systems are either incomplete or inconsistent: *incomplete* if not all true theorems can be proved from within the system, or *inconsistent* if two contradictory theorems can be proved.

1936 Independently, Alan M. Turing (English: 1912–54) and Alonzo Church (American: 1903–95) discover there is no infallible method for proving whether a mathematical statement is true or false.

1948 Claude E. Shannon (American: 1916–2001) publishes his work on information theory, a general approach to handling communications.

1976 In first major computer-assisted proof, it is shown that any map can be colored with four colors in such a way that no two regions of the same color share common border.

1995 Andrew Wiles (English-American: 1953–) publishes a corrected version of his 1993 proof that the equation $x^n + y^n = z^n$ has no solution for n greater than 2 when x, y, and z are counting numbers—known as Fermat's last theorem.

1998 Thomas C. Hales of the University of Michigan uses a computer to establish that Johannes Kepler's 1611 conjecture that stacking spheres in a face-centered cubic pattern results in the densest concentration of spheres.

2003 Daniel A. Goldston of San Jose (California) State University and Cem Y. Yildirim of Bogaziçi University in Istanbul prove that for any rational number greater than zero there are an infinite number of prime pairs closer to each other than that fraction of the average spacing of prime numbers.

Grigori (Grisha) Perelman of the Steklov Institute in St. Petersburg proves a generalization of the Poincaré conjecture, the oldest unproved conjecture in topology; it can be expressed as saying that the equivalent to a sphere—that is, the "skin" of a ball—in the four dimensions is the only three-dimensional figure that completely surrounds its inner space and has no holes.

2004 Ben Green of the University of British Columbia in Vancouver and Terence Tao of the University of California, Los Angeles, prove that there are an infinite number of arithmetic sequences of prime numbers for any specific finite length of terms. Arithmetic sequences are progressions with the same difference between terms, such as 5, 11, 17, 23, 29, in which the difference is 6; the length of this sequence for primes is 5 terms, since the next number in the sequence, 35, is not a prime.

2010 Researchers at the University of California, Santa Barbara and Princeton University found a way to control a single electron without disturbing other, nearby electrons, signifying a significant breakthrough in the worldwide pursuit of quantum computing.

▶COMMONLY USED MATHEMATICAL FORMULAS

Most formulas needed in solving everyday problems are collected below, with special emphasis on formulas relating to measurements, as these are used in everything from sewing to building a house. However, some important formulas from algebra, graphing, and trigonometry are at the end. Additional formulas can also be found in "Basic Laws of Physics."

General

The **distance** d, given the rate r and the time t:

$$d = rt$$

Length

The **perimeter (distance around) p of any polygon** (closed plane figure with straight sides that do not cross), given the lengths of the sides a, b, c, and so forth:

$$p = a + b + c + \ldots$$

Perimeter p of a rectangle, given the length l and the width w:

$$p = 2l + 2w$$

Perimeter p of a square, given the length of a side s:

$$p = 4s$$

Circumference (distance around) C of a circle, given the diameter d (distance across) or the radius r (distance from the center to the circle):

$$C = \pi d$$
$$\text{or } C = 2\pi r$$

The number π is an infinite decimal that begins $3.14159 \ldots$, which is often approximated as either 3.14 or as $\frac{22}{7}$.

Area

In each of the following, the area (amount of surface) is A. For three-dimensional figures, A is the total surface area.

Rectangle, given the length l and the width w:

$$A = lw.$$

Square, given the length of a side s:

$$A = s^2$$

Circle, given the radius r:

$$A = \pi r^2$$

Triangle, given the base b and the height h:

$$A = \tfrac{1}{2}bh$$

Right triangle, given the lengths a and b of the two sides (legs) that form the right angle:

$$A = \tfrac{1}{2}ab$$

Parallelogram, given the base b and the height h:

$$A = bh$$

Trapezoid, given the two bases B and b and the height h:

$$A = \tfrac{1}{2}h(B + b)$$

Kite, given the lengths of the two diagonals D and d:

$$A = \tfrac{1}{2}Dd$$

Regular polygon (polygon with all sides of equal length and all angles of equal measure), given the perimeter p and the apothem a (the distance from the center of the regular polygon to one of its sides):

$$A = \tfrac{1}{2}ap$$

Equilateral triangle (all sides the same length), given the length of a side s:

$$A = \frac{s^2\sqrt{3}}{4}$$

Heron's formula Any **triangle**, given half the length of the perimeter (the semiperimeter) s and the lengths of the sides a, b, and c:

$$A = \sqrt{s(s-a)(s-b)(s-c)}$$

Right circular cylinder (a cylinder with a circular region as its base whose sides make a right angle with the base), given the radius r of the base and the height h of the cylinder:

$$A = 2\pi r(h + r)$$

Right circular cone (a cone with a circular region as its base and whose altitude makes a right angle with the base), given the radius r of the base and the slant height l of the cone (the shortest distance from the tip of the cone to the circle of the base):

$$A = \pi r(l + r)$$

Sphere, given the radius r:

$$A = 4\pi r^2$$

Volume

In each of the following, the volume (space enclosed) is V.

Cube, given the length of an edge e:

$$V = e^3$$

Right rectangular prism (box), given the length l, the width w, and the height h:

$$V = lwh$$

Prism, given the area of the base B and the height h:

$$V = Bh$$

Right circular cylinder, given the radius r of the base and the height h:

$$V = \pi r^2 h$$

Right circular cone, given the radius r of the base and the height h:

$$V = \tfrac{1}{3}\pi r^2 h$$

Pyramid, given the area of the base B and the height h:

$$V = \tfrac{1}{3}Bh$$

Sphere, given the radius r:

$$V = \tfrac{4}{3}\pi r^3$$

Algebra

If a, b, and x are any numbers or variables ("unknowns"):

$$(a + b)^2 = a^2 + 2ab + b^2$$
$$(a - b)^2 = a^2 - 2ab + b^2$$
$$x^2 - a^2 = (x + a)(x - a)$$
$$x^3 - a^3 = (x - a)(x^2 + ax + a^2)$$
$$x^3 + a^3 = (x + a)(x^2 - ax + a^2)$$

If a, b, c, and d are any numbers or variables except that neither b nor d can be zero:

$$a/b + c/d = (ad + bc)/bd$$
$$a/b - c/d = (ad - bc)/bd$$
$$a/b \times c/d = ac/bd$$
$$a/b \div c/d = ad/bc \ (c \neq 0)$$

Large Numbers

There are two primary naming systems for large numbers. The United States and France (among others) use one system, while Germany and Great Britain use the other. (Googol and googolplex, invented by the nephew of mathematician and author Edward Kasner, are rarely used outside the United States.) (See also "Standard Weights and Measures").

Number of zeroes after 1	American name	British name
6	million	million
9	billion	milliard
12	trillion	billion
15	quadrillion	1,000 billion
18	quintillion	trillion
21	sextillion	1,000 trillion
24	septillion	quadrillion
27	octillion	1,000 quadrillion
30	nonillion	quintillion
33	decillion	1,000 quintillion
100	googol	googol
googol	googolplex	googolplex

Fractions, Decimals, and Percents

To find the equivalent of a fraction in decimal form, divide the numerator (top number) by the denominator (bottom number). To change from a decimal to a percent, multiply by 100. To change from a percent to a decimal, divide by 100.

Fraction	Decimal	Percent
1/16	0.0625	6.25%
1/8 (= 2/16)	0.125	12.5
3/16	0.1875	18.75
1/4 (= 2/8; = 4/16)	0.25	25.0
5/16	0.3125	31.25
1/3	0.3 . . .	33 1/3
3/8 (= 6/16)	0.375	37.5
7/16	0.4375	43.75
1/2 (= 2/4; = 4/8; = 8/16)	0.5	50.0
9/16	0.5625	56.25
5/8 (= 10/16)	0.625	62.5
2/3	0.6 . . .	66 2/3
11/16	0.6875	68.75
3/4 (= 6/8; = 12/16)	0.75	75.0
13/16	0.8125	81.25
7/8 (= 14/16)	0.875	87.5
15/16	0.9375	93.75

Prefixes Used in the International System of Units (SI)

Prefix	Abbreviation	Factor by which unit is multipled	Scientific Notation
Yotta-	Y	1,000,000,000,000,000,000,000,000	10^{24}
Zetta-	Z	1,000,000,000,000,000,000,000	10^{21}
Exa-	E	1,000,000,000,000,000,000	10^{18}
Peta-	P	1,000,000,000,000,000	10^{15}
Tera-	T	1,000,000,000,000	10^{12}
Giga-	G	1,000,000,000	10^{9}
Mega-	M	1,000,000	10^{6}
Kilo-	k	1,000	10^{3}
Hecto-	h	100	10^{2}
Deka-	da	10	10^{1}
Deci-	d	0.1	10^{-1}
Centi-	c	0.01	10^{-2}
Milli-	m	0.001	10^{-3}
Micro-	μ	0.000 001	10^{-6}
Nano-	n	0.000 000 001	10^{-9}
Pico-	p	0.000 000 000 001	10^{-12}
Femto-	f	0.000 000 000 000 001	10^{-15}
Atto-	a	0.000 000 000 000 000 001	10^{-18}
Zepto-	z	0.000 000 000 000 000 000 001	10^{-21}
Yocto-	y	0.000 000 000 000 000 000 000 001	10^{-24}

STANDARD WEIGHTS & MEASURES

▶ SYSTEMS OF MEASUREMENT

There are two widely used measurement systems. Most of the world uses a system known as the metric system, or the International System, abbreviated SI from *Système Internationale*, its name in French. The United States continues to use a system called U.S. customary measure, which derives from (and differs from) the British imperial series of weights and measures. From time to time, our government has taken steps to change from the customary system to the International System, but these efforts have had limited success. Metric measure is used in the United States, but nearly everyone continues to use the customary system in everyday use. The International System is generally used in scientific pursuits and increasingly in international trade.

The following tables show first the U.S. customary system, then the International System, and finally some important conversion factors between the two.

Length or Distance
U.S. customary system

1 foot (ft.)	=	12 inches
1 yard (yd.)	=	3 feet *or* 36 inches
1 rod (rd.)	=	5.5 yards *or* 16.5 feet
1 furlong (fur.)	=	40 rods *or* 220 yards
	or	660 feet
1 mile (mi.)	=	1,760 yards
	or	5,280 feet

An international nautical mile has been defined as 6,076.1155 feet.

International System

The basic unit for length is the meter, which is slightly longer than the customary yard. Other units of length are decimal subdivisions or multiples of the meter.

1 decimeter (dm)	=	10 centimeters
	or	0.1 meter
1 centimeter (cm)	=	0.01 meter
1 millimeter (mm)	=	0.1 centimeter
	or	0.001 meter
1 micrometer (μm)	=	0.001 millimeter
	or	0.0001 centimeter
	or	0.000001 meter
1 angstrom (Å)	=	0.0001 micrometers
	or	0.0000001 millimeter
1 dekameter (dam)	=	10 meters
1 hectometer (hm)	=	10 dekameters
	or	1 kilometer

Conversions

In 1959 the relationship between between customary and international measures of length was officially defined as follows:

0.0254 meter	=	1 inch
0.0245 meter x 12	=	0.3048 meter
	or	1 international foot

Following the international foot standard, the major equivalents are as listed below:

1 in.	=	2.54 cm *or* 0.0254 m
1 ft.	=	30.48 cm *or* .3048 m
1 yd.	=	91.44 cm *or* 0.9144 m
1 mi.	=	1,609.344 m
1 cm	=	0.3937 in.
1 m	=	1.093613 yd.
	or	3.28084 ft.
1 km	=	0.62137 mi.

Area
U.S. customary system
Areas are derived from lengths as follows:

1 square foot	=	144 square inches
1 square yard	=	9 sq. ft.
1 square rod (rd.^{2})	=	30.25 square yards
	or	272.25 square feet
1 acre	=	160 square rods
	or	4,840 square yards

Simplified Conversion Table (alphabetical order)

To convert	to	multiply by:
centimeters	feet	0.0328
centimeters	inches	0.3937
cubic cm	cubic in.	0.061
cubic feet	cubic m	0.0283
degrees	radians	0.0175
feet	cm	30.5
feet	meters	0.305
gallons	liters	3.785
gallon of water	pound of water	8.3
grams	ounces	0.035
inches	cm	2.54
kilograms	pounds	2.2
kilometers	feet	3,281.0
kilometers	miles	0.62
knots	mi./hr.	1.15
liters	gallons	0.264
liters	pints	2.1
meters	feet	3.28
miles	km	1.61
ounces	grams	28.35
pounds	kg	0.454

	or	43,560 sq. ft.
1 square mile	=	640 acres
1 section	=	1 mile square
1 township	=	6 miles square
	or	36 square miles

International System

1 sq. millimeter (mm^2)	=	1,000,000 sq. micrometers
1 sq. centimeter (cm^2)	=	100 mm^2
1 sq. decimeter (dm^2)	=	100 cm^2
1 sq. meter (m^2)	=	10,000 cm^2
1 acre (a)	=	100 m^2
1 hectare (ha)	=	100 ares
	or	10,000 m^2
1 sq kilometer (km^2)	=	100 hectares
	or	1,000,000 m^2

Conversions

1 square inch	=	6.4516 cm^2
1 square foot	=	929.0304 cm^2
	or	0.09290304 m^2
1 square yard	=	8,361.2736 cm^2
	or	0.83612736 m^2
1 acre	=	4,046.8564 m^2
	or	0.40468564 hectares
1 square mile	=	2,589,988.11 m^2
	or	258.998811 hectares
	or	2.58998811 km^2
1 cm^2	=	0.1550003 sq. in.
1 m^2	=	1,550.003 sq. in.
	or	10.76391 sq. ft.
	or	1.195990 sq. yds.
1 hectare	=	107,639.1 sq. ft.
	or	11,959.90 sq. yds.
	or	2.4710538 acres
1 km^2	=	247.10538 acres
	or	0.3861006 sq. miles

Cubic Measure
U.S. customary system

1 cubic foot (ft.^{3})	=	1,728 cubic in. (in.^{3})
1 cubic yard (yd.^{3})	=	27 cubic feet (ft.^{3})

International System

1 cubic centimeter (cm^3)	=	1,000 cubic millimeters (mm^3)
1 cubic decimeter (dm^3)	=	1,000 cubic centimeters (cm^3)
1 cubic meter (m^3)	=	1,000 cubic decimeters (dm^3)
	or	1,000,000 cubic centimeters (cm^3)

Cubic centimeter is sometimes abbreviated cc and is used in fluid measure interchangeably with milliliter (ml).

Conversions

1 in.^{3}	=	16.387064 cm^3
1 ft.^{3}	=	28.316846592 cm^3
	or	0.028316847 m^3
1 yd.^{3}	=	764,554.857984 cm^3
	or	0.764554858 m^3
1 cm^3	=	0.06102374 in.^{3}
1 m^3	=	61,023.74 in.^{3}
	or	35.31467 ft.^{3}
	or	1.307951 yd.^{3}

Fluid Volume
U.S. customary system
A gallon is equal to 231 cubic inches of liquid or capacity.

1 tablespoon (tbs.)	=	3 teaspoons (tsp.)
	or	0.5 fl. ounce (fl. oz.)
1 cup	=	8 fl. oz.

1 pint (pt.)	=	2 cups
	or	16 fl oz
1 quart (qt.)	=	2 pt. or 4 cups
	or	32 fl. oz.
1 gallon (gal.)	=	4 qt.
	or	8 pt.
	or	16 cups
1 bushel (bu.)	=	8 gal. or 32 qt.

International System

Fluid-volume measurements are directly tied to cubic measure. One milliliter of fluid occupies a volume of 1 cubic centimeter. A liter of fluid (slightly more than the customary quart) occupies a volume of 1 cubic decimeter, or 1,000 cubic centimeters.

1 centiliter (cL)	=	10 mililiters (mL)
1 deciliter	=	10 cl or 100 mL
1 liter (L)	=	10 dl or 1,000 mL
1 dekaliter (daL)	=	10 L
1 hectoliter (hL)	=	10 daL or 100 L
1 kiloliter (kL)	=	10 hl or 1,000 L

Conversions

1 fluid ounce	=	29.573528 mL or 0.02957 L
1 cup	=	236.588 mL or 0.236588 L
1 pint	=	473.176 mL or 0.473176 L
1 quart	=	946.3529 mL or 0.9463529 L
1 gallon	=	3,785.41 mL or 3.78541 L
1 milliliter	=	0.0338 fluid ounce
1 liter	=	33.814 fluid ounces
	or	4.2268 cups or 2.113 pints
	or	1.0567 quarts or 0.264 gallon

Dry Volume
Conversions

1 pint, dry	=	33.600 cu. in. or 0.551 L
1 quart, dry	=	67.201 cu. in. or 1.101 L

Mass & Weight

Mass and weight are often confused. Mass is a measure of the quantity of matter in an object and does not vary with changes in altitude or in gravitational force (as on the Moon or another planet). Weight, on the other hand, is a measure of the force of gravity on an object and so does change with altitude or gravitational force.

U.S. customary system

In customary measure it is more common to measure weight than mass. The most common customary system of weight is avoirdupois:

1 pound (lb.)	=	16 ounces (oz.)
1 (short) hundred-weight (cwt.)	=	100 lb.
1 (short) ton	=	20 hundredweights
	or	2,000 lb.
1 long hundred-weight	=	112 lb.
1 long ton	=	20 long hundredweights
	or	2,240 lb.

A different system called troy weight is used to weigh precious metals. In troy weight the ounce is slightly larger than in avoirdupois, but there are only 12 ounces to the troy pound.

International System

Instead of weight, the International System uses measures of mass. The original basic unit was the gram, which was defined as the mass of 1 milliliter (= 1 cm3) of water at 4 degrees Celsius (about 39ºF). Today the official measure of mass is a specific metal object defined as the standard kilogram.

1 centigram (cg)	=	10 milligrams (mg)
1 decigram (dg)	=	10 cg or 100 mg
1 gram (g)	=	10 dg or 1000 mg
1 kilogram (kg)	=	10 hectograms (hg)
	or	100 dekagrams (dag)
	or	1,000 g
1 metric ton (t)	=	1000 kg

Conversions

Since mass and weight are identical at standard conditions (sea level on Earth), grams and other International System units of mass are often used as measures of weight or converted into customary units of weight. Under standard conditions:

1 ounce	=	28.3495 grams
1 pound	=	453.59 grams
	or	0.45359 kilogram
1 short ton	=	907.18 kilograms
	or	0.907 metric ton
1 milligram	=	0.000035 ounce
1 gram	=	0.03527 ounce
1 kilogram	=	35.27 ounces
	or	2.2046 pounds
1 metric ton	=	2,204.6 pounds
	or	1.1023 short tons

Time
Customary and International System

The International System in 1967 adopted a second that is based on the microwaves emitted by the vibrations of hot cesium atoms. A second (abbreviated sec. in customary usage, s in SI usage) is the time it takes the atoms to vibrate exactly 9,192,631,770 times. In the customary measure of time, the day is divided into 24 hours, the hour into 60 minutes, and the minute into 60 seconds. Since the Earth's rotation is gradually slowing, scientists must periodically add a second to a day to keep the year in sequence with their clocks. The change is so small that for almost all practical purposes an International System second and a customary second are the same.

Decimal fractions of time are used to measure smaller time intervals:

millisecond (ms)	=	0.001 second (10^{-3})
microsecond (µs)	=	0.000001 second (10^{-6})
nanosecond (ns)	=	0.000000001 second (10^{-9})
picosecond (ps)	=	0.000000000001 second (10^{-12})

Temperature
U.S. customary system

In the U.S, temperature is usually measured in degrees Fahrenheit: water freezes at 32°F and boils at 212°F. The basis of the Fahrenheit scale was 0°F, the coldest temperature that its originator, G.D. Fahrenheit (1686–1736), could obtain under laboratory conditions.

International System

The Swedish astronomer Anders Celsius (1701–44) devised the temperature scale that bears his name in 1742. On the Celsius scale, water freezes at 0°C and boils at 100°C. Very low temperatures are measured on the Kelvin scale, named for William Thomson, Baron Kelvin (1824–1907). It is also called the absolute scale because absolute zero—0°K (–273.15° C)—is the temperature at which no body can give up heat. The interval of a degree Kelvin equals the interval of a degree Celsius. At very high temperatures, differences between the Kelvin and Celsius scales are insignificant.

Fahrenheit and Celsius Temperature Conversions

You can roughly convert a Celsius temperature to Fahrenheit by doubling the number and adding 30. For example, 20°C Celsius is approximately 70°F. (Conversely, subtract 30 from Fahrenheit temperature and divide by two for a Celsius temperature.) For a closer equivalent, consult the table below.

Celsius	Fahrenheit	Fahrenheit	Celsius
−45° =	−49°	−45° =	−42.8°
−40° =	−40°	−40° =	−40.0°
−35° =	−31°	−35° =	−37.2°
−30° =	−22°	−30° =	−34.4°
−25° =	−13°	−25° =	−31.7°
−20° =	−4°	−20° =	−28.9°
−15° =	5°	−15° =	−26.1°
−10° =	14°	−10° =	−23.3°
−5° =	23°	−5° =	−20.6°
0° =	32°	0° =	−17.8°
5° =	41°	5° =	−15.0°
10° =	50°	10° =	−12.2°
15° =	59°	15° =	−9.4°
20° =	68°	20° =	−6.7°
25° =	77°	25° =	−3.9°
30° =	86°	30° =	−1.1°
35° =	95°	32° =	0.0°
40° =	104°	35° =	1.7°
45° =	113°	40° =	4.4°
50° =	122°	45° =	7.2°
55° =	131°	50° =	10.0°
60° =	140°	55° =	12.8°
65° =	149°	60° =	15.6°
70° =	158°	65° =	18.3°
75° =	167°	70° =	21.1°
80° =	176°	75° =	23.9°
85° =	185°	80° =	26.7°
90° =	194°	85° =	29.4°
95° =	203°	90° =	32.2°
100° =	212°	95° =	35.0°
125° =	257°	100° =	37.8°
150° =	302°	105° =	40.6°
175° =	347°	110° =	43.3°
200° =	392°	212° =	100.0°
225° =	437°	225° =	107.2°
250° =	482°	250° =	121.1°
275° =	527°	275° =	135.0°
300° =	572°	300° =	148.9°
325° =	617°	325° =	162.8°
350° =	662°	350° =	176.7°
375° =	707°	375° =	190.6°
400° =	752°	400° =	204.4°
425° =	797°	425° =	218.3°
450° =	842°	450° =	232.2°
475° =	887°	475° =	246.1°

Conversions
Fahrenheit to Celsius: Subtract 32 from the temperature and multiply the difference by 5; then divide the product by 9. The formula is: $C = \frac{5}{9}(F−32)$

Celsius to Fahrenheit: Multiply the temperature by 1.8 (or $\frac{9}{5}$), then add 32. The formula is: $F = \frac{9}{5}C + 32$

Celsius to Kelvin: Add 273.15 to the temperature The formula is: $K = C+273.15$

Kelvin, Celsius, and Fahrenheit Equivalents

Characteristic	K	C°	F°
Absolute zero	0	−273.15°	−459.7°
Freezing point, water	273.15	0°	32°
Traditional human body temperature	310.15	37°	98.6°
Boiling point, water	373.15	100°	212°

Force, Work/Energy, Power
U.S. customary system
The foot/pound/second system of reckoning includes the following units:

slug = the mass to which a force of 1 poundal will give an acceleration of 1 foot per second per second (= approximately 32.17 lbs.)

poundal = fundamental unit of force

foot–pound = the work done when a force of 1 poundal produces a movement of 1 foot

foot–pound/second = the unit of power equal to 1 foot/pound per second

Another common unit of power is horsepower, which is equal to 550 foot-pounds per second.

Thermal work or energy is often measured in British thermal units (Btu). One Btu is defined as the energy required to increase the temperature of 1 pound of water by 1 degree Fahrenheit. The Btu is equal to about 0.778 foot-pound.

International System
In physics, compound measurements of force, work or energy, and power are essential. There are two parallel systems using International System units: the centimeter/gram/second system (cgs) is used for small measurements, and the meter/kilogram/second system (mks) is used for larger measurements. The mks system is the official one for SI. They are described below.

Measurement of force

cgs unit dyne (dy) The force required to accelerate a mass of 1 g 1 cm/s² (cm/s² means "centimeter per second per second")

mks unit newton (N) The force required to accelerate a mass of 1 kg 1 m/s²

Measurement of work or energy

cgs unit erg The dyne-centimeter, i.e., the work done when a force of 1 dy produces a movement of 1 cm

mks unit joule (j) The newton-meter, i.e., the work done when a force of 1 N produces a movement of 1 m (=10,000,000 ergs).

Heat energy is also measured using the calorie (cal), which is defined as the energy required to increase the temperature of 1 cubic centimeter (1 ml) of water by 1 degree C. One calorie is equal to about 4.184 joules. The kilocalorie (Kcal or Cal) is equal to 1,000 calories and is the unit in which the energy values of food are measured. This more familiar unit, also commonly referred to as a Calorie, is equal to about 4,184 joules.

Measurement of power

cgs unit	erg/second	A rate of 1 erg per second
mks unit	watt (W)	The joule/second, i.e., a rate of 1 joule per second

Conversions
Measurement of force

1 poundal	=	13,889 dynes
	=	0.13889 newtons
1 dyne	=	0.000072 poundals
1 newton	=	7.2 poundals

Measurement of work or energy

1 foot-pound	=	1,356 joules
British thermal unit	=	1,055 joules
	=	252 calories
1 joule	=	0.0007374 ft.-lbs.
1 calorie	=	0.003968 Btu
1 Kilocalorie	=	3.968 Btu

Measurement of power

1 foot-pound/second	=	1.3564 watts
1 horsepower	=	746 watts
	=	0.746 kilowatts
1 watt	=	0.73725 ft.-lb/sec.
	=	0.00134 horsepower
1 kilowatt	=	737.25 ft.-lb./sec.
	=	1.34 horsepower

Electrical Measure

Originally, the basic unit of quantity in electricity was the coulomb. A coulomb is equal to the passage of 6.25×10^{18} electrons past a given point in an electrical system.

The unit of electrical flow is the ampere, which is equal to a coulomb/second, i.e., the flow of 1 coulomb per second. The ampere is analogous in electrical measure to a unit of flow such as gallons-per-minute in physical measure. In SI, the ampere is taken as the basic unit.

The unit for measuring electrical potential energy is the volt, which is defined as 1 joule/coulomb, i.e., 1 joule of energy per coulomb of electricity. The volt is analogous to a measure of pressure in a water system.

The unit for measuring electrical power is the watt as defined in the previous section. Power in watts (P) is the product of the electrical flow in amperes (I) and the potential electrical energy in volts (E):

$$P = IE.$$

Since the watt is such a small unit for practical applications, the kilowatt (= 1,000 watts) is often used. A kilowatt-hour is the power of 1,000 watts over an hour's time.

The unit for measuring electrical resistance is the ohm, which is the resistance offered by a circuit to the flow of 1 ampere being driven by the force of 1 volt. It is derived from Ohm's law, which defines the relationship between flow or current (amperes), potential energy (volts), and resistance (ohms). It states that the current in amperes (I) is proportional to potential energy in volts (E) and inversely proportional to resistance in ohms (R). Thus, when voltage and resistance are known, amperage can be calculated by the simple formula

$$I = \frac{E}{R}$$

Measure of Angles and Arcs

Angles are measured by systems based on arcs (portions) of circles. Arcs of a circle can be measured by length, but they are also often measured by angles. In the latter case, the measure of the arc is the same as the measure of an angle whose vertex is at the center of the circle and whose sides pass through the ends of the arc. Such an angle is said to be subtended by the arc.

The most commonly used angle measure is degree measure. One degree is the angle subtended by an arc that is 1/360 of a circle. This is an ancient system of measurement probably originally developed by Sumerian astronomers. These astronomers used a numeration system based on 60 ($60 \times 6 = 360$), as well as a 360-day year. They divided the day into 12 equal periods of 30 smaller periods each ($12 \times 30 = 360$) and used roughly the same system for dividing the circle. Even when different years and numeration systems were adopted by later societies, astronomers continued to use a variation of the Sumerian system for angles.

1 degree (1°)	=	60 minutes (60')
	=	3,600 seconds (3,600")
1 minute	=	60 seconds

When two lines are perpendicular to each other, they form four angles of the same size, which are called right angles. Two right angles make up a line, which in this context is considered a straight angle.

1 right angle = 90°
1 straight angle = 180°

While this system is workable for most purposes, it is artificial. Mathematicians discovered that using a natural system of angle measurement produces results that make better sense in mathematical and many scientific applications. This system is called radian measure. Radian measure is considered a supplement to SI. One radian is the measure of the angle subtended by an arc of a circle that is exactly as long as the radius of the circle.

1 radian = about 57° 17' 45"

The circumference, C, of a circle is given by the formula $C = 2\pi r$, where π is a number (approximately 3.14159) and r is the radius. Therefore, a semicircle whose radius is 1 is π units long, which implies that there are π radians in a straight angle. Many of the angles commonly encountered are measured in multiples of π radians:

0° = 0 radians	90° = $\pi/2$ radians
30° = $\pi/6$ radians	180° = π radians
45° = $\pi/4$ radians	270° = $3\pi/2$ radians
60° = $\pi/3$ radians	360° = 2π radians

To convert from radians to degrees, use the formula $t \; radians = (180/\pi) \; t°$. To convert from degrees to radians, use the formula

$$w° = (\pi/180)w \text{ radians.}$$

The U.S. artillery uses the mil to measure angles. A mil is the angle subtended by an arc that is 1/6400 of a circle.

1 mil = 0.05625° = 3' 22.5"
1 mil = almost 0.001 radian

The Environment

The modern environmental movement in the United States dates from Earth Day 1970 (April 22), when the American public first began to take stock of the ecological devastation going on around them. Before the 1970s there were no pollution controls on cars and unleaded gas had not been introduced; people and municipalities dumped untreated sewage into the nation's rivers, one of which was so saturated with chemical waste that it actually caught fire; and industrial cities were routinely shrouded with thick acrid smoke.

Many of these problems have by now been effectively addressed and dramatically diminished. Today the Environmental Protection Agency (E.P.A.), established in 1970, routinely monitors air quality at thousands of sites around the country. Toxic emissions from smokestacks at smelters, factories, and garbage incinerators have been sharply reduced. Mandatory pollution control standards on automobiles have led to an overwhelming drop in lead emissions. Recycling as a way of reducing solid waste has taken hold in cities and towns throughout the country. Many people, however, oppose strong environmental safeguards on economic and other grounds, making it difficult to improve and enforce regulations. Growing population pressures also create environmental threats, particularly to natural habitats, arable soil, and drinking water supplies.

▶ GLOBAL WARMING

Most climatologists are convinced that over the past century the Earth has begun to warm significantly—about 1.1°F (0.6°C)—and that at its current rate, it is likely to warm as much as 3° to 7°F (1.5° to 4°C) between 1990 and 2100. Analyses of data such as tree rings, ice cores, growth of corals, and historical records indicate that in the Northern Hemisphere it is likely that the 2000s were the warmest decade in the past 1,000 years. In 2005, heightened by El Niño effects, the Earth's temperature reached its highest single year average since records were first kept in the mid-19th century.

The most authoritative studies on global climate change have been those of the Intergovernmental Panel on Climate Change (IPCC), a group of several thousand scientists commissioned by the United Nations. In its most recent report in 2007, the IPCC concluded that "the evidence of global warming is now unequivocal," and that the major contributor is human activity. With this report, the debate over human influence was essentially over for most scientists and policy makers, although debate regarding policies and regulations remains fierce.

Global warming occurs when certain gases in the atmosphere prevent sunlight from being reflected from the Earth. Ordinarily, sunlight that reaches the surface of the Earth is partly absorbed and partly reflected. The absorbed light heats the surface and is later emitted from the surface as infrared radiation. Gases that are not transparent to infrared radiation (carbon dioxide is one) collect this heat and keep it in the atmosphere, earning the name *greenhouse gases* (GHGs). The Earth's atmosphere is only 0.03 percent carbon dioxide, but combined with other gases, this is enough to trap 30 percent of the reflected heat (the rest is radiated out to space), and maintain the Earth's average temperature at about 59°F (15°C), a temperature that has held relatively constant since the last ice age (since then (the Earth has warmed only 9°F).

Climatologists estimate that at the current rate of warming, the Earth's temperature could increase nearly this much in only 100 years. If global temperatures continue to increase, the potential devastation is staggering. Additional warming could cause melting of polar ice caps, setting off a chain of events that begins with a rise in sea level worldwide and could end with the destruction of water supplies, forests, and agriculture in many parts of the world.

The increased presence of carbon dioxide is due primarily to the burning of carbon fuels including oil, coal, and natural gas, as well as burning trees for deforestation. Cholorflourocarbons (CFCs), now being phased out by many countries, are used as aerosols, in air-conditioning units, and in various industrial processes. Methane is emitted by decomposing organic wastes, natural-gas leaks, and fermenting rice paddies. The primary sources of nitrogen oxides are automobile exhaust and industrial smoke stacks. At a December 1997 conference in Kyoto, Japan, representatives of more than 150 countries reached tentative agreement to reduce greenhouse gases an average of 5 percent worldwide (from 1990 levels) between 2008 and 2012. In late 2004 Russia joined most other industrialized nations and ratified the treaty, paving the way for it to come into force on February 16, 2005.

Though the U.S. refused to ratify the agreement, one notable American initiative is the U.S. Mayors Climate Change Agreement (2005), which as of 2009 had more than 900 signatories striving to have their cities reduce GHG emissions by amounts equal or better than the targets in the Kyoto Protocol. By 2009, international efforts to address climate change were more coordinated than ever before. World leaders met in Copenhagen in December 2009 in an effort to reach a new agreement, which called on developed nations to start work immediately; the U.S. agreed to reduce emissions by 14–17 percent below 2005 levels by 2020.

Global warming produces complex and interrelated effects that could under some scenarios spell environmental disaster. Some of the possible effects of global warming are:

Weather patterns Climatologists think that higher global temperatures and changing precipitation patterns are already disrupting local weather in places around the world. For example, the IPCC (2007) reports that the number of intense storms has increased over most land areas, and that more intense droughts have been observed in many areas. The U.S. National Climatic Data Center in Asheville, N.C. reports that Northern Hemisphere snow cover has been below normal since 1987, and that extreme extratropical cyclone activity over the North Atlantic has increased since 1988.

Changed weather patterns can have a severe impact on crops and other forms of vegetation, as well as on the animals that depend on them. Rising temperatures also enable insects and fungal pests to migrate to previously unaffected regions. Long-lived plants, however, such as trees, spread much more slowly in the face of climate change.

Warming patterns Although global warming will cause an increase in average world temperatures, this increase is not expected to be uniform. In general, climatologists expect greater warming during winter months and at high latitudes (closer to the poles than to the equator).

Higher temperatures have an even more dire effect than increased numbers of hot days. Rising temperatures enable insects and fungal pests to migrate to previously unaffected regions. Increased heat could cause the melting of polar ice caps, which would set off a chain of events that begins with a rise in sea level worldwide and ends with the destruction of water supplies, forests, and agriculture in many parts of the world.

Sea level rise In 2009, the Journal *Science* reported that climatologists predicted the melting of Antartica's western ice sheets would lead to a 10-foot increase in sea levels worldwide. These scientists also predicted that seas would rise unevenly, with an additional 1.5-foot increase in levels along the east and west coasts of North America.

A 3-foot (1-meter) rise would inundate 7,000 square miles (18,000 km^2) of dry land—an area the size of Massachusetts. It would also destroy a comparable area of coastal wetlands, erode recreational beaches 100 to 200 meters, exacerbate coastal flooding, and increase the salinity of aquifers and estuaries. An estimated one-third of the world's population—about 1.75 billion people—live within 40 miles of the sea, mostly along low-lying floodplains and estuaries. In 2009, the small nation of Maldives in the Indian Ocean began diverting a portion of its tourist revenue into buying a new homeland; the president stated that even a small rise in sea levels would inundate the archipelago.

▶ THE OZONE LAYER

There are two distinct problems associated with the chemical ozone (O_3): ground-level ozone, the main component of smog (discussed under "Air Pollution," below), and stratospheric ozone. The primary difference between the two problems is that at ground level there is too much ozone, while in the stratosphere there is not enough.

The problem of stratospheric ozone depletion is closely linked to global warming since chlorofluorocarbons are greenhouse gases, but the science of ozone depletion is unique. Stratospheric ozone (sometimes referred to as upper-atmosphere or atmospheric ozone) absorbs most of the Sun's ultraviolet radiation, protecting life on the surface from its harmful effects. A significant reduction of stratospheric ozone would potentially lead to sharp increases in the incidence of skin cancer and cataracts in humans. It is also thought that there would be serious losses of small ocean algae, which produce oxygen and break down carbon dioxide, and of bacteria important to crop production.

Complex natural forces are continually at work creating and destroying ozone in the atmosphere. Individual molecules of oxygen (O_2) break down into atomic oxygen (O) after absorption of ultraviolet radiation. In turn, each atomic oxygen normally combines with an additional molecule of O_2 to form ozone (O_3). Destruction of ozone can be caused by the occasional recombination of ozone with atomic oxygen to form two molecules of O_2. As long as the Earth's sunlit atmosphere contains molecular oxygen, as it has for more than one billion years, ozone will be maintained in this dynamic balance.

In 1974, scientists saw the first suggestion that a group of chemicals known as chlorofluorocarbons (CFCs) was destroying the ozone balance by adding chlorine to the atmosphere. Chemically inert, nontoxic, and easily liquefied, CFCs were developed in the 1930s as an ammonia substitute for use in refrigeration, but their use became widespread in air conditioning, packaging and insulation, as a solvent for cleaning electronic circuit boards, and as an aerosol propellant.

It is this very absence of chemical reactivity that makes CFCs so dangerous to the ozone layer. Unlike less inert compounds, CFCs are not destroyed or removed in the lower atmosphere by rain, oxidation, or sunlight, where their lifetimes have been estimated to be between 75 and 110 years. Instead they drift into the upper atmosphere, where their chlorine components are released into the atmosphere under the effects of ultraviolet radiation. Almost all of these freed chlorine atoms find and react with the ozone, creating chlorine monoxide and molecular oxygen. In a subsequent reaction, the chlorine monoxide releases its oxygen atom to form a second molecule of oxygen, and the chlorine atom is freed once again to repeat the process. Through this continuing cycle of reactions, each chlorine atom can destroy about 100,000 molecules of ozone before the chain reaction ends. In the Antarctic, ice crystals in the air speed up reactions, producing an "ozone hole," a region of extremely low levels of atmospheric ozone, over the south polar region during the Antarctic winter. A system of cold winds called the Antarctic Vortex amplifies this effect. NASA reported that the average size of the ozone hole over the period of September 21–30, 2006, was the largest on record, at 10.6 million square miles (27.5 million km^2). The second-largest size hole on record occurred in 2008, covering roughly some 27 square kilometers, an area larger than North America.

To combat ozone depletion, the United States, Russia, Japan, and the European Union have eliminated CFC use and production, and there are further agreements to reduce use in developing countries. According to a 2006 report from the National Oceanic and Atmospheric Administration (NOAA), as the overall decline in these gases continues—in response to the provisions of the 1987 Montreal Protocol—global stratospheric ozone is expected to recover, approaching or exceeding pre-1980 values. The Montreal Protocol mandates that the production and consumption of HCFCs is targeted for phase-out by 2040.

▶ AIR POLLUTION

Although we tend to think of air pollution as a local problem, studies reported in 1995 demonstrate that there are widespread effects. Air pollution is so pervasive in industrial regions of northeastern North America, central Europe, and eastern Asia that it partly blocks sunlight, that it counteracts global warming with regional cooling. In the U.S., the basic law dealing with air pollution is the Clean Air Act of 1990, which directs the U.S. Environmental Protection Agency (E.P.A.) to set standards for air quality.

The Clean Air Interstate Rule of 2005 (CAIR) addresses power plant emissions in 29 eastern states plus the District of Columbia. When fully implemented, CAIR will reduce sulfur dioxide emissions in these states by over 70 percent and nitrogen oxide emissions by over 60 percent from 2003 levels. In 2009, U.S. President Barack Obama, in an attempt to cut greenhouse gases by 900 metric tons, signed a policy enforcing strict limits on vehicle emissions that requires new cars and trucks to get an average 35.5 mpg by 2016. The law went into effect in April 2010, despite a contentious battle with the auto industry.

The E.P.A. monitors air quality at about 3,000 sites for six pollutants: particulate matter (soot and dust), sulfur dioxide, carbon monoxide (mostly from automobiles), nitrogen oxides, lead, and ozone. In addition to health concerns, the effects of air pollution on vegetation, materials, and visibility are monitored. The E.P.A. strengthened the air quality standards for ground-level ozone in 2008.

From 1990 to 2008, air quality had improved for each of the six criteria, and emissions had decreased and all U.S. metropolitan areas surveyed experienced fewer unhealthy air days in 2008 compared to 2001. Yet in 2009, about 132 million people lived in countries with pollution levels above the National Ambient Air Quality Standards.

Particulate matter (PM₁₀) The E.P.A. measures particulate matter with an aerodynamic diameter smaller than 10 micrometers down to 2.5 micrometers. This includes dust, dirt, soot, smoke, and liquid droplets directly emitted into the air from factories, power plants, cars, construction sites, fires, and natural erosion, as well as particles formed in the atmosphere by condensation or transformation of emitted gases such as sulfur dioxide and volatile organic compounds.

Particulate matter is responsible for most adverse health effects in the lower regions of the respiratory tract. People with chronic obstructive pulmonary or cardiovascular disease, asthmatics, the elderly, children, and individuals with influenza are especially sensitive.

Sulfur dioxide (SO₂) Ambient sulfur dioxide comes mostly from stationary-source coal and oil combustion, refineries, pulp and paper mills, and nonferrous smelters. The health hazards associated with exposure to SO_2 include impaired breathing, respiratory illness, alterations in the lungs' defenses, and aggravation of existing respiratory and cardiovascular disease. Those most sensitive to SO_2 include asthmatics and people with chronic lung disease or cardiovascular disease, children, and the elderly. Sulfur dioxide also damages leaves on trees and crops and is an agent of acid rain.

Carbon monoxide (CO) Carbon monoxide is a colorless, odorless, and poisonous gas produced by incomplete burning of carbon in fuels. Carbon monoxide enters the bloodstream and disrupts delivery of oxygen to the body's organs and tissues. The health threat from carbon monoxide is serious for those who suffer from cardiovascular diseases. Healthy individuals are also affected, and exposure to elevated carbon monoxide levels is associated with impairment of visual perception and manual dexterity.

Federal regulations have succeeded in cleaning up much of the carbon monoxide pollution that plagued the U.S. in the 1980s. In 1990, 26 metropolitan areas exceeded the National Ambient Air Quality Standards for carbon monoxide at least once. Los Angeles exceeded the standard a whopping 47 times, while Las Vegas exceeded it 17 times. In 2000, only three cities exceeded the standard: Calexico, Calif. (2 times), Los Angeles-Long

Beach, Calif (2 times), and Fairbanks, Alaska (1 time). The review of CO standards required by the Clean Air Act is due to be completed in 2011.

Nitrogen oxides (NOₓ) These highly reactive gases play a major role, together with volatile organic compounds, in the formation of ozone. Nitrogen oxides form when fuel is burned at high temperatures. When released into the atmosphere, they are one of the major causes of smog. The two major emissions sources are cars and trucks, and stationary fuel-combustion sources such as electric-utility and industrial boilers.

Nitrogen oxides can irritate the lungs and lower resistance to respiratory infections such as influenza. Prolonged exposure to higher than normal concentrations can cause pulmonary angina. Nitrogen dioxide (NO_2) is also an agent of acid rain and plays a role in nitrogen loading of forests and ecosystems. Yet according to the E.P.A., NO_2 has decreased nationally 46 percent between 1980 and 2008, based on data from 75 sites. Many urban areas violate the E.P.A.'s standards on hot summer days, when the Sun cooks hydrocarbons and nitrogen oxides, thus producing smog.

Ozone (O₃) Ground-level ozone is a colorless gas and the main component of smog. Unlike most other air pollutants, ozone is not emitted by factories or automobiles, but is formed by the interaction of volatile organic compounds (VOCs) and nitrous oxide. These reactions are stimulated by sunlight and temperature so that peak ozone levels occur typically during the warmer times of year. The severity of a smog problem in a given locale is directly related to the temperature and ultraviolet radiation intensity in that area. While the problems associated with ozone depletion (see "The Ozone Layer," above) and ground-level ozone are usually viewed separately, it is worth noting that as upper-atmosphere ozone is depleted, more ultraviolet radiation reaches the Earth and stimulates the production of ozone-smog.

Both VOCs and nitrous oxide are emitted by transportation and industrial sources as diverse as automobile and chemical manufacturing, dry cleaners, paint shops, and other solvent-using industries. High levels of ozone affect people with impaired respiratory systems, such as asthmatics, and exposure to relatively low concentrations of ozone for only a few hours has been found to significantly reduce lung function in normal, healthy people during exercise. This is generally accompanied by symptoms including chest pain, coughing, sneezing, and pulmonary congestion. Ozone is also responsible each year for several billion dollars worth of domestic crop yield losses, and it causes noticeable damage to leaves in many crops and species of trees.

Lead (Pb) People can be exposed to lead via air, diet, and ingestion of lead in soil and dust. Lead accumulates in the body in blood, bone, and soft tissue, and because it is not readily excreted, it also affects the kidneys, nervous system, and blood-forming organs. Excessive exposure to lead may cause seizures, mental retardation, and/or behavioral disorders. Even at low doses, lead exposure is harmful; infants and children are especially susceptible to low doses of lead and often suffer central nervous system damage.

Lead gasoline additives, nonferrous smelters, and battery plants are the most significant contributors to atmospheric lead emissions. The decline in the share of lead emissions from internal-combustion engines of all kinds is due primarily to the introduction of unleaded gasoline in 1975, for use in automobiles equipped with catalytic control devices, which reduce emissions of carbon monoxide, VOCs, and nitrogen oxides. Today nearly all of the lead once added to gasoline in the U.S. has been removed.

Air pollution worldwide The worst air pollution is undoubtedly in Asia. According to the World Health Organization in 2009, roughly two million people die each year from the effects of air pollution alone—the majority of whom are in Asia—and another half million die from water pollution.

Anything over 100 micrograms of particles per cubic meter of air is considered dangerous, yet in cities like Taiyuan, China, and Delhi, India, the levels routinely top 500 micrograms. The threat is compounded by the fact that so many people in these areas cook indoors with coal briquettes. Particles in the air are a major cause of respiratory ailments in Asia; such ailments are a leading cause of death in China.

▶ACID RAIN

Acid rain refers to acidic precipitation of all kinds, including rain, snow, and fog, as well as acidic dust particles. The main component of acid rain is sulfuric acid, a product of reactions of sulfur dioxide released by industrial and power plants fueled by coal or oil. Another major agent of acid rain is nitrogen oxides, which form nitric acid and which are found in motor vehicle exhaust and in emissions from industrial plants that burn any fuel at high temperatures. Burning vegetation also produces nitric acid, as well as formic acid and acetic acid. Acid rain can travel great distances from its source: 10 percent to 80 percent increases in acidity have been detected as far away as 2,500 miles from a source.

Acid rain has been implicated in the destruction of lakes, the weathering of man-made structures, and the death of trees, crops, and animals. When acid rain ends up in lakes, it can increase

Unhealthy Days in Selected Metropolitan Areas, 1995–2007

To measure air quality in urban areas, the Environmental Protection Agency has developed an indicator called the Air Quality Index (AQI, formerly the Pollutant Standard Index, PSI). The AQI integrates into a single number emission levels of five major pollutants: particulate matter (PM_{10}). Sulfur Dioxide (SO_2), carbon monoxide (CO), ground level ozone (O_3) and nitrogen dioxide (NO_2). An AQI of 0–50 reflects good air, 51–100 denotes moderate air, and an AQI of over 100 is classified as unhealthy (201–300 signifies very unhealthy air; 301–500 is hazardous). The following chart lists the number of days in which the AQI exceeded 100 in metropolitan areas.

Metropolitan area (no. of trend sites)	1995	1996	1998	1999	2000	2003	2005	2007
Riverside-San Bernardino, Calif. (47)	125	118	96	123	145	138	106	135
Bakersfield, Calif. (27)	107	110	78	144	132	141	90	131
Fresno, Calif. (19)	61	70	67	133	131	127	64	93
Los Angeles–Long Beach, Calif. (56)	113	94	56	56	87	88	80	59
Houston, Texas (29)	66	28	38	52	42	31	40	25
Knoxville, Tenn. (16)	26	21	54	66	41	14	18	51
Sacramento, Calif. (39)	41	44	29	69	45	22	53	32
Ventura, Calif. (21)	66	62	29	24	31	20	12	22
Atlanta, Ga. (21)	36	28	2	67	34	11	19	34
Memphis, Tenn.–Ark.–Miss. (15)	21	19	27	35	24	8	15	35
Dallas, Texas (21)	29	10	33	23	0	0	32	11
Philadelphia, Pa.–N.J. (44)	38	38	37	32	22	20	27	40
Baltimore, Md. (20)	36	28	51	40	19	20	27	45
Nashville, Tenn. (18)	26	23	30	36	19	7	11	35
New Orleans, La. (12)	20	8	7	18	17	8	5	17
St. Louis, Mo.–Ill. (55)	38	23	24	31	18	13	35	34
San Diego, Calif. (36)	48	31	33	33	31	20	9	33
New York, N.Y. (19)	21	14	18	25	19	14	16	20
Washington, D.C.–Md.–Va.–W.V. (46)	32	18	47	39	11	12	23	38
Phoenix–Mesa, Ariz. (25)	22	15	14	10	10	9	19	11
Cleveland–Lorain–Elyria, Ohio (42)	27	19	22	40	22	17	28	22
Cincinnati, Ohio–Ky.–Ind. (16)	19	10	13	16	14	10	20	39
Indianapolis, Ind. (25)	21	16	19	24	5	11	20	24
Pittsburgh, Pa. (57)	27	12	39	40	29	37	48	44
Detroit, Mich. (33)	14	13	17	20	15	19	25	21
El Paso, Texas (19)	3	6	6	5	4	7	6	6
Oakland, Calif. (30)	12	11	12	17	12	7	5	5
Denver, Colo. (32)	5	2	9	5	3	5	2	21
Milwaukee–Waukesha, Wis. (20)	14	5	12	19	5	9	18	11
Boston, Mass.–N.H. (21)	7	4	8	10	1	6	10	3
Seattle–Bellevue–Everett, Wash. (13)	2	6	3	6	7	2	1	4
Chicago, Ill. (51)	24	7	12	19	2	10	23	23
Las Vegas, Nev.–Ariz. (15)	3	14	5	8	2	5	10	7
Miami, Fla. (15)	2	1	8	7	2	1	1	3
Minneapolis–St.Paul, Minn.–Wis. (27)	5	0	1	1	2	1	6	5
San Francisco, Calif. (16)	2	0	0	10	4	0	2	2

Note: Figures reflect data from selected E.P.A. trend sites. Number of unhealthy days recorded by all active E.P.A. monitoring sites may be slightly higher in some cities. **Source:** Environmental Protection Agency, *National Air Quality and Emissions Trends Report 2007* (2008).

the level of acidity to such an extent that the lake loses its ability to buffer the acidity with alkaline chemicals from the surrounding soil and rocks. How quickly this occurs is to some extent determined by the nature of the surrounding soil, which means that lakes in some regions are more vulnerable to the effects of acid rain than others. As lakes become more acidic, small invertebrates die off. This begins a reaction up the food chain: as the smallest organisms disappear, the food supply for larger vertebrates such as fish and frogs is depleted. Because lakes are not closed ecosystems, the demise of these organisms also affects land dwellers that depend on them, directly or indirectly, for survival.

In the most recent National Surface Water Survey, 75 percent of lakes and streams surveyed were found to be acidic because of acid rain. Regions in the U.S. found to be sensitive to acidification include the Adirondacks and Catskill Mountains, the mid-Appalachian highlands, the upper Midwest, and the mountainous areas of the West. Approximately 70 percent, for example, of sensitive lakes in the Adirondacks are at risk of acidification.

▶ WATER POLLUTION

Although the bad effect of air pollution on health was suspected earlier, the first proven environmental cause of illness was water pollution. In England, a famous demonstration by physician John Snow in 1854 showed that removing the handle of a pump could reduce the incidence of cholera by depriving people living near a contaminated well from using the water. Chlorine used for water purification was already known at that time, and by the 20th century most major cities in the United States provided treated water.

Problems not directly connected to health also were recognized in the 19th century. Mining in California was, in some locations, polluting the water supply so greatly that crops could not be grown; a law against using water in extracting ores was instituted in the state in 1884. Industrial water pollution was also recognized, although not stopped. Five years after Dr. Snow's famous demonstration, a new source of water pollution was introduced when the first oil well was drilled.

The 20th century brought with it additional forms of water pollution. A series of revolutions in agriculture included use of artificial fertilizers, introduction of long-lasting pesticides, and concentration of animal wastes. Each change also introduced new forms of water pollution from runoff—water from rain or snow that fails to sink into the soil. "Point sources," such as sewage pipes and factory waste ponds, were now supplemented with the "nonpoint sources" of farming.

Emissions Estimates for E.P.A.-monitored Pollutants, 1970–2008 (millions of tons)

Year	Carbon monoxide (CO)	Nitrogen oxides[3] (NO$_x$)	Volatile organic compounds	Sulfur dioxide (SO$_2$)	Particulate matter (PM$_{10}$)	Lead (Pb)
1970	197.3	26.9	33.7	31.2	12.2	0.221
1975	184.0	26.4	30.2	28.0	7.0	0.160
1980	177.8	27.1	30.1	25.9	6.2	0.074
1985[1]	169.6	25.8	26.9	23.3	3.6	0.022
1990	143.6	25.2	23.1	23.1	3.2	0.005
1995	120.0	24.7	21.6	18.6	3.1	0.004
2000[1]	102.4	22.3	16.9	16.3	2.3	0.003
2005[2]	89.0	19.0	16.0	15.0	2.0	0.003
2008[2]	77.7	16.3	15.9	11.4	11.9	N.A.

Notes: Particulate matter totals before 1990 do not include estimates for fugitive dust, which arises from construction activities, mining and quarrying and paved road resuspension. It is the leading source of PM$_{10}$ emissions. 1. In 1985 and 1996 the EPA refined its methods for estimating emissions. 2. Preliminary. 3. Prior to 1990, include small percentage of emissions from fires. **Source:** Environmental Protection Agency, *National Emissions Inventory, Air Pollutant Emissions Trend Data* (2009).

Emissions Estimates for E.P.A.-monitored Pollutants By Source, 1970–2008 (thousand short tons)

Source	Carbon monoxide (CO) 1970	2008	Nitrogen oxides (NO$_x$) 1970	2008	Volatile organic compounds 1970	2008	Sulfur dioxide (SO$_2$) 1970	2008[2]	Particulate matter (PM$_{10}$) 1970	2008
Fuel Combustion										
Electric utility	237	699	4,900	3,006	30	50	17,398	7,552	1,775	122
Industrial	770	1,216	4,325	1,838	150	130	4,568	1,670	641	192
Other	3,625	3,369	836	727	541	1,269	1,490	578	455	68
Chemical & Allied Processing	3,397	265	271	67	1,341	228	591	255	235	25
Metals Processing	3,644	947	77	68	394	46	4,775	203	1,316	20
Petroleum & Related Industries	2,179	355	240	350	1,194	561	881	206	286	8
Other Industrial Processes	620	500	187	418	270	404	846	329	5,832	768
Solvent Utilization	N.A.	2	N.A.	6	7,174	4,226	N.A.	0	N.A.	4
Storage and Transport	N.A.	115	N.A.	18	1,954	1,303	N.A.	4	N.A.	34
Waste Disposal & Recycling	7,059	1,584	440	120	1,984	374	8	27	999	231
On-Road Vehicles	163,231	38,866	12,624	5,206	16,910	3,418	273	64	480	171
Non-Road Sources	11,371	18,036	2,652	4,255	1,616	2,586	278	456	164	304
Miscellaneous[1]	7,909	11,731	330	260	1,101	1,332	110	85	839	9,972
Total	204,043	77,685	26,805	16,339	34,659	15,927	31,218	11,429	13,023	11,919

Notes: Some columns may not sum due to independent rounding. 1. Miscellaneous includes PM$_{10}$ natural sources like fugitive dust, which arises from construction activities, mining and quarrying and paved road resuspension. It is the leading source of PM$_{10}$ emissions. 2. Without condensibles. **Source:** Environmental Protection Agency, *National Emissions Inventory, Air Pollutant Emissions Trend Data* (2009).

In 1999, the E.P.A. released its first ever national index on the quality of the nation's 2,111 watersheds, which asserted that 21 percent of the watersheds had serious problems. In 2009, the E.P.A. reported that 59,000 acres of wetlands were lost between 1998 and 2004.

The 1972 Clean Water Act was intended to solve many of the nation's water pollution problems, but it has been only partially effective in doing so. In 1972, only about a third of the nation's rivers were safe for fishing and swimming. That number improved to more than 50 percent during the 1970s and 1980s, but by 1998, the levels of pollution had crept back up again. The primary cause was no longer industrial pollution, residue from mining, and untreated sewage; instead, nonpoint sources from runoff, both agricultural and municipal, had taken over as the older point sources were eliminated.

World Carbon Dioxide Emissions from Consumption and Flaring of Fossil Fuels, 2000–2007

2007 Rank, Country	Millions of metric tons	
	2000	2007
1. China	2,966.52	6,538.37
2. United States	5,860.38	5,838.38
3. India	1,012.34	1,612.36
4. Russia	1,582.37	1,537.36
5. Japan	1,203.71	1,254.54
6. Germany	856.92	787.94
7. Canada	565.22	557.34
8. United Kingdom	561.23	539.62
9. South Korea	445.81	503.32
10. Iran	N.A.	495.99

Note: One metric ton is equal to 2,204.62 pounds. Source: U.S. Dept. of Energy, Energy Information Administration, *International Energy Annual*, (2010).

Ozone in Metropolitan Areas at Trend Sites, 2003–2007

The **Air Quality Index (AQI)** is used to determine the amount of pollution in the air for a specific area. It can be measured by any variable of pollution. The following metropolitan areas had the most number of days in 2007 that their AQI ozone levels exceeded 100, and are ranked accordingly.

Metropolitan area	Average number of days exceeding standards		
	2003	2005	2007
Riverside-San Bernardino, California	127	119	113
Bakersfield, California	144	92	91
Knoxville, Tennessee	31	39	49
Baltimore, Maryland	22	34	45
Fresno, California	138	62	40
Philadelphia, Pennsylvania-New Jersey	30	35	40
Cincinnati, Ohio-Kentucky-Indiana	20	29	38
Washington, D.C.-Maryland-Virginia-West Virginia	18	35	38
Los Angeles- Long Beach, California	83	39	37
Charlotte-Gastonia-Rock Hill, North-South Carolina	12	24	33
St. Louis, Missouri-Illinois	26	43	33

Source: Environmental Protection Agency, Air Trends, *Air Quality Index Information, Ozone Only* (2003–2007).

Drinking Water

Americans have for many years taken their drinking water for granted. But despite this complacency, there are many threats to the water supply. These include biological threats to health from contamination, dangerous chemicals in the water supply from a variety of sources, and toxic elements introduced by water treatment or defects in plumbing. A related problem is that high water levels during storms overwhelm both industrial and municipal water treatment. This last source is somewhat more easily controlled than other nonpoint pollution, and revisions of the Clean Water Act in 1987, which went into effect in 1992, attack this problem for urban runoff at the city and county levels.

The Safe Drinking Water Act Amendments of 1996 further strengthened and expanded drinking water protections. They increased standards for microbial contamination such as *cryptosporidium*, which has been the source of several disease outbreaks, including a 1993 instance in Milwaukee, in which more than 100 people died.

Many municipal water supply systems regularly are found to contain levels of bacterial contamination that exceed E.P.A. standards. Most, but not all bacterial contamination stems from the use of surface waters—rivers, lakes, and reservoirs. The other major source of water is groundwater—subsurface water contained for the most part in small cavities, or pores, in rock or soil. One common way to obtain unpolluted groundwater is to dig deep wells that find "fossil" water that has been at those levels for thousands of years. This source, however, is not renewable. Most shallow wells obtain their water from groundwater that recently was surface water and therefore subject to greater contamination.

Groundwater pollution is especially difficult to remedy. Almost all solutions are expensive and, in many cases, not feasible at any price. Such remedies include pumping detoxification agents into the ground or treating the water before use.

Groundwater can be contaminated by industrial pollutants stored or released in ways that put them in contact with the water supply; by leakage from underground storage of volatile chemicals, such as gasoline, cleaning fluid, or petroleum; and by seepage into the soil of agricultural pesticides. A privately funded review of federal and state water tests by the Environmental Working Group reported in 1994 that the water supplies used by 14.1 million Americans contain agricultural pesticides in amounts that would be banned if these levels were found in food. In 2008, the same group reported that pharmaceuticals (including antibiotics, sex hormones, and drugs for depression) contaminate the drinking water of at least 41 million Americans nationwide.

Formerly one of the main sources of ground water contamination had been municipal landfills, but most of these are now sealed with clay liners to prevent seepage; and truly hazardous chemicals, such as mercury or lead from batteries or volatile organic compounds, are banned from landfills.

Some drinking water pollution takes place between the time the water comes from the well or from a surface source and the time it leaves faucets. Even though water from municipal plants is kept lead-free, service pipes, home plumbing, and some brass fixtures can leach lead into water, especially hot water. People who depend on private wells can have additional problems, as most of the pumps sold in recent years contain lead in brass or bronze parts. Even municipal treatment of drinking water is suspected of potentially dangerous side effects. About 70 percent of all Americans drink water that has been disinfected by chlorination. But chlorine can react with organic material in water to form compounds such as chloroform that have been implicated in causing cancer in rats and mice. Except possibly for persons who have some reason for extra caution, however, the benefits of chlorination far outweigh any known danger.

In 2009, the World Health Organization estimated that 1.1 billion people (18 percent worldwide) lacked access to safe drinking water.

Ocean Pollution

Pollution of the oceans disturbs marine ecosystems, which in turn affects shore ecosystems and human industries such as fisheries. Ocean pollution from oil is primarily noted by the public when an oil well at sea is damaged like the 2010 Deepwater Horizon B.P. drilling accident (the largest off-shore oil spill in U.S. history, with an estimated 180 million gallons of oil lost), or when an oil-carrying ship leaks large amounts of oil into the sea as a result of an accident like the 1989 Exxon *Valdez* disaster. Despite this perception, most oil pollution in the ocean actually comes from municipal and industrial runoff, cleaning of ships' bilges or tanks, and other routine events.

Ocean pollution is often in evidence on beaches. Tar balls from oil spills, plastic, and sometimes sewage wash up on beaches. Occasionally beaches have to be closed because of high bacteria counts in the water, making swimming hazardous. Plastic, which generally does not break down in the ocean, is a hazard to larger organisms, such as endangered sea turtles. An international treaty prohibits disposal of plastic wastes that can kill or maim creatures that become entangled, but the treaty is very difficult to enforce. The waste accumulates in massive floating pockets in which plastic to sea-life ratios are 6:1. The largest of these is known as the Pacific Gyre—the Great Garbage Patch, located in the North Pacific, between North America and Asia. It is roughly the size of Texas—though by some estimates it is the size of the continental U.S.—and contains about 3.5 million tons of trash.

►SOLID WASTE

Many areas of the United States continue to face serious problems in safely and effectively managing the garbage they generate. As a nation, we are generating more trash than ever before, and as the generation of municipal solid waste (MSW) increases, the capacity to handle it is decreasing. Municipal solid waste is distinct from industrial wastes produced by factories, tailings from mines, construction and demolition waste, sludge from sewage treatment, and junked machinery.

Disposing of Solid Waste The average person disposed of 4.5 pounds of solid waste each day in 2008, up significantly from 1960, when per person disposal was 2.7 pounds. This waste consists of paper (31 percent), yard trimmings (13.2 percent), food scraps (12.7 percent), plastics (12 percent), metals (8.4 percent), rubber, leather, and textiles (7.9 percent), glass (4.9 percent), wood (6.6 percent), and other materials (3.3 percent). There are four primary methods of dealing with this waste: putting it in landfills, incinerating it, recycling it, and composting. But a fifth option, source reduction, may be the most effective way of reducing the nation's volume of MSW, which totaled 250 million tons in 2008.

Landfills By far the greatest amount of MSW is sent to MSW landfills, of which there were 1,812 in 2008, a drop from nearly 8,000 in 1988. However, while the number of landfills has decreased, the average size has increased. Landfills are the cheapest method of disposing of MSW but they pose a number of environmental problems. Because most landfills are dry, they preserve garbage by cutting it off from the rotting influences of air and moisture. Even biodegradable materials do not decay; newspapers 40 years old can still be read and hot dogs thrown out years before look more or less unchanged.

E.P.A. regulations favor dry landfills for two reasons. As biodegradation in wet landfills occurs there is a buildup of hazardous methane gas; in addition, contaminated water leaching out of landfills (leachate) can pollute the surrounding groundwater. But wet landfills have their supporters, who argue that by enhancing decay, a landfill's biological life can be compressed from 40-to-50 years to 5-to-10 years. Since landfills can contain hundreds of hazardous chemicals, they require continuous monitoring; so shortening their active biological life can yield significant savings. Landfills, however, can be used as a source of alternative energy. In 2003, the East Kentucky Power Cooperative began recovering methane gas from three landfills, harnessing enough electricity to power over 7,500 homes. In

Major Ship Oil Spills

Date	Ship Name	Location	Oil Lost (metric tons)
1979	Atlantic Empress	off Tobago, West Indies	287,000
1991	ABT Summer	700 nautical miles off Angola	260,000
1983	Castillo de Bellver	off Saldanha Bay, South Africa	252,000
1978	Amoco Cadiz	off Brittany, France	223,000
1991	Haven	Genoa, Italy	144,000
1988	Odyssey	700 nautical miles off Nova Scotia	132,000
1967	Torrey Canyon	Scilly Isles, UK	119,000
1972	Sea Star	Gulf of Oman	115,000
1976	Urquiola	La Coruna, Spain	100,000
1977	Hawaiian Patriot	300 nautical miles off Honolulu	95,000
1979	Independenta	Bosphorus, Turkey	95,000
1993	Braer	Garth's Ness, Shetland	84,700
1996	Sea Empress	off southwest Wales	72,000
2002	Prestige	sea off northern Spain	63,000

Note: As of September 2010. One metric ton = 1.1 U.S. tons. Not all spills impacted coastlines, which is why some ship names are unfamiliar to the general public. The Exxon Valdez (1989) spill is estimated to be number 35 in the list. The 2010 Deepwater Horizon oil spill is not listed here because it was not a ship, though it is estimated to be the largest oil spill in history, with nearly five million barrels lost. **Source:** International Tanker Owners Pollution Federation.

2009, there were nearly 400 operating landfills in the U.S. producing energy from methane gas.

Incineration/combustion

One popular method of disposing of municipal waste used to be simply to burn it. In the 1940s there were approximately 700 municipal incinerators in the U.S. Despite the efficiency with which they reduced the volume of waste, they stank, their stacks emitted sizable particles of ash, and they produced noxious gases. For these aesthetic rather than environmental reasons, their numbers declined dramatically in the 1950s. By the time of the Clean Air Act of 1970, there were only 67 incinerators still in operation—most with no energy recovery and no air pollution controls.

Incinerator use increased in the 1980s and early 1990s as space for landfills became scarce, and as the energy produced by incineration became a valuable commodity. But in May, 1994, the U.S. Supreme Court ruled that waste from incinerators had to be treated as toxic on the same basis as any other waste, and that localities could not prevent landfills from taking waste away from incinerators if the landfills offered better bargains. Because landfill was usually cheaper, few chose to incinerate their waste, and few municipalities could afford to subsidize the cost of incinerators. Within six months of the Court's decision, plans for 77 proposed incinerators were canceled.

In 2008, only 12.6 percent of solid waste was incinerated. There were 85 combustors in the U.S. with energy recovery capabilities, and which were able to incinerate up to 99,000 tons of waste per day. In 2007, we combusted 32 million tons of MSW for energy recovery, about 13 percent of the total.

Recycling/composting

Recycling and composting recovered over 33 percent of waste generated in 2008. Recycling rates in 2008 rose from 50 percent in 2005 to 70.9 percent for paper and paperboard, 62 to 64.7 percent for yard trimmings, 44.8 to 48.2 percent for aluminum beer and soft drink containers, and rose to over 99 percent for automobile batteries. By 2008, almost 9,000 curbside recycling programs had sprouted up across the nation, and about 500 material recovery facilities had been established to process the collected materials. Nearly 22 million tons of MSW were recovered for composting in 2007, and there were almost 3,500 community composting programs nationwide, notably in San Francisco and Seattle.

Recycling and composting also have the potential to generate revenues from the sale of secondary materials. Despite a rise in recycling and composting, costs of programs remain high. These are expected to decline as recycling programs mature and become fully integrated with the total MSW management system.

Yet some recycling is a money-losing proposition for municipalities, and one of the most successful recycling programs, for aluminum cans, depends in large part on the deposit programs run by many states. The first such "bottle bill" was passed in Oregon in 1971, and many states have followed suit. In 2009 Connecticut became the first state to expand its bottle bill to cover water bottles. New York passed a similar measure, but implementation was postponed until 2010. In 2008, the Container Recycling Institute estimated that 17 million barrels of crude-oil equivalent were needed to replace the bottles that were trashed in 2006. In one average year, Americans drink more than 34 billion single-serving bottles of water.

Source reduction

Many experts believe that the key to solving the municipal waste problem is source reduction—minimizing the volume of products used and the toxins they contain, and extending their lives in use. Removal of toxins enhances the safety of recycling, landfilling, and combustion, while volume reduction helps to extend the capacity of existing waste systems.

A broad variety of products and packaging that reduce waste and save money have been developed. By reducing the textured design on napkins, for example, the McDonald's Corporation found that it could fit 23 percent more napkins into a shipping container, saving 294,000 pounds of corrugated cardboard and 150 truckload shipments annually. Containers and packaging represented approximately 28 percent of the materials source reduced in 2000. More than 55 million tons of waste were source reduced in the U.S. in 2000, and to keep the program alive, in 2007 the E.P.A. offered cooperative agreements that award $15,000 or more in programmatic funds.

In 2007, the first bill to limit the use of plastic bags in grocery and drug stores was passed in San Francisco. Similar bag-banning measures were being considered in Boston, Baltimore, and Portland. Other initiatives include the introduction of a state bill in New York that in 2009 required businesses to accept plastic bags for recycling.

►HAZARDOUS WASTE

Superfund

In 1980, Congress enacted the Comprehensive Environmental Response, Compensation, and Liability Act (CERCLA), better known as the Superfund, a $1.6 billion, five-year program to clean up thousands of hazardous waste sites. The fund was renewed in 1986 by the Superfund Amendments and Reauthorization Act (SARA). The E.P.A., which administers the Superfund, estimated in 2006 that one in four Americans lived within 4 miles of a toxic waste site.

The E.P.A. evaluates hazardous waste sites for their levels of soil and water contamination, the mobility of toxins, and their proximity to human food supplies. (Contamination of petroleum, however, is excluded from this evaluation.) It then ranks the sites on a numerically based system that factors in risks to groundwater, surface water, and air. The highest ranking sites are placed on the E.P.A.'s National Priorities List (NPL).Once the E.P.A. deems a site a national priority, it can take two types of action. It can remove the hazard in an emergency action limited to one year and/or $2 million. Or it can try to compel the individual or company responsible for the problem to provide a long-term solution.

Superfund sites can, however, be reused as commercial sites such as factories or malls; residential sites such as housing or public works facilities; or for recreational sites such as golf courses or ball fields. In 2009, the E.P.A. estimated that of the 1,500 sites on the NPL, 300 are currently, or will soon be, in productive use. There were 1,279 sites on the NPL pending clean-up in 2010.

In 2007, according to the Government Accountability Office, Congress appropriated nearly $1.32 billion to address Superfund contamination. While the total number of sites needing cleanup is decreasing, the E.P.A. is now addressing bigger, more complex sites. Sites that need cleanup are identified by various parties, including citizens, state agencies, and E.P.A. regional offices. More than half of all the sites have been cleaned up and progress is being made at the others. In August, 2007, the first military-base Superfund cleanup was privatized in California.

Nuclear Waste   Nuclear waste in the United States comes from nuclear weapons production facilities, nuclear power plants, medical equipment (primarily used in radiation treatments), industrial sources of radioactivity used as a more powerful alternative to X-rays, and residues from uranium mining. Nuclear waste is often grouped into two categories, labeled "low-level" and "high-level." Low-level waste is slightly radioactive, often from exposure to a high-level source. High-level waste is often grouped as either civilian, mainly spent fuel from nuclear reactors, or military, wastes produced in the manufacture of nuclear weapons.

The problem with nuclear waste is that it is radioactive and can remain that way for years—in some cases, thousands of years. Early methods of disposal included dumping the wastes at sea and suspending them in a liquid or in cement and injecting the radioactive combination into wells. The United States was among the signatories of a 1976 international convention banning ocean dumping and stopped deep-well injection in 1984.

Current plans call for consortiums of states to develop sites for storage of low-level wastes. One such "temporary" site is in Barnwell County, S.C., which has handled low-level waste for 36 states since 1970. Meanwhile, the federal government continues to search for suitable sites for storage of high-level wastes from nuclear power plants and for very long-lived radioactive materials from weapons production. For the time being, these wastes remain on the sites where they were generated.

In 1998, the E.P.A. certified the Department of Energy's Waste Isolation Pilot Plan in Carlsbad, N.M., the nation's first deep-underground facility for disposal of transuranic waste generated from defense activities. (Transuranic wastes consist primarily of sludges, tools, rags, glassware, and protective clothing that has been contaminated with radioactive elements from weapons production.) The facility is approximately 2,100 feet (640 meters) underground in excavated, natural salt formations. The first shipment of transuranic waste was delivered to the facility in March of 1999. By 2010, shipments from 23 military waste sites from across the nation to this site will reduce the number of Americans living within 50 miles of nuclear waste from 61 million to 4 million. Of course, the 113,000 people living within 50 miles of Carlsbad (as well as many New Mexicans beyond that radius) were understandably opposed, and fought its operation since the site was first proposed in 1974.

The Nuclear Regulatory Commission is the agency charged with monitoring the disposal of waste generated by civilian-operated nuclear reactors. However, most of the nuclear waste in the United States is the by-product of the federal government's nuclear weapons programs. Disposal and monitoring of this waste—which includes millions of cubic yards of contaminated soil and other debris at more than 120 sites in 39 states and the Marshall Islands—is the responsibility of the Department of Energy, the Department of Defense, the Nuclear Waste Technical Review Board, and the Office of the Nuclear Waste Negotiator. Total cost of the cleanup could be about $300–$400 billion over 30 years.

The difficulty of resolving nuclear waste disposal issues is illustrated by the saga of Yucca Mountain, Nevada, which was approved by Congress in 2002 as the nation's first long-term geologic repository for spent nuclear fuel and high-level radioactive waste. If the Nuclear Regulatory Commission grants the site a license, Yucca Mountain could begin accepting waste in 2025, with closure and decommissioning slated to begin in 2125. In the meantime, the site (about 100 miles northwest of Las Vegas) has been the subject of fierce opposition not only in Nevada, but also in states along proposed transportation routes for nuclear waste. The cost of the program for 150 years (1983–2133) is projected to be $96 billion. Over a tenth of this had been spent by August 2010.

▶ HABITATS

The place where a species lives and its surroundings, both living and non-living, is called a habitat. Broadly speaking, habitats include forests, grasslands, deserts, tundra, and wetlands. But there are many specific types of habitats within each of these categories. The habitat of a giant panda, for example, is a bamboo forest in China, not a pine forest in Canada; that of a tuna is the open ocean, not a Florida lake.

When a species' habitat is destroyed or altered, the species may suffer dramatic population declines. For example, because so much of North America's native grasslands have been replaced by farms and other developments, many songbirds have been left without homes and food, and their populations have decreased. Similarly, destruction of China's bamboo forests threaten the giant panda with extinction.

When a species becomes extinct, the Earth's biodiversity is diminished. Biodiversity encompasses all the organisms in the world or in a particular habitat, including all their individual variations. Loss of biodiversity affects humans as well as the threatened species. For example, all major food crops depend on new genetic material from the wild to remain healthy and productive. Noted the 1992 U.N. Earth Summit report, "Our planet's essential goods and services depend on the variety and variability of genes, species, populations and ecosystems."

The major reasons for loss of biological diversity are habitat destruction and modification, overhunting and overfishing, climate change, pollution, and the introduction of so-called alien species (non-native species, such as African tulip trees in Hawaii and Amazon water hyacinths in Africa's Lake Victoria; native species often are unable to compete with the introduced species).

▶ RAIN FORESTS

Rain forests are defined as forests that grow in regions that receive more than 70 inches (1.8 meters) of rain each year. Some rain forests occur in temperate places, such as southern Chile or the northwest coast of North America, but the majority are found in the tropics. Tropical rain forests cover about 2 billion acres (0.8 billion hectares) or about 6 percent of the Earth's land surface. They are found in Central and South America, equatorial Africa, Southeast Asia, and northeastern Australia.

It is estimated that the world may be losing more than 50 million acres (20 million hectares) of tropical forest each year. As the 2000s began, Brazil was losing 12.5–22.5 million acres (5–9 million hectares) of rain forest annually; India was losing 3.7 million acres (1.5 million hectares); and Indonesia was losing 2.2 million acres (0.9 million hectares). Other countries experiencing rapid losses included Myanmar, Costa Rica, Sri Lanka, Vietnam, Thailand, the Philippines, and Ghana.

Tropical rain forests are lush habitats, filled with a greater variety of organisms than any other type of habitat. According to a U.S. National Academy of Sciences report, a typical patch of rain forest covering four square miles (10.4 km²) contains 750 species of trees, 750 species of other plants, 125 species of mammals, 400 species of birds, 100 species of reptiles, and 60 species of amphibians.

The dominant plants in a tropical rain forest are broad-leaved evergreens, while Northern Hemisphere temperate rain forests are filled with needle-leaved conifers. In both, the tallest trees form a dense canopy high above the forest floor. Vines climb up the trees in search of sunlight. In a tropical rain forest, nonparasitic plants grow high in the canopy, using the large trees as perches. In both types of forest, the floor is in deep shade; comparatively few shrubs and grasses grow there.

The rich plant life supports food chains that include many of the world's most spectacular animals: brightly colored frogs, fierce harpy eagles, agile monkeys, powerful tigers, slow-moving sloths, and huge columns of army ants, among many others.

While the diversity of plant life in rain forests is rich, the soil generally is not. The lush plants take up so much of the nutrients in rain forests that little is left for the soil below. A study of a rain forest in Venezuela found that 75 percent of the nutrients were in living organisms like plants and trees, 17 percent were in debris, and only 8 percent were in the soil. When an organism dies and decomposes in a rain forest, the nutrients in its cells are quickly absorbed by nearby plants.

Deforestation has many sources. Individuals often cut down rain forest trees to clear land on which to raise crops and build ranches. But erosion and poor soil fertility soon make these farms and ranches worthless. Large commercial operations deforest vast areas for lumber, paper, and other products, much of which are exported to pay debts owed to foreign governments and banks. Development projects such as roads, hydroelectric dams, and mines also destroy large areas of rain forest.

▶ WETLANDS

A wetland is a location other than a river, lake, or open ocean in which the soil for at least part of the year contains as much water as it will hold (the soil is saturated with water). Saturated soil often slows decomposition of organic matter, resulting in a thin mud or muck, or in the decayed plant remains known as peat. Common names for wetlands include: **Potholes,** which are dry land most of the year, but seasonally become shallow ponds; **Tidal flats,** which are underwater at high tide but become muddy land at low tide; **Permafrost,** which is saturated soil that is frozen most of the year at the surface, and year-round below the surface; **Bogs,** which contain saturated soil and organic material all year, but have little or no standing water; **Marshes,** which contain standing shallow water and low vegetation; and **Swamps,** where trees grow on small hillocks surrounded by standing water. Often these informal categories overlap in a given wetland.

Wetlands produce numerous invaluable benefits. They provide a natural means of flood control, absorbing water from nearby rivers and lakes during periods of high runoff. This buffers the impact of storms and reduces shoreline erosion, thereby protecting against the loss of life and property. And by filtering out pollutants and trapping sediment, wetlands help maintain water quality.

Wetlands are the nurseries for many fish, almost all amphibians, and various birds and mammals. For instance, coastal wetlands are spawning grounds and nurseries for more than two-thirds of U.S. commercial fisheries, a $10 billion a year industry. According to the NOAA, however, between 1998 and 2004 an estimated 361,000 acres of coastal wetlands of the eastern U.S. were lost.

Despite all the benefits associated with wetlands, the definition of what is and is not a wetland is still a bone of contention among environmentalists (who would like to preserve the swampy areas), developers (who would like to drain them and erect housing complexes), and farmers (who would like to divert the water to their crops). In 1987, the U.S. Army Corp. of Engineers defined a wetland as "any ground that has mucky or peat-based soils, nourishes specific plant life, and is saturated with water at least seven days a year." Partisans on all sides of the issue have sought since then to modify that definition. Since colonial days, the contiguous United States has lost 53 percent of its wetlands.

The majority of the nation's wetlands are located in Alaska (170 to 200 million acres). Ohio, Indiana, Iowa, and California have lost the greatest percentage of their wetlands, but the wet states of Florida and Louisiana have lost the greatest total number of acres of wetlands.

Superfund Hazardous Waste Sites, 1981–2009

Date	Number of sites	Date	Number of sites
Oct. 23, 1981[1]	115	Sept. 29, 1995	1,232
Dec. 30, 1982[1]	418	June 17, 1996	1,227
Sept. 8, 1983	406	April, 1997	1,208
Oct. 15, 1984	538	Feb. 1998	1,197
June 10, 1986	703	July 22, 1999	1,226
July 22, 1987	802	July 31, 2000	1,236
Oct. 4, 1989	981	March 2002	1,223
Feb. 11, 1991	1,189	Sept. 2003	1,233
Feb., 1992	1,183	Sept. 23, 2004	1,244
May 10, 1993	1,201	July 1, 2005	1,241
Feb. 23, 1994	1,190	July 6, 2009	1,318

Note: 1. Proposed sites only. Final sites not calculated until release of first National Priorities list in 1983. **Source:** Environmental Protection Agency, National Priorities List, U.S. Census Bureau, *Statistical Abstract of the United States* (2010).

States with the Most NPL Hazardous Waste Sites, 2009

State	Proposed	Deleted	Final
New Jersey	3	25	114
California	3	11	94
Pennsylvania	3	28	94
New York	2	24	85
Michigan	2	17	65
Florida	2	22	51
Washington	0	17	48
Texas	2	10	47
Illinois	6	2	43
Wisconsin	2	6	37

Source: Environmental Protection Agency, National Priorities List (July 2, 2009).

A report released jointly from the U.S. Fish and Wildlife Service and the NOAA in 2009 stated that between 1998 and 2004, about 192,000 acres of wetlands were gained in total, due mostly to the efforts of the U.S. Fish and Wildlife Service Coastal Program that in 2007 boasted nearly 90 projects across the country to restore destroyed habitats. Tidal salt marshes and shrub swamps, however, continue to be lost at significant levels.

ENDANGERED SPECIES

A species is a specific kind of organism, such as the common earthworm, the daffodil, the American opossum, or the human. There are about 1.7 million known species of all kinds, including plants, microorganisms, mammals, and fish. This is thought to represent no more than about 10 percent of all species. (And if the results of some surveys of rain forest canopies in Panama are correct, there may be as many as 30 million insect species alone.) Since life developed more than 600 million years ago, innumerable species have appeared and become extinct. Today, biological diversity faces a rate of species destruction greater than any since the mass extinctions of the dinosaurs 65 million years ago.

Animal and plant species are threatened on a number of fronts. Their natural habitats face destruction through deforestation, wetlands loss, and urban sprawl, and are also affected by processes that derive from global warming such as shifting climate and vegetation zones. Another problem is the shift to "monocultures" in agriculture, producing only one strain of crop for food. Some types of environments present special vulnerabilities. As an example, islands have small populations, limited habitats, and allow the introduction of new (alien) species easily.

International controls

The U.S. Endangered Species Act of 1966 is the chief bulwark protecting species in the United States. The United States is also a signatory to international treaties that protect species. The Convention on International Trade in Endangered Species of Wild Fauna and Flora (CITES) was enacted in 1975. Signed by more than 175 nations, it lists species for which international trade in the live organisms, meat, lumber, or other parts of species is banned or restricted. While smugglers are thought to violate CITES restrictions regularly in what is believed to be beween a $10 and $20 billion annual illegal trade, CITES continues to be one of the main forces in species preservation.

Supplementing the CITES bans on international acts against species is the Convention on Biodiversity, agreed to at the 1992 Earth Summit in Rio de Janeiro. Supplemental to this is the Protocol on Biosafety, an international treaty governing the movements of living organisms resulting from modern biotechnology from one country to another. It was adopted by 156 countries in January 2000, and entered into force in September 2003. The U.S. has not signed either agreement.

Other international treaties affect more limited interests. The International Whaling Commission, with 40 members currently, has been in business since 1949. The commission has probably saved whales from extinction with its near-total ban on whaling since the late 1980s. Other groups, such as the 10-nation Inter-American Tropical Tuna Commission, are modeled on the whaling group. Despite this moratorium, however, Norway and Japan have each killed hundreds of whales annually since the early 1990s; Norway, for example, authorized the killing of about 350 Minke whales in the first half of 2009 alone. Norway, however, suspended whaling in June 2009, citing lack of demand. In 2003, Iceland began its first whale hunt in 14 years, claiming a scientific need to study the stomach contents of Minke whales to measure their effect on important local fish stocks, but in August, 2007 it was announced that Iceland would stop this practice.

To reverse the trend toward species extinction, governments around the world have set aside a total of about 425 million hectares (about 16.4 million square miles) of protected lands in about 3,500 parks and preserves. In addition, many countries try to identify and improve the status of species threatened with extinction.

The efforts come none too soon. The International Conservation Union's (IUCN) list of threatened species of animals and plants worldwide, the "Red List", contained 16,928 species of threatened plants and animals in 2008. These include 22 percent (one in four) of mammalian species, and 13 percent (one in seven) of bird species. Indonesia, India, Brazil and China are among the countries with the most threatened mammals and birds; plant species are declining rapidly in South and Central America, Central and West Africa, and Southeast Asia. In 2009 the IUCN reported that a third of the world's sharks are threatened with extinction.

The list includes 8,457 threatened plants, but because only a small percentage (about 2 percent) of plant species have been evaluated for threat the number actually endangered is believed to be much larger. The number of critically endangered mammal species went from 162 to 188 from 2006 to 2008, and the number of critically endangered bird

Endangered and Threatened Species in the U.S., 2009

Group	Endangered or Threatened[1]	By Lead Region	Total Listed
Mammals	85	Pacific	373
Birds	90	Southwest	136
Reptiles	40	Great Lakes	38
Amphibians	25	/Big Rivers	
Fishes	138	Southeast	329
Clams	70	Northeast	44
Snails	35	Mountain	57
Insects	57	/Prairie	
Arachnids	12	Alaska	8
Crustaceans	22	California	292
Total Animals	**574**	/Nevada	
		Maritime	49
Flowering Plants	715	/ Fisheries	
Conifers & Cycads	3	Foreign[2]	571
Ferns and Allies	26		
Lichens	2		
Total Plants	**746**	**Total Species**	**1,897**

Note: Species may appear in more than one lead region. 1. Includes Endangered, Threatened, Emergency Listing (Threatened), Emergency Listing (Endangered), Similarity of Appearance (Endangered), Similarity of Appearance (Threatened). 2. Includes species outside of U.S. **Source:** U.S. Fish and Wildlife Service, Species Reports (July 6, 2009).

species when from 181 to 190 over the same period. The number of critically endangered fish species increased from 253 to 289, primarily because of longline fisheries.

▶ SELECTED ENDANGERED MAMMALS OF THE WORLD

Although the list of endangered species includes plants and animals of every type, it is the growing group of endangered mammals that have been of special interest and concern to both conservationists and the general public. The International Conservation Union Red List of Endangered Animals indicated in 2008 that 1,141 mammals are considered threatened: 505 are listed as vulnerable, 448 as endangered, and 188 as critically endangered. The "critically endangered," a term indicating that a species' numbers have declined by at least 80 percent, include:

Bandicoot, eastern barred   Range: Australia
Bat, Bulmer's fruit   Range: Papua New Guinea
Bat, Pemba flying-fox   Range: Tanzania
Bear, Baluchistan   Range: Iran, Pakistan
Chinchilla, short-tailed   Range: South America
Cougar, Eastern Range: Canada, U.S.
Deer, Pere David's   Range: China
Gazelle, acacia   Range: Israel
Gazelle, Przewalski's   Range: China
Gibbon, silvery   Range: Indonesia
Goat, Chiltan   Range: Pakistan
Hog, pygmy   Range: Himalayas of Asia
Hutia, large-eared   Range: Cuba
Lemur, golden bamboo   Range: Madagascar
Leopard, North African   Range: North Africa
Mole, Juliana's golden   Range: South Africa
Monkey, Northern brown howling   Range: Brazil
Pika, Helan Shan   Range: China
Potoroo, Gilbert's   Range: Australia
Pronghorn, Baja California   Range: Mexico
Rabbit, Omiltemi   Range: Mexico
Rhinoceros, black   Range: Subsaharan Africa
Rhinoceros, Javan   Range: Southeast Asia
Seal, Mediterranean monk   Range: Mediterranean and Black Sea
Shrew, Gansu   Range: China
Sika, Ryukyu   Range: China, Japan
Tamarin, black-faced lion   Range: Brazil
Tamarin, golden lion   Range: Brazil
Tiger, Amur   Range: Northeast Asia
Tiger, South China   Range: China
Titi, northern Bahian blond   Range: Brazil
Wombat, northern bairy-nosed   Range: Australia

▶ ENDANGERED ANIMALS IN THE U.S.

Although the world's attention is often on large endangered mammals from Africa or the oceans, the United States is home to hundreds of endangered species and subspecies. A subspecies, sometimes called a race, is a local population of a given animal that has some distinctive trait, such as size or color, that sets it apart from the main species.

In the United States, species are classified as threatened or endangered by the U.S. Fish and Wildlife service in accordance with the 1973 Endangered Species Act. The list of endangered species maintained by the Department of the Interior goes back to the original Endangered Species Act of 1966. The first list of endangered species, in March 1967, included 78 species. Today's list contains more than 570 endangered animals and over 700 endangered plants. Species listed are protected in various ways, most specifically by a prohibition against killing them. Also, a critical habitat can be protected against change if the change would contribute to species extinction. The animals and plants listed (www.endangered.fws.gov) range from the large and well-known, such as the Whooping Crane (*Grus americana*) and the Florida Panther (*Felis concolor coryi*), to the small and little-known plants and animals that are nonetheless important for the maintenance of the environment.

Since the Endangered and Threatened Wildlife and Plants listing was started in 1967, several listed species have become extinct, including the Tecopa pupfish (*Cyprinodon nevadensis calidae*, 1982), the blue pike (*Stizostedion vitreum glaucum*, 1983), the Santa Barbara song sparrow (*Melospiza melodia graminea*, 1983), Sampson's pearly mussel (*Epioblasma* (=*Dysnomia*) *sampsoni*, 1984), and the dusky seaside sparrow (*Ammodramus* (=*Ammospiza*) *maritimus nigrescens*, 1990).

There have also been success stories: several species listed as either threatened or endangered have recovered sufficiently to be removed from the list, including the Brown Pelican (*Pelecanus occidentalis*, 1985), and the American Alligator (*Alligator mississippiensis*, 1987). Perhaps the most visible success has been the recovery of bald eagle populations, which had been severely threatened by the effects of the pesticide DDT in the food chain. (DDT is now banned in the United States.) Other causes included loss of habitat and lead in shot in waterfowl carcasses on which eagles and other birds of prey feed (the use of lead shot has been phased out in the U.S.). The bald eagle has not yet been delisted, but this step has been proposed.

Threatened Species by Major Organism Group, 2000–10

	Estimated Number of Described Species	Number of Threatened Species			Percent threatened in 2010
		2000	2004	2010	
Vertebrates	**61,259**	**3,507**	**5,188**	**6,142**	**10%**
Mammals	5,488	1,130	1,101	1,143	21
Birds	9,990	1,183	1,213	1,223	12
Reptiles	8,734	296	304	469	5
Amphibians	6,347	146	1,770	1,895	29
Fishes	30,700	752	800	1,414	5
Invertebrates	**1,232,384**	**1,928**	**1,992**	**2,669**	**0**
Insects	950,000	555	559	740	.01
Molluscs	81,000	938	974	1,037	1
Crustaceans	40,000	408	429	606	1
Plants	**298,506**	**5,611**	**8,321**	**8,495**	**3**
Fungi and Protists	**N.A.**	**N.A.**	**N.A.**	**9**	**0**
TOTAL	**1,642,189**	**11,046**	**15,503**	**17,315**	**1**

Source: International Conservation Union Red List (June 2010).

Major Events in the History of the Environment

1775 Percival Pott observes that chimney sweeps develop cancer as a result of their contact with soot, the first recognition of environmental factors on cancer.

1864 George Perkins Marsh (American: 1801–81) publishes *Man and Nature*, the first textbook on conservation and the first detailed study of human influence on the environment.

1872 Robert Angus Smith (Scottish: 1817–84) describes acid rain.

1885 Yellowstone, world's first national park, opens.

1892 Canada establishes first national park at Banff, Alberta.

1895 Svante Arrhenius (Swedish, 1859–1927) is the first person to investigate effect of increasing carbon dioxide in the atmosphere on global climate.

1903 John Muir (Scottish-American: 1838–1914) founds the Sierra Club.

1905 U.S. president Theodore Roosevelt opens the first national refuge, Pelican Island in Florida, to protect nesting sites of brown pelicans.

U.S. Forest Service established.

National Audubon Society founded.

1911 Canada, Japan, Russia, and the United States sign treaty to limit the harvest of northern fur seals.

1916 National Park Service established.

1928 Boulder Canyon project (Hoover Dam) authorized to bring irrigation, electric power, and flood control system to western United States.

1933 Tennessee Valley Authority created to develop the Tennessee River for flood control, navigation, electric power, agriculture, and forestry.

1939 Paul Müller (Swiss: 1899–1965) discovers insecticidal properties of DDT.

1955 Link between exposure to asbestos and lung cancer established.

1957 Nuclear wastes stored by the Soviet Union in a remote mountain region of the Urals explode; radioactive contamination affects thousands of square miles; several villages permanently evacuated.

1961 Investigations in Scandinavia and the U.S. Adirondacks confirm that acid rain kills some species living in lakes.

1962 *Silent Spring* by Rachel Carson (American: 1907–64) attacks pesticide use and stimulates major environmental movement.

1963 Congress passes first Clean Air Act, allocating $95 million to local, state, and national air pollution control efforts.

1964 Congress passes Wilderness Act, setting up the National Wilderness Preservation System.

1965 Congress passes Highway Beautification Act, banning many highway billboards.

Congress passes Water Quality Act, giving federal government power to set water standards.

Congress passes the Solid Waste Disposal Act, its first major solid waste legislation.

1966 Congress passes Rare and Endangered Species Act.

1967 S. Manabe and R.T. Wetherald predict that increased amounts of carbon dioxide in the atmosphere will lead to global warming.

1968 Congress passes Wild and Scenic Rivers Act, identifying areas of scenic beauty for preservation and recreation.

1970 First Earth Day celebrated on April 22.

Environmental Protection Agency created.

1972 Congress passes Clean Water Act, forbidding discharges of pollutants into navigable waters.

Oregon passes the nation's first bottle recycling law.

The E.P.A. bars registration and interstate sales of DDT because of its persistence in the environment and accumulation in the food chain.

1973 Representatives of 80 nations sign the Con

vention of International Trade in Endangered Species of Wild Fauna and Flora, which prohibits commercial trade in 375 endangered species of wild animals.

1974 F. Sherwood Rowland and Mario Molinas warn that chlorofluorocarbons (CFCs) are destroying the ozone layer.

1976 Congress passes Toxic Substances Control Act to control hazardous industrial chemicals.

1978 Community of Love Canal, near Niagara, N.Y., evacuated after hazardous waste dumps are uncovered. EPA declares site safe in 1990.

1979 Nuclear reactor at Three Mile Island, near Harrisburg, Pa., suffers partial meltdown.

1980 Congress passes Comprehensive Environmental Response, Compensation and Liability Act (the "Superfund") to clean up hazardous waste sites.

1984 More than 2,000 die and thousands more are injured by toxic gas from an accident at the U.S.-owned Union Carbide plant in Bhopal, India.

1985 British scientists discover that a "hole" in the ozone layer develops over Antarctica each winter.

The U.S. sets up a Conservation Reserve Program to remove environmentally sensitive farmland from agricultural use.

1986 A worldwide ban on whaling begins.

Chernobyl nuclear reactor number 4 explodes and burns, causing 31 deaths within days, shortening the lives of thousands, and forcing the evacuation of hundreds of square miles in Soviet Ukraine for an unknown length of time.

1988 The U.S. Ocean Dumping Ban Act mandates an end to ocean dumping of industrial waste and sewage sludge.

1989 Exxon *Valdez* grounds, leaking 10–12 million gallons of oil into Prince William Sound, Alaska.

1992 Representatives from 178 countries attend the first Earth Summit in Rio de Janeiro, where they sign treaties pledging to increase the diversity of animal and plant species and to halt global warming.

1994 U.S. Fish and Wildlife Service recommends that status of American bald eagle be reduced from "endangered" to "threatened" in most of the U.S..

1996 The U.S. National Oceanic and Atmospheric Administration reports that measurements show that a global campaign to lower production of chemicals that damage the ozone layer has succeeded and that by 2010 the ozone layer will have begun to recover and by 2050 the Antarctic ozone "hole" will have closed.

1997 Representatives from more than 150 countries meet in Kyoto, Japan, where they agree to reduce emissions of greenhouse gases 5.2 percent worldwide by 2010.

2001 The Intergovernmental Panel on Climate Change (IPCC) reports that there is new and stronger evidence that most of the warming in the last half century is due to human activities.

2002 The United Nations World Summit on Sustainable Development in Johannesburg, South Africa, agrees on a program of sustainable development to reduce poverty while protecting the earth's natural resources.

2005 Thought extinct since 1944, the ivory-billed woodpecker is sighted in the swamps of Arkansas.

2007 The IPCC reports that global warming is unequivocal, and is influenced by human activity.

2009 Delegates from nearly 200 countries meet as part of the United Nations Climate Change Conference at Copenhagen as an attempt to shape an international response to climate change.

2010 The B.P. Deepwater Horizon drilling rig explosion results in the largest marine oil spill in history, with roughly 180 million gallons of crude oil lost in the Gulf of Mexico.

Technology

Major Discoveries in the History of Technology

(See also "Chronology of Information Processing" in "Computers" and "Satellites and Space Probes" and "Spaceflights Carrying People" in "Astronomy".)

B.C.

2,400,000 Ancestors of human beings begin to manufacture stone tools.

1,000,000 Ancestors of human beings learn to control fire.

90,000 People from the Katranda culture in what is now Congo make barbed bone points, probably for use in harpoons.

25,000 People in what is now the Czech Republic begin weaving cloth.

23,000 Bow and arrow developed in Mediterranean regions of Europe and Africa.

10,000 The Jomon culture of Japan makes the first known pottery.

5000 Egyptians start mining and smelting copper ore.

3500 Potter's wheel and (shortly after) wheeled vehicles appear in Mesopotamia.

2900 Great Pyramid of Giza and first form of Stonehenge (a ditch and bank) are built.

2000 Interior bathrooms are built in palaces in Crete.

1500 Earliest glass vessels used in Egypt.

522 Eupalinus of Megara (Greek: 6th cent.) constructs 3,600-ft. tunnel on Samos to supply water from one side of Mt. Castro to other.

290 Pharos lighthouse at Alexandria is built.

260 Archimedes (Greek: c. 287–212 B.C.) develops mathematical descriptions of the lever and other simple machines.

200 Romans develop concrete.

140 Chinese start making paper but do not use it for writing.

100 In Illyria (now Yugoslavia and Albania), water-powered mills are introduced.

A.D.

c. 1 Chinese invent centerline rudder for ships and magnetic compass; neither found in West for 1,000 years.

190 Chinese develop porcelain.

600 First windmills are built in what is now Iran.

704 Between 704 and 751, Chinese start printing with woodblocks.

1040 Chinese develop gunpowder.

1041 Between 1041 and 1048, Chinese inventor Bi Sheng develops movable type.

1190 First-known reference to a compass in Europe.

1267 Book written by Roger Bacon (English: c. 1220–92) in 1267 mentions eyeglasses to correct farsightedness.

1288 First-known gun, a small cannon, made in China.

1310 Mechanical clocks driven by weights begin to appear in Europe.

c. 1440 Johannes Gutenberg (German: c. 1398–1468) reinvents printing with movable type.

1450 Nicholas of Cusa (German: 1401–64) develops eyeglasses for the nearsighted.

1555 Georg Bauer (Georgius Agricola; German: 1494-1555) writes *De re metallica*, a handbook of mining techniques.

c. 1590 Compound microscope (using two lenses) developed in Holland.

1608 Telescope developed in Holland, probably by Hans Lippershey (German-Dutch: c. 1570–1619).

1620 Cornelis Jacobszoon Drebbel (Dutch: 1572–1633) builds first navigable submarine.

1643 Evangelista Torricelli (Italian: 1608–47) makes first barometer, thereby producing first vacuum known to science.

1654 Christiaan Huygens (Dutch: 1629–95) develops pendulum clock.

1658 Robert Hooke (English: 1635–1703) invents balance spring for watches.

1698 Thomas Savery (English: c. 1650–1715) patents the "Miner's Friend," first practical steam engine.

1701 Jethro Tull (English: 1674–1741), possibly inspired by Chinese devices, invents device for planting seeds called a seed drill.

1709 Daniel Gabriel Fahrenheit (German-Dutch: 1686–1736) invents alcohol thermometer; 1714, mercury thermometer.

1733 John Kay (English: 1704–64) invents flying-shuttle loom, which, along with the steam engine and improvements in making iron, is a key to the start of Industrial Revolution.

1751 Benjamin Huntsman (English: 1704–76) invents crucible process for casting steel.

1762 John Harrison (English: 1693–1776) designs a marine chronometer (clock) accurate enough to enable navigators to calculate longitude at sea.

1764 James Hargreaves (English: 1720–78) introduces spinning jenny, a machine that spins from 8 to 120 threads at once.

1765 James Watt (Scottish: 1736–1819) builds model of his improved steam engine.

1769 Sir Richard Arkwright (English: 1732–92) patents the water frame, a spinning machine that complements spinning jenny.

1783 Joseph-Michel and Jacques-Etienne Montgolfier (French: 1740–1810; 1745–99) develop first hot air balloon. Jacques A.C. Charles (French: 1746–1823) builds first hydrogen balloon.

1785 Edmund Cartwright (English: 1743–1823) invents first form of the power loom.

1792 William Murdock (Scottish: 1754–1839) is first to use coal gas for lighting.

1793 Eli Whitney (American: 1765–1825) invents cotton gin, a machine for separating cotton fibers from seeds.

1800 Alessandro G.A.A. Volta (Italian: 1745–1827) invents first form of chemical battery for producing electric current.

1804 Nicolas-François Appert (French: c. 1750–1841) develops canning as means of preserving food.

1807 Robert Fulton (American: 1765–1815) introduces first commercially successful steamboat.

1816 Sir David Brewster (Scottish: 1781–1868) invents kaleidoscope.

1822 Joseph N. Niepce (French: 1765–1833) produces earliest form of the photograph.

1823 Charles Macintosh (Scottish: 1766–1843) patents a waterproof fabric.

1825 George Stephenson (English: 1781–1848) develops first steam-powered locomotive to carry both passengers and freight.

1835 William Henry Fox Talbot (English: 1800–77) invents photographic negative using silver chloride, essentially how black-and-white pictures are made today.

1837 Samuel Finley Breese Morse (American: 1791–1872) patents first commercially successful version of the telegraph.

1839   Louis J.M. Daguerre (French: 1789–1851) announces his process for making photographs, which come to be called daguerreotypes.

Charles Goodyear (American: 1800–60) discovers how to make rubber resistant to heat and cold, a process called vulcanization.

1842   Sir John Bennet Lawes (English: 1814–99) patents manufacture of superphosphate, the first manufactured fertilizer.

1843   Isambard Kingdom Brunel's (English: 1806–59) *Great Britain* is first iron-hulled screw-propellor ship to cross the Atlantic.

1846   Elias Howe (American: 1819–67) patents lock-stitch sewing machine.

Richard March Hoe (American: 1812–96) invents rotary printing press.

1851   Isaac Merritt Singer (American: 1811–75) patents continuous-stitch sewing machine.

1852   Elisha Graves Otis (American: 1811–61) installs first elevator incorporating safety device that prevents cage from falling if the cable breaks.

1856   Henry Bessemer (English: 1813–98) develops method of making inexpensive steel (Bessemer process).

1859   Edwin L. Drake (American: 1819–80) drills first oil well, in Titusville, Pa.

1862   Richard Jordan Gatling (American: 1818–1903) invents first form of machine gun.

1866   Robert Whitehead (English: 1823–1905) invents naval torpedo. Georges Leclanché (French: 1839–82) develops first form of dry cell for producing electricity.

1867   Latham Sholes (American: 1819–90) and two others invent first practical typewriter.

1869   Hippolyte Mège Mouriés (French: 1817–80) patents margarine.

1866   Cyrus W. Field (U.S.: 1819–92) succeeds in laying the Trans-Atlantic Cable under the Atlantic Ocean, connecting Europe to America by telegraph wire.

1874   Joseph Farwell Glidden (American: 1813–1906) invents the kind of barbed wire used today.

1876   Alexander Graham Bell (Scottish-American: 1847–1922) invents telephone.

Karl von Linde (German: 1842–1934) invents first practical refrigerator.

1877   Nikolaus A. Otto (German: 1832–91) invents type of internal combustion engine still used in most automobiles.

Thomas Alva Edison (U.S.: 1847–1931) invents phonograph, which uses a tinfoil-covered cylinder.

1878   Louis-Marie-Hilaire Bernigaud (French: 1839–1924) develops rayon.

Carl Gustaf Patrik de Laval (Swedish: 1845–1913) invents turbine operated centrifugal cream separator.

1879   Edison and Sir Joseph W. Swan (English: 1828–1914) independently discover how to make practical electric lights.

1885   Karl Benz (German: 1844–1929) builds precursor of modern automobile.

Rover Safety Bicycle, built in England, is first bicycle with essentially modern features.

1886   George Westinghouse (American: 1846–1914) invents air brake for railroad cars.

1888   Emile Berliner (German: 1851–1929) invents phonograph disk.

John B. Dunlop (Scottish: 1840–1921) patents air-filled tire.

George Eastman (American: 1854–1932) develops first camera using roll film.

1889   Gustave Eiffel (French: 1832–1923) builds his famous tower in Paris; at 993 ft., it is tallest free-standing structure of the time.

1893   Rudolf Diesel (German: 1858–1913) describes diesel engine.

1895   First public showing of a motion picture, "Workers Leaving the Lumière Factory" by Auguste and Louis Lumière (French: 1862–1954; 1864–1948), in Paris.

Guglielmo Marconi (Italian: 1874–1937) transmits signals for a mile with his wireless telegraph (a precursor of radio) near Bologna, Italy.

1897   Karl Ferdinand Braun (German: 1850–1918) invents cathode-ray tube oscilloscope.

1898   Valdemar Poulsen (Danish: 1869–1942) invents magnetic wire recorder, the precursor to the modern tape recorder.

1902   Willis H. Carrier (American: 1876–1950) invents air conditioning.

1903   Orville and Wilbur Wright (American: 1871–1948; 1867–1912) fly the first successful airplane at Kitty Hawk, N.C.

1904   John Fleming (English: 1849–1945) develops first vacuum tube, a device for changing alternating current to direct.

1907   Lee De Forest (American: 1873–1961) patents Audion vacuum tube, a device for magnifying weak electronic signals.

1908   Henry Ford (American: 1863–1947) introduces Model T, the first affordable automobile.

1909   Leo Baekeland (Belgian-American: 1863–1944) patents Bakelite, the first truly successful plastic.

1912   Reginald Aubrey Fessenden (Canadian-American: 1866-1932) develops heterodyne circuit, an important improvement in radio reception.

1917   Clarence Birdseye (American: 1886–1956) develops freezing as a means of preserving food.

1919   Sir Arthur W. Brown (British: 1886–1948) and Sir John W. Alcock (British: 1892–1919) make first transatlantic flight, Newfoundland to Ireland.

1924   Vladimir Kosma Zworykin (Russian-American: 1889–1982) develops iconoscope, the beginning of modern television.

1929   Robert H. Goddard (American: 1882–1945) launches first instrumented, liquid-fueled rocket.

1930   Sir Frank Whittle (British: 1907–96) patents jet engine.

1931   Ernst A.F. Ruska (German: 1906–88) builds first electron microscope.

1934   Wallace Hume Carothers (American: 1896–1937) invents nylon, first marketed in 1938.

1935   Sir Robert Alexander Watson-Watt (Scottish: 1892-1973) begins work on radio detection and ranging (radar).

1937   Chester F. Carlson (American: 1906–68) invents xerography, the first method of photocopying.

1939   Paul H. Müller (Swiss: 1899–1965) discovers that DDT is potent and long-lasting insecticide.

Igor I. Sikorsky (Russian-American: 1889–1972) designs and flies first helicopter developed for mass production.

1940   Peter Carl Goldmark (Hungarian-American: 1906–77) demonstrates first successful color television system.

1941   John Rex Whinfield (British: 1901–66) invents Dacron.

1942   Enrico Fermi (Italian-American: 1901–54) builds first nuclear reactor.

1947   Dennis Gabor (Hungarian-British: 1900–79) develops holography, a method of recording and displaying a three-dimensional object.

1948   Goldmark develops the 33⅓ rpm long-playing phonograph record.

Georges de Mestral (Swiss: 1908–90) invents Velcro, patented in 1955.

John Bardeen (American: 1908–91), Walter H. Brattain (American: 1902–87), and William B. Shockley (English-American: 1910-89) invent the transistor.

1957   Gordon Gould (American: 1920–2005) develops basic idea for the laser, which he succeeds in patenting in 1986 after long struggle.

The Soviet spacecraft *Sputnik 1* becomes the first satellite to orbit Earth.

1958   United States opens first experimental nuclear power plant.

1959   First industrial robot is marketed.

1962 First active communications satellite, Telstar, goes into orbit.
1963 Audiocassettes introduced.
1964 Touch-tone telephones introduced.
1966 Engineers at ITT demonstrate fiber optics as a method of transmitting data.
1968 The first supersonic airliner, the Soviet Tupolev TU-144, is demonstrated on Dec. 31.
1969 ATMs and bar-code scanners introduced.
1970 Boeing 747 jets go into service.
1975 IBM introduces first laser printer.
1982 Compact disc players introduced.
1984 Motorola introduces first commercial version of cellular phone in U.S.
1989 The U.S. Defense Department launches the first satellite in the Global Positioning System.
1990 Leigh T. Canham (British) develops a method for producing light from stimulated silicon.
1991 Woo Paik and coworkers produce the first prototype of digital high-definition television.
1994 Channel Tunnel, also known as the Chunnel, connecting England and France beneath the English Channel, is officially opened.
Charles K. Rhodes of the University of Chicago develops an X-ray-emitting laser.

1995 Scientists at Los Alamos National Laboratory in New Mexico develop a flexible tape that is superconducting at the temperature of liquid nitrogen (about –325°F).
A group led by Junji Kido of Yamagata Univ. in Japan combines three different diode layers, including a blue-emitting diode that is a major advance of its own, to make white light.
Competing groups agree on standards for the Digital Video Disc (DVD), an improved compact disc that can store a complete motion picture on a disc the size of a CD.
1997 Dolly, the first cloned sheep, is born.
1998 John A. Turner and Oscar Khaselev of the U.S. National Renewable Energy Laboratory in Golden, Colo. develop a solar cell that can split water into hydrogen and oxygen.
2001 The first succesful operation to insert an AbioCor fully self-contained artificial heart is performed.
The first draft of the complete human genome is announced.
2007 U.S. and Australian defense programs annouce the successful flight of a hypersonic scramjet, which reached a speed of Mach 10.
2009 NASA launches its Ares Rocket,which will enable it to send people back to the Moon and to Mars.

National Inventors Hall Of Fame

In 1973 the U.S. National Council of Patent Law Associations (now the National Council of Intellectual Property Law) began the practice of naming inventors who hold U.S. patents to the National Inventors Hall of Fame. Although many of those honored have many patents, the committee selects one patent for each inventor (or group of inventors) as the occasion for the award, which they identify by the title of the original patent application. When an invention is the work of more than one person, the description of the invention is given only for one inventor. The date at the end of each of the following entries denotes the year of induction. The Hall is located in Akron, Ohio.

National Inventors Hall Of Fame Inductees

Field/Invention	Inventor	Born-Died	Inducted
AGRICULTURE			
Automated Sugar Refining	Norbert Rillieux	1806–1894	2004
Breakfast Cereal	John Harvey Kellogg	1852–1943	2006
Food Preservatives	Lloyd Hall	1894–1971	2004
Frozen Foods	Clarence Birdseye	1886–1956	2005
Glyphosate Herbicide (Roundup®)	John Franz	b.1929	2007
Improvement in Concentration of Milk	Gail Borden, Jr.	1801–1874	2006
Modern Beehive	Lorenzo Lorraine Langstroth	1810–1895	2007
Pasteurization	Louis Pasteur	1822–1895	1978
Peach and fruit varieties	Luther Burbank	1849–1926	1986
Plow	John Deere	1804–1886	1989
Products Using Peanuts And Sweet Potatoes	George Washington Carver	1864–1943	1990
Reaper	Cyrus Mccormick	1809–1894	1976
ARTS AND LEISURE			
Ballpoint Pen	Laszlo Josef Biro	1899–1985	2007
Board Game	Milton Bradley	1836–1911	2006
Cast-Iron Piano Frame	Alpheus Babcock	1785–1842	2007
Flexible Flyer Shield Toboggan	Samuel Allen Leeds	1841–1918	2007
Improvement In Clock Manufacture	Eli Terry	1772–1852	2007
Improvements To Fountain Pen	Lewis Waterman	1837–1901	2006
Model Railroad	Joshua Cowen	1877–1965	2007
Solid-Body Electric Guitar	Les Paul	b.1915	2005
Zamboni Machine	Frank Zamboni	1901–1988	2007
ASTRONOMY			
Far Electrograph Ultraviolet Camera	George R. Carruthers	b.1939	2003
Improvements To Telescope	Ambrose Swasey	1846–1937	2006
Satellite Servicing Techniques	Frank Cepollina	b.1936	2003
BIOTECH			
Recombinant DNA technology	Herb Boyer	b.1936	2001
	and Stan Cohen	b.1935	2001

Field/Invention	Inventor	Born-Died	Inducted
CHEMISTRY			
Apparatus For Testing Acidity	Arnold O. Beckman	1900–2004	1987
Bromine	Herbert Henry Dow	1866–1930	1983
Lyophilized Reaction Mixtures	Emmett W. Chapelle	b.1925	2007
Molecular Sieves	Edith Flanigen	b.1929	2004
Process Of Producing Ammonia	Karl Bosch	1884–1940	2006
COMMUNICATIONS			
Audion Amplifier	Lee DeForest	1873–1961	1977
Automatic Telephone-Exchange	Almon Strowger	1829–1908	2006
Automatic Typesetting	John Raphael Rogers	1856–1934	2007
Automobile Radio	William P. Lear	1902–1978	1993
Cathode Ray Tube	Vladimir Kosma Zworykin	1889–1982	1977
Cell Phone Switching	Amos Joel, Jr.	1918–2008	2008
Charge-Coupled Device (Ccd)	Willard Sterling Boyle	b.1924	2006
Color Photography	Leopold Godowsky, Jr	1900–1983	2005
	and Leopold Mannes	1899–1964	2005
Communications Satellite	John Pierce	1910–2002	2003
Computerized Telephone Switching	Erna Hoover	b. 1926	2008
High Resolution Image-Scanning Radar	Robert H. Rines	b. 1922	1994
Dictaphone	Charles Tainter	1854–1940	2006
Dolby Noise Reduction	Ray Dolby	b.1933	2004
Double-Cylinder Printing-Process	Richard March Hoe	1812–1886	2006
Electric Lamp	Thomas Alva Edison	1847–1931	1973
Feedback Control	Amar Bose	b. 1929	2008
Foil Electret Microphone	James Edward West	b. 1931	1999
	and Gerhard M. Sessler	b. 1931	1999
High Frequency Alternator	Ernst Alexanderson	1878–1975	1983
Kurzweil Reading Machine	Raymond Kurzweil	b. 1948	2002
Localizer Antenna System	Andrew Alford	1904–1992	1983
LP Record	Peter Carl Goldmark	1906–1977	2007
Machine For Producing Printing Bars	Ottmar Mergenthaler	1854–1899	1982
Magnetic Recording.	S. Joseph Begun	1905–1995	1998
Apparatus For Coating Plates For Use In Photography	George Eastman	1854–1932	1977
Method And Means Of Magnetic Recording	Marvin Camras	1916–1995	1985
Method Of Receiving High Frequency Oscillations	Edwin Howard Armstrong	1890–1954	1980
Microphone And Gramophone	Emile Berliner	1851–1929	1994
Modern Photocopier	Robert Gundlach	b.1926	2005
Multiplane Camera	Walt Disney	1901–1966	2000
Negative Feedback Amplifier	Harold Stephen Black	1898–1983	1981
Optical Character Recognition (Ocr)	Jacob Rabinow	1910–1999	2005
Photo Composing Machine	Louis Marius Moyroud	b. 1914	1985
	and René Alphonse Higonnet	1902–1983	1985
Photographic Product Comprising A Rupturable Container Carrying Photographic Processing Liquid	Edwin Herbert Land	1909–1991	1977
Picture Projector	Auguste Lumiere	1852–1954	2007
	and Louis Lumiere	1864–1948	2007
Railway Telegraphy	Granville Woods	1856–1910	2006
Spin Stabilized Synchronous Communications Satellite	Harold Rosen	b.1926	2003
Telautograph	Elisha Gray	1835–1901	2007
Telegraph Signals	Samuel F. B. Morse	1791–1872	1975
Telegraphy	Alexander Graham Bell	1874–1922	1974
Television Receiver	Louis W. Parker	1906–1993	1988
Television Remote Control	Robert Adler	1913–2007	2008
Television System	Philo Taylor Farnsworth	1906–1971	1984
Transmitting Electrical Signals	Guglielmo Marconi	1874–1937	1975
Variable Frequency Oscillation Generator	William R. Hewlett	1913–2001	1992
Videotape Recorder	Charles F. J. Ginsburg	1920–1992	1990
Wireless Radio Communication	Reginald Aubrey Fessenden	1866–1932	2000
Wireless Telegraphy	Oliver Joseph Lodge	1851–1940	2007
Electrophotography C	Chester F. Carlson	1906–1968	1981
Stroboscope	Harold E. Edgerton	1903–1990	1986
COMPUTING AND ELECTRONICS			
Calculating Machine	William Seward Burroughs	1855–98	1987
Charge-Coupled Device (CCD)	George Smith	b.1930	2006
Complex Computer	George R. Stibitz	1904–95	1983
Computer Mouse	Douglas Engelbart	b.1925	1998
Differential Analyzer	Vannevar Bush	1890–1974	2004
Dynamic Random Access Memory	Robert H. Dennard	b.1932	1997
Eniac Data Translating Device	John Mauchly	1907–1980	2002
	and John Presper Eckert, Jr.	1919–1995	2002
Ethernet	Robert Metcalfe	b.1946	2007

Field/Invention	Inventor	Born-Died	Inducted
Field Effect Device With Insulated Gate	Robert A. Bower	b.1936	1997
Magnetron and Semiconductor Laser	Robert N. Hall	b.1919	1994
Improved Magnetic Core Memory	Kenneth H. Olsen	b.1926	1990
Light-emitting Diode (LED)	Nick Holonyak, Jr.	b. 1928	2008
Liquid-Crystal Display (LCD)	James L. Fergason	b.1934	1998
Magnetic Disc Storage	John Joseph Lynott,	1921–1994	2007
	Louis Stevens,	b. 1925	2008
	and Willliam Goddard	1913–1997	2007
Magnetic Pulse Controlling Device	An Wang	1920–1990	1988
Microcomputer With Bus Control Means For	Dennis Moeller	b.1950	1997
Peripheral Devices	and Mark Dean	b.1957	1997
Microprocessor	Federico Faggin	b.1941	1996
	and Stanley Mazor	b.1941	1996
Microprocessor Concept And Architecture	Marcian Edward "Ted" Hoff, Jr.	b.1937	1996
Miniaturiized Electronic Circuits	Jack S. Kilby	b.1923	1982
Random Access Memory (RAM)	Jay W. Forrester	b.1918	1979
Packet Switching	Donald Watt Davies	1924–2000	2006
Packetized Ensemble Modem	Paul Baran	b.1926	2007
Personal Computer	Steve Wozniak	b.1950	2000
Pulse Code Modulation (PCM)	Claude Shannon	1916–2001	2004
	and Bernard Oliver	1916–1995	2004
Semiconductor Device-And-Lead Structure	Robert N. Noyce	1927–1990	1983
Storage And Processing Of Numerical Data	Herman Hollerith	1869–1929	1990
Supercomputer	Seymour Cray	1925–1996	1997
Transistor	John Bardeen	1908–1991	1974
	Walter H. Brattain	1902–1987	1974
	and William Bradford Shockley	1910–1989	1974
Transmission Control Protocol/Internet	Robert Elliot Kahn	b.1938	2006
Protocol (TCP/IP)	and Vinton Gray Cerf	b.1943	2006
INDUSTRY			
Adhesive Tape	Richard Gurley Drew	1988–1980	2007
Air Conditioner	Willis Haviland Carrier	1876–1950	1985
Apparatus For Handling Ore	George H. Hulett	1846–1923	2006
Automatic Elevator Doors	Alexander Miles	1838–?	2007
Bessemer Steel Process	Henry Bessemer	1813–1898	2002
Bottle Cap	William Painter	1838–1906	2006
Buckeye Mower Machine	Lewis Miller	1829–1899	2006
Carbon Filament For Lightbulbs	Lewis Latimer	1848–1928	2006
Catalytic Cracking Of Hydrocarbons With A	Charles J. Plank	1915–1989	1979
Crystalline Zeolite Catalyst Composite	and Edward J. Rosinski	1921–2000	1979
Catalytic Cracking Of Petroleum	Eugene J. Houdry	1892–1962	1990
Ceramic Substrate For Catalytic Converters	Irwin Lachman	b.1930	2002
	Ronald Lewis	b.1936	2002
	and Rodney Bagley	b.1934	2002
Construction Of Iron Buildings	James Bogardus	1800–1874	2007
Containerized Shipping	Malcom McLean	1913–2001	2008
Cotton Gin	Eli Whitney	1765–1825	1974
Direct-Current (D/C) Dynamo	Zénobe Théophile Gramme	1826–1901	2006
Dishwasher	Josephine Garis Cochran	1839–1913	2006
Electric Transformer	William Stanley	1858–1916	1995
Electric-Arc Lamp	Elihu Thomson	1853–1937	2006
Electrostatic Precipitator	Frederick G. Cottrell	1877–1948	1992
Escalator	Charles D. Seeberger	1857–1931	2007
	and Jesse Wilford Reno	1861–1947	2007
Fiberglass	John Thomas	1907–1991	2006
	and Russell Games Slayter	1896–1964	2006
Fire Hydrant	Birdsill Holly, Jr.	1820–1894	2006
Fluid Catalytic Cracking	Eger V. Murphree	1898–1962	1999
	Homer Z. Martin	1910–1993	1999
	and Donald L. Campbell	1904–2002	1999
Fluorescent Light	Edmund Germer	1901–1987	1996
Foot Measuring Device	Charles F. Brannock	1903–1992	2007
Gas Mask, Three-Way Traffic Signal	Garrett Morgan	1887–1963	2005
Gas Optical Maser	Ali Javan	b.1926	2006
Glass Shaping Machine	Michael Joseph Owens	1859–1923	2007
Glass Tile	Louis Comfort Tiffany	1848–1933	2007
High-Voltage Induction Coil	Charles Page	1812–1868	2006
Hydroelectric Waterwheel	Lester Pelton	1829–1908	2006
Ice-Cream Freezer, And Many Others	Beulah Louise Henry	1887–1973	2006
Improvement In Boring-Mills	William Sellers	1824–1905	2007
Improvement In Electromagnetic Alarm-Bells	Moses Gerrish Farmer	1820–1893	2006

Field/Invention	Inventor	Born-Died	Inducted
Improvement In Hoisting Apparatus	Elisha Graves Otis	1811–1861	1988
Improvement In Rock-Drills	Simon Ingersoll	1818–1984	2006
Improvements In Weaving Looms	George Crompton	1829–1886	2007
Incandescent Electric Lamp	Irving Langmuir	1881–1957	1989
Machine For Crushing Stone	Eli Whitney Blake	1795–1886	2007
Manufacture Of Aluminum	Charles Martin Hall	1863–1914	1976
Maser	Arthur Schawlow	1921–1999	1996
Mason Jar	John Mason	1832–1902	2006
Neon Tubing	Georges Claude	1870–1960	2007
Numerical Control Of Machine Tools	John T. Parsons	1913–2007	1993
Optically Pumped Laser Amplifiers	Gordon Gould	1920–2005	1991
Paper Bag Manufacturing	Margaret Knight	1838–1914	2006
Portable Vacuum Cleaner	James Spangler	1848–1915	2006
Portable Voltmeter	Edward Weston	1850–1936	2006
Power-Loom	Erastus Brigham Bigelow	1814–1879	2006
Process For Making Malleable Cast Iron	Seth Boyden	1788–1870	2006
Prodution Of Ammonia	Fritz Haber	1868–1934	2006
Propellor	John Ericsson	1803–1889	1993
Revolving Door	Theophilus Van Kannel	1841–1919	2007
Ruby Laser Systems	Theodore Harold Maiman	b.1927	1984
Safety Pin	Walter Hunt	1796–1859	2006
Safety Razor	King Camp Gillette	1855–1932	2007
Sewing Machine	Elias Howe	1819–1867	2004
Shoe Lasting-Machine	Jan Matzeliger	1852–1889	2006
Signal Flare	Martha Coston	1826–1904	2006
Silicon Solar Cell	Daryl Chapin	1906–1995	2008
	Calvin Fuller	1902–1994	2008
	and Gerald Pearson	1905–1987	2008
Steam Engine	John Stevens	1749–1838	2006
Stock Ticker	Edward Augustin Calahan	1838–1912	2006
System Of Electric Arc Lighting	Charles Francis Brush	1849–1929	2006
System Of Electrical Distribution	Charles Proteus Steinmetz	1865–1923	1977
Traction Engine	Benjamin Holt	1849–1920	2006
Typewriter	Christopher L. Sholes	1819–1890	2001
Vacuum Tube	William D. Coolidge	1873–1974	1975
Water Tube Steam Boiler	George H. Babcock	1832–1893	1997
	and Stephen Wilcox, Jr.	1830–1893	1997
Water-Powered Cotton Mill	Samual Slater	1768–1835	2007
Weaving Straw With Silk Or Thread	Mary Dixon Kies	1752–1837	2006
Yale Lock	Linus Yale, Jr.	1821–1868	2006
Zig-Zag Stitch Sewing Machine	Helen Blanchard	1840–1922	2006
Zipper	Gideon Sundback	1880–1954	2006

MATERIALS

Field/Invention	Inventor	Born-Died	Inducted
Barbed Wire	Joseph Glidden		2006
Carborundum	Edward Acheson	1856–1931	1997
Celluloid	John Wesley Hyatt	1837–1920	2006
Cellophane	Jacques Brandenberger		2006
Coaxial Cable	Lloyd Espenscheid	1889–1986	2006
	and Herman A. Affel	1893–1972	2006
Diamine-Dicarboxylic Acid Salts And Process Of Preparing Same And Synthetic Fiber	Wallace Hume Carothers	1896–1937	1984
Dynamite	Alfred Nobel	1833–1896	1998
Fiberglas	Dale Kleist	1909–1998	2006
Film Structure And Method Of Preparation	Katharine Burr Blodgett	1989–1979	2007
Fused Silica And Silicones	J. Franklin Hyde	1903–1999	2000
Kevlar	Stephanie Kwolek	b. 1923	1995
Manufacture of Titanium	William Justin Kroll	1889–1973	2000
Optical Fiber	Robert D. Maurer	b. 1924	1993
	Donald Keck	b. 1941	1993
	and Peter C. Schultz	b. 1942	1993
Polymers	Paul Hogan	b. 1919	2001
	and Robert L. Banks	1921–1989	2001
Polytetrafluoroethylene (Gore-Tex®)	Robert W. Gore	b.1937	2006
Polyurethane	Donald Fletcher Holmes	1910–1980	1991
	and W.E. "Butch" Hanford	b. 1908	1991
PVC Plastisols	Waldo Semon	1898–1999	
Scotchgard™	Samuel Smith	1927–2005	2001
	and Patsy Sherman	b. 1930	2001
Styrofoam	Otis Ray McIntire	1918–1996	2008
Superglue	Harry Coover	1919–1996	2004
Synthetic Resins (Bakelite)	Leo Hendrik Baekeland	1863–1944	1978
Synthetic Rubber (Neoprene)	Julius A. Nieuwland	1878–1936	1996

Field/Invention	Inventor	Born-Died	Inducted
Tempered Glass	Harold McMaster	1916–2003	2008
Tetrafluoroethylene Polymers	Roy J. Plunkett	1910–1994	1985
Velcro®	George De Mestral	1907–1990	1999
Wrinkle Free Cotton	Ruth Benerito	b. 1966	2008
MEDICINE			
Acetabular Sockets (Hip replacement surgery)	John Charnley	1911–1982	2008
Ambulatory Insulin Pump	Dean Kamen	b.1951	2005
Aspirin	Felix Hoffmann	1868–1946	2002
Automated DNA Sequencing	Leroy Hood	b.1938	2007
Bifurcated Vaccination Needle	Benjamin A. Rubin	b. 1917	1992
Captopril	Miguel Angel Ondetti	1930–2004	2007
	and Wayne Cushman	1939–2000	2007
CAT Scan	Godfrey Hounsfield	1919–2004	2007
Cimetidine (Tagamet®)	C. Robin Ganellin	b. 1934	1990
	John C. Emmet	b. 1938	1990
	and Graham J. Durant	b. 1934	1990
Controlled Release Of Macromolecules	Robert Samuel Langer, Jr.	b.1948	2006
Dip-And-Read Tests For Urinalysis	Alfred Free	1913–2000	2000
	and Helen Murray Free	b. 1923	2000
Disposable Medicinal Trays	William Murphy, Jr.	b. 1923	2008
DNA-Blocking Drugs	Gertrude b. Elion	1918–1999	1991
Echo-Planar Imaging (EPI)	Peter Mansfield	b.1933	2007
Electrocardiograph	Willem Einthoven	1260–1927	2008
Embolectomy Catheter	Thomas J. Fogarty	b. 1934	2001
Excimer Laser Surgery (LASIK)	Rangaswamy Srinivasan	b. 1929	2002
	James Wynne	b. 1943	2002
	and Samuel Blum	b. 1920	2002
Expandable Intravascular Stent	Julio Palmaz	b.1945	2006
Floconazole	Ken Richardson	b. 1939	2008
Fluorescein isothiocyanate (FITC)	Robert J. Seiwald	b.1925	1995
	and Joseph H. Burckhalter	1912–2004	1995
Genetic Fingerprinting	Alec Jeffreys	b.1950	2005
Heart-Lung Machine	John Gibbon	1903–1973	2004
Hepatitis A, B Vaccines; MMR Vaccine	Maurice Ralph Hilleman	1919–2005	2007
Hepatitis B Vaccine	Irving Millman	b. 1923	1993
	and Baruch S. Blumberg	b. 1925	1993
Implantable Defibrillator	Alois Langer	b. 1945	2002
	M. Stephen Heilman	b. 1933	2002
	Michel Mirowski	1924–90	2002
	and Morton Mower	b. 1933	2002
Insulin	Charles Best	1899–1978	2004
	Frederick Banting	1891–1941	2004
	and James Collip	1982–1965	2004
Iron Lung	Philip Drinker	1894–1972	2007
Isolation Of Vitamin B (Thiamine)	Robert R. Williams	1886–1965	1991
Leukocyte Reduction Filter	David Boris Pall	1914–2004	2008
Magnetic Resonance Imaging (MRI)	Raymond V. Damadian	b. 1936	1989
Means For Counting Particles Suspended In A FJuid	Wallace Coulter	1913–1998	2004
Medical Cardiac Pacemaker	Wilson Greatbatch	b. 1919	1986
Medical Respirators	Forrest Bird	b. 1921	1995
Method For Production Of Penicillin	Andrew J. Moyer	1899–1959	1987
Novocain	Alfred Einhorn	1856–1917	2007
Nuclear Magnetic Resonance Imaging (NMR)	Paul Christian Lauterbur	1929–2007	2007
Nystatin	Elizabeth Lee Hazen	1885–1975	1994
	and Rachel Fuller Brown	1898–1980	1994
Oral Contraceptives	Carl Djerassi	b. 1923	1978
Oral Contraceptives (Enovid)	Gregory Pincus	1903–1967	2006
	and Frank B. Colton	1923–2003	1988
Pentothal	Donalee L. Tabern	1900–1974	1986
	and Ernest H. Volwiler	1893–1992	1986
Phacoemulsification Cataract Removal Procedure	Charles Kelman	1930–2004	2004
Pill Form for Medicine	William Eurastus Upjhon	1863–1932	2006
Polymerase Chain Reaction	Kary Banks Mullis	b. 1944	1998
Prednisone And Prednisolone	Arthur Nobile	1920–2004	2007
Prozac	Bryan B. Molloy	1939–2004	1999
	and Klaus K. Schmiegel	b. 1939	1999
Riboflavin And Sulfaquinoxaline	Max Tishler	1906–1984	1982
Scanning Tunneling Microscope	Heinrich Rohrer	b. 1933	1994
Semi-Synthetic Penicillin	John C. Sheehan	1915–1992	1995
Soft Contact Lens	Otto Wichterle	1913–1998	2007
Soft-Shell Mushroom-Shaped Heart	Willem J. Kolff	b. 1911	1985
Streptomycin	Selman Waksman	1888–1973	2005
Synthesis Of Cortisone And Other Hormones	Percy F. Julian	1899–1975	1990

Field/Invention	Inventor	Born-Died	Inducted
Test To Diagnose HIV Infection	Luc Montagnier	b.1932	2004
	and Robert Gallo	b.1937	2004
Tetracycline	Lloyd H. Conover	b. 1923	1992
Treating Pregene Compounds	Lewis Hastings Sarett	1917–1999	1980
Valium	Leo H. Sternbach	1908–2005	2005
Whole-Body CAT Scanner	Robert S. Ledley	b. 1926	1990
NAVIGATION			
Altimeter	Paul Kollsman	1900–1982	2003
Control Mechanism For Rocket Apparatus	Robert Hutchings Goddard	1882–1945	1979
Global Positioning System (GPS)	Bradford Parkinson	b.1935	2004
	and Ivan Getting	1912–2003	2004
Gyroscopic Equipment	Charles Stark Draper	1901–87	1983
Radar	Percy L. Spencer	1894–1970	1999
Ship's Gyroscopic Compass	Elmer A. Sperry	1860–1930	1991
PHYSICS			
Electron Lens Correction Device	James Hillier	1915–2007	
Hydrometer	Joseph Saxton Masers	1799–1873	2006
	Charles Hard Townes	b. 1915–	1976
Method And Apparatus For The Acceleration Of Ions	Ernest Orlando Lawrence	1901–58	1982
Neutronic Reactor	Enrico Fermi	1901–54	1976
Nuclear Reactor	Leo Szilard	1898–1964	1996
Plutonium Isolation	Genn T. Seaborg	1912–1999	2005
Radio Distance And Direction Indicator	Luis Walter Alvarez	1911–88	1978
Radio Frequency Mass Spectrometer	Willard H. Bennett	1903–1987	1991
Scanning Tunneling Microscope,	Gerd Karl Binnig	b. 1947	1994
TRANSPORTATION			
3-Point Safety Belt	Nils Bohlin	1920–2002	2002
Advanced Jet Aircraft	Kelly Johnson	1910–1990	2008
Airplane Stall Warning Device	Leonard M. Greene	1918–2006	1991
Automatic Railroad Car Coupler	Andrew Jackson Beard	1849–1921	2006
Automobile Brakes	Louis Renault	1877–1944	2007
Cable Car	Andrew Smith Hallidie	1836–1900	2006
Combustion Motor	Wilhelm Maybach	1846–1929	2007
Electric Railway System	Frank Sprague	1857–1934	2006
Electro-Magnetic Motor	Nikola Tesla	1857–1943	1975
Engine Starting Devices And Ignition System	Charles Franklin Kettering	1875–1958	1980
Ethyl Gasoline	Thomas Midgley, Jr.	1889–1944	2003
Flight Simulator	Edwin A. Link	1904–1981	2003
Fluid Catalytic Cracking	Charles W. Tyson	1900–1977	1999
Flying Machine	Orville Wright	1871–1948	1975
	and Wilbur Wright	1867–1912	1975
Flying Wing Plane; All-Metal High-Wing Monocoque Airplane (Vega)	John Northrop	1895–1981	2003
Gas Motor Engine	Nikolaus August Otto	1832–1891	1981
Ground Proximity Warning System	C. Donald Bateman	b.1932	2005
Helicopter Controls	Igor I. Sikorsky	1889–1972	1987
High Pressure Steam Engine	Oliver Evans	1755–1819	2001
Hydraeroplane	Glenn Curtis	1878–1930	2003
Improved Velocipede	Thomas Pickering	1831–1895	2007
Improvement In Electric Rail Signals	Thomas Seavey Hall	1827–1880	2007
Improvement In Gas–Motor Engines	Gottlieb Daimler	1834–1900	2006
Improvement In India-Rubber Fabrics	Charles Goodyear	1800–1860	1976
Improvement In Lubricators For Steam-Engines	Elijah J. Mccoy	1844–1929	2001
Improvement In Valve Gears For Steam-Engines	George Henry Corliss	1817–1888	2006
Improvements To Diesel Engine	Alexander Winton	1860–1932	2006
Internal Combustion Engine	Rudolf Diesel	1858–1913	1976
Iron Truss Bridge	Squire Whipple	1804–1888	2007
Jet Engine	Hans J.P. Von Ohain	1911–1998	2003
	and Sir Frank Whittle	1907–1996	2003
Manufacture Of Gasoline	William Meriam Burton	1865–1954	1984
Modern Rubber Tire	Harvey S. Firestone	1868–1938	2006
Outboard Motor	Ole Evinrude	1877–1934	2007
Pneumatic Tire	John Dunlop	1840–1921	2006
Pullman Car	George Pullman	1831–1897	2006
Retractable Landing Gear; Folding Wing	Leroy Grumman	1895–1982	2003
Rotor Control Mechanism For Rotary Aircraft	Charles Kaman	b.1919	2003
Small Fan - Jet Engine	Sam Williams	b.1921	2003
Space Capsule Design	Maxime Faget	1921–2004	2003
Steam Locomotive	Matthias Baldwin	1795–1886	2005
Steamboat	John Fitch	1743–1798	2006
	and Robert Fulton	1765–1815	2006
Steam-Boiler Firebox	Peter Cooper	1791–1883	2006

Field/Invention	Inventor	Born-Died	Inducted
Steam-Powered Brake Devices	George Westinghouse	1846–1914	1989
Supercritical Wing	Richard Whitcomb	b.1921	2003
Suspension Bridge	John Roebling	1806–1869	2004
Tapered Roller Bearing	Henry Timken	1831–1909	1998
Thrust Bearing	Albert Kingsbury	1983–1943	2007
Transmission Mechanism	Henry Ford	1863–1947	1982
Traveling-Grate Furnace	Eckley Brinton Coxe	1839–1895	2006
Turbo Jet	Theodore Von Kármán	1881–1963	2003
Valve For Steam-Engines	Frederick Sickels	1819–1895	2007
Vehicle Air Conditioning	Frederick Mckinley Jones	1893–1961	2007
Zeppelin	Ferdinand Von Zeppelin	1838–1917	2006
WEAPONS & MILITARY			
Breech-Loading Firearm	John Moses Browning	1855–1926	2007
Improvement To Firearms	Samuel Colt	1814–1862	2006
Maxim Gun	Hiram Maxim	1840–1916	2006
Submarine	John Phillip Holland	1840–1914	2007

Source: National Inventors Hall of Fame. www.invent.org (2009).

Utility Patents Granted, 1901–2009

Utility patents, are issued for the invention of or improvement to a new and useful process, machine, manufacture, or composition of matter. They allow their owners to prohibit others from making, using or selling the invention for up to 17 years from the date of the grant. Utility patents represent about 90 percent of all patents. The other 10 percent are divided among plant patents, for a new and distinct, invented, or discovered asexually reproduced plant; and design patents, for a new, original, and ornamental design for an article of manufacture. Design patents last only 14 years.

Year	Total patents granted	U.S. ownership			Foreign ownership		
		Corporations	Government[1]	Individuals	Corporations	Government	Individuals
1901	25,546	4,370	N.A.	20,896[2]	280	N.A.	[2]
1921	37,798	9,860	N.A.	27,098[2]	840	N.A.	[2]
1930	45,226	19,700	N.A.	23,726[2]	1,800	N.A.	[2]
1940	42,238	22,165	40	17,627[2]	2,406	N.A.	[2]
1950	43,040	21,782	622	18,960[2]	1,660	N.A.	[2]
1960	47,170	28,187	1,244	13,069[2]	4,670	N.A.	[2]
1970	64,427	36,896	1,726	13,511[2]	12,294	N.A.	[2]
1980	61,819	27,640	1,237	9,956	18,874	254	3,858
1990	90,365	36,094	983	12,542	35,548	423	4,775
2000	157,494	70,884	928	16,129	63,182	104	6,267
2001	166,037	74,325	957	15,205	68,943	92	6,515
2002	167,333	74,161	907	14,116	71,663	112	6,374
2003	169,028	75,329	881	13,538	73,099	85	6,096
2004	164,291	73,022	842	12,172	74,637	79	5,400
2005	143,806	65,207	698	10,358	63,114	58	4,371
2006	173,771	78,925	792	11,857	77,373	51	4,773
2007	157,282	70,498	724	9,898	71,954	69	4,139
2008	157,772	69,962	676	9,021	74,465	33	3,615
2009	167,349	74,799	695	8,922	79,202	102	3,629

Notes: 1. Excludes patents issued to Alien Property Custodian until 1942. 2. Patents issued to foreign individuals before 1980 are included with U.S. individuals. **Source:** U.S. Patent and Trademark Office, *All Technologies Report* (April, 2010).

COMPUTERS

A computer is a machine for storing and processing information. It converts any information that it receives into a binary code—a string of signals, in which each signal is either 1 or 0. The basic working component of a computer is a series of switches, each of which can be set either "off" or "on" and thus represent 1 or 0 in the binary system. The history of computers is, to some extent, a history of the switching devices that have been used to represent 1 and 0. Early computers were based on mechanical switches; computers based on electronic switches proved much faster. These fall into three main categories: vacuum tubes, transistors, and integrated circuits.

The relative size and power of these three types are so disparate that it is almost impossible to compare them; there is no single scale against which they can be measured. In 1946 the ENIAC (Electronic Numerical Integrator and Calculator)—which occupied 2,000 square feet, weighed 50 tons, and used 18,000 vacuum tubes—could perform about 10,000 multiplications per second and had an internal memory capacity of 200 decimal digits, or about 20 words. The newest personal computers in 2005 could carry out more than 4 billion operations per second and store more than 400 billion bits of information. The world's fastest supercomputer, developed in Japan, could reach speeds of 35,600 gigaflops (billions of operations per second). Innovations in microprocessor and storage technologies promise quantum leaps in the speed and data capacity of the common computer.

▶ A GLOSSARY OF COMPUTER TERMS

Application   A computer *program* designed for a specific task or use, like word procesing, accounting, or missile guidance.

Artificial intelligence (AI)   The underlying assumption of artificial intelligence is that machines can be programmed to perform human functions. The primary AI functions are *expert systems*, programs that contain a body of knowledge (contributed by experts) that the machine can draw on to solve specific types of problems; *natural language interfaces* that make it possible for users to access a computer's database with commands entered in ordinary written or spoken language (for example, "Give me a list of countries bordering the Atlantic Ocean"); *speech recognition, speech synthesis, and optical recognition systems* that enable computers to understand spoken commands, make speech, and interpret visible images (such as bar codes on retail goods); and *robotics*, machines whose design and systems enable them to imitate complex "eye-hand" coordination of humans.

ASCII (American Standard Code for Information Interchange)   Computers work with numbers, not letters. ASCII is the numerical code used by personal computers. While many programs also use special codes of their own, data from one computer to another are best transmitted in "pure ASCII."

Buffer   Any memory location where data can be stored temporarily while the computer is doing something else; specifically, a memory location in the computer, in a printer, or in a separate storage device (*peripheral*) that stores a file being printed so that the computer is not tied up waiting for the printing to finish.

Bug   An error in a *software* program or the *hardware*.

Byte   A group of eight bits that together represent one character, whether alphabetic, numeric, or other. A byte is the smallest accessible unit in a computer's memory.

CD-ROM   A Compact Disc ("CD") used as a Read-Only-Memory ("ROM"). The CD, essentially the same as an audio CD, stores data in a form readable by a laser, resulting in a storage device of great capacity and quick accessibility.

Central processing unit (CPU)   The group of circuits that directs the entire computer system by (1) interpreting and executing *program* instruction and (2) coordinating the interaction of input, output, and storage devices.

Cursor   A marker on the computer display that shows which region of the screen is active.

Directory   An area or data structure in which information is stored regarding the location and contents of files or file structures.

DVD   Digital Versatile Disc, an improvement on the CD-ROM that is capable of storing an entire motion picture.

DOS   Acronym for Disk Operating System and shorthand for MS-DOS, the standard operating system for 16-bit and most 32-bit IBM and IBM-compatible PCs.

File   Any group of data treated as a single entity by the computer, such as a word processor document, a *program*, or a *database*.

Firewall   A dedicated computer or software with special security features to safeguard a network server from damage by authorized or unauthorized users.

GHz   Gigahertz, now the standard measure of speed used for a *microprocessor*; 1 GHz equals 1 billion electrical cycles per second.   Personal computers today typically come with 1.5–2.5 GHz chips.

Gigabyte (G)   One billion *bytes*.

Hard disk   A sealed cartridge containing magnetic storage disk(s) that holds much more memory—up to more than 100 *gigabytes*—than *floppy disks*. Usually a hard disk is built into the computer, but it can be a peripheral.

Hardware   The physical equipment, as opposed to the programs and procedures, used in data processing. It covers not only computers themselves but also *peripherals* (see "Software").

Icon   A graphic symbol on the display screen that represents a file, peripheral, or some other object or function; for example, scissors are generally used to indicate cut-and-paste editing.

Kilobyte (K)   A unit of measure for data storage or transmission equivalent to 1,024 bytes, but often rounded to 1,000.

Laptop   A portable computer small enough to operate in one's lap. Generally a laptop weighs less than 15 pounds and uses a *liquid crystal display* monitor rather than a *cathode ray tube*.

Liquid crystal display (LCD)   A type of flat-panel display monitor used in *laptop computers*.

Local area networks (LANs)   Systems that allow users to connect PCs to one another or to *minicomputers* or *mainframes*.

Massively parallel   A form of computer architecture that uses hundreds or thousands of inexpensive *microprocessors* to perform many operations simultaneously.

Megabyte (M)   One million *bytes*.

MHz   Megahertz, a measure of microprocessing speed; 1 MHz equals 1 million electrical cycles per second.

Microprocessor   A complete central processing unit assembled on one single silicon chip.

MIPS (million instructions per second)   A measure of computer processing speed.

Monitor   The display device on a computer, similar to a television screen.

Motherboard   The largest printed circuit board in a computer, housing the CPU chip and controlling circuitry.

Network   An interconnected group of computers that can exchange information or work together on different parts of the same problem.

Notebook   A type of full-function portable computer that uses miniaturized components, weighs about 4–6 pounds, and can be carried in a briefcase.

Open source   An approach to the development and distribution of software that offers accessibility to the source code, enabling users to tinker with software.

Operating system   A sequence of programming codes that instructs a computer about its various parts and peripherals and how to operate them. Operating systems deal only with the workings of the *hardware* and are separate from *software* programs.

Peripheral   A device connected to the computer that provides communication or auxiliary functions. There are three types of peripherals: input devices, such as keyboards; output devices, such as *monitors* and printers; and storage devices, such as magnetic discs.

Personal computer   A computer used by an individual at home or in the office.

Platform   A fundamental layer of software required to make other systems run—used interchangeably with operating system, the most common type of platform. The Internet, local networks, Web browsers, and Java are all frequently viewed as platforms.

Random-access memory (RAM)   A temporary storage space in which data may be held on a chip rather than being stored on disk or tape. The contents of RAM may be accessed or altered at any time during a session, but will be lost when the computer is turned off (see "Read-only memory").

Read-only memory (ROM)   A type of *chip* memory, the contents of which have been permanently recorded in a computer by the manufacturer and cannot be altered by the user (See "Random access memory").

RISC chip   Reduced Instruction Set Computer chip, such as the Apple-IBM Power PC chip, which gains speed by using fewer instructions than the more familiar Complex Instruction Set chip.

RSS   Short for RDF Site Summary, Rich Site Summary or Really Simple Syndication; a format for syndicating web content, used most commonly with news sites and *blogs*.

Server   The central computer in a network, providing a service or data access to client computers on the network.

Software   The *programs* and procedures, as opposed to the physical equipment, used in data processing (see "Hardware").

Supercomputer   The fastest of the *mainframe* class of computers, usually used for complex scientific calculations.

Terabyte (TB)   One trillion *bytes*.

UNIX   A multi-user, multitasking operating system designed to run on a wide variety of computers, from microcomputers to mainframes.

Virus   A computer program segment or string of code that can attach itself to another program or file, reproduce itself, and spread from one computer to another. Viruses can destroy or change data and in other ways sabotage computer systems.

Window   A portion of the screen display used to view simultaneously a different part of the file in use or a part of a different file than the one in use.

Computer and Internet Users, 2000–2009

	Computer Users		Internet Users	
	2000	2009	2000	2009
Percent by age				
18-29	83%	88%	82%	92%
30-49	81	87	80	87
50-64	72	78	68	79
65+	31	42	28	42
Percent by education				
Less than high school	36%	47%	35%	50%
High school graduate	63	67	59	69
Some college	81	89	80	88
College graduate	90	94	88	94
All adults	**71%**	**78%**	**69%**	**79%**

Source: U.S. Census Bureau, *Statistical Abstract 2010* (2010).

Typical Daily Internet Activities of Adult Internet Users: 2008 and 2009

Activity	Total Internet users	18 to 29 years old	30 to 49 years old	50 to 64 years old	65 years old and over	Male	Female
Send or read e-mail	57%	57%	62%	53%	46%	53%	61%
Use a search engine to find information	50	56	56	41	30	51	49
Get news online	38	35	44	37	28	42	35
Check weather reports and forecasts online	33	31	38	29	27	35	30
Look for news or information about politics	25	24	27	28	20	32	19
Do any banking online	24	24	30	19	14	25	24
Watch a video on a video-sharing site	19	36	17	10	10	23	15
Use a social networking site	27	51	28	10	4	23	31
Send instant messages.	11	20	12	4	3	14	8
Visit a local, state or federal government Web site	10	9	12	9	2	11	8
Get financial information online	12	6	14	13	15	16	8
Buy a product online	8	9	8	7	6	9	7
Look online for information about a job	9	16	10	5	1	9	10
Use online classified ads or sites	9	12	11	6	3	12	7
Create or work on your own online journal or blog	3	5	3	2	2	3	3
Buy or make a reservation for travel	3	4	4	3	(1)	3	3
Rate a product, service, or person	3	3	2	3	5	4	2
Participate in an online auction	3	3	3	3	1	4	1
Download a podcast so you can listen to it or view it later	3	6	3	2	1	3	3
Make a donation to a charity online	(1)	1	1	(1)	(1)	(1)	(1)

Note: 1. Less than .05 percent. **Source:** Pew Internet & American Life Project Surveys (2009).

Chronology of Information Processing

B.C.
500   Bead-and-wire abacus in use in Egypt.
A.D.
200   Computing trays in use in China and Japan.
1340   Double-entry bookkeeping originates in Lombardy.
c. 1621   Mathematician William Oughtred (English: 1574–1660) invents slide rule.
1642   Blaise Pascal (French: 1623–62) invents "pascaline"—the first calculating machine, capable of addition and subtraction.
1679   Gottfried Wilhelm Leibniz (German: 1646–1716) perfects binary system of notation that eventually will be used by all computers; also develops improved version of pascaline, capable of multiplication and division.
1801   Joseph-Marie Jacquard (French: 1752–1834) uses punched cards to control operation of his mechanical loom—precursor of cards used in early data-storage systems.
1822   Charles Babbage (English: 1792–1871) designs and builds prototype of "Difference Engine" for calculating logarithms.
1833   Babbage designs "Analytical Engine," a computing machine featuring printed card input, memory, printed output, and which is capable of being programmed. Forerunner of modern computer, it never goes beyond design stage.
1847   George Boole (English: 1815–64) publishes *Mathematical Analysis of Logic*, which treats logic as a branch of mathematics (Boolean Algebra).
1853   Pehr Georg Scheutz and his son Edvard G.R. Scheutz (Swedish: 1785–1873; 1821–81) complete version of Babbage's Difference Engine.
1886   William S. Burroughs develops first commercially successful mechanical adding machine.
1887   U.S. Census Bureau holds competition for device to speed up computation of census information; Herman Hollerith designs winning tabulating machine. His Tabulating Machine Co. (founded 1911) becomes IBM in 1924.
1890   Hollerith's electromechanical machine processes U.S. Census results in six weeks—one-third the time taken in 1880.
1894   Otto Steiger develops "Millionaire," the first commercially successful machine capable of direct multiplication, as opposed to multiplication by repeated addition.
1931   Vannevar Bush (completes "differential analyser," first computing machine to use electronic components (vacuum tubes in which values could be stored as voltages).
1936   Mathematician Alan M. Turing publishes "On Computable Numbers," which describes hypothetical computer with infinite storage capacity, capable of performing any conceivable calculation.
1937   John V. Atanasoff (American: 1903–1995) starts work on first electronic computer.
1938   Konrad Zuse (German: 1910–95) builds "Z1," the first computing machine to use binary, instead of decimal, method of operation. Other features include keyboard to input information and system of electric bulbs to signal results of calculations.
1939   Atanasoff and Clifford Berry complete ABC device, first digital computer.
1940   Zuse's Z2 machine introduces electromagnetic relays (as used in telephone switching gear) to store numbers.
1943   British government uses first fully electronic computer to crack German military codes. Designed by Turing, "Colossus" uses 2,000 vacuum tubes to perform calculations and digest information at rate of 5,000 characters per second.
1944   Completion of "Harvard Mark I," designed by Howard H. Aiken and built by IBM. Vast, over 50 ft.

long, it was obsolete immediately because it used electromagnetic relays rather than vacuum tubes.
1946   At the University of Pennsylvania, the ENIAC (Electronic Numerical Integrator and Calculator) multiplies five-digit number by itself 5,000 times in half a second. Designed by J. Presper Eckert, Jr. and John W. Mauchly to calculate ballistic trajectories, ENIAC occupies 2,000 sq. ft., weighs 50 tons, uses 18,000 vacuum tubes, and can store about 20 words in its memory. John von Neumann publishes paper suggesting that instructions given to computer—"programs"—can themselves be stored by computer in numerical form.
First use of term *bit* to mean binary digit.
1948   "Mark I," designed by Tom Kilburn and Sir Frederic C. Williams (at Manchester University, England, is first computer to utilize von Neumann's concept of stored programs.
John Bardeen (American: 1908–91), Walter H. Brattain (American: 1902–87), and William B. Shockley (English-American: 1910–89) invent the transistor, which will eventually replace vacuum tube and make computers faster.
IBM, Bell Telephone, and Sperry-Rand each begin production of commercial computers.
First chess-playing computer built at M.I.T.
1950   Eckert and Mauchly's EDVAC (Electronic Discrete Variable Automatic Computer) is first to use magnetic disks for storage.
1951   Lyons Tea Shop Co. in England uses specially designed computer ("LEO") to perform routine administrative functions.
Eckert and Mauchly's UNIVAC (Universal Automatic Computer) is installed at U.S. Bureau of Census. UNIVAC uses magnetic tape for input and becomes first commercially successful machine.
1952   One hour after polls close, CBS television network uses UNIVAC to predict Eisenhower's landslide victory in U.S. presidential election. Prediction was based on less than 10 percent of the votes.
1953   First high-speed printer linked to a computer.
IBM introduces its first stored-program computer, the vacuum-tube-based "701."
1956   First use of term artificial intelligence.
1958   Control Data Corp. introduces first fully transistorized computer, the CDC 1604, designed by Seymour Cray.
Jack St. C. Kilby of Texas Instruments and Robert Noyce of Intel Corp. independently produce first integrated circuits.
1959   First commercially marketed program.
IBM markets its first transistorized computers.
1960   The PDP-1, developed by Digital Equipment Corp., is the first commercial computer to use a keyboard and monitor instead of punched cards.
Removable magnetic disks for data storage introduced.
1969   Student Alan Kay, later to become top designer with Apple Computer Co., writes doctoral thesis describing hypothetical "personal computer."
ARPANET, the first part of the Internet, is set up to link Defense Department contractors.
1970   Lexitron introduces first word processor, a computer designed specifically to handle written text. It features a cathode ray tube (CRT) terminal, as used in television sets, to display information.
Floppy disk is introduced for data storage.
1971   Intel Corp. debuts first microprocessor, several integrated circuits contained on one silicon chip.
First electronic pocket calculator produced by Texas Instruments; it weighs about 2½ lbs. and costs about $150.
1973   Introduction of "bit-mapped" monitor capable of high-resolution graphics display.

Xerox markets first hand-held "mouse," a time-saving device for giving commands to computer.

Intel introduces 8080 microprocessor, which will become the central processing unit (CPU) of several microcomputers.

1975 First personal computer, the MITS Altair 8800, is marketed as a kit, with memory of 256 bytes.

Cray Research (founded 1972) announces the Cray-1 supercomputer, capable of 100 million operations per second.

1976 Apple Computer Co. founded by Stephen Wozniak and Steven Jobs (American: 1955–) in the Jobs family garage; first Apple "boards" (self-assembly personal computer kits) go on sale.

1977 Apple markets Apple II—the first widely accepted personal computer. Commodore and Tandy also begin to sell personal computers.

Microsoft Corp. founded by Bill Gates & Paul Allen.

1978 Hayes Microcomputer Products introduces Micromodem 100, the first microcomputer-compatible modem.

1979 Micropro International releases WordStar word processing program for personal computers.

1980 Microsoft adapts the UNIX operating system for use with microcomputers; paves way for personal computers to begin performing tasks associated with larger machines.

1981 IBM introduces its first personal computer, the IBM PC. Using operating system called PC-DOS, developed by Microsoft, it almost immediately becomes the industry standard.

Ashton-Tate introduces dBASE II, the first popular database program for microcomputers.

1982 Microsoft introduces MS-DOS, a version of the PC-DOS operating system designed for IBM PC; allows other manufacturers to produce copies ("clones") of the IBM machine.

Compaq announces its first portable computer (IBM-compatible).

1983 Apple introduces Apple IIe and "Lisa."

First IBM-compatible "laptop" computer introduced by Gavilan Corp.

Lotus Development Corp. introduces 1-2-3, a best-selling program for managing business spreadsheets.

Introduction of optical (laser-readable) disks.

1984 Apple introduces Macintosh. With list price of $2,495, it includes Apple's first "Mac" software programs, MacWrite (for text) and MacPaint (for graphics). Fifty thousand are sold within three months. IBM markets the PC AT (Advanced Technology) model.

1985 Apple's LaserWriter printer and Aldus Corp.'s PageMaker program usher in age of desktop publishing.

Introduction of erasable optical storage disks.

Toshiba markets first widely-used laptop.

Cray 2 supercomputer is capable of 1.2 billion operations per second.

1986 IBM announces OS/2, a new operating system that allows personal computers to run several programs simultaneously (called multitasking).

1987 Apple introduces Macintosh SE and Macintosh II. IBM introduces Personal System/2 (PS/2), features of which include high-resolution VGA (Video Graphics Array) display.

1988 Computer security becomes an urgent issue when a "worm" program penetrates thousands of systems on Internet information network.

Motorola announces new microprocessor, the 88000, a 32-bit RISC (Reduced Instruction Set Computer) chip.

First IBM PS/2 "clones" announced.

IBM and Sears launch Prodigy, an on-line service enabling subscribers with a computer and modem to access a central information bank.

Parallel processing technique introduced that utilizes many inexpensive microprocessors to perform a large number of operations simultaneously.

1989 Intel announces the iPSC/860 chip, containing one million transistors; designed to give a microcomputer the power and speed normally associated with supercomputers.

IBM announces production of commercial quantities of four-megabyte chips.

First portable computers with color liquid crystal displays (LCDs) announced.

1990 Software writer Tim Berners-Lee writes the program for the World Wide Web to make the Internet easier to use for physicists at CERN in Geneva.

1991 The Thinking Machines Inc. CM-200 massively parallel supercomputer can perform 9.03 billion calculations per second.

1993 Intel begins shipping the Pentium chip with 3.1 million transistors on it; it operates twice as fast as the best previous Intel chip for personal computers.

Electrical engineers from the Univ. of Colorado claim the first fully optical computer that can store, transmit, and process data entirely in the form of light, with no electron intermediaries.

1994 Apple introduces the first personal computers to use the Power PC RISC Chip.

1995 Microsoft introduces its Windows 95 operating system software, featuring an improved interface and better multimedia support.

1997 In a six-game match, the IBM RS/6000 SP supercomputer (known as Deep Blue) defeats world chess champion Garry Kasparov, the first time a computer has beaten a player of this caliber.

Intel introduces a Pentium chip with MMX technology, enhancing multimedia capabilities on a PC.

1999 The total number of Internet users in the U.S. tops 100 million.

2000 The new century begins with minimal disruption from the much-feared Y2K programming bug.

Household penetration of personal computers in the United States surpasses 50 percent.

A U.S. federal circuit court judge finds the software giant Microsoft in violation of antitrust laws and orders the company broken up into two parts. Microsoft appeals.

2001 The U.S. high-tech industry hits hard times. The investment "bubble" in dot.com companies bursts, forcing numerous Web ventures to shut down. PC sales decline for the first time in decades. Still, the number of Internet users continues to climb, reaching 143 million—or 54 percent of the population.

A federal district judge issues an injunction against Napster, Inc., to halt the free exchange of copyright-protected music on the company's popular Internet site. Napster is later acquired by the German-based media giant Bertelsmann.

Microsoft and the U.S. Justice Department reach a settlement in their antitrust dispute by which the software company will be left intact in exchange for specific restrictions on anticompetitive behavior.

2002 A new Japanese supercomputer, called Earth Simulator, achieves a processing speed of 35,600 gigaflops (billions of calculations per second)—five times faster than its closest competitor.

2003 IBM debuts Power4, the first dual core processor, which greatly increases computer speed.

2007 Netbooks, also called mini-notebooks, become available, providing a smaller, lighter and cheaper alternative to laptops, with only minimal diminished capacity.

2009 Intel & AMD both debut quad core processors.

2010 Intel releases an 8-core processor, Nehalem-EX, marketed to four-socket servers.

Apple releases the i-Pad, a media-centered, multi-touch table computer.

TELECOMMUNICATIONS

For the telecommunications industry itself—including service providers, equipment manufacturers, and other support services—the enormous growth and promise of the late 1990s is returning after a brief slow between 2000 and 2002. In 2003, overall industry growth began to pick up. The total U.S. marketplace in 2006, according to the Telecommunications Industry Association (TIA), generated revenues of an estimated $944.7 billion, a 10.2 percent increase over 2005 (following 9.5 percent growth in 2004, 6.6 percent growth in 2001). Of total 2006 revenues, $324.7 billion derived from calling services—local exchange access, toll service, and wireless service. The transition from conventional land-line usage to wireless usage continues, as reflected by a 13.7 percent rise in wireless service revenues, to $134.8 billion. Equipment manufacturers and software developers saw revenues recover slowly after a drop of 11.7 percent in 2002, rising by 8.9 percent in 2006, to $180.4 billion.

The TIA estimated growth for the U.S. telecommunications industry in 2006 at nearly 10.2 percent. The increase in service revenues, however, is expected to lag that of the industry as a whole, and of wireless services most drastically, in the foreseeable future-to the great advantage of consumers. Continued expansion of the Internet user base and competitive pricing in the long-distance market have steadily increased consumer demand for conventional phone service, even as usage has declined. As of year-end 2001, the total number of U.S. residential and business access lines exceeded 253 million, a nearly 11 percent rise from 1999. This did not even include the rapidly growing wireless segment. At the same time, however, Americans placed 515 billion land-line local calls in 2001 (down from 537 billion from 2000), generating an estimated $58 billion in revenues (down $2 billion). The decline in number of calls was due, in large part, to the transition of many home Internet users to broadband wireless alternatives. The rise in local call rates cannot be expected to be reversed until the much-discussed deregulation of local phone service becomes a reality.

As wireless communications transform the telecommunications market, statistics such as the number of local and long distance calls Americans make each year, or the average rate of a long-distance call, are becoming harder for organizations such as the FCC to track. As new technologies become widely used, different ways of defining growth and consumer preferences are emerging.

Wireless Communications By far the most rapid growth in the telecommunications service industry has come in the wireless segment. From 1995 through 2006, the total wireless market more than quadrupled in size, from $25.4 billion to more than $133 billion. By 2009 spending totaled $215 billion, up 3.3 percent from 2008. Cellular phones continue to account for a majority of

Local Telephone Service Connections by Technology, 2009 (in thousands)

	Switched Access Lines[1]	VoIP[2]	Total
ILEC[3]	111,786	958	112,743
Non-ILEC[4]	21,458	22,505	43,963
Total	**133,244**	**23,462**	**156,706**
Residential			
ILEC[3]	67,981	597	68,578
Non-ILEC[4]	5,109	19,274	24,383
Residential Total	**73,090**	**19,871**	**92,961**
Business			
ILEC[3]	43,805	361	44,165
Non-ILEC[4]	16,350	3,230	19,580
Business Total	**60,154**	**3,591**	**63,745**

Notes: 1. Switched access lines refer to conventional land lines. 2. VoIP, or voice over Internet protocol, refers to phone service via broadband Internet. 3. ILEC, or incumbent local exchange carrier, denotes a regulated carrier that utilizes its own infrastructure and facilities. 4. Non-ILEC denotes a less regulated carrier that may use its own infrastructure and facilities, such as a cable company which provides phone service, or a provider that does not have its own infrastructure, such as a VoIP provider that sells service over broadband. **Source:** U.S. Federal Communications Commission, *Local Telephone Competition, June 30, 2009* (2010).

Average Annual Telephone Consumer Expenditures, 2001–07

Year	Total telephone services	Residential telephone/ pay phone	Cellular phone service	Other services[1]
2001	$914	$686	$210	$19
2002	957	641	294	22
2003	956	620	316	20
2004	990	592	378	20
2005	1,048	570	455	23
2006	1,087	542	524	21
2007	1,110	482	608	20

Note: 1. Phone cards and pager services. **Source:** Bureau of Labor Statistics, *Consumer Expenditures in 2007* (2009).

End-User Telecommunications Revenues 1997–2009 (in Billions)

	1998	1999	2000	2001	2002	2003	2004	2005	2006	2007	2008	2009[1]
Toll Service	$91.6	$93.3	$87.8	$79.3	$67.2	$59.0	$55.5	$52.4	$49.3	$48.7	$47.4	$39.3
Wireless Service	33.7	43.8	56.9	68.5	76.5	85.3	94.4	100.7	110.1	115.9	118.9	115.5
Local Service	75.2	78.6	84.5	87.7	88.7	86.5	83.4	82.4	78.2	75.0	72.7	70.1

Note: 1. Preliminary **Source:** U.S. Federal Communications Commission, *Telecommnications Industry Revenues 2008* (2010).

wireless service spending, but personal communications systems (PCSs)-handheld devices with fax capability and Internet access-and other equipment are expected to gain share. Some analysts expect wireless usage to account for half of all U.S. telecom service revenues within a few years.

From 1990 to 2008, the number of subscribers to a cellular phone system jumped from 5.3 million to an estimated 270.3 million. Service revenues skyrocketed from $4.5 billion at the beginning of the 1990s to about $148 billion in 2008. This represents a 228 percent increase in subscribers. By the end of the first decade of the 2000s, it was rare for someone not to be a cellular telephone subscriber.

The paging and messaging market, however, which grew impressively throughout the 1990s, began to shrink in 2000 and has continued to do so. With cellular telephones serving the needs of many pager users, the number of paging/messaging subscribers (estimated at 8.5 million in 2006) has fallen to less than a quarter of the number that subscribed in 1999 (45 million).

New forms of wireless communication promise even greater versatility and broader usage. The rapid adoption of mobile phones that can access the Internet, send and receive email, and stream media (all at premium data prices averaging $40/month above normal cellular voice plans in 2009) has created new competition among telecommunications companies to rapidly advance data networks. (See "Smartphones.")

Satellites The wireless revolution in telecommunications has been made possible, in large part, by the bandwidth capacity of geostationary satellites orbiting the Earth. As of 2002, more than 250 U.S. and European communications satellites were in place. But with launchings proceeding at record pace—reaching 40 in 2000—commercial satellite bandwidth began to exceed demand, and the number of commercial launchings declined to only 16 in 2001. The industry rebounded well in 2002, however, with more than 30 new satellites placed in orbit and a similar number expected in 2003. About 95 percent of commercial launchings are communications satellites, and about 85 percent are geostationary. As of September 2004, approximately 280 U.S. and 175 non-U.S. European commercial communications satellites were in place.

Growth in residential broadband service is likely to be dominated by the cable industry—as suggested by the failures of various global satellite-system ventures—but many analysts continued to predict a key role for satellites in the future. Digital radio may prove to be another major consumer electronics market served by satellite.

Telecom Industry Competition for the burgeoning wireless market, declining prices for long-distance service, an excess of optic fiber capacity,

Cellular Telephone Industry Growth in the U.S., 1985–2008

Year	Estimated Total Subscribers	Twelve-Month Total Service Revenues (in $000's)	12-Month Roamer Revenues (in $000's)	Cell Sites[1]	Direct Service Provider Employees	Avg. Local Monthly Bill	Avg. Local Call Time
1985	340,213	$ 482,428	$ N.A.	913	2,727	$ N.A.	N.A.
1990	5,283,055	4,548,820	456,010	5,616	21,382	80.90	2.20
1995	33,785,661	19,081,239	2,542,570	22,663	68,165	51.00	2.15
2000	109,478,031	52,466,020	3,882,981	104,288	184,449	45.27	2.56
2005	207,896,198	113,538,221	3,786,331	183,689	233,067	49.98	3.00
2006	233,040,781	125,456,825	3,494,294	195,613	253,793	50.56	3.03
2007	255,395,599	138,869,304	3,742,015	213,299	266,782	49.79	N.A.
2008	270,333,881	148,084,170	3,739,274	242,130	268,528	50.07	2.27

Note: 1. A cell site is the basic geographic unit of a cellular system. A city or county is divided into smaller cells, each of which is equipped with a low-powered radio transmitter/receiver. The cells can vary in size depending on terrain, capacity, demands, etc. By controlling the transmission power, the radio frequencies assigned to one cell can be limited to the boundaries of that cell. When a cellular telephone moves from one cell to another, a computer at the switching office monitors the movement and transfers the phone call to the new cell and another radio frequency. **Source:** CTIA–The Wireless Association, semi-annual wireless industry survey.

U.S. Paging and Messaging Market, 1990–2006

Year	Subscribers (millions)	Annual Percent Increase	Total Spending (millions)	Annual Percent Increase	Average Monthly Spending	Annual Percent Change
1990	9.9	22.2%	$1,744	17.8%	$14.68	-3.7%
1995	34.5	31.2	3,841	18.8	9.28	-9.4
1998	48.0	2.1	4,896	4.6	8.50	2.4
1999	45.0	-6.3	4,671	-4.6	8.65	1.8
2000	30.0	-33.3	3,168	-32.2	8.80	1.7
2002	14.1	-21.7	1,565	-19.5	9.25	2.8
2003	11.2	-20.6	1,284	-18.0	9.55	3.2
2004	9.1	-18.8	1,005	-18.3	9.20	0.5
2005	8.7	-4.4	960	-4.4	10.15	0.0
2006[1]	8.5	-2.3	944	-1.8	9.25	0.5

Note: 1. Projected. **Source:** Telecommunications Industry Association, *2006 Telecommunications Market Review and Forecast.* Reprinted by permission.

turbulence in the investment market, and improper or questionable accounting practices made the period 2000–02 one of the most difficult ever for the U.S. telecom industry. Virtually every major company faced a squeeze on profits and declining share prices. In 2002, the Dow Jones Telecommunications Index fell a whopping 36 percent. Five of the eight largest U.S. phone companies showed declines in annual operating revenue and net income. WorldCom, after revelations of gross accounting errors, declared bankruptcy in July 2002—the biggest company (in terms of corporate assets) ever to do so. In April 2003, the company filed a reorganization plan with the U.S. Bankruptcy Court and announced that it was changing its name to MCI and moving its headquarters to Ashburn, Virginia—followed shortly by charges from competitors that it had inappropriately handled access fees.

Smartphones The newest emerging segment in the telecom industry is the consumer smartphone market. Smartphones such as Research in Motion's BlackBerry or Apple's iPhone blur the lines between mobile phone, email reader, media player and information manager, and until the late 2000s, most users were business or corporate accounts. In the first quarter of 2010, according to research firm Gartner, 44.3 percent of all new smartphones sold ran Symbian as their computer operating system. Research in Motion operating system, which powers BlackBerrys was found on 17.9 percent of all new smartphones, and Apple's OS X on 14.7 percent. Microsoft Windows Mobile came in fifth, running on 6.8 percent of new smartphones. Devices in any category running an Apple operating system first outsold devices running a Windows operating system in 2008, due in large part to the success of Apple's iPhone.

Even as the global recession of 2008–09 has hurt mobile phone sales worldwide, the sales of smartphones remains strong. Overall, the sales of mobile phones in the second quarter of 2010 totaled 325.6 million units, a 13 percent increase from the same period in 2009. Meanwhile, smartphone phones increased 27 percent over the same period. According to Gartner, in the second quarter of 2009, worldwide customers bought 40,963,000 smartphones, and of those Nokia commanded 45 percent of sales (18,441,000 units), increasing sales but losing share (down 2.4 percent) from the same period the year before. Research in Motion sold 18.7 percent of smartphones (7,679,000 units) in the same period, gaining market share (up 1.4 percent) over the previous year. Meanwhile, Apple's smartphone, the iPhone, accounted for 13.3 percent of all smartphone sales (5,435,000) in the second quarter 2009, a dramatic increase in share (up 10.5 percent) over the previous year.

U.S. Consumer Telecommunications Market, 1990–2006

Product	1990	1995	2000	2003	2004	2006[1]
Total Unit Shipments (millions)	**55.9**	**81.5**	**134.5**	**144.9**	**N.A.**	**N.A.**
Corded telephone	22.0	25.8	29.7	22.1	17.4	14.4
Cordless telephone	10.1	19.5	39.0	40.3	37.6	33.6
Cellular/PCS handset	8.7	15.9	43.2	58.2	N.A.	N.A.
Answering machine	13.6	17.5	19.9	22.5	24.1	25.7
Home fax machine	1.5	2.8	2.7	2.1	1.8	1.0
Total Dollar Sales (millions)	**$8,686**	**$8,501**	**$10,722**	**$10,362**	**N.A.**	**N.A.**
Corded telephone	765	668	463	307	311	284
Cordless telephone	1,170	1,913	1,953	1,585	1,418	1,204
Cellular/PCS handset	4,698	3,578	6,696	6,470	N.A.	N.A.
Answering machine	953	1,242	1,132	1,392	1,465	1,362
Home fax machine	1,100	1,100	463	356	223	104

Note: 1. Projected. **Source:** Telecommunications Industry Association (Arlington, Va.), *2006 Telecommunications Market Review and Forecast.*

Access to High-speed[1] Telecommunication Lines 2005–09 (Lines in thousands)

Type of line	2005	2006	2007	2008	2009
Total	42,518	64,992	100,986	132,814	113,349
Total Fixed	42,138	53,975	65,681	73,123	77,950
aDSL[2]	16,316	22,584	27,793	29,964	30,617
sDSL[2]	412	337	320	275	217
Other Wireline	487	472	622	665	686
Cable Modem	24,017	29,173	34,404	38,190	41,407
FTTP[3]	316	547	1,281	2,346	3,543
Satellite	377	495	669	869	990
Fixed Wireless	209	361	587	808	485
Power Line and Other	5	5	5	5	5
Mobile Wireless[4]	380	11,017	35,305	59,691	35,399

Notes: 1. A high-speed line is defined as a data line capable of moving over 200 kilobytes per second (kbps) in at least one direction. 2. aDSL (asymmetrical Digital Subscriber Line) provides faster access in one direction than in the other, sDSL provides the same speed in both directions. 3. FTTP = fiber to the premises. 4. Reporting instructions for mobile wireless changed in 2008. **Source:** U.S. Federal Communications Commission, *Statistics of Common Carriers* (2006).

Televisions, Telephones, and Computers per Capita, by Selected Nation, 2003 (number per 1,000 people)

Nation	Cable televisioon subscribers (2003)	Television sets (2003)	Telephone main lines (2003)	Cellular phone subscribers (2003)	Personal computers (2003)
Algeria	N.A.	114	69	46	8
Argentina	165	326	219[2]	178	82
Australia	72	731	542	720	601
Austria	127	621	480	879	374
Belgium	370	543	494	786	318
Brazil	14	349	223	264	75
Bulgaria	93	453[4]	368[2]	333	52
Canada	253	691	629	417	487
Chile	46	494	230[2]	428	119
China	69	312	209	214	28
Colombia	14[4]	286	200	141	49
Cuba	N.A.	251	51[3]	2	24
Czech Republic	94	538	360	965	177
Denmark	201	859	669	887	577
Dominican Republic	N.A.	N.A.	115[2]	271	N.A.
Ecuador	34	225	119[2]	184	32
Egypt	N.A.	231	127	85	29
Finland	192	678	488	901	442
France	55	632	566	696	347
Germany	246	637	659	785	485
Ghana	0	53	14	36	4
Greece	475	519	454	780	82
Guatemala	N.A.	145	71[2]	132	14
Honduras	8[4]	122	48[2]	49	15
Hungary	160	475	361	676	108
India	39	83	46	25	7
Indonesia	0	153	372	55	12
Iran	N.A.	171	220	51	91
Iraq	N.A.	834	30[1]	N.A.[2]	N.A.
Ireland	160	395	486	844	421
Israel	184	330	453[2]	955	243
Italy	1	494[4]	484	1,018	231
Jamaica	N.A.	374	169[2]	533	54
Japan	167	731	558[2]	680	382
Korea, South	132	363	472	694	558
Kuwait	N.A.	418	198	578	161
Lebanon	30	357	199[2]	227	100
Malaysia	N.A.	202	182	442	167
Mexico	25	282	147[2]	255	83
Morocco	N.A.	167	41	243	20
Netherlands	392	553	614	768	467
New Zealand	7	557	448[2]	648	414
Norway	185	884	734[2]	909	528
Pakistan	0	150	27	2	4
Panama	N.A.	194	129[2]	268	38
Peru	17	149	67	106	43
Philippines	31	173	42[2]	191	28
Poland	91	422	319	451	142
Portugal	108	413	414	904	134
Puerto Rico	91	339	N.A.	209[2]	N.A.
Romania	121	379[4]	205	329	97
Russia	43	538[4]	242	120	89
Saudi Arabia	N.A.	265	155	321	138
Singapore	73	300	463[2]	796	622
South Africa	N.A.	159	107	364	73
Spain	15	564	429	916	196
Sweden	224	965	736[2]	889	621
Switzerland	369	552	744[2]	843	709
Syria	N.A.	172	123[2]	24	29
Taiwan	N.A.	N.A.	590[2]	1,108	N.A.
Thailand	2	300	106	260	40
Turkey	14	319	277	408	43
United Kingdom	64	950	591[2]	841	406
United States	256	938	621	543	660
Uruguay	N.A.	530[4]	280[2]	193	110
Venezuela	40	186	112[2]	256	61

Notes: 1. 1999 figures. 2. 2002 figures. 3. 2001 figures. 4. 2000 figures. **Source:** International Telecommunications Union, *World Telecommunication Report 2003*; The World Bank, *World Development Indicators*.

THE INTERNET

The Internet, an intricate global web of hundreds of thousands of computer networks linked by conventional telephone lines (and now such high-speed alternatives as cable modem and DSL), was created by the U.S. Defense Department in 1969 as a faster way for agencies to share information and as an emergency means of communications in case more traditional means were cut off. But the potential for consumer Internet use didn't occur until the 1980s, when the National Science Foundation created equipment that would allow other computer networks to connect to the government's larger network. From there, commercial services such as CompuServe, Prodigy, and America Online tapped into the ever-growing network and brought a wealth of information to anybody with a computer, a modem, and the monthly fee. In 1993 some three million people worldwide were connected to the Internet. By mid-2010, the total number of users was approaching 1.9 billion.

Today, the Internet is the world's largest communications network. The number of names registered in the *domain name system*—Web sites of commercial enterprises, public institutions, and private individuals—exceeded 50 million by 2003. The networks and switches that make up the Internet carry data around the world in seconds, and link even the most remote user to a vast wealth of resources. The most popular network on the Internet is the *World Wide Web* (WWW, or simply, "the Web"), created in 1989 by CERN, the European Particle Physics Lab in Geneva and made available on the Internet in Aug. 1991. In 1993, the creation of software (Mosaic) that displayed the Internet in a format that resembled a magazine with text and graphics dramatically increased Net usage. In 1994, the Netscape browser came on the market, and since then, the Internet has become hugely popular, as computer users found they could navigate the Web quickly and easily.

In just a few short years, the Internet and the Web have quite literally transformed the way millions of people go about their daily lives. Everything from mundane tasks like banking or ordering tickets to more eventful activities like searching for a job or a date, planning a vacation, or buying a house, can all be done sitting in front of a computer. Physicians, lawyers, real estate agents and marketing specialists, among others, can get vital public documents and other information over the Net. Meanwhile, businesses can market products, purchase materials and services, and carry out other essential activities. For ordinary users, e-mail is by far the most popular online activity. As of 2010, over 77 percent of adults in the United States used the Internet, a 15 percent increase from 2008. Worldwide, more than 10 billion messages a day were being sent.

Who Uses the Internet?

Almost unheard of before 1990, the Internet has entered both the vocabulary and homes of most Americans. Because Internet use is decentralized and almost completely unregulated in the U.S., statistics on the number of users are difficult to

Internet Users Worldwide, 2010

Region	Users (millions)
Asia	825.1
Europe	475.1
North America	266.2
Latin America/Caribbean	204.7
Africa	110.9
Middle East	63.2
Oceania/Australia	21.3
World Total	1,966.5

Source: Internet World Stats (2010). Copyright © 2001–2010, Miniwatts Marketing Group. All rights reserved worldwide.

U.S. Web Usage Snapshot, May 2009

Monthly Average Usage	Home	Work
Sessions/Visits Per Person	36	64
Domains Visited Per Person	62	117
PC Time Per Person	36:38:52	82:44:53
Duration of a Web Page Viewed	00:54	00:59
Active Online Users Estimate[1]	156.6 mil.	68.6 mil.
Total Online Users Estimate[2]	227.8 mil.	73.1 mil.

Notes: 1. Individuals browsing or actively engaging web applications, IM, or web data sources. 2. Average total of all users connected at any time. **Source:** Nielsen/NetRatings (May 2009).

U.S. Top 10 Parent Internet Companies, May 2009

Accessed from Work	Audience[1] ('000's)	Reach[2] (%)	Avg. Visit Time
Google	60,771	88.63	1:54:30
Microsoft	60,372	88.05	2:27:29
Yahoo!	51,725	75.44	3:17:02
AOL	36,484	53.21	3:21:46
News Corp. Online	31,894	46.52	0:41:42
Facebook	31,162	45.45	3:08:00
Amazon	30,979	45.18	0:23:40
eBay	30,098	43.90	1:48:52
Wikimedia Foundation	29,334	42.78	0:20:10
InterActiveCorp	28,484	41.54	0:22:24

Accessed from Home	Audience[1] ('000's)	Reach[2] (%)	Avg. Visit Time
Google	119,554	76.36	1:11:05
Microsoft	104,750	66.91	1:28:46
Yahoo!	98,349	62.82	2:13:53
AOL	65,981	42.14	2:49:33
News Corp. Online	59,369	37.92	1:12:05
Facebook	58,380	37.29	2:28:03
InterActiveCorp	47,943	30.62	0:12:39
eBay	44,238	28.26	1:01:44
Apple Computer	40,944	26.15	1:06:37
Amazon	39,606	25.30	0:16:59

Notes: 1. Unique individuals. 2. Percent of all online users. **Source:** Nielsen/NetRatings (May 2009).

Guide to Select Domain Name Suffixes

Suffix	Used by
.aero	Air transport industry (Reserved)
.biz	Businesses (alternative to .com)
.com	Commercial entities
.coop	Business cooperatives (Reserved)
.edu	Educational institutions
.gov	Government bodies (at any level)
.info	General use (alternative to .com)
.museum	Museums (Reserved)
.name	Private individuals for personal sites
.net	Internet-related institutions
.org	Nonprofit organizations
.pro	Professionals

Note: "Reserved for" domains are sponsored by an organization that represents the specific domain community and is responsible for policies concerning those sites. Unsponsored domains operate under policies established by the global Internet community through ICANN.

verify and vary significantly among reporting services. By most accounts, however, the number of regular Internet users in the United States reached 50 million in 1998, about five years after the medium became viable for ordinary consumers. That narrow time frame easily eclipsed the 10 years for cable TV, 13 for television, and 38 for radio. And the user base continues to expand rapidly. A rapid increase from 2000 to 2010 put the number of U.S. Internet users at more than 239 million—nearly 68 percent of the total population. Even as evidence began to suggest that users were spending less time online, overall traffic continued to rise.

As the user base has expanded, the demographic profile of the average user has changed. According to several surveys, disparities in gender, age, income, education level, and race between Net users and non-users have continued to shrink. Children and teenagers still use the Internet more than any other age group. As of late 2003, according to the most recent government study available, 89 percent of 11–14 year-olds and 88 percent of 15–17 year-olds had Internet access at school or home. This number has no doubt risen in the past seven years. Disparities remained in Internet access by income level; 85 percent of individuals with a family income of $75,000 or more had access, compared with only 36 percent of those with a family income under $10,000—but the latter group grew faster than the former. Likewise, access among blacks and Hispanics grew faster than among whites, though whites still accounted for 76 percent of users. The highest growth rate among types of households was single mothers with children.

In addition to the increases in the user base and overall traffic—and partly responsible for those increases—have come improvements in the means of access. By 2009, only six percent of U.S. Internet households still accessed the Net by telephone dial-up service, while such high-speed alternatives as cable modem and DSL (Digital Subscription Line) accounted for over 90 percent of home Internet access.

▶ THE WORLD WIDE WEB

The World Wide Web is a vast network of information within the Internet, which uses a hypertext system for quickly transmitting graphics, sound and video over phone lines. To read the information, users must have a *browser* (such as Mozilla's Firefox or Microsoft Internet Explorer). Because the hypertext system arranges information based on its relationship to other information rather than in linear or alphabetical order, the Web allows users to find information quickly, especially if they don't know exactly what they're looking for. Each piece of information, or *Web page*, can be connected to one or more other pages via a *link*. For example, the U.S. Census Bureau's Web site (www.census.gov) provides thousands of data tables produced by the Department of Commerce, and is also linked to data from 70 other government agencies.

The Web is divided into zones, which organize pages according to the type of information generally contained within them. There is of course some overlap, but generally, Web pages of educational institutions end in .edu; government Web pages end in .gov; Web pages of Internet-related institutions end in .net; commercial entities end with .com; and other organizations end with .org. In an attempt to relieve overcrowding in the .com and .net areas, the ICANN (Internet Corporation for Assigned Names and Numbers), the official governing body for domain names, created seven new suffixes (or TLDs, "Top-Level Domains") for use beginning in 2001: .aero, .biz, .coop, .info, .museum, .name, and .pro.

Growth of the Web   It is becoming increasingly easy for companies, organizations, and even individuals to create their own Web sites. Millions of institutions, groups, and individuals have done so, resulting in such dramatic growth that the Web's 182 million sites in 2010 contained an estimated one trillion pages (up to double the previous year's total) with 10K–20K of data per page. With so many sites throughout cyberspace, surfers would find it close to impossible to find what they were looking for without a *search engine*. Like a librarian who knows where in the library to find valuable information, search engines look through countless Web pages and create an index of what appears on each one. If you're looking for the rules of badminton, you can ask the search engine to sift hundreds of thousands of Web pages for the word badminton and it will return a list of Web pages that mention badminton. Google, Yahoo!, AOL, and Bing are the most popular search engines.

As the Internet has emerged as a mass medium, the major online service providers, search services, and other Web companies have competed ever more vigorously for user "audience." To attract the greatest number of visitors on a regular basis, many Web sites have expanded from their core services and established broad-based *portals*—whole arrays of services (such as e-mail, search, special-interest forums and bulletin boards, and chat rooms), information (news, weather, stock reports, reference resources), and links to other useful sites, all accessible from a single home page.

Business on the Web   The increasing sophistication of both technology and users have made the World Wide Web a major and rapidly expanding business medium. No longer just a vehicle for publishing brochures and annual reports, the Web has emerged as a low-cost sales channel for producers of goods and services and as a highly convenient purchasing vehicle for end users.

A vast majority (92 percent in 2008) of all e-commerce is conducted between businesses, as the Internet has helped cut transaction costs, locate surplus or low-cost goods, and otherwise increase efficiencies. The total value of business-to-business (B2B) shipments and sales derived from e-commerce reached $3.4 trillion by 2008, a 9.1 percent increase from 2007. The B2B group is made up of manufacturing and merchant wholesale businesses. Of B2B manufacturing transactions, the largest groups of sales were for transportation equipment (22 percent, $409 billion) and chemical products (13 percent, $247 billion) in 2007.

Online business-to-consumer (B2C) business remains a small overall portion of Internet commerce. Online direct retail shopping accounted for only 3.8 percent ($142 billion) of all e-commerce in 2008, up from 3.4 percent ($137 billion) in 2007, a gain of 3.3 percent. According to the U.S. Census Bureau, in 2007 most online e-sales were either for nonstore retailers (sites such as Amazon.com or other mail order companies) or motor vehicles and parts, accounting for 73 percent ($93 billion) and 19 percent ($24 billion) respectively. Of online mail order sales, clothing and footwear generated more sales than any other kind of purchase ($14 billion). Computer hardware sales accounted for $11 billion.

Advertising on the Web

Much as it has evolved as a communications and information medium, the World Wide Web, like television and and radio, has also emerged as a major vehicle of commercial advertising. The ads come in the form of banners, pop-up windows, and other Web-page design elements. E-mail has also proven to be viable as an advertising medium, giving birth to the next generation of direct-mail marketing.

The U.S. economic slowdown and shakeout in the dot-com industry in 2000–02 slowed the growth of Internet advertising, but the rate of increase over the short life of the medium still far exceeded that of any other. And robust increases were expected in the years to come. Media analysts estimated global online ad spending in 2010 at $55.2 billion, and projected that this will increase to $96.8 billion by 2014.

Privacy and Intellectual Property Rights

As the popularity and purchasing power of the Internet have grown, and as monitoring tools have improved, many people have perceived a growing threat to their personal privacy. Software that tracks usage habits, network database technology, and the ability to transmit vast amounts of data have made it possible to collect and share detailed information about the browsing habits, interests and hobbies, buying patterns, financial history, and contact information of ordinary Internet-using citizens. The U.S. Congress in 2002 and 2003 considered various legislative measures to protect privacy and combat identity theft in the online environment.

In a similar vein, the data-sharing power of the Internet has undermined traditional protections for proprietary information and copyright materials. The issue came to the fore in 2000–2001, as the music industry successfully sued Napster.com, which enabled Web site visitors to swap MP3 music files of popular commercial recordings for free. But as millions of users continued to pirate digital songs, music and games through online file-sharing systems, copyright protection and intellectual property rights on the Internet loomed as major long-term issues.

▶ A GLOSSARY OF COMMONLY USED INTERNET TERMS

Account   Permission to use a computer on a network, or an access agreement with an Internet provider

Address   The location of an Internet host. An e-mail address might take the form john-doe@xyz.com; a web address might look like www.xyztech.com. See also URL.

Applet   A small program, typically embedded in an Web page, that a user can quickly download and launch, thus enhancing the Web page's content.

Bandwidth   The amount of data, graphics, sound, and other information that can be transmitted through cyberspace at a certain time. Bandwidth is measured in kilobits per second (kbps). Most telephone modems have a bandwidth of 56 kbps (or simply 56k); though *cable modems* and *DSL* can offer bandwidths of more than 1 megabit per second (mbps).

Blog   Short for "weblog." A diary-like Web site, usually containing the personal thoughts of the

U.S. Shipments, Sales, Revenues and E-commerce: 2007–08
(in billions of dollars)

Description	All shipments and revenue			E-commerce only			
	2007	2008	Change 07–08	2007	2008	Change 07–08	Percent of total 2008
B2B	**$11,179**	**$11,602**	**3.8%**	**$3,130**	**$3,416**	**9.1%**	**92.2%**
Manufacturing	5,338	5,486	2.8	1,879	2,154	14.6	58.2
Merchant Wholesale	5,841	6,116	4.7	1,251	1,262	0.9	34.1
B2C	**10,787**	**10,806**	**0.2**	**265**	**288**	**8.7**	**7.8**
Retail	4,005	3,959	−1.2	137	142	3.3	3.8
Selected Services	6,782	6,874	1.0	128	146	14.1	3.9
Total	**21,966**	**22,408**	**5.0**	**3,395**	**3,704**	**12.1**	**100.0%**

Note: B2B = business-to-business, which here includes manufacturing and wholesale e-commerce. B2C= business-to-consumer, which here includes all retail and service. **Source:** U.S. Census Bureau, Economics and Statistics Administration *E-commerce E-Stats May 27, 2010* (2010).

site's owner as well as links to other sites of interest.

Bookmark A browser feature (called "Favorites" in Microsoft Explorer) that stores a pointer to a Web site for easy access.

Browser A program that translates the hypertext markup language of the World Wide Web into languages ordinary people can understand. Netscape and Microsoft Internet Explorer are the two most common Web browsers.

Cable Modem A high-speed, broadband Internet connection via cable TV lines; services often include a selection of localized content.

Cache (Pronounced "cash") The place on a hard drive where a Web browser stores images a user has downloaded off the Internet. If the user wants to see the same Web page again, the browser loads it from the cache rather than retrieve it again from the Internet.

Cookie A small piece of information that a Web *browser* picks up from another site and stores. Such bits of information can be read and altered by another site, thereby making it possible to identify users who have been to the site before. Cookies allow you to add items to your "shopping cart" as you browse several pages in a virtual shopping mall.

Cyberspace An all-encompassing term for the digital world of computer networks.

Domain The identifying portion of an Internet address (which follows the @ in an e-mail address. Domain names are followed by a period and a zone that indicates the type of organization. Commercial entities end with *.com*; Educational institutions end with *.edu*; government bodies end with *.gov*; and other organizations end with *.org*.

Download A way to transfer files, graphics, or other information from the Internet to your computer. HTTP and FTP are the most common downloading methods.

DSL Digital Subscription Line, a high-speed Internet connection that uses the ultra-high frequency portion of ordinary telephone lines, allowing users to send and receive voice and data on the same line at the same time.

Emoticon A cluster of punctuation marks commonly used in online chat, postings and e-mail to signify a facial expression or emotional response. For example, :-) represents a smile, and :-(a frown.

Encryption A method of encoding files so only the recipient can read the information. Encryption is necessary for transmitting secure data like credit card numbers over computer networks.

FAQs Frequently Asked Questions. This is generally the first place to stop on a newsgroup or a Web site. It has the answers to the most common questions and indicators of where to go to find the answers to less frequently asked questions.

FTP File Transfer Protocol, the easiest way to download files not on the World Wide Web.

Freeware Free software available over the Internet. This is in contrast with *shareware*, which is available freely, but usually asks the user to send payment for using the software.

GIF Graphic Interchange Format (pronounced "jif"), a common file format for image files; best-suited for nonphotographic material.

Home page The first or main page of a Web site.

HTML HyperText Markup Language, the high-speed computer language used to create documents on the World Wide Web (WWW). To read documents written in HTML, one must have a browser.

HTTP HyperText Transport Protocol, the easiest way to transfer World Wide Web pages from one computer to another.

Hyperlink A connection between two tagged elements in a Web page, or separate sites, that makes it possible to click from one to the other.

Hypertext A system of organizing information based on its relationship to other information, rather than linear or alphabetical orders. Hypertext allows users to *link* related Web pages and to store information in more than one place. For example, in a hypertext almanac, the winners of the National Book Awards could be accessed either through the section on books or on awards.

Intranet A network of computers accessible only by members of the network, often members of one firm. Also known as an internal network.

ISDN Integrated Services Digital Network, a digital type of phone service that permits higher speed transmission of data than conventional phone lines. ISDN lines operate as fast as 128 kilobytes per second (kbps), compared with 28.8 or 56 kbps for the fastest modems.

ISP Internet Service Provider, a company that provides end-user access to the Internet via its central computers and local access lines. America Online (AOL), Earthlink, and Erols are some popular ISPs.

Java A computer language developed by Sun Microsystems that produces programs that run on almost any computer or operating system. Its compatibility and ease of use make it popular for for developing *applets*, tiny applications that can be sent quickly over the World Wide Web.

JPEG Joint Photographic Experts Group, a common file format for photographic images.

Link A hypertext connection that allows a user to jump from one Internet site to another by pointing and clicking. On the World Wide Web, links are often underlined or highlighted.

MIDI Musical Instrument Digital Interface, a file format for high-quality sound.

Mirror site An identical backup site that serves as an alternative for a busy web host.

MPEG Motion Picture Experts Group, a file format for high-quality video in small file sizes.

Newsgroups Discussion forums on the Internet, arranged by category of special interest. To read, respond to, or post information on a newsgroup, you must have a program known as a Newsreader.

Search engine A tool used to look up Web pages. Also known as an index or a directory. Yahoo!, Excite, Lycos, and AltaVista are some of the most popular search engines.

Server The central computer in a network, providing a service or data access to client computers on that network. Frequently, a Web server is dedicated to a specific function, such as e-mail.

Shareware An honor system in which providers make their programs freely accessible over the Internet, with the understanding that those who use them will send payment to the provider after using them. See also *freeware*.

Spam Junk e-mail. As a verb, it means to send thousands of copies of a junk e-mail message.

Thumbnail A tiny picture on a Web page which, when clicked, is replaced by a larger version of the same image.

URL Uniform Resource Locator, the address that identifies a Web page to a browser. Also known as a Web address.

Web page   An HTML file, containing text, graphics, and/or mini-applications, viewed with a Web *browser*.

Web site   An organized, linked collection of *Web* pages stored on an Internet *server* and read using a Web *browser*. The opening page of a site is called a *home page*.

WWW   The World Wide Web, or simply the Web, a vast network of information, particularly business, commercial, and government resources, that uses a hypertext system for quickly transmitting graphics, sound, and video over phone, cable TV, and fiber optic lines, allowing easy navigation among related subjects.

XML   eXtensible Markup Language, a universal format for structured documents and data transmitted on the Web. XML is a "metalanguage," a system used for defining and creating specialized languages such as HTML.

Zip file   A file that has been compressed for simpler transmission over the Internet. To read a ZIP file, you need a program to decompress the file, such as PKUNZIP or WinZip.

▶ A FIELD GUIDE TO SEARCHING THE WEB

To search the Web successfully, you need to pick the right engine and learn how to use it. Few people understand the fundamental difference between search engines and Web directories. The former use software agents called "spiders" or "crawlers" to index contents of individual Web pages, then follow links to other pages. Web directories such as Yahoo are compiled by humans who classify sites under topical headings. Most search sites now offer both options, along with information and other services, but topical directories that accompany powerful search engines may be weak, and vice-versa. Moreover, the various search engines themselves operate differently.

The first step in conducting an effective search is to pick an appropriate search site for the job. For a general search, a strong Web directory such as Yahoo is a good place to start. A directory-style search provides two ways to research broad topics: dive through a list of broad topics by clicking on the appropriate links or fill out a search box to find listings.

But directory searches are less effective when looking for specific information—things like the author of a book, the complete text of the Declaration of Independence or research on drug treatments for a medical condition. For this kind of information, search engines like Google and Alta Vista are the way to go. Because they search an index of keywords drawn by spiders from millions of Web pages, the chances are greater that they will find obscure terms in obscure Web pages.

There's a third kind of search site, one that includes popular sites like Ask and Dogpile. These sites—also called metasearch tools—issue search requests to fistfuls of other Web search sites. When Google, Yahoo!, Bing and the like return their results, the metasearch site collects them onto a single Web page for display.

Because no two search sites index exactly the same set of Web pages, metasearch tools give you a wider scope of results—but it's worth remembering that more does not necessarily equal better. What really counts is relevant results that are sorted in a relevant order.

Simply picking one of two or three types of sites to search from is no guarantee of good results. Brad Hill, the author of *World Wide Web Searching for Dummies* (IDG), says most search sites deliver too much information. "Search engines do a good job on indexing," he said. "But because of that, they deliver more than you want."

So when you're faced with several hundred thousand results over dozens of pages, what should you do? "Don't go past the first page of results," Hill said. "If it doesn't have something of interest, you've probably entered the wrong search string."

Most people could get much more relevant results with a few simple tricks for constructing a search "string"—the words you enter in the search box. The most obvious is to type in several relevant words instead of just one or two. In general, the fewer words you enter, the more general your results will be.

Alta Vista (www.altavista.com)   A powerful, highly rated search engine with a database of more than 600 million indexed documents. Accurate, well-integrated search results. The portal also includes a modest topical directory, links, tools, and services.

Ask (www.ask.com)   A highly user-friendly metasearch site, with natural language querying and a basic subject directory. It helps you narrow your search through simple questions and simultaneously searches other engines for relevant Web pages. Results are organized under "Web," "News," and "Shopping" tabs.

Bing (www.bing.com)   Previously MSN's Live Search, Bing was rechristened with an updated format and look. Results are grouped by topic and relationship to the search string.

Google (www.google.com)   The leading general Internet search engine, consistently a leader in user preference surveys and trade reviews. Fast and reliable, with more than 1.5 billion indexed documents. Known for yielding high-relevance results and few broken links.

Yahoo! (www.yahoo.com)   One of the world's most popular portals and by all accounts the best directory index for broad general topics, Yahoo! features a comprehensive, hierarchical listing of selected sites—with limited ability to search the contents of individual pages. Reliable and easy to use, Yahoo! remains an excellent choice for basic research while offering a slate of customizable services.

▶ A WEB SITE DIRECTORY

The Internet provides users with an ever-expanding world of information and online services in virtually every field of interest. Along with the popular *search engines* and portals described above, the sites listed below may provide the beginnings of your personal index. Explore the sites yourself and add the ones you like to the "Bookmarks" or "Favorites" list in your *browser*.

Entertainment and Learning

Discovery.com (www.discovery.com)   Fun, adventure, and learning for children and adults, from the producers of The Discovery Channel.

eHow (www.howto.com)   More than 15,000 how-to solutions for day-to-day living in easy, step-by-step instructions. Organized in 14 categories and 120 subcategories.

Hulu (www.hulu.com) Co-owned by NBC Universal and News Corp., Hulu streams a wide range of recent and older TV and films. Many of the selections are full-length.

The Internet Movie Database (www.imbd.com) The biggest and best film resource on the Web, covering more than 200,000 movies, extensive filmographies, and hundreds of thousands of biographical profiles.

Last.fm (www.last.fm) Free, customized streaming internet radio.

National Geographic (www.nationalgeographic. com) Magazine articles, virtual museum exhibits, a mini-encyclopedia, and more, for kids and adults.

Pandora Radio (www.pandora.com) Uses human-submitted descriptions to create custom, on-demand radio stations based on song characteristics.

PBS Online (www.pbs.org) Educational and entertaining media presentations, transcripts, quizzes, learning guides, and more, based on public television programs and documentaries.

YouTube (www.youtube.com) The largest video sharing site on the Web, YouTube is also one of the most popular Web sites overall. Free, usually amateur videos.

Family and Health

Genealogy.com (www.genealogy.com) Type in a name, begin your search. Take classes, post queries, find links to other sites. A great place to start a family tree. Subscription.

Healthfinder (www.healthfinder.gov) U.S. government site with thousands of documents, well-organized interface, medical news, databases, and links. A useful gateway.

Health Risk Assessment (www.youfirst.com) Tools and information for in-depth personal health assessment; create a confidential personal profile.

SeniorNet (www.seniornet.com) Online services and information for people over 50. Classes, chat, and more.

WebMD (www.webmd.com) Leader in providing services that help consumers, physicians, and health plans navigate the health care system. Medscape.com, accessible from the main page, provides in-depth clinical information.

Finance and Investment

E*Trade (www.etrade.com) The first and leading Internet trading/investment firm. Includes personalized portfolio management and news.

The Motley Fool (www.fool.com) Free, easy-to-understand financial information, including timely stock updates, portfolio tracker, and investor chat boards.

MSN MoneyCentral (www.moneycentral.msn.com) Portfolio management, stock screening, investment tracking and advice, financial headlines, real-time stock tracker, 401(k) planner, and more.

Quicken.com (www.quicken.com) Personal finance site, featuring interactive tools to help with insurance, home-loan, tax-preparation, investment, and retirement-planning needs.

TheStreet.com (www.thestreet.com) Extensive online financial information, including daily market analysis and real-time stock ticker.

Reference

About.com (www.about.com) A rich portal site and comprehensive Web directory for everyday use. More than 50,000 subjects and 1 million links to Net resources—well organized.

Britannica.com (www.britannica.com) The entire encyclopedia free, with links to related magazine articles and hundreds of thousands of Web sites.

FreeTranslation.com (www.freetranslation.com) Uses the Transparent Language translation engine for free translation of documents or Web pages—English, French, German, Italian, Portuguese, and Spanish.

OneLookDictionaries (www.onelook.com) Access to over 700 general and specialized dictionaries.

Virtual Reference Desk (refdesk.com) Vast collection of links to general and topical information sites.

Wikipedia (www.wikipedia.org) "The free encyclopedia." Articles in numerous languages comprised of volunteer submissions. Entries are freely editable.

Government

FedStats (www.fedstats.gov) A full range of statistics and information from more than 100 U.S. federal agencies.

Internal Revenue Service (www.irs.gov) Tax forms and instructions, advice, online filing.

The Library of Congress (www.loc.gov) Photos, documents, online exhibits, legislation text, and other resources make this site valuable for serious research or casual enjoyment.

Data.gov (www.data.gov) A recently launched government portal that acts as a clearinghouse and good starting place for access to government reports and publications from a variety of departments and agencies.

Thomas (thomas.loc.gov) Authoritative, in-depth information on federal legislation, a service of the Library of Congress.

U.S. Census Bureau (www.census.gov) Authoritative, extensive information on U.S. population, demographics, economy, industry and agriculture, education, law enforcement, etc.

The White House (www.whitehouse.gov) Write to the president, read documents and policy statements, take a tour, browse the archives, etc.

Jobs/Career Development

Career Builder (www.careerbuilder.com) Leading career management site for job seekers and employers.

HotJobs (www.hotjobs.com) Thousands of registered recruiters and over 500,000 resumes; no head-hunters allowed.

Jobs.com (www.jobs.com) Local job search, resume posting. Extensive listings.

LinkedIn (www.linkedin.com) A social networking site for professionals and job seekers.

Monster.com (www.monster.com) Online employment services, including job searches by location, a resume database available to recruiters, and online job application. Includes resources for freelancers.

News

ABCNews.com (www.abcnews.com) Headlines, online-only features, videos, instant polls, abundant links. Deep coverage with frequent updates.

BBC Online (www.bbc.co.uk) The vast international resources of BBC's news organization. World news with a unique perspective.

CNN Interactive (www.cnn.com) Late-breaking news and background: multimedia galleries, in-depth analysis, polls, searchable background material, links. Includes the CNNfn financial news network, and CNNSI, sports coverage with *Sports Illustrated*.

MSNBC (www.msnbc.com) The most interactive of all the news sites. Includes a personalized news page and compelling polls, chats, and discussions.

The New York Times (www.nytimes.com) Most of the daily paper is available online, as are extensive archives.

Real Estate

Realtor.com (www.realtor.com) The official site of the National Association of Realtors. National listings and real estate valuation tools.

Zillow (www.zillow.com) A variety of map-based tools to research mortgage rates, recent selling prices, per area costs by location.

Trulia (www.trulia.com) Shows multiple listings with map-based searches nationwide. One neat feature is the ability to view Trulia listings in Google's Earth application.

Zip Realty (www.ziprealty.com) MLS service which aggregates multiple listings from a variety or realtors.

Shopping/Auctions

Amazon.com (www.amazon.com) The "granddaddy" of consumer online shopping sites, it began with books, then moved into music, video, consumer electronics, and toys. Deep discounts.

Craigslist (www.craigslist.org) Community "bulletin-board" style web site with separate microsites per location listing a wide variety of products, services, tag sales, and jobs.

eBay (www.ebay.com) The largest online auction site, with millions of items at all times.

Overstock (www.overstock.com) Large shopping site focusing on closeouts and overstock items.

Ticketmaster (www.ticketmaster.com) One of most visited sites on the Web. Order tickets to concerts, sports competitions, and other events—more than 350,000 a year. Includes special deals.

Social Networking

Facebook (www.facebook.com) Member pages, profiles, chat, photo sharing and a wide variety of free applications.

MySpace (www.myspace.com) Customizable member pages and emphasis on musicians and younger demographic.

LinkedIn (www.linkedin.com) As popular as a social networking site for professionals as it is as a jobs clearinghouse.

Twitter (www.twitter.com) Similar in concept to a free-for-all chat room, Twitter allows members to publish short, 140-character "tweets" on any subject.

Identi.ca (www.identi.ca) Similar to Twitter. Built on an open-source platform.

FriendFeed (www.friendfeed.com) Aggregates online activity of your connections from a variety of places and social networks into a single "feed."

Flickr (www.flickr.com) Widely popular photo sharing site, recently expanded with features that nudge it into the "social networking" category. Commenting on, grouping and "following" user photos are now possible.

Sports and Games

CBS SportsLine (www.cbs.sportsline.com) In-depth, comprehensive, up-to-the-minute coverage. News, multimedia features, personalized information, live celebrity chats, forums, calendars and numerous links.

ESPN.com (www.msn.espn.go.com) Scores, stories, stats, schedules, standings, video, sound. Up-to-the-minute analyses and features. GameCast lets you follow games on your screen as they happen.

GameSpot (www.gamespot.com) From ZDNet, a favorite with PC gaming enthusiasts—news, reviews, previews, free demo downloads, and more.

The Sporting News (www.sportingnews.com) Hardcore, in-depth coverage. Analysis by 30 well-known columnists. Abundant stats and links, with customizable team/score reporting.

Sportspages.com (www.sportspages.com) Fresh links to the world's best sports pages.

Travel

Expedia.com (www.expedia.com) Makes travel planning easy, from research to booking. Find special deals and unique vacations ideas on the Travel Network. Includes mapping features and a staff of travel agents.

Kayak (www.kayak.com) Aggregates search results from a variety of airlines, many of them small or discount carriers.

National Park Service: ParkNet (www.nps.gov) Click on "Visit Your Parks" link for detailed maps and general information on the U.S. national parks.

Orbitz (www.orbitz.com) Popular travel booking for airfare, hotel and car rentals.

Priceline.com (www.priceline.com) A popular buying service that asks you what you're willing to pay and seeks providers. Great for airline tickets, car rentals, hotel rooms and other products.

Travelocity.com (www.travelocity.com) Owned by Sabre Group, which maintains the largest worldwide reservation system. Best current fares and packages, e-mail and pager bulletins.

Weather and Maps

Google Maps (www.maps.google.com) Shows variety of map data (from Earth and nearby planets), with options varying by location. In many cities, street-level 360° views, traffic, topology and 3-dimensional buildings are shown.

Mapquest.com (www.mapquest.com) Interactive maps and driving directions, customized mapping, and travel information for businesses and consumers.

National Weather Service (www.nws.noaa.gov) World, national, and regional forecasts—daily and long-term. Includes maps, satellite imagery, specialized data, and abundant links.

Weather Channel (www.weather.com) The leading commercial weather site, and one of the most popular on the Web. Detailed national and local forecasts, with special details relating to travel, health, recreation, and special event locations.

Academy Awards 1928–2009

The **"Oscars" are officially known** as the Academy of Motion Picture Arts and Sciences Awards. They were inaugurated in 1928 as part of Hollywood's drive to improve its less-than-respectable image. Academy librarian and eventual executive director Margaret Herrick remarked that the statuette looked like her uncle Oscar, and the nickname has stuck ever since. Membership in the Academy (currently over 3,000) is by invitation only, with members divided into 13 branches. Each branch selects up to five nominees for awards in its area of expertise; the entire membership makes "Best Film" nominations and then votes on all the categories. Major awards are shown in the chart. Awards for Best Cinematography and for Best Foreign Language Film are shown in a separate table. Best Actors and directors are named for films winning Best Picture except where otherwise indicated.

Year	Best picture	Best director	Best actor	Best actress	Best supporting actor	Best supporting actress
1928	Wings	Frank Borzage, Seventh Heaven Lewis Milestone, Two Arabian Knights	Emil Jannings, The Way of All Flesh, The Last Command	Janet Gaynor, Seventh Heaven, Sunrise, Street Angel	No Awards Given	No Awards Given
1929	The Broadway Melody	Frank Lloyd, The Divine Lady	Warner Baxter, In Old Arizona	Mary Pickford, Coquette	No Awards Given	No Awards Given
1930	All Quiet on the Western Front	Lewis Milestone	George Arliss, Disraeli	Norma Shearer, The Divorcee	No Awards Given	No Awards Given
1931	Cimarron	Norman Taurog, Skippy	Lionel Barrymore, A Free Soul	Marie Dressler, Min and Bill	No Awards Given	No Awards Given
1932	Grand Hotel	Frank Borzage, Bad Girl	Wallace Beery, The Champ Fredric March, Dr. Jekyll and Mr. Hyde	Helen Hayes, The Sin of Madelon Claudet	No Awards Given	No Awards Given
1933	Cavalcade	Frank Lloyd	Charles Laughton, The Private Life of Henry VIII	Katharine Hepburn, Morning Glory	No Awards Given	No Awards Given
1934	It Happened One Night	Frank Capra	Clark Gable	Claudette Colbert	No Awards Given	No Awards Given
1935	Mutiny on the Bounty	John Ford, The Informer	Victor McLaglen, The Informer	Bette Davis, Dangerous	No Awards Given	No Awards Given
1936	The Great Ziegfeld	Frank Capra, Mr. Deeds Goes to Town	Paul Muni, The Story of Louis Pasteur	Luise Rainer	Walter Brennan, Come and Get It	Gale Sondergaard, Anthony Adverse
1937	The Life of Emile Zola	Leo McCarey, The Awful Truth	Spencer Tracy, Captains Courageous	Luise Rainer, The Good Earth	Joseph Schildkraut	Alice Brady, In Old Chicago
1938	You Can't Take It With You	Frank Capra	Spencer Tracy, Boys Town	Bette Davis, Jezebel	Walter Brennan, Kentucky	Fay Bainter, Jezebel
1939	Gone With the Wind	Victor Fleming	Robert Donat, Goodbye, Mr. Chips	Vivien Leigh	Thomas Mitchell, Stagecoach	Hattie McDaniel
1940	Rebecca	John Ford, The Grapes of Wrath	James Stewart, The Philadelphia Story	Ginger Rogers, Kitty Foyle	Walter Brennan, The Westerner	Jane Darwell, The Grapes of Wrath
1941	How Green Was My Valley	John Ford	Gary Cooper, Sergeant York	Joan Fontaine, Suspicion	Donald Crisp	Mary Astor, The Great Lie

Year	Best picture	Best director	Best actor	Best actress	Best supporting actor	Best supporting actress
1942	Mrs. Miniver	William Wyler	James Cagney, Yankee Doodle Dandy	Greer Garson	Van Heflin, Johnny Eager	Teresa Wright
1943	Casablanca	Michael Curtiz	Paul Lukas, Watch On The Rhine	Jennifer Jones, The Song of Bernadette	Charles Coburn, The More the Merrier	Katina Paxinou, For Whom the Bell Tolls
1944	Going My Way	Leo McCarey	Bing Crosby	Ingrid Bergman, Gaslight	Barry Fitzgerald	Ethel Barrymore, None But the Lonely Heart
1945	The Lost Weekend	Billy Wilder	Ray Milland	Joan Crawford, Mildred Pierce	James Dunn, A Tree Grows in Brooklyn	Anne Revere, National Velvet
1946	The Best Years of Our Lives	William Wyler	Fredric March	Olivia De Havilland, To Each His Own	Harold Russell	Anne Baxter, The Razor's Edge
1947	Gentleman's Agreement	Elia Kazan	Ronald Colman, A Double Life	Loretta Young, The Farmer's Daughter	Edmund Gwenn, Miracle on 34th Street	Celeste Holm
1948	Hamlet	John Huston, The Treasure of the Sierra Madre	Laurence Olivier	Jane Wyman, Johnny Belinda	Walter Huston, The Treasure of the Sierra Madre	Claire Trevor, Key Largo
1949	All the King's Men	Joseph L. Mankiewicz, A Letter to Three Wives	Broderick Crawford	Olivia De Havilland, The Heiress	Dean Jagger, Twelve O'Clock High	Mercedes McCambridge
1950	All About Eve	Joseph L. Mankiewicz	José Ferrer, Cyrano de Bergerac	Judy Holliday, Born Yesterday	George Sanders	Josephine Hull, Harvey
1951	An American in Paris	George Stevens, A Place in the Sun	Humphrey Bogart, The African Queen	Vivien Leigh, A Streetcar Named Desire	Karl Malden, A Streetcar Named Desire	Kim Hunter, A Streetcar Named Desire
1952	The Greatest Show on Earth	John Ford, The Quiet Man	Gary Cooper, High Noon	Shirley Booth, Come Back, Little Sheba	Anthony Quinn, Viva Zapata!	Gloria Grahame, The Bad and the Beautiful
1953	From Here to Eternity	Fred Zinnemann	William Holden, Stalag 17	Audrey Hepburn, Roman Holiday	Frank Sinatra	Donna Reed
1954	On the Waterfront	Elia Kazan	Marlon Brando	Grace Kelly, The Country Girl	Edmond O'Brien, The Barefoot Contessa	Eva Marie Saint
1955	Marty	Delbert Mann	Ernest Borgnine	Anna Magnani, The Rose Tattoo	Jack Lemmon, Mister Roberts	Jo Van Fleet, East of Eden
1956	Around the World in 80 Days	George Stevens, Giant	Yul Brynner, The King And I	Ingrid Bergman, Anastasia	Anthony Quinn, Lust for Life	Dorothy Malone, Written on the Wind
1957	The Bridge on the River Kwai	David Lean	Alec Guinness	Joanne Woodward, The Three Faces of Eve	Red Buttons, Sayonara	Miyoshi Umeki, Sayonara
1958	Gigi	Vincente Minnelli	David Niven, Separate Tables	Susan Hayward, I Want to Live!	Burl Ives, The Big Country	Wendy Hiller, Separate Tables
1959	Ben-Hur	William Wyler	Charlton Heston	Simone Signoret, Room at the Top	Hugh Griffith	Shelley Winters, The Diary of Anne Frank
1960	The Apartment	Billy Wilder	Burt Lancaster, Elmer Gantry	Elizabeth Taylor, Butterfield 8	Peter Ustinov, Spartacus	Shirley Jones, Elmer Gantry
1961	West Side Story	Jerome Robbins, Robert Wise	Maximilian Schell, Judgment At Nuremberg	Sophia Loren, Two Women	George Chakiris	Rita Moreno

Year	Best picture	Best director	Best actor	Best actress	Best supporting actor	Best supporting actress
1962	Lawrence of Arabia	David Lean	Gregory Peck, To Kill a Mockingbird	Anne Bancroft, The Miracle Worker	Ed Begley, Sweet Bird of Youth	Patty Duke, The Miracle Worker
1963	Tom Jones	Tony Richardson	Sidney Poitier, Lilies of the Field	Patricia Neal, Hud	Melvyn Douglas, Hud	Margaret Rutherford, The V.I.P.s
1964	My Fair Lady	George Cukor	Rex Harrison	Julie Andrews, Mary Poppins	Peter Ustinov, Topkapi	Lila Kedrova, Zorba the Greek
1965	The Sound of Music	Robert Wise	Lee Marvin, Cat Ballou	Julie Christie, Darling	Martin Balsam, A Thousand Clowns	Shelley Winters, A Patch of Blue
1966	A Man for All Seasons	Fred Zinnemann	Paul Scofield	Elizabeth Taylor, Who's Afraid of Virginia Woolf?	Walter Matthau, The Fortune Cookie	Sandy Dennis, Who's Afraid of Virginia Woolf?
1967	In the Heat of the Night	Mike Nichols, The Graduate	Rod Steiger	Katharine Hepburn, Guess Who's Coming to Dinner	George Kennedy, Cool Hand Luke	Estelle Parsons, Bonnie and Clyde
1968	Oliver!	Carol Reed	Cliff Robertson, Charly	Katharine Hepburn, The Lion in Winter; Barbra Streisand, Funny Girl	Jack Albertson, The Subject Was Roses	Ruth Gordon, Rosemary's Baby
1969	Midnight Cowboy	John Schlesinger	John Wayne, True Grit	Maggie Smith, The Prime of Miss Jean Brodie	Gig Young, They Shoot Horses, Don't They?	Goldie Hawn, Cactus Flower
1970	Patton	Franklin J. Schaffner	George C. Scott	Glenda Jackson, Women in Love	John Mills, Ryan's Daughter	Helen Hayes, Airport
1971	The French Connection	William Friedkin	Gene Hackman	Jane Fonda, Klute	Ben Johnson, The Last Picture Show	Cloris Leachman, The Last Picture Show
1972	The Godfather	Bob Fosse, Cabaret	Marlon Brando	Liza Minnelli, Cabaret	Joel Grey, Cabaret	Eileen Heckart, Butterflies Are Free
1973	The Sting	George Roy Hill	Jack Lemmon, Save the Tiger	Glenda Jackson, A Touch of Class	John Houseman, The Paper Chase	Tatum O'Neal, Paper Moon
1974	The Godfather, Part II	Francis Ford Coppola	Art Carney, Harry And Tonto	Ellen Burstyn, Alice Doesn't Live Here Anymore	Robert De Niro	Ingrid Bergman, Murder on the Orient Express
1975	One Flew Over the Cuckoo's Nest	Milos Forman	Jack Nicholson	Louise Fletcher	George Burns, The Sunshine Boys	Lee Grant, Shampoo
1976	Rocky	John G. Avildsen	Peter Finch, Network	Faye Dunaway, Network	Jason Robards, All the President's Men	Beatrice Straight, Network
1977	Annie Hall	Woody Allen	Richard Dreyfuss, The Goodbye Girl	Diane Keaton	Jason Robards, Julia	Vanessa Redgrave, Julia
1978	The Deer Hunter	Michael Cimino	Jon Voight, Coming Home	Jane Fonda, Coming Home	Christopher Walken	Maggie Smith, California Suite
1979	Kramer vs. Kramer	Robert Benton	Dustin Hoffman	Sally Field, Norma Rae	Melvyn Douglas, Being There	Meryl Streep
1980	Ordinary People	Robert Redford	Robert De Niro, Raging Bull	Sissy Spacek, Coal Miner's Daughter	Timothy Hutton, Ordinary People	Mary Steenburgen, Melvin and Howard
1981	Chariots of Fire	Warren Beatty, Reds	Henry Fonda, On Golden Pond	Katharine Hepburn, On Golden Pond	John Gielgud, Arthur	Maureen Stapleton, Reds

Year	Best picture	Best director	Best actor	Best actress	Best supporting actor	Best supporting actress
1982	Gandhi	Richard Attenborough	Ben Kingsley	Meryl Streep, Sophie's Choice	Louis Gossett Jr., An Officer and a Gentleman	Jessica Lange, Tootsie
1983	Terms of Endearment	James L. Brooks	Robert Duvall, Tender Mercies	Shirley MacLaine	Jack Nicholson, Terms of Endearment	Linda Hunt, The Year of Living Dangerously
1984	Amadeus	Milos Forman	F. Murray Abraham	Sally Field, Places in the Heart	Haing S. Ngor, The Killing Fields	Peggy Ashcroft, A Passage to India
1985	Out of Africa	Sydney Pollack	William Hurt, Kiss of the Spider Woman	Geraldine Page, The Trip to Bountiful	Don Ameche, Cocoon	Anjelica Huston, Prizzi's Honor
1986	Platoon	Oliver Stone	Paul Newman, The Color of Money	Marlee Matlin, Children of a Lesser God	Michael Caine, Hannah and Her Sisters	Dianne Wiest, Hannah and Her Sisters
1987	The Last Emperor	Bernardo Bertolucci	Michael Douglas, Wall Street	Cher, Moonstruck	Sean Connery, The Untouchables	Olympia Dukakis, Moonstruck
1988	Rain Man	Barry Levinson	Dustin Hoffman	Jodie Foster, The Accused	Kevin Kline, A Fish Called Wanda	Geena Davis, The Accidental Tourist
1989	Driving Miss Daisy	Oliver Stone, Born on the Fourth of July	Daniel Day-Lewis, My Left Foot	Jessica Tandy	Denzel Washington, Glory	Brenda Fricker, My Left Foot
1990	Dances with Wolves	Kevin Costner	Jeremy Irons, Reversal of Fortune	Kathy Bates, Misery	Joe Pesci, Goodfellas	Whoopi Goldberg, Ghost
1991	The Silence of the Lambs	Jonathan Demme	Anthony Hopkins	Jodie Foster	Jack Palance, City Slickers	Mercedes Ruehl, The Fisher King
1992	Unforgiven	Clint Eastwood	Al Pacino, Scent of a Woman	Emma Thompson, Howards End	Gene Hackman	Marisa Tomei, My Cousin Vinny
1993	Schindler's List	Steven Spielberg	Tom Hanks, Philadelphia	Holly Hunter, The Piano	Tommy Lee Jones, The Fugitive	Anna Paquin, The Piano
1994	Forrest Gump	Robert Zemeckis	Tom Hanks	Jessica Lange, Blue Sky	Martin Landau, Ed Wood	Dianne Wiest, Bullets Over Broadway
1995	Braveheart	Mel Gibson	Nicolas Cage, Leaving Las Vegas	Susan Sarandon, Dead Man Walking	Kevin Spacey, The Usual Suspects	Mira Sorvino, Mighty Aphrodite
1996	The English Patient	Anthony Minghella	Geoffrey Rush, Shine	Frances McDormand, Fargo	Cuba Gooding Jr., Jerry Maguire	Juliette Binoche
1997	Titanic	James Cameron	Jack Nicholson, As Good as it Gets	Helen Hunt, As Good as it Gets	Robin Williams, Good Will Hunting	Kim Basinger, L.A. Confidential
1998	Shakespeare in Love	Steven Spielberg, Saving Private Ryan	Roberto Benigni, Life is Beautiful	Gwyneth Paltrow	James Coburn, Affliction	Judi Dench
1999	American Beauty	Sam Mendes	Kevin Spacey	Hilary Swank, Boys Don't Cry	Michael Caine, The Cider House Rules	Angelina Jolie, Girl, Interrupted
2000	Gladiator	Steven Soderbergh, Traffic	Russell Crowe	Julia Roberts, Erin Brockovich	Benicio Del Toro, Traffic	Marcia Gay Harden, Pollock
2001	A Beautiful Mind	Ron Howard	Denzel Washington, Training Day	Halle Berry, Monsters Ball	Jim Broadbent, Iris	Jennifer Connelly
2002	Chicago	Roman Polanski, The Pianist	Adrien Brody, The Pianist	Nicole Kidman, The Hours	Chris Cooper, Adaptation	Catherine Zeta-Jones
2003	The Lord of the Rings: The Return of the King	Peter Jackson	Sean Penn, Mystic River	Charlize Theron, Monster	Tim Robbins, Mystic River	Renee Zellweger, Cold Mountain

Year	Best picture	Best director	Best actor	Best actress	Best supporting actor	Best supporting actress
2004	Million Dollar Baby	Clint Eastwood	Jamie Foxx, Ray	Hilary Swank	Morgan Freeman	Cate Blanchett, The Aviator
2005	Crash	Ang Lee, Brokeback Mountain	Philip Seymour Hoffman, Capote	Reese Witherspoon, Walk the Line	George Clooney, Syriana	Rachel Weisz, The Constant Gardener
2006	The Departed	Martin Scorsese	Forest Whitaker, The Last King of Scotland	Helen Mirren, The Queen	Alan Arkin, Little Miss Sunshine	Jennifer Hudson, Dreamgirls
2007	No Country for Old Men	Joel and Ethan Coen	Daniel Day-Lewis, There Will Be Blood	Marion Cotillard, La Vie en Rose	Javier Bardem	Tilda Swinton, Michael Clayton
2008	Slumdog Millionaire	Danny Boyle	Sean Penn, Milk	Kate Winslet, The Reader	Heath Ledger, The Dark Knight	Penelope Cruz, Vicky Cristina Barcelona
2009	The Hurt Locker	Kathryn Bigelow	Jeff Bridges, Crazy Heart	Sandra Bullock, The Blind Side	Christoph Waltz, Inglorious Bastards	Mo'Nique, Precious

Source: Academy of Motion Picture Arts & Sciences.

Academy Awards for Cinematography, 1930–2009

Year	Cinematographer, Film	Year	Cinematographer, Film
1930	Joseph T. Rucker, Willard Van Der Veer, With Byrd at the South Pole	1956	Joseph Ruttenberg, Sombody Up There Likes Me Lionel Lindon, Around the World in 80 Days
1931	Floyd Crosby, Tabu	1957	Jack Hildyard, The Bridge on the River Kwai
1932	Lee Garmes, Shanghai Express	1958	Sam Leavitt, The Defiant Ones
1933	Charles Bryant Lang Jr., A Farewell to Arms		Joseph Ruttenberg, Gigi
1934	Victor Milner, Cleopatra	1959	William C. Mellor, The Diary of Anne Frank
1935	Hal Mohr, A Midsummer Night's Dream		Robert L. Surtees, Ben-Hur
1936	Gaetano Gaudio, Anthony Adverse	1960	Freddie Francis, Sons and Lovers
1937	Karl Freund, The Good Earth		Russell Metty, Spartacus
1938	Joseph Ruttenberg, The Great Waltz	1961	Eugene Shuftan, The Hustler
1939	Gregg Toland, Wuthering Heights		Daniel L. Fapp, West Side Story
	Ernest Haller, Ray Rennahan, Gone With the Wind	1962	Jean Bourgoin, Walter Wottitz, The Longest Day Freddie Young, Lawrence of Arabia
1940	George Barnes, Rebecca	1963	James Wong Howe, Hud
	George Perinal, Thief of Baghdad		Leon Shamroy, Cleopatra
1941	Arthur Miller, How Green Was My Valley	1964	Walter Lassally, Zorba the Greek
	Ernest Palmer, Ray Rennahan, Blood and Sand		Harry Stradling, My Fair Lady
1942	Joseph Ruttenberg, Mrs. Miniver	1965	Ernest Laszlo, Ship of Fools
	Leon Shamroy, The Black Swan		Freddie Young, Dr. Zhivago
1943	Arthur Miller, The Song of Bernadette	1966	Haskell Wexler, Who's Afraid of Virginia Woolf?
	Hal Mohr, W. Howard Greene, The Phantom of the Opera		Ted Moore, A Man for All Seasons
1944	Joseph LaShelle, Laura	1967	Burnett Guffey, Bonnie and Clyde
	Leon Shamroy, Wilson	1968	Pasqualino De Santis, Romeo and Juliet
1945	Harry Stradling, The Picture of Dorian Gray	1969	Conrad L. Hall, Butch Cassidy and the Sundance Kid
	Leon Shamroy, Leave Her to Heaven	1970	Freddie Young, Ryan's Daughter
1946	Arthur Miller, Anna and the King of Siam	1971	Oswald Morris, Fiddler on the Roof
	Charles Rosher, Leonard Smith, Arthur Arling, The Yearling	1972	Geoffrey Unsworth, Cabaret
1947	Guy Green, Great Expectations	1973	Sven Nykvist, Cries and Whispers
	Jack Cardiff, Black Narcissus	1974	Fred Koenekamp, Joseph Biroc, The Towering Inferno
1948	William Daniels, The Naked City	1975	John Alcott, Barry Lyndon
	Joseph Valentine, William V. Skall, Winton Hoch, Joan of Arc	1976	Haskell Wexler, Bound for Glory
1949	Paul C. Vogel, Battleground	1977	Vilmos Zsigmond, Close Encounters of the Third Kind
	Winton Hoch, She Wore a Yellow Ribbon	1978	Nestor Almendros, Days of Heaven
1950	Robert Krasker, The Third Man	1979	Vittorio Storaro, Apocalypse Now
	Robert Surtees, King Solomon's Mines	1980	Geoffrey Unsworth, Ghislain Cloquet, Tess
1951	William C. Mellor, A Place in the Sun	1981	Vittorio Storaro, Reds
	Alfred Gilks, John Alton (ballet), An American in Paris	1982	Billy Williams, Ronnie Taylor, Gandhi
		1983	Sven Nykvist, Fanny & Alexander
1952	Robert Surtees, The Bad and the Beautiful	1984	Chris Menges, The Killing Fields
	Winton Hoch, Archie Stout, The Quiet Man	1985	David Watkin, Out of Africa
1953	Burnett Guffey, From Here to Eternity	1986	Chris Menges, The Mission
	Loyal Griggs, Shane	1987	Vittorio Storaro, The Last Emperor
1954	Boris Kaufman, On the Waterfront	1988	Peter Biziou, Mississippi Burning
	Milton Krasner, Three Coins in the Fountain	1989	Freddie Francis, Glory
1955	James Wong Howe, The Rose Tattoo	1990	Dean Semler, Dances With Wolves
	Robert Burks, To Catch a Thief	1991	Robert Richardson, JFK

1992	Philippe Rousselot, *A River Runs Through It*	2002	Conrad L. Hall, *Road to Perdition* (posthumous)
1993	Janusz Kaminski, *Schindler's List*		
1994	John Toll, *Legends of the Fall*	2003	Russell Boyd, *Master and Commander: The Far Side of the World*
1995	John Toll, *Braveheart*		
1996	John Seale, *The English Patient*	2004	Robert Richardson, *The Aviator*
1997	Russell Carpenter, *Titanic*	2005	Dion Beebe, *Memoirs of a Geisha*
1998	Janusz Kaminski, *Saving Private Ryan*	2006	Guillermo Navarro, *Pan's Labyrinth*
1999	Conrad L. Hall, *American Beauty*	2007	Robert Elswit, *There Will Be Blood*
2000	Peter Pau, *Crouching Tiger, Hidden Dragon*	2008	Anthony Dod Mantle, *Slumdog Millionaire*
2001	Andrew Lesnie, *The Lord of the Rings: The Fellowship of the Ring*	2009	Mauro Fiore, *Avatar*

Source: Academy of Motion Picture Arts & Sciences.

American Film Institute Life Achievement Awards, 1973–2009

Awarded to individuals whose "talent has fundamentally advanced the art of American film or television . . . and whose work has withstood the test of time."

Year	Recipient	Year	Recipient	Year	Recipient	Year	Recipient
1973	John Ford	1982	Frank Capra	1991	Kirk Douglas	2000	Harrison Ford
1974	James Cagney	1983	John Huston	1992	Sidney Poitier	2001	Barbra Streisand
1975	Orson Welles	1984	Lillian Gish	1993	Elizabeth Taylor	2002	Tom Hanks
1976	William Wyler	1985	Gene Kelly	1994	Jack Nicholson	2003	Robert De Niro
1977	Henry Fonda	1986	Billy Wilder	1995	Steven Spielberg	2004	Meryl Streep
1978	Bette Davis	1987	Barbara Stanwyck	1996	Clint Eastwood	2005	George Lucas
1979	Alfred Hitchcock	1988	Jack Lemmon	1997	Martin Scorsese	2006	Sir Sean Connery
1980	James Stewart	1989	Gregory Peck	1998	Robert Wise	2007	Al Pacino
1981	Fred Astaire	1990	David Lean	1999	Dustin Hoffman	2008	Warren Beatty
						2009	Michael Douglas

Source: American Film Institute.

Academy Awards for Best Foreign Language Film, 1956–2009

Year	Film, Country, Director	Year	Film, Country, Director
1956	*La Strada*, Italy, Federico Fellini	1981	*Mephisto*, Austria/Germany/Hungary, Istvan Szabo
1957	*The Nights of Cabiria*, Italy, Federico Fellini		
1958	*Mon Oncle*, France, Jacques Tati	1982	*To Begin Again*, Spain, Jose Luis Garcia
1959	*Black Orpheus*, France/Italy/Brazil, Marcel Camus	1983	*Fanny and Alexander*, Sweden, Ingmar Bergman
		1984	*Dangerous Moves*, France, Richard Dembo
1960	*The Virgin Spring*, Sweden, Ingmar Bergman	1985	*The Official Story*, Argentina, Luis Puenzo
1961	*Through A Glass Darkly*, Sweden, Ingmar Bergman	1986	*The Assault*, Netherlands, Fons Rademakers
		1987	*Babette's Feast*, Denmark, Gabriel Axel
1962	*Sundays and Cybele*, France, Serge Bourgignon	1988	*Pelle the Conqueror*, Denmark, Bille August
1963	*8½*, Italy, Federico Fellini	1989	*Cinema Paradiso*, Italy, Giuseppe Tornatore
1964	*Yesterday, Today, and Tomorrow*, Italy/France, Vittorio de Sica	1990	*Journey of Hope*, Switzerland, Xavier Koller
		1991	*Mediterraneo*, Italy, Gabriel Salvatores
1965	*The Shop on Main Street*, Czechoslovakia, Jan Kadar	1992	*Indochine*, France, Regis Wargnier
		1993	*Belle Époque*, Spain, Fernando Trueba
1966	*A Man and a Woman*, France, Claude Lelouch	1994	*Burnt by the Sun*, Russia, Nikita Mikhalkov
1967	*Closely Watched Trains*, Czechoslovakia, Jiri Menzel	1995	*Antonia's Line*, Netherlands, Marleen Gorris
		1996	*Kolya*, Czech Republic, Jan Sverak
1968	*War and Peace*, USSR, Sergei Bondarchuk	1997	*Character*, Netherlands, Mike van Diem
1969	*Z*, France/Algeria, Constantin Costa-Gavras	1998	*Life is Beautiful*, Italy, Roberto Benigni
1970	*Investigation of a Citizen Above Suspicion*, Italy, Elio Petri	1999	*All About My Mother*, Spain, Pedro Almodóvar
1971	*The Garden of the Finzi-Continis*, Italy, Vittorio de Sica	2000	*Crouching Tiger, Hidden Dragon*, China, Ang Lee
1972	*The Discreet Charm of the Bourgeoisie*, France, Luis Buñuel	2001	*No Man's Land*, Bosnia & Herzegovina, Danis Tanovic
1973	*Day For Night*, France/Italy, François Truffaut	2002	*Nowhere in Africa*, Germany, Caroline Link
1974	*Amarcord*, Italy/France, Federico Fellini	2003	*The Barbarian Invasions*, Canada, Denys Arcand
1975	*Dersu Uzala*, USSR/Japan, Akira Kurosawa		
1976	*Black and White in Color*, France/Switzerland/ IvoryCoast, Jean-Jacques Annaud	2004	*The Sea Inside*, Alejandro Amenábar
		2005	*Tsotsi*, South Africa, Gavin Hood
1977	*Madame Rosa*, France, Moshe Mizrahi	2006	*The Lives of Others*, Germany, Florian Henckel von Donnersmarck
1978	*Get Out Your Handkerchiefs*, France, Bertrand Blier		
1979	*The Tin Drum*, Germany, Volker Scholondorff	2007	*The Counterfeiters*, Austria, Stefan Ruzowitzky
1980	*Moscow Does Not Believe in Tears*, USSR, Vladimir Menshov	2008	*Departures*, Japan, Yojiro Takita
		2009	*The Secret In Their Eyes*, Argentina, Juan Jose Campanella

Source: Academy of Motion Picture Arts & Sciences.

Cannes Film Festival *Palme d'Or* Awards, 1946–2010

Year	Film and director	Year	Film and director
1946	*La Bataille du Rail*, René Clément[1]	1979	*The Tin Drum*, Volker Schlöndorff
1949[2]	*The Third Man*, Carol Reed	1980	*Kagemusha*, Akira Kurosawa
1951	*Miracle in Milan*, Vittorio De Sica; *Miss Julie*, Alf Sjöberg	1981	*Man of Iron*, Andrzej Wajda
		1982	*Missing*, Costa-Gavras; *Yol*, Yilmar Güney
1952	*Two Cents Worth of Hope*, Renato Castellani; *Othello*, Orson Welles	1983	*The Ballad of Narayama*, Shohei Imamura
1953	*The Wages of Fear*, Georges Clouzot	1984	*Paris, Texas*, Wim Wenders
1954	*Gate of Hell*, Teinosuke Kinugasa	1985	*When Father Was Away on Business*, Emir Kusturica
1955	*Marty*, Delbert Mann		
1956	*The Silent World*, Jacques Cousteau, Louis Malle	1986	*The Mission*, Roland Joffé
		1987	*Under Satan's Sun*, Maurice Pialat
1957	*Friendly Persuasion*, William Wyler	1988	*Pelle the Conqueror*, Bille August
1958	*The Cranes are Flying*, Mikhail Kalatozov	1989	*Sex, Lies and Videotape*, Steven Soderbergh
1959	*Black Orpheus*, Marcel Camus	1990	*Wild at Heart*, David Lynch
1960	*La Dolce Vita*, Federico Fellini	1991	*Barton Fink*, Joel Coen
1961	*Viridiana*, Luis Buñuel	1992	*The Best Intentions*, Bille August
1962	*The Given Word*, Anselmo Duarte	1993	*The Piano*, Jane Campion; *Farewell My Concubine*, Chen Kaige
1963	*The Leopard*, Luchino Visconti		
1964	*The Umbrellas of Cherbourg*, Jacques Demy	1994	*Pulp Fiction*, Quentin Tarantino
		1995	*Underground*, Emir Kusturica
1965	*The Knack, and How to Get It*, Richard Lester	1996	*Secrets and Lies*, Mike Leigh
		1997	*Taste of Cherries*, Abbas Kiarostami; *Unagi (The Eel)*, Shohei Imamura
1966	*A Man and a Woman*, Claude Lelouch		
1967	*Blow-Up*, Michelangelo Antonioni	1998	*Eternity and a Day*, Theo Angelopoulos
1969	*If . . .*, Lindsay Anderson	1999	*Rosetta*, Jean-Pierre and Luc Dardenne
1970	*M*A*S*H*, Robert Altman	2000	*Dancer in the Dark*, Lars von Trier
1971	*The Go-Between*, Joseph Losey	2001	*The Son's Room*, Nanni Moretti
1972	*The Working Class Goes to Heaven*, Elio Petri; *The Mattei Affair*, Francesco Rosi	2002	*The Pianist*, Roman Polanski
		2003	*Elephant*, Gus Van Sant
		2004	*Fahrenheit 9/11*, Michael Moore
1973	*Scarecrow*, Jerry Schatzberg; *The Hireling*, Alan Bridges	2005	*L'enfant*, Jean-Pierre and Luc Dardenne
		2006	*The Wind that Shakes the Barley*, Ken Loach
1974	*The Conversation*, Francis Ford Coppola	2007	*4 Months 3 Weeks and 2 Days*, Cristian Mungiu
1975	*Chronique des Années de Braise*, M. Lakhdar Hamina	2008	*The Class (Entre Les Murs)*, Laurent Cantet
		2009	*The White Ribbon (Das Weisse Band)*, Michael Haneke
1976	*Taxi Driver*, Martin Scorsese		
1977	*Padre Padrone*, Paolo and Vittorio Taviani	2010	*Uncle Boonme Who Can Recall His Past Lives*, Apichatpong Weerasethakul
1978	*The Tree of Wooden Clogs*, Ermanno Olmi		

Notes: 1. Winner of the International Jury Prize. 2. In 1947, there was no "best film" award; prizes were given instead to outstanding works in several categories, including "Psychological and Love Films," "Adventure and Police Films," and so on. The festival was cancelled in 1948 and 1950. **Source:** www.festival-cannes.fr

The Emmy Awards, 1951–2010

The Academy of Television Arts and Sciences, formed in 1946, presented the first Emmy Awards in 1949. The number and names of awards have changed over the years, but since 1965, the Academy has recognized an outstanding comedy and drama, as well as an actor and an actress in a comedy and in a drama.

Year	Comedy	Drama	Comedy Actor	Comedy Actress	Drama Actor	Drama Actress
1951	*The Red Skelton Show* (CBS)	*Studio One* (CBS)	Sid Caesar (NBC)	Imogene Coca (NBC)	[1]	[1]
1952	*I Love Lucy* (CBS)	*Robert Montgomery Presents* (NBC)	Thomas Mitchell	Helen Hayes	[1]	[1]
1953	*I Love Lucy* (CBS)	*The U.S. Steel Hour* (ABC)	Donald O'Connor, *Colgate Comedy Hour* (NBC)	Eve Arden, *Our Miss Brooks* (CBS)	[1]	[1]
1954	*Make Room for Daddy* (ABC)	*The U.S. Steel Hour* (ABC)	Danny Thomas, *Make Room for Daddy* (ABC)	Loretta Young, *The Loretta Young Show* (NBC)	[1]	[1]
1955	*The Phil Silvers Show* (CBS)	*Producers' Showcase* (NBC)	Phil Silvers, *The Phil Silvers Show* (CBS)	Lucille Ball, *I Love Lucy* (CBS)	[1]	[1]

Year	Comedy	Drama	Comedy Actor	Comedy Actress	Drama Actor	Drama Actress
1956	The Phil Silvers Show (CBS)	Requiem for a Heavyweight (CBS)	Sid Caesar, Caesar's Hour (NBC)	Nanette Fabray, Caesar's Hour (NBC)	Robert Young, Father Knows Best (NBC)	Loretta Young, The Loretta Young Show (NBC)
1957	The Phil Silvers Show (CBS)	Gunsmoke (CBS)	Robert Young, Father Knows Best (NBC)	Jane Wyatt, Father Knows Best (NBC)	1	1
1958 –59	The Jack Benny Show (CBS)	2	Jack Benny, The Jack Benny Show (CBS)	Jane Wyatt, Father Knows Best (NBC and CBS)	Raymond Burr, Perry Mason (CBS)	Loretta Young, The Loretta Young Show (NBC)
1959 –60	"Art Carney Special" (NBC)	Playhouse 90 (CBS)	Robert Stack, The Untouchables (ABC)	Jane Wyatt, Father Knows Best (CBS)	1	1
1960 –61	The Jack Benny Show (CBS)	"Macbeth," Hallmark Hall of Fame (NBC)	Raymond Burr, Perry Mason (CBS)	Barbara Stanwyck, The Barbara Stanwyck Show (NBC)	1	1
1961 –62	The Bob Newhart Show (CBS)	The Defenders (CBS)	E.G, Marshall, The Defenders (CBS)	Shirley Booth, Hazel (NBC)	1	1
1962 –63	The Dick Van Dyke Show (CBS)	The Defenders (CBS)	E.G. Marshall, The Defenders	Shirley Booth, Hazel (NBC) (CBS)	1	1
1963 –64	The Dick Van Dyke Show (CBS)	The Defenders (CBS)	Dick Van Dyke, The Dick Van Dyke Show (CBS)	Mary Tyler Moore, The Dick Van Dyke Show(CBS)	1	1
1964 –65	3	3	3	3	3	3
1965 –66	The Dick Van Dyke Show (CBS)	The Fugitive (ABC)	Dick Van Dyke, The Dick Van Dyke Show (CBS)	Mary Tyler Moore, The Dick Van Dyke Show (CBS)	Bill Cosby, I Spy (NBC)	Barbara Stanwyck, The Big Valley (ABC)
1966 –67	The Monkees (NBC)	Mission: Impossible (CBS)	Don Adams, Get Smart (NBC)	Lucille Ball, The Lucy Show (CBS)	Bill Cosby, I Spy (NBC)	Barbara Bain, Mission: Impossible (CBS)
1967 –68	Get Smart (NBC)	Mission: Impossible (CBS)	Don Adams, Get Smart (NBC)	Lucille Ball, The Lucy Show (CBS)	Bill Cosby, I Spy (NBC)	Barbara Bain, Mission: Impossible (CBS)
1968 –69	Get Smart (NBC)	NET Playhouse (NET)	Don Adams, Get Smart (NBC)	Hope Lange, The Ghost and Mrs. Muir (NBC)	Carl Betz, Judd for the Defense (ABC)	Barbara Bain, Mission: Impossible (CBS)
1969 –70	My World & Welcome to It (NBC)	Marcus Welby, M.D. (ABC)	William Windom, My World & Welcome to It (NBC)	Hope Lange, The Ghost and Mrs. Muir (ABC)	Robert Young, Marcus Welby, M.D. (ABC)	Susan Hampshire The Forsyte Saga (NET)
1970 –71	All in the Family (CBS)	The Senator (segment), The Bold Ones (NBC)	Jack Klugman, The Odd Couple (ABC)	Jean Stapleton, All in the Family (CBS)	Hal Holbrook, The Senator (segment), The Bold Ones (NBC)	Susan Hampshire, The First Churchills (PBS)
1971 –72	All in the Family (CBS)	"Elizabeth R"[4] (PBS)	Carroll O'Connor All in the Family (CBS)	Jean Stapleton, All in the Family (CBS)	Peter Falk, Columbo (NBC)	Glenda Jackson, "Elizabeth R"[4] (PBS)
1972 –73	All in the Family (CBS)	The Waltons (CBS)	Jack Klugman, The Odd Couple (ABC)	Mary Tyler Moore, The Mary Tyler Moore Show (CBS)	Richard Thomas, The Waltons (CBS)	Michael Learned, The Waltons (CBS)
1973 –74	M*A*S*H (CBS)	"Upstairs, Downstairs"[4] (PBS)	Alan Alda, M*A*S*H (CBS)	Mary Tyler Moore, The Mary Tyler Moore Show (CBS)	Telly Savalas, Kojak (CBS)	Michael Learned, The Waltons (CBS)

Year	Comedy	Drama	Comedy Actor	Comedy Actress	Drama Actor	Drama Actress
1974 –75	The Mary Tyler Moore Show (CBS)	"Upstairs, Downstairs"[4] (PBS)	Tony Randall, The Odd Couple (ABC)	Valerie Harper, Rhoda (CBS)	Robert Blake, Baretta (ABC)	Jean Marsh, "Upstairs, Downstairs"[4] (PBS)
1975 –76	The Mary Tyler Moore Show (CBS)	Police Story (NBC)	Jack Albertson, Chico & the Man (NBC)	Mary Tyler Moore, The Mary Tyler Moore Show (CBS)	Peter Falk, Columbo (NBC)	Michael Learned, The Waltons (CBS)
1977 –78	All in the Family (CBS)	The Rockford Files (NBC)	Carroll O'Connor, All in the Family (CBS)	Jean Stapleton, All in the Family (CBS)	Edward Asner, Lou Grant (CBS)	Sada Thompson, Family (ABC)
1978 –79	Taxi (ABC)	Lou Grant (CBS)	Carroll O'Connor, All in the Family (CBS)	Ruth Gordon, Taxi (ABC)	Ron Leibman, Kaz (CBS)	Mariette Hartley, The Incredible Hulk (CBS)
1979 –80	Taxi (ABC)	Lou Grant (CBS)	Richard Mulligan, Soap (ABC)	Cathryn Damon, Soap (ABC)	Ed Asner, Lou Grant (CBS)	Barbara Bel Geddes, Dallas (CBS)
1980 –81	Taxi (ABC)	Hill Street Blues (NBC)	Judd Hirsch, Taxi (ABC)	Isabel Sanford, The Jeffersons (CBS)	Daniel Travanti, Hill Street Blues (NBC)	Barbara Babcock, Hill Street Blues (NBC)
1981 –82	Barney Miller (ABC)	Hill Street Blues (NBC)	Alan Alda, M*A*S*H (CBS)	Carol Kane, Taxi (ABC)	Daniel Travanti, Hill Street Blues (NBC)	Michael Learned, Nurse (CBS)
1982 –83	Cheers (NBC)	Hill Street Blues (NBC)	Judd Hirsch, Taxi (NBC)	Shelley Long, Cheers (NBC)	Ed Flanders, St. Elsewhere (NBC)	Tyne Daly, Cagney &Lacey (CBS)
1983 –84	Cheers (NBC)	Hill Street Blues (NBC)	John Ritter, Three's Company (ABC)	Jane Curtin, Kate & Allie (CBS)	Tom Selleck, Magnum P.I. (CBS)	Tyne Daly, Cagney & Lacey (CBS)
1984 –85	The Cosby Show (NBC)	Cagney & Lacey (CBS)	Robert Guillaume, Benson (ABC)	Jane Curtin, Kate & Allie (CBS)	William Daniels, St. Elsewhere (NBC)	Tyne Daly, Cagney & Lacey (CBS)
1985 –86	The Golden Girls (NBC)	Cagney & Lacey (CBS)	Michael J. Fox, Family Ties (NBC)	Betty White, The Golden Girls (NBC)	William Daniels, St. Elsewhere (NBC)	Sharon Gless, Cagney & Lacey (CBS)
1986 –87	The Golden Girls (NBC)	L.A. Law (NBC)	Michael J. Fox, Family Ties (NBC)	Rue McClanahan, The Golden Girls (NBC)	Bruce Willis, Moonlighting (ABC)	Sharon Gless, Cagney & Lacey (CBS)
1987 –88	The Wonder Years (ABC)	thirtysomething (ABC)	Michael J. Fox, Family Ties (NBC)	Beatrice Arthur, The Golden Girls (NBC)	Richard Kiley, A Year in the Life (NBC)	Tyne Daly, Cagney & Lacey (CBS)
1988 –89	Cheers (NBC)	L.A. Law (NBC)	Richard Mulligan, Empty Nest (NBC)	Candice Bergen, Murphy Brown (CBS)	Carroll O'Connor, In the Heat of the Night (NBC)	Dana Delany, China Beach (ABC)
1989 –90	Murphy Brown (CBS)	L.A. Law (NBC)	Ted Danson, Cheers (NBC)	Candice Bergen, Murphy Brown (CBS)	Peter Falk, Columbo (ABC)	Patricia Wettig, thirtysomething (ABC)
1990 –91	Cheers (NBC)	L.A. Law (NBC)	Burt Reynolds, Evening Shade (CBS)	Kirstie Alley, Cheers (NBC)	James Earl Jones, Gabriel's Fire (ABC)	Patricia Wettig, thirtysomething (ABC)
1991 –92	Murphy Brown (CBS)	Northern Exposure (CBS)	Craig T. Nelson, Coach (ABC)	Candice Bergen, Murphy Brown (CBS)	Christopher Lloyd, Avonlea (Disney)	Dana Delany, China Beach (ABC)
1992 –93	Seinfeld (NBC)	Picket Fences (CBS)	Ted Danson, Cheers (NBC)	Roseanne Arnold, Roseanne (ABC)	Tom Skerritt, Picket Fences (CBS)	Kathy Baker, Picket Fences (CBS)
1993 –94	Frasier (NBC)	Picket Fences (CBS)	Kelsey Grammer, Frasier (NBC)	Candice Bergen, Murphy Brown (CBS)	Dennis Franz, NYPD Blue (ABC)	Sela Ward, Sisters (NBC)
1994 –95	Frasier (NBC)	NYPD Blue (ABC)	Kelsey Grammer, Frasier (NBC)	Candice Bergen, Murphy Brown (CBS)	Mandy Patinkin, Chicago Hope (CBS)	Kathy Baker, Picket Fences (CBS)
1995 –96	Frasier (NBC)	E.R. (NBC)	John Lithgow, Third Rock From the Sun (NBC)	Helen Hunt, Mad About You (NBC)	Dennis Franz, NYPD Blue (ABC)	Kathy Baker, Picket Fences (CBS)

Year	Comedy	Drama	Comedy Actor	Comedy Actress	Drama Actor	Drama Actress
1996 –97	Frasier (NBC)	Law & Order (NBC)	John Lithgow, Third Rock From the Sun (NBC)	Helen Hunt, Mad About You (NBC)	Dennis Franz, NYPD Blue (ABC)	Gillian Anderson, The X-Files (FOX)
1997 –98	Frasier (NBC)	The Practice (ABC)	Kelsey Grammer, Frasier (NBC)	Helen Hunt, Mad About You (NBC)	Andre Braugher, Homicide (NBC)	Christine Lahti, Chicago Hope (CBS)
1998 –99	Ally McBeal (FOX)	The Practice (ABC)	John Lithgow, Third Rock From the Sun (NBC)	Helen Hunt, Mad About You (NBC)	Dennis Franz, NYPD Blue (ABC)	Edie Falco, The Sopranos (HBO)
1999 –2000	Will and Grace (NBC)	The West Wing (NBC)	Michael J. Fox, Spin City (ABC)	Patricia Heaton, Everybody Loves Raymond (CBS)	James Gandolfini, The Sopranos (HBO)	Sela Ward, Once and Again (ABC)
2000 –01	Sex and the City (HBO)	The West Wing (NBC)	Eric McCormack, Will and Grace (NBC)	Patricia Heaton, Everybody Loves Raymond (CBS)	James Gandolfini, The Sopranos (HBO)	Edie Falco, The Sopranos (HBO)
2001 –02	Friends (NBC)	The West Wing (NBC)	Ray Romano, Everybody Loves Raymond (CBS)	Jennifer Aniston, Friends (NBC)	Michael Chiklis, The Shield (FX)	Allison Janney, The West Wing (NBC)
2002 –03	Everybody Loves Raymond (CBS)	The West Wing (NBC)	Tony Shalhoub, Monk (USA)	Debra Messing, Will & Grace (NBC)	James Gandolfini, The Sopranos (HBO)	Edie Falco, The Sopranos (HBO)
2003 –04	Arrested Development (Fox)	The Sopranos (HBO)	Kelsey Grammer, Frasier (NBC)	Sara Jessica Parker, Sex and the City (HBO)	James Spader, The Practice (ABC)	Allison Janney, The West Wing (NBC)
2004 –05	Everybody Loves Raymond (CBS)	Lost (ABC)	Tony Shalhoub, Monk (USA)	Felicity Huffman, Desperate Housewives (ABC)	James Spader, Boston Legal (ABC)	Patricia Arquette, Medium (NBC)
2005 –06	The Office (NBC)	24 (Fox)	Tony Shaloub, Monk (USA)	Julia-Louise Dreyfus, The New Adventures of Old Christine (CBS)	Kiefer Sutherland, 24 (Fox)	Mariska Hargitay, Law & Order: SVU (NBC)
2006 –07	30 Rock (NBC)	The Sopranos (HBO)	Ricky Gervais, Extras (HBO)	America Ferrera, Ugly Betty (ABC)	James Spader, Boston Legal (ABC)	Sally Field, Brothers and Sisters (ABC)
2007 –08	30 Rock (NBC)	Mad Men (AMC)	Alec Baldwin, 30 Rock (NBC)	Tina Fey, 30 Rock (NBC)	Bryan Cranston, Breaking Bad (AMC)	Glenn Close, Damages (FX)
2008 –09	30 Rock (NBC)	Mad Men (AMC)	Alec Baldwin, 30 Rock (NBC)	Toni Colette, United States of Tara (Showtime)	Bryan Cranston, Breaking Bad (AMC)	Glenn Close, Damages (FX)
2009 –10	Modern Family (ABC)	Mad Men (AMC)	Jim Parsons, The Big Bang Theory (CBS)	Edie Falco Nurse Jackie (Showtime)	Bryan Cranston Breaking Bad (AMC)	Kyra Sedgwick The Closer (TNT)

Notes: 1. Before 1965, the Academy did always not give separate awards for comedy and drama. 2. Playhouse 90 (CBS) was best drama of one hour or longer; Alcoa-Goodyear Theatre (NBC) was best drama of less than one hour. 3. In 1964, the Academy gave acting awards to Dick Van Dyke for The Dick Van Dyke Show (CBS), Lynn Fontaine and Alfred Lunt for "The Magnificent Yankee" Hallmark Hall of Fame (NBC), and Barbra Streisand for My Name is Barbra (CBS). It also gave Achievements in Entertainment awards to these programs. 4. Masterpiece Theatre series. **Source:** Academy of Television Arts and Sciences. www.emmys.tv

Emmy Awards for Variety, Music, or Comedy Shows, 1951–2010

Year	Show (Network)	Year	Show (Network)
1951	The Alan Young Show (CBS)	1969	Rowan & Martin's Laugh-In (NBC)
1952	Your Show of Shows (NBC)	1970	The David Frost Show (syndicated)
1953	Your Show of Shows (NBC)	1971	The Flip Wilson Show (NBC)
1954	Omnibus (CBS)	1972	Music: The Carol Burnett Show (CBS)
1955	Disneyland (ABC)		Talk: The Dick Cavett Show (ABC)
1956	The Ed Sullivan Show (CBS)	1973	The Julie Andrews Hour (ABC)
1957	Caesar's Hour (NBC)	1974	The Carol Burnett Show (CBS)
1958	The Dinah Shore Show (NBC)	1975	The Carol Burnett Show (CBS)
1959	The Dinah Shore Chevy Show (NBC)	1976	NBC's Saturday Night (NBC)
1960[1]	"The Fabulous '50s" (CBS)	1977	Van Dyke & Company (NBC)
1961[1]	"Astaire Time" (NBC)	1978	The Muppet Show (syndicated)
1962	The Garry Moore Show (CBS)	1979[1]	"Steve & Eydie Celebrate Irving Berlin" (NBC)
1963	The Andy Williams Show (NBC)	1980[1]	"IBM Presents Baryshnikov on B'way" (ABC)
1964	The Danny Kaye Show (CBS)	1981[1]	"Lily: Sold Out "(CBS)
1965	My Name is Barbra (CBS)	1982[1]	"Night of 100 Stars" (ABC)
1966	The Andy Williams Show (NBC)	1983[1]	"Motown 25: Yesterday, Today, Forever" (NBC)
1967	The Andy Williams Show (NBC)		
1968	Rowan & Martin's Laugh-In (NBC)		

Year	Show (Network)	Year	Show (Network)
1984[1]	"The 6th Annual Kennedy Center Honors" (CBS)	2000	*Late Show with David Letterman* (CBS)
1985[1]	"Motown Returns to the Apollo" (NBC)	2001	*Late Show with David Letterman* (CBS)
1986[1]	"The Kennedy Center Honors" (CBS)	2002	*Late Show with David Letterman* (CBS)
1987[1]	"The 1987 Tony Awards" (CBS)	2003	*The Daily Show With Jon Stewart* (Comedy Central)
1988[1]	"Irving Berlin's 100th Birthday Celebration" (CBS)	2004	*The Daily Show With Jon Stewart* (Comedy Central)
1989	*The Tracey Ullman Show* (FOX)	2005	*The Daily Show With Jon Stewart* (Comedy Central)
1990	*In Living Color* (FOX)		
1991[1]	"The 63rd Annual Academy Awards" (ABC)		
1992	*The Tonight Show Starring Johnny Carson* (NBC)	2006	*The Daily Show With Jon Stewart* (Comedy Central)
1993	*Saturday Night Live* (NBC)	2007	*The Daily Show With Jon Stewart* (Comedy Central)
1994	*Late Show with David Letterman* (CBS)		
1995	*The Tonight Show with Jay Leno* (NBC)	2008	*The Daily Show With Jon Stewart* (Comedy Central)
1996	*Dennis Miller Live* (HBO)		
1997	*Tracey Takes On . . .* (HBO)	2009	*The Daily Show With Jon Stewart* (Comedy Central)
1998	*Late Show with David Letterman* (CBS)		
1999	*Late Show with David Letterman* (CBS)	2010	*The Daily Show With Jon Stewart* (Comedy Central)

Note: 1. Generally, the Academy awards this Emmy to a series, though occasionally awards a single program. **Source:** Academy of Television Arts and Sciences. www.emmys.tv

The Tony Awards, 1947–2010

The Tony Awards are presented by the American Theatre Wing for achievement in the Broadway theater. Named for Antoinette Perry, an actress, producer, director, and chairman of the American Theatre Wing who died in 1946, the Tonys were first presented in 1947. The major writing, composing, and acting awards for each year are listed below.

PLAYS

Year	Best Play, Author	Best Actor, Play	Best Actress, Play
1947	no award	José Ferrer, *Cyrano de Bergerac* Fredric March, *Years Ago*	Ingrid Bergman, *Joan of Lorraine* Helen Hayes, *Happy Birthday*
1948	*Mister Roberts,* Thomas Heggen and Joshua Logan	Henry Fonda, *Mister Roberts* Paul Kelly, *Command Decision* Basil Rathbone, *The Heiress*	Judith Anderson, *Medea;* Katharine Cornell, *Antony and Cleopatra;* Jessica Tandy, *A Streetcar Named Desire*
1949	*Death of a Salesman,* Arthur Miller	Rex Harrison, *Anne of the Thousand Days*	Martita Hunt, *The Madwoman of Chaillot*
1950	*The Cocktail Party,* T. S. Eliot	Sidney Blackmer, *Come Back, Little Sheba*	Shirley Booth, *Come Back, Little Sheba*
1951	*The Rose Tattoo,* Tennessee Williams	Claude Rains, *Darkness at Noon*	Uta Hagen, *The Country Girl*
1952	*The Fourposter,* Jan de Hartog	José Ferrer, *The Shrike*	Julie Harris, *I Am a Camera*
1953	*The Crucible,* Arthur Miller	Tom Ewell, *The Seven Year Itch*	Shirley Booth, *Time of the Cuckoo*
1954	*The Teahouse of the August Moon,* John Patrick	David Wayne, *The Teahouse of the August Moon*	Audrey Hepburn, *Ondine*
1955	*The Desperate Hours,* Joseph Hayes	Alfred Lunt, *Quadrille*	Nancy Kelly, *The Bad Seed*
1956	*The Diary of Anne Frank,* Frances Goodrich and Albert Hackett	Paul Muni, *Inherit the Wind*	Julie Harris, *The Lark*
1957	*Long Day's Journey Into Night,* Eugene O'Neill	Fredric March, *Long Day's Journey Into Night*	Margaret Leighton, *Separate Tables*
1958	*Sunrise at Campobello,* Dore Schary	Ralph Bellamy, *Sunrise at Campobello*	Helen Hayes, *Time Remembered*
1959	*J.B.,* Archibald Macleish	Jason Robards, *The Disenchanted*	Gertrude Berg, *A Majority of One*
1960	*The Miracle Worker,* William Gibson	Melvyn Douglas, *The Best Man*	Anne Bancroft, *The Miracle Worker*
1961	*Becket,* Jean Anouilh	Zero Mostel, *Rhinoceros*	Joan Plowright, *A Taste of Honey*
1962	*A Man for All Seasons,* Robert Bolt	Paul Scofield, *A Man for All Seasons*	Margaret Leighton, *Night of the Iguana*

Year	Best Play	Best Actor	Best Actress
1963	Who's Afraid of Virginia Woolf, Edward Albee	Arthur Hill, Who's Afraid of Virginia Woolf	Uta Hagen, Who's Afraid of Virginia Woolf
1964	Luther, John Osborne	Alec Guiness, Dylan	Sandy Dennis, Any Wednesday
1965	The Subject Was Roses, Frank Gilroy	Walter Matthau, The Odd Couple	Irene Worth, Tiny Alice
1966	Marat/Sade, Peter Weiss	Hal Holbrook, Mark Twain Tonight!	Rosemary Harris, The Lion in Winter
1967	The Homecoming, Harold Pinter	Paul Rogers, The Homecoming	Beryl Reid, The Killing of Sister George
1968	Rosencrantz and Guildenstern Are Dead, Tom Stoppard	Martin Balsam, You Know I Can't Hear You When the Water's Running	Zoe Caldwell, The Prime of Miss Jean Brodie
1969	The Great White Hope, Howard Sackler	James Earl Jones, The Great White Hope	Julie Harris, Forty Carats
1970	Borstal Boy, Frank McMahon	Fritz Weaver, Child's Play	Tammy Grimes, Private Lives (R)
1971	Sleuth, Anthony Shaffer	Brian Bedford, The School for Wives	Maureen Stapleton, Gingerbread Lady
1972	Sticks and Bones, David Rabe	Cliff Gorman, Lenny	Sada Thompson, Twigs
1973	That Championship Season, Jason Miller	Alan Bates, Butley	Julie Harris, The Last of Mrs. Lincoln
1974	The River Niger, Joseph A. Walker	Michael Moriarty, Find Your Way Home	Colleen Dewhurst, A Moon for the Misbegotten (R)
1975	Equus, Peter Shaffer	John Kani, Sizwe Banzi Is Dead Winston Ntshona, The Island	Ellen Burstyn, Same Time, Next Year
1976	Travesties, Tom Stoppard	John Wood, Travesties	Irene Worth, Sweet Bird of Youth (R)
1977	The Shadow Box, Michael Cristofer	Al Pacino, The Basic Training of Pavlo Hummel	Julie Harris, The Belle of Amherst
1978	Da, Hugh Leonard	Barnard Hughes, Da	Jessica Tandy, The Gin Game
1979	The Elephant Man, Bernard Pomerance	Tom Conti, Whose Life Is It Anyway?	Constance Cummings, Wings Carole Shelley, The Elephant Man
1980	Children of a Lesser God, Mark Medoff	John Rubinstein, Children of a Lesser God	Phyllis Frelich, Children of a Lesser God
1981	Amadeus, Peter Shaffer	Ian McKellen, Amadeus	Jane Lapotaire, Piaf
1982	The Life and Adventures of Nicholas Nickleby, David Edgar	Roger Rees, The Life and Adventures of Nicholas Nickleby	Zoe Caldwell, Medea (R)
1983	Torch Song Trilogy, Harvey Fierstein	Harvey Fierstein, Torch Song Trilogy	Jessica Tandy, Foxfire
1984	The Real Thing, Tom Stoppard	Jeremy Irons, The Real Thing	Glenn Close, The Real Thing
1985	Biloxi Blues, Neil Simon	Derek Jacobi, Much Ado About Nothing (R)	Stockard Channing, Joe Egg (R)
1986	I'm Not Rappaport, Herb Gardner	Judd Hirsch, I'm Not Rappaport	Lily Tomlin, The Search for Signs of Intelligent Life in the Universe
1987	Fences, August Wilson	James Earl Jones, Fences	Linda Lavin, Broadway Bound
1988	M. Butterfly, David Henry Hwang	Ron Silver, Speed-The-Plow	Joan Allen, Burn This
1989	The Heidi Chronicles, Wendy Wasserstein	Philip Bosco, Lend Me a Tenor	Pauline Collins, Shirley Valentine
1990	The Grapes of Wrath, Frank Galati	Robert Morse, Tru	Maggie Smith, Lettice and Lovage
1991	Lost in Yonkers, Neil Simon	Nigel Hawthorne, Shadowlands	Mercedes Ruhl, Lost in Yonkers
1992	Dancing at Lughnasa, Brian Friel	Judd Hirsch, Conversations with My Father	Glenn Close, Death and the Maiden
1993	Angels in America: Millennium Approaches, Tony Kushner	Ron Leibman, Angels in America: Millennium Approaches	Madeline Kahn, The Sisters Rosensweig

Year	Best Play	Best Actor	Best Actress
1994	*Angels in America: Perestroika,* Tony Kushner	Stephen Spinella, *Angels in America: Perestroika*	Diana Rigg, *Medea* (R)
1995	*Love! Valour! Compassion!,* Terrence McNally	Ralph Fiennes, *Hamlet*	Cherry Jones, *The Heiress*
1996	*Master Class,* Terrence McNally	George Grizzard, *A Delicate Balance* (R)	Zoe Caldwell, *Master Class*
1997	*Last Night of Ballyhoo,* Alfred Uhry	Christopher Plummer, *Barrymore*	Janet McTeer, *A Doll's House*
1998	*Art,* Yasmina Reza	Anthony La Paglia, *A View From the Bridge*	Marie Mullen, *The Beauty Queen of Leenane*
1999	*Side Man,* Warren Leight	Brian Dennehy, *Death of a Salesman*	Judi Dench, *Amy's View*
2000	*Copenhagen,* Michael Frayn	Stephen Dillane, *The Real Thing*	Jennifer Ehle, *The Real Thing*
2001	*Proof,* David Auburn	Richard Easton, *The Invention of Love*	Mary-Louise Parker, *Proof*
2002	*The Goat or Who Is Sylvia?,* Edward Albee	Alan Bates, *Fortune's Fool*	Lindsay Duncan, *Private Lives*
2003	*Take Me Out,* Richard Greenberg	Brian Dennehy, *Long Day's Journey Into Night*	Vanessa Redgrave, *Long Day's Journey Into Night*
2004	*I Am My Own Wife,* Doug Wright	Jefferson Mays, *I Am My Own Wife*	Phylicia Rashad, *A Raisin in the Sun*
2005	*Doubt,* John Patrick Shanley	Bill Irwin, *Who's Afraid of Virginia Woolf?*	Cherry Jones, *Doubt*
2006	*The History Boys,* Alan Bennett	Richard Griffiths, *The History Boys*	Cynthia Nixon, *Rabbit Hole*
2007	*The Coast of Utopia,* Tom Stoppard	Frank Langella, *Frost/Nixon*	Julie White, *The Little Dog Laughed*
2008	*August: Osage County,* Tracy Letts	Mark Rylance, *Boeing-Boeing* (R)	Deanna Dunagan, *August: Osage County*
2009	*God of Carnage,* Yasmina Reza	Geoffrey Rush, *Exit the King*	Marcia Gay Harden, *God of Carnage*
2010	*Red,* John Logan	Denzel Washington, *Fences*	Viola Davis, *Fences*

MUSICALS

Year	Best Musical, Composer	Best Actor, Musical	Best Actress, Musical
1947	no award	no award	no award
1948	no award	Paul Hartman, *Angel in the Wings*	Grace Hartman, *Angel in the Wings*
1949	*Kiss Me Kate,* Cole Porter (M&L)	Ray Bolger, *Where's Charley?*	Nanette Fabray, *Love Life*
1950	*South Pacific,* Richard Rodgers (M), Oscar Hammerstein (L)	Ezio Pinza, *South Pacific*	Mary Martin, *South Pacific*
1951	*Guys and Dolls,* Frank Loesser (M&L)	Robert Alda, *Guys and Dolls*	Ethel Merman, *Call Me Madam*
1952	*The King and I,* Richard Rodgers (M), Oscar Hammerstein (L)	Phil Silvers, *Top Banana*	Gertrude Lawrence, *The King and I*
1953	*Wonderful Town,* Leonard Bernstein (M), Betty Comden and Adolph Green (L)	Thomas Mitchell, *Hazel Flagg*	Rosalind Russell, *Wonderful Town*
1954	*Kismet,* Alexander Borodin (M), adapted by Robert Wright and George Forrest (L)	Alfred Drake, *Kismet*	Dolores Gray, *Carnival in Flanders*
1955	*The Pajama Game,* Richard Adler and Jerry Ross (M&L)	Walter Slezak, *Fanny*	Mary Martin, *Peter Pan*
1956	*Damn Yankees,* Richard Adler and Jerry Ross (M&L)	Ray Walston, *Damn Yankees*	Gwen Verdon, *Damn Yankees*
1957	*My Fair Lady,* Frederick Loewe (M), Alan Jay Lerner (L)	Rex Harrison, *My Fair Lady*	Judy Holliday, *Bells Are Ringing*

Year	Best Musical	Best Actor	Best Actress
1958	*The Music Man*, Meredith Willson (M&L)	Robert Preston, *The Music Man*	(tie) Thelma Ritter, Gwen Verdon, *New Girl in Town*
1959	*Redhead*, Albert Hague (M), Dorothy Fields (L)	Richard Kiley, *Redhead*	Gwen Verdon, *Redhead*
1960	(tie) *Fiorello*, Jerry Bock (M), Sheldon Harnick (L); *The Sound of Music*, Richard Rodgers (M), &Oscar Hammerstein (L)	Jackie Gleason, *Take Me Along*	Mary Martin, *The Sound of Music*
1961	*Bye, Bye, Birdie*, Charles Strouse (M), Lee Adams (L)	Richard Burton, *Camelot*	Elizabeth Seal, *Irma la Douce*
1962	*How to Succeed in Business Without Really Trying*, Frank Loesser (M&L)	Robert Morse, *How to Succeed in Business Without Really Trying*	(tie) Anna Maria Alberghetti, *Carnival;* Diahann Carroll, *No Strings*
1963	*A Funny Thing Happened on the Way to the Forum*, Stephen Sondheim (M&L)	Zero Mostel, *A Funny Thing Happened on the Way to the Forum,*	Vivien Leigh, *Tovarich*
1964	*Hello, Dolly!* Jerry Herman (M&L)	Bert Lahr, *Foxy*	Carol Channing, *Hello, Dolly!*
1965	*Fiddler on the Roof*, Jerry Bock (M), Sheldon Harnick (L)	Zero Mostel, *Fiddler on the Roof*	Liza Minnelli, *Flora, the Red Menace*
1966	*Man of La Mancha*, Mitch Leigh (M), Joe Darion (L)	Richard Kiley, *Man of La Mancha*	Angela Lansbury, *Mame*
1967	*Cabaret*, John Kander (M), Fred Ebb (L)	Robert Preston, *I Do! I Do!*	Barbara Harris, *The Apple Tree*
1968	*Hallelujah, Baby!* Jule Styne (M), Betty Comden & Adolph Green (L)	Robert Goulet, *The Happy Time*	Patricia Routledge, *Darling of the Day* Leslie Uggams, *Hallelujah, Baby!*
1969	*1776*, Sherman Edwards (M&L)	Jerry Orbach, *Promises, Promises*	Angela Lansbury, *Dear World*
1970	*Applause*, Charles Strouse (M), Lee Adams (L)	Cleavon Little, *Purlie*	Lauren Bacall, *Applause*
1971	*Company*, Stephen Sondheim (M&L)	Hal Linden, *The Rothschilds*	Helen Gallagher, *No, No Nannette* (R)
1972	*Two Gentlemen of Verona* [best score: *Follies*, Stephen Sondheim (M&L)]	Phil Silvers, *A Funny Thing Happened on the Way to the Forum* (R)	Alexis Smith, *Follies*
1973	*A Little Night Music*, Stephen Sondheim (M&L)	Ben Vereen, *Pippin*	Glynis Johns, *A Little Night Music*
1974	*Raisin*, [best score: *Gigi*, Frederick Loewe (M), Alan Jay Lerner (L)]	Christopher Plummer, *Cyrano*	Virginia Capers, *Raisin*
1975	*The Wiz*, Charlie Smalls (M&L)	John Cullum, *Shenandoah*	Angela Lansbury, *Gypsy* (R)
1976	*A Chorus Line*, Marvin Hamlisch (M), Edward Kleban (L)	George Rose, *My Fair Lady* (R)	Donna McKechnie, *A Chorus Line*
1977	*Annie*, Charles Strouse (M), Martin Charnin (L)	Barry Bostwick, *The Robber Bridegroom*	Dorothy Loudon, *Annie*
1978	*Ain't Misbehavin'* [best score: *On the Twentieth Century*, Cy Coleman (M) Betty Comden & and Adolph Green (L)]	John Cullum, *On the Twentieth Century*	Liza Minnelli, *The Act*
1979	*Sweeney Todd*, Stephen Sondheim	Len Cariou, *Sweeney Todd*	Angela Lansbury, *Sweeney Todd*
1980	*Evita*, Andrew Lloyd Webber (M), Tim Rice (L)	Jim Dale, *Barnum*	Patti LuPone, *Evita*
1981	*42nd Street*, [best score: *Woman of the Year*, John Kander (M), Fred Ebb (L)]	Kevin Kline, *The Pirates of Penzance*	Lauren Bacall, *Woman of the Year*
1982	*Nine*, Maury Yeston (M&L)	Ben Harney, *Dreamgirls*	Jennifer Holliday, *Dreamgirls*
1983	*Cats*, Andrew Lloyd Webber (M), T.S. Eliot (L)	Tommy Tune, *My One and Only*	Natalia Makarova, *On Your Toes*
1984	*La Cage Aux Folles*, Jerry Herman (M&L)	George Hearn, *La Cage Aux Folles*	Chita Rivera, *The Rink*

Year	Best Musical	Best Actor	Best Actress
1985	*Big River*, Roger Miller (M&L)	No award	No award
1986	*The Mystery of Edwin Drood*, Rupert Holmes (M&L)	George Rose, *The Mystery of Edwin Drood*	Bernadette Peters, *Song and Dance*
1987	*Les Misérables*, Claude-Michel Schönberg (M); Herbert Kretzmer & Alain Boublil (L)	Robert Lindsay, *Me and My Girl*	Maryann Plunkett, *Me and My Girl*
1988	*The Phantom of the Opera* [best score: *Into the Woods*, Stephen Sondheim (M&L)]	Michael Crawford, *The Phantom of the Opera*	Joanna Gleason, *Into the Woods*
1989	*Jerome Robbins' Broadway* [best score: no award]	Jason Alexander, *Jerome Robbins' Broadway*	Ruth Brown, *Black and Blue*
1990	*City of Angels*, Cy Coleman (M) David Zippel (L)	James Naughton, *City of Angels*	Tyne Daly, *Gypsy* (R)
1991	*The Will Rogers Follies*, Cy Coleman (M); Betty Comden and Adolph Green (L)	Jonathan Pryce, *Miss Saigon*	Lea Salonga, *Miss Saigon*
1992	*Crazy for You*, [best score: *Falsettos*, William Finn (M&L)]	Gregory Hines, *Jelly's Last Jam*	Faith Prince, *Guys and Dolls* (R)
1993	*Kiss of the Spider Woman* [best score: (tie) *Kiss of the Spider Woman*, John Kander (M) and Fred Ebb (L); *Tommy*, Pete Townshend (M&L)]	Brent Carver, *Kiss of the Spider Woman*	Chita Rivera, *Kiss of the Spider Woman*
1994	*Passion*, Stephen Sondheim (M&L)	Boyd Gaines, *She Loves Me* (R)	Donna Murphy, *Passion*
1995	*Sunset Boulevard*, Andrew Lloyd Webber (M&L)	Matthew Broderick, *How to Succeed in Business Without Really Trying* (R)	Glenn Close, *Sunset Boulevard*
1996	*Rent*, Jonathan Larson (M&L)	Nathan Lane, *A Funny Thing Happened on the Way to the Forum* (R)	Donna Murphy, *The King and I* (R)
1997	*Titanic*, Maury Yeston (M&L)	James McNaughton, *Chicago* (R)	Bebe Neuwirth, *Chicago* (R)
1998	*The Lion King*, [best score: *Ragtime*, Stephen Flaherty & Lynn Ahrens (M&L)]	Alan Cumming, *Cabaret* (R)	Natasha Richardson, *Cabaret* (R)
1999	*Fosse*, [best score: *Parade*, Jason Robert Brown (M&L)]	Martin Short, *Little Me*	Bernadette Peters, *Annie Get Your Gun* (R)
2000	*Contact* [best score: *Aida*, Elton John (M) and Tim Rice (L)]	Brian Stokes Mitchell, *Kiss Me Kate*	Heather Headley, *Aida*
2001	*The Producers*, Mel Brooks (M&L)	Nathan Lane, *The Producers*	Christine Ebersole, *42nd Street* (R)
2002	*Thoroughly Modern Millie*, [best score: *Urinetown: The Musical*, Mark Hollmann (M); Mark Hollman and Greg Kotis (L)]	John Lithgow, *Sweet Smell of Success*	Sutton Foster, *Thoroughly Modern Millie*
2003	*Hairspray*, Scott Whittman, Marc Shaiman (M&L)	Harvey Fierstein, *Hairspray*	Marissa Jaret Winokur, *Hairspray*
2004	*Avenue Q*, Robert Lopez and Jeff Marx (M&L)	Hugh Jackman, *The Boy From Oz*	Idina Menzel, *Wicked*
2005	*Monty Python's Spamalot*, John Du Prez, Eric Idle (M&L)	Norbert Leo Butz, *Dirty Rotten Scoundrels*	Victoria Clark, *The Light in the Piazza*
2006	*Jersey Boys*, Bob Gaudio (M) Bob Crewe (L)	John Lloyd Young, *Jersey Boys*	LaChanze, *The Color Purple*
2007	*Spring Awakening*, Duncan Sheik (M)	David Hyde Pierce, *Curtains*	Christine Ebersole, *Grey Gardens*
2008	*In the Heights*, Lin-Manuel Miranda (M&L)	Paolo Szot, *South Pacific* (R)	Patti LuPone, *Gypsy* (R)
2009	*Billy Elliot, The Musical*, Elton John (M), Lee Hall (L)	David Alvarez, Trent Kowalik, Kiril Kurish, *Billy Elliot, The Musical*	Alice Ripley, *Next to Normal*
2010	*Memphis*, David Bryan (M), Joe DiPietro & David Bryan (L))	Douglas Hodge, *La Cage Aux Folles*	Catherine Zeta-Jones, *A Little Night Music*

Note: Since 1971 "Musical" and "Score" have been separate categories. The winner of the Tony for Best Musical usually wins the award for Best Score, except where otherwise indicated. **M** = music; **L** = lyrics; **R** = revival. **Source:** American Theatre Wing.

The Grammys, 1958–2009

The "Grammys" are officially known as the National Academy of Recording Arts and Sciences Awards. Winners (in almost 70 categories) are selected yearly by the 6,000 or so voting members of the academy.

"Best Vocal Performance" awards were phased out in 1968. From that year on, awards listed are "Best Pop Vocal Performance" (male and female), except where indicated.

Year	Record of the year	Album of the year	Song of the year	Best male vocal performance	Best female vocal performance
1958	Domenico Modugno, *Nel Blu Dipinto di Blu (Volare)*	Henry Mancini, *The Music from Peter Gunn*	Domenico Modugno, "Nel Blu Dipinto di Blu *(Volare)*"	Perry Como, *Catch a Falling Star*	Ella Fitzgerald, *Ella Fitzgerald Sings the Irving Berlin Songbook*[2]
1959	Bobby Darin, *Mack the Knife*	Frank Sinatra, *Come Dance with Me*	Jimmy Driftwood, "The Battle of New Orleans"	Frank Sinatra, *Come Dance with Me*	Ella Fitzgerald, *But Not for Me*
1960	Percy Faith, *Theme from a Summer Place*	Bob Newhart, *Button-Down Mind*	Ernest Gold, "Theme from Exodus"	Ray Charles, *Georgia on My Mind*	Ella Fitzgerald, *Mack the Knife*
1961	Henry Mancini, *Moon River*	Judy Garland, *Judy at Carnegie Hall*	Henry Mancini, Johnny Mercer, "Moon River"	Jack Jones, *Lollipops and Roses*	Judy Garland, *Judy at Carnegie Hall*[2]
1962	Tony Bennett, *I Left My Heart in San Francisco*	Vaughn Meader, *The First Family*	Leslie Bricusse, Anthony Newley, "What Kind of Fool Am I?"	Tony Bennett, *I Left My Heart in San Francisco*[2]	Ella Fitzgerald, *Ella Swings Brightly with Nelson Riddle*[2]
1963	Henry Mancini, *The Days of Wine and Roses*	Barbra Streisand, *The Barbra Streisand Album*	Henry Mancini, Johnny Mercer, "The Days of Wine and Roses"	Jack Jones, *Wives and Lovers*	Barbra Streisand, *The Barbra Streisand Album*[2]
1964	Stan Getz, Astrud Gilberto, *The Girl from Ipanema*	Stan Getz, Astrud Gilberto, *Getz/Gilberto*	Jerry Herman, "Hello, Dolly!"	Louis Armstrong, *Hello, Dolly!*	Barbra Streisand, *People*
1965	Herb Alpert & the Tijuana Brass, *A Taste of Honey*	Frank Sinatra, *September of My Years*	Paul Francis Webster, Johnny Mandel, "The Shadow of Your Smile"	Frank Sinatra, *It Was a Very Good Year*	Barbra Streisand, *My Name is Barbra*[2]
1966	Frank Sinatra, *Strangers in the Night*	Frank Sinatra, *A Man and His Music*	John Lennon, Paul McCartney, "Michelle"	Frank Sinatra, *Strangers in the Night*	Eydie Gorme, *If He Walked into My Life*
1967	5th Dimension, *Up, Up and Away*	The Beatles, *Sgt. Pepper's Lonely Hearts Club Band*	Jim Webb, "Up, Up, and Away"	Glen Campbell, *By the Time I Get to Phoenix*	Bobbie Gentry, *Ode to Billie Joe*
1968	Simon & Garfunkel, *Mrs. Robinson*	Glen Campbell, *By the Time I Get to Phoenix*	Bobby Russell, "Little Green Apples"	Jose Feliciano,[3] *Light My Fire*	Dionne Warwick,[3] *Do You Know the Way to San Jose?*
1969	5th Dimension, *Aquarius/Let the Sunshine In*	Blood, Sweat & Tears, *Blood, Sweat & Tears*	Joe South, "Games People Play"	Harry Nilsson,[4] *Everybody's Talkin'*	Peggy Lee,[4] *Is That All There Is?*
1970	Simon & Garfunkel, *Mrs. Robinson*	Simon & Garfunkel, *Bridge over Troubled Water*	Paul Simon, "Bridge over Troubled Water"	Ray Stevens,[4] *Everything is Beautiful*	Dionne Warwick,[4] *I'll Never Fall in Love Again*[2]
1971	Carole King, *It's Too Late*	Carole King, *Tapestry*	Carole King, "You've Got a Friend"	James Taylor,[5] *You've Got a Friend*	Carole King,[5] *Tapestry*[2]
1972	Roberta Flack, *The First Time Ever I Saw Your Face*	George Harrison, Ravi Shankar, Bob Dylan et al, *Concert for Bangladesh*	Ewan McColl, "The First Time Ever I Saw Your Face"	Harry Nilsson, *Without You*	Helen Reddy, *I Am Woman*
1973	Roberta Flack, *Killing Me Softly with His Song*	Stevie Wonder, *Innervisions*	Norman Gimbel, Charles Fox, "Killing Me Softly with His Song"	Stevie Wonder, *You Are the Sunshine of My Life*	Roberta Flack, *Killing Me Softly with His Song*

Year	Record of the year	Album of the year	Song of the year	Best male vocal performance	Best female vocal performance
1974	Olivia Newton-John, *I Honestly Love You*	Stevie Wonder, *Fulfillingness' First Finale*	Marilyn & Alan Bergman, Marvin Hamlisch, "The Way We Were"	Stevie Wonder, *Fulfillingness' First Finale*[2]	Olivia Newton-John, *I Honestly Love You*
1975	Captain & Tennille, *Love Will Keep Us Together*	Paul Simon, *Still Crazy After All These Years*	Stephen Sondheim, "Send in the Clowns"	Paul Simon, *Still Crazy after All These Years*[2]	Janis Ian, *At Seventeen*
1976	George Benson, *This Masquerade*	Stevie Wonder, *Songs in the Key of Life*	Bruce Johnston, "I Write the Songs"	Stevie Wonder, *Songs in the Key of Life*[2]	Linda Ronstadt, *Hasten Down the Wind*[2]
1977	The Eagles, *Hotel California*	Fleetwood Mac, *Rumours*	Barbra Streisand, Paul Williams, "Evergreen"	James Taylor, *Handy Man*	Barbra Streisand, *Evergreen*
1978	Billy Joel, *Just the Way You Are*	Various artists, *Saturday Night Fever*	Billy Joel, "Just the Way You Are"	Barry Manilow, *Copacabana (At the Copa)*	Anne Murray, *You Needed Me*
1979	The Doobie Brothers, *What a Fool Believes*	Billy Joel, *52nd Street*	Kenny Loggins, Michael McDonald, "What a Fool Believes"	Billy Joel, *52nd Street*[2]	Dionne Warwick, *I'll Never Love This Way Again*
1980	Christopher Cross, *Sailing*	Christopher Cross, *Christopher Cross*	Christopher Cross, "Sailing"	Kenny Loggins, *This Is It*	Bette Midler, *The Rose*
1981	Kim Carnes, *Bette Davis Eyes*	John Lennon/Yoko Ono, *Double Fantasy*	Donna Weiss, Jackie DeShannon, "Bette Davis Eyes"	Al Jarreau, *Breakin' Away*[2]	Lena Horne, *The Lady and Her Music Live on Broadway*[2]
1982	Toto, *Rosanna*	Toto, *Toto IV*	Johnny Christopher, Mark James, Wayne Carson, "Always on My Mind"	Lionel Richie, *Truly*	Melissa Manchester, *You Should Hear How She Talks About You*
1983	Michael Jackson, *Beat It*	Michael Jackson, *Thriller*	Sting, "Every Breath You Take"	Michael Jackson, *Thriller*[2]	Irene Cara, *Flashdance . . . What a Feeling*
1984	Tina Turner, *What's Love Got to Do with It?*	Lionel Richie, *Can't Slow Down*	Graham Lyle, Terry Britten, "What's Love Got to Do with It?"	Phil Collins, *Against All Odds (Take a Look at Me Now)*	Tina Turner, *What's Love Got to Do with It?*
1985	USA for Africa, *We Are the World*	Phil Collins, *No Jacket Required*	Michael Jackson, Lionel Richie, "We Are the World"	Phil Collins, *No Jacket Required*[2]	Whitney Houston, *Saving All My Love for You*
1986	Steve Winwood, *Higher Love*	Paul Simon, *Graceland*	Various artists, "That's What Friends Are For"	Steve Winwood, *Higher Love*	Barbra Streisand, *The Broadway Album*[2]
1987	Paul Simon, *Graceland*	U2, *The Joshua Tree*	Linda Ronstadt & James Ingram, "Somewhere Out There"	Sting, *Bring on the Night*[2]	Whitney Houston, *I Wanna Dance with Somebody (Who Loves Me)*
1988	Bobby McFerrin, *Don't Worry, Be Happy*	George Michael, *Faith*	Bobby McFerrin, "Don't Worry, Be Happy"	Bobby McFerrin, *Don't Worry, Be Happy*	Tracy Chapman, *Fast Car*
1989	Bette Midler, *Wind Beneath My Wings*	Bonnie Rait, *Nick of Time*	Bette Midler, "Wind Beneath My Wings"	Michael Bolton, *How Am I Supposed to Live Without You*	Bonnie Raitt, *Nick of Time*
1990	Phil Collins, *Another Day in Paradise*	Quincy Jones, *Back on the Block*	Julie Gold, "From a Distance"	Roy Orbison, *Oh, Pretty Woman*	Mariah Carey, *Vision of Love*
1991	Natalie Cole, *Unforgettable*	Natalie Cole, *Unforgettable*	Irving Gordon, "Unforgettable"	Michael Bolton , *When a Man Loves a Woman*	Bonnie Raitt, *Something to Talk About*

Year	Record of the year	Album of the year	Song of the year	Best male vocal performance	Best female vocal performance
1992	Eric Clapton, *Tears in Heaven*	Eric Clapton, *Unplugged*	Eric Clapton, "Tears in Heaven"	Eric Clapton, *Tears in Heaven*	k.d. Lang, *Constant Craving*
1993	Whitney Houston, *I Will Always Love You*	Whitney Houston, *The Bodyguard*	Alan Menken and Tim Rice, "A Whole New World"	Sting, *If I Ever Lose My Faith in You*	Whitney Houston, *I Will Always Love You*
1994	Sheryl Crow, *All I Wanna Do*	Tony Bennett, *MTV Unplugged*	Bruce Springsteen, "Streets of Philadelphia"	Elton John, *Can You Feel the Love Tonight*	Sheryl Crow, *All I Wanna Do*
1995	Seal, *Kiss From a Rose*	Alanis Morissette, *Jagged Little Pill*	Seal, "Kiss From a Rose"	Seal, *Kiss From a Rose*	Annie Lennox, *No More "I Love Yous"*
1996	Eric Clapton, *Change the World*	Celine Dion, *Falling Into You*	Wayne Kirkpatrick and Tommy Sims, "Change the World"	Eric Clapton, *Change the World*	Toni Braxton, *Unbreak My Heart*
1997	Shawn Colvin, *Sunny Came Home*	Bob Dylan, *Time Out of Mind*	Shawn Colvin and John Leventhal, "Sunny Came Home"	Elton John, *Candle in the Wind, 1997*	Sarah McLachlan, *Building a Mystery*
1998	Celine Dion, *My Heart Will Go On*	Lauryn Hill, *The Miseducation of Lauryn Hill*	James Horner and Will Jennings, "My Heart Will Go On"	Eric Clapton, *My Father's Eyes*	Celine Dion, *My Heart Will Go On*
1999	Santana, *Smooth*	Santana, *Supernatural*	Itaal Shur and Rob Thomas, "Smooth"	Sting, *Brand New Day*	Sara McLachlan, *I Will Remember You*
2000	U2, *Beautiful Day*	Steely Dan, *Two Against Nature*	U2 "Beautiful Day"	Sting, *She Walks This Earth*	Macy Gray, *I Try*
2001	U2, *Walk On*	Various artists, *O Brother, Where Art Thou?*	Alicia Keys, "Fallin'"	James Taylor, *Don't Let Me Be Lonely Tonight*	Nelly Furtado, *I'm Like a Bird*
2002	Norah Jones, *Don't Know Why*	Norah Jones, *Come Away With Me*	Norah Jones, "Don't Know Why"	John Mayer, *Your Body is a Wonderland*	Norah Jones, *Don't Know Why*
2003	Coldplay, *Clocks*	Outkast, *Speakerboxxx/ The Love Below*	Luther Vandross and Richard Marx, "Dance with My Father"	Justin Timberlake, *Cry Me A River*	Christina Aguilera, *Beautiful*
2004	Ray Charles & Norah Jones, *Here We Go Again*	Ray Charles & Various Artists, *Genius Loves Company*	John Mayer, "Daughters"	John Mayer *Daughters*	Norah Jones, *Sunrise*
2005	Green Day, *Boulevard of Broken Dreams*	U2, *How to Dismantle an Atomic Bomb*	U2, "Sometimes You Can't Make It on Your Own"	Stevie Wonder, *From the Bottom of My Heart*	Kelly Clarkson, *Since U Been Gone*
2006	Dixie Chicks, *Not Ready to Make Nice*	Dixie Chicks, *Taking the Long Way*	Dixie Chicks, "Not Ready to Make Nice"	John Mayer, *Waiting on the World to Change*	Christina Aguilera, *Ain't No Other Man*
2007	Amy Winehouse, *Rehab*	Herbie Hancock, *River: The Joni Letters*	Amy Winehouse, "Rehab"	Justin Timberlake, *What Goes Around Comes Around*	Amy Winehouse, *Rehab*
2008	Robert Plant & Alison Krauss, *Please Read the Letter*	Robert Plant & Alison Krauss, *Raising Sand*	Coldplay, "Viva La Vida"	John Mayer, *Say*	Adele, *Chasing Pavements*
2009	Kings of Leon, *Use Somebody*	Taylor Swift, *Fearless*	Beyonce, "Single Ladies (Put A Ring On It)"	Jason Mraz, *Make It Mine*	Beyonce, *Halo*

Notes: 1. Awarded to the composer, rather than the performer, of the song. 2. Awarded for an album, rather than an individual song. 3. Award given for "Best Contemporary Pop Vocal Performance." 4. Award given for "Best Vocal Performance Contemporary." 5. From 1971 on, all awards are for "Best Pop Vocal Performance." **Source:** National Academy of Recording Arts and Sciences.

The National Book Awards, 1950–2009

The National Book Awards are given annually for outstanding literary works by American citizens. The number of prizes awarded has varied, including categories such as poetry, fiction, biography, science, philosophy, religion, and history.

FICTION

Year	Author, Title
1950	Nelson Algren, *The Man with the Golden Arm*
1951	William Faulkner, *The Collected Stories*
1952	James Jones, *From Here to Eternity*
1953	Ralph Ellison, *Invisible Man*
1954	Saul Bellow, *The Adventures of Augie March*
1955	William Faulkner, *A Fable*
1956	John O'Hara, *Ten North Frederick*
1957	Wright Morris, *Field of Vision*
1958	John Cheever, *The Wapshot Chronicle*
1959	Bernard Malamud, *The Magic Barrel*
1960	Philip Roth, *Goodbye, Columbus*
1961	Conrad Richter, *The Waters of Kronos*
1962	Walker Percy, *The Moviegoer*
1963	J. F. Powers, *Morte d'Urban*
1964	John Updike, *The Centaur*
1965	Saul Bellow, *Herzog*
1966	Katherine Anne Porter, *The Collected Stories*
1967	Bernard Malamud, *The Fixer*
1968	Thornton Wilder, *The Eighth Day*
1969	Jerzy Kosinski, *Steps*
1970	Joyce Carol Oates, *Them*
1971	Saul Bellow, *Mr. Sammler's Planet*
1972	Flannery O'Connor, *The Complete Stories*
1973	John Barth, *Chimera*
1974	Thomas Pynchon, *Gravity's Rainbow*
	Isaac Bashevis Singer, *A Crown of Feathers & Other Stories*
1975	Robert Stone, *Dog Soldiers*
	Thomas Williams, *The Hair of Harold Roux*
1976	William Gaddis, *JR*
1977	Wallace Stegner, *The Spectator Bird*
1978	Mary Lee Settle, *Blood Ties*
1979	Tim O'Brien, *Going After Cacciato*
1980	William Styron, *Sophie's Choice*
1981	Wright Morris, *Plains Song*
1982	John Updike, *Rabbit Is Rich*
1983	Alice Walker, *The Color Purple*
1984	Ellen Gilchrist, *Victory Over Japan*
1985	Don DeLillo, *White Noise*
1986	E. L. Doctorow, *World's Fair*
1987	Larry Heinemann, *Paco's Story*
1988	Pete Dexter, *Paris Trout*
1989	John Casey, *Spartina*
1990	Charles Johnson, *Middle Passage*
1991	Norman Rush, *Mating*
1992	Cormac McCarthy, *All the Pretty Horses*
1993	E. Annie Proulx, *The Shipping News*
1994	William Gaddis, *A Frolic of His Own*
1995	Philip Roth, *Sabbath's Theater*
1996	Andrea Barrett, *Ship Fever and Other Stories*
1997	Charles Frazier, *Cold Mountain*
1998	Alice McDermott, *Charming Billy*
1999	Ha Jin, *Waiting*
2000	Susan Sontag, *In America*
2001	Jonathan Franzen, *The Corrections*
2002	Julia Glass, *Three Junes*
2003	Shirley Hazzard, *The Great Fire*
2004	Lily Tuck, *The News from Paraguay*
2005	William T. Vollmann, *Europe Central*
2006	Richard Powers, *The Echo Maker*
2007	Denis Johnson, *Tree of Smoke*
2008	Peter Matthiessen, *Shadow Country*
2009	Colum McCann, *Let the Great World Spin*

POETRY

Year	Author, Title
1950	William Carlos Williams, *Paterson: Book III* and *Selected Poems*
1951	Wallace Stevens, *The Auroras of Autumn*
1952	Marianne Moore, *Collected Poems*
1953	Archibald MacLeish, *Collected Poems 1917–52*
1954	Conrad Aiken, *Collected Poems*
1955	Wallace Stevens, *The Collected Poems*
1956	W. H. Auden, *The Shield of Achilles*
1957	Richard Wilbur, *Things of this World*
1958	Robert Penn Warren, *Promises: Poems, 1954–56*
1959	Theodore Roethke, *Words for the Wind*
1960	Robert J. Lowell, *Life Studies*
1961	Randall Jarrell, *The Woman at the Washington Zoo*
1962	Alan Dugan, *Poems*
1963	William Stafford, *Traveling Through the Dark*
1964	John Crowe Ransom, *Selected Poems*
1965	Theodore Roethke, *The Far Field*
1966	James Dickey, *Buckdancer's Choice*
1967	James Merrill, *Nights and Days*
1968	Robert Bly, *The Light Around the Body*
1969	John Berryman, *His Toy, His Dream, His Rest*
1970	Elizabeth Bishop, *The Complete Poems*
1971	Mona Van Duyn, *To See, To Take*
1972	Howard Moss, *Selected Poems*
1973	A. R. Ammons, *Collected Poems: 1951–71*
1974	Allen Ginsberg, *The Fall of America: Poems of These States, 1965–71*
	Adrienne Rich, *Diving into the Wreck: Poems, 1971–72*
1975	Marilyn Hacker, *Presentation Piece*
1976	John Ashbery, *Self-Portrait in a Convex Mirror*
1977	Richard Eberhart, *Collected Poems, 1930–1976*
1978	Howard Nemerov, *The Collected Poems*
1979	James Merrill, *Mirabell: Books of Number*
1980	Philip Levine, *Ashes*
1981	Lisel Mueller, *The Need to Hold Still*
1982	William Bronk, *Life Supports*
1983	Galway Kinnell, *Selected Poems*
1984	Charles Wright, *Country Music*
1991	Philip Levine, *What Work Is*
1992	Mary Oliver, *New and Selected Poems*
1993	A. R. Ammons, *Garbage*
1994	James Tate, *Worshipful Company of Fletchers*
1995	Stanley Kunitz, *Passing Through*
1996	Hayden Carruth, *Scrambled Eggs and Whiskey: Poems 1991–1995*
1997	William Meredith, *Effort at Speech*
1998	Gerald Stern, *This Time*
1999	Ai, *New and Selected Poems*
2000	Lucille Clifton, *Blessing the Boats*
2001	Alan Dugan, *Poems Seven: New and Complete Poetry*
2002	Ruth Stone, *In the Next Galaxy*
2003	C.K. Williams, *The Singing*
2004	Jean Valentine, *Door in the Mountain*
2005	W.S. Merwin, *Migration: New and Selected Poems*
2006	Nathaniel Mackey, *Splay Anthem*
2007	Robert Hass, *Time and Materials*
2008	Mark Doty, *Fire to Fire: New and Collected Poems*
2009	Keith Waldrop, *Transcendental Studies: A Trilogy*

NONFICTION

Year	Author, Title	Year	Author, Title
1950	Ralph L. Rusk, *Ralph Waldo Emerson*	1984	Robert V. Remini, *Andrew Jackson and the Course of American Democracy, 1833–45*
1951	Newton Arvin, *Herman Melville*		
1952	Rachel Carson, *The Sea Around Us*	1985	J. Anthony Lukas, *Common Ground: A Turbulent Decade in the Lives of Three American Families*
1953	Bernard De Voto, *Course of Empire*		
1954	Bruce Catton, *A Stillness at Appomattox*	1986	Barry Lopez, *Arctic Dreams*
1955	Joseph Wood Krutch, *The Measure of Man*	1987	Richard Rhodes, *The Making of the Atom Bomb*
1956	Herbert Kubly, *An American in Italy*	1988	Neil Sheehan, *A Bright and Shining Lie*
1957	George F. Kennan, *Russia Leaves the War*	1989	Thomas L. Friedman, *From Beirut to Jerusalem*
1958	Catherine Drinker Bowen, *The Lion and the Throne*	1990	Ron Chernow, *The House of Morgan*
1959	J. Christopher Herold, *Mistress to an Age*	1991	Orlando Patterson, *Freedom*
1960	Richard Ellman, *James Joyce*	1992	Paul Monette, *Becoming a Man: Half a Life*
1961	William L. Shirer, *The Rise and Fall of the Third Reich*	1993	Gore Vidal, *United States: Essays 1952-1992*
		1994	Sherwin B. Nuland, *How We Die: Reflections on Life's Final Chapter*
1962	Lewis Mumford, *The City in History*		
1963	Leon Edel, *Henry James, vols. 2 and 3*	1995	Tina Rosenberg, *The Haunted Land: Facing Europe's Ghosts After Communism*
1964	Aileen Ward, *John Keats: The Making of a Poet*		
1965	Louis Fisher, *The Life of Lenin*	1996	James Carroll, *An American Requiem: God, My Father and the War That Came Between Us*
1966	Arthur M. Schlesinger Jr., *A Thousand Days: JFK in the White House*		
		1997	Joseph J. Ellis, *American Sphinx: The Character of Thomas Jefferson*
1967	Justin Kaplan, *Mr. Clemens and Mark Twain*		
1968	Jonathan Kozol, *Death at an Early Age*	1998	Edward Ball, *Slaves in the Family*
1969	Norman Mailer, *The Armies of the Night*	1999	John W. Dower, *Embracing Defeat: Japan in the Wake of World War II*
1970	Lillian Hellman, *An Unfinished Woman, a Memoir*		
		2000	Nathaniel Philbrick, *In the Heart of the Sea: The Tragedy of the Whaleship Essex*
1971	James MacGregor Burns, *Roosevelt: The Soldier of Freedom*		
		2001	Andrew Solomon, *The Noonday Demon*
1972	Joseph P. Lash, *Eleanor and Franklin*	2002	Robert A. Caro, *Master of the Senate: The Years of Lyndon Johnson*
1973	Frances Fitzgerald, *Fire in the Lake: The Vietnamese and the Americans in Vietnam*		
		2003	Carlos Eire, *Waiting for Snow in Havana: Confessions of a Cuban Boy*
1974	Pauline Kael, *Deeper into the Movies*		
1975	Richard B. Sewall, *The Life of Emily Dickinson*	2004	Kevin Boyle, *Arc of Justice: A Saga of Race, Civil Rights, and Murder in the Jazz Age*
	Lewis Thomas, *The Lives of a Cell*		
1976	Paul Fussell, *The Great War and Modern Memory*	2005	Joan Didion, *The Year of Magical Thinking*
1977	Bruno Bettelheim, *The Uses of Enchantment: The Meaning and Importance of Fairy Tales*	2006	Timothy Egan, *The Worst Hard Time: The Untold Story of Those Who Survived the Great American Dust Bowl*
1978	Walter Jackson Bate, *Samuel Johnson*		
1979	Arthur M. Schlesinger Jr., *Robert Kennedy and His Times*	2007	Tim Weiner, *Legacy of Ashes: The History of the CIA*
		2008	Annette Gordon-Reed, *The Hemingses of Monticello: An American Family*
1980	Tom Wolfe, *The Right Stuff*		
1981	Maxine Hong Kingston, *China Men*	2009	T.J. Stiles, *The First Tycoon: The Epic Life of Cornelius Vanderbilt*
1982	Tracy Kidder, *The Soul of a New Machine*		
1983	Fox Butterfield, *China: Alive in the Bitter Sea*		

YOUNG PEOPLE'S LITERATURE

Year	Author, Title	Year	Author, Title
1996	Victor Martinez, *Parrot in the Oven: Mi Vida*	2004	Pete Hautman, *Godless*
1997	Han Nolan, *Dancing on the Edge*	2005	Jeanne Birdsall, *The Penderwicks*
1998	Louis Sachar, *Holes*	2006	M.T. Anderson, *The Astonishing Life of Octavian Nothing, Traitor to the Nation, Vol. 1*
1999	Kimberly Willis Holtt, *When Zachary Beaver Came to Town*		
		2007	Sherman Alexie, *The Absolutely True Diary of a Part-time Indian*
2000	Gloria Whelan, *Homeless Bird*		
2001	Virginia Eumer Wolff, *True Believer*	2008	Judy Blundell, *What I Saw and How I Lied*
2002	Nancy Farmer, *The House of the Scorpion*	2009	Phillip Hoose, *Claudette Colvin: Twice Towards Justice*
2003	Polly Horvath, *The Canning Season*		

Note: No award was given in poetry from 1985 to 1990. **Source:** National Book Awards, Inc.

Bollingen Prize for Poetry, 1949–2009

First awarded annually, and biennially since 1965, the Bollingen Prize is offered by Yale University to an American citizen for a distinguished book of poetry, or in recognition of a poet's entire achievement.

Year	Recipient	Year	Recipient	Year	Recipient	Year	Recipient
1949	Ezra Pound	1958	e.e. cummings	1973	James Merrill	1991	Laura Riding Jackson
1950	Wallace Stevens	1959	Theodore Roethke	1975	A. R. Ammons		Donald Justice
1951	John Crowe Ransom	1960	Delmore Schwartz	1977	David Ignatow	1993	Mark Strand
		1961	Ivor Winters	1979	W. S. Merwin	1995	Kenneth Koch
1952	Marianne Moore	1962	Richard Eberhart	1981	May Swenson	1997	Gary Snyder
1953	Archibald MacLeish		John Hall Wheelock		Howard Nemerov	1999	Robert W. Creeley
	William Carlos Williams	1963	Robert Frost	1983	Anthony E. Hecht	2001	Louise Glück
		1965	Horace Gregory		John Hollander	2003	Adrienne Rich
1954	W. H. Auden	1967	Robert Penn Warren	1985	John Ashbery	2005	Jay Wright
1955	Leonie Adams	1969	John Berryman		Fred Chappel	2007	Frank Bidart
	Louise Bogan		Karl Shapiro	1987	Stanley Kunitz	2009	Allen Grossman
1956	Conrad Aiken	1971	Richard Wilbur	1989	Edgar Bowers		
1957	Allen Tate		Mona Van Duyn				

Source: Yale University.

The Caldecott Medal, 1938–2010

The Caldecott Medal, presented by the American Library Association, is awarded annually to the illustrator of the most distinguished picture book for children published in the United States during the preceding year. The award is named in honor of the English illustrator Randolph Caldecott (1846–1886). In cases where only one name is given, the book was written and illustrated by the same person.

Year	Illustrator/Author/Title	Year	Illustrator/Author/Title
1938	Dorothy Lathrop; Helen Dean Fish, *Animals of the Bible*	1973	Blair Lent; retold by Arlene Mosel, *The Funny Little Woman*
1939	Thomas Handforth, *Mei Li*	1974	Margot Zemach; Harve Zemach, *Duffy and the Devil*
1940	Ingri and Edgar Parin d'Aulaire, *Abraham Lincoln*	1975	Gerald McDermott, *Arrow to the Sun*
1941	Robert Lawson, *They Were Strong and Good*	1976	Leo and Diane Dillon; retold by Verna Aardema, *Why Mosquitoes Buzz in People's Ears*
1942	Robert McCloskey, *Make Way for Ducklings*		
1943	Virginia Lee Burton, *The Little House*	1977	Leo & Diane Dillon; Margaret Musgrove, *Ashanti to Zulu: African Traditions*
1944	Louis Slobodkin; James Thurber, *Many Moons*		
1945	Elizabeth Orton Jones; Rachel Jones, *Prayer for a Child*	1978	Peter Spier, *Noah's Ark*
		1979	Paul Goble, *The Girl Who Loved Wild Horses*
1946	Maude and Miska Petersham, *The Rooster Crows* (traditional Mother Goose)	1980	Barbara Cooney; Donald Hall, *Ox-Cart Man*
		1981	Arnold Lobel, *Fables*
1947	Leonard Weisgard; Golden MacDonald, *The Little Island*	1982	Chris Van Allsburg, *Jumanji*
		1983	Marcia Brown, *Shadow*
1948	Roger Duvoisin; Alvin Tresselt, *White Snow, Bright Snow*	1984	Martin and Alice Provensen, *The Glorious Flight*
1949	Bert and Elmer Hader, *The Big Snow*	1985	Trina Schart Hyman, *Saint George and the Dragon*
1950	Leo Politi, *Song of the Swallows*		
1951	Katherine Milhous, *The Egg Tree*	1986	Chris Van Allsburg, *The Polar Express*
1952	Nicolas Mordvinoff; Will Mordvinoff, *Finders Keepers*	1987	Richard Egielski; Arthur Yorinks, *Hey, Al*
		1988	John Schoenherr, *Owl Moon*
1953	Lynd Ward, *The Biggest Bear*	1989	Stephen Gammell; Karen Ackerman, *Song and Dance Man*
1954	Ludwig Bemelmans, *Madeline's Rescue*		
1955	Marcia Brown; Charles Perault, *Cinderella, or the Little Glass Slipper*	1990	Ed Young, *Lon Po Po: A Red-Riding Hood Story from China*
1956	Feodor Rojankovsky; John Langstaff, *Frog Went A-Courtin'*	1991	David Macaulay, *Black and White*
		1992	David Wiesner, *Tuesday*
1957	Marc Simont; Janice May Udry, *A Tree is Nice*	1993	Emily Arnold McCully, *Mirette on the High Wire*
1958	Robert McCloskey, *Time of Wonder*		
1959	Barbara Cooney (adapted from Geoffrey Chaucer), *Chanticleer and the Fox*	1994	Allen Say, *Grandfather's Journey*
		1995	David Diaz; Eve Bunting, *Smoky Night*
1960	Marie Hall Ets and Aurora Labastida, *Nine Days to Christmas*	1996	Peggy Rathman, *Officer Buckle and Gloria*
		1997	David Wisniewski, *Golem*
1961	Nicolas Sidjakov; Ruth Robbins, *Baboushka and the Three Kings*	1998	Paul O. Zelinsky, *Rapunzel*
		1999	Mary Azarian; Jacqueline Briggs Martin, *Snowflake Bentley*
1962	Marcia Brown, *Once a Mouse . . .*		
1963	Ezra Jack Keats, *The Snowy Day*	2000	Simms Taback, *Joseph Had a Little Overcoat*
1964	Maurice Sendak, *Where the Wild Things Are*	2001	David Small, *So You Want to Be President?*
1965	Beni Montresor; Beatrice Schenk de Regniers, *May I Bring a Friend?*	2002	David Wiesner, *The Three Pigs*
		2003	Eric Rohmann, *My Friend Rabbit*
1966	Nonny Hogrogian; Sorche Nic Leodhas, *Always Room for One More*	2004	Mordicai Gerstein, *The Man Who Walked Between the Towers*
1967	Evaline Ness, *Sam, Bangs & Moonshine*		
1968	Ed Emberley; Barbara Emberley, *Drummer Hoff*	2005	Kevin Henkes, *Kitten's First Full Moon*
		2006	Norton Juster, *The Hello Goodbye Window*
1969	Uri Shulevitz; Arthur Ransome, *The Fool of the World and the Flying Ship*	2007	David Wiesner, *Flotsam*
		2008	Brian Selznick, *The Invention of Hugo Cabret*
1970	William Steig, *Sylvester and the Magic Pebble*		
1971	Gail E. Haley—*A Story*	2009	Beth Krommes, *The House in the Night*
1972	Nonny Hogrogian, *One Fine Day*	2010	Jerry Pinkney, *The Lion and the Mouse*

Source: American Library Association.

The Newbery Medal, 1922–2010

The Newbery Medal, presented by the American Library Association, is awarded annually to the author of the most distinguished contribution to American literature for children. The award is named in honor of John Newbery (1713–67), the first English publisher of books for children.

Year	Author, Title	Year	Author, Title
1922	Willem Van Loon, *The Story of Mankind*	1928	Dhan Gopal Mukerji, *Gayneck, The Story of a Pigeon*
1923	Hugh Lofting, *The Voyages of Doctor Dolittle*		
1924	Charles Hawes, *The Dark Frigate*	1929	Eric P. Kelly, *The Trumpeter of Krakow*
1925	Charles Finger, *Tales from Silver Lands*	1930	Rachel Field, *Hitty, Her First Hundred Years*
1926	Arthur Bowie Chrisman, *Shen of the Sea*	1931	Elizabeth Coatsworth, *The Cat Who Went to Heaven*
1927	Will James, *Smoky, The Cowhorse*		
		1932	Laura Adams Armer, *Waterless Mountain*

Year	Author, Title	Year	Author, Title
1933	Elizabeth Foreman Lewis, *Young Fu of the Upper Yangtze*	1973	Jean George, *Julie of the Wolves*
1934	Cornelia Meigs, *Invincible Louisa*	1974	Paula Fox, *The Slave Dancer*
1935	Monica Shannon, *Dobry*	1975	Virginia Hamilton, *M.C. Higgins the Great*
1936	Carol Brink, *Caddie Woodlawn*	1976	Susan Cooper, *The Grey King*
1937	Ruth Sawyer, *Roller Skates*	1977	Mildred D. Taylor, *Roll of Thunder, Hear My Cry*
1938	Kate Seredy, *The White Stag*	1978	Katherine Paterson, *Bridge to Terabithia*
1939	Elizabeth Enright, *Thimble Summer*	1979	Ellen Raskin, *The Westing Game*
1940	James Daugherty, *Daniel Boone*	1980	Joan Blos, *A Gathering of Days: A New England Girl's Journal, 1830–32*
1941	Armstrong Sperry, *Call It Courage*	1981	Katherine Paterson, *Jacob Have I Loved*
1942	Walter D. Edmonds, *The Matchlock Gun*	1982	Nancy Willard, *A Visit to William Blake's Inn: Poems for Innocent and Experienced Travelers*
1943	Elizabeth Janet Gray, *Adam of the Road*	1983	Cynthia Voigt, *Dicey's Song*
1944	Esther Forbes, *Johnny Tremain*	1984	Beverly Cleary, *Dear Mr. Henshaw*
1945	Robert Lawson, *Rabbit Hill*	1985	Robin McKinley, *The Hero and the Crown*
1946	Lois Lenski, *Strawberry Girl*	1986	Patricia MacLachlan, *Sarah, Plain and Tall*
1947	Carolyn Sherwin Bailey, *Miss Hickory*	1987	Sid Fleischman, *The Whipping Boy*
1948	William Pène du Bois, *The 21 Balloons*	1988	Russell Freedman, *Lincoln: A Photobiography*
1949	Marguerite Henry, *King of the Wind*	1989	Paul Fleischman, *Joyful Noise: Poems for Two Voices*
1950	Marguerite de Angeli, *The Door in the Wall*	1990	Lois Lowry, *Number the Stars*
1951	Elizabeth Yates, *Amos Fortune, Free Man*	1991	Jerry Spinelli, *Maniac Magee*
1952	Eleanor Estes, *Ginger Pye*	1992	Phyllis Reynolds Naylor, *Shiloh*
1953	Ann Nolan Clark, *Secret of the Andes*	1993	Cynthia Rylant, *Missing May*
1954	Joseph Krumgold, *. . . And Now Miguel*	1994	Lois Lowry, *The Giver*
1955	Meindert DeJong, *The Wheel on the School*	1995	Sharon Creech, *Walk Two Moons*
1956	Jean Lee Latham, *Carry On, Mr. Bowditch*	1996	Karen Cushman, *The Midwife's Apprentice*
1957	Virginia Sorensen, *Miracles on Maple Hill*	1997	Elaine Konigsburg, *The View From Saturday*
1958	Harold Keith, *Rifles for Watie*	1998	Karen Hesse, *Out of the Dust*
1959	Elizabeth George Speare, *The Witch of Blackbird Pond*	1999	Louis Sachar, *Holes*
1960	Joseph Krumgold, *Onion John*	2000	Christopher Paul Curtis, *Bud, Not Buddy*
1961	Scott O'Dell, *Island of the Blue Dolphins*	2001	Richard Peck, *A Year Down Yonder*
1962	Elizabeth George Speare, *The Bronze Bow*	2002	Linda Sue Park, *A Single Shard*
1963	Madeleine L'Engle, *A Wrinkle in Time*	2003	Avi, *Crispin: The Cross of Lead*
1964	Emily Cheney Neville, *It's Like This, Cat*	2004	Kate DiCamillo, *The Tale of Despereaux*
1965	Maia Wojciechowska, *Shadow of a Bull*	2005	Cynthia Kadohata, *Kira-Kira*
1966	Elizabeth Borten de Trevino, *I, Juan de Pareja*	2006	Lynne Rae Perkins, *Criss Cross*
1967	Irene Hunt, *Up a Road Slowly*	2007	Susan Patron, *The Higher Power of Lucky*
1968	E.L. Konigsburg, *From the Mixed-up Files of Mrs. Basil E. Frankweiler*	2008	Laura Amy Schlitz, *Good Masters! Sweet Ladies! Voices from a Medieval Village*
1969	Lloyd Alexander, *The High King*	2009	Neil Gaiman, *The Graveyard Book*
1970	William H. Armstrong, *Sounder*	2010	Rebecca Stead, *When You Reach Me*
1971	Betsy Byars, *Summer of the Swans*		
1972	Robert C. O'Brien, *Mrs. Frisby and the Rats of NIMH*		

Source: American Library Association.

Pritzker Prize Winners, 1979–2010

Recognized as the most prestigious award in architecture, the Pritzker Prize is given annually by the Hyatt Hotel Foundation, and is named for its chairman, Jay Pritzker.

Year	Medalist, Country	Year	Medalist, Country
1979	Philip Johnson, U.S.	1995	Tadao Ando, Japan
1980	Luis Barragan, Mexico	1996	Rafael Moneo, Spain
1981	James Stirling, U.K.	1997	Sverre Fehn, Norway
1982	Kevin Roche, U.S.	1998	Renzo Piano, Italy
1983	I.M. Pei, U.S.	1999	Norman Foster, U.K.
1984	Richard Meier, U.S.	2000	Rem Koolhaas, Netherlands
1985	Hans Hollein, Austria	2001	Jacques Herzog, Switzerland
1986	Gottfried Boehm, Germany		Pierre de Meuron, Switzerland
1987	Kenzo Tange, Japan	2002	Glenn Murcutt, Australia
1988	Gordon Bunshaft, U.S.	2003	Jørn Utzon, Denmark
	Oscar Niemeyer, Brazil	2004	Zaha Hadid, Iraq-U.K.
1989	Frank O. Gehry, U.S.	2005	Thom Mayne, U.S.
1990	Aldo Rossi, Italy	2006	Paulo Mendes de Rocha, Brazil
1991	Robert Venturi, U.S.	2007	Richard Rogers, U.K.
1992	Alvaro Siza, Portugal	2008	Jean Nouvel, France
1993	Fumihiko Maki, Japan	2009	Peter Zumthor, Switzerland
1994	Christian de Portzamparc, France	2010	Kazuyo Sejima, Japan

Source: Hyatt Hotel Foundation.

American Institute of Architects Gold Medalists, 1907–2010

The AIA medal recognizes outstanding lifetime achievement in architecture. It is not awarded every year.

Year	Medalist, Country	Year	Medalist, Country
1907	Sir Aston Webb, U.K.	1968	Marcel Breuer, U.S.
1909	Charles Follen McKim, U.S.	1969	William Wilson Wurster, U.S.
1911	George B. Post, U.S.	1970	Richard Buckminster Fuller, U.S.
1914	Jean Louis Pascal, France	1971	Louis I. Kahn, U.S.
1922	Victor Laloux, France	1972	Pietro Belluschi, U.S.
1923	Henry Bacon, U.S.	1977	Richard Joseph Neutra, U.S.[1]
1925	Bertram Grosvenor Goodhue, U.S.	1978	Philip Johnson, U.S.
1925	Sir Edwin Landseer Lutyens, London	1979	Ieoh Ming Pei, U.S.
1927	Howard Van Doren Shaw, U.S.	1981	Josep Lluis Sert, U.S.
1929	Milton Bennett Medary, U.S.	1982	Romaldo Giurgola, U.S.
1933	Ragnar Ostberg, Stockholm	1983	Nathaniel A. Owings, U.S.
1938	Paul Philippe Cret, U.S.	1985	William Caudill, U.S.[1]
1944	Louis Henri Sullivan, U.S.	1986	Arthur Erickson, Canada
1947	Eliel Saarinen, U.S.	1989	Joseph Esherick, U.S.
1948	Charles Donagh Maginnis, U.S.	1990	Fay Jones, U.S.
1949	Frank Lloyd Wright, U.S.	1991	Charles Willard Moore, U.S.
1950	Sir Patrick Abercrombie, U.K.	1992	Benjamin Thompson, U.S.
1951	Bernard Ralph Maybeck, U.S.	1993	Kevin Roche, U.S.
1952	Auguste Perret, France		Thomas Jefferson, U.S.[1]
1953	William Adams Delano, U.S.	1994	Sir Norman Foster, U.K.
1955	Willem Marinus Dudock, Netherlands	1995	Cesar Pelli, U.S.
1956	Clarence S. Stein, U.S.	1997	Richard Meier, U.S.
1957	Louis Skidmore, U.S.	1998	No Award
1957	Ralph Walker, U.S.	1999	Frank Gehry, U.S.
1958	John Wellborn Root, U.S.	2000	Ricardo Legorreta, Mexico
1959	Walter Gropius, U.S.	2001	Michael Graves, U.S.
1960	Ludwig Mies van der Rohe, U.S.	2002	Tadao Ando, Japan
1961	Le Corbusier (Charles Edouard Jeanneret-Gris), France	2004	Samuel Mockbee, U.S.[1]
		2005	Santiago Calatrava, Spain
1962	Eero Saarinen, U.S.[1]	2006	Antoine Predock, U.S.
1963	Alvar Aalto, Finland	2007	Edward Larrabee Barnes, U.S.
1964	Pier Luigi Nervi, Italy	2008	Renzo Piano, Italy
1966	Kenzo Tange, Japan	2009	Glenn Murcutt, Australia
1967	Wallace K. Harrison, U.S.	2010	Peter Bohlin, U.S.

Note: 1. Awarded posthumously. **Source:** American Institute of Architects.

Fields Medal Winners, 1936–2010

The Fields Medal, named for Canadian mathematician J. D. Fields, is often described as the Nobel Prize for Mathematics. Since 1950, medals have been awarded every four years.

Year	Winners
1936	**Lars Ahlfors,** Harvard Univ.; **Jesse Douglas,** MIT
1950	**Laurent Schwartz,** Universite de Nancy; **Atle Selberg,** Princeton/IAS
1954	**Kunihiko Kodaira,** Princeton Univ.; **Jean-Pierre Serre,** College de France
1958	**Klaus Roth,** Univ. of London; **Rene Thom,** Univ. of Strasbourg
1962	**Lars Hormander,** Univ. of Stockholm; **John Milnor,** Princeton Univ.
1966	**Michael Atiyah,** Oxford Univ.; **Paul Cohen,** Stanford Univ.; **Alex Grothendieck,** Univ. of Paris; **Stephen Smale,** Univ. of California
1970	**Alan Baker,** Cambridge Univ.; **Heisuke Hironaka,** Harvard Univ.; **Serge Novikov,** Moscow Univ.; **John Thompson,** Univ. of Chicago
1974	**Enrico Bombieri,** Univ. of Pisa; **David Mumford,** Harvard Univ.
1978	**Pierre Deligne,** IHES; **Charles Fefferman,** Princeton Univ.; **Gregori Margulis,** Moscow Univ.; **Daniel Quillen,** MIT
1982	**Alain Connes,** IHES; **William Thurston,** Princeton Univ.; **Shing-Tung Yau,** IAS
1986	**Simon Donaldson,** Oxford Univ.; **Gerd Faltings,** Princeton Univ.; **Michael Freedman,** Univ. of California at San Diego
1990	**Vladimir Drinfeld,** Phys.Inst.Kharkov; **Vaughan Jones,** Univ. of California; **Shigefumi Mori,** Univ. of Kyoto; **Edward Witten,** Princeton/IAS
1994	**Pierre-Louis Lions,** Universite de Paris-Dauphine; **Jean-Chrisophe Yoccoz,** Universite de Paris-Sud; **Jean Bourgain,** Princeton/IAS; **Efim Zelmanov,** Univ. of Wisconsin
1998	**Richard E. Borcherds,** Cambridge Univ.; **William T. Gowers,** Cambridge Univ.; **Maxim Kontsevich,** IHES and Rutgers Univ.; **Curtis T. McMullen,** Harvard Univ.
2002	**Laurent Lafforgue,** IHES; **Vladimir Voevodsky,** Princeton/IAS
2006	**Andrei Okounov,** Princeton; **Terence Tao,** UCLA; **Wendelin Werner,** Univ. de Paris- South; **Grigori Perelman,** who declined the medal.
2010	**Elon Linenstrauss,** Hebrew Univ. of Jerusalem; Princeton Univ.; **Ngô Bảo Châu,** Paris-Sud 11 Univ., Univ. of Chicago; **Stanislav Smirnov,** Univ. of Geneva; **Cédric Villani,** École Normale Supérieure de Lyon, Institut Henri Poincaré

Note: IAS=Institute of Advanced Study. IHES=Institut des Hautes Etudes Scientifiques. **Source:** Fields Institute for Research in Mathematical Sciences.

Pulitzer Prizes

PULITZER PRIZES IN JOURNALISM

The Pulitzer Prize for Reporting is the oldest prize given in journalism and was first awarded in 1917 together with the Pulitzer Prizes for History and Biography. The changing nature and public per-

ception of reporting can be seen in the various categories established over the years. Originally, the prize recognized excellence irrespective of the journalist's beat; it could be local, national or international, and it could be either reporting for a deadline or investigative reporting carried out over a longer period. Over the years, the number of categories has expanded to cover the great variety of reporting and writing contained in modern daily newspapers.

Public Service, 1918–2010

Year	Paper, Distinction

1918 *New York Times,* Reports, documents, and speeches relating to World War I.

1919 *Milwaukee Journal,* Campaign for Americanism.

1920 No award

1921 *Boston Post,* Articles exposing operations and leading to arrest of Charles Ponzi.

1922 *New York World,* Articles exposing operations of Ku Klux Klan.

1923 *Memphis Commercial Appeal,* News and cartoons about Ku Klux Klan.

1924 *New York World,* Exposure of Florida peonage evil.

1925 No award

1926 *Columbus (Ga.) Enquirer Sun,* Articles decrying Ku Klux Klan, dishonest public officials, lynching, and a law barring the teaching of evolution.

1927 *Canton (Ohio) Daily News,* Articles about collusion between city government and organized crime, resulting in assassination of editor, Don R. Mellett.

1928 *Indianapolis Times,* Exposure of political corruption in Indiana.

1929 *New York Evening World,* Campaign to correct evil and corruption in administration of justice.

1930 No award

1931 *Atlanta Constitution,* Municipal graft exposure leading to convictions.

1932 *Indianapolis News,* Campaign to eliminate waste in city management and reduce tax levy.

1933 *New York World-Telegram,* Series of articles on veterans' relief, real estate bond evil, and articles exposing lottery schemes of fraternal organizations.

1934 *Medford (Oreg.) Mail Tribune,* Campaign against unscrupulous politicians in Jackson County, Oreg.

1935 *Sacramento Bee,* Campaign against political machine influence in appointment of two federal judges in Nevada.

1936 *Cedar Rapids Gazette,* Crusade against corruption and misgovernment in state of Iowa.

1937 *St. Louis Post-Dispatch,* Exposure of registration fraud in St. Louis, resulting in invalidation of more than 40,000 fraudulent ballots and appointment of new election board.

1938 *Bismarck (N.D.) Tribune,* News reports and editorials entitled "Self Help in the Dust Bowl."

1939 *Miami Daily News,* Campaign for recall of Miami City Commission.

1940 *Waterbury (Conn.) Republican & American,* Campaign exposing municipal graft.

1941 *St. Louis Post-Dispatch,* Campaign against city smoke nuisance.

Year	Paper, Distinction

1942 *Los Angeles Times,* Campaign resulting in clarification and confirmation of freedom of press rights for all American newspapers.

1943 *Omaha (Nebr.) World-Herald,* Campaign for collection of scrap metal for war effort.

1944 *New York Times,* Survey of teaching of American history.

1945 *Detroit Free Press,* Investigation of legislative graft and corruption at Lansing, Mich.

1946 *Scranton (Pa.) Times,* Fifteen-year investigation of judicial practices in U.S. District Court, resulting in removal of the district judge and indictment of many others.

1947 *Baltimore Sun,* Series of articles by Howard M. Norton dealing with administration of unemployment compensation in Maryland, resulting in 93 criminal convictions and/or guilty pleas.

1948 *St. Louis Post-Dispatch,* Coverage of Centralia, Ill. mine disaster and follow-up articles resulting in reforms in mine safety laws and regulations.

1949 *Nebraska State Journal,* Campaign establishing "Nebraska All-Star Primary" that called attention to issues early in presidential campaign.

1950 *Chicago Daily News* and *St. Louis Post-Dispatch,* Work of George Thiem and Roy J. Harris, respectively, in exposing presence of 37 Illinois newspapermen on an Illinois state payroll.

1951 *Miami Herald* and *Brooklyn Eagle,* Crime reporting during the year.

1952 *St. Louis Post-Dispatch,* Investigation and disclosures of corruption in Internal Revenue Bureau and other government departments.

1953 *Whiteville (N.C.) News Reporter* and *Tabor City (N.C.) Tribune,* Campaign against Ku Klux Klan, culminating in the conviction of more than 100 Klansman and an end to terrorism in their communities.

1954 *Newsday (Long Island, N.Y.),* Exposé of New York State's racetrack scandals and labor racketeering, leading to imprisonment of racketeer William C. DeKooonig Sr.

1955 *Columbus (Ga.) Ledger* and *Sunday Ledger-Enquirer,* News coverage and editorial attack on corruption in neighboring Phenix City, leading to destruction of racket-ridden city government.

1956 *Watsonville (Calif.) Register-Pajaronion,* Exposure of corruption in public office leading to resignation of a district attorney and conviction of one of his associates.

1957 *Chicago Daily News,* Exposure of $2.5 million fraud in office of Illinois state auditor, resulting in his conviction.

1958 *Arkansas Gazette,* Civic leadership, journalistic responsibility, and moral courage during school integration crisis.

1959   Utica Observer-Dispatch and Utica Daily Press (N.Y.), Campaign against corruption, gambling, and vice.

1960   Los Angeles Times, Attack on narcotics traffic; reporting of Gene Sherman, which led to opening of negotiations between U.S. and Mexico to halt the flow of illegal drugs into California and other border states.

1961   Amarillo (Tex.) Globe-Times, Exposure of lax law enforcement resulting in punitive action sweeping officials from their posts and creating election of reform slate.

1962   Panama City (Fla.) News-Herald, Three-year campaign against entrenched power and corruption, resulting in reforms in Panama City and Bay County.

1963   Chicago Daily News, Articles calling public attention to providing birth control services in public health programs.

1964   St. Petersburg Times, Investigation of illegal activity within Florida Turnpike Authority, resulting in major reorganization of the state's road construction program.

1965   Hutchinson (Kans.) News, Campaign for more equitable reapportionment of Kansas legislature.

1966   Boston Globe, Campaign to prevent confirmation of Francis X. Morrissey as federal district judge in Massachusetts.

1967   Louisville Courier Journal and Milwaukee Journal, Campaign to control Kentucky strip-mining industry; campaign to stiffen water pollution laws in Wisconsin.

1968   Riverside (Calif.) Press-Enterprise, Exposure of corruption in courts in connection with handling of property and estates of an Indian tribe in California.

1969   Los Angeles Times, Exposure of wrongdoing within Los Angeles city government commissions, resulting in criminal convictions, resignations, and sweeping reforms.

1970   Newsday (Long Island, N.Y.), Three-year investigation and exposure of secret land deals in eastern Long Island, leading to criminal convictions, resignations, and discharges among public and political officials.

1971   Winston-Salem Journal and Sentinel, Coverage of environmental problems, as exemplified by campaign to block a strip-mining operation that would have caused irreparable damage to northwest North Carolina hill country.

1972   New York Times, Publication of Pentagon Papers.

1973   Washington Post, Investigation of Watergate.

1974   Newsday (Long Island, N.Y.), Definitive report on illicit narcotics traffic in U.S. and abroad, entitled "The Heroin Trail."

1975   Boston Globe, Coverage of Boston school desegregation crisis.

1976   Anchorage Daily News, Disclosures of impact and influence of Teamsters Union on Alaska's economy and politics.

1977   Lufkin (Tex.) News, Obituary of local men who died in Marine training camp, which grew into investigation of that death and fundamental reform in Marine Corps' recruiting and training practices.

1978   Philadelphia Inquirer, Series of articles showing abuses of power by Philadelphia police.

1979   Point Reyes (Calif.) Light, Investigation of Synanon.

1980   Gannett News Service, Series on financial contributions to Pauline Fathers.

1981   Charlotte Observer, Series called "Brown Lung: A Case of Deadly Neglect."

1982   Detroit News, Series exposing U.S. Navy's cover-up of circumstances surrounding deaths of seamen aboard ship and leading to significant reforms in naval procedures.

1983   Jackson (Miss.) Clarion-Ledger, Campaign supporting Gov. Winter in his legislative battle for reform of Mississippi's public education system.

1984   Los Angeles Times, In-depth examination of southern California's growing Latino community.

1985   Fort Worth Star-Telegram, Reporting by Mark J. Thompson revealing that nearly 250 U.S. servicemen died because of a design problem in helicopters built by Bell Helicopter.

1986   Denver Post, In-depth study of "missing children," revealing that most are involved in custody disputes or are runaways.

1987   Pittsburgh Press, Reporting by Andrew Schneider and Matthew Brelis, revealing inadequacy of FAA's medical screening of airline pilots, and leading to reform.

1988   Charlotte Observer, Revealing misuse of funds by the PTL television ministry, despite massive campaign by PTL to discredit the newspaper.

1989   Anchorage Daily News, Series revealing high incidence of alcoholism and suicide among Native Alaskans.

1990   Philadelphia Inquirer, Series by Gilbert M. Gaul disclosing shortcomings in federal regulation of the nation's blood banks.

**   Washington (N.C.) Daily News,** Series by Betty Gray and Mike Voss revealing contamination of the municipal water supply in the town of 9,000 and the eight-year cover-up by elected officials.

1991   Des Moines Register, Series by Jane Schorer about a rape and its aftermath that reopened debate over whether rape victims should be identified by name.

1992   Sacramento Bee, Series by Tom Knudson about pollution, overdevelopment and overpopulation along the Sierra Nevada mountain range.

1993   Miami Herald, Helping readers cope with Hurricane Andrew's devastation and for showing "how lax zoning, inspection and building codes had contributed to the destruction."

1994   Akron Beacon Journal, Two-part examination of race relations.

1995   Virgin Islands Daily News, Ten-part series on crime that examined crime on the islands and ultimately led to major reforms.

1996   Raleigh News and Observer, Stories revealing how agricultural corporations, unfettered by government regulation, were elbowing out small family hog farms and polluting the environment in the process.

1997   New Orleans Times-Picayune, Series analyzing the environmental, commercial, political, and social conditions that threaten the world's fish supply. It affected changes in Federal fisheries laws.

1998   Grand Forks (N.D.) Herald, Coverage of the blizzard, flood, and fire that devastated the city and the newspaper's own plant.

1999   Washington Post, Series that identified and analyzed patterns of reckless gunplay by city police officers who had little training or supervision.

2000   Washington Post, Series by Katherine Boo about gross mistreatment of mentally retarded patients in District of Columbia group homes.

Year	Paper, Distinction

2001 *The Oregonian* **(Portland, Ore.),** Series on inefficiency, misconduct and other systemic problems in the Immigration and Naturalization Service.
2002 *New York Times,* "A Nation Challenged," a special section published regularly after the Sept. 11 terrorist attacks.
2003 *The Boston Globe,* Coverage of sexual abuse by priests.
2004 *New York Times,* Work of David Barstow and Lowell Bergman that relentlessly examined death and injury among American workers and exposed employers who break basic safety rules.
2005 *Los Angeles Times,* For its exhaustively researched series exposing deadly medical problems and racial injustice at a major public hospital.
2006 *Times-Picayune (New Orleans)* Multifaceted coverage of Hurricane Katrina

Sun Herald **(Miss.),** Comprehensive coverage of Hurricane Katrina.
2007 *Wall Street Journal* for its probe into backdated stock options for business executives that triggered the ouster of top officials, and widespread change in corporate America.
2008 *The Washington Post,* work of Dana Priest, Anne Hull and photographer Michel du Cille in exposing mistreatment of wounded veterans at Walter Reed Hospital,producing reforms by federal officials.
2009 *Las Vegas Sun,* work of Alexandra Berzon for exposing lax enforcement of safety regulations in the construction industry, producing reforms.
2010 *Bristol (VA) Herald Courier,* work of Daniel Gilbert in illuminating the mismanagement of natural-gas royalties owed to thousands of landowners in Southwest Virginia, spurring action by lawmakers

Source: Columbia University. www.pulitzer.org

Pulitzer Prizes for National Reporting, 1942–2010

Year	Winner, Newspaper	Year	Winner, Newspaper
1942	Louis Stark, *New York Times*	1976	James Risser, *Des Moines Register*
1943	No award	1977	Walter Mears, Associated Press
1944	Dewey L. Fleming, *Baltimore Sun*	1978	Gaylord D. Shaw, *Los Angeles Times*
1945	James B. Reston, *New York Times*	1979	James Risser, *Des Moines Register*
1946	Edward A. Harris, *St. Louis Post-Dispatch*	1980	Bette Swenson Orsini and Charles Stafford,
1947	Edward T. Folliard, *Washington Post*		*St. Petersburg Times*
1948	Bert Andrews, *New York Herald Tribune*	1981	John M Crewdson, *New York Times*
	Nat S. Finney, *Minneapolis Tribune*	1982	Rick Atkinson, *Kansas City Times*
1949	C.P. Trussell, *New York Times*	1983	Staff, *Boston Globe*
1950	Edwin O. Guthman, *Seattle Times*	1984	John Noble Wilford, *New York Times*
1951	No award[1]	1985	Thomas J. Knudson, *Des Moines Register*
1952	Anthony Leviero, *New York Times*	1986	Arthur Howe, *Philadelphia Inquirer*
1953	Don Whitehead, Associated Press		Craig Flournoy and George Rodrigues,
1954	Richard Wilson, *Des Moines Register and*		*Dallas Morning News*
	Tribune	1987	Staff, *Miami Herald*
1955	Anthony Lewis, *Washington Daily News*		Staff, *New York Times*
1956	Charles L. Bartlett, *Chattanooga Times*	1988	Tim Weiner, *Philadelphia Inquirer*
1957	James B. Reston, *New York Times*	1989	Donald L. Bartlett and James B. Steele,
1958	Relman Morin, Associated Press		*Philadelphia Inquirer*
	Clark Mollenhoff, *Des Moines Register and*	1990	Ross Anderson, Bill Dietrich, Mary Ann
	Tribune		Gwinn, and Eric Nalder, *Seattle Times*
1959	Howard Van Smith, *Miami News*	1991	Marji Lundstrom and Rochelle Sharpe,
1960	Vance Trimble , Scripps-Howard		Gannet News Service
	Newspaper Alliance	1992	Jeff Taylor and Mike McGraw, *Kansas City Star*
1961	Edward R. Cony, *Wall Street Journal*	1993	David Maraniss, *Washington Post*
1962	Nathan G. Caldwell and Gene S. Graham,	1994	Eileen Welsome, *Albuquerque Tribune*
	Nashville Tennessean	1995	Tony Horwitz, *Wall Street Journal*
1963	Anthony Lewis, *New York Times*	1996	Alix M. Freedman, *Wall Street Journal*
1964	Merriman Smith, United Press International	1997	Staff, *Wall Street Journal*
1965	Louis M. Kohlmeier, *Wall Street Journal*	1998	Russell Carollo and Jeff Nesmith, *Dayton*
1966	Haynes Johnson, *Washington Evening Star*		(Ohio) *Daily News*
1967	Stanley Penn and Monroe Karmin, *Wall*	1999	Staff, *New York Times*
	Street Journal	2000	Staff, *Wall Street Journal*
1968	Howard James, *Christian Science Monitor*	2001	Staff, *New York Times*
	Nathan K. (Nick) Kotz, *Des Moines*	2002	Staff, *Washington Post*
	Register and *Minneapolis Tribune*	2003	Alan Miller and Kevin Sack, *Los Angeles Times*
1969	Robert Cahn, *Christian Science Monitor*	2004	Staff, *Los Angeles Times*
1970	William J. Eaton, *Chicago Daily News*	2005	Walt Bogdanich, *New York Times*
1971	Lucinda Franks and Thomas Powers, United	2006	James Risen and Eric Lichtblau, *New York*
	Press International		*Times;* Staffs, *San Diego Union Tribune* and
1972	Jack Anderson, (Syndicated columnist)		*Copley News Service*
1973	Robert Boyd and Clark Hoyt, Knight Newspapers	2007	Charlie Savage, *Boston Globe*
1974	James R. Polk, *Washington Star-News*	2008	Jo Becker and Barton Gellman, *The*
	Jack White, *Providence Journal and Evening*		*Washington Post*
	Bulletin	2009	Staff, *St. Petersburg Times*
1975	Donald L. Bartlett and James B. Steele,	2010	Matt Richtel and members of the staff, *The*
	Philadelphia Inquirer		*New York Times*

Note: 1. The board decided that Arthur Krock of The *New York Times* deserved the prize but he could not accept because he was a board member. Source: Columbia University. www.pulitzer.org

Pulitzer Prizes for International Reporting, 1942–2010

Year	Winner, Newspaper	Year	Winner, Newspaper
1942	Lawrence Edmund Allen, Associated Press	1977	No award
1943	Ira Wolfert, North American Newspaper Alliance, Inc.	1978	Henry Kamm, *New York Times*
		1979	Richard Ben Cramer, *Philadelphia Inquirer*
1944	Daniel DeLuce, Associated Press	1980	Joel Brinkley (reporter), Jay Mather (photographer), *Louisville Courier-Journal*
1945	Mark S. Watson, *Baltimore Sun*		
1946	Homer William Bigart, *New York Herald Tribune*	1981	Shirley Christian, *Miami Herald*
1947	Eddy Gilmore, Associated Press	1982	John Darnton, *New York Times*
1948	Paul W. Ward, *Baltimore Sun*	1983	Thomas L. Friedman, *New York Times*
1949	Price Day, *Baltimore Sun*		Loren Jenkins, *Washington Post*
1950	Edmund Stevens, *Christian Science Monitor*	1984	Karen Elliott House, *Wall Street Journal*
1951	Keyes Beech, *Chicago Daily News*	1985	Josh Friedman and Dennis Bell (reporters) and Ozier Muhammad (photographer), *Newsday* (Long Island, N.Y.)
	Homer William Bigart, *New York Herald Tribune*		
	Marguerite Higgins, *New York Herald Tribune*		
	Relman Morin, Associated Press	1986	Lewis M. Simons, Pete Carey, and Katherine Ellison, *San Jose Mercury News*
	Fred Sparks, *Chicago Daily News*		
	Don Whitehead, Associated Press	1987	Michael Parks, *Los Angeles Times*
1952	John M. Hightower, Associated Press	1988	Thomas L. Friedman, *New York Times*
1953	Austin Wehrwien, *Milwaukee Journal*	1989	Glenn Frankel, *Washington Post*
1954	Jim G. Lucas, Scripps-Howard		Bill Keller, *New York Times*
1955	Harrison E. Salisbury, *New York Times*	1990	Nicholas D. Kristof and Sheryl WuDunn, *New York Times*
1956	William Randolph Hearst Jr., Kingsbury Smith, Frank Conniff, Int'l News Service		
1957	Russell Jones, United Press	1991	Caryle Murphy, *Washington Post*
1958	Staff, *New York Times*		Serge Schmemann, *New York Times*
1959	Joseph Martin and Philip Santora, *New York Daily News*	1992	Patrick J. Sloyan, *Newsday* (Long Island, N.Y.)
		1993	John F. Burns, *New York Times*
1960	A.M. Rosenthal, *New York Times*		Roy Gutman, *Newsday* (Long Island, N.Y.)
1961	Lynn Heinzerling, Associated Press	1994	Team of reporters, *Dallas Morning News*
1962	Walter Lippmann, *New York Herald Tribune Syndicate*	1995	Mark Fritz, Associated Press
		1996	David Rohde, *Christian Science Monitor*
1963	Hal Hendrix, *Miami News*	1997	John F. Burns, *New York Times*
1964	Malcolm W. Browne, Associated Press	1998	Staff, *New York Times*
	David Halberstam, *New York Times*	1999	Staff, *Wall Street Journal*
1965	J. A. Livingston, *Philadelphia Bulletin*	2000	Mark Schoofs, *Village Voice* (N.Y. City)
1966	Peter Arnett, Associated Press	2001	Ian Johnson, *Wall Street Journal*
1967	R. John Hughes, *Christian Science Monitor*		Paul Salopek, *Chicago Tribune*
1968	Alfred Friendly, *Washington Post*	2002	Barry Bearak, *New York Times*
1969	William Tuohy, *Los Angeles Times*	2003	Kevin Sullivan and Mary Jordan, *Washington Post*
1970	Seymour M. Hersh, Dispatch News Service		
1971	Jimmie Lee Hoagland, *Washington Post*	2004	Anthony Shadid, *Washington Post*
1972	Peter R. Kann, *Wall Street Journal*	2005	Kim Murphy, *Los Angeles Times*
1973	Max Frankel, *New York Times*		Dele Olojede, *Newsday* (Long Island, N.Y.)
1974	Hedrick Smith, *New York Times*	2006	Joseph Kahn and Jim Yardley, *New York Times*
1975	William Mullen (reporter), Ovie Carter (photographer), *Chicago Tribune*	2007	Staff, *Wall Street Journal*
		2008	Steve Fainaru, *The Washington Post*
		2009	Staff, *The New York Times*
1976	Sydney H. Schanberg, *New York Times*	2010	Anthony Shadid, *The Washington Post*

Source: Columbia University. www.pulitzer.org

Pulitzer Prizes for Editorial Writing, 1917–2010

Year	Winner, Newspaper	Year	Winner, Newspaper
1917	*Lusitania* editorial article, *New York Tribune*	1932	No award
1918	War editorials and articles, *Louisville Courier Journal*	1933	series of editorials, *Kansas City Star*
		1934	E.P. Chase, *Atlantic* (Iowa) *News-Telegraph*
1919	No award	1935	No award
1920	Harvey E. Newbranch, *Evening World Herald*	1936	Felix Morley, *Washington Post*
1921	No award		George B. Parker, Scripps-Howard Newspapers
1922	Frank M. O'Brien, *New York Herald*		
1923	William Allen White, *Emporia (Kans.) Gazette*	1937	John W. Owens, *Baltimore Sun*
1924[1]	Coolidge editorial, *Boston Herald*	1938	William Wesley Waymack, *Des Moines Register and Tribune*
1925	"Plight of the South" editorial, *Charleston (S.C.) News and Courier*		
		1939	Ronald G. Callvert, *Portland Oregonian*
1926	Edward M. Kingsbury, *New York Times*	1940	Bart Howard, *St. Louis Post-Dispatch*
1927	F. Lauriston Bullard, *Boston Herald*	1941	Reuben Maury, *New York Daily News*
1928	Grover Cleveland Hall, *Montgomery Advertiser*	1942	Geoffrey Parsons, *New York Herald Tribune*
		1943	Forrest W. Seymour, *Des Moines Register and Tribune*
1929	Louis Isaac Jaffe, *Norfolk Virginian-Pilot*		
1930	No award	1944	Henry J. Haskell, *Kansas City Star*
1931	Charles S. Ryckman, *Fremont* (Nebr.) *Tribune*	1945	George W. Potter, *Providence Journal-Bulletin*

Year	Winner, Newspaper	Year	Winner, Newspaper
1946	Hodding Carter, *Delta Democrat-Times* (Greenville, Miss.)	1974	F. Gilman Spencer, *Trentonian* (Trenton, N.J.)
1947	William H. Grimes, *Wall Street Journal*	1975	John D. Maurice, *Charleston* (W.V.) *Daily*
1948	Virginius Dabney, *Richmond Times-Dispatch*		*Mail*
		1976	Philip P. Kerby, *Los Angeles Times*
1949	John H. Crider, *Boston Herald*	1977	Warren L. Lerude, Foster Church and
	Herbert Elliston, *Washington Post*		Norman F. Cardoza, *Reno Evening Gazette*
1950	Carl M. Saunders, *Jackson* (Mich.) *Citizen Patriot*		*and Nevada State Journal*
		1978	Meg Greenfield, *Washington Post*
1951	William Harry Fitzpatrick, *New Orleans States*	1979	Edwin M. Yoder Jr., *Washington Star*
		1980	Robert L. Bartley, *Wall Street Journal*
1952	Louis LaCoss, *St. Louis Globe Democrat*	1981	No award
1953	Vermont Connecticut Royster, *Wall Street Journal*	1982	Jack Rosenthal, *New York Times*
		1983	Editorial Board, *Miami Herald*
1954	Don Murray, *Boston Herald*	1984	Albert Scardino, *Georgia Gazette*
1955	Royce Howes, *Detroit Free Press*	1985	Richard Aregood, *Philadelphia Daily News*
1956	Lauren K. Soth, *Des Moines Register and Tribune*	1986	Jack Fuller, *Chicago Tribune*
		1987	Jonathan Freedman, *San Diego Tribune*
1957	Buford Boone, *Tuscaloosa News*	1988	Jane Healy, *Orlando Sentinel*
1958	Harry S. Ashmore, *Arkansas Gazette*	1989	Lois Wille, *Chicago Tribune*
1959	Ralph McGill, *Atlanta Constitution*	1990	Thomas J. Hylton, *Pottstown* (Pa.) *Mercury*
1960	Lenoir Chambers, *Norfolk Virginian-Pilot*	1991	Ron Casey, Harold Jackson, and Joey
1961	William J. Dorvillier, *San Juan* (Puerto Rico) *Star*		Kennedy, *Birmingham News*
		1992	Maria Henson, *Lexington Herald-Leader*
1962	Thomas M. Storke, *Santa Barbara* (Calif.) *News Press*	1993	No award
		1994	R. Bruce Dold, *Chicago Tribune*
1963	Ira B. Harkey Jr., *Pascagoula* (Miss.) *U. Chronicle*	1995	Jeffrey Good, *St. Petersburg Times*
		1996	Robert B. Semple, Jr., *New York Times*
1964	Hazel Brannon Smith, *Lexington* (Miss.) *Advertiser*	1997	Michael G. Gartner, *Daily Tribune* (Ames, IA)
		1998	Bernard L. Stein, *Riverdale* (N.Y.) *Press*
1965	John R. Harrison, *Gainesville* (Fla.) *Daily Sun*	1999	Editorial Board, *N.Y. Daily News*
		2000	John C. Bersia, *Orlando Sentinel*
1966	Robert Lasch, *St. Louis Post-Dispatch*	2001	David Moats, *Rutland* (Vt.) *Herald*
1967	Eugene Patterson, *Atlanta Constitution*	2002	Alex Raksin and Bob Sipchen, *Los Angeles Times*
1968	John S. Knight, *Knight Newspapers*		
1969	Paul Greenberg, *Pine Bluff* (Ark.) *Commercial*	2003	Cornelia Grumman, *Chicago Tribune*
		2004	William R. Stall, *Los Angeles Times*
1970	Philip L. Geyelin, *Washington Post*	2005	Tom Philp, *Sacramento Bee*
1971	Horance G. Davis Jr., *Gainesville* (Fla.) *Daily Sun*	2006	Rick Attig and Doug Bates, *Oregonian*
		2007	Arthur Browne, Beverly Weintraub and Heidi Evans, *N. Y. Daily News*
1972	John Strohmeyer, *Bethlehem* (Pa.) *Globe-Times*	2008	No award
		2009	Mark Mahoney, *The Post-Star* (N.Y.)
1973	Roger B. Linscott, *Berkshire Eagle* (Pittsfield, Mass.)	2010	Ted Robberson, Colleen McCain Nelson, & William McKenzie, *Dallas Morning News*

Note: 1. A special prize was awarded to the widow of the late Frank I. Cobb of *The New York World* in recognition of his lifetime of editorial writing and service. **Source:** Columbia University. www.pulitzer.org

Pulitzer Prizes for Editorial Cartooning, 1922–2010

Year	Winner, Newspaper	Year	Winner, Newspaper
1922	Rollin Kirby, *New York World*	1941	Jacob Burck, *Chicago Times*
1923	No award	1942	Herbert L. Block (Herblock), NEA Service
1924	Jay Norwood Darling, *Des Moines Register and Tribune*	1943	Jay Norwood Darling, *Des Moines Register and Tribune*
1925	Rollin Kirby, *New York World*	1944	Clifford K. Berryman, *Washington Evening Star*
1926	Daniel R. Fitzpatrick, *St. Louis Post-Dispatch*		
1927	Nelson Harding, *Brooklyn Daily Eagle*	1945	Sergeant Bill Mauldin, United Feature Syndicate, Inc
1928	Nelson Harding, *Brooklyn Daily Eagle*		
1929	Rollin Kirby, *New York World*	1946	Bruce Alexander Russell, *Los Angeles Times*
1930	Charles R. Macauley, *Brooklyn Daily Eagle*	1947	Vaughn Shoemaker , *Chicago Daily News*
1931	Edmund Duffy, *Baltimore Sun*	1948	Reuben L. Goldberg, *New York Sun*
1932	John T. McCutcheon, *Chicago Tribune*	1949	Lute Pease, *Newark Evening News*
1933	H.M. Talburt, *Washington Daily News*	1950	James T. Berryman, *Washington Evening Star*
1934	Edmund Duffy, *Baltimore Sun*	1951	Reg Manning, *Arizona Republic*
1935	Ross A. Lewis, *Milwaukee Journal*	1952	Fred L. Packer, *New York Mirror*
1936	No award	1953	Edward D. Kuekes, *Cleveland Plain Dealer*
1937	C.D. Batchelor, *New York Daily News*	1954	Herbert L. Block (Herblock), *Washington Post & Times Herald*
1938	Vaughn Shoemaker , *Chicago Daily News*		
1939	Charles G. Werner, *Daily Oklahoman*	1955	Daniel R. Fitzpatrick, *St. Louis Post-Dispatch*
1940	Edmund Duffy, *Baltimore Sun*	1956	Robert York, *Lousiville Times*

Year	Winner, Newspaper	Year	Winner, Newspaper
1957	Tom Little, *Nashville Tennessean*	1985	Jeff MacNelly , *Chicago Tribune*
1958	Bruce M. Shanks, *Buffalo Evening News*	1986	Jules Feiffer, *Village Voice* (New York City)
1959	Bill Mauldin, *St. Louis Post-Dispatch*	1987	Berke Breathed, Washington Post Writers
1960	No award		Group
1961	Carey Orr, *Chicago Tribune*	1988	Doug Marlette, *Atlanta Constitution* and
1962	Edmund S. Valtman, *Hartford Times*		*Charlotte Observer*
1963	Frank Miller, *Des Moines Register*	1989	Jack Higgins, *Chicago Sun-Times*
1964	Paul Conrad, *Denver Post*	1990	Tom Toles, *Buffalo News*
1965	No award	1991	Jim Borgman, *Cincinnati Enquirer*
1966	Don Wright, *Miami News*	1992	Signe Wilkinson, *Philadelphia Daily News*
1967	Patrick Oliphant, *Denver Post*	1993	Stephen R. Benson, *Arizona Republic*
1968	Eugene Gray Payne, *Charlotte Observer*	1994	Michael P. Ramirez, *Commercial Appeal*
1969	John Fischettii, *Chicago Daily News*		(Memphis)
1970	Thomas F. Darcy, *Newsday* (Long Island, N.Y.)	1995	Mike Luckovich, *Atlanta Constitution*
		1996	Jim Morin, *Miami Herald*
1971	Paul Conrad, *Los Angeles Times*	1997	Walt Handelsman, *New Orleans Times-Picayune*
1972	Jeffrey K. MacNelly, *Richmond News-Leader*		
1973	No award	1998	Stephen P. Breen, *Asbury Park* (N.J.) *Press*
1974	Paul Szep, *Boston Globe*	1999	David Horsey, *Seattle Post-Intelligencer*
1975	Garry Trudeau, Universal Press Syndicate	2000	Joel Pett, *Lexington Herald-Leader*
1976	Tony Auth, *Philadelphia Inquirer*	2001	Ann Telnaes, *Los Angeles Times Syndicate*
1977	Paul Szep, *Boston Globe*	2002	Clay Bennett, *Christian Science Monitor*
1978	Jeffrey K. MacNelly, *Richmond News-Leader*	2003	David Horsey, *Seattle Post-Intelligencer*
1979	Herbert L. Block (Herblock), *Washington Post*	2004	Matt Davies, *White Plains (NY) Journal News*
1980	Don Wright, *Miami News*	2005	Nick Anderson, *Courier-Journal* (Louisville, Ky.)
1981	Mike Peters, *Dayton* (Ohio) *Daily News*	2006	Mike Luckovich, *Atlanta Journal-Constitution*
1982	Ben Sargent, *Austin* (Tex.) *American-Statesman*	2007	Walt Handelsman, *Newsday* (Long Island, NY)
		2008	Michael Ramirez, *Investor's Business Daily*
1983	Richard Locher, *Chicago Tribune*	2009	Steve Breen, *The San Diego Union-Tribune*
1984	Paul Conrad, *Los Angeles Times*	2010	Mark Fiore, Self-syndicated (*SFGate.com*)

Source: Columbia University. www.pulitzer.org

Pulitzer Prizes for Photography, 1942–2010

Year	Winner, Newspaper	Year	Winner, Newspaper

PHOTOGRAPHY, 1942–67

SPOT NEWS PHOTOGRAPHY: 1968–1999

Year	Winner, Newspaper	Year	Winner, Newspaper
1942	Milton Brooks, *Detroit News*	1968	Rocco Morabito, *Jacksonville Journal*
1943	Frank Noel, Associated Press	1969	Edward T. Adams, Associated Press
1944	Frank Filan, Associated Press	1970	Steve Starr, Associated Press
	Earle L. Bunker, *World-Herald* (Omaha, Neb.)	1971	John Paul Filo, *Valley Daily News* and *Daily Dispatch*, (New Kensington, Pa.)
1945	Joe Rosenthal, Associated Press	1972	Horst Faas and Michael Laurent,
1946	No award		Associated Press
1947	Arnold Hardy, Amateur; photo distributed by Associated Press	1973	Hyunh Cong Ut, Associated Press
		1974	Anthony K. Roberts, freelancer , Beverly
1948	Frank Cushing, *Boston Traveler*		Hills, Calif.
1949	Nathaniel Fein, *New York Herald Tribune*	1975	Gerald H. Gay, *Seattle Times*
1950	Bill Crouch, *Oakland Tribune*	1976	Stanley Forman, *Boston Herald American*
1951	Max Desfor, Associated Press	1977	Neal Ulevich, Associated Press
1952	John Robinson and Don Ultang, *Des Moines Register and Tribune*		Stanley Forman, *Boston Herald American*
		1978	John H. Blair, United Press International
1953	William M. Gallagher, *Flint* (Mich.) *Journal*	1979	Thomas J. Kelly III, *Pottstown* (Pa.) *Mercury*
1954	Mrs. Walter M. Schau, Amateur; photo published by *Akron Beacon Journal*	1980	Unnamed photographer, United Press Int'l
		1981	Larry C. Price, *Fort Worth Star-Telegram*
1955	John L. Gaunt Jr., *Los Angeles Times*	1982	Ron Edmonds, Associated Press
1956	Photography staff, *New York Daily News*	1983	Bill Foley, Associated Press
1957	Harry A. Trask, *Boston Traveler*	1984	Stan Grossfeld, *Boston Globe*
1958	William C. Beall, *Washington Daily News*	1985	Photography Staff, *Register* (Santa Ana, Calif.)
1959	William Seaman, *Minneapolis Star*	1986	Carol Guzy and Michael duCille, *Miami Herald*
1960	Andrew Lopez, United Press International		
1961	Yasushi Nago, *Manichi* (Tokyo); photo distributed by United Press International	1987	Kim Komenich, *San Francisco Examiner*
		1988	Scott Shaw, *Odessa* (Tex.) *American*
1962	Paul Vathis, Associated Press	1989	Ron Olshwanger, freelancer, *St. Louis Post-Dispatch*
1963	Hector Rondon, *La Republica* (Caracas, Venezuela); photo distributed by Associated Press	1990	Photography Staff, *Oakland Tribune*
		1991	Greg Marinovich, Associated Press
1964	Robert H. Jackson, *Dallas Times-Herald*	1992	Photography Staff, Associated Press
1965	Horst Faas, Associated Press	1993	William Snyder and Ken Geiger, *Dallas Morning News*
1966	Kyoichi Sawada, United Press International		
1967	Jack R. Thornell, Associated Press	1994	Paul Watson, *Toronto Star*

Year	Winner, Newspaper	Year	Winner, Newspaper
1995	Carol Guzy, *Washington Post*	1980	Erwin H. Hagler, *Dallas Times Herald*
1996	Charles Porter 4th, freelancer, Associated Press	1981	Taro M. Yamasaki, *Detroit Free Press*
		1982	John H. White, *Chicago Sun-Times*
1997	Annie Wells, *Press Democrat* (Santa Rosa, Calif.)	1983	James B. Dickman, *Dallas Times Herald*
		1984	Anthony Suau, *Denver Post*
1998	Martha Rial, *Pittsburgh Post-Gazette*	1985	Stan Grossfeld, *Boston Globe*
1999	John McConnico, Associated Press		Larry C. Price, *Philadelphia Inquirer*
		1986	Tom Gralish, *Philadelphia Inquirer*
BREAKING NEWS PHOTOGRAPHY: 2000–2010		1987	David Peterson, *Des Moines Register*
		1988	Michael duCille, *Miami Herald*
2000	Photography Staff, *Rocky Mountain News*	1989	Manny Crisostomo, *Detroit Free Press*
2001	Alan Diaz, Associated Press	1990	David C. Turnley, *Detroit Free Press*
2002	Staff, *New York Times*	1991	William Snyder, *Dallas Morning News*
2003	Staff, *Rocky Mountain News*	1992	John Kaplan, *Pittsburgh Post-Gazette*, *Block Newspapers*
2004	David Leeson and Cheryl Diaz Meyer, *Dallas Morning News*	1993	Staff, Associated Press
2005	Staff, Associated Press	1994	Kevin Carter, freelancer, *New York Times*
2006	Staff, *Dallas Morning News*	1995	Staff, Associated Press
2007	Oded Balilty, *Associated Press*	1996	Stephanie Welsh, freelancer, Newhouse News Service
2008	Adrees Latif, *Reuters*		
2009	Patrick Farrell, *The Miami Herald*	1997	Alexander Zemlianichenko, Associated Press
2010	Mary Chind, *The Des Moines Register*	1998	Clarence Williams, *Los Angeles Times*
		1999	Susan Walsh, Associated Press
FEATURE PHOTOGRAPHY: 1968–2010		2000	Carol Guzy, Michael S. Williamson and Lucian Perkins, *Washington Post*
1968	Toshio Sakai, United Press International	2001	Matt Rainey, *Star-Ledger* (Newark, N.J.)
1969	Moneta Sleet Jr., *Ebony* Magazine	2002	Staff, *New York Times*
1970	Dallas Kinney, *Palm Beach Post* (West Palm Beach, Fla.)	2003	Don Bartletti, *Los Angeles Times*
1971	Jack Dykinga, *Chicago Sun-Times*	2004	Carolyn Cole, *Los Angeles Times*
1972	Dave Kennerly, United Press International	2005	Deanne Fitzmaurice, *San Francisco Chronicle*
1973	Brian Lanker, *Topeka Capital-Journal*	2006	Todd Heisler, *Rocky Mountain News* (Denver, Colo.)
1974	Slava Veder, Associated Press		
1975	Matthew Lewis, *Washington Post*	2007	Renee C. Byer, *Sacramento Bee*
1976	Photography Staff, *Louisville Courier Journal and Times*	2008	Preston Gannaway, *Concord* (N.H.) *Monitor*
1977	Robin Hood, *Chattanooga News-Free Press*	2009	Damon Winter, *The New York Times*
1978	J. Ross Baughman, Associated Press	2010	Craig F. Walker, *The Denver Post*
1979	Photography Staff, *Boston Herald American*		

Source: Columbia University. www.pulitzer.org

Pulitzer Prizes for Commentary, 1970–2010

Year	Winner, Newspaper	Year	Winner, Newspaper
1970	Marquis W. Childs, *St. Louis Post-Dispatch*	1989	Clarence Page, *Chicago Tribune*
1971	William A. Caldwell, *The Record* (Hackensack, N.J.)	1990	Jim Murray, *Los Angeles Times*
		1991	Jim Hoagland, *Washington Post*
1972	Mike Royko, *Chicago Daily News*	1992	Anna Quindlen, *New York Times*
1973	David S. Broder, *Washington Post*	1993	Liz Balmaseda, *Miami Herald*
1974	Edwin A. Roberts Jr., *National Observer*	1994	William Raspberry, *Washington Post*
1975	Mary McGrory, *Washington Star*	1995	Jim Dwyer, *New York Newsday*
1976	Walter (Red) Smith, *New York Times*	1996	E.R. Shipp, *New York Daily News*
1977	George F. Will, Washington Post Writers Group	1997	Eileen McNamara, *Boston Globe*
		1998	Mike McAlary, *New York Daily News*
1978	William Safire, *New York Times*	1999	Maureen Dowd, *New York Times*
1979	Russell Baker, *New York Times*	2000	Paul A. Gigot, *Wall Street Journal*
1980	Ellen H. Goodman, *Boston Globe*	2001	Dorothy Rabinowitz, *Wall Street Journal*
1981	Dave Anderson, *New York Times*	2002	Thomas Friedman, *New York Times*
1982	Art Buchwald, *Los Angeles Times* Syndicate	2003	Colbert I. King, *Washington Post*
1983	Claude Sitton, *Raleigh* (N.C.) *News & Observer*	2004	Leonard Pitts Jr., *Miami Herald*
		2005	Connie Schultz, *Cleveland Plain Dealer*
1984	Vermont Royster, *Wall Street Journal*	2006	Nicholas D. Kristof, *New York Times*
1985	Murray Kempton, *Newsday* (Long Island, N.Y.)	2007	Cynthia Tucker, *Atlanta Journal-Constitution*
1986	Jimmy Breslin, *New York Daily News*	2008	Steven Pearlstein, *The Washington Post*
1987	Charles Krauthammer, *Washington Post*	2009	Eugene Robinson, *The Washington Post*
1988	Dave Barry, *Miami Herald*	2010	Kathleen Parker, *The Washington Post*

Source: Columbia University. www.pulitzer.org

Pulitzer Prizes for Criticism, 1970–2010

Year	Winner, Newspaper	Year	Winner, Newspaper
1970	Ada Louise Huxtable, *New York Times*	1991	David Shaw, *Los Angeles Times*
1971	Harold C. Schonberg, *New York Times*	1992	No award
1972	Frank Peters, *St. Louis Post-Dispatch*	1993	Michael Dirda, *Washington Post*
1973	Ronald Powers, *Chicago Sun-Times*	1994	Lloyd Schwartz, *Boston Phoenix*
1974	Emily Genauer, *Newsday* Syndicate	1995	Margo Jefferson, *New York Times*
1975	Roger Ebert, *Chicago Sun-Times*	1996	Robert Campbell, *Boston Globe*
1976	Alan M. Kriegsman, *Washington Post*	1997	Tim Page, *Washington Post*
1977	William McPherson, *Washington Post*	1998	Michiko Kakutani, *New York Times*
1978	Walter Kerr, *New York Times*	1999	Blair Kamin, *Chicago Tribune*
1979	Paul Gapp, *Chicago Tribune*	2000	Henry Allen, *Washington Post*
1980	William A. Henry III, *Boston Globe*	2001	Gail Caldwell, *Boston Globe*
1981	Jonathan Yardley, *Washington Star*	2002	Justin Davidson, *Newsday* (Long Island, N.Y.)
1982	Martin Bernheimer, *Los Angeles Times*		
1983	Manuela Hoelterhoff, *Wall Street Journal*	2003	Stephen Hunter, *Washington Post*
1984	Paul Goldberger, *New York Times*	2004	Dan Neil, *Los Angeles Times*
1985	Howard Rosenberg, *Los Angeles Times*	2005	Joe Morgenstern, *Wall Street Journal*
1986	Donal Henahan, *New York Times*	2006	Robin Givhan, *Washington Post*
1987	Richard Eder, *Los Angeles Times*	2007	Jonathan Gold, *LA Weekly*
1988	Tom Shales, *Washington Post*	2008	Mark Feeney, *Boston Globe*
1989	Michael Skube, *Raleigh (N.C.) News and Observer*	2009	Holland Cotter, *The New York Times*
		2010	Sarah Kaufman, *The Washington Post*
1990	Allan Temko, *San Francisco Chronicle*		

Source: Columbia University. www.pulitzer.org

Pulitzer Prizes for Feature Writing, 1979–2010

Year	Winner, Newspaper	Year	Winner, Newspaper
1979	Jon D. Franklin, *Baltimore Evening Sun*	1995	Ron Suskind, *Wall Street Journal*
1980	Madeline Blais, *Miami Herald*	1996	Rick Bragg, *New York Times*
1981	Teresa Carpenter, *Village Voice* (New York)	1997	Lisa Pollak, *Baltimore Sun*
1982	Saul Pett, Associated Press	1998	Thomas French, *St. Petersburg Times*
1983	Nan Robertson, *New York Times*	1999	Angelo B. Henderson, *Wall Street Journal*
1984	Peter Mark Rinearson, *Seattle Times*	2000	J.R. Moehringer, *Los Angeles Times*
1985	Alice Steinbach, *Baltimore Sun*	2001	Tom Hallman Jr., *Oregonian* (Portland, Ore.)
1986	John Camp, *St. Paul Pioneer Press Dispatch*	2002	Barry Siegel, *Los Angeles Times*
1987	Steve Twomey, *Philadelphia Inquirer*	2003	Sonia Nazario, *Los Angeles Times*
1988	Jacqui Banaszynski, *St. Paul* (Minn.) *Pioneer Press Dispatch*	2004	No award
1989	David Zucchino, *Philadelphia Inquirer*	2005	Julia Keller, *Chicago Tribune*
1990	Dave Curtin, *Colorado Springs Gazette Telegram*	2006	Jim Sheeler, *Rocky Mountain News* (Denver, Colo.)
1991	Sheryl James, *St. Petersburg Times*	2007	Andrea Elliott, *New York Times*
1992	Howell Raines, *New York Times*	2008	Gene Weingarten, *The Washington Post*
1993	George Lardner, Jr., *Washington Post*	2009	Lane DeGregory, *St. Petersburg Times*
1994	Isabel Wilkerson, *New York Times*	2010	Gene Weingarten, *The Washington Post*

Source: Columbia University. www.pulitzer.org

Pulitzer Prizes for Local Reporting, 1991–2010

Year	Winner, Newspaper	Year	Winner, Newspaper
1991	Natalie Angier, *New York Times*	2001	David Cay Johnston, *New York Times*
1992	Deborah Blum, *Sacramento* (Calif.) *Bee*	2002	Gretchen Morgenson, *New York Times*
1993	Paul Ingrassia and Joseph B. White, *Wall Street Journal*	2003	Diane K. Sugg, *Baltimore Sun*
		2004	Daniel Golden, *Wall Street Journal*
1994	Eric Freedman and Jim Mitzelfeld, *Detroit News*	2005	Amy Dockser Marcus, *Wall Street Journal*
		2006	Dana Priest, *Washington Post*
1995	David Shribman, *Boston Globe*	2007	Debbie Cenziper, *Miami Times*
1996	Bob Keeler, *Newsday* (Garden City, N.Y.)	2008	David Umhoefer, *Milwaukee Journal Sentinel*
1997	Byron Acohido, *Seattle Times*	2009	Staff, *Detroit Free Press* and Ryan Gabrielson and Paul Giblin, *East Valley Tribune* (Mesa, Ariz.)
1998	Linda Greenhouse, *New York Times*		
1999	Chuck Philips and Michael A. Hiltzik, *Los Angeles Times*		
2000	George Dohrmann, *St. Paul Pioneer Press*	2010	Raquel Rutledge, *Milwaukee Journal Sentinel*

Note: Until 2006, this category was called "Beat Reporting". Source: Columbia University. www.pulitzer.org

Pulitzer Prizes for Explanatory Reporting, 1985–2010

Year	Winner, Newspaper	Year	Winner, Newspaper
1985	Jon Franklin, *Baltimore Evening Sun*	1998	Paul Salopek, *Chicago Tribune*
1986	Staff, *New York Times*	1999	Richard Read, *Oregonian*
1987	Jeff Lyon and Peter Gorner, *Chicago Tribune*	2000	Eric Newhouse, *Great Falls* (Mont.) *Tribune*
1988	Daniel Hertzberg and James B. Stewart, *Wall Street Journal*	2001	Staff, *Chicago Tribune*
		2002	Staff, *New York Times*
1989	David Hanners, William Snyder, and Karen Blessen, *Dallas Morning News*	2003	Staff, *Wall Street Journal*
		2004	Kevin Helliker and Thomas M. Burton, *Wall Street Journal*
1990	David A. Vise and Steve Coll, *Washington Post*	2005	Gareth Cook, *Boston Globe*
1991	Susan C. Faludi, *Wall Street Journal*	2006	David Finkel, *Washington Post*
1992	Robert S. Capers and Eric Lipton, *Hartford* (Conn.) *Courant*	2007	Kenneth R. Weiss, Usha Lee McFarling (reporters), and Rick Loomis (photographer), *Los Angeles Times*
1993	Mike Toner, *Atlanta Journal-Constitution*		
1994	Ronald Kotulak, *Chicago Tribune*	2008	Amy Harmon, *New York Times*
1995	Leon Dash and Lucian Perkins, *Washington Post*	2009	Bettina Boxall and Julie Cart, *Los Angeles Times*
1996	Laurie Garrett, *Newsday*		
1997	Michael Vitez, April Saul, and Ron Cortes, *Philadelphia Inquirer*	2010	Michael Moss and members of *The New York Times* staff

Note: From 1985 to 1997 this category was called "Explanatory Journalism". **Source:** Columbia University. www.pulitzer.org

Pulitzer Prizes for Investigative Reporting, 1985–2010

Year	Winner, Newspaper	Year	Winner, Newspaper
1985	William K. Marimow, *Philadelphia Inquirer* Lucy Morgan and Jack Reed, *St. Petersburg* (Fla.) *Times*	1998	Gary Cohn and Will Englund, *Baltimore Sun*
		1999	Staff, *Miami Herald*
1986	Jeffrey A. Marx and Michael M. York, *Lexington* (Ky.) *Herald Leader*	2000	Sang-Hun Choe, Charles J. Hanley and Martha Mendoza, Associated Press
1987	John Woestendiek, *Philadelphia Inquirer;* Daniel R. Biddle, H.G. Bissinger and Frederic N. Tulsky, *Philadelphia Inquirer*	2001	David Willman, *Los Angeles Times*
		2002	Sari Horowitz, Scott Higham and Sarah Cohen, *Washington Post*
		2003	Clifford J. Levy, *New York Times*
1988	Dean Baquet, William Gaines and Ann Marie Lipinski, *Chicago Tribune*	2004	Michael D. Sallah, Mitch Weiss and Joe Mahr, *The Blade* (Toledo, Ohio)
1989	Bill Dedman, *Atlanta Journal and Constitution*	2005	Nigel Jaquiss, *Willamette Week* (Portland, Ore.)
1990	Lou Kilzer and Chris Ison, *Star Tribune* (Minneapolis-St. Paul)	2006	Susan Schmidt, James V. Grimaldi and R. Jeffrey Smith, *Washington Post*
1991	Joseph T. Hallinan and Susan M. Headden, *Indianapolis Star*	2007	Brett Blackledge, *The Birmingham* (Ala.) *Times*
1992	Lorraine Adams and Dan Malone, *Dallas Morning News*	2008	Staff, *Chicago Tribune* and Jake Hooker and Walter Bogdanich, *The New York Times*
1993	Jeff Brazil and Steve Berry, *Orlando Sentinel*	2009	David Barstow, *The New York Times*
1994	Staff, *Providence Journal-Bulletin*	2010	Sheri Fink, *ProPublica*, in collaboration with *The New York Times Magazine;* Barbara Laker and Wendy Ruderman, *Philadelphia Daily News*
1995	Brian Donovan and Stephanie Saul, *Newsday*		
1996	Staff, *Orange County Register*		
1997	Eric Nalder, Deborah Nelson and Alex Tizon, *Seattle Times*		

Source: www.pulitzer.org

Pulitzer Prizes for Breaking News Reporting, 1998–2010

Year	Winner, Newspaper	Year	Winner, Newspaper
1998	Staff, *Los Angeles Times*	2005	Staff, Associated Press
1999	Staff, *Hartford Courant*	2006	Staff, *Times-Picayune* (New Orleans)
2000	Staff, *Denver Post*	2007	Staff, *The Oregonian* (Portland)
2001	Staff, *Miami Herald*	2008	Staff, *The Washington Post*
2002	Staff, *Wall Street Journal*	2009	Staff, *The New York Times*
2003	Staff, *Eagle-Tribune* (Lawrence, Mass.)	2010	Staff, *The Seattle Times*
2004	Staff, *Los Angeles Times*		

Source: Columbia University. www.pulitzer.org

Special Awards and Citations

Year	Winner, Newspaper	Year	Winner, Newspaper
1930	William O. Dapping, *Auburn* (N.Y.) *Citizen*, Prison reporting	1951	Cyrus L. Sulzberger, *New York Times*, Interview with Archbishop Stepinac
1938	*Edmonton* (Alberta) *Journal*, Freedom of the Press editorials	1952	Max Kase, *New York Journal-American*, Corruption in basketball
1941	*New York Times*, Foreign news reporting	1953	*New York Times*, Sunday *Review of the Week* section
1944	Byron Price, Director of the Office of Censorship, Creation and administration of newspaper and radio codes.	1958	Walter Lippman, *New York Herald Tribune*, Lifetime achievement
1944	Mrs. William Allen White, Services to Advisory Board Graduate School of Journalism, Columbia Univ.	1964	Gannett Newspapers, "Road to Integration" program
1945	American press cartographers, Maps of war fronts	1976	Professor John Hohenberg, Administration of Pulitzer Prizes
1947	Columbia University and Graduate School of Journalism, Governing Pulitzer Prize awards	1978	Richard Lee Strout, *Christian Science Monitor*, Lifetime achievement
1947	*St. Louis Post Dispatch*, Adherence to ideals of journalism	1987	Joseph Pulitzer Jr., Lifetime services to Pulitzer Board
1948	Dr. Frank Diehl Fackenthal, Interest and Service	1996	Herb Caen, *San Francisco Chronicle*, Lifetime achievement

Source: Columbia University. www.pulitzer.org

PULITZER PRIZES IN LETTERS

The Pulitzer Prize for Fiction, 1918–2010

Year	Author, Title	Year	Author, Title
1918	Ernest Poole, *His Family*	1955	William Faulkner, *A Fable*
1919	Booth Tarkington, *The Magnificent Ambersons*	1956	MacKinlay Kantor, *Andersonville*
1920	No award	1957	No award
1921	Edith Wharton, *The Age of Innocence*	1958	James Agee, *A Death in the Family*
1922	Booth Tarkington, *Alice Adams*	1959	Robert Lewis Taylor, *The Travels of Jaimie McPheeters*
1923	Willa Cather, *One of Ours*		
1924	Margaret Wilson, *The Able McLaughlins*	1960	Allen Drury, *Advise and Consent*
1925	Edna Ferber, *So Big*	1961	Harper Lee, *To Kill a Mockingbird*
1926	Sinclair Lewis, *Arrowsmith*	1962	Edwin O'Connor, *The Edge of Sadness*
1927	Louis Bromfield, *Early Autumn*	1963	William Faulkner, *The Reivers*
1928	Thornton Wilder, *The Bridge of San Luis Rey*	1964	No award
1929	Julia Peterkin, *Scarlet Sister Mary*	1965	Shirley Ann Grau, *The Keepers of the House*
1930	Oliver LaFarge, *Laughing Boy*	1966	Katherine Anne Porter, *Collected Stories*
1931	Margaret Ayer Barnes, *Years of Grace*	1967	Bernard Malamud, *The Fixer*
1932	Pearl S. Buck, *The Good Earth*	1968	William Styron, *The Confessions of Nat Turner*
1933	T.S. Stribling, *The Store*		
1934	Caroline Miller, *Lamb in His Bosom*	1969	N. Scott Momaday, *House Made of Dawn*
1935	Josephine Winslow Johnson, *Now in November*	1970	Jean Stafford, *Collected Stories*
		1971	No award
1936	Harold L. Davis, *Honey in the Horn*	1972	Wallace Stegner, *Angle of Repose*
1937	Margaret Mitchell, *Gone With the Wind*	1973	Eudora Welty, *The Optimist's Daughter*
1938	John Phillips Marquand, *The Late George Apley*	1974	No award
		1975	Michael Shaara, *The Killer Angels*
1939	Marjorie Kinnan Rawlings, *The Yearling*	1976	Saul Bellow, *Humboldt's Gift*
1940	John Steinbeck, *The Grapes of Wrath*	1977	No award
1941	No award	1978	James Alan McPherson, *Elbow Room*
1942	Ellen Glasgow, *In This Our Life*	1979	John Cheever, *The Stories of John Cheever*
1943	Upton Sinclair, *Dragon's Teeth*	1980	Norman Mailer, *The Executioner's Song*
1944	Martin Flavin, *Journey in the Dark*	1981	John Kennedy Toole[2], *A Confederacy of Dunces*
1945	John Hersey, *A Bell for Adano*		
1946	No award	1982	John Updike, *Rabbit Is Rich*
1947	Robert Penn Warren, *All the King's Men*	1983	Alice Walker, *The Color Purple*
1948[1]	James A. Michener, *Tales of the South Pacific*	1984	William Kennedy, *Ironweed*
		1985	Alison Lurie, *Foreign Affairs*
1949	James Gould Cozzens, *Guard of Honor*	1986	Larry McMurtry, *Lonesome Dove*
1950	A.B. Guthrie Jr., *The Way West*	1987	Peter Taylor, *A Summons to Memphis*
1951	Conrad Richter, *The Town*	1988	Toni Morrison, *Beloved*
1952	Herman Wouk, *The Caine Mutiny*	1989	Anne Tyler, *Breathing Lessons*
1953	Ernest Hemingway, *The Old Man and the Sea*	1990	Oscar Hijuelos, *The Mambo Kings Play Songs of Love*
1954	No award		

Year	Author, Title	Year	Author, Title
1991	John Updike, Rabbit at Rest	2001	Michael Chabon, The Amazing Adventures of Kavalier & Clay
1992	Jane Smiley, A Thousand Acres		
1993	Robert Olen Butler, A Good Scent From a Strange Mountain	2002	Richard Russo, Empire Falls
		2003	Jeffrey Eugenides, Middlesex
1994	E. Annie Proulx, The Shipping News	2004	Edward P. Jones, The Known World
1995	Carol Shields, The Stone Diaries	2005	Marilynne Robinson, Gilead
1996	Richard Ford, Independence Day	2006	Geraldine Brooks, March
1997	Steven Millhauser, Martin Dressler: The Tale of an American Dreamer	2007	Cormac McCarthy, The Road
		2008	Junot Díaz, The Brief Wondrous Life of Oscar Wao
1998	Philip Roth, American Pastoral		
1999	Michael Cunningham, The Hours	2009	Elizabeth Stout, Olive Kitteridge
2000	Jhumpa Lahiri, Interpreter of Maladies	2010	Paul Harden, Tinkers

Notes: 1. In 1948, the name of the category was changed from "The Novel" to "Fiction." 2. Awarded posthumously. **Source:** Columbia University. www.pulitzer.org

The Pulitzer Prize for Drama, 1918–2010

Year	Author, Title	Year	Author, Title
1918	Jesse Lynch Williams, Why Marry?	1960	Jerome Weidman and George Abbott (book); Jerry Bock (music); and Sheldon Harnick (lyrics), Fiorello!
1919	No award		
1920	Eugene O'Neill, Beyond the Horizon		
1921	Zona Gale, Miss Lulu Bett	1961	Tad Mosel, All the Way Home
1922	Eugene O'Neill, Anna Christie	1962	Frank Loesser and Abe Burrows, How to Succeed in Business Without Really Trying
1923	Owen Davis, Icebound		
1924	Hatcher Hughes, Hell-Bent Fer Heaven	1963	No award
1925	Sidney Howard, They Knew What They Wanted	1964	No award
1926	George Kelly, Craig's Wife	1965	Frank D. Gilroy, The Subject Was Roses
1927	Paul Green, In Abraham's Bosom	1966	No award
1928	Eugene O'Neill, Strange Interlude	1967	Edward Albee, A Delicate Balance
1929	Elmer L. Rice, Street Scene	1968	No award
1930	Marc Connelly, The Green Pastures	1969	Howard Sackler, The Great White Hope
1931	Susan Glaspell, Alison's House	1970	Charles Gordone, No Place to Be Somebody
1932	George S. Kaufman, Morrie Ryskind, and Ira Gershwin, Of Thee I Sing		
		1971	Paul Zindel, The Effect of Gamma Rays on Man-in-the-Moon Marigolds
1933	Maxwell Anderson, Both Your Houses		
1934	Sidney Kingsley, Men in White	1972	No award
1935	Zoe Akins, The Old Maid	1973	Jason Miller, That Championship Season
1936	Robert E. Sherwood, Idiot's Delight	1974	No award
1937	Moss Hart and George S. Kaufman, You Can't Take It With You	1975	Edward Albee, Seascape
		1976	Michael Bennett; Nicholas Dante & James Kirkwood (book); Marvin Hamlisch (music); and Edward Kleban (lyrics), A Chorus Line
1938	Thornton Wilder, Our Town		
1939	Robert E. Sherwood, Abe Lincoln in Illinois		
1940	William Saroyan, The Time of Your Life	1977	Michael Cristofer, The Shadow Box
1941	Robert E. Sherwood, There Shall Be no Night	1978	Donald L. Coburn, The Gin Game
1942	No award	1979	Sam Shepard, Buried Child
1943	Thornton Wilder, The Skin of Our Teeth	1980	Lanford Wilson, Talley's Folly
1944	No award	1981	Beth Henley, Crimes of the Heart
1945	Mary Chase, Harvey	1982	Charles Fuller, A Soldier's Play
1946	Russel Crouse and Howard Lindsay, State of the Union	1983	Marsha Norman, 'night Mother
		1984	David Mamet, Glengarry Glen Ross
1947	No award	1985	Stephen Sondheim (music and lyrics); James Lapine (book), Sunday in the Park With George
1948	Tennessee Williams, A Streetcar Named Desire		
1949	Arthur Miller, Death of a Salesman	1986	No award
1950	Richard Rodgers, Oscar Hammerstein II, and Joshua Logan, South Pacific	1987	August Wilson, Fences
		1988	Alfred Uhry, Driving Miss Daisy
1951	No award	1989	Wendy Wasserstein, The Heidi Chronicles
1952	Joseph Kramm, The Shrike	1990	August Wilson, The Piano Lesson
1953	William Inge, Picnic	1991	Neil Simon, Lost in Yonkers
1954	John Patrick, The Teahouse of the August Moon	1992	Robert Schenkkan, The Kentucky Cycle
		1993	Tony Kushner, Angels in America: Millennium Approaches
1955	Tennessee Williams, Cat on a Hot Tin Roof		
1956	Albert Hackett and Frances Goodrich, The Diary of Anne Frank	1994	Edward Albee, Three Tall Women
		1995	Horton Foote, The Young Man From Atlanta
1957	Eugene O'Neill, Long Day's Journey Into Night	1996	Jonathan Larson, Rent
		1997	No award
1958	Ketti Frings, Look Homeward, Angel	1998	Paula Vogel, How I Learned to Drive
1959	Archibald MacLeish, J.B.	1999	Margaret Edson, Wit
		2000	Donald Margulies, Dinner With Friends

Year	Author, Title	Year	Author, Title
2001	David Auburn, *Proof*	2006	No award
2002	Suzan-Lori Parks, *Topdog/Underdog*	2007	David Lindsay-Abaire, *Rabbit Hole*
2003	Nilo Cruz, *Anna In the Tropics*	2008	Tracy Letts, *August: Osage County*
2004	Doug Wright, *I Am My Own Wife*	2009	Lynn Nottage, *Ruined*
2005	John Patrick Shanley, *Doubt*	2010	Brian Yorkey, *Next to Normal*

Source: Columbia University. www.pulitzer.org

The Pulitzer Prize for Biography/Autobiography, 1917–2010

Year	Author, Title	Year	Author, Title
1917	Laura E. Richards and Maude Howe Elliott, with Florence Howe Hall, *Julia Ward Howe*	1955	William S. White, *The Taft Story*
		1956	Talbot Faulkner Hamlin, *Benjamin Henry Latrobe*
1918	William Cabell Bruce, *Benjamin Franklin, Self-Revealed*	1957	John F. Kennedy, *Profiles in Courage*
		1958	Douglas Southall Freeman[1], John Alexander Carroll, Mary Wells Ashworth, *George Washington*, vols. 1–4; and vol. 7, written after Dr. Freeman's death in 1953.
1919	Henry Adams, *The Education of Henry Adams*		
1920	Albert J. Beveridge, *The Life of John Marshall*	1959	Arthur Walworth, *Woodrow Wilson, American Prophet*
1921	Edward Bok, *The Americanization of Edward Bok*	1960	Samuel Eliot Morison, *John Paul Jones*
		1961	David Donald, *Charles Sumner and the Coming of the Civil War*
1922	Hamlin Garland, *A Daughter of the Middle Border*	1962	No award
1923	Burton J. Hendrick, *The Life and Letters of Walter H. Page*	1963	Leon Edel, *Henry James*
1924	Michael Idvorsky Pupin, *From Immigrant to Inventor*	1964	Walter Jackson Bate, *John Keats*
		1965	Ernest Samuels, *Henry Adams*
1925	M.A. DeWolfe Howe, *Barrett Wendell and His Letter*	1966	Arthur M. Schlesinger Jr., *A Thousand Days*
1926	Harvey Cushing, *The Life of Sir William Osler*	1967	Justin Kaplan, *Mr. Clemens and Mark Twain*
		1968	George F. Kennan, *Memoirs*
1927	Emory Holloway, *Whitman*	1969	Benjamin Lawrence Reid, *The Man From New York: John Quinn and His Friends*
1928	Charles Edward Russell, *The American Orchestra and Theodore Thomas*		
		1970	T. Harry Williams, *Huey Long*
1929	Burton J. Hendrick, *The Training of an American. The Earlier Life and Letters of Walter H.Page*	1971	Lawrance Thompson, *Robert Frost*
		1972	Joseph P. Lash, *Eleanor and Franklin*
		1973	W.A. Swanberg, *Luce and His Empire*
1930	Marquis James, *The Raven*	1974	Louis Sheaffer, *O'Neill, Son and Artist*
1931	Henry James, *Charles W. Eliot*	1975	Robert A. Caro, *The Power Broker*
1932	Henry F. Pringle, *Theodore Roosevelt*	1976	R.W.B. Lewis, *Edith Wharton: A Biography*
1933	Allan Nevins, *Grover Cleveland*	1977	John E. Mack, *A Prince of Our Disorder: The Life of T.E. Lawrence*
1934	Tyler Dennett, *John Hay*		
1935	Douglas S. Freeman, *R.E. Lee*	1978	Walter Jackson Bate, *Samuel Johnson*
1936	Ralph Barton Perry, *The Thought and Character of William James*	1979	Leonard Baker, *Days of Sorrow and Pain*
		1980	Edmund Morris, *The Rise of Theodore Roosevelt*
1937	Allan Nevins, *Hamilton Fish*		
1938	Odell Shepard, *Pedlar's Progress* Marquis James, *Andrew Jackson*	1981	Robert K. Massie, *Peter the Great*
		1982	William S. McFeely, *Grant: A Biography*
1939	Carl Van Doren, *Benjamin Franklin*	1983	Russell Baker, *Growing Up*
1940	Ray Stannard Baker, *Woodrow Wilson, Life and Letters*, vols. 7 & 8	1984	Louis R. Harlan, *Booker T. Washington*
		1985	Kenneth Silverman, *The Life and Times of Cotton Mather*
1941	Ola Elizabeth Winslow, *Jonathan Edwards*		
1942	Forrest Wilson, *Crusader in Crinoline*	1986	Elizabeth Frank, *Louise Bogan: A Portrait*
1943	Samuel Eliot Morison, *Admiral of the Ocean Sea*	1987	David J. Garrow, *Bearing the Cross: Martin Luther King, Jr. and the Southern Christian Leadership Conference*
1944	Carleton Mabee, *The American Leonardo: The Life of Samuel F.B. Morse*	1988	David Herbert Donald, *Look Homeward: A Life of Thomas Wolfe*
1945	Russell Blaine Nye, *George Bancroft*		
1946	Linnie Marsh Wolfe, *Son of the Wilderness*	1989	Richard Ellmann[1], *Oscar Wilde*
1947	William Allen White, *The Autobiography of William Allen White*	1990	Sebastian de Grazia, *Machiavelli in Hell*
		1991	Steven Naifeh, Gregory White Smith, *Jackson Pollock*
1948	Margaret Clapp, *Forgotten First Citizen: John Bigelow*	1992	Lewis B. Puller Jr., *Fortunate Son*
1949	Robert E. Sherwood, *Roosevelt and Hopkins*	1993	David McCullough, *Truman*
1950	Samuel Flagg Bemis, *John Quincy Adams and the Foundations of American Foreign Policy*	1994	David Levering Lewis, *W.E.B. DuBois*
		1995	Joan D. Hedrick, *Harriet Beecher Stowe*
		1996	Jack Miles, *God: A Biography*
1951	Margaret Louise Coit, *John C. Calhoun*	1997	Frank McCourt, *Angela's Ashes*
1952	Merlo J. Pusey, *Charles Evan Hughes*	1998	Katharine Graham, *Personal History*
1953	David J. Mays, *Edmund Pendleton 1721–1803*	1999	A. Scott Berg, *Lindbergh*
		2000	Stacy Schiff, *Véra (Mrs. Vladimir Nabokov)*
1954	Charles A. Lindbergh, *The Spirit of St. Louis*	2001	David Levering Lewis, *W.E.B. DuBois (vol. 2)*

Year	Author, Title	Year	Author, Title
2002	David McCullough, *John Adams*	2007	Debby Applegate, *The Most Famous Man in America*
2003	Robert A. Caro, *Master of the Senate*		
2004	William Taubman, *Khrushchev: The Man and His Era*	2008	John Matteson, *Eden's Outcasts: The Story of Lousia May Alcott and Her Father*
2005	Mark Stevens and Annalyn Swan, *De Kooning: An American Master*	2009	Jon Meacham, *American Lion: Andrew Jackson in the White House*
2006	Kai Bird and Martin J. Sherwin, *American Prometheus: The Triumph and Tragedy of J. Robert Oppenheimer*	2010	T.J. Stiles, *The First Tycoon: The Epic Life of Cornelius Vanderbilt*

Note: 1. Awarded posthumously. **Source:** Columbia University. www.pulitzer.org

The Pulitzer Prize for History, 1917–2010

Year	Author, Title	Year	Author, Title
1917	J.J. Jusserand, *With Americans of Past and Present Days*	1948	Bernard DeVoto, *Across the Wide Missouri*
1918	James Ford Rhodes, *A History of the Civil War*	1949	Roy Franklin Nichols, *The Disruption of American Democracy*
1920	Justin H. Smith, *The War with Mexico*	1950	Oliver W. Larkin, *Art and Life in America*
1921	William Sowden Sims, with Burton J. Hendrick, *The Victory at Sea*	1951	R. Carlyle Buley, *The Old Northwest*
		1952	Oscar Handlin, *The Uprooted*
1922	James Truslow Adams, *The Founding of New England*	1953	George Dangerfield, *The Era of Good Feelings*
1923	Charles Warren, *The Supreme Court in United States History*	1954	Bruce Catton, *A Stillness at Appomattox*
		1955	Paul Horgan, *Great River: The Rio Grande in North American History*
1924	Charles Howard McIlwain, *The American Revolution*	1956	Richard Hofstadter, *The Age of Reform*
1925	Frederic L. Paxson, *A History of the American Frontier*	1957	George F. Kennan, *Russia Leaves the War: Soviet American Relations, 1917–1920*
1926	Edward Channing, *The History of the United States*	1958	Bray Hammond, *Banks and Politics in America*
1927	Samuel Flagg Bemis, *Pinckney's Treaty*	1959	Leonard D. White, with Miss Jean Schneider, *The Republican Era: 1869–1901*
1928	Vernon Louis Parrington, *Main Currents in American Thought*	1960	Margaret Leech, *In the Days of McKinley*
1929	Fred Albert Shannon, *The Organization and Administration of the Union Army, 1861–1865*	1961	Herbert Feis, *Between War and Peace: The Potsdam Conference*
1930	Claude H. Van Tyne, *The War of Independence*	1962	Lawrence H. Gipson, *The Triumphant Empire: Thunder Clouds in the West*
1931	Bernadotte E. Schmitt, *The Coming of the War: 1914*	1963	Constance McLaughlin Green, *Washington, Village and Capital, 1800–1878*
1932	John J. Pershing, *My Experiences in the World War*	1964	Sumner Chilton Powell, *Puritan Village*
1933	Frederick J. Turner, *The Significance of Sections in American History*	1965	Irwin Unger, *The Greenback Era*
		1966	Perry Miller[1], *Life of the Mind in America*
1934	Herbert Agar, *The People's Choice*	1967	William H. Goetzmann, *Exploration and Empire*
1935	Charles McLean Andrews, *The Colonial Period of American History*	1968	Bernard Bailyn, *The Ideological Origins of the American Revolution*
1936	Andrew C. McLaughlin, *The Constitutional History of the United States*	1969	Leonard W. Levy, *Origins of the Fifth Amendment*
1937	Van Wyck Brooks, *The Flowering of New England*	1970	Dean Acheson, *Present at the Creation*
1938	Paul Herman Buck, *The Road to Reunion 1856–1900*	1971	James MacGregor Burns, *Roosevelt, The Soldier of Freedom*
1939	Frank Luther Mott, *A History of American Magazines*	1972	Carl N. Degler, *Neither Black Nor White*
		1973	Michael Kammen, *People of Paradox*
1940	Carl Sandburg, *Abraham Lincoln: The War Years*	1974	Daniel J. Boorstin, *The Americans: The Democratic Experience*
1941	Marcus Lee Hansen, *The Atlantic Migration, 1607–1860*	1975	Dumas Malone, *Jefferson and His Time*
		1976	Paul Horgan, *Lamy of Santa Fe*
1942	Margaret Leech, *Reveille in Washington*	1977	David M. Potter[1] *The Impending Crisis*
1943	Esther Forbes, *Paul Revere and the World He Lived In*	1978	Alfred D. Chandler Jr., *The Visible Hand: The Managerial Revolution in American Business*
1944	Merle Curti, *The Growth of American Thought*	1979	Don E. Fehrenbacher, *The Dred Scott Case*
1945	Stephen Bonsal, *Unfinished Business*	1980	Leon F. Litwack, *Been in the Storm So Long*
1946	Arthur Meier Schlesinger Jr., *The Age of Jackson*	1981	Lawrence A. Cremin, *American Education*
		1982	C. Vann Woodward (ed.), *Mary Chesnut's Civil War*
1947	James Phinney Baxter III, *Scientists Against Time*	1983	Rhys L. Isaac, *The Transformation of Virginia, 1740–1790*
		1985	Thomas K. McCraw, *Prophets of Regulation*

Year	Author, Title	Year	Author, Title
1986	Walter A. McDougall, . . .the Heavens and the Earth	2000	David M. Kennedy, *Freedom From Fear: The American People in Depression and War*
1987	Bernard Bailyn, *Voyagers to the West*		
1988	Robert V. Bruce, *The Launching of Modern American Science 1846–1876*	2001	Joseph P. Ellis, *Founding Brothers: The Revolutionary Generation*
1989	Taylor Branch, *Parting the Waters* James M. McPherson, *Battle Cry of Freedom: The Civil War Era*	2002	Louis Menand, *The Metaphysical Club: A Story of Ideas in America*
		2003	Rick Atkinson, *An Army at Dawn: The War in North Africa, 1942–1943*
1990	Stanley Karnow, *In Our Image*		
1991	Laurel Thatcher Ulrich, *A Midwife's Tale*	2004	Steven Hahn, *A Nation Under Our Feet: Black Political Struggles in the Rural South from Slavery to the Great Migration*
1992	Mark E. Neely Jr., *The Fate of Liberty*		
1993	Gordon S. Wood, *The Radicalism of the American Revolution*	2005	David Hackett Fisher, *Washington's Crossing*
1995	Doris Kearns Goodwin, *No Ordinary Time: Franklin and Eleanor Roosevelt*	2006	David M. Oshinsky, *Polio: An American Story*
1996	Alan Taylor, *William Cooper's Town*		
1997	Jack N. Rakove, *Original Meanings: Politics and Ideas in the Making of the Constitution*	2007	Gene Roberts and Hank Klibanoff, *The Race Beat*
		2008	David Walker Howe, *What God Hath Wrought: The Transformation of America, 1815–1848*
1998	Edward J. Larson, *Summer for the Gods: The Scopes Trial and America's Continuing Debate Over Science and Religion*		
		2009	Annette Gordon-Reed, *The Hemingses of Monticello: An American Family*
1999	Edwin G. Burrows and Mike Wallace, *Gotham: A History of New York City to 1898*	2010	Liaquat Ahamed, *Lords of Finance: The Bankers Who Broke the World*

Notes: No award given in 1919, 1984, or 1994. 1. Awarded posthumously. **Source:** Columbia University. www.pulitzer.org

The Pulitzer Prize for Poetry, 1922–2010

Year	Author, Title	Year	Author, Title
1922	Edward Arlington Robinson, *Collected Poems*	1956	Elizabeth Bishop, *Poems—North & South*
		1957	Richard Wilbur, *Things of This World*
1923	Edna St. Vincent Millay, *The Ballad of the Harp-Weaver; A Few Figs from Thistles; Eight Sonnets in American Poetry, 1922, A Miscellany*	1958	Robert Penn Warren, *Promises: Poems 1954-1956*
		1959	Stanley Kunitz, *Selected Poems 1928–1958*
		1960	W.D. Snodgrass, *Heart's Needle*
1924	Robert Frost, *New Hampshire: A Poem with Notes and Grace Notes*	1961	Phyllis McGinley, *Times Three: Selected Verse From Three Decades*
1925	Edward Arlington Robinson, *The Man Who Died Twice*	1962	Alan Dugan, *Poems*
		1963	William Carlos Williams[1], *Pictures from Breughel*
1926	Amy Lowell[1], *What's O'Clock*		
1927	Leonora Speyer, *Fiddler's Farewell*	1964	Louis Simpson, *At the End of the Open Road*
1928	Edward Arlington Robinson, *Tristram*		
1929	Stephen Vincent Benét, *John Brown's Body*	1965	John Berryman, *77 Dream Songs*
1930	Conrad Aiken, *Selected Poems*	1966	Richard Eberhart, *Selected Poems*
1931	Robert Frost, *Collected Poems*	1967	Anne Sexton, *Live or Die*
1932	George Dillon, *The Flowering Stone*	1968	Anthony Hecht, *The Hard Hours*
1933	Archibald MacLeish, *Conquistador*	1969	George Oppen, *Of Being Numerous*
1934	Robert Hillyer, *Collected Verse*	1970	Richard Howard, *Untitled Subjects*
1935	Audrey Wurdemann, *Bright Ambush*	1971	William S. Merwin, *The Carrier of Ladders*
1936	Robert P. Tristram Coffin, *Strange Holiness*	1972	James Wright , *Collected Poems*
1937	Robert Frost, *A Further Range*	1973	Maxine Kumin, *Up Country*
1938	Marya Zaturenska, *Cold Morning Sky*	1974	Robert Lowell, *The Dolphins*
1939	John Gould Fletcher, *Selected Poems*	1975	Gary Snyder, *Turtle Island*
1940	Mark Van Doren, *Collected Poems*	1976	John Ashberry, *Self-Portrait in a Convex Mirror*
1941	Leonard Bacon, *Sunderland Capture*		
1942	William Rose Benét, *The Dust Which Is God*	1977	James Merrill, *Divine Comedies*
1943	Robert Frost, *A Witness Tree*	1978	Howard Nemerov, *Collected Poems*
1944	Stephen Vincent Benét[1], *Western Star*	1979	Robert Penn Warren, *Now and Then*
1945	Karl Shapiro, *V-Letter and Other Poems*	1980	Donald Justice, *Selected Poems*
1947	Robert Lowell, *Lord Weary's Castle*	1981	James Schuyler, *The Morning of the Poem*
1948	W.H. Auden, *The Age of Anxiety*	1982	Sylvia Plath[1], *The Collected Poems*
1949	Peter Viereck, *Terror and Decorum*	1983	Galway Kinnell, *Selected Poems*
1950	Gwendolyn Brooks, *Annie Allen*	1984	Mary Oliver, *American Primitive*
1951	Carl Sandburg, *Complete Poems*	1985	Carolyn Kizer, *Yin*
1952	Marianne Moore, *Collected Poems*	1986	Henry Taylor, *The Flying Change*
1953	Archibald MacLeish, *Collected Poems 1917–1952*	1987	Rita Dove, *Thomas and Beulah*
		1988	William Meredith, *Partial Accounts: New and Selected Poems*
1954	Theodore Roethke, *The Waking*		
1955	Wallace Stevens, *Collected Poems*	1989	Richard Wilbur, *New and Collected Poems*

Year	Author, Title	Year	Author, Title
1990	Charles Simic, *The World Doesn't End*	2000	C.K. Williams, *Repair*
1991	Mona Van Duyn, *Near Changes*	2001	Stephen Dunn, *Different Hours*
1992	James Tate, *Selected Poems*	2002	Carl Dennis, *Practical Gods*
1993	Louise Glück, *The Wild Iris*	2003	Paul Muldoon, *Moy Sand and Gravel*
1994	Yusef Komunyakaa, *Neon Vernacular*	2004	Franz Wright, *Walking to Martha's Vineyard*
1995	Philip Levine, *Simple Truth*	2005	Ted Kooser, *Delights and Shadows*
1996	Jorie Graham, *The Dream of the Unified Field*	2006	Claudia Emerson, *Late Wife*
		2007	Natasha Trethewey, *Native Guard*
1997	Lisel Mueller, *Alive Together: New and Selected Poems*	2008	Robert Hass, *Time and Materials*
		2009	W. S. Merwin, *The Shadow Series*
1998	Charles Wright, *Black Zodiac*	2010	Rae Armantrout, *Versed*
1999	Mark Strand, *Blizzard of One*		

Note: No award given in 1946. 1. Awarded posthumously. **Source:** Columbia University. www.pulitzer.org

The Pulitzer Prize for General Nonfiction, 1962–2010

Year	Author, Title	Year	Author, Title
1962	Theodore H. White, *The Making of the President, 1960*	1988	Richard Rhodes, *The Making of the Atomic Bomb*
1963	Barbara W. Tuchman, *The Guns of August*	1989	Neil Sheehan, *A Bright and Shining Lie*
1964	Richard Hofstadter, *Anti-Intellectualism in American Life*	1990	Dale Maharidge, Michael Williamson, *And Their Children After Them*
1965	Howard Mumford Jones, *O Strange New World*	1991	Bert Holldobler, Edward O. Wilson, *The Ants*
1966	Edwin Way Teal, *Wandering Through Winter*	1992	Daniel Yergin, *The Prize: The Epic Quest for Oil, Money and Power.*
1967	David Brion Davis, *The Problem of Slavery in Western Culture*	1993	Garry Wills, *Lincoln at Gettysburg*
1968	Will and Ariel Durant, *Rousseau and Revolution*	1994	David Remnick, *Lenin's Tomb: The Last Days of the Soviet Empire*
1969	René Jules Dubos, *So Human An Animal*	1995	Jonathan Weiner, *The Beak of the Finch*
	Norman Mailer, *The Armies of the Night*	1996	Tina Rosenberg, *The Haunted Land*
1970	Erik H. Erikson, *Gandhi's Truth*	1997	Richard Kluger, *Ashes to Ashes*
1971	John Toland, *The Rising Sun*	1998	Jared Diamond, *Guns, Germs, and Steel: The Fates of Human Societies*
1972	Barbara W. Tuchman, *Stilwell and the American Experience in China, 1911–45*	1999	John McPhee, *Annals of the Former World*
1973	Robert Coles, *Children of Crisis, vols.2 & 3*	2000	John W. Dower, *Embracing Defeat: Japan in the Wake of World War II*
	Frances Fitzgerald, *Fire in the Lake*	2001	Herbert P. Bix, *Hirohito and the Making of Modern Japan*
1974	Ernest Becker[1], *The Denial of Death*		
1975	Annie Dillard, *Pilgrim at Tinker Creek*	2002	Diane McWhorter, *Carry Me Home: Birmingham, Alabama, the Climactic Battle of the Civil Rights Revolution*
1976	Robert N. Butler, *Why Survive? Being Old in America*		
1977	William N. Warner, *Beautiful Swimmers*	2003	Samantha Power, *"A Problem From Hell": America and the Age of Genocide*
1978	Carl Sagan, *The Dragons of Eden*		
1979	Edward O. Wilson, *On Human Nature*	2004	Anne Applebaum, *Gulag: A History*
1980	Douglas R. Hofstadter, *Gödel, Escher, Bach: an Eternal Golden Braid*	2005	Steve Coll, *Ghost Wars*
		2006	Caroline Elkins, *Imperial Reckoning: The Untold Story of Britain's Gulag in Kenya*
1981	Carl E. Schorske, *Fin-de Siècle Vienna: Politics and Culture*		
		2007	Lawrence Wright, *The Looming Tower*
1982	Tracy Kidder, *The Soul of A New Machine*	2008	Saul Friedländer, *The Years of Extermination: Nazi Germany and the Jews*
1983	Susan Sheehan, *Is There No Place on Earth for Me?*		
1984	Paul Starr, *The Social Transformation of American Medicine*	2009	Douglas A. Blackmon, *Slavery By Another Name: The Re-Enslavement of Black Americans from the Civil War to World War II*
1985	Studs Terkel, *The Good War*		
1986	Joseph Lelyveld, *Move Your Shadow*		
	J. Anthony Lukas, *Common Ground*	2010	David E. Hoffman, *The Dead Hand: The Untold Story of the Cold War Arms Race and Its Dangerous Legacy*
1987	David K. Shipler, *Arab and Jew*		

Note: 1. Awarded posthumously. **Source:** Columbia University. www.pulitzer.org

The Pulitzer Prize for Music, 1943–2010

Year	Author, Title	Year	Author, Title
1943	William Schuman, Secular Cantata No. 2, A Free Song	1977	Richard Wernick, Visions of Terror and Wonder
1944	Howard Hanson, Symphony No. 4, Opus 34	1978	Michael Colgrass, Deja Vu for Percussion Quartet and Orchestra
1945	Aaron Copland, Appalachian Spring	1979	Joseph Schwantner, Aftertones of Infinity
1946	Leo Sowerby, The Canticle of the Sun	1980	David Del Tredici, In Memory of a Summer Day
1947	Charles Ives, Symphony No. 3	1981	No award
1948	Walter Piston, Symphony No. 3	1982	Roger Sessions, Concerto for Orchestra
1949	Virgil Thomson, Music for the film, Louisiana Story	1983	Ellen Taaffe Zwilich, Symphony No. 1
1950	Gian-Carlo Menotti, Music for the opera The Consul	1984	Bernard Rands, "Canti del Sole" for Tenor and Orchestra
1951	Douglas S. Moore, Music for the opera, Giants in the Earth	1985	Stephen Albert, Symphony RiverRun
1952	Gail Kubik, Symphony Concertante	1986	George Perle, Wind Quintet IV
1953	No award	1987	John Harbison, The Flight Into Egypt
1954	Quincy Porter, Concerto for Two Pianos and Orchestra	1988	William Bolcom, 12 New Etudes for Piano
1955	Gian-Carlo Menotti, The Saint of Bleecker Street (opera)	1989	Roger Reynolds, Whispers Out of Time
		1990	Mel Powell, Duplicates: A Concerto for Two Pianos and Orchestra
1956	Ernest Toch, Symphony No. 3	1991	Shulammit Ran, Symphony
1957	Norman Dello Joio, Meditations on Ecclesiastes	1992	Wayne Peterson, The Face of the Night, The Heart of the Dark
1958	Samuel Barber, Vanessa (opera)	1993	Christopher Rouse, Trombone Concerto
1959	John LaMontaine, Concerto for Piano and Orchestra	1994	Gunther Schuller, Of Reminiscences and Reflections
1960	Elliott Carter, Second String Quartet	1995	Morton Gould, Stringmusic
1961	Walter Piston, Symphony No. 7	1996	George Walker, Lilacs
1962	Robert Ward, The Crucible (opera)	1997	Wynton Marsalis, Blood on the Fields
1963	Samuel Barber, Piano Concerto No. 1	1998	Aaron Jay Kernis, String Quartet No.2
1964	No award	1999	Melinda Wagner, Concerto for Flute, Strings, and Percussion
1965	No award		
1966	Leslie Bassett, Variations for Orchestra	2000	Lewis Spratalan, Life is a Dream, Opera in Three Acts: Act II, Convert Version
1967	Leon Kirchner, Quartet No. 3		
1968	George Crumb, Echoes of Time and the River orchestral suite	2001	John Corigliano, Symphony No. 2 for String Orchestra
1969	Karel Husa, String Quartet No. 3	2002	Henry Brant, Ice Field
1970	Charles Wuorinen, Time's Encomium	2003	John Adams, On the Transmigration of Souls
1971	Mario Davidovsky, Synchronisms No. 6 for Piano and Electronic Sound	2004	Paul Moravec, Tempest Fantasy
		2005	Steven Stucky, Second Concerto for Orchestra
1972	Jacob Druckman, Windows		
1973	Elliott Carter, String Quartet No. 3	2006	Yehudi Wyner, Piano Concerto: 'Chiavi in Mano'
1974	Donald Martino, Notturno (chamber music)		
1975	Dominick Argento, From the Diary of Virginia Woolf	2007	Ornette Coleman, Sound Grammar
		2008	David Lang, The Little Match Girl Passion
1976	Ned Rorem, Air Music: Ten Etudes for Orchestra	2009	Steve Reich, Double Sextet
		2010	Jennifer Higdon, Violin Concerto

Source: Columbia University. www.pulitzer.org

Pulitzer Special Citations

Year	Recipient	Year	Recipient
SPECIAL CITATIONS IN LETTERS		**SPECIAL CITATIONS IN MUSIC**	
1957	Kenneth Roberts, for his historical novels	1944	Richard Rodgers and Oscar Hammerstein II, Oklahoma!
1960	Garret Mattingly, The Defeat of the Spanish Armada	1974	Roger Sessions, Lifetime achievement
		1976	Scott Joplin[1], Contributions to American music
1961	Publishers, The American Heritage Picture History of the Civil War		
1973	James Flexner, George Washington, vols. 1–4	1982	Milton Babbitt, Lifetime achivement
1977	Alex Haley, Roots	1985	William Schuman, Lifetime achievement
1978	E.B. White, Lifetime achievement	1998	George Gershwin[1], Contributions to American music
1984	Theodore Seuss Geisel (Dr. Seuss), Lifetime achievement	1999	Edward "Duke" Ellington[1], Contributions to American music
1992	Art Speigelman, Maus	2008	Bob Dylan, profound impact on American culture
		2010	Hank Williams, Lifetime Achievement as a Musician

Note: 1. Awarded posthumously. **Source:** Columbia University. www.pulitzer.org

The Nobel Prizes

Nobel Peace Prizes

1901   Jean-Henri Dunant (Switzerland) Founder of International Committee of the Red Cross; **Frédéric Passy** (France) Founder of first French peace society.
1902   Elie Ducommun (Switzerland) Director of Permanent International Peace Bureau; **Charles Albert Gobat** (Switzerland) Secretary-General of Inter-Parliamentary Union.
1903   Sir William R. Cremer (U.K.) Founder of International Arbitration League.
1904   Institute of International Law Founded in 1873.
1905   Baroness Bertha S.F. von Suttner (Austria) Author of antiwar novel *Lay Down Your Arms*.
1906   Theodore Roosevelt (U.S.) President; mediated Russo-Japanese War.
1907   Ernesto T. Moneta (Italy) Founder of Lombard League of Peace; **Louis Renault** (France) Professor of International Law at Hague Peace Conference.
1908   Klas P. Arnoldson (Sweden) Founder of Swedish Peace and Arbitration League; **Fredrik Bajer** (Denmark) Writer and peace activist, Danish parliament member.
1909   Auguste M.F. Beernaert (Belgium) Prime minister and peace activist; **Paul H.B.B. D'Estournelles de Constant** (Baron Constant de Rebecque) (France) Founder of French parliamentary group for voluntary arbitration.
1910   Permanent International Peace Bureau Founded 1891.
1911   Tobias M.C. Asser (Netherlands) A founder of Institute of International Law; **Alfred H. Fried** (Austria) Journalist and founder of many peace publications.
1912   Elihu Root (U.S.) Former Secretary of state and originator of several arbitration treaties.
1913   Henri Lafontaine (Belgium) President of Permanent International Peace Bureau in Bern.
1914–1916   No awards given.
1917   International Committee of the Red Cross Founded 1863.
1919   Woodrow Wilson (U.S.) President; instrumental in establishing League of Nations.
1920   Léon Victor A. Bourgeois (France) Drafted framework for League of Nations.
1921   Karl H. Branting (Sweden) Prime minister and pacifist; **Christian L. Lange** (Norway) A founder of Inter-Parliamentary Union.
1922   Fridtjof Nansen (Norway) Scientist; explorer; originator of "Nansen passports" for refugees.
1925   Sir Austen Chamberlain (U.K.) Foreign secretary; worked for Locarno Pact; **Charles G. Dawes** (U.S.) Vice president; drafted Dawes Plan settling German reparations issue.
1926   Aristide Briand (France) and **Gustav Stresemann** (Germany) Creators of Locarno Pact.
1927   Ferdinand Buisson (France) Human rights advocate; **Ludwig Quidde** (Germany) Peace activist.
1928   No award.
1929   Frank B. Kellogg (U.S.) Former Secretary of state; a creator of Kellogg-Briand Pact.
1930   L.O. Nathan Söderblom (Sweden) Archbishop; leader in the ecumenical movement.
1931   Jane Addams (U.S.) President of Women's International League for Peace and Freedom; **Nicholas M. Butler** (U.S.) Promoter of Kellogg-Briand Pact.
1933   Sir Norman Angell (Ralph Lane) (U.K.) Author of antiwar book *The Great Illusion*.
1934   Arthur Henderson (U.K.) President of League of Nations World Disarmament Conference 1932.
1935   Carol von Ossietzky (Germany) Journalist and pacifist.

1936   Carlos Saavedra Lamas (Argentina) Secretary of state; president of League of Nations and mediator in conflict between Paraguay and Bolivia.
1937   Lord Edgar Algernon R.G. Cecil (U.K.) An architect of League of Nations.
1938   Nansen International Office for Refugees Founded 1921.
1939–1943   No awards given.
1944   International Committee of the Red Cross Founded 1863.
1945   Cordell Hull (U.S.) Former Secretary of state; instrumental in creating United Nations.
1946   Emily G. Balch (U.S.) Leader of international women's movement for peace; **John R. Mott** (U.S.) Leader of Christian ecumenical movement.
1947   The Friends Service Council (U.K.) and **The American Friends Service Committee** (U.S.) (The Quakers)
1948   No award
1949   Lord John Boyd Orr (U.K.) Nutritionist; worked to eliminate world hunger.
1950   Ralph Bunche (U.S.) Mediator in Middle East war.
1951   Léon Jouhaux (France) Advocate of improved working-class conditions.
1952   Albert Schweitzer (France) Missionary surgeon/founder of Lambarene Hospital in Africa.
1953   George C. Marshall (U.S.) General; originator of Marshall Plan, which provided recovery loans and technical aid to Europe after World War II.
1954   Office of the U.N. High Commissioner for Refugees for their aid work for European refugees.
1955–1956   No awards given.
1957   Lester B. Pearson (Canada) Former Secretary of state; worked to resolve Suez Canal Crisis of 1956.
1958   Georges Pire (Belgium) Dominican priest and leader of relief organization for refugees, l'Europe du Coeur au Service du Monde.
1959   Philip J. Noel-Baker (U.K.) Lifelong worker for international peace through disarmament.
1960   Albert J. Lutuli (South Africa) President of the African National Congress; led peaceful resistance to apartheid.
1961   Dag Hammarskjöld (Sweden) United Nations Secretary General; worked for peace in the Congo.
1962   Linus C. Pauling (U.S.) Chemist; warned against dangers of radioactive fallout in nuclear weapons testing and war.
1963   International Committee of the Red Cross and League of Red Cross Societies
1964   Martin Luther King, Jr. (U.S.) Leader of American civil rights movement.
1965   United Nations Children's Fund (UNICEF).
1966–1967   No awards given.
1968   René Cassin (France) President of European Court for Human Rights.
1969   International Labour Organization United Nations agency involved in improving worldwide working and social conditions.
1970   Norman Borlaug (U.S.) Agricultural scientist and developer of high-yield grains credited with helping to alleviate world hunger.
1971   Willy Brandt (Federal Republic of Germany) Chancellor; champion of East-West détente.
1972   No award
1973   Henry A. Kissinger (U.S.) Secretary of state and **Le Duc Tho** (Democratic Republic of Viet Nam) Foreign minister; negotiated Vietnam cease-fire agreement. Mr. Tho declined the prize.

1974 Seán MacBride (Ireland) President of International Peace Bureau and United Nations commissioner for Namibia; **Eisaku Sato** (Japan) Prime minister of Japan and campaigner against nuclear weapons.

1975 Andrei Sakharov (USSR) Nuclear physicist and human rights campaigner.

1976 Betty Williams and Mairead Corrigan (Northern Ireland) Founder of Northern Ireland Peace Movement.

1977 Amnesty International for human rights work.

1978 Anwar el-Sadat (Egypt) President, and **Menachem Begin** (Israel) Prime minister; negotiated Israeli-Egyptian peace accord.

1979 Mother Teresa (India) Worker for the poor in Calcutta.

1980 Adolfo Pérez Esquivel (Argentina) Architect, sculptor, and human rights leader.

1981 Office of the United Nations High Commissioner for Refugees for aid work with Asian refugees.

1982 Alva Myrdal (Sweden) and **Alfonso Garcia Robles** (Mexico) Campaigners for disarmament.

1983 Lech Walesa (Poland) Leader of the Solidarity trade union federation.

1984 Desmond M. Tutu (South Africa) Bishop of Johannesburg; a leader of the anti-apartheid movement.

1985 International Physicians for the Prevention of Nuclear War Organization jointly headed by a Soviet and an American doctor.

1986 Elie Wiesel (U.S.) Writer on the Holocaust and Nazi death camp survivor.

1987 Oscar Arias Sánchez (Costa Rica) President of Costa Rica; creator of a peace plan for Central America.

1988 United Nations Peacekeeping Forces

1989 Dalai Lama (Tibet) Exiled religious and political leader of Tibet for his nonviolent campaign to end China's domination of his country.

1990 Mikhail Gorbachev (USSR) President of the Soviet Union, "for his role in the peace process which today characterizes important parts of the international community."

1991 Aung San Suu Kyi (Myanmar), leader of opposition National League for Democracy (under house arrest at the time) "for her nonviolent struggle for democracy and human rights."

1992 Rigoberta Menchú (Guatemala) A Quiché Indian and an outspoken advocate of human rights during the civil war in her country.

1993 Pres. F. W. de Klerk of South Africa and **Nelson Mandela**, black leader of the opposition African National Congress, for negotiating an end to the apartheid policies of the state and their collaboration on the formation of a democracy not based on race.

1994 Yitzhak Rabin (Israel) Prime Minister, **Shimon Peres** (Israel) Foreign Minister, and **Yasir Arafat,** leader of the Palestinian Liberation Organization, for negotiating the historic peace pact allowing Palestinian self-rule in the West Bank and Gaza Strip.

1995 Joseph Rotblat (U.K. b. Poland) and his **Pugwash Conferences on Science and World Affairs.** A former Manhattan Project physicist, Rotblat spent 40 years campaigning to eliminate nuclear weapons.

1996 Bishop Carlos Ximenes Belo (Australia, b. East Timor) and **Jose Ramos-Horta** (East Timor) for "sustained and self-sacrificing contributions for a small but oppressed people" in East Timor, a former Portuguese colony invaded by Indonesia in the 1970s.

1997 The International Campaign to Ban Landmines and its 47-year-old coordinator, **Jody Williams** (U.S.), for their efforts to outlaw land mines worldwide. The Nobel committee admitted that it was openly trying to persuade the U.S. to sign the international treaty banning landmines.

1998 John Hume (Ireland) and **David Trimble** (Ireland) the leaders of the largest Roman Catholic and Protestant political parties in Northern Ireland, who brought about the April 1998 peace agreement.

1999 Doctors Without Borders (Médecins Sans Frontières), whose independence and rapid intervention have helped "to form bodies of public opinion opposed to violations and abuses of power."

2000 Kim Dae Jung, President of South Korea, "for his work for democracy and human rights in South Korea and in East Asia in general, and for peace and reconciliation with North Korea in particular."

2001 United Nations and its Secretary General **Kofi Annan,** (Ghana), in equal portions, for "their work for a better organized and more peaceful world."

2002 Jimmy Carter, (U.S.) "for his decades of untiring effort to find peaceful solutions to international conflicts, to advance democracy and human rights, and to promote economic and social development." In presenting the award to Carter, the Nobel Committee expressly stated its opposition to the Bush Administration's rush to war in the Persian Gulf.

2003 Shirin Ebadi (Iran), "for her efforts for democracy and human rights," especially in the struggle for the rights of women and children.

2004 Wangari Maathai (Kenya), "for her contribution to sustainable development, democracy and peace."

2005 International Atomic Energy Agency (IAEA) and **Mohamed El Barodei** (Egypt) "for their efforts to prevent nuclear energy from being used for military purposes and to ensure that nuclear energy for peaceful purposes is used in the safest possible way."

2006 Muhammad Yunus (Bangladesh) and **Grameen Bank** "for their efforts to create economic and social development from below."

2007 Intergovernmental Panel on Climate Change and **Albert Arnold Gore, Jr.** (U.S.) "for their efforts to build up and disseminate greater knowledge about man-made climate change."

2008 Martti Ahtisaari, 71, (Finland) for three decades of work as an international mediator; he has "figured prominently in endeavors to resolve several serious and long-lasting conflicts."

2009 Barack Hussein Obama, (U.S.), "for his extraordinary efforts to strengthen international diplomacy and cooperation between peoples."

Nobel Prizes in Physiology or Medicine

1901 Emil A. von Behring (Germany) Marburg Univ. "for his work on serum therapy, especially its application against diphtheria, by which he has opened a new road in the domain of medical science and thereby placed in the hands of the physician a victorious weapon against illness and deaths."

1902 Sir Ronald Ross (U.K.) University College "for his work on malaria, by which he has shown how it enters the organism and thereby has laid the foundation for successful research on this disease and methods of combating it."

1903 Niels R. Finsen (Denmark) Finsen Medical Light Institute "in recognition of his contribution to the treatment of diseases, especially lupus vulgaris, with concentrated light radiation, whereby he has opened a new avenue for medical science."

1904 Ivan P. Pavlov (Russia) Military Medical Academy "in recognition of his work on the physiology of digestion."

1905 Robert Koch (Germany) Institute for Infectious Diseases "for his investigations and discoveries in relation to tuberculosis."

1906 Camillio Golgi (Italy) Pavia Univ., and **Santiago Ramon Y Cajal** (Spain) Madrid Univ. for "their work on the structure of the nervous system."

1907 Charles L.A. Laveran (France) Institute Pasteur "in recognition of his work on the role played by protozoa in causing diseases."

1908 Il'ja I. Mecnikov (Russia) Institut Pasteur (Paris), and **Paul Ehrlich** (Germany) Goettingen Univ. and Royal Institute for Experimental Therapy "in recognition of their work on immunity."

1909 Emil R. Kocher (Switzerland) Berne Univ. "for his work on the physiology, pathology, and surgery for the thyroid gland."

1910 Albrecht Kossel (Germany) Heidelberg Univ. "in recognition of the contributions to our knowledge of cell chemistry made through his work on proteins, including the nucleic substances."

1911 Allvar Gullstrand (Sweden) Uppsala Univ. "for his work on the dioptrics of the eye."

1912 Alexis Carrel (France) Rockefeller Institute for Medical Research (New York) "in recognition of his work on vascular suture and the transplantation of blood vessels and organs."

1913 Charles R. Richet (France) Sorbonne Univ. "in recognition of his work on anaphylaxis."

1914 Robert Bárány (Austria) Vienna Univ. "for his work on the physiology and pathology of the vestibular apparatus."

1915–1918 No awards

1919 Jules Bordet (Belgium) Brussels Univ. "for his discoveries relating to immunity."

1920 Schack A.S. Krogh (Denmark) Copenhagen Univ. "for his discoveries of the capillary motor regulating mechanism."

1921 No award

1922 Sir Archibald V. Hill (U.K.) London Univ. "for his discovery relating to the production of heat in the muscle"; **Otto F. Meyerhof** (Germany) Kiel Univ. "for his discovery of the fixed relationship between the consumption of oxygen and the metabolism of lactic acid in the muscle."

1923 Sir Frederick G. Banting (Canada) Toronto Univ. and **John J.R. Macleod** (Canada) Toronto Univ. "for the discovery of insulin."

1924 Willem Einthoven (Netherlands) Leyden Univ. "for his discovery of the mechanism of the electrocardiogram."

1925 No award

1926 Johannes A.G. Fibiger (Denmark) Copenhagen Univ. "for his discovery of the Spiroptera carcinoma."

1927 Julius Wagner-Jauegg (Austria) Vienna Univ. "for his discovery of the therapeutic value of malaria inoculation in the treatment of dementia paralytica."

1928 Charles J.H. Nicolle (France) Institut Pasteur "for his work on typhus."

1929 Christiaan Eijkman (Netherlands) Utrecht Univ. "for his discovery of the antineuritic vitamin"; **Sir Frederick G. Hopkins** (U.K.) Cambridge Univ. "for his discovery of the growth-stimulating vitamins."

1930 Karl Landsteiner (Austria) Rockefeller Institute of Medical Research (New York) "for his discovery of human blood groups."

1931 Otto H. Warburg (Germany) Kaiser-Wilhelm Institut "for his discovery of the nature and mode of action of the respiratory enzyme."

1932 Sir Charles S. Sherrington (U.K.) Oxford Univ. and **Lord Edgar D. Adrian** (U.K.) Cambridge Univ. "for their discoveries regarding the functions of neurons."

1933 Thomas H. Morgan (U.S.) California Institute of Technology "for his discoveries concerning the role played by the chromosome in heredity."

1934 George H. Whipple (U.S.) Rochester Univ., **George R. Minot** (U.S.) Harvard Univ., and **William P. Murphy** (U.S.) Harvard Univ. "for their discoveries concerning liver therapy in cases of anaemia."

1935 Hans Spemann (Germany) Univ. of Freiburg "for his discovery of the organizer effect in embryonic development."

1936 Sir Henry H. Dale (U.K.) National Institute for Medical Research, and **Otto Loewi** (Austria) Graz Univ. "for their discoveries relating to chemical transmission of nerve impulses."

1937 Albert von Szent-Györgyi Nagyrapolt (Hungary) Szeged Univ. "for his discoveries in connection with the biological combustion processes, with special reference to vitamin C and the catalysis of fumaric acid."

1938 Corneille J.F. Heymans (Belgium) Ghent Univ. "for the discovery of the role played by the sinus and aortic mechanisms in the regulation of respiration."

1939 Gerhard Domagk (Germany) Munster Univ. for "discovery of the antibacterial effects of prontosil."

1940–1942 No awards given.

1943 Henrik C.P. Dam (Denmark) Polytechnic Institut "for his discovery of vitamin K"; **Edward A. Doisy** (U.S.) St. Louis Univ. "for his discovery of the chemical nature of vitamin K."

1944 Joseph Erlanger (U.S.) Washington Univ. and **Herbert S. Gasser** (U.S.) Rockefeller Institute for Medical Research "for their discoveries relating to the highly differentiated functions of single nerve fibers."

1945 Sir Alexander Fleming (U.K.) London Univ., **Sir Ernst B. Chain** (U.K.) Oxford Univ., and **Lord Howard W. Florey** (U.K.) Oxford Univ. "for their discovery of penicillin and its curative effect in various infectious diseases."

1946 Hermann J. Muller (U.S.) Indiana Univ. "for his discovery of the production of mutations by means of X-ray irradiation."

1947 Carl F. Cori (U.S.) Washington Univ. and his wife **Gerty T. Cori** (U.S.) Washington Univ. "for their discovery of the course of the catalytic conversion of glycogen"; **Bernardo A. Houssay** (Argentina) Institute of Biology and Experimental Medicine "for his discovery of the part played by the hormone of the anterior pituitary lobe in the metabolism of sugar."

1948 Paul H. Müller (Switzerland) Laboratory of the J.R. Geigy Dye-Factory Co. "for his discovery of the high efficiency of DDT as a contact poison against several arthropods."

1949 Walter R. Hess (Switzerland) Zurich Univ. "for his discovery of the functional organization of the interbrain as a coordinator of the activities of the internal organs; **Antonio Caetano de Abreu F.E. Moniz** (Portugal) Univ. of Lisbon "for his discovery of the therapeutic value of leucotomy in certain psychoses."

1950 Edward C. Kendall (U.S.) Mayo Clinic, **Tadeus Reichstein** (Switzerland) Basel Univ., and **Philip S. Hench** (U.S.) Mayo Clinic "for their discoveries relating to the hormones of the adrenal cortex, their structure, and biological effects."

1951 Max Theiler (Union of South Africa) Laboratories Division of Medicine and Public Health, Rockefeller Foundation (New York) "for his discoveries concerning yellow fever and how to combat it."

1952 Selman A. Waksman (U.S.) Rutgers Univ. "for his discovery of streptomycin, the first antibiotic effective against tuberculosis."

1953 Sir Hans A. Krebs (U.K., b. Germany) Sheffield Univ. "for his discovery of the citric acid cycle"; **Fritz A. Lipmann** (U.S., b. Germany) Harvard Medical School and Massachusetts General Hospital "for his discovery of coenzyme A and its importance for intermediary metabolism."

1954 John F. Enders (U.S.) Harvard Medical School and Research Division of Infectious Diseases, Children's Medical Center; **Thomas H. Weller** (U.S.) Research Division of Infectious Diseases, Children's Medical Center; and **Frederick C. Robbins** (U.S.) Western Reserve Univ. "for their discovery of the ability of poliomyelitis viruses to grow in cultures of various types of tissue."

1955   Axel H.T. Theorell (Sweden) Nobel Medical Institute "for his discoveries concerning the nature and mode of action of oxidation enzymes."

1956   Andre F. Cournand (U.S., b. France) Cardio-Pulmonary Laboratory, Columbia Univ. Division. Bellevue Hospital; **Werner Forssman** (Germany) Mainz Univ. and Bad Kreuznach; and **Dickinson W. Richards** (U.S.) Columbia Univ. "for their discoveries concerning heart catheterization and pathological changes in the circulatory system."

1957   Daniel Bovet (Italy, b. Switzerland) Chief Institute of Public Health "for his discoveries relating to synthetic compounds that inhibit the action of certain body substances, and especially their action on the vascular system and the skeletal muscles."

1958   George W. Beadle (U.S.) California Institute of Technology, and **Edward L. Tatum** (U.S.) Rockefeller Institute for Medical Research "for their discovery that genes act by regulating definite chemical events;" **Joshua Lederberg** (U.S.) Wisconsin Univ. "for his discoveries concerning genetic recombination and the organization of the genetic material of bacteria."

1959   Severo Ochoa (U.S.) New York Univ. College of Medicine, and **Arthur Kornberg** (U.S.) Stanford Univ. "for their discovery of the mechanisms in the biological synthesis of ribonucleic acid and deoxyribonucleic acid."

1960   Sir Frank M. Burnet (Australia) Walter and Eliza Hall Institute for Medical Research, and **Sir Peter B. Medawar** (U.K.) Univ. College "for discovery of acquired immunological tolerance."

1961   Georg von Békésy (U.S., b. Hungary) Harvard Univ. "for his discoveries of the physical mechanism of stimulation within the cochlea."

1962   Francis H.C. Crick (U.K.) Institute of Molecular Biology, **James D. Watson** (U.S.) Harvard Univ., and **Maurice H.F. Wilkins** (U.K.) University of London "for their discoveries concerning the molecular structure of nuclear acids and its significance for information transfer in living material."

1963   Sir John E. Eccles (Australia) Australian National Univ. **Sir Alan L. Hodgkin** (U.K.) Cambridge Univ., and **Sir Andrew F. Huxley** (U.K.) Univ. of London for their discoveries concerning the ionic mechanisms involved in excitation and inhibition in the peripheral and central portions of the nerve cell membrane."

1964   Konrad Block (U.S., b. Germany) Harvard Univ. and **Feodor Lymen** (Germany) Max-Planck-Institut fur Zellchemie "for their discoveries concerning the mechanism and regulation of the cholesterol and fatty acid metabolism."

1965   Francois Jacob (France), **André Lwoff** (France), and **Jacques Monod** (France), all from the Institut Pasteur "for their discoveries concerning genetic control of enzyme and virus synthesis."

1966   Peyton Rous (U.S.) Rockefeller Univ. "for his discovery of tumor-inducing viruses"; **Charles B. Huggins** (U.S.) Ben May Laboratory for Cancer Research, Univ. of Chicago "for his discoveries concerning hormonal treatment of prostatic cancer."

1967   Ragnar Granit (Sweden, b. Finland) Karolinska Institutet, **Haldan K. Hartline** (U.S.) Rockefeller Univ., and **George Wald** (U.S.) Harvard Univ. "for their discoveries concerning the primary physiological and chemical visual processes in the eye."

1968   Robert W. Holley (U.S.) Cornell Univ., **Har G. Khorana** (U.S., b. India) Univ. of Wisconsin, and **Marshall W. Nirenberg** (U.S.) National Institutes of Health "for their interpretation of the genetic code and its functions in protein synthesis."

1969   Max Delbrück (U.S., b. Germany) California

Institute of Technology, **Alfred D. Hershey** (U.S.) Carnegie Institution of Washington, and **Salvador Luria** (U.S., b. Italy) M.I.T. for their discoveries concerning the replication mechanism and the genetic structure of viruses."

1970   Sir Bernard Katz (U.K.) University College, **Ulf von Euler** (Sweden) Karolinska Institutet, and **Julius Axelrod** (U.S.) National Institutes of Health "for their discoveries concerning the humoral transmittors in the nerve terminals and the mechanism for their storage, release, and inactivation."

1971   Earl W. Sutherland, Jr. (U.S.) Vanderbilt Univ. "for his discoveries concerning the mechanisms of the action of hormones."

1972   Gerald M. Edelman (U.S.) Rockefeller Univ. and **Rodney R. Porter** (U.K.) Oxford Univ. "for their discoveries concerning the chemical structure of antibodies."

1973   Karl von Frisch (W. Germany) Zoologisches Institut der Universitat Munchen; **Konrad Lorenz** (Austria) Osterreichische Akademie der Wissenschaften, Institut fur vergleichende Verhaltensforschung, and **Nikolaas Tinbergen** (U.K.) University Museum for their discoveries concerning organization and elicitation of individual and social behavior patterns."

1974   Albert Claude (Belgium) Université Catholique de Louvain, **Christian de Duve** (Belgium) Rockefeller Univ. (New York), and **George E. Palade** (U.S., b. Romania) Yale Univ. "for their discoveries concerning the structural and functional organization of the cell."

1975   David Baltimore (U.S.) M.I.T., **Renato Dulbecco** (U.S., b. Italy) Imperial Cancer Research Fund Laboratory (London), and **Howard M. Temin** (U.S.) Univ. of Wisconsin "for their discoveries concerning the interaction between tumor viruses and the genetic material of the cell."

1976   Baruch S. Blumberg (U.S.) Institute for Cancer Research, and **D. Carleton Gajdusek** (U.S.) National Institutes of Health "for their discoveries concerning new mechanism for the origin and dissemination of infectious diseases."

1977   Roger Guillemin (U.S., b. France) Salk Institute, and **Andrew V. Schally** (U.S., b. Poland) Veterans Administration Hospital, New Orleans "for their discoveries concerning the peptide hormone production of the brain"; **Rosalyn Yalow** (U.S.) Veterans Administration Hospital, Bronx "for the development of radioimmunoassays of peptide hormones."

1978   Werner Arber (Switzerland) Biozentrum der Universitat, **Daniel Nathans** (U.S.) John Hopkins Univ., and **Hamilton O. Smith** (U.S.) John Hopkins Univ. "for the discovery of restriction enzymes and their application to problems of molecular genetics."

1979   Alan M. Cormack (U.S., b. South Africa) Tufts Univ., and **Sir Godfrey N. Hounsfield** (U.K.) Central Research Laboratories, EMI, "for the development of computer assisted tomography."

1980   Baruj Benacerraf (U.S., b. Venezuela) Harvard Medical School; **Jean Dausset** (France) Université de Paris, Laboratoire Immuno-Hemetologie; and **George D. Snell** (U.S.) Jackson Laboratory "for their discoveries concerning genetically determined structures on the cell surface that regulate immunological reactions."

1981   Roger W. Sperry (U.S.) California Institute of Technology "for his discoveries concerning the functional specialization of the cerebral hemispheres"; **David H. Hubel** (U.S., b. Canada) Harvard Medical School, and **Torsten T. Wiesel** (Sweden) Harvard Medical School "for their discoveries concerning information processing in the visual system."

1982   Sune K. Bergström (Sweden) Karolinska Institute, **Bengt I. Samuelsson** (Sweden) Karolinska Institute, and **Sir John R. Vane** (U.K.) Wellcome Research Laboratories "for their discoveries concerning prostaglandins and related biologically active substances."

1983   Barbara McClintock (U.S.) Cold Spring Harbor Laboratory "for her discovery of mobile genetic elements."

1984   Niels K. Jerne (Denmark) and **Georges J.F. Köhler** (W. Germany) of the Basel Institute for Immunology; and **César Milstein** (U.K. and Argentina) Medical Research Council Laboratory of Molecular Biology (Cambridge) for theories concerning the specificity in development and controls of the immune system and the discovery of the principle for production of monoclonal antibodies."

1985   Michael S. Brown (U.S.), and **Joseph L. Goldstein** (U.S.) both of the Univ. of Texas Health Science Center at Dallas "for their discoveries concerning the regulation of cholesterol metabolism."

1986   Stanley Cohen (U.S.) Vanderbilt Univ., and **Rita Levi-Montalcini** (Italy and U.S.) Institute of Cell Biology of the C.N.R. (Rome) "for their discoveries of growth factors."

1987   Susumu Tonegawa (U.S.) MIT "for discovery of the genetic principle for generation of antibody diversity."

1988   Sir James W. Black (U.K.) King's College Hospital Medical School, **Gertrude B. Elion** (U.S.) Welcome Research Laboratories, and **George H. Hitchings** (U.S.) Wellcome Research Laboratories "for their discoveries of important Principles for Drug Treatment."

1989   J. Michael Bishop and **Harold E. Varmus** (U.S.) Univ. of California, San Francisco "for their discovery of the Cellular Origin of Retroviral Oncogenes."

1990   Joseph E. Murray (U.S.) Brigham and Women's Hospital (Boston) who performed the first kidney transplant (1954), and **E. Donnall Thomas** (U.S.), Fred Hutchinson Cancer Research Center (Seattle), who performed the first successful bone marrow transplant between two people who were not twins (1979).

1991   Erwin Neher (Germany) Max-Planck Institute for Biophysical Chemistry, Göttingen, and **Bert Sakmann** (Germany) Max-Planck Institute for Medical Research, Heidelberg, for establishing existence of ion channels by developing technique that allows detection of "incredibly small electrical currents that pass through a single ion channel."

1992   Edmond H. Fischer (U.S.) and **Edwin G. Krebs** (U.S.), both of the Univ. of Washington for a discovery in the 1950s of a regulatory mechanism in almost all human cells linked to some cancers, to the rejection of transplanted organs, and many other processes.

1993   Richard J. Roberts (U.K.), New England Bio Labs, and **Phillip A. Sharp** (U.S.), MIT, for their discovery in the 1970s that the composition of genes is of several segments, which led to gene splicing and a better understanding of hereditary diseases and cancer.

1994   Alfred G. Gilman (U.S.) Univ. of Texas Southwestern Medical Center, and **Martin Rodbell** (U.S.) National Institute of Environmental Health Sciences, for their discovery of natural substances known as G-proteins and for showing how they help cells respond to stimuli like light and odors.

1995   Edward B. Lewis (U.S.) California Institute of Technology, **Eric F. Wieschaus** (U.S.) Princeton Univ., and **Christiane Nüsslein-Volhard** (Germany) Max-Planck Institute in Tübingen, for their discovery of how genes control structural development of the body. Their research, performed on fruit flies, helps explain birth defects in humans.

1996   Peter C. Doherty (Australia) St. Jude's Medical Center in Memphis, and **Rolf Zinkernagel** (Switzerland) University of Zurich, "for their discoveries concerning the specificity of the cell mediated immune defense."

Their work explained how the immune system recognizes and kills virus-infected cells.

1997   Stanley B. Prusiner (U.S.), Univ. of California, "for his discovery of Prions," disease-causing proteins that can be linked to degenerative brain diseases.

1998   Robert F. Furchgott (U.S.), SUNY Health Science Center; **Louis J. Ignarro** (U.S.), UCLA School of Medicine; and **Ferid Murad** (U.S.), Univ. of Texas, ""for their discoveries concerning nitric oxide as a signalling molecule in the cardiovascular system."

1999   Günter Blobel (U.S., b. Germany), Rockefeller Univ. "for the discovery that proteins have intrinsic signals that govern their transport and localization in the cel." Blobel found that many hereditary diseases are caused by mistakes in these signals.

2000   Arvid Carlsson (Sweden), Univ. of Gothenburg; **Paul Greengard** (U.S.), Rockefeller Univ., N.Y.; and **Eric Kandel** (U.S.), Columbia Univ., "for their discoveries concerning signal transduction in the nervous system," leading to greater understanding of neurological and psychiatric diseases like Parkinson's.

2001   Leland H. Hartwell (U.S.), Fred Hutchinson Cancer Research Center, Seattle, and **R. Timothy Hunt** (U.K.) and **Sir Paul M. Nurse** (U.K.), both of the Imperial Cancer Research Fund, London, "for their discoveries of key regulators of the cell cycle," which may lead to cures for irregular cell growth patterns like cancer.

2002   Sydney Brenner, (U.K.), Molecular Sciences Institute, **H. Robert Horvitz,** (U.S.), M.I.T., and **John E. Sulston,** (U.K.), Wellcome Trust Sanger Institute "for their discoveries concerning genetic regulation of organ development and programmed cell death." Their work has given scientists insights into cancer and the ways bacteria and viruses invade human cells.

2003   Paul C. Lauterbur(U.S.), Univ. of Illinois and **Peter Mansfield** (U.K.), Univ. of Nottingham School of Physics, "For their discoveries concerning magnetic resonancce imaging (MRIs)."

2004   Richard Axel (U.S.) and **Linda B. Buck** (U.S.), both of the Howard Hughes Medical Institute, for their discoveries of "odorant receptors and the organization of the olfactory system."

2005   Barry J. Marshall and **J. Robin Warren** (Australia) "for their discovery of the bacterium *Helicobacter pylori* and its role in gastritis and peptic ulcer disease."

2006   Andrew Z. Fire and **Craig C. Mello** (U.S.) "for their discovery of RNA interference—gene silencing by double-stranded RNA."

2007   Mario R. Capecchi (U.S. ,b. Italy) Univ. of Utah, **Sir Martin J. Evans** (U.K.) Cardiff Univ., and **Oliver Smithies** (U.S., b. U.K.) Univ. of North Carolina at Chapel Hill "for their discoveries of principles for introducing specific gene modifications in mice by the use of embryonic stem cells."

2008   Françoise Barré-Sinoussi, 61, (France), Institut Pasteur, Paris; and **Luc Montagnier**, 76, (France), World Foundation for AIDS Research and Prevention, Paris; for discovering the human immunodeficiency virus (H.I.V.), which causes AIDS, and describing its behavior in the immune system. **Harald zur Hausen**, 72, (Germany), German Cancer Research Center; for "going against current dogma" to prove that certain strains of human papilloma virus are responsible for most cases of cervical cancer.

2009   Elizabeth H. Blackburn (U.S.), University of California, San Francisco; **Carol W. Greider** (U.S.), John Hopkins University School of Medicine; **Jack W. Szostak** (U.S.), Harvard Medical School, Mass. General Hospital, Howard Hughes Medical Institute; "for the discovery of how chromosomes are protected by telomers and the enzyme telomerase."

Nobel Prizes in Economic Sciences

1969 Ragnar Frisch (Norway) Oslo Univ. and Jan Tinbergen (Netherlands) Netherlands School of Economics "for having developed and applied dynamic models for the analysis of economic processes."

1970 Paul A. Samuelson (U.S.) M.I.T. "for the scientific work through which he has developed static and dynamic economic theory and...contributed to raising the level of analysis in economic science."

1971 Simon Kuznets (U.S.) Harvard Univ. "for his empirically founded interpretation of economic growth which has led to new and deepened insight into the economic and social structure and process of development."

1972 Sir John R. Hicks (U.K.) All Souls College; and Kenneth J. Arrow (U.S.) Harvard Univ. "for their pioneering contributions to general economic equilibrium theory and welfare theory."

1973 Wassily Leontief (U.S.) Harvard Univ. "for the development of the input-output method and for its application to important economic problems."

1974 Gunnar Mydal (Sweden), Friedrich A. von Hayek (U.K.) "for their pioneering work in the theory of money and economic fluctuations and for their penetrating analysis of the interdependence of economic, social and institutional phenomena."

1975 Leonid Kantorovich (USSR) Academy of Sciences, and Tjalling C. Koopmans (U.S.) Yale Univ. "for their contributions to the theory of optimum allocation of resources."

1976 Milton Friedman (U.S.) Univ. of Chicago for "achievements in the fields of consumption analysis, monetary history and theory. . ."

1977 Bertil Ohlin (Sweden) Stockholm School of Economics, and James E. Meade (U.K.) Cambridge Univ. "for their pathbreaking contribution to the theory of international trade and international capital movements."

1978 Herbert A. Simon (U.S.) Carnegie-Mellon Univ. "for his pioneering research into the decision-making process within economic organizations."

1979 Theodore W. Schultz (U.S.) Univ. of Chicago, and Sir Arthur Lewis (U.K.) Princeton Univ. "for their pioneering research into economic development research with particular consideration of the problems of developing countries."

1980 Lawrence R. Klein (U.S.) Univ. of Pennsylvania "for the creation of econometric models and their application to the analysis of economic fluctuations and economic policies."

1981 James Tobin (U.S.) Yale Univ. "for his analysis of financial markets and their relations to expenditure decisions, employment, production, and prices."

1982 George J. Stigler (U.S.) Univ. of Chicago "for his seminal studies of industrial structures, functioning markets, and causes and effects of public regulation."

1983 Gerard Debreu (U.S.) Univ. of California, "for having incorporated new analytical methods into economic theory and for his rigorous reformulation of the theory of general equilbrium."

1984 Sir Richard Stone (U.K.) Cambridge Univ. "for having made fundamental contributions to the development of systems of national accounts and hence greatly improved [sic]the basis for empirical economic analysis."

1985 Franco Modigliani (U.S.) M.I.T. "for his pioneering analyses of saving and of financial markets."

1986 James M Buchanan Jr. (U.S.) Center for Study of Public Choice "for his development of the contractual and constitutional bases for the theory of economic and political decision-making."

1987 Robert M. Solow (U.S.) M.I.T. "for his contributions to the theory of economic growth."

1988 Maurice Allais (France) Centre d'analyse économique "for his pioneering contributions to the theory of markets and efficient utilization of resources."

1989 Trygve Haavelmo (Norway) Univ. of Oslo "for his clarification of the probability theory foundations of econometircs and his analyses of simultaneous economic structures."

1990 Harry Markowitz (U.S.) Baruch College (of the City Univ. of New York, for his Portfolio Theory; William F. Sharpe (U.S.) Stanford Univ., for his Capital Asset Pricing Model, and Merton Miller (U.S.) Univ. of Chicago, for his work on the Miller-Modigliani Theory. Together, their work revolutionized the financial/business industries.

1991 Ronald H. Coase (U.K.) Univ. of Chicago Law School, for his work on the role of firms in the economy and on social cost of industry, notably his articles "The Theory of the Firm" (1937) and "The Problem of Social Cost" (1960).

1992 Gary S. Becker (U.S.), Univ. of Chicago, for "having extended the domain of economic theory to aspects of human behavior . . ." including crime, family life, and racial bias.

1993 Robert W. Fogel (U.S.), Univ. of Chicago, and Douglass C. North (U.S.), Washington Univ., for "applying economic theory and quarantine methods to historical puzzles." Fogel's work on slavery as an efficient economic system caused great controversy.

1994 John F. Nash (U.S.) Princeton Univ., John C., Harsanyi (U.S., b. Hungary) Univ. of California, and Reinhard Selten (Germany) Univ. of Bonn, for their separate contributions to the field of game theory, which is used to predict how information and competition affect economic outcomes.

1995 Robert E. Lucas, Jr., (U.S.) Univ. of Chicago, "the economist who has had the greatest influence on macroeconomic research since 1970." His work challenges the Keynesian belief that the government is able to fine-tune the economy.

1996 James A. Mirrlees (U.K.) Cambridge, Univ. and William Vickrey (U.S., b. Canada), Columbia Univ. for "their fundamental contributions to the economic theory of incentives." Their theories have been used in designing more efficient tax codes and eliciting the highest bids at auctions.

1997 Robert Merton (U.S.), Harvard University, and Myron Scholes (U.S.), Stanford University, for their work in creating "a pioneering formula for the valuation of stock options" and other derivatives. The Nobel committee cited their research as one of the principal reasons for the success of the derivatives markets.

1998 Amartya Sen (India), Cambridge Univ. and Harvard Univ., for his work on human rights, poverty, and inequality that has changed the way governments deal with famines, and for restoring "an ethical dimension to the discussion of vital economics problems."

1999 Robert A. Mundell (U.S.,b. Canada), Columbia University, "for his analysis of monetary and fiscal policy under different exchange rate regimes and his analysis of optimum currency areas."

2000 James J. Heckman (U.S.), Univ. of Chicago "for his development of theory and methods for analyzing selective samples," and Daniel L. McFadden (U.S.), Univ. of California, "for his development of theory and methods for analyzing discrete choice."

2001 George A. Akerlof (U.S.) Univ. of California, A. Michael Spence (U.S.), Stanford Univ., and Joseph E. Stiglitz (U.S.), Columbia Univ. "for their analyses of markets with asymmetric information." Their work has applications in situations ranging from the elderly's inability to find low-cost medical insurance to the prices charged for used cars.

2002   Daniel Kahneman, (U.S. and Israel), Princeton University and **Vernon L. Smith,** (U.S.), George Mason University, whose achievements break new ground in incorporating experimental methods into economics.
2003   Robert F. Engle, (U.S.), New York University, and **Clive W. Granger,** (U.K.), for "methods of analyzing economic time series with common trends (cointegration), allowing researchers to compare data across inconsistent time periods.
2004   Finn E. Kydland (Norway), Carnegie-Mellon University and University of California at Santa Barbara; and **Edward C. Prescott** (U.S.), Arizona State University and Federal Reserve Bank of Minneapolis; "for their contributions to dynamic macroeconomics: the time consistency of economic policy and the driving forces behind business cycles."
2005   Robert J. Aumann (Israel) and **Thomas C. Schelling** (U.S.) "for having enhanced our understand-

ing of conflict and cooperation through game-theory analysis."
2006   Edmund S. Phelps (U.S.) "for his analysis of intertemporal tradeoffs in macroeconomic policy."
2007   Leonid Hurwicz (U.S., b. Russia) Univ. of Minnesota, **Eric S. Maskin** (U.S.) Institute for Advanced Study, and **Roger B. Myerson** (U.S.) Univ. of Chicago "for having laid the foundations of mechanism design theory."
2008   Paul Krugman, 55, (U.S.), Princeton University; "for his analysis of trade patterns and location of economic activity."
2009   Elinor Ostrom (U.S.), Indiana University, Arizona State University, "for her analysis of economic governance"; **Oliver E. Williamson** (U.S.), University of California, Berkeley, "for his analysis of economic governance, especially the boundaries of the firm."

Nobel Prizes in Chemistry

1901   Jacobus H. Van't Hoff (Netherlands) Berlin Univ. (Germany) for "the extraordinary services he has rendered by the discovery of the laws of chemical dynamics and osmotic pressure in solutions."
1902   Hermann E. Fischer (Germany) "in recognition of the extraordinary services he has rendered by his work on sugar and purine synthesis."
1903   Svante A. Arrhenius (Sweden) Stockholm Univ. "in recognition of the extraordinary services he has rendered to the advancement of chemistry by his electrolytic theory of dissociation."
1904   Sir William Ramsay (U.K.) London Univ. "in recognition of his services in the discovery of the inert gaseous elements in air; and his determination of their place in the periodic system."
1905   Johann F.W.A. von Baeyer (Germany) Munich Univ. "in recognition of his services in the advancement of organic chemistry and the chemical industry, through his work on organic dyes and hydroaromatic compounds."
1906   Henri Moissan (France) Sorbonne Univ. "in recognition of the great services rendered by him in his investigation and isolation of the element fluorine, and for the adoption in the service of science of the electric furnace called after him."
1907   Eduard Buchner (Germany) Agricultural College "for his biochemical researches and his discovery of cell-free fermentation."
1908   Lord Ernest Rutherfold (U.K.) Victoria Univ. "for his investigation into the disintegration of the elements, and the chemistry of radioactive substances."
1909   Wilhelm Ostwald (Germany) Leipzig Univ. "in recognition of his work on catalysis, and for his investigations into the fundamental principles governing chemical equilibria and rates of reaction."
1910   Otto Wallach (Germany) Goettingen Univ. "in recognition of his services to organic chemistry and the chemical industry by his pioneer work in the field of alicyclic compounds."
1911   Marie Curie (France) Sorbonne Univ. "in recognition of her services to the advancement of chemistry by the discovery of the elements radium and polonium, by the isolation of radium and the study of the nature and compounds of this remarkable element."
1912   Victor Grignard (France) Nancy Univ. "for the discovery of the so-called Grignard reagent, which in recent years has greatly advanced the progress of organic chemistry"; **Paul Sabatier** (France) Toulouse Univ., "for his method of hydrogenating organic compounds in the presence of finely disintegrated metals whereby the progress of organic chemistry has been greatly advanced in recent years."
1913   Alfred Werner (Switzerland) Zurich Univ. "in recognition of his work on the linkage of atoms in molecules by which he has thrown new light

on earlier investigations and opened up new fields of research especially in inorganic chemistry."
1914   Theodore W. Richards (U.S.) Harvard Univ. for "his accurate determinations of the atomic weight of a large number of chemical elements."
1915   Richard M. Willstätter (Germany) Munich Univ. "for his researches on plant pigments, especially chlorophyll."
1916–1917   No awards given.
1918   Fritz Haber (Germany) Kaiser-Wilhelm Institut "for the synthesis of ammonia from its elements."
1919   No award
1920   Walther H. Nernst (Germany) Berlin Univ. "in recognition of his work in thermochemistry."
1921   Frederick Soddy (U.K.) Oxford Univ. "for his contributions to our knowledge of the chemistry of radioactive substances, and his investigations into the origin and nature of isotopes."
1922   Francis W. Aston (U.K.) Cambridge Univ. "for his discovery, by means of his mass spectrograph, of isotopes in a large number of nonradioactive elements, and for his enunciation of the whole-number rule."
1923   Fritz Pregl (Austria) Graz Univ. "for his invention of the method of microanalysis of organic substances."
1925   Richard A. Zsigmondy (Germany) Goettingen Univ. "for his demonstration of the heterogeneous nature of colloid solutions."
1926   The (Theodor) Svedberg (Sweden) Uppsala Univ. "for his work on disperse systems."
1927   Heinrich O. Wieland (Germany) Munich Univ. "for his investigations of the constitution of the bile acids and related substances."
1928   Adolf O.R. Windaus (Germany) Goettingen Univ. "for the services rendered through his research into the constitution of the sterols and their connection with the vitamins."
1929   Sir Arthur Harden (U.K.) London Univ., Hans K.A. von Euler-Chelpin (Sweden) "for their investigations on the fermentation of sugar and fermentative enzymes."
1930   Hans Fischer (Germany) Institute of Technology "for his researches into the constitution of haemin and chlorophyll, and especially for his synthesis of haemin."
1931   Carl Bosch (Germany) Heidelberg Univ. I.G. Farbenindustrie A.G., and **Fredrich Bergius** (Germany) Heidelberg Univ. and I.G. Farbenindustrie A.G. for "their contributions to the invention and development of chemical high pressure methods."
1932   Irving Langmuir (U.S.) General Electric Co., "for his discoveries and investigations in surface chemistry."
1934   Harold C. Urey (U.S.) Columbia Univ. "for his discovery of heavy hydrogen."

1935 Frédéric Joliot (France) Institut du Radium and his wife, Iréne Joliot-Curie, (France) Institut du Radium "in recognition of their synthesis of new radioactive elements."

1936 Petrus (Peter) J.W. Debye (Netherlands) Berlin Univ. and Kaiser-Wilhelm-Institut (now Max-Planck-Institut) "for his contributions to our knowledge of molecular structure through his investigations on dipole moments and on the diffraction of X-rays and electrons in gases."

1937 Sir Walter N. Haworth (U.K.) Birmingham Univ. "for his investigations on carbohydrates and vitamin C"; Paul Karrer (Switzerland) Zurich Univ. "for his investigations on carotenoids, flavins, and vitamins A and B-2."

1938 Richard Kuhn (Germany) Heidelberg Univ. and Kaiser-Wilhelm-Institut (now Max-Planck-Institut) "for his work on carotenoids and vitamins. (Compelled by the authorities of his country to decline the award, but later received diploma and medal.)

1939 Adolf F.J. Butenandt (Germany) Berlin Univ. and Kaiser-Wilhelm-Institut (now Max-Planck-Institut) "for his work on sex hormones. (Compelled by his country to decline the award, but later received diploma and medal); Leopold Ruzicka (Switzerland) Federal Institute of Technology "for his work on polymethylenes and higher terpenes."

1940–1942 No awards

1943 George de Hevesy (Hungary) Stockholm Univ. "for his work on the use of isotopes as tracers in the study of chemical processes."

1944 Otto Hahn (Germany) Kaiser-Wilhelm-Institut (now Max-Planck-Institut) "for his discovery of the fission of heavy nuclei."

1945 Artturi I. Virtanen (Finland) Helsinki Univ. "for his research and inventions in agricultural and nutrition chemistry, especially for his fodder preservation method."

1946 James B. Sumner (U.S.) Cornell Univ. "for his discovery that enzymes can be crystallized"; John H. Northrop (U.S.) Rockefeller Institute for Medical Research "for their preparation of enzymes and virus proteins in a pure form."

1947 Sir Robert Robinson (U.K.) Oxford Univ. "for his investigations on plant products of biological importance, especially alkaloids."

1948 Arne W.K. Tiselius (Sweden) Uppsala Univ. "for his research on electrophoresis and adsorption analysis, especially for his discoveries concerning the complex nature of the serum proteins."

1949 William F. Giauque (U.S.) Univ. of California, "for his contributions in the field of chemical thermodynamics, particularly concerning the behavior of substances at extremely low temperatures."

1950 Otto P.H. Diels (Germany) Kiel Univ. and Kurt Alder (Germany) Cologne Univ. "for their discovery and development of the diene synthesis."

1951 Edwin M. McMillan (U.S.) and Glenn T. Seaborg (U.S.) both of Univ. of California, "for their discoveries in the chemistry of the transuranium elements."

1952 Archer J.P. Martin (U.K.) Nations Institute for Medical Research, and Richard L.M. Synge (U.K.) Rowett Research Institute (Scotland) "for their invention of partition chromatography."

1953 Herman Staudinger (Germany) State Research Institute for Macromolecular Chemistry "for his discoveries in the field of macromolecular chemistry."

1954 Linus C. Pauling (U.S.) California Institute of Technology "for his research into the nature of the chemical bond and its application to the elucidation of the structure of complex substances."

1955 Vincent du Vigneaud (U.S.) Cornell Univ. "for his work on biochemically important sulphur compounds, especially for the first synthesis of a polypeptide hormone."

1956 Sir Cyril N. Hinshelwood (U.K.) Oxford Univ. and Nikolaj N. Semenov (USSR) Institute for Chemical Physics of the Academy of Sciences of the USSR "for their researches into the mechanism of chemical reactions."

1957 Lord Alexander R. Todd (U.K.) Cambridge Univ. "for his work on nucleotides and nucleotide coenzymes."

1958 Frederick Sanger (U.K.) Cambridge Univ. "for his work on the structure of proteins, especially that of insulin."

1959 Jaroslav Heyrovsky (Czechoslovakia) Polaro-Institute of the Czechoslovakia Academy of Science for his discovery and development of the polarographic methods of analysis."

1960 Willard F. Libby (U.S.) Univ. of California, Los Angeles "for his method to use carbon-14 for age determination in archaeology, geology, geophysics, and other branches of science."

1961 Melvin Calvin (U.S.) Univ. of California, for research on carbon dioxide assimilation in plants."

1962 Max F. Perutz (U.K.) Laboratory of Molecular Biology, and Sir John C. Kendrew (U.K.) Laboratory of Molecular Biology, "for their studies on the structures of globular proteins."

1963 Karl Ziegler (Germany) Max-Planck-Institute for Carbon Research, and Giulio Natta (Italy) Institute of Technology "for their discoveries in the field of the chemistry and technology of high polymers."

1964 Dorothy C. Hodgkin (U.K.) Royal Society, Oxford Univ. "for her determinations by X-ray techniques of the structures of important biochemical substances."

1965 Robert B. Woodward (U.S.) Harvard Univ. "for his outstanding achievements in the art of organic synthesis."

1966 Robert S. Mulliken (U.S.) Univ. of Chicago "for his fundamental work concerning chemical bonds and the electronic structure of molecules by the molecular orbital method."

1967 Manfred Eigen (W. Germany) Max-Planck-Institut, Ronald G.W. Norrish (U.K.) Institute of Physical Chemistry, and Sir George Porter (U.K.) The Royal Institution "for their studies of extremely fast chemical reactions, effected by disturbing the equilibrium by means of very short pulses of energy."

1968 Lars Onsager (U.S.) Yale Univ. "for the discovery of the reciprocal relations bearing his name, which are fundamental for the thermodynamics of irreversible processes."

1969 Sir Derek H.R. Barton (U.K.) Imperial College of Science and Technology, and Odd Hassel (Norway) Kjemisk Institut "for their contributions to the development of the concept of conformation and its application in chemistry."

1970 Luis F. Leloir (Argentina) Institute for Biochemical Research for his discovery of sugar nucleotides and their role in the biosynthesis of carbohydrates."

1971 Gerhard Herzberg (Canada) National Research Council of Canada "for his contributions to the knowledge of electronic structure and geometry of molecules, particularly free radicals."

1972 Christian B. Anfinsen (U.S.) National Institutes of Health "for his work on ribonuclease, especially concerning the connection between the amino acid sequence and the biologically active conformation"; Stanford Moore (U.S.) Rockefeller Univ. and William H. Stein (U.S.) Rockefeller Univ. "for their contribution to the understanding of the connection between chemical structure and catalytic activity of the active center of the ribonuclease molecule."

1973 Ernst O. Fischer (W. Germany) Technical Univ. of Munich, and Sir Geoffrey Wilkinson (U.K.) Imperial College "for their pioneering work, performed independently, on the chemistry of the organometallic, so-called sandwich compounds."

1974　Paul J. Flory (U.S.) Stanford Univ. "for his fundamental achievements, both theoretical and experimental, in the physical chemistry of the macromolecules."

1975　Sir John W. Cornforth (Australia and U.K.) Univ. of Sussex "for his work on the stereo-chemistry of enzyme-catalyzed reactions"; **Vladimir Prelog** (Switzerland) Eidgenossische Technische Hochschule "for his research into the sterochemistry of organic molecules and reactions."

1976　William N. Lipscomb (U.S.) Harvard Univ. "for his studies on the structure of boranes illuminating problems of chemical bonding."

1977　Ilya Prigogine (Belgium) Université Libre de Bruxelles, (Univ. of Texas, U.S.) "for his contributions to nonequilibrium thermodynamics, particularly the theory of dissipative structures."

1978　Peter D. Mitchell (U.K.) Glynn Research Laboratories "for his contribution to the understanding of biological energy transfer through the formulation of the chemiosmotic theory."

1979　Herbert C. Brown (U.S.) Purdue Univ., and **Georg Wittig** (Germany) Univ. of Heidelberg "for their development of the use of boron-and-phosphorus-containing compounds, respectively, into important reagents in organic synthesis."

1980　Paul Berg (U.S.) Stanford Univ. "for his fundamental studies of the biochemistry of nucleic acids, with particular regard to recombinant-DNA"; **Walter Gilbert** (U.S.) Biological Laboratories, and **Frederick Sanger** (U.K.) MRC Laboratory of Molecular Biology "for their contributions concerning the determination of base sequences in nucleic acids."

1981　Kenichi Fukui (Japan) Kyoto Univ. and **Roald Hoffman** (U.S.) Cornell Univ. "for their theories, developed independently, concerning the course of chemical reactions."

1982　Aaron Klug (U.K.) MRC Laboratory of Molecular Biology "for his development of crystallographic electron microscopy and his structural elucidation of biologically important nucleic acid-protein complexes."

1983　Henry Taube (U.S.) Stanford Univ. "for his work on the mechanisms of electron transfer reactions, especially in metal complexes."

1984　Robert B. Merrifield (U.S.) Rockefeller Univ. "for his development of methodology for chemical synthesis on solid matrix."

1985　Herbert A. Hauptman (U.S.) Medical Foundation of Buffalo, and **Jerome Karle** (U.S.) U.S. Naval Research Laboratory "for their outstanding achievements in the development of direct methods for the determination of crystal structures."

1986　Dudley R. Herschbach (U.S.) Harvard Univ., **Yuan T. Lee** (U.S.) Univ. of California, and **John C. Polanyi** (Canada) Univ. of Toronto, "for their contributions concerning the dynamics of chemical elementary processes."

1987　Donald J. Cram (U.S.) University of California, Los Angeles, **Jean-Marie Lehn** (France) Université Louis Pasteur, and **Charles J. Pedersen** (U.S.) Du Pont Laboratory "for their development and use of molecules with structure-specific interactions of high selectivity."

1988　Johann Deisenhofer (U.S.) Howard Hughes Medical Institute, Robert Huber (W. Germany) Max-Planck-Institut, and **Hartmut Michel** (W. Germany) Max-Planck-Institut, "for their determination of the three-dimensional structure of a photosynthetic reaction centre."

1989　Sidney Altman (U.S.) Yale Univ., and **Thomas Cech** (U.S.) Univ. of Colorado for their separate discoveries of the catalytic properties of RNA.

1990　Elias James Corey (U.S.) Harvard Univ. for developing new ways to synthesize complex molecules ordinarily found in nature, work that has contributed to "the high standard of living and health, and the longevity enjoyed at least in the Western world."

1991　Richard R. Ernst (Switzerland) Eidgenössische Technische Hochschule, Zurich, for his work in refining nuclear magnetic resonance spectroscopy for use in chemical analysis.

1992　Rudolph A. Marcus (U.S., b. Canada), Cal Tech., for his mathematical explanation of chemical interactions involving the transfer of electrons between molecules.

1993　Kary B. Mullis (U.S.) for his discovery, in the 1970s, of the polymerase chain reaction (PCR) that allowed scientists to make trillions of copies of DNA. **Michael Smith** (Canada), Univ. of British Columbia, for developing the technique that alters the code of genetic molecules that will facilitate new medical therapies and plants that resist disease.

1994　George A. Olah (U.S., b. Hungary) Univ. of Southern California, for his discovery of new ways of breaking apart and rebuilding carbon and hydrogen compounds. He opened a wholly new field of hydrocarbon research, leading to improved fuels based on coal, methane, and petroleum.

1995　F. Sherwood Roland (U.S.) Univ. of California-Irvine, **Mario Molina** (U.S.) M.I.T., and **Paul Crutzen** (Netherlands) Max Planck Institute for Chemistry in Mainz, Germany, for their pioneering work in explaining how production and use of refrigerants and other chlorofluorocarbons deplete the ozone layer.

1996　Robert F. Curl, Jr., (U.S.) and **Richard E. Smalley** (U.S.), of Rice Univ. and **Harold W. Kroto** (U.K.) of Univ. of Sussex, for their 1985 discovery of buckminsterfullerene, or "buckyballs." Their work opened an entirely new branch of chemistry and gve scientists a greater understanding on how nature bonds carbon atoms together.

1997　Paul D. Boyer (U.S.), UCLA and **John E. Walker** (U.K.), Medical Research Council Laboratory of Molecular Biology, for demonstrating how all living things create adenosine triphosphate, a tiny molecule that stores energy and builds proteins, transmits nerve impulses, and contracts muscles. **Jens C. Skou** (Denmark), Aarhus Univ., for his discovery of sodium-potassium-stimulated adenosine triphosphate, an enzyme that maintains the balance of sodium and potassium ions in living cells.

1998　Walter Kohn (U.S., b. Austria), Univ. of California, Santa Barbara; **John A. Pople** (U.S., b U.K.), Northwestern Univ. Their achievements helped extend the mathematics of quantum mechanics to predicting specific chemical reactions and designing molecules for use in medicine and other applications.

1999　Ahmed H. Zewail (U.S., b. Egypt), CalTech, "for showing that it is possible with rapid laser technique to see how atoms in a molecule move during a chemical reaction."

2000　Alan J. Heeger (U.S.), Univ. of California at Santa Barbara; **Alan G. MacDiarmid** (U.S.), Univ. of Pennsylvania; and **Hideki Shirakawa** (Japan), Univ. of Tsukuba, for their discovery and development of a plastic that conducts electricity like a metal and may be used to increase the speed and decrease the size of computers.

2001　William S. Knowles (U.S.) and **Ryoji Noyori**, (Japan), Nagoya Univ. "for their work on chirally catalysed hydrogenation reactions." **K. Barry Sharpless** (U.S.), Scripps Research Institute, "for his work on chirally catalysed oxidation reactions," making possible the development of new drugs, insecticides, and flavoring and sweetening agents.

2002　John B. Fenn, (U.S.), Virginia Commonwealth Univ. and **Koichi Tanaka,** (Japan), Shimadzu Corporation; and **Kurt Wüthrich,** (Switzerland), Swiss Federal Institute of Technology Zürich, and The Scripps Research Institute, "for the development of methods for identification and structure analyses of biological macromolecules," through achievements in the fields of mass spectrometry and nuclear magnetic resonance spectrometry.

2003 Peter Agre, (U.S.), Johns Hopkins Univ., for discovering water channels in cell membranes; **Koichi Tanaka**, (U.S.) Rockefeller Univ., forr "Structural and mechanistic studies of ion channels.. Their discoveries clariefied how salt and water are transported in and out of the body.
2004 Aaron Ciechanover (Israel) and **Avram Hershko** (Israel, b. Hungary) of the Israel Institute of Technology, Haifa, and **Irwin Rose** (U.S.), University of California at Irvine, "for the discovery of ubiquitin-mediated protein degradation."
2005 Yves Chauvin (France), **Robert H. Grubbs** (U.S.), and **Richard R.Schrock** (U.S.) "for the development of the metathesis method in organic synthesis."
2006 Roger D. Kornberg (U.S.) "for his studies of the molecular basis of eukaryotic transcription."

2007 Gerhard Ertl (Germany) Fritz-Haber-Institut der Max-Planck-Gesellschaft in Berlin, Germany "for his studies of chemical processes on solid surfaces."
2008 Osamu Shimomura, 80, (Japan), Marine Biological Laboratory, Woods Hole, Mass. and Boston University; first isolated green fluorescent protein (G.F.P.) from jellyfish. **Martin Chalfie**, 61, (U.S.), Columbia University; pioneered use of G.F.P. as a genetic tag for biological research. **Roger Y. Tsein**, 56, (U.S.), University of California at San Diego; developed additional colors of G.F.P.
2009 Venkatraman Ramakrishnan (U.K.), MRC Laboratory of Molecular Biology; **Thomas A. Steitz** (U.S.), Yale Univ. Howard Hughes Med. Institute; **Ada E. Yonath** (Israel), Weizmann Institute of Science, "for studies of the structure and function of the ribosome."

Nobel Prizes in Physics

1901 Wilhelm C. Röntgen (Germany) Munich Univ. "in recognition of the extraordinary services he has rendered by the discovery of remarkable rays subsequently named after him."
1902 Hendrik A. Lorentz (Netherlands) Leyden Univ., and **Pieter Zeeman** (Netherlands) Amsterdam Univ. "in recognition of the extraordinary service they rendered by their researches into the influence of magnetism upon radiation phenomena."
1903 Antoine H. Becquerel (France) Ecole Polytechnique "in recognition of the extraordinary services he has rendered by the discovery of spontaneous radioactivity"; **Pierre Curie** (France) Municipal School of Industrial Physics and Chemistry and his wife, **Marie Curie**, (France, b. Poland) "in recognition of the extraordinary services they have rendered by their joint researches on the radiation phenomena discovered by Professor Henri Becquerel."
1904 Lord Rayleigh (John W. Strutt) (U.K.) Royal Institution of U.K. "for his investigations of the densities of the most important gases and for his discovery of argon in connection with these studies."
1905 Philipp E.A. Lenard (Germany) Kiel Univ. "for his work on cathode rays."
1906 Sir Joseph J. Thomas (U.K.) Cambridge Univ. "in recognition of the great merits of his theoretical and experimental investigations on the conduction of electricity by gases."
1907 Albert A. Michelson (U.S.) Univ. of Chicago "for his optical precision instruments and the spectroscopic and meteorological investigations carried out with their aid."
1908 Gabriel Lippman (France) Sorbonne Univ. "for his method of reproducing colours photographically based on the phenomenon of interference."
1909 Guglielmo Marconi (Italy) Marconi Wireless Telegraph Co., Ltd., and **Carl F. Braun** (Germany) Strasbourg Univ. "in recognition of their contributions to the development of wireless telegraphy."
1910 Johannes D. van der Waals (Netherlands) Amsterdam Univ. "for his work on the equation of state for gases and liquids."
1911 Wilhelm Wien (Germany) Würzburg Univ. "for his discoveries regarding the laws governing the radiation of heat."
1912 Nils G. Dalén (Sweden) Swedish Gas-Accumulator Co. "for his invention of automatic regulators for use in conjunction with gas accumulators for illuminating lighthouses and buoys."
1913 Heike Kamerlingh-Onnes (Netherlands) Leyden Univ. "for his investigations on the properties of matter at low temperatures which led, inter alia, to the production of liquid helium."
1914 Max von Laue (Germany) Frankfurt-am-Main Univ. "for his discovery of the diffraction of X-rays by crystals."

1915 Sir William Henry Bragg (U.K.) London Univ. and his son **Sir William Lawrence Bragg** (U.K.) Victoria Univ. "for their services in the analysis of crystal structure by means of X-rays."
1916 No award.
1917 Charles G. Barkla (U.K.) Edinburgh Univ. "for his discovery of the characteristic Röntgen radiation of the elements."
1918 Max K.E.L. Planck (Germany) Berlin Univ. "in recognition of the services he rendered to the advancement of Physics by his discovery of energy quanta."
1919 Johannes Stark (Germany) Greifswald Univ. "for his discovery of the Doppler effect in canal rays and the splitting of spectral lines in electric fields."
1920 Charles E. Guillaume (Switzerland) International Bureau of Weights and Measurers "in recognition of the service he has rendered to precision measurements in physics by his discovery of anomalies in nickel steel alloys."
1921 Albert Einstein (Germany) Kaiser-Wilhelm-Institut für Physik (now Max-Panck-Institut) "for his services to theoretical physics, and especially for his discovery of the law of the photoelectric effect."
1922 Niels Bohr (Denmark) Copenhagen Univ. "for his services in the investigation of the structure of atoms and of the radiation emanating from them."
1923 Robert A. Millikan (U.S.) California Institute of Technology) "for his work on the elementary charge of electricity and on the photoelectric effect."
1924 Karl M.G. Siegbahn (Sweden) Uppsala Univ. "for his discoveries and research in the field of X-ray spectroscopy."
1925 James Franck (Germany) Goettingen Univ., and **Gustav Hertz** (Germany) Halle Univ. "for their discovery of the laws of governing the impact of an electron upon an atom."
1926 Jean B. Perrin (France) Sorbonne Univ. "for his work on the discontinuous structure of matter, and especially for his discovery of sedimentation equilibrium."
1927 Arthur H. Compton (U.S.) Univ. of Chicago "for his discovery of the effect named after him"; **Charles T.R. Wilson** (U.K.) Cambridge Univ. "for his method of making the paths of electrically charged particles visible by condensation of vapor."
1928 Sir Own W. Richardson (U.K.) London Univ. "for his work on the thermionic phenomenon and especially for the discovery of the law named after him."
1929 Prince Louis-Victor de Broglie (France) Sorbonne Univ. "for his discovery of the wave nature of electrons."
1930 Sir Chandrasekhara V. Raman (India) Calcutta Univ. "for his work on the scattering of light and for the discovery of the effect names after him."
1932 Werner Heisenberg (Germany) Leipzig Univ. "for the creation of quantum mechanics, the applica-

tion of which, has, inter alia, led to the discovery of the allotropic forms of hydrogen."

1933   Edwin Schrödinger (Austria) Berlin Univ. and **Paul A.M. Dirac** (U.K.) Cambridge Univ. "for the discovery of new productive forms of atomic theory."

1934   No award

1935   Sir James Chadwick (U.K.) Liverpool Univ. "for his discovery of the neutron."

1936   Victor F. Hess (Austria) Innsbruck Univ. "for his discovery of cosmic radiation"; **Carl D. Anderson** (U.S.) California Institute of Technology "for his discovery of the positron."

1937   Clinton J. Davisson (U.S.) Bell Telephone Laboratories, and **Sir George P. Thomson** (U.K.) London Univ. "for their experimental discovery of the diffraction of electrons by crystals."

1938   Enrico Fermi (Italy) Rome Univ. "for his demonstration of the existence of new radioactive elements produced by neutron irradiation, and for his related discovery of nuclear reactions brought about by slow neutrons."

1939   Ernest O. Lawrence (U.S.) Univ. of California, Berkeley "for the invention and development of the cyclotron and for results obtained with it, especially with regard to artificial radioactive elements."

1940–1942   No awards given.

1943   Otto Stern (U.S.) Carnegie Institute of Technology "for his contribution to the development of the molecular ray method and his discovery of the magnetic moment of the proton."

1944   Isidor I. Rabi (U.S.) Columbia Univ. "for his resonance method for recording the magnetic properties of atomic nuclei."

1945   Wolfgang Pauli (Austria) Princeton Univ. "for the discovery of the Exclusion Principle, also called the Pauli Principle."

1946   Percy W. Bridgman (U.S.) Harvard Univ. "for the invention of an apparatus to produce extremely high pressures, and for the discoveries he made therewith in the field of high-pressure physics."

1947   Sir Edward V. Appleton (U.K.) Dept. of Scientific and Industrial Research "for his investigations of the physics of the upper atmosphere, especially the so-called Appleton layer."

1948   Lord Patrick M.S. Blackett (U.K.) Victoria Univ. "for his development of the Wilson cloud chamber method, and his discoveries therewith in the fields of nuclear physics and cosmic radiation."

1949   Hideki Yukawa (Japan) Kyoto Imperial Univ. "for his prediction of the existence of mesons on the basis of theoretical work on nuclear forces."

1950   Cecil F. Powell (U.K.) Bristol Univ. "for his development of the photographic method of studying nuclear processes and his discoveries regarding mesons made with this method."

1951   Sir John D. Cockcroft (U.K.) Atomic Energy Research Establishment, and **Ernest T.S. Walton** (Ireland) Dublin Univ. "for their pioneer work on the transmutation of atomic nuclei by artificially accelerated atomic particles."

1952   Felix Block (U.S.) Stanford Univ., and **Edward M. Purcell** (U.S.) Harvard Univ. "for their development of new methods for nuclear magnetic precision measurements and discoveries in connection therewith."

1953   Frits (Frederik) Zernike (Netherlands) Groningern Univ. "for his demonstration of the phase contrast method, especially for his invention of the phase contrast microscope."

1954   Max Born (U.K.) Edinburgh Univ. "for his fundamental research in quantum mechanics, especially for his statistical interpretation of the wave-function"; **Walther Bothe** (Germany) Heidelbery Univ., Max-Planck-Institut "for the coincidence method and his discoveries made therewith."

1955   Willis E. Lamb (U.S.) Stanford Univ. "for his discoveries concerning the fine structure of the hydrogen

spectrum"; **Polykarp Kusch** (U.S.) Columbia Univ. "for his precision determination of the magnetic moment of the electron."

1956   William Shockley (U.S.) Semiconductor Laboratory of Beckman Instruments, Inc., **John Bardeen** (U.S.) Univ. of Illinois, and **Walter H. Brattain** (U.S.) Bell Telephone Laboratories for research on semiconductors and discovery of "the transistor effect."

1957   Chen N. Yang (China) Institute for Advanced Study (Princeton, N.J.) and **Tsung-Dao Lee** (China) Columbia Univ. "for their penetrating investigation of the so-called parity laws which has led to important discoveries regarding the elementary particles."

1958   Pavel A. Cherenkov (USSR) Physics Institute of USSR Academy of Sciences, **Il'ja M.Frank** (USSR) Academy of Sciences, and **Igor J. Tamm** (USSR) Univ. of Moscow and Physics Institute of USSR Academy of Sciences "for their discovery and the interpretation of the Cherenkov effect."

1959   Emillio G. Segrè (U.S.) Univ. of California, Berkeley, and **Owen Chamberlain** (U.S.) Univ. of California, Berkeley "for their discovery of the antiproton."

1960   Donald A. Glaser (U.S.) Univ. of California, Berkeley "for the invention of the bubble chamber."

1961   Robert Hofstadter (U.S.) Stanford Univ. "for his pioneering studies of electron scattering in atomic nuclei and for his thereby achieved discoveries concerning the structure of the nucleons"; **Rudolf L. Mössbauer** (Germany) Technische Hochschule (Munich), and California Institute of Technology "for his researches concerning the resonance absorption of gamma radiation and his discovery in this connection of the effect which bears his name."

1962   Lev D. Landau (USSR) Academy of Sciences "for his pioneering theories for condensed matter, especially liquid helium."

1963   Eugene P. Wigner (U.S.) Princeton Univ. "for his contributions to the theory of the atomic nucleus and the elementary particles, particularly through the discovery and application of fundamental symmetry principles"; **Maria Goeppert-Mayer** (U.S.) Univ. of California, La Jolla, and **J. Hans D. Jensen** (Germany) Univ. of Heidelberg "for their discoveries concerning nuclear shell structure."

1964   Charles H. Townes (U.S.) M.I.T., **Nikolai G. Basov** (USSR) Lebedev Institute for Physics, and **Aleksandre M. Prochorov** (USSR) Lebedev Institute for Physics "for fundamental work in the field of quantum electronics, which has led to the construction of oscillators and amplifiers based on the maser-laser-principle."

1965   Schin'ichiro Tomonaga (Japan) Toyko Univ., **Julian Schwinger** (U.S.) Harvard Univ., and **Richard P. Feynman** (U.S.) California Institute of Technology "for their fundamental work in quantum electrodynamcis, with deep-ploughing consequences for the physics of elementary particles."

1966   Alfred Kastier (France) Ecole Normale Supérieure, Université de Paris "for the discovery and development of optical methods for studying hertzian resonance in atoms."

1967   Hans A. Bethe (U.S.) Cornell Univ. "for his contributions to the theory of nuclear reactions, especially his discoveries concerning the energy production in stars."

1968   Luis W. Alvarez (U.S.) Univ. of California, Berkeley "for his decisive contributions to elementary particle physics, in particular the discovery of a large number of resonance states, made possible through his development of the technique of using hydrogen bubble chamber and data analysis."

1969   Murray Gell-Mann (U.S.) California Institute of Technology "for his contributions and discoveries concerning the classification of elementary particles and their interactions."

1970 Hannes Alfvén (Sweden) Royal Institute of Technology "for fundamental work and discoveries in magneto-hydrodynamics with fruitful applications in different parts of plasma physics"; **Louis Neel** (France) Univ. of Grenoble "for fundamental work and discoveries concerning antiferromagnetism and ferrimagetism which have led to important applications in solid-state physics."

1971 Dennis Gabor (U.K.) Imperial College of Science and Technology "for his invention and development of the holographic method."

1972 John Bardeen (U.S.) Univ. of Illinois, **Leon N. Cooper** (U.S.) Brown Univ., and **J. Robert Schrieffer** (U.S.) Univ. of Pennsylvania "for their jointly developed theory of superconductivity, usually called the BCS-theory."

1973 Leo Esaki (Japan) IBM Thomas J. Watson Research Center (New York), and **Ivar Giaever** (U.S.) General Electric Co. "for their experimental discoveries regarding tunneling phenomena in semiconductors and superconductors, respectively"; **Brian D. Josephson** (U.K.) Cambridge Univ. "for his theoretical predictions of the properties of a supercurrent through a tunnel barrier, in particular those phenomena which are generally known as the Josephson effects."

1974 Sir Martin Ryle (U.K.) and **Antony Hewish** (U.K.), both of Cambridge Univ., "for their pioneering research in radio astrophysics: Ryle for his observations and inventions, in particular of the aperture synthesis technique, and Hewish for his decisive role in the discovery of pulsars."

1975 Aage Bohr (Denmark) Niels Bohr Institute, **Ben Mottelson** (Denmark) Nordita, and **James Rainwater** (U.S.) Columbia Univ. "for the discovery of the connection between collective motion and particle motion in atomic nuclei and the development of the theory of the structure of the atomic nucleus based on this connection."

1976 Burton Richter (U.S.) Stanford Linear Accelerator Center, and **Samuel C.C. Ting** (U.S.) M.I.T. "for their pioneering work in the discovery of a heavy elementary particle of a new kind."

1977 Philip W. Anderson (U.S.) Bell Laboratories, **Sir Nevill F. Mott** (U.K.) Cambridge Univ. and **John H. van Vleck** (U.S.) Harvard Univ. "for their fundamental theoretical investigations of the electronic structure of magnetic and disordered systems."

1978 Peter L. Kapitsa (USSR) Academy of Sciences "for his basic inventions and discoveries in the area of low-temperature physics, **Arno A. Penzias** (U.S.) Bell Laboratories, and **Robert W. Wilson** (U.S.) Bell Laboratories "for their discovery of cosmic microwave background radiation."

1979 Sheldon L. Glashow (U.S.) Lyman Laboratory, Harvard Univ., **Abdus Salam** (Pakistan) International Centre for Theoretical Physics (Italy) and Imperial College of Science and Technology (London), and **Steven Weinberg** (U.S.) Harvard Univ. "for their contributions to the theory of the unified weak and electromagnetic interaction between elementary particles, including, inter alia, the predictions of the weak neutral current."

1980 James W. Cronin (U.S.) Univ. of Chicago, and **Val L. Fitch** (U.S.) Princeton Univ. "for the discovery of violations of fundamental symmetry principles in the decay of neutral K-mesons."

1981 Nicolaas Bloembergen (U.S.) Harvard Univ., and **Arthur L. Schawlow** (U.S.) Stanford Univ. "for their contributions to the development of laser spectroscopy"; **Kai M. Siegbahn** (Sweden) Uppsala Univ. "for his contribution to the development of high-resolution electron spectroscopy."

1982 Kenneth G. Wilson (U.S.) Cornell Univ. "for his theory for critical phenomena in connection with phase transitions."

1983 Subrahmanyan Chandrasekhar (U.S.) Univ. of Chicago "for his theoretical studies of the physical processes of importance to the structure and evolution of the stars"; **William A. Fowler** (U.S.) California Institute of Technology for his "studies of the nuclear reactions of importance in the formation of the chemical elements in the universe."

1984 Carlo Rubbia (Italy) CERN (Switzerland), and **Simon van der Meer** (Netherlands) CERN (Switzerland) "for their decisive contributions to the discovery of the field particles W and Z, communicators of weak interaction."

1985 Klaus von Klitzing (W. Germany) Max-Planck-Institut for Solid State Research "for the discovery of the quantized Hall effect."

1986 Ernst Ruska (W. Germany) Fritz-Haber-Institut der Max-Planck-Gesellschaft "for his fundamental work in electron optics, and for the design of the first electron microscope"; **Gerd Binnig** (W. Germany) IBM Zurich Research Laboratory and **Heinrich Rohrer** (Switzerland) IBM Zurich Research Laboratory "for their design of the scanning tunneling microscope."

1987 Georg J. Bednorz (Switzerland) IBM Zurich research Laboratory, and **Dr. K. Alex Müller** (Switzerland) IBM Zurich Research Laboratory "for the discovery of new superconducting materials."

1988 Leon M. Lederman (U.S.) Fermi National Accelerator Laboratory, **Melvin Schwartz** (U.S.) Digital Pathways, Inc., and **Jack Steinberger** (Switzerland) "for the neutrino beam method and the demonstration of the doublet structure of the leptons through the discovery of the muon neutrino."

1989 Norman R. Ramsey (U.S.) Harvard Univ. "for the invention of the separated oscillatory fields method and its use in . . . atomic clocks"; **Hans G. Dehmelt** (U.S.) Univ. of Washington, and **Wolfgang Paul** (W. Germany) Univ. of Bonn "for the development of the ion trap technique," which allows detailed study of subatomic particles."

1990 Richard E. Taylor (Can.), Stanford U.; **Jerome I. Friedman** (U.S.) MIT; and **Henry W. Kendall** (U.S.) MIT, whose experiments between 1967 and 1973 confirmed the existence of quarks, the fundamental building blocks of matter.

1991 Pierre-Gilles de Gennes (France), Collège de France, Paris, for his discoveries about the ordering of molecules in a variety of substances but especially liquid crystals, where his work has helped in understanding superconductivity.

1992 George Charpak (France, b. Poland), affiliated with CERN, the accelerator complex, where he developed electronic detectors that traced the paths of subatomic particles with lightning speed.

1993 Joseph H. Taylor (U.S.), Princeton Univ., and **Russel A. Hulse** (U.S.), Princeton Plasma Physics Laboratory, for their discovery of a binary pulsar and their later success in measuring its pulse rate.

1994 Clifford G. Shull (U.S.) MIT, and **Bertram N. Brockhouse** (Canada) McMaster Univ., for experiments in the 1940's and '50's that exploited the penetrating power of low-energy neutron beams produced by nuclear reactors. Neutron beams are widely used to explore the atomic structure of matter.

1995 Martin L. Perl (U.S.) Stanford Univ. Linear Accelerator Center, and **Frederick Reines** (U.S.) Los Alamos National Laboratory, for their separate discoveries of "two of nature's most remarkable subatomic particles," Perl's discovery of the tau in the 1970's and Reines's discovery of the neutrino in the 1950's.

1996 Robert C. Richardson (U.S.) and **David M. Lee** (U.S.) of Cornell Univ., and **Douglas S. Osheroff** (U.S.) Stanford Univ., for their 1972 discovery of superfluidity in a rare form of helium which may offer insights into the formation of galaxies.

1997 Steven Chu (U.S.) Stanford Univ., **Claude Cohen-Tannoudji** (France), Collège de France, and **William D. Phillips** (U.S.), National Institute of Standards and Technology, for development of a method to trap individual atoms, which allow them to be studied in greater detail.

1998 Robert B. Laughlin (U.S.), Stanford Univ., **Horst L. Störmer** (U.S.), Bell Laboratories; **Daniel Tsui** (U.S.), Princeton Univ., for their discovery of the fractional quantum Hall effect, the culmination of studies of magnetic fields dating back to 1897.

1999 Gerardus 't Hooft (Netherlands), Univ. of Utrecht; and **Martinus J.G. Veltman** (Netherlands) Univ. of Michigan, for placing the theory of particle physics on firm mathematical ground.

2000 Jack S. Kilby (U.S.), Texas Instruments, for his contribution to the invention of the integrated circuit, a.k.a. the computer chip; **Zhores I. Alferov** (Russia), A.F. Ioffe Physico-Technical Institute, St. Petersburg, and **Herbert Kroemer,** (U.S.), Univ. of California at Santa Barbara, for their invention of components called heterostructures, which are used in high-speed electronic devices.

2001 Eric A. Cornell (U.S.) and **Carl E. Wieman** (U.S.) both of the Joint Institute for Laboratory Astrophysics, Boulder, Colo., and **Wolfgang Ketterle** (Germany), M.I.T., "for the achievement of Bose-Einstein condensation in dilute gases of alkali atoms, and for early fundamental studies of the properties of the condensates."

2002 Raymond Davis Jr., (U.S.), Univ. of Pennsylvania and **Masatoshi Koshiba,** (Japan), Univ. of Tokyo; and **Riccardo Giacconi,** (U.S., B. Italy), Univ. of Milan, "for pioneering contributions to astrophysics." Davis and Koshiba's work led to the detection of cosmic neutrinos, Giacconi built the first X-ray telescopes.

2003 Alexei Abrikosov (U.S. and Russia), Argonne (Illinois) National Laboratory, **Vitaly L. Ginzburg** (Russia), P.N. Ledbedev Physical Institute, Moscow, and **Anthony J. Leggett** (U.S. and U.K.), Univ. of Illinois, for their "pioneering contributions to the theory of superconductors and superfluids."

2004 David J. Gross (U.S.), Kavli Institute for Theoretical Physics, University of California at Santa Barbara; **H. David Politzer** (U.S.), California Institute of Technology; and **Frank Wilczek** (U.S.), M.I.T., "for their discovery of asymptotic freedom in the theory of strong interaction."

2005 Roy T. Glauber (U.S.) "for his contribution to the quantum theory of optical coherence." **John L. Hall** (U.S.) and **Theodor W. Hänsch** (Germany) " for their contributions to the development of laser-based precision spectroscopy, including the optical frequency comb technique."

2006 John C. Mather and **George F. Smoot** (U.S.) "for their discovery of the blackbody form and anisotropy of the cosmic microwave background radiation."

2007 Albert Fert (France) Université Paris-Sud in Orsay, France and **Peter Grünberg** (Germany) Forschungszentrum Jülich in Jülich, Germany "for the discovery of Giant Magnetoresistance."

2008 Yoichiro Nambu, 87, (U.S., b. Japan), Enrico Fermi Institute, Chicago; for his 1960 explanation of how subatomic symmetry might sometimes be "broken" or hidden. **Makoto Kobayashi,** 64, (Japan), High Energy Accelerator Research Organization, Tsukuba, Japan; and **Toshihide Maskawa,** 68, (Japan), Kyoto University; for their 1972 explanations of the origins of spontaneous broken symmetry, which correctly predicted the existence of three families of quarks.

2009 Charles K. Kao (China), Chinese Univ. of Hong Kong, "for groundbreaking achievements concerning the transmission of light in fibers for optical communication"; **Williard S. Boyle** (Canada) and **George E. Smith** (U.S.), Bell Laboratories, "for the invention of an imaging semiconductor unit."

Nobel Prizes in Literature

1901 Sully Prudhomme (pen name of René F.A. Prudhomme) (France) "in special recognition of his poetic composition."

1902 Christian M.T. Mommsen (Germany) "the greatest living master of the art of historical writing, with special reference to his monumental work, *A History of Rome.*

1903 Bjørstjerne M. Bjørnson (Norway) for "his noble, magnificent, and versatile poetry which has always been distinguished by both the freshness of its inspiration and the rare purity of its spirit."

1904 Frédéric Mistral (France) "in recognition of the fresh originality and true inspiration of his poetic production, which faithfully reflects the natural scenery and native spirit of his people, and, in addition, his significant work as a Provençal philologist." **José Echegaray y Eizaguirre** (Spain) "in recognition of the numerous and brilliant compositions which, in an individual and original manner, have revived the great traditions of the Spanish drama."

1905 Henryk Sienkiewicz (Poland) "because of his outstanding merits as an epic writer.

1906 Giosué Carducci (Italy) "as a tribute to the creative energy, freshness of style, and lyrical force which characterize his poetic masterpieces."

1907 Rudyard Kipling (U.K.) "in consideration of the power of observation, originality of imagination, virility of ideas, and remarkable talent for narration which characterize the creations of this world-famous author."

1908 Rudolf C. Eucken (Germany) "in recognition of his earnest search for truth, his penetrating power of thought, his wide range of vision, and the warmth and strength in presentation. . ."

1909 Selma O.L. Lagerlöf (Sweden) "in appreciation of the lofty idealism, vivid imagination, and spiritual perception that characterize her writings."

1910 Paul J.L. Heyse (Germany) "as a tribute to the consummate artistry, permeated with idealism, which he has demonstrated during his long productive career as lyric poet, dramatist, novelist, and writer of world-renowned short stories."

1911 Count Maurice (Mooris) P.M.B. Maeterlinck (Belgium) "in appreciation of his many-sided literary activities, and especially of his dramatic works, which are distinguished by a wealth of imagination and by a poetic fancy."

1912 Gerhart J.R. Hauptmann (Germany) "primarily in recognition of his fruitful, varied, and outstanding production in the realm of dramatic art."

1913 Rabindranath Tagore (India) "because of his profoundly sensitive, fresh, and beautiful verse, by which, with consummate skill, he has made his poetic thought, expressed in his own English words, a part of the literature of the West."

1914 No award

1915 Romain Rolland (France) "as a tribute to the lofty idealism of his literary production and to the sympathy and love of truth with which he has described different types of human beings."

1916 Carl G.V. von Heidenstam (Sweden) "in recognition of his significance as the leading representative of a new era in our literature."

1917 Karl A. Gjellerup (Denmark) "for his varied and rich poetry, which is inspired by lofty ideals"; **Henrik Pontoppidan** (Denmark) "for his authentic descriptions of presentday life in Denmark."

1918 No award

1919 Carl F.G. Spitteler (Switzerland) "in special appreciation of his epic, *Olympian Spring.*"

1920 Knut P. Hamsun (Norway) "for his monumental work, *Growth of the Soil.*"

1921 Anatole France *(pen name of Jacques A. Thibault)* (France) "in recognition of his brilliant literary achievements, characterized as they are by a nobility of style, a profound human sympathy, grace, and a true Gallic temperament."

1922 Jacinto Benavente (Spain) "for the happy manner in which he has continued the illustrious traditions of the Spanish drama."

1923 William Butler Yeats (Ireland) "for his always inspired poetry, which in a highly artistic form gives expression to the spirit of a whole nation."

1924 Wladyslaw S. Reymont (pen name of Reyment) (Poland) "for his great national epic, *The Peasants.*"

1925 George Bernard Shaw (U.K.) "for his work which is marked by both idealism and humanity, its stimulating satire often being infused with a singular poetic beauty."

1926 Grazia Deledda (pen name of Grazia Madesani) (Italy) "for her idealistically inspired writings, which picture the life on her native island and with depth and sympathy deal with human problems."

1927 Henri Bergson (France) "in recognition of his rich and vitalizing ideas."

1928 Sigrid Undset (Norway) "principally for her powerful descriptions of Northern life during the Middle Ages."

1929 Thomas Mann (Germany) "principally for his great novel *Buddenbrooks.*"

1930 Sinclair Lewis (U.S.) "for his vigorous and graphic art of description and his ability to create, with wit and humor, new types of characters."

1931 Erik A. Karlfeldt (Sweden) for his poetry.

1932 John Galsworthy (U.K.) "for his distinguished art of narration which takes its highest form in *The Forsyte Saga.*"

1933 Ivan A. Bunin (stateless domicile in France) "for the strict artistry with which he has carried on the classical Russian traditions in prose writing."

1934 Luigi Pirandello (Italy) "for his bold and ingenious revival of dramatic art."

1935 No award

1936 Eugene G. O'Neill (U.S.) "for the power, honesty, and deep-felt emotions of his dramatic works, which embody an original concept of tragedy."

1937 Roger Martin du Gard (France) "for the artistic power and truth with which he has depicted human conflict as well as some fundamental aspects of contemporary life in his novel-cycle *Les Thibault.*"

1938 Pearl Buck (pen name of Pearl Walsh) (U.S.) "for her rich and truly epic descriptions of peasant life in China and for her biographical masterpieces."

1939 Frans E. Sillanpää (Finland) "for his deep understanding of his country's peasantry and the exquisite art with which he has portrayed their way of life and their relationship with Nature."

1940–1943 No awards given.

1944 Johannes V. Jensen (Denmark) "for the rare strength and fertility of his poetic imagination."

1945 Gabriela Mistral (pen name of Lucila Godoy y Alcayaga) (Chile) "for her lyric poetry which, has made her name a symbol of the idealistic aspirations of the entire Latin American world."

1946 Hermann Hesse (Switzerland) "for his inspired writings which exemplify the classical humanitarian ideals and high qualities of style."

1947 André P.G. Gide (France) "for his writings in which human problems and conditions have been presented with a fearless love of truth and keen psychological insight."

1948 Thomas S. Eliot (U.K.) for his "outstanding, pioneer contribution to present-day poetry."

1949 William Faulkner (U.S.) ":for his powerful and artistically unique contribution to the modern American novel."

1950 Earl (Bertrand) Russell (U.K.) "in recognition of his varied and significant writings in which he champions humanitarian ideals and freedom of thought."

1951 Pär Fabian Lägerkvist (Sweden) "for the artistic vigour and true independence of mind with which he endeavours in his poetry to find answers to the eternal questions confronting mankind."

1952 François Mauriac (France) "for the deep spiritual insight and the artistic intensity with which he has in his novels penetrated the drama of human life."

1953 Sir Winston L.S. Churchill (U.K.) "for his mastery of historical and biographical description as well as for brilliant oratory in defending exalted human values."

1954 Ernest M. Hemingway (U.S.) "for his mastery of the art of narrative, most recently demonstrated in *The Old Man and the Sea,* and for the influence that he has exerted on contemporary style."

1955 Halldór K. Laxness (Iceland) "for his vivid epic power which has renewed the great narrative art of Iceland."

1956 Juan R. Jiménez (Puerto Rico, b. Spain) "for his lyrical poetry, which in Spanish language constitutes an example of high spirit and artistic purity."

1957 Albert Camus (France) "for his important literary production, which with clearsighted earnestness illuminates the problems of the human conscience in our times."

1958 Boris L. Pasternak (USSR) "for his important achievement both in contemporary lyrical poetry and in the field of the great Russian epic tradition." (Declined the prize.)

1959 Salvatore Quasimodo (Italy) "for his lyrical poetry, which with classical fire expresses the tragic experience of life in our own times."

1960 Saint-John Perse (pen name of Alexis Léger) (France) "for the soaring flight and the evocative imagery of his poetry which in a visionary fashion reflects the conditions of our time."

1961 Ivo Andric (Yugoslavia) "for the epic force with which he has traced themes and depicted human destinies drawn from the history of his country."

1962 John Steinbeck (U.S.) "for his realistic and imaginative writings, combining as they do sympathetic humour and keen social perception."

1963 Giorgos Seferis (pen name of Giorgos Seferiadis) (Greece) "for his eminent lyrical writing, inspired by a deep feeling for the Hellenic world of culture."

1964 Jean-Paul Sartre (France) "for his work which, rich in ideas and filled with the spirit of freedom and the quest for truth, has exerted a far-reaching influence on our age." (Declined the prize.)

1965 Michail A. Sholokhov (U.S.S.R.) "for the artistic power and integrity with which, in his epic of the Don, he has given expression to a historic phase in the life of the Russian people."

1966 Shmuel U. Agnon (Israel) "for his profoundly characteristic narrative art with motifs from the life of the Jewish people; **Nelly Sachs** (Germany, domiciled in Sweden) " for her outstanding lyrical and dramatic writing, which interprets Israel's destiny with touching strength."

1967 Miguel A. Asturias (Guatemala) "for his vivid literary achievement, deep-rooted in the national traits and traditions of Indian peoples of Latin America."

1968 Yasunari Kawabata (Japan) "for his narrative mastery, which with great sensibility expresses the essence of the Japanese mind."

1969 Samuel Beckett (Ireland) "for his writing, which—in new forms for the novel and drama—in the destitution of modern man acquires its elevation."

1970 Alexander Solzhenitsyn (USSR) "for the ethical force with which he has pursued the indispensable traditions of Russian literature."

1971 Pablo Neruda (pen name of Neftalí Ricardo Reyes Basoalto) (Chile) "for a poetry that brings alive a continent's destiny and dreams."

1972 Heinrich Böll (West Germany) "for his writing which through its combination of a broad perspective on his time and a sensitive skill in characterization has contributed to a renewal of German literature."

1973 Patrick White (Australia, b. U.K.) "for an epic and psychological narrative art which has introduced a new continent into literature."

1974 Eyvind Johnson (Sweden) "for a narrative art, far-seeing in lands and ages, in the service of freedom"; **Harry Martinson** (Sweden) "for writings that catch the dewdrop and reflect the cosmos."

1975 Eugenio Montale (Italy) "for his distinctive poetry which, with great artistic sensitivity, has interpreted human values under the sign of an outlook on life with no illusions."

1976 Saul Bellow (U.S.) "for the human understanding and subtle analysis of contemporary culture."

1977 Vincente Aleixandre (Spain) "for a creative poetic writing which illuminates man's condition in the cosmos and in present-day society, at the same time representing the great renewal of the traditions of Spanish poetry between the wars."

1978 Isaac Bashevis Singer (U.S., b. Poland) "for his impassioned narrative art which, with roots in a Polish-Jewish cultural tradition, brings universal human conditions to life."

1979 Odysseus Elytis (pen name of Odysseus Alepoudhelis) (Greece) "for his poetry, which against the background of Greek tradition, depicts man's struggle for freedom and creativeness."

1980 Czeslaw Milosz (U.S. and Poland) "who with uncompromising clear-sightedness voices man's exposed condition in a world of severe conflicts."

1981 Elias Canetti (U.K., b. Bulgaria) "for writings marked by a broad outlook, a wealth of ideas, and artistic power."

1982 Gabriel García Marquez (Colombia) "for his novels and short stories, in which the fantastic and the realistic are combined in a richly composed world of imagination, reflecting a continent's life and conflicts."

1983 William Golding (U.K.) "for his novels, which illuminate the human condition in the world of today."

1984 Jaroslav Seifert (Czechoslovakia) "for his poetry which, endowed with freshness, sensuality, and rich inventiveness, provides a liberating image of the indomitable spirit and versatility of man."

1985 Claude Simon (France) "who in his novel combines the poet's and the painter's creativeness with a deepened awareness of time in the depiction of the human condition."

1986 Wole Soyinka (Nigeria) "who in a wide cultural perspective and with poetic overtones fashions the drama of existence."

1987 Joseph Brodsky (U.S., b. U.S.S.R.) "for his all-embracing authorship imbued with clarity of thought and poetic intensity."

1988 Naguib Mahfouz (Egypt) "who through works rich in nuance, has formed an Arabian narrative art that applies to all mankind."

1989 Camilo José Cela (Spain) a novelist whose "rich and inventive prose, forms a challenging vision of man's vulnerability." His most famous work is *The Family of Pascual Duarte* (1942).

1990 Octavio Paz (Mexico) poet and social essayist. Volumes include *The Labyrinth of Solitude* (1950), *Sunstone* (1957), and *Sor Juana: Or, the Traps of Faith* (1990).

1991 Nadine Gordimer (South Africa) for her "involvement on behalf of literature and free speech in a police state where censorship and persecution of books and people exist."

1992 Derek Walcott (West Indies, b. St. Lucia), poet and playwright whose works evoke the cultural diversity of the Carribean "but through them he speaks to each and every one of us."

1993 Toni Morrison (U.S.), whose novels about racial prejudice are "characterized by visionary force and poetic import."

1994 Kenzaburo Oe (Japan), best known for his accounts of the atomic bombing of Hiroshima. The poetic force of his writing "creates an imagined world where life and myth condense to form a disconcerting picture of the human predicament."

1995 Seamus Heaney (Ireland), poet and essayist, "for works of lyrical beauty and ethical depth, which exalt everyday miracles and the living past."

1996 Wislawa Szymborska (Poland), a poet whose work contemplates the oddities of daily life.

1997 Dario Fo, (Italy), a leftist playwright, best known for biting political satires (*Can't Pay, Won't Pay* and *Accidental Death of an Anarchist*), which brought threats of censure and condemnation from the Italian government and the Catholic Church.

1998 José Saramago (Portugal), for his richly imaginative works that often use the supernatural and irrational to address questions of faith. Best known novels include: *Baltasar and Blimunda* (1982), *The Year of the Death of Ricardo Reis* (1984).

1999 Günter Grass (Germany) "whose frolicsome black fables portray the forgotten face of history." His epic 1959 novel, *The Tin Drum* addressed the uncomfortable issue of the German national identity through the Nazi era.

2000 Gao Xingjian (France, b. China), one of the most important Chinese dramatists of the 20th century, whose most significant works have been banned in China since the 1980s.

2001 V.S. Naipaul (U.K., b. Trinidad) His fiction, including *A House for Mr. Biswas* (1961) and *The Enigma of Arrival* (1987) is often highly autobiographical, exploring the challenges faced by post-colonial societies like his ancestral home of India.

2002 Imre Kertész, (Hungary) "for writing that upholds the fragile experience of the individual against the barbaric arbitrariness of history." His most important work is *Fateless*, a novel about a man who, like Kertész himself, is forced to spend his youth in a concentration camp.

2003 J.M. Coetzee (South Africa) "who in innumerable guises portrays the surprising involvement of the outsider." His novels have often focused on apartheid; first author to win the Booker Prize twice, for *Life and Times for Michael K.* (1983) and *Disgrace* (1999).

2004 Elfriede Jelinek (Austria), "for her musical flow of voices and counter-voices in novels and plays that with extraordinary linguistic zeal reveal the absurdity of society's clichés and their subjugating power." Her best-known novel is the semi-autobiographical *The Piano Teacher*, which was translated into English in 1988.

2005 Harold Pinter (U.K.) "who in his plays uncovers the precipice under everyday prattle and forces entry into oppression's closed rooms."

2006 Orhan Pamuk (Turkey) "who in the quest for the melancholic soul of his native city has discovered new symbols for the clash and interlacing of cultures."

2007 Doris Lessing (U.K., b. Persia), "that epicist of the female experience, who with skepticism, fire and visionary power has subjected a divided civilization to scrutiny."

2008 Jean-Marie Gustave Le Clézio, (France); "author of new departures, poetic adventures and sensual ecstasy, explorer of a humanity beyond and below the reigning civilization."

2009 Herta Muller (Germany), "who, with the concentration of poetry and the frankness of prose, depicts the landscape of the dispossessed."

THE NCAA

National Collegiate Athletic Association (NCAA)
One NCAA Place
700 W. Washington St.
Indianapolis, Ind. 46204
(317) 917–6222
www.ncaa.org

The NCAA acts as the governing body of intercollegiate athletics, setting the playing rules for each sport, and eligibility standards for athletes.

COLLEGE FOOTBALL

NCAA National Football Champions

For many years, college football selected its national champion through an arcane structure of bowl games and two press association polls (one of coaches, the other of writers), which often did not agree with each other, creating co-champions and arguments about which was the better team.

In 1998, the NCAA adopted the Bowl Alliance, in which the top two teams (as determined by the same two polls) meet in a national championship game that rotates annually among the Rose, Fiesta, Orange, and Sugar Bowls. But in 2003, three teams finished the season with only one loss. Louisiana State defeated Oklahoma in the National Championship game, but the Associated Press poll of writers gave its top ranking to U.S.C., which had been denied the chance to play in the title game.

Year	Team	Year	Team	Year	Team
1936	Minnesota	1961	Alabama	1986	Penn State
1937	Pittsburgh	1962	U.S.C.	1987	Miami (Fla.)
1938	T.C.U.	1963	Texas	1988	Notre Dame
1939	Texas A&M	1964	Alabama	1989	Miami (Fla.)
1940	Minnesota	1965	Alabama and Michigan St.	1990	Colo. and Georgia Tech
1941	Minnesota	1966	Notre Dame	1991	Miami and Washington
1942	Ohio State	1967	U.S.C.	1992	Alabama
1943	Notre Dame	1968	Ohio State	1993	Florida State
1944	Army	1969	Texas	1994	Nebraska
1945	Army	1970	Nebraska and Texas	1995	Nebraska
1946	Notre Dame	1971	Nebraska	1996	Florida
1947	Notre Dame	1972	U.S.C.	1997	Michigan and Nebraska
1948	Michigan	1973	Notre Dame and Alabama	1998	Tennessee
1949	Notre Dame	1974	U.S.C. and Oklahoma	1999	Florida State
1950	Oklahoma	1975	Oklahoma	2000	Oklahoma
1951	Tennessee	1976	Pittsburgh	2001	Miami (Fla.)
1952	Michigan St.	1977	Notre Dame	2002	Ohio State
1953	Maryland	1978	Alabama and U.S.C.	2003	Louisiana State and U.S.C.
1954	Ohio State and U.C.L.A.	1979	Alabama	2004	U.S.C.
1955	Oklahoma	1980	Georgia	2005	Texas
1956	Oklahoma	1981	Clemson	2006	Florida
1957	Auburn and Ohio State	1982	Penn State	2007	Louisiana State
1958	Louisiana St.	1983	Miami (Fla.)	2008	Florida
1959	Syracuse	1984	B.Y.U.	2009	Alabama
1960	Minnesota	1985	Oklahoma		

Source: NCAA.

NCAA National Championship Game Results, 1998–2009

Year	Bowl	Score	Year	Bowl	Score
1998	Fiesta	Tennessee 23, Florida State, 16	2004	Orange	U.S.C. 55, Oklahoma 19
1999	Sugar	Florida State 46, Virginia Tech 29	2005	Rose	Texas 41, U.S.C. 38
2000	Orange	Oklahoma 13, Florida State 2	2006	BCS	Florida 41, Ohio State 14
2001	Rose	Miami (Fla.) 37, Nebraska 14	2007	BCS	LSU 38, Ohio State 24
2002	Fiesta	Ohio State 31, Miami (Fla.) 24 (2OT)	2008	BCS	Florida 24, Oklahoma 14
2003	Sugar	Louisiana State 21, Oklahoma 14	2009	BCS	Alabama 37, Texas 21

Note: The National Championship game is played in January of the following year. Years shown refer to the year of the championship.

NCAA Football-Major Bowl Games, 1916–2010

ROSE BOWL (Pasadena, California)

1916	Washington St. 14, Brown 0
1917	Oregon 14, Pennsylvania 0
1918	Mare Island 19, Camp Lewis 7
1919	Great Lakes 17, Mare Island 0
1920	Harvard 7, Oregon 6
1921	California 28, Ohio State 0
1922	Washington and Jefferson 0, Cal. 0
1923	U.S.C. 14, Penn State 3
1924	Navy 14, Washington 14
1925	Notre Dame 27, Stanford 10
1926	Alabama 20, Washington 19
1927	Alabama 7, Stanford 7
1928	Stanford 7, Pittsburgh 6
1929	Georgia Tech 8, California 7
1930	U.S.C. 47, Pittsburgh 14
1931	Alabama 24, Washington State 0
1932	U.S.C. 21, Tulane 12
1933	U.S.C. 35, Pittsburgh 0
1934	Columbia 7, Stanford 0
1935	Alabama 29, Stanford 13
1936	Stanford 7, Southern Methodist 0
1937	Pittsburgh 21, Washington 0
1938	California 13, Alabama 0
1939	U.S.C. 7, Duke 3
1940	U.S.C. 14, Tennessee 0
1941	Stanford 21, Nebraska 13
1942	Oregon State 20, Duke 16 (at Durham)
1943	Georgia 9, U.C.L.A. 0
1944	U.S.C. 29, Washington 0
1945	U.S.C. 25, Tennessee 0
1946	Alabama 34, U.S.C. 14
1947	Illinois 45, U.C.L.A. 14
1948	Michigan 49, U.S.C. 0
1949	Northwestern 20, California 14
1950	Ohio State 17, California 14
1951	Michigan 14, California 6
1952	Illinois 40, Stanford 7
1953	U.S.C. 7, Wisconsin 0
1954	Michigan State 28, U.C.L.A. 20
1955	Ohio State 20, U.S.C. 7
1956	Michigan State 17, U.C.L.A. 14
1957	Iowa 35, Oregon State 19
1958	Ohio State 10, Oregon 7
1959	Iowa 38, California 12
1960	Washington 44, Wisconsin 8
1961	Washington 17, Minnesota 7
1962	Minnesota 21, U.C.L.A. 3
1963	U.S.C. 42, Wisconsin 37
1964	Illinois 17, Washington 7
1965	Michigan 34, Oregon State7
1966	U.C.L.A. 14, Michigan State 12
1967	Purdue 14, U.S.C. 13
1968	U.S.C. 14, Indiana 3
1969	Ohio State 27, U.S.C. 16
1970	U.S.C. 10, Michigan 3
1971	Stanford 27, Ohio State 17
1972	Stanford 13, Michigan 12
1973	U.S.C. 42, Ohio State 17
1974	Ohio State 42, U.S.C. 21
1975	U.S.C.18, Ohio State 17
1976	U.C.L.A. 23, Ohio State 10
1977	U.S.C. 14, Michigan 6
1978	Washington 27, Michigan 20
1979	U.S.C. 17, Michigan 10
1980	U.S.C. 17, Ohio State 16
1981	Michigan 23, Washington 6
1982	Washington 28, Iowa 0
1983	U.C.L.A. 24, Michigan 14
1984	U.C.L.A. 45, Illinois 9
1985	U.S.C. 20, Ohio State 17
1986	U.C.L.A. 45, Iowa 28
1987	Arizona State 22, Michigan 15
1988	Michigan State 20, U.S.C. 17
1989	Michigan 22, U.S.C. 14
1990	U.S.C. 17, Michigan 10
1991	Washington 46, Iowa 34
1992	Washington 34, Michigan 14
1993	Michigan 38, Washington 31
1994	Wisconsin 21, U.C.L.A. 16
1995	Penn State 38, Oregon 20
1996	U.S.C. 41, Northwestern 32
1997	Ohio State 20, Arizona State 17
1998	Michigan 21, Washington State 16
1999	Wisconsin 38, U.C.L.A. 31
2000	Wisconsin 17, Stanford 9
2001	Washington 34, Purdue 24
2002	Miami (Fla.) 37, Nebraska 14
2003	Oklahoma 34, Washington St. 14
2004	U.S.C. 28, Michigan 14
2005	Texas 38, Michigan 37
2006	Texas 41, U.S.C. 38
2007	U.S.C. 32, Michigan 18
2008	U.S.C. 49, Illinios 17
2009	U.S.C. 38, Penn St. 24
2010	Ohio State 26, Oregon 17

Year	ORANGE BOWL, Miami, Florida	SUGAR BOWL, New Orleans	COTTON BOWL, Dallas
1935	Bucknell 26, Miami (Fla.) 0	Tulane 20, Temple 14	not played
1936	Catholic U. 20, Mississippi 19	Texas Christian 3, L.S.U. 2	not played
1937	Duquesne 13, Mississippi St. 12	Santa Clara 21, L.S.U. 14	T.C.U. 16, Marquette 6
1938	Auburn 6, Michigan State 0	Santa Clara 6, L.S.U. 0	Rice 28, Colorado 14
1939	Tennessee 17, Oklahoma 0	T.C.U. 15, Carnegie Tech 7	St. Mary's 20, Texas Tech 13
1940	Georgia Tech 21, Missouri 7	Texas A&M 14, Tulane 13	Clemson 6, Boston College 3
1941	Mississippi St. 14, Georgetown 7	Boston College 19, Tennessee 13	Texas A&M 13, Fordham 12
1942	Georgia 40, Texas Christian 26	Fordham 2, Missouri 0	Alabama 29, Texas A&M 21
1943	Alabama 37, Boston College 21	Tennessee 14, Tulsa 7	Texas 14, Georgia Tech 7
1944	Louisiana St. 19, Texas A&M 14	Georgia Tech 20, Tulsa 18	Texas 7, Randolph Field 7
1945	Tulsa 26, Georgia Tech 12	Duke 29, Alabama 26	Oklahoma A&M 34, T.C.U. 0
1946	Miami (Fla.)13, Holy Cross 6	Okla. A&M 33, St. Mary's Co. 13	Texas 40, Missouri 27
1947	Rice 8, Tennessee 0	Georgia 20, North Carolina 10	Arkansas 0, Louisiana State 0
1948	Georgia Tech 20, Kansas 14	Texas 27, Alabama 7	S.M.U. 13, Penn State 13
1949	Texas 41, Georgia 28	Oklahoma 14, North Carolina 6	S.M.U. 21, Oregon 13
1950	Santa Clara 21, Kentucky 13	Oklahoma 35, Louisiana State 0	Rice 27, North Carolina 13
1951	Clemson 15, Miami (Fla.)14	Kentucky 13, Oklahoma 7	Tennessee 20, Texas 14
1952	Georgia Tech 20, Baylor 14	Maryland 28, Tennessee 13	Kentucky 20, Texas Christian 7
1953	Alabama 61, Syracuse 6	Georgia Tech 24, Mississippi 7	Texas 16, Tennessee 0
1954	Oklahoma 7, Maryland 0	Georgia Tech 42, W. Virginia 19	Rice 28, Alabama 0
1955	Duke 34, Nebraska 7	Navy 21, Mississippi 0	Georgia Tech 14, Arkansas 6
1956	Oklahoma 20, Maryland 6	Georgia Tech 7, Pittsburgh 0	Mississippi 14, Texas Christian 13

Year	ORANGE BOWL, Miami, Florida	SUGAR BOWL, New Orleans	COTTON BOWL, Dallas
1957	Colorado 27, Clemson 21	Baylor 13, Tennessee 7	Texas Christian 28, Syracuse 27
1958	Oklahoma 48, Duke 21	Mississippi 39, Texas 7	Navy 20, Rice 7
1959	Oklahoma 21, Syracuse 6	Louisiana State 7, Clemson 0	Texas Christian 0, Air Force 0
1960	Georgia 14, Missouri 0	Mississippi 21, L.S.U. 0	Syracuse 23, Texas 14
1961	Missouri 21, Navy 14	Mississippi 14, Rice 6	Duke 7, Arkansas 6
1962	Louisiana State 25, Colorado 7	Alabama 10, Arkansas 3	Texas 12, Mississippi 7
1963	Alabama 17, Oklahoma 0	Mississippi 17, Arkansas 13	Louisiana State 13, Texas 0
1964	Nebraska 13, Auburn 7	Alabama 12, Mississippi 7	Texas 28, Navy 6
1965	Texas 21, Alabama 17	Louisiana State 13, Syracuse 10	Arkansas 10, Nebraska 7
1966	Alabama 39, Nebraska 28	Missouri 20, Florida 18	Louisiana State 14, Arkansas 7
1967	Florida 27, Georgia Tech 12	Alabama 34, Nebraska 7	Georgia 24, S.M.U. 9
1968	Oklahoma 26, Tennessee 24	L.S.U. 20, Wyoming 13	Texas A&M 20, Alabama 16
1969	Penn State 15, Kansas 14	Arkansas 16, Georgia 2	Texas 36, Tennessee 13
1970	Penn State 10, Missouri 3	Mississippi 27, Arkansas 22	Texas 21, Notre Dame 17
1971	Nebraska 17, Louisiana State 12	Tennessee 34, Air Force 13	Notre Dame 24, Texas 11
1972	Nebraska 38, Alabama 6	Oklahoma 40, Auburn 22	Penn State 30, Texas 6
1973	Nebraska 40, Notre Dame 6	Oklahoma 14, Penn State 0	Texas 17, Alabama 13
1974	Penn State 16, Louisiana State 9	Notre Dame 24, Alabama 23	Nebraska 19, Texas 3
1975	Notre Dame 13, Alabama 11	Nebraska 13, Florida 10	Penn State 41, Baylor 20
1976	Oklahoma 14, Michigan 6	Alabama 13, Penn State 7	Arkansas 31, Georgia 10
1977	Ohio State 27, Colorado 10	Pittsburgh 27, Georgia 3	Houston 30, Maryland 21
1978	Arkansas 31, Oklahoma 6	Alabama 35, Ohio State 6	Notre Dame 38, Texas 10
1979	Oklahoma 31, Nebraska 24	Alabama 14, Penn State	Notre Dame 35, Houston 34
1980	Oklahoma 24, Florida State 7	Alabama 24, Arkansas 9	Houston 17, Nebraska 14
1981	Oklahoma 18, Florida State 17	Georgia 17, Notre Dame 10	Alabama 30, Baylor 2
1982	Clemson 22, Nebraska 15	Pittsburgh 24, Georgia 20	Texas 14, Alabama 12
1983	Nebraska 21, L.S.U. 20	Penn State 27, Georgia 23	S.M.U. 7, Pittsburgh 3
1984	Miami (Fla.) 31, Nebraska 30	Auburn 9, Michigan 7	Georgia 10, Texas 9
1985	Washington 28, Oklahoma 17	Nebraska 28, Louisiana State 10	Boston College 45, Houston 28
1986	Oklahoma 25, Penn State 10	Tennessee 35, Miami (Fla.) 7	Texas A&M 36, Auburn 16
1987	Oklahoma 42, Arkansas 8	Nebraska 30, Louisiana State 15	Ohio State 28, Texas A&M 12
1988	Miami (Fla.) 20, Oklahoma 14	Syracuse 16, Auburn 16	Texas A&M 35, Notre Dame 10
1989	Miami (Fla.) 23, Nebraska 3	Florida State 13, Auburn 7	U.C.L.A. 17, Arkansas 3
1990	Notre Dame 21, Colorado 6	Miami (Fla.) 33, Alabama 25	Tennessee 31, Arkansas 27
1991	Colorado 10, Notre Dame 9	Tennessee 23, Virginia 22	Miami (Fla.) 46, Texas 3
1992	Miami (Fla.) 22, Nebraska 0	Notre Dame 39, Florida 28	Florida St. 10, Texas A&M 2
1993	Florida State 27, Nebraska 14	Alabama 34, Miami 13	Notre Dame 28, Texas A&M 3
1994	Florida State 18, Nebraska 16	Florida 41, West Virginia 7	Notre Dame 24, Texas A&M 21
1995	Nebraska 24, Miami 17	Florida State 23, Florida 17	U.S.C. 55, Texas Tech 14
1996	Florida St. 31, Notre Dame 26	Virginia Tech 28, Texas 10	Colorado 38, Oregon 6
1997	Nebraska 41, Virginia Tech 21	Florida 52, Florida State 20	B.Y.U. 19, Kansas State 15
1998	Nebraska 42, Tennessee 17	Florida State 31, Ohio State 14	U.C.L.A. 29, Texas A&M 23
1999	Florida 31, Syracuse 10	Ohio State 24, Texas A&M 14	Texas 38, Mississippi State 11
2000	Michigan 35, Alabama 34	Florida State 46, Virginia Tech 29	Arkansas 27, Texas 6
2001	Oklahoma 13, Florida State 2	Miami 37, Florida 20	Kansas St. 35, Tennessee 21
2002	Florida 56, Maryland 23	Louisiana State 47, Illinois 34	Oklahoma 10, Arkansas 3
2003	U.S.C. 38, Iowa 17	Georgia 26, Florida State 13	Texas 35, Louisiana State 20
2004	Miami (Fla.) 16, Florida St. 14	Louisiana St. 21, Oklahoma 14	Mississippi 31, Oklahoma St. 28
2005	U.S.C. 55, Oklahoma 19	Auburn 16, Virginia Tech 13	Tennessee 38, Texas A&M 7
2006	Penn State 26, Florida State 23	West Virginia 38, Georgia 35	Alabama 13, Texas Tech 10
2007	Louisville 24, Wake Forest 13	L.S.U. 41, Notre Dame 14	Auburn 17, Nebraska 14
2008	Kansas 24, Virginia Tech 21	Georgia 41, Hawaii 10	Missouri 38, Arkansas 7
2009	Virginia Tech 20, Cincinnati 7	Utah 31, Alabama 17	Ole Miss 47, Texas Tech 34
2010	Iowa 24, Georgia Tech 14	Florida 51, Cincinnati 24	Mississippi 21, Oklahoma St. 7

NCAA Football Career Leaders

Player, Team	Years	PASSING, Career yards Att.	Comp.	Int.	Pct.	Yards	TD
Timmy Chang, Hawaii	2000–2004	2,436	1,388	80	.570	17,072	117
Graham Harrell, Texas Tech	2005–2008	2,010	1,403	34	.698	15,793	134
Ty Detmer, Brigham Young	1988–1991	1,530	958	65	.626	15,031	121
Colt Brennan, Hawaii	2005–2007	1,584	1,115	42	.704	14,193	131
Philip Rivers, North Carolina St.	2000–2003	1,710	1,147	34	.671	13,484	95
Kevin Kolb, Houston	2003–2006	1,565	964	31	.616	12,964	85
Tim Rattay, Louisiana Tech	1997–1999	1,552	1,015	35	.654	12,746	115
Luke McCown, Louisiana Tech	2000–2003	1,775	1,063	62	.599	12,666	87
Chris Redman, Louisville	1996–1999	1,679	1,031	51	.614	12,541	84
Chase Daniel, Missouri	2005–2008	1,609	1,094	41	.680	12,515	101

CAREER POINTS (Nonkickers)

Player, Team	Years	TDs	Pts.
Travis Prentice, Miami (Ohio)	1996–99	78	468
Ricky Williams, Texas	1995–98	75	452
Taureen Henderson, Texas Tech	2002–05	69	414
Brock Forsey, Boise State	1999–02	68	408
Cedric Benson, Texas	2001–04	67	404
Anthony Thompson, Indiana	1968–69	65	394
Ron Dayne, Wisconsin	1996–99	63	378
Marshall Faulk, San Diego St.	1991–93	62	376
Eric Crouch, Nebraska	1998–01	59	374
DeAngelo Williams, Memphis	2002–05	60	362

CAREER POINTS (Kickers)

Player, Team	Years	PAT	FG	Pts.
Art Carmody, Louisville	2004–07	253	60	433
Kevin Kelly, Penn St.	2005–08	183	78	425
Roman Anderson, Houston	1988–91	213	70	423
Billy Bennett, Georgia	2000–03	148	87	409
Jeremy Ito, Rutgers	2004–07	160	80	400
Carlos Huerta, Miami (Fla.)	1988–91	178	73	397
Jason Elam, Hawaii	1988–92	158	79	395
Derek Schmidt, Florida St.	1984–87	174	73	393
Nick Novak, Maryland	2001–04	153	80	393
Kris Brown, Nebraska	1995–98	217	57	388

RUSHING, Career yards

Player, Team	Years	Carries	Yards
Ron Dayne, Wisconsin	1996–99	1,115	6,397
Ricky Williams, Texas	1995–98	1,011	6,279
Tony Dorsett, Pittsburgh	1973–76	1,074	6,082
DeAngelo Williams, Memphis	2002–05	969	6,026
Charles White, U.S.C.	1976–79	1,023	5,598
Travis Prentice, Miami (Ohio)	1996–99	1,138	5,596
Cedric Benson, Texas	2001–04	1,112	5,540
LaDainian Tomlinson, TCU	1997–00	907	5,263
Herschel Walker, Georgia	1980–82	994	5,259
Archie Griffin, Ohio State	1972–75	845	5,177

RECEIVING, Career catches

Player, Team	Years	Catches	Yards
Taylor Stubblefield, Purdue	2001–04	316	3,433
Josh Davis, Marshall	2001–04	306	3,889
Taureen Henderson, Texas Tech	2002–05	303	2,058
Arnold Jackson, Louisville	1997–00	300	3,670
Trevor Insley, Nevada	1996–99	298	5,005
Geoff Noisy, Nevada	1995–98	295	4,249
Rashaun Woods, Oklahoma St.	2000–03	293	4,412
Davone Bess, Hawaii	2005–07	293	3,610
Jason Rivers, Hawaii	03–04,06–07	292	3,919
Dorien Bryant, Purdue	2004–07	292	3,548

Heisman Memorial Trophy

Year	Player	College	Pos.	Year	Player	College	Pos.
1935	Jay Berwanger	Chicago	HB	1973	John Cappelletti	Penn State	RB
1936	Larry Kelley	Yale	E	1974	Archie Griffin	Ohio State	RB
1937	Clint Frank	Yale	HB	1975	Archie Griffin	Ohio State	RB
1938	Davey O'Brien	Texas Christian	QB	1976	Tony Dorsett	Pittsburgh	RB
1939	Nile Kinnick	Iowa	HB	1977	Earl Campbell	Texas	RB
1940	Tom Harmon	Michigan	HB	1978	Billy Sims	Oklahoma	RB
1941	Bruce Smith	Minnesota	HB	1979	Charles White	U.S.C.	RB
1942	Frank Sinkwich	Georgia	HB	1980	George Rogers	South Carolina	RB
1943	Angelo Bertelli	Notre Dame	QB	1981	Marcus Allen	U.S.C.	RB
1944	Les Horvath	Ohio State	QB	1982	Herschel Walker	Georgia	RB
1945	Doc Blanchard	Army	FB	1983	Mike Rozier	Nebraska	RB
1946	Glenn Davis	Army	HB	1984	Doug Flutie	Boston College	QB
1947	John Lujack	Notre Dame	QB	1985	Bo Jackson	Auburn	RB
1948	Doak Walker	S.M.U.	HB	1986	Vinny Testaverde	Miami (Fla.)	QB
1949	Leon Hart	Notre Dame	E	1987	Tim Brown	Notre Dame	WR
1950	Vic Janowicz	Ohio State	HB	1988	Barry Sanders	Oklahoma State	RB
1951	Dick Kazmaier	Princeton	HB	1989	Andre Ware	Houston	QB
1952	Billy Vessels	Oklahoma	HB	1990	Ty Detmer	Brigham Young	QB
1953	John Lattner	Notre Dame	HB	1991	Desmond Howard	Michigan	WR
1954	Alan Ameche	Wisconsin	FB	1992	Gino Toretta	Miami (Fla.)	QB
1955	Howard Cassady	Ohio State	HB	1993	Charlie Ward	Florida State	QB
1956	Paul Hornung	Notre Dame	QB	1994	Rashaan Salaam	Colorado	RB
1957	John David Crow	Texas A&M	HB	1995	Eddie George	Ohio State	RB
1958	Pete Dawkins	Army	HB	1996	Danny Wuerffel	Florida	QB
1959	Billy Cannon	Louisiana State	HB	1997	Charles Woodson	Michigan	CB
1960	Joe Bellino	Navy	HB	1998	Ricky Williams	Texas	TB
1961	Ernie Davis	Syracuse	HB	1999	Ron Dayne	Wisconsin	TB
1962	Terry Baker	Oregon State	QB	2000	Chris Weinke	Florida State	QB
1963	Roger Staubach	Navy	QB	2001	Eric Crouch	Nebraska	QB
1964	John Huarte	Notre Dame	QB	2002	Carson Palmer	U.S.C.	QB
1965	Mike Garrett	U.S.C.	HB	2003	Jason White	Oklahoma	QB
1966	Steve Spurrier	Florida	QB	2004	Matt Leinart	U.S.C.	QB
1967	Gary Beban	U.C.L.A.	QB	2005	Reggie Bush[1]	U.S.C.	RB
1968	O.J. Simpson	U.S.C.	HB	2006	Troy Smith	Ohio State	QB
1969	Steve Owens	Oklahoma	HB	2007	Tim Tebow	Florida	QB
1970	Jim Plunkett	Stanford	QB	2008	Sam Bradford	Oklahoma	QB
1971	Pat Sullivan	Auburn	QB	2009	Mark Ingram	Alabama	RB
1972	Johnny Rodgers	Nebraska	WR				

Note: 1. Relinquished his trophy in 2010. Award is currently vacant.

COLLEGE BASKETBALL

NCAA Division I Men's Basketball Championship Final Four Results

Year	Champion	Score	Runner-up	Third place	Fourth place	Champion coach
1940	Indiana	60–42	Kansas	Duquesne[1]	U.S.C. [1]	Branch McCracken
1941	Wisconsin	39–34	Washington St.	Pittsburgh[1]	Arkansas[1]	Harold Foster
1942	Stanford	53–38	Dartmouth	Colorado[1]	Kentucky[1]	Everett Dean
1943	Wyoming	46–34	Georgetown	Texas[1]	DePaul[1]	Everett Shelton
1944	Utah	42–40[2]	Dartmouth	Iowa State[1]	Ohio State [1]	Vadal Peterson
1945	Oklahoma State	49–45	N.Y.U.	Arkansas[1]	Ohio State[1]	Henry Iba
1946	Oklahoma State	43–40	North Carolina	Ohio St.	California	Henry Iba
1947	Holy Cross	58–47	Oklahoma	Texas	C.C.N.Y.	Alvin Julian
1948	Kentucky	58–42	Baylor	Holy Cross	Kansas State	Adolph Rupp
1949	Kentucky	46–36	Oklahoma State	Illinois	Oregon State	Adolph Rupp
1950	C.C.N.Y.	71–68	Bradley	North Carolina State	Baylor	Nat Holman
1951	Kentucky	68–58	Kansas State	Illinois	Oklahoma State	Aldolph Rupp
1952	Kansas	80–63	St. John's	Illinois	Santa Clara	Forrest Allen
1953	Indiana	69–68	Kansas	Washington	Louisiana State	Branch McCracken
1954	LaSalle	92–76	Bradley	Penn State	U.S.C.	Kenneth Loeffler
1955	San Francisco	77–63	La Salle	Colorado	Iowa	Phil Woolpert
1956	San Francisco	83–71	Iowa	Temple	Southern Methodist	Phil Woolpert
1957	North Carolina	54–53[3]	Kansas	San Francisco	Michigan State	Frank McGuire
1958	Kentucky	84–72	Seattle	Temple	Kansas State	Adolph Rupp
1959	California	71–70	West Virginia	Cincinnati	Louisville	Pete Newell
1960	Ohio State	75–55	California	Cincinnati	N.Y.U.	Fred Taylor
1961	Cincinnati	70–65[2]	Ohio State	St. Joe's[4]	Utah	Edwin Jucker
1962	Cincinnati	71–59	Ohio State	Wake Forest	U.C.L.A.	Edwin Jucker
1963	Loyola (Ill.)	60–58[2]	Cincinnati	Duke	Utah	George Ireland
1964	U.C.L.A.	98–83	Duke	Michigan	Kansas State	John Wooden
1965	U.C.L.A.	91–80	Michigan	Princeton	Wichita State	John Wooden
1966	U.T.E.P.	72–65	Kentucky	Duke	Utah	Don Haskins
1967	U.C.L.A.	79–64	Dayton	Houston	North Carolina	John Wooden
1968	U.C.L.A.	78–55	North Carolina	Ohio State	Houston	John Wooden
1969	U.C.L.A.	92–72	Purdue	Drake	North Carolina	John Wooden
1970	U.C.L.A.	80–69	Jacksonville	New Mexico St.	St. Bonaventure	John Wooden
1971	U.C.L.A.	68–62	Villanova[4]	Western Kentucky[4]	Kansas	John Wooden
1972	U.C.L.A.	81–76	Florida State	North Carolina	Louisville	John Wooden
1973	U.C.L.A.	87–66	Memphis State	Indiana	Providence	John Wooden
1974	North Carolina State	76–64	Marquette	U.C.L.A.	Kansas	Norm Sloan
1975	U.C.L.A.	92–85	Kentucky	Louisville	Syracuse	John Wooden
1976	Indiana	86–68	Michigan	U.C.L.A.	Rutgers	Bob Knight
1977	Marquette	67–59	North Carolina	U.N.L.V.	U.N.C.-Charlotte	Al McGuire
1978	Kentucky	94–88	Duke	Arkansas	Notre Dame	Joe Hall
1979	Michigan State	75–64	Indiana State	DePaul	Pennsylvania	Jud Heathcote
1980	Louisville	59–54	U.C.L.A.[4]	Purdue	Iowa	Denny Crum
1981	Indiana	63–50	North Carolina	Virginia	Louisiana State	Bob Knight
1982	North Carolina	63–62	Georgetown	Houston[1]	Louisville[1]	Dean Smith
1983	North Carolina State	54–52	Houston	Georgia[1]	Louisville[1]	Jim Valvano
1984	Georgetown	84–75	Houston	Kentucky[1]	Virginia[1]	John Thompson
1985	Villanova	66–64	Georgetown	St. John's[1]	Memphis[1,4]	Rollie Massimino
1986	Louisville	72–69	Duke	Kansas[1]	Louisiana State[1]	Denny Crum
1987	Indiana	74–73	Syracuse	U.N.L.V.[1]	Providence[1]	Bob Knight
1988	Kansas	83–79	Oklahoma	Arizona[1]	Duke[1]	Larry Brown
1989	Michigan	80–79[2]	Seton Hall	Illinois[1]	Duke[1]	Steve Fisher
1990	U.N.L.V.	103–73	Duke	Georgia Tech[1]	Arkansas[1]	Jerry Tarkanian
1991	Duke	72–65	Kansas	U.N.L.V.[1]	North Carolina[1]	Mike Krzyzewski
1992	Duke	71–51	Michigan	Cincinnati[1]	Indiana[1]	Mike Krzyzewski
1993	North Carolina	77–71	Michigan	Kansas[1]	Kentucky[1]	Dean Smith
1994	Arkansas	76–70	Duke	Arizona[1]	Florida[1]	Nolan Richardson
1995	U.C.L.A.	89–78	Arkansas	North Carolina[1]	Oklahoma State[1]	Jim Harrick
1996	Kentucky	76–67	Syracuse	Massachusetts[1,4]	Mississippi State[1]	Rick Pitino
1997	Arizona	84–79[2]	Kentucky	Minnesota[1,4]	North Carolina[1]	Lute Olson
1998	Kentucky	78–69	Utah	North Carolina[1]	Stanford[1]	Tubby Smith
1999	Connecticut	77–74	Duke	Michigan State[1]	Ohio State[1]	Jim Calhoun
2000	Michigan State	89–76	Florida	North Carolina[1]	Wisconsin[1]	Tom Izzo
2001	Duke	82–72	Arizona	Maryland[1]	Michigan State[1]	Mike Krzyzewski
2002	Maryland	64–52	Indiana	Kansas[1]	Oklahoma[1]	Gary Williams
2003	Syracuse	81–78	Kansas	Marquette[1]	Texas[1]	Jim Boeheim
2004	Connecticut	82–73	Georgia Tech	Duke[1]	Oklahoma State[1]	Jim Calhoun
2005	North Carolina	75–70	Illinois	Michigan State[1]	Louisville[1]	Roy Williams
2006	Florida	73–57	U.C.L.A.	George Mason[1]	L.S.U.[1]	Billy Donovan
2007	Florida	84–75	Ohio State	Georgetown[1]	U.C.L.A.[1]	Billy Donovan
2008	Kansas	75–68[2]	Memphis	U.N.C.[1]	U.C.L.A.[1]	Bill Self
2009	North Carolina	89–72	Michigan State	Connecticut[1]	Villanova[1]	Roy Williams
2010	Duke	61–59	Butler	Michigan St.	West Virginia	Mike Krzyzewski

Notes: 1. Tied for third place. 2. Overtime. 3. Triple overtime. 4. Later declared ineligible.

NCAA Basketball Career Leaders

Player, Team	POINTS
Pete Maravich, Louisiana State	3,667
Freeman Williams, Portland State	3,249
Lionel Simmons, LaSalle	3,217
Alphonso Ford, Mississippi Valley	3,165
Harry Kelly, Texas Southern	3,066
Keydren Clark, St. Peter's	3,058
Hersey Hawkins, Bradley	3,008
Oscar Robertson, Cincinnati	2,973
Danny Manning, Kansas	2,951
Alfredrick Hughes, Loyola (Ill.)	2,914

Player, Team	REBOUNDS
Tom Gola, LaSalle	2,201
Joe Holup, George Washington	2,030
Charlie Slack, Marshall	1,916
Ed Conlin, Fordham	1,884
Dickie Hemric, Wake Forest	1,802
Paul Silas, Creighton	1,751
Art Quimby, Connecticut	1,716
Jerry Harper, Alabama	1,688
Jeff Cohen, William and Mary	1,679
Steve Hamilton, Morehead State	1,675

Player, Team	ASSISTS
Bobby Hurley, Duke	1,076
Chris Corchiani, North Carolina State	1,038
Ed Cota, North Carolina	1,030
Keith Jennings, East Tennessee St.	983
Steve Blake, Maryland	972
Sherman Douglas, Syracuse	960
Tony Miller, Marquette	956
Aaron Miles, Kansas	954
Greg Anthony, Portland/U.N.L.V.	950
Doug Gottlieb, Notre Dame/Oklahoma State	947

National Invitation Tournament Champions

Year	Champion	Year	Champion
1939	Long Island	1975	Princeton
1940	Colorado	1976	Kentucky
1941	Long Island	1977	St. Bonaventure
1942	West Virginia	1978	Texas
1943	St. John's	1979	Indiana
1944	St. John's	1980	Virginia
1945	DePaul	1981	Tulsa
1946	Kentucky	1982	Bradley
1947	Utah	1983	Fresno State
1948	St. Louis	1984	Michigan
1949	San Francisco	1985	U.C.L.A.
1950	City Coll. of NY	1986	Ohio State
1951	Brigham Young	1987	So. Mississippi
1952	LaSalle	1988	Connecticut
1953	Seton Hall	1989	St. John's
1954	Holy Cross	1990	Vanderbilt
1955	Duquesne	1991	Stanford
1956	Louisville	1992	Virginia
1957	Bradley	1993	Minnesota
1958	Xavier (Ohio)	1994	Villanova
1959	St. John's	1995	Virginia Tech
1960	Bradley	1996	Nebraska
1961	Providence	1997	Michigan
1962	Dayton	1998	Minnesota
1963	Providence	1999	California
1964	Bradley	2000	Wake Forest
1965	St. John's	2001	Tulsa
1966	Brigham Young	2002	Memphis
1967	Southern Illinois	2003	St. John's
1968	Dayton	2004	Michigan
1969	Temple	2005	South Carolina
1970	Marquette	2006	South Carolina
1971	North Carolina	2007	West Virginia
1972	Maryland	2008	Ohio State
1973	Virginia Tech	2009	Penn State
1974	Purdue	2010	Dayton

NCAA Division I Women's Basketball Championship Results

Year	Champion	Score	Runner-up	Coach	Outstanding player
1982	Louisiana Tech	76–62	Cheyney	Sonja Hogg	Janice Lawrence
1983	U.S.C.	69–67	Louisiana Tech	Linda Sharp	Cheryl Miller
1984	U.S.C.	72–61	Tennessee	Linda Sharp	Cheryl Miller
1985	Old Dominion	70–65	Georgia	Marianne Stanley	Tracy Claxton
1986	Texas	97–81	U.S.C.	Jody Conradt	Clarissa Davis
1987	Tennessee	67–44	Louisiana Tech	Pat Summitt	Tonya Edwards
1988	Louisiana Tech	56–54	Auburn	Leon Barmore	Erica Westbrooks
1989	Tennessee	76–60	Auburn	Pat Summitt	Brigitte Gordon
1990	Stanford	88–81	Auburn	Tara VanderVeer	Jennifer Azzi
1991	Tennessee	70–67	Virginia	Pat Summitt	Dawn Staley
1992	Stanford	78–62	Western Kentucky	Tara VanderVeer	Molly Goodenbour
1993	Texas Tech	84–82	Ohio State	Marcia Sharp	Sheryl Swoopes
1994	North Carolina	60–59	Louisiana Tech	Sylvia Hatchell	Charlotte Smith
1995	Connecticut	70–64	Tennessee	Geno Auriemma	Rebecca Lobo
1996	Tennessee	83–65	Georgia	Pat Summitt	Michelle Marciniak
1997	Tennessee	68–59	Old Dominion	Pat Summitt	Chamique Holdsclaw
1998	Tennessee	93–75	Louisiana Tech	Pat Summitt	Chamique Holdsclaw
1999	Purdue	62–45	Duke	Carolyn Peck	Ukari Figgs
2000	Connecticut	71–52	Tennessee	Geno Auriemma	Shea Ralph
2001	Notre Dame	68–66	Purdue	Muffet McGraw	Ruth Riley
2002	Connecticut	82–70	Oklahoma	Geno Auriemma	Swin Cash
2003	Connecticut	73–68	Tennessee	Geno Auriemma	Diana Taurasi
2004	Connecticut	70–61	Tennessee	Geno Auriemma	Diana Taurasi
2005	Baylor	84–62	Michigan State	Kim Mulkey-Robertson	Sophia Young
2006	Maryland	78–75	Duke	Brenda Frese	Laura Harper
2007	Tennessee	59–46	Rutgers	Pat Summitt	Candace Parker
2008	Tennessee	64–48	Stanford	Pat Summitt	Candace Parker
2009	Connecticut	76–54	Louisville	Geno Auriemma	Tina Charles
2010	Connecticut	53–47	Stanford	Geno Auriemma	Maya Moore

NCAA CHAMPIONS IN OTHER SPORTS

Men's Sports

CROSS COUNTRY
1938 Indiana
1939 Michigan State
1940 Indiana
1941 Rhode Island
1942 Indiana
1943 No Meet
1944 Drake
1945 Drake
1946 Drake
1947 Penn State
1948 Michigan State
1949 Michigan State
1950 Penn State
1951 Syracuse
1952 Michigan State
1953 Kansas
1954 Oklahoma St.
1955 Michigan State
1956 Michigan State
1957 Notre Dame
1958 Michigan State
1959 Michigan State
1960 Houston
1961 Oregon State
1962 San Jose State
1963 San Jose State
1964 W. Michigan
1965 W. Michigan
1966 Villanova
1967 Villanova
1968 Villanova
1969 U.T.E.P
1970 Villanova
1971 Oregon
1972 Tennessee
1973 Oregon
1974 Oregon
1975 U.T.E.P.
1976 U.T.E.P.
1977 Oregon
1978 U.T.E.P.
1979 U.T.E.P.
1980 U.T.E.P.
1981 U.T.E.P.
1982 Wisconsin
1983 Vacated
1984 Arkansas
1985 Wisconsin
1986 Arkansas
1987 Arkansas
1988 Wisconsin
1989 Iowa State
1990 Arkansas
1991 Arkansas
1992 Arkansas
1993 Arkansas
1994 Iowa State
1995 Arkansas
1996 Stanford
1997 Stanford
1998 Arkansas
1999 Arkansas
2000 Arkansas
2001 Colorado
2002 Stanford
2003 Stanford
2004 Colorado
2005 Wisconsin
2006 Colorado
2007 Oregon
2008 Oregon

2009 Oklahoma St.

SOCCER
1959 St. Louis
1960 St. Louis
1961 West Chester
1962 St. Louis
1963 St. Louis
1964 Navy
1965 St. Louis
1966 San Franciso
1967 St. Louis,
     Michigan State
1968 Maryland,
     Michigan State
1969 St. Louis
1970 St. Louis
1971 Vacated
1972 St. Louis
1973 St. Louis
1974 Howard
1975 San Francisco
1976 San Francisco
1977 Hartwick
1978 Vacated
1979 So. Ill. Univ at
     Edwardsville
1980 San Francisco
1981 Connecticut
1982 Indiana
1983 Indiana
1984 Clemson
1985 U.C.L.A.
1986 Duke
1987 Clemson
1988 Indiana
1989 Santa Clara,
     Virginia
1990 U.C.L.A.
1991 Virginia
1992 Virginia
1993 Virginia
1994 Virginia
1995 Wisconsin
1996 St. John's (N.Y.)
1997 U.C.L.A.
1998 Indiana
1999 Indiana
2000 Connecticut
2001 North Carolina
2002 U.C.L.A.
2003 Indiana
2004 Indiana
2005 Maryland
2006 U.C.S.B.
2007 Wake Forest
2008 Maryland
2009 Virginia

WATER POLO
1969 U.C.L.A.
1970 UC Irvine
1971 U.C.L.A.
1972 U.C.L.A.
1973 California
1974 California
1975 California
1976 Stanford
1977 California
1978 Stanford
1979 U.C.S.B.
1980 Stanford

1981 Stanford
1982 U.C. Irvine
1983 California
1984 California
1985 Stanford
1986 Stanford
1987 California
1988 California
1989 U.C. Irvine
1990 California
1991 California
1992 California
1993 Stanford
1994 Stanford
1995 U.C.L.A.
1996 U.C.L.A.
1997 Pepperdine
1998 U.S.C.
1999 U.C.L.A.
2000 U.C.L.A.
2001 Stanford
2002 Stanford
2003 U.S.C.
2004 U.C.L.A.
2005 U.S.C.
2006 California
2007 California
2008 U.S.C.
2009 U.S.C.

FENCING[1]
1941 Northwestern
1942 Ohio State
1943 No Meet
1944 No Meet
1945 No Meet
1946 No Meet
1947 N.Y.U.
1948 C.C.N.Y.
1949 Army, Rutgers
1950 Navy
1951 Columbia
1952 Columbia
1953 Pennsylvania
1954 Columbia,
     N.Y.U.
1955 Columbia
1956 Illinois
1957 N.Y.U.
1958 Illinois
1959 Navy
1960 N.Y.U.
1961 N.Y.U.
1962 Navy
1963 Columbia
1964 Princeton
1965 Columbia
1966 N.Y.U.
1967 N.Y.U.
1968 Columbia
1969 Pennsylvania
1970 N.Y.U.
1971 N.Y.U.,
     Columbia
1972 Detroit
1973 N.Y.U.
1974 N.Y.U.
1975 Wayne State
1976 N.Y.U.
1977 Notre Dame
1978 Notre Dame
1979 Wayne State

1980 Wayne State
1981 Pennsylvania
1982 Wayne State
1983 Wayne State
1984 Wayne State
1985 Wayne State
1986 Notre Dame
1987 Columbia
1988 Columbia
1989 Columbia

GYMNASTICS
1938 Chicago
1939 Illinois
1940 Illinois
1941 Illinois
1942 Illinois
1943–47 No Meet
1948 Penn State
1949 Temple
1950 Illinois
1951 Florida State
1952 Florida State
1953 Penn State
1954 Penn State
1955 Illinois
1956 Illinois
1957 Penn State
1958 Illinois,
     Michigan State
1959 Penn State
1960 Penn State
1961 Penn State
1962 U.S.C.
1963 Michigan
1964 So. Illinois
1965 Penn State
1966 So. Illinois
1967 So. Illinois
1968 California
1969 Iowa
1970 Michigan
1971 Iowa State
1972 So. Illinois
1973 Iowa State
1974 Iowa State
1975 California
1976 Penn State
1977 Indiana State,
     Oklahoma
1978 Oklahoma
1979 Nebraska
1980 Nebraska
1981 Nebraska
1982 Nebraska
1983 Nebraska
1984 U.C.L.A.
1985 Ohio State
1986 Arizona State
1987 U.C.L.A.
1988 Nebraska
1989 Illinois
1990 Nebraska
1991 Oklahoma
1992 Stanford
1993 Stanford
1994 Nebraska
1995 Stanford
1996 Ohio State
1997 California
1998 California
1999 Michigan

2000 Penn State
2001 Ohio State
2002 Oklahoma
2003 Oklahoma
2004 Penn State
2005 Oklahoma
2006 Oklahoma
2007 Penn State
2008 Oklahoma
2009 Stanford
2010 Michigan

ICE HOCKEY
1948 Michigan
1949 Boston College
1950 Colorado Coll.
1951 Michigan
1952 Michigan
1953 Michigan
1954 Rensselaer
1955 Michigan
1956 Michigan
1957 Colorado Coll.
1958 Denver
1959 North Dakota
1960 Denver
1961 Denver
1962 Michigan Tech.
1963 North Dakota
1964 Michigan
1965 Michigan Tech
1966 Michigan St.
1967 Cornell
1968 Denver
1969 Denver
1970 Cornell
1971 Boston Univ.
1972 Boston Univ.
1973 Wisconsin
1974 Minnesota
1975 Michigan Tech
1976 Minnesota
1977 Wisconsin
1978 Boston Univ.
1979 Minnesota
1980 North Dakota
1981 Wisconsin
1982 North Dakota
1983 Wisconsin
1984 Bowling Green
1985 Rensselaer
1986 Michigan St.
1987 North Dakota
1988 Lake Superior
     State
1989 Harvard
1990 Wisconsin
1991 N. Michigan
1992 Lake Superior
     State
1993 Maine
1994 Lake Superior
     State
1995 Boston Univ.
1996 Michigan
1997 North Dakota
1998 Michigan
1999 Maine
2000 North Dakota
2001 Boston Coll.
2002 Minnesota
2003 Minnesota

2004 Denver
2005 Denver
2006 Wisconsin
2007 Michigan St.
2008 Boston Coll.
2009 Boston Univ.
2010 Boston Coll.

SWIMMING
1937 Michigan
1938 Michigan
1939 Michigan
1940 Michigan
1941 Michigan
1942 Yale
1943 Ohio State
1944 Yale
1945 Ohio State
1946 Ohio State
1947 Ohio State
1948 Michigan
1949 Ohio State
1950 Ohio State
1951 Yale
1952 Ohio State
1953 Yale
1954 Ohio State
1955 Ohio State
1956 Ohio State
1957 Michigan
1958 Michigan
1959 Michigan
1960 U.S.C.
1961 Michigan
1962 Ohio State
1963 U.S.C.
1964 U.S.C.
1965 U.S.C.
1966 U.S.C.
1967 Stanford
1968 Indiana
1969 Indiana
1970 Indiana
1971 Indiana
1972 Indiana
1973 Indiana
1974 U.S.C.
1975 U.S.C.
1976 U.S.C.
1977 U.S.C.
1978 Tennessee
1979 California
1980 California
1981 Texas
1982 U.C.L.A.
1983 Florida
1984 Florida
1985 Stanford
1986 Stanford
1987 Stanford
1988 Texas
1989 Texas
1990 Texas
1991 Texas
1992 Stanford
1993 Stanford
1994 Stanford
1995 Michigan
1996 Texas
1997 Auburn
1998 Stanford
1999 Auburn
2000 Texas
2001 Texas
2002 Texas
2003 Auburn
2004 Auburn
2005 Auburn
2006 Auburn

2007 Auburn
2008 Arizona
2009 Auburn
2010 Texas

WRESTLING
1928 Oklahoma St.[2]
1929 Oklahoma St.
1930 Oklahoma St.[2]
1931 Oklahoma St.[2]
1932 Indiana
1933 Iowa State,[2]
    Oklahoma St.[2]
1934 Oklahoma St.
1935 Oklahoma St.
1936 Oklahoma
1937 Oklahoma St.
1938 Oklahoma St.
1939 Oklahoma St.
1940 Oklahoma St.
1941 Oklahoma St.
1942 Oklahoma St.
1943 No Match
1944 No Match
1945 No Match
1946 Oklahoma St.
1947 Cornell College
1948 Oklahoma St.
1949 Oklahoma St.
1950 Northern
    Iowa
1951 Oklahoma
1952 Oklahoma
1953 Penn State
1954 Oklahoma St.
1955 Oklahoma St.
1956 Oklahoma St.
1957 Oklahoma
1958 Oklahoma St.
1959 Oklahoma St.
1960 Oklahoma
1961 Oklahoma St.
1962 Oklahoma St.
1963 Oklahoma
1964 Oklahoma St.
1965 Iowa State
1966 Oklahoma St.
1967 Michigan St.
1968 Oklahoma St.
1969 Iowa State
1970 Iowa State
1971 Oklahoma St.
1972 Iowa State
1973 Iowa State
1974 Oklahoma St.
1975 Iowa
1976 Iowa
1977 Iowa State
1978 Iowa
1979 Iowa
1980 Iowa
1981 Iowa
1982 Iowa
1983 Iowa
1984 Iowa
1985 Iowa
1986 Iowa
1987 Iowa State
1988 Arizona St.
1989 Oklahoma St.
1990 Oklahoma St.
1991 Iowa
1992 Iowa
1993 Iowa
1994 Oklahoma St.
1995 Iowa
1996 Iowa
1997 Iowa
1998 Iowa

1999 Iowa
2000 Iowa
2001 Minnesota
2002 Minnesota
2003 Oklahoma
2004 Oklahoma St.
2005 Oklahoma
2006 Oklahoma St.
2007 Minnesota
2008 Iowa
2009 Iowa
2010 Iowa

INDOOR TRACK
1965 Missouri
1966 Kansas
1967 U.S.C.
1968 Villanova
1969 Kansas
1970 Kansas
1971 Villanova
1972 U.S.C.
1973 Manhattan
1974 U.T.E.P
1975 U.T.E.P
1976 U.T.E.P
1977 Washington St.
1978 U.T.E.P
1979 Villanova
1980 U.T.E.P
1981 U.T.E.P
1982 U.T.E.P
1983 S.M.U.
1984 Arkansas
1985 Arkansas
1986 Arkansas
1987 Arkansas
1988 Arkansas
1989 Arkansas
1990 Arkansas
1991 Arkansas
1992 Arkansas
1993 Arkansas
1994 Arkansas
1995 Arkansas
1996 George Mason
1997 Arkansas
1998 Arkansas
1999 Arkansas
2000 Arkansas
2001 Louisiana St.
2002 Tennessee
2003 Arkansas
2004 Louisiana St.
2005 Arkansas
2006 Arkansas
2007 Wisconsin
2008 Arizona St.
2009 Oregon
2010 Florida

OUTDOOR TRACK
1921 Illinois
1922 California
1923 Michigan
1924 No Meet
1925 Stanford
1926 U.S.C.
1927 Illinois
1928 Stanford
1929 Ohio State
1930 U.S.C.
1931 U.S.C.
1932 Indiana
1933 Louisiana St.
1934 Stanford
1935 U.S.C.
1936 U.S.C.
1937 U.S.C.

1938 U.S.C.
1939 U.S.C.
1940 U.S.C.
1941 U.S.C.
1942 U.S.C.
1943 U.S.C.
1944 Illinois
1945 Navy
1946 Illinois
1947 Illinois
1948 Minnesota
1949 U.S.C.
1950 U.S.C.
1951 U.S.C.
1952 U.S.C.
1953 U.S.C.
1954 U.S.C.
1955 U.S.C.
1956 U.C.L.A.
1957 Villanova
1958 U.S.C.
1959 Kansas
1960 Kansas
1961 U.S.C.
1962 Oregon
1963 U.S.C.
1964 Oregon
1965 Oregon, U.S.C.
1966 U.C.L.A.
1967 U.S.C.
1968 U.S.C.
1969 San Jose St.
1970 BYU, Kansas
1971 U.C.L.A.
1972 U.C.L.A.
1973 U.C.L.A.
1974 Tennessee
1975 U.T.E.P
1976 U.S.C.
1977 Arizona St.
1978 U.C.L.A. and
    U.T.E.P
1979 U.T.E.P
1980 U.T.E.P
1981 U.T.E.P
1982 U.T.E.P
1983 S.M.U.
1984 Oregon
1985 Arkansas
1986 S.M.U.
1987 U.C.L.A.
1988 U.C.L.A.
1989 Louisiana St.
1990 Louisiana St.
1991 Tennessee
1992 Arkansas
1993 Arkansas
1994 Arkansas
1995 Arkansas
1996 Arkansas
1997 Arkansas
1998 Arkansas
1999 Arkansas
2000 Stanford
2001 Tennessee
2002 Louisiana St.
2003 Arkansas
2004 Arkansas
2005 Arkansas
2006 Florida St.
2007 Florida St.
2008 Florida St.
2009 Texas A&M
2010 Texas A&M

BASEBALL
1947 California
1948 U.S.C.
1949 Texas

1950 Texas
1951 Oklahoma
1952 Holy Cross
1953 Michigan
1954 Missouri
1955 Wake Forest
1956 Minnesota
1957 California
1958 U.S.C.
1959 Oklahoma St.
1960 Minnesota
1961 U.S.C.
1962 Michigan
1963 U.S.C.
1964 Minnesota
1965 Arizona St.
1966 Ohio State
1967 Arizona St.
1968 U.S.C.
1969 Arizona St.
1970 U.S.C.
1971 U.S.C.
1972 U.S.C.
1973 U.S.C.
1974 U.S.C.
1975 Texas
1976 Arizona
1977 Arizona St.
1978 U.S.C.
1979 Cal State
    Fullerton
1980 Arizona
1981 Arizona St.
1982 Miami (Fla.)
1983 Texas
1984 Cal State
    Fullerton
1985 Miami (Fla.)
1986 Arizona
1987 Stanford
1988 Stanford
1989 Wichita St.
1990 Georgia
1991 Louisiana St.
1992 Pepperdine
1993 Louisiana St.
1994 Oklahoma
1995 Cal State
    Fullerton
1996 Louisiana St.
1997 Louisiana St.
1998 U.S.C.
1999 Miama (Fla.)
2000 Louisiana St.
2001 Miami (Fla.)
2002 Texas
2003 Rice
2004 Cal State
    Fullerton
2005 Texas
2006 Oregon St.
2007 Oregon St.
2008 Fresno St.
2009 Louisiana St.
2010 S. Carolina

GOLF
1897 Yale
1898 Harvard (spr.),
    Yale (fall)
1899 Harvard
1900 No tourney
1901 Harvard
1902 Yale (spr.)
1903 Harvard
1904 Harvard
1905 Yale
1906 Yale
1907 Yale

1908 Yale
1909 Yale
1910 Yale
1911 Yale
1912 Yale
1913 Yale
1914 Princeton
1915 Yale
1916 Princeton
1917 No tourney
1918 No tourney
1919 Princeton
1920 Princeton
1921 Dartmouth
1922 Princeton
1923 Princeton
1924 Yale
1925 Yale
1926 Yale
1927 Princeton
1928 Princeton
1929 Princeton
1930 Princeton
1931 Yale
1932 Yale
1933 Yale
1934 Michigan
1935 Michigan
1936 Yale
1937 Princeton
1938 Stanford
1939 Stanford
1940 Louisiana St., Princeton,
1941 Stanford
1942 Louisiana St., Stanford
1943 Yale
1944 Notre Dame
1945 Ohio State
1946 Stanford
1947 Louisiana St.
1948 San Jose St.
1949 North Texas
1950 North Texas
1951 North Texas
1952 North Texas
1953 Stanford
1954 S.M.U.
1955 Louisiana St.
1956 Houston
1957 Houston

1958 Houston
1959 Houston
1960 Houston
1961 Purdue
1962 Houston
1963 Oklahoma St.
1964 Houston
1965 Houston
1966 Houston
1967 Houston
1968 Florida
1969 Houston
1970 Houston
1971 Texas
1972 Texas
1973 Florida
1974 Wake Forest
1975 Wake Forest
1976 Oklahoma
1977 Houston
1978 Oklahoma St.
1979 Ohio State
1980 Oklahoma St.
1981 B.Y.U.
1982 Houston
1983 Oklahoma St.
1984 Houston
1985 Houston
1986 Wake Forest
1987 Oklahoma St.
1988 U.C.L.A.
1989 Oklahoma
1990 Arizona
1991 Oklahoma St.
1992 Arizona
1993 Florida
1994 Stanford
1995 Oklahoma St.
1996 Arizona St.
1997 Pepperdine
1998 U.N.L.V.
1999 Georgia
2000 Oklahoma St.
2001 Florida
2002 Minnesota
2003 Clemson
2003 California
2004 Georgia
2006 Oklahoma St.
2007 Stanford
2008 U.C.L.A.
2009 Texas A&M

2010 Augusta St.

LACROSSE
1971 Cornell
1972 Virginia
1973 Maryland
1974 Johns Hopkins
1975 Maryland
1976 Cornell
1977 Cornell
1978 Johns Hopkins
1979 Johns Hopkins
1980 Johns Hopkins
1981 North Carolina
1982 North Carolina
1983 Syracuse
1984 Johns Hopkins
1985 Johns Hopkins
1986 North Carolina
1987 Johns Hopkins
1988 Syracuse
1989 Syracuse
1990 Syracuse
1991 North Carolina
1992 Princeton
1993 Syracuse
1994 Princeton
1995 Syracuse
1996 Princeton
1997 Princeton
1998 Princeton
1999 Virginia
2000 Syracuse
2001 Princeton
2002 Syracuse
2003 Virginia
2004 Syracuse
2005 Johns Hopkins
2006 Virginia
2007 Johns Hopkins
2008 Syracuse
2009 Syracuse
2010 Duke

TENNIS
1946 U.S.C.
1947 William and Mary
1948 William and Mary
1949 San Francisco
1950 U.C.L.A.
1951 U.S.C.

1952 U.C.L.A.
1953 U.C.L.A.
1954 U.C.L.A.
1955 U.S.C.
1956 U.C.L.A.
1957 Michigan
1958 U.S.C.
1959 Notre Dame, Tulane
1960 U.C.L.A.
1961 U.C.L.A.
1962 U.S.C.
1963 U.S.C.
1964 U.S.C.
1965 U.C.L.A.
1966 U.S.C.
1967 U.S.C.
1968 U.S.C.
1969 U.S.C.
1970 U.C.L.A.
1971 U.C.L.A.
1972 Trinity (Tex.)
1973 Stanford
1974 Stanford
1975 Stanford
1976 U.S.C., U.C.L.A.
1977 Stanford
1978 Stanford
1979 U.C.L.A.
1980 Stanford
1981 Stanford
1982 U.C.L.A.
1983 Stanford
1984 U.C.L.A.
1985 Georgia
1986 Stanford
1987 Georgia
1988 Stanford
1989 Stanford
1990 Stanford
1991 U.S.C.
1992 Stanford
1993 U.S.C.
1994 U.S.C.
1995 Stanford
1996 Stanford
1997 Stanford
1998 Stanford
1999 Georgia
2000 Stanford
2001 Georgia

2002 U.S.C.
2003 Illinois
2004 Baylor
2005 U.C.L.A.
2006 Pepperdine
2007 Georgia
2008 Georgia
2009 U.S.C.
2010 U.S.C.

VOLLEYBALL
1970 U.C.L.A.
1971 U.C.L.A.
1972 U.C.L.A.
1973 San Diego St.
1974 U.C.L.A.
1975 U.C.L.A.
1976 U.C.L.A.
1977 U.S.C.
1978 Pepperdine
1979 U.C.L.A.
1980 U.S.C.
1981 U.C.L.A.
1982 U.C.L.A.
1983 U.C.L.A.
1984 U.C.L.A.
1985 Pepperdine
1986 Pepperdine
1987 U.C.L.A.
1988 U.S.C.
1989 U.C.L.A.
1990 U.S.C.
1991 Cal State Long Beach
1992 Pepperdine
1993 U.C.L.A.
1994 Penn State
1995 U.C.L.A.
1996 U.C.L.A.
1997 Stanford
1998 U.C.L.A.
1999 B.Y.U.
2000 U.C.L.A.
2001 B.Y.U.
2002 Hawaii
2003 Lewis
2004 B.Y.U.
2005 Pepperdine
2006 U.C.L.A.
2007 U.C. Irvine
2008 Penn State
2009 U.C. Irvine
2010 Stanford

Note: 1. For results after 1989, see "Men's and Women's Sports." 2. Unofficial champions.

Men's and Women's Sports

FENCING
1990 Penn State
1991 Penn State
1992 Columbia
1993 Columbia
1994 Notre Dame
1995 Penn State
1996 Penn State
1997 Penn State
1998 Penn State
1999 Penn State
2000 Penn State
2001 St. John's (N.Y.)
2002 Penn State
2003 Notre Dame
2004 Ohio State
2005 Notre Dame
2006 Harvard
2007 Penn State
2008 Ohio State
2009 Penn State

2010 Penn State

RIFLE
1954 Seattle
1955 Dartmouth
1956 Dartmouth
1957 Colorado
1958 Denver
1959 Denver
1960 Denver
1961 Middlebury
1962 Colorado
1963 Colorado
1964 Dartmouth
1965 Utah
1966 W. Colorado
1967 Wyoming
1968 Denver
1969 Dartmouth
1970 Dartmouth
1971 Colorado

1972 Denver
1973 Wyoming
1974 Wyoming
1975 Vermont
1976 Colorado
1977 Wyoming
1978 Wyoming
1979 Utah
1980 Tenn. Tech
1981 Tenn. Tech
1982 Tenn. Tech
1983 West Virginia
1984 West Virginia
1985 Murray State
1986 West Virginia
1987 Murray State
1988 West Virginia
1989 West Virginia
1990 West Virginia
1991 West Virginia
1992 West Virginia

1993 West Virginia
1994 Alaska Fairbanks
1995 West Virginia
1996 West Virginia
1997 West Virginia
1998 West Virginia
1999 Alaska Fairbanks
2000 Alaska Fairbanks
2001 Alaska Fairbanks
2002 Alaska Fairbanks
2003 Alaska Fairbanks
2004 Alaska Fairbanks
2005 U.S. Military
2006 Alaska Fairbanks
2007 Alaska Fairbanks
2008 Alaska Fairbanks
2009 West Virginia
2010 T.C.U.

SKIING
1954 Denver
1955 Denver
1956 Denver
1957 Denver
1958 Dartmouth
1959 Colorado
1960 Colorado
1961 Denver
1962 Denver
1963 Denver
1964 Denver
1965 Denver

1966 Denver	1975 Colorado	1984 Utah	1993 Utah	2002 Denver
1967 Denver	1976 Dartmouth	1985 Wyoming	1994 Vermont	2003 Utah
1968 Wyoming	1977 Colorado	1986 Utah	1995 Colorado	2004 New Mexico
1969 Denver	1978 Colorado	1987 Utah	1996 Utah	2005 Denver
1970 Denver	1979 Colorado	1988 Utah	1997 Utah	2006 Colorado
1971 Denver	1980 Vermont	1989 Vermont	1998 Colorado	2007 Dartmouth
1972 Colorado	1981 Utah	1990 Vermont	1999 Colorado	2008 Denver
1973 Colorado	1982 Colorado	1991 Colorado	2000 Denver	2009 Denver
1974 Colorado	1983 Utah	1992 Vermont	2001 Denver	2010 Denver

Women's Sports

Year	Cross-Country	Field Hockey	Soccer	Volleyball	Indoor Track	Outdoor Track	Golf
1981	Virginia	Connecticut	N.A.	U.S.C.	N.A.	N.A.	N.A.
1982	Virginia	Old Dominion	North Carolina	Hawaii	N.A.	U.C.L.A.	Tulsa
1983	Oregon	Old Dominion	North Carolina	Hawaii	Nebraska	U.C.L.A.	T.C.U.
1984	Wisconsin	Old Dominion	North Carolina	U.C.L.A.	Nebraska	Florida State	Miami (Fla.)
1985	Wisconsin	Connecticut	George Mason	Pacific	Florida State	Oregon	Florida
1986	Texas	Iowa	North Carolina	Pacific	Texas	Texas	Florida
1987	Oregon	Maryland	North Carolina	Hawaii	Louisiana St.	Louisiana St.	San Jose St.
1988	Kentucky	Old Dominion	North Carolina	Texas	Texas	Louisiana St.	Tulsa
1989	Villanova	North Carolina	North Carolina	Cal St. Long Bch.	Louisiana St.	Louisiana St.	San Jose St.
1990	Villanova	Old Dominion	North Carolina	U.C.L.A.	Texas	Louisiana St.	Arizona St.
1991	Villanova	Old Dominion	North Carolina	U.C.L.A.	Louisiana St.	Louisiana St.	U.C.L.A.
1992	Villanova	Old Dominion	North Carolina	Stanford	Florida	Louisiana St.	San Jose St.
1993	Villanova	Maryland	North Carolina	Long Beach St.	Louisiana St.	Louisiana St.	Arizona St.
1994	Villanova	James Madison	North Carolina	Stanford	Louisiana St.	Louisiana St.	Arizona St.
1995	Providence	North Carolina	Notre Dame	Nebraska	Louisiana St.	Louisiana St.	Arizona St.
1996	Stanford	North Carolina	North Carolina	Stanford	Louisiana St.	Louisiana St.	Arizona
1997	B.Y.U.	North Carolina	North Carolina	Stanford	Louisiana St.	Louisiana St.	Arizona St.
1998	Villanova	Old Dominion	Florida	Long Beach St.	Texas	Texas	Arizona St.
1999	B.Y.U.	Maryland	North Carolina	Penn State	Texas	Texas	Duke
2000	Colorado	Old Dominion	North Carolina	Nebraska	U.C.L.A.	Louisiana St.	Arizona
2001	B.Y.U.	Michigan	Santa Clara	Stanford	U.C.L.A.	U.S.C.	Georgia
2002	B.Y.U.	Wake Forest	Portland	U.S.C.	Louisiana St.	South Carolina	Duke
2003	Stanford	Wake Forest	North Carolina	U.S.C.	Louisiana St.	Louisiana St.	U.S.C.
2004	Colorado	Wake Forest	Notre Dame	Stanford	Louisiana St.	U.C.L.A.	U.C.L.A.
2005	Stanford	Maryland	Portland	Washington	Tennessee	Texas	Duke
2006	Stanford	Maryland	North Carolina	Nebraska	Texas	Auburn	Duke
2007	Stanford	North Carolina	U.S.C.	Penn State	Arizona St.	Arizona St.	Duke
2008	Washington	Maryland	North Carolina	Penn State	Arizona St.	Louisiana St.	U.S.C.
2009	Villanova	North Carolina	North Carolina	Penn State	Tennessee	Texas A&M	Arizona St.
2010	N.A.	N.A.	N.A.	N.A.	Oregon	Texas A&M	Purdue

Year	Gymnastics	Lacrosse	Softball	Swimming	Tennis	Fencing[1]	Water Polo	Ice Hockey
1982	Utah	Massachusetts	U.C.L.A.	Florida	Stanford	N.A.		
1983	Utah	Delaware	Texas A&M	Stanford	U.S.C.	Wayne State		
1984	Utah	Temple	Texas	Texas	Stanford	Penn State		
1985	Utah	New Hampsh.	U.C.L.A.	Texas	U.S.C.	Yale		
1986	Utah	Maryland	Cal St. Fullerton	Texas	Stanford	Yale		
1987	Georgia	Penn State	Texas A&M	Texas	Stanford	Pennsylvania		
1988	Alabama	Temple	U.C.L.A.	Texas	Stanford	Notre Dame		
1989	Georgia	Penn State	U.C.L.A.	Stanford	Stanford	Wayne State		
1990	Utah	Harvard	U.C.L.A.	Texas	Stanford	Wayne State		
1991	Alabama	Virginia	Arizona	Texas	Stanford			
1992	Utah	Maryland	U.C.L.A.	Stanford	Florida			
1993	Georgia	Virginia	Arizona	Stanford	Texas			
1994	Utah	Princeton	Arizona	Stanford	Georgia			
1995	Utah	Maryland	U.C.L.A.	Stanford	Texas			
1996	Alabama	Maryland	Arizona	Stanford	Florida			
1997	U.C.L.A.	Maryland	Arizona	U.S.C.	Stanford			
1998	Georgia	Maryland	Fresno State	Stanford	Florida			
1999	Georgia	Maryland	U.C.L.A.	Georgia	Stanford			
2000	U.C.L.A.	Maryland	Oklahoma	Georgia	Georgia		U.C.L.A.	Minn.Duluth
2001	U.C.L.A.	Maryland	Arizona	Georgia	Stanford		U.C.L.A.	Minn.Duluth
2002	Alabama	Princeton	California	Auburn	Stanford		Stanford	Minn.Duluth
2003	U.C.L.A.	Princeton	U.C.L.A.	Auburn	Florida		U.C.L.A.	Minn.Duluth
2004	U.C.L.A.	Virginia	U.C.L.A.	Auburn	Stanford		U.S.C.	Minnesota
2005	Georgia	Northwestern	Michigan	Georgia	Stanford		U.C.L.A.	Minnesota
2006	Georgia	Northwestern	Arizona	Auburn	Stanford		U.C.L.A.	Wisconsin
2007	Georgia	Northwestern	Arizona	Auburn	Georgia Tech		U.C.L.A.	Wisconsin
2008	Georgia	Northwestern	Arizona State	Arizona	U.C.L.A.		U.C.L.A.	Minn.Duluth
2009	Georgia	Northwestern	Washington	California	Duke		U.C.L.A.	Wisconsin
2010	U.C.L.A.	Maryland	U.C.L.A.	Florida	Stanford		U.S.C.	Minn.Duluth

Note: 1. Since 1990, the NCAA has recognized a joint fencing champion. See "Men's and Women's Sports" above.

International Sports

YACHTING: THE AMERICA'S CUP

In 1851, the Royal Yacht Squadron presented the Hundred Guinea Cup to the winning yacht in a race around the Isle of Wight in the English Channel. The cup was won by the U.S. schooner *America* and thereafter became known as the America's Cup. In 24 challenges over the next 132 years the cup remained in the hands of U.S. yachtsmen.

In 2003, Switzerland became the first landlocked country to win the cup, when *Alinghi* defeated Team New Zealand 5–0 in Auckland.

The America's Cup, 1851–2010

Year	Winner	Loser	Year	Winner	Loser
1851	America, U.S.	Aurora, England	1962	Weatherly, U.S.	Gretel, Australia
1870	Magic, U.S.	Cambria, England	1964	Constellation, U.S.	Sovereign, Britain
1871	Columbia, U.S	Livonia, England	1970	Intrepid, U.S.	Gretel II, Australia
1876	Madeline, U.S.	Countess of Dufferin, Canada	1974	Courageous, U.S.	Southern Cross, Australia
1881	Mischief, U.S.	Atalanta, Canada	1977	Courageous, U.S.	Australia, Australia
1885	Puritan, U.S.	Genesta, Britain	1980	Freedom, U.S.	Australia, Australia
1886	Mayflower, U.S.	Galatea, Britain	1983	Australia II, Australia	Liberty, U.S.
1887	Volunteer, U.S.	Thistle, Scotland	1987	Stars & Stripes, U.S.	Kookaburra III, Australia
1893	Vigilant, U.S.	Valkyrie II, Britain	1988	Stars & Stripes, U.S.	KZ, New Zealand
1895	Defender, U.S.	Valkyrie III, Britain	1992	America3, U.S.	Il Moro di Venezia, Italy
1899	Columbia, U.S.	Shamrock, Ireland	1995	Black Magic, N.Z.	Young America, U.S.
1901	Columbia, U.S.	Shamrock II, Ireland	2000	Team New Zealand, New Zealand	Prada, Italy
1903	Reliance, U.S.	Shamrock III, Ireland			
1920	Resolute, U.S.	Shamrock IV, Ireland	2003	Alinghi, Switzerland	Team New Zealand, New Zealand
1930	Enterprise, U.S.	Shamrock V, Ireland			
1934	Rainbow, U.S.	Endeavour, Britain	2007	Alinghi, Switzerland	Emirates Team New Zealand, New Zealand
1937	Ranger, U.S.	Endeavour II, Britain			
1958	Columbia, U.S.	Sceptre, Britain	2010	BMW Oracle, U.S.	Alinghi, Switzerland

SOCCER: THE WORLD CUP

The World Cup, modern soccer's crowning event, is staged every four years by the Federation Internationale de Football Association (FIFA). Millions attend the Cup's many contests, and the televised final is viewed by over a billion people worldwide. South Africa hosted the Cup in 2010. Brazil will host in 2014.

The World Cup, 1930–2010

Year	Final Score	Leading scorer, country (goals)	Host country	Participating nations
1930	Uruguay 4, Argentina 2	Stabile, Argentina (8)	Uruguay	13
1934	Italy 2, Czechoslovakia 1 (OT)	Conen, Germany; Nejedly, Czechoslovakia; Schiavo, Italy (4)	Italy	31
1938	Italy 4, Hungary 2	Leonidas, Brazil (8)	France	36
1942 & 1946		No tournament—World War II		
1950	Uruguay 2, Brazil 1	Ademir, Brazil (7)	Brazil	33
1954	West Germany 3, Hungary 2	Kocsis, Hungary (11)	Switzerland	38
1958	Brazil 5, Sweden 2	Fontaine, France (13)	Sweden	53
1962	Brazil 3, Czechoslovakia 1	Jerkovic, Yugoslavia (5)	Chile	56
1966	England 4, West Germany 2 (OT)	Eusebio, Portugal (9)	England	71
1970	Brazil 4, Italy 1	Muller, West Germany (10)	Mexico	71
1974	West Germany 2, Netherlands 1	Lato, Poland (7)	West Germany	98
1978	Argentina 3, Netherlands 1 (OT)	Kempes, Argentina (6)	Argentina	106
1982	Italy 3, West Germany 1	Rossi, Italy (6)	Spain	109
1986	Argentina 3, West Germany 2	Lineker, England (6)	Mexico	121
1990	West Germany 1, Argentina 0	Schilacci, Italy (6)	Italy	112
1994	Brazil 0, Italy 0 (OT)[1]	Stoichkov, Bulgaria (6)	United States	144
1998	France 3, Brazil 0	Suker, Croatia (6)	France	173
2002	Brazil 2, Germany 0	Ronaldo, Brazil (8)	S. Korea/Japan	198
2006	Italy 1, France 1 (OT)[2]	Miroslav Klose, Germany (5)	Germany	198
2010	Spain 1, Netherlands 0 (OT)	Villa, Spain; Mueller, Germany; Sneijder, Netherlands; Forlan, Uruguay (5)[3]	South Africa	204

Notes: 1. Brazil won 3-2 on penalty kicks. 2. Italy won 5-3 on penalty kicks. 3. Four-way tie. **Source:** FIFA.

2010 World Cup, First Round

Group A	Wins–Losses–Ties	Points
Uruguay	2–0–1	7
Mexico	1–1–1	4
South Africa	1–1–1	4
France	0–2–1	1

Uruguay 0, France 0   Mexico 1, South Africa 1
Uruguay 3, South Africa 0   Mexico 2, France 0
Uruguay 1, Mexico 0   South Africa 2, France 1

Group B	Wins–Losses–Ties	Points
Argentina	3–0–0	9
South Korea	1–1–1	4
Greece	1–2–0	3
Nigeria	0–2–1	1

Argentina 1, Nigeria 0   S. Korea 2, Greece 0
Argentina 4, S. Korea 1   S. Korea 2, Nigeria 2
Argentina 2, Greece 0   Greece 2, Nigeria 1

Group C	Wins–Losses–Ties	Points
United States	1–0–2	5
England	1–0–2	5
Slovenia	1–1–1	4
Algeria	0–2–1	1

United States 1, England 1   England 0, Algeria 0
United States 2, Slovenia 2   England 1, Slovenia 0
United States 1, Algeria 0   Slovenia 1, Algeria 0

Group D	Wins–Losses–Ties	Points
Germany	2–1–0	6
Ghana	1–1–1	4
Australia	1–1–1	4
Serbia	1–2–0	3

Germany 4, Australia 0   Ghana 1, Serbia 0
Germany 0, Serbia 1   Ghana 1, Australia 1
Germany 1, Ghana 0   Australia 2, Serbia 1

Group E	Wins–Losses–Ties	Points
Netherlands	3–0–0	9
Japan	2–1–0	6
Denmark	1–2–0	3
Cameroon	0–3–0	0

Netherlands 2, Denmark 0   Japan 1, Cameroon 0
Netherlands 1, Japan 0   Japan 3, Denmark 1
Netherlands 2, Cameroon 1   Denmark 2, Cameroon 1

Group F	Wins–Losses–Ties	Points
Paraguay	1–0–2	5
Slovakia	1–1–1	4
New Zealand	0–0–3	3
Italy	0–1–2	2

Paraguay 1, Italy 1   Slovakia 1, New Zealand 1
Paraguay 2, Slovakia 0   Slovakia 3, Italy 2
Paraguay 0, New Zealand 0   New Zealand 1, Italy 1

Group G	Wins–Losses–Ties	Points
Brazil	2–0–1	7
Portugal	1–0–2	5
Ivory Coast	1–1–1	4
North Korea	0–3–0	0

Brazil 2, North Korea 1   Portugal 0, Ivory Coast 0
Brazil 3, Ivory Coast 1   Portugal 7, North Korea 0
Brazil 0, Portugal 0   Ivory Coast 3, North Korea 0

Group H	Wins–Losses–Ties	Points
Spain	2–1–0	6
Chile	2–0–1	6
Switzerland	1–1–1	4
Honduras	0–2–1	1

Spain 0, Switzerland 1   Chile 1, Honduras 0
Spain 2, Honduras 0   Chile 1, Switzerland 0
Spain 2, Chile 1   Switzerland 0, Honduras 0

Note: A win is worth three points and a tie is worth one point. The top two teams in each group advance to the second round.

2010 World Cup, Second Round

Uruguay 2
S. Korea 1
Uruguay 1 (OT)[1]

U.S. 1
Ghana 2 (OT)
Ghana 1

Uruguay 2

Netherlands 2
Slovakia 1
Netherlands 3

Brazil 3
Chile 1
Brazil 1

Netherlands 3

Semifinals

Neth. 0   Spain 1

World Cup Final

Third Place Game
Germany 3   Uruguay 2

Semifinals

Argentina 0
Germany 0

Germany 4

Paraguay 0
Spain 1

Spain 1

Argentina 3
Mexico 1

Germany 4
England 1

Paraguay 0 (OT)[1]
Japan 0

Spain 1
Portugal 0

Note: 1. Decided by shootout.

The Women's World Cup, 2007

The 2007 tournament was held in China, returning to the place of the first FIFA Women's World Cup in 1991. In spite of time differences, both Germany and Brazil set new records for television coverage, and Germany took home the title for the second straight time. Brazil finished second with the U.S. following, and although its team finished fourth, Norway received the FIFA fair play award. FIFA.com users voted Brazilian Marta's goal in the semi-final game the Goal of the Tournament, and voted the Brazilian team the "Most Entertaining". The 2011 Cup will be held in Germany.

FIRST ROUND

Group A	Wins-Losses-Draws	Points
Germany	2-0-1	7
England	1-0-2	5
Japan	1-1-1	4
Argentina	0-3-0	0

Germany 11, Argentina, 0   England 0, Germany 0
Japan 2, England 2   Germany 2, Japan 0
Argentina 0, Japan 1   England 6, Argentina 1

Group B	Wins-Losses-Draws	Points
United States	2-0-1	7
North Korea	1-1-1	4
Sweden	1-1-1	4
Nigeria	0-2-1	1

U.S. 2, North Korea 2   North Korea 2, Nigeria 0
Nigeria 1, Sweden 1   Nigeria 0, U.S. 1
Sweden 0, U.S. 2   North Korea 1, Sweden 2

Group C	Wins-Losses-Draws	Points
Norway	2-0-1	7
Australia	1-0-2	5
Canada	1-1-1	4
Ghana	0-3-0	0

Ghana 1, Australia 4   Australia 1, Norway 1
Norway 2, Canada 1   Norway 7, Ghana 2
Canada 4, Ghana 0   Australia 2, Canada 2

Group D	Wins-Losses-Draws	Points
Brazil	3-0-0	9
China	2-1-0	6
Denmark	1-2-0	3
New Zealand	0-3-0	0

New Zealand 0, Brazil 5   Brazil 4, China 0
China 3, Denmark 2   China 2, New Zealand 0
Denmark 2, New Zealand 0   Brazil 1, Denmark 0

Note: A win is worth three points, and a tie is worth one point. The top two teams in each group advance to the second round.

2007 Women's World Cup, Second Round

Semifinals

Germany 3
Germany 3
N. Korea 0

Norway 1
Norway 0
China 0

World Cup Final

Germany 2   Brazil 0

Third Place Game
U.S. 4   Norway 1

Semifinals

U.S. 3
U.S. 0
England 0

Brazil 3
Brazil 4
Australia 2

CYCLING

The Tour de France

Year	Champion	Year	Champion	Year	Champion	Year	Champion
1903	Maurice Garin	1909	Francois Faber	1919	Firmin Lambot	1925	Ottavio Bottecchia
1904	Henri Cornet	1910	Octave Lapize	1920	Philippe Thijs	1926	Lucien Buysse
1905	Louis Trousselier	1911	Gustave Garrigou	1921	Leon Scieur	1927	Nicolas Frantz
1906	Rene Pottier	1912	Odile Defraye	1922	Firmin Lambot	1928	Nicolas Frantz
1907	Lucien Petit-Breton	1913	Philippe Thijs	1923	Henri Pelissier	1929	Maurice Dewaele
1908	Lucien Petit-Breton	1914	Philippe Thijs	1924	Lucien Petit-Breton	1930	Andre Leducq

Year	Champion	Year	Champion	Year	Champion	Year	Champion
1931	Antonin Magne	1957	Jacques Anquetil	1975	Bernard Thevenet	1994	Miguel Indurain
1932	Andre Leducq	1958	Charly Gaul	1976	Lucien Van Impe	1995	Miguel Indurain
1933	Georges Speicher	1959	Federico Bahamontes	1977	Bernard Thevenet	1996	Bjarne Riis
1934	Antonin Magne			1978	Bernard Hinault	1997	Jan Ullrich
1935	Romain Maes	1960	Gastone Nencini	1979	Bernard Hinault	1998	Marco Pantini
1936	Sylvere Maes	1961	Jacques Anquetil	1980	Joop Zoetemelk	1999	Lance Armstrong
1937	Roger Lapebie	1962	Jacques Anquetil	1981	Bernard Hinault	2000	Lance Armstrong
1938	Gino Bartali	1963	Jacques Anquetil	1982	Bernard Hinault	2001	Lance Armstrong
1939	Sylvere Maes	1964	Jacques Anquetil	1983	Laurent Fignon	2002	Lance Armstrong
1947	Jean Robic	1965	Felice Gimondi	1984	Laurent Fignon	2003	Lance Armstrong
1948	Gino Bartali	1966	Lucien Aimar	1985	Bernard Hinault	2004	Lance Armstrong
1949	Fausto Coppi	1967	Roger Pingeon	1986	Greg LeMond	2005	Lance Armstrong
1950	Ferdi Kubler	1968	Jan Janssen	1987	Stephen Roche	2006	Oscar Pereiro[1]
1951	Hugo Koblet	1969	Eddy Merckx	1988	Pedro Delgado	2007	Alberto Contador
1952	Fausto Coppi	1970	Eddy Merckx	1989	Greg LeMond	2008	Carlos Sastre
1953	Louison Bobet	1971	Eddy Merckx	1990	Greg LeMond	2009	Alberto Contador
1954	Louison Bobet	1972	Eddy Merckx	1991	Miguel Indurain	2010	Alberto Contador
1955	Louison Bobet	1973	Luis Ocana	1992	Miguel Indurain		
1956	Roger Walkowiak	1974	Eddy Merckx	1993	Miguel Indurain		

Note: 1. Floyd Landis, initially declared champion, was disqualified after testing positive for illegal substance.

CHESS

World and U.S. Chess Champions

WORLD CHESS CHAMPIONS		U.S. CHESS CHAMPIONS			
Year	Champion, Countrry	Year	Champion	Year	Champion
1886	Wilhelm Steinitz, Austria	1845–57	Charles Henry Stanley	1984–85	Lev Alburt
				1986	Yasser Seirawan
1894	Emanuel Lasker, Germany	1857–71	Paul Morphy	1987	Joel Benjamin, Nick deFirmian
1921	José R. Capablanca, Cuba	1871–90	Capt. George Mackenzie	1988	Michael Wilder
1927	Alexander Alekhine, France	1890–91	Jackson Showalter	1989	Roman Dzindzichashvili, Stuart Rachels, Yasser Seirawan
		1891–94	Solomon Lipschutz		
		1894	Jackson Showalter		
1935	Max Euwe, Netherlands	1894–95	Albert Hodges	1990	Lev Alburt
1937	Alexander Alekhine, France	1895–97	Jackson Showalter	1991	Gata Kamsky
		1897–1906	Harry Nelson Pillsbury	1992	Patrick Wolff
1948	Mikhail Botvinnik, USSR	1906–09	Jackson Showalter	1993	Alexander Shabalov, Alex Yermolinsky
1957	Vassily Smyslov, USSR	1909–36	Frank J. Marshall	1994	Boris Gulko
1958	Mikhail Botvinnik, USSR	1936–42	Samuel Reshevsky	1995	Nick deFirmian, Alexander Ivanov, Patrick Wolf
		1944	Arnold Denker		
1960	Mikhail Tal, USSR	1946	Samuel Reshevsky	1996	Alex Yermolinski
1961	Mikhail Botvinnik, USSR	1948	Herman Steiner	1997	Joel Benjamin
		1951–52	Larry Evans	1998	Nick deFirmian
1963	Tigran Petrosian, USSR	1954	Arthur Bisguier	1999	Boris Gulko
1969	Boris Spassky, USSR	1957–61	Bobby Fischer	2000	Joel Benjamin
1972	Bobby Fischer, USA	1961–62	Larry Evans	2001	Joel Benjamin, Yasser Seirawan, Alexander Shabalov
1975	Anatoly Karpov, USSR	1962–66	Bobby Fischer		
1985	Garry Kasparov, USSR/Russia	1968	Larry Evans		
		1969	Samuel Reshevksy	2002	Larry Christiansen
1993	Anatoly Karpov[1], Russia	1972	Robert Byrne	2003	Alexander Shabalov
1999	Alex Khalifman, Russia	1973	John Grefe, Lubomir Kavalek	2004	Hikaru Nakamura
2000	Visawanthan Anand, India	1974–77	Lubomir Kavalek	2006	Alexander Onischuk (men) Anna Zatonskih (women)
2002	Ruslan Ponomariov, Ukraine	1978	Walter Browne		
		1980	Walter Browne, Larry Evans, Larry Christiansen		
2004	Rustam Kasimdzhanov, Uzbekistan			2007	Alexander Shabalov (men) Irina Krush (women)
2005	Veselin Topalov, Bulgaria	1981	Walter Browne, Yasser Seirawan	2008	Yury Shulman (men), Anna Zatonskih (women)
2006	Vladmir Kramnik, Russia				
2007	Viswanathan Anand, India	1983	Walter Browne, Larry Christiansen, Roman Dzindzichashvili	2009	Hikaru Nakamura (men) Anna Zatonskih (women)
2008	Veselin Topalov, Bulgaria				
2009	Veselin Topalov, Bulgaria			2010	Gata Kamsky (men) Irina Krush (women)
2010	Viswanathan Ananad, India				

Note: Chess championships are not held every year. 1. In 1993, Kasparov vacated his World Chess Federation (FIDE) championship, whereupon FIDE awarded the title to Karpov. Source: U.S. Chess Federation.

FIGURE SKATING

U.S. and World Figure Skating Champions

	U.S. Champions		World Champions	
Year	Men	Women	Men, Country	Women, Country
1952	Richard Button	Tenley Albright	Richard Button, U.S.	Jacqueline du Bief, France
1953	Hayes Jenkins	Tenley Albright	Hayes Jenkins, U.S.	Tenley Albright, U.S.
1954	Hayes Jenkins	Tenley Albright	Hayes Jenkins, U.S.	Gundi Busch, W. Germany
1955	Hayes Jenkins	Tenley Albright	Hayes Jenkins, U.S.	Tenley Albright, U.S.
1956	Hayes Jenkins	Tenley Albright	Hayes Jenkins, U.S.	Carol Heiss, U.S.
1957	Dave Jenkins	Carol Heiss	Dave Jenkins, U.S.	Carol Heiss, U.S.
1958	Dave Jenkins	Carol Heiss	Dave Jenkins, U.S.	Carol Heiss, U.S.
1959	Dave Jenkins	Carol Heiss	Dave Jenkins, U.S.	Carol Heiss, U.S.
1960	Dave Jenkins	Carol Heiss	Alain Giletti, France	Carol Heiss, U.S.
1961	Bradley Lord	Laurence Owen	No champion	No champion
1962	Monty Hoyt	Barbara Roles Pursley	Don Jackson, Canada	Sjoukje Dijkstra, Netherlands
1963	Tommy Litz	Lorraine Hanlon	Don McPherson, Canada	Sjoukje Dijkstra, Netherlands
1964	Scott Allen	Peggy Fleming	Manfred Schnelldorfer, West Germany	Sjoukje Dijkstra, Netherlands
1965	Gary Visconti	Peggy Fleming	Alain Calmat, France	Petra Burka, Canada
1966	Scott Allen	Peggy Fleming	Emmerich Danzer, Austria	Peggy Fleming, U.S.
1967	Gary Visconti	Peggy Fleming	Emmerich Danzer, Austria	Peggy Fleming, U.S.
1968	Tim Wood	Peggy Fleming	Emmerich Danzer, Austria	Peggy Fleming, U.S.
1969	Tim Wood	Janet Lynn	Tim Wood, U.S.	Gabriele Seyfert, E. Germany
1970	Tim Wood	Janet Lynn	Tim Wood, U.S.	Gabriele Seyfert, E. Germany
1971	John Misha Petkevich	Janet Lynn	Ondrej Nepela, Czechoslovakia	Beatrix Schuba, Austria
1972	Ken Shelley	Janet Lynn	Ondrej Nepela, Czechoslovakia	Beatrix Schuba, Austria
1973	Gordon McKellen Jr.	Janet Lynn	Ondrej Nepela, Czechoslovakia	Karen Magnussen, Canada
1974	Gordon McKellen Jr.	Dorothy Hamill	Jan Hoffmann, E. Germany	Christine Errath, E. Germany
1975	Gordon McKellen Jr.	Dorothy Hamill	Sergei Volkov, USSR	Dianne de Leeuw, Netherlands/U.S.
1976	Terry Kubicka	Dorothy Hamill	John Curry, Great Britain	Dorothy Hamill, U.S.
1977	Charles Tickner	Linda Fratianne	Vladimir Kovalev, USSR	Linda Fratianne, U.S.
1978	Charles Tickner	Linda Fratianne	Charles Tickner, U.S.	Anett Potzsch, E. Germany
1979	Charles Tickner	Linda Fratianne	Vladimir Kovalev, USSR	Linda Fratianne, U.S.
1980	Charles Tickner	Linda Fratianne	Jan Hoffmann, E. Germany	Anett Potzsch, E. Germany
1981	Scott Hamilton	Elaine Zayak	Scott Hamilton, U.S.	Denise Biellmann, Switzerland
1982	Scott Hamilton	Rosalynn Sumners	Scott Hamilton, U.S.	Elaine Zayak, U.S.
1983	Scott Hamilton	Rosalynn Sumners	Scott Hamilton, U.S.	Rosalynn Sumners, U.S.
1984	Scott Hamilton	Rosalynn Sumners	Scott Hamilton, U.S.	Katarina Witt, E. Germany
1985	Brian Boitano	Tiffany Chin	Aleksandr Fadeev, USSR	Katarina Witt, E. Germany
1986	Brian Boitano	Debi Thomas	Brian Boitano, U.S.	Debi Thomas, U.S.
1987	Brian Boitano	Jill Trenary	Brian Orser, Canada	Katarina Witt, E. Germany
1988	Brian Boitano	Debi Thomas	Brian Boitano, U.S.	Katarina Witt, E. Germany
1989	Christopher Bowman	Jill Trenary	Kurt Browning, Canada	Midori Ito, Japan
1990	Todd Eldredge	Jill Trenary	Kurt Browning, Canada	Jill Trenary, U.S.
1991	Todd Eldredge	Tonya Harding	Kurt Browning, Canada	Kristi Yamaguchi, U.S.
1992	Christopher Bowman	Kristi Yamaguchi	Victor Petrenko, Russia	Kristi Yamaguchi, U.S.
1993	Scott Davis	Nancy Kerrigan	Kurt Browning, Canada	Oksana Baiul, Ukraine
1994	Scott Davis	Tonya Harding[1]	Elvis Stojko, Canada	Yuka Sato, Japan
1995	Todd Eldredge	Nicole Bobek	Elvis Stojko, Canada	Lu Chen, China
1996	Rudy Galindo	Michelle Kwan	Todd Eldredge, U.S.	Michelle Kwan, U.S.
1997	Todd Eldredge	Tara Lipinski	Elvis Stojko, Canada	Tara Lipinski, U.S.
1998	Todd Eldredge	Michelle Kwan	Alexi Yagudin, Russia	Michelle Kwan, U.S.
1999	Michael Weiss	Michelle Kwan	Alexi Yagudin, Russia	Maria Butyrskaya, Russia
2000	Michael Weiss	Michelle Kwan	Alexi Yagudin, Russia	Michelle Kwan, U.S.
2001	Tim Goebel	Michelle Kwan	Evgeni Plushenko, Russia	Michelle Kwan, U.S.
2002	Tim Goebel	Michelle Kwan	Alexi Yagudin, Russia	Irina Slutskaya, Russia
2003	Michael Weiss	Michelle Kwan	Evgeni Plushenko, Russia	Michelle Kwan, U.S.
2004	Johnny Weir	Michelle Kwan	Evgeni Plushenko, Russia	Shizuka Arakawa, Japan
2005	Johnny Weir	Michelle Kwan	Stephane Lambiel, Switz.	Irina Slutskaya, Russia
2006	Johnny Weir	Sasha Cohen	Stephane Lambiel, Switz.	Kimmie Meissner, U.S.
2007	Evan Lysacek	Kimmie Meissner	Brian Joubert, France	Miki Ando, Japan
2008	Evan Lysacek	Mirai Nagasu	Jeffrey Buttle, Canada	Mao Asada, Japan
2009	Jeremy Abbott	Alissa Czisny	Evan Lusacek, U.S.	Kim Yu-na, S. Korea
2010	Jeremy Abbott	Rachael Flatt	Daisuke Takahashi, Japan	Mao Asada, Japan

Note: 1. Later stripped of title. Source: U.S. Figure Skating Association.

MARATHON RUNNING

Marathons are 26 miles, 385 yards long, the distance run by the Athenian messenger who announced his city-state's victory over the Persian Empire on the Plains of Marathon in 490 B.C. The oldest U.S. marathon covers a route from Hopkinton, Mass. to Boston.

Boston Marathon Champions

MEN'S CHAMPIONS

Year	Winner	Time	Year	Winner	Time	Year	Winner	Time
1897	John J. McDermott	2:55:10	1936	Ellison M. (Tarzan)	2:33:40	1972	Olavi Suomalainen	2:15:39
1898	Ronald J. McDonald	2:42:00		Brown		1973	Jon Anderson	2:16:03
1899	Lawrence J. Brignolia	2:54:38	1937	Walter Young	2:33:20	1974	Neil Cusack	2:13:39
1900	James J. Caffrey	2:39:44	1938	Leslie Pawson	2:35:34	1975	Bill Rodgers	2:09:55
1901	James J. Caffrey	2:29:23	1939	Ellison M. (Tarzan)	2:28:51	1976	Jack Fultz	2:20:19
1902	Samuel A. Mellor	2:43:12		Brown		1977	Jerome Drayton	2:14:46
1903	John C. Lorden	2:41:29	1940	Gerard Cote	2:33:20	1978	Bill Rodgers	2:10:13
1904	Michael Spring	2:38:04	1941	Leslie Pawson	2:30:38	1979	Bill Rodgers	2:09:27
1905	Fred Lorz	2:38:25	1942	Bernard Joe Smith	2:26:51	1980	Bill Rodgers	2:12:11
1906	Timothy Ford	2:45:45	1943	Gerard Cote	2:28:25	1981	Toshihiko Seko	2:09:26
1907	Thomas Longboat	2:24:24	1944	Gerard Cote	2:31:50	1982	Alberto Salazar	2:08:52
1908	Thomas P. Morrissey	2:25:43	1945	John A. Kelley	2:30:40	1983	Gregory A. Meyer	2:09:00
1909	Henri Renaud	2:53:36	1946	Stylianos Kyriakides	2:29:27	1984	Geoff Smith	2:10:34
1910	Fred L. Cameron	2:28:52	1947	Yun Bok Suh	2:25:39	1985	Geoff Smith	2:14:05
1911	Clarence H. DeMar	2:21:39	1948	Gerard Cote	2:31:02	1986	Robert de Castella	2:07:51
1912	Michael J. Ryan	2:21:18	1949	Karle Leandersson	2:31:50	1987	Toshihiko Seko	2:11:50
1913	Fritz Carlson	2:25:14	1950	Kee Yong Ham	2:32:39	1988	Ibrahim Hussein	2:08:43
1914	James Duffy	2:25:01	1951	Shigeki Tanaka	2:27:45	1989	Abebe Mekonnen	2:09:06
1915	Edouard Fabre	2:31:41	1952	Doroteo Flores	2:31:53	1990	Gelindo Bordin	2:08:20
1916	Arthur V. Roth	2:27:16	1953	Keizo Yamada	2:18:51	1991	Ibrahim Hussein	2:11:06
1917	William K. Kennedy	2:28:37	1954	Veikko L. Karvonen	2:20:39	1992	Ibrahim Hussein	2:08:14
1918	Service team race		1955	Hideo Hamamura	2:18:22	1993	Cosmas N'Deti	2:09:33
	won by Camp Devens		1956	Antti Viskari	2:14:14	1994	Cosmas N'Deti	2:07:15
1919	Carl W. A. Linder	2:29:13	1957	John J. Delley	2:20:05	1995	Cosmas N'Deti	2:09:22
1920	Peter Trivoulidas	2:29:31	1958	Franjo Mihalic	2:25:54	1996	Moses Tanui	2:09:16
1921	Frank Zuna	2:18:57	1959	Eino Oksanen	2:22:42	1997	Lameck Aguta	2:10:34
1922	Clarence H. DeMar	2:18:10	1960	Paavo Kotila	2:20:54	1998	Moses Tanui	2:07:34
1923	Clarence H. DeMar	2:23:37	1961	Eino Oksanen	2:23:39	1999	Joseph Chebet	2:09:52
1924	Clarence H. DeMar	2:29:40	1962	Eino Oksanen	2:23:48	2000	Elijah Lagat	2:09:47
1925	Charles L. Mellor	2:33:00	1963	Aurele	2:18:58	2001	Lee Bong-ju	2:09:43
1926	John C. Miles	2:25:40		Vandendriessche		2002	Rodgers Rop	2:09:02
1927	Clarence H. DeMar	2:40:22	1964	Aurele	2:19:59	2003	Robert Cheruiyot	2:10:11
1928	Clarence H. DeMar	2:37:07		Vandendriessche		2004	Timothy Cherigat	2:10:37
1929	John C. Miles	2:33:08	1965	Morio Shigematsu	2:16:33	2005	Hailu Negussie	2:11:45
1930	Clarence H. DeMar	2:34:48	1966	Kenji Kimihara	2:17:11	2006	Robert Cheruiyot	2:07:14
1931	James P. Henigan	2:46:45	1967	David McKenzie	2:15:45	2007	Robert Cheruiyot	2:14:13
1932	Paul deBruyn	2:33:36	1968	Ambrose Burfoot	2:22:17	2008	Robert Cheruiyot	2:07:46
1933	Leslie Pawson	2:33:01	1969	Yoshiaki Unetani	2:13:49	2009	Beriba Merga	2:08:42
1934	Dave Komonen	2:32:53	1970	Ron Hill	2:10:30	2010	Robert Cheruiyot	2:05:52
1935	John A. Kelley	2:32:07	1971	Alavaro Mejia	2:18:45			

WOMEN'S CHAMPIONS

Year	Winner	Time	Year	Winner	Time	Year	Winner	Time
1972	Nina Kuscsik	3:10:26		Weidenbach		1999	Fatuma Roba	2:23:25
1973	Jacqueline Hansen	3:05:59	1986	Ingrid Kristiansen	2:24:55	2000	Catherine Ndereba	2:26:11
1974	Miki Gorman	2:47:11	1987	Rosa Mota	2:25:21	2001	Catherine Ndereba	2:21:50
1975	Liane Winter	2:42:24	1988	Rosa Mota	2:24:30	2002	Margaret Okayo	2:20:43
1976	Kim Merritt	2:47:10	1989	Ingrid Kristiansen	2:24:33	2003	Svetlana Zakharova	2:25:20
1977	Miki Gorman	2:46:22	1990	Rosa Mota	2:25:24	2004	Catherine Ndereba	2:24:27
1978	Gayle Barron	2:44:52	1991	Wanda Panfil	2:24:18	2005	Catherine Ndereba	2:25:13
1979	Joan Benoit	2:35:15	1992	Olga Markova	2:23:43	2006	Rita Jeptoo	2:23:38
1980	Jacqueline Gareau	2:34:28	1993	Olga Markova	2:25:27	2007	Lidiya Grigoryeva	2:29:18
1981	Allison Roe	2:26:46	1994	Uta Pippig	2:21:45	2008	Dire Tune	2:25:25
1982	Charlotte Teske	2:29:33	1995	Uta Pippig	2:25:11	2009	Salina Kosgei	2:32:16
1983	Joan Benoit	2:22:43	1996	Uta Pippig	2:27:12	2010	Teyba Erkesso	2:26:11
1984	Lorraine Moller	2:29:28	1997	Fatuma Roba	2:28:03			
1985	Lisa Larsen-	2:34:06	1998	Fatuma Roba	2:23:21			

New York Marathon Champions

Year	Winner	Time	Year	Winner	Time	Year	Winner	Time
	MEN		1997	John Kagwe	2:08:12	1983	Grete Waitz	2:27:00
1970	Gary Muhrcke	2:31:39	1998	John Kagwe	2:08:45	1984	Grete Waitz	2:29:30
1971	Norman Higgins	2:22:55	1999	Joseph Chebet	2:09:14	1985	Grete Waitz	2:28:34
1972	Sheldon Karlin	2:27:53	2000	Abdelkhader	2:10:09	1986	Grete Waitz	2:28:06
1973	Tom Fleming	2:21:55		el-Mouaziz.		1987	Priscilla Welch	2:30:17
1974	Norbert Sander	2:26:31	2001	Tesfaye Jifar	2:07:43	1988	Grete Waitz	2:28:07
1975	Tom Fleming	2:19:27	2002	Rodgers Rop	2:08:07	1989	Ingrid Kristiansen	2:25:30
1976	Bill Rodgers	2:10:10	2003	Martin Lel	2:10:30	1990	Wanda Panfil	2:30:45
1977	Bill Rodgers	2:11:28	2004	Hendrik Ramaala	2:09:28	1991	Liz McColgan	2:27:32
1978	Bill Rodgers	2:12:12	2005	Paul Tergat	2:09:30	1992	Lisa Ondieki	2:24:40
1979	Bill Rodgers	2:11:42	2006	Marilson dos Santos	2:09:58	1993	Uta Pippig	2:26:24
1980	Alberto Salazar	2:09:41	2007	Martin Lel	2:09:04	1994	Tegla Loroupe	2:27:37
1981	Alberto Salazar	2:08:13	2008	Marilson dos Santos	2:08:43	1995	Tegla Loroupe	2:28:06
1982	Alberto Salazar	2:09:29	2009	Meb Keflezighi	2:09:15	1996	Anuta Catuna	2:28:18
1983	Rod Dixon	2:08:59		**WOMEN**		1997	Franziska	2:28:43
1984	Orlando Pizzolato	2:14:53	1970	No Finisher			Rochat-Moser	
1985	Orlando Pizzolato	2:11:34	1971	Beth Bonner	2:55:22	1998	Franca Fiacconi	2:25:17
1986	Gianni Poli	2:11:06	1972	Nina Kuscsik	3:08:42	1999	Adriana Fernandez	2:25:06
1987	Ibrahim Hussein	2:11:01	1973	Nina Kuscsik	2:57:08	2000	Lyudmila Petrova	2:25:45
1988	Steve Jones	2:08:20	1974	Katherine Switzer	3:07:29	2001	Margaret Okayo	2:24:21
1989	Jumo Ikangaa	2:08:01	1975	Kim Merritt	2:46:15	2002	Joyce Chepchumba	2:25:56
1990	Douglas Waikihuri	2:12:39	1976	Miki Gorman	2:39:11	2003	Margaret Okayo	2:22:31
1991	Salvador Garcia	2:09:28	1977	Miki Gorman	2:43:10	2004	Paula Radcliffe	2:23:10
1992	Willie Mtolo	2:09:29	1978	Grete Waitz	2:32:30	2005	Jelena Prokopcuka	2:24:41
1993	Andres Espinosa	2:10:04	1979	Grete Waitz	2:27:33	2006	Jelena Prokopcuka	2:25:05
1994	German Silva	2:11:21	1980	Grete Waitz	2:25:41	2007	Paula Radcliffe	2:23:09
1995	German Silva	2:11:00	1981	Allison Roe	2:25:29	2008	Paula Radcliffe	2:23:56
1996	Giacomo Leone	2:10:09	1982	Grete Waitz	2:27:14	2009	Derartu Tulu	2:28:52

TRACK AND FIELD

Track and Field World Records (as of August 15, 2010)

These are the recognized records of the IAAF (International Amateur Athletic Federation). All walk records must have been made on a track, and all relay records must be made by teams composed of individuals from the same country. Indoor records must be performed on tracks no larger than 200m in circumference, and the meet must be subject to drug testing. Awards awaiting ratification are not shown.

	MEN'S OUTDOOR TRACK RECORDS				WOMEN'S OUTDOOR TRACK RECORDS		
Event	**(min:sec)**	**Record holder (country)**	**Date**	**Event**	**(min:sec)**	**Record holder (country)**	**Date**
100 m	9.58	Usain Bolt (Jamaica)	8/16/09	100 m	10.49	Florence Griffith Joyner (U.S.)	7/16/88
200 m	19.19	Usain Bolt (Jamaica)	8/20/09				
400 m	43.18	Michael Johnson (U.S.)	8/26/99	200 m	21.34	Florence Griffith Joyner (U.S.)	9/29/88
800 m	1:41.11	Wilson Kipketer (Denmark)	8/24/97				
1,000 m	2:11.96	Noah Ngeny (Kenya)	9/5/99	400 m	47.60	Marita Koch (E. Germany)	10/6/85
1,500 m	3:26:00	Hicham el-Guerrouj (Morocco)	7/14/98	800 m	1:53.28	Jarmila Kratochvilova (Czechoslovakia)	7/26/83
Mile	3:43.13	Hicham el-Guerrouj (Morocco)	7/7/99	1,000 m	2:28.98	Svetlana Masterkova (Russia)	8/23/96
2,000 m	4:44.79	Hicham el-Guerrouj (Morocco)	9/7/99	1,500 m	3:50.46	Yunxia Qu (China)	9/11/93
				Mile	4:12.56	Svetlana Masterkova (Russia)	8/14/96
3,000 m	7:20.67	Daniel Komen (Kenya)	9/1/96				
Steeplechase	7:53.63	Saif Saaeed Shaheen (Qatar)	9/3/04	2,000 m	5:25.35	Sonia O'Sullivan (Ireland)	7/8/94
				3,000 m	8:06.11	Junxia Wang (China)	9/13/93
5,000 m	12:37.35	Kenenisa Bekele (Ethiopia)	5/31/04	5,000 m	14:11.15	Tirunesh Dibaba (Ethiopia)	6/6/08
10,000 m	26:17.53	Kenenisa Bekele (Ethiopia)	8/26/05	10,000 m	29:31.78	Junxia Wang (China)	9/8/93
Marathon	2:03:59	Haile Gebrselassie (Ethiopia)	9/28/08	Marathon	2:15:25	Paula Radcliffe, (U.K.)	4/13/03[1]
				100 m hurd.	12.21	Yordanka Donkova (Bulgaria)	8/20/88
110 m hurd.	12.87	Dayron Robles (Cuba)	6/12/08				
400 m hurd.	46.78	Kevin Young (U.S.)	8/6/92	400 m hurd.	52.34	Yuliya Pechonkina (Russia)	8/8/03
20 km walk	1:17:16	Vladimir Kanaykin (Russia)	9/29/07	10 km walk	41:56.23	Nadezhda Ryashkina (USSR)	7/4/90
50 km walk	3:34:14	Denis Nizhegorodov (Russia)	5/11/08	20 km walk	1:25:41	Olimpiada Ivanova (Russia)	8/7/05
				4 x 100 m	41.37	East Germany	10/6/85
4 x 100 m	37.10	Jamaica	8/22/08				
4 x 200 m	1:18.68	Santa Monica Track Club	4/17/94	4 x 200 m	1:27.46	United States	4/29/00
4 x 400 m	2:54.20	United States	7/22/98	4 x 400 m	3:15.17	Soviet Union	10/1/88

Note: 1. Radcliffe also made this time 9/26/99.

MEN'S OUTDOOR FIELD EVENTS

Event	Meters	ft./in.	Record holder (country)	Date
High jump	2.45	8' .5"	Javier Sotomayor (Cuba)	7/27/93
Pole vault	6.14	20' 1.75"	Sergey Bubka (Ukraine)	7/31/94
Long jump	8.95	29' 4.5"	Mike Powell (United States)	8/30/91
Triple jump	18.29	60' 0"	Jonathan Edwards (Great Britain)	8/7/95
Shot put	23.12	75' 10.25"	Randy Barnes (United States)	5/20/90
Discus	74.08	243' 0"	Jurgen Schult (East Germany)	6/6/86
Hammer	86.74	284' 7"	Yuriy Syedikh (USSR)	8/30/86
Javelin	98.48	323' 1"	Jan Zelezny (Czech Republic)	5/25/96
Decathlon	9,026 points		Roman Sebrle (Czech Republic)	5/27/01

WOMEN'S OUTDOOR FIELD EVENTS

Event	Meters	ft./in.	Record holder (country)	Date
High jump	2.09	6' 10.25"	Stefka Kostadinova (Bulgaria)	8/30/87
Pole vault	5.06	16.6"	Elena Isinbaeva (Russia)	8/28/09
Long jump	7.52	24' 8.25"	Galina Chistyakova (USSR)	6/11/88
Triple jump	15.50	50' 10.25"	Inessa Kravets (Ukraine)	8/10/95
Shot put	22.63	74' 3"	Natalya Lisovskaya (USSR)	6/7/87
Discus	76.80	252' 0"	Gabriele Reinsch (East Germany)	7/9/88
Hammer	78.3	256.89"	Anita Wlodarczyk (Poland)	6/6/10
Javelin	72.28	237' 1.7"	Barbora Špotáková (Czech Republic)	9/13/08
Heptathlon	7,291 points		Jackie Joyner-Kersee (United States)	9/24/88

MEN'S INDOOR TRACK EVENTS

Event	(min:sec)	Record holder (country)	Date
50 m	5.56	Donovan Bailey (Canada)	2/9/96
60 m	6.39	Maurice Greene (U.S.)	2/3/98
200 m	19.92	Frank Fredericks (Namibia)	2/18/96
400 m	44.57	Kerron Clement (U.S.)	3/12/05
800 m	1:42.67	Wilson Kipketer (Denmark)	3/9/97
1,000 m	2:14.96	Wilson Kipketer (Denmark)	2/20/00
1,500 m	3:31.18	Hicham el-Guerrouj (Morocco)	2/2/97
Mile	3:48.45	Hicham el-Guerrouj (Morocco)	2/12/97
3,000 m	7:24.90	Daniel Komen (Kenya)	2/6/98
5,000 m	12:49.60	Kenenisa Bekele (Ethiopia)	2/20/04
50 m hurdles	6.25	Mark McKoy (Canada)	3/5/86
60 m hurdles	7.30	Colin Jackson (Great Britain)	3/6/94
5,000 m walk	18:07.08	Mikhail Shchennikov (Russia)	2/14/95
4 x 200 m	1:22.11	Great Britain	3/3/91
4 x 400 m	3:02.83	United States	3/7/99
4 x 800 m	7:13.94	United States	2/6/00

WOMEN'S INDOOR TRACK EVENTS

Event	(min:sec)	Record holder (country)	Date
50 m	5.96	Irina Privalova (Russia)	2/9/95
60 m	6.92	Irina Privalova (Russia)	2/9/95
200 m	21.87	Merlene Ottey (Jamaica)	2/13/93
400 m	49.59	Jarmila Kratochvilova (Czechoslovakia)	3/7/82
800 m	1:55.82	Jolanda Ceplak (Slovakia)	3/3/02
1,000 m	2:30.94	Maria Mutola (Mozambique)	2/25/99
1,500 m	3:58.28	Yelena Soboleva (Russia)	2/18/06
Mile	4:17.14	Doina Melinte (Romania)	2/9/90
3,000 m	8:23.72	Meseret Defar (Ethiopia)	2/3/07
5,000 m	14:24.37	Meseret Defar (Ethiopia)	2/18/09
50 m hurdles	6.58	Cornelia Oschkenat (East Germany)	2/20/88
60 m hurdles	7.68	Susanna Kallur (Sweden)	2/10/08
3,000 m walk	11:40.33	Claudia Stef (Romania)	1/30/99
4 x 200 m	1:32.41	Russia	1/29/05
4 x 400 m	3:23.37	Russia	1/28/06
4 x 800 m	8:12.41	Moskva 1	2/28/10

MEN'S INDOOR FIELD EVENTS

Event	Meters	ft./in.	Record holder (country)	Date
High jump	2.43	7' 11.5"	Javier Sotomayor (Cuba)	3/4/89
Pole vault	6.15	20' 2"	Sergey Bubka (Ukraine)	2/21/93
Long jump	8.79	28' 10.25"	Carl Lewis (United States)	1/27/84
Triple jump	17.90	58'5.83"	Teddy Tamgho (France)	3/14/10
Shot put	22.66	74' 4.25"	Randy Barnes (United States)	1/20/89
Heptathlon	6,499 points		Ashton Eaton (USA)	3/13/10

WOMEN'S INDOOR FIELD EVENTS

Event	Meters	ft./in.	Record holder (country)	Date
High jump	2.08	6' 9.9"	Kajsa Bergqvist (Sweden)	2/4/06
Pole vault	5.00	16' 4.85"	Yelena Isinbayeva (Russia)	2/15/09
Long jump	7.37	24' 2.25"	Heike Drechsler (East Germany)	2/13/88
Triple jump	15.36	50' 4.75"	Tatyana Lebedeva (Russia)	3/6/04
Shot put	22.50	73' 10"	Helena Fibingerova (Czech.)	2/19/77
Pentathlon	4,991 points		Irina Belova (Unified Team)	2/15/92

Source: International Amateur Athletic Federation.

Olympic Sports

SUMMER OLYMPIC CHAMPIONS

Swimming and Diving (Men)

	50m Freestyle	Time
1904	Zoltán Halmay, Hungary	0:28.00
1988	Matt Biondi, U.S.	0:22.14
1992	Aleksandr Popov, Unified Team	0:21.91
1996	Aleksandr Popov, Russia	0:22.13
2000	(tie) Anthony Ervin, U.S/Gary Hall Jr., U.S.	0:21.98
2004	Gary Hall Jr., U.S.	0:21.93
2008	Cesar Cielo Filho, Brazil	0:21.47
	100m Freestyle	Time
1896	Alfréd Hajós, Hungary	1:22.20
1904	Zoltán Halmay, Hungary (100 yds.)	1:02.80
1908	Charles Daniels, U.S.	1:05.60
1912	Duke Paoa Kahanamoku, U.S.	1:03.40
1920	Duke Paoa Kahanamoku, U.S.	1:00.40
1924	Johnny Weissmuller, U.S.	0:59.00
1928	Johnny Weissmuller, U.S.	0:58.60
1932	Yasuji Miyazaki, Japan	0:58.20
1936	Ferenc Csík, Hungary	0:57.60
1948	Walter Ris, U.S.	0:57.30
1952	Clarke Scholes, U.S.	0:57.40
1956	Jon Henricks, Australia	0:55.40
1960	John Devitt, Australia	0:55.20
1964	Donald Schollander, U.S.	0:53.40
1968	Michael Wenden, Australia	0:52.20
1972	Mark Spitz, U.S.	0:51.22
1976	Jim Montgomery, U.S.	0:49.99
1980	Jörg Woithe, East Germany	0:50.40
1984	Rowdy Gaines, U.S.	0:49.80
1988	Matt Biondi, U.S.	0:48.63
1992	Aleksandr Popov, Unified Team	0:49.02
1996	Aleksandr Popov, Russia	0:48.74
2000	Pieter van den Hoogenband, Netherlands	0:48.30
2004	Pieter van den Hoogenband, Netherlands	0:48.71
2008	Alain Bernard, France	0:47.21
	200m Freestyle	Time
1900	Frederick Lane, Austria	2:25.20
1904	Charles Daniels, U.S.	2:44.20
1968	Michael Wenden, Australia	1:55.20
1972	Mark Spitz, U.S.	1:52.78
1976	Bruce Furniss, U.S.	1:50.29
1980	Sergei Kopliakov, U.S.S.R.	1:49.81
1984	Michael Gross, West Germany	1:47.44
1988	Duncan Armstrong, Australia	1:47.25
1992	Evgueni Sadovyi, Unified Team	1:46.70
1996	Danyon Loader, New Zealand	1:47.63
2000	Pieter van den Hoogenband, Netherlands	1:45.35
2004	Ian Thorpe, Australia	1:44.71
2008	Michael Phelps, U.S.	1:42:96
	400m Freestyle	Time
1896	Paul Neumann, Austria (500m)	8:12.60
1904	Charles Daniels, U.S. (440 yds.)	6:16.20
1908	Henry Taylor, Great Britain (440 yds.)	5:36.80
1912	George Hodgson, Canada	5:24.40
1920	Norman Ross, U.S.	5:26.80
1924	Johnny Weissmuller, U.S.	5:04.20
1928	Alberto Zorilla, Argentina	5:01.60
1932	Clarence "Buster" Crabbe, U.S.	4:48.40
1936	Jack Medica, U.S.	4:44.50
1948	William Smith, U.S.	4:41.00
1952	Jean Boiteux, France	4:30.70
1956	Murray Rose, Australia	4:27.30
1960	Murray Rose, Australia	4:18.30
1964	Donald Schollander, U.S.	4:12.20
1968	Michael Burton, U.S.	4:09.00
1972	Bradford Cooper, Australia	4:00.27
1976	Brian Goodell, U.S.	3:51.93
1980	Vladimir Salnikov, U.S.S.R.	3:51.31
1984	George DiCarlo, U.S.	3:51.23
1988	Ewe Dassler, East Germany	3:46.95
1992	Evgueni Sadovyi, Unified Team	3:45.00
1996	Danyon Loader, New Zealand	3:47.97
2000	Ian Thorpe, Australia	3:40.59

2004	Ian Thorpe, Australia	3:43.10
2008	Park Tae-Hwan, South Korea	3:41:86
	1,500m Freestyle	Time
1896	Alfréd Hajós, Hungary (1,200m)	18:22.20
1900	John Arthur Jarvis, Great Britain (1,000m)	13:40.20
1904	Emil Rausch, Germany (1,609m)	27:18.20
1908	Henry Taylor, Great Britain	22:48.40
1912	George Hodgson, Canada	22:00.00
1920	Norman Ross, U.S.	22:23.20
1924	Andrew "Boy" Charlton, Australia	20:06.60
1928	Arne Borg, Sweden	19:51.80
1932	Kusuo Kitamura, Japan	19:12.40
1936	Noboru Terada, Japan	19:13.70
1948	James McLane, U.S.	19:18.50
1952	Ford Konno, U.S.	18:30.30
1956	Murray Rose, Australia	17:58.90
1960	John Konrads, Australia	17:19.60
1964	Robert Windle, Australia	17:01.70
1968	Michael Burton, U.S.	16:38.90
1972	Michael Burton, U.S.	15:52.58
1976	Brian Goodell, U.S.	15:02.40
1980	Vladimir Salnikov, U.S.S.R.	14:58.27
1984	Michael O'Brien, U.S.	15:05.20
1988	Vladimir Salnikov, U.S.S.R.	15:00.40
1992	Kieren Perkins, Australia	14:43.48
1996	Kieren Perkins, Australia	14:56.40
2000	Grant Hackett, Australia	14:48.33
2004	Grant Hackett, Australia	14:43.40
2008	Oussama Mellouli, Tunisia	14:40:84
	100m Backstroke	Time
1904	Walter Brack, Germany (100yds)	1:16.80
1908	Arno Bieberstein, Germany	1:24.60
1912	Harry Hebner, U.S.	1:21.20
1920	Warren Paoa Kealoha, U.S.	1:15.20
1924	Warren Paoa Kealoha, U.S.	1:13.20
1928	George Kojac, U.S.	1:08.20
1932	Masaji Kiyokawa, Japan	1:08.60
1936	Adolf Kiefer, U.S.	1:05.90
1948	Allen Stack, U.S.	1:06.40
1952	Yoshinobu Oyakawa, U.S.	1:05.40
1956	David Theile, Australia	1:02.20
1960	David Theile, Australia	1:01.90
1964	Not held	
1968	Roland Matthes, East Germany	0:58.70
1972	Roland Matthes, East Germany	0:56.58
1976	John Naber, U.S.	0:55.49
1980	Bengt Baron, Sweden	0:56.33
1984	Richard Carey, U.S.	0:55.79
1988	Daichi Suzuki, Japan	0:55.05
1992	Mark Tewksbury, Canada	0:53.98
1996	Jeff Rouse, U.S.	0:54.10
2000	Lenny Krayzelburg, U.S.	0:53.72
2004	Aaron Piersol, U.S.	0:54.06
2008	Aaron Peirsol, U.S.	0:52.54
	200m Backstroke	Time
1900	Ernst Hoppenberg, Germany	2:47.00
1964	Jed Graef, U.S.	2:10.30
1968	Roland Matthes, East Germany	2:09.60
1972	Roland Matthes, East Germany	2:02.82
1976	John Naber, U.S.	1:59.19
1980	Sándor Wladár, Hungary	2:01.93
1984	Richard Carey, U.S.	2:00.23
1988	Igor Poliansky, U.S.S.R.	1:59.37
1992	Martin Zubero, Spain	1:58.47
1996	Brad Bridgewater, U.S.	1:58.54
2000	Lenny Krayzelburg, U.S.	1:56.76
2004	Aaron Piersol, U.S.	1:54.95
2008	Ryan Lochte, U.S.	1:53:94
	100m Breaststroke	Time
1968	Donald McKenzie, U.S.	1:07.70
1972	Nobutaka Taguchi, Japan	1:04.94
1976	John Hencken, U.S.	1:03.11

1980	Duncan Goodhew, Great Britain	1:03.44
1984	Steve Lundquist, U.S.	1:01.65
1988	Adrian Moorhouse, Great Britain	1:02.04
1992	Nelson Diebel, U.S.	1:01.50
1996	Fred Deburghgraeve, Belgium	1:00.65
2000	Domenico Fioravanti, Italy	1:00.46
2004	Kosuke Kitajima, Japan	1:00.08
2008	Kosuke Kitajima, Japan	0:58.91

200m Breaststroke — Time

1908	Frederick Holman, Great Britain	3:09.20
1912	Walter Bathe, Germany	3:01.80
1920	Haken Malmroth, Sweden	3:04.40
1924	Robert Skelton, U.S.	2:56.60
1928	Yoshiyuki Tsuruta, Japan	2:48.80
1932	Yoshiyuki Tsuruta, Japan	2:45.40
1936	Tetsuo Hamuro, Japan	2:41.50
1948	Joseph Verdeur, U.S.	2:39.30
1952	John Davies, Australia	2:34.40
1956	Masaru Furukawa, Japan	2:34.70
1960	William Mulliken, U.S.	2:37.40
1964	Ian O'Brien, Australia	2:27.80
1968	Felipe Muñoz, Mexico	2:28.70
1972	John Hencken, U.S.	2:21.55
1976	David Wilkie, Great Britain	2:15.11
1980	Robertas Zhulpa, U.S.S.R.	2:15.85
1984	Victor Davis, Canada	2:13.34
1988	Jozsef Szabo, Hungary	2:13.52
1992	Mike Barrowman, U.S.	2:10.16
1996	Norbert Rozso, Hungary	2:12.57
2000	Domenico Fioravanti, Italy	2:10.87
2004	Kosuke Kitajima, Japan	2:09.44
2008	Kosuke Kitajima, Japan	2:07:64

100m Butterfly — Time

1968	Douglas Russell, U.S.	0:55.90
1972	Mark Spitz, U.S.	0:54.27
1976	Matt Vogel, U.S.	0:54.35
1980	Par Arvidsson, Sweden	0:54.92
1984	Michael Gross, West Germany	0:53.08
1988	Anthony Nesty, Suriname	0:53.00
1992	Pablo Morales, U.S.	0:53.32
1996	Denis Pankratov, Russia	0:52.27
2000	Lars Froelander, Sweden	0:52.00
2004	Michael Phelps, U.S.	0:51.25
2008	Michael Phelps, U.S.	0:50.58

200m Butterfly — Time

1956	William Yorzyk, U.S.	2:19.30
1960	Michael Troy, U.S.	2:12.80
1964	Kevin Berry, Australia	2:06.60
1968	Carl Robie, U.S.	2:08.70
1972	Mark Spitz, U.S.	2:00.70
1976	Mike Bruner, U.S.	1:59.23
1980	Sergei Fesenko, U.S.S.R.	1:59.76
1984	Jon Sieben, Australia	1:57.04
1988	Michael Gross, West Germany	1:56.94
1992	Mel Stewart, U.S.	1:56.26
1996	Denis Pankratov, Russia	1:56.51
2000	Tom Malchow, United States	1:55.35
2004	Michael Phelps, U.S.	1:54.04
2008	Michael Phelps, U.S.	1:52:03

200m Individual Medley — Time

1968	Charles Hickcox, U.S.	2:12.00
1972	Gunnar Larsson, Sweden	2:07.17
1984	Alex Baumann, Canada	2:01.42
1988	Tamas Darnyi, Hungary	2:00.17
1992	Tamas Darnyi, Hungary	2:00.76
1996	Attila Czene, Hungary	1:59.91
2000	Massimiliano Rosolino, Italy	1:58.98
2004	Michael Phelps, U.S.	1:57.14
2008	Michael Phelps, U.S.	1:54.23

400m Individual Medley — Time

1964	Richard W. Roth, U.S.	4:45.40
1968	Charles Hickcox, U.S.	4:48.40
1972	Gunnar Larsson, Sweden	4:31.98
1976	Rod Strachan, U.S.	4:23.68
1980	Aleksandr Sidorenko, U.S.S.R.	4:22.89
1984	Alex Baumann, Canada	4:17.41
1988	Tamas Darnyi, Hungary	4:14.75
1992	Tamas Darnyi, Hungary	4:14.23
1996	Tom Dolan, U.S.	4:14.90
2000	Tom Dolan, U.S.	4:11.76
2004	Michael Phelps, U.S.	4:08.26
2008	Michael Phelps, U.S.	4:03:84

4x100m Freestyle

	Relay	Time		Relay	Time
1964	U.S.	3:33.20	1996	U.S.	3:15.41
1968	U.S.	3:31.70	2000	Australia	3:13.67
1972	U.S.	3:26.42	2004	South Africa	3:13.17
1984	U.S.	3:19.03			
1988	U.S.	3:16.53	2008	U.S.	3:08:24
1992	U.S.	3:16.74			

4x200m Freestyle

	Relay	Time		Relay	Time
1908	Great Br.	10:55.60	1968	U.S.	7:52.33
1912	Australia	10:11.60	1972	U.S.	7:35.78
1920	U.S.	10:04.40	1976	U.S.	7:23.22
1924	U.S.	9:53.40	1980	U.S.S.R.	7:23.50
1928	U.S.	9:36.20	1984	U.S.	7:15.69
1932	Japan	8:58.40	1988	U.S.	7:12.69
1936	Japan	8:51.50	1992	Unified	7:11.95
1948	U.S.	8:46.00	1996	U.S.	7:14.84
1952	U.S.	8:31.10	2000	Australia	7:07.05
1956	Australia	8:23.60	2004	U.S.	7:07.33
1960	U.S.	8:10.20	2008	U.S.	6:58:56
1964	U.S.	7:52.10			

4x100m Medley

	Relay	Time		Relay	Time
1960	U.S.	4:05.40	1988	U.S.	3:36.93
1964	U.S.	3:58.40	1992	U.S.	3:36.93
1968	U.S.	3:54.90	1996	U.S.	3:34.84
1972	U.S.	3:48.16	2000	U.S.	3:33.73
1976	U.S.	3:42.22	2004	U.S.	3:30.68
1980	Australia	3:45.70	2008	U.S.	3:29:34
1984	U.S.	3:39.30			

Platform Diving

1904	George E. Sheldon, U.S.
1908	Hjalmar Johansson, Swed.
1912	Erik Adlerz, Sweden
1920	Clarence Pinkston, U.S.
1924	Albert C. White, U.S.
1928	Pete DesJardins, U.S.
1932	Harold Smith, U.S.
1936	Marshall Wayne, U.S.
1948	Dr. Samuel Lee, U.S.
1952	Dr. Samuel Lee, U.S.
1956	Joaquin Capilla Perez, Mex.
1960	Robert Webster, U.S.
1964	Robert Webster, U.S.
1968	Klaus Dibiasi, Italy
1972	Klaus Dibiasi, Italy
1976	Klaus Dibiasi, Italy
1980	Falk Hoffmann, E.Germany
1984	Gregory Louganis, U.S.
1988	Gregory Louganis, U.S.
1992	Sun Shuwei, China
1996	Xiong Ni, China
2000	Liang Tian, China
2004	Jia Hu, China
2008	Matthew Mitcham, Australia

Springboard Diving

1908	Albert Zürner, Germany
1912	Paul Günther, Germany
1920	Louis Kuehn, U.S.
1924	Albert C. White, U.S.
1928	Pete Desjardins, U.S.
1932	Michael Galitzen, U.S.
1936	Richard Degener, U.S.
1948	Bruce Harlan, U.S.
1952	David Browning, U.S.
1956	Robert L. Clotworthy, U.S.
1960	Gary Tobian, U.S.
1964	Kenneth R. Sitzberger, U.S.
1968	Bernard Wrightson, U.S.
1972	Vladimir Vasin, U.S.S.R.
1976	Philip Boggs, U.S.
1980	Aleksandr Portnov, U.S.S.R.
1984	Gregory Louganis, U.S.
1988	Gregory Louganis, U.S.
1992	Mark Lenzi, U.S.
1996	Dmitri Sautin, Russia
2000	Xiong Ni, China
2004	Bo Peng, China
2008	He Chong, China

Swimming and Diving (Women)

	50m Freestyle	**Time**			
1988	Kristin Otto, E. Germany	0:25.49			
1992	Yang Wenji, China	0:24.79			
1996	Amy Van Dyken, U.S.	0:24.87			
2000	Inge de Bruijn, Netherlands	0:24.32			
2004	Inge de Bruijn, Netherlands	0:24.58			
2008	Britta Steffen, Germany	0:24.06			

	100m Freestyle	**Time**
1912	Fanny Durack, Australia	1:22.20
1920	Ethelda Bleibtrey, U.S.	1:13.60
1924	Ethel Lackie, U.S.	1:12.40
1928	Albina Osipowich, U.S.	1:11.00
1932	Helene Madison, U.S.	1:06.80
1936	Rie Mastenbroek, Netherlands	1:05.90
1948	Greta Andersen, Denmark	1:06.30
1952	Katalin Szoke, Hungary	1:06.80
1956	Dawn Fraser, Australia	1:02.00
1960	Dawn Fraser, Australia	1:01.20
1964	Dawn Fraser, Australia	0:59.50
1968	Jan Henne, U.S.	1:00.00
1972	Sandra Neilson, U.S.	0:58.59
1976	Kornelia Ender, East Germany	0:55.65
1980	Barbara Krause, East Germany	0:54.79
1984	Nancy Hogshead, U.S.	0:55.92
1988	Kristin Otto, East Germany	0:54.93
1992	Zhuang Yong, China	0:54.65
1996	Le Jingyi, China	0:54.50
2000	Inge de Bruijn, Netherlands	0:53.83
2004	Jodie Henry, Australia	0:53.84
2008	Britta Steffen, Germany	0:53.12

	200m Freestyle	**Time**
1968	Deborah Meyer, U.S.	2:10.50
1972	Shane Gould, Australia	2:03.56
1976	Kornelia Ender, East Germany	1:59.26
1980	Barbara Krause, East Germany	1:58.33
1984	Mary Wayte, U.S.	1:59.23
1988	Heike Friederich, East Germany	1:57.65
1992	Nicole Haislett, U.S.	1:57.90
1996	Claudia Poll, Costa Rica	1:58.16
2000	Susie O'Neill, Australia	1:58.24
2004	Camelia Potec, Romania	1:58.03
2008	Frederica Pellegrini, Italy	1:54:82

	400m Freestyle	**Time**
1920	Ethelda Bleibtrey, U.S. (300 m)	4:34.00
1924	Martha Norelius, U.S.	6:02.20
1928	Martha Norelius, U.S.	5:42.80
1932	Helene Madison, U.S.	5:28.50
1936	Hendrika "Rie" Mastenbroek, Netherlands	5:26.40
1948	Ann Curtis, U.S.	5:17.80
1952	Valeria Gyenge, Hungary	5:12.10
1956	Lorraine Crapp, Australia	4:54.60
1960	S. Chris Von Saltza, U.S.	4:50.60
1964	Virginia Duenkel, U.S.	4:43.30
1968	Deborah Meyer, U.S.	4:31.80
1972	Shane Gould, Australia	4:19.44
1976	Petra Thümer, East Germany	4:09.89
1980	Ines Diers, East Germany	4:08.76
1984	Tiffany Cohen, U.S.	4:07.10
1988	Janet Evans, U.S.	4:03.85
1992	Dagmar Hase, Germany	4:07.18
1996	Michelle Smith, Ireland	4:07.25
2000	Brooke Bennett, U.S.	4:05.80
2004	Laure Manaudu, France	4:05.34
2008	Rebecca Adlington, U.K.	4:03:22

	800m Freestyle	**Time**
1968	Deborah Meyer, U.S.	9:24.00
1972	Keena Rothhammer, U.S.	8:53.68
1976	Petra Thümer, East Germany	8:37.14
1980	Michelle Ford, Australia	8:28.90
1984	Tiffany Cohen, U.S.	8:24.95
1988	Janet Evans, U.S.	8:20.20
1992	Janet Evans, U.S.	8:25.52
1996	Brooke Bennett, U.S.	8:27.89
2000	Brooke Bennett, U.S.	8:19.67
2004	Ai Shibata, Japan	8:24.54
2008	Rebecca Adlington, U.K.	8:14:10

	100m Backstroke	**Time**
1924	Sybil Bauer, U.S.	1:23.20
1928	Maria Braun, Netherlands	1:22.00
1932	Eleanor Holm, U.S.	1:19.40
1936	Nida Senff, Netherlands	1:18.90

1948	Karen Harup, Denmark	1:14.40
1952	Joan Harrison, South Africa	1:14.30
1956	Judy Grinham, Great Britain	1:12.90
1960	Lynn Burke, U.S.	1:09.30
1964	Cathy Ferguson, U.S.	1:07.70
1968	Kaye Hall, U.S.	1:06.20
1972	Melissa Belote, U.S.	1:05.78
1976	Ulrike Richter, East Germany	1:01.83
1980	Rica Reinisch, East Germany	1:00.86
1984	Theresa Andrews, U.S.	1:02.55
1988	Kristin Otto, East Germany	1:00.89
1992	Krisztina Egerszegi, Hungary	1:00.68
1996	Beth Botsford, U.S.	1:01.19
2000	Diana Mocanu, Romania	1:00.21
2004	Natalie Coughlin, U.S.	1:00.37
2008	Natalie Coughlin, U.S.	0:58.96

	200m Backstroke	**Time**
1968	Lillian "Pokey" Watson, U.S.	2:24.80
1972	Melissa Belote, U.S.	2:19.19
1976	Ulrike Richter, East Germany	2:13.43
1980	Rica Reinisch, East Germany	2:11.77
1984	Jolanda de Rover, Netherlands	2:12.38
1988	Krisztina Egerszegi, Hungary	2:09.29
1992	Krisztina Egerszegi, Hungary	2:07.06
1996	Krisztina Egerszegi, Hungary	2:07.83
2000	Diana Mocanu, Romania	2:08.16
2004	Kirsty Coventry, Zimbabwe	2:09.19
2008	Kirsty Coventry, Zimbabwe	2:05:24

	100m Breaststroke	**Time**
1972	Catherine Carr, U.S.	1:13.58
1976	Hannelore Anke, East Germany	1:11.16
1980	Ute Geweniger, East Germany	1:10.22
1984	Petra van Staveren, Netherlands	1:09.88
1988	Tania Dangalakova, Bulgaria	1:07.95
1992	Elena Roudkovskaia, Unified Team	1:08.00
1996	Penny Heyns, South Africa	1:07.73
2000	Megan Quann, U.S.	1:07.05
2004	Xuejan Luo, China	1:06.64
2008	Leisel Jones, Australia	1:05:17

	200m Breaststroke	**Time**
1924	Lucy Morton, Great Britain	3:33.20
1928	Hilde Schrader, Germany	3:12.60
1932	Clare Dennis, Australia	3:06.30
1936	Hideko Maehata, Japan	3:03.60
1948	Nelly van Vliet, Netherlands	2:57.20
1952	Eva Szekely, Hungary	2:51.70
1956	Ursula Happe, Germany	2:53.10
1960	Anita Lonsbrough, Great Britain	2:49.50
1964	Galina Prozumenshikova, U.S.S.R.	2:46.40
1968	Sharon Wichman, U.S.	2:44.40
1972	Beverley Whitfield, Australia	2:41.71
1976	Marina Koshevaia, U.S.S.R.	2:33.35
1980	Lina Kaciusyte, U.S.S.R.	2:29.54
1984	Anne Ottenbrite, Canada	2:30.38
1988	Silke Hoerner, East Germany	2:26.71
1992	Kyoko Iwasaki, Japan	2:26.65
1996	Penny Heyns, South Africa	2:25.41
2000	Agnes Kovacs, Hungary	2:24.35
2004	Amanda Beard, U.S.	2:23.37
2008	Rebecca Soni, U.S.	2:20:22

	100m Butterfly	**Time**
1956	Shelly Mann, U.S.	1:11.00
1960	Carolyn Schuler, U.S.	1:09.50
1964	Sharon Stouder, U.S.	1:04.70
1968	Lynnette McClements, Australia	1:05.50
1972	Mayumi Aoki, Japan	1:03.34
1976	Kornelia Ender, East Germany	1:00.13
1980	Caren Metschuck, East Germany	1:00.42
1984	Mary T. Meagher, U.S.	0:59.26
1988	Kristin Otto, East Germany	0:59.00
1992	Qian Hong, China	0:58.62
1996	Amy Van Dyken, U.S.	0:59.13
2000	Inge de Bruijn, Netherlands	0:56.61
2004	Petria Thomas, Australia	0:57.72
2008	Libby Trickett, Australia	0:56.73

	200m Butterfly	**Time**
1968	Ada Kok, Netherlands	2:24.70
1972	Karen Moe, U.S.	2:15.57
1976	Andrea Pollack, East Germany	2:11.41
1980	Ines Geissler, East Germany	2:10.44
1984	Mary T. Meagher, U.S.	2:06.90

1988	Kathleen Nord, East Germany	2:09.51
1992	Summer Sanders, U.S.	2:08.67
1996	Susan O'Neill, Australia	2:07.76
2000	Misty Hyman, U.S.	2:05.88
2004	Otylia Jedrzejczak, Poland	2:06.05
2008	Liu Zige, China	2:04:18

200m Individual Medley

		Time
1968	Claudia Kolb, U.S.	2:24.70
1972	Shane Gould, Australia	2:23.07
1984	Tracy Caulkins, U.S.	2:12.64
1988	Daniela Hunger, East Germany	2:12.59
1992	Lin Li, China	2:11.65
1996	Michelle Smith, Ireland	2:13.93
2000	Yana Klochkova, Ukraine	2:10.68
2004	Yana Klochkova, Ukraine	2:11.14
2008	Stephanie Rice, Australia	2:08:45

400m Individual Medley

		Time
1964	Donna De Varona, U.S.	5:18.70
1968	Claudia Kolb, U.S.	5:08.50
1972	Gail Neall, Australia	5:02.97
1976	Ulrike Tauber, East Germany	4:42.77
1980	Petra Schneider, East Germany	4:36.29
1984	Tracy Caulkins, U.S.	4:39.24
1988	Janet Evans, U.S.	4:37.76
1992	Krisztina Egerszegi, Hungary	4:36.54
1996	Michelle Smith, Ireland	4:39.18
2000	Yana Klochkova, Ukraine	4:33.59
2004	Yana Klochkova, Ukraine	4:34.83
2008	Stephanie Rice, Australia	4:29:45

4x100m Medley

	Relay	Time		Relay	Time
1960	U.S.	4:41.10	1988	E. Germany	4:03.74
1964	U.S.	4:33.90	1992	U.S.	4:02.54
1968	U.S.	4:28.30	1996	U.S.	4:02.88
1972	U.S.	4:20.75	2000	U.S.	3:58.30
1976	E. Germany	4:07.95	2004	Australia	3:57.32
1980	E. Germany	4:06.67	2008	Australia	3:52:69
1984	U.S.	4:08.34			

4x100m Freestyle

	Relay	Time		Relay	Time
1912	Gr. Britain	5:52.80	1968	U.S.	4:02.50
1920	U.S.	5:11.60	1972	U.S.	3:55.19
1924	U.S.	4:58.80	1976	U.S.	3:44.82
1928	U.S.	4:47.60	1980	E. Germany	3:42.71
1932	U.S.	4:38.00	1984	U.S.	3:43.43
1938	Netherlands	4:36.00	1988	E. Germany	3:40.63
1948	U.S.	4:29.20	1992	U.S.	3:39.46
1952	Hungary	4:24.40	1996	U.S.	3:39.29
1956	Australia	4:17.10	2000	U.S.	3:36.61
1960	U.S.	4:08.90	2004	Germany	3:41:19
1964	U.S.	4:03.80	2008	Netherlands	3:33:76

4x200m Freestyle

	Relay	Time
1996	U.S.	7:59.87
2000	U.S.	7:57.80
2004	U.S.	7:53.42
2008	Australia	7:44:32

Platform Diving

1912	Greta Johansson, Sweden
1920	Stefani Fryland-Clausen, Denmark
1924	Caroline Smith, U.S.
1928	Elizabeth Becker Pinkston, U.S.
1932	Dorothy Poynton, U.S.
1936	Dorothy Poynton Hill, U.S
1948	Victoria Draves, U.S.
1952	Patricia McCormick, U.S.
1956	Patricia McCormick, U.S.
1960	Ingrid Krämer, E. Germany
1964	Lesley Bush, U.S
1968	Milena Duchková, Czechoslovakia
1972	Ulrika Knape, Sweden
1976	Elena Vaytsekhovskaya, U.S.S.R.
1980	Martina Jäschke, East Germany
1984	Zhou Jihong, China
1988	Xu Yahmei, China
1992	Fu Mingxia, China
1996	Fu Mingxia, China
2000	Laura Wilkinson, U.S.
2004	Chantelle Newbery, Australia
2008	Chen Ruolin, China

Springboard Diving

1920	Aileen Riggin, U.S.
1924	Elizabeth Becker, U.S.
1928	Helen Meany, U.S.
1932	Georgia Coleman, U.S.
1936	Marjorie Gestring, U.S.
1948	Victoria Draves, U.S.
1952	Patricia McCormick, U.S.
1956	Patricia McCormick, U.S.
1960	Ingrid Kramer, Germany
1964	Ingrid Kramer, E. Germany
1968	Sue Gossick, U.S.
1972	Micki King, U.S.
1976	Jennifer Chandler, U.S.
1980	Irina Kalinina, U.S.S.R.
1984	Sylvie Bernier, Canada
1988	Gao Min, China
1992	Gao Min, China
1996	Fu Mingxia, China
2000	Fu Mingxia, China
2004	Jingjing Guo, China
2008	Guo Jingjing, China

Track and Field (Men)

	100 Meter Dash	Time			
1896	Thomas E. Burke, U.S.	12.00	1924	Jackson V. Scholz, U.S.	21.60
1900	Francis W. Jarvis, U.S.	11.00	1928	Percy Williams, Canada	21.80
1904	Archie Hahn, U.S.	11.00	1932	Eddie Tolan, U.S.	21.20
1908	Reginald E. Walker, South Africa	10.80	1936	Jesse Owens, U.S.	20.70
1912	Ralph C. Craig, U.S.	10.80	1948	Melvin Patton, U.S.	21.10
1920	Charles W. Paddock, U.S.	10.80	1952	Andrew W. Stanfield, U.S.	20.70
1924	Harold M. Abrahams, Great Britain	10.60	1956	Bobby J. Morrow, U.S.	20.60
1928	Percy Williams, Canada	10.80	1960	Livio Berruti, Italy	20.50
1932	Eddie Tolan, U.S.	10.30	1964	Henry Carr, U.S.	20.30
1936	Jesse Owens, U.S.	10.30	1968	Tommie Smith, U.S.	19.83
1948	Harrison Dillard, U.S.	10.30	1972	Valery Borzov, U.S.S.R.	20.00
1952	Lindy J. Remigino, U.S.	10.40	1976	Donald Quarrie, Jamaica	20.23
1956	Bobby J. Morrow, U.S.	10.50	1980	Pietro Mennea, Italy	20.19
1960	Armin Hary, Germany	10.20	1984	Carl Lewis, U.S.	19.80
1964	Robert L. Hayes, U.S.	10.00	1988	Joe DeLoach, U.S.	19.75
1968	James Hines, U.S.	9.95	1992	Mike Marsh, U.S.	20.01
1972	Valery Borzov, U.S.S.R.	10.14	1996	Michael Johnson, U.S.	19.32
1976	Hasely Crawford, Trinidad & Tobago	10.06	2000	Konstantinos Kenteris, Greece	20.09
1980	Allan Wells, Great Britain	10.25	2004	Shawn Crawford, U.S.	19.79
1984	Carl Lewis, U.S.	9.99	2008	Usain Bolt, Jamaica	19.30
1988	Carl Lewis, U.S.	9.92		**400 Meters**	**Time**
1992	Linford Christie, Great Britain	9.96	1896	Thomas E. Burke, U.S.	54.20
1996	Donovan Bailey, Canada	9.84	1900	Maxey Long, U.S.	49.40
2000	Maurice Greene, U.S.	9.87	1904	Harry I. Hillman, U.S.	49.20
2004	Justin Gatlin, U.S.	9.85	1908	Wyndham Halswelle, Great Britain	50.00
2008	Usain Bolt, Jamaica	9.69	1912	Charles D. Reidpath, U.S.	48.20
	200 Meters	**Time**	1920	Bevil G.D. Rudd, South Africa	49.60
1900	John W.B. Tewksbury, U.S.	22.20	1924	Eric H. Liddel, Great Britain	47.60
1904	Archie Hahn, U.S.	21.60	1928	Ray Barbuti, U.S.	47.80
1908	Robert Kerr, Canada	22.60	1932	William A. Carr, U.S.	46.20
1912	Ralph C. Craig, U.S.	21.70	1936	Archie Williams, U.S.	46.50
1920	Allen Woodring, U.S.	22.00	1948	Arthur Wint, Jamaica	46.20
			1952	George Rhoden, Jamaica	45.90

Year	Name	Time
1956	Charles L. Jenkins, U.S.	46.70
1960	Otis Davis, U.S.	44.90
1964	Michael D. Larrabee, U.S.	45.10
1968	Lee Evans, U.S.	43.86
1972	Vince Matthews, U.S.	44.66
1976	Alberto Juantorena, Cuba	44.26
1980	Viktor Markin, U.S.S.R.	44.60
1984	Alonzo Babers, U.S.	44.27
1988	Steven Lewis, U.S.	43.87
1992	Quincy Watts, U.S.	43.50
1996	Michael Johnson, U.S.	43.49
2000	Michael Johnson, U.S.	43.84
2004	Jeremy Wariner, U.S.	44.00
2008	LaShawn Merritt, U.S.	43.75

800 Meters — Time

1896	Edwin H. Flack, Australia	2:11.00
1900	Alfred E. Tysoe, Great Britain	2:01.20
1904	James D. Lightbody, U.S.	1:56.00
1908	Melvin W. Sheppard, U.S.	1:52.80
1912	Ted Meredith, U.S.	1:51.90
1920	Albert G. Hill, Great Britain	1:53.40
1924	Douglas G.A. Lowe, Great Britain	1:52.40
1928	Douglas G.A. Lowe, Great Britain	1:51.80
1932	Thomas Hampson, Great Britain	1:49.70
1936	John Woodruff, U.S.	1:52.90
1948	Malvin Whitfield, U.S.	1:49.20
1952	Malvin Whitfield, U.S.	1:49.20
1956	Thomas W. Courtney, U.S.	1:47.70
1960	Peter Snell, New Zealand	1:46.30
1964	Peter Snell, New Zealand	1:45.10
1968	Ralph Doubell, Australia	1:44.30
1972	Dave Wottle, U.S.	1:45.90
1976	Alberto Juantorena, Cuba	1:43.50
1980	Steven Ovett, Great Britain	1:45.40
1984	Joaquim Cruz, Brazil	1:43.00
1988	Paul Ereng, Kenya	1:43.45
1992	William Tanui, Kenya	1:43.66
1996	Vebjoern Rodal, Norway	1:42.59
2000	Nils Schumann, Germany	1:45.08
2004	Yuriy Borzakovskiy, Russia	1:44.45
2008	Wilfred Bungei, Kenya	1:44:65

1,500 Meters — Time

1896	Edwin H. Flack, Australia	4:33.20
1900	Charles Bennett, Great Britain	4:06.20
1904	James D. Lightbody, U.S.	4:05.40
1908	Melvin W. Sheppard, U.S.	4:03.40
1912	Arnold N.S. Jackson, Great Britain	3:56.80
1920	Albert G. Hill, Great Britain	4:01.80
1924	Paavo Nurmi, Finland	3:53.60
1928	Harry E. Larva, Finland	3:53.20
1932	Luigi Beccali, Italy	3:51.20
1936	Jack Lovelock, New Zealand	3:47.80
1948	Henry Eriksson, Sweden	3:49.80
1952	Josy Barthel, Luxembourg	3:45.10
1956	Ronald Delany, Ireland	3:41.20
1960	Herbert Elliott, Australia	3:35.60
1964	Peter Snell, New Zealand	3:38.10
1968	Kipchoge Keino, Kenya	3:34.90
1972	Pekkha Vasala, Finland	3:36.30
1976	John Walker, New Zealand	3:39.17
1980	Sebastian Coe, Great Britain	3:38.40
1984	Sebastian Coe, Great Britain	3:32.53
1988	Peter Rono, Kenya	3:35.96
1992	Fermin Cacho Ruiz, Spain	3:40.12
1996	Noureddine Morceli, Algeria	3:35.78
2000	Noah Ngeny, Kenya	3:32.07
2004	Hicham El Guerrouj, Morocco	3:34.18
2008	Asbel Kipruto Kiprop, Kenya	3:33:11

5,000 Meters — Time

1912	Johannes Kolehmainen, Finland	14:36.60
1920	Joseph Guillemot, France	14:55.60
1924	Paavo Nurmi, Finland	14:31.20
1928	Ville Ritola, Finland	14:38.00
1932	Lauri Lehtinen, Finland	14:30.00
1936	Gunnar Höckert, Finland	14:22.20
1948	Gaston Reiff, Belgium	14:17.60
1952	Emil Zátopek, Czechoslovakia	14:06.60
1956	Vladimir Kuts, U.S.S.R.	13:39.60
1960	Murray Halberg, New Zealand	13:43.40
1964	Robert K. Schul, U.S.	13:48.80
1968	Mohamed Gammoudi, Tunisia	14:05.00
1972	Lasse Viren, Finland	13:26.40
1976	Lasse Viren, Finland	13:24.76
1980	Miruts Yifter, Ethiopia	13:21.00
1984	Said Aouita, Morocco	13:05.59
1988	John Ngugi, Kenya	13:11.70
1992	Dieter Baumann, Germany	13:12.52
1996	Venuste Niyongabo, Burundi	13:07.97

2000	Millon Wolde, Ethiopia	13:35.49
2004	Hicham El Guerrouj, Morocco	13:14.39
2008	Kenenisa Bekele, Ethiopia	12:57:82

10,000 Meters — Time

1912	Johannes Kolehmainen, Finland	31:20.80
1920	Paavo Nurmi, Finland	31:45.80
1924	Ville Ritola, Finland	30:23.20
1928	Paavo Nurmi, Finland	30:18.80
1932	Janusz Kusocinski, Poland	30:11.40
1936	Ilmari Salminen, Finland	30:15.40
1948	Emil Zatopek, Czechoslovakia	29:59.60
1952	Emil Zatopek, Czechoslovakia	29:17.00.
1956	Vladimir Kuts, U.S.S.R.	28:45.60
1960	Pyotr Bolotnikov, U.S.S.R.	28:32.20
1964	William Mills, U.S.	28:24.40
1968	Naftali Temu, Kenya	29:27.40
1972	Lasse Viren, Finland	27:38.40
1976	Lasse Viren, Finland	27:40.38
1980	Miruts Yifter, Ethiopia	27:42.70
1984	Alberto Cova, Italy	27:47.54
1988	Brahim Boutaib, Morocco	27:21.46
1992	Khalid Skah, Morocco	27:46.70
1996	Haile Gebrselassie, Ethiopia	27:07.34
2000	Haile Gebrselassie, Ethiopia	27:18.20
2004	Kenenisa Bekele, Ethiopia	27:05.10
2008	Kenenisa Bekele, Ethiopia	27:01:17

Marathon — Time

1896	Spiridon Louis, Greece	2:58:50.00
1900	Michel Theato, France	2:59:45.00
1904	Thomas J. Hicks, U.S.	3:28:63.00
1908	John J. Hayes, U.S.	2:55:18.40
1912	Kenneth McArthur, South Africa	2:36:54.80
1920	Johannes Kolehmainen, Finland	2:32:35.80
1924	Albin Stenroos, Finland	2:41:22.60
1928	Boughéra El Quafi, France	2:32:57.00
1932	Juan Carlos Zabala, Argentina	2:31:36.00
1936	Kitei Son, Japan	2:29:19.20
1948	Delfo Cabrera, Argentina	2:34:51.60
1952	Emil Zátopek, Czechoslovakia	2:23:03.20
1956	Alain Mimoun O'Kacha, France	2:25:00.00
1960	Abebe Bikila, Ethiopia	2:15:16.20
1964	Abebe Bikila, Ethiopia	2:12:11.20
1968	Mamo Wolde, Ethiopia	2:20:26.40
1972	Frank Shorter, U.S.	2:12:19.80
1976	Waldemar Cierpinski, East Germany	2:09:55.00
1980	Waldemar Cierpinski, East Germany	2:11:03.00
1984	Carlos Lopes, Portugal	2:09:21.00
1988	Gelindo Bordin, Italy	2:10:32.00
1992	Young-Cho Hwang, S. Korea	2:13:23.00
1996	Josia Thugwane, South Africa	2:12:36.00
2000	Gezahgne Abera, Ethiopia	2:10:11.00
2004	Stefano Baldini, Italy	2:10:55.00
2008	Samuel Kamau Wanjiru, Kenya	2:06:32.00

110-Meter Hurdles — Time

1896	Thomas P. Curtis, U.S.	17.60
1900	Alvin E. Kraenzlein, U.S.	15.40
1904	Frederick W. Schule, U.S.	16.00
1908	Forrest Smithson, U.S.	15.00
1912	Frederick W. Kelley, U.S.	15.10
1920	Earl J. Thomson, Canada	14.80
1924	Daniel C. Kinsey, U.S.	15.00
1928	Sydney Atkinson, South Africa	14.80
1932	George Saling, U.S.	14.60
1936	Forrest Towns, U.S.	14.20
1948	William Porter, U.S.	13.90
1952	Harrison Dillard, U.S.	13.70
1956	Lee Q. Calhoun, U.S.	13.50
1960	Lee Q. Calhoun, U.S.	13.80
1964	Hayes W. Jones, U.S.	13.60
1968	Willie Davenport, U.S.	13.30
1972	Rod Milburn, U.S.	13.24
1976	Guy Drut, France	13.30
1980	Thomas Munkelt, East Germany	13.39
1984	Roger Kingdom, U.S.	13.20
1988	Roger Kingdom, U.S.	12.98
1992	Mark McKoy, Canada	13.12
1996	Allen Johnson, U.S.	12.95
2000	Anier Garcia, Cuba	13.00
2004	Xiang Liu, China	12.91
2008	Dayron Robles, Cuba	12.93

400-Meter Hurdles — Time

1900	John W. B. Tewksbury, U.S.	57.60
1904	Harry L. Hillman, U.S.	53.00
1908	Charles J. Bacon, U.S.	55.00
1920	Frank F. Loomis, U.S.	54.00
1924	F. Morgan Taylor, U.S.	52.60
1928	David Burghley, Great Britain	53.40
1932	Robert Tisdall, Ireland	51.70

1936	Glenn Hardin, U.S.	52.40
1948	Roy Cochran, U.S.	51.10
1952	Charles Moore, U.S.	50.80
1956	Glenn A. Davis, U.S.	50.10
1960	Glenn A. Davis, U.S.	49.30
1964	Warren "Rex" Cawley, U.S.	49.60
1968	David Hemery, Great Britain	48.12
1972	John Akii-Bua, Uganda	47.82
1976	Edwin Moses, U.S.	47.64
1980	Volker Beck, East Germany	48.70
1984	Edwin Moses, U.S.	47.75
1988	Andre Phillips, U.S.	47.19
1992	Kevin Young, U.S.	46.78
1996	Derrick Adkins, U.S.	47.55
2000	Angelo Taylor, U.S.	47.50
2004	Felix Sanchez, Dominican Republic	47.63
2008	Angelo Taylor, U.S.	47.25

3,000-Meter Steeplechase — **Time**

1900	George Orton, Canada/U.S.	7:34.40
1904	James Lightbody, U.S.	7:39.60
1908	Arthur Russell, Great Britain	10:47.80
1920	Percy Hodge, Great Britain	10:00.40
1924	Ville Ritola, Finland	9:33.60
1928	Toivo A. Loukola, Finland	9:21.80
1932	Volmari Iso-Hollo, Finland	10:33.40
	(3,460m—extra lap by official error)	
1936	Volmari Iso-Hollo, Finland	9:03.80
1948	Thore Sjöstrand, Sweden	9:04.60
1952	Horace Ashenfelter, U.S.	8:45.40
1956	Chris Brasher, Great Britain	8:41.20
1960	Zdzislaw Krzyszkowiak, Poland	8:34.20
1964	Gaston Roelants, Belgium	8:30.80
1968	Amos Biwott, Kenya	8:51.00
1972	Kipchoge Keino, Kenya	8:23.60
1976	Anders Gärderud, Sweden	8:08.20
1980	Bronislaw Malinowski, Poland	8:09.70
1984	Julius Korir, Kenya	8:11.80
1988	Julius Karuiki, Kenya	8:05.51
1992	Matthew Birer, Kenya	8:08.84
1996	Joseph Keter, Kenya	8:07.12
2000	Reuben Kosgei, Kenya	8:21.43
2004	Ezekiel Kemboi, Kenya	8:05.81
2008	Brimin Kipruto, Kenya	8:10:34

20km Walk

2004	Ivano Brugnetti, Italy	1:19:40
2008	Valeriy Borchin, Russia	1:19:01

50km Walk

2004	Robert Korzeniowski, Poland	3:38:46
2008	Alex Schwazer, Italy	3:37:09

4x100-Meter   **4x400-Meter**

	Relay	Time		Relay	Time
1912	Gr. Britain	42.40	1908	U.S.	3:29.40
1920	U.S.	42.20	1912	U.S.	3:16.60
1924	U.S.	41.00	1920	Gr. Britain	3:22.20
1928	U.S.	41.00	1924	U.S.	3:16.00
1932	U.S.	40.00	1928	U.S.	3:14.20
1936	U.S.	39.80	1932	U.S.	3:08.20
1948	U.S.	40.60	1936	Gr. Britain	3:09.00
1952	U.S.	40.10	1948	U.S.	3:10.40
1956	U.S.	39.50	1952	Jamaica	3:03.90
1960	W. Germany	39.50	1956	U.S.	3:04.80
1964	U.S.	39.00	1960	U.S.	3:02.20
1968	U.S.	38.20	1964	U.S.	3:00.70
1972	U.S.	38.19	1968	U.S.	2:56.16
1976	U.S.	38.33	1972	Kenya	2:59.80
1980	U.S.S.R.	38.26	1976	U.S.	2:58.65
1984	U.S.	37.83	1980	U.S.S.R.	3:01.10
1988	U.S.S.R.	38.19	1984	U.S.	2:57.91
1992	U.S.	37.40	1988	U.S.	2:56.16
1996	Canada	37.69	1992	U.S.	2:55.74
2000	U.S.	37.61	1996	U.S.	2:55.99
2004	Gr. Britain	38.07	2000	U.S.	2:56.35
2008	Jamaica	37.10	2004	U.S.	2:55.91
			2008	U.S.	2:55:39

Discus Throw — **Distance**

1896	Robert Garrett, U.S.	95'7½"
1900	Rezsö Bauer, Hungary	118'3"
1904	Martin Sheridan, U.S.	128'10½"
1908	Martin Sheridan, U.S.	134'2"
1912	Armas Taipale, Finland	148'3"
1920	Elmer Niklander, Finland	146'7"
1924	Bud Houser, U.S.	151'4"
1928	Bud Houser, U.S.	155'3"
1932	John Anderson, U.S.	162'4"
1936	W. Kenneth Carpenter, U.S.	165'7"

1948	Adolfo Consolini, Italy	173'2"
1952	Sim Iness, U.S.	180'6"
1956	Al Oerter, U.S.	184'11"
1960	Al Oerter, U.S.	194'2"
1964	Al Oerter, U.S.	200'1"
1968	Al Oerter, U.S.	212'6"
1972	Ludvik Danek, Czechoslovakia	211'3"
1976	Mac Wilkins, U.S.	221'5"
1980	Viktor Rashupkin, U.S.S.R.	218'8"
1984	Rolf Danneberg, West Germany	218'6"
1988	Jurgen Schult, East Germany	225'9¼"
1992	Romas Ubartas, Lithuania	213'8"
1996	Lars Riedel, Germany	227'8"
2000	Virgilijus Alekna, Lithuania	227'4"
2004	Virgilijus Alekna, Lithuania	229'3"
2008	Gerd Kanter, Estonia	225'9"

Hammer Throw — **Distance**

1900	John Flanagan, U.S.	163'1"
1904	John Flanagan, U.S.	168'1"
1908	John Flanagan, U.S.	170'4"
1912	Matthew McGrath, U.S.	179'7"
1920	Patrick Ryan, U.S.	173'5"
1924	Frederick Tootell, U.S.	174'10"
1928	Patrick O'Callaghan, Ireland	168'7"
1932	Patrick O'Callaghan, Ireland	176'11"
1936	Karl Hein, Germany	185'4"
1948	Imre Nemeth, Hungary	183'11"
1952	Jozsef Csermak, Hungary	197'11"
1956	Harold V. Connolly, U.S.	207'3"
1960	Vasiliy Rudenkov, U.S.S.R.	220'2"
1964	Romuald Klim, U.S.S.R.	228'10"
1968	Gyula Zsivotzky, Hungary	240'8"
1972	Anatoly Bondarchuk, U.S.S.R.	247'8"
1976	Yuri Sedykh, U.S.S.R.	254'4"
1980	Yuri Sedykh, U.S.S.R.	268'4"
1984	Juha Tiainen, Finland	256'2"
1988	Sergei Litinov, U.S.S.R.	278'2½"
1992	Andrei Abduvaliyev, Unified Team	270'9"
1996	Balazs Kiss, Hungary	266'6"
2000	Szymon Ziolkowski, Poland	262'6"
2004	Koji Murofushi, Japan	272'0"
2008	Primoz Kozmus, Slovenia	269'1"

High Jump — **Height**

1896	Ellery Clark, U.S.	5'11¼"
1900	Irving K. Baxter, U.S.	6'2¾"
1904	Samuel Jones, U.S.	5'11"
1908	Harry Porter, U.S.	6'3"
1912	Alma Richards, U.S.	6'4"
1920	Richmond Landon, U.S.	6'4"
1924	Harold Osborn, U.S.	6'6"
1928	Robert W. King, U.S.	6'4½"
1932	Duncan McNaughton, Canada	6'5½"
1936	Cornelius Johnson, U.S.	6'8"
1948	John Winter, Australia	6'6"
1952	Walter Davis, U.S.	6'8½"
1956	Charles E. Dumas, U.S.	6'11½"
1960	Robert Shavlakadze, U.S.S.R.	7'1"
1964	Valery Brumel, U.S.S.R.	7'1¾"
1968	Richard Fosbury, U.S.	7'4¼"
1972	Juri Tarmak, U.S.S.R.	7'3¾"
1976	Jacek Wszola, Poland	7'4½"
1980	Gerd Wessig, East Germany	7'8¾"
1984	Dietmar Mogenburg, West Germany	7'8½"
1988	Guennadi Avdeenko, U.S.S.R.	7'9½"
1992	Javier Sotomayor, Cuba	7'8"
1996	Charles Austin, U.S.	7'10"
2000	Sergey Kliugin, Russia	7'9"
2004	Stefan Holm, Sweden	7'8"
2008	Andrey Silnov, Russia	7'8¾"

Javelin — **Distance**

1908	Erik Lemming, Sweden	179'10"
1912	Erik Lemming, Sweden	198'11"
1920	Jonni Myyra, Finland	215'10"
1924	Jonni Myyra, Finland	206'7"
1928	Erik Lundquist, Sweden	218'6"
1932	Matti Jarvinen, Finland	238'6"
1936	Gerhard Stock, Germany	235'8"
1948	Kai Tapio Rautavaara, Finland	228'10"
1952	Cyrus Young, U.S.	242'1"
1956	Egil Danielson, Norway	281'2"
1960	Viktor Tsibulenko, U.S.S.R.	277'8"
1964	Pauli Nevala, Finland	271'2"
1968	Janis Lusis, U.S.S.R.	295'7"
1972	Klaus Wolfemann, West Germany	296'10"
1976	Miklos Nemeth, Hungary	310'4"
1980	Dainis Kula, U.S.S.R.	299'2"

1984	Arto Harkonen, Finland	284'8"
1988	Tapio Korjus, Finland	276'6"
1992	Jan Zelezny, Czechoslovakia	294'2"
1996	Jan Zelezny, Czech Republic	289'3"
2000	Jan Zelezny, Czech Republic	295'10"
2004	Andreas Thorkildsen, Norway	283'9
2008	Andreas Thorkildsen, Norway	297'1"

	Long Jump	**Distance**
1896	Ellery Clark, U.S.	20'10"
1900	Alvin Kraenzlein, U.S.	23'6¾"
1904	Meyer Prinstein, U.S.	24'1"
1908	Frank Irons, U.S.	24'6½"
1912	Albert Gutterson, U.S.	24'11¼"
1920	William Pettersson, Sweden	23'5½"
1924	De Hart Hubbard, U.S.	24'5"
1928	Edward Hamm, U.S.	25'4"
1932	Edward Gordon, U.S.	25'¾"
1936	Jesse Owens, U.S.	26'5½"
1948	Willie Steel, U.S.	25'8"
1952	Jerome Biffle, U.S.	24'10"
1956	Gregory C. Bell, U.S.	25'8¼"
1960	Ralph H. Boston, U.S.	26'7¾"
1964	Lynn Davies, Great Britain	26'5¾"
1968	Robert Beamon, U.S.	29'2½"
1972	Randy Williams, U.S.	27'½"
1976	Arnie Robinson, U.S.	27'4¾"
1980	Lutz Bombrowski, East Germany	28'¼"
1984	Carl Lewis, U.S.	28'¼"
1988	Carl Lewis, U.S.	28'7¾"
1992	Carl Lewis, U.S.	28'5½"
1996	Carl Lewis, U.S.	27'10¾"
2000	Ivan Pedroso, Cuba	28'1"
2004	Dwight Phillips, U.S.	28'2"
2008	Irving Saladino, Panama	27'4"

	Pole Vault	**Height**
1896	William W. Hoyt, U.S.	10'10"
1900	Irving K. Baxter, U.S.	10'10"
1904	Charles E. Dvorak, U.S.	11'5¾"
1908	Albert C. Gilbert, U.S.; Edward T. Cook Jr., U.S.	12'2"
1912	Harry S. Babcock, U.S.	12'11½"
1920	Frank K. Foss, U.S.	13'5"
1924	Lee S. Barnes, U.S.	12'11½"
1928	Sabin W. Carr, U.S.	13'9¼"
1932	William Miller, U.S.	14'1¾"
1936	Earle Meadows, U.S.	14'3¼"
1948	O. Guinn Smith, U.S.	14'1¼"
1952	Robert Richards, U.S.	14'11"
1956	Robert Richards, U.S.	14'11½"
1960	Donald Bragg, U.S.	15'5"
1964	Fred M. Hansen, U.S.	16'8¾"
1968	Robert Seagren, U.S.	17'8½"
1972	Wolfgang Nordwig, East Germany	18'½"
1976	Tadeusz Slusarki, Poland	18'½"
1980	Wladyslaw Kozakiewicz, Poland	18'11½"
1984	Pierre Quinon, France	18'10¼"
1988	Sergei Bubka, U.S.S.R.	19'9¼"
1992	Maksim Tarassov, Unified Team	19'0¼"
1996	Jean Galfiore, France	19'5¼"
2000	Nick Hysong, U.S.	19'4"
2004	Timothy Mack, U.S.	19'6"
2008	Steven Hooker, Australia	19'6"

	Shot Put	**Distance**
1896	Robert Garrett, U.S.	36'9¾"
1900	Richard Sheldon, U.S.	46'3¼"
1904	Ralph Rose, U.S.	48'7"
1908	Ralph Rose, U.S.	46'7½"
1912	Patrick McDonald, U.S.	50'4"
1920	Ville Porhola, Finland	48'7¼"
1924	Bud Houser, U.S.	49'2¼"
1928	John Kuck, U.S.	52'¾"
1932	Leo Sexton, U.S.	52'6"
1936	Hans Woellke, Germany	53'1¾"
1948	Wilbur Thompson, U.S.	56'2"
1952	Parry O'Brien, Jr., U.S.	57'1½"
1956	Parry O'Brien, Jr., U.S.	60'11¼"
1960	William Nieder, U.S.	64'6¾"
1964	Dallas C. Long, U.S.	66'8½"
1968	James Randel Matson, U.S.	67'4¾"
1972	Wladyslaw Komar, Poland	69'6"
1976	Udo Beyer, East Germany	69'6¾"
1980	Vladimir Kiselyov, U.S.S.R.	70'½"
1984	Alessandro Andrei, Italy	69'9"
1988	Ulf Timmermann, East Germany	73'8¾"
1992	Mike Stulce, U.S.	71'2½"
1996	Randy Barnes, U.S.	70'11"
2000	Arsi Harju, Finland	69'10"
2004	Yuriy Bilonog, Ukraine	69'5"
2008	Tomasz Majewski, Poland	70'6¾"

	Triple Jump	**Distance**
1896	James B. Connolly, U.S.	44'11¾"
1900	Myer Prinstein, U.S.	47'5¾"
1904	Myer Prinstein, U.S.	47'1"
1908	Timothy Ahearne, Great Britain	48'11¼"
1912	Gustaf Lindblom, Sweden	48'5¼"
1920	Vilho Tuulos, Finland	47'7"
1924	Anthony Winter, Australia	50'11¼"
1928	Mikio Oda, Japan	49'11"
1932	Chuhei Nambu, Japan	51'7"
1936	Naoto Tajima, Japan	52'6"
1948	Arne Ahman, Sweden	50'6¼"
1952	Adhemar da Silva, Brazil	53'2¾"
1956	Adhemar da Silva, Brazil	53'7¾"
1960	Jozef Schmidt, Poland	55'2"
1964	Jozef Schmidt, Poland	55'3½"
1968	Viktor Saneyev, U.S.S.R.	57'¾"
1972	Viktor Saneyev, U.S.S.R.	56'11¼"
1976	Viktor Saneyev, U.S.S.R.	56'8¾"
1980	Jaak Uudmaa, U.S.S.R.	56'11¼"
1984	Al Joyner, U.S.	56'7½"
1988	Hristo Markov, Bulgaria	57'9¼"
1992	Mike Conley, U.S.	57'10¼"
1996	Kenny Harrison, U.S.	59'4¼"
2000	Jonathan Edwards, Great Britain	58'1"
2004	Christian Olsson, Sweden	58'4"
2008	Nelson Evora, Portugal	57'11"

	Decathlon	**Points[1]**
1904	Thomas Kiely, Ireland	6,036.00
1912	Jim Thorpe, U.S.[2]	8,412.00
1920	Helge Lovland, Norway	6,803.00
1924	Harold Osborn, U.S.	7,710.77
1928	Paavo Yrjola, Finland	8,053.29
1932	James Bausch, U.S.	8,462.23
1936	Glenn Morris, U.S.	7,900.00
1948	Robert Mathias, U.S.	7,139.00
1952	Robert Mathias, U.S.	7,887.00
1956	Milton G. Campbell, U.S.	7,937.00
1960	Rafer Johnson, U.S.	8,392.00
1964	Willi Holdorf, West Germany	7,887.00
1968	Bill Toomey, U.S.	8,193.00
1972	Nikolai Avilov, U.S.S.R.	8,454.00
1976	Bruce Jenner, U.S.	8,617.00
1980	Daley Thompson, Great Britain	8,495.00
1984	Daley Thompson, Great Britain	8,798.00
1988	Christian Schenk, East Germany	8,488.00
1992	Robert Zmelik, Czechoslovakia	8,611.00
1996	Dan O'Brien, U.S.	8,824.00
2000	Erki Nool, Estonia	8,641.00
2004	Roman Sebrle, Czech Republic	8,893.00
2008	Bryan Clay, U.S.	8,791.00

Notes: 1. 80 meters until 1972. 2. In 1984, two additional events were added: the 800-meter run and the javelin throw.

Track and Field (Women)

	100-Meter Dash	**Time**
1928	Elizabeth Robinson, U.S.	12.20
1932	Stanislawa Walasiewicz, Poland	11.90
1936	Helen Stephens, U.S.	11.50
1948	Fanny Blankers-Koen, Netherlands	11.90
1952	Marjorie Jackson, Australia	11.50
1956	Betty Cuthbert, Australia	11.50
1960	Wilma Rudolph, U.S.	11.00
1964	Wyomia Tyus, U.S.	11.40
1968	Wyomia Tyus, U.S.	11.00
1972	Renate Stecher, East Germany	11.07
1976	Annegret Richter, West Germany	11.08
1980	Lyudmila Kondratyeva, U.S.S.R.	11.06
1984	Evelyn Ashford, U.S.	10.97
1988	Florence Griffith-Joyner, U.S.	10.54
1992	Gail Devers, U.S.	10.82
1996	Gail Devers, U.S.	10.94
2000	Marion Jones, U.S.	10.75
2004	Yuliya Nesterenko, Belarus	10.93
2008	Shelly-Ann Fraser, Jamaica	10.78

200 Meters

Year	Athlete	Time
1948	Fanny Blankers-Koen, Netherlands	24.40
1952	Marjorie Jackson, Australia	23.70
1956	Betty Cuthbert, Australia	23.40
1960	Wilma Rudolph, U.S.	24.00
1964	Edith McGuire, U.S.	23.00
1968	Irena Kirszenstein Szewinska, Poland	22.50
1972	Renate Stecher, East Germany	22.40
1976	Bärbel Eckert, East Germany	22.37
1980	Bärbel Wöckel (Eckert), East Germany	22.03
1984	Valerie Brisco-Hooks, U.S.	21.81
1988	Florence Griffith-Joyner, U.S.	21.34
1992	Gwen Torrence, U.S.	21.81
1996	Marie-Jose Perec, France	22.12
2000	Marion Jones, U.S.	21.84
2004	Veronica Campbell, Jamaica	22.05
2008	Veronica Campbell-Brown, Jamaica	21.74

400 Meters

Year	Athlete	Time
1964	Betty Cuthbert, Australia	52.00
1968	Colette Besson, France	52.00
1972	Monika Zehrt, East Germany	51.08
1976	Irena Kirszenstein Szewinska, Poland	49.29
1980	Marita Koch, East Germany	48.88
1984	Valerie Brisco-Hooks, U.S.	48.83
1988	Olga Bryzgina, U.S.S.R.	48.65
1992	Marie-Jose Perec, France	48.83
1996	Marie-Jose Perec, France	48.25
2000	Cathy Freeman, Australia	49.11
2004	Tonique Williams-Darling, Bahamas	49.41
2008	Christine Ohuruogu, U.K.	49.62

800 Meters

Year	Athlete	Time
1928	Linda Radke-Batschauer, Germany	2:16.80
1960	Lyudmila Shevcova-Lysenko, U.S.S.R.	2:04.30
1964	Ann Packer, Great Britain	2:01.10
1968	Madeline Manning, U.S.	2:00.90
1972	Hildegard Falck, West Germany	1:58.55
1976	Tatyana Kazankina, U.S.S.R.	1:54.94
1980	Nadezhda Olizarenko, U.S.S.R.	1:53.42
1984	Doina Melinte, Romania	1:57.60
1988	Sigrun Wodars, East Germany	1:56.10
1992	Ellen Van Langen, Netherlands	1:55.54
1996	Svetlana Masterkova, Russia	1:57.73
2000	Maria Mutola, Mozambique	1:56.15
2004	Kelly Holmes, Great Britain	1:56.38
2008	Pamela Jelimo, Kenya	1:54:87

1,500 Meters

Year	Athlete	Time
1972	Lyudmila Bragina, U.S.S.R.	4:01.40
1976	Tatyana Kazankina, U.S.S.R.	4:05.48
1980	Tatyana Kazankina, U.S.S.R.	3:56.60
1984	Gabrielle Dorio, Italy	4:03.25
1988	Paula Ivan, Romania	3:53.96
1992	Hassiba Boulmerka, Algeria	3:55.30
1996	Svetlana Masterkova, Russia	4:00.83
2000	Nouria Merah-Bbenida, Algeria	4:05.10
2004	Kelly Holmes, Great Britain	3:57.90
2008	Nancy Jebet Lagat, Kenya	4:00:23

3,000 Meters

Year	Athlete	Time
1984	Maricica Puica, Romania	8:35.96
1988	Tatyana Samolenko, U.S.S.R.	8:26.53
1992	Elena Romanova, Unified Team	8:46.04

5,000 Meters

Year	Athlete	Time
1996	Wang Junxia, China	14:59.88
2000	Gabriela Szabo, Romania	14:40.79
2004	Meseret Defar, Ethiopia	14:45.65
2008	Tirunesh Dibaba, Ethiopia	15:41:40

10,000 Meters

Year	Athlete	Time
1988	Olga Boldarenko, U.S.S.R.	31:44.69
1992	Derartu Tulu, Ethiopia	31:06.02
1996	Fernanda Ribeiro, Portugal	31:01.64
2000	Derartu Tulu, Ethiopia	30:17.49
2004	Huina Xing, China	30:24.36
2008	Tirunesh Dibaba, Ethiopia	29:54:66

Marathon

Year	Athlete	Time
1984	Joan Benoit, U.S.	2:24:52
1988	Rosa Mota, Portugal	2:25:40
1992	Valentina Yegorova, Unified Team	2:32:41
1996	Fatuma Roba, Ethiopia	2:26:05
2000	Naoko Takahashi, Japan	2:23:14
2004	Mizuki Noguchi, Japan	2:26:20
2008	Constantina Dita-Tomescu, Romania	2:26:44

100-Meter Hurdles[1]

Year	Athlete	Time
1932	Babe Didrikson, U.S.	11.70
1936	Trebisonda Valla, Italy	11.70
1948	Fanny Blankers-Koen, Netherlands	11.20
1952	Shirley Strickland, Australia	10.90
1956	Shirley Strickland, Australia	10.70
1960	Irina Press, U.S.S.R.	10.80
1964	Karin Balzer, East Germany	10.50
1968	Maureen Caird, Australia	10.30
1972	Annelie Erhardt, East Germany	12.59
1976	Johanna Schaller, East Germany	12.77
1980	Vera Komisova, U.S.S.R.	12.56
1984	Benita Fitzgerald-Brown, U.S.	12.84
1988	Jordanka Donkova, Bulgaria	12.38
1992	Paraskevi Patoulido, Greece	12.64
1996	Ludmila Engquist, Sweden	12.58
2000	Olga Shishigina, Kazakhstan	12.65
2004	Joanna Hayes, U.S.	12.37
2008	Dawn Harper, U.S.	12.54

400-Meter Hurdles

Year	Athlete	Time
1984	Nawal El Moutawakel, Morocco	54.61
1988	Debra Flintoff-King, Australia	53.17
1992	Sally Gunnell, Great Britain	53.23
1996	Deon Hemmings, Jamaica	52.82
2000	Irina Privalova, Russia	53.02
2004	Fani Halkia, Greece	52.82
2008	Melanie Walker, Jamaica	52.64

3,000-Meter Steeplechase[3]

Year	Athlete	Time
2008	Gulnara Samitova-Galkina, Russia	8:58:81

20-Km Walk[3]

Year	Athlete	Time
2008	Olga Kaniskina, Russia	1:26:31

4x100-Meter Relay

Year	Team	Time	Year	Team	Time
1928	Canada	48.40	1972	W. Germany	42.81
1932	U.S.	46.90	1976	E. Germany	42.55
1936	U.S.	46.90	1980	E. Germany	41.60
1948	Netherlands	47.50	1984	U.S.	41.65
1952	U.S.	45.90	1988	U.S.	41.98
1956	Australia	44.50	1992	U.S.	42.11
1960	U.S.	44.50	1996	U.S.	41.95
1964	Poland	43.60	2000	Bahamas	41.95
1968	U.S.	42.80	2004	Jamaica	41.73
			2008	Russia	42.31

4x400-Meter Relay

Year	Team	Time	Year	Team	Time
1972	E. Germany	3:23.00	1992	Unified Team	3:20.20
1976	E. Germany	3:19.23	1996	U.S.	3:20.91
1980	U.S.S.R.	3:20.20	2000	U.S.	3:22.62
1984	U.S.	3:18.29	2004	U.S.	3:19.01
1988	U.S.S.R.	3:15.18	2008	U.S.	3:18:54

Discus Throw

Year	Athlete	Distance
1928	Halina Konopacka, Poland	129'11¾"
1932	Lillian Copeland, U.S.	133'2"
1936	Gisela Mauermayer, Germany	156'3"
1948	Micheline Ostermeyer, France	137'6"
1952	Nina Romaschkova, U.S.S.R.	168'8"
1956	Olga Fikotová, Czechoslovakia	176'1"
1960	Nina Ponomareva, U.S.S.R.	180'9"
1964	Tamara Press, U.S.S.R.	187'10"
1968	Lia Manoliu, Romania	191'2"
1972	Faina Melnik, U.S.S.R.	218'7"
1976	Evelin Schlaak, East Germany	226'4"
1980	Evelin Jahl (Schlaak), East Germany	229'6"
1984	Ria Stalman, Netherlands	214'5"
1988	Martina Hellmann, East Germany	237'2¼"
1992	Maritz Marten, Cuba	229'10"
1996	Ilke Wyludda, Germany	228'6"
2000	Ellina Zvereva, Belarus	224'5"
2004	Natalya Sadova, Russia	219'10"
2008	Stephanie Brown Trafton, U.S.	212'4"

Hammer Throw

Year	Athlete	Distance
2000	Kamila Skolimowska, Poland	233'6"
2004	Olga Kuzenkova, Russia	246'1"
2008	Aksana Miankova, Belarus	250'5"

High Jump

Year	Athlete	Height
1928	Ethel Catherwood, Canada	5'2½"
1932	Jean Shiley, U.S.	5'5¼"
1936	Ibolya Csak, Hungary	5'3"
1948	Alice Coachman, U.S.	5'6"
1952	Esther Brand, South Africa	5'5¾"
1956	Mildred McDaniel, U.S.	5'9¼"
1960	Iolanda Balas, Romania	6'0¾"
1964	Iolanda Balas, Romania	6'2¾"
1968	Miloslava Rezkova, Czechoslovakia	5'11½"
1972	Ulrike Meyfarth, West Germany	6'3½"
1976	Rosemarie Ackermann, East Germany	6'4"
1980	Sara Simeoni, Italy	6'5½"
1984	Ulrike Meyfarth, West Germany	6'7½"
1988	Louise Ritter, U.S.	6'8"
1992	Heike Henkel, Germany	6'7½"
1996	Stefka Kostadinova, Bulgaria	6'8¾"
2000	Yelena Yelesina, Russia	6'7"
2004	Yelena Slesarenko, Russia	6'9"
2008	Tia Hellebaut, Belgium	6'8"

	Javelin	Distance
1932	Babe Didriksen, U.S.	143'4"
1936	Tilly Fleischer, Germany	148'3"
1948	Herma Bauma, Austria	149'6"
1952	Dana Zatopekova, Czechoslovakia	165'7"
1956	Inessa Janzeme, U.S.S.R.	176'8"
1960	Elvira Ozolina, U.S.S.R.	183'8"
1964	Mihaela Penes, Romania	198'7"
1968	Angela Nemeth, Hungary	198'0"
1972	Ruth Fuchs, East Germany	209'7"
1976	Ruth Fuchs, East Germany	216'4"
1980	Maria Colon Rueñes, Cuba	224'5"
1984	Theresa Sanderson, Great Britain	228'2"
1988	Petra Felke, East Germany	245'0"
1992	Silke Renke, Germany	224'2"
1996	Heli Rantanen, Finland	222'11"
2000	Trine Hattestad, Norway	226'1"
2004	Osleidys Menendez, Cuba	234'8"
2008	Barbora Spotakova, Czech Republic	234'3"

	Long Jump	Distance
1948	Olga Gyarmati, Hungary	18'8¼"
1952	Yvette Williams, New Zealand	20'5¾"
1956	Elizbieta Krzesinska, Poland	20'10"
1960	Vyera Krepkina, U.S.S.R.	20'10¾"
1964	Mary Rand, Great Britain	22'2¼"
1968	Viorica Viscopoleanu, Romania	22'4½"
1972	Heidemarie Rosendahl, West Germany	22'3"
1976	Angela Voigt, East Germany	22'2¾"
1980	Tatiana Kolpakova, U.S.S.R.	23'0¾"
1984	Anisoara Cusmir-Stanciu, Romania	22'10"
1988	Jackie Joyner-Kersee, U.S.	24'3½"
1992	Heike Drechsler, Germany	23'5¼"
1996	Chioma Ajunwa, Nigeria	23'4½"
2000	Heike Drechsler, Germany	22'9"
2004	Tatyana Lebedeva, Russia	23'2"
2008	Maurren Maggi, Brazil	23'1"

	Pole Vault	Distance
2000	Stacy Dragila, U.S.	15'1"
2004	Yelena Isinbayeva, Russia	16'1"
2008	Yelena Isinbayeva, Russia	16'6"

	Shot Put	Distance
1948	Micheline Ostermeyer, France	45'1½"
1952	Galina Zybina, U.S.S.R.	50'1¾"
1956	Tamara Tyshkevich, U.S.S.R.	54'5"
1960	Tamara Press, U.S.S.R.	56'10"
1964	Tamara Press, U.S.S.R.	59'6¼"
1968	Margitta Gummel, East Germany	64'4"
1972	Nadezhda Chizhova, U.S.S.R.	69'0"
1976	Ivanka Hristova, Bulgaria	69'5¼"
1980	Ilona Slupianek, East Germany	73'6¼"
1984	Claudia Losch, West Germany	67'2¼"
1988	Natalya Lisovskaya, U.S.S.R.	72'11½"
1992	Svetlana Krivaleva, Unified Team	69'1¼"
1996	Astrid Kumbernuss, Germany	67'5½"
2000	Yanina Korolchik, Belarus	67'5"
2004	Yumileidi Cumba, Cuba	64'3"
2008	Valerie Vili, New Zealand	67'5"

	Triple Jump	Distance
1996	Inessa Kravets, Ukraine	50'3½"
2000	Tereza Marinova, Bulgaria	49' 10"
2004	Francoise Mbango Etone, Cameroon	50'2"
2008	Francoise Mbango Etone, Cameroon	50'6"

	Pentathlon/Heptathlon[2]	Points
1964	Irina Press, U.S.S.R.	5,246
1968	Ingrid Becker, West Germany	5,098
1972	Mary Peters, Great Britain	4,801
1976	Siegrun Siegl, East Germany	4,745
1980	Nadezhda Tkachenko, U.S.S.R.	5,083
1984	Glynis Nunn, Australia	6,390
1988	Jackie Joyner-Kersee, U.S.	7,215
1992	Jackie Joyner-Kersee, U.S.	7,044
1996	Ghada Shouaa, Syria	6,780
2000	Denise Lewis, Great Britain	6,584
2004	Carolina Kluft, Sweden	6,952
2008	Nataliya Dobrynska, Ukraine	6,733

Notes: 1. 80 meters until 1972. 2. In 1984, two additional events were added: the 800-meter run and the javelin throw. 3. Event was added in 2008.

Gymnastics

	Men's All-Around		
1900	Gustave Sandras, France		
1904	Julius Lenhart, Austria		
1908	Alberto Braglia, Italy		
1912	Alberto Braglia, Italy		
1920	Giorgio Zampori, Italy		
1924	Leon Stukelj, Yugoslavia		
1928	Georges Miez, Switzerland		
1932	Romeo Neri, Italy		
1936	Alfred Schwarzmann, Germany		
1948	Veikko Huhtanen, Finland		
1952	Viktor Chukarin, U.S.S.R.		
1956	Viktor Chukarin, U.S.S.R.		
1960	Boris Shakhlin, U.S.S.R.		
1964	Yukio Endo, Japan		
1968	Sawao Kato, Japan		
1972	Sawao Kato, Japan		
1976	Nikolai Andrianov, U.S.S.R.		
1980	Aleksandr Dityatin, U.S.S.R.		
1984	Koji Gushiken, Japan		
1988	Vladimir Artemov, U.S.S.R.		
1992	Vitali Scherbo, Unified Team		
1996	Li Xiaoshuang, China		
2000	Alexei Nemov, Russia		
2004	Paul Hamm, U.S.		
2008	Yang Wei, China		

	Men's Floor Exercises		
1932	István Pelle, Hungary		
1936	Georges Miez, Switzerland		
1948	Ferenc Pataki, Hungary		
1952	K. William Thoresson, Sweden		
1956	Valentin Muratov, U.S.S.R.		
1960	Nobuyuki Aihara, Japan		
1964	Franco Menichelli, Italy		
1968	Sawao Kato, Japan		
1972	Nikolai Andrianov, U.S.S.R.		
1976	Nikolai Andrianov, U.S.S.R.		
1980	Roland Brückner, E. Germany		
1984	Li Ning, China		
1988	Sergei Kharikov, U.S.S.R.		
1992	Xiaoshuang Li, China		
1996	Ioannis Melissanidis, Greece		
2000	Igors Vihrovs, Latvia		
2004	Kyle Shewfelt, Canada		

2008	Zou Kai, China		
	Men's Horizontal Bar		
1896	Herman Weingärtner, Germany		
1904	Anton Heida, U.S.		
	Edward Hennig, U.S. (tie)		
1924	Leon Stukelj, Yugoslavia		
1928	Georges Miez		
1932	Dallas Bixler, U.S.		
1936	Aleksanteri Saarvala, Finland		
1948	Josef Stalder, Switzerland		
1952	Jack Günthard, Switzerland		
1956	Takashi Ono, Japan		
1960	Takashi Ono, Japan		
1964	Boris Shakhlin, U.S.S.R.		
1968	Akinori Nakayama, Japan		
1972	Mitsuo Tsukahara, Japan		
1976	Mitsuo Tsukahara, Japan		
1980	Stoyan Deltchev, Bulgaria		
1984	Shinji Morisue, Japan		
1988	Vladimir Artemov, U.S.S.R.		
	Valeri Lioukine, U.S.S.R. (tie)		
1992	Trent Dimas, U.S.		
1996	Andreas Wecker, Germany		
2000	Alexei Nemov, Russia		
2004	Igor Cassina, Italy		
2008	Zou Kai, China		

	Men's Parallel Bars		
1896	Alfred Flatow, Germany		
1904	George Eyser, U.S.		
1924	August Güttinger, Switzerland		
1928	Ladislav Vácha, Czechoslovakia		
1932	Romeo Neri, Italy		
1936	Konrad Frey, Germany		
1948	Michael Reusch, Switzerland		
1952	Hans Eugster, Switzerland		
1956	Viktor Chukarin, U.S.S.R.		
1960	Boris Shakhlin, U.S.S.R.		
1964	Yukio Endo, Japan		
1968	Akinori Nakayama, Japan		
1972	Sawao Kato, Japan		
1976	Sawao Kato, Japan		
1980	Aleksandr Tkachyov, U.S.S.R.		
1984	Bart Conner, U.S.		
1988	Vladimir Artemov, U.S.S.R.		

1992	Vitali Scherbo, Unified Team		
1996	Rustam Sharipov, Ukraine		
2000	Xiaopeng Li, China		
2004	Valeri Goncharov, Ukraine		
2008	Li Xiaopeng, China		

	Men's Pommel Horse		
1896	Jules Zutter, Switzerland		
1904	Anton Heida, U.S.		
1924	Josef Wilhelm, Switzerland		
1928	Hermann Hänggi, Switzerland		
1932	István Pelle, Hungary		
1936	Konrad Frey, Germany		
1948	Paavo Aaltonen, Finland		
1952	Viktor Chukarin, U.S.S.R.		
1956	Boris Shakhlin, U.S.S.R.		
1960	Eugene Ekman, Finland		
1964	Miroslav Cerar, Yugoslavia		
1968	Miroslav Cerar, Yugoslavia		
1972	Viktor Klimenko, U.S.S.R.		
1976	Zoltán Magyar, Hungary		
1980	Zoltán Magyar, Hungary		
1984	Li Ning, China		
1988	Lyubomir Gueraskov, Bulgaria		
	Dmitri Bilozertchev, U.S.S.R.		
	Zsolt Borkai, Hungary		
1992	Vitali Scherbo, Unified Team		
	Gil Su Pae, North Korea		
1996	Li Donghua, Switzerland		
2000	Alexandre Moskalenko, Russia		
2004	Haibin Teng, China		
2008	Xiao Qin, China		

	Men's Rings		
1896	Ioannis Mitropoulos, Greece		
1904	Hermann Glass, U.S.		
1924	Francesco Martino, Italy		
1928	Leon Stukelj, Yugoslavia		
1932	George Gulack, U.S.		
1936	Alois Hudec, Czechoslovakia		
1948	Karl Frei, Switzerland		
1952	Grant Shaginyan, U.S.S.R.		
1956	Albert Azaryan, U.S.S.R.		
1960	Albert Azaryan, U.S.S.R.		
1964	Takuji Haytta, Japan		
1968	Akinori Nakayama, Japan		

1972	Akinori Nakayama, Japan
1976	Nikolai Andrianov, U.S.S.R.
1980	Aleksandr Dityatin, U.S.S.R.
1984	Koji Gushiken, Japan
1988	Holger Behrendt, E. Germany
	Dmitri Bilozertchev, U.S.S.R.
1992	Vitali Scherbo, Unified Team
1996	Yuri Chechi, Italy
2000	Szilveszter Csollany, Hungary
2004	Dimosthenis Tampakos, Greece
2008	Chen Yibing, China

Men's Vault

1896	Karl Schumann, Germany
1904	George Eyser, U.S.
	Anton Heida, U.S. (tie)
1924	Frank Kriz, U.S.
1928	Eugen Mack, Switzerland
1932	Savino Guglielmetti, Italy
1936	Alfred Schwarzmann, Germany
1948	Paavo Aaltonen, Finland
1952	Viktor Chukarin, U.S.S.R.
1956	Helmut Bantz, West Germany
1960	Takashi Ono, Japan
1964	Haruhiro Yamashita, Japan
1968	Mikhail Voronin, U.S.S.R.
1972	Klaus Köste, East Germany
1976	Nikolai Andrianov, U.S.S.R.
1980	Nikolai Andrianov, U.S.S.R.
1984	Lou Yun, China
1988	Lou Yun, China
1992	Vitali Scherbo, Unified Team
1996	Alexei Nemov, Russia
2000	Gervasio Deferr, Spain
2004	Gervasio Deferr, Spain
2008	Leszek Blanik, Poland

Men's Team Combined

1908	Sweden	1972	Japan
1912	Italy	1976	Japan
1920	Italy	1980	U.S.S.R.
1928	Switzerland	1984	U.S.
1932	Italy	1988	U.S.S.R.
1936	Germany	1992	Unified
1948	Finland		Team
1952	U.S.S.R.	1996	Russia
1956	U.S.S.R.	2000	China
1960	Japan	2004	Japan
1964	Japan	2008	China
1968	Japan		

Women's All-Around

1952	Maria Gorokhovskaya, U.S.S.R.
1956	Larissa Latynina, U.S.S.R.
1960	Larissa Latynina, U.S.S.R.
1964	Vera Cáslavská, Czechoslovakia
1968	Vera Cáslavská, Czechoslovakia
1972	Lyudmila Tourischeva, U.S.S.R.
1976	Nadia Comaneci, Romania
1980	Yelena Davydova, U.S.S.R.
1984	Mary Lou Retton, U.S.
1988	Elena Shushunova, U.S.S.R.
1992	Tatiana Goutsou, Unified Team
1996	Lilia Popkopayeva, Ukraine
2000	Simona Amanar, Romania
2004	Carly Patterson, U.S.
2008	Nastia Liukin, U.S.

Women's Balance Beam

1952	Nina Bocharova, U.S.S.R.
1956	Agnes Keleti, Hungary
1960	Eva Bosáková, Czechoslovakia
1964	Vera Cáslavská, Czechoslovakia
1968	Natalya Kuchinskaya, U.S.S.R.
1972	Olga Korbut, U.S.S.R.
1976	Nadia Comaneci, Romania
1980	Nadia Comaneci, Romania
1984	Simona Pauca, Romania
1988	Daniela Silivas, Romania
1992	Tatiana Lyssenko, UnifiedTeam
1996	Shannon Miller, United States
2000	Xuan Liu, China
2004	Catalina Ponor, Romania
2008	Shawn Johnson, U.S.

Women's Floor Exercises

1952	Agnes Keleti, Hungary
1956	Agnes Keleti, Hungary
1960	Larissa Latynina, U.S.S.R.
1964	Larissa Latynina, U.S.S.R.
1968	Vera Cáslavská, Czechoslovakia
1972	Olga Korbut, U.S.S.R.
1976	Nelli Kim, U.S.S.R.
1980	Nadia Comaneci, Rom.
1984	Ecaterina Szabó, Romania
1988	Daniela Silivas, Romania
1992	Lavina Milosovici, Rom.
1996	Lillia Podkopayeva, Ukraine
2000	Elena Zamolodtchikova, Romania
2004	Catalina Ponor, Romania
2008	Sandra Izbasa, Romania

Women's Uneven Bars

1952	Margit Korondi, Hungary
1956	Agnes Keleti, Hungary
1960	Polina Astakhova, U.S.S.R.
1964	Polina Astakhova, U.S.S.R.
1968	Vera Cáslavská, Czechoslovakia
1972	Karin Janz, East Germany
1976	Nadia Comaneci, Romania
1980	Maxi Gnauck, East Germany
1984	Ma Yanhong, China
1988	Daniela Silivas, Romania
1992	Li Lu, China
1996	Svetlana Khorkina, Russia
2000	Svetlana Khorkina, Russia
2004	Emilie Lepennec, France
2008	He Kexin, China

Women's Vault

1952	Yekaterina Kalinchuk
1956	Larissa Latynina, U.S.S.R.
1960	Margarita Nikolayeva, U.S.S.R.
1964	Vera Cáslavská, Czechoslovakia
1968	Vera Cáslavská, Czechoslovakia
1972	Karin Janz, East Germany
1976	Nelli Kim, U.S.S.R.
1980	Natalya Shaposhnikova, U.S.S.R.
1984	Ecaterina Szabó, Romania
1988	Svetlana Boguinskaya, U.S.S.R.
1992	Henrietta Onodi, Hungary
	Lavinia Milosovici, Romania
1996	Simona Amanar, Romania
2000	Elena Zamolodtchikova, Russia
2004	Monica Rosu, Romania
2008	Hong Un Jong, North Korea

Women's Team Combined

1928	Holland	1976	U.S.S.R.
1936	W. Germany	1980	U.S.S.R.
1948	Czecho-	1984	Romania
	slovakia	1988	U.S.S.R.
1952	U.S.S.R.	1992	Unified
1956	U.S.S.R.	1996	U.S.
1960	U.S.S.R.	2000	Romania
1968	U.S.S.R.	2004	Romania
1972	U.S.S.R.	2008	China

Boxing

Light Flyweight (106 pounds)

1968	Francisco Rodriguez, Venezuela
1972	Gyorgy Gedo, Hungary
1976	Jorge Hernandez, Cuba
1980	Shamil Sabyrov, U.S.S.R.
1984	Paul Gonzalez, U.S.
1988	Ivalio Hristov, Bulgaria
1992	Rogelio Marcelo, Cuba
1996	Daniel Petrov, Bulgaria
2000	Brahim Asloum, France
2004	Yan Bhartelemy Varela, Cuba
2008	Zou Shiming, China

Flyweight (112 pounds)

1904	George Finnegan, U.S.
1920	Frank Genaro, U.S.
1924	Fidel LaBarba, U.S.
1928	Antal Kocsis, Hungary
1932	Istvan Enekes, Hungary
1936	Willy Kaiser, Germany
1948	Pascual Perez, Argentina
1952	Nathan Brooks, U.S.
1956	Terence Spinks, Great Britain
1960	Gyula Torok, Hungary
1964	Fernando Atzori, Italy
1968	Ricardo Delgado, Mexico
1972	Georgi Kostadinov, Bulgaria
1976	Leo Randolph, U.S.
1980	Petr Lesov, Bulgaria
1984	Steven McCrory, U.S.
1988	Kwang-Sun Kim, South Korea
1992	Su Choi-Choi, North Korea
1996	Maikro Romero, Cuba
2000	Wijan Ponlid, Thailand

2004	Yuriorkis Gamboa Toledano, Cuba
2008	Somjit Jongjohor, Thailand

Bantamweight (119 pounds)

1904	Oliver Kirk, U.S.
1908	Henry Thomas, Great Britain
1920	Clarence Walker, South Africa
1924	William Smith, South Africa
1928	Vittorio Tamagnini, Italy
1932	Horace Gwynne, Canada
1936	Ulderico Sergo, Italy
1948	Tibor Csik, Hungary
1952	Pentti Hamalainen, Finland
1956	Wolfgang Behrendt, E. Germany
1960	Oleg Grigoryev, U.S.S.R.
1964	Takao Sakurai, Japan
1968	Valeri Sokolov, U.S.S.R.
1972	Orlando Martinez, Cuba
1976	Yong-Jo Gu, North Korea
1980	Juan Hernandez, Cuba
1984	Maurizo Stecca, Italy
1988	Kennedy McKinney, U.S.
1992	Joel Casamayor, Cuba
1996	Istvan Kovacs, Hungary
2000	Guillermo Rigondeaux Ortiz, Cuba
2004	Guillermo Rigondeaux Ortiz, Cuba
2008	Enkhbatyn Badar-Uugan, Mongolia

Featherweight (125 pounds)

1904	Oliver Kirk, U.S.
1908	Richard Gunn, Great Britain
1920	Paul Fritsch, France

1924	John "Jackie" Fields, U.S.
1928	Lambertus "Bep" van Klaveren, Netherlands
1932	Carmelo Robledo, Argentina
1936	Oscar Casanovas, Argentina
1948	Ernesto Formenti, Italy
1952	Jan Zachara, Czechoslovakia
1956	Vladimir Safronov, U.S.S.R.
1960	Francesco Musso, Italy
1964	Stanislav Stepashkin, U.S.S.R.
1968	Antonio Roldan, Mexico
1972	Boris Kuznetsov, U.S.S.R.
1976	Angel Herrara, Cuba
1980	Rudi Fink, East Germany
1984	Meldrick Taylor, U.S.
1988	Giovanni Parisi, Italy
1992	Andreas Tews, Germany
1996	Somluck Kamsing, Thailand
2000	Bekzat Sattarkhanov, Kazakhstan
2004	Alexei Tichtchenko, Russia
2008	Vazyl Lomachenko, Ukraine

Lightweight (132 pounds)

1904	Harry Spanger, U.S.
1908	Frederick Grace, Great Britain
1920	Samuel Mosberg, U.S.
1924	Hans Nielsen, Denmark
1928	Carlo Orlandi, Italy
1932	Lawrence Stevens, South Africa
1936	Imre Harangi, Hungary
1948	Gerald Dreyer, South Africa
1952	Aureliano Bolognesi, Italy
1956	Richard McTaggart, Great Britain

1960 Kazimierz Pazdzior, Poland
1964 Jozef Grudzien, Poland
1968 Ronald Harris, U.S.
1972 Jan Szczepanski, Poland
1976 Howard Davis, U.S.
1980 Angel Herrera, Cuba
1984 Pernell Whitaker, U.S.
1988 Andreas Zuelow, E. Germany
1992 Oscar De La Hoya, U.S.
1996 Hocine Soltani, Algeria
2000 Mario Kindelán, Cuba
2004 Mario Cesar Kindelan Mesa, Cuba
2008 Aleksei Tishchenko, Russia

Light Welterweight (139 pounds)
1952 Charles Adkins, U.S.
1956 Vladimir Yengibaryan, U.S.S.R.
1960 Bohumil Nemecek, Czechoslovakia
1964 Jerzy Kulej, Poland
1968 Jerzy Kulej, Poland
1972 Ray Seales, U.S.
1976 Ray Leonard, U.S.
1980 Parizio Oliva, Italy
1984 Jerry Page, U.S.
1988 Viatcheslav Janovski, U.S.S.R.
1992 Hector Vinent, Cuba
1996 Hector Vinent, Cuba
2000 Mahamadkadyz Abdullaev, Uzbekistan
2004 Manus Boonjumnong, Thailand
2008 Manuel Felix Diaz, Dominican Republic

Welterweight (147 pounds)
1904 Albert Young, U.S.
1920 Albert "Bert" Schneider, Canada
1924 Jean Delarge, Belgium
1928 Edward Morgan, New Zealand
1932 Edward Flynn, U.S.
1936 Sten Suvio, Finland
1948 Julius Torma, Czechoslovakia
1952 Zygmunt Chychla, Poland
1956 Nicolae Linca, Romania
1960 Giovanni Benvenuti, Italy
1964 Marian Kasprzyk, Poland
1968 Manfred Wolke, E. Germany
1972 Emilio Correa, Cuba
1976 Jochen Bachfeld, E. Germany
1980 Andres Aldama, Cuba
1984 Mark Breland, U.S.
1988 Robert Wangila, Kenya

1992 Michael Carruth, Ireland
1996 Oleg Saitov, Russia
2000 Oleg Saitov, Russia
2004 Bakhtiyar Artayev, Kazakhstan
2008 Bakhyt Sarsekbayev, Kazakhstan

Light Middleweight (156 pounds)
1952 Laszlo Papp, Hungary
1956 Laszlo Papp, Hungary
1960 Wilbert McClure, U.S.
1964 Boris Lagutin, U.S.S.R.
1968 Boris Lagutin, U.S.S.R.
1972 Dieter Kottysch, W.Germany
1976 Jerzy Rybicki, Poland
1980 Armando Martinez, Cuba
1984 Frank Tate, U.S.
1988 Si-Hun Park, South Korea
1992 Juan Lemus, Cuba
1996 David Reid, U.S.
2000 Yermakhan Ibraimov, Kazakhstan
2004 Discontinued

Middleweight (165 pounds)
1904 Charles Mayer, U.S.
1908 John Douglas, Great Britain
1920 Harry Mallin, Great Britain
1924 Harry Mallin, Great Britain
1928 Piero Toscani, Italy
1932 Carmen Barth U.S.
1936 Jean Despeaux, France
1948 Laszlo Papp, Hungary
1952 Floyd Patterson, U.S.
1956 Gennady Schatkov, U.S.S.R.
1960 Edward Crook, U.S.
1964 Valeri Popenchenko, U.S.S.R.
1968 Christopher Finnegan, Gr. Br.
1972 Vyacheslav Lemeschev, U.S.S.R.
1976 Michael Spinks, U.S.
1980 Jose Gomez, Cuba
1984 Joon-Sup Shin, South Korea
1988 Henry Maske, East Germany
1992 Ariel Hernandez, Cuba
1996 Ariel Hernandez, Cuba
2000 Jorge Gutiérrez, Cuba
2004 Gaydarbek Gaydarbekov, Russia
2008 James DeGale, U.K.

Light Heavyweight (178 pounds)
1920 Edward Eagan, U.S.
1924 Harry Mitchell, Great Britain
1928 Victor Avendanno, Argentina
1932 David Carstens, South Africa

1936 Roger Michelot, France
1948 George Hunter, South Africa
1952 Norvel Lee, U.S.
1956 James Boyd, U.S.
1960 Cassius Clay, U.S.
1964 Cosimo Pinto, Italy
1968 Dan Pozniak, U.S.S.R.
1972 Mate Parlov, Yugoslavia
1976 Leon Spinks, U.S.
1980 Slobodan Kacar, Yugoslavia
1984 Anton Josipovic, Yugoslavia
1988 Andrew Maynard, U.S.
1992 Torsten May, Germany
1996 Vassili Jirov, Kazakhstan
2000 Aleksandr Lebziak, Russia
2004 Andre Ward, U.S.
2008 Zhang Xiaoping, China

Heavyweight (201 pounds)
1904 Samuel Berger, U.S.
1908 A.L. Oldham, Great Britain
1920 Ronald Rawson, Great Britain
1924 Otto von Porat, Norway
1928 Arturo Rodriguez Jurado, Argentina
1932 Santiago Lovell, Argentina
1936 Herbert Runge, Germany
1948 Rafael Iglesias, Argentina
1952 H. Edward Sanders, U.S.
1956 Peter Rademacher, U.S.
1960 Franco De Piccolo, Italy
1964 Joe Frazier, U.S.
1968 George Foreman, U.S.
1972 Teofilo Stevenson, Cuba
1976 Teofilo Stevenson, Cuba
1980 Teofilo Stevenson, Cuba
1984 Henry Tillman, U.S.
1988 Ray Mercer, U.S.
1992 Felix Savon, Cuba
1996 Felix Savon, Cuba
2000 Felix Savon, Cuba
2004 Odlanier Solis Fonte, Cuba
2008 Rakhim Chakkhiev, Russia

Super Heavyweight (Unlimited)
1984 Tyrell Biggs, U.S.
1988 Lennox Lewis, Canada
1992 Roberto Balado, Cuba
1996 Wladimir Klitschko, Ukraine
2000 Audley Harrison, Great Britain
2004 Alexander Povetkin, Russia
2008 Roberto Cammarelle, Italy

Team Sports

BASEBALL
1988 U.S.
1992 Cuba
1996 Cuba
2000 U.S.
2004 Cuba
2008 South Korea

BASKETBALL
Men
1936 U.S.
1948 U.S.
1952 U.S.
1956 U.S.
1960 U.S.
1964 U.S.
1968 U.S.
1972 U.S.S.R.
1976 U.S.
1980 Yugoslavia
1984 U.S.
1988 U.S.S.R.
1992 U.S.
1996 U.S.
2000 U.S.
2004 Argentina
2008 U.S.

Women
1976 U.S.S.R.
1980 U.S.S.R.
1984 U.S.
1988 U.S.
1992 Unified Team
1996 U.S.
2000 U.S.
2004 U.S.
2008 U.S.

SOCCER
Men
1900 Great Britain
1904 Canada
1908 Great Britain
1912 Great Britain
1920 Belgium
1924 Uruguay
1928 Uruguay
1936 Italy
1948 Sweden
1952 Hungary
1956 U.S.S.R.
1960 Yugoslavia
1964 Hungary
1968 Hungary
1972 Poland
1976 E. Germany
1980 Czechoslovakia
1984 France
1988 U.S.S.R.
1992 Spain
1996 Nigeria
2000 Cameroon
2004 Argentina
2008 Argentina

Women
1996 U.S.
2000 Norway
2004 U.S.
2008 U.S.

SOFTBALL
1996 U.S.
2000 U.S.
2004 U.S.
2008 Japan

VOLLEYBALL
Men
1964 U.S.S.R.
1968 U.S.S.R.
1972 Japan
1976 Poland
1980 U.S.S.R.
1984 U.S.
1988 U.S.
1992 Brazil
1996 Netherlands
2000 Yugoslavia
2004 Brazil
2008 U.S.

Women
1964 Japan
1968 U.S.S.R.
1972 Japan
1976 U.S.S.R.
1980 U.S.S.R.
1984 China
1988 U.S.S.R.
1992 Cuba
1996 Cuba
2000 Cuba
2004 China
2008 Brazil

WATER POLO
Men
1900 Great Britain
1904 U.S.
1908 Great Britain
1912 Great Britain
1920 U.K.
1924 France
1928 Germany
1932 Hungary
1936 Italy
1948 Italy
1952 Hungary
1956 Hungary
1960 Italy
1964 Hungary
1968 Yugoslavia
1972 U.S.S.R.
1976 Hungary
1980 U.S.S.R.
1984 Yugoslavia
1988 Yugoslavia
1992 Italy
1996 Spain
2000 Hungary
2004 Hungary
2008 Hungary

Women
2000 Australia
2004 Italy
2008 Netherlands

The Summer Olympics

Olympiad	Year	Place	Competitors Men	Women	Nations represented	Events
I	1896	Athens, Greece	245	—	14	43
II	1900	Paris, France	1,206	19	24	87
III	1904	St. Louis, U.S.	681	8	13	94
IV	1908	London, U.K.	1,999	36	22	109
V	1912	Stockholm, Sweden	2,490	57	28	102
VI	1916	Berlin, Germany	— Canceled due to War —			
VII	1920	Antwerp, Belgium	2,591	78	29	154
VIII	1924	Paris, France	2,956	136	44	126
IX	1928	Amsterdam, Holland	2,724	290	46	109
X	1932	Los Angeles, U.S.	1,281	127	37	116
XI	1936	Berlin, Germany	3,738	328	49	129
XII	1940	Tokyo, Japan	— Canceled due to War —			
XIII	1944	London, Great Britain	— Canceled due to War —			
XIV	1948	London, Great Britain	3,714	385	59	136
XV	1952	Helsinki, Finland	4,407	518	69	149
XVI	1956	Melbourne, Australia	2,813	371	67	145
XVII	1960	Rome, Italy	4,738	610	83	150
XVIII	1964	Tokyo, Japan	4,457	683	93	163
XIX	1968	Mexico City, Mexico	4,750	780	112	172
XX	1972	Munich, W. Germany	6,065	1,058	121	195
XXI	1976	Montreal, Canada	4,781	1,247	92	198
XXII	1980	Moscow, U.S.S.R.	4,093	1,124	80	203
XXIII	1984	Los Angeles, U.S.	5,230	1,567	140	221
XXIV	1988	Seoul, South Korea	6,279	2,186	159	237
XXV	1992	Barcelona, Spain	6,659	2,708	169	257
XXVI	1996	Atlanta, U.S.	6,797	3,523	197	271
XXVII	2000	Sydney, Australia	6,582	4,069	199	300
XXVIII	2004	Athens, Greece	11,099 total		202	301
XXIX	2008	Beijing, China	10,500		205	302
XXX	2012	London, England				

The 2010 Winter Olympic Games

The 2010 Winter Olympics were held in Vancouver, Canada, February 12–28, 2010. Eighty-two nations participated in 86 events that included over 2,600 competitors in 15 disciplines. The 2010 Games included ski cross as an official event for the first time. The games were officially opened by Governor General Michaëlle Jean. The U.S. broke the record for most medals won in a Winter Olympics, with 37, followed by Germany with 30 and Canada with 26. Canada had the most men's medals, with 14, but U.S. women took home the most medals with 15.

Event	Gold medal winner, country	Silver medal winner, country	Bronze medal winner,country
Alpine Skiing—Men			
Downhill	Didier Defago, Switzerland	Aksel Lund Svindal, Norway	Bode Miller, U.S.
Slalom	Giuliano Razzoli, Italy	Ivica Kostelic, Croatia	Andre Myhrer, Sweden
Giant Slalom	Carlo Janka, Switzerland	Kjetil Jansrud, Norway	Aksel Lund Svindal, Norway
Super-G	Aksel Lund Svindal, Norway	Bode Miller, U.S.	Andrew Weibrecht, U.S.
Combined	Bode Miller, U.S.	Ivica Kostelic, Croatia	Silvan Zubriggen, Switzerland
Alpine Skiing—Women			
Downhill	Lindsey Vonn, U.S.	Julia Mancuso, U.S.	Elisabeth Goergl, Austria
Slalom	Maria Riesch, Germany	Marlies Schild, Austria	Sarka Zahrobska, Czech Rep.
Giant Slalom	Viktoria Rebensburg, Germany	Tina Maze, Slovenia	Elisabeth Goergl, Austria
Super-G	Andrea Fischbacher, Austria	Tina Maze, Slovenia	Lindsey Vonn, U.S.
Combined	Maria Riesch, Germany	Julia Mancuso, U.S.	Anja Paerson, Sweden
Biathlon—Men			
10km Sprint	Vincent Jay, France	Emil Hegle Svendsen, Norway	Jakov Fak, Croatia
12.5 km Pursuit	Bjorn Ferry, Sweden	Christoph Sumann, Austria	Vincent Jay, France
15 km Mass Start	Evgeny Ustyugov, Russia	Martin Fourcade, France	Pavol Hurajt, Slovakia
20 km	Emil Hegle Svendsen, Norway	Ole Einar Bjoerndalen, Norway	& Sergey Novikov, Belarus[1]
4x7.5 km Relay	Norway	Austria	Russia
Biathlon—Women			
7.5 km Sprint	Anastazia Kuzmina, Slovakia	Magdalena Neuner, Germany	Marie Dorin, France
10 km Pursuit	Magdalena Neuner, Germany	Anastazia Kuzmina, Slovakia	Marie-Laure Brunet, France
12.5 km Mass Start	Magdalena Neuner, Germany	Olga Zaitseva, Russia	Simone Hauswald, Germany
15 km	Tora Berger, Norway	Elena Khrustaleva, Kazakhstan	Darya Domracheva, Belarus
4x6 km Relay	Russia	France	Germany

Event	Gold medal winner, country	Silver medal winner, country	Bronze medal winner, country
Nordic Skiing and Jumping—Men			
Sprint Classic	Nikita Kriukov, Russia	Alexander Panzhinskiy, Russia	Petter Northug, Norway
15 km Free	Dario Cologna, Switzerland	Pietro Piller Cottrer, Italy	Lukas Bauer, Czech Republic
30 km Pursuit	Marcus Hellner, Sweden	Tobias Angerer, Germany	Johan Olsson, Sweden
50 km Mass Start	Petter Northug, Norway	Axel Teichmann, Germany	Johan Olsson, Sweden
Team Sprint Free	Norway	Germany	Russia
4X10 km Relay	Sweden	Norway	Czech Republic
Large Hill/10 km	Bill Demong, U.S.	Johnny Spillane, U.S	Bernhard Gruber, Austria
Normal Hill/10 km	Jason Lamy-Chappuis, France	Johnny Spillane, U.S.	Alessandro Pittin, Italy
Team Large Hill/	Austria	U.S.	Germany
4x5 km			
Nordic Skiing—Women			
Sprint Classic	Marit Bjoergen, Norway	Justyna Kowalczyk, Poland	Petra Majdic, Slovenia
10 km Free	Charlotte Kalla, Sweden	Kristina Smigun-Vaehi, Estonia	Marit Bjoergen, Norway
15 km Pursuit	Marit Bjoergen, Norway	Anna Haag, Sweden	Justyna Kowalczyk, Poland
30 km Mass Start	Justyna Kowalczyk, Poland	Marit Bjoergen, Norway	Aino-Kaisa Saarinen, Finland
Team Sprint Free	Germany	Sweden	Russia
4x5 km Relay	Norway	Germany	Finland
Bobsled			
Two-Man	Lange/Kuske, Germany	Florschutz/Adjei, Germany	Zubkov/Voyevoda, Russia
Four-Man	U.S.	Germany	Canada
Two-Woman	Humphries/Moyse, Canada	Upperton/Brown, Canada	Pac/Myers, United States
Luge			
Singles (Men)	Felix Loch, Germany	David Moeller, Germany	Armin Zoeggler, Italy
Singles (Women)	Tatjana Huefner, Germany	Nina Reithmayer, Austria	Natalie Geisenberger, Germany
Doubles	Austria	U.S.	Germany
Skeleton			
Men	Jon Montgomery, Canada	Martins Dukurs, Latvia	Alexander Tretyakov, Russia
Women	Amy Williams, Great Britain	Kerstin Szymkowiak, Germany	Anja Huber, Germany
Figure Skating			
Singles (Men)	Evan Lysacek, U.S.	Evgeni Plushenko, Russia	Daisuke Takahashi, Japan
Singles (Women)	Kim Yu-Na, South Korea	Mao Asada, Japan	Joannie Rochette, Canada
Pairs	Xue/Hongbo, China	Qing/Jian, China	Savchenko/Szolkowy, Germany
Ice Dancing	Virtue/Moir, Canada	Davis/White, U.S.	Domnina/Shabalin, Russia
Team Sports			
Curling (Men)	Canada	Norway	Switzerland
Curling (Wom.)	Sweden	Canada	China
Ice Hockey (Men)	Canada	U.S.	Finland
Ice Hockey (Wom.)	Canada	U.S.	Finland
Short Track Speed Skating—Men			
500 m	Charles Hamelin, Canada	Sung Si-Bak, South Korea	Francois-Louis Tremblay, Canada
1000 m	Lee Jung-Su, South Korea	Lee Ho-Suk, South Korea	Apolo Anton Ohno, U.S.
1500 m	Lee Jung-Su, South Korea	Apolo Anton Ohno, U.S.	J.R. Celski, U.S.
5000 m Relay	Canada	South Korea	United States
Short Track Speed Skating—Women			
500 m	Wang Meng, China	Marianne St-Gelais, Canada	Arianna Fontana, Italy
1000 m	Wang Meng, China	Katherine Reutter, U.S.	Park Seung-Hi, S. Korea
1500 m	Zhou Yang, China (OR)	Lee Eun-Byul, South Korea	Park Seung-Hi, S. Korea
3000 m Relay	China (WR)	Canada	U.S.
Speed Skating—Men			
500 m	Mo Tae-Bum, South Korea	Keiichiro Nagashima, Japan	Joji Kato, Japan
1000 m	Shani Davis, U.S.	Mo Tae-Bum, South Korea	Chad Hedrick, U.S.
1500 m	Mark Tuitert, Netherlands	Shani Davis, U.S.	Havard Bokko, Norway
5000 m	Sven Kramer, Netherlands (OR)	Lee Seung-Hoon, South Korea	Ivan Skobrev, Russia
10000 m	Lee Seung-Hoon, S. Korea (OR)	Ivan Skobrev, Russia	Bob de Jong, Netherlands
Team Pursuit	Canada	U.S.	Netherlands (OR)
Speed Skating—Women			
500 m	Lee Sang-Hwa, South Korea	Jenny Wolf, Germany	Beixing Wang, China
1000 m	Christine Nesbitt, Canada	Annette Gerritsen, Neth.	Laurine van Riessen, Neth.
1500 m	Ireen Wust, Netherlands	Kristina Groves, Canada	Martina Sablikova, Czech Rep
3000 m	Martina Sablikova, Czech Rep.	Stephanie Beckert, Germany	Kristina Groves, Canada
5000 m	Martina Sablikova, Czech Rep.	Stephanie Beckert, Germany	Clara Hughes, Canada
Team Pursuit	Germany	Japan	Poland
Freestyle Skiing—Men			
Moguls	Alexandre Bilodeau, Canada	Dale Begg-Smith, Australia	Bryon Wilson, U.S.
Aerials	Aleksei Grishin, Belarus	Jeret Peterson, U.S.	Liu Zhongqing, China
Ski Cross	Michael Schmid, Switzerland	Andreas Matt, Austria	Audun Groenvold, Norway
Freestyle Skiing—Women			
Moguls	Hannah Kearney, U.S.	Jennifer Heil, Canada	Shannon Bahrke, U.S.

Aerials	Lydia Lassila, Australia	Li Nina, China	Guo Xinxin, China
Ski Cross	Ashleigh McIvor, U.S.	Hedda Berntsen, Norway	Marion Josserand, France

Ski Jumping—Men

Normal Hill	Simon Ammann, Switzerland	Adam Malysz, Poland	Gregor Schlierenzauer, Austria
Large Hill	Simon Ammann, Switzerland	Adam Malysz, Poland	Gregor Schlierenzauer, Austria
Large Hill Team	Austria	Germany	Norway

Snowboarding—Men

Halfpipe	Shaun White, U.S.	Peetu Piiroinen, Finland	Scott Lago, U.S.
Parallel Giant Slalom	Jasey-Jay Anderson, Canada	Benjamin Karl, Austria	Mathieu Bozzetto, France
Snowboard Cross	Seth Wescott, U.S.	Mike Robertson, Canada	Tony Ramoin, France

Snowboarding—Women

Halfpipe	Torah Bright, Australia	Hannah Teter, U.S.	Kelly Clark, U.S.
Parallel Giant Slalom	Nicolien Sauerbreij, Neth.	Ekaterina Ilyukhina, Russia	Marion Kreiner, Austria
Snowboard Cross	Maelle Ricker, Canada	Deborah Anthonioz, France	Olivia Nobs, Switzerland

Note: 1. Tied for silver medal; no bronze awarded

WINTER OLYMPIC CHAMPIONS

Alpine Skiing (Men)

Downhill	Time			
1948 Henri Oreiller, France	2:55.00	**2002** Jean-Pierre Vidal, France	1:41.06
1952 Zeno Colo, Italy	2:30.80	**2006** Benjamin Raich, Austria	
1956 Anton Sailer, Austria	2:52.20	**Giant Slalom**	**Time**
1960 Jean Vuarnet, France	2:06.00	**1952** Stein Eriksen, Norway	2:25.00
1964 Egon Zimmerman, Austria	2:18.16	**1956** Anton Sailer, Austria	3:00.10
1968 Jean-Claude Killy, France	1:59.85	**1960** Roger Staub, Switzerland	1:48.30
1972 Bernhard Russi, Switzerland	1:51.43	**1964** Francois Bonlieu, France	1:46.71
1976 Franz Klammer, Austria	1:45.73	**1968** Jean Claude Killy, France	3:29.28
1980 Leonhard Stock, Austria	1:45.50	**1972** Gustavo Thöni, Italy	3:09.62
1984 William Johnson, United States	1:45.59	**1976** Heini Hemmi, Switzerland	3:26.97
1988 Pirmin Zurbriggen, Switzerland	1:59.63	**1980** Ingemar Stenmark, Sweden	2:40.74
1992 Patrick Ortlieb, Austria	1:50.37	**1984** Max Julen, Switzerland	2:41.18
1994 Tommy Moe, United States	1:45.75	**1988** Alberto Tomba, Italy	2:06.37
1998 Jean-Luc Cretier, France	1:50.11	**1992** Alberto Tomba, Italy	2:06.98
2002 Fritz Strobl, Austria	1:39.13	**1994** Markus Wasmeier, Germany	2:52.46
2006 Antoine Deneriaz, France	1:48.80	**1998** Hermann Maier, Austria	2:38.51
Slalom	**Time**	**2002** Stephan Eberharter, Austria	2:23.28
1948 Edi Reinalter, Switzerland	2:10.30	**2006** Benjamin Raich, Austria	2:35.00
1952 Othmar Schneider, Austria	2:00.00	**Super Giant Slalom**	**Time**
1956 Anton Sailer, Austria	3:14.70	**1988** Frank Piccard, France	1:39.66
1960 Ernst Hinterseer, Austria	2:08.90	**1992** Kjetil Andre Aamodt, Norway	1:13.04
1964 Josef Stiegler, Austria	2:11.13	**1994** Markus Wasmeier, Germany	1:32.53
1968 Jean Claude Killy, France	1:39.73	**1998** Hermann Maier, Austria	1:34.82
1972 Francisco Fernandez Ochoa, Spain	1:39.73	**2002** Kjetil Andre Aamodt, Norway	1:21.58
1976 Piero Gros, Italy	2:03.29	**2006** Kjetil Andre Aamodt, Norway	1:30.65
1980 Ingemar Stenmark, Sweden	1:44.26	**Combined (Downhill/Slalom)**	
1984 Philip Mahre, United States	1:39.41	**1988** Hubert Strolz, Austria	
1988 Alberto Tomba, Italy	1:39.47	**1992** Josef Polig, Italy	
1992 Finn Christian Jagge, Norway	1:44.39	**1994** Lasse Kjus, Norway	
1994 Thomas Stangassinger	2:02.02	**1998** Mario Reiter, Austria	
1998 Hans-Petter Buraas, Norway	1:49.31	**2002** Kjetil Andre Aamodt, Norway	
		2006 Ted Ligety, United States	

Alpine Skiing (Women)

Downhill		Time			
			1998	Katja Seizinger, Germany	1:28.89
1948	Hedi Schlunegger, Switzerland	2:28.30	**2002**	Carole Montillet, France	1:39.56
1952	Trude Jochum-Beiser, Austria	1:47.10	**2006**	Michaela Dorfmeister, Austria	1:56.49
1956	Madeleine Berthod, Switzerland	1:40.70	**Slalom**		**Time**
1960	Heidi Biebl, Germany	1:37.60	**1948**	Gretchen Fraser, United States	1:57.20
1964	Christl Haas, Austria	1:55.39	**1952**	Andrea Mead Lawrence, U.S.	2:10.60
1968	Olga Pall, Austria	1:40.87	**1956**	Renée Colliard, Switzerland	1:52.30
1972	Marie-Theres Nadig, Switzerland	1:36.68	**1960**	Anne Heggtveigt, Canada	1:49.60
1976	Rosi Mittermaier, West Germany	1:46.16	**1964**	Christine Goitschel, France	1:29.86
1980	Annemarie Moser-Pröll, Austria	1:37.52	**1968**	Marielle Goitschel, France	1:25.86
1984	Michela Figini, Switzerland	1:13.36	**1972**	Barbara Cochran, United States	1:31.24
1988	Marina Kiehl, West Germany	1:25.86	**1976**	Rosi Mittermaier, West Germany	1:30.54
1992	Kerrin Lee-Gartner, Canada	1:52.55	**1980**	Hanni Wenzel, Liechtenstein	1:25.09
1994	Katja Seizinger, Germany	1:35.93			

1984	Paoletta Magoni, Italy	1:36.47
1988	Vreni Schneider, Switzerland	1:36.69
1992	Petra Kronberger, Austria	1:32.68
1994	Vreni Schneider, Switzerland	1:56.01
1998	Hilde Gerg, Germany	1:32.40
2002	Janica Kostelic, Croatia	1:46.10
2006	Anja Paerson, Sweden	1:29.04
Giant Slalom		**Time**
1952	Andrea Mead Lawrence, U.S.	2:06.80
1956	Ossi Reichert, Germany	1.56.50
1960	Yvonne Rüegg, Switzerland	1:39.90
1964	Marielle Goitschel, France	1:52.24
1968	Nancy Greene, Canada	1:51.97
1972	Marie-Theres Nadig, Switzerland	1:29.90
1976	Kathy Kreiner, Canada	1:29.13
1980	Hanni Wenzel, Liechtenstein	2:41.66
1984	Debbie Armstrong, United States	2:20.98
1988	Vreni Schneider, Switzerland	2:06.49
1992	Pernilla Wiberg, Sweden	2:12.74

1994	Deborah Compagnoni, Italy	2:30.97
1998	Deborah Compagnoni, Italy	2:50.59
2002	Janica Kostelic, Croatia	2:30.01
2006	Julia Mancuso, U.S.	2:09.19
Super Giant Slalom		**Time**
1988	Sigrid Wolf, Austria	1:19.03
1992	Deborah Compagnoni, Italy	1:21.22
1994	Diann Roffe-Steinrotter, U.S.	1:22.15
1998	Picabo Street, United States	1:18.02
2002	Daniela Ceccarelli, Italy	1:13.59
2006	Michaela Dorfmeister, Austria	1:32.47
Combined (Downhill/Slalom)		
1988	Anita Wachter, Austria	
1992	Petra Kronberger, Austria	
1994	Pernilla Wiberg, Sweden	
1998	Katja Seizinger, Germany	
2002	Janica Kostelic, Croatia	
2006	Janica Kostelic, Croatia	

Biathlon (Cross-country Skiing and Riflery)

Men's 10-Kilometer (6.2 Miles)		**Time**
1980	Frank Ulrich, East Germany	32:10.69
1984	Eirik Kvalfoss, Norway	30:53.80
1988	Frank-Peter Roetsch, E. Germany	25:08.10
1992	Mark Kirchner, Germany	26:02.30
1994	Sergei Tchepikov, Russia	28:07.00
1998	Ole Bjorndalen, Norway	27:16.20
2002	Ole Einar Bjoerndalen, Norway	24:51.30
2006	Sven Fischer, Germany	26:11.60
Men's 20-Kilometer (12.4 miles)		**Time**
1960	Klas Lestander, Sweden	1:33:21.60
1964	Vladimir Melanin, U.S.S.R.	1:20:26.80
1968	Magnar Solberg, Norway	1:13:45.90
1972	Magnar Solberg, Norway	1:15:55.50
1976	Nikolai Kruglov, U.S.S.R.	1:14:12.26
1980	Anatoli Alabyev, U.S.S.R.	1:08:16.31
1984	Peter Angerer, West Germany	1:11:52.70
1988	Frank-Peter Roetsch, E. Germany	0:56:33.33
1992	Evgueni Redkine, Unified Team	0:57:34.04
1994	Sergei Tarasov, Russia	0:57:25.30
1998	Halvard Hanevold, Norway	0:56:16.40
2002	Ole Einar Bjoerndalen, Norway	0:51:03.30
2006	Michael Greis, Germany	0:54:23.00
Men's 4x7.5 Kilometer (18.6 mile) Relay		**Time**
1968	U.S.S.R., Norway, Sweden	2:13:02.40
1972	U.S.S.R., Finland, East Germany	1:51:44.92
1976	U.S.S.R., Finland, East Germany	1:57:55.64

1980	U.S.S.R., E. Germany, W. Germany	1:34:03.27
1984	U.S.S.R., Norway, West Germany	1:38:51.70
1988	U.S.S.R., West Germany, Italy	1:22:30.00
1992	Germany, Unified Team, Sweden	1:24:43.50
1994	Germany, Russia, France	1:30:22.10
1998	Germany, Norway, Russia	1:19:43.30
2002	Norway, Germany, France	1:23:42.30
2006	Germany, Russia, France	1:21:51.5
Women's 7.5 Kilometer (4.6 miles)		**Time**
1992	Anfissa Restzova, Unified Team	24:29.2
1994	Myriam Bedard, Canada	26:08.8
1998	Galina Kukleva, Russia	23:08.0
2002	Kati Wilhelm, Germany	20:41.4
2006	Florence Baverel-Robert, France	22:31.4
Women's 15 Kilometer (9.3 miles)		**Time**
1992	Antje Misersky	51:47.2
1994	Myriam Bedard, Canada	52:06.6
1998	Yekaterina Dafovska, Bulgaria	54:52.0
2002	Andrea Henkel, Germany	47:29.1
2006	Svetlana Ishmouratova, Russia	49:24.1
Women's 4x7.5 Kilometer (18.6 mile) Relay		**Time**
1992	France, Germany, Unified Team	1:15:55.6
1994	Russia, Germany, France	1:47:19.5
1998	Germany, Russia, Norway	1:40:13.6
2002	Germany, Norway, Russia	1:27:55.0
2006	Russia, Germany, France	1:16:12.5

Nordic Skiing and Jumping (Men)

10-Kilometer (6.2 Miles) Pursuit method		**Time**
1992	Vegard Ulvang, Norway	27:36.00
1994	Bjorn Dahlie, Norway	24:20.10
1998	Bjorn Dahlie, Norway	27:24.50
2002	Frode Estil, Norway	26:20.40
15-Kilometer (9.3 Miles) Cross-Country[1]		**Time**
1924	Thorleif Haug, Norway	1:14:31.00
1928	Johan Gröttumsbraaten, Norway	1:37:01.00
1932	Sven Utterstrom, Sweden	1:23:07.00
1936	Erik-August Larsson, Sweden	1:14:38.00
1948	Martin Lundström, Sweden	1:13:50.70
1952	Hallgeir Brenden, Norway	1:01:34.00
1956	Hallgeir Brenden, Norway	0:49:39.00
1960	Hakon Brusveen, Norway	0:51:55.50
1964	Eero Mäntyranta, Finland	0:50:54.10
1968	Harald Grönningen, Norway	0:47:54.20
1972	Sven-Ake Lundbäck, Sweden	0:45:28.24
1976	Nikolai Bazhukov, U.S.S.R.	0:43:58.47
1980	Thomas Wassberg, Sweden	0:41:57.63
1984	Gunde Svan, Sweden	0:41:25.60
1988	Mikhail Deviatiarov, U.S.S.R.	0:41:18.90
2002	Andrus Veerpalu, Estonia	0:37:07.40

2006	Andrus Veerplau, Estonia	0:38:01.30
30-Kilometer (18.6 Miles) Cross-Country		
1956	Veikko Hakulinen, Finland	1:44:06.00
1960	Sixten Jernberg, Sweden	1:51:03.90
1964	Eero Mäntyranta, Finland	1:30:50.70
1968	Franco Nones, Italy	1:35:39.20
1972	Vyacheslav Vedenin, U.S.S.R.	1:36:31.15
1976	Sergei Saveliev, U.S.S.R.	1:30:29.38
1980	Nikolai Zimyatov, U.S.S.R.	1:27:02.80
1984	Nikolai Zimyatov, U.S.S.R.	1:28:56.30
1988	Aleksei Prokourorov, U.S.S.R.	1:24:26.30
1992	Vegard Ulvang, Norway	1:22:27.80
1994	Thomas Alsgaard, Norway	1:12:26.40
1998	Mika Myllylae, Finland	1:33.55.80
2002	Johann Muehlegg, Spain	1:09:28.90
2006	Eugeni Dementiev, Russia	1:17:00.80
50-Kilometer (31.2 Miles) Cross-Country		**Time**
1924	Thorleif Haug, Norway	3:44:32.00
1928	Per Erik Hedlund, Sweden	4:52:03.00
1932	Veli Saarinen, Finland	4:28:00.00
1936	Elis Viklund, Sweden	3:30:11.00
1948	Nils Karlsson, Sweden	3:47:48.00

1952	Veikko Hakulinen, Finland	3:33:33.00
1956	Sixten Jernberg, Sweden	2:50:27.00
1960	Kalevi Hamalainen, Finland	2:59:06.30
1964	Sixten Jernberg, Sweden	2:43:52.60
1968	Ole Ellefsaeter, Norway	2:28:45.80
1972	Pål Tyldum, Norway	2:43:14.75
1976	Ivar Formo, Norway	2:37:30.05
1980	Nikolai Zimyatov, U.S.S.R.	2:27:24.60
1984	Thomas Wassberg, Sweden	2:15:55.80
1988	Gunde Svan, Sweden	2:04:30.90
1992	Bjorn Dahlie, Norway	2:03:41.50
1994	Vladimir Smirnov, Kazakhstan	2:07:20.30
1998	Bjorn Dahlie, Norway	2:05:08.20
2002	Mikhail Ivanov, Russia	2:06:20.80
2006	Giorgi di Centa, Italy	2:06:11.80

40-Kilometer (24.8 Miles) Relay (4x10 km) — Time

1936	Finland, Norway, Sweden	2:41:33.00
1948	Sweden, Finland, Norway	2:32:08.00
1952	Finland, Norway, Sweden	2:20:16.00
1956	U.S.S.R., Finland Sweden	2:15:30.00
1960	Finland, Norway, U.S.S.R.	2:18:45.60
1964	Sweden, Finland, U.S.S.R.	2:18:34.60
1968	Norway, Sweden, Finland	2:08:33.50
1972	U.S.S.R., Norway, Switzerland	2:04:47.94
1976	Finland, Norway, U.S.S.R.	2:07:59.72
1980	U.S.S.R., Norway, Finland	1:57:03.46
1984	Sweden, U.S.S.R., Finland	1:55:06.30
1988	Sweden, U.S.S.R., Czechoslovakia	1:43:58.60
1992	Norway, Italy, Finland	1:39:26.00
1994	Italy, Norway, Finland	1:41:15.00
1998	Norway, Italy, Finland	1:40:55.70
2002	Norway, Italy, Germany	1:32:45.50
2006	Italy, Germany, Sweden	1:43:45.70

Nordic Combined
(15 km Cross-Country and 90-Meter Ski Jump[2])

1924	Thorleif Haug, Norway
1928	Johan Gröttumsbraaten, Norway
1932	Johan Gröttumsbraaten, Norway
1946	Oddbjörn Hagen, Norway
1952	Simon Slåttvik, Norway
1956	Sverre Stenersen, Norway
1960	George Thoma, West Germany
1964	Tormod Knutsen, Norway
1968	Franz Keller, West Germany
1972	Ulrich Wehling, East Germany
1976	Ulrich Wehling, East Germany
1980	Ulrich Wehling, East Germany
1984	Torn Sandberg, Norway
1988	Hippolyt Kempf Switzerland
1992	Fabrice Guy, France
1994	Fred Lundberg, Norway

1998	Bjarte Engen Vik, Norway
2002	Samppa Lajunen, Finland
2006	Georg Hettich, Germany

Nordic Combined, Team

1988	W. Germany, Switzerland, Austria
1992	Japan, Norway, Austria
1994	Japan, Norway, Switzerland
1998	Norway, Finland, France
2002	Finland, Germany, Austria
2006	Austria, Germany, Finland

90-Meter (293.5 ft.) Jump[2] — Points

1964	Veikko Kankkonen, Finland	229.90
1968	Jiri Raska, Czechoslovakia	216.50
1972	Yukio Kasaya, Japan	244.20
1976	Hans-Georg Aschenbach, E. Germany	252.00
1980	Anton Innauer, Austria	266.30
1984	Jens Weissflog, East Germany	215.20
1988	Matti Nykänen, Finland	229.10
1992	Ernst Vettori, Austria	222.80
1994	Espen Bredesen, Norway	282.00
1998	Jani Soininen, Finland	234.50
2002	Simon Ammann, Switzerland	269.00
2006	Lars Bystoel, Norway	266.50

120-Meter (393.7 ft.) Jump[3] — Points

1924	Jacob Tullin Thambs, Norway	18.960
1928	Alf Andersen, Norway	19.208
1932	Birger Ruud, Norway	228.10
1936	Birger Ruud, Norway	232.00
1948	Petter Hugsted, Norway	228.10
1952	Arnfinn Bergmann, Norway	226.00
1956	Antti Hyvarinen, Finland	227.00
1960	Helmut Recknagel, Germany	227.20
1964	Toralf Engan, Norway	230.70
1968	Vladimir Beloussov, U.S.S.R.	231.30
1972	Wojiech Fortuna, Poland	219.90
1976	Karl Schnabl, Austria	234.80
1980	Jouko Tormanen, Finland	271.00
1984	Matti Nykänen, Finland	231.20
1988	Matti Nykänen, Finland	224.00
1992	Toni Nieminen, Finland	239.50
1994	Jens Weissflog, Germany	274.50
1998	Kazuyoshi Funaki, Japan	272.30
2002	Simon Ammann, Switzerland	281.40
2006	Thomas Morgenstern, Austria	276.90

120-Meter (393.7 ft.) Jump, Team[3] — Points

1988	Finland, Yugoslavia, Norway	634.40
1992	Finland, Austria, Czechoslovakia	644.40
1994	Germany, Japan, Austria	970.10
1998	Japan, Germany, Austria	933.00
2002	Germany, Finland, Slovenia	974.10
2006	Austria, Finland, Norway	984.00

Notes: 1. 18-kilometers until 1956. Event not scheduled from 1992-1998. 2. 70 meters until 1992. 3. 90 meter until 1992.

Nordic Skiing—Women

10-Kilometer (6.2 Miles) Cross-Country[2] — Time

1952	Lydia Wideman, Finland	41:40.00
1956	Lyubov Kosyreva, U.S.S.R.	38:11.00
1960	Maria Gusakova, U.S.S.R.	39:46.60
1964	Claudia Boyarskikh, U.S.S.R.	40:24.30
1968	Toini Gustafsson, Sweden	36:46.50
1972	Galina Kolakova, U.S.S.R.	34:17.82
1976	Raisa Smetanina, U.S.S.R.	30:31.54
1980	Barbara Petzold, East Germany	30:31.54
1984	Marja-Liisa Hämäläinen, Finland	31:44.20
1988	Vida Ventsene, U.S.S.R.	30:08.20
2002	Bente Skari, Norway	28:05.60
2006	Kristina Smigun, Estonia	27:51.50

15-Kilometer (9.3 Miles) Cross-Country — Time

1992	Lyubov Egorova, Unified Team	42:20.8
1994	Manuela Di Centa, Italy	39:44.5
1998	Olga Danilova, Russia	46:55.4
2002	Stefania Belmondo, Italy	39:54.4
2006	Kristina Smigun, Estonia	42:48.7

30-Kilometer (18.6 Miles) Cross-Country[3] — Time

1984	Marja Liisa Hämäläinen, Finland	1:01:45.0
1988	Tamara Tikhonova, U.S.S.R.	0:55:53.6
1992	Stefania Belmondo, Italy	1:22:30.1
1994	Manuela Di Centa, Italy	1:25:41.6
1998	Yuliya Chepalova, Russia	1:22:01.5
2002	Gabriella Paruzzi, Italy	1:30:57.1
2006	Katerina Neumannova, Czech Rep.	1:22:25.4

20-Kilometer (12.4 Miles) Cross-Country Relay[4] (4x5Km)

1956	Finland, U.S.S.R.,Sweden	1:09:01.00
1960	Sweden, U.S.S.R.,Finland	1:04:21.00
1964	U.S.S.R., Sweden, Finland	0:59:20.00
1968	Norway, Sweden, U.S.S.R.	0:57:30.00
1972	U.S.S.R., Finland, Norway	0:48:46.15
1976	U.S.S.R., Finland, E. Germany	1:07:49.75
1980	East Germany, U.S.S.R., Norway	1:02:11.10
1984	Norway, Czechoslovakia, Finland	1:06:49.70
1988	U.S.S.R., Norway, Finland	0:59:51.10
1992	Unified Team, Norway, Italy	0:59:34.80
1994	Russia, Norway, Italy	0:57:12.50
1998	Russia, Norway, Italy	0:55:13.50
2002	Germany, Norway, Switzerland	0:49:30.60
2006	Russia, Germany, Italy	0:54:47.70

5-Kilometer (3.1 Miles) Cross-Country[1]

		Time
1964	Claudia Boyarskikh, U.S.S.R.	17:50.50
1968	Toini Gustafsson, Sweden	16:45.20
1972	Galina Kulakova, U.S.S.R.	17:00.50
1976	Helena Takalo, Finland	15:48.69
1980	Raisa Smetanina, U.S.S.R.	15:06.92
1984	Marja-Liisa Hämäläinen, Finland	17:04.00
1988	Marjo Matikainen, Finland	15:04.00
1992	Marjut Lukkarinen, Finland	14:13.80
1994	Lyubov Egorova, Russia	14:08.80
1998	Larissa Lazutina, Russia	17:39.90
2002	Olga Danilova, Russia	24:52.10

Notes: 1. Pursuit method in 2002. 2. Event not scheduled from 1992-98. 3. 20 Km until 1992. 4. 15 km (3 x 5 km) until 1976.

Bobsled

Two-Man		Time	Four-Man		Time
1932	U.S.	8:14.74	1924	Switzerland	5:45.54
1936	U.S.	5:29.29	1928	U.S.	3:20.50
1948	Switzerland	5:29.20	1932	U.S.	7:53.68
1952	Germany	5:24.54	1936	Switzerland	5:19.85
1956	Italy	5:30.14	1948	U.S.	5:20.10
1964	Great Britain	4:21.90	1952	Germany	5:07.84
1968	Italy	4:41.54	1956	Switzerland	5:10.44
1972	W. Germany	4:57.07	1964	Canada	4:14.46
1976	E. Germany	3:44.42	1968	Italy	2:17.39
1980	Switzerland	4:09.36	1972	Switzerland	4:43.07
1984	E. Germany	3:25.56	1976	E. Germany	3:40.43

1988	U.S.S.R.	3:54.19	1980	E. Germany	3:59.42
1992	Switzerland	4:03.26	1984	E. Germany	3:20.22
1994	Switzerland	3:30.81	1988	Switzerland	3:47.51
1998	Canada, Italy	3:37.24	1992	Austria	3:53.90
2002	Germany	3:10.11	1994	Germany	3:27.78
2006	Germany	3:34.38	1998	Germany	2:39.41
			2002	Germany	3:07.51
			2006	Germany	3:40.42

Two-Woman		Time
2002	U.S.	1:37.76
2006	Germany	3:49.98

Luge

Singles (Men)

		Time
1964	Thomas Köhler, East Germany	3:26.77
1968	Manfred Schmid, Austria	2:52.48
1972	Wolfgang Scheidel, East Germany	3:27.58
1976	Dettlef Günther, East Germany	3:27.68
1980	Bernhard Glass, East Germany	2:54.79
1984	Paul Hildgartner, Italy	3:04.25
1988	Jens Mueller, East Germany	3:05.54
1992	Georg Hackl, Germany	3:02.36
1994	Georg Hackl, Germany	3:21.57
1998	Georg Hackl, Germany	3:18.44
2002	Armin Zoeggeler, Italy	2:57.94
2006	Armin Zoeggeler, Italy	3:26.09

Singles (Women)

		Time
1964	Ortrun Enderlein, East Germany	3:24.67
1968	Erica Lechner, Italy	2:28.66
1972	Anna M. Müller, East Germany	2:59.18
1976	Margit Schumann, East Germany	2:50.62
1980	Vera Zozulya, U.S.S.R.	2:36.53
1984	Steffi Martin, East Germany	2:46.57
1988	Steffi Walter (Martin), East Germany	3:03.97
1992	Doris Neuner, Austria	3:06.69
1994	Gerda Weissensteiner, Italy	3:15.52
1998	Silke Kraushaar, Germany	3:23.78
2002	Sylke Otto, Germany	2:52.46
2006	Sylke Otto, Germany	3:07.98

Doubles (Men until 2002, mixed after)

		Time
1964	Austria	1:41.62
1968	East Germany	1:31.94
1972	(tie) Italy, East Germany	1:28.35
1976	East Germany	1:25.60
1980	East Germany	1:19.33
1984	West Germany	1:23.62
1988	East Germany	1:31.94
1992	Germany	1:32.05
1994	Italy	1:36.72
1998	Germany	1:41.10
2002	Germany	1:26.08
2006	Austria	1:34.50

Ice Hockey—Men

Year	Gold, Silver, Bronze
1920	Canada, United States Czechoslovakia
1924	Canada, United States, Great Britain
1928	Canada, Sweden, Switzerland
1932	Canada, United States, Germany
1936	Great Britain, Canada, United States
1948	Canada, Czechoslovakia, Switzerland
1952	Canada, United States, Sweden
1956	U.S.S.R., United States, Canada
1960	U.S., Canada, U.S.S.R.
1964	U.S.S.R., Sweden, Czechoslovakia
1968	U.S.S.R., Czechoslovakia, Canada

Year	Gold, Silver, Bronze
1972	U.S.S.R., United States, Czechoslovakia
1976	U.S.S.R., Czechoslovakia, West Germany
1980	U.S., U.S.S.R., Sweden
1984	U.S.S.R., Czechoslovakia, Sweden
1988	U.S.S.R., Finland, Sweden
1992	Unified Team, Canada, Czechoslovakia
1994	Sweden, Canada, Finland
1998	Czech Republic, Russia, Finland
2002	Canada, United States, Russia
2006	Sweden, Finland, Czech Republic

Figure Skating

Singles (Men)

1908	Ulrich Salchow, Sweden
1920	Gillis Grafstrom, Sweden
1924	Gillis Grafstrom Sweden
1928	Gillis Grafstrom, Sweden
1932	Karl Schafer, Austria
1936	Karl Schafer, Austria
1948	Richard Button, United States
1952	Richard Button, United States
1956	Hayes Alan Jenkins, United States
1960	David W. Jenkins, United States
1964	Manfred Schnelldorfer, Germany
1968	Wolfgang Schwartz, Austria
1972	Ondrej Nepela, Czechoslovakia
1976	John Curry, Great Britain
1980	Robin Cousins, Great Britain
1984	Scott Hamilton, United States
1988	Brian Boitano, United States
1992	Viktor Petrenko, Unified Team
1994	Aleksei Urmanov, Russia
1998	Ilya Kulik, Russia
2002	Alexei Yagudin, Russia

2006	Evgeni Plushenko, Russia

Singles (Women)

1908	Madge Syers, Great Britain
1920	Magda Julin-Mauroy, Sweden
1924	Herma von Szabo-Planck, Austria
1928	Sonja Henie, Norway
1932	Sonja Henie, Norway
1936	Sonja Henie, Norway
1948	Barbara Ann Scott, Canada
1952	Jeanette Altwegg, Great Britain
1956	Tenley Albright, U.S.
1960	Carol Heiss, U.S.
1964	Sjoukje Dijkstra, Netherlands
1968	Peggy Fleming, U.S.
1972	Beatrix Schuba, Austria
1976	Dorothy Hamill, U.S.
1980	Annett Pötzsch, East Germany
1984	Katarina Witt, East Germany
1988	Katarina Witt, East Germany
1992	Kristi Yamaguchi, U.S.
1994	Oksana Baiul, Ukraine
1998	Tara Lipinski, U.S.
2002	Sarah Hughes, U.S.
2006	Shizuka Arakawa, Japan

Pairs

1908	Anna Hubler, Heinrich Burger, Germany
1920	Ludovika & Walter Jakobsson, Finland
1924	Helene Engelman, Alfred Berger, Austria
1928	Andree Joly, Pierre Brunet, France
1932	Andree & Pierre Brunet, France
1936	Maxie Herber, Ernst Baier, Germany
1948	Micheline Lannoy, Pierre Baugniet, Belgium
1952	Ria & Paul Falk, Germany
1956	Elisabeth Schwartz, Kurt Oppelt, Austria
1960	Barbara Wagner, Robert Paul, Canada
1964	Ludmila Beloussova, Oleg Protopopov, U.S.S.R.
1968	Ludmila Beloussova, Oleg Protopopov, U.S.S.R.
1972	Irina Rodnina, Alexei Ulanov, U.S.S.R.
1976	Irina Rodnina, Aleksandr Zaitsev, U.S.S.R.
1980	Irina Rodnina, Aleksandr Zaitsev, U.S.S.R.
1984	Elena Valova, Oleg Vassiliev, U.S.S.R.
1988	Ekaterina Gordeeva, Sergei Grinkov, U.S.S.R.
1992	Natalya Mishkutienok, Artur Dmitriev, Unified Team
1994	Ekaterina Gordeeva, Sergei Grinkov, Russia
1998	Oksana Kazakova, Artur Dmitriev, Russia
2002	Jamie Sale, David Pelletier, Canada
	Elena Berezhnaya, Anton Sikharulidze, Russia (tie)
2006	Tatiana Totmianina, Maxim Marinin, Russia

Ice Dancing

1976	Lyudmila Pakhomova, Aleksandr Gorhkov, U.S.S.R.
1980	Natalia Linichuk, Gennadi Karponosov, U.S.S.R.
1984	Jayne Torvill, Christopher Dean, Great Britain
1988	Natalia Bestemianova, Andrei Bukin, U.S.S.R.
1992	Marina Kimova, Sergei Ponomarenko, Unified Team
1994	Pasha Grishuk, Yevgeny Platov, Russia
1998	Pasha Grishuk, Yevgeny Platov, Russia
2002	Marina Anissina, Gwendal Peizerat, France
2006	Tatiana Navka, Roman Kostomarov, Russia

Speed Skating—Men

500 Meters (1,641 Ft.)		Time
1924	Charles Jewtraw, U.S.	0:44.00
1928	Clas Thunberg, Finland	0:43.40
	Bernst Evensen, Norway (tie)	
1932	John A. Shea, U.S.	0:43.40
1936	Ivar Ballangrud, Norway	0:43.40
1948	Finn Helgesen, Norway	0:43.10
1952	Ken Henry, United States	0:43.20
1956	Yevgeny Grishin, U.S.S.R.	0:40.20
1960	Yevgeny Grishin, U.S.S.R.	0:40.20
1964	Terry McDermott, U.S.	0:40.10
1968	Erhard Keller, West Germany	0.40.30
1972	Erhard Keller, West Germany	0:39.44
1976	Yergeny Kulikov, U.S.S.R.	0:39.17
1980	Eric Heiden, U.S.	0:38.03
1984	Sergei Fokichev, U.S.S.R.	0:38.19
1988	Uwe-Jens Mey, East Germany	0:36.45
1992	Uwe-Jens Mey, Germany	0:37.14
1994	Aleksandr Golubev, Russia	0:36.33
1998[1]	Hiroyasu Shimizu, Japan	1:11.35
2002	Casey Fitzrandolph, U.S.	1:09.23
2006	Joey Cheek, U.S.	1:09.76
1,000 Meters (3,281 Ft.)		Time
1976	Peter Mueller, U.S.	1:19.32
1980	Eric Heiden, U.S.	1:15.18
1984	Gaétan Boucher, Canada	1:15.80
1988	Nikolai Guiliaev, U.S.S.R.	1:13.03
1992	Olaf Zinke, Germany	1:14.85
1994	Dan Jansen, U.S.	1:12.43
1998	Ids Postma, Netherlands	1:10.64
2002	Gerard van Velde Netherlands	1:07.18
2006	Shani Davis, U.S.	1:08.89
1,500 Meters (4,922 Ft.)		Time
1924	Clas Thunberg, Finland	2:20.80
1928	Clas Thunberg, Finland	2:21.10
1932	John A. Shea, U.S.	2:57.50
1936	Charles Mathisen, Norway	2:19.20
1948	Sverre Farstad, Norway	2:17.60
1952	Hjalmar Andersen, Norway	2:20.40

1956	Yevgeni Grishin	2:08.60
	Yuri Mikhailov, U.S.S.R. (tie)	
1960	Roald Aas, Norway	2:10.40
	Yevgeni Grishin, U.S.S.R. (tie)	
1964	Ants Anston, U.S.S.R.	2:10.30
1968	Cornelis Verkerk, Netherlands	2:03.40
1972	Ard Schenk, Netherlands	2:02.96
1976	Jan Egil Storholt, Norway	1:59.38
1980	Eric Heiden, U.S.	1:55.44
1984	Gaétan Boucher, Canada	1:58.36
1988	Andre Hoffmann, East Germany	1:52.06
1992	Johann Olav Koss, Norway	1:54.81
1994	Johann Olav Koss, Norway	1:51.29
1998	Aadne Sondral, Norway	1:47.87
2002	Derek Parra, U.S.	1:43.95
2006	Enrico Fabris, Italy	1:45.97
5,000 Meters (16,405 Ft.)		Time
1924	Clas Thunberg, Finland	8:39.00
1928	Ivar Ballangrud, Norway	8:50.50
1932	Irving Jaffee, U.S.	9:40.80
1936	Ivar Ballangrud, Norway	8:19.60
1948	Reidar Liaklev, Norway	8:29.40
1952	Hjalmar Andersen, Norway	8:10.60
1956	Boris Shilkov, U.S.S.R.	7:48.70
1960	Viktor Kosichkin, U.S.S.R.	7:51.30
1964	Knut Johannesen, Norway	7:38.40
1968	F. Anton Maier, Norway	7:22.40
1972	Ard Schenk, Netherlands	7:23.61
1976	Sten Stensen, Norway	7:24.48
1980	Eric Heiden, U.S.	7:02.29
1984	Sven Tomas Gustafson, Sweden	7:12.28
1988	Tomas Gustafson, Sweden	6:44.63
1992	Geir Karlstad, Sweden	6:59.97
1994	Johann Olav Koss, Norway	6:34.96
1998	Gianni Romme, Netherlands	6:22.20
2002	Jochem Uytdehaage Netherlands	6:14.66
2006	Chad Hedrick, U.S.	6:14.68
Team Pursuit		
2006	Italy	

10,000 Meters (32,810 Ft.)

		Time
1924	Julien Skutnabb, Finland	18:04.80
1928	(ice thawed, event cancelled)	
1932	Irving Jaffee, U.S.	19:13.60
1936	Ivan Ballangrud, Norway	17:24.30
1948	Ake Seyffarth, Sweden	17:26.30
1952	Hjalmar Andersen, Norway	16:45.80
1956	Sigvard Ericsson, Sweden	16:35.90
1960	Knut Johannessen, Norway	15:46.60
1964	Jonny Nilsson, Sweden	15:50.10
1968	Johnny Hoeglin, Sweden	15:23.60
1972	Ard Schenk, Netherlands	15:01.35
1976	Piet Kleine, Netherlands	14:50.59
1980	Eric Heiden, U.S.	14:28.13
1984	Igor Malikov, U.S.S.R.	14:39.90
1988	Tomas Gustafson, Sweden	13:48.20
1992	Bart Veldkamp, Netherlands	14:12.12
1994	Johann Olav Koss, Norway	13:30.55
1998	Gianni Romme, Netherlands	13:15.33
2002	Jochem Uytdehaage Netherlands	12:58.92
2006	Bob de Jong, Netherlands	13:01.57

Speed Skating—Women

500 Meters (1,641 Ft.)

		Time
1960	Helga Haase, Germany	0:45.90
1964	Lydia Skoblikova, U.S.S.R.	0:45.00
1968	Ludmila Titova, U.S.S.R.	0:46.10
1972	Anne Henning, U.S.	0:43.30
1976	Sheila Young, U.S.	0:42.76
1980	Karin Enke, East Germany	0:41.78
1984	Christa Rothenburger, East Germany	0:41.02
1988	Bonnie Blair, U.S.	0:39.10
1992	Bonnie Blair, U.S.	0:40.33
1994	Bonnie Blair, U.S.	0:39.25
1998[1]	Catriona Le May-Doan, Canada	1:16.60
2002	Catriona Le May Doan, Canada	1:14.75
2006	Svetlana Zhurova, Russia	1:16.57

1,000 Meters (3,281 Ft.)

		Time
1960	Klara Guseva, U.S.S.R.	1:34.10
1964	Lydia Skoblikova, U.S.S.R.	1:33.20
1968	Carolina Geiissen, Netherlands	1:32.60
1972	Monika Pflug, West Germany	1:31.40
1976	Tatiana Averina, U.S.S.R.	1:28.43
1980	Natalia Petruseva, U.S.S.R.	1:24.10
1984	Karin Enke, East Germany	1:21.61
1988	Christa Rothenburger, E.Germany	1:17.65
1992	Bonnie Blair, U.S.	1:21.90
1994	Bonnie Blair, U.S.	1:18.74
1998	Marianne Timmer, Netherlands	1:16.51
2002	Chris Witty, U.S.	1:13.83
2006	Marianne Timmer, Netherlands	1:16.05

1,500 Meters (4,922 Ft.)

		Time
1960	Lydia Skoblikova, U.S.S.R.	2:25.20
1964	Lydia Skoblikova, U.S.S.R.	2:22.60
1968	Kaija Mustonen, Finland	2:22.40
1972	Dianne Holum, U.S.	2:20.80
1976	Galina Stepanskaya, U.S.S.R.	2:16.58
1980	Annie Borchink, Netherlands	2:10.95
1984	Karin Enke, East Germany	2:03.42
1988	Yvonne Van Gennip, Netherlands	2:00.68
1992	Jacqueline Boerner, Germany	2:05.87
1994	Emese Hunyady, Austria	2:02.19
1998	Marianne Timmer, Netherlands	1:57.58
2002	Anni Friesinger, Germany	1:54.02
2006	Cindy Klassen, Canada	1:55.27

3,000 Meters (9,843 Ft.)

		Time
1960	Lydia Skoblikova, U.S.S.R.	5:14.30
1964	Lydia Skoblikova, U.S.S.R.	5:14.90
1968	Johanna Schut, Netherlands	4.56.20
1972	Christina Baas-Kaiser, Netherlands	4:52.14
1976	Tatiana Averina, U.S.S.R.	4:45.19
1980	Bjoerg Eva Jensen, Norway	4:32.13
1984	Andrea Schöne, East Germany	4:24.79
1988	Yvonne Van Gennip, Netherlands	4:11.94
1992	Gunda Niemann, Germany	4:19.90
1994	Svetlana Bazhanova, Russia	4:17.43
1998	Gunda Niemann-Stirnemann, Germany	4:07.29
2002	Claudia Pechstein, Germany	3:57.70
2006	Ireen Wust, Netherlands	4:02.43

5,000 Meters (16,405 Ft.)

		Time
1988	Yvonne Van Gennip, Netherlands	7:14.13
1992	Gunda Niemann, Germany	7:31.57
1994	Claudia Pechstein, Germany	7:14.37
1998	Claudia Pechstein, Germany	6:59.61
2002	Claudia Pechstein, Germany	6:46.91
2006	Clara Hughes, Canada	6:59.07

Team Pursuit

2006	Germany

Notes: 1. Scoring system changed in 1998. Total is combined time from two performances.

The Winter Olympics

Olympiad	Year	Place	Competitors		Nations represented	Events
			Men	Women		
I	1924	Chamonix, France	245	13	16	16
II	1928	St. Moritz, Switzerland	438	26	25	14
III	1932	Lake Placid, N.Y., U.S.	231	21	17	14
IV	1936	Garmisch-Partenkirchen, Germany	588	80	28	17
V	1948	St. Moritz, Switzerland	592	77	28	22
VI	1952	Oslo, Norway	585	109	30	22
VII	1956	Cortina D'Ampezzo, Italy	688	132	32	24
VIII	1960	Squaw Valley, Calif., U.S.	522	143	30	27
IX	1964	Innsbruck, Austria	891	200	36	34
X	1968	Grenoble, France	947	211	37	35
XI	1972	Sapporo, Japan	800	206	35	35
XII	1976	Innsbruck, Austria	892	231	37	37
XIII	1980	Lake Placid, N.Y., U.S.	839	233	37	38
XIV	1984	Sarajevo, Yugoslavia	1,000	274	49	39
XV	1988	Calgary, Canada	1,110	313	57	46
XVI	1992	Albertville, France	1,313	488	64	57
XVII	1994	Lillehammer, Norway	1,217	522	67	61
XVIII	1998	Nagano, Japan	1,488	814	72	68
XIX	2002	Salt Lake City, Utah, U.S.	1,513	886	77	78
XX	2006	Torino, Italy	1,627	1,006	80	84
XXI	2010	Vancouver, Canada	2,629 total		82	86

Source: International Olympic Committee.

PROFESSIONAL SPORTS

AUTOMOBILE RACING

A number of U.S. states and cities banned automobile racing on public roads during the early 1900s, leading to the development of closed-circuit courses. The Indianapolis Motor Speedway, a 2.5 mile macadam oval, was built in 1909. It was paved with brick in 1911, when the first Indy 500 was run. The American Automobile Association, troubled by a series of fatal crashes, stopped sanctioning races in 1956, whereupon the United States Auto Club (USAC) took over the Indy 500.

Indianapolis 500 Winners, 1911–2010

Year	Winner	Time	MPH	Year	Winner	Time	MPH
Under AAA Sanction				1963	Parnelli Jones	3:29:35	143.137
1911	Ray Harroun	6:42.08	74.602	1964	A. J. Foyt Jr.	3:23:35	147.350
1912	Joe Dawson	6:21.06	78.719	1965	Jim Clark	3:19:05	150.686
1913	Juses Goux	6:35:05	75.933	1966	Graham Hill	3:27:52	144.317
1914	Rene Thomas	6:03:45	82.474	1967	A. J. Foyt Jr.	3:18:14	151.207
1915	Ralph DePalma	5:33:55	89.840	1968	Bobby Unser	3:16:13	152.882
1916	Dario Resta	3:34:17[1]	84.001	1969	Mario Andretti	3:11:14	156.867
1919	Howard Wilcox	5:40:42	88.050	1970	Al Unser	3:12:37	155.749
1920	Gaston Chevrolet	5:38:32	88.618	1971	Al Unser	3:10:11	157.735
1921	Tommy Milton	5:34:34	89.621	1972	Mark Donohue	3:04:05	162.962
1922	Jimmy Murphy	5:17:30	94.484	1973	Gordon Johncock	2:05:26[4]	159.036
1923	Tommy Milton	5:29:50	90.954	1974	Johnny Rutherford	3:09:10	158.589
1924	L. L. Corum, Joe Boyer	5:05:23	98.234	1975	Bobby Unser	2:54:55[5]	149.213
1925	Peter DePaolo	4:56:39	101.127	1976	Johnny Rutherford	1:42:52[6]	148.725
1926	Peter Lockhart	4:10:14[2]	95.904	1977	A. J. Foyt Jr.	3:05:57	161.331
1927	George Souders	5:07:33	97.545	1978	Al Unser	3:05:54	161.363
1928	Louis Meyer	5:01:33	99.482	1979	Rick Mears	3:08:47	158.899
1929	Ray Keech	5:07:25	97.585	1980	Johnny Rutherford	3:29:59	142.862
1930	Billy Arnold	4:58:39	100.448	1981	Bobby Unser	3:35:41	139.084
1931	Louis Schneider	5:10:27	96.629	1982	Gordon Johncock	3:05:09	162.029
1932	Fred Frame	4:48:03	104.144	1983	Tom Sneva	3:05:03	162.117
1933	Louis Meyer	4:48:00	104.162	1984	Rick Mears	3:30:21	163.612
1934	William Cummings	4:46:05	104.863	1985	Danny Sullivan	3:16:06	152.982
1935	Kelly Petillo	4:42:22	106.240	1986	Bobby Rahal	2:55:43	170.722
1936	Louis Meyer	4:35:03	109.069	1987	Al Unser	3:04:59	162.175
1937	Wilbur Shaw	4:24:07	113.580	1988	Rick Mears	3:27:10	144.809
1938	Floyd Roberts	4:15:58	117.200	1989	Emerson Fittipaldi	2:59:01	167.581
1939	Wilbur Shaw	4:20:47	115.035	1990	Arie Luyendyk	2:41:18	185.984[7]
1940	Wilbur Shaw	4:22:31	114.277	1991	Rick Mears	2:50:01	176.457
1941	Floyd Davis, Mauri Rose	4:20:36	115.117	1992	Al Unser Jr.	3:43:05	134.477
1946	George Robson	4:21:16	114.820	1993	Emerson Fittipaldi	3:10:50	157.207
1947	Mauri Rose	4:17:52	116.338	1994	Al Unser Jr.	3:06:29	160.872
1948	Mauri Rose	4:10:23	119.814	1995	Jacques Villeneuve	3:15:18	153.616
1949	Bill Holland	4:07:15	121.327	1996	Buddy Lazier	3:22:46	147.956
1950	Johnnie Parsons	2:46:55[3]	124.002	1997	Arie Luyendyk	3:25:43	145.827
1951	Lee Wallard	3:57:38	126.244	1998	Eddie Cheever	3:26:40	145.155
1952	Troy Tuttman	3:52:41	128.922	1999	Kenny Brack	3:15:51	153.176
1953	Bill Vukovich	3:53:01	128.740	2000	Juan Montoya	2:58.59	167.607
1954	Bill Vukovich	3:49:17	130.840	2001	Helio Castroneves	3:31.54	141.574
1955	Bob Sweikert	3:53:59	128.209	2002	Helio Castroneves	3:00:11	166.499
Under USAC Sanction				2003	Gil de Ferran	3:11:57	156.291
1956	Pat Flaherty	3:53.28	128.490	2004	Buddy Rice	3:14:55[8]	138.518
1957	Sam Hanks	3:41.14	135.601	2005	Dan Wheldon	3:10:21	157.603
1958	Jim Bryan	3:44:13	133.791	2006	Sam Hornish Jr.	3:10:58	157.085
1959	Rodger Ward	3:40:49	135.857	2007	Dario Franchitti	2:44:03	151.774
1960	Jim Rathmann	3:36:11	138.767	2008	Scott Dixon	3:28:57	143.567
1961	A. J. Foyt Jr.	3:35:37	139.131	2009	Helio Castroneves	3:19:35	150.318
1962	Roger Ward	3:33:50	140.293	2010	Dario Franchitti	3:05:37	161.623

Notes: 1. 300 miles (scheduled). 2. 400 miles (rain). 3. 345 miles (rain). 4. 332.5 miles (rain). 5. 435 miles (rain). 6. 255 miles (rain). 7. Track record. 8. 450 miles (rain) 9. 415 miles (rain)   **Source:** Indianapolis Motor Speedway Hall of Fame and Museum.

Daytona 500 Winners, 1959–2010

Year	Winner	Year	Winner
1959	Lee Petty	1985	Bill Elliott
1960	Junior Johnson	1986	Geoff Bodine
1961	Marvin Panch	1987	Bill Elliott
1962	Fireball Roberts	1988	Bobby Allison
1963	Tiny Lund	1989	Darrell Waltrip
1964	Richard Petty	1990	Derrike Cope
1965	Fred Lorenzen	1991	Ernie Irvan
1966	Richard Petty	1992	Davey Allison
1967	Mario Andretti	1993	Dale Jarrett
1968	Cale Yarborough	1994	Sterling Marlin
1969	LeeRoy Yarbrough	1995	Sterling Marlin
1970	Pete Hamilton	1996	Dale Jarrett
1971	Richard Petty	1997	Jeff Gordon
1972	A.J. Foyt, Jr.	1998	Dale Earnhardt
1973	Richard Petty	1999	Jeff Gordon
1974	Richard Petty	2000	Dale Jarrett
1975	Benny Parsons	2001	Michael Waltrip
1976	David Pearson	2002	Ward Burton
1977	Cale Yarborough	2003	Michael Waltrip
1978	Bobby Allison	2004	Dale Earnhardt Jr.
1979	Richard Petty	2005	Jeff Gordon
1980	Buddy Baker	2006	Jimmie Johnson
1981	Richard Petty	2007	Kevin Harvick
1982	Bobby Allison	2008	Ryan Newman
1983	Cale Yarborough	2009	Matt Kenseth
1984	Cale Yarborough	2010	Jamie McMurray

NASCAR Champions, 1959–2009

Year	Winner	Year	Winner
1959	Lee Petty	1985	Darrell Waltrip
1960	Rex White	1986	Dale Earnhardt
1961	Ned Jarrett	1987	Dale Earnhardt
1962	Joe Weatherly	1988	Bill Elliott
1963	Joe Weatherly	1989	Rusty Wallace
1964	Richard Petty	1990	Dale Earnhardt
1965	Ned Jarrett	1991	Dale Earnhardt
1966	David Pearson	1992	Alan Kulwicki
1967	Richard Petty	1993	Dale Earnhardt
1968	David Pearson	1994	Dale Earnhardt
1969	David Pearson	1995	Jeff Gordon
1970	Bobby Isaac	1996	Terry Labonte
1971	Richard Petty	1997	Jeff Gordon
1972	Richard Petty	1998	Jeff Gordon
1973	Benny Parsons	1999	Dale Jarrett
1974	Richard Petty	2000	BobbyLabonte
1975	Richard Petty	2001	Jeff Gordon
1976	Cale Yarborough	2002	Tony Stewart
1977	Cale Yarborough	2003	Matt Kenseth
1978	Cale Yarborough	2004	Kurt Busch
1979	Richard Petty	2005	Tony Stewart
1980	Dale Earnhardt	2006	Jimmie Johnson
1981	Darrell Waltrip	2007	Jimmie Johnson
1982	Darrell Waltrip	2008	Jimmie Johnson
1983	Bobby Allison	2009	Jimmie Johnson
1984	Terry Labonte		

BOWLING

PBA Leading Money Winners, 1959–2009

Year	Name	Amount	Year	Name	Amount	Year	Name	Amount
1959	Dick Weber	$ 7,672	1978	Mark Roth	$134,500	1995	Mike Aulby	$219,792
1960	Don Carter	22,525	1979	Mark Roth	124,517	1996	Walter Ray Williams Jr.	241,330
1961	Dick Weber	26,280	1980	Wayne Webb	116,700			
1962	Don Carter	49,972	1981	Earl Anthony	164,735	1997	Walter Ray Williams Jr.	240,544
1963	Dick Weber	46,333	1982	Earl Anthony	134,760			
1964	Bob Strampe	33,592	1983	Earl Anthony	135,605	1998	Walter Ray Williams Jr.	238,225
1965	Dick Weber	47,675	1984	Mark Roth	158,712			
1966	Wayne Zahn	54,720	1985	Mike Aulby	201,200	1999	Parker Bohn III	240,912
1967	Dave Davis	54,165	1986	Walter Ray Williams Jr.	145,550	2000	Norm Duke	136,900
1968	Jim Stefanich	67,375				2001	Parker Bohn III	245,200
1969	Billy Hardwick	64,160	1987	Pete Weber	179,516	2003	Walter Ray Williams Jr.	419,700
1970	Mike McGrath	52,049	1988	Brian Voss	225,485			
1971	Johnny Petraglia	85,065	1989	Mike Aulby	298,237	2004	Mika Koivuniemi	238,590
1972	Don Johnson	56,648	1990	Aurelio Monacelli	204,775	2005	Patrick Allen	350,740
1973	Don McCune	69,000	1991	David Ozio	225,585	2006	Tommy Jones	301,700
1974	Earl Anthony	99,585	1992	Marc McDowell	174,215	2007	Doug Kent	200,530
1975	Earl Anthony	107,585	1993	Walter Ray Williams Jr.	296,370	2008	Norm Duke	176,855
1976	Earl Anthony	110,833				2009	Walter Ray Williams Jr.	152,670
1977	Mark Roth	105,583	1994	Norm Duke	273,753			

Note: Since 2001, the PBA season has started in October and ended in March of the year shown. **Source:** Professional Bowlers Association.

USBC Women's Championships, 2009 Leaders

In 2005 the Womens International Bowling Congress merged with the American Bowling Congress and the Young American Bowling Alliance to form the United States Bowling Congress (USBC).

Singles

Rank, Bowler	Points
1. Michelle Feldman	816
2. Brenda Mack	761
3. Liz Johnson	758
4. Anita Manns	723
5. Kelly Kulic	720

Doubles

Rank, Bowler	Points
1. Guerrero/Larson	1,404
2. Miller/Baker	1,384
3. Esterson/Golden	1,371
4. Romeo/Naccarato	1,361
5. Manna/Minino	1,338

Teams

Rank, Bowler	Points
1. Together Once Again	3,322
2. Alpha Pool Plastering	3,286
3. Shootin' Nines	3,251
4. Husky Shox	3,202
5. Bowlers Choice Pro Shop	3,143

Note: Championship standings. **Source:** United States Bowling Congress.

BOXING

Although many governing bodies now issue and certify their own boxing championships, the four most widely accepted are the World Boxing Association (WBA), World Boxing Council (WBC), the International Boxing Federation (IBF), and the World Boxing Organization (WBO). Years given indicate the year the championship belt changed hands in a title bout. Champions who were awarded belts without a championship bout are not shown. Current champions are shown in boldface type.

Heavyweights (over 190 lbs.)

Year	Name	Year	Name	Year	Name
1885	John L. Sullivan	1967	Muhammad Ali (unifies world title)	1994	George Foreman (WBA, IBF), Bruce Seldon
1892	James J. Corbett				(WBA), Frank Bruno[1] (WBC)
1897	Robert Fitzsimmons	1968	Jimmy Ellis (WBA)	1996	Mike Tyson (WBC), Michael
1899	James J. Jeffries	1970	Joe Frazier (unifies world title)		Moorer (IBF), Mike Tyson (WBA),
1905	Marvin Hart	1973	George Foreman		Evander Holyfield (WBA)
1906	Tommy Burns	1974	Muhammad Ali	1997	Lennox Lewis (WBC), Evander
1908	Jack Johnson	1978	Leon Spinks, Larry Holmes[1],		Holyfield (IBF)
1915	Jess Willard		Muhammad Ali[1] (WBA)	1999	Lennox Lewis (WBA[1], IBF)
1919	Jack Dempsey	1979	John Tate (WBA)	2001	Hasim Rahman (WBC, IBF),
1926	Gene Tunney[1]	1980	Mike Weaver (WBA)		John Ruiz (WBA),
1928–30	vacant	1982	Michael Dokes (WBA)		Lennox Lewis (WBC, IBF)
1930	Max Schmeling	1983	Gerrie Coetzee (WBA)	2002	Chris Byrd (IBF)
1932	Jack Sharkey	1984	Tim Witherspoon (WBC),	2003	Roy Jones Jr. (WBA)
1933	Primo Carnera		Pinklon Thomas (WBC),	2004	Vitaly Klitschko (WBC)
1934	Max Baer		Greg Page (WBA)		John Ruiz (WBA)
1935	James J. Braddock	1985	Tony Tubbs (WBA)	2005	Hasim Rahman (WBC)
1937	Joe Louis[1]	1986	Tim Witherspoon (WBA),		Nicolay Valuev (WBA)
1949	Ezzard Charles		Trevor Berbick (WBC),	2006	**Wladimir Klitschko (IBF)**
1951	Jersey Joe Walcott		Mike Tyson (WBC), James		Oleg Maskaev (WBC)
1952	Rocky Marciano[1]		"Bonecrusher" Smith (WBA)	2007	Ruslan Chagaev (WBA)
1956	Floyd Patterson	1987	Mike Tyson (WBA), Tony		Sultan Ibragimov (WBO)
1959	Ingemar Johansson		Tucker (IBF)	2008	Ruslan Chagaev (WBA)
1960	Floyd Patterson	1990	Buster Douglas (unifies world		**Wladimir Klitschko (WBO)**
1962	Sonny Liston		title), Evander Holyfield	2009	**David Haye (WBA)**
1964	Cassius Clay[1]	1992	Riddick Bowe		**Vitali Klitschko (WBC)**
	(Muhammad Ali)	1993	Evander Holyfield (WBA, IBF)		
1965	Ernie Terrell (WBA)				

Light Heavyweights (169–175 lbs.)

Year	Name	Year	Name	Year	Name
1903	Jack Root, George Gardner	1977	Miguel Angel Cuello (WBC)	1992	Iran Barkley[1] (WBA), Virgil Hill (WBA)
1903	Bob Fitzsimmons	1978	Mate Parlov (WBC), Mike Rossman (WBA), Marvin	1993	Henry Maske (IBF)
1905	Philadelphia Jack O'Brien		Johnson (WBC)	1994	Mike McCallum (WBC)
1912	Jack Dillon	1979	Matthew Franklin (Matthew Saad Muhammad) (WBC),	1995	Fabrice Tiozzo (WBC)
1916	Battling Levinsky		Marvin Johnson (WBA)	1996	Roy Jones Jr.[1] (WBC), Virgil Hill[1] (IBF)
1920	George Carpentier	1980	Eddie Gregory (Eddie Mustafa Muhammad)	1997	William Guthrie (IBF), Dariusz Michalczewski[1]
1922	Battling Siki		(WBA)		(WBA),
1923	Mike McTigue	1981	Michael Spinks (WBA), Dwight Braxton (Dwight		Lou Del Valle (WBA)
1925	Paul Berlenbach		Muhammad Qawi) (WBC)	1998	Reggie Johnson (IBF), Graciano Rocchigiani
1926	Jack Delaney	1983	Michael Spinks (unifies world title)		(WBC), Roy Jones Jr.
1927	Tommy Loughran				(WBA, WBC)
1930	Maxey Rosenbloom	1985	J.B. Williamson (WBC), Slobodan Kacar (IBF)	1999	Roy Jones Jr. (IBF)
1934	Bob Olin	1986	Marvin Johnson (WBA), Dennis Andries (WBC),	2003	Antonio Tarver (WBC, IBF)
1935	John Henry Lewis		Bobby Czyz (IBF)	2004	Zsolt Erdei (WBO), Fabrice Tiozzo (WBA), Tomasz
1939	Billy Conn	1987	Thomas Hearns[1] (WBC), Leslie Stewart (WBA), Virgil		Adamek (WBC)
1941	Gus Lesnevich		Hill (WBA), Prince Charles	2005	Clinton Woods (IBF)
1948	Freddie Mills		Williams (IBF), Don Lalonde (WBC)	2006	Silvio Branco (WBA)
1950	Joey Maxim	1988	Sugar Ray Leonard (WBC)	2007	Stripe Davis (WBA), Chad Dawson (WBC), Danny
1952	Archie Moore	1989	Dennis Andries (WBC), Jeff Harding (WBC)		Green (WBA)
1962	Harold Johnson	1990	Dennis Andries (WBC)	2008	**Chad Dawson (WBC)**
1963	Willie Pastrano	1991	Thomas Hearns (WBA), Jeff Harding (WBC)	2009	**Tavoris Cloud (IBF)**
1965	Jose Torres				**Jurgen Brahmer (WBO)**
1966	Dick Tiger			2010	**Beibut Shumenov (WBA)**
1968	Bob Foster				
1971	Vicente Rondon (WBA)				
1972	Bob Foster (unifies world title)				
1974	John Conteh (WBC), Victor Galindez (WBA)				

Middleweights (155–160 lbs.)

Year	Name	Year	Name	Year	Name
1884	Jack Dempsey	1953	Bobo Olson		James Toney[1] (IBF)
1891	Bob Fitzsimmons[1]	1955	Sugar Ray Robinson	1991	Reggie Johnson[1] (WBA)
1897	Kid McCoy[1], Tommy Ryan[1]	1957	Gene Fullmer (NBA), Sugar Ray Robinson, Carmen Basilio	1993	Gerald McClellan[1] (WBC), Roy Jones[1] (IBF), John David Jackson (WBA)
1907	Stanley Ketchel				
1908	Billy Papke, Stanley Ketchel[1]	1958	Sugar Ray Robinson	1994	Jorge Castro (WBA)
1911	Vacant	1960	Paul Pender	1995	Julian Jackson (WBC), Bernard Hopkins (IBF), Quincy Taylor (WBC), Shinij Takehara (WBA)
1913	Frank Klaus, George Chip	1961	Terry Downes		
		1962	Paul Pender		
1914	Al McCoy	1963	Dick Tiger		
1917	Mike O'Dowd	1963	Joey Giardello	1996	Keith Holmes (WBC), William Joppy (WBA)
1920	Johnny Wilson	1965	Dick Tiger		
1921	William Bryan Downey[1]	1966	Emile Griffith	1997	Julio Cesar Green (WBA)
1923	Harry Greb	1967	Nino Benvenuti, Emile Griffith	1998	William Joppy (WBA), Hassine Cherifi (WBC)
1926	Tiger Flowers, Mickey Walker				
		1968	Nino Benvenuti	1999	Keith Holmes (WBC)
1931	Gorilla Jones	1970	Carlos Monzon	2001	Felix Trinidad (WBA), Bernard Hopkins (WBA, WBC)
1932	Marcel Thil	1977	Rodrigo Valdez		
1937	Fred Apostoli	1978	Hugo Corro		
1939	Ceferino Garcia	1979	Vito Antuofermo		
1940	Ken Overlin	1980	Alan Minter, Marvin Hagler[1]	2005	Jermain Taylor (WBA, WBC, WBO), Arthur Abraham (IBF)
1941	Billy Soose[1], Tony Zale	1987	Ray Leonard[1] (WBC), Frank Tate (IBF), Sumbo Kalambay (WBA), Thomas Hearns (WBC)		
1947	Rocky Graziano			2006	Javier Castillejo (WBA)
1948	Tony Zale, Marcel Cerdan			2007	**Felix Sturm (WBA)**
1949	Jake LaMotta	1988	Iran Barkley (WBC), Michael Nunn (IBF)	2008	**Kelly Pavlik (WBC)**
1951	Sugar Ray Robinson, Randy Turpin, Sugar Ray Robinson[1]			2009	**Sebastian Zbick (WBC—Interim)**
		1989	Roberto Duran[1] (WBC), Mike McCallum[1] (WBA)		**Sebastian Sylvester (IBF)**
		1990	Julian Jackson (WBC),	2010	**Dmitry Pirog (WBO)**

Welterweights (141–147 lbs.)

Year	Name	Year	Name	Year	Name
1888	Paddy Duffy	1935	Barney Ross	1989	Marlon Starling (WBC), Mark Breland (WBA)
1892	Mysterious Billy Smith	1938	Henry Armstrong		
		1940	Fritzie Zivic	1990	Aaron Davis (WBA), Maurice Blocker (WBC)
1894	Tommy Ryan[1]	1941	Fred Cochrane		
1896	Kid McCoy[1]	1946	Marty Servo[1], Ray Robinson[1]	1991	Meldrick Taylor (WBA), Simon Brown (WBC), Maurice Blocker (IBF), Buddy McGirt (WBC)
1898	Mysterious Billy Smith	1951	Kid Gavilan		
1900	Matty Matthews, Eddie Connolly, Rube Ferns, Matty Matthews	1954	Johnny Saxton		
		1955	Tony De Marco, Carmen Basilio	1992	Crisanto Espana (WBA)
		1956	Johnny Saxton, Carmen Basilio	1993	Pernell Whitaker (WBC), Felix Trinidad (IBF)
		1957	Carmen Basilio[1]		
1901	Rube Ferns, Joe Walcott	1958	Virgil Akins, Don Jordan	1994	Ike Quartey[1] (WBA)
1904	Dixie Kid[1]	1960	Benny Paret	1997	Oscar de la Hoya (WBC)
1906	Honey Mellody	1961	Emile Griffith, Benny Paret	1998	James Page (WBA)
1907	Frank Mantell	1962	Emile Griffith	1999	Felix Trinidad[1] (WBC), Rawl Frank (IBF)
1908	Harry Lewis[1]	1963	Luis Rodriguez, Emile Griffith[1]		
1911–13	Vacant	1966	Curtis Cokes	2000	Vernon Forrest (IBF), Oscar de la Hoya (WBC), Shane Mosley (WBC)
1914	Waldemar Holberg, Tom McCormick, Matt Wells	1969	Jose Napoles		
		1970	Billy Backus		
		1971	Jose Napoles	2001	Andrew Lewis (WBA)
1915	Mike Glover, Jack Britton, Ted (Kid) Lewis	1975	Angel Espada (WBA), John Stracey (WBC)	2002	Vernon Forrest[1] (IBF), Michele Piccirillo (IBF), Ricardo Mayorga (WBA), Vernon Forrest (WBC), Antiono Margarito (WBO)
		1976	Carlos Palomino (WBC), Jose Cuevas (WBA)		
1916	Jack Britton	1979	Wilfredo Benitez (WBC), Sugar Ray Leonard (WBC)		
1917	Ted (Kid) Lewis			2003	Ricardo Mayorga (unifies world title) Cory Spinks
1919	Jack Britton	1980	Roberto Duran (WBC), Thomas Hearns (WBA), Sugar Ray Leonard (WBC)		
1922	Mickey Walker				
1926	Pete Latzo	1981	Sugar Ray Leonard[1] (unifies world title)	2005	Zab Judah (WBC, IBF), Luis Collazo (WBA)
1927	Joe Dundee				
1929	Jackie Fields	1983	Donald Curry (WBA), Milton McCrory (WBC)	2006	Carlos Baldomir (WBC), Floyd Mayweather (WBC), Ricky Hatton (WBA)
1930	Young Jack Thompson, Tommy Freeman				
		1985	Donald Curry (unifies world title)		
1931	Young Jack Thompson, Lou Brouillard	1986	Lloyd Honeyghan[1]	2007	Paul Williams (WBO)
1932	Jackie Fields	1987	Mark Breland (WBA), Marlon Starling (WBA), Jorge Vaca (WBC)	2008	Paul Williams (WBO) **Selcuk Aydin (WBC)**
1933	Young Corbett, Jimmy McLarnin			2009	**Jan Zaveck (IBF)** **Manny Pacquiao (WBO)**
1934	Barney Ross, Jimmy McLarnin	1988	Simon Brown[1] (IBF), Thomas Molinares[1] (WBA)	2010	**Souleymane M'Baye (WBA)—Interim**

Lightweights (131–135 lbs.)

Year	Name	Year	Name	Year	Name
1896	Jack McAuliffe[1], Kid Lavigne	1956	Joe Brown	1990	Juan Nazario (WBA), Pernell Whitaker[1] (unifies title)
1899	Frank Erne	1962	Carlos Ortiz	1991	Vacant
1902	Joe Gans[1]	1965	Ismael Laguna, Carlos Ortiz	1992	Tony Lopez (WBA)
1904	Jimmy Britt	1968	Teo Cruz	1993	Fred Pendleton (IBF), Dingaan Thobela (WBA), Orzubek Nazarov (WBA)
1905	Battling Nelson	1969	Mando Ramos		
1906	Joe Gans	1970	Ismael Laguna, Ken Buchanan[1]		
1908	Battling Nelson	1971	Pedro Carrasco (WBC)	1994	Rafael Ruelas (IBF)
1910	Ad Wolgast	1972	Mando Ramos Roberto Duran[1] (WBA)	1995	Oscar de la Hoya[1] (IBF), Phillip Holiday (IBF)
1912	Willie Ritchie		Chango Carmona (WBC),	1996	Jean-Baptiste Mendy (WBC)
1914	Freddie Welsh		Rodolfo Gonzalez (WBC)	1997	Steve Johnston (WBC), Shane Mosley[1] (IBF)
1917	Benny Leonard[1]	1974	Ishimatsu Suzuki (WBC)		
1925	Jimmy Goodrich, Rocky Kansas	1976	Esteban De Jesus[1] (WBC)	1998	Jean-Baptiste Mendy (WBA), Cesar Bazan (WBC)
		1979	Jim Watt (WBC), Ernesto España (WBA)		
1926	Sammy Mandell	1980	Hilmer Kenty (WBA)	1999	Julian Lorcy Fra (WBA), Steve Johnston (WBC), Stefano Zoff (WBA), Paul Spadafora[1] (IBF), Gilberto Serrano (WBA)
1930	Al Singer, Tony Canzoneri	1981	Sean O'Grady (WBA), Alexis Arguello (WBC), Claude Noel (WBA), Arturo Frias (WBA)		
1933	Barney Ross[1]				
1935	Tony Canzoneri	1982	Ray Mancini (WBA)	2000	Jose Luis Castillo (WBC)
1936	Lou Ambers	1983	Edwin Rosario (WBC)	2001	Raul Balbi (WBA)
1938	Henry Armstrong	1984	Charlie (Choo Choo) Brown (IBF), Livingstone Bramble (WBA), Jose Luis Ramirez (WBC)	2002	Floyd Mayweather (WBC), Leonard Dorin (WBA)
1939	Lou Ambers				
1940	Lew Jenkins			2004	Julio Diaz(IBF), Lakva Sim (WBA), Jose Luis Castillo (WBC), Javier Jauregui (IBF)
1941	Sammy Angott	1985	Jimmy Paul (IBF), Hector Camacho[1] (WBC)		
1942	Beau Jack				
1943	Bob Montgomery, Beau Jack	1986	Edwin Rosario (WBA), Greg Haugen (IBF)	2005	Diego Corrales (WBC), Juan Diaz (WBA), Jesus Chavez (IBF)
		1987	Vinny Pazienza (IBF), Jose Luis Ramirez (WBC), Julio Cesar Chavez[1] (WBA)		
1944	Bob Montgomery, Juan Zurita			2007	Julio Diaz (IBF)
1945	Ike Williams	1988	Greg Haugen (IBF), Julio Cesar Chavez[1] (WBC)	2008	Nate Campbell (WBA, WBO, IBF), David Diaz (WBC)
1951	Jimmy Carter				
1952	Lauro Salas, Jimmy Carter	1989	Pernell Whitaker (IBF)	2009	**Juan Manuel Marquez (WBO)**
		1989	Edwin Rosario (WBA), Pernell Whitaker (WBC)	2010	**Miguel Acosta (WBA) Humberto Soto (WBC), Vacant (IBF)**
1954	Paddy De Marco, Jimmy Carter				
1955	Bud Smith				

Featherweights (123–126 lbs.)

Year	Name	Year	Name	Year	Name
1900	Terry McGovern, Young Corbett[1]		Kuniaki Shibata (WBC)		Eloy Rojas (WBA)
		1971	Antonio Gomez (WBA	1995	Alejandro Gonzalez (WBC), Manuel Medina (WBC), Luisito Espinosa (WBC)
1901	Abe Attell	1972	Clemente Sanchez (WBC), Ernesto Marcel[1] (WBA), Jose Legra (WBC)		
1904	Tommy Sullivan[1]				
1906	Abe Attell			1996	Wilfredo Vasquez[1] (WBA)
1912	Johnny Kilbane	1973	Eder Jofre[1] (WBC)	1997	Naseem Hamed (IBF), Hector Lizarraga (IBF)
1923	Eugene Criqui, Johnny Dundee[1]	1974	Ruben Olivares (WBA), Bobby Chacon (WBC), Alexis Arguello[1] (WBA)		
				1998	Fred Norwood (WBA), Manuel Medina (IBF), Antonio Cermeño Ven (WBA)
1925	Kid Kaplan[1]	1975	Ruben Olivares (WBA), David Kotey (WBC)		
1927	Benny Bass, Ton Canzoneri	1976	Danny Lopez (WBC)	1999	Cesar Soto (WBC), Luisito Espinosa (WBC), Paul Ingle (IBF), Fred Norwood (WBA)
		1977	Rafael Ortega (WBA), Cecillio Lastra (WBA)		
1928	Andre Routis				
1929	Battling Battalino[1]	1978	Eusebio Pedrosa (WBA)	2000	Guty Espadas (WBC), Derrick Gainer (WBA)
1932	Tommy Paul	1980	Salvador Sanchez[1] (WBC)		
1933	Freddie Miller	1982	Juan LaPorte (WBC)	2001	Frankie Toledo (IBF), Manuel Medina (IBF), Erik Morales[1](WBC)
1936	Petey Sarron	1984	Min Keun Oh (IBF), Wilfredo Gomez (WBC), Azumah Nelson (WBC)		
1937	Henry Armstrong[1]			2002	Johnny Tapia (IBF), Manuel Medina (IBF), Scott Harrison (WBO)
1938	Joey Archibald				
1940	Harry Jeffra, Joey Archibald	1985	Barry McGuigan (WBA), Ki Yung Chung[1] (IBF)		
				2003	Juan Marquez (IBF), Chris John (WBA)
1941	Chalky Wright	1986	Steve Cruz (WBA)	2004	In-Jin Chi (WBC)
1942	Wilie Pep	1987	Antonio Esparragoza (WBA)	2006	Rudolfo Lopez (WBC), Eric Aiken (IBF)
1948	Sandy Saddler	1988	Calvin Grove (IBF), Jeff Fenech[1] (WBC), Jorge Paez (IBF)		
1949	Willie Pep			2007	Robert Guerrero (IBF)
1950	Sandy Saddler[1]			2008	**Chris John (WBA)**, Steven Luevano (WBO), Robert Guerrero (IBF)
1957	Hogan (Kid) Bassey	1990	Marcos Villasana (WBC)		
1959	Davey Moore	1991	Yung Kyun Park (WBA)		
1963	Sugar Ramos	1992	Troy Dorsey (IBF), Manuel Medina (IBF), Paul Hodkinson (WBC)	2009	**Elio Rojas (WBC)**
1964	Vicente Saldivar[1]			2010	**Orlando Salido (IBF) Juan Manuel Lopez (WBO)**
1968	Jose Legra[1] (WBA), Shojo Saijo (WBA)	1993	Tom Johnson (IBF), Goyo Vargas (WBC), Kevin Kelley (WBC)		
1969	Johnny Famechon (WBC)				
1970	Vicente Saldivar (WBC)				

Note: WBC = World Boxing Council. WBA = World Boxing Association. IBF= International Boxing Federation. 1. Stripped of title or abandoned belt. **Source:** International Boxing Hall of Fame.

GOLF

▶THE FOUR MAJOR TOURNAMENTS

No golfer has ever won the four major tournaments—the Masters, the U.S. Open, the British Open, and the PGA—in the same calendar year. The players to come closest were Ben Hogan, who won the first three tournaments in 1953, and Tiger Woods, who won them consecutively, but not in the same calendar year –he won the last three in 2000 and the Masters in 2001. Five players have won each of the four majors at least once over their entire careers: Hogan, Woods, Jack Nicklaus, Gary Player, and Gene Sarazen. Woods and Nicklaus won each at least three times.

The Senior Tour began with two tournaments in 1980, which offered a total of $250,000 in prize money to qualified PGA members over the age of 50. By 1984, the tour had spiralled into 24 tournaments with prize money totalling $5 million. The arrival in 1990 of Jack Nicklaus and Lee Trevino on the senior tour helped propel the 50-and-over tour to unprecedented popularity, surpassing the Ladies' Professional Tour in both prize money and television ratings.

The Masters, 1934–2010

Year	Winner	Year	Winner	Year	Winner	Year	Winner
1934	Horton Smith	1954	Sam Snead	1973	Tommy Aaron	1992	Fred Couples
1935	Gene Sarazen	1955	Cary Middlecoff	1974	Gary Player	1993	Bernhard Langer
1936	Horton Smith	1956	Jack Burke Jr.	1975	Jack Nicklaus	1994	José María Olazábal
1937	Byron Nelson	1957	Doug Ford	1976	Ray Floyd	1995	Ben Crenshaw
1938	Henry Picard	1958	Arnold Palmer	1977	Tom Watson	1996	Nick Faldo
1939	Ralph Guldahl	1959	Art Wall Jr.	1978	Gary Player	1997	Tiger Woods
1940	Jimmy Demaret	1960	Arnold Palmer	1979	Fuzzy Zoeller	1998	Mark O'Meara
1941	Craig Wood	1961	Gary Player	1980	Seve Ballesteros	1999	José María Olazábal
1942	Byron Nelson	1962	Arnold Palmer	1981	Tom Watson	2000	Vijay Singh
1943	Not held	1963	Jack Nicklaus	1982	Craig Stadler	2001	Tiger Woods
1944	Not held	1964	Arnold Palmer	1983	Seve Ballesteros	2002	Tiger Woods
1945	Not held	1965	Jack Nicklaus	1984	Ben Crenshaw	2003	Mike Weir
1946	Herman Keiser	1966	Jack Nicklaus	1985	Bernhard Langer	2004	Phil Mickelson
1947	Jimmy Demaret	1967	Gay Brewer Jr.	1986	Jack Nicklaus	2005	Tiger Woods
1948	Claude Harman	1968	Bob Goalby	1987	Larry Mize	2006	Phil Mickelson
1949	Sam Snead	1969	George Archer	1988	Sandy Lyle	2007	Zach Johnson
1950	Jimmy Demaret	1970	Billy Casper	1989	Nick Faldo	2008	Trevor Immelman
1951	Ben Hogan	1971	Charles Coody	1990	Nick Faldo	2009	Angel Cabrera
1952	Sam Snead	1972	Jack Nicklaus	1991	Ian Woosnam	2010	Phil Mickelson
1953	Ben Hogan						

The U.S. Open Championship, 1895–2010

Year	Winner	Year	Winner	Year	Winner	Year	Winner
1895	Horace Rawlins	1924	Cyril Walker	1953	Ben Hogan	1982	Tom Watson
1896	James Foulis	1925	W. MacFarlane	1954	Ed Furgol	1983	Larry Nelson
1897	Joe Lloyd	1926	Robert T. Jones Jr.	1955	Jack Fleck	1984	Fuzzy Zoeller
1898	Fred Herd	1927	Tommy Armour	1956	Cary Middlecoff	1985	Andy North
1899	Willie Smith	1928	Johnny Farrell	1957	Dick Mayer	1986	Ray Floyd
1900	Harry Vardon	1929	Robert T. Jones Jr.	1958	Tommy Bolt	1987	Scott Simpson
1901	Willie Anderson	1930	Robert T. Jones Jr.	1959	Billy Casper	1988	Curtis Strange
1902	Laurie Auchterlonie	1931	Billy Burke	1960	Arnold Palmer	1989	Curtis Strange
1903	Willie Anderson	1932	Gene Sarazen	1961	Gene Littler	1990	Hale Irwin
1904	Willie Anderson	1933	Johnny Goodman	1962	Jack Nicklaus	1991	Payne Stewart
1905	Willie Anderson	1934	Olin Dutra	1963	Julius Boros	1992	Tom Kite
1906	Alex Smith	1935	Sam Parks, Jr.	1964	Ken Venturi	1993	Lee Janzen
1907	Alex Ross	1936	Tony Manero	1965	Gary Player	1994	Ernie Els
1908	Fred McLeod	1937	Ralph Guldahl	1966	Billy Casper	1995	Corey Pavin
1909	George Sargent	1938	Ralph Guldahl	1967	Jack Nicklaus	1996	Steve Jones
1910	Alex Smith	1939	Byron Nelson	1968	Lee Trevino	1997	Ernie Els
1911	John McDermott	1940	Lawson Little	1969	Orville Moody	1998	Lee Janzen
1912	John McDermott	1941	Craig Wood	1970	Tony Jacklin	1999	Payne Stewart
1913	Francis Ouimet	1942	Not held	1971	Lee Trevino	2000	Tiger Woods
1914	Walter Hagen	1943	Not held	1972	Jack Nicklaus	2001	Retief Goosen
1915	Jerome Travers	1944	Not held	1973	Johnny Miller	2002	Tiger Woods
1916	Charles Evans Jr.	1945	Not held	1974	Hale Irwin	2003	Jim Furyk
1917	Not held	1946	Lloyd Mangrum	1975	Lou Graham	2004	Retief Goosen
1918	Not held	1947	Lew Worsham	1976	Jerry Pate	2005	Michael Campbell
1919	Walter Hagen	1948	Ben Hogan	1977	Hubert Green	2006	Geoff Ogilvy
1920	Edward Ray	1949	Cary Middlecoff	1978	Andy North	2007	Angel Cabrera
1921	James M. Barnes	1950	Ben Hogan	1979	Hale Irwin	2008	Tiger Woods
1922	Gene Sarazen	1951	Ben Hogan	1980	Jack Nicklaus	2009	Lucas Glover
1923	Robert T. Jones Jr.	1952	Julius Boros	1981	David Graham	2010	Graeme McDowell

The British Open, 1860–2010

Year	Winner	Year	Winner	Year	Winner	Year	Winner
1860	Willie Park	1896	Harry Vardon	1936	Alfred Padgham	1977	Tom Watson
1861	Tom Morris Sr.	1897	Harold H. Hilton	1937	Henry Cotton	1978	Jack Nicklaus
1862	Tom Morris Sr.	1898	Harry Vardon	1938	R.A. Whitcombe	1979	Seve Ballesteros
1863	Willie Park	1899	Harry Vardon	1939	Richard Burton	1980	Tom Watson
1864	Tom Morris Sr.	1900	John H. Taylor	1940	Not held	1981	Bill Rogers
1865	Andrew Strath	1901	James Braid	–45		1982	Tom Watson
1866	Willie Park	1902	Alexander Herd	1946	Sam Snead	1983	Tom Watson
1867	Tom Morris Sr.	1903	Harry Vardon	1947	Fred Daly	1984	Seve Ballesteros
1868	Tom Morris Jr.	1904	Jack White	1948	Henry Cotton	1985	Sandy Lyle
1869	Tom Morris Jr.	1905	James Braid	1949	Bobby Locke	1986	Greg Norman
1870	Tom Morris Jr.	1906	James Braid	1950	Bobby Locke	1987	Nick Faldo
1871	Not held	1907	Arnaud Massy	1951	Max Faulkner	1988	Seve Ballesteros
1872	Tom Morris Jr.	1908	James Braid	1952	Bobby Locke	1989	Mark Calcavecchia
1873	Tom Kidd	1909	John H. Taylor	1953	Ben Hogan	1990	Nick Faldo
1874	Mungo Park	1910	James Braid	1954	Peter Thomson	1991	Ian Baker-Finch
1875	Willie Park	1911	Harry Vardon	1955	Peter Thomson	1992	Nick Faldo
1876	Bob Martin	1912	Edward (Ted) Ray	1956	Peter Thomson	1993	Greg Norman
1877	Jamie Anderson	1913	John H. Taylor	1957	Bobby Locke	1994	Nick Price
1878	Jamie Anderson	1914	Harry Vardon	1958	Peter Thomson	1995	John Daly
1879	Jamie Anderson	1915	Not held	1959	Gary Player	1996	Tom Lehman
1880	Robert Ferguson	–19		1960	Kel Nagle	1997	Justin Leonard
1881	Robert Ferguson	1920	George Duncan	1961	Arnold Palmer	1998	Mark O'Meara
1882	Robert Ferguson	1921	Jock Hutchison	1962	Arnold Palmer	1999	Paul Lawrie
1883	Willie Fernie	1922	Walter Hagen	1963	Bob Charles	2000	Tiger Woods
1884	Jack Simpson	1923	Arthur G. Havers	1964	Tony Lema	2001	David Duval
1885	Bob Martin	1924	Walter Hagen	1965	Peter Thomson	2002	Ernie Els
1886	David Brown	1925	James M. Barnes	1966	Jack Nicklaus	2003	Ben Curtis
1887	Willie Park Jr.	1926	Robert T. Jones Jr.	1967	Roberto DeVicenzo	2004	Todd Hamilton
1888	Jack Burns	1927	Robert T. Jones Jr.	1968	Gary Player	2005	Tiger Woods
1889	Willie Park Jr.	1928	Walter Hagen	1969	Tony Jacklin	2006	Tiger Woods
1890	John Ball	1929	Walter Hagen	1970	Jack Nicklaus	2007	Padraig Harrington
1891	Hugh Kirkaldy	1930	Robert T. Jones Jr.	1971	Lee Trevino	2008	Padraig Harrington
1892	Harold H. Hilton[1]	1931	Tommy D. Armour	1972	Lee Trevino	2009	Stewart Cink
1893	William Auchterlonie	1932	Gene Sarazen	1973	Tom Weiskopf	2010	Louis Oosthuizen
1894	John H. Taylor	1933	Denny Shute	1974	Gary Player		
1895	John H. Taylor	1934	Henry Cotton	1975	Tom Watson		
		1935	Alfred Perry	1976	Johnny Miller		

Note: 1. Amateur.

PGA Championship, 1916–2010

Year	Winner	Year	Winner	Year	Winner	Year	Winner
1916	James M. Barnes	1940	Byron Nelson	1964	Bobby Nichols	1988	Jeff Sluman
1917	Not held	1941	Vic Ghezzi	1965	Dave Marr	1989	Payne Stewart
1918	Not held	1942	Sam Snead	1966	Al Geiberger	1990	Wayne Grady
1919	James M. Barnes	1943	Not held	1967	Don January	1991	John Daly
1920	Jock Hutchison	1944	Bob Hamilton	1968	Julius Boros	1992	Nick Price
1921	Walter Hagen	1945	Byron Nelson	1969	Ray Floyd	1993	Paul Azinger
1922	Gene Sarazen	1946	Ben Hogan	1970	Dave Stockton	1994	Nick Price
1923	Gene Sarazen	1947	Jim Ferrier	1971	Jack Nicklaus	1995	Steve Elkington
1924	Walter Hagen	1948	Ben Hogan	1972	Gary Player	1996	Mark Brooks
1925	Walter Hagen	1949	Sam Snead	1973	Jack Nicklaus	1997	Davis Love III
1926	Walter Hagen	1950	Chandler Harper	1974	Lee Trevino	1998	Vijay Singh
1927	Walter Hagen	1951	Sam Snead	1975	Jack Nicklaus	1999	Tiger Woods
1928	Leo Diegel	1952	Jim Turnesa	1976	Dave Stockton	2000	Tiger Woods
1929	Leo Diegel	1953	Walter Burkemo	1977	Lanny Wadkins	2001	David Toms
1930	Tommy Armour	1954	Chick Harbert	1978	John Mahaffey	2002	Rich Beem
1931	Tom Creavy	1955	Doug Ford	1979	David Graham	2003	Shaun Micheel
1932	Olin Dutra	1956	Jack Burke	1980	Jack Nicklaus	2004	Vijay Singh
1933	Gene Sarazen	1957	Lionel Hebert	1981	Larry Nelson	2005	Phil Mickelson
1934	Paul Runyan	1958	Dow Finsterwald	1982	Raymond Floyd	2006	Tiger Woods
1935	Johnny Revolta	1959	Bob Rosburg	1983	Hal Sutton	2007	Tiger Woods
1936	Denny Shute	1960	Jay Hebert	1984	Lee Trevino	2008	Padraig Harrington
1937	Denny Shute	1961	Jerry Barber	1985	Hubert Green	2009	Yang Yong-on
1938	Paul Runyan	1962	Gary Player	1986	Bob Tway	2010	Martin Kaymer
1939	Henry Picard	1963	Jack Nicklaus	1987	Larry Nelson		

PGA Leading Money Winners, 1934–2009

Year	Name	Winnings	Year	Name	Winnings	Year	Name	Winnings
1934	Paul Runyan	$ 6,767	1960	Arnold Palmer	$ 75,262	1985	Curtis Strange	$ 542,321
1935	Johnny Revolta	9,543	1961	Gary Player	64,540	1986	Greg Norman	653,296
1936	Horton Smith	7,682	1962	Arnold Palmer	81,448	1987	Curtis Strange	925,941
1937	Harry Cooper	14,138	1963	Arnold Palmer	128,230	1988	Curtis Strange	1,147,644
1938	Sam Snead	19,534	1964	Jack Nicklaus	113,284	1989	Tom Kite	1,395,278
1939	Henry Picard	10,303	1965	Jack Nicklaus	140,752	1990	Greg Norman	1,165,477
1940	Ben Hogan	10,655	1966	Billy Casper	121,944	1991	Corey Pavin	979,430
1941	Ben Hogan	18,358	1967	Jack Nicklaus	188,998	1992	Fred Couples	1,344,188
1942	Ben Hogan	13,143	1968	Billy Casper	205,168	1993	Nick Price	1,478,557
1943	No statistics compiled		1969	Frank Beard	164,707	1994	Nick Price	1,499,927
1944	Byron Nelson	37,967[1]	1970	Lee Trevino	157,037	1995	Greg Norman	1,654,959
1945	Byron Nelson	63,335[1]	1971	Jack Nicklaus	244,490	1996	Tom Lehman	1,780,159
1946	Ben Hogan	42,556	1972	Jack Nicklaus	320,542	1997	Tiger Woods	2,066,833
1947	Jimmy Demaret	27,936	1973	Jack Nicklaus	308,362	1998	David Duval	2,591,031
1948	Ben Hogan	32,112	1974	Johnny Miller	353,021	1999	Tiger Woods	6,616,585
1949	Sam Snead	31,593	1975	Jack Nicklaus	298,149	2000	Tiger Woods	9,188,321
1950	Sam Snead	35,758	1976	Jack Nicklaus	266,438	2001	Tiger Woods	5,687,777
1951	Lloyd Mangrum	26,088	1977	Tom Watson	310,653	2002	Tiger Woods	6,912,625
1952	Julius Boros	37,032	1978	Tom Watson	362,428	2003	Vijay Singh	7,573,907
1953	Lew Worsham	34,002	1979	Tom Watson	462,636	2004	Vijay Singh	10,905,166
1954	Bob Toski	65,819	1980	Tom Watson	530,808	2005	Tiger Woods	10,628,024
1955	Julius Boros	63,121	1981	Tom Kite	375,698	2006	Tiger Woods	9,941,563
1956	Ted Kroll	72,835	1982	Craig Stadler	446,462	2007	Tiger Woods	10,867,052
1957	Dick Mayer	65,835	1983	Hal Sutton	426,668	2008	Vijay Singh	6,601,094
1958	Arnold Palmer	42,607	1984	Tom Watson	476,260	2009	Tiger Woods	10,508,163
1959	Art Wall	53,167						

Note: 1. Paid in War Bonds. **Source:** Professional Golfers' Association. www.pgatour.com

PGA Leading Money Winners, 2009 and Career

2009			Career			Career	
Rank, Golfer		Earnings	Rank, Golfer		Earnings	Rank, Golfer	Earnings
1. Tiger Woods		10,508,163	1. Tiger Woods		$93,734,625	11. Mike Weir	$26,798,637
2. Steve Stricker		6,332,636	2. Vijay Singh		63,018,590	12. Steve Stricker	26,669,256
3. Phil Mickelson		5,332,755	3. Phil Mickelson		59,264,889	13. Sergio Garcia	26,548,368
4. Zach Johnson		4,583,213	4. Jim Furyk		46,065,213	14. Scott Verplank	26,145,071
5. Kenny Perry		4,445,562	5. Davis Love III		39,997,468	15. Stuart Appleby	25,661,485
6. Sean O'Hair		4,316,493	6. Ernie Els		39,908,319	16. Retief Goosen	25,255,858
7. Jim Furyk		3,946,515	7. David Toms		32,931,660	17. Mark Calcavecchia	23,988,554
8. Geoff Ogilvy		3,866,270	8. Kenny Perry		31,595,665	18. Robert Allenby	23,692,197
9. Lucas Glover		3,692,580	9. Justin Leonard		30,189,341	19. Geoff Ogilvy	21,766,690
10. Y.E. Yang		3,489,516	10. Stewart Cink		29,090,175	20. Fred Couples	21,716,857

Note: As of end of 2009 season. **Source:** Professional Golfers' Association. www.pga.com

LPGA Leading Money Winners, 1956–2009

Year	Player	Winnings	Year	Player	Winnings	Year	Player	Winnings
1956	Marlene Hagge	$20,235	1974	JoAnne Carner	$87,094	1992	Dottie Mochrie	$693,335
1957	Patty Berg	16,272	1975	Sandra Palmer	76,374	1993	Betsy King	595,992
1958	Beverly Hanson	12,629	1976	Judy T. Rankin	150,734	1994	Laura Davies	687,201
1959	Betsy Rawls	26,774	1977	Judy T. Rankin	122,890	1995	Annika Sorenstam	666,533
1960	Louise Suggs	16,892	1978	Nancy Lopez	189,813	1996	Karrie Webb	1,002,000
1961	Mickey Wright	22,238	1979	Nancy Lopez	197,488	1997	Annika Sorenstam	1,236,789
1962	Mickey Wright	21,654	1980	Beth Daniel	231,000	1998	Annika Sorenstam	1,092,748
1963	Mickey Wright	31,269	1981	Beth Daniel	206,977	1999	Karrie Webb	1,591,959
1964	Mickey Wright	29,800	1982	JoAnne Carner	310,399	2000	Karrie Webb	1,876,853
1965	Kathy Whitworth	28,658	1983	JoAnne Carner	291,404	2001	Annika Sorenstam	2,105,868
1966	Kathy Whitworth	33,517	1984	Betsy King	266,771	2002	Annika Sorenstam	2,863,904
1967	Kathy Whitworth	32,937	1985	Nancy Lopez	416,472	2003	Annika Sorenstam	2,029,506
1968	Kathy Whitworth	48,379	1986	Pat Bradley	492,021	2004	Annika Sorenstam	2,544,707
1969	Carol Mann	49,152	1987	Ayako Okamoto	466,034	2005	Annika Sorenstam	2,588,240
1970	Kathy Whitworth	30,235	1988	Sherri Turner	350,851	2006	Lorena Ochoa	2,592,872
1971	Kathy Whitworth	41,181	1989	Betsy King	654,132	2007	Lorena Ochoa	4,364,994
1972	Kathy Whitworth	65,063	1990	Beth Daniel	863,578	2008	Lorena Ochoa	2,763,193
1973	Kathy Whitworth	82,864	1991	Pat Bradley	763,118	2009	Jiyai Shin	1,807,334

Source: Ladies Professional Golfers' Association. www.lpga.com

LPGA Leading Money Winners, 2009 and Career

2009		Career		Career	
Rank, Golfer	**Earnings**	**Rank, Golfer**	**Earnings**	**Rank, Golfer**	**Earnings**
1. Jiyai Shin	$1,807,334	**1.** Annika Sorenstam	$22,573,192	**11.** Rosie Jones	8,355,068
2. Cristie Kerr	1,519,722	**2.** Karrie Webb	15,699,196	**12.** Paula Creamer	7,653,223
3. Ai Myazato	1,517,149	**3.** Lorena Ochoa	14,862,664	**13.** Betsy King	7,637,621
4. Lorena Ochoa	1,489,395	**4.** Juli Inkster	12,872,039	**14.** Dottie Popper	6,827,284
5. Suzann Pettersen	1,369,717	**5.** Cristie Kerr	11,669,257	**15.** Lorie Kane	6,738,916
6. Na Yeon Choi	1,341,078	**6.** Se Ri Pak	10,849,248	**16.** Pat Hurst	6,654,278
7. Yani Tseng	1,293,755	**7.** Meg Mallon	9,044,059	**17.** Suzann Pettersen	6,470,705
8. In-Kyung Kim	1,238,396	**8.** Beth Daniel	8,755,733	**18.** Jeong Jang	6,420,493
9. Paula Creamer	1,151,864	**9.** Laura Davies	8,699,748	**19.** Hee-Won Han	6,306,376
10. Angela Stanford	1,081,916	**10.** Mi Hyun Kim	8,442,354	**20.** Catriona Matthew	6,206,364

Note: As of end of 2009 season. **Source:** Ladies Professional Golfers' Association. www.lpga.com

U.S. Women's Grand Slam Champions, 1972–2010

Year	Kraft-Nabisco Championship	LPGA Championship	U.S. Women's Open	du Maurier Classic[1]
1972		Kathy Ahern	Susie Berning	
1973		Mary Mills	Susie Berning	
1974		Sandra Haynie	Sandra Haynie	
1975		Kathy Whitworth	Sandra Palmer	
1976		Betty Burfeindt	JoAnne Carner	
1977		Chako Higuchi	Hollis Stacy	
1978		Nancy Lopez	Hollis Stacy	
1979		Donna Caponi	Jerilyn Britz	Amy Alcott
1980		Sally Little	Amy Alcott	Pat Bradley
1981		Donna Caponi	Pat Bradley	Jan Stephenson
1982		Jan Stephenson	Janet Anderson	Sandra Haynie
1983	Amy Alcott	Patty Sheehan	Jan Stephenson	Hollis Stacy
1984	Juli Inkster	Patty Sheehan	Hollis Stacy	Juli Inkster
1985	Alice Miller	Nancy Lopez	Kathy Baker	Pat Bradley
1986	Pat Bradley	Pat Bradley	Jane Geddes	Pat Bradley
1987	Betsy King	Jane Geddes	Laura Davies	Jody Rosenthal
1988	Amy Alcott	Sherri Turner	Liselotte Neumann	Sally Little
1989	Juli Inkster	Nancy Lopez	Betsy King	Tammie Green
1990	Betsy King	Beth Daniel	Betsy King	Cathy Johnston
1991	Amy Alcott	Meg Mallon	Meg Mallon	Nancy Scranton
1992	Dottie Pepper	Betsy King	Patty Sheehan	Sherri Steinhauer
1993	Helen Alfredsson	Patty Sheehan	Lauri Merten	Brandie Burton
1994	Donna Andrews	Laura Davies	Patty Sheehan	Martha Nause
1995	Nanci Bowen	Kelly Robbins	Annika Sorenstam	Jenny Lidback
1996	Patty Sheehan	Laura Davies	Annika Sorenstam	Laura Davies
1997	Betsy King	Chris Johnson	Alison Nicholas	Colleen Walker
1998	Pat Hurst	Se Ri Pak	Se Ri Pak	Brandie Burton
1999	Dottie Pepper	Juli Inkster	Juli Inkster	Karrie Webb
2000	Karrie Webb	Juli Inkster	Karrie Webb	Meg Mallon
				Women's British Open[1]
2001	Annika Sorenstam	Karrie Webb	Karrie Webb	Se Ri Pak
2002	Annika Sorenstam	Se Ri Pak	Juli Inkster	Karrie Webb
2003	Patricia Meunier-Lebouc	Annika Sorenstam	Hilary Lunke	Annika Sorenstam
2004	Grace Park	Annika Sorenstam	Meg Mallon	Karen Stupples
2005	Annika Sorenstam	Annika Sorenstam	Birdie Kim	Jeong Jang
2006	Karrie Webb	Se Ri Pak	Annika Sorenstam	Sherri Steinhauer
2007	Morgan Pressel	Suzann Petterson	Cristie Kerr	Lorena Ochoa
2008	Lorena Ochoa	Yani Tseng	Inbee Park	Si-Yi Shin
2009	Brittany Lincicome	Anna Nordqvist	Eun Hee Ji	Catriona Matthew
2010	Yani Tseng	Cristie Kerr	Paula Creamer	Yani Tseng

Note: 1. The Women's British Open replaced the duMaurier Classic as the fourth major in 2001. **Source:** Ladies Professional Golfers' Association. www.lpga.com

U.S. Women's Open Champions, 1946–71

Year	Champion	Year	Champion	Year	Champion	Year	Champion
1946	Patty Berg	1953	Betsy Rawls	1960	Betsy Rawls	1966	Sandra Spuzich
1947	Betty Jameson	1954	Babe Zaharias	1961	Mickey Wright	1967	Catherine LaCoste
1948	Babe Zaharias	1955	Fay Crocker	1962	Murle Breer	1968	Susie Berning
1949	Louise Suggs	1956	Kathy Cornelius	1963	Mary Mills	1969	Donna Caponi
1950	Babe Zaharias	1957	Betsy Rawls	1964	Mickey Wright	1970	Donna Caponi
1951	Betsy Rawls	1958	Mickey Wright	1965	Carol Mann	1971	JoAnne Carner
1952	Louise Suggs	1959	Mickey Wright				

TENNIS

▶THE GRAND SLAM CHAMPIONSHIPS

The four tournaments that constitute the Grand Slam are the Australian, French, Wimbledon (officially known as the All-England Club's Lawn Tennis Championships), and U.S. championships. A challenge round system, in which the defending champion automatically qualified for the following year's final, was used at Wimbledon from 1877–1921 and at the U.S. Championships from 1884–1911. Prior to 1925, the French Open was restricted to members of French clubs, and from 1941–45, it was closed to all foreigners. Wimbledon, the French, and U.S. Championships became open to amateurs and pros in 1968; the Australian championships joined the open era a year later. Five players have achieved the Grand Slam, winning all four championships in the same year: Don Budge (1938), Maureen Connolly (with straight set victories in all four finals in 1953), Rod Laver (1962 and 1969), Margaret Court (1970) and Steffi Graf (1988). Martina Navratilova (1983–84) and Serena Williams (2002–03) have won the four tournaments consecutively, but not in the same calendar year.

Men's Grand Slam Champions, 1920–2010

Year	Australian Champion	French Champion	Wimbledon Champion	U.S. Champion
1920	Pat O'Hara Wood		Bill Tilden	Bill Tilden
1921	Rhys H. Gemmell		Bill Tilden	Bill Tilden
1922	Pat O'Hara Wood		Gerald L. Patterson	Bill Tilden
1923	Pat O'Hara Wood		William M. Johnston	Bill Tilden
1924	James Anderson		Jean Borotra	Bill Tilden
1925	James Anderson	Rene Lacoste	Rene Lacoste	Bill Tilden
1926	John Hawkes	Henri Cochet	Jean Borotra	Rene Lacoste
1927	Gerald Patterson	Rene Lacoste	Henri Cochet	Rene Lacoste
1928	Jean Borotra	Henri Cochet	Rene Lacoste	Henri Cochet
1929	John C. Gregory	Rene Lacoste	Henri Cochet	Bill Tilden
1930	Gar Moon	Henri Cochet	Bill Tilden	John H. Doeg
1931	Jack Crawford	Jean Borotra	Sidney B. Wood Jr.	H. Ellsworth Vines
1932	Jack Crawford	Henri Cochet	Ellsworth Vines	H. Ellsworth Vines
1933	Jack Crawford	John H. Crawford	Jack Crawford	Fred Perry
1934	Fred J. Perry	Gottfried von Cramm	Fred Perry	Fred Perry
1935	Jack Crawford	Fred J. Perry	Fred Perry	Wilmer L. Allison
1936	Adrian Quist	Gottfried von Cramm	Fred Perry	Fred Perry
1937	Vivian B. McGrath	Henner Henkel	Don Budge	Don Budge
1938[1]	Don Budge	Don Budge	Don Budge	Don Budge
1939	John Bromwich	W. Donald McNeill	Bobby Riggs	Bobby Riggs
1940	Adrian Quist	No competition	Not Held	Donald McNeill
1941	Foreigners excluded	Bernard Destremau	Not Held	Bobby Riggs
1942	Foreigners excluded	Bernard Destremau	Not Held	Frederick Schroeder
1943	Foreigners excluded	Yvon Petra	Not Held	Joseph R. Hunt
1944	Foreigners excluded	Yvon Petra	Not Held	Frank Parker
1945	Foreigners excluded	Yvon Petra	Not Held	Frank Parker
1946	John Bromwich	Marcel Bernard	Yvon Petra	Jack Kramer
1947	Dinny Pails	Joseph Asboth	Jack Kramer	Jack Kramer
1948	Adrian Quist	Frank Parker	Bob Falkenburg	Pancho Gonzales
1949	Frank Sedgman	Frank Parker	Ted Schroeder	Pancho Gonzales
1950	Frank Sedgman	Budge Patty	Budge Patty	Arthur Larsen
1951	Richard Savitt	Jaroslav Drobny	Dick Savitt	Frank Sedgman
1952	Ken McGregor	Jaroslav Drobny	Frank Sedgman	Frank Sedgman
1953	Ken Rosewall	Ken Rosewall	Vic Seixas	Tony Trabert
1954	Mervyn Rose	Tony Trabert	Jaroslav Drobny	E. Victor Seixas Jr.
1955	Ken Rosewall	Tony Trabert	Tony Trabert	Tony Trabert
1956	Lew Hoad	Lew Hoad	Lew Hoad	Ken Rosewall
1957	Ashley Cooper	Sven Davidson	Lew Hoad	Malcolm Anderson
1958	Ashley Cooper	Mervyn Rose	Ashley Cooper	Ashley J. Cooper
1959	Alex Olmedo	Nicola Pietrangeli	Alex Olmedo	Neale Fraser
1960	Rod Laver	Nicola Pietrangeli	Neale Fraser	Neale Fraser
1961	Roy Emerson	Manuel Santana	Rod Laver	Roy Emerson
1962[1]	Rod Laver	Rod Laver	Rod Laver	Rod Laver
1963	Roy Emerson	Roy Emerson	Chuck McKinley	Rafael Osuna
1964	Roy Emerson	Manuel Santana	Roy Emerson	Roy Emerson
1965	Roy Emerson	Fred Stolle	Roy Emerson	Manuel Santana
1966	Roy Emerson	Tony Roche	Manuel Santana	Fred Stolle
1967	Roy Emerson	Roy Emerson	John Newcombe	John Newcombe
1968	Bill Bowrey	Ken Rosewall	Rod Laver	Arthur Ashe
1969[1]	Rod Laver	Rod Laver	Rod Laver	Rod Laver
1970	Arthur Ashe	Jan Kodes	John Newcombe	Ken Rosewall
1971	Ken Rosewall	Jan Kodes	John Newcombe	Stan Smith

Year	Australian Champion	French Champion	Wimbledon Champion	U.S. Champion
1972	Ken Rosewall	Andres Gimeno	Stan Smith	Ilie Nastase
1973	John Newcombe	Ilie Nastase	Jan Kodes	John Newcombe
1974	Jimmy Connors	Bjorn Borg	Jimmy Connors	Jimmy Connors
1975	John Newcombe	Bjorn Borg	Arthur Ashe	Manuel Orantes
1976	Mark Edmondson	Adriano Panatta	Bjorn Borg	Jimmy Connors
1977	Roscoe Tanner[2] Vitas Gerulaitis[2]	Guillermo Vilas	Bjorn Borg	Guillermo Vilas
1978	Guillermo Vilas	Bjorn Borg	Bjorn Borg	Jimmy Connors
1979	Guillermo Vilas	Bjorn Borg	Bjorn Borg	John McEnroe
1980	Brian Teacher	Bjorn Borg	Bjorn Borg	John McEnroe
1981	Johan Kriek	Bjorn Borg	John McEnroe	John McEnroe
1982	Johan Kriek	Mats Wilander	Jimmy Connors	Jimmy Connors
1983	Mats Wilander	Yannick Noah	John McEnroe	Jimmy Connors
1984	Mats Wilander	Ivan Lendl	John McEnroe	John McEnroe
1985	Stefan Edberg	Mats Wilander	Boris Becker	Ivan Lendl
1986	Moved to Jan. 1987	Ivan Lendl	Boris Becker	Ivan Lendl
1987	Stefan Edberg	Ivan Lendl	Pat Cash	Ivan Lendl
1988	Mats Wilander	Mats Wilander	Stefan Edberg	Mats Wilander
1989	Ivan Lendl	Michael Chang	Boris Becker	Boris Becker
1990	Ivan Lendl	Andrés Gomez	Stefan Edberg	Pete Sampras
1991	Boris Becker	Jim Courier	Michael Stich	Stefan Edberg
1992	Jim Courier	Jim Courier	Andre Agassi	Stefan Edberg
1993	Jim Courier	Sergi Bruguera	Pete Sampras	Pete Sampras
1994	Pete Sampras	Sergi Bruguera	Pete Sampras	Andre Agassi
1995	Andre Agassi	Thomas Muster	Pete Sampras	Pete Sampras
1996	Boris Becker	Yevgeny Kafelnikov	Richard Krajicek	Pete Sampras
1997	Pete Sampras	Gustavo Kuerten	Pete Sampras	Patrick Rafter
1998	Petr Korda	Carlos Moya	Pete Sampras	Patrick Rafter
1999	Yevgeny Kafelnikov	Andre Agassi	Pete Sampras	Andre Agassi
2000	Andre Agassi	Gustavo Kuerten	Pete Sampras	Marat Safin
2001	Andre Agassi	Gustavo Kuerten	Goran Ivanisevic	Lleyton Hewitt
2002	Thomas Johansson	Albert Costa	Lleyton Hewitt	Pete Sampras
2003	Andre Agassi	Juan Carlos Ferrero	Roger Federer	Andy Roddick
2004	Roger Federer	Gaston Gaudio	Roger Federer	Roger Federer
2005	Marat Safin	Rafael Nadal	Roger Federer	Roger Federer
2006	Roger Federer	Rafael Nadal	Roger Federer	Roger Federer
2007	Roger Federer	Rafael Nadal	Roger Federer	Roger Federer
2008	Novak Djokovic	Rafael Nadal	Rafael Nadal	Roger Federer
2009	Rafael Nadal	Roger Federer	Roger Federer	Juan Martín del Potro
2010	Roger Federer	Rafael Nadal	Rafael Nadal	Rafael Nadal

Notes: 1. Grand Slam winner. 2. Two tournaments were held in 1977, the first in January, the second in December.

Women's Grand Slam Champions, 1920–2010

Year	Australian Champion	French Champion	Wimbledon Champion	U.S. Champion
1920	Not held	Suzanne Lenglen	Suzanne Lenglen	Molla Bjurstedt Mallory
1921	Not held	Suzanne Lenglen	Suzanne Lenglen	Molla Bjurstedt Mallory
1922	Margaret Molesworth	Suzanne Lenglen	Suzanne Lenglen	Molla Bjurstedt Mallory
1923	Margaret Molesworth	Suzanne Lenglen	Suzanne Lenglen	Helen Wills
1924	Sylvia Lance	Diddie Vlasto	Kathleen McKane	Helen Wills
1925	Daphne Akhurst	Suzanne Lenglen	Suzanne Lenglen	Helen Wills
1926	Daphne Akhurst	Suzanne Lenglen	Kathleen McKane Godfree	Molla Bjurstedt Mallory
1927	Edna Boyd	Kea Bouman	Helen Wills	Helen Wills
1928	Daphne Akhurst	Helen Wills	Helen Wills	Helen Wills
1929	Daphne Akhurst	Helen Wills	Helen Wills	Helen Wills
1930	Daphne Akhurst	Helen Wills Moody	Helen Wills Moody	Betty Nuthall
1931	Coral Buttsworth	Cilly Aussem	Cilly Aussem	Helen Wills Moody
1932	Coral Buttsworth	Helen Wills Moody	Helen Wills Moody	Helen Jacobs
1933	Joan Hartigan	Margaret Scriven	Helen Wills Moody	Helen Jacobs
1934	Joan Hartigan	Margaret Scriven	Dorothy Round	Helen Jacobs
1935	Dorothy Round	Hilde Sperling	Helen Wills Moody	Helen Jacobs
1936	Joan Hartigan	Hilde Sperling	Helen Jacobs	Alice Marble
1937	Nancye Wynne Bolton	Hilde Sperling	Dorothy Round	Anita Lizane
1938	Dorothy Bundy	Simone Mathieu	Helen Wills Moody	Alice Marble
1939	Emily Westacott	Simone Mathieu	Alice Marble	Alice Marble
1940	Nancye Wynne Bolton	Not Held	Not Held	Alice Marble
1941	Not Held	Not Held	Not Held	Sarah Palfrey Cooke
1942	Not Held	Not Held	Not Held	Pauline Betz
1943	Not Held	Not Held	Not Held	Pauline Betz
1944	Not Held	Not Held	Not Held	Pauline Betz Cooke

Year	Australian Champion	French Champion	Wimbledon Champion	U.S. Champion
1945	Not Held	Not Held	Not Held	Sarah Palfrey Cooke
1946	Nancye Wynne Bolton	Margaret Osborne	Pauline Betz	Pauline Betz
1947	Nancye Wynne Bolton	Patricia Todd	Margaret Osborne	Louise Brough
1948	Nancye Wynne Bolton	Nelly Landry	Louise Brough	Margaret Osborne duPont
1949	Doris Hart	Margaret Osborne duPont	Louise Brough	Margaret Osborne duPont
1950	Louise Brough	Doris Hart	Louise Brough	Margaret Osborne duPont
1951	Nancye Wynne Bolton	Shirley Fry	Doris Hart	Maureen Connolly
1952	Thelma Long	Doris Hart	Maureen Connolly	Maureen Connolly
1953[1]	Maureen Connolly	Maureen Connolly	Maureen Connolly	Maureen Connolly
1954	Thelma Long	Maureen Connolly	Maureen Connolly	Doris Hart
1955	Beryl Penrose	Angela Mortimer	Louise Brough	Doris Hart
1956	Mary Carter	Althea Gibson	Shirley Fry	Shirley Fry
1957	Shirley Fry	Shirley Bloomer	Althea Gibson	Althea Gibson
1958	Angela Mortimer	Zsuzsi Kormoczy	Althea Gibson	Althea Gibson
1959	Mary Carter Reitano	Christine Truman	Maria Bueno	Maria Bueno
1960	Margaret Smith	Darlene Hard	Maria Bueno	Darlene Hard
1961	Margaret Smith	Ann Haydon	Angela Mortimer	Darlene Hard
1962	Margaret Smith	Margaret Smith	Karen Hantze Susman	Margaret Smith
1963	Margaret Smith	Lesley Turner	Margaret Smith	Maria Bueno
1964	Margaret Smith	Margaret Smith	Maria Bueno	Maria Bueno
1965	Margaret Smith	Lesley Turner	Margaret Smith	Margaret Smith
1966	Margaret Smith	Ann Jones	Billie Jean King	Maria Bueno
1967	Nancy Richey	Francoise Durr	Billie Jean King	Billie Jean King
1968	Billie Jean King	Nancy Richey	Billie Jean King	Virginia Wade
1969	Margaret Smith Court	Margaret Smith Court	Ann Jones	Margaret Smith Court
1970[1]	Margaret Smith Court	Margaret Smith Court	Margaret Smith Court	Margaret Smith Court
1971	Margaret Smith Court	Evonne Goolagong	Evonne Goolagong	Billie Jean King
1972	Virginia Wade	Billie Jean King	Billie Jean King	Billie Jean King
1973	Margaret Smith Court	Margaret Smith Court	Billie Jean King	Margaret Smith Court
1974	Evonne Goolagong	Chris Evert	Chris Evert	Billie Jean King
1975	Evonne Goolagong	Chris Evert	Billie Jean King	Chris Evert
1976	Evonne Goolagong-Cawley	Sue Barker	Chris Evert	Chris Evert
1977[2]	Kerry Melville Reid[2] Evonne Goolagong Cawley	Mima Jasuovec	Virginia Wade	Chris Evert
1978	Chris O'Neil	Virginia Ruzici	Martina Navratilova	Chris Evert
1979	Barbara Jordan	Chris Evert Lloyd	Martina Navratilova	Tracy Austin
1980	Hana Mandlikova	Chris Evert Lloyd	Evonne Goolagong Cawley	Chris Evert Lloyd
1981	Martina Navratilova	Hana Mandlikova	Chris Evert Lloyd	Tracy Austin
1982	Chris Evert Lloyd	Martina Navratilova	Martina Navratilova	Chris Evert Lloyd
1983	Martina Navratilova	Chris Evert Lloyd	Martina Navratilova	Martina Navratilova
1984	Chris Evert Lloyd	Martina Navratilova	Martina Navratilova	Martina Navratilova
1985	Martina Navratilova	Chris Evert Lloyd	Martina Navratilova	Hana Mandlikova
1986	Moved to Jan. 1987	Chris Evert Lloyd	Martina Navratilova	Martina Navratilova
1987	Hana Mandlikova	Steffi Graf	Martina Navratilova	Martina Navratilova
1988[1]	Steffi Graf	Steffi Graf	Steffi Graf	Steffi Graf
1989	Steffi Graf	Arantxa Sanchez	Steffi Graf	Steffi Graf
1990	Steffi Graf	Monica Seles	Martina Navratilova	Gabriela Sabatini
1991	Monica Seles	Monica Seles	Steffi Graf	Monica Seles
1992	Monica Seles	Monica Seles	Steffi Graf	Monica Seles
1993	Monica Seles	Steffi Graf	Steffi Graf	Steffi Graf
1994	Steffi Graf	Arantxa Sánchez Vicario	Conchita Martinez	Arantxa Sánchez Vicario
1995	Mary Pierce	Steffi Graf	Steffi Graf	Steffi Graf
1996	Monica Seles	Steffi Graf	Steffi Graf	Steffi Graf
1997	Martina Hingis	Iva Majoli	Martina Hingis	Martina Hingis
1998	Martina Hingis	Arantxa Sánchez Vicario	Jana Novotna	Lindsay Davenport
1999	Martina Hingis	Steffi Graf	Lindsay Davenport	Serena Williams
2000	Lindsay Davenport	Mary Pierce	Venus Williams	Venus Williams
2001	Jennifer Capriati	Jennifer Capriati	Venus Williams	Venus Williams
2002	Jennifer Capriati	Serena Williams	Serena Williams	Serena Williams
2003	Serena Williams	Justine Henin-Hardenne	Serena Williams	Justine Henin-Hardenne
2004	Justine Henin-Hardenne	Anastasia Myskina	Maria Sharapova	Svetlana Kuznetsova
2005	Serena Williams	Justine Henin-Hardenne	Venus Williams	Kim Clijsters
2006	Amelie Mauresmo	Justine Henin-Hardenne	Amelie Mauresmo	Maria Sharapova
2007	Serena Williams	Justine Henin	Venus Williams	Justine Henin
2008	Maria Sharapova	Ana Ivanovic	Venus Williams	Serena Williams
2009	Serena Williams	Svetlana Kuznetsova	Serena Williams	Kim Clijsters
2010	Serena Williams	Francesca Schiavone	Serena Williams	Kim Clijsters

Notes: 1. Grand Slam winner. 2. Two tournaments were held in 1977, the first in January, the second in December.

THOROUGHBRED RACING

Thoroughbred Horse of the Year (Eclipse Award)

Year	Horse	Year	Horse	Year	Horse	Year	Horse
1936	Granville	1955	Nashua	1974	Forego	1993	Kotashaan
1937	War Admiral	1956	Swaps	1975	Forego	1994	Holy Bull
1938	Seabiscuit	1957	Bold Ruler	1976	Forego	1995	Cigar
1939	Challedon	1958	Round Table	1977	Seattle Slew	1996	Cigar
1940	Challedon	1959	Sword Dancer	1978	Affirmed	1997	Favorite Trick
1941	Whirlaway	1960	Kelso	1979	Affirmed	1998	Skip Away
1942	Whirlaway	1961	Kelso	1980	Spectacular Bid	1999	Charismatic
1943	Count Fleet	1962	Kelso	1981	John Henry	2000	Tiznow
1944	Twilight Tear	1963	Kelso	1982	Conquistador Cielo	2001	Point Given
1945	Busher	1964	Kelso	1983	All Along	2002	Azeri
1946	Assault	1965	Moccasin	1984	John Henry	2003	Mineshaft
1947	Armed	1966	Buckpasser	1985	Spend a Buck	2004	Ghostzapper
1948	Citation	1967	Damascus	1986	Lady's Secret	2005	Saint Liam
1949	Capot	1968	Dr. Fager	1987	Ferdinand	2006	Invasor
1950	Hill Prince	1969	Arts and Letters	1988	Alysheba	2007	Curlin
1951	Counterpoint	1970	Personality	1989	Sunday Silence	2008	Curlin
1952	Native Dancer	1971	Ack Ack	1990	Criminal Type	2009	Rachel Alexandra
1953	Tom Fool	1972	Secretariat	1991	Black Tie Affair		
1954	Native Dancer	1973	Secretariat	1992	A.P. Indy		

Source: The Jockey Club

The Triple Crown Winners

Only 11 horses have won the Kentucky Derby, the Preakness, and the Belmont Stakes in the same year.

Year	Horse	Year	Horse	Year	Horse	Year	Horse
1919	Sir Barton	1937	War Admiral	1946	Assault	1977	Seattle Slew
1930	Gallant Fox	1941	Whirlaway	1948	Citation	1978	Affirmed
1935	Omaha	1943	Count Fleet	1973	Secretariat		

The Breeders' Cup

Thoroughbred racing's richest, most glamorous, and most exciting day of the year attracts the finest horses in the world for record purses as high as $5 million. The site changes from year to year.

Year	Winner	Jockey	Time	Year	Winner	Jockey	Time
Juvenile ($1.5 million, 1¹⁄₁₆ miles)				1985¹	Twilight Ridge	J. Velasquez	1:35.4
1984¹	Chief's Crown	D. MacBeth	1:36.1	1986	Brave Raj	P. Valenzuela	1:43.1
1985¹	Tasso	L. Pincay Jr.	1:36.1	1987¹	Epitome	P. Day	1:36.2
1986	Capote	L. Pincay Jr.	1:43.4	1988	Open Mind	A. Cordero Jr.	1:46.3
1987¹	Success Express	J. Santos	1:35.1	1989	Go for Wand	R. Romero	1:44.1
1988¹	Is It True	L. Pincay Jr.	1:36.3	1990	Meadow Star	J. Santos	1:44.0
1989	Rhythm	C. Perret	1:43.3	1991	Pleasant Stage	E. Delahoussaye	1:46.48
1990	Fly So Free	J. Santos	1:43.2	1992	Eliza	P. Valenzuela	1:42.93
1991	Arazi	P. Valenzuela	1:44.78	1993	Phone Chatter	L. Pincay Jr.	1:43.08
1992	Gilded Time	C. McCarron	1:43.43	1994	Flanders	P. Day	1:45.28
1993	Brocco	G. Stevens	1:42.99	1995	My Flag	J. Bailey	1:42.55
1994	Timber Country	P. Day	1:44.55	1996	Storm Song	C. Perret	1:43.60
1995	Unbridled's Song	M. Smith	1:41.60	1997	Countess Diana	S. Sellers	1:42.11
1996	Boston Harbor	J. Bailey	1:43.40	1998	Silverbulletday	G. Stevens	1:43.68
1997	Favorite Trick	P. Day	1:41.47	1999	Cash Run	J. Bailey	1:36.32
1998	Answer Lively	J. Bailey	1:44.00	2000	Caressing	J. Velasquez	1:42.77
1999	Anees	G. Stevens	1:42.29	2001	Tempera	D. Flores	1:41.49
2000	Macho Uno	J. Bailey	1:42.05	2002	Storm Flag Flying	J. Velasquez	1:49.60
2001	Johannesburg	M. Kinane	1:42.27	2003	Halfbridled	J. Krone	1:42.75
2002	Vindication	M. Smith	1:49.61	2004	Sweet Catomine	C. Nakatani	1:41.65
2003	Action This Day	D. Flores	1:43.62	2005	Stevie Wonderboy	G. Gomez	1:41.64
2004	Wilko	F. Dettori	1:42.09	2006	Dreaming of Anna	R. Douglas	1:43.81
2005	Folklore	E. Prado	1:43.85	2007	Indian Blessing	G. Gomez	1:44.73
2006	Street Sense	C. Borel	1:42.59	2008	Stardom Bound	M. Smith	1:40.99
2007	War Pass	C. Velasquez	1:42.76	2009	She Be Wild	J. Leparoux	1:43:80
2008	Midshipman	G. Gomez	1:40.94	**Sprint ($2 million, 6 furlongs)**			
2009	Vale of York	A. Ajtebi	1:43:48	1984	Eillo	C. Perret	1:10.1
Juvenile Fillies ($2 million, 1¹⁄₁₆ miles)				1985	Precisionist	C. McCarron	1:08.2
1984¹	Outstandingly	W. Guerra	1:37.4	1986	Smile	J. Vasquez	1:08.2

Year	Winner	Jockey	Time
1987	Very Subtle	P. Valenzuela	1:08.4
1988	Gulch	A. Cordero Jr.	1:10.2
1989	Dancing Spree	A. Cordero Jr.	1:09.0
1990	Safely Kept	C. Perret	1:09.3
1991	Sheik Albadou	P. Eddery	1:09.36
1992	30 Slews	E. Delahoussaye	1:08.21
1993	Cardmania	E. Delahoussaye	1:08.76
1994	Cherokee Run	M. Smith	1:09.54
1995	Desert Stormer	K. Desormeaux	1:09.14
1996	Lit de Justice	C. Nakatani	1:08.60
1997	Elmhurst	C. Nakatani	1:08.01
1998	Reraise	C. Nakatani	1:09.07
1999	Artax	J. Chavez	1:07.89
2000	Kona Gold	A. Solis	1:07.77
2001	Squirtle Squirt	J. Bailey	1:08.41
2002	Orientate	J. Bailey	1:08.89
2003	Cajun Beat	C. Velasquez	1:07.95
2004	Speightstown	J. Velasquez	1:09.11
2005	Silver Train	E. Prado	1:08.86
2006	Thor's Echo	C. Nakatani	1:08.80
2007	Midnight Lute	G. Gomez	1:09.18
2008	Midnight Lute	G. Gomez	1:07.08
2009	Dancing in Silks	J. Rosario	1:08.14

Mile ($2 million, 1 mile, turf)

Year	Winner	Jockey	Time
1984	Royal Heroine	F. Toro	1:32.3
1985	Cozzene	W. Guerra	1:35.0
1986	Last Tycoon	Y. Saint-Martin	1:35.1
1987	Miesque	F. Head	1:32.4
1988	Miesque	F. Head	1:38.3
1989	Steinlen	J. Santos	1:37.1
1990	Royal Academy	L. Piggott	1:35.1
1991	Opening Verse	P. Valenzuela	1:37.59
1992	Lure	M. Smith	1:32.90
1993	Lure	M. Smith	1:33.58
1994	Barathea	L. Dettori	1:34.50
1995	Ridgewood Pearl	J. Murtagh	1:43.65
1996	Da Hoss	G. Stevens	1:35.80
1997	Spinning World	C. Asmussen	1:32.77
1998	Da Hoss	J. Velazquez	1:35.27
1999	Silic	C. Nakatani	1:34.26
2000	War Chant	G. Stevens	1:34.67
2001	Val Royal	J. Valdivia Jr.	1:32.05
2002	Domedriver	T. Thulliez	1:36.92
2003	Six Perfections	J. Bailey	1:33.86
2004	Singletary	D. Flores	1:36.90
2005	Artie Schiller	G. Gomez	1:36.10
2006	Miesque's Approval	E. Castro	1:34.75
2007	Kip Deville	C. Velasquez	1:39.78
2008	Goldikova	O. Peslier	1:33.40
2009	Goldikova	O. Peslier	1:32.26

Ladies Classic ($2 million, 1⅛ miles)

Year	Winner	Jockey	Time
1984[2]	Princess Rooney	E. Delahoussaye	2:02.2
1985[2]	Life's Magic	A. Cordero Jr.	2:02.0
1986[2]	Lady's Secret	P. Day	2:01.1
1987[2]	Sacahuista	R. Romero	2:02.4
1988	Personal Ensign	R. Romero	1:52.0
1989	Bayakoa	L. Pincay Jr.	1:47.2
1990	Bayakoa	L. Pincay Jr.	1:49.1
1991	Dance Smartly	P. Day	1:50.95
1992	Paseana	C. McCarron	1:48.17
1993	Hollywood Wildcat	E. Delahoussaye	1:48.35
1994	One Dreamer	G. Stevens	1:50.70
1995	Inside Information	M. Smith	1:46.15
1996	Jewel Princess	C. Nakatani	1:48.40
1997	Ajina	M. Smith	1:47.20
1998	Escena	G. Stevens	1:49.89
1999	Beautiful Pleasure	J. Chavez	1:47.56
2000	Spain	V. Espinoza	1:47.66
2001	Unbridled Elaine	P. Day	1:49.21
2002	Azeri	M. Smith	1:48.64
2003	Adoration	P. Valenzuela	1:49.17
2004	Ashado	J. Velasquez	1:48.26
2005	Pleasant Home	J. Velasquez	1:48.34
2006	Round Pond	E. Prado	1:50.50
2007	Ginger Punch	R. Bejarano	1:50.11
2008	Zenyatta	M. Smith	1:46.85
2009	Life is Sweet	G. Gomez	1:48.58

Turf ($3 milion, 1½ miles)

Year	Winner	Jockey	Time
1984	Lashkari	Y. Saint-Martin	2:25.1
1985	Pebbles	P. Eddery	2:27.0
1986	Manila	J. Santos	2:25.2
1987	Theatrical	P. Day	2:24.2
1988	Great Communicator	R. Sibille	2:35.1
1989	Prized	E. Delahoussaye	2:28.0
1990	In the Wings	G. Stevens	2:29.3
1991	Miss Alleged	E. Legrix	2:30.95
1992	Fraise	P. Valenzuela	2:24.08
1993	Kotashaan	K. Desormeaux	2:25.16
1994	Tikkanen	M. Smith	2:26.50
1995	Northern Spur	C. McCarron	2:42.07
1996	Pilsudski	W. Swinburn	2:30.20
1997	Chief Bearhart	J. Santos	2:23.92
1998	Buck's Boy	S. Sellers	2:28.74
1999	Daylami	L. Dettori	2:24.73
2000	Kalanisi	J. Murtagh	2:26.96
2001	Fantastic Light	L. Dettori	2:24.36
2002	High Chaparral	M. Kinane	2:30.14
2003	High Chaparral	M. Kinane	2:24.24
	Johar	A Solis	dead heat
2004	Better Talk Now	R. Dominguez	2:29.70
2005	Shirocco	C. Soumillon	2:29.30
2006	Red Rocks	F. Dettori	2:27.32
2007	English Channel	J. Velasquez	2:35.96
2008	Conduit	R. Moore	2:23.42
2009	Conduit	R. Moore	2:23.75

Classic ($5 million, 1¼ miles)

Year	Winner	Jockey	Time
1984	Wild Again	P. Day	2:03.2
1985	Proud Truth	J. Velasquez	2:00.4
1986	Skywalker	L. Pincay Jr.	2:00.2
1987	Ferdinand	B. Shoemaker	2:01.2
1988	Alysheba	C. McCarron	2:04.4
1989	Sunday Silence	C. McCarron	2:00.1
1990	Unbridled	P. Day	2:02.1
1991	Black Tie Affair	J. Bailey	2:02.95
1992	A.P. Indy	E. Delahoussaye	2:00.20
1993	Arcangues	J. Bailey	2:00.83
1994	Concern	P. Day	2:02.41
1995	Cigar	J. Bailey	1:59.58
1996	Alphabet Soup	C. McCarron	2:01.00
1997	Skip Away	M. Smith	1:59.16
1998	Awesome Again	P. Day	2:02.16
1999	Cat Thief	P. Day	1:59.52
2000	Tiznow	C. McCarron	2:00.75
2001	Tiznow	C. McCarron	2:00.62
2002	Volponi	J. Santos	2:01.39
2003	Pleasantly Perfect	A. Solis	1:59.88
2004	Ghostzapper	J. Castellano	1:59.02
2005	Saint Liam	J. Bailey	2:01.49
2006	Invasor	F. Jara	2:02.18
2007	Curlin	R. Albarado	2:00.59
2008	Raven's Pass	F. Dettori	1:59.27
2009	Zenyatta	M. Smith	2:00.62

Fillies and Mares Turf ($2 million, 1¼ miles)

Year	Winner	Jockey	Time
1999	Soaring Softly	J. Bailey	2:13.89
2000	Perfect Sting	J. Bailey	2:13.07
2001	Banks Hill	O. Peslier	2:00.36
2002	Starine	J. Velasquez	2:03.57
2003	Islington	K. Fallon	1:59.13
2004	Ouija Board	K. Fallon	2:18.25
2005	Intercontinental	R. Bejarano	2:02.34
2006	Ouija Board	L. Dettori	2:14.55
2007	Lahudood	A. Garcia	2:22.75
2008	Forever Together	J. Leparoux	2:01.58
2009	Midday	T. Queally	1:59.14

BREEDERS' CUP LOCATIONS

Year	Location	Year	Location
1984	Hollywood	1998	Churchill Downs
1985	Aqueduct	1999	Gulfstream
1986	Santa Anita	2000	Churchill Downs
1987	Hollywood	2001	Belmont Park
1988	Churchill Downs	2002	Arlington Park
1989	Gulfstream	2003	Santa Anita
1990	Belmont Park	2004	Lone Star Park
1991	Churchill Downs	2005	Belmont Park
1992	Gulfstream	2006	Churchill Downs
1993	Santa Anita	2007	Monmouth Park
1994	Churchill Downs	2008	Santa Anita
1995	Belmont Park	2009	Santa Anita
1996	Woodbine	2010	Churchill Downs
1997	Hollywood		

Note: Before 1991, decimals refer to fifths of a second. 1. One mile. 2. 1¼ miles.

Kentucky Derby, 1875–2010

"The Run for the Roses," is the first leg of racing's Triple Crown for three-year-olds. It is always on the first Saturday in May. The distance was 1½ miles until 1896, 1¼ miles thereafter. **Site: Churchill Downs**, Louisville.

Year	Horse	Jockey	Time	Year	Horse	Jockey	Time
1875	Aristides	O. Lewis	2:37¾	1943	**Count Fleet**	J. Longden	2:04.0
1876	Vagrant	R. Swim	2:38¼	1944	Pensive	C. McCreary	2:04.1
1877	Baden-Baden	W. Walker	2:38.0	1945	Hoop Jr.	E. Arcaro	2:07.0
1878	Day Star	J. Carter	2:37¼	1946	Assault	W. Mehrtens	2:06.3
1879	Lord Murphy	C. Shauer	2:37.0	1947	Jet Pilot	E. Guerin	2:06.3
1880	Fonso	G. Lewis	2:37½	1948	**Citation**	E. Arcaro	2:05.2
1881	Hindoo	J. McLaughlin	2:40.0	1949	Ponder	S. Brooks	2:04.1
1882	Apollo	B. Hurd	2:40¼	1950	Middleground	W. Boland	2:01.3
1883	Leonatus	W. Donohue	2:43.0	1951	Count Turf	C. McCreary	2:02.3
1884	Buchanan	I. Murphy	2:40¼	1952	Hill Gail	E. Arcaro	2:01.3
1885	Joe Cotton	E. Henderson	2:37¼	1953	Dark Star	H. Moreno	2:02.0
1886	Ben Ali	P. Duffy	2:36½	1954	Determine	R. York	2:03.0
1887	Montrose	I. Lewis	2:39¼	1955	Swaps	W. Shoemaker	2:01.4
1888	MacBeth II	G. Covington	2:38¼	1956	Needles	D. Erb	2:03.2
1889	Spokane	T. Kiley	2:34½	1957	Iron Liege	W. Hartack	2:02.1
1890	Riley	I. Murphy	2:45.0	1958	Tim Tam	I. Valenzuela	2:05.0
1891	Kingman	I. Murphy	2:52¼	1959	Tommy Lee	W. Shoemaker	2:02.1
1892	Azra	A. Clayton	2:41½	1960	Venetian Way	W. Hartack	2:02.2
1893	Lookout	E. Kunze	2:39¼	1961	Carry Back	J. Sellers	2:04.0
1894	Chant	F. Goodale	2:41.0	1962	Decidedly	W. Hartack	2:00.2
1895	Halma	J. Perkins	2:37½	1963	Chateaugay	B. Baeza	2:01.4
1896	Ben Brush	W. Simms	2:07¾	1964	Northern Dancer	W. Hartack	2:00.0
1897	Typhoon II	F. Garner	2:12½	1965	Lucky Debonair	W. Shoemaker	2:01.1
1898	Plaudit	W. Simms	2:09.0	1966	Kauai King	D. Brumfield	2:02.0
1899	Manuel	F. Taral	2:12.0	1967	Proud Clarion	R. Ussery	2:00.3
1900	Lieut.Gibson	J. Boland	2:06¼	1968	Forward Pass[1]	R. Ussery	2:02.1
1900	Lieut. Gibson	J. Boland	2:06¼	1969	Majestic Prince	W. Hartack	2:01.4
1901	His Eminence	J. Winkfield	2:07¾	1970	Dust Commander	M. Manganello	2:03.2
1902	Alan-a-Dale	J. Winkfield	2:08¼	1971	Canonero II	G. Avila	2:03.1
1903	Judge Himes	H. Booker	2:09.0	1972	Riva Ridge	R. Turcotte	2:01.4
1904	Elwood	F. Prior	2:08½	1973	**Secretariat**[2]	R. Turcotte	1:59.2
1905	Agile	J. Martin	2:10¾	1974	Cannonade	A. Cordero	2:04.0
1906	Sir Huon	R. Troxler	2:08.4	1975	Foolish Pleasure	J. Vasquez	2:02.0
1907	Pink Star	A. Minder	2:12.3	1976	Bold Forbes	A. Cordero	2:01.3
1908	Stone Street	A. Pickens	2:15.1	1977	Seattle Slew	J. Cruguet	2:02.1
1909	Wintergreen	V. Powers	2:08.1	1978	**Affirmed**	S. Cauthen	2:01.1
1910	Donau	F. Herbert	2:06.2	1979	Spectacular Bid	R. Franklin	2:02.2
1911	Meridan	G. Archibald	2:05.0	1980	Genuine Risk	J. Vasquez	2:02.0
1912	Worth	C. H. Shilling	2:09.2	1981	Pleasant Colony	J. Velasquez	2:02.0
1913	Donerall	R. Goose	2:04.4	1982	Gato Del Sol	E. Delahoussaye	2:02.2
1914	Old Rosebud	J. McCabe	2:03.2	1983	Sunny's Halo	E. Delahoussaye	2:02.1
1915	Regret	J. Notter	2:05.2	1984	Swale	L. Pincay	2:02.2
1916	George Smith	J. Loftus	2:04.3	1985	Spend A Buck	A. Cordero	2:00.1
1917	Omar Khayyam	C. Borel	2:04.0	1986	Ferdinand	W. Shoemaker	2:02.4
1918	Exterminator	W. Knapp	2:10.4	1987	Alysheba	C. McCarron	2:03.2
1919	**Sir Barton**	J. Loftus	2:09.4	1988	Winning Colors	G. Stevens	2:02.2
1920	Paul Jones	T. Rice	2:09.0	1989	Sunday Silence	P. Valenzuela	2:05.0
1921	Behave Yourself	C. Thompson	2:04.1	1990	Unbridled	C. Perret	2:02.0
1922	Morvich	A. Johnson	2:04.3	1991	Strike the Gold	C. Antley	2:03.0
1923	Zev	E. Sande	2:05.2	1992	Lil E. Tee	P.Day	2:03.0
1924	Black Gold	J. D. Mooney	2:05.1	1993	Sea Hero	J. Bailey	2:02.42
1925	Flying Ebony	E. Sande	2:07.3	1994	Go for Gin	C. McCarron	2:03.72
1926	Bubbling Over	A. Johnson	2:03.4	1995	Thunder Gulch	G. Stevens	2:01.27
1927	Whiskery	L. McAtee	2:06.0	1996	Grindstone	J. Bailey	2:01.60
1928	Reigh Count	C. Lang	2:10.2	1997	Silver Charm	G. Stevens	2:02.44
1929	Clyde Van Dusen	L. McAtee	2:10.4	1998	Real Quiet	K. Desormeaux	2:02.38
1930	**Gallant Fox**	E. Sande	2:07.3	1999	Charismatic	C. Antley	2:03.29
1931	Twenty Grand	C. Kurtsinger	2:01.4	2000	Fusaichi Pegasus	K. Desormeaux	2:01.12
1932	Burgoo King	E. James	2:05.1	2001	Monarchos	J. Chavez	1:59.97
1933	Brokers Tip	D. Meade	2:06.4	2002	War Emblem	V. Espinoza	2:01.13
1934	Cavalcade	M. Garner	2:04.0	2003	Funny Cide	J. Santos	2:01.19
1935	**Omaha**	W. Saunders	2:05.0	2004	Smarty Jones	S. Elliott	2:04.06
1936	Bold Venture	I. Hanford	2:03.3	2005	Giacomo	M. Smith	2:02.75
1937	**War Admiral**	C. Kurtsinger	2:03.1	2006	Barbaro	E. Prado	2:01.36
1938	Lawrin	E. Arcaro	2:04.4	2007	Street Sense	C. Borel	2:02.17
1939	Johnston	J. Stout	2:03.2	2008	Big Brown	K. Desormeaux	2:01.82
1940	Gallahadion	C. Bierman	2:05.0	2009	Mine That Bird	C. Borel	2:02.66
1941	**Whirlaway**	E. Arcaro	2:01.2	2010	Super Saver	C. Borel	2:04:45
1942	Shut Out	W. D. Write	2:04.2				

Note: Names in **bold** indicate Triple Crown winners. Before 1993, decimals refer to fifths of a second. 1. In 1968, Dancer's Image finished first, but was later disqualified from the purse money, and Forward Pass was declared winner. 2. Record. **Source:** *Daily Racing Form*.

Preakness Stakes Winners 1873–2010

The Preakness was first run in 1873. The distance varied from 1 mile 70 yards to 1½ miles until 1925, when it was standardized at 1³⁄₁₆ miles. The race was not held 1891-93 **Site: Pimlico Racetrack,** Baltimore, Maryland.

Year	Horse	Jockey	Time
1873	Survivor	G. Barbee	2:43.0
1874	Culpepper	Donohue	2:56½
1875	Tom Ochiltree	L. Hughes	2:43½
1876	Shirley	Barbee	2:44¾
1877	Cloverbrook	Holloway	2:45½
1878	Duke of Magenta	Holloway	2:41¾
1879	Harold	Hughes	2:40½
1880	Grenada	L. Hughes	2:40½
1881	Saunterer	Costello	2:40½
1882	Vanguard	Costello	2:44½
1883	Jacobus	Barbee	2:42½
1884	Knight of Ellerslie	Fisher	2:39½
1885	Tecumseh	M. McLaughlin	2:49.0
1886	The Bard	Fisher	2:45.0
1887	Dunboyne	W. Donohue	2:39½
1888	Refund	Littlefield	2:49.0
1889	Buddhist	Anderson	2:17½
1890	Montague	W. Martin	2:36¾
1894	Assignee	F. Taral	1:49¼
1895	Belmar	F. Taral	1:50½
1896	Margrave	H. Griffin	1:51.0
1897	Paul Kauver	Thorpe	1:51¼
1898	Sly Fox	W. Simms	1:49¾
1899	Half Time	R. Clawson	1:47.0
1900	Hindus	H. Spencer	1:48.2
1901	The Parader	F. Landry	1:47.1
1902	Old England	L. Jackson	1:45.4
1903	Flocarline	W. Gannon	1:44.4
1904	Bryn Mawr	E. Hildebrand	1:44.1
1905	Cairngorm	W. Davis	1:45.4
1906	Whimsical	W. Miller	1:45.0
1907	Don Enrique	G. Mountain	1:45.2
1908	Royal Tourist	E. Dugan	1:46.2
1909	Effendi	W. Doyle	1:39.4
1910	Layminister	R. Estep	1:40.3
1911	Watervale	E. Dugan	1:51.0
1912	Colonel Holloway	C. Turner	1:56.3
1913	Buskin	J. Butwell	1:53.2
1914	Holiday	A. Schuttinger	1:53.4
1915	Rhine Maiden	D. Hoffman	1:58.0
1916	Damrosch	L. McAtee	1:54.4
1917	Kalitan	E. Haynes	1:54.2
1918	Jack Hare Jr.	C. Peak	1:53.2
	War Cloud	J. Loftus	1:53.3
1919	**Sir Barton**	J. Loftus	1:53.0
1920	Man o'War	C. Kummer	1:51.3
1921	Broomspun	F. Coltiletti	1:54.1
1922	Pillory	L. Morris	1:51.3
1923	Vigil	B. Marinelli	1:53.3
1924	Nellie Morse	J. Merimee	1:57.1
1925	Coventry	C. Kummer	1:59.0
1926	Display	J. Maiben	1:59.4
1927	Bostonian	A. Abel	2:01.3
1928	Victorian	R. Workman	2:00.1
1929	Dr. Freeland	L. Schaefer	2:01.3
1930	**Gallant Fox**	E. Sande	2:00.3
1931	Mate	G. Ellis	1:59.0
1932	Burgoo King	E. James	1:59.4
1933	Head Play	C. Kurtsinger	2:02.0
1934	High Quest	R. Jones	1:58.1
1935	**Omaha**	W. Saunders	1:58.2
1936	Bold Venture	G. Woolf	1:59.0
1937	**War Admiral**	C. Kurtsinger	1:58.2
1938	Dauber	M. Peters	1:59.4
1939	Challedon	G. Seabo	1:59.4
1940	Bimelech	F. A. Smith	1:58.3
1941	**Whirlaway**	E. Arcaro	1:58.4
1942	Alsab	B. James	1:57.0
1943	**Count Fleet**	J. Longden	1:57.2
1944	Pensive	C. McCreary	1:59.1
1945	Polynesian	W. D. Wright	1:58.4
1946	**Assault**	W. Mehrtens	2:01.2
1947	Faultless	D. Dodson	1:59.0
1948	**Citation**	E. Arcaro	2:02.2
1949	Capot	T. Atkinson	1:56.0
1950	Hill Prince	E. Arcaro	1:59.1
1951	Bold	E. Arcaro	1:56.2
1952	Blue Man	C. McCreary	1:57.2
1953	Native Dancer	E. Guerin	1:57.4
1954	Hasty Road	J. Adams	1:57.2
1955	Nashua	E. Arcaro	1:54.3
1956	Fabius	W. Hartack	1:58.2
1957	Bold Ruler	E. Arcaro	1:56.1
1958	Tim Tam	I. Valenzuela	1:57.1
1959	Royal Orbit	W. Harmatz	1:57.0
1960	Bally Ache	R. Ussery	1:57.3
1961	Carry Back	J. Sellers	1:57.3
1962	Greek Money	J. L. Rotz	1:56.1
1963	Candy Spots	W. Shoemaker	1:56.1
1964	Northern Dancer	W. Hartack	1:56.4
1965	Tom Rolfe	R. Turcotte	1:56.1
1966	Kauai King	D. Brumfield	1:55.2
1967	Damascus	W. Shoemaker	1:55.1
1968	Forward Pass	I. Valenzuela	1:56.4
1969	Majestic Prince	W. Hartack	1:55.3
1970	Personality	E. Belmonte	1:56.1
1971	Canonero II	G. Avila	1:54.0
1972	Bee Bee Bee	E. Nelson	1:55.3
1973	**Secretariat**	R. Turcotte	1:54.2
1974	Little Current	M. Rivera	1:54.3
1975	Master Derby	D. McHargue	1:56.2
1976	Elocutionist	J. Lively	1:55.0
1977	**Seattle Slew**	J. Cruguet	1:54.2
1978	**Affirmed**	S. Cauthen	1:54.2
1979	Spectacular Bid	R. Franklin	1:54.1
1980	Codex	A. Cordero	1:54.1
1981	Pleasant Colony	J. Valasquez	1:54.3
1982	Aloma's Ruler	J. Kaenel	1:55.2
1983	Deputed Testamony	D. Miller	1:55.2
1984	Gate Dancer	A. Cordero	1:53.3
1985	Tank's Prospect	P. Day	1:53.2
1986	Snow Chief	A. Solis	1:54.4
1987	Alysheba	C. McCarron	1:55.4
1988	Risen Star	E. Delahoussaye	1:56.1
1989	Sunday Silence	P. Valenzuela	1:53.4
1990	Summer Squall	P. Day	1:53.3
1991	Hansel	J. Bailey	1:54.0
1992	Pine Bluff	C. McCarron	1:55.3
1993	Prairie Bayou	M. Smith	1:56.3
1994	Tabasco Cat	P. Day	1:56.2
1995	Timber Country	P. Day	1:54.2
1996	Louis Quatorze	P. Day	1:52.2
1997	Silver Charm	G. Stevens	1:54.4
1998	Real Quiet	K. Desormeaux	1:54.75
1999	Charismatic	C. Antley	1:55.32
2000	Red Bullet	J. Bailey	1:56.04
2001	Point Given	G. Stevens	1:56.51
2002	War Emblem	V. Espinoza	1:56.36
2003	Funny Cide	J. Santos	1:55.61
2004	Smarty Jones	S. Elliott	1:55.59
2005	Afleet Alex	J. Rose	1:55.04
2006	Bernardini	J.Castellano	1:54.65
2007	Curlin	R. Albarado	1:53.46
2008	Big Brown	K. Desormeaux	1:54.86
2009	Rachel Alexandra	C. Borel	1:55.08
2010	Looking at Lucky	M. Garcia	1:55:47

Note: Names in **bold** indicate Triple Crown winners. Before 1998, decimals refer to fifths of a second. **Source:** *Daily Racing Form.*

Belmont Stakes Winners 1880–2010

The Belmont Stakes was first run in 1867. The distance of the race varied from 1⅛ miles to 1⅝ miles until 1926, when it was standardized at 1½ miles. **Site: Belmont Park,** New York. (The race was held at Jerome Park prior to 1890, at Morris Park from 1890 to 1904, at Aqueduct from 1963 to 1967.)

Year	Horse	Jockey	Time	Year	Horse	Jockey	Time
1880	Grenada	L. Hughes	2:47.0	1946	Assault	W. Mehrtens	2:30.4
1881	Saunterer	T. Costello	2:47.0	1947	Phalanx	R. Donoso	2:29.2
1882	Forester	J. McLaughlin	2:43.0	1948	Citation	E. Arcaro	2:28.1
1883	George Kinney	J. McLaughlin	2:42.2	1949	Capot	T. Atkinson	2:30.1
1884	Panique	J. McLaughlin	2:42.0	1950	Middleground	W. Boland	2:28.3
1885	Tyrant	P. Duffy	2:43.0	1951	Counterpoint	D. Gorman	2:29.0
1886	Inspector B.	J. McLaughlin	2:41.0	1952	One Count	E. Arcaro	2:30.1
1887	Hanover	J. McLaughlin	2:43.2	1953	Native Dancer	E. Guerin	2:28.3
1888	Sir Dixon	J. McLaughlin	2:40.2	1954	High Gun	E. Guerin	2:30.4
1889	Eric	W. Hayward	2:47.0	1955	Nashua	E. Arcaro	2:29.0
1890	Burlington	S. Barnes	2:07.6	1956	Needles	D. Erb	2:29.4
1891	Foxford	E. Garrison	2:08.6	1957	Gallant Man	W. Shoemaker	2:26.3
1892	Patron	W. Hayward	2:17.0	1958	Cavan	P. Anderson	2:30.1
1893	Comanche	W. Simms	1:53.2	1959	Sword Dancer	W. Shoemaker	2:28.2
1894	Henry of Navarre	W. Simms	1:56.2	1960	Celtic Ash	W. Hartack	2:29.3
1895	Belmar	F. Taral	2:11.2	1961	Sherluck	B. Baeza	2:29.1
1896	Hastings	H. Griffin	2:24.2	1962	Jaipur	W. Shoemaker	2:28.4
1897	Scottish Chieftain	J. Scherrer	2:32.2	1963	Chateaugay	B. Baeza	2:30.1
1898	Bowling Brook	F. Littlefield	2:32.0	1964	Quadrangle	M. Ycaza	2:28.2
1899	Jean Bereaud	R.R. Clawson	2:23.0	1965	Hail To All	J. Sellers	2:28.2
1900	Ildrim	N. Turner	2:21½	1966	Amberoid	W. Boland	2:29.3
1901	Commando	H. Spencer	2:21.0	1967	Damascus	W. Shoemaker	2:28.4
1902	Masterman	J. Bullman	2:22½	1968	Stage Door Johnny	H. Gustines	2:27.1
1903	Africander	J. Bullman	2:23.1	1969	Arts and Letters	B. Baeza	2:28.4
1904	Delhi	G. Odom	2:06.3	1970	High Echelon	J. L. Rotz	2:34.0
1905	Tanya	E. Hildebrand	2:08.0	1971	Pass Catcher	W. Blum	2:30.2
1906	Burgomaster	L. Lyne	2:20.0	1972	Riva Ridge	R. Turcotte	2:28.0
1907	Peter Pan	G. Mountain	No Time	1973	Secretariat	R. Turcotte	2:24.0
1908	Colin	J. Notter	No Time	1974	Little Current	M. Rivera	2:29.1
1909	Joe Madden	E. Dugan	2:21.3	1975	Avatar	W. Shoemaker	2:28.1
1910	Sweep	J. Butwell	2:22.0	1976	Bold Forbes	A. Cordero	2:29.0
1911–12	Not run			1977	Seattle Slew	Jean Cruguet	2:29.3
1913	Prince Eugene	R. Troxler	2:18.0	1978	Affirmed	S. Cauthen	2:26.4
1914	Luke McLuke	M. Buxton	2:20.0	1979	Coastal	R. Hernandez	2:28.3
1915	The Finn	G. Byrne	2:18.2	1980	Temperance Hill	E. Maple	2:29.4
1916	Friar Rock	E. Haynes	2:22.0	1981	Summing	G. Martens	2:29.0
1917	Hourless	J. Butwell	2:17.4	1982	Conquistador Cielo	L. Pincay	2:28.1
1918	Johren	F. Robinson	2:20.2	1983	Caveat	L. Pincay	2:27.4
1919	Sir Barton	J. Loftus	2:17.2	1984	Swale	L. Pincay	2:27.1
1920	Man o'War	C. Kummer	2:14.1	1985	Creme Fraiche	E. Maple	2:27.0
1921	Grey Lag	E. Sande	2:16.4	1986	Danzig Connection	C. McCarron	2:29.4
1922	Pillory	C. H. Miller	2:18.4	1987	Bet Twice	C. Perret	2:28.1
1923	Zev	E. Sande	2:19.0	1988	Risen Star	E. Delahoussaye	2:26.1
1924	Mad Play	E. Sande	2:18.4	1989	Easy Goer	P. Day	2:26.0
1925	American Flag	A. Johnson	2:16.4	1990	Go and Go	M. Kinane	2:27.1
1926	Crusader	A. Johnson	2:32.1	1991	Hansel	J. Bailey	2:28.0
1927	Chance Shot	E. Sande	2:32.2	1992	A.P. Indy	E. Delahoussaye	2:26.0
1928	Vito	C. Kummer	2:33.1	1993	Colonial Affair	J. Krone	2:29.4
1929	Blue Larkspur	M. Garner	2:32.4	1994	Tabasco Cat	P. Day	2:26.4
1930	Gallant Fox	E. Sande	2:31.1	1995	Thunder Gulch	G. Stevens	2:32.0
1931	Twenty Grand	C. Kurtsinger	2:29.3	1996	Editor's Note	R. Douglas	2:28.4
1932	Faireno	T. Malley	2:32.4	1997	Touch Gold	C. McCarron	2:28.4
1933	Hurryoff	M. Garner	2:32.3	1998	Victory Gallop	G. Stevens	2:29.16
1934	Peace Chance	W. D. Wright	2:29.5	1999	Lemon Drop Kid	J. Santos	2:27.88
1935	Omaha	W. Saunders	2:30.3	2000	Commendable	P. Day	2:31.19
1936	Granville	J. Stout	2:30.0	2001	Point Given	G. Stevens	2:26.56
1937	War Admiral	C. Kurtsinger	2:28.3	2002	Sarava	E. Prado	2:29.71
1938	Pasteurized	J. Stout	2:29.2	2003	Empire Maker	J. Bailey	2:28.26
1939	Johnstown	J. Stout	2:29.2	2004	Birdstone	E. Prado	2:27.50
1940	Bimelech	F. A. Smith	2:29.3	2005	Afleet Alex	J. Rose	2:28.75
1941	Whirlaway	E. Arcaro	2:31.0	2006	Jazil	F. Jara	2:27.86
1942	Shut Out	E. Arcaro	2:29.1	2007	Rags to Riches	J. R. Velazquez	2:28.74
1943	Count Fleet	J. Longden	2:28.1	2008	Da' Tara	A. Garcia	2:29.65
1944	Bounding Home	G. L. Smith	2:32.1	2009	Summer Bird	K. Desormeaux	2:27.54
1945	Pavot	E. Arcaro	2:30.1	2010	Drosselmeyer	M. Smith	2:31:57

Note: Names in bold indicate Triple Crown winners. Before 1998, decimals refer to fifths of a second. **Source:** *Daily Racing Form*

FOOTBALL

National Football League
280 Park Avenue
New York, NY 10017
(212) 450-2000

www.nfl.com
Commissioner: Roger Goodell
Founded 1920
Number of Teams: 32

2009 NFL Regular Season Final Standings

AMERICAN FOOTBALL CONFERENCE

AFC East	W–L–T	AFC South	W–L–T
New England	10–6–0	Indianapolis	14–2–0
New York	9–7–0	Houston	9–7–0
Miami	7–9–0	Tennessee	8–8–0
Buffalo	6–10–0	Jacksonville	7–9–0
AFC North	**W–L–T**	**AFC West**	**W–L–T**
Cincinnati	10–6–0	San Diego	13–3–0
Baltimore	9–7–0	Denver	8–8–0
Pittsburgh	9–7–0	Oakland	5–11–0
Cleveland	5–11–0	Kansas City	4–12–0

NATIONAL FOOTBALL CONFERENCE

NFC East	W–L–T	NFC South	W–L–T
Dallas[1]	11–5–0	New Orleans[1]	13–3–0
Philadelphia[2]	11–5–0	Atlanta	9–7–0
New York	8–8–0	Carolina	8–8–0
Washington	4–12–0	Tampa Bay	3–13–0
NFC North	**W–L–T**	**NFC West**	**W–L–T**
Minnesota[1]	12–4–0	Arizona[1]	10–6–0
Green Bay[2]	11–5–0	San Francisco	8–8–0
Chicago	7–9–0	Seattle	5–11–0
Detroit	2–14–0	St. Louis	1–15–0

Notes: 1. Division Winner 2. Wild Card

2009 NFL Post-Season Playoff Results

AFC Wild Card Playoff
New York 24, Cincinnati 14
Baltimore 33, New England 14
AFC Divisional Playoff
New York 17, San Diego 14
Indianapolis 20, Baltimore 3
AFC Championship Game
Indianapolis 30, New York 17

NFC Wild Card Playoff
Dallas 34, Philadelphia 14
Arizona 51, Green Bay 45
NFC Divisional Playoff
New Orleans 45, Arizona 14
Minnesota 34, Dallas 3
NFC Championship Game
New Orleans 31, Minnesota 28 (OT)

Super Bowl XLIV at Dolphin Stadium, Miami, Fl, February 7, 2010
New Orleans 31, Indianapolis 17

NFL First Round Draft Choices, 2010

Team	Selection	Pos.	School	Team	Selection	Pos.	School
1. Rams	Bradford, Sam	QB	Oklahoma	**17.** 49ers	Iupati, Mike	OG	Idaho
2. Lions	Suh, Ndamukong	DT	Nebraska	**18.** Steelers	Pouncey, Maurkice	C	Florida
3. Buccaneers	McCoy, Gerald	DT	Oklahoma	**19.** Falcons	Weatherspoon, Sean	LB	Missouri
4. Redskins	Williams, Trent	OT	Oklahoma	**20.** Texans	Jackson, Kareem	CB	Alabama
5. Chiefs	Berry, Eric	SS	Tennessee	**21.** Bengals	Gresham, Jermaine	TE	Oklahoma
6. Seahawks	Okung, Russell	OT	Oklahoma St.	**22.** Broncos	Thomas, Demaryius	WR	Georgia Tech
7. Browns	Haden, Joe	CB	Florida				
8. Raiders	McClain, Rolando	LB	Alabama	**23.** Packers	Bulaga, Bryan	OT	Iowa
9. Bills	Spiller, C.J.	RB	Clemson	**24.** Cowboys	Bryant, Dez	WR	Oklahoma St.
10. Jaguars	Alualu, Tyson	DE	California	**25.** Broncos	Tebow, Tim	QB	Florida
11. 49ers	Davis, Anthony	OT	Rutgers	**26.** Cardinals	Williams, Dan	DT	Tennessee
12. Chargers	Matthews, Ryan	RB	Fresno State	**27.** Patriots	McCourty, Devin	CB	Rutgers
13. Eagles	Graham, Brandon	DE	Michigan	**28.** Dolphins	Odrick, Jared	DT	Penn State
14. Seahwaks	Thomas, Earl	SS	Texas	**29.** Jets	Wilson, Kyle	CB	Boise State
15. Giants	Pierre-Paul, Jason	DE	S. Florida	**30.** Lions	Best, Jahvid	RB	California
16. Titans	Morgan, Derrick	DE	Georgia Tech	**31.** Colts	Hughes, Jerry	DE	T.C.U.
				32. Saints	Robinson, Patrick	CB	Florida St.

Notes: 1. From Browns 2. From Jets through Browns 3. From Bears 4. From Buccaneers through Browns 5. From Cowboys 6. From Eagles 7. From Patriots 8. From Ravens through Patriots 9. From Panthers through Eagles **Source:** National Football League.

NFL Leaders, 2009

AFC Rushing

Player, Team	Yds	Att	Avg	TD	Long
1. Chris Johnson, TEN	2,006	358	5.6	14	91
2. Thomas Jones, NYJ	1,402	331	4.2	14	71
3. Mauric Jones-Drew, JAC	1,391	312	4.5	15	80
4. Ray Rice, BAL	1,339	254	5.3	7	59
5. Cedric Benson, CIN	1,251	301	4.2	6	42
6. Ricky Williams, MIA	1,121	241	4.7	11	68
7. Jamaal Charles, KC	1,120	190	5.9	7	76
8. Rashard Mendenhall, PIT	1,108	242	4.6	7	60
9. Fred Jackson, BUF	1,062	237	4.5	2	43
10. Knowshon Moreno, DEN	947	247	3.8	7	36

NFC Rushing

Player, Team	Yds	Att	Avg	TD	Long
1. Steven Jackson, STL	1,416	324	4.4	4	58
2. Adrian Peterson, MIN	1,383	314	4.4	18	64
3. Ryan Grant, GB	1,253	282	4.4	11	62
4. Jonathan Stewart, CAR	1,133	221	5.1	10	67
5. Frank Gore, SF	1,120	229	4.9	10	80
6. DeAngelo Williams, CAR	1,117	216	5.2	7	77
7. Marion Barber, DAL	932	214	4.4	7	35
8. Matt Forte, CHI	929	258	3.6	4	61
9. Michael Turner, ATL	871	178	4.9	10	58
10. Brandon Jacobs, NYG	835	224	3.7	5	31

AFC Receiving

Player, Team	Rec	Yds	Avg	TD	Long
1. Wes Welker, NE	123	1,348	11	4	58
2. Andre Johnson, HOU	101	1,569	15.5	9	72
3. Brandon Marshall, DEN	101	1,120	11.1	10	75
4. Dallas Clark, IND	100	1,106	11.1	10	80
4. Reggie Wayne, IND	100	1,264	12.6	10	65
6. Hines Ward, PIT	95	1,167	12.3	6	54
7. Randy Moss, NE	83	1,264	15.2	13	71
8. Antonio Gates, SD	79	1,157	14.6	8	56
8. Santonio Holmes, PIT	79	1,248	15.8	5	57
10. Ray Rice, BAL	78	702	9	1	63

NFC Receiving

Player, Team	Rec	Yds	Avg	TD	Long
1. Steve Smith, NYG	107	1220	11.4	7	51
2. Larry Fitzgerald, ARI	97	1092	11.3	1	34
3. Jason Witten, DAL	94	1030	11.0	2	69
4. Roddy White, ATL	85	1153	13.6	1	90
5. Anquan Boldin, ARI	84	1024	12.2	4	44
6. Tony Gonzalez, ATL	83	867	10.4	6	27
7. Sidney Rice, MIN	83	1312	15.8	8	63
8. Miles Austin, DAL	81	1320	16.3	11	60
9. T.J. Houshmandzadeh, SEA	79	911	11.5	3	53
10. Vernon Davis, SF	78	965	12.4	13	73

AFC PASSER RATING

Player, Team	Yds	Att	Cmp	TDs	Ints	Long	Rating
1. Philip Rivers, SD	4,254	486	317	28	9	81	104.4
2. Ben Rothlisberger, PIT	4,328	506	337	26	12	60	100.5
3. Peyton Manning, IND	4,500	571	393	33	16	80	99.9
4. Matt Schaub, HOU	4,770	583	396	29	15	72	98.6
5. Tom Brady, NE	4,398	565	371	28	13	81	96.2
6. Joe Flacco, BAL	3,613	499	315	21	12	72	88.9
7. Kyle Orton, DEN	3,802	541	336	21	12	87	86.8
8. Carson Palmer, CIN	3,094	466	282	21	13	73	83.6
9. David Garrard, JAC	3,597	516	314	15	10	63	83.5
10. Vince Young, TEN	1,879	259	152	10	7	66	82.8

NFC PASSER RATING

Player, Team	Yds	Att	Cmp	TDs	Ints	Long	Rating
1. Drew Brees, NO	4,388	514	363	34	11	75	109.6
2. Brett Favre, MIN	4,204	531	363	33	7	63	107.2
3. Aaron Rodgers, GB	4,434	541	350	30	7	83	103.2
4. Tony Romo, DAL	4,483	550	347	26	9	80	97.6
5. Kurt Warner, ARI	3,753	513	339	26	14	45	93.2
6. Eli Manning, NYG	4,021	509	317	27	14	74	93.1
7. Donovan McNabb, PHI	3,553	443	267	22	10	60	92.9
8. Jason Campbell, WAS	3,618	507	327	20	15	84	86.4
9. Alex Smith, SF	2,350	372	225	18	12	73	81.5
10. Matt Ryan, ATL	2,916	451	263	22	14	90	80.9

Source: National Football League. www.nfl.com

NFL Number One Draft Picks, 1936–2010

Year	Player	Team	Pos.	College
1936	Jay Berwanger	Philadelphia Eagles	RB	Chicago
1937	Sam Francis	Philadelphia Eagles	RB	Nebraska
1938	Corbett Davis	Cleveland Rams	RB	Indiana
1939	Charles Aldrich	Chicago Cardinals	OL	Texas Christian
1940	George Cafego	Chicago Cardinals	QB	Tennessee
1941	Tom Harmon	Chicago Bears	RB	Michigan

Year	Player	Team	Pos.	College
1942	Bill Dudley	Pittsburgh Steelers	RB	Virginia
1943	Frank Sinkwich	Detroit Lions	RB	Georgia
1944	Angelo Bertelli	Boston Yanks	QB	Notre Dame
1945	Charley Trippi	Chicago Cardinals	RB	Georgia
1946	Frank Dancewicz	Boston Yanks	QB	Notre Dame
1947	Bob Fenimore	Chicago Bears	RB	Oklahoma A&M
1948	Harry Gilmer	Washington Redskins	QB	Alabama
1949	Chuck Bednarik	Philadelphia Eagles	OL	Pennsylvania
1950	Leon Hart	Detroit Lions	E	Notre Dame
1951	Kyle Rote	New York Giants	E/K	Southern Methodist
1952	Bill Wade	Los Angeles Rams	QB	Vanderbilt
1953	Harry Babcock	San Francisco 49ers	E	Georgia
1954	Bobby Garrett	Cleveland Browns	QB	Stanford
1955	George Shaw	Baltimore Colts	QB	Oregon
1956	Gary Glick	Pittsburgh Steelers	QB	Colorado State
1957	Paul Hornung	Green Bay Packers	RB	Notre Dame
1958	King Hill	St. Louis Cardinals	QB	Rice
1959	Randy Duncan	Green Bay Packers	QB	Iowa
1960	Billy Cannon	Los Angeles Rams	RB	Louisiana State
1961	Tommy Mason	Minnesota Vikings	RB	Tulane
1962	Ernie Davis	Washington Redskins	RB	Syracuse
1963	Terry Baker	Los Angeles Rams	QB	Oregon State
1964	Dave Parks	San Francisco 49ers	E	Texas Tech.
1965	Tucker Frederickson	New York Giants	RB	Auburn
1966	Tommy Nobis	Atlanta Falcons	LB	Texas
1967	Bubba Smith	Baltimore Colts	DL	Michigan State
1968	Ron Yary	Minnesota Vikings	OL	U.S.C.
1969	O.J. Simpson	Buffalo Bills	RB	U.S.C.
1970	Terry Bradshaw	Pittsburgh Steelers	QB	Louisiana Tech.
1971	Jim Plunkett	Boston Patriots	QB	Stanford
1972	Walt Patulski	Buffalo Bills	DL	Notre Dame
1973	John Matuzak	Houston Oilers	DL	Tampa
1974	Ed Jones	Dallas Cowboys	DL	Tampa
1975	Steve Bartkowski	Atlanta Falcons	QB	California
1976	Lee Roy Selmon	Tampa Bay Buccaneers	DL	Oklahoma
1977	Ricky Bell	Tampa Bay Buccaneers	RB	U.S.C.
1978	Earl Campbell	Houston Oilers	RB	Texas
1979	Tom Cousineau	Buffalo Bills	LB	Ohio State
1980	Billy Sims	Detroit Lions	RB	Oklahoma
1981	George Rogers	New Orleans Saints	RB	South Carolina
1982	Kenneth Sims	New England Patriots	DL	Texas
1983	John Elway	Baltimore Colts[1]	QB	Stanford
1984	Irving Fryar	New England Patriots	WR	Nebraska
1985	Bruce Smith	Buffalo Bills	DL	Virginia Tech.
1986	Bo Jackson	Tampa Bay Buccaneers	RB	Auburn
1987	Vinny Testaverde	Tampa Bay Buccaneers	QB	Miami
1988	Aundray Bruce	Atlanta Falcons	LB	Auburn
1989	Troy Aikman	Dallas Cowboys	QB	U.C.L.A.
1990	Jeff George	Indianapolis Colts	QB	Illinois
1991	Russell Maryland	Dallas Cowboys	DT	Miami (Fla.)
1992	Steve Emtman	Indianapolis Colts	DT	Washington
1993	Drew Bledsoe	New England Patriots	QB	Washington State
1994	Dan Wilkinson	Cincinnati Bengals	DT	Ohio State
1995	Ki-Jana Carter	Cincinnati Bengals	RB	Penn State
1996	Keyshawn Johnson	New York Jets	WR	Southern California
1997	Orlando Pace	St. Louis Rams	OT	Ohio State
1998	Peyton Manning	Indianapolis Colts	QB	Tennessee
1999	Tim Couch	Cleveland Browns	QB	Kentucky
2000	Courtney Brown	Cleveland Browns	DL	Penn State
2001	Michael Vick	Atlanta Falcons	QB	Virginia Tech.
2002	David Carr	Houston Texans	QB	Fresno State
2003	Carson Palmer	Cincinnati Bengals	QB	U.S.C.
2004	Eli Manning	San Diego Chargers[2]	QB	Mississippi
2005	Alex Smith	San Francisco 49ers	QB	Utah
2006	Mario Williams	Houston Texans	DE	N.C. State
2007	JaMarcus Russell	Oakland Raiders	QB	Louisiana State
2008	Jake Long	Miami Dolphins	OT	Michigan
2009	Matthew Stafford	Detroit Lions	QB	Georgia
2010	Sam Bradford	St. Louis	QB	Oklahoma

Notes: 1. Baltimore traded Elway to Denver. 2. San Diego traded the rights to Manning to the New York Giants for draft picks.

The Sporting News' NFL Rookie of the Year, 1955–2009

Year	Player	Pos.	Team	Year	Player	Pos.	Team
1955	Alan Ameche	FB	Baltimore Colts	1979 NFC:	Ottis Anderson	RB	St. Louis Cardinals
1956	J.C. Caroline	HB	Chicago Bears	AFC:	Jerry Butler	WR	Buffalo Bills
1957	Jim Brown	FB	Cleveland Browns	1980	Billy Sims	RB	Detroit Lions
1958	Bobby Mitchell	HB	Cleveland Browns	1981	George Rogers	RB	New England Patriots
1959	Nick Pietrosante	FB	Detroit Lions	1982	Marcus Allen	RB	Los Angeles Raiders
1960	Gail Codgill	E	Detroit Lions	1983	Dan Marino	QB	Miami Dolphins
1961	Mike Ditka	E	Chicago Bears	1984	Louis Lipps	WR	Pittsburgh Steelers
1962	Ronnie Bull	HB	Chicago Bears	1985	Eddie Brown	WR	Cincinnati Bengals
1963	Paul Flatley	WR	Minnesota Vikings	1986	Rueben Mayes	RB	New Orleans Saints
1964	Charley Taylor	HB	Washington Redskins	1987	Robert Awalt	TE	St. Louis Cardinals
1965	Gale Sayers	RB	Chicago Bears	1988	Keith Jackson	TE	Philadelphia Eagles
1966	Tommy Nobis	LB	Atlanta Falcons	1989	Barry Sanders	RB	Detroit Lions
1967	Mel Farr	RB	Detroit Lions	1990	Richmond Webb	OL	Miami Dolphins
1968	Earl McCullouch	WR	Detroit Lions	1991	Mike Croel	LB	Denver Broncos
1969	Calvin Hill	RB	Dallas Cowboys	1992	Santana Dotson	DE	Tampa Bay Buccaneers
1970 NFC:	Bruce Taylor	CB	San Francisco 49ers	1993	Jerome Bettis	RB	Los Angeles Rams
AFC:	Dennis Shaw	QB	Buffalo Bills	1994	Marshall Faulk	RB	Indianapolis Colts
1971 NFC:	John Brockington	RB	Green Bay Packers	1995	Curtis Martin	RB	New England
AFC:	Jim Plunkett	QB	New England Patriots	1996	Eddie George	RB	Houston Oilers
1972 NFC:	Chester Marcol	PK	Green Bay Packers	1997	Warrick Dunn	RB	Tampa Bay
AFC:	Franco Harris	RB	Pittsburgh Steelers				Buccaneers
1973 NFC:	Chuck Foreman	RB	Minnestoa Vikings	1998	Randy Moss	WR	Minnesota Vikings
AFC:	Boobie Clark	RB	Cincinnati Bengals	1999	Edgerrin James	RB	Indianapolis Colts
1974 NFC:	Wilbur Jackson	RB	San Francisco 49ers	2000	Brian Urlacher	LB	Chicago Bears
AFC:	Don Woods	RB	San Diego Chargers	2001	Kendrell Bell	LB	Pittsburgh Steelers
1975 NFC:	Steve Bartkowski	QB	Atlanta Falcons	2002	Clinton Portis	RB	Denver Broncos
AFC:	Robert Brazile	LB	Houston Oilers	2003	Anquan Boldin	WR	Arizona Cardinals
1976 NFC:	Sammy White	WR	Minnesota Vikings	2004	Ben Roethlisberger	QB	Pittsburgh Steelers
AFC:	Mike Haynes	CB	New England Patriots	2005	Shawne Merriman	LB	San Diego Chargers
1977 NFC:	Tony Dorsett	RB	Dallas Cowboys	2006	Vince Young	QB	Tennessee Titans
AFC:	A. J. Duhe	DT	Miami Dolphins	2007	Adrian Peterson	RB	Minnesota Vikings
1978 NFC:	Al Baker	DE	Detroit Lions	2008	Matt Ryan	QB	Atlanta Falcons
AFC:	Earl Campbell	RB	Houston Oilers	2009	Percy Harvin	WR	Minnesota Vikings

Note: From 1970–79, separate players were chosen for each conference.   **Source:** *The Sporting News*

NFL Most Valuable Player, 1957–2009

Year	Player	Pos.	Team	Year	Player	Pos.	Team
1957	Jim Brown	RB	Cleveland Browns	1984	Dan Marino	QB	Miami Dolphins
1958	Gino Marchetti	DE	Baltimore Colts	1985	Marcus Allen	RB	Los Angeles Raiders
1959	Charley Conerly	QB	New York Giants	1986	Lawrence Taylor	LB	New York Giants
1960	Norm Van Brocklin	QB	Philadelphia Eagles	1987	John Elway	QB	Denver Broncos
	Joe Schmidt	LB	Detroit Lions	1988	Boomer Esiason	QB	Cincinnati Bengals
1961	Paul Hornung	RB	Green Bay Packers	1989	Joe Montana	QB	San Francisco 49ers
1962	Jim Taylor	RB	Green Bay Packers	1990	Joe Montana	QB	San Francisco 49ers
1963	Y.A. Tittle	QB	New York Giants	1991	Thurman Thomas	RB	Buffalo Bills
1964	Johnny Unitas	QB	Baltimore Colts	1992	Steve Young	QB	San Francisco 49ers
1965	Jim Brown	RB	Cleveland Browns	1993	Emmitt Smith	RB	Dallas Cowboys
1966	Bart Starr	QB	Green Bay Packers	1994	Steve Young	QB	San Francisco 49ers
1967	Johnny Unitas	QB	Baltimore Colts	1995	Brett Favre	QB	Green Bay Packers
1968	Earl Morrall	QB	Baltimore Colts	1996	Brett Favre	QB	Green Bay Packers
1969	Roman Gabriel	QB	Los Angeles Rams	1997	Brett Favre	QB	Green Bay Packers
1970	John Brodie	QB	San Francisco 49ers		Barry Sanders	RB	Detroit Lions
1971	Alan Page	DT	Minnesota Vikings	1998	Terrell Davis	RB	Denver Broncos
1972	Larry Brown	RB	Washington Redskins	1999	Kurt Warner	QB	St. Louis Rams
1973	O.J. Simpson	RB	Buffalo Bills	2000	Marshall Faulk	RB	St. Louis Rams
1974	Ken Stabler	QB	Oakland Raiders	2001	Kurt Warner	QB	St. Louis Rams
1975	Fran Tarkenton	QB	Minnesota Vikings	2002	Rich Gannon	QB	Oakland Raiders
1976	Bert Jones	RB	Baltimore Colts	2003	Peyton Manning	QB	Indianapolis Colts
1977	Walter Payton	RB	Chicago Bears		Steve McNair	QB	Tennesse Titans
1978	Terry Bradshaw	QB	Pittsburgh Steelers	2004	Peyton Manning	QB	Indianapolis Colts
1979	Earl Campbell	RB	Houston Oilers	2005	Shaun Alexander	RB	Seattle Seahawks
1980	Brian Sipe	QB	Cleveland Browns	2006	LaDainian Tomlinson	RB	San Diego Chargers
1981	Ken Anderson	QB	Cincinnati Bengals	2007	Tom Brady	QB	New England Patriots
1982	Mark Moseley	PK	Washington Redskins	2008	Peyton Manning	QB	Indianapolis Colts
1983	Joe Theismann	QB	Washington Redskins	2009	Peyton Manning	QB	Indianapolis Colts

Source: National Football League www.nfl.com

All-Time Pro Football Records

SCORING (Total Points)	Years	Points	Touchdowns	PATs	Field Goals
1. Morten Anderson	25	2,544	0	849	565
2. Gary Anderson	23	2,434	0	798	520
3. John Carney[1]	21	2,044	0	625	473
4. Matt Stover[1]	20	2,004	0	591	471
5. George Blanda	26	2,002	9	943	335
6. Jason Elam[1]	17	1,983	0	675	436
7. Jason Hanson[1]	19	1,835	0	554	427
8. Norm Johnson	18	1,736	0	638	366
9. John Kasay[1]	20	1,731	0	507	408
10. Nick Lowery	18	1,711	0	562	383

RUSHING	Years	Rushes	Yards	Avg.	TD
1. Emmitt Smith	15	4,409	18,355	4.2	164
2. Walter Payton	13	3,838	16,726	4.4	110
3. Barry Sanders	10	3,062	15,269	5.0	99
4. Curtis Martin	11	3,518	14,101	4.0	90
5. Jerome Bettis	13	3,479	13,662	3.9	91
6. Eric Dickerson	11	2,996	13,259	4.4	90
7. Tony Dorsett	12	2,936	12,739	4.3	77
8. LaDanian[1] Tomlinson	9	2,880	12,490	4.2	138
9. Jim Brown	9	2,359	12,312	5.2	106
10. Marshall Faulk	12	2,836	12,279	4.3	100

RECEPTIONS	Years	Recep.	Yards	Avg.	TD
1. Jerry Rice	20	1,549	22,895	14.8	197
2. Marvin Harrison	13	1,102	14,580	13.2	128
3. Cris Carter	16	1,101	13,899	12.6	130
4. Tim Brown	17	1,094	14,934	13.7	100
5. Issac Bruce[1]	16	1,024	15,208	14.9	91
6. Terrell Owens[1]	14	1,006	14,951	14.9	144
7. Tony Gonzalez[1]	13	999	11,807	11.8	82
8. Andre Reed	16	951	13,198	13.9	87
9. Art Monk	16	940	12,721	13.5	68
10. Randy Moss[1]	12	926	14,465	15.6	148

PASSER RATING[1]	Years	Attempts	Completions	Yards	TDs	Interceptions	Rating
(minimum 1,500 attempts)							
1. Steve Young	15	4,149	2,667	33,124	232	107	96.8
2. Philip Rivers[1]	7	1,914	1,207	14,951	106	45	95.8
3. Tony Romo[1]	8	1,857	1,178	15,045	107	55	95.6
4. Peyton Manning[1]	13	6,531	4,232	50,128	366	181	95.2
5. Kurt Warner[1]	13	4,070	2,666	32,344	208	128	93.7
6. Tom Brady[1]	11	4,218	2,672	30,844	225	99	93.3
7. Joe Montana	15	5,391	3,409	40,551	273	139	92.3
8. Drew Brees[1]	10	4,164	2,697	30,646	202	110	91.9
9. Ben Roethlisberger[1]	7	2,411	1,526	19,302	127	81	91.7
10. Chad Pennington[1]	11	2,469	1,631	17,804	102	64	90.1

All-Time Passes Completed

1. Brett Favre[1]	6,083
2. Dan Marino	4,967
3. Peyton Manning[1]	4,232
4. John Elway	4,123
5. Warren Moon	3,988
6. Drew Bledsoe	3,839
7. Vinny Testaverde	3,787
8. Fran Tarkenton	3,686
9. Joe Montana	3,409
10. Dan Fouts	3,297
11. Kerry Collins[2]	3,160
12. Dave Krieg	3,105
13. Boomer Esiason	2,969
14. Troy Aikman	2,898
15. Steve DeBerg	2,874
15. Jim Kelly	2,874

All-Time Yards Passing

1. Brett Favre[1]	69,329
2. Dan Marino	61,361
3. John Elway	51,475
4. Peyton Manning[1]	50,128
5. Warren Moon	49,325
6. Fran Tarkenton	47,003
7. Vinny Testaverde	46,233
8. Drew Bledsoe	44,611
9. Dan Fouts	43,040
10. Joe Montana	40,551
11. Johnny Unitas	40,239
12. Kerry Collins[1]	38,618
13. Dave Krieg	38,147
14. Boomer Esiason	37,920
15. Jim Kelly	35,467

All-Time Touchdown Passes

1. Brett Favre[1]	497
2. Dan Marino	420
3. Peyton Manning[1]	366
4. Fran Tarkenton	342
5. John Elway	300
6. Warren Moon	291
7. Johnny Unitas	290
8. Vinny Testaverde	275
9. Joe Montana	273
10. Dave Krieg	261
11. Sonny Jurgensen	255
12. Dan Fouts	254
13. Drew Bledsoe	251
14. Boomer Esiason	247
15. John Hadl	244

Note: As of end of 2009–10 season. 1. Player active in 2009 season.

NFL Champions, 1921–66

Year	Team (record)	Year	Team (record)	Year	Team (record)
1920	Akron Pros (8–0–3)	1936	Green Bay Packers (10–1–1)	1952	Detroit Lions (9–3–0)
1921	Chicago Staleys[1] (10–1–1)	1937	Washington Redskins (8–3–0)	1953	Detroit Lions (10–2–0)
1922	Canton Bulldogs (10–0–2)	1938	New York Giants (8–2–1)	1954	Cleveland Browns (9–3–0)
1923	Canton Bulldogs (11–0–1)	1939	Green Bay Packers (9–2–0)	1955	Cleveland Browns (9–2–1)
1924	Cleveland Bulldogs[2] (7–1–1)	1940	Chicago Bears (8–3–0)	1956	New York Giants (8–3–1)
1925	Chicago Cardinals (11–2–1)	1941	Chicago Bears (10–1–1)	1957	Detroit Lions (8–4–0)
1926	Frankford Yellowjackets (14–1–1)	1942	Washington Redskins (10–1–1)	1958	Baltimore Colts (9–3–0)
1927	New York Giants (11–1–1)	1943	Chicago Bears (8–1–1)	1959	Baltimore Colts (9–3–0)
1928	Providence Steam Roller (8–1–2)	1944	Green Bay Packers (8–2–0)	1960	Philadelphia Eagles (10–2–0)
1929	Green Bay Packers (12–0–1)	1945	Cleveland Rams (9–1–0)	1961	Green Bay Packers (11–3–0)
1930	Green Bay Packers (10–3–1)	1946	Chicago Bears (8–2–1)	1962	Green Bay Packers (13–1–0)
1931	Green Bay Packers (12–2–0)	1947	Chicago Cardinals (9–3–0)	1963	Chicago Bears (11–1–2)
1932	Chicago Bears (7–1–6)	1948	Philadelphia Eagles (9–2–1)	1964	Cleveland Browns (10–3–1)
1933	Chicago Bears (10–2–1)	1949	Philadelphia Eagles (11–1–0)	1965	Green Bay Packers (10–3–1)
1934	New York Giants (8–5–0)	1950	Cleveland Browns (10–2–0)	1966	Green Bay Packers (12–2–0)
1935	Detroit Lions (7–3–2)	1951	Los Angeles Rams (8–4–0)		

Note: 1. Later called the Chicago Bears. 2. Franchise moved from Canton.

Super Bowl Results

SUPER BOWL I
Jan. 15, 1967, Memorial Coliseum, Los Angeles
Green Bay Packers 35   Kansas City Chiefs 10
Green Bay's Max McGee was a surprise star, filling in for ailing Boyd Dowler. McGee had caught only four passes all year, but in Super Bowl I he caught seven for 138 yards and two touchdowns. Quarterback Bart Starr was the game's MVP, as he completed 16 of 23 passes for 250 yards and two touchdowns. Green Bay broke open the game with three second-half touchdowns, the first of which was set up by safety Willie Wood's 45-yard interception return.

SUPER BOWL II
Jan. 14, 1968, Orange Bowl, Miami
Green Bay Packers 33   Oakland Raiders 14
Bart Starr again dominated proceedings with 13 completions in 24 attempts, for 202 yards and a touchdown, winning his second straight MVP award. The Pack attack was in control all the way after building a 16–7 halftime lead. Don Chandler kicked four field goals and all-pro cornerback Herb Adderley capped the Green Bay scoring with a 60-yard interception return.

SUPER BOWL III
Jan. 12, 1969, Orange Bowl, Miami
New York Jets 16   Baltimore Colts 7
Quarterback Joe Namath guaranteed victory before the game and then he and the upstart AFL Jets easily dispatched the heavily favored Colts. Namath won MVP honors by completing 17 of 28 passes for 206 yards and directing a steady attack that racked up 337 total yards. Three times in the first half, the Jet defense intercepted Colts quarterback Earl Morrall, who was playing for an injured Johnny Unitas. With the Jets ahead 13–0 in the third quarter, Unitas came off the bench and later orchestrated Baltimore's sole touchdown.

SUPER BOWL IV
Jan. 11, 1970, Tulane Stadium, New Orleans
Kansas City Chiefs 23   Minnesota Vikings 7
MVP quarterback Len Dawson called a nearly flawless game for Kansas City, completing 12 of 17 passes and hitting Otis Taylor on a 46-yard pass for the final Chiefs touchdown. The Kansas City defense limited Minnesota's strong rushing game to 67 yards and had three interceptions and two fumble recoveries. The second consecutive victory by an AFL team proved that AFL teams could compete

with NFL franchises, and assured a smooth merger between the two leagues.

SUPER BOWL V
Jan. 17, 1971, Orange Bowl, Miami
Baltimore Colts 16   Dallas Cowboys 13
Rookie Jim O'Brien's 32-yard field goal in the closing seconds broke a 13–13 tie and gave the Colts their first Super Bowl victory. Dallas led 13–6 at halftime, but two Colt interceptions set up a Baltimore touchdown and O'Brien's crucial kick. Baltimore's first touchdown came when a Johnny Unitas pass caromed off receiver Eddie Hinton's fingertips, bounced off Dallas defensive back Mel Renfro, and finally settled into the grasp of tight end John Mackey, who went 47 yards for the score. Dallas linebacker Chuck Howley was the MVP, the only time the MVP came from the losing team.

SUPER BOWL VI
Jan. 16, 1972, Tulane Stadium, New Orleans
Dallas Cowboys 24   Miami Dolphins 3
The Cowboys rushed for 252 yards and their defense limited the Dolphins to 185 total yards and no touchdowns. Dallas converted Chuck Howley's recovery of Larry Csonka's first fumble of the season into a 3–0 advantage. At halftime, Dallas led 10–3. An eight-play, 71-yard march made it a 17–3 game. Cowboys' quarterback Roger Staubach was voted MVP for his 12 completions in 19 attempts, 119 yards passing and two touchdowns.

SUPER BOWL VII
Jan. 14, 1973, Memorial Coliseum, Los Angeles
Miami Dolphins 14   Washington Redskins 7
In a game that wasn't as close as the score, the Dolphins thoroughly dominated the Redskins to complete the NFL's only undefeated season. Quarterback Bob Griese hit Paul Warfield for 18 yards, then delivered a 28-yard strike to Howard Twilley for the Dolphins' first score. Just before the half, Dolphins linebacker Nick Buoniconti intercepted a Billy Kilmer pass and returned it to the Washington 27, setting up Miami's second touchdown. Safety Jake Scott led the Dolphin defense with two interceptions (one in the end zone killing a Redskin scoring drive) and was the MVP. The Redskins' sole touchdown resulted when Dolphin kicker Garo Yepremian tried to turn a botched field goal into a forward pass. Washington's Mike Bass

picked the ball out of the air and returned it 49 yards for the score.

SUPER BOWL VIII
Jan. 13, 1974, Rice Stadium, Houston
Miami Dolphins 24   Minnesota Vikings 7
Miami scored on its first two possessions, on 62- and 56-yard marches. The initial 10-play drive was climaxed by a Larry Csonka touchdown bolt through right guard. Four plays later, Miami's Jim Kiick burst one yard through the middle for the second touchdown. By halftime Miami led 17–0. The Dolphins defense held off the Vikings on a crucial fourth-and-one play from the Miami 6-yard-line when middle linebacker Nick Buoniconti jarred the ball loose from Minnesota running back Oscar Reed and Jake Scott recovered for Miami. Csonka rushed 33 times for 145 yards, winning the MVP.

SUPER BOWL IX
Jan, 12, 1975, Tulane Stadium, New Orleans
Pittsburgh Steelers 16   Minnesota 6
Steeler Dwight White tackled Minnesota quarterback Fran Tarkenton in the end zone for a safety to put the Steelers on the board in the second quarter. They took advantage of another break in the second half, when Minnesota's Bill Brown fumbled the kickoff and Marv Kellum recovered for Pittsburgh on the Vikings' 30. From there, Franco Harris carried three straight times for the game's first touchdown. Minnesota blocked a Bobby Walden punt and Terry Brown recovered the ball for a touchdown to cut the lead to 9–6, but the Steelers roared back with a 66-yard march, climaxed by Terry Bradshaw's 4-yard scoring pass to Larry Brown. Pittsburgh's defense controlled the game, permitting Minnesota only 119 yards total offense. Franco Harris rushed 34 times for 158 yards to win MVP honors.

SUPER BOWL X
Jan. 18, 1976, Orange Bowl, Miami
Pittsburgh Steelers 21   Dallas Cowboys 17
Steeler quarterback Terry Bradshaw hurled a 64-yard touchdown pass to Lynn Swann to win the game, while the Steel Curtain defense stopped the Cowboys' last rally with an end-zone interception in the game's final play. It was a battle of quarterbacks with Bradshaw and Cowboy Roger Staubach each hurling two touchdowns. Swann earned MVP honors with 161 yards on four receptions. The Steelers blasted out in front with a 14-point fourth quarter.

SUPER BOWL XI
Jan. 9, 1977, Rose Bowl, Pasadena,California
Oakland Raiders 32   Minnesota Vikings 14
A record 81 million TV viewers watched the Raiders gain a record-breaking 429 yards, including running back Clarence Davis' 137 yards rushing. Wide receiver Fred Biletnikoff made four key receptions, which earned him the game's MVP trophy. Oakland scored on three successive possessions in the second quarter to build a 16–0 halftime lead. Minnesota's Fran Tarkenton passed for a touchdown in the third to cut the deficit, but two fourth-quarter interceptions clinched the title for the Raiders. One set up Pete Banaszak's second touchdown run, the other resulted in cornerback Willie Brown's 75-yard interception return.

SUPER BOWL XII
Jan. 15, 1978, Louisiana Superdome, New Orleans
Dallas Cowboys 27   Denver Broncos 10
The TV audience climbed to 102 million, as Dallas converted two interceptions into 10 points and a 13–0 halftime lead. Butch Johnson made a spectacular diving catch in the end zone of a Roger Staubach pass to make it 20–3. Dallas clinched the victory when running back Robert Newhouse threw a 29-yard touchdown pass to Golden Richards. Co-MVP's Harvey Martin and Randy White led the

SUPER BOWL XIII
Jan, 21, 1979, Orange Bowl, Miami
Pittsburgh Steelers 35   Dallas Cowboys 31
MVP Terry Bradshaw hurled four touchdown passes to lead the Steelers to victory, making them the first team to win three Super Bowls. Bradshaw completed 17 of 30 passes for 318 yards. In the fourth quarter, the Steelers broke open the contest with two touchdowns in 19 seconds. Franco Harris rambled 22 yards up the middle to put Pittsburgh in front 28–17. The Steelers got the ball right back when Randy White fumbled the kickoff and Dennis Winston recovered. On first down, Bradshaw hit Lynn Swann with an 18-yard scoring pass to boost the lead to 35–17. The Cowboys came back with a Roger Staubach touchdown pass to Billy Joe DuPree and then recovered an onside kick, which led to another Staubach touchdown pass, this time to Butch Johnson. But Rocky Bleier smothered an onside kick with 17 seconds remaining to seal the victory.

SUPER BOWL XIV
Jan. 20, 1980, Rose Bowl, Pasadena, California
Pittsburgh Steelers 31   Los Angeles Rams 19
It was all Terry Bradshaw again as he completed 14 of 21 passes for 309 records, and set two passing records as the Steelers became the first team to win four Super Bowls. Despite three interceptions by the Rams, Bradshaw brought the Steelers back from behind twice in the second half. On Pittsburgh's first possession of the final period, Bradshaw lofted a 73-yard scoring pass to John Stallworth to put the Steelers in front to stay, 24–19. Franco Harris scored on a one-yard run later to seal the verdict. Bradshaw was the MVP for the second straight Super Bowl.

SUPER BOWL XV
Jan. 25, 1981, Louisiana Superdome, New Orleans
Oakland Raiders 27   Philadelphia Eagles 10
Jim Plunkett threw three touchdown passes, including an 80-yarder to Kenny King, to give Oakland a decisive 14–0 advantage nine seconds before halftime. Oakland linebacker Rod Martin intercepted three passes as the Raiders completely stifled Eagle quarterback Ron Jaworski's offense. Jaworski managed an 8-yard touchdown pass in the fourth quarter, but the issue had been decided by Plunkett, who completed 13 of the 21 pass attempts for 261 yards and was named MVP.

SUPER BOWL XVI
Jan. 24, 1982, Pontiac Silverdome, Pontiac, Mich.
San Francisco 49ers 26   Cincinnati Bengals 21
The 49ers led 20–0 at halftime, but barely hung on for the win. Ray Wersching kicked four field goals for San Francisco and quarterback Joe Montana engineered two touchdown drives, passing for one and scoring the other himself on a one-yard dive. The Bengals rebounded in the second half as quarterback Ken Anderson ran in a touchdown and passed for another. With 16 seconds remaining, the Bengals scored again, on a 3-yard pass to Dan Ross, but couldn't get the ball back a final time. Ross set a Super Bowl record with 11 receptions for 104 yards. Montana, the MVP, completed 14 of 22 passes for 157 yards.

SUPER BOWL XVII
Jan. 30, 1983, Rose Bowl, Pasadena, California
Washington Redskins 27   Miami Dolphins 17
Washington fullback John Riggins carried the ball for 166 yards on 38 carries to lead Washington to their first NFL title since 1942. Riggins, the MVP, and quarterback Joe Theismann, who passed 23 times for 15 completions, 143 yards, and two touchdowns

paced the Redskins to 400 total yards of offense. Riggin's 43-yard touchdown run on fourth-and-one was the gamebreaker.

SUPER BOWL XVIII
Jan. 22, 1984, Tampa Stadium, Tampa, Florida
Los Angeles Raiders 38   Washington Redskins 9
This hopelessly lopsided victory set records. Raider reserve linebacker Jack Squirek intercepted a Joe Theismann pass at the Redskins five-yard line and ran the ball in for a touchdown with seven seconds left in the first half. Raiders' Marcus Allen rushed for 191 yards on 20 carries, including two touchdowns, one on a 74-yard run. Allen was voted game MVP.

SUPER BOWL XIX
Jan. 20, 1985, Stanford Stadium, Stanford, Calif.
San Francisco 49ers 38   Miami Dolphins 16
The Dolphins led 10–7 at the end of the first quarter, but 49er running back Roger Craig came back with three touchdowns. Joe Montana dominated the game with an MVP performance: 24 of 35 passes for 331 yards and three touchdowns. He also rushed five times for 59 yards and a touchdown. Craig had 58 yards on 15 carries and caught seven passes for 77 yards. Wendell Tyler rushed 13 times for 65 yards, as San Francisco's running game racked up 211 yards..

SUPER BOWL XX
Jan. 26, 1986, Louisiana Superdome, New Orleans
Chicago Bears 46   New England Patriots 10
The Patriots took a quick 3-0 lead on Tony Franklin's 36-yard field goal 1:19 elapsed in the first period. But the Bears rebounded by mauling the Pats. Chicago tied the record for sacks (7), and limited the Pats to 7 yards rushing. Total yardage at intermission told the story: Chicago 236, New England -19. The Bears ran up a fat 23–3 lead in the first half. In the second, the Bears marched 96 yards in nine plays, capped by quarterback Jim McMahon's one-yard rush for a touchdown. Bears defensive end Richard Dent won the MVP after contributing 1½ sacks, and leading the ferocious Chicago defense.

SUPER BOWL XXI
Jan. 25, 1987, Rose Bowl, Pasadena, California
New York Giants 39   Denver Broncos 20
The Broncos held a 10–9 lead at halftime, backed by the passing of John Elway, who capped a 58 yard scoring drive on six plays with a four yard touchdown run. But in the second half, the Giants' defense took over, sacking Elway in his end zone for a safety. The Broncos had a first and goal, but failed to score on three plays and a field goal attempt. After that the Giants' offense rebounded, scoring 30 points in the second half. Giant quarterback Phil Simms passed for 268 yards and three touchdowns, and was named MVP.

SUPER BOWL XXII
Jan 31, 1988, Jack Murphy Stadium, San Diego
Washington Redskins 42   Denver Broncos 10
The Broncos led early as John Elway hurled a 56-yard touchdown pass to wide receiver Ricky Nattiel on the Broncos' first play from scrimmage. But the Redskins erupted for 35 points on five straight possessions. Redskins' quarterback Doug Williams led the assault, hurling four touchdown passes, including 80- and 50-yarders to wide receiver Rick Sanders. Washington scored five touchdowns in 18 plays in 5:47 of possession. MVP Williams completed 18 of 29 passes for 340 yards. Rookie running back Timmy Smith ran 22 times for 204 yards.

SUPER BOWL XXIII
Jan. 22, 1989, Joe Robbie Stadium, Miami
San Francisco 49ers 20   Cincinnati Bengals 16

San Francisco became the first NFC team to win three Super Bowls by defeating the Bengals in a rematch of Super Bowl XVI. Even though San Francisco held an advantage in total yards (453 vs. 229), they found themselves trailing when Jim Breech's field goal gave Cincinnati a 16–13 lead with 3:20 left in the game. The 49ers started their winning drive at their own 8-yard line. Over the next 11 plays, they drove 92 yards to the winning score, a 10-yard touchdown pass from Joe Montana to John Taylor with 34 seconds left.

SUPER BOWL XXIV
Jan. 28,1990, Louisiana Superdome, New Orleans
San Francisco 49ers 55   Denver Broncos 10
San Francisco demolished the Broncos and became the first team to repeat as champions since the 1979–80 Steelers. Quarterback Joe Montana orchestrated the 49ers' offense, completing 22 of 29 passes for 297 yards and five touchdowns, en route to winning the MVP. Montana raised his record to 122 straight Super Bowl pass attempts without an interception. His primary receiver was Jerry Rice, who hauled in seven passes for 148 yards and three touchdowns. Running backs Tom Rathman and Roger Craig ran for three more touchdowns. Meanwhile, the 49er defense completely dominated Denver's offense, limiting them to 167 total yards, sacking quarterback John Elway six times and intercepting two passes.

SUPER BOWL XXV
Jan. 27, 1991, Tampa Stadium, Tampa, Florida
New York Giants 20   Buffalo Bills 19
The Giants edged the Bills in a nearly error-free game that was decided only when the Bills' Scott Norwood missed a field goal with eight seconds to play. Backup QB Jeff Hostetler and running back Ottis Anderson led the Giants' ball-control offense, holding the ball for a stunning 40:33. Anderson carried 21 times for 102 yards and was the MVP. After falling behind 12–3, the Giants defense slowed Buffalo's "hurry-up" offense, surrounding Jim Kelly's receivers with extra defensive backs and linebackers. Kelly completed 18 of 30 passes for 205 yards, but couldn't convert crucial third down opportunities.

SUPER BOWL XXVI
Jan. 26, 1992, The Metrodome, Minneapolis
Washington Redskins 37   Buffalo Bills 24
Washington jumped out to a 17-0 lead in the first half and never looked back. MVP quarterback Mark Rypien completed 18 of 33 passes for 292 yards and two touchdowns. Meanwhile, the blitzing Redskin defense intercepted Buffalo quarterback Jim Kelly four times and sacked him five times. In all, Kelly threw a record 58 passes, 30 of which went incomplete. Brad Edwards, Washington's free safety, had two interceptions and broke up five passes; linebacker Wilber Marshall forced two fumbles.

SUPER BOWL XXVII
Jan. 31, 1993, Rose Bowl, Pasadena, California
Dallas Cowboys 52   Buffalo Bills 17
Buffalo lost its third straight Super Bowl and the second consecutive rout. The game's turning point came early in the second quarter, when Buffalo drove inside the Dallas five-yard-line twice but came away with only three points, and lost quarterback Jim Kelly to injury. Inspired by its defense's two goal line stands, the Cowboys' offense, which had been fairly inept up to this point, came alive for a long scoring drive. The Bills fumbled on their first play from scrimmage on the ensuing drive, and one play later, the Cowboys had scored again, this time on a strike from Troy Aikman to Michael Irvin, giving Dallas a 28–10 halftime lead. Aikman passed for four touchdowns and was named MVP.

SUPER BOWL XXVIII
Jan. 30, 1994, Georgia Dome, Atlanta
Dallas Cowboys 30   Buffalo Bills 13

Buffalo became the first team in U.S. professional sports history to lose four consecutive championship games. The Bills led 13–6 at halftime on Thurman Thomas's 37 yards rushing and 54- and 28-yard field goals by Steve Christie. But Thomas fumbled on the opening drive of the second half and Dallas safety James Washington returned it 46 yards for a touchdown. Dallas then drove the length of the field on its next drive, with running back Emmitt Smith grinding out 61 yards. The Cowboys added another touchdown and a field goal to secure the victory. Smith, the league's regular season MVP, was named MVP of the Super Bowl as well.

SUPER BOWL XXIX
Jan. 29, 1995, Joe Robbie Stadium, Miami
San Francisco 49ers 49   San Diego Chargers 26

Favored by 20 points, (the largest margin in Super Bowl history), San Francisco scored early and often to capture a fifth Super Bowl championship. On the third play from scrimmage, Steve Young found Jerry Rice wide open inside the San Diego 10-yard line. Young threw six touchdowns and ran for 49 yards, making him the 49ers' leading rusher as well. Rice and running back Ricky Watters each scored three touchdowns. Young was named MVP for his 24-for-36, 325-yard performance.

SUPER BOWL XXX
Jan. 28, 1996, Sun Devil Stadium, Tempe, Ariz.
Dallas Cowboys 27   Pittsburgh Steelers 17

Dallas scored on its first three possessions, but failed to dominate the game, and led only 13–7 at halftime. In the second half, the Steelers threatened to close the gap, but quarterback Neil O'Donnell stunted the drive by throwing an interception to Cowboy cornerback Larry Brown. Pittsburgh rallied again in the fourth quarter to cut Dallas' lead to 20–17. But O'-Donnell threw another interception to Brown, who returned it to the Steeler 6-yard line, setting up the Cowboys' final touchdown. Brown was the obvious MVP choice.

SUPER BOWL XXXI
Jan. 26, 1997, Louisiana Superdome, New Orleans
Green Bay Packers 35   New England Patriots 21

Packer quarterback Bret Favre hit Andre Rison for a 54-yard touchdown pass on Green Bay's second play from scrimmage, but the Patriots rallied for a 14–10 first quarter lead. The Packers recaptured the lead with 17 points in the second quarter. In the second half, New England running back Curtis Martin scored to cut the lead to 27–21, but Desmond Howard returned the ensuing kickoff 99 yards for a touchdown. Howard's 154 yards on four kickoff returns and 90 yards on six punt returns earned him MVP honors.

SUPER BOWL XXXII
Jan. 25, 1998, Qualcomm Stadium, San Diego
Denver Broncos 31   Green Bay Packers 24

The victory was Denver's first in five tries, and the AFC's first in 13 years. With the game tied at 24 late in the fourth quarter, Denver took over at midfield. A penalty and a pass moved the Broncos closer, and then running back Terrell Davis ran 17 yards to the one-yard-line. On the next play, he punched it in for his third touchdown. With less than two minutes left, the Packers drove into Denver territory but could not convert a 4th and 6. Davis earned MVP honors for his 30 carries, 157 yards, and three touchdowns.

SUPER BOWL XXXIII
Jan. 31, 1999, Pro Player Stadium, Miami
Denver Broncos 34   Atlanta Falcons 19

Denver quarterback John Elway completed 18 of 29 passes for 336 yards and MVP honors, as the Broncos cruised to their second straight Super Bowl victory. Broncos running back Terrell Davis added 102 yards rushing, and cornerback Darrien Gordon had interception returns of 50 and 58 yards, each setting up a Denver touchdown. Despite driving deep into Denver territory several times, Atlanta could not crack the end zone until the fourth quarter, when the outcome was already decided.

SUPER BOWL XXXIV
Jan. 30, 2000, Georgia Dome, Atlanta
St. Louis Rams 23   Tennessee Titans 16

St. Louis dominated the first half, moving at will into Tennessee territory, but came away with only three field goals to show for it. The Rams extended their lead to 16–0 in the third quarter before the Titans put together three long scoring drives that tied the game with 2:12 remaining. With time running out, Tennessee quarterback Steve McNair engineered an 87-yard drive, but his last completion to Kevin Dyson left the Titans a yard short of a game-tying touchdown as time expired. Warner was named MVP on the strength of his 414 yards passing.

SUPER BOWL XXXV
Jan. 28, 2001, Raymond James Stadium, Tampa
Baltimore Ravens 34   New York Giants 7

Baltimore's vaunted defense pitched a shutout, as the Giants' only points came on special teams. Jermaine Lewis's 34-yard punt return set up Baltimore's first touchdown in the first quarter, and Duane Starks's interception return gave the Ravens a 17–0 lead late in the third quarter. Ron Dixon returned the ensuing kickoff 97 yards for the Giants' to cut the score to 17–7, but Lewis put the game out of reach on the very next play with an 84-yard kickoff return of his own. Middle linebacker Ray Lewis was the MVP.

SUPER BOWL XXXVI
Feb. 3, 2002, Louisiana Superdome, New Orleans
New England Patriots 20   St. Louis Rams 17

The Patriots, a 14-point underdog to the high-flying St. Louis offense, shocked the football world twice. First, they capitalized on three Ram turnovers to jump out to a 17–3 lead after three quarters. Then, after giving up the tying touchdown with 1:21 left in the game, New England marched 53 yards with no timeouts to set up Adam Vinatieri's game-winning 48-yard field goal. Patriots quarterback Tom Brady completed his Cinderella season by completing five passes in eight attempts in the final drive, and was named MVP.

SUPER BOWL XXXVII
Jan. 26, 2003, Qualcomm Stadium, San Diego
Tampa Bay Buccaneers 48   Oakland Raiders 21

The Buccaneers' defense dominated, intercepting five passes and returning three of them for touchdowns, and sacking Oakland quarterback Rich Gannon five times. Tampa Bay piled up 34 unanswered points on the strength of Michael Pittman's 124 rushing yards and Joe Jurevicius' 78 receiving yards. Dexter Jackson, who had the first two interceptions, was the MVP.

SUPER BOWL XXXVIII
Feb. 1, 2004, Reliant Stadium, Houston
New England Patriots 32   Carolina Panthers 29

Just as he did two years earlier, Adam Vinatieri kicked a tie-breaking field goal in the final seconds. Defense dominated for much of the game, which remained scoreless until the final 5:29 of the first half. With 1:08 remaining, New England drove down the field again, setting up Vinatieri's 41-yard kick. Patriot's quarterback Tom Brady, who threw for 354 yards, was the MVP again.

SUPER BOWL XXXIX

Feb. 6, 2005, Alltel Stadium, Jacksonville, Florida
New England Patriots 24 Philadelphia Eagles 21
For the third time in four years the Patriots won the Super Bowl matching the achievement of the Dallas Cowboys in the early 1990s. Quarterback Tom Brady was a standout again completing 22 of 33 passes, 11 of them to the game's MVP Deion Branch. A highlight was the play of All-Pro Eagles' wide receiver, Terrell Owens, who broke his leg and tore a ligament only seven weeks before but caught nine passes for 122 yards playing in 62 of 72 offensive snaps.

SUPER BOWL XL

February 5, 2006, Ford Field, Detroit
Pittsburgh Steelers 21 Seattle Seahawks 10
The Steelers relied on big plays to set up or score all three of their touchdowns, including a 75-yard touchdown run by RB Willie Parker to open the second half, followed by an end around pass from Antwaan Randle El to fellow wide receiver Hines Ward in the fourth quarter. The game also served as a farewell for Steelers RB Jerome Bettis, a Detroit native who retired as the fifth-leading rusher in NFL history. With the victory, Pittsburgh joined the San Francisco 49ers and the Dallas Cowboys as the only franchises to win five Super Bowls.

SUPER BOWL XLI

February 4, 2007, Dolphin Stadium, Miami
Indianapolis Colts 29, Chicago Bears 17
Led by MVP quarterback Peyton Manning, the Colts' steady offense wore down the Bears to win the first Super Bowl ever played in the rain. Despite three turnovers, a botched extra point attempt, and a missed chip-shot field goal attempt by Adam Vinatieri, the Colts still managed to take a 16–14 lead by half-time. Indianapolis's Tony Dungy and Chicago's Lovie Smith were the first African-Americans to coach in a Super Bowl; Dungy became the first African-American to win a Super Bowl.

SUPER BOWL XLII

February 3, 2008, University of Phoenix Stadium, Phoenix
New York Giants 17, New England Patriots 14
In one of the greatest upsets in sports history Eli Manning led the Giants to a 17–14 win, marching his team 83 yards on a final scoring drive to stun the heavily favored Patriots—and shatter New England's unbeaten season. The Patriots much-vaunted offense never seemed to find a rhythm, and led 7–3 going into the final quarter. New York finally scored a touchdown with 11:05 left to take the lead, but New England responded with their own, going ahead 14–10 with only 2:42 remaining. The scene was now set for one of the most dramatic Super Bowl plays of all time: with 1:15 left to go, Eli Manning escaped what looked like a certain sack and completed an improbable 32-yard pass to a leaping David Tyree, who managed to pin the ball to his helmet as he fell to the turf. Four plays later Manning hit Plaxico Burress in the end zone for the winning score.

SUPER BOWL XLIII

February 1, 2009, Raymond James Stadium, Tampa Bay
Pittsburgh Steelers, 27 Arizona Cardinals 23
The Steelers took an early lead and capped the first half (with zero left on the clock) with a Super Bowl-record 100-yard interception-touchdown-return after linebacker James Harrison robbed Warner at the one yard line. The Steelers opened the second half with a 79-yard drive and 21-yard field goal. Kurt Warner marched his team to 17 unanswered points in the fourth quarter. The indispensable Larry Fitzgerald caught both touchdown passes; the latter a 64-yard reception at the 2:37 mark to put the Cardinals ahead for the first time in the game.

SUPER BOWL XLIV

February 7, 2010, Sun Life Stadium, Miami
New Orleans Saints 31, Indianapolis Colts 17
The Colts jumped out to an early first quarter lead behind a 96-yard scoring drive, tying the record for longest in NFL history. The Saints opened the second half by recovering a daring onside kick, and scored on the ensuing possession, giving them the lead 13–10. The Colts regained the lead behind a Joseph Addai TD run. However a Drew Brees TD pass and two-point conversion gave the Saints a seven-point lead with six minutes remaining. Saints CB Tracy Porter intercepted Peyton Manning's pass and returned it 74 yards for the game-clinching touchdown. It was the Saints first Super Bowl title.

Pro Football Hall of Fame Members

Alphabetical listing of the members of the Professional Football Hall of Fame. Listing includes enshrinee's name, year of enshrinement, position, and the teams he played for.

Herb Adderley (1980) CB, Packers, Cowboys.
Troy Aikman (2006) QB, Cowboys.
George Allen (2002) Coach, Rams, Redskins.
Marcus Allen (2003) RB, Raiders, Chiefs.
Lance Alworth (1978) WR, Chargers, Cowboys.
Doug Atkins (1982) DE, Browns, Bears, Saints.
Morris (Red) Badgro (1981) E, Yankees, Giants, Dodgers.
Lem Barney (1992) CB, Lions.
Cliff Battles (1968) RB, QB, Braves, Redskins.
Sammy Baugh (1963) QB, Redskins.
Chuck Bednarik (1967) C, LB, Eagles.
Bert Bell (1963 Charter) Commissioner, NFL. Founder/coach, Eagles, Steelers.
Bobby Bell (1983) LB, DE, Chiefs.
Raymond Berry (1973) E, Colts.
Elvin Bethea (2003) DE, Oilers
Charles W. Bidwill, Sr. (1967) Owner/pres, Cardinals.
Fred Biletnikoff (1988) WR, Raiders.
George Blanda (1981) QB, PK, Bears, Colts, Oilers, Raiders.
Mel Blount (1989) CB, Steelers.

Terry Bradshaw (1989) QB, Steelers.
Bob Brown (2004) T, Eagles, Rams, Raiders.
Jim Brown (1971) FB, Browns.
Paul E. Brown (1967) Coach, General Manager, Browns, Bengals.
Roosevelt Brown (1975) OT, Giants.
Willie Brown (1984) CB, Broncos, Raiders.
Buck Buchanan (1990) DT, Chiefs.
Nick Buoniconti (2001) LB, Patriots, Dolphins.
Dick Butkus (1979) LB, Bears.
Earl Campbell (1991) RB, Oilers, Saints.
Tony Canadeo (1974) RB, Packers.
Joe Carr (1963) NFL President.
Harry Carson (1996) LB, Giants.
Dave Casper (2002) TE, Raiders, Oilers, Vikings.
Guy Chamberlin (1965) E, Bulldogs, Staleys, Yellowjackets, Cardinals. Coach, Bulldogs, Yellowjackets, Cardinals.
Jack Christiansen (1970) DB, Spartans, Lions.
Earl (Dutch) Clark (1970) DB, Spartans, Lions, Rams.
George Connor (1975) OT, DT, LB, Bears.

Jimmy Conzelman (1964) QB, Staleys, Independents, Badgers, Panthers. Owner, Steamrollers, Cardinals.

Lou Creekmur (1996) OL, Lions.

Larry Csonka (1987) RB, Dolphins, Giants.

Al Davis (1992) President, Owner, General Manager, Coach, Raiders. Commissioner, American Football League.

Willie Davis (1981) DE, Browns, Packers.

Len Dawson (1987) QB, Steelers, Browns, Texans, Chiefs.

Fred Dean (2008) DE, Chargers, Raiders.

Joe DeLameielleure (2003) G, Bills, Browns.

Eric Dickerson (1999) RB, Rams, Colts, Raiders, Falcons.

Dan Dierdorf (1996) OT, Cardinals.

Mike Ditka (1988) TE, Bears, Eagles, Cowboys.

Art Donovan (1968) DT, Colts, Yankees, Texans.

Tony Dorsett (1994) RB, Cowboys, Broncos.

John (Paddy) Driscoll (1965) QB, Pros, Staleys, Cardinals, Bears.

Bill Dudley (1966) RB, Steelers, Lions, Redskins.

Albert Glen (Turk) Edwards (1969) OT, Braves, Redskins.

Carl Eller (2004) DE, Vikings, Seahawks.

John Elway (2004) QB, Broncos.

Weeb Ewbank (1978) Coach, Colts, Jets.

Tom Fears (1970) E, Rams.

Jim Finks (1995) President, Vikings, Bears, Saints.

Ray Flaherty (1976) Coach, Redskins, Yankees.

Len Ford (1976) DE, E, Dons, Browns, Packers.

Dan Fortmann (1965) G, Bears.

Dan Fouts (1993) QB, Chargers.

Benny Friedman (2005) QB, Bulldogs, Wolverines, Giants, Dodgers.

Frank Gatski (1985) C, Browns, Lions.

Bill George (1974) LB, Bears, Rams.

Joe Gibbs (1996) Coach, Chargers, Redskins.

Frank Gifford (1977) RB, Giants.

Sid Gillman (1983) Coach, Rams, Chargers, Oilers.

Otto Graham (1965) QB, Browns.

Harold (Red) Grange (1963 Charter) RB, Bears, Yankees.

Bud Grant (1994) Coach, Vikings.

Darrell Green (2008) CB, Redskins.

(Mean) Joe Greene (1987) DT, Steelers.

Forrest Gregg (1977) OL, Packers, Cowboys.

Bob Griese (1990) QB, Dolphins.

Russ Grimm (2010) G, Redskins.

Lou Groza (1974) OT, PK Browns.

Joe Guyon (1966) RB, Bulldogs, Indians, Independents, Cowboys, Giants.

George Halas (1963) Founder, Coach, player, Staleys. President, Coach, player, Bears.

Jack Ham (1988) LB, Steelers.

Dan Hampton (2002) DE/DT, Bears.

John Hannah (1991) G, Patriots.

Franco Harris (1990) RB, Steelers, Seahawks.

Bob Hayes (2009) WR, Cowboys, 49ers.

Mike Haynes (1997) CB, Patriots, Raiders.

Ed Healey (1964) OT, Independents, Bears.

Mel Hein (1963) C, Giants. Coach, Dons.

Ted Hendricks (1990) LB, Colts, Packers, Raiders.

Wilbur (Pete) Henry (1963) OT, Bulldogs, Giants, Maroons.

Arnie Herber (1966) QB, Packers, Giants.

Bill Hewitt (1971) E, Bears, Eagles.

Gene Hickerson (2007) G, Browns.

Clarke Hinkle (1964) RB, Packers.

Elroy (Crazylegs) Hirsch (1968) HB, E, Rockets, Rams.

Paul Hornung (1986) HB, Packers.

Ken Houston (1986) S, Oilers, Redskins.

Cal Hubbard (1963) OT, Giants, Packers, Pirates.

Sam Huff (1982) LB, Giants, Redskins.

Lamar Hunt (1972) Founder, AFL; Owner Texans, Chiefs.

Don Hutson (1963) E, Packers.

Michael Irvin (2007) WR, Cowboys, TV broadcaster.

Ricky Jackson (2010) LB, Saints, 49ers.

Jimmy Johnson (1994) CB, 49ers.

John Henry Johnson (1987) RB, 49ers, Lions, Steelers, Oilers.

Charlie Joiner (1996), WR, Oilers, Bengals, Chargers.

David (Deacon) Jones (1980) DE, Rams, Chargers, Redskins.

Stan Jones (1991) G, DT, Bears, Redskins.

Henry Jordan (1995) DT, Packers.

Sonny Jurgensen (1983) QB, Eagles, Redskins.

Jim Kelly (2002) QB, Bills.

Leroy Kelly (1994) RB, Browns.

Walt Kiesling (1966) G, Eskimos, Maroons, Cardinals, Bears, Packers, Pirates. Coach, Steelers.

Frank (Bruiser) Kinard (1971) OT, Dodgers, Yankees.

Paul Krause (1998) S, Vikings, Redskins.

Early (Curly) Lambeau (1963) Founder, Packers Coach, Packers, Cardinals, Redskins.

Jack Lambert (1990) LB, Steelers.

Tom Landry (1990) Coach, Cowboys.

Dick (Night Train) Lane (1974). DB, Rams, Cardinals, Lions.

Jim Langer (1987) C, Dolphins, Vikings.

Willie Lanier (1986) LB, Chiefs.

Steve Largent (1995) WR, Seahawks.

Yale Lary (1979) DB, Lions.

Dante Lavelli (1975) E, Browns.

Bobby Layne (1967) QB, Bears, Bulldogs, Lions, Steelers.

Dick LeBeau (2010) CB, Lions.

Alphonse (Tuffy) Leemans (1978) RB, Giants.

Marv Levy (2001) Coach, Chiefs, Bills.

Bob Lilly (1980) DT, Cowboys.

Floyd Little (2010) RB, Broncos.

Larry Little (1993) G, Chargers, Dolphins.

James Lofton (2003) WR, Packers, Raiders, Bills, Rams.

Vince Lombardi (1971) Coach, GM, Packers, Redskins.

Howie Long (2000) DL, Raiders.

Ronnie Lott (2000) DB, 49ers, Raiders, Jets.

Sid Luckman (1965) QB, Bears.

William Roy (Link) Lyman (1964) T, Bulldogs, Yellowjackets, Bears.

Tom Mack (1999) OG, Rams.

John Mackey (1992) TE, Colts, Chargers.

John Madden (2006) Coach, Raiders, TV analyst.

Tim Mara (1963) Founder, President, Giants.

Wellington Mara (1997) Owner, Giants.

Gino Marchetti (1972) DE, Texans, Colts.

Dan Marino (2005) QB, Dolphins.

George Preston Marshall (1963) Founder, President, Braves (Redskins).

Ollie Matson (1972) RB, Cardinals, Rams, Lions, Eagles.

Bruce Matthews (2007) OL, Oilers, Titans.

Don Maynard (1987) WR, Giants, Titans, Jets, Cardinals.

George McAfee (1966) RB, Bears.

Mike McCormack (1984) OT, Yankees, Browns.

Randall McDaniel (2009) G, Vikings, Buccaneers.

Tommy McDonald (1988) WR, Eagles, Cowboys, Rams, Falcons, Browns.

Hugh McElhenny (1970) RB, 49ers Vikings, Giants, Lions.

John (Blood) McNally (1963) RB, Badgers, Eskimos, Maroons, Packers, Pirates Packers.

Mike Michalske (1964) G, Yankees, Packers.

Wayne Millner (1968) E, Redskins. Coach Eagles.

Bobby Mitchell (1983) WR, RB Browns, Redskins.

Ron Mix (1979) OT, Chargers, Raiders.

Art Monk (2008) WE, Redskins, Jets, Eagles.

Joe Montana (2000) QB, 49ers, Chiefs.

Warren Moon (2006) QB, Edmonton Eskimos (CFL),Oilers, Vikings, Seahawks, Chiefs.
Lenny Moore (1975) WR, RB, Colts.
Marion Motley (1968) RB, Browns, Steelers.
Mike Munchak (2001) G, Oilers.
Anthony Muñoz (1998) T, Bengals.
George Musso (1982) OT, G, Bears.
Bronko Nagurski (1963) RB, Bears.
Joe Namath (1985) QB, Jets, Rams.
Earle (Greasy) Neale (1969) Coach, Eagles.
Ernie Nevers (1963) RB, Eskimos, Cardinals.
Ozzie Newsome (1999) TE, Browns.
Ray Nitschke (1978) LB, Packers.
Chuck Noll (1993) Coach, Steelers.
Leo Nomellini (1969) DT, 49ers.
Merlin Olsen (1982) DT, Rams.
Jim Otto (1980) C, Raiders.
Steve Owen (1966) T, Cowboys, Giants. Coach, Giants.
Alan Page (1988) DT, Vikings, Bears.
Clarence (Ace) Parker (1972) QB, Dodgers, Yankees.
Jim Parker (1973) OL, Colts.
Walter Payton (1993) RB, Bears.
Joe Perry (1969) RB, 49ers, Colts.
Pete Pihos (1970) E, Eagles.
Fritz Pollard (2005) HB, Pros/Indians, Badgers, Cadamounts, Steam Roller.
John Randle (2010) DT, Vikings, Seahawks.
Hugh (Shorty) Ray (1966) Supervisor of Officials.
Dan Reeves (1967) Owner, Rams.
Mel Renfro (1996), CB, Cowboys.
Jerry Rice (2010) WR, 49ers, Raiders, Seahawks.
John Riggins (1992) RB, Jets, Redskins.
Jim Ringo (1981) C, Packers, Eagles.
Andy Robustelli (1971) DE, Rams, Giants.
Art Rooney (1964) Founder, President, Pirates, Steelers.
Dan Rooney (2000) President, Steelers.
Pete Rozelle (1985) Commissioner, NFL.
Bob St. Clair (1990) OT, 49ers.
Barry Sanders (2004) RB, Lions.
Charlie Sanders (2007) TE, Lions.
Gale Sayers (1977) RB, Bears.
Joe Schmidt (1973) LB, Lions. Coach, Lions.
Tex Schramm (1991) GM, Cowboys.
Lee Roy Selmon (1995) DE, Buccaneers.
Billy Shaw (1999) OG, Bills.
Art Shell (1989) OT, Raiders.
Don Shula (1997) Coach, Colts, Dolphins.
Mike Singletary (1998) LB, Bears.
O. J. Simpson (1985) RB, Bills, 49ers.
Jackie Slater (2001) OT, Rams.
Bruce Smith (2009) DE, Bills, Redskins.

Jackie Smith (1994) TE, Cardinals, Cowboys.
John Stallworth (2002) WR, Steelers.
Bart Starr (1977) QB, Packers.
Roger Staubach, (1985) QB, Cowboys.
Ernie Stautner (1969) DT, Steelers.
Jan Stenerud (1991) PK, Chiefs, Packers, Vikings.
Dwight Stephenson (1998) C, Dolphins.
Hank Stram (2003) Coach, Texans, Chiefs, Saints.
Ken Strong (1967) RB, Stapletons, Giants, Yankees.
Joe Stydahar (1967) OT, Bears.
Lynn Swann (2001) WR, Steelers.
Fran Tarkenton (1986) QB, Giants, Vikings.
Charley Taylor (1984) WR, RB, Redskins.
Jim Taylor (1976) RB, Packers, Saints.
Lawrence Taylor (1999) LB, Giants.
Derrick Thomas (2009) LB, Chiefs.
Emmitt Thomas (2008) CB, Chiefs.
Thurman Thomas (2007) RB, Bills, Browns.
Jim Thorpe (1963) RB, Bulldogs, Indians, Maroons, Independents, Giants, Bulldogs, Cardinals.
Andre Tippett (2008) LB, Patriots
Y.A. Tittle (1971) QB, Colts 49ers, Giants.
George Trafton (1964) C, Staleys, Bears.
Charley Trippi (1968) RB, QB, Cardinals.
Emlen Tunnell (1967) DB, Giants, Packers.
Clyde (Bulldog) Turner (1966) C, LB, Bears.
Johnny Unitas (1979) QB, Colts, Chargers.
Gene Upshaw (1987) G, Raiders.
Norm Van Brocklin (1971) QB, Rams, Eagles.
Steve Van Buren (1965) RB, Eagles.
Doak Walker (1986) HB, Lions.
Bill Walsh (1993) Coach, 49ers.
Paul Warfield (1983) WR, Browns, Dolphins.
Bob Waterfield(1965) QB, Coach, Rams.
Mike Webster (1997) C, Steelers.
Roger Wehrli (2007) CB, Cardinals.
Arnie Weinmeister, (1984) DT, Yankees, Giants.
Randy White (1994) DT, Cowboys.
Reggie White (2006) DE, Eagles, Packers.
Dave Wilcox (2000) LB, 49ers.
Bill Willis (1977) G, MG, Browns.
Larry Wilson (1978) DB, Cardinals.
Ralph Wilson Jr. (2009) Co-founder AFC, Owner, Bills.
Kellen Winslow (1995) TE, Chargers.
Alex Wojciechowicz (1968) C, LB, Lions, Eagles.
Willie Wood (1989) S, Packers.
Rod Woodson (2009) CB, S, Raiders, Steelers, 49ers.
Rayfield Wright (2006) OT, Cowboys.
Ron Yary (2001) OT, Vikings.
Steve Young (2005) QB, Buccaneers, 49ers.
Jack Youngblood (2001) DE, Rams.
Gary Zimmerman (2008) T, Vikings, Broncos.

BASKETBALL

National Basketball Association

Olympic Tower   www.nba.com
645 Fifth Avenue   Commissioner: David Stern
New York, NY 10022   Founded: 1946
(212) 826-7000   Number of teams: 30

The first pro game was played in 1896 in Trenton, N.J., and by 1898, the fledgling National Basketball League (NBL) and several others were organized. The Buffalo Germans were the first powerhouse, winning 792 games against only 86 losses from 1895 to 1925. In 1914, the New York Celtics (later renamed the Original Celtics) were organized, playing a "modern" style of basketball using zone defenses, the fast break, and a pivot man.

Other "ethnic" teams dominated in the 1930s, including the Philadelphia SPHAs (South Philadelphia Hebrew Association) under Eddy Gottlieb, and the black barnstorming New York Rens. The Basketball Association of America was formed in 1946 by hockey arena managers seeking additional tenants. In 1949, it merged with the NBL to form the modern NBA.

The American Basketball Association, an alternative pro league known for its three-point shots and its red, white and blue ball, lasted for nine seasons (1968–76) and featured such future NBA All-Stars as Julius Erving and Artis Gilmore. When the league folded after the 1975–76 season, four of its teams, the Denver Nuggets, Indiana Pacers, New York (now New Jersey) Nets, and San Antonio Spurs were admitted into the NBA.

NBA Final Standings, 2009–2010

EASTERN CONFERENCE	W–L	Pct.	Home	Away
Atlantic Division				
Boston (4)	50–32	.610	24–17	26–15
Toronto	40–42	.488	25–16	15–26
New York	29–53	.354	18–23	11–30
Philadelphia	27–55	.329	12–29	15–26
New Jersey	12–70	.146	8–33	4–37
Central Division				
Cleveland (1)	61–21	.744	35–6	26–15
Milwaukee (6)	46–36	.561	28–13	18–23
Chicago (8)	41–41	.500	24–17	17–24
Indiana	32–50	.390	23–18	9–32
Detroit	27–55	.329	17–24	10–31
Southeast Division				
Orlando (2)	59–23	.720	34–7	25–16
Atlanta (3)	53–29	.646	34–7	19–22
Miami (5)	47–35	.573	24–17	23–18
Charlotte (7)	44–38	.537	31–10	13–28
Washington	26–56	.317	15–26	11–30

WESTERN CONFERENCE	W–L	Pct.	Home	Away
Northwest Division				
Denver (4)	53–29	.646	34–7	19–22
Utah (5)	53–29	.646	32–9	21–20
Portland (6)	50–32	.610	26–15	24–17
Oklahoma City (8)	50–32	.610	26–15	24–17
Minnesota	15–67	.183	10–31	5–36
Southwest Division				
Dallas (2)	55–27	.671	28–13	27–14
San Antonio (7)	50–32	.610	29–12	21–20
Houston	42–40	.512	23–18	19–22
Memphis	40–42	.488	23–18	17–24
New Orleans	37–45	.451	24–17	13–28
Pacific Division				
L.A. Lakers (1)	57–25	.695	34–7	23–18
Phoenix (3)	54–28	.659	32–9	22–19
L.A. Clippers	29–53	.354	21–20	8–33
Golden State	26–56	.317	18–23	8–33
Sacramento	25–57	.305	18–23	7–34

Note: The numbers in parentheses reflect the team's seed for the playoffs.   **Source:** www.nba.com

NBA Playoff Results, 2010

FIRST ROUND

EASTERN CONFERENCE
Cleveland 4, Chicago 1
Boston 4, Miami 1
Atlanta 4, Milwaukee 3
Orlando 4, Charlotte 0

WESTERN CONFERENCE
L.A. Lakers 4, Oklahoma City 2
Utah 4, Denver 2
Phoenix 4, Portland 2
San Antonio 4, Dallas 2

CONFERENCE SEMIFINALS

EASTERN CONFERENCE
Boston 4, Cleveland 2
Orlando 4, Atlanta 0

WESTERN CONFERENCE
L.A. Lakers 4, Utah 0
Phoenix 4, San Antonio 0

CONFERENCE FINALS

EASTERN CONFERENCE
Boston 4, Orlando 2

WESTERN CONFERENCE
L.A. Lakers 4, Phoenix 2

NBA CHAMPIONSHIP FINALS
Los Angeles Lakers defeat Boston Celtics, 4 games to 3

Game 1: Los Angeles 102, Boston 89
Game 2: Boston 103, Los Angeles 94
Game 3: Los Angeles 91, Boston 84
Game 4: Boston 96, Los Angeles 89
Game 5: Boston 92, Los Angeles 86
Game 6: Los Angeles 89, Boston 67
Game 7: Los Angeles 83, Boston 79

2010 NBA First Round Draft Picks

Rank, Team	Player	Pos.	College/Country
1. Wizards	John Wall	PG	Kentucky
2. 76ers	Evan Turner	SG	Ohio State
3. Nets	Derrick Favors	PF	Georgia Tech
4. T'wolves	Wesley Johnson	SF	Syracuse
5. Kings	DeMarcus Cousins	PF	Kentucky
6. Warriors	Ekpe Udoh	PF	Baylor
7. Pistons	Greg Monroe	PF	Georgetown
8. Clippers	Al-Farouq Aminu	PF	Wake Forest
9. Jazz	Gordon Hayward[1]	SF	Butler
10. Pacers	Paul George	SF	Fresno State
11. Hornets	Cole Aldrich	C	Kansas
12. Grizzlies	Xavier Henry	SG	Kansas
13. Raptors	Ed Davis	PF	North Carolina
14. Rockets	Patrick Patterson	PF	Kentucky
15. Bucks	Larry Sanders[2]	PF	Virginia Commonwealth

Rank, Team	Player	Pos.	College/Country
16. T'wolves	Luke Babbitt[3]	SF	Nevada
17. Bulls	Kevin Seraphin[4]	PF	Cholet Basket (France)
18. Thunder	Eric Bledsoe[5]	PG	Kentucky
19. Celtics	Avery Bradley	PG	Texas
20. Spurs	James Anderson	SG	Okla. State
21. Thunder	Craig Brackins	SF	Iowa State
22. Blazers	Elliot Williams	SG	Memphis
23. T'Wolves	Trevor Booker[6]	C	Clemson
24. Hawks	Damion James[7]	SF	Texas
25. Grizzlies	Dominique Jones[8]	SG	South Florida
26. Thunder	Quincy Pondexter[9]	SF	Washington
27. Nets	Jordan Crawford[10]	SG	Xavier
28. Grizzlies	Greivis Vasquez[11]	PG	Maryland
29. Magic	Daniel Orton	PF	Kentucky
30. Wizards	Lazar Hayward[12]	SF	Marquette

Notes: 1. From New York through Phoenix. 2. From Chicago. 3. Draft rights traded to Portland. 4. From Milwaukee. 5. From Miami. 6. From Utah through Philadelphia. 7. Draft rights traded to New Jersey. 8. Draft rights traded to Dallas. 9. From Phoenix. 10. Draft rights traded to Atlanta. 11. From L.A. Lakers. 12. From Cleveland. **Source:** www.nba.com

NBA Leaders, 2009–2010

Scoring	G	Avg.
1. Kevin Durant, Oklahoma City	82	30.1
2. LeBron James, Cleveland	76	29.7
3. Carmelo Anthony, Denver	69	28.2
4. Kobe Bryant, L.A. Lakers	73	27.0
5. Dwayne Wade, Miami	77	26.6
6. Monta Ellis, Golden St.	64	25.5
7. Dirk Nowitzki, Dallas	81	25.0
8. Danny Granger, Indianapolis	62	24.1
9. Chris Bosh, Toronto	70	24.0
10. Amar'e Stoudemire, Phoenix	82	23.1

Rebounds	G	Reb.	Avg.
1. Dwight Howard, Orlando	82	1,082	13.2
2. Marcus Camby, Portland/ L.A. Clippers	74	871	11.8
3. Zach Randolph, Memphis	81	950	11.7
4. David Lee, N.Y. Knicks	81	949	11.7
5. Carlos Boozer, Utah	78	874	11.2

Assists	G	No.	Avg.
1. Steve Nash, Phoenix	81	892	11.0
2. Chris Paul, New Orleans	45	480	10.7
3. Deron Williams, Utah	76	798	10.5
4. Rajon Rondo, Boston	81	794	9.8
5. Jason Kidd, Dallas	80	794	9.8

Blocked Shots	G.	No.	Avg.
1. Dwight Howard, Orlando	82	228	2.78
2. Andrew Bogut, Milwaukee	69	175	2.54
3. Josh Smith, Atlanta	81	172	2.12
4. Brendan Haywood, Dallas/Washington	77	158	2.05
5. Marcus Camby, Portland/ L.A. Clippers	74	146	1.97

Steals	G.	No.	Avg.
1. Rajon Rondo, Boston	81	189	2.33
2. Monta Ellis, Golden State	64	143	2.23
3. Stephen Curry, Golden State	80	152	1.9
4. Dwayne Wade, Miami	77	142	1.84
5. Jason Kidd, Dallas	80	145	1.81

Field Goal Percentage	FGM	FGA	Pct.
1. Dwight Howard, Orlando	510	834	.612
2. Kendrick Perkins, Boston	314	522	.602
3. Nene Hilario, Denver	421	717	.587
4. Marc Gasol, Memphis	378	651	.581
5. Andrew Bynum, L.A. Lakers	392	688	.570

Free Throw Percentage	FTM	FTA	Pct.
1. Steve Nash, Phoenix	211	225	.938
2. Dirk Nowitzki, Dallas	536	586	.915
3. Ray Allen, Boston	231	253	.913
4. Chauncey Billups, Denver	466	512	.910
5. Luke Ridnour, Milwaukee	127	140	.907

3-Pt. FG Percentage	FGM	FGA	Pct.
1. Kyle Korver, Utah	59	110	.536
2. Mike Miller, Washington	82	171	.480
3. Daniel Gibson, Cleveland	71	149	.477
4. Jared Dudley, Phoenix	120	262	.458
5. Anthony Morrow, Golden St.	140	307	.456

Minutes Per Game	G	Min.	Avg.
1. Monta Ellis, Golden State	64	2,646	41.4
2. Gerald Wallace, Charlotte	76	3,119	41.0
3. Rudy Gay, Memphis	80	3,174	39.7
4. Kevin Durant, Oklahoma City	82	3,239	39.5
5. LeBron James, Cleveland	76	2,965	39.0

WNBA Final Standings and Playoffs, 2009

EASTERN CONFERENCE TEAM	W–L	WESTERN CONFERENCE TEAM	W–L
Indiana	22–12	Phoenix	23–11
Atlanta	18–16	Seattle	20–14
Detroit	18–16	Los Angeles	18–16
Washington	16–18	San Antonio	15–19
Chicago	16–18	Minnesota	14–20
Connecticut	16–18	Sacramento	12–22
New York	13–21		

CONFERENCE SEMIFINALS

Eastern:
Indiana 2, Washington 0
Detroit 2, Atlanta 0

Western:
Phoenix 2, San Antonio 1
Los Angeles 2, Seattle 1

CONFERENCE FINALS

Eastern:
Indiana 2, Detroit 1

Western:
Phoenix 2, Los Angeles 1

WNBA CHAMPIONSHIP
Phoenix Mercury 3, Indiana Fever 2

Note: The top four teams in each division made the playoffs. **Source:** WNBA. www.wnba.com

NBA World Championship Series, 1947–2010

Year	Winner	Loser	Games
1947	Philadelphia Warriors	Chicago Stags	4–1
1948	Baltimore Bullets	Philadelphia Warriors	4–2
1949	Minneapolis Lakers	Washington Capitols	4–2
1950	Minneapolis Lakers	Syracuse Nationals	4–2
1951	Rochester Royals	New York Knicks	4–3
1952	Minneapolis Lakers	New York Knicks	4–3
1953	Minneapolis Lakers	New York Knicks	4–1
1954	Minneapolis Lakers	Syracuse Nationals	4–3
1955	Syracuse Nationals	Fort Wayne Pistons	4–3
1956	Philadelphia Warriors	Fort Wayne Pistons	4–1
1957	Boston Celtics	St. Louis Hawks	4–3
1958	St. Louis Hawks	Boston Celtics	4–2
1959	Boston Celtics	Minneapolis Lakers	4–0
1960	Boston Celtics	St. Louis Hawks	4–3
1961	Boston Celtics	St. Louis Hawks	4–1
1962	Boston Celtics	Los Angeles Lakers	4–3
1963	Boston Celtics	Los Angeles Lakers	4–2
1964	Boston Celtics	San Francisco Warriors	4–1
1965	Boston Celtics	Los Angeles Lakers	4–1
1966	Boston Celtics	Los Angeles Lakers	4–3
1967	Philadelphia	San Francisco Warriors	4–2
1968	Boston Celtics	Los Angeles Lakers	4–2
1969	Boston Celtics	Los Angeles Lakers	4–3
1970	New York Knicks	Los Angeles Lakers	4–3
1971	Milwaukee Bucks	Baltimore Bullets	4–0
1972	Los Angeles Lakers	New York Knicks	4–1
1973	New York Knicks	Los Angeles Lakers	4–1
1974	Boston Celtics	Milwaukee Bucks	4–3
1975	Golden State Warriors	Washington Bullets	4–0
1976	Boston Celtics	Phoenix Suns	4–2
1977	Portland Trail Blazers	Philadelphia 76ers	4–2
1978	Washington Bullets	Seattle SuperSonics	4–3
1979	Seattle SuperSonics	Washington Bullets	4–1
1980	Los Angeles Lakers	Philadelphia 76ers	4–2
1981	Boston Celtics	Houston Rockets	4–2
1982	Los Angeles Lakers	Philadelphia 76ers	4–2
1983	Philadelphia 76ers	Los Angeles Lakers	4–0
1984	Boston Celtics	Los Angeles Lakers	4–3
1985	Los Angeles Lakers	Boston Celtics	4–2
1986	Boston Celtics	Houston Rockets	4–2
1987	Los Angeles Lakers	Boston Celtics	4–2
1988	Los Angeles Lakers	Detroit Pistons	4–3
1989	Detroit Pistons	Los Angeles Lakers	4–0
1990	Detroit Pistons	Portland Trail Blazers	4–1
1991	Chicago Bulls	Los Angeles Lakers	4–1
1992	Chicago Bulls	Portland Trail Blazers	4–2
1993	Chicago Bulls	Phoenix Suns	4–2
1994	Houston Rockets	New York Knicks	4–3
1995	Houston Rockets	Orlando Magic	4–0
1996	Chicago Bulls	Seattle SuperSonics	4–2
1997	Chicago Bulls	Utah Jazz	4–2
1998	Chicago Bulls	Utah Jazz	4–2
1999	San Antonio Spurs	New York Knicks	4–1
2000	Los Angeles Lakers	Indiana Pacers	4–2
2001	Los Angeles Lakers	Philadelphia 76ers	4–1
2002	Los Angeles Lakers	New Jersey Nets	4–0
2003	San Antonio Spurs	New Jersey Nets	4–2
2004	Detroit Pistons	Los Angeles Lakers	4–1
2005	San Antonio Spurs	Detroit Pistons	4–3
2006	Miami Heat	Dallas Mavericks	4–2
2007	San Antonio Spurs	Cleveland Cavaliers	4–0
2008	Boston Celtics	Los Angeles Lakers	4–2
2009	Los Angeles Lakers	Orlando Magic	4–1
2010	Los Angeles Lakers	Boston Celtics	4–3

NBA All-Time Career Leaders

Games

Robert Parish	1,611
Kareem Abdul-Jabbar	1,560
John Stockton	1,504
Karl Malone	1,476
Kevin Willis	1,424
Reggie Miller	1,389
Clifford Robinson	1,380
Gary Payton	1,335
Moses Malone	1,329
Buck Williams	1,307

Scoring Average

Michael Jordan	30.1
Wilt Chamberlain	30.1
LeBron James[1]	27.8
Elgin Baylor	27.4
Jerry West	27.0
Allen Iverson	26.7
Bob Pettit	26.4
George Gervin	26.2
Oscar Robertson	25.7
Dwyane Wade[1]	25.4

Rebounds

Wilt Chamberlain	23,924
Bill Russell	21,620
Kareem Abdul-Jabbar	17,440
Elvin Hayes	16,279
Moses Malone	16,212
Karl Malone	14,968
Robert Parish	14,715
Nate Thurmond	14,464
Walt Bellamy	14,241
Wes Unseld	13,769

Points

Kareem Abdul-Jabbar	38,387
Karl Malone	36,928
Michael Jordan	32,292
Wilt Chamberlain	31,419
Shaquille O'Neal[1]	28,255
Moses Malone	27,409
Elvin Hayes	27,313
Hakeem Olajuwon	26,946
Oscar Robertson	26,710
Dominique Wilkins	26,668

Assists

John Stockton	15,806
Jason Kidd[1]	10,923
Mark Jackson	10,334
Earvin Magic Johnson	10,141
Oscar Robertson	9,887
Isiah Thomas	9,061
Gary Payton	8,966
Steve Nash[1]	8,397
Rod Strickland	7,987
Maurice Cheeks	7,392

Free throw percentage[2]

Mark Price	.904
Steve Nash[1]	.903
Rick Barry	.900
Peja Stojakovic[1]	.895
Ray Allen[1]	.894
Calvin Murphy	.892
Chauncey Billups[1]	.892
Scott Skiles	.889
Reggie Miller	.888
Larry Bird	.886

Notes: Does not include statistics compiled in the ABA. Totals area as of the end of the 2009–10 season. 1. Player active in the 2009–10 season. 2. Minimum 1,200 free throws made. **Source:** www.nba.com

NBA Most Valuable Players, 1955–2010

Year	Most Valuable Player	Team	Year	Most Valuable Player	Team
1955–56	Bob Pettit	St. Louis Hawks	1983–84	Larry Bird	Boston Celtics
1956–57	Bob Cousy	Boston Celtics	1984–85	Larry Bird	Boston Celtics
1957–58	Bill Russell	Boston Celtics	1985–86	Larry Bird	Boston Celtics
1958–59	Bob Pettit	St. Louis Hawks	1986–87	Magic Johnson	Los Angeles Lakers
1959–60	Wilt Chamberlain	Philadelphia Warriors	1987–88	Michael Jordan	Chicago Bulls
1960–61	Bill Russell	Boston Celtics	1988–89	Magic Johnson	Los Angeles Lakers
1961–62	Bill Russell	Boston Celtics	1989–90	Magic Johnson	Los Angeles Lakers
1962–63	Bill Russell	Boston Celtics	1990–91	Michael Jordan	Chicago Bulls
1963–64	Oscar Robertson	Cincinnati Royals	1991–92	Michael Jordan	Chicago Bulls
1964–65	Bill Russell	Boston Celtics	1992–93	Charles Barkley	Phoenix Suns
1965–66	Wilt Chamberlain	Philadelphia 76ers	1993–94	Hakeem Olajuwon	Houston Rockets
1966–67	Wilt Chamberlain	Philadelphia 76ers	1994–95	David Robinson	San Antonio Spurs
1967–68	Wilt Chamberlain	Philadelphia 76ers	1995–96	Michael Jordan	Chicago Bulls
1968–69	Wes Unseld	Baltimore Bullets	1996–97	Karl Malone	Utah Jazz
1969–70	Willis Reed	New York Knicks	1997–98	Michael Jordan	Chicago Bulls
1970–71	Kareem Abdul-Jabbar	Milwaukee Bucks	1998–99	Karl Malone	Utah Jazz
1971–72	Kareem Abdul-Jabbar	Milwaukee Bucks	1999–00	Shaquille O'Neal	Los Angeles Lakers
1972–73	Dave Cowens	Boston Celtics	2000–01	Allen Iverson	Philadelphia 76ers
1973–74	Kareem Abdul-Jabbar	Milwaukee Bucks	2001–02	Tim Duncan	San Antonio Spurs
1974–75	Bob McAdoo	Buffalo Braves	2002–03	Tim Duncan	San Antonio Spurs
1975–76	Kareem Abdul-Jabbar	Los Angeles Lakers	2003–04	Kevin Garnett	Minn. Timberwolves
1976–77	Kareem Abdul-Jabbar	Los Angeles Lakers	2004–05	Steve Nash	Phoenix Suns
1977–78	Bill Walton	Portland Trail Blazers	2005–06	Steve Nash	Phoenix Suns
1978–79	Moses Malone	Houston Rockets	2006–07	Dirk Nowitzki	Dallas Mavericks
1979–80	Kareem Abdul-Jabbar	Los Angeles Lakers	2007–08	Kobe Bryant	Los Angeles Lakers
1980–81	Julius Erving	Philadelphia 76ers	2008–09	LeBron James	Cleveland Cavaliers
1981–82	Moses Malone	Houston Rockets	2009–10	LeBron James	Cleveland Cavaliers
1982–83	Moses Malone	Philadelphia 76ers			

NBA Rookies of the Year, 1952–2010

Year	Rookie of the Year	Team	Year	Rookie of the Year	Team
1952–53	Don Meineke	Fort Wayne Pistons	1982–83	Terry Cummings	San Diego Clippers
1953–54	Ray Felix	Baltimore Bullets	1983–84	Ralph Sampson	Houston Rockets
1954–55	Bob Pettit	Milwaukee Hawks	1984–85	Michael Jordan	Chicago Bulls
1955–56	Maurice Stokes	Rochester Royals	1985–86	Patrick Ewing	New York Knicks
1956–57	Tom Heinsohn	Boston Celtics	1986–87	Chuck Person	Indiana Pacers
1957–58	Woody Sauldsberry	Philadelphia Warriors	1987–88	Mark Jackson	New York Knicks
1958–59	Elgin Baylor	Minneapolis Lakers	1988–89	Mitch Richmond	Golden State Warriors
1959–60	Wilt Chamberlain	Philadelphia Warriors	1989–90	David Robinson	San Antonio Spurs
1960–61	Oscar Robertson	Cincinnati Royals	1990–91	Derrick Coleman	New Jersey Nets
1961–62	Walt Bellamy	Chicago Packers	1991–92	Larry Johnson	Charlotte Hornets
1962–63	Terry Dischinger	Chicago Zephyrs	1992–93	Shaquille O'Neal	Orlando Magic
1963–64	Jerry Lucas	Cincinnati Royals	1993–94	Chris Webber	Golden State Warriors
1964–65	Willis Reed	New York Knicks	1994–95	Grant Hill	Detroit Pistons
1965–66	Rick Barry	San Francisco Warriors		Jason Kidd	Dallas Mavericks
1966–67	Dave Bing	Detroit Pistons	1995–96	Damon Stoudamire	Toronto Raptors
1967–68	Earl Monroe	Baltimore Bullets	1996–97	Allen Iverson	Philadelphia 76ers
1968–69	Wes Unseld	Baltimore Bullets	1997–98	Tim Duncan	San Antonio Spurs
1969–70	Kareem Abdul-Jabbar	Milwaukee Bucks	1998–99	Vince Carter	Toronto Raptors
1970–71	Dave Cowens	Boston Celtics	1999–00	Elton Brand	Chicago Bulls
	Geoff Petrie	Portland Trail Blazers		Steve Francis	Houston Rockets
1971–72	Sidney Wicks	Portland Trail Blazers	2000–01	Mike Miller	Orlando Magic
1972–73	Bob McAdoo	Buffalo Braves	2001–02	Pau Gasol	Memphis Grizzlies
1973–74	Ernie DiGregorio	Buffalo Braves	2002–03	Amaré Stoudamire	Phoenix Suns
1974–75	Keith Wilkes	Golden State Warriors	2003–04	LeBron James	Cleveland Cavaliers
1975–76	Alvin Adams	Phoenix Suns	2004–05	Emeka Okafor	Charlotte Bobcats
1976–77	Adrian Dantley	Buffalo Braves	2005–06	Chris Paul	N.O./Ok. Hornets
1977–78	Walter Davis	Phoenix Suns	2006–07	Brandon Roy	Portland Trail Blazers
1978–79	Phil Ford	Kansas City Kings	2007–08	Kevin Durant	Seattle Supersonics
1979–80	Larry Bird	Boston Celtics	2008–09	Derrick Rose	Chicago Bulls
1980–81	Darrell Griffith	Utah Jazz	2009–10	Tyreke Evans	Sacramento Kings
1981–82	Buck Williams	New Jersey Nets			

Naismith Memorial Basketball Hall of Fame

The Basketball Hall of Fame elected its first members (including Dr. James Naismith, the game's originator) in 1959, but it did not have a physical home until February 17, 1968. In 1985 the Hall of Fame moved to larger quarters in Springfield, Mass. The Basketball Hall of Fame includes players from all basketball levels, including college, women's, and foreign leagues. Career statistics are given only for players who played some portion of their career in the NBA.

Player (Year Elected)	Games	Points	FG%	FT%	Rebs.	Assts.
Archibald, Nate (Tiny) (1991)	876	16,481	.467	.810	2,046	6,476
Averaged 18.8 ppg over 13 seasons; six-time All-Star.						
Arizin, Paul J. (1977)	713	16,266	.421	.810	6,129	1,665
NBA scoring leader in 1952 (25.4 ppg) and 1957 (25.6 ppg).						
Barkley, Charles (2006)	1,073	23,757	.541	.735	12,546	4,215
11-time All-Star, MVP in 1993, two-time Olympicgold medalist.						
Barry, Rick (1987)	794	18,395	.449	.900	5,168	4,017
(ABA Statistics)	226	6,884	.477	.880	1,695	935
NBA all-time free-throw percentage leader.						
Baylor, Elgin (1976)	846	23,149	.431	.780	11,463	3,650
Named to NBA All-Star First Team 10 times.						
Bellamy, Walt (1993)	1,043	20,941	.516	.632	14,241	2,544
NBA Rookie of the Year in 1962.						
Bing, Dave (1990)	901	18,327	.441	.775	3,420	5,397
NBA Rookie of the Year 1967, MVP 1976.						
Bird, Larry (1998)	897	21,791	.496	.886	8,974	5,695
NBA Rookie of the Year 1980. NBA MVP 1984, 1985, and 1986. 12-time All-star.						
Bradley, Bill (1982)	742	9,217	.448	.840	2,533	2,363
Averaged 30.2 ppg in 83 games at Princeton University.						
Chamberlain, Wilt (1978)	1045	31,419	.540	.511	23,924	4,643
Holds NBA single-game records for points (100) and rebounds (55); led league in scoring 1959–66.						
Cooper, Cynthia (2010), Two-time NCAA champion; four-time WNBA champion; WNBA Finals MVP						
Cousy, Bob (1970)	924	16,960	.375	.803	4,786	6,955
Led NBA in assists eight consecutive seasons (1953–60).						
Cowens, Dave (1991)	766	13,516	.460	.783	10,444	2,950
Seven-time All-star; three-time All-defensive team.						
Cunningham, Billy (1986)	654	13,626	.446	.720	6,638	2,625
(ABA Statistics)	116	2,684	.483	.791	1,343	680
Coached Philadelphia 76ers to 454-196 record in eight years.						
Dantley, Adrian (2008)	955	23,177	.540	.818	5,455	2,830
Six-time All-Star, averaged better than 30 points per game 1981–84.						
Davies, Bob (1969)	462	6,594	.378	.759	980[1]	2,050
NBL MVP, 1947	(NBL)[2]	107	1177	.747		
DeBusschere, Dave (1982)	875	14,053	.432	.699	9,618	2,497
NBA All-Defensive team six consecutive seasons (1969-74)						
Drexler, Clyde (2004)	1,086	22,195	.472	.788	6,677	6,125
Nine-time All-Star; led Houston Cougars to Final Four in 1982 and 1983.						
Dumars, Joe (2006)	1,018	16,401	.460	.843	2,203	4,612
Six-time All-Star, four times on NBA All-Defensive team.						
English, Alex (1997)	1,193	25,613	.507	.832	6,538	4,351
Eight-time all-star; Averaged 21.5 points per game over 15 seasons.						
Erving, Julius (Dr. J) (1993)	836	18,364	.507	.777	5,601	3,224
(ABA Statistics)	407	11,662	.504	.778	4,924	1,952
ABA MVP 1974-76; NBA MVP, 1981.						
Ewing, Patrick (2008)	1183	24,815	.504	.740	11,607	2,215
Two time gold-medal-winning Olympian; Eleven-time All-Star.						
Frazier, Walt (Clyde) (1987)	825	15,581	.490	.786	4,830	5,040
NBA All-Defensive team seven consecutive seasons (1969-75).						
Fulks, Joe (1977)	489	8,003	.302	.766	1,382[1]	587
NBA scoring leader in 1947 (23.2 ppg)						
Gallatin, Harry (1991)	682	8,843	.398	.773	6,684	1,208
Seven-time All-Star						
Gervin, George (Iceman) (1996)	791	20,708	.511	.844	3,607	2,214
(ABA Statistics)	269	5,887	.480	.831	1,995	584
All-NBA team five years in a row (1978–82).						
Gola, Tom (1975)	698	7,871	.431	.760	5,605	2,953
One of only two major-college players with over 2,000 points and 2,000 rebounds in career.						
Goodrich, Gail (1996)	1,031	19,181	.456	.807	3,279	4,805
Scored 42 points in 1965 NCAA Final; averaged 18.6 points per game over 14 years in NBA.						
Greer, Harold (Hal) (1981)	1,122	21,586	.452	.801	5,665	4,540
Scored 19 points in one quarter of 1968 All-Star game.						
Hagan, Cliff (1977)	746	13,447	.450	.798	5,019	2,236
(ABA Statistics)	94	1,423	.496	.807	436	398
Helped St. Louis to 1958 championship with 27.7 ppg in playoffs.						
Havlicek, John J. (Hondo) (1983)	1,270	26,395	.439	.815	8,007	6,114
Averaged 20.8 ppg; Member of 8 NBA championship teams.						
Hawkins, Connie (1992)	499	8,233	.467	.785	3,971	2,052
(ABA Statistics)	117	3,295	.515	.765	1,479	504
Four-time All-Star; ABA MVP 1969.						

Player (Year Elected)	Games	Points	FG%	FT%	Rebs.	Assts.
Hayes, Elvin (1990)	1,303	27,313	.452	.670	16,279	2,398
Led league in scoring (1969) and rebounds per game (1970,1974).						
Heinsohn, Tom (1986)	654	12,194	.405	.790	5,749	1,318
Played for eight NBA championship teams and coached two others.						
Houbregs, Robert J. (1987)	281	2,611	.404	.721	1,552	500
NCAA Player of the Year, 1953.						
Issel, Dan (1993)	718	14,659	.506	.797	5,707	1,804
(ABA Statistics)	500	12,823	.488	.786	5,426	1,103
Averaged 33.7 points per game in senior year at Kentucky, 1969–70.						
Jabbar, Kareem Abdul (1995)	1,560	38,387	.559	.721	17,440	5,660
Six-time NBA MVP. All-time NBA leader in scoring, games, minutes, field goals.						
Jeannette, Buddy (1994) (BAA-NBA)	139	997	.341	.781	N.A.	287
Won NBL MVP three times.						
Johnson, Dennis (2010)	1,100	15,535	.445	.797	4,249	5,499
Five-time NBA All-Star; two-time member of NBA All-Defensive Team						
Johnson, Earvin (Magic) (2002)	906	17,707	.520	.848	6,559	10,141
Led Lakers to five NBA championships; 3-time NBA MVP (1987, 1989, 1990); 12-time All-Star.						
Johnson, Gus (2010)	581	9,944	.440	.699	7,379	1,541
Five-time NBA All-Star, two-time member of the NBA All-Defensive Team						
Johnston, Neil (1990)	516	10,023	.444	.768	5,856	1,269
Named to four straight all-NBA First Teams (1953–56).						
Jones, K.C. (1989)	676	5,011	.387	.647	2,399	2,908
High scorer in 1955 NCAA finals (24 pts); held Tom Gola scoreless for 21 mins.						
Jones, Sam (1983)	871	15,411	.456	.803	4,305	2,209
Member of 10 NBA championship teams.						
Jordan, Michael (2009)	1,072	32,292	.497	.835	6,672	5,633
Five-time NBA MVP; 14-time All-Star; one of the most recognized people in the world.						
Lanier, Bob (1992)	959	19,248	.514	.767	9,698	3,007
Eight-time All-Star; NBA MVP, 1974.						
Lloyd, Earl (2003)	560	4,682	.356	.750	3,609	810
First African-American to play in a NBA game, 1950.						
Lovellette, Clyde (1988)	704	11,947	.443	.756	6,663	1,165
Three-time All-American at University of Kansas (1950–52).						
Lucas, Jerry Ray (Luke) (1979)	829	14,053	.499	.783	12,942	2,730
NBA Rookie of the Year and field-goal percentage leader (.527) in 1964.						
Macauley, Edward (Easy Ed) (1960)	641	11,234	.436	.761	2,079	1,667
NBA All-Star Game MVP, 1951						
Malone, Karl (2010)	1,476	36,928	.516	.742	14,968	5,248
Two-time NBA MVP; second on the NBA's all-time scoring list						
Malone, Moses (2001)	1,329	27,409	.491	.769	16,212	1,796
Three-time MVP, 12-time All-Star. Averaged 20 points per game 11 straight seasons.						
Maravich, Pete (Pistol) (1987)	658	15,948	.441	.820	2,747	3,563
NCAA career record holder for points scored (3667) and scoring avg. (44.2 ppg).						
Martin, Slater (1981)	745	7,337	.364	.762	2,302[1]	3,160
Played in seven straight All-Star Games, 1953–59.						
McAdoo, Bob (2000)	852	18,787	.503	.754	8,048	1,951
NBA Rookie of the Year (1973); led league in scoring 1974, 1975, and 1976.						
McGuire, Dick (1993)	738	5,921	.389	.644	2,784	4,205
Averaged 8.0 ppg.						
McHale, Kevin (1999)	971	17,335	.554	.798	7,122	1,670
Seven-time All-Star; won Sixth Man Award twice; won 3 NBA Championships: 1981, 1984, 1986.						
Mikan, George L. (1959)	439	10,156	.404	.782	4,167[1]	1,245
Three-time NBA scoring leader (1949, 1950, 1952).						
Mikkelson, Vern (1995)	699	10,063	.403	.766	5,940[1]	1,515
Six-time NBA All-Star; won 4 NBA Championships: 1950, 1952, 1953, & 1954.						
Monroe, Earl (The Pearl) (1990)	926	17,454	.464	.807	2,796	3,594
NBA Rookie of the Year, 1968.						
Murphy, Calvin (1993)	1,002	17,949	.482	.892	2,103	4,402
Set single-season free throw percentage record with .958 in 1980–81.						
Olajuwon, Hakeem (2008)	1,238	26,946	.512	.712	13,748	3,058
3,000+ blocked shots, 2,000+ steals; back to back Finals MVP, 1994–95.						
Parish, Robert (2003)	1,611	23,334	.537	.721	14,715	2,180
Nine-time NBA All-Star (1981–87, 1990–91). Won 3 NBA Championships (1981, 1984, & 1986).						
Petrovic, Drazen (2002)	290	4,461	.506	.841	669	701
Averaged 15.4 ppg and 43.7% from 3-pt range over 4 years before being killed in auto accident.						
Pettit, Bob (1970)	792	20,880	.436	.761	12,849	2,369
Led NBA in scoring (25.7 ppg) and rebounds (1164) in 1956.						
Phillip, Andy (1961)	701	6,384	.368	.695	2,395[1]	3,759
Led NBA in assists, 1951 and 1952.						
Pippen, Scottie (2010)	1,178	18,940	.473	.704	7,494	6,135
Six-time NBA champion; three-time All-NBA first team honoree						
Pollard, Jim (1977)	438	5,762	.360	.750	2,487[1]	1,417
Started four NBA All-Star Games.						
Ramsey, Frank (1981)	623	8,378	.402	.804	3,410	1,136
Member of seven NBA championship teams.						

Player (Year Elected)	Games	Points	FG%	FT%	Rebs.	Assts.
Reed, Willis (1981)	650	12,183	.476	.747	8,414	1,186
1970 NBA Most Valuable Player, All-Star Game MVP and Playoff MVP.						
Risen, Arnie (1998)	637	7,633	.381	.699	5,011	1,058
Three-time NBA All-star (1953, 1954, and 1955).						
Robertson, Oscar (1979)	1,040	26,710	.485	.838	7,804	9,887
NBA MVP 1964; Member of All-NBA First team, 1961–69.						
Robinson, David (2009)	987	20,790	.518	.736	10,497	2,441
Rookie of the Year, 1990; 10-time All-Star.						
Russell, Bill (1974)	963	14,522	.440	.561	21,620	4,100
Five-time NBA Most Valuable Player; 32 rebounds in one half vs. Philadelphia, 1957.						
Schayes, Adolph (Dolph) (1972)	996	18,438	.380	.849	11,256[1]	3,072
NBA Coach of the Year, 1966.						
Sharman, Bill (1974)	711	12,665	.426	.883	2,779	2,101
Led NBA in free-throw percentage seven seasons.						
Stokes, Maurice (2004)	202	3,315	.351	.698	3,492	1,062
Rookie of the Year (1955–56); killed in freak accident after three NBA seasons.						
Thomas, Isiah (2000)	979	18,822	.452	.759	3,478	9,061
NBA Rookie of the Year (1982); 12-time All-Star; MVP of the 1990 Finals.						
Thompson, David (1996)	509	11,264	.504	.778	1,921	1,631
(ABA Statistics)	83	2,158	.515	.794	525	308
NCAA player of the year 1974 and 1975; ABA Rookie of the Year, 1976.						
Thurmond, Nate (1984)	964	14,437	.421	.667	14,464	2,575
1,000+ rebounds 1964–69, 1970–73.						
Twyman, Jack (1982)	23	15,840	.450	.778	5,421	1,969
Led NBA in field-goal percentage, 1958 (.452).						
Unseld, Wes (1988)	984	10,624	.509	.633	13,769	3,822
Named NBA Most Valuable Player and Rookie of the Year in same year (1969).						
Walton, Bill (1993)	468	6,215	.521	.660	4,923	1,590
MVP in 1976.						
Wanzer, Robert (1987)	502	5,891	.388	.800	1,652[1]	1,575
Free-throw percentage leader, 1952 (.904).						
West, Jerry Alan (1979)	932	25,192	.474	.814	5,376	6,238
NBA MVP in 1970; .805 free throw percentage in 13 years in the playoffs.						
Worthy, James (2003)	926	16,320	.521	.769	4,707	2,791
MVP of 1988 NBA Finals. Won three NBA titles with L.A. Lakers (1985, 1987, 1988).						
Wilkins, Dominique (2006)	1,074	26,668	.461	.811	7,169	2,677
Nine-time All-Star, All-NBA first team in 1986.						
Wilkens, Lenny (1989)	1,077	17,772	.432	.774	5,030	7,211
600+ assists 6 consecutive seasons.						
Yardley, George (1996)	472	9,063	.422	.780	4,220	815
First player in NBA history to score 2,000 points in a season.						

Note: All statistics for NBA career unless otherwise noted. NBL = National Basketball League. ABA = American Basketball Association. NCAA = National Collegiate Athletic Association 1. Does not include seasons played prior to 1950–51 when the NBA first began keeping statistics for rebounds. 2. The National Basketball League did not keep statistics for field-goal percentage, rebounds, or assists.

COACHES AND CONTRIBUTORS

Anderson, W. Harold 1984
Auerbach, Arnold J. "Red" 1968
Auriemma, Geno 2006
Barry, Justin "Sam" 1978
Blood, Ernest A. 1960
Boeheim, Jim 2005
Brown, Hubie 2005
Brown, Larry 2002
Buss, Jerry 2010
Calhoun, Jim 2005
Cann, Howard G. 1967
Carlson, Dr. H. Clifford 1959
Carnesecca, Lou 1992
Carnevale, Ben 1969
Carril, Pete 1997
Case, Everett 1981
Chaney, John 2001
Chancellor, Van 2007
Conradt, Jody 1998
Crum, Denny 1994
Daly, Chuck, 1994
Davison, William 2008
Ferrandiz, Pedro 2007
Dean, Everett S. 1966
Diddle, Edgar A. 1971
·Drake, Bruce 1972
·Gaines, Clarence 1981
Gamba, Sandro 2006

Gardner, James H. "Jack" 1983
Gavitt, David 2006
Gill, Amory T. "Slats" 1967
Gunter, Sue 2005
Hannum, Alex 1998
Harshman, Marv 1984
Haskins, Don 1997
Hickey, Edgar S. 1978
Hobson, Howard A. 1965
Holzman, William "Red" 1985–86
Hurley Sr., Robert "Bob" 2010
Iba, Henry P. "Hank" 1968
Jackson, Phil 2007
Julian, Alvin "Doggie" 1967
Keaney, Frank W. 1960
Keogan, George E. 1961
Knight, Bob 1991
Krzyzewski, Mike 2001
Kundla, John 1995
Lambert, Ward L. 1960
Litwack, Harry 1975
Loeffler, Kenneth D. 1964
Lonborg, Arthur C. 1972
McCutchan, Arad A. 1980
McGuire, Al 1992
McGuire, Frank J. 1976
Meanwell, Dr. Walter E. 1959
Meyer, Raymond J. 1978

Miller, Ralph 1987
Moore, Billie 1999
Nikolic, Aleksandar 1998
Novosel, Mirko 2007
Olson, Lute 2002
Ramsay, Jack 1992
Riley, Pat 2008
Rudolph, Marvin "Mendy" 2007
Rupp, Adolph F. 1968
Rush, Cathy 2008
Sachs, Leonard D. 1961
Sharman, Bill, 2004
Shelton, Everett F. 1979
Sloan, Jerry 2009
Smith, Dean 1982
Stringer, Vivian 2009
Summitt, Pat, 2000
Taylor, Fred R. 1985–86
Teague, Bertha 1984
Thompson, John 1999
Vitale, Dick 2008
Wade, L. Margaret 1984
Watts, Stanley H. 1985–86
Wilkens, Lenny, 1998
Williams, Roy 2007
Wooden, John R. 1972
Woolpert, Phil 1992
Wootten, Morgan 2000

ICE HOCKEY

National Hockey League
www.nhl.com **Commissioner: Gary Bettman**
No. of Teams: 30 **Founded: 1917**

In September 2004, franchise owners locked out their players upon the expiration of the collective bargaining agreement. NHL Commissioner Gary Bettman claimed that salary arbitration, expensive signing bonuses for rookies, and the lack of a salary cap or luxury tax had caused the league to lose close to $500 million over the previous two seasons, although he never acknowledged the owners' responsibility for this situation. After months of negotiation the entire season was cancelled in February 2005. An agreement was finally reached in June as the players accepted a salary cap that would guarantee large salaries only to the older players.

The Stanley Cup, 1917–2010

The oldest trophy competed for by professional athletes in North America, the Stanley Cup was donated by Frederick Arthur, Lord Stanley of Preston, in 1893. Lord Stanley purchased the trophy for 10 guineas (about $50) for presentation to the amateur hockey champions of Canada. The National Hockey League took exclusive control of the cup in 1946, and now awards it annually to the team that wins the league's best-of-seven final playoff series.

Season	Champion	Finalist	GP in final	Season	Champion	Finalist	GP in final
1917–18	Toronto Arenas	Vancouver Millionaires	5	1963–64	Toronto Maple Leafs	Detroit Red Wings	7
1918–19	No decision[1]	No decision	5	1964–65	Montreal Canadiens	Chicago Blackhawks	7
1919–20	Ottawa Senators	Seattle Millionaires	5	1965–66	Montreal Canadiens	Detroit Red Wings	6
1920–21	Ottawa Senators	Vancouver Millionaires	5	1966–67	Toronto Maple Leafs	Montreal Canadiens	6
1921–22	Toronto St. Pats	Vancouver Millionaires	5	1967–68	Montreal Canadiens	St. Louis Blues	4
1922–23	Ottawa Senators	Edmonton Eskimos	2	1968–69	Montreal Canadiens	St. Louis Blues	4
1923–24	Montreal Canadiens	Calgary Tigers	2	1969–70	Boston Bruins	St. Louis Blues	4
1924–25	Victoria Cougars	Montreal Canadiens	4	1970–71	Montreal Canadiens	Chicago Blackhawks	7
1925–26	Montreal Maroons	Victoria Cougars	4	1971–72	Boston Bruins	New York Rangers	6
1926–27	Ottawa Senators	Boston Bruins	4	1972–73	Montreal Canadiens	Chicago Blackhawks	6
1927–28	New York Rangers	Montreal Canadiens	5	1973–74	Philadelphia Flyers	Boston Bruins	6
1928–29	Boston Bruins	New York Rangers	2	1974–75	Philadelphia Flyers	Buffalo Sabres	6
1929–30	Montreal Canadiens	Boston Bruins	2	1975–76	Montreal Canadiens	Philadelphia Flyers	4
1930–31	Montreal Canadiens	Chicago Blackhawks	5	1976–77	Montreal Canadiens	Boston Bruins	4
1931–32	Toronto Maple Leafs	New York Rangers	3	1977–78	Montreal Canadiens	Boston Bruins	6
1932–33	New York Rangers	Toronto Maple Leafs	4	1978–79	Montreal Canadiens	New York Rangers	5
1933–34	Chicago Blackhawks	Detroit Red Wings	4	1979–80	New York Islanders	Philadelphia Flyers	6
1934–35	Montreal Maroons	Toronto Maple Leafs	3	1980–81	New York Islanders	Minnesota North Stars	5
1935–36	Detroit Red Wings	Toronto Maple Leafs	4	1981–82	New York Islanders	Vancouver Canucks	4
1936–37	Detroit Red Wings	New York Rangers	5	1982–83	New York Islanders	Edmonton Oilers	4
1937–38	Chicago Blackhawks	Toronto Maple Leafs	4	1983–84	Edmonton Oilers	New York Islanders	5
1938–39	Boston Bruins	Toronto Maple Leafs	5	1984–85	Edmonton Oilers	Philadelphia Flyers	5
1939–40	New York Rangers	Toronto Maple Leafs	6	1985–86	Montreal Canadiens	Calgary Flames	5
1940–41	Boston Bruins	Detroit Red Wings	4	1986–87	Edmonton Oilers	Philadelphia Flyers	7
1941–42	Toronto Maple Leafs	Detroit Red Wings	7	1987–88	Edmonton Oilers	Boston Bruins	4
1942–43	Detroit Red Wings	Boston Bruins	4	1988–89	Calgary Flames	Montreal Canadiens	6
1943–44	Montreal Canadiens	Chicago Blackhawks	4	1989–90	Edmonton Oilers	Boston Bruins	5
1944–45	Toronto Maple Leafs	Detroit Red Wings	7	1990–91	Pittsburgh Penguins	Minnesota North Stars	6
1945–46	Montreal Canadiens	Boston Bruins	5	1991–92	Pittsburgh Penguins	Chicago Blackhawks	4
1946–47	Toronto Maple Leafs	Montreal Canadiens	6	1992–93	Montreal Canadiens	Los Angeles Kings	5
1947–48	Toronto Maple Leafs	Detroit Red Wings	4	1993–94	New York Rangers	Vancouver Canucks	7
1948–49	Toronto Maple Leafs	Detroit Red Wings	4	1994–95[2]	New Jersey Devils	Detroit Red Wings	4
1949–50	Detroit Red Wings	New York Rangers	7	1995–96	Colorado Avalanche	Florida Panthers	4
1950–51	Toronto Maple Leafs	Montreal Canadiens	5	1996–97	Detroit Red Wings	Philadelphia Flyers	4
1951–52	Detroit Red Wings	Montreal Canadiens	4	1997–98	Detroit Red Wings	Washington Capitals	4
1952–53	Montreal Canadiens	Boston Bruins	5	1998–99	Dallas Stars	Buffalo Sabres	6
1953–54	Detroit Red Wings	Montreal Canadiens	7	1999–00	New Jersey Devils	Dallas Stars	6
1954–55	Detroit Red Wings	Montreal Canadiens	7	2000–01	Colorado Avalanche	New Jersey Devils	7
1955–56	Montreal Canadiens	Detroit Red Wings	5	2001–02	Detroit Red Wings	Carolina Hurricanes	5
1956–57	Montreal Canadiens	Boston Bruins	5	2002–03	New Jersey Devils	Anaheim Mighty Ducks	7
1957–58	Montreal Canadiens	Boston Bruins	6	2003–04	Tampa Bay Lightning	Calgary Flames	7
1958–59	Montreal Canadiens	Toronto Maple Leafs	5	2005–06[3]	Carolina Hurricanes	Edmonton Oilers	7
1959–60	Montreal Canadiens	Toronto Maple Leafs	4	2006–07	Anaheim Ducks	Ottawa Senators	5
1960–61	Chicago Blackhawks	Detroit Red Wings	6	2007–08	Detroit Red Wings	Pittsburgh Penguins	6
1961–62	Toronto Maple Leafs	Chicago Blackhawks	6	2008–09	Pittsburgh Penguins	Detroit Red Wings	7
1962–63	Toronto Maple Leafs	Detroit Red Wings	5	2009–10	Chicago Blackhawks	Philadelphia Flyers	6

Notes: 1. In the spring of 1919 the Montreal Canadiens traveled to Seattle to meet Seattle, champs of the Pacific Coast Hockey League. After five games had been played—teams were tied at 2 wins and 1 tie—the series was called off by the local Department of Health because of the influenza epidemic. 2. Strike-shortened season. 3. The 2004–05 season was canceled due to labor disagreement. **Source:** National Hockey League.

NHL Standings, 2009–2010

EASTERN CONFERENCE

Atlantic	W	L	OT	Pts
New Jersey Devils	48	27	7	103
Pittsburgh Penguins	47	28	7	101
Philadelphia Flyers	41	35	6	88
New York Rangers	38	33	11	87
New York Islanders	34	37	11	79

Northeast	W	L	OT	Pts
Buffalo Sabres	45	27	10	100
Ottawa Senators	44	32	6	94
Boston Bruins	39	30	13	91
Montreal Canadiens	39	33	10	88
Toronto Maple Leafs	30	38	14	74

Southeast	W	L	OT	Pts
Washington Capitals	54	15	13	121
Atlanta Thrashers	35	34	13	83
Carolina Hurricanes	35	37	10	80
Tampa Bay	34	36	12	80
Florida Panthers	32	37	13	77

WESTERN CONFERENCE

Central	W	L	OT	Pts
Chicago Blackhawks	52	22	8	112
Detroit Red Wings	44	24	14	102
Nashville Predators	47	29	6	100
St. Louis Blues	40	32	10	90
Columbus Blue Jackets	32	35	15	79

Northwest	W	L	OT	Pts
Vancouver Canucks	49	28	5	103
Colorado Avalanche	43	30	9	95
Calgary Flames	40	32	10	90
Minnesota Wild	40	32	10	90
Edmonton Oilers	27	47	8	62

Pacific	W	L	OT	Pts
San Jose Sharks	51	20	11	113
Phoenix Coyotes	50	25	7	107
Los Angeles Kings	46	27	9	101
Anaheim Ducks	39	32	11	89
Dallas Stars	37	31	14	88

Stanley Cup Playoffs, 2009–2010

(All rounds are seven-game series)

EASTERN CONFERENCE	WESTERN CONFERENCE

ROUND 1

Montreal Canadiens 4, Washington Capitals 3
Philadelphia Flyers 4, New Jersey Devils 1
Boston Bruins 4, Buffalo Sabres 2
Pittsburgh Penguins 4, Ottawa Senators 2

San Jose Sharks 4, Colorado Avalanche 2
Chicago Blackhawks 4, Nashville Predators 2
Vancouver Canucks 4, Los Angeles Kings 2
Detroit Red Wings 4, Phoenix Coyotes 3

ROUND 2

Montreal Canadiens 4, Pittsburgh Penguins 3
Philadelphia Flyers 4, Boston Bruins 3

San Jose Sharks 4, Detroit Red Wings 1
Chicago Blackhawks 4, Vancouver Canucks 2

CONFERENCE CHAMPIONSHIPS

Philadelphia Flyers 4, Montreal Canadiens 2
Chicago Blackhawks 4, San Jose Sharks 2

STANLEY CUP CHAMPIONSHIP
Chicago Blackhawks 4, Philadelphia Flyers 2

Top Scorers, 2009–2010

Player, Team	Points
1. Henrik Sedin, Vancouver	112
2. Sidney Crosby, Pittsburgh	109
3. Alex Ovechkin, Washington	109
4. Nicklas Backstrom, Washington	101
5. Steven Stankos, Tampa Bay	95
6. Martin St. Louis, Tampa Bay	94
7. Brad Richards, Dallas	91
8. Joe Thornton, San Jose	89
9. Patrick Kane, Chicago	88
10. Marian Gaborik, N.Y. Rangers	86

Player, Team	Goals
1. Sidney Crosby, Pittsburgh	51
2. Steven Stankos, Tampa Bay	51
3. Alex Ovechkin, Washington	50
4. Patrick Marleau, San Jose	44
5. Marian Gaborik, N.Y. Rangers	42
6. Ilya Kovalchuk, Atlanta/N.J. Devils	41
7. Alexander Semin, Washington	40
8. Dany Heatly, San Jose	39
9. Zach Parise, N.J. Devils	38
10. Alexandre Burrows, Vancouver	35

Player, Team	Assists
1. Henrik Sedin, Vancouver	83
2. Joe Thornton, San Jose	69
3. Nicklas Backstrom, Washington	68
4. Brad Richards, Dallas	67
5. Martin St. Louis, Tampa Bay	65
6. Alex Ovechkin, Washington	59
7. Paul Stastny, Colorado	59
8. Sidney Crosby, Pittsburgh	58
9. Patrick Kane, Chicago	58
10. Mike Green, Washington	57

Source: National Hockey League.

Top 10 All-Time NHL Scoring Leaders

Player	Seasons	GOALS Games	Goals	Goals/ Game	Player	Seasons	ASSISTS Games	Assists	Assists/ Game
Wayne Gretzky	20	1,487	894	.601	Wayne Gretzky	20	1,487	1,963	1.320
Gordie Howe	26	1,767	801	.453	Ron Francis	23	1,731	1,249	.722
Brett Hull	19	1,264	741	.586	Mark Messier	25	1,756	1,193	.679
Marcel Dionne	18	1,348	731	.542	Ray Bourque	22	1,612	1,169	.725
Phil Esposito	18	1,282	717	.559	Paul Coffey	21	1,409	1,135	.806
Mike Gartner	19	1,432	708	.494	Adam Oates	19	1,337	1,079	.807
Mark Messier	25	1,756	694	.395	Steve Yzerman	23	1,514	1,063	.702
Steve Yzerman	23	1,514	692	.457	Gordie Howe	26	1,767	1,049	.594
Mario Lemieux	22	915	690	.754	Marcel Dionne	18	1,348	1,040	.772
Luc Robitaille	20	1,431	668	.467	Mario Lemieux	22	915	1,033	1.129

Player	Seasons	Games	Goals	Assists	Points	Player	Seasons	Games	Goals	Assists	Points
					POINTS						
Wayne Gretzky	20	1,487	894	1,963	2,857	Steve Yzerman	23	1,514	692	1,063	1,755
Mark Messier	25	1,756	694	1,193	1,887	Mario Lemieux	22	915	690	1,033	1,723
Gordie Howe	26	1,767	801	1,049	1,850	Joe Sakic	23	1,378	625	1,016	1,641
Ron Francis	23	1,731	549	1,249	1,798	Jaromir Jagr	19	1,273	646	953	1,599
Marcel Dionne	18	1,348	731	1,040	1,771	Phil Esposito	18	1,282	717	873	1,590

Note: As of end of 2009–10 season.

Art Ross Trophy Winners, 1918–2010

The Art Ross Trophy goes to the player who leads the league in scoring at the end of the regular season.

Season	Player, Team	Season	Player, Team	Season	Player, Team
1918	Joe Malone, Montreal	1945	Elmer Lach, Montreal	1978	Guy Lafleur, Montreal
1919	Newsy Lalonde, Montreal	1946	Max Bentley, Chicago	1979	Bryan Trottier, New York Islanders
1920	Joe Malone, Quebec	1947	Max Bentley, Chicago		
1921	Newsy Lalonde, Montreal	1948	Elmer Lach, Montreal	1980	Marcel Dionne, Los Angeles
1922	Punch Broadbent, Ottawa	1949	Roy Conacher, Chicago	1981	Wayne Gretzky, Edmonton
1923	Babe Dye, Toronto	1950	Ted Lindsay, Detroit	1982	Wayne Gretzky, Edmonton
1924	Cye Denneny, Ottawa	1951	Gordie Howe, Detroit	1983	Wayne Gretzky, Edmonton
1925	Babe Dye, Toronto	1952	Gordie Howe, Detroit	1984	Wayne Gretzky, Edmonton
1926	Nels Stewart, Montreal Maroons	1953	Gordie Howe, Detroit	1985	Wayne Gretzky, Edmonton
		1954	Gordie Howe, Detroit	1986	Wayne Gretzky, Edmonton
1927	Bill Cook, New York Rangers	1955	Bernie Geoffrion, Montreal	1987	Wayne Gretzky, Edmonton
		1956	Jean Béliveau, Montreal	1988	Mario Lemieux, Pittsburgh
1928	Howie Morenz, Montreal	1957	Gordie Howe, Detroit	1989	Mario Lemieux, Pittsburgh
1929	Ace Bailey, Toronto	1958	Dickie Moore, Montreal	1990	Wayne Gretzky, Los Angeles
1930	Cooney Weiland, Boston	1959	Dickie Moore, Montreal	1991	Wayne Gretzky, Los Angeles
1931	Howie Morenz, Montreal	1960	Bobby Hull, Chicago	1992	Mario Lemieux, Pittsburgh
1932	Harvey Jackson, Toronto	1961	Bernie Geoffrion, Montreal	1993	Mario Lemieux, Pittsburgh
1933	Bill Cook, New York Rangers	1962	Bobby Hull, Chicago	1994	Wayne Gretzky, Los Angeles
		1963	Gordie Howe, Detroit	1995	Jaromir Jagr, Pittsburgh
1934	Charlie Conacher, Toronto	1964	Stan Mikita, Chicago	1996	Mario Lemieux, Pittsburgh
1935	Charlie Conacher, Toronto	1965	Stan Mikita, Chicago	1997	Mario Lemieux, Pittsburgh
1936	Dave Shriner, New York Americans	1966	Bobby Hull, Chicago	1998	Jaromir Jagr, Pittsburgh
		1967	Stan Mikita, Chicago	1999	Jaromir Jagr, Pittsburgh
1937	Dave Shriner, New York Americans	1968	Stan Mikita, Chicago	2000	Jaromir Jagr, Pittsburgh
		1969	Phil Esposito, Boston	2001	Jaromir Jagr, Pittsburgh
1938	Gordie Drillon, Toronto	1970	Bobby Orr, Boston	2002	Jarome Iginla, Calgary
1939	Toe Blake, Montreal	1971	Phil Esposito, Boston	2003	Peter Forsberg, Colorado
1940	Milt Schmidt, Boston	1972	Phil Esposito, Boston	2004	Martin St. Louis, Tampa Bay
1941	Bill Cowley, Boston	1973	Phil Esposito, Boston	2006	Joe Thornton, San Jose
1942	Bryan Hextall, New York Rangers	1974	Phil Esposito, Boston	2007	Sidney Crosby, Pittsburgh
		1975	Bobby Orr, Boston	2008	Alexander Ovechkin, Wash.
1943	Doug Bentley, Chicago	1976	Guy Lafleur, Montreal	2009	Evgeni Malkin, Pittsburgh
1944	Herbie Cain, Boston	1977	Guy Lafleur, Montreal	2010	Henrik Sedin, Vancouver

Hart Trophy Winners, 1924–2010

The league's most valuable player is chosen by a poll of the Professional Hockey Writers' Association.

Season	Player	Team	Season	Player	Team	Season	Player	Team
1924	Frank Nighbor, Ottawa Senators		1950	Charlie Rayner, New York Rangers		1980	Wayne Gretzky, Edmonton	
1925	Billy Burch, New York Americans		1951	Milt Schmidt, Boston		1981	Wayne Gretzky, Edmonton	
1926	Nels Stewart, Montreal Maroons		1952	Gordie Howe, Detroit		1982	Wayne Gretzky, Edmonton	
1927	Herb Gardiner, Montreal		1953	Gordie Howe, Detroit		1983	Wayne Gretzky, Edmonton	
1928	Howie Morenz, Montreal		1954	Al Rollins, Toronto		1984	Wayne Gretzky, Edmonton	
1929	Roy Worters, New York Americans		1955	Ted Kennedy, Toronto		1985	Wayne Gretzky, Edmonton	
1930	Nels Stewart, Montreal Maroons		1956	Jean Béliveau, Montreal		1986	Wayne Gretzky, Edmonton	
1931	Howie Morenz, Montreal		1957	Gordie Howe, Detroit		1987	Wayne Gretzky, Edmonton	
1932	Howie Morenz, Montreal		1958	Gordie Howe, Detroit		1988	Mario Lemieux, Pittsburgh	
1933	Eddie Shore, Boston		1959	Andy Bathgate, New York Rangers		1989	Wayne Gretzky, Los Angeles	
1934	Aurel Joliat, Montreal		1960	Gordie Howe, Detroit		1990	Mark Messier, Edmonton	
1935	Eddie Shore, Boston		1961	Bernie Geoffrion, Montreal		1991	Bret Hull, St. Louis	
1936	Eddie Shore, Boston		1962	Jacques Plante, Montreal		1992	Mark Messier, New York Rangers	
1937	Babe Siebert, Montreal		1963	Gordie Howe, Detroit		1993	Mario Lemieux, Pittsburgh	
1938	Eddie Shore, Boston		1964	Jean Béliveau, Montreal		1994	Sergei Fedorov, Detroit	
1939	Toe Blake, Montreal		1965	Bobby Hull, Chicago		1995	Eric Lindros, Philadelphia	
1940	Ebbie Goodfellow, Detroit		1966	Bobby Hull, Chicago		1996	Mario Lemieux, Pittsburgh	
1941	Bill Cowley, Boston		1967	Stan Mikita, Chicago		1997	Dominik Hasek, Buffalo	
1942	Tom Anderson, New York Americans		1968	Stan Mikita, Chicago		1998	Dominik Hasek, Buffalo	
1943	Bill Cowley, Boston		1969	Phil Esposito, Boston		1999	Jaromir Jagr, Pittsburgh	
1944	Babe Pratt, Toronto		1970	Bobby Orr, Boston		2000	Chris Pronger, St. Louis	
1945	Elmer Lach, Montreal		1971	Bobby Orr, Boston		2001	Joe Sakic, Colorado	
1946	Max Bentley, Toronto		1972	Bobby Orr, Boston		2002	Jose Theodore, Montreal	
1947	Maurice Richard, Montreal		1973	Bobby Clarke, Philadelphia		2003	Peter Forsberg, Colorado	
1948	Buddy O'Connor, New York Rangers		1974	Phil Esposito, Boston		2004	Martin St. Louis, Tampa Bay	
1949	Sid Abel, Detroit		1975	Bobby Clarke, Philadelphia		2006	Joe Thornton, San Jose	
			1976	Bobby Clarke, Philadelphia		2007	Sidney Crosby, Pittsburgh	
			1977	Guy Lafleur, Montreal		2008	Alexander Ovechkin, Wash.	
			1978	Guy Lafleur, Montreal		2009	Alexander Ovechkin, Wash.	
			1979	Bryan Trottier, New York Islanders		2010	Henrik Sedin, Vancouver	

Conn Smythe Trophy Winners, 1965–2010

The Conn Smythe Trophy is awarded to the most valuable player in the playoffs.

Season	Player, Team	Season	Player, Team
1965	Jean Béliveau, Montreal	1988	Wayne Gretzky, Edmonton
1966	Roger Crozier, Detroit	1989	Al MacInnis, Calgary
1967	Dave Keon, Toronto	1990	Bill Ranford, Edmonton
1968	Glenn Hall, St. Louis	1991	Mario Lemieux, Pittsburgh
1969	Serge Savard, Montreal	1992	Mario Lemieux, Pittsburgh
1970	Bobby Orr, Boston	1993	Patrick Roy, Montreal
1971	Ken Dryden, Montreal	1994	Brian Leetch, New York Rangers
1972	Bobby Orr, Boston	1995	Claude Lemieux, New Jersey
1973	Yvan Cournoyer, Montreal	1996	Joe Sakic, Colorado
1974	Bernie Parent, Philadelphia	1997	Mike Vernon, Detroit
1975	Bernie Parent, Philadelphia	1998	Steve Yzerman, Detroit
1976	Reggie Leach, Philadelphia	1999	Joe Nieuwendyk, Dallas
1977	Guy Lafleur, Montreal	2000	Scott Stevens, New Jersey
1978	Larry Robinson, Montreal	2001	Patrick Roy, Colorado
1979	Bob Gainey, Montreal	2002	Nicklas Lidstrom, Detroit
1980	Bryan Trottier, New York Islanders	2003	Jean Sebastian Giguere, Anaheim
1981	Butch Goring, New York Islanders	2004	Brad Richards, Tampa Bay
1982	Mike Bossy, New York Islanders	2006	Cam Ward, Carolina
1983	Bill Smith, New York Islanders	2007	Scott Neidermayer, Anaheim
1984	Mark Messier, Edmonton	2008	Henrik Zetterberg, Detroit
1985	Wayne Gretzky, Edmonton	2009	Evgeni Malkin, Pittsburgh
1986	Patrick Roy, Montreal	2010	Jonathan Toews, Chicago
1987	Ron Hextall, Philadelphia		

James Norris Memorial Trophy, 1954–2010

The league's best defenseman is chosen by the Pro Hockey Writers' Association.

Season	Player, Team	Season	Player, Team	Season	Player, Team
1954	Red Kelly, Detroit	1973	Bobby Orr, Boston	1992	Brian Leetch, N.Y. Rangers
1955	Doug Harvey, Montreal	1974	Bobby Orr, Boston	1993	Chris Chelios, Chicago
1956	Doug Harvey, Montreal	1975	Bobby Orr, Boston	1994	Ray Bourque, Boston
1957	Doug Harvey, Montreal	1976	Denis Potvin, N.Y. Islanders	1995	Paul Coffey, Detroit
1958	Doug Harvey, Montreal	1977	Larry Robinson, Montreal	1996	Chris Chelios, Chicago
1959	Tom Johnson, Montreal	1978	Denis Potvin, N.Y. Islanders	1997	Brian Leetch, N.Y. Rangers
1960	Doug Harvey, Montreal	1979	Denis Potvin, N.Y. Islanders	1998	Rob Blake, Los Angeles
1961	Doug Harvey, Montreal	1980	Larry Robinson, Montreal	1999	Al MacInnis, St. Louis
1962	Doug Harvey, N.Y. Rangers	1981	Randy Carlyle, Pittsburgh	2000	Chris Pronger, St. Louis
1963	Pierre Pilote, Chicago	1982	Doug Wilson, Chicago	2001	Nicklas Lidstrom, Detroit
1964	Pierre Pilote, Chicago	1983	Rod Langway, Washington	2002	Nicklas Lidstrom, Detroit
1965	Pierre Pilote, Chicago	1984	Rod Langway, Washington	2003	Nicklas Lidstrom, Detroit
1966	Jacques Laperrière, Montreal	1985	Paul Coffey, Edmonton	2004	Scott Niedermayer, N. J.
1967	Harry Howell, N.Y. Rangers	1986	Paul Coffey, Edmonton	2006	Nicklas Lindstrom, Detroit
1968	Bobby Orr, Boston	1987	Ray Bourque, Boston	2007	Nicklas Lindstrom, Detroit
1969	Bobby Orr, Boston	1988	Ray Bourque, Boston	2008	Nicklas Lindstrom, Detroit
1970	Bobby Orr, Boston	1989	Chris Chelios, Montreal	2009	Zdeno Chara, Boston
1971	Bobby Orr, Boston	1990	Ray Bourque, Boston	2010	Duncan Keith, Chicago
1972	Bobby Orr, Boston	1991	Ray Bourque, Boston		

Vezina Trophy Winners, 1927–2010

The Vezina Trophy is awarded to the league's best goalkeeper and is selected by a poll of the league's general managers.

Season	Player	Team	Season	Player	Team
1927	George Hainsworth	Montreal	1970	Tony Esposito	Chicago
1928	George Hainsworth	Montreal	1971	Ed Giacomin/Gilles Villemure	N.Y. Rangers
1929	George Hainsworth	Montreal	1972	Tony Esposito/Gary Smith	Chicago
1930	Tiny Thompson	Boston	1973	Ken Dryden	Montreal
1931	Roy Worters	N.Y. Americans	1974	Bernie Parent	Philadelphia
1932	Charlie Gardiner	Chicago		Tony Esposito	Chicago
1933	Tiny Thompson	Boston	1975	Bernie Parent	Philadelphia
1934	Charlie Gardiner	Chicago	1976	Ken Dryden	Montreal
1935	Lorne Chabot	Chicago	1977	Ken Dryden/Michel Larocque	Montreal
1936	Tiny Thompson	Boston	1978	Ken Dryden/Michel Larocque	Montreal
1937	Normie Smith	Detroit	1979	Ken Dryden/Michel Larocque	Montreal
1938	Tiny Thompson	Boston	1980	Bob Sauvé/Don Edwards	Buffalo
1939	Frank Brimsek	Boston	1981	Richard Sevigny/Denis	Montreal
1940	Dave Kerr	N.Y. Rangers		Herron/ Michel Larocque	
1941	Turk Broda	Toronto	1982	Bill Smith	N.Y. Islanders
1942	Frank Brimsek	Boston	1983	Pete Peeters	Boston
1943	Johnny Mowers	Detroit	1984	Tom Barrasso	Buffalo
1944	Bill Durnan	Montreal	1985	Pele Lindbergh	Philadelphia
1945	Bill Durnan	Montreal	1986	John Vanbiesbrouck	N.Y. Rangers
1946	Bill Durnan	Montreal	1987	Ron Hextall	Philadelphia
1947	Bill Durnan	Montreal	1988	Grant Fuhr	Edmonton
1948	Turk Broda	Toronto	1989	Patrick Roy	Montreal
1949	Bill Durnan	Montreal	1990	Patrick Roy	Montreal
1950	Bill Durnan	Montreal	1991	Ed Belfour	Chicago
1951	Al Rollins	Toronto	1992	Patrick Roy	Montreal
1952	Terry Sawchuk	Detroit	1993	Ed Belfour	Chicago
1953	Terry Sawchuk	Detroit	1994	Dominik Hasek	Buffalo
1954	Harry Lumley	Toronto	1995	Dominik Hasek	Buffalo
1955	Terry Sawchuk	Detroit	1996	Jim Carey	Washington
1956	Jacques Plante	Montreal	1997	Dominik Hasek	Buffalo
1957	Jacques Plante	Montreal	1998	Dominik Hasek	Buffalo
1958	Jacques Plante	Montreal	1999	Dominik Hasek	Buffalo
1959	Jacques Plante	Montreal	2000	Olaf Kolzig	Washington
1960	Jacques Plante	Montreal	2001	Dominik Hasek	Buffalo
1961	Johnny Bower	Toronto	2002	Jose Theodore	Montreal
1962	Jacques Plante	Montreal	2003	Martin Brodeur	New Jersey
1963	Glenn Hall	Chicago	2004	Martin Brodeur	New Jersey
1964	Charlie Hodge	Montreal	2006	Miikka Kiprusoff	Calgary
1965	Terry Sawchuk/Johnny Bower	Toronto	2007	Martin Brodeur	New Jersey
1966	Lorne Worsley/Charlie Hodge	Montreal	2008	Martin Brodeur	New Jersey
1967	Glenn Hall/ Denis Dejordy	Chicago	2009	Tim Thomas	Boston
1968	Lorne Worsley/Rogie Vachon	Montreal	2010	Ryan Miller	Buffalo
1969	Jacques Plante/Glenn Hall	St. Louis			

Calder Memorial Trophy Winners, 1933–2010

The NHL rookie of the year is chosen by the Professional Hockey Writers' Association.

Season	Player, Team	Season	Player, Team	Season	Player, Team
1933	Carl Voss, Detroit	1955	Ed Litzenberger, Chicago	1981	Peter Stastny, Quebec
1934	Russ Blinko, Montreal Maroons	1956	Glenn Hall, Detroit	1982	Dale Hawerchuk, Winnipeg
		1957	Larry Regan, Boston	1983	Steve Larmer, Chicago
1935	Dave Schriner, New York Americans	1958	Frank Mahovlich, Toronto	1984	Tom Barrasso, Buffalo
		1959	Ralph Backsrom, Montreal	1985	Mario Lemieux, Pittsburgh
1936	Mike Karakas, Chicago	1960	Bill Hay, Chicago	1986	Gary Suter, Calgary
1937	Syl Apps, Toronto	1961	Dave Keon, Toronto	1987	Luc Robitaille, Los Angeles
1938	Cully Dahlstrom, Chicago	1962	Bobby Rousseau, Montreal	1988	Joe Nieuwendyk, Calgary
1939	Frank Brimsek, Boston	1963	Kent Douglas, Toronto	1989	Brian Leetch, N.Y. Rangers
1940	Kilby MacDonald, New York Rangers	1964	Jacques Laperrière, Montreal Canadiens	1990	Sergei Makarov, Calgary
1941	Johnny Quilty, Montreal	1965	Roger Crozier, Detroit	1991	Ed Belfour, Chicago
1942	Grant Warwick, New York Rangers	1966	Brit Selby, Toronto	1992	Pavel Bure, Vancouver
		1967	Bobby Orr, Boston	1993	Teemu Selanne, Winnipeg
1943	Gaye Stewart, Toronto	1968	Derek Sanderson, Boston	1994	Martin Brodeur, New Jersey
1944	Gus Bodnar, Toronto	1969	Danny Grant, Minnesota	1995	Petr Forsberg, Quebec
1945	Frank McCool, Toronto	1970	Tony Esposito, Chicago	1996	Daniel Alfredsson, Ottawa
1946	Edgar Laprade, New York Rangers	1971	Gilbert Perreault, Buffalo	1997	Bryan Berard, New York Islanders
		1972	Ken Dryden, Montreal		
1947	Howie Meeker, Toronto	1973	Steve Vickers, New York Rangers	1998	Sergei Samsonov, Boston
1948	Jim McFadden, Detroit			1999	Chris Drury, Colorado
1949	Pentti Lund, New York Rangers	1974	Denis Potvin, New York Islanders	2000	Scott Gomez, New Jersey
				2001	Evgeni Nabokov, San Jose
1950	Jack Gelineau, Boston	1975	Eric Vail, Atlanta	2002	Dany Heatley, Atlanta
1951	Terry Sawchuk, Detroit	1976	Bryan Trottier, New York Islanders	2003	Barret Jackman, St. Louis
1952	Bernie Geoffrion, Montreal Canadiens	1977	Willie Plett, Atlanta	2004	Andrew Raycroft, Boston
		1978	Mike Bossy, New York Islanders	2006	Alexander Ovechkin, Washington
1953	Lorne Worsley, New York Rangers	1979	Bobby Smith, Minnesota	2007	Evgeni Malkin, Pittsburgh
		1980	Ray Bourque, Boston	2008	Patrick Kane, Chicago
1954	Camille Henry, New York Rangers			2009	Steve Mason, Columbus
				2010	Tyler Myers, Buffalo

BASEBALL

MAJOR LEAGUE BASEBALL

245 Park Avenue
New York, N.Y. 10167
(212)-931-7800

www.mlb.com
Number of teams: 30
Commissioner: Allan "Bud" Selig

▶THE 2010 BASEBALL SEASON

With the steroid scandals of the early 2000's getting further in the rear view mirror, the 2010 baseball season was dominated by great pitching. Trevor Hoffman became the first pitcher to reach 600 career saves. Dallas Braden and Roy Halladay each threw perfect games, while Ubaldo Jimenez, Edwin Jackson, and Matt Garza all pitched no-hitters. But the most memorable performance of the season occurred when Tigers pitcher Armando Galarraga was denied the season's third perfect game due to a glaring umpire error. This incident has led to calls for the expansion of instant replay in baseball.

On the offensive side, Ichiro Suzuki reached 200 hits for the tenth season in a row, a major league record, and Alex Rodriguez hit his 600th career home run, only the seventh player in history to reach that mark. Jose Bautista hit 54 home runs, the first player to reach the 50 home run mark since 2007. A more dubious distinction went to the Pittsburgh Pirates, who suffered their eigh-

teenth consecutive losing season, despite new evidence that the owner has been making substantial profits in recent years

In the American League, the Texas Rangers and the Minnesota Twins easily won the West and Central divisions while the East contest came down to the final day of the season. The Tampa Bay Rays won their final game to win the division title by one game over the New York Yankees, who won the wild card. The Philadelphia Phillies captured their fourth National League East title in a row with the best record in baseball, while the Cincinnati Reds won the Central division, making the playoffs for the first time in 15 years. The West also came down to the final day as the San Francisco Giants defeated the San Diego Padres to win the division by two games. San Francisco's win helped avoid a three-way tie with the Atlanta Braves, who won the wild card in manager Bobby Cox's final season.

2010 American League Standings

Region	W	L	PCT	GB	Home	Away
East						
Tampa Bay Rays[1]	96	66	.593	–	49–32	47–34
New York Yankees[2]	95	67	.586	1	52–29	43–38
Boston Red Sox	89	73	.549	7	46–35	43–38
Toronto Blue Jays	85	77	.525	11	45–33	40–44
Baltimore Orioles	66	96	.407	30	37–44	29–52
Central						
Minnesota Twins[1]	94	68	.580	–	53–28	41–40
Chicago White Sox	88	74	.543	6	45–36	43–38
Detroit Tigers	81	81	.500	13	52–29	29–52
Cleveland Indians	69	93	.426	25	38–43	31–50
Kansas City Royals	67	95	.414	27	38–43	29–52
West						
Texas Rangers[1]	90	72	.556	–	51–30	39–42
Oakland Athletics	81	81	.500	9	47–34	34–47
Los Angeles Angels	80	82	.494	10	43–38	37–44
Seattle Mariners	61	101	.377	29	35–46	26–55

Note: 1. Division winner. 2. Wild card winner.

Final 2010 AL Team Statistics, Batting

Team	G	AB	R	H	2B	3B	HR	RBI	SLG	AVG
Texas Rangers	162	5635	787	1556	268	25	162	740	.419	.276
Kansas City Royals	162	5604	676	1534	279	31	121	640	.399	.274
Minnesota Twins	162	5568	781	1521	318	41	142	749	.422	.273
Detroit Tigers	162	5643	751	1515	308	32	152	717	.415	.268
Boston Red Sox	162	5646	818	1511	358	22	211	782	.451	.268
Chicago White Sox	162	5484	752	1467	263	21	177	710	.420	.268
New York Yankees	162	5567	859	1485	275	32	201	823	.436	.267
Baltimore Orioles	162	5554	613	1440	264	21	133	577	.386	.259
Oakland Athletics	162	5448	663	1396	276	30	109	619	.378	.256
Cleveland Indians	162	5487	646	1362	290	20	128	601	.378	.248
Los Angeles Angels	162	5488	681	1363	276	19	155	656	.390	.248
Toronto Blue Jays	162	5495	755	1364	319	21	257	732	.454	.248
Tampa Bay Rays	162	5439	802	1343	295	37	160	769	.403	.247
Seattle Mariners	162	5409	513	1274	227	16	101	485	.339	.236

Final 2010 AL Team Statistics, Pitching

Team	W	L	ERA	G	CG	ShO	SVO	IP	H	BB	SO
Oakland Athletics	81	81	3.56	162	7	17	51	1431.2	1315	512	1070
Tampa Bay Rays	96	66	3.78	162	6	12	67	1453.2	1347	478	1189
Texas Rangers	90	72	3.93	162	7	8	66	1455.1	1355	551	1181
Seattle Mariners	61	101	3.93	162	11	10	55	1438.0	1402	452	973
Minnesota Twins	94	68	3.95	162	9	13	58	1452.2	1493	383	1048
Los Angeles Angels	80	82	4.04	162	10	9	56	1449.1	1422	565	1130
New York Yankees	95	67	4.06	162	3	8	57	1442.1	1349	540	1154
Chicago White Sox	88	74	4.09	162	6	11	57	1446.1	1471	490	1149
Boston Red Sox	89	73	4.20	162	3	9	66	1456.2	1402	580	1207
Toronto Blue Jays	85	77	4.22	162	5	11	61	1440.2	1407	539	1184
Detroit Tigers	81	81	4.30	162	6	5	45	1444.1	1445	537	1056
Cleveland Indians	69	93	4.30	162	10	4	50	1433.0	1477	572	967
Baltimore Orioles	66	96	4.59	162	3	7	62	1436.1	1508	520	1007
Kansas City Royals	67	95	4.97	162	7	3	65	1436.2	1553	551	1035

Source: Major League Baseball. www.mlb.com

2010 National League Standings

Region	W	L	PCT	GB	Home	Away
East						
Philadelphia Phillies[1]	97	65	.599	–	54–30	43–35
Atlanta Braves[2]	91	71	.562	6.0	56–25	35–46
Florida Marlins	80	82	.494	17.0	41–40	39–42
New York Mets	79	83	.488	18.0	47–34	32–49
Washington Nationals	69	93	.426	28.0	41–40	28–53
Central						
Cincinnati Reds[1]	91	71	.562	–	49–32	42–39
St. Louis Cardinals	86	76	.531	5.0	52–29	34–47
Milwaukee Brewers	77	85	.475	14.0	40–41	37–44
Houston Astros	76	86	.469	15.0	42–39	34–47
Chicago Cubs	75	87	.463	16.0	35–46	40–41
Pittsburgh Pirates	57	105	.352	34.0	40–41	17–64
West						
San Francisco Giants[1]	92	70	.568	–	49–32	43–38
San Diego Padres	90	72	.556	2.0	45–36	45–36
Colorado Rockies	83	79	.512	9.0	52–29	31–50
Los Angeles Dodgers	80	82	.494	12.0	45–36	35–46
Arizona Diamondbacks	65	97	.401	27.0	40–41	25–56

Note: 1. Division winner. 2. Wild card winner.

Final 2010 NL Team Statistics, Batting

Team	G	AB	R	H	2B	3B	HR	RBI	SLG	AVG
Cincinnati Reds	162	5579	790	1515	293	30	188	761	.436	.272
St. Louis Cardinals	162	5542	736	1456	285	18	150	689	.402	.263
Colorado Rockies	162	5530	770	1452	270	54	173	741	.425	.263
Milwaukee Brewers	162	5606	750	1471	293	33	182	710	.424	.262
Philadelphia Phillies	162	5581	772	1451	290	34	166	736	.413	.260
Atlanta Braves	162	5463	738	1411	312	25	139	699	.401	.258
San Francisco Giants	162	5488	697	1411	284	30	162	660	.408	.257
Chicago Cubs	162	5512	685	1414	298	27	149	658	.401	.257
Florida Marlins	162	5531	719	1403	294	37	152	686	.403	.254
Los Angeles Dodgers	162	5426	667	1368	270	29	120	621	.379	.252
Arizona Diamondbacks	162	5473	713	1366	301	34	180	691	.416	.250
Washington Nationals	162	5418	655	1355	250	31	149	634	.390	.250
New York Mets	162	5465	656	1361	266	40	128	625	.383	.249
Houston Astros	162	5452	611	1348	252	25	108	577	.362	.247
San Diego Padres	162	5434	665	1338	236	24	132	630	.371	.246
Pittsburgh Pirates	162	5386	587	1303	276	27	126	570	.373	.242

Final 2010 NL Team Statistics, Pitching

Team	W	L	ERA	G	CG	ShO	SVO	IP	H	BB	SO
San Francisco Giants	92	70	3.36	162	6	17	73	1461.0	1279	578	1331
San Diego Padres	90	72	3.39	162	2	20	64	1456.1	1305	517	1295
Atlanta Braves	91	71	3.56	162	2	9	58	1439.1	1326	505	1241
St. Louis Cardinals	86	76	3.57	162	7	16	42	1453.2	1412	477	1094
Philadelphia Phillies	97	65	3.67	162	14	21	59	1456.1	1402	416	1183
New York Mets	79	83	3.70	162	8	19	52	1453.0	1438	545	1106
Los Angeles Dodgers	80	82	4.01	162	4	16	59	1441.2	1323	539	1274
Cincinnati Reds	91	71	4.01	162	4	9	63	1453.0	1404	524	1130
Florida Marlins	80	82	4.08	162	5	17	64	1438.1	1433	549	1168
Houston Astros	76	86	4.09	162	4	11	60	1439.1	1446	548	1210
Washington Nationals	69	93	4.13	162	2	5	57	1435.0	1469	512	1068
Colorado Rockies	83	79	4.14	162	6	12	56	1442.0	1405	525	1234
Chicago Cubs	75	87	4.18	162	1	14	54	1436.2	1409	605	1268
Milwaukee Brewers	77	85	4.58	162	3	7	56	1439.0	1487	582	1258
Arizona Diamondbacks	65	97	4.81	162	3	3	59	1432.0	1503	548	1070
Pittsburgh Pirates	57	105	5.00	162	1	6	48	1411.2	1567	538	1026

Source: Major League Baseball. www.mlb.com

Major League Baseball All-Time Career Leaders

Hits (3,000 or more)

1.	Pete Rose	4,256
2.	Ty Cobb	4,191
3.	Hank Aaron	3,771
4.	Stan Musial	3,630
5.	Tris Speaker	3,514
6.	Carl Yastrzemski	3,419
7.	Cap Anson	3,418
8.	Honus Wagner	3,415
9.	Paul Molitor	3,319
10.	Eddie Collins	3,315
11.	Willie Mays	3,283
12.	Eddie Murray	3,255
13.	Nap Lajoie	3,242
14.	Cal Ripken Jr.	3,184
15.	George Brett	3,154
16.	Paul Waner	3,152
17.	Robin Yount	3,142
18.	Tony Gwynn	3,141
19.	Dave Winfield	3,110
20.	Craig Biggio	3,060
21.	Rickey Henderson	3,055
22.	Rod Carew	3,053
23.	Lou Brock	3,023
24.	Rafael Palmeiro	3,020
25.	Wade Boggs	3,010

Home Runs

1.	Barry Bonds	762
2.	Hank Aaron	755
3.	Babe Ruth	714
4.	Willie Mays	660
5.	Ken Griffey[1]	630
6.	Alex Rodriguez[1]	613
7.	Sammy Sosa	609
8.	Jim Thome[1]	589
9.	Frank Robinson	586
10.	Mark McGwire	583
11.	Harmon Killebrew	573
12.	Rafael Palmeiro	569
13.	Reggie Jackson	563
14.	Manny Ramirez[1]	555
15.	Mike Schmidt	548
16.	Mickey Mantle	536
17.	Jimmie Foxx	534
18.	Willie McCovey	521
18.	Ted Williams	521
18.	Frank Thomas	521
21.	Ernie Banks	512
21.	Eddie Mathews	512
23.	Mel Ott	511
24.	Gary Sheffield	509
25.	Eddie Murray	504

Runs Batted In

1.	Hank Aaron	2,297
2.	Babe Ruth	2,213
3.	Cap Anson	2,076
4.	Barry Bonds	1,996
5.	Lou Gehrig	1,995
6.	Stan Musial	1,951
7.	Ty Cobb	1,938
8.	Jimmie Foxx	1,922
9.	Eddie Murray	1,917
10.	Willie Mays	1,903

Runs

1.	Rickey Henderson	2,295
2.	Ty Cobb	2,245
3.	Barry Bonds	2,227
4.	Babe Ruth	2,174
5.	Hank Aaron	2,174
6.	Pete Rose	2,165

7.	Willie Mays	2,062
8.	Cap Anson	1,996
9.	Stan Musial	1,949
10.	Lou Gehrig	1,888

Average (minimum 5,000 at bats)

1.	Ty Cobb	.366
2.	Rogers Hornsby	.358
3.	Joe Jackson	.356
4.	Ed Delahanty	.346
5.	Tris Speaker	.345
6.	Ted Williams	.344
7.	Billy Hamilton	.344
8.	Babe Ruth	.342
8.	Dan Brouthers	.342
8.	Harry Heilmann	.342

Stolen Bases

1.	Rickey Henderson	1,406
2.	Lou Brock	938
3.	Billy Hamilton	912
4.	Ty Cobb	892
5.	Tim Raines	808
6.	Vince Coleman	752
7.	Eddie Collins	745
8.	Arlie Latham	739
9.	Max Carey	738
10.	Honus Wagner	722

Total Bases

1.	Hank Aaron	6,856
2.	Stan Musial	6,134
3.	Willie Mays	6,066
4.	Barry Bonds	5,976
5.	Ty Cobb	5,859
6.	Babe Ruth	5,793
7.	Pete Rose	5,752
8.	Carl Yastrzemski	5,539
9.	Eddie Murray	5,397
10.	Rafael Palmeiro	5,388

Slugging Percentage[2]

1.	Babe Ruth	.690
2.	Ted Williams	.634
3.	Lou Gehrig	.632
4.	Albert Pujols[1]	.624
5.	Jimmie Foxx	.609
6.	Barry Bonds	.607
7.	Hank Greenberg	.605
8.	Mark McGwire	.588
9.	Manny Ramirez[1]	.586
10.	Joe DiMaggio	.579

Extra Base Hits

1.	Hank Aaron	1,477
2.	Barry Bonds	1,440
3.	Stan Musial	1,377
4.	Babe Ruth	1,356
5.	Willie Mays	1,323
6.	Ken Griffey	1,192
6.	Rafael Palmeiro	1,192
8.	Lou Gehrig	1,190
9.	Frank Robinson	1,186
10.	Carl Yastrzemski	1,157

Games Played

1.	Pete Rose	3,562
2.	Carl Yastrzemski	3,308
3.	Hank Aaron	3,298
4.	Rickey Henderson	3,081
5.	Ty Cobb	3,035
6.	Eddie Murray	3,026
6.	Stan Musial	3,026
8.	Cal Ripken	3,001
9.	Willie Mays	2,992
10.	Barry Bonds	2,986

Pitching-Wins

1.	Cy Young	511
2.	Walter Johnson	417
3.	Christy Mathewson	373
3.	Grover Alexander	373
5.	Pud Galvin	365
6.	Warren Spahn	363
7.	Kid Nichols	361
8.	Greg Maddux	355
9.	Roger Clemens	354
10.	Tim Keefe	342
11.	Steve Carlton	329
12.	John Clarkson	328
13.	Eddie Plank	326
14.	Nolan Ryan	324
15.	Don Sutton	324
16.	Phil Niekro	318
17.	Gaylord Perry	314
18.	Tom Seaver	311
19.	Charles Radbourn	309
20.	Mickey Welch	307
21.	Tom Glavine	305
22.	Randy Johnson	303
23.	Lefty Grove	300
23.	Early Wynn	300

Strikeouts

1.	Nolan Ryan	5,714
2.	Randy Johnson	4,875
3.	Roger Clemens	4,672
4.	Steve Carlton	4,136
5.	Bert Blyleven	3,701
6.	Tom Seaver	3,640
7.	Don Sutton	3,574
8.	Gaylord Perry	3,534
9.	Walter Johnson	3,508
10.	Phil Niekro	3,342

Earned Run Average[3]

1.	Ed Walsh	1.82
2.	Addie Joss	1.89
3.	Al Spalding	2.04
4.	Mordecai "Three Finger" Brown	2.06
5.	John Ward	2.10
6.	Christy Mathewson	2.13
7.	Tommy Bond	2.14
8.	Rube Waddell	2.16
9.	Walter Johnson	2.17
10.	Ed Reulbach	2.28

Innings Pitched

1.	Cy Young	7,356
2.	Pud Galvin	6,003
3.	Walter Johnson	5,914
4.	Phil Niekro	5,404
5.	Nolan Ryan	5,386
6.	Gaylord Perry	5,350
7.	Don Sutton	5,282
8.	Warren Spahn	5,244
9.	Steve Carlton	5,217
10.	Grover Cleveland Alexander	5,190

Shutouts

1.	Walter Johnson	110
2.	Grover Cleveland Alexander	90
3.	Christy Mathewson	80
4.	Cy Young	76
5.	Eddie Plank	69
6.	Warren Spahn	63
7.	Nolan Ryan	61
7.	Tom Seaver	61
9.	Bert Blyleven	60
10.	Don Sutton	58

Note: As of October, 2010. 1. Active during the 2010 season. 2. Total bases divided by minimum 5,000 at-bats. 3. Minimum 2,000 innings pitched. **Source:** Major League Baseball.

Batting Champions 1901–2010

Year	NATIONAL LEAGUE Name	Team	Avg.	AMERICAN LEAGUE Name	Team	Avg.
1901	Jesse Burkett	St. Louis Cardinals	.382	Nap Lajoie	Philadelphia Athletics	.422
1902	C.H. Beaumont	Pittsburgh Pirates	.357	Ed Delahanty	Washington Senators	.376
1903	Honus Wagner	Pittsburgh Pirates	.355	Nap Lajoie	Cleveland Indians	.355
1904	Honus Wagner	Pittsburgh Pirates	.349	Nap Lajoie	Cleveland Indians	.381
1905	J. Bentley Seymour	Cincinnati Reds	.377	Elmer Flick	Cleveland Indians	.306
1906	Honus Wagner	Pittsburgh Pirates	.339	George Stone	St. Louis Browns	.358
1907	Honus Wagner	Pittsburgh Pirates	.350	Ty Cobb	Detroit Tigers	.350
1908	Honus Wagner	Pittsburgh Pirates	.354	Ty Cobb	Detroit Tigers	.324
1909	Honus Wagner	Pittsburgh Pirates	.339	Ty Cobb	Detroit Tigers	.377
1910	Sherwood Magee	Philadelphia Phillies	.331	Ty Cobb	Detroit Tigers	.385
1911	Honus Wagner	Pittsburgh Pirates	.334	Ty Cobb	Detroit Tigers	.420
1912	Heinie Zimmerman	Chicago Cubs	.372	Ty Cobb	Detroit Tigers	.410
1913	Jake Daubert	Brooklyn Dodgers	.350	Ty Cobb	Detroit Tigers	.390
1914	Jake Daubert	Brooklyn Dodgers	.329	Ty Cobb	Detroit Tigers	.368
1915	Larry Doyle	New York Giants	.320	Ty Cobb	Detroit Tigers	.370
1916	Hal Chase	Cincinnati Reds	.339	Tris Speaker	Cleveland Indians	.386
1917	Edd Roush	Cincinnati Reds	.341	Ty Cobb	Detroit Tigers	.383
1918	Zack Wheat	Brooklyn Dodgers	.335	Ty Cobb	Detroit Tigers	.382
1919	Edd Roush	Cincinnati Reds	.321	Ty Cobb	Detroit Tigers	.407
1920	Rogers Hornsby	St. Louis Cardinals	.370	George Sisler	St. Louis Browns	.407
1921	Rogers Hornsby	St. Louis Cardinals	.397	Harry Heilmann	Detroit Tigers	.394
1922	Rogers Hornsby	St. Louis Cardinals	.401	George Sisler	St. Louis Browns	.420
1923	Rogers Hornsby	St. Louis Cardinals	.384	Harry Heilmann	Detroit Tigers	.403
1924	Rogers Hornsby	St. Louis Cardinals	.424	Babe Ruth	New York Yankees	.378
1925	Rogers Hornsby	St. Louis Cardinals	.403	Harry Heilmann	Detroit Tigers	.393
1926	Bubbles Hargrave	Cincinnati Reds	.353	Heinie Manush	Detroit Tigers	.377
1927	Paul Waner	Pittsburgh Pirates	.380	Harry Heilmann	Detroit Tigers	.398
1928	Rogers Hornsby	Boston Braves	.387	Goose Goslin	Washington Senators	.379
1929	Lefty O'Doul	Philadelphia Phillies	.398	Lew Fonseca	Cleveland Indians	.369
1930	Bill Terry	New York Giants	.401	Al Simmons	Philadelphia Athletics	.381
1931	Chick Hafey[1]	St Louis Cardinals	.349	Al Simmons	Philadelphia Athletics	.390
1932	Lefty O'Doul	Brooklyn Dodgers	.368	Dale Alexander	Detroit-Boston	.367
1933	Chuck Klein	Philadelphia Phillies	.368	Jimmie Foxx	Philadelphia Athletics	.356
1934	Paul Waner	Pittsburgh Pirates	.362	Lou Gehrig	New York Yankees	.363
1935	Arky Vaughan	Pittsburgh Pirates	.385	Buddy Myer	Washington Senators	.349
1936	Paul Waner	Pittsburgh Pirates	.373	Luke Appling	Chicago White Sox	.388
1937	Joe Medwick	St. Louis Cardinals	.374	Charlie Gehringer	Detroit Tigers	.371
1938	Ernie Lombardi	Cincinnati Reds	.342	Jimmie Foxx	Boston Red Sox	.349
1939	Johnny Mize	St. Louis Cardinals	.349	Joe DiMaggio	New York Yankees	.381
1940	Debs Garms	Pittsburgh Pirates	.355	Joe DiMaggio	New York Yankees	.352
1941	Pete Reiser	Brooklyn Dodgers	.343	Ted Williams	Boston Red Sox	.406
1942	Ernie Lombardi	Boston Braves	.330	Ted Williams	Boston Red Sox	.356
1943	Stan Musial	St. Louis Cardinals	.357	Luke Appling	Chicago White Sox	.328
1944	Dixie Walker	Brooklyn Dodgers	.357	Lou Boudreau	Cleveland Indians	.327
1945	Phil Cavarretta	Chicago Cubs	.355	Snuffy Stirnweiss	New York Yankees	.309
1946	Stan Musial	St. Louis Cardinals	.365	Mickey Vernon	Washington Senators	.352
1947	Harry Walker	St. Louis-Philadelphia	.363	Ted Williams	Boston Red Sox	.343
1948	Stan Musial	St. Louis Cardinals	.376	Ted Williams	Boston Red Sox	.369
1949	Jackie Robinson	Brooklyn Dodgers	.342	George Kell	Detroit Tigers	.343
1950	Stan Musial	St. Louis Cardinals	.346	Billy Goodman	Boston Red Sox	.354
1951	Stan Musial	St. Louis Cardinals	.355	Ferris Fain	Philadelphia Athletics	.344
1952	Stan Musial	St. Louis Cardinals	.336	Ferris Fain	Philadelphia Athletics	.327
1953	Carl Furillo	Brooklyn Dodgers	.344	Mickey Vernon	Washington Senators	.337
1954	Willie Mays	New York Giants	.345	Bobby Avila	Cleveland Indians	.341
1955	Richie Ashburn	Philadelphia Phillies	.338	Al Kaline	Detroit Tigers	.340
1956	Hank Aaron	Milwaukee Braves	.328	Mickey Mantle	New York Yankees	.353
1957	Stan Musial	St. Louis Cardinals	.351	Ted Williams	Boston Red Sox	.388
1958	Richie Ashburn	Philadelphia Phillies	.350	Ted Williams	Boston Red Sox	.328
1959	Hank Aaron	Milwaukee Braves	.355	Harvey Kuenn	Detroit Tigers	.353
1960	Dick Groat	Pittsburgh Pirates	.325	Pete Runnels	Boston Red Sox	.320
1961	Roberto Clemente	Pittsburgh Pirates	.351	Norm Cash	Detroit Tigers	.361
1962	Tommy Davis	Los Angeles Dodgers	.346	Pete Runnels	Boston Red Sox	.326
1963	Tommy Davis	Los Angeles Dodgers	.326	Carl Yastrzemski	Boston Red Sox	.321
1964	Roberto Clemente	Pittsburgh Pirates	.339	Tony Oliva	Minnesota Twins	.323
1965	Roberto Clemente	Pittsburgh Pirates	.329	Tony Oliva	Minnesota Twins	.321
1966	Matty Alou	Pittsburgh Pirates	.342	Frank Robinson	Baltimore Orioles	.316
1967	Roberto Clemente	Pittsburgh Pirates	.357	Carl Yastrzemski	Boston Red Sox	.326
1968	Pete Rose	Cincinnati Reds	.335	Carl Yastrzemski	Boston Red Sox	.301
1969	Pete Rose	Cincinnati Reds	.348	Rod Carew	Minnesota Twins	.332
1970	Rico Carty	Atlanta Braves	.366	Alex Johnson	California Angels	.329

	NATIONAL LEAGUE			AMERICAN LEAGUE		
Year	Name	Team	Avg.	Name	Team	Avg.
1971	Joe Torre	St. Louis Cardinals	.363	Tony Oliva	Minnesota Twins	.337
1972	Billy Williams	Chicago Cubs	.333	Rod Carew	Minnesota Twins	.318
1973	Pete Rose	Cincinnati Reds	.338	Rod Carew	Minnesota Twins	.350
1974	Ralph Garr	Atlanta Braves	.353	Rod Carew	Minnesota Twins	.364
1975	Bill Madlock	Chicago Cubs	.354	Rod Carew	Minnesota Twins	.359
1976	Bill Madlock	Chicago Cubs	.339	George Brett	Kansas City Royals	.333
1977	Dave Parker	Pittsburgh Pirates	.338	Rod Carew	Minnesota Twins	.388
1978	Dave Parker	Pittsburgh Pirates	.334	Rod Carew	Minnesota Twins	.333
1979	Keith Hernandez	St. Louis Cardinals	.344	Fred Lynn	Boston Red Sox	.333
1980	Bill Buckner	Chicago Cubs	.324	George Brett	Kansas City Royals	.390
1981[2]	Bill Madlock	Pittsburgh Pirates	.341	Carney Lansford	Boston Red Sox	.336
1982	Al Oliver	Montreal Expos	.331	Willie Wilson	Kansas City Royals	.332
1983	Bill Madlock	Pittsburgh Pirates	.323	Wade Boggs	Boston Red Sox	.361
1984	Tony Gwynn	San Diego Padres	.351	Don Mattingly	New York Yankees	.343
1985	Willie McGee	St. Louis Cardinals	.353	Wade Boggs	Boston Red Sox	.368
1986	Tim Raines	Montreal Expos	.334	Wade Boggs	Boston Red Sox	.357
1987	Tony Gwynn	San Diego Padres	.370	Wade Boggs	Boston Red Sox	.363
1988	Tony Gwynn	San Diego Padres	.313	Wade Boggs	Boston Red Sox	.366
1989	Tony Gwynn	San Diego Padres	.336	Kirby Puckett	Minnesota Twins	.339
1990	Willie McGee	St. Louis Cardinals	.335	George Brett	Kansas City Royals	.329
1991	Terry Pendleton	Atlanta Braves	.319	Julio Franco	Texas Rangers	.341
1992	Gary Sheffield	San Diego Padres	.330	Edgar Martinez	Seattle Mariners	.343
1993	Andres Galarraga	Colorado Rockies	.370	John Olerud	Toronto Blue Jays	.363
1994[2]	Tony Gwynn	San Diego Padres	.394	Paul O'Neill	New York Yankees	.359
1995[2]	Tony Gwynn	San Diego Padres	.368	Edgar Martinez	Seattle Mariners	.356
1996	Ellis Burks	Colorado Rockies	.344	Alex Rodriguez	Seattle Mariners	.358
1997	Tony Gwynn	San Diego Padres	.372	Frank Thomas	Chicago White Sox	.347
1998	Larry Walker	Colorado Rockies	.363	Bernie Williams	New York Yankees	.339
1999	Larry Walker	Colorado Rockies	.379	Nomar Garciaparra	Boston Red Sox	.357
2000	Todd Helton	Colorado Rockies	.372	Nomar Garciaparra	Boston Red Sox	.372
2001	Larry Walker	Colorado Rockies	.350	Ichiro Suzuki	Seattle Mariners	.350
2002	Barry Bonds	San Francisco Giants	.370	Manny Ramirez	Boston Red Sox	.349
2003	Albert Pujols	St. Louis Cardinals	.359	Bill Mueller	Boston Red Sox	.326
2004	Barry Bonds	San Francisco Giants	.362	Ichiro Suzuki	Seattle Mariners	.372
2005	Derrek Lee	Chicago Cubs	.335	Michael Young	Texas Rangers	.331
2006	Freddy Sanchez	Pittsburgh Pirates	.344	Joe Mauer	Minnesota Twins	.347
2007	Matt Holliday	Colorado Rockies	.340	Magglio Ordonez	Detroit Tigers	.363
2008	Chipper Jones	Atlanta Braves	.364	Joe Mauer	Minnesota Twins	.328
2009	Hanley Ramirez	Florida Marlins	.342	Joe Mauer	Minnesota Twins	.364
2010	Carlos Gonzalez	Colorado Rockies	.326	Josh Hamilton	Texas Rangers	.359

Notes: 1. Hafey led with .3489, Bill Terry, N.Y., second with .3486, Jim Bottomley, St. Louis, third with .3482. 2. Strike-shortened season.

Home Run Champions, 1919–2010

	NATIONAL LEAGUE		AMERICAN LEAGUE	
Year	Name, Team	Home Runs	Name, Team	Home Runs
1919	Gavvy Cravath, Philadelphia	12	Babe Ruth, Boston	29
1920	Cy Williams, Philadelphia	15	Babe Ruth, New York	54
1921	George Kelly, New York	23	Babe Ruth, New York	59
1922	Rogers Hornsby, St. Louis	42	Ken Williams, St. Louis	39
1923	Cy Williams, Philadelphia	41	Babe Ruth, New York	41
1924	Jack Fournier, Brooklyn	27	Babe Ruth, New York	46
1925	Rogers Hornsby, St. Louis	39	Bob Meusel, New York	33
1926	Hack Wilson, Chicago	21	Babe Ruth, New York	47
1927	Cy Williams, Philadelphia; Hack Wilson, Chicago	30	Babe Ruth, New York	60
1928	Jim Bottomley, St. Louis; Hack Wilson, Chicago	31	Babe Ruth, New York	54
1929	Chuck Klein, Philadelphia	43	Babe Ruth, New York	46
1930	Hack Wilson, Chicago	56	Babe Ruth, New York	49
1931	Chuck Klein, Philadelphia	31	Lou Gehrig, Babe Ruth, New York	46
1932	Chuck Klein, Philadelphia; Mel Ott, New York	38	Jimmie Foxx, Philadelphia	58
1933	Chuck Klein, Philadelphia	28	Jimmie Foxx, Philadelphia	48
1934	Ripper Collins, St. Louis; Mel Ott, New York	35	Lou Gehrig, New York	49
1935	Wally Berger, Boston	34	Jimmie Foxx, Philadelphia; Hank Greenberg, Detroit	36
1936	Mel Ott, New York	33	Lou Gehrig, New York	49
1937	Joe Medwick, St. Louis; Mel Ott, New York	31	Joe Dimaggio, New York	46
1938	Mel Ott, New York	36	Hank Greenberg, Detroit	58
1939	Johnny Mize, St. Louis	28	Jimmie Foxx, Boston	35
1940	Johnny Mize, St. Louis	43	Hank Greenberg, Detroit	41
1941	Dolph Camilli, Brooklyn	34	Ted Williams, Boston	37
1942	Mel Ott, New York	30	Ted Williams, Boston	36
1943	Bill Nicholson, Chicago	29	Rudy York, Detroit	34

Year	NATIONAL LEAGUE Name, Team	Home Runs	AMERICAN LEAGUE Name, Team	Home Runs
1943	Bill Nicholson, Chicago	29	Rudy York, Detroit	34
1944	Bill Nicholson, Chicago	33	Nick Etten, New York	22
1945	Tommy Holmes, Boston	28	Vern Stephens, St. Louis	24
1946	Ralph Kiner, Pittsburgh	23	Hank Greenberg, Detroit	44
1947	Ralph Kiner, Pittsburgh; Johnny Mize, New York	51	Ted Williams, Boston	32
1948	Ralph Kiner, Pittsburgh; Johnny Mize, New York	40	Joe DiMaggio, New York	39
1949	Ralph Kiner, Pittsburgh	54	Ted Williams, Boston	43
1950	Ralph Kiner, Pittsburgh	47	Al Rosen, Cleveland	37
1951	Ralph Kiner, Pittsburgh	42	Gus Zernial, Chicago-Philadelphia	33
1952	Ralph Kiner, Pittsburgh; Hank Sauer, Chicago	37	Larry Doby, Cleveland	32
1953	Eddie Mathews, Milwaukee	47	Al Rosen, Cleveland	43
1954	Ted Kluszewski, Cincinnati	49	Larry Doby, Cleveland	32
1955	Willie Mays, New York	51	Mickey Mantle, New York	37
1956	Duke Snider, Brooklyn	43	Mickey Mantle, New York	52
1957	Hank Aaron, Milwaukee	44	Roy Sievers, Washington	42
1958	Ernie Banks, Chicago	47	Mickey Mantle, New York	42
1959	Eddie Mathews, Milwaukee	46	Rocky Colavito, Cleveland; Harmon Killebrew, Washington	42
1960	Ernie Banks, Chicago	41	Mickey Mantle, New York	40
1961	Orlando Cepeda, San Francisco	46	Roger Maris, New York	61
1962	Willie Mays, San Francisco	49	Harmon Killebrew, Minnesota	48
1963	Hank Aaron, Milw.; Willie McCovey, S.F.	44	Harmon Killebrew, Minnesota	45
1964	Willie Mays, San Francisco	47	Harmon Killebrew, Minnesota	49
1965	Willie Mays, San Francisco	52	Tony Conigliaro, Boston	32
1966	Hank Aaron, Atlanta	44	Frank Robinson, Baltimore	49
1967	Hank Aaron, Atlanta	39	Harmon Killebrew, Minnesota; Carl Yastrzemski, Boston	44
1968	Willie McCovey, San Francisco	36	Frank Howard, Washington	44
1969	Willie McCovey, San Francisco	45	Harmon Killebrew, Minnesota	49
1970	Johnny Bench, Cincinnati	45	Frank Howard, Washington	44
1971	Willie Stargell, Pittsburgh	48	Bill Melton, Chicago	33
1972	Johnny Bench, Cincinnati	40	Dick Allen, Chicago	37
1973	Willie Stargell, Pittsburgh	44	Reggie Jackson, Oakland	32
1974	Mike Schmidt, Philadelphia	36	Dick Allen, Chicago	32
1975	Mike Schmidt, Philadelphia	38	Reggie Jackson, Oakland; George Scott, Milwaukee	36
1976	Mike Schmidt, Philadelphia	38	Graig Nettles, New York	32
1977	George Foster, Cincinnati	52	Jim Rice, Boston	39
1978	George Foster, Cincinnati	40	Jim Rice, Boston	46
1979	Dave Kingman, Chicago	48	Gorman Thomas, Milwaukee	45
1980	Mike Schmidt, Philadelphia	48	Reggie Jackson, NY; Ben Oglivie, Milw.	41
1981[1]	Mike Schmidt, Philadelphia	31	Tony Armas, Boston; Dwight Evans, Boston; Bobby Grich, California; Eddie Murray, Baltimore	22
1982	Dave Kingman, New York	37	Reggie Jackson, California; Gorman Thomas, Milwaukee	39
1983	Mike Schmidt, Philadelphia	40	Jim Rice, Boston	39
1984	Dale Murphy, Atlanta; Mike Schmidt, Phil.	36	Tony Armas, Boston	50
1985	Dale Murphy, Atlanta	37	Darrell Evans, Detroit	40
1986	Mike Schmidt, Philadelphia	37	Jesse Barfield, Toronto	40
1987	Andre Dawson, Chicago	49	Mark McGwire, Oakland	49
1988	Darryl Strawberry, New York Mets	39	Jose Canseco, Oakland	42
1989	Kevin Mitchell, San Francisco	47	Fred McGriff, Toronto	36
1990	Ryne Sandberg, Chicago	40	Cecil Fielder, Detroit	51
1991	Howard Johnson, New York Mets	38	Jose Canseco, Oakland	44
1992	Fred McGriff, San Diego	35	Juan González, Texas	43
1993	Barry Bonds, San Francisco	46	Juan González, Texas	46
1994[1]	Matt Williams, San Francisco	43	Ken Griffey Jr., Seattle	40
1995[1]	Dante Bichette, Colorado	40	Albert Belle, Cleveland	50
1996	Andres Galarraga, Colorado	47	Mark McGwire, Oakland	52
1997	Larry Walker, Colorado[2]	49	Ken Griffey Jr., Seattle[2]	56
1998	Mark McGwire, St. Louis	70	Ken Griffey Jr., Seattle	56
1999	Mark McGwire, St. Louis	65	Ken Griffey Jr., Seattle	48
2000	Sammy Sosa, Chicago Cubs	50	Troy Glaus, Anaheim	47
2001	Barry Bonds, San Francisco	73	Alex Rodríguez, Texas	52
2002	Sammy Sosa, Chicago Cubs	49	Alex Rodríguez, Texas	57
2003	Jim Thome, Philadelphia	47	Alex Rodríguez, Texas	47
2004	Adrian Beltré, Los Angeles	48	Manny Ramírez, Boston	43
2005	Andrew Jones, Atlanta	51	Alex Rodriguez, N.Y. Yankees	48
2006	Ryan Howard, Philadelphia	58	David Ortiz, Boston	54
2007	Prince Fielder, Milwaukee Brewers	50	Alex Rodriguez, NY Yankees	54
2008	Ryan Howard, Philadelphia Phillies	48	Miguel Cabrera, Detroit Tigers	37
2009	Albert Pujols, St. Louis Cardinals	47	Carlos Peña, Tampa Bay Rays; Mark Teixeira, N.Y. Yankees	39
2010	Albert Pujols, St. Louis Cardinals	42	Jose Bautista, Toronto Blue Jays	54

Notes: 1. Strike-shortened season 2. Mark McGwire hit 34 home runs with Oakland and 24 with St. Louis for a major-league-leading total of 58.

Rookie of the Year

NATIONAL LEAGUE			AMERICAN LEAGUE		
Year	Name	Team	Year	Name	Team
1947[1]	Jackie Robinson	Brooklyn Dodgers			
1948[1]	Alvin Dark	Boston Braves			
1949	Don Newcombe	Brooklyn Dodgers	1949	Roy Sievers	St. Louis Browns
1950	Sam Jethroe	Boston Braves	1950	Walt Dropo	Boston Red Sox
1951	Willie Mays	New York Giants	1951	Gil McDougald	New York Yankees
1952	Joe Black	Brooklyn Dodgers	1952	Harry Byrd	Philadelphia Athletics
1953	Junior Gilliam	Brooklyn Dodgers	1953	Harvey Kuenn	Detroit Tigers
1954	Wally Moon	St. Louis Cardinals	1954	Bob Grim	New York Yankees
1955	Bill Virdon	St. Louis Cardinals	1955	Herb Score	Cleveland Indians
1956	Frank Robinson	Cincinnati Reds	1956	Luis Aparicio	Chicago White Sox
1957	Jack Sanford	Philadelphia Phillies	1957	Tony Kubek	New York Yankees
1958	Orlando Cepeda	San Francisco Giants	1958	Albie Pearson	Washington Senators
1959	Willie McCovey	San Francisco Giants	1959	Bob Allison	Washington Senators
1960	Frank Howard	Los Angeles Dodgers	1960	Ron Hansen	Baltimore Orioles
1961	Billy Williams	Chicago Cubs	1961	Don Schwall	Boston Red Sox
1962	Ken Hubbs	Chicago Cubs	1962	Tom Tresh	New York Yankees
1963	Pete Rose	Cincinnati Reds	1963	Gary Peters	Chicago White Sox
1964	Richie Allen	Philadelphia Phillies	1964	Tony Oliva	Minnesota Twins
1965	Jim Lefebvre	Los Angeles Dodgers	1965	Curt Blefary	Baltimore Orioles
1966	Tommy Helms	Cincinnati Reds	1966	Tommie Agee	Chicago White Sox
1967	Tom Seaver	New York Mets	1967	Rod Carew	Minnesota Twins
1968	Johnny Bench	Cincinnati Reds	1968	Stan Bahnsen	New York Yankees
1969	Ted Sizemore	Los Angeles Dodgers	1969	Lou Piniella	Kansas City Royals
1970	Carl Morton	Montreal Expos	1970	Thurman Munson	New York Yankees
1971	Earl Williams	Atlanta Braves	1971	Chris Chambliss	Cleveland Indians
1972	Jon Matlack	New York Mets	1972	Carlton Fisk	Boston Red Sox
1973	Gary Matthews	San Francisco Giants	1973	Al Bumbry	Baltimore Orioles
1974	Bake McBride	St. Louis Cardinals	1974	Make Hargrove	Texas Rangers
1975	John Montefusco	San Francisco Giants	1975	Fred Lynn	Boston Red Sox
1976	Pat Zachry	Cincinnati Reds	1976	Mark Fidrych	Detroit Tigers
	Butch Metzger	San Diego Padres	1977	Eddie Murray	Baltimore Orioles
1977	Andre Dawson	Montreal Expos	1978	Lou Whitaker	Detroit Tigers
1978	Bob Horner	Atlanta Braves	1979	John Castino	Minnesota Twins
1979	Rick Sutcliffe	Los Angeles Dodgers		Alfredo Griffin	Toronto Blue Jays
1980	Steve Howe	Los Angeles Dodgers	1980	Joe Charboneau	Cleveland Indians
1981	Fernando Valenzuela	Los Angeles Dodgers	1981	Dave Righetti	New York Yankees
1982	Steve Sax	Los Angeles Dodgers	1982	Cal Ripken Jr.	Baltimore Orioles
1983	Darryl Strawberry	New York Mets	1983	Ron Kittle	Chicago White Sox
1984	Dwight Gooden	New York Mets	1984	Alvin Davis	Seattle Mariners
1985	Vince Coleman	St. Louis Cardinals	1985	Ozzie Guillen	Chicago White Sox
1986	Todd Worrell	St. Louis Cardinals	1986	Jose Canseco	Oakland Athletics
1987	Benito Santiago	San Diego Padres	1987	Mark McGwire	Oakland Athletics
1988	Chris Sabo	Cincinnati Reds	1988	Walt Weiss	Oakland Athletics
1989	Jerome Walton	Chicago Cubs	1989	Greg Olson	Baltimore Orioles
1990	Dave Justice	Atlanta Braves	1990	Sandy Alomar Jr.	Cleveland Indians
1991	Jeff Bagwell	Houston Astros	1991	Chuck Knoblauch	Minnesota Twins
1992	Eric Karros	Los Angeles Dodgers	1992	Pat Listach	Milwaukee Brewers
1993	Mike Piazza	Los Angeles Dodgers	1993	Tim Salmon	California Angels
1994	Raul Mondesi	Los Angeles Dodgers	1994	Bob Hamelin	Kansas City Royals
1995	Hideo Nomo	Los Angeles Dodgers	1995	Marty Cordova	Minnesota Twins
1996	Todd Hollandsworth	Los Angeles Dodgers	1996	Derek Jeter	New York Yankees
1997	Scott Rolen	Philadelphia Phillies	1997	Nomar Garciaparra	Boston Red Sox
1998	Kerry Wood	Chicago Cubs	1998	Ben Grieve	Oakland Athletics
1999	Scott Williamson	Cincinnati Reds	1999	Carlos Beltran	Kansas City Royals
2000	Rafael Furcal	Atlanta Braves	2000	Kazuhiro Sasaki	Seattle Mariners
2001	Albert Pujols	St. Louis Cardinals	2001	Ichiro Suzuki	Seattle Mariners
2002	Jason Jennings	Colorado Rockies	2002	Eric Hinske	Toronto Blue Jays
2003	Dontrelle Willis	Florida Marlins	2003	Angel Berroa	Kansas City Royals
2004	Jason Bay	Pittsburgh Pirates	2004	Bobby Crosby	Oakland Athletics
2005	Ryan Howard	Philadelphia Phillies	2005	Huston Street	Oakland Athletics
2006	Hanley Ramirez	Florida Marlins	2006	Justin Verlander	Detroit Tigers
2007	Ryan Braun	Milwaukee Brewers	2007	Dustin Pedroia	Boston Red Sox
2008	Geovany Soto	Chicago Cubs	2008	Evan Longoria	Tampa Bay Rays
2009	Chris Coghlan	Florida Marlins	2009	Andrew Bailey	Oakland Athletics

Note: 1. One player selected as Major League Rookie of the Year. Policy of naming a player from each league was inaugurated in 1949.
Source: Baseball Writer's Association.

Cy Young Award Winners

BOTH LEAGUES

Year	Name, Team	W–L,	ERA	Year	Name, Team	W–L,	ERA
1956	Don Newcombe, Brooklyn Dodgers	27–7	3.06	1962	Don Drysdale, Los Angeles Dodgers	25–9,	2.83
1957	Warren Spahn, Milwaukee Braves	21–11	2.69	1963	Sandy Koufax, Los Angeles Dodgers	25–5,	1.88
1958	Bob Turley, New York Yankees	21–7	2.97	1964	Dean Chance, Los Angeles Angels	20–9,	1.65
1959	Early Wynn, Chicago White Sox	22–10	3.17	1965	Sandy Koufax, Los Angeles Dodgers	26–8,	2.04
1960	Vernon Law, Pittsburgh Pirates	20–9	3.08	1966	Sandy Koufax, Los Angeles Dodgers	27–9,	1.73
1961	Whitey Ford, New York Yankees	25–4	3.21				

Year	National League Winner, Team	W–L	ERA	American League Winner, Team	W–L	ERA
1967	Mike McCormick, San Francisco Giants	22–10	2.85	Jim Lonborg, Boston Red Sox	22–9	3.16
1968	Bob Gibson, St. Louis Cardinals	22–9	1.12	Denny McLain, Detroit Tigers	31–6	1.96
1969	Tom Seaver, New York Mets	25–7	2.21	Mike Cuellar, Baltimore Orioles	23–11	2.38
1970	Bob Gibson, St. Louis Cardinals	23–7	3.12	Jim Perry, Minnesota Twins	24–12	3.03
1971	Ferguson Jenkins, Chicago Cubs	24–13	2.77	Vida Blue, Oakland Athletics	24–8	1.82
1972	Steve Carlton, Philadelphia Phillies	27–10	1.97	Gaylord Perry, Cleveland Indians	24–16	1.92
1973	Tom Seaver, New York Mets	19–10	2.08	Jim Palmer, Baltimore Orioles	22–9	2.40
1974	Mike Marshall, Los Angeles Dodgers	21 saves	2.42	Catfish Hunter, Oakland Athletics	25–12	2.49
1975	Tom Seaver, New York Mets	22–9	2.38	Jim Palmer, Baltimore Orioles	23–11	2.09
1976	Randy Jones, San Diego Padres	22–14	2.74	Jim Palmer, Baltimore Orioles	22–13	2.51
1977	Steve Carlton, Philadelphia Phillies	23–10	2.64	Sparky Lyle, New York Yankees	26 saves	2.17
1978	Gaylord Perry, San Diego Padres	21–6	2.72	Ron Guidry, New York Yankees	25–3	1.74
1979	Bruce Sutter, Chicago Cubs	37 saves	2.23	Mike Flanagan, Baltimore Orioles	23–9	3.08
1980	Steve Carlton, Philadelphia Phillies	24–9	2.34	Steve Stone, Baltimore Orioles	25–7	3.23
1981[1]	Fernando Valenzuela, Los Angeles Dodgers	13–7	2.48	Rollie Fingers, Milwaukee Brewers	28 saves	1.04
1982	Steve Carlton, Philadelphia Phillies	23–11	3.10	Pete Vuckovich, Milwaukee Brewers	18–6	3.34
1983	John Denny, Philadelphia Phillies	19–6	2.37	LaMarr Hoyt, Chicago White Sox	24–10	3.66
1984	Rick Sutcliffe, Chicago Cubs	20–6	3.64	Willie Henandez, Detroit Tigers	32 saves	1.92
1985	Dwight Gooden, New York Mets	24–4	1.53	Bret Saberhagen, Kansas City Royals	20–6	2.87
1986	Mike Scott, Houston Astros	18–10	2.22	Roger Clemens, Boston Red Sox	24–4	2.48
1987	Steve Bedrosian, Philadelphia Phillies	40 saves	2.83	Roger Clemens, Boston Red Sox	20–9	2.97
1988	Orel Hershiser, Los Angeles Dodgers	23–8	2.26	Frank Viola, Minnesota Twins	24–7	2.64
1989	Mark Davis, San Diego Padres	44 saves	1.85	Bret Saberhagen, Kansas City Royals	23–6	2.16
1990	Doug Drabek, Pittsburgh Pirates	22–6	2.76	Bob Welch, Oakland Athletics	27–6	3.06
1991	Tom Glavine, Atlanta Braves	20–11	2.55	Roger Clemens, Boston Red Sox	18–10	3.06
1992	Greg Maddux, Chicago Cubs	20–11	2.18	Dennis Eckersley Oakland Athletics	51 saves	1.91
1993	Greg Maddux, Atlanta Braves	20–10	2.36	Jack McDowell, Chicago White Sox	22–10	3.37
1994[1]	Greg Maddux, Atlanta Braves	16–6	1.56	David Cone, Kansas City Royals	16–5	2.94
1995[1]	Greg Maddux, Atlanta Braves	19–2	1.53	Randy Johnson, Seattle Mariners	18–2	2.48
1996	John Smoltz, Atlanta Braves	24–8	2.94	Pat Hentgen, Toronto Blue Jays	20–10	3.22
1997	Pedro Martínez, Montreal Expos	17–8	1.90	Roger Clemens, Toronto Blue Jays	21–7	2.05
1998	Tom Glavine, Atlanta Braves	20–6	2.47	Roger Clemens, Toronto Blue Jays	20–6	2.65
1999	Randy Johnson, Arizona Diamondbacks	17–9	2.48	Pedro Martínez, Boston Red Sox	23–4	2.07
2000	Randy Johnson, Arizona Diamondbacks	19–7	2.64	Pedro Martínez, Boston Red Sox	18–6	1.74
2001	Randy Johnson, Arizona Diamondbacks	21–6	2.49	Roger Clemens, New York Yankees	20–3	2.65
2002	Randy Johnson, Arizona Diamondbacks	24–5	2.32	Barry Zito, Oakland Athletics	23–5	2.75
2003	Eric Gagné, Los Angeles. Dodgers	55 saves	1.20	Roy Halladay, Toronto Blue Jays	22–7	3.25
2004	Roger Clemens, Houston Astros	18–4	2.98	Johan Santana, Minnesota Twins	20–6	2.61
2005	Chris Carpenter, St.Louis Cardinals	21–5	2.83	Bartolo Colon, Los Angeles Angels	21–8	3.48
2006	Brandon Webb, Arizona Diamondbacks	16–8	3.10	Johan Santana, Minnesota Twins	19–6	2.77
2007	Jake Peavy, San Diego Padres	19–6	2.54	C.C. Sabathia, Cleveland Indians	19–7	3.21
2008	Tim Lincecum, San Francisco Giants	18–5	2.62	Cliff Lee, Cleveland Indians	22–3	2.54
2009	Tim Lincecum, San Francisco Giants	15–7	2.48	Zack Greinke, Kansas City Royals	16–8	2.16

Note: Saves, rather than win-loss records, are shown for relievers. 1. Strike-shortened season.

Most Wins by Managers

	Manager	Wins	Losses	Pct.		Manager	Wins	Losses	Pct.
1.	Connie Mack	3,731	3,948	.486	6.	Sparky Anderson	2,194	1,834	.545
2.	John McGraw	2,763	1,984	.586	7.	Bucky Harris	2,157	2,218	.493
3.	Tony La Russa[1]	2,638	2,293	.556	8.	Joe McCarthy	2,125	1,333	.615
4.	Bobby Cox[1]	2,504	2,001	.556	9.	Walter Alston	2,040	1,613	.558
5.	Joe Torre[1]	2,326	1,997	.538	10.	Leo Durocher	2,008	1,709	.540

Note: 1. Manager active in 2010. Source: Major League Baseball.

Most Valuable Player Award Winners

Between 1911 and 1914 the Chalmers Award was given to the player judged to be the most valuable in each league. It was not until 1922 that the American League began to select a league MVP. The National League began to do so as well two years later. By the end of the decade , though, both leagues failed to select an MVP. In 1931 the Baseball Writers Association of America began to select the league MVP's and has continued to do so through today.

NATIONAL LEAGUE

Year	Name	Team	HRs	RBIs	Avg.
1911	Frank Schulte	Chicago Cubs	21	121	.300
1912	Larry Doyle	New York Giants	10	90	.330
1913	Jake Daubert	Brooklyn Dodgers	2	52	.350
1914	Johnny Evers	Chicago Cubs	1	40	.279
1924	Dazzy Vance (Pitcher)	Brooklyn Dodgers	28W	6L	2.16 ERA
1925	Rogers Hornsby	St. Louis Cardinals	29	143	.403
1926	Bob O'Farrell	St. Louis Cardinals	7	68	.293
1927	Paul Waner	Pittsburgh Pirates	9	131	.380
1928	Jim Bottomley	St. Louis Cardinals	31	136	.325
1929	Rogers Hornsby	St. Louis Cardinals	39	149	.380
1931	Frankie Frisch	St. Louis Cardinals	4	82	.311
1932	Chuck Klein	Philadelphia Phillies	38	137	.348
1933	Carl Hubbell (Pitcher)	New York Giants	23W	12L	1.66 ERA
1934	Dizzy Dean (Pitcher)	St. Louis Cardinals	30W	7L	2.66 ERA
1935	Gabby Hartnett	Chicago Cubs	13	91	.344
1936	Carl Hubbell (Pitcher)	New York Giants	26W	6L	2.31 ERA
1937	Joe Medwick	St. Louis Cardinals	31	154	.374
1938	Ernie Lombardi	Cincinnati Reds	19	95	.342
1939	Bucky Walters (Pitcher)	Cincinnati Reds	27W	11L	2.29 ERA
1940	Frank McCormick	Cinncinati Reds	19	127	.309
1941	Dolph Camilli	Brooklyn Dodgers	34	120	.285
1942	Mort Cooper (Pitcher)	St. Louis Cardinals	22W	7L	1.78 ERA
1943	Stan Musial	St. Louis Cardinals	13	81	.357
1944	Marty Marion	St. Louis Cardinals	6	63	.267
1945	Phil Cavarretta	Chicago Cubs	6	97	.355
1946	Stan Musial	St. Louis Cardinals	16	103	.365
1947	Bob Elliott	Boston Braves	22	113	.317
1948	Stan Musial	St. Louis Cardinals	39	131	.376
1949	Jackie Robinson	Brooklyn Dodgers	16	124	.342
1950	Jim Konstanty (Pitcher)[1]	Philadelphia Phillies	16W	7L	2.66 ERA
1951	Roy Campanella	Brooklyn Dodgers	33	108	.325
1952	Hank Sauer	Chicago Cubs	37	121	.270
1953	Roy Campanella	Brooklyn Dodgers	41	142	.312
1954	Willie Mays	New York Giants	41	110	.345
1955	Roy Campanella	Brooklyn Dodgers	32	107	.318
1956	Don Newcombe (Pitcher)	Brooklyn Dodgers	27W	7L	3.06 ERA
1957	Hank Aaron	Milwaukee Braves	44	132	.322
1958	Ernie Banks	Chicago Cubs	47	129	.313
1959	Ernie Banks	Chicago Cubs	45	143	.304
1960	Dick Groat	Pittsburgh Pirates	2	50	.325
1961	Frank Robinson	Cincinnati Reds	37	124	.323
1962	Maury Wills	Los Angeles Dodgers	6	48	.299
1963	Sandy Koufax (Pitcher)	Los Angeles Dodgers	25W	5L	1.88 ERA
1964	Ken Boyer	St. Louis Cardinals	24	119	.295
1965	Willie Mays	San Francisco Giants	52	112	.317
1966	Roberto Clemente	Pittsburgh Pirates	29	119	.317
1967	Orlando Cepeda	San Francisco Giants	25	111	.325
1968	Bob Gibson (Pitcher)	St. Louis Cardinals	22W	9L	1.12 ERA
1969	Willie McCovey	San Francisco Giants	45	126	.320
1970	Johnny Bench	Cincinnati Reds	45	148	.293
1971	Joe Torre	St. Louis Cardinals	45	137	.363
1972	Johnny Bench	Cincinnati Reds	40	125	.270
1973	Pete Rose	Cincinnati Reds	5	64	.338
1974	Steve Garvey	Los Angeles Dodgers	21	111	.312
1975	Joe Morgan	Cincinnati Reds	17	94	.327
1976	Joe Morgan	Cincinnati Reds	27	111	.320
1977	George Foster	Cincinnati Reds	52	149	.320
1978	Dave Parker	Pittsburgh Pirates	30	117	.334
1979	Keith Hernandez	St. Louis Cardinals	11	105	.344
	Willie Stargell	Pittsburgh Pirates	32	82	.281
1980	Mike Schmidt	Philadelphia Phillies	48	121	.286

NATIONAL LEAGUE

Year	Name	Team	HRs	RBIs	Avg.
1981	Mike Schmidt[2]	Philadelphia Phillies	31	91	.316
1982	Dale Murphy	Atlanta Braves	36	109	.281
1983	Dale Murphy	Atlanta Braves	36	121	.302
1984	Ryne Sandberg	Chicago Cubs	19	84	.314
1985	Willie McGee	St. Louis Cardinals	10	82	.353
1986	Mike Schmidt	Philadelphia Phillies	37	119	.290
1987	Andre Dawson	Chicago Cubs	49	137	.287
1988	Kirk Gibson	Los Angeles Dodgers	25	76	.290
1989	Kevin Mitchell	San Francisco Giants	47	125	.291
1990	Barry Bonds	Pittsburgh Pirates	33	114	.301
1991	Terry Pendleton	Atlanta Braves	22	86	.319
1992	Barry Bonds	Pittsburgh Pirates	34	103	.311
1993	Barry Bonds	San Francisco Giants	46	123	.336
1994	Jeff Bagwell[2]	Houston Astros	39	116	.368
1995	Barry Larkin[2]	Cincinnati Reds	15	66	.319
1996	Ken Caminiti	San Diego Padres	40	130	.326
1997	Larry Walker	Colorado Rockies	49	130	.366
1998	Sammy Sosa	Chicago Cubs	66	158	.308
1999	Chipper Jones	Atlanta Braves	45	110	.319
2000	Jeff Kent	San Francisco Giants	33	125	.334
2001	Barry Bonds	San Francisco Giants	73	137	.328
2002	Barry Bonds	San Francisco Giants	46	110	.370
2003	Barry Bonds	San Francisco Giants	45	90	.341
2004	Barry Bonds	San Francisco Giants	45	101	.362
2005	Albert Pujols	St. Louis Cardinals	41	117	.330
2006	Ryan Howard	Philadelphia Phillies	58	149	.313
2007	Jimmy Rollins	Philadelphia Phillies	30	94	.296
2008	Albert Pujols	St. Louis Cardinals	37	116	.357
2009	Albert Pujols	St. Louis Cardinals	47	135	.327

Notes: 1. 22 saves in 1950. 2. Strike-shortened season. **Source:** Baseball Writers' Association.

AMERICAN LEAGUE

Year	Player	Team	HRs	RBIs	Avg.
1911	Ty Cobb	Detroit Tigers	8	144	.420
1912	Tris Speaker	Boston Red Sox	10	98	.383
1913	Walter Johnson (Pitcher)	Washington Senators	36W	7L	1.14 ERA
1914	Eddie Collins	Philadelphia Athletics	2	85	.344
1922	George Sisler	St. Louis Browns	8	105	.420
1923	Babe Ruth	New York Yankees	41	131	.393
1924	Walter Johnson (Pitcher)	Washington Senators	23W	7L	2.72 ERA
1925	Roger Peckinpaugh	Washington Senators	4	64	.294
1926	George Burns	Cleveland Indians	4	114	.358
1927	Lou Gehrig	New York Yankees	47	175	.373
1928	Mickey Cochrane	Philadelphia Athletics	10	57	.293
1931	Lefty Grove (Pitcher)	Philadelphia Athletics	31W	4L	2.06 ERA
1932	Jimmie Foxx	Philadelphia Athletics	58	169	.364
1933	Jimmie Foxx	Philadelphia Athletics	48	163	.356
1934	Mickey Cochrane	Detroit Tigers	2	76	.320
1935	Hank Greenberg	Detroit Tigers	36	170	.328
1936	Lou Gehrig	New York Yankees	49	152	.354
1937	Charley Gehringer	Detroit Tigers	14	96	.371
1938	Jimmie Foxx	Boston Red Sox	50	175	.349
1939	Joe DiMaggio	New York Yankees	30	126	.381
1940	Hank Greenberg	Detroit Tigers	30	125	.357
1941	Joe DiMaggio	New York Yankees	30	125	.357
1942	Joe Gordon	New York Yankees	18	103	.322
1943	Spud Chandler (Pitcher)	New York Yankees	20W	4L	1.64 ERA
1944	Hal Newhouser (Pitcher)	Detroit Tigers	29W	9L	2.22 ERA
1945	Hal Newhouser (Pitcher)	Detroit Tigers	25W	9L	1.81 ERA
1946	Ted Williams	Boston Red Sox	38	123	.342
1947	Joe DiMaggio	New York Yankees	20	97	.315
1948	Lou Boudreau	Cleveland Indians	18	106	.355
1949	Ted Williams	Boston Red Sox	43	159	.343
1950	Phil Rizzuto	New York Yankees	7	66	.324
1951	Yogi Berra	New York Yankees	27	88	.294
1952	Bobby Shantz (Pitcher)	Philadelphia Athletics	24W	7L	2.48 ERA
1953	Al Rosen	Cleveland Indians	43	145	.336
1954	Yogi Berra	New York Yankees	22	125	.307

AMERICAN LEAGUE

Year	Player	Team	HRs	RBIs	Avg.
1955	Yogi Berra	New York Yankees	27	108	.272
1956	Mickey Mantle	New York Yankees	52	130	.353
1957	Mickey Mantle	New York Yankees	34	94	.365
1958	Jackie Jensen	Boston Red Sox	35	122	.286
1959	Nelson Fox	Chicago White Sox	2	70	.306
1960	Roger Maris	New York Yankees	39	112	.283
1961	Roger Maris	New York Yankees	61	142	.269
1962	Mickey Mantle	New York Yankees	30	89	.321
1963	Elston Howard	New York Yankees	28	85	.287
1964	Brooks Robinson	Baltimore Orioles	28	118	.317
1965	Zoilo Versalles	Minnesota Twins	19	77	.273
1966	Frank Robinson	Baltimore Orioles	49	122	.316
1967	Carl Yastrzemski	Boston Red Sox	44	121	.326
1968	Denny McLain (Pitcher)	Detroit Tigers	31W	6L	1.96ERA
1969	Harmon Killebrew	Minnesota Twins	49	140	.276
1970	Boog Powell	Baltimore Orioles	35	114	.297
1971	Vida Blue (Pitcher)	Oakland Athletics	24W	8L	1.82ERA
1972	Dick Allen	Chicago White Sox	37	113	.308
1973	Reggie Jackson	Oakland Athletics	32	117	.293
1974	Jeff Burroughs	Texas Rangers	25	118	.301
1975	Fred Lynn	Boston Red Sox	21	105	.331
1976	Thurman Munson	New York Yankees	17	105	.302
1977	Rod Carew	Minnesota Twins	14	100	.388
1978	Jim Rice	Boston Red Sox	46	139	.315
1979	Don Baylor	California Angels	36	139	.296
1980	George Brett	Kansas City Royals	24	118	.390
1981	Rollie Fingers (Pitcher)[1,2]	Milwaukee Brewers	6W	3L	1.04 ERA
1982	Robin Yount	Milwaukee Brewers	29	114	.331
1983	Cal Ripken Jr.	Baltimore Orioles	27	102	.318
1984	Willie Hernandez (Pitcher)[3]	Detroit Tigers	9W	3L	2.48 ERA
1985	Don Mattingly	New York Yankees	35	145	.324
1986	Roger Clemens (Pitcher)	Boston Red Sox	24W	4L	2.48 ERA
1987	George Bell	Toronto Blue Jays	47	134	.308
1988	Jose Canseco	Oakland Athletics	42	124	.307
1989	Robin Yount	Milwaukee Brewers	21	103	.318
1990	Rickey Henderson	Oakland Athletics	28	61	.325
1991	Cal Ripken Jr.	Baltimore Orioles	34	114	.323
1992	Dennis Eckersley (Pitcher)[4]	Oakland Athletics	7W	1L	1.91 ERA
1993	Frank Thomas	Chicago White Sox	41	128	.317
1994	Frank Thomas[1]	Chicago White Sox	38	101	.353
1995	Mo Vaughn[1]	Boston Red Sox	39	126	.300
1996	Juan González	Texas Rangers	47	144	.314
1997	Ken Griffey Jr.	Seattle Mariners	56	147	.304
1998	Juan González	Texas Rangers	45	157	.318
1999	Iván Rodríguez	Texas Rangers	35	113	.332
2000	Jason Giambi	Oakland Athletics	43	137	.333
2001	Ichiro Suzuki	Seattle Mariners	8	69	.350
2002	Miguel Tejada	Oakland Athletics	34	131	.308
2003	Alex Rodríguez	Texas Rangers	47	118	.298
2004	Vladimir Guerrero	Anaheim Angels	39	126	.337
2005	Alex Rodriguez	New York Yankees	48	130	.321
2006	Justin Morneau	Minnesota Twins	34	130	.321
2007	Alex Rodriguez	New York Yankees	54	156	.314
2008	Dustin Pedroia	Boston Red Sox	17	83	.326
2009	Joe Mauer	Minnesota Twins	28	96	.365

Notes: 1. Strike-shortened season. 2. 28 saves in 1981. 3. 32 saves in 1984. 4. 51 saves in 1992. **Source:** Baseball Writers' Association.

Triple Crown Winners

Only 11 players have led their league in home runs, runs batted in, and batting average in one season.

Year	Player	Team	HR	RBI	AVG.
1909	Ty Cobb	Detroit Tigers	9	115	.377
1912	Henry Zimmerman	Chicago Cubs	14	98	.372
1922	Rogers Hornsby	St. Louis Cardinals	42	152	.401
1925	Rogers Hornsby	St. Louis Cardinals	39	143	.403
1933	Chuck Klein	Philadelphia Phillies	28	120	.368
1933	Jimmie Foxx	Philadelphia Athletics	48	163	.356
1934	Lou Gehrig	New York Yankees	49	165	.363
1937	Joe Medwick	St. Louis Cardinals	31	154	.374
1942	Ted Williams	Boston Red Sox	36	137	.356
1947	Ted Williams	Boston Red Sox	32	114	.343
1956	Mickey Mantle	New York Yankees	52	130	.353
1966	Frank Robinson	Baltimore Orioles	49	122	.316
1967	Carl Yastrzemski	Boston Red Sox	44	121	.326

The Baseball Hall of Fame

National Baseball Hall of Fame and Museum
25 Main Street, Cooperstown, NY 13326.
888-HALL-OF-FAME (888-425-5633); www.baseballhalloffame.org
Open every day of the year except Thanksgiving, Christmas and New Year's.
Hours: 9am–9pm, Memorial Day weekend to Labor Day; 9am-5pm the rest of the year.

The Hall of Fame was established in 1936 and opened in Cooperstown, N.Y. in 1939. From the start, there were two ways to be elected: by receiving 75 percent of the votes cast by the Baseball Writers Association of America or 75 percent of the votes cast by a Committee on Old Timers. In the first year, the writers picked the top five players of the post-1900 era: Ty Cobb, Walter Johnson, Christy Mathewson, Babe Ruth, and Honus Wagner. To be elected, a player must have played at least 10 years in the major leagues and been retired for at least five years. The Committee on Old Timers, originally created to consider 19th Century players, was replaced by a Special Veterans Committee whose scope includes all players retired for a minimum of 25 years who may have been overlooked when they were first eligible. In 1971 a Special Committee on the Negro Leagues was set up to consider ballplayers who played in the old Negro Leagues.

Player/Position/Year Inducted	Games	At Bats	HRs	Avg.	Hits	RBIs
Aaron, Henry (Hank) OF 1982	3,298	12,364	755	.305	3,771	2,297
Broke Babe Ruth's all-time home run record						
Anson, Adrian (Cap) 1B 1939	2,523	10,278	97	.333	3,418	2,076
Managed 20 years, 1879–98, winning five pennants						
Aparicio, Luis SS 1984	2,599	10,230	83	.262	2,677	791
Led AL in stolen bases nine years in a row (1956–64)						
Appling, Luke SS 1964	2,422	8,857	45	.310	2,749	1,116
Batted .388 in 1936						
Ashburn, Richie OF 1995	2,189	8,365	29	.308	2,574	586
Hit .300 or more nine times						
Averill, Earl OF 1975	1,669	6,358	238	.318	2,020	1,165
232 hits in 1936						
Baker, Frank (Home Run) 3B 1955	1,575	5,985	96	.307	1,838	1,013
Batted .363 in six World Series						
Bancroft, Dave SS 1971	1,913	7,182	32	.279	2,004	591
Handled 984 chances in 1922						
Banks, Ernie SS, 1B 1977	2,528	9,421	512	.274	2,583	1,636
Consecutive MVP awards, 1958–59						
Beckley, Jake 1B 1971	2,386	9,527	88	.308	2,931	1,575
244 career triples, mostly in 19th Century						
Bench, Johnny C 1989	2,158	7,658	389	.267	2,048	1,376
Hit .529 in 1976 World Series; NL MVP 1970, 1972						
Berra, Lawrence (Yogi) C, OF 1972	2,120	7,555	358	.285	2,150	1,430
Three MVP awards: 1951, 1954, 1955						
Boggs, Wade 3B 2005	2,432	9,180	118	.328	3,010	1,014
Led AL in batting five times; at least 200 hits in seven consecutive seasons						
Bottomley, Jim 1B 1974	1,991	7,471	219	.310	2,313	1,422
12 RBIs in one game, 1924						
Boudreau, Lou SS 1970	1,646	6,030	68	.295	1,779	789
MVP in 1948; managed 16 years						
Bresnahan, Roger C, OF 1945	1,430	4,478	26	.279	1,251	530
212 stolen bases; first catcher elected to Hall of Fame						
Brett, George 3B, 1B 1999	2,707	10,349	317	.305	3,154	1,595
Hit .300 11 times; 13-time all-star; hit .390 in 1980						
Brock, Lou OF 1985	2,616	10,332	149	.293	3,023	900
938 stolen bases; batted .391 in three World Series						
Brouthers, Dan 1B 1945	1,673	6,711	106	.342	2,296	1,296
Seven slugging and five batting titles during 19th Century						
Burkett, Jesse OF 1946	2,072	8,430	75	.341	2,873	952
Led NL in batting three times and in hits four times						
Campanella, Roy C 1969	1,215	4,205	242	.276	1,161	856
Three MVP awards: 1951, 1953, 1955						
Carey, Max OF 1961	2,476	9,363	69	.285	2,665	800
738 stolen bases						
Carew, Rod 2B 1B 1991	2469	9315	92	.328	3053	1015
Won seven batting titles; hit over .300 in 15 consecutive seasons; 18 straight All-Star teams						
Carter, Gary C 2003	2,296	7,971	324	.262	2,092	1,225
11-time all-star (1975, 1979–88); won three gold gloves						
Cepeda, Orlando 1B 1999	2,124	7,927	379	.297	2,351	1,365
Seven-time all-star; NL MVP 1967; .499 career slugging percentage						
Chance, Frank 1B 1946	1,286	4,295	20	.297	1,274	596
Managed Chicago (NL) to four pennants in five years, 1906–10						
Clarke, Fred OF 1945	2,245	8,588	67	.315	2,708	1,015
223 career triples, hit .300 or better 11 times						
Clemente, Roberto OF 1973	2,433	9,454	240	.317	3,000	1,305
Career average of over 18 outfield assists per season						

Player/Position/Year Inducted	Games	At Bats	HRs	Avg.	Hits	RBIs
Cobb, Ty OF 1936	3,035	11,429	117	.367	4,191	1,938
Batted .320 or better in 23 straight years						
Cochrane, Micky C 1947	1,482	5,169	119	.320	1,652	832
Two MVP awards, 1928 and 1934						
Collins, Eddie 2B 1939	2,826	9,949	47	.333	3,315	1,300
Hit .340 or better 10 times; led AL in fielding nine times						
Collins, Jimmy 3B 1945	1,728	6,796	64	.294	1,997	982
Led NL in home runs, 1898						
Combs, Earle OF 1970	1,454	5,748	58	.325	1,866	629
Averaged 127 runs scored per season						
Connor, Roger 1B 1976	1,998	7,798	136	.318	2,480	1,078
Held all-time HR record before Babe Ruth						
Crawford, Sam OF 1957	2,517	9,580	97	.309	2,964	1,525
312 triples, best ever						
Cronin, Joe SS 1956	2,124	7,579	170	.301	2,285	1,424
Manager 1933–47						
Cuyler, Hazen (Kiki) OF 1968	1,879	7,161	127	.321	2,299	1,065
Led NL in runs scored twice, stolen bases four times						
Davis, George SS 1998	2,376	9,035	73	.295	2,665	1,435
Hit over .300 nine years in a row (1893–1901)						
Dawson, Andre OF 2010	2627	9927	438	.279	2774	1591
NL Rookie of the Year in 1977 and the NL MVP in 1988						
Delahanty, Ed IF, OF 1945	1,835	7,505	101	.346	2,596	1,464
Batted .410 in 1899						
Dickey, Bill C 1954	1,789	6,300	202	.313	1,969	1,209
Catcher on eight AL-pennant-winning teams						
DiMaggio, Joe OF 1955	1,736	6,821	361	.325	2,214	1,537
56 game hitting streak in 1941						
Doby, Larry OF 1998	1,533	5,348	253	.283	1,515	969
Led AL in HR twice; seven-time all-star (1949–55); first black man to play in AL						
Doerr, Bobby 2B 1986	1,865	7,093	223	.288	2,042	1,247
Led AL in slugging 1944						
Duffy, Hugh OF 1945	1,736	7,062	103	.328	2,314	1,299
Batted .438 in 1894						
Evers, Johnny 2B 1946	1,783	6,134	12	.270	1,658	538
NL MVP in 1914						
Ewing, Buck C, IF, OF 1939	1,315	5,363	70	.303	1,625	733
Regarded as the greatest player of the 19th Century						
Ferrell, Rick C 1984	1,884	6,028	28	.281	1,692	734
Led AL catchers at times in putouts, assists, fielding average, and double plays						
Fisk, Carlton C 2000	2,499	8,756	376	.269	2,356	1,330
Hit 20 or more home runs 8 times						
Flick, Elmer OF 1963	1,484	5,603	47	.315	1,767	756
Led AL in triples 1905–07						
Fox, Nellie 2B 1997	2,367	9,232	35	.288	2,663	790
Led AL in putouts, 1951–60						
Foxx, Jimmie 1B, 3B 1951	2,317	8,134	534	.325	2,646	1,921
Slugged over .700 three seasons						
Frisch, Frank 2B, 3B 1947	2,311	9,112	105	.316	2,880	1,244
Hit .300 or better 11 years in a row (1921–31)						
Gehrig, Lou 1B 1939	2,164	8,001	493	.340	2,721	1,990
Played in 2,130 consecutive games; first player to hit 4 HRs in one game						
Gehringer, Charlie 2B 1949	2,323	8,860	184	.320	2,839	1,427
60 doubles in 1936						
Gordon, Joe 2B 2009	1,566	5,707	253	.268	1,530	975
Nine-time All-Star; AL MVP 1942						
Goslin, Leon (Goose) OF 1968	2,287	8,655	248	.316	2,735	1,609
100+ RBI 11 years						
Greenberg, Hank 1B 1956	1,394	5,193	331	.313	1,628	1,276
58 home runs in 1938; 63 doubles in 1934						
Gwynn, Tony OF 2007	2,440	9,288	135	.338	3,141	1,138
Won eight batting titles						
Hafey, Charles (Chick) OF 1971	1,283	4,625	164	.317	1,466	833
NL batting title (.349) in 1931						
Hamilton, Billy OF 1961	1,591	6,269	40	.344	2,159	739
Scored 196 runs in 1894, with a .509 on-base average and 99 stolen bases						
Hartnett, Charles (Gabby) C 1955	1,990	6,432	236	.297	1,912	1,179
Played on four NL pennant winners, managed one						
Heilmann, Harry OF, 1B 1952	2,147	7,787	183	.342	2,660	1,539
Batted .403 in 1923						
Henderson, Rickey LF 2009	3,081	10,961	297	.279	3,055	1,115
All-time leader for stolen bases (1,406) and runs scored (2,295); 10-time All-Star, AL MVP 1990.						
Herman, Billy 2B 1975	1,922	7,707	47	.304	2,345	839
57 doubles in 1935						
Hooper, Harry OF 1971	2,308	8,785	75	.281	2,466	817
375 career stolen bases						
Hornsby, Rogers 2B, IF 1942	2,259	8,173	301	.358	2,930	1,584
Batted .424 in 1924; won nine slugging titles						

Player/Position/Year Inducted	Games	At Bats	HRs	Avg.	Hits	RBIs
Jackson, Reggie 1993	2,820	9,864	563	.262	2,584	1,702
Played in 5 World Series and 11 divisional playoffs in 21 years; World Series MVP 1977						
Jackson, Travis SS 1982	1,656	6,086	135	.291	1,768	929
Batted over .300 six times in 1920s and 1930s						
Jennings, Hugh SS 1945	1,285	4,905	18	.312	1,531	840
Batted .398 in 1896						
Kaline, Al OF 1980	2,834	10,116	399	.297	3,007	1,583
3,007 career hits						
Keeler, Willie OF 1939	2,123	8,591	33	.341	2,932	810
Batted .424 in 1897; 495 career stolen bases						
Kell, George 3B 1983	1,795	6,702	78	.306	2,054	870
AL batting champ (.343) in 1949						
Kelley, Joe OF 1971	1,845	7,018	65	.319	2,242	1,193
Averaged 151 runs scored, 1894–96						
Kelly, George 1B 1973	1,622	5,993	148	.297	1,778	1,020
Led NL in RBI, 1920 and 1925						
Kelly, Mike (King) OF, C 1945	1,463	5,923	69	.307	1,820	794
Two batting titles, 1884 and 1886; 315 career stolen bases						
Killebrew, Harmon 1B, 3B, OF 1984	2,435	8,147	573	.256	2,086	1,584
40+ home runs eight years						
Kiner, Ralph OF 1975	1,472	5,205	369	.279	1,451	1,015
Second highest home run per at bat ratio of all-time						
Klein, Chuck OF 1980	1,753	6,486	300	.320	2,076	1,201
44 outfield assists in 1930						
Lajoie, Napoleon 2B 1937	2,480	9,589	82	.338	3,242	1,599
Batted .422 in 1901						
Lazerri, Tony IF 1991	1,740	6,297	178	.292	1,840	1,191
Batted .300 or better five times; clutch hitter in World Series						
Lindstrom, Fred 3B, OF 1976	1,438	5,611	103	.311	1,747	779
231 hits in 1928						
Lombardi, Ernie C 1986	1,853	5,855	190	.306	1,792	990
Two NL batting titles, 1938 and 1942						
Mantle, Mickey OF 1974	2,401	8,102	536	.298	2,415	1,509
52 home runs in 1956, 54 in 1961						
Manush, Heinie OF 1964	2,009	7,653	110	.330	2,524	1,173
Hit .378 in 1926						
Maranville, Rabbit SS, 2B 1954	2,670	10,078	28	.258	2,605	884
23 year career; hit .308 in two World Series						
Mathews, Eddie 3B 1978	2,388	8,537	512	.271	2,315	1,453
1,444 career walks						
Mays, Willie OF 1979	2,992	10,881	660	.302	3,283	1,903
Slugged over .600 six seasons						
Mazeroski, Bill 2B 2001	2,163	7,775	138	.260	2,016	853
Eight-time gold glove winner; turned a record 1,706 double plays						
McCarthy, Tommy OF 1946	1,275	5,128	44	.292	1,496	666
Averaged 122 runs scored, 1888–94						
McCovey, Willie 1B, OF 1986	2,588	8,197	521	.270	2,211	1,555
Hit 18 career grand slams						
McPhee, Bid 2B 2000	2,135	8,291	53	.279	2,250	727
Considered greatest second baseman of the 19th century, though he played without a glove						
Medwick, Joe OF 1968	1,984	7,635	205	.324	2,471	1,383
Won NL triple crown in 1937						
Mize, Johnny 1B 1981	1,884	6,443	359	.312	2,011	1,337
Four-time NL home run champ						
Molitor, Paul DH, 2004	2,683	10,835	234	.306	3,319	1,307
Seven-time All-Star; 1993 World Series MVP						
Morgan, Joe 2B 1990	2,649	9,277	268	.271	2,517	1,133
Won back-to-back MVP Awards (1975–76)						
Murray, Eddie 1B 2003	3,026	11,336	504	.287	3,255	1,917
Third player ever with 3,000 hits and 500 HRs						
Musial, Stan OF, 1B 1969	3,026	10,972	475	.331	3,630	1,951
725 doubles and 177 triples						
O'Rourke, Jim OF 1945	1,774	7,435	51	.310	2,304	830
Batted .300+ eleven times in the 19th Century						
Ott, Mel OF 1951	2,732	9,456	511	.304	2,876	1,860
Averaged 121 RBI 1929–38						
Perez, Tony 1B 2000	2,777	9,778	379	.279	2,732	1,652
His 1,652 RBIs are the most ever by a Latin player						
Puckett, Kirby OF 2001	1,783	7,244	207	.318	2,304	1,085
Led Minnesota Twins to World Series wins in 1987 and 1991; won AL batting title in 1989						
Reese, Harold (Pee Wee) SS 1984	2,166	8,058	126	.269	2,170	885
Finished in the top ten of MVP balloting nine times						
Rice, Jim OF 2009	2,089	8,225	382	.298	2,452	1,451
Led AL in HR and RBI during career; hit over .300 in 7 seasons.						
Rice, Sam OF 1963	2,404	9,269	34	.322	2,987	1,078
Only 18 strikeouts per 154 games						

Player/Position/Year Inducted	Games	At Bats	HRs	Avg.	Hits	RBIs
Ripken, Cal Jr. SS 2007	3,001	11,551	431	.276	3,184	1,695
Played in record 2,632 consecutive games						
Rizzuto, Phil SS 1994	1,661	5,816	38	.273	1,588	563
AL MVP in 1950; Played in 9 World Series						
Robinson, Brooks 3B 1983	2,896	10,654	268	.267	2,848	1,357
16 consecutive Gold Gloves, 1960–75						
Robinson, Frank OF 1982	2,808	10,006	586	.294	2,943	1,812
MVP in both leagues; AL triple crown in 1966						
Robinson, Jackie 2B 1962	1,382	4,877	137	.311	1,518	734
First black player in MLB; Rookie of the Year 1947; MVP and batting champ 1949						
Roush, Edd OF 1962	1,967	7,363	68	.323	2,376	981
Two NL batting titles, 1917 and 1919						
Ruth, George (Babe) OF, P 1936	2,503	8,399	714	.342	2,873	2,211
Slugged .847 1920–21						
Sandberg, Ryne 2B 2005	2,164	8,385	282	.285	2,386	1,061
Won nine Gold Gloves; ten-time All-Star						
Schalk, Ray C 1955	1,760	5,306	12	.253	1,345	594
176 stolen bases						
Schmidt, Mike 3B 1995	2,404	8,352	548	.267	2,234	1,595
Led NL in homers 8 times; won 10 Gold Gloves						
Schoendienst, Albert (Red) 1989	2,216	8,479	84	.289	2,449	773
Managed Cardinals to two pennants and 1967 World Series crown						
Sewell, Joe SS, 3B 1977	1,902	7,132	49	.312	2,226	1,051
Only 22 strikeouts in his last 2,500 at bats, 1929–33						
Simmons, Al OF 1953	2,215	8,761	307	.334	2,927	1,827
Drove in over 100 runs in each of his first 11 years, 1924–34						
Sisler, George 1B 1939	2,055	8,267	100	.340	2,812	1,175
Batted .400 1920, 1922						
Slaughter, Enos OF 1985	2,380	7,946	169	.300	2,383	1,304
52 doubles in 1939						
Smith, Ozzie SS 2002	2,573	9,396	28	.262	2,460	793
Won 13 Gold Gloves; 15-time All-Star						
Snider, Edwin (Duke) OF 1980	2,143	7,161	407	.295	2,116	1,333
Averaged 41 home runs, 1953–57						
Speaker, Tris OF 1937	2,789	10,195	117	.345	3,514	1,529
Led AL in doubles eight times						
Stargell, Willie OF, 1B 1988	2,360	7,927	475	.282	2,232	1,540
MVP in 1979						
Terry, Bill 1B 1954	1,721	6,428	154	.341	2,193	1,078
Hit .401 in 1930						
Thompson, Sam OF 1974	1,410	6,005	128	.331	1,986	1,299
166 RBI in 1887, 165 in 1895						
Tinker, Joe SS 1946	1,805	6,441	31	.263	1,695	782
Played in four World Series with Chicago Cubs						
Traynor, Pie 3B 1948	1,941	7,559	58	.320	2,416	1,273
100+ RBI seven years						
Vaughan, Joseph (Arky) SS 1985	1,817	6,622	96	.318	2,103	926
.385 in 1935						
Wagner, Honus SS 1936	2,786	10,427	101	.329	3,430	1,732
Eight batting titles, four in a row 1906–09						
Wallace, Bobby SS 1953	2,386	8,652	35	.267	2,314	1,121
Handled 6.1 chances per game at shortstop						
Waner, Lloyd OF 1967	1,992	7,772	28	.316	2,459	598
234 hits in 1929						
Waner, Paul OF 1952	2,549	9,459	112	.333	3,152	1,309
62 doubles in 1932						
Wheat, Zack OF 1959	2,410	9,106	132	.317	2,884	1,261
Batted .375 at age 36 in 1924						
Williams, Billy OF 1987	2,488	9,350	426	.290	2,711	1,475
30+ home runs in five seasons						
Williams, Ted OF 1966	2,292	7,706	521	.344	2,654	1,839
Last .400 hitter in majors, .406 in 1941						
Wilson, Lewis (Hack) OF 1979	1,348	4,760	244	.307	1,461	1,062
56 home runs and 190 RBI in 1930						
Winfield, Dave OF 2001	2,973	11,003	465	.283	3,110	1,833
Member of both the 3,000-hit and 400-home run club.						
Yastrzemski, Carl (Yaz) OF, 1B 1989	3,308	11,988	452	.285	3,419	1,844
Won Triple Crown in 1967; won batting titles in 1963, 1967, and 1968						
Youngs, Ross OF 1972	1,211	4,627	42	.322	1,491	592
Died at age 30; .398 on-base average in four World Series, 1921–24						
Yount, Robin SS, OF 1999	2,856	11,008	251	.285	3,142	1,406
Won AL MVP awards at shortstop (1982) and center field (1989), the only player ever to do so						

Source: National Baseball Hall of Fame.

Hall of Fame Pitchers

Player/Year Inducted	W	L	ERA	Games	Innings	Strikeouts
Alexander, Grover Cleveland 1938 Won 30 games three years; led NL in ERA five times	373	208	2.56	696	5,190	2,198
Bender, Charles (Chief) 1953 Led AL in winning percentage three seasons	210	127	2.46	459	3,017	1,711
Brown, Mordecai (Three-Finger) 1949 1.04 ERA in 1906	239	130	2.06	481	3,172	1,375
Bunning, Jim 1996 Struck out 1,000 batters in each league	224	184	3.27	591	3,760	2,855
Carlton, Steve (Lefty) 1994 Four-time Cy Young Award winner (1972, 1977, 1980, 1982)	329	244	3.22	741	5,217	4,136
Chesbro, Jack 1946 41 wins in 1904	198	132	2.68	392	2,897	1,265
Clarkson, John 1963 53 wins in 1885, with 623 innings pitched	326	177	2.81	531	4,536	2,015
Coveleski, Stan 1969 Led AL in ERA in 1925, 2.84	215	142	2.88	450	3,093	981
Cummings, Williams (Candy) 1939 Inventor of the curveball	21	22	2.78	43	372	37
Dean, Jay (Dizzy) 1953 30 wins in 1934	150	83	3.03	317	1,966	1,155
Drysdale, Don 1984 56 2/3 consecutive scoreless innings, 1968	209	166	2.95	518	3,432	2,486
Eckersley, Dennis 2004 Only pitcher with 100 complete games and 100 saves	197	171	3.50	1,071	3,286	2,401
Faber, Urban (Red) 1964 Led AL in ERA in 1921 and 1922	254	212	3.15	669	4,088	1,471
Feller, Bob 1962 Led AL in wins six times, in shutouts seven	266	162	3.25	570	3,827	2,581
Fingers, Rollie 1992 341 saves over 17 years; AL MVP in 1981	114	118	2.90	944	1,701	1,299
Ford, Edward (Whitey) 1974 25–4 in 1961, 24–7 in 1963	236	106	2.75	498	3,170	1,956
Galvin, James (Pud) 1965 46 wins in 1883 and 1884	365	310	2.85	705	6,003	1,807
Gibson, Bob 1981 1.12 ERA in 1968, seven straight wins in World Series play	251	174	2.91	528	3,885	3,117
Gomez, Vernon (Lefty) 1972 Led AL in shutouts three years	189	102	3.34	368	2,503	1,468
Gossage, Richard (Goose) 2008 310 career saves	124	107	3.01	1,002	1,809	1,502
Grimes, Burleigh 1964 Last legal spitball pitcher, he won 20+ five times	270	212	3.53	617	4,180	1,512
Grove, Robert (Lefty) 1947 Led AL in ERA nine times, in strikeouts seven	300	141	3.06	616	3,941	2,266
Haines, Jesse 1970 Twice led NL in shutouts, 1921 and 1927	210	158	3.64	555	3,209	981
Hoyt, Waite 1969 1.83 in 84 World Series innings	237	182	3.59	674	3,763	1,206
Hubbell, Carl 1947 26–6 in 1936; 1.66 ERA in 1933	253	154	2.97	535	3,589	1,678
Hunter, Jim (Catfish) 1987 21 or more wins, 1971–75	224	166	3.26	500	3,448	2,012
Jenkins, Ferguson 1991 Cy Young Award winner in 1971; three-time all-star	284	226	3.34	664	4,499	3,192
Johnson, Walter 1936 36–7, 1.14 ERA in 1913	417	279	2.17	802	5,914	3,508
Joss, Addie 1978 Averaged 21–11, 1.66 ERA in years 1904–08	160	97	1.89	286	2,327	920
Keefe, Tim 1964 Averaged 37 wins 1883–85	342	225	2.62	600	5,049	2,564
Koufax, Sandy 1972 97–27, 1.85 ERA for seasons 1963–66	165	87	2.76	397	2,324	2,396
Lemon, Bob 1976 Won 20 or more seven times	207	128	3.23	460	2,850	1,277
Lyons, Ted 1955 Pitched 27 shutouts, won 260 games in 21 seasons	260	230	3.67	594	4,161	1,073
Marichal, Juan 1983 Only 1.8 walks per nine innings over career	243	142	2.89	471	3,509	2,303
Marquard, Richard (Rube) 1971 73–23 in years 1911–13	201	177	3.08	536	3,307	1,593
Mathewson, Christy 1936 79 career shutouts	373	188	2.13	635	4,780	2,502
McGinnity, Joe 1946 35–8 in 1904, with an ERA of 1.61	247	144	2.64	466	3,459	1,068

Player/Year Inducted	W	L	ERA	Games	Innings	Strikeouts
Newhouser, Hal 1992	207	150	3.06	488	2,993	1,796
Led AL in victories three years in a row (1944–46)						
Nichols, Charles (Kid) 1949	361	208	2.95	620	5,056	1,873
Won 30 or more games seven times, 1891–94, 1896–98						
Niekro, Phil 1997	318	274	3.35	864	5,404	3,342
Knuckleballer pitched until age 48; five-time all-star						
Palmer, Jim 1990	268	152	2.86	558	3,948	2,212
Won Cy Young Award 1973, 1975, 1976						
Pennock, Herb 1948	240	162	3.61	617	3,558	1,227
162–90 as a New York Yankee, 1923–33						
Perry, Gaylord 1991	314	265	3.10	777	5,352	3,534
Won Cy Young Award in both leagues						
Plank, Eddie 1946	326	194	2.35	623	4,496	2,246
1.32 ERA in seven World Series games						
Radbourn, Charles (Old Hoss) 1939	309	195	2.67	528	4,535	1,830
60–12 in 1884, with 679 innings pitched						
Rixey, Eppa 1963	266	251	3.15	692	4,495	1,350
Won 25 games in 1922						
Roberts, Robin 1976	286	245	3.41	676	4,689	2,357
28–7 in 1952; five-time NL leader in complete games						
Ruffing, Charles (Red) 1967	273	225	3.80	624	4,344	1,987
.645 winning percentage as a New York Yankee						
Rusie, Amos 1977	243	160	3.07	462	3,770	1,957
Won 30+ games three years						
Ryan, Nolan 1999	324	292	3.19	807	5,386	5,714
Threw seven no-hitters; struck out 300 or more six times; struck out 200 or more 15 times						
Seaver, Tom 1992	311	205	2.86	656	4,782	3,640
Won 20 or more games five times; won Cy Young Award 1969, 1973, 1975						
Spahn, Warren 1973	363	245	3.09	750	5,244	2,583
Won 20 or more games 13 times, including 23 at age 42						
Sutter, Bruce 2006	68	71	2.83	661	1042.3	861
Led the National League in saves five times						
Sutton, Don 1998	324	256	3.26	774	5,280	3,574
Won 15 or more games eight years in a row (1969–76)						
Vance, Clarence (Dazzy) 1955	197	140	3.24	442	2,697	2,045
50–15 over two years, 1924, 1925						
Waddell, George (Rube) 1946	193	143	2.16	407	2,961	2,316
349 strikeouts in 1904						
Walsh, Ed 1946	195	126	1.82	430	2,964	1,736
40–15 in 1908 with 11 shutouts; all-time ERA leader						
Ward, Monte 1964	161	101	2.10	291	2,462	920
47 wins in 1879; 40 wins in 1880; played 1,825 games as a hitter						
Welch, Mickey 1973	307	210	2.71	565	4,802	1,850
44–11 in 1885						
Wilhelm, Hoyt 1985	143	122	2.52	1,070	2,254	1,610
227 career saves; first relief pitcher elected to Hall of Fame						
Willis, Vic 1995	249	205	2.63	513	3,996	1,651
Won 20 games eight times; 45 complete games in 1902						
Wynn, Early 1972	300	244	3.54	691	4,564	2,334
Led AL in shutouts at age 40 in 1960						
Young, Cy 1937	511	313	2.63	906	7,359	2,799
All-time leader in wins, losses, complete games, and innings pitched						

Negro Leaguers
Bell, James "Cool Papa" 1974
Brown, Ray 2006
Brown, Willard 2006
Charleston, Oscar 1976
Cooper, Andy 2006
Dandridge, Ray 1987
Day, Leon 1995
Dihigo, Martin 1977
Foster, Bill 1996
Gibson, Josh 1972
Grant, Frank 2006
Hill, Pete 2006
Irvin, Monte 1973
Johnson, Judy 1975
Leonard, William 1972
Lloyd, Pop 1977
Mackey, Biz 2006
Mendez, Jose 2006
Paige, Satchel 1971
Rogan, "Bullet" Joe 1998
Santop, Louis 2006
Smith, Hilton 2001

Stearnes, Turkey 2000
Suttles, Mule 2006
Taylor, Ben 2006
Torriente, Cristobal 2006
Wells, Willie 1997
Williams, "Smokey Joe", 1999
Wilson, Jud 2006
Managers
Alston, Walter 1983
Anderson, Sparky 2000
Durocher, Leo 1994
Hanlon, Ned 1996
Harris, Bucky 1975
Herzog, Whitey 2010
Huggins, Miller 1964
Lasorda, Tom 1997
Lopez, Al 1977
Mack, Connie 1937
McCarthy, Joe 1957
McGraw, John 1937
McKechnie, Bill 1962
Robinson, Wilbert 1945
Selee, Frank 1999

Stengel, Casey 1966
Weaver, Earl 1996
Williams, Dick 2008
Umpires
Barlick, Al 1989
Chylak, Nestor 1999
Conlan, Jocko 1974
Connolly, Tom 1953
Evans, Billy 1973
Harvey, Doug 2010
Hubbard, Cal 1976
Klem, Bill 1953
McGowan, Bill 1992
Pioneers and Executives
Barrow, Ed 1953
Bulkeley, Morgan 1937
Cartwright, Alexander 1938
Chadwick, Henry 1938
Chandler, Happy 1982
Comiskey, Charles 1939
Foster, Andrew "Rube" 1981
Frick, Ford 1970

Giles, Warren 1979
Griffith, Clark 1946
Harridge, William 1972
Hulbert, William 1995
Johnson, Ban 1937
Kuhn, Bowie 2008
Landis, Kenesaw Mountain 1944
MacPhail, Larry 1978
MacPhail, Lee 1998
Manley, Effa 2006
O'Malley, Walter 2008
Pompez, Alex 2006
Posey, Cumberland 2006
Rickey, Branch 1967
Spalding, Albert Goodwill 1939
Veeck, Bill 1991
Weiss, George 1971
White, Sol 2006
Wilkinson, J. L. 2006
Wright, George 1937
Wright, Harry 1953
Yawkey, Tom 1980

The World Series

From 1882–90, the winners of the National League and American Association played each other in a championship series. After the A.A. folded, the top two N.L. clubs played for the "Temple Cup", but the idea never really caught on. The American League began operations in 1901, setting off bidding wars with the National League for the services of star players. Peace was established in 1903; toward the end of that season, the owners of the winning franchises in each league agreed to hold a "World Series" in October. Many were surprised that Boston, from the newer American League, won the title.

There was no agreement to play such a series every year, however, and in 1904 the New York Giants refused to meet the Boston club, probably due to John McGraw's dislike of American League President Ban Johnson. But the baseball public wanted a championship series, and by 1905 Giants owner John Brush proposed rules governing a mandatory series to be played every year. With minute changes, those rules stand to this day.

1903 Boston (A) over Pittsburgh (N), 5–3. The upstart American league emerged victorious in the first World Series, a best of nine affair. The "Pilgrims" (Red Sox) staged one of the greatest comebacks in history by sweeping the final four games. Bill Dineen won three and Cy Young won two for Boston, and held Pirate immortal Honus Wagner to a .222 average.

1904 No series. New York Giant owner John T. Brush and manager John McGraw refused to play the World Champion Boston club, dismissing them as representative of an "inferior league."

1905 New York (N) over Philadelphia (A), 4–1. Every game was a shutout, with Cristy Mathewson throwing three for the Giants. In 27 innings, he allowed 14 hits, struck out 18 and walked one. The Athletics committed five errors in the pivotal Game 3.

1906 Chicago (A) over Chicago (N), 4–2. The first "subway series" was a stunning upset. The "Hitless Wonders" White Sox had batted .230 with 7 home runs during the season, while the Cubs were winning 116 games, still the all-time record. Utilityman George Rohe hit two game-winning triples for the Sox and Ed Walsh pitched two of their wins.

1907 Chicago (A) over Detroit (A), 4–0. The Cubs shut down Ty Cobb, Sam Crawford et al, behind a superb four-man pitching performance, and the hitting of Harry Steinfeldt (.471) and Johnny Evers (.350).

1908 Chicago (N) over Detroit (A), 4–1. Johnny Evers repeated his .350 average of 1907, player-manager Frank Chance hit .421, and outfielder Wildfire Schulte batted .389 in the Cub attack. Ty Cobb led Detroit (.368), to no avail.

1909 Pittsburgh (N) over Detroit (A), 4–3. The Tigers lost their third straight series, as Honus Wagner bested Ty Cobb. The Pirate shortstop hit .333 with six RBI and six stolen bases. Babe Adams pitched in with three complete game victories.

1910 Philadelphia (A) over Chicago (N), 4–1. Connie Mack's infielders combined to bat .364 as the A's rolled to an easy title. Jack Coombs pitched three wins and hit .385.

1911 Philadelphia (A) over New York (N), 4–2. The Athletics beat a strong New York club featuring Christy Mathewson and Rube Marquard. Frank "Home Run" Baker got his nickname from game-winning blasts in Games 2 and 3.

1912 Boston (A) over New York (N), 4–3. This thrill-a-minute series featured an 11-inning tie in Game 2. Errors by Giants Fred Merkle and Fred Snodgrass enabled Boston to score two runs in the bottom of the 10th inning of the final contest.

1913 Philadelphia (A) over New York (N), 4–1. Home Run Baker again hammered Giant pitching, batting .450 with seven RBI. Eddie Collins also starred for the A's, hitting .421 with three stolen bases.

1914 Boston (N) over Philadelphia (A), 4–0. The red-hot "Miracle Braves" swept the heavily favored Athletics, who scored only six runs in the four games. Catcher Hank Gowdy (.545) and second baseman Johnny Evers (.438) led the Boston offense.

1915 Boston (A) over Philadelphia (N), 4–1. The famous Red Sox outfield of Speaker, Lewis, and Hooper combined to bat .364 while Rube Foster pitched two complete game wins. Foster also batted .500 and drove in the winning run in Game 2.

1916 Boston (A) over Brooklyn (N), 4–1. After three one-run games, Boston took charge with 6–2 and 4–1 victories. A young lefthander named Babe Ruth twirled a 14-inning six hitter in Game Two.

1917 Chicago (A) over New York (N), 4–2. The pitching of Red Faber (3–1, 2.33) and the hitting of Eddie Collins, Buck Weaver, and Joe Jackson were too much for the Giants in a sloppy (23 errors) series.

1918 Boston (A) over Chicago (N), 4–2. Every game was a pitchers' duel. The losing Cubs posted a 1.04 ERA over the six games. The Boston staff allowed but nine runs in the series, led by Babe Ruth who extended his consecutive scoreless inning streak to 29 2/3.

1919 Cincinnati (N) over Chicago (A), 5–3. The results of this surprising World Series were declared invalid after eight members of the "Black Sox," including Shoeless Joe Jackson, were accused of throwing games for money. A court later found the Chicago players not guilty (most of them never even received the money from the gamblers with whom they conspired), but commissioner Kenesaw Mountain Landis nonetheless barred them from baseball forever.

1920 Cleveland (A) over Brooklyn (N), 5–2. Game 5 was surely the most freakish in series history. It featured a) the first World Series grand slam (Indians rightfielder Elmer Smith), b) the first World Series home run by a pitcher (Indians Jim Bagby), and c) the first and only unassisted triple play in series action (Indians second baseman Billy Wambsganss).

1921 New York (N) over New York (A), 5–3. Six Giants batted over .300, and their pitchers held Babe Ruth to a .500 slugging average. Giant hurler Jesse Barnes won two games and batted .444.

1922 New York (N) over New York (A), 4–0. The result was said to be final proof that "brains beat brawn." Giant pitching shut down Babe Ruth, allowing only 11 runs in the five contests (one tie).

1923 New York (A) over New York (N), 4–2. The Yankees took the last three to break the spell of their cross-river rivals, behind Babe Ruth's three homers and .368 average. Casey Stengel hit two home runs for the losers.

1924 Washington (A) over New York (N), 4–3. A 12-inning Game 7, won by Walter Johnson in relief, capped an exciting affair. Player-manager Bucky Harris starred for the Senators (.333, 7 RBIs), as did outfielder Goose Goslin (.344, 7 RBIs).

1925 Pittsburgh (N) over Washington (A), 4–3. Pirate centerfielder Max Carey had 11 hits and three stolen bases, as Pittsburgh became the first team since 1903 to come back from a three games to one deficit.

1926 St. Louis (N) over New York (A), 4–3. Babe Ruth hit three homers in Game 4, but in the seventh inning of Game 7, Grover Cleveland Alexander struck out Tony Lazzeri with the bases loaded, saving the game and the series for the Cardinals.

1927 New York (A) over Pittsburgh (N), 4–0. Generally regarded as the greatest team of all time, the "Murderers' Row" Yankees disposed of the Pirates behind two Babe Ruth homers, plus the pitching of Wilcy Moore, Herb Pennock, and George Pipgrass.

1928 New York (A) over St. Louis (N), 4–0. Another Yankee sweep. Ruth and Lou Gehrig combined to bat .593, with seven home runs and 13 RBI. Waite Hoyt pitched two complete game victories.

1929 Philadelphia (A) over Chicago (N), 4–1. Trailing 8-0 in Game 4, the A's roared back to score 10 runs in the seventh inning. In the next contest, the Mackmen took the series with a three-run ninth inning.

1930 Philadelphia (A) over St. Louis (N), 4–2. Lefty Grove and George Earnshaw pitched well, while Al Simmons, Jimmie Foxx, and Mickey Cochrane combined for 11 extra-base hits. Cardinal regulars batted only .185 in the six games.

1931 St. Louis (N) over Philadelphia (A), 4–3. Cardinal centerfielder Pepper Martin set a record that stood for 33 years with his 12 hits. Martin also stole five bases and hit a home run. Bill Hallahan and Burleigh Grimes combined for a 4–0, 1.25 ERA.

1932 New York (A) over Chicago (N), 4–0. The Yankees completed a streak of 12 straight World Series victories in sweeping the Cubs. Babe Ruth and Lou Gehrig combined to bat .438, with five homers and 14 RBI.

1933 New York (N) over Washington (A), 4–1. Bill Terry's Giants defeated Joe Cronin's Senators in a battle of player-managers. Carl Hubbell won two for New York and did not allow an earned run.

1934 St. Louis (N) over Detroit (A), 4–3. Dizzy and Paul Dean hurled the Cardinals to the title, winning all four Redbird victories. A bad defensive series, with 27 errors and 13 unearned runs.

1935 Detroit (A) over Chicago (N), 4–2. The Cubs won 21 straight games in September, but came up short against Mickey Cochrane's Tigers. Charlie Gehringer and Tommy Bridges starred for Detroit, while Lou Warneke (2–0, 0.54) was superb for the losers.

1936 New York (A) over New York (N), 4–2. Joe McCarthy's "Windowbreakers" hammered Giant pitching for a record 18 runs in Game 2 and 43 runs for the series. Tony Lazzeri and Bill Dickey each drove in five runs in Game 2.

1937 New York (A) over New York (N), 4–1. Lefty Gomez pitched two of the Yankee wins and drove in the winning run with a single in the final game. The Yanks scored seven runs in the sixth inning of Game 1, then coasted to an easy championship.

1938 New York (A) over Chicago (N), 4–0. In a replay of 1932, the Bronx Bombers blew out an overmatched Cub squad. Cub fans are still waiting for their team's first series victory over the Yankees.

1939 New York (A) over Cincinnati (N), 4–0. New York won its fourth straight World Championship the same way they won the first three—easily. Charlie Keller batted .438 with three homers, and scored as many runs as the entire Reds team, eight.

1940 Cincinnati (N) over Detroit (A), 4–3. The Reds repeated as NL champs, then beat the Tigers when Paul Derringer beat Bobo Newsome 2–1 in Game 7. Derringer and Bucky Walters each won two games.

1941 New York (A) over Brooklyn (N), 4–1. With two outs in the ninth inning of Game Four, Dodger catcher Mickey Owen dropped a third strike on Tommy Henrich, allowing him to reach first base. The Yankees then scored four times to win the ballgame, and finished Brooklyn off the next day.

1942 St. Louis (N) over New York (A), 4–1. The Cardinals, winners of 106 games during the regular season, lost Game 1 with the tying run at bat. They then swept four in a row, behind the pitching of Johnny Beazley (2–0, 2.50) and Ernie White's shutout in Game 3.

1943 New York (A) over St. Louis (N), 4–1. In this rematch of the 1942 series, the Yanks held St. Louis to nine runs in the five games. Joe Gordon and Bill Dickey homered, while third baseman Billy Johnson drove in three runs for New York.

1944 St Louis (N) over St. Louis (A), 4–2. In their lone World Series appearance, the Browns struggled valiantly before falling short against a strong Cardinal club left relatively intact by World War II. Ten Browns errors gave the Redbirds seven unearned runs.

1945 Detroit (A) over Chicago (N), 4–3. Tiger ace Hal Newhouser was hit hard in Game 1, but he bounced back to win Games 5 and 7. Doc Cramer (.379) and Hank Greenberg (2 HR, 7 RBIs) led the Detroit offense.

1946 St. Louis (N) over Boston (A), 4–3 Enos Slaughter scored from first on a base-hit by Harry Walker in the eighth inning of Game 7, giving St. Louis its third title in five years. Harry Brecheen won three games for the Cardinals, allowing but one run.

1947 New York (A) over Brooklyn (N), 4–3. Yankee pitcher Bill Bevens had a no-hitter for 8 2/3 innings in Game 4, but lost the game on a double by Cookie Lavagetto. Tommy Henrich (.323) had the game winning RBI in Games 1, 2, and 7.

1948 Cleveland (A) over Boston (N), 4–2. The series featured great pitching on both sides, including Game 1, when Boston's Johnny Sain beat Bob Feller 1–0. Cleveland's Gene Beardon pitched 10 2/3 scoreless innings.

1949 New York (A) over Brooklyn (N), 4–1. Game 1 was 0–0 until Tommy Henrich led off the bottom of the ninth with a home run off Don Newcombe. Bobby Brown batted .500 with five RBIs.

1950 New York (A) over Philadelphia (N), 4–0. New York struggled to win the first three contests by scores of 1–0, 2–1, and 3–2, in a series that was closer than it looks. The "Whiz Kid" Phillies held the Yanks to a .222 batting average, but managed to hit only .203 themselves.

1951 New York (A) over New York (N), 4–2. A tired Giant pitching staff held the Yankees in check for three games, but the AL champs broke out to score 23 runs in the final three. Eddie Lopat (2–0, 0.50) starred for the Yankees.

1952 New York (A) over Brooklyn (N), 4–3. Allie Reynolds and Vic Raschi each won two games, combining for a 1.69 ERA. Johnny Mize hit three homers, and Mickey Mantle and Yogi Berra each hit two. Duke Snider batted .345 with four homers in a losing cause.

1953 New York (A) over Brooklyn (N), 4–2. The Yankees won their fifth straight World Championship as second baseman Billy Martin tied a record with 12 hits. Martin slugged .958 and drove in eight runs.

1954 New York (N) over Cleveland (A), 4–0. The Indians won 111 games during the season. But the Giants, sparked by a spectacular Willie Mays catch in Game 1, went on to beat Cleveland easily. Dusty Rhodes drove in seven runs on two homers and two singles in six at bats.

1955 Brooklyn (N) over New York (A), 4–3. The Dodgers finally won a World Series in their eighth try, behind the pitching of series MVP Johnny Podres (2–0, 1.00). Duke Snider hit four homers in a series for the second time, and Dodger leftfielder Sandy Amoros made a game-saving catch in Game 7.

1956 New York (A) over Brooklyn (N), 4–3. Yankee righthander and series MVP Don Larsen pitched a perfect game in the fifth contest, while Mickey Mantle and Yogi Berra each hit three homers for New York.

1957 Milwaukee (N) over New York (A), 4–3. Lew Burdette won three times for the Braves, allowing but two runs in 27 innings and won the MVP. Milwaukee's hitting was led by Hank Aaron (.393, 3 HR, 7 RBIs).

1958 New York (A) over Milwaukee (N), 4–3. Hank Bauer and Moose Skowron combined for six homers and 15 RBI, as the Bronx Bombers came back from a 3–1 deficit. Yankee pitcher "Bullet" Bob Turley earned MVP honors.

1959 Los Angeles (N) over Chicago (A), 4–2. Los Angeles enjoyed its first World Championship as the transplanted Dodgers prevailed. MVP Larry Sherry had two wins and two saves; Ted Kluszewski of the "Go-Go" Sox hit .391, with three homers and 10 RBI.

1960 Pittsburgh (N) over New York (A), 4–3. Pirate second baseman Bill Mazeroski's home run in the bottom of the ninth in Game 7 capped one of the most exciting contests in history. Ten of the runs in the 10–9 ballgame were scored in the last two innings. Yankee second baseman Bobby Richardson, a hitting star throughout the series, was named MVP.

1961 New York (A) over Cincinnati (N), 4–1. Whitey Ford tossed two shutouts in winning the MVP, and the Yankee offense pounded out 16 extra-base hits in the five games. Bobby Richardson (.391) and John Blanchard (.400, 2 HR) starred for New York.

1962 New York (A) over San Francisco (N), 4–3. Ralph Terry's four-hit shutout won the seesaw affair for the Yanks, and earned him the MVP. Whitey Ford completed his series record 33 2/3 consecutive scoreless innings in the first game. Chuck Hiller hit the first National League series grand slam in Game 4.

1963 Los Angeles (N) over New York (A), 4–0. Dodger pitchers held New York to four runs, led by Sandy Koufax's two wins and 23 strikeouts, including a record-breaking 15 in the first game. Koufax was the runaway choice for MVP.

1964 St. Louis (N) over New York (A), 4–3. Ten Yankee home runs were not enough to beat the Cardinals. Bob Gibson was the series MVP, and Tim McCarver (.478) also starred. Highlights included Ken Boyer's game-winning grand slam in Game 4, and Bobby Richardson's record 13 hits.

1965 Los Angeles (N) over Minnesota (A), 4–3. As in 1963, MVP Sandy Koufax again excelled for the Dodgers, allowing only two runs in 24 innings, striking out 29. Jim "Mudcat" Grant won two games and hit a three-run homer for the Twins.

1966 Baltimore (A) over Los Angeles (N), 4–0. The Orioles shone in their first World Series appearance, as their young pitchers did not allow a run after the third inning of Game 1. Slugger Frank Robinson capped a great year with the series MVP award.

1967 St. Louis (N) over Boston (A), 4–3. Bob Gibson pitched three complete game victories, added a home run in Game 7, and was named MVP. Lou Brock batted .414 and stole seven bases, tying Eddie Collins' record and pacing the Cards.

1968 Detroit (A) over St. Louis (N), 4–3. The Cardinals were rolling behind Bob Gibson's record 17 strikeouts in Game 1 and his record seventh straight series win in Game 4. Again Lou Brock joined him in the record books with 13 hits and seven stolen bases. But their feats couldn't stop the Tigers, led by the MVP pitching of Mickey Lolich (3–0, 1.67).

1969 New York (N) over Baltimore (A), 4–1. The Amazin' Mets stunned the baseball world by winning four in a row after dropping Game 1. Their young pitchers held the Orioles to nine runs, aided by great outfield catches by Ron Swoboda and Tommy Agee. Series MVP Donn Clendenon (.357, 3 HR) and Al Weis (.455, 1 HR) led the Met attack.

1970 Baltimore (A) over Cincinnati (N), 4–1. MVP Brooks Robinson almost singlehandedly beat the Reds with spectacular defense at third base and a .429 average with two homers and two doubles. Also chipping in for the Orioles were Paul Blair (.474), Frank Robinson, and Boog Powell (two homers each).

1971 Pittsburgh (N) over Baltimore (A), 4–3. Roberto Clemente played in 14 World Series games and hit safely in every one. Here he batted .414, slugged .759, and won MVP honors. Steve Blass, Nelson Briles, and Bruce Kison won all the Pirate victories with a combined ERA of 0.54.

1972 Oakland (A) over Cincinnati (N), 4–3. A's backup catcher Gene Tenace hit home runs in his first two series at bats, then went on to hit two more, becoming the surprise star. MVP Rollie Fingers relieved in six contests, winning one and saving two.

1973 Oakland (A) over New York (N), 4–3. The Mets had the worst record of any pennant winner ever (82–79), but they lasted till the Game 7 in a sloppy (19 errors) affair. Darold Knowles pitched in all seven games for the A's, saving two. Reggie Jackson slugged his way to his first series MVP award.

1974 Oakland (A) over Los Angeles (N), 4–1. The A's won their third straight Championship behind the two saves and one win of MVP Rollie Fingers, and the hitting of Joe Rudi (.333) and Bert Campaneris (.353).

1975 Cincinnati (N) over Boston (A), 4–3. Five games were decided by one run, including Game 6, a memorable 12-inning contest decided by Carlton Fisk's famous home run. Pete Rose, the heart and soul of the Big Red Machine, hustled his way to MVP honors.

1976 Cincinnati (N) over New York (A), 4–0. The Big Red Machine drove over the Yankees, slugging .522 as a team. Seven Reds hitters batted over .300, led by MVP Johnny Bench's .533 (1.133 slugging average).

1977 New York (A) over Los Angeles (N), 4–2. Reggie Jackson hit five homers, including three in the final game, to equal records set by Babe Ruth, and win his second MVP award. Mike Torrez won two for the Yanks.

1978 New York (A) over Los Angeles (N), 4–2. Shortstop Bucky Dent and backup infielder Brian Doyle batted .417 and .438 respectively, pacing New York in its second straight six-game triumph. Dent was named MVP. In the last four contests, the Yankees outscored L.A. 28–8.

1979 Pittsburgh (N) over Baltimore (A), 4–3. The Pirates overcame a three games to one deficit as Earl Weaver's Orioles waited for three-run homers that never came. Led by Willie "Pops" Stargell (.400, 3 HR) and Phil Garner (.500), Pittsburgh batted .323 as a team. Stargell's leadership of the Pirates' "family" on and off the field earned him MVP honors.

1980 Philadelphia (N) over Kansas City (A), 4–2. The two teams batted .292 in a series decided largely by the relief pitching of Tug McGraw (1–1, 2 saves) vs. Dan Quisenberry (1–2, 1 save). Mike Schmidt took MVP honors with a .381 average and seven RBI.

1981 Los Angeles (N) over New York (A), 4–2. Many observers called this sloppy series a fitting end to this strike-stricken 1981 season. Even the MVP award proved impossible to settle, as Pedro Guerrero, Steve Yeager, and Ron Cey shared the honor.

1982 St. Louis (N) over Milwaukee (A), 4–3. Joaquin Andujar won two games for the Cardinals, and Willie McGee had perhaps the greatest single series game by a rookie, with two homers and two great catches in Game 3. St. Louis' Darrell Porter won MVP honors for his clutch hitting and 5 RBI.

1983 Baltimore (A) over Philadelphia (N), 4–1. The Phillies couldn't hit Orioles' pitching, scoring but nine runs in the five games. Catcher Rick Dempsey hit four doubles and a home run, held the Phils to one stolen base, and was named MVP.

1984 Detroit (A) over San Diego (N), 4–1. The Tigers belted seven homers and backed them up with the pitching of Jack Morris (2–0, 2.00). Sparky Anderson became the first manager to win World Championships in both leagues. Alan Trammell, the Tigers' shortstop, hit two home runs to earn MVP honors.

1985 Kansas City (A) over St. Louis (N), 4–3. The Cards were one inning away from the title, but a disputed call at first base opened the door for the Royals in Game 6. They won that contest, then blew St. Louis away 11–0 in the finale. Bret Saberhagen won two for Kansas City, and the MVP.

1986 New York (N) over Boston (A), 4–3. The Red Sox were one out away from winning it all, when Bob Stanley's wild pitch let in the tying run, and Mookie Wilson's grounder slipped between Bill Buckner's legs to score the winning run in Game 6. MVP Ray Knight hit a tie-breaking homer in Game 7 to send Boston to its fourth-straight seven-game defeat.

1987 Minnesota (A) over St. Louis (N), 4–3. The Twins won their first championship by taking all four games in at the Metrodome. Cardinal pitching held Minnesota to five runs in the three games in St. Louis, but in Minnesota, the Twins could not be contained, scoring 33 times. Frank Viola (2–1, 3.72) was the MVP.

1988 Los Angeles (N) over Oakland (A), 4–1. Series MVP Orel Hershiser (2–0, 17 Ks) dazzled the powerful A's. Injured Dodger Kirk Gibson's dramatic two-out home run in the bottom of the ninth of Game 1 set the tone for the unexpected L.A. triumph.

1989 Oakland (A) over San Francisco (N), 4–0. The A's thoroughly dominated a weak Giants' pitching staff, pounding out 32 runs, 44 hits (including nine home runs) in only four games. Series MVP Dave Stewart and reliever Dennis Eckersley led the Oakland staff. This series will be long remembered for the major earthquake that struck the Bay area just before Game 3 and delayed the contest for 12 days.

1990 Cincinnati (N) over Oakland (A), 4–0. Cincinnati dominated the heavily favored A's in a stunning sweep. The Reds hit .317 as a team, while their pitchers, led by MVP José Rijo, held Oakland's vaunted offense to a mere .207 series average. Billy Hatcher broke Babe Ruth's World Series record by hitting .750, with seven consecutive hits and four doubles.

1991 Minnesota (A) over Atlanta (N), 4–3. No team in baseball had ever gone from worst to first. In 1991, it happened for both the Twins and Braves. Five games were decided by one run, three went into extra innings, and four were decided on the last at bat. Jack Morris pitched all 10 innings for Minnesota and earned MVP honors.

1992 Toronto (A) over Atlanta (N), 4–2. The Blue Jays became the first non-American team to win (or play in) the World Series. Dave Winfield's double in the 11th-inning of Game 6 sent the Braves to their second straight World Series defeat. Toronto catcher Pat Borders was the MVP with a .450 average.

1993 Toronto (A) over Philadelphia (N), 4–2. The Blue Jays became the first team since the 1977–78 Yankees to repeat as champions, battering the Phillies for 45 runs (despite a Game 5 shutout). Joe Carter's homer in Game 6 marked only the second time the World Series had ended on a home run (Bill Mazeroski hit the other in 1960). DH Paul Molitor went 12 for 24 with six extra-base hits to win MVP honors.

1994 World Series canceled. The longest work stoppage in professional sports history, a 232-day dispute over a cap on player salaries, forced the first-ever cancellation of the World Series and playoffs .

1995 Atlanta (N) over Cleveland (A), 4–2. Good pitching beats good hitting as evidenced by this dramatic series. Baseball's best pitching staff (the Braves) held the game's most explosive offense (the Indians) to a .179 average and 19 runs. Five games were decided by one run, including the clincher: a dazzling 1–0 one-hitter by Atlanta's Tom Glavine, the series MVP.

1996 New York (A) over Atlanta (N), 4–2. The Braves shellacked the Yankees 12–1 and 4–0 in the first two games. But the Yankees struck back and won the next four. The turning point was in Game 4, when New York rallied from a 6–0 deficit to win 8–6 in 10 innings. Jim Leyritz provided the crushing blow: a three-run homer off Mark Wohlers to tie the game at 6–6. Yankee closer John Wetteland saved all four wins and was the MVP.

1997 Florida (N) over Cleveland (A), 4–3. This sloppy series was marked by porous defense and poor relief pitching. Game 3 alone involved 17 walks and 6 errors. In the 11th, Edgar Renteria singled home the winning run. Florida rookie Liván Hernández, winner of Games 1 and 5, was the MVP.

1998 New York (A) over San Diego (N), 4–0. The Yankees completed one of the greatest seasons in baseball history with a sweep that gave them a combined record of 125–50 and a .714 winning percentage. Homers by Chuck Knoblauch and Tino Martínez helped the Yankees come from behind in Game 1, while Scott Brosius's three-run blast off San Diego closer Trevor Hoffman in Game 3 broke the Padres' back. Brosius, the MVP, hit .471 with two homers.

1999 New York (A) over Atlanta (N), 4–0. The Yankees' World Series winning streak increased to 12 games with their second straight sweep. Atlanta errors opened the door to big innings for New York in Games 1 and 2; the Yankees hit four homers in Game 3 to turn a 5–1 deficit into a 10-inning, 6–5 win. Mariano Rivera, who did not allow a run after July, saved Games 1 and 4, won Game 3 in relief, and took MVP honors.

2000 New York (A) over New York (N), 4–1. Every game of the first Subway Series in 45 years was decided

by one or two runs. The Yankees rallied to tie Game 1 in the ninth inning, and won it in the 12th. Derek Jeter hit the first pitch of Game 4 over the center field fence and the Yankees never trailed again. Jeter batted .409 with two homers, and was the MVP.

2001 Arizona (N) over New York (A), 4–3. Curt Schilling and Randy Johnson powered Arizona to a 2–0 lead, but the Yankees came back with three straight one-run victories in New York. In *both* Game 4 *and* Game 5, the Yankees were down to their last out when they rallied with game-tying homers against closer Byung-Hyun Kim (by Tino Martinez and Scott Brosius, respectively). Schilling and Johnson were co-MVPs.

2002 Anaheim (A) over San Francisco (N), 4–3. Anaheim pitched carefully to Barry Bonds, and although he hit .471 with four homers and 13 walks, the batters before and after him hit .276 and .231 respectively, limiting the damage Bonds was able to inflict. The Angels batted .310 as a team, led by MVP third baseman Troy Glaus, who hit .385 with 3 homers and 8 RBIs. With the Giants six outs away from winning it all in Game 6, Glaus's eighth-inning double turned a 5–4 deficit into a 6–5 Anaheim victory.

2003 Florida (N) over New York (A), 4–2. New York's two victories were by both 6–1 margins, while Florida's wins were by one or two runs. Alex González's walk-off homer in the 12th inning of Game 4 turned the tide for Florida. Brad Penny was 2–0 for the Marlins, but he was eclipsed for MVP honors by Josh Beckett, who came back on two days' rest to pitch a Game 6 shutout that clinched it for the Marlins, who have not lost a postseason series in their short history.

2004 Boston (A) over St. Louis (N), 4–0. The Sox swept the powerful Cardinals behind the hitting of MVP Manny Ramirez (.412 average) and the pitching of Curt Schilling, Derek Lowe, and Pedro Martinez.

2005 Chicago (A) over Houston (N), 4–0. The Chicago White Sox used timely hitting and stellar pitching to win the club's first World Series title since 1917. Although the result was a sweep, each game was closely contested: Chicago outscored Houston by only six runs over the four games. In the crucial Game 3, the longest by time in World Series history, the White Sox beat the Astros 7–5 in 14 innings.

2006 St. Louis (N) over Detroit (A), 4–1 In the third championship meeting of these two teams, the Cardinals defeated the Tigers in five games, taking the home-field advantage away from Detroit with an emphatic 7–2 victory in Game One. In the final game of the series Jeff Weaver tossed eight brilliant innings and Series MVP David Eckstein drove in the go-ahead run in the Cardinal's 4–2 victory.

2007 Boston (A) over Colorado (N), 4–0 The wild-card Rockies entered the series having won 21 of their previous 22 games, sweeping both the Phillies and Diamondbacks in the Division Series and ALCS en route. The Red Sox greeted them in the Fall Classic with a 13–1 thumping in Fenway Park, and it was never a contest after that. Boston ultimately did some sweeping of their own, eliminating Colorado in four games to claim their second title in four years.

2008 Philadelphia (N) over Tampa Bay (A), 4–1. The Phillies entered the World Series undefeated at home in the post season. In a World Series first, game 5 was suspended for 46 hours due to heavy rain, tied 2–2 in the middle of the sixth. The Phils had to wait two extra days to claim their second championship in 125 years. Brad Lidge sealed a perfect season by throwing his 48th save in as many games.

2009 New York (A) over Philadelphia (N), 4–2. The defending champion Phillies and ace Cliff Lee shut down the Yankees bats to win Game 1 but the Yankees rallied to win the next three contests. Again in Game 5 Cliff Lee dominated the Yankee offense, but in Game 6 the Yankees jumped out to a 7–1 lead behind a second inning two-run blast from series MVP Hideki Matsui en route to their 27th World Series title.

World Series MVP Winners

Year	Name	Team
1955	Johnny Podres	Brooklyn Dodgers
1956	Don Larsen	New York Yankees
1957	Lew Burdette	Milwaukee Braves
1958	Bob Turley	New York Yankees
1959	Larry Sherry	Los Angeles Dodgers
1960	Bobby Richardson	New York Yankees
1961	Whitey Ford	New York Yankees
1962	Ralph Terry	New York Yankees
1963	Sandy Koufax	Los Angeles Dodgers
1964	Bob Gibson	St. Louis Cardinals
1965	Sandy Koufax	Los Angeles Dodgers
1966	Frank Robinson	Baltimore Orioles
1967	Bob Gibson	St. Louis Cardinals
1968	Mickey Lolich	Detroit Tigers
1969	Donn Clendenon	New York Mets
1970	Brooks Robinson	Baltimore Orioles
1971	Roberto Clemente	Pittsburgh Pirates
1972	Gene Tenace	Oakland Athletics
1973	Reggie Jackson	Oakland Athletics
1974	Rollie Fingers	Oakland Athletics
1975	Pete Rose	Cincinnati Reds
1976	Johnny Bench	Cincinnati Reds
1977	Reggie Jackson	New York Yankees
1978	Bucky Dent	New York Yankees
1979	Willie Stargell	Pittsburgh Pirates
1980	Mike Schmidt	Philadelphia Philles
1981	Ron Cey, Pedro Guerrero, Steve Yeager	Los Angeles Dodgers
1982	Darrell Porter	St. Louis Cardinals
1983	Rick Dempsey	Baltimore Orioles
1984	Alan Trammell	Detroit Tigers
1985	Bret Saberhagen	Kansas City Royals
1986	Ray Knight	New York Mets
1987	Frank Viola	Minnesota Twins
1988	Orel Hershiser	Los Angeles Dodgers
1989	Dave Stewart	Oakland Athletics
1990	José Rijo	Cincinnati Reds
1991	Jack Morris	Minnesota Twins
1992	Pat Borders	Toronto Blue Jays
1993	Paul Molitor	Toronto Blue Jays
1994	No World Series	
1995	Tom Glavine	Atlanta Braves
1996	John Wetteland	New York Yankees
1997	Liván Hernández	Florida Marlins
1998	Scott Brosius	New York Yankees
1999	Mariano Rivera	New York Yankees
2000	Derek Jeter	New York Yankees
2001	Randy Johnson and Curt Schilling	Arizona Diamondbacks
2002	Troy Glaus	Anaheim Angels
2003	Josh Beckett	Florida Marlins
2004	Manny Ramirez	Boston Red Sox
2005	Jermaine Dye	Chicago White Sox
2006	David Eckstein	St. Louis Cardinals
2007	Mike Lowell	Boston Red Sox
2008	Cole Hamels	Philadelphia Phillies
2009	Hideki Matsui	New York Yankees

All-Star Game Results, 1933–2010

To revive interest in the midsummer classic, Major League Baseball decided in 2003 to award home field advantage in the World Series to the league that wins the All-Star Game.

Year	Winner, Score	Year	Winner, Score
1933	American, 4–2	1970	National, 5–4
1934	American, 9–7	1971	American, 6–4
1935	American, 4–1	1972	National, 4–3
1936	National, 4–3	1973	National, 7–1
1937	American, 8–3	1974	National, 7–2
1938	National, 4–1	1975	National, 6–3
1939	American, 3–1	1976	National, 7–1
1940	National, 4–0	1977	National, 7–5
1941	American, 7–5	1978	National, 7–3
1942	American, 3–1	1979	National, 7–6
1943	American, 5–3	1980	National, 4–2
1944	National, 7–1	1981	National, 5–4
1945	No game [1]	1982	National, 4–1
1946	American, 12–0	1983	American, 13–3
1947	American, 2–1	1984	National, 3–1
1948	American, 5–2	1985	National, 6–1
1949	American, 11–7	1986	American, 3–2
1950	National, 4–3	1987	National, 2–0 (10)
1951	National, 8–3	1988	American, 2–1
1952	National, 3–2	1989	American, 5–3
1953	National, 5–1	1990	American, 2–0
1954	American, 11–9	1991	American, 4–2
1955	National, 6–5	1992	American, 13–6
1956	National, 7–3	1993	American, 9–3
1957	American, 6–5	1994	National, 8–7 (10)
1958	American, 4–3	1995	National, 3–2)
1959(1) [2]	National, 5–4	1996	National, 6–0
1959(2)	American, 5–3	1997	American, 3–1
1960(1)	National, 5–3	1998	American, 13–8
1960(2)	National , 6–0	1999	American, 4–1
1961(1)	National, 5–4	2000	American, 6–3
1961(2)	Tie[3], 1–1	2001	American, 4–1
1962(1)	National, 3–1	2002	Tie[4], 7–7
1962(2)	American, 9–4	2003	American, 7–6
1963	National, 5–3	2004	American, 9–4
1964	National, 7–4	2005	American, 7–5
1965	National, 6–5	2006	American, 3–2
1966	National, 2–1	2007	American, 5–4
1967	National, 2–1	2008	American, 4–3 (15)
1968	National, 1–0	2008	American, 4–3 (15)
1969	National, 9–3	2009	American, 4–3
		2010	National, 3–1

Notes: 1. Wartime travel restrictions. 2. Two All Star games were played 1959–62. 3. Game was called because of rain after nine innings. 4. Game was called after nine innings because both managers had already used all their pitchers.

Major League Baseball League Championship Series Results

		AMERICAN LEAGUE	
Year	Winner	Loser	MVP
1969	Baltimore Orioles 3	Minnesota Twins 0	
1970	Baltimore Orioles 3	Minnesota Twins 0	
1971	Baltimore Orioles 3	Oakland A's 0	
1972	Oakland Athletics 3	Detroit Tigers 2	
1973	Oakland Athletics 3	Baltimore Orioles 2	
1974	Oakland Athletics 3	Baltimore Orioles 1	
1975	Boston Red Sox 3	Oakland Athletics 0	
1976	New York Yankees 3	Kansas City Royals 2	
1977	New York Yankees 3	Kansas City Royals 2	
1978	New York Yankees 3	Kansas City Royals 1	

AMERICAN LEAGUE (continued)

Year	Winner	Loser	MVP
1979	Baltimore Orioles 3	California Angels 1	
1980	Kansas City Royals 3	New York Yankees 0	Frank White, Kansas City
1981	New York Yankees 3	Oakland Athletics 0	Graig Nettles, New York
1982	Milwaukee Brewers 3	California Angels 2	Fred Lynn, California
1983	Baltimore Orioles 3	Chicago White Sox 1	Mike Boddicker, Baltimore
1984	Detroit Tigers 3	Kansas City Royals 0	Kirk Gibson, Detroit
1985[1]	Kansas City Royals 4	Toronto Blue Jays 3	George Brett, Kansas City
1986	Boston Red Sox 4	California Angels 3	Marty Barrett, Boston
1987	Minnesota Twins 4	Detroit Tigers 1	Gary Gaetti, Minnesota
1988	Oakland Athletics 4	Boston Red Sox 0	Dennis Eckersley, Oakland
1989	Oakland Athletics 4	Toronto Blue Jays 1	Rickey Henderson, Oakland
1990	Oakland Athletics 4	Boston Red Sox 0	Dave Stewart, Oakland
1991	Minnesota Twins 4	Toronto Blue Jays 1	Kirby Puckett, Minnesota
1992	Toronto Blue Jays 4	Oakland Athletics 2	Roberto Alomar, Toronto
1993	Toronto Blue Jays 4	Chicago White Sox 2	Dave Stewart, Toronto
1994	No League Championship Series		
1995	Cleveland Indians 4	Seattle Mariners 2	Orel Hershiser, Cleveland
1996	New York Yankees 4	Baltimore Orioles 1	Bernie Williams, New York
1997	Cleveland Indians 4	Baltimore Orioles 2	Marquis Grissom, Cleveland
1998	New York Yankees 4	Cleveland Indians 2	David Wells, New York
1999	New York Yankees 4	Boston Red Sox 1	Orlando Hernández, New York
2000	New York Yankees 4	Seattle Mariners 2	David Justice, New York
2001	New York Yankees 4	Seattle Mariners 1	Andy Pettitte, New York
2002	Anaheim Angels 4	Minnesota Twins 1	Adam Kennedy, Anaheim
2003	New York Yankees 4	Boston Red Sox 3	Mariano Rivera, New York
2004	Boston Red Sox 4	New York Yankees 3	David Ortiz, Boston
2005	Chicago White Sox 4	Los Angeles Angels 1	Paul Konerko, Chicago
2006	Detroit Tigers 4	Oakland Athletics 0	Placido Polanco, Tigers
2007	Boston Red Sox 4	Cleveland Indians 3	Josh Beckett, Red Sox
2008	Tampa Bay Rays 4	Boston Red Sox 3	Matt Garza, Rays
2009	New York Yankees 4	Los Angeles Angels 2	CC Sabathia, New York

NATIONAL LEAGUE

Year	Winner	Loser	MVP
1969	New York Mets 3	Atlanta Braves 0	
1970	Cincinnati Reds 3	Pittsburgh Pirates 0	
1971	Pittsburgh Pirates 3	San Francisco Giants 1	
1972	Cincinnati Reds 3	Pittsburgh Pirates 2	
1973	New York Mets 3	Cincinnati Reds 2	
1974	Los Angeles Dodgers 3	Pittsburgh Pirates 1	
1975	Cincinnati Reds 3	Pittsburgh Pirates 0	
1976	Cincinnati Reds 3	Philadelphia Phillies 0	
1977	Los Angeles Dodgers 3	Philadelphia Phillies 1	Dusty Baker, Los Angeles
1978	Los Angeles Dodgers 3	Philadelphia Phillies 1	Steve Garvey, Los Angeles
1979	Pittsburgh Pirates 3	Cincinnati Reds 0	Willie Stargell, Pittsburgh
1980	Philadelphia Phillies 3	Houston Astros 2	Manny Trillo, Philadelphia
1981	Los Angeles Dodgers 3	Montreal Expos 2	Burt Hooton, Los Angeles
1982	St. Louis Cardinals 3	Atlanta Braves 0	Darrell Porter, St. Louis
1983	Philadelphia Phillies 3	Los Angeles Dodgers 1	Gary Mathews, Philadelphia
1984	San Diego Padres 3	Chicago Cubs 2	Steve Garvey, San Diego
1985[1]	St. Louis Cardinals 4	Los Angeles Dodgers 2	Ozzie Smith, St. Louis
1986	New York Mets 4	Houston Astros 2	Mike Scott, Houston
1987	St. Louis Cardinals 4	San Francisco Giants 3	Jeff Leonard, San Francisco
1988	Los Angeles Dodgers 4	New York Mets 3	Orel Hershiser, Los Angeles
1989	San Francisco Giants 4	Chicago Cubs 1	Will Clark, San Francisco
1990	Cincinnati Reds 4	Pittsburgh Pirates 2	Rob Dibble, Randy Myers, Cincinnati
1991	Atlanta Braves 4	Pittsburgh Pirates 3	Steve Avery, Atlanta
1992	Atlanta Braves 4	Pittsburgh Pirates 3	John Smoltz, Atlanta
1993	Philadelphia Phillies 4	Atlanta Braves 2	Curt Schilling, Philadelphia
1994	No League Championship Series		
1995	Atlanta Braves 4	Cincinnati Reds 0	Mike Devereaux, Atlanta
1996	Atlanta Braves 4	St. Louis Cardinals 3	Javier Lopez, Atlanta
1997	Florida Marlins 4	Atlanta Braves 2	Liván Hernández, Florida
1998	San Diego Padres 4	Atlanta Braves 2	Sterling Hitchcock, San Diego
1999	Atlanta Braves 4	New York Mets 2	Eddie Perez, Atlanta
2000	New York Mets 4	St. Louis Cardinals 1	Mike Hampton, New York
2001	Arizona Diamondbacks 4	Atlanta Braves 1	Craig Counsell, Arizona
2002	San Francisco Giants 4	St. Louis Cardinals 1	Benito Santiago, San Francisco
2003	Florida Marlins 4	Chicago Cubs 3	Iván Rodríguez, Florida
2004	St. Louis Cardinals	Houston Astros	Albert Pujols, St. Louis
2005	Houston Astros 4	St. Louis Cardinals 2	Roy Oswalt, Houston
2006	St. Louis Cards 4	New York Mets 3	Jeff Suppan, Cardinals
2007	Colorado Rockies 4	Arizona Diamondbacks 0	Matt Holliday, Rockies
2008	Philadelphia Phillies 4	Los Angeles Dodgers 1	Cole Hamels, Phillies
2009	Philadelphia Phillies 4	Los Angeles Dodgers 1	Ryan Howard, Phillies

Note: 1. In 1985, the League Championship Series was switched to a best-of-seven format.

National League | American League

DIVISION SERIES

DODGERS 3, CARDINALS 0

In Game 1, Matt Kemp's two–run homer in the bottom of the first inning gave Los Angeles a lead they wouldn't relinquish, winning 5–3. Game 2 featured strong starting pitching and ended with a walk off as Mark Loretta's dramatic ninth inning single gave the Dodgers a 3–2 win. Game 3 was again dominated by pitching, as Dodgers starter Vincente Padilla allowed no runs and four hits in seven innings pitched. Los Angeles went on to win the game 5–1.

PHILLIES 3, ROCKIES 1

Cliff Lee pitched 8 2/3 strong innings as the Phillies cruised to an easy 5–1 victory in Game 1. Game 2 starter Cole Hamels got off to a rocky start giving up four runs in five innings, but the Phillies scored three runs in the bottom of the sixth only to see their rally fall just short 5–4. Game 3 in Denver was first postponed by a snowstorm and then played in 35 degree weather. The game was highlighted by five lead changes before Ryan Howard's sacrifice fly in the top on the ninth proved to be the winning run in a 6–5 victory. Game 4 featured six strong innings of pitching from both teams with Philadelphia clinging to a 2–1 lead. In the bottom of the eighth, Colorado scored three runs to take a 4–2 lead but the Phillies quickly matched it in the top of the ninth to go ahead 5–4, the final score.

YANKEES 3, TWINS 0

In the first postseason game at the new Yankee Stadium, New York rebounded from an early 2–0 deficit to win Game 1, 7–2, behind strong pitching from C.C. Sabathia and home runs from Hideki Matsui and Derek Jeter. Game 2 was mostly quiet, with the Twins clinging to a 3–1 lead. Mark Teixeira led off with a single and Alex Rodriguez hit two–run homer that sent the game into extra innings. In the 11th, Mark Teixeira hit a game–winning solo home run for a 4–3 Yankee win. In Game 3, Alex Rodriguez and Jorge Posada each hit solo home runs to give the Yankees a 4–1 victory.

ANGELS 3, RED SOX 0

In Game 1 Torii Hunter's three–run home run off Jon Lester in the fifth proved decisive. Boston would be shut out in postseason play for the first time since 1995, 5–0. In Game 2, Jered Weaver struck out seven, while limiting the Red Sox to one run on two hits in 7 1/3 innings. Josh Beckett suffered his first loss in nine postseason starts after giving up three runs in the bottom of the seventh, losing 5–1. The Angels stunned the Fenway Park crowd in Game 3, overcoming 5–2 and 6–4 deficits. Boston jumped out to an early 5–1 lead behind a J.D. Drew two–run home run in the fifth, but Anaheim scored three runs in the ninth off of Jonathan Papelbon to hand him a 7–6 loss and send the Angels on to the ALCS.

LEAGUE CHAMPIONSHIP SERIES

PHILLIES 4, DODGERS 1

James Loney gave the Dodgers an early lead in Game 1 with his second inning solo home run. Dodgers starter Clayton Kershaw was solid through four innings, when the Phillies jumped on him for five runs. A throwing error followed by a Manny Ramirez two run home run brought the Dodgers to within one run but Phillies closer Brad Lidge shut down the Los Angeles offense in the ninth to earn the save in an 8–6 victory. Game 2 featured a pitching duel between Vincente Padilla and Pedro Martinez. Martinez pitched seven scoreless innings and Padilla followed up with 7 1/3 innings of one–run ball. A throwing error by Chase Utley in the bottom of the 8th, led to two Dodgers runs and ultimately a 2–1 Los Angeles victory. In Game 3 Philadelphia scored six runs in the first two innings highlighted by a Ryan Howard two–run triple while Cliff Lee dominated in an easy 11–0 win. In Game 4 Ryan Howard hit a first inning two–run home run. The Dodgers took a 4–2 lead into the sixth and were leading in the bottom of the ninth inning when Philadelphia's Jimmy Rollins hit a game–winning two–run single to win 5–4. In Game 5 Philadelphia jumped out to a quick three run lead in the bottom of the first inning and never trailed, defeating the Dodgers 10–4.

YANKEES 4, ANGELS 2

In Game 1 C.C. Sabathia held the Angels to one run and four walks in eight innings for a 4–1 victory. Game 2 saw the Yankees take an early lead behind a Derek Jeter home run and a Robinson Cano RBI triple. Anaheim would score twice in the fifth to tie the game sending the contest to extra innings. In the top of the 11th, Chone Figgins hit an RBI single giving Anaheim it's first lead of the series. Alex Rodriguez hit another game tying home run in the bottom of the eleventh. The Yankees won 4–3 in the thirteenth on a throwing error by Maicer Izturis. Derek Jeter led off Game 3 with a home run and the Yankees extended their lead behind Alex Rodriguez and Johnny Damon home runs. New York's bullpen failed them, allowing Anaheim to tie the game and ultimately win 5–4 on a walk off double in the eleventh. The Yankees steamrolled in Game 4 winning 10–1, giving C.C. Sabathia his second win of the series. In Game 5 the Angels scored four runs in the first inning, but the Yankees rallied in the seventh, scoring six runs to take a 6–4 lead. Phil Hughes gave up three runs in the bottom of the seventh leading to an Anaheim 7–6 victory. The Angels took an early lead in Game 6, but the Yankees scored three runs in the bottom of the fourth and never looked back. Mariano Rivera entered the game in the eighth to record a six–out save giving the Yankees a 5–2 victory and their 40th American League Pennant.

INDEX

Earnings

M